Softwai
Engineer
Reference Book

CW00524744

Software Engineer's Reference Book

Edited by
John A McDermid

With specialist contributors

Butterworth-Heinemann Ltd
Linacre House, Jordan Hill, Oxford OX2 8DP

 A member of the Reed Elsevier group

OXFORD   LONDON   BOSTON
MUNICH   NEW DELHI   SINGAPORE   SYDNEY
TOKYO   TORONTO   WELLINGTON

First published 1991
First published as a paperback edition 1993
Reprinted 1994

© Butterworth-Heinemann 1991
except chapters 1, 4, 17, 29, 37 © the authors
except chapters 18, 59 © Crown copyright

All rights reserved. No part of this publication
may be reproduced in any material form (including
photocopying or storing in any medium by electronic
means and whether or not transiently or incidentally
to some other use of this publication) without the
written permission of the copyright holder except in
accordance with the provisions of the Copyright,
Designs and Patents Act 1988 or under the terms of a
licence issued by the Copyright Licensing Agency Ltd,
90 Tottenham Court Road, London, England W1P 9HE.
Applications for the copyright holder's written
permission to reproduce any part of this publication
should be addressed to the publishers

British Library Cataloguing in Publication Data
Software engineer's reference book
  1. Computer systems. Software packages
  I. McDermid, John A.
  005.3

ISBN 0 7506 0813 7

Front cover illustration courtesy of The Image Bank
Printed and bound in Great Britain
by Hartnolls Ltd, Bodmin, Cornwall

679

COVENTRY TECHNICAL
COLLEGE L.R.C.

ACCESSION NO.   717

CLASS NO.   RR 005.1 MAC

DATE   -4 AUG 1994

WITHDRAWN TECHNICAL COLLEGE

Preface

Introduction

The production of a book is really a form of software project – and it shares many of the technical and managerial problems of typical software developments. The project manager (the publisher) wants the project completed on time and to budget. The technical architect (the editor) wants to 'do it right', and always needs just a little bit longer to add some really important functionality (chapters). The project is constrained by hardware limitations – how can one do justice to the subject in *only* 1000 pages? Once you get most of it implemented, you begin to see clearly how you *ought* to have designed the system (defined the contents list) and so on. However many software projects fail to deliver anything at all, so perhaps we didn't do so badly!

The project wasn't *very* late and it came in quite close to the agreed budget. Many of the authors of the individual chapters (modules) recognized the errors and omissions in my definitions of their chapters (module specifications) and were able to correct them before they started writing (coding). Perhaps most importantly, the organization (module structure) of the book was such that I managed to accommodate most of the changes, and additions, that I wanted without unduly confusing the authors who had already started work on their chapters (the programmers who were already working on their modules)!

The book is like a software project in another important respect – it is almost impossible to draw a hard boundary around the book (system), i.e. to decide what should be included, and what should be left out; it is also very difficult to decide how information should be presented. In addressing this problem I have tried to apply two of the most important principles of quality management in software systems design – assess the knowledge and capability of the users (readers), and establish a set of key principles, or objectives, for guiding and assessing the design of the system (book). I hope that the result is a quality product.

The audience for the Software Engineer's Reference Book (*SERB*)

The intention in planning the book was that the primary audience for the *SERB* would be practising software engineers, or software project managers, who would look to the *SERB* as a source of information to help them with practical development problems. Since universities have only fairly recently started teaching computer science, and related subjects, on a wide scale, it is reasonable to assume that few of these readers will have had a sound grounding in the fundamentals of computer science or software engineering. This means that it is necessary to cover basic principles of the subject, but also to show how these principles relate to industrial practice.

Further, although many new recruits to the industry have had a relevant academic education, the discipline is developing very

quickly so the knowledge gained in academia rapidly becomes out of date. Hence there is a need to provide up-to-date information, but assuming that the reader does have a good grasp of the basic principles of computer science and software engineering.

It was intended that the reference book would have, as a secondary audience, research workers, consultants, etc. who need a reference work to 'get them started' when studying a new technical field for the first time. Thus part of the audience may be very knowledgeable in the general area of computer science and software engineering, but wish to gain a relatively deep understanding of some topic which is currently outside their domain of expertise.

This suggests that the book must deal with individuals with quite widely differing technical backgrounds, and with quite different needs in terms of the depth in which the material is covered.

Principles and key objectives for the *SERB*

I indicated above that I expected the readers of the *SERB* to have quite widely varying objectives in reading the book, and that I also expected the background knowledge and experience of the readers to be quite diverse. The problems which this diversity creates for the *SERB* authors are compounded by the rate of change of the computer and software development technology. I have adopted a number of principles to (endeavour to) overcome these problems.

First, the *SERB* focuses on material which is relatively non-volatile. That is, it stresses principles and general approaches to software development problems, rather than concentrating on the details of some particular software development method or tool. For example, it discusses general strategies for the design and analysis of software systems which should be applicable regardless of the design notation, or design method, adopted. Further, many of the chapters discuss the fundamental limits of the sort of technology they describe, and discuss the capabilities of current tools and techniques in terms of these limits. This reduces, although it cannot eliminate, the volatility of the material.

Second, the book focuses on material which is relatively mature so, although there are descriptions of current tools and techniques, there is a reasonable expectation that these techniques will remain current for some time to come. In this way we hope to provide topical information whilst avoiding having too much material which is subject to rapid change.

Third, the material is presented, as far as is possible, as pragmatic guidance, rather than as an academic study. This is not to say that the *SERB* does not contain some basic material on computer science, but rather that an attempt is made throughout the reference book to relate the basic material to the problems faced by practitioners. Thus the bias is perhaps rather more towards the practitioner than the researcher.

Fourth, the book aims to give the reader a sound understanding of the material covered, rather than risking giving a superficial understanding of a vast range of topics. Thus most of the chapters start at a relatively basic level, or make explicit their dependence on an understanding of material in other chapters, and proceed to give a sound grounding in the key issues in the subject. The aim is to enable the reader to be able to start work in that area, but also to be able to comprehend the more detailed papers and books on the subject. Further, most chapters contain a comprehensive set of references, or a bibliography, which enables the reader (especially the researcher) to find the more detailed technical literature relevant to the subject.

Fifth, the aim has been to make the chapters as self-contained as possible, without unnecessarily duplicating material. Thus it should be possible for readers to 'dip into' the book without having to read the book assiduously from cover to cover. Inevitably this means that there is some overlap between chapters – but part of my job as editor has been to keep this overlap to a minimum.

The adoption of a common set of principles for the chapters does not mean that they are all presented in a similar style. The diversity of material calls for a range of styles from informal introduction of basic concepts, through to detailed technical treatises. The former treatment is used particularly where a topic is still evolving, e.g. formal refinement, or the topic is unlikely to be familiar to software engineers, e.g. computer integrated manufacture. The latter approach is used where there is a stable and mature body of theory which will probably have been studied by the reader, at some time, but where a comprehensive '*aide memoire*' is needed. This style is exemplified by the material on discrete mathematics and basic computer science.

The choice of principles outlined above has also influenced the definition of the scope for the *SERB*.

Scope and structure of the *SERB*

The scope of the *SERB* is:

1. All aspects of computer science and the methods, techniques and technology for developing the software of computer systems – this forms the bulk of the book.
2. Hardware, only to the extent that it is necessary to help those engaged in producing embedded systems.
3. Information on computer architectures, especially as they affect design of programs, etc.
4. Information on how to design generic classes of application, e.g. databases, real-time systems, process control systems.

The *SERB* also covers topics which are thought of as 'AI' or 'IKBS' as well as more 'conventional' software engineering but, due to limitations on space, this material is given relatively brief treatment. This leads us on to the gross structure of the *SERB*.

The *SERB* comprises three main parts plus this introductory material, an epilogue, and a comprehensive index.

Part I: theory and mathematics

This is a dissertation on the theory of computer science and other basic mathematics, e.g. statistics, which is used in the rest of the *SERB*. This covers logic, set theory, theory of computation, computational complexity, Turing Machines, finite state automata, graph theory, etc. The emphasis is on those topics which underlie formal specification techniques, program analysis, systematic testing and other software development technologies.

This part of the book is expected to be of most interest to

consultants and researchers. It is also expected to be fairly stable, although it may become clear, at some stage, that additional material is needed as further mathematical domains become applicable to software engineering.

Part II: methods, techniques and technology

This is a discussion of software development methods, techniques and technology primarily based around a conventional view of the software life cycle. It discusses techniques applicable at each stage of the software life cycle. It covers both the more traditional 'structured' methods such as CORE, SSADM, and SREM, and formal methods including VDM and Z. Attention is also given to other technical activities in the life cycle including testing and prototyping.

This part of the book also covers 'managerial' aspects of software development such as configuration control and quality assurance. It also covers the large numbers of programming languages in common use but tries to explain the principles on which the design of programming languages is based, rather than simply giving a catalogue of language features. Finally it covers the 'operational environment' for software dealing with issues of hardware interfacing, operating systems, and so on.

This part of the book is aimed primarily at practising software engineers looking for techniques to help them with a particular problem. It should also assist consultants in finding relevant techniques to recommend to clients. Large parts of this material will be stable, but it is recognized that it will be subject to some degree of change, e.g. as various software development methods come into and go out of fashion.

Part III: principles of applications

The purpose of this section is not to describe particular applications, e.g. the air traffic control system at Heathrow, but more the techniques, standards, etc. which are relevant in producing particular classes of application. This material is intended to be complementary to Part II. Thus, for example, treatment of real-time systems will discuss timeliness as it affects every stage of the life cycle, rather than focusing on one stage of software development.

It is intended that this material should also be of use to practising software engineers. It is expected that the basis of this material will be fairly stable, but that it will be extended from time to time as computers become more pervasive in their application.

This brief outline sets out the principal contents and aim of each part of the reference book. Each part contains an introduction which describes its aim and content in more detail. Further assistance in finding relevant material can be gleaned from the contents list and index. However I would like to draw the reader's attention to the epilogue. This discusses the nature of a professional approach to software engineering and outlines the steps which need to be taken for software development to evolve into a true engineering discipline. I believe that this epilogue contains some interesting insights into the future of our profession.

Conclusions

I have no delusions that it is possible for a book of this nature to be 'perfect' – it is simply too difficult to define the scope, to achieve the right balance between contributions, and so on. I hope, however, that I have helped to make the *SERB* informative, stimulating, and generally useful to a wide class of professionals and that there aren't any glaring omissions in coverage.

If this goal has been achieved, in the eyes of the readers of the *SERB*, then much of the credit goes to the individual authors for the quality of their contributions. I will feel I have made my contribution as editor if the whole is viewed as being more than the sum of its parts.

Finally, I have noted that many traditional engineers are dismissive of software engineering due to the poor quality of much commercially available software, and the difficulties of delivering software to specification, and on time. I hope that this reference book will go some way to counter this scepticism, and to make software developers believe that they are members of a true engineering discipline, by making people aware of the vast range of applicable methods and management practices which can assist in the production of quality software. Perhaps it will also act as a spur to practising software developers to seek to learn more about the scientific and technical basis of their discipline, and to carry out their work in a more professional and disciplined manner.

John McDermid
York, July 1990

Acknowledgements

It would obviously have been impossible to produce this reference book without contributions and assistance from a large number of people. The greatest thanks must go to the authors for their contributions and, for the most part, for producing their material on time. I am immensely grateful to all the authors, especially those that I did not know personally prior to the production of this book but who nevertheless responded enthusiastically to my request for contributions. Perhaps the most pleasant 'side-effect' of my job as editor of the *SERB* is that I now feel that I have a much-enhanced set of professional colleagues (on whom I can call for the second edition!).

I have been most fortunate to be supported by two excellent secretaries during the production of the reference book. Jenny Turner helped me in the early days with the book, and Rebecca Wise has been of immense assistance during the past year. In particular, Rebecca has helped in collating the chapters, managing a burgeoning filing system, and preparing the text for my personal contributions to the book. Without her efficient and tireless support the *SERB* might not have seen the light of day.

I have also been greatly assisted (and harassed, albeit politely) by the staff at Butterworth Scientific. Ann Berne as commissioning editor was the driving force behind the production of the book, but was ably assisted by many other people including Nick Bliss and Karen Panaghiston.

Finally I must thank my family for their tolerance of the long hours spent working on the reference book, particularly in reviewing and editing the submitted manuscripts for each chapter. My wife Heather has always been supportive and my daughter, Ailsa, has been very tolerant of a father who spends inexplicably long hours in the study when there are important things to do like play with Lego and jigsaws.

List of
Contributors

Albert Alderson, BSc, PhD, CEng, MBCS
Chief Designer, IPSYS Software plc, Macclesfield

Martin C Atkins, BA, DPhil
Department of Computer Science, University of York

Giorgio Ausiello
Full Professor of Computer Science of the University "La Sapienza" of Rome

Ruth Aylett, BSc
Knowledge Engineering Group, AIAI, Edinburgh

Robert Laurence Baber, SM, CEng
Management Consultant and Software Engineer, Bad Homburg

Howard Beck, MSc
Knowledge Engineering Group, AIAI, Edinburgh

Professor Keith H Bennett, MSc, PhD, FBCS, CEng, FIEE
Science Laboratories, Durham

Dr Phil Bennett, PhD, FIEE, FBCS, FIQA
Managing Director of The Centre for Software Engineering Ltd; Chairman of IEE Safety Critical Systems Committee

Cornelia Boldyreff, BA, MPhil
Research Fellow, Department of Computer Science, Brunel University, Uxbridge

Alan W Brown, BSc, PhD
Lecturer in Computer Science, University of York

Professor Dr Manfred Broy
Institut für Informatik Technische, Universität München

Professor J N Buxton, MA, CEng, FBCS
Professor of Information Technology, Kings College, London

Paddy Byers, BSc
University of Surrey, Guildford

Bernard A Carré, MA, BSc, PhD, CEng, MIEE, FBCS
Managing Director, Program Validation Ltd, Southampton

Paul Wai Hing Chung, BSc, PhD, MPCS
Knowledge Engineering Group, AIAI, Edinburgh

Barry Cornelius, BSc, MSc
Lecturer in Computer Science, Centre for Software Maintenance, University of Durham

Dan Craigen, BSc, MSc
Odyssey Research Associates, Ottawa

James Davenport, MA, PhD, FIMA, MBCS
Professor of Information Technology, University of Bath

Tim Denvir
Principal Consultant, Praxis Systems plc, Bath; Associate Reader, Brunel University, Uxbridge

Dr R Dowsing
School of Information Systems, University of East Anglia

John Fraser, BSc, MSc
Knowledge Engineering Group, AIAI, Edinburgh

William Freeman
Department of Computer Science, University of York

Professor Marie-Claude Gaudel
LRI, Université de Paris Sud

Carlo Ghezzi
Professor of Software Engineering, Politecnico di Milano, Dipartimento di Elettronica, Milano

Hugh Glaser, BSc
Senior Lecturer, Department of Electronics & Computer Science, University of Southampton

Dorothy Graham, AB, MSc
Independant Software Engineering Consultant, Grove Consultants, Macclesfield

Anthony Hall, MA, DPhil
Principal Consultant, Praxis Systems plc, Bath

Patrick A V Hall, BSc, MA, DIC, PhD
Professor of Computer Science, Brunel University, Uxbridge

D J Hand, MA, MSc, PhD
Professor of Statistics, Statistics Department, The Open University, Milton Keynes

John Henderson, MA, MSc, FBCS, FRSA
Senior Research Fellow, King's College London

Peter Henderson, BSc, PhD
Professor of Computer Science, Electronics and Computer Science, University of Southampton

Christopher John Hogger
Senior Lecturer, Department of Computing, Imperial College of Science, Technology and Medicine, London

D C Ince, BSc, PhD, MIEE, CEng
Department of Computing, Open University, Milton Keynes

Professor Agnes Kaposi, Dipl Ing, PhD, CEng, FIEE
Senior Partner, Kaposi Associates, London

Chris F Kemerer, PhD
Douglas Drane Career Development Assistant Professor of
Information Technology and Management, Massachusetts
Institute of Technology

Barbara Kitchenham, PhD
The National Computing Centre, Manchester

Professor Dr H Kopetz
Institut für Technische Informatik, Wein

Laurie S Keller, BA, MSc, MBCS
Lecturer in Computer Science at the Open University, Faculty
of Mathematics, Milton Keynes

John K C Kingston, BSc, MSc
Knowledge Engineering Group, AIAI, Edinburgh

Bev Littlewood, BSc, PhD
Professor of Software Engineering, Centre for Software
Reliability, City University, London

Martin Loomes
Principal Lecturer, School of Information Science, Hatfield
Polytechnic

Eur Ing John A McDermid, MA, PhD, CEng, FIEE, FBCS
Professor of Software Engineering, University of York;
Director, York Software Engineering Ltd

Andrew D McGettrick
Department of Computer Science, University of Strathclyde,
Glasgow

Brian L Meek, MSc, FBCS, FRAS
Director of Information Technology, Computer Centre,
Goldsmiths' College, London

Dr Isi Mitrani
Reader in Computing Science, Computing Laboratory,
University of Newcastle

Brian Q Monahan, PhD, MBCS, CEng
Research Fellow, University of Manchester

Andrew F Monk, BSc, PhD
Senior Lecturer in Psychology, University of York

Malcolm Munro, BSc, MSc
Lecturer in Computer Science, Centre for Software
Maintenance, University of Durham

Martyn A Ould, MA, CEng, MBCS
Quality and Technical Director, Praxis plc, Bath

David Pitt, BSc, PhD, MSc
University of Surrey, Guildford

Professor V J Rayward-Smith, MA, Dip MIP, PhD, FIMA,
FBCS
School of Information Systems, University of East Anglia,
Norwich

D J Robson, BSc, MSc, PhD
Lecturer in Computer Science, Centre for Software
Maintenance, University of Durham

Paul Rook, MSc
Independent Consultant; Centre for Software Reliability,
London

C T Sennett, MA, DPhil
RSRE, Malvern

Helen Sharp, MSc, PhD
Mathematics Faculty, The Open University, Milton Keynes

Roger Shaw, GIMA, MBCS
Section Head, Systems Assessment and Development
Lloyd's Register of Shipping, Croydon

S K Shrivastava, ME, PhD
Professor of Computer Science, Computing Laboratory,
University of Newcastle upon Tyne

Keith Southwell, BSc
Director, Software Engineering, Logica Cambridge Ltd,
Cambridge

David A Stokes, MEng
Department of Computer Science, University of York

Harold Thimbleby
Professor of Information Technology, Stirling University,
Department of Computing Science, Stirling University

Steven Vickers
Lecturer in Computing, Department of Computing, Imperial
College, London

Peter J L Wallis, BSc, ARCS, DPhil, FBCS
School of Mathematical Sciences, University of Bath

I C Wand, PhD, CEng, FIEE
Professor of Computer Science, Department of Computer
Science, University of York

M I Wardlaw, MSc
British Telecom Research Laboratories, Ipswich

Dr R P Whittington, CEng
Hand, Whittington & Associates Ltd, York

Peter Whysall, MEng
Department of Computer Science, University of York

Dr B A Wichmann, DPhil, BSc, FBCS, CEng
National Physical Laboratory, Teddington

Professor Steve R Wilbur, CEng, FIEE
Department of Computer Science, University College,
London

David J Williams, BSc, PhD, CEng, MIMechE, MIM
Professor of Manufacturing Processes, Department of
Manufacturing Engineering, Loughborough University of
Technology

Contents

Part I

Theory and Mathematics

Introduction and overview to Part I

John McDermid and Tim Denvir

Engineers from 'traditional' engineering disciplines would all recognize that their work is based on scientific and mathematical underpinnings. Typically these underpinnings are physics and various aspects of continuous mathematics such as the calculus of real numbers.

If software engineering is to become a true engineering discipline it too must have an appropriate foundation in science and mathematics – albeit a rather different foundation due to the different nature of the 'materials' and artefacts used and studied.

Computer and software systems are usually modelled by discrete mathematics and the scientific basis for the discipline includes automata theory and formal language theory – abstract sciences since we are mainly concerned with the abstract properties of computers, not their physical manifestation.

Few software engineers are, or have been, educated to have an engineering ethos – consequently practising software engineers are less likely to appreciate the need for these theoretical foundations than their counterparts in, say, civil or mechanical engineering. Thus this preface has two aims:

1. To explicate the role of mathematics (and other relevant theory) in software engineering.
2. To introduce the material covered in Part 1, and relate it to the rest of the book.

We address the first point from the perspectives of the practical problems of software engineering, and education in software engineering.

1 Discrete mathematics and software engineering

What is the connection between discrete mathematics and software engineering? Three separate observations can be made. Firstly, the topics of discrete mathematics to be found in undergraduate computer science degree and software engineering curricula are remarkably diverse so there is little agreement as to what is relevant. Secondly, many respected authorities in computer science, such as Dijkstra and Hoare, have for a long time asserted that programming is a 'mathematical' activity. The third observation arises from problems perceived by those who are responsible for the production of software artefacts, namely problems of software errors, of poor productivity in the process of developing software and of expensive maintenance after software has been delivered. A more 'mathematical' approach to software development, usually embodied in a 'formal method', is frequently proposed as a solution, or at least a partial solution, to these problems.

1.1 Software development problems and solutions

Problems, or 'crises', of software developments have become a perennial lament, and these days are beginning to have a familiar, almost prophetic quality: cries in the wilderness of high technology. The complaints are that software is late, over budget, incorrect, incomplete and does not meet requirements. As a result managers responsible for software development projects lack confidence in the quality of the products and have concerns about the controlability of their projects. There are three, almost independent, perceived solutions. These are:

1. To improve quality assurance procedures.
2. To organize the development process more systematically.
3. To adopt a more 'scientific' or 'mathematical' approach.

These solutions are by no means exclusive. One may attempt to implement all three. The first, quality assurance, consists of management rules and procedures. These require that the products resulting from the development process (feasibility study documents, specifications, designs, test plans, test data, programs, etc.) are examined by designated individuals according to a defined procedure and are 'signed off' when found to be satisfactory. The procedures generally require records to be kept, so that a history of the project can be accessed to ensure that the procedures have been followed. The procedures may not, however, require any particular specific technical verification to be applied to the development products.

The second solution, systematic organization, consists of designing adequate management and organizational procedures to handle the many variants and versions of all the products of the development process, ensuring that the interrelationship of co-existing variants, superseding editions, and their compatibilities are all recorded and understood. It is typical of large software projects that these issues of software configuration management become extremely complex and benefit from the use of, essentially clerical, support tools. These organizational procedures are often subsumed under the quality procedures. These classes of solution are addressed in Part II of the reference book.

The third 'solution', a scientific or mathematical approach, is the one of interest in the bulk of this part of the reference book and several chapters in Part II. If we adopt a scientific approach to software development, where does mathematics play a part?

It is becoming accepted wisdom that computer programming is, or should be, viewed as a mathematical activity. Authorities such as E. W. Dijkstra (1976) and C. A. R. Hoare have been proclaiming this principle since at least the 1970s; Hoare's seminal paper (1969), giving mathematical axioms for computer programs, was published in the late 1960s and expressed an attitude, if not an understanding, which was current for some years before then.

The principle that programming is mathematics, which Hoare describes as 'general philosophical and moral' principles, are most succinctly and expressively summarized in his inaugural lecture at the University of Oxford (1986): 'Computers are mathematical machines; computer programs are mathematical expressions; a programming language is a mathematical theory; programming, like other branches of applied mathematics and engineering, is a mathematical activity.'

These principles are beginning to be accepted in practice. They form the basis of so-called 'formal methods' of software development, which are in turn starting to be used in practical projects. Thus we can further clarify the role of mathematics in software development by considering formal methods in the development process, but first it is constructive to look at a more general issue – the role of mathematics in science.

1.2 Mathematics and science

In many science and engineering text books, one may find a somewhat simplistic description of the role of mathematics in science along the lines shown in *Figure 1*.

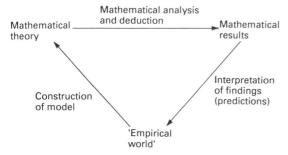

Figure 1 Role of mathematics in science

An abstract mathematical model is hypothesized in which the mathematical constructs have an interpretation in the observable, empirical, world domain. Then by following abstract rules of mathematics, the model is analysed and various results are deduced. These mathematical results are interpreted back into the empirical world domain as predictions. Then experimental observations can be made to confirm or refute the predictions and the model from which they are deduced. Much has been written about the methodology of this cycle of theory construction, deduction, interpretation and prediction: see for example Lakatos (1978) and Popper (1972). This topic is also discussed in Chapter 12 on measurement theory.

Is this kind of connection between mathematics and science valid when applied to computer science or software engineering, and if so how does it apply? These questions concern the role of mathematics in the software development process, and to determine this we first need to examine the life cycle of software development.

1.3 The software life cycle

This is illustrated in stylized form in *Figure 2*. We discuss more realistic life cycle models in Chapter 15 in Part II. The 'Application' is the empirical, 'real-world' domain which is the subject matter of the software being developed. For a computerized airline reservation system, the application would be airline reservations and all their ramifications. For a public telephone network, the application domain would be telephony, etc.

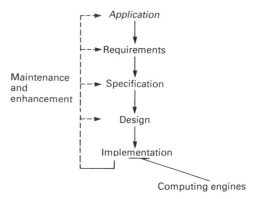

Figure 2 Stylized life cycle model

The requirements are a statement of what the software or computer system is required to do. This is usually first expressed in natural language, except in those rare cases where the application domain has a well-established and widely recognized theory (mathematical model) already. The requirements may describe the environmental need which the proposed software is to satisfy.

The specification is a statement of what the proposed software is supposed to do, i.e. its function or behaviour. The specification may also prescribe various properties of the software, which depend on its design or implementation; for example, its performance or the equipment or operating system to which it must interface. Taking the 'scientific view', the specification, especially that part which specifies functional behaviour, is best written in a formal language, that is, a language with precisely defined semantics. Such languages in this context normally have a semantics defined in mathematical terms.

Several levels of design may in fact take place. Each level should satisfy all the prescriptions given in the design or specification at the level above it, and will normally incorporate more decisions about the means of construction of the software system.

The implementation is a level of design which can be processed and executed by computer, so as to carry out all the required functions in accordance with the specification. As techniques and the tools which reflect them become increasingly more sophisticated, the level of design which can stand as an implementation rises. Sometimes higher levels of design can be executed as a prototype which does not conform to all the constraints prescribed by the specification, for example the performance constraints.

The language(s) in which the designs and the implementations are expressed are in general formal languages, with a defined semantics. The language of the implementation is invariably formal, its semantics being at least implicitly defined by the computing engine.

The solid arrows in Figure 2 represent a satisfaction, conformance or fulfilment relation. The design must satisfy the specification, that is, it must exhibit all the properties prescribed by the specification, or it must prescribe them itself so that the lower levels of design are obliged to fulfil them. This satisfaction relation becomes a formal relation when applied to the specifications, designs and implementation expressed in a formal language. See also *Figure 3*. In the development process, these formal relationships hold between the generated specifications, designs, etc. If the required relationship does not hold, an error has occurred in the development process, and parts of the development are recast. This constitutes 'maintenance' (or corrective work in development) and is indicated by the dotted lines in Figure 2.

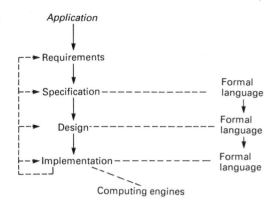

Figure 3   Formal languages in software development

Assuming that the requirements (and possibly certain aspects of the specification) are stated in informal language, there is also a corresponding informal relationship between specifications, designs, etc., and requirements. Being informal, these cannot be proved, and indeed the requirements may not be fully agreed or understood. Improving the development to conform better to requirements, or to upgrade requirements, constitutes 'enhancement' and is part of the development process similar to maintenance. This can be facilitated by exercising or demonstrating the properties of the design and implementation by prototyping and running tests.

The documents are not necessarily generated in the order indicated in Figures 2 and 3. These may be regarded as a 'rational reconstruction' of the actual development process. It is not unknown in practice for the specification to be written after the design, and the requirements after the specification!

1.4 Mathematical models

We can identify three different kinds of role for mathematical models in the life cycle described above.

Over many years mathematical theories of computation have been developed. These comprise such topics as automata theory, the theory of computability, formal languages (Chomsky classifications, formal grammars, etc.) and theories of algorithmic complexity. Such theories treat abstract properties of computing engines, implementations and low-level designs in the life cycle (see *Figure 4*).

Secondly, at the other end of the life cycle, mathematics can be used to model theories of the phenomena of the application domain. The task of the systems analyst may indeed be considered to be essentially the same as that of the scientist, in that it involves constructing an abstract mathematical model of a real-world domain of phenomena. In Figure 4 this kind of model is called the 'phenomenological theory'.

In fact, this abstract modelling of the application-domain phenomena often takes place in two stages. The first stage consists of a direct model of the application domain, and the second consists of a computational model in terms of finitary algorithms and information structures which can be implemented directly in a programming language. For example, in Newtonian mechanics, differential and integral calculus is used to model the phenomena; to translate this into a computer implementation a computational model is required. This would comprise such techniques as iterative methods, numerical algorithms, etc. In applications involving certain traffic problems, queuing theory would be the mathematical model and queuing algorithms the computational model. In data encryption,

number theory would be required to formulate the mathematical model and the computational model would comprise data encryption algorithms.

It is perhaps worth emphasizing at this point that 'formal methods' of software development have nothing to say about the 'correctness' of phenomenological theory, even though the mathematics they involve may be closely related to the mathematics used to express that theory. A phenomenological theory is a hypothesis that a certain specific mathematic construction models aspects of behaviour of a real-world situation and its phenomena. Formal methods may enable one to demonstrate the mathematical consistency of the model, or to show that other particular constructions conform to it. However, formal methods cannot demonstrate that the model is accurate, i.e. valid, and if it is not so, all the mathematical rigour brought to bear in the subsequent stages of development will be of no avail. If the model is inappropriate, the program may work well, but will not fit its environment, with possibly disastrous results.

The third role for mathematical models concerns the development process itself which is subject to a scientific analysis using the models. The formal languages have a semantics which defines an abstract mathematical model for each specification or design (each 'sentence') in the language. The mathematical semantics of these languages are frequently based on domain theory and other more basic topics in discrete mathematics – in particular, set theory and recursive functions. Process algebras are used to model the semantics of concurrent or dynamic languages. The specification languages themselves are often based on set theory or the fundamentals of universal algebra. Various forms of logic, typically propositional and predicate calculus, are used to reason about formal specifications, to infer properties of them and to show that one specificaton satisfies another (i.e. that the theorems of one include all the theorems of the other). Various modal logics are sometimes used to define temporal conditions which programs are required to fulfil. Finally, to provide a complete explanation of the meanings and relationships of a coherent set of specifications in a development, category theory has been found useful. (More recent research has been investigating the use of topology in this kind of role.)

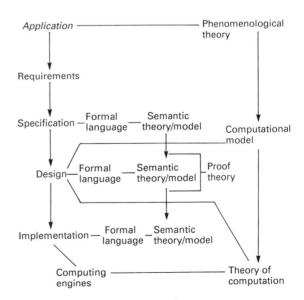

Figure 4   Mathematical models in software engineering

1.5 Classes of mathematical explanation

The first and third of these forms of modelling, namely the theory of computation and the theories of the software development process, lie firmly within the accepted boundaries of theoretical computer science. Yet they have markedly different characters. The following characteristics of the relationship between these two kinds of model can be put forward.

Firstly, we have 'computation' standing, as it were, as a naturally occurring phenomenon. One may object, saying that surely the vehicles of computation, namely computers and computer programs, are human artefacts and must therefore be treated rather differently from the phenomenon of natural science. However, the constraints which, we assume, must apply to computations, namely that they must be finite in various respects and that each step of a computational process occupies a non-zero period of time, are derived from natural physical properties of the world in which the actual computations will take place. In this respect the mathematical modelling of computations play the same scientific role as the mathematical models of electromagnetic theory, quantum mechanics or relativity.

In any scientific theory, the models put forward play (at least) two parallel roles. They form bases for predictions, which are subject to potential refutation by experimental observation. They also act as media of explanation, clarifying our understanding of the phenomena and forming the language we use to describe them and communicate facts about them. Explanations in their turn can be at a variety of levels and purposes. Their objective is to answer questions of the form: 'Why. . .?' and as such can provide answers from very different viewpoints.

In particular one can identify a spectrum of explanations from 'reductionist' at one end to 'holistic' at the other. A reductionist explanation is one which presupposes that the whole is explained by explaining all its parts. For example a reductionist explanation of electrical phenomena would concentrate on the 'atomic' mechanisms which produce electrical behaviour, i.e. Maxwell's equations, electromagnetic theory, etc. On the other hand a 'holistic' explanation would be more specific to the domain of usage of electricity and would comprise, say, the theory of waveguide or filter design, principles of electrical power engineering, the theory of telecommunication systems or whatever. All these are 'electrical phenomena', depending on the reductionist Maxwell's equations for their operations and existence, but are by no means wholly explained by them. Broadly, holistic explanations deny, or at any rate do not rely on the possibility, that the whole is explicable in terms of its parts.

Of the three forms of mathematical modelling which have been identified in the pictures of software engineering shown, theories of computation can be classed as reductionist models and theories of the development process more as holistic models. Furthermore, within the latter there seem to be varying degrees of holism; the category-theoretic accounts, for example, strike one as being more holistic than the individual logics of particular specification languages.

1.6 Modelling the phenomena

One might regard the third usage of discrete mathematics in software engineering, namely the modelling of application phenomena, to be out on a limb, not properly part of software engineering per se, and only coincidentally connected. This is not entirely the case. The presence of 'self-referential applications' explained below seems a plausible explanation for the frequent coalescing of the three kinds of modelling role for discrete mathematics.

There appear to be three distinct kinds of application. These do not fall neatly into any kind of orderly spectrum, and do not seem to be obviously related. This may not be a complete categorization in that some applications may not fall easily into any of the three categories. The categories do, however, seem to be reasonably distinct, with little or no overlap. The three categories of application identified are 'specialist', 'self-referential' and 'familiar'. The choice of terminology may leave something to be desired.

1.6.1 Specialist applications

An application is called 'specialist' if it is linked with computers principally because of the application's context. For example, some applications contain problems the solution of which is greatly facilitated, or even made possible, by the power of computers. Large-scale statistical or combinatorial problems for which the study and knowledge of statistics and combinatorics is required, fall into this category. Other applications lend themselves to the use of computers because they lie in a neighbouring engineering field. Examples of these are communication networks, data encryption, signal processing, and many other similar applications.

Specialist applications are thus associated with particular topics in mathematics including: combinatorics, statistics, graph theory, encryption, error correcting codes, hashing algorithms and others. It is also reasonable to include in specialist applications those which have an existing scientific theory with a mathematical model which is already accepted. Newtonian mechanics has calculus as its mathematical model, for example, and although computational models (methods) have been devised for this, the subject is not particularly conducive to solution or analysis by computer programming.

Pragmatically, therefore, the mathematical basis of the phenomenological theory may be discrete mathematics, but it may also be in continuous mathematics such as mechanics or fluid dynamics. Thus this class of problems can only be addressed by (groups of) people who have knowledge of both mathematical and phenomenological domains.

1.6.2 Self-referential applications

The software development process itself is, in principle, highly amenable to being supported by computer-based tools. This is because the intermediate results from the process are well defined, having a theory couched in mathematical terms. Indeed, this results from that part of computer science which studies the nature of software (from a holistic viewpoint) and provides mathematical models of the syntax and semantics of programming and specification languages. Thus the 'application' is itself computation, or parts of the software development process, and the phenomenological theory of the application is itself part of computation theory.

Examples of self-referential applications are compilers, language processors, proof checkers for specification languages, and related tools. The mathematics which underpins their theory includes formal languages, transformations of algorithms and the proof theory of formal specification languages.

Clearly, work can be done in these applications with a knowledge of discrete mathematics and the relevant theory of computer science, but without knowledge of other domains. Many projects undertaken in universities are of this self-referential nature and it is perhaps this remoteness from 'real-world' issues which has caused much of the industrial disregard for some academic work. It is hoped that this discussion has helped clarify why there is this divergence between some academic and industrial work and indicates the need for computer scientists and software engineers to co-operate with specialists from other disciplines if they are to be able to apply their ideas outside self-referential applications.

1.6.3 Familiar applications

Familiar applications are those where the 'scientific theory' is so simple, or so much part of our cultural background, or perhaps so indisputable, that no-one would ever proclaim the mathematical model as a 'scientific theory'. For example, numbers have been part of all cultures since before recorded history, because they form an acceptable theory for many of the immediately observable phenomena people encounter. Numbers are a convenient model for the physical properties of length, mass or weight, velocity, periods of time, rates of growth or other dynamic events, money, prices, volumes and so on. Much is conserved and much is oblivious in measuring such phenomena, in the ways that the properties of numbers can express. For example, if one measures the width of an object – a piece of wood, say – from left to right, one will obtain the same results as if one measured from right to left. Other properties of conservation apply. (Although in fact all is not as simple as it appears. Books have been written which explore the scientific justification of using numbers to model such familiar properties as length, and theories of error need to be formulated. See, for example, Kyburg (1984). This topic is dealt with in more detail in Chapter 12 on measurement theory.)

In a computing context, the familiar applications are those in which set theory generally provides a model. The allocation of crews (drawn from a set of staff) to (a set of) buses which are to travel along a set of routes; a manufacturer's database in which a set of orders is to be matched with the stock, which comprises numbers of items belonging to a set of merchandise. A personnel file comprises a set of records, each of which is a member of a Cartesian product of employee names, ages, national insurance numbers, salaries, grades, etc. Each of these is likewise a member of some other set.

It is the systems analyst's task to put forward what is usually called a 'data model' of the application domain. If this is expressed in the slightly more abstract terms of set theory rather than in the more restricted repertoire of program language data types, the systems analyst is in fact playing the part of a true scientist. (It is doubtless no coincidence that as programming languages have evolved, their available data types have approached increasingly closely the constructs offered by traditional set theory.) A systems analyst observes the phenomena of the application domain and their important properties, and proposes an abstract mathematical model which stands as the phenomenological theory (see Figure 4).

Pragmatically, there is no need to develop, and perhaps no need to articulate, the relevant phenomenological theory when dealing with such applications.

1.7 Mathematical foundation for software engineering

Having considered the analysis of how and why mathematics is used in different parts of the development process, we now have an opportunity to itemize the essential topics of mathematics for computer science and software engineering with more clarity and on a more rational basis. This should make clearer the structure and scope of this part of the book which we view as providing a basic course in mathematics and other foundational topics in computer science and software engineering.

The specialized applications will be of importance to those working in those particular fields, and will have little impact on others. The topics particular to such specialized applications typically comprise:

1. Statistics
2. Combinatorics
3. Graphs, etc.

To limit the scope of the reference book we have restricted ourselves to 'specialized applications', as we have defined them, which can be treated within discrete mathematics.

General applications, classified here as 'familiar', are the kind of application domains in which very many software engineers may find themselves working in their subsequent professional lives. The mathematical topic which is appropriate for modelling such applications is, predominantly, set theory. A simple account of set theory with an emphasis of its use in modelling application-specific information is therefore a core of the discrete mathematics for software engineering, and is where our treatment starts.

The software development process links the phenomenological theory of the application domain to the computational models which are expressed by the implementation of the developed software system. The most general treatment of the development process requires sets, functions and logic, and this should be present in the core of any computer science or software engineering curriculum. This forms the basis for more specific topics dealt with in Part II, such as:

1. Algebraic specifications (e.g. OBJ or CLEAR).
2. Model-oriented specifications (e.g. VDM or Z).
3. Process algebras (e.g. CSP or CCS).

Sets, functions and logic are all treated in Chapter 1.

A more specialist and advanced treatment of software engineering would include the more global theories of the development process, involving:

1. Domain theory
2. Universal algebra
3. Category theory
4. Topology

At present these topics are really only relevant to research and are not treated here.

The above mathematical bases of the software development process help to provide a holistic explanation of computation. At the other end of the scale, the subject generally given the name of 'theory and computation' provides reductionist explanations. The canonical topics here are:

1. Formal languages
2. Automata
3. Theory of computability
4. Algorithmic complexity

These should all be a mandatory part of any course of computer science as distinct from software engineering, since they – or at least the first three – collectively form the basic theory of computing machines. They fulfil the same role in computer science as electromagnetic theory does in electricity. Those specializing in the particular branches of electrical engineering such as digital systems or power engineering may well be able to carry on their profession in an entirely competent way without having learned Maxwell's equations. Nonetheless, they are necessary for a proper formulation of the science of the subject and therefore are desirable as scientific background for all branches of electrical engineering. Likewise the topics of the theory of computation are not essential for software engineers, in this role, but are a desirable scientific foundation.

However, one should go further for two of the above topics: formal languages and automata. These have a dual role as the phenomenological theory of some very important 'self-referential' applications, namely language compilers and other support tools. These tools are such a necessary and universal component of almost every development process that they are an essential part of every software engineer's fundamental toolset. So formal languages and automata should be mandatory topics in all courses, whether for computer science or software engineering. For that reason they are covered here in some depth.

Contents of Part I

Having set out the role of mathematics in software engineering, and having roughly identified the set of topics which should be addressed, we are now in a position to outline the contents of Part I. Thus the following gives an overview of each chapter and, for those topics not addressed above, indicates our reasons for covering the topic.

There is no absolute logical order for treating the material, but we have organized the chapters so that the later chapters are dependent on earlier ones, but not vice versa. The chapters are divided into three main groups, *viz*:

1. Applicable mathematics.
2. Fundamental computer science.
3. Other relevant science and theory.

These subdivisions are not entirely clear cut, but hopefully they are indicative of the contents. We discuss the groups and content in order.

2.1 Applicable mathematics

This group of chapters is restricted to the domain of discrete mathematics. It focuses on those topics which form a basis for various phenomenological theories, and for the semantic models of formal specification languages. It does not address issues of the theory of computation.

Arguably Chapter 2, on programming logics and proof, is out of place and would be better treated under fundamental computer science. We include it here because the principles do underpin various approaches to formal specification and development and, of course, it forms the phenomenological theory for work on program verification systems.

2.1.1 Discrete mathematics

As should be clear from the above the basic topics in discrete mathematics – sets, logic, functions and relations – underpin all the other mathematical topics covered in Part I of the reference book, and all the formal material in Part II (especially the group of chapters on formal development).

The material is treated from first principles, and the account is kept at an elementary level. The chapter should therefore be accessible to any reasonably numerate reader, yet it covers enough material to enable the reader to go on to study specification languages such as Z without recourse to further tutorial material.

This material is built on in perhaps 20 further chapters. The strongest links in Part I are with Chapter 2, which applies the concepts to specification of, and reasoning about programs, and Chapter 3 which extends the concepts to deal with basic algebraic properties. Chapters 21–26 in Part II are all dependent on this fundamental material.

2.1.2 Logics and proof of correctness

In order to treat programming as a mathematical discipline it is necessary to be able to use set theory, etc. to specify the desired behaviours of programs, and logic to show that the program behaves as specified (or otherwise). This latter activity is usually referred to as proof of correctness.

This chapter explains the role of logic and proof in programme development, then explains the basic principles of program specification and proofs of correctness, building directly on the work of Chapter 1. The chapter then shows how to apply these principles to declarative (functional or logic) programs, before considering the more difficult case of procedural

programs. This treatment covers both Dijkstra's weakest preconditions and Hoare's axiomatic approach.

This work is directly relevant to Chapters 25 and 26 on formal implementation and verification environments. To a lesser extent it supports the treatment of refinement in Chapter 24.

2.1.3 Introduction to algebra

Abstract algebra has two distinct but related uses in software engineering. First it can be used directly (perhaps with some syntactic sugar) to specify behaviour of some program or system. Second it can be used to compare, e.g. for equivalence, different specifications in a sound manner. Thus it is a tool both in specification and in the analysis of specifications.

The chapter introduces the basic concepts of algebra where an algebra consists of a set of sorts (types) and operations on objects of these sorts. This is the basic framework required for algebraic specification.

The chapter then covers key properties of algebras, e.g. the notion of a homomorphism, which is a mapping between two algebras so that the operations in one elgebra have counterparts which 'do the same thing' under the mapping. These concepts form the basis of the capability for comparing specifications.

This chapter directly underpins Chapter 22 on algebraic specifications. The notions of algebras and homomorphisms are also employed elsewhere, e.g. in Chapter 12 on measurement theory.

2.1.4 Graph theory

Graphs, as well as being important in many application domains, have a significant role in 'self-referential' applications. Examples include optimization in compilers, assessment of the effectiveness of testing, and program analysis and verification.

The chapter introduces the basic notions of a graph as a set of nodes, connected by a set of arcs. This builds directly on the idea of sets and relations described in Chapter 1. The chapter then introduces measures (properties) of graphs and operations on graphs which relates to the practical applications of graph theory.

The notions of graphs are employed directly in measures of test efficacy, see Chapter 19. They also, less manifestly, support the material on compilation and verification.

2.1.5 Introduction to probability

Probability theory is concerned with predictions about the future. It is thus important in topics such as reliability modelling, but it also underpins information theory. Through these two 'applications' it is also pertinent to topics such as fault tolerance and telephony.

The chapter introduces the basic concepts of probability as a way of modelling the likelihood of the outcome of a future 'experiment', e.g. the execution of some program, based on the concepts in Chapter 1. It then derives the ideas of stochastic processes, conditional probability, predictive techniques and discusses decision procedures for relating causes and effects.

This material is used directly in Chapter 7 on queuing theory, Chapter 14 on information theory and in Chapter 31 on reliability modelling. It is also relevant to metrics and measurement (Chapter 30), and several application areas such as telecommunication (Chapter 58) and safety (Chapter 60).

2.1.6 Statistics

Descriptive statistics gives us ways of modelling observations of behaviour, and predictive statistics enable us to produce hypotheses about the future operation of systems. Statistics is clearly important as a phenomenological theory, e.g. in stochastic control, but it is also used in assessing and estimating properties of systems, such as reliability.

The chapter extends the basic concepts of probability distributions introduced in the previous chapter and introduces the concept of estimation based on distributions. The chapter then describes common probability distribution functions, and ways of sampling behaviour to estimate distributions. This is useful in testing.

The ideas of simulation, based on Monte Carlo methods, are also considered. This is useful in many applications, for example modelling the behaviour of queuing systems.

The direct uses of this material are in information theory (Chapter 14) and reliability models (Chapter 31). The techniques are also applicable in many other application domains although the material is not directly used in other chapters.

2.1.7 *Queuing theory*

Many application problems such as road traffic systems and communication systems can be modelled by queues, so queuing theory has a phenomenological role. Queuing theory can also be used as an abstract model of performance of a computer system, so it also functions in the role of an abstract model of computation.

The chapter introduces the concepts of queuing theory which can model any system where multiple clients compete for access to finite resources. It studies issues of performance in queuing systems, e.g. average response time, relying on the earlier material on probability and statistics. The chapter deals with various forms of queuing systems, including open and closed networks, and also illustrates the application of the theory to computing problems, e.g. the analysis of the performance of various job scheduling algorithms.

This material is relevant to networks and distributed systems (Chapter 53), telecommunications (Chapter 58) and the analysis of software system architectures (Chapter 17).

2.1.8 *Numerical computing*

Integers, real numbers and arithmetic, are an example of a familiar domain which we would normally take for granted. However, computer arithmetic is of limited precision, is subject to rounding errors, and so on. Consequently, it is necessary to consider the issues of numerical computing as opposed to arbitrary precision arithmetic.

The chapter covers the basic issues of number representation, precision and accuracy of numerical computation. It also discusses design of algorithms to minimize numeric errors.

This material is little used elsewhere in the reference book, but it is fundamental to the design of all numerical programs.

2.2 Fundamental computer science

There are many important topics in computer science, relevant to software engineering, but limitations on space force us to concentrate on the central issues. We have chosen three related topics as they allow us to focus on important aspects of the theory of computation, *viz*:

1. Computability – whether or not it is possible to solve a problem on a machine.
2. Computational complexity – the cost of solving a problem on a machine.
3. Language syntax and semantics – the formalization of syntax and semantics to facilitate the generation of parsers and other language processing tools.

These issues are fundamental in the design of almost any software system.

2.2.1 *Automata theory*

Automata theory is concerned with mathematical models of real computing devices. This material is fundamental as it enables us to investigate computability and space and time complexity, as well as providing a basis for analysing the 'parsability' of languages.

The chapter develops models of various classical types of automata, leading on to the analysis of Turing Machines which are simple computational models of stored program computers. The models are developed to derive standard results in terms of linguistic theory, and the classic notion of undecidability. (Loosely, an undecidable problem is one which cannot be solved by a single computer program.) The chapter also deals with space and time complexity, i.e. the amount of memory and CPU time needed by a given algorithm.

This material is directly used by the other two chapters in this group. It is essential for modelling the (space–time) cost of any proposed computer program, and thus underpins work described in many of the other chapters, e.g. work on analysis of architectures in Chapter 17. Automata are also used as the basis of many design notations.

2.2.2 *Language theory*

In order to develop a compiler for a programming language it is necessary to have well-defined syntax and semantics for that language. Language theory is better developed in the realm of syntax, but there are also formal bases for defining language semantics. Study of this material is therefore essential for the designers of programming languages and compilers, but it is also important for everyone who is involved in designing languages and analysers for those languages – which includes many designers of computer systems with a human interface.

The chapter introduces a number of different models of the syntax of languages, based on the fundamental work of Chomsky and the mathematical concepts introduced in the chapters on automata theory and algebra. This theory is used to subdivide languages into classes, dependent on the way in which they may be parsed. This work is of practical significance because most practical parser generators for languages are restricted to dealing with one or other of these language classes.

The chapter briefly describes a number of different formal approaches to modelling the semantics of programming languages.

This material is used directly in Chapter 52 on compiler construction, and is of direct practical use in many software engineering projects.

2.2.3 *Data structures and algorithms*

It is a truism that the detailed design of programs reduces to the selection of data structures for representing information, and the choice for development of algorithms. In practice the choice of data structures and algorithms should be illuminated by knowledge of a number of their properties including space and time complexity. A full treatment of even the commonly used algorithms would require a volume the size of this reference work, not just a single chapter, so the chapter focuses on principles and some of the most common algorithms.

The chapter extends the concepts of space and time complexity developed in the chapter on automata theory to define a number of different measures of computational complexity. For example, the concepts of expected and worst-case execution time are introduced. These principles are illustrated by analysis of common algorithms, e.g. various classes of sorting algorithms. To clarify the practical role of these analyses the chapter also includes thorough treatments of data structures and algorithms for maintaining dictionaries and priority queues.

This material is not used directly in other chapters in the reference book, but the techniques it describes should be part of the analytic repertoire of any practising software engineer.

2.3 Other relevant science and theory

Given the wide range of applicability of computer systems, there are very many other topics which could be considered to be relevant to a treatise on software engineering. However, we have confined ourselves to three topics which have particular bearing on software engineering.

2.3.1 Measurement theory

It has long been recognized that one of the difficulties of managing software projects arises from the fact that software is somewhat nebulous, and therefore difficult to control. In order to gain control over the software development process it is necessary to establish a measurement system covering both software, as a product, and its development process. To establish valid measurement systems, it is important to understand the theory and principles behind measurement – and this is the purpose of this chapter. It should be pointed out, however, that this material is not only relevant to those who will develop elaborate systems of metrics. It is also relevant on a day-to-day basis in project management to those who wish validate the pragmatic measures which they set up in order to control their projects.

The chapter gives an overview of the principles of measurement theory, starting with basic concepts of the meaning of valid measurements. It proceeds from dealing with simple measurements of a single property of some artefact, through the measurement of groups of related projects, to the treatment of complete subject domains such as software engineering. Throughout the material is illustrated with examples from familiar 'real-world' domains and software engineering.

This material is not used directly elsewhere in the reference book but it is of importance in ensuring that the measures dealt with in several of the chapters on software development management are indeed valid. Consequently the principles of measurement theory should be viewed as applying to Chapter 28 on estimation, Chapter 30 on metrics and measurement and Chapter 31 on reliabilty modelling. Also, as indicated above, the principles should be used to guide the development of any pragmatic measureent program put in place to run a project.

2.3.2 Cognitive psychology

Most computer systems developed today have interfaces for use by human beings. Whilst there are many guidelines and approaches for the development of human interfaces to computer systems, they all should be guided and constrained by knowledge of basic human cognitive processes. The purpose of this chapter is to set out the basic perceptive and cognitive skills of typical human beings in order to provide a scientific basis for those engaged in designing interactive systems, particularly special-purpose human interfaces.

In order to use interfaces people have to make judgements with respect to some perceptive attribute. The chapter sets out the basic perceptive capabilities of humans with respect to temporal and spatial resolution, and draws out the major distinctions in capability when dealing with relative as opposed to absolute judgement. The chapter also deals with simple models of human memory and discusses the way in which skill is acquired both in a qualitative and quantitative manner.

Again this material is little used, directly, within the rest of the reference book. However, it does represent valuable information which should be understood by all those engaged in developing interactive systems.

2.3.3 Information theory

Computers store information, and the algorithms developed by program designers process information in a variety of ways. However, typically, little regard is given for the nature of this 'material' that our programs process. This seems analogous to civil engineers not understanding the stress and strain properties of steel or concrete. The principles of information theory are used directly in a number of domains, e.g. communication theory and cryptography. However, the material seems to be of much broader, cultural, value in explicating the nature of the 'material' manipulated by programs, for example, information is transferred across interfaces to computer programs and an understanding of information theory should aid in making their transfer efficient.

The chapter deals with the basic concept of the amount of information generated or conveyed by some event in terms of the general principle that information reduces possibilities. This builds on the basic concepts of probability theory introduced earlier. The chapter then builds up more sophisticated ideas of information theory inducing the concepts of entropy and conditional entropy which allows, for example, two observers to extract different amounts of information from the same message. It is this idea of conditional entropy that gives us the basis of cryptographic techniques for protecting data from unauthorized interpretation.

The material on information theory is used directly in Chapter 58 on digital communications and telephony. However, as we said earlier, it has much broader importance in setting out the fundamental nature of the 'material' processed by programs.

3 Conclusions

Even within the confines of such a major reference work it is clearly impossible to cover all topics which may be relevant to practising software engineers. We are aware that we have not dealt with issues in discrete mathematics, such as category theory, which are now becoming relevant in many research projects. Similarly we have not dealt, at all, with any of the vast quantity of continuous mathematics which is concerned with the many applications of computers. However, we do believe that the fundamental material which is central to the subject has been covered, at least to some level of detail, in these chapters.

4 References

Dijkstra, E. W. (1976) *A Discipline of Programming*, Prentice Hall.

Hoare, C. A. R. (1969) An axiomatic basis for computer programming. *CACM*, **12**.

Hoare, C. A. R. (1986) *The Mathematics of Programming*, Clarendon Press.

Kyburg, H. E. (1984) *Theory and Measurement*, Cambridge University Press.

Lakatos, I. (1978) *Proofs and Refutations*, Cambridge University Press.

Popper, K. (1972) *Conjectures and Refutations*, Routeledge and Kegan Paul.

Applicable
Mathematics

1

Discrete mathematics

Tim Denvir
Praxis Systems and Brunel University

Contents

1.1 Introduction

This chapter gives a summary of the discrete mathematics which underlies the process of software engineering. Topics covered are those that a software engineer needs to know in order to produce formal specifications, either algebraic (e.g. OBJ or CLEAR), model-oriented (e.g. VDM or Z), or using a process algebra or calculus (e.g. CSP, CCS or LOTOS).

Sections of this chapter are on logic, set theory, functions, relations, and algebras. The account is kept at an elementary level. A more advanced and specialist treatment would probably embark on domain theory, universal algebra, category theory, and topology, which are used to explain the semantics of specification languages such as those mentioned above, and also of some aspects of programming languages. These advanced topics are not covered here, but a final section of this chapter provides a link through homomorphisms to categories, for those who wish to pursue this in greater depth. Algebra is covered further in Chapter 3.

The discrete mathematics which are fundamental to computation, formal languages and automata, are covered in Chapters 9 and 10.

1.2 Logic

1.2.1 Propositions and predicates

Logic – the calculus of propositions and the calculus of predicates – is an essential part of discrete mathematics for software engineering. A logic of propositions is needed to make assertions about properties of objects in the application domain which the software is to model. Propositional and predicate calculus are needed to make statements about programs, in particular to assert that they meet specifications, and that parts of programs have certain effects, such as establishing a relationship between the values of particular variables.

A proposition is a statement which is either true or false. A predicate is a formula such that when its variables are assigned values (of an appropriate type) it becomes a proposition. Examples of propositions are:

Proposition	Value
$7 > 3$	True
$4 = 5$	False
$\{3, 4\} \subseteq \{4, 3, 6\}$	True
The sun is shining	?

Examples of predicates are:

$$x > 3$$
$$y = z - 7$$
$$S1 \subseteq S2$$

A good treatment of propositional and predicate calculus can be found in Manna and Waldinger (1985).

1.2.2 Logical connectives

Propositions can be formed from other propositions by means of logical operators or connectives. The logical connectives are:

$\neg$	not
$\wedge$	and
$\vee$	or
$\Rightarrow$	implies
$\Leftrightarrow$	equivalence

The logical connectives in general capture the intuitive linguistic ideas of 'not', 'and', 'or', 'implies' or 'if ... then ...', and 'if and only if'. Their meanings can be defined by truth tables. If P, Q, R are propositions, then so are:

$$\neg P$$
$$P \wedge Q$$
$$P \vee Q$$
$$P \Rightarrow Q$$
$$P \Leftrightarrow Q$$

Hence compound propositions can be constructed:

$$P \wedge Q \wedge R$$
$$P \wedge (Q \Rightarrow R)$$

etc.

The precedence conventions are in the order given above, so that:

$$\neg P_1 \wedge P_2 \vee P_3 \Rightarrow P_4 \Leftrightarrow P_5$$

is taken as:

$$((((\neg P_1) \wedge P_2) \vee P_3) \Rightarrow P_4) \Leftrightarrow P_5$$

However, it is good practice to insert brackets even where it is unnecessary, if this improves readability.

The meanings of the connectives are defined by the following tables:

P	$\neg P$
true	false
false	true

P	Q	$P \wedge Q$	$P \vee Q$	$P \Rightarrow Q$	$P \Leftrightarrow Q$
true	true	true	true	true	true
true	false	false	true	false	false
false	true	false	true	true	false
false	false	false	false	true	true

The meaning given to implication sometimes causes difficulty when the operand on the left is false. It may help to consider such colloquialisms as 'If it rains today I'll eat my hat', where both component propositions are false, but the compound proposition is considered true. Likewise if one is given a request 'If you're driving to Birmingham today will you take this package with you?', then one is complying with the request by not driving to Birmingham and not taking the package. Likewise, one is also complying by travelling to Birmingham by train and taking the package anyway.

The variable letters such as P, P_1, Q etc. may also stand as propositions. In that case the proposition has a truth value only when its constituent variables are 'interpreted' by being assigned a truth value themselves. However, a proposition may have the same value for all interpretations of its constituent propositional variables. If a proposition is true for all interpretations, it is called a tautology. If a proposition is false for all interpretations, it is called a contradiction.

The following are examples of tautologies:

$$P \vee \neg P$$
$$P \Rightarrow P$$

The following are examples of contradictions:

$$P \wedge \neg P$$
$$\text{true} \Rightarrow \text{false}$$

The truth values of compound propositions can conveniently be calculated by means of truth tables. The technique is to construct a table containing a number of lines, the number being 2^n where n is the number of propositional variables in the proposition; this is the number of possible combinations of the truth values of the propositional variables. A column is drawn for each propositional subexpression, ending with a column for the total proposition. The truth values for each column are then filled in, using the truth tables for the primitive operators.

For example, suppose we wish to establish that:

$$(\neg P \vee Q) \Leftrightarrow (P \Rightarrow Q)$$

is a tautology. We proceed as follows:

P	Q	$\neg$P	$\neg$P$\vee$Q	P$\Rightarrow$Q	($\neg$P$\vee$Q)$\Leftrightarrow$(P$\Rightarrow$Q)
true	true	false	true	true	true
true	false	false	false	false	true
false	true	true	true	true	true
false	false	true	true	true	true

The final column containing 'true' for all combinations of truth values for P and Q shows that it is a tautology.

Truth tables can be used to verify a number of well-known laws. These state that each member of a pair of propositions have the same truth value. The most well known of these are as follows:

P, $\neg\neg$P	idempotence
P, P $\wedge$ P	idempotence
P, P $\vee$ P	
$\neg$P $\vee$ Q, P$\Rightarrow$Q	De Morgan's law
P $\wedge$ Q, $\neg(\neg$P $\vee \neg$Q)	De Morgan's law
P $\vee$ Q, $\neg(\neg$P $\wedge \neg$Q)	Distributive laws
R $\wedge$ (P $\vee$ Q), (R $\wedge$ P) $\vee$ (R $\wedge$ Q)	Distributive laws
R $\vee$ (P $\wedge$ Q), (R $\vee$ P) $\wedge$ (R $\vee$ Q)	Commutativity
P $\wedge$ Q, Q $\wedge$ P	Commutativity
P $\vee$ Q, Q $\vee$ P	Commutativity
P$\Leftrightarrow$Q, Q$\Leftrightarrow$P	Associativity
P $\wedge$ (Q $\wedge$ R), (P $\wedge$ Q) $\wedge$ R	Associativity
P $\vee$ (Q $\vee$ R), (P $\vee$ Q) $\vee$ R	
P $\vee \neg$P, true	
P $\wedge \neg$P, false	

All these laws can be proved from the truth tables. The meanings of the operators can alternatively be given by means of axioms, in which case the above laws can be proved from the axioms by natural deduction.

A sentence in predicate calculus is a proposition which may contain variables, constants, functions, and predicate symbols which stand for truth-valued functions. In addition to the logical operators of propositional logic, in predicate calculus one may also construct sentences using universal and existential quantifiers.

A sentence in predicate calculus consists of any of the following:

1. the truth values true or false

2. a predicate $p(t_1, \ldots, t_n)$ where p is a predicate symbol of arity n, and $t_1, \ldots, t_n$ are terms
   $\neg$P where P is a sentence
   P $\wedge$ Q where P, Q are sentences
   P $\vee$ Q where P, Q are sentences
   P$\Rightarrow$Q where P, Q are sentences
   P$\Leftrightarrow$Q where P, Q are sentences
   $\forall x . P$ where x is any variable and P is a sentence
   $\exists x . Q$ where x is any variable and Q is a sentence
   $\exists ! x . Q$ where x is any variable and Q is a sentence

The last three forms are called 'quantified expressions'. $\forall x . P$ means that P is true for all values of x, and $\exists x . P$ means that P is true for some value of x and $\exists ! x . Q$ means that there is a unique x such that Q is true. $\forall$ is called the universal quantifier, and $\exists$ and $\exists !$ are called existential quantifiers.

Terms may be built from variables, constants, functions and predicates; a term is any of the following:

1. A constant.
2. A variable.
3. A function application $f(t_1, \ldots, t_n)$ where f is a function symbol of arity n and $t_1, \ldots, t_n$ are terms.

Generalizing, predicates may be regarded as special cases of functions and the truth values as particular constants. Function, and predicate symbols may be infix (in which case $\wedge$, $\vee$ etc. are predicate and hence function symbols) and a term may also be a sentence. Predicate calculus is usually typed, in which case variables are designated as being of a particular type, and arguments of functions have to match the types expected. Then the quantified expressions are of form:

$$\forall x : T . P$$
$$\exists x : T . P$$

where T is a type.

A sentence in predicate calculus has a truth value when all free variables are assigned values conforming to their type. This is analogous to the proposition symbols in propositional logic being assigned truth values, resulting in the proposition which contains them having a value.

Examples of predicates are:

$$x > 3$$
$$y = z - 7$$
$$S1 \subseteq S2$$
$$\forall x : \mathbb{Z} . x * x \geqslant 0$$
$$\exists y : \mathbb{R} . y * y = 2$$

where $\mathbb{Z}$ and $\mathbb{R}$ are the sets of integer and real numbers respectively.

In the above, x, y, z would have numeric types and S1, S2 would have types whose members were sets. The symbols $>$ and $\subseteq$ are examples of predicate symbols.

Predicates are used to express conditions in many contexts in computer science: in assertions about the values of variables in a program, in pre- and post-conditions in VDM and other techniques based on Dijkstra's weakest pre-conditions, in loop invariants, and elsewhere. See Dijkstra (1976), Gries (1981), Jones (1986) etc. So, for example, in a relational database, if a relation R is transitive, i.e. is such that whenever, for entities in E, $e_1 R e_2$ and $e_2 R e_3$ we have $e_1 R e_3$, this can be expressed in predicate calculus:

$$\forall e_1, e_2, e_3 : E . (e_1 R e_2 \wedge e_2 R e_3) \Rightarrow e_1 R e_3$$

1.3 Set theory

Set theory is relevant to software engineering for many reasons. It is one of the principal foundations of mathematics. It provides a useful model of various styles of type theory which, in turn, are the basis of abstract data types and data types in programming languages.

Sets can be defined axiomatically, and this is the best formal treatment of the subject. It is also intuitively helpful to think of sets as collections of objects, and this is the approach we shall take in this brief account. Those who wish to pursue an axiomatic treatment are referred to Enderton (1975) or Halmos (1960). In fact the mathematically defined theory of sets can stand as a theory of collections of objects, just as the mathematically defined theory of numbers can stand as a theory of measurable quantities such as mass and length.

A set may be thought of as a collection of any objects of any kind. The collection is unordered, and no distinguishable object can occur in it more than once, i.e. all objects in a set can be distinguished one from another.

There is thus a relation 'belongs to', written as an infix symbol $\in$; we write:

$$x \in S$$

to indicate that x is a member, or belongs to, the set S. x may or may not be a set. The operator $\in$ is thus a predicate symbol, since an expression of the form $x \in S$ is either true or false.

Throughout this account, the words 'element' and 'member' are used interchangeably.

One also denotes the negation of set membership by $\notin$. Thus:

$$x \notin S$$

means the same as:

$$\neg (x \in S)$$

A set is identified by its members. This means that two sets S1 and S2 are equal, i.e. the same set, if and only if they have the same members.

A set with a finite number of members $x_1, x_2, \ldots, x_n$ can be denoted:

$$\{x_1, \ldots, x_n\}$$

Since the members of a set are in no particular order, the order of the $x_1, \ldots, x_n$ is irrelevant. Also, since there is no concept of repetition of the elements, repetitions of any of the values x are irrelevant. Thus the following all denote the same set:

$$\{1, 2, 3\}$$
$$\{3, 1, 2\}$$
$$\{3, 1, 3, 2, 2\}$$

and the set they denote has three members. (Note that the last form may not be legal in some specification or programming languages.)

It follows that the empty set, that set which has no members, is denoted:

$$\{\}$$

Other forms are also written, for example $\bigcirc$. Since a set is identified by its members, it follows that there is just one empty set, the identity of which is independent of the way in which it is defined. Thus, for example, the set of numbers greater than two and less than one is the same set as the set of planets in the solar system which are larger than Jupiter.

Sets may also be defined implicitly, by means of the properties of their members. If $P(x)$ is a predicate in which the variable x occurs free (see next section), then:

$$\{x \mid P(x)\}$$

denotes the set of all values x such that $P(x)$ is true.

1.3.1 Free and bound

The value of an expression like $x \wedge y$ depends on the values of the variables x and y. In such a case x and y are said to occur 'free' in the expression. On the other hand, in an expression like $\{x \mid P(x)\}$, x is said to occur 'bound'; the value of the expression does not depend on any value which x might have in its surrounding context. The variable x plays much the same role as it does in the (more familiar) expression:

$$\sum_{x=1}^{n} A_x$$

A more rigorous definition follows:

A variable x is said to occur free or bound in an expression e under the following circumstances:

1. x occurs free in the expression x, i.e. the expression which consists solely of the variable x.
2. If x occurs free in the expression e, then it occurs free in the expression (e).
3. If x occurs free in the expression e, then it occurs free in the expression $f(e_1, e_2, \ldots, e_n)$ where one of $e_1, \ldots, e_n$ is e, and f is a function or predicate symbol. This is also true for infix forms of the function or predicate symbol.
4. If x occurs free in the expression p, and x and y are different variable symbols, then x occurs free in each of:
   (a) $\forall y . p$
   (b) $\exists y . p$
   (c) $\{y \mid p\}$.
5. If x occurs free in e, then x occurs free in $\{e_1, \ldots e_n\}$ where $e = e_i$ for some i, $1 \leqslant i \leqslant n$.
6. x occurs bound in each of:
   (a) $\forall x . p$
   (b) $\exists x . p$
   (c) $\{x \mid p\}$.
7. If x occurs bound in e, then x occurs bound in (e).
8. If x occurs bound in the expression e, then it occurs bound in the expression $f(e_1, \ldots, e_n)$ where one of $e_1, \ldots, e_n$ is e, and f is a function or predicate symbol. This is also true for infix forms of the function or predicate symbol.
9. If x occurs bound in the expression p, and x and y are different variable symbols, then x occurs bound in each of:
   (a) $\forall y . p$
   (b) $\exists y . p$
   (c) $\{y \mid p\}$.
10. If x occurs bound in e, then x occurs bound in $\{e_1, \ldots e_n\}$ where $e = e_i$ for some i, $1 \leqslant i \leqslant n$.

If the variable y does not occur free in p, then the following pairs of expressions are equal and interchangeable:

$$\begin{array}{ll} \forall x . p & \forall y . p_{[x \to y]} \\ \exists x . p & \exists y . p_{[x \to y]} \\ \{x \mid p\} & \{y \mid p_{[x \to y]}\} \end{array}$$

Where $p_{[x \to y]}$ denotes the expression p with all free occurrences of x replaced by y.

1.3.1.1 Examples

Logic and set theory are useful for formally expressing assertions about, for example, the desired effect of a program:

$$\forall i, j \in \{x \,|\, x \in \mathbb{N} \wedge x \leqslant \text{len file}\} . i \leqslant j \Rightarrow$$
$$\text{KEY (file}(i)) \leqslant \text{KEY (file}(j))$$

All the items in the file are ordered by their KEY fields.

$$\forall p \in \text{Personnel} . \text{Job\_title}(p) = \text{``supervisor''} \Rightarrow \text{Grade}(p) \geqslant 6$$

Everyone in the personnel database whose Job-title is 'supervisor' has a grade of at least 6.

1.3.2 Set operators

Operators on sets allow new sets to be defined in terms of existing sets. Again, the meaning of the set operators can be defined axiomatically, and that approach is taken in Enderton (1975) and Halmos (1960). Here we shall define ε ⌐perations constructively, in terms of their membership relations, since this matches more easily the intuitive view of sets as collections of objects which is already taken.

1. *Set union.* $S \cup T$ where S and T are sets, is the set satisfying:

   $$x \in (S \cup T) \text{ if and only if } x \in S \text{ or } x \in T$$

2. *Set intersection.* $S \cap T$ where S and T are sets, is the set satisfying:

   $$x \in (S \cap T) \text{ if and only if } x \in S \text{ and } x \in T$$

3. *Set difference.* $S - T$ where S and T are sets, is the set satisfying:

   $$x \in (S - T) \text{ if and only if } x \in S \text{ and } x \notin T$$

The effect of these set operators can be depicted by so-called 'Venn diagrams'. These are shown in *Figures 1.1–1.3*.

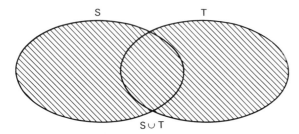

Figure 1.1 Union

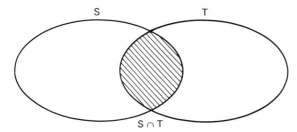

Figure 1.2 Intersection

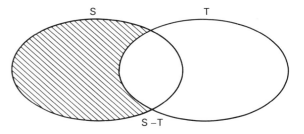

Figure 1.3 Set subtraction

Certain facts are easily proved from the definitions:

$S \cup T = T \cup S$	Commutativity
$S \cap T = T \cap S$	Commutativity
$(S \cup T) \cup R = S \cup (T \cup R)$	Associativity
$(S \cap T) \cap R = S \cap (T \cap R)$	Associativity
$S \cap (T \cup R) = (S \cap T) \cup (S \cap R)$	Distributivity
$S \cup (T \cap R) = (S \cup T) \cap (S \cup R)$	Distributivity

$$(S \cup T) - R = (S - R) \cup (T - R)$$
$$(S \cap T) - R = (S - R) \cap (T - R)$$
$$R - (S \cup T) = (R - S) - T$$

$$\{x_1, \ldots, x_n\} \cup \{y_1, \ldots, y_m\} = \{x_1, \ldots, x_n, y_1, \ldots, y_m\}$$

$$\{x\,|\,p\} \cup \{x\,|\,q\} = \{x\,|\,p \vee q\}$$
$$\{x\,|\,p\} \cap \{x\,|\,q\} = \{x\,|\,p \wedge q\}$$
$$\{x\,|\,p\} - \{x\,|\,q\} = \{x\,|\,p \wedge \neg q\}$$

Since the set operators $\cup$ and $\cap$ are associative and commutative, distributed forms of these are often used. Given an index range $1 .. n$, one may write:

$$\bigcup_{i=1}^{n} S_i \quad \bigcap_{i=1}^{n} S_i$$

Likewise, given an index set I, one may write:

$$\bigcup_{i \notin I} S_i \quad \bigcap_{i \notin I} S_i$$

The meaning is, for each respective case:

$$\{x \,|\, \exists i \in I . x \in S_i\} \quad \text{for distributed union}$$
$$\{x \,|\, \forall i \in I . x \in S_i\} \quad \text{for distributed intersection}$$

For the $1 .. n$ forms, the index set I can be taken as $\{i \,|\, i \in \mathbb{Z} \wedge 1 \leqslant i \leqslant n\}$. Distributed and $\wedge$ and distributed or $\vee$ can be defined in an analogous way

1.3.3 Set relations

Three set relation operators are in common use. These are $\subseteq$ (subset), $\subset$ (proper subset), $=$ (equality). If S1, S2 are sets, then the expressions:

$$S1 \subseteq S2$$
$$S1 \subset S2$$
$$S1 = S2$$

each have the value *true* or *false*.

The subset relation is defined as follows:

S1 ⊆ S2 if and only if all members of S1 are also members of S2.

The proper subset relation is defined:

S1 ⊂ S2 if and only if S1 ⊆ S2 and there is at least one member of S2 which is not a member of S1.

Equality of sets has already been defined:

S1 = S2 if all members of S1 are members of S2 and all members of S2 are members of S1.

The subset relation can be illustrated by the Venn diagram shown in *Figure 1.4.*

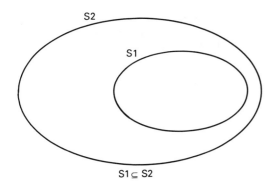

Figure 1.4   Subset

The following facts follow immediately from the definitions:

$$S1 \subset S2 \Leftrightarrow S1 \subseteq S2 \land \neg(S2 \subseteq S1)$$
$$\Leftrightarrow S1 \subseteq S2 \land S1 \neq S2$$
$$S1 = S2 \Leftrightarrow S1 \subseteq S2 \land S2 \subseteq S1$$
$$S1 \subseteq S2 \Leftrightarrow \forall x . x \in S1 \Rightarrow x \in S2$$
$$S1 = S2 \Leftrightarrow \forall x . x \in S1 \Leftrightarrow x \in S2$$

If S1 ⊆ S2 then S1 ∪ S3 ⊆ S2 ∪ S3
If S1 ⊆ S2 then S1 ∩ S3 ⊆ S2 ∩ S3

1.3.4 Cardinality

For finite sets, the cardinality of the set is equal to the number of its members. A unary (or monadic) operator is used for this:

card S   is the number of distinct members of S, when S is finite.

'card' is not defined for infinite sets. Various symbols are in common use for this operator, in particular:

|S|
and
#S

The following facts can easily be shown:

card {} = 0

card S1 + card S2 = card (S1 ∪ S2) + card (S1 ∩ S2)

1.3.5 Powersets

The powerset operator applied to a set S gives the set of all its subsets. We write:

$$\mathscr{P}S$$

which is defined:

$$\mathscr{P}S = \{x \mid x \subseteq S\}$$

Since, for any set S, S ⊆ S and {} ⊆ S, it follows that:

{} ∈ 𝒫S
S ∈ 𝒫S

In computer science (and software engineering) it is often useful to consider the set of all finite subsets of a set S. This is easy to define, and is sometimes written:

$$\mathscr{F}S$$

The definition will be given when we have dealt with functions. Of course if S is itself finite, then its powerset will also be finite, and so 𝒫S and ℱS will be the same. For a finite set S, the cardinality of its powerset bears the following relationship to the cardinality of the set itself:

$$\text{card } \mathscr{P}S = 2^{\text{card } S}$$

1.3.6 Cartesian product

If S and T are sets, a further set can be constructed which is the set of ordered pairs of members of S and T. We write:

S × T

to denote the set of pairs (x, y) such that $x \in S$ and $y \in T$.

Since 'pairs' have not yet been defined, this definition is strictly not meaningful. An intuitive concept of ordered pair is that the order of the elements of the pair is significant and that repetition may perhaps be allowed. To give this idea more formal substance, we need to define operators on the set which is denoted S × T. First a constructor of pairs of any two sets S, T (and indeed, S and T may be the same set) can be defined, 'make$_{S,T}$' takes a member of the set S and a member of the set T, and yields a member of the set S × T.

The second operator, 'first$_{S,T}$', takes a member of the set S × T (i.e. a 'pair') and yields a member of S:

$$\text{first}_{S,T}(\text{make}_{S,T}(x, y)) = x$$

Likewise, a third operator, 'second$_{S,T}$', takes a member of the set S × T and yields a member of T:

$$\text{second}_{S,T}(\text{make}_{S,T}(x, y)) = y$$

When the context is clear, and this is more usual, the subscripts S, T are omitted. Also the 'make' operator is not normally named, and the mix–fix notation:

$$(\_,\_)$$

is used to construct pairs. The underline symbols indicate the positions of the arguments when the operator is applied to specific values. Thus the above may be rewritten in a more abbreviated way:

$second((x, y)) = y$

Occasionally for pair-construction, other brackets are used, for example, $[\_,\_]$ or $\langle\_,\_\rangle$.

Example. The complex numbers may be regarded as the Cartesian product $\mathbb{R} \times \mathbb{R}$ of pairs of real numbers.

We can generalize the foregoing concept by constructing multiple Cartesian products. If $S_1, S_2, \ldots, S_n$ are sets, then the Cartesian product of n-tuples is written:

$$S_1 \times S_2 \times \ldots \times S_n$$

or

$$\underset{i=1}{\overset{n}{\times}} S_i$$

A corresponding 'make' operator is defined:

$$\text{make}_T(x_1, \ldots, x_n)$$

where $x_i \in S_i$, $1 \leqslant i \leqslant n$, and:

$$T = S_1 \times S_2 \times \ldots \times S_n$$

Selection operators are likewise defined:

$$\text{select}_{T,i}(x_1, \ldots, x_n) = x_i$$

for $1 \leqslant i \leqslant n$. If k is a tuple which is a member of T, instead of writing:

$$\text{select}_{T,i} k$$

one more often writes $k(i)$ or $k[i]$. The selection operators are often known as 'projections'.

The cardinality of a Cartesian product is related to the cardinality of its components:

$$\text{card } (S \times T) = \text{card } S * \text{card } T$$

In general:

$$\text{card } \underset{i=1}{\overset{n}{\times}} S_i = \prod_{i=1}^{n} \text{card } S_i$$

1.3.6.1 Examples

There are numerous examples of Cartesian products, and tuples which are members of them, in software engineering. Arrays in programming languages are one. An array of n integers is a representation of a member of the Cartesian product:

$$\times_{i=1}^{n} \mathbb{Z}$$

where $\mathbb{Z}$ is the set of integers.

1.3.7 Labelled Cartesian products

An elaboration of multiple Cartesian products, whose members are n-tuples or tuples, is the concept of 'labelled' or 'tagged' Cartesian product. This concept is used mainly in computer science contexts rather than in mathematical ones, since it provides a convenient mathematical model of files, tuples in databases, Pascal-style records, etc.

Let L be an arbitrary set of labels or tags. It is convenient for L not to be of finite cardinality, so as to provide an unlimited source of labels. Then a labelled or tagged Cartesian product T can be constructed from a number of constituent sets $S_1, \ldots, S_n$ and the same number of distinct labels $L_1, \ldots, L_n$ where $L_i \in L$, $1 \leqslant i \leqslant n$, and defined by the following notation:

$$T = L_1 : S_1 \times L_2 : S_2 \times \ldots \times L_n : S_n$$

When T is defined as above, it denotes a set with operators 'make-T' and 'select-T'; 'make-T' takes members of the sets S_1, $\ldots, S_n$ as arguments and yields a result which is a member of T:

$$\text{make-T}(s_1, s_2, \ldots, s_n)$$

where

$$s_i \in S_i, 1 \leqslant i \leqslant n$$

The select-T operator takes a member of T as its first argument and a member of L as its second argument. To be well defined, the member of L must be one of the $L_1, \ldots, L_n$ occurring in the definition of T. The select-T operator yields as a result a member of the set S_i which corresponds to the label which stands as its second parameter; this will be the selected component of the tuple which is a member of T.

The definition of the operators and the set T is captured by the following rule. If $t \in T$ is such that:

$$t = \text{make-T}(s_1, \ldots, s_n)$$

where $T = L_1 : S_1 \times \ldots \times L_n : S_n$, then:

$$\text{select-T}(t, L_i) = s_i$$

for each $1 \leqslant i \leqslant n$.

1.3.7.1 Notation

In the definition of a tagged Cartesian product the product symbols ' $\times$ ' are frequently omitted.

The 'select-T' operator is often simply written as $\_.\_$ or $\_(\_)$, so that in the above definition one would write:

$$t . L_i = s_i$$

or:

$$L_i(t) = s_i$$

The set T is determined from context, by the term t.

1.3.7.2 Example

Pers = NAME: Text
           AGE: $\mathbb{N}$
           OCC: Text
           SALARY: $\mathbb{N}$

Let:

fred = make-Pers("Fred", 40, "Hacker", 8000)

then:

fred.NAME = "Fred"
fred.AGE = 40

1.4 Functions

Given two sets, S, T there is a set of functions from S to T, denoted S → T. If f is such a function, then f belongs to this set, i.e.:

$$f \in S \rightarrow T$$

So S → T is the set of all functions of this type.

Given a function f as above, and a member x of S, then f may be *applied* to x to yield a member t of T. t is often said to be the 'image' of x under f. Function application is an operator whose usual syntax is _(_), e.g.:

$$f(x) = t$$

(In texts following an older tradition, function application is sometimes written: xf.)

Functions are usually considered as 'total', which means that for every $x \in S$, the application $f(x)$ of f to x is defined. Functions which are not total are said to be 'partial'. Familiar examples of partial functions are 'square-root' applied to real numbers, which is not defined for negative numbers, and division, which is not defined for a second argument of zero.

The notation S → T is usually taken to mean the set of total functions from S to T. Another often used notation is T^S. The set of partial and total functions is sometimes written:

$$S \nrightarrow T$$

although S → T is often used with this meaning.

The collection of values in S for which f yields a value in T is called the 'domain' of f. Thus:

$$\text{dom} f = \{x \mid x \in S \land \exists y \in T . f(x) = y\}$$

Likewise the collection of members of T to which f maps some member of S is called the 'range' of f. Thus:

$$\text{ran} f = \{y \mid y \in T \land \exists x \in S . f(x) = y\}$$

For $f \in S \rightarrow T$, T is called the 'codomain' of f. There is no accepted term for S, although if f is total, then $S = \text{dom} f$. For partial f, the term 'source' has been suggested for S. Unfortunately, there is little general agreement about many of these terms; for example, 'range' is often used to mean 'codomain' as defined above.

Associated with any function $f \in S \rightarrow T$, there is a set of pairs called the 'graph' of f, defined:

$$\text{graph} f = \{(x, y) \mid (x, y) \in S \times T \land f(x) = y\}$$

Because any function f applied to a member x of its domain yields a unique value, the set of pairs which constitute the graph of f has the following uniqueness property:

$$\forall x \in \text{dom} f, y_1, y_2 \in \text{ran} f .$$
$$(x, y_1) \in \text{graph} f \land (x, y_2) \in \text{graph} f \Rightarrow y_1 = y_2$$

Conversely, any subset of S × T which conforms to this condition is associated with a unique function. Because there is very close association between a function and its graph, they are sometimes considered identical. In the Z notation, for example, functions are defined as being their graphs.

For $f \in S \rightarrow T$ and $S1 \subseteq S$, a function restriction operator can be defined, which restricts the domain of f to $S1 \cap \text{dom} f$. The function $f \mid S1$ is defined such that:

$$\text{dom} (f \mid S1) = S1 \cap \text{dom} f$$

$$(f \mid S1)(x) = f(x) \text{ for } x \in S1 \cap \text{dom} f$$
$$(f \mid S1)(x) \text{ is not defined for } x \in S - (S1 \cap \text{dom} f)$$

An extended function can be defined, given $f : S \rightarrow T$. The extended function, usually also denoted by f (by 'abuse of notation'), is of type $\mathscr{P}S \rightarrow \mathscr{P}T$, and is defined such that, for $S1 \subseteq S$:

$$f(S1) = \{y \mid \exists x \in S1 . y = f(x)\}$$

If $T1 = f(S1)$, T1 is sometimes called the 'image' of S1 under f.

In some computer science contexts, it can be useful to consider the 'finite functions' from S to T, that is, partial functions whose domains are finite. For example, such finite functions can be an abstraction of arrays. An n-dimensional array whose elements are of type T and whose indices range from l to m is a representation of a finite function which is a member of $\mathbb{N} \rightarrow T$ (or, synonymously, TN). There is no accepted notation for distinguishing finite partial functions from general partial functions. In the Z notation the symbol $\mapsto\mkern-14mu\to$ is used, but this is not widely recognized.

Thus, given sets S, T, we can construct new sets $S \nrightarrow T, S \rightarrow T$, being the set of total and partial functions respectively from S to T. These can again stand as abstractions of data types in computing, as well as abstractions of computations, i.e. algorithms, and programs whose executions calculate the results of applying the abstract functions. This gives rise to questions as to whether we need to distinguish finite functions as abstractions of finitary data types, i.e. types whose values contain finite information, or even whether we should distinguish computable functions at the abstract level.

These are debatable questions. Provided a function is finitely representable, for example, by an algorithm with a finite description, there is no reason why it should not be an abstraction of a value of some data type. Indeed, in several high-level languages, procedures are treated as first-class data objects, for which non-finite functions would be required as abstractions.

It is certainly not possible to represent non-computable functions in a computer program, and so one might think that restricting the class of functions in a specification to computable functions would make it more difficult to specify unimplementable requirements. However, this is not usually done. To enable general proofs that any given function definition defines a computable function would require excessive restrictions on the expressibility of the logical calculus used for the definitions, to the point of negating their usefulness.

1.4.1 Function composition

Given functions $f \in R \rightarrow S$ and $g \in S \rightarrow T$, a 'function composition' operator o is defined:

$$g \circ f \in R \rightarrow T$$
$$\forall x \in \text{dom} f . (g \circ f)(x) = g(f(x))$$

Function composition is associative, i.e. given $f \in R \rightarrow S$, $g \in S \rightarrow T$, $h \in T \rightarrow U$, then:

$$h \circ (g \circ f) = (h \circ g) \circ f$$

since, for any $x \in \text{dom} f$:

$$(h \circ (g \circ f))(x) = ((h \circ g) \circ f)(x) = h(g(f(x)))$$

A statement in a programming language can be regarded as a

function which transforms values of the variables in whose scope the statement lies. Given two such statements S1 and S2, their sequence:

S1; S2

has the effect of $f2 \circ f1$ where S1 has the effect of the function $f1$ and S2 has the effect of $f2$. For this reason, in some contexts, the statement combinator ';' has been adopted as a mathematical notation, so that:

$f1; f2$

means the same as:

$f2 \circ f1$

1.4.2 Functions of more than one argument

Functions can in general have more than one argument. A function f with two arguments, each of which belongs to a set S, T respectively, is characterized:

$f: S, T \rightarrow R$

where R is the codomain of f. f is then applied to two (or more) arguments, by writing:

$f(x, y)$

where $x \in S$, $y \in T$. This notation is traditional and familiar from school mathematics. It can be explained in terms of functions of one argument in two separate ways. The first is to treat the arguments as a tuple belonging to a Cartesian product, thus:

$f: S \times T \rightarrow R$

Then the function application uses the tuple construction (x, y). The second way of explaining a function of more than one argument is by 'Currying', named after the mathematician H. B. Curry, but in fact due to Schönfinkel (1958). A Curried function takes the arguments one at a time and produces a new function, until the last argument is taken. Thus:

Curry $f: S \rightarrow (T \rightarrow R)$

When Curry f is applied to an element of S it yields a function which, when applied to an element of T, yields an element of R. This technique can be extended to any number of arguments. Currying functions enables them to be treated in terms of λ-expressions, and also gives rise to a more succinct explanation of partial functions.

1.4.3 Properties of functions

For the set of functions $S \rightarrow S$ mapping a set S to itself, there is a special function called the 'identity' mapping or function, id, which maps each member of S to itself. Thus:

$id(x) = x$ for all $x \in S$

It follows that for all functions $f \in S \rightarrow S$:

$id \circ f = f = f \circ id$

If $f, g \in S \rightarrow S$ are such that $f \circ g = id$, then g is called the 'inverse' of f. It follows that f is also the inverse of g because:

$g \circ (f \circ g) = g \circ id = g$
$g \circ (f \circ g) = (g \circ f) \circ g$

so:

$g \circ f = id$

The inverse of a function f is written f^{-1}.

A function $f \in S \rightarrow T$ is called 'one–one' or an 'injection' if, for each $y \in ran f$, there is at most one $x \in dom f$ such that $y = f(x)$. This is expressible as:

$\forall x_1, x_2 \in dom f . f(x_1) = f(x_2) \Rightarrow x_1 = x_2$

It follows that, for an injection f, if f is finite:

card dom f = card ran f

A function $f \in S \rightarrow T$ which is such that ran f = T is called a 'surjection' and is said to map S onto T.

A total function which is an injection and a surjection is called a 'bijection' or a 'one–one correspondence'. A bijection has the property that its domain and range are of equal cardinality. This fact can be used as a definition of cardinality: a set S is of cardinality n if there is a bijection from S to the range of natural numbers $\{1:n\}$. We can then extend the idea of cardinality to define cardinality of infinite sets: two sets S and T have the same cardinality if there is a bijection from S to T. A set S is said to be countable if either S is finite or if there is a bijection from S to $\mathbb{N}$. A set is said to be uncountable if it is not countable.

The following standard results are easily proved:

$\mathbb{Z}$ is countable
$\mathscr{P}\mathbb{N}$ is uncountable
$\mathbb{N} \rightarrow \mathbb{N}$ is uncountable
$\mathbb{N} \rightarrow \mathbf{B}$ is uncountable
$\mathbb{R}$ is uncountable
$\mathscr{F}\mathbb{N}$ is countable

where:

1. $\mathbb{Z}$ is the set of integers
2. $\mathbb{N}$ is the set of natural numbers
3. $\mathbf{B}$ is the set of truth values, true and false
4. $\mathbb{R}$ is the set of real numbers
5. $\mathscr{P}$ stands for powerset
6. $\mathscr{F}$ stands for finite powerset

Any Cartesian product of countable sets is countable.

Since, in general, computer programs transform input values to output values in a predictable, definable, and deterministic way, functions are abstractions of computer programs and of many of the constructs which occur in computer programs. In general any construct in a program is an implementation of a function which transforms values of inputs and variables in whose scope the construct lies, to new values of those variables, and possibly output values. Examples of such constructs include statements, 'functions' (e.g. Pascal functions), procedures, expressions.

1.4.4 Disjoint union

A further way of constructing a set from existing sets is by means of the 'disjoint union', 'discriminated union', or, simply, 'sum' operator (all of these being synonymous).

Given two sets, S, T, a new set can be constructed which is usually denoted:

$$S \oplus T$$

or simply:

$$S + T$$

(Note the symbol $\oplus$ is used for other purposes in the $\mathbb{Z}$ language.) This set is intuitively like set union, except that if S and T share members, then these are represented in $S \oplus T$ by distinct copies of themselves. Thus $S \oplus T$ can be modelled by the union of disjoint copies of S and T. However, the definition of $S \oplus T$ is given by axioms relating the operators which can be applied to it. These operators are:

inj1: $S \rightarrow S \oplus T$
inj2: $T \rightarrow S \oplus T$
proj1: $S \oplus T \rightarrow S$
proj2: $S \oplus T \rightarrow T$

The operators above are related by the rules:

For $x \in S$, $y \in T$:

proj1(inj1(x)) = x
proj2(inj2(y)) = y

Frequently, when the context permits no risk of ambiguity, the injection and projection function applications are omitted.

Disjoint union can be modelled by constructing the union of isomorphic copies of S and T, by, for example, labelling the copies of the members of S with the label '1', and the copies of the members of T with the label '2'. Thus if $x \in S \cap T$, then $1:x$ and $2:x$ will separately be members of $S \oplus T$. These can be modelled in a computer program by records which have an appropriate label field.

Clearly:

card $(S \oplus T)$ = card S + card T

It also makes sense to talk about $S \oplus S$, and card $(S \oplus S)$ = $2*$card S.

Like (Cartesian) products, disjoint unions, or sums, can be extended to a multiplicity:

$$\bigoplus_{i=1}^{n} S_i$$

denotes the disjoint union of n sets, and:

$$\bigoplus_{i \in I} S_i$$

denotes the disjoint union of an I-indexed family of sets. The corresponding injection and projection functions are, in both cases:

inj$_i$: $S_i \rightarrow \bigoplus S_i$
proj$_i$: $\bigoplus S_i \rightarrow S_i$

with the set of rules:

proj$_i$(inj$_i$(x)) = x for $x \in S_i$

It is, of course, perfectly possible, and straightforward, to define a concept of labelled or tagged disjoint union, with the injection and projection functions being distinguished from each other by the tag which labels the component set S_i, in an analogous way to tagged Cartesian products. This is slightly less common, however, and we shall not pursue the details here.

1.4.5 Sequences

The multiple Cartesian product:

$$\overset{n}{\underset{i=1}{\times}} S_i$$

can be further extended to a general sequence, in the case where all the S_i are the same set S. The following abbreviation is used:

$$S^n = \overset{n}{\underset{i=1}{\times}} S$$

A sequence S* of elements over S is defined:

$$S^* = \bigcup_{n \geq 0} S^n$$

Thus S* contains as elements all tuples of the form:

make$_{S^n}(x_1, \ldots, x_n)$

where $x_1, \ldots, x_n \in S$. These elements of S* are more often abbreviated:

$[x_1, \ldots, x_n]$

The context usually determines to what set S^n the sequence belongs. S^0 is taken to be that set containing just one member, the empty sequence. So:

$S^0 = \{[\,]\}$

Other brackets for delimiting sequences are in common use: $\langle \rangle$ and ( ).

The empty sequence, abbreviated $[\,]$, is strictly:

make$_S($)

for some S. However, it is usual practice to consider all such empty sequences identical, i.e.:

make$_S($) = make$_T($)

even when $S \neq T$. However, the semantic situations in which the distinction arises are infrequent in practice, and it is possible to define the semantics of the empty sequences either as being distinguished by their type or not.

The same selection operator is defined on sequences as is defined on multiple tuples. If $[x_1, \ldots, x_n] \in S^*$, then select$_S$:S*, $\mathbb{N} \rightarrow S$ is defined:

select$_S([x_1, \ldots, x_n], i) = x_i$

for $1 \leq i \leq n$. This operator is usually abbreviated; if $t = [x_1, \ldots, x_n]$:

$t(i) = x_i$

or:

$t_i = x_i$

Other operators are defined on sequences. Assuming $t = [x_1, \ldots, x_n]$, hd:S* $\rightarrow$ S and tl:S* $\rightarrow$ S* are defined:

hd $t = x_1$
tl $t = [x_2, \ldots, x_n]$

The above are not defined when applied to empty sequences.

1.4.6 Concatenation

$\|: S^*, S^* \rightarrow S^*$ is defined:

$(t\|u)(i) = t(i)$ for $1 \leqslant i \leqslant n$ where $t = [x_1, \ldots x_n]$
$= u(i - n)$ for $n < i$

A length operator len, $|\_|$ or $\#$, where len: $S^* \rightarrow N$ is defined:

len $t = n$

Some obvious observations can be made:

len $(t\|u) = $ len $t + $ len u
len tl $t = $ len $t - 1$
$t(i) = ($ tl $t)(i - 1)$ for $i > 1$
$t\|[\,] = t = [\,]\|t$
len $[\,] = 0$

All these operators, and hence sequences themselves, can be defined in an axiomatic style.

1.4.6.1 Examples

Composite sets constructed using the various set operations can be used to define abstractions of the many different program language data types such as arrays, records, files, etc.

1.5 Relations

A relation R between two sets A, B is a subset of the Cartesian product $A \times B$. Thus any such relation is a set of pairs (a, b) with $a \in A$, $b \in B$.

A relation is thus, in general, a many–many correspondence. It can be used to capture the possession of attributes by individuals. The database for a telephone accounts system, for example, could indicate the possession of various facilities by subscribers by means of a relation between the set of subscribers and the set of facilities.

Another intuitively immediate example is the various relationships between members of a population. The relation 'is a cousin of' is a many–many relation from the set of members of the population to itself.

A relation R from a set S to the same set S is said to be 'on' S.

Functions are, as already stated, closely associated with their graphs. For a function $f: A \rightarrow B$, the graph of f is indeed a set of pairs and is a relation:

graph $f \subseteq A \times B$

For this reason, in some disciplines (Z for example) functions are regarded as special cases of relations.

We normally write aRb for $(a, b) \in R$.

1.5.1 Properties of relations

There are a number of special properties and classes of relations on a set. A relation R on a set S is defined to be:

1. *Symmetric*, if, for all $a, b \in S$, $aRb \Rightarrow bRa$.
2. *Reflexive* if, for all $a \in S$, aRa.
3. *Transitive* if for all $a, b, c \in S$, $aRb \wedge bRc \Rightarrow aRc$.
4. *Antisymmetric*, if for all distinct $a, b \in S$, $aRb \Rightarrow \neg bRa$.
5. *Irreflexive*, if for all $a \in S$, $\neg aRa$.

1.5.2 Equivalence relations

A relation R on a set S is called an 'equivalence relation' if R is reflexive, transitive, and symmetric.

Such a relation conveniently captures ideas of equivalence, or possessing the same properties. For example, in a database of subscribers for a telephone system, there is an equivalence relation relating subscribers who have the same facilities. There is an equivalence relation between terms in an algebra which evaluate to the same value, or between computer programs which calculate the same function.

Two degenerate equivalence relations on a set S can be distinguished. The maximal relation relates each member of S to every other:

R1 $= \{(a, b) | a, b \in S\}$

The other degenerate relation is the minimal equivalence relation in which each member of S is related only to itself:

R2 $= \{(a, a) | a \in S\}$

1.5.3 Equivalence classes

Every equivalence relation R on a set S induces a set of 'equivalence classes', which comprise a partition of S. That is, each equivalence class is a subset of S, they are pair-wise disjoint, and every member of S belongs to some equivalence class. Each equivalence class is such that all the members of the equivalence class are related to each other by R. Thus the definition of the equivalence classes induced by R on S is:

$\{SS | SS \subseteq S \wedge \forall a \in SS. \forall b \in S. aRb \Leftrightarrow b \in SS\}$

Transitivity of the equivalence relation R ensures that the equivalence classes are pair-wise disjoint.

An example is the relation of equality modulo n for some number n, over the integers. This partitions the integers into n equivalence classes. The numbers in each class will give the same remainder when divided by n.

A common notation for the unique equivalence class to which an element a belongs is $[a]$.

1.5.4 Partial orders

A relation which is reflexive, transitive, and antisymmetric is called a 'partial order'. A set S with a partial order R is called a 'partially ordered set' or 'poset', and written (S, R).

Many examples of partially ordered sets exist: for example, $(\mathscr{P}S, \subseteq)$ for any set S, $(\mathbb{N}, \leqslant)$, $(\mathbb{R}, \leqslant)$, $(\mathbb{R}, \geqslant)$.

Given a poset $(S, \subseteq)$, the relation $\subseteq$ can be extended to subsets of S thus:

$x \subseteq T$
$P \subseteq y$

where $P, T \subseteq S$, means that:

$\forall z \in T. x \subseteq z$
$\forall z \in P. z \subseteq y$

respectively. In those cases, x is a lower bound of T, and y is an upper bound of P.

The greatest lower bound (glb) written $\sqcap T$ and least upper bound (lub) written $\sqcup T$ of a subset T of S are defined:

$(\sqcap T) \subseteq T \wedge \forall x \in S. x \subseteq T \Rightarrow x \subseteq (\sqcap T)$
$T \subseteq (\sqcup T) \wedge \forall x \in S. T \subseteq x \Rightarrow (\sqcup T) \subseteq x$

The lub $\sqcup\{x, y\}$ of a pair of elements x, y can be written as an operator $x \sqcup y$. Likewise the glb can be written $x \sqcap y$. These are called the 'join' and 'meet' respectively. These operators can easily be proved to be commutative and associative, i.e.:

$$x \sqcup y = y \sqcup x$$
$$x \sqcap y = y \sqcap x$$
$$x \sqcup (y \sqcup z) = (x \sqcup y) \sqcup z$$
$$x \sqcap (y \sqcap z) = (x \sqcap y) \sqcap z$$

Also:

$$x \sqcup x = x$$
$$x \sqcap x = x$$

A poset in which every pair of elements has a meet and a join is called a 'lattice'. It follows by induction that in a lattice every finite subset has a lub and a glb.

A lattice can be defined in terms of the meet and join operators, in which case:

$$x \sqsubseteq y \Leftrightarrow x \sqcap y = x \wedge x \sqcup y = y$$

A set of propositions closed under $\wedge$ and $\vee$ forms such a lattice with $\sqcap$ corresponding to $\wedge$, $\sqcup$ corresponding to $\vee$, and $\sqsubseteq$ corresponding to $\Rightarrow$.

A lattice in which every subset has a lub and a glb is called a 'complete lattice'.

If $(S, \sqsubseteq)$ is such a lattice, then $\sqsubseteq S$ is written $\top$, and $\sqcap S$ is written $\bot$, the top and bottom elements respectively. Thus $\bot \sqsubseteq S, S \sqsubseteq \top$.

An example of a complete lattice is the set of all functions of type $A \to B$ where A is any set and where $\sqsubseteq$ is defined:

$$f \sqsubseteq g \Leftrightarrow \forall x \in A . f(x) \Rightarrow g(x)$$

Then $f \sqcap g$ is:

$$(f \sqcap g)(x) = f(x) \wedge g(x)$$
$$(f \sqcup g)(x) = f(x) \vee g(x)$$

Further, for a set of functions $F \subseteq A \to B$:

$$\sqcap F(x) = \forall f \in F . f(x)$$
$$\sqcup F(x) = \exists f \in F . f(x)$$

Lattices are fundamental to domain theory, which forms the theory of denotational semantics. See, for example, Schmidt (1986), Gordon (1979), or Stoy (1977).

1.5.5 Algebras

An algebra consists of a finite number of sets (its carriers) together with a finite number of functions or (synonymously) operations defined on those sets. Constants can be considered as operations with no arguments.

1.5.5.1 Examples

1. The Boolean algebra consisting of the set $\mathbf{B}$ with constants true, false, and operations:

$$\neg: \mathbf{B} \to \mathbf{B}$$
$$\wedge: \mathbf{B}, \mathbf{B} \to \mathbf{B}$$
$$\vee: \mathbf{B}, \mathbf{B} \to \mathbf{B}$$
$$\Rightarrow: \mathbf{B}, \mathbf{B} \to \mathbf{B}$$
$$\Leftrightarrow: \mathbf{B}, \mathbf{B} \to \mathbf{B}$$

The operations can be defined by axioms. Axioms for the Booleans (not the usual ones) could be expressed:

$$\neg \, \text{true} = \text{false}$$
$$\neg \, \text{false} = \text{true}$$

For $x \in \mathbf{B}$:

$$\text{true} \wedge x = x$$
$$\text{false} \wedge x = \text{false}$$
$$\text{true} \vee x = \text{true}$$
$$\text{false} \vee x = x$$
$$\text{true} \Rightarrow x = x$$
$$\text{false} \Rightarrow x = \text{true}$$

etc.

2. The Natural numbers consisting of the set $\mathbb{N}$ with constants 0, 1 and operations $+$, $*$.
3. The above two algebras can be combined together. Axioms for $\mathbb{N}$ may be expressed:

$$x + 0 = x$$
$$x + (y + 1) = (x + y) + 1$$
$$x \times 0 = 0$$
$$x \times (y + 1) = (x \times y) + x$$

We can then define additional operators:

$$\geqslant: \mathbb{N}, \mathbb{N} \to \mathbf{B}$$
$$\leqslant: \mathbb{N}, \mathbb{N} \to \mathbf{B}$$
$$>: \mathbb{N}, \mathbb{N} \to \mathbf{B}$$
$$<: \mathbb{N}, \mathbb{N} \to \mathbf{B}$$

with axioms:

$$x \geqslant x = \text{true}$$
$$(x + 1) \geqslant x = \text{true}$$
$$x \geqslant y = \text{true} \wedge y \geqslant z = \text{true} \Rightarrow x \geqslant z = \text{true}$$
$$x \leqslant y = y \geqslant x$$
$$x < y = \neg \, x \geqslant y)$$
$$x > y = y < x$$

4. A classical example of an algebra is a Group. A group has a carrier S, operations $+: S, S \to S$, $-: S \to S$, and a constant 0: S. The axioms are:

$$x, y, z \in S$$
$$0 + x = x$$
$$x = x + 0$$
$$x + (y + z) = (x + y) + z$$
$$x + (-x) = 0$$
$$(-x) + x = 0$$

In fact the above does not specify a single algebra, but a whole class of algebras, all of which are groups. For example, the integers with $+$, $-$ and 0; the strictly positive Real numbers with $*$, reciprocal and 1; the integers modulo n with $+$, $-$ (defined as $-x = n - x$), 0; and numerous others.

If one is given the symbols for operations and carrier sets, and axioms, but the carriers themselves are not specified, one has an 'algebraic specification'. In general many algebras conform to such a specification, and the specification can be used as a specification for a program. A comprehensive treatment of algebraic specifications can be found in Ehrig and Mahr (1985). Algebras are dealt with more fully in Chapter 3.

If, on the other hand, the carriers are specified precisely and the operations defined either by axioms or more constructively, then the algebra can stand as a so-called 'model-based' specification for a program. The techniques VDM (Jones, 1986) and Z (Spivey, 1988, 1989) use such model-based approaches.

1.6 Homomorphisms and categories

Given two algebras A, B with carriers $CA_1, \ldots, CA_n, CB_1, \ldots CB_n$ respectively, and operations $OPA_1, \ldots OPA_k, OPB_1, \ldots, OPB_k$ respectively, a general 'homomorphism' from A to B is a family of functions:

$$f_1: CA_1 \to CB_1$$
$$\vdots$$
$$f_n: CA_n \to CB_n$$

which preserve the effect of the operations. This means that for each operation OPA_i in A and the corresponding operation in OPB_i in B, where:

$$OPA_i: CA_{i1}, \ldots, CA_{im} \to CA_{ir}$$
$$OPB_i: CB_{i1}, \ldots, CB_{im} \to CB_{ir}$$

the following holds:

$$OPB_i(f_{i1}(a_1), \ldots, f_{im}(a_m)) =$$
$$f_{ir}(OPA_i(a_1, \ldots, a_m))$$

for any $a_j \in CA_{ij}, 1 \leqslant j \leqslant m$ where $f_{ij}: CA_{ij} \to CB_{ij}, 1 \leqslant j \leqslant m$.

Given algebras A, B, C with homomorphisms $f: A \to B$, $g: B \to C$, f and g compose, like functions, to form another homomorphism:

$$g \circ f: A \to C$$

defined as the family of composed functions:

$$g_1 \circ f_1: CA_1 \to CC_1$$
$$g_n \circ f_n: CA_n \to CC_n$$

Under appropriate circumstances, there is a homomorphism from the algebra inherent in a program in a particular language to the algebra embodied in the specification which that program fulfils. Also the 'retrieve' functions defined in VDM by Jones (1986) and the refinement operator defined in Z (Spivey, 1989) are homomorphisms.

The definition of a homomorphism over general multi-sorted algebras as above is cumbersome and difficult to deal with. Category theory (see, e.g., Blyth (1986)) provides a general theory which can encompass homomorphisms of general algebras in a tractable way. Category theory has also been used to explain generic procedures in high-level programming languages and parametrized specifications. See, for example, Rydeheard and Burstall (1988) and Thatcher et al. (1978). This is one example of how an advanced mathematical concept has been used to explain and give insight into powerful and useful programming techniques.

1.7 Truth, Models, and Theories

Various topics in mathematics, especially discrete mathematics, can be used to express a theory of the phenomena with which a computer program is planned to interact. Expressions in those mathematical topics can be used to specify the intended behaviour of the program. In particular set theory can be used as a theory of collections of various objects and the relationships between them, and other aspects of mathematics can be used to express other kinds of phenomenological theory.

Propositional and predicate calculus can be used to prove that a program meets (i.e. is a model of) its specification. The specification is couched in terms of the properties of the phenomenological theory.

Mathematics cannot prove or disprove the accuracy ('truth') of this theory. If the theory is wrong, then the program will be deficient, even if proved correct. However, a mathematical analysis of the specification using predicate calculus can display its properties and thereby help to assess the accuracy of the theory.

At the end of the day, however, certainty will always evade us (Wittgenstein, 1969).

1.8 References

Blyth, T. S. (1986) *Categories*, Longman

Dijkstra, E. W. (1976) *A Discipline of Programming*, Prentice-Hall, Englewood Cliffs, NJ, USA

Ehrig, H. and Mahr, B. (1985) *Fundamentals of Algebraic Specification, Volume 1*, EATCS Monographs 6, Springer Verlag

Enderton, H. (1975) *Elements of Set Theory*, Academic Press

Gordon, M. J. C. (1979) *The Denotational Description of Programming Languages*, Springer Verlag

Gries, D. (1981) *The Science of Programming*, Springer Verlag

Halmos, P. R. (1960) *Naive Set Theory*, Van Nostrand

Hoare, C. A. R. (1969) The axiomatic basis of computer programming, *Communications of ACM*, **12,** 576–583

Hoare, C. A. R. (1985) *The Mathematics of Programming*, lecture, Clarendon Press, Oxford

Jones, C. B. (1986) *Systematic Software Developing Using VDM*, Prentice Hall

Kyburg, H. E. (1984) *Theory and Measurement*, Cambridge University Press

Lakatos, I. (1978) *The Methodology of Scientific Research Programmes*, Cambridge University Press

Manna, Z. and Waldinger, R. (1985) *The Logical Basis for Computer Programming*, Addison Wesley, Reading, Mass., USA

Popper, K. (1972) *Conjectures and Refutations*, Routledge and Kegan Paul

Rydeheard, D. and Burstall, R. (1988) *Computational Category Theory*, Prentice Hall

Schmidt, D. (1986) *Denotational Semantics*, Allyn & Bacon, Newton, Mass., USA

Schönfinkel, M. (1924) Uber die Vausteine der Mathematischen Logik, *Math. Anal.*, **92,** 305

Stoy, J. (1977) *Denotational Semantics*, MIT Press, Cambridge, Mass., USA

Thatcher, J., Wagner, E. and Wright, J. (1978) An initial algebra approach to the specification, correctness and implementation of abstract data types. In *Current Trends in Programming Methodology*, Vol. 4 (ed. R. T. Yeh), Prentice Hall, pp. 80–149

Wittgenstein, L. (1969) *On Certainty*, Blackwell, Oxford

2

Logics and proofs of correctness

Martin Loomes
School of Information Science, Hatfield Polytechnic

Contents

It is often said that the process of software design needs to become more scientific. One of the dimensions usually included in this statement is that software designers should be able, and prepared, to prove properties of their software, rather than trusting solely to testing strategies and good fortune.

However, it is also inherent in the adoption of the name 'software engineering' that software designers should conform to some of the established standards of engineering. One of the more universal of these is that engineers should ensure that artefacts constructed are fit for purpose.

The purpose of this chapter is to discuss part of the problem of proving that an artefact is fit for purpose, by proving its correctness with respect to some specification. The chapter starts by introducing the concept of program correctness, and demonstrating how correctness can be viewed in a wider engineering context. This is necessary because the term is frequently misunderstood, and 'correctness' is raised to the status of 'fitness for purpose'. This misunderstanding lies at the heart of many of the disagreements between the proponents and opponents of formal methods.

The chapter then discusses the notion of a formal proof, and formal systems within which formal proofs occur. This will be done by providing proof mechanisms for the logics introduced in the previous chapter.

Finally, the chapter discusses how the concept of correctness can be formalized, and how formal systems can be constructed within which correctness can be proved for particular programming paradigms.

It is important that the reader bears in mind that the intention is to discuss the ideas behind formal proofs of program correctness, not to introduce definitive methods for carrying out such proofs. It is also not an attempt to persuade software engineers to use formal proofs of correctness in their professional activities. This decision properly belongs in the context of each project, and responsibility rests with the engineers in charge. It is the intention, however, to provide sufficient background for this decision to be taken in an informed manner.

2.1 Fitness for purpose

There are a number of aspects of fitness for purpose that need to be considered by any company wishing to construct an artefact with the intention of it being a commercial success. For example, packages to run on personal computers might well give rise to questions such as the following:

1. Can one produce a product whose cost will be commensurate with the price its potential buyers will be prepared to pay? This price will be largely determined by the buyer's perception of the product's fitness for purpose.
2. Are the potential users' views of fitness for purpose understood, and is this understanding sufficiently refined for it to form the basis of a design?
3. Can a product be produced which will be reliable to an appropriate degree? It should survive reasonable misuse, such as pressing multiple keys, and environmental problems, e.g. power failures, but probably does not need to be constructed to survive total immersion in water.
4. Are the time-scales for its production sensible? Will the purpose still be the same when the artefact is finally constructed?
5. Is the functionality a potential user would require of the system known, and can a system with this functionality be provided?

There are also a number of issues that will probably not be

made explicit, but which are subsumed under good engineering practice, such as adherence to safety standards.

For many systems, judging the fitness for purpose of a delivered system is intuitively quite simple; most people, when faced with a word processor, can judge whether it meets their needs. For many other systems the judgement may be rather harder; the complexity of the problem being addressed may be such that the notion of purpose can never be universally agreed, or the complexity of the artefact might be such that a true judgement of fitness is never really made.

All this merely endorses the view, of course, that software design is an inherently difficult process. It involves building an artefact that meets exacting standards, and doing so in an optimal way, where both the standards to be met and also the optimization function being used are often difficult to make explicit.

A desideratum of software design, however, is to improve the quality and efficiency of software production. This involves finding ways of predicting and verifying an artefact's fitness for purpose before it is built and delivered. Indeed, in an ideal world, one would like to prove that an artefact built to a particular design will be fit for purpose. This means one must find ways of handling the complexity of both the problems to be solved and also the artefacts to be produced.

It is common engineering, and scientific, practice to consider complex systems via a number of abstraction mechanisms. In constructing a hydro-electric dam, for example, the dam may be considered as a static structure acted upon by forces – a surface subject to erosion or as an intrusion upon an eco-system. The ways in which these various abstractions are brought into contact depends to a large extent upon the nature of the abstractions themselves. Spotting necessary interactions and ignoring irrelevant ones is part of the professional judgement of an engineer. For example, failure to note that changes to the eco-system will alter the chemical constitution of the water being held back, and hence the erosion properties of the dam itself, are errors in engineering judgement.

Abstractions of software systems can be viewed in very similar ways. Common models of such artefacts include reliability models, performance models of both algorithms and systems, abstract data types and state transitional systems. Models of the problem are less generally applicable, but include such things as entity–attribute relations, data-flow diagrams and metrics for performance and reliability.

One aspect of this abstraction process is usually referred to as 'correctness'. This may be considered an unfortunate choice of term, because it carries connotations of 'goodness' or 'adherence to a standard', and is often, erroneously, taken to mean that a correct system is one which is well designed and meets *all* its requirements. In fact, using the term correctness in the technical sense introduced below, a 'correct' system may be badly designed, totally unfit for purpose, and generally unusable. Proving a system correct is only a stepping stone on the way to demonstrating that the system is fit for purpose; removing that stone just makes the journey that bit more hazardous.

This misunderstanding of terms, unfortunately, is at the heart of one of the major misconceptions of software engineering, namely that a proof of *correctness* is a proof of *fitness for purpose*.

This misconception is very damaging to software engineering for two reasons. First, those who realise the impossibility of proving the fitness for purpose of most real systems are tempted to dismiss proofs of correctness, believing the two to be the same. Second, those who believe that proofs of correctness can be done are tempted to believe that they have proved fitness for purpose, or at least, the published literature on the subject rarely points out the limitations of what has been achieved when such a proof has been carried out.

2.2 Correctness

Intuitively, an implementation is a 'correct' realisation of a specification if it satisfies the specification. This is extremely vague, of course, and is of no real use for introducing rigour into software engineering. One way in which this idea can be made more precise, however, is to restrict attention to particular kinds of specification and implementation, and to define more carefully what we mean by a satisfaction relation.

For specifications here, the required system will be considered as transforming an initial state into a final state. Moreover, a black-box approach will be adopted that does not describe *how* this transformation might take place, but simply expresses the relationship between the initial and final states. Such a specification is sometimes referred to as a functional specification. This is also a dangerous term, as it carries connotations of purpose again. These are the only sort of specifications considered here, but the reader should remember that these specifications are only addressing one small, if important, aspect of the problem.

One point which often leads to confusion with specifications of this kind is the way in which inputs and outputs become bundled into the initial and final states respectively. If a system is required to read the contents of a magnetic tape and to produce suitably formatted output on a printer, then one captures this information statically by using state variables. Once again, note that *how* the information is being represented on a particular device is not being made explicit, only *what* information is being represented. Of course, the mere act of writing down what information is being captured means that one must choose a representation for it, but one is free to choose the most suitable vehicle for representation, rather than being constrained by issues such as the physical characteristics of devices.

In general, most systems are only expected to operate with defined behaviours for an identified set of initial states, although defensive programming may well be deployed to make this a very large set. For the sake of clarity, no defensive strategies will be used here. If a program to add two numbers is wanted, there will be no discussion as to what happens if it is given a string and an array. In fact, one school of thought says that such issues should always be subsumed under good engineering practice, and so need never be made explicit.

The initial states for which a system does have a defined behaviour can be characterized by a predicate which is satisfied by precisely those states. Such a predicate is usually referred to as a pre-condition. Similarly a predicate can be used to express the relation between valid initial states and acceptable final states. This is usually referred to as the post-condition. Some authors prefer to make the post-condition a predicate over final state alone, carrying forward relevant initial state values as variables which cannot be changed. This is a fine distinction which need not be of concern here.

For these predicates to be meaningful, one needs to associate types with data items in both the initial and final states; otherwise the predicates would need to range over a domain of interest which is too large to be managed by simple logics.

The specifications can now be viewed as functions, or more generally relations, between initial and final states. A specification will be a function if the required system is deterministic, that is, an initial state uniquely identifies a final state, otherwise it will be a relation. The pre-condition serves to define the domain of the function or relation. For a total function, the pre-condition will be *true*, which is a predicate satisfied by all states of the appropriate type. For further details of this style of specification, see Jones (1986).

Example 1. A system, *max*, to find the maximum of two given natural numbers, *a* and *b* say, which are both less than 100. We will assume that the result is represented by *r* in the final state:

$$max: \mathbb{N} \times \mathbb{N} \;\nrightarrow \mathbb{N}$$
$$pre\text{-}max(a,b) \triangleq (a < 100) \wedge (b < 100)$$
$$post\text{-}max(a,b,r) \triangleq$$
$$((a > b) \wedge (a = r)) \vee ((a \leqslant b) \wedge (b = r))$$

The system is being modelled here as a partial function, hence the need for a pre-condition.

Example 2. A system, *bigmax*, to accept any two natural numbers, *a* and *b*, and output *either*:

the greater of *a* and *b*, if either *a* or *b* is less than 100,

or

a or *b* if both *a* and *b* are greater than or equal to 100:

$$bigmax: \mathbb{N} \times \mathbb{N} \leftrightarrow \mathbb{N}$$
$$pre\text{-}bigmax(a,b) \triangleq true$$
$$post\text{-}bigmax(a,b,r) \triangleq$$
$$(((a < 100) \vee (b < 100))$$
$$\wedge (((a > b) \wedge (a = r)) \vee ((a \leqslant b) \wedge (b = r))))$$
$$\vee ((a \geqslant 100) \wedge (b \geqslant 100) \wedge ((r = a) \vee (r = b)))$$

Example 3. The pre- and post-conditions of a sublist routine need to reflect a number of decisions, such as what types of list the routine is to work with, what form the sublist delimiters are to take, what will happen if the routine is called upon an empty list, and so on. One possible specification of such a routine is as follows:

$$sublist: ListOfItems \times \mathbb{N} \times \mathbb{N} \;\rightarrow ListOfItems$$
$$pre\text{-}sublist(l,i,j) \triangleq \;\leqslant i \leqslant j \leqslant length(l)$$
$$post\text{-}sublist(l,i,j,r) \triangleq length\,(r) = j - i + 1$$
$$\wedge \; \exists p,q: ListOfItems\,.(p@r@q = l \wedge length(p) = i - 1)$$

where @ denotes string catenation and length is a function which returns the number of items in a list of items.

One important aside should be made at this point. Once the specification has been formalized in this way one can prove properties of the system being described. This is not directly related to the proving of correctness, but it is a valuable aid to ensuring fitness for purpose. It allows the exploration of the implications of those aspects of the systems behaviour made explicit in the specification without actually having to construct the system. In particular, one can prove that desirable properties follow and undesirable properties are positively excluded. For example, an obvious desirable property of our sublist routine above is that the length of a resulting sublist should not be greater than the length of the list presented as an argument.

First, we can assume that the pre-condition holds, for we certainly cannot guarantee any properties of the routine if it is called erroneously, thus:

$$1 \leqslant i \leqslant j \leqslant length(l) \tag{2.1}$$

Second, we can assume that the post-condition holds, and in particular:

$$length(r) = j - i + 1 \tag{2.2}$$

Then a proof might follow. From Equation (2.1) we get:

$$j \leqslant length(l)$$

Since i is positive, also from Equation (2.1), then:

$$j - i < length(l)$$

and so:

$$j - i + 1 \leqslant length(l)$$

but, from Equation (2.2) we have:

$$length(r) = j - i + 1$$

and so:

$$length(r) \leqslant length(l)$$

This proof may appear trivial, but in actual fact many complicated things have been done. First, a strategy has been discovered for carrying out the proof. Second, strings of symbols have been manipulated according to very precise rules, although these rules have not been made explicit. Third, an attempt has been made to present the proof in such a way as to convince readers that the property does indeed hold. When it comes to proving programs correct, however, the proofs seldom seem trivial. This is because one is dealing with objects and rules which are less familiar. For this reason the next section discusses exactly what constitutes a proof.

Returning to the task of defining correctness, a refined notion is needed now of what constitutes an implementation. It will be assumed that this is simply the text of a program written in a suitable programming language, together with some definition of how the text will cause its target machine to behave. The following is a definition of program correctness:

A program is correct with respect to a pre- and post-condition specification if the execution of the program on a machine whose initial state satisfies the pre-condition will result in the machine terminating in a state which satisfies the post-condition.

Sometimes it is convenient to separate out the notion of correctness into two parts, making use of a concept called partial correctness:

A program is partially correct with respect to a pre- and post-condition specification if the execution of the program on a machine whose initial state satisfies the pre-condition will never result in the machine terminating in a state which violates the post-condition.

This is a subtle change: a partially correct program is *safe*, in the sense that it will never produce incorrect result, but it may not be *live* because it may produce no results at all.

Now an alternative definition of correctness can be given:

A program is correct with respect to a pre- and post-condition specification if it is partially correct with respect to the specification, and it terminates.

This provides a possible strategy for proving correctness; one can prove partial correctness and termination separately. If the term 'partial correctness' is being used in a particular context, then the term 'total correctness' is sometimes used instead of just 'correctness'.

The notation:

$$\{pre\text{-}condition\}P\{post\text{-}condition\}$$

will be used as a shorthand notation for the proposition:

The program P is partially correct with respect to the specification (pre-condition, post-condition)

For example:

$$\{0 < a < 99 \wedge 0 < b < 99\}\, begin\; program;$$
$$r := a + b; end\; program\{r > a \wedge r > b\}$$

is a proposition which, assuming a sensible implementation of the programming language, one would expect to be true.

Unfortunately, this notation, although widely used, is not a standard. It is sometimes used to denote total correctness, and a variety of alternative notations exist for both partial and total correctness.

It is important to note that correctness, as stated here, does not suggest a software development strategy or method. If we relax our notation of correctness slightly, however, and allow statements of the form:

$$\{pre\}P\{post\}$$

where P can be a program or *another specification*, then the way has been paved for a technique known as refinement. If one can provide a sequence of statements of the form:

$$\{pre_i\}P_i\{post_i\} \quad \text{where} \quad i \geqslant 1$$

such that:

$$\forall i . (pre_1 \Rightarrow pre_i) \wedge (post_i \Rightarrow post_1)$$

then one can chain together a number of correctness arguments to provide a systematic way of moving from a specification to an implementation. This idea is further developed in later chapters.

2.3 Logic and proofs

A proof is a convincing argument of the truth of something. Sometimes arguments are convincing because of one's knowledge of the world:

'If you pour boiling water over your hand it will hurt, therefore you should take great care not to pour boiling water over your hand.'

Often such arguments are used persuasively, rather than scientifically, especially when dealing with children:

'If you go out in the rain then you will catch a cold, therefore you cannot play outside.'

Sometimes such arguments are shown to be dramatically flawed because of poor understanding of the world:

'If you try to sail westward for too long then you will fall off the edge of the world'

and, moreover, such arguments are purely subjective; anyone who still believes the world is flat will be convinced by the above.

Using such arguments in engineering practice is inherently dangerous. Designers will often attempt persuasion rather than proof, and misunderstandings which cause design errors will often manifest themselves in correctness arguments based on the same misunderstandings. One way around this is to subject designs to reviews by individuals who are not intimately concerned with the design process itself. If this is to be a valuable exercise, however, the design must be presented in such a way that the chain of reasoning which leads to it can be appreciated by the newcomers without them needing to understand the problem to the same extent as the original design team.

One way in which this can be achieved is by utilizing formal proofs, which depend on the form of the argument rather than its semantic content. For example, the validity of the argument:

'If P is true then Q is true. P is true, therefore Q is true'

would be accepted by most people independently of the meanings of the terms P and Q.

Great care must be taken when using such forms to reason about the real world, as the choice of form must be appropriate for the particular problem being addressed. Of course, this choice of formalism is itself a subjective process. Pragmatically, the value of the formal approach is that it reduces subjectivity in arguments about program behaviour, but there will always be an element of subjectivity in any design process. Fortunately, a number of useful formalisms have been developed by experts which can be applied by software engineers in much the same way as differential equations can be applied by mechanical engineers.

Formal proofs must take place within formal systems, just as informal proofs take place within an implicit understanding of the world. Frequently the formal systems themselves are not made explicit because they are widely used, such as the formal systems underpinning arithmetic and traditional algebra. As the engineer is ultimately responsible for the choice of formal system, however, it is important that the subject of formal systems is addressed here sufficiently to support this selection process.

A formal system comprises a formal language, which defines the admissible strings of symbols that can be used in arguments, and also a deductive apparatus, which provides the formal rules that can be used in manipulating these strings to mirror reasoning.

A formal language was introduced in Chapter 1 called propositional logic, which allowed simple and compound propositions to be formally described, such as:

$P \wedge \neg Q$

A deductive apparatus will now be added to this language, thus creating a formal system. There are a number of choices of suitable deductive systems that are suitable for this language and intended purpose. One known as a natural deduction system is used here. In such a system the rules introduced map closely onto intuitive understanding of the formal strings being manipulated.

The rules are expressed in the form:

$$\frac{antecedent_1, antecedent_2 \ldots antecedent_n}{consequent}$$

where the antecedents and consequents are valid sentences of the formal language, or other derivations carried out within the formal system. Informally, the rules can be read as:

Given the set of antecedents we can infer the consequent.

Formally, the interest here is only in whether or not the antecedents, or derivations, have already been written down. If they have, then the consequent may be written down.

There are two forms of arguments that can be expressed in a formal system: theorems, which are properties of the formal system, and can be established without the assumption of any premises; and derivations, which are of the form:

If we assume the following premises, $P_1, P_2, \ldots P_n$ then we can prove C.

Derivations and proofs are usually denoted by:

$P_1, P_2, \ldots P_n \vdash C$ and $\vdash T$

respectively. The symbol $\vdash$ is called the syntactic turnstile.

There is obviously a close connection between a derivation and a rule of the formal system. The distinction, however, is that rules need not, and usually cannot, be proved, but form part of the statement of the formal system; derivations need to be proved, and form part of the emergent properties of the formal system. Once a derivation, or a theorem, has been proved, however, it is usual to allow it to be elevated to the status of a rule within the formal system, and to allow its subsequent reuse in new proofs and derivations.

2.3.1 Rules of propositional calculus

The deductive apparatus for propositional logic has ten rules, corresponding to the introduction and elimination of the five symbols $\wedge$, $\vee$, $\Rightarrow$ $\Leftrightarrow$ and $\neg$. What follows will use α, β and γ to denote sentences in propositional logic.

If we have α and we also have β then we have $\alpha \wedge \beta$, and also $\beta \wedge \alpha$:

$$\frac{\alpha, \beta}{\alpha \wedge \beta} \quad \text{and} \quad \frac{\alpha, \beta}{\beta \wedge \alpha} \quad (\wedge\text{-introduction rule})$$

Similarly, if we have $\alpha \wedge \beta$ then we clearly have them both separately:

$$\frac{\alpha \wedge \beta}{\alpha} \quad \text{and} \quad \frac{\alpha \wedge \beta}{\beta} \quad (\wedge\text{-elimination rule})$$

If we have $\neg \neg \alpha$ then we have α:

$$\frac{\neg \neg \alpha}{\alpha} \quad (\neg\text{-elimination rule})$$

If we have α and also $\alpha \Rightarrow \beta$ then we have β:

$$\frac{\alpha, \alpha \Rightarrow \beta}{\beta} \quad (\Rightarrow\text{-elimination rule})$$

If we have a then we have $a \vee \beta$ for any choice of β:

$$\frac{a}{a \vee \beta} \quad \text{and} \quad \frac{a}{\beta \vee a} \quad (\vee\text{-introduction rule})$$

The sentence $\alpha \Leftrightarrow \beta$ is just a shorthand for:

$$(\alpha \Rightarrow \beta) \wedge (\beta \Rightarrow \alpha)$$

which gives rise to the following rules:

$$\frac{\alpha \Leftrightarrow \beta}{\alpha \Rightarrow \beta} \quad \text{and} \quad \frac{\alpha \Leftrightarrow \beta}{\beta \Rightarrow \alpha} \quad (\Leftrightarrow\text{-elimination rule})$$

and:

$$\frac{\alpha \Rightarrow \beta, \beta \Rightarrow \alpha}{\alpha \Leftrightarrow \beta} \quad \text{and} \quad \frac{\alpha \Rightarrow \beta, \beta \Rightarrow \alpha}{\beta \Leftrightarrow \alpha} \quad (\Leftrightarrow\text{-introduction rule})$$

We can now illustrate these rules in a simple derivation.

Derivation 1. Show that:

$$P, P \Leftrightarrow Q, Q \Rightarrow R \vdash R \vee S$$

Derivation:

1.	P	Premise
2.	$P \Leftrightarrow Q$	Premise
3.	$Q \Rightarrow R$	Premise
4.	$P \Rightarrow Q$	2, $\Leftrightarrow$-elimination
5.	Q	1,4 $\Rightarrow$-elimination
6.	R	3,5 $\Rightarrow$-elimination
7.	$R \vee S$	6 $\vee$-introduction

QED

Note that this derivation contains only strings from the formal language, except for the addition of line numbers and a note of which rules are being used and which lines are being taken as antecedents.

The next three rules are rather more complex as they make use of assumptions. These assumptions should not be confused with the premises of a derivation, they are devices used within particular rules. These assumptions are discharged by particular statements within the rules, thus the scope of the assumption runs from its introduction to the line which discharges it. During this scope, any line which is derived as a consequence of the assumption, directly or indirectly, is not available outside of this scope. The scope of assumptions are marked by a line next to the proof.

If we wish to show that $\alpha \Rightarrow \beta$ then we can assume α and show that β can be derived. Note that β itself is derived in the scope of an assumption, so it is not to be used outside of this scope. In any derivation using assumptions we are also entitled to use strings already written down (including other assumptions that are in scope); we will denote this collection of strings by Φ.

$$\frac{\alpha, \Phi \vdash \beta}{\alpha \Rightarrow \beta} \quad (\Rightarrow\text{-introduction rule})$$

Example 4. Here is a theorem of propositional logic:

$$\vdash P \Rightarrow P \vee Q$$

Proof:

1.	P	Assumption
2.	$P \vee Q$	1 $\vee$-introduction
3.	$P \Rightarrow P \vee Q$	1,2 $\Rightarrow$-introduction

QED

Another use of assumptions is in introducing negations. If we wish to derive or prove $\neg \alpha$ then we can sometimes assume α and show it leads to a contradiction. Since either α or $\neg \alpha$ must be the case and α leads to a contradiction then we must have $\neg \alpha$:

$$\frac{a, \Phi \vdash \beta \wedge \neg \beta}{\neg a} \quad (\neg\text{-introduction rule})$$

The final use of assumptions is to remove disjunctions. If we have $\alpha \vee \beta$ then we clearly have either α or β, but we do not know which. We can consider a case analysis, however, proceeding from α and β in turn. If we can find a common result then that result is a consequence of both α and β, and since we have at least one of these it must be a consequence of $\alpha \vee \beta$:

$$\frac{\alpha, \Phi \vdash \gamma, \beta, \Phi \vdash \gamma, \alpha \vee \beta}{\gamma} \quad (\vee\text{-elimination rule})$$

Example 5. Show that:

$$Q \Rightarrow R, P \Rightarrow R, P \vee Q \vdash R$$

Derivation:

1.	$P \Rightarrow R$	Premise
2.	$Q \Rightarrow R$	Premise
3.	$P \vee Q$	Premise
4.	P	Assumption
5.	R	1,4 $\Rightarrow$-elimination
6.	Q	Assumption
7.	R	2,6 $\Rightarrow$-elimination
8.	R	1–7, $\vee$-elimination

QED

2.3.2 Rules of predicate calculus

One can add to these rules four additional rules for the introduction and elimination of the quantifiers, and hence arrive at a deductive apparatus for predicate calculus.

To eliminate the universal quantification from:

$$\forall x . P(x)$$

we can observe that this is really a convenient notation for the (possibly infinite) conjunction:

$$P(a_1) \wedge P(a_2) \wedge P(a_3) \ldots$$

where $a_1, a_2 \ldots$ are the specific names of objects in the domain of discourse. This gives a weak elimination rule, that from $\forall x . P(x)$ we can infer $P(a_n)$ for some specific n. We can strengthen this rule, however, by allowing the use of an arbitrary name, denoting a typical, but unspecified, particular object. Then:

$$\frac{\forall x . P(x)}{P(a)} \quad \text{where } a \text{ is arbitrary} \quad (\forall\text{-elimination rule})$$

Now, to reintroduce universal quantification, all we need is a statement of the form $P(a)$, where a is arbitrary, but care must be taken that this is really the case. In particular, a must not be involved in any assumptions currently in scope, or it will no longer be truly arbitrary, since properties of it are being assumed:

$$\frac{P(a)}{\forall x . P(x)} \quad \text{where } a \text{ is arbitrary} \quad (\forall\text{-introduction rule})$$

To introduce existential quantification, it is sufficient to have $P(x)$ being asserted for any object, particular or arbitrary:

$$\frac{P(a)}{\exists x . P(x)} \quad (\exists\text{-introduction rule})$$

To remove existential quantification, we can observe that it is really a shorthand for the (possibly infinite) disjunction:

$$P(a_1) \vee P(a_2) \vee P(a_3) \ldots$$

The rule for $\vee$-elimination can now be extended to give:

$$\frac{\exists x . P(x), \forall x . (P(x) \Rightarrow Q)}{Q} \quad (\exists\text{-elimination rule})$$

The following is an example of these rules in action.

Derivation 2. Show that:

$$\forall x \cdot (P(x) \Rightarrow Q(x)), \exists y \cdot P(y) \vdash \exists z \cdot Q(z)$$

Derivation:

1.	$\forall x \cdot P(x) \Rightarrow Q(x)$	Premise
2.	$\exists y \cdot P(y)$	Premise
3.	$P(a) \Rightarrow Q(a)$	1 $\forall$-elimination
4.	$P(a)$	Assumption
5.	$Q(a)$	3,4 $\Rightarrow$-elimination
6.	$\exists z \cdot Q(z)$	5 $\exists$-introduction
7.	$P(a) \Rightarrow \exists z \cdot Q(z)$	4–6 $\Rightarrow$-introduction
8.	$\forall x \cdot (P(x) \Rightarrow \exists z \cdot Q(z))$	7 $\forall$-introduction
9.	$\exists z \cdot Q(z)$	2,8 $\exists$-elimination

QED

2.3.3 Equality

One very common predicate is that of equality, which allows the use of different names for the same object. Although this is just a predicate, it is often useful to build some of its special properties into the formal system as additional axioms of rules. For example:

$$\forall x . x = x \quad \text{(Axiom of Reflexivity)}$$

It is also useful to be able to substitute equal things and know that the resulting expression will have the same meaning. We use the notation $P[m/n]$ to denote P with some or all of the free occurrences of n replaced by m:

$$\frac{m = n, P(n)}{P[m/n]}$$

and

$$\frac{m = n, P(m)}{P[n/m]} \quad \text{(Rule of Substitution)}$$

The following is a simple derivation which uses equality.

Derivation 3. Show that:

$$s = t \vdash (s = u) \Rightarrow (t = u)$$

Derivation:

1.	$s = t$	Premise
2.	$s = u$	Assumption
3.	$t = u$	1,2 substitution
4.	$(s = u) \Rightarrow (t = u)$	2,3 $\Rightarrow$-introduction

QED

2.3.4 Further reading

There are many excellent texts on logic. Good introductions include Lemmon (1965) and Newton-Smith (1985). A more advanced treatment of the topic can be found in Andrews (1986).

2.4 Proofs of correctness

Some examples can now be given of formal systems that can be used for proving program correctness. Clearly the formal system used must be capable of capturing relevant aspects of both the specification and the implementation, if one is to show some form of satisfaction relation between the two. This means that different formal systems are needed for different specification styles and implementation languages. Note that this means that proofs will consist of an intermingling of terms which are drawn from logic, the problem domain and also programming languages. Strictly, however, the formal language comprises sentences which may contain terms of all three kinds.

Attention will be restricted to specifications written as pre- and post-conditions, and only two programming paradigms will be considered: declarative and traditional procedural. Declarative, or functional, programming provides a fairly easy paradigm within which to prove correctness, because of the referential transparency possessed by the program code. Procedural programming is not so easy to handle, and the formal systems are somewhat more complex. We will explore two approaches to this problem, Dijkstra's weakest pre-conditions (1976) and Hoare Logics (Hoare, 1989a).

2.4.1 Declarative paradigms

Consider the simple declarative program:

```
fun f x = x + 3;
```

This program will compute the value of $x + 3$ for any given argument. The formal system for such a programming paradigm can simply be constructed from predicate logic with equality, by including the program text itself as an axiom of equality, or more properly, an axiom schema as an infinite number of axioms can be generated by instantiations of x. The proof will seem very similar to normal mathematical proofs, as the latter are usually centred on the use of such equalities, and so we will present the proof with a similar degree of formality rather than making it totally formal.

For example, given the pre- and post-conditions:

$$pre\text{-}prog(x) \triangleq 0 \leqslant x \leqslant 100$$
$$post\text{-}prog(x,r) \triangleq 3 \leqslant r \leqslant 103$$

where $r = f x$, we can prove correctness as follows.

First, we note that the pre-condition must hold, so we can take it as axiomatic:

$$0 \leqslant x \leqslant 100$$

Now we can add 3 throughout the inequality:

$$3 \leqslant x + 3 \leqslant 103$$

But using our program as an axiom of equality, we can rewrite $x + 3$ as $f x$, or r, giving:

$$3 \leqslant r \leqslant 103$$

and we have derived the post-condition as a theorem in our formal system. Note that we have imported a number of results into our proof from the nature of the data types under consideration, such as the use of the rule for inequalities. This is common practice in mathematics, and also in proofs of program correctness, but where we are using non-standard data types great care must be taken before their properties are assumed. The next chapter discusses ways in which properties of data types can be formalized and proved.

As another example, consider the *sublist* specification given above:

$$sublist: ListOfItems \times \mathbb{N} \times \mathbb{N} \rightarrow ListOfItems$$
$$pre\text{-}sublist(l,i,j) \triangleq 1 \leqslant i \leqslant j \leqslant length(l)$$
$$\triangleq length(r) = j - i + 1$$
$$\exists p, q: ListOfItems . (p@r@q = l \wedge length(p) = i - 1)$$

Here is an implementation that meets this specification:

```
val rec sublist l i j =
if not((1<=i)&(i<=j)&(j<=length l)) then escape
"invalid call to sublist"
else if i>1 then sublist (tl l) (i−1) (j−1)
    else if i=1 & j>1 then hd(l)::sublist (tl l) 1 (j−1)
        else [hd(l)];
```

To prove this implementation correct with respect to its specification, we will assume the pre-condition and program text as axioms, and attempt to prove the post-condition as a theorem. As the post-condition is of the form $P \wedge Q$ we can prove $\vdash P$ and $\vdash Q$ individually.

First, we will prove that $length(sublist\ l\ i\ j) = j - i + 1$. This proof will be inductive on l. We start with the smallest possible list, which is the singleton list $[e]$, where e is an arbitrary element. For this list, the pre-condition forces $i = j = 1$, so using the program text as a rule of equality:

$$sublist\ l\ i\ j = sublist[e]\ 1\ 1 = [hd[e]]$$

thus:

$$length(sublist\ l\ i\ j) = length([hd[e]]) = \\ 1 = 1 - 1 + 1 = j - i + 1$$

as required.

For the inductive step, we assume that $length(sublist\ x\ i\ j) = j - i + 1$ for some arbitrary list x, of length n, and for all valid i and j, then show it must hold true for the list $a::x$, which is of length $n + 1$. We need to consider three cases:

Case $i > 1$

Using our program text as an axiom of equality:

$$sublist\ a::x\ i\ j = sublist\ x\ i-1\ j-1$$

So, using our inductive hypothesis:

$$length(sublist\ a::x\ i\ j) = length(sublist\ x\ i-1\ j-1) = \\ (j-1) - (i-1) + 1 = j - i + 1$$

Case $i = 1 \wedge j > 1$

Using our program text as an axiom of equality:

$$sublist\ a::x\ 1\ j = [hd\ a::x]@sublist\ x\ 1\ j-1$$

so:

$$length(sublist\ a::x\ i\ j) = length([hd\ a::x]@sublist\ x\ 1\ j-1)$$

A property of the data type *list* is that, for any lists p and q:

$$length([hd\ p]@q) = 1 + length\ q$$

so:

$$length(sublist\ a::x\ i\ j) = 1 + length(sublist\ x\ 1\ j-1)$$

which, using the inductive hypothesis, is:

$$1 + ((j-1) - 1 + 1) = j - 1 + 1 = j - i + 1$$

Case $i = 1 \wedge j = 1$

Using the program text as an axiom of equality:

$$sublist\ a::x\ 1\ 1 = [hd\ a::x]$$

but:

$$length([hd\ a::x]) = 1 = 1 - 1 + 1 = j - i + 1$$

Hence, in all three cases:

$$length(sublist\ l\ i\ j) = j - i + 1$$

as required.

Now we need to prove the second part of the post-condition, namely:

$$\exists p,q : ListOfItems\ .\ p@sublist\ l\ i\ j@q = l \wedge length\ (p) = i - 1$$

we will again use induction. For the inductive step the strategy is to carry out a case analysis again, and find suitable values for p and q in each case.

For the basis of the induction we again let l be the singleton list, $[e]$, and note that $i = j = 1$ is forced upon us by the pre-condition. Using the program text:

$$sublist[e]\ 1\ 1 = [hd[e]] = [e]$$

but:

$$[]@[e]@[] = [e]\ and\ length\ ([]) = 0$$

and so the condition is satisfied.

For the inductive step, we assume that $\exists p,q : ListOfItems$. $p@sublist\ x\ i\ j@q = l$ for some arbitrary list x, of length n, then show it must hold true for the list $a::x$, which is of length $n + 1$.

The following lemma is rather useful in this proof:

$$\forall i.(sublist\ a::l\ i+1\ n+1 = sublist\ l\ i\ n)$$

where i ranges only over those values for which the pre-condition is satisfied. The proof of this lemma is left as an exercise.

Again, the proof proceeds by cases. Just one case is considered here, as they all follow along very similar lines:

Case $i > 1 \wedge j < n + 1$

Here we can see that suitable values for p and q in the post-condition are:

$$p = sublist\ a::x\ 1\ i-1$$

and:

$$q = sublist\ a::x\ j+1\ n+1$$

So we are required to prove that:

$$sublist\ a::x\ 1\ i-1@sublist\ a::x\ i\ j@sublist \\ a::x\ j+1\ n+1 = a::x$$

by assuming that:

$$sublist\ x\ 1\ i-1@sublist\ x\ i\ j@sublist\ x\ j+1\ n = x$$

for arbitrary i and j.

Rewriting the first sublist gives:

$$(a::sublist \ x \ 1 \ i - 2)@sublist \ a::x \ i \ j@sublist \ a::x \ j + 1 \ n + 1$$

but $(a::p)@q = a::(p@q)$, so we obtain:

$$a::(sublist \ x \ 1 \ i - 2@sublist \ a::x \ i \ j@sublist \ a::x \ j + 1 \ n + 1)$$

but since $i > 1$ we can use our lemma on the second and third sublists, to obtain:

$$a::(sublist \ x \ 1 \ i - 2@sublist \ x \ i - 1 \ j - 1@sublist \ x \ j \ n)$$

but by our induction hypothesis, the bracketed expression is just x, remembering that i and j were arbitrary, so expressing them as $i - 1$ and $j - 1$ is valid, as the pre-condition will still hold in this case. So we have proved that:

$$sublist \ a::x \ 1 \ i - 1@sublist \ a:x \ i \ j@sublist$$
$$a::x \ j + 1 \ n + 1 = a::x$$

and hence:

$$\exists p,q : List \ OfItems . p@sublist \ l \ i \ j@q = l$$

as required. The $length \ (p) = i - 1$ follows from the first result proved.

We have only proved partial correctness at this stage, however, as we have not shown that the recursion will necessarily terminate. To do this we define a function f which takes as argument function calls which may or may not involve i and j, such that:

$$f(g(i,j)) = i + j$$
$$f(g(i)) = i$$
$$f(g(j)) = j$$
$$f(g(\ )) = 0 \quad \text{that is, } g \text{ is independent of } i \text{ and } j$$

This function assigns a unique natural number, an f-value say, to each call of a function. We want to show that any invocation of *sublist* results only in calls whose f-value is less than the f-value of the initial call to sublist. Then, since f has range $\mathbb{N}$, and 0 is a lower bound on $\mathbb{N}$, then the function *sublist* must terminate.

Once again the proof is by induction. The base case is the singleton list $[e]$. Here the invocation must be $sublist[e] \ 1 \ 1$ whose f-value is 2. The implementation of *sublist*, however, results in a call to the function hd, namely $[hd[e]]$, whose f-value is 0 (as it is independent of i and j), which is less than 2.

The inductive step proceeds by assuming that all calls to sublist for some list x result only in calls with lower f-values, and showing this property also holds true for calls involving $a::x$. Again we proceed by cases, and will give just one example to illustrate the technique.

Case $i > 1$

$$sublist \ a::x \ i \ j = sublist \ x \ i - 1 \ j - 1$$

and

$$f(sublist \ a::x \ i \ j) = i + j > f(sublist \ x \ i - 1 \ j - 1) = i + j - 2$$

but since, by our induction hypothesis, $sublist \ x \ i - 1 \ j - 1$ results in calls with lower f-values, all resulting calls from *sublist* $a::x \ i \ j$ must have lower f-values, and the result is proved.

2.5 Procedural paradigms

There are two famous approaches to proving program correctness for pre- and post-condition specifications and procedural implementations. These two approaches have many similarities, but for the sake of clarity will be treated separately here. For a development of the two systems in parallel, and a discussion of how they are related, see Backhouse (1986).

2.5.1 Weakest pre-conditions

This approach, developed by Dijkstra (1976), treats a program P as a predicate transformer. Consider a program P designed to meet a specification with post-condition $post_p$. In general, there will be many pre-conditions that define states from which P could execute and terminate in acceptable final states. The weakest pre-condition is the pre-condition that is implied by all others, it is defined precisely by the program P and the post-condition $post_p$. We denote it as:

$$wp(P, post_p)$$

Thus a given program P has the effect of transforming any post-condition $post_p$ into the appropriate weakest pre-condition. We require weakest pre-conditions for individual programming language statements, as well as whole programs, but we shall refer to all such constructs as P, since a program is itself a valid program statement. Indeed, we will calculate the weakest pre-condition for a program by calculating the weakest pre-conditions for the statements that make it up.

For a given specification $(pre_p, post_p)$, a program P is (totally) correct with respect to this specification iff:

$$pre_p \Rightarrow wp(P, post_p)$$

Note that if P is only partially correct, then we will not in general be able to prove this implication, because pre_p alone will be too weak to ensure termination.

A program is partially correct, that is:

$$\{pre_p\}P\{post_p\}$$

if we can prove that:

$$(pre_p \land wp(P, true)) \Rightarrow wp(P, post_p)$$

since $wp(P, true)$ is the weakest pre-condition ensuring termination in any state.

This technique assumes that we are able to calculate $wp(P, post_p)$ for all P and $post_p$, and the core of this method is the provision of such a calculus. This calculus can be presented as a number of laws, which can be treated as axioms in our formal system. Some of these laws are general, in the sense that they are independent of the details of the program statement P, others are specific to particular programming language constructs, and so need to be defined for specific languages.

Since $wp(P, post_p)$ is a proposition, we should be careful of writing $wp(P, post_p) = Q$, since equality is normally reserved for identity between objects in the world being discussed, and not equivalence of truth values. We should write either $wp(P, post_p) \Leftrightarrow Q$ or $wp(P, post_p) \equiv Q$, to denote equivalence of truth values. In practice, however, most authors on weakest pre-conditions allow the overloading of ' = ', allowing the context in which it is being used to disambiguate its meaning. This use of ' = ' will be followed, and it reinforces the notion that a calculus of weakest pre-conditions is being developed.

First the general laws, which hold true for all program statements are introduced.

2.5.1.1 Law of the excluded miracle

There are no initial states for which a statement can be guaranteed to terminate in no state (it would certainly be a miracle if any statement could terminate without ending up in some state!):

$$wp(P, false) = false$$

Note that there is no corresponding law for $wp(P, true)$: it is tempting to believe that a suitable weakest pre-condition here is *true*, but this would mean that all statements P would be guaranteed to terminate, and this is clearly not the case, otherwise infinite loops would not be programmable.

2.5.1.2 Law of monotonicity

$$(Q \Rightarrow R) \Rightarrow (wp(P,Q) \Rightarrow wp(P,R))$$

Any state s which satisfies Q must also satisfy R. Any initial state that guarantees termination in a state satisfying Q also guarantees termination in a state satisfying R.

2.5.1.3 Distribution of conjunctions

$$wp(P, Q \wedge R) = wp(P,Q) \wedge wp(P,R)$$

Consider a state s which satisfies $wp(P, Q \wedge R)$. If we execute P from this state then clearly we end up in a state which satisfies Q and also satisfies R (since it satisfies $Q \wedge R$). Thus $wp(P, Q \wedge R) \Rightarrow wp(P,Q) \wedge wp(P,R)$. Now consider a state s which satisfies $wp(P,Q) \wedge wp(P,R)$, execution from this state must result in a state which satisfies P and also satisfies R, thus $wp(P,Q) \wedge wp(P,R) \Rightarrow wp(P,Q \wedge R)$. Hence we can see that $wp(P, R \wedge R) = wp(P, W) \wedge wp(P,R)$ (remembering that we are using '=' here as a synonym for $\Leftrightarrow$).

2.5.1.4 Distribution of disjunction

$$wp(P,Q) \vee wp(P,R) \Rightarrow wp(P, Q \vee R)$$

Consider a state s which satisfies $wp(P,Q) \vee wp(P,R)$, if we execute P from this state then clearly we end up in a state which satisfies $Q \vee R$. The converse is not true, in general, as we can have a non-deterministic statement. Consider a random number generator, G, which outputs integers. The output must satisfy one of the predicates $even(r)$ or $odd(r)$. Thus $wp(G, even \vee odd) = true$, but $wp(G, odd) = false$, as there are no states that can guarantee the random number generated will be *odd*, similarly $wp(G, even) = false$. Now, $false \Rightarrow true$ but it is not the case that $true \Rightarrow false$, so we cannot, in general, replace the $\Rightarrow$ with an $=$ in the above law.

For a deterministic statement, however, where every valid initial state corresponds to a unique final state, the equality will hold. Consider a state which satisfies $wp(P,Q) \vee wp(P,R)$. If we execute P from this state we must end up in a unique state which satisfies either Q or R or both. Thus $wp(P, Q \wedge R) \Rightarrow wp(P,Q) \vee wp(P,R)$, and so the $\Rightarrow$ in the above law could become an $=$.

Now for the laws which are specific to a particular programming language. To explain these properly, it is necessary to introduce a simple programming language as a vehicle for discussion. This language is a trivial subset of many real languages, although the syntax may differ slightly. To utilize this technique on a real problem, of course, it is necessary to find the appropriate calculus for the particular programming language being used.

2.5.1.5 Assignment statements

Consider the statement:

    x:= e

where x is a variable and e is an expression, and their types are compatible. First, note that there is no problem of termination with this statement; we can expect it to terminate for any pre-condition. Second, if we want the post-condition Q to hold after execution, and Q is written in terms of x, then this will only be the case if Q holds with e textually replacing all free occurrences of x in Q before the assignment. We will write this as $Q[e/x]$, although you will often see it written as Q_e^x. Thus:

$$wp(x:= e, Q) = Q[e/x]$$

Strictly, this is not enough. We should also include conditions to the effect that x and e are of compatible types, and that e is well defined, and hence can be evaluated. In practice, attempting to include too much in the calculus makes for a formal clutter which renders the technique useless, and it is often easier to reason about the type compatibilities and other such issues separately, and many compilers will perform such checks anyway.

An example of the use of this law is:

$$wp(x:= 7, x > 5) = x > 5[7/x] = 7 > 5 = true$$

Thus this assignment statement will terminate with $x > 5$ for all initial states.

Another example is:

$$wp(x:= x + y, x > 0) = x > 0[x + y/x] = x + y > 0 = x > -y$$

Thus this assignment statement will terminate with $x > 0$ provided that initially $x > -y$.

It is tempting, however, to expect too much from this simple law, and use it for more complex assignments. Consider assignment to an array element, for example, we might ask what is:

$$wp(a[i]:= a[i] + 1, \forall x . 0 \leqslant x \leqslant i \Rightarrow even(a[x]))$$

where $even(x)$ is a predicate that returns *true* if x is an even number. Now, if we use the law for assignment given above, then we get:

$$wp(a[i]:= a[i] + 1, \forall x . 0 \leqslant x \leqslant i \Rightarrow even(a[x]))$$
$$= \forall x . 0 \leqslant x \leqslant i \Rightarrow even(a[x])[a[i] + 1/a[i]]$$

but since $\forall x . 0 \leqslant x \leqslant i \Rightarrow even(a[x])$ does not contain the string 'a[i]', no substitution takes place, and the pre-condition is the same as the post-condition. This is patently absurd, as the post-condition states that $a[i]$ must be even, if the statement being executed adds one then clearly $a[i]$ cannot be even before execution.

Array elements, like other complex data structures, cannot be handled with the law for simple assignment, and need their own laws devised. For example, we might treat arrays as functions, thus we can think of the array:

$$b[1] = 3, b[2] = 5, b[3] = 7$$

as the function:

$$b = \{1 \mapsto 3, 2 \mapsto 5, 3 \mapsto 7\}$$

Assignment to an array element now corresponds to function overriding, so that:

$b[2] := 9$ corresponds to $b \oplus \{2 \mapsto 9\}$

and thus returns a new array.

In the literature on correctness, this overriding is often written as:

$b;2:9$

especially when the substitution notation:

$Q^b_{b;2:9}$

is being used.

Using this idea, we can produce a law for assignment to an array variable

$wp(b[i] := e, Q) = Q[b;i:e/b]$

thus:

$wp(a[i] := a[i] + 1, \forall x . 0 \leqslant x \leqslant i \Rightarrow even(a[x]))$
$= \forall x . 0 \leqslant x \leqslant i \Rightarrow even(a[x])[a;i:a[i] + 1/a]$
$= \forall x . 0 \leqslant x \leqslant i \Rightarrow even((a;i:a[i] + 1)[x])$

That is, all the values in the array must be even, except for the ith, which must be odd. Strictly, we should enhance this law, to include assertions that the array index is within range, but this is usually treated separately.

2.5.1.6 Law of statement composition

The programming language allows statements to be composed into larger statements by writing:

$P_1;P_2$

The semicolon is associative, so $P_1;(P_2;P_3)$ is the same as $(P_1;P_2);P_3$ and we can omit the brackets if we wish. The law for this construct is:

$wp(P_1;P_2, Q) = wp(P_1, wp(P_2, Q))$

That is, the weakest pre-condition for the composite of P_1 and P_2 is found by calculating the weakest pre-condition which will force P_2 to terminate satisfying Q, and then calculating the weakest pre-condition that will force P_1 to terminate in a state which meets the weakest pre-condition for P_2.

For example:

$wp(x := y + z; x := x + x, x > 20)$
$= wp(x := y + z, wp(x := x + x, x > 20))$
$= wp(x := y + z, x > 20[x + x/x])$
$= wp(x := y + z, 2x > 20) = 2x > 20[y + z/x]$
$= 2(y + z) > 20$
$= y + z > 10$

2.5.1.7 Laws of conditionals

Consider the statement:

if B then P_1 else P_2

The weakest pre-condition for this statement, with respect to some post-condition Q, can be seen by considering the two possible execution paths through the statement. If the Boolean B is true then we execute P_1, whereas if it is false (i.e. $\neg B$ is true) then we execute P_2:

$wp(\text{if } B \text{ then } P_1 \text{ else } P_2, Q)$
$= (B \Rightarrow wp(P_1, Q)) \wedge (\neg B \Rightarrow wp(P_2, Q))$

For example:

$wp(\text{if } k < 0 \text{ then } x := -k \text{ else } x := k, x \geqslant 0)$
$= (k < 0 \Rightarrow wp(x := -k, x \geqslant 0)) \wedge ((\neg (k < 0) \Rightarrow$
$\quad\quad\quad\quad\quad\quad\quad\quad\quad\quad wp(x := k, x \geqslant 0)))$
$= (k < 0 \Rightarrow x \geqslant 0[-k/x]) \wedge (k \geqslant 0 \Rightarrow x \geqslant 0[k/x])$
$= (k < 0 \Rightarrow -k \geqslant 0) \wedge (k \geqslant 0 \Rightarrow k \geqslant 0)$
$= true \wedge true$
$= true$

so this conditional statement will always result in a state which satisfies the post-condition.

A similar consideration leads to the law:

$wp(\text{if } B \text{ then } P, Q) = (B \Rightarrow wp(P, Q)) \wedge (\neg B \Rightarrow Q)$

2.5.1.8 Law of iteration

This can be illustrated with a while statement of the form:

while B do P done

where B is a Boolean expression and P is a statement.

Now, if we unravel this statement, we find that its execution corresponds to a, possibly empty, sequence $P; P; P; \ldots; P$. If the required post-condition is Q, then we can say that if the sequence is empty, the required weakest pre-condition must be:

$W_0 = \neg B \wedge Q$

B must be false, otherwise the body of the while loop would have been executed at least once, and as the body is not executed, the post-condition must already be satisfied. If the sequence contains just one execution of P, then the weakest pre-condition must be:

$W_1 = B \wedge wp(P, W_0)$

B must now be true, otherwise P will not be executed, and after P has been executed we are back at the top of the loop, but now the body will not be entered, and so $wp(P, W_0)$ must hold true to ensure we end up satisfying the post-condition Q.

Carrying on in this vein, we can obtain a sequence of weakest pre-conditions, whose general case is:

$W_k = B \wedge wp(P, W_{k-1})$ where $k \geqslant 2$

Now we do not know in advance how many times the body will be executed, but we do know that if the loop is to terminate then it must execute a finite number of times. Thus our general weakest pre-condition asserts that there must be a finite number for which a particualar weakest pre-condition is satisfied:

$wp(\text{while } B \text{ do } P \text{ done}, Q) = \exists k : \mathbb{N} . W_k$

To illustrate this law, consider the following program:

t := a;
r := 1;

while t > 1 do
    r:= t*r
    t:= 1 − 1
    done

with the required post-condition:

$$r = a!$$

Since the while loop is the last statement executed, its post-condition must be the post-condition of the whole program. We can write down its weakest pre-condition by constructing W_k. To see this, we will construct the first few values in the sequence $W_0, W_1, W_2, \ldots$. One can see in this example that the symbol '=' is being overloaded:

$$
\begin{aligned}
W_0 &= \neg(t > 1) \land r = a! \\
&= t \leqslant 1 \land r = a! \\
W_1 &= t > 1 \land wp(r:= t*r;t:= t − 1, W_0) \\
&= t > 1 \land wp(r:= t*r;t:= t − 1, t \leqslant 1 \land r = a!) \\
&= t > 1 \land wp(r:= t*r, wp(t:= t − 1, t \leqslant 1 \land r = a!)) \\
&= t > 1 \land wp(r:= t*r, t − 1 \leqslant 1 \land r = a!) \\
&= t > 1 \land t − 1 \leqslant 1 \land t*r = a! \\
&= (t = 2) \land t*r = a! \\
W_2 &= t > 1 \land wp(r:= t*r;t:= t − 1, W_1) \\
&= t > 1 \land wp(r:= t*r;t:= t − 1, t = 2 \land t*r = a!) \\
&= t > 1 \land wp(r:= t*r, wp(t:= t − 1, t = 2 \land t*r = a!)) \\
&= t > 1 \land wp(r:= t*r, t − 1 = 2 \land (t − 1)*r = a!) \\
&= t > 1 \land t − 1 = 2 \land (t − 1)*t*r = a! \\
&= (t = 3) \land (t − 1)*t*r = a! \\
&\vdots \\
W_k &= (t = k + 1) \land t*(t − 1)*(t − 2)*\ldots*(t − k + 1)*r = a!
\end{aligned}
$$

So now the weakest pre-condition for our while loop is:

$$wp_{while} = \exists k:\mathbf{N}.(t = k + 1) \land t*(t − 1)*(t − 2)*\ldots*(t − k + 1)$$
$$*r = a!$$

Using this as the post-condition for the statement $t:= a;r:= 1$ yields a weakest pre-condition for the program of:

$$
\begin{aligned}
&wp(t:= a;r:= 1, wp_{while}) = wp(t:= a, wp(r:= q, wp_{while})) \\
&= wp(t:= a, wp(r:= 1, \exists k:\mathbf{N}.(t = k + 1) \land t*(t − 1)*(t − 2) \\
&\qquad\qquad\qquad\qquad\qquad\qquad *\ldots* (t − k + 1)*r = a!)) \\
&= wp(t:= a, \exists k:\mathbf{N}.(t = k + 1) \land t*(t − 1)*(t − 2) \\
&\qquad\qquad\qquad\qquad\qquad *\ldots*(t − k + 1)*1 = a!) \\
&= \exists k:\mathbf{N}.(a = k + 1) \land a*(a − 1)*(a − 2) \\
&\qquad\qquad\qquad\qquad *\ldots*(a − k + 1)*1 = a! \\
&= a > 0
\end{aligned}
$$

2.5.1.9 Laws for procedures

Procedures are too complex to treat with any sort of generality in this short introduction, but the approach adopted to calculating suitable weakest pre-conditions is usually along the following lines.

It is assumed that each procedure has a body to be executed, and a list of formal parameters. These parameters can be considered to be of three classes: in parameters, which contain meaningful values of entry which cannot be changed by the procedure; out parameters, which contain no meaningful values on entry to the procedure but will be assigned meanings by the procedure body; and in–out parameters, which contain meaningful values on entry but can also be changed by the procedure body.

Procedure definitions will look something like:

procedure P(in:x; in–out:y; out:z)

where **x**, **y** and **z** are vectors of formal parameters (that is, parameters used in the definition).
Procedure calls will look like:

*P(**a**,**b**,**c**)*

where we assume that the types and numbers of the actual parameters contained in **a**, **b** and **c** are appropriate, and the same name is never used twice.

Now, we can consider a procedure call as performing the following actions:

1. Substitute the actual parameters **a** and **b** for the formal in and in–out parameters **x** and **y**. This can be viewed as two assignments.
2. Execute the body, *B*, of the procedure call.
3. Substitute the formal in–out and out parameters **y** and **z** for the actual parameters **b** and **c**.

This gives rise to the law:

$$wp(P(\mathbf{a},\mathbf{b},\mathbf{c}),Q) = wp(x:= \mathbf{a}; y:= \mathbf{b}; B; \mathbf{b}:= y; \mathbf{c}:= z, Q)$$

To illustrate this, let us turn the factorial program developed above into a procedure:

procedure factorial (a:in; r:out)
    t:= a;
    r:= 1;
    while t > 1 do
        r:= t*r;
        t:= 1 − 1
        done
end procedure

We will denote the body of the procedure by *F*. Remember that we know $wp(F, r = a!) = a > 0$.
Now let us call the procedure as follows:

factorial(7,j)

Clearly the desired post-condition is $j = 7!$, but what is the weakest pre-condition?

$$
\begin{aligned}
wp(factorial(7,j), j = 7!) &= wp(a:= 7; F; j:= r, j = 7!) \\
&= wp(a:= 7; F, wp(j:= r, j = 7!)) \\
&= wp(a:= 7; F, r = 7!) \\
&= wp(a:= 7, wp(F, r = 7!)) \\
&= wp(a:= 7, 7 > 0) \\
&= 7 > 0 \\
&= true
\end{aligned}
$$

Thus this procedure call will always succeed.

In practice, however, most procedure mechanisms are not this straightforward. We need laws to handle calls by name, reference and value, and preferably laws that are easier to use than the one given above. Restrictions placed on the use of procedures may well allow simplifications to the laws. For a more detailed account of the problems associated with procedures see Gries (1981).

2.5.1.10 Further reading

There are two main sources of information on weakest pre-conditions. The original source by Dijkstra, *A Discipline of Programming* (1976), contains a more detailed account of the calculus of weakest pre-conditions, and also many examples of its use on quite complex problems. Gries's book, *The Science of Programming* (1981), contains a section on weakest pre-conditions which develops some of the ideas presented by Dijkstra, and also attempts to show how these ideas can be used in the development of programs.

2.5.2 Hoare logics

Hoare logics are very explicitly formal systems within which proofs of program correctness take place. Whereas the use of weakest pre-conditions seems like fairly conventional mathematics, because it centres on the use of the substitution of equal quantities, Hoare logics introduce new inference rules into the formal system of predicate logic.

A more significant difference between Hoare logics and the use of weakest pre-conditions is that the former are usually only used for proving partial correctness, proofs of termination being treated separately. This is not necessarily the case, and Hoare logics for proving total correctness have been developed, but they will not be considered here. An introduction to such logics may be found in Manna (1974).

There is one general rule which is independent of any particular programming language:

2.5.2.1 Rule of consequence

$$\frac{P \Rightarrow S, \{S\}Q\{R\}}{\{P\}Q\{R\}} \quad \text{and} \quad \frac{R \Rightarrow T, \{S\}Q\{R\}}{\{S\}Q\{T\}}$$

We can always replace a pre-condition by a stronger condition, or a post-condition by a weaker condition. For example, if a program is defined for all $n \geqslant 0$ then it is also defined for all $n > 0$, because $n \geqslant 0 \Rightarrow n > 0$. Similarly, if a program is guaranteed to terminate such that $n > 0$ then it is guaranteed to terminate such that $n \geqslant 0$.

2.5.2.2 Axiom (schema) of assignment

$$\{P[e/x]\} x := e\{P\}$$

This is really saying that:

$$\{wp(x := e, P\} x := e\{P\}$$

which should come as no surprise.

This is called an axiom schema because it allows us to generate an infinite number of axioms, by varying the values of x, e and P.

For example:

$$\{x \geqslant 0[-x/x]\} x := -x\{x \geqslant 0\}$$

is an axiom, which can be rewritten as:

$$\{x \leqslant 0\} x := -x\{x \geqslant 0\}$$

If we want a statement of partial correctness with a stronger pre-condition, then we can use the rule of consequence to generate one. Using the fact that $x < 0 \Rightarrow x \leqslant 0$ we can apply the law of consequence to get:

$$\{x < 0\} x := -x\{x \geqslant 0\}$$

2.5.2.3 Rule of composition

$$\frac{\{P\}A\{Q\}, \{Q\}B\{S\}}{\{P\}A; B\{S\}}$$

Note that we can only apply the rule of composition if the inner conditions, Q match: the rule of consequence allows us to achieve this.

2.5.2.4 Rules of conditionals

For the statement:

if B then P

there are two possible execution paths. Consider a specification with pre-condition Q and post-condition R. Either B is false, and this fact together with the pre-condition Q is sufficient to imply the post-condition R, or B is true, and the execution of P must ensure the post-condition is met:

$$\frac{Q \wedge \neg B \Rightarrow R, \{Q \wedge B\}P\{R\}}{\{Q\}\text{if } B \text{ then } P_1 \text{ else } P\{R\}}$$

A similar argument leads to:

$$\frac{\{Q \wedge B\}P_1\{R\}, \{Q \wedge \neg B\}P_2\{R\}}{\{Q\}\text{if } B \text{ then } P_1 \text{ else } P_2\{R\}}$$

For example, to prove the correctness of the program:

if $x < 0$ then $y := -x$ else $y := x$

with respect to the specification:

prog: $Int \rightarrow Int$
pre-prog $\triangleq true$
post-prog $\triangleq (y \geqslant 0) \wedge ((y = x) \vee (y = -x))$

we need to show that:

$\{true\}$if $x < 0$ then $y := -x$ else
$y := x\{(y \geqslant 0) \wedge ((y = x) \vee (y = -x))\}$

Proof:

1. $\{(x \geqslant 0) \wedge ((x = x) \vee (x = -x))\} y := x$
   $\{(y \geqslant 0) \wedge (y = x) \vee (y = -x)\}$
   Axiom of assignment
2. $(true \wedge \neg (x < 0)) \Rightarrow (x \geqslant 0) \wedge ((x = x) \wedge (x = -x))$
   Lemma
3. $\{(true \wedge \neg (x < 0))\} y := x\{(y \geqslant 0) \wedge ((y = x) \vee (y = -x))\}$
   1,2 consequence
4. $\{(-x \geqslant 0) \wedge ((-x = x) \vee (-x = -x))\} y := -x\{(y \geqslant 0)$
   $\wedge ((y = x) \vee (y = -x))\}$
   Axiom of assignment
5. $(true \wedge (x < 0)) \Rightarrow (-x \geqslant 0) \wedge ((-x = x) \vee (-x = -x))$
   Lemma
6. $\{(true \wedge (x < 0))\} y := -x\{(y \geqslant 0) \wedge ((y = x) \vee (y = -x))\}$
   4,5 consequence
7. $\{true\}$if $x < 0$ else $y := -x$ else $y := x$
   $\{(y \geqslant 0) \wedge ((y = x) \vee (y = -x))\}$
   3,6 conditionals

QED

Note that we again had to introduce a number of lemmas corresponding to properties of the data types being used, here the properties of integers and inequalities. In practice, considerable skill and experience is required to derive suitable lemmas.

2.5.2.5 *Rule of iteration*

The rule for handling:

while B do P done

is rather simpler than the corresponding law for calculating the weakest pre-condition, because we are only dealing with partial correctness, and so we do not need to ensure termination using the rule.

This law hinges on finding the loop invariant for the construct, that is, an assertion I which is true both before P is executed and after, and hence this invariant must hold regardless of the number of times that the loop is executed. This gives rise to the rule:

$$\frac{\{I \wedge B\}P\{I\}}{\{I\}\text{while }B\text{ do }P\text{ done}\{I \wedge \neg B\}}$$

Notice that we do not need to include terms to handle the case when B is initially false as an antecedent, because this would just introduce $(I \wedge \neg B) \Rightarrow (I \wedge \neg B)$ which is tautologous.

For example, here is a program to meet the following specification:

$prog: \mathbb{N} \rightarrow \mathbb{N}$
$pre\text{-}prog \triangleq y > 0$
$post\text{-}prog \triangleq 2^{n-1} < y \leqslant 2^n$

n: = 0;
k: = 1;
while y > k do
    k: = k*2;
    n: = n + 1
    done

For convenience, we will refer to the body of the loop as W. The loop invariant is:

$(y > 2^{n-1}) \wedge (k = 2^n)$

We need to show that:

$\{y > 1\}prog\{2^{n-1} < y \leqslant 2^n\}$

Proof:

1. $\{(y > 2^n) \wedge (k = 2^{n+1})\}n := n + 1\{(y > 2^{n-1}) \wedge (k = 2^n)\}$
   Axiom of assignment
2. $\{(y > 2^n) \wedge (k*2 = 2^{n+1})\}k := k*2\{(y > 2^n) \wedge (k = 2^{n+1})\}$
   Axiom of assignment
3. $\{(y > 2^n) \wedge (k*2 = 2^{n+1})\}k := k*2; n := n + 1$
   $\{(y > 2^{n-1}) \wedge (k = 2^n)\}$
   1,2 composition
4. $((y > 2^{n-1}) \wedge (k = 2^n) \wedge (y > k)) \Rightarrow ((y > 2^n) \wedge (k*2 = 2^{n+1}))$
   Lemma
5. $\{(y > 2^{n-1}) \wedge (k = 2^n) \wedge (y > k)\}k := k*2; n := n + 1$
   $\{(y > 2^{n-1}) \wedge (k = 2^n)\}$
   3,4 consequence
6. $\{(y > 2^{n-1}) \wedge (k = 2^n)\}W\{(y > 2^{n-1}) \wedge (k = 2^n) \wedge \neg (y > k)\}$
   5 iteration

7. $((y > 2^{n-1}) \wedge (k = 2^n) \wedge \neg (y > k)) \Rightarrow 2^{n-1} < y \leqslant 2^n$
   Lemma
8. $\{(y > 2^{n-1}) \wedge (k = 2^n)\}W\{2^{n-1} < y \leqslant 2^n\}$
   6,7 consequence
9. $\{(y > 2^{n-1}) \wedge (1 = 2^n)\}k := 1\{(y > 2^{n-1}) \wedge (k = 2^n)\}$
   Axiom of assignment
10. $\{(y > 2^{-1}) \wedge (1 = 2^0)\}n := 0\{(y > 2^{n-1}) \wedge (1 = 2^n)\}$
   Axiom of assignment
11. $y > 1 \Rightarrow ((y > 2^{n-1}) \wedge (1 = 2^0))$
   Lemma
12. $\{y > 1\}n := 0\{(y > 2^{n-1}) \wedge (1 = 2^n)\}$
   10,11 consequence
13. $\{y > 1\}n := 0; k := 1\{(y > 2^{n-1}) \wedge (k = 2^n)\}$
   9,12 composition
7. $\{y > 1\}prog\{2^{n-1} < y \leqslant 2^n\}$
   8,13 composition

QED

2.5.2.6 *Further reading*

There are a number of sources of further information on Hoare logics. In particular, there is a paper on the use of these for procedures (Hoare, 1989e), an embryonic logic for Pascal (Hoare, 1989b), an introduction to the use of such logics for parallel programming (Hoare, 1989d), the extension of such logics for parallel programming to provide proofs of total correctness (Hoare, 1989c), and a survey of Hoare logics in use (Apt 1981).

2.6 Conclusions

This chapter has only illustrated the principles of proving the correctness of programs with simple problems using small subsets of programming languages. It should be clear, however, that these principles can be extended to deal with larger problems and complete programming languages, although certain aspects of modern languages, such as concurrency, can be difficult to treat formally.

In practice, however, it is hard to carry out formal proofs without some automated support. Some of these automated verification environments are discussed in Chapter 26. Unfortunately, current technology is still only able to support relatively modest programs (circa 5000 lines). This does not mean that the techniques are without value. They provide a theoretical basis for reasoning about the correctness of programs, and thus are an essential tool for the software engineer in showing fitness for purpose, whether formally or informally. As discussed in the epilogue, these techniques must become part of our engineering culture.

2.7 References

Andrews, P. B. (1986) *An Introduction To Mathematical Logic and Type Theory: To Truth through Proof*, Academic Press

Apt, K. R. (1981) Ten years of Hoare logic, a survey, part 1. *ACM Transactions on Programming Languages and Systems*, 3, 431–483

Backhouse, R. C. (1986) *Program Construction and Verification*, Prentice Hall

Dijkstra, E. W. (1976) *A Discipline of Programming*, Prentice Hall

Gries, D. (1971) *The Science of Programming*, Springer-Verlag

Hoare, C. A. R. (1989a) An axiomatic basis for computing programming. In *Essays in Computing Science* (eds C. A. R. Hoare and C. B. Jones), Prentice Hall

Hoare, C. A. R. (1989b) An axiomatic definition of the programming language Pascal. In *Essays in Computing Science* (eds C. A. R. Hoare and C. B. Jones), Prentice Hall

Hoare, C. A. R. (1989c) A calculus of total correctness for communicating sequential processes. In *Essays in Computing Science* (eds C. A. R. Hoare and C. B. Jones), Prentice Hall

Hoare, C. A. R. (1989d) Parallel programming: an axiomatic approach. In *Essays in Computing Science* (eds C. A. R. Hoare and C. B. Jones), Prentice Hall

Hoare, C. A. R. (1989e) Procedures and parameters: an axiomatic approach. In *Essays in Computing Science* (eds. C. A. R. Hoare and C. B. Jones), Prentice Hall

Jones, C. B. (1980) *Systematic Software Developing Using VDM*, Prentice Hall

Lemmon, E. J. (1965) *Beginning Logic*, Nelson

Manna, Z. (1974) *Mathematical Theory of Computation*, McGraw-Hill

Newton-Smith, W. H. (1985) *Logic – An Introductory Course*, Routledge & Kegan Paul

3

Introduction to algebra

David Pitt
Paddy Byers
University of Surrey, Guildford

Contents

3.1 Introduction

Computer programming is primarily concerned with abstraction. An abstraction of a 'real world' problem, albeit simple arithmetic, the dynamics of some physical system or a large information system, must be modelled and manipulated in a machine. The notion of a type is paramount in most modern programming languages and even in BASIC we have the notion of integer variables, Boolean variables, etc. In its simplest form a type is a set of values, which will have to be represented internally (and externally) together with a family of operations which may be carried out on them. For example, a type integer may involve the operations, addition, subtraction, multiplication, each of which take two integer arguments and yield an integer result. Types may be more complicated, involving more than one sort of value. In our example we may also have the operations 'greater than' and 'less than', each of which take two integer arguments and yield a Boolean result. However, here, for simplicity, we shall focus on types with only one sort of value, but all the results that are presented easily generalize to the many-sorted case.

The description of integers is a simple abstraction from many 'real world' problems. Its utility need not be debated. However, just as, historically, various representations of such a system were formulated on tablet, papyrus, or paper, the implementor of a language incorporating such a type must find an internal representation of the values and the operations. These implemented operations must then behave in a manner which is consistent with our external representation.

To address such issues we need a framework within which we can formalize the abstraction of the system in such a way that:

1. The notion of a 'representation'.
2. The constraints which representations must satisfy.
3. The concepts involved in comparing representations.
   may all be made precise.

Abstract algebra provides just such a framework.

3.2 Signatures and structures

In the type integer discussed above we have only one sort of value:

Sort   integer

Three operations were mentioned:

Operations   plus: integer, integer $\rightarrow$ integer

                  minus: integer, integer $\rightarrow$ integer

                  multiply: integer, integer $\rightarrow$ integer

Each of these takes two arguments of sort integer and yields a result of sort integer. Where we only have one sort the number of arguments of an operation is referred to as its 'arity'. Thus the three operations listed above each have arity two. An operation of arity one will take a single argument of sort integer and yield a result of sort integer. So, for example, we might include:

negate: integer $\rightarrow$ integer

We may also require that our sort has some specific named values in its representations, for example zero or one. These constants could be thought of as operations of arity zero (with no arguments) simply returning a constant value. Thus we could include them in our purely syntactic listing of sort and operation symbols either as:

zero: integer

or as:

one: $\rightarrow$ integer

The listing of the sort symbols (names) and operation symbols (names) together with the sort names of their arguments and results is called a 'signature'.

Definition. A *single sorted signature*, $\Sigma = (S, \alpha)$ is a sort name S together with a sequence $\alpha = (K_0, K_1, \ldots, K_n, \ldots)$ of sets of operation symbols, K_n being the collection of operation symbols of arity n. (If we wish to avoid name clashes, we may require these to be disjoint.)

Thus if we require our type to have only one sort (and henceforth we shall), together with one 'binary operation', that is, an operation which takes two arguments of sort S and 'combines them' to yield a result of sort S, our signature would include a name for the sort, say S, and a name for the binary operation, say 'combine'. Thus we would have:

Sort   S
Operation   combine: S, S $\rightarrow$ S

Signature 2a

We would also present this single-sorted signature as:

$$\Sigma = (S, \alpha)$$

where $\alpha = (K_0, K_1, K_2, K_3, \ldots)$

and $K_0 = \emptyset$,

        $K_1 = \emptyset$,

        $K_2 = \{combine\}$,

        $K_3 = \emptyset$,

        . . .

Signature 2b

The intended meaning of signature 2 is that S should be represented by some set of values, S_M say, and combine should be interpreted as a function, $combine_M$, which given two values from S_M will yield a third. Any set S_M with a binary operation $combine_M$ is called a structure over signature 2. The set S_M is called the carrier of the sort symbol S, and the function $combine_M$ is called the interpretation of the operation combine.

The first such structures to come to mind are arithmetic in nature, in which the carrier for S is a set of numbers and the interpretation of combine is an arithmetic operation:

Structure N_1 $S_{N_1} = $ $\leq$ the set of real numbers

            $combine_{N_1} = $ $+$ addition

Here the carrier for S is the set of real numbers and combine is interpreted as addition.

Structure N_2 $S_{N_2} = $ $\leq^+$ the set of positive real numbers

            $combine_{N_1} = $ $\times$ multiplication

Structure N_3 $S_{N_3} = $ $\mathbb{Z}$ the set of integers

            $combine_{N_3} = $ $-$ subtraction

The list of 'arithmetic structures' could continue; however, there are many other familiar and equally important signature 2 structures:

Structure L_1 $\qquad S_{L_1} =$ {true, false}

$\qquad\qquad$ combine$_{L_1} = \quad \wedge \qquad$ and

If we choose any set A then there are various signature 2 structures associated with A which are of interest:

Structure A_1 $\qquad S_{A_1} = \quad$ A* $\quad$ the set of all strings
$\qquad\qquad\qquad\qquad\qquad\qquad$ (finite sequences) over
$\qquad\qquad\qquad\qquad\qquad\qquad$ some alphabet A

$\qquad\qquad$ combine$_{A_1} = \quad \hat{} \qquad$ concatenation

e.g. $\qquad\qquad\qquad$ A = {a, b, c}

$\qquad\qquad\qquad\qquad$ A* = {$\langle\,\rangle$, $\langle$a$\rangle$, $\langle$ab$\rangle$, $\langle$b$\rangle$, $\langle$bca$\rangle$,
$\qquad\qquad\qquad\qquad\qquad\quad$ ...}

Structure A_2 $\qquad S_{A_2} = \quad \mathbb{P}(A) \quad$ the set of all finite
$\qquad\qquad\qquad\qquad\qquad\qquad\qquad$ subsets of A

$\qquad\qquad$ combine$_{A_2} = \quad \cup \qquad$ union

e.g. with A as above, $\mathbb{P}(A) = \{\Phi, \{a\}, \{b\}, \{c\}, \{a, b\}, \ldots\}$

Structure A_3 $\qquad S_{A_3} = \quad$ Tr A $\quad$ the set of all
$\qquad\qquad\qquad\qquad\qquad\qquad\qquad$ non-empty binary
$\qquad\qquad\qquad\qquad\qquad\qquad\qquad$ trees whose leaves
$\qquad\qquad\qquad\qquad\qquad\qquad\qquad$ are labelled with
$\qquad\qquad\qquad\qquad\qquad\qquad\qquad$ elements of A,

$\qquad\qquad\qquad\qquad$ Tr A =

$\qquad\qquad$ combine$_{A_3} = \quad$ 'join' $\quad$ as illustrated below:

In each case we have a set, S_M, of values associated with the sort S and, associated with each operation symbol $f \in K_n$, we have a function, f_M, which takes an appropriate number of arguments:

$$f_M: \ S_M \times S_M \times \ldots \times S_M \to S_M$$

where:

$S_M \times S_M \times \ldots \times S_M$ is the set of n-tuples of elements of S_M. Returning to the type of integers discussed earlier,

$$\Sigma = (\text{Integer}, (K_0, K_1, K_2, \emptyset, \emptyset, \ldots)),$$

$$K_0 = \{\text{zero, one}\},$$

$$K_1 = \{\text{negate}\},$$

$$K_2 = \{\text{plus, minus, multiply}\},$$

an implementation may involve an 'internal' structure, the carrier for integer being the set of possible stored values for an integer variable, integer$_{internal}$. The values corresponding to zero and one and the functions corresponding to the implementations of negate, plus, minus, and multiply will be the interpretations of these operations. The user of this implementation will also have an 'external' structure in mind. Ignoring the limitations of storage space, each value in the external structure will be represented internally.

We therefore have a function

$\qquad$ representation of: integer$_{external} \to$ integer$_{internal}$

carrying each external integer value to its internal counterpart. To be useful the function must respect our operations; it must 'simulate' the external structure in the internal structure. If we enter '5' and '7' and then add them internally, the result should be the same as adding them externally and then entering the resulting '12'.

Formally:

$\qquad$ add$_{internal}$(representation of(5), representation of(7))
$\qquad\qquad\qquad$ = representation of(add$_{external}$(5,7))

This property must hold for all external values and each operation symbol, and motivates the following definition:

Definition. Given a pair of structures M and N for a signature $\Sigma = (S, (K_0, K_1, \ldots))$, a homomorphism, ϕ, from M to N is a function $\phi: S_M \to S_N$ such that for each $f \in K_n$ (operation of n-arguments) and every n-tuple $(x_1, x_2, \ldots, x_n)$ of elements of S_M we have:

$$\phi(f_M(x_1, x_2, \ldots, x_n)) = f_N(\phi(x_1), \phi(x_2), \ldots, \phi(x_n))$$

i.e. it does not matter whether we apply the operation, (f), and then 'translate' using ϕ or we translate and then apply the operation. As in the example, ϕ can be thought of as simulating M in N.

Here are some further examples of homomorphisms based on signature 2 structures. Consider the signature 2 structures A_1 and A_3. Recall that S_{A_3} comprised trees whose leaves were labelled by elements of the set A and S_{A_2} had finite sequences over A as elements. We can simulate the trees as lists simply by mapping a tree to the list of its leaves, mapping, for example,

$\qquad$ to $\qquad \langle$a b c$\rangle$.

The reader is left to convince him or herself that this does define a homomorphism, *sequence_of*, say, from the tree structure A_3 to the list structure A_1. For example,

A frequently used homomorphism from strings A_1 to numbers N_1 is 'length_of'. It is the function which, given a string, returns its length. It is not hard to see that

$$\text{length\_of}(s_1 \hat{} s_2) = \text{length\_of}(s_1) + \text{length\_of}(s_2).$$

If we now consider the composition of length_of with sequence_of, length_of ∘ sequence_of: Tr A → ℝ,

from trees to numbers, defined by

length_of ∘ sequence_of(tr) = length_of(sequence_of(tr)),

we see that it is also a homomorphism. Given a tree, length_of ∘ sequence_of returns the number of leaves of the tree, so we might call it number_of_leaves_of. The fact that this composition is a homomorphism is no coincidence – in fact we have the following theorem:

Theorem. If N, M, and R are structures over a signature $\Sigma = (S, (K_0, K_1, \ldots))$ and both $\phi: S_N \to S_M$ and $\psi: S_M \to S_R$ are homomorphisms, then so is $\psi \circ \phi: S_N \to S_R$.

Proof. Let $f \in K_n$ and $x_1, x_2, \ldots, x_n$ be elements from S_N. Then

$\psi \circ \phi(f(x_1, x_2, \ldots, x_n))$

$= \psi(\phi(f(x_1, x_2, \ldots, x_n)))$ by definition of $\psi \circ \phi$

$= \psi(f(\phi(x_1), \phi(x_2), \ldots, \phi(x_n)))$ ϕ a homomorphism

$= f(\psi(\phi(x_1), \phi(x_2), \ldots, \phi(x_n)))$ ψ a homomorphism

$= f(\psi \circ \phi(x_1), \psi \circ \phi(x_2), \ldots, \psi \circ \phi(x_n))$ by definition of $\psi \circ \phi$

Effectively this means that if we simulate structure M in structure N, and then separately simulate structure M in structure R, the simulations may be combined to obtain a simulation of structure N in structure R.

Recall that structures N_1 and N_2 for signature 2 involved the real numbers with addition and the positive real numbers with multiplication. The slide rule was based on the ability to simulate multiplication by addition using log (logarithms to the base 10):

log: ℝ⁺ → ℝ

and:

$\log(a \times b) = \log(a) + \log(b)$

That is:

log: $S_{N_2} \to S_{N_1}$

and:

$\log(a \text{ combine}_{N_2} b) = \log(a) \text{ combine}_{N_1} \log(b)$

Thus, log is a homomorphism from N_2 to N_1. In fact, log is rather more than simply a homomorphism; what makes it so useful is the fact that it is 1–1 and onto (a bijection), and, in consequence, there is an 'inverse function':

inv_log: ℝ → ℝ⁺

defined by

inv_log: $x \mapsto 10^x$

such that for every real number x:

$\log(\text{inv\_log}(x)) = x$

and for every positive real number y:

inv_log (log(y)) = y

In addition, the function inv_log is a homomorphism, since:

$10^{x+z} = 10^x \times 10^z$

for all real numbers x and z.

Thus the simulation of N_2 in N_1 using log is 'perfect' in the sense that:

1. No information is lost – this might be the case if, for example, log(3) were to equal log(4).
2. There are no values in S_{N_1} which cannot be retrieved to N_2 (using inv_log (x)).

A homomorphism $\phi: S_1 \to S_2$ (such as log) which is 1–1 and onto (and whose inverse is thus a homomorphism), is called an isomorphism; in this case we say S_1 and S_2 are isomorphic. An isomorphism is the strongest possible form of simulation – effectively it is a relabelling of the names of the elements of one structure by the names of the elements of another. In practice, in order to show that two structures are isomorphic, it is necessary to exhibit an isomorphism between them. But how may we demonstrate that two structures are *not* isomorphic?

To do this we go back to the example sequence_of from trees to lists we had earlier. We can see that sequence_of is not 1–1, since:

$$\text{sequence\_of}(\overset{\bullet}{\underset{a \quad b}{\bigwedge}}{}_c) = \langle a\, b\, c \rangle = \text{sequence\_of}({}_a\overset{\bullet}{\underset{b \quad c}{\diagup\bigwedge}})$$

Therefore sequence_of is not an isomorphism. In fact, there is no isomorphism between these two structures. We demonstrate this by showing that any homomorphism, ϕ from A_3 to A_1 cannot be 1–1.

Let ϕ be a homomorphism from A_3 to A_2 and let a be an element of A. If we denote the singleton tree by a then $\phi(a)$ is a sequence, seq, say (not necessarily $\langle a \rangle$), since we wish to consider any possible ϕ). Since ϕ is a homomorphism we have

$$\phi(\overset{\bullet}{\underset{a \quad a}{\bigwedge}}{}_a) = \phi(\text{joint}(\text{join}(a, a), a))$$

$$= (\text{seq} \,\hat{}\, \text{seq}) \,\hat{}\, \text{seq}$$

$$= \text{seq} \,\hat{}\, (\text{seq} \,\hat{}\, \text{seq}) \qquad (*)$$

$$= \phi(\text{join}(a, \text{join}(a, a)))$$

$$= \phi({}_a\overset{\bullet}{\underset{a \quad a}{\diagup\bigwedge}})$$

But $\overset{\bullet}{\underset{a \quad a}{\bigwedge}}{}_a$ and ${}_a\overset{\bullet}{\underset{a \quad a}{\diagup\bigwedge}}$ are *not* equal trees, so ϕ is not 1–1.

The above hinges on the fact, (*), that for any three sequences $x, y, z \in S_{N_2}$,

$x \,\hat{}\, (y \,\hat{}\, z) = (x \,\hat{}\, y) \,\hat{}\, z$

i.e. concatenation is associative, whereas join is not.

The structures N_1 and N_2 are isomorphic to each other whereas A_1 and A_3 are not. We could see that A_1 and A_3 were not because the interpretation of combine in A_1, concatenate, was associative whereas the interpretation of combine in A_3, join, was not. If two structures are isomorphic we expect them to have the same 'properties'; if they don't then they will not be isomorphic. The property which distinguished between A_2 and A_3 could be expressed in the 'equation':

(E₁) combine(x, combine(y, z)) = combine(combine(x, y), z)

The interpretation of combine in a structure is said to be associative if the equation (E_1) is satisfied in the structure for all possible interpretations of x, y, and z in the carrier set. In the following sections these ideas will be made more precise. First we list two more properties of this kind:

(E₂) combine(x, y) = combine(y, x)

(E₃) combine(x, x) = x

E_2 is known as commutativity and E_3 as idempotency.

The reader is invited to determine which of the signature 2 structures given satisfy these equations. If A has more than one element then no two of the structures given, other than N_1 and N_2, are isomorphic. The reader is again invited to formulate properties which distinguish them.

In order to formalize notions of equations and satisfaction, it is necessary to go back to the definition of a signature. As already stated, we can also include constant operations into our signature. Suppose we wished to include an 'alphabet' of basic symbols from which all our objects are constructed.

The extended signature might look like this (signature 3):

Sort	S
Operations:	a, b, . . ., z: → S
	combine: S, S → S

Signature 3

This means that in every structure we will be able to identify the elements corresponding to a, b, . . ., z *and* that for every homomorphism ϕ: S → S', we will have $\phi(a) = a'$, $\phi(b) = b'$, and so on. In addition to this, however, we will in every structure be able to identify the elements corresponding to a, b, combine(a, b), combine(combine(a, b), c), etc. This leads us to the idea that this collection of elements is always present in every structure – such elements are called terms.

Definition. Given a signature $\Sigma = (S, \alpha)$ and a set of variable names X, the set of *terms over* Σ on X, $\Sigma_T(X)$, is defined inductively such that:

1. Every element of X is a term.
2. Every constant operation in Σ is a term.
3. Whenever $f \in K_n$, and $t_1, \ldots, t_n$ are terms, then $ft_1 \ldots t_n$ is a term.
4. That's all.

(Formally, what condition (4) means is that the set $\Sigma_T(X)$ is the intersection of all sets satisfying the closure properties (1), (2) and (3).)

The set $\Sigma_T(X)$ is called the Σ free algebra on X. Elements of $\Sigma_T(\Phi)$ (written simply as Σ_T) are called closed terms, and these are the terms, not involving variables, which we started to enumerate above.

We can think of closed terms as being trees, as, for both Σ_T and Tr A (the binary trees introduced earlier), each element contains within it the information about the way it has been built up. For example, consider the closed terms of signature 2. To each closed term we can associate a binary tree: the term which is just the constant a would be identified with the tree consisting of a single leaf, a;

the term *combine combine a b c*, or combine(combine(a, b), c), would correspond to the tree:

This leads to the idea that the terms form a structure just as the trees do.

Formally, given a signature Σ, for any X, $\Sigma_T(X)$ can be given a natural Σ structure, by defining:

a: ↦ a

b: ↦ b

and, for every n, $f \in K_n$, $f: t_1, \ldots, t_n \mapsto ft_1 \ldots t_n$

Regarded as a structure, Σ_T is called the term algebra.

Now, as hinted at earlier, given a Σ-structure S, there is actually a mapping:

$$\phi: \Sigma_T \to S_M$$

given by $\phi: a \mapsto a_M$

$$\phi: ft_1 \ldots t_n \mapsto f_M(t_{1_M}, \ldots, t_{n_M}).$$

In addition, ϕ is now a homomorphism from the structure Σ_T to the structure S, since

$$\phi(f(t_1, \ldots, t_n)) = \phi(ft_1 \ldots t_n)$$

$$\text{by definition of } f \text{ on } \Sigma_T$$

$$= f_M(\phi(t_1), \ldots \phi(t_n))$$

$$\text{by definition of } \varphi \text{ on } ft_1 \ldots t_n$$

for any f in Σ.

Given a closed term t, the image $\phi(t)$ of t under ϕ is called the interpretation of t. In the case of signature 2, this mapping into the structure of trees is precisely the identification we mentioned.

It can be seen that ϕ is the only homomorphism $\Sigma_T \to S$, and we call ϕ the evaluation homomorphism for S. Evaluation homomorphisms into different structures can be regarded as performing computation on the terms. For example, consider the following structure of signature 3:

Structure N₄	$S_{N_4} = \mathbb{N}$ the set of natural numbers
	$a_{N_4}, b_{N_4}, \ldots, z_{N_4} = 1$
	$\text{combine}_{N_4} = +$ addition

The evaluation homomorphism for this structure takes a term and delivers a number, equal to the number of constants in the term. If we go back to thinking of each term as a tree, this is the function number_of_leaves_of discussed earlier. So in evaluating a term, we are actually performing some computation on it.

Here is another structure:

Structure N₅	$S_{N_5} = \mathbb{N}$ the set of natural numbers
	$a_{N_5}, b_{N_5}, \ldots, z_{N_5} = 1$
	$\text{combine}_{N_5} = \text{max} + 1$ a function, which, given two numbers, returns the larger plus one.

It is left to the reader to verify that evaluation in this structure corresponds to the computation of the depth of a tree.

3.3 Theories and models

We can extend the idea of interpretation to include interpretation of terms which include variables. In this case, the interpretation of a term will be a function taking n arguments if there are n variables in the term. The result of the function will be the element of S_M obtained by substituting the arguments for the variables in the term.

We are now in a position to observe that the equations we wrote down earlier, for example:

$$join(x, join(y, z)) = join(join(x, y), z)$$

comprised a pair of terms from $\Sigma_T(X)$ where X is the set of variable names used in the equation. A structure satisfies the equation if those two terms have the same interpretation. In the context of the list structure, A_1, the interpretation of combine$(x, combine(y, z))$ is the function $(S_1, S_2, S_3) \to S_1\hat{\ }(S_2\hat{\ }S_3)$ and the interpretation of combine$(combine(x, y), z)$ is the function $(S_1, S_2, S_3) \mapsto (S_1\hat{\ }S_2)\hat{\ }S_3)$.

These two functions are equal; that is, for any given values of the arguments they yield the same result. Thus A_1 satisfies the equation; the structure A_3, on the other hand, does not.

Formally, given a signature, Σ, and a set of variable names X, an equation is simply a pair (t_1, t_2) where $t_1, t_2 \in \Sigma_T(X)$. We will often write this as the equation $(t_1 = t_2)$.

We can make more use of equations than just using them to distinguish between structures. In practice, we may not be interested in all signature 2 structures, but only those in which, for example, the interpretation of combine is both associative and commutative. These are precisely those structures which satisfy equations (E_1) and (E_2), where, as before:

(E_1) combine$(x, combine(y, z)) = $ combine$(combine(x, y), z)$

and (E_2) combine$(x, y) = $ combine(y, x)

The information required to define such structures is embodied in the signature together with the two equations (theory 1):

Sort	S
Operation	combine: $S, S \to S$
Variables	x, y, z: S
Equations	combine$(x, y) = $ combine(y, x)
	combine$(x, combine(y, z)) = $ combine$(combine(x, y), z)$

Theory 1

A triple, Th $= (\Sigma, X, E)$, where Σ is a signature, X is a set (of variable names which should be distinct from any names in Σ), and E is a set of equations, is called a theory presentation. Structures over Σ which satisfy the equations in E are called models of (or algebras over) the theory presentation Th, or, more simply, models of Th.

In the following examples, binary operations will be declared:

$$\_*\_:\ S, S \to S$$

rather than $*:\ S, S \to S$

to indicate infix usage. Then we write $x * y$ rather than $*(x, y)$.

Here is another example of a theory (theory 2):

Sort	Mon
Operations	e: Mon
	$\_*\_:$ Mon, Mon $\to$ Mon
Variables	x, y, z: Mon
Equations	$x * (y * z) = (x * y) * z$
	$x * e = x$
	$e * x = x$

Theory 2

A model M of theory 2 is called a Monoid. It has a carrier set Mon_M, together with an associative binary operation $*_M$ and an element $e_M \in Mon_M$ which is an identity for $*_M$. Such models include the integers, $\mathbb{Z}$, with addition, together with zero as an identity.

Other theories which can be set in this framework include the theories of Groups, Rings and Boolean Algebras; some theories cannot be described using equations alone, notably the theory of Fields (see Bibliography for suitable references).

Now, natural questions to ask are:

1. Given a signature Σ, which equations are satisfied in the term algebra Σ_T?
2. Given a theory presentation, will Σ_T be a model of that theory?

The answer to the first question is not very many.

We can see, in fact, that the term algebra Σ_T satisfies the fewest equations of any structure of S of Σ. An equation $(t_1 = t_2)$ is satisfied in Σ_T only when t_1 and t_2 are the same term; and any equation $(t = t)$ is automatically satisfied in every structure.

This gives us the answer to the second question. In general, Σ_T will not be a model of a theory, and, if it is, the theory is 'trivial' in that then every structure is a model of it.

In the same way as we were able to 'generically' obtain a structure Σ_T from every signature Σ, can we obtain a generic model for a theory presentation Th $= (\Sigma, X, E)$? The answer is yes, and such a model is the quotient term model, or initial model of Th, $\Sigma_{T/E}$. We will describe how to construct $\Sigma_{T/E}$, and then outline its most important properties. The term algebra Σ_T is the most useful starting point for construction of $\Sigma_{T/E}$.

Essentially, what we need to do is identify, or regard as being equal, terms whenever an equation of the theory says they must be equal. Given a theory presentation Th, our strategy will be to group together the terms into 'bunches' such that the set of bunches can be made into a structure *and* in such a way that this structure is then a model of Th.

Formally, what we require is a partition of Σ_T, and this is most easily described by an equivalence relation on Σ_T. This is a binary relation, $\sim$, on Σ_T which is:

1. Reflexive, i.e. $x \sim x$ for all $x \in \Sigma_T$.
2. Symmetric, i.e. $x \sim y$ whenever $y \sim x$.
3. Transitive, i.e. if $x \sim y$ and $y \sim z$ for some $x, y, z \in \Sigma_T$, then $x \sim z$.

These properties serve to ensure that the equivalence classes (the bunches of related objects) partition Σ_T; the set of bunches is called the quotient of Σ_T by $\sim$, written $\Sigma_T/\sim$. Given $x \in \Sigma_T$, we will write the equivalence class of x in $\Sigma_T/\sim$ as $[x]_\sim$.

That is: $[x]_\sim = \{t \in \Sigma_T \mid t \sim x\}$.

Now we wish to interpret the operations of Σ on $\Sigma_T/\sim$ to make $\Sigma_T/\sim$ a structure of Σ; we would like to be able to do this by using the structural information contained in Σ_T. Given an n-ary operation f of Σ and elements $x_1, x_2, \ldots, x_n$ of Σ_T, one possibility would be to define $f([x_1]_\sim, [x_2]_\sim, \ldots, [x_n]_\sim)$ to be the equivalence class $[fx_1 x_2 \ldots x_n]_\sim$. However, there is a problem here. How can we be sure that the outcome of f on $\Sigma_T/\sim$ does not depend on which representatives we choose for the equivalent classes of $x_1, x_2, \ldots, x_n$? The property we require of $\sim$ is that equivalent arguments give equivalent results; that is, for each n and each $f \in K_n$,

4. $x_1 \sim y_1, x_2 \sim y_2, \ldots, x_n \sim y_n \Rightarrow fx_1 x_2 \ldots x_n \sim fy_1 y_2 \ldots y_n$

If $\sim$ has this property we say it is a congruence with respect to Σ_T.

Given such a congruence $\sim$ we can form a structure of Σ from $\Sigma_T/\sim$.

Finally, we must ensure that $\Sigma_T/\sim$ satisfies the equations E. The requirement is that whenever t_1 and t_2 are terms, and $t_1 = t_2$ is an equation of E, then it is satisfied in $\Sigma_T/\sim$. That is, given any association of elements of $\Sigma_T/\sim$ with the variables in t_1 and t_2, the elements of $\Sigma_T/\sim$ then corresponding to t_1 and t_2 are equal. If we define a closed equation from E to be an equation obtained by substituting closed terms for the variables in an equation from E, we can reformulate this requirement as follows:

5. $t_1 \sim t_2$ whenever $t_1 = t_2$ is a closed equation of E.

A model of a theory presentation which can be obtained as a quotient of Σ_T in this way is called a term-model.

Now all we have to do is find such a $\sim$. In fact, we do more than that. We find the 'weakest' one: that is, a relation $\sim_E$ such that if $\approx$ is another relation satisfying (1)–(2) and $t_1 \sim_E t_2$ then $t_1 \approx t_2$.

The relation $\sim_E$ is (as you might expect) obtained from E and defined inductively such that:

1. If $t \in \Sigma_T$, then $t \sim_E t$.
2. If $t_1 \sim_E t_2$ and $t_2 \sim_E t_3$ then $t_1 \sim_E t_3$.
3. If $t_1 \sim_E t_2$ then $t_2 \sim_E t_1$.
4. If $f \in K_n$ and $t_1 \sim_E t_{1'}, t_2 \sim_E t_{2'}, \ldots, t_n \sim_E t_{n'}$ then
   $ft_1 t_2 \ldots t_n \sim_E ft_{1'} t_{2'} \ldots t_{n'}$.
5. If $t_1 = t_2$ is a closed equation of E, then $t_1 \sim_E t_2$.
6. That's all.

Theorem
(a) $\sim_E$ satisfies requirements (1)–(5).
(b) if $\approx$ satisfies requirements (1)–(5) and $t_1 \approx t_2$ for some $t_1, t_2 \in \Sigma_T$, then $t_1 \sim_E t_2$.

Proof
(a) Clauses (1)–(5) of the definition ensure conditions (1)–(5) respectively.
(b) Since $\approx$ satisfies conditions (1)–(5), it is closed under clauses (1)–(5) of definition of $\sim_E$.

Then we define $\Sigma_{T/E}$ to be the model $\Sigma_T/\sim_E$.

We observed when discussing term algebras that given a structure S of Σ, the evaluation homomorphism is the unique homomorphism $\phi: \Sigma_T \to S$. Now, the initial model $\Sigma_{T/E}$ is a structure of Σ_T, so let ϕ_E be the evaluation homomorphism $\phi_E: \Sigma_T \to \Sigma_{T/E}$. Also, given a model S of T, we have the evaluation homomorphism $\phi_S: \Sigma \to S$.

An interesting property of $\Sigma_{T/E}$ is that there is a unique homomorphism $\theta: \Sigma_{T/E} \to S$ and $\phi_S = \theta \circ \phi_E$.

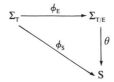

The uniqueness of θ can be seen by considering the diagram; any other homomorphism $\theta': \Sigma_{T/E} \to S$ would give rise to another homomorphism $\phi': \Sigma_T \to S$, (ϕ' will be genuinely different because ϕ_E is surjective) but since the evaluation homomorphism is unique, so θ must be unique.

The existence of the homomorphism θ can be seen by first considering the image $\phi_S(\Sigma_T)$ of Σ_T by ϕ_S in S. This is the set $Im\phi_S = \{s \in S \mid \exists t \in \Sigma_T . \phi_S(t) = s\}$. The operations as defined on S are closed on this set since it is a structure. It is also a model of T whenever S is a model of T since if an equation $t_1 = t_2$ is satisfied in S (the interpretations of t_1 and t_2 are the same functions on S) then it is certainly satisfied on $Im\phi_S$ (those functions restricted to $Im\phi_S$ are also the same). (These results easily generalize to the results that the homomorphic image of any structure is also a structure, and the homomorphic image of any model is also a model.) We can define the relation $\approx$ on Σ_T by $t_1 \approx t_2$ if $\phi_S(t_1) = \phi_S(t_2)$. Then $Im\phi_S$ is the model $\Sigma_T/\sim$, so $\approx$ has properties (1)–(5), and is no weaker than $\sim_E$. This then guarantees that the map:

$$\theta: \quad \Sigma_{T/E} \to S$$

given by $\quad \theta: \quad [x]_\sim \mapsto \phi_S(x)$

is well defined; this is the θ required.

Thus, given any model S of a theory T, there is a unique homomorphism:

$$\theta: \quad \Sigma_{T/E} \to S$$

(This motivates use of the term 'initial' to describe $\Sigma_{T/E}$.)

Going back to our examples, we can see that for the empty theory (where every structure is a model), the initial model is isomorphic to the set of trees under join, structure A_3.

If we add the axiom of associativity:

(E_1) combine(x, combine(y, z)) = combine(combine(x, y), z)

our initial model is the set of trees but with trees such as:

identified. This is isomorphic to the set of sequences under concatenation.

Taking the structure N_4 we had earlier, there is then a unique homomorphism from the set of trees to this structure. This function is the one already described, number_of_leaves_of. The results of the last section tell us that it should be possible to decompose this function into the composition of two functions; one from trees to the initial model (sequences), and one from the initial model to structure N_3. In fact we have already seen this decomposition: the function from trees to sequences is sequence_of and the function from sequences to numbers is length_of. As we have already seen, this gives

number_of_leaves_of = length_of sequence_of.

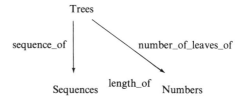

If we go back to the theory, and add the axiom of commutativity:

(E$_2$) combine(x, y) = combine(y, x)

we obtain a different initial model in which order information is ignored, the only concern is the number of each type of constant present in the sequence. This is the structure which is given by multi-sets (or bags) under union.

Finally, adding the axiom of idempotency:

(E$_3$) combine(x, x) = x

we obtain an initial model in which even the number of each type of constant is ignored; only which ones are present is important. This is isomorphic to the structure of sets under union.

Thus we have a chain of initial models and homorphisms:

Trees → Sequences → Bags → Sets

$$\Sigma_{T/\Phi} \to \Sigma_{T/E_1} \to \Sigma_{T/E_2} \to \Sigma_{T/E_3}$$

where:

E$_1$ = {combine(x, combine(y, z)) =
$\qquad\qquad\qquad$ combine(combine(x, y), z)},

E$_2$ = E$_1 \cup$ {combine(x, y) = combine(y, x)},

E$_3$ = E$_2 \cup$ {combine(x, x) = x}.

3.4 Extensions

It may be that at some time we need to take a certain signature and 'extend' it, such as if we want to add more operations or constants. Some examples have already appeared. One was the introduction of constant symbols to the signature 2 to obtain signature 3.

Formally, a signature $\Sigma' = (S, \alpha')$ is an extension of signature $\Sigma = (S, \alpha)$ if $K_i \subseteq K_i'$ for each i, where $\alpha = (K_0, K_1, \ldots, K_i, \ldots)$ and $\alpha' = (K_0', K_1', \ldots, K_i', \ldots)$. In the example, $K_i = K_i'$ for all $i > 0$ and $K_0' = \{a, b, c, \ldots, z\}$ whereas $K_0 = \Phi$.

Similarly, we may want to take a theory presentation over a signature and extend it to another theory presentation over an extended signature.

For example, we may take signature 2 and extend it by adding a new constant symbol, e, and the axioms:

combine(x, e) = x

combine(e, x) = x

(e will then be an identity with respect to combine).

Formally, again, a theory presentation Th' = (Σ', X', E') is an *extension* of a theory presentation Th = (Σ, X, E) if Σ' is an extension of Σ, $X \subseteq X'$, and $E \subseteq E'$.

Two things may happen when a theory presentation is extended:

1. The additional operations introduce 'new' elements.
2. Some of the 'old' elements which were previously disjoint become equal.

The term algebra will always be extended if new operations are introduced; the issue is whether or not the new operations can be 'defined' in terms of the existing operations. That is, whether or not the initial model is extended.

Let $\Sigma'_{T/E'}$ be the initial model of Th'. This is a structure of Σ' satisfying E'; in particular, we can think of it as a structure of Σ, simply by ignoring the new sorts and operations added in Σ', and as such it satisfies E, i.e. it is a model of Th. Thus there is a unique homomorphism ϕ mapping $\phi: \Sigma_{T/E} \to \Sigma'_{T/E'}$.

Of the above possibilities, (1) occurs when ϕ is not onto (surjective), and (2) occurs when ϕ is not 1–1 (injective).

New elements introduced by (1) may be regarded as 'junk' (at least with respect to Σ) and additional equations being satisfied as in (2) may be regarded as 'confusion'. Extensions in which neither is present (then ϕ is a bijection and hence an isomorphism) are called conservative extensions or enrichments.

Consider the following theory (theory 3):

Sort	N	
Operations	zero: $\to N$	
	succ: $N \to N$	(Theory 3)

(There are no equations in this theory)

This describes Peano Arithmetic.

Let theory 4 be the following:

Sort	N	
Operations	zero: $\to N$	
	succ: $N \to N$	
	add: $N, N \to N$	
Variables	x, y: N	
Equations	add(zero, x) = x	
	add(succ x, y) = add(x, succ y)	(Theory 4)

Then theory 4 is a conservative extension of theory 3.

We can further extend theory 4 to get theory 5:

Sort	N	
Operations	zero: $\to N$	
	succ: $N \to N$	
	add: $N, N \to N$	
	multiply: $N, N \to N$	
Variables	x, y: N	
Equations	add(zero, x) = x	
	add(succ x, y) = add(x, succ y)	
	multiply(zero, x) = zero	
	multiply(succ x, y) = add(multiply(x, y), y)	
		(Theory 5)

then theory 5 is a conservative extension of theory 4.

One significant property of conservative extensions is that they can be 'chained together' as follows:

Theorem. Let Th = (Σ, X, E) be a theory; let Th' = (Σ', X', E') be a conservative extension of Th, and let Th″ = (Σ″, X″, E″) be a conservative extension of Th′. Then Th″ is a conservative extension of Th.

Proof. From the definition of extension, it is clear that Th″ is in fact an extension of Th. Now consider the following diagram:

$$\Sigma_{T/E} \xrightarrow{\phi_{E'}} \Sigma'_{T/E'} \xrightarrow{\phi_{E''}} \Sigma''_{T/E''}$$

The map $\phi_{E'}$ is the unique homomorphism from the initial model of Th to $\Sigma'_{T/E'}$ regarded as a model of Th. The map $\phi_{E''}$ is the unique homomorphism from the initial model of Th′ to $\Sigma''_{T/E''}$ regarded as a model of Th′. Now we can think of both $\Sigma_{T/E}$ and $\Sigma''_{T/E''}$ as models of Th, and as such, $\phi_{E'}$ will be a Σ-homomorphism. Thus the composite of these maps $\psi = \phi_{E'}\,\phi_{E''}$ will also be a Σ-homomorphism; so it must be the unique homomorphism from the initial model of Th to $\Sigma''_{T/E''}$. Furthermore, since both maps $\phi_{E'}$ and $\phi_{E''}$ are 1–1 and onto (they are isomorphisms because each of the extensions are conservative), their composite ψ is also 1–1 and onto. Thus ψ is an isomorphism, and Th″ is a conservative extension of Th.

Thus, in the examples given, we have that theory 5 is a conservative extension of theory 3. This means that if we write a specification of a datatype, and subsequently wish to enrich it by adding more operations and equations, we can extend the theory piece by piece (checking correctness at each stage), rather than having to make the extension all in one go. This is essential for structured development to be possible, and is fundamental to algebraic specification/development practices in use.

For further reading on the subject, its applications to specification, and discussion of the issues raised here, the reader is referred to the bibliography and to other related chapters of this book.

3.5 Bibliography

The references listed here are divided according to the depth of the material covered.

3.5.1 Introductory, algebra/discrete mathematics

Gersting, J. L., 1982. *Mathematical Structures for Computer Science*, W. H. Freeman & Co., San Francisco, USA

Johnsonbaugh, R., 1990. *Discrete Mathematics*, Macmillan Publishing Co., New York, USA

Skvarcius, R. and Robinson, W. B., 1986. *Discrete Mathematics with Computer Science Applications*, Benjamin Cummings, San Francisco, USA.

3.5.2 Intermediate, basic algebra and logic

Allenby, R. B. J. T., 1983. *Rings, Fields and Groups*, Arnold, East Kilbride, Scotland.

Fraleigh, J. B., 1988. *A First Course in Abstract Algebra*, Addison Wesley, Reading, MA, USA.

Herstein, I. N., 1987. *Abstract Algebra*, Macmillan Publishing Co.

Johnstone, P. T. 1987. *Notes on Logic and Set Theory*, Cambridge University Press, Cambridge.

3.5.3 Intermediate, algebraic data types

Burstall, R. M. and Goguen, J. A., 1984. Putting Theories Together to Make Specifications. In *Proc. Fifth International Joint Conference on Artificial Intelligence*

Colman, D. and Gallimore, R. M., 1982. *Software Engineering Using Executable Specifications*, Lecture Notes, Dept. of Computation, University of Manchester Institute of Science and Technology

Ehrig, H. and Mahr, B., 1985. *Fundamentals of Algebraic Specification 1*, Springer Verlag, Berlin, West Germany

3.5.4. Advanced algebraic and related topics

Birkoff, S. and Maclane, G., 1967. *Algebra*, Macmillan Publishing Co.

Cohn, P. M., 1965. *Universal Algebra*, Harper and Row, New York, USA

Maclane, S., 1971. *Categories for the Working Mathematician*, Springer Verlag, New York, USA

4

Graph theory

Bernard Carré
Program Validation Ltd

Contents

This chapter presents some concepts of graph theory which are particularly relevant to software engineering. After introducing basic terminology, it discusses various forms of connectedness of graphs, and properties of some important classes of graphs such as acyclic graphs and trees. The concepts are illustrated with examples from program analysis.

Following this rather general presentation, the control-flow graphs of sequential algorithms are considered in some detail (in Section 4.7). Such graphs are of direct practical relevance, of course, and it is hoped that the reader will find the results of interest. However, this section is also intended to serve as a little case study, showing how relatively simple graph-theoretic argumentation can be useful – in this instance bringing to light the essential features of a 'well-formed' control structure.

The conditions imposed on control structures here, essentially in terms of the existence of particular kinds of paths on a graph, are sufficient for the notion of a 'program loop' to be meaningful. However, for static analysis techniques such as data-flow and information-flow analysis to give useful results and for formal verification to be tractable, there are stronger requirements. These are most conveniently expressed in terms of graph grammars, which are discussed in Section 4.8.

4.1 The notion of graph

A graph $G = (X,U)$ consists of:

1. A finite set $X = \{x_1, x_2, \ldots, x_n\}$ the elements of which are called nodes.
2. A subset U of the Cartesian product $X \times X$, the elements of which are called arcs.

A graph can be depicted by a diagram in which nodes are represented by points in the plane, and each arc (x_i, x_j) is indicated by the arrow drawn from the point representing x_i to the point representing x_j.

Example 1. Flowcharts and control-flow Graphs. A hardware integer division procedure is shown in *Figure 4.1*, and a familiar flowchart representation of this procedure is shown in *Figure 4.2(a)*. The latter has been derived by decomposing the conditional and repetitive statements of the procedure into rudimentary test and assignment statements, which correspond to elements of a flowchart (see *Figure 4.3*). A flowchart is an example of a graph in which the nodes, and possibly arcs, are labelled in some way. The (unlabelled) graph corresponding to Figure 4.2(a) is shown in Figure 4.2(b); this graph is called the control-flow graph of the procedure.

```
procedure division (x,y: integer; var q,r: integer);
pre (x > 0) and (y > 0);
post (x = q*y + r) and (0 < = r < y);
var w: integer;
begin
    r: = x; q: = 0; w: = y;
    while w < = x do w: = 2*w;
    while w < > y do
    begin
        q: = 2*q; w: = w div 2;
        if w < = r then
            begin
                r: = r - w; q: = 1 + q
            end
    end
end;
```

Figure 4.1 Hardware integer division algorithm

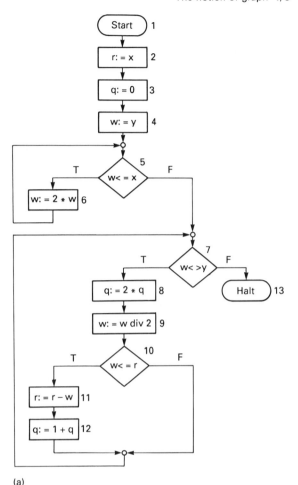

(a)

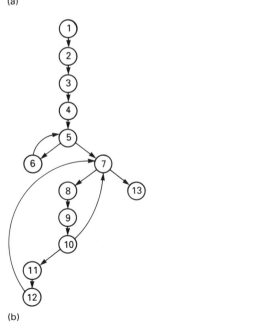

(b)

Figure 4.2 Flowchart and control-flow graph of hardware integer-division algorithm: (a) flowchart, (b) control-flow graph

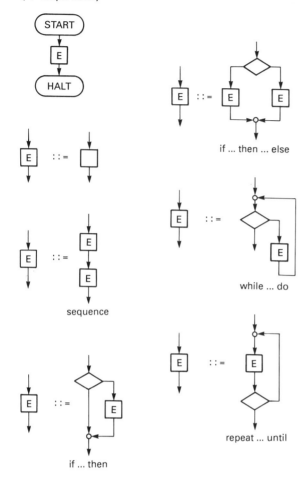

Figure 4.3 A grammar of a class of flow charts

Since the arc set U of a graph $G = (X,U)$ is a subset of the Cartesian product $X \times X$ of its node set X, we could describe a graph $G = (X,U)$ as a finite set X together with a binary relation U on X; every graph defines a relation on its node-set, and every binary relation on a set can be represented by a graph. As an illustration of this correspondence between graphs and relations, a control-flow graph represents the relation 'may transfer control to' on a set of program statements.

4.2 Basic terminology

In discussing graphs the following terminology will be used:

Initial and terminal end-points of an arc. For an arc (x_i,x_j), the node x_i is the initial end-point and the node x_j is the terminal end-point.

Adjacent nodes, adjacent arcs. Two nodes are said to be adjacent if they are joined by an arc. Two arcs are adjacent if they have at least one common end-point.

Successors and predecessors of a node. In a graph $G = (X,U)$, a node x_j is called a successor of a node x_i if $(x_i,x_j) \in U$; the set of all successors of x_i is denoted by $\Gamma^+(x_i)$. Similarly, a node x_j is called a predecessor of x_i if $(x_j,x_i) \in U$, and the set of all predecessors of x_i is denoted by $\Gamma^-(x_i)$. In the graph of *Figure 4.4*, the node x_3 has the set of successors $\Gamma^+(x_3) = \{x_1,x_4\}$ and the set of predecessors $\Gamma^-(x_3) = \{x_2,x_4\}$.

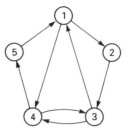

Figure 4.4

Arcs incident to and from a node. If an arc u has node x_i as its initial end-point, we say that the arc is incident from x_i; whereas if an arc u has node x_i as its terminal end-point we say that arc u is incident to x_i. The number of arcs incident from a node x_i is called the out-degree of x_i and it is denoted by $\rho^+(x_i)$; while the number of arcs incident to x_i is called the in-degree of x_i and is denoted by $\rho^-(x_i)$.

Partial graphs. If we remove from a graph $G = (X,U)$ a subset of its arcs, we are left with a graph of the form:

$$H = (X,V), \text{ where } V \subseteq U$$

which is called a partial graph of G. The graph of *Figure 4.5* is a partial graph of that shown in Figure 4.4.

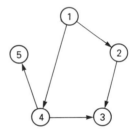

Figure 4.5

Subgraphs. If we remove from a graph $G = (X,U)$ a subset of its nodes, together with all the arcs incident to or from those nodes, we are left with a graph of the form:

$$H = (Y,U_y),$$

where

$$Y \subseteq X \text{ and } U_y = U \cap (Y \times Y)$$

which is called a subgraph of G. We may describe H more precisely, as the subgraph of G generated by Y. As an example, *Figure 4.6* shows a subgraph of the graph of Figure 4.4, in particular the subgraph generated by $\{x_1,x_3,x_4\}$.

Figure 4.6

Condensations. Let $P = \{X_1, X_2, \ldots, X_n\}$ be a partition of the node-set of a graph $G = (X, U)$. Then the condensation of G induced by P is the graph $G_p = (P, U_p)$ where:

$$U_p = \{(X_r, X_s) \in P \times P | X_r \neq X_s \wedge (\exists x_i \in X_r, x_j \in X_s | (x_i, x_j) \in U)\}$$

In pictorial terms, G_p is obtained from G by coalescing the nodes of each member of P, and then removing any loops. The condensation of the graph of Figure 4.4 induced by the partition $\{\{x_1, x_2\}, \{x_3, x_4\}, \{x_5\}\}$ is shown in *Figure 4.7*.

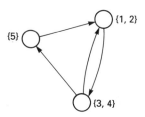

Figure 4.7

4.3 Paths on graphs

4.3.1 Paths and cycles

A path is a finite sequence of arcs of the form:

$$\mu = (x_{i_0}, x_{i_1}), (x_{i_1}, x_{i_2}), \ldots, (x_{i_{r-1}}, x_{i_r})$$

i.e. a finite sequence of arcs in which the terminal node of each arc coincides with the initial node of the following arc; the number r of arcs in the sequence is called the order of the path. The initial end-point of the first arc and the terminal end-point of the last arc of a path are called respectively the initial and terminal end-points of the path. A path whose end-points are distinct is said to be open, whereas a path whose end-points coincide is called a closed path, or cycle. A path is elementary if it does not traverse any node more than once, i.e. if all the initial end-points (or all the terminal end-points) of its arcs are distinct.

It is evident that a path is completely determined by the sequence of nodes $x_{i_0}, x_{i_1}, \ldots, x_{i_r}$ which it visits; we shall sometimes find it convenient to specify a path by listing this node sequence rather than the arc sequence.

Example 2. In the graph of Figure 4.4, the arc sequence:

$$(x_2, x_3), (x_3, x_1), (x_1, x_4), (x_4, x_3), (x_3, x_4)$$

is a non-elementary path of order 5, from x_2 to x_4. The arc sequence:

$$(x_2, x_3), (x_3, x_1), (x_1, x_4)$$

is an elementary path from x_2 to x_4, and the arc sequence:

$$(x_1, x_4), (x_4, x_3), (x_3, x_1)$$

is an elementary cycle.

Example 3. The call graph of a program. Let X be the set of procedures of a program, and let $G = (X, U)$ be the graph in which each pair of nodes x_i and x_j are joined by an arc (x_i, x_j) if and only if the body of procedure x_i contains a direct call of procedure x_j. This graph is described as the call graph of the program. If the execution of a procedure x_i may involve a direct or indirect call of a procedure x_j, then the call graph will contain a path from x_i to x_j. In particular, if a procedure may be used recursively, then on the call graph it will be traversed by a cycle.

4.3.2 Accessibility

Let $G = (X, U)$ be a graph, and let x_i be one of its nodes. Then any node x_j (not necessarily distinct from x_i) such that there exists a path from x_i to x_j is called a descendant of x_i; while any node x_j (not necessarily distinct from x_i) such that there exists a path from x_j to x_i is called an ascendant of x_i. It will be observed that a node x_j can be both a descendant and an ascendant of x_i: this occurs whenever there exists a cycle passing through both x_i and x_j. We shall denote the set of descendants of a node x_i by $\hat{\Gamma}^+(x_i)$, and the set of its ascendants by $\hat{\Gamma}^-(x_i)$.

A node x_j is said to be accessible from a node x_i if x_j is a descendant of x_i or $x_j = x_i$; similarly, x_j is said to be converse-accessible from x_i if x_j is an ascendant of x_i or $x_j = x_i$. The sets of nodes which are accessible and converse-accessible from x_i will be denoted by $\overset{*}{\hat{\Gamma}}{}^+(x_i)$ and $\overset{*}{\hat{\Gamma}}{}^-(x_i)$ respectively. Clearly:

$$\overset{*}{\hat{\Gamma}}{}^+(x_i) = \{x_i\} \cup \hat{\Gamma}^-(x_i)$$

and

$$\overset{*}{\hat{\Gamma}}{}^-(x_i) = \{x_i\} \cup \hat{\Gamma}^+(x_i)$$

Example 4. Accessibility conditions for control-flow graphs. Let $G = (X, U)$ be the control-flow graph of a program, and let x_s and x_t be the nodes of G which represent the program's START and HALT statements respectively. It is evident that (a) every statement of the program should be accessible from the START statement, and (b) the HALT statement should be accessible from every statement. In graph-theoretic terms these conditions are expressed by:

(a) $\quad \overset{*}{\hat{\Gamma}}{}^+(x_s) = X$

and

(b) $\quad \overset{*}{\hat{\Gamma}}{}^-(x_t) = X$

4.4 Two forms of connectivity of graphs

4.4.1 Weak connectivity

A chain of a graph is a sequence of nodes such that each pair of consecutive nodes in the sequence are adjacent. For instance, in the graph of Figure 4.4 the node sequence x_2, x_1, x_3, x_4 is a chain (although it is not a path).

For any graph $G = (X, U)$ we define a binary relation called the connectivity relation γ on the node set X by the rule:

$$x_i \gamma x_j \Leftrightarrow x_i \text{ and } x_j \text{ are joined by a chain}$$

When $x_i \gamma x_j$, we say that x_i is connected to x_j.

The relation γ is obviously reflexive, symmetric and transitive, and since it has these properties it is an equivalence relation. Consequently it induces a partition X/γ of the node-set of G, the members of which are the equivalence classes with respect to γ. The subgraphs of G which are generated by these equivalence classes are called the connected components of G.

If a graph has only one connected component, we say that the graph is connected. We note that the control-flow graph of a (well-formed) sequential program is always connected.

Example 5. The basic blocks of a control-flow graph. The first step in analysing a control-flow graph is to simplify the graph by 'compressing straight-line code'. In graph-theoretic terms this process can be described precisely, as follows. Let G be a control-flow graph, in which all nodes are accessible from the START node, and the HALT node is accessible from all other nodes. Also, let H be the partial graph of G obtained by removing:

1. All arcs incident to nodes of in-degree greater than unity.
2. All arcs incident to or from nodes of out-degree greater than unity (the 'test' nodes).
3. The arc incident from the START node.
4. All arcs incident to the HALT node.

(As an illustration, *Figure 4.8*(a) shows the graph H derived from the control-flow graph of Figure 4.2.)

Each connected component of H is a subgraph of G; either it has only one node (and no arcs), or its nodes and arcs form an open elementary path. We describe these components as the blocks of the control-flow graph; the node of each block which has no predecessors (resp. successors) on H is called the head (resp. tail) of its block.

To study, for instance, the loop structure of a program, it is convenient to use, in place of G, the condensation G' of G whose nodes correspond to the blocks of G. (In other words, we construct G' simply by 'shrinking' each block of G to a single node.) For the control-flow graph G of Figure 4.2, the condensation G' is shown in Figure 4.8(b); the numbers on nodes of G' are the numbers of the heads of their corresponding blocks in G.

4.4.2 Strong connectivity

Again, let $G = (X,U)$ be any graph, and let us define another binary relation σ on the node-set X of G, by the rule:

$$x_i \sigma x_j \Leftrightarrow \text{each of } x_i \text{ and } x_j \text{ is accessible from the other}$$

The relation σ is called the strong connectivity relation on G, and when $x_i \sigma x_j$ we say that x_i is strongly connected to x_j.

It is easily verified that like γ, the relation σ is an equivalence relation. The subgraphs of G which are generated by the equivalence classes with respect to σ are called the strongly connected components of G. If G contains only one strongly connected component, we say that G is strongly connected. Clearly, every strongly connected graph is connected.

In studying the properties of a graph $G = (X,U)$ it is often helpful to determine the set of equivalence classes X/σ, and then to construct the condensation of G induced by X/σ (as defined in Section 4.2). This particular condensation, which is called the reduced graph G^R of G, shows clearly the form of connectivity between each pair of nodes on G. In particular, it is easily verified that if x_i and x_j are nodes of G, which belong respectively to members X_a and X_b of X/σ, then:

1. x_i is connected to x_j on G if and only if X_a is connected to X_b on G^R.
2. x_j is accessible from x_i on G if and only if X_b is accessible from X_a on G^R.

Finally, it is important to note that for any graph G, the reduced graph G^R does not contain any cycles. This can be proved by contradiction, as follows. Suppose G^R contains a cycle, and let (X_a, X_b) be one of its arcs. Then on G^R, X_a is strongly connected to X_b, which implies that in G there exist nodes $x_i \in X_a$ and $x_j \in X_b$ which are strongly connected. Now the

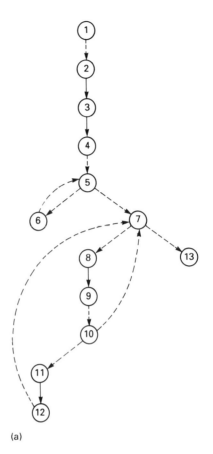

(a)

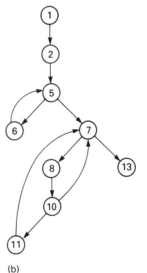

(b)

Figure 4.8

nodes x_i and x_j belong to the same member of X/σ and so $X_a = X_b$. But then, by the method of construction of G^R this graph cannot contain the arc (X_a, X_b), which contradicts our assumption that G^R contains a cycle.

An efficient algorithm for finding strong components is given by Aho *et al.* (1974).

4.5 Acyclic graphs

An acyclic graph is a graph which does not contain any cycles. The purpose of this section is to establish some properties of acyclic graphs in general; some particular kinds of acyclic graphs will be considered in later sections.

First, it will be demonstrated that any acyclic graph contains at least one node which has no successors, and at least one node which has no predecessors.

The first part is proved by contradiction, as follows. Let $G = (X,U)$ be an acyclic graph, and let us assume that every node on G has at least one successor. Then, starting from any node x_{i_0}, we can find a successor of x_{i_0}, say x_{i_1}, and then a successor of x_{i_1}, say x_{i_2}, and so on, and hence we may construct a path $x_{i_0}, x_{i_1}, x_{i_2}, \ldots, x_{i_r}$ of arbitrarily high order. But since the number of nodes of G is finite, on a path of sufficiently high order some node x_{i_k} say will be encountered twice. Hence x_{i_k} lies on a cycle, which contradicts the assumption that G is acyclic. The second part can be proved by a similar argument (we trace a path 'backwards', rather than 'forwards', from some node x_{i_0}).

This result leads to the concept of node rank, which is defined as follows. Let $G = (X,U)$ be an acyclic graph, and let N_0 be the set of nodes without predecessors on G:

$$N_0 = \{x_i \in X \mid \Gamma^-(x_i) = \varnothing\}$$

Now consider the subgraph G_0 of G which is generated by $X - N_0$, i.e. the subgraph obtained by removing from G all nodes in N_0, and all arcs incident from those nodes. If G_0 contains any nodes, then it must contain at least one node without predecessors (since all subgraphs of G are acyclic), and collecting together all such nodes we obtain a non-empty set:

$$N_1 = \{x_i \in X - N_0 \mid \Gamma^-(x_i) \subseteq N_0\}$$

Now consider the subgraph G_1 of G_0 which is generated by $X - (N_0 \cup N_1)$. Again, if G_1 contains any nodes, then it contains at least one node without predecessors, and collecting together all such nodes we obtain:

$$N_2 = \{x_i \in X - (N_0 \cup N_1) \mid \Gamma^-(x_i) \subseteq N_1\}$$

Continuing in this manner until all the nodes of G have been removed, we construct successively the (non-empty) sets:

$$N_3 = \{x_i \in \left(X - \bigcup_{k=0}^{2} N_k\right) \mid \Gamma^-(x_i) \subseteq \bigcup_{k=0}^{2} N_k\}$$

$$\vdots$$

$$N_q = \{x_i \in \left(X - \bigcup_{k=0}^{q-1} N_k\right) \mid \Gamma^-(x_i) \subseteq \bigcup_{k=0}^{q-1} N_k\}$$

where q is the smallest integer such that:

$$X - \bigcup_{k=0}^{q-1} N_k = \varnothing$$

From the method of construction of these sets, it is evident that the set $\{N_0, N_1, \ldots, N_q\}$ is a partition of X.

Let us now assign to each node x_i of G an integer $r(x_i)$, through the rule:

$$x_i \in N_k \Leftrightarrow r(x_i) = k$$

We call $r(x_i)$ the rank of node x_i. Clearly, for each node x_i of G:

1. $r(x_i) < r(x_j)$, for all $x_j \in \Gamma^+(x_i)$.

2. If $r(x_i) > 0$, then x_i has at least one predecessor of rank $r(x_i) - 1$.

The concept of rank can be important in scheduling interrelated activities. The ranking algorithm given here can also be extended in an obvious way, to the determination of whether or not a graph is acyclic – which will be relevant to the discussion of skeletons of control flow graphs in Section 4.7.

4.6 Spanning trees

A tree is an acyclic graph $G = (X,U)$ in which one node x_r has no predecessors and every other node has exactly one predecessor. The node x_r is called the root of the tree.

Quite generally, a node x_k of a graph $G = (X,U)$ is called a root of G if every node is accessible from x_k. For instance, the START node of a control-flow graph should be a root of this graph. If a graph G has a root, then it has at least one partial graph which is a tree. Such a tree is called a spanning tree of G. As an illustration, *Figure 4.9*(b) is one of the spanning trees of Figure 4.9(a). Trees of this kind will be used in the next section, which considers control flow in programs.

The arc set V of a spanning tree, with a specified root x_k, can be constructed by the algorithm of *Figure 4.10*.

4.7 Control-flow graphs

The graph-theoretic study of program control structures began in the early 1960s, in the course of development of data flow analysis techniques for optimizing compilers. The control structures of the programs to be compiled at that time (written in languages such as FORTRAN, allowing unrestrained use of goto statements) could be quite 'disorderly'. Compiler authors introduced such optimizations as they could, in the face of this impediment, but in so doing they identified properties of control-flow graphs (the most important being 'reducibility' – or equivalently, the absence of the 'forbidden subgraph' – discussed in Section 4.7.2) which seemed essential for data flow analysis to give strong results. Very fast (low-order polynomial-time) algorithms were found for the data flow analysis of reducible programs. Reducibility also seemed essential to the clarification of what we might mean by a 'program loop', which is not captured either by the notion of a cycle or that of a strong component.

At much the same time, those studying the systematic construction of programs in such a way that one could reason about the functions they performed were encouraging the same choices of control structures (Dijkstra, 1968; Knuth, 1974). Meanwhile, FORTRAN practitioners, from their painful experiences of program testing, had coined the maxim 'Avoid upward gotos' – which was later found to be a sufficient condition for reducibility of FORTRAN programs.

The need for orderliness of control structures is little emphasized today, because the better high-level languages and 'structured assemblers' now strongly encourage it, or even impose it, through their syntax rules (for instance by providing case statements and loop statements with multiple exits, but not goto statements). However, the graph-theoretic justification for the choices of structured statements in such languages is of interest; the nature of requirements and the possibility of checking that they are met also remains relevant to the use of assembly languages where conditional and unconditional jump statements are still necessary.

Throughout this section the term 'flow graph' is used to describe a control-flow graph in which (1) every node is accessible from the START node and (2) the HALT node is accessible from every node.

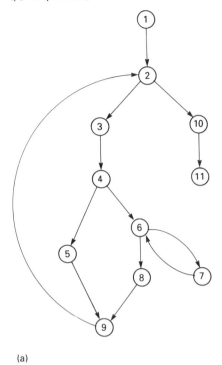

(a)

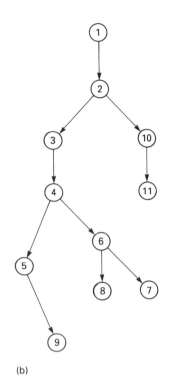

(b)

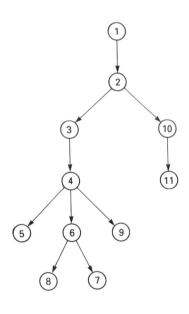

(c)

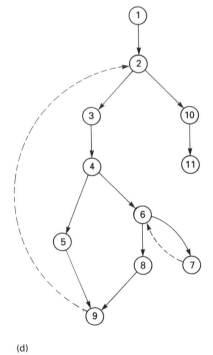

(d)

Figure 4.9

```
begin
    A:={x_k}; B:={x_k}; V:=∅;
    while B≠∅ do
    begin
        select arbitrarily a node x_i in B;
        B:=B−{x_i};
        for each successor x_j of x_i do
            if x_j∉A then
            begin
                A:=A∪{x_j};
                B:=B∪{x_j};
                V:=V∪{(x_i,x_j)}
            end
    end
end;
```

Figure 4.10 Algorithm to construct a spanning tree of a graph with root x_k. On termination A is the accessible set of x_k and V is the arc set of a spanning tree rooted at x_k

4.7.1 Dominance

Let G be a flow graph with start node s, and let x and y be any two (not necessarily distinct) nodes of G. We say that x dominates y if every path from s to y traverses x. To indicate that x dominates y we may use the notation $x\delta y$. If x dominates y and $x\neq y$, we say that x properly dominates y.

We say that x directly dominates y if:

1. x properly dominates y.
2. If z properly dominates y and $z\neq x$, then z (properly) dominates x.

It will be observed that the dominance relation δ of a flow graph is a partial ordering. Indeed:

1. δ is reflexive. From the definition of dominance it follows immediately that $x\delta x$, for every node x.
2. δ is antisymmetric. The proof is by contradiction. Let us suppose that δ is not antisymmetric. Then there exist nodes x and y such that $x\delta y$ and $y\delta x$ and $x\neq y$. Since $x\neq y$ neither x nor y can be the node s (for s is not dominated by any node other than itself). Now every node of G is accessible from s, hence there exists an elementary path μ say from s to x. Since $y\delta x$, the node y must lie on μ; and since $x\delta y$, node x must also lie on μ, between s and y. But then node x occurs twice on an elementary path, which is a contradiction.
3. δ is transitive. Let us assume that $x\delta y$ and $y\delta z$, and let μ be any path from s to z. Then μ contains y, since $y\delta z$, and the segment of μ from s to y contains x, since $x\delta y$. Hence x lies on every path from s to z, and therefore $x\delta z$, as required.

It can be shown furthermore that the dominators of a node form a linear ordering. To prove this it suffices to show that for any three distinct nodes x, y and z, the conditions $x\delta z$ and $y\delta z$ together imply that either $x\delta y$ or $y\delta x$. So let us suppose that the conditions $x\delta z$ and $y\delta z$ hold, and let μ be any path from s to z. Since $x\delta z$ and $y\delta z$, the nodes x and y both lie on μ; without loss of generality we may suppose that x precedes y on this path. But then $x\delta y$; for if there existed another path from s to y, which did not contain x, then this path concatenated with the segment of μ from y to z would form a path from s to z which did not contain x. This would contradict our initial assumption that $x\delta z$.

From the definition of direct dominance, and the fact that the dominators of a node are linearly ordered, it follows immediately that every node other than s has a unique direct dominator. Thus for any flow graph $G=(X,U)$ with start node s, the graph of the direct-dominance relation on X is a tree, rooted at s. This tree contains an arc (x_i,x_j) if and only if x_i directly dominates x_j; and it contains a path from x_i to x_j if and only if x_i

dominates x_j (directly or indirectly). As an illustration, the dominance tree of the graph of Figure 4.9(a) is shown in Figure 4.9(c).

The two following observations lead to a method of constructing the dominance tree of a flow graph:

1. If a flow graph G is a tree, then the dominance tree of G is identical to G.
2. Let G be a flow graph and let T be its dominance tree. Also, let G' be the graph obtained by adding some arc (x_i,x_j) to G. Then the dominance tree T' of G' can be derived from T as follows:
   (a) If T contains a path from x_i to x_j, then remove from T its arc incident to x_j, and insert the arc (x_i,x_j).
   (b) If T contains a path from x_j to x_i, then T' is identical to T.
   (c) If T does not contain any paths between x_i and x_j then find, on T, the node x_k which is of highest rank in the set $\hat{\Gamma}^-(x_i)\cap\hat{\Gamma}^-(x_j)$; remove from T the arc incident to x_j, and insert the arc (x_k,x_j).

One simple way of applying these rules is as follows. First we construct a spanning tree H of G, by the algorithm of Figure 4.10. We then obtain the dominance tree of G by making a succession of modifications to H, as prescribed above, to take account of the arcs of G which were not assigned to H initially. Further details of techniques for constructing dominance trees are given by Hecht (1977).

4.7.2 Reducibility

Let G be a flow graph with entry node s. If any strongly connected subgraph H of G has a node x which dominates all other nodes of H, we say that H is single-entry, and we describe x as the entry node of H. If all the strongly-connected subgraphs of G are single-entry we say that G is reducible; otherwise G is said to be irreducible.

Now let us consider a flow graph of the form shown in *Figure 4.11*, where the wavy lines represent arc-disjoint paths; the nodes a, b, c and s (the initial node) are distinct, except that a and s may be the same. Clearly, no reducible flow graph contains a (partial) subgraph of this form, for the loop between b and c constitutes a strongly connected subgraph, which is not single-entry. On the other hand, every irreducible flow graph does have a subgraph of this form. To prove this, let us suppose that G is an irreducible flow graph. Then G contains a strongly connected subgraph H which is not single-entry, hence G has a subgraph of the form shown in *Figure 4.12*; here the wavy lines again represent arc-disjoint paths, and the nodes a, x, y and s are distinct, except that a and s may be the same. Now since H is strongly connected, it contains a path μ say from x to y, and a path μ' say from y to x. If these paths are arc-disjoint, then obviously G contains a subgraph of the form of Figure 4.11,

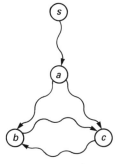

Figure 4.11 The forbidden subgraph

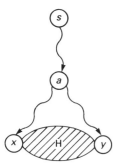

Figure 4.12

with b = x and c = y. Otherwise, let z be the first node on μ' which is encountered in traversing μ from x towards y. Then G has a subgraph of the form shown in Figure 4.11, with b = x and c = z.

In summary, a flow graph is reducible if and only if it does not have a (partial) subgraph of the form shown in Figure 4.11. For obvious reasons we may refer to such a subgraph as a 'forbidden subgraph'.

4.7.3 Skeletons of flow graphs

Let $G = (X, U)$ be a flow graph, with dominance relation δ. Then we may partition the arc set U of G into two sets:

$$U_f = \{(x_i, x_j) \in U | x_j \bar{\delta} x_i\}$$

and

$$U_b = \{(x_i, x_j) \in U | x_j \delta x_i\}$$

The arcs in U_f are called the forward arcs of G, whereas the arcs in U_b are called backward arcs. As an illustration, Figure 4.9(d) shows the flow graph of Figure 4.9(a), with its backward arcs drawn as broken lines.

For any flow graph $G = (X, U)$, we describe the partial graph $G_f = (X, U_f)$ of G as the skeleton of G. It will be observed that:

1. If a flow graph is reducible then its skeleton is acyclic. Indeed, let G be a flow graph and let us suppose that its skeleton contains a cycle, γ say. Then γ also belongs to G, and since G is reducible γ has one node which dominates all its other nodes. But then γ contains at least one backward arc, which contradicts our initial assumption that G_f contains γ.
2. If a flow graph is irreducible then its skeleton contains a cycle. For if a flow graph G is irreducible, then it contains a forbidden subgraph. Since none of the arcs of the elementary cycle of the forbidden subgraph are backward arcs, this elementary cycle appears in the skeleton of G.

From these results we conclude that a flow graph is reducible if and only if its skeleton is acyclic.

4.7.4 Loops of reducible flow graphs

In a reducible graph, a node is called a loop head if it is the terminal end-point of one or more backward arcs. Now let x be a loop head in a reducible graph $G = (X, U)$, let $\beta(x)$ be the set of initial end-points of backward arcs of G which are incident to x:

$$\beta(x) = \{x' \in X | (x', x) \in U \text{ and } x\delta x'\}$$

and let $\pi(x)$ be the set of nodes:

$$\pi(x) = \{x' \in X | G \text{ has a path from } x' \text{ to some node in } \beta(x), \text{ which does not traverse } x\}$$

We describe the subgraph of G generated by $\{x\} \cup \beta(x) \cup \pi(x)$ as the loop with head x. As an illustration the graph of Figure 4.9(d) has two loops, (1) the subgraph generated by $\{x_2, x_3, x_4, x_5, x_6, x_7, x_8, x_9\}$, whose head is x_2, and (2) the subgraph generated by $\{x_6, x_7\}$, whose head is x_6.

Now let $L_1 = (X_1, U_1)$ and $L_2 = (X_2, U_2)$ be two loops in a flow graph. We say that L_1 envelops L_2 (or that L_2 is enveloped or nested in L_1), and write $L_1 \triangleright L_2$, if $X_2 \subseteq X_1$. It is evident that the enveloping relation $\triangleright$ on the set of loops of a program is a partial ordering (since the set inclusion relation has this property). Furthermore, for any two loops $L_1 = (X_1, U_1)$ and $L_2 = (X_2, U_2)$, the condition $X_1 \cap X_2 \neq \emptyset$ implies that either $L_1 \triangleright L_2$ or $L_2 \triangleright L_1$. To prove this let us suppose that the loops L_1 and L_2 have heads x_1 and x_2 respectively, and that the condition $X_1 \cap X_2 \neq \emptyset$ applies. Then for any node $y \in X_1 \cap X_2$, we have both $x_1 \delta y$ and $x_2 \delta y$. Hence (as the dominators of a node are linearly ordered), either $x_1 \delta x_2$ or $x_2 \delta x_1$. Since the graph $(X_1 \cup X_2, U_1 \cup U_2)$ is strongly connected, it follows that either $X_1 \subseteq X_2$ or $X_2 \subseteq X_1$, as required. From this result we conclude that for any loop, the set of loops which envelop it form a linear ordering.

The definition of a 'loop' here accords well with our understanding of loop statements in high-level languages; it also has the properties sought in code optimization (see Aho *et al.* (1986), who describe a loop as defined here as a 'natural loop').

4.8 Graph grammars

Figure 4.3 presented an informal graph grammar for a class of flow graphs (or more precisely for flowcharts) corresponding to Dijkstra's original concept of 'structured programming'. In this figure nodes are depicted by rectangles and diamonds; a rectangle containing an 'E' is an 'expansible' node (the only nonterminal symbol of the grammar), empty rectangles and diamonds are non-expansible (i.e. terminal symbols). An expansible node can be replaced by the right-hand side of any of the productions. Thus, just as a BNF definition of the syntax of a programming language can be regarded as a generator of sentences (or programs) in the language, the grammar of Figure 4.3 is a generator of 'structured flow graphs'.

A parsing process can also be applied to a graph, in much the same way as parsing is performed by a compiler. Employing a bottom-up parsing method, production rules are applied 'in reverse' to the graph, repeatedly condensing a subgraph which corresponds to the right-hand side of a production to a single node. If a graph is grammatically correct it is eventually condensed to a single node (the sentence symbol). Its grammatical structure can be defined by recording the sequence of reductions performed, either in the form of a syntax tree, or as an extended regular expression representing all the paths through the graph. (For this process to be meaningful, and practicable, the graph grammar must form a finite Church–Rosser transformation (Hecht, 1977), meaning that its rules can only be applied a finite number of times to any flow graph, and that the final result is independent of the order in which they are applied.)

Of course the grammar of Figure 4.3 is not rich enough to describe all the kinds of flow graphs one may wish to employ in practice. In particular, it is desirable to allow the use of case statements with multiple alternatives, and loops having multiple exits as in Modula-2 and Ada. Examples of graph grammars which accommodate such structures, whilst still possessing the finite Church–Rosser property, are described by Kennedy (1981). As a concrete example, the control structures which can be produced in the programming language SPARK, a sublanguage of Ada designed to support rigorous program development (Carré, 1989a), all satisfy the rules of a 'semi-structured flow-graph grammar (SSFG)' similar to that of Farrow *et al.* (1975). The SSFG requirements are met simply by eliminating

Ada's goto statement (which is rather superfluous, since Ada is otherwise rich in control structures) and imposing reasonable restrictions on the placement of loop exit and subprogram return statements.

To explain now the practical relevance of graph grammars to programming, the data flow analysis of a program involves the construction of certain binary relations from the set V of its variables to the set E of instances of expressions in its statements. As an example, to detect data flow errors (i.e. references to undefined variables) we construct for the program a relation θ_s: $V \rightarrow E$, where for any statement s (which may be an 'atomic' statement such as an assignment statement, or a conditional or iterative statement, or the composition of a number of statements, possibly even the entire program), $v\theta_s e$ means 'the value of the variable v immediately prior to the execution of s may be employed in the evaluation of the expression e in s'. The θ-relation for the program is obtained by calculating and combining the θ-relations of the statements that make it up, in a manner similar in some respects to that described by Loomes in Chapter 2, for calculating the weakest precondition of a program in terms of the weakest preconditions of its constituents. (An important difference, however, is that here, we do not require complete knowledge of the semantics of the program statements, but only the names of the variables which each statement defines and references.)

For some programming languages whose syntax rules only allow the use of 'well-formed' control structures, such as Modula-2 and SPARK, rules of construction of the θ-relations can be associated with productions of the language grammar, making it possible to compute the θ-relation for a program in the course of a traversal of its syntax tree. However, data flow and information flow analysis is often required for programs written in languages whose syntax rules do not allow this (assembly languages being important examples). Nevertheless, if the control structure of a program satisfies the rules of an appropriate graph grammar (such as an SSFG grammar), its flow analysis can still be performed by constructing its flowchart model, parsing this, and then calculating the θ-relation for the program parsed in this way. The same technique can be applied to other forms of flow analysis, such as the determination of input–output dependencies of program variables (Bergeretti and Carré, 1985). Some details of the implementation of these techniques in a program analysis and verification system are given by Carré (1989b).

4.9 Further reading

The notions of flowcharts and flowchart schemas were formalized and studied in detail by Manna (1974). Program flow analysis is described by Hecht (1977) and the contributors to Muchnick and Jones (1981). Of the latter, Kennedy (1981) in particular discusses graph grammars and graph parsing, in the context of data flow analysis. For a further discussion of graph-theoretic concepts and their applications, see Carré (1979).

4.10 References

Aho, A. V., Hopcroft, J. E. and Ullman, J. D. (1974) *The Design and Analysis of Computer Algorithms*, Addison-Wesley

Aho, A. V., Sethi, R. and Ullman, J. D. (1986) *Compilers – Principles, Techniques, and Tools*, Addison-Wesley

Bergeretti, J.-F. and Carré, B. A. (1985) Information-flow and data-flow analysis of while programs. *ACM Transactions on Programming Languages and Systems*, **7**, 37–61

Carré, B. A. (1979) *Graphs and Networks*, Oxford University Press

Carré, B. A. (1989a) Reliable programming in standard languages. In *High-Integrity Software* (ed. C. T. Sennett), Pitman

Carré, B. A. (1989b) Program analysis and verification. In *High-Integrity Software* (ed. C. T. Sennett), Pitman

Dijkstra, E. W. (1968) Goto statements considered harmful. *Communications of ACM*, **11**, 147–8

Farrow, R., Kennedy, K. and Zucconi, L. (1975) Graph grammars and global program flow analysis. In *Proceedings 17th Annual IEEE Symposium on Foundations of Computer Science*

Hecht, M. S. (1977) *Flow Analysis of Computer Programs*, North-Holland

Kennedy, K. (1981) A survey of data flow analysis techniques. In *Program Flow Analysis* (eds S. S. Muchnick and N. D. Jones), Prentice-Hall

Knuth, D. E. (1974) Structured programming with goto statements. *Computing Surveys*, **6**, 261–301

Manna, Z. (1974) *Mathematical Theory of Computation*, McGraw-Hill

Muchnick, S. S. and Jones, N. D. (1981) *Program Flow Analysis*, Prentice-Hall

5

Probability theory

W. Freeman
Department of Computer Science, University of York

Contents

5.1 Introduction

Probability theory is a way of modelling expectations about the future. In no way does it allow us to assert the correctness of those expectations. Rather, it enables us to calculate the consequences of hypotheses. It is of the form: *if* the hypotheses are correct, *then* the following will be the case. Probability theory is quite distinct from statistics, which is a way of organizing, presenting and exploiting past observations of the world. There is a logical sequence here: descriptive statistics is a way of summarizing observations; predictive statistics is a way of using models based on those observations to erect plausible hypotheses about the future; and probability theory allows the deduction of the consequences of those hypotheses, rigorously and precisely, conditional only on those hypotheses being the case. Notice, though, that statistical observations are only one source of predictive hypotheses. All kinds of informal and indirect observation, hunches and experience of the past can go into making hypotheses. Their creation is a matter for human judgement, while deduction from them is a matter for mathematical rigour. Rigour tells us what we may or may not deduce, whereas our judgement tells us what it is we want to deduce. This is to give each kind of thought its proper sphere of action, and to prevent confusion and muddled thinking.

In what follows, therefore, probabilities will be defined in an abstract mathematical way, without any necessary reference to the 'real world'. For a discussion of the ways in which mathematical probabilities can be used to model the real world, see Nagel (1939) and Kyburg (1961). Fine (1973) has made a comparative study of rival and radical bases and interpretations. Venn (1888) and Keynes (1921) are of historical interest, and for a history of the subject, see Todhunter (1865), Maistrov (1974) and Hacking (1975).

5.2 Rational model of probability

Probability theory may be founded on different sets of axioms, depending on (1) whether we assume that the number of possible outcomes of any future experiment will be finite, or that it may be countably, or uncountably, infinite and (2) whether we allow the numerical values of the probabilities involved to take on values that are rational or irrational. In its simplest, rational form, it uses the relationships among the regions of a partition of a finite set, or between one such partition and another, to model the probabilistic relationships between events in the real world; and represents probabilities as rational numbers. The treatment of probability according to this assumption must be regarded as non-standard, except as a means of introducing the subject. (It is used for that purpose by Kyburg (1969), for example.) All standard treatments allow probabilities to be irrational. We shall introduce that possibility, and also that of the number of outcomes being infinite, in a later section. In the following it is assumed that the reader is familiar with the concepts and notation set out in Chapter 1, on discrete mathematics.

5.2.1 Partitions and refinements of partitions

First, we need to define the set of all subsets of a given size, k, of a set, S:

$$\mathcal{Q}_k(S) \triangleq \{x : x \subseteq S \wedge \#x = k\}$$

as, for example: $\mathcal{Q}_2(\{a, b, c\}) = \{\{a, b\}\{b, c\}\{c, a\}\}$; the set of singletons of S:

$$\mathscr{S}(S) \triangleq \mathcal{Q}_1(S),$$

as, for example: $\mathscr{S}(\{a, b, c\}) = \{\{a\}, \{b\}, \{c\}\}$, and the *powerset* of

$$\mathscr{P}(S) \triangleq \bigcup_{k=0}^{\#S} \mathcal{Q}_k = \{x : x \subseteq S\}$$

as, for example, $\mathscr{P}(\{a, b, c\}) = \{\{\}, \{a\}, \{b\}, \{c\}, \{a, b\}, \{b, c\}, \{c, a\}, \{a, b, c\}\}$. Notice that $\#\mathcal{Q}_k(S) = \binom{\#S}{k}$, $\#\mathscr{S}(S) = \#S$, and $\#\mathscr{P}(S) = 2^{\#S}$.

Then, a partition is a way of chopping up a set into subsets. More formally, a partition of a set S is defined to be a set of disjoint non-empty subsets of S, called regions, such that every element of S belongs also to one of those regions. Equivalently, P is a partition of S iff:

$$P \subseteq \mathscr{P}(S) \backslash \{\varnothing\} \text{ and } s \in S \Rightarrow \exists! x : s \in x \wedge x \in P$$

Here, S is called the base set of the partition. As an example, $\{\{a, c\}, \{b\}\}$ is a partition of the base set $\{a, b, c\}$. If $P = \{S\}$, then it is the trivial partition of S; otherwise, it is proper. If $P = \mathscr{S}(S)$, then it is the ultimate partition of S. As examples, $\{\{a, b, c\}\}$ is the trivial partition, and $\{\{a\}, \{b\}, \{c\}\}$ is the ultimate partition, of $\{a, b, c\}$. Notice that membership of the same region of a given partition is an equivalence relation on the base set.

A partition, R, is a refinement of a partition, P (and, conversely, P is an encoarsement of R), of the same base set iff:

$$x \in R \Rightarrow \exists y : x \subseteq y \wedge y \in P$$

We then write $R \Rightarrow P$ to mean 'R is a refinement of P', or 'R encoarses to P', and write $\Leftarrow$ for the converse. As an example, $\{\{a, e\}, \{c\}, \{b\}, \{d\}\} \Rightarrow \{\{a, c, e\}, \{b, d\}\}$. Also, we can write 'P $\Rightarrow \{S\}$' to mean 'P is a partition of S'. If $R \Rightarrow P$ and $R \neq P$, then R is a proper refinement of P; otherwise, it is trivial. Notice that '$\Rightarrow$' induces a partial ordering on the set of all partitions of a given base set S, thereby forming a lattice: with $\{S\}$, their ultimate encoarsement, as the unique maximal element, and $\mathscr{S}(S)$, their ultimate refinement, as the unique minimal element.

Finally, we define two pieces of notation for row and column sequences:

$$[x_i]_{i=0}^{2} \triangleq x_0, x_1, x_2 \text{ and } [\![x_i]\!]_{i=0}^{2} \triangleq \begin{matrix} x_0 \\ x_1 \\ x_2 \end{matrix}$$

We shall write '†' for matrix transposition, '$\triangle$' for 'equals by definition', '$\triangleq$' for 'iff by definition'; and '$\rightarrow$' as a right-associative guard placed in front of a theorem or definition, following a condition under which it holds. 'a $\lessgtr$ b$\leftrightarrow$y $\lessgtr$ z' means 'a < b$\leftrightarrow$y < z and a = b$\leftrightarrow$y = z and a > b$\leftrightarrow$y > z'. Much of the terminology and notation developed in this chapter will be used also in Chapter 14, on information theory.

5.2.2 Stochastic spaces

We can now define probabilities in terms of a finite set, Ω, which represents certainty. We can construct a certainty set of size N, say, as:

$$\Omega \triangle \quad \{[\omega_h]_{h=0}^{N-1}\}$$

whose elements, the number and distinctness of which are important, but whose nature is otherwise irrelevant, are called its atoms. We define the stochastic space, or probability space, whose base is Ω, to be $\mathscr{S}(\Omega)$.

We use the word 'experiment' to describe any set of possible future outcomes, whose probabilities (of becoming an actual future outcome) we wish to model. Formally, an experiment, X, is an encoarsement of a stochastic space, $\mathscr{S}(\Omega)$; and the regions of that encoarsement are called the outcomes of X.

We might, for example, have the certainty set:

$$\Omega = \{\omega_0, \omega_1, \omega_2, \omega_3, \omega_4, \omega_5, \omega_6\}$$

This creates the stochastic space:

$$\mathscr{S}(\Omega) = \{\{\omega_0\}, \{\omega_1\}, \{\omega_2\}, \{\omega_3\}, \{\omega_4\}, \{\omega_5\}, \{\omega_6\}\}$$

and an example of an experiment on this space would be the following encoarsement of it:

$$X = \{x_0, x_1, x_2\} = \{\{\omega_0, \omega_1\}, \{\omega_2\}, \{\omega_3, \omega_4, \omega_5, \omega_6\}\}$$

A 'trial' of an experiment is the actual occurrence of one of its possible outcomes; a throw of a die, for example, is a trial of an experiment with six possible outcomes, these being the faces of the die. We can think of a trial as the happening of one of the atoms. We are then told which outcome contains the atom that happened, but not the identity of the actual atom itself. The probability $p(X_t = x)$, that trial t of experiment X will have an outcome x, is defined as the sum of the probabilities of all the atomic outcomes contained within x. An atomic outcome, $\{\omega_h\}$ for example, is an element of the stochastic space $\mathscr{S}(\Omega)$. We define the probability of an atomic outcome by a mapping $p : \mathscr{S}(\Omega) \to \mathbf{Q}$, from a stochastic space to the rational numbers, such that all the atomic outcomes of a given stochastic space have the same probability, and that their probabilities collectively sum to unity. If the probabilities are the same from trial to trial, and there can be no confusion, we write $p(x)$ for $p(X_t = x)$. Then, recalling that $\mathscr{S}\Omega \Rightarrow X \Rightarrow \{\Omega\}$, we have:

$$\bigwedge_{\substack{\omega \in \Omega \\ \omega' \in \Omega}} [p(\{\omega\}) \triangle p(\{\omega'\})] \text{ and } \sum_{\omega \in \Omega} p(\{\omega\}) \triangle 1$$

so that:

$$\bigwedge_{\omega \in \Omega} \left[p(\{\omega\}) = \frac{1}{\#\Omega} \right] \text{ and } p(x) = \sum_{\omega \in X} p(\{\omega\}) = \frac{\#x}{\#\Omega}$$

and, finally and importantly:

$$\bigwedge_{x \in X} [0 \leqslant p(x) \leqslant 1] \quad \text{and} \quad \sum_{x \in X} p(x) = 1$$

We call $m \triangle \#X$ the multiplicity of the experiment $X \triangle \{[x_i]_{i=0}^{m-1}\}$; the vector:

$$\hat{X} \triangle ([p(x_i)]_{i=0}^{m-1})$$

is called the probability vector, or distribution, of X. (It is an example of a stochastic vector. This term is used to mean any vector whose components are non-negative and sum to unity.) Continuing with the previous example, suppose that $X = \{x_0, x_1, x_2\} = \{\{\omega_0, \omega_1\}, \{\omega_2\}, \{\omega_3, \omega_4, \omega_5, \omega_6\}\}$. Then $\hat{X} = (\frac{2}{7}, \frac{1}{7}, \frac{4}{7})$. If $\hat{X} = ([\frac{1}{m}]_{i=0}^{m-1})$, then $\hat{X}$ is called a uniform distribution. Particular examples of uniformly distributed experiments are the null, or trivial experiment $X = \{\Omega\}$, which has $\hat{X} = (1)$; and the ultimate experiment, $\hat{X} = \mathscr{S}(\Omega)$, which has $\hat{X} = ([\frac{1}{\#\Omega}]_{i=0}^{\#\Omega-1})$.

An element (i.e. region) of any encoarsement of X is called an event of X. This includes the trivial and ultimate encoarsements.

In order that the set of events of an experiment shall be closed under complementation relative to Ω, the empty set is also, by definition, an event. Notice that the outcomes of an experiment are among its events, but that, while any two distinct outcomes of the same experiment are disjoint, two events are not necessarily so, even if distinct. Formally, the set of events of an experiment X is given by:

$$\mathscr{F}(X) \triangle \{\emptyset\} \cup \bigcup_{P \Leftarrow X} P$$

(Such sets are conventionally called fields of events but beware that, although $(\mathscr{F}(X), \cup)$ is a monoid, with identity $\emptyset$, and has a dual monoid, $(\mathscr{F}(X), \cap)$, with identity Ω, neither of these is a 'field' in the usual sense of abstract algebra. Beware also that, for any two experiments, X and Y, $\mathscr{F}(X) \cap \mathscr{F}(Y)$ is always a field of events, but $\mathscr{F}(X) \cup \mathscr{F}(Y)$ need not be.) There is an obvious bijection between $\mathscr{F}(X)$ and $\mathscr{P}(X)$, in that each set of outcomes ultimately encoarses to a distinct event; and, among the refinements of each event, there is exactly one that is a set of outcomes. So $\#\mathscr{F}(X) = \#\mathscr{P}(X) = 2^m$.

Continuing with the previous example, the events of X are:

$$\text{empty} = \{\} = \emptyset$$

$$x_0 = \{\omega_0, \omega_1\}$$

$$x_1 = \{\omega_2\}$$

$$x_0 \cup x_1 = \{\omega_0, \omega_1, \omega_2\}$$

$$x_2 = \{\omega_3, \omega_4, \omega_5, \omega_6\}$$

$$x_0 \cup x_2 = \{\omega_0, \omega_1, \omega_3, \omega_4, \omega_5, \omega_6\}$$

$$x_1 \cup x_2 = \{\omega_2, \omega_3, \omega_4, \omega_5, \omega_6\}$$

$$x_0 \cup x_1 \cup x_2 = \{\omega_0, \omega_1, \omega_2, \omega_3, \omega_4, \omega_4, \omega_6\} = \Omega$$

The probability, $p(\xi)$, of an event, ξ, is defined to be equal to the sum of the probabilities of the outcomes included within it, that is:

$$p(\xi) \triangle p(X_t \subseteq \xi) \triangle \sum_{\substack{x \subseteq \xi \\ x \subseteq \xi}} p(x) = \frac{\#\xi}{\#\Omega}$$

It is therefore the case that $p(\xi \cup \xi') = p(X_t \subseteq \xi \cup \xi') = p(X_t \subseteq \xi \vee X_t \subseteq \xi')$, and that $p(\xi \cap \xi') = p(X_t \subseteq \xi \cap \xi') = p(X_t \subseteq \xi \wedge X_t \subseteq \xi')$. Of the events of an experiment, $\emptyset$ is the impossible event, Ω is the certain event, those that coincide with outcomes are elementary events, and those that are unions of distinct outcomes are composite events. Notice that $p(\emptyset) = 0$, and that $p(\Omega) = 1$.

As an example, suppose we consider that the probability of rain at noon tomorrow is $\frac{2}{7}$, and of snow at noon tomorrow is $\frac{1}{7}$, and that it cannot rain and snow at the same time. Then this can be modelled by the example experiment, X, given above, with $x_0 = $ 'rain at noon', $x_1 = $ 'snow at noon', and $x_2 = $ 'neither of these' (noting that we have assumed that 'both' cannot occur). Then we have the following probabilities of events.

p('not rain at noon, and not snow at noon, and not either of these') $= p(\emptyset) = 0$

p('rain at noon') $= p(x_0) = \frac{2}{7}$

p('snow at noon') $= p(x_1) = \frac{1}{7}$

$p(\text{'rain at noon, or snow at noon'}) = p(x_0 \cup x_1) = \tfrac{3}{7}$

$p(\text{'neither rain nor snow at noon'}) = p(x_2) = \tfrac{4}{7}$

$p(\text{'rain at noon, or neither'}) = p(x_0 \cup x_2) = \tfrac{6}{7}$

$p(\text{'snow at noon, or neither'}) = p(x_1 \cup x_2) = \tfrac{5}{7}$

$p(\text{'rain at noon, or snow at noon, or neither'}) = p(x_0 \cup x_1 \cup x_2)$
$= p(\Omega) = 1$

Given that the only possibilities are rain, snow or neither; and given that, here, Ω is the universal set, we can usefully employ complementary sets as complementary events. For example:

$p(\text{'not rain at noon'}) = p(\bar{x}_0) = p(\Omega \backslash x_0) = p(x_1 \cup x_2) = \tfrac{5}{7}$

$p(\text{'not snow at noon'}) = p(\bar{x}_1) = p(\Omega \backslash x_1) = p(x_0 \cup x_2) = \tfrac{6}{7}$

$p(\text{'not (rain at noon or snow at noon)'}) = p(\overline{x_0 \cup x_1}) = p(\Omega \backslash (x_0 \cup x_1)) = p(x_2) = \tfrac{4}{7}$

5.2.3 Conditional probability and dependence of events

The example experiment discussed above ('rain/snow/neither') can be specified in a diagram such as the following:

$x_i = \quad x_0 \ x_1 \ x_2$

$\#x_i = \quad 2 \ 1 \ 4$

The row of numbers, if normalized by dividing by $\#\Omega_X$ (which we shall write, for clarity, in place of $\#\Omega$), would yield the distribution $\hat{X}$. Now suppose that the probabilities of 'warm' and 'cold' are $\tfrac{11}{12}$ and $\tfrac{10}{21}$ respectively, and we say that $Y = \{y_0, y_1\}$, with $y_0 = $ 'warm' and $y_1 = $ 'cold', and $\#\Omega_Y = 21$:

$y_j = \quad y_0 \ y_1$

$\#y_j = \quad 11 \ 10$

Then, what is the probability of 'rain and warm at noon tomorrow'? From the information given so far, *we cannot tell*. But suppose that all of the *mn* outcomes of the compound experiment:

$(X,Y) \triangleq ([[x_i \cap y_j]_{j=0}^{n-1}]_{i=0}^{m-1})$

were specified. For this example, we specify them in the form of a table, $[[\#x_i \cap y_j]_{j=0}^{n-1}]_{i=0}^{m-1}$, of sizes of outcomes:

	y_0	y_1
x_0	1	5
x_1	0	3
x_2	10	2

$\#x_i \cap y_j$

where X,Y and (X,Y) are all based on a stochastic space with $\#\Omega = \#\Omega_{X,Y} = \mathrm{lcm}(\#\Omega_X, \#\Omega_Y) = 21$. (Indeed, any other common multiple of $\#\Omega_X$ and $\#\Omega_Y$ would do.) Then, for example, $p(\text{'rain and warm'}) = p(x_0 \cap y_0) = \tfrac{1}{21}$. Notice that $p(x_0) = p(x_0 \cap (y_0 \cup y_1)) = p(x_0 \cap y_0) + p(x_0 \cap y_1)$, and is thus expressed in terms of outcomes of (X,Y), which are of course disjoint. Notice also that $p(x_0) = \tfrac{1}{21} + \tfrac{5}{21} = \tfrac{2}{7}$, as before; but that x_0, although an

outcome of X, is a composite event of (X,Y). In general, the x_i, being outcomes of X, are disjoint; but they are composite events of (X,Y). Similarly, the y_j, although disjoint, are composite events of (X,Y). It is the $x_i \cap y_j$ that are the outcomes of (X,Y). (The outcome $x_1 \cap y_0$ is allowed to be a region of a partition, even though it is empty, because it is merely empty in practice, contingently, and not in principle, analytically.)

We can now express the probabilities of composite events represented by arbitrary set expressions. For example, if $\xi_a = x_2 \cup y_1 \cap x_1$ and $\xi_b = x_2 \cap y_0 \cup x_0 \cap y_1$, then:

$p(\xi_a \cup \xi_b) = p(x_2 \cap y_0) + \sum_{i=0}^{2} p(x_i \cap y_1) = \tfrac{20}{21}$

This has served to illustrate the following important point. We have:

$\Omega_{X,Y} = \bigcup_{x \in X} \bigcup_{y \in Y} x \cap y$ and $\#\Omega_{X,Y} = \sum_{x \in X} \sum_{y \in Y} \#x \cap y$

Now let $\xi \in \mathcal{F}(X)$ and $\upsilon \in \mathcal{F}(Y)$, then:

$\xi \cap \upsilon = \bigcup_{\substack{y \in Y \\ y \subseteq \upsilon}} \xi \cap y = \bigcup_{\substack{x \in X \\ y \subseteq \xi}} \bigcup_{\substack{y \in Y \\ y \subseteq \upsilon}} x \cap y$

and

$\#\xi \cap \upsilon = \sum_{\substack{y \in Y \\ y \subseteq \upsilon}} \#\xi \cap y = \sum_{\substack{x \in X \\ x \subseteq \xi}} \sum_{\substack{y \in Y \\ y \subseteq \upsilon}} \#x \cap y$

This is called the total probability rule.

A stochastic space, variously encoarsed as two experiments X and Y, can be used to answer questions such as 'given that it will be cold at noon tomorrow (and given our hypotheses), what is the probability that it will snow at noon tomorrow?' In considering the answer to such a question, we should have regard to the $Y_t = y_1$ column, only, of the diagram of (X,Y); and if this forms its own stochastic space, partitioned as 5:3:2, we have the probability distribution $\hat{Y} = (\tfrac{5}{10}, \tfrac{3}{10}, \tfrac{2}{10})$. These probabilities are then conditional, being of the form 'given that $Y_t = y_1, \ldots$'; and we write them as $p(x_0|y_1) = \tfrac{1}{2}$, $p(x_1|y_1) = \tfrac{3}{10}$, and $p(x_2|y_1) = \tfrac{1}{5}$. In general, we define the conditional probability of an event ξ, given a non-empty event υ, by:

$\upsilon \neq \varnothing \rightarrow p(\xi|\upsilon) \triangleq p(X_t \subseteq \xi | X_t \subseteq \upsilon) \triangleq \dfrac{p(\xi \cap \upsilon)}{p(\upsilon)}$

where $p(\upsilon) = \sum_{i=0}^{m-1} p(x_i \cap \upsilon)$. So $p(\xi|\upsilon) = \#\xi \cap \upsilon / \#\upsilon$, provided that $\upsilon \neq \varnothing$. Conditional probabilities are particularly simple in cases where $\xi \subseteq \upsilon$. For example:

$p(X_t \subseteq x_0 | X_t \subseteq x_0 \cup x_2) = \dfrac{p(x_0)}{p(x_0 \cup x_2)} = \tfrac{1}{3}$

Notice that, in the example above, $p(x_0|y_0) = \tfrac{1}{11}$, but that $p(y_0|x_0) = \tfrac{1}{6}$. Such inversions of conditional probabilities can be obtained generally by means of Bayes' theorem:

$\xi \neq \varnothing \rightarrow \upsilon \neq \varnothing \rightarrow p(\upsilon|\xi) = \dfrac{p(\upsilon \cap \xi)}{p(\xi)} = \dfrac{p(\upsilon)}{p(\xi)} p(\xi|\upsilon)$

where $p(\xi) = \sum_{j=0}^{n-1} p(\xi \cap y_j)$.

Repeated use of the definition of conditional probability gives:

$$p(\xi\cap\upsilon\cap\zeta) = p(\xi\cap\upsilon)p(\zeta\,|\,\xi\cap\upsilon) = p(\xi)p(\upsilon\,|\,\xi)p(\zeta\,|\,\xi\cap\upsilon)$$

and generally, on a subset $\{[\xi_i]_{i=0}^{k-1}\}$ of $\mathscr{F}(X)$:

$$p(\bigcap_{i=0}^{k-1}\xi_i) = \prod_{i=0}^{k-1}p(\xi_i\,|\,\bigcap_{j=0}^{i-1}\xi_j)$$

noting that any vacuous intersections take the value Ω, and that any vacuous products take the value 1.

Referring again to the example, $p(y_1) = \frac{10}{21}$, $p(y_1\,|\,x_0\cup x_1) = \frac{8}{9}$, and $p(y_1\,|\,\overline{x_0\cup x_1}) = \frac{1}{6}$. So:

1. Knowledge that $X_t \subseteq x_0\cup x_1$ would *raise* our estimate of the probability of $Y_t \subseteq y_1$, from $\frac{30}{63}$ to $\frac{56}{63}$;
2. Knowledge that $X_t \nsubseteq x_0\cup x_1$ would *lower* it, from $\frac{20}{42}$ to $\frac{7}{42}$.

These two observations are in fact equivalent to one another, as is shown by the theorem of contrary dependence on the complementary event:

$$\upsilon \ne \varnothing \to \upsilon \ne \Omega \to p(\xi) \lesseqgtr p(\xi\,|\,\upsilon)\Leftrightarrow p(\xi\,|\,\overline{\upsilon}) \lesseqgtr p(\xi)$$

(Recall that '$\lesseqgtr$' expands to give three propositions, with '$<$', '$=$', and '$>$' substituted consistently throughout.) Since, in the example, $p(y_1\,|\,x_0\cup x_1)$ is *greater* that $p(y_1)$, we say that y_1 is positively dependent on $x_0\cup x_1$. Actually, we can say that y_1 and $x_0\cup x_1$ are positively dependent on one another, since the relation is symmetric, as is shown by the following theorem:

$$\xi \ne \varnothing \to \upsilon \ne \varnothing \to p(\upsilon) \lesseqgtr p(\upsilon\,|\,\xi)\Leftrightarrow p(\xi) \lesseqgtr p(\xi\,|\,\upsilon)$$

which follows immediately from:

$$\xi \ne \varnothing \to \upsilon \ne \varnothing \to \frac{p(\upsilon\,|\,\xi)}{p(\upsilon)} = \frac{p(\xi\cap\upsilon)}{p(\xi)p(\upsilon)} = \frac{p(\xi\,|\,\upsilon)}{p(\xi)}$$

We then define positive (stochastic) dependence, independence and negative dependence of events ξ and υ according as $p(\xi\cap\upsilon)$ is greater than, equal to, or less than $p(\xi)p(\upsilon)$ respectively:

$$\left.\begin{array}{c}\xi\,\blacktriangle\,\upsilon\\[4pt]\xi\,\blacksquare\,\upsilon\\[4pt]\xi\,\blacktriangledown\,\upsilon\end{array}\right\} \triangleq p(\xi\cap\upsilon)\left\{\begin{array}{c}>\\[4pt]=\\[4pt]<\end{array}\right\}p(\xi)p(\upsilon)$$

These notations should, however, be used with some circumspection owing to the existence of problems such as Simpson's paradox, which shows by example that one can have $(\xi\,\blacktriangledown\,\upsilon) \wedge (\xi'\,\blacktriangledown\,\upsilon)$ and yet $(\xi\cup\xi')\,\blacktriangle\,\upsilon$. See, for example, Romano and Siegel (1986). Do not confuse independence with mutual exclusion, $\xi\,\blacktriangle\mkern-14mu\text{-}\,\upsilon$, of ξ and υ:

$$\xi\,\blacktriangle\mkern-14mu\text{-}\,\upsilon \triangleq X_t \subseteq \xi\,\blacktriangle\mkern-14mu\text{-}\,X_t \subseteq \upsilon \triangleq \xi\cap\upsilon = \varnothing$$

Among important pathological cases, it should be noticed that

$$(\xi\,\blacktriangle\mkern-14mu\text{-}\,\upsilon) \wedge (\xi\,\blacksquare\,\upsilon)\Leftrightarrow\xi = \varnothing\,\text{V}\,\upsilon = \varnothing$$

$$\xi\,\blacktriangle\mkern-14mu\text{-}\,\xi\Leftrightarrow\xi = \varnothing, \text{ and:}$$

$$\xi\,\blacksquare\,\xi\Leftrightarrow\xi = \varnothing\,\text{V}\,\xi = \Omega$$

More generally:

$$\xi \ne \varnothing \to \upsilon \ne \varnothing \to \xi\,\blacktriangle\mkern-14mu\text{-}\,\upsilon\Rightarrow\xi\,\blacktriangledown\,\upsilon$$

but compare this with:

$$\xi \ne \varnothing \to \upsilon \ne \varnothing \to \upsilon \ne \Omega \to \xi \subseteq \upsilon\Rightarrow\xi\,\blacktriangle\,\upsilon$$

The events ξ in a subset $\Sigma\subseteq\mathscr{F}(X)$ are said, as a whole, to be independent (or, we may say for definiteness and clarity, *collectively* independent), if and only if

$$\bigwedge_{\Xi\subseteq\Sigma}\left[p(\cap\,\Xi) = \prod_{\xi\in\Xi}p(\xi)\right]$$

If this condition is expressed in the form

$$\bigwedge_{\Xi\in\mathscr{P}(\Sigma)}[\ldots],$$

and then again in the form

$$\bigwedge_{k=0}^{\#\Sigma}\bigwedge_{\Xi\in\mathscr{P}_k(\Sigma)}[\ldots],$$

it will be apparent that independence among the events in the subset requires independence in all collections taken k at a time, for all sensible k. Beware, therefore, that the events in Σ can obey

$$\bigwedge_{\Xi\in\mathscr{P}_k(\Sigma)}\left[p(\cap\,\Xi) = \prod_{\xi\in\Xi}p(\xi)\right],$$

for one or more k, $3 \le k$, and yet not even be *pairwise* independent among themselves. Conversely, they may be pairwise independent, $\xi \ne \xi'\Rightarrow\xi\,\blacksquare\,\xi'$, and yet not be independent in any collections taken three or more at a time. (Notice that they always obey the rule when taken one at a time or none at a time.) For a discussion of this, with examples, see Romano and Siegel (1986).

Two experiments are defined to be independent (of each other) iff their outcomes are independent in all their respective pairings:

$$X\,\blacksquare\,Y \triangleq \bigwedge_{\substack{x\in X\\y\in Y}}x\,\blacksquare\,y$$

It may, of course, happen that two experiments X and Y coincide in some or all of their outcomes, or that one experiment refines the other. If $X \Rightarrow Y$, then knowledge of the outcome of X determines the outcome of Y absolutely; on the other hand, knowledge of the outcome of Y leaves X with some stochastic freedom. We then say that Y is totally dependent on X, and note that:

$$X \Rightarrow Y\Leftrightarrow\mathscr{F}(Y) \subseteq \mathscr{F}(X)$$

For instance, $(X,Y) \Rightarrow X$ and $(X, Y) \Rightarrow Y$ and $\mathscr{F}(X) \subseteq \mathscr{F}((X,Y))$ and $\mathscr{F}(Y) \subseteq \mathscr{F}((X,Y))$.

5.3 Causes and effects

5.3.1 Prediction and retrodiction

The compound experiment:

$$(X,Y) \triangle ([[x_i\cap y_j]_{j=0}^{n-1}]_{i=0}^{m-1})$$

whose distribution we shall call:

$$\hat{S} \triangle ([[p(x_i\cap y_j)]_{j=0}^{n-1}]_{i=0}^{m-1})$$

was represented in the example above by a table of integers each of the form $\#x_i \cap y_j$. Recall that:

$$p(x_i \cap y_j) = \frac{\#x_i \cap y_j}{\#\Omega_{X,Y}}$$

and let us write the distribution as a *synoptic matrix*, **S**, composed of these probabilities of joint occurrence of outcomes:

$$\mathbf{S} \triangleq (\llbracket [p(x_i \cap y_j)] \rrbracket_{j=0}^{n-1} \rrbracket_{i=0}^{m-1})$$

We define a stochastic matrix as one whose every row is a stochastic vector; that is, is a vector of non-negative components that sum to unity. Notice that, although $\hat{X}$, $\hat{Y}$ and $\hat{S}$ are all stochastic *vectors*, nevertheless the matrix **S** is not a stochastic *matrix*, since *all* of its mn components, rather than those in each and every row, sum to unity. As a further example, which we shall use from now on, consider:

$$\mathbf{S} = \begin{bmatrix} \frac{3}{40} & \frac{2}{40} & \frac{3}{40} & \frac{1}{40} \\ \frac{2}{40} & \frac{0}{40} & \frac{5}{40} & \frac{7}{40} \\ \frac{2}{40} & \frac{2}{40} & \frac{6}{40} & \frac{7}{40} \end{bmatrix}$$

or, equivalently, $\hat{S} = (\frac{3}{40}, \frac{2}{40}, \frac{3}{40}, \frac{1}{40}, \frac{2}{40}, \frac{0}{40}, \frac{5}{40}, \frac{7}{40}, \frac{2}{40}, \frac{2}{40}, \frac{6}{40}, \frac{7}{40})$. We can get $\hat{S}$ immediately from **S**, and, given m or n, get **S** immediately from $\hat{S}$. We shall therefore work with **S** instead, as being more convenient. By adding the rows of **S**, column by column, we get $\hat{Y}$; or, by adding the columns, we get $\hat{X}^\dagger$ (that is, $\hat{X}$ as a column vector). In the example, we have $\hat{Y} = (\frac{7}{40}, \frac{4}{40}, \frac{14}{40}, \frac{15}{40})$ and $\hat{X} = (\frac{9}{40}, \frac{14}{40}, \frac{17}{40})$. So, we can deduce $\hat{X}$ and $\hat{Y}$ from **S**, but cannot deduce **S** from $\hat{X}$ and $\hat{Y}$. This is because **S** contains $mn - 1$ numerically independent components, whereas $\hat{X}$ and $\hat{Y}$ between them contain only $(m - 1) + (n - 1)$ numerically independent components. The set of outcomes of the compound experiment (X,Y) is, in an obvious sense, the Cartesian product of the sets, X and Y, of outcomes of its constituent experiments; but if and only if the two experiments X and Y are stochastically independent, as defined at the end of the previous section, is the distribution of (X,Y) (most conveniently represented here by **S**), constrained to equal the tensor product of $\hat{X}$ and $\hat{Y}$:

$$X \blacksquare Y \Leftrightarrow \mathbf{S} = (\hat{X}^\dagger)(\hat{Y})$$

We often need to answer the question, 'Given the distribution of X, what is the distribution of Y?' This is of course unanswerable if we cannot have access to, and make use of, some of the information in **S** that is not given by $\hat{X}$ alone. What we need is the matrix:

$$\mathbf{T} \triangleq (\llbracket [p(y_j | x_i)] \rrbracket_{j=0}^{n-1} \rrbracket_{i=0}^{m-1})$$

whose components, of the form $p(y_j | x_i)$, are easily obtained from **S** by normalizing each of its rows individually to sum to unity: that is, by using $p(y_j | x_i) = p(y_j \cap x_i)/p(x_i)$. (Clearly, in order that $p(x_i) \neq 0$, all zero rows of **S**, that is, impossible outcomes of X, must have been deleted before the exercise is begun.)

We then have what we required, in the form of the equation:

$$\hat{Y} = \hat{X}\mathbf{T}$$

Similarly, we can define:

$$\mathbf{R} \triangleq (\llbracket [p(x_i | y_j)] \rrbracket_{i=0}^{m-1} \rrbracket_{j=0}^{n-1})$$

and obtain it by normalizing the columns of **S** each to sum to unity. By using **R**, we can now say that:

$$\hat{X}^\dagger = \mathbf{R}\,\hat{Y}^\dagger$$

or, in a form more convenient for our purposes, $\hat{X} = \hat{Y}\mathbf{R}^\dagger$. Note that **T** is $m \times n$ and is (row-)stochastic, whereas **R** is also $m \times n$, but is column-stochastic, in that its columns sum each to unity. Its transpose is $n \times m$, but is row-stochastic, and so will be used from now on. In the example, therefore, we have:

$$\mathbf{T} = \begin{bmatrix} \frac{3}{9} & \frac{2}{9} & \frac{3}{9} & \frac{1}{9} \\ \frac{2}{14} & \frac{0}{14} & \frac{5}{14} & \frac{7}{14} \\ \frac{2}{17} & \frac{2}{17} & \frac{6}{17} & \frac{7}{17} \end{bmatrix} \quad \text{and} \quad \mathbf{R}^\dagger = \begin{bmatrix} \frac{3}{7} & \frac{2}{7} & \frac{2}{7} \\ \frac{1}{2} & \frac{0}{2} & \frac{1}{2} \\ \frac{3}{14} & \frac{5}{14} & \frac{6}{14} \\ \frac{1}{15} & \frac{7}{15} & \frac{7}{15} \end{bmatrix}$$

So far, X and Y have been treated as being of equal status and in principle interchangeable; but, very often, we need to treat one of them (X, say) as corresponding to a set of possible causes, and the other (Y, therefore) as corresponding to a set of possible effects. Accordingly, we shall call **T** the predictive matrix, and $\mathbf{R}^\dagger$ the retrodictive matrix, of the compound experiment synoptically represented by **S**. We shall use **T** to find the distribution of effects as a function of the distribution of causes (i.e. prediction); and $\mathbf{R}^\dagger$ to find the converse, that is, causes as a function of effects (i.e. retrodiction). Our identification of X with causes, and Y with effects, breaks the formal symmetry between them: we are thereby asserting that we will generally be *given* $\hat{X}$ and **T**, and have to *deduce* $\hat{Y}$, (and, where necessary, $\mathbf{R}^\dagger$) from them.

Given $\hat{X}$ and **T**, we can easily find $\hat{Y}$, since $\hat{Y} = \hat{X}\mathbf{T}$. If we then need to know **S** or $\mathbf{R}^\dagger$, we can calculate:

$$\mathbf{S} = (\llbracket [p(x_i)][p(y_j | x_i)] \rrbracket_{j=0}^{n-1} \rrbracket_{i=0}^{m-1})$$

and

$$\mathbf{R}^\dagger \triangleq \mathbf{R}^\dagger(\hat{X},\mathbf{T}) = (\llbracket [p(x_i \cap y_j)]_{i=0}^{m-1}/p(y_j) \rrbracket_{j=0}^{n-1})$$

$$= (\llbracket [p(x_i)p(y_j | x_i)]_{i=0}^{m-1}/p(y_j) \rrbracket_{j=0}^{n-1})$$

There is a danger of circularity here. It may well be asked: what, if we need to know $\hat{X}$ in order to find $\mathbf{R}^\dagger$, is the point of calculating $\mathbf{R}^\dagger$, when its only use appears to be in employing $\hat{X} = \hat{Y}\mathbf{R}^\dagger$ to calculate $\hat{X}$, which we knew, and had to know, in the first place? The answer to this lies in the order of our observations. We call $\hat{X}$, whose value we have hypothesized on the basis of whatever prior knowledge we may have possessed, the prior distribution of X. From it, and from **T**, we obtain the best estimate we can at this stage of the distribution of Y, by using $\hat{Y} = \hat{X}\mathbf{T}$. But now suppose that we make a direct observation of a trial of Y, and find that $Y_t = y_j$, say, where y_j is some specific outcome. We are now in a position to make a more informed, and therefore better, estimate of the distribution of X, given y_j, for this trial. We may write this conditional experiment as $X | y_j$. It is easy to see that its distribution, $\hat{X} | y_j$, the posterior distribution of X given our observation that $Y = y_j$, is given by the jth row of $\mathbf{R}^\dagger$. That is why $\mathbf{R}^\dagger$ is worth considering; we can calculate it before our observation of the tth trial of Y, and make use of it afterwards. This point is taken up in the next section, on decision methods. (Borrowing ahead from the section on random variables, we may note that the expected value of $\hat{X} | y_j$ is calculated as $\hat{Y}\mathbf{R}^\dagger = \hat{X}$, as we should expect). Sometimes, *in extremis*, we may be asked to estimate $\hat{Y}$ or $\mathbf{R}^\dagger$, given **T**, but in ignorance of $\hat{X}$. The best course then is to assume a uniform prior distribution, that is, assume that $\hat{X} = \hat{U} \bigtriangleup U(m) \bigtriangleup ([\frac{1}{m}]_{i=0}^{m-1})$, and use $\hat{Y}|U \bigtriangleup \hat{U}T$ and $\mathbf{R}^\dagger|U \bigtriangleup \mathbf{R}^\dagger(\hat{U}, T)$, for want of anything better. Using the example, these would be:

$$\hat{Y}|U = \left(\tfrac{1272}{6426}, \tfrac{728}{6426}, \tfrac{2235}{6426}, \tfrac{2191}{6426} \right) \text{ and } \mathbf{R}^\dagger|U = \begin{bmatrix} \tfrac{119}{212} & \tfrac{51}{212} & \tfrac{42}{212} \\ \tfrac{17}{26} & \tfrac{0}{26} & \tfrac{9}{26} \\ \tfrac{714}{2235} & \tfrac{765}{2235} & \tfrac{756}{2235} \\ \tfrac{34}{313} & \tfrac{153}{313} & \tfrac{126}{313} \end{bmatrix}$$

For a discussion of this point, see, for example, Fine (1973).

5.3.2 Most likely causes and effects: decision methods

If X is a set of causes, and Y is a set of effects, we shall often wish to know the most likely effect(s) of each cause (MLEC), or the most likely cause(s) of each effect (MLCE). Accordingly, we define as follows. MLEC is the mapping $X \rightarrow \mathscr{F}(Y)$ given by finding the greatest components(s) in each row of T (or, equivalently, of S):

$$\text{MLEC: } x \mapsto \bigcup_{y \in Y} [y : p(y|x) = \max_{y' \in Y} p(y'|x)]$$

For example,

$$T = \begin{bmatrix} \tfrac{3}{9} & \tfrac{2}{9} & \tfrac{3}{9} & \tfrac{1}{9} \\ \tfrac{2}{14} & \tfrac{0}{14} & \tfrac{5}{14} & \tfrac{7}{14} \\ \tfrac{2}{17} & \tfrac{2}{17} & \tfrac{6}{17} & \tfrac{7}{17} \end{bmatrix} \Rightarrow \text{MLEC: } \begin{cases} x_0 \mapsto y_0 \cup y_2 \\ x_1 \mapsto y_3 \\ x_2 \mapsto y_3 \end{cases}$$

Conversely, MLCE is the mapping $Y \rightarrow \mathscr{F}(X)$ given by finding the greatest components(s) in each row of $\mathbf{R}^\dagger$ (or, equivalently, of $S^\dagger$):

$$\text{MLCE: } y \mapsto \bigcup_{x \in X} [x : p(x|y) = \max_{x' \in X} p(x'|y)]$$

For example:

$$\mathbf{R}^\dagger = \begin{bmatrix} \tfrac{3}{7} & \tfrac{2}{7} & \tfrac{2}{7} \\ \tfrac{1}{2} & \tfrac{0}{2} & \tfrac{1}{2} \\ \tfrac{3}{14} & \tfrac{5}{14} & \tfrac{6}{14} \\ \tfrac{1}{15} & \tfrac{7}{15} & \tfrac{7}{15} \end{bmatrix} \Rightarrow \text{MLCE: } \begin{cases} y_0 \mapsto x_0 \\ y_1 \mapsto x_0 \cup x_2 \\ y_2 \mapsto x_2 \\ y_3 \mapsto x_1 \cup x_2 \end{cases}$$

In predictive and retrodictive problems, by hypothesis, we are given T but are not given $\mathbf{R}^\dagger$. It is easy to see that MLEC can be obtained directly from T; but MLCE requires that we calculate $\mathbf{R}^\dagger = \mathbf{R}^\dagger(\hat{X}, T)$. So MLCE (although not MLEC) depends upon $\hat{X}$, and we need to calculate a new MLCE for every prior distribution $\hat{X}$ that is of interest. Here, again, we may need to assume a uniform prior distribution, and use $\mathbf{R}^\dagger|U$ to give MLCE$|U$.

We are often faced with the practical problem of making the best guess at what was the cause of each observed effect. Unable, by hypothesis, to observe X directly, we can think of T as an imperfect channel of communication, back down which we look when trying to observe X: and Y is what we actually see. Prior to our observations, we must have set up a decision method to make the best use of them. One possible scheme is obviously the MLCE method described above. It can be shown that it minimizes the probability that a wrong decision will be made: it is therefore also called the minimum-error or ideal observer decision method (IODM).

Another scheme, the maximum-likelihood decision method (MLDM), tries to maximize the conditional probability of each effect, over all possible causes; it is a mapping $Y \rightarrow \mathscr{F}(X)$, given by:

$$\text{MLDM: } y \mapsto \bigcup_{x \in X} [x : p(y|x) = \max_{x' \in X} p(y|x')]$$

Clearly, IODM is the 'better' of these, simply because it minimizes the probability of a wrong decision. Equally clearly, though, since it is identical with the MLCE scheme discussed earlier, it requires that $\hat{X}$ be known; or, failing that, that a uniform prior distribution be assumed, thereby calling into question the minimum-error property, which may well be very sensitive to $\hat{X}$. It is easily shown that IODM$|U$ coincides with MLDM.

MLDM, which is always applicable, is simpler to calculate than IODM; it may, even though it lacks the minimum-error property, be worth considering. It involves finding the greatest component(s) in each row of $T^\dagger$. The following example has, for clarity, the rows of $T^\dagger$ each expressed with a consistent denominator: but beware that it is *column*, not *row*, stochastic:

$$T^\dagger = \begin{bmatrix} \tfrac{119}{357} & \tfrac{51}{357} & \tfrac{42}{357} \\ \tfrac{34}{153} & \tfrac{0}{153} & \tfrac{18}{153} \\ \tfrac{238}{714} & \tfrac{255}{714} & \tfrac{252}{714} \\ \tfrac{34}{306} & \tfrac{153}{306} & \tfrac{126}{306} \end{bmatrix} \Rightarrow \text{MLDM: } \begin{cases} y_0 \mapsto x_0 \\ y_1 \mapsto x_0 \\ y_2 \mapsto x_1 \\ y_3 \mapsto x_1 \end{cases}$$

Notice that the rows of $T^\dagger$ are proportional to the rows of $\mathbf{R}^\dagger|U$, as set out above: and that that is because MLDM coincides with IODM$|U$.

5.4 Markov chains

Probability theory can be used to model an autonomous machine (that is, one with no inputs), whose current state can be observed, and whose successive future states are related probabilistically to a finite fixed-length segment of its most recent history. Consistent with our present consideration of finite probability, we restrict ourselves to discrete-time, finite-state, machines. These are called Markov chains.

Let the set of states in such a machine be $X = \{[x_i]_{i=0}^{m-1}\}$, and the current state be X_t. We assume here that the distribution of the immediate successor state, X_{t+1}, given the current state, X_t, is independent of all earlier states; that is, that:

$$0 \leqslant r \rightarrow \bigwedge_{x \in X} [p(X_{t+1} = x | X_{t-r}, X_{t-r+1}, \ldots, X_{t-1}, X_t) = p(X_{t+1} = x | X_t)]$$

This is called the Markov property. We also assume that

$$([p(X_{t+1} = x_j | X_t = x_i]_{j=0}^{m-1})$$

is independent of t (although, of course, dependent on i), so we can write it as

$$([p(x_j | x_i)]_{j=0}^{m-1})$$

Since in general we are dealing not with a known current state, x_i, but rather with a distribution,

$$\hat{X} = ([p(x_i)]_{i=0}^{m-1})$$

we are operating with m succession vectors, or, in effect, an $m \times m$ succession matrix:

$$\mathbf{T} \triangleq ([[p(x_j|x_i)]_{j=0}^{m-1}]_{i=0}^{m-1})$$

which is called the transition matrix of the Markov chain. Exploiting the terminology used earlier, this is a prediction matrix for the chain, since it predicts the successor distribution as a probabilistic function of the current distribution. So, given an initial distribution $\hat{X}$ at time $t = 0$, the distributions predicted for successive times $t = 0, 1, 2, 3, 4, \ldots$ are $\hat{X}, \hat{X}\mathbf{T}, \hat{X}\mathbf{T}^2, \hat{X}\mathbf{T}^3, \hat{X}\mathbf{T}^4, \ldots$ and in general $\hat{X}\mathbf{T}^r$ at time $t = r$.

A Markov chain can also be represented by a directed graph (digraph), whose points correspond to its states, and whose arcs correspond to its possible transitions between them (and are marked with their probabilities). This is called a transition diagram. The adjacency matrix of such a digraph is equal to $\lceil \mathbf{T} \rceil$, which is derived from $\mathbf{T}$ by replacing each non-zero element with unity. The strongly-connected components (SCs) of a digraph form a partition of its point set; the structure of the transition diagram, in terms of SCs, is important in deciding the behaviour of the chain. No cyclic path can exist among any of the SCs, since otherwise they would all be one SC. An SC that has at least one arc leading from it is said to be transient: otherwise, it is persistent. A chain with exactly one persistent SC (PSC) is said to be pure (or irreducible); otherwise, it is mixed (or reducible). In a pure chain, the greatest common divisor of all the cycle lengths within the unique PSC is called its, and the chain's, period; if the period is unity, the chain is aperiodic. A chain that is pure and aperiodic is said to be ergodic. Ergodicity is a guarantee of good behaviour, in that a chain will eventually forget its past (including its initial state) completely, iff it is ergodic. On the other hand, a mixed chain will end up trapped permanently in just one of its PSCs; but which one that will be, or even the distribution among them, cannot be known *a priori*, since the starting state is unknown; and a pure but periodic chain, of period τ, will exhibit good behaviour only if it is observed after every τ transition. Ergodic chains, therefore, are more tractable objects than non-ergodic. They are, in practice, sufficient for modelling most stochastic processes. *Figure 5.1* shows the transition diagram of an ergodic chain; and *Figure 5.2* shows a mixed chain with two PSCs of periods 1 and 2. The transition matrices of these chains are:

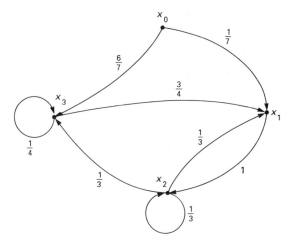

Figure 5.1

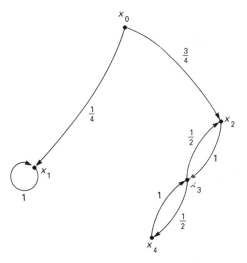

Figure 5.2

$$\mathbf{T} = \begin{bmatrix} 0 & \frac{1}{7} & 0 & \frac{6}{7} \\ 0 & 0 & 1 & 0 \\ 0 & \frac{1}{3} & \frac{1}{3} & \frac{1}{3} \\ 0 & \frac{3}{4} & 0 & \frac{1}{4} \end{bmatrix} \quad \text{and} \quad \mathbf{T} = \begin{bmatrix} 0 & \frac{1}{4} & \frac{3}{4} & 0 & 0 \\ 0 & 1 & 0 & 0 & 0 \\ 0 & 0 & 0 & 1 & 0 \\ 0 & 0 & \frac{1}{2} & 0 & \frac{1}{2} \\ 0 & 0 & 0 & 1 & 0 \end{bmatrix}$$

respectively. An aperiodic chain, then, asymptotically approaches a steady-state distribution, $\hat{X}$, and this can be found by solving the eigendistribution equation:

$$\hat{X}\mathbf{T} = \hat{X}$$

If $\mathbf{T}$ is $m \times m$, this provides only $m - k$ linearly independent

equations, where k is the number of PSCs; but we have to hand the further equation

$$\sum_{i=0}^{m-1} p(x_i) = 1$$

and so there are $k - 1$ undetermined coefficients in the distribution $\hat{X}$, these representing the unknowable distribution among the k PSCs. But, for an ergodic chain, we know that $k = 1$; and so then the eigendistribution equation is exactly soluble. As an example, the chain of Figure 5.1 has the eigendistribution $\hat{X} = (0, \frac{6}{19}, \frac{9}{19}, \frac{4}{19})$.

Observation of states should not be confused with observation of transitions. If a hitherto unobserved ergodic Markov chain has achieved a steady state distribution $\hat{X}$, then, if we observe the next transition, this will, prior to the observation of the current state, have the m^2-component distribution $([[p(x_i)p(x_j|x_i)]_{j=0}^{m-1}]_{i=0}^{m-1})$, where the $p(x_i)$ are the components of $\hat{X}$, and the $p(x_j|x_i)$ are the components of $\mathbf{T}$; and, following the observation of the current state, x_i, the m-component distribution:

$$([p(x_j|x_i)]_{j=0}^{m-1})$$

Now, if we want the probability of the successor to depend on the λ most recent states, rather than on just the one current state (that is, to be λ-dependent), all that is necessary is to set up a chain with state set $\{[w_i]_{i=0}^{\lambda-1}\} \triangle W \triangle X^\lambda$, that is, representing all the m^λ sequences of states of X, of length λ. The transition probabilities will then be of the form $p(W_{t+1} = w_j | W_t = w_i)$, which can be seen to have the Markov property. Such a chain is called a λth extension of the original, simple, chain.

In a simple Markov chain (with $\lambda = 1$), all of the m^2 arcs in the Cartesian product X^2 are logically possible, even if some are allocated zero probability of transition; but, in a Markov chain whose states represent sequences of length λ, where there will be m^λ states (all of which are logically possible, even if some can only be starting states), each state can still have no more than m successors (all of which are logically possible, even if some have zero probability): and so the number of arcs cannot exceed $m^{\lambda+1}$. (A digraph showing all the m^λ logically possible states, with all the $m^{\lambda+1}$ logically possible arcs drawn in, is called a Good-de Bruijn diagram. The transition diagram of a λ-dependent of a Markov chain is a sub-digraph of the corresponding Good-de Bruijn diagram, since not all arcs may be stochastically possible, and its transition matrix will be $m^\lambda \times m^\lambda$ with no more than m non-zero entries in each row.) In all other respects, the treatment of λ-dependent Markov chains follows that of single chains, as outlined above.

For more on Markov chains, see Grimmett and Stirzaker (1985); or, for more specialist treatments, Rosenblatt (1974), and, including a discussion of pure periodic chains, Romanovsky (1970).

5.5 Random variables

Suppose that some numerical variable, $\tilde{V}$, observed at trial t, takes a value V_t drawn from a finite or countable set of numbers $V = \{[v_i]_{i=0}^{m-1}\}$, such that there are well-defined probabilities of the form $p(V_t = v_i)$, and that these are independent of t. Such a random variable (RV) may be constructed by an injection from the set of outcomes of an experiment to a suitable set of numbers: for example, $\tilde{V}: X \to V$. (This is injective so that there will be an inverse partial mapping from values in V to the *outcomes* in X representing their probability; otherwise, there would be an inverse partial mapping from values to *events* representing their probability.) Then we define the expected value of $\tilde{V}$ to be:

$$\mathcal{E}\tilde{V} \triangle \sum_{i=0}^{m-1} p(V_t = v_i) \cdot v_i$$

(We shall see later that $\#\Omega$ can become countably infinite: in that case, the expectation is defined only if this sum is absolutely convergent.) Where $\tilde{V}$ is understood, we may write:

$$\mathcal{E}\tilde{V} = \overset{m-1}{\underset{i=0}{\mathcal{E}}} v_i$$

whenever it is useful to do so. Notice that $\mathcal{E}$ is a linear operator. Also, although not at all obvious, it can in fact be shown that:

$$\mathcal{E}f(\tilde{V}) = \sum_{i=0}^{m-1} p(V_t = v_i) \cdot f(v_i)$$

for any finite or countable numerical function $f(-)$, for example $f: V \to V'$. In the case of two RVs, $\tilde{U}$ and $\tilde{V}$, it will be understood that:

$$\mathcal{E}\tilde{U}\tilde{V} = \sum_{i=0}^{m-1} \sum_{j=0}^{m-1} p(U_t = u_i \wedge V_t = v_j) \cdot u_i v_j$$
$$= \sum_{i=0}^{m-1} p(U_t = u_i) \cdot u_i \sum_{j=0}^{m-1} p(V_t = v_j | U_t = u_i) \cdot v_j$$

Two RVs may or may not be (stochastically) independent, and may or may not be uncorrelated, in senses now to be defined. These are distinct, if related, ideas. From earlier consideration of independence of experiments, we can say that independence of $\tilde{U}$ and $\tilde{V}$ is given by:

$$\tilde{U} \blacksquare \tilde{V} \Leftrightarrow \underset{\substack{u \in U \\ v \in V}}{\wedge} [p(U_t = u \wedge V_t = v) = p(U_t = u)p(V_t = v)]$$

On the other hand, $\tilde{U}$ and $\tilde{V}$ are said to be uncorrelated iff:

$$\mathcal{E}(\tilde{U}\tilde{V}) = \mathcal{E}(\tilde{U}) \cdot \mathcal{E}(\tilde{V})$$

Uncorrelated RVs need not be independent; it is easy to show, though, that the independence of two RVs implies their uncorrelation.

Having previously defined the concepts of positive and negative dependence, we shall now find it useful to obtain the equivalent ideas for correlation. First, we remove any additive bias by transforming a RV into a deviation from its expected value:

$$\Delta\tilde{V} \triangle \tilde{V} - \mathcal{E}\tilde{V}$$

so that $\mathcal{E}\Delta\tilde{V} = 0$; and then define the covariance of two RVs, and the variance and standard deviation of a single RV, respectively as follows:

$$\text{cov}(\tilde{U},\tilde{V}) \triangle \mathcal{E}(\Delta\tilde{U} . \Delta\tilde{V}) = \mathcal{E}\tilde{U}\tilde{V} - \mathcal{E}\tilde{U} \cdot \mathcal{E}\tilde{V}$$

$$\text{var}(\tilde{V}) \triangle \text{cov}(\tilde{V},\tilde{V}) = \mathcal{E}(\Delta\tilde{V})^2 = \mathcal{E}(\tilde{V})^2 - (\mathcal{E}\tilde{V})^2, \text{ and}$$

$$|\tilde{V}| \triangle \sqrt{\text{var}(\tilde{V})}$$

The variance is always non-negative, and is a measure of the likely 'spread' of the value of a RV; the standard deviation is similar (but is a linear operator if $\mathcal{E}\tilde{V} = 0$). The covariance is equal to zero for uncorrelated RVs, and it will be found that its sign accurately reflects intuitive ideas of positive and negative correlation. It can be made even more useful by removing any multiplicative bias, to produce the normalized covariance, or coefficient of correlation:

$$\rho_{\tilde{U},\tilde{V}} \triangle \frac{\text{cov}(\tilde{U},\tilde{V})}{|\tilde{U}| . |\tilde{V}|}$$

which then lies in the range $-1 \leqslant \rho_{\tilde{U},\tilde{V}} \leqslant +1$. If the coefficient of correlation takes the values $+1$ or -1, then the RVs are said to be perfectly correlated or perfectly anti-correlated respectively. (In particular, if $\tilde{V} = a\tilde{U} + b$, then $\rho_{\tilde{U},\tilde{V}} = \text{sgn } a$. Moreover, if $\rho_{\tilde{U},\tilde{V}} = \pm 1$, then $\tilde{V} = a\tilde{U} + b$ for some a, b.)

There is an instructive and fruitful geometric interpretation of this result. Consider the mapping to V, not from the m outcomes of X, but rather from the $\#\Omega$ atomic outcomes of $\mathscr{S}(\Omega)$: we can then represent $\Delta\tilde{V}$ as a $\#\Omega$-tuple position vector:

$$\vec{\tilde{V}} \triangle ([V_h]_{h=0}^{\#\Omega-1}) \triangle ([[v_i - \mathcal{E}\tilde{V}]_{h=0}^{\#x_i-1}]_{i=0}^{m-1})$$

which is rooted at the origin of $\#\Omega$-dimensional Euclidean space ($\mathbf{E}^{\#\Omega}$). Its length is given by $\|\vec{\tilde{V}}\| = \sqrt{\langle \vec{\tilde{V}} | \vec{\tilde{V}} \rangle}$, where $\langle \vec{\tilde{U}} | \vec{\tilde{V}} \rangle = \sum_h U_h V_h$ is the scalar (or inner) product of two vectors $\vec{\tilde{U}}$ and $\vec{\tilde{V}}$. Then we have:

$$\mathcal{E}\Delta\tilde{V} = \frac{1}{\#\Omega}\sum_{h=0}^{\#\Omega-1} V_h$$

$$\mathrm{cov}(\tilde{U},\tilde{V}) = \frac{1}{\#\Omega^2}\sum_{h=0}^{\#\Omega-1} U_h V_h = \frac{1}{\#\Omega^2}\langle\tilde{U}|\tilde{V}\rangle, \text{ and}$$

$$|\hat{V}| = \frac{1}{\#\Omega}\sqrt{\langle\hat{V}|\hat{V}\rangle} = \frac{1}{\#\Omega}\|\hat{V}\|$$

But, if two vectors $\tilde{U}$ and $\hat{V}$ make an angle $\theta_{0,\varphi}$, we know that $\langle\tilde{U}|\hat{V}\rangle = \|\tilde{U}\|.\|\hat{V}\|.\cos\theta_{0,\varphi}$. So:

$$\rho_{0,\varphi} = \frac{\langle\tilde{U}|\hat{V}\rangle}{\|\tilde{U}\|.\|\hat{V}\|} = \cos\theta_{0,\varphi}$$

Uncorrelated RVs have $\cos\theta_{0,\varphi} = 0$, and so $\theta_{0,\varphi} = \pi/2$: such RVs are therefore said to be orthogonal to one another. Perfectly (anti-)correlated RVs are represented by (anti-)collinear vectors, as is shown by the fact that, for them, $\cos\theta_{0,\varphi} = \pm 1$. For more on random variables, and their distributions, see for example Blake (1979) or Grimmett and Stirzaker (1985).

5.6 Irrational probabilities and infinite spaces

So far, we have supposed that all probabilities are rational numbers. The *standard* treatment of probability, however, expresses the numerical values of probabilities as 'real' numbers: that is, irrational probabilities are permitted. The reason for this is as follows. Suppose that we are modelling the throw of a particular die, a physical object whose faces have probabilities that are not $\frac{1}{6}, \frac{1}{6}, \frac{1}{6}, \frac{1}{6}, \frac{1}{6}, \frac{1}{6}$, but rather, to some specified degree of precision, 0.166, 0.168, 0.160, 0.167, 0.167, and 0.172. It would still be possible to use rational numbers for the probabilities (in this case, with 1000 as denominator), but that could become rather artificial and inconvenient. Although all physical measurements are of finite precision, and therefore it is never *necessary* to use 'real' numbers in order to model them mathematically, the freedom from manipulation of a possibly artificial denominator, and the freedom to differentiate and integrate supposedly continuous quantities, have led to the adoption of a real model for probabilities. We can then no longer represent probabilities by ratios of sizes of sets: we must replace that definition by one that is an arbitrarily specified mapping, from the set of events, to a set (finite, countable or uncountable) of numbers. Such a mapping is called a *measure*, and the set of numbers (the image of the set of events) is called its *support*. Now suppose that each trial of a certain experiment consisted in tossing a coin repeatedly until it showed 'heads', the outcome being determined by the number of tails preceding that occurrence. There would then be exactly as many possible outcomes as there are natural numbers: and that is countably infinite. In the stochastic spaces so far considered, with $\Omega = \{[\omega_h]_h\}$, suppose that we do indeed let $\#\Omega$ become countably infinite. That would in turn allow $\#\mathcal{S}(\Omega)$, the maximum number of possible outcomes, to become countably infinite. If $\#X$, the number of outcomes, actually became countably infinite, then, since $\#\mathcal{F}(X) = \#\mathcal{P}(X) = 2^{\#\Omega}$, the number of events would become uncountably infinite. That is, if $\#X$ took the value $\aleph_0$ (the countable cardinality of the natural numbers), then $\#\mathcal{F}(X)$ would take the value c (the uncountable cardinality of the continuum). This would not in itself cause any great problems except that, although we could still sum over all the $\aleph_0$ outcomes, we could not sum over all the c events.

An even more serious problem arises if we want, for reasons of convenience in constructing mathematical models, to be able freely to integrate and differentiate distributions of probability and random variables as functions of a 'real' variable. That would entail $\#\Omega$ itself becoming uncountably infinite, so that, if nothing else were done, $\mathcal{F}(X)$ could have cardinality $2^c = 2^{2^{\aleph_0}}$. This is so large it can cause difficulties, and something must be done. What is done is to restrict $\mathcal{F}(X)$ to contain a subset only of the set of all regions of encoarsements of X, such that it is still closed under complementation, but is closed under countably iterated unions only. That is, $(\mathcal{F}(X),\cup)$ is countable, and is therefore still a field of events, but is based on an uncountable set of atoms. Such a construct is called a Borel field. For more on this, see Kolmogorov (1933), Gnedenko (1968) or Rosenblatt (1974).

5.7 Applications

In the context of software engineering, and especially of this book, probability theory is of the essence in information theory (Chapter 14), at least in the classical formulation of that subject. It is also important in the study of many of the topics in software development management (Chapters 27–34); in particular, Chapter 30 on metrics and measurement, and Chapter 31, on reliability modelling; and the non-deterministic aspects of process control (Chapter 51), networks and distributed systems (53), real-time systems (56), digital communications and telephony (58), and security, safety and fault-tolerant systems (59–61). In the last of these, probability theory occupies a central position, along with combinatorics: a pairing of ideas that is common throughout the study of non-deterministic discrete systems.

5.8 Bibliography

Ash, R. B. (1970) *Basic Probability Theory*, John Wiley, New York

Blake, I. F. (1979) *An Introduction to Applied Probability*, John Wiley, New York

Feller, W. (1968) *An Introduction to Probability Theory and its Applications, Vol. I*, (3rd edn), Wiley, New York

Fine, T. L. (1973) *Theories of Probability: an Examination of Foundations*, Academic Press, New York

Galambos, J. (1974) *Introductory Probability Theory*, Marcel Dekker, New York

Gnedenko, B. V. (1968) *The Theory of Probability*, 4th edn. Chelsea Publishing Company, New York

Grimmett, G. R. and Stirzaker, D. R. (1985) *Probability and Random Processes*, Clarendon Press, Oxford

Grimmett, G. R. and Welsh, D. (1982) *Probability: an Introduction*, Clarendon Press, Oxford

Hacking, I. (1975) *The Emergence of Probability: a Philosophical Study of Early Ideas about Probability, Inductions and Statistical Inference*, Cambridge University Press, Cambridge

Keynes, J. M. (1921) *A Treatise on Probability*, Macmillan, London

Kolmogorov, A. N. (1933) *Foundations of the Theory of Probability*, (2nd English Edn, 1956), Chelsea Publishing Company, New York, USA

Kyburg, H. E. (1961) *Probability and the Logic of Rational Belief*, Wesleyan University Press, Middleton CT

Kyburg, H. E. (1969) *Probability Theory*, Prentice-Hall, Englewood Cliffs, NJ, USA

Maistrov, L. E. (1974) *Probability Theory: a Historical Sketch*, Academic Press, New York

Nagel, E. (1939) *Principles of the Theory of Probability*, University of Chicago Press, Chicago, IL, USA

Romano, J. P. and Siegel, A. F. (1986) *Counterexamples in Probability and Statistics*, Wadsworth and Brooks, Monterey, CA

Romanovsky, V. I. (1970) *Discrete Markov Chains*, Wolters-Noordhoff Publishing, Groningen

Rosenblatt, M. (1974) *Random Processes*, 2nd edn. Springer-Verlag, New York

Todhunter, I. (1865) *A History of the Theory of Probability from the Time of Pascal to that of Laplace*, Chelsea Publishing Company, New York, Reprinted (1949, 1965)

Venn, J. (1888) *The Logic of Chance*, 3rd edn. Chelsea Publishing Company, New York, Reprinted as 4th edn. (1962)

6

Statistics

D J Hand
The Open University

Contents

6.1 Introduction

Statistics is a broad discipline, subsuming the practical application of the theory of probability to phenomena in the real world as well as informal methods of data description and reduction. Both these aspects have a relevance to software engineering, either in building formal models of the behaviour of systems or in summarizing results so that general conclusions can be inferred and putative explanations suggested. In addition, of course, researchers make very heavy use of statistical packages – so much so that in many academic and research environments statistical analysis is the single most extensive use to which computers are put.

This chapter attempts to provide an overview of statistical and probabilistic concepts for software engineers. Clearly, in the space available there cannot be much detail. Thus an effort has been made to supplement the overview by references to material where more details may be sought. Chapter 5 gives a more formal introduction to probability. This chapter concentrates particularly on techniques which allow the estimation of properties of systems, e.g. programs, from observations (samples) of their behaviour.

The first part of this chapter discusses the basics of probability, including an outline of some probability distributions of relevance to software engineering. The second half describes statistical concepts and techniques. In this part ideas are unified to some extent, so that the common underlying basis of techniques which may superficially seem different can be perceived. This is in contrast to many elementary texts, which present the methods as discrete and apparently disconnected concepts. The aim here is to show that statistics, far from being a collection of isolated methods, is in fact a technical language designed for a particular purpose.

Before proceeding it is perhaps worth remarking that statistics is a very young discipline. Although it has its foundations in the distant past, it was not until the 1940s that it really began as a separate science. Reflecting its youth, it is a subject that is making rapid progress. In part this is a consequence of growing theoretical maturity and in part it is a product of increasingly powerful computer systems permitting the practical development of methods which require extensive amounts of numerical manipulation. These are referred to briefly below.

6.2 Basic probability

Imagine a sequence of trials or operations, each one of which results in an outcome from a common set of possible outcomes. An example would be a set of programs written by a class of trainee programmers. The outcome of each might be classified as belonging to the set of possible outcomes {succeed, fail}. Alternatively, one might enlarge the classification to the set {succeed, failure type 1, failure type 2,...} according to a classification of program bugs.

The number of times a particular outcome occurs is called its frequency, and the proportion of times it occurs is its relative frequency. If one arbitrarily increases the number of trials in such a sequence (in the example above, if one takes an arbitrarily large number of trainee programmers) then empirical observation shows that the relative frequency tends to converge to a constant value. This value is called the probability of the outcome. In the example, there is a probability that a randomly selected trainee programmer will write a successful program, and so on.

More generally, one can group outcomes into classes of outcomes, called events – similar failure types in the example might be grouped into a single class for those types. If A

represents the event in question – the set of outcomes comprising the event – then the notation $p(A)$ is used to signify the probability that event A will occur – that one of the outcomes comprising A will occur.

This is the frequency or frequentist definition of probability. There are other definitions. An important alternative is the subjective definition, which views the probability of an event as the degree of belief that someone has in the event. This alternative interpretation has led to the development of an alternative school of statistical inference, Bayesian inference, which is growing in importance.

There are two general points to note from this. First, since statistics is a science it is perhaps not surprising that there are different schools of thought. What science does not progress by virtue of internal tensions produced by differing viewpoints or theories? Second, the different definitions of probability describe how one maps the formal mathematical structure of probability to the real world. Both definitions use the same mathematical structure – the same calculus of probability – based on axioms developed by Kolmogorov in the 1930s.

Readers interested in pursuing the difference further, and the implications for statistical inference and scientific inference in general, will find an excellent introduction in Barnett (1982). Returning to probability itself, note that, as the discussion of the frequency definition shows, probabilities must lie between 0 and 1 and the total probability that some event occurs must be 1.

The basic notion of probability has a number of important extensions. The joint probability of two events A and B is the probability that both occur together, denoted $p(A,B)$. The conditional probability of A given B, $p(A|B)$, is the probability that A will occur given that B has occurred. In the example above, let B signify the event that a failure has occurred and let A be the event that it was in fact a failure of the first type. Then $p(A|B)$ is the probability that a failure of the first type occurred, given that one knows a failure of some kind occurred. This may be quite different from $p(A)$. If very few failures occurred, but when they did they were almost all of the first type then $p(A)$ (being less than $p(B)$) will be small whereas $p(A|B)$ will be large.

These notions of probability, joint probability, and conditional probability can be extended to continuous outcome spaces. For example, one may be interested in the probability that the run-time of a particular program will lie between 30 and 40 seconds. More generally, one may want to know the overall distribution of run times – so that one can ask other questions. The mathematical function $F(x)$ showing the probability that the run time takes a value less than or equal to x is called the cumulative probability distribution, or cumulative distribution function, of x. Its derivative $f(x) = F'(x)$ is the probability density function of x. In effect $f(x)$ shows the probability that run time lies in an infinitesimal interval around x. Informally, this text will refer to a probability distribution or simply a distribution, and this may include continuous and discrete components.

The general term random variable, or random variate, is used to denote variables which may take various values according to a probability distribution.

The notation $f(x,y)$ and $f(x|y)$ will be used to indicate joint and conditional distributions in general – for discrete, continuous, or mixed random variables.

The joint distribution of x and y gives the probability that a pair (x,y) will occur together. One can decompose $f(x,y)$ as:

$$f(x,y) = f(x|y)f(y)$$

which simply says that the probability that x and y take a particular pair of values is the product of the probability that y takes the value in question and the probability that x takes its value, given that y has its value.

We could alternatively express this as:

$$f(x,y) = f(y|x)f(x)$$

Putting these two expressions together allows us to state:

$$f(x|y) = \frac{f(y|x)f(x)}{f(y)}$$

or alternatively:

$$f(x|y) = \frac{f(y|x)f(x)}{\int f(y|x)f(x)dx}$$

The last two expressions are alternative forms of Bayes theorem, a relationship which is widely used in statistics. In particular, this theorem lies at the root of Bayesian statistics, referred to above. In Bayesian statistics, $f(x)$ represents a distribution of prior belief that x takes each value and $f(y|x)$ is a measure of the likelihood of observed data y given each possible x value. Bayes theorem permits these two to be combined to yield a posterior measure of belief, $f(x|y)$, that x takes each value.

From the relationship $f(x,y) = f(x|y)f(y)$ we can see that if the distribution of x does not depend on y, i.e. if $f(x|y) = f(x)$, then $f(x,y) = f(x)f(y)$. Put another way, if x and y are independent, then the joint distribution of x and y can be factorized into the product of the two marginal distributions:

$$f(x) = \int f(x,y)dy \text{ and } f(y) = \int f(x,y)dx$$

The probability distribution is a mathematical function giving a complete description of the probability that the random variable will take any value. Often, however, it is useful to summarize the distribution. Two important summarizing values are the mean and standard deviation.

The (arithmetic) mean of a random variable x (also called the expected value) is defined as:

$$E(x) = \int f(x)xdx$$

It is thus a weighted sum of the possible outcomes, where the weights are the probabilities of the outcomes. It can be interpreted as an average or representative value of x because $E(x)$ is the value of z which minimizes:

$$\int (x - z)^2 f(x)dx$$

which is the weighted sum of squared deviations.

This weighted sum of squared deviations is itself a measure of how widely dispersed the probability distribution is. From the above it takes its minimum value when $z = E(x)$ and:

$$V(x) = \int [x - E(x)]^2 f(x)dx = E[x - E(x)]^2$$

is called the variance of x.

Variance is measured in the square of the units of x and it is often useful to transform it back to the basic units. The standard deviation of x is simply the square root of the variance.

The definitions of mean and standard deviation given above refer to the distribution of the random variable x. In real life one never actually knows what shape the overall population distribution has, of course (although one may assume that it has a particular form). In practice one has a sample of x values from the distribution and one can use this to make inferences about the underlying population distribution. In particular, one can plot a histogram or bar chart showing the proportion of

observed values taking particular values of x (for x discrete) or lying within certain ranges of x (for x continuous).

Similarly, just as the histogram is a sample approximation to the shape of $f(x)$, so one can calculate a sample mean:

$$\bar{x} = \sum x_i/n$$

from the n values $x_1, \ldots, x_n$ in the sample, and a sample standard deviation:

$$s = \sqrt{\frac{\sum(x_i - \bar{x})^2}{n}}$$

(Often the n here is replaced by $(n-1)$. This represents the difference between the maximum likelihood and an unbiased estimator – see Section 6.6.)

$\bar{x}$ and s here can be regarded as estimates of the corresponding population values.

More advanced statistical ideas permit further statements to be made about distributional forms and properties. One important idea is the law of large numbers, which says:

$$p(|\bar{x} - \mu| > \varepsilon) < \frac{\sigma^2}{\varepsilon^2 n}$$

That is, the probability that the difference between the sample mean $\bar{x}$ and the population mean μ exceeds ε is less than $\sigma^2/\varepsilon^2 n$, where σ^2 is the variance of the distribution and n is the sample size. We see in particular that by increasing the sample size we can make the probability that $\bar{x}$ is far from μ as small as we like.

Before leaving this section it is necessary to define mode and median, since these are terms the reader is quite likely to encounter.

The mode of a distribution is its most likely value – the value of x taken by more cases than is any other x value.

The median is the value of x such that $F(x) = 1/2$. Thus 50% of the population has an x value less than the median and 50% greater.

6.3 Some important probability distributions

6.3.1 The binomial distribution

In some situations there are just two mutually exclusive possible outcomes (a simple example is tossing a coin, which can result in just a head or a tail). If we denote the outcomes by A and B, then outcome A will have a probability $p = p(A)$ associated with it and outcome B will have a probability $q = 1 - p$ associated with it. Now suppose that n identical trials of this situation are conducted, each with the same two possible outcomes and with $p(A) = p$. Then the probability that A will occur x times is:

$$p(x) = \binom{n}{x} p^x (1 - p)^{n-x}$$

Because of its elementary nature, this distribution, known as the binomial distribution, finds widespread application. The mean and variance of this distribution are $\mu = np$ and $\sigma^2 = npq$ respectively.

6.3.2 The Poisson distribution

A process in which events occur 'randomly' over time is a Poisson process. Formally, a Poisson process is a process in which the probability density function of x, the number of events occurring in a time t is:

$$f(x) = \begin{cases} e^{-\lambda t}(\lambda t)^x x! & x = 0, 1, 2 \ldots \\ 0 & \text{otherwise} \end{cases}$$

The parameter λ is the rate of the Poisson process. The mean and variance of the number of events occurring in time t are both λt. An example might be the number of hardware failures occurring over time. Note, however, that the underlying continuum need not be time – one could model the number of mispunched figures in a set of data as a Poisson process.

The Poisson and binomial distributions have a useful relationship. A binomial distribution with sample size n and probability p can be approximated by a Poisson distribution with parameter $\lambda = np$, if n is large and p is small, with the approximation improving as $n \to \infty$ and $p \to 0$.

6.3.3 The normal distribution

The binomial and Poisson distributions are examples of discrete distributions – x can only take values from a discrete set. The most important continuous distribution – where x comes from a continuum (in fact the entire real line) – is the normal distribution. This has the probability density function:

$$f(x) = \frac{1}{\sigma\sqrt{2\pi}} \exp\left[-\frac{1}{2}\left(\frac{x - \mu}{\sigma}\right)^2 \right]$$

where μ and σ are parameters identifying a particular member of the family of normal distributions (as were n, p, λ, and t for the binomial and Poisson distributions), and the mean and variance of the normal distribution are μ and σ^2 respectively.

There are many reasons for the importance of the normal distribution. One is the central limit theorem, which states that the distribution of the mean of a sample of size n from a distribution with mean μ and variance σ^2 can be made arbitrarily close to a normal distribution with mean μ and variance σ^2/n, by taking n sufficiently large. Thus, whatever distribution the sample originates from (continuous or discrete) if n is large enough, the distribution of the sample mean is approximately normal. Since much statistical theory is concerned with the distribution of sample means it follows that very great simplification is possible – and the results are valid even though one does not know the original population distribution.

6.3.4 The uniform distribution

A random variable x is said to follow the uniform distribution between two limits a and b if it has an identical probability of taking each value between a and b. The most common range for uniform distributions is the interval $[0, 1]$. Such a uniform distribution has a mean $1/2$ and variance $1/12$.

6.4 Sampling

It was noted above that samples could be used to yield estimates of parameters of distributions, such as their mean and variance. More generally, samples can be used to study processes and structures. By making use of concepts such as the law of large numbers, referred to above, statements can be made about the probable accuracy of the conclusions.

The simplest and most common sampling method is simple random sampling. If a population has N objects and a sample size n is to be drawn, then a simple random sample is one in which each subset of size n has an equal probability of being drawn. (So once an object has been chosen it cannot be chosen again – this is said to be sampling without replacement.)

With a simple random sample each object has a probability of n/N of being chosen and sample statistics (e.g. of mean and variance) can be easily calculated and used as estimates of the corresponding population (underlying distribution) values. Note, however that allowance must be made for the finite size, N, of the population when calculating the variance, unless N is large. See Kish (1965) for details.

Sometimes improvements can be made over the basic simple random sampling method. A common such modification is stratified sampling. Suppose that the population being studied falls into several distinct strata, e.g. there may be a few distinct types of program being run. In this case, if each stratum is relatively homogeneous – i.e. there is little within stratum variability on the variable being studied – then very accurate estimates can be made within each stratum separately. These can then be combined (weighting appropriately by the size of the strata) to yield a very accurate overall estimate. Simple random samples can be taken separately within each stratum. The result will be more accurate than merely an overall simple random sample provided the strata have sufficient internal homogeneity.

There are variants on this principle of stratification. In proportionate sampling, the sampling fraction n_i/N_i in the ith stratum (n_i objects being chosen out of the N_i in the stratum) is set equal to the overall sampling fraction n/N. In disproportionate sampling, different sampling fractions may be used in each stratum, and these can be chosen to make the overall estimate as accurate as possible. For example, one can draw proportionally more cases from strata with higher internal variability. It is also possible to apply the mathematics of stratification after the data have been collected – in post-stratification.

A related sample design which is sometimes confused with stratified sampling, but which is in fact quite different, is cluster sampling. For this the population being studied is grouped into distinct classes called clusters and a subset of clusters is chosen for further sampling. For example, one might be surveying the quality of software in an organization which has many programmers. To keep the cost of interrupting work to a minimum one might choose (by an appropriate sampling method) just a few of these programmers and then take a sample of the programs each has produced. Here the programs would be the cases and the clusters would be the programmers.

Note that all of the above use some kind of 'random' procedure in selecting the objects to be included in the sample. They are all probability sampling methods. The advantage of using such methods is that they permit formal statistical methods to be applied so that one can make valid statistical inferences. One can contrast such methods with purposive sampling where the objects are chosen by the engineer. While this may seem superficially more sensible than random selection, in fact it means that probability-based statistical methods cannot be applied. One cannot make probability statements and the results may well be worthless. This point is significant when trying to estimate software reliability, see Chapter 31.

A qualitatively different kind of sampling is sequential sampling, in which the objects are chosen one at a time or in a sequence of groups. An important difference between this approach and the above is that the sample size is not fixed beforehand but sampling stops when a sufficiently accurate conclusion is reached.

Acceptance sampling describes the strategy of accepting or rejecting a product lot on the basis of an examination of a sample. In manufacturing industry rejection will probably mean scrapping the lot from which the sample was taken. In software development one may well attempt to remove from the system the errors causing the 'lot' to be defective.

For software, the product is the output of a program, so attention can be focused on the quality of that output and samples of output can be drawn. This may well be a more fruitful way of looking at software quality than focusing attention on the software system itself, since even a bug-free program does not guarantee that the output will satisfy the user's requirements. In a statistical package, for example, highly correlated input variables could lead to unstable matrix inversion, producing parameter estimates with very large variances. See Cho (1980) for further details.

The operating characteristic curve of a sampling plan is a curve relating the probability of accepting the lot $A(\theta)$ to θ the proportion of defectives in the lot. A typical shape for such a curve is shown in *Figure 6.1*.

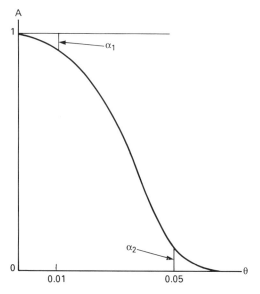

Figure 6.1   A typical operating characteristic curve

In this figure α_1 represents the probability that a good lot (i.e. with low θ) will be rejected, while α_2 represents the probability that a poor lot (with high θ) will be accepted. For specified values of α_1 and α_2, and corresponding θ_1 and θ_2 at which these α_1 are to occur, a sanmpling plan (in terms of sample size and number of defectives which lead to rejection) can be drawn up. This approach can be developed for both single samples and sequential sampling methods.

6.5 Simulation, Monte Carlo methods and random number generators

Monte Carlo methods use random numbers to solve problems. These problems fall into two classes: probabilistic ones, in which the random numbers are used to simulate some stochastic phenomenon in the real world, and deterministic ones, which may be mathematically translated into an equivalent probabilistic problem which can then be tackled through simulation.

An example of the first class of problem would be job queuing in a computer. This is an intrinsically stochastic process and one could experiment by generating random numbers to represent job lengths (perhaps in terms of CPU time). Parameters of the model could then be altered to see how the overall process was affected (see also Chapter 7).

Many deterministic problems, especially in operational research and nuclear physics, cannot be tackled by existing analytic mathematical theory. In other cases the theory exists but the practicalities of finite computing power impose restrictions on what can be done. A simple example of this sort of problem is multivariate integration. In high dimensions, quadrature type approaches break down and an alternative is to reformulate the problem as an expectation (see Section 6.2). This expectation can then be approximated by a sample mean, where a random sample of values of the function is simply averaged.

Digital computers cannot, of course, generate random numbers, since they do not contain internal chance mechanisms. Instead algorithms have been developed which generate sequences of numbers which pass tests for randomness. (Such sequences are called pseudo-random numbers.) Thus, although the generators are in fact deterministic, they give the impression of producing a random sequence.

An early technique for generating uniformly distributed pseudo-random numbers was the 'mid-square' method. This begins with a two-digit number, squares it, takes the middle two digits as the next number, squares these and takes the middle two digits, and so on. This has been found to perform poorly, and the most commonly used method nowadays is the multiplicative congruential method. Beginning with a starting number x_0 (a seed) the $(i + 1)$th pseudo-random number is generated from the ith, using the relationship:

$$x_{i+1} = ax_i \bmod(n)$$

where n is a large integer (typically 2^s, s being the computer's word size in bits) and a and x_0 are integers between 0 and $(n - 1)$. The sequence is then given by the numbers x_i/n.

It is obvious that this is only pseudo-random, not truly random, since it must be cyclic with a period no greater than n. Therefore it is very important to ensure that the period is longer than the number of numbers which will be used.

An extension of the above is to use:

$$x_{i+1} = ax_i + c \bmod(n)$$

where c is again an integer between 0 and $(n - 1)$. Now a cycle of length n is achieved if c and n have no common divisor, a is congruent to 1 (mod p) for every prime factor of n, and a is congruent to 1 (mod 4) if n is a multiple of 4.

Of course, many problems require the numbers to follow distributions other than the uniform. Rather than producing different generators for each distribution, the approach adopted is to generate uniformly distributed pseudo-random numbers and then transform the distribution. In principle this is straightforward. If $f(x)$ is the desired density function, with cumulative distribution function $F(x)$, then we generate uniformly distributed y and calculate x as $x = F^{-1}(y)$.

For binomial random variables, we can generate uniformly distributed x and then score the outcome as A or B according to whether x is less than or equal to p or not.

A common method for generating normally distributed random variables is the Box-Muller (1958) transform. If x and y are independent uniform random variables then:

$$X = (- 2 \log x)^{\frac{1}{2}} \cos(2\pi y)$$

and:

$$Y = (- 2 \log x)^{\frac{1}{2}} \sin(2\pi y)$$

are independent, normally distributed random variables.

To conclude this section, there is a general principle of Monte

Carlo methods – that one should always try to restate and reformulate the problem so that as accurate results as possible are obtained, rather than blindly tackling the problem as initially stated. For example, the technique of stratified sampling, outlined above, might be used to break the problem into sub-problems which can later be combined to yield a more accurate result.

Since the numbers produced by a pseudo-random number generator are not truly random it is always possible that they may have some pattern which will invalidate the conclusions. For this reason it is important to test the output stream of numbers. Of course, even rigorous testing is not a guarantee; one can only apply a few tests in practice.

Several tests are in common use, including the frequency test, the poker test, the serial test, and the gap test.

The frequency test checks to see that each of the digits 0–9 occurs about equally often. That is, in terms of the hypothesis test formulation (see Section 6.7), the null hypothesis is that the digits follow the multinomial distribution with $p(i) = 0.1$ for $i = 0, 1, \ldots, 9$. The chi-squared test (Section 6.7) can be used to examine this.

In the poker test, the sequence is partitioned into blocks of m digits (where m is a small number, such as 4) and the frequencies of blocks containing m identical digits, $(m - 1)$ identical digits, etc. down to all digits different are calculated. These frequencies are then compared with the expected values – again using a chi-squared goodness of fit test.

In the serial test, the frequencies with which each digit follows each other are calculated and compared with the expected values.

The gap test is based on the gaps between identical digits – i.e. the number of other digits occurring between occurrences of the same digit. Again the distribution of these gaps is compared with the expected distribution under the hypothesis that the digits are uniformly randomly distributed.

Sometimes, violation of some of the tests of randomness will not affect the conclusions. In such cases it may be possible to use a non-random sequence which satisfies only the properties which are deemed necessary. Such sequences are termed quasi-random.

6.6 Estimation

It was pointed out in Section 6.2 that the sample mean could be regarded as an estimate of a corresponding population value. This notion of estimate can be put on a more formal basis.

First, one can distinguish point estimation from interval estimation. A point estimate is a single number which serves as an estimate of the population parameter in question. The use of a sample mean as a point estimate of population mean was discussed earlier. An interval estimate is an interval of the real line within which the population parameter is expected to lie. The interpretation of this is quite subtle and is outlined below.

Beginning with point estimation, the first question to ask is what criteria one might use to judge whether or not an estimator is a good one.

One such criterion is that of unbiasedness. An estimator $\hat{\theta}$ of a population parameter θ is said to be unbiased if $E(\hat{\theta}) = \theta$. That is, the mean value of the estimator is equal to the true value of the parameter being estimated. Note that this says nothing about the particular estimate arising from the particular sample drawn – but merely about average performance in repeated sampling.

A second important criterion is that as one increases the sample size towards infinity, so the mean squared error of the estimator should tend to zero. If this is the case the estimator is said to be consistent; so consistency states that one can increase

confidence in one's estimate to an arbitrary extent by increasing the sample size sufficiently.

It is possible to compare two alternative estimators of the same parameter in terms of relative efficiency. Estimator $\hat{\theta}_1$ is said to be more efficient than estimator $\hat{\theta}_2$ if the variance of $\hat{\theta}_1$ is less than that of $\hat{\theta}_2$.

A more abstract criterion is that of sufficiency. An estimator $\hat{\theta}$ is said to be sufficient for parameter θ if the distribution of the sample given $\hat{\theta}$ does not depend on θ. That is, all of the information about θ contained in the data is contained in $\hat{\theta}$. Aspects of the data not involved in $\hat{\theta}$ (e.g. the sample variance when estimating the mean) are irrelevant to the estimation of θ.

So much for criteria by which competing estimators might be compared. Now it is necessary to know how such competitors might be constructed.

One widely used method is maximum likelihood. Suppose the sample arises from a distribution $f(x;\theta)$, where θ is a parameter to be estimated and which indexes a family of distributions. Then, assuming that the n sample points have been independently sampled, the overall distribution of the sample is:

$$l = \prod_{i=1}^{n} f(x_i; \theta)$$

Regarded as a function of θ, this is called the likelihood function. Then the Maximum Likelihood Principle is to take as the best estimator of θ the value for which the obtained data would have had the highest probability of occurring. (Note, this is not the same as regarding l as providing a probability distribution for θ. Under the frequency interpretation of probability this is meaningless, although it is meaningful under a subjective interpretation (Section 6.2).)

Rather than working with l directly it is usual to work with $L = \log l$ since:

$$\log l = \sum_{i=1}^{n} \log f(x_i; \theta)$$

and sums are easier to manipulate than products. Since log is a monotonic function, the value of θ which maximizes l is also the value which maximizes L.

Maximum likelihood estimators have a number of nice properties. For example, under fairly general conditions the maximum likelihood estimator is consistent (though it is often biased) and a function of a maximum likelihood estimator is the maximum likelihood estimator of that function.

Another common estimation technique uses the least squares principle. Here the parameter value is chosen which minimizes the sum of squared deviations between predicted values and the data. An example of this, regression analysis, involving two or more parameters, is described in Section 6.8, but note here that the sample mean is the least squares estimate of the population mean – as remarked in Section 6.2.

So far only point estimates have been discussed. These are the best estimates, in some sense, of the value of the parameter in question. It is known, however, that a point estimate is unlikely to be exactly accurate – and what a point estimate fails to convey is any sense of how accurate it is. Interval estimates do just this by specifying an interval within which the true value is likely to lie. Thus one seeks two numbers a and b which satisfy:

$$P(a < \theta < b) = 1 - \alpha$$

where $(1 - \alpha)$ is the confidence coefficient (e.g. 95%). Since a and b, and hence the interval $[a,b]$, will be calculated from the data, they are random variables. Thus we can interpret the confidence interval as saying that the probability is 0.95 that the random interval $[a, b]$ contains the true value of θ. Note, however, that once we have calculated numerical values for a and b, we cannot interpret this as saying that the probability is 0.95 that the true θ lies in this interval. For a given interval θ either does or does not lie within it. θ is not a random variable (unless one adopts a Bayesian approach).

In principle, calculating confidence intervals is straightforward, although the computations may be involved. One simply obtains the cumulative distribution function of $\hat{\theta}$, $F(\hat{\theta})$, in terms of θ, chooses α, and solves for θ the two equations:

$$F(\hat{\theta}) = \frac{\alpha}{2} \qquad 1 - F(\hat{\theta}) = \frac{\alpha}{2}$$

Whichever θ value is the smaller is taken as the lower bound of the interval.

6.7 Hypothesis testing

Based on a theoretical understanding of some phenomenon or process, one will build a model. Using the estimation procedures outlined above one will fit the model to the data. The next step is to test it – to see how good a fit it is. The discussion will be kept simple by being focused on hypothesis testing for single parameters.

The first step is to formulate the hypothesis to be tested – the null hypothesis. For example, one may state the hypothesis that the mean value of a population distribution is 50, or that the mean productivity (in terms of lines of code per day) is greater for employees of company A than of company B.

A test statistic is then chosen, for which the sampling distribution (i.e. the distribution of the statistic over repeated samples) can be specified. Using this sampling distribution, a rejection region is chosen: a region such that if the sample statistic falls in that region then the null hypothesis would be rejected. Clearly the rejection region will cover values which are extreme in some sense – if the null hypothesis is true then one would not expect to obtain such values of the sample statistic very often.

Only at this point does one draw the sample, calculate the obtained value of the sample statistic, and reject or not reject the null hypothesis according to whether or not the test statistic does or does not fall in the rejection region.

Examples given below put this abstract description on a more concrete footing, but before that some more definitions should be given.

The rejection region will be chosen so that if the null hypothesis is true then it will be incorrectly rejected with some (low) probability – typically 1% or 5%. This is the significance level of the test. Such an error – an incorrect rejection of a true null hypothesis – is known as a type 1 error.

Conversely, if the null hypothesis is false there will be a finite probability of incorrectly failing to reject the false null hypothesis. An error of this kind is a type 2 error. The power of a test is defined as $1 - P$ (type 2 error). Thus the greater the probability that a test will correctly reject a false null hypothesis, the greater its power. Clearly power can be used as a basis on which to compare tests.

The first example will be a test to compare the mean value of a distribution with some hypothesized mean value.

Suppose that the null hypothesis is that the population has a mean of 100. The sample gives $\bar{x}$ as the sample mean, and if the sample did come from a population with mean 100 then we would not expect this to be too far from 100. Thus we begin by looking at $(\bar{x} - 100)$. This alone, however, is not enough. If the underlying population has a very large standard deviation then differences as large as $(\bar{x} - 100)$ might be common. Conversely, if the population has a small standard deviation such a difference may be extremely unusual. To take this into account we must compare $(\bar{x} - 100)$ with the population standard deviation. That is, we consider using $(\bar{x} - 100)/\sigma$ as a test statistic. This is all very well, but σ will be unknown, and will have to be estimated from the sample, yielding $(\bar{x} - 100)/s$.

To use this as a test statistic we must find its distribution. Section 6.3.3 described the central limit theorem, which says that if the sample size is large enough one can assume that $\bar{x}$ is normally distributed. We shall assume this to be the case (or that the underlying population is normal, in which case $\bar{x}$ follows a normal distribution whatever the sample size). Adding constants and dividing by constants do not affect the normality of a normal distribution (though obviously they change the mean and standard deviation) so if we were using $(\bar{x} - 100)/\sigma$, we could use the widespread tables of the normal distribution. Unfortunately, replacing σ by s changes the distribution so that outlying values of $(\bar{x} - \mu)/s$ are more likely than those of $(\bar{x} - \mu)/\sigma$ – it no longer follows a normal distribution. The distribution that $(\bar{x} - \mu)/s$ follows is called the t-distribution, and tables of this are also widely available. Unfortunately, these tables are slightly more complicated than those of the normal distributions, there being one such table for each sample size n involved. The tables are in fact indexed by $(n - 1)$, the number of degrees of freedom.

These tables state how likely it is that a value of $(\bar{x} - 100)/s$ as extreme or more extreme than that observed will occur.

For the second example, consider the very common situation of wishing to compare the means of two independent groups. The null hypothesis may be that the means are equal: $\mu_1 = \mu_2$. A sample size n_i is taken from population i and we wish to compare $(\bar{x}_1 - \bar{x}_2)$ with $(\mu_1 - \mu_2)$, that is, with zero. Again we shall assume that the n_i are large enough for us to adopt normal approximations and we shall now make the additional assumption that the two populations have the same variance. Using the results that variance $(\sum x_i) = \sum$ (variance x_i) for independent observations x_i and variance $(a\,x) = a^2 \times$ variance (x), we find that variance $(\bar{x}_1 - \bar{x}_2) = \sigma_1^2/n_1 + \sigma_2^2/n_2$, where σ_i^2 is the variance of population i $(i = 1, 2)$. Thus we can parallel the earlier single sample test and adopt the test statistic:

$$t = \frac{(\bar{x}_1 - \bar{x}_2) - (\mu_1 - \mu_2)}{\sqrt{s_1^2/n_1 + s_2^2/n_2}}$$

which simplifies to:

$$t = (\bar{x}_1 - \bar{x}_2)/s \left(\frac{1}{n_1} + \frac{1}{n_2} \right)^{1/2}$$

using the assumed common values of σ_1^2 and σ_2^2 to obtain a single estimate s of within group standard deviation. If the assumptions are correct then, under the null hypothesis the statistic t follows the t-distribution with $(n_1 + n_2 - 2)$ degrees of freedom.

Two forms of t-test have been described above. Other important cases are where the null hypothesis is less than (or greater than) some value and where, in the two groups case, the two samples are not independent but are matched in some way. For example, one might be comparing the performance of two different programs for tackling a certain numerical operation and one might test each on the same 30 data sets. Clearly the two sets of 30 results will not be independent and this should be allowed for in the analysis (typically, matching in this way improves the power of the test). Extensions such as these are described in many elementary texts (e.g. Hays, 1963).

Another basic statistical test which finds very widespread application is the chi-squared goodness of fit test.

Section 6.5 outlined tests for randomness which compared observed frequencies with those expected if the null hypothesis of uniform random numbers was true. Let us look in detail at how the chi-squared test is used with the frequency test.

Suppose that 100 supposedly random digits have been generated. If these have come from a uniform distribution, then the expected frequencies are $100 \times 0.1 = 10$ for each digit (0.1 being the probability that a particular digit occurs). Let A_i be the actual observed frequency for the ith digit ($i = 0, \ldots, 9$). The deviation between observed and actual values is $(A_i - 10)$ but we cannot simply add these over all digits (can the reader see why?) and in fact we use $\sum(A_i - 10)^2$.

So that the largest frequencies do not dominate excessively we divide by the expected values, yielding $\sum(A_i - 10)^2/10$. If the null hypothesis (of a uniform distribution) is true this will follow a chi-squared distribution. Once again, tables are available, and also once again there are different tables according to the number of frequencies involved. In this case there are $n = 10$ different digits and we will use the chi-squared table with $n - 1 = 9$ degrees of freedom.

The chi-squared goodness of fit test has very wide application, the general form of the test statistic being $\sum(A_i - E_i)^2/E_i$, where A_i is the actual observed frequency and E_i is the expected frequency. One particularly common application is to test two categorical variables for independence (e.g. one may wish to see if the error type distribution is identical for four different programmers or whether error type and programmer are independent). The expected values in such a test are obtained by multiplying together the marginal frequencies, and now the chi-squared statistic has $(p - 1)(e - 1)$ degrees of freedom (with p programmers and e error types). Details and examples are given in any elementary statistics text.

The t-tests which are outlined above rely either on the assumption that the sample sizes are sufficiently large for the normal approximation to the distribution of $\bar{x}$ to hold or make the assumption that the underlying populations are normal. Tests which rely on such distributional assumptions are called parametric tests. Another class of statistical techniques relaxes these assumptions, and these are naturally known as non-parametric or distribution-free methods.

Distribution-free tests are often based on ranking the observations (so that the original distribution is irrelevant), and then calculating significance levels by permuting the data and seeing, amongst all permutations, how often a test statistic as extreme as or more extreme than that actually observed occurs.

Distribution-free methods are widely used in certain sciences where distributional assumptions are dubious. Generally, however, if the distributional assumptions are correct then an appropriate parametric test will be more powerful.

6.8 Correlation and regression

One might define science as being concerned with understanding the relationships between variables describing aspects of the world. Thus it is hardly surprising that well-developed statistical methods exist for describing and inferring relationships. The simplest such techniques concern the relationship between just two variables. For example, one might wish to explore the relationship between program complexity, in terms of length, and program development time.

The correlation coefficient is a measure of the extent to which there exists a simple linear relationship between two variables. If (x_i, y_i) represent measures of length and time respectively for the ith program in a sample of n programs then the sample correlation coefficient is defined as:

$$r = \frac{\sum(x_i - \bar{x})(y_i - \bar{y})}{\sqrt{\sum(x_i - \bar{x})^2 \sum(y_i - \bar{y})^2}}$$

where the summations are over the n programs in the sample.

This coefficient will be larger to the extent that large values of length are associated with large values of time and small values of length are associated with small values of time. It lies between $+1$, indicating perfect association, 0, indicating total lack of association, and -1, indicating perfect negative association (large time values associated with small length values).

It is perhaps worth drawing attention to the word 'linear' in the above. If time were initially to increase and then decrease as length increased, then the correlation coefficient could be small even though there was a strong relationship.

The correlation coefficient, as defined above, is all very well, but it takes experience before a value is very meaningful. It is therefore helpful to note that r^2 can be interpreted as the proportion of variance in one variable which may be attributed to the other. In the example we might find that 80% of the variance in development time could be explained by differences in program length.

As it stands, the distribution of r is markedly non-normal, even if x and y are each normally distributed. Fortunately, however, the transformation:

$$z = \frac{1}{2} ln \frac{1+r}{1-r}$$

yields a distribution which is approximately normal, with mean $1/2 \, l n \, (1 + \rho)/(1 - \rho)$ and standard deviation $1/\sqrt{(n - 3)}$, where n is the sample size and ρ is the correlation coefficient in the underlying population from which the samples were drawn. This can be used for hypothesis tests about ρ.

Correlation provides a measure of strength of a symmetric relationship between variables but often one is interested in how accurately one can predict one variable from another. This is the realm of regression analysis. Using the same example as in the description of correlation above, we seek an equation which will permit us to predict time, y, from a measured length value x. The basic model we shall adopt is:

$$y_i = a_0 + a_1 x_i + e_i$$

meaning that the ith time value in the sample is a linear function $(a_0 + a_1 x_i)$ of the ith length value (x_i) plus a random error component unique to the ith pair of observations, e_i. The a_0 and a_1 parameters will be common to all pairs and the reason that the function $y_i = a_0 + a_1 x_i$ does not fit perfectly is the random e_i term.

Clearly we will now seek a_0 and a_1 values which minimize the prediction error between a predicted value given by $\hat{y}_i = a_0 + a_1 x_i$ and the observed y_i. The most common measure of prediction error is a sum of squared errors. That is, we will choose a_0 and a_1 to minimize:

$$\sum(y_i - \hat{y}_i)^2 = \sum(y_i - a_0 - a_1 x_i)^2 = \sum e_i^2$$

Some fairly straightforward algebra shows that the prediction error is minimized when:

$$\hat{a}_1 = \Sigma(x_i - \bar{x})(y_i - \bar{y})/\Sigma(x_i - \bar{x})^2$$

and

$$\hat{a}_0 = \bar{y} - \hat{a}_1 \bar{x}$$

This idea of predicting one variable from another can be extended to the prediction of a variable from a set $(x_1, x_2, \ldots, x_p)$ of others – in multiple regression. The prediction equation is then of the form:

$$\hat{y} = a_0 + a_1 x_1 + \ldots + a_p x_p$$

and the a_i parameters are again estimated by minimizing the sum of squared errors between the predicted $\hat{y}_i$ values and the observed y_i values in a sample.

6.9 Analysis of variance and covariance

The model used in regression analysis is an example of a linear model because it involves a mathematical structure which is linear in the a_i. Another closely related linear model, for situations where the predictor variables are categorical, is analysis of variance.

Suppose first we have just one predictor which is categorical with four categories. Then the analysis of variance model expresses an individual's score as:

$$y_{ij} = \mu + a_j + e_{ij}$$

where μ is an overall mean, a_j is the effect of being in category j (e.g. being in category j might add something to or subtract something from the overall response variable mean score μ) and e_{ij} is a random error term uniquely associated with the ith case in the jth group. This clearly has the same basic form as the regression model.

In analysis of variance models one is typically interested in whether the categories have different effects on the response variable, or whether particular patterns of differences appear. For example, one might wish to explore whether categories 2, 3, and 4 differ from category 1, the latter corresponding to some kind of standard.

Tests in analysis of variance are based on comparing the variability between group means with the variability within groups. This is precisely the same principle as the t-tests outlined above, which compared differences between means $(\bar{x}_1 - \bar{x}_2)$ with variability within groups(s). Analysis of variance tests are formulated in terms of sums of squares between and within groups and instead of a t-distribution the test statistics follow an F-distribution when the null hypothesis is true. Once again tables are readily available.

Just as simple regression can be extended to multiple regression, so analysis of variance can be extended to include more categorical predictor variables, termed factors. The analysis is then not merely a question of repeating the single factor tests for each factor but becomes qualitatively more complex. One must consider whether the effect of a factor varies according to the level of other factors (i.e. whether or not there is an interaction) and, if the cells of the factorial cross-classification have different numbers of observations, it is probable that the estimated effect of one factor will be related to the estimated effect of other factors. Some allowance has to be made for this.

Analysis of variance and regression are based on the same linear model, the difference being that the first is for continuous predictors and the second for categorical predictors. Often, of course, problems arise in which both types of predictors are needed together. Analysis of covariance represents a merger of the two techniques.

A generalized linear model has three components:

1. A systematic component in which a linear predictor ζ is related to covariates $x_1, \ldots, x_p$:

$$\zeta = \Sigma \beta_i x_i$$

2. A random component y, with mean value:

$$E(y) = \mu$$

3. The link function relating the systematic and random components:

$$\zeta = g(\mu)$$

An example of a generalized linear model which has made a dramatic impact on statistical analysis in the last decade is the log-linear model. This model is a model for multiple categorical variables and involves the link function $\zeta = \ln \mu$ – transforming a multiplicative model into an additive linear model.

Survival analysis can also be formulated as a linear model. Here the dependent variable – that being predicted – is the length of time until some event occurs.

Generalized linear models, and log-linear models in particular, owe their development in large part to the power of the computer. Another class of techniques for which this is also true is that of multivariate methods. Examples of such methods include:

1. Principal component analysis, which seeks the linear combination of variables which yields greatest variance.
2. Factor analysis, which seeks linear combinations which parsimoniously explain the covariance structure between the variables. For example, it might be that the relationships between the ten variables measured can be explained in terms of three latent unmeasured variables. This has been extended to linear structural relational models, formulated in terms of a measurement model, relating the observed measurements to hypothesized latent variables, and a structural equation model, which specifies the structure of the latent variables.
3. Discriminant analysis, where the objective is to classify an object on the basis of a set of measurements made on it. The classification rule is designed (parameters estimated) using a sample of cases with known classes.
4. Cluster analysis, in which the problem is to partition a set of cases into natural classes or clusters, again using information on a set of measurements taken on each case.
5. Multivariate analysis of variance, which parallels analysis of variance but with multiple response variables.
6. Recursive partitioning algorithms, which build classification trees using a sample of cases.

Finally, a third class of statistical techniques which makes extensive use of computers and which would have been infeasible without them is the class of resampling methods such as bootstrap techniques. These are general methods for exploring variability in complex (or simple) estimation problems and are based on the idea of repeatedly subsampling from the obtained data.

6.10 More advanced methods

Regression analysis and analysis of variance are amongst the most widely used of statistical methods. They are both examples of techniques based on a linear model. Other statistical techniques also make use of this model and the idea has been extended to generalized linear models.

6.11 Further reading

Most elementary statistics texts contain introductions to the elements of probability calculus. Examples are Hays (1963) and Folks (1981). A description of subjective probability may be found in Barnett (1982), an excellent overview of different statistical schools, including the Bayesian approach.

Sampling techniques are described in Kish (1965) and the application of acceptance sampling to software quality control in Cho (1980).

Monte Carlo and simulation methods, as well as the associated random number techniques, are described in Hammersley and Handscomb (1979).

Estimation methods and hypothesis testing are described in many elementary texts, with a more advanced description being given in van der Waerden (1969). Non-parametric methods are described in Marascuilo and McSweeney (1977).

There are many texts on analysis of variance and regression, including Scheffé (1959), Wonnacott and Wonnacott (1981), and Hand and Taylor (1987).

Generalized linear models are described in McCullagh and Nelder (1983) and log-linear models in particular in Bishop, Fienberg, and Holland (1975).

Multivariate techniques are described in Tabachnick and Fidell (1983), recursive partitioning algorithms in Breiman *et al.* (1984), and resampling methods in Efron (1982).

6.12 References

Barnett, V. (1982) *Comparative Statistical Inference*, Wiley, Chichester

Bishop, Y. M. M., Fienberg, S. E., and Holland, W. (1975) *Discrete Multivariate Analysis*, MIT Press, Cambridge, Mass, USA

Box, G. E. P. and Muller, M. E. (1958) A note on the generation of random normal deviates. *Ann. Math. Statist.*, **29**, 610–11

Breiman, L., Friedman, J. H., Olshen, R. A., and Stone, C. J. (1984) *Classification and Regression Trees*, Wadsworth, Belmont, CA, USA

Cho, C-K. (1980) *An Introduction to Software Quality Control*, Wiley, New York

Efron, B. (1982) *The Jacknife, the Bootstrap, and Other Resampling Plans*, SIAM, Philadelphia, USA

Folks, J. L. (1981) *Ideas of Statistics*, Wiley, New York

Hammersley, J. M. and Handscomb, D. C. (1979) *Monte Carlo Methods*, Chapman & Hall, London

Hand, D. J. and Taylor, C. C. (1987) *Multivariate Analysis of Variance and Repeated Measures*, Chapman & Hall, London

Hays, W. L. (1963) *Statistics*, Holt, Rinehart & Winston, New York, USA

Jansson, B. (1966) *Random Number Generators*, Victor Pettersons Bokindustri Aktiebolog, Stockholm, Sweden

Kish, L. (1965) *Survey Sampling*, Wiley, New York

Marascuilo, L. A. and McSweeney, M. (1977) *Nonparametric and Distribution-Free Methods for the Social Sciences*, Brooks-Cole Publishing Company, CA, USA

McCullagh, P. and Nelder, J. A. (1983) *Generalized Linear Models*, Chapman & Hall, London

Scheffé, H. (1959) *The Analysis of Variance*, Wiley, New York

Tabachnick, B. G. and Fidell, L. S. (1983) *Using Multivariate Statistics*, Harper & Row, New York

van der Waerden, B. L. (1969) *Mathematical Statistics*, George Allen & Unwin, London

Wonnacott, T. H. and Wonnacott, R. J. (1981) *Regression: a Second Course in Statistics*, Wiley, New York

7

Queuing theory

I Mitrani
Computing Laboratory, University of Newcastle-upon-Tyne

Contents

7.1 Introduction

The objects of interest in this chapter are queuing systems. These are systems where service demands of one or more types arrive according to some random pattern and compete with each other for possession of the available resources. Typically, that competition causes some demands to be delayed, or perhaps lost. The amounts of service required from the resources are generally also random. In the fields of computing and communication, the demands are usually jobs submitted for execution, messages sent for transmission or calls requiring links; the service resources may be processors, input/output (I/O) devices, communication channels or software modules; waiting room is provided by central or peripheral memories. In different contexts, the demands might be product components, airline passengers or hospital casualties; the service resources could be industrial robots, booking clerks or brain scanners.

From now on, unless it is important to be specific about the nature of the demands and the service resources, we shall refer to them as 'jobs' and 'servers', respectively.

The behaviour of a queuing system can be studied by constructing and analysing a model which captures its essential characteristics. The mathematical discipline that deals with such models is called queuing theory. It emerged as a separate subject in the early 1920s, through the works of Erlang, Pollaczek and other pioneers. Although the original motivation for the research came from various problems in telephony, it was soon realised that the range of applications of the theory is in fact very wide. When computers appeared on the scene, both the number and the importance of the problems that could be tackled by the methods of queuing theory increased considerably.

Consider, as an example, a simple queueing system such as the one illustrated in *Figure 7.1*.

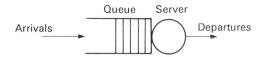

Arrivals → Queue Server → Departures

Figure 7.1

Jobs arrive at a station containing a single server. They remain there until their service is completed, and then depart. The server works whenever there are jobs present, and there is no limit to the number of jobs that may be present at any one time. This station could be a counter in a bank; the jobs are the customers and the server is the teller behind the window. Alternatively, it may be a network gateway; the jobs are messages that have to be sent across the network, and the server is a computer executing a communication protocol.

To define a model for this system, or for any other queuing system, one would have to make specific assumptions concerning the following three fundamental components:

1. The pattern of arrivals. Do jobs arrive singly or in batches? What is the distribution of the intervals between consecutive arrival instants? Does that distribution depend on the time of day? Does the time of the next arrival depend on the number of jobs present?
2. The service process. What is the distribution of service times? Are the latter independent of each other and of the arrival instants? Do they depend on the number of jobs present?
3. The scheduling strategy. This prescribes the order in which jobs are selected for service, whether they are served to completion or whether, and under what circumstances, interruptions of service may occur.

Having defined the model, it should be possible to carry out a mathematical analysis, with the object of determining various performance characteristics that may be of interest. For example, one may wish to find the utilization of a server (the fraction of time that it is busy), the average queue size, the average response time (the interval between the arrival of a job and its departure), the probability that a delay time will exceed a given threshold, etc. The analysis may be exact or approximate, and the solution may be easy or difficult to obtain, depending on the objectives and on the assumptions that are made. The most commonly sought performance metrics, and the only ones of interest in this chapter, concern steady-state behaviour. That is, the system is assumed to have been running for a sufficiently long time that it has settled down into a regime of statistical equilibrium that is independent of the starting conditions.

Certain aspects of steady-state performance can be quantified without any complicated analysis, and under very general assumptions. The principal tool that enables us to do this is introduced in the following section.

7.2 Little's theorem and its applications

Consider an arbitrary queuing system, or part of a system, in the steady state. No particular structure is postulated. For the purpose of this discussion, it is just a place where jobs of some sort arrive, remain for some time, and then depart. Let L be the average number of jobs observed in the system at a random point in time, W be the average time a job spends in the system (the average response time) and λ be the job arrival rate, i.e. the average number of arrivals per unit time. This is also equal to the average number of departures per unit time, or the system throughput. Then the following relation holds:

$$L = \lambda W \tag{7.1}$$

This result is known as 'Little's theorem' (Little, 1961). It is important to emphasize that the validity of Relation 7.1 is not restricted by any assumptions about the distribution of the intervals between consecutive arrivals, or about their independence (the mean of those intervals must of course be $1/\lambda$, so that the arrival rate is λ). Nor is anything assumed about the operations performed on the jobs in the system, the number of servers, the distributions of service times, or the scheduling strategy.

Certain fundamental properties possessed by many queuing systems are immediate consequences of Little's theorem. Let us examine, for example, the class of single-server systems illustrated in *Figure 7.1*. Suppose that the job arrival rate, λ, and the average required service time, b, are known. The scheduling strategy is immaterial and may involve arbitrary interleaving of services. However, no job leaves the system before it is completed.

We can apply Little's theorem to the sub-system consisting of the service position only; a job is said to be in that sub-system if it is receiving service. Clearly, the throughput of the service subsystem is also λ, while the average amount of time that jobs spend there is b. Hence, by 7.1, the average number of jobs in service, which in the case of a single server is the same as the probability that the server is busy, is equal to λb. This product of the throughput and the average service time can be interpreted as the average amount of work (measured in units of required service time), that arrives into the system per unit time. It is usually referred to as the 'offered load'.

Thus we reach the conclusion that the steady-state utilization of the server, denoted by U, is equal to the offered load:

$$U = \lambda b \tag{7.2}$$

Relation 7.2 is known as the Utilization Law. A trivial corollary of that law is the fact that, for the steady-state to exist, the offered load should satisfy the inequality $\lambda b \leqslant 1$ (a deeper analysis shows that the inequality should in fact be strict, except when both the arrival and the service processes are deterministic).

The above results generalize easily to systems with multiple job types and multiple parallel servers (*Figure 7.2*).

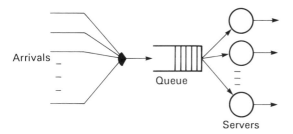

Figure 7.2

Suppose that there are C job types and m identical parallel servers. Jobs of type i arrive at the rate of λ_i per unit time and their required service times are b_i, on the average. In other words, the offered load of type i is $\lambda_i b_i$ ($i = 1, 2, \ldots, C$). Then applying Little's theorem to the sub-system consisting of the servers only, we can assert that in the steady-state, the average number of type i jobs in service, i.e. the average number of servers serving type i jobs, U_i, is equal to:

$$U_i = \lambda_i b_i, \quad i = 1, 2, \ldots, C \tag{7.3}$$

Moreover, for steady-state to exist, it is necessary that the total offered load is less than the number of servers:
$$\lambda_1 b_1 + \lambda_2 b_2 + \ldots + \lambda_C b_C < m.$$
Consider now a class of systems where, rather than arriving externally in streams with known rates, jobs are submitted by a finite number, K, of users (e.g. terminals) connected to a central service facility. Assume, to start with, that all users are statistically identical and that there is a single server (*Figure 7.3*).

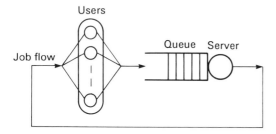

Figure 7.3

Each user, having submitted a job, waits until that job is completed, then 'thinks' for a period of time, then submits a new job, etc. This behaviour can be represented by having K jobs circulating for ever between their respective users and the server, experiencing think delays at the former and queuing and service delays at the latter. Let the average think times and the average service times be a and b, respectively.

Suppose that the performance measures of interest in this system are:

L: the average number of active jobs (queueing or in service).
W: the average response time (interval between a job leaving its terminal and returning to it).
T: the throughput (average number of jobs arriving at, or leaving the server per unit time).
U: the utilization of the server.

These quantities are closely interrelated. Applying Little's theorem to the sub-system consisting of the queue and server, we get:

$$L = TW \tag{7.4}$$

The same theorem, applied to the group of users, yields:

$$K - L = Ta \tag{7.5}$$

Eliminating L from 7.4 and 7.5 provides a very important relation between response time and throughput:

$$W = (K/T) - a \tag{7.6}$$

This is known as the 'Response Time Law' for finite-source systems. Another version of the law is obtained by combining 7.6 with the Utilization Law, according to which $U = Tb$. This yields:

$$W = b(K/U) - a \tag{7.7}$$

Relations 7.6 and 7.7 imply that, given the parameters K, a and b, the objective of minimizing the average response time is equivalent to that of maximizing the throughput, or the server utilization. When the system is heavily loaded, e.g. when K is large, or b is large, or a is small, the utilization of the server is close to 1 and the throughput is close to $1/b$. In such cases, the average response time increases approximately linearly with the number of users: $W \approx bK - a$.

The Response Time Law, too, can be generalized by allowing multiple job types and multiple parallel servers. Suppose that there are K_i users of type i, ($i = 1, 2, \ldots, C$), with average think times a_i and average service times b_i. Denote the throughput of type i jobs by T_i and their average response time by W_i. These quantities are related as follows:

$$W_i = (K_i/T_i) - a_i, \quad i = 1, 2, \ldots, C \tag{7.8}$$

Moreover, if U_i is the average number of types i jobs in service, i.e., the average number of servers serving type i jobs, then:

$$W_i = b_i(K_i/U_i) - a_i, \quad i = 1, 2, \ldots, C \tag{7.9}$$

We have now introduced, and examined in a general way, two rather different kinds of systems. The first kind, exemplified by Figures 7.1 and 7.2, is 'open'. Jobs arrive from the outside world in streams whose rates are independent of the system state. Those arrival rates, which in the steady state are also the throughputs, are usually known parameters. Together with the average service times, they determine the utilization of servers, via the Utilization Law. However, knowing the utilization is not sufficient to determine the average response times.

The second kind of systems, of which a special case is illustrated in Figure 7.3, is 'closed'. Here the demand is generated by a fixed number of users who submit jobs one at a time, with think periods in between. The known parameters include the numbers of users of different types, the average think times and the average service times. Neither the throughputs (or, equivalently, the server utilizations), nor the average response times can be obtained from these parameters alone. However, the throughputs determine the response times uniquely (and *vice versa*), via the Response Time Law.

To derive the performance measures of interest it is necessary to make specific assumptions regarding the distributions of relevant random variables and the job scheduling strategy, and to carry out an analysis of the resulting model. That will be the aim of subsequent sections, for various open and closed systems.

7.3 Residual lifetime and the FIFO queue

We shall start by studying the performance of open single-server queuing systems of the kind shown in Figure 7.1. The performance measures L (average number of jobs in the system) and W (average response time for a job), will be determined by obtaining a second relation between them, in addition to the one provided by Little's theorem.

This section will concentrate on a model that satisfies the following three assumptions:

1. The stream of job arrivals is Poisson distributed, with rate λ; in other words, the intervals between consecutive arrival instants are independent of each other and are distributed exponentially with mean $1/\lambda$.
2. Jobs remain in the queue until served to completion. Service is given in order of arrival, and without interruption. This scheduling strategy is usually referred to as FIFO (first-in-first-out), or FCFS (first-come-first-served).
3. Job service times are independent and identically distributed, with some general distribution function, $F(x)$, and mean b.

This model is known in the literature as the 'M/G/1 queue' (Markov arrivals, General service times, 1 server). Assumption (1), which appears the most artificial and restrictive of the three, is made for two reasons: first, Poisson arrival streams arise naturally in practice as a result of merging many independent sources of demand; second, these streams possess a number of 'nice' properties which facilitate the analysis considerably.

Particularly important is the fact that the jobs from a Poisson arrival stream behave like random observers. In other words, the system state seen by an incoming job is statistically identical to the one that would be seen if the observation point was selected at random. This very useful property is referred to as PASTA (Poisson Arrivals See Time Averages).

Let us 'tag' a job arriving into the system in the steady state, and consider its average response time. The latter can be represented as the sum of three components:

$$W = W_0 + W_q + b \tag{7.10}$$

where W_0 is the average interval until the departure of the job currently in service (if any); W_q is the total average service time of the jobs currently waiting; and b is the average service time of the tagged job itself. Now, according to the PASTA property and the Utilization Law, the tagged job sees an average of L jobs in the system on arrival, of which λb are being served (i.e., there is a job in service with probability λb), and $L - \lambda b$ are waiting. If there is a job in service, it will remain there for some period whose average we shall denote by R. On the other hand, each of the waiting jobs will occupy the server for time b, on the average. Hence, we have $W_0 = \lambda b R$, and $W_q = (L - \lambda b)b$. These two expressions, substituted into equation 7.10, provide a new relation between W and L. Eliminating L with the aid of $L = \lambda W$ (Little's theorem), and denoting the offered load, λb, by ρ, we obtain

$$W = b + \rho R/(1 - \rho) \tag{7.11}$$

Thus the average response time has been expressed in terms of R. This last quantity is quite important in its own right, and is worth defining in a more general context. Consider a sequence of repeated realisations of some random activity, e.g., life cycles of a particular species of bacteria, or operations performed by a worker in an assembly line. At a randomly chosen point in time, one of those realisations is observed to be in progress. Then the interval between the observation point and the termination of the current realisation is called the 'residual lifetime' of the activity. In this terminology, R is the average residual lifetime of a job's service time.

Intuition might suggest that the average residual lifetime is equal to half the average duration of the activity (in our case, $R = b/2$). However, that intuition is wrong, in general. When periods of varying lengths are being observed, a random observation point is more likely to fall into a longer period than into a short one. The effect of this 'random observer bias', is to make the average residual lifetime longer than half the average lifetime of the activity. Moreover, the difference can be arbitrarily large.

The correct expression for R involves not just the mean, but also the second moment, M_2, or the variance, σ^2, of the service time distribution $F(x)$. That expression has the following form (e.g., see Kleinrock (1975)):

$$R = M_2/(2b) = (b/2)(\sigma^2 + b^2)/b^2 = (b/2)(C^2 + 1) \tag{7.12}$$

where C^2, defined as the ratio between the variance and the square of the mean, is called the 'squared coefficient of variation' of the service times. It is clear from Relation 7.12 that $R \geqslant b/2$, with equality only when $C^2 = 0$, i.e. when all service times have exactly the same length.

Substituting Relation 7.12 into 7.11, we find the average response time in terms of three basic parameters: the offered load, the average service time and the squared coefficient of variation of the service time:

$$W = b + \rho(b/2)(C^2 + 1)/(1 - \rho) \tag{7.13}$$

This result is known as 'Khinchine-Pollaczeck's formula'. It illustrates two important aspects of the performance of queuing systems. The first is the rather obvious one that the system performance deteriorates when the offered load increases, and becomes arbitrarily bad when the latter approaches 1. The second, less obvious but equally crucial aspect is that even when the system is lightly loaded its performance may be arbitrarily bad provided that the variation of the required service times is sufficiently high.

The average number of jobs in the system is of course given by Relation 7.13, together with the relation $L = \lambda W$.

In some applications it is of interest to know the conditional average response time of a job, $W(x)$, given that its required service time is x. Under the FIFO scheduling strategy, the job's waiting time is independent of its required service; therefore, repeating the argument leading to Relation 7.13, we get:

$$W(x) = x + \rho(b/2)(C^2 + 1)/(1 - \rho) \tag{7.14}$$

One particular case of this model deserves a special mention. This is the M/M/1 queue, where both the interarrival periods and the service times are exponentially distributed. In this case, we have $C^2 = 1$ and $R = b$. The fact that the average residual service time is equal to the average service time is due to the 'memoryless', or 'Markov' property of the exponential distribution (Kleinrock, 1975): given that a service time is observed to be in progress, the amount already elapsed has no influence on what remains.

For the M/M/1 queue, Relation 7.10 has a rather simple form:

$$W = (L + 1)b \qquad (7.15)$$

The performance measures are now given by

$$W = b/(1 - \rho) \qquad (7.16)$$

$$L = \rho/(1 - \rho) \qquad (7.17)$$

$$W(x) = x + \rho b/(1 - \rho) \qquad (7.18)$$

We shall return to the M/M/1 queue, and to some of the above results, when we discuss queuing networks. In particular, Relation 7.15 will provide the basis for a recursive solution method for closed networks.

7.4 Processor-sharing scheduling strategy

Many multiprogrammed computer systems employ a job-scheduling strategy which allocates service in quanta of fixed size, Q. Having received a quantum of service, the job at the head of the queue either departs (if its requirement has been satisfied), or returns to the end of the queue and awaits its turn again. Thus, if there are n jobs present, each of them occupies the server for one out of every n quanta. This strategy is called 'Round-Robin'. It is illustrated in *Figure 7.4*.

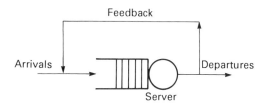

Feedback

Arrivals   Departures

Server

Figure 7.4

A good idea of the behaviour of the Round-Robin strategy is obtained by considering the limiting case when the quantum size Q is allowed to shrink to 0. The smaller the quantum, the more frequently each of the waiting jobs visits the processor. In the limit $Q \rightarrow 0$, all competing jobs proceed in parallel, each receiving an equal fraction of the available processing capacity. That limiting scheduling strategy is called 'processor-sharing' (PS). As well as being of interest in its own right, it provides a good approximation to the Round-Robin strategy with a small quantum size.

A more direct definition of the PS strategy can be given by saying that if there are n jobs in the system at time t, then in the infinitesimal interval $(t, t + dt)$ each of those jobs receives an amount of service equal to dt/n. Alternatively, the time necessary for every one of the n jobs to increase its attained service by an infinitesimal amount, ds, is equal to $n\,ds$.

We are still in the context of the M/G/1 system, i.e., jobs arrive from the outside in a Poisson stream with rate λ, and the required service times have some general distribution function, $F(x)$, with mean b. As in any other single-server system, in order that steady state may exist, it is necessary that the offered load, $\rho = \lambda b$, should be less than 1.

A rather interesting property of the PS scheduling strategy is that it is 'insensitive' with respect to the distribution of the

required service times. That is, the average response time, W, the average number of jobs in the system, L, and the conditional average response time, $W(x)$, do not in fact depend on the shape of $F(x)$. The corresponding formulae are:

$$W = b/(1 - \rho) \qquad (7.19)$$

$$L = \rho/(1 - \rho) \qquad (7.20)$$

$$W(x) = x/(1 - \rho) \qquad (7.21)$$

Note, that W and L have the same values under PS with arbitrarily distributed service times, as they do under FIFO with exponentially distributed service times. Comparing for example 7.19 with 7.13, we see that for a given distribution function $F(x)$, the average performance of the PS scheduling strategy is better than that of FIFO if $C^2 > 1$, while FIFO is better if $C^2 < 1$.

It is clear from Relation 7.21 that PS has a tendency to favour short jobs at the expense of long ones. Whether jobs of a given length are better off under that scheduling strategy or under FIFO, depends on the value of C^2. For instance, if $C^2 = 1$ (e.g., if the service times are distributed exponentially), then jobs for which $x < b$, i.e. those that are shorter than average, are better off under PS. Conversely, if $x > b$, then FIFO is better.

The processor-sharing strategy can be applied where the job population is not homogeneous. Suppose that there are K job types, arriving in independent Poisson streams with different rates (λ_i for type i) and different distributions of required service times ($F_i(x)$ for type i; mean b_i). All jobs in the system, regardless of their type, share the processor and receive equal fractions of the service capacity.

Let W, L and $W(x)$ be the overall average response time (all jobs combined), the total average number of jobs in the system and the average response time for a job length x (regardless of type), respectively. Due to the insensitive property of the PS strategy, Formulae 7.19–7.21 continue to hold, with the overall average service time, b, and the total load, ρ, now given by:

$$b = (\lambda_1 b_1 + \lambda_2 b_2 + \ldots + \lambda_K b_K)/(\lambda_1 + \lambda_1 + \lambda_2 + \ldots + \lambda_K)$$

$$\rho = \lambda_1 b_1 + \lambda_2 b_2 + \ldots + \lambda_K b_K = \rho_1 + \rho_2 + \ldots + \rho_K$$

The average response time for a job of type i, W_i, and the average number of type i jobs in the system, L_i, are equal to

$$W_i = b_i/(1 - \rho) \qquad (7.22)$$

$$L_i = \rho_i/(1 - \rho) \qquad (7.23)$$

Note, that as far as the average type i performance is concerned, the influence of the other job types is expressed only through their total load. A similar statement can be made about the distribution of type i jobs in the system.

A further generalization of the PS model with non-homogeneous job population is to make the strategy 'discriminatory', rather than 'egalitarian'. A larger fraction of the service capacity could be allocated to one job type, and a smaller one to another, while still allowing all jobs in the system to receive service in parallel. In terms of the Round-Robin strategy, a larger quantum of service would be given to jobs of one type, and a smaller quantum to those of another. Then all quanta would shrink to zero in the same ratios. Unfortunately, such a generalization destroys the insensitivity property of the strategy and the results presented here are no longer valid. The discriminatory PS model is much more difficult to analyse than the egalitarian one (see Fayolle *et al.*, 1980).

7.5 Systems with priorities

It is often desirable to treat jobs of different types unequally, giving a better quality of service to some jobs at the expense of others. This is usually done by operating some sort of priority scheduling strategy. Such a strategy is characterized by the fact that its scheduling decisions are based on a set of priority indices, one of which is allocated to each job type.

We shall consider an M/G/1 model with K job types numbered $1,2,\ldots,K$. Jobs of type i arrive in a Poisson stream with rate λ_i and have generally distributed service times with mean b_i and second moment $M_{2i}(i=1,2,\ldots K)$. There is a separate queue for each job type, and a single server (*Figure 7.5*).

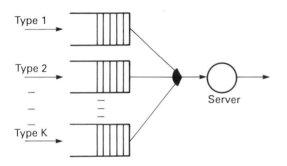

Figure 7.5

The job type numbers serve as priority indices: type 1 has top priority, type 2 second top, etc. Whenever a new service is to be started, the job selected is the one at the head of the highest priority (lowest index) non-empty queue. Hence, a type i job may start service only if queues $1,2,\ldots,i-1$ are empty ($i=2,3,\ldots,K$). Within each queue, jobs wait in FIFO order.

Priority scheduling strategies differ in the actions they take when a higher priority job arrives and finds a lower priority one in service. One possibility is simply to place the new job in its queue and await the scheduling decision that will be made on completing the current service. Such a strategy is called 'non-preemptive', or 'head-of-the-line' priority scheduling strategy. If, on the other hand, a new arrival is allowed to interrupt the current service and occupy the server immediately, then the strategy is called 'preemptive'.

The preemptive priority scheduling strategies are further classified according to the way they deal with interrupted jobs. The latter remain at the heads of their respective queues until the server can attend to them again. If, when that happens, the interrupted service is continued from the point of interruption, the strategy is said to be 'preemptive-resume'. If the service is restarted from the beginning, then the strategy is 'preemptive-repeat'. Preemptive-repeat scheduling strategies can be 'with re-sampling' or 'without re-sampling', depending on whether the restarted service is a new random one from the same distribution, or exactly the same one as before.

The most commonly used priority scheduling strategies are the non-preemptive and the preemptive-resume ones. We shall examine first the performances of the non-preemptive priority strategy, by generalizing the approach used in the analysis of the single M/G/1 queue.

Let us tag an incoming job of type i, and consider the delays to which it may be subjected. The tagged job may find a service in progress, in which case it will have to wait until the latter is completed. Denote the average of that delay by W_0. Also, there may be jobs of priority i, or, higher, already queued. Let their

total average service time be W_{qi}. Furthermore, all jobs of priority higher than i that arrive while the tagged job is waiting in its queue, will be served before it. Denote that average delay by W_{pi}. Finally, there is the tagged job's own service time. Thus, the average response time for a job of type i, W_i, can be expressed as a sum of four components:

$$W_i = W_0 + W_{qi} + W_{pi} + b_i , \quad i = 1,2,\ldots,K \qquad (7.24)$$

Of course, the component W_{pi} does not exist for $i=1$.

At the arrival instant of the tagged job, there is an average of L_j jobs of type j in the system, of which $\rho_j = \lambda_j b_j$ are in service and $L_j - \rho_j$ are waiting in queue j, for $j=1,2,\ldots,K$ (PASTA property and the Utilization Law). The quantities L_j are related to the response times W_j by Little's theorem: $L_j = \lambda_j W_j$. If a job of type j is found in service, then its average remaining service time, or residual lifetime, is equal to $M_{2j}/(2b_j)$ (see Equation 7.12). Hence we can write

$$W_0 = \sum_{j=1}^{K} \rho_j M_{2j}/(2b_j) = (1/2) \sum_{j=1}^{K} \lambda_j M_{2j} \qquad (7.25)$$

Similarly, since each of the waiting type j jobs takes an average of b_j to serve, we have:

$$W_{qi} = \sum_{j=1}^{i} (L_j - \rho_j)b_j = \sum_{j=1}^{i} (\lambda_j W_j - \rho_j)b_j \qquad (7.26)$$

To find the average delay imposed by higher priority jobs which arrive while the tagged job is waiting, we argue as follows. The average waiting time of the tagged job is $W_i - b_i$; during that time, an average of $\lambda_j(W_i - b_i)$ jobs of type j arrive ($j < i$); each of these jobs takes an average of b_j to serve. Therefore:

$$W_{pi} = (W_i - b_i) \sum_{j=1}^{i-1} \rho_j \qquad (7.27)$$

Substituting Relations 7.26 and 7.27 into 7.24 yields a set of linear equations for the unknown quantities W_i. That set is triangular and can easily be solved by consecutive elimination. The resulting solution is as follows:

$$W_i = b_i + W_0 [(1 - \sum_{j=1}^{i-1} \rho_j)(1 - \sum_{j=1}^{i} \rho_j)]^{-1} , \quad i = 1,2,\ldots,K \quad (7.28)$$

where W_0 is given by Relation 7.25 (the first sum in the right-hand side vanishes when $i=1$).

The above expressions are known as 'Cobham's formulae', (Cobham, 1954; Conway *et al.*, 1967). They have some important implications for the performance of the non-preemptive scheduling strategy. First, it is clear that a steady state exists for the entire system if the total load, $\rho_1 + \rho_2 + \ldots + \rho_K$, is less than 1. However, because of the priority scheduling, it is possible for job types $1,2,\ldots,i$ to have finite average response times, while those for types $i+1, i+2,\ldots,K$ are infinite. This happens if $\rho_1 + \rho_2 + \ldots + \rho_i < 1$, but $\rho_1 + \rho_2 + \ldots + \rho_i + \rho_{i+1} > 1$.

The second consequence of Cobham's formulae is that, as far as the performance of type i jobs is concerned, all jobs of types $1,2,\ldots,i-1$ can be lumped together into a single 'high priority' type, and all jobs of types $i+1, i+2,\ldots,K$ can be lumped together into a single 'low priority' type. Changing the scheduling strategy within the high priority type, and/or within the low priority type, has no influence on jobs of type i.

Suppose now that the priority strategy is preemptive-resume. Consider, once more, the average response time of a tagged job of type i. It is convenient to express this as a sum of two components:

$$W_i = V_i + R_i, \ i = 1, 2, \ldots, K \tag{7.29}$$

where V_i and R_i are the average intervals between the arrival of the tagged job and the start of its service, and between the start and the end of the service, respectively. The latter interval includes all service interruptions. We shall call V_i the 'waiting time', and R_i the 'residence time', of the tagged job.

Since jobs of types $i + 1, i + 2, \ldots 2, \ldots, K$ can be interrupted by the tagged job, they have no effect at all on W_i. On the other hand, until the tagged job starts its service, the fact that the priorities of types $1, 2, \ldots, i - 1$ are preemptive, is immaterial. Therefore, the waiting time of the tagged job is the same as it would have been if the priorities were non-preemptive and if types $i + 1, i + 2, \ldots, K$ did not exist. Modifying Relation 7.28 appropriately, we get:

$$V_i = W_{0i} [(1 - \sum_{j=1}^{i-1} \rho_j)(1 - \sum_{j=1}^{i} \rho_j)]^{-1} \tag{7.30}$$

where W_{0i} is a suitably restricted from of Relation 7.25:

$$W_{0i} = (1/2) \sum_{j=1}^{i} \lambda_j M_{2j} \tag{7.31}$$

To find the residence time, R_i, note that it consists of the service time of the tagged job, plus all service times of higher priority jobs that arrive during the residence time. Hence:

$$R_i = b_i + R_i \sum_{j=1}^{i-1} \rho_j, \text{ or } R_i = b_i (1 - \sum_{j=1}^{i-1} \rho_j)^{-1} \tag{7.32}$$

Substituting Relations 7.30–32 into 7.29, we obtain the desired result for preemptive-resume priorities:

$$W_i = [b_i + W_{0i}(1 - \sum_{j=1}^{i} \rho_j)^{-1}](1 - \sum_{j=1}^{i-1} \rho_j)^{-1}, \ i = 1, 2, \ldots, K \tag{7.33}$$

The overall average response time, W, under either the non-preemptive or preemptive priority scheduling strategy, is obtained easily from the above results. It suffices to note that an arbitrary incoming job is of type i with probability λ_i / λ, where $\lambda = \lambda_1 + \lambda_2 + \ldots + \lambda_K$ is the total arrival rate. Hence, W can be expressed as a weighted average of the form:

$$W = (1/\lambda) \sum_{i=1}^{K} \lambda_i W_i \tag{7.34}$$

An interesting optimization problem arises in these scheduling strategies. Given the arrival and service requirement characteristics of the K job types, how should priorities be assigned to them in order to minimize a cost function which is a linear combination of the average response times:

$$C = \sum_{i=1}^{K} c_i W_i \tag{7.35}$$

(the coefficients c_i reflect the relative importance of the different job types). It turns out that the optimal non-preemptive priority assignment is obtained as follows. Renumber the job types, so that they satisfy the inequalities $(c_1/\rho_1) \geqslant (c_2/\rho_2) \geqslant \ldots \geqslant (c_K/\rho_K)$. Then give top priority to type 1, second to type 2, ..., bottom

priority to type K. The same recipe is valid in the preemptive priority case, provided that the required service times are exponentially distributed (for a more extensive discussion of this problem, see Gelenbe and Mitrani (1980) and Walrand (1988)).

In the special case when the cost function is the linear combination 7.34, i.e., when the object is to minimize the overall average response time, the above result indicates that the optimal priority assignment is the one for which $b_1 \leqslant b_2 \leqslant \ldots \leqslant b_K$. In other words, the shortest jobs should be given top priority, the next shortest second top, etc. That scheduling strategy is known as 'Shortest-Expected-Processing-Time' (SEPT).

7.6 Open queuing networks

In the models considered so far, the processing of jobs has taken place at a single service centre; completion of a service there has meant the completion of a job. It is important, however, to be able to model systems where processing is distributed over a number of service centres, or nodes. A job may need service at one of the nodes, then go to another node and ask for more service there, etc. At every node there could be congestion and delays caused by other jobs competing for the local server or servers. An appropriate tool for modelling such systems is a network of queues.

A queuing network can be thought of as a connected directed graph, where the nodes represent service centres and the arcs indicate one-step moves that jobs may take from node to node. Each node has its own queue, served according to some scheduling strategy. Jobs may be of different types and may follow different routes through the network. An arc without origin leading into a node indicates that jobs arrive externally into that node. Similarly, an arc without destination leading out of a node indicates that jobs may leave the system after completing service at that node. If it is possible to move in one step from node i to node j, and also from node j to node i, then those nodes are connected by two arcs in opposite directions. A feedback arc indicates that jobs may rejoin a node after completing service there, and ask for a new service. Figure 7.6 illustrates a four-node network, with external arrivals into nodes 1 and 2, departures from nodes 1 and 3, bi-directional flow between nodes 1 and 3 and feedback from node 2 into itself.

To complete the specification of a queuing network model, it is necessary to make assumptions about the nature of the

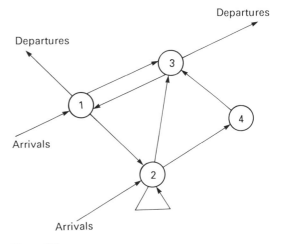

Figure 7.6

external arrival streams, the routing of jobs among nodes and, for each node, the number of parallel servers available, the required service times and the scheduling strategy. Not all such assumptions lead to numerically tractable models, but when they do not, approximate solutions are often possible.

A queuing network is said to be 'open', if there are external arrivals and departures, and if out of every node there is a path that leads eventually to the outside world (e.g. Figure 7.6). A network without external arrivals and departures, but with a fixed numer of jobs circulating forever among the nodes, is 'closed'. If the network is open with respect to some job types and closed with respect to others, then it is called 'mixed'.

Let us consider now the most basic open queuing network model. There are N nodes, numbered 1, 2, ..., N, each containing a single server. (We make this last assumption for simplicity; it is not difficult to relax it by allowing different numbers of parallel servers at the different nodes.) Service times at node i are distributed exponentially with mean b_i; the scheduling strategy is FIFO ($i = 1,2, \ldots, N$).

All jobs are statistically identical and independent of each other. Jobs arrive externally into node i in a Poisson stream with rate γ_i. Whenever a job completes service at node i, it goes to node j with probability q_{ij} ($i,j = 1, 2, \ldots, N$), regardless of its past history. All such transfers are assumed to be instantaneous (in cases where this last assumption appears unreasonable, it is quite easy to introduce transfer delays by means of artificial intermediate nodes). The probabilities q_{ij} are called the 'routing probabilities' of the network; they satisfy the inequalities $q_{i1} + q_{i2} + \ldots + q_{iN} \leqslant 1$, for all i. A job leaves the network after node i with probability $q_{i0} = 1 - (q_{i1} + q_{i2} + \ldots + q_{iN})$.

The above assumptions define a 'Jackson queuing network', (Jackson, 1957). We are interested in evaluating the behaviour of that network in the steady state. Among the performance measures that could be of interest in this connection are: the utilization of node i, U_i: the average number of jobs at node i, L_i; the average time a job spends at node i per visit there, w_i; the average number of visits a job makes to node i, V_i; the conditional average time a job spends in the network, given that it has just joined node i, W_i; the overall average time a job spends in the network, W.

As a first step towards determining those performance measures, it is necessary to find the total arrival rates of jobs into node i, λ_i, for $i = 1,2, \ldots, N$ (that total includes arrivals from other nodes and feedbacks, as well as external arrivals). Bearing in mind that, in the steady state, the total arrival rate into a node is equal to the total departure rate from that node, and that, out of all departures from node j, a fraction q_{ji} go to node i, we can write:

$$\lambda_i = \gamma_i + \sum_{j=1}^{N} \lambda_j q_{ji} , \ i = 1,2, \ldots, N \tag{7.36}$$

Equations 7.36 are called the 'traffic equations' of the queuing network. In an open network, the arrival rates λ_i are determined uniquely by the traffic equations. Note that the required service times do not appear in Equations 7.36; only the external arrival rates and the routing probabilities. Moreover, the validity of these equations does not depend on the external arrival streams being Poisson.

Having obtained λ_i by solving the set of traffic equations, the offered load at node i, ρ_i, is given by $\rho_i = \lambda_i b_i$. Since there is a single server at each node, the condition for existence of steady state is $\rho_i < 1$, $i = 1,2, \ldots, N$. When that condition is satisfied, the probability that the server at node i is busy is equal to the offered load, according to the Utilization Law (Section 7.2). Thus, $U_i = \rho_i$, $i = 1,2, \ldots, N$.

The average number of visits that a job makes to node i is found by arguing as follows. The total average number of

external jobs that arrive into the network per unit time is equal to $\gamma = \gamma_1 + \gamma_2 + \ldots + \gamma_N$. Each of these jobs makes an average of v_i visits to node i. Therefore, the total average number of arrivals to node i per unit time is γv_i, which must be equal to λ_i Hence:

$$v_i = \lambda_i /(\gamma_1 + \gamma_2 + \ldots + \gamma_N) , \ i = 1,2, \ldots, N \tag{7.37}$$

All of the above results are valid for arbitrary distributions of interarrival and service times. However, to find the performance measures L_i and W_i, one has to use the assumptions of the Jackson model. Then the following property provides the solution:

Theorem (Jackson). Node i in a Jackson queuing network behaves like an independent M/M/I queue with arrival rate λ_i and average required service times b_i, where λ_i is the solution of the traffic Equations 7.36.

(If, instead of a single server, node i contains n_i parallel servers, that number being either finite or infinite, then M/M/1 should be replaced by M/M/n_i.)

Despite its apparent simplicity, this theorem is rather remarkable. The fact that the queue sizes at any pair of nodes, even directly connected ones, are independent of each other, is somewhat counter-intuitive. Also, it can be demonstrated that when the internal and external arrivals into a node are merged together, the resulting stream is not, in general, Poisson. Yet the node behaves as if it was!

Using Jackson's theorem, along with the M/M/I results (7.16) and (7.17), we can write:

$$w_i = b_i /(1 - \rho_i) , \ i = 1,2, \ldots, N \tag{7.38}$$

and

$$L_i = \rho_i /(1 - \rho_i) , \ i = 1,2, \ldots, N \tag{7.39}$$

The total average number of jobs in the network, L, is determined by summing Equation 7.39 over all nodes. Then the overall average response time, W, can be obtained by applying Little's theorem to the entire network: $W = L/\gamma$. Alternatively, since a job makes an average of v_i visits to node i, and on each visit remains for an average period of w_i, one could write:

$$W = \sum_{i=1}^{N} v_i w_i \tag{7.40}$$

The two expressions are equivalent, in view of Equation 7.37.

Let us now tag a job that has just joined node i, and consider the average time that it will remain in the network, W_i. Because the routing is memoryless, it does not matter whether the arrival was external, or from another node. First, the tagged job has to pass through node i, which takes an average of w_i. Then, if it goes to node j (which happens with probability q_{ij}), its average remaining time in the network will be W_j. Hence:

$$W_i = w_i + \sum_{j=1}^{N} q_{ij} W_j , \ i = 1,2, \ldots, N \tag{7.41}$$

This set of equations determines the W_is uniquely.

The results of this section can be generalized in several directions. The service rate at a node can be an arbitrary function of the number of jobs present there. Jobs could be of different types, with different external arrival rates, routing matrices and (perhaps) required service times. Certain non-FIFO scheduling strategies may be allowed. For details on these and other generalizations see, for instance, Gelenbe and Mitrani (1980), Kelly (1979) and Walrand (1988).

7.7 Closed queuing networks

It is often desirable to evaluate systems where processing may take place at a number of nodes, and where the total number of jobs circulating among those nodes is kept constant over long periods of time. Such systems are modelled by closed queueing networks. Examples of applications include distributed systems with a fixed number of users and heavily loaded multiprogrammed systems operating a restrictive admission policy.

Consider a closed queuing network with N nodes and K jobs. Each node contains either a single server, or at least K parallel servers. In the latter case, the node is called a 'delay node', to emphasize the fact that jobs do not queue there. They are just delayed independently of each other. A delay node typically models a collection of user terminals with associated think periods.

The average service time at node i is b_i, $i = 1,2, \ldots , N$. The corresponding distribution is assumed to be exponential in the case of the single-server nodes, but may be general for the delay nodes. After completing service at node i, a job goes to node j with probability q_{ij}, regardless of past history. Since jobs do not leave the network, the routing probabilities satisfy $q_{i1} + q_{i2} + \ldots + q_{iN} = 1$, for all i. There are no external arrivals.

Denoting, as before, the total arrival rate into node i by λ_i, and repeating the argument leading to Relation 7.36, we obtain the closed network version of the traffic equations:

$$\lambda_i = \sum_{j=1}^{N} \lambda_j q_{ji} , \ i = 1,2, \ldots , N \tag{7.42}$$

Unfortunately, these equations are now homogeneous and their coefficient matrix is singular (all its row sums are zero). Consequently, the arrival rates λ_i can no longer be determined uniquely by solving the traffic equations. However, if any one of those rates is fixed, then the others would be determined in terms of it.

To solve the closed network model, we shall transform it into a conceptually open one, without disturbing its behaviour in any essential way. In a real system where the number of jobs is kept constant, it is not necessarily the same jobs that are present at all times. When a job is completed, it departs and is immediately replaced by a new one from outside. This is what will happen in our model. A special point, called the 'entry point', is introduced on one of the arcs in the network – say the arc from node j to node k. Whenever a job traverses that particular arc and passes through the entry point, it changes identity and becomes a new job. In other words, the job that left node j departs from the network, a new job enters immediately from outside and goes to node k. This exchange is illustrated in Figure 7.7.

Clearly, this modification of the model has no effect on performance measures like node utilizations, queue sizes or node delays. However, since jobs are now temporary entities, it is possible to talk about the average time a job spends in the network, W, the average number of visits a job makes to node i, v_i, and the network throughput, T (the average number of jobs entering, and leaving, the network per unit time). These 'open' performance measures depend in general, on where the entry point is. Also, W and T depend on the number of jobs in the network, K.

Let us restate the Relation 7.37 between the arrival rate and the visit number for a node (the total external arrival rate is now replaced by the throughput):

$$v_i = \lambda_i/T ; \ i = 1,2, \ldots , N \tag{7.43}$$

The fact that the v_is are proportional to the λ_is implies that the former also satisfy the traffic Equation 7.42. Thus, if one of the visit numbers could be obtained somehow, all the others would be determined by those equations. However, we do know that each job makes exactly one passage through the entry point (or along the arc from node j to node k) during its life in the network. On the other hand, each visit to node j is followed by such a passage with probability q_{jk}. Hence, $v_j q_{jk} = 1$, or:

$$v_j = 1/q_{jk} \tag{7.44}$$

This, together with Relation 7.42, determines all visit numbers. It is clear from the above procedure that those numbers depend on the position of the entry point, but not on the number of jobs, K.

A relation between the average number of jobs at node i, L_i, and the average time jobs spend there per visit, w_i, is provided by Little's theorem:

$$L_i = \lambda_i w_i = T v_i w_i ; \ i = 1,2, \ldots , N \tag{7.45}$$

Summing these over all nodes, and remembering that the total number of jobs in the network is K, we can write an expression for the throughput:

$$T = K/[\sum_{i=1}^{N} v_i w_i] \tag{7.46}$$

Consider now the average time a job spends at node i per visit. In the case of a delay node, when there is no queuing, w_i is equal to the average service time, b_i. If it is a single-server node, and the job finds an average of Y_i jobs already present, then w_i is equal to $(Y_i + 1)b_i$. Both cases can be combined by writing:

$$w_i = b_i(1 + \delta_i Y_i) ; \ i = 1,2, \ldots , N \tag{7.47}$$

where $\delta_i = 0$ if node i is a delay node, and $\delta_i = 1$ if it is a single-server node.

Equations 7.45, 7.46 and 7.47 would be sufficient to determine all performance measures if the averages L_i and Y_i could be related to each other. They are not equal. A job coming into a node of a closed network sees fewer jobs there, on the average, than a random observer looking at the same node. This is because the incoming job always sees at most $K - 1$ jobs at the node (it never sees itself). The desired relation is provided by the following result:

Arrival theorem (Sevcik and Mitrani, 1981). Let $S(K)$ be the state of a closed network with K jobs, seen by a random observer in the steady state. Also let $S^*(K)$ be the network state seen by a job in transit from one node to another (that job is considered to have left the former node but not to have joined the latter). Then $S^*(K)$ has the same distribution as $S(K-1)$.

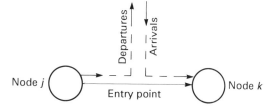

Figure 7.7

This rather intuitive assertion allows us to develop a solution for the model, based on a recurrence with respect to the job population size, K. From now on, the fact that the performance measures T, w_i, L_i and Y_i depend on K will be acknowledged explicitly by including that last parameter in parenthesis. As an immediate corollary of the arrival theorem, we can write:

$$Y_i(K) = L_i(K - 1) \; ; \; i = 1,2, \ldots , N \tag{7.48}$$

Then Equations 7.47, 7.46, and 7.45 can be rewritten in the form of recurrence relations in terms of K:

$$w_i(K) = b_i[1 + \delta_i L_i(K - 1)] \; ; \; i = 1,2, \ldots , N \tag{7.49}$$

$$T(K) = K/[\sum_{i=1}^{N} v_i w_i(K)] \tag{7.50}$$

$$L_i(K) = v_i T(K) w_i(K) \; ; \; i = 1,2, \ldots , N \tag{7.51}$$

The obvious initial conditions for an iterative solution procedure based on the above equations, are $L_i(0) = 0$ $(i = 1,2,\ldots, N)$. The first iteration yields $w_i(1)$, $T(1)$, and $L_i(1)$; the second gives $w_i(2)$, $T(2)$ and $L_i(2)$, and so on, until the desired population size is reached.

The total average time that a job spends at node i during its life in the network, $B_i(K)$, is given by:

$$B_i(K) = v_i w_i(K) \; ; \; i = 1,2, \ldots , N \tag{7.52}$$

Similarly, the total average service time that a job requires from node i, D_i, is equal to:

$$D_i = v_i b_i \; ; \; i = 1,2, \ldots , N \tag{7.53}$$

Sometimes the total average service requirements D_i can be estimated quite easily, either, by monitoring the real system or by extrapolating from other measurements. Those averages can then be given as model parameters, instead of the service times per visit, b_i, and the routing probabilities, q_{ij}. In that case, it is not necessary to solve the traffic equations and find the visit numbers. Indeed, combining Equations 7.52 and 7.53 with 7.49, 7.50 and 7.51, leads to a somewhat simpler recurrence schema which does not involve v_i, and where $w_i(K)$ and b_i are replaced by $B_i(K)$ and D_i, respectively:

$$B_i(K) = D_i[1 + \delta_i L_i(K - 1)] \; ; \; i = 1,2, \ldots , N \tag{7.54}$$

$$T(K) = K/[\sum_{i=1}^{N} B_i(K)] \tag{7.55}$$

$$L_i(K) = T(K) B_i(K) \; ; \; i = 1,2, \ldots , N \tag{7.56}$$

The average response time for the network (the total time a job spends in it), $W(K)$, can be obtained from any one of the following equations:

$$W(K) = \sum_{i=1}^{N} v_i w_i(K) = \sum_{i=1}^{N} B_i(K) = K/T(K) \tag{7.57}$$

Another performance measure which may be of interest in the context of a closed network is the utilization of node i, $U_i(K)$. According to the Utilization Law, this is equal to the offered load at node i, and may be evaluted from:

$$U_i(K) = \lambda_i b_i = T(K) v_i b_i = T(K) D_i \; ; \; i = 1,2, \ldots , N \tag{7.58}$$

This last result provides a simple upper bound on the network throughput in the steady state. Since the utilization of a server cannot exceed 1, we must have:

$$T(K) \leqslant \min(1/v_i b_i) = \min(1/D_i) \tag{7.59}$$

where the minimum is taken over all single-server nodes. In other words, the 'bottleneck' node limiting the network throughout is the single-server one for which the total average service requirement is the largest. Moreover, the above inequality becomes an equality when the population size K approaches infinity.

If node i is a delay note, then Relation 7.58 yields the average number of jobs, or busy servers there.

The solution procedures that we have described here are known in the literature as 'mean value analysis' (MVA) (Reiser and Lavenberg, 1980). There are other algorithms that can be used to solve closed queuing networks (see, for example, Bruell and Balbo (1980)). Whatever method is employed, the solution is likely to be computationally expensive when the model is large. For instance, the MVA recurrences require K iterations, with the evaluation of $2N + 1$ quantities at each iteration.

The numerical complexity of the solution can be reduced considerably if one is prepared to accept an approximate solution instead of an exact one. The idea is to eliminate the recursion altogether, by finding an approximate relation between the job-observed and random-observed averages, Y_i and L_i, at the same population level. One such relation that has been shown to work well is:

$$Y_i(K) = [(K - 1)/K] L_i(K) \; ; \; i = 1,2, \ldots , N \tag{7.60}$$

This expression is of course exact for $K = 1$. It is also asymptotically exact for large values of K. In the intermediate cases, it provides a reasonable approximation.

Substituting Relation 7.60 into 7.47 yields, together with 7.46 and 7.45, a set of $2N + 1$ non-linear equations with $2N + 1$ unknowns. These can be solved by existing methods.

The closed queuing network models that are amenable to analysis can be generalized both with respect to node structure and job behaviour. Among the texts that could be consulted in this connection are Kelly (1979), Mitrani (1987) and Walrand (1988). Solutions exist also for certain mixed networks, i.e. networks with external arrivals and departures for some job types, and fixed populations of other types.

7.8 Markov chains and processes, and their applications

It should be evident from the preceding sections that quite a lot can be learned about the performance of a system by considering only various averages, and the relations between them. However, it must be pointed out that there are many interesting questions which cannot be answered in this way. Those are questions concerning the distributions of certain random variables, e.g., 'What is the probability that there are n jobs in the queue?' or 'What is the probability that the response time of a job will (will not) exceed x seconds?'

To be able to address questions of this sort, it is necessary to study the evolution of the system state as a function of time. The appropriate tool for modelling such dynamic behaviour is a 'stochastic process'. This is defined as a family of random variables, $\{S_t, t \geq 0\}$, depending on a parameter t. The variable S_t represents the state of the system at time t, and the set of values that it takes is assumed to be finite or denumerable. Thus, the possible states of the process can be identified with (a subset of) the non-negative integers $0, 1, \ldots$

To characterize the short-term behaviour of the system, one would have to find the conditional distribution of S_t, given the initial state, S_0. If, on the other hand, the object of interest is the long-run, or steady-state behaviour, then the aim of the analysis would be to determine the limiting distribution of S_t as $t \to \infty$. The latter is independent of the initial state and is therefore easier to obtain.

The stochastic processes most commonly used in modelling are those possessing the 'Markov property', which can be stated in general terms as follows:

Given the state of the process at any moment in time, its subsequent behaviour is independent of its past history.

In other words, if u is an arbitrary moment in time, then the distribution of S_t for $t > u$ is completely determined by the state S_u, and is independent of the states S_t for $t < u$. When this property holds, the family $\{S_t, t \geq 0\}$ is called a 'Markov process'. In fact, the term 'Markov process' is usually reserved for the case when the time parameter is continuous, i.e. when a change of state may occur at any instant. When the time parameter is discrete, i.e. when the system state is observed at a sequence of time instants numbered 0, 1, ..., then the term 'Markov chain' is used instead. We shall examine this latter case first.

A Markov chain, $S = \{S_n, n = 0, 1, ...\}$, is completely described by a matrix $Q = (q_{ij})$, where the indices i and j range over the possible states of S. The element q_{ij} is the probability that S will be in state j at time $n + 1$, given that it was in state i at time n. These 'one-step transition probabilities' are assumed not to depend on n. Since every state transition brings the chain into one of its feasible states, each row of Q must sum up to 1.

A convenient diagrammatic representation of S is provided by a directed graph whose nodes correspond to the states of S. An arc from node i to node j indicates that the corresponding one-step transition probability is non-zero. That probability, q_{ij}, is shown on the arc. Such a graph is called the state diagram of the Markov chain. It should be emphasized perhaps, that despite a superficial similarity between a state diagram and a queuing network graph (Figure 7.6), the two are fundamentally different. The transitions that we are concerned with now are changes of state, whereas before they were physical movements of jobs.

As an example, consider a finite buffer with M locations, where items of information are inserted and removed at random. More precisely, during the nth time unit, one new item is placed into the buffer (if there is an empty location) with probability α. Such an insertion takes place independently of past history. Also one of the items present (if any) is removed with probability β, again independently of past history. Moreover, insertions and removals are independent of each other. However, if both an insertion and a removal event occur during the same time unit, the former is assumed to take place before the latter.

This buffer can be modelled by a Markov chain whose state at time n is the number of currently occupied locations in the buffer ($n = 0, 1, ...$). The above assumptions imply that if the chain is in state i at time n ($i = 0, 1, ..., M$), then at time $n + 1$ it may be in state $i + 1$ (an insertion occurs, but no removal; $i < M$), state $i - 1$ (a removal occurs, but no insertion; $i > 1$), or state i (all other cases). The corresponding state diagram is shown in Figure 7.8.

Thus, to construct a Markov chain model, one has to specify the state space and the one-step transition probability matrix. Having done that, the next object of interest is usually the probability distribution vector $p = (p_0, p_1, ...)$, where p_i is the long-term, or steady-state probability that the chain is found in state i ($i = 0, 1, ...$). The aim is to decide whether the steady-state distribution exists, and if so, to determine it. That aim is served

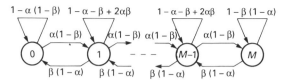

Figure 7.8

by the following fundamental result, which applies in most cases of practical interest:

Steady-state theorem for Markov chains. Let Q be the one-step transition probability matrix of a Markov chain. If the set of simultaneous linear equations

$$p = pQ \qquad (7.61)$$

has a non-negative solution whose elements sum up to 1, then that solution is unique and is the steady-state distribution of the Markov chain. Conversely, if the steady-state distribution exists, then it satisfies Relation 7.61.

For this theorem to be valid, the Markov chain should be 'irreducible' and 'aperiodic'. Irreducibility means that the chain should be able to pass from every state to every other state in a finite number of steps, with non-zero probability. Aperiodicity refers to the times of consecutive visits to a given state. These must not occur with a fixed interval (greater than 1) between successive visits. Most Markov chains used in modelling satisfy these two conditions.

Equation 7.61 is called the 'balance equation' of the Markov chain, whereas the requirement that the elements of p should sum up to 1 is referred to as the 'normalizing equation'. In practice, when solving for p, one of the balance equations is usually discarded and is replaced by the normalizing equation.

Balance equations have a simple and rather intuitive probabilistic interpretation, which also justifies their name. Perhaps the easiest way to explain it is in terms of the state diagram. Imagine that an arc from state i to state j carries a 'flow' of $p_i q_{ij}$ (this is the average number of transitions from i to j per unit time). Then the ith balance equation states that the probability p_i is equal to the total flow associated with all arcs leading into state i (including the feedback from i to i). Alternatively, it expresses the fact that the total flow into state i from other states (excluding state i), is equal to the total flow out of state i to other states.

Let us apply the steady-state theorem to the buffer example given above. Using the state diagram in Figure 7.8, we can easily write the set of balance equations:

$$\alpha(1 - \beta)p_0 = \beta(1 - \alpha)p_1 \qquad (7.62a)$$

$$[\alpha(1 - \beta) + \beta(1 - \alpha)]p_i = \alpha(1 - \beta)p_{i-1} + \beta(1 - \alpha)p_{j+1};$$
$$i = 1, 2, ..., M - 1 \qquad (7.62b)$$

$$\beta(1 - \alpha)p_M = \alpha(1 - \beta)p_{M-1} \qquad (7.62c)$$

The solution of these equations, with the addition of the normalizing equation, is readily seen to be a truncated geometric distribution:

$$p_i = (1 - r)r^i/(1 - r^{M+1}), \; i = 0, 1, ..., M - 1 \qquad (7.63)$$

where $r = \alpha(1 - \beta)/[\beta(1 - \alpha)]$. Having got the steady-state distribution, one can easily obtain various performance measures like average number of items present, throughput, probability of rejecting an item etc.

Consider now the case when changes of state occur in continuous time subject to the Markov property, i.e. when the system behaviour is modelled by a Markov process, $S = \{S_t, t \geq 0\}$. This is perhaps the more important case from our point of view, since continuous time models arise more frequently in queueing theory applications.

The Markov property in continuous time is closely related to the exponential distribution. The latter is 'memoryless', in the following sense: if the duration of some activity is distributed exponentially with parameter a, i.e. if its distribution function is:

$$F(x) = 1 - e^{-ax}$$

and if that activity is observed to be in progress, then the time until completion is distributed exponentially with parameter a, regardless of how much time has already elapsed (see the discussion on residual lifetimes Section 7.3). Moreover, the exponential distribution is the only continuous distribution which has the memoryless property. Thus, in order to model a queueing system as a Markov process, various random variables like required service times, interarrival times, etc., have to be assumed to be exponentially distributed.

In characterizing a Markov process, the role of the one-step transition probabilities is played by the so-called 'instantaneous transition rates', a_{ij}. For $j \neq i$, these rates are defined by saying that if at time t the process is in state i, then a short time later, at time $t + \Delta t$, it will be in state j with probability $a_{ij}\Delta t + o(\Delta t)$ where $o(\Delta t)$ is a quantity that tends to 0 faster than Δt $(i, j = 0, 1, \ldots, j \neq i)$. The sum $a_i = a_{i0} + a_{i1} + \ldots$, is called the 'instantaneous transition rate out of state i'. The matrix $\mathbf{A}$, whose off-diagonal elements are the instantaneous transition rates a_{ij} and the ith diagonal element is by definition equal to $-a_i$, is called the 'generator matrix' of the Markov process. Each row of the generator matrix sums up to 0.

The evolution of a Markov process with a generator matrix $\mathbf{A}$ can be described as follows: having entered a state, say i, the process remains in it for a period of time which is distributed exponentially with parameter a_i; then the process moves to a different state, j, with probability a_{ij}/a_i; remains in the new state for an exponentially distributed period with parameter a_j, etc.

The state diagram of a Markov process, like that of a Markov chain, is a directed graph with nodes representing states and arcs representing possible transitions between them. An arc from state i to state j is now marked with the instantaneous transition rate, a_{ij}. There is no arc leading from state i to state i, because a transition out of a state necessarily implies an entry into a different state.

To study the long-term behaviour of a Markov process, we have a tool which is analogous to the steady-state theorem for Markov chains. The process is specified by its generator matrix, $\mathbf{A}$, and the object of interest is the vector $\boldsymbol{p} = (p_0, p_1, \ldots)$, where p_i is the steady-state probability that is found in state i($i = 0, 1, \ldots$).

Steady-state theorm for Markov processes. If the set of simultaneous linear equations:

$$\boldsymbol{p}\mathbf{A} = 0 \tag{7.64}$$

has a non-negative solution whose elements sum up to 1, then that solution is unique and is the steady-state distribution of the Markov process. Conversely, if the steady-state distribution exists, then it satisfies Relation 7.64.

Again there is a requirement that the process should a be irreducible, i.e., that starting in any state, there should be non-

zero probability of eventually reaching any other state. The question of aperiodicity does not arise in continuous time.

Equation 7.64 is the 'balance equation' of the Markov process. If we define the 'flow' associated with the arc from state i to state j as $p_i a_{ij}$ (i.e., the average number of transitions from state i to state j per unit time), then the ith balance equation can be interpreted as saying that the total flow out of state i is equal to the total flow into state i.

The fact that the elements of $\boldsymbol{p}$ sum up to 1 supplies the normalizing equation which ensures that the solution of Equation 7.64 is unique.

Let us examine now a rather special, yet non-trivial, Markov process which has had numerous applications in modelling various queuing systems. This is the 'birth-and-death' process, which can be thought of as representing the size of some changing population. The possible transitions out of state i are to state $i + 1$ (birth), with instantaneous rate λ_i, or to state $i - 1$ (death; $i > 1$), with instantaneous rate μ_i; $i = 0, 1, \ldots$. The state diagram of the birth-and-death process is shown in Figure 7.9.

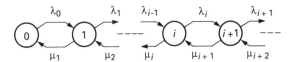

Figure 7.9

The steady-state probabilities, p_i, that the process is in state i, satisfy the following set of balance equations (total flow out of state i equals flow into state i):

$$\lambda_0 p_0 = \mu_1 p_1 \tag{7.65a}$$

$$(\lambda_i + \mu_i)p_i = \lambda_{i-1}p_{i-1} + \mu_{i+1}p_{i+1}, \ i = 1, 2, \ldots \tag{7.65b}$$

From these equations, by successive elimination, all probabilities p_i can be expressed in terms of p_0:

$$p_i = p_0 \prod_{j=1}^{i} r_j, \ i = 1, 2, \ldots \tag{7.66}$$

where $r_j = \lambda_{j-1}/\mu_j$. The normalizing equation then yields:

$$p_0 = \left[1 + \sum_{i=1}^{\infty} \prod_{j=1}^{i} r_j\right]^{-1} \tag{7.67}$$

Clearly Relation 7.67 will only produce a non-zero value for p_0 (and hence for all other probabilities), if the infinite series which appears in its right-hand side converges. That convergence is therefore the necessary and sufficient condition for existence of steady state.

Consider a few applications of the birth-and-death process. If the birth and death rates are independent of the state, i.e. if $\lambda_i = \lambda$, $\mu_i = \mu$ for all i, then we have a model of the $M/M/1$ queue with arrival rate λ and average service times $1/\mu$. The process is in state i when there are i jobs in the system. Transitions from state i to state $i + 1$ correspond to arrivals of new jobs, while those from state i to state $i - 1$ correspond to departures. The formulae for the steady-state probabilities, 7.66 and 7.67, reduce to:

$$p_i = (1 - \rho)\rho^i, \ i = 0, 1, \ldots, \tag{7.68}$$

where $\rho = \lambda/\mu$ is the offered load. The condition for existence of steady-state is $\rho < 1$.

Thus, the steady-state number of jobs in the $M/M/1$ system is distributed geometrically. The performance measures that were obtained by mean value arguments in Section 7.3 can also be derived from Equation 7.68. In addition, the latter implies that the distribution of the response time of a job in the $M/M/1$ queue is exponential with parameter $\mu - \lambda$ (mean $1/(\mu - \lambda)$).

Suppose now that the rates of death depend on the state in the following special way: $\mu_i = i\mu$ for $i < n$, and $\mu_i = n\mu$ for $i \geq n$ (the birth rates are still state-independent, $\lambda_i = \lambda$). This is a model of the $M/M/n$ queue: job arrival rate λ, average required service time $1/\mu$ and n parallel servers. When the number of jobs in the system, i, is less than n, the instantaneous departure rate is $i\mu$ because there are i busy servers; when i is greater than or equal to n, the departure rate is $n\mu$ because all n servers are busy.

The steady-state distribution of the number of jobs in the $M/M/n$ queue is given by:

$$p_i = (\rho^i/i!)p_0 , \quad i = 0, 1, \ldots, n-1 \tag{7.69a}$$

$$p_i = (\rho^i n^{n-i}/n!)p_0, \quad i = n, n+1, \ldots \tag{7.69b}$$

where

$$p_0 = \left\{ \sum_{j=0}^{n-1} (\rho^j/j!) + \rho^n/[(n-1)!(n-\rho)] \right\}^{-1} \tag{7.70}$$

The condition for existence of steady-state is $n - \rho > 0$ (see also Section 7.2).

Various performance measures, such as average number of jobs in the system, average response time, etc., can be derived from this distribution. Another quantity of interest in this context is the probability, q, that an incoming job will find at least n jobs in the system and will therefore have to wait. We have:

$$q = \sum_{j=n}^{\infty} p_j = p_0 \rho^n/[(n-1)!(n-\rho)] \tag{7.71}$$

with p_0 given by Equation 7.70. This expression is known as 'Erlang's delay formula'.

Finally, consider a finite birth-and-death model. The birth rates are constant, $\lambda_i = \lambda$, for $i \leq n$, and are 0 for $i > n$. The death rates are $\mu_i = i\mu$ for $i \leq n$, and are 0 for $i > n$. This is a model of a telephone exchange with n lines, call arrival rate λ and average call duration $1/\mu$. Up to n calls may be in progress, and when all lines are busy, new arrivals are rejected and are lost.

The steady-state distribution of the number of calls in progress is given by Equation 7.69a including $i = n$, with:

$$p_0 = \left\{ \sum_{j=0}^{n} (\rho^j/j!) \right\}^{-1} \tag{7.72}$$

The probability that an incoming call will find all lines busy and will be lost, is equal to:

$$p_n = (\rho^n/n!) \left\{ \sum_{j=0}^{n} (\rho^j/j!) \right\}^{-1} \tag{7.73}$$

This is the 'Erlang's loss formula'.

7.9 Further study

There are many books covering different aspects of queuing theory and its applications. A self-contained introduction to the subject that does not assume much mathematical background can be found in Mitrani (1987). A somewhat more advanced and considerably more extensive presentation (but pre-dating many of the queuing network developments), is that of Kleinrock (1975). There are also various specialized texts. A unified methodology for analysing queuing systems with priorities and service interruptions is described in Conway, Maxwell and Miller (1967). The fullest and most mathematically rigorous treatment of single-server queuing systems is in Cohen (1982). The most recent and thorough coverage of queuing networks is that of Walrand (1988), while Kelly (1979) gives many of the earlier theoretical advances. The three last mentioned books require quite a solid mathematical background of the reader.

The basis for queuing theory is in probability and stochastic processes. There is of course a large literature on both of these subjects, but here it is enough to mention one book for each. Perhaps the best introduction to probability theory is Feller (1968). The theory of stochastic processes, including renewal, Poisson and Markov, is well presented in Cinlar (1975).

7.10 References

Bruell, S. C. and Balbo, G. (1980) *Computational Algorithms for Closed Queuing Networks,* North-Holland

Cobham, A. (1954) Priority assignments in waiting line problems. *Operations Research,* **2**

Cinlar, E. (1975) *Introduction to Stochastic Processes,* Prentice-Hall

Cohen, J. W. (1982) *The Single Server Queue,* 2nd. ed., North-Holland

Conway, R. W., Maxwell, W. L. and Miller, L. W. (1967) *Theory of Scheduling,* Addison-Wesley

Fayolle, G., Mitrani, I. and Iasnogorodski, R. (1980) Sharing a processor among many job classes, *J.A.C.M.,* **27**

Feller, W. (1968) *An Introduction to Probability Theory and Its Applications,* John Wiley

Gelenbe, E and Mitrani, I. (1980) *Analysis and Synthesis of Computer Systems,* Academic Press

Jackson, J. R. (1957) Networks of waiting lines. *Operations Research,* **5**

Kelly, F. P. (1979) *Reversibility and Stochastic Networks,* John Wiley

Kleinrock, L. (1975) *Queuing Systems,* Vol. 1, John Wiley

Little, J. D. C. (1961) A proof of the queuing formula $L = \lambda W$. *Operations Research,* **9**

Mitrani, I. (1987) *Modelling of Computer and Communication Systems,* Cambridge University Press

Reiser, M. and Lavenberg, S. S. (1980) Mean value analysis for closed multichain queuing networks. *J.A.C.M.,* **27**

Sevcik, K. C. and Mitrani, I. (1981) The distribution of queuing network states at input and output instants. *J.A.C.M.,* **28**

Walrand, J. (1988) *An Introduction to Queuing Networks,* Prentice-Hall

8

Numerical computation

Peter J L Wallis
University of Bath

Contents

8.1 Introduction

Many important computer applications fall into the category of numerical (scientific) computation, which broadly embraces any computing in which a substantial amount of numerical processing takes place. Applications of numerical computation range from simple, everyday engineering computations to huge computations for such applications as weather forecasting. In larger applications, the numerical performance attainable with large special-purpose computers ('number crunchers') is a limiting factor on what can be achieved. The field may be characterized as concerned with numerical calculations derived from problems that are mathematically formulated.

Software production for numerical computation differs from conventional software engineering in at least two respects. First, there is an understandable preoccupation with choice of algorithm. Indeed, the whole of the related discipline of numerical analysis is concerned with the development of suitable algorithms for the computation of numerical results corresponding to various mathematically-formulated problems. Second, the details of number representation and the precise properties of the available arithmetic operations are far more important than in most software engineering practice.

The overall design of software for numerical computation inevitably involves several skills that are beyond the training of the typical software engineer. The selection of an appropriate algorithm for a given numerical computation requires specialist skills in numerical analysis. Even in apparently straightforward applications appropriate specialist help can be very useful. Discussion of numerical analysis is outside the scope of this chapter, although some idea of the variety of techniques that might be applied in finding suitable algorithms is provided by Section 8.7 below.

Once an algorithm has been selected, special care in programming may be needed as non-integer quantities are typically represented with limited accuracy within computers. Here again specialist assistance should be sought where possible, although basic principles of such programming are explicable in terms of the characteristics of floating-point arithmetic. An introduction to this subject is given here.

The rest of this chapter is devoted to a discussion of computer arithmetic, with a particular emphasis on floating-point arithmetic and how it should affect the detailed programming of numerical computations. In considering issues affecting the use, first, of single arithmetic operations and then of sequences of such operations, we will be led to a discussion of some numerical analysis issues. Full consideration of these issues is quite outside both the present scope and the area of competence of the typical software engineer.

8.2 Computer arithmetic systems

A very wide variety of different kinds of computer arithmetic is currently available. For example, virtually all computers offer integer arithmetic, while one or more floating-point systems (such as single- and double-length floating-point arithmetic) are frequently featured. There are also more specialized forms of computer arithmetic, such as interval computation (discussed later), and numerous experimental arithmetic systems. In general, a particular arithmetic system can be supported by hardware, software, or some software/hardware combination. So a computer arithmetic system can be any specific combination of the hardware or software for the arithmetic operations and the associated scheme for representing numbers as bit strings within the machine.

Virtually all computers support the four basic integer arithmetic operations, if only because these are required for indexing and addressing. Computer integer arithmetic is typically exact, with two exceptions. First, the range of integers that can be represented is not infinite but is bounded above and below. Second, the result of an integer division is usually given as a quotient and remainder, since fractions are not representable within a scheme for integers only. Note that as only a finite range of integers can be represented, the product of two integers may be too large for the representation scheme. In such cases an overflow condition is usually signalled. Integer arithmetic is adequate for many computing applications, provided care is taken to keep the integer quantities concerned within the available range. Furthermore, any rounding or inaccuracies that do arise must be handled carefully in a consistent way. For example, calculations involving currencies can be handled using integer arithmetic and working in terms of the smallest unit involved, provided rounding errors like those involved in currency conversions and interest calculations are properly handled. Suitable methods for rounding and for keeping the integer quantities concerned within the representable range are generally quite easily devised once the problems are fully appreciated, and integer arithmetic is perfectly satisfactory for many software engineering applications.

The handling of currency quantities in terms of multiples of the smallest unit involved suggests a variant of integer arithmetic, in which quantities are still represented as integers but with an implied decimal (binary) point at some fixed place within them. For example, a length in metres might be represented as an integer number of millimetres, with an implied point in the appropriate position. This type of working is known as fixed-point arithmetic, with the fixed point most frequently being taken to be at the left-most end of the representable integers, so all fixed-point quantities lie between 0 and 1. Fixed-point addition and substraction are exactly like their integer counterparts, but multiplication and division are different. In fixed-point multiplication the most significant half of the double-length product is retained, instead of the least significant half. This means that overflow is impossible but underflow (the returning of a zero result to indicate a quantity too small to represent) is a possibility. In fixed-point division, overflow occurs unless the divisor is greater in magnitude than the dividend.

Fixed-point arithmetic has been used successfully for many numerical computations, but the constant need for the scaling of results to avoid overflow and underflow makes its use tedious and error-prone. It is rarely used for numerical computation, except in special cases, e.g. for the few computers that do not offer floating-point instructions. The use of floating-point arithmetic, in which the operations themselves take care of scaling within the available range and accuracy of representable numbers, is far simpler, and floating-point arithmetic is the preferred choice for the vast majority of contemporary numerical computations. For this reason, the following sections of this chapter are concerned exclusively with floating-point arithmetic.

It is important at this point to note one major difference between integer arithmetic on the one hand, and fixed- and floating-point arithmetic on the other.

In integer arithmetic, all the basic arithmetic operations are accurate, in the sense that they all deliver exactly the same result as the corresponding mathematical operations, provided only that the operands and the result of the operation are within the range of representable integers. Further, there are no representation errors involved in integer arithmetic. For integers within the representable range there is no possible loss of accuracy in conversions between an integer quantity on an external medium and its representation as a bit string within a computer

These properties are not true of fixed- and floating-point arithmetic, because these support fixed numbers of significant digits of accuracy. Thus they are typically prone both to representation errors and to errors associated with the basic arithmetic operations. Such errors can be avoided in special cases – for example, many floating-point systems incorporate accurate arithmetic for small integers – but in general they are unavoidable. These basic facts about inaccuracy are at the heart of most, if not all, of the problems of numerical computation, and will be discussed further in the following sections.

Having introduced numerical computation and computer arithmetic systems in general, much more detailed consideration of floating-point arithmetic follows, as it is of central importance for numerical computations. Floating-point arithmetic is introduced in detail, both in general terms and in terms of typical implementations. Subsequently the problems of error control in numerical computation are addressed.

8.3 Floating-point arithmetic in theory

This section describes the basic properties of floating-point arithmetic as it is commonly implemented on computers. An idealised view is given, removed from the details of the implementation of floating-point arithmetic or any particular machine, in an endeavour to show how errors in numerical computation may arise at the level of the basic arithmetic operations themselves.

Starting with the way floating-point numbers are represented, this idea should be familiar from the 'scientific' notation for numbers in terms of a mantissa and an exponent. The idea of a floating-point number representation as used within computers is just the same, a quantity n being represented by the pair of quantities (f,e) where:

$$n = f.b^c$$

and b is a machine-dependent constant called the base of the representation. Here f is called the fraction part (or mantissa) of the representation and e is an integer called the exponent of the representation. For a given machine, the floating-point base, b, is fixed (some typical values being 2, 10 or 16). Also fixed are the number of base-b digits of f and the range of possible values of e; these last quantities determine the range and accuracy of the arithmetic offered. The range of representable numbers is given by the range of values of e, an overflow condition arising if e_{max} is exceeded and an underflow condition resulting if e takes a smaller value than e_{min}. These parameters for a floating-point number system are summarised in *Figure 8.1* and some representative parameter values for different floating-point arithmetic systems are given in *Table 8.1*.

A characteristic of the scientific notation for numbers is that a given number may be represented in more than one way, for example:

$$3.14159E0 = 0.314159E1 = 0.0314159E2 = 3.14159$$

In floating-point number representations used on computers, the representation satisfying:

$$b^{-1} \leqslant |f| < 1$$

is generally taken to be standard, f being represented as a string of base-b digits with an implicit radix point at the left-most end. Floating-point representations satisfying this condition (giving a unique representation for each number) are said to be normalized. So if we use base-10 and the conventional notation for scientific numbers, the normalized representation of 3.14159 is 0.314159E1, while that of 27000 is 0.27E5.

Any particular floating-point representation is characterized by the base, precision and exponent range. In other words, the basic parameters of all integers are:

1. The base, b.
2. The precision, p.
3. The maximum exponent, e_{max}.
4. The minimum exponent, e_{min}.

These define a system of floating-point numbers consisting of zero and all numbers of the form:

$$x = f.b^c$$
$$\text{where: } f = \pm (f_1 b^{-1} + ... + f_p b^{-p})$$
$$\text{with: } f_1 = 1, ... , b-1$$
$$f_2, ... , f_p = 0, ... , b-1$$
$$e_{min} \leqslant e \leqslant e_{max}$$

Figure 8.1 Floating-point numbers: basic parameters

Table 8.1 Characteristics of some floating-point systems

System	Base, b	Precision, p (number of base b digits)	Minimum Exponent (e_{min})	Maximum Exponent (e_{max})
IBM 370/168:				
Single	16	6	− 64	63
Double	16	14	− 64	63
DEC VAX:				
Single	2	24	− 127	127
Double	2	56	− 127	127
Honeywell 6000:				
Single	2	27	− 128	127
Double	2	63	− 128	127
IEEE Binary Standard:				
Single	2	24	− 126	127
Single Extended	2	⩾ 32	⩽ − 1 022	⩾ 1 023
Double	2	53	− 1 022	1 023
Double Extended	2	⩾ 64	⩽ − 16 382	⩾ 16 383

Most of the floating-point arithmetic operations offered on current computers give their results in normalized form, so it is usual for all floating-point quantities arising within a computation to be held in that form. However, unnormalized arithmetic is occasionally useful and some machines offer it, although this is always in addition to the conventional normalized operations. Unnormalized arithmetic extends the range of representable numbers, albeit with some loss of accuracy. Also, it may be possible to use unnormalized arithmetic to provide an indication of the amount of accuracy in a floating-point result, although this is exceedingly difficult in general (Knuth 1981i).

The previous remarks about errors in numerical computation may be amplified in the case of floating-point computation by making it clear that an extremely important characteristic of floating-point numbers, from the programmer's point of view, is that they should always be regarded as potentially inaccurate.

This inaccuracy has several sources. It may stem initially from the fact that the floating-point representation used in the computer cannot match the known accuracy of the input data, or the input data may not be exactly representable as a floating-point number within the computer. For example, the decimal constant 0.1 is not exactly representable as a floating-point number unless the base b has 10 as a factor. This excludes the common cases $b = 2$ and $b = 16$. A further frequent source of error is rounding. A number of different rounding methods have been implemented with some floating-point units offering a choice of rounding method.

Additional errors may be introduced during floating-point computations as a result of roundings and cancellations during the execution of the individual arithmetic operations. A full discussion of errors in the basic floating-point arithmetic operations is given in Knuth (1981ii). This material is too complicated to summarize adequately here but a few examples of error effects follow.

Consider purely as an example a decimal floating-point system with five significant digits of accuracy. Rounding errors in addition are unavoidable. In fact, if the quantities being added are too different in magnitude the smaller may be treated as if it were zero.

Example 1

$$0.50000E1 + 0.10000E-7 = 0.50000E1$$

Cancellation may lead to loss of accuracy in addition or subtraction.

Example 2

$$0.50000E1 - 0.49999E1 = 0.10000E-3$$

Further comment on Example 2 may be helpful. If the two operands represent exact floating-point quantities, then the result of the operation reflects the difference between them and no further comment is necessary. However, bearing in mind the earlier remark that floating-point quantities should always be regarded as potentially inaccurate, if the operands represent approximate values, the loss of significance is serious since it greatly decreases the number of significant digits (i.e. increases the rounding error) in the result of the operation. The point is excellently summarized by Knuth (1981iii): cancellation in the calculation of a sum $u + v$ reveals *previous* errors in the computation of u and v.

Having illustrated very briefly the kinds of errors that may result from the naive use of the basic floating-point arithmetic operations, it remains to consider how their effects may be minimized by the use of careful programming. This topic is further discussed in a later section. First to be considered is the question of how the floating-point units of actual computers may differ from the somewhat idealized model of floating-point arithmetic presented here.

8.4 Floating-point arithmetic in practice

The last section discussed the characteristics of floating-point arithmetic in a fairly abstract way. This section considers the differences in floating-point arithmetic offered by various computers. One way of coping with the differences between floating-point units is to consider the issues involved in portable floating-point programming, a topic addressed later in this section.

8.4.1 Machine floating-point arithmetic

A wide range of floating-point number formats have been used in different computers; some idea of the variability can be gained from Table 8.1. For example, the overall length of a floating-point number (which governs both the exponent range and the accuracy offered) ranges at least from 32 to 128 bits. Further, there is no standardization of the base, b, of the representation used. Values of 2, 10 and 16 are found among contemporary systems, with decimal ($b = 10$) floating-point arithmetic featured on many calculators, and hexadecimal ($b = 16$) floating-point arithmetic offered on the IBM System/360 and its subsequent developments. Precise details of the signalling of overflow vary, as do those of the occurrence of underflow, which may be signalled or ignored, with some machines simply replacing underflowed quantities with zero without informing the programmer. Normalized arithmetic is generally offered, but sometimes unnormalized arithmetic is available too, if only for the provision of 'gradual underflow' in which quantities slightly smaller in modulus than the smallest attainable normalized floating-point number are stored with diminished accuracy.

In characterizing overflow and underflow as the *bêtes noires* of portability, Brown (1981) includes the following examples:

1. If the machine has an asymmetric range, the statement y := −x may cause overflow or underflow.
2. On some machines the statement y := x/x may cause overflow or underflow.
3. If x is very small, the statement y:= 1.0*x may cause underflow on an attempted normalization, and the statement **if** (x ≠ 0) **then** y:= 1/x may cause division by zero, x being regarded as non-zero by the comparison but not by the division! This example illustrates the general principle that comparisons for the equality or inequality of floating-point numbers should not be used because of the inherent inaccuracy of all floating-point quantities.

Further variations between different floating-point hardware units may be found in the areas of the accuracy of arithmetic operations (some units improve accuracy by the use of extended-precision registers internal to the floating-point unit), or in details of the rounding conventions used.

Besides such variations in the arithmetic offered, there are other problems, possibly caused by design errors in the floating-point hardware concerned. (Those interested in this subject may refer to Knuth (1981iv).) For example, Cody (1982) quotes the fact that on some computers there are small, representable and computable floating-point numbers x satisfying:

$$x \neq 0$$

which also satisfy one of the identities:

$$1.0 * x = 0 \text{ or } x + x = 0$$

This means, for example, that a parameter representing the underflow threshold (the smallest representable and computable floating-point number supported by the machine) can be seriously misleading, in that this quantity does not behave in the way the programmer might feel entitled to expect. Further examples of unexpected machine behaviour can also be given. For example, some floating-point hardware units contain an error that sets the least significant bit of a floating-point number to 0 when multiplying it by 1.0 (Brown and Feldman, 1980).

An important response to the wide variation and numerous shortcomings of floating-point units was the development of the IEEE standards for floating-point arithmetic (IEEE, 1985; Cody *et al.*, 1984). These standards were designed with great care by experts in the field and have been implemented for a number of different machines. Features include guaranteed accuracy for arithmetic operations, a variety of rounding modes and a selection of traps and other exceptional conditions. As intended, these standards are becoming widespread and their general use should do much to raise standards in floating-point programming. The IEEE standards are discussed at greater length by Wallis (1990i).

8.4.2 Floating-point portability

In the absence of similar universal (i.e. universally applied) standards, writers of portable numerical software need a way to write floating-point programs that provide equivalent numerical performance on different floating-point units. An approach that has been widely tried is to write programs using a set of parameters that characterizes the available floating-point arithmetic. However, as already briefly illustrated, the disadvantage of this approach is that there is no way of avoiding machine-dependent irregularities in the arithmetic.

A more comprehensive approach to this problem is manifested by the idea of 'model' floating-point arithmetic due to Brown (1981). The basic idea is to introduce a regular and realistic model of floating-point arithmetic that can be fitted to existing floating-point units in such a way as to minimize the effects of any machine-dependent irregularities in the arithmetic. This is done by identifying for each floating-point unit a subset of the arithmetic capabilities offered by the floating-point hardware, typically identified by reduced range and/or accuracy, for which the arithmetic performance is guaranteed to be sufficiently regular for the application of conventional error analyses (see Section 8.6.1). In other words, machines exhibiting unsatisfactory behaviour are 'penalized' by reductions in the range and/or accuracy for which conventionally regular behaviour is obtained.

For example, take the case of the machine irregularity mentioned earlier where a floating-point multiplication by 1.0 clears the bottom bit of the fraction of the resulting floating-point number. In this case, the bottom bit of the fraction part of a floating-point number is clearly unreliable, so Brown advocates taking the fraction part to be one bit shorter than is actually the case. Corresponding to this 'penalization', there is a more pessimistic view of the error behaviour of arithmetic operations which provides a realistic measure of the applicability of conventional error analysis to the behaviour of this unit. Other machine irregularities such as defective rounding performance are handled similarly. For example, an appropriate response to deficiencies in rounding behaviour would be to 'penalize' a floating-point unit by quoting for the Brown Model characteristics of the unit an accuracy that was lower than details of the floating-point hardware representation might lead one to expect. For the actual and model characteristics of a number of current floating-point units see Brown and Feldman (1980).

Brown's model is an excellent quantitative description of the reliability of floating-point arithmetic on many different machines, the 'penalization' associated with it being an effective way of masking machine-dependent irregularities. Unfortunately, this assessment of Brown's achievement conceals the fact that the model is very difficult to use correctly. The problem is that the programmer receives no help from the computer hardware in keeping within the model boundaries. For example, the model overflow and underflow thresholds frequently differ from those detected by the machine hardware, so the user must test to see that they are not violated.

It is of some interest to note that Brown's model was used as the basis for the floating-point arithmetic incorporated in the Ada programming language. The design of the Ada language broke new ground in addressing questions of floating-point portability with unwonted seriousness, although some features of the resulting design are somewhat contentious. See Wallis (1990) for a more extensive discussion of the Brown model and the Ada approach to floating-point, together with further references.

8.4.3 Floating-point arithmetic and formal specification

It follows from the preceding discussion that the detailed characteristics of any floating-point system are far from straightforward, which militates against the prospect of being able to use such arithmetic in any software that is formally specified in a reasonably straightforward way. However, if one discounts floating-point units exhibiting machine-dependent irregularities, there is no reason in principle why floating-point arithmetic should not be used in a rigorous way. The complexities involved make this rather a daunting prospect. For example, a full formal specification of the arithmetic of the Brown Model is implicit in the results of Brown (1981). The arithmetic provided by the IEEE standard for binary floating-point arithmetic has been fully described using the specification language Z. See Barrett (1987) for an account of this work. For a formal definition of floating-point arithmetic using VDM, see Wichman (1989).

8.5 Floating-point programming techniques

Enough has been written already to indicate that floating-point programming is full of pitfalls for the unwary, and that specialized techniques may be necessary to get the most accurate results from a given combination of problem and floating-point unit. The purpose of this section is to give a few examples of the kinds of programming techniques that are sometimes used. Only the very briefest of surveys can be given. There are further examples in Knuth (1981) and Cody and Waite (1980) which give a fascinating compendium of programming techniques of this kind, rewarding careful study by any numerical programmer.

8.5.1 Some tricks of the trade

Sometimes special measures are needed because of the characteristics of the floating-point arithmetic in use. An example is the avoidance of machine-dependent irregularities in arithmetic of the kinds mentioned in Section 8.4.1. Another example, discussed by Cody and Waite (1980), concerns a multiplication by $\pi/2$ in a trigonometric functional routine. On hexadecimal machines, the normalized representation of $\pi/2$ starts with three zeros, whereas that of $2/\pi$ does not. The result is that division by $2/\pi$ is almost one significant decimal digit more accurate than multiplication by $\pi/2$ on such a machine.

A related problem is that of range reduction for functions such as $\sin(x)$ with arguments in radians. The requirement is to reduce the argument modulo 2π, which must be done with great care, especially for large arguments. Again, Cody and Waite (1980) discuss this problem in detail. The solution involves holding an appropriate constant to extended precision, and also raising an error condition if the argument given is too large for the range reduction, as programmed, to deliver acceptable accuracy in the final result.

Sometimes rearrangement of expressions or scaling of intermediate results is necessary to avoid loss of information by cancellation, or termination of a calculation due to overflow or underflow. As an example, consider the evaluation of the roots of a quadratic equation:

$$ax^2 + bx + c = 0$$

using the familiar formula:

$$x = \frac{-b \pm \sqrt{(b^2 - 4ac)}}{2a}$$

Some of the hazards that may attend a naive evaluation of this formula are;

1. If b is very large, overflow may occur during evaluation of b^2.
2. If $b^2 \approx 4ac$, there may be an unacceptable loss of accuracy in forming the discriminant $(b^2 - 4ac)$.
3. If $b^2 \geqslant 4ac$ there may be unacceptable loss of accuracy in forming one of the roots.

This list is not exhaustive, simply serving as an illustration of the kinds of programming problems that may arise.

The types of technique which might be brought to bear on such problems depend both on the computer arithmetic in use and the precise circumstances of a particular case, but typical responses might comprise such suggestions as:

1. Use of alternative arithmetic (eg double-length floating-point) for evaluation of the discriminant.
2. Radical rearrangement of the formula, for example as a rational approximation or a power series.
3. Reformulation of the whole problem (of which the solution of the quadratic equation formed one small step) to avoid the need to solve the equation explicitly.

Numerous other examples of these kinds of rearrangement can be quoted. For example, if we have evaluated $f(x)$ and $f(a + \varepsilon)$ for given f, x and small ε, cancellation will frequently occur when evaluating $(f(x + \varepsilon) - f(x))$. Such cancellation may often be avoided by the device of finding symbolically an expression for $g(x) = (f(x + \varepsilon) - f(x))/\varepsilon$ and the calculating $\varepsilon * g(x)$. This is a simple example of how the symbolic rearrangement of an expression can help in its accurate computation.

Further examples of this kind of rearrangement are discussed by Knuth (1981) and by Cody and Waite (1980).

8.5.2 Alternatives to floating-point arithmetic

Because of the difficulties of accurate floating-point programming, it is natural to ask whether alternatives to the conventional floating-point operations can be devised to provide better performance in terms of error propagation. Two of the many possible alternatives are introduced now, with their possible use in algorithms discussed in Section 8.6.3.

Since all floating-point quantities are inherently inaccurate, it is possible to represent such quantities not as single numbers but as intervals within which their true values lie. Then an algorithm delivering a single numerical result would instead produce an interval within which its result is known to lie, a technique sometimes called 'guaranteed inclusion' of results. This is obviously a very attractive idea, but straightforward replacement of all floating-point operations by their interval equivalents rarely produces satisfactory results. A much more sophisticated approach is necessary, as Section 8.6.3 indicates.

Another alternative to conventional floating-point arithmetic, and in fact one that can be used to implement the basic operations of interval arithmetic, is the Karlsruhe Accurate Arithmetic (KAA). The idea here is that the basic conventional floating-point operations with good error behaviour are augmented with a new operation that allows scalar products to be calculated with a single rounding error. Improved error behaviour of many algorithms can result if the method is properly used, but again naive use of the technique may well not produce any significant improvement in the accuracy of the delivered results of complete algorithms.

8.6 Error control in extended numerical computations

Extended numerical computations comprise long sequences of floating-point arithmetic operations, each of which is subject to the types of error discussed already. The study of error propagation in such calculations is an important aspect of numerical analysis, the discipline concerned with the development of effective numerical algorithms for various mathematically formulated problems. A detailed discussion of numerical analysis lies outside the scope of this chapter, but the way error propagation is typically handled by numerical analysts is discussed here briefly.

An alarming phenomenon in numerical analysis is the existence of so called ill-conditioned problems, which are exceedingly sensitive to small changes in the input data. Ill-conditioning is instructive, if only to serve as a reminder of how important error analysis can be if any reliance at all is to be placed on the results of a computation. An example of ill-conditioning is given below. Finally, the section looks briefly at the scope for error control in extended computations afforded by various alternatives to conventional floating-point arithmetic.

8.6.1 Error analysis

Any discussion of the error behaviour of algorithms resulting from the basic shortcomings of floating-point arithmetic should certainly be related to the conventional error analysis featured in the numerical analysis literature, which is now very briefly introduced.

If a quantity $\hat{x}$ approximates the value of an exact quantity x, it is common to define the terms absolute error, referring to quantity:

$$\eta = x - \hat{x}$$

and the relative error given by:

$$\hat{x} = x(1 + \varepsilon)$$

or:

$$\varepsilon = \frac{\hat{x} - x}{x}$$

Conventional error analysis is usually formulated in terms of the relative error, taking as basic the equation:

$$X \mathrm{o} f y = (x \mathrm{o} y)(1 + \delta)$$

where o denotes any of the basic arithmetic operators $(+, -, \times, \div)$ and of denotes the corresponding floating-point arithmetic operation. The error term, δ, is then assumed to reflect satisfactory rounding behaviour; in terms of the quantities defined in Figure 8.1, the term δ is given by the equation:

$$|\delta| < \varepsilon$$

where:

$$\varepsilon = b^{1-p}$$

represents a 'unit in the last place' (ulp) of the fraction part of the floating-point representation used.

Starting from this point, the conventional treatment of errors in numerical analysis follows a well-defined path expounded in many introductory numerical analysis texts such as Fox and

Mayers (1968). A distinction is drawn between forward and backward error analysis. In forward analysis, an equation equivalent to the relative error equation above is applied repeatedly to the steps of a calculation, bounding the accumulated error at each step and hence eventually the error of the final result. Backward analysis, on the other hand, starts with the computed solution and works backwards to reconstruct the perturbed problem of which it is an exact solution. Backward analyses are usually easier to perform than forward ones, and generally lead to more useful evaluations of the numerical methods in use. Examples of forward and backward error analyses are to be found throughout the numerical analysis literature, the definitive references for the error analysis of algebraic processes being Wilkinson (1963 and 1965).

8.6.2 Ill-conditioning

A problem or algorithm is said to be ill-conditioned when the computed results are extremely sensitive to small changes in the input data. Since the input data is conventionally handled as floating-point numbers, and hence is subject to errors, it is in the handling of ill-conditioned problems that the effects of floating-point arithmetic inaccuracies are likely to be most dramatic.

It is important to distinguish between ill-conditioned *problems*, where the ill-conditioning is inherent in the problem itself, and ill-conditioned *algorithms*, where a particular proposed computing method is likely to be badly conditioned. Sometimes numerical analysts will use the terms inherent or induced ill-conditioning in referring respectively to ill-conditioned problems and ill-conditioned algorithms. In practice this distinction is not clear-cut, because it may be possible to improve the conditioning of a problem by changing the way it is posed. However, ill-conditioning does deserve some mention here, if only because references to ill-conditioning in the numerical analysis literature serve to highlight points at which the need for accurate floating-point programming is potentially of the greatest concern.

A classic example of an ill-conditioned numerical problem is due to Wilkinson (Wilkinson 1963; Fox and Mayers 1968). The polynomial:

$$p_{20}(z) = (z - 1)(z - 2) \ldots (z - 20) = z^{20} - 210z^{19} + \ldots + 20!$$

obviously has roots 1 .. 20, but if the coefficient of z^{19} is changed to $(210 + 2^{-23})$ and the polynomial is otherwise unchanged, the roots 16 and 17 are replaced by the complex pair:

$$z_{16}, z_{17} \approx 16.73 \pm 2.81i$$

This example illustrates vividly the problems that can be encountered in ill-conditioned problems, since even small errors in floating-point computation in finding the roots of such a polynomial could clearly render the computed results quite meaningless.

8.6.3 Use of alternative arithmetic

Two possible alternatives to the use of conventional floating-point arithmetic – interval arithmetic and the Karlsruhe Accurate Arithmetic – were introduced earlier. It is instructive to consider briefly what prospect their use, either separately or in conjunction with conventional floating-point arithmetic, can offer for improved error behaviour in extended numerical computations.

Interval arithmetic is a highly attractive idea, but has an unfortunate drawback in practice in that its naive use in extended computations leads to a rapid widening of intervals, rendering the delivered results of little value. However, more elaborate interval analysis, in which the arithmetic is used in a more elaborate fashion to guide the execution of algorithms, can remedy this situation to some extent. For more details see Alefeld and Herzberger (1983) and Moore (1966).

Similar problems are associated with the Karlsruhe Accurate Arithmetic. Although it provides the prospect of greatly improved error behaviour of numerical algorithms it is naive to expect its uninformed use necessarily to lead to any noticeable improvements (Kulisch and Miranker, 1981 and 1983). However, recent studies involving the redesign of complete algorithms to realise the full potential of KAA have led to the development of a number of new algorithms for a wide variety of numerical problems that provide guaranteed error bounds on the computed results (Wallis 1990; Ullrich and Wolff von Gudenberg, 1989).

The conclusion is quite clear, and also relates to other forms of alternative kinds of arithmetic. Informed use of an alternative arithmetic by skilled numerical analysts can indeed lead to significantly improved error behaviour of algorithms, but no such arithmetic can possibly offer a direct pathway to improved accuracy for numerically naive users. Perhaps for this reason such arithmetics remain largely experimental. While they are occasionally featured as hardware or software options for particular machines, they are not generally available to the software engineer and should be used only in conjunction with expert guidance.

8.7 Reformulation of problems

This chapter has been laced with warnings that many of the issues involved in numerical computation are outside the skills of the typical software engineer, and that expert guidance in such matters should be sought from a numerical analyst. Perhaps the point can be driven home by explaining that the answer to problems with inadequate numerical performance sometimes turns out to entail a complete reformulation of the problems as posed. Such a possibility has already been suggested in discussing the use of the formula for solving a quadratic equation.

Fox and Mayers (1968) have a story that illustrates this point. One of the authors was once asked to tabulate a given set of function values, and ended up constructing an elliptic partial differential equation satisfied by the required function and suggesting a numerical technique for solving the equation. It turned out that this derivation of the equation had led to a reconstruction of the original formulation of the client's problem!

Further examples are provided by the algorithms for elementary functions given by Cody and Waite (1980). A typical computation comprises a range reduction, the use of a special rational approximation for the reduced range, and a derivation of the required result. The point here is that the choice of the reduced range and of the rational approximation to be used are intimately linked.

A further example concerns the solution of simultaneous linear algebraic equations. Although standard numerical subroutines for this task (and for hosts of others) are easily obtainable, the choice of method in such a case can depend on such factors as the size of the system to be solved, whether it is known to be ill-conditioned, the sparseness or otherwise of the matrix of coefficients and whether solutions are needed for several different right-hand sides. All this means that intimate knowledge of the possibilities available may be needed, even to the extent of suggesting reformulation of the problem as originally posed in order to facilitate the use of the most satisfactory method.

To summarize again, the typical software engineer encountering a substantial numerical computation should enlist the services of someone with knowledge of numerical analysis. Failure to appreciate the importance of such limits to personal professional competence can lead to much misguided effort.

8.8 Conclusion

Many important applications of computers depend on numerical computation, yet the world of scientific computation is traditionally regarded as somewhat removed from mainstream software engineering. The reasons for this are to be found in its esoteric flavour. Many numerical computations require extensive background in numerical analysis and the use of unusual programming techniques to ensure that the best possible results are delivered from given computer hardware. The basic causes are inherent in the subject itself.

As the illustration of ill-conditioning shows, even a tiny error in the numerical specification of a numerical problem can make a huge difference to the delivered results. All floating-point operations are inherently inaccurate and effective, while reliable numerical programming will always remain a highly specialized field. Fortunately, a number of excellent libraries of numerical software exist which are frequently helpful, but, as with the use of alternatives to conventional floating-point arithmetic, there is no substitute for specialized knowledge of the field.

8.9 References

Alefeld, G. and Herzerberger, J. (1983) *Introduction to Interval Computation*, Academic Press, New York, USA

Barrett, G. (1987) Formal methods applied to a floating point system. *Programming Research Group Technical Monograph PRG-58*, Computing Laboratory, Oxford University

Brown, W. S. (1981) A simple but realistic model of floating point computation. *ACM Transactions on Mathematical Software*, 7, 445–480

Brown, W. S. and Feldman, S. I. (1980) Environment parameters and basic functions for floating-point computation. *ACM Transactions on Mathematical Software*, 6, 510–523

Cody, W. J. (1982) Floating point parameters, models and standards. In: *The Relationship Between Numerical Computation and Programming Languages* (ed. J. K. Reid) North-Holland, Amsterdam, pp 50–67

Cody, W. J. and Waite, W. M. (1980) *Software Manual for the Elementary Functions*, Prentice-Hall, Englewood Cliffs, USA

Cody, W. J., Coonen, J. T., Gay, D. M. *et al.* (1984) A proposed radix- and wordlength-independent standard for floating point arithmetic. *IEEE Micro*, 8, 86–99

IEEE P754:1985 Standard for Binary Floating-point Arithmetic, IEEE Inc., New York

Knuth, D. E. (1981) *The Art of Computer Programming, Vol. 2, Seminumeral Algorithms*, Addison-Wesley, Reading, Mass., USA, (i) p 233 (ii) pp 213–223 (iii) p 574 (iv) pp 205–207

Kulisch, U. and Miranker, W. L. (1981) *Computer Arithmetic in Theory and Practice*, Academic Press, New York, USA

Kulisch, U. and Miranker, W. L. (1983) *A New Approach to Scientific Computation*, Academic Press, New York, USA

Moore, R. (1966) *Interval Analysis*, Prentice-Hall, Englewood Cliffs, NY, USA

Ullrich, C. and Wolff von Gudenberg (eds) (1989) *Accurate Numerical Algorithms, Research Reports ESPRIT, Project 1072 DIAMOND*, Vol. 1, Springer-Verlag

Wallis, P. J. L. (ed.) (1990) *Improving Floating-Point Programming*, J. Wiley, Chichester (i) Chapter 2

Wichman, B. A. (1989) Towards a formal specification of floating point. *Computer Journal*, 32, 432–436

Wilkinson, J. H. (1963) *Rounding Errors in Algebraic Processes*, HMSO, London and Prentice-Hall, Englewood Cliffs, USA

Wilkinson, J. H. (1965) *The Algebraic Eignevalue Problem*, Clarendon Press, Oxford.

Acknowledgement

The author wishes to acknowledge the permission of John Wiley and Sons Limited for the reproduction of material from Wallis (1990).

Fundamental
Computer
Science

9

Automata theory

Professor V J Rayward-Smith
University of East Anglia, Norwich

Contents

9.1 Introduction

Automata theory is concerned with the construction and application of mathematical models of computing devices. By studying such models, the computer scientist is able to answer fundamental questions such as: 'What is a computer capable of computing?', 'Are there important problems which cannot be solved on a computer?', or 'Is some specified problem so difficult that we will always need exponential time to solve it?'. The origins of the subject can be found in the work of various logicians published in the 1930s (Church, 1936; Kleene, 1936; Post, 1936; Turing, 1936). The relevance of this work to computer science is now widely accepted and considerable further research has been undertaken. There are now a large number of texts available covering various aspects; most of the results cited in this chapter are to be found in the classic and scholarly texts (Hopcroft and Ullman, 1969 and 1979). A more elementary introduction is in Rayward-Smith (1983 and 1986). Other recommended texts for general reading are Arbib (1963), Davis (1958), Hennie (1977), Hermes (1969), Lewis and Papadimitrou (1981), Mandrioli and Ghezzi (1987), Manna (1974) and Minsky (1967).

One can view a (programmed) computing device, M, as a 'black box', as in *Figure 9.1*. Some input x is provided and the computing device provides a corresponding output, y. For any given M, the output, y, will often depend solely upon the input, x. Moreover, in many of the models discussed in this chapter, each time the input, x, is given, the same output, y, will result and we can thus view the black box as computing a function f_M: $x \to y$. Depending upon the nature of the operations performed within the black box, certain functions may or may not be capable of being computed.

Figure 9.1 The 'black box'

Programmers are accustomed to handling a wide range of different types of input and output. For example, one program might accept an array of reals and produce an integer whilst another might take a file of records and produce another such file. Automata theory usually assumes the input and output are in some encoded form. The most commonly used encodings are natural numbers or strings over some finite alphabet. The computer scientist is used to a binary string representation whilst mathematical logicians are used to integer representations constructed using Gödel numbering.

9.1.1 Gödel numbering

A Gödel numbering, g, of the elements in a set, S, is an assignment g: $S \to N$ of natural numbers to the elements which satisfy the following conditions:

1. Different Gödel numbers are assigned to different elements (i.e. g is one–one).
2. There is an algorithm to calculate the Gödel number of any element (i.e. g can be effectively calculated).
3. Given any natural number, there is an algorithm to test whether that number is a Gödel number of some element in the set and, if so, to determine that corresponding element (i.e., g^{-1} can be effectively calculated).

In practice, Gödel numbering exploits prime factorization. Let $p_1 = 2$, let $p_2 = 3, \ldots$ denote the increasing sequence of prime numbers. Consider g(x), a Gödel numbering of x. Then if p_n divides g(x) always implies p_m divides g(x) for all $m < n$, prime factorization of g(x) is a simple task. For this reason, this is a usual property of Gödel numbering. As an example, a Gödel numbering of B = {0, 1}* can be defined as follows:

g(x) = 1   if x = ε, but otherwise

$$g(x) = p_1^{a_1} \times p_2^{a_2} \ldots \times p_n^{a_n} \text{ where } x = b_1 b_2 \ldots b_n, b_i \in \{0, 1\} \text{ for } 1 \leqslant i \leqslant n \text{ and } a_i = b_i + 1$$

In this chapter, both functions on binary strings and on natural numbers are considered. A result about functions on strings will have obvious parallels for natural numbers and *vice versa*.

9.2 Finite state automata

An initial attempt at modelling a computer begins with the observation that at any time the machine is in a certain 'state' and only changes this state as it processes the input. Moreover, since the total hardware in any machine is finite, the total number of different states must also be finite. The study of finite state systems originated in McCulloch and Pitts (1943) and was later developed by Kleene (1956), Mealy (1955), Moore (1956) and others.

9.2.1 Deterministic finite state automata

A deterministic finite state automaton (DFSA) is formally defined as a 5-tuple M = (K, T, δ, k_0, F) where K is a finite set of states; T is a finite input alphabet; δ: K × T → K is a (possibly partial) transition function; $k_0 \in K$ is the start state; F ⊆ K is the set of final states.

The DFSA computes a function using the following algorithm.

```
state: = k₀; {the state is initialized to the start state}
while there exists more input
do begin read the next input symbol (a, say);
     state: = δ (state, a)
   end;
if state ∈ F then output (1)
else output (0)
```

Thus the DFSA, M, computes a function f_M: T* → {0, 1}. If an input x∈T* results in an output of 1, x is said to be accepted by M; otherwise x is said to be rejected by M. Note that since δ may be partial, δ (state, a) may not be defined in which case there is no output. Hence x can be rejected by producing either a zero as output or by producing no output. The set of strings accepted by a DFSA, M, is the language accepted by M, *viz* {x∈T* | M accepts x} and is denoted by T(M).

More formally, δ: K × T → K is extended to a function δ: K × T* → K by recursively defining δ(k, ε) = k where ε is the empty string, and δ(k, ax) = δ(δ(k, a), x) where a∈T and x∈T*. Then T(M) = {x | δ(k_0, x)∈F}.

A language is regular if and only if it is accepted by a deterministic finite state automaton. Such languages are exactly those generated by regular grammars (see Section 10.9). A regular language is also known as a regular set.

If L ⊆ T is accepted by a DFSA, M = (K, T, δ, k_0, F), with a partial transition function δ, then it is also accepted by the DFSA, M' = (K ∪ {d}, T, δ', k_0, F), where d∉K is a new 'dummy' state and δ' is a total transition function defined by

$$\delta'(k, a) = \begin{cases} \delta(k, a) & \text{if } \delta(k, a) \text{ is defined,} \\ d & \text{otherwise} \end{cases}$$

and δ'(d, a) = d for all a∈T.

For any regular language $L \subseteq T^*$ there is a DFSA with a minimum number of states which accepts L. Moreover, the Myhill–Nerode theorem (Nerode, 1958) proves that this minimum state automaton is unique up to isomorphism (i.e. renaming of the states) and can be constructed by a simple algorithm. For this and other algorithms concerning DFSAs, the reader is referred to Hopcroft and Ullman (1969 and 1979) and Rabin and Scott (1959).

9.2.2 Transition matrix and directed graph representation

Given a DFSA, $M = (K, T, \delta, k_0, F)$, the transition function can be represented as a transition matrix where the rows are indexed by K and the columns by T. Entry (k, a) of the matrix is the value $\delta(k, a)$ (where defined). For example, consider the DFSA with $K = \{1, 2, 3, 4, 5\}$, $T = \{a, b\}$, $k_0 = 1$, $F = \{4, 5\}$ and (partial) transition function defined by the following:

$(1, a) \rightarrow 2$ $(1, b) \rightarrow 3$ $(2, a) \rightarrow 4$ $(2, b) \rightarrow 2$

$(3, a) \rightarrow 4$ $(3, b) \rightarrow 3$ $(4, b) \rightarrow 5$ $(5, a) \rightarrow 5$

The corresponding transition matrix with rows indexed 1 . . . 5 and columns indexed a, b is:

$$\begin{bmatrix} 2 & 3 \\ 4 & 2 \\ 4 & 3 \\ - & 5 \\ 5 & - \end{bmatrix}$$

If a dummy state (6, say) is introduced to ensure δ is total, the corresponding transition matrix is:

$$\begin{bmatrix} 2 & 3 \\ 4 & 2 \\ 4 & 3 \\ 6 & 5 \\ 5 & 6 \\ 6 & 6 \end{bmatrix}$$

A DFSA can also be represented as a labelled directed graph. Each node represents a state, the start state being distinguished by an arrow ($\downarrow$) and final states by being represented by a square rather than a circle. There is a directed arc from state k to state k' labelled a iff $\delta(k, a) = k'$. *Figure 9.2* gives a graphical representation of the above DFSA.

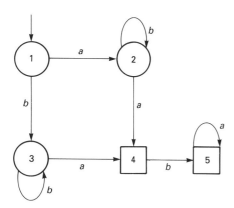

Figure 9.2

It is relatively easy to see from this example that $T(M) = \{a, b\}.\{b\}^*.\{a\}.(\{\epsilon\} \cup \{b\}.\{a\}^*)$ where ϵ denotes the empty string, . denotes set concatenation and * denotes Kleene closure, so $\{a\}^* = \{\epsilon, a, aa, aaa, \ldots\}$.

9.2.3 Regular expressions

Regular expressions provide a neat way of describing regular sets. The regular expressions over the alphabet, T, each represent a regular set in T and are defined recursively as follows.

1. 0, representing the empty set, and 1, representing $\{\epsilon\}$, are both regular expressions over T. [It is assumed that neither 0 nor 1 are elements of T but, if so, alternative symbols need to be defined.]
2. For each $a \in T$, a itself is a regular expression over T and represents $\{a\}$.
3. If r_1 and r_2 are regular expressions over T, representing L_1 and L_2 respectively, then $(r_1 + r_2)$, representing $L_1 \cup L_2$, $(r_1.r_2)$, representing $L_1.L_2$, and (r_1^*), representing L^*, are all regular expressions over T.
4. Only expressions defined by (1), (2) and (3) are regular expressions over T.

When writing regular expressions, parentheses may be omitted according to the rule that * is the highest priority operator, then . (concatenation), then + (union).

Moreover, the symbol . is often omitted and r_1r_2 written for $r_1.r_2$. For example, T(M) of Figure 9.2 is represented by the regular expression $(a + b)b^*a(1 + ba^*)$.

Any regular language in T^* can be represented by a regular expression and, conversely, any regular expression over T always describes a regular language. Given a DFSA, there is a simple technique for determining a corresponding regular expression and *vice versa*.

9.2.4 Non-deterministic finite state automata

In Section 9.2.1, the transition function within the definition of a DFSA ensured that if the machine was in state k and received an input a then there was *at most* one state to which it could move. Relating this to the graphical representation, this means that at most one directed arc with a given label can leave any vertex. Thus, the finite state machine depicted in *Figure 9.3* is not a DFSA according to the definition. In state 3, an input of b does not uniquely determine the next state. To allow for this, non-determinism is introduced into the model.

A non-deterministic finite state automaton (NFSA) is defined as a 5-tuple $M = (K, T, \delta, k_0, F)$ where:

1. K is a finite set of states.
2. T is a finite input alphabet.
3. $\delta: K \times T \rightarrow 2^K$ is a (total) transition function.
4. $k_0 \in K$ is the start state.
5. $F \subseteq K$ is the set of final states.

For the NFSA represented in *Figure 9.3*,

$\delta(1, a) = \{2\}$ $\delta(1, b) = \{3\}$ $\delta(2, a) = \{2\}$ $\delta(2, b) = \{4\}$

$\delta(3, a) = \Phi$ $\delta(3, b) = \{3, 4\}$ $\delta(4, a) = \{2\}$ $\delta(4, b) = \Phi$

$\delta: K \times T \rightarrow 2^K$ is extended to a function $\delta: 2^K \times T \rightarrow 2^K$ in the obvious way by defining $\delta(A, a) = \bigcup_{k \in A} \delta(k, a)$.

Then δ is yet further extended to a function $2^K \times T^* \rightarrow 2^K$ by recursively defining $\delta(A, \epsilon) = A$ and $\delta(A, ax) = \delta(\delta(A, a), x)$, $a \in T$, $x \in T^*$. Then if $M = (K, T, \delta, k_0, F)$ is a NFSA, the set of strings accepted by M is denoted by T(M) and defined by $T(M) = \{x \in T^* | \delta(\{k_0\}, x) \cap F \neq \Phi\}$. Thus the set of strings accepted by M is precisely that set of strings labelling paths from the

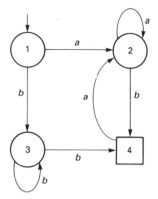

Figure 9.3

start state k_0 to some final state in the graphical representation of M.

A fundamental result in finite state automata theory is that L is accepted by a DFSA iff L is accepted by a NFSA. There is a simple algorithm for constructing a DFSA accepting the same language as a given NFSA.

9.2.5 Finite state automata with ε moves

If the definition of a NFSA is altered so that transitions from one state to another can be accomplished without necessitating any input, we say the NFSA has ε moves. The definition of the transition function δ is changed to a function $K \times (T \cup \{\epsilon\}) \to 2^K$. Even with this modification, the language accepted by the NFSA remains regular.

9.2.6 Complexity of finite state automata

If $M = (K, T, \delta, k_0, F)$ is a DFSA with a total function δ and $x \in T^*$ then $T_M(x)$ denotes the number of moves required by M to process x. Since a FSA performs exactly one move per input symbol, $T_M(x) = length(x)$ and this provides the time-complexity measure for a DFSA. Since a FSA has no memory capability (except through the finite number of states), the space-complexity measure is simply zero.

9.2.7 Mealy/Moore machines

The DFSA of Section 9.2.1 computes a (possibly partial) function $f_M: T^* \to \{0, 1\}$. Both Mealy and Moore machines are modifications of the basic DFSA model which compute more general functions $T_1^* \to T_2^*$ for some input alphabet, T_1, and some output alphabet, T_2. In a Mealy machine (1955), an output is associated with each transition, whilst in a Moore machine (1956), an output is associated with each state.

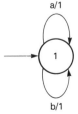

a/1

1

b/1

Figure 9.4 A simple Mealy machine

Figure 9.4 gives a directed graph representation of a Mealy machine which computes the length (in unary notation) of an input string in {a, b}*. A label x/y on an arc from state k to k′ is used to represent the fact that an input x causes a transition from k to k′ and an associated output of y.

Formally, a Mealy machine is a 5-tuple $(K, T_1, T_2, \delta, k_0)$ where:

1. K is a finite set of states.
2. T_1 is a finite input alphabet.
3. T_2 is a finite output alphabet.
4. $\delta: K \times T_1 \to K \times T_2$ a (possibly partial) transition function.
5. $k_0 \in K$ is the start state.

Note that final states do not feature in Mealy machines.

$\delta_1: K \times T_1 \to K$ denotes the first projection of δ and $\delta_2: K \times T_1 \to T_2$ denotes the second projection. Then, δ_1 and δ_2 are extended in the obvious way to produce functions $\delta_1: K \times T_1^* \to K$ and $\delta_2: K \times T_1^* \to T_2^*$, *viz* by defining $\delta_1(k, \epsilon) = k$, $\delta_1(k, ax) = \delta_1(\delta_1(k, a), x)$ for $a \in T_1$, $x \in T_1^*$, and, similarly, $\delta_2(k, \epsilon) = \epsilon$, $\delta_2(k, ax) = concat(\delta_2(k, a), \delta_2(\delta_1(k, a), x))$ for $a \in T_1$, $x \in T_1^*$.

Given a Mealy machine $M = (K, T_1, T_2, \delta, k_0)$ and an input string $x \in T^*$, the associated output, $y = f_M(x)$, is equal to $\delta_2(k_0, x)$. Note that if δ is a partial function then y may be undefined, i.e. f_M may also be partial. However, if y is defined then $length(y) = length(x)$.

A Moore machine is defined similarly to a Mealy machine, but output is associated with each state. Thus, a Moore machine is a 6-tuple $(K, T_1, T_2, \delta, \eta, k_0)$ where:

1. K is a finite set of states.
2. T_1 is a finite input alphabet.
3. T_2 is a finite output alphabet.
4. $\delta: K \times T_1 \to K$ is a transition function.
5. $\eta: K \to T_2$ is an output function.
6. $k_0 \in K$ is the start state.

The DFSA of Section 9.2.1 can be viewed as a special case of a Moore machine where $T_2 = \{0, 1\}$ and k is a final state iff $\eta(k) = 1$.

The transition function δ is extended to a function $\delta^*: K \times T_1^* \to K^*$ by recursively defining it by: $\delta^*(k, \epsilon) = k$, $\delta^*(k, a) = \delta(k, a)$ and $\delta^*(k, ax) = concat(k, \delta^*(\delta(k, a), x))$, $a \in T_1$, $x \in T_1^*$. Thus, $\delta^*(k, x)$ represents the sequence of states visited during the processing of string x given the initial state k. The length of the string $\delta(k, x)$ is one greater than the length of x.

The output function is also extended by recursively defining $\eta^*: K^* \to T_2^*$ in the same manner as $\delta^* \eta^*(\epsilon) = \epsilon$ and $\eta^*(kx) = concat(\eta(k), \eta^*(x))$, $k \in K$, $x \in K^*$. The output of a Moore machine $M = (K, T_1, T_2, \delta, p, k_0)$ given an input x is then defined by $y = f_M(x) = \eta^*(\delta^*(k_0, x))$. If y is defined it will always be a string of length one greater than x.

If $y = f_M(x)$ is defined then y is necessarily of the form $\eta(k_0)y'$ for some string y′ of the same length as x. A Mealy machine M and a Moore machine M′ are equivalent iff, for all inputs $x \neq \epsilon$, $\eta(k_0)f_M(x) = f_{M'}(x)$. For any Moore machine there is an equivalent Mealy machine and *vice versa*, see, for example, Hopcroft and Ullman (1979).

9.2.8 Generalized sequential machine

The Mealy machine model can be generalized so that it is non-deterministic and is permitted to output any string of symbols (including ε) at each move rather than just a single symbol. Such a machine is called a generalized sequential machine (GSM) and is defined as a 6-tuple $M = (K, T_1, T_2, \delta, k_0, F)$ where K, T_1, T_2, k_0 and F are defined as for Mealy machines but δ is a function from $K \times T_1$ to finite subsets of $K \times T_2^*$. If $(k', w) \in \delta(k, a)$ then M, in state k, given input a, can move to state k' and output $w \in T_2^*$. The domain of δ is extended to $K \times T_1^*$ by defining $\delta(k, \varepsilon) = \{(k, \varepsilon)\}$ and for $a \in T_1^*$, $x \in T_1^*$, $\delta(k, ax) = \{(k', \omega) \mid \omega = \omega_1 \omega_2 \text{ such that for some } k'', (k'', \omega_1) \in \delta(k, a) \text{ and } (k', \omega_2) \in \delta(k'', x)\}$.

Let $A_M(x)$ denote the set $\{y \mid (k, y) \in \delta(k_0, x) \text{ for some } k \in F\}$ and $L \subseteq \Sigma^*$ then $A_M(L)$ denotes $\{y \mid y \in A_M(x) \text{ for some } x \in L\}$. $A_M(L)$ is called a GSM mapping. Properties of GSM mapping and their inverses are to be found in Hopcroft and Ullman (1969 and 1979).

9.2.9 Two-way finite state automata

With the conventional FSA, the input is scanned symbol by symbol from left to right. A two-way finite automaton can move both forwards and backwards over an input string during processing. Formally, a two-way finite state automaton is defined as a DFSA except that $\delta: K \times T \rightarrow K \times \{L, R, 0\}$ defines the transition function. The interpretation of $\delta(k, a) = (k', X)$, $k' \in K$, $X \in \{L, R, 0\}$ is that M, in state k, scanning an input of a within the input string, will change to state k' and move its input head L(eft), R(ight) or 0 (stay where it is).

The two-way automaton M starts in state k_0 scanning the left-most symbol in the input string, x. Should M ever move off the end of x, M halts. An input x is accepted by M iff M eventually moves off the right-hand end of x and, at the same time, M enters a final state. Thus x can be rejected by moving off the left end of x, moving off the right end of x in a non-final state, or by looping.

Two-way automata accept exactly the same class of languages as DFSA, i.e. the regular languages (Rabin and Scott, 1959).

9.2.10 Applications of finite automata

One of the major application areas of the theory of finite automata is in the design of lexical analysers. The tokens of a programming language are generally recognizable by finite state machines and the initial lexical analysis module of compiler is constructed using a Moore machine (see Chapter 52).

The use of finite automata in switching circuit design is discussed in Kohavi (1970). There are also numerous applications in the design of text editors and text processing programs. References to these and other applications can be found in Hopcroft and Ullman (1979).

9.2.11 Limitations of finite automata

The essential aim of automata theory is to construct mathematical models of a 'computing device'. Any computer can only be in one of a finite number of states and any input can alter the machine from one state to another. Thus the FSA approach does indeed appear to model the situation. However, in practice, the number of states required to model a machine is very large; if the machine has x bits, it can be in any of 2^x states. Moreover, finite state automata cannot even compute simple arithmetic functions. For example, the language of $\{a^i b^j c^k \mid k = i + j\}$ is not regular. If a FSA cannot be designed to accept strings of this form, how can it be expected to do simple addition? The essential problem is the finiteness criterion. A FSA cannot 'remember' arbitrarily large numbers, i.e. numbers larger than the number of states. Its only 'memory' is the current state. In the next sections, more general automata are designed which more accurately model computing devices. It is not until a potentially infinite store is provided that functions such as addition can be computed in their full generality.

In Chapter 10, formal languages are discussed and the regular languages are seen to be strictly contained within other classes of languages (Chomsky, 1959). The most general such class of languages is the class of recursively enumerable (r.e.) languages. If an automaton is to model the most general of computing device then it can surely be expected to recognize such languages. This further supports the argument that the FSA model, although useful for many applications, is not suitable as a general model for a computing device.

9.3 Push-down automata

A push-down automaton (PDA) is equipped with a stack (i.e. a push-down store). The original formulation has been credited to Oettinger (1961) although the model was also used by several other researchers in the early 1960s (Chomsky, 1962; Evey, 1963; Schutzenberger, 1963). The content of the stack can be represented by a string of symbols over the stack alphabet, S. If $X = s_1 s_2 \ldots s_n \in S^*$ represents the stack content, then the stack contains symbols s_1 (at the top), s_2 next, etc., through to the bottom element, s_n.

There are two types of move a PDA can make. The first type takes the next symbol from the input and, depending upon this, the current state, and the top symbol popped off the stack, makes a transition. A transition corresponds to a possible change of state and pushing a string of symbols onto the stack. The second type (called an ε-transition) is used to manipulate the stack content without reading input. Depending merely upon the current state and the top symbol popped off the stack, the PDA can change state and push a new string of symbols onto the stack. No input is required.

9.3.1 Non-deterministic push-down automata

A non-deterministic push-down automata (NPDA) is a 7-tuple $(K, T, S, \delta, k_0, s_0, F)$ where:

1. K is a finite set of states.
2. T is a finite input alphabet.
3. S is a finite stack alphabet.
4. δ is a transition function from $K \times (T \cup \{\varepsilon\}) \times S$ to finite subsets of $K \times S^*$.
5. $k_0 \in K$ is the start state.
6. $s_0 \in S$ is the start stack symbol.
7. $F \subseteq K$ is a set of final states.

If $\delta(k, a, s) = \{(k_1, x_1), (k_2, x_2), \ldots, (k_n, x_n)\}$ then, if M is in state k, with s at the top of the stack, and a is input, M will pop s, push x_i and move to state k_i, for some $1 \leqslant i \leqslant n$. The left-most symbol of x_i will then be placed highest in the stack.

If $\delta(k, \varepsilon, s) = \{(k_1, x_1), (k_2, x_2), \ldots, (k_n, x_n)\}$ then the NPDA M, in state, k, with s at the top of the stack, can move to state k_i, pop s and push $x_i (1 \leqslant i \leqslant n)$ without requiring any input.

At any time, the NPDA will be in a configuration (k, z) where k is the current state and z the current stack contents. If $a \in T \cup \{\varepsilon\}$ can change configuration (k, z) to (k', z') then this is written as a: $(k, z) \vdash_M (k', z')$. Thus, a: $(k, z) \vdash_M (k', z')$ iff $z = s\zeta$ $(s \in S, \zeta \in S^*)$, $z' = z_i \zeta$ and $(k', z_i) \in \delta(k, a, s)$.

If $x = a_1 a_2 \ldots a_n$ (each $a_i \in T \bigcup \{\varepsilon\}$) then x: $(k_1, z_1) \vdash_M (k_{n+1}, z_{n+1})$ denotes that for some sequence $k_1, k_2, \ldots, k_{n+1}$ of states and for some sequence $z_1, z_2, \ldots, z_{n+1}$ of strings in S^*, a_i: $(k_i, z_i) \vdash_M (k_{i+1}, z_{i+1})$ for $1 \leqslant i \leqslant n$.

A NPDA, M, can accept a language either by empty store or by final state. T(M) denotes the set of strings accepted by final state and is defined by $T(M) = \{x \in T^* \mid x: (k_0, s_0) \vdash_M^* (k, z) \text{ for some } k \in F\}$. N(M) denotes the set of strings accepted by empty store and is defined by $N(M) = \{x \in T^* \mid x: (k_0, s_0) \vdash_M^* (k, \varepsilon) \text{ for any } k \in K\}$.

A major result concerning NPDAs is that $L = T(M)$ for some NPDA, M, iff $L = N(M')$ for some NPDA, M'. Moreover, the class of languages so accepted is precisely the context-free languages. Push-down automata are thus capable of recognizing a larger class of languages than finite state machines. However, the last-in–first-out constraint on the store of a PDA still imposes significant constraints. For example, a PDA is not capable of recognizing such simple languages as $\{0^n 1^n 0^n \mid n \geqslant 1\}$. All these results can be found in standard texts such as Hopcroft and Ullman (1969 and 1979).

9.3.2 Deterministic push-down automata

A push-down automaton is said to be deterministic iff there is at most one possible move from any configuration. The definition of a deterministic PDA (DPDA) is thus the same as for a non-deterministic PDA but with the additional constraints:

1. For each $k \in K$ and $s \in S$, whenever $\delta(q, \varepsilon, s) \neq \Phi$ then $\delta(k, a, s) = \Phi$ for all $a \in T$.
2. For no $k \in K$, $s \in S$ and $a \in T \cup \{\varepsilon\}$ does $\delta(k, a, s)$ contain more than one element.

For FSAs, the deterministic and non-deterministic models are equivalent in the sense that any language accepted by some DFSA is accepted by some NFSA and *vice versa*. This is not the case for PDAs, however. By definition, any language accepted by a DPDA is accepted by some NPDA but the converse is not true. For example, if x^r denotes the reverse of a string, the set of palindromes $\{xx^r \mid x \in \{0, 1\}^*\}$ is accepted by a NPDA but not by any DPDA.

A language is said to be deterministic if and only if it is accepted by a DPDA. Since a DFSA can be viewed as a DPDA which ignores its stack, every regular language is deterministic. However, there are deterministic languages which are not regular. An example is $\{0^n 1^n \mid n \geqslant 1\}$. Thus regular – deterministic – context-free forms a proper hierarchy of language classes. A DPDA is said to be in normal form if the only stack operations are to erase the top symbol or to push one symbol. Any deterministic language can be recognized by a DPDA in normal form (Hopcroft and Ullman, 1979).

9.3.3 Push-down transducers

The basic model of a PDA can be extended to produce output. A push-down transducer (PDT) is defined as a 9-tuple $(K, T_1, T_2, S, \delta, \eta, k_0, s_0, F)$ where $K, S, \delta, k_0, s_0, F$ are defined as in the definition of a NPDA, T_1 is the finite input alphabet, T_2 is the finite output alphabet and η is the output function $\eta: K \times (T_1 \cup \{\varepsilon\}) \times S \to T_2^*$ defined whenever δ is defined.

With any sequence of valid moves the PDT thus associates an output string. If $x \in T_2^*$ can result in an output of $y \in T_2^*$, x and y are related by M. This relation is a function whenever the transducer is deterministic. Push-down transducers and their associated relations are studied in a sequence of papers published in the 1960s (Evey, 1963; Fischer, 1963; Ginsburg *et al.*, 1967; Ginsburg and Rose, 1966; Lewis and Stearns, 1968).

9.3.4 Complexity of push-down automata computations

Let M = $(K, T, S, \delta, k_0, s_0, F)$ be a NPDA. Let $C_0 = (k_0, s_0)$ be the initial configuration. Say an input x results in the sequence of configurations $C_0 \vdash_M C_1 \vdash_M \ldots \vdash_M C_n$ where C_n is either an accepting or rejecting configuration. In this case, n is a measure of the time spent in processing x. In some cases, however, because of the non-deterministic nature of M, more or less time might be required. It may even be the case that M might not halt at all when processing a given input, in which case, the time complexity measure is infinite. Given $x \in T^*$, let $T_M(x)$ denote the length of the longest possible sequence of configurations required to process x. The time complexity function $T_M: N \to N$ for M is then defined by:

$$T_M(n) = \max\{T_M(x) \mid length(x) = n\}$$

The space complexity measure is given by the maximum size of the stack during processing. $S_M(x) = \max\{length(z) \mid y:(k_0, s_0) \mid \vdash_M^* (k, z) \text{ for some prefix } y \text{ of } x\}$. The space complexity function $S_M: N \to N$ for M is then defined by:

$$S_M(n) = \max\{S_M(x) \mid length(x) = n\}$$

Any deterministic language can be recognized by some PDA with both time and space complexity linear in the length of the input string (Lewis *et al.*, 1965).

9.3.5 Applications of push-down automata to compiler design

Since the syntax of many programming languages is defined by a context-free grammar, many compilers are stack based. DPDAs are used within LR parsers. LR(1) grammars have great importance in compiler design since they are general enough to include the syntax of most programming languages yet parsers can be constructed from them that are essentially DPDAs.

9.4 Turing machines

Turing machines, originally proposed by the logician Alan Turing (1936), provide a model simple enough for easy analysis yet powerful enough to compute all the functions which, from experience, can be expected to be computable – such functions are said to be 'effectively computable'. A formal definition of 'effectively computable' is impossible to give because the term is used for a conceptual class of functions, i.e. that class of functions for which a computer scientist would expect to be able to write programs. There are a large number of texts which use the Turing machine approach (e.g. Davis, 1958; Eilenberg and Elgot, 1980; Hermes, 1969; Hopcroft and Ullman, 1969 and 1979; Manna, 1974; Mendelson, 1964; Minsky, 1967; Rayward-Smith, 1983 and 1986; Rogers, 1967). Most of the results cited in this section can be found in any one of these.

From earlier discussion, any machine capable of computing all effectively computable functions must be equipped with potentially infinite store. Of course, in any finite calculation only a finite amount of this store will be used. However, if an upper limit is placed *a priori* on the store then situations can arise where some input or string of values required during computation exceeds the storage limitations.

9.4.1 Turing machines

The Turing machine (TM) is equipped with limitless store which can be viewed as a tape divided into a number of locations indexed $\ldots -2, -1, 0, 1, 2, \ldots$ as in *Figure 9.5*. In each location, a symbol from some prescribed alphabet can be written. Initially, the tape will be blank, i.e. each location will hold the blank symbol, here denoted by $\wedge$. An initial input of $x = a_1 a_2 \ldots a_n$ will be written one symbol at a time in locations $1, 2, \ldots, n$.

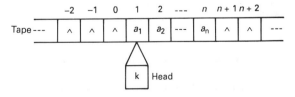

Figure 9.5

The TM has a (tape) head which moves backwards and forwards across the tape, scanning the locations and inserting and deleting symbols. The head can be in any one of a finite number of states, K. Initially, the head will be in a prescribed start state, $k_0 \in K$, and will be scanning location 1. The machine will only halt successfully if the tape head reaches any one of a number of final states, $F \subseteq K$.

At any time during the computation, the head is in some state, k (say), and scans some symbol in the tape, a (say), called the current tape symbol. The next step of the TM depends upon these values. If $k \notin F$, the head can overwrite the current tape symbol and possibly move to the adjacent location to the left or to the right. At the same time the state k may or may not change. If there is at most one possible move the TM can make from any configuration, the TM is said to be deterministic. If, eventually, the TM head is in state $k \in F$, the computation halts and the output is taken to be the string of symbols in locations $1, 2, \ldots, m$ where $m + 1$ is the left-most location greater than 0 which contains a blank symbol. The precise action to be taken by a deterministic TM at each step of a computation is determined by a program. The program can be tabulated as a list of 5-tuples of the form given in *Figure 9.6*.

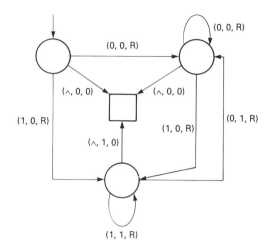

Figure 9.7 A TM computing cons0

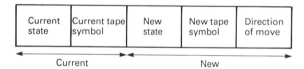

Current state	Current tape symbol	New state	New tape symbol	Direction of move

Current — New

Figure 9.6

Formally, a deterministic Turing machine (TM) is a 6-tuple, $M = (K, \Sigma, T, \delta, q_0, F)$ where:

1. K is a finite set of states.
2. Σ is a finite set of tape symbols, i.e. symbols which can appear on the tape, one of which is denoted by $\wedge$ and is called the blank symbol.
3. $T \subseteq \Sigma - \{\wedge\}$ is the set of input symbols.
4. δ is the program, i.e. a (possibly partial) transition function δ: $(K - F) \times \Sigma \to K \times \Sigma \times \{L, R, 0\}$.
5. $k_0 \in K$ is the start state.
6. $F \subseteq K$ is the set of final states.

Symbols which appear on the tape which are not input symbols nor the blank symbol are called auxiliary symbols. The auxiliary alphabet, V, is $\Sigma - T - \{\wedge\}$.

If $\delta(k, a) = (k', a', X)$, this is interpreted to mean that the TM when in state k scanning a will change to state k', overwrite a by a', and move the tape head in direction X (L for left, R for right, 0 for no move).

9.4.2 Graphical representation of Turing machines

A TM, $M = (K, \Sigma, T, \delta, q_0, F)$, can be represented by a labelled directed graph. The vertices are states, K. If $\delta(k, a) = (k', a', X)$ then vertex k is connected by a directed arc to vertex k' and this arc is labelled (a, a', X). The start state is highlighted by a single arrow and final states by being in squares rather than circles. The TM represented in *Figure 9.7* computes the elementary function *cons0*: $x \to 0x$ for all $x \in \{0, 1\}^*$.

9.4.3 Turing machine computations

Say at some stage the TM's head is in state k, scanning symbol a and in location i. Let λ denote the left-most location on the tape holding a non-blank symbol and ρ the right-most such location.

The string to the left of the head, denoted by α, equals ε if $i \leqslant \lambda$ but, otherwise, is the string in locations λ through $i - 1$. Similarly, β, the string to the right of the head equals ε if $i \geqslant \rho$ but, otherwise, is the string in locations $i + 1$ through ρ. The configuration of the TM is thus defined by the 5-tuple (k, i, α, a, β) (see *Figure 9.8*).

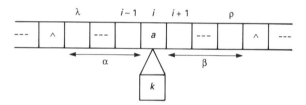

Figure 9.8 A TM configuration

Given an input of $x = \varepsilon$, the initial configuration is $C_0 = (k_0, 1, \varepsilon, \varepsilon, \varepsilon)$ but, otherwise, the input is $x = ay$, $a \in T$, $y \in T^*$, and initial configuration is $(k_0, 1, \varepsilon, a, y)$. The program dictates how the TM changes its configuration. The sequence of configurations, $C_0, C_1, \ldots$ is called the computation sequence for M with input x. Given $C_n = (k, i, \alpha'b, a, c\beta')$, C_{n+1} is defined by:

$$C_{n+1} = \begin{cases} (k', i-1, \alpha', b, a'c\beta') & \text{if } \delta(k, a) = (k', a', L), \\ (k', i+1, \alpha'ba, c, \beta') & \text{if } \delta(k, a) = (k', a', R), \\ (k', i, \alpha'b, a', c\beta') & \text{if } \delta(k, a) = (k', a', 0). \end{cases}$$

If the string to the left or right of a is ε these definitions have to be modified in the obvious way.

If the TM reaches a configuration, C_m, for which the state is a final state, the TM halts and succeeds and the output is computed as described in Section 9.4.1. However, if a configuration, C_m, is reached for which the state is not a final state but for which there is no move, i.e. for which $\delta(k, a)$ is undefined, the TM halts and fails and the output is undefined. The other possibility is that the TM loops infinitely never reaching a final state and never computing any output.

Providing M halts and succeeds in a configuration C_m, the computation sequence for x, comprising C_0, C_1, ..., C_m is said to be successful. The resulting output is $y = f_M(x)$. Since M is deterministic, f_M is a (possibly partial) function and is called the function computed by M.

9.4.4 Turing computability and Church's thesis

A function $f: T^* \rightarrow \Sigma^*$ is Turing-computable iff there is some Turing machine, M, such that $f = f_M$. Church's thesis states that 'every effectively computable function is Turing computable'. Of course, this cannot be proved since 'effectively computable' cannot even be defined. However, there is much to support the thesis. Nobody has ever produced a function computable on any other computing device which is not Turing-computable (see Section 9.5).

There are countably infinite Turing machines which compute partial functions $T^* \rightarrow \Sigma^*$ for any finite alphabets, T, Σ. Thus the Turing-computable functions $T^* \rightarrow \Sigma^*$ are also countably infinite and diagonalization arguments can be used to construct non-computable functions.

9.4.5 Multi-tape Turing machines

A multi-tape Turing machine consists of $n(> 1)$ infinite tapes over which n tape heads move. The tape heads are connected to a control unit which can be in any one of a finite number of states. The program specifies the next move which depends upon the state of the control and the n scanned symbols. Depending upon these values, the control can change state, each of the n scanned symbols can be overwritten and any or all of the tape heads can independently be moved one location left or right. In support of Church's thesis, multi-tape TMs compute exactly the same class of functions as single-tape TMs.

9.4.6 Deterministic two-push-down tape machines

A deterministic two-push-down tape machine is a multi-tape, deterministic TM with a read-only input and two storage tapes. If a head moves left on either of these storage tapes, a blank symbol is printed on that tape. Such a machine can simulate an arbitrary single-tape TM, M. The symbols of the left of the head of M can be stored on one push-down list whilst the symbols on the right are in the other push-down list.

9.4.7 One-way infinite Turing machines

If the tape is limited so that instead of being indexed ... −2, −1, 0, 1, 2, ..., it is simply indexed 1, 2, ..., the TM is said to be one-way infinite. The TM program is executed as for a two-way infinite tape but if a left move is attempted when the head is scanning location 1 then the machine halts and fails. The restriction, however, does not affect the class of funtions computed, i.e. a one-way infinite tape TM is capable of computing any Turing-computable function.

9.4.8 Counter machines

There are other restrictions that can be made to the TM model without affecting the computing power. For example, the TM can be viewed as a 2-tape device, the first tape being used for input/output and the second tape as a work tape. Even if the alphabet used on the work tape comprises just one symbol other than the blank, all Turing-computable functions can still be computed. Such a machine is sometimes called a counter machine. For this and other similar results see Fischer (1963) and Hopcroft and Ullman (1979).

9.4.9 Universal Turing machine

The Universal Turing machine, U, takes as input on its tape, e(M), some encoding of a TM, $M = (K, \Sigma, T, \delta, q_0, F)$, followed by a separator symbol, * (say), followed by a string $x \in T^*$. Then U simulates the action of M on x. Thus if M halts so does U and if M loops forever given input x so does U given input e(M)*x.

9.4.10 Non-deterministic Turing machines

When defining TMs in Section 9.4.1, the program was determined by a partial function $(K - F) \times \Sigma \rightarrow K \times \Sigma \times \{L, R, 0\}$. By insisting that the program was a function it was ensured that $\delta(k, a)$, $k \in K - F$, $a \in \Sigma$, could have at most one value. Thus the TM was deterministic. However, if this constraint is relaxed so that a TM may have several choices for a next move, that TM is said to be non-deterministic.

A non-deterministic Turing machine (NDTM) is formally defined as for the deterministic case except that δ becomes a function $(K - F) \times \Sigma \rightarrow 2^{K \times \Sigma \times \{L, R, 0\}}$. Thus given $k \in K - F$, $a \in \Sigma$, $\delta(k, a)$ is a set of possible moves. Since this set may be empty, δ is always a total function.

9.4.11 Recursive and recursively enumerable languages

A language $L \subseteq T^*$ is called recursive iff there exists a TM with input alphabet T which computes the characteristic function of L, *viz*:

$$\chi_L(x) = \begin{cases} 1 & \text{if } x \in L, \\ 0 & \text{if } x \in T^* - L \end{cases}$$

Note that this TM is not allowed to have an undefined output for any input $x \in T^*$. The TM must always be able to decide whether or not $x \in L$.

Recursively enumerable (r.e.) languages in T^* are those languages $L \subseteq T^*$ for which there exists a TM which computes the partial characteristic function of L, *viz*:

$$\chi'_L(x) = \begin{cases} 1 \text{ if } x \in L, \\ \text{undefined if } x \in T^* - L \end{cases}$$

Such a TM will be able to confirm if $x \in L$ but, if $x \notin L$, no output will be produced.

Every recursive language is recursively enumerable but not every r.e. language is recursive. However, if $L \subseteq T^*$ and $T^* - L$ are both recursively enumerable, then clearly L is recursive.

A string $x \in T^*$ is accepted by a non-deterministic or deterministic TM, M, iff there is some sequence of moves which leads M given x as input to eventually enter a final state. L is accepted by a non-deterministic or deterministic TM if L is recursively enumerable. The recursively enumerable languages are those languages generated by phrase structure grammars, i.e. Chomsky type 0 grammars. This gives yet further support to Church's thesis.

9.4.12 Linear-bounded automata and context-sensitive languages

A non-deterministic TM which for all inputs x will only use at most $k_1 length(x) + k_2$ locations for some fixed integers, k_1, k_2, is called a linear-bounded automaton (LBA). The linear-bounded automata are the acceptors for the context-sensitive (Chomsky type I) languages.

9.4.13 Unsolvable/undecidable problems; the halting problem for Turing machines

An algorithm can be defined as a Turing machine which always halts. If an algorithm exists which solves a given problem that problem is said to be solvable but, otherwise, it is unsolvable. If a problem is a decision problem, i.e. has a yes/no answer, the term decidable is usually used to replace solvable and correspondingly undecidable for unsolvable.

A classic undecidable problem is the halting problem for Turing machines, *viz* the problem: 'Given a TM, $M = (K, \Sigma, T, \delta, q_0, F)$, and an input $x \in T^*$, will M eventually halt?' The decidability of this problem is established by showing that the TM of *Figure 9.9* cannot possibly exist. The input is similar to that given to the Universal TM of Section 9.4.9, but H behaves differently from U because it is required to recognize when M is looping forever. Thus a simple simulation of M will not suffice.

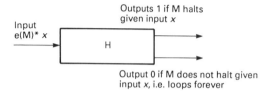

Figure 9.9

9.4.15 Post's correspondence problem

Post's correspondence problem (PCP) is yet another undecidable problem. Its undecidability is used extensively to prove a range of undecidability problems in formal language theory.

PCP is a decision problem which can be defined using a standard format (Garey and Johnson, 1978) as follows.

Post's correspondence problem (PCP)
Instance: A finite alphabet, T, and two *n*-tuples ($n > 0$) of strings in T^+, $x_n = (x_1, x_2, \ldots, x_n)$ and $y = (y_1, y_2, \ldots, y_n)$.
Question: Is there a sequence of integers, $i1, i2, \ldots, im$ ($m > 1$) such that $x_{i1}x_{i2} \ldots x_{im} = y_{i1}y_{i2} \ldots y_{im}$?

9.4.16 A technique for establishing unsolvability/undecidability

Results concerning unsolvability are usually about decision problems and, since most problems can be re-expressed as decision problems, this is no real disadvantage. Consider two decisions problems Π_1 and Π_2. Π_1 is said to reduce to Π_2 iff an algorithm to solve Π_2 can be directly used to solve Π_1. More formally, Π_1 reduces to Π_2 iff there is a TM that will take as input $e_1(I_1)$, an encoding of an instance of Π_1, and yield as output $e_2(I_2)$, an encoding of an instance of Π_2, such that I_1 is a YES-instance of Π_1 iff I_2 is a YES-instance of Π_2. If Π_1 reduces to Π_2 and Π_1 is undecidable then so is Π_2. Thus, for example, any decision problem to which the halting problem or PCP reduces must be undecidable. There is now a large collection of known undecidable problems, and many of these results have fundamental repercussions within computer science.

9.5 Alternative characterizations of computable functions

Through Turing machines, a class of functions – the Turing-computable functions – has been formally defined, and

Church's thesis states this is to be taken as the class of effectively computable functions. There are other approaches which have also been attempted and the fact that they all prove equivalent to the Turing machine approach strongly supports Church's thesis. These alternative approaches are either via alternative machines or use a constructive approach to build a class of functions which are intuitively computable.

9.5.1 Post-computable functions

Post (1936) introduced the concept of Post-system which generates sets of strings by application of certain simple rules. From such sets, the notion of a Post-computable function is derived.

A Post-system S over T is a 3-tuple, $S = (T, A, P)$, where:

1. T is a finite alphabet.
2. $A \subseteq T^*$ is a finite set of strings, the axioms of S.
3. P is a finite set of productions of the form

$$x_0 X_1 x_1 X_2 x_2 \ldots x_{m-1} X_m x_m \to y_0 X_{i1} y_1 X_{i2} y_2 \ldots X_{in} y_n$$

where:

(a) $x_0, x_1, \ldots, x_m, y_0, y_1, \ldots, y_n$ are strings in T^*,
(b) the subscripts $i1, \ldots, in$ are all in $\{1, 2, \ldots, m\}$ but need not be distinct.

If v, $w \in T^*$ is such that w can be obtained from v by a finite number of applications of productions in P, then this is written as $v \Rightarrow^P w$. If $v \Rightarrow^P w$ for some $v \in A$ then w is said to be generated by the Post-system S and this is written $\vdash_S w$. The set of all strings generated by S is $T_S = \{w \in T^* \vdash_S w\}$. A subset $L \subseteq T^*$ is Post-generable iff there is an alphabet $T_1 \supseteq T$ and a Post-system S over T_1 such that $L = T_S \cap T^*$.

A set of productions P (and any Post-system in which P occurs) is said to be normal if all productions in P have the form $xS \to Sy$. Any Post-generable set can be generated by a normal system.

Now consider the partial function f: $T^* \to T^*$. Let \$ be a new symbol not in T and define the set of strings $T(f) = \{w\$f(w) | w \in \text{domain } (f)\}$. Then f: $T^* \to T^*$ is said to be Post-computable iff T(f) is Post-generable. The Post-computable functions are precisely the same class of functions as the Turing-computable functions.

An alternative way of defining Post-computability is via deterministic (or monogenic) Post-systems. A set of productions P is monogenic iff at most one production on P can be applied to any given string. Let f: $T^* \to T^*$ be a partial function and let $\uparrow$ and $\downarrow$ be two new symbols not in T used to distinguish input strings from output strings. The function f is then Post-computable iff there is a monogenic set of productions P over $T \cup \{\uparrow, \downarrow\}$ such that for $w \in \text{domain } (f)$, $\uparrow w \Rightarrow^P \downarrow f(w)$ and no production in P applies to $\downarrow f(w)$.

9.5.2 Post machines

Post machines owe their origin to normal Post-systems. However, they were not defined by Post but by Arbib (1963) and independently by Shepherdson and Sturgess (1963). A Post machine takes an input $x \in T^*$ but can also use an auxiliary symbol, \$, not in T. The program is constructed from (a) test statements which are applied to the left-most symbol of the current string x, that symbol then being deleted, and (b) assignment statements allowing the concatenation of symbols in $T \cup \{\$\}$ to the right of x. An elementary introduction using flowcharts can be found in Manna (1974). The class of functions computable by Post machines is precisely the class of functions computable by Turing machines.

9.5.3 Markov computability

The Markov approach to computability (1954) has many similarities to that of Post. Rather than restrict attention to monogenic systems, Markov uses rules to determine uniquely which of the available productions should next be applied. Once again, the class of function so defined, i.e. the Markov-computable functions, correspond exactly to the Turing-computable functions.

9.5.4 Unlimited register machines

The unlimited register machine (URM) is a model of a computation device designed to compute functions over the natural numbers (Shepherdson and Sturgis, 1963). The URM has an infinite number of registers $R_1, R_2, \ldots$ each of which contains a natural number. Once these registers have been initialized, a program is run constructed from instructions of the following forms:

1. *Zero instructions.* Z_i meaning set contents of R_i to 0.
2. *Successor instruction.* S_i meaning set contents of R_i to previous contents plus one, i.e., $R_i := R_i + 1$.
3. *Jump instruction.* $J_{i,j,k}$ meaning **if** $R_i = R_j$ **then goto** kth instruction in the program but otherwise go onto the next instruction.
4. *Stop instruction.* STOP.

For example, the program given in *Figure 9.10* will add the contents of R_2 to R_1.

1	Z_3	$\{R_3 := 0\}$
2	$J_{2,3,6}$	$\{$if $R_2 = R_3$ then goto 6$\}$
3	S_3	$\{R_3 := R_3 + 1\}$
4	S_1	$\{R_1 := R_1 + 1\}$
5	$J_{2,2,2}$	$\{$if $R_2 = R_2$ then goto 2$\}$
6	STOP	

Figure 9.10

When using URMs, it is customary to extend the basic instruction set using a suite of developed programs (Cutland, 1980; Fischer, 1982). As with normal programming, this greatly enhances the ease of software development.

If f: $N^n \to N$ is a partial function defined on the natural numbers then f is said to be URM-computable iff for all n-tuples $(a_1, a_2, \ldots, a_n)$ in the domain of f, there is some URM which given $R_1 = a_1, \ldots, R_n = a_n$, and all other registers zero will compute $f(a_1, a_2, \ldots, a_n)$ and halt with that value in R_1.

The URM-computable functions in the natural numbers are precisely the TM-computable functions (subject to a suitable encoding). Thus URMs compute the partial recursive functions over the natural numbers (see below).

9.5.5 Primitive and partial recursive functions

Gödel, Herbrand and Kleene developed the theory of recursive functions using an equational calculus in the 1930s. More recent references are Hermes (1969), Kleene (1952), Mendelson (1964), Péter (1967) and Rayward-Smith (1986). The idea is to construct a class of effectively computable functions from a collection of base functions using accepted techniques such as function composition and recursion.

9.5.5.1 Primitive recursive functions over binary strings

Using B to denote $\{0, 1\}^*$, the primitive recursive functions $B^n \to B$ ($n \geq 1$) are constructed according to the following rules.

1. *Base functions.* The following are primitive recursive functions:

   (a) $nil: B \to B$ defined by $nil(x) = \varepsilon$ for all $x \in B$;
   (b) $cons0$ and $cons1$: $B \to B$ defined by $cons0(x) = 0x$ and $cons1(x) = 1x$ for all $x \in B$;
   (c) the selector functions δ_n^i: $B^n \to B$ ($1 \leq i \leq n$) where $\delta_n^i(x_1, x_2, \ldots, x_n) = x_i$ for all n-tuples $(x_1, \ldots, x_n) \in B^n$.

2. From known primitive recursive functions new primitive recursive functions are constructed using:

   (a) *Function composition.* If the functions $h: B^m \to B$ and $g_1, g_2, \ldots, g_m: B^n \to B$ are primitive recursive then so is the n-ary function, $f: B^n \to B$ defined by
   $$f(x_1, \ldots, x_n) = h(g_1(x_1, \ldots, x_n), \ldots, g_m(x_1, \ldots, x_n)).$$
   (b) *Primitive recursion.* If $h_1, h_2: B^2 \to B$ are primitive recursive so too is any $f: B \to B$ defined by the following rules:

   $$f(\varepsilon) = w \quad \text{\{some constant string\}}$$
   $$f(0x) = h_1(x, f(x))$$
   $$f(1x) = h_2(x, f(x))$$

   Similarly, a function $f: B^n \to B$ can be defined in terms of known primitive recursive functions $g: B^{n-1} \to B$ and $h_1, h_2: B^{n+1} \to B$ as follows:
   $$f(\varepsilon, x_2, \ldots, x_n) = g(x_2, \ldots, x_n)$$
   $$f(0x_1, x_2, \ldots, x_n) = h_1(x_1, \ldots, x_n, f(x_1, \ldots, x_n))$$
   $$f(1x_1, x_2, \ldots, x_n) = h_2(x_1, \ldots, x_n, f(x_1, \ldots, x_n))$$

3. No other functions except the base functions and those constructed by repeated use of (2) above are primitive recursive.

Since all the base functions are total TM-computable functions and since both composition and primitive recursion preserve these properties, all primitive recursive functions are TM-computable total functions. However, the converse is not true, i.e. there are total TM-computable functions that are not primitive recursive the classic example being Ackermann's functions see, for example, Hermes (1969).

9.5.5.2 Primitive recursive functions over the natural numbers

The primitive recursive functions $N^n \to N$ ($n \geq 1$) are defined as above with the following modifications. The base functions are redefined so that instead of nil, $cons0$ and $cons1$, the functions $zero: N \to N$ and $succ: N \to N$ are used where $zero(x) = 0$ and $succ(x) = x + 1$ for $x \in N$. A primitive recursive definition of $f: N \to N$ requires a definition of $f(0)$ as some constant and $f(x + 1)$ in terms of known primitive recursive functions whose arguments may include $f(x)$. Similarly, $f: N^n \to N$ ($n \geq 1$) proceeds by just defining $f(0, x_2, \ldots, x_n)$ as a known primitive recursive function applied to arguments $x_2, \ldots, x_n$, and then defining $f(x_1 + 1, x_2, \ldots, x_n)$ as a known primitive recursive functions applied to arguments $x_1, x_2, \ldots, x_n, f(x_1, x_2, \ldots, x_n)$.

9.5.5.3 Partial recursive functions over binary strings

To define the partial recursive functions, the μ-operator must be introduced. A partial function $P: B^n \to B$ is a partial predicate iff $P(x_1, \ldots, x_n)$ is either undefined or evaluates to 0 or 1. If $P(x_1, \ldots, x_n)$ is a partial predicate ($n \geq 2$), then $\mu y. P(x_1, \ldots, x_{n-1}, y)$ equals y' if $P(x_1, \ldots, x_{n-1}, y') = 1$ and $P(x_1, \ldots, x_{n-1}, y'') = 0$ for all predecessors y'' of y' in the natural lexicographic ordering, ε, 0, 1, 00, ... Otherwise, $\mu y. P(x_1, \ldots, x_n, y)$ is undefined. If P is any n-ary predicate that is TM-computable and f is the $(n-1)$-ary function defined by $f(x_1, \ldots, x_{n-1}) = \mu y. P(x_1, \ldots, x_{n-1}, y)$ then f is also TM-computable. A function constructed in this way is said to be constructed by unbounded minimization.

The class of partial recursive functions over binary strings are functions $B^n \to B$ ($n \geq 1$) constructed from the base functions nil, *cons0*, *cons1* and δ_n^i ($1 \leqslant i \leqslant n$) using just composition, recursion and unbounded minimization. Details can be found in Ray-ward-Smith (1986). The partial recursive functions $B^n \to B$ are precisely the TM-computable functions $B^n \to B$. This result is generally known as Kleene's theorem.

9.5.5.4 *Partial recursive functions over the natural numbers*

This is a class of functions equivalent to the TM-computable functions over the natural numbers (given a suitable encoding). They are defined in terms of base functions *zero*, *succ* and δ_n^i using composition, recursion and unbounded minimization. In this case $\mu y . P(x_1, \ldots, x_{n-1}, y)$ is the smallest natural number y', such that $P(x_1, \ldots, x_{n-1}, y') = 1$ but $P(x_1, \ldots, x_{n-1}, y'') = 0$ for all $y'' < y'$ if such a y' exists and is undefined otherwise.

9.6 Complexity theory

There are two types of complexity measure, time complexity and space complexity. In most situations the complexity of a computation will depend upon the size of the input, and for Turing machines, the length of the input string is thus used. Time complexity depends upon the length of a computation sequence and space complexity on the amount of tape used.

9.6.1 Time complexity of a Turing machine computation

Consider a TM, M, with an arbitrary number of two-way infinite storage tapes one of which is also used for input. If for every input string of length n, M makes at most $T(n)$ moves before halting then M is said to be a $T(n)$ time-bounded Turing machine or to be of time complexity $T(n)$. Time complexity defined in this way applies to both deterministic and non-deterministic TMs. A $T(n)$ time-bounded NDTM is such that no sequence of moves can be made which causes the machine to exceed its $T(n)$ limit for any input string of length n.

The language accepted by a TM of time complexity $T(n)$ is also said to be of time complexity $T(n)$. The class of languages of deterministic time complexity $T(n)$ is denoted by $DTIME(T(n))$ and that of non-deterministic time complexity $T(n)$ by $NTIME(T(n))$. These classes of languages are examples of complexity classes. The relationship between these complexity classes as $T(n)$ varies is discussed in Hopcroft and Ullman (1979). In particular, a corollary of a result established in Hartmanis and Stearns (1965) is that if:

$$\operatorname*{Inf}_{n \to \infty} \frac{T(n)}{n} = \infty \quad \text{and} \quad c > 0$$

then $DTIME(T(n)) = DTIME(cT(n))$. Also, if $f(n) = cn$ for some $c > 1$ and $g(n) = (1 + \varepsilon)n$ for any $\varepsilon > 0$ then $DTIME(f) = DTIME(g)$. Analogous results also hold for NDTMs.

The definition of time complexity uses a TM with an arbitrary number of tapes. The number of tapes cannot be fixed in the definition without altering the complexity classes. However, it can be shown that if L is in $DTIME(T(n))$ then L is accepted in time $T^2(n)$ by a one-tape TM and a similar analogous result exists for $NTIME(T(n))$. Also if L is accepted by a k-tape $T(n)$ time-bounded TM, M_1, then L is also accepted by a two-storage tape TM, M_2, in time $T(n) \log T(n)$ (Hennie and Stearns, 1966). These and other results are well described in Hopcroft and Ullman (1979).

9.6.2 P, NP and NP-complete

The languages recognizable in deterministic polynomial time are denoted by P. Thus $P = \bigcup_{i \geqslant 1} DTIME(n^i)$. Similarly, the languages recognizable in non-deterministic polynomial time is denoted by $NP = \bigcup_{i \geqslant 1} NTIME(n^i)$. If Π is a decision problem then the set of instances of Π is denoted by D_Π. Assume there is an encoding, e, of instances $I \in D_\Pi$ into strings of T^*, i.e. e: $D_\Pi \to T^*$. A deterministic algorithm which solves Π is then a DTM which recognizes whether or not e(I) is in the language $L[\Pi, e] = \{e(I) | I \in Y_\Pi\}$, where $Y_\Pi \subseteq D_\Pi$ is the subset of YES-instances of Π. The encoding used must be a sensible, concise encoding, i.e. it must contain no spurious 'padding', must be uniquely and effectively decodable and must represent numbers etc. in binary (or octal, decimal, etc., but *not* unary) notation. $\Pi \in P$ is then used to mean $L[\Pi, e] \in P$ for some such encoding.

If Π is solved by a non-deterministic TM which accepts $L[\Pi, e]$ then the time taken to determine if I in Y_Π is the maximum length of a computation sequence accepting e(I). If I is not in Y_Π then no sequence of moves should result the acceptance of e(I).

Clearly, $P \subseteq NP$ and it is believed that $P \neq NP$. Whether this is correct or not, is one of the great open problems of theoretical computer science.

A decision problem, Π_1, polynomially transforms to a decision problem, Π_2, written $\Pi_1 \propto \Pi_2$, iff there exists a function f: $D_{\Pi_1} \to D_{\Pi_2}$ such that:

1. for each $I \in D_{\Pi_1}$, $I \in Y_{\Pi_1}$ iff $f(I) \in Y_{\Pi_2}$;
2. f can be computed in polynomial time.

In a more formal language theoretic context, $L_1 \subseteq T_1^*$ polynomially transforms to $L_2 \subseteq T_2^*$, written $L_1 \propto L_2$, iff there exists f: $T_1^* \to T_2^*$ such that:

1. for all $x \in T_1^*$, $x \in L_1$ iff $f(x) \in L_2$;
2. there is a polynomial time DTM that computes f.

Thus $\Pi_1 \propto \Pi_2$, iff there exist (sensible, concise) encodings e_1, e_2, such that $L[\Pi_1, e_1] \propto L[\Pi_2, e_2]$.

It is easy to show that $\propto$ is a transitive relation and that $L_1 \propto L_2$, $L_2 \in P$ implies $L_1 \in P$.

A language L is NP-complete iff (1) $L \in NP$ and (2) for all $L' \in NP$, $L' \propto L$.

A decision problem Π is NP-complete iff for some sensible, concise encoding, e, $L[\Pi, e]$ is NP-complete. Informally, Π is NP-complete iff (1) $\Pi \in NP$ and (2) for all $\Pi' \in NP$, $\Pi' \propto \Pi$.

If any NP-complete problem can be solved in polynomial time then $NP = P$. The NP-complete problems have proved an important class of problems all of which can be solved by a non-deterministic polynomial time algorithm but not apparently by a deterministic polynomial time algorithm. The first problem known to be NP-complete is satisfiability, this result being established by Cook (1971).

Satisfiability
Instance: A finite set, U, of Boolean variables and a finite set, C, of clauses over U.
Question: Is there a satisfying truth assignment for C?

If $\Pi' \in NP$ then Π' can be shown to be NP-complete by establishing $\Pi \propto \Pi'$ for any Π known to be NP-complete. This provides a simple technique for establishing new NP-completeness results. From the seminal result that satisfiability is NP-complete, a large number of other problems have now also been shown to be NP-complete (Garey and Johnson, 1978; Traub, 1976). The known NP-complete problems are listed in the classic text by Garey and Johnson (1978) and this list has since been regularly updated in a series of articles in the *Journal of Algorithms*.

In the definition of an encoding, the use of unary notation

was specifically excluded. A number problem (i.e., a decision problem including numbers) is said to be unary NP-complete or NP-complete in the strong sense if it remains NP-complete even if unary encoding is adopted. Some number problems are unary NP-complete whilst others are not.

9.6.3 Complementary problems

If Π is some decision problem, it will have the general format: 'given an instance, I, is some condition, B, true for I?'. The complement of the problem Π, denoted by Π^c, is identical to Π except that the question asked is whether the condition, B, is false for I. Thus $D_{\Pi^c} = D_\Pi$ and $Y_{\Pi^c} = D_\Pi - Y_\Pi$. At the language level, the complexity class co-P is defined to be $\{T^* - L \mid L \subseteq T^*$ is in P$\}$ and clearly co-P = P. However, if co-NP is defined analogously, co-NP is unlikely to be equal to NP. Certainly $P = NP \Rightarrow NP = co\text{-}NP$ but the converse has not been established. However, it is easily shown that $P \subseteq NP \cap co\text{-}NP$ and that $NP \neq co\text{-}NP \Rightarrow NP\text{-complete} \subseteq NP - co\text{-}NP$ and co-NP-complete $\subseteq co\text{-}NP - NP$. These properties are summarized in *Figure 9.11*.

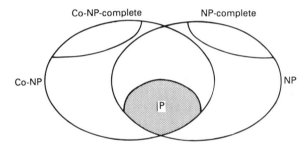

Co-NP-complete   NP-complete

Co-NP   P   NP

Figure 9.11

9.6.4 NP-easy, NP-hard and the polynomial hierarchy

Consider a TM equipped with the following extra facility known as an oracle. A TM with an oracle for L is a TM equipped with an oracle input tape on which can be written any string $x \in T^*$ and, in one time unit, the oracle can then report whether or not $x \in L$. The oracle corresponds to a subroutine which can solve some sub-problem, but each time the subroutine is used, only one time unit is required.

A decision problem Π is said to be NP-easy if it can be solved in polynomial time by a DTM equipped with an oracle for some language in NP (i.e. which solves some problem in NP). Any problem in NP is thus trivially NP-easy.

If X is any class of problems, P^X is defined to be the class of problems which can be solved in polynomial time by a DTM equipped with an oracle solving some problem $\Pi' \in X$. NP^X is defined similarly.

The NP-easy problems are thus P^{NP}. Moreover, $NP^{NP} \supseteq P^{NP} \supseteq NP \cup co\text{-}NP$. The NP-easy problems are so-called because, in some sense, they are no harder than any problem in NP.

On the other hand, NP-hard problems are those problems which could be used to solve NP-complete problems. A problem Π is NP-hard if there exists an NP-complete problem Π' which could be solved by a polynomial time DTM provided it is equipped with an oracle to solve Π.

The hierarchy $NP^{NP} \supseteq P^{NP} \supseteq NP \cup co\text{-}NP$ is the beginning of an infinite hierarchy of complexity known as the polynomial hierarchy. This is defined recursively as $\Sigma_0 = \Pi_0 = \Delta_0 = P$.

For all $k \geqslant 0$:

$$\Delta_{k+1} = P^{\Sigma_k}, \; \Sigma_{k+1} = NP^{\Sigma_k} \text{ and } \Pi_{k+1} = co\text{-}\Sigma_{k+1}$$

Then for any k, $\Delta_k \subseteq \Pi_k \cap \Sigma_k$ and $\Pi_k \cup \Sigma_k \subseteq \Delta_{k+1}$
The complexity class:

$$PH = \bigcup_{k=1}^{\infty} \Sigma_k$$

denotes all problems (languages) in this hierarchy. Details of this hierarchy are to be found in Stockmeyer (1976).

9.6.5 Space complexity of a Turing machine computation

When discussing space complexity the length of the input is discounted and thus the basic model of the TM used differs slightly from that of Section 9.6.1.

Consider a TM, M, with one finite read-only tape equipped with end markers and an arbitrary number of semi-infinite storage tapes. If for every input word of length n, M scans at most $S(n)$ locations on any individual storage tape, M is said to be $S(n)$ space-bounded or of space complexity $S(n)$. The language recognized by M is also said to be of space complexity $S(n)$. Since every TM uses at least one location on all its inputs, $S(n) \geqslant 1$ for all n. It is thus customary to interpret the phrase 'space complexity $S(n)$' to mean the space complexity is max $(1, [S(n)])$.

DSPACE($S(n)$) denotes the class of languages of deterministic space complexity $S(n)$ and correspondingly NSPACE($S(n)$) the class of languages of non-deterministic space complexity $S(n)$. From a result established in Hartmanis *et al.* (1965):

$$L \in NSPACE(S(n)) \Rightarrow L \in NSPACE(cS(n)) \text{ for any } c > 0$$

If L is accepted by an $S(n)$ space-bounded TM with k storage tapes, it is also accepted by an $S(n)$ space-bounded TM with a single storage tape. Hence, when discussing space-bounded TMs it is safe to assume the usual model of a single-tape TM provided $S(n) \geqslant n$.

Further results on DSPACE($S(n)$), NSPACE($S(n)$) are to be found in Hartmanis *et al.* (1965), Hopcroft and Ullman (1979), Seiferas (1977a and b).

9.6.6 PSPACE, POLYLOGSPACE, DLOGSPACE and PSPACE-complete

PSPACE is the class of language recognizable in deterministic polynomial space, i.e.

$$PSPACE = \bigcup_{i \geqslant 1} DSPACE(n^i)$$

By a result of Savitch (1970), PSPACE = NSPACE. Also, it is then clear that $NP \subseteq PSPACE$ but whether this containment is strict is an open problem.

Within PSPACE, there are two hierarchies of complexity classes, *viz*:

$$DSPACE(\log n) \subseteq DSPACE(\log^2 n) \subseteq \ldots \text{ and}$$

$$NSPACE(\log n) \subseteq NSPACE(\log^2 n) \subseteq \ldots$$

Now, $DSPACE(\log^k n) \subseteq NSPACE(\log^k n)$ and, by Savitch, $\bigcup_{k \geqslant 1} NSPACE(\log^k n) = \bigcup_{k \geqslant 1} DSPACE(\log^k n)$. This complexity class is denoted by POLYLOGSPACE. Although POLYLOGSPACE $\neq P$ is known, it is not known whether either of these classes is contained within the other. The complexity class DLOGSPACE denotes DSPACE($\log n$) and is a sub-space of P. Again, it is not known whether it is a proper sub-space or not. However, since DLOGSPACE $\neq$ PSPACE, one of the containments in DLOGSPACE $\subseteq$ P $\subseteq$ NP $\subseteq$ PSPACE must be proper.

A language L is said to be PSPACE-complete iff L$\in$PSPACE and for all L'$\in$PSPACE, L' $\propto$ L. As with the NP-complete complexity class, this definition is extended to include decision problems. Although there are many known PSPACE-complete problems (Garey and Johnson, 1978), they are fewer in number than the known NP-complete problems.

9.6.7 Log-space transformations, log-space complete for P

Let L_1, L_2 be two languages over alphabets T_1, T_2, respectively. A log-space transformation from L_1 to L_2, denoted $L_1 \propto_{\log} L_2$, is a function $f: T_1^* \to T_2^*$ such that:

1. $x \in L_1$ iff $f(x) \in L_2$.
2. f can be computed by a log-space transducer, i.e. a multiple TM with read-only input which always halts and has space complexity $\log n$.

Then $\alpha_{\log}$ is transitive and $L_1 \propto_{\log} L_2$ implies both
$L_2 \in$ DLOGSPACE $\Rightarrow L_1 \in$ DLOGSPACE and
$L_2 \in$ POLYLOGSPACE $\Rightarrow L_1 \in$ POLYLOGSPACE.

A Language L is log-space complete for P if and only if:

1. $L \in P$.
2. For all $L' \in P$, $L' \propto_{\log} L$.

If any such language belonged to POLYLOGSPACE then P $\subseteq$ POLYLOGSPACE which is assumed not to be the case. All the above definitions can be extended from languages to problems in the obvious way. It is widely believed that a dramatic speed-up from polynomial to polylogarithmic time can only be obtained by parallelism for those problems in P that belong to POLYLOGSPACE. This assertion has become known as the parallel computation hypothesis. A problem that is log-space complete for P is thus very unlikely to yield to such a dramatic speed-up.

9.6.8 Stack automata

The stack automaton (SA) is a restricted type of two-tape non-deterministic TM which can also be viewed as an extension of a non-deterministic push-down automaton. The SA has an input tape and a work tape, i.e. the stack. The head on the input can move both ways over this tape. Symbols can only be added to or removed from the top of the stack but the stack head can traverse the whole of the stack in a read-only mode.

Stack automata were originally defined in Ginsburg et al. (1967). Important restrictions on stack automata are (1) making the machine deterministic, (2) making it non-erasing, i.e. ensuring no stack symbol is ever erased and (3) insisting the input head never moves left, i.e. that the SA is one-way.

The primary results (Hopcroft and Ullman, 1979) are:

1. L is accepted by a non-erasing deterministic SA iff L$\in$DSPACE($n \log n$).
2. L is accepted by a non-erasing non-deterministic SA iff L$\in$NSPACE(n^2).
3. L is accepted by a non-deterministic SA iff L$\in \bigcup_{c>0}$ DTIME(c^{n^2}).
4. L is accepted by a deterministic SA iff L$\in \bigcup_{c>0}$DTIME(n^{cn}).
5. If L is accepted by a one-way non-deterministic stack automaton then L$\in$DSPACE(n).

9.7 References and bibliography

Arbib, M. A. (1963) Monogenic normal systems are universal. *Journal of the Australian Mathemat. Society*, **3**, 301–306

Arbib, M. A. (1969) *Theories of Abstract Automata*, Prentice Hall, Englewood Cliffs, NJ

Chomsky, N. (1959) On certain formal properties of grammars, *Information and Control*, **2**, 137–167

Chomsky, N. (1962) Context-free grammars and pushdown storage. *Quarterly Prog. Report, MIT Research Laboratory*, No. 65, 187–194

Church, A. (1936) An unsolvable problem of elementary number theory. *Amer. J. Math.*, **58**, 345–363

Cook, S. A. (1971) The complexity of theorem proving procedures. In *Proc. Third Annual ACM Symposium on the Theory of Computing*, 151–158

Cutland, N. J. (1980) *Computability: An Introduction to Recursive Function Theory*, Cambridge University Press, Cambridge

Davies, M. (1958) *Computability and Unsolvability*, McGraw-Hill, New York

Eilenberg, S. and Elgot, C. C. (1980) *Recursiveness*, Academic Press, New York

Evey, J. (1963) Applications of pushdown store machines. In *Proc. 1963 Fall, Joint Comp. Conf.*, AFIPS Press, Montvale, NJ, pp. 215–227

Fischer, P. C. (1963) On the computability by certain classes of restricted Turing machine. In *Proc. Fourth Annual Symposium on Switching Circuit Theory & Logical Design*, Chicago, Ill., 23–32

Fischer, A. E. (1982) *Formal Number Theory and Computability: a Workbook*, Oxford University Press, Oxford

Garey, M. R. and Johnson, D. S. (1978) *Computers and Intractability: A Guide to the Theory of NP-Completeness*, W. H. Freeman, San Francisco

Ginsburg, S., and Greibach, S. A. (1966) Mappings which preserve context-sensitive languages. *Information and Control*, **9**, 563–582

Ginsburg, S., Greibach, S. A. and Harrison, M. A. (1967) Stack automata and compiling. *Journal of the ACM*, **14**, 172–201

Ginsburg, S., and Rose, G. F. (1966) Preservation of languages by transducers. *Information and Control*, **9**, 153–176

Hartmanis, J., Lewis, P. M.,II, and Stearns, R.E. (1965) Hierarchies of memory limited computations. In *Proc, Sixth Annual IEEE Symposium on Switching Circuit Theory and Logical Design*, pp. 179–190

Hartmanis, J., and Stearns, R. E. (1965) On the computational complexity of algorithms. *Trans. AMS*, **117**, 285–306

Hennie, F. C. (1977) *Introduction to Computability*, Addison-Wesley, Reading, MA

Hennie, F. C., and Stearns, R. E. (1966) Two-tape simulation of multiple Turing machines, *Journal of the ACM*, **13**, 533–546

Hermes, H. (1969) *Enumerability, Decidability, Computability*, translated by G. T. Hermann and O. Plassman, Springer-Verlag, New York

Hopcroft, J. E., and Ullman, J. D. (1969) *Formal Languages and their Relation to Automata*, Addison-Wesley, Reading, MA

Hopcroft, J. E., and Ullman, J. D. (1979) *Introduction of Automata Theory, Languages and Computation*, Addison-Wesley, Reading, MA

Kleene, S. C. (1936) General recursive functions of natural numbers. *Mathematisches Annalen*, **112**, 727–742

Kleene, S. C. (1952) *Introduction to Metamathematics*, North Holland, Amsterdam

Kleene, S. C. (1956) Representation of events in nerve nets and finite automata. In *Automata Studies*, Princeton Univ. Press, Princeton, NJ, pp. 3–42

Kohavi, Z. (1970) *Switching and Finite Automata Theory*, McGraw-Hill, New York

Kuroda, S. Y. (1964) Classes of languages and linear bounded automata. *Information and Control*, **7**, 207–223

Lewis, H. R., and Papadimitriou, C. H. (1981) *Elements of the Theory of Computation*, Prentice-Hall, Englewood Cliffs, NJ

Lewis, P. M. II, and Stearns, R. E. (1968) Syntax directed transduction. *Journal of the ACM*, **15**, 465–488

Lewis, P. M., II, Stearns, R. E. and Hartmanis, J. (1965) Memory bounds for recognition of context-free and context-sensitive languages. In *Proc. Sixth Annual IEEE Symposium on Switching Circuit Theory and Logical Design*, pp. 191–202

McCulloch, W. S., and Pitts, W. (1943) A logical calculus of the ideas imminent in nervous activity. *Bull. Math. Biophysics*, **5**, 115–133

McNaughton, R. (1982) *Elementary Computability, Formal Languages and Automata*, Prentice-Hall, Englewood Cliffs, NJ

Mandrioli, D., and Ghezzi, C. (1987) *Theoretical Foundations of Computer Science*, J. Wiley, New York

Manna, Z. (1974) *Mathematical Theory of Computation*, McGraw-Hill, New York

Markov, A. (1954) The theory of algorithms. *Trans. Math. Inst. Steklow*, **42**

Mealy, G. H. (1955) A method for synthesizing sequential circuits. *Bell System Tech. Journal*, **34**, 1045–1079

Mendelson, E. (1964) *Introduction to Mathematical Logic*, Van Nostrand Reinhold, New York

Minsky, M. L. (1967) *Computation: Finite and Infinite Machines*, Prentice-Hall, Englewood Cliffs, NJ

Moore, E. F. (1956) Gedanken experiments on sequential machines. In *Automata Studies*, Princeton Univ. Press, Princeton, NJ, pp. 129–153

Nerode, A. (1958) Linear automation transformation, *Proc. AMS, 9*, 541–544

Oettinger, A. G. (1961) Automatic syntactic analysis and the pushdown store. In *Proc. Symposia in App. Math., 12,* Amer. Math. Soc., Providence, RI

Péter, R. (1967) *Recursive Functions*, translated by I. Földes, Academic Press, New York

Post, E. (1936) Finite combinatory process – formulation I. *Journal of Symbolic Logic*, **1**, 103–105

Post, E. (1946) A variant of a recursive unsolvable problem. *Bull. AMS*, **52**, 264–268

Rabin, M. O., and Scott, D. (1959) Finite automata and their decision problems. *IBM J. Res., 3*, 115–125

Rayward-Smith, V. J. (1983) *A First Course in Formal Language Theory*, Blackwell Scientific, Oxford

Rayward-Smith, V. J. (1986) *A First Course in Computability*, Blackwell Scientific, Oxford

Rogers, H. Jr. (1967) *The Theory of Recursive Functions and Effective Computability*, McGraw-Hill, New York

Savitch, W. J. (1970) Relationships between nondeterministic and deterministic tape complexities. *Journal of Computer and Systems Sciences, 4*, 177–192

Schutzenberger, M. P. (1963) On context-free languages and pushdown automata. *Info. and Control, 6*, 246–264

Seiferas, J. I. (1977) Techniques for separating space complexity classes. *Journal of Computer and Systems Sciences, 14*, 73–99

Seiferas, J. I. (1977) Relating referred complexity classes. *Journal of Computer and Systems Sciences, 14*, 100–129

Shepherdson, J. C., and Sturgis, H. E. (1963) Computability of recursive functions, *Journal of the ACM, 10*, 217–255

Stockmeyer, L. J. (1976) The polynomial time hierarchy, *Theoretical Computer Science, 3*, 1–22

Traub, J. F. (ed.) (1976) *Algorithms and Complexity: New Directions and Recent Results*, Academic Press, New York

Turing, A. M. (1936) On computable numbers with an application to the entscheidungsproblem, *Proc. London Math Soc., 2*, 230–265

10 Language theory

Professor V J Rayward-Smith
University of East Anglia, Norwich

Contents

10.1 Introduction

10.1.1 Syntax and Semantics

Within both natural languages and programming languages, there are two specific components that can immediately be recognized. The first is the syntax, or the rules of grammar, which determines whether a sentence is well formed. The second is the semantics or meaning which determines how one interprets the sentence. Thus the two English sentences, 'the dog bites the man' and 'the man is bitten by the dog', both have the same semantic interpretation but differ syntactically. On occasions in English, a syntactic analysis may aid the semantic interpretation. For example, the English sentence 'they are flying planes' has two distinct parses, see *Figure 10.1*, and associated with each is a different meaning. Examples such as this are relatively rare in English since the association between syntax and semantics is not of overriding importance.

they   are flying planes   they   are flying planes

Noun Verb phrase Noun   Noun Verb Adjective Noun

Noun phrase

Figure 10.1

However, the association is much stronger within computing languages. Programming languages usually have a rigorous, but sometimes only partial, formal syntactic definition either formally or informally linked with their semantic definition. A key step in compiling is to take a program and parse it according to the rules of the programming language. In this chapter, the formal theory behind the syntactic and semantic definition of programming languages is reviewed.

In this first section, some necessary mathematical notation is introduced together with the simple language generators known as OL systems. In subsequent sections, the concept of a phrase structure grammar and its variants are studied. Most of this material stems from the pioneering work of Chomsky dating back to the 1950s (Chomsky, 1956 and 1959) and can be found in various texts on formal language theory (Ginsburg, 1966; Hopcroft and Ullman, 1969, 1979; Mandrioli and Ghezzi, 1987; Rayward-Smith, 1983; Salomaa, 1973, for example). These grammars are used to formally define the syntax of programming languages. The formal definition of semantics has proved a much more difficult task and it is only since the latter half of the 1960s that significant progress has been made. This is reviewed in the later part of the chapter.

10.1.2 Alphabets and strings

An alphabet is a finite (totally ordered), non-empty set of characters. A string over an alphabet is a finite sequence of characters from the alphabet with possible repetitions and written in juxtaposition. Thus, 011 is a string over the alphabet $\{0,1\}$. The number of characters in a string, counted according to multiplicity, is the length of that string. If x is a string, $|x|$, denotes the length of that string, for example, $|011| = 3$. The string of length 0 is usually denoted by ε (although some authors use λ).

If T is an alphabet then T* denotes the sets of all strings over T. T* always contains the empty string. $T^+ = T^* - \{\varepsilon\}$ denotes the strings of length > 0. Any string in T^+ is of the form $x = ay$ where $a \in T$, $y \in T^*$. The first character, a, of such a string, x, is denoted by head(x) and the remaining characters, y, by tail(x).

There is a natural ordering of T* called the lexicographic ordering, which can be inferred from the ordering of T. If $<$ denotes the ordering of T, the lexicographic ordering, $<_{lex}$, is defined recursively as follows:

$$x <_{lex} y \text{ iff } \quad \textbf{either} \quad |x| < |y|$$
$$\textbf{or} \quad |x| = |y| \textbf{ and } \text{head}(x) < \text{head}(y)$$
$$\textbf{or} \quad |x| = |y| \textbf{ and } \text{head}(x) = \text{head}(y) \textbf{ and}$$
$$\text{tail}(x) <_{lex} \text{tail}(y)$$

Thus, if T = $\{0,1\}$ with $0 < 1$, then the elements of T* can be listed in lexicographic ordering as ε, 0, 1, 00, 01, 10, 11, 000, 001, 010, 011, 100, 101, etc.

If x,y are strings in T* then their concatenation is the string $xy \in T^*$. The identity with respect to this operation is thus the empty string ε. If $x \in T^*$, then $x^0 = \varepsilon$, $x^2 = xx$, $x^3 = xx^2, \ldots$, and, in general, $x^k = xx^{k-1}$, $(k \geqslant 1)$.

A string $x \in T^*$ is a substring of $y \in T^*$ iff y can be written $y = y_0 x y_1$ where $y_0, y_1 \in T^*$. If y_0 is empty, x is said to be a prefix of y and if y_1 is empty, x is said to be a postfix of y. If $y_0 y_1 \neq \varepsilon$ then x is said to be a proper substring of y. A proper prefix is a prefix which is a proper substring and, similarly, a proper postfix is a postfix which is a proper substring.

The reversal of a string $x \in T^*, x'$, is defined recursively by $\varepsilon' = \varepsilon$, and if $x = ay$, $a \in T$, $y \in T^*$ then $x' = y'a$.

10.1.3 Formal (string) languages

A (formal, string) language over T is a subset of T*. Note that it may be empty, finite or infinite.

If L_1, L_2 are two languages over T then their (set) concatenation is $L_1 L_2 = \{xy \mid x \in L_1 \text{ and } y \in L_2\}$. With respect to set concatentation, $\emptyset$ is a zero since for all L, $L\emptyset = \emptyset L = \emptyset$ and $\{\varepsilon\}$ is the identity since for all L, $L\{\varepsilon\} = \{\varepsilon\}L = L$.

If L is a language in T* then $L^0 = \{\varepsilon\}$, $L^2 = LL$, $L^3 = LL^2, \ldots$, and, in general, $L^k = LL^{k-1}$ $(k \geqslant 1)$. The positive closure of L is defined by:

$$L^+ = \bigcup_{i=1}^{\infty} L^i$$

and the Kleene closure of L by:

$$L^* = \bigcup_{i=0}^{\infty} L^i$$

Note that T^i denotes the set of strings of length i and T^+ and T* under this definition conform to earlier established usage.

The complement of a language L in T* is $L^c = T^* - L$. Two other unary operations on languages, MIN and MAX, are defined by:

1. MIN(L) = $\{x \mid x \in L \text{ and no } w \in L \text{ is a proper prefix of } x\}$
2. MAX(L) = $\{x \mid x \in L \text{ and } x \text{ is not a proper prefix of any } w \in L\}$

As well as the binary operation of set concatenation defined above, the set theoretic binary operations of union, intersection and (set) difference are also used. Also, if L_1, L_2 are two languages, the quotient of L_1 with respect to L_2, denoted by L_1/L_2 is the language $L_1/L_2 = \{x \mid \exists y \in L_2 \text{ such that } xy \in L_1\}$.

10.1.4 String homomorphisms and DOL systems

If T_1, T_2 are alphabets then a mapping $h: T_1^* \to T_2^*$ is called a homomorphism iff $h(xy) = h(x)h(y)$ for all $x, y \in T_1^*$. To define a homomorphism it is only necessary to specify $h(a)$ for all $a \in T_1$. It follows from the definition that if $x = a_1 a_2 \ldots a_n (a_i \in T_1)$ then $h(x) = h(a_1)h(a_2) \ldots h(a_n)$.

If $h: T_1^* \to T_2^*$ is a homomorphism then h can be extended to act on languages in T_1^* by defining $h(L) = \bigcup\{h(x)\,|\,x \in L\}$ for any $L \subseteq T_1^*$.

A DOL system is a triple $G = (T,h,x)$ where T is an alphabet, $h: T^* \to T^*$ is a homomorphism and x is a string in T^*. A DOL system is one of the simplest finite devices for language definition. Associated with G is the sequence of strings, $x = h^0(x), h(x), h^2(x) = h(h(x)), h^3(x) = h(h(h(x))), \ldots$, and hence the language $L(G) = \{h^i(x)\,|\,i \geq 0\}$. Properties of DOL systems can be found in Rozenberg and Salomaa (1969) and Salomaa (1981).

If $h: T_1^* \to T_2^*$ is a homomorphism then the inverse homomorphic image of a string $y \in T_2^*$ is defined to be the language $\{x\,|\,h(x) = y\}$. This language is denoted by $h^{-1}(y)$ and is contained in T_1^*. The inverse homomorphic image of a language $L \subseteq T_2^*$, $h^{-1}(L)$, is defined by $h^{-1}(L) = \bigcup\{h^{-1}(y)\,|\,y \in L\}$.

10.1.5 Substitutions and OL systems

A substitution, σ, is a mapping $T_1 \to 2^{T_2^*}$ for some alphabets, T_1, T_2. Such a substitution associates a language in T_2^* with each element of T_1. The mapping can be extended to strings in the obvious way by recursively defining $\sigma(\varepsilon) = \{\varepsilon\}$ and $\sigma(ax) = \sigma(a)\sigma(x)$, $a \in T_1, x \in T_1^*$. Then the extension of σ to a function:

$$\sigma: 2^{T_1^*} \to 2^{T_2^*}$$

is obtained by defining:

$$\sigma(L) = \bigcup_{x \in L} \sigma(x)$$

A substitution:

$$\sigma: T_1 \to 2^{T_2^*}$$

is finite if $\sigma(a)$ is finite for all $a \in T_1$. A homomorphism can thus be regarded as a finite substitution where $\sigma(a)$ is always a singleton set.

A substitution:

$$\sigma: T_1 \to 2^{T_2^*}$$

is said to be ε-free if for each $a \in T_1$, $\varepsilon \notin \sigma(a)$.

Just as homomorphisms are used to define DOL systems so the more general finite substitutions are used to define OL systems. An OL system is a triple $G = (T, \sigma, x)$ where σ is a finite substitution, $T \to 2^{T^*}$, and $x \in T^*$. The language defined by G, $L(G)$ is:

$$\bigcup_{i \geq 0} \sigma^i(x).$$

DOL and OL systems are special types of L systems, named after the biologist Lindenmayer, who used such systems in developmental biology (1968, 1971). L systems are fully discussed in Rozenberg and Salomaa (1980).

10.2 Grammars

10.2.1 Phrase structure grammars

In the 1950s, Chomsky defined a technique for generating languages known variously as a phrase structure, type 0, semi-Thue or unrestricted grammar. Chomsky used two distinct alphabets, the terminal alphabet and the non-terminal alphabet. Strings in the language are over the terminal alphabet while the

non-terminal alphabet is used by the grammar internally during generation of terminal strings.

Formally a phrase structure grammar (PSG) is a 4-tuple $G = (N, T, P, S)$ where:

1. N is an alphabet of non-terminals.
2. T is an alphabet of terminals, $N \cap T = \varnothing$.
3. P is a finite set of productions where a production is an expression of the form $\alpha \to \beta$, $\alpha \in (N \cup T)^+$, $\beta \in (N \cup T)^*$.
4. $S \in N$ is a designated start symbol.

To define the language, $L(G)$, generated by G, the relation, $\underset{G}{\Rightarrow}$, is defined.

If $\gamma_1 \alpha \gamma_2 \in (N \cup T)^+$ and $\alpha \to \beta$ is a production in G, then $\gamma_1 \alpha \gamma_2$ generates $\gamma_1 \beta \gamma_2$, written $\gamma_1 \alpha \gamma_2 \underset{G}{\Rightarrow} \gamma_1 \beta \gamma_2$. If $\gamma_1 \alpha \gamma_2 \underset{G}{\Rightarrow} \gamma_1 \beta \gamma_2$ then $\gamma_1 \beta \gamma_2$ is said to be derived from $\gamma_1 \alpha \gamma_2$.

The subscript, G, is often dropped when the grammar, G, is clear from context. The relation $\underset{G}{\overset{+}{\Rightarrow}}$ is the transitive closure of $\underset{G}{\Rightarrow}$ and $\underset{G}{\overset{*}{\Rightarrow}}$ is the reflexive, transitive closure of $\underset{G}{\Rightarrow}$.

The language generated by $G = (N, T, P, S)$ is defined to be $L(G) = \{x \in T^*\,|\,S \overset{*}{\Rightarrow} x\}$. If x is in T^* then $x \in L(G)$ iff there exists a derivation of x from S, $S \underset{G}{\Rightarrow} \gamma_1 \underset{G}{\Rightarrow} \gamma_2 \underset{G}{\Rightarrow} \cdots \underset{G}{\Rightarrow} \gamma_n = x$, where $\gamma_i \in (N \cup T)^+$, $1 \leq i < n$ and $n \geq 1$. Any string $\gamma \in (N \cup T)^+$ such that $S \overset{*}{\Rightarrow} \gamma$ is called a sentential form of G. The strings in $L(G)$ are thus exactly the sentential forms contained in T^*; such strings are known as sentences.

Figure 10.2 provides an example of a phrase structure grammar. The language generated by this grammar is $\{a^i\,|\,i$ is a positive power of 2$\}$. The derivation of a^2 is provided as an illustration.

As in this example, a convention is used whereby elements of N are denoted by (possibly subscripted) upper case roman letters whilst elements of T are generally (possible subscripted) lower case roman letters. The symbol, S, is then used to denote the start symbol. Providing these conventions are used, grammars can be described merely by stating their productions and this is how they are most commonly presented.

G = ({A,B,C,D,E,S}, {a},P,S) where P comprises the following productions

$S \to ACaB$ $aD \to Da$

$Ca \to aaC$ $AD \to AC$

$CB \to DB$ $aE \to Ea$

$CB \to E$ $AE \to \varepsilon$

$S \Rightarrow ACaB \Rightarrow AaaCB \Rightarrow AaaE \Rightarrow AaEa \Rightarrow AEaa \Rightarrow aa$

Figure 10.2 An example phrase structure grammar and derivation

If L_1, L_2 are both type 0 languages then so is $L_1 \cup L_2$. Thus the type 0 languages are closed under union. They are closed under concatenation, Kleene closure, reversal, MIN, intersection, substitution, also ε-free substitution and inverse homomorphism. Type 0 languages are precisely the recursively enumerable (r.e.) languages accepted by Turing machines (see Section 9.4.11).

10.2.2 Context-sensitive grammars

A context-sensitive grammar or Chomsky type-1 grammar is a PSG, $G = (N, T, P, S)$, where all the productions, $\alpha \to \beta$, in P are constrained so that $|\alpha| \leq |\beta|$. Thus, in particular, the empty string cannot occur on the right hand side of any production in a CSG.

Any context-sensitive grammar (CSG) can be rewritten in a

normal form in which each production is a form $\alpha_1 A \alpha_2 \to \alpha_1 \beta \alpha_2$ with $\beta \neq \varepsilon$. Thus, the nonterminal, A, is 'expanded' to β in the 'context' of α_1 and α_2. It is for this reason that this class of grammars is called context-sensitive.

A language is called context-sensitive language (CSL) iff there is some CSG which generates it. By definition, every CSL is recursively enumerable. In fact, every CSL is recursive (see Section 9.4.11) but there are recursive languages which are not context-sensitive.

Any CSL can be accepted by some linear bounded automaton (see Landweber (1963) and Section 9.4.12). Moreover, if L denotes any language accepted by such a machine then $L - \{\varepsilon\}$ is necessarily context-sensitive. Thus the linear bounded automata are the acceptors for context-sensitive languages just as the Turing machines are acceptors for the r.e. languages. Context-sensitive languages are closed under union, concatenation, positive closure, reversal, inverse homomorphism intersection and ε-free (but not general) substitution. For these and other results concerning context-sensitive grammars and languages the reader is referred to Ginsburg and Greibach (1966a), Hopcroft and Ullman (1969, 1971).

10.3 Context-free grammars

10.3.1 Definitions

A phrase structure grammar $G = (N, T, P, S)$ is said to be context-free or type-2 when all its productions are constrained to be of the form $A \to \alpha$, $A \in N$, $\alpha \in (N \cup T)^*$. Thus a nonterminal, A, can be expanded to corresponding string $\alpha \in (N \cup T)^*$ regardless of the context in which A appears.

The language generated by a context-free grammar (CFG) is called a context-free language (CFL). The study of context-free languages has proved important within computer science because of the use of CFGs to define programming languages (see Sections 10.3.5 and 10.3.6).

The definition of CFG allows the possibility of the use of ε-productions, i.e. productions of the form $A \to \varepsilon$, $A \in N$. However, if a grammar $G = (N,T,P,S)$ contains such productions, it is possible to construct a second grammar G' which contains no such productions and generates $L(G') = L(G) - \{\varepsilon\}$.

10.3.2 Left-most and right-most derivations

Let $G = (N, T, P, S)$ denote a CFG. If $\gamma_1, \gamma_2 \in (N \cup T)^*$ are such that:

1. $\gamma_1 = xA\beta$, $x \in T^*$, $A \in N$, $\beta \in (N \cup T)^*$
2. $\gamma_2 = x\alpha\beta$, $x \in T^*$, $\alpha, \beta \in (N \cup T)^*$
3. $A \to \alpha$ is a production in P

then γ_1 generates γ_2 by a single left-most derivation. Thus it is always the left-most non-terminal that is expanded. For any CFG, $G = (N, T, P, S)$, $x \in L(G)$ iff there exists a left-most derivation of x from S. Similarly, a right-most derivation can be defined and a similar result holds for right-most derivations.

10.3.3 Parse-trees, derivation trees

A derivation of a terminal string from a CFG can be represented diagrammatically using a parse (or derivation) tree. Let $G = (N, T, P, S)$ be a CFG. Then the root of a parse tree must be labelled with S. Each interior vertex is labelled with some nonterminal (A, say) and then its children must be labelled $X_1, X_2, \ldots, X_n$ $(X_i \in N \cup T)$ where $A \to X_1 X_2 \ldots X_n$ is a production in P. The exterior nodes are labelled with terminals and the tree is a derivation tree for $x \in L(G)$ iff these labels read $x = a_1 a_2 \ldots a_m$ from left to right. An example parse tree is given in *Figure 10.3*.

$S \to AaBS \mid AA$

$A \to aA \mid a$

$B \to bAB \mid b$

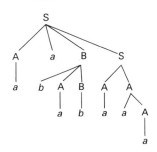

Figure 10.3 Derivation tree for *aababaaa*

In this example, the grammar is presented using a convention whereby the $n(>1)$ productions $A \to \alpha_1$, $A \to \alpha_2, \ldots, A \to \alpha_n$ are written $A \to \alpha_1 \mid \alpha_2 \mid \ldots \mid \alpha_n$.

10.3.4 Ambiguity and inherent ambiguity

A CFG, G, is said to be ambiguous iff there is some $x \in L(G)$ which has two or more distinct derivation trees or equivalently two or more distinct left-most (or right-most) derivations. Clearly, if a semantic interpretation is to be deduced from a derivation tree then it is desirable that the derivation tree is unique. Grammars defining programming languages should thus be unambiguous.

Unfortunately, it is undecidable whether an arbitrary CFG is ambiguous (Cantor, 1962; Chomsky and Schutzenberger, 1963; Floyd, 1962).

If a CFL, L, has no unambiguous grammar then it is called inherently ambiguous. Such languages do exist (see Hopcroft and Ullman (1979) for an example). Inherent ambiguity is another unsolvable problem (see Section 10.4.2).

10.3.5 Backus Naur Form

Backus Naur Form (Backus Normal Form, BNF) is a notation, equivalent to that of CFGs. In the early 1960s, it was successfully used to describe the programming language, Algol 60, and considerably enhanced the production of Algol 60 compilers. BNF was a major development because it enabled the syntax of the language to be formally defined. The semantics of Algol 60, however, was not formally defined but largely presented as English text. The historical development of Algol 60 is discussed in Naur (1978).

In BNF, nonterminals are represented as strings of characters surrounded by '<' and '>', e.g. < identifier >. Terminals such as **begin**, := , **if**, ×, +, etc. are referred to as basic symbols. The production symbol $\to$ of context-free grammars is replaced by ::= . A BNF definition of a subset of simple arithmetic expressions is given in *Figure 10.4*.

< expression > ::= < expression > + < term >
                   | < expression > − < term > | < term >

< term > ::= < term > × < factor > | < term > / < factor > | < factor >

< factor > ::= < identifier > | (< expression >)

< identifier > ::= a | b | c

Figure 10.4

BNF is now widely used to define the syntax of programming languages and the notation has been continually refined and updated by its users. Much of this usage is nonstandard but some variants are widely used, see McGettrick (1980).

10.3.6 Syntax charts

Syntax charts (or graphs) provide a graphical description of the rules of a context-free grammar. They are now widely used to describe programming languages syntax. The chart in *Figure 10.5* is taken from *Pascal: User Manual and Report* (Jensen and Wirth, 1975).

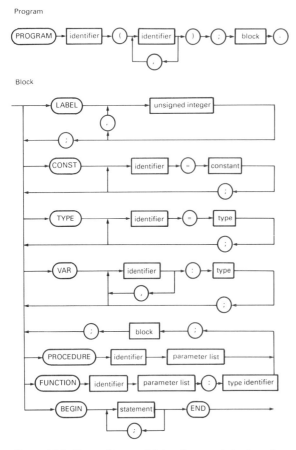

Figure 10.5 Syntax diagrams defining the general structure of a program

10.3.7 Pumping lemma

Let L be any CFL. The pumping lemma (or *uvwxy* theorem) states that there exists some n (depending on L) such that if $z \in L$ and $|z| \geqslant n$ then z can be expressed as $z = uvwxy$ such that:

1. $|vx| \geqslant 1$
2. $|vwx| \leqslant n$
3. for all $i \geqslant 0$, $uv^iwx^iy \in L$

This result is obtained by considering the derivation tree for *vwx*. It can be used to prove certain languages, e.g. $\{a^nb^nc^n \mid n \geqslant 1\}$, and $\{a^p \mid p$ is prime$\}$, are not context-free, for example, see Hopcroft and Ullman (1969). A stronger version of the pumping lemma known as Ogden's lemma is given in Ogden (1968).

10.3.8 Closure properties of context-free languages

Context-free languages are closed under union, concatenation, Kleene closure, reversal, substitution, ε-free substitution and inverse homomorphism. They are not closed under intersection, MIN, MAX, inverse substitution nor under complement. However, if L is context-free and R is regular (see Section 10.4) then $L \cap R$ is context-free.

10.3.9 Acceptors

For any CFL, L, there exists a non-deterministic pushdown automation (NPDA), M, such that $L = N(M)$ (see Schutzenberger (1963) and Section 9.3.1). Moreover, any language accepted by an NPDA is context-free. Thus NPDAs are the acceptors for context-free languages (Chomsky, 1962).

10.3.10 Normal forms for CFGs

A CFG, $G = (N, T, P, S)$, is said to be in Chomsky normal form if every production in P is of either the form $A \rightarrow BC$, $A,B,C \in N$ or of the form $A \rightarrow a$, $A \in N$, $a \in T$. If G generates an ε-free language then there is an equivalent grammar to G which is in Chomsky normal form (Chomsky, 1959).

A CFG, $G = (N, T, P, S)$ is said to be in Greibach normal form if every production in P is of the form $A \rightarrow ax$, $A \in N$, $a \in T$, $x \in (N \cup T)^*$. As above, for any G generating an ε-free language, there is an equivalent grammar in Greibach normal form (Greibach, 1965).

10.3.11 Dyck languages

A Dyck language is a CFL generated by a CFG with productions:

$$S \rightarrow SS \mid \varepsilon$$
$$S \rightarrow a_1Sb_1 \mid a_2Sb_2 \mid \ldots \mid a_nSb_n$$

where $n \geqslant 1$. The language thus consists of strings of balanced parentheses of various types (a_1 and b_1, a_2 and b_2, ..., a_n and b_n).

Every CFL can be expressed as a $h(D \cap R)$ where h is a homomorphism, D is a Dyck language and R is a regular set (Chomsky, 1962; Ginsburg, 1966).

10.3.12 Context-free languages as fixed points

Consider the following system of equations:

$$X_1 = f_1(X_1, X_2, \ldots, X_n)$$
$$X_2 = f_2(X_1, X_2, \ldots, X_n)$$
$$\cdots$$
$$X_n = f_n(X_1, X_2, \ldots, X_n)$$

where each $f_i(X_1, X_2, \ldots, X_n)$ is constructed from finite sets of strings in T^* and the variables $X_1, X_2, \ldots, X_n$ using the operations of union and set concatenation only.

Such a system of equations is called a system of set equations over T^*. Writing $\mathbf{X}$ for the n-tuple $(X_1, X_2, \ldots, X_n)$, the system of set equations can be written as $\mathbf{X} = f(\mathbf{X})$. A solution to $\mathbf{X} = f(\mathbf{X})$ is any n-tuple of sets in T^*, $\mathbf{S} = (S_1, S_2, \ldots, S_n)$ which satisfies $\mathbf{S} = f(\mathbf{S})$. If $\mathbf{T} = (T_1, T_2, \ldots, T_n)$ then $\mathbf{S} \subseteq \mathbf{T}$ iff $S_i \subseteq T_i$ for $1 \leqslant i \leqslant n$. Any system of set equations over T^* has a unique least solution according to the ordering $\subseteq$ (Blickle, 1972) *viz*:

$$\mathbf{S} = \bigcup_{i=1}^{\infty} f^i(\varnothing)$$

Moreover, each component of **S** is a CFL and for any CFL, L, there exists a system of equations where L is a component of the unique least solution. For example, the CFG:

$S \rightarrow AaBS \mid AA$
$A \rightarrow aA \mid a$
$B \rightarrow bAB \mid b$

has a corresponding set of equations:

$S = A\{a\}BS \cup AA$
$A = \{a\}A \cup \{a\}$
$B = \{b\}AB \cup \{b\}$

The first component of the solution to this set of equations is L(G).

10.3.13 Decision problems relating to CFGs

Given an arbitrary CFG, G = (N, T, P, S), there are simple algorithms to determine if L(G) is empty, finite or infinite. However, it is unsolvable to determine whether L(G) = T* or whether L(G) is regular. Similarly, if G_1, G_2 are arbitrary CFGs, the following are unsolvable: Are G_1, G_2 equivalent? Is $L(G_1) \subseteq L(G_2)$? Is $L(G_1) \cap L(G_2)$ empty, finite, infinite and/or context-free? These and other similar results are discussed in Hopcroft and Ullman (1969, 1979).

10.3.14 The Parikh map

Let I denote the non-negative integers and Q the rational numbers. I^n is a subset of the vector space of Q^n over Q. A subset S of I^n is a linear set iff there exists $\mathbf{a}, \mathbf{b}_1, \ldots, \mathbf{b}_m \in I^n$ such that $S = \{\mathbf{x} \mid \mathbf{x} = \mathbf{a} + n_1\mathbf{b}_1 + \ldots + n_m\mathbf{b}_m, n_1, \ldots, n_m \in I\}$. S is said to be semilinear iff S is a finite union of linear sets.

Let L be a language over the (ordered) alphabet $T = \{a_1, a_2, \ldots a_n\}$. Define a map $\chi: L \rightarrow I^n$ recursively by $\chi(\varepsilon) = (0,0,\ldots,0)$, $\chi(a_1) = (1,0,\ldots,0)$, $\chi(a_2) = (0,1,\ldots,0)$, $\ldots, \chi(a_n) = (0,0,\ldots,1)$ and $\chi(xy) = \chi(x) + \chi(y)$ for any $x, y \in L$. $\chi(L) = \cup \{\chi(x) \mid x \in L\}$ is called the Parikh map with respect to T.

Parikh (1966) showed that a necessary condition for $L \subseteq T^*$ to be context-free is that $\chi(L)$ is semi-linear. However, the condition is not a sufficient condition for L to be context-free.

10.4 Deterministic languages

10.4.1 Definition

Context-free languages are precisely those accepted by non-deterministic pushdown automata. A proper subclass of the context-free languages is the class of deterministic languages. This is the class of languages accepted by deterministic pushdown automata (see Section 9.3.2).

Given a string x in a deterministic language L, it has been shown that there exists a DPDA accepting L which will recognize any $x \in L$ in time $0(|x|^3)$ (Younger, 1987).

10.4.2 Properties of deterministic languages

Every deterministic language is context-free and every regular language is deterministic. Whereas context-free languages are not closed under complement, MAX or MIN, the deterministic languages are closed under all of these operations (Ginsburg and Greibach, 1966). Hence the deterministic languages form a proper subclass of the context-free languages. For example, $\{x \in \{a,b\}^* \mid x$ contains an equal number of a s and b s$\}$ is shown to

be deterministic in Hopcroft and Ullman (1969) but this language is not regular.

As with context-free languages, there are many undecidable properties associated with deterministic languages (Ginsburg and Greibach, 1966b). If L_1, L_2 are arbitrary deterministic languages then the following are all undecidable. Is $L_1 \cap L_2 = \emptyset$? Is $L_1 \subseteq L_2$? Is $L_1 \cap L_2$ a deterministic language? Is it context-free? Is $L_1 \cup L_2$ deterministic? If L is an arbitrary CFL, it is unsolvable to determine if L is deterministic. Thus it is unsolvable to determine whether a language is inherently ambiguous (Ginsburg and Ullian, 1966).

10.4.3 Top-down parsing and LL(k) grammars

There are two basic ways to approach the problem of parsing a string $a_1a_2 \ldots a_n \in L(G)$. Firstly, the derivation tree can be built top-down, i.e. start with the root node, S, and develop a tree from the top in such a way that its external nodes are $a_1, a_2, \ldots, a_n$. Alternatively, a bottom-up approach can be used, i.e. start with $a_1a_2 \ldots a_n$ and try to deduce the internal nodes of the tree from the bottom right up to the root node, S.

LL parsing is a top-down method used for a class of grammars known as LL(k) grammars. These grammars generate deterministic languages. The first L in LL stands for 'left-to-right' scanning' and the second L for 'constructing a left-most derivation'.

Informally, an LL(k) grammar ($k \geq 1$) is a CFG, G = (N, T, P, S), where given a sentential form $wA\gamma$, $w \in T^*$, $A \in N$, $\gamma \in (N \cup T)^*$, generated by a left-most derivation, at most a k symbol lookahead into the unmatched part of the input string is required to uniquely determine which of the productions with A on the left-hand side should next be applied. With an LL(k) grammar, the next production to apply can thus be uniquely determined by:

1. The left-most nonterminal, A.
2. The next k unmatched input symbols.
3. The string $w \in T^*$ appearing before A and the string $\gamma \in (N \cup T)^*$ appearing after A in the sentential form.

If the next production can always be determined uniquely from just (1) and (2), the grammar is said to be strong LL (k). These concepts are defined formally as follows:

$\text{FIRST}_k: T^* \rightarrow T^*$ is defined by:

$$\text{FIRST}_k(x) = \begin{cases} x \text{ if } |x| \leq k, \\ y \text{ if } x = yz, y \in T^k, z \in T^* \end{cases}$$

Then, FIRST_k is extended to act on languages by defining $\text{FIRST}_k(L) = \{\text{FIRST}_k(x) \mid x \in L\}$ for all $L \subseteq T^*$.

Let G = (N, T, P, S) be a CFG. G is said to LL(k)($k \geq 1$) if, whenever there exist two left-most derivations, $S \overset{*}{\Rightarrow} wA\gamma \Rightarrow w\alpha\gamma \overset{*}{\Rightarrow} wy \in T^*$ and $S \overset{*}{\Rightarrow} wA\gamma \Rightarrow w\beta\gamma \overset{*}{\Rightarrow} wz \in T^*$, then $\text{FIRST}_k(y) = \text{FIRST}_k(z)$ implies $\alpha = \beta$. G is said to be strong LL(k)($k \geq 1$) whenever there exist two left-most derivations, $S \overset{*}{\Rightarrow} wA\gamma \Rightarrow w\alpha\gamma \overset{*}{\Rightarrow} wy \in T^*$ and $S \overset{*}{\Rightarrow} xA\delta \Rightarrow x\beta\delta \overset{*}{\Rightarrow} xz \in T^*$, then $\text{FIRST}_k(y) = \text{FIRST}_k(z)$ implies $\alpha = \beta$.

Every LL(k) grammar is unambiguous. By definition, every strong LL(k) grammar is LL(k) but for k > 1, there are LL(k) grammars which are not strong LL(k). For the case k = 1, though, the two definitions are equivalent. However, the class of languages generated by LL(k) grammars is precisely the class of languages generated by strong LL(k) grammars for any $k \geq 1$ (Rosenkrantz and Stearns, 1970).

LL(1) grammars are of particular use in compiling and much of the syntax of many programming languages can be defined using an LL(1) grammar. Foster's Syntax Improving Device (SID) is an early transformation tool designed to transform an arbitrary grammar into an equivalent LL(1) grammar whenever possible (Foster, 1968). LL(1) grammars lead naturally to recursive descent compilers.

If $G = (N, T, P, S)$ is an arbitrary CFG, the augmented grammar is $G' = (N', T', P', S')$ where $N' = N \cup \{S'\}$, $S' \notin N$, $T' = T \cup \{\$\}$, $\$ \notin T$ and $P' = P \cup \{S' \rightarrow S\$\}$. Thus, $L(G') = \{x\$ | x \in L(G)\}$ comprises strings of $L(G)$ terminated by an end-of-input marker, $\$$. The following functions are then defined on $N' \cup T'$:

$$\text{EMPTY}(X) = \begin{cases} \text{true if } X \overset{*}{\Rightarrow} \varepsilon, \\ \text{false otherwise} \end{cases}$$

$\text{FIRST}(X) = \{a | a \in T' \text{ and } X \overset{*}{\Rightarrow} ax \text{ for some } x \in (T')^*\}$

$\text{FOLLOW}(X) = \{a | a \in T' \text{ and } S' \overset{*}{\Rightarrow} xXay \text{ for some } x \in T^* \text{ and } y \in (T')^*\}$.

The function EMPTY is extended to be a function on $(N' \cup T')^*$ by defining $\text{EMPTY}(\varepsilon) = \text{true}$, $\text{EMPTY}(X\alpha) = \text{EMPTY}(X)$ **and** $\text{EMPTY}(\alpha)$, $X \in N' \cup T'$, $\alpha \in (N' \cup T')^*$.

Then, the function LOOKAHEAD on productions of G is defined by:

$\text{LOOKAHEAD } (A \rightarrow X_1 X_2 \ldots X_n)$
$= \bigcup \{\text{FIRST}(X_i) | 1 \leqslant i \leqslant n \text{ and } \text{EMPTY}(X_1 X_2 \ldots X_{i-1})\}$
$\cup \text{ if } \text{EMPTY}(X_1 X_2 \ldots X_n) \text{ then } \text{FOLLOW}(A) \text{ else } \varnothing$

From these definitions, an augmented CFG is (strong) LL(1) iff for each pair of distinct productions $A \rightarrow \alpha$, $A \rightarrow \beta$, both with the same left-hand side, $\text{LOOKAHEAD } (A \rightarrow \alpha) \cap \text{LOOKAHEAD } (A \rightarrow \beta) = \varnothing$. Once LOOKAHEAD sets are determined, a parser for an LL(1) grammar follows easily (see, for example Aho and Ullman (1972, 1977); Backhouse (1979) and Rayward–Smith (1983)).

10.4.4 Bottom-up parsing

Given an unambiguous CFG, G, and a string $x \in L(G)$, both the top-down and the bottom-up parsing techniques (if applicable) must yield identical derivation trees. The distinction between the methods lies in the way the trees are constructed. The bottom-up method starts with the leaf nodes, i.e. the input string x and works towards the root, S. The input string is initially scanned to find substrings which match the right-hand side of some production of G. Once one of these substrings is found, it can be replaced by, or reduced to, the non-terminal on the left-hand side of a production to obtain a sentential form of the grammar. The process is repeated, working with this sentential form again seeking a substring to be reduced. Continuing in this way, a sequence of reductions is found resulting in the start symbol, S. Usually, practical bottom-up techniques use this method to construct right-most derivations (but in reverse). The substring which is reduced at each stage is called the handle of the right-most derivation. The central problem with the bottom-up technique is to find and suitably reduce the handle at each step.

10.4.5 Simple precedence grammars

One class of grammars for which finding the handle is a particularly easy task is the simple precedence grammars.

Let $G = (N, T, P, S)$ be a CFG and let $\alpha XY\beta$ be a right-most sentential form, $\alpha, \beta \in (N \cup T)^*$, $X, Y \in N \cup T$. At some point in the reduction of this sentential form to S, one of the three following possibilities arise:

1. X is part of the handle but Y is not. Thus X is the tail of the handle. In this case, we say X has precedence over Y and write $X \gtrdot Y$.

2. X and Y are both in the handle. We then say X and Y have equal precedence and write $X \doteq Y$.
3. Y is part of the handle but X is not. Thus Y is the head of the handle and we say it has precedence over X, written $X \lessdot Y$.

The relations $\gtrdot$, $\doteq$ and $\lessdot$ are called simple precedence relations. It follows from these definitions that:

1. $X \gtrdot T$ iff Y is a terminal symbol (remember that $\alpha XY\beta$ is a sentential form in a right-most derivation) and there exists some production $A \rightarrow \gamma_1 BZ\gamma_2$, $A, B \in N, Z \in N \cup T$, $\gamma_1, \gamma_2 \in (N \cup T)^*$ such that $B \overset{*}{\Rightarrow} \delta_1 X$ and $Z \overset{*}{\Rightarrow} Y\delta_2$, $\delta_1, \delta_2 \in (N \cup T)^*$.
2. $X \doteq Y$ iff there exists some production $A \rightarrow \gamma_1 XY\gamma_2$, $A \in N$, $\gamma_1\gamma_2 \in (N \cup T)^*$.
3. $X \lessdot Y$ iff there exists some production $A \rightarrow \gamma_1 XB\gamma_2$, $B \in N$, $\gamma_1\gamma_2 \in (N \cup T)^*$ such that $B \overset{*}{\Rightarrow} Y\delta, \delta \in (N \cup T)^*$.

A CFG, $G = (N, T, P, S)$, is called a simple precedence grammar provided:

1. No two rules of the grammar have identical right parts.
2. There is at most one simple precedence relation between any pair of symbols in $(N \cup T) \times (N \cup T)$.

If a CFG is a simple precedence grammar, the handle of any rightmost sentential form can be uniquely determined and a simple parsing technique follows. The sentential form is scanned for the left-most pair of symbols X_j and X_{j+1} such that $X_j \gtrdot X_{j+1}$. X_j is then the tail of the handle. The sentential form is scanned from right to left starting at X_j until a pair X_{i-1}, X_i is found such that $X_{i-1} \lessdot X_i$. X_i is the head of the handle and so the handle is $\beta = X_i \ldots X_j$. Having found the handle, there must be a unique production of form $A \rightarrow \beta$ and so the handle can be reduced to A. The only problem with this approach arises when the tail of the handle is the last symbol or the head of the handle is the first symbol. This is overcome by introducing an endmarker, $\$ \notin N \cup T$ (say), to be used at both ends of the sentential form. Setting $\$ \lessdot X$ and $X \gtrdot \$$ for all $X \in N \cup T$ ensures that by repeated reduction of handles, the input string $\$x\$$ can be reduced to $\$S\$$.

A convenient way to implement the reduction of handles is to use a stack and an input buffer. The primary operations will be a push (or shift) action and the reduce action. Parsers implemented in this way are known as shift-reduce parsers. For an example shift reduce parser for a simple precedence grammar see Rayward-Smith (1983).

10.4.6 Operator (precedence) grammars

An operator grammar is a CFG with no productions of the form $A \rightarrow \alpha BC\beta$, $A, B, C \in N$, $\alpha, \beta \in (N \cup T)^*$. For operator grammars, the relations $\gtrdot$, $\doteq$ and $\lessdot$ are only defined between terminal symbols, as follows:

1. $a \gtrdot b$ if there is a production of the form $A \rightarrow \alpha Bb\beta$, $A, B \in N$, $\alpha, \beta \in (N \cup T)^*$ and $B \overset{*}{\Rightarrow} \gamma a$ or $B \overset{*}{\Rightarrow} \gamma aC$ for some $\gamma \in (N \cup T)^*$, $C \in N$.
2. $a \doteq b$ if there is a production of the form $A \rightarrow \alpha ab\beta$ or $A \rightarrow \alpha aBb\beta$, $A, B \in N$, $\alpha, \beta \in (N \cup T)^*$.
3. $a \lessdot b$ if there is a production of the form $A \rightarrow \alpha aB\beta$, $A, B \in N$, $\alpha, \beta \in (N \cup T)^*$ and $B \overset{*}{\Rightarrow} b\gamma$ or $B \overset{*}{\Rightarrow} Cb\gamma$, $B, C \in N$, $\gamma \in (N \cup T)^*$.

An operator precedence grammar is an operator grammar where a unique relationship ($\gtrdot$, $\doteq$ or $\lessdot$) occurs between pairs of terminal symbols. For such grammars, a simple shift reduce parser is easily constructed (for an example, see Hopgood (1969)).

10.4.7 LR grammars

The bottom-up parsing technique most widely used in practical compilers is the LR technique, a shift-reduce technique initially developed by Knuth (1965) and, with later developments, surveyed in Aho and Johnson (1974). The L in LR stands for 'left-to-right scanning' and the R for 'constructing a right-most derivation in reverse'. The method is applicable to LR(k) grammars; for such grammars any sentence can be parsed in a single scan from left to right with no backtracking and using at most k symbols of lookahead.

An LR(0) grammar is characterized by the following two properties:

1. Its start symbol does not appear on the right-hand side of any production.
2. If there are two right-most derivations:

$$S \overset{*}{\Rightarrow} \gamma Axy \Rightarrow \gamma \beta xy \text{ and } S \overset{*}{\Rightarrow} \delta By \Rightarrow \delta \beta' y = \gamma \beta xy$$

where $\gamma, \delta, \beta, \beta' \in (N \cup T)^*$, $A, B \in N$ and $x, y \in T^*$, then $\gamma = \delta$, $A = B$, $\beta = \beta'$ and $x = \varepsilon$.

The set of strings which can appear on the stack prior to a reduction using a production $A \to \beta$ is called the LRCONTEXT set of $A \to \beta$. Formally, LRCONTEXT $(A \to \beta) = \{\alpha | \alpha = \gamma \beta \in (N \cup T)^* \text{ where } S \overset{*}{\Rightarrow} \gamma Ax \Rightarrow \gamma \beta x \text{ is a right-most derivation, } x \in T^*, \gamma \in (N \cup T)^*\}$.

Condition (2) above can be replaced by:

2. If $\alpha \in$ LRCONTEXT $(A \to \beta')$ and $\alpha x \in$ LRCONTEXT $(B \to \beta')$ where $A \to \beta$, $B \to \beta'$ are productions in P, $\alpha \in (N \cup T)^*$ and $x \in T^*$ then $x = \varepsilon$, $A = B$ and $\beta = \beta'$.

Every string in LRCONTEXT $(A \to \beta)$ is of the form $\gamma \beta$ for some $\gamma \in (N \cup T)^*$. Hence, defining LEFT(A) = $\{\gamma | S \overset{*}{\Rightarrow} \gamma Ax$ is a right-most derivation, $x \in T^*\}$, it follows that LRCONTEXT $(A \to \beta) = $ LEFT(A)·$\{\beta\}$. The LEFT sets are easily evaluated and both these and the LRCONTEXT sets are regular. These properties are used in the construction of a shift-reduce parser. For examples, see Backhouse (1979) and Rayward-Smith (1983).

The use of LR(1) grammars has been widely exploited by compiler writers. Let G = (N, T, P, S) be an arbitrary CFG which has been augmented with an end-of-input marker, $. Thus the only production in P which involves S is the single production S → E$ for some E∈N. The LR(1)CONTEXT set of a production A → β in P is defined by:

LR(1)CONTEXT $\quad (A \to \beta) = \{\alpha | \alpha = \gamma \beta a \in (N \cup T)^* \quad$ where $S \overset{*}{\Rightarrow} \gamma Aax \Rightarrow \gamma \beta ax$ is a right-most production for some $a \in T$, $x \in T^*, \gamma \in (N \cup T)^*\}$.

If $\alpha \in$ LR(1)CONTEXT $(A \to \beta)$ then $\alpha = \alpha' a$ for some $\alpha' \in$ LRCONTEXT $(A \to \beta)$ and $a \in T$, the one symbol lookahead.

If G = (N, T, P, S) is an augmented CFG, G is LR(1) provided the following condition holds: $a \in$ LR(1)CONTEXT $(A \to \beta)$ and $\alpha x \in$ LR(1)CONTEXT $(B \to \beta')$, $A \to \beta$, $\to \beta' \in P$, $\alpha \in (N \cup T)^*$, $x \in T^* \Rightarrow x = \varepsilon$, $A = B$ and $\beta = \beta'$.

This definition can be generalized to obtain a definition of an LR(k) grammar ($k > 1$) (Backhouse, 1979). Every LL(k) grammar is necessarily LR(k). Moreover, every deterministic language can be defined by an LR(1) grammar and, since every LR(k) grammar necessarily defines a deterministic language, it follows that a language is generated by an LR(k) grammar ($k \geqslant 1$) iff it is generated by an LR(1) grammar. The LR(0) grammars define exactly those deterministic languages which satisfy the prefix property, i.e. whenever $x \in L$ no proper prefix of x is in L. Thus, if an end-of-input marker, $ is used every deterministic language L$ satisfies the prefix property and hence can be generated by an LR(0) grammar. All these results can be found in Hopcroft and Ullman (1979).

A stronger condition than the LR(1) condition is sometimes used. A simple LR(1) context of a production $A \to \beta$ in a modified CFG is defined by SLR(1)CONTEXT$(A \to \beta) = $ LRCONTEXT$(A \to \beta) \cdot$ FOLLOW(A) where FOLLOW(A) is as defined in Section 10.4.3. An augmented CFG, G = (N, T, P, S), is a simple LR(1) grammar (SLR(1) grammar) provided the following condition holds: $\alpha \in$ SLR(1)CONTEXT $(A \to \beta)$ and $\alpha x \in$ SLR(1)CONTEXT $(\beta \to \beta')$, $A \to \beta$, $B \to \beta' \in P$, $\alpha \in (N \cup T)^*$, $x \in T^* \Rightarrow x = \varepsilon$, $A = B$ and $\beta = \beta'$. By definition, every SLR(1) grammar is LR(1) but there are grammars that are LL(1) but not SLR(1).

A practical approach to LR parsing techniques is to be found in Aho and Ullman (1977). There, another variation of LR grammars known as LALR grammars is discussed. SLR(1) and LALR(1) grammars are due to De Remer (1969, 1971).

10.5 Regular languages

10.5.1 Definition

A PSG, G = (N, T, P, S) is called a regular, or type 3, grammar provided that:

1. If there exists an ε-production in P then it is S → ε and in this case S does not appear as a substring of the right-hand side of any other production in P.
2. All other productions are of the form A → a or A → aB, A, B∈N, a∈T.

Alternatively, condition (2) can be replaced by:

2. All other productions are of the form A → a or A → Ba, A, B∈T, a∈T.

A language is called regular iff it is generated by some regular grammar. A regular language is sometimes called a regular set.

10.5.2 Properties of regular languages

A language is regular iff it is accepted by a (deterministic or non-deterministic) finite state automaton (see Section 9.2). Regular languages are closed under union, concatenation, Kleene closure, reversal, MIN, MAX, intersection, complement, (ε-free) substitutions and quotient. Since every regular language is accepted by some deterministic finite state automation (Salomaa, 1981), regular languages are clearly deterministic (and obviously context-free) but there are deterministic languages that are not regular.

Regular grammars and languages are particularly easy to handle and there are simple algorithms to answer the vast majority of questions likely to arise, e.g. is $L(G_1) \subseteq L(G_2)$? Is $L(G_1) \cap L(G_2)$ empty, finite or infinite? None of these particular questions are solvable for deterministic languages. These and other results can be found in many of the texts surveying material on regular grammars and finite automata (e.g. Ginsburg, 1966; Hopcroft and Ullman, 1969, 1979; Rayward-Smith, 1983).

10.5.3 Left linear and right linear grammars

If every production in a PSG, G = (N, T, P, S) is either of the form A → x or A → xB, A, B∈N, x∈T*, the grammar is called right-linear. Similarly, if every production is of the form A → x or A → Bx, A, B∈N, x∈T*, the grammar is called left-linear.

L ⊆ T* is generated by a right-linear grammar iff L is regular iff L is generated by a left-linear grammar.

10.5.4 Regular expressions

Regular expressions are particularly neat ways of representing regular languages. The rules defining regular expressions over T can be summarized as follows:

1. 0 represents the empty set and 1 represents $\{\varepsilon\}$.
2. If $L = \{x_1, x_2, \ldots, x_n\}$ is a finite set of strings where $x_i \in T^+$, $i = 1, \ldots, n$, then L is represented by $(x_1 + x_2 + \ldots + x_n)$.
3. If r_1 is a regular expression representing a regular language L_1 and r_2 is a regular expression representing a regular language L_2, then:

   (a) $(r_1 + r_2)$ represents $L_1 \cup L_2$.
   (b) $(r_1 \cdot r_2)$ represents $L_1 L_2$.
   (c) (r_1^k) represents $L_1^k (k \geqslant 0)$.
   (d) $(r_1)^*$ represents L_1^*.

4. Only those expressions defined by (1), (2) and (3) are regular expressions.

Parentheses in regular expressions can be omitted according to the rule that the unary operators have the highest priority, then $\cdot$ and lastly $+$. As with normal algebra, $(r_1 r_2)$ is commonly written for $(r_1 \cdot r_2)$.

Since every finite set of strings is a regular language and since regular languages are closed under union, set concatenation and Kleene closure, it follows that every regular expression over T describes a regular language in T^*. The converse of this result is also true, viz. every regular set can be described by a regular expression (Kleene, 1956).

Regular expressions as a descriptive mechanism for regular sets were first introduced by Kleene (1956) and many results concerning them can be found in Brzozowski (1962) and McNaughton and Yamada (1960).

10.5.5 Pumping lemma

Based upon the fact that for every regular set there exists a deterministic finite state automation which accepts it, a pumping lemma for regular sets can be established (Bar-Hillel *et al.*, 1961). This states that there is a constant, n, such that if z is a string in a regular set, L, with $|z| \geqslant n$ then z can be written as uvw where $|uv| \leqslant n$, $|v| \geqslant 1$ and such that for all $i \geqslant 0$, uv^iw is in L.

10.6 Families of languages

A family of languages is a collection of languages containing at least one non-empty language.

10.6.1 The Chomsky hierarchy

Regular languages, context-free languages, context-sensitive languages and recursively enumerable languages are all families of languages. They are also known, respectively, as the Chomsky type 3, type 2, type 1 and type 0 languages.

The regular languages are a proper sub-family of the context-free languages; the ε-free context-free languages are a proper sub-family of the context-sensitive languages which, in turn, are a proper sub-family of the recursively enumerable languages. This hierarchy of languages with their associated acceptors, finite state automata, non-deterministic push-down automata, linear bounded automata and Turing machines, is called the Chomsky hierarchy of (families of) languages.

10.6.2 Trios and full trios

A trio is a family of languages closed under intersection with regular set, inverse homomorphism and ε-free homomorphism. If the family is also closed under arbitrary homomorphisms, then it is a full trio. Chomsky type 3, type 2 and type 0 languages are full trios, whilst Chomsky type 1 languages are a trio but not a full trio. In fact, the regular languages are the smallest full trio

since every full trio contains all regular languages. Similarly, the ε-free regular languages are the smallest trio (Ginsburg and Greibach, 1969). For closure properties of trios and full trios, see Section 10.6.5.

10.6.3 Generalized sequential machines

A generalized sequential machine (GSM) is a generalization of the Mealy machine (Section 9.2.7) whereby any output string, rather than just a single symbol, can be output at each move. Formally, it is defined as a 6-tuple $M = (K, T_1, T_2, \delta, k_0, F)$ where:

1. K is a finite set of states.
2. T_1 is the input alphabet.
3. T_2 is the output alphabet.
4. δ is a mapping from $K \times T_1$ to finite subsets of $K \times T_2^*$.
5. $k_0 \in K$ is the initial state.
6. $F \subseteq K$ is the final state.

The first projection of δ is δ_1, a mapping from $K \times T_1$ to finite subsets of K whilst the second projection of δ is δ_2, a mapping from $K \times T_1$ to finite subsets of T_2^*. The domain of δ is extended to $K \times T_1^*$ by recursively defining $\delta(k,\varepsilon) = \{(k,\varepsilon)\}$ and $\delta(k,xa) = \{(k',y) \mid k' \in \delta_1(k'',a)$ and $y = vw$ where $(k'',v) \in \delta(k,x)$ and $w \in \delta_2(k'',a)\}$.

If $M = (K, T_1, T_2, \delta, k_0, F)$ is a GSM and $x \in T_1^*$ then $M(x)$ denotes the set $\{y \mid (k',y) \in \delta(k_0,x)$ and $k' \in F\}$. If $L \subseteq T_1^*$ then $M(L) = \bigcup \{M(x) \mid x \in L\}$. $M(L)$ is called a GSM mapping. M is thus regarded as a mapping:

$$2^{T_1^*} \to 2^{T_2^*}$$

If δ maps $K \times T_1$ to finite subsets of $K \times T_2^+$ then the GSM is said to be ε-free and the associated mapping is an ε-free GSM mapping.

Defining $M^{-1}(x) = \{y \mid M(y)$ contains $x\}$, and $M^{-1}(L) = \bigcup \{M^{-1}(x) \mid x \in L\}$, an inverse GSM mapping:

$$M^{-1}: 2^{T_2^*} \to 2^{T_1^*}$$

is obtained. Note that it is not necessarily the case that $M^{-1}(M(L)) = M(M^{-1}(L)) = L$ so M^{-1} is not a true inverse.

10.6.4 Abstract families of languages

A class of languages is called an abstract family of languages (AFL) if it is a trio and is closed under union, concatenation and positive closure. A class of languages is called a full abstract family of languages (full AFL) if it is a full trio and is closed under union, concatenation and Kleene closure. Independence of the various AFL operations is discussed in Greibach and Hopcroft (1969).

The r.e. languages, context-free languages and regular languages are all full AFLs; the context-sensitive languages are an AFL.

10.6.5 Closure properties

The closure properties of trios, full trios, AFLs and full AFLs are given in *Table 10.1*, a modified version of a figure from Hopcroft and Ullman (1979).

10.6.6 Other language classes

During the 1970s, considerable research was undertaken into classes of languages lying between the context-free languages and the context-sensitive languages. Examples are (context-free) programmed languages (Rosenkrantz, 1969), simple matrix

Table 10.1 Closure Properties

	Trio	Full trio	AFL	Full AFL
Union			√	√
Concatenation			√	√
Positive closure			√	√
Kleene closure				√
Inverse homomorphism	√	√	√	√
ε-free homomorphism	√	√	√	√
Homomorphism		√		√
Intersection with regular set	√	√	√	√
ε-free GSM mapping	√	√	√	√
GSM mapping		√		√
Inverse GSM mapping	√	√	√	√
Quotient with regular set		√		√
Substitution into regular sets			√	√
Substitution by ε-free regular sets	√	√	√	√
Substitution by regular sets		√		√

(Ibarra, 1970), indexed languages (Aho, 1968), inside-out and inside-in macro languages (Fischer, 1968), quoted languages (Fischer, 1968) and inside-out and inside-in hyperlanguages (Rayward-Smith, 1977). Of these, the class of indexed languages is known to be a full AFL. The class of inside-out macro languages do not form an AFL since they are not closed under inverse homomorphism although they are closed under union, concatenation, closure and intersection with regular sets. The class of outside-in macro languages is identical to the class of indexed languages and to the class of outside-in hyperlanguages. The class of inside-out hyperlanguages equals the class of quoted languages.

10.7 Formal techniques for programming language definition

10.7.1 Introduction

The BNF definition of the Algol 60 syntax and the syntax charts for Pascal (see Section 10.3) were early attempts at the formal definition of programming languages. They only define the context-free syntax of the language and have to be supported by prose descriptions of the context-sensitive restrictions and the semantics. As stated in Marcotty *et al.* (1976), such an approach has serious consequences, *viz*:

1. Language designers do not have good tools for careful analysis of their decisions.
2. Standardization efforts are impeded by a lack of an adequate formal notation.
3. Despite the fact that standards exist for programming languages, it is still risky to move a program from one implementation to another, even on the same hardware.
4. It is impossible to make a contract with a vendor for a compiler and be assured that the product will be an exact implementation of the language.

5. It is difficult to write reference manuals and tutorial texts without glossing over critical details that may change from implementation to implementation.
6. The answers to detailed questions about a programming language frequently have to be obtained by trying an implementation or hoping for a consensus from several implementations.

There have been several attempts at designing techniques for the formal definition of all aspects of a programming language. In this section various methods are reviewed. Marcotty, *et al.* (1976) compare some of these methods applying them to a simple language, ASPLE, and some of the material in this section is based on their excellent survey.

W-grammars and attribute grammars are used primarily for defining the (context-free and context-sensitive) syntax of programming languages but they can also be used to define semantics. These methods are discussed in Sections 10.7.2 and 10.7.3.

Three main methods have been developed for the formal definition of the semantics of programming languages. With the operational approach, an abstract machine is defined and the semantics of the language is given in terms of that machine. The Vienna Definition Language (Section 10.7.4) uses this approach. The second approach associates an axiom with each kind of statement in the programming language. This axiomatic approach is briefly discussed in Section 10.7.5 together with an application in 10.7.6. The basic ideas have already been covered in Chapter 2. The third approach, denotational semantics, which appears best suited to functional programming languages, is covered in Section 10.7.7.

10.7.2 W-Grammars, two-level grammars

Van Wijngaarden used a two-level grammar known as a W-grammar to describe Algol 68. A simple introduction to W-grammars can be found in McGettrick (1980).

A W-grammar consists of two finite sets of rules, the meta productions and the hyperrules. The hyperrules provide a blue print for context-free productions and, together with the meta-productions, describe how the user can derive a conceptually infinite set of productions. The infinite set of context-free productions is able to specify the context-sensitive restrictions and semantics of a language.

Metaproductions are context-free productions, the nonterminals of which are called metanotions (written as upper case strings) and the terminals of which are called protonotions (written as lower case strings). For example:

ALPHA::a; b; ...; z.
NOTION::ALPHA;
       NOTION ALPHA.

are two metaproductions following the W-grammar conventions where ':::' replaces ':: =' of BNF, ';' replaces '|' and every metaproduction is terminated by a full stop.

A hyperrule is used to generate context-free productions. For example, the hyperrule below is a blueprint for typed sequences. It contains both metanotions and protonotions. The notation is similar to that for metaproductions except ':' replaces ':::' and a comma is used to separate different protonotions within the same alternative:

NOTION sequence:
NOTION;
NOTION sequence,
NOTION.

The earlier metaproductions enable the generation of an infinite set of protonotions from the metanotion **NOTION,** e.g. **integer.** Replacing **NOTION** by this protonotion in the preceding hyperrule provides a definition of **integer sequence,** *viz*:

> **integer sequence:**
> **integer;**
> **integer sequence,**
> **integer.**

Using a W-grammar, it is possible to define all aspects of the context-free and context-sensitive syntax as well as the semantics of a programming language. Even though W-grammars are essentially simple to understand, it is often claimed that they prove too unwieldy in practice and do not readily provide an easily read, clearly defined syntax or semantics.

10.7.3 Attribute grammars

Attribute grammars, originated by Knuth (1968, 1971), are an adaptation of a BNF definition whereby attributes are associated with the nodes of a parse tree. They have become increasingly important over the last decade because of their potential use with automatic compiler generation. A good introduction to attribute grammars and their use can be found in McGettrick (1980).

There are two kinds of attributes. Inherited attributes are attributes acquired by a node from its parent; the synthesized attributes, on the other hand, are attributes obtained from the node's immediate descendants and the production generating these. Thus a production in an attribute grammar has to specify the inherited attributes of the right-hand side and the synthesized attributes of the left-hand side. There are various ways of specifying how the attributes are to be evaluated. To use attribute grammars as a formal definition tool some method must be adopted. Action symbols (Lewis *et al.*, 1973) are used in Marcotty *et al.* (1976) to define ASPLE. Action symbols are needed whenever the evaluation of an attribute value requires more than a simple value transfer.

As a simple example of an attribute grammar using action symbols, consider the definition of < number > given in *Figure 10.6* (taken from Marcotty *et al.* (1976)). Two attributes are

< number > ↑numdigits₁ ↑value₁ ::=

    < digit > ↑ value₁

    <u>give value to attribute</u> ↓*one-digit* ↑num-digits₁

    | < number > ↑numdigits₂ ↑value₂

    < digit > ↓value₃

    <u>multiply</u> ↓value₂ + *10* ↑value₄

    <u>add</u> ↓ value₄ ↓value₃ ↑value₁

    <u>add one digit</u> ↓num-digits₂ ↑ num-digits₁

< digit > ↑value ::= *0*

    <u>give value to attribute</u>↓ *0* ↑value

    | *1*

    <u>give value to attribute</u>↓*1* ↑value

    ...

    | *9*

    <u>*give value to attribute*</u>↓ *9* ↑value

Figure 10.6 An attribute grammar definition of < number >

specified: num-digits and value. By convention, the terminal symbols are written in italic characters and each symbol of the right-hand side of a production starts a new line. Attributes are represented by names written on the same line following the syntactic symbol to which they apply. Synthesized attributes are prefixed by an arrow pointing upwards and inherited ones by an arrow pointing downwards. Subscripts on attribute names distinguish different instances of attributes of the same type. These distinguished attributes may have different values which can be used within an evaluation specified by the action symbols. Action symbols are shown within the grammar by underlining.

10.7.4 The operational approach and the Vienna Definition Language

The operational approach to formal definition describes an implementation on some (formal) computing device. For example, the Vienna Definition Language uses an abstract machine (see *Figure 10.7*) and is fully described in Wegner (1972). It was used in the late 1960s to define PL/1 formally (Lucas *et al.*, 1968; Lucas and Walk, 1969).

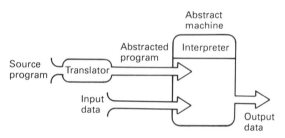

Figure 10.7 Schematic of a programming language definition in VDL

The meaning of a program is defined by the sequence of changes in the state of the abstract machine as the program is executed. The rules of execution are defined by an algorithm, the Interpreter. To make a distinction between those properties of a program that can be determined statically and those that are intrinsically connected to the dynamics of the program's execution, the original program is transformed into an abstracted form before execution. This transformation is performed by another algorithm, the Translator, which corresponds to the early phases of a compiler in a real computer system. During the transformation, the context-sensitive requirements on syntax can be checked.

10.7.5 The axiomatic approach to semantics

The axiomatic approach (Hoare, 1974; Hoare and Wirth, 1973) is based upon first-order predicate calculus and has already been discussed in Chapter 2. Assuming the context-free and context-sensitive syntax of the programming language is already established, an axiomatic approach can be used to define the semantics. Essentially, the approach establishes assertions about the program and these assertions can be used to define the semantics. The problem is thus to establish a correspondence between programs and relevant assertions.

There are two basic parts to this correspondence. Some assertions can be generated directly from the program text but there are also points where either the user must derive new assertions from those already generated or else rely upon some sort of automatic generation. The major use of Hoare's ideas has been in program verification. If a programming language is designed to support the use of this approach to program verification then an axiomatic approach to semantic definition can work well. One such language is Euclid. When a programming language is not so designed, the axiomatic approach will generally prove quite a difficult exercise.

10.7.6 Production systems

Ledgard (1977) has developed the production systems of Post (see Section 9.5.1 and Post (1943)) into a technique for the formal definition of programming languages. Like attribute grammars, they are a generative grammar developed from BNF. They have additional power which allows the definition of sets of n-tuples and the naming of specific components of n-tuples. These capabilities are sufficiently powerful to enable the description of any recursively enumerable set yet preserve readability.

In Marcotty *et al.* (1976), Ledgard's production systems technique is combined with the axiomatic approach to give a formal definition of the syntax and semantics of ASPLE. The production systems are used to define the syntax and a specification of a mapping from legal programs into a target language (based on the axiomatic approach) defines the semantics.

10.7.7 Denotational semantics

Defining the semantics of a programming language axiomatically can be difficult and defining them operationally, i.e. in terms of state transformations, is not always appropriate. For example, functional languages provide a tool by which functions are defined without recourse to the use of explicit computation steps. Accordingly, the formal semantics of such languages does not yield naturally to the operational approach but is more fittingly described using denotational semantics. This technique, rather than relying on (a model of) a particular implementation, describes the semantics of functional definitions in terms of a fixed point of a set of equations.

As a very simple example, consider the domain of integers, N, and the recursive program to compute the factorial function, f: $N \rightarrow N$,

$$f(n) \equiv \text{ if } n = 0 \text{ then } 1 \text{ else } n*f(n-1)$$

Given any function, f: $N \rightarrow N$, the right-hand side of this definition, *viz*. **if** $n = 0$ **then** 1 **else** $n*f(n-1)$, will construct a new function $N \rightarrow N$. The right-hand side can thus be viewed as defining a higher order function, φ: $(N \rightarrow N) \rightarrow (N \rightarrow N)$ by:

$$\varphi(f) \equiv \text{ if } n = 0 \text{ then } 1 \text{ else } n*f(n-1)$$

The factorial function then satisfies $f = \varphi(f)$, i.e. it is a fixed point of φ.

The work of Scott and Strachey (1971) provided the necessary theoretical background to show that this fixed point approach can be used to formally define semantics. Providing care is taken with undefined values, a unique fixed point can always be obtained and thus the semantics can be precisely defined. In Mandrioli and Ghezzi (1987), this approach is used to define the semantics of McCarthy's formalism. Detailed discussion and further applications of the method can be found in Stoy's widely cited text (Stoy, 1977).

The theory relies on the use of partially ordered sets (posets). Let D_1, D_2 be two posets with partial ordering, $\subseteq$. f: $D_1 \rightarrow D_2$ is monotonic iff $x \subseteq y$ implies $f(x) \subseteq f(y)$ for all $x,y \in D_1$. The composition of any two monotonic functions can easily be shown to be monotonic.

Let D be any domain extended to contain a bottom (undefined) element, ω. A partial ordering, $\subseteq$, on the extended domain (denoted by $\mathbb{D}$) is defined by $\omega \subseteq x$ for all x and $x \subseteq y$

implies either $x = \omega$ or $x = y$. A partial function, f: $D \rightarrow R$, can be extended to a total function, f: $\mathbb{D} \rightarrow \mathbb{R}$, by defining $f(\omega) = \omega$ and $f(x) = f(x)$ if $f(x)$ is defined but ω otherwise.

If $D_1, D_2, \ldots, D_n$ are arbitrary domains then the ordering, $\subseteq$, is extended to $\mathbb{D}_1 \times \mathbb{D}_2 \times \ldots \times \mathbb{D}_n$ by defining $(x_1 x_2, \ldots, x_n) \subseteq (y_1, y_2, \ldots, y_n)$ iff $x_1 \subseteq y_1, x_2 \subseteq y_2, \ldots, x_n \subseteq y_n$. The set of all monotonic functions from $\mathbb{D}_1 \times \mathbb{D}_2 \times \ldots \times \mathbb{D}_n$ to $\mathbb{R}$ is denoted by $[\mathbb{D}_1 \times \mathbb{D}_2 \times \ldots \times \mathbb{D}_n \rightarrow \mathbb{R}]$.

A function f: $\mathbb{D}_1 \times \mathbb{D}_2 \times \ldots \times \mathbb{D}_n \rightarrow \mathbb{R}$ is called a natural extension iff $f(x_1, x_2, \ldots, x_n) = \omega$ implies at least one x_i equals ω. Every natural extension is necessarily monotonic and, in general, functions are assumed to be naturally extended. However, this is not always the case. Constant functions, $f(x) = k$ for all x, are extended to monotonic functions by defining $f(\omega) = k$. The **if** ... **then** ... **else** function also requires special treatment. If $B = \{T, F\}$ then the monotonic function, **if** ... **then** ... **else**: $B \times D \times D \rightarrow D$ is defined as follows:

1. **if** T **then** x **else** $y \equiv x$ for any x and y (including ω).
2. **if** F **then** x **else** $y \equiv y$ for any x and y (including ω).
3. **if** ω **then** x **else** $y \equiv \omega$ for any x and y (including ω).

Note that this is not the natural extension of **if** ... **then** ... **else** but that it does intuitively conform to general programming practice.

Let $\mathbb{D} = \mathbb{D}_1 \times \mathbb{D}_2 \times \ldots \times \mathbb{D}_n$. Say $f, g \in [\mathbb{D} \rightarrow \mathbb{R}]$ then $f \subseteq g$ denotes that for all $x \in D$, $f(x) \subseteq g(x)$ and $f \equiv g$ denotes that $f \subseteq g$ and $g \subseteq f$, i.e. $f(x) = g(x)$ for all $x \in \mathbb{D}$. Ω: $\mathbb{D} \rightarrow \mathbb{R}$ denotes the everywhere undefined function, $\Omega(x) = \omega$ for all $x \in \mathbb{D}$. Ω is monotonic and $\Omega \subseteq f$ for any $f \in [\mathbb{D} \rightarrow \mathbb{R}]$.

Let $\{f_i\}$ be a sequence of functions in $[\mathbb{D} \rightarrow \mathbb{R}]$, then $\{f_i\}$ is a chain iff $f_i \subseteq f_{i+1}$ for all $i \geqslant 1$. $f \in [\mathbb{D} \rightarrow \mathbb{R}]$ is an upper bound of the chain iff $f_i \subseteq f$ for all i, and a least upper bound iff any other upper bound, g, satisfies $f \subseteq g$. Every chain, $\{f_i\}$, has a unique least upper bound denoted by $\bigcup f_i$.

A functional is a mapping $[\mathbb{D} \rightarrow \mathbb{R}]^n \rightarrow [\mathbb{D} \rightarrow \mathbb{R}]^n$. For example, the higher order function, φ, met in the introduction to this section defines a functional $[N \rightarrow N] \rightarrow [N \rightarrow N]$. A functional τ: $[\mathbb{D} \rightarrow \mathbb{R}]^n \rightarrow [\mathbb{D} \rightarrow \mathbb{R}]^n$ is monotonic iff $f \subseteq g$ implies $\tau(f) \subseteq \tau(g)$. It is continuous iff for any chain $\{f_i\}$ in $[\mathbb{D} \rightarrow \mathbb{R}]^n$, $\tau(\bigcup f_i) = \bigcup \tau(f_i)$. If τ is continuous then $\{\tau^i(\Omega)\}$ forms a chain and $\bigcup \tau^i(\Omega)$ is the least fixed point of τ. This fixed point theorem, variously attributable to Tarski, Knaster and Kleene, is the central result which enables the semantics to be uniquely defined in terms of fixed points.

Thus the semantic interpretation of the example factorial function:

$$f(n) \equiv \text{ if } n = 0 \text{ then } 1 \text{ else } n*f(n-1)$$

is uniquely defined to be $\bigcup \varphi^i(\Omega)$ where $\Omega(n) = \omega$ for all n and φ: $[N \rightarrow N] \rightarrow [N \rightarrow N]$ is defined by:

$$\varphi(f) \equiv n \rightarrow \text{if } n = \omega \text{ then } \omega$$
$$\text{else if } n = 0 \text{ then } 1 \text{ else } n*f(n-1)$$

The values of $\varphi^i(\Omega)$ can be tabulated as in *Figure 10.8*.

	ω	1	2	3	4	5	6	...
Ω	ω	ω	ω	ω	ω	ω	ω	...
$\varphi(\Omega)$	ω	1	ω	ω	ω	ω	ω	...
$\varphi^2(\Omega)$	ω	1	2	ω	ω	ω	ω	...
$\varphi^3(\Omega)$	ω	1	2	6	ω	ω	ω	...
$\varphi^4(\Omega)$	ω	1	2	6	24	ω	ω	...
$\varphi^5(\Omega)$	ω	1	2	6	24	120	ω	...
.	.	.	.	.	.	.	.	...
.	.	.	.	.	.	.	.	...
.	.	.	.	.	.	.	.	...

Figure 10.8

10.8 Use of the theory

The theory relating to programming language syntax is widely used and most practical parser generators are based on LR(k) or LL(k) principles (see Chapter 50). The formal approaches to definition of language semantics are less often used. Most programming languages semantics are defined informally, or only the static semantics are defined formally. A notable counter example is m-EVES (see Chapter 22).

10.9 References and bibliography

Aho, A. V. (1968) Indexed grammars – an extension of context-free grammars. *Journal of the ACM*, **15**, 647–671

Aho, A. V. and Johnson, S. C. (1974) LR parsing. *Computing Surveys*, **6**, 99–124

Aho, A. V. and Ullman, J. D. (1972) *The Theory of Parsing, Translation and Compiling, Vol I: Parsing*, Prentice Hall, Englewood Cliffs, NJ, USA

Aho, A. V. and Ullman, J. D. (1977) *Principles of Compiler Design*, Addison-Wesley, Reading, Mass., USA

Backhouse, R. C. (1979) *Syntax of Programming Languages: Theory and Practice*, Prentice-Hall, Englewood Cliffs, NJ, USA

Bar-Hillel, Y., Perles, M. and Shamir, E. (1961) On formal properties of simple phrase structure grammars. *Zeitschrift fuer Phonetik, Sprachwissenschaft, und Kommunikationsforschung.*, **14**, 143–172

Blickle, A. (1972) Equational languages. *Information and Control*, **21**, 134–147

Brzozowski, J. A. (1962) A survey of regular expressions and their applications. *IEEE Transactions on Electronic Computers*, **11**, 324–335

Cantor, D. C. (1962) On the ambiguity problem of Backus systems. *Journal of the ACM*, **9**, 477–479

Chomsky, N. (1956) Three models for the description of language, *IEEE Transactions on Information Theory*, **2**, 113–124

Chomsky, N. (1959) On certain formal properties of grammars, *Information and Control*, **2**, 137–167

Chomsky, N. (1962) Context-free grammars and pushdown storage. *Quarterly Progress Report. No. 65.* MIT Research Laboratories, Cambridge, Mass., pp 187–194

Chomsky, N. (1963) Formal properties of grammars. In *Handbook of Mathematical Psychology*, Vol 2. John Wiley and Sons, New York, pp 323–418

Chomsky, N. and Schutzenberger, M. P. (1963) The algebraic theory of context free languages. In *Computer Programming and Formal Systems*, North Holland, Amsterdam, pp 118–161

DeRemer, F. L. (1969) Generating parsers for BNF grammars. In *Proceedings 1969 Spring Joint Conference*, AFIPS Press, Montvale, NJ, USA, pp 793–799

DeRemer, F. L. (1971) Simple LR(k) grammars. *Communications of the ACM*, **14**, 453–460

Fischer, M. J. (1968) Grammars with macro-like productions. In *Proceedings of Ninth Annual IEEE Symposium on Switching and Automata Theory*, IEEE, pp. 131–142

Floyd, R. W. (1962) On the ambiguity in phrase structure languages. *Communications of the ACM*, **5**, 526–534

Foster, J. M. (1963) A syntax improving device. *The Computer Journal*, **11**, 31–34

Ginsburg, S. (1960) *The Mathematical Theory of Context-free Languages*, McGraw Hill, New York, USA

Ginsburg, S. and Greibach, S. A. (1966a) Mappings which preserve context-sensitive languages. *Information and Control*, **9**, 6, 563–582

Ginsburg, S. and Greibach, S. A. (1966b) Deterministic context-free languages, *Information and Control*, **9**, 620–648

Ginsburg, S. and Greibach, S. A. (1969) Abstract families of languages. In *Studies in Abstract Families of Languages.* Memoir No 87, American Mathematical Society, Providence RL, USA, pp. 1–32

Ginsburg, S. and Ullian, J. S. (1966) Ambiguity in context-free languages. *Journal of the ACM*, **13**, 62–88

Greibach, S. A. (1965) A new normal form theorem for context-free phrase structure grammars. *Journal of the ACM*, **12**, 42–52

Greibach, S. A. and Hopcroft, J. E. (1969) Independence of AFL operations. In *Studies in Abstract Families of Languages*, Memoir No 87, American Mathemtical Society, Providence, RI, USA, 33–40

Hoare, C. A. R. (1974) Consistent and complementary formal theories of the semantics of programming languages. *Acta Informatica*, **3**, 135–153

Hoare, C. A. R. and Wirth, N. (1973) An axiomatic definition of the programming language PASCAL. *Acta Informatica*, **2**, 335–355

Hopcroft, J. E. and Ullman, J. D. (1969) *Formal Languages and Their Relation to Automata*, Addison-Wesley, Reading, Mass., USA

Hopcroft, J. E. and Ullman, J. D. (1979) *Introduction to Automata Theory, Languages and Computation*, Addison-Wesley, Reading, Mass., USA

Hopgood, F. R. A. (1969) *Compiling Techniques*, American Elsevier, New York, USA

Ibarra, O. H. (1970) Simple matrix languages. *Information and Control*, **17**, 359–394

Jensen, K. and Wirth, N. (1975) *PASCAL: User Manual and Report*, Springer-Verlag, Berlin, FRG

Kleene, S. C. (1956) Representation of events in nerve nets and finite automata. *Automata Studies*, Princeton University Press, Princeton, NJ, USA, pp. 3–42

Knuth, D. E. (1965) On the translation of languages from left to right. *Information and Control*, **8**, 607–639

Knuth, D. E. (1968 and 1971) Semantics of context-free languages. *Mathematical Systems Theory*, **2**, 127–145 and **5**, 95

Landweber, P. S. (1963) Three theorems on phrase structure grammars of type 1. *Information and Control*, **6**, 131–136

Ledgard, H. F. (1977) Production systems: a notation for defining syntax and translation of programming languages. *IEEE Transactions on Software Engineering*, SE-3, 105–124

Lewis, P. M., Rosenkrantz, D. J. and Sterns, F. E. (1973) Attributed translations. *ACM Symposium on Theory of Computing*, Austin, Texas, USA

Lindenmayer, A. (1968) Mathematical models for cellular interactions in development, parts I and II. *Journal of Theoretical Biology*, **18**, 280–315

Lindenmayer, A. (1971) Developmental systems without cellular interaction, their languages and grammars. *Journal of Theoretical Biology*, **30**, 455–484

Lucas, P., Lauer, P. and Sigleitner, H. (1968) Method and notation for the formal definition of programming languages. *IBM Technical Report 25.087*, IBM Laboratory, Vienna, Austria

Lucas, P. and Walk, K. (1969) On the formal description of PL/I. *Annual Review of Automatic Programming*, **6**, 105–182

McGettrick, A. D. (1980) *The Definition of Programming Languages*, Cambridge University Press, Cambridge

McNaughton, R. and Yamada, H. (1960) Regular expressions and state graphs for automata. *IEEE Transactions on Electronic Computers*, **9**, 39–47

Mandrioli, D. and Ghezzi, C. (1987) *Theoretical Foundations of Computer Science*, John Wiley

Marcotty, M., Ledgard, H. F. and Bochmann, G. V. (1976) A sampler of formal definitions. *Computing Surveys*, **8**, 191–276

Naur, P. (1978) The European side of the last phase of the development of Algol. *ACM SIGPLAN Notices*, **13**, 15–44

Ogden, W. (1968) A helpful result for proving inherent ambiguity. *Mathematical Systems Theory*, **2**, 191–194

Parikh, R. J. (1966) On context-free languages. *Journal of the ACM*, **13**, 570–581

Post, E. L. (1943) Formal reductions of the general combinatorial decision problem. *American Journal of Mathematics*, **65**, 197–215

Rabin, M. O. and Scott, D. (1959) Finite automata and their decision problems. *IBM Journal of Research and Development.*, **3**, 115–125

Rayward-Smith, V. J. (1983) *A First Course in Formal Language Theory*, Blackwell, Oxford

Rayward-Smith, V. J. (1977) Hypergrammars: an extension of macro-grammars. *Journal of Computer Systems Science*, **14**, 130–149

Rozenberg, G. and Salomaa, A. (1980) *The Mathematical Theory of L Systems*, Academic Press

Rosenkrantz, D. J. (1969) Programmed grammars and classes of formal languages. *Journal of the ACM*, **16**, 107–131

Rosenkrantz, D. J. and Stearns, R. E. (1970) Properties of deterministic top-down grammars. *Information and Control*, **17**, 226–256

Salomaa, A. (1973) *Formal Languages*, Academic Press, USA

Salomaa, A. (1981) *Jewels of Formal Language Theory*, Computer Science Press, Rockville, MD, USA

Schutzenberger, M. P. (1963) On context-free languages and pushdown automata. *Information and Control*, **6**, 246–264

Scott, D. and Strachey, C. (1971) Towards a mathematical semantics for computer language. *PRG-6*, Programming Language Research Group, Oxford

Stoy, J. E. (1977) *Denotational Semantics: The Scott-Strachey Approach to Programming Language Theory*, MIT Press, Cambridge, Mass., USA

Wegner, P. (1972) The Vienna definition language. *Computing Surveys*, **4**, 5–63

van Wijngaarden, A., Mailloux, B. J., Peck, J. E. and Koster, C. H. A. (1969) *Report on the Algorithmic language Algol68*, Mathematisch Centrum, Amsterdam

Younger, D. H. (1967) Recognition and parsing of context-free languages in time n³. *Information and Control*, **10**, 189–208

11

Data structures and algorithms

Giorgio Ausiello
Dipartimento di Informatica e Sistemistica,
La Sapienza University, Rome, Italy

Contents

11.1 Introduction

The design and analysis of data structures and algorithms play a very important role in software engineering. If the first two main goals in software development are reliability and maintainability, the third one is definitely efficiency (Ghezzi and Jazayeri, 1987). It is well known that in several applications, such as real-time systems and defence, efficiency is a critical issue. But it is worth stressing that efficiency is also a key issue in several other areas where users need fast and powerful interaction with complex systems (very large databases, expert systems, computer-aided design (CAD) and computer-aided software engineering (CASE) systems etc.). This chapter is devoted to the design of efficient algorithms and data structures.

According to the most widespread view of software design, based on the principles of modularity and abstraction (Ehrig and Mahr, 1985), a software system can be viewed as a collection of data types, each one composed of a set of data items together with operations on such items. This approach has several advantages, the main one being the provision of a certain degree of independence between the logical specification of the operations and their physical implementation by means of different data structures. This allows the adoption of the particular implementation of a data type that is most suited to meeting the efficiency requirements.

Starting from this point of view, efficiency considerations should not be seen as being in contrast to other design principles. No clear difference can be established between designing algorithms and designing data structures. On the one hand, the efficient performance of an algorithm may derive from the appropriate choice of the implementation of the supporting data type, while on the other, ingenious algorithm design techniques may be exploited to provide efficient implementation of complex operations on a data structure.

This section provides an overview of the basic techniques for analysing and designing algorithms and data structures with application to searching and sorting.

11.2 Analysis techniques

To evaluate the performance of algorithms various aspects have to be defined: the machine model on which the algorithm is supposed to run, the complexity measure to evaluate, and the type of analysis to be performed.

11.2.1 Machine models and complexity measures

The concept of computational complexity was introduced in Chapter 9 in terms of abstract machines (Turing machines, universal register machines etc.) and of the corresponding time and space complexity measures (in the case of Turing machines these respectively are the number of computation steps performed and the number of tape cells visited).

According to the literature (Hopcroft and Ullman, 1979), Turing machines are mostly used for studying abstract properties of computations (such as space-time trade-offs or intrinsic power of time and space bounded computations). As a machine model for analysing the complexity of algorithms, Turing machines and related kinds of automata are essentially applied in the analysis of string algorithms (recognition and syntax analysis of formal languages, pattern matching etc.).

In other areas of algorithms different types of machine models are used, ranging from natural (computer-like) models, such as the register machines (also called random access machines (RAMs)), to *ad hoc* models, defined with the specific aim of studying particular classes of algorithms, such as directed acyclic graphs (DAGs), which are applied in the study of

compilers for describing code optimization techniques (see Chapter 52).

In its simplest version a RAM consists of a control unit, capable of performing the instructions of a very simple machine language, and of an unlimited set of registers (memory cells), each one containing an arbitrarily large non-negative integer. Additionally, the machine has a few special registers:

1. *Accumulator*, which contains data processed by the instructions.
2. *Input* and *output* registers.
3. *Program counter*, which contains the address of the instruction to be performed next by the machine.

A schematic representation of a RAM is given in *Figure 11.1*.

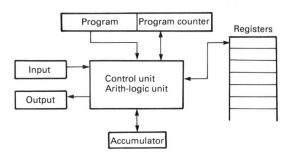

Figure 11.1

The instructions of a RAM are performed on various kinds of operands:

1. *Integers*. The integer n is denoted $= n$ and the operation is directly performed on the integer n.
2. *Registers*. The ith register is denoted Ri and the operation involves the content of register Ri.
3. *Indirectly accessed registers*. The operand is denoted [Ri] and the operation involves the content of the register addressed by the content of register Ri.

We will call data an operand of type (1), (2) and (3) and register an operand of type (2) and (3). A label is simply an integer denoting the (progressive) number of an instruction (that is the instruction whose label is n is the nth instruction of a program). All registers that have not yet been accessed are set to 0.

The basic instructions of a RAM are:

1. I/O instructions
   READ ⟨register⟩ read from input into register
   PRINT ⟨register⟩ print output from register
2. Copy from/to accumulator and registers:
   LOAD ⟨data⟩ load data into accumulator
   STORE ⟨register⟩ save content of accumulator into register
3. Arithmetic operations
   ADD ⟨data⟩ add data to the content of accumulator
   SUB ⟨data⟩ subtract data from content of accumulator
   MULT ⟨data⟩ multiply content of accumulator by data
4. Flow control instructions
   JZERO ⟨label⟩ jump to label if content of accumulator equal to zero
   JGTZ ⟨label⟩ jump to label if content of accumulator greater than zero
   JUMP ⟨label⟩ jump to label unconditionally
   HALT the execution of the program stops

A program stops either when it comes to a HALT instruction or when it would otherwise jump to a non-existent instruction.

When an algorithm is described by a RAM program its performance may be measured in two different ways:

1. *Uniform costs* The cost of any instruction that is performed is equal to 1 and the overall cost of the execution of the algorithm is equal to the number of instructions that are performed; this way of evaluating computation costs is simple but leads to rather unnatural effects since it allows access to an arbitrarily large memory and the manipulation of arbitrarily large integers with unitary costs.
2. *Logarithmic costs* The cost of an instruction depends upon the size of the accessed storage and the size of processed data (content of accumulator and content of registers). Since we imagine all integers expressed in binary notation the 'size' of an integer corresponds to its logarithm in base 2. For example, if the content of the ith register is n and the content of the accumulator is m, the cost of the instruction 'ADD Ri' is: $\log i + \log n + \log m$. Though more complex, this cost measure is more accurate and realistic since it takes into account the physical limitations of the abstract model.

Example 11.1

Let us consider the simple algorithm for the sum of n integers a_1, $a_2, \ldots, a_n$, given in *Figure 11.2*. Let us suppose that the integers are stored in the registers R4, R5, $\ldots$, R$(3 + n)$ and that register R1 contains a pointer to such registers. In addition, register R2 contains the sum of the n integers and register R3 contains the integer n.

1	LOAD	$= 3$
2	STORE	R1
3	LOAD	R1
4	ADD	$= 1$
5	STORE	R1
6	LOAD	[R1]
7	ADD	R2
8	STORE	R2
9	LOAD	R3
10	SUB	$= 1$
11	STORE	R3
12	JGTZ	3
13	HALT	

Figure 11.2 RAM program for the sum of n integers

If we use the uniform cost criterion, since the loop is repeated n times, the program takes time $a n + b$ to be performed, where a and b are constants depending respectively on the length of the loop (10) and on the number of instructions (3) of the initialization and termination phases. If we use the logarithmic cost criterion instead, we have to consider that the sums at instruction 7 have a cost depending on the largest among the n integers (say a_{MAX}) and that the number of registers that have to be accessed is dependent on n. Hence the overall cost determined in this more precise way will be $c n (\log n + \log a_{MAX}) + d$ where again c and d are suitable values which depend on all other constant costs.

Its realism and accuracy mean that the RAM model also provides a good point of departure for the analysis of algorithms expressed in a high-level language or even in natural language. In this case the analysis is based on finding a dominant operation (that is, an operation whose contribution to the overall cost of the algorithm is at least of the same order of magnitude as the cost of all other operations) and in determining the cost of the algorithm in terms of this operation, as a function of some meaningful parameter of the input. For example, a sorting algorithm may quite reasonably be evaluated in terms of the number of comparisons executed as a function of the number of elements to be sorted. For these reasons, the analysis of an algorithm is often performed starting from a high-level description of the algorithm and only when one needs a very precise estimate of cost is it necessary to refer to a specific machine model.

11.2.2 Asymptotic analysis

The performance evaluation of algorithms and programs is usually based on an asymptotic analysis of the time (more rarely, space) execution costs as the size of the input tends to infinity. This means that, in an example such as the preceding one, we might have avoided determining the precise values of the constants (a, b and c, d), and have simply said that the cost grows like n according to the first cost criterion, and like $n \log n$ according to the second, as n tends to infinity.

The drawback of asymptotic analysis is that in several practical cases we are not interested in the limit behaviour of an algorithm so much as in the behaviour for instances with small size. In these cases ignoring the constants may not be correct. For example, in comparing two algorithms for small-size data we may prefer using an algorithm which takes time $2 n^2$ than one that takes time $10 000 n \log n$. Still asymptotic analysis provides a first approximate evaluation of the efficiency of an algorithm.

To express asymptotic analysis a specific notation has been introduced, called 'big-oh' notation. If two positive functions $t(n)$ and $g(n)$ are given we say that:

$$t(n) \text{ is } O(g(n))$$

if there are two positive constants c and n_0 such that, for all $n \geqslant n_0$:

$$t(n) \geqslant c\, g(n)$$

For example, the function $t(n) = a n \log n + bn + c$ is O ($n \log n$).

The big-oh notation is usually applied for expressing both the worst-case behaviour of an algorithm and the average-case behaviour.

Let us denote by $t_A(x)$ the cost of executing algorithm A on input x. Let:

$$t_A(n) = \max \{t_A(x) \mid \text{size } (x) = n\}$$

In the worst-case asymptotic analysis we are interested in determining the asymptotic growth of $t_A(n)$.

In several cases, when we do not have severe efficiency constraints, we may use average-case asymptotic analysis instead of worst case. In this case we examine the growth of the function:

$$t_A(n) = E \{t_A(x) \mid \text{size } (x) = n\}$$

where $E\{t_A(x) \mid \text{size } (x) = n\}$ denotes the expected cost of executing the algorithm on an instance x of size n, assuming that we know the probability distribution of the instances of size n.

Example 11.2

Let us consider two algorithms for sorting an array of n elements: SELECTION-SORT and INSERTION-SORT, respectively shown in *Figures 11.3* and *11.4*.

```
procedure SelectionSort (var vect: array [1 .. N] of integer);

var i, j, index_to_min, tmp: integer

begin { SelectionSort }
  for i := 1 to N − 1 do
    begin
      index_to_min := i;
      for j := i + 1 to N do
        if vect[j] < vect[index_to_min] then index_to_min := j;
      tmp := vect[index_to_min];
      vect[index_to_min] := vect[i];
      vect[i] := tmp
    end
end; { SelectionSort }
```

Figure 11.3 SELECTION-SORT

```
procedure InsertionSort (var vect: array [1 .. N] of integer);

var i, j, tmp: integer;

begin { InsertionSort }
  for i := 2 to N do
    begin
      tmp := vect[i];
      j := i − 1;
      while (j > = 1) and (tmp < vect[j]) do
        begin
          vect[j + 1] := vect[j];
          j := j − 1
        end;
      vect[j + 1] := tmp
    end
end; { InsertionSort }
```

Figure 11.4 INSERTION-SORT

In the case of SELECTION-SORT both the worst-case and the average-case analysis are very simple. Since the algorithm essentially consists of determining the smallest key among n, $n − 1, \ldots, 2$ keys, the overall number of comparisons to sort the elements of the array is:

$$\sum_{i=2}^{n} (i - 1) = n(n - 1)/2$$

that is, $O(n^2)$, whatever the previous ordering of the array. This means that in all cases, and hence also in the average case, the execution cost of the algorithm is the same.

The situation with the INSERTION-SORT algorithm is quite different. In this algorithm the second, third, ..., nth keys are checked against the preceding ones in the array until the proper place is found. The cost is hence determined by (actually exactly equal to) the number of inversions in the array, that is, the number of pairs $A[i]$, $A[j]$ in the array such that $i < j$ while $A[i] > A[j]$. Let us denote by $inv(j)$ the number of inversions with respect to element $A[j]$. Then the overall number of inversions is:

$$INV (n) = \sum_{j=2}^{n} inv(j)$$

Clearly in the best case (the array is already sorted) the number of inversions is 0, while in the worst case it will be $n(n-1)/2$. It turns out that in the worst case the algorithm again takes time $0(n^2)$. The analysis of the average case complexity shows instead a better performance. To derive such an analysis

we have to make some reasonable hypothesis about the distribution of the possible permutations of an array with n elements and compute the average number of inversions according to such a distribution. If we assume that all permutations are equally likely we have that for every element j:

$$\begin{aligned}Prob\{inv(j) = 1\} = Prob\{inv(j) = 2\} = \ldots \\ = Prob\{inv(j) = j - 1\} = 1/j\end{aligned}$$

Hence, if we denote $E(inv(j))$ the expected value of $inv(j)$ we have:

$$E(inv(j)) = (j - 1)/2$$

and consequently:

$$E(INV(n)) = \sum_{j=2}^{n} E(inv(j)) = 1/2 \sum_{j=2}^{n} (j - 1) = n(n-1)/4$$

This means that, while being still $O(n^2)$, the average cost of INSERTION-SORT is one half the worst case cost.

11.2.3 Analysis based on recurrence relations

Several problems may be efficiently solved by making use of a design technique consisting of decomposing the problem into subproblems and then recombining the solutions to obtain the solution to the original problem. This technique is called *divide et impera* (divide and conquer).

Beside being important for algorithm design, this technique is also useful in the analysis phase because its inherent recursion allows the derivation of cost equations in the form of recurrence relations. A recurrence relation is an equation in which a function is recursively defined in terms of the values that the function itself takes for smaller values of the argument.

Example 11.3

Let us consider again the problem of sorting an array. A classical method based on *divide et impera* is the algorithm MERGE-SORT, shown in *Figure 11.5*.

Suppose we are given an array with $2n$ elements. To determine the number $T(2n)$ of comparisons needed to sort the array we may simply observe that such a number is given by the solution of the following equation:

$$T(2n) = 2T(n) + n$$

since to sort the array of size $2n$ we have to sort two arrays of size n and we need n comparisons to merge the two sorted arrays. The solution of the equation gives:

$$T(n) = \log n$$

This shows that the MERGE-SORT algorithm is asymptotically more efficient than the two algorithms that were presented before.

The *divide et impera* technique has been widely used to derive efficient algorithms in various fields of computer science, such as algebraic algorithms (Aho *et al.*, 1974) and computational geometry (Mehlhorn, 1984). As a design technique it is particularly advantageous under suitable conditions: not too many subproblems, balanced decomposition, low cost of recombining the partial solutions. A very important result that has been achieved by a careful application of the technique is the famous Strassen's matrix multiplication algorithm – the first matrix multiplication algorithm with a less than cubic ($O(n^{2.81})$) running time.

```
procedure Merge (vl, v2: array [1 .. N] of integer;
                i1, j1, i2, j2: integer;
                var v_out: array [1 .. N] of integer;
                i_out: integer);
{ merges vl[i1 .. j1] and v2[i2 .. j2] into: v_out [i_out ..
(j1 + j2 − i1 − i2 + 1 + i_out)] }

var i: integer;

begin { Merge }
    while (i1 < = j1) and (i2 < = j2) do
        begin
            if vl[i1] < = v2[i2]
                then begin
                    v_out[i_out] := vl[i1];
                    i1 := i1 + 1
                end
            else begin
                    v_out[i_out] := v2[i2];
                    i2 := i2 + 1
                end;
            i_out := i_out + 1
        end
    if i1 > j1
        then for i := i2 to j2 do
            begin
                v_out[i_out] := v2[i];
                i_out := i_out + 1
            end
        else for i := i1 to j1 do
            begin
                v_out[i_out] := vl[i];
                i_out := i_out + 1
            end
end; { Merge }


procedure MergeSort1 (var vect: array [1 .. N] of integer;
i, j: integer);

var half: integer;

begin { MergeSort1 }

    if i < j then
        begin
            half := (i + j) div 2;
            MergeSort1(vect, i, half);
            MergeSort1(vect, half + 1, j);
            Merge(vect, vect, i, half, half + 1, j, vect, i)
        end
end; { MergeSort1 }

procedure MergeSort (var vect: array [1 .. N] of integer);

begin { MergeSort }
    MergeSort1(vect, 1, N)
end; { MergeSort }
```

Figure 11.5 MERGE-SORT

A fairly general class of algorithms based on the *divide et impera* paradigm consists in decomposing a problem of size n into subproblems of size n/c. In many cases the cost of recombining the result of the given problem from the partial solutions of the subproblems is linear. In all these cases the recurrence relations have the following general form:

$$T(n) = \begin{cases} b & \text{if } n = 1 \\ a\,T(n/c) + bn & \text{if } n > 1 \end{cases}$$

By solving the equation we may determine the computational cost of the solution in the various cases:

1. If $a < c$ then $T(n)$ is $O(n)$.
2. If $a = c$ then $T(n)$ is $O(n \log n)$.
3. If $a > c$ then $T(n)$ is $O(n^{\log_c a})$.

The second case is the MERGE-SORT case where we have $a = c = 2$.

In the case of the matrix multiplication algorithm the problem of computing the product of two $n \times n$ matrices may be reduced to the problem of computing seven products of matrices of size $n/2 \times n/2$. This corresponds to the third case and leads to a running time $O(n^{\log_2 7})$.

Recurrence relations with the same structure arise in the analysis of many other algorithms. In several other cases the application of the *divide et impera* technique leads to more complex recurrence relations whose algebraic solution requires sophisticated mathematical tools (Greene and Knuth, 1981).

11.2.4 Analysis of lower bounds

Beside giving information on the running time of a particular algorithm for the solution of a given problem, the formal asymptotic worst-case analysis also provides an upper bound on the complexity of the given problem, that is, with information on the amount of resource (time, space) that is sufficient to solve the problem.

The notation that is currently used to express a complexity upper bound is again the big-oh. When we say that 'a problem P has a complexity $O(g(n))$' this means that there exists at least one algorithm A for solving problem P whose running time $t_A(n)$ is $O(g(n))$.

In order to assess the intrinsic complexity of a problem a second item of information is needed: the amount of resource that is necessary to solve it, no matter what algorithm we choose. This information is called the complexity lower bound.

To express a complexity lower bound a specific notation has been introduced, called omega notation. If two positive functions $t(n)$ and $g(n)$ are given we say that:

$$t(n) \text{ is } \Omega(g(n))$$

if there are two positive constants c and n_0 such that, for all $n \geq n_0$:

$$t(n) \geq c\,g(n)$$

For example, the function $t(n) = a\,n \log n + b\,n + c$ is $\Omega(n)$ and also $\Omega(n \log n)$.

The omega notation is usually applied for expressing the amount of resource that is necessary to solve a problem. We say that the complexity of a given problem P is $\Omega(g(n))$ if any algorithm A for solving problem P has a running time $t_A(n)$ which is $\Omega(g(n))$, that is asymptotically as large as $g(n)$.

The difficulty of determining a complexity lower bound derives from the fact that it is a characteristic property of the problem and hence it does not depend on a specific algorithm used for the solution. In other words, it is related to the intrinsic computational nature of the problem. This means that the techniques that are used for proving complexity lower bounds (which may be algebraic, geometric, combinatorial, information theoretic techniques etc.) have to be chosen depending on the nature of the given problem.

A technique commonly used for searching and sorting problems, where the complexity is often measured in terms of number of comparisons, is the information theoretic technique. If we are given a problem such that for an input of size n the number of possible outcomes is $h(n)$, by means of a simple information theoretic argument we may state that the complexity of such problem is $\Omega(\log h(n))$. In fact, since identifying an object in a set containing $h(n)$ objects requires $\log h(n)$ bits of information and since of any comparison provides a yes-or-no answer (corresponding to one bit of information), no algorithm based on comparisons can solve the given problem with less than $\log h(n)$ comparisons.

Example 11.4

By means of the information theoretic argument we can prove that searching for a key in a structure with n keys has a complexity lower bound $\Omega(\log n)$ comparisons.

When the complexity of a problem is neatly characterized by means of an upper bound $O(g(n))$ and a lower bound $\Omega(g(n))$ that are assymptotically coincident, we may say that we have an asymptotically optimal solution of the problem. In this case we use again a specific notation, the theta notation and we say that the complexity of the problem is $\theta(g(n))$.

Example 11.5

Since the well-known binary search method (see next section) provides an $O(\log n)$ algorithm for searching for a key in an array with n keys we may say that searching has a complexity $\theta(\log n)$.

Example 11.6

Sorting an array with n keys has a complexity $\theta(n \log n)$. In fact we have seen that the MERGE-SORT algorithm gives an $O(n \log n)$ upper bound for sorting. Alternatively, using the information theoretic argument, we may derive that sorting takes $\Omega(n \log n)$ comparisons. In fact since the possible outcomes of a sorting algorithm are the $n!$ permutations of the array, the number of comparisons needed by any sorting algorithm are $\Omega(\log n!)$, that is $\Omega(n \log n)$ by Stirling's approximation. Since the upper bound and the lower bound coincide, this means that the complexity of sorting is precisely characterized and is $\theta(n \log n)$ and that MERGE-SORT is an (asymptotically) optimal algorithm.

11.3 Design of efficient data structures and algorithms

In this section fundamental data structures for the implementation of two data types with wide application in software systems will be considered: dictionaries (both in the static and in the dynamic case) and priority queues.

11.3.1 Dictionaries

Let us consider a collection of items (or records), each one consisting of two parts: the key (consisting of that data that characterizes the item, e.g. name and birth date in an employee information system) and the information (consisting of all supplementary data, e.g. the salary). The data type dictionary is a collection of items on which we want to perform the following operations:

1. *insert* (item).
2. *delete* (item).
3. *search* (key), in order to retrieve the associated information.

To implement a dictionary we may use various data structures. Their efficiency depends on the frequency of update operations (insert, delete) with respect to queries (search). If the latter are more frequent we speak of a static case, otherwise we speak of a dynamic case. This describes some of the most relevant data structures both for the static and for the dynamic case.

To make the exposition simpler the items will be considered as consisting only of an integer key and, unless otherwise specified, the way the associated information is stored will not be considered.

11.3.1.1 Static case

The typical structure used for implementing a dictionary in the static case is the array. If the array is maintained as sorted the well-known binary search method allows the search to be achieved for a key with a logarithmic number of comparisons. The drawback of this implementation, which makes it convenient only in the static case, is the high cost of maintaining the ordering under insertion and deletions.

A second possible implementation is based on lists. It is slightly more convenient for updating but its poor searching performance makes it useful only for small collections of items.

The table in *Figure 11.6* shows the costs of the dictionary operations on an array (both in the sorted and in the unordered case) and on a list (the ordering does not affect the efficiency in this case). Note that the costs of insertion and deletion do not include the cost of first searching for the item.

	Insert	Delete	Search
Sorted array	0(n)	0(n)	0(log n)
Unordered array	0(1)	0(1)	0(n)
List	0(1)	0(1)	0(n)

Figure 11.6 Execution cost of dictionary operations on tables and lists

When the keys in the array are uniformly distributed the so-called 'interpolation search' technique (Knuth, 1973b) may provide a better average access time ($O(\log \log n)$) but in the worst case (that is if the uniform distribution hypothesis is not satisfied) the access time is $O(n)$.

A different table based approach to static dictionary management is the direct access method known as 'hashing'.

Let K be the set of possible keys and V the set of addresses in the table. A hash function is a mapping h: $K \to V$. In an ideal situation this would allow access to a key with a single operation. Since, in general, the size of K is much larger than the size of V, the mapping cannot be injective. Hence for two different keys k_1, k_2 we may have $h(k_1) = h(k_2)$. Such a situation is called a collision. Colliding keys may be treated in two ways (see *Figure 11.7*):

1. In open hashing, they are put in overflow buckets.
2. In closed hashing they have to be reallocated in the table.

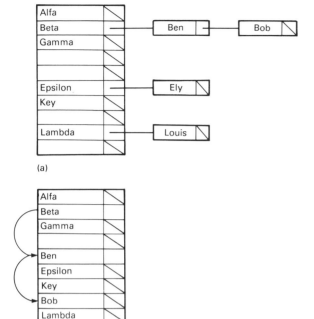

(a)

(b)

Figure 11.7 Hash table (a) open hashing (b) closed hashing

In both cases insertion and search for a key may require several accesses and this may cause a performance degradation.

The performance of hashing techniques (Mauer and Lewis, 1975) mainly depends on the following two aspects:

1. Quality of the randomization performed by the hash function over the keys (keys should be uniformly distributed over the physical addresses to reduce collision probability).
2. Efficient management of collisions and (in the case of closed hashing) of reallocation of colliding keys (reallocated keys should not increase the probability of collisions too much).

Let $B(k)$ be the binary string corresponding to the key k and let $|V| = 2^v$ be the size (number of rows) of the table. The most typical hash functions are obtained in the following ways:

1. Cut $B(k)$ in substrings $B_1, B_2, \ldots$ of v bits each and sum over all B_is mod 2^v.
2. Compute $B(k)^2$ and extract v bits from the middle of the result.
3. Compute the remainder of $B(k)/|V|$ (note that in this case $|V|$ should be odd).

The reallocation strategies in closed hashing are based on various probing techniques:

1. *Linear probing*, with constant step d: after collision in position $h(k)$ key is allocated in the first empty position among $h(k) + d$, $h(k) + 2d$, $\ldots$, $h(k) + n\,d$. This technique has the inconvenience of causing what is called 'primary clustering': two keys k_1 and k_2 such that $h(k_2) = h(k_1) + n\,d$ will have the same probing sequence, and hence a high collision probability.
2. *Quadratic probing*. The probing sequence is $h(k) + d$, $h(k) + d + (d + 1)$, $\ldots$, $h(k) + n\,d + n(n-1)/2$. Primary clustering is eliminated but secondary clustering still happens: two keys k_1 and k_2 such that $h(k_1) = h(k_2)$ still have the same probing sequence.

3. *Rehashing*. At each step the value of a new hash function is computed depending on the key and on the number of previous collisions. In this way both primary and secondary clustering are eliminated.

11.3.1.2 Dynamic case

When the frequency of updates is high the table-based implementations of a dictionary are unsatisfactory, especially if operations on secondary storage are required. In this case the most widely used implementations are based on various kinds of trees.

To use trees in the efficient implementation of dictionaries in the dynamic case two conditions have to be satisfied. First, keys have to be associated with nodes in such a way that searching for a key requires access at most nodes from the root to the leaves. Since it is well known that the depth of a complete binary (*m*ary) tree is $O(\log_2 n)$ $(O(\log_m n))$ where n is the number of nodes of the tree (see *Figure 11.8*) this condition would guarantee a logarithmic search time.

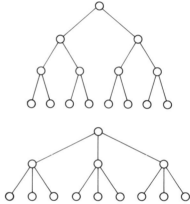

Figure 11.8 Complete binary and ternary trees

On the other hand, under insertions and deletions, the tree structure cannot be maintained complete but has, at least, to be maintained in a balanced way, that is, the subtrees branching from a node should contain 'approximately' the same number of keys. If this condition is satisfied logarithmic access time may still be guaranteed.

The main differences between tree implementations of dictionaries depend on how these two conditions are satisfied.

Let us first consider the binary case. A binary search tree is a tree where the key associated with an internal node is smaller than all keys in the right subtree branching from the node and larger than all keys associated with the left subtree (see *Figure 11.9*).

Historically the first tree structure that has been proposed for implementing dictionaries are AVL-trees (Adelson Velskii and Landis, 1962). AVL-trees are binary search trees that are maintained balanced according to the following condition: at any internal node the absolute value of the difference between the depth of the right and of the left subtrees is at most one (see *Figure 11.9b*)).

If the balancing condition is satisfied it turns out that the minimum number of nodes $N(h)$ in a tree of depth h is given by the following recurrence relation:

$$N(1) = 1$$
$$N(2) = 2$$
$$N(h) = N(h-1) + N(h-2) + 1 \text{ for } h \geqslant 3$$

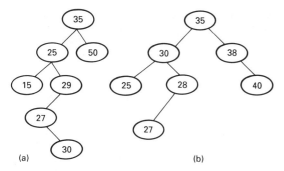

(a)   (b)

Figure 11.9 Binary tree searches (a) unbalanced (b) balanced

By solving the relation it can be shown that in a balanced tree with n nodes the depth is O(log n) and hence the number of comparisons needed to search for a key is also O(log n).

To maintain balanced AVL-trees we proceed as follows. When as a consequence of an insert or delete operation the balance condition is violated, a rotation is performed, that is, the nodes in the tree and their associated keys are reorganized in such a way that the balance is recovered. In *Figure 11.10* two different trivial cases are considered in which an insert(3) operation might unbalance the tree and rotations are required to recover the balance.

To deal with more complex cases a balancing factor equal to -1, 0, 1 and corresponding to the difference between the depth of the left subtree and the depth of the right subtree is associated with all nodes in an AVL-tree. A suitable use of the balance factors allows the maintenance of balance, while performing insertion and deletion of keys, with a number of node accesses and (possibly) of rotations that is proportional to the depth of the tree and, hence, O(log n) again (Horowitz and Sahni, 1976).

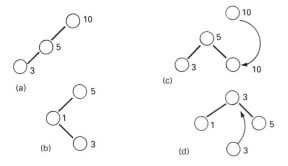

Figure 11.10 (a) (b) Two unbalanced trees determined by insert (3), (c) (d) the balanced trees resulting from rotation

In conclusion we may assert that AVL-trees allow the management of all operations on a dictionary of n items in time O(log n).

A simple application of AVL-trees in sorting derives from the observation that visiting an AVL-tree in symmetric order accesses all keys in ascending order. To sort an array A[1 ... n] the algorithm, named TREE-SORT, performs the following two steps:

1. For all $i = 1$ to n in the array do insert A[i] on an AVL-tree.
2. Visit the tree in symmetric order and return all accessed keys.

Since both steps take time O(n log n) TREE-SORT is asymptotically optimal.

Despite the fact that AVL-trees allow a complete implementation of dictionaries in the dynamic case in logarithmic time, their performance is still rather poor if implementations on secondary storage are considered. A better performance is obtained by means of a widely adopted structure: the B-tree.

A B-tree (Bayer and McCreight, 1972) is an $m$ary search tree that satisfies the following properties (let us assume m even for sake of clarity:

1. Every internal node (except the root) has d subtrees with $m/2 \geqslant d \geqslant m$.
2. The root has at least 2 subtrees.
3. Starting from the root all branches have the same length.
4. To an internal node with d subtrees $T_1, T_2, \ldots, T_d, d-1$ keys $k_1, k_2, \ldots, k_{d-1}$ are associated, with the property that for all $i(i = 1, \ldots, d-1)$ k_i is larger than all keys associated with T_i and smaller than all keys associated with T_{i+1}.
5. No keys are associated with the leaves.

In *Figure 11.11* an example of quaternary B-tree is given.

In contrast to the case of AVL-trees, where balance among subtrees is obtained by introducing a condition on their depth, with B-trees balance is based on a condition on the degree d of the nodes. If the condition is maintained the time to search for a key on a B-tree is determined by the number of nodes accessed (bounded by O($\log_{m/2} n$)) and the cost of searching inside a node (bounded by O(log m)). The overall search cost is therefore O($\log_{m/2} n$ log m).

To maintain the balance condition under insertions and deletions, when an attempt is made to insert a new key in a node that already contains $m - 1$ keys (that is a node with m subtrees), the node is split into two sub-nodes one containing the $m/2$ smaller keys and the other one containing the $m/2 - 1$ larger keys. The intermediate key is moved to the superior node (see *Figure 11.12*). If the superior node is also already full the splitting is repeated until either a non-full node is reached or, eventually, the root of the B-tree is also split.

Using the node splitting technique, an insertion in a B-tree can be made without violating the balance condition, in time proportional to the depth of the tree.

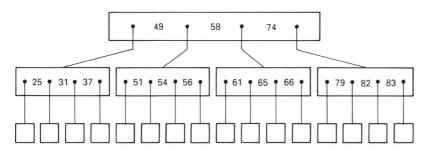

Figure 11.11 Quaternary B-tree

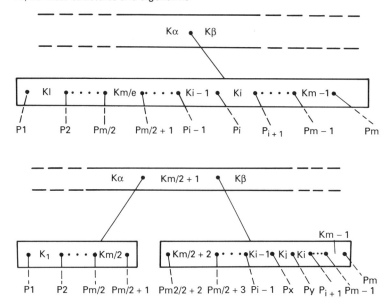

Figure 11.12 Node splitting in a B-tree

The case of the deletion operation is treated in a similar way. When we attempt to delete a key from a node with the minimum allowed number of subtrees $(m/2)$, a recombination of the node together with the other adjacent nodes takes place and may lead to a decrease by one level in the depth of the tree. This operation may be performed in logarithmic time.

In conclusion, a B-tree provides an efficient implementation of a dictionary, allowing the performance of all operations in the dynamic case with a cost:

$$O(\log_{m/2} n \log m)$$

Several variants of B-tree exist (B$^+$-trees, B*-trees etc.) and are frequently used for file management on secondary storage (Smith and Barnes, 1987).

In real applications there is a need to keep the number of node accesses as small as possible (that is, m as large as possible, e.g. equal to 100) because node accesses correspond to disk accesses and are the most expensive contribution to the above indicated overall search cost. Besides, it is often the case that the information associated with keys is kept on secondary storage while the B-tree structure (or variants of it) are used as a directory in main storage.

A last class of tree structures for implementing dictionaries are variants of hashing (known as a 'dynamic hashing') which are suitable for dynamic data management on secondary storage.

In dynamic hashing overflow buckets are organized as leaves in a tree structure and keys are distributed among them on the basis of randomization (see *Figure 11.13*). When a new insertion means that a bucket is going to overflow, it is split in two and keys are randomly distributed in the two twin buckets. In case of underflow two twin buckets may be recombined into one.

Various implementations of dynamic hashing are based on different techniques for randomizing the keys and for managing the directory in main storage (Larson, 1978; Litwin, 1978; Fagin *et al.*, 1978).

11.3.2 Priority queues

In several combinatorial problems such as job scheduling, shortest paths in graphs, and partial ordering the concept of priority has to be efficiently managed. A priority queue is a collection of items characterized by a property (priority) consisting of an integer value ranging over a suitable interval. The operations that we want to perform on a priority queue are:

1. insert (item).
2. find-max.
3. delete-max.

If the cardinality of the collection is small a priority queue may be implemented by means of naive structures such as arrays and lists. As in dictionary management, such implementations are rather poor (that is, linear) in terms of the efficiency of maintaining the arrays and sorting lists, and so we keep them unordered (see *Figure 11.14*).

Both AVL-trees and B-trees, the tree structures that efficiently implement dictionaries, may be used for implementing priority queues with logarithmic costs for every operation. In fact we already know that insertions and deletions can be performed in logarithmic time; at the same time the find-max (or find-min) operations can both be performed in logarithmic time because the largest (or the smallest) keys in the dictionary are located at the extreme left (or at the extreme right) in the tree.

Unfortunately, for both AVL-trees and B-trees the management of the tree structures is expensive in time (even though optimal from the asymptotic point of view) and, since explicit tree structures need pointers, costly in terms of space. A data structure that provides an efficient and, in both time and space, optimal implementation of a priority queue, is based on an implicit tree organization and is known as a 'heap'.

A heap of n elements is an array $A[1 \ldots n]$ satisfying the property that for every i:

1. If $2i \geqslant n$ then $A[i] \geqslant A[2i]$.
2. If $2i + 1 \leqslant n$ then $A[i] \geqslant A[2i + 1]$.

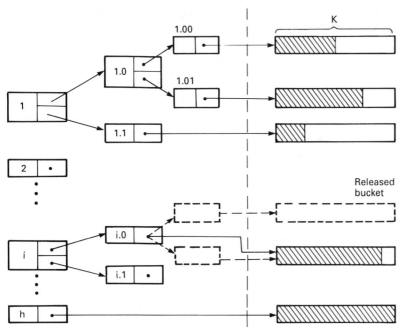

Figure 11.13 Dynamic hashing structure

	Insert	Del-: max	Find – max
Sorted array	0(n)	0(1)	0(1)
Unordered array	0(1)	0(n)	0(n)
Sorted list	0(n)	0(1)	0(1)

Figure 11.14 Execution costs of priority queue operations on lists and arrays

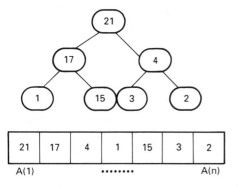

Figure 11.15 A heap and its corresponding tree representation

```
procedure InsertIntoHeap (var vect: array [1 .. N] of integer;
                                          k, dim: integer);
{ dim is the dimension of the heap after inserting the new value }

var   father, son, tmp: integer;
      end_flag: boolean;

begin { InsertIntoHeap }
   vect[dim] := k;
   son := dim;
   end_flag := false;
   while (son > 1) and not end_flag do
      begin
         father := son div 2;
         if vect[son] > vect[father]
            then begin
               tmp := vect[son];
               vect[son] := vect[father];
               vect[father] := tmp;
               son := father
            end
            else end_flag: = true
      end
end; { InsertIntoHeap }


procedure CreateHeap (var vect: array [1 .. N] of integer):

var i: integer;

begin { CreateHeap }
   for i := 2 to N do InsertIntoHeap(vect, vect[i], i);
end; { CreateHeap }
```

Figure 11.16 Procedure Insert-into-heap and Create-heap

procedure ExtractMax (**var** vect: **array** [1 .. N] **of integer**;
　　　　　　　　　　　var max: **integer**; dim: **integer**);

{ dim is the dimension of the heap before extracting the max }

var　left_son, right_son, max_son, father, tmp: **integer**;
　　　end_flag: **boolean**;

begin { ExtractMax }
　max := vect[1];
　vect[1] := vect[dim];
　end_flag := **false**;
　father := 1;
　while (father * 2 < dim) **and not** end_flag **do**
　　begin
　　　left_son := 2 * father;
　　　if left_son < dim − 1
　　　　then right_son := left_son + 1
　　　　else right_son := 0; { it does not exist! }
　　　if right_son > 0
　　　　then if vect[right_son] > vect[left_son]
　　　　　　then max_son := right_son
　　　　　　else max_son := left_son
　　　　else max_son := left_son;
　　　if vect[father] < vect[max_son]
　　　　then begin
　　　　　　　tmp := vect[father];
　　　　　　　vect[father] := vect[max_son];
　　　　　　　vect[max_son] := tmp;
　　　　　　　father := max_son
　　　　　end
　　　　else end_flag := **true**
　　end
end; { ExtractMax }

Figure 11.17　Procedure Extract-max

procedure HeapSort (**var** vect: **array** [1 .. N] **of integer**);

var i, max: **integer**;

begin { HeapSort }
　CreateHeap(vect);
　for i := N **down to** 2 **do**
　　begin
　　　ExtractMax(vect, max, i);
　　　vect[i] := max
　　end
end; { HeapSort }

Figure 11.18　Procedure Heap Sort

A heap may be considered to be the level-by-level representation of a binary tree in which all levels are complete except, at most, the lowest one and in which the integer associated with a node is always greater than or equal to the integers associated with both sons. In *Figure 11.15* a heap and its corresponding tree representation are shown.

Since, in a heap, the root element has the largest priority, the find-max operation may be performed in constant time O(1). The programs for executing the other two operations are given in *Figures 11.16* and *11.17*.

Both operations may be performed by simply proceeding along one branch from the root to the leaf in the case of extract-max, or *vice versa* in the case of insert. Since a heap is an almost complete binary tree (where at most the lowest level is incomplete) and hence its depth is logarithmic with respect to the number of nodes, it follows that both operations require a number of comparisons O(log *n*).

As well as its applications in the implementation of priority queues, a heap may be applied to derive yet another asymptotically optimal sorting algorithm HEAP-SORT. Given an array A[1 ... *n*], to sort it the algorithm proceeds in the following way.

First, the given array is transformed into a heap by repeatedly applying the insert procedure. Subsequently, by repeatedly applying the extract-max procedure the heap is transformed into a sorted array. By making use of the primitive operations defined above the HEAP-SORT algorithm may easily be expressed (see *Figure 11.18*).

11.4 Summary and conclusions

The subject of data structures and algorithms is very broad, and this chapter has only been able to cover a small part of the material relevant to software engineering. This chapter has focused on the principles of analysing algorithmic complexity, and data structures and algorithms for some of the more commonly encountered design problems.

There are many other classes of algorithm, e.g. string searching and sorting, and these are well covered in the literature. Clear definition and analyses of some important algorithms are given by Knuth (1973a) and Sedgewick (1989). Booch (1987) discusses the implementation of many standard algorithms in Ada.

11.5 References

Adelson Velskii, G. M. and Landis, Y. M. (1962) An algorithm for the organization of information. *Dokl. Akad. Nauk.*, **146**, 263–266

Aho, A. V., Hopcroft, J. E. and Ullman, J. D. (1974) *The Design and Analysis of Computer Algorithms*, Addison-Wesley

Bayer, R. and McCreight, E. (1972) Organization and maintenance of large ordered indexes. *Acta Informatica*, **1**, 173–189

Booch, G. (1987) *Software Components with Ada*, Benjamin Cummings

Ehrigh, H. and Mahr, B. (1985) *Fundamentals of Algebraic Specification 1*, Springer Verlag

Fagin, R., Nievergelt, J., Pippenger, N. and Strong, H. R. (1978) Extendible hashing. A fast access method for dynamic files, *IBM Res. Rep. RJ2305*

Ghezzi, C. and Jazayeri, M. (1987) *Programming Language Concepts*, 2nd Edition, John Wiley & Sons

Greene, D. H. and Knuth, D. E. (1981) *Mathematics for the Analysis of Algorithms*, Birkhäuser

Hopcroft, J. E. and Ullman, J. D. (1979) *Introduction to Automata Theory, Languages and Computation*, Addison Wesley

Horowitz, E. and Sahni, S. (1976) *Fundamentals of Data Structures*, Computer Science Press, Potomac

Knuth, D. E. (1973a) *The Art of Computer programming, Vol 1, Fundamental Algorithms*, Addison-Wesley

Knuth, D. E. (1973b) *The Art of Computer Programming, Vol 3, Sorting and Searching*, Addison-Wesley

Larson, P. (1978) Dynamic hashing. *Bit*, **18**, 184–201

Litwin, W. (1978) Virtual hashing. A dynamically changing hashing. In: *Proceedings of Symposium on Very Large Databases*

Maurer, W. and Lewis, T. (1975) Hash table methods *ACM Computing Surveys*, **7**, 5–20

Mehlhorn, K. (1984) *Data Structures and Algorithms 3: Multi-dimensional Searching and Computational Geometry*, Springer Verlag

Sedgewick, R. (1989) *Algorithms*, 2nd edition, Addison-Wesley

Smith, P. D. and Barnes, G. M. (1987) *Files and Databases. An Introduction*, Addison-Wesley

Other Relevant Science and Theory

12

Measurement theory

Agnes A Kaposi
Kaposi Associates

Contents

12.1 Introduction

The mature disciplines of natural science and engineering are unified bodies of knowledge; they distil empirical observations into formal theories, and express them in mathematical notation. To achieve this, they make use of measurement theory and metrological practice, on which we draw not only in science and engineering but in every sphere of daily life.

The new discipline of software engineering is yet to achieve unification of formal theory and empirical observation. This lack of cohesion impedes the penetration of theoretical advances into industrial practice, hinders the quality and safety of software and software-related systems, and creates dis-unity within the profession.

This chapter is primarily intended for software practitioners, but it also addresses practising engineers in other disciplines who are interested in software engineering. Its approach is to consider software as an engineered artefact, the quality of which must be assured and which must be efficiently produced. It assumes that the twin aims of engineering quality and productivity can only be served by characterizing entities formally, and this must mean much more than assigning numbers and collecting data. The description must be objective, accurate, reproducible, reliable and meaningful. In short, the characterization must amount to measurement which has integrity and unimpeachable quality.

The purpose of this chapter is three-fold:

1. To present the structure of the domain of knowledge related to measurement.
2. To outline the theoretical and practical foundations of scientific/engineering measurement, generalizing concepts if necessary to embrace software.
3. To introduce the concepts and methods of measurement theory as foundation for the quality assurance of measurement.

Although the reader's familiarity with industrial environments is assumed, the treatment of the material is introductory throughout. The only formalism used is the notation of elementary set theory.

Section 12.2 of the chapter outlines the measurement process, describes the structure of the subject domain of measurement, and examines the role of measurement theory. Sections 12.3 and 12.4 introduce the concepts of measurement theory in the simplest and narrowest case: when measurement is directed at a single property. Section 12.5 extends the scope to the characterization of objects which require the measurement of several properties and the aggregation of the measured results. Section 12.6 broadens the scope further, presenting the notion of a measurement system capable of covering an entire subject domain, and outlining the problems of developing a measurement system for software and for systems engineering. Emphasis is given throughout to the quality of measurement.

12.2 Measurement, metrology and measurement theory

Galileo is reported to have said: 'Measure the measurable and try to render measurable what is not yet measurable'. Bunge (1967) says: 'The history of science has been, in good part, the story of quantification of initially qualitative concepts'. Bunge goes as far as arguing that all concepts are quantifiable once our ideas are well formed, and that the dominant use of measurement in the natural sciences and the relative lack of use of measurement in other fields (such as the life sciences, the social sciences and the arts) stems from tradition and historical accident rather than from any fundamental characteristic of these subject domains.

We turn to measurement for the orderly and reliable representation of observations. The need for measurement arises because one or more key property is identified, in terms of which an important class of objects (things, events, entities in general) may be described, identified, categorized or ordered. Measurement is the means of recording this property with integrity: objectively, reliably, repeatably, efficiently, and without bias or ambiguity.

Measurement has been the basis of the empirical scientist's conduct of enquiry into the understanding of the world. It is an essential means of obtaining and recording factual information systematically, so that knowledge could be brought under general laws, and trustworthy methods could be devised for obtaining new truths. Thus, measurement is central to the 'scientific method' of observation, hypothesis generation and independent confirmation/refutation of hypotheses. Measurement has also underpinned the technologist's efforts in shaping the world, and has supported the exploitation of the results of scientific discovery by means of practical pursuits.

Measurement has always been essential in business. It is the means of setting trading standards, enforcing norms, and assuring fair dealing between purchaser and vendor. Measurement standards promote compatibility, interchangeability and the availability of alternative sources of supply. In this way they benefit the public, encouraging healthy competition, and facilitating the flow of goods and information through society. Measurements are the basis of characterizing artefacts and drawing up contracts between supplier and vendor; they are the ultimate impartial arbiter in settling disputes.

Measurement is thus part of all aspects of daily life: business and commerce, finance and medicine, communication and education, management, administration and law.

Measurement is central to the engineering professions. Measures are needed in all phases of the life cycle of products and processes, from the capturing of customer requirements, through all phases of the product life cycle of specification, design, production, operation and maintenance. They are used in classifying, characterizing and appraising existing and future systems and components, formulating problems precisely and experimenting with variant solutions, evaluating alternative designs, assuring the quality of products and services and the cost-effectiveness of bringing them about, and ascertaining that they are safe to use. Measurement is implicit in many of the activities of the 'quality loop', illustrated in the national and international standard (BS5750, 1987) which defines the principles of the quality system guarding products and services.

In these and other applications measurements are needed as:

1. Descriptors, which characterize an entity already in existence. Descriptors may serve the evaluation of an entity against a specification, or appraise it in comparison with other entities of the same class.
2. Prescriptors, setting norms which a future entity must meet once implemented, setting bounds for tolerance of admissible deviations from the norm, or laying down national, international and local standards which all entities of a certain class must satisfy.
3. Predictors, used in the course of design for estimating or calculating future properties of an entity yet to be implemented. Predictions are made from formal theory or from empirical laws and allow the engineer to decide upon the trade-off between one property and another.

12.2.1 Definition of measurement

The BSI standard (BS 5233) defines measurement in terms of its immediate purpose, as: 'the operations having the object of determining the value of a quantity'.

The operations of measurement involve collecting and recording data from observation; however, these activities form only part of the process. Measurement also means identifying the class of entities to which the measurement relates, defining the selected property precisely, and describing it objectively and repeatably, within set bounds of uncertainty. The results of measurement must be independent of the views and preferences of the measurer, and must not be corrupted by an incidental unrecorded circumstance which might influence the outcome.

The popular expectation is that measurement will result in the quantification of properties of things and events by means of the real numbers. This expectation is re-inforced by the quotation from Lord Kelvin's writings which has become a motto of many books on measurement and most papers on software metrics:

> ... if you can measure what you are speaking about and express it in numbers you know something about it; but when you cannot measure it, when you cannot express it in numbers, your knowledge of it is of a meagre and unsatisfactory kind.

A wider interpretation of measurement is admitted by Finkelstein (1975a) who offers the definition that measurement is:

> ... the process of empirical, objective assignment of *numbers* to the properties of objects and events of the *real world* so as to describe them [author's emphasis].

Finkelstein's definition does not confine measurement to the use of real numbers; it allows one to record observations in other kinds of numerical structures, including complex numbers (used for example in the measurement of electrical impedance), and encode numbers variously, for example, in hexadecimal notation.

In many situations, such as those arising in software engineering, even this definition requires further generalization and broader interpretation in two respects:

1. Measurement must be able to characterize abstract entities as well as to describe properties of real-world objects and events.
2. Measurement need not mean assignment of a numerical value; indeed measurement may not need to involve numbers at all; the results of measurement may be captured in terms of any well-defined formal system.

Accordingly, the definition adopted here is:

> Measurement is the process of empirical, objective encoding of some property of a selected class of entities in a formal system of symbols so as to describe them.

12.2.2 The 'architecture' of the subject domain of measurement

This section starts with the simple, informative, authoritative definition of a useful term which is alien to the software metrics community. It is rarely used in its fullest sense even by scientists and engineers.

> Metrology is the field of knowledge concerned with measurement. (BS 5233, 1986).

Accordingly, metrology embraces the whole body of theoretical and pragmatic knowledge on and around measurement. The matrix of Figure 12.1 (which is a development and extension of ideas suggested by Fiok *et al.*, 1988) is offered as an example of a conceptual framework required for organizing and classifying the subject matter of this vast domain.

Spheres of concern

Aspects	Quanti-tative metrology	Object-oriented metrology	Subject domain-oriented metrology	General metrology
Theoretical metrology				
Methodology of metrology				
Technology of metrology (instrumentation)				
Legal metrology (including standards and quality)				

Figure 12.1 A structure for representing the subject domain of metrology

The rows of the matrix indicate 'aspects' of metrology:

1. Theoretical metrology:
   (a) The philosophy and method of empirical science.
   (b) The logical foundations of measurement, including classification and conceptualization.
   (c) The formation of hypotheses and models.
   (d) Testability.
   (e) The general theory of experimentation, scale formation and interpretation of data as evidence.
   (f) Error theory.
2. Methodology of metrology:
   (a) Measurement strategies.
   (b) The organization and execution of measurement and the interpretation of results.
3. Technology of metrology:
   (a) The design or judicious choice of measuring instruments/measurement systems for sensing, processing, storing and displaying measurement data.
4. Legal metrology:
   (a) The system of procedures, codes of practice, regulations and laws concerning the development and maintenance of the units and standards of measurement, together with the standards and other support structures for monitoring and maintaining conformance to standards.

The columns of the matrix represent 'spheres of concern' of metrology, listed here in order from the most specific to the most general:

1. Quantitative (or property-oriented) metrology:
   (a) The determination of the value of a particular parameter of some entity.
2. Object-oriented metrology:
   (a) The characterization of an entity in terms of the parameters of its selected model.
3. Subject-domain-oriented metrology:
   (a) The parametric characterization of the class of all entities within a specific domain of science, engineering, technology or other discipline.

4. General metrology:
   (a) The study, without reference to any particular subject domain, of the way in which measurable concepts are formed, entities parametrically characterized, and metrological systems developed, operated and maintained.

The structure of the subject of measurement is reflected in the organization of this chapter. Interest is centred on measurement theoretic aspects; only brief mention is made of methodological, technological and legal aspects, and that only when these have bearing on theoretical considerations. Quantitative metrology – the case with the narrowest sphere of concern – is treated in some detail, as a vehicle for introducing ideas of wider applicability. Object-oriented and subject domain oriented metrology are also discussed, with particular reference to their software engineering implications. Mention is made from time to time of issues which fall in the domain of general metrology but the topic is not addressed here.

12.2.3 The measurement process

To set the context and define the role attributed to measurement theory, the measurement process is outlined below. The process has two main aspects: management and execution. Only the first holds interest from our viewpoint here.

Management of measurement itself has three interlinked parts:

1. Planning the measurement. This includes plans for devising and conducting the measurement, as well as planning the validation and quality assurance of the results. This is of major interest in this chapter and will be discussed in Section 12.2.4 and subsequently.
2. Organization of the execution of measurement, covering such issues as the provision of human resources and training of personnel, the design and procurement of equipment and instrumentation, the accommodation and environment of measurement, the design of the procedures of measurement and calibration, and the provision of appropriate administrative structures and legal support. All of these important considerations are beyond the scope of this chapter.
3. Control and oversight of the execution of measurement, extending to the management of personnel and resources used in conducting the measurement, assurance that measurement practice is consistent with plans, and review of organizational arrangements to assure that they are adequate. This too is outside this chapter's concern.

This description of the measurement process assumes that measurement takes place in a mature subject domain where the measurement can draw on established conceptual foundations, measurement systems and legal support structures. The chapter gives consideration to the problems of measurement in a developing subject domain, such as software engineering, where these conditions do not obtain.

12.2.4 Quality of measurement

This definition of measurement admits the encoding of observations in numbers and other symbol systems. For the sake of simplicity, the following refers mostly to numerical representations, although much of the discussion is also valid for other symbol systems.

Numerical encoding of observations can have great value in specific contexts and well-controlled environments. However, casual allocation of numbers to things seldom meets those demands which would assure the reliability, authority, universal validity – in short, the quality – of measurement. Taken out of context, intuitive quantitative descriptions of entities may be invalid or open to misinterpretation; they may obscure rather than assist understanding, retard rather than promote the development of industrial and trading standards, and may harbour serious dangers of misplaced confidence by decision makers who act upon them.

A brief outline is given here of the intuitive notions most frequently used in describing the quality of measurement. As the chapter goes on to show, the role of measurement theory is to conceptualize and formalize some of the important desirable features of measurement and provide methods in support of their realization:

1. Measurement must be valid for the intended purpose and should yield meaningful results with reference to its purpose. The validity of measurement can be promoted by good management and execution, but validity can only be confirmed empirically, once the data is available.

   Validity and meaningfulness are general requirements which are fulfilled through other, detailed quality considerations.
2. The numerical encoding of observation by measurement must not be arbitrary. The purpose of measurement reflects subjective judgment, but its results must uniquely represent the properties under observation.
3. Measurement must not be obtrusive. The act of measurement should not interfere unduly with the observed properties. In engineering environments measuring instruments should not 'load' the system to the point where the measured quantity is no longer representative. In human situations, such as continuous assessment of students, the assignment of grades should not bias future performance.
4. Measurement should be accurate. The error and uncertainty of the measurement must be kept within bounds.
5. Measurement must be reproducible (Sydenham, 1982). It must be stable and objective, such that the same results should be obtained when the same measurement is carried out at a different time by different persons, possibly using different apparatus.
6. Measurement must also be feasible to perform and should be effective in its resource utilization. Measurement should be focused on providing the required information, without wasting resources on irrelevancies. It must be possible to conduct the measurement without it imposing excessive overheads.
7. Measured results should have integrity. It must be possible to ensure and demonstrate the impartiality of the measurement; otherwise it is hard to enforce its conclusions if the need arises.

12.2.5 Role of measurement theory

It is useful to distinguish five parts of the planning processes where measurement theory contributes significantly to the validity and quality of measurement:

1. *Problem definition.* Defining the measurement problem involves designating the set of objects (programs, specifications, user manuals, etc.) which form the target of the measurement, and selecting the key properties which must be measured.
2. *Modelling.* Providing a frugal description of the target set, focusing attention on the key properties (cost, size, structure, etc). This is termed the 'model' of the target set with reference to the key properties.
3. *Forming the empirical relational system.* Describing the model by means of the observable relations between objects in terms of the selected key properties (distinguishing programs by size, structure, etc.).
4. *Defining the formal relational system.* Selecting the formal

(numerical or other) systems in which the measured results are to be represented, and creating in this formal system an image of the empirical relational system.

5. *Validating the results* of the measurement.

Problem definition is often regarded as being outside the domain of measurement theory. Apart from Jevons (1877; reissued by Nagel in 1958), who covers all aspects of measurement and whose books remain invaluable sources of insight, Leaning and Finkelstein (1985) are among the few who refer specifically to modelling; usually this step is implicit or is subsumed in the formation of the empirical relational system. The rest of this section is devoted to the discussion of these two parts of the process.

The formation of empirical relational systems, their mapping into a formal system, and the meaningfulness of the measured data are central concerns of measurement theory, and these will be discussed in the next three sections of this chapter. From the viewpoint of general metrology and engineering, Finkelstein (1975, 1982), Leaning and Finkelstein (1985) and Sydenham (1982) cover the subject comprehensively. Roberts (1979) provides an excellent introduction and deep treatment of measurement theory and its applications in fields other than the natural sciences and their technologies. His concern is the extension of classical measurement theory to new subject areas in the social sciences, and the examples reflect this subject interest. However, most of the discussion is highly relevant for other new subject domains, such as software engineering. Kyburg (1984) also provides a persuasive introductory text which argues the case for the theoretical foundations of measurement and illustrates the difference between measurement (as practised in the mature sciences) and casual quantification (as may still occur in some domains). This paper builds much of its material on the ideas expressed in the work of these authors.

12.2.5.1 Definition of the measurement problem

Planning measurement involves the statement of the problem, the analysis of the requirements, and the specification of the purpose of the measurement. This then leads to the isolation of the set of target objects at which the measurement is to be directed. This problem definition phase is often neglected, on the assumption that 'we all know what we want to measure'. The difficulties which arise from such a casual approach are similar to those of developing software without a clearly stated specification.

The first part of problem definition is to decide on the 'target set' $A = \{a, b, \ldots, z\}$. The definition may be given in various ways, such as by enumeration or by stating the criteria of set membership. The identification of the target set from a large potential population may involve formal experimental design, as would be the case if the purpose of the measurement were to provide data for a survey in an investigation of the nutritional problems of the children of some region. In a field such as software engineering, the definition of a target set begs the difficult question of how to define criteria of an adequate classification scheme, capable of isolating unambiguously the target set of measurement, such as the set of 'safety-critical software', or the set of 'software life cycle phases'.

Just one instance is given here to illustrate the importance of the precise definition of the target set and the stability of the set membership over the period of conducting the measurement. The target membership, and consequently the meaningfulness of the measured result, must be in doubt when errors in a program are counted by taking observations on various versions during a period of successive modifications, the data obtained from the different versions is aggregated, and the results are used to characterize the final version.

The second task in this phase is to decide on the set of 'key properties' K (sometimes referred to as the 'quality manifestations') in terms of which the objects in the target set A are to be characterized.

In practice, some key property or properties are often the motivators of the measurement process. For example, there may be concern about the rising cost of software maintenance in some company's industrial products, or about the country's increasing dependency on software reliability in the performance of social services. In another context, there may be concern expressed about the physical and educational development of the schoolchildren of some region falling below the national norm, as evidenced by their examination performance and growth. Measurement is required as the means of establishing objectively whether or not there is cause for concern, and is the basis of a strategy for detecting the existence of the problem. If it is established that there is a problem, measurement would also help in diagnosing the root.

The definition of the set of key properties is an important and often intricate task, requiring not just competence in measurement, but inspiration, judgment and understanding of the application domain itself. The difficulty of the task is compounded by the complexity of real-life entities which display many observable properties simultaneously, and many of their key properties are intricately interrelated. The isolation of the set of key properties of a class of objects requires abstraction: the replacement of the objects of the target set by a simplified model. Modelling is fundamental to measurement; without an empirical model for describing observations, measurement is not possible; without a model on which to interpret the results, measured data amounts to a jumble of meaningless symbols.

12.2.5.2 Modelling the target set

Models are deliberate, purposeful simplifications of reality. They are the stock-in-trade of technologists and empirical scientists, allowing them to recognize the fundamental similarities and organizing principles which link apparently different entities. Models are the means of obtaining useful generalizations and creating predictive theories.

Modelling in problem solving is the means of turning a complex problem into a tractable one. The simplifying assumptions carry implications which define the bounds of validity of the solution. The assumptions must be explicitly stated, and must be revised if a broader problem is to be tackled, or if a refined solution is required.

Technologists use models of many types: scale models of physical objects, maps and other pictorial and diagrammatic representations, various forms of linguistic characterizations and mathematical/logical descriptions of many types. The judicious choice of model frequently makes the difference between success and failure in problem solving.

There are no general methods for modelling. Choosing a model is a creative step, drawing on the inspiration and experience of the problem solver. The quality of models is not absolute: the 'best' model is the simplest which suffices for the purpose. However, there is danger in oversimplification and inappropriate usage. Error frequently arises from constructing a model for one purpose and using it for another. Taking a software engineering example, flowcharts were specifically devised to model control flow in programs; they subsequently gained a bad name among software practitioners because they did not describe information flow – a purpose for which they were never intended!

Let us turn now to the example of child development, and let the whole classful of children be represented by the set $A = \{a, b \ldots, z\}$, where each letter from a to z denotes an individual child. There may be many manifestations of the adequacy or otherwise of these children's development, and the diagnosis of this problem by measurement would require the multivariate characterization of each child. However, if the measurement task indicates that height is the only property to be measured, then it is necessary and sufficient for each child to be characterized by just this single property. For the purpose of the measurement, a child may be replaced by a pole of the same height, a piece of string of the same length as the height of the child, or indeed any arbitrary object, such as a wall or a cupboard, only provided that one of its dimensions preserves the height of the child.

At the end of the modelling process we can represent the target set $A = \{ a, b, \ldots, z \}$ by the set $A = \{ a, b, \ldots, z \}$, where each element of A is a model of the corresponding element of A in terms of the set K of selected key properties.

Before leaving the subject of modelling, it is necessary to conclude on a note of principle. The view has been expressed by some authors that the word 'model' is used in the technical literature in two different ways, conveying fundamentally different meanings (Turski and Maibaum, 1987; Cohen, Harwood and Jackson, 1986):

1. Movement from the general to the particular, when the model is the manifestation of a theory in practice and a 'concrete exemplification of generally stated principles'. This meaning is often adopted in mathematics and computer science.
2. Movement from the particular to the general by abstraction – the sense in which the term is used here, and is defined in the dictionary (e.g. Bullock *et al.*, 1988) and the literature of problem solving (e.g. Ashby, 1964).

In the measurement context the two meanings are not incompatible and both are utilized. The model is an abstraction from the particular target set to its representation by the key properties, as described in the empirical relational system. The formal relational system (the mapping of the empirical relational system) is the concrete exemplification of the entire theory of relations and operations of the chosen formal system.

12.3 Direct measurement of a single property

This section focuses on the case when measurement records a single directly observable property of a class of objects. Roberts refers to this as 'fundamental measurement', and remarks that such single-minded measurement may arise in the early stage of development of some subject area. It will be seen later that single-property direct measurement is also the basis of determining the value of a property indirectly, and forms part of comprehensive programmes of object-oriented measurement.

This section describes the construction of the empirical and formal relational systems for single-parameter direct measurement, and discusses some of the implications of these notions of measurement theory from the practical viewpoint.

The concepts of measurement theory are new to most software practitioners. An attempt is made to introduce them with reference to examples which are relevant to software engineering. However, it would be futile to try to elucidate concepts on examples which themselves contain ambiguous, problematical and contentious notions. This would confuse the reader rather than help comprehension. There is such a danger with most software engineering examples at the present state of the art. To avoid this difficulty, many ideas are introduced with the aid of simple, neutral, everyday examples.

12.3.1 The empirical relational system

Let $A = \{ a, b, \ldots, z \}$ be our target set and K the chosen key property. For example, let A be the set of schoolchildren enrolled to a class, and let K be the property of their height. Now let $A = \{ a, b, \ldots, z \}$ be the model of A which describes each child in terms of the property of height. The empirical relational system comprises this model set, together with all the operations and relations which our observations define over the elements.

One may make several direct observations about the height of children relative to each other. For example, we may note that:

1. Child a is *taller than* child b.
2. Children c and d appear to be of *the same height*.
3. The height of child e is *head and shoulders above* that of f.
4. The combined height of v and w, even when v is *standing on the head of w*, is a head and a shoulder above the height of y, etc.

On the basis of these and similar observations one may draw various conclusions about the height of the children. For example, one may be able to sort them according to height, or find the child in the middle of the line of children ordered by height. Note that the same group of children may be ordered quite differently if, instead of height, the key property had been weight, IQ, blood pressure, age, number of siblings, travelling time between home and school, or something else.

One may also have observed that some children are taller than the cupboard or just as tall as the bookcase of the classroom. If it is the intention to aggregate these observations with the previous ones where children were compared with each other, this would imply that the cupboard and the bookcase have now been added to the target set A for the purpose of recording the key property K. For the purpose of height measurement, a sensible combined target set can be formed of children and furniture. However, such a target set would be meaningless if the key property were to be blood pressure, examination marks or IQ. From these considerations, the existence of an empirical relational system which is complete, in the sense of including *all* the members of the target set in the set of observable and meaningful relations, emerges as a quality requirement of the measurement.

Continuing now with the formation of the empirical relational system, the next task is to record our empirical observations as:

1. A set R of n-ary relations.
2. A set O of binary operations.

These are defined on the model set A.

In the example of the height of schoolchildren, let us consider only three relations:

1. r1 as 'taller than'.
2. r2 as 'the same height as'.
3. r3 as 'head and shoulders above'.

These form the set R of empirical relations.

Our observations also involved the operation of creating a new 'object' of observable height. The set O of operations comprises the single operation o; this is the concatenation operation defined over two children:

o is the operator 'standing on the head of'.

In all, nine children were involved in the observations: a, b, c, d, e, f, v, w and y. These form the object set. Thus, the model set of our example is $A = \{ a, b, c, d, e, f, v, w, y \}$.

We can now attempt to describe the empirical relational system for the measurement as an ordered set:

$$E = (A, R, O) = (A, \{ r1, r2, r3 \}, \{ o \}).$$

This set models the classroom of children and their observed interrelations in terms of the property of height.

12.3.2 The formal relational system

The next step in the process is to select a suitable formal system A′, together with a suitable mapping, to create a formal relational system representative of our empirical relational system. This formal system is the nested ordered set F = (A′, R′, O′).

Measurement requires that the following conditions should be satisfied:

1. The formal system must be capable of expressing all of the relations and operations of the empirical relational system E, and must also support any meaningful conclusions from the data which is required for fulfilling the original purpose of the measurement.
2. The mapping from E to F must actually represent all of the observations, preserving all the relations and operations of the empirical relational system.

To satisfy the first of these requirements, the formal relational system must be a mathematical object with an underlying set which has appropriate 'built-in' relations and operations. In this example, the positive real numbers (or even the natural numbers) would be quite suitable for expressing the children's height, the operation of concatenation and the relations of comparison and equality. The number system is also likely to be able to support any relation or operation one might define over the children's height in the future, or any statistics one might seek to derive about height.

Let us turn now to the second requirement. If E = (A, R, O) and F = (A′, R′, O′), and if all the relations R and operations O on A are preserved by the relations R′ and operations O′ on A′, then we say that the mapping $m : A \rightarrow A'$ is a homomorphism, and that F is homomorphic to E.

In general, a mapping is a homomorphism if the following two conditions are satisfied:

For all i ∈ A and rh ∈ R, with corresponding rh′ ∈ R′,
rh (a,b, ... , z) ⟺ rh′ (m(a), m(b), ... ,m(z))
For all i, j ∈ A and og ∈ O with corresponding og′ ∈ O′,
m(og (i, j)) ⟺ m(i) og′ m(j)

From the viewpoint of measurement we may express this as follows:

Given that A is a model of A with respect to the key property κ, and given also that m is a homomorphism from E to F, then we call m a measure of the property κ of the objects of A. For any i ∈ A, m(i) is a measure of the extent to which the object i ∈ A manifests the property κ.

Consider again the example of the height of schoolchildren and the choice for A′ values from the positive integers. Then, to satisfy the above homomorphism conditions we require the following:

1. To satisfy the conditions for the relations in R over the model objects a, b, c, d, e, f, v, w, ∈ A :
   (a) Given that r1 is the empirical relation 'taller than', then:

   a r1 b ⟺ m(a) > m(b)

   (b) Given that r2 is the empirical relation 'of the same height as', then:

   r2 (c, d) ⟺ m(c) = m(d)

   (c) Given that r3 is the empirical relation 'head and shoulders above', then we must query the definition of

the empirical relation because one is unable to assign any kind of numerical relation to such a vague observation.

Let us assume now that, by scrutinizing the children's height more closely, the observer determines that r3 may be refined to 'much taller than'. This means that the relation can be expressed as:

r3 (e, f) ⟺ m(e) >> m(f)

Note however that this relation is superfluous because it is already included in the relation r1.

Assume instead that the observer notes that child e is 'at least a third as tall again as' child f. Then we may say that:

r3 (e, f) ⟺ m(e) ⩾ 1.3 × m(f)

2. To satisfy the operation o on v,w ∈ A :
   Given that o is the concatenation of the height of v and w, then:

$$m (v \text{ o } w) \Leftrightarrow m (v) + m (w)$$

Choosing the first option for r3, and omitting it because of its redundancy, we may now describe the mapping m from the empirical to the formal relational system in this example as:

$$m : (A, \{r1, r2\}, \text{o }) \rightarrow (A', \{ >, = \}, +)$$

where

1. A is the set { a,b,c,d,e,f,v,w,y } which is the model of the set of children { a,b,c,d,e,f,v,w,y} with respect to height.
2. r1, r2, stand for the empirical relations 'taller than' and 'as tall as', defined on A.
3. o is the operation 'standing on the head of', also defined on A.
4. A′ is the set of positive integers.
5. >, =, + have the usual meaning in arithmetic.

12.3.3 Some comments and observations

Apart from illustrating the planning of the two crucial phases of the measurement process – the formation of the empirical and formal relational systems – this simple example draws attention to several interesting points, some of which concern the validity of measurement and will be formalized and detailed later:

1. The example shows, in case of the relation r3, how the mapping into a well-chosen formal system can detect vagueness and how it can stimulate the refinement of empirical observations.
2. If the sole purpose of the measurement had been to sort the children according to height then the formal system need not have been numerical. Any symbol system capable of expressing succession and precedence (such as the alphabet) would have sufficed. Finkelstein (1975b) draws attention to the need to the use of such symbol systems in measurement.

   Lexicographic systems of some sort are widely used in measuring examination results and they are also used for assessment of course work. For example, letters A–E may be marks to denote course work attainment at about equal steps and in reverse order of merit, with F added for good measure to represent failure. The disadvantages of a formal relational system built on such alphabetic grades are several, including unsuitability for calculating mean values of attainment. Any advantage of simplicity is promptly spoilt, and the alphabet domain transgressed, by teachers subsequently inventing an unspecified system of in-between and out-of-bounds grades, such as C +, B − −, A + and even α.

3. In the example of the height of children we took advantage of a well-defined target set (the register of children enrolled to the class), and the availability of the well-established concept of length, used in the notion of height. It was also meaningful to model length on the real numbers, and make use of the 'built-in' operations of the number systems when describing observations of relative length as multiplications by a constant (in the second alternative of r3) and operations such as concatenation into addition over numbers.

In new and developing subject domains, such as the social sciences and software engineering, many important properties are too weakly defined to warrant their representation by numerical measurement. In many cases the empirical relational system contains relations but has no operations at all, and the measurement has the modest aim of expressing preference or relative utility. In such cases the assignment of numbers is arbitrary and can even be misleading, implying greater precision than the concepts and observations warrant, and inviting numerical conclusions, such as summation or multiplication, which can be readily made in the formal system but have no meaning in practice.

12.3.4 Approach to indirect measurement

In practice, relatively few properties of interest admit readily to direct measurement; many measurements are made indirectly, where the required property is inferred from another related property which is easier or more convenient to observe. This chapter deals with the important problem of indirect measurement of a single property in some detail, treating it as a case of object-oriented measurement.

12.4 Quality of single property direct measurement

The aim of this section is to describe principles and methods which measurement theory provides for guarding the quality of the direct measurement of a single property. To do this, it is necessary to explore in greater detail the notion of the validity of measurement, and its foundations in the concepts of scale, uniqueness, representation and meaningfulness. These will also be the basis of the quality assurance of object-oriented measurement, where the purpose is to characterize a class of objects by direct or indirect measurements.

12.4.1 Scale

Assume that the following are given:

1. The set A which models the target set A with respect to the key property κ.
2. The empirical relational system E, and F, the formal relational system.
3. m, which is a mapping $A \to A'$, a homomorphism from E to the formal system F.

Then $S = (\,E, F, m\,)$ is called the scale of measurement for the key property κ of the target set A.

Assume now that the formal relational system F is defined over some subset of the real numbers. Within the scale, measurement maps the key property of each object of the target set into a number. If the mapping from E to F is a homomorphism then the measured data will be representative of the key property of the corresponding object, and the empirical relations and operations on the properties will also have correct representations on the corresponding numbers. If now, to satisfy the purpose of the measurement, one must draw empirical deductions from the observations, then these deductions can

be drawn from the data by appropriate operations on the real numbers. The homomorphism assures that these formal conclusions, drawn in the number domain, will have corresponding conclusions in the empirical domain, and will therefore fulfil the purpose of the measurement.

12.4.2 Scaling, scale types and uniqueness

This section shows that in almost every type of measurement the planner has some freedom to choose the numbers which are assigned to measured data. However, this cannot mean that the measurement is arbitrary because the key property which the data represents (such as the height of a child) is *unique* within the bounds of our powers of observation. The choice of numbers must be curbed by some conditions of invariance which guarantee that they represent the unique property faithfully.

The freedom of choice in the numerical representation of the observed property arises because the scale calls for a homomorphism between E and F, and a homomorphism is seldom unique. There are many sets of numbers which can express the key property under homomorphism. For example, one may quote the cost of software in £, $ or various other convertible currencies; one may express the height of a child in yards, centimetres or microns; one may measure temperature in Centigrade, Fahrenheit, Degrees Kelvin or other scales. The choice is guided by convenience: the currency in usage, the habits of the measurer and the availability of the yardstick, thermometer or other instrument. Given that we know how to convert correctly between different scales, the choice does not affect the description of the unique property.

Preservation of unique representation of the real-life property demands that the various valid manifestations of measurement should be deducible from each other by means of appropriate re-scaling transformations. For a given measurement, the uniqueness condition specifies the set of all re-scaling transformations which are admissible under homomorphisms.

Within the guidelines of measurement theory, the planner of the process can design the scale most suited to the purpose of the measurement. Described here are the most frequently used scales and their admissible transformations (which shall be denoted by φ). This classification of scales follows from the theoretical work of Stevens (1946, 1959). Accordingly, measurement theory distinguishes five main types of scale. These are outlined below in ascending order of 'strength', each permitting less freedom of choice and imposing stricter conditions than the previous:

1. *Nominal scales.* Such scales can be used in denoting membership of a class for purposes such as labelling and colour matching. There are no operations of E and F, and the only relation is the equivalence relation (which is transitive, reflexive and symmetric). Uniqueness is preserved by any one-to-one mapping.

2. *Ordinal scales* are used when measurement expresses comparative judgement, imposing an order over the items of the class, sorting them according to ascending/descending order of the chosen attribute. The relationship in E and F is transitive, asymmetric and irreflexive. The scale is preserved under any monotonic transformation. For weak orders, the transformations are of the form $x \geqslant y \Leftrightarrow \varphi(x) \geqslant \varphi(y)$, or else $x > y \Leftrightarrow \varphi(x) > \varphi(y)$ for strict simple orders (where no two items of the target set can have the same value).

Examples of the use of ordinal scales are the grading of goods or rating candidates at job interviews, and generally expressing preference. Myers (1989) demonstrates ordinal scales in characterizing tree structure models of software specifications, ordering trees according to their maximum root-leaf distance.

3. *Interval scales* are applied for measuring 'distances' between pairs of items of a class according to the chosen attribute. The scale is preserved under positive linear transformations of the form $\varphi(x) = \alpha m + \beta$, $\alpha > 0$, when the transformation may alter the origin as well as the steepness of the scale. Examples of the use of this scale and its admissible transformations are the measurement of temperature (e.g in degrees C and degrees F, but not degrees K) and calendar time (e.g. in the Christian to the Jewish calendar, excluding leap years).

4. *Ratio scales* are the most frequently used in measurement. The numbers they assign to each object of the target class denote the degree, in relation to a standard, to which the objects manifest the chosen property. The transformation must preserve the origin, but may alter the slope of the scale by the similarity transformation $\varphi(x) = \alpha m$, $\alpha > 0$. Examples are measurement of mass, length (simple distance measurements such as the height of children in centimetres, metres or nautical miles), elapsed time intervals (measurable in hours, years or microseconds, as opposed to calendar time), and absolute temperature.

5. *Absolute scales* are ratio scales which include a 'standard' unit. Such scales are usually based on the positive integers and are used when counting items of the class which satisfy the class membership criterion. Absolute scales give no freedom to the measurer: the scale is only preserved under the identity transformation $\varphi(x) = x$; in practical terms, this type of scale is not transformable.

Note that the list above does not exhaust the possible scale types: it gives representative examples of the most commonly used scales. Roberts offers further examples of scale types, which include:

6. The *log-interval scale*, reported to be useful in psychophysical measurement where the sensed effect of physical stimuli on people or animals is not a linear function of the cause. The admissible scaling transformations take the form $\varphi(x) = \alpha x^{\beta}$, $\alpha, \beta > 0$.

In all the above discussion the use of 'regular scales' is assumed, for which the theorem of Roberts and Franke holds:

The scale (E, F, m) is regular if and only if for every other homomorphism (E, F, g), and for all a, b in A, $m(a) = m(b)$ implies $g(a) = g(b)$.

The regular scale guards uniqueness in the following sense. If, when measured on one scale, two objects yield the same measure for the key property κ, then they will also give the same measure on any other scale which his homomorphic.

To summarize, with the exception of measurement on the absolute scale, there is a certain degree of freedom which the measurer may exercise when choosing the scale in which to express the data. To preserve the integrity of the measurement in regard to uniqueness, the scale must be regular, and any subsequent scaling transformation must preserve homomorphism between the empirical relational system and the formal relational system which represents it.

12.4.3 Meaningfulness

Meaningfulness is a wide notion and it will occur several times in different contexts when discussing the quality of measurement. In the present context, meaningfulness demands that the scale of measurement should be appropriate to the type of property measured such that, once measurement has been performed and data expressed on some scale, sensible conclusions could be drawn from it.

Roberts discusses a 'theory of meaningfulness' for various scales of single-property direct measurement. In case of regular scales, he offers the following definition:

A statement involving (numerical) scales is meaningful if and only if its truth or falsity is unchanged under admissible transformations.

In the context discussed here, meaningfulness may be assured 'constructively', by definition of an appropriate scale at the early stage of planning. Alternatively, meaningfulness may be deduced 'retrospectively', at the later stage of validating the scale. This is referred to by Leaning and Finkelstein (1985) as typing of the scale by analysis and '*post-facto* rationalization'. Roberts also discusses this, and supplies examples of the difficulty of retrospective typing, especially in new discipline areas where the empirical concept of the key property is not yet well established. These emphasize the need for deliberate planning of scales in the interest of assuring the meaningfulness of measurement.

Table 12.1 gives examples of meaningful and meaningless statements. The idea of compiling such a table originates from Fenton (1988), and some statements of the table are quoted directly from his useful collection.

Table 12.1 Illustrative examples of meaningful and meaningless statements

---

• **Point A is twice as far as Point B**. Distance is ratio scale, but position is not. Without the definition of the point of reference, the statement is meaningless.

• **Point A is twice as far from point X as Point B**. The statement is meaningful.

• **Point A is closer to point X than point B**. The statement is meaningful if measured on an ordinal scale; it can also refer to measurement on the stronger interval and ratio scales.

• **The cost of producing program A is twice that of producing program B**. The statement is meaningful, given that cost is defined on a ratio scale.

• **Program A is an Ada program**. The statement is meaningful, given that 'Ada program' is defined on a nominal scale.

• **Program A took 3 months to write**. The statement is meaningful to time interval defined on a ratio scale.

• **The quality of program A is higher than program B**. The statement is meaningless; there is no consensus on the scale of measurement for quality and the statement gives no reference to scale. It could be meaningful if quality were to be defined on an ordinal, interval or ratio scale.

• **The quality of program A is 97%**. The statement is meaningless; there is still no reference to scale. This statement could only stand if quality were to be ratio scale.

• **The cyclic order of graph A is 1**. The statement is meaningful: cyclic order (Myers, 1988) is measured on an absolute scale.

• **The complexity of this program is 42**. The statement is meaningless: no scale is given and the concept of complexity has not been defined.

• **Software A is more re-usable than software B**. The statement is meaningless: the scale and concept of reusability of software has not been defined.

• **Program A is twice as long as program B**. The statement may be meaningful on a ratio scale, provided that some established concept of length measurement applies. This could mean printing out the programs and measuring the length of the paper. If this length measure is not appropriate and an alternative is not given then the statement is meaningless.

• **Program A is 50 lines longer than program B**. The statement is meaningful under the concept of length measurable on a ratio scale, provided that there is a definition of 'line'. Note however that there is no standard definition at present, and the literature records as much as 150% difference in the lines-of-code measure assigned to the same program code by people using different assumptions.

12.4.4 Representation

As has been seen, measurement uses a formal system in which to describe observable properties. The representation problem of measurement defines the properties of the mapping from the empirical to the formal system which must assure the correspondence between the observed property and the numbers which describe it. Hence the representation problem addresses the question: under what conditions is the measurement possible?

The answer is required as a formal statement of necessary and sufficient testable conditions which assure homomorphism. These conditions are the representation axioms of the measurement.

The representation problem can be approached in two ways: retrospectively or constructively. In most practical cases of software engineering, measurement is used on an intuitive basis; measures are produced without measurement theoretic preparation. In such cases only a retrospective approach is possible to the quality assurance of the measures, and this is the case to which most of these discussions refer:

1. In the constructive case one works forwards, devising the representation and uniqueness conditions with the aid of measurement theory before starting the data collection. The quality of measurement is predictable: it is assured in advance.
2. In the retrospective case one works backwards. Here a formal (numerical) system is already given and data may have been gathered already, but the condition of representation, and the corresponding condition of uniqueness, are not known, or may not be stated explicitly. Quality assurance can only be applied 'post facto', at the validation stage of measurement.

Formulating the representation condition demands setting up tests on the data such that the conditions of the measurement and the type of scale could be articulated. Alternatively, one may set up tests of existence to ascertain that a homomorphic mapping is possible.

Data testing is illustrated later in this section. Here the case is demonstrated of testing existence by referring to the earlier example of measuring the height of children.

Retrospective tests of representation must be set up on each of the two relations (r1, r2) and on the single operation o. If any of these fail, the measurement is not representative. Concentrating here only on the operation, one needs to devise a test to show that the formal operation of addition of numbers has corresponding empirical operation on the children's heights – as indeed it has: a child can stand on the head of another to form a meaningful composite entity of measurable height. Had the same formal operation of addition been defined in another numerical measurement relating to the children's blood pressure or IQ, it is unlikely that there would be any meaning to a corresponding empirical operation and representation would fail.

Two further illustrations are given. First, the use of measurement for recording preference in procuring software is discussed with an indication of how one may retrospectively formalize the representation axioms for measurements of this kind. The second case touches on the representation conditions for 'extensive' measurement.

12.4.4.1 Characterizing 'usability' by expressing preference – an example

Assume now that the purpose of measurement is to make sound decisions on software procurement. Various candidate software products on the market have already been assembled and modelled by the single parameter of 'usability'. The prospective purchaser's staff had already appraised each of the candidate software products of the set A = a to z, and they have assigned to each product a positive integer of value between 1 and 100, according to their perception of the product's usability. What would be the conditions of representation and uniqueness in this case?

The chosen formal set can readily support comparison relations between number pairs. We can now set up an empirical data-testing exercise, to check whether or not the numbers have been 'reasonably' assigned.

For example, if a had been judged 'more usable' than b, and a larger number had been assigned to a than to b, and if b had been judged 'more usable' than c, then we would have the right to expect that a larger number should be given to b than to c. Moreover, we have the right to expect that *all* software products should have been given numerical descriptions on the basis of such 'sensible' assignments.

The first question is: what is the prospective buyers' meaning of the phrase 'more usable'? Is it the intention that there should always be a strict preference of one item over the other, or can there be indifference? At the start of the data test this question must be settled: in the chosen formal structure of numbers, a different relation corresponds to the two cases.

Let us assume now that the question is settled and the intention is that the empirical relation should be strict preference (there would be no point in reaching tied decisions if only one product is to be procured). Then the corresponding formal preference relation must be $>$. The data can now be tested; if there are two or more programs for which the same value has been given, representation has already failed.

If the data passes this first test, we may try to define other necessary conditions of representation on the basis of common sense. Ultimately one requires proof that, together, the set of necessary conditions are sufficient to assure homomorphism.

Many authors have shown (e.g. Finkelstein and Leaning (1984)) that the following three representation axioms are necessary and sufficient to set up a homomorphic mapping from a finite set of target objects under the relation r of strict preference to the positive real numbers under the relation $>$. Describing this in the 'usability' case we get:

1. a r b & b r c $\Rightarrow$ a r c, for all a, b, c $\in$ A
   (Transitivity; if a is more usable than b and b is more usable than c then a is more usable than c.)
2. $\neg$ a r a, for all a $\in$ A
   (Irreflexivity; it is not true that a is more usable than itself.)
3. i r j $\Rightarrow$ j r i, for all i, j $\in$ A
   (Asymmetry; if i is more usable than j then it is not true that j is more usable than i.)

These conditions state the representation theorem for any strict simple order. Given such a set, Roberts proves the corresponding uniqueness theorem that E (A, r) $\rightarrow$ F (A', $>$) is regular, and that (E, F, m) is an ordinal scale.

For weak order, the homomorphic mapping of the relation p (which may stand for 'more usable than or just as usable as', or for 'preferred or equal to') into $\geqslant$, the conditions (1), (2) and (3) above are modified to:

1'. a p b & b p c $\Rightarrow$ a p c, for all a, b, c $\in$ A
    (Transitivity: if a is preferred or equal to b and b is preferred or equal to c then a is preferred or equal to c.)
2'. a p a, for all $\in$ A
    (Reflexivity: a is equal to itself.)
3'. a p b or b p a, for all a, b $\in$ A
    (Completeness: either a is preferred (or equal) to b or b is preferred (or equal) to a.)

If it turns out from analysing the data of the 'usability'

example that conditions (1), (2), (3) are not valid for every data item, then some of the numbers have been recorded incorrectly, represent inconsistency in expressing preference, or cannot have been assigned rationally. Measurement theory flags the problem at the stage of validation by retrospective quality assurance. It would be precipitate to make purchasing decisions on the basis of such doubtful data.

In this example one can note again the freedom of choice available to the measurer. The uniqueness and representation conditions would still be the same for a different domain of numbers, or if the ordering relations were to be systematically reversed, and numbers would be assigned in reverse order of preference. The scale is not at all unique but it is far from being arbitrary.

The retrospective approach is often applied intuitively in practice, in cases such as assessing a sizeable population of applicants for a post, or marking a large number of examination scripts. As experience is accumulated with performing the measurement task, grades given at the beginning may later prove to be too harsh or too lenient, and using the 'raw' data may lead to irrational decisions. To avoid this, adjustments are frequently applied later, on the basis of pairwise comparisons.

Returning to the 'usability' example, recall now that ordinal scales only permit a very limited range of meaningful conclusions to be drawn from data. One can state such things as 'software a is the third most usable', or 'software b is at the middle of the bunch', but there would be no meaning to the statement 'software c is twice as usable as software d', nor could we assign any meaning to a number which represented a product of the measures of software a and software b, or claimed to represent 'the average usability of programs a, b, c'. If the purpose of the measurement is to draw such conclusions from the data then the axioms of ordinal measurement do not suffice; one needs to define conditions necessary and sufficient for extensive measurement.

12.4.4.2 Extensive measurement

Extensive measurement is called for when the empirical relational system includes an operation which creates a new item for the target set. We have met this situation already in the case for the concatenation operator for the height of children: the operation produced a new composite item of measurable height. More formally, extensive measurement requires that the set should be a group, see e.g. Franksen (1977).

(Note that, strictly speaking, the group property of extensive measurement raises a problem for the operator in our example of measuring children's height. If each element of the object set is defined as 'a child', concatenation cannot be allowed, because the composite object will not be 'a child'.)

The most usual (although not the only) case of extensive measurement is one where the empirical relational system $E = (A, R, O)$ contains the single relation r which is one of the ordering relations, the single operation o is some kind of concatenation, and the representation condition demands that the numerical operation should be addition:

$$m (a\ o\ b) = m(a) + m(b)$$

Illustrated informally is the Archimedean axiom and the conditions of representation and uniqueness for extensive measurement. The axiom requires that measurement should be possible by means of a finite standard sequence. No matter how 'large' h is, and how 'small' is the standard of reference q, it must be possible to build an entity even larger than h by creating a large enough number of copies of q and combining these in accord with r a finite number of times. For extensive measurement there must always be a finite positive integer N such that $Nq > h$.

If A is the model of a target set A under a chosen key property, r is a binary relation on A, o is a binary operation on A, and m is a real-valued function for which it holds that:

$$a\ r\ b \Leftrightarrow m(a) > m(b) \text{ and } m(a\ o\ b) = m(a) + m(b)$$

then $E = (A, r, o) \rightarrow f = (A', >, +)$ is regular, and (E, F, m) is a ratio scale.

Assume now that we have a well-defined software engineering concept of 'line-of-code', and consider the task of measuring software size in terms of this. The Archimedean axiom will hold for any software object: the size of any item of software will be measurable as a finite integer multiple of the length of a line of code. Concatenation of two programs a and b of size a and b should yield a new program c whose size is $c = (a + b)$. Extensive measurement on a ratio scale means that, given a well-defined size measure, statements like 'program c is twice as long as program d', or 'the length of program module e is twice the average module size' are meaningful.

12.4.5 Case study of using measurement theory to assure the quality of measurement

An interesting and extensive case study is provided by Zuse (Zuse and Bollman, 1989) who, over a period of some years, has developed a technique for analysing the properties of 'complexity measures' of software control structure.

The study addresses questions such as: given that the data about programs is obtained by use of a complexity metric (such as that of McCabe, for example), what can one do with the numbers? Do the numbers provide a trustworthy basis of comparing programs? What kind of statistics can be derived from the numbers? Do the complexity metrics devised by different people give consistent appraisals of the complexity of the same set of programs?

The scope of the study extends to some 75 complexity metrics of control structure, including the widely used metrics of McCabe, Halstead, Belady, Gilb, and recently proposed metrics of Hausen, Fenton, and Zuse himself.

Zuse calls the empirical observations which are embodied in the metric 'viewpoints', decomposes them, and lists the 'elementary viewpoints' expressed in each metric. For example, McCabe's metric is defined as: $m(g) = K - N + 2$, where g is the control flow graph of program P, K and N are the number of arcs and nodes and $m(g)$ is the complexity metric.

This implies elementary viewpoints such as: 'if Q results from P by adding an edge to g then Q is more complex than P', and 'if Q results from P by adding an edge and a node then Q and P are equally complex'. The empirical validity of these statements follows from the definition of the metric, and the statements themselves are used by Zuse to derive retrospectively the representation and uniqueness conditions.

The results of the study show that, although all the metrics claim to characterize the same key property (program control structure), they measure very different things and yield widely inconsistent results. Once again, this raises the question of conceptualization as a prerequisite of measurement; perhaps what the measures show is that the designers of the different metrics had quite different concepts in mind.

Note also that in practice two (or more) programs are often combined (by concatenation or nesting), to form other programs. All such programs are composed from elementary control structures. This would imply that, for measuring control structures, extensive measurement is called for. However, by no means are all the metrics extensive. Zuse's study is highly recommended for anyone who collects control complexity measures and uses these as bases of technical, managerial or business decisions.

One may draw some important general conclusions from Zuse's case study. There are many software measures in use which have been derived from experience and validated through practice. Many practitioners *know* from experience that these measures 'work'; they form the basis of meaningful conclusion and perhaps even prediction. This field experience is too valuable to ignore but too subjective to trust. What is needed now is extensive measurement-theoretic analysis of these measures so that one can use them discerningly and attribute the appropriate industrial significance. However, retrospective quality assurance is often very difficult; there is no general method for reconstructing the representation and uniqueness conditions from data. This indicates the need for constructive quality assurance of measurement, appealing to the support of measurement theory at the stage of planning.

12.4.6 Validity revisited

In the light of the discussions above, and in conclusion to this section on the quality of measurement, it is worth examining again the notions of validity and meaningfulness, interpreting these notions in the broader sense. Such a view has been put forward in the literature in an informative and amusing paper by Brakel (1985) and also by Fenton and Kaposi (1989).

Recall that validity as a general notion means that the measurement is applicable to the circumstances. For purposes here, validity, like quality itself, must be defined with reference to purpose. A measurement is valid if it serves the purpose.

12.4.6.1 Validity and accuracy

Measurement often demands costly and delicate instruments. Measurement may be invalid for various practical reasons: the instrument may be faulty, misused, wrongly calibrated or inappropriate for the purpose. Measurement may also be inaccurate because of perturbation caused to the system, as is often the case in software engineering. These and other technological considerations are firmly within the domain of metrology, and the estimation and containment of error is an important and difficult branch of measurement theory. However, for the purpose of these discussions we exclude them from further consideration.

12.4.6.2 Validity and the target group

The relationship between measurement and classification has already been mentioned. The idea will be reinforced here to confirm the role of classification in determining the validity of measurement – a serious problem in software engineering.

Measurement should be seen as the refinement of classification. The target group represents the class under investigation, and measurement identifies the relative position of individuals within the class. If the class is ill-defined and membership is uncertain or unstable then measurement will suffer; it may either not be able to take place at all, or it will lead to unreliable and false conclusions. The results will also be misleading in the sense that they may have the appearance of meaningfulness in the technical sense but not in the deeper sense of meaningfulness coupled to validity.

12.4.6.3 Validity and concept

Recall that measurement relies on the modelling of objects of the target group with reference to a chosen key property or properties. Without adequate definition of the key concept, a model cannot be formed and valid measurement cannot take place.

Returning to the familiar example, consider that the purpose of the measurement is to answer the question whether the children of a region are adequately nourished, and the answer is to be provided by measuring height as a single parameter. It is an open question, to be addressed through the theory of nutrition rather than the theory of measurement, whether or not valid conclusions can be drawn from measurements of height alone. However, if the purpose of measurement is changed and the question is whether the children of the neighbourhood reach the national norm in height, it can be asserted that the *same* measurement will have sound conceptual foundations.

Similar queries about conceptual validity are raised in software engineering, for example, when control structure (or data flow structure) on its own is treated as an indicator of program complexity. This begs the question (to be answered by psychology rather than measurement theory) as to the meaning (and the measurability) of cognitive complexity, and the relationship between program structure and cognitive difficulty. When the purpose of the measurement is changed to the characterization of structure by means of measurement, the conceptual problem disappears.

12.4.6.4 Validity and stability

The problem associated with poor stability has already been mentioned and must be re-emphasized. Validity will be undermined if the notional 'single-key property' changes during the time required to conduct the measurement and the characteristics of the individuals in the target group will be biased according to the order in which the measurement is taken. In this case time assumes the role of a second key property and the methods of single-property measurement lead to invalid results.

12.4.6.5 Validity and representation

It has been seen that validity will suffer if empirical observations are vague, the empirical relational system is poorly constructed, the formal relational system is poorly chosen, or if the meaninglessness of the conclusion drawn from the data remains undetected.

An aspect not yet mentioned is the 'quantization error', arising from the choice of too coarse a scale. For comparing the height of local children with the national average, probably an integral scale based on the unit of the centimetre would be adequate. In any case, observation and instrumentation errors would not warrant a finer scale than this. However, an integral scale based on the unit of a foot will be almost certainly inadequate because the poor resolution of the scale would mask the conclusion.

12.4.6.6 Validity and environmental factors

Of the many other factors which can adversely affect the validity of measurement, only one is mentioned here – that of unrecorded changes in 'environmental factors'. The problem is very similar to the stability problem just discussed. Direct measurement of a single property can only yield valid results if all the factors which could influence the measurement are kept invariant. To assure that invariance is maintained, all the relevant factors must be identified and monitored in the interest of guarding the validity of measurement. Lack of appreciation of this is one of the main causes of faulty conclusions drawn from misleading data.

12.5 Object-oriented measurement

In earlier sections the assumption was made that the purpose of measurement could be fulfilled by observing a single property.

Such measurement is based on a model of the target set which preserved only the chosen key property, excluding all others.

Measurement of a single property is seldom adequate for the purpose of the measurement. There are two main reasons, and these can also occur in combination:

1. Direct measurement of the required property is often costly, inconvenient, and, at a given state-of-the-art, perhaps even impossible. Instead, measured results may be better achieved indirectly, observing one or more other property directly, deriving the measurement of the required property from these.
2. Measurement is seldom focused on a single property; the scope is usually far wider. It may be necessary to characterize a class of objects by the combination of several properties. The process of obtaining such 'object profiles' is often incremental. Only a few properties may be chosen at first (or even just a single one), but the picture is gradually built up by adding some more 'primitive' properties which are to be measured directly, and deriving from these further properties by indirect measurement.

As an example, no sensible procurement decision would ever be taken about software products on just one property (usability in the earlier example); decision would be based on the whole product profile composed of properties such as correctness of function, cost, data security, compatibility with existing equipment and software, reliability, performance, etc. Some of these would be directly measured, others indirectly.

This section deals with both of the cases above. The sphere of concern is extended from the direct measurement of a single property to object-oriented metrology: the characterization of the entity by means of a model which retains all relevant dimensions of the target object, as well as their interrelations. This means building up a profile of objects by measuring a set of their key properties directly or indirectly. Object profiles can then support informed decision making, based on the aggregation of the properties of the profile in 'conjoint measurement'.

12.5.1 Modelling in object-oriented measurement

It was seen in Section 12.2 that the single-property modelling process strips away all features of the target objects, with the exception of the chosen key property. Object-oriented measurement looks for the characterization of each object of the target set $A = \{ a, b, \ldots, z \}$ by a whole family of key properties $K = \{ \kappa1, \kappa2, \ldots, \kappa n, \ldots, \kappa q \}$. The objects and the measures $M = \{ m1, m2, \ldots, mn, \ldots, mq \}$ of their key properties may be represented by a matrix structure such as shown in *Figure 12.2*. The matrix is referred to as the profile of the object-oriented model. For a given target set, such a matrix represents a database; it stores properties which have already been found important, provides information for deriving new indirectly measured properties of importance, and offers a framework for adding new primitive properties when these come to light.

Properties of the set K are usually of two types: those which are directly measured on what Roberts calls a 'primitive scale', and indirectly measured properties whose scale is 'deduced' from primitive scales. In Figure 12.2 it is assumed that properties measured on a primitive scale are denoted $\kappa1$ to κn; the measures themselves are shown on the figure as $m1$ to mn. The rest of the key properties up to κq are indirectly measured. Such indirect measurement requires that the model should only retain all primitive properties of the object system but also all their interrelations: these give the basis for finding the representation conditions of indirect measurement.

A typical example of object-oriented measurement is the characterization of the quality of a software product. The principle is that quality is a composite property which is not

observed directly but is deduced from a set of other properties which themselves are ultimately obtained from directly measurable properties. Various multi-level 'quality models' are defined in the literature which link the measurands to the measurables (see e.g. Hausen (1989a) and McCall *et al.* (1977)). To assure functional relationships between quality (the property of ultimate interest termed the 'measurand') and its constituent 'measurables', Hausen calls for the quality model to be an acyclic graph. Similar object-oriented measurement leads to the characterization of the profile of the productivity of the software process.

Indirect measurement is very frequently used, not only in software engineering but also in everyday life and in all branches of science and technology. The speed of a motorcar is measured on the milometer by observing angular displacement; ambient temperature is measured on a linear scale, by thermal expansion on a length of a column of mercury (or other, safer, fluids); high temperatures can be measured by observing colour change of heat-sensitive paints, etc. In many cases the choice between direct and indirect measurement, and indeed the choice among alternative media in which to express indirect measurement, is not related to the purpose of the measurement but to convenience, expediency and cost. If some of the properties of interest can be deduced from others, it is wasteful to measure them all directly even when this is possible, unless the redundant direct measurement serves some explicit purpose of independent validation.

Kyburg (1984) devotes a great deal of attention to indirect measurement, discussing it in the practical as well as the historical context. He argues that good understanding of the concepts of length and angular displacement, and relatively weak understanding of the idea of temperature, velocity and current, influenced the development of traditional measuring instruments, and led to the indirect measurement of the former through the direct measurement of the latter. Kyburg also gives some interesting examples. He says:

> There are quantities, such as speed, which admit of direct measurement, but which, as directly measured, can only be placed in an ordinal scale. As indirectly measured, speed can be placed in a ratio scale. . . . Such a scale is much more useful than the mere ordinal scale.

The example of the indirect measurement of electrical current is discussed in more detail, to illustrate the importance of object-oriented modelling, and some difficulties which indirect measurement can present in practice.

Current amplitude i is frequently the subject of indirect measurement. It is a 'through-variable' whose measurement involves the interruption of the circuit which can be a matter of great inconvenience. Instead, one can more directly observe the voltage v (an 'across-variable') which is created by the current i on a standard resistor (a physical object) whose resistance ρ (its model in terms of resistance as the key property) had already been measured. Current is then indirectly measured, its value deduced from the model of the object which preserves all three key properties and links them by Ohm's well-known law: $i = v/\rho$. In Hausen's terms, this is an acyclic graph, indeed a tree with v and ρ as leaves and i as the root.

So far, indirect measurement appeared as a simple matter. The problem becomes more complicated, and the notion of object-oriented modelling comes into its own, when the value of the resistance cannot be adequately modelled by a constant. Experience tells us that the resistance ρ of a real-life resistor is not invariant but changes with many factors, one of which is temperature. This requires the inclusion of temperature τ among the key properties of the object-oriented measurement. The current i may now be deduced from the model as $i = g (v, \rho (\tau))$. This would indicate that indirect measurement is represented by

Objects of the model set A	Measures of key properties of the model objects					
	$m1$	$m2$	$\ldots$	mn	$\ldots$	mq
a	$m1\,(a)$	$m2\,(a)$		$mn\,(a)$		$mq\,(a)$
b	$m1\,(b)$	$m2\,(b)$		$mn\,(b)$		$mq\,(b)$
.						
.						
.						
z	$m1\,(z)$	$m2\,(z)$		$mn\,(z)$		$mq\,(z)$

Figure 12.2 Profile of the object-oriented model

a tree, with v and τ as leaves, i as the root and ρ as an intermediate node. However, the laws of empirical science tell us about the heating effect which current has on a resistor. This means that temperature τ is not an independent variable but has dependence on current; $\tau(i)$, destroying not just the tree but the acyclic structure of indirect measurement. We spare the reader further elaboration, such as non-linearity of the model, caused by the variance of resistance with the voltage coefficient of the resistor, and its sensitivity to the frequency of the current, which requires it to be modelled by a frequency-dependent complex impedance instead of the real-valued resistance ρ. All such factors must be accounted for in the interest of validity of the indirect measurement, either by including them in the object-oriented model A of the target set A, or be explicitly excluding them, postulating their invariance.

The above notions are now discussed more formally, in preparation for addressing the question: what are the representation and uniqueness conditions to be satisfied for assuring the quality of indirect measurement?

Let $A = \{\,a, b, \ldots, z\,\}$ be the target set of objects as before. Assume now that the indirect measurement requires the model of objects of A to be described in terms of n directly measured key properties.

Let $Ai = \{\,ai, bi, \ldots, zi\,\}$ be a model of A with respect to the ith key property. Then the empirical relational system $Ei = \{\,Ai, Ri, Oi\,\}$ models the set A with respect to the ith property, preserving the relations and operations which the property imposes on the objects of A. $Si = (Ei, Fi, mi)$ will be a scale for the ith property. Now the set A will be an n-dimensional model of A: $A = \{\,A1, A2, \ldots, An\,\}$, each with its own scale.

Assume now that $M = \{\,m1, m2, \ldots, mn\,\}$ is the set of the real-valued functions on A, composed of measures of one of the directly measured key properties according to properly defined conditions of representation and uniqueness. If one can define a real-valued function g on A in terms of the primitive measures of M, then g will be an 'indirect measure' of the set of objects of A in terms of the chosen set of key properties. Note that these definitions are consistent with that proposed by Hausen for software quality (1989), and also with those put forward by Kaposi and Kitchenham (1987) and Stockman (1988).

12.5.2 Meaningfulness

Indirect measures are easy to define. One can impose some arbitrary real-valued function over the numbers yielded by the formal representation system. However, the scales must not be arbitrary; measurement must always serve some practical purpose. Indirect measures must represent meaningful empirical properties. They should reflect some theoretical or empirical law which is valid over the primitive measures of all of the target objects of A. These laws must be embodied in the model A,

which describes the objects of the target set A with respect to their selected and related key properties. The representation and uniqueness conditions of object-oriented indirect measurement must therefore be of two kinds: 'inherited' conditions .which each primitive measure must individually satisfy, and 'interrelation' conditions which permit one to deduce the meaningful indirect measure as a function of the primitive measures, according to the laws imposed by the model.

12.5.3 Representation

The notation adopted by Roberts gives the representation condition of a single indirect measure g in a form C($m1$, $m2$, ..., mn, g), where the symbols in the argument are as above, and C is the set of necessary and sufficient conditions which the indirect measure g must satisfy. These specify the empirical relations of the model A as an n-ary 'interrelation' operation $g = g(\,m1, m2, \ldots, mn\,)$, additional to the 'inherited' representation condition which each of the direct measures $m1$ to mn must individually satisfy. If the object-oriented measurement requires the characterization of the object by more than one indirectly measured property, such as shown on Figure 12.2, individual representation conditions must be set up for each such measure, in the form just given.

As an example, consider the indirect measurement of electrical power, with all complications removed by assuring invariance. Only three key properties enter the object-oriented model: current, voltage and power. The reason for adopting indirect measurement is practical – power is observed by its effects (such as heat generated in a unit of time) rather than directly, or else it is deduced by calculation (as the product of current and voltage). In the latter case the representation condition for indirect measurement arises from the model of A which must express DC power p as the product $v \times i$. Accordingly, C (v, i, p) is the condition $p = v \times i$.

Further practical examples of object-oriented indirect measurement, relevant to software engineering, would be the summative aggregation of total process costs or processing times from primitive measures of the cost or durations of part-processes, and the measurement of the efficiency of resource utilization as the ratio of the useful resources produced to the total resources absorbed. The representation condition of the indirect measure is readily given in each case by the model which preserves the operations on the primitive measures.

12.5.4 Uniqueness

The uniqueness of the primitive measures gives the permissible scaling transformations of the measures of M. From these, the scale of any indirect measure is deduced by means of the interrelation condition.

In the case of the power measurement example, we know that current and voltage are measurable on ratio scale. Given α and β as scaling factors for v and i respectively, the rescaling for p = v × i is the product α × β.

Many interesting and difficult scaling problems arise in indirect measurement, of which two are mentioned here:

1. Given the task of measuring the position in space of a set of communications satellites, the position of points in space may be measured by setting up a Cartesian coordinate system at some point of reference (such as a controlling ground station) and measuring three distances in the axial directions on a ratio scale. If these coordinate systems may themselves be transposed (e.g. if the ground station is liable to be relocated), the measurement of the same distance is set up on an interval scale, allowing transformations of the sort: φ(x) − αx + β, α > 0. However, position in space may also be measured in coordinate systems other than Cartesian, such as polar, cylindrical, etc. In case of a polar coordinate system, two of the three parameters defining position will be angles, and the admissible transformations between the polar and Cartesian measures will include trigonometric functions.

2. Scaling problems arise in telecommunications when some properties of signals may be described in the time domain, others in the frequency domain, and, to draw the required conclusions from the measurement, one must aggregate these. Measure-preserving transformations between the two domains must be set up by use of appropriate transform calculi.

12.5.5 Dimensional invariance as an indicator of the quality of measurement

The concept under observation is reflected in the dimensions of the measured property. The quantitative result of the measurement is expressed in the magnitude of the number; the qualitative description of the concept captured by the property is reflected in the dimensions of the unit of measurement. Thus, any measured result consists of a numerical and dimensional part. Length is measured in metres, cost in pounds sterling, volume in cubic inches, velocity in miles per hour, or in dimensional units which represent valid transformations of these. 'Dimensionless' quantities (such as the number of objects in the target set, or the number of nodes of a graph) are said to be measured in scalar units, normally on an absolute scale.

The analysis of dimensions (as opposed to magnitudes) is a powerful aid for assuring the quality of measurement. If there is incompatibility between the dimensions of the property sought and the result obtained, this flags a qualitative error – an error of principle. Dimensional errors of measurement must be uncovered; they show that the measured result is flawed, even if the numerical value of the data is plausible. From a practical viewpoint, checking results for dimensional errors is effective because such errors are much more readily detectable than numerical ones.

Once the error is detected, its cause must be diagnosed. Here again, dimensions give a powerful guide to quality assurance. The discipline of designating each quantity with its dimension through all steps and phases of the measurement process assists in tracing the error to its root by qualitative means.

Indirect measurement is particularly prone to dimensional error. The primitive measures embedded in the deduction of indirect measures carry their own dimensions which qualitatively express the constituent concepts; the representation condition of indirect measurement must be checked to ensure that the measurement has correct dimensional structure, composing the dimensions of the primitive measures into a dimension appropriate for the measurement of the property in question.

Dimensional incompatibility indicates error in representation, scaling, or both.

When the indirect measure is constructed as a sum, this allows an easy and effective way to check the dimensional homogeneity of all constituents. In other cases the check may not be quite so obvious.

Kyburg (1984) treats the subjects of the algebra of quantities and dimensional analysis comprehensively. He demonstrates the value of these methods in assuring the quality of object-oriented indirect measurement. Even more importantly, he emphasizes the potential of dimensional analysis and dimensional structures in concept formation for new discipline domains.

12.5.6 Conjoint measurement

Object-oriented measurement builds up a picture of the class of objects property-by-property. The motivation for this can be to support decision making about the object. The decision may be based on a single property. However, the decision maker usually bases judgment on some kind of aggregation of several properties. The new composite property may represent the values and priorities of the measurer, defined as a function over the other (directly and indirectly measured) properties of the object set. The new measure may itself be regarded as just another indirect measure. In some cases it may also be seen as having more general significance: some kind of 'emergent property', characterizing the object as a whole. This is the interpretation given to the measures of software quality (see e.g. Hausen, 1989a) and productivity. The composition of aggregate functions and the definition of their measures is referred to as 'conjoint measurement'.

Roberts discusses the representation and uniqueness conditions of conjoint measurement in several interesting practical cases. Among these, he provides a detailed discussion of a simple case of conjoint measurement when:

1. The aggregating function is an un-weighted sum over all measures of the object profile.
2. The conjoint measurement defines a preference relation over the aggregates such that the new property is measured on an ordinal scale.

This type of additive conjoint measurement is illustrated on a more elaborate version of the earlier example of software procurement.

Assume that {a, b, . . . , z} is the candidate set of programs and {m1, m2, . . . mq} is the set of measures of their key parameters. The profile of the object set is given in a matrix such as that of Figure 12.2. Assume now that each individual measure is so defined that the higher the merit of the program, the higher the numerical value of the measure. If the measurer decides that all of the measured properties are equally important, and if the measures for these properties are additive, then the order over the value of the sum of the measures would express the priority order of the programs which are candidates for procurement.

Alternatively, an ordinal utility function may be defined over a weighted sum of the measures, where a positive scalar multiplier would describe the relative value assigned by the measurer to each constituent property of the profile.

Of course, conjoint measurement need not be additive. Performance indices and figures of merit are defined in many fields; these are typical instances giving rise to conjoint object oriented measurement. In software engineering, quality models are the basis of defining the relationship between profile parameters and the emergent property, and here again, conjoint measurement may not be additive. The theory of conjoint measurement provides guidelines and methods for defining appropriate representations and scales, and assuring the quality of the aggregated appraisal of objects.

12.6 Subject domain-oriented measurement

When approaching the issue of object-oriented measurement, it was necessary to broaden the perspective from a single property to the many-featured characterization of objects. When considering subject domain-oriented measurement, one must widen one's horizons once more, to consider the problem of characterizing by measurement *any* of the objects of a discipline.

One may attempt to envisage subject domain-oriented metrology as an enormous matrix of the type of Figure 12.2, covering all target objects and all of the key properties which the discipline had identified or produced in the past. The notion of subject domain-oriented measurement is even wider than that. It also embodies the expectation of covering all objects and all properties which the discipline domain is likely to produce in the future. Subject domain-oriented measurement demands that the practical implementation of measurement should be feasible over the whole subject domain. Since disciplines do not recognize geographical boundaries, subject domain-oriented metrology must have global scope, and its concept and methods must have international recognition.

What are the theoretical and practical implications of subject domain-oriented metrology?

Subject domain-oriented metrology must offer a theoretical framework for representation and scaling, adaptable to any individual measurement problem of the domain. Such a framework must provide for the discipline:

1. A comprehensive set of basic concepts, defined on measurable terms.
2. A system of coherent theories linking these concepts and deriving from them new concepts for object oriented measurement.

If the theoretical framework is to support measurement in practice, it must have measurement methods and procedures to cover the whole discipline domain, and instrumentation technologies for implementing the execution of measurement. It must also have a comprehensive system of standards, together with legal and administrative structures. If the measurement is to have global validity, the units and standards must be internationally recognized and their usage globally enforced.

In summary, subject domain-oriented measurement must provide a comprehensive measurement system, covering all of the aspects of the metrology domain outlined in Figure 12.1.

Assuming for a moment that it is possible to develop such a measurement system for some important subject domain, such as software engineering, what advantage would such a system offer?

The potential theoretical and practical power of such a measurement system is enormous:

1. The measurement system would serve the unity of the discipline, providing for practising professionals (scientists and technologists) a 'common culture', captured in generally accepted concepts, codified in empirically validated theories of the discipline domain, expressed in recognized notations, with measurement results recorded in internationally agreed standard units.
2. Through the common culture, the measurement system would serve the education and training of young professionals; the common culture would assure lasting skills of global value.
3. The measurement system would serve business and commerce, aiding effective management in the supply industries, providing a basis for trading standards and enforceable contracts between vendor and client, and promoting international trade.

4. Most importantly, the measurement system would be a servant of the public, being an instrument of the measurement-based quality assurance of all the goods and services derived from the discipline domain.

Is it feasible to develop such a measurement system for any significant subject domain?

There is an overwhelmingly impressive example to prove the feasibility of a measurement system for a whole subject domain of universal proportions. The most important (and perhaps the only) comprehensive measurement system is the one covering the application domain of the natural sciences. This system also forms the basis of measurement in all the technologies of classical engineering. While it is impossible to prove that the system can sustain all future measurement in the sciences and technologies of the domain, its maintainability and its robustness to withstand new demands have been empirically proven.

The measurement system incorporates internationally agreed units (SI: *Systeme Internationale d'Unites*). SI provides measures for characterizing observable entities of the physical universe by means of only seven orthogonal base units:

1. length (metre)
2. mass (kilogram)
3. time (second)
4. temperature (degrees Kelvin)
5. electric current (ampere)
6. luminous intensity (candela)
7. the amount of substance (mole)

Other physical quantities are measured in units derived from these, such as velocity measured in metre/second ($m s^{-1}$) or force measured in metre $\times$ kilogram/second^2 ($m(ks^{-2})$).

So accustomed are we to this measurement system that we tend to take it for granted. The enormous scope and extraordinary frugal elegance of the measurement system must be consciously appreciated. Frugality of the base set of SI is of great practical importance. The small number of base units facilitates the maintenance of base standards and the operation of an international calibration system for measuring instruments. Kyburg (1984) gives an enlightening discussion on the development of measurement systems with minimal sets of base units. International standards have been defined and physically established for all seven base units of SI.

The example of SI must be remembered when setting goals for developing standards and measures for new disciplines. Problem solvers have the natural tendency to regard their task as unique, or at least very highly specialized, not related to the experience of others but requiring entirely new concepts, methods and measures. In software engineering there is evidence that such introspective attitudes have prevailed in the past, and led to fragmentation of the discipline, repetitious and inefficient use of effort, and isolation of groups of workers who would achieve a great deal more by collaboration. Fragmentation, and the lack of a discipline-wide measurement system, harbours dangers that weakly defined concepts may be accepted as valid, poorly tested designs may be implemented in situations of high risk, productivity suffers and projects run out of time and budget, and the progress of the entire science, technology and business of the discipline suffers.

Natural science, with its measurement system demonstrates an opposite approach to isolation and introspection. It illustrates the merits of a discipline-wide common culture on examples of breathtaking variety from the cosmic to the sub-atomic, that a boundless variety of problems can be characterized, and their solution expressed, in structures over only seven base measures.

All scientific advance and technological achievement of the domain is 'grounded' in this measurement system. The problem solver works within a discipline which demands depth of thought in expressing the problem and the solution in the general framework, rather than each person rushing out each time to invent entire worlds of new concepts and measures.

Two practical extensions of the measurement system must be noted.

1. Technology's goal is to enhance welfare (Kaposi, AA, 1989). It is concerned with cost-effective utilization of scientific advance. In the practice of engineering and business, the base measures of SI are complemented with the unit of money.
2. The 'information era' of this century presented a new challenge for engineers: information could not be measured within the SI framework. Shannon and his associates came forward with the 'bit' as a new measure of the quantity of information. Modern communication theory incorporates the bit into the engineer's measurement system. Thus for example we can combine old and new to measure the rate of information flow in units of bits per second (bit/s) and one can evaluate by measurement the suitability of communication channels, installed for old-style analogue communication, for the transmission of bit-streams of information.

How far has software measurement progressed and what is the way ahead?

At present, software engineering is still in need of stronger discipline-wide conceptual foundations and more comprehensive formal theories and empirical laws. The subject domain is not ready for the formulation of a comprehensive measurement system, along the lines of SI. However, there is now widespread recognition of the need for measurement-based characterization of software, stemming from discontent about the quality of software and the productivity of the industry. There is growing anxiety about the safety of software-related systems and concern about the security of data entrusted to software. Convincing evidence of safety and security can only be provided by measurement. This has stimulated interest in measurement in software engineering. People are also beginning to realize that it is not enough to measure: one must measure *well*.

Two different measurement approaches have been pursued in the past. Their purpose is the same: providing numerical data about the 'measurands' of software – the important properties which we need to know. To highlight the difference between the two ways of going about this task, they are labelled here as the 'goal-directed' and the 'method-driven' approach:

1. The goal-directed approach to software measurement proposes 'metrics' as numerical representations for the measurands, and gathers field data about these. Empirical validation is attempted, and interrelationships sought between the various measurands. Collections of important properties, on several levels of resolution, have been proposed. An example is the quality model of McCall *et al.* (1977), already quoted. The measurands are popularly referred to as the 'ilities' of software engineering. Definitions of such properties are also being created as part of current activities of international standards bodies.

   The goal-directed approach is highly practical and has proved to be of substantial value in individual organizations and specific situations. However, the approach has limitations. The definitions of properties proposed so far leave room for wide variation of interpretation. In most cases the data recorded is not related to a well-defined model of the product or process, the circumstances of measurement are not explicitly stated, and hence it is not possible to guard the invariants of the measurement. The 'tuning' of the metrics to every situation creates obstacles to repeating measurement results and establishing measures applicable in different organizations.

   The goal-directed approach, on its own, cannot provide the depth of insight necessary for establishing a measurement

system for software engineering. Kyburg (1984) devotes his entire book to arguing this point, and does so convincingly, and with eloquence.

2. The method-driven approach starts by defining 'measurables': observable properties implicit in the software which can be precisely captured in models and measured according to the dictates of measurement theory. However, this approach too has limitations as the properties that can be measured are not necessarily those about which information is needed. The hope is that the measurables of the method-driven approach may prove to be 'measurands' of empirical significance in themselves, or that their models may lead to firmer definitions of the 'ilities' by linking the primitive measurables of the object profile indirectly to the 'measurands'.

   The method-driven approach can provide deep insights and sound measures for properties such as those of size, structure, complexity (in the classical sense), and some aspects of performance. Nevertheless, on its own, without thorough empirical validation, the measures have no practical meaning and the approach is little more than an academic curiosity.

For software engineering, the way forward must lie in combining the practical insights of the goal-directed approach with the theoretical soundness of the method driven approach. Classical measurement theory must be reviewed, extended and systematically applied in support of the current practice and future development of software engineering. It can offer powerful support in appraising and retrospectively enhancing current 'software metrics', as has been shown on the example of Zuse's case study, and as is currently pursued through the ESPRIT Project METKIT (see e.g. Hausen, 1989b). Measurement theory is already used constructively, such as in the development of new measures for characterizing static and animated specifications (e.g. Kaposi and Myers, 1989). Extension of the constructive use of measurement theory in the planning and systematic design of new measures will help in defining firmer concepts, promoting the development of the discipline, and laying the foundations of a future measurement system for the subject domain of software engineering.

What should be the future scope of subject domain oriented measurement?

The demarcation between the subject domains of the classical engineering disciplines and software engineering is not tenable. Software is entrusted with tasks of increasing scope and importance: the design of new products, the control of industrial production, and essential services such as transport, communication, health care, government administration and defence. The software is the controller of the hardware on which it is implemented. It is no longer adequate to assure that the software meets its quality targets and assume that the hardware is perfect (Dyer, 1989). Satisfactory operation of the system depends on the quality of both, and the quality assurance process must treat hardware and software 'symmetrically' (Kaposi, J F, 1989).

Even this is not enough in itself. The quality of the specification and design of the system as a whole, as an interrelation and effective cooperation between hardware and software, must be assured (Kaposi and Myers, 1989). Before complex computer-based systems are put in charge of sensitive services, the public is entitled to know that their quality has been assured. Convincing evidence can only be supplied by means of measurement. The measurement system must be comprehensive, embracing both of the relevant disciplines (Kaposi, AA, 1989).

At the moment we are without a measurement system which can meet these demands; we are even short of a measurement system for software alone. However, the foundations are already there in the measurement system of the natural sciences, measurement theory, and in the well-publicised achievements of goal-directed and method-driven software engineering measurement. When developing software standards and measures, it is essential to assure their measurement-theoretic foundations and their compatibility with the established measurement system of SI. The more distant aim must be to unify and consolidate these foundations and develop them into a comprehensive metrological system for systems engineering.

12.7 Acknowledgements

The author is indebted to the scientists, philosophers and engineers who have laid the foundations of the subject of measurement theory, and in particular to Jevons, Bunge, Finkelstein and Roberts, whose ideas have had a major influence on much of this chapter. Thanks are due to Professor Finkelstein, Professor Pyle and Professor Dobson for their comments and criticisms of the ideas and details of the text, and for their many valuable suggestions for improvement, and also to Professor McDermid for his careful editorial scrutiny.

The chapter reflects recent work carried out by the author and her colleagues under the sponsorship of British Telecommunications Research Laboratories, and in the context of the ESPRIT project METKIT. These programmes have contributed greatly to the development of the subject of measurement and its application to software, and created a community for fruitful collaboration between researchers and practitioners. The author is obliged to the sponsors of these research programmes, and to all her colleagues in Britain and Europe, particularly to Margaret Myers.

John Kaposi's engineering insight, and his deep understanding of measurement and quality assurance in industrial practice, has enriched every aspect of the text. Without his support and encouragement the chapter would never have been written.

12.8 References

Ashby, W. R. (1964) *An Introduction to Cybernetics*, Methuen

van Brakel, J. (1985) Measurement and meaningfulness. *Acta IMECO 1985*, 319–333

BS 5233:1986 British standard glossary of terms used in Metrology (incorporating BS 2643), British Standards Institution

BS 5750: Part 0; Section 0.2: 1987 ISO 9004–1987 Quality systems; Part 0; Principal concepts and applications; Section 0.2; Guide to quality management and quality system elements, British Standards Institution

Bullock, A., Stallybrass, O. and Trombley, S. (1988) (eds) *The Fontana Dictionary of Modern Thought*, Fontana Press

Bunge, M. (1967) *Scientific Research I and II*, Springer Verlag

Cohen, B., Harwood, W. T. and Jackson, M. I. (1986) *The Specification of Complex Systems*, Addison Wesley

Dyer, M. (1989) The cleanroom software development process. In *Measurement for Software Control and Quality Assurance* (eds. B. A. Kitchenham and B. Littlewood) Elsevier Applied Science, pp 1–26

Fenton, N. E. (1988) Software measurement. In *Software Reliability and Metrics Newsletter*, (ed. B. Littlewood) 7, Centre for Software Reliability, City University, London

Fenton, N. E. and Kaposi, A. A. (1989) An engineering theory of structure and measurement. In *Measurement for Software Control and Quality Assurance*, (eds. B. A. Kitchenham and B. Littlewood) Elsevier Applied Science, pp 289–319

Finkelstein, L. (1975a) Fundamental concepts of measurement: definition and scales. *Measurement and Control*, **8**, 105–111

Finkelstein, L. (1975b) Representation by symbol systems as an extension of the concept of measurement. *Kybernetes*, **4**, 215–223

Finkelstein, L. and Leaning, M. S. (1984) A review of the fundamental concepts of measurement. *Measurement*, **2**, 25–34

Fiok, A. J., Jaworski, J. M., Morawski, R. Z., Oledzki, J. S. and Urban, A. C. (1988) Theory of measurement in teaching metrology in engineering faculties. *Measurement*, **6**, 63–68

Franksen, O. E. (1977) On measurements and their group-theoretic foundations. In *Problem analysis in science and engineering*, (eds. F. H. Branin and K. Huseyn) Academic Press

Hausen, H. L. (1989a) Generic modelling of software quality. In *Measurement for Software Control and Quality Assurance* (eds. B. A. Kitchenham and B. Littlewood) Elsevier Applied Science, pp 201–241

Hausen, H. L. (1989b) Rule-based handling of software quality and productivity models. In *Proceedings of the 2nd European Software Engineering Conference 1989* (ed. J. McDermid) Springer Verlag

Jevons, W. S. (written in 1871, published 1958) *The Principles of Science—a Treatise on Logic and Scientific Method*, Dover Publications

Kaposi, A. A. (1989) *Software Measurement – an Engineering Approach*, ESPRIT Project METKIT working paper

Kaposi, A. A. and Kitchenham, B. (1987) The architecture of system quality. *Software Engineering Journal*, 2–8

Kaposi, A. A. and Myers, M. (1989) *Quality assuring specification and design. Software Engineering Journal*, January 1990, pp. 11–26

Kaposi, J. F. (1989) *Software Quality Measurement, System Quality Measurement – a Practitioner's View of Future Developments*, ESPRIT Project MUSE working paper

Kyburg, H. E. (1984) *Theory and Measurement*, Cambridge University Press

Leaning, M. S. and Finkelstein, L. (1985) Towards an applied theory of measurement. *Acta IMEKO*, 287–296

McCall, J. A., Richards, P. K. and Walters, G. F. (1977) Concepts and definitions of software quality. *Factors in Software Quality*, **1**, NTIS, Springfield, VA, USA

Myers, M. (1989) *Quality Assurance of Specifications and Design of Software*, PhD Thesis, South Bank Polytechnic, London

Roberts, F. S. (1979) *Measurement Theory, Encyclopedia of Mathematics and its Applications, Vol 7*, Addison-Wesley

Stevens, S. S. (1946) On the theory of scales of measurement. *Science*, **103**, 677–680

Stevens, S. S. (1959) Measurement, empirical meaningfulness and three-valued logic. In *Measurement: Definitions and Theories* (eds. C. W. Churchman and P. Ratoosh) John Wiley, pp 129–143

Stockman, S. G. (1988) A constructive approach to software quality assurance. Paper presented at 1er Seminaire E O Q C sur la Qualite des Logiciels, Brussels, 25–27 April 1988

Sydenham, P. H. (1982) Measurement, models and systems, and Standardization of measurement fundamentals and practices. In *Handbook of Measurement Science, Vol 1* (ed. P. H. Sydenham) John Wiley, pp 31–47, 49–94

Turski, W. M. and Maibaum, T. S. E. (1987) *The Specification of Computer Programs* Addison Wesley

Zuse, H. (1990) *Software Complexity. Measures and Methods*, de Gruyter

13

Cognitive psychology

Andrew Monk
Department of Psychology, University of York

Contents

13.1 How to use this chapter

Managers and professional users demand systems which are easy to use and easy to learn. Small improvements in usability can result in large cumulative gains in productivity. A 5% improvement achieved by adding, say, half a man-month to a small design, where the system is to be used by 20 operators for one year, represents a 24-fold return in time. Perhaps more importantly, a well-engineered system will be easy to learn. By reducing training time one increases the flexibility with which operators can be assigned to jobs.

User-centred design involves understanding the problems faced by a user and then adapting the system to minimize them. The first step in this direction is to understand how people process information. This is the subject of cognitive psychology. This chapter describes some basic characteristics of human information processing, including perception, memory and motor control. Software engineers familiar with this material will understand that usability problems may be due to problem processing information and not just 'bloody-mindedness' on the part of the operator. They will be in a better position to recognize the nature of problems as they arise and the changes that need to be made.

It is only possible to cover some of the more salient concepts from cognitive psychology in a single chapter. While the data upon which a concept is based will be outlined, detailed experiments will not be described. Similarly, it is not possible to discuss any of the theoretical models in cognitive psychology. However, while there are models which make quantitative predictions we are still a long way from being able to provide predictive models that would allow an engineer to calculate usability metrics in advance of implementing a design.

The last point has implications for the way the material in this chapter is to be used. Software engineering is different from other branches of engineering in many respects. The arguments above suggest that the software engineer's task in fitting the system to its users is as important as fitting it to the hardware.

Yet, the specification given to the designer of how the system is to be used is often very poor. Fortunately, compared with other engineering disciplines, prototyping is relatively easy. Trial users are generally not expensive to recruit. Simulations can be used and software can be built so that user interface is easy to change (see Chapter 36 on Prototyping). An iterative approach to the design of the user interface is necessary as the most experienced and knowledgeable designer will not be able to anticipate precisely how a user will behave. The material in this chapter may help to avoid some problems in the first place but its major use will be to recognize the cause of problems, after the event, so that the appropriate changes can be made.

13.2 Temporal and spatial resolution

The first topic to be considered is perception, how one inputs information. In particular, what are the limits of temporal and spatial resolution of the human perceptual system? From the point of view of the engineer this is relevant to the design of 'output' devices such as visual displays and sound generators.

13.2.1 Temporal frequency sensitivity function

The human auditory apparatus can usefully be thought of as a low-pass filter. *Figure 13.1* plots the minimum intensity of sound which can be reliably detected at different frequencies. The type of experiment in which this data is collected requires people to listen during two time periods. One contains a very faint tone and the other does not. After listening during both periods they have to say which was which. On such a task chance performance is 50% correct responses. The intensity resulting in 75% correct is the intensity plotted. Notice that above about 20 kHz the tone will not be detected whatever the intensity. The perceived loudness of a pure tone follows the same curve so as well as being maximally sensitive to tones of about 3 kHz, tones of this frequency will also appear loudest for a given energy level.

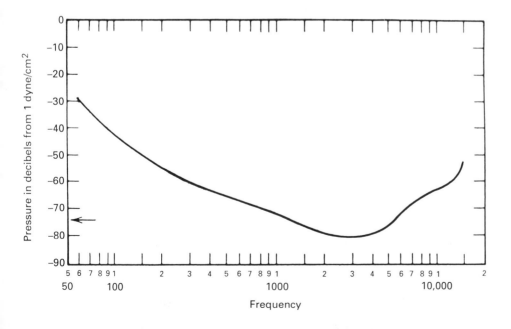

Figure 13.1 Minimum audible pressure, at different frequencies (adapted from Schiffman, 1976)

Analogous experiments have been done with sinusoidally flickering lights. *Figure 13.2* was derived by finding the minimum amplitude of flicker which can be reliably detected at different frequencies. In these experiments the comparison stimulus is a steady light. The observer has to say which period contained the steady stimulus and which the flickering stimulus. The inverse of the minimum amplitude at which flicker can be detected is the 'sensitivity' at that frequency and it is sensitivity that is plotted in Figure 13.2. Above about 60 Hz a steadily shining light is seen whatever the amplitude of modulation. This curve depends on the background luminance the flicker is imposed on. A higher background luminance results in a higher sensitivity to flicker.

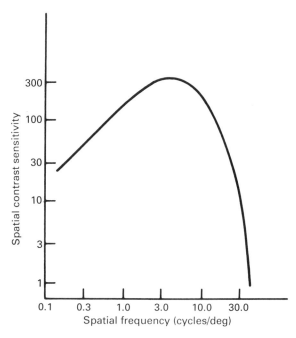

Figure 13.3 Human spatial contrast sensitivity function (from Thompson, 1985)

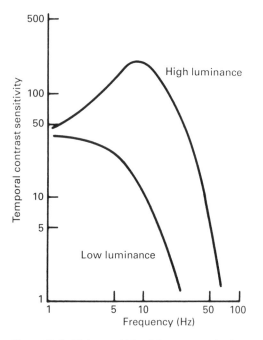

Figure 13.2 Flicker sensitivity of the eye at two luminances (from Thompson, 1985)

13.2.2 The spatial frequency sensitivity function

As well as being a low-pass temporal frequency filter the visual system is also a low-pass spatial filter. *Figure 13.3* is the spatial equivalent of Figure 13.2. It was plotted by finding the minimum amplitude which can be detected at various spatial frequencies. Spatial frequency is measured in cycles/degree. The stimulus used in these experiments are the spatial equivalents of a pure tone; that is gratings whose intensity varies sinusoidally. The width of the stripe in these gratings and their distance from the viewer define the spatial frequency. A spatial frequency of one cycle/degree is a grating whose intensity changes from bright to dark and back in 1 cm when viewed at a distance of 57 cm. Doubling the width of the stripes or halving the viewing distance will both have the same effect of changing the spatial frequency to 0.5 cycles/degree. Figure 13.3 is again plotted with the ordinate sensitivity, i.e., the inverse of the minimum amplitude of modulation which can be detected. It shows that even very high contrast changes cannot be resolved at spatial frequencies greater than 30 cycles/degree (three stripes to a mm viewed from a distance of 57 cm).

13.2.3 Practical considerations – flicker, aliasing, acuity, the use of movement

CRT (Cathode Ray Tube) displays depend on the low-pass characteristics of the visual system. A raster display consists of a rectangular grid of picture elements each of which is caused to fluoresce briefly by a scanning electron beam. Temporal blurring gives the illusion of a steady image even though each point is only brightened periodically. Spatial blurring give the illusion of smooth curves, lines of arbitrary slope and so on, even though the picture elements are arranged in a rectangular array.

These illusions will only be maintained while the spatial and temporal frequencies are outside of the range where changes are perceived. Breakdown of the temporal illusion is seen as flicker and is very disturbing to some users. The most common refresh rate for a visual display is the mains frequency, 50 Hz (60 Hz in the USA). This is perilously close to the limit. Peripheral vision is more temporally sensitive than central vision and we are also more sensitive with bright background illumination. A bright display seen 'out of the corner of the eye' will often appear to flicker. Flicker may be cured by decreasing the overall intensity but this will reduce legibility as it also increases the spatial blurring. A better solution is to increase the refresh rate.

Break down of the spatial illusion is known as aliasing. Curves or slanting lines are seen as being made up of discontinuous steps. Again spatial resolution is higher the brighter the display and so dimming it may prevent aliasing. Aliasing is best prevented by introducing more picture elements (better screen resolution). Alternatively, anti-aliasing is a technique by which the contrast of changes is reduced by introducing picture elements of intermediate intensities to restore the illusion of a smooth curve or straight line. This is of course only possible when the frame buffer codes brightness with more than one bit, a feature which is rare in most monochrome displays but may be available in a colour display which is being used to provide a monochrome image.

Problems can arise because temporal or spatial resolution is insufficient. The most common examples of this are letters which subtend too small a visual angle to be read or gaps and other visual imperfections which cannot be detected. In this context spatial resolution is referred to as acuity. Acuity drops off very rapidly in peripheral vision. For example, a letter presented only 5° from central vision needs to be five times as large to be named reliably. Thus the area of high acuity vision is remarkably small and in most tasks the eye must scan a visual display to pick up the high spatial frequency information.

Fortunately, the increase in temporal frequency sensitivity in the periphery means that a change in the stimulus can usually direct attention to the new information. This sensitivity to movement is used in displays that have flashing cursors or flashing alerts. Similarly, a standard trick for finding the mouse cursor in a page of a text is to move the mouse.

Problems in this area are generally straightforward to detect. The visual systems of different individuals are remarkably similar. Users will quickly pinpoint the problem if a display flickers or critical information is difficult to see or find.

13.3 Relative and absolute judgement

13.3.1 The just noticeable difference

The data described above was obtained in experiments where people had to detect the presence or absence of a stimulus. It is also possible to test our ability to discriminate a difference between two levels of some psychophysical scale. For example, an observer might be shown two patches of light in such a way that they can be directly compared. The task is to say which has the higher intensity. As before, chance performance is 50%. The difference in intensity between the two patches is increased until 75% correct performance is achieved. This just noticeable difference (JND) depends on the average intensity of the two patches according to a simple function.

$$JND = KI$$

I is the average intensity and K is known as the Weber fraction. K for light intensity is $1/60$. Thus two light patches one of which is 1.7% more intense than the other can reliably be discriminated. For most other psychophysical scales the Weber fraction is similarly small and so we can discriminate many different pitches, loudnesses, tastes and so on. When the stimuli are multi-dimensional, e.g., pitch and intensity, then even more distinctions are possible. While the human ability to make this kind of comparative judgement is extremely good, our ability to make absolute judgements, where stimuli have to be put into arbitrary categories, is much poorer.

13.3.2 Naming and categorizing stimuli

Imagine an experiment where a listener is asked to identify tones by their pitch. Perhaps four tones are played each of which have to be identified by a number. After each one is heard and its number guessed, the correct answer is supplied. This task is practised until no more improvement is observed and then a new task introduced with, say, 14 tones. This task, to associate names with the different values on a scale, is described as absolute judgement to contrast it with the relative judgement task described above. People can cope with four tones or four categories of tone without difficulty, but it is surprisingly difficult to learn 'names' for more than about six pure tones.

The data from such experiments has been interpreted in terms of information theory. The information present in the stimulus depends on the number of alternatives. Thus each stimulus in a four tone task contains two bits of information. In an eight-tone task it is three bits, and so on. The correspondence between the stimulus information (the correct name for the stimulus) and the response information (the name given by the observer) can be expressed as information transmitted. *Figure 13.4* plots the results of an experiment where the number of tones varies between two and 14 (1–3.8 bits). With up to two bits of stimulus information the correspondence between stimulus and response is perfect i.e., all the stimulus information is transmitted. However, with larger stimulus sets mistakes are made and the information transmitted asymptotes at about 2.5 bits. The 2.5 bits correspond to about six equally likely alternatives. The results show that it is not possible to pick more than about six different tones a listener will never confuse. These sets of tones covered the range from 100 Hz to 8 kHz in equal logarithmic steps but the same results are obtained if the range is restricted to say 6–8 kHz. Being able to discriminate say five high pitch tones in one series and five low pitch tones in another does not mean one can combine all ten into a single series.

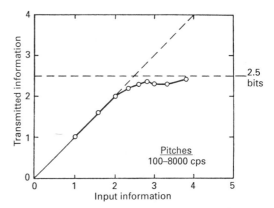

Figure 13.4 Data on the amount of information transmitted by listeners making absolute judgements of auditory pitch (from Miller, 1956)

The limit of about six is very small compared with the thousands of JNDs of pitch which can be discriminated in a relative judgement task, but the finding is robust and general. For loudness for example, the limit is 2.3 bits or about five perfectly discriminable alternatives. For points on a line it is 3.25 bits (nine categories) and for concentrations of saline solution 1.9 bits (four categories).

The experiments were carried out with randomly selected volunteers who were practised with each stimulus set until their performance showed no sign of improvement. The limits on absolute judgement can be extended with month or years of practice. A competent musician for example can identify 50 or 60 different pitches. Also, the stimuli used only varied on a single dimension. A stimulus set which varies on two or more dimensions can transmit more information, although the gain is not additive. For example, the maximum information transmitted by points on a line is 3.25 bits so one might expect the information transmitted by positions in a square to be 6.5 bits. In fact it is 4.6 bits or 24 positions accurately categorized. One experiment used six acoustic dimensions and achieved a transmission rate of 7.2 bits equivalent to 150 equally likely categories.

13.3.3 Practical considerations: auditory warnings, inspection tasks

The distinction developed above is of clear practical importance. We can discriminate between different levels of a stimulus dimension very well, if they can be directly compared. However, if the task is to associate names or classes with particular stimuli then our ability is much more limited. For uni-dimensional stimuli it is very poor indeed.

Consider the problem of devising a set of auditory warning signals. This is a problem of absolute judgement so that the operator should not be required to learn a large number of different signals. In addition the task can be make easier by using signals that vary on a number of dimensions, e.g., pitch, interruption rate, on time and so on.

An inspection task might involve absolute or relative judgement. Imagine a computer-controlled inspection task involving the estimation of some uni-dimensional property such as length. If the operator has to remember the tolerance limits then this can be viewed as an absolute judgement task with three categories: too short, acceptable and too long. Alternatively, the operator may be given, as standards, an example of the minimum acceptable length and an example of the maximum acceptable length. This turns it into a task of relative judgement.

Any task which involves making judgements about the levels of stimulus dimensions will be subject to the limitations described above. As with the limitations in our ability to resolve high temporal and spatial frequencies, the problems resulting from these limitations will be relatively easy to diagnose and devise a cure for.

13.3.4 Practical considerations: colour displays, colour deficiencies

Colour is generally considered to be a multi-dimensional attribute and it is usual to specify a colour by its position in some 'colour space'. There are various colour spaces in common use. One uses the dimensions hue, saturation and brightness. Hue corresponds most closely to the wavelength of light. *Table 13.1* gives some wavelengths and the colour terms most people agree best exemplify the colour specified. Saturation describes the amount of white light added. A highly saturated colour has no white light added, a highly unsaturated colour is mostly white. Thus pink can be described as an unsaturated red. Brightness corresponds closely to the physical scale of intensity.

Other colour spaces are based on the fact any colour can be created by mixing some proportion of single wavelength red, green and blue. These may be more technically useful because they are numerically precise.

Table 13.1 Ten spectral colours which can be reliably identified without extended training

Wavelength (nm)	Label
642	red
610	orange
596	orange-yellow
582	yellow
556	yellow green
515	green
504	green-blue
494	blue-green
476	blue
430	violet

About 8% of the male population and 0.4% of the female population suffer from some kind of colour deficiency. It is somewhat confusing to call this colour blindness. People with the most common deficit, described as red/green colour blindness, have difficulty discriminating colours formed by mixing red and green light (shades of yellow and brown). Clearly people with an abnormally large JND for such colours will also have difficulty associating different names with them.

Problems with colour displays may be difficult to diagnose. That there is a problem will usually be readily apparent. Users will report a particular colour or colour combination is unpleasant, difficult to read or whatever. However, correcting the problem may require expert advice. In general, saturated reds, greens and blues give rise to more problems than de-saturated mixtures of these colours. Where users may have colour deficits it is also difficult to anticipate the problems which will arise. If the designer has colour deficits it is particularly important to prototype the display.

13.4 Human memory

13.4.1 Recognition and recall

Memory experiments have traditionally taken one or two forms. In a recall test the testee is required to produce the to-be-remembered material. So, a list of randomly chosen digits might be read out and after a short delay recalled, i.e., reproduced. In a recognition test the task is to distinguish between material presented in an earlier learning phase from new stimuli or 'lures'. For example, one might have been asked to read a list of sentences including sentences S1 and S2:

S1: The debutante was kissed by the hippy in the park.
S2: The policeman lectured the mayor in the street.

After a delay of one hour one would be presented with a further list of sentences, including:

S3: The policeman lectured the mayor in the street.
S4: The hippy kissed the debutante in the park.

The task is to assign a number between one and five to each sentence. If the testee feels it was definitely in the original list he or she should give it five and, if they feel it was definitely not, one. S3 should be rated five and S4, which is a lure, one.

The difficulty of a recall task depends on the effectiveness of the recall cue. 'Recall the list you just read' is less specific as a recall cue than 'recall the names of the animals in the list you just read' or 'which word was printed in red?'. If the testee makes the association used in the recall cue at the time of learning then a specific recall cue will generally be more effective than a general one. The difficulty of a recognition test depends on the nature of the lures. For example, people tend to remember the gist of a sentence rather than its precise wording. Lures like S4 (c.f. S1) are particularly effective. People tend to give sentences with same meaning as old sentences a high rating even when they are instructed to pay attention to the exact wording of the sentence. However, people are surprisingly good at some recognition tasks. One experiment involved showing 2560 colour slides for ten seconds each. Recognition was above 90% correct after a delay of several days.

It is commonly believed that recognition is always better than recall, so that the amount of learning required to give 100% recognition will always be less than that required to give 100% recall. However, it is possible to devise recall tasks which are easier than recognition tasks with the same materials.

Few everyday tasks are anything like the recognition task. When we say that we recognize a face, what we usually mean is that we can recall the context in which we previously saw it or the name of the person whose face it is. An identity parade is one of the few occasions where people are required to distinguish familiar stimuli from lures.

13.4.2 Short-term memory

Short-term memory for randomly chosen digits has been intensively studied by cognitive psychologists. A typical experiment involves writing down a sequence of digits immediately after hearing them. The task is repeated using the same digits in different orders. The longest sequence someone can recall in this way is described as their digit span. For adults this will be around seven. The immediate memory span for binary digits is slightly larger at nine and for monosyllabic words it is five. Notice that information theory cannot help us predict immediate memory span. The information contained in nine binary digits is much less than that in five randomly chosen words. Indeed the memory span for binary digits can be improved if one learns to recode sequences of binary digits. For example, a sequency of 16 binary digits can be recoded to four hexadecimal digits as it is read out, rehearsed as four hexadecimal digits and then recalled as a binary sequence.

As well as having a limited capacity, short-term memory requires active rehearsal to maintain it. If for example, one has just looked up a telephone number and is forced to pay attention to something else, perhaps by someone asking a question, one will forget the number. One way of demonstrating this characteristic of short-term memory is to have people do some task which prevents rehearsal. The data in *Figure 13.5* is from an experiment where people were asked to remember three consonants while counting backwards in threes. Less than 20% of the consonant sequences could be remembered after 12 seconds.

13.4.3 Long-term memory

Long-term memory function is quite different. There does not seem to be any limit on the quantity of information that can be stored, and once it is stored, it requires little conscious activity to keep it accessible. Long-term memory depends very much on relationships and structure. It is easy to store away and later retrieve some fact if it relates clearly to something we already know. Things that are completely novel or meaningless are very difficult to remember using long-term memory. This is what one might expect given the enormous quantities of information we all carry around with us. We all know the meaning of many thousand words and phrases, we know procedures for manipulating many kinds of objects and what to expect in many different kinds of situations. Like any large information store this knowledge has to be structured and organized. If some piece of information does not fit into that structure then it will be difficult to store and difficult to retrieve later.

There are a number of demonstrations of this characteristic of long-term memory. *Figure 13.6* depicts the results of an experiment which looked at the memory of experts, in this case, expert chess players. Chess masters were able to remember much more about the position of pieces on a board than club players. Their greater experience of chess allowed them to 'see' and remember more.

In one experiment, one could read the following passage. The reader should then write down what he or she can remember of it.

The procedure is actually quite simple. First you arrange items into different groups. Of course one pile might be sufficient depending on how much there is to do. If you have to go somewhere else due to lack of facilities, that is the next step; otherwise, you are pretty well set. It is important not to overdo things. That is, it is better to do too few things at once than too many. In the short run this may not seem important, but complications can easily arise. A mistake can be expensive as well. At first the whole procedure will seem complicated.

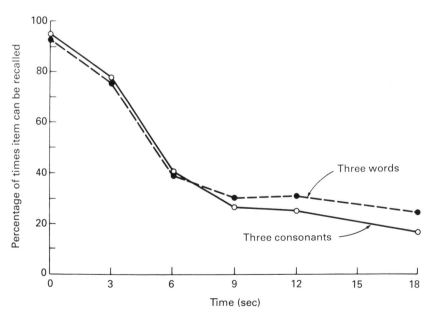

Figure 13.5   Recall of three words or three consonants when rehearsal is prevented by requiring the testee to count backwards in threes (from Lindsay and Norman, 1972)

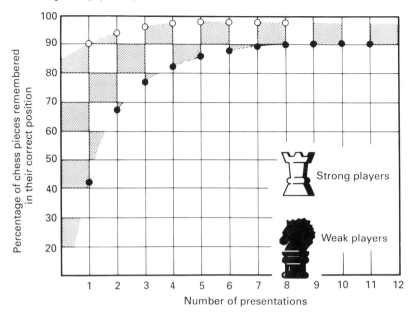

Figure 13.6 Recall of the position of chess pieces after some number of five second glimpses (from Baddeley, 1983). After only one five-second glimpse of a game in progress, expert chess players can remember the position of 90 per cent of the pieces on the board. Weaker players take five glimpses to reach this level. (Adapted from de Groot, 1966).

Soon, however, it will become just another fact of life. It is difficult to forsee any end to the necessity for this task in the immediate future, but then one never can tell. After the procedure is completed one arranges the material into different groups again. They can then be put into their appropriate places. Eventually they will be used once more and the whole cycle will then have to be repeated. However, that is a part of life. (Baddeley, 1983)

This passage was used in a memory experiment. Half of the people tested read it without a title just as you did. The other half were given the title 'Doing the washing' beforehand. The latter group rated the passage as being much more meaningful and were able to recall twice as much of it. Once one knows it is about doing the washing one can relate the actions described to an existing framework. This property of long-term memory can also work against you. *Figure 13.7* shows how drawings become corrupted in memory. The first drawing, an Egyptian hieroglyph, was presented to one person. After ten minutes study that person attempted to redraw it. The result is the second drawing. To amplify the changes made that drawing was then given to a second person to learn and redraw. His drawing was given to another, and so on. In the last drawing the hieroglyph has metamorphosed into a cat with a bow. This demonstration shows how meaningless features are remembered by relating them to meaningful frameworks and how this process can distort memory towards more meaningful memories. This has been called 'the effort after meaning'.

The above demonstrations show how long-term memory is intimately related to comprehension and meaning. Meaning can be thought of as a pattern of relationships and comprehension as the process of relating some stimulus to existing patterns of relationships stored in long-term memory. Long-term memory is modified by changing or adding to existing patterns of relationships. Knowledge is retrieved from long-term memory by activating patterns of relationships. Variation in the effectiveness of different recall cues and the difference between recall

and recognition can be explained in terms of differences in the way these patterns of relationships are activated. Much work in artificial intelligence and cognitive psychology has been devoted to devising representations capable of describing these processes.

Figure 13.7 Progressive distortions in the recall of a drawing (from Bartlett, 1932)

13.4.4 Practical considerations: menus, working memory

It is generally harder to recall and type the command needed to accomplish some task with a computer than to choose it from a list of possible commands presented on a menu. This is not just a matter of recognition being easier than recall because the same is probably true when a user is trying to guess the command, never having seen it before. Command sequences can be effective for novices and experts alike if aids to memory and learning are provided e.g., command summaries or 'help'.

Some human factors experts, who should know better, have recommended that menus should be limited to seven items on the basis that a larger number would exceed the immediate memory span. The short-term memory load when choosing an item from a menu is of course negligible. One might have to remember the key to be pressed for the time it takes to find it on the keyboard but if the selection is made via a pointing device, such as a mouse, there is not even this to remember. Experiments have shown that what limits the size of a menu is simply the space available. If the items in a menu are laid out so that the one required can be found without difficulty, then the larger the menu the better. In fact, immediate memory span is rarely a problem. If operators have difficulty remembering something they will jot it down on a scrap of paper. This sort of behaviour is probably symptomatic of a poorly engineered system. It should not be necessary for operators to read information simply to enter it again into another part of the system.

Short-term memory, as investigated in the experiments described above, has been identified with 'working memory'. Working memory holds information temporarily when it is necessary to do so as part of some cognitive task. Here the relevant property of short-term memory is that it requires active maintenance. For example, working memory may be used to keep track of where we are in some sequence of sub-tasks needed to perform some larger task. So, while dealing with our electronic mail we are distracted by a telephone call. Can the information that is lost from working memory about which messages have and have not been read be reconstructed after the phone call? In most systems this is possible because the messages are read in a fixed sequence and the most recently read message remains on the screen. Imagine a system where a list or 'directory' of messages is displayed after each message has been read, replacing all trace of the message on the display. To avoid the problem described above such a system would need to have some way of flagging which messages had and had not been read.

Working memory problems may be hard to diagnose. Users may report 'getting lost' or finding the system 'difficult' or 'requiring a lot of concentration'. They are unlikely to be able to tell you that the contents of their working memory have been lost because they have been prevented from rehearsal!

13.4.5 Practical considerations: rapid prototyping, metaphor

Most of the memory problems that users face have to do with long-term memory. The experiment with 'doing the washing' passage may seem contrived but the experience of the group not given a title may be very similar to that of novice computer users. People learning to use a system often do not have a suitable conceptual framework to which they can relate the menus, prompts and documentation. Further, they will make an 'effort after meaning' and draw all sorts of false conclusions. The problem for the designer and technical writer is to see the system through the eyes of the user. They might guess that the user will have a very different background but because they are not told precisely what the user does and does not know they are rarely in a position to do anything about it. The temptation is to design a system, or system documentation, for people like oneself. A user who is lacking concepts such as files, input buffers and so on will have great difficulty understanding and remembering how to use a system designed for someone who takes such concepts for granted. On the other hand, the user is likely to have a much richer understanding of the problem domain than the designer giving rise to further problems of communication.

The only really effective solution to this is for the designer to observe and inverview users working with prototypes and simulations. For example, one very effective way of refining the usability of a functional specification is to use it to write prototype documentation. Typical users then perform typical tasks using that documentation in a paper simulation. Users are taken through what screen will look like if they take certain actions and then asked what they should do next e.g., 'when you click here the screen will look like this . . . how would you move the cursor to the next data entry field?'. Where the documentation, prompts, menus, or even the way the task is structured does not correspond to the users' expectations they will make errors. They can then be questioned about the problem and suitable changes made. All this can be done before a single line of code is written. The experience of seeing at first hand the problems that users have will often provide genuine insights about how to improve the system.

Prototyping methods offer a way of detecting problems in referencing long-term memory and will often suggest solutions to those problems. When users have difficulty comprehending new concepts a metaphor may be useful. The most famous example is the desktop metaphor. A graphic display is used to represent files as 'documents' scattered on a surface. Files may be put into 'folders' or deleted by dragging them to a 'trash bin'. A metaphor works by suggesting a body of existing knowledge about one domain that can serve as a framework or structure for learning about a new domain. In this case the two domains are an office and an office information processing system. In any metaphor the analogy only applies to some of the properties of the two domains and the boundaries of any metaphor must be made clear. No one would expect to have to dust or polish the metaphorical desktop, but they might expect to find documents in the same position if they leave the desktop and then come back to it. However, if there is some good reason for violating the metaphor, *and it is apparent to the user*, there should be no problem in doing so. For example, one might explain how 'when you press this button or leave the desktop the documents are automatically put into a neat stack in order of priority'.

13.5 Quantitative changes in skill

13.5.1 The learning curve

Much of the work on human skills has been concerned with repetitive tasks of the kind that might be performed in an assembly line. However, the principles discussed in this section have also been shown to apply to skills which are predominantly perceptual e.g., transcribing Morse code or predominantly cognitive, for example, programming and mental arithmetic.

One such principle is the power law of practice. If the logarithm of the time it takes to perform some task is plotted against the logarithm of the number of times it has been performed a straight line will generally result. *Figure 13.8* was obtained by measuring the time it takes a skilled operative to make a cigar. The line only levels off after about four years of experience when performance approaches the minimum cycle time of the machine. This power function, rapid improvement at first which quickly (but not entirely) levels off is characteristic of all kinds of skill from golf to playing chess.

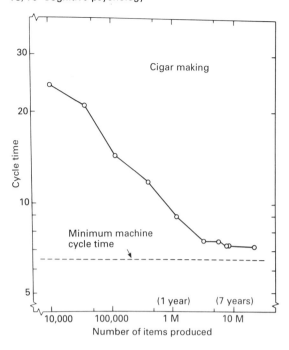

Figure 13.8 A learning curve (from Fitts and Posner, 1968)

13.5.2 Transfer

The starting point of a learning curve depends on many factors. One important one is whether there is positive or negative transfer from previous experience. If one imagines one is designing a graphic display used to control the flow through pumps in a chemical plant. The operator controls the pumps by manipulating a 'slider' (see Figure 13.9(a)). The knob on the slider is manipulated with a mouse to change the flow. Would one program the system so that moving the slider up increases or decreases flow? Most people would say up goes with more and down goes with less with this kind of control. Our experience is with controls which work this way rather than the other. If we choose the up-for-more arrangement then this experience will help operators to learn the new task. We say that there is positive transfer from previous experience with this kind of control. If we choose the down-for-more arrangement then the operator's previous experience will interfere with learning the new task, there will be negative transfer. Even when they have learned to work the controllers old habits may occasionally break through and errors will result, particularly in times of stress or after other distractions.

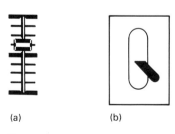

(a)   (b)

Figure 13.9 (a) a slider, (b) a switch

13.5.3 Practical considerations: population stereotypes, stimulus – response compatibility, consistency

When designing for positive transfer it should be remembered that different populations of users will have different experience. For example, the switch depicted in *Figure 13.9(b)* will be most commonly judged to be off in the USA and judged to be on in the UK. In the skills literature these conventions are known as 'population stereotypes'.

Stimulus–response compatibility is another kind of convention developed by experience. The earliest experiments on this involved pressing buttons when lights came on. The experiments varied the number of lights and buttons and the mapping between them. It was found that the simpler the spatial mapping the quicker the reponse was learned. In extreme cases the difference in speed of response was maintained after considerable amounts of practice. *Figure 13.10* depicts two experimental conditions which vary in stimulus–response compatibility. In *Figure 13.10(a)* the spatial mapping between lights and button is straightforward. The button to be pressed is the one immediately below the light that comes on. In *Figure 13.10(b)* the spatial mapping is more arbitrary, there is less stimulus response compatibility. An arrangement which looked like Figure 13.10(a) but where light was randomly assigned to buttons represents very poor stimulus response compatibility and would result in negative transfer. A similar problem arises if menu choices are signalled by pressing special function keys on the keyboard. Let us say that the function keys are arranged in two

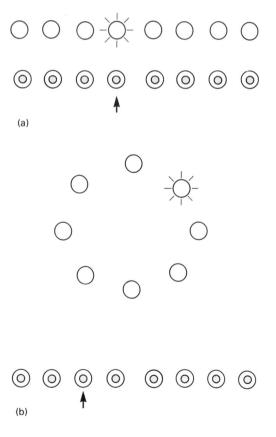

(a)

(b)

Figure 13.10 (a) lights and buttons with high stimulus–response compatibility, (b) lower stimulus response compatibility

vertical columns as on some IBM keyboards. It would make sense to maximize stimulus–response compatibility by arranging the menu items similarly in two columns instead of the more conventional single list.

Learning is facilitated by consistency within a system because it leads to positive transfer from one task to another. If a skill learned in one task context can be applied, without modification, in another task then the skills needed for the second task are already partially learned before one starts to do it. Conversely, problems will arise if a different procedure is followed when doing the same sub-task in different system contexts. As an example of the benefits of consistency, consider a user who has learned a procedure for selecting text in order to delete it. If the same procedure is used to select text which is to have its font changed, then the skills learned in the first task context can be transferred directly to the second. As an example of problems arising from inconsistency consider a bibliographic database known to the author. When searching the database the user can press <esc> at any point to return to the main menu from which all the main tasks are accessed. The user learns to signal 'I have finished this task and am ready to start another' by pressing this key. However for one task, updating a reference, task completion has to be signalled in another way or the file is not updated. Users have great difficulty with this and regularly go through long sequences of modifications only to find that no permanent changes have been made. The problem could possibly be fixed by having a 'done' and an 'abort' command, and making them available in all task contexts.

Transfer is seen by user organizations as an important issue in the design of new software. They demand that any new system should be 'upwardly compatible' with the systems it replaces. This applies to the user interface as much as it does to data files and hardware. Having trained a large population of operators they need to capitalize on that training and not to have it work against them. It may take considerable ingenuity to achieve this requirement without sacrificing the internal consistency needed to maximize the transfer of skills from one task to another.

13.6 Qualitative changes in skill

13.6.1 Phases of skill acquisition

As well as the quantitative changes with practice described by a learning curve, there are certain qualitative changes which can be described as phases of skill acquisition. The earliest stage is characterized by its cognitive nature. The problem is to understand the task; to work out what perceptual information is relevant to the task and what is not relevant, to break it down into sub-tasks and individual actions. This can be contrasted with the final phase where there is very little conscious processing required. Here thinking about what one is doing can be very disruptive to the smooth performace of the skill. This final phase has been called the autonomous phase. In between the early cognitive and the late autonomous phases there is an intermediate 'associative' phase. Here errors of various kinds are suppressed and sub-skills perfected.

Of course any higher level task, e.g., using a word processor, will involve acquiring a number of skills each of which can be broken down into various sub-skills. Each of these will have its cognitive, associative and autonomous phases which will last different periods of time. It is the large number of component skills which go to make up skilled performance that gives rise to a relatively smooth learning curve.

Computer analogies have proved useful when thinking about the changes that occur in the acquisition of skill. The early cognitive phase has been visualized as a program executed by a central executive. Components of this program are gradually separated out as subroutines which can be compiled for execution by independent processors, thus freeing the central executive for other work. More recent theories have identified the early phase with the operation of general cognitive processes on declarative knowledge. Declarative knowledge consists of facts and propositions. Work has to be done on this knowledge to infer a procedure which will achieve the task goal. The autonomous phase is identified with procedural knowledge. Here the procedures generated in the cognitive phase have been learned along with the conditions that call for their use. They no longer have to be inferred from declarative knowledge each time they are needed.

It would take many pages to develop the evidence for and history of these ideas. They rest on four reasonably well accepted principles:

1. There are general-purpose cognitive processes used to deal with novel situations. They are applied to declarative knowledge and seem to correspond to conscious thought or attention.
2. Our capacity to process information in this way is limited. We can only attend to one thing at a time and the speed and fluency of response is generally inferior to that in the autonomous phase.
3. Procedures can be learned so that we can respond rapidly and appropriately to the environment without engaging the slower general purpose mechanisms.
4. Attention or processing by some central executive is still required to sequence and trigger individual procedures. This means there is an advantage to composing several small procedures into a larger procedure. Before composition attentional control would be required to initiate each procedure. After composition there is only one procedure to be initiated.

13.6.2 Practical considerations: incremental learning

When we are learning a skill it may take all of our attention. So a learner driver will not be able to conduct a conversation and drive at the same time. Practised drivers have no difficulty in doing both these rather different tasks at the same time. Learning a complex skill may be beyond our attentional capacity altogether. The solution is to practise component skills separately until they become automated. The cognitive effort is then reduced to integrating these component skills. This is the idea behind many training schedules which use artificial exercises to practice individual skills before real tasks are attempted. However, in general, users prefer to do real tasks from the beginning. A well-engineered system can be learned in a piecemeal fashion. The functionality should be organized so that it is possible for users to learn the basic function needed to perform core tasks in some domain without concerning themselves with the rest of the system. Having automated the skills needed to perform those tasks they are then in a position to learn more advanced functions in the same domain or the core functionality of some other domain. For example, when learning to use a word processor it should be possible to learn the functions needed to create a minimally formatted one page text, e.g., a short memo, without having to consider browsing mechanisms, rulers and so on.

Many learners like to learn by exploration. This can be facilitated by hiding some of the more esoteric functionality from beginners. This prevents them from going down blind alleys and generally helps them to guess which command is needed. One popular word processor has implemented this idea as 'long' and 'short menus'. Beginners are advised to work with the cut down 'short menus'. When they are confident with the system they can switch on the 'long menus'.

13.6.3 Practical considerations: avoiding errors

Consider a commercial data entry system known to the author. This used the same responses to perform the different functions depending on whether the user was creating a new file ('data entry mode') or modifying an old one ('update mode'). In the former case pressing the right-arrow key caused the field to be filled with a default string. In the latter case it ended the updating session. From the point of view of the user looking at a single record the task was identical in each of these two modes, that was to see that each field contained the appropriate material. The display was also very similar with just a small visual signal to indicate which mode the system was in. It was thus not surprising that users found this system hard to learn and even after many hours of use regularly pressed the wrong keys.

The error described above can be thought of as a mode error. That is, the action taken could have been appropriate if the system had been in a different state or mode. The classic mode error occurred with early text editors which had replace and insert modes. A user typing when the system was in replace mode when he thought it was in insert mode could end up overwriting a large amount of text. As an example of an everyday mode error consider the following slip which is one of a large number collected by Reason (1979):

'My office phone rang. I picked up the receiver and bellowed "Come in" at it.'

Modes in computer systems are not necessarily a problem particularly if:

1. The user sees the purpose of the actions as being very different when taken in the different modes.
2. The mode change is effectively signalled.

So for example, a paint package may use the same mouse actions to perform very different functions such as free-hand drawing, drawing squares and filling areas with colour. Each of these 'tools' represents a different mode in which the mouse may be used. This is not a problem because the user sees each of these tasks as being very different and the mode change is clearly signalled by changing the mouse cursor. Since one cannot operate a mouse without looking at the mouse cursor this is an effective signal.

Mode errors may appear in the cognitive or autonomous phases of skill acquisition. A novice user is prevented from learning, an expert user is caught out when momentarily distracted or when working under stress.

Other errors are the result of the way procedural knowledge is organized and triggered and so only occur with well-practised skills. 'Capture errors' are a good example of this kind of problem. One's route home from work may be so well practised that the procedure followed requires almost no attentional monitoring. One day one sets off somewhere else, but the first part of the route is the same as the route home. The correct procedure is 'captured' by the 'going home procedure' and one takes the wrong turn and ends up at home instead of the intended destination.

A similar capture error may have been experienced by readers who used early versions of the Unix vi editor. The normal way of leaving this editor is to type :wq < return > . This response is very well practised. To save the file without exiting the editor one types :w < return > . The tasks are similar enough that the latter procedure will occasionally be 'captured' by the former and the user will find they have inadvertently left the editor. Capture errors can be cured by avoiding overlapping command sequences. Later versions of vi allows users to type ZZ in place of :wq < return > . There is no overlap between the procedures :w < return > and ZZ.

The framework developed in this section should allow a designer to classify and devise a cure for errors observed when prototyping or in the operation of an existing system which is to be updated. However, anticipating or avoiding errors in skilled usage is very difficult. It is also difficult to design systems which facilitate the acquisition of skill. The prototyping techniques described in Section 13.4.4 are effective in detecting mismatches in the way user and designer think about the system. This evaluation using simulations is relatively inexpensive to do and may be crucial in designing a system which has the right functionality and is comprehensible to the user. However, skilled performance can only develop with considerable practice with a working system. This makes errors in skilled performance expensive to detect. Also, by this stage in the design process major changes in the user interface may be very expensive to make. Very often the best one can do is to look carefully for internal inconsistencies (the same action having different meanings in similar task circumstances or the same sub-task requiring different actions depending on the larger task context) and to check that the consistencies with other systems and population sterotypes assumed actually apply to one's users.

13.7 Discussion

It is important to note that the viewpoint taken by cognitive psychologists is only one perspective on human behaviour. Viewing people as information processing mechanisms is no more dehumanizing than viewing them as organisms. Each perspective has its uses, just as each perspective necessarily presents a very narrow view of what a person is.

The same point applies to the view of usability presented in this chapter. Many computer applications come to grief not because there are cognitive problems in their use but rather because they give rise to social or organizational problems. One can think about this in terms of the scope of the system to be designed. A very narrow engineering point of view will only consider the hardware and software. The computer has input and output, some of which will come from or go to operators but worrying about the way the operator works is beyond the scope of design. This viewpoint is summarized in *Figure 13.11(a)*. The aim of this chapter is to broaden the scope of the system considered to include the operator (see *Figure 13.11(b)*). Rather than thinking about input and output devices we can now think about the user interface as a channel of communication between user and machine. But even this is a definition of very limited scope. To be really effective the system designed must include all the other individuals who interact with the operator and the organization within which they reside. An example will illustrate this point:

A British company installed a computerized cold store, which created new jobs requiring people to monitor the status of the cold store using visual display units, and to issue orders for moving and refilling pallets via a computer. The job was designed as manual work and given the highest wage grade in the factory. In order to minimize disruption to wage levels, the workers selected to carry out the work – which could involve sitting watching a VDU screen for up to eight hours – were those who were previously paid the highest existing manual grades, fork-lift truck drivers! (Clegg *et al.* 1988).

Of course, this short cut led to dissatisfaction and low productivity. If those responsible had viewed pay structures in the organization as properly within the scope of the system to be designed they might not have made this mistake.

Jobs need to be designed as carefully as any other component of the system. An operator who feels his job is too demanding or

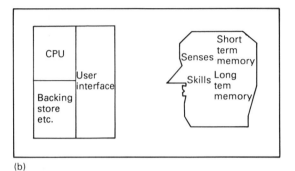

(a)

(b)

Figure 13.11 System components, (a) narrow scope, (b) broader scope

that he has been de-skilled is a symptom of design error quite as important as any of those discussed in this chapter. Information systems can also have subtle effects at an organizational level. They may cause shifts of power by centralizing or decentralizing control. Such shifts must be considered i.e., designed, and not occur as accidental side effects.

Figure 13.11(b) is misleading in another way. Talking about communication between computer and user may imply some sort of intention on the part of the machine. Intention is more reasonably ascribed to the designer of the machine. One can view the designer as communicating with the user through the medium of the machine, just as the author of a book communicates with a reader through the medium of print. The designer is not present when the machine is eventually used but neither is the author when a book is read. The importance of this analogy is that it suggests that we should judge computer applications in the same way as we judge a book such as an encyclopedia. While it is undoubtedly important to format the page properly, provide high quality printing and lots of illustrations, the encyclopedia will be judged on the correctness of the information it provides and the ability of the author to communicate the ideas it contains.

13.8 Further study

This chapter was concerned with how ideas from cognitive psychology might help in the design of effective computer systems and not a chapter on designing the user interface *per se*. Having read it one may be interested in reading more about the research on human–computer interaction. Schneiderman (1987) presents a coherent body of advice on the design of menus,

command languages and so on. Baecker and Buxton (1987) have collected an extensive and most useful set of readings. The text they have written to introduce each group of papers constitutes a clear and authoritative review of the area.

The need for iterative design has been a theme of the chapter. Ideas from cognitive psychology are to be used to diagnose and cure problems observed in prototypes and simulations. The reader interested in finding out more about rapid prototyping and iterative design techniques is referred to the two influential case studies provided by Gould and Lewis (1985) and Gould *et al.* (1987). A first step in design should be to evaluate the usability of the current methods for doing the job. Clegg *et al.* (1988) gives practical advice on 'how to evaluate your company's new technology'. As well as examining issues of usability it considers equipment, working conditions, job quality and organizational effectiveness.

Readers who are interested in finding out more about the human visual and auditory systems are referred to chapters in Monk (1984) by Thompson (1984) and Bailey (1984) respectively. Baddeley (1983) has written an informative and entertaining guide to human memory entitled *Your Memory – A User's Guide*. Research on the acquisition of skill is well reviewed by Hammond (1987) who also relates the findings in this area to guidelines for the design of interactive systems. Norman's (1981) review of action slips and Miller's (1956) review of absolute judgement and short-term memory are also well worth reading.

13.9 References

Baddeley, A. D. (1983) *Your Memory – A User's Guide*, Penguin

Baecker, R. M. and Buxton, A. S. (1987) *Readings in Human–Computer Interaction: a Multidisciplinary Approach*, Morgan Kaufman

Bailey, P. (1984) Speech communication: the problem and some solutions. In A. F. Monk (ed), *Fundamentals of Human–Computer Interaction*, Academic Press, pp. 193–220

Bartlett, F. C. (1932) *Remembering*, Cambridge University Press

Clegg, C., Warr, P., Green, T. *et al.* (1988) *People and Computers: How to Evaluate Your Company's New Technology*, Ellis Horwood

Fitts, P. M. and Posner, M. I. (1968) *Human Performance*, Brooks Cole

Gould, J. D. and Lewis, C. (1985) Designing for usability: key principles and what designers think. *Communications of the ACM*, **28**, 300–311

Gould, J. D., Boies, S. J., Levy, S., Richards, J. T. and Schoonard, J. (1987) The 1984 Olympic message system: a test of behavioural principles of system design. *Communications of the ACM*, **30**, 758–769

Hammond, N. V. (1987) Principles from the psychology of skill acquisition. In M. M. Gardiner and B. Christie (eds.) *Applying Cognitive Psychology to User–Interface Design*, Wiley, pp. 163–187

Lindsay, P. H. and Norman, D. A. (1972) *Human Information Processing*, Academic Press

Miller, G. A. (1956) The magical number seven, plus or minus two: some limits on our capacity for processing information. *Psychological Review*, **63**, 81–97

Monk, A. F. (1984) *Fundamentals of Human–Computer Interaction*, Academic Press

Norman, D. A. (1981) Categorization of action slips. *Psychological Review*, **88**, 1–15

Reason, J. T. (1979) Actions not as planned. In G. Underwood and R. Stevens (eds) *Aspects of Consciousness*, Academic Press

Schiffman, H. R. (1976) *Sensation and Perception: an Integrated Approach*, John Wiley

Schneiderman, B. (1987) *Designing the User Interface: Strategies for Effective Human–Computer Interaction*, Addison-Wesley

Thompson, P. (1984) Visual perception: an intelligent system with limited bandwidth. In A. F. Monk (ed), *Fundamentals of Human–Computer Interaction*, Academic Press, pp. 5–33

14

Information theory

W. Freeman
University of York

Contents

14.1 Introduction

Information theory involves the definition of a measure of information, which enables one to model, usefully and precisely, the ways in which information can be stored, retrieved, transmitted, transformed, corrupted and lost. The term 'information theory' has been applied to several theories that are purely mathematical, thus differing from physical theories such as those of optics, radio and transmission lines.

The classical form of the theory, due to Shannon (1948, 1949, 1950, 1951), can usefully be regarded as a branch of the theory of probability. A probabilistic function, called entropy, is developed as a measure of the quantity of information obtained per trial of an experiment which is regarded as an information source. The entropy function can be developed to measure the entropy of two experiments, regarded as the components of a compound experiment, with the components being, possibly, independent, or partially or totally dependent. This extension immediately generalizes to as many experiments as are required. By applying the entropy function to the state sequences of a Markov chain, it is possible to model ergodic information sources with finite internal memory. Also, by applying it to the input and output of a communication channel, it is possible to model the properties (throughput, loss, noise) of such a channel either without or with internal memory – the former case only being considered here.

Straightaway it must be said that the scope of application of Shannon's information theory is universal (all systems must obey its rules, just as they must obey the second law of thermodynamics); and its scope of usefulness is large. Beyond helping one to achieve efficient and reliable telecommunications, it judges and limits the effectiveness of data compression techniques applied to files, databases and indeed any other data structures. From its very earliest days, the theory has been applied very widely: technically, to psychology, as in Attneave (1959), and suggestively, to the process of literary translation, as in Richards (1951) – this last example coming complete with Shannon's diagram of a channel! For a recent treatment of its application to abstract structures that are of use in the social sciences, see Krippendorff (1986). It is not sensible to try to list the areas of useful application; it is best to leave it that all systems, including of course those engineered in software, are constrained by information theory, and most can have their design guided both by its ideas and by its equations.

It is likely, though, that 'alternative' information theories will become ever more important, especially in applications where the data held are fuzzy or incomplete or partially inconsistent, and where the algorithms are heuristic. The real-life extraction of information from the human and physical world is a messy business, and its representation, processing and presentation – and especially its uses in decision-making, such as with expert systems – call for new ways of computing its properties. These points are taken up in Section 14.8.

Section 14.8, and the ends of several other sections, provide pointers into the literature for further reading, but the following introductory texts may be mentioned here: Chambers (1985), Cattermole (1986), Llewellyn (1987) – this one particularly aimed at the software specialist – and Welsh (1988).

14.1.1 Notation

For the meanings of the symbols $\emptyset$, Ω, $\mathscr{P}$, $\Rightarrow$, $\rightarrow$, A, $[.]_i$, $[\![.]\!]_i$, $\dagger$, $\mathcal{E}$, $\underline{\mathcal{E}}$, $\blacktriangle$, $\blacksquare$, and $\blacktriangledown$, see Chapter 5, above, on probability theory.

Some inter-related items of notation will be defined here. The Kronecker product, $A \otimes B$, of two matrices A and B is given by:

$$A \otimes B \triangleq ([\![[a_{i,j} B]_j]\!]_i)$$

For example:

$$
\begin{bmatrix} p & q \\ r & s \end{bmatrix} \otimes \begin{bmatrix} u & v \\ w & x \\ y & z \end{bmatrix} =
\begin{bmatrix}
pu & pv & qu & qv \\
pw & px & qw & qx \\
py & pz & qy & qz \\
ru & rv & su & sv \\
rw & rx & sw & sx \\
ry & rz & sy & sz
\end{bmatrix}
$$

This product is associative, but not commutative. Notice that there is no conformity requirement; any pair of matrices can form a Kronecker product. The definition just given applies, most obviously, to matrices of numbers. When forming the Kronecker product of matrices of sets, their components should be multiplied by intersection, as, for example:

$$(a\, b\, c) \otimes (r\, s) = (a \cap r\ a \cap s\ b \cap r\ b \cap s\ c \cap r\ c \cap s)$$

The kth Kronecker power, $A^{[k]}$, of a matrix A, for non-negative integral k, is given by $A^{[0]} \triangleq 1$ (or $A^{[0]} \triangleq \Omega$, as appropriate) and:

$$1 \leqslant \lambda \ \rightarrow\ A^{[\lambda]} \triangleq A^{[\lambda-1]} \otimes A$$

For more on Kronecker operations, see Graham (1981).

In Chapter 5, an experiment, X, say, was regarded as a *set of* outcomes, $X \triangleq \{[x_i]_{i=0}^{l-1}\}$. Here, however, it will often be more convenient to regard it as a *vector*, $X \triangleq ([x_i]_{i=0}^{l-1})$. Then we can write:

$$X \otimes Y = ([[x_i \cap y_j]_{j=0}^{n-1}]_{i=0}^{m-1})$$

By convention, X^{Λ} will refer to Λ *successive* observations of X, thus:

$$0 \leqslant \Lambda \ \rightarrow\ X^{\Lambda} \triangleq \overset{\Lambda}{\underset{r=1}{\bigotimes}} X_{-\Lambda+r}$$

We shall define PD(X) as giving the probability distribution of X:

$$\text{PD}(X) \triangleq ([p(x_i)]_{i=0}^{m-1})$$

and continue to write $\hat{X}$ for PD(X) where a single variable is involved. It is important to take notice of the distinction between the typical components of:

$$\text{PD}(X \otimes Y) \ - \ \text{typical component: } p(x_i \cap y_j)$$

on the one hand, and:

$$\hat{X} \otimes \hat{Y} \ - \ \text{typical component: } p(x_i)p(y_j)$$

on the other. Furthermore:

$$\hat{X} \otimes \hat{Y} = \text{PD}(X \otimes Y) \Leftrightarrow X \blacksquare Y$$

14.2 Surprise and dependence

The fundamental assumptions upon which Shannon's measure is founded are (1) that we know *a priori* the set of all possible messages that can be sent from the source on a given occasion, and the probabilities of their being chosen for sending, and (2) that improbable messages are more informative than probable ones. This latter assertion can be pushed further: what is more improbable than something else will be a greater surprise to us when it happens; so, we may say that surprise is a measure of information. If an event, ξ, has probability $p(\xi)$, then we may express improbability either as its complement: $1 - p(\xi)$, or as its reciprocal: $1/p(\xi)$. Since we prefer that the impossible event, $\varnothing$, be infinitely improbable, we employ the measure $1/p(\xi)$. Moreover, the latter measure will permit us to define the surprise, $\sigma(\xi)$, of an event ξ in such a way that it satisfies the following relationships that experience should lead us to demand of any such measure:

$$\sigma(\xi) = +\infty \Leftrightarrow \xi = \varnothing$$

$$0 \leqslant \sigma(\xi) \quad \text{with equality iff } \xi = \Omega$$

$$\sigma(\xi \cap \upsilon) \leqslant \sigma(\xi) + \sigma(\upsilon) \quad \text{w.e.iff } \xi \blacksquare \upsilon$$

The last of these inequalities, which expresses the important property of sub-additivity, says that the surprise from the joint occurrence of two events cannot exceed the sum of their surprises observed separately, and attains equality with it if and only if the events are independent. It follows that such a measure can be constructed by defining:

$$\sigma_\beta(\xi) \triangle \log_\beta \left(\frac{1}{p(\xi)} \right)$$

where β is greater than unity. It is of interest to ask, when does $\sigma_\beta(\xi) = 1$? The answer is that this occurs when $p(\xi) = 1/\beta$. The logarithmic base, β, is a scale factor that we can choose in order to adjust the level of improbability that we wish to regard as causing unit surprise.

Unless otherwise stated, we shall assume natural logarithms, and, having chosen $\beta = e$, we write $\sigma(\xi) \triangle \sigma_e(\xi)$. So, here, $\sigma(\xi) = 1$ when $p(\xi) = 1/e$. By convention, the choice of $\beta = e$ is made explicit by stating quantities in 'natural units'. Had we chosen $\beta = 2$, the units would have been 'bits'; and for $\beta = 10$, 'Hartleys' (cf. Hartley, 1928). Of course, all these 'units' are physically dimensionless.

The relationship between $p(\xi)$, $\sigma(\xi)$ and $p(\xi)\sigma(\xi)$ is shown in *Figure 14.1*. The importance of the last of these quantities will be seen later. For the moment, we note that we shall require, and therefore define:

$$p(\varnothing)\sigma(\varnothing) \triangle \lim_{p \to +0} p \log \frac{1}{p} = 0$$

Almost all significant statements about information involve either the information in one event given the outcome of another, or the information in common between two events. So it is useful to define corresponding surprises: conditional surprise and joint surprise. Nevertheless, as the joint surprise can be negative in value, we should call it the 'synergy' between the two events. We therefore define, as the conditional surprise of the event υ given the outcome of ξ:

$$\sigma(\upsilon|\xi) \triangle \log \frac{1}{p(\upsilon|\xi)} = \log \frac{p(\xi)}{p(\xi \cap \upsilon)}$$

and, as the synergy between ξ and υ:

$$\sigma(\xi,\upsilon) \triangle \log \frac{p(\xi \cap \upsilon)}{p(\xi)p(\upsilon)}$$

The 'ways up' of the ratios whose logarithm is taken may seem somewhat arbitrary. Formally, indeed, they are. In an axiomatic treatment, such choices would be implicit in the axioms. Here,

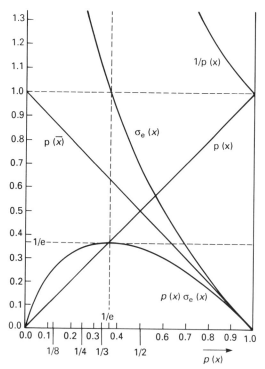

Figure 14.1 Complementary probability, improbability, surprise and weighted surprise, to base e, of an event x

however, in this heuristic treatment, the way up is chosen in each case simply to give the surprise or synergy a sign appropriate for its use as a model of the behaviour of information in the real world. These measures are then related in ways that are intuitively satisfying. For example:

$$0 \leqslant \sigma(\upsilon|\xi) \quad \text{w.e.iff } \xi \subseteq \upsilon$$

$$\sigma(\upsilon|\xi) = +\infty \Leftrightarrow \xi \mathbf{A} \upsilon$$

$$\sigma(\upsilon|\xi) = 1 \Leftrightarrow \frac{p(\xi \cap \upsilon)}{p(\xi)} = \frac{1}{e}$$

$$\sigma(\upsilon|\xi) = \sigma(\xi \cap \upsilon) - \sigma(\xi)$$

$$\sigma(\xi \cap \upsilon) = \sigma(\xi) + \sigma(\upsilon|\xi)$$
$$= \sigma(\upsilon) + \sigma(\xi|\upsilon)$$

$$\sigma(\upsilon|\xi) \leqslant \sigma(\xi \cup \upsilon) \quad \text{w.e.iff } (\xi = \Omega) \vee (\upsilon = \varnothing)$$

$$\sigma(\xi, \upsilon) = \sigma(\upsilon, \xi)$$

$$\sigma(\xi, \upsilon) = \sigma(\upsilon) \Leftrightarrow \xi \subseteq \upsilon$$

$$\sigma(\xi, \upsilon) = -\infty \Leftrightarrow \xi \mathbf{A} \upsilon$$

$$\sigma(\xi, \upsilon) = \sigma(\upsilon) - \sigma(\upsilon|\xi)$$
$$= \sigma(\xi) - \sigma(\xi|\upsilon)$$
$$= \sigma(\xi) + \sigma(\upsilon) - \sigma(\xi \cap \upsilon)$$

$$\sigma(\xi, \upsilon) \begin{cases} <0 \\ =0 \\ >0 \end{cases} \Leftrightarrow \begin{cases} \xi \blacktriangledown \upsilon \\ \xi \blacksquare \upsilon \\ \xi \blacktriangle \upsilon \end{cases}$$

It is especially worth the reader's while to contemplate the last two of these.

14.3 Entropy and information

We now regard an experiment as a source of information. Strictly speaking, it is a discrete memoryless source (DMS), since our assumptions about simple probability distributions (derived from Section 5.2.2) still stand. We define the entropy, $H(X)$, of such a source, X, or of its distribution, $\hat{X}$, to be the expected value of the surprise of that distribution:

$$H(X) \triangleq H(\hat{X}) \triangleq \mathop{\mathcal{E}}_{i=0}^{m-1} \sigma(x_i) = \sum_{i=0}^{m-1} p(x_i) \log \frac{1}{p(x_i)}$$

where $\hat{X} = ([p(x_i)]_{i=0}^{m-1})$. Hence:

$$0 \leqslant H(X) \quad \text{w.e.iff } X \text{ is deterministic}$$

that is, with equality if and only if $p(x_k) = 1$ for some k: whereupon $p(x_i) = 0$, for all $i \neq k$. By invoking the convexity of the logarithm function, it can easily be shown that:

$$H(X) \leqslant \log m \quad \text{w.e.iff } X \text{ is uniform}$$

Moreover:

$$H([p(x_i)]_i) = H([p(x_{\pi(i)})]_i)$$

for any permutation $\pi(.)$, and:

$$H([p(x_i)]_i) = H([p(x_i)]_i, 0)$$

If two sources X and Y have the same entropy, then we say that they (or, equivalently, their distributions) are isentropic, and write $X \curvearrowright Y$ (or $\hat{X} \curvearrowright \hat{Y}$).

It will be convenient to define $D(m, k)$ to be a deterministic source of multiplicity m whose outcome d_k is certain, that is:

$$\hat{D}(m, k) \triangleq ([\delta_{i,k}]_{i=0}^{m-1})$$

where δ is Kronecker's delta. When they are arbitrary, or can be deduced from the context, we shall omit k, or both m and k. Similarly, we define $U(m)$ to be a uniform source of multiplicity m:

$$\hat{U}(m) \triangleq ([1/m]_{i=0}^{m-1})$$

and omit m when it is arbitrary or deducible. We then have:

$$0 = H(D) \leqslant H(X) \leqslant H(U(m)) = \log m$$

We shall show 'X is deterministic' by writing $X \curvearrowright D$, and 'X is uniform' by $X \curvearrowright U$.

Notice that entropies are expressed in the same units as were used for surprise. Here, we use natural units, indicating that all logarithms, surprises and entropies are to base e. (If we wish to use another base on some occasion, then we shall write $H_\beta(X) \triangleq \mathcal{E}\sigma_\beta(x)$.) The following two example distributions are taken from Section 5.2.3:

$$H(X) = H\left(\frac{2}{7}, \frac{1}{7}, \frac{4}{7}\right) \approx 0.9557 \text{ natural units}$$

$$H(Y) = H\left(\frac{11}{21}, \frac{10}{21}\right) \approx 0.6920 \text{ natural units}$$

Compare these with the uniform sources of similar multiplicities: $H(U(3)) \approx 1.0986$ and $H(U(2)) \approx 0.6932$ natural units. As a further example, with a countable infinity of outcomes, consider

the coin-tossing experiment discussed in Section 5.6. We are to toss a fair coin, and repeat the process as long as it keeps on showing 'tails'; when 'heads' occurs, we are to stop. Suppose that we have to convey to someone the number of tails, N, that occurs before the first head. How much information shall we transfer in doing so? Every number is permitted. If all were equally probable, then the statement of the number of tails would have infinite information content. Yet that is clearly not the case here. At each toss, if the coin is fair, tails will occur with probability $1/2$. The probability distribution is therefore given by $p(N = i) = 2^{-i-1}$, so that:

$$H(N) = \sum_{i=0}^{\infty} p(N = i) \log \frac{1}{p(n = i)}$$

$$= \sum_{i=1}^{\infty} 2^{-i} i \log 2 = 2 \log 2 \approx 1.3863 \text{ natural units}$$

Graphs of entropy against distribution are given in *Figures 14.2* and *14.3*, for experiments of two and three outcomes respectively. Notice that the locus of the distribution is contained, by the condition $0 \leqslant p(x)$, within a regular simplex of m vertices, in the $m-1$ dimensions that remain of its degrees of freedom after the constraint

$$\sum_{i=0}^{m-1} p(x_i) = 1$$

has been applied (see Kendall, 1961). The entropy $(m-1)$-variety is symmetric under interchange of vertices, but is not spherically symmetric except, trivially, when $m \leqslant 2$. (In particular, in Figure 14.3, the isentropes are symmetric under rotation through $2\pi/3$, but they are not circles.) The isentropes are, nevertheless, everywhere convex, whatever the number of dimensions. It is easily shown, for any m, letting $\hat{X} = (\cdots, p, q)$, with $p \leqslant q$ and $0 < \delta < q - p$, that:

$$H(\hat{X}) \leqslant H(\cdots, p + \delta, q - \delta)$$

The apex of the entropy $(m-1)$-variety, representing maximum entropy, lies above the centroid of the simplex, which represents uniformity of the experiment's distribution. Although the sur-

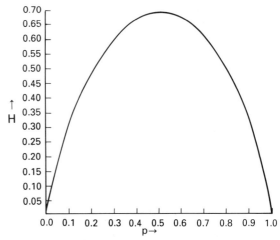

Figure 14.2 Entropy in one dimension (two outcomes, one degree of freedom)

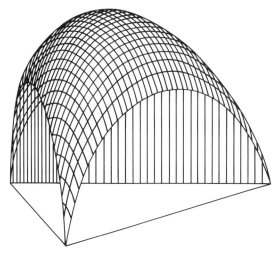

Figure 14.3 Entropy in two dimensions (three outcomes, two degrees of freedom)

face rises with infinite gradient at the vertices, nevertheless in the broad neighbourhood of the apex it is relatively flat and level – flat, that is, in the sense of having little curvature, and level as having a gradient of small magnitude. This means that an experiment need not be accurately uniform in order to have an entropy near to the maximum possible.

Given the inequality $0 \leqslant H(X) \leqslant \log m$, and the fact that both extrema are in general attainable, it is useful to define the following:

$$\eta(X) \triangleq \frac{H(X)}{\log m} \qquad \text{the efficiency of } X$$

$$\bar{H}(X) \triangleq \log m - H(X) \qquad \text{the absolute redundancy of } X$$

$$\bar{\eta}(X) \triangleq \frac{\bar{H}(X)}{\log m} = 1 - \eta(X) \qquad \text{the relative redundancy of } X$$

Notice that $H(.)$ and $\log(.)$ must always be expressed to the same base, and that $\eta(.)$ and $\bar{\eta}(.)$ are then independent of that base. Clearly:

$$0 = \eta(D) \leqslant \eta(X) \leqslant \eta(U) = 1$$

and:

$$0 = \bar{\eta}(U) \leqslant \bar{\eta}(X) \leqslant \bar{\eta}(D) = 1$$

Notice that $H_m(X) = H_e(X)/(\log_e m)$, so that the efficiency of a source is equal to its entropy expressed to a base equal to its multiplicity. The three examples given earlier have efficiencies $\eta(X) \approx 0.8699$, $\eta(Y) \approx 0.9983$ and $\eta(N) = 0$ respectively. The last of these shows that, while $X \sim D \Leftrightarrow H(X) = 0$, and $X \sim D \Rightarrow \eta(X) = 0$, the latter has '$\Leftarrow$' only if the number of outcomes, $m = \#X$, is finite. Taking up the earlier point about flatness near the apex, consider the following:

$$H\left(\frac{4}{12}, \frac{4}{12}, \frac{4}{12}\right) \approx 1.0986 \qquad \eta\left(\frac{4}{12}, \frac{4}{12}, \frac{4}{12}\right) \approx 1.0000$$

$$H\left(\frac{3}{12}, \frac{4}{12}, \frac{5}{12}\right) \approx 1.0776 \qquad \eta\left(\frac{3}{12}, \frac{4}{12}, \frac{5}{12}\right) \approx 0.9808$$

$$H\left(\frac{3}{12}, \frac{3}{12}, \frac{6}{12}\right) \approx 1.0397 \qquad \eta\left(\frac{3}{12}, \frac{3}{12}, \frac{6}{12}\right) \approx 0.9464$$

$$H\left(\frac{2}{12}, \frac{4}{12}, \frac{6}{12}\right) \approx 1.0114 \qquad \eta\left(\frac{2}{12}, \frac{4}{12}, \frac{6}{12}\right) \approx 0.9206$$

Now, as mentioned previously, the entropies of two partly dependent sources are of profound practical importance – especially in data compression, transmission and security. We can define the total entropy of two sources, X and Y, without any new principle being involved, as $H(X \cup Y) \triangleq H(X \otimes Y)$. Then, taking $m = \#X$ and $n = \#Y$, we have:

$$H(X \cup Y) = \sum_{i=0}^{m-1} \sum_{j=0}^{n-1} \sigma(x_i \cap y_j) = H(Y \cup X)$$

$$0 \leqslant H(X \cup Y) \quad \text{w.e.iff } X \otimes Y \curvearrowright D(mn)$$

$$H(X \cup Y) \leqslant \log mn \quad \text{w.e.iff } X \otimes Y \curvearrowright U(mn)$$

$$H(X) \leqslant H(X \cup Y) \quad \text{w.e.iff } X \Rrightarrow Y$$

$$H(X \cup Y) \leqslant H(X) + H(Y) \quad \text{w.e.iff } X \blacksquare Y$$

Notice that $X \otimes Y \curvearrowright U(mn)$ implies that $X \curvearrowright U(m)$ and $Y \curvearrowright U(n)$, but the converse does not hold.

Quite pragmatically, we define the conditional entropy of source Y, given the outcome of source X, by:

$$H(Y|X) \triangleq H(X \cup Y) - H(X)$$

Then:

$$H(Y|X) = \sum_{i=0}^{m-1} \sum_{j=0}^{n-1} \sigma(y_j|x_i)$$

$$0 \leqslant H(Y|X) \quad \text{w.e.iff } X \Rrightarrow Y$$

$$H(Y|X) \leqslant H(Y) \quad \text{w.e.iff } X \blacksquare Y$$

Similarly, we define the mutual entropy of sources X and Y by:

$$H(X \cap Y) \triangleq H(X) + H(Y) - H(X \cup Y)$$

Then:

$$H(X \cap Y) = \sum_{i=0}^{m-1} \sum_{j=0}^{n-1} \sigma(x_i, y_j) = H(Y \cap X)$$

$$0 \leqslant H(X \cap Y) \quad \text{w.e.iff } X \blacksquare Y$$

$$H(X \cap Y) \leqslant H(Y) \quad \text{w.e.iff } X \Rrightarrow Y$$

The joint entropy is a measure of the information that we are told by X or by Y (or by both of them), whereas the mutual entropy measures what we are told by X and Y. Mutual entropy is equal to expectation of synergy. It is symmetric between the two sources, and represents the informaton that is in common between them. If it is to be non-zero (in which case it is positive), the sources must be at least partially dependent (see Section 5.2.3).

A great number of useful and pleasing inequalities now

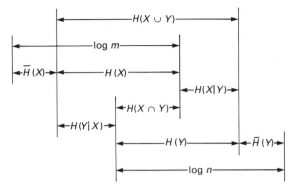

Figure 14.4 Total, conditional and common entropies of two sources

follow, but rather than list some of them, it is easier to illustrate all of them. They can be derived from *Figure 14.4*, in which, by convention, each pair of vertical lines may coincide, but may not be strictly reversed in order. All the quantities illustrated are non-negative.

As an example, consider the following space, which was used in Section 5.2.3:

$$
\begin{array}{cc}
 & y_0 \quad y_1 \\
x_0 & 1 \quad 5 \\
x_1 & 0 \quad 3 \\
x_2 & 10 \quad 2
\end{array} \Biggr\} \#x_i \cap y_j
$$

Here:

$$H(X) = H\left(\frac{6}{21}, \frac{3}{21}, \frac{12}{21}\right) \approx 0.9557$$

$$H(Y) = H\left(\frac{11}{21}, \frac{12}{21}\right) \approx 0.6920$$

$$H(X \cup Y) = H\left(\frac{1}{21}, \frac{5}{21}, \frac{3}{21}, \frac{10}{21}, \frac{2}{21}\right) \approx 1.3419$$

$$H(X|Y) = H(X \cup Y) - H(Y) \approx 0.6499$$

$$H(Y|X) = H(X \cup Y) - H(X) \approx 0.3862$$

$$H(X \cap Y) = H(X) + H(Y) - H(X \cup Y) \approx 0.3058$$

It is important to realize that $H(Y|X)$ is *not* a measure of 'the entropy of Y once we know X'. That would be $H(Y|X_t = x_0)$, $H(Y|X_t = x_1)$ or $H(Y|X_t = x_2)$, according to what is that value of X that we actually know. Rather, $H(Y|X)$ is our expectation *now*, ignorant of X, of what will be the entropy of Y when, at some time in the future, we shall have known X.

For use in the next section, we shall need entropies defined on more than two sources. These are defined in an obvious way, so that:

$$H(X \cup Y \cup Z) \triangleq H(X \otimes Y \otimes Z)$$

$$H(Z|X \cup Y) \triangleq H(X \cup Y \cup Z) - H(X \cup Y)$$

$$
\begin{aligned}
H(X \cap Y \cap Z) &\triangleq H(Y \cap Z) - H(Y \cap Z|X) \\
&= H(Z) - H(Z|Y) - H(Z|X) \\
&\quad + H(Z|X \cup Y) \\
&= H(X) + H(Y) + H(Z) \\
&\quad - H(X \cup Y) - H(X \cup Z) - H(Y \cup Z) \\
&\quad + H(Z \cup Y \cup Z)
\end{aligned}
$$

and so on. But beware that quantities involving the mutual entropy of three or more sources can be negative. As an example, consider the following refinement of the previous space:

$$
\begin{array}{ccccc}
 & y_0 \cap z_0 & y_0 \cap z_1 & y_1 \cap z_0 & y_1 \cap z_1 \\
x_0 & 1 & 0 & 1 & 4 \\
x_1 & 0 & 0 & 2 & 1 \\
x_2 & 3 & 7 & 2 & 0
\end{array}
$$

This gives:

$$H(X) + H(Y) + H(Z) \approx 2.3306$$

$$H(X \cup Y) + H(X \cup Z) + H(Y \cup Z) \approx 4.3239$$

$$H(X \cup Y \cup Z) \approx 1.8429$$

$$H(X \cap Y \cap Z) \approx -0.1504$$

For a discussion of the reasons for this fact, and its interpretation, see Abramson (1963).

It will not have escaped the reader's notice that, if we take any equation or inequality among the sizes of arbitrary sets X, Y and Z, then if the sets are replaced by similarly named sources, set difference by '|', and set size $\#(.)$ by the entropy operation $H(.)$, all the equations and inequalities will continue to hold. For example, the result concerning $H(X \cap Y \cap Z)$ can be obtained by applying these changes to a statement of the inclusion–exclusion principle. This has no practical significance, but is of tremendous mnemonic usefulness; see also Feinstein (1958).

Finally, a composite information source $(X \otimes Y)$ may, in an obvious way, be regarded as comprising the three independent sources $(X|Y)$, $(Y|X)$ and $(X \cap Y)$. It is of interest to ask whether there is a coding system (see Section 14.6) that can actually separate out the mutual information $(X \cap Y)$ from the total information $(X \cup Y)$. Gács and Körner (1973) have shown that this is possible only to a very small extent.

14.4 Models of discrete sources with memory (DSMs)

Discrete information sources with memory are most conveniently modelled by means of Markov chains (see Section 5.3), and, as a direct development from them, Markov sources. Using Markov chains, suppose that we observe the successive states of the chain Λ at a time, allowing the dependencies of the probabilities of successive states to influence the probabilities of the words of length Λ (called Λ-grams) that we observe, but ignoring dependencies between such words. We then say that we are observing the Λth extension, $X^\wedge$, of the original chain, X. If $m = \#X$, then the multiplicity of the Λth extension is $m^\wedge = \#X^\wedge$.

It is useful to distinguish four kinds of entropy of such an extended chain. First, the Λ-gram entropy, $H(X^\wedge)$, is given by:

$$H(X^\wedge) = H\left(\bigcup_{r=0}^{\Lambda-1} X_{t-r}\right)$$

entropy units per Λ-gram; from this we immediately derive the specific Λ-gram entropy, $H(X^\wedge)/\Lambda$ entropy units per single-symbol observation; next, the Λth marginal entropy, $H^\wedge(X)$, is defined by:

$$1 \leqslant \Lambda \rightarrow H^\wedge(X) \triangleq H\left(X_t \Big| \bigcup_{r=1}^{\Lambda-1} X_{t-r}\right) = H(X^\wedge) - H(X^{\wedge-1})$$

entropy units per single-symbol observation; and finally the asymptotic entropy, $H^\infty(X)$, is defined by:

$$H^\infty(X) \triangleq \lim_{\Lambda \to \infty} H^\Lambda(X)$$

entropy units per single-symbol observation, if such a limit exists.

Of these, the Λ-gram entropy measures the amount of information expected from an observation of one Λ-gram (i.e. the total of Λ successive single-symbol observations, or, equivalently, one observation of the Λth extension) of a hitherto unobserved chain. The specific Λ-gram entropy is that same measure averaged over the Λ single symbols in the Λ-gram. The Λth marginal entropy is the measure of the information which we expect to gain from a Λth single-symbol observation once the preceding $\Lambda - 1$ symbols have been observed and taken into account. Finally, when the entire history of an immemorially ancient chain is to be taken into account, the appropriate measure for the information expected from one further observation is the asymptotic entropy.

It follows immediately that $H(X^0) = 0$. (Notice that $H^0(X)$ is not defined.) Writing $\hat{X}$ for the eigendistribution of the chain, it is easy to see that $H(X^1) = H^1(X) = H(\hat{X})$, so that we may write $H(X)$ indifferently. Furthermore:

$$H(X^\Lambda) = \sum_{r=1}^{\Lambda} H^r(X) \leqslant \Lambda \log m$$

$$H^{\Lambda+1}(X) \leqslant H^\Lambda(X) \leqslant H(X) \leqslant \log m$$

$$H^\infty(X) = \sum_{i=0}^{m-1} H(\hat{T}_i) \leqslant \log m$$

where $\hat{T}_i$ is the ith row of the transition matrix T of the chain X. From the Markov property (see Section 5.3) it then follows that:

$$H^\Lambda(X) = \begin{cases} H(X) & \text{when } \Lambda = 1 \\ \\ H^\infty(X) & \text{when } 2 \leqslant \Lambda \end{cases}$$

so that:

$$\frac{H(X^\Lambda)}{\Lambda} \to H^\infty(X) \quad \text{as } \Lambda \to \infty$$

As an example, consider the chain illustrated in *Figure 14.5*, whose transition matrix is:

$$\begin{bmatrix} \frac{2}{3} & \frac{1}{3} & 0 \\ \frac{1}{4} & 0 & \frac{3}{4} \\ 1 & 0 & 0 \end{bmatrix}$$

It will be found that the eigendistribution of this chain is:

$$\hat{X} = \left(\frac{12}{19}, \frac{4}{19}, \frac{3}{19} \right)$$

This gives $H(\hat{X}) \approx 0.9097$ natural units. Writing $p(x_h x_k) \triangleq p(X_{t-1} = x_h \cap X_t = x_k)$, etc., we have $p(x_h x_k) = p(x_h)p(x_k|x_h)$, and $p(x_h x_k x_l) = p(x_h)p(x_k|x_h)p(x_l|x_k)$, etc., all as guaranteed by the Markov property. Hence the following distributions and entropies:

$$H(X^2) = H\left(\frac{8}{19}, \frac{4}{19}, \frac{1}{19}, \frac{3}{19}, \frac{3}{19} \right) \approx 1.4301$$

and:

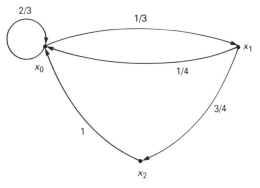

Figure 14.5 Graph of a Markov chain

$$H(X^3) = H\left(\frac{16}{57}, \frac{8}{57}, \frac{3}{57}, \frac{9}{57}, \frac{2}{57}, \frac{1}{57}, \frac{9}{57}, \frac{6}{57}, \frac{3}{57} \right) \approx 1.9505$$

and so on. Moreover:

$$H^\infty(X) = \frac{12}{19} H\left(\frac{2}{3}, \frac{1}{3} \right) + \frac{4}{19} H\left(\frac{1}{4}, \frac{3}{4} \right) + \frac{3}{19} H(1) \approx 0.5204$$

and generally, that is, as in *Table 14.1*.

Now we extend these ideas by incorporating a mapping, φ: $X \to S$, from the set, X, of states of the chain, to a set, S, of symbols. We shall write $m = \#X$ and $k = \#S$, and note that $k \leqslant m$. The structure (X, T, S, φ) is called a Markov source; for short, we write $S \triangleq (X, T, S, \varphi)$. (Again, we assume that (X, T) represents an ergodic Markov chain.) We regard X as a set of *internal* states, that are, by hypothesis, not directly observable. S will be called the *external* alphabet of the chain, and we suppose that the arrival of the chain at a particular internal state x, where $x \in X$, causes the emission of its external symbol, $\varphi(x)$, into the outside world where it can be observed. Clearly, $H(S) \leqslant \log k$. Also, since φ is not in general injective, $H(S) \leqslant H(X)$.

When observing a Markov *chain*, the initial single-symbol observation gives an entropy that is in general greater than that of any subsequent observation. It is the subsequent observations that each give the 'true' entropy, since that is, in the long term, a way in which the asymptotic entropy may be regarded. Now, though, when we observe a Markov *source*, the chain is being observed through the 'filter' of the mapping, φ. (This mapping is actually a noiseless, and possibly lossy, channel; see the next section.) Not only will the previous effect of initial and asymptotic entropies operate, but now there will be the effects of another kind of incompleteness of observation; that is, those owing to the fact that the only knowledge we possess about the *internal* states of the chain is gained by observation of the *external* symbols from the source. In order to make a more complete observation, we try to deduce the internal from the external; at best that will take time, and at worst it may be impossible.

To simplify the problem, we shall look at well-behaved

Table 14.1

Λ	$H(X^\Lambda)$	$H^\Lambda(X)$	$\frac{1}{\Lambda}H(X^\Lambda)$
0	0	—	—
1	0.9097	0.9097	0.9097
2	1.4301	0.5204	0.7151
3	1.9505	0.5204	0.6502
$\vdots$	$\vdots$	$\vdots$	$\vdots$
∞	∞	0.5204	0.5204

sources only. We proceed in two stages. First, we require that, given the internal state at a particular time, we shall be able to track the subsequent sequence of internal states merely by observing the corresponding external symbols. We therefore define a source as unifilar if each and every one of its internal states has all of its possible distinct successors mapped to distinct external letters, that is, if:

$$0 < p(x'|x) \wedge 0 < p(x''|x) \Rightarrow x' = x'' \vee \phi(x') \neq \phi(x'')$$

for all $x \in X$. This clearly gives the desired property. We can say, for each internal state of a unifilar source, that its possible successors are distinctly 'labelled' by the mapping ϕ.

Next, given a unifilar source, we require that we shall be able to deduce the internal state after observing a sufficiently long sequence of external symbols only; that is, *without* our having been given any internal information at all. (Once that deduction can be made, unifilarity will guarantee perfect tracking thereafter.) So, we define the order, $\mu(S)$, of a source S as the length of the shortest sequence of possible successive external observations whose string will determine a unique final internal state, and say that the source is of infinite order if no such length exists. Let $F(\Sigma)$ be the set of final internal states possible after the emission of an external string Σ. (Note that $F(\Sigma)$ may be empty.) Then:

$$\mu(S) \triangleq \min\{\lambda: \Sigma \in S^\lambda \Rightarrow \#F(\Sigma) \leqslant 1\}$$

The search for a value of μ need not be protracted indefinitely, since it can be shown (see Ash, 1965) that either $\mu \leqslant (m(m-1))/2$, or μ is infinite. For discrete memoryless sources, we take $m=1$, so that $\mu(\text{DMS}) \triangleq 0$.

As an example, the chain shown in Figure 14.5 can have exactly the following mappings:

1. $x_0 \mapsto$ 'a', $x_1 \mapsto$ 'a', $x_2 \mapsto$ 'a': so $k=1$; this is deterministic, and all the entropies of the source are zero.
2. $x_0 \mapsto$ 'b', $x_1 \mapsto$ 'a', $x_2 \mapsto$ 'a': so $k=2$; this is unifilar.
3. $x_0 \mapsto$ 'a', $x_1 \mapsto$ 'b', $x_2 \mapsto$ 'a': so $k=2$; this is not unifilar, as the possible successors to x_1 are not distinctly labelled by the mapping.
4. $x_0 \mapsto$ 'a', $x_1 \mapsto$ 'a', $x_2 \mapsto$ 'b': so $k=2$; this also is not unifilar, since the possible successors to x_0 are not distinctly labelled.
5. $x_0 \mapsto$ 'a', $x_1 \mapsto$ 'b', $x_2 \mapsto$ 'c': so $k=3$; here, the mapping is a bijection: unifilarity is automatically fulfilled, and the order of the source is automatically unity. All the entropies of the source are identical with those of the chain. The mapping is a perfect channel (see later), so external observation gives immediate and complete information about the internal state.

Mapping (5) is useful, but needs no new consideration. Mappings (1), (3) and (4) can be written off as useless or badly-behaved. We now have to consider whether the order of the source with mapping (2) is finite and, if so, what are its entropies.

Before doing so, we may remark that the number of possible mappings that we have to consider in general is equal to the number of partitions that can be made of m objects, or, equivalently, the number of equivalence relations definable on m objects; that is, the Bell number given by:

$$B(m) \triangleq \sum_{k=1}^{m} S_2(m, k)$$

where $S_2(m, k)$ is the Stirling number of the second kind, given by $S_2(m, 1) \triangleq 1$ and $S_2(m, m) \triangleq 1$ and:

$$1 < k < m \rightarrow S_2(m, k) \triangleq S_2(m-1, k-1) + k\,S_2(m-1, k)$$

Considering the example source generated by mapping (2), above, we have $F('a') = \{x_1, x_2\}$ and $F('b') = \{x_0\}$. So, while this is unique for 'b', it is not so for 'a', and the order must be greater than 1. We have $m(m-1)/2 = 3$, so we would only need to try $\mu = 2$ and $\mu = 3$ before giving up and saying that the order was infinite; but, in fact, $F('aa') = \{x_2\}$, $F('ab') = \{x_0\}$, $F('ba') = \{x_1\}$ and $F('bb') = \{x_0\}$. So, with strings of length two, none of the sets contains more than one member. That was not so for strings of length one. So the order is $\mu = 2$.

Now, for a unifilar source, S, of order μ, containing an ergodic chain, X, we have:

$$H^{\mu+1}(S) = H^\infty(S) = H^\infty(X)$$

and so:

$$H^\Lambda(S) \begin{cases} = H(\hat{S}) & \text{when } \Lambda = 1 \\[4pt] \leqslant H(\hat{S}) & \text{when } 2 \leqslant \Lambda \leqslant \mu \\[4pt] = H^\infty(X) & \text{when } \mu + 1 \leqslant \Lambda \end{cases}$$

Moreover:

$$H^\infty(X) \leqslant H^{\Lambda+1}(S) \leqslant H^\Lambda(S) \leqslant H(S) \leqslant \log k$$

$$\frac{H(S^\Lambda)}{\Lambda} \rightarrow H^\infty(X) \quad \text{as } \Lambda \rightarrow \infty$$

$$\mu \leqslant \Lambda \Rightarrow H(S^\Lambda) = H(S^\mu) + (\Lambda - \mu)H^\infty(X)$$

Pursuing the previous example, we now have

$$\hat{S} = (p('a'), p('b')) = (p(x_1 \cup x_2), p(x_0)) = \left(\frac{7}{19}, \frac{12}{19}\right)$$

so that $H(\hat{S}) \approx 0.6581$ natural units. From examination of the distribution of 2-grams (that is, the second extension of S), we can find $H(S^2) \approx 1.3117$. It is instructive to compare the distribution, $\text{PD}(S^3)$, of the third extension of S with the distribution, $\hat{S}^{[3]}$, of 3-grams from a memoryless source with the same 1-gram distribution, $\hat{S}$. The former has $p('abb') = p('a')p('b'|'a')p('b'|'b')$, etc.; the latter has $p('abb') = p('a')p('b')p('b')$, etc.:

	$\text{PD}(S^3)$	$\hat{S}^{[3]}$
aaa	0	$\dfrac{343}{6859}$
aab	$\dfrac{9}{57}$	$\dfrac{588}{6859}$
aba	$\dfrac{4}{57}$	$\dfrac{588}{6859}$
abb	$\dfrac{8}{57}$	$\dfrac{1008}{6859}$
baa	$\dfrac{9}{57}$	$\dfrac{588}{6859}$
bab	$\dfrac{3}{57}$	$\dfrac{1008}{6859}$
bba	$\dfrac{8}{57}$	$\dfrac{1008}{6859}$
bbb	$\dfrac{16}{57}$	$\dfrac{1728}{6859}$

From which, $H(S^3) \approx 1.8431$, whereas $H(\hat{S}^{[3]}) \approx 1.9743$. For the extensions of S, see the results shown in *Table 14.2*.

Table 14.2

Λ	$H(S^\Lambda)$	$H^\Lambda(S)$	$\dfrac{1}{\Lambda}H(S^\Lambda)$
0	0	–	–
1	0.6581	0.6581	0.6581
$2 = \mu$	1.3117	0.6536	0.6559
$3 = \mu+1$	1.8321	0.5204	0.6107
$4 = \mu+2$	2.3525	0.5204	0.5881
$\vdots$	$\vdots$	$\vdots$	$\vdots$
$\infty = \mu+\infty$	∞	0.5204	0.5204

Efficiencies of Markov chains and sources can be defined in an obvious way: the Λ-gram efficiencies as

$$\eta(X^\Lambda) \triangleq \frac{H(X^\Lambda)}{\Lambda \log m} \quad \text{and} \quad \eta(S^\Lambda) \triangleq \frac{H(S^\Lambda)}{\Lambda \log k}$$

the Λth marginal efficiencies as:

$$\eta^\Lambda(X) \triangleq \frac{H^\Lambda(X)}{\log m} \quad \text{and} \quad \eta^\Lambda(S) \triangleq \frac{H^\Lambda(S)}{\log k}$$

and the asymptotic efficiencies as:

$$\eta^\infty(X) \triangleq \frac{H^\infty(X)}{\log m} \quad \text{and} \quad \eta^\infty(S) \triangleq \frac{H^\infty(S)}{\log k}$$

All of these efficiencies lie within $0 \leqslant \eta \leqslant 1$.
For the examples given above:

$\eta(X) \approx 0.8280$ $\eta(S) \approx 0.9495$
$\eta(X^2) \approx 0.6509$ $\eta(S^2) \approx 0.9463$
$\eta(X^3) \approx 0.5918$ $\eta(S^3) \approx 0.8811$

$\eta^2(X) \approx 0.4737$ $\eta^2(S) \approx 0.9430$
$\eta^3(X) \approx 0.4737$ $\eta^3(S) \approx 0.7508$
$\eta^\infty(X) \approx 0.4737$ $\eta^\infty(S) \approx 0.7508$

These will be useful in judging the performance of compression codes, given in Section 14.6.1

For more on discrete sources with memory, see Ash (1965), Paz (1971) and McEliece (1977). For ways of working all this backwards, that is, deriving the Markov model from data hypothesized to be 'typical', see for example, Lee *et al.* (1970).

14.5 Models of discrete memoryless channels (DMCs)

A discrete memoryless channel (DMC) is a system for conveying information that conveys one symbol each time it is used. The symbol that is output on each occasion is dependent on the symbol that was input, and on the memoryless stochastic properties of the channel itself, but not at all on any of the symbols previously transmitted. There are a number of discrete inputs (the input alphabet, X), and likewise of outputs (the output alphabet, Y). The actual letters used in these alphabets are, of course, immaterial, but the alphabets may or may not be of the same size, and either one may be larger than the other. We shall write $m = \#X$ and $n = \#Y$. Then m/n is the aspect ratio of the channel, and a square channel has $m = n$.

The stochastic properties of a DMC may be modelled by a transfer matrix of m rows and n columns, whose typical component is $p(y_j|x_i) \triangleq p(Y_t = y_j | X_t = x_i)$, so that $\hat{Y} = \hat{X}T$; for example:

$$T = \begin{bmatrix} 0 & \frac{1}{3} & 0 & \frac{2}{3} \\ 1 & 0 & 0 & 0 \\ \frac{1}{7} & 0 & \frac{4}{7} & \frac{2}{7} \end{bmatrix}$$

or by a stochastically scaled bipartite directed graph, with that in *Figure 14.6*, for example, being equivalent to the matrix just given. The broad properties of a DMC are seen most clearly in the graph form, where the outputs that are possible for a given input are shown by its pattern of adjacency. If the transfer matrix T, is $m \times n$, then the $(m+n) \times (m+n)$ adjacency matrix of the $(m+n)$-point digraph is given by:

$$\begin{bmatrix} O_{m \times m} & \lceil T \rceil \\ O_{n \times m} & O_{n \times n} \end{bmatrix}$$

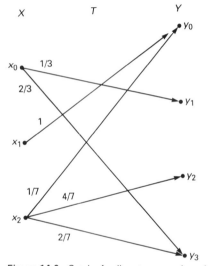

Figure 14.6 Graph of a discrete memoryless channel

where $\lceil T \rceil$ is derived from T by replacing each non-zero component with unity.

There are two 'channel problems'. One is the decision problem: given that a particular output has occurred, what input is most likely to have caused it? That was discussed in Sections 5.3.1 and 5.3.2, although it will be re-visited here, later, in the guise of the decoding problem, which also includes the probability of making a wrong decision. The other is the information capacity problem: how much entropy is there in common between input and output, how large can that quantity be, and how can that maximum be achieved? That is the problem that will now be addressed.

Various entropies of the DMC can be defined as follows:

    $H(X)$ input entropy.
    $H(Y)$ output entropy.
  $H(X \cup Y)$ total entropy (input together with output).
  $H(X|Y)$ loss entropy (input, given output).
  $H(Y|X)$ noise entropy (output, given input).
  $H(X \cap Y)$ throughput entropy (in common between input and output).

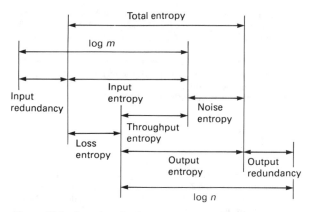

Figure 14.7 Entropies of a discrete memoryless channel

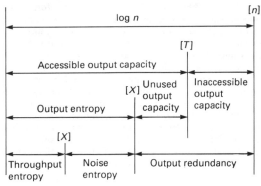

Figure 14.8 Output entropies and capacity of a discrete memoryless channel

and the inequalities connecting these entropies may conveniently be obtained from *Figure 14.7*.

If $H(X|Y)=0$, the channel is lossless. If $H(Y|X)=0$, it is noiseless. A channel is perfect if it is lossless and noiseless. If $H(X\cap Y)=0$, it is useless. In all cases, a channel specifies a mapping $X\to\mathscr{P}(Y)$.

1. In a lossless channel, there is at most one non-zero component in each column of T; equivalently, no two arcs in the bipartite digraph converge on the same (output) point. A lossless channel induces a partition on the set of possible outputs: it can therefore be decoded with no possibility of error.
2. In a noiseless channel, every row of T is deterministic, and the digraph defines a mapping $X\to Y$.
3. In a perfect channel, the mapping $X\to Y$ is an injection. A perfect channel must have $m\leqslant n$. Indeed, if there are no impossible outputs, it will be square: and then the mapping will be a bijection, and T will be a permutation matrix.
4. A square channel that is not perfect must be both lossy and noisy.

(In general, a channel that is not formally lossless may nevertheless have zero loss for some input distributions, and one that is not formally noiseless may have zero noise for some input distributions. In these cases, some of the inputs will necessarily be impossible. Then it may be feasible to re-write the transfer matrix with the impossible rows omitted. If that is done, the channel can be re-classified as lossless, or noiseless as appropriate.)

It is easily seen that

$$H(Y|X)=\sum_{i=0}^{m-1} H(\hat{T}_i)$$

where T_i is the ith row of T. On the other hand, $H(X|Y)$ is not so easily expressed, and is in any case a function not only of T but also of X. (This situation is similar to that involving MLEC and MLCE in Section 5.3.)

We are interested in the capacity that a channel possesses for the transmission of information between its input and its output. We ask how much entropy the input and output have in common, that is, what is the throughput; how much they *can* have in common when the input distribution is, by hypothesis, subject to our control; and what is the distribution that will cause that maximum to be achieved. The capacity, $C(T)$, of a DMC whose transfer matrix is T will be equal to its throughput maximized over all possible input distributions:

$$C(T)\triangleq \max_{\hat{x}} H(X\cap Y)=\max_{\hat{x}}(H(Y)-H(Y|X))$$

(The r.h.s. is expressed in terms of $H(Y)$ and $H(Y|X)$, rather than $H(X)$ and $H(X|Y)$, for the reasons given above.) The problem is as shown in Figures 14.7 and 14.8. In *Figure 14.8*, the top of each vertical line is marked with the quantity that controls its horizontal position; that is, n, T or $\hat{X}$. Of these, n and T are constants that define the problem; but, by hypothesis, $\hat{X}$, the input distribution, is variable and subject to our control by suitable coding of the input (see Section 14.6 on coding). Clearly, we should like to reduce the output redundancy to zero (that is, increase its entropy to the maximum, $\log n$, and thus increase its efficiency to unity). If the output redundancy were indeed always reducible to zero, we would then know that the full output capacity, of value $\log n$, was available to be partitioned between the noise and the throughput. If, in addition, this reduction of the output redundancy could be carried through independent of the input distribution, then we should merely have to adjust $\hat{X}$ to minimize the noise. However, the situation is in general not nearly that simple. $\hat{X}$ is the only lever of control that we possess, and while *it* can be made to take any value in its $(m-1)$-dimensional simplex, there is no guarantee that any particular value of $\hat{Y}$ is attainable merely by the adjustment of $\hat{X}$. The given transfer matrix T may preclude it, rendering parts of the $\hat{Y}$ simplex inaccessible. Moreover, even if the whole of the range of $H(Y)$ were accessible, from 0 to $\log n$, there would still be no guarantee that a value of $\hat{X}$ that maximized the output entropy would also minimize the noise. The root cause of this is the fact that, of the vertical lines in Figure 14.8, *two* are marked with 'X' as their controlling factor. We then have the problem of maximizing a difference under constraints. In the general case, this becomes a convex problem in numerical analysis (see, for example, Ash (1965), and, specifically, Arimoto (1972)).

There are, however, fortunate cases in which the problem admits of an analytical solution. Many practical channels exhibit certain kinds of symmetry or regularity that render them analytical, and so we shall now proceed by imposing ever stronger such conditions upon a channel, and see the expression for its capacity become progressively simpler.

It would, in particular, be fortunate if

$$\max_{\hat{x}} H(Y) \quad \text{and} \quad \min_{\hat{x}} H(Y|X)$$

both occurred at the same value of the input distribution, $\hat{X}$. This condition could arise, realistically, if either $H(Y)$ or $H(Y|X)$ were independent of $\hat{X}$. There would then, in effect, be only one simple extremum to find. Now, if $H(Y)$ were indeed independent of $\hat{X}$, we should have $H(Y)=H(Y|X)$, and so $C(T)=0$ and the channel would be useless. On the other hand, if it were $H(Y|X)$ that was independent of $\hat{X}$, the problem not only would be tractable, but would have a useful solution. We therefore define an isentropic channel as one for which $H(Y|X)$ is constant; that is, one for which the noise is a function of the channel only (represented by T), and not of the input applied to it at any particular time. We can write this condition as, say, $\hat{T}_i \curvearrowright \hat{T}_0$ for all relevant i, where $\hat{T}_i$ is the ith row of T. It is easy to check a DMC for the property of isentropy, to any desired precision, by evaluating the entropy of each of the rows of its transfer matrix. However, constructing a synthetic example of such a matrix admits both of an easy though restricted solution, in which each row is a permutation of every other, and of a general but difficult solution in which each partly specified row can be completed, if at all, only by a process of numerical iteration.

The noise generated within an isentropic channel is given by

$$H(Y|X) = \sum_{i=0}^{m-1} H(\hat{T}_i) = H(\hat{T}_0)$$

and the channel's capacity therefore by:

$$C(T) = (\max_{\hat{x}} H(Y)) - H(\hat{T}_0)$$

Since $H(Y) \leqslant \log n$, this capacity is bounded by:

$$C(T) \leqslant \log n - H(\hat{T}_0)$$

and, if $H(Y)$ ever reached its bound, it would do so when $\hat{Y}$ was uniform. We should wish this bound actually to be accessible (by the adjustment of $\hat{X}$, which is by hypothesis the only means permitted); and, given such accessibility of the maximum, we should want to know what would be the value of $\hat{X}$ that would cause it actually to be achieved.

In order to discuss a case in which such an adjustment is certainly feasible, we define an isobaric channel as one for which each column of its transfer matrix has the same weight as every other.

$$\sum_{i=0}^{m-1} p(y_j|x_i) = \sum_{i=0}^{m-1} p(y_0|x_i)$$

for all relevant j. It is easily seen that each of the columns of a $m \times n$ isobaric transfer matrix has weight m/n, and that, in particular, a square isobaric transfer matrix is doubly (i.e. row- and column-) stochastic. The properties of an isobaric channel that are important for present purposes are that its output distribution can be made uniform, and that this will happen when its input distribution is uniform. It follows that the capacity of a channel that is both isentropic and isobaric is given by the actual equality:

$$C(T) = \log n - H(\hat{T}_0)$$

and that this capacity is attained when $X \curvearrowright U$.

As with isentropy alone, the construction of a synthetic example of a channel that is both isentropic and isobaric is in general a problem in numerical iteration. More usefully, it is often the case that consideration of the symmetry and regularity of a given practical channel will show *a priori* that it has these properties. An important such case is the weakly symmetric channel (WSC), which is defined as one whose transfer matrix has the property that each of its rows is a permutation of every other row, and each of its columns is a permutation of every other column. Here is an example:

$$T = \begin{bmatrix} \frac{1}{24} & \frac{1}{3} & \frac{1}{8} & \frac{1}{8} & \frac{1}{24} & \frac{1}{3} \\ \frac{1}{8} & \frac{1}{24} & \frac{1}{3} & \frac{1}{24} & \frac{1}{3} & \frac{1}{8} \\ \frac{1}{3} & \frac{1}{8} & \frac{1}{24} & \frac{1}{3} & \frac{1}{8} & \frac{1}{24} \end{bmatrix}$$

If a channel is weakly symmetric, then it is both isentropic and isobaric and its capacity is therefore equal to $\log n - H(\hat{T}_0)$. The example just given has $H(\hat{T}_0) \approx 1.5171$ and $C(T) \approx 0.2747$ natural units.

The channel of greatest importance in information engineering, and the one most frequently referred to in books on information and coding theory, is the binary symmetric channel (BSC). This is a WSC with $m = n = 2$, so that:

$$T = \begin{bmatrix} \bar{\varepsilon} & \varepsilon \\ \varepsilon & \bar{\varepsilon} \end{bmatrix}$$

where $\bar{\varepsilon} = 1 - \varepsilon$. Clearly, $C(\text{BSC}) = \log 2 - H(\varepsilon, \bar{\varepsilon})$. This is at its maximum value, $\log 2$, when either $\varepsilon = 0$ or $\varepsilon = 1$; and at its minimum, 0, when $\varepsilon = 1/2$. Since, by a suitable indexing of rows and columns, we can always arrange that $\varepsilon \leqslant 1/2$, we can regard $p(y_i|x_i) = \bar{\varepsilon}$ as the probability of 'correct' transmission, and $p(y_{1-i}|x_i) = \varepsilon$ as that of 'incorrect' transmission; that is, of error.

The idea of correct and incorrect transmission through a square channel can, with appropriate indexing of its rows and columns, give rise immediately to an $n \times n$ channel in which $x_i \mapsto y_j$ is 'correct' when $j = i$, and 'incorrect' when $j \neq i$. It is then easiest to drop the distinction between the input and output alphabets and consider that the channel is transmitting index numbers from the ring $\mathbf{Z}_n \triangleq \{0, 1, \dots, n-1\}$. We can then write a typical component of T as $p(j|i)$. If such a channel is to be a WSC (so that we shall know its capacity), then this will be the case most usefully when:

$$p(j|i) = q(j - i \bmod n)$$

for some function $q(.)$ that depends on $j - i$, but not on i alone. This defines an additive noise channel (ANC). Here, we consider the channel to be adding, modulo n, a 'noise signal' of amplitude $\psi = j - i$ to the input signal of amplitude i; that is, $T(i): i \mapsto i + \psi$ mod n, where $p(\Psi_t = \psi)$ is a component of the noise distribution $\hat{\Psi}$, and where $\#\Psi = n$. The 'modulo n' ensures that we have a WSC; row $\hat{T}_i$ is then a cyclic shift, by i places, of row $\hat{T}_0$, and so T is a circulant matrix. Here is an example of an ANC:

$$T = \begin{bmatrix} \frac{8}{14} & \frac{2}{14} & \frac{3}{14} & \frac{1}{14} \\ \frac{1}{14} & \frac{8}{14} & \frac{2}{14} & \frac{3}{14} \\ \frac{3}{14} & \frac{1}{14} & \frac{8}{14} & \frac{2}{14} \\ \frac{2}{14} & \frac{3}{14} & \frac{1}{14} & \frac{8}{14} \end{bmatrix}$$

Clearly, $\psi = 0$ represents correct transmission; and $\psi \neq 0$ represents an error: one of the $n - 1$ errors that may be possible for any given input. Such a channel has capacity $C(\text{ANC}) = \log n - H(\Psi)$.

A common special case of this is the uniform symmetric channel (USC), which has $p(\Psi_t = 0) = \bar{\varepsilon}$, and $p(\Psi_t = i) = \varepsilon/(n-1)$ for each $i \neq 0$, so that $p(\Psi_t \neq 0) = \varepsilon$, and $\text{PD}(\Psi_t | \Psi_t \neq 0) \curvearrowright \hat{U}(n-1)$. Here, $C(\text{USC}) = \log n - H(\varepsilon, \bar{\varepsilon}) - \varepsilon \log(n-1)$. (Notice that, although T for the USC is a 'symmetric matrix' in the usual sense, such is not necessarily the case for an ANC in general.)

The ANC may be extended to model channels in which, although a given 'noise amplitude' j always causes the same displacement off the main diagonal of T, independent of i, nevertheless the noise source, Ψ, is a general ergodic Markov source. That is, Ψ may have memory. Then the capacity of this λth extension of an ANC is given by $\lambda \log n - H(\Psi^\lambda)$. One particular form of extended ANC has a noise source containing a 'quiet region' of low entropy, and a 'noisy region' of high entropy – but with both belonging to the unique permanent strong component of the chain, being coupled by a very low p(noisy|quiet) transition probability and a moderate p(quiet|noisy) transition probability. This can be used to model additive channels in which noise is slight except in bursts during which it is nearly saturating. Such is called a Gilbert channel (Gilbert, 1960a).

Finally, before proceeding to a brief consideration of the composition of channels, it should be noted that all square WSCs, including the ANC and the USC, reduce to the BSC when $n = 2$.

It is often helpful to consider a complicated DMC as being composed from simpler ones that may be more easily analysed. First, any one of the previous forms of channel can function as the useful constituent part of an erasure channel. This is rather unfortunately named, as symbols are not actually deleted from the transmitted sequence, but rather may be output as a common 'don't know' symbol of fixed probability. In an erasure channel, if the useful constituent has $m' \times n'$ transfer matrix T', and the probability of 'don't know' is ε, then the overall effective transfer matrix is $m' \times (n' + 1)$ and is given by $T = [\bar{\varepsilon}T', [\![\varepsilon]\!]_{i=0}^{m'-1}]$. Its capacity is $\bar{\varepsilon}C(T')$. Here is an example, with $\varepsilon = 1/12$:

$$T' = \begin{bmatrix} \frac{1}{11} & \frac{2}{11} & \frac{8}{11} \\ \frac{6}{11} & \frac{3}{11} & \frac{2}{11} \end{bmatrix} \text{ and } T = \begin{bmatrix} \frac{1}{12} & \frac{2}{12} & \frac{8}{12} & \frac{1}{12} \\ \frac{6}{12} & \frac{3}{12} & \frac{2}{12} & \frac{1}{12} \end{bmatrix}$$

The commonest example of an erasure channel is the binary (symmetric) erasure channel (BEC), in which $m' = n' = 2$, and $T' = I$. Then:

$$T = \begin{bmatrix} \bar{\varepsilon} & 0 & \varepsilon \\ 0 & \bar{\varepsilon} & \varepsilon \end{bmatrix}$$

and $C(\text{BEC}) = \bar{\varepsilon} \log 2$.

Second, suppose that the output from a $m' \times n'$ channel, T', is plugged into the input of a $m'' \times n''$ channel, T''. This can happen with perfect fit only if $n' = m''$, so that T' and T'' conform for multiplication; the overall effective transfer matrix is then $T'T''$. This is called the cascade product of the constituent channels, and it can clearly be extended to an indefinite cascade of conforming channels. The cascade product of isobaric channels is itself isobaric, but the cascade product of isentropic channels is not necessarily isentropic.

Third, consider two channels T' and T'', not necessarily conforming in any way, but operated so that each input symbol is sent either through T', or through T'', *but not both*. Then the effective channel has a transfer matrix

$$\begin{bmatrix} T' & O \\ O & T'' \end{bmatrix}$$

This is called the sum of the channels, and its capacity is

$$\log_e[e^{C(T')} + e^{C(T'')}].$$

Finally, suppose that each symbol is sent partly through T' and partly, in parallel, through T''. The effective channel then deals in ordered pairs of symbols, and it is called the Cartesian product of the constituent channels. Its capacity is simply $C(T') + C(T'')$, and its transfer matrix is given by $T' \otimes T''$.

If the same DMC is used repeatedly in order to transmit the symbols in a block of data serially, or if several identical DMCs are so used in parallel, then the overall effective channel is a Cartesian power of the simple DMC. Its effective transfer matrix, when processing λ-grams of input, is called the λth extension of the DMC, and is given by the λth Kronecker power, $T^{[\lambda]}$, of T. We shall apply this in block coding for memoryless channels, discussed later. (Notice that it does not

apply to the extended ANC, discussed earlier, unless the noise source is memoryless.)

14.6 Coding systems

A coding system is an algorithm by which symbols from one text (the source text) are processed, deterministically, and usually without loss of information, to form a new text (the object text), possibly of a different length and possibly over a different alphabet. The constraints of determinism and, usually, losslessness imply a one-to-one correspondence between the source and object texts. This in turn means that, to the encoding process, which maps source to object, there corresponds an inverse: a decoding process, which maps object back to source. (It will be apparent that encoders and decoders are examples of perfect channels; although it will be seen later that, in specific circumstances and for specific reasons, encoders and decoders may sometimes be designed to be lossy.)

In its most general form, a coding system can be defined so that the encoder accepts the entire source text and replaces it by an arbitrarily defined object. More practically, an encoder will be designed to accept a finite portion of the source – of fixed or varying length – and replace it by a corresponding portion of object text, doing this in each one of a sequence of iterations of the encoding operation. At each iteration, the window of acceptance will move a certain distance along the source. The window cannot move by more than its own width, or information would be lost (contrary to hypothesis). If its moves are by a distance exactly equal to its own width, we are said to have a block code, and if by a lesser distance, we have a convolutional code. If all or part of the most recently generated portion of the object text is also fed into the encoding window, then we have a recursive code. Here, we shall consider block codes only.

Three cases may conveniently be distinguished, according as the redundancy of the source is reduced, increased or maintained by the encoding operation:

1. Codes that enable redundancy to be *reduced* are used for data compression. The aim is then to represent a supposed inefficiently represented source by a more efficient object text; that is, assuming alphabets of equal size, a shorter one.
2. Codes that deliberately *increase* the redundancy of the text are used to enable the detection, and perhaps the correction, of errors that occur when a text is transmitted through a channel. The extra capacity that is implied by the redundancy allows the codewords to absorb a certain amount of noise entropy without any loss of information necessarily being incurred thereby. These codes that increase the redundancy can be used for the protection of data not only against accidental corruption, as in a channel, but also against deliberate amendment, extension, re-ordering or replacement. We shall call these codes data protection codes, whether used for any of these purposes.
3. Codes that *maintain* the existing level of redundancy are used for data security; that is, the safeguarding of encoded data against unauthorized decoding. (The allied topic of security against the unauthorized copying or storage of a plain or encrypted text is not considered here.) One caveat must be entered: classically, data security systems have operated with a maintained level of redundancy, that is, in normal circumstances, without altering the message length. Nevertheless, on the one hand it is possible to gain in security by precompressing the data in order to remove as much as is feasible of its redundancy; and also, it is possible to use data protection codes, that increase the redundancy, together with deliberately introduced errors, to provide data security.

Just as the segment (sourceword) of source text accepted at

each iteration of the encoding operation may be of fixed or varying length, so the corresponding codeword appended to the object text may be of fixed or varying length. Consequently, there are fixed-to-fixed-length (FTFL), fixed-to-variable-length (FTVL), variable-to-fixed-length (VTFL) and variable-to-variable-length (VTVL) codes. A perfect decoder for an FTFL code will also be FTFL, that for FTVL must be VTFL, and so on. (Note that the term 'block code' is sometimes applied not in opposition to 'convolutional', but rather to mean specifically FTFL.) For data compression, it is clearly essential that at least one side of the mapping be variable-length. A FTFL code cannot work, at least, unless some loss is tolerated (see later). Conversely, codes for data protection and for security are almost without exception FTFL.

When particular sourcewords or codewords have to be recognized in a stream of symbols, as when encoding for VTFL, or decoding for FTVL, or either of these for VTVL, there arises the question of whether this can be done unambiguously. For example, if 'a', 'ab', 'bc' and 'c' all count as recognizable words, then 'abc' could be interpreted as 'a' followed by 'bc', or as 'ab' followed by 'c'. For simplicity, we shall now consider FTVL codes only. The uniqueness problem then arises during decoding, when the decoder is faced with a stream of codewords. (Notice that it is *not* faced with a stream of arbitrary symbols, albeit from the correct alphabet.) If such a decoding operation is possible, giving a unique result, then the code is said to be uniquely decodable (UD). An algorithm – due to Sardinas and Patterson (1953) – for testing that a given code has the UD property is given, proved and discussed in Ash (1965).

The decoding algorithm may well require the use of a buffer: the codewords 'a' and 'aaaaaab', for example, cannot be distinguished until seven symbols have been read. The length of the shortest necessary buffer is called the delay of the code, and a code with zero delay is said to be instantaneous, or instantaneously decodable (ID). It is also called a prefix-free code, since it will be found to have no codeword a prefix of another. Since 'being a prefix of' is reflexive and transitive, and 'having as an immediate prefix' defines a unique word, it is possible to place all words over the alphabet on a rooted tree, with words of length λ at depth λ, and with the leaves of the tree representing codewords. It is possible to generate a prefix-free code (that is, allocate leaves on the tree) with a family of lengths $[\lambda_i]_{i=0}^{c-1}$, over an alphabet of size n, if and only if the family obeys Kraft's inequality:

$$\sum_{i=0}^{c-1} \frac{1}{n^{\lambda_i}} \leqslant 1$$

with equality if and only if all the leaves of the tree are allocated to codewords. (This was extended to UD codes in general by McMillan (1956).) It is possible to show that prefix-free codes are 'adequate' in the sense that nothing is to be gained by the use of UD (but non-ID) codes. The practical ease of generation and of use, especially the more efficient decoding, of ID codes, together with the lack of any theoretical advantage in the use of UD codes, means that ID codes are to be preferred generally. For further discussion, see Ash (1965) and McEliece (1977).

The question of synchronization of encoder and decoder – its initial establishment, supposing that to be necessary, and its re-acquisition if lost – has not yet been mentioned. Its nature varies according as the code involved has fixed or variable-length codewords; and according as the transmission regime is noise-less (as for compression), noisy (as for protection) or mainly noiseless but perhaps not wholly reliable (as for security). A code is said to be synchronizable if, synchronization having been lost, the decoder will recognize a codeword in the stream of symbols of the object text only when that codeword was indeed generated as such by the encoder (i.e. and was not formed accidentally by the concatenation of other, genuine, code-

words), and also if the decoder can be guaranteed to perform such a recognition when a finite number of symbols have been received. That finite number is called the synchronization delay of the code. A brute-force method of ensuring synchronization would be for the codewords to be separated by a special extra-alphabetic character, which is technically called a comma (The inclusion of a comma would actually have wider implications. Not only would it render any code re-synchronizable with unit delay, but any such code would automatically be UD, and indeed, ID.) Obviously it will be preferable for a code to be designed so that a comma is not necessary. A code is said to be 'comma-free' if it is synchronizable with a delay of at most one codeword. This phrase occurs in the titles of much of the literature: Crick, Griffith and Orgel (1957), Golomb *et al.* (1958a and b), Gilbert (1960b), Jiggs (1963), Eastman (1965), Levy (1966), Scholtz (1969) and Guibas and Odlyzko (1978). The topic of synchronization tends to be poorly served in textbooks, but, for a notable exception, see Stiffler (1971) and, for a treatment in the compression case, with a software emphasis, see Llewellyn (1987).

14.6.1 Coding for data compression

Data compression can be accomplished by means of a fixed-to-variable-length (FTVL) code, arranged so that the most probable Λ-grams in the source stream produce the shortest words in the object stream. Alternatively, a variable-to-fixed-length (VTFL), or even a variable-to-variable-length (VTVL) code may be used, again according to the principle that the benefit of probable long-to-short encodings will need only partly to be paid for by the cost of improbable short-to-long encodings. In either case, the intention is that, after allowing for different alphabet sizes, the expected length of an object text will be less than that of the corresponding source. More accurately, one should say that the efficiency of the object will be greater than that of the source, and that the effectiveness of a code for a given source may be measured by the closeness of approach of this efficiency to unity.

The most important information-theoretic result relating to data compression is Shannon's source-coding theorem, which is as follows. Suppose that S^Λ, the Λth extension of an ergodic source S, whose alphabet is of size $k = \#S$, has c possible sourcewords, where $c \leqslant k^\Lambda$. (In practice, if may be convenient to set $c = k^\Lambda$, and to allocate zero probability to any impossible sourcewords.) Then if this source is encoded by a FTVL code over an alphabet of size n, it can be shown that the expected codeword length:

$$\mathcal{E}\lambda \triangleq \sum_{i=0}^{c-1} \lambda_i$$

is subject to the lower bound:

$$\frac{H(S^\Lambda)}{\log n} \leqslant \mathcal{E}\lambda$$

and that this bound is attained if and only if $\lambda_i = \sigma(x_i)/(\log n)$ for all relevant i. Notice that the condition for attainment can also be written $\lambda_i = \sigma_n(x_i)$. When this condition holds, we say that the code is perfect (i.e. perfectly matched to the source).

It is useful to define the symbol compression factor, κ, of a given encoding of a given source by $\kappa \triangleq \mathcal{E}\lambda/\Lambda$. The output of such a given encoding of a given source may itself be regarded as a source, E, of symbols from the output alphabet, so that $\#E = n$. This source will have memory – not, of course, between codewords, but between the symbols in each codeword. Since the encoder is a perfect channel, we can equate the asymptotically expected entropy per encoding *in* with that *out*. Noting that, once the source is observed in Λ-grams, no subsequent observation of those Λ-grams, however extended, can recover the asymptotic entropy of the source, we then have:

$$H(S^\Lambda) = \mathcal{E}\lambda H^\infty(E)$$

so that:

$$\eta^\infty(E) = \frac{H^\infty(E)}{\log n} = \frac{\Lambda \log k}{\mathcal{E}\lambda \log n} \eta(S^\Lambda) = \frac{1}{\kappa} \frac{\log k}{\log n} \eta(S^\Lambda)$$

Such an encoding has an efficiency improvement factor, or *rate*, ρ, given by:

$$\rho \triangleq \frac{\eta^\infty(E)}{\eta(S^\Lambda)} = \frac{\Lambda \log k}{\mathcal{E}\lambda \log n} = \frac{1}{\kappa} \frac{\log k}{\log n}$$

The attainable bound in Shannon's source-coding theorem can now be expressed as an upper bound on the object efficiency:

$$\eta^\infty(E) \leqslant 1$$

or as a lower bound on the symbol compression ratio:

$$\frac{\log k}{\log n} \eta(S^\Lambda) \leqslant \kappa$$

or as an upper bound on the rate:

$$\rho \leqslant \frac{1}{\eta(S^\Lambda)}$$

Notice that $\rho = 1/\kappa$ when, as often happens, the source and object alphabets are of the same size.

For a given source, S, and object alphabet size, n, but with a free choice of code, it is useful to define $\kappa_o(S^\Lambda)$, the *optimal compression factor*, as being the smallest compression factor obtainable for any constructable FTVL code on the Λth extension of the source; and the *perfect* compression factor, $\kappa_p(S^\Lambda) \triangleq (\log k/\log n)\eta(S^\Lambda)$, as one which attains Shannon's lower bound; and also to call

$$\kappa_p(S^\infty) \triangleq \lim_{\Lambda \to \infty} \kappa_p(S^\Lambda)$$

the *asymptotic* compression factor. It is easily shown that $\kappa_o(S^\Lambda) \to \kappa_p(S^\Lambda)$ as $\Lambda \to \infty$. This tendency is owing to the ever closer approximation to perfect codeword lengths enabled by their greater number and length. Combined with ever more extended observations of the source, this gives $\kappa_o(S^\Lambda) \to \kappa_p(S^\infty)$ as $\Lambda \to \infty$. For more on this, see Ash (1965) and McEliece (1977).

Here are three examples of FTVL codes being used for data compression. In all these cases, $\Lambda = 3$ and $k = 2$. First, the source is the third extension, $\hat{S}^{[3]}$, of a discrete *memoryless* source (DMS), with alphabet $\{a, b\}$ and distribution

$$\hat{S} = \left(\frac{7}{19}, \frac{12}{19} \right)$$

It is encoded over an alphabet $\{\alpha, \beta\}$, so that $n = 2$. The columns are in the order: probability, sourceword, codeword:

$\dfrac{1728}{6859}$	$bbb \to \beta a$
$\dfrac{1008}{6859}$	$abb \to a\beta\beta$
$\dfrac{1008}{6859}$	$bab \to \alpha\alpha\alpha$
$\dfrac{1008}{6859}$	$bba \to \alpha\alpha\beta$

$\dfrac{588}{6859}$	$aab \to \beta\beta\alpha$
$\dfrac{588}{6859}$	$aba \to \beta\beta\beta$
$\dfrac{588}{6859}$	$baa \to \alpha\beta\alpha\alpha$
$\dfrac{343}{6859}$	$aaa \to \alpha\beta\alpha\beta$

This gives $\mathcal{E}\lambda \approx 2.8838$ and $\kappa \approx 0.9613$.

Next, the third extension, S^3, of the discrete source with memory (DSM) used in the example in Section 14.4 is encoded over the same alphabet, so that again $n = 2$:

$\dfrac{16}{57}$	$bbb \to \alpha\beta$
$\dfrac{9}{57}$	$aab \to \beta\beta$
$\dfrac{9}{57}$	$baa \to \alpha\alpha\alpha$
$\dfrac{8}{57}$	$abb \to \alpha\alpha\beta$
$\dfrac{8}{57}$	$bba \to \beta\alpha\alpha$
$\dfrac{4}{57}$	$aba \to \beta\alpha\beta\alpha$
$\dfrac{3}{57}$	$bab \to \beta\alpha\beta\beta$

This gives $\mathcal{E}\lambda \approx 2.6842$ and $\kappa \approx 0.8947$.

Finally, the same source is encoded over the alphabet $\{\alpha, \beta, \gamma\}$, so that now $n = 3$:

$\dfrac{16}{57}$	$bbb \to \beta$
$\dfrac{9}{57}$	$aab \to \alpha\alpha$
$\dfrac{9}{57}$	$baa \to \alpha\beta$
$\dfrac{8}{57}$	$abb \to \alpha\gamma$
$\dfrac{8}{57}$	$bba \to \gamma\alpha$
$\dfrac{4}{57}$	$aba \to \gamma\beta$
$\dfrac{3}{57}$	$bab \to \gamma\gamma$

This gives $\mathcal{E}\lambda \approx 1.7193$ and $\kappa \approx 0.5731$.

The effects of these three example compression encodings on the various entropies and efficiencies are given in *Table 14.3*.

One of the earliest data compression codes was the FTVL code of Fano (1949). This was later eclipsed, for most of the applications where a FTVL code was suitable, by that of Huffman (1952), which, remarkably, is optimal. That is, given the assumption that a FTVL code is to be used, and that all the source probabilities are known, there can be no more effective code. (Nevertheless, when all the probabilities are *not* known, the Fano code is still of use.) For a proof of Huffman's optimality, see Huffman (1952), Ash (1965) or McEliece (1977). The codes in the examples just given were all constructed using Huffman's algorithm.

The theoretical optimality of the Huffman code is not always exploitable in practice. First, it may be that not all of the source probabilities are known: it cannot then be argued that the code

Table 14.3

Source	$\hat{S}^{[\Lambda]}$	$S^\wedge$	$S^\wedge$
k	2	2	2
Λ	3	3	3
$\Lambda \log k$	2.0794	2.0794	2.0794
n	2	2	3
$\mathcal{E}\lambda$	2.8838	2.6842	1.7193
$\mathcal{E}\lambda \log n$	1.9989	1.8605	1.8888
κ	0.9613	0.8947	0.5731
ρ	1.0403	1.1177	1.1009
H (source)	1.9743	1.8321	1.8321
η (source)	0.9495	0.8811	0.8811
$\eta^x(E)$	0.9877	0.9848	0.9700

is optimal (see, for example, Golomb (1966)). Second, the very 'fine tuning' of codeword lengths that enables the optimality (i.e. in object length) to be achieved causes the decoding algorithm to be inefficient in processing time. A third problem, which applies to data compression codes in general, is that either the output from, or the input to, the encoder has to be buffered, and the buffer must eventually overflow. Fourth, and taking a very different view of things from that with which we have been concerned so far, compression may be based not on probability, but on statistics. This happens with the non-time-critical compression of computer files. Instead of compressing 'on the fly', on the assumption of pre-determined probabilities, each block of source text is analysed statistically, and the block is compressed using a compression code based on the statistics. However, there is a catch. The decoding table for each block must be included in the object text, and that lowers the effectiveness of the compression. A Huffman code may not be suitable for such an application. All of these problems have led to increased attention being paid to the choice between FTVL, VTFL and VTVL codes, and to the details of their implementation rather than their theoretical optimality of object length. For a discussion of all of these problems, and possible solutions, see Jelinek (1968a), Jelinek and Schneider (1972), Cover (1973), Davisson (1973), Ziv and Lempel (1977 and 1978), Jakobsson (1978), Reghbati (1981) and Welch (1984). A properly designed statistical compression code will be asymptotically optimal: it is said to be 'universal'. Probablistic codes that are asymptotically optimal for *any* distribution are also called universal. See for example Elias (1975). For more on data compression in general, see Schwartz and Kleiboemer (1967), Longo and Sgarro (1985) and Benelli *et al.* (1985a, d and e). For applications of compression in general, see, for example, Cappellini (1985b), and, for compression of images in particular, Huang (1977). Wilkins and Wintz (1971) give a comprehensive early bibliography both of data compression in general and, particularly, of picture compression.

In circumstances where it is known how many errors would be caused by a certain degree of over-compression, and where also the cost of erroneous decompression of data can be quantified, it is possible to make a rational decision in favour of over-compression when the cost (in errors) is exceeded by the benefit (in compression effectiveness). This, the subject of rate-distortion theory, was introduced by Shannon (1959). For more on the topic, see Berger (1971) and Gray and Davisson (1974).

One solution to the buffer-overflow problem is to attempt compression with a fixed-rate (i.e. FTFL) code, for which there is no buffer and so it cannot overflow; the corollary being that some loss due to over-compression takes place instead (see, for example, Davisson (1973)).

Many texts, notably Davisson (1973) and Davisson and Gray (1976), reserve the term 'data compression' for the case when strict over-compression is being carried out; otherwise, they refer to 'noiseless coding'. This is useful, and justified. If the purpose of the code is merely to change the alphabet size of a source of unit efficiency, then the coding is certainly noiseless (in the sense that it is not intended to protect the data against the effects of noise) and lossless, but it does not involve compression. Conversely, strict over-compression involves not only the loss of information during encoding, but also, eventually, either the acceptance of the now lower entropy after deterministic over-decompression, or the introduction of noise through stochastic over-decompression.

14.6.2 Coding for data protection

When a stream of data is sent through a discrete memoryless channel (DMC), it is necessary in principle for the receiver to make a decision, for each symbol received, about what was most likely to have been sent. (This is the decision problem, addressed in Section 5.2.5.)

For a given channel, the question arises: even if the most likely input is chosen on each occasion, how often will it be wrong? Furthermore, supposing that the redundancy of the blocks of data were to be increased sufficiently, but by no more than necessary, before transmission, would the cost of the then less efficient throughput be paid for by increased reliability? Yet further, suppose that we demand a specific level of reliability (expressed as probability of error), how close to the raw capacity of the channel can we then come, through the careful choice of code? Once a specific code has been chosen, the first of these questions is easily answered from probability theory. The second and third questions are answered by Shannon's channel coding theorem, which will be stated after we have seen an example of channel coding.

For simplicity, let us assume a square channel, with $n \times n$ transfer matrix T. We should have a source, S, of multiplicity $k = \#S$, of which we would observe the Λth extension, $S^\wedge$. Then we should have a $k^\wedge \times n^\lambda$ encoding matrix, Θ, where the channel is used to transfer blocks of length λ; a $n^\lambda \times n^\lambda$ effective channel transfer matrix, $T^{[\lambda]}$, being the λth extension of T. Then we should have a $n^\lambda \times k^\wedge$ decoding matrix, Φ. The Λth extension of the source would be encoded by forming $X = S^\wedge\Theta$. This would be input to the extended channel, whose output would be $Y = S^\wedge\Theta T^{[\lambda]}$. This would then be decoded by Φ, to form the receiver's estimate of the source Λ-gram, as $(S^\wedge)' = S^\wedge\Theta T^{[\lambda]}\Phi$. Notice that Θ is, in itself, a perfect DMC, but that Φ, while noiseless (because deterministic), is lossy. We design Φ precisely so as to lose as much as possible of the noise that was introduced by the channel, while losing as little as possible of the input.

As a simple numerical example, with $k = n = 2$, $S = \{a, b\}$ and $\Lambda = 1$, let $\lambda = 3$ and $T = BSC$ (see earlier), and take the 'triple repetition code' $(a \rightarrow aaa, b \rightarrow bbb)$. Then, with rows corresponding to the sourcewords:

$$\begin{bmatrix} a \\ b \end{bmatrix}$$

and the columns to the channel words (aaa, aab, aba, ..., bbb) – only the first and last of these being *code*words – we have:

$$\Theta = \begin{bmatrix} 1 & 0 & 0 & 0 & 0 & 0 & 0 & 0 \\ 0 & 0 & 0 & 0 & 0 & 0 & 0 & 1 \end{bmatrix}$$

Also:

$$T^{[\lambda]} = \begin{bmatrix} \bar{\varepsilon} & \varepsilon \\ \varepsilon & \bar{\varepsilon} \end{bmatrix}^{[3]}$$

and Φ is constructed as a majority-vote decision matrix, whose columns correspond to (a, b):

$$\Phi = \begin{bmatrix} 1 & 0 \\ 1 & 0 \\ 1 & 0 \\ 0 & 1 \\ 1 & 0 \\ 0 & 1 \\ 0 & 1 \\ 0 & 1 \end{bmatrix} \quad \text{from} \quad \begin{cases} aaa \\ aab \\ aba \\ abb \\ baa \\ bab \\ bba \\ bbb \end{cases}$$

The overall encoder-channel-decoder equivalent channel can be written:

$$\Theta T^{[\lambda]} \Phi = \begin{bmatrix} \bar{\delta} & \delta \\ \delta & \bar{\delta} \end{bmatrix}$$

where, it will be found, $\delta = 2\varepsilon^2(3 - 2\varepsilon)$. This decrease in the probability of error, from ε to δ (that is, by a factor of about 2ε) has been bought by a reduction in capacity from $\log 2 - H(\varepsilon, \bar{\varepsilon})$ to $1/3(\log 2 - H(\delta, \bar{\delta}))$. Clearly, triple repetition is not a very efficient code.

As an example in which errors are merely detected – leaving correction to take place by re-transmission on request rather than on-the-fly – consider a simple parity check on S^Λ with $\Lambda = 2$, in which the number of 'b's in the codewords is made even. That is $(aa \mapsto aaa, ab \mapsto abb, ba \mapsto bab, bb \mapsto bba)$, as given by:

$$\Theta = \begin{bmatrix} 1 & 0 & 0 & 0 & 0 & 0 & 0 & 0 \\ 0 & 0 & 0 & 1 & 0 & 0 & 0 & 0 \\ 0 & 0 & 0 & 0 & 0 & 1 & 0 & 0 \\ 0 & 0 & 0 & 0 & 0 & 0 & 1 & 0 \end{bmatrix}$$

where the rows of Θ correspond to the sourcewords:

$$\begin{bmatrix} aa \\ ab \\ ba \\ bb \end{bmatrix}$$

and its columns to the channel words $(aaa, aab, aba, abb, \ldots, bbb)$, as also do the rows of Φ:

$$\Phi = \begin{bmatrix} 1 & 0 & 0 & 0 & 0 \\ 0 & 0 & 0 & 0 & 1 \\ 0 & 0 & 0 & 0 & 1 \\ 0 & 1 & 0 & 0 & 0 \\ 0 & 0 & 0 & 0 & 1 \\ 0 & 0 & 1 & 0 & 0 \\ 0 & 0 & 0 & 1 & 0 \\ 0 & 0 & 0 & 0 & 1 \end{bmatrix} \quad \text{from} \quad \begin{cases} aaa \\ aab \\ aba \\ abb \\ baa \\ bab \\ bba \\ bbb \end{cases}$$

The columns of Φ, which is now $n^\lambda \times (k^\Lambda + 1)$, correspond to $(aa, ab, ba, bb, ??)$ – the last of these components meaning, of course, 'error'. Here, Φ is acting as a parity-checker rather than (as previously) as a majority-voter, but beware that the term 'parity check matrix' has quite a different technical meaning in the theory of linear codes.

Notice that in these examples λ symbols had to be sent through the channel for every Λ delivered from the source to the destination. We say that the rate of the code is $\rho \triangleq \Lambda \log k / (\lambda \log n)$. For triple repetition, we had $\rho = 1/3$; and, for the two-symbol parity check, $\rho = 2/3$. (The latter ignores the 'error' output, which conveys no information about the input.) For a given rate, and given alphabet sizes, both Λ and λ can increase together, and the range and variety of codes from which we can choose will increase with them. Notice that a given rate implies a

given reduction in source-to-destination throughput, so that only a given fraction of the entropic capacity of the channel can be used for source-to-destination transmission (the rest being used to carry the deliberately introduced redundant entropy of the codewords). Shannon's channel coding theorem states that, for any discrete memoryless channel, and using MLEC decoding, there exists a sequence of codes (with increasing Λ) such that, for any given acceptable positive probability of error, however low, and for any given acceptable strict reduction in capacity, however small, there exists a member of that sequence that will prove sufficient. This is a remarkable result. It is, however, not constructive. No guidance is given on how to find such codes, other than a further result that randomly chosen codes are as good as any others. (For a discussion of MLEC decoding, see Section 5.2.5.) For elementary proofs of Shannon's channel coding theorem, see Abramson (1963); for intermediate proofs see Ash (1965); for advanced proofs see Wolfowitz (1964). The explanation given by Abramson is especially clear. Once given the entropic formulation of information theory, Shannon's source coding theorem follows quite easily; his channel coding theorem, however, is more difficult to prove. However, it is worth the effort of understanding, since it can reasonably be considered the single most important result in the theory of communication. For another view of the problem, see Wyner (1970).

The random coding result does not, however, mean that randomly chosen codes are useful in practice. One cannot rely on a randomly chosen code for any required level of protection. It could turn out that one had made an unfortunate choice, and, although improbable, one would like it to be certain that it was not the case. More seriously, there can be no neat and efficient way of encoding and decoding for a randomly chosen code. One is stuck with the manipulation of huge tables or matrices, and these are of a size that in practice makes them infeasible to store or to search. It is better to adopt some mathematical principle (usually algebraic or combinatoric) which enables one to assert a guaranteed level of protection, and also provides one with an algorithm for efficient and effective encoding and decoding. The study of the construction of codes for data protection was begun by Golay (1949) and Hamming (1950). The absence of an optimal constructive solution (like that of Huffman for compression codes) has meant that the subject has grown explosively since then. The literature is enormous. Here, we may mention Berlekamp (1968) as a classic on algebraic codes and Blake and Mullin (1976) on combinatorial as well as algebraic techniques. For brief treatments of particular topics, see Benelli *et al.* (1985b, c and d) and Cappellini (1985b). More compendious treatments include Peterson and Weldon (1972), MacWilliams and Sloane (1977), Clark and Cain (1981) – notable for emphasizing algorithms and eschewing proofs – and Lin and Costello (1983).

The last two of these incorporate extensive treatments of convolutional codes. Technically, block codes are especially suited for protection against sparse ('diffuse' or 'random') errors, and convolutional codes for protection against burst errors (although there are several burst-error-correcting block codes). For further discussion of convolutional coding, see also Massey (1963 and 1977), Omura (1977), Schalkwijk (1977) and Viterbi and Omura (1978).

14.6.3 Coding for data security

There are very many aspects to data security. Coding is considered in this section, and dissemination and containment in the following section. For a wider treatment of the subject, see, for example, Denning (1983) and Davies and Price (1984).

Within the ambit of data security, the study of coding, and of its security, is called cryptology. Codes are called ciphers; encoding is encryption, or encipherment; and decoding is decryption or decipherment. A text in encrypted form is called a cryptogram, or ciphertext. In its original form, before encryption (and, if all goes well, after decryption), it is a plaintext. Of course, decryption may be legitimate (by the intended recipient) or illegitimate (by someone else). It is assumed that legitimate and illegitimate recipients differ in more than what they are intended, by the sender, to be. It is usually hoped that they differ in the means, especially information, at their disposal. The business of constructing ciphers is called cryptography, and the art of illegitimate decryption is called cryptanalysis. So, cryptology = cryptography + cryptanalysis.

A cryptographer is concerned about the efficiency of algorithms for encryption and (legitimate) decryption, and about the security of data while it is in encrypted form. It is considered good practice not to rely on the continued secrecy of any algorithm (a principle of Kerkhhoffs: see, for example, Kahn (1967)). So, encryption is usually carried out by means of a publicized (or presumably compromised) algorithm to which are fed two pieces of data which together form the sourcetext: they are (1) the plaintext message, and (2) a key.

For convenience, a message may be broken up into blocks, and each encrypted using the same key. If a different key were used for each block, then each block would be considered as a separate cryptogram and as a separate problem for the cryptanalyst, whose job would be made more difficult. Unfortunately, key economy may require not only that all the blocks of one message, but that several messages, use the same key. The analyst's job is therefore easier, and a decryption may be made using only some of the earlier blocks, or earlier messages.

A recipient may or may not know the plaintext (M), may or may not know the key (K), and may or may not know the ciphertext (Y). The usual circumstances of cryptanalysis are:

1. *Ciphertext only*: from Y we try to deduce K and therefore M.
2. *Known plaintext*: we know a matching (M, Y) pair, and try to deduce K for future use.
3. *Chosen plaintext*: having chosen M, we obtain Y and then try to deduce K for future use.

It would be easy for cryptographers to assert, *a priori*, that their latest creation 'must' be difficult to break (i.e. cryptanalyse), and to justify such an assertion by reference to certain features of the algorithm, whose size or subtlety are considered to provide the necessary evidence. It would even be possible for them to quantify these features, and to state – equally *a priori* – that the degree of difficulty of analysis is of a certain magnitude. Yet all that would be false and in vain. One cannot assert that one has thought of all possible analytical techniques, and so one may not make *a priori* assertions about security. The only acceptable gauge of security – of the difficulty, that is, of breaking a cipher – is the *a posteriori* estimate that is derived from trial by ordeal of cryptanalysis. While mathematical theorems are of use in cryptanalysis, the opposite, absence of a theorem, cannot be used in cryptography. The cases are not symmetric. As in the paradox of the Cretan liar, the opposite of 'proved' is not 'proved false', but rather 'not proved'. Conversely, one supporting example does not prove true, but one counter-example does prove false. The assertion of security is a mere conjecture that may fall at any time. Just as people gain confidence in a conjecture the longer it survives the search for a counter-example, so a cipher may gain in credibility the longer it survives the deliberate and sustained efforts of cryptanalysts to break it. The cryptanalysts are, of course, trying to disprove the conjecture 'this cipher is secure'. It is as well to remember that, for *any* cipher, they may do so at any moment. A cipher will be considered strongest when it has resisted efforts at breaking it in the chosen-plaintext case (3) above.

A cipher can be regarded as a channel whose capacity (as estimated by the recipient) is dependent upon the recipient's knowledge of the key. If the receiver is ignorant of the key, then, ideally, the channel should have zero capacity. Then the channel is useless and the system is secure. If, on the other hand, the recipient has total knowledge of the key, K, then we should want the capacity to be $\Lambda \log n$, where n is the size of the alphabet (common to the plaintext, the key and the ciphertext), and Λ is the length of the message (that is, both of the plaintext and of the ciphertext). Then the channel is perfect. In both cases, the plaintext and the ciphertext are of the same length, Λ, and the cipher algorithm is deterministic (noiseless). But in the case where the key is unknown, the input consists of the pair (plaintext, key), and this exceeds the ciphertext in multiplicity, so the channel will be lossy. On the other hand, when the key is known, it makes a deterministic selection from a number of possible algorithms (the general algorithm, with all possible keys), so the multiplicities of input and output are equal and the channel is perfect. If the channel is indeed totally obscure to an illegitimate receiver, and transparent to a legitimate one, we consider the cryptographic system to be ideally secure and reliable.

Shannon (1949b) published the first information-theoretical – indeed, *theoretical* of any kind – study of cryptographic security. Prior to that, there had been some notable codifications of experience, that of Kerchhoffs (see Kahn, 1967) being of vital importance to good cryptographic practice, but Shannon's was the first to seek a firm mathematical foundation. Since then, two important contributions have been made by Hellman (1977) and by Jürgensen and Matthews (1983), both of which tackle the principal difficulty inherent in Shannon's treatment: namely, the lack of clarity of definition of certain stochastic spaces. See also Deavours (1977) or Reeds (1977).

Consider case (1), where the cryptanalyst knows the ciphertext only. It is necessary also to assume (the worst case for the cryptographer) that the cryptanalyst knows the language in which the plaintext messages are written; that is to say, the analyst can make a good guess at a model (perhaps a Markov model) of the generator of plaintext messages. Then Shannon's analysis shows that enough information will have been gained from the ciphertext for the entropy $H(K|Y)$ of the key, given the ciphertext, to fall to zero, when a certain number, Λ_U, of cipher symbols have been received. This would mean that then the key selection, initially (by hypothesis) uniformly distributed, will have become deterministic from the point of view of the cryptanalyst. This critical length, Λ_U, is called the unicity point, since it is the point in the ciphertext at which the estimate of the key becomes unique, for a given ciphertext. The unicity point is characteristic of the cipher (algorithm) and language (of plaintext) being employed. Its value was shown to be $\Lambda_U = L \log n / (\bar{H}(M))$, whose numerator is the entropy of the entire key – supposed to be of length L – and whose denominator is the absolute redundancy per symbol of the language of the plaintext message. Equivalently, $\Lambda_U = L/(\bar{\eta}(M))$, whose denominator is the relative redundancy of the language.

So, in a protracted, but ultimately successful, exercise in cryptanalysis, $H(K|Y)$ – the entropy of the whole key, as estimated by the analyst in possession of a ciphertext – will decrease gradually from $L \log n$ to zero; that is, $\eta(K)$ will decrease gradually from 1 to 0. In words, the efficiency of the key will dwindle from its full value to nothing. So we must rely on the effectiveness of the algorithm to prevent such a successful attack by making Λ_U as large as possible, or at least exceed the length of the ciphertext. This can be done, for example, by making the key very long, or by making the plaintext language much less redundant. It would be ideal to have a key as long as the message – of the same length as the plaintext, in the case of the 'one-time-pad' (see Welsh, 1988) – but that is not always practicable. It also calls into question the method for making its distribution uniform (see, for example, Lempel and Ziv (1976), Reeds (1977a) and Fischer (1981)). Clearly, the sender would have been wise to destroy all the linguistic information by compressing the message to unit efficiency (zero redundancy) before encipherment. But that is problematic, in so far as it supposes a perfect model of the language upon which to base the compression code. More to the point, such a step is not always practical. It is generally considered more cost-effective to put the time and effort into the design and operation of the cipher (i.e. algorithm) itself. It may, of course, be argued that a statistical, rather than probabilistic, compression could be used (see towards the end of Section 14.6.1.) But then the decompression tables would have to be included in the plaintext, and, in encrypted form, in the ciphertext, and that would cause more problems than it solved. For a discussion, see Reeds (1977b).

These results, while information-theoretically sound, do not take into account the fact that a cipher that is insecure from the point of view of information theory may nevertheless be secure in practice. The memory size, processor power and time necessary to exploit a weakness that is visible to information theory may well exceed the mass, available energy and lifetime of the solar system, and so can reasonably be counted as infeasible. More realistically, even the cost of decryption may be beyond the gross national product of the world; and it need only exceed the value (to the illegitimate recipient) of the thus disclosed data to be uneconomic. The purely information-theoretic approach of Shannon, Hellman, and Jürgensen and Matthews is reliable in setting bounds, and is profoundly suggestive, but is of limited practical use. Unfortunately, the complementary approach, via computational complexity, must await more study of best-case, as opposed to average or worst-case, complexity. That is because the best case for the illegitimate-recipient cryptanalyst is the worst case for the cryptographer in search of security. For a discussion of this topic, see, specifically, Fischer (1981), Yao (1988), and, more generally, Welsh (1988).

For further reading in cryptology, Diffie and Hellman (1976 and 1979), Lempel (1979), Denning (1983), Davies and Price (1984) Welsh (1988).

14.7 Dissemination and containment of information

Since the diffusion of information is often used as a model for secrecy and security, it will be as well to make clear how information may or may not be created, destroyed, disseminated or contained. Consider an example: data can be replicated at negligible cost, but does copying a document increase the amount of information? In fact, no new information is created in common with that of the message in the document, but some new, independent, information is observable: namely, the information that the document *has* been copied, and how many times. If I can write to or read from filing system, and if you may not do either of these but may look at the table of contents, then we may penetrate the security of the system by *my* adjusting the number of copies of a previously agreed file that are stored in it, according to a code agreed between us: and *your* examining the contents to discover that number thereby receiving some information from me. For a discussion of problems of this kind, see Denning (1983).

Taking a more general view, there are two main types of law that can apply to the difference in the total amount of some measurable quantity, $M(t)$, at two times t_1 and t_2 (with $t_1 < t_2$):

(C) $M(t_1) = M(t_2)$

which is usually given in the form $M(t) = constant$, and:

(D) $M(t_1) \geqslant M(t_2)$

with equality under some special condition. (The converse, $M(t_1) \leqslant M(t_2)$, is only trivially distinct, since we may define $M' = -M$.)

Of these laws, (C) is a conservation law. It applies, for example, to all the electric charge in the universe; also to all the energy (including mass-energy) in the universe; and also to the total angular momentum of the component parts of the solar system. Instead of to 'the universe', the law may be applied to any closed system contained by a boundary impervious to the passage of the measured quantity, or to any system sufficiently decoupled by distance from the effects of other systems. Mere containment or decoupling is not in itself sufficient for any quantity to be conserved: the quantity itself must be one that is innately conserved. Some are, and some are not. Electric charge, for instance, is conserved if we take account of sign. A closed conducting container that starts neutral will remain neutral. Electric field is also conserved in any such container within which the charges are stationary. See, for example, Brillouin (1951). The positive and negative charges can be represented as sources and sinks of electric field, so that the conservation can be expressed for sub-regions of the container.

Law (D), on the other hand, is a dissipation law. It applies, for example, to the negative of the physical entropy ('negentropy') of the universe. See, for example, Brillouin (1951). The purely numerical (i.e. physically dimensionless) entropy, $H(X)$, of a physical system, X, is given by $H(X) = \log N$, where N is the number of possible internal arrangements of the system when it is observed to be in a given external state, and where all those N arrangements are equally probable. This number is then linked to the physical entropy by:

$$S(X) = k\,H(X)$$
$$\qquad = k \log N \text{ (units of energy/temperature)}$$

where k, Boltzmann's constant, has the approximate value $1.38 \times 10^{-23}\,\text{JK}^{-1}$. Physical entropy can never be destroyed, and its magnitude is left unchanged only by reversible processes; otherwise, it increases with time. (So, reversible processes provide the equality condition for the law in its form as at (D) above.) For a thumbnail history, invoking the names of Boltzmann, Planck, Gibbs, Shannon and Wiener, see the Foreword to Levine and Tribus (1979).

Put the other way around, negentropy can never be created. The universe is provided with a fixed quantity of it, which all spontaneous (and therefore irreversible) processes are gradually squandering (see, for example, Bent (1965)). Even if a living process causes a local increase in negentropy, that must be paid for by an even greater decrease elsewhere, so that there is a net loss over the entire universe.

Informational entropy behaves like physical (neg)entropy in that it is dissipative. The same measure, entropy, is used for information and for noise. What matters is the amount of entropy in common between any arbitrary signal and some data that we have selected as a 'message' that we wish to transmit or store. The physical configuration of any part of the universe (including an idea held in a human brain), however arrived at, may be counted as a message whose information can be conveyed elsewhere (transmitted through space) or stored for later use (transmitted through time). Although we regard our selection process ('*this* is a *message*') as designating a source of information, we have not created any new information thereby; and, because entropy is dissipative, there are no sinks of information.

Information cannot travel faster than the speed of light, so in order to move through space it must take time. The history of the universe is a channel from the past to the future. It is not a perfect channel, and in general the evolution of any physical configuration will involve loss and noise. Among the physical configurations that are subject to these effects are both human and computer memory systems. We carry forward information imperfectly from past to future. The same applies to all records; the process of recording, storing and retrieving are all imperfect. Even if we perform archaeological experiments to try to discover the past, albeit only probabilistically, we get less information than was there originally. More accurately, we should say that the entropy in common between us (now) and the past system that existed (then) is in general less than, and certainly not greater than, the absolute entropy of either of those systems on its own. This can work the other way round. It is instructive to regard science – that is, the performing of experiments in order to form and test theories about the future – as an attempt to communicate through a channel from the future to the present. The channel is noisy and lossy, and there is only limited entropy in common between its ends. Just as with a channel between A and B in everyday life, where you can walk round from the receiver to the transmitter to find out how good your past decoding actually was, so with theories. You can perform experiments, involving a wait for the elapse of time, to see how good your predictions were. In neither case is it much help for the next time round, except as more information to be fed into your model of the channel; that is, as a correction to your estimates of the stochastic spaces themselves. We cannot go back to the past, but, on the other hand, we can never know that the information that we have in our possession about the past is *all* the information about it that now exists (and that could in principle come into our possession). A surprising discovery of information may be made at any moment.

This is all to point out the difficulty not only of *retaining* information, but also of *destroying* it. If we were sure that an 'opponent' was going to use a certain channel, we could perhaps arrange for the capacity of that channel to be set to zero. But we are not sure. And even so, that would merely block transmission on this one occasion, leaving the source untouched. In the context of data security, we are in the position of a blackmail victim. We hand over money (a conserved quantity) in exchange for a photograph (information: a dissipative quantity). We can never know that we have bought all copies of the photograph, in whatever form. We do know that copies may be made, without important limit, at negligible cost. The discovery of an unadmitted copy will not bring our money back. Information is dissipative, but money is conserved. There are no sinks for information.

14.8 Bibliography and development of the subject

The *locus classicus* is Shannon (1948). This is reprinted in book form in Shannon and Weaver (1949) and also, together with an important paper by McMillan (1953), in a survey by Slepian (1974). For the allied (and partly dependent) topic of coding theory, see the surveys by Blake (1973) and Berlekamp (1974). The first textbooks to use the term 'information theory' in their titles were Bell (1953) and Goldman (1953). Advanced treatments include Feinstein (1958), Fano (1961), Gallager (1964 and 1968) and Jelinek (1968b). The present author recommends McEliece (1977) as a general introduction to information and coding theory, although Ash (1965) is better on some topics.

The early history of information theory – when general principles were gradually teased out of a collection of special cases, when a clear distinction began to be drawn between physical and mathematical theories, and the relationship between them came to be articulated – can be traced through the work of Nyquist (1924 and 1928), Hartley (1928), Wiener (1949), Gabor (1946 and 1950), Shannon (1948 and 1949a), Brillouin (1951), Woodward and Davies (1952), Woodward (1953) and Ashby (1956). Brillouin (1956 and 1964) has also studied the extent to which physical phenomena – principally

the effects of the laws of thermodynamics – limit the extent to which information can be stored or transmitted reliably, even given the constraints of the Shannon theory. Beware that this line of discussion, as with many 'applications' of information theory, can pass through the fanciful to the misleading: a useful corrective is supplied by Denbigh and Denbigh (1985). See also Kubát and Zeman (1975).

There have been many essays in strengthening the philosophical foundations of Shannon's classical model; see, for example, Fadiev (1956), Khinchin (1957), Golomb (1961) and Lee (1964), the latter dealing with the continuous distribution of probability. For an approach that deals with the question 'how random is a given finite string?', evolving into the subject of *algorithmic information theory*, see Selfridge (1956) – who defined a pattern as equivalent to a set of rules for recognizing it – Brown (1956) – including the ensuing discussions by Good, Hutten, Mayne and Bar-Hillel – see Solomonov (1964), Kolmogorov (1965 and 1968), Martin-Löf (1966), Chaitin (1966, 1969, 1974, 1975, 1990), Lempel and Ziv (1976), and various discussions in Székely (1986). For historical reviews of the classical theory, see Weaver (1949), Cherry (1950 and 1953), Gabor (1953), Gilbert (1966), Pierce (1973), Slepian (1973), Viterbi (1973) and Tribus (1979).

Most of the alternative theories of information are to be found among:

1. Those that keep Shannon's entropy, but attempt to take into account the finite resources (processor power, memory space, time and money) available for encoding and decoding.
2. Those that retain a probabilistic basis, but define alternative entropies, upon it, perhaps for example not requiring that all outcomes have their probabilities known.
3. Those that define information measures in terms of non-probabilistic representations of uncertainty: belief, plausibility, possibility and suchlike.

For examples of (1), see Yao (1988), Orlitsky and El Gamal (1988) and Traub (1988). For (2), see Rényi (1961), Aczél and Daróczy (1975), Behara and Chawla (1975), Kannapan (1975) and Mathai and Rathie (1975). For (3), see, discursively, Good (1971), technically, Klir and Folger (1988). Most of the works that come into category (2) above include a study of characterizations – that is, menus containing many possible axioms, from which an operative selection may be made – and considerations of the consequences of several such possible selections. In this way, Hobson and Cheng (1973), Aczél, Forte and Ng (1974), Forte (1975) and Aczél (1975) compare Shannon's characterization with several alternatives.

A fruitful alternative theory of probability and decision-making involves standing the whole discussion on its head, taking the maximum-entropy principle as axiomatic, and deriving probability theory and decision theory from it (see, essentially, Jaynes (1979)).

14.9 References

Abramson, N. (1963) *Information Theory and Coding*, McGraw-Hill, New York

Abu-Mostafa, Y. S. (ed.) (1988) *Complexity in Information Theory*, Springer-Verlag, New York

Aczél, J. (1975) On Shannon's inequality, optimal coding, and characterisations of Shannon's and Rényi's entropies. *Symposia Mathematica*, **15**, 153–179

Aczél, J., Behara, M., Chawla, J. M. S. *et al.* (1975) *Entropy and Ergodic Theory*, Hindustan Publishing Corporation, Delhi, India

Aczél, J., Forte, B. and Ng, C. T. (1974) Why the Shannon and Hartley entropies are 'natural'. *Advances in Applied Probability*, **6**, 131–146

Aczél, J. and Daróczy, Z. (1975) *On Measures of Information and Their Characterisations*, Academic Press, New York

Arimoto, S. (1972) An algorithm for computing the capacity of arbitrary discrete memoryless channels. *IEEE Transactions on Informa-*

tion Theory, **IT-18**, 14–20

Ash, R. (1965) *Information Theory*, John Wiley, New York

Ashby, W. R. (1956) *An Introduction to Cybernetics*, Chapman and Hall, London

Attneave, F. (1959) *Applications of Information Theory: a Summary of Basic Concepts, Methods and Results*, Henry Holt, New York

Behara, M. and Chawla, J. M. S. (1975) Generalised gamma-entropy. In Aczél *et al.* (1975) *Entropy and Ergodic Theory*, Hindustan Publishing Corporation, Delhi, India

Bell, D. A. (1953) *Information Theory*, Pitman, London

Benelli, G., Del Re, E., Cappellini, V. and Lotti, F. (1985a) Data compression techniques. In *Data Compression and Error Control Techniques with Applications* (ed. V. Capellini), Academic Press, London

Benelli, G. and Biancardi, C. (1985b) Channel models and channel coding. In *Data Compression and Error Control Techniques with Applications* (ed. V. Cappellini), Academic Press, London

Benelli, G., Biancardi, C. and Cappellini, V. (1985c) Error control coding techniques. In *Data Compression and Error Control Techniques with Applications* (ed. V. Cappellini), Academic Press, London

Benelli, G., Del Re, E. and Cappellini, V. (1985d) Joint source and channel coding. In *Data Compression and Error Control Techniques with Applications* (ed. V. Cappellini), Academic Press, London

Benelli, G., Del Re, E. and Lotti, F. (1985e) Software implementation of data compression and error control techniques. In *Data Compression and Error Control Techniques with Applications* (ed. V. Cappellini), Academic Press, London

Bent, H. A. (1965) *The Second Law: an Introduction to Classical and Statistical Thermodynamics*, Oxford University Press, New York

Berger, T. (1971) *Rate Distortion Theory: a Mathematical Basis for Data Compression*, Prentice-Hall, Englewood Cliffs, NJ, USA

Berlekamp, E. R. (1968) *Algebraic Coding Theory*, McGraw-Hill, New York

Berlekamp, E. R. (ed.) (1974) *Key Papers in the Development of Coding Theory*, IEEE Press, New York

Billingsley, P. (1965) *Ergodic Theory and Information*, John Wiley, New York

Blake, I. F. (ed.) (1973) *Algebraic Coding Theory: History and Development*, Dowden, Hutchinson and Ross, Stroudsberg, PA, USA

Blake, I. F. and Mullin, R. C. (1976) *An Introduction to Algebraic and Combinatorial Coding Theory*, Academic Press, New York

Brillouin, L. (1951) Information and entropy: I and II. *Journal of Applied Physics*, **22**, 334–337 and 338–343

Brillouin, L. (1956) *Science and Information Theory*, Academic Press, New York

Brillouin, L. (1964) *Scientific Uncertainty, and Information*, Academic Press, New York

Cappellini, V. (ed.) (1985a) *Data Compression and Error Control Techniques with Applications*, Academic Press, London

Cappellini, V. (1985b) Applications of data compression and error control techniques. In *Data Compression and Error Control Techniques with Applications*, Academic Press, London

Cattermole, K. W. (1986) *Mathematical Foundations for Communication Engineering; Volume 2: Statistical Analysis and Finite Structures*, Pentech Press, London

Chaitin, G. J. (1966) On the lengths of programs for computing finite binary sequences. *Journal of the ACM*, **13**, 547–569. Also in Chaitin (1990) below

Chaitin, G. J. (1969) On the lengths of programs for computing finite binary sequences: statistical considerations. *Journal of the ACM*, **16**, 145–159. Also in Chaitin (1990) below

Chaitin, G. J. (1974) Information-theoretic computational complexity. *IEEE Transactions on Information Theory*, **IT-20**, 10–15

Chaitin, G. J. (1975) A theory of program size formally identical to information theory. *Journal of the ACM*, **22**, 329–340. Also in Chaitin (1990) below

Chaitin, G. J. (1990) *Information, Randomness and Incompleteness: Papers on Algorithmic Information Theory*. 2nd edition, Singapore: World Scientific

Chambers, W. G. (1985) *Basics of Communications and Coding*, Clarendon Press, Oxford

Chaum, D. (ed.) (1983) *Advances in Cryptology: Proceedings of Crypto 83*, Plenum Press, New York

Cherry, E. C. (1950) A history of the theory of information. In *Proceedings of the (First London) Symposium on Information Theories 1950* (ed. Jackson, W. D.) Ministry of Supply, London and (1951) *Proceedings of the IEE*, **98-III**, 383–393

Cherry, E. C. (1953). *On Human Communication*, Chapman and Hall, London

Cherry, E. C. (ed.) (1956) *Proceedings of the Third London Symposium on Information Theory, 1955*, Butterworth Scientific, London

Clark, G. C. and Cain, J. B. (1981) *Error-correcting Coding for Digital Communications*. Plenum Press, New York

Cover, T. M. (1973) Enumerative source encoding. *IEEE Transactions on Information Theory*, **IT-19**, 73–77. Also in *Data Compression* (eds L. D. Davisson and R. M. Gray), Dowden, Hutchinson and Ross, Stroudsberg, PA, USA

Crick, F. H. C., Griffiths, J. S. and Orgel, L. E. (1957) Codes without commas. *Proceedings of the [US] National Academy of Science*, **43**, 416–421

Davies, D. W. and Price, W. L. (1984) *Security for Computer Networks: an Introduction to Data Security in Teleprocessing and Electronic Funds Transfer*, Wiley, Chichester

Davisson, L. D. (1973) Universal noiseless coding. *IEEE Transactions on Information Theory*, **IT-19**, 783–795

Davisson, L. D. and Gray, R. M. (eds) (1976) *Data Compression*, Dowden, Hutchinson and Ross, Stroudsberg, PA, USA

Deavours, C. A. (1977). Unicity points in cryptanalysis. *Cryptologia*, **1**, 46–68. Also in *Cryptology: Yesterday, Today and Tomorrow* (1987) (eds. C. A. Deavours *et al.*), Artech House, Norwood, MA, USA

Deavours, C. A., Kahn, D., Kruh, L., Mellen, G. and Winkel, B. (1987) *Cryptology: Yesterday, Today and Tomorrow*, Artech House, Norwood, MA, USA

Denbigh, K. G. and Denbigh, J. S. (1985) *Entropy in Relation to Incomplete Knowledge*, Cambridge University Press, Cambridge

Denning, D. E. R. (1983) *Cryptography and Data Security*, Addison-Wesley, Reading, MA, USA

Diffie, W. and Hellman, M. (1976) New directions in cryptography. *IEEE Transactions on Information Theory*, **IT-22**, 644–654

Diffie, W. and Hellman, M. (1979) Privacy and authentication: an introduction to cryptography. *Proceedings of the IEEE*, **67**, 397–427

Eastman, W. L. (1965) On the construction of comma-free codes. *IEEE Transactions on Information Theory*, **IT-11**, 263–267

Elias, P. (1975) Universal codeword sets and representations of the integers. *IEEE Transactions on Information Theory*, **IT-21**, 194–203

Fadiev, D. K. (1956) On the notion of entropy of a finite probability space. *Uspekhi matematieskikh nauk*, **11**, 227–231 [in Russian]

Fano, R. M. (1949) *Technical Report No. 65*, MIT Research Laboratory of Electronics, Cambridge, MA, USA

Fano, R. M. (1961) *Transmission of Information*, MIT Press, Cambridge, MA, USA

Feinstein, A. (1958) *Foundations of Information Theory*, McGraw-Hill, New York

Fischer, E. (1981) A theoretical measure of cryptographic performance. *Cryptologia*, **5**, 59–62. Also in *Cryptology: Yesterday, Today and Tomorrow* (1987) (eds C. A. Deavours *et al.*), Artech House, Norwood, MA, USA

Forte, B. (1975) Why Shannon's entropy. *Symposia Mathematica*, **15**, 137–152

Gabor, D. (1946) Theory of communication. *Journal of the IEE*, **93-III**, 429–457

Gabor, D. (1950) *Communication theory and physics*. In Jackson (1950) and, expanded, in *Philosophical Magazine*, **41**, 1161–1187 (1950)

Gabor, D. (1953) A summary of communication theory. In *Proceedings of the Second London Symposium on Information Theory*, 1952 (ed. W. D. Jackson), Butterworth Scientific, London

Gács, P. and Köner, J. (1973) Common information is far less than mutual information. *Problems of control and information theory*, **2**, 149–162

Gallager, R. G. (1964) Information theory. In *The Mathematics of Physics and Chemistry, Vol. 2* (eds H. Margenau and C. M. Murphy), Van Nostrand, Princeton, NJ, USA

Gallager, R. G. (1968) *Information Theory and Reliable Communication*, Wiley, New York

Gilbert, E. N. (1960a) Capacity of a burst noise channel. *Bell System Technical Journal*, **39**, 1253–1265

Gilbert, E. N. (1960b) Synchronization of binary messages. *IEEE Transactions on Information Theory*, **IT-6**, 470–477

Gilbert, E. N. (1966) Information theory after 18 years. *Science*, **152**, 320–326

Godambe, V. P. and Sprott, D. A. (eds) (1971) *Foundations of Statistical Inference*, Holt, Rinehart and Winston, Toronto, Canada

Golay, M. J. E. (1949) Notes on digital coding. *Proceedings of the IRE*, **37**, p. 657. Also in Blake (1973) and Berlekamp (1974) above

Goldman, S. (1953) *Information Theory*, Prentice-Hall, Englewood Cliffs, NJ, USA

Golomb, S. W. (1961) A new derivation of the entropy expressions. *IRE Transactions on Information Theory*, **IT-7**, 166–167

Golomb, S. W. (1966) Run-length encodings. *IEEE Transactions on Information Theory*, **IT-12**, 399–401

Golomb, S. W., Gordon, B. and Welch, L. R. (1958a) Comma-free codes. *Canadian Journal of Mathematics*, **10**, 202–209

Golomb, S. W., Welch, L. R. and Delbrück, M. (1958b) Construction and properties of comma-free codes. *Biologiske medelelser udgivet af det Kongelige Danske videnskabernes selskab*, **23**, 1–34

Good, I. J. (1971) The probabilistic explication of information, evidence, surprise, causality, explanation and utility. In *Foundations of Statistical Inference* (eds V. P. Godambe and D. A. Sprott), Holt, Rinehart and Winston, Toronto, Canada

Graham, A. (1981) *Kronecker Products and Matrix Calculus with Applications*, Ellis Horwood, Chichester

Gray, R. M. and Davisson, L. D. (1974) A mathematical theory of data compression. In *Proceedings of the 1974 International Conference on Communications*. Also USCEE report 477, University of Southern California Electronic Sciences Laboratory, Los Angeles

Gray, R. M. and Davisson, L. D. (eds) (1977) *Ergodic and Information Theory*, Dowden, Hutchinson and Ross, Stroudsberg, PA, USA

Guiaşu, S. (1977) *Information Theory with Applications*, McGraw-Hill International, London

Guibas, L. J. and Odlyzko, A. M. (1978). Maximal prefix-synchronized codes. *SIAM Journal of Applied Mathematics*, **35**, 401–418

Hamming, R. W. (1950) Error correcting and error detecting codes. *Bell System Technical Journal*, **29**, 147–160. Also in Blake (1973) and Berlekamp (1974) above

Hartley, R. V. L. (1928) Transmission of information. *Bell System Technical Journal*, **7**, 535–563

Hellman, M. E. (1977) An extension of the Shannon theory approach to cryptography. *IEEE Transactions on Information Theory*, **IT-23**, 289–294

Hobson, A. and Cheng, B-K. (1973) A comparison of the Shannon and Kullback information measures. *Journal of Statistical Physics*, **7**, 301–310

Huang, T. S. (1977) Efficient coding of graphics [and] efficient coding of continuous-tone images. In *The Information Theory Approach to Communications* (ed. G. Longo), Springer-Verlag, Vienna, Austria

Huffman, D. A. (1952) A method for the construction of minimum redundancy codes. In *Proceedings of the IRE*, **40**, pp. 1098–1101. Also in Jackson (1953) and Slepian (1974) below

Jackson, W. D. (ed.) (1950) *Proceedings of the [First London] Symposium of Information Theory, 1950*, Ministry of Supply, London

Jackson, W. D. (ed.) (1953) *Communication Theory: Proceedings of the Second London Symposium on Information Theory, 1952*, Butterworths Scientific, London

Jakobsson, M. (1978) Huffman coding in bit-vector compression. *Information Processing Letters*, **7**, 304–307

Jaynes, E. T. (1979) Where do we stand on maximum entropy? In *The Maximum Entropy Formalism* (eds R. D. Levine and M. Tribus), MIT Press, Cambridge, MA, USA

Jelinek, F. (1968a) Buffer overflow in variable length coding of fixed rate sources. *IEEE Transactions on Information Theory*, **IT-14**, 490–501. Also in Davisson and Gray (1976) above

Jelinek, F. (1968b) *Probabilistic Information Theory: Discrete and Memoryless Models*, McGraw-Hill, New York

Jelinek, F. and Schneider, K. S. (1972) On variable-length-to-block coding. *IEEE Transactions on Information Theory*, **IT-18**, 765–774. Also in Davisson and Gray (1976) above

Jiggs, B. H. (1963) Recent results on comma-free codes. *Canadian Journal of Mathematics*, **15**, 178–187

Jürgensen, H. and Matthews, D. E. (1983) Some results on the information-theoretic analysis of cryptosystems. In *Advances in Cryptology: Proceedings of Crypto 83* (ed. D. Chaum), Plenum Press, New York

Kahn, D. (1967) *The Codebreakers*, Macmillan, New York, USA

Kannapan, P. (1975) On Réyni–Shannon entropy and related measures. In *Entropy and Ergodic Theory* (eds J. Aczél *et al.*), Hindustan Publishing Corporation, Delhi, India

Kendall, M. G. (1961) *A Course in the Geometry of* n *Dimensions*, Charles Griffin, London

Khinchin, A. I. (1957) *Mathematical Foundations of Information Theory*, Dover, New York

Klir, G. J. and Folger, T. A. (1988) *Fuzzy Sets, Uncertainty, and Information*, Prentice-Hall International, London

Kolmogorov, A. N. (1965) Three approaches for defining the concept of information quantity. *Information Transmission*, **1**, 1–8. [Tri podhoda k opredeleniju ponjatija 'kolidestvo informacii'. *Problemy peredači informacii*, **1**, 3–11]

Kolmogorov, A. N. (1968) Logical basis for information theory and probability theory, *IEEE Transactions on Information Theory*, **IT-14**, 662–664

Krippendorff, K. (1986) *Information Theory: Structural Models for Qualitative Data*, Sage Publications, Beverly Hills, CA, USA

Kubát, L. and Zeman, J. (eds) (1975) *Entropy and Information in Science and Philosophy*, Elsevier Scientific, Amsterdam

Kullback, S. (1959) *Information Theory and Statistics*, Wiley, New York

Lee, P. M. (1964) On the axioms of information theory. *Annals of Mathematical Statistics*, **35**, 415–418

Lee, T. C., Judge, G. G. and Zellner, A. (1970) *Estimating the Parameters of the Markov Probability Model from Aggregate Time Series Data*, North-Holland, Amsterdam

Lempel, A. (1979) Cryptology in transition. *Computing Surveys*, **11**, 285–303

Lempel, A. and Ziv, J. (1976) On the complexity of finite sequences. *IEEE Transactions on Information Theory*, **IT-22**, 75–81

Levine, R. D. and Tribus, M. (eds) (1979) *The Maximum Entropy Formalism*, MIT Press, Cambridge, MA, USA

Levy, J. E. (1966) Self-synchronizing codes derived from binary cyclic codes. *IEEE Transactions on Information Theory*, **IT-12**, 286–290

Lin, S. and Costello, D. J. (1983) *Error Control Coding: Fundamentals and Applications*, Prentice-Hall, Englewood Cliffs, NJ, USA

Llewellyn, J. A. (1987) *Information and Coding*, Chartwell-Bratt, Bromley

Longo, G. (ed.) (1977) *The Information Theory Approach to Communications*, Springer-Verlag, Vienna, Austria

Longo, G. and Sgarro, A. (1985) Source coding. In *Data Compression and Error Control Techniques with Applications* (ed. V. Cappellini), Academic Press, London

MacWilliams, F. J. and Sloane, N. J. A. (1977) *The Theory of Error-Correcting Codes*, North-Holland, Amsterdam

Margenau, H. and Murphy, G. M. (eds) (1964) *The Mathematics of Physics and Chemistry, Vol. II*, Van Nostrand, Princeton, NJ, USA

Martin-Löf, P. (1966) The definition of random sequences. *Information and Control*, **9**, 602–619

McEliece, R. J. (1977) *The Theory of Information and Coding: a Mathematical Framework for Communication*, Addison-Wesley, Reading, MA, USA

McMillan, B. (1953) The basic theorems of information theory. *Annals of Mathematical Statistics*, **24**, 196–219

McMillan, B. (1956) Two inequalities implied by unique decipherability. *IRE Transactions on Information Theory*, **IT-2**, 115–116

Mathai, A. M. and Rathie, P. N. (1975) *Basic Concepts in Information Theory and Statistics*, Wiley Eastern, New Delhi, India

Nyquist, H. (1924) Certain factors affecting telegraph speed. *Bell System Technical Journal*, **3**, 324–346

Nyquist, H. (1928) Certain topics in telegraph transmission theory. *AIEE Transactions*, **47**, 617

Omura, J. K. (1977) Source and channel coding with block and convolutional codes. In *The Information Theory Approach to Communications* (ed. G. Longo), Springer-Verlag, Vienna, Austria

Orlitsky, A. and El Gamal, A. (1988) Communication complexity. In *Complexity in Information Theory* (ed. Y. S. Abu-Mostafa), Springer-Verlag, New York

Paz, A. (1971) *Introduction to Probablistic Automata*, Academic Press, New York

Peterson, W. W. and Weldon, E. J. (1972) *Error correcting codes* (2nd edn), MIT Press, Cambridge, MA

Pierce, J. R. (1973) The early days of information theory. *IEEE Transactions on Information Theory*, **IT-19**, 3–8

Reeds, J. (1977a) 'Cracking' a random number generator. *Cryptologia*, **1**, 20–26. Also in Deavours *et al.* (1987) above

Reeds, J. (1977b) Entropy calculations and particular methods of cryptanalysis. *Cryptologia*, **3**, 235–254. Also in Deavours *et al.* (1987) above

Reghbati, H. K. (1981) An overview of data compression techniques. *IEEE Computer*, **14** (April), 71–76

Rényi, A. (1961) On measures of entropy and information. In *Proceedings of the Fourth Berkeley Symposium on Mathematical Statistics and Probability, 1960, Vol. I*, pp. 547–561, University of California Press, Berkeley, CA, USA

Reza, F. M. (1961) *An Introduction to Information Theory*, McGraw-Hill, New York

Richards, I. A. (1951) *The Wrath of Achilles: the* Iliad *of Homer, Shortened and in a New Translation*, Routledge and Kegan Paul, London

Sardinas, A. A. and Patterson, G. W. (1953) A necessary and sufficient condition for the decomposition of coded messages. *IRE Convention Record*, 104–108

Schalkwijk, J. P. M. (1977) Convolutional codes: a state–space approach. In *The Information Theory approach to Communications* (ed. G. Longo), Springer-Verlag, Vienna, Austria

Scholtz, R. A. (1969) Maximal and variable word-length comma-free codes. *IEEE Transactions on Information Theory*, **IT-15**, 300–306

Schwartz, E. S. and Kleiboemer, A. J. (1967) A language element for compression coding. *Information and Control*, **10**, 315–333

Shannon, C. E. (1948) A mathematical theory of communication. *Bell System Technical Journal*, **27**, 379–423 and 623–656. Also in Shannon and Weaver (1949) and Slepian (1974) below

Shannon, C. E. (1949a) Communication in the presence of noise. *Proceedings of the IRE*, **37**, 10–21. Also in Slepian (1974) below

Shannon, C. E. (1949b) Communication theory of secrecy systems. *Bell System Technical Journal*, **28**, 656–715

Shannon, C. E. (1951) Prediction and entropy of printed English. *Bell System Technical Journal*, **30**, 50–64 Also in Slepian (1974) below

Shannon, C. E. (1959) Coding theorems for a discrete source with a fidelity criterion. *IRE National Convention Record*, part 4, 142–163 Also in Slepian (1974) below

Shannon, C. E. and Weaver, W. (1949) *The Mathematical Theory of Communication*, Illinois University Press, Urbana, IL, USA

Stiffler, J. J. (1971) *Theory of Synchronous Communication*. Prentice-Hall, Englewood Cliffs, NJ, USA

Slepian, D. (1973) Information theory in the fifties. *IEEE Transactions on Information Theory*, **IT-19**, 145–147

Slepian, D. (ed.) (1974) *Key Papers in the Development of Information Theory*, IEEE Press, New York

Solomonov, R. J. (1964) A formal theory of inductive inference. *Information and Control*, **7**, 1–22, 224–254

Székely, G. J. (1986) *Paradoxes in Probability Theory and Mathematical Statistics*, Reidel, Dordrecht

Traub, J. (1988) Introduction to information-based complexity. In *Complexity in Information Theory* (ed. Y. S. Abu-Mostafa), Springer-Verlag, New York

Tribus, M. (1979) Thirty years of information theory. In *The Maximum Entropy Formalism* (eds R. D. Levine and M. Tribus), MIT Press, Cambridge, MA, USA

Viterbi, A. J. (1973) Information theory in the sixties. *IEEE Transactions on Information Theory*, **IT-19**, 257–262

Viterbi, A. J. and Omura, J. (1978) *Digital Communication and Coding*, McGraw-Hill, New York

Weaver, W. (1949) Recent contributions to the mathematical theory of communication. In *The Mathematical Theory of Communication* (eds C. E. Shannon and W. Weaver), Illinois University Press, Urbana, IL, USA

Welch, T. A. (1984) A technique for high-performance data compression. *IEEE Computer*, **17** (June), 8–19

Welsh, D. (1988) *Codes and Cryptography*, Clarendon Press, Oxford

Wiener, N. (1949) *The Extrapolation, Interpolation and Smoothing of Stationary Time Series*, Wiley, New York

Wilkins, L. C. and Wintz, P. A. (1971) Bibliography on data compression, picture properties, and picture coding. *IEEE Transactions on Information Theory*, **IT-17**, 180–197

Wolfowitz, J. (1964) *The Coding Theorems of Information Theory* (2nd edn), Prentice-Hall, Englewood Cliffs, NJ, USA

Woodward, P. M. (1953) *Probability and Information Theory, with Application to Radar*, Pergamon, London

Woodward, P. M. and Davies, I. L. (1952) Information theory and inverse probability in telecommunication. *Proceedings of the IEE*, **99-III**, 37–44

Wyner, A. D. (1970) Another look at the coding theorem of information theory – a tutorial. *Proceedings of the IEEE*, **58**, 894–913

Yao, A. (1988) Computational information theory. In *Complexity in Information Theory* (ed. Y. S. Abu-Mostafa), Springer-Verlag, New York

Ziv, J. and Lempel, A. (1977) A universal algorithm for sequential data compression. *IEEE Transactions on Information Theory*, **IT-23**, 337–343

Ziv, J. and Lempel, A. (1978) Compression of individual sequences via variable-rate coding. *IEEE Transactions on Information Theory*, **IT-24**, 530–536

Part II

Methods, Techniques and Technology

Introductory Material

Introduction and overview to Part II

John A. McDermid

1 Introduction

Engineering is not *just* applied science. Engineering is a creative and innovative undertaking. The relevant science provides the basis for *analysing* designs and systems but, in general, it provides only limited guidance for creating designs and for managing engineering projects.

These general principles are true for software engineering. Thus software engineering is not *just* applied computer science. More pertinently, it is not just the application of the science and mathematics set out in Part I. It is therefore helpful to discuss definitions of engineering and software engineering in order to define the scope of Part II of the reference book and to set out its relationship to Part I.

1.1 Definition of software engineering

There are many definitions of engineering. One of the most common is that:

> Engineering is the application of science and mathematics to the design and construction of artefacts which are useful to man.

Given our discussion above, this seems to be rather a narrow definition. A more appealing definition (within a more limited context) comes from the journal entitled *The Structural Engineer*, published by the Institution of Structural Engineers in the UK:

> Structural engineering is the science and art of designing and making, with economy and elegance, buildings, bridges, frameworks and other structures so that they can safely resist the forces to which they may be subjected.

The reference to 'art' addresses the issue of creativity and the term 'economy' at least hints at management, but the definition, as stated, is clearly not applicable to software engineering.

In order to adapt this definition to software engineering we first need a definition of software. Following the thrust of the general definition of engineering a broad definition might be that:

> Software consists of the programs, documentation and operating procedures by which computers can be made useful to man.

The definition of structural engineering did not address issues of specification, issues of delivery schedules nor of post-delivery maintenance. Addressing these limitations, we arrive at a new definition:

> Software engineering is the science and art of specifying, designing, implementing and evolving – with economy, timeliness and elegance – programs, documentation and operating procedures whereby computers can be made useful to man.

Whilst this definition may not cover all facets of the term it does seem to capture the essential spirit and breadth of the notion of 'software engineering'.

Implicity, this definition also sets out the basic goal of software engineering as being:

> (to facilitate) specification, design, implementation and evolution of programs, documentation and operating procedures which are useful to man, in an economic, timely and elegant manner (using the appropriate science and art).

The aim of Part II is to set out means of acheiving this goal (or coming as close as to it was we know how). However, before we consider what means are relevant it is constructive to consider the impediments to achieving this goal.

1.2 Problems of software development

In considering the problems of software development it is helpful to discuss both the symptoms of the problems and their underlying causes.

1.2.1 Symptoms of the problems

Stories of failed software projects are legion and the cliché 'the software crisis' has now acquired the status of Peter's cries of 'wolf'. However, as in Peter's case there is some substance behind the cries and there is a problem which may yet reach crisis proportions. Perhaps one of the best summaries of the problem comes from a survey of US government projects published by the US Government Accounting Office in 1979. Based on nine software projects the cost and destiny of the software was:

- Paid for but never delivered: $3.2M.
- Delivered but not used: $2.0M.
- Abandoned or reworked: $1.3M.
- Used after changes: $0.2M.
- Used as delivered: $0.1M.

It is tempting to believe that these were problems of the 1970s and that everything is now much better. Indeed, the situation does seem much better, but there are still horrendous problems. We need only consider a few.

In the 1970s the UK MoD embarked on the procurement of the Nimrod airborne early warning (AEW) system intended to provide warning of airborne attacks on western Europe from the east. Requirements and design evolved through countless versions and, although much functional software was produced for the complex multi-processor system, the project was cancelled in 1986 and a decision made to purchase the US AWACS system instead. This technico-political decision was, in essence, based on greater confidence that the working AWACS system could be modified to the UK requirements than that the AEW system could be completed. Cancellation effectively wrote off hundreds of millions of pounds worth of development. The primary problem seems to have been continual and substantive change in detailed requirements, but see Malcolm (1990) for a deeper analysis of the problems, including some of the difficulties that arose from inappropriate design decisions.

Another, more recent, example of an unsuccessful project is that of a secure office information system, known as Folios, developed for the UK Government. Folios was intended to automate much of the existing paper-based message and document handling functions of part of a UK government department, and to do so whilst enforcing the rules for handling classified documents. The project was cancelled in 1989 after four years work and £3.5M had been spent. Further, the contractors were instructed to repay most of the money they had received from the Government. Press reports at the time (*Computer Weekly*, Nov. 1989) indicated that the main reason for cancelling the project was the poor performance and response of the system which was caused, at least in part, by use of outdated hardware. This case is not as well documented as Nimrod but from my experience in the early stages of the project it would appear that many of the problems stemmed from incompatibility between functional and security requirements (the latter of which constrained the choice of hardware).

In the commercial sphere there have also been problems. For example, in 1988, the press reported cancellation of a project at the Bank of America which had spent $60M in ten months – failing to solve a problem. According to reports (*Computing*, Feb. 1988) the Bank was failing to get out statements to customers on time due to (computer) resource (capacity) problems. After failing to solve the problem the bank moved the accounts to a system run by another bank (part of the same overall group). Whilst detailed data on the project is not available it seems to the outside observer to be a classic case of 'Brook's Law' – adding more people to a late software project makes it even later (Brooks, 1975). (How else could they have spent so much money in so short a space of time to such little effect?)

At the time of writing (May 1990) there are reports of Boeing 747-400 aircraft suffering from computer-related faults (Learmount, 1990). According to reports, in over 20 cases, an engine has been throttled down whilst the aircraft was on auto-pilot and without pilot intervention. No cause for the problem has yet been identified (in public) but the symptoms indicate a design/implementation fault in the auto-pilot software.

There are many other examples which could be quoted, including several where human life was endangered or lost. (The interested reader with access to the InterNet News facility is recommended to subscribe to comp.risks.) However, the examples quoted so far are sufficient to show that there are problems with respect to all the main aspects of our definitions of software engineering:

- Specification – Nimrod, Folios.
- Design – probably a factor in all cases.
- Implementation – probably a factor in all cases.
- Evolution – possibly a problem with the 747-400, but none of the others got this far!
- Economic – Nimrod, Folios, Bank of America.
- Timeliness – Nimrod, Bank of America.
- Elegance – probably an inappropriate epithet in all cases.

The aim of the above is not to lambast software system developers, merely to indicate that we still have severe development problems. Before considering solutions (ameliorations) to these problems it is informative to consider their nature or underlying causes.

1.2.2 Nature of the problems

The developers of large-scale software systems face many difficult technical and managerial problems. A number of the commonly occurring problems are self-inflicted – for example, due to failure to apply known good practices – but many are inherent. Whilst it is possible in principle, to eliminate the self-inflicted problems, it is only possible to ameliorate the inherent problems – so it is helpful to identify which problems fit into which category. In doing this I follow Brooks (1987) who gives a clear and insightful analysis of the above dichotomy, although my perspective on the issues is slightly different from that of Brooks.

For the sake of brevity we focus on the inherent, or essential – in the Aristotlean sense – problems. This author believes that there are five issues which subsume Brooks' four:

- Complexity.
- Difficulty of establishing and stabilizing requirements.
- Changeability or malleability of software.
- Invisibility.
- Development of a theory for the problem domain.

We treat each point in turn.

1.2.2.1 Complexity Software systems are necessarily complex because of the applications in which we choose to use computerized solutions. In particular, they are complex because of the need to interface to complex engineered (e.g. mechanical and electronic) systems and to complex social or organizational systems (e.g. companies or Government bodies which have strict rules about data access). This form of complexity is what Brooks calls conformance.

Complexity also arises from the nature of software 'as a material'. Software does not have a regular structure, unlike other engineering artefacts. If we need to carry out a function more than once then we implement it as a procedure or subroutine – thus good design *removes* regularity.

Software systems are too large to be understood in their entirety by a single individual. Modules can be assimilated independently but (typically) as systems grow the interactions between modules increase non-linearly, thus making complexity grow faster than size.

1.2.2.2 Establishment of requirements It is notoriously difficult to establish an adequate and stable set of requirements for a software system. Some of the problems in developing requirements are set out in Chapter 16, but we draw out some of the more significant points here.

Requirements analysts usually find that users 'don't know what they want'. This problem arises because many users do not fully appreciate the capabilities and limitations of computer systems (and of course it is unreasonable to expect that they do). The introduction of a computer system will typically perturb the way people currently work and therefore they cannot simply extrapolate from current activities. Various aspects of the way they carry out their work are 'second nature' and these form hidden assumptions in trying to elicit requirements for a system, and so on.

There are often also communication problems between requirements analysts and the system's potential users because their experience and education are different. Specifically this means that the analysts and users do not have a common understanding of terms that are used, so they have different interpretations of the requirements specification.

The notion of 'completeness' of a requirement specification is problematic. There is no analytic procedure for determining when the users have told the developers everything that they need to know in order to produce the system required. This is true both because there is no easy way of telling what are *all* the functions that the system is expected to do, and because there is no simple way of determining when the requirements contain enough information to overcome the difference in experience and education between the users and the development team.

Finally, requirements are never stable. Changes in the environment in which the system has to work may change the requirements for the system, e.g. because of amendments in legislation to which the system has to conform. Also, once the system is deployed, the users will find new ways in which the system can help them in their jobs, but some of these may require the implementation of additional functionality. In practice it is quite common for requirements to change even before the system is installed due to changes in its intended operational environment.

1.2.2.3 Malleability of software It is deceptively easy to write, or to change, small programs. Consequently, in a complex system the pressure for change always focuses on the software rather than the hardware or any other aspects of the system. Unfortunately, changing software in a large system is much less straightforward than in a small system.

In practice the interaction between the different parts of a system make change difficult – at least change which does not introduce further errors or 'bugs'. Our ability to maintain and evolve software is distinctly limited so software 'decays', i.e. the structure and intelligibility of the software worsens as it is modified over the years. This makes it still more difficult to modify and can sometimes result in software which even the originators 'dare not change' for fear of what will happen if they make modifications.

Interestingly, the desire to change software is not only found with faulty software, but also with good quality software which is highly successful. It is a fact of life that highly successful programs are widely used and therefore more applications and requirements are found for the software, leading to a pressure to change it. Thus it is the perception of the ease of change, as opposed to the reality that large software systems are very hard to change, that is the essential problem.

1.2.2.4 Invisibility All other engineering disciplines produce physical artefacts which we can see and touch. Even in VLSI design, where the physical structures are small and difficult to see, we can still rely on physical analogy and, in the limit, we do have tools such as electron microscopes that allow us to see the structure of circuits. Software, though, is essentially 'thought stuff' and, in addition, much of what is important about software, i.e. the reasons for making design decisions that led to the particular programs, is not manifest in the programs themselves.

There are ways of at least partially visualizing the structure of programs, e.g. using techniques such as structured analysis, but these techniques are inherently limited. We need to understand the structure of programs from a number of different points of view, e.g. scope of variables, concurrent structure, sequential and temporal execution behaviour, exception handling structure, and so on. In practice there is no single (geometrical or regular) structure about which to base our visualization of the program. Whilst we can attempt to visualize them from a number of different points of view, they are inherently multi-dimensional objects and there is a considerable intellectual difficulty in establishing relationships between the different views and perspectives of a program. In many ways this problem of visualization is closely linked with the issue of complexity.

1.2.2.5 Problem domain theories In most engineering disciplines the development of a new system involves the application of existing theory, not the derivation of new theories. Thus the development of bridges involves the use of existing theory about stress and strain and the ability of structures to bear load. It is relatively rare for new theories to be developed, although, for example new theoretical results were needed for the first time curved concrete beams were used for a bridge. By contrast, with software systems new theories are being developed all the time – although probably without the derivation of the software engineers being aware that this is what they are doing.

A requirements specification for a system and the programs in a system contain, perhaps implicitly, a model of the application domain. Thus a specification for an air traffic control system contains or implies a model of the way in which air traffic is marshalled and scheduled, the flight separation rules and so on – and this is, in effect, a theory of (information processing for) air traffic control. Every time a system is developed in a new problem domain we are faced with developing a new theory. In principle we should be able to transport problem domain theories from one application to another, e.g. from one payroll program to another. In practice it is very rare for problem domain theories to be re-used and this is an area where our current practices exacerbate the inherent problem.

This may sound like a rather abstract, or theoretical problem. However, it is of profound pragmatic importance. It has long been recognized that the bulk of systems software problems arise from inadequacy in specification, not from errors in implementation. Development of problem domain theories is very difficult (simply consider how long it has taken to evolve some of our current understanding of physics) yet we undertake this exercise, perhaps unwittingly, for every new problem domain to which we apply computers. Again the difficulty is exacerbated by the fact that we are often dealing with social, or other engineered, systems and as they change with time so our theory or model must change. See Checkland (1981) for a deep and detailed discussion on this topic.

1.2.3 Summary

My aim here has not been to give a thorough and detailed account of the problems of developing large-scale software systems, as it is likely that awareness of these problems is one of the major factors in bringing readers to the book. However, it does seem important to draw out two facts. The first is that the symptoms of the problems are really quite different in nature from their underlying causes. Second, some of the underlying causes are inescapable. All we can do in developing software systems is to be aware of these problems and to try to ameliorate their effects. As Brooks put it, 'there are no silver bullets'. However, we now turn to a discussion of some of the evolving approaches to addressing these problems, and to addressing the man-made problems caused by going about software development in an appropriate or ineffective manner.

1.3 Evolving solutions

In my view the two key intellectual weapons we have for mastering the difficulties of building large-scale software systems are *structuring* and *abstraction*. Superficially it would appear that the key advance in software engineering over the last two decades is in automation – the provision of computer-based tools to assist the development of large scale software systems. However, the tools would, I believe, prove much less effective, if not nugatory, if they were not based on appropriate abstractions and ways of structuring systems, and their development process. Further, I believe that these twin principles of structuring and abstraction can be seen both in the technical and managerial domains.

Structuring and abstraction are key intellectual weapons because they give us a way of handling complexity. Structuring enables us to decompose systems into components, or views, and to understand the system a little at a time – yet still understand how the components or views relate one to another. Abstraction gives us a way of 'drawing away from' the details of a system and, again, this aids comprehension. Given the prevalence of terms such as 'structured programming' and 'abstract data types', it is unsurprising that these should be viewed as key ways of addressing technical problems. However, software processes are themselves complex entities and abstraction and structuring, for example in the form of Pert and Gantt charts, provide means for addressing the complexity of the development process. Thus they are an aid to management.

We now briefly discuss the evolution of the technical and managerial solutions to the problems of developing large scale software systems to set the scene for a discussion of the contents of Part II of the reference book.

1.3.1 Technical solutions

Most of the improvements in our technology for developing large-scale software systems have depended on finding improved abstractions or improved structuring techniques for writing or specifying programs. Rather than try to present an accurate chronology of events, we simply identify some key advances.

One of the earliest, and arguably still the most important, abstractions was the move away from programming at the machine level to programming in 'higher level' languages which are oriented towards understanding by people, rather than by machines. Early high-level languages preserved the essentially procedural view of program execution embodied in the underlying machine. Thus although the high-level languages were abstractions away from the machine, in the sense of containing less detail, they were still based on the same concepts, or abstractions. More recent languages have been oriented towards different conceptual frameworks, e.g. expressing programs declaratively in a logical or functional framework. Here we see the introduction of new, more powerful, abstractions and the consequent ability to think about the problems being solved in a different, and often more effective way. Much current research focuses on the use of higher order functions, i.e. functions which can take functions as parameters. The expressive power of these languages is such that it is possible to solve problems that are infeasible, or at best very clumsy, in the earlier procedural languages.

From the point of view of structuring of programs, we have seen a change in concerns from the structure of fairly low-level programming constructs to the level of major program components such as modules and packages. Early work introduced the idea of structured control statements such as 'if ... then ... else' and 'while ... do' in the place of unconstrained jumps through the program. These ideas of structured programming are now so ingrained in our culture we would find it very strange if these basic ideas were not supported in a programming language or, at any rate, in a procedural programming language. The introduction of the ideas of modules, or packages, of programs gave us a structure in which we would develop and test parts of programs independently of one another before integrating them to form the finished software product. Interestingly, the early functional and logic languages were rather poorly structured. Although the ideas of structured programming are of limited applicability within the functional and logical programming paradigms, the ideas of modules or packages of programs still

seem entirely appropriate, yet it is only recently that they have been reintroduced into the mainstream functional and logic languages. Whilst it is hard to see what the next step in abstraction might be within the realm of programming languages, it seems clear that there is still much mileage in research into better techniques for structuring the more modern programming languages.

A different class of technical solutions to the problems of software engineering arose with the appreciation that it was possible to write specifications which abstracted away from the detailed implementation in any programming language. The most significant work in this area, almost undoubtedly, is what has come to be known as structured analysis (SA) or structured analysis/structured design (SA/SD). The great benefit of these techniques is that they give both a way of abstracting away from the details of programs and a way of structuring the description of a system. For example, in data flow diagrams (DFDs) which form a part of SA and SA/SD, the main processing entities and the data flows between the entities are shown – but no details are given about the representation of the data structures or the processing that transforms the data structures. These abstract structures enable the 'gross-level' behaviour of the system to be defined without cluttering the definitions with unnecessary detail.

These so-called structured techniques have evolved from their early, rather simple, beginnings into an enormous array of techniques and methods (often incorrectly called methodologies). These methods cover the design of databases, including the normalization of data structures, the structured development of programs from high-level designs, the development of real-time systems using models based on a notion of state machines, and so on. A key advance amongst the latter structured techniques is the ability to represent hierarchical composition, or decomposition, within the notation. This enables the users of the method to 'control the level of abstraction' at which they model the system under development.

Within the context of system and software specification, the recent advances have seen the introduction of the so-called formal methods which are mathematically-based techniques. These techniques enable specifications to be produced which, whilst being abstract, enable more facets of the software to be specified than is possible with structured techniques. For example, it is typically possible to be much more precise about system functionality with a formal technique than is possible with a structured technique. Ironically, rather like the advent of modern high-level languages, the formal methods are relatively poor at describing system structure and, arguably, there would be considerable benefit from linking formal and structured techniques to overcome these limitations.

We could extend the above discussion to cover techniques of verification and validation, e.g. testing, but hopefully enough has now been done to illustrate our basic point. However, there are two more trends which are worth noting. First, there has been a trend to move attention away from 'low-level' issues concerned with programming languages back into the earlier stages of software development, e.g. design and requirements analysis. Indeed, it could have been argued that there are no longer really significant research issues at the level of programming languages and that the important issues to be addressed are those relevant early in the life cycle, however it seems that we might now be coming 'full circle'. Many of the concepts and ideas that can be modelled using the new specification abstractions available to us do not map down efficiently on to commonly available programming languages. In my view this will lead to a new drive to develop and adapt more sophisticated programming languages, e.g. based on more sophisticated type theories and offering more elaborate techniques for program structuring. Perhaps the best way to summarize the trend would be to say that it seems likely that there will be a reunification of abstractions and structuring techniques throughout the life cycle, from requirements down to implementation.

Second, although we feel it is appropriate to de-emphasize the role of tools, it is clear that tools are important in software engineering. Historically, most of the tools have been aimed at supporting a single individual carrying out a specific task, e.g. producing an SA/SD diagram. There seem to be two important discernible trends. One is the development of more broadly based tools, often called support environments, which support teams working on a project rather than individuals. The second is the greater use of transformational techniques for generating lower level design descriptions or programs from higher level, or abstract, problem descriptions. There are still many technical problems to be addressed before support environments and transformational tools can be widely used for a broad class of problems. However, it seems to me that there is a major and important trend towards the development of this sort of tool technology. Of course, the provision of this sort of automation will free software engineers from having to deal with certain classes of implementation detail and thus open the way for new abstractions and new structuring techniques to deal with new classes of problems. . . .

1.3.2 Managerial solutions

Management in software development is primarily concerned with planning, decision making including allocation of resources, progress monitoring and estimation. Whilst there have been improvements in these individual technical areas, *per se*, over the last two decades, all of them depend on having an appropriate model of the software development process – and this, of course, depends on having appropriate structuring and abstractions.

Our ability to provide appropriate abstractions and structuring for the software process is almost synonymous with improvements in our ability to produce life cycle models. The earliest model, the so-called Waterfall model, gave a simple abstraction of the process identifying a sequential set of stages dealing with requirements analysis, design, implementation, testing, and so on. Whilst the Waterfall model is adequate for describing some projects, it has a number of severe limitations. First, it equates a technical activity, such as requirements analysis, with a sequential phase of the development process, whereas in practice activities from different stages of the process may go on at the same time, e.g. design activities may be carried out in requirement analysis as the basis of a feasibility study. In addition, the model does not adequately show iteration, i.e. moving backwards and forwards between stages to correct errors made at early stages that are only found later in the development process. There have been a number of enhancements to the Waterfall model, but in recent years the trend has been towards the development of much more sophisticated models.

The primary advance came from the realization that it was appropriate to structure, or model, the process differently from a managerial as opposed to a technical point of view. This led to the production of separate, but related, abstractions dealing with the technical development activities, including iteration, and the management processes which seek to control the technical development activities. Most of the technically-oriented models recognize different classes of activity such as development, or synthesis, and verification and validation. The same is true of the management models, most notably Boehm's (1988) spiral model, which identify different management activities such as planning, risk assessment and control. These models, whilst still being abstract, are now rich enough to give a framework into which we can fit the basic managerial activities identified above. For example, Boehm's spiral model explicitly shows planning and various forms of decision making.

It seems clear that the notions of structuring and abstraction

give us good ways of thinking about the managerial aspects of the software development process, but it is much less clear that they actually aid us in management of the process. However, there are a number of ways where our ability to provide good structuring and to provide appropriate abstractions is of direct benefit.

Most obviously, the ability to structure the process into phases and to structure the work to be undertaken, i.e. through a work breakdown structure, gives the basis necessary for good project control. Without clearly delineated phases, activities and deliverables it is not possible for managers to assess progress and to exercise the necessary control over the process. Without such structuring one only has chaos.

In the context of software cost estimation, progress has relied on good structuring but, more significantly, on finding good abstractions. For example the COCOMO cost estimation model (Boehm, 1981) relies on a number of so-called cost drivers which are essentially abstractions from the technical detail of the project to factors which drive the overall cost and development schedules for projects. These abstractions are the essential basis for being able to make accurate predictions without knowledge of the details of the project.

In order to monitor progress in software projects we need appropriate metrics for different aspects of the products and the process itself. Here abstractions such as test coverage for modules give a basis for measurement and control in certain parts of the process. However, it is quite clear that this is one area where we have an inadequate set of abstractions for proper project control. This therefore remains an important area of research.

A final area which is briefly worth considering is that of risk management. Software development is inherently a risky process but good management relies on being able to identify the sources of the most significant risks and being able to organize the development so as to minimize, or ameliorate, the possible effects of these risks. Again work has been undertaken on this problem trying to find appropriate abstractions, rather like the cost drivers for the cost estimation models, which identify commonly found classes of risk. Current work, however, is concerned with identifying an appropriate way of structuring the overall development process in order to control risks, rather than trying to identify costs. Again this is an area of active research, but one that shows how the notions of abstraction and structuring come together, i.e. the abstractions used in assessing risk lead to ways of choosing appropriate structuring for the process. All of these points are discussed in more detail in Chapter 15.

Whilst these notions of abstraction and structuring are, I believe, fundamental, clearly they do not address all the management issues. For example, it is of paramount importance to have good communications within the project team and between the project manager and the team members. Similarly it is necessary for managers to have good interpersonal skills and, again, these do not really derive from any notion of abstraction and structuring. However, we have focused on these particular issues in order to stress their importance in giving a basis for a controllable project and to indicate that our ability to control projects has advanced, and will continue to advance, by finding better forms of structuring for projects and better abstractions from the details of the projects.

Finally, we should not forget automation. Within the technical activities many of the advances have been supported by the provision of tools which facilitate activities undertaken by a single designer or programmer, e.g. compilation or unit testing. The crux for management is to deal with software development by a team. A considerable amount of work has been undertaken on the design of integrated project support environments. These are particularly relevant from a managerial point of view as they provide a framework for dealing with teams, rather than just providing the functionality required by individuals. Unfortunately for practising software project managers, the currently available environments have many technical limitations. Again this remains an area for research and for future developments.

1.3.3 Other trends

There are a number of other discernible trends in the technology for developing complex software systems and in the principles and techniques for managing such development programmes. We focused on the notions of abstractions and structuring in order to make a point – that these two principles underlie many of the detailed advances made in technical and managerial aspects of software development. Specifically they give ways of addressing the five problems identified earlier, not just complexity. However, we can identify a number of other trends. For the sake of brevity, we focus on four classes of development which are now influencing commercial developments.

First, there is the increased use of formal approaches to software and system development. The use of formal, i.e. mathematically based, methods has been a popular academic research topic now for many years. Within the last few years there has been an increasing trend to use these techniques within industry. We have now moved from a position of almost total scepticism to a situation where a number of industrial developers are reporting real benefits from the use of techniques. Of course it can be argued that the great benefit of the formal techniques is that they enable us to produce abstract specifications of programs whilst still preserving precision. However, it is also clear that other properties of formal techniques, e.g. the ability to manipulate formal specifications in order to carry out proofs or to perform animation, are also significant benefits. Interestingly, although formality has primarily affected technical developments, use is also being made of formal approaches in modelling software processes. Indeed, it is possible that some forthcoming support environments will make use of the formally based software process models in order to define and control the overall development processes.

Second, there is the influence of so-called 'artificial intelligence' or 'knowledge based systems' (KBS). A common underlying factor in these techniques is that they give a way of explicitly modelling the problem domain which the program is intended to address. This is a direct 'attack' on the problem identified earlier, under the heading of problem domain theories. These techniques have had an effect on deployed systems both directly, e.g. through so-called 'expert systems', and indirectly through interactive development environments and by providing implementation techniques for formal methods, and other, support tools. In my view KBS approaches have not lived up to their promise, but I believe that benefit will come from an (already discernible) trend towards unification of ideas in KBS and 'mainstream' software engineering.

Third, considerable advances have been made through re-use of software. Re-use is currently viewed as an important research area and is often seen as a problem – it is common for people to claim that there is a very poor level of software re-use. There are major practical counter-arguments to this position, e.g. the widespread use of relational databases and libraries of numerical routines. However, it is quite clear that much 'new' software is developed unnecessarily as the appropriate functionality already exists. Therefore, although re-use is on the increase, this again seems to be a major research area where we would hope for benefits in the future. Again, in my view, a primary issue here is one of abstraction – finding the appropriate abstractions from the solution functionality and the problem domain requirements which we can 'match' in order to find appropriate components to re-use. Pragmatically, it seems that a combi-

nation of formal and knowledge based techniques may give us the appropriate technology for achieving re-use in practice.

Fourth, there is an increasing trend to quantify and measure aspects of software and the development process. This is a key trend in making software development more repeatable and controllable. At present our primary capability seems to be to make comparative measurements, i.e. to be able to compare one artefact or development with another. It is to be hoped that, in the longer run, the trend will be towards more direct and absolute measurements as we develop an appropriate set of metrics for the process and product. These issues are discussed more fully in Chapter 30.

It is impossible within such a short introduction to give a full and detailed summary of the main issues and trends in software engineering. This is one of the primary reasons I have focused on two principles which I feel are, all too often, forgotten. The final point that should be stressed, though, is that of integration. Techniques for software engineering do not, and cannot work effectively in isolation. Our aim must be to produce a coherent set of techniques which fit together across the whole life cycle and provide links between technical and managerial activities. At present, despite the marketing 'hype', we see relatively little evidence that there is a trend towards developing integrated solutions to software engineering problems. Provision of such solutions, would mean, for example, knowing the comparative cost of deploying formal and structured techniques in a particular problem domain and being able to choose a process accordingly. We still seem to be a long way away from being able to provide true integration either in a technical sense or between technical and managerial activities. I hope that when the time comes to release the second edition of this book that I will be able to include integration as one of the trends in software engineering.

1.4 Structure of Part II

The structure of Part II of the reference book is determined, to a large extent, by the foregoing discussion. It starts with a chapter on life-cycle models and the software process which lays a framework for the following material on software development techniques and on project management.

The introduction to the reference book as a whole stated that one of the objectives was to present material that was stable, rather than to discuss research results. Formal methods cannot really be considered to be mature and stable technology yet, but, quite clearly, there is a great trend towards the use of these techniques and they are likely to be very important in the coming decade. Consequently, I chose to cover both the widely used conventional techniques and the 'up and coming' formal techniques. Thus, the first major group of chapters in Part II of the reference book, entitled *Conventional development*, deals with what are essentially 'structured methods' for each stage of the development process. The second section, that on 'Formal development,' surveys different classes of formal method. The presentation is essentially categorized by technology, rather than life cycle stage, as this reflects the current state of development and application of formal methods.

The third major group of chapters, entitled 'Software development management', is concerned with the main managerial activities such as planning and control, together with the wider range of issues alluded to above, e.g. personnel management and integrated project support environments. The intention is that Chapters 15–20 and 27–34 (groups 1 and 3) between them reflect the best industrial software engineering practice from a technical and managerial point of view.

The remaining sections of this part of the reference book cover other approaches to software development and other information which is relevant to practical software engineering.

As indicated above, AI/KBS technology is already relevant for many software projects and it is likely that they will become integrated with 'mainstream' software engineering in the fullness of time. The group of chapters entitled 'AI/IKBS approaches' addresses some of the available technologies and briefly discusses the two classes of programming language which are most widely used for implementing systems with an AI/IKBS component.

There are a number of other trends in software development including a drive towards software re-use, and the increased uses of prototyping and object-oriented design techniques. The group of chapters entitled 'Other approaches to software development' draws together these disparate, but important, contributions towards current software development technology.

Whilst much of a software development project is concerned with specifications, ultimately we need to produce programs if we are to develop working systems! The group of chapters on 'Programming languages' addresses both practical issues, such as low-level programming and linking and loading, and gives a survey of current programming languages. The language survey is in three parts covering early high-level languages, modern conventional, i.e. procedural or imperative, languages and non-conventional programming, e.g. functional and logical, languages.

The final group of chapters, dealing with 'The operational environment', surveys a number of issues which are relevant to the development of working programs. Specifically, it deals with the hardware and operating system environment of which the software engineer must be aware if he is to produce working and effective programs.

2 Contents of Part II

We have set the scene for Part II by describing the problems and goals of software engineering, discussing trends in the techniques and technology of software engineering and briefly delineating the scope of Part II of the reference book. Our aim here is to give a slightly more detailed overview of each of the chapters in the reference book to assist the reader in finding relevant material and in understanding the relationships between the chapters.

2.1 Life-cycle models and the software process

The preceding discussion should have made clear the importance of life cycle models to practical developments.

This chapter by John McDermid and Paul Rook plays an important role in Part II of the reference book as it establishes a framework into which many of the subsequent chapters fit. It discusses the software development life cycle from the technical point of view and identifies a set of canonical stages in the development process. These canonical stages represent technically distinct activities such as requirements analysis and architectural design. These stages also define the scope of the chapters in the following group dealing with conventional development. The chapter also discusses life-cycle and process models from the management point of view, in particular identifying phases of software development which are the basic structuring required for management control. The chapter finishes with a discussion of the issues in designing, or choosing, a process for a given software project. As indicated above, the selection of an appropriate process is critical to the success of the software project.

This material is relevant to most of the remainder of Part II and in particular to the groups of chapters on conventional development and software development management.

2.2 Conventional development

The group of chapters (16–20) covering conventional development aims to give an overview of the best current industrial practice in software systems development. It is structured around the stages of the life cycle defined in Chapter 15 and deals with the maintenance of software once it is delivered and installed. Each chapter can be read in isolation but there is a natural flow of the chapters through the software development life cycle, so they can also be read in sequence to gain an impression of the new issues that need to be addressed at each stage in the development process.

2.2.1 Requirements analysis

Requirements analysis is typically the first stage of the development process, primarily concerned with eliciting from potential users of the system their views on its intended functionality and other properties. It has long been recognized that requirements analysis is a very difficult activity and that mistakes made in requirements can have a profound effect on the usability of the eventual system.

David Stokes analyses the primary sources of difficulty in producing requirements, considers desirable properties of requirements specifications and goes on to discuss two classes of technique for addressing these problems. The first are general techniques applicable across a wide range of applications, e.g. for validating specifications. The second are more specific methods, e.g. CORE, for carrying out requirements analysis. Although the bulk of the techniques described use diagrammatic notations, Stokes also discusses some formal approaches to requirement analysis.

There is an interesting comparison between requirements analysis and the techniques of knowledge elicitation in Chapter 38.

2.2.2 Architectural design

The first stage of the software system design process is concerned with definition of the system architecture, or 'grand plan' for the system, identifying the major system components and their inter-relationships. Like requirements analysis, architectural design is pivotal in the system development process and errors made at this stage, but not caught until implementation, are likely to be very expensive and very difficult to rectify.

John Buxton and John McDermid discuss the fundamental difficulties of developing system architectures and particularly stress the role of 'non-functional' requirements, e.g. timeliness and quality, in the design process. They define in some detail the different sorts of information that are necessary to provide a complete architectural specification for a system and consider the analyses that are required to show specification consistency and implementability. As with the discussion of requirements, they then go on to identify generally applicable techniques and specific design methods. General techniques include definitions of module structure and data-flow modelling. Specific design methods include HOOD, an approach to object-oriented design.

The chapter builds on some of the theory set out in Chapters 7, 9 and 11 and is also related to Chapter 39 which discusses object-oriented techniques.

2.2.3 Implementation

Implementation is the final development stage that is largely creative, being concerned with detailed program design and the production of program source code. Architectural design will have identified modules which can be implemented by individual software engineers. Implementation is concerned with the production of these individual modules.

Brian Wichmann addresses the issues of design analysis required before production of the final code and goes on to identify a number of different ways of structuring the implementation. In particular, he covers general principles of program design such as information hiding and the use of abstract data types. He then illustrates the use of the techniques of stepwise refinement for developing well structured, high quality programs. The illustrations are given in Ada.

This chapter provides an interesting contrast to Chapters 24 and 25 on refinement and formal implementation.

2.2.4 Software testing

In traditional software developments, testing is the primary means for showing that the implementation has the requisite functionality and other non-functional properties. However, testing, and other forms of verification and validation, are important at all stages of the software development process.

Darrel Ince first discusses the role of testing in the software life cycle, stressing the importance of the testing activities in requirements analysis and design. He then goes on to discuss a number of testing techniques, e.g. structural testing and mutation testing. This survey gives a comprehensive view of available testing techniques and provides pragmatic advice on when the different techniques are applicable. The chapter concludes with an overview of the capabilities of some available testing tools and an indication of likely future developments in testing techniques.

This chapter is largely self-contained although it draws, to some extent, on the material on graph theory in Chapter 6.

2.2.5 Software maintenance

It is now widely recognized that the maintenance, i.e. post-delivery development activity, often accounts for the major costs associated with the production and use of a software system. Hitherto little attention has been given to maintenance as a technical software engineering activity in its own right, however, given its economic importance, research is now being focused on this topic.

Keith Bennett and his colleagues give an overview of the nature, role and importance of maintenance before discussing particular maintenance techniques. They identify different sorts of maintenance concerned with fixing 'bugs' in the software and adapting it to new requirements. They discuss the relationships with software project management (see Chapter 27) and aspects of configuration and release management (see Chapter 34). The discussion of techniques covers ideas such as reverse engineering and re-engineering as well as discussing the capability of available maintenance tools. Finally, they discuss issues of quality in maintenance and designing new software to ease the maintenance burden.

2.3 Formal development

Formal methods can be used in a number of different ways in software development. The simplest distinction is between the use of formal methods purely for the production of specifications in order to clarify what a system is required or intended to do and formal derivation of programs from specifications. In the first instance specifications are usually written at an abstract level; in the second case the specifications tend to be very close to the level of programs, although these low-level specifications may have been derived by a process of refinement from the higher level specification.

There are a number of different approaches to writing abstract formal specifications. We discuss here two of the most commonly used and described approaches, the so-called model-based and algebraic approaches. In essence the distinction

between these two approaches is the extent to which an explicit model of the state of the programs being specified is produced. We also address issues of formal specification of concurrency.

The final three chapters are concerned with the derivation of implementations from specifications, within the formal framework. The first looks at the general issue of refinement including the relationship between low-level and high-level specifications. The last two chapters look at formal implementation from two different points of view: formally deriving programs from the specifications and carrying out *post hoc* verification of the correspondence between programs and specifications.

This 'technique-oriented' as opposed to life-cycle oriented approach to this group of chapters was taken because the discipline is not yet mature enough to be able to describe a set of formal techniques for use at each stage in the development process. It is to be hoped that, as formal methods increase in their maturity, it does become possible to describe the techniques on the basis of the conventional development life cycle.

2.3.1 Model-based specifications

Using model-based approaches to specifications, an abstract model of the system, or program, state is developed then operations which transform or modify the state are specified. This style of formal specification is probably the most widely used in industry, perhaps because it has a fairly obvious mapping into procedural programming languages.

Roger Shaw and Brian Monahan give an extensive introduction to the production of model based specifications illustrated primarily using the specification language Z. They first describe the basic mathematical language for Z, building on the basic notions of discrete mathematics set out in Chapter 1. They then describe the schema language in Z which is a way of modularizing specifications and building larger specifications out of small parts, followed by an example specification in Z. The chapter concludes with a brief description of the other widely used model-based specification approach, VDM, and gives a comparison between the two methods, together with a brief historical account of the development of the two methods.

This chapter builds on the basic mathematical foundations in Part I, particularly on Chapter 1. It also underpins some of the ideas on refinement set out in Chapter 24 and on computer security in Chapter 59.

2.3.2 Algebraic specification

Algebraic specifications have a similar role in software development to model-based approaches but they do not use an explicit model of the system state. They are, perhaps, less widely used than model-based approaches but have a number of attractive properties, e.g. they are naturally amenable to execution as a form of 'rapid prototyping'.

The production of algebraic specification builds on the material on algebra set out in Chapter 3, but a rather more extensive mathematical underpinning is required. Consequently Marie-Claude Gaudel builds up the underlying theory to a point where it is possible to produce representations of algebraic data types, which are very similar in spirit to the notion of abstract data types, and to show how to represent refinements between different algabraic specifications within a specification hierarchy. This leads on to a brief description of existing algebraic specification languages and the presentation of a small example in the language PLUSS.

This chapter builds on the theory in Part I, particularly on Chapters 1 and 3. It provides a complement both to Chapter 21 on model-based specification and, to a lesser extent, to Chapter 24 on refinement.

2.3.3 *Formal treatment of concurrency and time*

The algebraic and model-based approaches to not explicitly model concurrency, although this does not mean that they can only specify sequential systems. However, there are many circumstances where it is necessary, and appropriate, to produce explicit models of concurrent systems, e.g. for specifying communication systems.

There are a number of technical difficulties to be addressed in specifying concurrent systems, for instance dealing with non-determinism and asynchronous behaviour. Manfred Broy builds up the basic mathematical structures for dealing with concurrency, showing how to model processes and their inter-communication. This work is extended to deal with timing in concurrent systems and treatment of state in distributed systems. This leads on to a discussion of programming languages for distributed systems and a brief discussion of semantics for specification languages for concurrent systems.

Again this work builds on the foundational mathematics set out in Part I. It also underpins aspects of the material on networks and distributed systems set out in Chapter 53 and is relevant to other chapters in Part III, e.g. that on digital telephony and switching (Chapter 58).

2.3.4 *Refinement*

Refinement is concerned with showing that some low-level specification is consistent with, or satisfies, some more abstract specification. Whilst still a nascent discipline, refinement is a critical component of a full formal development method.

Peter Whysall discusses the nature and use of refinement before going on to lay out the basic theory of refinement, covering what it means for one specification to 'satisfy' another. The theory is presented in an algebraic framework although the concepts are equally applicable to model based approaches. A simple example of a refinement is given followed by a brief discussion of tools for supporting the refinement process.

Again this chapter builds on the foundational mathematics in Chapters 1 and 3. It complements Chapters 21 and 22 on model-based and algebraic specifications, and provides a partial contrast with the views of refinement set out in Chapter 22. It can also be seen as a precursor to Chapters 25 and 26 which deal with the final stage of refinement from low level specifications to programs.

2.3.5 *Formal implementation*

In order to complete a formal development it is necessary to be able to derive programs formally from low level specifications. There are a number of technical difficulties in carrying out this exercise, not least of which is mapping between the semantics of programming languages and the specification languages.

Steven Vickers starts by discussing the role and value of the formal construction of programs from low-level specifications. He then gives an introduction to the basic technical material of this chapter – program logic. Program logic is concerned with the mapping between the semantics of the specification and programming languages and, in essence, makes it possible to reason about programs within the specification formalism. Vickers uses merge sort to give an example of formal program construction, concluding with a brief survey of other formal implementation techniques.

This chapter builds on the basic notions set out in Chapter 2, and complements the next chapter on verification environments.

2.3.6 *Verification environments*

In carrying out formal implementation it is necessary, in principle, to carry out proofs to verify that the program produced does implement its specification. Management of proofs becomes difficult as program size increases, so much research effort is being devoted to building program verification environments which, as far as possible, automate the process of establishing proofs.

Dan Craigen describes the basic structure and functionality of program verification environments building on the material in the preceding chapter and in Chapter 12. He then goes on to give a fairly extensive example of a program verification using a system known as m-EVES. He contrasts the description of m-EVES by describing a similar verification exercise with two other systems, namely Gypsy and Affirm. Craigen concludes by discussing limitations with existing tools and discussing areas for future work.

This chapter builds on a number of the chapters in Part I, particularly Chapter 2 on logics and proofs of correctness. It complements most of the other chapters in this group, especially that on formal implementation. It is also relevant to a number of the other chapters, for example Chapter 59 on computer security.

2.4 Software development management

This group of chapters is concerned with a broad range of managerial issues covering both strict project management issues and technical aspects of the management of large-scale projects. Chapters 27–31 cover some of the fundamental management activities. The first three cover the activities of planning and control, estimation of the cost and duration of projects and achievement of quality in software development. The next two deal with issues of measurement in the process, the first chapter taking a broad perspective and the second focusing on the important topic of software reliability. Next, Chapter 32 deals with personnel management, particularly looking at the issues of managing teams on a software development project.

The last two chapters deal with ways of supporting team developments. The first chapter deals with integrated support environments which are meant to provide automated support to the bulk of the technical and managerial activities in software development. The final chapter in the group has a rather narrower scope, dealing specifically with configuration and release management, and discussing automated support for these activities.

2.4.1 *Project planning and control*

The fundamental activities in software project management are planning and control. Thus this chapter addresses both the central issue in software project management and also sets the framework for the following chapters.

Paul Rook builds on the life-cycle model described in Chapter 15 to set out the basic objectives and activities in software project management and control. This leads on to a more detailed discussion of risk management and the important issue of choosing and establishing a software development process for a project. Rook then discusses more detailed managerial activities, those of project planning, progress monitoring and reporting, and the relationships between management and technical methods for achieving quality and productivity.

This chapter naturally complements and extends Chapter 15 on software life-cycle models and provides a framework and background for the remaining chapters in this group.

2.4.2 *Software cost estimation models*

One of the biggest difficulties facing software project managers is the ability to estimate accurately the cost and duration of projects. Recognizing this difficulty, researchers have developed a number of cost estimation models which can be calibrated, based on past experience, to give ways of developing more reliable cost and time scale estimates. These models are now entering reasonably widespread industrial use.

Chris Kemerer describes the basic role and purpose of software cost estimation models largely by elaborating on the above management problems. He then describes the three basic streams of cost model, namely the economic, Rayleigh and function point streams. One of the difficulties facing a software project manager is how to select an appropriate model for his projects, so Kemerer goes on to describe work in evaluating and validating the various models. He concludes with some recommendations on model selection and an extensive bibliography on relevant research and practical results.

The material in this chapter is largely self-contained but it complements the previous chapter by filling out in some detail the available techniques for software cost estimation.

2.4.3 Quality control and assurance

One of the crucial tasks for a software project manager is to achieve an appropriate level of quality in the software that is produced. Assessment and control of quality is notoriously difficult, hence this is a very demanding task for the software project manager.

Martyn Ould starts by addressing the nature of quality and considers the definition of quality attributes and the establishment of measures of quality. He then goes on to discuss ways of developing an effective quality management system. This discussion covers both general quality, planning and management issues and more detailed techniques such as structured walk-throughs and Fagan inspections. Ould concludes by summarising the primary issues in achieving effective quality management procedures.

Again this material is largely self-contained and it amplifies on one particular aspect of project planning and control as outlined in Chapter 27.

2.4.4 Metrics and measurement

It has often been said that 'one cannot control what one cannot measure', so metrics and measurement are central to the task of software project management.

Barbara Kitchenham introduces this topic by identifying two different uses of metrics and measurement: for control over the software process and for the prediction of qualities of the software product. These distinctions are important as they define the way in which metrics should be selected and applied. She goes on to describe the practical problems of collecting and interpreting metric data and to recommend a practical approach to establishing a measurement scheme. She then focuses on metrics for the project control and gives an example of metrics analysis and interpretation in this context. Finally, she gives some advice on the choice and selection of metrics.

This chapter amplifies on a topic discussed in Chapter 27 on project planning and control and also links strongly to Chapters 28 and 29. It is complemented by Chapter 12 which discusses the difficulties of establishing a measurement system from the point of view of measurement theory.

2.4.5 Software reliability modelling

Software reliability figures are merely a specific class of software quality attribute, or software metric. However, achievement and assessment of reliability is so central to software engineering that it is appropriate to address this specific metric in detail.

Bev Littlewood explains why software reliability models have to be based on statistical measures, illustrating this by looking at some publicly available software failure rate data. He then discusses a number of different reliability models shows how to use some of the commonest forms of model, namely software reliability growth models, in practice. Littlewood concludes by giving some guidance on how to select an appropriate software reliability modelling technique for a given project and discussing the difficulties of assessing very high levels of reliability (very low failure rates) by means of these statistically based reliability models.

This chapter forms an interesting complement to Chapters 29 and 30 dealing with quality control and metrics and measurement in general. There are also interesting similarities with Chapter 28 which addresses a similar problem of choosing appropriate models for a project albeit in the context of cost estimation.

2.4.6 Managing software engineering teams

Software development projects are people projects and a key management skill is the ability to manage and motivate teams of individuals. Whilst staff management is certainly not a science, it is an important engineering discipline which deserves proper consideration.

Keith Southwell first addresses two central personnel management responsibilities: delegation and motivation. He then discusses the central issue for software project managers, that of organizing, managing and motivating a project team. He also looks at pragmatic problems such as the organization and running of meetings, dealing with staff turnover and managing conflicts within projects. He discusses the working environment for software development covering both the office environment and the technical facilities provided, and then concludes with an overview of how technical issues such as the methods and tools used on a project interact with team management.

This chapter essentially stands alone but nonetheless it is of central importance for practical software engineering management.

2.4.7 Integrated project support environments

Many tools have been developed to support individual software engineers and the purpose of an integrated project support environment (IPSE) is to provide a unifying framework which facilitates teamwork. This involves both co-ordinating tools and providing a co-operative framework for team working.

IPSEs are an emergent, rather than an industrially mature, technology, so Anthony Hall starts by discussing the concepts and requirements of IPSEs, focusing on three important topics: support for the complete life cycle, support for methodical development and support for development in the large. He then describes basic principles of IPSE design and discusses current approaches, technologies and products, concentrating mainly on general purpose environments. He then discusses current trends in IPSE development, including the convergence between IPSEs and computer aided software engineering tools before turning to longer term trends, e.g. support for mathematically based software development and knowledge-based approaches to software development.

This chapter complements many of the other chapters in this group and in the two preceding groups, as it sets out a framework in which the individual technologies can be brought together to provide proper support for large-scale software engineering projects.

2.4.8 Configuration management

It is impossible to manage a large-scale software development project unless one can find and keep track of all the specification and program units produced by the development team. The role of configuration management procedures and tools is to help identify, track and control modification to such software development products.

Albert Alderson introduces the basic concepts of configuration management and gives definitions of configuration items, versions and variants, configurations and system building. This leads on to a discussion of basic configuration management procedures, covering configuration identification, and configuration control through baselines and through configuration status accounting. Alderson discusses a number of practical issues in configuration management, such as merging variants and building configuration items from their components. The chapter concludes with an extensive survey of available configuration management tools.

Again this chapter is largely complementary to the other material. It is most strongly related to the preceding chapter as a major function of an IPSE is to provide configuration and management support.

2.5 AI/IKBS approaches

Systems incorporating concepts of artificial intelligence (sometimes referred to as intelligent knowledge-based systems) differ from 'conventional' systems in that they embody some explicit model of application domain knowledge in the programs. This leads to an ability to produce applications with characteristics not achievable by conventional techniques but it has also, perhaps coincidentally, led to a rather different approach to software development. Traditional software engineering has espoused a staged approach to software development, whereas AI/IKBS typically embodies a more iterative and interactive development process, which is not to say that the processes are not methodological.

This group of chapters aims therefore to give an illustration of the capability of typical AI/IKBS systems and also to give an understanding of the characteristics of development environments for such systems.

Typically, this class of systems has been developed in non-procedural programming languages, e.g. functional or logic languages. Although it would be possible to deal with these topics under the general heading of programming languages, we have chosen to deal with them here as being particularly relevant to this class of application.

2.5.1 Functional programming

The primary characteristic of functional programming is that values are derived purely by function application, or function call, and there are no 'side effects' such as assignment to variables. This style of programming has a number of attractions including being amenable to formal verification.

Peter Henderson and Hugh Glaser give a brief introduction to the basic concepts of functional programming, dealing particularly with the use of functions as an abstraction mechanism and the treatment of functions as first class objects, i.e. the ability to treat them as parameters and results of other functions like ordinary data objects. They then illustrate the functional programming style, before discussing the place of functional programming in the context of software engineering. They conclude with a look at developments in functional programming languages which are likely to lead to their wider use.

This chapter primarily forms a complement to the material on programming languages in Chapters 42–46.

2.5.2 Logic programming

The primary characteristic of logic programming is that it involves expressing programs in a restricted form of propositional or predicate logic which is capable of being interpreted on a computer. Like functional programming, it is closer in nature to the underlying mathematics than procedural programming languages, but the details of the way programs are constructed are quite different.

Christopher Hogger introduces the concepts of logic programming by showing how to use logic languages to represent knowledge of particular application domains and thus to solve problems in these domains. He then explains how logic languages are interpreted in a procedural senses, and compares them with procedural programming languages. The bulk of the chapter gives an overview of Prolog, probably the most widely used logic language, and illustrates some of the features of the language that facilitate the production of efficient programs. Hogger concludes with a discussion of the significance of logic languages for software engineering, including the ability to verify properties of programs and transforming programs within the single formalism.

This chapter builds on the basic mathematics set out in Chapter 1 although it can be read alone. Like the chapter on functional languages, it complements the other material on programming languages and also illustrates one basic implementation mechanism for AI/IKBS systems, and it is thus relevant to the following two chapters.

2.5.3 Development environments

AI systems are usually developed in an incremental and iterative style, so their development environments need to support this mode of working. Arguably, the development environments are one of the most significant contributions of AI to software engineering.

Paul Chung and his colleagues give an introduction to the topic by discussing the facilities of an 'ideal' development environment for AI systems. This covers obvious facilities such as strong tool integration, offering efficient edit-compile-execute cycles, and the less obvious, such as program analysis and monitoring tools. They then discuss the capability of existing environments in terms of this ideal, covering language-based environments, e.g. those based round Lisp, expert system shells and more broadly based tool kits. The chapter concludes with a survey of knowledge acquisition tools which are aids to the establishment of the domain knowledge necessary to build into AI systems.

This chapter complements the succeeding one which deals with AI development components and techniques. It also provides a contrast with Chapter 33 on integrated project support environments which focuses more directly on support for 'conventional' software development.

2.5.4 AI/IKBS development components/techniques

Most AI/IKBS systems used in industry are built using some standard component, such as an expert system shell. They have to be developed with specialized techniques, e.g. for knowledge acquisition, and these tend to be determined by the components or tools used, so it is appropriate to consider these aspects of AI/IKBS system development together.

Helen Sharp discusses four primary aspects of the development of AI systems. She discusses techniques for knowledge acquisition and contrasts these with more conventional requirements analysis. She discusses knowledge representation, i.e. data structures for storing knowledge representations which facilitate problem domain modelling and inference. This leads on naturally to a discussion of inference techniques, i.e. the way of deriving conclusions from the stored knowledge base. The fourth aspect to be discussed is that of explanation systems, i.e. facilities for explaining to the user how the system derived particular conclusions. This leads finally to a discussion of expert system shells. Throughout the chapter Sharp gives valuable pragmatic advice on the selection of techniques and identification of problems amenable to the IKBS treatment.

This chapter complements the others in the group and gives an interesting contrast with the group on conventional development, particularly contrasting with Chapter 16 on requirements analysis.

2.6 Other approaches to software development

There are a number of developments which are influencing the way 'mainstream' software engineering is carried out and which might, in the long run, form a major part of conventional software development processes. Whilst it is impossible to give an exhaustive list of possible influential technologies, I have selected three which I believe are likely to prove the most significant over the next few years.

The term 'object-oriented' is now in widespread use, although the origins of the techniques are over 20 years old. In essence, object orientation is a form of structuring and abstraction initially based on the idea that program 'objects' should mirror the functionality and behaviour of 'real world' entities. Although some of the technical bases of object-oriented approaches are often obscured by excessive hyperbole, there seems to be considerable substance to the approach and it is possible that it will offer a unifying basis for a number of otherwise diverse approaches, e.g. artificial intelligence and functional programming.

It is common in most engineering disciplines to build prototypes, that is functional models of systems which are deficient in some important way, e.g. performance. There is considerable benefit in using prototyping in software engineering, e.g. to provide experimental versions of user interfaces. Again, it seems likely that the use of prototypes will become much more widespread, particularly as the sophistication of interactive systems increases.

We have already discussed the value and importance of software re-use in the introduction. Although software re-use is currently relatively uncommon, it offers, in principle, a route towards much greater productivity and quality in software products.

2.6.1 Principles of object-oriented systems

The term 'object-oriented' was initially developed in the context of programming languages, although more recently it has come to be used for a wide range of development techniques. There is also some confusion over what the term means and many widely different systems lay claim to this epithet.

Martin Atkins and Alan Brown explain the meaning of 'object-oriented' by identifying a number of fundamental characteristics of the approach. A common characteristic of object-oriented systems is that it is possible for one object to inherit properties from another. This is both beneficial in problem structuring and in achieving efficient implementations. The authors describe the basic concepts of inheritance and discuss the properties of the different 'flavours' of inheritance. This leads on to a discussion of some existing object-oriented systems, including those built on top of existing functional languages, such as Lisp. In order to illustrate the concepts of object-oriented programming, the authors develop a small example in C++, one of the most widely used object-oriented languages. They conclude with a discussion of some approaches to requirements and design specification based on the object-oriented model of systems.

This chapter has relationships to many others, including those on conventional development and AI/IKBS approaches, but the strongest links are probably with Chapters 44 and 45, dealing with modern programming languages.

2.6.2 Prototyping

Prototyping can be used either as an adjunct to a more conventional development process (perhaps to reduce the risk of error in a specification) or it can also be used as a development technique in its own right to produce a final system by refining a series of prototypes.

Darrel Ince discusses the rationale for prototyping, contrasting the throw away, incremental and evolutionary uses of prototypes. He then gives a comprehensive survey of techniques for producing prototypes, explaining which techniques are suitable in the incremental throw away and evolutionary contexts. He then separately discusses prototyping techniques for the user interface before discussing issues in managing prototyping projects.

This chapter has links with several others, most notably Chapter 57 on design of interactive systems and Chapter 27 on project planning and control.

2.6.3 Software re-use

Despite the obvious advantages, software re-use is not widely practised. There are several impediments to re-use, including the problems of designing software so it may be widely re-used and finding appropriate software components to deploy on a particular project.

Patrick Hall and Cornelia Boldyreff discuss the potential benefits of software re-use and then describe a number of re-use processes. These processes deal with the issues of finding suitable components for use in a project and ways of cataloguing components produced by a project for potential future re-use. Re-use is much easier within particular programming paradigms and the authors discuss the relationship between language style and opportunities for re-use. This leads on to a discussion of practical examples of large-scale software re-use and systems that have been developed in order to facilitate re-use. The chapter concludes with a discussion of non-technical methods of achieving re-use, and also some non-technical hindrances to use, e.g. programmer psychology.

Again there are wide dependencies with other chapters in this part of the reference book, most particularly with Chapter 27 on project planning and control and the group of chapters on programming languages.

2.7 Programming languages

A characteristic of many software development projects is that insufficient attention is given to the early stages of the process, e.g. requirements analysis and architectural design, and that there is an urge to 'get on with the job' and to start programming before the developers have a clear idea of the overall task in hand. Being aware of this tendency I was very tempted to leave out the topic of programming languages altogether in order to make the point that more attention needs to be given to other issues! This temptation was further strengthened by the knowledge that the one thing I could be certain that all readers of the book would be familiar with was programming languages. However, discretion being the better part of valour, I decided to include the topic but to focus primarily on the concepts and principles that influence current language design and are likely to influence future programming language developments. The group of chapters also includes some rather more pragmatic information.

The ideas of programming in lower level languages and practical development issues, such as linking and loading, are often picked up 'on the job'. There are still valuable principles to apply in low-level programming and in other practical endeavours such as debugging. Consequently, the first and last chapters in the group deal with low-level programming and practical program development issues respectively.

The remaining three chapters are focused on principles and issues in early and current day programming languages. The first chapter deals largely with the evolution of early high-level programming languages from the level of machine programs, although it also illustrates principles behind many current day languages. The other two chapters in this group deal with modern languages but from the point of view of procedural languages and non-conventional programming languages respectively.

2.7.1 Low-level programming

Nowadays it is relatively uncommon to write programs in low-level languages, e.g. assemblers, but occasionally it is still necessary, either as inserts in high-level language programs to achieve efficiency, or when writing low-level system routines. Although low-level programs are, in a sense, unstructured, there are still good principles of program design which can be applied.

John Henderson discusses the issues of low-level programming, primarily in the context of classical von Neumann architectures. First he looks at general characteristics of central processing units, and then discusses issues of data representation and addressing. One of the keys to writing good low-level programs is to make appropriate use of the machine addressing structures, so there is an extensive discussion of both logical and physical addressing modes. Henderson also discusses input/output processing, interrupts and trap mechanisms before briefly examining the properties of other architectures. The chapter concludes with an overview of properties of assemblers and other programming tools, addressing such issues as conditional assembly and inter-module communication.

This chapter can be read alone but it also links quite strongly to Chapter 47 which gives a basic description of computer hardware.

2.7.2 Early high-level languages

Probably the most significant contribution to software development productivity and program quality has been the advent of the high-level language. Early high-level languages abstracted away from the details of the underlying machine but still preserved the basic machine concepts, e.g. control flow mechanisms and machine-oriented data, rather than giving pure functional or logical abstractions.

Brian Meek discusses the evolution of early high-level languages largely from the point of view of conceptual advances rather than as a strict chronology. He first addresses data types, initially dealing with purely machine dependent data such as integers and characters, and then discusses the introduction of type constructors that enable programmers to build composite objects, such as records, sets and unions. This leads from the basic ideas encapsulated in early languages such as FORTRAN through to the sorts of data structures found in programming languages such as Pascal. Similarly, Meek traces the development of control constructs, first the hiding of the notorious GOTO with more structured control flow constructs, leading on to modern views of conditional statements and loop constructs. This is followed by a brief discussion of higher level program structuring concepts, such as blocks, procedures and modules. Other concepts such as parallel processing and generic procedures are also briefly discussed.

This chapter primarily acts as a precursor to Chapters 44 and 55, dealing with modern programming languages.

2.7.3 Modern non-conventional programming language concepts

The primary characteristic that makes a language 'non-conventional' is that it is not based on the von Neumann model of computation. Thus non-conventional languages embrace issues such as functional logic and object oriented programming.

Carlo Ghezzi introduces the concepts of non-conventional programming languages and discusses functional and logic languages in some detail, but from a rather different perspective than that adopted in Chapters 35 and 36. Ghezzi deals with the fundamental language principles underlying functional and logic languages and discusses a broad range of programming languages in each paradigm, rather than focusing on a more detailed definition of how to develop programs in the functional or logical style. Ghezzi also briefly addresses what are termed 'data-intensive' languages, which are primarily concerned with modelling data rather than directly expressing computation.

The chapter clearly has a direct relationship with Chapters 35 and 36, giving a broader perspective on the issues covered in those chapters. Many of the languages discussed also have a direct relevance to AI and IKBS developments as discussed in Chapters 37 and 38.

2.7.4 Features of modern imperative programming languages

The most dramatic advances in programming languages over the last decade have been in the context of non-conventional languages. However, there are a number of significant developments in imperative, or procedural, programming languages over this period. The common feature underlying many of these developments has been support for 'programming in the large' within the programming language themselves.

Ian Wand discusses four key characteristics of modern imperative programming languages: types, modularity, exceptions and concurrency. He deals with the basic concepts and properties of type systems, then covers more modern type constructs both for data structures and for functions and procedures, including the notion of polymorphism. Modules have evolved over the years from the basic notions of program blocks, through procedures and functions, to separate compilation units such as packages supported by Ada. Exceptions, i.e. ways of treating unexpected events in programs, have evolved from very *ad hoc* beginnings through to well defined mechanisms in modern languages such as Ada. There are a variety of different ways of achieving concurrency in programming languages and, more significantly, achieving communication and co-ordination between parallel processes. Wand discusses both the basic principles and illustrates how to realize the different mechanisms in common programming languages. Comprehensive examples, primarily in Ada, are presented throughout the chapter.

This chapter complements the others in this group and also has a strong relationship with Chapter 18 which deals with conventional implementation techniques.

2.7.5 Practical program development issues

There are a number of practical problems to be addressed when developing programs, including how to remove 'bugs' from the program and how to build an appropriate load image to run on the machine. Other issues, such as configuration management and testing, are dealt with in other chapters.

John Henderson, Roy Dowsing and Dorothy Graham focus on program linking, loading and debugging. Software engineers can often be unaware of linking and loading issues, but are directly exposed to the concepts when working on a 'bare' machine without an operating system. The authors cover basic issues such as the production of a bootstrap loader, through program relocation, to dynamic loading and down-line loading as required in host target software development. The discussion will be useful both for users of loading facilities and for would-be designers of linkers and loaders. Debugging is often a chaotic activity undertaken under pressure at the end of a project yet is much more effective if planned and managed in a methodical way. The authors discuss the issues of managing the debugging process and procedures to be followed to isolate bugs, make them reproducible and later to verify that they have been eliminated properly. The chapter closes with a brief discussion of mixed language working and program portability.

The material in this chapter relates to the discussion of configuration management in Chapter 34 and operating systems in Chapter 49. It also complements the material on testing in Chapter 19.

2.8 Operational environment

Software development is not carried out in isolation, but is constrained by a number of factors including the capabilities of computer hardware, the nature of available interfaces, and so on. The purpose of this group of chapters is to survey some of the more important aspects of the operational environment which constrain and influence program development.

Clearly a primary factor is the capability of assisting processors and memory systems, particularly modern VLSI central processing units. A similar class of constraint comes from interfacing techniques both in terms of communication lines and to standard classes of peripherals. Whilst it is not possible to give a comprehensive survey of such issues, it is feasible to illustrate the characteristics of common processors and common classes of peripheral interfaces.

Very few programs are developed to run on 'bare' machines, so the characteristics of the operating system are a major constraint on software developers.

From a rather different point of view, software development is also constrained by a number of standards both for software development itself and for other pertinent issues such as machine to machine communication.

2.8.1 Computer hardware – introduction and overview

The characteristics of computer hardware are more a constraint on compiler writers and operating system developers than on the application programmer. However, it is still necessary for application developers to understand the underlying capabilities and limitations of the hardware they use, particularly in the realm of peripheral interfacing and memory management.

Roy Dowsing gives an historical introduction to computer architectures briefly describing the five generations of computer technology. He then discusses the parallel evolution of processor capability and characteristics, leading to a more detailed discussion of typical current architectures. These concepts are illustrated by descriptions of the Motorola 6800 range of processors and the Digital Equipment Corporation Vax range of computers. Dowsing also discusses modern developments in processor design and technology and gives consideration to the dependencies of software engineering techniques on computer architecture.

This chapter is most strongly related with those on operating systems (Chapter 49) and low-level programming (Chapter 42).

2.8.2 Computer interfacing

The available interface techniques and technologies influence software engineers in much the same ways as the basic computer architecture itself, i.e. they are more directly relevant to operating system and compiler developers than application developers. However, both the low level characteristics and the higher level control of interfaces constrain the way in which software is developed.

Roy Dowsing deals with processor-to-interface communication, covering both the nature and characteristics of computer

buses and techniques for mapping processor addresses on to peripherals and interfaces. He discusses the basic interface control mechanisms of polling, interrupts and direct memory (DMA). This leads on to a discussion of more sophisticated modern interface devices, including programmable I/O devices. Dowsing also briefly discusses analogue-to-digital conversion as it is a common requirement to interface processors to analogue devices.

This chapter can best be thought of as an extension of Chapter 47 on computer hardware and it has a similar set of relationships to the other chapters.

2.8.3 Operating systems

Most software engineers develop programs with the support of an operating system and in the knowledge that they will be run under the control of an operating system. Thus operating systems are a very significant constraint on the work of a software engineer, yet clearly it is difficult to give a comprehensive survey of such systems.

Laurie Keller gives a survey of the characteristics of the most common classes of operating system and illustrates this with examples from some of the most widely found operating systems. She discusses operating systems for single-user machines, multi-programmed machines and multi-processing or distributed systems. The primary issues addressed in each case are memory management, disc and file organisation and control of access to machine resources. The main systems discussed are MS-DOS, CP-M, Unix, MVS and VMS. The chapter concludes with a discussion of ways of gaining access to operating system facilities from modern programming languages and with a bibliography of information on the main operating systems.

Again this chapter largely stands alone, but it relates strongly to the material on computer hardware in Chapter 47 and on low level programming in Chapter 42.

2.8.4 Standards

The software engineer's work is constrained by standards relating to products, e.g. programming language compilers, and processes, e.g. the way he carries out program validation. There is a plethora of standards-making bodies, many of whom produce standards relevant to software engineers.

Patrick Hall and Maurice Resnick give a summary of the standards-making process with the major international standards bodies, and with the national bodies in the UK and the USA. They also identify the primary standards bodies relevant to software engineering on a world wide basis. They then discuss and itemize relevant product and process standards produced by the major international and national standards making bodies. The chapter closes with a brief discussion of testing conformance to standards.

This chapter is an invaluable source of reference information for the practising software engineer and is directly relevant to almost all the other chapters in the reference book.

3 Conclusions

The technologies and management skills relevant to large-scale industrial software engineering are many and varied. This part of the reference book covers a very large number of issues focusing on both stable and mature technology and dealing, to a lesser extent, with evolving techniques.

My aim was to focus on the most important issues and, to a large extent, I believe and hope that I have done this. However, with hindsight there are a number of other important issues, e.g. risk management, system integration and system documentation, which probably deserved chapters of their own. I hope that these omissions do not detract from the value of the remaining material and that I will have the opportunity to redress these omissions in the second edition!

4 References

Boehm, B. W. (1981) *Software Engineering Economics*, Prentice Hall

Boehm, B. W. (1988) A spiral model of software development and enhancement. *ACM Software Engineering Notes*, **11**(4)

Brooks, F. P. (1975) *The Mythical Man-Month: Essays on Software Engineering*, Addison Wesley Publishing Company

Brooks, F. P. (1987) No silver bullet: essence and accidents of software engineering *Computer*, **20**(4)

Checkland, P. (1981) *Systems Thinking, Systems Practice*, J. Wiley & Sons

Learmount, D. (1990) Throttle hitch hits 747-400'. *Flight International*, 11 April, 4–5

Malcolm, R. E. (1990) A large embedded system case study. in *Proceedings CSR Conference 1989* (ed. B. Kitchenham) Elsevier

15

Software development process models

John McDermid
University of York and York Software Engineering Ltd

Paul Rook
Independent Consultant and Centre for Software Reliability

Contents

15.1 Introduction

Software development is, or should be, an engineering discipline. One of the characteristics of established engineering disciplines is that they embody a structured, methodical approach to developing and maintaining artefacts. In software development one often talks about the software 'life cycle' (borrowing the term from biology). By common usage life cycle models (LCMs) are abstract descriptions of the structured, methodical development and modification process typically showing the main stages in producing and maintaining executable software. Although the target of the development process is the production of working software, the models have a much wider scope, being concerned with requirements, design specification, verification activities, and so on.

It is valuable to discuss life-cycle models in order to understand the development process as a whole, to see relationships between different activities in software development, and to understand the requirements for methods and tools to support each aspect of the life cycle. The main aim of this chapter is to illuminate the above three topics in order to set the scene for the more detailed discussion of software development and management in the subsequent chapters. A subsidiary aim is to indicate how to design the software development process in order to reduce and control software development risk.

By definition the term life cycle covers use and maintenance (post-delivery evolution) of a system. Maintenance is often viewed as being vastly different from development because it involves adapting existing systems, not creating them anew. However, in principle the distinction is not so great as many of the technical activities are common to development and maintenance. Also, much development involves modifying existing software modules and subsystems. In practice, though, maintenance often has to include the results of an ill-managed, or ill-documented, developments, so there are often activities in maintenance, e.g. software identification, which have no counterpart in development. These issues are addressed in Chapter 20, on maintenance. Similarly, no model of software operation is given here, so the term software development process model (SDPM) is given as the chapter title, and the term software process, rather than life cycle, is used for much of the rest of the chapter.

In producing an SDPM, detail from the development process has to be omitted and it is a difficult value judgement to decide which 'details' to leave out of the models. Consequently, there are a number of 'alternative' models proposed in the literature. This chapter discusses and describes in some detail two approaches to modelling: one treating the software life cycle from a technical point of view, and the other taking a managerial viewpoint. These approaches clearly relate to the same underlying process, and the aim towards the end of the chapter is to draw them together by discussing canonical models of the process and process selection, or design.

The primary distinction between the two approaches is that the technical models are concerned with stages of development, i.e. technically related collections of activities such as the elicitation and validation activities in requirements analysis. Typical stages include requirements analysis, architectural design, detailed design and implementation. They are each characterized by being at a particular level of abstraction with respect to the executable software to be produced by the development project.

Management models are concerned with phases, i.e. temporally related groups of activities. Typically, phases start and stop at well-defined points in time, and terminate with a review of some products. These products may relate to more than one stage. Some groups of activities, e.g. acceptance testing, might be referred to both as a technical stage and as a phase. However,

in general there will be a complex relationship between stages and phases which depends on the methods used for software development. Much of this discussion will focus on these relationships.

The authors chose to discuss technical development models first although, inevitably, there are some forward references to management issues. Section 15.2 discusses the two most common forms of technical process model, then discusses ways in which iteration and risk is managed in the technical development process.

Section 15.3 discusses process selection from a technical point of view which is (almost) synonymous with selection of technical development methods. The primary concern here is to identify those factors which must be taken into consideration when selecting methods for a project.

Section 15.4 discusses a number of the available management models of software development, and draws out the links between the software development activities and phases. It also discusses managerial approaches to reduction of software development risk.

This discussion leads on to a description of the 'canonical' development model in Section 15.5 – this time operation and maintenance are included so it is a true life cycle model. Section 15.6 discusses the selection of process models from a management point of view, and also from the point of view of the customer.

By way of conclusion the relationships between this chapter and the remainder of this part of the reference book are discussed, drawing out the most salient points raised in the chapter about software process design.

15.2 Software development process models from the technical development viewpoint

As indicated above, the technical process models focus on the technical stages of development. There are essentially two ways of structuring such a model – focusing on activities, or focusing on products. First we discuss an activity-oriented, transformational model, then a product-oriented, contractual model is considered.

15.2.1 Transformational model

The software 'life cycle' is concerned with the development of software from initial concepts through delivery, use and so-called maintenance. The transformational model is based on an abstract view of the activities carried out in software development and maintenance.

The initial concept for a proposed system will usually be some brief indication of its function and purpose, such as:

'It would be a good idea to automate the accounts department to ensure that we get invoices out on time.'

The aim of development and management methods is to ensure (increase the likelihood) that the process will terminate with a working implementation, satisfied users, and the initial expectations fully satisfied.

The first observation to be made is that, except for trivial systems, it is not possible to proceed directly from the initial concepts to executable software. Instead, a number of intermediate system 'descriptions' are produced, e.g. requirements specifications, and design specifications. We refer to them as descriptions, although we previously used the term representations (McDermid and Ripken, 1984).

The early descriptions typically describe the system from the user's point of view, and later descriptions represent the designer's and implementor's points of view. In addition, the change between the levels of description involves adding design detail, giving further information about algorithms, data structures, and so on – in general, making commitments to particular ways of satisfying the stated requirements.

Development generally proceeds from concepts through requirements, etc., with one description being developed by some intellectual or automated process from the preceding description or descriptions. This process is referred to as a transformation, although there is no implication that this is a purely automatable process. Arguably, synthesis is a more satisfying term.

The transformations add information of a number of types, and arising from a number of different sources. At the higher levels the information may derive mainly from the designer's experience and will relate to overall system structure (architecture), styles of interaction with users, etc. Quality attributes such as maintainability, reliability and safety may drive the design process, and thus influence the transformations. At the lower levels the transformations are more familiar, for example, adding detail by producing an executable algorithm from a pseudocode specification.

In an ideal world the transformations would yield a sequence of descriptions, resulting in executable programs which satisfied their requirements and the initial concepts. In practice errors and infelicities are discovered during development (and maintenance) which cause iteration, i.e. repetition of the current transformation or rework of earlier descriptions. The term verification and validation (V & V) is used for the checking activities which can lead to iteration. The differences between verification and validation are discussed below. The model is summarized in graphical form in *Figure 15.1*.

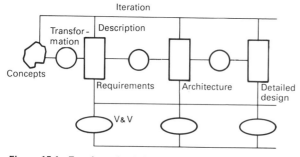

Figure 15.1 Transformational life cycle model

This model also encompasses maintenance. The main forms of maintenance activity are:

1. *Corrective.* Removing errors from the system.
2. *Perfective.* Finding better ways of implementing existing functions.
3. *Adaptive.* Modifying the system to satisfy new requirements.

These can all be seen as being iteration within the model. They differ from the processes of iteration in development in that the source of the request for change is different. Differences between the three activities concern whether or not the change involves the requirements as well as the design and implementation. Technically there is (or should be) no difference between these three activities and those carried out in development, although in terms of personnel, management, etc. there often is a distinction between development and maintenance (see Chapter 20).

The model can encompass a number of different development approaches or paradigms (see Section 15.2.4). Thus it can be used as the basis for comparing different development methodologies. On a smaller scale it is helpful as a basis for discussing methods, as it identifies the three major components of a method, *viz*:

1. The notation used for the description.
2. The rules (and guidelines) for V & V.
3. The guidelines for the transformation.

We use term rules for V & V as there should be a precise correspondence between descriptions. However, we use the term guidelines for transformations, recognizing that it is an intellectual process guided by general principles such as 'information hiding' (Parnas, 1972) and 'delaying design commitment'. More generally, we would expect to establish a number of quality objectives for a system, e.g. reliability and portability, and to guide development in terms of these objectives (Kitchenham and Walker, 1986).

The term V & V is often used loosely. More strictly we use the term verification to answer the question: 'are we building it right?', which implies checking the correspondence between descriptions. Similarly we associate validation with the question 'are we building the right thing?', which implies determining whether the descriptions are still consistent with the initial concepts. Thus we should talk about verification rules and guidelines for validation.

It is interesting to note that many so-called methods are deficient in terms of the model presented above. This is usually where the method defines a notation but no transformation guidelines, or rules for V & V. The absence of guidelines for transformation is a limitation of many current formal methods. This point is referred to when process design and method selection are discussed.

15.2.2 Contractual model

The contractual model views some of the specifications (descriptions) produced as being 'contracts' between the staff working on 'adjacent' stages in the software process, e.g. requirements analysts and designers. However, the contractual model clearly has to show development activities so one can view the transformational and contractual models as being duals.

The transformational model was described earlier in abstract terms to make it clear that it could be particularized to a variety of specific development approaches or models. (The appendix to McDermid and Kipken (1984) gives a number of examples.) By way of contrast, a rather concrete contractual model is given to illustrate the software process followed when using formal methods. This model is taken from Cohen (1982).

The principle is that of viewing specifications as contracts between teams, with alternations of specification and design, the result from one stage of design being then explicitly written as the contractual specification(s) for the next stage. It should be noted that this model views the implementors as suppliers with designers as customers; similarly, designers are suppliers with requirements analysts as customers.

The specifications correspond to the descriptions in the transformational model. The activities on the left-hand side of the diagram correspond to validation in the transformational model, and those on the right-hand side to verification.

Transformations are not explicit in the contractual model, (they are implicit in the progress made through the stages.) The theories and formal models in *Figure 15.2* have no explicit counterpart in the transformational model. Despite these differences it is clear that these two models represent a common perception of the nature of the (technical aspects of the) software development process.

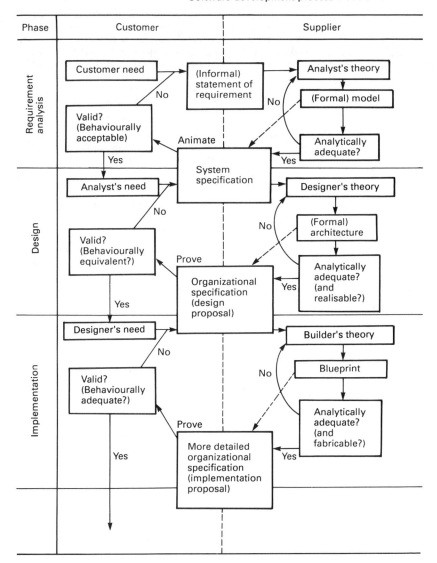

Phase	Customer	Supplier

Figure 15.2   Cohen's contractual model of software development

The contractual model is often viewed as an approach to the management of development risk. This view of the model is discussed in Section 15.2.4.

15.2.3   Iteration in software development

The contractual and transformational models show a rather 'static' view of the development process. In practice, as indicated above, iteration (rework of current and previous specifications) occurs as errors and infelicities are detected by verification and validation activities. Thus one can see that the process contains nested iterations, both within a stage dealing with 'local' errors and between stages due to belated realisations that earlier (design) decisions were inappropriate. This iterative structure is illustrated in *Figure 15.3*.

Here description N is the product of stage N in the development process. It undergoes evaluation, and, if necessary, some suggested modifications are passed on to the synthesis activity

(which is equivalent to our previous transformation). Synthesis develops (potentially) multiple putative output descriptions. These undergo analysis (*cf* the verification activities in the contractual and tranformational models) and are submitted, together with the outputs from the analysis, to evaluation.

Analysis will normally encompass at least syntactic and static semantic correctness, but may be of much wider scope. The results of the analysis might include, for example, the evaluation of control flow complexity. Thus evaluation is based on such analyses, together with direct assessment of the alternative descriptions. The direct assessment will often be by means of a review (Fagan, 1976) and will assess many issues, typically including quality attributes such as readability, modifiability, etc. as well as more objective factors. These issues are dealt with in greater detail in Chapter 29, on quality management.

Further iteration occurs, with indicated deviations (i.e. changes to the descriptions), until the descriptions are deemed suitable to pass on to the next stage. On any iteration, including

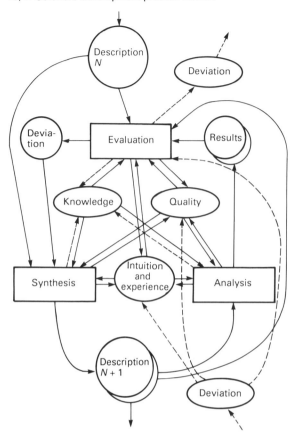

Figure 15.3 Model for stage *N*+1 of software development

the first, the evaluation can refer the description back to a previous stage because it is deemed to be inappropriate for further 'refinement' for some reason. Evaluation also incorporates the decision to proceed to the next stage.

There are three sources of information which inform the evaluation, analysis and synthesis activities. These are identified as ovals labelled knowledge, quality and intuition and experience in Figure 15.3. Knowledge is intended to represent hard knowledge to do with the syntax and semantics of notations used, e.g. the verification rules in the transformational model and the theories in the contractual model. Experience and intuition reflect the skills of the designers or analysts as applied to this particular task. Quality implies the quality attributes which are defined for the particular project, e.g. to do with maintainability, reliability, interoperability, etc.

The arrows from these three ovals represent the direct impact of these information sources on the activities. The reverse arrows show feedback influencing the information sources. Thus experience carrying out analysis and synthesis activities is shown feeding back into the designer's intuition, and into the representation of quality attributes for the system. The arrows to knowledge are shown as dotted reflecting the fact that changes to hard knowledge, e.g. method design, are much slower. There is, of course, feedback between stages. For example, discovery that what appeared to be a good architecture is in fact very poor, when carrying out detailed design, will (or at any rate should) significantly modify the designer's intuition.

This model is, of course, still abstract, and still something of an idealisation. One aspect that is worthy of discussion is the treatment of quality. Quality issues tend to be articulated first in requirements, then they 'migrate' during the design process into more direct functional specifications and implementations. For example, performance requirements may result in the choice of particular algorithms, and reliability requirements may lead to the use of redundant hardware and diverse (differently designed) implementations of software algorithms. Thus the 'flows' in the model between quality, the descriptions and the actions are more complex than indicated above.

Between them these three models serve to illustrate the complexity of the software development process and the interrelationships between the activities and products (descriptions) produced at each stage in development.

15.2.4 Management of technical risk

It is now well understood that there are considerable risks associated with software development. Indeed, it is all too common for software to be delivered late, at too high a cost, with inadequate quality or functionality. There are many solutions or ameliorations to these problems, most of which relate to the technical development methods or management practices, and do not affect one's perception of the overall software process. However, the gross-level structure of the development process, often called the development paradigm, does impinge on the process model. The authors choose to use the term approach rather than paradigm, and focus on the contractual approach and prototyping and incremental approaches as examples of approaches.

15.2.4.1 Contractual approach

In the simplest form of the contractual approach a series of specifications are produced and agreed to be (essentially) fixed baselines for future development. No work is done on a given stage (level of specification) until all the work on the previous stage is completed. The term contractual is used as the specifications take the form of (technical annexes to) 'contracts' between the producers of the level *N* and level *N* + 1 descriptions to supply a level *N* + 1 description consonant with the level *N* description. This is the most obvious interpretation of the transformational and contractual models presented above.

The primary approach to risk management is that sufficient effort should be put into verifying and validating a description before it is made into a baseline, and subsequently used, so that there is a very low probability that rework will be required. Further, since each stage is completed before the next is started, there are natural breakpoints at which to decide to stop the project. Clearly with the contractual approach the primary financial risk taken at any time is that the current stage will not be completed successfully. Risk is not eliminated but it *is* contained.

Clearly for a large project the specifications need not be monolithic. For example, it would be normal for individual module specifications to form 'contracts' between the system architect/designer and the programmer. In principle, the 'contracts' can relate to activities as well as products, so there could be contracts for integration, unit testing, etc. Thus the contractual approach is compatible with the normal concepts of work breakdown, and other standard aspects of software development. The contractual approach is supported by some commercial IPSEs, e.g. ISTAR (Dowson, 1987).

This contractual approach is an excellent basis for the technical controller to structure the technical complexity of the transformations from requirements specification through design and down through detailed design to modules for implementation. Properly used, it also provides the structured documentation basis for the interactions between teams, working on successive stages.

The contractual model of technical transformation and decomposition is orthogonal to the principle of progress through time-based life cycle phases and cannot of itself be relied upon as the basis for project control. Any attempt to do so for large projects founders on questions of predefined levels of decomposition, 'goodness' of design and when the design is 'finished'. This point is discussed further at the end of Section 15.4.5.

The contractual approach does not affect the process models in the sense of causing the addition of extra activities or products. It does, however, reinforce the role and importance of the specifications in the contractual model (see Figure 15.2).

15.2.4.2 Prototyping approach

Prototyping can be used in two ways. First, one can attempt to validate the accuracy of requirements or the acceptability of some design decisions. Second, one can investigate the feasibility of some proposed design strategy. Each type of use addresses a different form of risk.

The first form of prototyping is useful where it is difficult or impossible to get a clear statement of user requirements. This can arise where there are non-functional requirements which are difficult to clarify or quantify, e.g. the infamous 'user-friendly'. Used in this way prototyping should be seen as a way of gaining enough knowledge to be able to produce a requirement or design specification that will meet user needs. Thus one can say that prototyping can address specification risk.

The second use of prototyping is concerned with eliminating some of the technical risks in development, rather than reducing the specification risk. Here alternative designs can be explored and compared for performance, etc. Clearly this is strongly related to the principles embodied in the Boehm spiral model (see Section 15.6). Prototyping may be used at many stages in the development process, although it is most likely to be useful at the earlier stages when there is most design freedom, and least knowledge available on which to base design decisions.

Prototypes are only of value if they can be produced quickly – hence the common use of the term 'rapid prototyping'. The techniques used in prototyping should therefore be optimized for speed of implementation, not development of 'product quality' software. Hence, for example, the requirements for documenting the design would normally be relaxed. Consequently, inclusion of prototype software in deliverable products can cause problems in maintenance (or possibly earlier in the life cycle) unless exceptional efforts are made to turn software into product quality. It is often better to discard the prototype and to reimplement it to the (now known) specification. Prototyping is discussed in more detail in Chapter 40.

The term 'prototyping approach' is usually associated with the first use of prototypes, i.e. in clarifying requirements, although both are valid uses of the technology. Clearly the prototyping and contractual approaches are not incompatible, as prototypes can be used to gain confidence that a description can be used as a baseline. In practice the distinction is one of emphasis. With the contractual approach the stress is on producing well-engineered products based on clear, detailed specifications, validated by whatever means. With prototyping, more emphasis is placed on the means for achieving clarification of requirements and the prototypes may themselves stand as specifications. Also, prototyping is more compatible with a 'cardinal points' approach to specification where only the key requirements are precisely specified and the remaining aspects of the system are left as details to be clarified by the designers.

The prototyping approach affects the process models as extra activities are produced. *Figure 15.4* gives a model of a 'prototyping only' process addressing specification risk, but clearly the earlier models could be adapted to include prototyping activities.

The topic of prototyping as a basis for risk control is discussed further in Section 15.4.7.

15.2.4.3 Incremental approach

With the incremental approach the aim is to manage risk by only defining and developing a small part of the system at a time. Thus a 'core' system is first designed and implemented, then additional functionality is implemented in a series of further overlapping subprojects. Assuming that the 'core' is specified and implemented satisfactorily, then the risk is reduced to the possibility that some given stage of development may fail. A great attraction of this approach is that at most times there is an executable, usable system and it is possible for users to give early feedback on, and gain confidence in, the implemented system.

There are different ways in which the incremental approach can be used. For example, it would be possible to derive a complete set of requirements and an architecture, then use the incremental approach for detailed design and implementation. Alternatively, incremental approaches could be used from the outset and the requirements clarified for each new increment as the development proceeds. With this 'fully incremental' approach there is a risk that unknown requirements may render the 'core' design invalid. With the more conservative approach there is the risk, as with the contractual approach, that the requirements or architecture may be flawed. In practice it is difficult to undertake the incremental approach without a

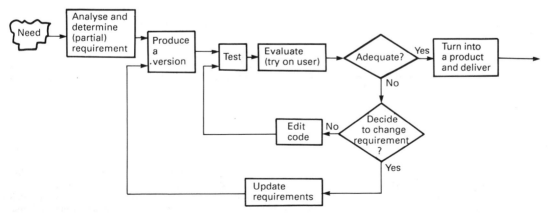

Figure 15.4 Prototyping development process

reasonable understanding of the complete requirements if for no other reason than this is an essential prerequisite to determining what constitutes the 'core' functionality.

It is clear that there is some commonality with the previous two approaches. Here the main distinction is that it would (normally) be deemed acceptable for different teams to be working in parallel on requirements, design and implementation for different increments. However, the increments should be made as independent as possible, e.g. a module should ideally be developed in one increment, but not modified in any subsequent increments. This reduces technical risk, and makes it easy for increments to proceed in parallel. In practice it is rarely possible to achieve this ideal and much of the skill in managing incremental development relates to handling (potentially) conflicting work in increments being undertaken (at least partially) in parallel.

Again the incremental approach does not impinge directly on the form of our models. However, it does change the interpretation of the models. Particularly, it indicates that the specifications should not be viewed as monolithic, but capable of controlled evolutionary development. One should accept that many, or indeed all, development activities may be carried out in parallel by different development teams.

The incremental approach is gaining popularity, and is discussed further in Section 15.4.8.

15.2.4.4 Experimental development and maintenance

There are, of course, other possible approaches to software development. For example, it is possible continuously to evolve, or modify, prototypes in order to produce a complete working system. As indicated above, the attendant risks are that the resultant software will be of low quality and hard to modify. This does not seem to be an approach to adopt intentionally for production quality software, but it is probably highly effective for 'experimental', e.g. research or prototype, software. This is also an approach often adopted for 'artificial intelligence' software.

However, it is clear that modifications made late in development and during maintenance take on much of the character of experimental development. A great risk here is that the initial design structures become diffuse and ill-defined as the system is progressively modified. This can lead to what is often called 'software decay' and a limited ability to make further changes to software. Clearly the biggest problems arise where the existing architecture is invalidated by some required change and the effort to carry out the restructuring is not available, or the need for the restructuring is not appreciated.

There are no really satisfactory development techniques or paradigms which deal with the maintenance aspects of the life cycle. There are tools and techniques for aiding in restructuring, but this is a cure for the symptoms, not a cure for the cause of the difficulties. The incremental approach is probably the most satisfactory from this point of view as there is a possibility if the system is well designed (see above) that the increments, apart from the core, can be modified independently. The only other remedy for software decay is to ensure that all changes are made starting at the highest level in the set of system descriptions which are affected by the (need for) change. This is *much* easier said than done. Maintenance problems and techniques are discussed further in Chapter 20.

15.2.5 Summary

Software development is a complex process. The four models illustrated above give different views of the process but they are essentially compatible, with the differences simply reflecting the desire to stress different facets of the process.

It is hoped that the models make clear the nature of the development process. They certainly indicate some of the factors which have to be considered when designing a process.

The choice of a development approach (transformational, contractual, evolutionary (prototyping or incremental) or a combination) is one parameter in controlling technical risk. The selection of the stages of the development process and the development methods to be employed are two further important parameters which we now discuss.

15.3 Selection of stages and methods

As indicated earlier, it is necessary for any development project to select, or design, its process, and both technical and managerial decisions have to be made. From a technical point of view the most important decisions are the choice of the set of stages, and the choice of methods to deal with each stage.

Note that there is a distinction between stages and levels of documentation. A project may decide to have an architectural design stage but, because of the size of the project, to have three levels of architectural design specification. The former is a technical decision and the latter is a managerial decision to do with the management of risk, setting of review points, and so on.

The authors believe that there is a set of development stages which are inherent in software development. However, structuring of these stages depends on the development paradigm chosen and, to some extent, the nature of the relationship with the customer for the system. These issues are briefly discussed below. Factors affecting each stage in the process are then considered, as are the choice of methods for each stage in the process.

15.3.1 Selection of stages

It should be stressed that the concern here is about the selection of *constructive* stages, i.e. those steps which produce descriptions. Thus, from the technical point of view, unit testing is part of the implementation stage even though, managerially, it may be a separate phase. This approach is adopted because (the authors believe that) the different stages deal with different forms of risk. First we discuss the canonical, or underlying, set of stages in development, then we consider how the set of stages varies with customer relationship and development paradigm.

Five development stages can be identified:

1. Requirements analysis ⎫
2. System specification ⎬ what
3. Architectural design ⎫
4. Detailed design ⎬ how
5. Implementation ⎭
6. (Maintenance or evolution)

The first two, requirements analysis and system specification, are in the domain of requirements, i.e. what the customer or user wants. The distinction between these two stages is that requirements are concerned with the operational environment for the system to be built, as well as the system itself, whereas system specification is not. Indeed, the system specification can be thought of as the interface definition between the system to be built and its environment.

The remaining three stages are in the design domain, i.e. how the system developer intends to satisfy the requirements. The architecture represents the overall system structure and other important characteristics such as resource usage. The two further stages represent progressively greater levels of detail until one reaches the level of executable code. In practice there may well be multiple levels of detailed design and the number of levels will be dictated by the scale of the system being developed and possibly other factors (see Section 15.3.4.2).

This set of stages and descriptions can be described as canonical as they each serve essential and different purposes. The requirements are a primary communication vehicle between user and computer specialist, and they identify the boundary between the system and its environment. This is an essential stage as one often does not know, *ab initio*, what functionality should be included in a system and which should not. This stage addresses the risk of specifying (and building) the wrong system.

The system specification defines precisely the interface at the system boundary to provide a basis for design and acceptance testing. This description addresses the (managerial and technical) risk that the system will be delivered and rejected as inappropriate. By contrast with the requirements, the system specification need not address the environment and it should be precise enough for acceptance testing against it to be unequivocal (the requirements need not.)

The architecture shows how to satisfy the requirements, including the non-functional attributes, by defining the overall system structure and essential functionality and resource requirements. This is a key stage as the structure of the architecture may need to be different from the requirements to deal with non-functional attributes, e.g. performance, or fault-tolerance. This stage addresses the (technical) risk that the whole design will prove ill-founded because it is infeasible to satisfy the requirements given the basic design, i.e. tinkering with implementation won't overcome basic design faults. (Note: the results of many projects are never used, with basic architectural faults probably a major contributory cause.)

The detailed design adds enough detail to separate pieces of the architecture so that a programmer can proceed to implement the programs which constitute the final system. This also addresses technical risk, albeit at a lower level.

In essence, descriptions associated with these canonical stages reflect interfaces between groups of individuals, e.g. users and requirements analysts, or analysts and designers. Thus they form a basis for intra-project communication as well as risk reduction or management. Clearly, therefore, the set of descriptions actually used will depend on the nature of the customer relationship.

If the developers are producing a unique system for a customer satisfying a 'new' need, e.g. automating some function which is currently carried out manually, then all stages are necessary. In particular, requirements analysis is essential to define the system boundary. However, if an existing system is to be replaced with, say, the same functionality but higher throughput, then it should be possible to proceed directly to system specification. Similar 'short cuts' will be possible in other circumstances, e.g. developing embedded systems where the design of the larger system has defined boundaries and requirements for the embedded system.

A rather different situation occurs where a system is developed for a perceived market need, or opportunity. Here there is no customer to ask so it is not really feasible to produce a requirements specification (at least in the normal way). This is particularly true for innovative, 'market creating', products, e.g. spreadsheets when they were first developed. Here it may be possible to go directly to an architectural specification from the perception of market opportunity or need (probably via feasibility studies). Alternatively, requirements and system specification documents may be produced albeit as 'frames of reference' for the designers, rather than as documents for communication with a customer. The choice may well depend on the development approach adopted.

The stages identified clearly map most directly on to the contractual model, and typically there would be a one to one mapping between stages and (sets of) contractual specifications.

A similar relationship will hold with an incremental approach but each contractual specification (within the framework of the overall development contract) will correspond to an increment.

With prototyping the mapping is less clear. For example, in developing a product for the market one might use a prototype to investigate the 'problem' and the design space and also to serve as a system specification and architectural model. Thus a prototype, with supporting documentation, may fulfill the role of the description for more than one stage. Thus prototyping can blur the distinctions between stages identified above.

The choice of stages and development paradigms is a precursor to choosing methods. Each of the 'canonical' stages has a role to play in development. If a stage is omitted it should be made clear how that role is to be fulfilled.

15.3.2 Canonical stages

We now illustrate technical issues to be addressed at each of the canonical stages in software development. There are two primary purposes in presenting this material. The first is to clarify the nature of the activities which have to be managed, and hence set the foundations for the development of the canonical life cycle model in Section 15.5. The second is to set the context for the more detailed discussion of requirements analysis, formal specification, and so on in later chapters.

Indicated below are requirements for methods to support each stage, with brief outlines of the relevant capabilities of existing formal and structured methods. It is useful to start by clarifying the distinction between these two classes of method.

The term 'formal method' is widely used, but with differing meanings. In this chapter, and the rest of the book, it is used to refer to methods with a sound basis in mathematics. The term 'structured method' refers here to methods which are well defined but which do not have a sound basis in mathematics. Typically structured methods use a well-defined diagrammatic notation, whereas formal methods employ notations based on discrete mathematics (e.g. set theory and predicate calculus). Technically, the most significant difference between the two classes of techniques is that formal methods permit functionality to be specified precisely whereas structured methods generally only allow system structure to be specified precisely.

The term 'informal method' describes those methods which have no formal basis, e.g. those using natural language system descriptions. Structured methods are used fairly widely in industry. Formal methods are used much less widely, but their use is on the increase. To avoid circumlocution the material here is largely presented in the terms of formal methods, but the concepts and criteria also apply equally to structured methods.

15.3.2.1 Requirements analysis

Requirements analysis is the first stage of the full development process concerned with documenting the user's or customer's perceived needs by 'transformation' from the (by definition undocumented) initial concepts. The distinguishing characteristic of requirements analysis is that it is primarily an information-gathering exercise which can only be validated, not verified.

The results of requirements analysis should describe both the *system* and the *environment* in which it operates. This is the case for two reasons:

1. The environment may change, affecting the functionality required of the system.
2. The boundary of the system is not known *a priori*.

It is hard to define precisely that part of the environment which should be considered in requirements analysis, but it should cover at least those systems, individuals, etc. which interact directly with the system to be developed. The need to represent the environment means that requirements descriptions must be able to represent concurrency explicitly (because the system and processes in the environment operate concurrently).

In requirements analysis, it must be possible to describe both functional and non-functional aspects of systems. By functional aspects we mean systematic relationships between values input to, and values output from, the system. Non-functional requirements are effectively constraints on how the functions are performed. These will typically relate to the volume of data to be handled, response times, reliability, response to hardware failures, etc.

Further, it is necessary to be able to record non-executable aspects/properties of systems. This is true for a number of reasons. Users may ask for unrealisable systems and it is desirable to be able to record their requests exactly, to analyse them, then to explain *why* their requests are unrealisable. Negative requirements, e.g. for safety and security, are essentially non-executable. Also, it must be possible to record partial requirements, or requirements based on the assumption of infinite resources, which may arise as part of the information gathering process. Thus the common desire to represent requirements entirely in an executable language seems misguided. However, recording suitable parts of the requirements in an executable form and using animation or rapid prototyping (see for example Hekmatpour and Ince (1986)) as a means of validating them is often very effective, especially with difficult aspects of requirements such as user interfaces.

The results of requirements analysis are the primary basis for communication with the users and customer for the system. For this reason it is desirable that the description should be as precise as possible, e.g. formal. However, it is rare for users to be educated to understand the necessary formalisms. Consequently, it seems that formal techniques either cannot be used at this stage, or if they are used some interpretation of the formalism is required for communication with the customer. The most obvious form of such an interpretation would be via prototyping or animation as indicated above.

Technically requirements analysis methods need to deal with causality, e.g. 'when this event occurs in the environment the system must perform the following actions', and other properties such as behaviour of the system under hardware failure conditions. Currently most requirements are specified informally. Structured methods such as CORE (Mullery, 1979) do address some of the technical problems alluded to above and are used in requirements analysis. There are few formal methods oriented towards requirements, although the work of the Alvey FOREST project (Maibaum *et al.*, 1986; Potts and Prinkelstein, 1986) is noteworthy as it deals with issues such as formally representing causality and giving guidelines for requirements capture. Existing requirements analysis techniques are described in Chapter 16.

There are a number of research problems which have to be overcome before formal techniques can be used widely for requirements analysis. Perhaps the most crucial of these is the development of notations rich enough to specify functional, causal and non-functional requirements but which can be presented to a user in an acceptable manner without (substantial) loss of precision. Of course, presentation can be via 'animation' or 'execution' rather than simply in terms of specification text. It seems that this tool based form of presentation is the most likely way of making formal methods applicable at this stage of the life cycle.

15.3.2.2 *System specification*

System specification is still in the requirements domain. It is concerned with what the system should do, not how it does it, although this is not always an easy distinction to make in practice (see below). The primary distinction between this and the previous stage is that it describes only the system, not the environment, and it gives precise definitions of the system interfaces. In practice the system specification may be an enriched subset of the requirement specification and it should encompass both the system interfaces and its functionality.

In the contractual model of the life cycle the system specification would be the basis of the contract for the development team. The implicit requirement for precision suggests that the specifications produced should be formal. Further the need to specify what, not how, suggests that it would be desirable to use algebraic specification techniques, i.e. techniques where the behaviour of a system is specified implicitly by equations relating inputs to outputs (see Chapter 22).

Algebraic specification techniques have been widely applied to small examples but there is little evidence yet that they are suitable for specifying large systems. It is worth trying to explain the problems of using algebraic specifications with a small example.

Imagine a system containing a database which we wish to update. If we model the database directly we can simply specify validity (the object to be updated exists, the type is correct, etc.). In an algebraic approach we would have to establish existence of an object by reasoning about the sequence of inputs to the system and determining whether the object had been created (successfully) since it was last deleted. This would make the specification obscure and cumbersome. In the authors' experience problems of this nature arise with the algebraic approach and such specifications tend to obfuscate rather than elucidate the problem being specified. Thus there is a conflict between the theoretical attractiveness of algebraic approaches and their apparent practical limitations.

As far as possible concurrency should be specified implicitly, not explicitly, so that the system developers are free to choose what level of concurrency to use in implementing the system. This is a contentious point and other authors, e.g. Zave (1982) would argue in favour of explicitly modelling concurrency. The primary argument in favour of the implicit approach is that it does not involve making premature design decisions.

There is another important issue related to system specification which can be illustrated by example. It is possible in an avionics system that some interfaces, for example, to radar subsystems, would be specified very precisely during requirements, perhaps down to the level of the meanings of bits at the interface. However interfaces to other devices, such as a head-up display, may be known in terms of the information to be displayed but not in terms of the data formats, etc. Defining these formats is a design exercise which should involve human factors experts. In producing a system specification the interface definition would have to be made precise so it will inevitably contain design information. The extent to which the system specification will (implicitly) contain design information will depend on the nature of the system being built.

It might be thought that this 'problem' of mingling requirements and design can be avoided by using a different development approach, such as prototyping. In fact, this does not avoid the need to produce a complete system specification. Instead, it simply (and possibly desirably) defers the point at which the specification is made precise until after validation of the proposed system specification by means of prototyping. It is desirable to avoid 'premature design', but it is clear that it is difficult to determine what is necessary design information and what is superfluous.

The system specification should be informally verified against the requirements. Since design information may have been added it is also desirable that it is validated against the initial concepts. It is possible that techniques of animation of specification execution (Coleman and Gallimore, 1987) can be used in validation, although, as pointed out above, system specification may not initially contain enough information to allow execution of all aspects of the specification.

There seem to be two possible ways in which formal techniques can evolve to become more applicable for this stage in the software development process. First, algebraic techniques can be developed so that they are applicable to large-scale systems. This will almost inevitably involve schemes for 'modularizing' specifications. Second, it may be possible to find ways of applying the more operational techniques so that they do not unduly compromise design.

There are a number of structured techniques which cover much of the life cycle, and many of the techniques start at this stage. Examples are JSD (Jackson, 1983), and SSADM. (SSADM is a method recommended by the CCTA which is closely based on LSDM developed by Learmonth and Burchett Management Systems.) These techniques assume that there is an existing system which one is trying to replace, and they base the system specification on an analysis of the functionality of the existing system. Within this limitation these methods have comparatively good transformation guidelines, and, particularly in the case of SSADM, powerful data analysis capabilities. When using the above structured methods validation would normally be via a design review with the 'customer' for the system.

The comparative strengths of the structured techniques are their transformation guidelines and their suitability for communication with the customer. The comparative strengths of the formal methods are the precision which they bring to specifying the system interfaces and functionality. Precision, and hence lack of ambiguity in communicating within the project team, are the main strengths of formal methods at each stage, so the observation will not be repeated in subsequent sections.

System specification using structured techniques is covered in Chapter 16 on requirements analysis and structured techniques are discussed further in Chapter 17. Both model-oriented (see below) and algebraic specifications may be used at this stage and they are described in Chapters 21 and 22 respectively.

15.3.2.3 Architectural design

Architectural design is the first 'pure' design stage. Architectural design is discussed in detail in Chapter 17 on high-level design.

The architectural design describes the system interfaces, functionality and structure as the designers intend to implement them. The architecture is distinct from the previous stage in that it discusses system structure and how the functionality will be achieved as well as what functionality is required. The level of detail contained in such a specification will vary from project to project. However, it is not the level of detail which characterizes architectural design, but the fact that this is the first description of the system from the developer's, rather than the user's, point of view.

Many different ways of producing formal specifications have been proposed, but the concept of architecture outlined above seems to match closely the ideas of model-oriented specifications, that is, producing a model of the system state and specifying the behaviour of operations by saying how they change the state. There are many other possible approaches to specifying architecture. Space does not permit a survey here, but a discussion of a number of relevant techniques is given in Chapter 17.

A primary characteristic of the transformation from system specification to architecture is that it may not be structure preserving. In other words, the structure of the design may have to be different to that of the requirement. This change in structure may be necessary so that the system performs suffi-

ciently quickly, or so that the customer can afford it. The authors have been surprised to find that even experienced software designers can find it difficult to accept this point, so a simple example is given by way of illustration. The example is necessarily rather simplistic; the real difficulty arises when much more sophisticated and/or subtle restructuring needs to be carried out to achieve an effective implementation.

Imagine a telephone exchange intended to handle 10 000 lines. The 'natural' way to specify this from the customer's point of view would be as 10 000 parallel processes, each carrying out the appropriate functions for their respective lines. (In practice there would be additional functions for producing customer's bills, fault finding, etc.) If the exchange were built with 10 000 processes (and, say, 100 processors to run the processes) then it would be prohibitively expensive. Instead, exchanges are built with a smaller number of specialized processes, each of which handles a part of the processing associated with handling each line. The number of processes is determined by a number of factors, including the expected density of call set-up requests, and the reliability of the processors to be used. Thus cost and the limitations of current hardware technology are primary factors in determining the design. A number of points can be drawn from this observation.

First, non-functional reasons are given for the change in structure. In other words, non-functional requirements, such as performance, cost and reliability, drive the design process. This is significant because, in general, neither formal nor structural specification methods enable this non-functional information to be recorded within the notation employed by the method.

Second, many formal methods support a concept known as refinement (see, for example, Jones (1986)), which enables one to define and verify the correctness of the relationships between two formal descriptions of the same system. However, the published refinement techniques are usually too restrictive to admit the sort of structural change identified above, although recent work in Oxford is addressing this problem (Hoare, 1986). A recent publication gives a survey of some current refinement techniques (McDermid, 1990), and Chapter 24 of this book explains the principles of refinement.

Third, quite a permissive interpretation of equivalence is needed between the levels of description. It must be possible to take into account non-determinism, asynchrony, etc. This would mean, *inter alia*, that the order of the outputs would not be determined entirely by the order of the inputs. The notion of behavioural equivalence, introduced in algebraic specification (see, for example, Sanella and Tarlecki (1984)) admits at least some of the requisite laxity in the meaning of equivalence.

As will be apparent from the example above, it is also necessary to be able to represent concurrency within the architectural design. The primary problem associated with applying formal methods at this stage in the life cycle is that there is no method, or notation, which encompasses all of the requirements identified above. At present the would-be user of formal methods must choose the technique which best supports the characteristics which are most critical in the application area, and find other ways, e.g. informal descriptions, of dealing with the remaining aspects of the design.

With the majority of structured methods it is easier to make the sorts of structural changes alluded to above as there are weaker rules governing the correspondence between descriptions. More positively, some techniques exist for making these structural changes. For example, JSD incorporates a technique known as 'inversion' which generates a parallel processing regime from the properties of a data structure in order to lead to efficient manipulation of data streams. However, in the authors' view, none of the techniques explicitly incorporates enough non-functional information into the design process.

Several structured methods give good guidelines for developing architectural specifications. Some, e.g. MASCOT3 (Bate, 1986), give a good basis for the design of concurrent and/or real-time computer systems. The handling of concurrency and the inherent flexibility are probably the main strengths of structured methods.

There are further important aspects of system architectures, such as the definition of a module structure for the system, and estimation of system resource usage. In fact there are issues of modularity, work breakdown, and so on, at each stage in the development process. This chapter focuses primarily on the technical capability of methods, rather than issues which are, to some extent, aspects of management. Nonetheless, these are important issues when selecting methods. Technical management issues are treated at some length in McDermid and Ripken (1984) and in Chapter 27, on project planning and control.

15.3.2.4 Detailed design

Detailed design is concerned with adding enough detail, e.g. in terms of data structures and algorithms, to the architecture to enable individual modules to be implemented subsequently.

It is the authors' view that detailed design should proceed from the architecture by the conventional process of (structure preserving) refinement. This is not a universally held view, indeed the phrase 'one man's design is another man's requirement' is often used with an inappropriate interpretation when discussing hierarchical specifications of systems. An appropriate interpretation of the phrase is that the designer has complete design freedom *within* the constraints imposed by the requirements, but none outside these constraints. An inappropriate, but common, interpretation is that any design that 'behaves the same' as specified by the requirements is acceptable. This latter interpretation means that the structure of the design and the details of the interfaces could be changed in each description. In the authors' opinion this is an unhealthy attitude from at least three points of view.

Technically, it implies that the architect did not have a complete (adequate) understanding of the system. This is particularly critical if the proposed changes involve modifying the process structure and hence impacting timing, etc. possibly to the extent that the system no longer meets its (non-functional) requirements. Clearly problems with the architecture may be found in detailed design. These should be resolved by updating the architecture, not by making low-level changes to the overall design.

Managerially, it implies that the project is not under adequate control. For example, modules common to several subsystems may have been identified for separate implementation and the basis on which this decision was made could be invalidated by allowing architectural changes in detailed design. Thus even if the restructuring preserves subsystem interfaces it could have 'knock-on' effects on the rest of the project and invalidate project plans, project resourcing, etc.

Philosophically it seems to contradict the whole nature of the development process. In proceeding from specification to implementation one is progressively adding information to the system descriptions. Concomitant with this is the fact that the designers are making *commitments* to design decisions. A major design decision made in the architectural stage is the system structure (module breakdown, etc.). Thus changing structure violates an earlier commitment, and is therefore unacceptable technically, managerially and philosophically.

This approach to detailed design is also fairly well supported. The structure preserving view is consistent with (capable of being supported by) current refinement techniques (see, for example, Jones (1986), and McDermid (1989)). The classical

refinement techniques apply for sequential systems. Some techniques for dealing with concurrency, e.g. CCS (Milner, 1980), support hierarchical decomposition of systems which is a form of refinement. So far as the authors are aware there is no satisfactory formalism for dealing with the simultaneous refinement of both the concurrent and sequential aspects of a system and this remains an active research area.

Many structured techniques support this form of refinement, although they do not normally use the term refinement. They often have powerful guidelines for handling this aspect of the design process. One example is SSADM which has well-developed, if somewhat complex, rules for developing 'data processing' applications centred on a database. The detailed design activities supported include logical and physical database design, as well as design of the functional aspects of the software. Detailed design and coding are discussed in Chapter 25, on formal implementation, and Chapter 18, on implementation.

15.3.2.5 Coding

Coding, or implementation, is the final stage of development concerned with producing programs and verifying them, e.g. by testing. There has been considerable work on formal treatment of the final stage of development, that is, formally relating a program to a low-level specification. Techniques include the so-called 'constructive' approach (see, for example, Backhouse (1986) and Chapter 25, in this book). They are sometimes supported by program verification environments (see, for example, Gypsy (Good, 1984) and Chapter 26). The constructive techniques are methods based on the idea of deriving the program from low-level specifications, and are intended to be applied manually. The verification environments are based on similar mathematical bases to the constructive techniques (see Hoare (1969) and Chapter 2). However, typically they are more concerned with giving automated assistance to proof of correspondence between a program and a specification. Techniques for formal implementation are most well developed for sequential programs, but some work has been carried out for concurrent programs. The techniques are expensive to use and most of their uses to date have been in highly critical systems, where the cost of failure justified the expense of applying the techniques in development. A considerable improvement in productivity using these techniques will be necessary before they can become more widely used.

The majority of these techniques are suited to the development of sequential programs, or at least programs which terminate. However, many critical applications where the use of these formal verification techniques would be justified on economic grounds are continuously running programs, monitoring the state of some (physical) process and taking the necessary remedial actions if the process is becoming dangerous, e.g. monitoring and controlling the flow of steel through a steel mill. Improvements in techniques for dealing with concurrency and continuously running programs will be necessary to handle this class of programs in a fully satisfactory manner.

Weaker forms of verification may be valuable under some circumstances. For example, tools such as Malpas can carry out various analyses on programs (Bramson, 1984), and these can be used to validate or verify the program. Capabilities of the tools include analysing control and data flow for undesirable features and establishment of the information flow in the program so it can be compared against the specification.

Compared with formal methods, structured methods that are applied manually use weaker techniques at this level, e.g. pseudocode and flowcharts. However, it is quite common with structured techniques for this final stage in development to be at least partially automated. Tools such as fourth generation languages (4GLs) generate code from high-level descriptions, and more limited tools generate program control structures from structure diagrams, but leave the programmer to fill in the 'action' code. Again, the power in tools such as 4GLs comes from the limitation to particular application areas, e.g. database transaction processing and online query.

In one sense it is unfair, and unhelpful, to compare the formal and structured techniques at this stage, as they are trying to solve rather different problems.

15.3.2.6 Commentary

The main stages of software development have been discussed here in some detail, as the technical issues to be addressed at each stage are major determinants in evaluating and selecting methods. Thus the above should be seen as setting out criteria against which methods can be judged.

To some extent the sources of some management problems have also been indicated. For example, the blurring between system specification and architectural design makes it difficult to define a precise phase boundary. In other words, some of the key problems of the process which has to be managed have been noted, thus identifying aspects of the activities which must be addressed by the managerial approach discussed in Section 15.4.

15.3.3 Issues affecting all life cycle stages

The methods chosen at each stage have to satisfy a number of criteria, e.g. effectiveness for the technical task. However, there are some general issues which equally affect all stages and which (should) influence our choice of methods.

As with the preceding section much of the material is presented from the perspective of formal methods, but comparisons are drawn between formal and structured approaches.

15.3.3.1 Descriptions

There are a number of issues which apply to all the descriptions which warrant discussion. Topics such as re-usability are dealt with elsewhere in this book (Chapter 41).

First, it is necessary to be able to 'modularize' specifications in order to be able to divide specification and implementation tasks among the members of a development team. Z (Hayes, 1986) has a form of modularization known as the schema calculus. This is analogous to the procedure in a programming language but, to the authors' knowledge, no formal or structured method supports modularity in the sense of, say, Ada packages. This is particularly a constraint on the application of formal methods. Similarly, it is a constraint on structured methods, but here it is rather less severe. This is because the semantic relationships between the different parts of the specification are weaker, and, in practice, there is better tool support for consistency checking.

Second, the different notations used throughout the life cycle need to relate to one another. This means that they should not be wantonly different in linguistic form and, more significantly, that they should be based on compatible models of the system. It is perhaps easiest to define compatibility by means of a counter-example! A description based on asynchronous communication by message passing would not, in general, be compatible with one based on synchronous communication via shared store. This is not to say that the two descriptions could not relate to the same system, more that there is a considerable conceptual change between the two descriptions which would impede understanding, especially of the way in which one description was meant to implement (refine) the other.

Third, there is benefit to be gained from having languages tailored to particular application areas. This may be achieved either through the design of a special-purpose language or by means of a 'library', used with a conventional formal specification language such as Z. The primary motivation behind this suggestion is the achievement of greater efficiency in the development of specifications. Here 4GLs are the most effective, commonly-used tools.

Fourth, it is necessary to be able to specify non-functional requirements and facets of the design. This is not possible within current formalisms. For this and other reasons it seems desirable that multiple (related) notations should be used for each description. This is analogous to other engineering disciplines where different notations are used to describe different aspects of the same artefacts, or different notations are used under different circumstances, c.f. high frequency and low frequency models of transistor behaviour.

15.3.3.2 Transformations

As explained above, transformation is primarily an intellectual process driven by non-functional requirements as much as by the functional requirements for a system. Guidelines for the transformations are as important for formal methods as they are for structured methods, although currently this is an area where formal methods are weak.

Some transformations can be automated. The most obvious example is the compilation of statements in a high-level language into assembly or machine code. However, it is possible to carry out transformations from higher level specifications to produce executable programs (Partsch and Steinbruggen, 1981). Formal methods are particularly amenable to transformation techniques because of the precise semantics of the notations used. It seems probable that these automated transformation tools will become more widely available in support of formal methods. Progress is likely to be slow, though, as there are significant technical problems to be overcome in producing efficient and effective tools.

Transformation tools for structured techniques are already quite common, e.g. 4GLs. These are less general-purpose than the experimental formal transformation systems, but much more practical. At least part of their power comes from automating common functions such as report generation, forms processing, and the generation of database queries. An alternative way of looking at these systems is that they give automated assistance to program re-use.

So far as the authors are aware a weakness of all current transformation systems is that they do not take into account the requisite non-functional information in generating the low-level descriptions.

15.3.3.3 Verification and validation

Verification is concerned with demonstrating consistency and completeness within a description, and that one description bears the correct relationship to another. Validation is concerned with demonstrating that the descriptions are consistent with initial system concepts, and high-level objectives. Typically these objectives, e.g. to take 40% of the world market in stored program telephone exchanges, are the 'real' requirements. It is essential to ensure that the requirements and design are valid in terms of these objectives.

Verification of consistency requires a demonstration that there are no contradictions in a particular description. Completeness is a more subtle concept. Ideally, one would like completeness to mean that a description covers every facet of the system. However, this implies perfect validation, hence it is not attainable. More practically, one might seek to achieve 'analytical completeness', where all facets of those objects and operations specified were covered. However, this prevents delay in design commitments, and has a number of other adverse characteristics. One is reduced to saying that the concept of completeness is subjective! This is one of the reasons that it is important to carry out reviews of the products of software development.

The detailed rules for demonstrating proper correspondence between descriptions depends on the refinement technique employed, i.e. on the rules for mapping from one level of description to the next. In general, refinement is concerned both with the data structures at two levels of description, and with the operations at two levels of description. The lower level (nearer to implementation) data structures need to be adequate for holding all the information which can be held by the higher level data structures. Similarly, the low-level operations need to satisfy the constraints placed on the high-level operations (with suitable interpretation of the meaning of the data structures). These concepts are set out for the refinement paradigm supported by VDM by Jones (1986) and are discussed in detail in Chapter 24 of this book.

Structured methods tend either to have well defined rules for transformation which obviate the need for explicit verification, or to be based on a much looser concept of correspondence between the descriptions. For these latter methods, verification implies production of informal arguments about the soundness of the transformation, or holding design reviews, structured walkthroughs, etc. These techniques have been shown to be very effective (see, for example, Fagan (1976)) and are equally applicable to formal methods. When using structured techniques much verification is carried out by testing (see Chapter 19). It is also valuable with formal methods, although the role is rather different.

As explained above, validation can be carried out by a number of techniques, including specification animation and execution. At least one system has been developed for executing a subset of a formal specification (Henderson, 1986). This may be used both for validation and for rapid prototyping. A limitation of this sort of validation technique is that it does not enable one to validate negative properties, e.g. 'the system shall not deadlock'. However, the proof techniques described above can be used in this way. In practice much validation is in the form of (peer) review. Testing is also valuable in validation, e.g. showing that the assumptions on which a specification is based are sound. The results of testing should be subject to review.

In V & V one is also concerned with quality. Thus a description may satisfy the V & V rules to do with refinement, but be unsatisfactory from the quality point of view. Typical quality criteria include maintainability, intelligibility/readability, and so on (Kitchenham and Walker, 1986). These criteria may be supported by metrics (see later) such as module coupling and strength (Myers, 1978) which indicate the effectiveness of the module structure (architecture) for ease of change in maintenance. Alternatively, they may simply be subjective judgements informed by previous experience of building similar systems. From this, and the above, it should be clear that the verification and validation activities are partially automatable, and partially the subject of human judgement.

Finally, one expects to modify descriptions both during development and during maintenance. Most verification techniques tend to be 'monolithic', i.e. a change in a description requires the whole V and V activity to be repeated. Considerable advantage would be gained from techniques which enabled re-verification to be carried out incrementally. In other words, the requirements for ease of change in maintenance apply to development also.

15.3.3.4 Metrics

It is clearly desirable to be able to measure facets of a system under development, and to measure and estimate productivity in order to be able to control a project. The requirement for metrics applies to all facets of software development, including productivity, error rates, and specification complexity – not just properties of the final implementation. The development of metrics is quite a controversial topic and a number of elaborate theories have been produced only to be discredited, e.g. Halstead's Software Science (Halstead, 1977). However, the lack of good metrics does not remove the requirement for metrics.

Even if soundly based complexity and productivity metrics cannot be produced, it is necessary for empirical measures to be developed and deployed, so that projects can be planned and controlled. Some experience with empirical measures of program maintenance, and an interpretation of how these techniques may be applied in integrated project support environments (IPSEs) – that is the infrastructure and toolset for supporting development – is given in Kitchenham and McDermid (1986). The general problems of measuring facets of software are discussed in Chapter 12, and Chapter 30 deals with existing metrics.

15.3.4 Selection of methods

The STARTS Guide gives some important and helpful criteria for choosing methods including maturity, level of tool support, etc. (DTI, 1987). The purpose of this section is to outline some additional technical issues which should also be taken into account in the selection of methods, and which are not adequately addressed in documents such as the STARTS guide.

The primary observation to be made is that some methods are good at dealing with particular classes of system, e.g. real-time systems, and poor with other classes, e.g. database systems. The technical characteristics of an application and of the available methods should drive the choice of methods for the project to develop that application. As illustrated above, these factors should also influence the choice of development approach.

First to be discussed are some desirable characteristics of 'joined-up' methods, that is, methods that span the full life cycle.

15.3.4.1 'Joined-up' methods

Many methods claim that they cover all of the life cycle, but few, if any, do so. This means that one has to consider combinations of methods for particular development projects. Some important aspects of 'joined-up' methods were identified above. They should cover the complete life cycle; they should be based on compatible system models; they need to encompass functional requirements. There are other properties which are worth mentioning.

There is no *a priori* reason why formal and structured methods should not be mixed. However, it may be easier to use a set of methods which are all based on compatible linguistic forms. There is benefit to be gained from using application-specific, rather than general-purpose, tools. For example, it is more beneficial to use a parser generator in producing a compiler than it is to do the whole design, say, in SSADM. It is important to consider the reasons for using the methods.

The primary reasons for having multiple system descriptions, and for employing methods, are to reduce the cost and risk, and to increase the reliability, of the development and maintenance processes. There may be some conflict between the objectives of reducing the cost of maintenance *and* development, so one should probably talk about reducing life cycle costs. Considering maintenance, one can see that the reduction in cost, and increase in reliability, comes from the provision of adequate information about the system, as this reduces the risk of making errors in modifying software. Given that most of development is concerned with modifying partially complete systems, not with creation, one can see that the same argument applies here also.

There is a conflict, however. The more information (descriptions) available, the greater the cost of making changes. Thus there is an optimization problem. One needs to balance the cost of changing descriptions with the costs that arise from having inadequate information about the system. There is another important factor – that of risk. In practice it may be necessary to have more than the optimal amount of information about the system (from the financial point of view) available to reduce the risk of errors arising in maintenance. In other words, one accepts higher necessary development and maintenance costs to reduce the risk of errors arising in maintenance. Unfortunately, the more information there is to change, the greater is the risk of making an error at some stage. Intuition says that the optimum situations for minimizing development and maintenance cost and unfortunately is is not possible to make quantitative judgements to validate this view. However, the balance between risk and cost should always be considered.

The above discussion may seem irrelevant to the selection of methods, but it does have a direct bearing. The current popularity of (structured) methods is giving rise to an attitude that it is good to have lots of methods (and descriptions). It has been shown here that this view is clearly wrong in principle. The intention here is to give guidelines which prevent developers being swamped with too many methods and descriptions. This view is certainly unconventional, if not heretical. However, the validity of the arguments should be clear, and the authors have personal experience of developments where the project was fettered by the need to update excessive volumes of documentation. Thus, when choosing methods to cover the whole life cycle, stress should be laid on controlling development risk and cost. The temptation to have a lot of methods because 'methods are good' should be avoided.

15.3.4.2 Choosing descriptions

The choice of stages was discussed above. Now we consider the related issue of the choice of descriptions, i.e. the number and types of specification produced. This relates both to the numbers of levels of documentation (corresponding to decomposition levels) and to the different facets of the design or requirements.

In any development it is essential to have some form of a statement of requirements and an architecture. Without the requirements one has no way of knowing when the project has been (successfully) completed. Without the architecture one has no way of controlling the development process, as the architecture will form the basis for dividing the system up in to work packages, and for carrying out integration and integration testing prior to acceptance and delivery. The choice of other descriptions (levels) is governed by:

1. The size of the application. In general the larger the application, the more descriptions are needed to handle the complexity. (Note: this might mean having several levels of description within one stage of the process.)
2. Whether the application area is new or old. In new areas there is likely to be a need for more explicit documentation to counteract unfamiliarity.
3. Whether the system is being developed for a specific customer or it is being developed against a general requirement for a perceived marketplace.
4. The skill of the project staff. In general higher levels of skill imply that one can use fewer descriptions (although one should not forget the issue of maintenance).

These four factors are probably the most important for choice of 'levels' of description, but other issues are also relevant, such

as the technical characteristics of the application. For example, for a safety critical system one would expect to produce far more descriptions, etc., than for a non-critical application, because of the cost of failure. However, these technical issues have more direct bearing on the choice of method.

Also as indicated above, one should seek to choose notations for descriptions that are modular, reflect non-functional characteristics, and perhaps are specific to the problem area. The notations chosen for each stage should be compatible. There are many circumstances where it is appropriate to take an eclectic approach to specification rather than to seek a ubiquitous notation, where each notation deals with a different facet of the system, e.g. timing, or functionality.

15.3.4.3 Choosing methods

The characteristics of each project that an organization undertakes are different. Hence, in principle, methods should be selected for each project. This 'ideal' is constrained by training costs, availability of suitable tools, etc., but it is still helpful to consider this ideal.

There are three primary technical factors which influence the section of methods:

1. Technical characteristics of the application.
2. Technical characteristics of the methods.
3. Life cycle coverage.

In principle one needs to choose methods for each stage of the life cycle which are good at dealing with the technical characteristics of the application and which 'join up' as described above.

Some of the characteristics which distinguish different classes of system can be explained using an automated teller machine (ATM) and a computer integrated manufacturing (CIM) system as examples (see *Table 15.1*). Several characteristics of applications are identified, and a numeric indication is given of the criticality of the characteristic to the application. The larger the numbers the more critical is the characteristic. A scale of one to five is used as an *illustration* of the approach. Note that these should not be taken as definitive judgements on the different classes of applications. In practice, a qualitative scale such as 'critical–important–relevent–irrelevant' is probably more appropriate.

Table 15.1 Application characteristics

	ATM	CIM
Real-time response	2	5
Distribution	4	3
Data structure	3	3
Dependability	2	5
MMI*/HCI[†]	2	4
Algorithmic complexity	1	3

*Man–machine interface. [†]Human–computer interaction.

One can make similar judgements about methods, but any reference to particular methods here could be viewed as libellous! A long discourse on the strengths and weaknesses of formal and structured methods has been given, but one can make a number of other useful general observations. Few, if any, methods deal well with human-computer interaction (HCI). Formal techniques are usually better for computationally complex systems as the mathematical basis gives a much more succinct basis for specifying algorithms. Methods can *hinder* the treatment of a particular characteristic by making it difficult to express the relevant concepts within the method's notation. For example, it is hard to deal with timing issues within the framework of an algebraic specification as definitions of operations are implicit.

One can also make judgements about the stages in the life cycle for which the methods apply. See, for example, *Table 15.2*. Again these are personal opinions and they may not accord with the views of the proponents of the methods. It should be noted, however, that this is a judgement on the method, not the notation. For example, the CORE notation can be used at the design level (and indeed has been used in this way on some avionics projects) but the method as described by Mullery (1979) does not give any guidelines for design.

Table 15.2 Method applicability

Stage	CORE	JSD	VDM
Requirements	Y	N	N
Specification	Y	Y	Y
Architecture	N	Y	Y
Design	N	Y	Y

Thus, in selecting methods for a new application one should seek a set of methods which:

1. Covers all the life cycle stages chosen for the project.
2. Minimizes the number of distinct methods.
3. Makes the best match of method and application characteristics.
4. Has compatible system models and similar notations.

In practice it is unlikely that a perfect match will be found. It will usually be necessary to 'strengthen' the chosen methods either by adding techniques from other methods, or by semimanagerial approaches such as instituting more thorough design reviews for critical projects.

Additionally, it is desirable to choose methods which give some guidelines for transformations and preferably give scope for automated transformation. However, care must be exercised to avoid getting caught in a 'straitjacket' by selecting a transformation tool which cannot be adopted to changing (non-functional) requirements.

A further criterion for selecting methods is that they should have well-defined rules and guidelines for verification and validation. (Surprisingly few methods do.) An associated criterion is that they should deal adequately with consistency, completeness and quality.

For many projects a positive decision is made to undertake incremental development. Pragmatically, a lot of work is undertaken incrementally anyway. In other words, much development is concerned with changing existing specifications or programs, not with creating them anew. Thus an important criterion is to select methods which support incremental change, and incremental (re)verification and validation. Sadly, few methods have this desirable characteristic.

15.3.4.4 Summary

The above gives an approach to the rational choice of methods for a particular project. It is clear that it is not always possible to find an ideal set of methods due both to the limitations of the methods, and to the practical constraints on projects such as the cost of training. The observation 'any method is better than none' is a fallacy, and it is possible that the use of inappropriate (or too many) methods may hinder a project more than help it.

Tools are important – indeed essential – for any large-scale development project. However, the tools should support the method, not *vice versa*, and it is necessary to focus on the choice of methods to ensure that coherent support is provided for the whole life cycle. The STARTS material provides copious advice on the selection of particular methods and tools, and the reader is referred to that for more concrete recommendations.

15.4 Software development process models from the project management viewpoint

The primary aim in software project management is to control the development process so that the resultant product is delivered:

1. On time.
2. Within budget.
3. Of acceptable quality and reliability.
4. Meeting customer's requirements and expectations.
5. Satisfying the specifications, etc.

Note that these latter two points are not equivalent and it is here that many of the problems of software development arise.

To achieve these objectives, it is necessary for project managers to prepare development plans, to monitor progress against the plans, to take remedial action if there are significant deviations from the plan, and so on. The 'technical' process models presented in the previous sections showed that iteration occurs in software development, for example, to correct errors or to satisfy the requirements for additional functionality in the system. Thus one of the most significant responsibilities, and major sources of difficulty, in project management is the achievement of control over the iterative nature of software development.

While management is thus strongly linked with technical activities, it is primarily concerned with:

1. Risk assessment, e.g. deciding whether or not a system is technically or economically feasible.
2. Planning and control, e.g. monitoring progress and replanning as necessary.
3. Decision making, e.g. selecting between alternative implementation strategies.

These issues are reflected in management-oriented models, which will be discussed from a semi-historical perspective, building up to the basis for the canonical life cycle model.

15.4.1 The waterfall model

The waterfall model was derived from the thinking in the late 1960s. One of the best papers describing the principles of the model is by Royce (1970), reprinted in Thayer (1988). Whilst the model has been overtaken by further development, the paper is still worth reading.

The first step from a totally unstructured process was to define a two-step structure consisting of deciding what to do and then doing it. This is shown for software development in *Figure 15.5*. This model is still valid for *very* small projects.

Refining this model produces *Figure 15.6*, with the justification for the different steps being based upon the distinctly different ways they are planned and staffed for best utilization of resources on a large project.

Clearly, simply following the sequence of steps in Figure 15.6 is simplistic for any practical software development. It is most unlikely that the required product can be completely specified and then completely designed without any realisation of need to

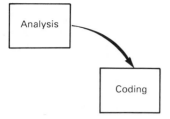

Figure 15.5 Implementation steps to deliver a small computer program for internal operations

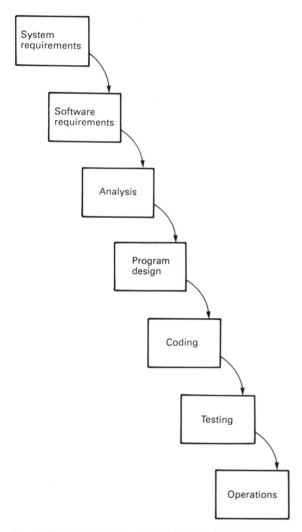

Figure 15.6 Implementation steps to develop a large computer program for delivery to customer

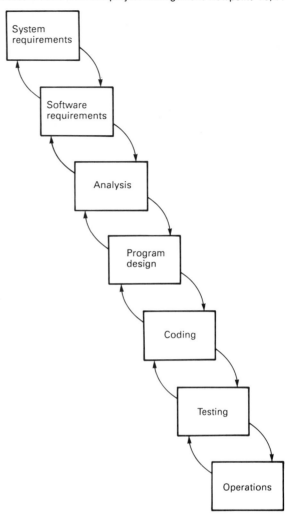

Figure 15.7 Classical waterfall model with the intention that iterative interactions between the various phases is confined to successive steps

The intention is that the process shown in Figure 15.7 remains under control if all rework needs only to go back one step for the team to retrieve the situation and then to have a basis for further progress. However, this is generally not so easily controllable. Design iterations may not be confined to successive stages, leading to the sort of situation shown in *Figure 15.8*, with consequent problems in the cost of correcting the software and loss of control of the project.

This model of the process of working makes perfectly good sense when the software is developed by an individual, or by a team acting cohesively as an individual. In this case the management perception is limited primarily to 'started', 'working' and 'finished product'. When there is a larger organization and more attempt to gain management insight and control of progress, then there is a significant problem in the meaning of the backwards arrows. Clearly the fact of rework is unarguable. But if the steps represent progress in time, then the backward arrows cannot represent reverse time. They must mean that any step can be revisited as required and anyone in the team can be working on any of the steps on any part of the product at any point in time. There is no control of such a software development team and management waits with bated breath until they

rework the specification. It will be necessary to review or rework early stages for clarification, even if there are no changes to customers' requirements in the meantime. Similarly, coding will usually involve sorting out unexpected problems in the design, and testing will find all sorts of surprises which require reworking of the previous steps. This leads then to the well-known, and often reproduced, Waterfall diagram, shown in *Figure 15.7*.

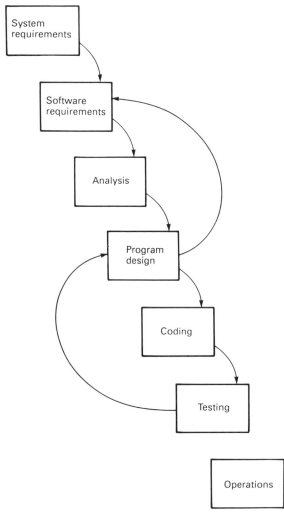

Figure 15.8 The uncontrollable model – the unfortunate situation where design iterations are not confined to the successive steps

The strongest early drive for definition of phases was based in the methods of working developed between the Department of Defense and its suppliers, and defined in American Military Standards. The resulting philosophy of a method of working has been extensively documented. The example in *Figure 15.9* is taken from a paper reporting work at TRW by Goldberg (1977).

Goldberg's paper lists sets of deliverable sub-products to be reviewed against checklists at each phase. This naturally leads to thorough definitions of the form of the reviews, the standards and procedures and a whole method of working which can be understood and supported by management and the customer. Also, the staff on the software development team can clearly see a structure of what is expected of them, and when it is expected. Additionally, they can expect training in an explicit way of working.

The set of phases shown in Figure 15.9, or something similar, is what has become known as the classical life cycle. Organizations which work on these principles refer to the life cycle model. These organizations know how to interpret the model and concentrate on developing the model by refining and interpreting the definitions and standards for the phase deliverables. They also use the model, and by carrying out thorough reviews typically find errors early in the process so that the software development process is effective.

However, there are still problems in trying to explain the process to management, thoroughly analyse the 'model', or investigate the process with the intention of improving what often continue to be inadequately controllable software development projects. These usually stem from relating the life cycle phases to the waterfall model and getting into complications and confusion with the idea of reworking based on 'iteration of phases'.

In the original waterfall model the team did indeed move a step (or more) back, as represented by the backward arrows, and rework before moving forward again. In Figure 15.9 the phases end at project milestones and the waterfall model is reinterpreted, as shown in *Figure 15.10* (Boehm, 1976), with the backward arrows representing *backreferences* for V & V against baselines. There is now no 'iteration of phases' implied in this new version of the waterfall model, since the end of a phase is a point in time and no-one is suggesting time travel.

Rework may be controlled within a phase when the phase-end review shows that the phase products are inadequate and further work must be done on them. The review is held again before the phase can be agreed to be finished. In fact, some organizations deliberately hold a series of informal reviews through which the work of completing the phase is really controlled. The product is then known to be acceptably complete and can be rubber-stamped at a formal phase-end review. Iteration of phase products in the following phases (rework to correct errors in the baselined phase products) is explained in Section 15.4.3 as a function of continuing activities.

Another basis for wishing to 'iterate phases' arises when the software project involves a significant element of research into what is wanted, and how it should be designed and implemented. However, the conclusion that should be drawn is that it is inappropriate to try to use the classical life cycle phases for such a project rather than to pretend to use them as a gloss on the actuality of a different process. The proper basis for feasibility studies, prototyping and incremental development for projects involving uncertainty and risk is worked out in later sections, the principles being combined in the spiral model (Section 15.6.1). For the next four sections, the discussion is illustrated by reference to the classical life cycle phases assuming projects for which this is a suitable development process. However, the value of defining phases and baselines, and the principle of continuing activities through the phases do apply to *all* software development processes, not just to those based on the classical life cycle.

have finished. This is the way many software projects were run, but by the late 1960s this was no longer acceptable and software development projects had to become better organized and more controllable.

Although some managers understood the principles of how to organize software projects, they had immense difficulty in putting it across to non-software management. This is reflected in the inability of the waterfall model to represent the more complex principles. Experts who successfully organized software development projects found themselves creating more and more complex extensions of the waterfall model diagram to illustrate the principles that they knew how to achieve in real projects. Royce's paper gives some examples of such constructions, but the development of a satisfactory model had to wait for two more principles to be established: precise phase-ends and continuing activities.

15.4.2 Classical life cycle phases

The idea of a phase is based on the simple but fundamental principle that it ends at a specific point in time with a pre-defined set of items which undergo a thorough review.

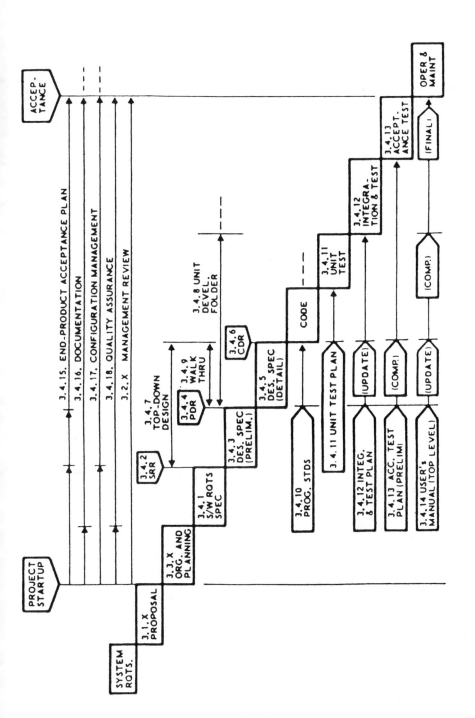

Figure 15.9 Software life cycle

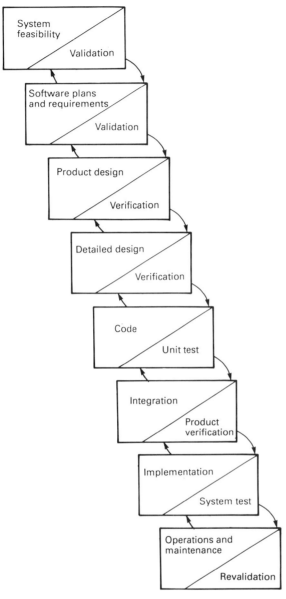

Figure 15.10 'Waterfall' model with stagewise V and V

Since staff on the project can relate to phases terminated with reviews as a helpful way of defining the software development process, the fact that there are management difficulties implies that understanding of the model is inadequate. It is therefore necessary to look at how the software development staff go about their work to find out how to improve the modelling of the process.

15.4.3 Interaction between teams

Every project of significant size has an organizational structure, which in turn is defined by the responsibilities of the parts of the organization. Such a structure normally defines teams, where teams will naturally be organized with responsibilities for the significant parts of the technical work, as seen by the senior technical staff. *Figure 15.11* shows the interaction between these teams.

Work products (deliverables from tasks) are produced by one team. The reaction of another team produces both work products for further teams and a response to the first team, generally requiring further work. A project is brought under control by the project manager setting a structure to these interactions which includes the need for making and recording decisions, allocation of responsibilities and control of changes.

This is the basis for defining the meaning of rework in the model. Each team performs an activity, and it is the iteration of work on specific deliverables between teams which is the essence of correcting problems in products which had been thought to be finished. If a phase product was thought to be correct at the phase-end review, but subsequently found to be faulty in the next, or even later, phase, then (subject to management decision and change control) the phase product is returned to the originating team to be corrected and updated. This goes on as an activity in parallel with the major activities of the phase. There is no iteration of phases, just iteration of work between teams, so that all activities associated with the teams carries on throughout all phases. It is natural to relate the stages discussed in Section 15.3 to the phases in the LCM, and it can be seen that work in a phase relates to the current stage and (potentially) rework of previous stages.

Confusion can arise, and it often does, from referring to the activities (and the teams) by the same names as the phases.

There should not be any serious thought that specification is only done in the specification phase. It is simply a primary activity of that phase. It does not stop at the end of that phase, but it carries on to update the specification documents during subsequent phases. These updates may be due to changes by the customer, realisation of errors or inconsistencies, or changes to the specification (with the customer's agreement) in the light of unexpected design difficulties.

Similarly, design (by design experts – namely the design team) is necessary before the specification phase-end review. This allows that review to be completed with the knowledge that it is thought possible to implement the specified product because enough design work has been done – a fundamental part of the review. This is iteration between specification and design activities within the specification phase.

If controllable progress is to be made through the development, then the weight of the interactions between the teams in Figure 15.11 will vary with time, with a 'rolling wave' progressing anti-clockwise round the diagram, starting and finishing at the top.

15.4.4 Software development activities

The activities which are the most important in each phase are defined, in principle, by the phase-end products. Thus, in the project initiation phase, the project manager must be concerned with sufficient analysis of requirements and design to be able to:

1. Plan the project.
2. Make decisions on methods, tools, procedures and standards.
3. Initiate strategies for configuration management, quality management, development facilities and testing.

In the requirements specification phase, although the major concern is with the capture and analysis of requirements and interface definitions, there is also considerable work required on updating the detail of the project plans. In the design phase, the emphasis must not only be on completing the design but also on the quality of the design for reliability, efficiency and maintainability with a major concentration on technical control.

Similar shifts in emphasis can be deduced for the subsequent phases. However, it must be clear that all activities continue across all phases of the project. Even if most of the attention of

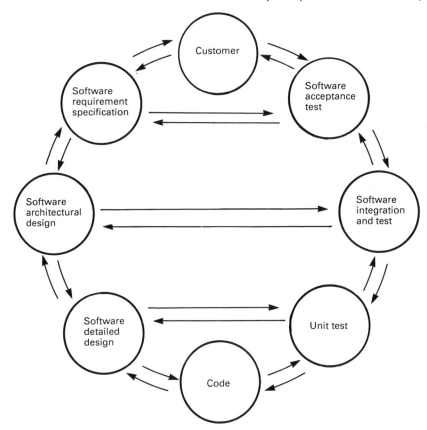

Figure 15.11 Team interaction in software development

the project is concentrated on the major concern of a phase, there must be staff working on other activities during each phase.

An obvious example is architectural design not only must significant work be carried out on this during the requirement specification phase, it is the primary activity in the architectural design phase and there must also be a continuing strong design control to maintain design integrity during the phases following completion of the review, at the end of the architectural design phase.

Although coding of a module does not properly commence before completion of the detailed design of that module, there are still programming activities to be performed during the early phases. These include planning the coding methods and facilities, acquisition and testing of tools and database development, and, in some cases, there may be exploratory investigations into algorithms and operations.

The primary activity of each of the phases should be thought of as continuing through the whole project; not as of fixed duration and stopping at the end of a phase. In a large software development, each activity should be staffed by a distinct group of people, whose numbers might grow and shrink, but whose existence is identifiable from project start to project end.

Figure 15.12 shows the allocation of effort to technical activities during development on a number of projects in the Yourdon survey (DeMarco, 1981). Whilst the shape of the curve and the balance between the activities will vary for different projects, the principle shown in the figure is valid for all software development projects. Note that Figure 15.12 only covers the activities of technical development. It does not

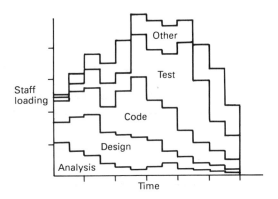

Figure 15.12 Allocation of effort to technical activities during development

include project management, configuration management or quality assurance. 'Other' in Figure 15.12 covers unanticipated and unclassified technical activities in the Yourdon survey data.

It can be seen that the activities are continuous throughout the development, although with the expected humps at the appropriate phases in the development life cycle. This spread of the activities assumes the inclusion of the preparation for a task within the execution of a task. This is entirely rational since the work is done by the same team and therefore the work of the team corresponds to the definition of an activity.

For a better understanding of the software development

process, a more precise definition of software development activities is needed than the simple terms used in Figure 15.12. The following definition, derived from one given by Boehm (1981), is an example of a suitable set of representative activities for software development:

1. *Project management*: project level management functions. These include project level planning and control, contract and subcontract management, customer interface, cost/schedule performance management, management reviews and audits, and includes acquisition of management tools.
2. *Technical control*: responsibility for the technical correctness and quality of the complete product and process. Covers responsibility for maintaining the integrity of the whole design during the detailed design, programming and testing phases. Specification, review and update of integration test and acceptance test plans and procedures. Acquisition of requirements and design verification and validation tools. Acquisition and support of test drivers, test tools and test data. Ensuring coherence of development process and tools.
3. *Requirements specification*: determination, specification, review and update of software functional, performance, interface and verification requirements, including acquisition of requirements analysis and specification tools. Development of requirement specification level documentation. A continuing responsibility for communication between customer requirements and the technical development staff.
4. *Architectural design*: determination, specification, review and update of hardware/software architecture, software design and database design, including acquisition of design tools. Development of structural design level documentation.
5. *Detailed design*: detailed design of individual computer program components. Development of detailed design-level documentation. When a significant number of staff is involved, includes team-level management functions.
6. *Code and unit test*: code, unit test and integration of individual computer program components, including tool acquisition. When a significant number of staff is involved, includes team-level management functions.

7. *Verification, validation and testing*: performance of independent requirements validation, design verification and validation, integration test and acceptance test, including production of test reports.
8. *Manuals production*: development and update of product support documentation: user manual, operations manual and maintenance manual.
9. *Configuration management*: product identification, operation of change control, status accounting, operation of program support library.
10. *Quality assurance*: consultancy on project standards and procedures, monitoring of project procedures in operation and quality audits of products.

The use of precise definitions of stages and activities such as those above (see Section 15.5 for a matching set of phase definitions) allows data to be collected and plans to be made with much more detail than the crude diagram shown in *Figure 15.12*. An example of planned staffing for a project, based on these detailed definitions, is shown in *Figure 15.13*. The sizes of the teams are shown through the project time-scale. It can be seen that the humps in the team-size curves represent peaks in their activities corresponding to the appropriate phase, with the emphasis shifting from activity to activity as the project proceeds through the phases.

15.4.5 Matrix of phases and activities

Having defined phases and activities, it is now possible to return to the software process model and see how it corresponds to the process of software development. Using the activities defined above and the classical life cycle phases, a matrix can be drawn out, as shown in *Figure 15.14*, defining tasks for the teams corresponding to the specific work of an activity in a phase. The tasks can be subdivided, where relevant, to subsystems and modules of the product.

Note that this is only a simple basis for seeing the definition of the tasks, the standards and procedures that should be in use and the appropriate tools, etc. for every box in the matrix. The

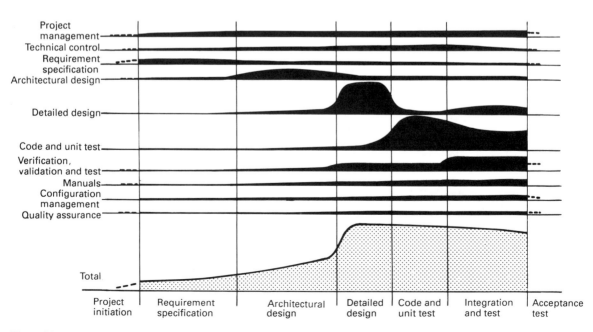

Figure 15.13 Software development teams

Activity \ Phase	Project initiation	Requirements specification	Architectural design	Detailed design	Code and unit test	Integration and test	Acceptance test	Maintenance
Project management	Project estimating planning, scheduling, procedures, organization, etc.	Project management, project planning contracts, liaison, etc.	Project management, status monitoring, contracts, liaison, etc.	Project management, status monitoring, contracts, liaison, etc.	Project management, status monitoring, contracts, liaison, etc.	Project management, status monitoring, contracts, liaison, etc.	Project management, status monitoring, contracts, liaison, etc.	Support management, status monitoring, contracts, liaison, etc.
Technical control	Technical strategy technical plans, technical standards	System models and risk analysis; acceptance test plan; acquire V and V tools for requirements and design. Top-level test plan	Design quality, models and risk analysis; draft test plans; acquire test tools	Design integrity; detailed test plans; acquire test tools	Design integrity; detailed test plans; install test tools	Design integrity; support test tools; monitor testing	Design integrity; support test tools; monitor acceptance	Design integrity; risk analysis; test plans
Requirement specification	Analyse requirements; determine user needs	Analyse existing system; determine user needs; integrate document and iterate requirements	Update requirements	Update requirements	Update requirements	Update requirements	Update requirements	Determine user needs and problems; update requirements
Architectural design	Design planning	Develop basic architecture, models, prototypes	Develop architectural design, models, prototypes	Update design	Update design	Update design	Update design	Update design
Detailed design	Identify programming methods and resources	Prototypes of algorithms; team planning	Models, algorithms investigation; team planning	Detailed design; component documentation	Update detailed design	Update detailed design	Update detailed design	Detailed design of changes and enhancements
Code and unit test	Identify programming methods and resources	Identify programming tools; team planning	Acquire programming tools and utilities; team planning	Integration planning	Code and unit test	Integrate software update code	Update code	Code and unit test of changes and enhancements
Verification, validation and test	V & V requirements	V & V specification	V & V structural design	V & V detailed design; V & V design changes	V & V top portions of code; V & V design changes	Perform product test; V & V design changes	Perform acceptance test; V & V design changes	V & V changes and enhancements
Manuals	Define user manual	Outline portions of user manual	Draft user and operator manuals; outline maintenance manual	Draft maintenance manual	Full draft user and operator manuals	Final user and operator and maintenance manuals	Acceptance of manuals	Update manual
Configuration management	CM plans and procedures	CM plans, procedures; identify CM tools	CM of requirements, design; acquire CM tools	CM of requirements; design; detailed design; install CM tools; set up library	CM of requirements; design, code, operate library	CM of requirements; design, code, operate library	CM of requirements; design, code, operate library	CM of all documentation; operate library
Quality assurance	QA plans, project procedures and standards	Standards, procedures; QA plans; identify QA tools	QA of requirements, design, project standards; acquire QA tools	QA of requirements, design, detailed design	QA of requirements; design, code	QA of requirements; design, code, testing	QA of requirements; design, code, acceptance	QA of maintenance updates

Figure 15.14 Software development tasks by activity and phase

matrix is not the software process model. It is only the outworking of the model for a particular set of phases and activities. The more precisely defined the phases and activities, the more precisely the process can be defined in the terms of a matrix.

However, even with good management and skilful, responsible, technical staff who wish to ensure that the intended process is actually followed, the matrix needs some interpretation in order to correspond to reality. The vertical lines for the ends of the first three phases do indeed correspond to phase ends for the whole of the project. Once past the end of the architectural design phase, the design is by definition now sufficiently baselined that it no longer has to be the property of a single team. Parts of the design can be worked on by separate teams, relying on defined interfaces. This, not some arbitrary level of design decomposition, is the distinction between the two design phases. The central design team will still have the activity of maintaining design integrity over the work of the teams working on the detailed designs, for example, participating in the detailed design walkthroughs. However, the work of the teams will proceed in parallel through detailed design, coding and unit test, producing their finished modules at different times. This would be deliberately planned, with the assignment of teams to the parts of the implementation organized so that they arrive in the required sequence for the integration and test team to proceed according to a planned (probably top-down) integration. Thus the ends of the two phases of detailed design and code and unit test in the matrix do not correspond to single points in time for the whole project. They are, though, very real points in time for the teams working on each group of modules, corresponding to thorough reviews (probably based on walkthroughs, code readings and unit test data).

Also, the phases of the software development process have a relationship that is not brought out in the linear progressions used in the diagrams shown so far. As can be seen in the V-diagram in the next section, there are tasks of producing test specifications, test plans, and test data derived from the specifications and designs in the earlier phases. These progress in parallel with, and independent of, the middle phases, but necessarily have to be completed for the work of the later testing phases. The appropriate matrix for the chosen phases and activities of any well-defined process is an excellent reference point, but must not be interpreted simplistically as being the model of the process.

The interactions between the activities and the phases determine the tasks and phase products to be baselined. This provides the technical basis to underpin the principles of project control described in Chapter 27. The more precise the definitions (backed by procedures) of the activities and the definitions (backed by standards) for the products to be reviewed at the end of each phase, the more precisely is the process defined and the more closely it can be planned with technically meaningful milestones, monitored and controlled. Similarly, the easier it is to collect data for project analysis. The matrix and the V-diagram are useful to illustrate the principles, but, for each specific project, it is necessary to work through the detail to a level such that a diagram like Figure 27.6 in Chapter 27 can be drawn before there is a sufficient basis for project control.

It should be emphasized that the principles of phases and activities discussed above are entirely general. Although the example uses the classical life cycle phases and the graphs show the type of curves usually associated with large real-time software projects using traditional coding languages, the principles apply just as well to different development methods and applications.

Use of a 4GL or a code generator leads naturally to less emphasis on coding and unit testing phases and more emphasis on analysis and design, with correspondingly different shapes in the curves. Small (even one-person) teams working on parts of the software in the sort of development process usually applied in commercial data processing require different definitions of activities and phases than those used for large, real-time projects. The resulting process will be defined by different versions of the diagrams exemplified in Figure 27.6, different definitions against which the project data is to be collected, and different staff-time profiles. However, the principles are universal. What is necessary is that, for the different processes used on different projects in different styles of development, they are fully worked out and defined in order to provide the basis for successful estimating, planning and project control.

The life cycle phases can be referred to as 'horizontal' time progression through suitable review milestones. The contractual approach, discussed in Section 15.2.4.1, is concerned with 'vertical' levels of abstraction and there is no requirement that there be a one-to-one mapping between them. There are usually six levels in Mascot. One normally only enters the detailed design with multiple teams when the design is reduced from parallel processes to purely procedural code. Prior to this point it is the responsibility of the design team to define the complete architecture. They do this by working up and down the six levels until a satisfactory architecture is achieved, thus completing the one phase of architectural design. The levels of abstraction in the chosen design method may be pre-planned, or their determination may be part of the design process itself. There should be no assumption that multiple life cycle phases are implied, although it is clearly wise to define phases and phase product

reviews at planned key achievements in the design process. It is the responsibility of the technical control team that the 'best' design techniques are used. The recursive nature of the contractual approach works with both data-based and control-based design techniques, provided the design team bring good design thinking to the task instead of allowing the levels of abstraction to be led merely by decomposing the functions.

Having said this, it should be clear that the contractual approach is not in conflict with the software process model. It is, in fact, an excellent way of representing the structuring of a good design as the technical side of the bridge between technical control and project management. The documents of the decomposed design structure are, of course, the task products for baselining which enables the phase-product based approach to give a measure of progress which includes technical quality.

15.4.6 Baselines and reviews

Each development phase is defined in terms of its outputs, or products. The products of the phases represent the points along the development path where there is a clear change in emphasis: where one definition of the emerging product is established, reviewed and used as the basis for the next derived definition. As such, they are the natural milestones of the development progression and offer objective visibility of that progression.

To use this visibility for effective management control, a software development process based on the model uses the concept of baselines. A 'baseline' established at any stage in the development process is a set of information which defines the product at that stage.

The completion of each phase is determined by the satisfactory review of the defined products of that phase and the products placed under configuration management. These products then form the baseline for the work in the next phase. The products of the next phase are measured and verified against previous baselines before themselves forming a new baseline. In this way confidence in project progress is progressively built on successive baselines.

It should be noted that the phase boundaries represent discontinuities in the product development. Representations or descriptions differ between phases. For example, a specification is very different from a design in terms of the viewpoint (what the system does versus how it does it) and hence the semantics and notation of the documentation. In a large project the staff involved in different phases are often different. Discontinuities are weak points in any process, so although phases provide the basis for managerial control points, extra care must be taken to avoid misunderstandings and undetected ambiguities. This is one area where technical control is essential.

A common representation of the phases of software development is the V-diagram, an example of which is shown in *Figure 15.15*. Here the rectangular boxes represent the phases and oval boxes represent the baselined phase products. The form of the diagram has the advantage of showing the symmetry between the successive decomposition of the design and the building of the product by successive stages of integration and test. Figure 15.15 also shows the verification and testing relationships. The product of each specification and design phase is verified against the previous baseline. The product of each integration phase is tested with test cases and the test data derived from the corresponding design or specification baseline on the left-hand side of the diagram. Validation occurs at many points in the process, particularly associated with reviews and testing.

The diagram is similar to that shown in The STARTS guide (DTI, 1987) and illustrates the same principles, though with some more detail. The simplified diagram in the STARTS guide matches the levels between the right-hand side and the left-hand side to correspond to tested compliance. (So, for example,

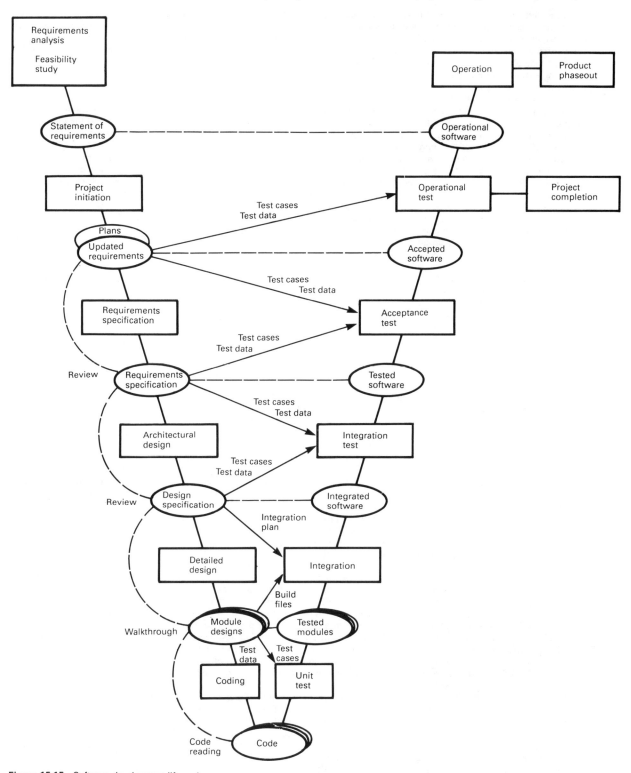

Figure 15.15 Software development life cycle

integrated test and software has been tested as fully meeting the intentions of the design.) With the extra detail showing the test relationships on this version of the diagram, it is more convenient to match the levels between the right-hand side and the left-hand side elements to correspond to claimed compliance ready to be tested. For example, integrated software is purported to match the design but has yet to be tested, and tested software is purported to match the specification but has yet to be checked in acceptance and operational tests. The form of the diagram gives visual recognition of testing and other aspects of verification as a fundamental part of the software development process. Refer to Chapter 19 for more coverage on testing.

Formal reviews at baseline stages of development are the most powerful determinant of the successful control of progress of a project. The review team should include not only development personnel but also experts from other projects and disciplines and, whenever possible, customer and user personnel.

The involvement of the user cannot be over-emphasized. One of the most frequent causes of unreliability or failure to achieve the required performance of a product is associated with the requirements and the users' expectations of their implementation in the final product. Getting the requirements right is arguably both the most essential and most difficult activity in a software project, and close involvement of the customer/user throughout the development process is essential, but nowhere is it more effective than at project reviews.

It can be seen from the V-diagram that verification takes the form of reviews when what is being reviewed refers to the project as a whole. This applies to the earlier phases on the left-hand side of the V-diagram, when prototypes, draft user manuals and test cases are very valuable in actualizing otherwise theoretical specifications.

Reviews are also used at the end of the phases of the right-hand side of the V-diagram, but here they are not so much the vehicle for discovering problems as reviews of the status of problems shown up in the testing, which is the primary basis for checking the correctness of the products of the phases.

In the lower part of the V-diagram, verification is on parts of the product (modules or groups of modules). Then walkthroughs, code readings and unit test inspections are much more appropriate, involving only the few staff immediately involved in a small efficient meeting. Walkthroughs are not just small reviews. They have a quite different format. Walkthroughs and code readings are better at finding different sorts of errors than reviews and where they are used staff should be explicitly trained in how to run them (Fagan, 1976; Freedman and Weinberg, 1982).

As an illustration of the classical software development process, the V-diagram is useful in a number of ways. It shows the time sequence of the phases (they do not overlap – the end of one phase corresponds to the start of the next), the principles of baselines, verification and test relationships, and major review points. The structural relationships of the various parts of the development process are seen in the context of progression towards achieving the required product, without any confusion about iterating between phases which may arise from a misinterpretation of the waterfall diagram.

However, the V-diagram provides only a high-level overview and is inadequate as a basis for planning and managing a project. A more detailed view is provided by the process definition diagram illustrated in Figure 27.6 in Chapter 27.

As will already be apparent from the V-diagram, most of the evident work in VV & T activities goes into verification and testing. It requires a specific determination to do validation, usually at the time of the phase reviews as part of the risk analysis.

VV & T should be carried out by staff within the project organization but, as far as possible, not by the originators of the

work. Verification may be the responsibility of a series of different teams as the project progresses through the life cycle phases. For testing, it is common practice to establish a separate text term with professional emphasis on the technical skills of testing and familiarity with the test tools.

15.4.7 Prototyping approach

So far in this section the product has been assumed to be a sufficiently well-defined and well known that the phases for the project can be predetermined in a form such as the classical life cycle. This is unrealistic for many large and complex software developments, which are usually tackling unprecedented problems at considerable risk from unknown technical and environmental factors. Increasingly, for large software development projects, the trend is to move away from the 'single-shot' approach to an evolutionary form of development. Where the project is dealing with unknown technology, or an uncertain statement of requirements or an unprecedented situation in any significant way, then, it is more suitable to use a process where either the phases are iterated around a cycle based on prototyping, or research followed by re-evaluation.

Prototyping may normally be thought of in the context of feasibility studies. However, the approach may also be used as the basis of product development, especially where the initial specification is difficult to determine. An example of such a process is shown in Figure 15.4. There are many forms of prototype ranging from a one-off version that will be thrown away when it has served its purpose, through a mock-up/simulation that will have its internal operations reprogrammed, and 4GL working models which, once proved, will be rewritten in a procedural language, to a basic system which will be enhanced and refined over time until it is user acceptable.

The emphasis on iteration is the strength of prototyping methods. It underlies the oft-expressed wish to 'iterate phases' in the waterfall model, mentioned in Section 15.4.2. It is the basis of the approach to minimizing the technical risk in producing a successful project. However, there are difficulties: scaling the methods up to very large systems (problems of spaghetti code, ensuring that the code is maintainable and flexible enough to accommodate unplanned evolution), avoiding the undisciplined hacker syndrome that the life cycle model has been trying to solve, and ensuring process visibility for project control.

15.4.8 Incremental approach

In choosing a process which gives a suitable basis for managing risk it is necessary to take into account not only technical risk but also the project environment and personnel risks shown in *Figure 15.16* to ensure reliable control of the development of a successful product. As discussed in Section 15.2.4.3, incremental development, like prototyping, is a good way of remaining in control of a project when the software development has technical risks which make it difficult to predict timescales. However, more than prototyping, the incremental approach is also capable of being used by a project manager to address project environment and personnel risks. *Figure 15.15* shows the principles of incremental development from the management point of view, with a series of overlapping developments and a series of staggered deliveries to the customer.

The team sizes shown in Figures 15.12 and 15.13 are based on the production of the software as a single delivery, and show the classic rise and fall in numbers of staff employed on the project. There is also a transfer of numbers of staff from design to programming to test as the project progresses through the phases (or alternatively a turnover of staff if different expertise is deemed to be required for work in the different teams). This can present problems simply in staffing the project, in addition to

Project environment	Personnel	Technical
Undefined responsibilities and authorities Undefined procedures Unknown quality of development products Inadequate control of development products Problems and errors detected late Inadequate technical approaches Inadequate support facilities and services Lack of visibility	Wrong people available: ● not the right grade. ● not the right training. ● not the right expertise. Wrong availability: ● too many people for the current tasks. ● too few people for the current tasks.	Requirement changes: ● genuine change of mind by customer. ● hidden implication emerges. Failure to meet requirement: ● cannot produce a feasible design. ● acceptance test fails. Problem or error detected: ● design inconsistent. ● missing component. ● inadequate computer time for testing.

Figure 15.16 Major components of risk

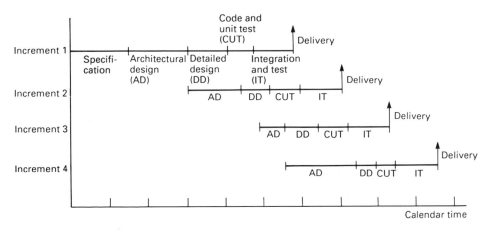

Figure 15.17 Incremental development sequence

the technical problems inherent in the single-shot approach to developing a software product.

If the software is developed incrementally, then provided proper top-down techniques are used, not only is the project under better technical control (especially when there is considerable technical uncertainty, and research is required) but also staffing problems are considerably eased. The design, programming and test teams can remain at relatively constant strengths, dealing with the work of each increment in turn. The main result is to level out the labour distribution curve on a software project. Instead of the classical Rayleigh curve distribution of labour over time, the labour distribution graph is much flatter (Boehm, 1981 pp 41–45).

If the increments of a large product development are very distinct, both in time and function, then the project organization approximates to a functional organization dealing with a series of projects going through. This implies that the full organizational structure needs to be permanently in operation and the manager needs then to be concerned with the span of control that this implies. Moreover, the manager has to attend to all the functions in parallel, whereas with a single development going through each phase in turn the project manager can give most attention to the primary activity corresponding to the current

phase. Thus, while incremental development decouples the project from the single driving pressure inherent in a single-shot development, when carried sufficiently far it may result in many pressures in parallel with all the dangers of a functional organization. When this threatens, the solution is either to strengthen the project office to deal with the increments separately, or to appoint sub-project managers for each increment to preserve the project-oriented drive. These problems only arise for a large project with very separate increments.

Although the diagram shows increments based on the classical life cycle phases, it is just as relevant to use prototyping methods in the development of the increments. Technical risk may also be dealt with by partitioning and moving, as far as possible, the less well understood parts of the functionality to later increments. Of course, this cannot be applied to anything that is crucial to the central design, which must be completed in the first increment. The splitting of the product into increments must not be done solely on consideration of priorities of user perceived functions. It must also be based on a 'first cut' at the architectural design, with the nucleus and primary structure designed and implemented in the first increment.

Another advantage of incremental development is that the increments of functional capability are much more helpful and easier to test than the intermediate products in a level-by-level top-down single-shot development. Further, the use of the successive increments provides a way to incorporate user experience into a refined product in a much less expensive way than by re-development following the first single-shot development. These are some of the reasons why incremental development is becoming so popular.

15.5 The canonical life cycle model

Section 15.2 introduced a set of 'canonical' stages of software development – the distinction between the stages primarily being one of their role in the development process. These stages, together with some fundamental management precepts, led to the design of a phase-based canonical life cycle model in Section 15.4. To clarify the relationship between technical and managerial activities each of the following so-called 'canonical' life cycle phases will be discussed.

1. Feasibility study.
2. Project initiation.
3. Requirement specification.
4. Architectural design.
5. Detailed design.
6. Coding.
7. Unit test.
8. Integration.
9. Integration test.
10. Acceptance test.
11. Operational test.
12. Project completion.
13. Operation (in-service and maintenance).
14. Product phaseout (replacement or disposal).

The phases follow in sequence, except project completion which occurs during operation. The term life cycle model can now be used as the list includes operation.

Not all projects have all of these phases. Small and simple projects may merge phases. Large and complex projects may need to have some of the phases divided. Where the software development is part of a system development, the software phases are generally interleaved with the system phases for hardware design and combined integration.

For many larger innovative projects, feasibility is a project in its own right, producing requirements, reports of options and even prototype products which will be precursors for the main development program. Often, and particularly when the designers of the software have experience of similar products, feasibility will be a very minor activity and will merge into project integration. Similarly incremental development will lead to a repetition of several phases and prototyping phases may be used to reduce technical risk. Thus the model cannot be viewed as definitive, but a description of the aim and conduct of each phase should clarify the issues which have to be taken into account when defining processes. Consequently the discussion of each phase in the following sections takes the form of:

- A brief description of key aspects of the activities in the phase.
- The phase products.
- The named review to complete the phase.

Note that for the reasons discussed in Section 15.3 and 15.4, the phase products will often relate to other technical activities in addition to the main activity of the phase.

15.5.1 Feasibility study

The first step in tackling a problematical software development is usually to carry out a feasibility study. The cost and duration of such a study will depend upon the size and complexity of the proposed development. The depth to which it goes in carrying out experimental work depends on what is needed to identify technical problems and to validate design assumptions, so that there is a basis for technical control in the development project. It may even be necessary to depend on a research contract. It is usually necessary to involve the customer/user to get the requirements right. This includes understanding the needs and exploring the limits of what is feasible to implement within the constraints of budget and design. The outcome of the feasibility study is not only whether the proposed development is feasible, but also an assessment of capability to do the job and a much better idea of the size of the job for predictions and initial estimates on which plans for the project can be based.

The feasibility study product is:

Feasibility report.

The feasibility review terminates the feasibility study, which should be treated as a project in its own right, terminated by the production and review of the report. It may be the necessary precursor to a subsequent development project, but it is not the first phase of, or an adequate foundation for, the development project – which must set up its own foundation in the project initiation phase.

15.5.2 Project initiation

There are many ways of embarking on a project, and entry into the initiation phase is often very ill defined. What is important is that the appointed project manager ensures that the *end* of this phase is well defined, with a thorough review of the foundation for control of the project in subsequent phases. The project manager must: set in place the basis of the project's adopted methods of working (process definition diagram, standards and procedures, technical methods and tools) and set in place the establishment of project control operations (work assignment, progress monitoring, metrics collection and analysis (quality monitoring), reporting and budget accountancy). It is also necessary for the project manager to ensure that external aspects are agreed, i.e. contractual issues and customer/user involvement during development, confirmation of requirements, technical control, the freedom to tackle technical risks by prototyping and incremental development, change control and commitments in the plans to deliveries and acceptance tests.

Project initiation phase products are:

1. Functional definition: high-level but precise statement of software requirements (e.g. cardinal points specification), including definition of the user manual, backed by an initial design study.
2. Contract (formal or informal).
3. Quality plan: approved strategy and resources for achieving the required quality.
4. Documentation plan.
5. Configuration management plan.
6. Initial design: derived from the approved, validated system architecture, with basic hardware-software allocations and concept of operation including boundaries between the users and the system, with definition of the technical strategy for implementation.
7. Test strategy and outline test plan.
8. Method of working on the project: approved process definition diagram showing how the project organization will develop the defined product together with specification of all the standards and procedures to be used, with particular emphasis on project control mechanisms.

9. Project plan: approved top level plan based on adequate estimates, milestones related to the process definition diagram and assignment of resources; showing organizational responsibilities and schedules for major elements of the work breakdown structure.

The project initiation review covers the above items (to project standards and following the project procedure) and also verifies that the method of working on the project is fully in operation. A satisfactory answer to the question 'do we have the project under control?' determines the completion of the phase and transition to the following development phases.

15.5.3 Requirements specification

Requirements specification is primarily concerned with finding out and documenting unambiguously 'what the user wants' and covers both requirements analysis and system specification as discussed in Section 15.2. This work, especially establishing a system boundary, may be intimately associated with continuing feasibility studies. Following Parnas, one can say that a requirement specification should tell the designer everything he or she needs to know in order to produce a system to satisfy the users, and nothing more. In other words if an 'ideal' specification could be produced, then the designer would need no further recourse to the users to clarify requirements. Clearly, as pointed out earlier and in Chapter 16, this ideal cannot be realised in practice.

This phase not only deals with fully capturing the requirements to produce the specification, but also involves a major emphasis on establishing the technical control, test strategy, test plans and tool support/development environment for subsequent phases. Increased precision in the detail of the specification and design enables estimates and plans to be refined, risks to be assessed (and the appropriate techniques of prototyping, customer involvement, simulation and incremental development invoked to deal with them). The change control procedures must be established and put into operation during this phase in order to control the cost of changes in subsequent phases.

Requirement specification phase products are:

1. Requirement specification: approved validated functional, performance, quality and interface specifications; verified for completeness, consistency, testability and feasibility and to a level of detail to deal with risk.
2. Outline user manual.
3. Draft design specification (including the basic software architecture).
4. Draft test plan: overall plans for verification and validation, excluding detailed test plans.
5. Detailed quality plan (including metrics to be used, data collection and analysis).
6. Detailed configuration management plan.
7. Detailed project plan: detailed development milestones, criteria, resource budgets, organization, responsibilities, work breakdown structure tasks, techniques, schedules, deliverables and plans for risk management.
8. Detailed plan for acceptance and usage: acceptance criteria, training, conversion, installation, operations and support related to development deliverables and schedules as set out in the project plan.
9. Confirmed contract.

The requirement specification review covers the above items and also verifies that product control (as defined in the quality, configuration management and test plans) is fully in operation. A satisfactory answer to the question 'do we have the technical

development under control?' determines completion of the phase. The updated plans require contractual confirmation with the customer.

15.5.4 Architectural design

Architectural design is the primary high-level design phase. The design team concentrates on the development of a good design to meet the requirements of functionality and performance. Transformation of the design to lower levels of detail and partitioning of the design into component specifications is the basis for definition of interfaces between components and subsequent assignment to a number of teams for implementation. This phase may lead to a revision of requirements based on an improved understanding of feasibility and/or cost.

Architectural design phase products are:

1. Design specification: verified for completeness, consistency, feasibility and traceability to requirements and with all high-risk technical issues identified and resolved; covering program component hierarchy, control structures and data interfaces through to unit level, physical and logical data structure through to field level, and data-processing resource budgets (timing, storage and accuracy).
2. Preliminary test specifications for integration testing, independent testing and acceptance testing.
3. Draft user manual.
4. Draft operations manual.
5. Outline maintenance manual.

The architectural design review on the above items poses the question 'is it now simply a matter of implementation?'. Of all the software design reviews, this review is the most crucial to the ultimate success of the project. Because the architectural design phase is the last opportunity to make changes and correct errors without a significant cost impact, the complete design should be carefully verified and validated before the project moves into the implementation phases (detailed design, coding and unit test).

15.5.5 Detailed design

This phase is characterized by multiple teams working on the parts of the designed software at the detailed level (down to algorithmic level). Technical control includes a central design authority to preserve design integrity. Project control is crucially dependent upon the previously established methods of working, reporting and product control. Thoroughgoing quality assurance in the preceding phases is necessary if the required quality of the product is to be assured as part of the process. The methods of working and their confirmation and strengthening by quality assurance are by now part of the project culture and very difficult to change under the increasing pressure and the technical drive of the team to get on with implementing the design. From this stage onwards quality assurance is increasingly ineffective in changing anything. It is only a matter of observation and discovery. Anything that is found with wider ramifications than a single module becomes a matter of debugging implemented software, which is notoriously costly and uncontrollable.

Detailed design phase products are:

1. Detailed design specification for each unit: verified for completeness, consistency, and traceability to requirements and system design specifications and size and speed budgets:
   (a) For each module (module size limitations as defined in the coding standard) specified name, purpose, assumptions, sizing, calling sequence, error exits, inputs, outputs, algorithms, and processing flow.

(b) Database description through parameter/character/bit level.
2. Unit test specifications (standalone test cases).
3. Completed and approved relevant parts of the integration and independent test plans and test data.
4. Completed relevant part of the draft maintenance manual.

A detailed design review satisfactorily completed (e.g. with a walkthrough) determines the completion of the phase for each module or group of modules. Note that previous phase ends were for the project as a whole, but for the detailed design, code and unit test the teams follow independent time paths for progress of their work on the modules.

15.5.6 Coding

Coding, or implementation, consists of production of programs implementing the functionality of each module.
Coding phase products are:

1. Coded module(s): verified as complying with programming standards.
2. Completion of module documentation.
3. Test data for unit testing: validated as covering all unit computations, using not only nominal values, but also singular and extreme values and exercising all input and output options, including error messages, all executable statements and all branch options.

The source code review usually takes the form of code reading (by another member of the team) or, in the case of critical modules, a walkthrough with a number of attendees.

15.5.7 Unit test

This involves exercising the units (modules) with representative data, testing singular and extreme values, and so on. Minor coding errors may be corrected in this phase.
Unit testing products are:

1. Unit testing results.
2. Verified modules.

The unit test review verifies that the unit test results show the unit performing correctly in all its operations, according to the unit test plan using test data derived from the detailed design.

15.5.8 Integration

The pre-requisite for this step is the integration test data and the first set of unit tested modules. Subsequent sets of modules will be available at intervals – planned to fit in with the integration strategy (such as top-down, critical processes first, etc.).
Integrated software items are:

1. Integration test data and results.
2. Development product (for central configuration management, from which new clean versions are installed for the independent test team and customer support team).
3. Installation notes.
4. Test data for independent testing.
5. Full draft user manual.
6. Full draft operations manual.
7. Draft maintenance manual.
8. Training needs analysis.
9. Stable reference version of the product (for production of manuals and training courses).

The integrated software review verifies that the integration test results show that the product is functionally integrated according to the integration test plan, using test data derived from the structural design.

15.5.9 Integration test

This is the real test of the integrated software. For thoroughness it is carried out by a test team independent of the development team(s). During the software implementation phases, this test team is responsible for the preparation of the test data from the structural design and the requirement specification. It takes the integrated software and the full draft user manual and thoroughly tests the product according to the plan for independent testing. Any faults found are passed back to the development team for correction and redelivery and re-installation of a new version of the product. This testing is internal and must be satisfactorily completed before delivery to the customer for acceptance testing.
Tested software items are:

1. Independent test results: satisfaction of planned test programme for the complete software product.
2. Quality and reliability report.
3. Deliverable product (initial release).
4. Installation notes (initial release).
5. User manual (initial release).
6. Operations manual (initial release).
7. Maintenance manual (initial release).

The tested software review poses the question 'do we have a properly functioning supported software product?'. This relies on verifying that the independent test results show the correct performance of the product in all its operations, according to the independent test plan. It also means checking that the above constituents of the tested software product and the analysis of the quality metrics in the quality and reliability report meet the criteria in the quality plan for release of the product for customer acceptance and that the support team is ready for the customer acceptance phase.

15.5.10 Acceptance test

This is evaluation and acceptance by the customer against the acceptance criteria, with acceptance tests using data derived from the requirements specification. Faults found by the customer are corrected by the development team (in the case of the software) and by the technical author (in the case of the manuals) with updated releases delivered to the customer by the support team.
Accepted software items are:

1. Acceptance test results: verification of satisfaction of software requirements, demonstration of acceptable off-nominal performance as specified.
2. Deliverable packaged software product.
3. Installation notes and trained installers.
4. Final accepted manuals for user, operations and maintenance.
5. Training courses and trained lecturers.

The customer acceptance review answers the question 'is the software product accepted and handed over to the customer?' by seeking confirmation of the customer's agreement that the product has met the original acceptance criteria and contractual acceptance of all deliverable software products including reports, manuals, as-built specifications and databases and that the product is satisfactorily supported.

15.5.11 Operational test

This deals with experience of initial operation of the product at the customer's site with continuing support from the development team to deal with problems. Analysis of the data from measurements of quality and reliability is used to determine the success of the product before the development project can be closed.

The operational test phase product is:

Quality and reliability report.

The product operation review determines the completion of all specified conversion, installation and training activities and verifies the operational readiness of the software, hardware, facilities and personnel. It also ensures that the product operation at the customer site is satisfactory and ready to be fully handed over to the support team for continuing in-service support and maintenance. If this phase is part of the contractual arrangements then there will usually be final formal confirmation of acceptance of all deliverable system products: hardware, software, documentation, training and facilities.

15.5.12 Project completion

The objectives of the project completion phase are to ensure that all technical information is properly available and to provide the planning and organization necessary to ensure a smooth handover to subsequent projects related to the project now completing. Depending on contracts and technology, these may be maintenance support, further product line development, or subsequent contractual stages in a large scale system development. The project completion phase also gathers and analyses quantitative data from the project, to improve the numerical basis of future project planning, estimating and control, and to capture for wider business use the commercial, technical and management experience gained on the project so that lessons are learned and methods updated where appropriate.

The project completion item is:

A completed project history document comparing estimates and plans with actual development schedule and costs.

The project completion review is an internal project management review, which confirms that all project actions are truly complete and that the project can indeed be closed. It also establishes that appropriate follow-on actions are identified through project and product analyses, that the information for these actions is available, and that responsibilities are assigned for their execution.

15.5.13 Operation (in-service and maintenance)

Corrections for implementation and specification errors, based on software problem reports (SPRs), and evolution of required functions are controlled by a series of releases of updated software. The goal of maintenance is a fully functioning version of the software at each release. Each release is based on a sequence of steps following the same phases as development, tailored to the magnitude and risks of the changes involved, with even greater emphasis on change control and configuration management.

15.5.14 Product phaseout (replacement or disposal)

The purpose of this phase is to address explicitly the need for a clean transition of the functions performed by the product to its successors (if any) at the end of its useful life. The phaseout product is:

Product phaseout plan and report on completion.

The product phaseout review verifies completion of all items in the phaseout plan: conversion, documentation, archiving and transition to new system(s).

15.6 Process selection

This section considers Boehm's spiral model. It is essentially as a meta-model of the development process. The alternative strategies for selecting a software process are discussed, followed by a brief consideration of the wider context of software (and system) procurement.

15.6.1 Spiral model

Figure 15.16 shows a 'spiral model' as a general meta-model for processes, which incudes most of the previously discussed models as special cases. It can be used to discuss the principles of processes to fit a wide variety of circumstances and provides guidance as to which sequence of phases best fits a given software situation. The spiral model has been developed at TRW over a number of years, based on experience on large government software projects (Boehm, 1988), updated and reprinted in Thayer (1988), which gives further details and describes the experience of applying the model to the TRW Software Productivity Project.

The radial dimension in Figure 15.16 represents the cumulative cost (with some artistic licence) incurred in accomplishing the steps to date; the angular dimension represents the progress made in completing each cycle of the spiral. The model holds that each cycle involves a progression through the same sequence of steps, for each portion of the product and for each of its levels of elaboration, from an overall concept of operation document down to the coding of each individual program.

Following the commitment to go ahead, each cycle of the spiral begins, in the top left-hand quadrant, with the determination of:

1. The objectives of the portion of the product being elaborated (performance, functionality, ability to accommodate change, etc.).
2. The alternative means of implementing this portion of the product (alternative designs, reuse, purchase, etc.).
3. The constraints imposed on the application of the alternatives (cost, schedule, interface, etc.).

The next step is to evaluate the alternatives with respect to the objectives and constraints. This evaluation must identify any areas of uncertainty which are significant sources of project risk, and formulate a cost-effective strategy for dealing with the sources of risk. This may involve prototyping, simulation, questioning users, analytic modelling, or combinations of these and other risk-resolution techniques.

Once the risks are evaluated, the next step is determined by the relative balance of the perceived risks. If technical (performance or user-interface) risks strongly dominate control (development project control or internal interface control) risks, the next step may be an evolutionary development step. This is a minimal effort to specify the overall nature of the product, a plan for the next level of prototyping, and the development of a more detailed prototype to continue to resolve the major risk issues. If this prototype is operationally useful, and robust enough to serve as a low-risk base for future project evolution, then the subsequent risk-driven steps would be the evolving series of evolutionary prototypes progressing to the right in Figure 15.16.

On the other hand, if previous prototyping efforts have already resolved all of the technical risks, and control risks dominate, the next step may follow the classical life cycle approach (concept of operation, software requirements, architectural design, etc.), modified as appropriate if incremental development is incorporated. Each level of specification through requirements and design is then followed by a validation step and the preparation of plans for the succeeding cycle.

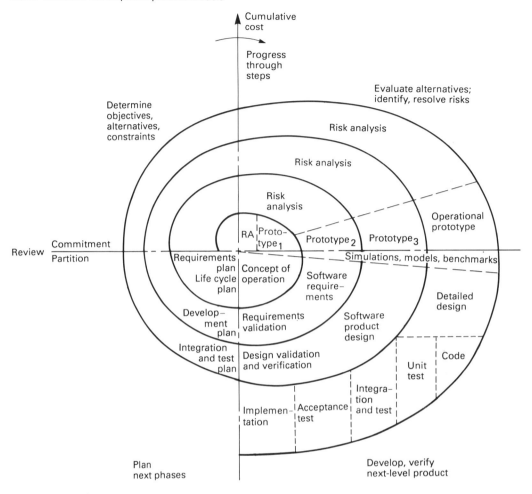

Figure 15.18 Spiral model of the software development process

The final development phases for each portion of the product are shown at the bottom of the lower right hand quadrant.

The major review to complete each full cycle is an important feature of the spiral model. It is shown as the left-hand axis in Figure 15.16, and involves the primary people or organizations concerned with the product. The review covers all of the products developed during the previous cycle, including the plans for the next cycle and the resources required to carry them out. The major objective is to ensure that all concerned parties are mutually committed to the approach to be taken for the next cycle. The plans for the succeeding phases may include a partition of the product into increments for successive development, or components to be developed by separate organizations, teams or individuals. Thus, the review and commitment step may range from an individual walkthrough of the design of a single programmer's component, to a major requirements review involving developer, customer, user and maintenance organizations.

The most significant emphasis of the diagram of the spiral model is on decision making to ensure management of *all* aspects of risk. The plans developed in the lower left-hand quadrant to achieve the commitment review decision undergo further analysis in the upper parts of the diagram before the

plans are finalized to a level of detail for the actual development. Planning, decision making, and determining, evaluating and resolving alternatives for detailed plans are not a simple linear progression but must be iterated for risk management planning in each cycle as necessary. The principle of the spiral model is valid without confusing the diagram with an attempt to show more detail of the decision making process. The emphasis of a large area of Figure 15.16 on decision making and risk analysis is consistent with the application of the model to determining processes for risky projects. Once risk is controlled for the development of all, or (more usually) a portion, of the product then that portion goes through into the lower right-hand part of the model to progress through a straightforward process to implementation. The lack of uncontrollable risk at this stage should mean that there is no need for a major review to commit to progress through each of these final phases.

The spiral model can be used to assist the choice of any appropriate mixture of specification-oriented, (automatic) transformation-oriented, simulation-oriented, prototype-oriented, incremental, or other approach to software development, where the appropriate mixed strategy is chosen by considering the relative magnitude of the program risks, and the relative effectiveness of the various techniques in resolving the risks. Risk management and the choice of a suitable process for a particular project from the risk management perspective are dealt with in Section 27.3 in Chapter 27.

Alternatively the spiral model can be seen as a process generator to create an *ad hoc* phase-by-phase process based on risk management to fit the specific situation of the project. An example of this is given in Boehm (1988) for the development of the TRW Software Productivity System. The principle of this alternative is shown in *Figure 15.17*, which shows an extended version of the spiral model (Boehm, 1989). A project using this version of the spiral model elaborates its definition of both the software product and the software process in a series of cycles. Each cycle of the spiral determines the product and process objectives and constraints; defines the alternative product and process solutions; evaluates and 'prioritizes' the alternative with respect to the objectives and constraints and identifies and resolves the major risks that a potential solution will satisfy the product and process objectives and constraints. Based on the results of the risk resolution, the project can then eliminate unpromising product and process alternatives, and refine the most attractive one(s). The process refinement constitutes a set of plans for future cycles. These are then reviewed and, given a commitment to proceed, further elaborated in the next cycle.

15.6.2 Process model alternatives

The main function of a software process model, from a project management point of view, is to establish the order in which a project performs its main stages (prototypes, specifications, increments, reviews, etc.) and to establish the transition criteria for proceeding from one main stage to the next. There are three strategies that can be followed in choosing from the alternative models for a specific project:

1. Treat the canonical model as an all-purpose model and tailor its use to fit every situation. This may be valid for a site where the projects do not get into unprecedented new developments. The strategy may be adopted, more unrealistically, in circumstances where the customer (or rather the procurer) appears to demand it as the prescribed process. Using an unsuitable process, or the alternative of pretending to use it as an overlay on an actually different process, are not recommended strategies.

2. Regard the various models as discrete alternatives, the most appropriate being selected for the specific project. *Figure 5.20*, from Boehm (1989) lays out such a set of alternatives with the reasons for deciding on the most appropriate for given circumstances. The same logical conclusions for choice

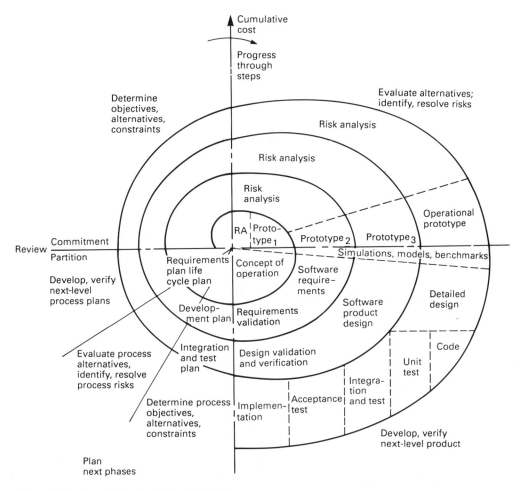

Figure 15.19 Extended version of the spiral model

Figure 15.20 Software development process model decision table

Objectives, constraints			State of the art		Process model	Example
Growth envelope	Understanding of requirements	Robustness	Available technology	Architecture understanding		
Limited			Commercial packages		Buy commercial package	Simple inventory control
Limited			4GL, Transform		Transform or evolutionary development	Small business – DP application
Limited	Low	Low		Low	Evolutionary prototype	Advanced pattern recognition
Limited to large	High	High		High	Pre-determined classical phases	Rebuild of old system
	Low	High			Risk reduction followed by classical phases	Complex situation assessment
		High		Low		High-performance avionics
Limited to medium	Low	Low to medium		High	Evolutionary development	New decision-support system
Limited to large			Large reusable components	Medium to high	Fit capabilities to requirements	Electronic publishing
Very large					Risk reduction plus classical phases	Air traffic control
Medium to large	Low	Medium	Some commercial packages	Low to medium	Spiral	Software support environment
Fixed budget or schedule available					Design to cost or design to schedule	
Early capability needed Limited staff or budget available Downstream requirements poorly understood High-risk system nucleus (Any one condition is sufficient) Large to very large application Required phasing with system increments					Incremental development	

of process can be derived from applying the first version, Figure 15.18, of the spiral model. The strategy consists of: determining process objectives and constraints, identifying the process model alternatives (from consideration of the state of the art), evaluating these with respect to the objectives and constraints; identifying and analysing the risks, and using the risk analysis results to determine the process model suitable for the project. This is a reasonable strategy when a specific alternative correctly fits the circumstances of a particular project – as will often be the case.

3. Create an *ad hoc* phase-by-phase process specifically for the project. This strategy is suitable for the circumstances where risks dominate the planning (rather than questions of accuracy of estimating for well understood software development). The necessary sequence would be to determine the objectives and constraints for the project and product, decide which are the critical process drivers and analyse the construction of process phases using the extended version of the spiral model (reference Figure 15.19) to develop a process which minimizes the risk of not satisfying the critical process drivers. The spiral model as used in this interpretation is suitable for complex, dynamic projects requiring a great deal of flexibility, but it provides more flexibility than is convenient for many situations. In a straightforward procurement of a low-risk system, the spiral model provides more degrees of freedom than most managers wish to deal with. In such cases, either an application of the canonical life cycle model, or an evolutionary development process (based on prototyping or on incremental development as appropriate) is easier for people to understand and work with. The simpler process model can be used to establish more specific up-front definitions for such items as contract provisions, product acceptance criteria, internal milestones, and cost-schedule control limits. The spiral model keeps these options open as long as possible, but the flexibility is achieved at the cost of simplicity and efficiency achievable by the more inflexibly prescribed approaches.

15.6.3 Procurement strategies

It is common for large-scale software systems to be developed by an organization or company other than the user organization. When this is the case, the procurement of the software will be governed by a legal contract. Even when development is carried out within the same organization, it is common to operate as if there were a legal contract between the users and developers. This is important as the way in which the software is specified and the contract is written can have a significant effect on the software development process. For example, a contract might enforce a 'contractual' approach by tying down the system specification, and acceptance tests, in the legal documents.

A primary aim in framing a contract should be to try to minimize financial *risk*, that is, the potential negative impact of the software development project on the company finances overall. In practice, it is often the case that contracts minimize financial *exposure*, that is, the amount that can be lost on the contract, e.g. by specifying that the work should be done at a fixed price or in a fixed timescale. However, this can *increase* technical and hence financial risk, as it can put undue and unrealistic pressures on staff to complete the creative development process. This will lead to shortcuts in development and consequent problems at acceptance or in maintenance. More disastrously, it can lead to a situation where customers do not pay for development work – but neither do they have the system they need to do their job, with major operational costs, e.g. lost business.

In general, financial risk can be reduced by allying the

procurement strategy to the most appropriate development approach for a given system. Thus, if incremental development is the most appropriate way to produce a system, then the contract structure should reflect this approach. It will probably still be necessary to have one overall contract, but the cost, duration and technical specification for each increment would be finalized as the project proceeded. This does not dramatically increase financial exposure. The customer has lots of opportunities at which to withdraw support. Defining the procurement strategy first and thus constraining which development paradigm can be adopted is to confuse cause and effect, and to run the risk of having exactly the opposite of the desired effect. This point is important as contractual issues can completely dominate a development project. The STARTS handbook (DTI, 1989) is one of the few sources of advice on this topic although it perhaps lays too much stress on fixed price procurement. Also Humphrey (1989) gives advice on process selection from the procurer's point of view. Perhaps the most important general point is that many organizations associated with a project, e.g. procurers, users and developers, face risks. The aim in selecting a process and a procurement strategy should be to reduce and balance risks, not to eliminate one risk at the expense of others – and thus run the risk of jeopardizing the whole project or one of the organizations involved.

15.7 Summary and conclusions

The difficulties of large-scale software development are now widely appreciated, if not well understood. One of the key factors in countering these difficulties is to establish an appropriate software development process. Specifically the process definition should ensure that all the major technical risks in development are addressed, and that the technical activities can be managed effectively. Thus there are technical and managerial inputs to process design or selection.

Two key roles in any software development are the project manager and the technical controller or system architect. Whilst these roles may, for small projects, be filled by the same individual it is important to keep the roles distinct (see Section 27.2.4). However, definition or selection of the process is a joint responsibility of the system architect and project manager. In addition it is usually necessary to agree the process with the customer or procurement authority, so that risks are jointly understood and managed.

The process may be defined in its entirety in project initiation, or it may evolve as part of a risk management strategy (see Section 15.6.1 and Chapter 27).

A primary purpose of the chapter has been to describe the software development process, from both the technical and managerial points of view, in order to clarify the issues which have to be addressed when selecting or designing a process. Process definition is discussed further in Chapter 27 which also illustrates a notation for describing software processes at a sufficient level of detail to facilitate effective project control.

This chapter is also intended to serve as a precursor to the discussion of particular approaches to software development, verification and validation. Specifically the intention has been to set out a framework for software development, and to clarify the role of the techniques discussed in other chapters in the overall process. The authors have also tried to indicate the requirements on methods for dealing with each stage in the development process to give some guidance on method, as well as process, selection.

In summary, there are considerable risks associated with software development. Understanding, selecting and controlling the process of software development is fundamental to reducing and managing development risks. Good process management is not a panacea but it is a key to project success.

15.8 References

Backhouse, R. (1986) *Program Construction and Verification*, Prentice-Hall International

Bate, D. G. (1986) MASCOT3: an informal introductory tutorial. *Software Engineering Journal*, **1**, 3

Boehm, B. W. (1976) Software engineering. *IEEE Transactions on Computers*, 1226–1241

Boehm, B. W. (1981) *Software Engineering Economics*, Prentice-Hall

Boehm, B. W. (1988) A spiral model of software development and enhancement. *IEEE Computer*, May, 61–72. Reprinted in Thayer, R. H. (ed) (1988) *IEEE Tutorial on Software Engineering Project Management*

Boehm, B. W. (1989) Software risk management. *IEEE Tutorial* EH 0291–5

Bramson, B. D. (1984) Malvern's program analysers. *RSRE Research Review*

Cohen, B. (1982) Justification of formal methods for system specification. *IEE Software and Microsystems*, **5**

Coleman, D. and Gallimore, R. M. (1987) *Software Engineering Using Executable Specifications*, Macmillan Computer Science Series

DeMarco, T. (1981) *Controlling Software Projects*, Yourdon Press

Dix, A. J., Harrison, M. D., Runciman, C. and Thimbleby, H. W. (1987) Interaction models and the principled design of interactive systems. In *Proceedings of ESEC '87*, Springer Verlag

Dowson, M. (1987) ISTAR and the contractual approach. In *Proceedings of 9th International Conference on Software Engineering*, IEEE Computer Society Press

DTI (1987) *The STARTS Guide, Second Edition*, Department of Trade and Industry. Available from the National Computing Centre, Manchester

DTI (1989) *STARTS Purchasers' Handbook*, 2nd edn., Department of Trade and Industry

Fagan, M. (1976) Design and code inspections to reduce errors in program development. *IBM Systems Journal*, **15**, 3, 182–211

Fagan, M. (1986) Advances in software inspection. *IEEE Transactions on Software Engineering*, 744–751

Freedman, D. P. and Weinberg, G. M. (1982) *Handbook of Walkthroughs, Inspections and Technical Reviews: Evaluating Programs, Projects and Products*, 3rd Edn., Little, Brown and Company, Boston, Mass, USA

Goldberg, E. A. (1977) *Applying Corporate Software Development Policies*, TRW Defense and Space Systems Group (December). Reprinted in Thayer, R. H. (ed) (1988) *IEEE Tutorial on Software Engineering Project Management*

Good, D. (1984) Mechanical Proofs about Computer Programs. *Report No. 41*, Institute for Computing Science, The University of Texas at Austin, USA

Halstead, M. (1977) *Elements of Software Science*, North Holland/Elsevier

Hayes, I. (ed.) (1986) *Specification Case Studies*, Prentice-Hall international.

Hekmatpour, S. and Ince, D. (1986) A formal specification-based prototyping system. In *Software Engineering*, Peter Peregrinus

Henderson, P. (1986) Functional programming, formal specification and rapid prototyping. *Transactions on Software Engineering*, **12**

Hoare, C. A. R. (1969) An axiomatic basis for computer programming. *Communications of the ACM*, **12**, 10

Hoare, C. A. R., He, H. and Sanders, J. W. (1986) *Data Refinement Refined*, Programming Research Group. University of Oxford

Humphrey, W. S. (1989) *Managing the Software process*, Addison-Wesley

Jackson, M. A. (1983) *System Development*, Prentice-Hall International

Jones, C. B. (1986) *Systematic Software Development Using VDM*, Prentice-Hall International

Kitchenham, B. A. and Walker, J. G. (1986) The meaning of quality. In *Software Engineering 86* (ed. P. J. Brown and D. J. Barnes) Peter Peregrinus

Kitchenham, B. A. and McDermid, J. A. (1986) Software metrics and integrated project support environments. *Software Engineering Journal* **1**, 1

Maibaum, T. S. E., Khosla, S. and Jeremaes, P. (1986) A modal [action] logic for requirements specification. In *Software Engineering 86* (ed. P. J. Brown and D. J. Barnes) Peter Peregrinus

McDermid, J. A. and Ripken, K. (1984) *Life Cycle Support in the Ada Environment*, Cambridge University Press

McDermid, J. A. (ed.) (1990) *The Theory and Practice of Refinement: Formal Approaches to the Development of Large Scale Software Systems*, Butterworths

Milner, A. J. R. G. (1980) Calculus of communicating systems. In *Lecture Notes in Computer Science No. 92* (ed. G. Goos and J. Hartmanis) Springer-Verlag

Mullery, G. P. (1979) CORE – a method for controlled requirements specification. In *Proceedings of 4th International Conference on Software Engineering*, IEEE Computer Society Press

Myers, G. J. (1978) *Composite/Structured Design*, Van Nostrand Reinhold

Parnas, D. L. (1972) On the criteria to be used in decomposing systems into modules. *Communications of the ACM*, **15**, 12

Partsch, H. and Steinbruggen, R. (1981) A comprehensive survey of program transformation systems. *Report No. I8108*, Institut für Informatik, Technical University of Munich, FRG

Potts, C. J. and Finkelstein, A. (1986) Structured common sense. In *Software Engineering 86* (ed. P. J. Brown and D. J. Barnes) Peter Peregrinus

Royce, W. W. (1970) Managing the development of large software systems. In *Proceedings of IEEE WESCON 1970, IEEE*, pp. 1–9. Reprinted in Thayer, R. H. (ed.) (1988) *IEEE Tutorial on Software Engineering Project Management*

Sanella, D. and Tarlecki, A. (1984) *On Observational Equivalence and Algebraic Specification*, Department of Computer Science, University of Edinburgh

Thayer, R. H. (1988) Software engineering project management. *IEEE Tutorial EH0263–4*

Weinberg, G. M. and Freedman, D. P. (1984) Reviews, walkthroughs and inspections. *IEEE Transactions on Software Engineering*, **10**, 1, 68–72. Reprinted in Thayer, R. H. (ed.) (1988) *IEEE Tutorial on Software Engineering Project Management*

Zave, P. (1982) An operational approach to requirements expression for embedded systems. *Transactions on Software Engineering*, **8**, 3.

Conventional Development

16

Requirements analysis

David Alan Stokes
University of York

Contents

16.1 Introduction

Requirements analysis is the first technical activity in software development and it is concerned with eliciting, clarifying and documenting the desired functionality of some system. This fact is recognized in most life-cycle models, and requirements analysis typically either comes as the first stage in the models, or follows immediately after project initiation. Many studies have shown that errors or omissions made at the requirements stage are very costly (or even impossible) to rectify. Nonetheless, requirements are often neglected or only partially completed (sometimes because managers naïvely think that their staff are not 'getting on with the job' if they are not producing code), leading to problems later in development. Further, current requirements analysis techniques are far from perfect. Consequently, the aim of this chapter is to explain the fundamental principles of requirements analysis and to evaluate the current tools and techniques in order to clarify the role, content and value of a requirements specification, and, it is hoped, to stimulate research into improved requirements analysis techniques.

First, however, it is important to explain a few terms and to consider a number of basic issues: what requirements are, why they are needed, who uses them, and what they are used for.

The term 'requirements analysis' (or requirements engineering) is a general term which refers to a collection of processes: elicitation, specification, verification and validation. The elicitation of requirements is an information-gathering exercise to ascertain exactly what it is that the customer or user requires. Specification is used to refer to both a process and the result of that process; it involves the presentation of the gathered information in a document referred to as the requirements specification. Verification is completed to ensure that this document does not contain any inconsistencies, and validation is carried out to ensure that the document describes accurately the artefact that the customer desires.

These processes involve a number of roles: the requirers, the facilitators, and the implementors. The requirers include customers and users, and represent the people that need or demand a system. The facilitators are analysts, and their role is to develop, through the application of appropriate elicitation, specification, verification and validation techniques, an accurate description of the system that the requirers want. Once the requirements specification has been produced, then the implementors, consisting of designers, engineers, and project managers (e.g. the contractors), build the system. Thus the facilitators write the specification for the implementors to build the system that the requirers need. Sometimes more than one role is filled by a given individual, or group of individuals, but requirements analysis is facilitated from both technical and managerial points of view if a clear distinction is made between these roles.

16.1.1 What are requirements?

The requirements are a collection of statements that should describe in a clear, concise, consistent and unambiguous manner all significant aspects of a proposed system. They should contain enough information to enable the designers and engineers to produce a system that will satisfy the customer and the users, *and nothing more*. Such a definition conveys the aim or purpose of requirements but gives little indication of exactly what information a requirements document should contain, nor to what level of detail and depth the requirements should be defined. Although it is clear from the definition that there must be some description of what the system should be capable of doing, the requirements usually have to include much more information.

The detailed contents of a requirements specification are considered in Section 16.3, but in general, there are six categories of information that are present in most requirements specifications.

1. *Functionality*. A set of statements describing the functionality of the system is always included. These requirements cover not only all externally observable behaviour, but may also define some internal functionality that is 'obviously' needed to support the external behaviour.
2. *Functional constraints*. In many applications, the results returned from any computation are only useful if they satisfy a number of constraints. These constraints should be included in the requirements specification, and they, typically, include performance, response times, capacities, numbers of users, safety standards, security standards and quality issues. These requirements do not alter the overall functionality of the system, but they do restrict the engineer to a limited subset of the possible implementations.
3. *Design constraints*. It is quite frequently the case that in addition to the functional constraints, customers will also stipulate a number of design constraints. These can cover a great variety of different things: system compatibility, the choice of hardware, the choice of operating system, and may even be as specific as the size and layout of bit patterns. Such constraints should be included in the requirements document, only where they are *essential* to customer satisfaction (a common fault in requirements documents is to stray too far into design – see Section 16.3).
4. *Data and communication protocols*. Most systems will communicate in some way with 'the outside world', and the content (and also possibly the form) of this communication will need to be recorded in the requirements specification. This information is usually of a very high-level nature; for example, the major inputs and outputs of the system.
5. *Project management*. To ensure that the development of the project runs smoothly, and that the system is delivered to the customer's satisfaction, it is helpful to include in the requirements specification information such as deadlines, deliverables, assumptions, expected changes, life-cycle aspects, installation details, manual standards, and training information. The detail and extent of this 'managerial' information will depend upon the application and the customer/contractor agreements.
6. *Environmental description/system objectives*. Design and development of the system is likely to be more successful if the designers and engineers are aware of the reason a computer system is required, and of how the system should interact with its eventual environment. This contextual information can be provided by including in the requirements specification a description of the environment and a statement of the main system objectives. These two topics are linked as objectives are normally most readily stated in terms of the system's environment.

Further details concerning what information should be present in a requirements specification, and how it should be presented can be found in a number of published standards (DTI and NCC, 1987) and these are considered in Section 16.3.

Cardinal points specifications are often used to guide system development. The cardinal points describe a set of technical objectives which must be met if the developed system is to satisfy the customer. It is important to realize that such specifications are not a replacement for requirements specifications. Cardinal points specifications state a number of high-level objectives for a system. However, it is not usually possible to (acceptance) test a system against a cardinal points specification, and the cardinal points specification will inevitably be incomplete, as it will make assumptions about the 'normal' functionality for a system of this nature. Thus, for a well-controlled development, it is necessary to produce a full requirements specification at some stage. The primary distinction with normal practice is that the design team will produce this specification and therefore there may be a greater blurring than usual between requirements and high-level design.

16.1.2 Why do we need requirements?

The benefits of establishing a firm statement of system requirements are numerous. By simply carrying out the processes involved in requirements analysis, both customer and analyst will have a better understanding of what is required and why it is needed. The analysis will improve communications between customer and contractor, and thus establish, at least at a technical level, good contractual relationships.

However, the overriding objective of requirements analysis is to provide necessary and sufficient information for subsequent design and implementation to be successful. As computer systems become more complex, errors are increasingly likely to be made in the design and construction of the systems. This problem is exacerbated by the fact that computer systems are now being used in many applications in which failure of the system cannot be tolerated, for example, in safety or security critical systems. If we are to avoid such errors, or at least reduce this incidence to an acceptable minimum, then it is absolutely vital that a complete and consistent set of requirements are developed; otherwise important functions may be omitted or important constraints, e.g. safety, may be neglected. This demands that once the requirements document has been produced, it always remains consistent and complete, so that the designers and engineers have a firm basis from which to work. This will only be the case if the requirements are completed with extreme care and discipline, and maintained throughout the development process.

The contractors must take steps to ensure that they are building the correct system, and that they are building the system correctly. Validation of requirements increases confidence that the correct system is being produced, and the requirements form the baseline against which it is possible to verify whether or not the system is being built correctly. Clearly consistent and complete requirements are essential in order to have effective validation and verification procedures.

To guarantee the smooth running of a project, project management must have a complete project plan, including costs, deadlines, resources, deliverables, and so on. Since a complete requirements specification will include information on targets for costs, deliverables, etc., it is again clear that thorough requirements analysis must be completed to make the development project manageable. Another important facet of the requirements is that they will provide the baseline for acceptance testing. Knowledge of objectives for acceptance testing greatly facilitates project management.

16.1.3 Who uses the requirements, and for what?

A variety of people, with differing backgrounds and technical capabilities, must read and understand the requirements: the customers and users, the analysts, the designers and engineers, and the project managers. The customer's and user's interest in the requirements is driven from a validatory position. The requirements are elicited and specified by analysts, and customer/user involvement during these stages is as an information source. Once the requirements have been written, the customers and users will wish to review them to ensure that they describe the 'right' system. It is during this review process that the customers and users validate the requirements, and it is vitally important for validation to be completed successfully. Clarity

and understandability of the requirements are therefore of paramount importance.

During the specification of the requirements, the analysts will be concerned with their consistency, completeness and correctness. Once the requirements specification has been finalized, the designers and engineers will construct the system it describes. The analyst's role will then be to ensure that the system is being developed correctly – although the onus of this task does not rest entirely with the analyst. The analyst's interest in the requirements is therefore one of analysis and interpretation. The analysis ensures consistency, and 'correctness', while interpretation helps with completeness and system development. For the analyst, formality (or precision) is important; the analysis can be carried out only in the context of a formal language, and its unambiguous nature helps to ensure that the analyst insists upon a consistent interpretation.

The designers and engineers design and build a system from the requirements. Their interest in the requirements is simply its use as a 'blueprint'; the requirements form the baseline for system development. Designers and analysts will, or at least should, prefer the use of more formal languages, since such languages tend to be unambiguous, consistent and concise, and thus the verification of the system with respect to the requirements is simpler and more reliable.

The project managers guide the development of the system to ensure that it is delivered on time, it conforms to any applicable standards, it is fully documented, and so on. Their interest in the requirements is therefore largely confined to the project management information. However, they will also be interested in ensuring that when the system is delivered, it satisfies the customer. This may mean that the project managers must be familiar with the full requirements to some degree so that they can be sure that the delivered system does in fact satisfy the requirements and therefore the customer. The general relationship between technical and managerial activities is discussed in Chapters 21–34 on the software process and on project management.

16.1.4 Current practice

Current practice in the field of requirements engineering varies a great deal, but in most cases it is different from the somewhat idealized process above, and is usually inadequate in terms of clarity, consistency and completeness. The requirements document is quite often an enormous work written in natural language, the structure of which is indicated by a series of paragraph numbers. The ambiguity of natural language, the difficulty involved in its verification and validation, the problems of ensuring consistency and completeness, and the misunderstandings between those concerned in system development all contribute to making natural language inappropriate for the specification of requirements from an analytical standpoint. For example, the use of natural language tends to lead to the over-specification of some aspects of the system, and the under-specification or omission of others. Furthermore, reading such a large document is a forbidding task, and any attempt to understand a natural language requirements specification completely is unlikely to succeed. It is not surprising that large system development based on textual requirements is a long, error-prone, and fraught exercise.

However, the analysts, designers and engineers are not entirely to blame. Natural language is frequently used because there is no real alternative. Although many formal methods exist, their use in large-scale projects is virtually untested, and thus designers and engineers are justifiably reluctant to use them. Of the formal methods that do exist, none are capable of expressing all the six types of requirement outlined above. In addition, there are areas of requirements which are currently inexpressible using any formal language; safety is an obvious example. Finally, there are few, if any, formal methods for requirements analysis which are accessible to customers and users. This illustrates one of the cruellest problems of requirements analysis – the needs for precision of specification imply the use of formal notations, yet the need for clarity and intelligibility mitigate against such techniques. We return to this problem in Section 16.2.

Ideally, requirements should not make a distinction between hardware and software, though it is usually the case that hardware design is carried out before the requirements are fully analysed. This will quite often place severe restrictions upon the implementors, since they must develop software that must be executable on the hardware. This could lead to the disastrous result of designing hardware that is simply incapable of supporting the required functionality. Pragmatically, requirements rarely take adequate cognizance of this class of constraint.

16.1.5 Chapter summary

Section 16.2 describes the problems that are frequently encountered during requirements analysis. These fall neatly into two sub-sections: the essence and the accidents. The essence describes those problems that are unavoidable because they arise as a direct result of the analysis process; the accidents describes those problems that are, or may be, encountered as a result of the approach that is adopted in carrying out requirements analysis.

Since such problems occur, it is important to realize how to distinguish between 'good' and 'bad' requirements specifications. Section 16.3 gives a relatively detailed description of what information should be present in a requirements specification, and why such information should be included, and briefly indicates a number of desirable properties that good specifications should satisfy.

Section 16.4 outlines current attempts to solve the problems, and indicates why such attempts have not been entirely successful. The attemps also fall into two sub-sections: the general and the specific. In the former, a number of different approaches are described, while the latter evaluates a number of specific tools (and techniques) that have been suggested as suitable for use in requirements analysis.

To bring the chapter to a close, and recapitulate the most important factors which influence the success of requirements analysis, Section 16.5 draws a few conclusions, and provides some general comments on requirements analysis.

16.2 Problems with requirements

As is the case with most problems of software engineering, the problems of requirements engineering have no panacea. Solutions will be developed gradually, as tools, methods, and techniques are steadily improved. But why should this be the case? Why is there no simple solution?

Following Brooks (1987), we can divide the problems of requirements into two categories: the essence and the accidents. Problems that are inherent in requirements and will always occur during requirements analysis are referred to as the 'essence'. Since these 'essential' problems are insoluble, (simple) solutions to them will not be found, although it is possible to develop techniques which will ameliorate this class of problems, as we shall see later. Problems that are not inherent in requirements, but arise through the application of a particular approach, are collectively referred to as the 'accidents'. While it is the case that greater improvements will be made in requirements engineering by addressing the essence rather than the accidents,

progress is more likely to be made on the essence only after the accidents have been removed, or reduced.

16.2.1 The essence

The essential problems of requirements analysis derive from two fundamental sources. First, the requirements are the interface between the customer/user and the analyst, and as such they must model (at least part of) the real world. Thus, they must be abstract representations of the real world through which we can describe and reason about a system and its interactions. Problems arising here have a philosophical basis, and include a number of issues concerning the language for expressing the requirements, completeness, and validation. Second, the requirements must be capable of describing large and complex systems. The problems encountered as a result of this include many issues of which the most significant are size, complexity and maintainability.

16.2.1.1 Languages for requirements analysis

The fact that the requirements are the interface between the customer/user and the analyst imposes severe demands upon the language that is used to express the requirements. Ideally, we would use languages which had a single interpretation, i.e. the language would be 'isomorphic with' the real world; each part (e.g. word) of the language would refer to only a single 'thing' in the real world. Such languages would allow the analyst to write system descriptions that would be entirely unambiguous, and which could be only correctly understood by both the customer/user and the designer/analyst. Furthermore, such languages would allow us to reason about the real world directly since all concepts (things, entities, etc) in the real world would be directly mapped onto specific parts of the language.

However, philosophers have for many years addressed the problem of developing methods of rational analysis which could allow a person to reason about the world directly. The problems they faced can be demonstrated by Kant's distinction between analytic and synthetic reasoning. In analytical reasoning any proposition, i.e. any statement which can be reduced to either true or false, can be evaluated purely within some logical framework. Conversely, in synthetic reasoning a proposition can be judged to be true or false only by making an observation of the real world. Such observations are subjective, i.e. different individuals may form different conclusions, and thus we cannot know, that is to say, give an absolute truth value to, any statements concerning the real world.

As an example, given a reasonable choice of a logical system including the symbols '2', '4', '+', and '=', the statement '$2 + 2 = 4$' can be found to be true without looking at the real world. But, the statement 'the Prime Minister is Winston Churchill' can be judged only by finding out who the Prime Minister actually is. Furthermore, the truth of synthetic statements is also dependent upon the statement's time and context. The statement concerning the Prime Minister, for example, was true for the UK in 1949, but has never been, and is unlikely to be, true for France.

This time aspect of synthetic statements suggests the inclusion of environment models in the requirements specification. Since it is the nature of environments to change with time, the validity of any requirements will be time-dependent. Any change in the environment will necessitate re-validation of the requirements. However, if we capture the environment in the requirements, then re-validation will be simpler because we can analyse the impact of this change in the environment on the requirements. In addition, if the change in the environment is reflected in an environment model, then the re-validation can be carried out in a much more controlled manner.

As we have seen above, single interpretation languages cannot exist, and languages that we employ to describe system requirements will thus use a representation of the real world. This representation should contain all the necessary and relevant real world information so that a language based upon it would allow the unique description of a system and its environment, and, in addition, would have a fixed and well-defined semantics. Through the use of the language, the analyst may write and then carry out analytical reasoning on the requirements. An example of such languages is formal languages. However, to understand and interpret the requirements and their relationship with the real world, we must relate the representation to the real world, i.e. we must indicate which features of the real world are captured in the representation. This, of course, requires observations of the real world. Thus, in attempting to understand and relate the representation and therefore the language to the real world, we must use synthetic reasoning.

An example may help to clarify this. Formal languages are usually based upon one of a number of representations, for example, set theory or first-order predicate calculus. Each language has a semantics which defines how we should interpret the notation and syntax of the language in terms of the underlying representation. Reasoning within the domain of the formal language is therefore analytical. However, in order to relate the language to the real world, a relationship between the formal notation and the real world must be established, i.e. we need to indicate what the terms in the formal language relate or refer to. This naturally requires an observation of the real world, and according to Kant, we again find that we are reduced to synthetic reasoning.

The essential problem that must be faced here is how to select an appropriate representation for a formal language in order to reduce the subjective nature of its interpretation. We need to force synthetic reasoning to be less subjective to bring the statement of requirements into an (almost) analytical framework. If we wish to use formal languages then the problem of misinterpretation must be reduced. How we might achieve this, perhaps by narrowing the 'bandwidth of the observations' that we must make to a minimum, and thereby controlling the degree of misinterpretation, will be discussed later.

16.2.1.2 Completeness

Completeness of a requirements specification demands that there are no 'gaps' in the requirements, i.e. that the requirements specification describes all, and only, the relevant facets of the desired system. The problem that must be faced is that establishing an answer to the question 'Are these requirements complete?' is entirely synthetic, and consequently subjective. Some of the more significant ramifications of this are discussed here.

First, since completeness is subjective, there can be no fixed limits imposed upon the extent of a particular system and thus there is no predetermined finish to the elicitation or specification of requirements. An answer to the above question can therefore always be 'Not yet'. Second, only the customer/user may judge the completeness of the requirements, and it is unfortunately the case that he or she is frequently unaware of *precisely* what he or she wants, outside major objectives and functionality. This can be because of a lack of understanding of computers and their capabilities. It can also be due to a lack of understanding of the 'problem' domain, or, more likely, a mistaken belief as to what is understood about the problem domain by the analyst/designer. Finally, we cannot describe processes or methods which, if followed carefully, guarantee that sufficient checks for completeness have been carried out. Thus the evaluation of completeness involves simply reading the requirements and making a judgement.

What we must attempt to do, if we are to have any degree of confidence in the completeness of the requirements, is ensure that the customer/user interprets the requirements as the analyst intends. Numerous techniques exist for improving the customer's understanding of the requirements, and a number of the more important of these are discussed in Section 16.4.

16.2.1.3 Validation

Validation is the process by which the customer must indicate the extent to which the requirements reflect his or her ideas. It is the process by which the customer ensures that the requirements describe the 'right' system. The problem here is that since validation, like completeness, is synthetic, its successfulness is entirely dependent upon the validator. If he or she does not interpret the requirements correctly, then it is quite possible that the validity of the requirements will be incorrectly judged, with the result that the final system will not be satisfactory. The problem is one of ensuring that the requirements are interpreted correctly.

As with completeness, we must develop techniques that will help the customer/user understand the requirements. Here the problem is simpler because we do not need to judge what is absent, but the correctness of what is present. Consequently, controlled processes may be used to ensure that at least all aspects of the requirements are validated. For example, it is possible to 'prove' the validity of the requirements by considering each requirement in relation to the real world and to the other requirements. Further examples of techniques for facilitating validation are discussed later.

One particularly interesting approach to validation is the use of an environmental model. By developing an environment model which captures all the relevant aspects of the application domain, we may be able to validate the requirements against the model rather than the real world. This would be useful because validation would then become more analytical, and less subjective. However, it is important to ensure that the model is itself validated and checked for consistency. Note that we have improved the validation situation, not simply moved the problem elsewhere, if the environment model can be re-used.

16.2.1.4 Size and complexity

If systems are large and complex, then the requirements are likely to reflect this; larger and more complex systems will demand larger and more complex requirements. Note, however, that this is not necessarily always the case. Some systems may be relatively easy to specify but hard to implement, and others may be easy to implement, but harder to specify.

As computer technology improves, and the capabilities of systems increases, then the demands that customers place on technology will also increase. Once we have developed tools and techniques for dealing with today's size and complexity problems, then the limit on size and complexity will be higher. Consequently, as technology improves there will always be systems that are larger and more complex than we can adequately deal with.

What we must aim to do is to develop tools for aiding the development and management of large and complex system requirements. Again, examples of such tools may be found in Section 16.4.

16.2.2 Accidents

The accidental problems of requirements stem from the language issues described in the essence. We use languages, based upon some representation of the real world, to describe and reason about system requirements, and it is the choice of representation (and language) that causes the following accidental problems.

16.2.2.1 Problems of expressing requirements

As seen in Section 16.2.1.1, one of the essential problems of requirements analysis is the selection or design of an appropriate representation for modelling the requirements, and a suitable language for describing the properties of systems. If the chosen representation or language is unsuitable, then (accidental) problems of expression will be encountered. For example, if we use set theory as our representation, then modelling time is exceedingly difficult (although it can be achieved), but if use is made of temporal logic, then the expression of (relative) time is much simpler.

Of the many different types of requirement: functional, functional constraints, design constraints, environment models, data and communication protocols and project management information, there exist tools and techniques for describing only the functional and data and communication protocol requirements. For the other types of requirement, there are few useful, elegant, or even satisfactory formal representations, and thus the representations, and languages, that are currently used to express such requirements cause a number of problems.

As an example, consider safety. Safety requirements, like some of the other functional constraints, are negative requirements. Rather than describing what should happen, they describe what should not happen. Since we do not have representations which are capable of modelling negative requirements, expressing safety policies for systems is currently onerous. The tendency is to describe the mechanisms for achieving or implementing the negative requirements, rather than the requirements themselves. Consequently, negative requirements are much harder to validate, and are not easily tested for completeness. In the case of safety requirements, this inadequacy of representation has led to many hazardous systems (Leveson, 1986).

There are two major hurdles to overcome. First, new and better formalisms for describing system requirements must be developed, and second, analysts, designers, and engineers must be persuaded to use them. The former problem is perhaps the most pressing, and is already being addressed by a number of research organizations. (Examples of such research are given in Section 16.4.2.)

The latter problem is one of attitude. One of the reasons natural language is so often used is that the existing formalisms for expressing the more subtle features of computer systems are in general too complex, and the demands for clarity and understandability of requirements means that such formalisms are rarely used. Of the developing formalisms, industrial experience with them is limited, and analysts, designers, and engineers are therefore unlikely to use them. This contrasts with some of the less formal methods which are sometimes used to express the functional requirements. These are usually quite simple and easy to understand and over a number of years, confidence, experience and expertise with them has grown. Consequently, there are several (semi-formal) methods which are used with the functional aspects of the system, but there are very few that are used with the non-functional aspects. However, it is important to note that there are already industry-linked research projects which are addressing this issue.

16.2.2.2 Verification

Verification is the process by which a system description at one level of abstraction is checked to ensure that it is consistent with another; for example, the design specification should be consistent with the requirements specification, and the imple-

mentation should be consistent with the design specification. Thus, verification is a purely analytical process. No observations of the real world are required to verify the consistency between two abstract descriptions of the system.

The accidental problem encountered during verification is that to verify one description with respect to another frequently requires each description to be interpreted before verification may take place. The descriptions are interpreted to bring them into a common semantic domain in which they can be compared. Clearly, if specifications are interpreted before verification, then there is the possibility that inconsistent specifications will be misinterpreted, and then verified as consistent.

Ideally, the languages used to write the various system descriptions would have direct mappings between them, so that one level of abstraction can be directly verified with respect to another. (Here, of course, there must be aspects of the less abstract descriptions which are not directly related to aspects of the more abstract descriptions, otherwise progress will not have been made in moving from one description to another.) The languages that are currently used typically do not have such direct mappings between them. For example, programming languages used to implement most large systems have control flow statements: loops, GOTOs, exceptions, and so on, whereas specification languages do not in general have such control statements.

However, since verification is (essentially) analytical, there is the possibility that mechanized verification techniques may be developed. By reducing verification to a number of analytical rules, and then automating the process on computer, greater confidence in the results of verification can be achieved, and the drudgery involved in carrying it out will be reduced. Such a solution clearly demands the use of more formal languages, and certain aspects of the requirements which we cannot yet describe formally cannot be verified in this manner.

16.2.2.3 Consistency

Establishing the consistency of a requirements document involves reviewing each statement to ensure that there are no statements with which any given statement is in conflict. Checking consistency, like verification, is a purely analytical process. Its successfulness depends on the language that is used to express the requirements, and while the representation and description of requirements remain a problem, checking consistency will also be problematical.

For example, consider again safety requirements. Since we lack formalisms for describing safety, ensuring that the safety requirements for a system are not in conflict with other requirements is difficult because there is no simple way of analysing the impact of what are essentially second-order requirements on the functional, first-order requirements. (Functional requirements are first order because they describe the behavioural properties of the system, whereas safety requirements, and some other functional constraints are second order, because they describe some required properties of the behavioural properties.)

Establishing analytical consistency of the functional requirements, although often hampered by the use of unsuitable languages and the size and complexity of many requirements specifications, is a mechanical task, and examples of systems which carry out consistency checks on requirements are already in existence (see Section 16.4). What is now needed is representations of the non-functional requirements which will allow these mechanical techniques to be used with the non-functional requirements.

16.2.2.4 Modifiability

Modifiability of requirements specifications demands that it is possible to change the requirements in a careful and controlled manner. It is usually needed because requirements are rarely captured in 'one sitting', and are frequently changed and revised, even after design and some coding may have taken place.

Problems that can be encountered here concern how consistency and correctness are maintained during the modifications. It would be unfortunate to have to re-validate all the requirements, or to re-check them for internal consistency, whenever a change, however small, is made. Thus, modifiability usually requires that some suitable structure is imposed upon the requirements so that the effects of any changes are confined to a limited portion of the requirements.

16.2.2.5 Coda

The aim of this section is not to depress readers and to make them think that production of requirements is impossible, or futile. It is rather to make clear the fundamental and pragmatic limitations of requirements analysis. The benefit of this discussion is that it should help the reader to be more effective in critically appraising requirements specifications and requirements analysis methods.

16.3 Requirements specifications

In the introduction, a brief indication of the contents of a requirements specification was given. Here, this description is expanded upon and a much fuller account of the sort of information that one would expect to find in a good requirements specification is given. In addition, a number of desirable properties are described that one would expect good requirements specifications to satisfy.

16.3.1 Contents of a requirements specification

Although the exact contents of a requirements specification will vary from situation to situation, there are essentially seven categories of information that are present in most requirements specifications, as shown in *Figure 16.1*. For each category we will consider what information it should include, why this information is needed, and how this information is related to the requirements in the other categories.

16.3.1.1 Functionality

All computer systems have some functionality that provides a number of services required by the customers and users, and it is the functional requirements that should accurately describe all aspects of this functionality. These requirements identify, from the customer's or user's point of view, the functional behaviour of the required system under all circumstances. The functional requirements therefore include descriptions of procedures for starting up and closing down the system, self-test procedures, operation under normal conditions, operation under abnormal conditions, procedures for controlling the mode of operation, recovery procedures, and procedures for continuing under reduced functionality. Such detail must be provided not only at the level of user/customer services, but at all levels of system description, so that the requirements explain not only what each function does, but also how these functions fit together. This usually requires that the relationship between functions, and the dependencies (control and data) that exist between them are also described.

The functional requirements, often (incorrectly) regarded as the most significant aspect of any requirements specification, are related to virtually all other requirements in one of two ways.

Figure 16.1 Contents of a requirements specification

The functionality that the system is to support must satisfy the original system objectives. The services that the functionality provides must operate within limits imposed by the functional constraints, and will consume and produce data. This data will be given to or taken from the environment. Thus the functional requirements are directly related to the system objectives, the environment description, the functional constraints and the data and communication protocols.

During system design, implementation, and testing, the design constraints and project management requirements will affect how the system is developed, but will not alter the functionality, and thus the functional requirements are only weakly related to these requirements.

16.3.1.2 Environment description and system objectives

The system objectives describe, at a reasonably abstract level, the fundamental reasons behind the desire for a computer system. An abstract example of a system objective might be 'To allow a fighter plane to enter enemy territory, destroy its target, and return safely'. Objectives can also be more specific and computer-oriented than this suggests, for example, 'To support low-level navigation over hostile territory'.

The environment description captures all relevant information concerning the environment in which the system is to operate and the application domain. This might include information such as: the physical attributes of the environment – e.g. size, shape, locality; organizational attributes – e.g. office application, military application; models of potential users; any safety or security hazards that may arise from the environment; changes in the environment that will impinge upon system operation; and so forth. An exhaustive list is difficult to provide because the exact content of this description is clearly dependent upon the application and the environment.

The environment description and system objectives have been considered together, because their reasons for inclusion in the requirements specification and their relationship with other requirements are similar. Both provide useful contextual information. For example, in cases where there is some confusion as to the meaning or interpretation of some requirements, the system objectives and environment model can be used to resolve the confusion. Furthermore, analysts, designers, and engineers will be better equipped to understand the significance of some requirements, for example, the functional or design constraints, if they are aware of why such requirements have been stipulated, and again it is the environment description and system objectives that provide such explanation.

In addition, since the system will communicate with the environment, it is useful to include in the requirements a description of that environment. Not only does this give a framework for carrying out analysis of any system interactions, but it also provides a mechanism for specifying a boundary to the requirements.

16.3.1.3 Project management

These requirements are included to ensure that the system development is carried out in a careful and controlled manner, and that the delivered system satisfies the customers/users in all respects. There are two major issues covered by project management: the development life cycle, and system delivery and installation. The life-cycle requirements describe how system development will proceed, and include information on topics such as system documentation standards, procedures for module testing and integration, procedures for controlling change, and assumptions/expected changes. System delivery and installation requirements are concerned with all processes that take place outside the scope of system development and

they include such things as deliverables, deadlines, acceptance criteria, training, manuals, support and maintenance.

In general, the project management requirements are largely orthogonal to the rest of the requirements, because although they guide system development and delivery, they have no direct impact upon the system itself; they do not in any way change the system described by the other requirements. However, since it is here that such things as acceptance criteria are defined, then clearly there must be some relationship between these and the other requirements. The properties described in the other requirements may be used as a measure of the acceptability of the system.

16.3.1.4 Functional constraints

In addition to providing the required functionality, any implemented system must operate within a number of constraints. For example, a computer system which provides information concerning the state of some system, e.g. a navigation system which presents information on aircraft position, must be able to evaluate the state in less time than it takes for the state to change significantly; otherwise the information that the computer provides will be of little use. Such functional constraints typically include performance, efficiency, safety, security, reliability, quality and dependability.

The functional constraints tend to be second order in nature. They describe the necessary properties of the system behaviour described in the functional requirements. The relationship between system functionality and the functional constraints can be exceedingly subtle, and it is not always clear whether a specific requirement is a functional requirement or a functional constraint. A reason for this is that quite abstract terms, for example security, are often used as functional constraints. Security embodies both explicit functionality such as auditing and authentication; it also embodies constraints such as restrictions on information flow in a system.

The functional requirements describe the behaviour of the system while the functional constraints typically provide information concerning the general structure of system operation. The functional requirements describe the possible operations, whereas the functional constraints would indicate when and how such operations may be carried out. For example, the functional requirements for a secure data processing system might describe how file access is achieved, but the functional constraints would indicate whether a particular file access is permitted.

16.3.1.5 Design constraints

It will often be the case that the customer/user wants a system which not only provides the required functionality, but also satisfies a number of (almost) arbitrary conditions. These usually include, *inter alia*, hardware and software standards, particular libraries and operating systems that must be used, and compatibility issues.

These requirements do not impinge upon other requirements, but on the design and development of the system from the requirements. For example, if a particular hardware interface is specified, e.g. the system must communicate through a particular bus, then this may alter the design and implementation, but will not alter the functionality of the interface, nor the functional constraints that have been imposed upon it.

A common failing on the part of customers is to specify too many design constraints. It is important to distinguish those design constraints which are essential, e.g. use of particular protocols for interoperability, from those which are over-specification, e.g. requests for the use of 'expert systems'. It is also worth noting that over-specification often reflects genuine non-functional requirements which the customer does not know how to articulate. For example, the insistence on the use of assembler is typically a substitute for constraints on performance or efficiency. Thus care is needed in analysing design constraints to see if they are essential, unnecessary, or necessary but in the wrong form.

16.3.1.3 Data and communication protocols

The data and communication protocol requirements describe all aspects of data flow between the functional components of the system, and between the system and its environment. This includes inputs, outputs, the relationships between them, and the interface and communication protocols.

The requirements described here relate the environment description, i.e. the real world, to the functional requirements, i.e. the system functionality. The data describes the information that the system uses and delivers, and this is produced and consumed by the environment respectively. The communication protocols describe how this flow of information between system and environment should take place.

16.3.2 Desirable properties of a requirements specification

Given that there are a number of problems with the production of requirements specifications, how can we be sure that we are developing good requirements specifications? From these discussions, it should be clear that there can be no simple method which will effectively characterize requirements, because if there were, many of the problems that have been described would simply disappear. However, it is possible to give a selection of properties that all good requirements specifications should satisfy, and to demonstrate that a given specification satisfies these properties by the application of one or more of the methods/approaches described in the next section.

For each property, an explanation of the property is given, together with an indication of which general approaches are particularly useful in judging whether a given specification satisfies a specific property.

1. *Unambiguous*. All specifications should ideally have only a single interpretation. We have seen that this is difficult to achieve, even through the application of formal methods, but the general approaches described in Sections 16.4.1.2–16.4.1.4 on rapid prototyping, animation, and reviews are particularly useful.
2. *Complete*. The requirements specification should describe every significant and relevant aspect of the system, and should include details concerning all the information described above. The subjective nature of completeness makes it impossible to guarantee, but the use of knowledge-based approaches (Section 16.4.1.6), rapid prototyping, animation, and reviews are useful.
3. *Consistent*. Consistency demands that there are no contradictory statements within the requirements specification. Consistency is often regarded as a purely analytical process which can be automated, but clearly the level of automation will depend upon the type of requirement and the language used to articulate that requirement.
4. *Verifiable*. Once a system has been designed and implemented, it must be possible to verify that the system design or implementation satisfies the original requirements. This typically demands the use of more formal methods, and some proof of system properties (Section 16.4.1.5) may be helpful.
5. *Validatable*. The customer/user should be able to read and understand the requirements specification, and then indicate the degree to which the requirements reflect his or her ideas.

This usually requires the use of less formal methods, which conflicts with the demands of some other properties. Approaches like rapid prototyping and animation are useful if formal methods are used, and reviews can be applied when less formal methods are used.

6. *Modifiable*. Since requirements are frequently subject to change, all requirements specifications must allow alterations to be made easily, without necessitating alterations to be made to the whole specification. This usually requires some structure to be imposed upon the specification, and thus separation of concerns (Section 16.4.1.7) is useful here.
7. *Understandable*. Customers, users, analysts, designers, and engineers must be able to read and understand the requirements. Because of their differing backgrounds, each might prefer a different representation of the requirements to be used. Again, separation of concerns may be of use.
8. *Testable*. If the requirements are to be used as a baseline against which the implementation is tested, then the requirements must be sufficiently quantitative so that testing may take place. From the selection of approaches described in Section 16.4, reviews may be the only way that the testability of the requirements may be judged.
9. *Traceable*. The requirements should allow referencing between aspects of the design or implementation and aspects of the requirements. The effects of modifications to requirements, design or implementation can then be controlled. Pragmatically this often means that individual 'requirements statements' are given a unique (numeric) reference.

Having set out desirable properties of a requirements specification we can now consider available requirements analysis techniques, and see to what extent they help in achieving these properties.

16.4 Solutions and approaches

Attempts to solve, or at least alleviate, the essential and accidental problems of requirements engineering can be divided into two categories: general and specific. In the former, the solutions described are not linked with any particular language or method; they are not limited to any particular application domain, and they are usually driven from a desire to alleviate one or more of the essential problems. Conversely, the specific solutions are simply various tools/systems/techniques that either have been, or are in the process of being, developed.

16.4.1 General solutions

Seven general solutions are discussed. Each solution is described and evaluated using three criteria: motivation, method and value. The motivation covers the reason for using the approach – this is usually a description of what problem the solution attempts to solve. What the solution involves, how it works, and how it is used constitute the method, and the value covers the advantages of using the approach and the problems that arise either during its application or as a result of its use.

16.4.1.1 Multiple techniques

It is clear that no tools or techniques exist now or in the foreseeable future which are capable of dealing satisfactorily with all facets of requirements. However, it is also clear that there are a number of tools and techniques which are capable of dealing effectively with part of the problem. Most of these are aimed at particular difficulties of requirements analysis, and most have specific advantages. Since not all these tools and techniques solve the same problems nor have the same deficiencies, it would seem sensible therefore to adopt an eclectic approach to requirements specification and combine a number of different techniques in the hope that we can solve a number of different problems, and that the deficiencies of the methods will 'cancel out'.

In this way, no new techniques need be defined, and one can simply apply the various techniques that one wishes to use, and then combine the results. Thus both formal and informal methods can be used where appropriate. In addition, viewing the requirements through a number of different presentations should ideally improve the confidence that the customer and contractor have in them. However, if *n* methods are used, then requirements analysis may need to be carried out *n* times, although the intention is that the methods would be applied to different aspects of the requirements, so the amount of effort should be much less, in practice.

If the different methods are highly incompatible, and the results they produce are difficult to relate, then using a number of methods may confuse rather than clarify. For example, attempting to establish the consistency between a number of different formal representations of the same system is likely to be time-consuming and unnecessary. The methods that are used must be selected with care to ensure that they complement each other. In particular they should all relate to some common framework, for example, a model of the system as a network of communicating processes, so that individual requirements statements can be related to one another.

16.4.1.2 Rapid prototyping

Rapid prototyping addresses two major problems of the essence: the difficulties involved in requirements validation, and the need for representations of the requirements that are understandable by a number of different readers. It involves developing an executable version of the functional and interface aspects of the system, usually in some language that will allow the prototype to be developed easily but will not have the performance characteristics of the implementation. So, the production of a prototype, or even a number of prototypes, that exhibit at least part of the functionality of the desired system simplifies validation, and allows the customer to understand the ramifications of the interactions between the requirements. In addition, since the customer may review the prototype rather than read the requirements, the requirements can be written in languages that suit the analyst and not the customer. Thus the problems of both validation and readers of different backgrounds can be reduced.

There are also other advantages to the production of prototypes. Since the customer has something that he or she can 'play with', it is much easier to see the progress that is being made. One of the problems inherent in software engineering is that there is little evidence of how things are going until virtually the end of the project. From the customer's point of view this can be a little unnerving; money is being spent and there seems to be little return. But, by providing the customer with a prototype, he or she can see at a relatively early stage how the development is proceeding.

It was suggested earlier that customers are often unaware of exactly what they want – they may be aware that a particular problem needs an automated solution, or that a system with various objectives must be developed, but the details of the system requirements may be unclear. By presenting customers with a prototype, they can clarify their ideas, and identify exactly what it is that they need. Furthermore, if there are visible gaps or deficiencies in the prototype, then the customer may be prompted to volunteer more information. The prototype may thus be used to aid in ensuring the completeness of the requirements.

It is to be expected that there are also disadvantages to using prototypes. Since a prototype is an implementation of the functional aspects of a computer system, then to implement the prototype, a certain amount of software design and coding must take place. If the system is large and complex, this is likely to take a great deal of effort. There are even some systems for which the production of a prototype is completely infeasible or at least exceedingly difficult, for example, embedded systems. These do not have user interfaces through which the functionality of the system may be tested, and they often involve control systems. To put a prototype control system in control of, say, a nuclear power station could prove to be dangerous!

Since the prototype may implement only part of the requirements, then clearly those aspects of the requirements that have not been included in the prototype cannot be validated through its use. Consequently, validating the prototype will validate only part of the requirements. As the languages and systems used to implement the prototype may not be the same as those used to implement the 'real system', then any 'non-functional' requirements cannot be validated through the prototype.

On a more theoretical level, validation through the evaluation of a prototype is not sufficient to guarantee the validity of the requirements for two reasons. First, it is unlikely that the customer will be able to carry out a systematic test of the prototype, i.e. test the prototype with all possible combinations of input values, and consequently there will be aspects of the prototype and thus the requirements that will not have been validated. Second, since the production of the prototype will involve interpretation of the requirements and a number of design decisions to be made, then validity of the prototype will not guarantee validity of the requirements, because in validating the prototype, the customer is validating the requirements *combined with the extra information needed to produce the prototype*. Unless the same interpretations and design decisions are made when the system is implemented, the customer's satisfaction with the prototype will not ensure that he or she is satisfied with the final system. This is even the case if the prototype is automatically produced from the requirements; unless the rules used to produce the prototype are also used to develop the system, then the system may not be consistent with the prototype. Control must be exercised over the development of the prototype and system so that validity of the prototype is necessary and sufficient to assume validity of the requirements.

As a final comment on prototypes, it is clear that although there are a number of significant advantages to the development of system prototypes, great care must be exercised during the production of the prototype and the system to ensure that they are consistent. Ideally, a simple rule by which validity of the prototype implies validity of the requirements is required.

16.4.1.3 Animation

Animation of requirements specifications is similar to rapid prototyping in that it addresses the same problems, but it differs from it in that instead of developing a prototype from the specifications, the specifications are simply 'executed'. This demands that either the requirements are written in an executable specification language, or that an animator exists which is capable of animating the language used to describe the requirements. Furthermore, animation differs from prototyping in another important respect. A prototype is an implementation, and thus describes many details concerning *how* the required system functionality is achieved, including algorithms, interface designs and so forth. Conversely, an animation, since it is so directly derived from the requirements, will not include such details. Additionally, animation may be weaker than prototyping in the sense that it may only demonstrate certain facets of the requirements, for example information flow through the system rather than functionality.

The strength of the animation can vary significantly. If the requirements are relatively abstract, then the animation will reflect this, and will be quite weak, and if the requirements are more detailed, then the animation will be more complex.

The animated specifications may be used in a similar manner to the way in which prototypes are used, but they are likely to suffer from a number of processing deficiencies because the specifications will describe *what* the system should do, and not *how* the system should do it. For example, functionality which uses complex algorithms or requires large amounts of computation will almost certainly demand that the animator must supply extra information which describes how particular results are achieved. Even so, there is less interpretation of the requirements and fewer design decisions to be made, and consequently the final system is more likely to be consistent with an animation than with a prototype.

However, there are also problems unique to specification animation. Animations can, of course, be carried out only on the more formal notations for expressing requirements. In many of these extra information must be added to the specification for it to be successfully animated, and, like rapid prototyping, if this extra information is not also used in the development of the system, then the customer's satisfaction with the animation will not necessarily guarantee his or her satisfaction with the final system. Furthermore, the development of animations might lead to the adoption of formalisms which are too 'operationally oriented', or even directly executable and thus less applicable to requirements specification and more applicable to design.

16.4.1.4 Reviews

Reviews are perhaps the simplest of the general approaches that one may use in addressing the problems of requirements. A review is simply a reading of the requirements. It may be carried out by any of the users of the requirements – the customer, the analyst, the designer, the engineer or a member of the project management team. In addition, a review can address any of the problems that are a result of requirements analysis: validation, consistency, completeness, and so forth. However, because a review is primarily a matter of reading the requirements, it does not enforce any great discipline, rigour or control and if the results of the review are to be useful, then the review must be completed with extreme care.

Since the confidence in the results of the review can be relatively small, a number of techniques have been defined to improve this situation (Weinberg and Freedman, 1984; Fagan, 1976). Ensuring that a number of different people of different backgrounds carry out the review, or demanding that the requirements are presented to the reviewer(s) in a number of different ways, are two simple techniques which will greatly improve the degree to which we can rely upon the results of the review.

However, there are many disadvantages to using reviews. Since a review must be carried out by hand, it will be very time-consuming, especially for large projects. An analysis of the interplay between requirements will be very hard, and will require the reviewer to 'carry around in his head' much of the requirements. These difficulties put a great deal of pressure on the reviewer, and consequently will increase his or her capacity to make errors.

In conclusion, although it is essential to carry out reviews of the requirements because human judgement is required to address synthetic issues such as completeness, they should not be the only method that is used to verify and validate the requirements. Of course, it is good practice for the results of other techniques, for example animation, to be the subject of reviews.

16.4.1.5 Proof of system properties

The increasing use of formal methods, and a belief that they provide 'the answer' to the problems of software engineering, has led to demands for proofs that systems will operate correctly, that they will be secure and safe, or that they will satisfy certain properties. In requirements, therefore, it would seem appropriate to prove that the requirements specification is valid, complete, correct and consistent. A formal development of a system from such requirements would then guarantee that the system would satisfy the customer. Thus, at least in theory, through the use of formal proof and formal development we may address many, perhaps even all, of the problems described in Section 16.2.

To carry out proof of system properties one needs to describe the requirements using some appropriate formalism, describe the system property that we hope the requirements will satisfy, and show that the requirements do indeed satisfy the property. For large sets of requirements, the complexity of these tasks is prohibitively high, which is just one of the reasons why proofs are rarely used outside academia, and small systems.

Such formal development has a price. Certain proofs are impossible. For example, validity and completeness are subjective issues and cannot be proven, and proofs, even of purely analytical concepts such as consistency, are often exceedingly difficult. For even the smallest of systems, complete proofs of just a few properties are computationally very expensive. Proofs have a way of 'exponentially exploding' so that what at first sight might appear a relatively simple proof may in fact require many proofs. Even if proof of a number of properties of requirements can successfully be carried out, it is then essential that the software development is completely formal, if the benefits of these proofs are not to be lost.

There are also a number of philosophical difficulties. The representation of the property to be proven in some formalism must be validated in much the same way as the requirements. If it is not, then there is no guarantee that the right proof is being carried out, and simply carrying out a number of inconsequential proofs is likely to reduce rather than improve the quality of software development.

If a proof fails, establishing exactly what is at fault will not be easy. While it is more likely that the requirements are at fault, it is also possible that the formalization of the property to be proven was incorrect, or that the proof itself was in error, or that the property chosen for proof is in fact neither a desirable nor a realizable property of the requirements specification. Although such considerations seem to approach proof over-cautiously, they are nevertheless things of which the analyst must be aware if he or she is to carry out proofs successfully.

Since proofs can be carried out only within a formal framework, the requirements specification must be written using some formalism, and since we cannot prove validity or completeness analytically and customers are rarely trained in formal notations, carrying out such tasks is made more difficult. If the customer is to validate or check the completeness of such requirements, then other techniques and methods described here, such as animation or prototyping, must be used. The only slight comfort is that animation or prototyping is much easier from a formal notation.

16.4.1.6 Knowledge-based approaches

To address the problems of synthetic reasoning and therefore of validation and completeness, use may be made of knowledge-based techniques. By modelling the environment in which the system is to operate eventually, the hope is that the 'real world' can be brought within the context of a formal framework. Then, analytical reasoning may be carried out upon the (representation of the) real world. Furthermore, since the knowledge base captures information concerning the application domain, it may also be used to force a particular, and, one hopes, unique, interpretation of the requirements.

Exactly how the model of the environment is constructed and stored in the knowledge base, how it is accessed, and how it is used, are still matters of research. One particularly interesting use of the model would be to 'bootstrap' formal languages. The model, which is a formal representation of some aspects of the real world, can be used by a formalism *as* the real world. The formal requirements specification would then be interpreted according to it, and pseudosynthetic reasoning would be carried out using it. The model would effectively be a static and pre-defined interface between formalisms and reality.

There appear to be two fundamental disadvantages of using a knowledge base containing a model. First, the development of a good model of the real world is very time-consuming, because, apart from the fact that its construction is hard, in order to have any real degree of confidence in the model it will need to be used and tested to ensure that it encapsulates the right information. Second, the development of a model will suffer from exactly the same problems as the development of a requirements specification. How can we be sure that it is consistent with the real world? Does it contain only relevant aspects of the real world? Does it say everything about the real world that it ought to, and so on? Although such issues must be addressed, it is hoped that it would be the case that models would need to be constructed for application domains only once, and then re-used. In addition, validating and verifying the model should be simpler than validating and verifying the requirements because the real world exists, and thus there is something against which we may judge the quality and adequacy of the model.

16.4.1.7 Separation of concerns

This deals with the 'different readers' problem. It is usually the case that different readers need to read only particular aspects of the requirements. To avoid forcing all readers to digest all of the requirements, it would seem sensible to partition the requirements into a number of different areas. Then, analysts will read only those sections containing the information in which they are interested, the engineers would read only the sections in which they were interested, and so on.

Eclecticism may be combined with separation of concerns, so that both formal and informal methods can be used where appropriate. Unfortunately, the customer will have to read most, if not all, of the requirements document to validate it and check if for completeness, and ensure that it is a suitable basis for contractual agreements. Consequently, any sections that might be read by the customer may need to be expressed in informal languages, and thus use of separation of concerns may be limited.

Finding a suitable division of the requirements, other than some very coarse categorization (for example, the categorization described in Section 16.1), is likely to be difficult because of the complex relationships between the various requirements. Making such a basic breakdown of the requirements is still probably useful, but it will not allow the analyst to produce formal requirements which the customer will not need to read, unless we are prepared to allow some duplication of information.

16.4.2 Current methods and tools

The number of different tools, techniques, and methods to aid in the production of requirements that are either already developed or are under development is surprisingly high. There are also methods which are simply corruptions of tools and tech-

niques that were developed to aid software design and development but have found applications in requirements analysis. The following list of methods is not an exhaustive list of the available methods, and others may be found in the literature (Boehm, 1984; Heitmeyer and McLean, 1983; Pyle, 1983; Roman, 1982; Kerner and Malhotra, 1983).

Generally, the methods have been motivated from the need to 'improve requirements engineering', although some are more specific about the problems that they attempt to solve. We shall consider the tools and techniques from three viewpoints: motivation, method, and value, as we did with the general approaches described above.

16.4.2.1 SREM (Software Requirements Engineering Methodology)

The management and consistency checking of large and complex software requirements was the primary reason for the development of SREM (Bell, Bixler and Dyer, 1977). In addition, it was felt that to be genuinely useful, SREM should have a flexible and natural input so that the analyst can express the requirements using familiar concepts, and that it should allow analysts to be creative while enforcing a degree of discipline to ensure that ambiguity is always reduced and consistency is always increased.

SREM is a tool based upon the requirements engineering and validation system (REVS), which is itself a set of tools for analysing requirements written in the requirements specification language (RSL). It consists of three basic components: a translator for RSL, an abstract system semantic model (ASSM), and a set of automated tools.

RSL, and its graphical counterpart R-Nets, are both based upon a finite state machine (FSM) model. (For a detailed description of automata theory, the reader is referred to Chapter 9.) The standard FSM model has been extended to allow a large FSM to be organized into a collection of smaller FSMs, or units. These units may be thought of as describing all the required responses to a given stimulus. Thus the requirements for a system are expressed as a collection of small FSMs which describe the system requirements in a stimulus–response manner.

RSL is an extensible language based upon just four primitive notions:

1. Elements, which are roughly equivalent to the nouns of natural language in that they encapsulate basic concepts.
2. Relationships, which are binary, non-commutative relations that are similar to natural language transitive verbs.
3. Attributes, which describe important properties of the elements, and can be thought of as adjectives.
4. Structures, which are a one-dimensional representation of the R-Net model that is used to express the requirements.

These four elements cannot be changed, but new elements, relationships, attributes and structures may be added to the requirements and used by any analyst. The translator for RSL simply takes RSL statements and adds the requirements they describe into the ASSM, checking that the additions are syntactically and semantically consistent with the current ASSM.

The ASSM is basically a relational database for storing requirements. Its abstract model decouples the RSL from the automated tools that use the requirements, thus facilitating the development and addition of new tools to SREM. The central locus of the ASSM allows analysts to develop their own requirements independently, and then insert them into the ASSM, and since the insertion process will ensure that consistency of the requirements is maintained, the analyst does not need to consider what other requirements are in the ASSM, unless the requirements he or she attempts to add will cause inconsistencies.

REVS, the set of automated tools, provides a number of tools which can be used to highlight areas of the requirements that need further resolution, to resolve problems and to evaluate inputs. Interactive graphics tools can be used for the production of R-Nets. These provide full editing capabilities for the R-Nets so that developing R-Nets can be done quickly and easily. Simulation tools exist to generate automatically discrete event-type simulators that are driven by external stimuli. These use either models to simulate processing, or real algorithms to compute any results that are needed (and thus are an example of the animation of specifications as described earlier). Static analysis tools can be used for checking consistency, structure, data-flow and hierarchy of the R-Nets.

Since the requirements language is based upon a FSM model, it is relatively easy to understand, for example, see *Figures 16.2 and 16.3* which describe a single system unit for the 'Dial 9' operation in a telephone exchange.

R Net: Process_digit_nine

    Structure:
    Input_interface digit_9_dialled_by_calling_party
    What_state
    Do (state = dial tone)
            Send_distinctive_dial_tone_to_calling_party
      (state = collecting 7 digits)
        Collect_digit
        Terminate
      (distinctive dial tone)
        Collect_digit
        Terminate
    End
End

Figure 16.2 RSL example (*Communications of the ACM, 31*, 1107)

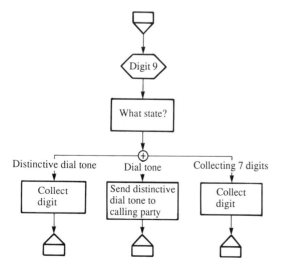

Figure 16.3 R-Net example (*Communications of the ACM, 31*,1107)

Conversely, the simplicity of the FSM means that the expressive power of RSL is limited to that of FSMs. For systems that have a great many possible states, or for which states are simply an inappropriate representation, RSL will not be able to describe their requirements. As SREM was developed for real-time applications that are stimulus-oriented, this is not surprising, and is perfectly acceptable.

Unfortunately, there are other aspects of requirements that are not addressed by SREM. RSL describes only the functional aspects of a system. The requirements which are not concerned directly with the description of function are not, and indeed cannot, be described by SREM. Included here are requirements such as timing issues, safety and security, design constraints and so forth. Since SREM was designed for describing the requirements for real-time systems, this could be a significant drawback. This, combined with the fact that it is only suited to a particular set of applications, means that SREM may be rather limited.

16.4.2.2 CORE (Controlled Requirements Expression)

CORE (Systems Designers, 1985) is a general method that aims to aid in the elicitation, specification, and analysis of requirements. It is in wide usage, and several different versions are now commercially available, some of which have automated support tools.

CORE is basically a diagrammatical method which is supported by natural language descriptions. The domain of discourse is bounded, and is partitioned into a number of viewpoints. This partitioning can be considered as providing a framework for considering the system requirements 'from the viewpoint' of each of the viewpoints, and each of them represents some organizational, human, software or hardware entities that exist within the boundary of the domain of discourse. Viewpoints can be classified as direct, parallel, or indirect. An indirect viewpoint (indicated in a viewpoint hierarchy by a dashed box) is of interest only as a source or destination of information, whereas direct and parallel viewpoints (indicated by solid and 'shadowed' boxes respectively) carry out some processing in which we are interested, and must be analysed further. *Figure 16.4* shows a possible viewpoint hierarchy for a safety monitoring system for a nuclear power station; the safety monitoring system would be an automated system for monitoring, displaying, and indicating errors in the state of a nuclear generator.

The analysis of the direct and parallel viewpoints is done in three stages: tabular collection, data structuring, and single viewpoint modelling. In tabular collection data flow around the system and its environment is gathered and analysed to produce a table which records the actions that a particular viewpoint carries out, the inputs and outputs of those actions, and the sources and destinations of those inputs and outputs. For example, *Figure 16.5* shows a tabular collection form for the safety monitor system from the above viewpoint structure; the actions describe the processes that the particular viewpoint carries out, and the inputs, sources (of input), outputs, and destinations (of output) describe exactly these pieces of information for each action. The sources and destinations of inputs and outputs are used to carry out simple consistency checks; each input must have a source, and each output a destination. Data structuring analyses the input and output data further, to produce a tree-like structure which describes the data items of a viewpoint and defines the order of their production. Single viewpoint modelling re-presents the information gathered during tabular collection together with some control flow and timing information in a third type of diagram.

Once all the information concerning individual viewpoints has been gathered, analysis across viewpoints is carried out.

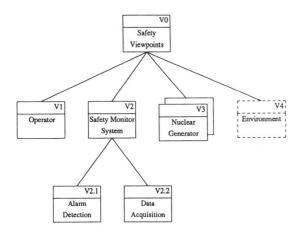

Figure 16.4 CORE viewpoint hierarchy

CORE is an informal method which is relatively easy to understand – even for non-technical staff – and can therefore be used for describing system requirements to the customer. However, using CORE well takes practice and experience because the breakdown of the system into viewpoints is conceptually quite hard, and, if an unsuitable division is chosen, then the rest of the specification, and the system development, suffers. Furthermore, the lack of formality and the excessive use of natural language may result in misinterpretation of the requirements.

The developers of CORE realized that requirements involve much more than just the specification of function, but unfortunately constraints analysis, included in the method to gather these extra requirements, is inadequate for correctly identifying all the 'non-functional' requirements. The analysis is basically of the 'what if . . .' approach, and thus relies upon the diligence and expertise of the analyst for its success.

16.4.2.3 PAISLey (process-oriented, applicative, and interpretable specification language)

The specification language PAISLey (Zave, 1982) has been developed in an attempt to provide a new and better approach to specifying the requirements for embedded systems.

The requirements are specified through the production of explicit, interacting models of the environment and system. Each model is a set of asynchronously interacting digital processes, and to represent some of the environment processes which are continuous in nature, a discrete simulation of each continuous process is used. The specification of the requirements involves writing PAISLey code (a set of applicative function definitions) for the processes that we wish to represent.

Combined viewpoint modelling is used to work out the responses within the domain of discourse to particular external stimuli; a combined viewpoint model corresponds roughly to a transaction in normal data processing terminology. Finally, constraints analysis is completed which attempts to provide a mechanism for gathering information about requirements which are not directly related to function, i.e. functional constraints.

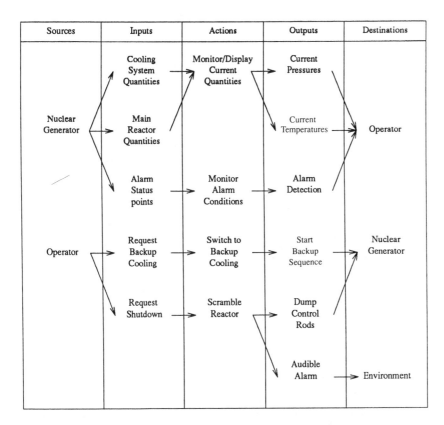

Figure 16.5 Tabular collection form example

An understanding of the requirements is then achieved by executing the specification.

As an example, consider the definition of a producer/consumer buffer. The process is defined by giving a successor function which takes the process from one state to the next. The process state is the current buffer contents, and the successor function is given in *Figure 16.6*. (In this example, square brackets are used for function application. The obliques are used to delimit predicate pairs; the expression before the colon represents the condition, and the expression after the colon describes what to do if the condition is true. 'xr-prod' and 'xr-cons' are used as very simple synchronization primitives between the processes using the buffer, and the buffer.)

It was stated in the introduction that the requirements for a system should describe all the significant aspects of a proposed system so that its recipient will be satisfied, with the emphasis placed upon *what* rather than *how*. The requirements should be an abstraction of the system so that the reader of the requirements can understand what the system should do without being directed towards a particular implementation. PAISLey, because it is executable, cannot specify what the system should do without specifying how the system should do it. Thus the authors believe that PAISLey cannot be viewed as a language for the specification of requirements. The nature of a PAISLey specification means that the design of the system is compromised, and this is not in keeping with the traditional philosophy of requirements engineering.

next-buffer: BUFFER → BUFFER;

next-buffer[b] = give_to_consumer[get-from-producer[b]];

get-from-producer: BUFFER → BUFFER;

get-from-producer[b] =
    /full[b] : b,
    'true' : put-on-tail[(b,xr-prod['null'])]
    /;

give-to-consumer: BUFFER → BUFFER;
    /empty[b] : b,
    'true' :put-on-head[(xr-cons[first[b]],rest[b])]
    /.

Figure 16.6 PAISLey example (*IEEE Transactions on Software Engineering*, **SE-8**, 262)

Zave (1982) defends PAISLey against criticism such as this by questioning the definition of requirements and design, and suggesting that the distinction between them is very subtle. Furthermore, she claims, like Boehm, that software development may proceed by a series of iterations, with the requirements at one level generated by the previous level, and thus a PAISLey specification specifies the requirements for the next stage in the software development process. However, the complexity of a PAISLey specification suggests that some analysis must be completed before PAISLey requirements can be written – perhaps a more traditional requirements analysis?

In Section 16.4.1, it was indicated that an aid to validation is the evaluation of some prototype system. Since PAISLey is an executable specification language, it would seem that it is better suited to prototype development rather than requirements specification. However, care must be taken when evaluating such a prototype. PAISLey is directed towards embedded systems in which timing issues are critical. Since the system is unlikely to be implemented in PAISLey, then any timing issues cannot be evaluated through the use of the prototype because the timing aspects of the implementation will be different from those of the PAISLey prototype.

16.4.2.4 SCS and MAL (Structured Common Sense and Modal Action Logic)

SCS (Finkelstein and Potts, 1986) has been developed as a prescriptive method for guiding the development of a formal specification from an application concept, and is directed towards the elicitation and formalization of requirements using the modal action logic, MAL (Maibaum, 1987). MAL has been defined in an attempt to produce a mathematical formalism for the specification of requirements which does not demand a mathematical background in order to be able to write and understand MAL specifications.

The modal action logic is based upon a many-sorted, first-order logic. This logic is defined as one would expect, and includes definitions of sorts, variables, logical symbols, predicates, function symbols, constant symbols, terms, atomic formulae, formulae, and a number of basic axioms and inference rules. This basic logic is then extended in a layered fashion by adding: two predefined sorts called 'actions' and 'agents', a modality, three deontic operators, three combinators, and a branching line temporal (interval) logic. The agents define entities in the real world in much the same way as the viewpoints of CORE, and the actions describe the processes that the agents may carry out. The modality allows the definition of formulae with the intuitive meaning: 'If an action is executed by an agent and the action terminates, then a specified predicate will hold'. This modality provides the notion of entities of the real world 'doing things', and the predicate may be considered as the post-condition or result of the action that was completed. The deontic operators allow control over what actions may be executed by the agents. These operators state whether particular agents are permitted, obliged, or not allowed to complete various actions. The modality allows the definition of the structure of the system, i.e. the definition of the consequences of particular actions, and the deontic operators allow the definition of the behaviour of the system, i.e. the definition of whether an agent is allowed to carry out particular actions. This dichotomy of structure versus behaviour is echoed in two of the steps of SCS. The combinators allow the sequential composition of actions, non-deterministic choice of actions, and parallel execution of actions to be defined. The interval logic is fairly standard, and is used to describe the timing aspects of requirements. The semantics of the logic is defined in terms of this interval logic.

Although the logic is very formal in nature, many of the statements that need to be made in requirements may easily be made within it, and have a relatively obvious meaning (provided the reader has a basic understanding of the notation that MAL uses), although to correctly capture many requirements may demand a better understanding of the underlying semantics. As an example, consider the following axioms extracted from the specification of a conference organization system.

[auth, ConsiderTopic(t)]
    $\exists$l,p (LetterSent(l) $\wedge \neg$ PaperSent(p))$\vee$
    ($\neg$ LetterSent(l) $\wedge$ PaperSent(p))

[pc, RequestPaper(auth)] $\neg$ per(pc, RequestPaper(auth))

The first axiom states that when an author, *auth*, carries out the action, *ConsiderTopic*, and then considers a topic, *t*, then he or she will either send a paper, *p*, or a letter of intent, *l*, to the programme committee. The second axiom states that once the programme committee, *pc*, has solicited a paper from an author, then they are not permitted to re-solicit a paper from that author.

The method, structured common sense, is based upon a number of exisiting methods including CORE, JSD, and ERA modelling, so that the time taken to familiarize oneself with the method should be relatively short if one understands these methods. It consists of a number of simple steps: identification of agents, data-flow analysis, action tabulation, ERA modelling, and causal tabulation. As these steps are carried out, the formal specification of the requirements is gradually constructed. The identification of agents is similar to the identification of viewpoints in CORE; the domain of discourse is partitioned into a number of relevant entities, which are defined as agents. Data-flow analysis does not add anything to the specification, but is included to aid the identification of actions by considering the communication and data flow between all the agents. Action tabulation is identical to the tabular collection stage of CORE; for each agent, the actions that agent may carry out, their inputs and outputs, and the sources and destinations of these inputs and outputs are collected together in a table. ERA modelling provides a method of analysing the static nature of the proposed system, and gives the analyst a handle on the definition of the constants, predicates, and functions that the specification will require. Finally, causal tabulation and special case analysis is used to specify control over the execution of actions and the preconditions for the actions. Causal tabulation and special case analysis therefore aids the development of the behavioural requirements, whereas the other steps aid in the development of the structural requirements.

While the logic has some attractive features, the links between the method and the specification are not always clear. For example, how the pre-conditions are defined from special case analysis is particularly obscure. In addition, SCS helps a great deal with the easier aspects of the formal specification, but unfortunately less help is provided for the more complex parts.

Time is a particularly difficult concept to capture successfully in requirements. Although standard interval logic has been used many times to describe time-related objects, it is not always obvious how to describe certain time relationships using the logic, nor is it always clear how to interpret statements in the logic. Since MAL uses an interval logic, it is not surprising that the expression of time-related issues is difficult.

SCS and MAL are part of the FOREST project, which is an ongoing research project to improve the development of formal requirements for embedded and real-time systems. Consequently, the method, SCS, and the logic, MAL, are constantly being revised and improved as experience with them grows, and their deficiencies become apparent. The project also includes the development of a number of tools for the validation and animation of MAL requirements (Finkelstein, 1988; Kramer and Ng, 1987). Future research topics include extending the logic to allow the specification of non-functional requirements, the development of greater tool support, for example, a MAL to English translator, improving the link between SCS and MAL, and so on (Quirk *et al.*, 1987).

16.4.2.5 *ERAE (Entity–Relation–Attribute–Event)*

ERAE (Hagelstein, 1988) addresses a number of problems. The motivation for its development arose from the desire to move the definition of requirements from a 'computer-oriented' to a 'problem-oriented' process. In doing so, more attention is paid to the environment, and the requirements for the system are stated in relationship to it, with the result that validation and checking for completeness are facilitated.

ERAE is based upon ERA modelling, enriched with the concept of an 'event'. ERA analysis usually involves the definition of entities and relationships between them, where an entity is an individual phenomenon perceived without reference to other concepts. Since in ERAE entities are understood to exist through time, we add to the notion of entities the concept of an instantaneous entity, which is termed an event. Pushing a lift button is an example of an event.

The method used with ERAE is also based upon ERA analysis. An ERAE model of the environment is constructed using basic ERA analysis. This model is then interpreted within a mathematical framework of multi-sorted first-order temporal logic. The events and entities are understood to describe the sets and constants of the sets, and the relationships between entities and events provide the predicates of the specification. This gives us a static model of the world. This model is then made dynamic, by using temporal logic statements to describe the static model with respect to time. In this way, a time-dependent model of the domain of discourse is described, and the requirements for a system are implicitly captured within the model.

As an example of the use of ERAE consider the ERAE diagram of the ubiquitous lift system, shown in *Figure 16.7*. The ERAE diagram uses a single box as an entity, a double box as an individual entity, an ellipse as an event, various arrows to indicate the time dependence of entities, relations, and attributes, and numbers to represent cardinality. The interpretation of this diagram would give us a number of constants and predicates, for example, the constants and predicates derived from Figure 16.7 are shown in *Figure 16.8.*

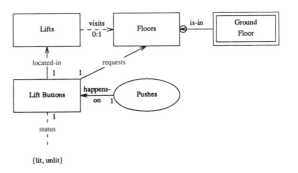

Figure 16.7 ERAE diagram example

Constants:

Ground-floor:	→ {Ground-floor}
Lifts:	→ {Lifts}
Floors:	→ {Floors}
Lift-buttons:	→ {Lift-buttons}
Pushes:	→ {Pushes}

Predicates:

visits:	Lifts × Floors
located-in:	Lift-buttons × Lifts
requests:	Lift-buttons × Floors
happens-on:	Pushes × Lift-buttons
status:	Lift-buttons × {lit, unlit}
is-in:	{Ground-floor} × Floors

Figure 16.8 Interpretation of an ERAE diagram

Once such constants and predicates are defined, then first-order temporal logic statements describing the static and dynamic properties of the system may be defined. The first predicate below describes a static property, and the latter, a dynamic property.

'A button must be unlit while its lift visits the corresponding floor'

> lb: Lift Buttons
> $\forall lb$: visits(lift(lb), floor(lb)) $\Rightarrow$ status(lb) = unlit

'After a button is pressed, the lift eventually visits the corresponding floor'

> p: Pushes
> $\forall p$: occurs(p)) $\Rightarrow$
> $\quad\Diamond$ visits(lift(button(p)), floor(button(p)))

where $\Diamond$ is the temporal logic symbol for 'some time', which roughly translates to the English 'eventually'.

Once the logic, and its relationship with ERA is understood, the method described above seems a very natural way to describe requirements. Because the requirements are described from the viewpoint of a model of the environment, it is relatively straightforward to avoid making design decisions within the specification. Although its formality may deter some analysts and customers, to help in the validation of the formal specification, use is made of deductions. The customer describes some of the features of the domain, which are translated into statements in the logic. From a number of statements, deductions are automatically generated. The statements resulting from the deductions are then translated back into natural language for the customer to validate them. Furthermore, since the features of the system are described in terms of the environment, it is more likely that the customer will ensure completeness, because the requirements are problem-oriented rather than computer-oriented.

As with many formal languages, because of the lack of suitable representations of the world, the 'non-functional' requirements are not considered, and formalizing the customer's requirements in first-order temporal logic can be an onerous task.

16.4.2.6 RML (Requirements Modelling Language)

As with ERAE, RML (Borgida, 1985) is motivated by the desire to bring more description of the environment into the requirements. The belief is that to facilitate the specification of the requirements, the analyst needs an understanding of the environment in which the software will be used. Such an understanding is thought to be gained by producing a model of the environment, and writing the requirements in terms of that model.

RML is a language designed to capture information about the real world, and to describe the requirements in relation to it. An RML requirements specification consists of a number of related objects, which are intended to represent some concepts of the real world. These objects may be organized into classes in order to capture common characteristics. For example, a *PATIENT* class might be represented as shown in *Figure 16.9*. This example also shows an object which describes the activity *ADMIT*. These classes can then be built into *generalization*, or *is-a* hierarchies. The is-a relation allows sub-classes to be defined, giving RML the power to express some notions of *inheritance*; the properties and constraints that are used to

PATIENT
parts
> name : PERSON_NAMES
> address : ADDRESSES
> hasPhysician : DOCTOR
> hasDiagnosis : DISEASE

ADMIT
participants
> newPatient : PERSON
> toWard : WARD
> admitter : DOCTOR

parts
> document: GET_INFO
> $\quad$ (from $\leftrightarrow$ newPatient)
> checkIn: ASSIGN_BED
> $\quad$ (toWhom $\leftrightarrow$ newPatient,
> $\quad$ onWard $\leftrightarrow$ toWard)

precondition
> canAdmit?: HAS_AUTHORITY
> $\quad$ (who $\leftrightarrow$ admitter,
> $\quad$ where $\leftrightarrow$ toWard)

Figure 16.9 Two simple RML objects (*IEEE Computer*, **18**, 85)

characterize the objects of a class can be inherited by the sub-class.

The principle of generalization presents an appropriate specification method: specification by step-wise refinement. The idea is that the more general classes are described first, and gradually, detail is added by developing appropriate sub-classes. The analyst would therefore build up his specification by selecting an abstract conceptual level, describing the details relevant at this level, and then moving on to the next, less abstract, level, constructing a taxonomy of related objects as specification proceeds. This taxonomy would capture the aspects of the world that were related to the system and its environment.

Time is also represented in RML; it is an infinite and dense sequence of time points. All objects, assertions, activities, and so on that are defined within the RML specification are described in relation to this sequence of time points. From this simple foundation, complex temporal descriptions can be constructed, including the description of time entities that can be used, to represent days, months and years for example. RML also adopts the interval relations described by Allen (1983), which can be neatly added to RML, without the need to extend the features of the language; predicates such as *during*, *before* and *overlaps* can all be defined as classes within RML.

RML is mainly based upon principles used in AI, and the method will suffer from some of the problems from which AI suffers. Of these, the most significant is the problem of over-abstraction. In a class of birds we might specify that *birds fly*, and that in a particular case, we might state that *a penguin is a bird*. This naturally raises the problem of *do penguins fly?* When dealing with descriptions of the real world through class hierarchies this problem always arises, because the real world objects do not fit into the simple categories that we might wish. In RML, the notion of excuses is added to resolve these difficulties; the fact that penguins do not fly excuses them from the assertion that birds fly.

One further fundamental difficulty of RML is the relationship between the world, the model and the system. How can we ensure that the model correctly represents the relevant issues of the real world? This is essentially the same as the problem of validation described in Section 16.2. The aim with RML is to provide an easier way of describing such relationships. The successfulness of this approach is yet to be analysed in depth, but a number of small systems have successfully been considered.

16.4.2.8 KBRA (Knowledge-Based Requirements Assistant)

KBRA (Czuchry and Harris, 1988) is a system which is part of a much larger system called the knowledge-based software assistant, the motivation for which arose from the desire to create a knowledge-based life-cycle paradigm, and to formalize software requirements for aiding the development of software.

The assistant is intended to be a tool which will allow the analyst/designer to work entirely on a computer, using any of a number of methods to both describe and present the requirements, including state-transition diagrams, an intelligent notepad, context diagrams, and a spreadsheet. In this way, any work that is carried out on the requirements is done so in a controlled manner, and is recorded.

While some knowledge-based approaches attempt to build a knowledge base of the world, KBRA builds a knowledge base of the actual requirements. A frame-based and constraint-based knowledge representation system is used to store the requirements so that the methods it supports can both read and update the requirements.

Of the many facilities that KBRA offers, its reasoning facilities are of most interest. Reasoning can be done in three ways: through inheritance, through automatic classification, and through constraint propagation. Inheritance allows particular instances of a generalized 'object' to inherit default and reasonable non-functional requirements. In automatic classification, all input requirements are classified under the most specific taxonomic group to allow greater inference to be carried out on the requirements. If the system is aware of the 'type' of the requirements, it is more able to reason about them, detect inconsistencies within them, and so on. To carry out constraint propagation, KBRA provides a deductive framework on top of a truth maintenance system. If contradictions are detected in the requirements, then KBRA provides for support, retraction, explanation, and culprit identification. This is supported by the truth maintenance system which records arbitrary dependencies between requirements.

Although it has a number of useful facilities, it is essentially a management system for the requirements, which allows a number of methods to be used for input/output of requirements. Thus it is limited to the power of expression of the languages it uses. Since these are relatively simple languages, a number of the problems described in Section 16.2 will arise.

16.4.2.9 RLP (Requirements Language Processor)

To attempt to alleviate the problem of different readers, RLP (Davis, 1982) is a system which allows the development of application-specific formal requirements languages. Since the languages are specific to the application domain, they should be readable and understandable by the customer, and since the languages are essentially formal in nature, then they should also be unambiguous, clear, and concise enough for subsequent software development.

RLP produces languages for the specification of requirements, by adjusting a built-in language to be application specific. The language, based upon finite state machines, uses features and stimulus-response sequences to organize and describe the requirements. Features are simply services that the customer envisages the system providing, and the stimulus-response sequences describe the dialogue between the system environment and the system. All the languages that RLP develops will be based upon this language, but will use different vocabulary. In addition, RLP also provides tools for processing the requirements written in different languages to detect any errors, such as inconsistencies and ambiguities, and tools for automatic test generation, system simulation, and automatic software synthesis.

Since all the languages have the same control structure, the same system model, and the same system organization, RLP can be used with only a specific set of applications, i.e. real-time applications that are feature-oriented. Furthermore, since the language is based upon finite state machines, the power of expression of the language is limited to that of finite state machines. Thus some of the information needed in requirements cannot be expressed; data structures and non-functional requirements, for example. However, there are a number of tools that can be used with RLP, and examples of the application of RLP to system requirements do exist (Chandrasekharan et al., 1985).

16.4.2.10 Other methods

The methods described here have, in general, not been developed specifically for the description of requirements, but have been found by some to be applicable. In addition to those described here, there are a number of other methods which have appeared in the literature. The reader is referred to the bibliography for information concerning these additional methods.

FSM (finite state machines). These describe hypothetical machines that can be in one of any of a given number of states. When provided with an appropriate input, the machine moves from one state to another, and may generate output. Two notations are usually used to describe FSMs: state transition diagrams (STDs) and state transition matrices (STMs). An STD is simply a directed graph with the nodes representing states, and the arcs representing the transition. The arcs are frequently embellished with labels describing the inputs and outputs of the transition. An STM is simply a matrix which has the possible states labelling the rows, and the possible stimuli labelling the columns. At the intersection of a row and a column, the next state and the output are indicated.

The simplicity of FSMs makes them attractive for the specification of functional requirements because they can be understood quickly by both customer and analyst, and yet they contain enough formalism to describe unambiguously system behaviour. However, pure FSMs describe the whole system in terms of a single diagram, which limits their usefulness to systems which are small enough to be describable in terms of a single diagram.

FSMs have a number of derivatives which extend the basic model to provide greater power of expression and to allow diagrams to be decomposed into a number of sub-diagrams. Statecharts are such a derivative. They extend FSMs to allow hierarchical decomposition and communication between concurrent (sub-) FSMs. The extensions include conditional change of state, and superstates which allow sets of states with common transitions to be collectively defined.

Extensions to the simple model have both advantages and disadvantages. The extensions usually increase the expressive power of the FSM and therefore make it more widely applicable, but they increase its complexity, with the result that it is much harder for customers to understand it. Thus they are perhaps inappropriate for the expression of requirements because if they are used unextended they cannot describe large systems, but if they are extended then they become more difficult to understand.

Decision tables and decision trees. A decision table is a matrix which relates all actions with all stimuli, and a decision tree is an acyclic directed graph of the same information. They are exceedingly simple, and therefore understandable without any training, but again they cannot be used with large systems, and they do not describe anything other than the basic functionality of the system. They do, however, have the advantage over FSMs in that they can describe what should happen when conflicting or confusing inputs arrive, whereas FSMs cannot.

SA/RT (Structured Analysis Real-Time). SA/RT consists of three different types of diagram which in combination can describe the requirements and design for a system. The first is a data-flow diagram (DFD) consisting of basically a number of processing nodes which are linked together by data-flow arcs. The second is similar to the first, but is termed a control flow diagram (CFD). Here, we still have nodes representing process, but now, the flow between the nodes represents control flows including such things as commands, or reports of events. The difference between DFDs and CFDs is immediately apparent because all CFDs are drawn with dotted circles and arcs, which contrasts with the solid circles and arcs of the DFDs. The final type of diagram is a state transition diagram.

Requirements written in SA/RT are relatively easy to understand, and can easily describe quite complex systems. However, it is also very easy to encroach upon design activities because of the lack of control over what is stated using the diagrams. This is not surprising because some of the versions of SA/RT were originally created for design. Again, only the functional activities may be described using SA/RT.

PDL (Program Design Language). PDL is unfortunately the *de facto* standard for describing software modules. It is essentially just structured natural language combined with a number of keywords which have specific meanings, for example: IF, THEN, ELSE. Clearly, because PDL is just natural language, then many of the problems associated with the use of natural language will occur here: ambiguity, over-specification, under-specification, inconsistency, and so forth. If PDL is to be used as a requirements specification language, then it must be used with extreme care, otherwise, the designers and engineers will not be able successfully to develop software from it.

Naturally, PDL may be applied to any system because it is just natural language, and in addition may even be able to address some aspects of the requirements other than just the system's function, although the usefulness of being able to do so is dubious because of the problems inherent in the use of natural language.

Petri-nets. Petri-nets (Peterson, 1977) are abstract virtual machines with a specific behaviour. A Petri-net specification consists of a number of circles and lines, termed places and transitions respectively, inter-connected by directed arcs, called arrows. Tokens are passed from place to place through the transitions by two simple rules. A clock pulse must have just occurred, and all the places that are connected to the transition must contain tokens. If these two rules are satisfied, then the tokens in places at the input to the transition are removed, and all the places that are the output of the transition receive tokens.

Understanding Petri-nets, and relating them to the real world is not very easy, and consequently the customer cannot easily understand them, and a certain amount of practice and experience is required with them if they are to be used successfully. Little support is provided for Petri-nets, though a number of animators do exist.

PSL/PSA (Problem Statement Language/Problem Statement Analyser). PSL/PSA (Teichroew and Hershey, 1977) consists of a notation and a tool. The notation is used for describing a system in terms of objects, and the relationships between them. Each object that is defined can have an arbitrary number of attributes associated with it which characterize the properties of that object, and can be related to other objects by a number of predefined relationships, which fall into a number of categories of relationships, including: system boundaries, data hierarchies, data derivation, system control, system dynamics, and project management. Thus the representation of the system is flexible, but limits the user to systems which can easily be described in this way.

PSA allows PSL descriptions to be entered into a database, and used to produce a number of reports. These reports cover such things as modifications to the database that have occurred, descriptions of the database from the perspective of a particular object, summaries of the database contents, and derivations of facts, for example gaps in system information flow, about the system from the information stored in the database.

The use of a database to store and maintain system descriptions has a number of advantages: maintaining consistency and coherence of the system description is made simpler, communication between users is simpler through the database, and so on. However, because there is no guidance provided for the development of a PSL system description, developing good requirements specifications using PSL/PSA will be dependent upon the experience and skill of the user.

16.5 Conclusions and comments

This chapter discusses three basic topics: the problems involved in requirements analysis, the content and properties of a good requirements specification, and a number of both general and specific approaches to requirements analysis.

Many of the problems discussed in Section 16.2 arise from a single source. To read and understand the requirements, to validate and verify them, and to check them for consistency and completeness, demands that the language used to express them is interpreted. It is this interpretation that causes problems in specification, verification, validation, consistency and completeness. These problems are exacerbated by the size and complexity of many requirements specifications.

As such problems arise, it is important to be able to distinguish between good and bad requirements specifications. From Section 16.3 it is clear that in general good requirements specifications will include information concerning system functionality, functional constraints, design constraints, system objectives, data and communication protocols and project management requirements, and will satisfy a number of properties. However, what is also clear is that establishing whether or not a given specification satisfies these properties is difficult, even using some of the approaches described in Section 16.4.

Even though the many different methods, tools, and techniques that have been discussed make use of techniques from numerous strands of computer science including artificial intelligence, object-oriented design, logic, databases and software engineering, many of them share two common deficiencies: a lack of facilities for expressing the non-functional requirements, and a problem of scale. Of these, the former is the more serious. The nebulous selection of non-functional requirements includes issues such as performance, efficiency, safety, security, fault-tolerance, reliability, and so forth. Although a few of these can be expressed using some formalisms, it is generally the case that they are not usually describable with as much formality as the functional requirements. As was seen in Section 16.2.2.1, there are not yet suitable formalisms for many of these system properties and, naturally, it is, at least for the moment, impossible to describe them formally. This problem of expression is exacerbated because analysts, designers, engineers, customers, project managers and users are often unaware of exactly what some requirements should state, and how they should be stated. For example, reliability requirements are often described by reference to some typically very small 'probability of failure', which is both impossible to prove and impossible to test. The usefulness of such requirements is debatable because if they can neither be proven nor tested, then how can we show that they have been satisfied by the developed software? Until it has been established what should be said and how we should say it, there will always be problems in describing the requirements, developing systems from them, and demonstrating to the customer/user that the final system satisfies them.

Some of the more formal approaches to requirements analysis do not scale well. With small systems that are a conceptual 'headful', formal methods can be shown to be effective. However, with larger systems, simply developing the requirements specification using the formal method is frequently prohibitively difficult; many formal methods are simply not tractable for 'real' systems. Analysts, designers and engineers will not then make use of such methods, and whatever benefits they may have will be lost.

In addition to deficiencies of method, there are also deficiencies in the attitudes of the people involved in requirements analysis. While there is in general an understanding of why requirements analysis should be carried out, there is insufficient belief in the value of carrying out a thorough and (hopefully more formal) elicitation, specification, verification and validation of requirements. It is all too often the case that requirements analysis is inadequately completed. Attitudes exemplified by 'we had better start coding because we are going to have a lot of debugging to do' are counter-productive, and must be replaced by an increased faith in controlled, disciplined and rigorous software development processes.

An important question that must be addressed here is what the future holds for requirements analysis. It has already been indicated that better attitudes towards requirements analysis are needed, but what of requirements analysis itself?

There are at least four areas that require attention. A greater understanding of what one wishes to express in requirements, and how one should express them, is clearly needed. Although there are a number of documented guidelines (DTI and NCC, 1987) which describe what general information should be present in a requirements specification, there is currently little knowledge of exactly what should be said about the non-functional requirements, and how such requirements should be expressed. Once one understands both the *what* and the *how*, it should be much easier to develop the representation that is needed to model requirements, and the languages that are needed to describe them. With better representations and languages available, practical and workable methods must be developed which should improve the development of requirements. To encourage the development of languages and methods that are practical for real systems requires links between the developers and the users of the methods to be forged. This demands industry-linked research projects to be set up. There are already a number of these in existence, and which are showing some success in the development of methods and tools.

16.6 References

Allen, J. F. (1983) Maintaining knowledge about temporal intervals. *Communications of the ACM*, **26**, 904–920

Bell, T. E., Bixler, D. C. and Dyer, M. E. (1977) An extendable approach to computer-aided software requirements engineering. *IEEE Transactions on Software Engineering*, **SE-3**, 849–60

Boehm, B. W. (1984) Verifying and validating software requirements and design specifications. *IEEE Software*, **1**, 75–88

Borgida, A., Greenspan, S. and Mylopoulos, J. (1985) Knowledge representation as the basis for requirements specifications. *IEEE Computer*, **18**, 82–91

Brooks, Jr., F. P. (1987) No silver bullet: essence and accidents of software engineering. *Computer*, April, 10–19

Chandrasekharan, M., Dasarathy, B. and Kishimoto, Z. (1985) Requirements-based testing of real-time systems: modeling for testability. *IEEE Computer*, **18**, 71–80

Czuchry, A. J. and Harris, D. R. (1988) KBRA: a new paradigm for requirements engineering. *IEEE Expert*, **3**, 21–35

Davis, A. M. (1982) The design of a family of application oriented requirements languages. *IEEE Computer*, **15**, 21–28

Davis, A. M. (1988) A comparison of techniques for the specification of external system behaviour. *Communications of the ACM*, **31**, 1098–1115

DTI and NCC (1987) *The Starts Guide*, 2nd edn, NCC Publications

Fagan, M. E. (1976) Design and code inspections to reduce errors in program development. *IBM Systems Journal*, **15**, 182–211

Finkelstein, A. (1986) Re-use of formatted requirements specifications. *Software Engineering Journal*, **1**, pp. 187–197

Finkelstein, A. and Potts, C. (1986) Structured common sense: the elicitation and formalization of requirements. In *Software Engineering '86* (ed. D. Barnes and P. Brown), Peter Peregrinus, pp. 236–250

Hagelstein, J. (1988) Declarative approach to information system requirements. *Knowledge Based Systems*, **1**, 211–220

Heitmeyer, C. L. and McLean, J. D. (1983) Abstract requirements specification: a new approach and its application. *IEEE Transactions on Software Engineering*, **SE-9**, 580–589

Kerner, D. V. and Malhotra, A. (1983) Generating requirements from enterprise analysis. *AFIPS National Computer Conference Proceedings*, pp. 255–260

Kramer, J. and Keng Ng (1987) Animation of requirements specification. *Research Report 87/17*, Imperial College

Leveson, N. (1986) Software safety: why, what and how. *ACM Computing Surveys*, **18**, 125–163

Maibaum, T. S. E. (1987) A logic for the formal requirements specification of real-time/embedded systems. *The FOREST Project (Alvey SE015)*, Deliverable R3

Peterson, J. L. (1977) Petri nets. *ACM Computing Surveys*, **9**, 223–252.

Pyle, I. C. (1983) Using Ada for specification of requirements and design. *York Report YCS.63*, University of York

Quirk, W. J., Booth, J. P., Horton, K., Cunningham, R. J., Jordan, D. and Tavendale, R. D. (1987) The role of validation in the FOREST method. *The FOREST Project (Alvey SE015)*, Deliverable R6

Roman, G. C. (1982) A rigorous approach to building formal system requirements. *WUCS-82-7*, Washington University, St. Louis

Systems Designers (1985) *CORE – The Method*, Systems Designers Scientific, Issue 1.0

Teichroew, D. and Hershey, III, E. A. (1977) PSL/PSA: a computer-aided technique for structured documentation and analysis of information processing systems. *IEEE Transactions on Software Engineering*, **SE-3**, 41–48

Weinberg, G. M. and Freedman, D. P. (1984) Reviews, walkthroughs, and inspections. *IEEE Transactions on Software Engineering*, **SE-10**, 68–72

Zave, P. (1982) An operational approach to requirements specification for embedded systems. *IEEE Transactions on Software Engineering*, **SE-8**, 250–269

17 Architectural design

John Buxton
Kings' College London

John McDermid
University of York

Contents

17.1 Introduction

Software development is a creative process and design activities permeate any software project. Although requirements should avoid design constraints as far as possible, in practice design decisions are made in requirements analysis and continue to be made until the last detail of a program is defined. However, this chapter is primarily concerned with the high-level design activities which come between the completion of requirements analysis (or specification) and detailed program design. By analogy with the building profession this activity will be referred to as architectural design.

17.1.1 Nature of design

Like many of the terms used in software engineering, design is both a (transitive) verb and a noun. Based on dictionary definitions, as a verb, design means 'to draw; to form a plan; to contrive; to intend . . .'. Similarly, as a noun it means 'a plan or scheme formed in the mind; pattern; relationship of parts to the whole . . .'. This chapter is concerned with design in both senses – specifically with processes and techniques for carrying out design, and with notations for expressing or representing designs.

These are good definitions as they draw out several important facets of design:

1. *Process*. It is an intellectual (creative) activity.
2. *Process and product*. It is concerned with breaking systems into parts and identifying the relationships between these parts.
3. *Product*. It is a plan in the sense of an architect's drawing to which a system will be built, and it also forms the basis for a plan in the managerial sense (see Chapter 27).

However, there is also an important sense in which the dictionary definitions *do not* capture the meaning of design. This relates to investigating the 'goodness' of a design.

In general, requirements are not concerned just with functionality but also with quality issues such as usability, modularity, reliability, and so on. Thus, investigating the goodness of a design involves demonstrating that the functional requirements are met, and that the design is of an appropriate quality. Common practice is adopted here and these investigative activities are referred to as verification and validation.

This chapter is therefore concerned with:

1. Notations for describing designs, including quality issues.
2. Guidelines and procedures for carrying out the creative aspects of the design process.
3. Guidelines and procedures for carrying out verification and validation.

This discussion is concerned with technical aspects of quality, and the reader is referred to Chapter 29 for a discussion of quality management.

17.1.2 Role and purpose of architectural design

The role of architectural design in the software development life cycle has been indicated briefly. The intention here is to clarify this role and to indicate the purpose of an architectural design from both a technical and a managerial point of view.

The requirements specification is concerned with the user's, or external, view of the system, and primarily with what the system should do, rather than how it should do it. In contrast, the architecture gives the designer's, or internal, point of view of the system and is concerned with both what should be done and how it should be done (albeit at an abstract level). In practice this distinction will normally be somewhat blurred as requirements will be contingent on what can be produced (at a reasonable price) and, for other reasons, may need to contain 'design' information. However, there is a fundamental change in *objective* when moving from requirements to architecture – from trying to document the user's needs to trying to show how to meet, or satisfy, these needs.

The architecture has a pivotal role in the development process. Many of the key design decisions are made in proceeding from the requirements to the architecture. The success of the project, particularly where there are stringent or conflicting quality requirements, can stand or fall on the effectiveness of the architecture. For example, it is unlikely that even extensive 'code optimization' will remedy performance problems if they are caused by inappropriate system structure (architecture).

The technical purpose of the architecture should be clear from the above. It is the definition of the structure, functionality, modules, resources, etc. of a system in such a manner that it enables the system to be built, ideally without further consultation with the users or requirements documentation, yet satisfying the requirements. In other words, it should contain everything the implementors need to know in order to produce a system which will satisfy the users (ignoring, for the moment, errors in requirements).

From a managerial point of view, the architecture should identify system components which can be designed, implemented and tested independently. Thus the work breakdown structure (see Chapter 27), which identifies the major independent work items in the project, should be derivable from the architecture. Typically, these items are referred to as modules. Despite their programming connotation this term will be used here, although it should be recognized that modules can include (lower level) specifications as well as program code.

In summary, the architecture, as a product:

1. Defines the structure of the system, its functionality, etc. in such a way that the system can be built.
2. Provides most of the information necessary to enable the remainder of the development process to be organized and planned.

This chapter concentrates primarily on the technical issues and the links to the management material discussed in Chapter 27 are essentially through the work breakdown structure.

17.1.3 Problems of architectural design

If requirements were purely concerned with functionality, then producing architectural designs would be comparatively straightforward. However, requirements typically contain design constraints such as 'it shall use an ERA database', quality requirements such as 'it shall conform to ISO 9001', and objectives for performance, reliability, etc. which are often referred to as 'non-functional' requirements. (The authors do not believe that this is a particularly good term as 'non-functional' issues can actually influence, or even conflict with, functional requirements. However the term is adopted here as it is in common usage.) The terms quality and non-functional will be used to refer to requirements that are not essentially descriptions of system functions.

In practice the complete set of requirements are normally, at least partially, in conflict. Thus the designer is faced both with a problem of conflict resolution, and with the added difficulty that he or she is not 'comparing like with like'. For example, faced with a trade-off between cost, performance, reliability and functionality, what priorities does the designer attribute to each factor in order to make the 'optimal' trade-off? In general, it is very difficult for the designer to make these decisions in isolation. Typically the trade-offs involve discussions with the customer and may involve making modifications to (weakening) the requirements. Thus non-functional and quality issues can force a re-think of the requirements, and they can also affect the structure of the design.

Architectural design can be straightforward. It is possible that the structure of the 'problem' as expressed in requirements can become the structure of the 'solution' as expressed in the architectural design. This can happen in systems with loosely coupled transactions sharing global data, e.g. a transaction processing system, where performance and quality attributes are not particularly demanding. It can also occur in embedded systems, but for a different reason, as the designer of the enclosing system will often take into account his or her understanding of the solution to the complete 'problem' in defining requirements for the software system.

Almost all of the structured methods assume that the requirements structure is preserved into the design. (JSD is a partial exception.) Most of the formal methods, or more pertinently rules for formal refinement (see Chapter 24), also assume the preservation of the system structure throughout the development process. However, there are cases where these assumptions are not valid and these are typically where there are stringent quality, or non-functional, requirements. This point seems not to be widely appreciated, so it is helpful to illustrate it with a simplified example.

Imagine a stored program telephone exchange intended to handle a large number of lines. The most 'natural' way to specify this from the customer's point of view would be as a set of parallel processes, each carrying out the complete set of functions for their respective lines. In practice those functions would include facilities for producing customers' bills, fault finding, etc. If the exchange were built with one process per line, and one process per processor, then it would in all probability be prohibitively expensive. Even with more processes per processor the cost is likely to be high, the flexibility low, and the efficiency poor, as most processes would be idle at any given time. Instead, exchanges are usually built with a smaller number of specialized processes, each of which handles a part of the processing associated with handling a line. The number of processes is determined by a number of factors, including the expected density of call set-up requests, and the speed and reliability of the processors to be used. Thus cost and the limitations of current hardware technology are primary factors in determining the design.

This is significant as non-functional reasons have been given for the change in structure. In other words, non-functional requirements such as performance, cost and reliability can *drive* the design process. A large part of this discussion will be concerned with taking into account non-functional and quality issues in design, and with resolving conflicts between these requirements.

17.1.4 Structure of the chapter

The remainder of the chapter is divided into four main parts. Section 17.2 clarifies the different types of requirements as they affect the design process and outlines some approaches to quantifying non-functional and quality requirements. Section 17.3 considers the main products of, and activities in, the design process and presents notations for describing architectures, guidelines for producing architectures, and techniques for analysing architectures, which are largely independent of any particular development method. By way of contrast, Section 17.4 discusses the characteristics of several of the more common development methods which are pertinent to architectural design. The discussion in Sections 17.3 and 17.4 is illustrated by a number of small examples. Section 17.5 draws conclusions and discusses a number of practical problems facing the system designer, e.g. choice of development method, and how to 'design the process' for software development. This latter material relates strongly to the topics covered in Chapter 15 on life cycle, or software process, models.

17.2 Objectives

The central objective in producing an architecture is to design an implementable system which meets the requirements described in the specification and delivers the functions required by the user within the imposed constraints. It was observed above that a specification may well describe different kinds of objectives. The distinctions now drawn are between functionality objectives, or requirements, and three different types of non-functional or quality objectives. Often requirements relate to both process and product. This text is restricted to dealing with aspects of the product.

17.2.1 Functions to be delivered by the system

Traditionally, the functionality required of the system has been specified in natural language text, and supported with diagrams and other notations, such as mathematics, where appropriate, on the grounds that a functional specification is the basis of a contract between user and supplier and so must be understood and agreed by both. More recently in some specific circumstances, e.g. for safety critical system components, formal notations for specification, e.g. Z or VDM, have begun to be used, together with executable prototypes derived from these specifications (see Chapter 40). Alternatively, an approach has been proposed by Parnas and others whereby functions are described in terms of system output. Here, each function determines values for one or more output data items and each output data item is given values by exactly one function. There are many different ways of specifying functionality and this topic is covered later in the chapter.

17.2.2 Directly quantifiable requirements

When identifying requirements it is clearly important to relate them to measurable properties whenever possible as compliance can then be determined by measurement. Typically, this applies to delivered performance parameters such as response times, throughput, down-time percentages, and so on.

There is a further class of requirements which is generally regarded as attempts to capture some aspects of quality which may also be crudely quantifiable, if only on a binary scale indicating presence or absence. One might include here the evaluation criteria for 'goodness' of software design, which were first proposed by Myers. These criteria attempt to categorize the properties of module coherence and coupling as central to good design. Qualitative scales of goodness, somewhat augmented from Myer's proposals are presented in *Table 17.1*, in order of 'goodness'.

A further and important category of requirement is related to high-integrity systems. Requirements on security and on safety levels for systems which contain software components are not sufficiently well understood and are an urgent area for research. For a summary of current work in the safety area see, for example, Leveson (1986).

Safety and security are difficult both to specify precisely (quantitatively) and to measure or evaluate. One of the primary difficulties is that the safety or security of a system depends on its operational context. For example, a supposedly secure system may be adequately secure, from the point of view of electromagnetic emanations, for use in the centre of a physically protected defence establishment but not in an office in a city centre. It is generally accepted that it is impossible to be sure that one has specified the safety properties of a system properly,

Table 17.1

Coherence within a module	Coupling between modules
Abstract Object oriented. Related to and encapsulating a single class of objects or abstract data type	*Abstract* By type checked procedure calls on services between modules
Functional Related to a single function	*Networked* With import/export interface between modules
Temporal e.g. all initializations	*Block structured* Nested blocks as in Pascal etc.
Logical e.g. all input functions	*Common* Via common data access as in FORTRAN
Coincidental The contents of the module are there by chance	*Direct* i.e. unrestricted references to code and data between modules

see, for example, Leveson (1986), and similar arguments apply to security.

The above suggests that specification/evaluation of safety and security are, in fact, unquantifiable. However, experience of developing and evaluating safety critical and secure systems has resulted in a body of knowledge which can be (and has been) used to develop standards for development and evaluation. Whilst they are not a panacea, these standards do reduce the uncertainties in developing and evaluating putatively safe or secure systems.

Standards typically used include the following:

1. *Security.* DoD Trusted System Evaluation Criteria (DoD, 1983). This sets out both an architecture and build qualities for different 'levels' of security.
2. *Avionics safety.* The Radio Technical Commissions for Aeronautics' document Software Considerations for Airborne Systems and Equipment Certification again covers aspects of architecture and development process and is widely used in the commercial aircraft industry (RTCA, 1984).

Because these standards are relatively well-defined, and because they identify quantitative 'levels of assurance' in systems, these can be thought of as quantifiable objectives.

There are also a considerable number of relevant publications on this topic. Sennett (1988) discusses a number of issues in developing high integrity systems. Pragmatic advice on selection of methods and tools for safety critical systems can be found in the STARTS Guide (DTI, 1989) and McDermid (1990).

17.2.3 Unquantifiable requirements

Users often specify requirements which are essentially unquantifiable. These are often given simply as lists of desirable properties. Typically they may fall into two areas: user interface-related and quality attributes, and long-term behaviour-related.

User interface-related properties and quality attributes include:

1. User friendliness.
2. Robustness.
3. Reliability.

Terms such as 'user-friendly' are essentially unquantifiable as they depend on subjective judgement ('I like this system – you do not'). Robustness can be partially quantified – but typically it is not. Quantification would involve identifying the classes of failure to which the system must be robust. This implies the availability of architectural knowledge in requirements – typically (desirably) this information is not available in requirements so the property cannot be quantified. Reliability requirements can be quantified but the difficulty here is measuring (reasonably high) levels of reliability in acceptably short timescales (Littlewood, 1988, *private communication*).

Long-term behaviour-related properties include:

1. Maintainability.
2. Modifiability.
3. Extensibility.
4. Reusability.

Note that one might expect good module coupling and coherence to lead to maintainable, modifiable, reusable and extensible software. However, there are other factors which affect these properties, so there is no guarantee that a system with abstract coherence and coupling will be easy to change given a particular requirements change. Pragmatically, these points cannot be quantified *during* a project so they cannot be used for project control and therefore are unquantifiable for practical purposes.

These properties are such that compliance of the design to the requirements is not straightforwardly measurable and so often they are demonstrated by exhortation rather than by proof. However, they express real needs and usually determine success or failure of the system in the real world. An unfriendly or unmaintainable system is unlikely to be well received.

17.2.4 Professional and legal requirements

Professional and legal requirements are typically implicit, not explicit, in a requirements specification or contract for software development. Professional standards really relate to codes of practice, etc. adopted by professional bodies such as the British Computer Society in the UK and the Association for Computing Machinery in the USA. These codes typically set out what is deemed to be ethical and professionally responsible behaviour, e.g. advising a client if development of a system is likely to be infeasible or to produce unsafe results. Whilst these codes may not have legal force, it is certainly reasonable for a customer to assume that they are followed in work undertaken for him. Thus they should be viewed as part of the requirement and should influence the design process.

Legal requirements vary enormously from country to country although after 1992 European legislation should be much more homogeneous. It is not possible to survey all the relevant legislation here, but one can draw out some important points.

In the UK, under the 1979 Sale of Goods Act, products sold should be of 'merchantable quality' and be 'fit for purpose'. Similar laws exist in other countries. These 'requirements' are very significant as they place on the designer the obligation to produce high-quality software, which is fit for its intended use, even if this means including facilities, features, etc. which are not explicitly referred to in the requirements.

The 1985 European Directive on Product Liability and the national enactments, e.g. the 1987 Consumer Protection Act in the UK, have made a dramatic change to the legal position with regard to product liability. Prior to this legislation, the designer of a product had to be shown negligent if he were to be successfully sued for damage caused by his products. Now negligence no longer has to be proved and one of the designer's few defences is that the 'state of the art' in the relevant technology was such when he produced the product that no one could reasonably have been expected to detect the flaw in the product which resulted in the damage. What is not yet clear is to what extent this so-called 'development risks defence' is a function of cost, i.e. is the state of the art interpreted in the light of the intended price of the product? Similarly it is not clear to what extent the act applies to software. The act does not mention software but the Department of Trade and Industry guidelines explicitly include software! These points will only become clear after several cases have been resolved in the courts.

Although the situation is far from clear, there are legal constraints affecting software design and development and these should be viewed as requirements on any system, especially those that can harm the public.

17.2.5 Meeting the requirements

Having thus outlined the different kinds of requirement, *viz* functional, quantifiable, unquantifiable (and legal, which we do not cover further here), it seems that compliance with requirements is perhaps only really demonstrable for quantifiable objectives that can be measured. As should be clear from the above, there are two related points: precision of specification, and precision of measurement or evaluation. Taken together these define 'how precisely/unequivocally one can tell if an objective has been met'. This point has been developed by Gilb in various papers on Design by Objectives (see, e.g. Gilb (1988)) to the effect that non-functional requirements must be specified quantitatively so that compliance can be verified by measurement. In principle this seems to be a good policy to follow. However, in practice it may not be fully achievable. For example, requirements that code produced be reusable are indeed measurable, but cannot be measured within the project producing the code; hence the measures cannot be used to control the development process.

Work has also been done by Parnas and others (Heninger *et al.*, 1978) on a more formal approach to specifying functional requirements, while refraining from the levels of formality in VDM (Jones, 1986) and Z (Hayes, 1986). In this approach, the system is specified by describing it as a set of functions which are associated with output data items. Each function determines values for one or more output data items; each output is given values by exactly one function. Inputs are treated as resources. This approach is extended for more general-purpose outputs, such as multi-purpose screens, by defining restored outputs or alternative modes. Other relevant work includes that of Dix *et al.* (1987) on formalizing principles for design of user interfaces.

The general drift of this work is to move requirements as far as possible into the quantifiable and clearly definable area. The purpose is to establish as clear a boundary as possible between the process of requirements specification on the one hand and the process of design on the other. However, the unquantifiable requirements – robustness, user-friendliness, maintainability and so on – restrain and strongly influence the system. It seems necessary to involve the user quite closely in the design process – not to do the design, but to evaluate the user acceptability of the proposals. In many cases this is done by prototyping the user interface or other aspects of the system where it is hard to quantify requirements at an early design stage.

Developing for long-term maintainability may well depend on the experience and skill of the designers. This is still, in the last analysis, a craft activity.

17.3 Design principles and notations

This section gives an idealized view of the design process, then considers situations where it is not possible to follow the ideal approach, in order to introduce pragmatic design principles and notations. In the most general terms the process of design in any field of engineering proceeds by hierarchical decomposition; that is, by a multi-level decomposition into components and sub-components. At each level, the system is described by the specifications of each component and their interactions; that is, by their function specifications and their interface specifications.

In programming terms the process was well described in the 1960s by Wirth under the title of 'stepwise refinement'. The process is to identify design as a sequence of refinement steps starting with a rough task definition and a rough solution method that achieves the principal result. Next one examines this rough solution more closely, taking the large steps of the solution and breaking them down into smaller steps. Each refinement in task definition leads to a refinement in the algorithm and in the data. This process leads to modules of the definition which are each developed independently. The process is aided if one uses, at each step, as high a level of notation as possible.

The decomposition process proceeds until the level reached is such that for each component:

1. It is obtainable 'from the shelf', or
2. It is achievable as a single work package.

The concept of re-usability is well understood in hardware and a designer's skill is to some extent measured by his success in re-using components; it is less widely used in software.

A 'single work package' is really where technical design meets the requirements of effective software management. Typically, it is a single fully-specified module of code and the detailed design and coding effort is of the order of a few days or weeks for a single software engineer.

17.3.1 Architectural design

One now faces the central problem in design methodology: how to perform the decomposition? The authors take the view that there seem to be three generic methods for this process of architectural design:

1. Functional decomposition.
2. Object-oriented decomposition.
3. Process-driven decomposition.

Each of these is described in more detail below, with examples.

The decomposition process can be viewed as taking place as a series of discrete steps as shown in *Figure 17.1*.

Each step represents a description of the system at that level of decomposition, described in a language L1, L2 ... which is suitable for that level. Of course, the idea of a language includes

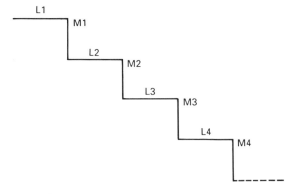

Figure 17.1 Languages and methods in development

graphical notations as well. The design progresses by applying at each stage a suitable method of decomposition, Mn, to advance the design from level Ln to Ln + 1. This somewhat idealized model does make the point that it may well be appropriate to use different methods at different levels. For example, a 'real-time system' could be viewed as a system of concurrent processes at the upper level; process-driven decomposition would be used to specify subsystems which could be treated later as separate sequential systems for functional or object-oriented decomposition.

A further general principle is that enunciated by Parnas under the term 'information hiding'. Parnas takes the view that 'a programmer is most effective if shielded from, rather than exposed to, the details of systems parts other than his own'. He goes on to propose that each module should encapsulate one, and only one, decision. This is a step towards long-term maintainability in that if a design decision has to be changed when, for example, new hardware becomes available, the consequential changes are restricted to one module of the system. Guidelines for what to hide include decisions on how to manage hardware interfaces, and decisions relating to requirements which are expected to change.

To a large extent the above principles tend to relate to a rather idealized view of the world. Some systems can be developed in a straightforward way by hierarchical decomposition, but often this process does not result in an effective architecture. In practice, the authors' view is that one embarks on a design with good intentions and so far as possible one proceeds by some version or other of the above 'good practice' methods. However, in many cases reviews and discussions will indicate that no obvious architectural decomposition will be adequate. When this happens it is often clear that some overriding requirements (such as the necessity to fit into 256K words of store) are the root cause of the problem. Such overriding concerns may drive the design into detailed and constrained craftsmanship to achieve this requirement, probably at the expense of many other requirements. In general, it is the non-functional requirements and design constraints which drive the design process when straightforward decomposition proves inadequate.

It is very frequently the case that the straightforward and testable requirements can be met by a range of possible designs. In practice the design choices are then driven by the non-quantifiable requirements and assessments of the result are very much by personal opinion. In this submission, little effective guidance can be given. In the last analysis good software engineering requires a measure of craft experience. However, analysing transactions through a system – that is, the complete path from input to the system through processing by the system to output – can often yield useful information to guide the architectural design. The reason for this is that many of the non-functional requirements, e.g. response time and reliability, which are the design drivers relate to transactions not specific functions or properties of the system.

The hierarchical approach to design is still useful – but as a way of representing and describing the design, not as a way of arriving at the design. This point is well made by Parnas (1986) in his paper 'The rational design process: how and why to fake it'.

This section now proceeds to more specific examples of architectural notations, etc., but first identifies the major components of an architecture definition. The term definition is used, rather than specification, to indicate that this is the information necessary to define the architecture – but that is not necessarily encapsulated in a single specification document, or a single architectural specification phase. Thus architecture definition refers to the totality of information needed to define an architecture. The term architectural specification is used to refer to deliverable documents or other forms of design representation.

17.3.2 An architecture definition

Architecture definitions are not simply concerned with the functionality of the system components. They are also concerned with process structures, the resources used by the processors and modules, and the inter-dependencies between the modules. Again, following the work of Parnas (Hester *et al.*, 1981), *Figure 17.2* shows a typical structure of an architecture definition.

Figure 17.2 shows the structure of an architecture in a stylized form of entity–relationship diagram, but does not indicate the attributes of the entities in the model. A brief overview of the nature and structure of the entities in the model is now given followed by a more detailed discussion of the more important entities.

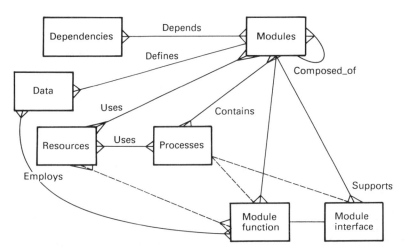

Figure 17.2 Structure of architecture definition

Assume that the basic unit of decomposition in the architecture is referred to as a module. The entity 'modules' represents this unit of decomposition, and the one to many relationship 'composed of' represents the hierarchical composition of modules. The attributes of the 'modules' entity as shown in the diagram are essentially only identification information, such as the name, and other attributes relating to the module as a whole e.g. coherence (see Section 17.2.2), reusability and other quality attributes. These attributes are discussed in detail elsewhere (e.g. Chapter 29), so will not be expanded upon here.

The entity 'dependencies' represents the different types of dependency between the modules. This does not include the composition relationship. The relationship 'depends' is shown as many to many because one module may depend on many others, and in turn be depended on by many others. Types of dependency include use of data definitions, calls of procedures, communication via message passing, and so on. The dependencies should also include the notion of module coupling (see Section 17.2.2).

The module structure represents the static construction of the system. The 'processes' represent the dynamic structure of the system, in terms of the set of potentially, or actually, concurrently executing threads in the program. There is a many to many relationship between modules and processes, because one module may contain many processes, and a process may in turn be broken down into many modules internally. One would expect the attributes of the 'processes' entity in the architectural model to be little more than a name, plus control information relating to creation, deletion, and invocation of the process. It is often useful to say more about the system dynamics – see below.

The 'resources' entity represents resources used both by the modules and by the processes. The resources represent aspects of the physical machine, or the machine execution, such as memory, CPU time, file store and peripherals. There are many to many relationships between modules and resources, and between processes and resources, because one module or process may use a number of resources, and similarly a resource may be shared by a number of processes or modules.

The entity 'module function' is intended to be a description of the functionality supported by the module. The details of this specification will depend on the method chosen to support software development. For example, it might be a formal specification in VDM or Z, it might be a diagrammatic representation such as that used by JSD, or it might simply be textual in the form of pseudo-code. The 'module interface' entity represents the information necessary to be able to call, or otherwise use, the module. This detailed information might not be available when the architecture definition is first produced, and may only be filled in during the detailed design stage. In practice it will often be useful for the interface to specify properties which can be relied on by other modules, e.g. data variants.

The 'data' entity represents (entries in) a conventional data dictionary. Thus it gives the type for a data item, its name, aliases, identifies the defining module, where the item is used, and so on.

The authors find it helpful to bear in mind the points made by Wirth (1976) in his choice of title for an early book on structured programming: *Algorithms + Data Structures = Programs* – it is necessary to pay attention to both. A common approach, e.g. in database designs, is to decouple these aspects and present the data structure designs for the system as a whole in a data dictionary, whereas algorithms may well be more meaningfully structured. One should not take too restrictive a view here – for many systems this may be adequate.

In a modular design, however, the authors prefer to address and describe in each module both its functionality (i.e. the algorithm) and the structure of the encapsulated data, perhaps by type definition. The example of the abstract data type

represents the ultimate stage in this approach. This issue is further discussed in Section 17.3.2.5.

Clearly, there are some consistency requirements on the architecture definition. For example, the resources required by a module should equate to those required by its constituent modules and processes. Similarly, the dependency types should correlate with the type of interface defined for the module.

It is also worth noting that the architecture will be represented by an evolving document, or set of documents. This is not only because errors occur in specification, but because there are many situations where it is not possible to determine accurately aspects of the architecture. Typically, this relates to the resources. In producing an initial architecture definition the resources will usually reflect estimates of usage by the modules and processes. Once the detailed design stage has begun it will be necessary to continue to review the resource usage of the modules and processes, and to update and revalidate the architecture definition as necessary.

The model effectively reflects the static structure of the design, i.e. those modules that have to be produced in order to implement the system. This choice is deliberate as it is essential information for subsequent stages, e.g. module design and module test specification, and it gives the basis for management control, e.g. processing a work break down structure. However, the module is lacking in one important way – it does not show how the system will work, i.e. execute. This can be shown via transactions and/or representations of data flow.

Transactions are often important in producing a design, as indicated above. They can also be invaluable in verifying an architecture against the requirements which will often be couched in terms of transactions or input/output relations. Taking this view transactions form part of the design rationale, not the architecture itself (no-one will actually directly implement a transaction). For this reason transactions are excluded from the model, but clearly it will often be important to document transactions which the system is expected to engage in.

Each facet of the architecture is now considered in more detail.

17.3.2.1 Processes

In essence, a process represents a single thread of control in a program. In principle, processes can run concurrently with each other. In practice, processes will run concurrently if they are executed by different processors in a distributed or multiprocessor computer system. In many cases, however, processes run in 'pseudo-concurrency' by being multiplexed onto a single shared CPU. One of the reasons for separating processes from the underlying resources is so that one can treat true and pseudo-concurrency in a unified logical framework, without being concerned, or confused, by whether or not the concurrency is real or artificial. Thus the process structure represents the logical concurrent behaviour of the system.

In drawing the architectural diagram it has been assumed that the functionality and interfaces of the processes are defined via the module function and the module interfaces. Essentially, this assumes that there is, at some level in the module hierarchy, a one-to-one mapping between modules and processes. If this is not the case then it will be necessary to introduce further relationships between the processes and module function and module interfaces in order to represent functionality and the communication interfaces for the processes.

The model also assumes that processes cannot be further subdivided into smaller scale processes. This is the reason there is no 'composed of' relationship from processes to processes. This is a slightly arbitrary design constraint, but one which is beneficial in simplifying the structure of software systems. The relationships between hierarchic and flat, i.e. non-hierarchic, process structures is discussed briefly and the authors outline their reasons for believing that flat process structures are more helpful to software system design.

In hierarchic process structures the hierarchy usually implies some relationship between the resources used by a particular process and its sub-processes. For example, the proportion of the CPU time allocated to a sub-process will usually be a fraction of that allocated to the parent process. Similar comments apply to the allocation of main memory, and so on. In general, hierarchic process structures introduce difficulties for process management and organization. For example, in a hierarchy, processes may well outlive their parents potentially causing problems in knowing when to release resources, what to do with resource quotas, knowing where to signal process failures, etc.

There are also (related but independent) problems in managing processes where there are shared data areas which need to be accessed in a disciplined manner in order to prevent erroneous program behaviour. The problems of shared data affect even modern programming languages such as Ada. In Ada there is a concept of a 'shared variable update' in which the language system does not have to guarantee that a process ('task' in Ada parlance) sees a consistent state of the data which is shared between a set of processes. With such program structures the software engineer is faced either with adding extra control mechanisms to synchronize access, or accepting that the data on which he operates may not always be consistent. There are standard solutions for shared variable update problems, see for example Hansen (1977). However, the approach should be used where its semantics is appropriate, rather than arising through thoughtless design.

Shared variable update problems can arise with flat process structures. However, they tend to be much worse with hierarchic structures as the pattern of access to shared data areas can be much more complex. It is always the case that these hierarchic process structures can be mapped onto a flat structure, with a rather different pattern of communication. In general, this organization makes programs easier to understand, and simpler to design. The only potential disadvantage is that access to data shared between particular processes may be somewhat inefficient. In general, the requirement that a sub-process has a subset of its parent's resources can be effected by means of resource quotas and priorities for processes.

There are some distinct advantages of using a flat process structure. For example, flat structures are much easier for designers to understand, and it is usually considerably easier to analyse the performance and space usage of flat process structures. Given these advantages, and the fact that any hierarchic process structure can effectively be flattened, it is assumed throughout the rest of this chapter that one is dealing with non-hierarchic process structures. For the reasons outlined above the authors believe that one can do this without loss of generality.

In many applications it is necessary to create and destroy processes on a dynamic basis. One obvious example of this is in an operating system where it is customary to create a process to support a new user when he logs in. This dynamism can be handled within the architectural structure already outlined, by making the process entity relate to a class of processes. Here additional control information will be required to indicate when individual processes may be created and destroyed. There may also be some additional constraints on the set of processes, e.g. indicating an upper bound on the number of processes which can be active, or created, at any one time.

It is usually also valuable to include information describing the way in which the processes are controlled. For example it is conventional in so-called real-time systems to distinguish between periodic and aperiodic processes. It is also useful to indicate the control mechanisms for initiating and terminating processes, for triggering a process to operate on some input data, and so on. This control information which describes process activation will usually relate to process to process messages. However, it may be necessary to indicate that the process is triggered in response to some interrupt. In this case the activation trigger would relate to the resource which generates the interrupt.

There are many applications for which there is no internal process structure. In this case the information on processes can clearly be omitted. The information on the functionality of the system then reduces to the definition of the modules, their functions, the resources which they use, and the interfaces by which the modules are invoked.

17.3.2.2 Resources

The resources part of the architectural definition indicates both the resources to which a module or process is allocated, and the resources which a particular module or process may use. In the cases where one is considering distributed systems the resources should therefore indicate the set of processors and memories available in the distributed system and indicate which module or modules and process or processes are allocated to each CPU, or CPU/memory pair. Where it is expected that processes will be allocated to resources dynamically, this should be indicated in the control information associated with the process.

In terms of resource usage the primary factors of consideration are space (in terms of memory), CPU time, and peripherals that may be attached to the processor. The information on space and time usage should, where possible, include both analytic and pragmatic information. Time is considered first.

In order to carry out timing and performance analysis of a system, it is useful to know the time complexity of each (function in each) module. The complexity will normally be a polynomial expression based on some property of the data stored in the module or received as parameters. The resource specification should define the complexity, e.g. linear, or $n \log n$, and indicate what attributes govern the complexity in practice, i.e. where the n comes from (see Chapter 9 on automata theory and Chapter 11 on data structures and algorithms for details). The information on the time complexity arises from an analysis of the algorithms to be executed by (functions in the) modules, and typically reflects the loop/control structure in the function or module.

Pragmatic timing information gives expected execution times for functions or parts thereof, based on estimates of instruction counts, etc., for the individual functions. This may be an absolute figure, e.g. 1 ms, but it is more likely to be given as an upper and lower bound on expected execution time.

This pragmatic information may supplant the complexity information entirely. For example, with an initialization routine which is always called under known conditions it may be possible to give an exact figure or narrow bounds on expected execution time. More usually the pragmatic information will provide constants in the complexity equations, e.g. k in kn, which relate the theoretical execution profile to actual durations. This can be seen most readily in the case of linear time complexity, i.e. complexity $= kn$, where the constant, k, represents the time necessary to process an extra unit of data. Again one would typically expect to get bounds on execution, e.g. $0.5n$ ms to $2n$ ms. Where possible it is also useful to estimate the range of values for, and hence the upper and lower bounds on, actual execution time.

It is worth making a few general observations. These estimates should reflect intrinsic execution times, not times which take into account possible resource conflicts, e.g. one process being blocked because two processes wish to write to the same file at once. These issues will be analysed elsewhere (see Section 17.3.5). In some cases it may only be possible to establish complexity, not absolute bounds on execution. For example, it is not possible to set execution bounds on a sort routine unless the size of the maximum data set which can be passed to the routine is known. Finally, it may be difficult to provide good time (and space) estimates when first defining the architecture. If this is the case then rough estimates should be made and these figures updated as detailed design proceeds.

The issues of space usage can be dealt with in a similar way. Space complexity of algorithms can be identified (see Chapters 9 and 11) and the absolute space figures represent estimates of the storage occupancy of particular data structures. The analysis should cover all 'levels' of memory, e.g. main memory, swap space and permanent file store.

The other resources represent logical or physical devices. Typically, at the physical level these will be magnetic or optical media, terminals or workstations, communication lines or specialized devices, such as radars or automatic teller machines. At the logical level these will typically be files or databases, virtual terminals or 'login sessions', and communication paths or channels. Typically, a module will act as a resource manager. For physical resources there will often be one module per resource, or class of resources. For logical resources there will typically be one module per class of resource, and the manager will create and destroy resources as necessary. Access to resources by other modules will be via invocation of interface functions in the manager modules.

At minimum, physical devices and their association with modules should be identified. If possible properties of the device should be specified, e.g. access time for a disc controller, and data rate for a data source such as a radar or temperature sensor. In general, it should be possible to establish some inherent characteristics for all physical devices, and it may be possible to find specific attributes such as data rates for active devices which are not controlled by the computer system. For devices controlled by the system, size and frequency of use information can probably only be derived by analysing the modules and processes which access it.

For logical devices the space and time properties of the device are determined by the analyses outlined above for the functions/modules which implement the resource.

It is also useful to indicate which device events trigger which functions, or processes, in the system, e.g. which function is invoked when a message arrives from a communications channel. This information should be presented at a logical level (i.e. it should not be at the level of interrupt vectors) but enough information should be presented here (and under process control) to enable transactions through the system to be identified. In other words it should be possible to trace the actions caused by some input through to output(s) from the system. This will be useful for subsequent analysis (see Section 17.3.5).

In practice, the system clock is always a very important device, and its relationship to other resources and processes should be identified.

17.3.2.3 Module function

This part of the architectural specification is concerned with what the modules, and the functions within the modules, actually do. In other words this part of the specification should indicate: given a system state and a set of inputs what new system state and set of outputs are produced by execution of the module or function. A number of approaches to specification of functions are discussed in Section 17.4, but some general observations are given here.

The role of the module function part of the architectural specification is rather different from that of the rest of the specification. The module function is the primary (but not only) source of information for detailed design and implementation. In contrast, the rest of the specification gives a framework into which the modules fit, and provides the information necessary to facilitate *analysis* of the architecture – to 'show that it works and to show how it works'. Clearly, the distinction is one of degree, and mode of use, not an absolute dichotomy in terms of the nature of the information presented. Also, information on how the module will be used is important to its designer, especially where there is internal concurrency in the module. These issues are discussed further under the heading of module interfaces and data.

Thus the architect will analyse the whole specification in order to assist in verification that the functional, performance, quality, etc. requirements for the system are met. The software engineer will use the module function, augmented by other parts of the specification, as the primary input to his design activities. This leads to a primary purpose of the module function.

In partitioning the system into modules, allocating resources to modules, and so on, the architect is making design decisions of various sorts. So that the implemented system will work (the analysis of the architecture remains valid in the implementation), the detailed design must honour, and observe, these design decisions. If these decisions are not observed, then, although individual modules may meet their functional requirements, the system as a whole may not satisfy *overall* requirements. For this reason these decisions are referred to as design *commitments*.

Thus the module function needs to specify, in addition to functionality in the conventional sense, commitments which might include data structures, scheduling algorithms, and the choice of synchronous or asynchronous communication between processes. One can draw out some consequences of these above observations.

First, the techniques described in Section 17.4 typically do not adequately identify design commitments, so they need to be augmented in this respect. Second, if using formal techniques, model-oriented approaches are more appropriate than algebraic approaches as they allow commitments to be made to particular (models of) system states. Alternatively, one can say that, if algebraic techniques are used, they may need to be augmented with additional information regarding data structures and algorithms. Third, as an extreme case, the identification of an algorithm (perhaps by reference to a technical paper or book) may be a perfectly adequate module function specification.

There are three further general issues worth highlighting. First, the Parnas tenet: 'a specification should tell you everything you need to know in order to satisfy the customer, and nothing more' applies here also, albeit in a rather different way. The module function should act in this role as a communication between architect and module implementor. The module function should contain all necessary information, or references to this information. Thus, for example, there is no need to copy an algorithm from a book or to reiterate parts of the requirements specification.

Second, this approach is *not* consistent with the view 'one man's design is another man's requirement'. To the authors, this implies that the designer is free to ignore certain commitments which the requirer (or architect) has made about system structure. If this attitude is taken there is a grave risk that the system as implemented will not be satisfactory for the reasons outlined above.

Third, the description does not mean that there is no scope for creativity, or questioning the architecture, in detailed design. The Parnas tenet ends '. . . and nothing more' so the designer/implementor should be given the maximum design freedom consistent with meeting the overall system requirements. On the issue of questioning the architecture the designer/implementor may indeed have a better idea of how to implement (part of) a system than the architect. However, the implementor *must* articulate these insights to the architect who, in turn, must ensure that the proposed changes are beneficial for the system as a whole. Without such discipline major problems will (almost inevitably) arise in system integration.

17.3.2.4 Module interfaces

The part of the architectural definition dealing with module interfaces contains essentially two sorts of information: that relating to the type and formats of parameters passing to the module functions, and that relating to the protocols governing the communications between the modules. This information is at the boundary between architecture and detailed design. In practice, it is likely that the basic information about protocols can be supplied at the architectural stage, but that the details of data formats and so on for calling functions in modules will only be supplied during detailed design.

The parameter part of this information should say everything that the designer of another module needs to know to be able to invoke the functions in a given module in a syntactically correct manner. The issues of semantic correctness relate both to the protocols and to the module function defined elsewhere. In practical terms this means that the information must cover whether parameters are passed either by value or by reference, whether they are read-only, write-only results, or read/write data areas, and so on. In many cases this information will be adequately catered for by definitions in the programming language of choice. If this is the case, then the appropriate programming language notation should be used to define these interfaces.

In many circumstances this information will be relatively straightforward to provide either at the architectural stage or early in the detailed design stage. It may be rather more complicated when one is developing a system which is programmed in a number of different languages. In this case, the interface definitions should deal with ways of mapping information from the structures of one language to another, e.g. FORTRAN arrays into Ada arrays.

Whilst this may seem rather detailed information, better suited for detailed design documents, it is valuable to have it included in the architectural specification for two primary reasons. First, it allows the definition of test sets and test harnesses for the individual modules to be carried out independently of the detailed module design. Second, it allows decisions to be made about the details of the integration strategy, and integration testing. Thus these two important activities can be planned, and perhaps started, in parallel with the detailed design of the individual modules.

The protocols reflect communication both within the program and, in effect, between the program and its user. Within a program where there are no concurrent processes, or where one is dealing with structure within an individual process, this part of the specification should be fairly straightforward to produce. In general the communication protocol will be via means of a procedure call or direct access to some globally visible data item. Where concurrent processes are involved the communication protocol may be much more complex.

There are many possible basic ways of communicating between processes. For example, it is possible for one process to send a message, then to carry on executing. Another possibility is where the message is passed, and the originating process waits until the recipient has dealt with its request and returned a reply, and so on. The protocol specification needs to deal with these forms of communication, and also to deal with other issues such as time out, exception handling, and the use of protocols intended to ensure reliability, e.g. two phase commit protocols

(see Chapter 53). It is also important to identify what constitutes 'well-formed' calls on the module function, e.g. open, intermingled reads and writes, then close on a file manager. This information may appear to be superfluous but in fact it is necessary both to design the internal logic of the modules and to be able to carry out an effective timing analysis of the system.

The protocols between the system and user cannot in fact be directly modelled in terms of the entities we have described for our architectural specification. However, in practice, the protocols will be manifest as communications between some process and a resource which manages the terminal, or set of virtual terminals, employed by a user. Thus the protocol defines the interaction between the process and the resource manager module.

In essence this protocol defines the dialogue between the user and the system. That is, it sets out the prompts issued to the users, the types of reply that may be returned, and so on. There are a number of simple dialogue specification languages which may be used for this task, although in many cases a simple form of BNF syntax or regular expression notations may suffice.

This information serves to define the form of the communication between the user and the computer. The details of the data displays, and so on, at the interface are dealt with when we consider the format of the data held and manipulated by the system. In general, it is also important to specify the 'look and feel' of the interface, i.e. the display and interaction styles. Thus the combination of the data descriptions and the protocol specifications give a full description of the user interface to the system. In other words this material, plus the data definitions, set out the logical specification of the human–computer interaction (HCI).

It may also be appropriate to include protocols that deal with access to remote machines. For example, this information would cover communication over local and wide area networks. In the spirit mentioned earlier, whereby algorithms could be specified merely by reference to standard works, one would expect this style of protocol to be defined primarily by reference to existing standards.

17.3.2.5 Data

The element of the architectural design which is concerned with data is very strongly analogous to the concept of a data dictionary as used in database development (and as supported by some 4GLs and CASE tools). The primary purpose of this part of the architecture is to specify the structure, relationship and usage of the data in the system.

At minimum it is necessary to indicate the type and structure of the individual data items, e.g. integer, list of strings, record with fields of particular types. There are many possible ways of representing data structures. It is quite common to use structure diagrams (see, for example, Section 17.3.2) or textual definitions based on a programming language or some form of pseudocode.

Where the structure of data is complex it is common to use techniques from database design, e.g. entity-relationship-attribute (ERA) models, of data (see Chapters 54 and 55). In these models the 'main' data objects are represented as entities, and values that they can hold are represented as attributes (rather like fields in a record). The relationships are fairly self-explanatory, but it is often useful to represent the cardinality of relationships (one to one, one to many, many to many) in order to give a clearer view of the use of the data.

In some programming languages the types of data items can form a hierarchy where one type is a subtype of another and thus associated entities can only hold a subset of the values, e.g. leap year is a subtype of year. It is often helpful to show subtype relationships on data in an architectural specification.

If the structured type definitions do not clearly determine the values which the data elements can hold then it is useful to expose such information explicity. Thus for a system to be implemented in FORTRAN it would be useful to explain that an integer could only be in the range of 1–10; in Ada one would expect the type definition to make this constraint explicit. Additionally, it is often useful to express integrity constraints on data, e.g. that the sum of two arrays of numbers should be equal, as might be necessary in a program handling a company's annual accounts.

Integrity constraints may be particularly valuable where a data item can be updated by more than one process. It may also be necessary to express explicit rules for accessing the data in order to ensure that data integrity is maintained. There is also clearly a strong link with the information on 'well-formed' access to a module identified under module interfaces. Representation of such issues may be addressed by the method used, e.g. MASCOT, or have to be handled by other techniques such as semaphores or monitors (see Hansen (1977) for a review of techniques).

It is always useful to have cross-reference information indicating where data is defined and used. This information is expressed by the relationships in Figure 17.1.

It is interesting to note that in the paper from Figure 17.1, Parnas did not include data. The reason for this is that Parnas believes it is appropriate to use Abstract Data Types (ADTs), which encapsulate data with the functions or procedures that are allowed to access the data, as a way of structuring specifications and systems. The authors believe that ADTs are very valuable, but that they are not *always* appropriate, so it is necessary to include data in a general model of an architectural design. In any event it will be necessary to specify the types and structure of the data used as parameters and results to the procedures and functions defined in the ADT.

17.3.2.6 Dependencies

The section on dependencies reflects two main related forms of data. One is simply the coupling between the modules, e.g. abstract or direct, and the other is the mechanistic way in which this coupling is achieved. This latter information could be, for example, a definition that the inter-module dependency is that of a function call, direct importation of data or type definition, access to shared data, and so on.

This information is primarily intended to help analyse and to verify the specification. Consequently, it is necessary to include reasons for choosing the level of module coupling if this is not abstract.

This aspect of the architectural specification is less complex than many of the other entities. Nonetheless, it is useful to separate this information as an easily identified part of the specification. The reason for this is that the dependencies make it relatively easy to determine the ramifications of proposed change. The information about the coupling, and the direct way in which the information in one module is used by another, give a very good basis for determining the effects of change on the program, and therefore to determining the likely costs and consequences of the proposed change.

17.3.2.7 General issues

There are a number of general issues which have not been drawn out via discussion of the individual entities and relationships in our model of an architecture definition. These are pragmatic issues to do with the way an architectural specification will be produced and used.

Typically, an architectural specification will be a document produced by one, or a number of, systems architects. In some cases the architectural specification may be produced by using one or a number of CASE tools. In this case the architectural specification might be in the form of a database, or a combination of electronically stored diagrams and text.

Although the contents of an architectural specification have been outlined using a stylized form of database schema for the specification, the authors do not intend that such schema should be viewed as an essential structure for an architectural specification. Instead, the intention is that the structure given above, and the discussion of each of the entities in the specification, should be viewed as forming a check list for the contents of an architectural specification. In other words, it does not matter if the information described is presented in a different form, or in a different structure. What is important is that the issues raised are addressed somewhere in the specification.

A very important class of information has been omitted from the description of the architecture definition. This class of information relates to the design rationale for the system. The design rationale should give reasons for choosing a particular structure, algorithm, etc. Typically, a statement in a design rationale will include the assumptions that were made in arriving at the decision, and may also indicate reasons for rejecting alternative possibilities. This information is of immense value in an architectural specification. It is inevitably the case that specifications are changed as the requirements for the system evolve. Clearly it is essential to understand how the system is intended to work when trying to change the system; it is often the design rationale which gives the maintenance engineers the greatest insight into the functioning of the system when they come to make their changes. In particular, if assumptions are recorded they can then determine whether or not their proposed way of modifying the system will violate any of these assumptions.

It has not been suggested that the design rationale should fit in at any particular 'point' in the architectural specification. This is partly because the authors do not believe that the description given should be treated as a contents list, and partly because this sort of design rationale is essentially all pervasive. In principle, every major design decision in a good architectural specification should be accompanied by a statement of a design rationale. In practice, it is very difficult to follow these general guidelines, but it is important that there is a consistent description of the design rationale, at least at some level in the module hierarchy for the whole system.

There is also another class of information missing from the description given of an architecture definition. This relates to links back from the architectural specification to the requirements, and links forward to the detailed design and implementation. In essence, these links should indicate which functions, or other requirements, in the requirements specification are satisfied by particular entities or attributes in the architectural specification. A dual set of relations should exist between the architecture and the detailed design and implementation information. In practice, this sort of information is very hard to provide and to maintain within purely textual specifications. This idealized view of a set of related specifications in the life cycle is unlikely to be practicable until there is much more widespread use of integrated project support environments (see Chapter 33).

In some circumstances it may also be useful to identify transactions in the architecture of the system. These are not included as part of the primary description of architecture because a transaction is essentially a dynamic facet of the system execution, rather than being part of the structure of the system which some software engineer would design and implement. Nonetheless, they can be very valuable in analysing the behaviour of a system.

For example, some classes of non-functional requirement, e.g. timing constraints, are typically expressed on a transaction basis. This might mean that the requirements specify the allowable time delay from some input arriving at the system and the associated output being generated by the system. In practice, it will only be possible to analyse a requirement for consistency with such constraints if it is possible to determine the transaction that is responsible for generating that output from its causal input. Where descriptions of transactions are useful they may either be included as part of the full architectural specification, or generated as transient objects during the process of analysis and verification.

The architecture definition as described here will be a redundant artefact. The authors believe that this is a good thing. The principle of using redundancy in specifying programs, and so on, is now well understood. The authors believe that the level of redundancy implicit in their description of an architecture is both acceptable in terms of the amount of effort required to produce the information, and useful in terms of the opportunities it creates for checking internal consistency of architecture definitions.

Furthermore, redundant descriptions may represent different viewpoints of a system, appropriate to different readers. Transactional analysis, for example, could be regarded as a viewpoint relevant to concerns with overall throughput.

There has been no guidance on the size of the module given so far. From a managerial point of view, a module ought to be the sort of unit which can be allocated to a software engineer and which can be designed and implemented within a few days or a few weeks. If the modules are much bigger than this, then it is extremely difficult to maintain good control over the running of the project.

However, this size of module may not correlate very well with the natural technical sub-divisions of the system. Typically, this is because it is useful to have modules which are much smaller than those which would be written over a matter of a few days or a few weeks. Thus it is possible that managerial decisions and allocation of work are made on the basis of modules which are some way up from the leaves of the module hierarchy. In practice, it may be the system architect who defines the full module hierarchy. Alternatively, the architect may define the structure down to the level of modules which are allocated as work items, and the individual implementor is then free to design his or her own module structure below that level. The main reason that the architect may want to go down to a lower level in the module structure would be to identify 'common use' modules. In other words, he may wish to make commitments to use particular modules in common between all major parts of the system.

In practice, it is often appropriate to take an eclectic approach to specification; in other words, one notation might be used for describing module structure and dependencies, another for describing the process structure of the system, another for defining the functionality of the modules, and so on. The authors do not believe that there is currently any method available for specifying architectures which adequately covers all of the aspects of architecture definition, as defined here. Consequently, they expect that it will be appropriate to use eclectic approaches to specification for some time to come, or possibly even indefinitely.

When using an eclectic approach to specification, however, it is essential that all the specifications written in the individual notations relate to a common model of the system structure and behaviour. Within the proposed model of an architectural specification, the module structure and the process structure form the common basis for all the individual specifications. In practice, it will be necessary to be very careful to ensure that all the notations used do relate to a common basis, otherwise there will be considerable scope for misinterpretation of the architectural specification.

Finally, it has long been accepted wisdom that it is desirable to develop, and to evaluate, a number of possible architectures for a system. The authors believe that this is a very sound principle, and that if this approach was taken fewer low-quality systems would be delivered to customers. They believe that the outlined approach to architectural specifications is entirely compatible with this approach. In practice, it may be possible, and desirable, to carry out evaluation of competing architectures on partially complete architectural specifications. If this is done then it is probably the case that the basic information on modules, module dependencies, resources, and processes form an adequate basis for such an evaluation. In other words one does not need to know the details of the functionality of the individual modules so long as one knows their basic non-functional attributes when carrying out evaluations. This point is discussed again in Section 17.3.4 on guidelines for design, and Section 17.3.5 on analysis techniques.

17.3.3 Notations for architecture definitions

There are many structured techniques e.g. JSD, and SSADM, which use a particular notation, or set of notations, for describing systems. The aim here is to illustrate a number of notations which are generally useful but which either are not used in any specific method, or which underpin a number of specific methods. Inevitably, only a sample of available diagrammatic notations is presented, and the reader is referred to McClure and Martin (1988) for a more comprehensive discussion of diagrammatic notations.

17.3.3.1 Myers' Structure Charts

In the mid 1970s Myers developed a notation for showing the module structure of software systems. *Figure 17.3.* shows the basic elements of the notation (slightly adapted).

Each rectangular box represents a module, and the modules are identified by a serial number in the top right-hand corner. The three-quarter circle symbols represent a function available in the operating environment of the program, e.g. a supervisor call (SVC) to an operating system, or interaction with a transaction processing monitor. The diagram represents the calling structure of the program and the numbered arrows represent the parameters (arguments) and results of function calls.

The internal structure of a module can be shown by decomposing the module 'box' into further boxes. Typically, these inner boxes carry 'decimal numbers', e.g. 4.2.7, to indicate the module hierarchy.

Further types of module can be defined. The rectangular box with double lines at the ends corresponds to a library function, e.g. a numerical routine. It is important to identify such modules as, managerially, it is necessary to know that some function does not need to be implemented but will be needed for integration and test.

When Myers developed the notation it was common to insist that modules had only one function within them. With the advent of the ideas of abstract data types and objects, where each operation on the object is a function in the module defining the object, it is useful to identify access to each function in the module (operation on the object). The module box with dashed sub-divisions represents an object, and each sub-division corresponds to a function in the module (operation on the object).

Myers also introduced notation for dealing with recursion and parallel execution (processes). The notation is rather poor so it is not presented here.

Myers' Structure Charts relate to the module hierarchy and dependencies identified in Section 17.3.2. Specifically, it covers module identification, module decomposition (the Composed_ of) relationship, and some of the dependency information.

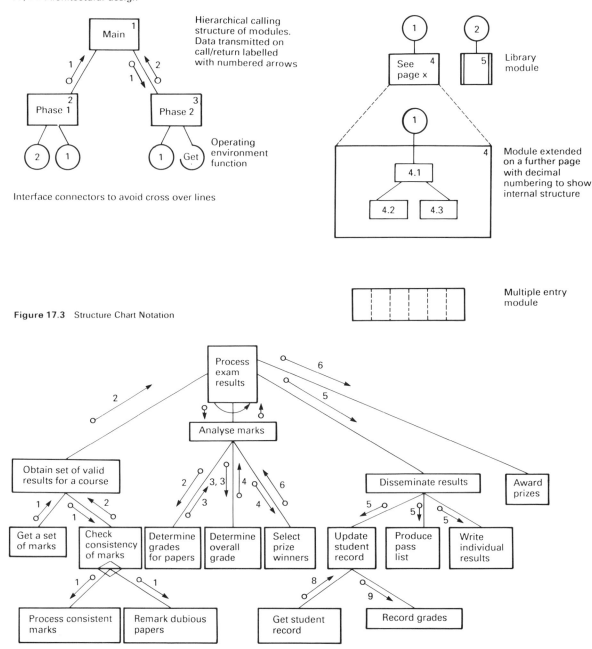

Figure 17.3   Structure Chart Notation

Figure 17.4   Structure chart annotated with data parameters. Key:
1 = Set of marks; 2 = Valid set of marks; 3 = Subject grades; 4 = Overall
course grade; 5 = 2,3 and 4; 6 = Prizewinners list; 7 = Student record;
8 = Updated student record

Information such as module coupling is not represented but could easily be added to the basic structure supported by the notation.

Figure 17.4 illustrates the use of the notation on a system for processing student examination marks.

The diagram shows the basic use of the calling hierarchy (without numbering the modules). There is one additional element of notation. The diamond shows that 'check validity of marks' calls either 'process valid marks' or 'process invalid marks', with some data but not both.

17.3.3.2 *Dataflow notation*

The dataflow notation was probably first introduced by Phillips (1968) but was brought into widespread industrial use by Yourdon (Yourdon and Constantine, 1985), De Marco (1978), and others. It is the basis of Structured Analysis (SA), sometimes known as the Yourdon Method, and many other derivative methods. Dataflow methods were originally developed for commercial data processing but (enhanced) versions of the method are now widely used, e.g. for real-time systems. The notation is illustrated in *Figure 17.5*.

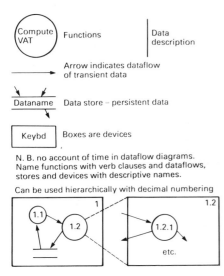

Figure 17.5 Dataflow Notation

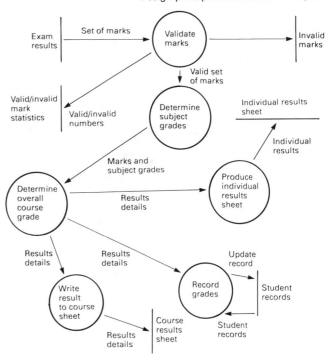

Figure 17.6 Examination marks processing in dataflow

Circles represent functions implemented, or to be implemented, by the system. Data objects, which are typically inputs to, and outputs from, the system, are represented by vertical lines. Arrows show the flow of transient data in the system, and parallel horizontal lines represent permanent data repositories, e.g. databases, files and in-store data structures. Boxes represent devices such as terminals or sensors. As with Myers' structure charts, the functions can be decomposed in an hierarchical fashion.

Figure 17.6 illustrates the use of the dataflow notation. The example used is the examination marks system illustrated in Figure 17.4. The two diagrams show that the two notations are fairly similar in terms of their expressive power, but that the dataflow notation tends to dictate what is viewed as a 'natural structure' for representing the system architecture. Note also that the dataflow diagrams do not indicate module structure. It is instructive to observe that the well-known data-transform design method uses just these two diagram forms and provides a simple rule to transform a dataflow diagram into a structure chart, see, for example, Myers (1975).

17.3.3.3 *MASCOT*

The dataflow diagrams do not explicitly represent concurrency, although there is nothing to stop functions being executed in parallel. Strictly MASCOT is a method, but the notation used in MASCOT2 (MASCOT, 1980) (now superseded by MASCOT3, see Section 17.4) is so simple and generally useful that it is worth including it in this section.

The notation used by MASCOT is illustrated in *Figure 17.7*. Superficially, this is very similar to the dataflow diagram. The process (referred to as an activity in MASCOT) corresponds to the dataflow function – except that all processes run concurrently, or at least in pseudo-concurrency on a single processor. The communication channels equate to the transient dataflows in the dataflow diagrams. Similarly, the pool corresponds to the

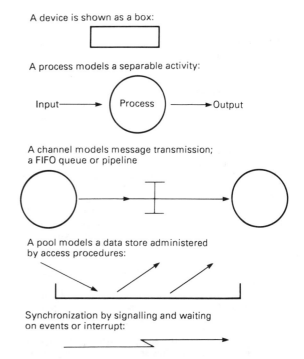

Figure 17.7 MASCOT diagram symbols

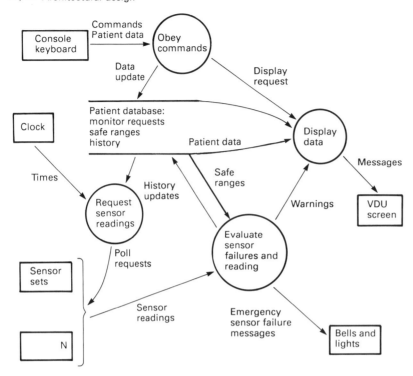

Figure 17.8 Hospital monitoring dataflow diagram

persistent data store. The indication of events or interrupts via the 'zig-zag arrow' shows MASCOT's origin in real-time systems design.

One can illustrate the use of MASCOT notation, and compare it with dataflow, by considering a health monitoring system for a hospital. Here sensors monitor patients for a number of vital signs, pulse rate, etc. These factors are checked periodically according to a timetable set for each patient, and the nurse is notified (via a VDU) if the values are outside the safe range for the patient. Sensor failures are also to be reported.

A possible representation in dataflow terms of such a system is shown in *Figure 17.8*. This shows the basic functions as set out above, and it is a little more specific about sensor failures, establishment of the timetable for checking that patient's state, and so on.

The MASCOT example (*Figure 17.9*) shows that there is relatively little difference in expressive power between the notations. However, from a methodological point of view the MASCOT diagram represents a design, whereas the SA diagram is much closer to an analysis of the problem. The use of the event arrow makes it clear that the clock triggers the (bulk of the) system activity. The sub-division of the patient databases into three parts makes the operation of the system rather clearer, but this is an effect of the way the system has been represented, not an inherent difference in the notation.

Note that, in both cases, some artifice has been used to represent the multiplicity of sensors, and certain aspects of the design are not clear, e.g. whether there are the same number of alarms as sensor sets, or only one for the system. Neither notation can deal with dynamic creation or destruction of processes or functions.

None of the functions described so far deals with representations of functionality or data structures, and data structures are discussed next.

17.3.3.4 *Data structure diagrams*

There are a number of techniques which are widely used for specifying data structures. The notation illustrated overleaf is based on that used in Jackson Structured Programming (JSP). (Similar notation is used in Jackson System Design (JSD) (Jackson, 1983) but for rather different purposes.)

The basic notation describes data by taking some 'complete' data item and decomposing it into its constituent parts, like fields in a record. The basic concepts are illustrated in *Figure 17.10*.

In this figure the data item A is composed of sub-parts A1, A2 and A3. Time-order of derivation goes from left to right, so A1 is derived before A2 which, in turn, is derived before A3. Where time-order of derivation is not known, or is indeterminate, the components of the data item are enclosed in a dotted box.

Iterated (repeated) items are represented by an asterisk, and alternatives by a circle. Both marks appear in the top right-hand corner of the boxes. It is normally required that, if one subcomponent is an alternative, then they all are. This means that the circle genuinely represents alternative, not optional, parts of the structure.

The use of the notation is illustrated in *Figure 17.11*. It is worth noting that indeterminate order actions are often iterated, as in this case. This reflects the fact that when components of data items are iterated, one often does not know how they will be interleaved.

This style of diagram is used in many methods, not just those developed by Jackson. There are other techniques in common use. Notations from database design, e.g. entity-relationship and entity-relationship attribute diagrams, are commonly used. A simple form of entity-relationship diagram was illustrated earlier in the chapter; further examples are given in Chapter 54. Syntax diagrams, or syntax descriptions in BNF (Backus Naur Form) are also commonly used, and are good for dealing with

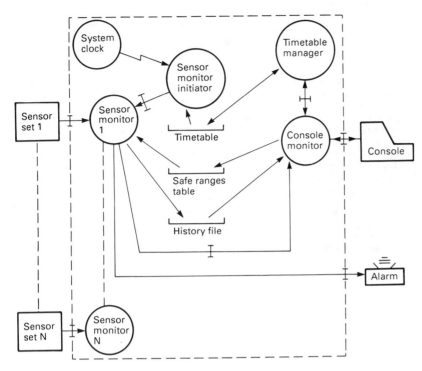

Figure 17.9 Hospital monitoring MASCOT diagram

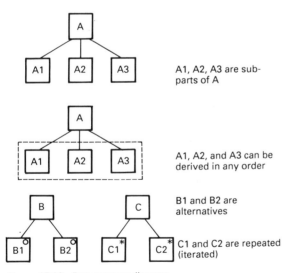

Figure 17.10 Data structure diagrams

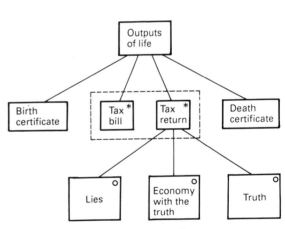

Figure 17.11 Example of data structure diagram

complex data structures, and can be adapted for representing the structure of dialogues at an interface.

17.3.3.5 Functionality

Graphical techniques are not particularly well suited to specifying functionality. They are quite well suited to showing *structure* of functions, e.g. the control structure and decision points, but is normally necessary to augment such diagrams with text.

Techniques such as pseudo-code, flowcharts, and design structure diagrams are quite well understood and are widely used at low levels of design to represent program structure (see BS6224). They are probably too detailed, as they represent quite detailed designs, except at the bottom of the module hierarchy. However, there are other useful techniques which are not so well understood.

Finite state machines, or finite state diagrams, which are based on models of automata (see Chapter 9) can be useful ways of showing the response of some systems to input stimuli. The diagrams essentially comprise circles, representing possible states of the (data or control flow in the) function, and arrows which represent transitions between states. The arrows are labelled with the input value(s) which cause(s) the transition. This notation is illustrated in *Figure 17.12* which shows a fragment of a finite state diagram for a UK telephone system.

The figure shows a possible set of states and transitions for a function carrying out call set-up in a telephone system (including the proposed new European emergency number). The system starts in the state standby/reset and the lifting of the receiver, followed by a sequence of digits, leads to a succession of states for the function as it sets up a call. The diagram is slightly artificial in that, for example, 'connect local call' and 'connect international' would have further internal structure based on the digit sequence from the handset. Similarly, the diagram does not show the return to standby/reset which can be caused by replacing the handset at any point.

Finite state diagrams can become complex and it is often necessary to structure them hierarchically, especially for large systems. These diagrams can also be augmented with 'output transitions', which show output generated by the function as it makes the transition from state to state. Finite state diagrams are the basis of, or a major component of, a large number of structured methods for specifying functionality. They are also widely used for specifying protocols. They can also be used with other methods, e.g. as ways of specifying the functionality of activities in MASCOT.

17.3.3.6 Commentary

A number of graphical notations have been illustrated which are capable of describing part of, or perhaps better facets of, an architectural specification. None of these notations of itself, covers all facets of the architectural specification as defined. To overcome these deficiencies the authors recommend an eclectic approach – that is, a variety of notations should be used to specify the system architecture. A number of issues are not addressed at all by the techniques outlined, so any diagrams would have to be further supplemented (probably simply by text) to deal with non-functional issues, resource usage, etc.

It is also interesting to note a possible area of synergy between formal (mathematical) and structured (graphical) methods. The structured methods are good at showing the organization and decomposition of a system, together with the communication between the system components. Formal methods are relatively weak at describing structure. (This is partly a consequence of notation and partly an issue of mode of use.)

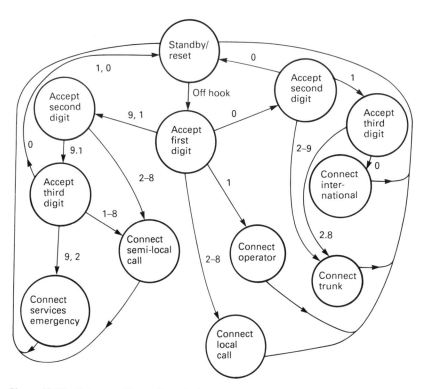

Figure 17.12 Finite state diagram for a telephone

On the other hand, formal methods are good at describing functionality, and structured methods are relatively weak in this area. Consequently the use of formal techniques for defining module functionality within an otherwise structured design representation may prove an effective form of hybrid specification. This may be particularly attractive where formal descriptions can be related to more conventional techniques for specifying functionality such as finite state diagrams. Indeed, the authors believe that, in the long run, formal and structured methods will 'evolve together' and it will become common to use the approaches in conjunction.

17.3.4 Guidelines for the design process

As indicated earlier design is, in the final analysis, a creative process. However, this does not mean that it is not possible to give some general guidlines for carrying out design. The guidelines briefly illustrated here relate to four different aspects of the design process. The first two essentially deal with ways of structuring the process, and the second two cover what might loosely be termed 'design heuristics'.

17.3.4.1 'First-cut' designs

It was explained earlier that there are essentially three different ways of carrying out hierarchical decomposition of systems. These are function-oriented, process-oriented, and object-oriented. The choice between these approaches will, to some extent, depend on the taste of the designer, or systems architect. However, the object-oriented approach is the most general and it should be possible to use object-oriented decomposition for any class of problem domain. The function-oriented decomposition applies best to sequential programs, e.g. compilers. Process-oriented decomposition is appropriate where it is clear from the outset that the design will have to be internally concurrent, either within a single processor, or running on multiple processors. In practice, however, the choice of decomposition strategy will be constrained by non-technical issues, such as the skill of the available staff, the availability of tool support, and so on. In general, however, it is the responsibility of the project manager and the technical architect for the system to design and choose an appropriate process. This idea of choice of process is discussed in Section 17.5, and the topic is also covered in Chapter 15 on software process models. It is also worth remembering that different processes may be appropriate at different levels in the design.

Having chosen a decomposition strategy, the architect should produce a 'first-cut' architecture, based simply on the decomposition rules. Having produced this outline architecture, he should then try to analyse the architecture in terms of the non-functional and quality attributes. As mentioned earlier, there are some types of system where a straightforward functional or process decomposition can produce satisfactory results. If it is clear from the analysis that the requirements can be satisfied with a straightforward decomposition, then the architect should simply complete his task by filling in the details of the architecture.

In general, it is not good practice to settle simply on the first satisfactory design. Consequently, it is desirable for the architect to produce outline designs for a number of possible ways of satisfying the requirements. Note that this is still compatible with the ideas of using, say, functional or process decomposition. What is required is that the granularity on which the functions are broken down, and the boundaries chosen between specific functions, are rather different. Another way of generating alternative designs to compare is to use more than one different decomposition strategy, e.g. object-oriented and function-oriented. Other approaches to producing alternative de-signs are to get more than one designer or design team to work in a 'semi-competitive' mode. In any event, it will be necessary and appropriate to evaluate the alternative designs. In the limit, if all of them satisfactorily meet the technical objectives laid out in the requirements, then the cheapest, or lowest risk, solution ought to be chosen.

17.3.4.2 *Relaxing the requirements*

In many circumstances, however, the architect will not be lucky enough to have a set of requirements which can all be met. He will carry out the 'obvious decompositions' and will end up with a design which, upon analysis, will prove to be inadequate. In other words, he will try a number of alternatives and discover that none of these satisfy both the functional objectives set out in the requirements, and the non-functional and quality objectives also imposed on the project. When this happens there is only one possible strategy available – to relax the requirements. In other words, it is necessary to weaken some of the constraints on the design, or to rescind a number of the requirements altogether, in order to produce a system which satisfies at least some of the requirements.

Usually the designer does not have the information, and he certainly does not have the responsibility, to decide between the various requirements set down by the customer for the system. This means that either the designer must go back to the system's customers, or it may be the case that he has already been supplied with some information about the priorities of the different objectives and constraints. Certainly, if one followed the principles of Gilb's design by objectives, then one would end up establishing a set of priorities over the non-functional and quality constraints for the system. In essence, the architect simply relaxes or abandons constraints until he is able to produce an architectural design which satisfies the remaining requirements and constraints. Even if the customer has not been involved in the process of determining which constraints should be ignored, or treated as low priority, he certainly should be involved in this stage. A review should be held with the customer making clear which of his initial set of requirements will no longer be met by the system design that has been proposed.

There are two points worth drawing out. If an architect has tried a number of different designs, and found that none of them is satisfactory in meeting the complete set of objectives, this does not mean that there is no satisfactory solution. Consequently, some degree of judgement is required to determine when the search for alternatives should be terminated, and the process of relaxing the requirements and constraints should be started. In general, such decisions will depend on the experience and intuition of the architect for the system, but this intuition can often be supported (or perhaps refuted) by considering other similar systems which have been developed or which are under development.

A second point concerns the risk associated with a particular development. It was indicated earlier that alternatives may be chosen on the basis of lowest cost, or lowest perceived risk. In general, risks are associated with development projects where one is undertaking design exercises in domains with which one is not familiar, or solving particular classes of problems for which one has no experience or expertise. It is possible, for example, that one design may use a bought-in component for some part of a system at quite high cost, whereas an alternative design may include custom developed software for that particular function, but the duration and cost of producing this additional functionality is rather uncertain. In this case, a design decision might be to purchase the software component, rather than to develop one anew, because this is a lower risk strategy even though the expected cost is rather higher. Again this sort of decision depends upon the experience, skill and intuition of the architect (and probably the project manager).

In summary, the approach to the design process is first of all to try straightforward architectures to satisfy the requirements and then, if no straightforward solution can be found, to try more imaginative solutions, progressively relaxing requirements and design constraints until an acceptable solution can be found. This makes this part of the design process highly iterative, with the client involved at each iteration, so it is rather difficult to predict the duration of the architectural design activities. However, once a satisfactory architectural design has been produced it should be fairly easy to produce good, and reliable, estimates of the time and duration for the rest of the design implementation project.

17.3.4.3 General design heuristics

It is interesting to consider a number of possible heuristics for aiding the design process. In general, these will be useful either in conjunction with a straightforward functional or process-oriented decomposition, or may be used more generally to guide more 'free form' design activities.

There are surprisingly few published guidelines on how to carry out the design process. Perhaps this is because design is viewed as being a creative process and that there is no structure or rationale in design. However, there are a number of published general design heuristics, and there are also a number of heuristics proposed for the design of interactive systems. A number of the more interesting heuristics from each of these two domains are illustrated here.

When writing requirements, it is good practice to note those areas of requirements that are expected to change. For example, this might include the number of terminals to be supported by a system or, in an accounting system, those aspects of company or tax law which are likely to change and affect the operation of the system. Similarly, it is good practice to hide the results of design decisions which may be affected by the expected changes. Typically, these design decisions therefore should be hidden inside a module and only visible either to that module itself, or to the subordinate modules in the module hierarchy.

Again, it is good practice to hide all the information concerned with management of each resource within one module. This is essentially because it is not necessary for other modules to understand the details of the techniques for operating the device, e.g. knowing what device control codes are used, and what interrupts are used, in order to exploit the resource. Failure to hide these details about manipulation of resources can lead to making programs much more complex than necessary.

It is also good practice to make a single major design decision, e.g. choice of a data structure for implementing some algorithm or related set of operations, within a single module. This guideline may be generalized to say that a set of related design decisions which determine the major characteristics of an abstract data type should be hidden within a module. Hiding information in this way will simplify the understanding of the program, and ease modifications that have to be made in maintenance. In effect, this is a way of achieving high module coherence and low module coupling.

A further general design heuristic is the idea of delaying commitments. It was indicated earlier that one of the activities undertaken by system architects is to make commitments to particular ways of implementing parts of systems. It was said that an architectural specification should contain everything that an implementor needs to know to satisfy the system architect, and nothing more. Consequently, when the architect does not have any particular reason to constrain some particular part of the design, then he ought to delay making a

commitment to that aspect of the design. So this general heuristic is essentially a consequence of the guidelines on writing specifications given by Parnas.

17.3.4.4 Design heuristics for interactive systems

It is generally accepted that one of the most difficult aspects of designing computer systems is to produce interfaces in such a way that the systems are easy to use, and can be used with relatively low error rates. There are a number of principles for guiding the designs of interactive systems. First, some general, rather philosophical, principles are illustrated, followed by some rather more detailed examples of design heuristics which derive from experience in designing interactive systems based on bit-mapped terminals.

One general heuristic for interactive systems is that the interface should be *predictable*; that is, there should be enough information on the screen for a user to predict exactly what will be the results of a command he issues, assuming he understands the behaviour or semantics of the command. Whilst this sounds a very obvious principle, many interactive systems fail to satisfy this heuristic. The Unix operating system is a notable example which violates this principle to quite a considerable degree.

Another general principle is that of *visibility*. This means that the results of carrying out some command on a system should be entirely visible within the display. Clearly, this is not always possible in general, although it is a nice principle to follow when it is feasible. Therefore, visibility is often weakened to say that it should be possible to make the result of some particular operation visible, without affecting the underlying state, e.g. the stored files and so on, in the system. Again, although this seems like an obvious principle it is quite often violated.

One can also look at some more specific guidelines for interactive systems. These derive from experience in developing a system known as MUX on bit-mapped displays. We illustrate a number of the insights gained by the designer of MUX, but suggest that the interested reader should read the full paper (Pike, 1988).

Pike's experience is that confirmation systems do not work. If the user tries to carry out some irrevocable, or dangerous operation, such as deleting a file or directory structure there is no benefit to be gained in giving him a little reminder asking for confirmation that he wishes to carry out this operation. The reason cited for this is that once users are experienced with the system they will hit the appropriate key for confirming the operation without stopping to consider whether or not they really meant to do the operation. It is argued that the irritation of having this extra operation to go through is not justified by the marginally reduced error rate gained through having the confirmation system.

This is a slightly surprising, and perhaps controversial, guideline but one that is based on a considerable amount of experience in using interactive systems. Pike also gives a number of other, rather less controversial, guidelines. For example, to carry out similar operations in different parts of the system, a set of consistent mechanisms should be used. Again, this seems like common sense, but many interactive systems do not follow this guideline. Another generally useful guideline, which is all too often violated, is to make common operations on a system easy (even at the expense of making the less common operations relatively difficult).

There are many more possible guidelines that one could quote. However, it seems more relevant to point the reader to Chapter 13, which deals with psychology as it relates to interface design, and Chapter 57 which gives more general guidelines on the design of interactive systems.

17.3.5 Analysis and review

In a contractual-style software development process, a complete architectural specification would be agreed before detailed design and implementation were started. In an incremental development, the initial 'core' architecture would be agreed early in the development process, and each increment would be agreed at subsequent times. Theses agrements will normally be reached at (design) reviews. The primary purpose of the analysis activities is to provide the information necessary for the review process.

The details of many of the analyses performed, e.g. consistency checking, will depend on the methods, and notations, used. Consequently, this section deals mainly with principles of the analysis activities.

The analyses should support reviews 'looking on both directions in the life cycle', that is, they should confirm that the architecture satisfies the requirements, and that it contains enough information for (trouble free) detailed design and development. General issues of consistency are illustrated first, then analyses which support reviews in each of the above 'directions in the life cycle' are discussed.

17.3.5.1 Consistency

Analysis for consistency is essentially a form of internal verification for the specification. 'Consistent' means that a specification is free from contradiction. Thus one expects names to be used consistently in a specification, and so on. The detailed consistency rules will depend on the methods employed. It is instructive to illustrate consistency in terms of resource usage.

The modules form a hierarchy and one would expect the usage of resources at one level in a module hierarchy to be circumscribed by the resources defined for the immediately superior level. The simplest possibility is that the sum of resources, e.g. time and memory, used at one level are equal to, or bounded by, those at the higher level. (The term 'bounded by' is used, as resource usage may be specified between upper and lower limits, not as an absolute figure.)

In practice, more complex relationships arise. For example, if two modules at one level are alternatives, that is, one or other, but not both, can be invoked for any one invocation of a parent module, then the resources defined at that level may exceed those specified at the parent level. Thus, in general, analysis of the consistency of resource usage in a module hierarchy requires considerable judgement to be exercised. In practice, it is probably acceptable to carry out the simple consistency checks automatically (e.g. bounds on resource usage being respected in the hierarchy) and simply documenting the reasons for any exception.

In practice, one needs to show internal consistency of all aspects of an architectural specification, e.g. resource usage, module dependencies and quality attributes, before one can consider the relationships to requirements and detailed design. Thus consistency analyses must be carried out first, and any inconsistencies rectified by the team responsible for the architecture before involving implementation staff or users. It may be desirable to carry out a review simply to ensure consistency.

17.3.5.2 Verification against requirements

Next, the architecture should be verified against the requirements. Some of the more important aspects of design verification are illustrated below, but note that design verification should be carried out for all facets of the requirements and architecture.

In requirements, system functionality is often specified in terms of transactions, that is, an activity leading from some input to the system to a set of outputs from the system. If the functionality does not depend on the history of inputs to the system, then the transaction function can be specified simply as a relationship between input values and output values. If history is significant, then the relationship will also refer to system state or input history. Even if requirements are not specified in terms of transactions, they are a useful concept in verifying the architecture against the requirements.

If the structure of the requirements is preserved into the architecture, then verification of module function, for example, will reduce to showing that the detail added in architecture is consistent with the function description in requirements. It was argued previously that non-functional and quality constraints lead to changes in system structure between requirements and architecture. Clearly, in cases where the structure changes, one cannot verify functionality on a module-by-module basis.

The set of inputs to, and outputs from, a system do not (must not) change from requirements to architecture. Similarly, the same inputs trigger the same outputs in both requirements and architecture. Thus the transactions form a 'fixed point' for verifying the consistency of architecture with requirements. Furthermore, if one analyses requirements and architecture on the basis of transactions, one can deal readily with most of the attributes of a specification described above.

For each transaction, the function specified in the architecture should be consistent with the function specified in the requirements, that is, whenever the requirements function is defined, i.e. the output is determined given some input value, then the mapping from input to output values should be equivalent in the two specifications. The architecture function may be specified more completely, e.g. in terms of error reports, than the requirements function, but it may not be specified less completely. In practice, the input and output data items may be specified in more detail (or in different ways) in the architecture, so an interpretation will be required between the two levels. The approach can perhaps best be illustrated by example.

Imagine a system required to read in positions of aircraft from a radar, to store the positions (plots) in a database, and to display those plots falling into a specified geographical area on a screen in front of an operator. Assume that the requirements specified radar plot and display in terms of true, and modelled latitude and longitude pairs, respectively. Assume further that the architecture defined the input plot in terms of range and angle, and the output in terms of (updates to) a bit map for display on a bit-mapped graphics display. Verification would then be concerned both with the translation between latitude/longitude position, range/angle position, and that between bit-map operations and modelled latitude/longitude. However, having taken into account these data item mappings, verification that the transactions are consistent is essentially straightforward (covering the cases when the plot is displayed, and when it is not).

Other properties of the architecture can be verified against the requirements in terms of transactions. For example, the execution time of a transaction in the architecture can be evaluated by summing the execution time of the functions in the transactions. This time can then be compared with the requirement.

If the transactions in the architecture are purely sequential and there are no resource clashes, then simple summation of function execution times will serve to derive the transaction response time. If, however, there are resource clashes, e.g. because parallel transactions (may) wish to use the same file, then the timing analysis will have to take into account the expected waiting time for the resource. In general, it is necessary to use queuing theory to calculate (estimate) these response times (see Chapter 7).

In general, analysis of the properties may have to be carried out on individual modules (functions), on individual transactions, or on the system as a whole. In some cases, depending on the detail of the requirements, it may be necessary to evaluate some system attribute, e.g. memory usage, at the module, transaction and system level.

In other cases, the attributes can be dealt with largely at one level. Many quality attributes will need to be verified only at module level, e.g. re-usability. The performance attributes, e.g. functionality, response time, need to be verified primarily at the transaction level. Dependability issues such as safety and security are archetypical systems issues, and can only be evaluated fully at the system level.

A further general system issue is *completeness*. Whilst one is concerned with completeness at a low level, e.g. dealing with all fuction inputs, the primary need for investigation of completeness of the architecture is at the system level. Put another way, ensuring completeness at the system level must *ipso facto*, ensure it at other levels.

17.3.5.3 Trade-offs and relaxation of requirements

It was stated earlier that two of the main issues in producing architectural specifications were to establish viable trade-offs between conflicting requirements and to evaluate alternative designs. Clearly, if alternative designs are produced, then it is necessary to analyse each design and to compare the results of the analyses. These analysis results, together with cost estimates, should provide the basic data for a comparative design review with the customer.

It is relatively uncommon to involve the customer in this sort of design review, so it is worthwhile amplifying slightly on the point. It is valuable to involve the customer at this point. The requirements say what the customer (thinks he) wants, but the architecture says what he will get. Especially where requirements have necessarily been compromised in design, it is very important that the customer agrees that he is willing to accept what is to be built. This leaves a problem of how the architecture can be made accessible, or intelligible, to the customer.

The key issue is to translate the architecture back into terms the user can understand, i.e. into the terms of the business or organization. The analyses, at least partly, help with this as they relate the architecture to the requirements, e.g. a necessary omission in the architecture can be related to functionality or transactions in the requirements. However, more may be needed. For example it may be helpful to explain that, say, a 20% reduction in transaction throughput means employing three more clerks. Whilst the architect may be able to make this sort of interpretation, it is probably valuable to involve the analyst who developed the initial requirements, at this stage, as he will have a better understanding of the link between the business and the system.

Stress is often laid on the value of prototyping for this sort of design verification activity. The authors believe that prototyping is of value, and that it should be used more widely (see Chapter 40). However, prototyping is not a panacea, and prototypes may still be mysterious to customers. Thus it is still necessary to interpret the results of prototyping in the business domain, and to say how to *scale* from the prototype to the finished system (*cf.* the use of prototypes in other engineering disciplines).

There is a further important aspect of involving the customer in the review when alternatives are being evaluated, or the software is being developed incrementally. Even assuming that the customer has expressed priorities for functions, etc., it may not be the case that the alternative (or first increment) which best meets these priorities is the right one to choose! Often choices of priorities reflect (hidden) assumptions about what functions can be provided easily, and which easily can be provided in conjunction. Especially where the structure of the

requirements and architecture are different, it is likely that these assumptions will be incorrect, so the customer should be given the opportunity to choose from 'what's on offer' in terms of design alternatives or increments.

17.3.5.4 Implementability

Once it has been established that the architecture is satisfactory *vis à vis* the requirements, it is sensible to turn to the utility of the architecture as an input to the design process. In essence, the issue here is to get agreement from the implementor that the modules for which he is responsible are defined adequately for the implementation task to be undertaken with relatively little risk. Thus, this form of review sounds like it should be simply an exercise in specification reading, but returning to the idea of implementor criticizing the architecture, another approach to the review can be seen.

If an implementor is to work on some module, or modules, at a fairly low level in the module hierarchy, the review should be based on a module one or two levels higher in the hierarchy (possibly with the implementors for all subordinate modules). The 'review' should then include a brainstorming session looking for better ways (in terms of all the requirements) of breaking down the module into its constituent parts.

This approach has three major benefits. First, it may find a better approach than the one suggested by the architect. Second, it will give the implementor an understanding of the context for the module, the reasons for design decisions implicit in the specification, and so on. This understanding will be *much better* than that which would have been gained by specification reading alone. Third, psychologically the implementor will feel much more involved in the design and should be much more willing to abide by the design commitments as he was involved in making them. In other words, it is good for motivation (see Chapter 32).

17.3.5.5 Role of the analyses and reviews

In summary, these analyses are carried out in support of reviews of the architecture. These reviews cover internal consistency, satisfaction of requirements, and suitability for implementation. Although the reviews have been described as taking place in this order, they may well take place in other orders, e.g. to check a crucial part of the system for implementability before showing it to the customer. The reviews will almost certainly take place iteratively. What is important is that the *roles* of the different types of review are not confused, and not combined. In other words, one must analyse and review the architecture to ensure it is satisfactory from these points of view: internal consistency, satisfaction of requirements, suitability for implementation.

17.3.6 Summary and conclusions

The nature of an architectural specification as a product, and the activities in the process of architectural specification have been discussed. Some of the difficulties of undertaking this process have been noted, and what the authors believe to be the most important and salient aspects of the contents of an architectural specification have been outlined.

This section also amplified on three aspects of the product and process. It outlined a number of generally useful notations which can be employed to describe different facets of an architecture. A number of guidelines were given for carrying out the process of architectural specification, including some general design heuristics. In the final analysis design is a creative, rather than a procedural, process so some stress has been laid on the analysis and review of architectural specifications.

Ideally, *requirements* for notations, guidelines, and analysis techniques for architectural specification would have been presented. However, the presentation would then have been rather more obscure, and it would also have been rather unsatisfactory, because it would have become clear that there were relatively few methods which actually satisfied the requirements. Thus the description of these various facets of an architectural specification has been rather more prescriptive. Consequently, they should be interpreted as being illustrative of the ways of specifying architecture, and carrying out the architectural design process, rather than being definitive ways of approaching the problems of architectural specification.

As indicated earlier, there are relatively few methods that address the full generality of problems that arise in architectural specification, and those methods that are relevant tend to deal relatively well with only a sub-set of the aspects of architectural specification. For example, many methods deal quite well with the issues of decomposition, and functional specification, but tend not to deal with the non-functional and quality issues associated with an architecture. Brief overviews of some interesting and relevant design methods are given in Section 17.4. However, it should be stressed that these methods do not deal with all the issues described here, and that any of the methods described will need to be augmented with techniques outlined in this section, or others, as appropriate.

17.4 Methods for architectural design

As explained earlier, there are many methods which deal with some facet or facets of architectural design but none, to the authors' knowledge, which adequately covers all facets of architectural design. This is one of the reasons for the extensive discussion of architectural specification notations and processes in Section 17.3.

However, the authors believe that it is useful to discuss some of the available methods. In Section 17.4.1 there is an overview of HOOD which the authors believe to be one of the more promising object-oriented design decomposition methods. Section 17.4.2 gives an overview of MASCOT3, a widely used real-time method. Section 17.4.3 gives a brief survey of some other available methods.

The chosen methods are somewhat biased towards technical/ embedded applications. However, the reader is directed to Chapter 55, which gives a good account of architectural design for database systems, or the database component of systems.

17.4.1 HOOD

HOOD (Hierarchical Object Oriented Design) is based on work on object-oriented design in relation to Ada carried out by Booch (1983 and 1986). In HOOD, objects are the basic unit of modularity, and they correspond to the module entity in the definition of the structure of an architectural specification in Section 17.3. Also HOOD enforces structuring of the objects according to three principles:

1. *Abstraction, information hiding and encapsulation*. Objects are defined by their external properties only (*cf.* algebraic specification), and the internal structure is hidden from users of the objects.
2. *Hierarchical decomposition and use*:
   (a) *Composition hierarchy*. Objects may be composed from other objects, so that a system can be constructed as 'parent' objects including 'child' objects.
   (b) *Use hierarchy*. Objects may use operations provided by other objects, so that a system can be constructed with 'senior' objects using 'junior' objects in the hierarchy (Stark, 1986).

3. *Control structuring*:
   (a) *Passive objects*. Passive objects are invoked via a form of procedure call and are strongly analogous with the concept of monitors (Hansen, 1977) or MASCOT IDAs (see Section 17.4.2).
   (b) *Active objects*. Active objects may operate on behalf of several client (calling) objects simultaneously in response to external stimuli. In the terminology here, active objects may include processes.

Most of this discussion focuses on the notation for describing these structures. An object binds together data and the operations working on the data. The basic object notation gives the object name and shows its 'incoming' and 'outgoing' interfaces. The interface falls into two parts (see *Figure 17.13*):

1. The provided interface defines the operations and resources provided by the object and their associated parameters and types.
2. The required interface defines the types and operations required from other objects.

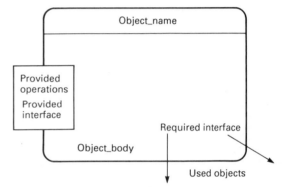

Figure 17.13 Basic HOOD object

The body implements the provided operations and resources (objects and types), as described in the interface, using external and internal operations and data, or using internal objects. As indicated earlier, objects can be passive or active, and this affects the control structure in the objects:

1. *Passive*. Control is transferred from the calling to the called object, and the operation is executed immediately. After completing the operation control is returned to the calling object. The flow of control is defined in an operation control structure (OPCS).

2. *Active*. Control is not transferred, and reaction to the stimulus will be serviced at a time determined by the internal state of the called object, as defined in a object control structure (OBCS).

The external influences on the top-level design object may 'trigger' an operation; to represent this case a 'zigzag arrow' is used. It may be annotated with the name of the associated (asynchronous) interrupt.

In either case, if the operation cannot be performed successfully, an exception can be raised and propagated to the user.

Figure 17.14 displays the graphical representations associated with active and passive objects.

17.4.1.1 Use relationship between objects (control flow)

An object is said to use another object if the former requires one or more of the operations provided by the latter. In HOOD, active objects can use other objects freely, but passive objects

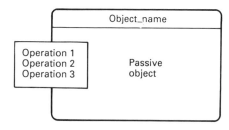

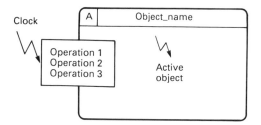

Figure 17.14 HOOD active and passive objects

can only use other passive objects. HOOD forbids cyclic use relationships between passive objects, but active objects may use one another in a cyclic manner. Thus active objects are at the top of the hierarchy and passive objects are at the bottom. Note that this is consistent with our previous suggestion of using process decomposition at the top of the hierarchy, and functional decomposition at the bottom. Typically there are use structures such as those shown in *Figure 17.15*.

HOOD encourages the principles of low coupling between, and high cohesion within, objects. In addition it suggests that the use interconnection graph should be of as low complexity as possible, i.e. objects should show low 'fan-out' (Kafura and Henry, 1984) (they should use as few other objects as possible) and high 'fan-in' (they should be used as much as possible), although this advice is clearly somewhat contradictory.

17.4.1.2 *Include relationship between objects (decomposition)*

To provide a top-down decomposition of a system, a parent object is composed from a set of child objects that collectively provide the functionality of the parent. Each of these child objects may in turn have internal objects. This decomposition is represented by the include relationship between objects, where one object, the parent, contains child objects. A system can be represented by a parent-child hierarchy with a top-level object (the system) and a number of different objects at the lower levels.

The graphical representation is shown in *Figure 17.16*, where:

1. The inclusion relationship is represented by showing the children inside the parent.
2. The implementation of operations at the parent level by operations at the child level is represented by a dashed arrow.
3. A child object may use another object at the parent level and this external object is represented by a box outside the parent object.

Figure 17.16 shows that a call to the provided operation Op3 is effectively mapped to call of Op2 in Child 3.

Parent operations may be implemented by operations provided by one child or combinations of those provided by several children. In this latter case, the parent operation controls the invocation order of the operations in its children. Control flow between operations is described at parent level by an OBCS which may take one of three forms:

1. The OBCS may be handled by one dedicated, active, child object.
2. The OBCS may be handled by several child objects.
3. The OBCS may be handled both by a dedicated active object and in several other child objects.

Figure 17.17 gives an example where one part of the object control structure is handled in CONTROL and other parts are handled in child objects Child1, Child2 and Child3. The trigger and use arrows show the nature of the control interactions. Note that the OBCS corresponds to the process control information identified in Section 17.3.

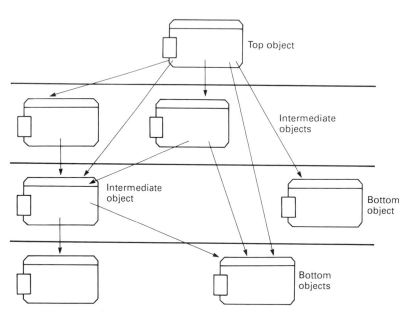

Figure 17.15 HOOD object use hierarchy

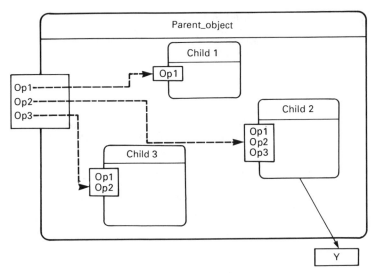

Figure 17.16 HOOD object decomposition hierarchy

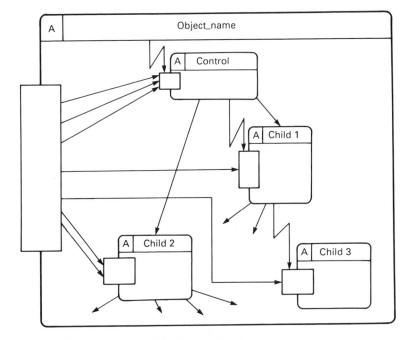

Figure 17.17 Representation of the object control structure

If an exception can be raised by an object, this is shown by a line crossing the use relationship. This line is annotated with the exception name or names, as shown in *Figure 17.18*. This completes the definition of the control structure notation.

17.4.1.3 Data flows

Figure 17.19 shows the flow of data, here a named arrow terminated with a circle is used, as illustrated earlier. Data may flow in the direction of the use relation, or in the opposite direction, or both. This notation is used to show the major data flows in a diagram which are the parameters and results of the provided operations of the used objects.

Thus there are now notations for showing module structure/ process structure, dependencies, control information and some aspects of module interfaces. Module function is not catered for by the diagrammatic notation.

17.4.1.4 Design heuristics

HOOD does not claim to define laws identifying 'good' objects and designs, but it defines heuristics for constructing and comparing alternative designs.

According to the HOOD manual, the intent of an object is to represent a problem domain entity, and it should also act as a 'black box' to facilitate testing, debugging and maintenance.

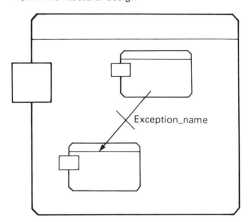

Figure 17.18 HOOD exception notation

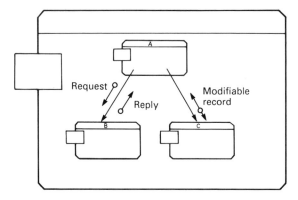

Figure 17.19 HOOD data flow notation

The principles of abstraction and information hiding articulated by Parnas provide the main guidelines for assessing an object, thus a 'good' object represents a problem domain entity and hides information that is likely to change, if design decisions relating to the object changes. In practice HOOD identifies several classes of object, only one of which corresponds to a 'real-world' entity:

1. *Entities*. These represent a problem domain entity or abstraction of an object in the 'real world'. Such an entity could be as concrete as a hardware sensing device, or more abstract such as an accounts department. Abstract data types fall into this category.
2. *Actions*. The manual says that these are: 'abstract properties of actions, instead of things, provide a generalised set of operations e.g. input_handler, math_processor. Procedures are elementary action abstractions. Action abstraction may be represented through HOOD active objects, where exported operations can operate concurrently'.
3. *Virtual machines*. These group together operations (common, lower level) which are all used at some superior level, or which all use some set of operations.

The distinction between entities and actions seems rather artificial, and perhaps would be better expressed as representing the difference between 'real-world' entities and those which are simply artefacts of the implementation, e.g. file handlers. In general, the published heuristics seem a little vague.

Note that there is a strong analogy here with the concept of module coherence introduced earlier.

The HOOD manual goes on to define a number of design principles based on these concepts.

17.4.1.5 Summary

This section has briefly illustrated the main notations and design guidelines used by HOOD. The interested reader is referred to the HOOD manual (1988) for further information.

The HOOD manual describes techniques for specifying object functionality based on an Ada-style pseudo-code. Thus HOOD deals with most facets of an architectural specification, as defined here; the primary exception is the handling of resources and interfaces. The main methodological weaknesses are the absence of sufficient analysis techniques, and the concept of transactions for supporting such analyses. The authors believe that HOOD is a very interesting method, and that the object-oriented approach is an attractive way of specifying architectures. However, the method is not very mature and some of the design guidelines and heuristics seem somewhat ill-formed. It is to be expected that the method will improve as experience is gained with its use.

17.4.2 MASCOT3

MASCOT (Modular Approach to Software Construction Operation and Test) was initially developed in the 1970s, and has evolved to its current form, MASCOT3, as a result of feedback from practical use of earlier versions of the method in real-time embedded systems. MASCOT3 embodies the notion that software is constructed, operated and tested according to a single modular scheme. This means that, once the design structure is completed, the implementation team work entirely in terms of this design structure without the need to change concepts. Thus the testing and debugging of systems developed using MASCOT is always performed in terms of the design components and concepts.

A brief overview of MASCOT3 is given here. Papers describing MASCOT3 in more detail can be found in a special issue of *Software Engineering Journal* (MASCOT, 1986) and an Official Handbook for MASCOT3 is available.

MASCOT3 assumes that there are six basic stages to the development process, but it provides notation and guidelines only for stages 2, 3 and 4:

1. Requirements and constraints.
2. Design proposal.
3. Network decomposition.
4. Element decomposition.
5. Algorithm definition.
6. Integration and test.

The design proposal is presented as a data flow network diagram containing three categories of components: active, passive and servers. Implicitly, process decomposition is used to produce the design proposal.

Active components are self-motivating and can take responsibility for implementing a specific set of cuntions and/or handling a specified set of external interactions. Passive components can store data required for communication between the active components. They also have responsibility for maintaining the integrity of their data in spite of data being simultaneously accessed by (potentially many) active components. Servers are responsible for controlling the embedded hardware devices connected to the system, and can be either passive or active depending upon the nature of the devices controlled.

The passive components are inter-communication data areas (IDAs). These may be either channels or pools as outlined in

Section 17.3 also, in MASCOT3, those may be more general communication areas such as HOOD passive objects. MASCOT3 is different from HOOD in that the synchronization requirements and mechanisms are well defined.

The active components may be either subsystems or activities, which are processes in this terminology. Subsystems are composite components containing other (lower level) components within them. These lower level components can be subsystems, IDAs, activities or servers, thus achieving a hierarchical representation. IDAs and servers may also be composite, but they are not allowed to contain active components. A MASCOT3 design proposal (as illustrated in *Figure 17.20*) is generic and must be instantiated to form a particular network (architectural design). This allows common design components, e.g. terminal servers, to be replicated in a simple fashion.

The design proposal illustrated above shows three devices, D1, D2 and D3, controlled by three servers, sv1, sv2 and sv3. These servers are instantiated from templates known as st1, st2 and st3. The subsystem ss1 is instantiated from the template subsys_1, and the set of components is configured to make the system, sys_ex. Communication within the network occurs via access interfaces ai1–3, and connect windows (w) on servers to ports (p1–3) on subsystems.

The access interfaces define a set of operations provided at the window and required at the port. It is worth noting that it is only possible to connect a window to a port if the types match, so we are guaranteed type correct system construction. Also, it is possible to have multiple MASCOT3 components satisfying the same interface, e.g. a device driver which drives a local device could be replaced by one which sends output to a device across a network without need to change the interface or the rest of the system.

The network decomposition stage of the MASCOT3 method is concerned entirely with establishing the hierarchical representation of the design down to a level of detail where the network components are either activities or non-composite IDAs and servers. At this stage the data to be held by each IDA, and the access facilities it must provide, have been determined, and the functions required of each server and activity have been defined.

The network decomposition uses the same notation as the design proposal and, for example, a decomposition of the network in Figure 17.20 could be as shown in *Figure 17.21*. Note that the communication paths – ports, windows and access interfaces – must be the same as shown in the higher level diagram.

Further decomposition (*Figure 17.22*) shows channels and pools. The element decomposition breaks activities down into a root (the main body) and subroots. This is equivalent to breaking a process into modules in the terminology of this chapter.

A design process for MASCOT3 has been described, although a common criticism of MASCOT is that it is largely a notation which offers little methodological guidance. Also guidance has been given on mapping MASCOT3 into Ada. Both aspects of this design approach are documented in the special issue of the *Software Engineering Journal* (MASCOT, 1986).

MASCOT3 was developed from MASCOT2 (the notation shown in Section 17.3), largely because of criticism over the non-hierarchic nature of the design representation. In terms of modelling hierachy MASCOT3 is similar to the methods based on SA/SD. It deals comparatively well with issues such as synchronization and control over communication, but is relatively weak in terms of function definition and representation of timing behaviour. However, the originators of MASCOT3 intended that it should be used with other notations, e.g. state machines for defining functionality, and MASCOT3 does provide a good framework for an architectural specification.

17.4.3 Other methods

There are many structured methods intended for use in the (architectural) design phase. Space does not permit us to give a thorough treatment of these methods. The following material should therefore be viewed as a form of annotated bibliography covering some of the better known and more widely used methods.

17.4.3.1 Structured analysis/structured design

The techniques of structured analysis and structured design (SA/SD) were pioneered by De Marco (1978), and Yourdon and Constantine (1985). Their original books, published in 1978 and 1979, still provide the best reference material for these methods.

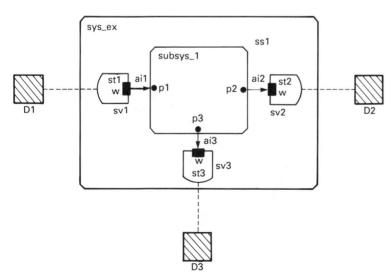

Figure 17.20   MASCOT3 design proposal

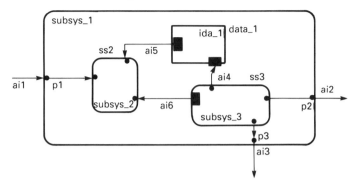

Figure 17.21 MASCOT3 network decomposition

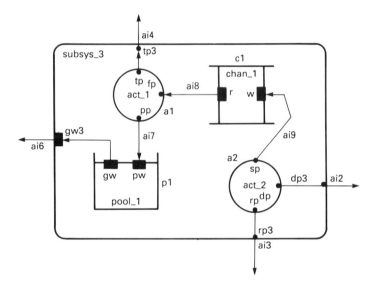

Figure 17.22 Further MASCOT3 network decomposition

Section 17.3 outlined the notation used by SA/SD, sometimes also known as the Yourdon method. Briefly illustrated here is the method by which this notation is intended to be used, and some of the more recent extensions to SA/SD to deal with the issues of real-time system design.

In applying the SA/SD method, most of the process is concerned with producing and refining the data flow diagrams. Initially a data flow diagram is produced which shows the whole system under consideration as a single process, with data flows going into and coming out of the system. This diagram is usually called the *context diagram*.

The context diagram is then refined or decomposed into a top-level data flow diagram, and this is subsequently decomposed into a number of further levels of design. As each level is produced, a number of additional data stores may be defined to hold data generated by the newly introduced functions or processes. This process stops when the individual functions or processes defined in the diagrams are believed to be small enough to be implemented simply from their specifications. These are usually referred to as primitive processes.

All the data flows and data stores in the diagram are included in a data dictionary. The data dictionary shows how the data elements are structured, or decomposed, into their component parts. There is a requirement that the flows should be consistent between the various levels of decomposition. Demonstrating consistency is usually referred to as achieving *balance* in the data flow diagrams.

The primitive processes are defined in more detail using the so-called *minispecs*. These are usually textual specifications of the functionality expected of the process. It is common to use structured English or pseudo-code for these specifications.

These diagrams provide much of the basic structural information called for in the definition of an architectural specification in Section 17.3. In particular, the techniques show quite well the process and inter-process communication structure. There is no explicit identification of modules, but it is usually assumed that the modules correspond to the lowest level processes in the hierarchy. Since SA/SD represents a process structure, it has been fairly common for these techniques to be applied in real-time systems. However, SA/SD does not cover all the important issues in specifying real-time systems, so a number of developments of SA/SD have been produced dealing with timing and other issues.

One of the most commonly used extensions of SA/SD for

real-time systems is that developed by Ward and Mellor (1985). More recently Hatley and Pirbhai (1987) have developed some fairly sophisticated extensions of SA/SD for dealing with real-time system specification. For example, their techniques include state transition diagrams for the processes, and process activation diagrams which define the control structures for the processes. The method also deals with timing issues, covering such properties as reception rates for periodic functions and the response time for aperiodic functions. The authors believe that this is one of the most effective structured techniques available for dealing with the specification of real-time systems architecture, although it does not deal with interfaces and other aspects of architecture as laid down in Section 17.3.

17.4.3.2 *Jackson System Development (JSD)*

JSD is another method that has evolved over many years of use. The original method had six steps, but JSD now comprises three basic stages: modelling, network and implementation. The notation used for JSD is conventional, and is similar to that of JSP and SA/SD described in Section 17.3. Consequently, this section will focus on the methodological aspects of JSD, rather than describing the notation in detail.

The characteristic principle of JSD is that it focuses on modelling the problem which the system is intended to address, rather than addressing the detailed specification of functionality directly. This apparently simple shift in view has a fairly profound effect on the nature of the analysis process. This may imply that JSD is concerned with requirements, but it is more properly concerned with modelling those aspects of the organization's behaviour that are going to be implemented in the system. Therefore it is properly an architectural design method rather than a requirements analysis method.

The modelling stage proceeds by looking for entities in the 'real world' and actions undertaken by those entities. An entity therefore represents some physical or logical object together with some associated actions which can modify the state of the object – in other words, it is closely analogous to the concept of object in object-oriented development. An example of such JSD entities might be a lift, which can be called, can move to a floor and so on.

The model of these entities is represented by a number of process structure diagrams (PSDs). These represent a process and its associated actions in a tree. The process is at the top of the tree and the individual actions are the leaves of the tree. With simple processes there will be only two levels in the tree – the process and the actions. For more complex processes, or entities, there will be an extended hierarchy where the intermediate nodes in the tree represent the groups of related actions. As indicated in Section 17.3 time ordering, alternatives, and iteration of actions are represented by simple diagrammatic conventions. More specifically, the events at the leaves form a regular grammar structure (albeit represented diagrammatically) which defines the allowable sequences of events. The state is represented by a data structure known as a state vector, and it must include enough information to support the actions and control over their ordering. Once the PSD is complete it is 'decorated' with actions and conditions, expressed as operations on the state vectors, which control selection and iteration in the regular grammar.

Determining suitable entities to form the basis of the model is an exercise which requires some skill and judgement. JSD gives some guidelines for finding suitable entities and particularly stresses the need to analyse the problem domain, rather than thinking about functionality that can be conveniently supported in a computer. However, the method recognizes that this is an area where the skill of the analyst, or system architect, is most needed.

At the network stage, sometimes called the system specification stage, the architect produces system structure diagrams (SSDs). These diagrams represent the flow of data through the system. The data can be of two sorts: data streams and state vectors. The data streams are messages passing between processes, e.g. requests or commands to the processes, or reports produced as the result of a request. These are very strongly analogous to the data flows in MASCOT3. State vectors represent the internal values held by the entities, e.g. the values stored in some database. Again, some skill is required in determining the distinction between data streams and state vectors, but, typically, data streams represent transient information and state vectors represent persistent information which is held over a long period of time by the system. Perhaps more importantly, the state vectors can be written only by the process with which they are associated, but read (inspected in JSD terms) by any process.

The first part of the network stage, known as the initial model phase, primarily adds information about data flows relating to the entities identified in the previous stage. The initial model phase provides one process per instance of a model entity, *cf.* the example about a process per line for a telephone exchange. Not surprisingly, this may yield more processes than are readily implementable. The issue of multiplicity of processes is dealt with in implementation. In addition, JSD provides ways of merging data flows between processes. The rules for merging give semantics for data access which are very similar to those for MASCOT channels and pools respectively.

The second part of this stage, known as the elaboration phase, may add new functions and processes to the system description. A number of new functions may be added to the entities or processes. Typically, these represent additional elementary operations which are needed to implement the existing model processes. These are often referred to as embedded functions.

The initial model phase identifies inputs and outputs to the system, but does not deal with any processing necessary to support input and output operations. As part of the elaboration phase, these additional functions, usually referred to as imposed functions, are added to the system model. Typical imposed functions include 'filters' on inputs which remove erroneous or invalid input from the user, and ensure that only valid inputs go through to the primary functions of the system which were identified at the entity modelling stage.

As part of the elaboration phase additional information is added about timing and synchronization of the system processes. A novel feature of JSD is that it has the concept of time grain markers (TGMs) which effectively represents periodic synchronization information. These TGMs are used to control the synchronization and interaction of processes to ensure that data integrity is preserved.

The third stage of JSD is concerned with implementation. Whilst this is strictly outside the remit of a study of architectural design methods, it is central to JSD, so it is worthwhile briefly discussing this stage. In theory, all JSD processes can run concurrently, assuming that there are enough processor resources to support concurrent operation. In practice, there will usually be fewer processors than processes, and it is usually necessary to multiplex several processes onto one processor. JSD approaches this issue by developing an explicit schedule for execution of the system processes. It also includes a number of devices, e.g. process inversion, which are intended to optimize the process structure. Inversion eliminates some of the overhead caused by communication between concurrent processes. For example, if two processes communicate only by passing an iterated data stream, there will be a context switch every time a data item is passed. Inversion with respect to this data stream would mean that one process called the other, passing the data item as a parameter of the call. Thus a pair of communicating processes has been reduced to a single process communicating internally by procedure call, and this eliminates a good deal of scheduling and context switching overhead.

Like other methods described in this chapter, JSD addresses certain aspects of the architectural specification. In particular, it deals with the process structure, process communication, synchronization and control, together with certain resource information, particularly timing. It is unusual in that it deals well with the 'protocol' aspect of architecture, determining the allowable order of events through the regular grammars. It does not directly address issues such as modularity, nor other aspects of resources such as space usage.

Once the basic entities have been identified, the method in JSD is essentially mechanistic and the proponents of JSD say that one of the great strengths is that no matter who uses the method, the same design should result, once the basic entities have been determined. This means that JSD can be very effective in certain circumstances but, if non-functional information is critical to the development, it is often very difficult to produce a satisfactory design. This is because there is no way of taking into account this information purely within the method as defined. Thus JSD is effective in many circumstances, but can become ineffective or unwieldy in other situations.

JSD is quite a sophisticated and subtle method, so it has not been possible to do it full justice here. The interested reader is referred to Sutcliffe's excellent book: *Jackson Systems Development* (1988) for a readable and up-to-date account of the method.

Also, interestingly, although JSD is clearly a structured method, it has a solid basis in automata theory, regular expressions, etc. Thus it provides evidence that the theoretical principles can be presented in such a way that the benefits of a rigorous foundation can be exploited without exposing the user to the underlying mathematics.

17.4.3.3 Structured System Analysis and Design Method (SSADM)

SSADM (Nicholls, 1987) has been developed by the Central Computing and Telecommunications Agency (CCTA) of the UK government for use in data processing applications. It was originally based on a proprietary method developed by Learmonth and Burchett Management Systems (LBMS). The method is widely used in government circles in the UK and also has a considerable degree of use in commerce.

The method falls into two major phases: analysis and design. Roughly speaking, analysis corresponds to the requirements phase, and design corresponds to the architectural phase that we are concerned with in this chapter. The method comprises six stages, three in each phase, and the interface between the two phases is the system specification. This method structure is illustrated in *Figure 17.23*.

In the analysis phase, the first stage looks at the current operational system, whether it is manual or automated, and investigates the problems of the system. The second stage determines the requirements for the system, and the third stage is concerned with selecting technical options for the system. That is, the third stage identifies priorities for the design and development process, and may determine major technical strategies based on results of a separate feasibility study.

In the design phase the detailed design of the data structures and of the individual processes can be carried out in parallel. After the logical design of the data and the processes, physical design, which gives a structure for implementation in some particular hardware/software environment, is carried out. In particular, physical design is concerned with ensuring that performance requirements for the system are satisfied.

Typical applications of SSADM are where there are large and complex data requirements. Consequently, SSADM depends very heavily on standard database analysis techniques (see Chapters 54 and 55). Thus SSADM employs fairly conventional notation for modelling entity relationship structures. It also employs fairly conventional notation for dealing with process decomposition, and more abstract data structures. Consequently, it seems more helpful to comment on the basic organization and structure of the method rather than going into details about the notation employed.

SSADM provides detailed guidance on the steps that must be carried out within each stage in the method. However, the repertoire of basic techniques used in each of these stages is relatively limited. Consequently, the main techniques used in SSADM are discussed briefly, but space does not permit illustration of the detailed organization of each of the method stages.

It should first be noted that SSADM is very much a datadriven method, and that one of the unique features of the method is the fact that it takes three different, but complementary, views of the data in the system. This text concentrates on the techniques for dealing with data modelling.

SSADM employs data flow diagrams, strongly analogous with those used in SA/SD. The notation employed in SSADM is slightly different from that employed in SA/SD, but the structure and content of the diagram are essentially equivalent.

SSADM supports the idea of logical data structures, which are stylized forms of entity-relationship diagrams. These diagrams are used at a number of stages in the software development life cycle, and are the basis for third normal form data analysis which provides logically sound data structures.

SSADM also has the concept of entity life histories, which provide a view of how the data is generated or evolves in the system. These are conceptually very similar to the process structure diagrams in JSD, and show the order of events which affect some entity or data item. As with JSD, iteration and alternatives are shown in the diagrams, together with basic ordering of events.

These three sets of diagrams represent different facets of the data and processing in the system and should be viewed as being complementary, rather than isolated, descriptions of system functionality. The data flow diagram shows how processes and system maintained data fit together, as well as how the system interfaces with processes in the real world. The logical data structure then shows the structure and inter-relationships of the data in the system, and also ways in which the data can be accessed. The entity life history shows the dynamics of the system operation in the sense that it indicates how the entity changes over time. The developers of SSADM believe that this complementary approach to modelling the data gives SSADM its strength in modelling and specifying systems.

The detailed definitions of each stage of SSADM draw upon these techniques and other standard techniques in data processing such as third normal form analysis. They also stress the role of reviews in the development process and explicitly include QA activities in the stage descriptions.

SSADM is widely used, but there have been several criticisms of the method, mostly to do with the volume of paperwork generated when applying the method. Some refinement of the techniques have already taken place and there is an SSADM 'fast path' which is a much less onerous way of using the method for fairly simple and small systems. However, SSADM has been used for a much shorter period of time than other techniques such as JSD and SA/SD. Consequently it is to be expected that the method will evolve further over time and as experience of use of the method increases.

There is copious literature on SSADM available both from the CCTA and LBMS. Perhaps the best simple introduction to

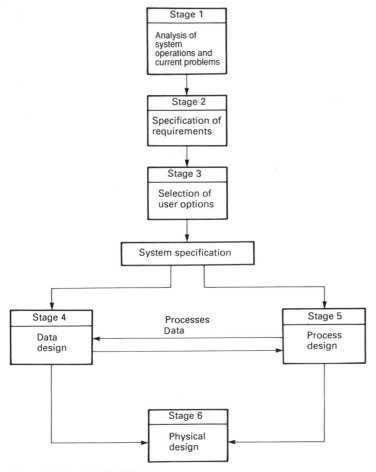

Figure 17.23 Basic SSADM structure

the method is an introduction produced by the CCTA (Nicholls, 1987).

17.4.3.4 Commentary

Only a very small number of structured methods which are intended to assist with the architectural design phase of software development have been discussed. However, some of the more important methods have been identified, including those which are probably most widely used in industry and commerce. As indicated earlier, there are perhaps a hundred structured methods in use, or at least described in the literature, and it is not possible to do justice to all these techniques in the space available. However, studies of structured methods indicate that there are a limited number of basic techniques underlying this wide range of structured methods and the above short survey has illustrated the majority of these basic techniques.

It should be clear from the examples that many of these techniques deal with a substantial part of the architectural specification as defined in Section 17.3. However, none of the techniques deals with all of the aspects of the architectural specification. Most of the techniques are fairly weak at dealing with non-functional and resource issues, and few, if any, deal in a satisfactory way with interfaces. Consequently, the authors

believe that, although it is useful to employ a structured method in architectural design, it is necessary to be aware of the limitations of the method chosen and to be sure that the diagrams produced using the method are supplemented with the appropriate information to cover the range of issues identified in Section 17.3.

17.5 Conclusions

The main purpose of these conclusions is to draw out some of the more important messages that have been covered in the preceding pages, and to relate what has been essentially a technical discourse to the associated management issues. A lot of information is required to define an architecture fully. Depending on the nature of the development process (including the methods used), this information may be established at a variety of stages in the process (from requirements to detailed design). To ensure clarity in these conclusions, the term architectural specification is used to refer to the stage, phase and product in development. Architecture definition is used to refer to the information necessary to define an architecture, as set out in Section 17.2, regardless of the stage at which the information is generated.

The history of software engineering shows that the development of large-scale software systems is a fraught and error-prone exercise. Many of the causes of problems in large-scale software development are technical. Almost by definition, the most critical technical activities in software development are the establishment and specification of requirements – without a set of requirements it is almost impossible to run a project as one has no basis against which to plan, nor any base line against which to judge success. However, it *is* possible to manage projects with very brief requirements specifications, e.g. cardinal point specifications. The architecture definition is probably the second most criticial technical aspect of a major software development project. However, here one cannot get away with outline specifications such as cardinal points.

The architecture definition occupies a pivotal role in the software development process. It is, or should be, the basis on which decisions about feasibility and implementability of a system are made. It provides a very strong link between technical and managerial activities. For example, the work breakdown structure and the modularization of the system for implementation should be derived from the architecture definition. Also, the architecture definition is pivotal from the point of view of the technical development activities. After architecture definition, development will proceed by means of a number of individuals or teams working in parallel. However, the software which they produce must inter-work, and the teams should be able to work in parallel without making design decisions which compromise, or conflict with, the decisions made by other teams. This means that the architecture, which by definition describes the system as a whole, must contain enough information to allow subsequent work to be carried on in parallel without major technical risk. As a consequence, it is very difficult, yet very important, to produce good architecture definitions. In the authors' view many of the problems of practical software development projects arise from poor architecture definitions.

Unfortunately, relatively few software development projects do produce high-level, or architectural, specifications. Where such specifications are produced they are often mistaken for work break down structures, or they contain very little technical detail beyond a module structure and a textual description of module functionality. The authors believe that the material described in Section 17.3.2 and outlined in Figure 17.2 form essential parts of an architectural specification. Perhaps the most constructive way to look at the material in Figure 17.2 and Section 17.3.2 is to say that it identifies an outline contents list, or check list for the contents, of an architectural specification.

The authors believe that this poor state of affairs arises from two interrelated causes: the lack of awareness of the problems and the absence of good methods for architectural specification. Clearly, these two points are mutually reinforcing. The pragmatic consequence of these observations is, in the view of the authors, that there is no entirely satisfactory method or notation for architectural specification which covers all the relevant issues. This causes problems for the would-be software architect in choosing methods for his project.

As was indicated in the discussion on software process models (Chapter 15), one of the joint responsibilities of the technical architect and project manager for a system is that they must define the process to be used in software development. This means, *inter alia*, that appropriate methods must be chosen for the various stages of software development. Given the above comments, it should be clear that this choice is difficult in practice, and that the system architect has to choose between a number of unsatisfactory alternatives.

It is perhaps helpful to give a fairly concrete example. It would be appropriate to use a technique such as SSADM for developing a transaction-oriented database system. However, it is extremely unlikely that the use of SSADM would prove appropriate for other classes of project, e.g. compiler development. Contrarily, the use of compiler specific tools, e.g. syntax analyser generators, are effective in the domain of language processors, but are likely to be a hindrance, not a help, if used in producing a database system. Consequently, the technical architect for the project must choose an appropriate tool. However, projects are rarely so simple. For example, it might be necessary to develop both database and language processing software in the same project. Whilst it is clearly appropriate to use the specific tools for detailed design and implementation of the relevant parts of a system, it is far from clear what should be chosen as the specification notation for the overall system architecture.

In general, the system architect has to make a compromise, and to choose a method and notation which is not equally well suited to all parts of the system. Further, the method chosen will inevitably not deal with all the issues of interest. For example, none of the widely available structured development methods deals well with interactive system design. Consequently, the system architect will also have to develop project specific standards or practices for dealing with these additional issues. The choice of development methods is also discussed in Chapter 15 on software process models.

There are managerial as well as technical issues to be decided when a complete system architecture has been specified. The architectural specification has to be produced, verified and validated (for the system) as a whole. This is true even where incremental development is used. Here one has to verify and validate all that has been specified so far, even if it does not constitute the complete system. However, beyond the architectural stage one could have higher levels of parallelism within the development process. Therefore, managerial decisions are required about how the remaining software should be developed and validated. In other words, some details of the process design must be carried out once the architectural specification is complete.

The main issue to be decided is the order in which the different parts of the software system will be implemented, tested and integrated. Whilst the architecture does not contain enough information to determine this order unequivocally, it does contain at least some of the information necessary for making these decisions. For example, the fan-in and fan-out between modules indicates modules which are widely used elsewhere, and which therefore might be considered for early implementation as they will be necessary in building and testing other modules. Similarly, low fan-out from a module will probably indicate a part of the system that can be developed and tested largely independently of the rest.

Additionally, the process structure can be helpful in determining units to be developed and tested independently. In general, it is quite straightforward to develop a process independently of the rest of the system, and to build a harness for evaluating the behaviour and performance of that process.

However, there are other factors which will influence the order of development and testing of the modules. These include problems of software development risk, which are not explicitly represented within the architectural specification. As was pointed out in Chapter 15 on software process models, the concepts of software development stage and phase should not be confused. In the development phase, which is concerned with producing architectural specifications, it is necessary to do some initial work on the detailed design stage. This should provide some of the necessary information on technical development risk to inform the process of determining the module implementation ordering. Consequently, the architectural design together with the results of these feasibility studies or investigations are adequate to determine this aspect of the work break down structure and the software development process, from a management point of view.

As was stated in the introduction to this chapter, software development is an exercise requiring considerable skill. Skills are required at all stages in the software development process, but it is perhaps in architectural design that skills are most critical and least well developed. It is hoped that the discussion of notations and methods for architectural design, together with the presentation of some general design guidelines, will help to improve this situation. Perhaps the best one can do, however, is to conclude with a very useful and very general design heuristic:

'Always design a thing by considering it in its next larger context – a chair in a room, a room in a house, a house in an environment, an environment in a city plan.' (Elial Saarinen, *Time* 2 July 1956).

17.6 Acknowledgements

The authors would like to thank Ken Jackson for his helpful and insightful comments on a draft of this chapter.

17.7 References

Booch, G. (1987) *Software Engineering with Ada*, 2nd edn, Benjamin Cummings

Booch, G. (1986) Object-oriented development. *IEEE Transactions on Software Engineering* **SE-12**

Dix, A. J., Harrison, M. D., Runciman, C. and Thimbleby, H. W. (1987) Interaction models and the principled design of interactive systems. In *Proceedings of ESEC '87*, Springer Verlag

DoD (1983) Trusted computer system evaluation criteria. *CSC-STD-001-83* Department of Defense, USA

DTI (1989) *STARTS Purchasers' Handbook,* (2nd edn) Department of Trade and Industry

Gilb, T. (1988) *Principles of Software Engineering Management*, Addison-Wesley

Hansen, P. B. (1977) *The Architecture of Concurrent Programs*, Prentice-Hall Series in Automatic Computation, Prentice-Hall

Hatley, D. J. and Pirbhai, I. A. (1987) *Strategies for Real-Time System Specification*, Dorset House

Hayes, I. (ed.) (1986) *Specification Case Studies*, Prentice-Hall International

Heninger, K. L., Kallander, J. W., Shore, J. E. and Parnas, D. L. (1978) *Software Requirements for the A-7E Aircraft*, Naval Research Laboratories, Washington DC, USA

Hester, S. D., Parnas, D. L. and Utter, D. F. (1981) Using documentation as a software design medium, *The Bell System Technical Journal*, **60**

HOOD (1988) *HOOD Manual* (revised P. J. Robinson), CISI Ingenerie

Jackson, M. A. (1983) *System Development*, Prentice-Hall International

Jones, C. B. (1986) *Systematic Software Development Using VDM*, Prentice-Hall International

Kafura and Henry, (1984) The evaluation of software systems structure using quantitative software metrics. *Software Practice and Experience*

Leveson, N. G. (1986) Software safety: what, why and how. *Computing Surveys*, **18**

De Marco, T. (1978) *Structured Analysis and System Specification*, Prentice-Hall

MASCOT (1980) *The Official Handbook of MASCOT*, MASCOT Suppliers Association

MASCOT (1986) *Software Engineering Journal*, **1** (No 3: Special Issue on MASCOT3)

McClure, C. and Martin, J. (1988) *Structured Techniques: the Basis for CASE*, (revised edn), Prentice-Hall

McDermid, J. A. (1990) Issues in developing software for safety critical systems. In *Reliability Engineering and System Safety*

Myers, G. J. (1975) *Reliable Software Through Composite Design*, Van Nostrand Reinhold

Nicholls, D. *Introducing SSADM – The NCC Guide*, NCC Publications, Manchester

Parnas, D. L. and Clements, P. C. (1986) A rational design process: how and why to fake it. *IEEE Transactions on Software Engineering*, **SE-12**

Phillips, C. S. E. (1968) Networks for real-time programming. *BCS Journal*

Pike, R. (1988) Window systems should be transparent. *Computing Systems ATOT Bell Labs*, **13**

RTCA (1984) Software considerations in airborne systems and equipment certification. In *Document No. RTCA/DO178A*, Radio Technical Commission for Aeronautics, USA

Sennett, C. T. (1988) *High Integrity Software*, Pitman

Stark, S. (1980) General object-oriented software development. *NASA Software Engineering Laboratory Series SEL-86-002*

Sutcliffe, A. (1988) *Jackson System Development*, Prentice-Hall

Ward, P. T. and Mellor, S. J. (1985) *Structured Development for Real-Time Systems*, Prentice Hall

Wirth, N. (1976) *Algorithms + Data Structures = Programs*, Prentice Hall

Yourdon, E. and Constantine, L. L. (1985) *Structured Design: Fundamentals of a Discipline of Computer Program and Systems Design*, Prentice-Hall

18

Implementation

B A Wichmann
National Physical Laboratory

Contents

18.1 Introduction

To be effective, the implementation phase in the life cycle must be seen as part of the total life cycle. This is a hard discipline since the pressure to complete the implementation on schedule encourages a narrow view in which only the immediate objectives are considered. Almost all software suffers from inadequate treatment of the longer-term goals in its design and implementation. Obviously, one cannot anticipate how software will be altered in the future, but a flexible design and implementation can ease the subsequent changes to an extent which far outweighs any initial costs.

This chapter takes a view of the implementation phase that is independent of the programming language in use. However, to illustrate specific points and to avoid a totally abstract presentation, the Ada programming language is used in examples (Ichbiah *et al.*, 1983). In general, the approach advocated can be achieved by disciplined use of other procedural languages.

It must be admitted that no attempt is made to cover the implementation of software in forms other than the mainstream programming languages. Examples which are therefore excluded from this chapter are:

1. *Small systems.* The well-known non-linear costs of information technology systems means that the greatest difficulties are to be faced with large systems. Therefore small systems which can be handled by one person are excluded.
2. *Fourth generation languages.* Such systems are typically designed with one application domain in mind and therefore present a different set of issues and problems to the implementor.
3. *Interactive systems.* Such systems can easily be dominated by considerations of the man–machine interface requiring rapid prototyping and experimentation to achieve an adequate implementation. See Chapter 57 on interactive systems for further details.
4. *Fifth generation languages.* Functional languages perhaps used as a specification tool are excluded as are languages used for 'artificial intelligence' applications (LISP, Prolog, etc). See Chapters 35 and 36 on functional and logic programming for further details.

This chapter considers the implementation process in the order encountered during the development: analysis of the design, understanding the implementation environment, structure of the implementation, trial implementation, full implementation, validation and testing. The implications of the (often vital) maintenance phase are omitted here since they are considered in Chapter 20 on maintenance.

18.2 Analysis of the design

The input to the implementation phase will be the module design. The form that the module takes will depend both upon the design method and upon the implementation technology. Numerous design methods, many supported by tools, are in widespread use. The advantage of this approach is in providing a fixed framework that the implementation process can exploit to reduce the work that needs to be undertaken. For instance, a 'box' in a diagram in the design could be a procedure in the implementation. A consistent method for a deriving the implementation from the design is a substantial assistance in understanding a large system since the design itself becomes an overview of the system's actual structure.

18.2.1 Design conflicts

Conflicts can arise between the design and implementation methods. As an example, consider a simple design method in which input and output variables are denoted by boxes. Such a diagrammatic form leads to a static view of data (the variable is that one, pointing to a specific box). This view is incorrect if recursion is used. Even if recursion is not actually used in the application, the implementation language may well dynamically allocate storage so that recursion can be supported.

Another example of conflict concerns concurrency. The MASCOT2 design method assumes a concurrent kernel to implement primitives for synchronization and data flow. This design method therefore conflicts with languages which do not support concurrency such as CORAL66. Since MASCOT2 is usually used with CORAL66 as the implementation language it seems we have a major conflict. This is resolved by MASCOT2 using a kernel in a CORAL66 system which provides the concurrency primitives by means of assembly language insertions.

Conflicts can also arise between the method used to specify a system and the ease with which an implementation can be provided. There is a school of thought that a specification should be an implementation in a functional language. This may be appropriate, but is certainly not universal. For instance, the specification of a sort routine is like to be very different from its implementation. In more detail, with the mathematical specification methods, the use of the universal and existential quantifiers causes conflicts which naturally increase implementation costs. For instance, to say that the result of sqrt$(x) = y$ should be such that $|x - y| < \varepsilon$ may be a perfectly good specification but does not state that one implements square root by extracting the floating point exponent, divide this by two to form an initial approximation and then perform two Newton iteration steps. A feature of many good specifications is that they have no implementation bias (see below) and hence provide no clues as to how an implementation should be produced.

18.2.2 Analysis checklist

Time spent carefully examining a design is likely to be rewarded in resolving conflicts before the major coding effort has to be undertaken. Some issues that should be considered are listed below.

1. *The environment.* The design will specify the inputs and outputs but will typically not specify inputs which are implicit in the environment provided to the application. For instance, operating systems calls can be undertaken to obtain other input, such as the time and date. However, if a test environment is to be used to allow the date to be set to an arbitrary value, then it is important that this implicit input should be obtained in a manner consistent with the overall design objective.
2. *Borderline cases.* Each clause in the specification should be noted for fixed limits. The corresponding borderline cases then need to be analysed. This analysis can form the basis of test cases.
3. *Capacity limits.* The capacity limits in an implementation are typically left unspecified. This should be noted and an appropriate strategy agreed with the design authority.
4. *Errors.* Are all the error situations noted in the design? Reporting omissions at this point may reveal more severe defects in the design.
5. *Problems areas.* Identification of potential problem areas may help even if specific defects in the design cannot be found at this stage. Indeed, a problem area could be caused by implementation issues rather than any defect in the specification. For instance, some problems often arise in interfacing hardware to software because of the need to use two potentially different systems. It has even been

known for problems to be caused by the software documentation numbering bits from the most significant end of the word, while the hardware documentation did the reverse! The largest and most complex component of the system can be expected to cause more problems.

6. *Experience from previous similar systems*. In practice, the computing industry depends to a large extent on previous experience in building similar systems. This should be taken into account in reviewing the design.

A practical point is that one should not expect to have all queries concerning the module specification resolved before starting the implementation phase. A quick acknowledgement by the design authority that a problem does exist, and must be resolved, is helpful since changes in a specific area can then be anticipated.

18.3 Understanding the implementation environment

This issue is sometimes forgotten since it is often the case that the programmer does have the necessary understanding of the environment and it is a common failing to ignore what one can assume to be understood. However, one needs to ensure that the environment is properly understood. Appropriate training may be needed, especially in specialist areas such as communication systems, databases etc.

The following issues need to be reviewed to ensure that there is no conflict between the requirements of the design and the implementation technology:

1. *Basic facilities*. Does the implementation environment have the necessary basic facilities? The design usually makes implicit assumptions here, but this needs to be made explicit. Hence if a numerical calculation is being undertaken, then it is important that the data types have sufficient precision. Similarly with file access facilities etc.

2. *Capacity limits*. Is the system likely to have some capacity limit which could jeopardise the implementation? This could be hard to determine in advance. The existence of another comparable system in the same environment is obviously a helpful positive indication. On MS-DOS systems, for example, the 64K addressing limitations can impose very significant problems which can even mean a major redesign. Similar problems can arise with any fixed limits in machines. For novel applications, it may be hard to determine in advance if such limits will cause problems and therefore some allowance must be made for this.

3. *Portability considerations*. For software which is designed to be portable, special issues arise. Can compiling options be used to ensure that only the portable subset of the language is used? Check that the design does not require extensions to the implementation language. See Nissen and Wallis (1983) for specific recommendations on the use of Ada to achieve portability.

4. *Host/target systems*. Special problems arise when the system is being developed on one system (the host) in order to run on another (the target). In general, this requires a good knowledge of both the host and the target. Typically the host is much larger than the target and hence there is a risk that the system will work correctly on the host but not meet implementation limits on the target. If the host system uses a simulator to mirror the functions of the target, then execution can be very slow and costly on the host which may cause cost overruns. On the other hand, if the host compiles the same source text, it is imperative that the same language dialect is used. (Typically this means

using a system designed for host/target development with the two compilers supplied by the same vendor.)

Communication and debugging systems are very important for host/target development. Systems which allow debugging to be done in a similar manner on the host and the target are obviously to be preferred.

5. *Conditional code for testing*. Good design anticipates that errors will remain in a completed system. Even if the unlikely situation occurs that no errors arise, it is very unlikely that such errors will not arise during maintenance (see below). One method of controlling the testing process is to insert additional code specifically for testing. A design will typically give pre-conditions and post-conditions on components (such as functions and procedures). If such conditions can be checked by means of executable code, then this should be included in the implementation. However, the cost in time and space of performing such checks may well be unacceptable (typically the case with real-time systems), and hence must be controlled by an option.

For an example of a suitable package for testing conditions, see below:

```
package Condition_Check is
    type Mode is (Log, Retro_Trace, Except, No_Check)
-- the package provides four modes of operations,
-- Log  -- all conditions logged onto standard
            -- output file
-- Retro_Trace  -- details of last few conditions logged if
                -- a failure occurs
-- Except -- exception raised on failure only
-- No_Check -- no check made on conditions

procedure Set_Mode(M: Mode);
-- by default the mode is Except.

procedure Assert( Message: String; Condition: Boolean);
-- the Condition should be True,
-- and the Message string gives an
-- identification of the condition being checked.

end Condition_Check;
```

6. *House styles*. Most organizations impose a style on code to aid readability and maintenance. If such styles are to be followed, then it is clearly important that they should be well-understood. If a programmer has reservations about a particular house style, this should result in a review of the style. Such styles should be reviewed on a regular basis to ensure they correspond to best practice. Styles such as layout should be enforced via tools, rather than requiring extra work from the programmer. Tools can also monitor coding styles to locate defects even if it is not possible to automatically correct the defects (as with layout tools). The house style should cover the question of testing conditions noted above.

18.4 Structure of the implementation

This section assumes that a systems analysis has been undertaken and that the checks upon this have been undertaken as noted above. For a form of analysis compatible with the treatment here, see DeMarco (1979) or Gane and Sarson (1979). For a short tutorial on data-flow diagrams, see Woodman (1988).

The major requirement from the analysis is to have a flow diagram giving the principal data flows and the transformations made upon the data. The main structured design methods produce this directly.

Given a data-flow diagram, then this can be realised in several different ways depending upon the programming paradigms and general design techniques in use. The major parameters in this area are illustrated below.

18.4.1 Information hiding

If a system can be designed and implemented so that only the necessary information is available at each level, then changes can be made much more easily. Unfortunately, most programming languages give only rather poor support for hiding which means that after the initial implementation has been completed, the subsequent maintenance will not be able to rely upon information being restricted on a need-to-know basis. Ada gives somewhat better support and hence the examples use this language.

The information hiding capabilities of the Ada language in addition to the usual procedure abstraction include encapsulation in a package, hiding details of a type via private and limited private types and hiding the representation via representation specifications. Understanding this capability is important since it is very easy to write in a subset of Ada that just corresponds to another language. (One must expect a programmer to take six months to become familiar enough with these features to use them properly which is why the training costs of Ada are high – although it is really a software engineering training cost.)

As a very simple example consider the implementation of a pseudo-random number generator. The flow diagram is just:

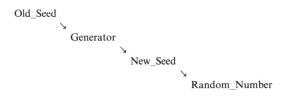

The key is clearly the form used to represent the Seed. The rule should be to hide as much as possible. Here one needs to know the other operations to be applied to Seeds. Let us say that these are to obtain the value of the current seed, and to give a value to the current seed. This implies that the world outside the abstraction can handle the 'seed' in some way. At this point, hiding becomes awkward rather than an advantage. A compromise is called for. The internal requirement of the algorithm for random number generation given in Hill and Wichmann (1982) is for three integers. Hence a compromise is to use a record type with three (visible) integer components as follows:

```
package Random_Numbers is
  type Seed is
    record
      X, Y, Z: Integer;
    end record;

  function Random Return Float;
    -- Returns a random number in range 0.0 ... 1.0.

  function Current_Seed return Seed;
    -- Returns the current value of the seed.

  procedure Restart(Restart_Seed: in Seed);
    -- Restarts from the given seed value.

end Random_Numbers;
```

For details of the implementation of such a package and for various alternative design strategies, see Wichmann and Meijerlink (1984) and Watt *et al.* (1987) (Example 19.11).

Guidelines can be given on aspects of a system which should be hidden:

1. *Will change.* If an aspect is known to be subject to change, then this should be hidden and placed in an isolated component. Care must be taken here for two reasons. Firstly, one's judgement of what is likely to change is unlikely to be totally reliable. Secondly, hiding can have costs in terms of performance and readability which must be taken into account.
2. *Lower level abstraction.* Here hiding is the natural method of describing the levels within the system.
3. *Lower level implementation.* In this case, portability considerations should require that machine specific components are identified, even if they are not strictly at a lower level of abstraction.
4. *External interfaces.* This is an important area of design. Clearly, such interfaces are unlikely to be entirely hidden, but some aspects of them which can be isolated should probably be hidden even if they are a key component of the total system design. This is because the view of the design from within one software component should be different.

18.4.2 Abstract data types

The example of the random number generator was dependent upon the type Seed. The decision was not to hide details of the type, but to hide the seed itself within the package body. With an abstract data type one hides details of the type itself so that an implementor has further freedoms in providing the code to satisfiy the specification. For instance, the decision that a seed could be represented by three integers might not have been appropriate which would force substantial changes upon the use of the Random-Numbers package.

As an example of the more abstract approach to types, consider a sorting package. Clearly such a facility is quite general and hence the solution should also be general to allow re-use when needed. The Ada method of allowing re-use is that of generics. Clearly we have a type which is to be sorted, and a function which determines the ordering relation on objects of the type. These two entities become parameters to our sorting facility, which can be written in Ada as:

```
generic
  type Names is private;
  with function ">" (L, R : Names)
       return Boolean is < >;
package Sort_Service is
  ...
end Sort_Service;
```

The type Names has been specified private to indicate that only assignment and equality need be used in the package body. Ada allows the function which determines the ordering to be called "〉" so that it can be used in the conventional infix manner. The "〈〉" is added to the specification of the function so that if a greater-than operation is already available for the type Names then no actual function need be provided.

We now need to decide the exact functions of the package. The problem here is one of implementation bias. If one assumes that all the Names are available in an array, then 'in-store' algorithms such as Quickersort (Scowen, 1965) are appropriate. On the other hand, if the Names can be accumulated in an appropriate data structure, then TreeSort is probably the best (Knuth, 1973). We give a set of procedures and functions which allow either approach:

```
generic
    type names is private;
    with function ">" (L, R : Names)
        return Boolean is < >;
package Sort_Service is
    procedure Make_List_Empty;
    procedure Insert (New_Name: in Names);
    procedure Prepare_Extraction;
    procedure Extract (Old_Name: out Names);
    function All_Extracted return Boolean;
    List_Full, List_Empty: exception;
end Sort_Service;
```

The package therefore accumulates the Names in a list and subsequently allows extraction in sorted order.

At this point, the package specification needs to be reviewed for potential defects. The package clearly has four states: before insertion, insertion, extraction and completed. Problems arise if insertion is attempted during extraction and *vice versa*. Hence at the very least, the documentation should note this potential danger, even if no specific remedy is taken. The fact that a package can be misused in ways like this is quite common and should not necessarily be taken as a design defect. In Ada, it would be easy to check that each procedure is called with the package being in the correct state and raise an exception if the check fails. The advantage of this approach is that no extra parameters or rules are needed for the correct usage of the package.

The coding of the package body from this point is easy and hence not elaborated here. However, it is worthwhile noting the potential implementation methods with their strengths and weaknesses:

1. *An array with insertion sort* (see page 162 of Watt *et al.* (1987)) This is slow, but easy to produce!
2. *An array which is sorted just before extraction.* This can use an efficient array sorting algorithm such as Quickersort. As in the previous case, a problem is to determine the size of the array in advance of the insertions.
3. *A binary tree constructed on insertion.* This does not need a fixed maximum size for the Names, but does require storage for pointers. Note that the pointers (access types in Ada) are not exported outside the package – this is important since pointers are basically an implementation device rather than an abstraction which should be visible outside the package.

Given such a package, we not only have some implementation freedom, but the facilities can be used for many applications by instantiation of the generic:

```
package Integer_Sort is new Sort_Service(Integer);
-- above uses the predefined ">" for sorting
package Real_Rev_Sort is new Sort_Service(Float, "<");
package Directory_Sort(Names, Directory_Order);
```

18.4.3 Object-oriented programming

This approach places emphasis on the objects rather than the types or the transformations. It is covered in more detail in Chapter 39 on object-oriented systems. If the high-level design is not expressed in this form, it may nevertheless be possible and appropriate to use object-oriented programming within the implementation of the single module.

18.4.4 Other design issues

Given a suitable strategy for choice of the programming paradigm, several other issues should be examined.

Cohesion and *coupling* need to be carefully considered in reviewing a decomposition stage. This is discussed in more detail in Chapter 17, on high-level design. Within a component, one should expect strong cohesion in the sense that the individual parts have common characteristics. On the other hand, weak cohesion could be an indication that the component boundaries are not drawn correctly. This is not an easy issue to resolve. For instance, most programming languages provide mathematical functions such as sine and square root. Given a module to provide these, where does one stop? What about arctangent, the hyperbolic functions, inverse hyperbolics, gamma function etc? One must expect a degree of arbitrariness. With coupling one is looking at the module decomposition from the complementary viewpoint. Given two modules which have tight coupling, it may be that these should be combined in one module. The danger of such an approach is that the resulting module becomes too big (and monolithic). The Ada language allows nested packages to overcome just this point. For an example of the issues involved in decomposition when only modest language support is available, see Parnas (1972).

```
with IO_Exceptions;
package Text_IO is
    type File_Type is limited private;
    type File_Mode is (In_File, Out_File);
    . . .
    procedure Put(Item : Character);
    . . .
    generic
        type Num is range < >;
    package Integer_IO is
        . . .
        procedure Put(. . .);
    . . .
    end Integer_IO;

    generic
        type Num is digits < >;
    package Float_IO is
        . . .
        procedure Put(. . .);
    . . .
    end Float_IO;
    . . .
end Text_IO;
```

The total number of procedures and functions inside Text_IO is quite large (more than a head full). However, by placing those related to integer input–output in a nested package, the total number in any one scope is reduced. In fact, the overloading rules in Ada helps here since the name Put can refer to several different versions without confusion. Without overloading, one can simply refer to Integer_IO.Put or Float_IO.Put.

Portability as a design objective has been noted. However, this impacts the entire implementation phase if it is to be fully realised. For instance, to ensure that the language dialect used has been as required, either a validated compiler with 'standards mode' so that all extensions are flagged, or a special tool should be used to achieve the same objective. Another strategy to increase portability is to port the code to another system as a check. With Ada, although the language is better standardized, the problem is that the use of low-level features can reduce portability since they depend upon non-standard properties of the underlying system. Hence tools should be used to ensure that these low-level features are only used in ways authorized in the design. See Nissen and Wallis (1983) for general guidelines for portability and style with Ada.

Enhanceability is an important property of software which is often forgotten in the rush to complete the first release. Hence the design and the implementation should be reviewed to see if the flaws will become apparent during subsequent enhancements. For very long-life software, it may be difficult to predict the nature of enhancements, but some attempt should be made.

Pre-packaged components can dramatically reduce software costs and hence every attempt should be made to use such components. Concerns about the quality of such components, the documentation, maintenance arrangements, etc. have reduced their use. The package mechanism in Ada is flexible enough to give a new impetus to this, which combined with the portability of the language could change the design process. The problem here is that the conventional top-down design does not lend itself to using pre-constructed packages at the lowest level. The solution is to produce an approximation to the requirements for the lowest level packages and then match these against the library packages available. If suitable packages are found, then the design must be adjusted to accommodate the available library components. See Chapter 41, on software re-use, for further details.

18.5 Trial implementation

In some difficult areas, it may not be possible to do a straightforward top-down design in the classical manner. Each step in the top-down design process depends upon an element of faith that the decomposition will be successful when the main coding phase is undertaken. For novel applications, this simplistic view can easily fail.

One approach to the dilemma of the conventional development method failing is to use prototyping. Since this technique is covered in a separate chapter (Chapter 40), no further details are given here.

Given that specific prototyping technology is not being used, then one approach is simply to produce a trial implementation in the full knowledge that it may have to be re-written (or more likely, re-designed) as a result of the trial. Naturally, this is an expensive process, but is typical of the research environment, and is increasing common of commercial practice as new application areas are explored.

As a further example, consider the development of a special test tool to check Pascal compilers (Wichmann and Davies, 1989). This tool is a standard Pascal program which uses a few integers, mainly the seeds of a pseudo-random number generator, to produce a correct, self-checking Pascal program. The idea behind this tool is to check a compiler in ways that cannot be accomplished by hand-written tests. The problem here is that the objective is very open-ended which makes the design process too unconstrained. Similar problems arise with any piece of software in a totally new application area. The appropriate method is to produce a trial implementation which has very restricted objectives. The objectives must be set large enough to cover at least some of the main problems to be faced with the full implementation, and yet small enough to be manageable. The current version of the Pascal tool is a trial system – it covers a significant part of the requirements but leaves out some major areas. In fact, it generates expressions reasonably fully and hence checks the code generator of the Pascal compiler. This experience has shown that there is a need for the tool (compilers fail the tests frequently). From this one can specify the full requirements with more confidence. To develop the full system, one must expect to have to rewrite parts of the trial system. In the case of this tool, the only form of loops that could be generated using the existing design would have simple properties which would probably make the testing too naive. Hence, although the existing tool is half the length of the full version, one must acknowledge that only about a third of the implementation has been completed.

A problem with producing a trial implementation is the cost, in that it could not be seen as a marketable product in itself. Not unnaturally, product companies like to produce new items which break new ground – but these are just the ones for which a trial implementation would make good sense. The commercial pressure to produce a marketable item then forces the move to a full implementation in advance of a full understanding of the requirements and implementation methods.

18.6 Full implementation

Given our decomposition into appropriate packages, functions and procedures, we then need to produce the statements from the dummy routines. The method advocated here is stepwise refinement. By this we mean adding detail to the implementation rather than to any aspect of the specification. We illustrate this by means of an example. We have already met the process of decomposition, which is continued further to produce the executable statements. The difference here is that there is inevitably a strong coupling between the refinement steps, which cannot be handled comprehensively via data-flow diagrams. Also, since we are now producing executable code, some more substantial checks can be performed upon the results.

The example is to develop a program to solve the quadratic equation:

$$Ax^2 + Bx + C = 0$$

where A, B and C are all integers, A being non-zero. The program is to simplify the solution as much as possible without using real arithmetic. Of course, we know the solution is given by:

$$x = \frac{-B \pm \sqrt{(B^2 - 4AC)}}{2A}$$

An initial step is to produce a very informal specification by giving some example output (which can subsequently become test cases):

Input			Output
A	B	C	
2	5	1	$x = -5 + - \mathrm{sqrt}(17) / 4$
1	2	-2	$x = -1 + - \mathrm{sqrt}(3)$
-4	0	1	$x = + -1 / 2$
1	2	1	$x = -1$
2	0	0	$x = 0$
1	0	7	$x = + - \mathrm{sqrt}(-7)$

At this stage, we have to admit that the exact form of the output has not been specified. However the initial requirements are clear: the computation requires the fixed part of the numerator $(-B)$, the discriminant $(B^2 - 4AC)$ and the denominator $(2A)$. Then the denominator must be made positive, and any common factors eliminated. Hence we arrive at an initial refinement:

```
procedure Solve_Quadratic_Equation is
  -- declarations
begin
  -- read A, B and C
  -- compute the fixed part of the numerator,
  -- the discriminant and the denominator
  -- make the denominator positive
  -- eliminate any common factors
  -- write the solution
end Solve_Quadratic_Equation;
```

Here we have used a form for the refinement which is acceptable to the Ada compiler by using comments to denote the steps still to be completed. These comments can be left in if the code itself is not self-explanatory.

The 'declarations' could clearly be refined further to include the declarations of *A*, *B* and *C* – however, since further declarations will be needed, this is delayed.

The 'compute the fixed part' can now be refined by introducing appropriate variables:

```
Num : = − B;
Discrim : = B**2 − 4 * A * C;
Denom : = 2 * A;
```

The 'make the denominator positive' step merely changes the sign of the top and bottom if the bottom is negative. (The discriminant need not be changed since both signs appear.)

```
if Denom < 0 then
    Denom : = − Denom;
    Num : = − Num;
end if;
```

The 'eliminate any common factors' must divide out the highest common factor from Denom,Num and the square in the discriminant. This computation can be done by working down from Denom until 1 is reached (since we know that Denom is greater than zero). This refinement, which is not expressed entirely in Ada, becomes:

```
HCF : = Denom;
while HCF > 1 and then (
        HCF 'is a factor of' Num and
        HCF 'is a factor of' Denom and
        HCF**2 'is a factor of' Discrim )
    loop HCF : = HCF − 1;
end loop;
Num : = Num / HCF;
Denom : = Denom / HCF;
Discrim : = Discrim / HCF**2;
```

Note that the use of 'is a factor of' explains what is required without expressing the method by which this is achieved. This should be done at each level of refinement. One frequent programming fault is to attempt two levels of refinement in one go, thereby introducing coding slips which are hard to locate since the purpose is no longer clear.

The refinement of 'write the solution' is straightforward but needs to handle degenerate cases of division by 1 and adding zero. Using an additional refinement step avoids any ambiguity in the steps to be performed:

```
Put ("x = ");
−−write the fixed part of the numerator, unless
−−    it is zero and the discriminant is nonzero
−−write the discriminant part, unless it is zero
−−write the denominator, unless it is 1
New_Line;
```

The completion of this refinement is straightfoward except that if the discriminant is a perfect square, the square root should be avoided.

Putting all the refinements together and completing the simple ones, the completed program as is shown opposite.

Note that the comments which refer to trivial refinement steps have been removed since the comment adds nothing when the code itself is present. On the other hand, some additional comments may be needed when a single refinement step is long

or if the code does not correspond to the requirement because some 'trick' is being used. Note also that the actual text contains much verbiage due to the language – such redundancy should help readability.

```
with Text_IO; use Text_IO;

procedure Solve_Quadratic_Equation is
    package Int_IO is new Integer_IO(Integer); use Int_IO;

    A, B, C : Integer;
    Num, Discrim, Denom : Integer;

    HCF, S: Natural;
begin
    Get(A); Get(B); Get(C);
    −−compute the fixed part of the numerator,
    −−the discriminant and the denominator
    Num : = − B;
    Discrim : = B**2 − 4 * A * C;
    Denom : = 2 * A;
    −−make the denominator positive
    if Denom < 0 then
        Denom : = − Denom;
        Num : = − Num;
    end if;
    −−eliminate any common factors
    HCF : = Denom;
    while HCF > 1 and then (
            Num mod HCF = 0 and
            Denom mod HCF = 0 and
            Discrim mod HCF**2 = 0)
    loop HCF : = HCF − 1;
    end loop;
    Num : = Num / HCF;
    Denom : = Denom / HCF;
    Discrim : = Discrim / HCF**2;
    −−write the solution
    Put ("x = ");
    −−write the fixed part of the numerator, unless
    −−it is zero and the discriminant is nonzero
    if not (Num = 0 and Discrim /= 0) then
        Put(Num, Width = > 1);
    end if;
    −−write the discriminant part, unless it is zero
    if Discrim /= 0 then
        Put (" + − ");
        −−compute the square root of Discrim
        S : = 1;
        while S**2 < Discrim loop
            S : = S + 1;
        end loop;
        if Discrim = S**2 then −−perfect square
            Put(S);
        else
            Put("sqrt("); Put(Discrim, Width = > 1); Put(")");
        end if;
    end if
    −−write the denominator, unless it is 1
    if Denom /= 1 then
        Put(" / "); Put(Denom, Width = > 1);
    end if;
    New_Line;
end Solve_Quadratic_Equation;
```

The process of stepwise refinement is very similar to that of modular decomposition in which cohesion and coupling were noted as key characteristics. In addition, for stepwise refinement we should have:

1. *Simplicity.* Each step should be a simple one – otherwise the risk of errors is increased dramatically.
2. *Consistency.* Internal consistency within a module is important to aid understanding. For instance, the refinement 'is a factor of' was required three times. All used the same coding method with mod, although to use rem would have been equally correct. (Note here that even correct programs can be hard to understand – style is often very important.)
3. *Delayed decisions.* Each refinement forces some decisions. However, the later a decision is made, the smaller will be the component which is influenced by the decision, and hence the more local will be its consequences. As an example, the decision on how to find out if the discriminant is a perfect square was delayed so that only a few lines of code involves this complexity.
4. *Documentation.* Consider what documentation should support the refinement step. Pre- and post-conditions might be appropriate, as well as invariants. Try to ensure consistency of style. Should there be a reference to standard algorithms? Any non-standard algorithms will need more refinement steps, more documentation and will be harder to maintain.

The above example has given a stepwise refinement of a single module (in this case, a complete program). In larger systems, several modules which will interact would require development. The obvious method is to do top-down refinement in parallel for each module. This concurrency will be essential for very large systems due to the size of the total task. However, in smaller systems, or medium sized subsystems, an incremental approach is probably better. With this approach part of the system is completed allowing some of the refinement steps to be validated before other parts are started.

With systems which are larger than can be illustrated here, the interaction between modules will be important and cannot be expected to be resolved during the modules' design process. A typical instance is that of a complex data structure which is used to describe the data across an interface. In Ada, this interface could be specified by means of a package which details the data type and the methods of provision by the data provider. The package specification can then be compiled before the implementation of the provider is completed. The user of the interface can then compile code using the interface knowing that the data is being used in a type secure fashion. Of course, before execution and testing can be performed, the data provider must complete the implementation (the package body). This approach supports concurrent development in a way which avoids the common mistake of two users of a data type having incompatible views of it.

The approach above can be carried a step further by starting with the specification of an interface which is incomplete (i.e. more than just the body of the package is to be provided). Recompilation of the package specification of the interface then needs to be synchronized between all the users, although if the interface is merely extended (which it should be), the change should be transparent to users not yet requiring the extension. Hence merely adding a procedure to a package, or adding a field to a data structure should be routine.

18.7 Validation

Several steps should be taken to validate the code before execution. The stepwise refinement process leads naturally to stepwise checking. Here we exploit the refinement steps by hand

executing with a few simple examples (we have those already). The shorter steps need not be hand executed for each case – one can use the refinement instead. This minimizes the work to be undertaken, and is vital with loops since complete hand execution is too time consuming. If errors are found, this indicates that the refinement steps were undertaken incorrectly. This may imply that the refinement steps were too big. This experience can be used to guide future choices for the size of refinement steps.

Almost all code will be maintained by somebody other than the author. Hence it is vital that coding styles encourage other people to understand the code. For this purpose, a review involving someone other than the author is desirable – preferably a complete code walk-through.

Given the quadratic equation solver developed in the last section, a code walk-through should reveal the following points:

1. There is no statement of the purpose of the program apart from the identifier used.
2. The program lacks any ability for re-use; should it use a procedure instead?
3. The identifiers Num, Discrim, Denom, HCF and S could be expanded to improve readability.
4. The calculation of Discrim could overflow even when the final value is in range; does that matter?
5. For large values of Denom, the loop to compute HCF will take some time; a faster version could be produced.
6. For large values of Discrim, the loop to compute S will take some time; a faster version could be produced.

In defence of the example concerning the last two points, an undue concern for efficiency can easily lead to obscure code which is incorrect or hard to check.

Apart from the text of the software, further documentation is usually required. The key to success in the production of such documentation is to have the reader clearly identified. For instance, entirely different documentation is needed for software maintenance than for operational use. This topic is not covered further here.

18.8 Unit testing/white-box testing

It is an unfortunate fact that the first step in the validation phase that can be adequately independently checked in the majority of software is that of unit testing. Here is a working software component for the first time, so it can be executed with appropriate test data to check its compliance with the specification. All too often flaws in the design are revealed at this stage which implies an expensive correction process. The temptation is to short-circuit the redesign stage so that the reliability of the program is impaired. For managerial remedies to such problems, see Chapter 27.

Techniques for testing are covered in Chapter 19 of this book and so are not developed further here. Note, however, that if special provision for checking pre- and post-conditions have been inserted, then we can substantially improve fault-finding. Consideration should be given to boundary value testing and random testing apart from conventional 'test data'. With complex systems, the fact that testing cannot be undertaken before the refinement process is complete is a significant drawback, since no real confidence can be gained of the system until very late in the development cycle. One approach to this is to perform some limited testing with an incomplete module in which only the completed parts are fully tested.

Consideration needs to be given to providing initial copies of the software to a few special clients (beta-testing), so that any mistakes which can be easily picked up by users are avoided in the full release. This does not need to be a formal process – merely getting a colleague to try out some software may be advantageous.

18.9 References

Gane, C. and Sarson, T. (1979) *Structured Systems Analysis*, Prentice-Hall

Hill, I. D. and Wichmann, B.A. (1982) An efficient and portable pseudo-random number generator. *Applied Statistics AS183*, **31**, 188–190

DeMarco, T. (1979) *Structured Analysis and System Specification*, Prentice-Hall

Ichbiah, J. D. *et al.* (1983) *Ada Programming Language*, ANSI/MIL-STD 181A, US Department of Defense (also ISO-8652)

Knuth, D. (1973) *The art of computer programming, Vol. 3 Sorting and Searching*, Addison Wesley

Nissen, J. C. D. and Wallis, P. (eds.) (1983) *Portability and Style in Ada*, CUP

Scowen, R. S. (1965) Quickersort. Algorithm 271. *CACM*, **8**, 669

Watt, D. A., Wichmann, B. A. and Findlay, W. (1987) *Ada: Language and Methodology*, Prentice-Hall

Wichmann, B. A. and Davies, M. (1989) *Experience with a Compiler Testing Tool*, NPL Report 138/89

Wichmann, B. A. and Meijerlink, J.G.J. (1984) Converting to Ada Packages. *Proceedings of 3rd Joint Ada Europe/AdaTec Conference*, CUP, pp 131–139

Woodman, M. (1988) Yourdon data flow diagrams: a tool for disciplined requirements analysis. *Information and Software Technology*, **30**, 515–534

Yourdon, E. and Constantine, L. (1978) *Structured Design*, Prentice-Hall

19

Software testing

Darrel Ince
The Open University

Contents

19.1 Role of testing

Validation and verification are two of the most important activities that occur on a software project. The former is concerned with ensuring that an evolving software system matches user requirements. The latter is concerned with ensuring that the output of a project phase is a correct reflection of the input to that phase. A good example of validation is the software requirements review. This takes place during system specification and its aim is to check that the system specification matches user requirements. A good example of verification is unit testing. Here, the conformance of a coded program unit (subroutine or procedure) is checked against its detailed design by executing it with test data.

Testing describes that subset of validation and verification activities which involve program code. There are two types of testing: white-box testing and black-box testing. In black-box testing the internal structure and behaviour of a system is not considered when test data is selected. In white-box testing the structure is considered.

An example of the black-box approach is acceptance testing, which is the testing of a software system to ensure that it meets user requirements, prior to it being handed over to the customer. Here the test data is chosen by means of a careful reading of the requirements specification.

An example of white-box testing is unit testing. Here a program unit (subroutine, procedure) is exercised with data, with the aim of ensuring that the code inside the unit implements its specification. In this form of testing a major aim is to ensure that a certain proportion of structural metrics are exercised, a typical target being the execution of 85% of the branches and 100% of all the statements in a program unit. In deriving test data the programmer has to develop test data sets which maximize the proportion of structural elements exercised. To do this the internal structure of a unit has to be examined. Thus, unit testing is primarily a white-box strategy.

It is fair, however, to point out that most testing in a software project has an element of both white-box and black-box testing. For example, in acceptance testing the quality assurance staff will predominantly select test data that confirms that functions in the system specification are implemented. However, they will also anticipate some of the architecture of the system to be developed and add in some extra tests which may pinpoint errors in the interface between program units in the system architecture.

19.2 Testing and the software life cycle

The aim of this section is to outline the testing tasks that should occur during the various phases of the software life cycle. These tasks are technical – for example, deriving acceptance test – or managerial – for example, planning for a test activity. In the description that follows it is assumed that the developer has one member of staff or a group of staff responsible for quality assurance. In large organizations such a function will be independent of the software project, while in smaller organizations the task will be delegated to project team members or the project manager. These phases correlate strongly with those defined in Chapter 15.

19.2.1 Testing and requirements analysis

The major developmental activities that take place during this phase are the elicitation and clarification of requirements and the subsequent construction of the system specification. The major testing activity that occurs during this phase is the derivation of the verification requirements. These are requirements which, during the latter stages of the project, are converted into the system and acceptance tests: tests which determine whether a system meets user requirements. Some examples of such verification requirements are shown below, for a system which produces information for water engineers about the level of water in a reservoir. Time duration stands for a period of time delimited by two times expressed using the 24-hour clock.

When the LEVEL-AVERAGE command is typed with a correct instrument name and with a valid time duration the average water level of the reservoir, as measured by the instrument, will be displayed on the originating VDU.

When the LEVEL-AVERAGE command is typed with an incorrect instrument name and with a valid time duration, an error message will be displayed.

When the LEVEL-AVERAGE command is typed with a correct instrument name, but with an invalid time duration, an error message will be displayed.

These verification requirements are at a high level of abstraction. As the software project proceeds they will be expanded into a number of tests. For example, the third verification requirement might be expanded into tests for the following:

1. When a time duration for which no water level data is available is executed, an error message will be displayed.
2. When the first time that delimits the time duration is later than the second time, an error message would be displayed.
3. When the first time is illegal, for example 25:33 or 17:66, an error message is displayed.
4. When the second time is illegal, an error message is displayed.

The expansion of the verification requirements usually takes place during the system design and detailed design phases. Normally most customers are happy to be presented with a system specification which is at a high level of abstraction and where there is a tacit understanding that phrases such as 'invalid time period' covers a multitude of cases.

Although the verification requirements can be established as late as the final stages of system design, it is important that they be established as early as possible during the requirements analysis stage. The reason for this is that requirements analysis is such a difficult task that the presence of a member of staff continually asking 'How do I test that?' can be an excellent check on the quality of a requirements specification.

It is during this phase that the test plan should be developed. The test plan should, eventually, be a very bulky document. However, at this stage it will only exist in outline. Often the outline test plan forms part of the contract for a software system and, occasionally, is used by a tendering board to judge the competence of competing developers. The test plan should eventually contain:

1. The organizational responsibilities for the various tasks in the testing program. In a large company this section differentiates those activities which are carried out by the development team and those carried out by an independent quality assurance organization, or by development staff in a project designated as having quality assurance functions.
2. The methods that are to be used to review documents associated with the test process. This includes:
   (a) When they are reviewed.
   (b) The staff who should carry out the review.
   (c) How unsatisfactory outcomes from a review are reported and follow-up actions taken.
   (d) How the execution of follow-up actions are checked.

(e) How the conduct of reviews is checked.

(f) What documents are associated with a review, i.e. which documents act as input to a review and which act as output.

(g) The skills of the reviewers.

(h) A description of any involvement of staff external to a project.

3. How the outcome of tests will be checked and monitored, and how discrepancies associated with tests will be acted on. This section will differentiate between tasks which are carried out by the developmental team and tasks carried out by an independent quality assurance function.

4. A description of the categories and levels of testing that will occur during the project. This chapter will describe a whole panorama of testing activities ranging from unit testing (testing individual program units) up to acceptance testing (the testing of a system to ensure that it meets user requirements). The test plan should detail these together with any standards that are to be applied.

5. The test schedule. This lists the tests that are to be carried out, together with the expected times that they will be executed. This test schedule should be presented in the standard form as an activity network such as a PERT chart. As with other project schedules, activities which are prone to delay should be marked, and alternative strategies to cope with possible delays should be outlined. For example, a developer might require a special test tool that needs to be built by a sub-contractor to a stringent timetable. The project plan should describe how the developer would cope with the late delivery of such a tool.

6. The various hardware configurations that are to be used when a test is executed. This is vitally important. One of the major reasons for project over-run is that developers underestimate the amount of hardware resource required for testing, particularly during the system and acceptance phase.

7. A description of each test that is to be carried out; and for each test a statement of the software configurations that will be needed to support the test together with the software tools required for the test. Normally simple software tools such as test harnesses are used. However, specialized tools such as simulators will occasionally be required.

8. A list of the verification requirements.

This document will be in outline, since much of this information will be unavailable at this stage of the software project. However, it is important that this document be created during this phase of the project, even if it largely contains section headings.

19.2.2 Testing and system design

There are a number of activities that are carried out during system (or architectural) design which are relevant to testing. First, the verification requirements will be expanded out so that they correspond more closely to individual tests. For example, the verification requirement:

4.3 When the DISPLAY command is typed with an invalid user identification, then an error message will be displayed on the originating console.

might be one of a number used to test an operating system. A valid user identification is a sequence of four alphabetic characters, ranging from AAAA to ZZZZ which has been allocated to the user of a system. This verification might be expanded to:

V4.3/1 When the DISPLAY command is typed, with a user identification A, then an error message will be displayed on the originating console.

V4.3/2 When the DISPLAY command is typed, with a user identification Z, then an error message will be displayed on the originating console.

V4.3/3 When the DISPLAY command is typed with a user identification which does not match a currently logged on user, then an error message will be displayed on the originating console.

V4.3/4 When the DISPLAY command is typed with a user identification which differs from a logged-on user identification by one character step in the first position, then an error message will be displayed on the originating console. For example, if a logged-on user had the identification ASFR the test should check that the user identification BSFR was incorrect.

V4.3/5 When the DISPLAY command is typed with a user identification which differs from a logged-on user identification by one character step in the fourth position then an error message will be displayed on the originating console. For example, if a logged-on user had the identification FRED the test should check that the user identification FREE was incorrect.

In general, as above, staff assigned to testing will generate tests which not only explore the normal behaviour of the system but will also check for extremal values such as the one referred to in V4.3/5. During this phase the verification requirements are considerably expanded. A second testing-related activity which should occur during this phase is to develop the test coverage matrix. This is a matrix which relates the expanded verification requirements to the modules which implement the requirements. An example of such a matrix, taken from a spreadsheet display, is shown in *Figure 19.1*.

Each row in this matrix relates the verification requirement to the program units that should be executed when a test corresponding to the verification requirement are carried out. For example, when a test corresponding to verification requirement 2.3 is carried out the program units *Update* and *Check* are executed.

There are five reasons for developing this matrix. First, towards the end of the software project, system and acceptance tests will be carried out, and these tests check that the completed software system is an adequate reflection of customer requirements. Occasionally the result of such a test will be coincidentally correct, i.e. the correct result will be given, but the wrong program units will be executed. By inserting print statements into simple program units, which type the name of the unit being executed, the staff carrying out system testing will be able to check, by referring to the test coverage matrix, whether the correct program units have been executed.

The second reason is that it provides a good check of the thoroughness of the system and acceptance testing. By examining those verification requirements which are selected for acceptance testing and system testing, quality assurance staff will be able to calculate the total number of program units which would be executed and whether any program units have been missed out.

The third reason is that it provides a check that the system design has been correctly developed. By tracing verification requirements against program units, staff charged with quality assurance are rapidly able to discover inconsistencies and omissions in the system design.

The fourth reason is that it checks whether the verification requirements which have been processed and expanded during system design have been expanded to the right level of detail. For example, a verification requirement may have been expanded to the point where one of two program units may be executed if certain items of data are input to the system. This cannot be expressed in the test coverage matrix; it assumes that

	A	B	C	D	E	F	G
2					Program units		
3							
4	Verification						
5	reqts		Update	Findx	Findy	Newest	Check
6							
7	1.1		X	X			X
8	1.2			X		X	
9	1.3				X	X	
10	2.1			X			
11	2.2				X		
12	2.3		X				X
13	2.4				X	X	X
14	2.5		X		X		
15	3.1			X			
16	3.2		X				

Figure 19.1 Example of a test coverage matrix

each test corresponds to the execution of a particular, fixed set of program units.

A final reason for constructing the test coverage matrix is that it provides useful information during the process of system modification. A software system is a dynamic entity; requirements change during project execution, and certainly change after release of the system. Such change is manifested in modifications to program code.

When the program code, in a specific unit or units, is changed the developer wants to know what other functions may be affected by that change. The usual reason for this is that he or she wishes to runs a series of tests to ensure that a modification due to a requirements change has not affected other functions of the system. The test coverage matrix gives this information.

For example, the test coverage matrix shown in Figure 19.1 shows that verification requirement 1.3 involves the execution of the program unit 'Findy'. If that requirement is changed and leads to a modification to Findy, then the developer should run tests that check that verification requirements 2.2, 2.4 and 2.5 are unaffected by the change.

A third activity that should be carried out during systems design is the development of the integration test strategy. This involves specifying the order in which the program units are added to the system which is being built up. There are essentially two strategies which are possible: a bottom-up strategy or a top-down strategy. In the latter the system is built from the topmost program units in a system; with the former the bottom level units are added first. The strategies are shown below for the simple system design described by Figure 19.2.

A top-down strategy would involve the order of integration:

A
AB
ABC
ABCD
ABCDE

while a typical bottom-up strategy would involve the sequence of integration:

D
DE
BDE
BDEC
BDECA

The advantages of each have been debated for the last 20 years (Myers, 1979). In general, the major advantage of a top-down approach is that it allows an early demonstration of a system and boosts morale. The major disadvantage is that stubs (dummy program units which replace program units which have not yet been programmed) have to be developed, whilst conceptually, it often seems easy to write such stubs, in practice it is often quite a difficult task.

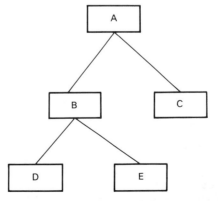

Figure 19.2 A simple system design

The major advantage of a bottom-up strategy is that it is easy to detect flaws that occur towards the bottom of a design. The major disadvantage is that it requires scaffold software. This is software which encloses a program unit and provides test data and prints out test results. In general a top-down strategy is to be preferred because of the importance of having an early version of a system which can be shown to a customer and which can enable the customer to detect any inconsistencies in the developers' perception of requirements. In practice the integration test plan needs to be defined taking into account the technical and schedule difficulties of integrating the product.

The integration test plan should include the order in which the integration takes place and the tests which need to be carried out after a program unit or groups of program units are added to a system. A major decision to be made before the integration plan is written is the granularity of the integration – whether tests are to occur after one program unit has been added or after a number of units have been added. In general, the granularity depends on the thoroughness with which the program units have been individually tested after they have been programmed. If they have been thoroughly tested then a high granularity might be employed; if they have been minimally tested then a granularity of one would be in order. Another factor in the granularity chosen is the complexity of the functionality delivered by the units to be integrated. For example, a developer may choose to integrate a large number of units at one time, where the units merely carry out the display of some data or error message, while units which carry out complex real-time processing would be integrated one at a time.

It is a fallacy to assume that the main function of the integration test should be to test that the interfaces between program units are correct. While this type of test is important, a number of other tests should be carried out. First, preliminary tests from the verification requirements should be executed. If, after integrating a set of program units, a verification requirement (or more accurately, software which can be checked by a specific verification requirement) has been implemented then a test should be carried out that the implementation has been correct. The reason, of course, is that it is a good principle in software development to check, as early as possible, that requirements have been implemented correctly. Carrying out such a test during integration, and discovering a fault, will save resources when compared with discovering the error during the final stages of testing.

Another type of test that should be carried out is a design function test. After the integration of a number of program units into system, a number of design functions (functions expressed in software terms), will have been implemented. A typical design function is:

When the program unit MOD-X is executed with a plane position, the position will be written into the flight database and the parameter FULL set to false. However, if the database is full then the parameter FULL is set to true.

Another important activity that should be carried out during integration testing is the testing of the response time of a real-time system. It is exceptionally difficult to predict the response time of a system during system design. Integration testing gives the first chance for the developer to check that real-time requirements have been met. This will only be a rough check because a partial system will only be executed and, hence, the full system will not be memory-resident. However, integration testing for response time does give the developer the confidence to assume that nothing has gone badly wrong with the real-time response of the system being constructed.

In summary, the set of integration tests will contain interface tests, design function tests, response tests and preliminary verification requirement tests. The set of integration tests should therefore include a description of the test, the outcome of the test, and the units that will have been integrated and the purpose of the test (interface, design function or preliminary verification requirement test).

19.2.3 Testing and detailed design

The next phase of the software project is detailed design. The main testing activity that occurs during this phase is the construction of the test procedures. A test procedure is a detailed step-by-step set of instructions for the staff who carry out the final stages of testing. A test procedure contains details of the software configuration used, the hardware configuration, the location of the job control language commands necessary for carrying out the test, the files containing test data, the expected outcomes of the tests and the location of the files which contain the test outcome.

A typical test procedure is:

TP 1/23 (Verification test V1.24)
Execute the test JCL commands stored in the file TP1/23.COM. This sets the test up. Connect the file TP1/23.FIL to the program held in the file TP1/23.PAS. The program should then be executed. During execution the program will halt four times with the prompt TEST⟩. Each time that the prompt is shown, type in an employee number between 1200 and 3200. When the execution has terminated, run the program FILE-MONITOR.OBJ. This will print out the employee database state after the employee numbers have been added. Check that the employee numbers are contained in the database.

Test procedures should be developed for both the system tests and the integration tests.

19.2.4 Testing and programming

The first, or primary, activity in this phase is programming or coding the individual units or modules. Work may also be carried out on producing test harnesses or stubs.

A second activity is the testing of the program units after they have been programmed. This process, normally called unit testing, is an informal process. The word 'informal' does not imply disorganized or unstructured. It means that the testing process is not under the control of a quality assurance organization; it is normally carried out by the programmer who produced the unit.

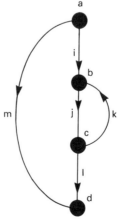

Figure 19.3 Directed graph of the procedure Init

The aim of unit testing is to check that a program unit matches the specification produced for it during system design. Unit testing is a structural testing activity, the aim being to ensure some degree of test thoroughness with respect to some measure of structural coverage. A typical measure is that the test data generated should ensure that 100% of the statements in a unit are executed. Although this is a common metric it is beginning to be regarded as inadequate, and the better metric of 100% statement coverage and 85% branch coverage is being gradually adopted in industry. Also, other more sophisticated test measures have been proposed (Woodward, 1980).

An important concept used, which is relevant to unit testing, is the directed graph. This is graphic description of the flow of control in a program or program unit. Nodes in a directed graph represent conditions or the destination of jumps, while lines represent flow of control. The directed graph for the Pascal procedure shown below is given in *Figure 19.3*.

```
Procedure Init (iter-times:integer; Check:boolean; a:arrayint);
var i:integer;
begin
if Check then
begin
  i: = 0;
  repeat
    i: = i + 1;
    a[i] : = 0
  until i = iter_times
end;
```

a, *b*, *c* and *d* are decision points of destinations of flow control. *d* is the exit point, *b* is the decision in the if statement, *c* is the decision in the repeat statement and *b* is the destination of the jump implied in the repeat statement.

An important concept in program testing is the program path. This is a trace of the flow of control through a program or program unit. One path through Init is *m* which occurs when the if statement evaluates to false. Another path is *ijl*, which occurs when the if condition evaluates to true and the repeat loop is only executed once. A further path is *ijkjkjkjkjl*, which occurs when the condition in the if statement is true and the repeat loop is executed four times. In general, a program or program unit contains an extremely high, if not infinite, number of paths and a high structural coverage during testing is usually the only practical test metric that can be aimed for.

An important document associated with unit testing is the unit folder or programmer's notebook. This is a document which describes the main features of a program unit. Normally it will contain the detailed design of a programming unit, the program code, the location of the test data used in testing the program unit and the files used to hold the test results. A useful piece of information which can be contained in the programmer's notebook is the rationale behind the choice of test data. The programmer must state why certain tests sets were used. For example, if a set of test data was used to check a program unit for the extremal values of the parameters of the unit then this must be stated. A company laying down such a standard will find that programmers will think more clearly about the choice of test data, as at present the choice of data tends to be governed by informal choices.

19.2.5 Testing and integration

Testing during the integration phase will follow the plans set out in system, or architectural, design. The primary aim of the testing activity is to verify the design, but a subsidiary aim is to begin to verify requirements functions.

During coding individual, tested program units will have been produced. These are then progressively integrated according to the agreed strategy, e.g. top-down or bottom-up. A number of specific facets of the design are tested, leading up to the testing of full design and requirements functions.

The first step is to check interface compatibility, i.e. that functions in units are correctly called by functions in the units that use them. This involves testing the validity of the parameters on all calls to functions, and the appropriateness of the response. As a minimum, parameter validity tests will ascertain that each parameter is of correct type and legal values. Ideally, testing should relate to a predicate defining the legal combinations of parameter values (see Section 19.3.4 on assertion testing). Checking the response is clearly a case of direct functional testing.

The notion of coverage extends to the invocation of function in the called unit, or module. The aim should be to ensure that the use, and operation, of the called function is valid for every possible call from the calling unit, i.e. there should be 100% call coverage. This, coupled with unit testing, should give high confidence in the interworking of the units if the programs are well structured.

In Chapter 17 the concepts of module coupling and cohesion were introduced. For well-structured programs coupling will be low, cohesion high and the interaction between the units will effectively be by function call and return. However, for less well-structured programs, especially where inter-module coupling is high, the above testing procedure will not be sufficient to give confidence that the modules will work well together. The testing strategy should be determined by the degree of module coupling. In the limit, where modules or units are content-coupled, i.e. one unit makes direct reference into another (see Chapter 17), then the pair of units have to be treated as if they were one, and unit tested in combination. This is clearly expensive and is one of the reasons for stressing the value of low module coupling in systems design.

At intermediate levels of coupling, other testing techniques, e.g. data flow-oriented (see Section 19.3.7), will be applicable as the coupling is likely to lead to data use errors. It may also be helpful to reapply the unit tests, as far as is possible, as a form of regression testing, to show that the integration has not adversely affected the functionality of the units.

As more units are integrated it will become possible to test individual design functions, i.e. major functional units defined in the system architecture. Once complete design functions have been integrated it will also be possible to check some of the non-functional requirements, e.g. space usage and response time.

If a given design function implements a requirements function in its entirety, then it will be possible to follow design function testing with preliminary evaluation using acceptance tests. With a more complex relationship between design and requirements functions, testing of requirements functions will only be possible later in the integration phase. The non-functional properties should be re-tested as more design functions are integrated.

To carry out integration testing, it will be necessary to build 'scaffolding' to exercise the partially integrated software. Producing the scaffolding, e.g. test harnesses and stubs, is expensive, especially as this software is likely to be of only temporary utility. One of the aims of test planning is to reduce the amount of scaffolding required. Another is to bring forward the times at which design and requirements functions can be tested.

Integration testing is a precursor to system and acceptance testing. If integration testing has been carried out effectively (and the necessary remedial work carried out) then the next phase should be relatively trouble-free.

19.2.6 System and acceptance testing

After programming and integration have been completed the (in some senses) most important testing activities occur. These are system testing and acceptance testing. In contrast to unit testing, both these activities are black-box activities. System testing is the process of executing the test procedures associated with the verification tests. Acceptance testing is the process of executing the test procedures associated with a subset of the verification requirements which are agreed by both the customer and the developer as being an adequate representation of user requirements. The major difference between system and acceptance testing is the fact that the former takes place in a simulated environment. It is usually carried out at the developer's premises, with items of equipment, or external sources or sinks of data, replaced by such tools as simulators or by stored data files.

System testing is a set of preliminary tests which are run to give the developer a high degree of confidence that the acceptance testing will be successful. They are executed for two reasons. First, it is very embarrassing when an acceptance test fails. Second, and more importantly, if an acceptance test fails the customer has every right to ask the developer to rerun all the acceptance tests after the error in a system has been remedied. The reason for this is that in modifying the system in response to an acceptance test error, the developer could have adversely affected some other part of the system and caused a further error which would only have been detected by an acceptance test that had already been executed. Thus, a failed acceptance test can cause the developer a large amount of expense.

19.2.7 Testing and maintenance

The final testing activity associated with the software life cycle is regression testing. This occurs during maintenance when a system has been modified. Regression testing is the execution of a series of tests which check that a modification, applied during maintenance, has not affected the code corresponding to those functions of the system which should be unaffected by the maintenance modification that had been carried out. A major item of documentation which is important during regression testing is the test coverage matrix described in Section 19.2.2. In practice it is also useful to carry out regression testing in earlier stages, e.g. when testing and rectifying faults in the programming phase.

19.3 Testing techniques

The aim of this section is to examine the various techniques which can be used to support the testing activities that were described in the previous section.

19.3.1 Mutation testing

Mutation testing can be used during system testing, acceptance testing or unit testing. However, as will be made clearer in this section, it is probably best employed during unit testing. An excellent description of the mutation testing process is described in Budd (1981) and Budd and Majoras (1978).

Once a series of tests have been carried out, a series of test files will have been constructed. These test files contain the data from these tests and a main concern of a tester is the adequacy of that data in terms of test effectiveness. Mutation testing is an attempt to quantify this adequacy. It is based on creating mutants of a program, a mutant being an original program which has been modified by inserting a small error. A typical error would be to replace an addition operator by a multiplication operator, or a less than operator by a greater than operator. A large number of such mutants are created and are then executed using the test data which was employed in testing the original program. If the

mutant gives a result which is different from the result of the test of the original program then the mutant is said to have died.

If the tests of the mutants result in all the mutants being killed off then the test data is adequate. However, if any mutants are still living then there is a problem. The test data that has been developed is unable to distinguish the original program from a program in which an artificial error has been inserted. Further test data is required which kills off any living mutants.

Mutation testing has one major advantage. It provides the tester with a target. He or she has to develop data which kills off a specific number of mutants. However, it has a major disadvantage, as in general there are a massive number of mutants that can be created. Even for a small program tens of thousands of mutants can be created. Since each of these mutants have to be compiled and executed it can be seen that it is a resource-intensive process.

However, limited forms of mutation testing are practical. For example, testing program units where only Boolean conditions are mutated is a powerful testing technique, since many errors in program code are due to programmer errors in the conditions in **if, while** and **repeat** statements. Because of the technique's potential for creating massive mutant sets it is only really practicable for unit testing where the size of the tested entities is small. Budd and Lipton (1978a) show how total correctness can be established for decision tables using mutation testing. Budd and Lipton (1978b) again show how total correctness can be achieved – for a subset of Lisp programs this time – by means of mutation testing. Budd *et al.* (1978) describe the architecture of a typical mutation system.

19.3.2 Random testing

Random testing is a technique which is only really practicable for unit testing as a useful adjunct to other testing techniques. It involves identifying the input data space for a program unit and randomly generating test data inside that space. For example, if a program unit processes an integer temperature between 0° and 100° C and an integer pressure between 0 mm and 1000 mm, then the data space would be characterized by the cross product {0..100} × {0..1000} and represented by ordered pairs taken from that space. Random testing involves the random sampling of this space to obtain pairs which are then executed by the program unit under test.

Random testing has a number of advantages. First, it is cheap in terms of tool support as all that is required is some form of random number generator. Second, it is extremely good at producing data which a human tester would not think of – often data which contains extreme values – and which stress tests a program unit. Third, it is possible to make reliability estimates from the response of a system to random testing (Duran and Wiorkowski, 1981). A good description of a project that adopted this testing technique can be found in Dyer (1989), and the topic is discussed further in Chapter 31.

There are a number of perceived disadvantages. First, random testing has been criticized on the basis that it would not lead to a high level of structural coverage; i.e. that it might not lead to a high number of statements or program branches being executed. A recent study (Duran and Ntafos, 1981) provides contrary evidence to this for small programs the size of program units. A second criticism is that if random testing resulted in a high structural coverage, then a large number of tests would need to be carried out and, consequently, a large amount of human resource is required for the examination of test results. A recent study (Ince, 1987) has demonstrated that it is possible to dispense with a large amount of examination of test results. Probably the most serious criticism of random testing, and the criticism which really ensures that it can be used in unit testing, is that for large programs the amount of data that needs to be generated is prohibitively large. The best advice that can be given about random testing is that it is a good strategy to use in conjunction with conventional testing techniques such as cause-effect graphing and can be used for the derivation of exceptional cases.

19.3.3 Structural testing

Structural testing involves testing a software system so that some structural metric is satisfied or a particular path is traversed. The latter is often referred to as path testing.

Path testing is normally employed during unit testing. During unit testing the programmer attempts to demonstrate that the functionality of a program unit reflects its specification. Test data is generated that checks out the function together with any error or exception cases.

Often the tester is faced with the problem of generating test data which traverses a particular path. The data for this can often be derived by looking at the program code. However, the code is occasionally so complex that the programmer needs to carry out a symbolic execution of the program unit to determine a predicate, expressed in terms of some set of input variables, which must be true for the path to be executed, and then solve that predicate. This predicate being known as a path predicate. An example of such a calculation is shown below. Consider the Pascal fragment which has two input variables a and b:

```
readln(a,b);
c: = a + b;
if c > 10 then
   begin
   d: = c↑2;
   e: = a − b
   end
else
   c: = b;
if d − e > 0 then
   writeln(d,e)
else
   writeln(d);
```

The path predicate which must be true for the path which includes both true branches of the if statements to be executed will be:

$$(a + b > 10) \wedge (((a + b)^2 - (a - b))) > 0$$

The first conjunct, $a + b > 10$, is derived from the fact that c is equal to $a + b$. The second conjunct is derived from the fact that d is equal to c^2 which, in turn, is equal to $(a + b)^2$, and e is equal to $a - b$. In order to derive the test data which executes the program path the predicate should be solved, the solution being given in terms of a and b. One solution would be to set a equal to 3 and b equal to 8.

The unit tester has not only to check that functionality has been implemented correctly, but has to ensure that his test data achieves a high structural coverage. That is, that a sufficiently high proportion of some structural feature of the program unit has been executed. Common structural metrics that are normally used in structural testing are statement coverage and branch coverage. In order to illustrate this consider the program unit shown below, expressed in Pascal:

```
Procedure Test1 ( val :integer; Var newval, oldval:integer);
begin
if val > 0 then newval: = 0
oldval: = 22
end;
```

Here the program unit contains two statements: an if state-ment and an assignment statement. It also contains two branches corresponding to the two outcomes from the if state-ment. A common industry standard in testing is required to achieve 100% statement coverage. Unfortunately, this is not adequate, as can be seen with reference to the program unit, where the data value 12 would achieve 100% coverage and yet not test the branch that is executed when val is greater less or equal to zero. Consequently, test thoroughness is often quanti-fied in terms of 100% statement coverage and some percentage of branch coverage, usually greater than 85%. Obviously it would be ideal to achieve 100% branch coverage but, in practice, it can be difficult to test particular cases (e.g. branches that correspond to fault recovery) so a lower figure is usually accepted.

Normally, structural testing is monitored by inserting soft-ware probes into the system or program being tested. A typical software probe will write to a history file the number of the branch or statement that has been executed. Such probes are normally automatically inserted by a software tool. A typical tool is described in Section 19.4.1.

Structural testing is normally employed during unit testing where the quality assurance function specifies particular levels of test coverage that individual programmers are meant to observe. However, structural testing is also useful during system testing where individual program units are instrumented with print statements that indicate that the unit has been executed. This ensures that when a system test gives a correct answer, that this was not due to coincidental correctness, but that the expected program units were executed.

Structural testing is also useful because, as a side-effect, it often provides information about which parts of a system are executed frequently. These are known as hot spots. Such hot spots occur in very localized parts of a system and a developer can, by applying limited resources to hot spots, drastically improve the run-time of a system. DeMillo et al. (1987) and Kaner (1988) provide good descriptions of structural testing. Beizer (1983) provides an excellent description of the theory that underlies structural testing. Huang (1978) is a good tutorial on instrumentation. Ramamoorthy and Ho (1975) describe how to place software probes into a system to minimize run-time overheads.

19.3.4 Assertion testing

An assertion is a predicate which relates the values of variables in a program and describes a condition which must be true during the execution of a program unit or a program. A typical assertion is:

old_value − new_value = 12* azimuth − initial_correction

which states a relation that must hold between the three variables used in the condition. Such conditions can be inserted by hand or by means of a software tool. A typical tool that uses assertions is described in Section 19.4.1. The mathematical techniques of software development, described in Chapters 2 and 21–26 of this book, have, as a by-product, data invariants which are similar to assertions.

Assertion testing is useful during the whole testing process up to system testing. It is an excellent technique whereby invalid variable values can be detected. It is probably at its most useful during integration and system testing. It can be used in conjunc-tion with defensive programming. This is a technique in which programming statements are inserted into a system which check that the relationship between program variables hold. For example, if after an input statement has been executed we know that the desired values of the variables a, b and c can be described by the predicate a + b < c then a program statement:

if a + b ⩾ c **then**
  writeln('assertion violated at statement 128')

would be included after the input statement. Such defensive programming statements are normally inserted after error prone code, e.g. after data items have been input, after a complex calculation has occurred, after some convoluted logic etc.

19.3.5 Adaptive testing

Adaptive testing is based on assertion testing. A program or program unit is placed in a test harness and is then instrumented by assertions. It is then executed with an initial set of test data. The number of assertions that have been violated is monitored and an optimization program is employed to derive further test data which violates more assertions. The theory behind adaptive testing is that the optimization routine automatically derives test data that increases the number of violations and hence the number of errors. A good introduction to adaptive testing is contained in Davis (1978). Apart from this paper there are no accounts which describe the success or otherwise of adaptive testing in an industrial environment.

19.3.6 Grammar-based testing

Grammar-based testing is based on describing the data set to be used in a test by means of some grammar formalism. The grammar formalisms that have been used are normally based on those used in compiling, for example BNF. The description of the test data is processed and test data produced which satisfies the description. The function of test tools based on a grammar formalism is the reverse of that of a compiler. A compiler takes a program and checks that it meets a formal description, while the test tools process a formal description and produce valid strings that meet the description.

A major use for grammar-based testing is in the development of compilers. Normally, the development of a grammar description of test data, for anything but the most trivial data, is a complex and laborious process. However, in compiler development the grammar description is mandatory and can be used directly. Normally grammar-based testing is employed during system and acceptance testing where large quantities of data are often required, particularly by compiler developers. Typical examples of grammar-based testing are described in Duncan and Hutchison (1981) and the architecture of a typical test data generator based on formal grammars is described in Bazzichi and Spadafora (1982).

19.3.7 Data flow-oriented testing

Some of the most common errors made in programming involve the assignment of inappropriate values to variables or inappropriate assignments. Such errors are also very difficult to detect. Data flow-oriented techniques involve the processing of a program in order to detect variable assignment anomalies. Typical anomalies are a variable being used, say, on the right-hand side of an assignment statement, without having been initialized, and a variable being assigned a value and then assigned another value without any intermediate uses of that variable.

Data flow-oriented testing requires software tools. Happily, the technology which is used to detect variable anomalies is mature; it is used in compiler writing. Data flow-oriented testing is best suited for unit testing or integration testing. A good description of data flow-oriented testing can be found in Laski (1982).

19.3.8 Symbolic execution

Normally, a program is executed with test data. However, a novel and effective technique involves the symbolic execution of a program. As an example of symbolic execution consider the Pascal fragment:

```
i: = 1; s: = 0;
while i ⩽ n do
  begin
  s: = s + a[i];
  i: = i + 1
  end;
print(s)
```

When this fragment is normally executed the sum of the first n elements of the array a will be displayed. However, when the fragment is symbolically executed the result which would be displayed for $n = 4$ would be:

$$\mathbf{a}[1] + \mathbf{a}[2] + \mathbf{a}[3] + \mathbf{a}[4]$$

Such a symbolic output is exceptionally useful for detecting program errors. As a validation technique it lies between the two end-points of program proving (as described in Chapters 2, 25 and 26 of this book) and pure testing. The former is general while the latter is very specific. It is useful as a testing technique during unit testing and requires quite a complex software tool for its operation.

There are a number of uses for symbolic execution. First, it is useful for debugging, as detailed above. Second, it can be used for the automatic generation of test data. A program or subroutine will consist of a number of paths each of which depend on a predicate, known as a path predicate, for execution. Such a predicate is expressed in terms of a number of input variables. When solved the predicate will give the values of the input variables that will cause the program path to be executed. The theory behind this form of testing can be found in Clarke (1976). It is described in more detail in Section 19.4 of this chapter.

A third use for symbolic execution is in program proving where assertions about the execution of a program are written in the program text and the path predicate compared with them to ascertain correctness. This use of symbolic execution is described in Darringer and King (1978) and King (1976).

A description of the architecture of a symbolic execution system is contained in King (1976). A rare paper describing the effectiveness of symbolic execution is Howden (1978).

19.3.9 Domain testing and input space partitioning

This is a technique whereby the input space of a program is partitioned into path domains – a subset of the program input domain that causes execution of each path. Thus, if the domain of a program is *employee_names* × *salary* × *hours_worked*, where *employee_names* is the set of all possible employee names, *salary* is an integer that represents an employee's salary and *hours_worked* is an integer which represents the number of hours worked. If the program under test carried out error processing when processing data which contains an integer value of *salary* greater than 1000 and less than 1500, *hours_worked* greater than 50 and less than 60, then the subset of the domain which causes the error processing to occur will be *employee_names* × 1001..1499 × 51..59.

One variant of input space partitioning is known as domain testing. Here test data is selected which lies on the boundary of the sub-domains. The theory is that errors such as loop variables off by one, or conditions being off by one, can be detected by examining test data which lies on the boundaries. This type of testing can be used during system testing, integration testing or unit testing. Good descriptions of domain testing techniques can be found in White (1981), Woodward *et al.* (1980) and Richardson and Clarke (1981).

19.3.10 Functional testing

Functional testing involves checking the functions of a computer system by means of examining either the system specification or the system design. With the former the functions are known as requirements functions while the latter are known as design functions. As an example of this process consider *Figure 19.4.*

This shows the architecture of a system which reads commands from a user and checks that the commands are correct, extracts the parameters of the command which are measuring instrument name and a time limit. It then checks that the instrument name is correct and that the time limit is valid. If the command is valid and the parameters are correct then the command is decoded and executed. There are four commands: *A, B, C* and *D*, all of them carry out the retrieval of data from a database. The units which accomplish command *A* are shown, but the other subsidiary units for the remaining commands are not. Typical (definitions for) requirements functions include:

1. A function which reads a command from a user and prints out an error if the command contains illegal parameters.

2. A function which reads a command from a user with correct parameters and carries out the actions associated with the command.

Such functions can be extracted by reading a system specification; the ease with which they can be extracted depends on the exactness of the notation used for the system specification. Typical design functions include:

1. A function which decodes a command and executes the correct program unit.
2. A function which retrieves data from the database.
3. A function which checks that the time limit given by an operator is correct.

In general, a requirement function can be expressed or implemented in terms of a design function. Normally, requirement functions are tested during system and acceptance testing and design functions during integration testing, although the wise developer will also carry out preliminary requirement function tests during integration testing.

Functional testing is the one testing activity that is poorly served by software tools. The reason for this is clear: functional testing requires an exact representation of a design or a functional specification. The vast majority of software projects still use semi-formal notations for these tasks where natural language is one of the components. To generate test data from natural language descriptions is well beyond even the most sophisticated artificial intelligence techniques.

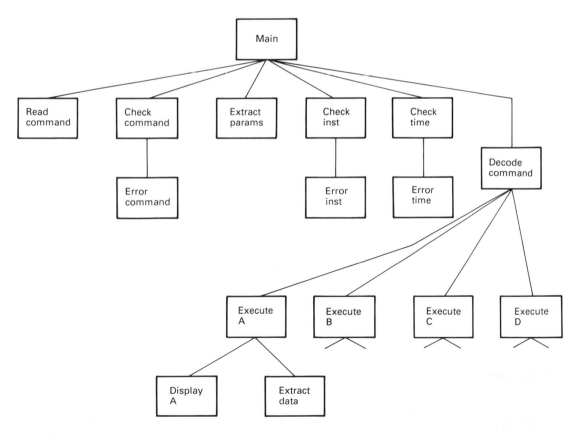

Figure 19.4 A system architecture

19.3.11 Real-time testing

There is very little literature concerning real-time testing. In general many of the techniques described in the previous ten sections are applicable to testing real-time systems. However, some extra testing is normally required. This testing arises from the properties of such systems. They have stringent response times and they involve temporal coordination between software modules and external devices. Consequently, there is a need for a large testing effort during system testing. Both adaptive testing and random testing are useful for this process as they can generate large amounts of data relatively easily and often generate data which the tester would not think of.

The testing of response time can be carried out by means of a technique known as thread testing. Thread testing occurs during integration testing, and involves the functions of the system being tested as the software system is being built up. In this way critical functions, which involve stringent time responses, can be tested early on in integration, and retested during later integration in order to check that increasing system size does not substantially degrade response time. Deutsch (1982) describes this process in detail.

19.3.12 Cause-effect testing

This is a technique for creating test cases that is primarily used during system testing. It has the advantage over other test generation techniques in that it is possible to consider combinations of circumstances that occur in a test. Its name comes from the graphical notation that it uses to specify tests. The elements of the notation are shown in *Figure 19.5*. On the left-hand side are causes which give rise to events in a system. Typical causes might be an operator typing a command, a valve closing, or delivery of stock being notified to a system. On the right-hand side are events that occur because of causes, for example, an alarm being sounded, a valve being closed or an error message being displayed on a screen.

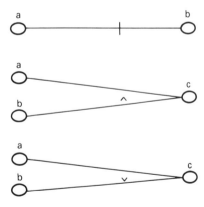

Figure 19.5

The first graph in Figure 19.5 states that event *b* will occur when event *a* does not. The second graph states that event *c* will occur when events *a* and *b* occur, and the third graph states that event *c* will occur when events *a* or *b* occur. An example of a simple cause-effect graph is shown in *Figure 19.6*.

Here event *f* will occur when either event *a* does not occur or events *b* and *c* occur or event *d* occurs. So, for example, if cause *a* stands for 'monitoring command typed in', cause *b* stands for 'system is in training mode', cause *c* stands for 'check command is typed in', cause *d* stands for 'global monitoring command is

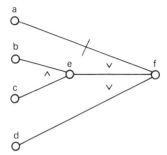

Figure 19.6

typed in' and event *f* is 'the system will be in a monitoring state', then the graph above stands for:

> if the monitoring command typed in or the system is in training mode and the check command is typed in or the global monitoring command is typed in then the system will be in a monitoring state.

The process of deriving test cases using cause-effect graphing is straightforward. First, the system is partitioned into manageable chunks. The reason for this is that attempting to derive a cause-effect graph for large parts of a system, or the whole system itself, requires a large amount of space on paper or a computer screen. The causes and effects are then identified from the system specification. The cause-effect graph is then built up and converted into a decision table which documents the test cases.

Myers (1979) provides an excellent example of cause-effect graphing in action. Cause-effect graphing has the major advantage that it is systematic. Unfortunately, it has never really been a popular technique. It is difficult to support when the only medium available is pencil and paper. However, the advent of cheap microcomputers with good quality, bit-mapped screens should ensure a renaissance.

19.4 Software tools for testing

As the previous section has indicated, testing requires the full use of software tools. In general software tools for testing have been built for code-level testing activities. There are few available tools for system and acceptance testing where the main input is the system specification. The reason for this is clear. Software engineering is still relatively undeveloped, to the point where natural language is still used as a descriptive medium for front-end activities such as system specification and system design. Since natural language lacks precision it is impossible to generate tests automatically which validate systems described using the medium. However, there are many tools which help with other aspects of testing. We summarize these below.

19.4.1 Program instrumentors

Program instrumentors insert program code into a unit or system under test. The most common instrumentor is the type used for dynamic analysis. The architecture of a typical dynamic analysis system is shown here as *Figure 19.7*. It contains a command processor (not shown), a pre-processor (or instrumentor), an executor and an analyser. The command processor takes commands from the user which determine the level and extent of the instrumentation that is required. For example, a

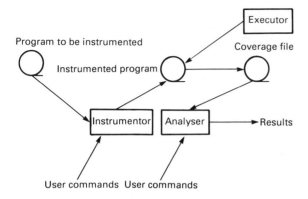

Figure 19.7 The architecture of an instrumentor

user may only want information that a program unit has been entered, say, during system testing when checking for coincidental correctness, or the user may want full branch coverage, say, during unit testing. The commands typed in by the user are then processed by the pre-processor or instrumentor. This reads in the program unit or system under test and inserts the probes which carry out the required level of testing.

The instrumentor establishes the syntactic structure of the program and inserts software probes into the program. A program unit and its instrumented version is:

```
procedure check_temp (temp:integer; Var flag:Boolean);
begin
if temp > 100 then flag: = true
else flag: = false
end;

procedure_check temp (temp:integer; Var flag:Boolean);
begin
writeprocname('check_temp')
if temp > 100 then
begin
writebranch('check_temp',1);flag: = true
end
else
begin
writebranch('check_temp',2);flag: = false
end;
```

The procedure *writeprocname*, inserted by the instrumentor, writes the name of the procedure that has been executed to an external file. Similarly, the procedure *writebranch* writes the procedure name and a branch number to the same external file.

The dynamic analysis system works as follows. The user communicates to the system the level of coverage that is required. For example, if integration testing was being carried out the user may only want to know what procedures have been entered; he or she may be uninterested in the branch coverage. The instrumentor then processes the program under test and inserts the software probes. The program is then executed and the probes write information to a coverage file. The user then interrogates the files in order to discover the coverage information that is of interest. The theory of program instrumentation is described in Huang (1979).

This is one form of program instrumentation known as coverage analysis. Other, less popular, forms also exist. For example, systems are in existence which insert monitors and assertions into a program; an assertion being a predicate which

reflects relationships bween the variables used in a program which must hold at that point. Assertion checking is primarily a debugging aid. It is also useful in the documentation of a program since many assertion processors have the ability to flag assertions as comments after a program has been fully tested.

Another form of instrumentation involves recording the minimum and maximum values of a variable, so that when an error in a variable value occurs it can be monitored, and debugging information provided. There are a large number of instrumentation tools on the market. Probably, the most sophisticated is PET (Stucki and Foshee, 1975). This provides both dynamic execution facilities and the ability to insert assertions and to monitor the values given to specified program variables. The only disadvantage with instrumentation systems is that since they insert code which accesses files into a program, the run time of the program is increased, and this increase can be as much as 100%. This is probably only a signficiant drawback for real-time systems.

19.4.2 Mutation systems

The vast majority of mutation systems operate on FORTRAN or COBOL programs. Their action is fairly similar. First, the program whose mutants are to be constructed is read in. It is syntactically analysed and converted to an internal form. The user then communicates the types of mutants that are required and mutant description records are then created which describe the type of mutant that is created. The original program is then run and the results monitored. The next step is for the mutants to be executed and the results from the runs compared with the results from the execution of the unmutated program.

A typical mutation system offers a number of facilities. The more important of these are: commands for allowing the user to select which types of mutants are to be created; output facilities which describe the quality of the test data numerically in terms of a ratio of dead mutants to the total number of mutants created; predicates which allow automatic comparison of the output from mutated programs; and commands which allow the user to designate parts of a system to be mutated.

There are a wide variety of mutants that current systems can create. They include: replacement of a constant; replacement of a variable; replacement of arithmetic operators; replacement of logical operators; statement deletion; label replacement; and modification of for loops.

The main problem with mutation systems is that they are capable of generating large numbers of mutants which can consume a large amount of resources when they are executed. Currently, they can only really be used for unit testing. However, they are powerful tools which are able to give an excellent indication of the quality of test data. They can also be constructed very easily. While many current mutation testing tools use a complicated system of deriving an internal form, a simpler tool with equivalent power can be constructed by using a programmable editor. This editor would contain instructions which told it to carry out changes to the system to be mutated. A description of a typical mutation system is contained in DeMillo *et al.* (1979).

19.4.3 Symbolic evaluators

Symbolic evaluators are software systems which take a program, or part of a program, and execute it symbolically. Instead of numerical values, symbolic values are produced. A major use of such tools is in routine debugging. However, they are also useful in automatic test data generation. During unit testing a major aim of the tester is to produce test data that results in a path being traversed, or in some high level of structural coverage being achieved. In order to show how a symbolic evaluator is able to support this process consider the procedure *test 1*:

```
Program test1;
Var a,b,c,d: integer;
begin
read(a,b,c,);
if a + b > c then d: = 2 + a↑2
    else d: = 4 + a;
if d  > 22*c then e: = 1
    else e: = 0
end
```

To illustrate how symbolic evaluation is able to help in this way, assume that the tester wishes to generate data which traverses the path through the program which executes the true branches of both if statements. The first true branch would be executed if $a + b > c$; when this is executed d becomes $2 + a^2$. The second branch is executed when $d > 22*c$ and since d has already been set to $2 + a^2$ then this means that $2 + a^2 > 22*c$. Thus in order for the path to be executed the two inequalities:

$$a + b > c$$
$$2 + a^2 > 22*c$$

must hold. These two inequalities can be solved using numerical analysis equation solving routines. The role of a symbolic evaluator in this case is to evaluate algebraic quantities, simplify them and present the inequalities to a numerical analysis program for solving the inequalities. Now the example above is trivial. In practice the inequalities are more numerous and are more complicated. However, the idea behind the use of symbolic evaluators is the same.

When using a symbolic evaluator to derive test data for achieving high structural coverage, a further pre-processing step is necessary. First, the control structure of the program or program unit under test is extracted. The paths which have to be executed in order for the structural coverage to be achieved are then calculated. Then, the symbolic evaluator calculates the data that is required to traverse each path using the process described in the previous two paragraphs. Clarke (1976) describes a typical system for test data generation based on symbolic execution.

19.4.4 Automatic test drivers

There is a large amount of routine work that is carried out during integration testing and unit testing. It involves setting up program code which provides the software under test with test data and also monitors the results from the software and displays it. Much of the work involved in this process is repetitive, so the process is susceptible to automation. Automatic test drivers, often called test harnesses, are software tools for simulating an environment for running tests. They usually provide a specific language for specifying tests and some systems. They additionally provide facilities for describing the result of a test, thus saving programmer resource when it comes to examining test outcomes. Typically a test driver manages the allocation of files to a tested system, initializes global variables with tester supplied values and displays values of variables after test execution. The majority of automatic test drivers use a special language for describing the test to be carried out. Typical test drivers are described in Sneed (1979) and Panzl (1978).

19.4.5 File comparators

These are software tools which compare the contents of two files. They are used to check the output of a test against a file constructed by the tester which contains the expected output.

They are most useful during the process of regression testing when maintenance changes have occurred, and the tester wants to ensure that these changes have not affected extant functions of the system.

19.4.6 Static analysers

A static analyser takes a program and, without executing it, reports on inconsistencies. Typical errors that static analysers are able to discover are: uninitialized variables; variables given a value but never used; code segments which can never be executed; departures from programming standards; and incorrect interfaces between program units. Rudimentary static analysers produce simple data such as cross-reference listings, profiles of programming statements categorized by type, and analysis of variable usage. Some typical static analysers are described in Brown and Johnson (1978) and Osterweil and Fosdick (1976). The theory of static analysis is described in Howden (1981).

19.5 Testing progress and prospects

The literature of testing is now quite considerable. Few books have been published which specifically address testing. However, those that have been written (Myers, 1979; DeMillo *et al.* 1987; Kaner, 1989) have been uniformly excellent. Also, the research literature on testing is as large as any other branch of software engineering. Unfortunately, there are still major weaknesses in testing research.

The first weakness is that little work has been carried out on a theory of testing. What has been written has been either technically flawed (Gourlay, 1983), or too general to be of application to current testing techniques (Goodenough and Gerhart, 1975).

A second weakness is the lack of research into *useful* automatic test data generation tools. The word *useful* is stressed because much research has been carried out into the generation of test data which is capable of exercising a path in a subroutine, for example, Bicevskis *et al.* (1979) and Ramamoorthy and Ho (1975). However, this work is of very limited value. Unit testing is not a particularly difficult process. The main feature of unit testing is that it is very repetitive and time-consuming. This arises less from the process of generating test data which exercises a path, but from the labour involved in writing scaffold software, developing test files and checking that test output is correct.

There is a serious lack of work on the automatic generation of design function tests that can be applied during integration testing, and function tests that can be applied during system and acceptance testing. The reason for this is that the notations used for both system testing and system design are not exact, and are incapable of being processed to generate test data. However, the advent of mathematical specification techniques should at least remove one barrier from researchers. Unfortunately, another barrier remains, as both the testing community and the formal methods community are culturally and geographically separate from each other.

The testing literature offers a strange phenomenon. Until 1982 the rate of publication of research articles on testing was very high. However, since then it has fallen quite drastically and now little new seems to be published. Almost certainly the interpretation to put on these figures is that many of the relatively easy problems in testing have been solved. For example, many of the design problems encountered with dynamic analysis tools have been solved, much of the applications of graph theory to testing have been successfully implemented, a large number of software tools which minimize the labour-intensive tasks of testing have been developed, and there is now a consensus on the management of testing process. It is the difficult problems discussed above that need to be solved and here the literature provides little, if any, guidance.

19.6 References

Bauer, J. A. and Finger, A. B. (1979) Test plan generation using formal grammars. In *Proceedings of 4th International Conference on Software Engineering*, Munich, IEEE Computer Society

Bazzichi, F. and Spadafora, I. (1982) An automatic generator for compiler testing. *IEEE Transactions on Software Engineering*, 8, 343–353

Beizer, B. (1983) *Software Testing Techniques*, Van Nostrand, New York, USA

Bicevskis, J. et al. (1975) SMOTL – A system to construct samples for data processing program debugging. *IEEE Transactions on Software Engineering*, 5, 60–66

Brown, J. C. and Johnson, D. B. (1978) FAST, a second generation program analysis system. In *Proceedings of the 3rd International Conference on Software Engineering*, IEEE Computer Society, pp 142–148

Budd, T. A. and Majoros, M. (1978) Experiences in a software test factory. In *Proceedings of IEEE Workshop on Software Testing and Test Documentation*, IEEE Computer Society, pp 112–136

Budd, T. A. and Lipton, R. J. (1978a) Proving LISP programs using test data. In *Proceedings of Workshop on Software Testing and Test Documentation*, IEEE Computer Society, pp 374–403

Budd, T. A. and Lipton, R. J. (1978b) Mutation analysis of decision table programs. In *Proceedings Conference on Information Science and Systems*, pp 346–349

Budd, T. A. *et al.* (1978) The design of a prototype mutation system for program testing. In *Proceedings NCC*, AFIPS Press, pp 623–627

Budd, T. A. *et al.* (1980) Theoretical and empirical studies on using program mutation to test the functional correctness of programs. In *Proceedings of 7th ACM Symposium on the Principles of Programming Languages*, ACM Press

Budd, T. A. (1981) Mutation analysis: ideas, examples, problems and prospects. In *Computer Program Testing* (eds B. Chandrasekaran and S. Radichi) North-Holland

Clarke, L. A. (1976) A system to generate test data and symbolically execute programs. *IEEE Transactions on Software Engineering*, 2, 215–222

Darringer, J. A. and King, J. C. (1978) Applications of symbolic execution to program testing. *Computer*, 11, 51–60

Davis, C. G. (1978) The testing of large real-time software systems. In *Proceedings 7th Texas Conference on Computing Systems*, Houston

DeMillo, R. A., Lipton, R. J. and Sayward, F. G. (1979) Program mutation: a new approach to program testing. In *Infotech State of the Art Report, Software Testing, Volume 2: Invited Papers*, Infotech International, pp. 107–126

DeMillo, R. A., McCracken, W. M., Martin, R. J. and Passafiume, J. F. (1987) *Software Testing and Evaluation*, Benjamin/Cummings, Menlo Park, CA, USA

Deutsch, M. S. (1982) *Software Verification and Validation–Realistic Project Approaches*, Prentice-Hall, Englewood Cliffs, NJ, USA

Duncan, A. G. and Hutchison, J. S. (1981) Using attribute grammars to test designs and implementations. In *Proceedings of 5th International Conference on Software Engineering*, IEEE Computer Society, pp 170–178

Duran, J. W. and Ntafos, S. (1981) A report on random testing. In *Proceedings of 5th International Conference on Software Engineering*, IEEE Computer Society, pp. 179–183

Duran, J. W. and Wiorkowski, J. J. (1981) Capture-recapture sampling for estimating software error content. *IEEE Transactions on Software Engineering*, 7, 147–148

Dyer, M. (1989) The clean-room-software development process. In *Measurement for Software Control and Assurance* (eds B. A. Kitchenham and B. Littlewood) Elsevier Applied Science, pp 1–62

Goodenough, J. B. and Gerhart, S. L. (1975) Toward a theory of test data selection. *IEEE Transaction on Software Engineering*, 9, 156–173

Gourlay, J. S. (1983) A Mathematical framework for the investigation of testing. *IEEE Transactions on Software Engineering*, 9, 686–710

Howden, W. E. (1978) An evaluation of the effectiveness of symbolic testing. *Software Practice and Experience*, 8, 381–397

Howden, W. E. (1981) A survey of static analysis methods. In *Tutorial: Software Testing and Validation Techniques*, IEEE

Huang, J. C. (1978) Program instrumentation and software testing. *Computer*, 11, 25–32

Huang, J. C. (1979) Program instrumentation: a tool for software testing. *Infotech State of the Art Report on Software testing, Volume 2*, Infotech International

Ince, D. C. (1987) The automatic generation of test data. *The Computer Journal*, 30, (1), 63–69

King, J. C. (1976) Symbolic execution and program testing. *Communications of the ACM*, 19, 385–394

Kaner, C. (1982) *Testing Computer Software*, TAB Books, Blue Ridge Summit, PA, USA

Laski, J. (1982) On data flow guided program testing. *SIGPLAN Notices*, 17

Myers, G. J. (1979) *The Art of Software Testing*, Wiley, New York, USA

Osterweil, L. J. and Fosdick, L. D. (1976) DAVE; a validation error detection and documentation system for FORTRAN programs. *Software Practice and Experience*, 6, 473–486

Paige, M. (1981) Data space testing. *Performance Evaluation Review*, 10

Panzl, D. J. (1978) Automatic software test drivers. *Computer*, 11, 44–50

Ramamoorthy, C. V. (1975) Optimal placement of software monitors aiding systematic testing. *IEEE Transactions on Software Engineering*, 1, 403–410

Ramamoorthy, C. V. and Ho, S. F. (1975) Testing large software with automated software evaluation systems. *IEEE Transactions on Software Engineering*, 1, 46–58

Richardson, D. J. and Clarke, L. A. (1981) A partition analysis method to increase program reliability. In *Proceedings of 5th International Conference on Software Engineering*, San Diego, IEEE Computer Society, pp 244–263

Sneed, H. M. (1979) Prufstand – a testbed for systems software components. *Infotech State of the Art Report on Software Testing, Volume 2*, Infotech International

Stucki, L. G. and Foshee, G. L. (1975) New assertion concepts for self-metric software validation. In *Proceedings of International Conference on Reliable Software*, IEEE Computer Society, pp 59–71

White, L. J. *et al.* (1981) A domain strategy for computer program testing. In *Computer Program Testing* (eds B. Chandrasekaran and S. Radicchi) Elsevier-North Holland, Amsterdam

Woodward, M. R. *et al.* (1980) Experience with path analysis and testing of programs. *IEEE Transactions on Software Engineering*, 6, 278–285

20

Software maintenance

Keith Bennett, Barry Cornelius, Malcolm Munro, Dave Robson
Centre for Software Maintenance,
University of Durham

Contents

20.1 Introduction

20.1.1 What is software maintenance?

Software maintenance has become established as a sub-discipline within the general field of software engineering. This has not always been the case, with software maintenance being given very low status by the software engineering community. Schneidewind in his survey paper (1987) concludes that there is general acknowledgement that the subject is an important one but at the same time that there has been a substantial technical neglect, while in a recent paper, Bennett *et al* (1988) argue that there is an urgent need to address the problems of software maintenance.

Software maintenance has been defined as:

the modification of a software product after delivery to correct faults, to improve performance or other attributes, or to adapt the product to a changed environment. (ANSI/IEEE, 1983)

Thus, maintenance refers to the activities that take place after a software product has been delivered to the customer.

The term 'software maintenance' is now well established in the computing profession, but in many ways it is an unfortunate choice of words, suggesting parallels or similarities with hardware maintenance. However, hardware maintenance is usually required because of the progressive degradation or wearing out of physical materials, while software is not subject to such factors.

Software maintenance activities have been classified into three categories by Lientz *et al.* (1978). First, there may be a fault in the software, so that it does not conform to its actual (or perceived) specification. Often the fault will have manifested itself in the form of an error when the program has run, and the fault (colloquially, a 'bug') must be removed. This is termed corrective maintenance. Under management pressure, emergency repairs may be undertaken ('patching') which often cause considerable problems later.

Even if a software system is fault-free, the environment in which it exists will be subject to change. For example, new versions of the operating system may be introduced, or the software may be moved to new or different hardware. This is termed adaptive maintenance.

The third category of maintenance is termed perfective maintenance, and is the consequence of a change in the requirements of the software. As a simple example, a tax program may need to be modified to reflect new tax laws but, usually, modifications are much more substantial.

Some authors also refer to preventive maintenance, which is work that is done in order to try to prevent malfunctions or improve maintainability (Arnold and Parker, 1982; Glass and Noiseux, 1981; Parikh, 1982a; Pressman, 1987; Swanson, 1976). For example, a section of the code that has had many alterations made to it may be completely rewritten, to improve its maintainability. Unlike the first three categories of software maintenance, preventive maintenance is not undertaken directly as a response to a user request. Typically, the need for preventive maintenance is stimulated from within the maintenance organization, although it is recognized that such a need can be a consequence of a major change request from a user, which is infeasible to implement using the software as it is.

It is also important to point out at this stage that there are many differences between software maintenance and initial development. In the latter, the project is undertaken within a timetable and to a budget, and an identifiable, specified product is seen (or should be seen) as the deliverable. In contrast, maintenance is usually open-ended, and may continue for many years. Indeed, it is often an objective to extend the life of a software system for as long as economically possible.

20.1.2 Economic consequences of maintenance

It is generally recognized that software maintenance consumes a huge budget. Despite this, only one major survey, by Lientz and Swanson (1980), has been undertaken to try to quantify the effort expended on software maintenance. Lientz and Swanson found the following distribution:

Perfective	50%
Adaptive	25%
Corrective	21%
Preventive	4%

This suggests that 'bug fixing' is a relatively small fraction of the total software maintenance activity.

Perhaps more significantly, Lientz and Swanson found that many organizations were spending between 20% and 70% of their software resource on maintenance. The distribution was attributed to the type of software, the application domain, etc., but it was not possible to determine the sensitivity of the results to the inherent maintainability of the software. Other results, such as those of Ditri *et al.* (1971) and Hoskyns Ltd (1973) provide reinforcement for these figures, although, frequently surveys measure different factors, such as: project cost, programmer time, programmer cost, and so on. Thus it is difficult directly to compare the results, and there are indications that in industries where the figure is very high, there is a reluctance to disclose detailed data. Although a comprehensive review of the survey data will not be provided, all reports agree that maintenance consumes a substantial proportion of the overall life cycle costs of a software project.

There is currently much research being undertaken to produce software through rigorous methods. Although this is expected to reduce the quantity of corrective maintenance needed, little empirical evidence exists. Rigorous methods may also assist perfective and adaptive maintenance, though here even less evidence exists. It is probable that such methods will introduce a new set of problems for the maintainer – see Section 20.6.

There is a further aspect of perfective maintenance that is having a serious economic impact. To maintain a competitive edge, a company must prepare new products, services, etc. Often this demands changes to the company's software and there is evidence that serious delays are occurring because the software cannot be modified easily, quickly and reliably. Delays of up to two years have been reported informally, with consequent effects upon the organization's marketing strategy. It would seem that the backlog is not simply attributable to poor project scheduling and planning; it is rather that changing existing software is a difficult and skilled task.

20.1.3 Characteristics of existing software

There is an enormous financial investment in existing software which has been produced through conventional (or *ad hoc*) software engineering methods. This includes almost all the software that is being produced today. Thus, industry and commerce are in the position of having to cope with huge quantities of software which it is economically infeasible to discard, because of the arrival of new methods or even new application packages. Some of this software will be required for many years yet, and much of this chapter is concerned with supporting such existing software.

Such software has been termed 'geriatric', referring to the technical challenge of looking after software written perhaps many years previously. The problem is accentuated typically by a lack of documentation or design information, *ad hoc* techniques used in production, and mixed language source codes (where they still exist).

A key issue in addressing the maintenance of this type of

software is the problem of scale. Methods which work for pilot, laboratory-sized, systems of a few hundred lines of code usually fail completely when faced with real systems comprising a million or more lines of code. A major concern in geriatric software is the control of the 'ripple effect': an apparently innocuous change in one part of the system has an unexpected side-effect in a completely different part, resulting in a faulty system. Thus testing and validation are central areas in software maintenance. These will form part of the quality assurance procedure in the software maintenance process.

It is characteristic of the perceived low status of software maintenance that capital investment is generally low. Tool support does exist, mainly in the form of cross-reference generators and in COBOL restructurers which transform a badly structured input into a well-structured output (see Section 20.4). To use such tools confidently, one needs reassurance that the transformations are correct. In general, however, there are no established maintenance methods, few tools, inadequate metrics and low financial rewards for personnel.

20.1.4 Maintenance and the software life cycle

Traditionally, maintenance has been regarded as not belonging to the software life cycle in the same sense as the earlier stages, but rather as occupying a detached position. However, it is inappropriate to regard it as a stage that is independent of the other stages of the life cycle. Sommerville (1985) states that: 'the maintenance activity may involve changes in requirements, design and implementation or it may highlight the need for further system testing'.

So the maintenance programmer may have to perform many of the activities that have been performed during the development stage.

There have been many criticisms of the classical software life cycle model (McCracken and Jackson, 1982; Gladden, 1982). In particular, it has been argued that the model stresses the importance of the development stages and yet maintenance is the main software engineering activity that takes place in the lifetime of a well-used large software system. Lehman (1980, 1984) suggests that large software systems are never completed and that such systems are always being maintained. He suggests that the term 'maintenance' should be avoided and that 'program evolution' be used. Such an approach recognizes that when a product is delivered to the customer, it is just the first of a number of releases in the evolution of the product.

20.1.5 Structure of the remaining sections

The next few sections focus on how the maintenance of existing software should be performed. There are four key themes:

1. A model of the maintenance process which identifies how all the different activities interconnect.
2. Techniques for the management of maintenance.
3. Techniques for each of the major activities of maintenance.
4. The establishment of quality assurance procedures.

Section 20.6 addresses how new software should be maintained; and Section 20.8 looks at how the maintenance process can be improved through further research.

20.2 Model of the maintenance process

20.2.1 Process models

The following definitions are provided by Dowson and Wileden (1985):

1. *Software process.* The collection of related activities, seen as a coherent process subject to reasoning, involved in the production of a software system.
2. *Software process model.* A purely descriptive representation of the software process. A software process model should represent attributes of a range of particular software processes and be sufficiently specific to allow reasoning about them.

Modelling the software process is an important current area for research (Tully, 1989). This is not surprising, since in order to understand and assess a software *product*, one needs to understand and study the *process* by which it was produced. Much of the work is addressing the initial software development, although some research is also including the evolution and more general maintenance of software. There would appear to be two approaches to work on software process models. In the first, existing software development is observed in real life, and empirical conclusions are abstracted from such analysis. In contrast, process models may be prescriptive, so that a model derived from theoretical or abstract considerations is imposed on the software development process. In practice, research is likely to move forward by a combination of these approaches, and this reflects the description of maintenance models given in this chapter.

20.2.2 Current models

The traditional life cycle model of software has always shown the software maintenance activity as a single step at the end of the cycle. This model is essentially:

requirements → design → code → install → operation and
maintenance

with possible feedback loops from each phase. The model does not portray the system life; it only shows the creation and development (or youth) of a system. It does not show the evolutionary development (or adulthood) that is the characteristic of most software systems. The final step needs to be replaced by a model that reflects this aspect of software evolution.

A number of authors have proposed a model of the software maintenance process (Liu, 1976; Boehm, 1976; Sharpley, 1977; Parikh, 1982a; Martin and McClure, 1983; Yau *et al.*, 1978; Osborne, 1987). These models range from the simple model of Boehm (1976) that outlines three phases of a maintenance effort:

1. Understanding the existing software.
2. Modification of the existing software.
3. Revalidation of the modified software.

to the more comprehensive phases identified by Osborne (1987):

1. Determination of need for change.
2. Submission of change request.
3. Requirements analysis.
4. Approval/rejection of change request.
5. Scheduling of task.
6. Design analysis.
7. Design review.
8. Code changes and their debugging.
9. Review of proposed code changes.
10. Testing.
11. Update documentation.
12. Standards audit.
13. Installation.
14. User acceptance.
15. Post-installation review of changes.
16. Completion of task.

Osborne points out that although the processes are presented in a linear fashion there are a number of iterative steps involved within the model itself. For example, the results of the design review may necessitate additional design analysis or even modification to the original change request. Rapid prototyping can easily be applied to such models.

20.2.3 Request-driven model

Elements from these models can be combined to produce a model that describes in detail the activities that take place during maintenance. This model is a request-driven model that attempts to portray the activities of software maintenance as dictated by users' requests for change. The model consists of three major processes, called:

Request control → Change control → Release control

It should be noted that the word 'control' has been deliberately used at the end of each process name to imply that the model will not work effectively without strict control from management of all the activities that take place. The activities that take place in each of these processes are now described.

20.2.3.1 Request control

The major activities are:

1. Collection of information about each request.
2. Setting up of mechanisms to categorize requests.
3. Using impact analysis to evaluate each request in terms of cost/benefit.
4. Assignment of a priority to each request.

It is this process that deals with the user's requests for change and has been a much neglected part of the maintenance activity. Collecting information about change requests plays an important role in that it will lay the foundation for measuring the activity and productivity of the maintenance operation leading to more effective management. This initial step of collection should be carried out by a 'help desk', manned by staff who will not be directly involved with the technical process of satisfying the request. It is preferable to have the help desk staffed by highly skilled systems analysts; such people can also distinguish genuine user change requests from queries arising from the misunderstanding of user documentation, etc.

A system to monitor all the requests and their progress through the system should be set up. It is recommended that a standard reporting mechanism be established (Pressman, 1987) utilizing standard maintenance request forms (MRFs) generated by the users and internally generated software change reports that will reflect the status of the request as it proceeds through the system. A problem monitoring system (PMS) has been reported in Gunn and Jolly (1988) which has been developed for the specific purpose of controlling customer queries and problems. The PMS is a PC-based system that holds customer and product information and is driven by a series of events that are date and time-stamped. PMS includes a flexible and powerful reporting facility that provides:

1. Statistics:
   (a) Time taken to resolve a change.
   (b) Programs most affected.
   (c) Requests outstanding.
2. Reports:
   (a) List by requests.
   (b) List by customers.

The first step is to categorize the request as either a perfective, adaptive, or corrective type of change operation. (It will be recalled that preventive maintenance requests are internally generated.) Then this needs to be further refined into the subject area of the requests so that the same or similar request can be spotted and amalgamated.

There are several questions that should be addressed when setting up the monitoring system:

1. What criteria are used in deciding the priority of a request?
2. How is the estimation of the cost of satisfying a request undertaken?
3. How are these requests managed?
4. What user interface should be presented to the users?

20.2.3.2 Change control

The activities are:

1. Selection from top of priority list.
2. Reproduction of the problem (if there is one).
3. Analysis of code (and specifications if available).
4. Design of changes and tests.
5. Quality assurance.

This is often seen as the key step in the process, the most expensive activity being the analysis of the existing code. The analysis takes place in order to gain an understanding of the operation of the current system so that the changes can be designed. There are tools available commercially that help with the analysis. In particular, there are cross-reference tools to help navigate around the source and code analysis tools that will provide information on control and data flow through the program.

Once an understanding of what needs to be done is achieved, then the necessary changes should be designed and test cases should be constructed. Note that at this stage no changes to the operational source should be allowed until the changes have been through the quality control procedure.

Quality control should be maintained throughout this process by the use of the recommended review or inspection procedures that were used in the development part of the cycle. There is no reason why this should be considered any different from a development activity.

There are several questions that need to be addressed in the process of change control:

1. How is the code analysis performed?
2. What tools should be used?
3. How can adequate documentation be produced?
4. How are the effects of the changes limited so that they do not interfere with other parts of the code (ripple effect limitation)?

20.2.3.3 Release control

The activities are:

1. Release determination.
2. Building of a new release.
   (a) Editing source.
   (b) Archival and configuration management.
   (c) Quality assurance.
3. Confidence testing.
4. Distribution.
5. Acceptance testing.

It is at this point that the requests which are to be included in a new release of the system are decided and the necessary changes to the source code are made. Once again, quality control procedures of reviews or inspections should be used at all stages to maintain the quality of the system, according to the quality plan in use.

20.3 Software maintenance management

20.3.1 Introduction

The requirements for the successful management of the software maintenance process are fundamentally not different from those needed for the management of other engineering activities. There are several constituent components (Reifer, 1979) (see also Chapter 27):

1. Planning.
2. Monitoring and controlling.
3. Organizing and implementing.
4. Human factors/staffing and leadership.

There are, however, significant differences in the way in which these components are implemented in software maintenance management, compared with the management of the earlier parts of the software engineering life cycle. These are important reasons for regarding software maintenance as a field in its own right. To support this, Lehman has argued that the software life cycle is inherently iterative (Lehman and Belady, 1976) and development is simply the initialization stage of this process. He has also argued that the evolution of a software system conforms to five 'laws', which he derived from empirical observations of several large systems (Lehman, 1980):

1. *Continuing change.* A program that is used and that, as an implementation of its specification, reflects some other reality, undergoes continuing change or becomes progressively less useful. The change or decay process continues until it is judged more cost effective to replace the program with a recreated value.
2. *Increasing complexity.* As an evolving program is continuously changed, its complexity, reflecting deteriorating structure, increases unless work is done to maintain it or reduce it.
3. *The fundamental law of program evolution.* Program evolution is subject to a dynamics which makes the programming process, and hence measures of global project and system attributes, self-regulating with statistically determinable trends and invariances. Thus, measurements of global system attributes may appear to be stochastic locally in time and space, but statistically they are self-regulating with well-defined, long-term trends.

   Thus, we are not free to set and achieve arbitrary design, work and performance targets. On the other hand, the third law suggests that models of large system evolution can be exploited as planning and control tools.
4. *Conservation of organizational stability.* The global activity rate in a project supporting an evolving program is statistically invariant. The law was originally termed the law of invariant work rate by Lehman, reflecting that in each of the systems he observed, the work rate in terms of the count of modules handled or changes made per unit of time, as averaged over each release interval, was statistically invariant.
5. *Conservation of familiarity.* The release content (changes, additions, deletions) of the successive releases of an evolving program is statistically invariant. Although the incremental growth of a program may vary widely from one release to the next, Lehman reported that the average over a relatively large number of releases remained remarkably constant (for the three systems investigated).

In practice, there often seems to be a discontinuity in management, methods, and technology between initial development and subsequent maintenance.

Attention will be focused on three aspects of software maintenance management:

1. The organizational context and objectives.
2. Inventory management.
3. A model of software maintenance management.

In this section, the above three issues will be amplified, and then the way in which they influence the overall management process analysed. It is not the intention to provide a 'management recipe book'. Instead the major issues to be considered in formulating a management policy and strategy are identified.

20.3.2 Organizational context

The initial development of software is usually project-based. It is undertaken to a budget and timescale. There is (it is hoped) a clear product defined through requirements analysis. The project exists because of an identified market (or other) need. The organization may have submitted a competitive tender to win the work. Prime objectives are expressed mainly in terms of functional and performance attributes of the software. In contrast, software maintenance is usually revenue based. In financial terms, it is seen as a continuing consumer of resource with a nebulous and unquantified benefit to the organization, and the objective is usually to achieve longevity of the software. The organizational support for software maintenance management is likely to be more forthcoming under the following conditions:

1. Senior management is aware of the importance of information technology to the organization.
2. Senior management views software as a corporate asset which often (and increasingly so) provides competitive edge.

Currently, it is not normal practice for software to be included as a capital asset in an organization's annual financial reports.

The existing literature has concentrated on internal software maintenance management issues. It is argued here that a high priority must be given to the organizational role, particularly in financial terms. The approach advocated is to justify the added value provided by software maintenance, and thus the financial benefits to be gained by investment in the maintenance process (for example, by buying better technology). This may require a concurrent change from maintenance as merely a survival activity, in which employees are expected to meet the on-going change load without frequent serious problems, to maintenance as a product management activity (Colter, 1988a and 1988b). Colter (1988b) argues that many software maintenance managers lack credibility in their organizations because 'they cannot speak the language of business', and that strong technical efforts will not succeed unless adequate funding for them is acquired. These will support the change to product management; changes are anticipated and planned for; maintainability of software is actively sustained instead of being allowed to degrade; staff are judged not simply on the rate of clearing changes, but on their support of improvements to system maintainability and quality.

It is sometimes advocated (but rarely implemented) that software services (including enhancements) should be provided to the rest of the organization on a full-cost basis. This can discourage users from making spurious change requests, but may result in much computing being undertaken by the end-users instead of the DP department.

20.3.3 Inventory management

A key feature of software maintenance is that the manager must take the software as it is. This typically means that there is lack of adequate product documentation, a poor record of historical evolution, highly variable quality attributes and so on. Unlike initial development, the manager has no control over an unsatisfactory inheritance. The cost of upgrading to an acceptable state through preventive maintenance may make such a change infeasible. The maintenance tools and techniques may be severely constrained. This represents a particularly difficult challenge for a theoretical approach to software maintenance (see later). Additionally, systems to be maintained are often large scale (more than 100 000 lines of source), and may contain very old code developed by out-of-date or *ad hoc* development technology. Over the lifetime of the software, the life cycle model used during software maintenance is itself likely to evolve.

It is sometimes argued that the solution to software maintenance is to discard all existing software and start again. Unfortunately:

1. The replacement software will itself require modification and enhancement, and it needs to be demonstrably more maintainable.
2. The rewrite will require effort, time and money.
3. The solution represents a casual management attitude to an organizational asset.
4. Existing systems embody in their design much information and knowledge about an organization. Rediscovering this from the partial and possibly inaccurate information otherwise available will be expensive.

Underlying this superficial view is a more serious point concerning the choice of strategy to be adopted in maintaining an item of software. This will be called inventory management.

A typical organization will have anything from a few to several thousand identifiable software items active. The approach advocated here involves the analysis of each to determine the best software maintenance policy. A spectrum of investment possibilities exists, including:

1. Discard the software immediately.
2. Retain the software, but do not enhance it further.
3. Continue to enhance the existing software.
4. Re-engineer the software.

The final alternative itself provides a range of choices, for example:

1. 'Rejuvenation' by restructuring the code, unifying data naming, insertion of standard comment headers in procedures, etc.
2. Partially, incrementally or fully rediscovering the design and reimplementing using modern software engineering techniques.
3. Incremental redocumentation of the system.

These techniques are described in more detail in Section 20.4. The first stage of the analysis involves the assessment of each item in terms of metrics such as:

1. Which are the important items of software to the business?
2. Which systems are anticipated to remain or become important within the planning timescales of the organization?
3. Which sections of the organization need the software?
4. What is the quality of the software system?

An advantage of this approach is that a top-down rationale for the collection of metrics and management statistics can be provided. It is also inherent in the analysis to seek an organization-wide approach, not simply the view of the DP department. For example, a software function might be considered very important to a section of the organization, yet the package actually available will be rated as highly unsatisfactory if it fails to meet the need. However good or bad the internal maintainability attributes of the software, the maintenance strategy should be determined by the organizational needs.

It will often be the case that a software system warrants further evolution. This will justify an internal analysis of the item to examine the feasibility and decide on a strategy. The issue of maintainability is discussed later in this chapter, but it includes: age of software; structural complexity; intermodule coupling; documentation; historical rate of modification. Other issues include the portability route (the software may have a restricted life because it cannot be ported economically to a new range of machines). In some cases, the analysis could be extended to the module level. We thus have positioned each item of software in an *n*-dimensional space (need, quality, importance, etc.). This can now provide the input to the decision-making process. For example, if software is very important to the organization both now and in the future, and is of high quality, this would suggest continued enhancement of the existing system. A similarly important package of very low quality may merit rewriting or re-engineering. Even very coarsely graduated metrics can be of considerable help to the decision process, especially if there is strong clustering.

To complete the analysis, a prediction of maintenance costs is needed. Cost estimation models such as COCOMO (Boehm, 1983 and 1981) have been shown to be useful, and Chapters 29 and 31 describe this further.

20.3.4 Software maintenance management activities

20.3.4.1 Planning

Effective software maintenance requires thorough planning. At one level, the objectives are to meet the demands specified by management or derived as described in Section 20.4. Software maintenance is predominantly change-driven, and planning will be based on this form of process model (as described in Section 20.3).

There is also a second level of planning that has been mentioned. This is planning the way in which maintenance is changed, perhaps from a survival mode to a product management mode. The former typifies many existing maintenance units. The work is change-control driven, and the main measure is timescale, in order to reduce the enormous backlog. Typically, the software suffers from a degradation in quality, poor personnel motivation, and unsatisfactory productivity. Planning (and monitoring) are perfunctory.

In the latter (which is often found in other branches of engineering), the work is characterized by a strategic, planned evaluation of the software in terms of its place in the organization's wider goals. The work is still mainly driven by change requests but there is an explicit life-cycle model (e.g. STARTS (DTI and NCC, 1987) and Chapter 27) with explicit quality review points and change control authorization. The incorporation of technology is explicitly addressed, for example, in the provision of an environment with full configuration management and versioning support.

Perry and Perry (1985) have identified five objectives in planning software maintenance:

1. A manager with clearly identified responsibility for software maintenance should be appointed.
2. Objectives for software maintenance should be clearly established.
3. The maintenance release mode method should be used.
4. The value added by software maintenance should be evaluated.
5. The maintenance tasks should be subject to full QA and control procedures.

20.3.4.2 Human factors

Much has been made of the perceived low status of software

maintenance and, by association, with those undertaking it (Cougar and Zawacki, 1980). It has been claimed that software maintenance is a more demanding task than development (Chapin, 1987), though this comparison is usually at the programmer level. The argument has been made that the name 'maintenance' is inappropriate (Lehman and Belady, 1976).

It seems clear that, whatever the reasons, the lack of status is a problem which must be addressed by management. As in other professions, quality of work is highly dependent upon recruiting skilled, intelligent, dedicated personnel. The US National Bureau of Standards (NBS, 1983) has suggested that:

1. Teams should include a mix of experienced and junior staff.
2. Maintenance should not be used as a training ground where junior staff are left to sink or swim (and to swim means to be promoted to development).
3. Staff should be rotated between maintenance and development.
4. Staff should be rotated between projects, to avoid individuals regarding the system as their private domain. (This has management advantages also, e.g. if the person leaves.)

There are more conventional reward mechanisms, such as:

1. Clearly showing the importance of maintenance to organizational goals.
2. Investing in technology, so that maintainers have similar facilities to developers.
3. Training.
4. Career structure.

Currently, few academic institutions address software maintenance in any level of their computer science courses, reinforcing the view of new graduates that the only significant software activity is initial development. Some training courses are now available for maintainers and their managers (see also Robson *et al*, 1988).

20.3.4.3 Monitoring and control

It is essential that information about the software being maintained and the maintenance process is collected and reported to management. Without this, control is lost, the effectiveness of maintenance procedures cannot be determined, and resource management becomes impossible. Without monitoring software quality, it will quickly degrade. It is not simply the code that requires monitoring, but documentation, design information etc.

Key process parameters include:

1. Response time to undertake changes.
2. Resource required to make a change.
3. The distribution of this resource across the several maintenance and QA activities.

A key indicator of software quality is the defect or error rate. Poor maintenance may cause this rate to rise, due to the ripple effects of a modification. Swanson (1976) and Pressman (1987) have provided a more detailed list of data that can usefully be recorded for each maintenance subproject:

1. Program identification.
2. Number of source statements.
3. Number of machine code instructions.
4. Programming language used.
5. Program installation date.
6. Number of program runs since installation.
7. Number of processing failures associated with item (6).
8. Program change level.
9. Number of source statements added by program change.
10. Number of person hours spent per change.

11. Program change date.
13. Identification of software engineer.
14. Change request identification.
15. Maintenance type.
16. Maintenance start and close dates.
17. Cumulative number of person-hours spent on maintenance.
18. Net benefits associated with maintenance performed.

These statistics are essential to provide evidence to more senior management of the maintenance group's activities. Swanson further lists useful metrics by which software maintenance may be evaluated, e.g.:

1. Average number of processing failures per program run.
2. Total person-hours spent in each maintenance category.
3. Average number of program changes made per program, per language, per maintenance type.
4. Average number of person-hours spent per source statement added or deleted due to maintenance.
5. Average person-hours spent per language.
6. Average turn-around time for a change request.
7. Percentage of maintenance requests by type.

Swanson's work is expressed principally in terms of source code. The ideas can be appropriately updated and extended to address, for example, design documentation, requirements, specifications etc.

20.3.4.4 Organization of maintenance teams

Software maintenance may be undertaken by the original development group, or responsibility may be given to a separate group. In the former case, there is a strong case to make the software maintainable, although documentation quality may suffer as staff see (even) less need for it. In the latter case, the development team may be able to move to new projects, as each group develops expertise. Fairley (1985) recommends that the minimum size for a maintenance team is two.

In larger teams, an identifiable quality assurance group should be established. There are strong advantages if this group has a separate reporting structure, to maximize its independence (see also Chapter 30).

20.3.4.5 Organization and implementation

A clear process model based on change requests is essential when implementing a maintenance plan. Change requests usually come from end users, and may involve any of those three types of maintenance activity. At times, emergency changes will be demanded, and these must, as a category, be anticipated and planned for. Such changes tend to short-circuit normal procedures, but they should lead to a change request for a permanent change which follows the standard procedure.

An important part of the organization is the Change Control Board which reviews requests and orders them by priority (see Section 20.2).

20.3.5 An abstract view

It is useful to take a more abstract view of the above activity. It is proposed here that it is often appropriate to change current software maintenance practice to an improved software maintenance practice. This can be regarded as evolution of the software maintenance process itself. It can be seen that the activities of perfective, adaptive, corrective and preventive maintenance on the software can also be considered valid activities on the software maintenance process. For example, one may have neglected to include in the software maintenance procedures a management review scheme following a code change. The process needs to be corrected. Secondly, one could find that the response time to changes can be improved by undertaking certain tasks in parallel rather than in series. This is adaptive maintenance on the process. As an example of perfective maintenance, one may wish to introduce a quality plan into the software maintenance process where none existed before. Finally, one may move from an implicit model of software maintenance to an explicit model. This (rather drastic) example should allow evolution of the software maintenance process to proceed more easily and more cheaply. It can be considered to be preventive maintenance of the process model.

If the software maintenance process is to evolve in time, then it is possible that the software being maintained by that process has to be transformed in some way. As an example, the new software maintenance process may require design information. (It is a reasonable step forward to maintain in terms of design information rather than merely source codes.) If that does not exist (one only has the source codes), then the information has to be extracted from the sources by a re-engineering task. It can now be seen that the inventory management is a particular instance of a more general management strategy. First, the evolution of the software maintenance process is planned. Then any re-engineering etc. is identified as a consequence of that evolution.

A particular technical problem may arise because process evolution might have to be undertaken while the software product is still being maintained. Another problem may be the committment to maintain old releases still extant on customer sites.

20.3.6 Summary

Good management techniques are central to effective software maintenance practice. Management techniques need to be based around a change control system. Even with limited technology, but with careful quality reviews and comprehensive monitoring, it is possible to move software maintenance from a survival activity to product management.

This section has also argued that software maintenance must be justified in terms of the organization and its business needs, in particular to attract capital investment which is surely needed.

20.4 Techniques

20.4.1 Preventive maintenance

20.4.1.1 Introduction

Unlike other types of software maintenance, preventive maintenance is not derived from a user change request. The objective of preventive maintenance is to alter software so that one or both of the following is met:

1. The altered software is of higher quality (e.g. in terms of detected defect rate). A system may exhibit so-called 'hotspots' where, statistically, the defect rate is poor and has remained so after modifications have been undertaken.
2. The altered software is more maintainable (see Section 20.6).

Management clearly need selection criteria to identify software which might benefit from preventive maintenance. The inventory management strategy described in Section 20.3 provides a means of making this decision. In terms of the n-dimensional decision space, a package or component will be a candidate for preventive maintenance if:

1. It is of strategic importance to the company both now and within the future planning period.
2. It is of acceptable quality now in terms of defect rate, complexity etc.
3. It is expected to be the subject of a continuing enhancement and modification programme.

Once a package or component which warrants preventive maintenance has been identified, several alternative actions may be taken. At one extreme, only the high-level design is retained (if it can be discovered) and the system is reimplemented and validated using modern software engineering techniques (original test suites, if they exist, may be reusable).

In practice, management statistics may show that only parts of the package are causing problems – the majority of the code has worked well for years, and has not been the subject of significant enhancements. Clearly, it is cost-effective to address only the former parts, and reimplement them. (Ideally, the modular structure of the system should be of help, but realistically, many older systems are not modular.)

Collins *et al.* (1987) have described a particularly interesting experiment in preventive maintenance. Subsystems of the IBM CICS system (a very widely used IBM software system) were specified using the Z notation. Discovery of the specification corresponding to an existing module was achieved by inspection. The module was then reimplemented from the Z specification, and Collins reports a significant improvement in the defect rate detected in the reimplemented modules.

Preventive maintenance would appear an expensive option to hard-pressed maintenance units who already have an extensive applications backlog. It is management's function to attempt to quantify the cost-benefit of a preventive maintenance strategy, based on the organization's software metrics and statistics. Pressman (1987) has identified the following points that support an active policy of preventive maintenance:

1. The cost to maintain one line of source code may be up to 40 times the cost of initial development of that line.
2. Redesign using modern software engineering techniques can facilitate maintainability.
3. Since the software already exists, development productivity should be higher than average.
4. The user has experience of the software, so that likely future changes can more easily be ascertained.
5. The system can be brought into a configuration management system if it is not there already.

Preventive maintenance is thus a positive response to Lehman's second law (see Section 20.3). This must be set against the third and fourth laws, in particular when scheduling preventive maintenance.

The terminology used in preventive maintenance is interpreted in different ways by different authors. In this chapter, the following definitions of preventive maintenance processes will be used:

1. *Inverse engineering.* The process of discovering the requirements specification for a software system or component, and then reimplementing using modern software engineering methods.
2. *Reverse engineering.* The process of redesigning parts or all of a software system, to improve its quality, and then reimplementing the design.
3. *Re-engineering* (also called rejuvenation). The modification of source code items (code, data structures, documentation etc.) based on modern software engineering principles to improve the maintainability of software.

In an hierarchical system, the design at one level is a specification for the next less abstract level of implementation. Hence the above terms need to be interpreted carefully in the context in which they are being used.

20.4.1.2 Inverse engineering using transformations

A useful technique in software maintenance is to reimplant part or all of a system using modern software maintenance techniques. This section describes a technique for formally deriving a specification from existing, probably undocumented, source code. 'Formal' means that each representation can be derived from the previous one by mechanical manipulation of symbols. The technique is based on Ward transformations (Ward, 1988; Ward and Munro, 1988). It has reached the stage of a research prototype, and appears very promising for software maintenance. Thus far, the theoretical work has addressed sequential systems only.

The basis of Ward's scheme is a system in which it is possible to prove that two versions of a program are equivalent. A transformation is a formal step in which a program is converted to an equivalent with identical semantics. Ward's formal system is independent of any particular programming language. Program transformations are used in program development (see, for example, Bauer, 1979; Bauer, 1976; Griffiths, 1976). However, the methods are not able to cope with generalized specifications or with transforming programs into their specifications. Ward uses a small 'kernel' language which has a simple mathematical semantics, associating a function with each program. This function maps each allowed initial state to the set of possible final states. Two programs are said to be equivalent if the associated functions are identical. The kernel consists of a small number of constructs, and others are added by defining them in terms of the kernel. In this way a complete programming language may be built up.

In practice, the kernel is extended to allow a source language (COBOL, C, etc.) to be converted to it using simple compiler writing techniques. Subsequently, transformations are performed on the extended kernel representation. Different source languages will, of course, be converted to different kernel extension languages. The kernel language contains both imperative constructs, and an 'atomic description' which allows the inclusion of statements expressed in first order logic. It is thus an example of a wide spectrum language.

Ward has produced a library of transformations which can successfully be applied. These transformations were proven before entry to the library. Inverse engineering is thus undertaken by applying a series of transformation steps to the original code (in its internal form), until a specification in (for example) first order logic is reached. This strong theoretical underpinning provides the confidence to apply transformations to a program which is not (as yet) well understood. An example of an extremely trivial transformation is the merging of two assignment statements into one. A more complex transformation converts a tail-recursive procedure to a loop equivalent.

It is envisaged that these transformations can assist software maintenance in the following ways:

1. Preventive maintenance can be achieved. A program which has become obscured through poor programming techniques together with accumulated modifications can be improved (incrementally if necessary) instead of discarding it.
2. Transforming code to an equivalent, but clearer form is an important tool for program comprehension.
3. By transforming a program to an equivalent specification, reimplementation using modern software engineering is possible.

It is not possible completely to automate the choice of which transformation to apply. However, empirically, humans become adept at making this selection, and once made, the application can be automated. Work is in progress on using AI techniques to provide an advisor to guide the expert maintainer in this selection (Ward and Munro, 1988). It is hoped that automation at lower levels of abstraction can predominate, while the maintainer can use his or her skills to suggest higher level transformations as understanding of the system becomes available.

20.4.1.3 Reverse engineering

A definition has already been provided of the term 'reverse engineering', but other interpretations are extant, e.g. reverse engineering is an attempt to bring an existing (old) software system under the control of a modern development method.

Another similar definition, seen from a different viewpoint is that reverse engineering is a process to support the analysis and understanding of data and processing in existing software systems.

In this definition a software system consists of the job control statements that construct and execute the software, the source code (COBOL, Assembler etc.), and any related databases.

This definition implies that a 'backwards' step is taken, to capture knowledge about an existing system, in order to proceed forward, making it less costly to make changes.

Work in this area has been carried out in two stages. The first step was the introduction of the concept of restructuring source code to make a program more understandable than the original. This is described in the following section.

The second step involved the rediscovery of design level knowledge, and two examples of this type of approach to reverse engineering have been reported by Warden (1988) and Sneed (1988) (Sneed and Jandriasics, 1987). The former is based on using existing software maintenance technology to improve the maintainability of software and the latter takes a more radical approach of extracting design information from source code. In commercial DP programs, the key design information required is often the macroscopic data structuring, given their microscopic implementation in the source code.

The term recycling is used by Sneed to describe his approach to reverse engineering, and consists of a set of tools to enable the recycling of old software by the method of static analysis, modularization, restructuring, backwards translation, design tuning and code regeneration.

The objectives of the technique are to:

1. Reuse as much as possible of the old code.
2. Create a new software architecture based on the principle of modular and structured programming.

The steps in the technique are:

1. Static analysis of the source code to produce a set of program tables that form an internal representation of the program.
2. Modularization to break large programs down into several small separate modules.
3. Restructuring of the flow of control within each module and the conversion of the code into a design language.
4. Adaptation of design language code to remove redundancies and problems that may have been introduced by previous steps, and to make any desired changes.
5. Code generation to produce a new version.

All the above steps are performed automatically except for the adaptation step, where the programmer, with the aid of the design language and a syntax driven editor, makes the changes. Some of the changes that need to be made will be as a result of problems introduced by the modularization and restructuring steps. There is currently no technique that can guarantee that the new version will perform in exactly the same way as the old version.

Some commercially available tools are appearing which can support reverse engineering to diagrammatic design notations. This allows computer-aided software engineering (CASE) technology to be used.

20.4.1.4 Re-engineering

This technique involves making simple changes to the software based on simple criteria that can be easily measured. The techniques use simple static analysis tools to produce reports that highlight potential problem areas in the source code that can then be manually modified.

Miller and Strauss (1987) claim that the restructuring process '... will not correct design flaws, but changes existing unstructured constructs into structured ones – which are more understandable and more maintainable'.

This statement infers that automatic restructurers solve the code readability and understandability problem that software maintainers face when they are confronted with an unfamiliar piece of code. The solution is not as simple as this, as has been pointed out by Calliss (1987). The use of automatic restructurers, while solving some problems, creates new ones in their place. These problems include:

1. Restricting the structure of the program to consist solely of a minimal set of valid program structures.
2. Making a program larger and the interacting sections of code more dispersed.
3. Adding sentinel variables and possibly paragraphs with meaningless names.
4. Making the program's comments untrustworthy.

The criteria used by Warden (1988) to justify re-engineering are to:

1. Reduce code complexity (McCabe measure used).
2. Simplify control flow.
3. Improve program structure.
4. Remove standards violations.
5. Remove redundant code and data.
6. Simplify file and data usage.
7. Improve performance.
8. Technically redocument the program (i.e. production of cross-reference listings, call graph data etc. in standard form).

From carrying out case studies Warden reports that the benefits of this technique were:

1. Improved maintainability.
2. Reduced risk to future change.
3. 40% reduction in code.
4. 15% improvement in performance.

An ambitious approach to comprehensive restructuring is being investigated by an ESPRIT II project called REDO (Katsoulakis, 1989). This project is investigating the design of an integrated toolset within an appropriate environment, to support the preventive maintenance and subsequent modification of existing software.

20.4.2 Program comprehension

Program comprehension is a vital part of the maintenance process. A software maintainer has to be able to understand the system to be modified before designing the modification. The system may not have any associated documentation, or if it has, it may not have been updated to include recent changes. Even worse, the documentation may also be incorrect. Relying on the

availability of the developers of the system is also not always possible as there is high turnover of staff in the industry. Thus the maintainer may only have the latest version of the source code as the only reliable authority on how the system is constructed. From the source code the maintainer needs to obtain an understanding of the various components of the system and their interaction.

Littman et al. (1986) have identified strategies for program comprehension and have conducted an experiment to investigate the relationship between these strategies and the knowledge acquired. They argue that there are two basic approaches to program comprehension of relatively small programs. First, there is the systematic approach where the maintainer examines the entire program and works out the interactions between various modules. The other approach is the 'as needed' strategy where the maintainer attempts to minimize the amount of studying prior to making a modification. Thus the maintainer tries to locate the section of the program which needs to be modified and then commences the modification. On the small program used in the experiment, it is clear that the systematic approach is superior, but on large programs this approach is infeasible and a (possibly adapted) 'as-needed' strategy must be employed.

Other theories of program comprehension have been proposed. Shneiderman and Mayer (1979) argue that comprehension is based on syntactic and semantic knowledge. Syntactic knowledge is the knowledge of the format of various statements in the language concerned. Semantic knowledge consists of more general concepts which are independent of the programming language. This semantic knowledge might be fairly low level and include concepts such as the function of each statement, or it may be high level and, for instance, include various sorting algorithms. The authors argue that comprehension involves applying the syntactic knowledge to develop an internal semantic representation. This internal representation can then be altered or translated into an alternative programming language.

Brooks (1983) puts forward a theory of program comprehension which is based on the hypothesis of a mapping between the problem domain and the programming domain. He argues that the developer produces these mappings and the maintainer has to reconstruct them. He views this reconstruction as a bottom-up approach rather than the more usual top-down approach to design. He also argues that the reconstruction of the mappings is an iterative, progressive activity. Thus a maintainer might start with an initial hypothesis which is adapted as more knowledge of the program is gained. He suggests that the initial hypothesis might be formed from just the name of a particular activity. For instance, an activity with the name 'sort the input' will immediately give the maintainer some ideas about the structure of the program. This initial hypothesis could be clarified once the actual sorting algorithm has been determined. Brooks also argues that one of the differences between programmers in their ability to comprehend programs is their domain knowledge. Thus in order to make comprehension easier, it is important not only to state the requirements, but also a history of the decisions that led to those requirements. This history may well contain important clues in the formulation of the correct hypothesis.

Letovsky (1986) describes an experiment in which maintenance programmers were given a program to modify and encouraged to think out aloud so that their thoughts could be recorded. From the recordings he focuses on two types of events, namely, questions and conjectures and develops taxonomies of these events. His taxonomy of questions leads him to suggest that a mixture of top-down and bottom-up strategies are employed during comprehension, where the top layer is the specification and the bottom is the implementation. These two layers are connected through various intermediate levels to form the programmer's mental model of the program. He argues that: 'the human understander is best viewed as an opportunist processor capable of exploiting both bottom-up and top-down cues as they become available'.

Tools can assist in the comprehension process. At the very lowest level, a simple cross-reference program which lists names and where they occur in the program can help a maintainer to keep track of the use of objects. There are also more sophisticated versions of these programs which are aware of the concepts included in the language in which the software is constructed. For instance, they are able to distinguish between uses of different variables with the same name. Research is also being undertaken into environments for program comprehension which couple language sensitive cross references to the source code. Hypertext front ends have been suggested as possible user interfaces for such systems (Fletton and Munro, 1988).

20.4.3 Tools and workbenches

There are a number of tools designed specifically for use in the software maintenance work environment. In general, the tools tend to be aimed at specific tasks and lack an ability to integrate with other tools or with existing project support environments.

To present the type of tool that is currently available, the category of tools devised by the General Service Administration's Office of Software Development and Information Technology (GSA) will be described. The full structure of the Programmers Workbench has been described in *Software Maintenance News* (1986) and reported in Munro and Calliss (1987).

20.4.3.1 GSA Programmer's Workbench

The GSA identified eleven categories of tools for software maintenance and brought them together in what is termed a Programmers Workbench (PWB). It should be noted that the GSA did not develop any of the tools described below; the tool categories were identified and third party tools were then bought in. The PWB sits on top of the Rand Development Center (RDC), although it should be noted that each tool can be used alone. The PWB was established specifically to deal with applications written in COBOL on IBM architectures. Since the PWB described below uses COBOL terminology, it is appropriate to provide very brief details of salient language features. COBOL programs are divided into four divisions: identification, environment, data, and procedure divisions. The data division contain declarations, in a highly formatted form in which some substructures and storage attributes (such as local working storage) are indicated by associated two-digit level numbers. Data type and initial values are indicated in such declarations by key words USAGE, PIC, VALUE.

The procedure division contains executable statements. COBOL has a primitive procedure mechanism known as CALL, and an iteration construct called PERFORM. Control transfers are provided by IF and ALTER constructs.

The categories of tools identified by the GSA were:

1. Test coverage monitor.
2. Source compare.
3. File compare.
4. Translator.
5. Reformatter.
6. Data standardization tool.
7. Restructuring tool.
8. Code analyser.
9. Cross-referencer.
10. Documentation and metric analyser.
11. Data manipulation tool.

The *test coverage monitor* is a tool to address the following important aspects of program testing:

1. Preparation of test data.
2. Measurement of test data coverage.

The tool should:

1. Compile and run programs with all available test data.
2. Identify and report any logical decision path or executable statements within the program that the test data fails to exercise.

With the information from this type of tool programmers can evaluate areas of a program that require further testing and software quality assurance personnel can make more accurate and reliable judgements of a program's readiness for production implementation.

The *source compare tool* can be used to compare:

1. New software releases to previous releases for debugging and documentation purposes.
2. Source code versions to provide audit trails.
3. Database files against backups to ensure integrity of the data.
4. Output files to ensure the results of source changes are installed as requested.

File compare tools are intended to compare object and load modules.

Translator tools perform the translation of one language to another or one dialect of a language to another.

The nominated tool performs a COBOL–COBOL translation and can be used to transform COBOL application programs, databases, and file and record systems in non-IBM to IBM and IBM to IBM environments. It will convert also COBOL 74 to COBOL 85, and the following non-IBM–IBM translations.

Reformatter tools are also known as pretty-printers, and as such will layout source code in a standard format. They transform old, large, or poorly written or documented programs into standardized formats that are more readily and easily maintained. Key words are aligned in the DATA and PROCEDURE divisions, including level numbers and compound and nested IF statements.

The *data name standardizer* tool standardizes data and paragraph names to:

1. Improve the overall readability of source programs.
2. Automatically enforce an installation style standard.
3. Provide all the necessary spacing and indentation in support of an installation's structured programming requirements.

Within a DATA division, the tool will:

1. Replace selected data names with more meaningful names.
2. Insert user-specified record prefixes.
3. Produce alphabetic sequencing of all working storage entries.
4. Convert USAGE, PICTURE, VALUE, and other specified clauses to standard forms and pre-defined positions.

Standardization within a PROCEDURE division can provide:

1. Sequencing, resequencing, or unsequencing of paragraph names.
2. Insertion and deletion of EJECT and SKIP statements, or of blank lines.
3. Multi-line indentation and alignment of COBOL reserved word pairs.

The *restructuring tool* transforms an unstructured program into a structured program. It takes unstructured COBOL code and replaces it with logically equivalent software consistent in style, format and structure. The transformations on the code include:

1. Reduction of GOTO logic.
2. Elimination of fall through confusion.
3. Increased use of the PERFORM construct.
4. Elimination of PERFORM THRU constructs and ALTER statements.
5. Conversion of NOTEs to comments.
6. Elimination of all unentered procedures ('dead code').

The *source code analyser* analyses programs to detect program structure, identify data usage and relationships, and trace data usage and logic flow. It is a tool that will greatly help in the understanding of how a program works.

This interactive tool assists the most difficult aspect of the software maintenance process – the evaluation and analysis of a program and program modifications.

Through the use of this tool the following essential steps in the maintenance process are fully automated:

1. *Task estimation.* Achieved by isolating program functions, allowing analysts to focus on program and I/O structures, control and data flow, and interaction between program modules.
2. *Analysis.* Achieved by highlighting complex and subtle logic and data relationships, and by predicting the outcome of changes proposed by the programmer prior to actual production tests.
3. *Testing.* Changes can be made and tested online.
4. *Documentation.* Automatically produced.
5. *Quality assurance.* Commands can be tailored to specific data processing environments, thus allowing the quality assurance analyst to determine standards compliance.

The *cross-reference* tool identifies all occurrences of data names, words or literals within a program. It is a useful tool for navigating around source code. The tool will:

1. Identify and trace data element modification, branch logic, program CALLs, and performed paragraph reference patterns.
2. Generate graphic record layouts to visually communicate data structures and formats.

The *documentation and metrics analyser* analyses source code and produces documentation reports of the results of the analysis.

The tool evaluates the logic paths of a program without executing it and stores metric information about the program, before or after a modification, for later reporting. It applies pre-established algorithms to compare the standards maintained in its summary statistics file to the various structural characteristics of programs. These algorithms are also used to derive practical metrics of a program's relative complexity and architecture.

The tool produces detailed and summary reports. These reports combine the measurements to assess overall asset quality at the system and program library levels.

The *data manipulation tool* allows data within records to be examined, modified, extracted, and printed for various file and record structures.

The tool is an interactive, full-screen data manipulation system designed to edit, browse, extract, reformat, and print VSAM, ISAM, PDS and sequential files. It checks the validity of data for each field in a record and identifies data that does not match related COBOL PICTURE and USAGE clauses.

20.4.3.2 SMN tools manual

Software Maintenance News (SMN) publishes a manual called *Software Maintenance Tools* (Zvegintzov, 1988). The manual contains a classification of tools from the viewpoint of the major activities of maintenance programmers, and a survey of known tools.

20.4.4 Maintenance environments

Most of the work on project software environments has been stimulated by the early development phases of the life cycle. There is little evidence available on their support of software maintenance, though the CADES system (Snowden, 1981) is an early notable exception.

It is clear that a basic minimum requirement is a good configuration management system which supports versions and variants of all life cycle components (see Chapter 34). It appears likely that as progressively more information about a system can be retained within such an environment, the maintainability will be enhanced.

A useful review of current European work on software engineering environments is given in Bennett (1989).

20.5 Quality assurance in maintenance

In earlier times, quality assurance focused on the elimination of errors by testing. It now has a wider interpretation as improved specification and design techniques can also lead to an increase in quality. Management practices can also influence the quality of the final product. Quality assurance is now an accepted term which is heard frequently during the development phase, but it is equally applicable in the maintenance phase. Quality assurance is addressed from a general point of view in Chapter 29, but the focus here is on quality assurance in maintenance.

One of the most general methods of quality assurance is the review. This can take several forms, and a number of alternative management techniques such as structured walkthroughs, inspections and active design reviews have been proposed. These reviews are as important in the maintenance phase as they are in the development phase, and should be used to filter out as many problems as possible. The emphasis should be on the effect on the system of any proposed change. Attention must of course be given to whether the proposed changes are correct, but there needs to be a particular study of the effect of a proposed change. It is extremely easy to forget that a change has to be made in more than one place and to ignore the effect of the change on functions which apparently are unconnected to the change.

There needs to be a clear management policy for handling changes to a system. In practical terms, this means that there should be a company model for making changes. There should be a maintenance group who produce the design for the change. This would then be given to a quality assurance group who are largely independent of the maintenance group and they would be responsible for evaluating the design and perhaps testing it after it has been implemented. There also needs to be a company method for producing the change, including details of the various stages of the change, the documents required and procedures for implementing the change. The latter would include details of which directories are to be used for implementing and testing the change, how backups of previous systems are to be saved and the progression to the altered system through the management process, so that it becomes the latest production version.

Testing also forms an important part of the quality assurance programme. Changes which involve new functions clearly need new test cases to be developed to exercise the new changes. However, tests also need to be executed to ensure that none of the unchanged functionality of the system has been corrupted by the new changes. This type of testing is known as regression testing. This form of testing requires the construction of a test suite that can be re-executed after changes have been made. Not only the test cases, but also their input and output need to be retained in the test suite. After a change has been made, the test cases are re-executed and the results compared to previous executions of the test suite.

Tools can assist in this process. The most basic is a file comparator which can highlight the difference between two sets of output from the test execution. Such tools can be relatively sophisticated and mask out differences such as the date and time, which would be expected to change on different executions. Such tools should also be required to be able to specify restart points and conditions to be waited for when comparing two files.

File comparators can work well for file-based systems, but for highly interactive systems containing window, icon and mouse interfaces another approach is required. A terminal spy is a program which is positioned between the user's terminal and the application. It may run on a separate machine which is between the terminal and the application computer. Such a program can record all movements produced on the user's terminal, pass them on to the application program and rerun the sequence of movements at a later date. Terminal spies can be completely independent of the system being tested. Such tools as these are rarely found on the open market at the time of writing, as they are often produced for internal use.

Another problem with regression testing is often the size of the test suite and deciding how frequently to carry out regression testing. With a very large test suite it is not always possible to re-execute the entire test suite every time a change is implemented. In this situation a subset of the test suite has to be selected. This can be done by hand, basing the selection criteria on the most likely parts of the system which could be affected by the change. This requires a method of linking test case to specific functions of the system, or in the case of white box tests to particular constructs within the software, such as procedures or functions. Such a method can be difficult to support in a system involving frequent change and it is an error-prone approach, because it is all to easy to omit a vital test case which could reveal a major flaw in the implementation of the change. There are few tools available to assist in this process and this is an area of current research. The emphasis of this research is to note which parts of the program are connected, so that when a change takes place in one part, all test cases in that part and all connected parts are re-executed.

However, a purely white-box approach to regression testing is insufficient. For instance, suppose a change is made to a system which decreases the performance of the system. The cause of the decrease may be system-related and might be due to the increase in the size of the program, resulting in its object version crossing a page boundary at some vital location. This may lead to a large increase in paging activity, thus leading to a decrease in performance. Detecting such situations is not possible solely using a white-box approach to regression tests. Thus, there needs to be a selection of tests which are functional in nature and which test vital characteristics of the functionality of the system. Such vital characteristics are sometimes omitted from requirements documents and are not always easy to detect.

Quality assurance is vital in the software maintenance phase to ensure that the software has not deteriorated due to the change. The quality assurance techniques which are present during the development phase can be equally applied during maintenance.

20.6 Maintainability and the maintenance of new software

20.6.1 Maintainability

The maintainability of a software system represents the ease with which it is possible to undertake software maintenance on that system. Currently, an adequate quantitative definition does not exist. Work on maintainability models has been undertaken by Boehm *et al.* (1978). Boehm regards maintainability as having three components: testability, modifiability and understandability. The two principal ideas running through this and other work are system complexity and system modularity (Harrison and Magel, 1981). Complexity may be regarded as having two components (Curtis and Sheppard, 1979): computational complexity and psychological complexity. According to Curtis and Sheppard, computational complexity is a property of the algorithm which makes proof of correctness difficult. Psychological complexity is a property which makes human understanding difficult. However, these two concepts have a substantial amount in common.

Modularity is concerned with the way in which a software system is decomposed into smaller subproblems. The hypothesis is that a program is more maintainable if the modules have minimum external coupling and maximum internal cohesiveness (Constantine *et al.*, 1974). (See also Chapter 17).

While these ideas are important, they are not the complete picture. A large system is continually evolving in time. How does a maintenance programmer retain an up-to-date mental model of the system, in terms of how it works, how it is constructed, and how it behaves? How should requirement, specification and design information be represented to ease maintenance? The source code represents the final design step, and ideally the maintenance staff should be acquiring the great majority of the knowledge of a system and performing changes to it at a much higher level of abstraction. Documentation produced during initial development may not be best suited for this. The ESPRIT II project MACS is investigating these issues (Georges, 1989).

It is clearly desirable to produce current software which is as good as possible using current technology. It is part of the nature of software that if one is concerned about the product, one must study the process by which it is produced. Thus, maintainability is not an attribute of the end product alone. One must address how the software is produced, and the way in which the information and knowledge used during the production is captured. A key technique is to prepare for maintenance both during initial development and during subsequent evolution. In other words, preparation for maintenance starts right at the requirements capture stage. This implies full consistent documentation at all levels of abstraction (with QA audits), change control procedures, version and release management, regression testing, internal standards and cost monitoring. It is difficult to see how any large-scale software project can succeed without strong management to implement these techniques. In small-scale developments (and small-scale enhancements to a large system), it is very tempting to take short cuts. The use of technology where available (such as data dictionaries, normal form data representation, use of metrics as a project control function) can make a substantial contribution. Modern design methods involving data hiding and abstractions should also be used. However, the specification and design of high maintainability systems still requires much research, and the work described in this section is still predominantly presented in terms of source code concepts.

There are thus a number of qualities that new software needs to possess for maintainability. Amongst these are flexibility, understandability and (for adaptive maintenance) portability.

Flexibility can be achieved by designing systems for change. Parnas (1972) developed the principle of information hiding as a method of designing for change, while more recently, object oriented design methods, which include information hiding, have been claimed as a suitable technique for increasing maintainability. On the other hand, inheritance mechanisms can easily degrade the cohesion of a large system, particularly if multiple inheritance is used. Practical experience with these systems over a long period is awaited. A major strength of a system which is highly modular lies in the potential for avoidance of multiple copies of data instances. As a very simple example, a program which involves the calculation of value added tax should define in a single place the current value of the tax. This is a well understood approach in the design of databases, but the principles are applicable to any maintainable program.

Understandability is an objective which is not easy to achieve. The crudest method of gaining knowledge about a system is to read the code. In the validation phase of the development cycle this is known as desk checking. It is also often undertaken during code reviews and the 'debugging' stages. Understanding code solely by reading is clearly a function of program size and complexity. Code understanding by reading can be effective, but it is difficult because there is a large amount of information in the code, and extracting the required knowledge is far from an easy task; it is also difficult because information (such as the rationale for design decisions) may be missing from the code.

The design method employed can effect readability. One experiment in this area is described by Woodfield et al. (1981) who performed an experiment to measure the effect of modularization techniques on program comprehension. Four different techniques were compared:

1. Monolithic modularization, where there was no modularization at all.
2. Functional modularization, where each module corresponded to a functional unit.
3. 'Super' modularization where modules consisted of very small internally cohesive routines.
4. Modularization based on the concept of abstract data types.

The conclusions were that modularization based on abstract data types was significantly easier to comprehend. This correlates well with Myers' views on module coherence (see Chapter 17).

Another factor affecting comprehension is the style in which the program is written. If the entire program is written in a consistent manner, either by a single programmer or by a team with all the members following a house style, then the program will be easier to comprehend than a similar program which does not have a consistent style. The question then arises as to what is good and bad style. A well-known text by Kernighan and Plauger (1978) describes various examples of good and bad style.

Experimental evidence has been collected to support some of the well-known techniques of good program style. Shneiderman (Shneiderman and Mayer, 1979) has investigated the effect of using meaningful identifiers on program comprehension and concluded that in terms of the syntactic/semantic model described earlier, the effect of meaningful variable names simplifies the conversion from a syntactic to a semantic representation. However, in a small experiment he did not find significant differences in comprehension between a program containing meaningful identifiers and an equivalent one which used non-mnemonic identifiers.

The effect of indentation on program comprehension has been studied by many investigators and a discussion of work in this area is given by Miara et al (1983). The general conclusion

of this work is that indented programs are easier to comprehend. They conducted their own experiments on the effect of levels of indentation and concluded that excessive indentation can slow the rate of comprehension. The optimal level seemed to be between two and four spaces indentation for each new block.

The experiment by Woodfield et al. (1981) also investigated the effect of comments on program comprehension. Their conclusion was that comments used in the proper manner can assist in program comprehension. However, their experiments used programs in which indentation had been removed and meaningful identifiers had been replaced by single character identifiers. A previous study by Weissman (1976) has shown that there has been no significant difference between commented and uncommented versions when indentation and meaningful identifiers were present. This could suggest that indentation, meaningful identifiers and comments are complementary in program comprehension, although it could also imply that comments are unnecessary if good indenting and naming are used. Van Tassel (1978) has given a description of the types of comments that should be used at various points within a program.

Basili and Mills (1982) have undertaken an interesting experiment in code reading. Their aim was to discover what a program does as opposed to how it does it and with this restriction they employed some of the techniques of program correctness proofs. For small parts of the program they employed direct cognition, but for medium-sized loops they used invariants. They analysed a small numerical analysis program written in FORTRAN in some detail using these techniques and though the results were interesting, it is not clear that such an approach would work on large software systems, or how this method could be automated.

20.6.2 Maintenance of new software

A characteristic of current work on software development is that the maintenance phase is either not considered seriously, or is considered as an afterthought. The authors strongly support the move to the use of formal specifications and transformational systems, but these will create new problems for maintenance which have not yet been addressed.

The argument is that an interesting approach to new software life cycle models is to give priority to the maintenance phase, and establish development methods to support maintenance, in particular perfective and adaptive maintenance. It would appear that software developers' views on techniques to help maintenance may differ from those of the persons who must actually manage and undertake the maintenance. For this reason, some development teams are partly constituted from staff who have had maintenance experience.

Perfective maintenance can be seen as applying a change in system requirement to an existing system. This will then demand the identification of those components that are unaltered by the new requirements and can be re-used, and those that must be altered or replaced. By 'component' is meant, for example, a specification, a transformation or a document; a component is not merely a module of source code.

It can be seen that maintenance is closely allied to reuse and it would be expected that an approach which addresses both issues will be worthwhile.

20.7 Other sources of information

20.7.1 Software maintenance in the USA

In the USA a section of the General Service Administration (GSA), the Federal Software Management Center, has identified software maintenance as a major problem area and established a task force to assess, select and support software maintenance tools. It identified 11 classes of maintenance tools and invited tool vendors to submit their existing tools as candidates for inclusions in a Programmers' Workbench aimed at providing tools for the maintenance of COBOL programs.

The categories of tools are described in Section 20.4.

Another US organization, the National Bureau of Standards, has been active in producing management guides which provide methods and procedures for conducting an effective maintenance programme (Martin and Osborne, 1983; McCall *et al.*, 1985).

20.7.2 Literature

Numerous textbooks have been published in the area of software engineering, but with very few specifically on the topic of software maintenance. The list of titles includes: *Software Maintenance Guidebook* (Glass and Noiseux, 1981); *Managing Software Development and Maintenance* (McClure, 1981); *Techniques of Program and System Maintenance* (Parikh, 1982a); *Tutorial on Software Maintenance* (Parikh and Zvegintzov, 1983); *Software Maintenance: The Problems and their Solutions* (Martin and McClure, 1983); and *Software Maintenance Management* (Lientz and Swanson, 1980). A new periodical has recently been published, entitled *The Journal of Software Maintenance: Research and Practice*, published by John Wiley.

20.7.3 Organizations

20.7.3.1 Software Maintenance Association

The Software Maintenance Association (SMA) is an independent special-interest group established in the USA with the objective of acting as a forum for practitioner topics in software maintenance. It organizes an annual conference, and the main discussion points revolve around the maintenance of DP-related software.

An independent publication that reports the activities of the SMA is *Software Maintenance News* published by Nicholas Zvegintzov. Further information can be obtained from: Software Maintenance Association, 56 Bay Street #400, Staten Island, New York, NY 10301, USA.

20.7.3.2 Centre for Software Maintenance

The Centre for Software Maintenance (CSM) was established at the University of Durham, England at Easter, 1987. The purpose of the Centre for Software Maintenance is to act as a focus for a major programme of research and development in the field of software maintenance.

For further information contact: Centre for Software Maintenance, School of Engineering and Applied Science, University of Durham, Durham DH1 3LE. UK.

20.7.4 Conferences

Recent conferences on Software Management include:

1983 Software Maintenance Workshop. Naval Postgraduate School, Monterey, CA. Sponsored by IEEE, National Bureau of Standards. Naval Postgraduate School and the ACM (Arnold *et al.*, 1984).
1985 Conference on Software Maintenance, Washington. Sponsored by the same organizations as above plus the Data Processing Management Association (IEEE, 1985).
1987 Software Maintenance Workshop, Durham, UK (Munro and Calliss, 1987).

1987 Conference on Software Maintenance, Austin, Texas (IEEE, 1987).
1988 Software Maintenance Workshop, Durham, UK (Calliss *et al.*, 1988).
1988 Conference on Software Maintenance, Phoenix, Arizona (IEEE, 1988).

The conferences organized by the IEEE and the Centre for Software Maintenance are now held annually.

20.8 Research directions

Despite the economic implications, very little research has been undertaken in software maintenance – in either the management of maintenance or in technical solutions to improve productivity and quality.

It is interesting to note that many projects concerned with the early stages of the software life cycle claim that 'new technique X will also assist maintenance'. Unfortunately, these claims are rarely substantiated. The authors argue that techniques and methods devised by system developers for maintainers are unlikely to be successful. Instead, the maintenance phase should be considered *a priori* and the development phase addressed with the objective of easing maintenance.

Compared with the early stages of the life cycle, there is generally a very poor breadth of tool support for maintenance, and no notion of an integrated support environment. Theoretical work on maintenance is almost completely lacking.

Hence research is expected to address the following major topics:

1. The protection of the investment in existing systems yet increasing the maintainability and life of those systems.
2. The acquisition of a better understanding of maintainability.
3. Investigation of the relationship between maintenance and reuse.
4. Environments and tools for software maintenance, from a better understanding of the associated process models.
5. Software maintenance of software developed by formal methods, and also the maintenance of artificial intelligence software.

There are very many practical problems in software maintenance which remain to be solved. For example, how should a database be moved from a hierarchical to a relational implementation while keeping the database live? How should software on board space satellites be maintained? In most cases, one is starting with raw material which is in a state that is far from ideal. This, however, is an inevitable characteristic of almost all the existing software that must be maintained.

20.9 Summary and conclusions

Software maintenance consumes most of the overall life cycle costs for much software. Predominantly, software maintenance is concerned with the evolution of software, perhaps over many years, and the more successful a software system is, the more likely it is to need maintenance.

It has been argued that software maintenance is not simply a technical issue. Section 20.3 explained that to protect software as a corporate asset, organization and management plans are needed too. A method addressing this was proposed and this was intended to help management formulate a strategy for software maintenance within the organization.

At the technical level, a change-control driven model of the maintenance process was described in Section 20.2. Currently, integrated toolsets to support such models are lacking, but details of some current tools and workbenches were presented in Section 20.4.

Considerable work is being undertaken to accomplish the preventative maintenance of software, either totally or incrementally, with the objective of improving the quality or the maintainability of the software system. By this means, geriatric software may have its life extended by bringing to bear on it modern software engineering techniques. A variety of approaches were described, ranging from simple operations on source code items, through to rediscovery of requirements specifications to allow re-implementation using modern techniques.

Quality assurance in the maintenance process is a key issue and efficient regression testing after changes have been made is essential. This was addressed in Section 20.5.

It is hoped that by finding solutions to the problems of maintaining existing software, it is possible to learn much more about writing new software which is *a priori* more maintainable. Much research remains to be done, and this is not easy because the results may only be evident after a long period. Section 20.7 provided additional useful factual information and some indications of key areas for research were given in Section 20.8.

20.10 Acknowledgements

The authors would like to thank all those in the Centre for Software Maintenance who have directly or indirectly contributed to this chapter. Their thanks are due too to Andrew Slade, who read early drafts, and Maureen Storey, who cheerfully coped with LaTeX.

The authors are also grateful to the following organizations, who are supporting the work of the Centre for Software Maintenance: Science and Engineering Research Council, Department of Trade and Industry, IBM (UK) Ltd, British Telecom Research Laboratories, K3 Software Services Ltd, The European Commission, Rank Xerox, AGS Information Systems Ltd and Lloyd's Register of Shipping.

20.11 References

ANSI/IEEE 729: 1983 IEEE standard glossary of software engineering terminology, *IEEE*

Arnold, R. S. and Parker, D. A. (1982) The dimensions of healthy maintenance. In *Proceedings of 6th International Conference Software Engineering*, 10–27

Arnold, R. S., Schneidewind, N. F. and Zvegintzov, N. (1984) A software maintenance workshop. *Communications of the ACM*, **27**, 1120–1121, 1158

Basili, V. R. and Mills, H. D. (1982) Understanding and documenting programs. *IEEE Transactions on Software Engineering*, **8**, 270–283

Bauer, F. L. (1976) Programming as an evolutionary process. *Lecture Notes in Computer Science, 46*, Springer-Verlag

Bauer, F. L. (1979) Program development by stepwise transformations the project CIP, *Lecture Notes in Computer Science, 69*, Springer-Verlag.

Bennett, K. H. (1989) *Software Engineering Environments: Research and Practice*, Ellis Horwood

Bennett, K. H., Cornelius, B. J., Munro, M. and Robson, D. J. (1988) Software maintenance: a key area for research. *University Computing*, **10**, 184–188

Boehm, B. W. (1976) Software engineering. *IEEE Transactions on Computing*, **25**, 1226–1242

Boehm, B. (1981) *Software Engineering Economics*, Prentice-Hall, Englewood Cliffs, NJ, USA

Boehm, B. (1983) The economics of software maintenance. In *Proceedings Software Maintenance Workshop*, IEEE, pp 9–37.

Boehm, B. W., Brown, J. R., Kaspar, H., Lipow, M., MacLeod, G. J. and Merritt, M. J. (1978) *Characteristics of Software Quality*, North-Holland

Brooks, R. (1983) Toward a theory of the comprehension of computer programs, *International Journal of Man-Machine Studies*, **18**, 543–554.

Calliss, F. W. (1987) *Problems with Automatic Restructurers SIGPLAN Notices*, **23**, 13–21.

Calliss, F. W., Cooper, S. D., Kenning, R. J. and Munro, M. (1988) *Notes of the Second Software Maintenance Workshop*, Centre for Software Maintenance, Durham

Chapin, N. (1987) The job of software maintenance. In *Proceedings of Conference on Software Maintenance*, IEEE, pp 4–12.

Collins, B. P., Nichols, J. E. and Sørensen, I. H. (1987) Introducing formal methods: the CICS experience with Z. *IBM Technical Report TR12.260*

Colter, M. A. (1988a) Strategies for software maintenance management. In *Proceedings of Conference on Software Maintenance, Chicago*, Software Maintainance Association.

Colter, M. A. (1988b) The business of software maintenance. *Second Software Maintenance Workshop Notes*, Centre for Software Maintenance, University of Durham

Constantine, L. L., Stevens, W. P. and Myers, G. J. (1974) Structured design. *IBM Systems Journal*, **2**, 115–139.

Cougar, E. and Zawacki, S. (1980) *Motivating and Managing Computer Personnel*, John Wiley

Curtis, B. and Sheppard, S. B. (1979) Identification and validation of quantitative measures of the psychological complexity of software. *Software Management Research Report*, General Electric.

Ditri, A. E., Shaw, J. C. and Atkins, W. (1971) *Managing the EDP Function*, McGraw-Hill

Dowson, M. and Wileden, J. C. (1985) A brief report on the international workshop on the software process and software environments. *ACM Software Engineering Notes*, **10**, 19–23

DTI and NCC (1987) *The STARTS Guide*, NCC

Fairley, R. (1985) *Software Engineering Concepts*, McGraw-Hill, NY, USA

Fletton, N. T. and Munro, M. (1988) Redocumenting software systems using Hypertext technology. In *Proceedings Conference on Software Maintenance*, IEEE, pp 54–59

Georges, M. (1989) The MACS project. In *Proceedings 3rd Durham Workshop on Software Maintenance*, University of Durham, Durham

Gladden, G. R. (1982) Stop the life cycle, I want to get off. *ACM Software Engineering Notes*, **7**, 35–39

Glass, R. L. and Noiseux, R. A. (1981) *Software Maintenance Guidebook*, Prentice-Hall

Griffiths, M. (1976) Program production by successive transformation. *Lecture Notes in Computer Science, 46*, Springer-Verlag

Gunn, C. and Jolly, D. (1988) Commercial software – development versus maintenance. *Second Software Maintenance Workshop Notes*, Centre for Software Maintenance, University of Durham

Harrison, W. and Magel, K. I. (1981) A complexity measure based on nesting level. *ACM SIGPLAN Notices*, **16**, 63–74

Hoskyns (1973) *Implications of Using Modular Programming*, Hoskyns Systems Research, London

IEEE (1985) *Proceedings of Conference on Software Maintenance – 1985*

IEEE (1987) *Proceedings of Conference on Software Maintenance – 1987*

IEEE (1988) *Proceedings of Conference on Software Maintenance – 1988*

Katsoulakis, T. (1989) The REDO project. In *Proceedings 3rd Durham Workshop on Software Maintenance*

Kernighan, B. and Plauger, P. (1978) *The Elements of Style*, McGraw-Hill

Lehman, M. M. (1980) Programs, life cycles, and laws of software evolution. In *Proceedings of IEEE*, **19**, 1060–1076

Lehman, M. M. (1984) Program evolution. *Information Processing Management*, **20**, 19–36

Lehman, M. M. and Belady, L. A. (1976) A model of large program development. *IBM Systems Journal*, **15**, 225–252

Letovsky, S. (1986) Cognitive processes in program comprehension. In *Empirical Studies of Programmers* (eds E. Soloway and S. Iyengar) Ablex, Norwood, pp 80–96

Lientz, B. and Swanson, E. B. (1980) *Software Maintenance Management*, Addison-Wesley

Lientz, B., Swanson, E. B and Tompkins, G. E. (1978) Characteristics of application software maintenance. *Communications of the ACM*, **21**, 466–471

Littman, D. C., Pinto, J., Levovsky, S. and Soloway, E. (1986) Mental models and software maintenance. In *Empirical Studies of Programmers* (eds E. Soloway and S. Iyengar) Ablex, Norwood, pp 80–96

Liu, C. C. (1976) A look at software maintenance. *Datamation*, **22**, 51–55

Martin, J. and McClure, C. (1983) *Software Maintenance: The Problems and its Solutions*, Prentice-Hall

Martin, R. J. and Osborne, W. M. (1983) Guidance of software maintenance. *NBS Special Publication 500–106*, National Bureau Standards, USA

McCall, J. A., Herdon, M. A. and Osborne, W. M. (1985) Software maintenance management. *NBS Special Publication 500–129*, National Bureau Standards, USA

McClure, C. L. (1981) *Managing Software Development and Maintenance*, Van Nostrand, New York, USA

McCracken, D. D. and Jackson, M. A. (1982) Life cycle concept considered harmful. *ACM Software Engineering Notes*, **7**, 29–32

Miller, J. C. and Strauss, III, B. M. (1987) Implications of automatic restructuring of COBOL. *ACM SIGPLAN Notices*, **22**, 41–49

Miara, R. J., Musselman, J. A., Navarro, J. A. and Shneiderman, B. (1983) Program indentation and comprehensibility. *Communications of the ACM*, **26**, 861–867

Munro, M. and Calliss, F. W. (1987) *Notes of the First Software Maintenance Workshop*, Centre for Software Maintenance, Durham

NBS (1983) *Guidance on Software Maintenance*, National Bureau of Standards, USA

Osborne, W. (1987) Building and sustaining software maintainability. *Proceedings of Conference on Software Maintenance*, IEEE Computer Society Press, pp 14–23

Parikh, G. (1982a) *Techniques of Program and System Maintenance*, Winthrop Publishers

Parikh, G. (1982b) Some tips, techniques and guidelines for program and system maintenance. In *Techniques of Program and System Maintenance*, Winthrop Publishers, pp 65–70

Parikh, G. and Zvegintzov, N. (1983) *Tutorial on Software Maintenance*, IEEE Computer Society

Parnas, D. (1972) On the criteria to be used in decomposing systems into modules. *Communications of the ACM*, **15**, 1053–1058

Perry, W. E. and Perry, S. M. N. (1985) A plan of action for software maintenance. *Data Management*, **23**

Pressman, R. S. (1987) *Software Engineering: A Practitioner's Approach*, McGraw Hill, NY, USA

Reifer, R. J. (1979) The nature of software management. *Tutorial: Software Management*, IEE, pp 2–5

Robson, D. J., Cornelius, B. J. and Munro, M. (1988) *An Approach to Software Maintenance Education*, Centre for Software Maintenance, University of Durham

Sharpley, W. K. (1977) Software maintenance planning for embedded computer systems. In *Proceedings of IEEE COMPSAC 77*, IEEE, pp 520–526

Schneidewind, N. F. (1987) The state of software maintenance. *IEEE Transactions on Software Engineering*, **13**, 303–310

Shneiderman, B. and Mayer, R. (1979) Syntactic semantic interactions in programming behaviour: a model. *International Journal of Computer and Information Science*, **8** 219–238

Sneed, H. and Jandrasics, J. (1987) Software recycling. In *Proceedings Conference on Software Maintenance*, IEEE, pp 82–90

Snowden, R. A. (1981) CADES and software development. In *Software Engineering Environments* (ed H. Huenke) North-Holland

Software Maintenance News (1986) GSA Launches the PWB (Sept. 86 and others)

Sommerville, I. (1985) *Software Engineering*, (2nd edn), Addison-Wesley

Swanson, E. B. (1976) The dimension of maintenance. In *Proceedings 2nd International Conference of Software Engineering*, IEEE, pp 492–497

Tully, C. (1989) Proceedings of 4th International Software Process Workshop. *ACM Software Engineering Notes*, **14**

van Tassel, D. (1978) *Program Style, Design, Efficiency, Debugging and Testing*, (2nd edn), Prentice-Hall

Ward, M. (1988) Transforming a program into a specification. *Centre for Software Maintenance Report 88/1*

Ward, M. and Munro, M. (1988) Intelligent program analysis tools for maintaining software. *The 1988 UK IT Conference*, University College, Swansea

Warden, R. (1988) Re-engineering for business change. *Second Software Maintenance Workshop Notes*, Centre for Software Maintenance, University of Durham

Weissman, L. (1976) Psychological complexity of computer programs: an experimental methodology. *ACM SIGPLAN Notices*, **9**, 25–36

Woodfield, S. N., Dunsmore, H. E. and Shen, V. Y. (1981) The effect of modularization and comments on program comprehension. *Working Paper*, Department of Computer Science, Arizona State University, USA

Yau, S., Colofello, J. S. and MacGregor, T. (1978) Ripple effect analysis of software maintenance. In *Proceedings IEEE COMPSAC 78*, pp 492–497

Zvegintzov, N. (ed) (1988) *Software Maintenance Tools*, Software Maintenance News

Formal
Development

21

Model-based specifications

Brian Monahan
University of Manchester

Roger Shaw
Lloyd's Register of Shipping

Contents

21.1 Introduction

This chapter introduces the topic of model-based specification and places it in a context relevant to practising software engineers. It begins with a discussion addressing the role of specifications within the software development process and what is meant by the terms 'model' and 'model-based specification'. There follows an extensive introduction to Z, a currently popular specification method, and the development of a specification for a heat sensing system. This is followed by a brief review of another model-based technique, VDM. The penultimate four sections provide a comparison between VDM and Z, an airing of some criticisms that are levelled at model-based specifications and a brief discussion on the topics of semantics and proof. The chapter ends with a short historical perspective of the two methods.

The reader of this chapter will be assumed to have studied Chapters 2 and 3 of this reference book, addressing discrete mathematics, and programming logics and proofs respectively. In addition, Chapter 15 examines the role of formal specification within the life cycle model and thus the reader should consult that chapter to find out how formal specifications may be used in a practical development setting. Finally, reification or refinement (the process of developing an abstract specification into an executable specification or implementation) is comprehensively covered in Chapter 24.

21.2 The task of specification

The task of specification arises in software engineering for several reasons. Following Jones (Jones, 1990; Jones and Shaw, 1990) as well as Turski and Maibaum (1987), the authors agree that specifications provide the criterion for establishing the acceptability of a piece of software to do some particular task (i.e. to say whether it is correct or not). Specifications therefore serve as the basis for a 'contract' of mutually agreed expectation between customer and supplier. Additionally, they document the essential aspects of the functionality of a system and its components. Such information will be useful when planning enhancements of the software, to re-use parts of the system in building other systems, to help in providing relevant user-level documentation, and so on.

So, in the world of software engineering, specifications will need to be written as part of the software development life cycle. Their purpose is to state definitively what is to be delivered by the software supplier. First, it is assumed that an appropriate study of system requirements has been performed to elicit the client's expectations about the system and that these have subsequently been recorded as part of the system requirements documentation.

Based upon these requirements, the specifier will set to work on trying to build a mathematically precise description of the overall functionality of the system which also is complete and consistent. 'Complete' is used to mean that the description should adequately cover all of the functionality apparently contained in the requirements. 'Consistent' means that the design forms a cohesive whole and that the description is logically consistent as a mathematical characterization of those requirements.

Whether or not a given specification is consistent with respect to a given set of requirements is a matter of discussion and informed debate between the parties concerned. Ultimately, some form of agreement is needed as to what must *necessarily* appear in the specification, based on the requirements. However, the logical consistency of a specification can always be confirmed by building a system that does manifestly satisfy it. This is because no software system could ever satisfy a logically inconsistent specification, and so any specification of a system which can be implemented somehow must therefore be consistent.

However, a major purpose of producing specifications of systems is to assess beforehand whether the system could ever be implemented adequately. This means that the specifier needs to do an analysis of the specification, to extract sufficient evidence for the existence of an implementation – without, of course, going to the effort of actually building one.

From this one can see that the specifier's primary role is to take the set of requirements and the client's expectations about the system, and from these to tease out the fundamental emergent properties of the software system. Sadly, it often turns out that the original requirement documents are full of loopholes and functional deficiencies, and may contain serious ambiguities and contradictions. If these issues are not discovered sufficiently early, they will only be found late, either during the implementation phase itself or, even worse, during beta-testing and operational use. Such a late discovery of functional deficiences brings well-known economic consequences.

So once any problems with the requirements have been identified, the specifier has to go back to the client to re-negotiate the requirements and reach some agreement that ensures that the mutually accepted requirements are consistent and reasonable and can be successfully implemented using the programming techniques and equipment available. In other words, the specifier is attempting to find out what the client *really* wanted from the system, given the client's original requirements as a starting point. The use of rapid prototyping (see Chapter 40) of system components can be an invaluable aid in helping both the client and the specifier to explore proposed alternatives in functionality.

Once a satisfactory specification has been obtained, it is passed to the system design team who use the document as the basis for their design and subsequent implementation.

Another way of looking at the specifier's task is to think of it as assessing the technical risk incurred in carrying out the software development to completion. This involves charting the consequences for the architecture of the system as implied by its functionality. The structure of the specification and its complexity may be good indicators of the ease with which a given system can be implemented. In particular, the technical feasibility case for constructing the system is especially clear if the system's specification can be expressed as straightforward combinations of components that have already been implemented. This issue also touches upon whether specifications should in general be executable and is discussed further in Hayes and Jones (1989).

The outcome of the specifier's work should therefore be a specification which is consistent and represents faithfully and completely the requirements that have been mutually agreed upon by the specifier and the client. In addition, the specification should be sufficiently precise for the design team to produce a system design meeting the agreed requirements.

21.3 Specification and mathematical models

Given this background to the role of specifications, it is clear that any specification should be precisely stated in terms that the client can accept as representing their requirements and that the system designers can use as a definitive starting point for their design task. This means that specifications will be stated at a higher level of abstraction than the design or its implementation, but also in a form that is more precise than the original statement of the requirements.

21.3.1 Property and model-oriented specification

In common with other engineering disciplines, specification can be seen as the result of a process involving the presentation and putting together of mathematically precise descriptions. There are several ways in which these mathematical specifications can be formulated and these are now discussed.

21.3.1.1 Property-oriented approach

One way is simply to write down as many pertinent logical properties and relationships of the mathematical objects that one has in mind and then determine if these properties are logically consistent or not. If they are inconsistent, one tries to decide which property to throw away and tries again to show the consistency of the remaining properties. On the other hand, if they are consistent, (ie. they possess a model), one then tries to minimize the basic collection of properties by throwing out properties that appear to be consequences of the remainder. Such a collection of properties is known as an axiomatization of a mathematical theory and each of the given properties are known as axioms. Technically speaking, a mathematical theory consists of the collection of all logical formulae which satisfy the collection of models as determined by the axioms.

The property-oriented approach is much favoured by mathematicians because it tries to extract fundamental sets of concepts needed to understand particular collections of mathematical objects. It does so by stating some characteristic properties that only the objects of interest possess, and then eliminating redundancy in the resulting description.

Algebraic specifications of software systems have a property-oriented character (see Chapter 18). This is because they describe systems in terms of their basic operators and the equational properties of their behaviour. These equational identities show how different combinations of the basic operators can achieve the same result. In general, a collection of equational properties will determine a collection of particular structures, one of which will be the system of interest. Usually (but not invariably), this system of interest is taken to be the 'least' or initial algebra satisfying the equations, whenever it exists.

21.3.1.2 Model-based approach

Another approach is to describe the objects of interest in terms of an *a priori* determined collection of fundamental objects, the existence of which may be taken for granted. The objects are then given existence by building them as compound structures, using the more fundamental objects as base material. This constructive, model-building approach suggests that for any (compound) object to exist it must be constructed by putting together a selection of fundamental objects in some way. As a consequence of this, the characteristic features of an object are manifested by the structural components used to build the object and the fundamental properties that these components possess. In other words, the properties of compound objects are derived as a consequence of how they were put together and of the underlying properties of the constituent components.

A recent article by the logician Jon Barwise (1989) contains a discussion of the distinction between property-oriented, axiomatically given descriptions of objects, on the one hand, and the more structured, model-based descriptions which are given relative to some *a priori* existing stock of useful objects, on the other. He argues that the prevalent method in applied mathematics is mainly the model construction approach, although he also admits that more often than not, a little of both is going on.

21.3.2 What is a model?

The word 'model' has been used so far as though it were an unambiguous and definitive term in its own right. However, this is not the case and it appears that there are (at least) three notions of 'model' that are often used in connection with software specifications.

21.3.2.1 Engineer's notion of 'model'

This is a prototype construction, smaller in scale than the real thing, but useful for testing out ideas and checking specific design calculations (*cf.* the use of wind tunnel models in aerodynamic design).

It is related to the way that a computer scientist would construct a software simulator (i.e. animation) of, say, a piece of hardware (or even of a piece of software) on which to test out aspects of a design or to validate certain predictions. Such a simulation will generally ignore various features of the system to be constructed and focus on those aspects that are relevant to a particular portion of the software's functionality.

For example, different prototypes might be constructed for experimenting with the kernel functionality of a system as opposed to the design of its user interface. Both are important aspects of any system and will often provide many possibilities for making engineering trade-offs. The simulations could then be used to explore which trade-offs are possible and to assess what consequences they may have for non-functional characteristics. The relationship between mathematical specifications and prototype simulations is discussed in greater depth in Hayes and Jones (1989).

21.3.2.2 Applied mathematician's notion of 'model'

This is a mathematical theory in which the more fundamental aspects of the system are formulated and discussed. This is useful in making predictions and in drawing conclusions about the system by the use of logical inference.

Again, such models are usually described at a more abstract level than any implementation that they may possess. They will generally have many possible implementations available, including the one that is eventually produced. One reason for having a fairly high level of abstraction (at least to start with) is that it is generally easier to change and to decide on the overall functionality of the system. However, there are no hard and fast rules about what a 'reasonable' level of abstraction is for any given system specification. This remains a matter of preference for the specifier and the client.

21.3.2.3 Mathematical logician's notion of 'model'

This is a basic technical construct used in formulating the semantics of logical languages. Technically, it is a relational structure consisting of a mapping from the (proper) names, or identifiers, to semantic meanings. Such a structure can then be used to determine the collection of logical formulae that are made true with respect to that structure. This relationship may then be turned around to determine the (class of all such) models which make a given collection of formulae true.

None of these meanings should be taken as being prior to, or more important than, any other. Each meaning has its place and proper usage within software engineering and computer science. However, when model-based specifications are discussed it is the applied mathematician's notion of model that is primarily intended. The important point to note is that there are several well-defined meanings given to the term 'model' and the reader should be alerted to these meanings and the possibility of confusion.

21.3.3 What is a model-based specification?

In software specific terms, a model-based specification is a description of the functionality of a software system presented in terms of a particular state space, together with a collection of operations and functions which act upon it. These operations and functions are expressed in terms of a standard collection of basic data types and other type constructors.

Mathematically, there will be a distinguished type Σ which represents the state space of the system, together with some further logical constraint, called the state invariant Inv: $\Sigma \rightarrow \mathbb{B}$ which restricts the state space to just the valid states. The operations should then preserve this state invariant when transforming the state and respect any pre-condition and post-condition predicates that are associated with it. For instance, a simplistic view of a library is that of two sets, one modelling those books on the library shelves and one modelling those books on loan. The state of the system would therefore be modelled by these two sets. A realistic restriction, or invariant, might be that the two sets should be disjoint – books should not be both on the shelves and on loan at the same time. Various library operations may be defined such as lending a book or adding a new book to the library's stock. A specification of the lend operation could reasonably assume that the book to be lent was not already on loan and was registered as being currently 'on the shelf'. This assumption is called the operation's pre-condition. The effect of the operation on the state would be to remove the book from the set of books available for loan and place it in the set of books recorded as being on-loan; this latter part of the specification would be known as the post-condition. The post-condition should yield a state that satisfies the state invariant, namely, that the two sets should be disjoint. Section 21.6 contains details of a Z specification and Sections 21.5 and 21.7 contain fragments of a further specification depicted in both VDM and Z which illustrate this approach.

It is no accident that the basic data types used in model-based specifications of software are useful in describing computer-oriented systems. These data types were carefully and deliberately chosen by the specification language designer as appropriate abstractions of familiar computer-oriented concepts which commonly arise in practice. As we shall see, the basic data types include sets, Cartesian products, various forms of relation, sequences, and so on.

Having these abstractions of computer-oriented concepts available means that model-based descriptions can be more easily interpreted by the design team. In this way, useful design information can be imparted to the designer, but without compromising the abstractions necessary for capturing the client's requirements.

It should now be evident that a model-based specification of a software system can be understood in the context of the constructive, model-building approach mentioned above. It is a description that is given in terms of a number of basic constituent structural features that are considered to be pre-given, or part of a mathematical library, and can therefore be taken for granted. In addition, a specification is like an applied mathematical theory of the intended system and from which pertinent consequences, in the form of theorems, should be deducible.

Finally, it should also be clear that model-based specifications involve some of the characteristics of each of the notions of 'model' mentioned above. They can describe simplified abstractions that are useful for engineering purposes as models; they are presentations of mathematical theories, corresponding to the models of applied mathematics; finally, they are also expressed in logical terms and so have a technical correspondence to the relational model structures in the sense of the mathematical logician.

21.4 The Z mathematical language

21.4.1 Introduction

This section, and the following two, will undertake a systematic, but not comprehensive, examination of the Z specification language. This section will briefly cover types and variables and show how variables are typed in declarations. It will then move on to review the way simple set and logical expressions are constructed and finally conclude with a quick review of relations and functions; comprehensive coverage of this material may be found in Diller (1990); McMorran and Nicholls (1989); Spivey (1989); Woodcock and Loomes (1988). Section 21.5 discusses the schema language and Section 21.6 walks through the development of a specification for a heat sensing system.

21.4.2 Types in Z

Every expression in Z has a decidable type and thus it is possible to check mechanically that expressions within the language are well typed. Types are maximal sets, that is, there is no sub-typing within the language. There are essentially four kinds of types within Z:

1. Basic types or given sets (including free types).
2. Set types.
3. Cartesian product types.
4. Schema types.

The first three of these are discussed below while schema types are described in Section 21.5.

21.4.2.1 Basic types or given sets

Basic types are either the integers ($\mathbb{Z}$) or atomic objects drawn from given sets that form the boundary of the specification and for which no internal structure is given. Consider, for instance, an employment agency database, where one might be interested in the set of companies subscribing to the database or the set of candidate employees. These sets might be called *COMPANY* and *PERSON* respectively. As the encoding of the elements of these sets is not important no additional structural information is provided. In Z we denote the integers by $\mathbb{Z}$ and other basic types are declared by placing square brackets around the names of the types; for example [*COMPANY*] and [*PERSON*], or, jointly, by [*COMPANY,PERSON*]. Using these basic types the remaining three more complex, or compound, types can be constructed and ever more complex hierarchies of types produced. Free types, which are discussed in Section 21.4.9, are a special form of basic type. However, it is necessary to introduce a little more notation before one can discuss them.

21.4.2.2 Set types

Given a basic or composite type, then sets containing objects of that type may be constructed. For example, a set of a potentially infinite collection of integers is of type $\mathbb{P}\,\mathbb{Z}$ and the set of companies in our database is of type $\mathbb{P}\,COMPANY$. Instances of this type can be explicitly or implicitly constructed, that is, their members may be identified explicitly or by defining a characteristic property:

$$\{1,2,3,5,8,13,21\} \in \mathbb{P}\,\mathbb{Z}$$
$$\{e : \mathbb{Z} \mid is\_even(e)\} \in \mathbb{P}\,\mathbb{Z}$$
$$\{c : COMPANY \mid employees(c) < 16\} \in \mathbb{P}\,COMPANY$$

21.4.2.3 Cartesian product types

A Cartesian product of two sets A and B is the set (denoted by $A \times B$) of all pairs (a,b) such that a is a member of A and b is a member of B. More generally Cartesian products are called n-tuples and may be defined over n sets where n is greater than or equal to 2. In the case above the type of the n-tuple would be $A \times B$. Instances of this type can, once again, be constructed explicitly or implicitly:

$(1,3) \in Z \times Z$
$\{(1,3),(3,6),(5,10),(7,14)\} \in \mathbb{P}(Z \times Z)$
$\{x,y,z: \mathbb{Z} \mid x^2 + y^2 + z^2 = c^2 \bullet (x,y,z)\} \in \mathbb{P}(Z \times Z \times Z)$

21.4.3 Variables and declarations

Variables are used throughout Z specifications in a number of roles as will be seen. Essentially a variable is a symbolic name for a value which may adopt different values in different models or may be constant in all models (here we are using model in the logician's sense). In addition, a variable has a scope which will be discussed further later. When a variable is introduced it is given a specific type and the association between the name and the type is known as a declaration. For instance, the following are all declarations:

$registered\_companies$: $\mathbb{P}(COMPANY \times \mathbb{Z})$
$number\_of\_candidates$: $\mathbb{Z}$
i,j,k: $\mathbb{Z}$
a,b,c: $\mathbb{Z}$; x: $COMPANY$; p: $PERSON$

As we will see subsequently, declarations may also constrain the values that variables can adopt.

21.4.4 The integers

Integer arithmetic and its operators should be familiar to most readers. *Table 21.1* summarizes Z's integer notation.

21.4.5 Set notation and expressions

Sets and the general form of set expressions have been introduced in Chapter 2. Z's set notation is summarized in *Table 21.2*.

Implicit set constructors require some explanation. The general form is shown below:

$\{declaration \mid constraint \bullet term\}$

The declaration part introduces bound local variables employed within the constraint and term expressions. The constraint part optionally introduces any restrictions on the bound variables that may apply and the term component denotes the form and construction of the elements in the set. For example, the set of squares of integers between 0 and 50 might

be specified as follows:

$\{e: \mathbb{Z} \mid e \geqslant 0 \wedge e \leqslant 50 \bullet e^2\}$

If there is no restriction then the following short form may be employed for the set of squared integers:

$\{e: \mathbb{Z} \bullet e^2\}$

Assuming that the declaration constitutes the term, subject to some restriction, then the term field may be left out:

$\{e: \mathbb{Z} \mid e \geqslant 100\}$

Finally, both the term and constraint may be omitted:

$\{c: COMPANY\}$ yields $COMPANY$

21.4.6 Cartesian products

Recall that Cartesian products are ordered n-tuples. Given an n-tuple of type $\mathbb{Z} \times \mathbb{Z}$, then:

$(x,y) \in \mathbb{Z} \times \mathbb{Z} \Leftrightarrow x \in \mathbb{Z} \wedge y \in \mathbb{Z}$

Table 21.3 summarizes the notation associated with Cartesian (cross) products. This notation should be included in the table of set notation; however, it has been separated out here for convenience of discussion.

21.4.7 Logic notation and logical expressions

Z's logic notation is summarized in *Table 21.4*. Note that quantified predicates are written in the same style as set comprehension expressions, that is they have the following general form:

$declaration \mid constraint \bullet predicate$

Here the predicate part holds for all, some or one case(s) determined by the quantified variable(s) and subject to the optional constraint. Some typical examples are set out below:

$\forall i,j: \mathbb{Z} \mid i \neq j \bullet name(i) \neq name(j)$
$\forall i,j: \mathbb{Z} \bullet i \neq j \Rightarrow name(i) \neq name(j)$
$\exists i: \mathbb{Z} \mid i > 1 \bullet i*i > 100$

The first expression states that for all integers i and j, subject to the constraint that i does not equal j, that $name(i)$ does not equal $name(j)$. The second expression removes the constraint part and introduces an implication stating that whenever it is true that i does not equal j then $name(i) \neq name(j)$ must also be true; the two expressions are equivalent.

Table 21.1 Summary of integer operators

Notation	Description
$\mathbb{Z}$	The set of integers – $\{\ldots -2, -1, 0, 1, 2, \ldots\}$
$\mathbb{N}$	The set of natural numbers – $\{0, 1, 2, \ldots\}$
	$\mathbb{N} = \{n: \mathbb{Z} \mid n \geqslant 0\}$
$\mathbb{N}_1$	The set of natural numbers excluding 0
$+, -, *$	Dyadic operators over the integers
$-$	Monadic negative operator
div, mod	Dyadic operators defined over $\mathbb{Z}$ and $\mathbb{Z}\backslash\{0\}$ respectively
$<, \leqslant, =, \neq, \geqslant, >$	Relational operators on the integers

Table 21.2 Summary of set notation

Notation	Description
$\mathbb{P}\,S$	The set of all subsets of S
$\mathbb{P}_1 S$	The set of all non-empty subsets of S
$\mathbb{F}\,S$	The set of all finite subsets of S
$\mathbb{F}_1 S$	The set of all non-empty finite subsets of S
$\bullet$	The empty set
$\{a,b,c,\ldots\}$	Explicit set construction – the set containing $a,b,c,\ldots$
$m\ldots n$	The set of integer numbers – $\{x:\mathbb{Z}\mid x\geqslant m \wedge x\leqslant n\}$
$\{x:T\mid P\}$	The set containing those elements of type T satisfying P
$\{x:T\mid P\bullet t\}$	The set of terms t for those elements of type T satisfying P
$S_1 = S_2$	Set equality – true if S_1 equals S_2
$S_1 \neq S_2$	Set inequality – true when S_1 does not equal S_2
$e \in S$	True if element e is a member of S
$e \notin S$	True if element e is not a member of S
$S_1 \subseteq S_2$	Subset – $\forall e:T\bullet e\in S_1 \Rightarrow e\in S_2$
$S_1 \subset S_2$	Proper subset – $S_1 \subseteq S_2 \wedge S_1 \neq S_2$
$S_1 \cup S_2$	Set union – $\{e:T\mid e\in S_1 \vee e\in S_2\}$
$S_1 \cap S_2$	Set intersection – $\{e:T\mid e\in S_1 \wedge e\in S_2\}$
$S_1 \backslash S_2$	Set subtraction – $\{e:T\mid e\in S_1 \wedge e\notin S_2\}$
$\bigcup SS$	Distributed union – $\{e:T\mid \exists S:SS\bullet e\in S\}$ where $SS:\mathbb{P}\,(\mathbb{P}\,T)$
$\bigcap SS$	Distributed intersection – $\{e:T\mid \forall S:SS\bullet e\in S\}$
$\#S$	The cardinality or size of the finite set S

Table 21.3 Summary of Cartesian product notation

Notation	Description
$S_1 \times S_2 \times \ldots \times S_n$	Cartesian product – $\{e_1\cdot S_1,\ldots,e_n\cdot S_n\mid (e_1,\ldots,e_n)\}$
(e_1,e_2)	Ordered pair
$(e_1,e_2,\ldots,e_n)$	Ordered n-tuple
$first(e_1,e_2)$	Projection function – $first(e_1,e_2)=e_1$
$second(e_1,e_2)$	Projection function – $second(e_1,e_2)=e_2$

Table 21.4 Summary of logic notation

Notation	Description
$\neg\, E$	The negation of E, not E
$E_1 \wedge E_2$	Conjunction of E_1 and E_2, E_1 and E_2
$E_1 \vee E_2$	Disjunction of E_1 and E_2, E_1 or E_2
$E_1 \Rightarrow E_2$	Implication, E_1 implies E_2
$E_1 \Leftrightarrow E_2$	Equivalence, E_1 if and only if E_2
$\forall e:T\mid P\bullet Q$	All e of type T which satisfy P also satisfy Q
$\forall e:T\bullet Q$	All e of type T satisfy Q
$\exists e:T\mid P\bullet Q$	Some e of type T which satisfy P also satisfy Q
$\exists_1 e:T\mid P\bullet Q$	Exactly one e of type T which satisfies P also satisfies Q

21.4.8 Global declarations and abbreviations

Declarations may be global to the whole specification. Such declarations introduce constants which may be used from the point of declaration onwards; predicates may be introduced along with the declaration. Global declarations are written as follows:

$$number\_of\_file\_servers: \mathbb{N}$$
$$number\_of\_file\_servers = 16$$

Declarations can introduce constants of any type, thus sets, cross-products, and so on, may be introduced and given constants in this way.

In a similar style an abbreviation introduces a global constant. For example:

$$\mathbb{N} == \{n:\mathbb{Z} \mid n \geq 0\}$$
$$\mathbb{N}_1 == \mathbb{N}\backslash\{0\}$$
$$Employment == \mathbb{P}(COMPANY \times \mathbb{Z})$$

The first abbreviation states that the natural numbers are the positive integers. The second example states that $\mathbb{N}_1$ is the same type as the expression $\mathbb{N}\backslash\{0\}$ and has the same value as the expression which, in this case, is the natural numbers less the value 0. The final example states that *Employment* is an abbreviation for the power set of cross products $(COMPANY \times \mathbb{Z})$. Like global declarations, the scope of abbreviations is from the point of definition onwards in the specification.

21.4.9 Free types

Free types were mentioned in Section 21.4.2. Essentially free types are basic types. A rather limited form of free type is presented here and the interested reader is referred to Diller (1990) or Spivey (1989) for a full definition of this type construct.

Often, when developing a specification, one would like to use an enumerated type. For instance one might like to model traffic lights using the following type:

$$TL\_colours = green \mid red\_amber \mid red \mid amber$$

and then introduce declarations of the following form meaning that *traffic_light* may adopt any of the values *green* or *red_amber* or *red* or *amber*:

$$traffic\_light : TL\_colours$$

The enumerated type *TL_colours* is actually defined using a number of global constants as shown below:

$$[TL\_colours]$$

$$green, red\_amber, red, amber : TL\_colours$$

$$disjoint(\langle\{green\},\{red\_amber\},\{red\},\{amber\}\rangle)$$

In other words, the free type is made up of disjoint constants of type *TL_colours*. From this definition one can see that free types are a special form of basic type.

21.4.10 Relations and functions

This section quickly reviews how relations, or more precisely binary relations, and functions are described in Z. Once again the basic mathematical ideas are explained in Chapter 2.

21.4.10.1 Relations

A relation is a set R of ordered pairs (x,y) such that x is related to y (sometimes written xRy or $(x,y)\in R$) if (x,y) is a member of R. A relation R between two sets X and Y is made up of elements of the form (x,y). Relations are introduced into Z specifications using the symbol $\leftrightarrow$. Thus, if we have a relation between two sets X and Y, the relation is written $X \leftrightarrow Y$.

A set of ordered pairs whose elements are taken from sets X and Y respectively is of type $\mathbb{P}(X \times Y)$, i.e. $X\leftrightarrow Y$ is the same as $\mathbb{P}(X \times Y)$. The type of the binary relation '$<$' for integers is therefore $\mathbb{P}(\mathbb{Z} \times \mathbb{Z})$. The type $\mathbb{P}(X \times Y)$ embraces many to many and one to many mappings. In Z these mappings are dis-

tinguished by using different symbols for the declaration of relations and functions.

A relation such as $<$, which pairs elements from a common set, that is where both values are drawn from the same type, is called homogeneous. We say that $<$ is a homogeneous relation on $\mathbb{Z}$. In contrast a relation between members of different types is called heterogeneous.

An element of a relation may be written as (x,y) or as $x\mapsto y$. The second form is called a maplet. Clearly, therefore, $(3,4)$ and $3\mapsto 4$ are both elements of the relation $<$ and are the same element.

Table 21.5 summarizes *some* of Z's relational calculus notation and a number of these operations require an explanation as they have not been defined in Chapter 2.

The relational image operator $R(S)$, as the definition indicates, produces the set of image points of R for those domain elements contained in the set S. For example:

$$R = \{(1,1),(1,2),(2,2),(2,3),(3,3),(3,4)\}$$
$$S = \{1,2,4\}$$

then $R(S)$ would be $\{1,2,3\}$. Note that S can contain elements not in the domain of R.

Domain restriction takes a relation R and a set S and yields a relation containing domain elements restricted to the values contained in S:

$$S \lhd R = \{(1,1),(1,2),(2,2),(2,3)\}$$

Domain anti-restriction yields a relation from R containing the domain elements that are not in S:

$$S \ntriangleleft R = \{(3,3),(3,4)\}$$

Range restriction and anti-restriction are similarly defined but operate on the range of R. Note that the constraining set is placed after the operator in these two cases making a natural analogy with the range of the relation:

$$R \rhd S = \{(1,1),(1,2),(2,2),(3,4)\}$$
$$R \ntriangleright S = \{(2,3),(3,3)\}$$

21.4.10.2 Functions

Functions are relations that are restricted to being one–one or many–one in form. As noted in Chapter 2, one can distinguish total functions, partial functions, one–one functions, onto functions and one–one and onto functions. Each can be defined precisely by using an appropriate predicate on the domain and range of sets of a relation. In Z a range of graphic symbols is provided to distinguish these different kinds of functions and associated with each symbol is an appropriate predicate restricting the function in some way. When one of these functions is used in a specification a proof obligation arises to show that the specification honours the precise form of the function.

Table 21.6 provides a summary of the main types of functions and the operations that may be used. Only function overriding should require some explanation. This operator is defined on two functions and yields a function. The resultant function contains all the functional pairings from the second function and only those pairings from the first function whose domain elements are not in the domain of the second function. An example will clarify this:

$$f_1 = \{(1,2),(3,9),(18,9),(5,20)\}$$
$$f_2 = \{(2,7),(18,6),(5,7),(7,14)\}$$

Table 21.5 Summary of relational operators

Notation	Description
$X \leftrightarrow Y$	A binary relation between X and Y is the same as $\mathbb{P}(X \times Y)$
(x,y)	The tuple containing x *and* y
$x \mapsto y$	A maplet from x to y – same as (x,y)
dom R	Domain of $R - \{x: X \mid \exists y: Y \bullet (x,y) \in R\}$
ran R	Range of $R - \{y: Y \mid \exists x: X \bullet (x,y) \in R\}$
$\tilde{R}$	Relational inverse $- \{x: X; y: Y \mid (x,y) \in R \bullet y \to x\}$
$R_1;R_2$	Relational composition $- \{x: X; z: Z \mid \exists y: Y \bullet (x,y) \in R_1 \wedge (y,z) \in R_2\}$
$R_1 \bullet R_2$	Reversed relational composition $- R_2;R_1$
$R(\!S\!)$	Relational image $- \{y: Y \mid \exists x: S \bullet (x,y) \in R\}$
$S \lhd R$	Domain restriction $- \{x: X; y: Y \mid x \in S \wedge (x,y) \in R\}$
$S \lhd R$	Domain anti-restriction $- \{x: X / y: Y \mid x \notin S \wedge (x,y) \in R\}$
$R \rhd S$	Range restriction $- \{x: X; y: Y \mid (x,y) \in R \wedge y \in S\}$
$R \rhd S$	Range anti-restriction $- \{x: X; y: Y \mid (x,y) \in R \wedge y \notin S\}$

Table 21.6 Summary of functional operators

Notation	Description
$X \nrightarrow Y$	Partial function $- \{f: X \leftrightarrow Y \mid \forall x: X; y_1,y_2: Y \bigcirc (x_1,y_1) \in f \wedge (x,y_2) \in f \Rightarrow y_1 = y_2\}$
$X \to Y$	Total function $- \{f: X \nrightarrow Y \mid \text{dom } f = X\}$
$X \nrightarrowtail Y$	Partial injection $- \{f: X \nrightarrow Y \mid \forall x_1,x_2: \text{dom } f \bigcirc f(x_1) = f(x_2) \Rightarrow x_1 = x_2\}$
$X \rightarrowtail Y$	Total injection $- (X \nrightarrowtail Y) \cap (X \to Y)$
$X \nrightarrow\!\!\!\!\to Y$	Partial surjection $- \{f: X \nrightarrow Y \mid \text{ran } f = Y\}$
$X \twoheadrightarrow Y$	Total surjection $- (X \nrightarrow\!\!\!\!\to Y) \cap (X \to Y)$
$X \rightarrowtail\!\!\!\!\to Y$	Bijection $- (X \nrightarrowtail Y) \cap (X \twoheadrightarrow Y)$
$f \oplus g$	Functional overriding $- ((\text{dom } g) \lhd f) \cup g$
fx or $f(x)$	Function application – function f applied to argument x

Then, $f_1 \oplus f_2$ will yield the function:

$$\{(1,2),(3,9),(18,6),(5,7),(2,7),(7,14)\}$$

Clearly $\#(f_1 \oplus f_2) = (\#f_1 + \#f_2) - \#(\text{dom} f_1 \cap \text{dom} f_2)$.

21.4.11 Type normalization

Types within Z are called maximal sets, that is, a type is either a basic type or a complex type made up from basic types; types are not defined over subsets of values.

Wherever subsetting is used, either through use of types $\mathbb{N}, \mathbb{N}_1$ or ranges of the form $m,..,n$, the type of the associated variable is an integer with an appropriate predicate asserting the range restriction. For relations and functions the type is a cross product of subsidiary types with appropriate restricting predicates.

For instance, a declaration of the form:

$x: \mathbb{N}$
$y: -20,..,-10$

would be seen as:

$x: \mathbb{Z}$
$y: \mathbb{Z}$

with the restricting predicate:

$(x \geqslant 0) \wedge (-20 \leqslant y) \wedge (y \leqslant -10)$

When type checking expressions involving x and y the types of these two variables would be taken as $\mathbb{Z}$. Types of the form $COMPANY \leftrightarrow \mathbb{N}$ and $COMPANY \to \mathbb{N}$ (for example) would be seen as belonging to the normalized (or base) type $\mathbb{P}(COMPANY \times \mathbb{Z})$, once again with an appropriate predicate restricting the values of the cross product. *Table 21.7* should make clear the distinctions drawn above.

Table 21.7

Declaration	Base types
$NAME \leftrightarrow DATE$	$\mathbb{P}(NAME \times DATE)$
$\mathbb{P}(NAME) \times DATE$	$\mathbb{P}(NAME) \times DATE$
$\mathbb{P}(NAME \nrightarrow DATE)$	$\mathbb{P}(\mathbb{P}(NAME \times DATE))$
$\mathbb{P}(NAME) \to DATE$	$\mathbb{P}(\mathbb{P}(NAME) \times DATE)$
$1...10$	$\mathbb{Z}$

21.5 Schema language and calculus

21.5.1 Introduction

The Z schema language provides a vehicle for modularizing the development and presentation of specifications. It is a mechanism for naming mathematical structures, and the schema calculus provides combinators for combining these structures in a systematic and mathematically tractable manner. Further information on schemas may be found in Diller (1990) and Woodcock (1989a).

The schema is used to factor out commonality in:

1. Describing states.
2. Describing operations.
3. Defining types.
4. Writing predicates.
5. Stating theorems.

It provides a powerful tool for structuring specifications. The advantages that accrue from the use of schemas are the same as those which accrue from introducing modularity features into programming languages, namely:

1. Subordination of complexity.
2. Highlighting the difference between similar structures.
3. Re-use of existing parts.
4. Simple modification of parts to make new parts.
5. Reduction of typographical errors.

The following discussion will start by examining schemas as states and operations. We will then introduce some aspects of the schema calculus and return to look at schemas as types, and the use of schemas for writing predicates and theorems. By no means all of the schema language and calculus is introduced here. A full definition of Z may be found in Spivey (1989).

21.5.2 A running example

When developing a model-based specification of a problem we aim to provide an abstract model of the problem using abstract structures such as relations, functions and Cartesian products. To illustrate the schema language we will develop a simple specification based on the following problem. A significantly larger example is discussed in Section 21.6.

Consider a simple employment agency database system. People apply for positions with companies; companies subscribe by offering employment positions. Companies may hire and fire people. A person may apply to the agency only once, thereby becoming a candidate, losing this status when hired by a company and regaining it when fired. A company may subscribe several times corresponding to the number of vacant positions. Finally, only people who are currently candidates may be hired and only by companies having vacant positions.

There are queries to check whether a person is a candidate, for finding out the company that someone works for (provided the person is not a candidate) and for finding out the number of vacant positions a company still has (provided the company is a subscriber).

Based on this simple set of requirements we can construct the entity–relationship diagram shown in *Figure 21.1*.

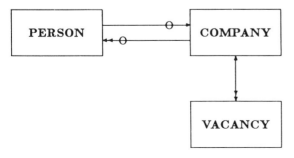

Figure 21.1 Employment agency database – entity–relationship diagram

21.5.3 Basic schema language

A schema may be viewed as a construct which allows us to introduce a declaration and an optional predicate. The declaration usually contains the names and types of one or more variables and the optional predicate places restrictions on the values that may be adopted by the variables. A schema may be written in either a horizontal or vertical form. The horizontal form has the following structure:

$$[declaration \mid predicate]$$

and the vertical form has the following structure:

$$\begin{array}{|l}
declaration \\
\hline
predicate \\
\end{array}$$

More usefully, we can name the schema; thus in horizontal form:

$$SchemaName \triangleq [declaration \mid predicate]$$

or, in vertical form:

$$\begin{array}{|l}
\hline
SchemaName \\
declaration \\
\hline
predicate \\
\end{array}$$

As we shall see, given a named schema, we can refer to the schema as a whole and make use of the declaration and predicates in different specification contexts. In the following text we will mostly write schemas using the vertical form.

21.5.3.1 The schema as a state

Returning to the employment agency database, we will develop a state model for the problem. The discussion in Section 21.3 on model-based specifications described the nature of state-based mathematical models. In this example the state variables that we choose to model and their mathematical structure are:

1. *Candidates.* A finite set will be used to model the set of people who have applied to the agency for work. This corresponds to the entity set **PERSON**, but only those not associated with a company.
2. *Employs.* A relation will be used to model the link between companies and employed people (one time candidates). This relationship models the link between the entities **COMPANY** and **PERSON**. The domain of the relationship models the entity set **COMPANY** and the pairs (company,person) models the entity set **PERSON** of those people employed by companies.
3. *Vacancies.* A partial function between companies and the number of vacancies each has. The domain of the function models the entity set **COMPANY**. The set of pairs (company, number) models the entity set **VACANCY**.

This information can all be expressed in a schema as follows, but first we need to introduce some basic types – the set of people and the set of companies from which particular individuals and companies will be drawn:

[*PERSON,COMPANY*]

```
┌─EADataBase────────────────
  candidates: 𝔽 PERSON
  employs: COMPANY↔PERSON
  vacancies: COMPANY⇸ℕ
├────────────────────────────
  ran employs ∩ candidates = {}
  dom employs ⊆ dom vacancies
  employs˜ ∈ PERSON⇸COMPANY
└────────────────────────────
```

Here we have a schema called *EADataBase*. In this case the declaration part models the state of the database and contains the state variables. The order in which the variables are expressed is unimportant and, more abstractly, a schema does not record the order of declaration of the state variables; only the names and underlying types are of import. The predicate part records restrictions that apply to the model; these restrictions are often call invariants. In this case it asserts that no person can be both a candidate and employed by a company, that the companies registered as employing people should be subscribers of the agency and that the inverse of the relation *employs* is a partial function thus stating that employees only work for one company. This, then, is our state abstraction for the problem expressed in terms of the schema *EADataBase*.

21.5.3.2 Schema inclusion

By naming a schema we can refer to it in varying contexts. One such context allows us to include the declaration and predicate of one schema within another, that is, we wish to define a new schema and include within it the same textual declaration and predicate parts that are already defined in another schema. This is called schema inclusion. Assume that we want to specialize our database so that it contains only management candidates; we may proceed as follows:

```
┌─ManagementDataBase──────────
  EADataBase
  management_candidates: 𝔽 PERSON
├──────────────────────────────
  candidates ⊆ management_candidates
└──────────────────────────────
```

Here the declaration contained in *EADataBase* is merged with the additional declaration contained in *ManagementData-Base* and the predicate of the former schema is conjoined with the additional predicate in the second schema. The following re-expression of *ManagementDataBase* is obtained by textual expansion:

```
┌─ManagementDataBase──────────
  candidates: 𝔽 PERSON
  employs: COMPANY↔PERSON
  vacancies: COMPANY→ℕ
  management_candidates: 𝔽 PERSON
├──────────────────────────────
  ran employs ∩ candidates = {}
  dom employs ⊆ dom vacancies
  employs˜ ∈ PERSON↔COMPANY
  candidates ⊆ management_candidates
└──────────────────────────────
```

When no identically named variables are shared between the merged schemas (as in this case) the resultant declaration is the union of the individual declarations. However, when named variables are held in common between the two schemas we have to be more careful. In Z a distinction is made between the terms declaration and signature. A declaration, as we have seen, introduces state variables and the sets from which they are drawn whereas a signature contains the names of the state variables and their normalized types (see Section 21.4.11). Thus, when we encounter two variables with the same name they will be merged into a single instance only if their signatures are the same. Normalization is the process that turns declarations into signatures. However, it should be borne in mind that a declaration is a syntactic object while a signature, a semantic object, is denoted by the declaration.

Having specified the state and its invariant we should consider the initial value of the state, that is, the values that the state variables should adopt when they are first created. Clearly the initial state must satisfy the state invariant. Conventionally the initial state is specified by writing a schema with the same name as that of the state schema to which it refers but prefixed by *Init*. Thus, for *EADataBase*, we might define the following initial state:

```
┌─InitEADataBase──────────────
  EADataBase
├──────────────────────────────
  candidates = {}
  employs = {}
  vacancies = {}
└──────────────────────────────
```

21.5.3.3 Schemas as operations

An examination of the employment agency database requirements reveals that a number of operations are identified. A person *Applies* to be a candidate, a company *Subscribes* to the database and *Hires* and *Fires* employees etc. These are all operations that require specification.

An operation specification has a number of interesting aspects:

1. *State change*. In specifying the effect of an operation we make use of the state variables. Model-based specification is based on the idea of stating what relationships hold between the values of state components before the operation is initiated and after the operation has completed. For instance, if a person wishes to become an employment candidate we will use the *Apply* operation. The effect of the operation, in terms of state changes, is that the value of the state variable *candidates* differs from the initial value by having one new entry, namely the new candidate. In order to state this relationship we need to refer to the initial and final values of any state variable. In Z, by convention, each state variable appears in a decorated and undecorated form. In the decorated form the state variable name has the symbol ' as a suffix and denotes the final state value. The initial state value is undecorated. In the example given above *candidates* refers to the initial state value and *candidates'* refers to the final state value.

2. *Arguments*. Operations often require arguments to be passed in (operationally this models our intuition of passing parameters into an abstract transaction, procedure or function). In Z, and once again by convention, an operation's arguments are modelled by variables decorated with the symbol ?. Arguments are viewed as constants and their values may not be changed.

3. *Results*. Operations may be required to produce results; these are modelled as variables decorated with the symbol ! .

With these conventions in mind we start by specifying the *Apply* operation:

```
┌─Apply──────────────────────────────────
│ candidates,candidates': 𝔽 PERSON
│ employs,employs': COMPANY ⇸ PERSON
│ vacancies,vacancies': COMPANY ⇸ ℕ
│ person?: PERSON
├─────────────────────────────────────────
│ ran employs ∩ candidates = {}
│ dom employs ⊆ candidates = {}
│ ran employs' ∩ candidates' = {}
│ dom employs' ⊆ dom vacancies'
│ employs ˜ ∈ PERSON ⇸ COMPANY
│ employs' ˜ ∈ PERSON ⇸ COMPANY
│ person? ∉ candidates
│ person? ∉ ran employs
│ candidates' = candidates ∪ {person?}
│ employs = employs'
│ vacancies = vacancies'
└─────────────────────────────────────────
```

The first thing to note is that the declaration contains two references to each state variable, one of which is decorated and is taken to refer to the final state value, and one of which is undecorated and taken to refer to the initial state. The predicate contains two copies of the invariant one asserting that it holds on the initial state and the other asserting that it holds on the final state. Additionally, the meaning of the operation is given by a further set of predicates. In this case we are told that the person seeking to be a candidate must not already be a candidate and must not be employed by one of the companies – these assumptions are known as pre-conditions. The effect of the operation is expressed in the following predicate which asserts that the final value of the set *candidates* is the same as the initial value but with *person?* added to it. Finally, we have to assert that the two state variables *employs* and *vacancies* are not changed by the operation. If the pre-condition is not satisfied then the operation is undefined, that is, in the logician's sense of the term, no model my be found to satisfy the specification. Later, we will see how to specify what should happen if our pre-conditions are not satisfied.

To avoid some of the duplication inherent in the style of specification shown above another Z convention has emerged. A schema, called *ΔEADataBase*, is defined as follows:

```
┌─ΔEADataBase────────────────────────────
│ candidates,candidates': 𝔽 PERSON
│ employs,employs': COMPANY ↔ PERSON
│ vacancies,vacancies': COMPANY ⇸ ℕ
├─────────────────────────────────────────
│ ran employs ∩ candidates = {}
│ dom employs ⊆ dom vacancies
│ ran employs' ∩ candidates' = {}
│ dom employs ⊆ dom vacancies'
│ employs ˜ ∈ PERSON ⇸ COMPANY
│ employs' ˜ ∈ PERSON ⇸ COMPANY
└─────────────────────────────────────────
```

Using schema inclusion we can respecify the apply operation using the Δ (delta) convention.

```
┌─Apply──────────────────────────────────
│ ΔEADataBase
│ person?: PERSON
├─────────────────────────────────────────
│ person? ∉ candidates
│ person? ∈ ran employs
│ candidates' = candidates ∪ {person}
│ employs = employs'
│ vacancies = vacancies'
└─────────────────────────────────────────
```

The Δ (delta) convention should be used in operations where a state change will take place, i.e. where one or more of the state variables is changed by the operation, and the definition of the Δ schema may be left implicit.

We will now turn our attention to an operation that does not cause a change to the state and in so doing we will discover another schema convention. The operation in question is *Number_of_vacancies*. Given a company name the operation yields the number of registered vacancies associated with the company:

```
┌─NumberOfVacancies──────────────────────
│ candidates,candidates': 𝔽 PERSON
│ employs,employs': COMPANY ↔ PERSON
│ vacancies,vacancies': COMPANY ⇸ ℕ
│ company?: COMPANY
│ result!: ℕ
├─────────────────────────────────────────
│ ran employs ∩ candidates = {}
│ dom employs ⊆ dom vacancies
│ ran employs' ∩ candidates' = {}
│ dom employs' ⊆ dom vacancies'
│ company? ∈ dom vacancies
│ result! = vacancies(company?)
│ candidates = candidates'
│ employs = employs'
│ vacancies = vacancies'
└─────────────────────────────────────────
```

This specification is shortened by introducing the Ξ (xi) convention which follows the form of the Δ convention but also includes predicates to assert that all of the state variables remain unchanged. We can therefore respecify the above operation as follows:

```
┌─NumberOfVacancies──────────────────────
│ ΞEADataBase
│ company?: COMPANY
│ result!: ℕ
├─────────────────────────────────────────
│ company? ∈ dom vacancies
│ result! = vacancies(company?)
└─────────────────────────────────────────
```

The Ξ convention should be used in operations where the state will not be changed by the operations.

21.5.3.4 *Schema decoration*

Schema decoration allows a new schema to be derived from an existing schema by systematically decorating all the variables and references to them in the predicates. Thus, if S is a schema, then S' is a schema with all the variables x_i in S appearing as x'_i in S' and with the types remaining unchanged. The properties of the two schemas are exactly the same. Decorations may be subscripted digits or elements drawn from the set {?,',!}.

Using schema decoration we can revisit the definition of the Δ convention:

```
┌─ΔSchemaName──────
  SchameName
  SchemaName'
```

Schema inclusion results in the declaration of the resulting schema containing both undashed and dashed state variables. The predicate will include assertions that the property holds for both the decorated and undecorated variables, i.e. the property holds both for the initial and final state values.

Revisiting ΔEADatabase we can specify it as follows using schema decoration:

```
┌─ΔEADatabase──────
  EADatabase
  EADatabase'
```

The expansion of the schema has already been shown.

The Ξ convention can be defined similarly but we will require a little more notation before it can be given.

21.5.4 Logical schema operators

The discussion so far has shown what schemas are, how to build them and how to model states and operations using them. In addition, using schema inclusion, we have seen how it is possible to define new schemas which contain the declaration and predicate parts of other schemas.

We will now examine how to combine schemas together using what are called the logical schema operators. These operators provide a flexible mechanism for combining schema fragments together into larger specification units. The operators that we will examine are shown in the *Table 21.8*.

Table 21.8

conjunction	$Schema_1 \wedge Schema_2$
disjunction	$Schema_1 \vee Schema_2$
existential quantification	$\exists declaration \bullet Schema$
universal quantification	$\forall declaration \bullet Schema$
hiding	$Schema \backslash (a_1, a_2, \ldots)$

Note that the logical schema operators are used only to combine schemas. These are not the same operators as those discussed in Section 21.4.

21.5.4.1 Schema conjunction

Schema inclusion, the device used to introduce the Δ and Ξ schemas, achieves exactly the same effect as schema conjunction; essentially it is a syntactic variant of schema conjunction.

When we conjoin two schemas the declarations are merged and the predicates are conjoined to. Schema conjunction has the following effect:

$$NewSchema \triangleq Schema_1 \wedge Schema_2$$

```
┌─New Schema──────
  declaration – derived by merging declarations from
      Schema₁ and Schema₂

  (Schema₁ predicate)
  ∧
  (Schema₂ predicate)
```

Clearly *NewSchema* will be satisfied when both the predicates from *Schema₁* and *Schema₂* are satisfied.

Consider the schema *NumberOfVacancies*. There are three aspects to this operation:

1. The introduction of the state variables and their associated predicates.
2. The introduction of the state variables and predicates, suitably decorated, to refer to the values of the final state variables and their invariant properties.
3. The argument and result variables of the operation together with any associated predicates.

Items (1) and (2) are addressed by the use of ΞEADataBase. Item (3) can be captured by the following schema:

```
┌─NumberOfVacanciesMain──────
  EADataBase
  company?: COMPANY
  result!: ℕ

  company? ∈ dom vacancies
  result! = vacancies(company?)
```

Using schema conjunction we can now re-specify *NumberOf-Vacancies* as follows:

$$NumberOfVacancies \triangleq \Xi EADataBase \wedge$$
$$NumberOfVacanciesMain$$

Here we define the schema *NumberOfVacancies* as the conjunction of the two schemas cited on the right-hand side of the ≜ symbol. If the schemas were expanded the resultant schema would be exactly the same as expanding the original version of *NumberOfVacancies*.

In similar style, using schema conjunction, we can re-visit the definition of the Δ convention:

$$\Delta SchemaName \triangleq SchemaName \wedge SchemaName'$$

21.5.4.2 Schema disjunction

This second operator works in an analogous manner to schema conjunction. However, rather than forming the conjunct of the two predicates, they are combined by disjunction. Declaration merging follows the familiar pattern. The predicate of the resulting schema will be satisfied if either disjunct is true or if both are true. We will now examine how disjunction is conventionally used. The effects of schema disjunction may be viewed as follows:

$$NewSchema = Schema_1 \vee Schema_2$$

```
┌─New Schema──────
  declaration – derived by merging declarations from
      Schema₁ and Schema₂

  (Schema₁ predicate)
  ∨
  (schema₂ predicate)
```

NewSchema will be satisfied when either *Schema₁* is satisfied or *Schema₂* is satisfied or when both are satisfied. In the latter case, that is, when both disjuncts are simultaneously true, the result determined by *NewSchema* is non-deterministic in that a result may be determined by either clause.

Consider the *NumberOfVacancies* operation again. Following the introduction of a new free type we could re-specify the operation as follows:

$$Error::= success \mid undefined\_company$$

```
┌─NumberOfVacancies────────
 ΞEADataBase
 company?: COMPANY
 vacs!: ℕ
 err!: Error
 ──────────────────────────
 (company? ∈ dom vacancies
 vacs! = vacancies(company?)
 err! = success)
 ∨ (company? ∉ dom vacancies
 err! = undefined_company)
```

Using schema disjunction this specification may be broken up by employing the following schemas:

```
┌─VacsOk───────────────────
 ΞEADataBase
 company?: COMPANY
 vacs!: ℕ
 err!: Error
 ──────────────────────────
 company? ∈ dom vacancies
 vacs! = vacancies(company?)
 err! = success
```

```
┌─VacsFailed───────────────
 ΞEADataBase
 company?: COMPANY
 err!: Error
 ──────────────────────────
 company? ∉ dom vacancies
 err! = undefined_company
```

$$NumberOfVacancies \triangleq VacsOk \lor VacsFailed$$

The value of *vacs!* is undefined in the case of the *VacsFailed* disjunct; all that can be said of the value is that it will be a natural number.

21.5.4.3 Using schema conjunction and disjunction

We will now consider a slightly larger example showing how schema disjunction and conjunction may be combined within a schema expression. The operation *Hire* is used where a company with vacancies hires a person. We will assume that the operation returns the number of remaining vacancies associated with a particular company.

As can be seen, we have a fairly extensive pre-condition associated with this operation. Now all of the operations we have specified so far have constraining pre-conditions. If these pre-conditions are *not* satisfied, then the operation is undefined. During the initial specification activity it is reasonable to ignore these conditions; nevertheless, we will need to address them

```
┌─BasicHire────────────────────────────
 ΔEADataBase
 company?: COMPANY
 person?: PERSON
 vacs!: ℕ
 ──────────────────────────────────────
 person? ∈ candidates
 company? ∈ dom vacancies
 person? ∉ ran employs
 vacancies(company?) > 0
 candidates' = candidates \ {person?}
 vacancies' = vacancies ⊕ {company? ↦
   vacancies(company?) − 1}
 employs' = employs ∪ {company? ↦ person?}
 vacs! = vacancies'(company?)
```

eventually. Taking the above example as a case in question let us introduce a new output called *result!* which will be set to *ok* if the pre-condition is satisfied and to a specific failure message if one or other pre-condition fails to be satisfied. Given the new output, we can produce a number of individual schemas each specifying what will happen if a given pre-condition is false.

We start by introducing a new type:

$$Response::= ok \mid invalid\_company \mid no\_vacancies \mid$$
$$not\_candidate \mid employed$$

The first schema asserts that *result!* is set to *ok*:

```
┌─HireOk Response─
 result!: Response
 ─────────────────
 result! = ok
```

The second schema deals with the case where the name of the company, provided as an argument, is not valid. In this case we assert that no change is made to the state and that *result!* is the same value as *invalid_company*:

```
┌─InvalidCompany───────────
 ΞEADataBase
 company?: COMPANY
 result!: Response
 ──────────────────────────
 company? ∉ dom vacancies
 result! = invalid_company
```

The following three schemas should be fairly self-evident as they follow the style employed above:

```
┌─No Vacancies─────────────
 ΞEADataBase
 company?: COMPANY
 result!: Response
 ──────────────────────────
 vacancies(company?) = 0
 result! = no_vacancies
```

```
┌─NotCandidate──────────
 ΞEADataBase
 person?: PERSON
 result!: Response
 ├─────────────────
 person? ∉ candidates
 result! = not_candidate
```

```
┌─Employed──────────
 ΞEADataBase
 person?: PERSON
 result!: Response
 ├─────────────────
 person? ∈ ran employs
 result! = employed
```

With this subsidiary schemas defined the *Hire* operation may be specified as follows:

$$Hire \triangleq Basic\,Hire \wedge HireOk\,Response \vee$$
$$InvalidCompany \vee NoVacancies \vee$$
$$NotCandidate \vee Employed$$

Schema conjunction and disjunction have been combined to provide the specification of a fairly complex operation. We have built the specification from a number of simpler parts, each developed in the form of a schema. In examining the final specification the following point should be noted. The exceptions are specified as four disjunctions. Examining each we see that they are not mutually exclusive, that is several may be true at the same time. For instance, the candidate may be invalid and the company may have no vacancies. How should these exceptions be reported? With what precedence? The answer is that the precedence is not determined and a would-be implementor can determine which exception to report. As discussed later on in this section the effect of *Hire*, in certain circumstances, is potentially non-deterministic.

21.5.4.4 Schema hiding

Name space management is an important consideration that must be taken into account when developing specifications. In modern programming languages and in many specification languages it is possible to develop specification fragments within their own internal name spaces. Names can be made visible by explicitly declaring them as being visible. A different convention has been employed in Z. When we investigated schema inclusion it was clear that the declaration name space of the included schema was made visible within the including schema. Similarly, the effect of the schema conjunction and disjunction was to produce a new schema where the constituent name spaces were merged together. In certain circumstances this may not be desirable and the ability to limit the visibility of names becomes a distinct advantage. To achieve this, Z provides a facility called schema hiding.

Consider the *BasicHire* operation. Assume we wish to specify a more limited operation that does not produce a result. One way of achieving this is to make *vacs!* invisible outside of the schema. This may be achieved as follows:

$$LimitedHire \triangleq BasicHire \backslash (vacs!)$$

This operation hides all the bracketed names. Hiding is achieved by removing the named variables from the declaration and making them part of the predicate by existentially quantifying them into the predicate. The effect is as follows:

```
┌─LimitedHire──────────────
 ΔEADataBase
 company?: COMPANY
 person?: PERSON
 ├──────────────────────
 person? ∈ candidates
 company? ∈ dom vacancies
 person? ∉ ran employs
 vacancies(company?) > 0
 candidates' = candidates \ {person?}
 vacancies' = vacancies ⊕ {company? ↦
    vacancies(company?) − 1}
 employs' = employs ∪ {company? ∪ person? ↦}
 ∃vacs!: ℕ •
    vacs! = vacancies'(company?)
```

As can be seen, *vacs!* becomes an existentially quantified variable which is only introduced into the predicate part of the schema. The name has been removed from the declaration part and is no longer visible outside of the schema *LimitedHire*.

The same effect can be achieved through the use of schema quantification, which has the effect of quantifying already named variables within the schema. Schema quantification is written as:

$$\forall declarations \bullet Schema$$
$$\exists declarations \bullet Schema$$

For instance, *LimitedHire* can be specified using schema quantification:

$$LimitedHire \triangleq \exists vacs!: \mathbb{N} \bullet BasicHire$$

The introduction of the quantifier binds the declaration of *vacs!* within *BasicHire* and thus makes it invisible outside *LimitedHire*.

21.5.5 Schemas within mathematical expressions

So far we have discovered what schemas are, what they are used for and how to construct them. We have used schemas to describe state and operations, and we have seen how to include one within another and how to employ some basic schema calculus operations. In this section we will examine how schemas can be used as part of our general mathematical language.

In what follows it is advisable to forget the idea of schemas modelling operations and states. Rather we should view them as a convenient way of bundling up a declaration and constraining predicates in a package to which we give a name.

21.5.5.1 Schemas as declarations

Consider the schema:

```
┌─S──────
 x: ℕ
 y: ℤ
 ├──────
 x > y
```

We can write quantified expressions involving S having the general form:

$\forall S \bullet predicate$ or $\forall S \,|\, constraint \bullet predicate$
$\exists S \bullet predicate$ or $\exists S \,|\, constraint \bullet predicate$

Here the schema S provides the declaration and constraint for the predicate (see Section 21.4). Thus:

$\forall S \bullet x^2 \geqslant y^2$

expands to the following quantified expression:

$\forall x: \mathbb{N};\ y: \mathbb{Z} \,|\, x > y \bullet x^2 \geqslant y^2$

This is true. Similarly:

$\exists S \,|\, y > 0 \bullet x \neq 0$

expands to:

$\exists x: \mathbb{N};\ y: \mathbb{Z} \,|\, x > y \wedge y > 0 \bullet x \neq 0$

In this latter case we are augmenting the existing schema constraint.

21.5.5.2 Schemas as predicates

A schema can be used wherever a predicate would be appropriate. Used in this context the schema is first normalized and the resulting signature discarded; the predicate part is retained. As the signature is discarded the names referred to in the predicate part must be bound either within the signature of an enclosing schema, or by having been introduced in a quantified or set comprehension expression which is more locally scoped. An example of using a schema as a predicate is shown below:

$\forall x \mathbb{Z} \bullet \exists y: \mathbb{Z} \bullet S$

which expands to:

$\forall x \mathbb{Z} \bullet \exists y: \mathbb{Z} \bullet x \in \mathbb{N} \wedge x > y$

21.5.5.3 Schemas in set comprehension expressions

Recall the general structure of set comprehension expressions outlined in Section 21.4.2:

$\{declaration \,|\, constraint \bullet term\}$

It follows from the discussion on schema quantification that a schema can be used to provide a declaration and constraint in a set comprehension expression. The set of pairs, (x,y), of positive integers may be specified as follows:

$Pairs = = \{S \,|\, y \geqslant 0 \bullet (x,y)\}$

This expands as follows:

$Pairs = = \{x: \mathbb{N};\ y: \mathbb{Z} \,|\, x > y \wedge y \geqslant 0 \bullet (x,y)\}$

21.5.5.4 Schemas defining unique values

μ-expressions have the following form and are best explained by an example:

μ $declaration \,|\, constraint \bullet expression$
μ $Schema \,|\, constraint \bullet expression$

For example, the expression:

$Value = = (\mu x: \mathbb{N};\ y: \mathbb{Z} \,|\, x > y \wedge y = 0 \wedge\ x - y = 2 \bullet x * y)$

has the value and type generated by expression. In order for a value to be generated there must be a unique assignment of values to the variables declared in the declaration which also must satisfy the constraint. For the example shown above the values assigned to x and y are 2 and 0 respectively; the value of the overall expression is 0 and its type is $\mathbb{Z}$. If there is no unique assignment then the μ-expression is undefined.

Using the schema S the μ-expression may be alternatively formulated as follows:

$Value = = (\mu S \,|\, y = 0 \wedge\ x - y = 2 \bullet x * y)$

Here the declaration within S introduces the variables x and y which must satisfy the predicate contained within S and the additional constraint imposed within the μ-expression.

21.5.5.4 Schemas and theorems

The axioms of a Z specification (i.e. those statements that are assumed to be true) include not only the axioms of predicate calculus and set theory but also the statements of the specification itself. We may attempt to prove properties of the specification by using these axioms.

Theorems in Z are stated as follows:

$hypothesis \vdash consequence$

This states that, under the assumptions contained in the *hypothesis*, we can prove the *consequence*.

Schemas may be used in theorems and in fact are commonly used to denote standard proof obligations. To illustrate the use of schemas for stating theorems we will consider two examples. The first is a proof obligation which requires us to show that the initial state value satisfies the state predicate, that is, the set of initial states is not empty. Using schema S and the following initial value for S the proof obligation may be stated as shown:

```
┌─InitS──────
│ S
│ ├──────────
│ x = 3 ∧ y = 1
└─
```

$\vdash \exists S \bullet InitS$

Expanding schemas yields the following:

$\vdash \exists x: \mathbb{N};\ y: \mathbb{Z} \,|\, x > y \bullet x = 3 \wedge y = 1$

The second theorem relates to a property of S:

$S \vdash x - y \geqslant 0$

Once again, expanding schemas reveals the following expression:

$x: \mathbb{N};\ y: \mathbb{Z} \,|\, x > y \vdash x - y \geqslant 0$

21.5.6 Schemas as types – schema variables

So far we have limited ourselves to examining what a schema is and showing how various schema operators work. Here we will examine how a schema may be used to define a type and allow the declaration of so called schema variables.

Before considering how to construct schema types we need to examine what is meant by the concepts of binding, type of a binding, type of a schema, a binding satisfying a schema and a binding formation. In the following discussion the notation used to describe binding and binding type are not part of Z, rather, they are used for descriptive purposes only.

A collection of named variables, (v_i), each with an associated type, (t_i), and typed value, (a_i), is known as a binding and is often written as follows:

$$v_1 \rightarrow a_1; \; v_2 \rightarrow :a_2; \ldots$$

A binding need only honour the underlying types of the variables and no ordering is implied, i.e. the binding associates values with the collection of variable names. A binding, therefore, is a value and has an associated type. The type of this binding is written:

$$\lhd v_1 : t_1; v_2 : t_2; \ldots \rhd$$

The signature (or type) of a schema is, once again, a collection of named and typed variables and thus the signature may be viewed as the type of a binding as described above. However, a schema also has a predicate which potentially further restricts values that the variables may adopt. A binding will only satisfy a schema when its values satisfy the predicate associated with the schema. In addition, the schema may be viewed as denoting a set of bindings, precisely those that satisfy the signature and predicate.

The following example should clarify some of these ideas. We start with *ASchema*:

```
┌─ASchema──────
│ a: ℕ
│ b: ℤ
├──────────────
│ b = 2*a
└──────────────
```

Applying the rules of normalization we can re-write the schema as follows:

```
┌─ASchema──────
│ a: ℤ
│ b: ℤ
├──────────────
│ a ⩾ 0
│ b = 2*a
└──────────────
```

The type of *ASchema* is therefore $\lhd a: \mathbb{Z}; \; b: \mathbb{Z} \rhd$. The following is a binding, $a \rightarrow 3; \; b \rightarrow 4$; its type is $\lhd a: \mathbb{Z}; \; b: \mathbb{Z} \rhd$. However, while this binding has the same type as *ASchema* it clearly does not satisfy the schema's predicate. On the other hand, the following binding has the same type and also satisfies the schema – $a \rightarrow 3; \; b \rightarrow 6$.

A binding formation, written θ*Schemaname*, is a binding which associates each variable x_i in *Schemaname* with the value of that variable currently in scope. The binding formation does not declare any variable names; all the names referenced in *Schemaname* must be in scope. The θ operator is often used with a decorated schema name, thus θ*Schemaname'*. In this context θ*Schemaname'* denotes a binding the type of which is the same as θ*Schemaname* but the value of which is determined by the decorated variables, x'_i, that are currently in scope.

Given an initialization schema:

```
┌─InitASchema──
│ ASchema
├──────────────
│ a = 4
│ b = 8
└──────────────
```

then θ*ASchema* would represent the binding $a \rightarrow 4; \; b \rightarrow 8$. Two bindings are said to be the same when they are of the same type and the correspondingly named components in each binding have the same value.

By way of a diversion we can now re-visit the definition of the Ξ schema naming convention. Using binding formations this convention can be defined as follows:

```
┌─ΞASchema──────────
│ ASchema
│ ASchema'
├───────────────────
│ θASchema = θASchema'
└───────────────────
```

The predicate asserts that the binding *ASchema* is the same as the binding *ASchema'*.

We can now examine how schema variables are constructed. We can define a declaration containing a schema variable. The type of this variable will be that of the underlying type of the schema and values of the variable will clearly be bindings. Given the following free type definition:

$$Skill ::= manual \mid clerical \mid management$$

a schema variable may be declared as follows:

```
┌─DataBases────────────────────
│ databases: Skill ⤚ EADataBase
└──────────────────────────────
```

As can be seen, we now have a database associated with each of the three different skill categories. How do we access the contents of these databases? The first approach involves selecting components from the database schema. The form of a selection is as follows:

$$schema\_variable.schema\_component$$

For instance, let us define an operation that returns the number of candidates by selected employment category.

```
┌─Category Count───────────────
│ ΞDataBases
│ skill?: Skill
│ numbers!: ℕ
├──────────────────────────────
│ numbers! = #(databases(skill?)).candidates
└──────────────────────────────
```

The expression *databases(skill?)* selects the database appropriate to the employment skill. We then extract the set of candidates by selecting the variable *candidates* using the notation, *(databases(skill?)).candidates*.

An alternative approach would be to specify *EADataBase* and its associated operations and then to use these specification components to build up higher level specifications. The following example, using these ideas, employs schemas within general mathematical expressions as explained in Section 21.5.5.

We start with an operation called *GeneralHire* which, given a skill category, company and person, will hire that person to the company within the indicated skill category database. We will make use of the already specified *LimitedHire* operation. We choose to re-name *LimitedHire* to avoid parameter name clashes:

```
┌─GeneralHire──────────────────────────────
 ΔDataBases
 skill?: Skill
 company?: COMPANY
 person?: PERSON
 ├──────────────────────────────────────
 databases' = database ⊕
   {LimitedHire₁ | θEADataBase₁ = databases(skill?) ∧
     company?₁ = company? ∧ person?₁ = person?•
     skill?↦θEADataBase'₁}
```

Alternatively, this operation may be specified as:

```
┌─GeneralHire──────────────────────────────
 ΔDataBases
 skill?: Skill
 company?: COMPANY
 person?: PERSON
 ├──────────────────────────────────────
 databases' = databases ⊕ {skill?↦
   (μLimitedHire₁ | θEADataBase₁ = databases(skill?) ∧
     company?₁ = company? ∧ person?₁ = person?•
     θEADataBase'₁)}
```

This style of specification employs schema types to construct what may be called abstract data types. A fuller discussion of this topic in the context of object-oriented specification may be found in Hall (1990).

21.5.7 Non-deterministic and loose specifications

This survey of Z is completed with a short discussion of non-deterministic and loose specifications. In producing a specification care must be taken to state only what is absolutely necessary and to avoid over specification. In so doing we encounter two particular situations that require careful consideration.

Consider the following specification:

```
┌─SetValue──────────────
 upper,upper': ℤ
 lower,lower': ℤ
 reading,reading': ℤ
 ├─────────────────────
 upper = upper'
 lower = lower'
 upper ⩾ reading' ∧ reading ⩾ lower
```

Here we are told that reading is to be between upper and lower; no specific value is given. This specification is non-deterministic in that the value chosen need only satisfy the predicate and the same value need not be chosen in identical circumstances. Essentially, non-determinism allows an arbitrary choice of value to be taken, subject to any constraining predicates, and in no two similar circumstances need the same value be selected, i.e. it is not determined which value will be taken.

What, then, is meant by a loose specification? Consider the same example again. Between the values of *upper* and *lower* there will be a potential range of values. Given an upper and lower limit we could always determine which value is chosen by specifying a function of the following form:

```
│ set_value: ℤ × ℤ → ℤ
│ ────────────────────
│ ∀t₁,t₂: ℤ •set_value(t₁,t₂)∈ℤ
```

Using this function, the value assigned to reading could be specified as follows:

$$reading' = set\_value(upper, lower)$$

It has been stated that the value of *reading'* is determined by the function *set_value*. What has not been stated is the particular value that will be chosen, that is, a family of potential functions is specified, one of which will consistently be chosen, i.e. given the same arguments the function will always return the same result. Looseness in specifications is therefore deterministic in that a particular value is specified. However, what is left open is which particular value is consistently selected.

21.5.8 Conclusion

This completes the walkthrough of the Z specification language. There are many aspects of the language that have not been covered and the interested reader is referred to Spivey (1989) for a complete definition of the language. However, sufficient of the language's features have been examined to allow investigation of the development of a reasonably comprehensive specification example.

21.6 A sensor system

This section follows the development of a model-based specification for a sensor system. The informal requirements may be stated as follows.

We are required to develop a heat sensing system for a building. The building comprises a number of rooms, each of which will contain one or more temperature sensors. Individual sensors have a number of attributes. First, a sensor has a unique identifier or code by which it will be known. Second, a sensor has two temperature threshold values, called 'upper' and 'lower', and a current recording of the ambient temperature. An ambient temperature reading which is higher than 'upper' or less than 'lower' will cause the sensor to signal a temperature threshold condition. Third, a sensor may be in one of two states – enabled or disabled. An enabled sensor is capable of reacting to temperature threshold conditions. A disabled sensor can record the current temperature reading but will not react to temperature threshold conditions. Sensors are scanned regularly at ten-second intervals.

In addition to the sensors the system has a logging function and an alarm function. The alarm function registers temperature threshold conditions for enabled sensors and records the presence of inoperable sensors. When a temperature threshold condition occurs in a room a light will be illuminated showing the room in which the condition has arisen and a buzzer will also be sounded. The light will remain on as long as a threshold condition exists in the room; the buzzer may be switched off by the operator. The log function records the state of the sensors and the alarms every ten minutes. In addition, the operator can force a logging action to take place at any time or force a recording of the state of a particular sensor.

From the operational point of view an operator may perform the following additional operations:

1. Add and remove a sensor to/from the system.
2. Enable and disable a sensor.
3. Display the state of all the sensors in a particular room.
4. Display the current temperature reading for a specified sensor together with its temperature threshold values.
5. Change the threshold temperature values on a particular sensor or for all of the sensors in a particular room.

Having examined the requirements, an entity relationship diagram, shown in *Figure 21.2*, is produced in order to gain an understanding of the important entities identified in the requirements and the significant relationships that hold between them. *Table 21.9* lists the important entities and relationships recorded in the diagram. At the end of this section, in *Table 21.10*, we will examine how these have been modelled within the specification. We now examine the attributes associated with each entity:

SENSOR(sensor-name, status, upper, lower, reading)
ROOM(room-name)
ALARMS(room-name, bell, light)
LOG(time)

The attributes of **SENSOR** are fairly straightforward and are clearly identified in the requirements. **ROOM** shows the asso-

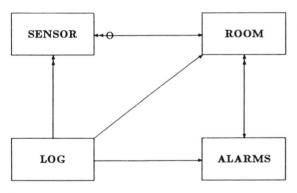

Figure 21.2 Entity relationship diagram for the sensor system

Table 21.9 Entities and relationships in the sensor system

Entity	Entity set
Sensor	Sensors
Room	Rooms
Alarms	Alarms
Log	Log

Source entity	Destination entity	Relationship
Sensor	Room	sensor_located_in
Room	Sensor	room_sensors
Room	Alarms	room_alarm
Alarms	Room	alarmed_rooms
Log	Sensor	logged_sensor
Log	Room	logged_room
Log	Alarms	logged_alarm

ciation between a room and the sensors in that room. The entity **ALARMS** associates rooms with alarm conditions. The attributes bell and light indicate if a temperature threshold condition is present or not in at least one sensor associated with the room. Lastly, the entity **LOG** records the state of the system on a regular basis. The log will contain either information on individual sensors or information on all sensors, their associations with particular rooms and the state of the alarms.

With this informal understanding of the problem we will approach the development of a formal specification of the sensor system.

21.6.1 Sensor

We start by introducing a given type, *SENSOR_ID*, of sensor names. Similarly, we need to specify what we mean by the status of a sensor:

[SENSOR_ID]
Status:: = *enabled* | *disabled*

We now specify the *Sensor* state – this has been derived directly from the list of sensor attributes identified above:

```
┌─Sensor──────────────────
│ sensor_name: SENSOR_ID
│ status: Status
│ lower: ℤ
│ upper: ℤ
│ reading: ℤ
│────────────────────────
│ lower ⩽ upper
└─────────────────────────
```

As a rule, when we define a state schema, we should consider its initial state values. In the case of a sensor the initial state values will be parameterized to the extent that when a sensor is created its upper and lower temperature threshold values will be set and a status assigned. As the temperature values will be provided by the user the initialization of the state may be viewed as being accomplished by an operation.

What operations do we require to perform on a sensor? Identifying all the operations required on a data item is not a straightforward task. We can often make a reasonably accurate guess at some of them but the task of developing a specification and discussing it with the customer and other interested parties often leads to a fuller understanding of the operations required. Here, then, is our first guess:

1. *InitSensor* – initialize a sensor.
2. *ChangeTempThresholds* – change the temperature threshold values on a sensor.
3. *ChangeStatus* – alter the status field of a sensor.
4. *ChangeReading* – alter the current values of the sensor reading

Note that none of these operations is directly available to the users of the system. User commands on sensors are all directed at the set of sensors, that is, they are all parameterized by the name of the sensor to which they apply. The following operations are specific to a single sensor and will be used in the specification of the user operations. In what follows, user-level operations will be prefixed by *User*.

We start with the initialization operation. Here we require to set the name of the sensor and the temperature readings together with the initial status setting. This specification is loose in the sense discussed in Section 21.5.7:

```
┌─InitSensor─────────────────
│ Sensor
│ name?: SENSOR_ID
│ upper?: ℤ
│ lower?: ℤ
├─────────────────────────────
│ sensor_name = name?
│ status = disabled
│ upper = upper?
│ lower = lower?
│ reading = set_value(upper,lower)
└─────────────────────────────
```

The next operation allows us to change the temperature threshold values of the sensor:

```
┌─ChangeTempThresholds────────
│ ΔSensor
│ upper?: ℤ
│ lower?: ℤ
├─────────────────────────────
│ upper' = upper? ∧ lower' = lower? ∧ reading' = reading
│ sensor_name' = sensor_name ∧ status' = status
└─────────────────────────────
```

The following two operations are fairly self-evident. *ChangeStatus* allows the status of a sensor to be changed while *ChangeReading* allows the currently recorded reading to be changed:

```
┌─ChangeStatus────────────────
│ ΔSensor
│ newstat?: Status
├─────────────────────────────
│ status' = newstat?
│ sensor_name' = sensor_name
│ ((status' = enabled ∧ reading' = set_value(upper,lower))
│ ∨
│ (status' = disabled ∧ reading' = reading))
│ lower' = lower ∧ upper' = upper
└─────────────────────────────
```

Note too that this operation is loose. Ideally, we would only like to state that *reading* is between *upper* and *lower*, rather than give it a specific value. This can be accomplished as discussed in Hall (1990) but requires a more detailed discussion of Z than has been given in this chapter.

```
┌─ChangeReading───────────────
│ ΔSensor
│ newreading?: ℤ
├─────────────────────────────
│ reading' = newreading?
│ sensor_name' = sensor_name ∧ status' = status
│ lower' = lower ∧ upper = upper'
└─────────────────────────────
```

These, then, are all the operations required on an individual sensor.

21.6.2 The entity set Sensors

The set of sensors can now be modelled using the following schema. Here we index each sensor by its unique name using a partial injection. The invariant states that each sensor is indexed by its unique sensor name:

```
┌─Sensors─────────────────────
│ sensors: SENSOR_ID ⇸ Sensor
│ ∀s: dom sensors • (sensors(s)).sensor_name = S
└─────────────────────────────
```

The initial state of *Sensors* is:

```
┌─InitSensors─────────────────
│ Sensors
├─────────────────────────────
│ sensors = {}
└─────────────────────────────
```

What operations apply to sensors alone? Essentially there are the following user operations, most of which were identified in the statement of requirements. Thus:

1. *UserEnableSensor* – set a specific sensor to enabled status.
2. *UserDisableSensor* – set a specific sensor to disabled status.
3. *UserDisplaySensorReading* – display the state of a particular sensor.
4. *UserChangeThresholds* – change the temperature threshold values on a particular sensor.

These operations can be specified using the basic sensor operations specified in the previous section. We start by ignoring exception conditions.

The *EnableSensor* operation makes use of the *ChangeStatus* operation defined on sensors:

```
┌─EnableSensor────────────────
│ ΔSensors
│ name?: SENSOR_ID
├─────────────────────────────
│ name? ∈ dom sensors
│ sensors' = sensors ⊕
│   {ChangeStatus | θSensor = sensors(name?) ∧
│     newstat? = enabled • name? ↦ θSensor'}
└─────────────────────────────
```

The operations *DisplaySensorReading* and *ChangeThresholds* are fairly straightforward and should present no problem:

```
┌─DisplaySensorReading────────
│ ΞSensors
│ name?: SENSOR_ID
│ upper!: ℤ
│ lower!: ℤ
│ reading!: ℤ
├─────────────────────────────
│ name? ∈ dom sensors
│ upper! = (sensors(name?)).upper
│ lower! = (sensors(name?)).lower
│ reading! = (sensors(name?)).reading
└─────────────────────────────
```

```
┌─DisableSensor───────────────
│ ΔSensors
│ name?: SENSOR_ID
├─────────────────────────────
│ name? ∈ dom sensors
│ sensors' = sensors ⊕
│   {ChangeStatus | θSensor = sensors(name?) ∧
│     newstat? = disabled • name? ↦ θSensor'}
└─────────────────────────────
```

$$
\begin{array}{|l}
\hline
\text{ChangeThresholds} \\
\Delta Sensors \\
name?: SENSOR\_ID \\
upper?: \mathbb{Z} \\
lower?: \mathbb{Z} \\
\hline
name? \in \text{dom } sensors \\
(sensors(name?)).status \neq enabled \\
upper? \geqslant lower? \\
sensors' = sensors \oplus \\
\quad \{ChangeTempThresholds_1 \,|\, \theta Sensor_1 = sensors(name?) \wedge \\
\quad\quad upper?_1 = upper? \wedge lower?_1 = lower? \bullet name? \mapsto \theta Sensor_1'\} \\
\hline
\end{array}
$$

All three operations require the named sensor to be valid. Additionally, *ChangeThresholds* requires that the upper temperature value is greater than or equal to the lower setting and that the status of the sensor is disabled, i.e. the temperature threshold settings may only be changed on disabled sensors.

A number of these operations have pre-conditions, that is, they make certain assumptions about the initial state and/or the arguments that are provided. If these assumptions are not true then the operation is undefined. We will now examine how to handle these pre-conditions. *EnableSensor* and *DisplaySensor-Reading* are only defined if the named sensor is in the domain of *sensors*. *ChangeThresholds* has a similar restriction but also requires that the upper temperature threshold setting is greater than or equal to the lower setting. These situations are dealt with as follows. We start with the introduction of a new type which will be used to signal exceptions:

$$SensorOpResponse ::= ok \,|\, invalid\_sensor\_name \,|$$
$$invalid\_temperature\_ranges \,|\, sensor\_enabled$$

We then specify the following schemas that state what happens in the case of satisfactory and unsatisfactory invocation of the operations.

The first schema asserts that the output parameter result is set to *ok*:

$$
\begin{array}{|l}
\hline
\text{SensorOkResponse} \\
result!: SensorOpResponse \\
\hline
result! = ok \\
\hline
\end{array}
$$

SensorEnabled establishes that a particular sensor is enabled and reports the fact:

$$
\begin{array}{|l}
\hline
\text{SensorEnabled} \\
\Xi Sensors \\
name?: SENSOR\_ID \\
result!: SensorOpResponse \\
\hline
name? \in \text{dom } sensors \\
(sensors(name?)).status = enabled \\
result! = sensor\_enabled \\
\hline
\end{array}
$$

The following schema asserts that the temperature parameters are wrongly set. It also asserts that the sensor name is valid:

$$
\begin{array}{|l}
\hline
\text{TemperatureRangeError} \\
\Xi Sensors \\
name?: SENSOR\_ID \\
upper?: \mathbb{Z} \\
lower?: \mathbb{Z} \\
result!1: SensorOpResponse \\
\hline
name? \in \text{dom } sensors \\
upper? < lower? \\
result! = invalid\_temperature\_ranges \\
\hline
\end{array}
$$

Finally, the schema *InvalidSensorName* asserts that the name of the sensor supplied is not defined within the state:

$$
\begin{array}{|l}
\hline
\text{InvalidSensorName} \\
\Xi Sensors \\
name?: SENSOR\_ID \\
result!: SensorOpResponse \\
\hline
name? \notin \text{dom } sensors \\
result! = invalid\_sensor\_name \\
\hline
\end{array}
$$

The user-level operations can now be specified employing the following combination of schemas:

$$UserEnableSensor \triangleq (EnableSensor \wedge SensorOkResponse) \vee$$
$$\quad InvalidSensorName$$
$$UserDisableSensor \triangleq (DisableSensor \wedge SensorOkResponse) \vee$$
$$\quad InvalidSensorName$$
$$UserDisplaySensorReading \triangleq (DisplaySensorReading \wedge$$
$$\quad SensorOkResponse) \vee InvalidSensorName$$
$$UserChangeThresholds \triangleq (ChangeThresholds \wedge$$
$$\quad SensorOkResponse) \vee$$
$$\quad InvalidSensorName \vee$$
$$\quad TemperatureRangeError \vee SensorEnabled$$

The last expression contains an instance of a specification which is non-deterministic. If invalid temperature settings are provided for an enabled sensor then the specification does not say which of the two relevant exceptions should be reported.

Finally, we will specify a function which will be used elsewhere in the specification. Given a set of sensors, we require a function that yields the names of those enabled sensors which have temperature threshold exceptions recorded:

$$
\begin{array}{|l}
\hline
sensor\_exception: \mathbb{P}\, Sensor \to \mathbb{P}\, SENSOR\_ID \\
\hline
\forall S: \mathbb{F}\, Sensor \bullet sensor\_exceptions(S) = \\
\quad \{s:S \,|\, s.status = enabled \wedge \\
\quad (s.reading > s.upper \vee s.reading < s.lower) \bullet s.sensor\_name\} \\
\hline
\end{array}
$$

21.6.3 The entity set Rooms

We could approach the specification of a **Room** in exactly the same way as we did for **Sensor**. However, we note that the only attributes of a room are its name and the names of the sensors linked to it. We will therefore only specifiy the entity set *Rooms*. This can be modelled as a relation between *ROOM_ID* and *SENSOR_ID*. Sensors associated with a specific room may be extracted by use of the relational image operator:

[*ROOM_ID*]

There are no operations that apply specifically to *Rooms*, and require no access to other state items, other than initialization of the rooms in the building. We will assume that the system is to be configured with a fixed number of rooms and that the *names* of these rooms are a system constant; to this end we introduce the following constant:

$$| names\_of\_rooms: \mathbb{F}\ ROOM\_ID$$

The schema *Rooms* models the relational association between room names and sensor names. Clearly the domain of the relation will always be a subset of the set of rooms in the building:

┌─ *Rooms* ──────────────
  rooms: $ROOM\_ID \leftrightarrow SENSOR\_ID$
├────────────────────────
  dom *rooms* $\subseteq$ *names_of_rooms*
└────────────────────────

We can now address the initial state. As, initially, no associations will have been made between room names and sensor names (performed by the *UserAddSensor* operation) this relation will be empty:

┌─ *InitRooms* ─
  Rooms
├──────────────
  rooms = {}
└──────────────

The remaining operations that relate to *Rooms* also require access to *Sensors*. We therefore introduce the following schema:

┌─ *RoomsAndSensors* ──────
  Rooms
  Sensors
├──────────────────────────
  ran *rooms* = dom *sensors*
└──────────────────────────

The operations required on rooms are:

1. *UserAddSensor* – to associate a specific sensor to a room.
2. *UserRemoveSensor* – to remove the association between a sensor and a room.
3. *UserDisplayRoomSensors* – display the state of the sensors in a particular room.
4. *UserChangeRoomThresholds* – change the temperature thresholds of all the sensors associated with a particular room.

In the following specifications no consideration has been given to the handling of exception conditions, that is, failures to meet pre-conditions:

┌─ *UserAddSensor* ──────────
  $\Delta RoomsAndSensors$
  name?: $SENSOR\_ID$
  room?: $ROOM\_ID$
  upper?: $\mathbb{Z}$
  lower?: $\mathbb{Z}$
├────────────────────────────
  name? $\notin$ dom *sensors*
  room? $\in$ *names_of_rooms*
  upper? $\geqslant$ *lower*?
  sensors' = *sensors* $\oplus$
    $\{InitSensor_1 \mid name?_1 = name? \wedge upper?_1 = upper? \wedge$
    $lower?_1 = lower? \bullet name? \mapsto \theta Sensor_1\}$
  rooms' = *rooms* $\oplus \{room? \mapsto name?\}$
└────────────────────────────

┌─ *UserRemoveSensor* ──────────
  $\Delta RoomsAndSensors$
  name?: $SENSOR\_ID$
  room?: $ROOM\_ID$
├───────────────────────────────
  room? $\in$ dom *rooms*
  name? $\in$ *rooms*{*room*?}
  (*sensors*(*name*?)).*status* = *disabled*
  rooms' = *rooms* $\rhd \{name?\}$
  sensors' = $\{name?\} \lhd$ *sensors*
└───────────────────────────────

┌─ *UserDisplayRoomSensors* ──────────
  $\Xi RoomsAndSensors$
  room?: $ROOM\_ID$
  sensor_states!: $\mathbb{F}\ Sensor$
├─────────────────────────────────────
  room? $\in$ *names_of_rooms*
  sensor_states! = (*rooms*;*sensors*)(\|{*room*?}\|)
└─────────────────────────────────────

┌─ *UserChangeRoomThresholds* ──────────
  $\Delta RoomsAndSensors$
  room?: $ROOM\_ID$
  upper?: $\mathbb{Z}$
  lower?: $\mathbb{Z}$
├───────────────────────────────────────
  room? $\in$ dom *rooms*
  upper? $\geqslant$ *lower*?
  $(\forall sen:Sensor \mid sen \in$
    $((rooms;sensors)(\|\{room?\}\|)) \bullet sen.status = disabled)$
  sensors' = *sensors* $\oplus$
  $\{sid:(rooms(\|\{room?\}\|));ChangeTempThresholds_1 \mid$
    $upper?_1 = upper? \wedge lower?_1 = lower? \wedge \theta Sensor_1$
    $= sensors'(sid) \bullet sid \mapsto \theta Sensor'_1\}$
  rooms' = *rooms*
└───────────────────────────────────────

The initialization of *RoomsAndSensors* can be defined in terms of the initialization operations specified on its constituent schemas:

$$InitRoomsAndSensors \triangleq InitRooms \wedge InitSensors$$

21.6.4 Alarms

The alarm system is primarily related to rooms. Whenever a sensor associated with a specific room encounters a temperature threshold condition then a visible warning light and audible bell will be activated. For the purposes of this example we will assume that there is a light and bell associated with each room. First, we require the following two free types:

$$Light ::= on \mid off$$
$$Bell ::= ringing \mid silent$$

Two partial functions model the associations between room names and lights and bells respectively. The invariant predicate states that the domains of the two functions are the same and that for any room with a bell ringing the alarm light should also be on – remember the requirement that the user can switch a bell off at any time so a light may be on but the bell off.

```
┌─Alarms──────────────────────────────────
│ signal_lights: ROOM_ID ⇸ Light
│ signal_bells: ROOM_ID ⇸ Bell
├──────────────────────────────────────────
│ dom signal_lights = dom signal_bells
│ ∀room: ROOM_ID | room∈dom signal_bells•
│     signal_bells(room) = ringing ⇒ signal_lights(room) = on
└──────────────────────────────────────────
```

The initial state provides no particular problems – all bells and lights are set to the non-active state:

```
┌─InitAlarms──────────────────────────────
│ Alarms
├──────────────────────────────────────────
│ signal_lights = {r:names_of_rooms • r↦off }
│ signal_bells = {r:names_of_rooms • r↦silent}
└──────────────────────────────────────────
```

There is only one alarm operation – *UserSilenceBell* – which allows a user to silence the bell associated with a specific sensor:

```
┌─UserSilenceBell─────────────────────────
│ ΔAlarms
│ room?: ROOM_ID
├──────────────────────────────────────────
│ room?∈dom signal_bells
│ signal_bells' = signal_bells ⊕ {room?↦silent} ∧
│     signal_light' = signal_light
└──────────────────────────────────────────
```

21.6.5 Building

Before we look at the log sub-system it is worth bringing together some of the components that we have already specified and noting a number of invariant properties that come into being as a result of combining these components. We will introduce a new schema called *Building* which unites *RoomsAndSensors* and *Alarm*:

```
┌─Building────────────────────────────────
│ RoomsAndSensors
│ Alarms
├──────────────────────────────────────────
│ dom rooms ⊆ dom signal_lights
│ (∀r: dom rooms•
│   #(sensor_exception((sensors∘rooms)(r))) > 0 ⇒
│   signal_lights(r) = on)
└──────────────────────────────────────────
```

The invariant associated with *Building* needs some careful consideration. It would be tempting to assert that whenever an enabled sensor in a room had a temperature exception then the respective room's alarm light would be on, and if there were no such exception then the room light would be off. However, life may not be quite so simple. Consider a room with one sensor causing a temperature exception; the light would be activated. If the sensor were then disabled the light would have to be immediately extinguished to preserve the invariant. Our current specification of *UserDisableSensor* does not say anything about lights being extinguished. If we required this to happen then we would need to re-structure the specifications so that *RoomsAndSensors* included *Alarms*. Here we will content ourselves with the light being extinguished at the next ten-second scan point. With this interpretation in mind it is clear that there is the possibility of a room light being on but there being no enabled sensor in that room with a temperature threshold condition. Based on this requirement we can insist on the weaker invariant

that if there is an enabled sensor with a temperature threshold condition then the light will be on or, alternatively, if the light is off then there will be no enabled sensor associated with the room which is recording a temperature exception.

The main operation at this level is:

1. *SensorTimeScan*, which takes place every 10 s on a sensor-by-sensor basis. This operation lies at the heart of the sensor system as it specifies how temperature threshold conditions are to be handled and how they interact with the alarm function. The frequency of invocation will be assumed informally.

In specifying the following operation we can build on the predicate associated with the *Building* schema. The operation must specify the following:

1. That the sensor data for the specific sensor being polled must be updated with the current reading.
2. That for each room:
   (a) If there is no enabled sensor with a temperature exception then the alarm light will be off. The *Alarm* schema predicate ensures that if the light is off then the bell will be off.
   (b) If, in the final state, there is a temperature exception recorded then, if initially the room warning light was on, the bell state will be left unchanged. However, if initially the light was off then the bell will be set ringing. Activation of the light in the presence of a temperature threshold condition is ensured by the *Building* schema predicate.
3. That rooms remains unchanged.

```
┌─SensorTimeScan──────────────────────────
│ ΔBuilding
│ name?: SENSOR_ID
│ newreading?: ℤ
├──────────────────────────────────────────
│ name?∈dom sensors
│ sensors' = sensors ⊕
│   {ChangeReading | θSensor = sensors(name?)•
│    name?→θSensor'}
│ (∀r: ROOM_ID | r∈dom rooms•
│   ((#(sensor_exception((sensors'∘rooms)({r}))) = 0) ∧
│   signal_lights'(r) = off)
│   ∨
│   ((#(sensor_exception((sensors'∘rooms)({r}))) > 0) ∧
│   ((signal_lights(r) = off ∧ signal_bells'(r) = ringing)
│   ∨
│   (signal_lights(r) = on ∧ signal_bells'(r)
│    = signal_bells(r)))))
│ rooms = rooms'
└──────────────────────────────────────────
```

The initial state of *Building* is specified using existing initial state specifications:

$$InitBuilding \triangleq InitRoomsAndSensors \land InitAlarms$$

21.6.6 Log

We can now approach the specification of the log sub-system. Recall that every ten minutes the log function records the state of the sensors, the alarm system and the relation between the sensors and rooms. In addition, the state of particular sensors can be recorded at will by the operators using the *UserSensorLog* operation. Log information will be time-tagged, showing when the log data was collected. We therefore need a new type with an ordering relation and, to achieve this, our notion of time is modelled on the natural numbers as follows:

$Time == \mathbb{N}$

The state includes two functions modelling system and sensor log events and a variable called *system_time* modelling an internal clock. No operation has been specified which increments *system_limit*; however, we will assume that it is progressively incremented:

```
┌─Log───────────────────────────
│ log_system: Time ⇸ Building
│ log_sensor: Time ⇸ Sensor
│ system_time: Time
│ ──────────────────────────────
│ ∀t:dom log_sensor • t ⩽ system_time
│ ∀t:dom log_system • t ⩽ system_time
└───────────────────────────────
```

The log operations are clearly:

1. *SystemGeneralLog* – logging initiated by the system.
2. *UserGeneralLog* – logging initiated by the operator.
3. *UserSensorLog* – operator initiated logging of a specific sensor.
4. Various analysis operations allowing statistical or specific enquiries to be made of the logged data. These operations will not be specified here.

The first operation, *SystemGeneralLog*, is initiated every ten minutes. We will assume, informally, that this operation takes place with the stated frequency:

```
┌─SystemGeneralLog──────────────────────
│ ΞBuilding
│ ΔLog
│ ───────────────────────────────────────
│ log_system' = log_system ⊕ {system_time↦θBuilding'}
│ log_sensor' = log_sensor
│ system_time' = system_time
└────────────────────────────────────────
```

UserGeneralLog follows exactly the same form and may be specified as follows:

```
┌─UserGeneralLog───────
│ SystemGeneralLog
└──────────────────────
```

UserSensorLog records the state of a particular sensor:

```
┌─UserSensorLog──────────────────────────
│ ΞBuilding
│ ΔLog
│ sensor?: SENSOR_ID
│ ────────────────────────────────────────
│ sensor? ∈ dom sensors
│ log_sensor' = log_sensor ⊕ {system_time↦sensors(sensor?)}
│ log_system' = log_system
│ system_time = system_time'
└─────────────────────────────────────────
```

Lastly, we consider the initial state of *Log*:

```
┌─InitLog────────
│ Log
│ ────────────────
│ log_system = {}
│ log_sensor = {}
│ system_time = 0
└────────────────
```

21.6.7 Sensor system initialization

The initialization of the sensor system is fairly straightforward, being built up from the initialization of the components:

$$InitSensorSystem \triangleq InitBuilding \wedge InitLog$$

21.6.8 Operation summary and entity–relationship modelling

Table 21.10 presents a summary of the main operations and functions specified within the sensor system while *Table 21.11* shows how the entities and relationships identifed at the beginning of this section, in Table 21.9, have been modelled within the specification.

21.6.9 Developing and documenting Z specifications

So far, we have said very little about how to develop and document a specification. The example presented in this section goes some way to indicating how a specification is derived and documented. However, many issues have been ignored, so brief mention should be made of them before we move on. Some of the topics raised here are discussed in detail elsewhere within the reference book; other discussions may be found in Diller (1990), King and Sørenson (1989) and Wordsworth (1987).

The primary aims of a specification should be to:

1. Present a succinct and abstract statement of the requirements combining both a natural language presentation of the issues and a formal representation; this combination of both formal and informal text is of the utmost importance.
2. Show how the specification has been derived from the requirements and how it satisfies the requirements.
3. Present correctness arguments of various forms aimed at establishing properties of the specification, demonstrating consistency etc.

In order to meet these objectives, a specification document should present the following information. However, it is important to realize that the development of a specification is an iterative exercise and during the development stages many of these points will be re-visited and revised.

1. *Identification of entities, attributes, relations and operations.* Here we are looking for an analysis of the requirements and an identification of the abstract entities, attributes and relationships that are to be modelled in the state together with the operations that are to be supported.
2. *Recording of the abstract state.* Based on the previous analysis, an abstract state model is constructed that should model the entities, attributes and relationships already identified. Invariants should also be specified at this point.
3. *Identification of the initial state.* Once the abstract state has been recorded, an initial state should be identified. A single unique state value or a set of potential initial values may be specified.
4. *Specification of the partial abstract operations.* The main system operations, identified during the analysis of the requirements, should now be specified; at this stage exception conditions should be ignored.
5. *Specification of total abstract operations.* Attention should now be given to stating what happens in the case of exception conditions, that is what is to happen when the pre-conditions of the partial operation specifications are not met.
6. *Addressing proof obligations.* Various proof obligations arise during the development of a specification. These should be

Table 21.10 Sensor system operations and functions

Schema name	System operation	User Operation
Sensor	*InitSensor* *ChangeTempThresholds* *ChangeStatus* *ChangeReading*	
Sensors	*sensor_exception*	*UserEnableSensor* *UserDisableSensor* *UserDisplaySensorReading* *UserChangeThreshold*
Rooms		
RoomsAndSensors		*UserAddSensor* *UserRemoveSensor* *UserDisplayRoomSensors* *UserChangeRoomThresholds*
Alarms		*UserSilenceBell*
Building	*SensorTimeScan*	
Log	*SystemGeneralLog*	*UserGeneralLog* *UserSensorLog*
SensorSystem		

Table 21.11 The modelling of entities and relationships in the specification

Entity	Entity set	Relationship	Modelled in
Sensor			*Sensor*
	Sensors		*Sensors*
	Rooms		*Rooms*
	Log		*Log*
	Alarms		*Alarms*
		room_sensors	*rooms*
		sensor_located_in	*rooms ˜*
		alarmed_room	*signal_lights* *signal_bells*
		room_alarm	*signal_lights* *signal_bells*
		logged_sensor	*log_system*
		logged_alarm	*log_system*
		logged_room	*log_system*

recorded as they arise and appropriately placed within the specification document. We will briefly review some of these proof obligations:

(a) *Consistency of state invariants.* In Z specifications we use one or more schemas, combined using the schema calculus, to define the state space of the specified system. A requirement arises to show that the state schema is not inconsistent, i.e. that the predicate does not reduce to 'false'. This proof obligation may be stated, rather oddly, as follows:

$$\vdash \exists State \bullet State$$

All that is required to prove this rather strange looking obligation is to find a particular assignment of values for the state components such that the state invariant is satisfied.

(b) *Existence of an initial state.* Given a schema defining a state space and another schema defining a set of initial states of the system, we must show that the set of initial states is not empty. This involves showing that the predicate part of the initial state schema does not reduce to 'false'. The general theorem to be proved is:

$$\vdash \exists State \bullet InitialState$$

(c) *Pre-conditions of state operations.* This proof obligation, discharged for each operation, shows that if the operation can occur (i.e. if the operation is applied to a legal state which satisfies the conditions specified by the operation) then at least one final state exists. In Z this task is performed by calculating the pre-condition schema of the operation and checking that it is consistent. We should also compare the pre-condition that we have calculated with the pre-condition that was recorded in the actual operation specification and ensure that the explicitly written pre-condition is no weaker than the calculated pre-condition.

(d) *Totality of operations.* When we specify how exceptions will be handled by our operations we effectively aim to make them total, that is, they are defined on all legal states and for all argument values. This proof obligation aims to show precisely this result, thus:

$$State; x:?\vdash \text{pre } TotalOperation$$

where pre *TotalOperation* is the calculated pre-condition of the specification of the schema *TotalOperation*.

7. *Data refinement.* The purpose of data refinement is to construct a more concrete representation of the state and operations in a specification. The process may continue for several stages until a design is attained which can easily be implemented. The data refinement process includes the following items:

(a) A schema to record the concrete state.
(b) A schema which describes the retrieve relation between the concrete and abstract states. (The retrieve relation provides a 'recipe' or 'algorithm' for recovering (retrieving) abstract states from concrete states, that is, given a concrete state representation the retrieve relation will yield its abstract representation.)
(c) A schema for the concrete initial state and a proof that it is correctly related to the abstract initial state.
(d) Schemas for the operations in terms of the concrete state and proofs of their correctness.

Once these steps have been undertaken two additional proof obligations arise:

(a) *The correctness of the initial state.* Here we need to show that the initial concrete state *CI*, when transformed into its abstract representation through the retrieve relation *R*, satisfies the abstract initial state schema *AI*, thus, given *CS* stands for a concrete state:

$$\vdash \forall CS \bullet CI \Rightarrow (\exists AS \bullet AI \wedge R)$$

(b) *Verifying the concrete operations.* In addition to proving a concrete representation for the data of the abstract state, we must also provide concrete representations for the operations. Furthermore, the concrete data states must 'behave like' the abstract states when subject to the concrete operations that correspond to the abstract operations. *Figure 21.3* provides a pictorial representation of some of the concepts outlined below.

Two theorems must be proved. The first states that whenever an abstract operation *AO* is legal in some abstract state *AS* the concrete operation *CO* is legal in any concrete state *CS* which represents the abstract state.

$$\vdash \forall AS; CS; x?: X \bullet (\text{pre } AO) \wedge R \Rightarrow \text{pre } CO$$

The second theorem states that the resulting final concrete state *CS'* of a concrete operation *CO* represents an abstract state *AS'* which must have been produced by the abstract operation *AO* which *CO* is a refinement of:

$$\vdash \forall AS; CS; CS'; x?: X; y!: Y \bullet$$
$$(\text{pre } AO) \wedge R \wedge CO \Rightarrow \exists AS' \bullet (AO \wedge R')$$

Once the refinement proofs have been discharged some of the information highlighted above should be produced for the refined state and its operations.

Data refinement will not be considered further here as it is addressed in Chapter 24 of the reference book. However, it should be borne in mind that if refinement is undertaken then the refinement steps and consequent proof obligations should all be recorded within the development history of the system.

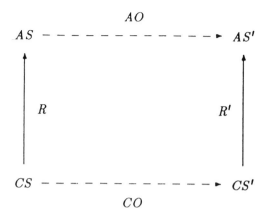

Symbol	Meaning
AS	Initial abstract state
AS'	Final abstract state
CS	Initial concrete state
CS'	Final concrete state
AO	Abstract operation relating an AS to an AS'
CO	Concrete operation relating to CS to a CS'
R	Retrieve relation between initial states
R'	Retrieve relation between final states

Figure 21.3 Diagrammatic depiction of operation modelling proof relations

8. *Operation refinement.* Data refinement produces a specification in which the data structures are easily implemented in a programming language. The purpose of operation refinement is to translate that specification into the implementation language, and in particular to find a sequential description which implements the functionality of the specification. For those interested in discovering more about this topic reference should be made to Gries (1981), King (1990), Morgan (1990) and Wordsworth (1987).

21.7 Overview of VDM

This section of the chapter provides a very brief introduction to VDM, sufficient, it is hoped, to enable a reasonable comparison to be made between VDM and Z. We start by re-visiting the Employment Agency Database example and specifying it in VDM. This is followed by a very brief examination of the way VDM approaches the specification of exceptions and the way VDM specifications may be structured.

21.7.1 The employment agency database re-visited

We will re-specify the employment agency database problem that we met in Section 21.5. When producing a VDM specification it is usual to follow much the same steps as we did when producing the Z specification. We start by developing a state model and identifying any invariant properties that hold. Our state model is similar to the Z model with the exception of *employs* which is now modelled as a function from *Person* to *Company*; VDM does not directly support a model for relations, only for functions. The VDM state, modelled as a tagged Cartesian product, is viewed as a type. The invariant property is a constraint on instances of the type. It is recorded as a truth valued function which restricts the set of values that an instance of the type may adopt. The following lexical conventions have been used. Type names start with an upper case letter which is followed by one or more lower case letters. Variable names, function names and elements of enumerated sets are shown using lower case names and operation names are all in upper case. Here then is the VDM state and invariant:

$$Ea\_database :: candidates: Person\text{-}set$$
$$employs: Person \xrightarrow{m} Company$$
$$vacancies: Company \xrightarrow{m} \mathbb{N}$$
$$\text{inv } mk\text{-}Ea\_database(candidates, employs, vacancies) \triangleq$$
$$candidates \cap \text{dom } employs = \{\} \wedge$$
$$\text{rng } employs \subseteq \text{dom } vacancies$$
$$\text{init } mk\text{-}Ea\_database(\{\},\{\},\{\})$$
$$Company, Person \text{ is not yet defined}$$

The types *Company* and *Person* are said to be not yet defined. This is analogous to basic types in Z. Essentially they are sets of distinguished values, the internal structure of which we are not interested in. The initial value of the state is specified along with the invariant. The initial state value, in this case the empty values for each of the state variables, may be viewed as the initial value of any instance of type *Ea database*. The data type invariant asserts that every value adopted by instances of this type must satisfy the given predicate.

We now turn to specifying the operations. An operation may be viewed as an abstract procedure which, given appropriately typed arguments and access to components of the state, may produce results and cause changes to the state. Operations may be used at varying levels of abstraction – capturing the semantics of anything from program-level fragments to complex system-level interactions. An operation specification has three parts: a signature (a declaration in Z), a pre-condition and a post-condition:

1. *Operation signature*. The signature provides information about the arguments and results of the operation and also tells us, through the *ext* (external clause), what components of the state the operation wishes to read (**rd**) or read/write (**wr**) access to.

2. *Pre-condition*. The pre-condition of an operation is a predicate that records what assumptions are being made about the arguments and state components accessed by the operation. The pre-condition must evaluate to true in order that the operation be guaranteed to terminate.

3. *Post-condition*. This is a predicate that states the relation that must hold between the input values, output values and the accessed state values. A putative implementation must be such as to produce results, based on a possible set of states and input values, that result in the post-condition relation holding true. Within a post-condition we may wish to refer to the value of state variables both before the invocation of the operation and after the completion of the operation. When referring to the value of a state variable as it was prior to the invocation of the operation we decorate the variable name with a hook, for example, $\overset{\frown}{variable\text{-}name}$, i.e. *we only decorate variable names in post-condition expressions*.

The operations that we require are as follows:

1. *APPLY(p: Person)*. Registers a person as a candidate employee in the database.

2. *EMPLOYED_BY(p: Person)c: Company*. Given the name of a person this operation yields the company that employs that person.

3. *EMPLOYS(c: Company)e: Person-set*. Returns the set of names of people registered as employed by the company.

4. *FIRE(c: Company; p: Person)*. The indicated person is noted as no longer working for the company and is returned to being a candidate employee in the database.

5. *HIRE(c: Company; p: Person)*. Hires the person, who must be a candidate, to the subscribing company.

6. *IS_CANDIDATE(p: Person)r: $\mathbb{B}$*. Returns true if the person is already a candidate; otherwise false.

7. *NUMBER_OF_VACANCIES(c: Company)n: $\mathbb{N}$*. Returns the number of vacancies registered to the nominated company.

8. *SUBSCRIBE(c: Company; n: $\mathbb{N}$)*. A company subscribes to the database. This operation will record either an initial subscription to the database with a corresponding number of vacancies or an additional number of vacancies for an already subscribing company.

Specifications of the individual operations are:

$$APPLY(p: Person)$$
$$\text{ext wr } candidates: Person\text{-}set$$
$$\text{rd } employs: Person \xrightarrow{m} Company$$
$$\text{pre } p \notin candidates \wedge p \notin \text{dom } employs$$
$$\text{post } candidates = \overset{\frown}{candidates} \cup \{p\}$$

The pre-condition asserts that the person applying must not already be a candidate employee and must not be working for a particular company. The post-condition asserts that the final value of *candidates* is the same as the initial value but with *p* added to it.

The meaning of the following operation should be fairly clear:

$$EMPLOYED\_BY(p: Person)c: Company$$
$$\text{ext rd } employs: Person \xrightarrow{m} Company$$
$$\text{pre } p \in \text{dom } employs$$
$$\text{post } c = \overset{\frown}{employs}(p)$$

$$EMPLOYS(c: Company)e: Person\text{-}set$$
$$\text{ext rd } employs: Person \xrightarrow{m} Company$$
$$\text{pre } c \in \text{rng } employs$$
$$\text{post } e = \{p \mid p \in \text{dom } employs \wedge employs(p) = c\}$$

This operation returns the set of people currently employed by the company. The company must be registered.

$$FIRE(c: Company; p: Person)$$
$$\text{ext wr } candidates: Person\text{-}set$$
$$\text{wr } employs: Person \xrightarrow{m} Company$$
$$\text{pre } p \in \text{dom } employs \wedge employs(p) = c$$
$$\text{post } employs = \overset{\frown}{employs} - \{p\} \wedge$$
$$candidates = \overset{\frown}{candidates} \cup \{p\}$$

The *FIRE* operation applies to agency members who are employed by subscribing companies. A person who is fired from a company is automatically re-entered as a candidate employee and removed from the set of employees associated with the company.

$$HIRE(c: Company; p: Person)$$
$$\text{ext wr } candidates: Person\text{-}set$$
$$\text{wr } employs: Person \xrightarrow{m} Company$$
$$\text{wr } vacancies: Company \xrightarrow{m} \mathbb{N}$$
$$\text{pre } p \in candidates \wedge c \in \text{dom } vacancies \wedge vacancies(c) > 0$$
$$\text{post } candidates = \overset{\frown}{candidates} - \{p\} \wedge$$
$$employs = \overset{\frown}{employs} \cup \{p \mapsto c\} \wedge$$
$$vacancies = \overset{\frown}{vacancies} \dagger \{c \mapsto \overset{\frown}{vacancies}(c) - 1\}$$

The operation is only defined if the company is registered and has vacancies and the person is a candidate.

HIRE results in the removal of the candidate from *candidates*, the inclusion of the candidate into the set of people known to be working for the company and a reduction in the companies vacancies by one.

> $IS\_CANDIDATE(p: Person)r: \mathbb{B}$
> ext rd *candidates*: *Person*-set
> post $r \Leftrightarrow p \in candidates$

The result of this operation is a Boolean value which will be true if the person is a candidate or false otherwise.

> $NUMBER\_OF\_VACANCIES(c: Company)n: \mathbb{N}$
> ext rd *vacancies*: $Company \xrightarrow{m} \mathbb{N}$
> pre $c \in \text{dom } vacancies$
> post $n = \overleftarrow{vacancies}(c)$

The result of this operation, defined only for subscribing companies, is the number of vacancies currently associated with that company.

> $SUBSCRIBE(c:Company;n:\mathbb{N})$
> ext wr *vacancies*: $Company \xrightarrow{m} \mathbb{N}$
> pre *true*
> post $(c \in \text{dom } vacancies \land vacancies =$
> $\qquad \overleftarrow{vacancies} \dagger \{c \mapsto \overleftarrow{vacancies}(c) + n\})$
> $\qquad \lor$
> $\qquad (c \notin \text{dom } vacancies \land vacancies =$
> $\qquad \overleftarrow{vacancies} \cup \{c \mapsto n\})$

Where an operation is total, that is, where there are no restrictions on the use of the operation, the pre-condition is considered to be vacuously true. We may explicitly state this or leave out the pre-condition altogether.

If the company is already a subscriber then the new vacancies are added onto the existing vacancies. Alternatively, if the company is not a subscriber, then an association is placed in the map *vacancies* linking the company with the indicated number of vacancies.

The initial state of the database may be established either by operation or an assertion in the state definition. We have seen how an initialization predicate can be associated with a state definition. Here we show the initial state being established by an operation:

> $INIT$
> ext wr *candidates*: *Person*-set
> $\quad$ wr *employs*: $Person \xrightarrow{m} Company$
> $\quad$ wr *vacancies*: $Company \xrightarrow{m} \mathbb{N}$
> post $candidates = \{\} \land employs = \{\} \land vacancies = \{\}$

21.7.2 Specification of exceptions

We have seen how schemas and the schema calculus are used to specify exceptions in Z. Exceptions can be specified in VDM either directly in the post-condition, much in the manner that we discussed for Z, or use may be made of the error specification mechanism provided in the language. The following example shows how exceptions may be handled for the *HIRE* operation. First, we need to introduce a new type:

> $Error = \{ok, invalid\_candidate, invalid\_company,$
> $\qquad no\_vacancies\}$

> $HIRE(c: Company; p: Person)err: Error$
> ext wr *candidates*: *Person*-set
> $\quad$ wr *employs*: $Person \xrightarrow{m} Company$
> $\quad$ wr *vacancies*: $Company \xrightarrow{m} \mathbb{N}$

> pre $p \in candidates \land c \in \text{dom } vacancies \land vacancies(c) > 0$
> post $candidates = \overleftarrow{candidates} - \{p\} \land$
> $\quad employs = \overleftarrow{employs} \cup \{p \mapsto c\} \land$
> $\quad vacancies = \overleftarrow{vacancies} \dagger \{c \mapsto \overleftarrow{vacancies}(c) - 1\} \land$
> $\quad err = ok$
> errs $INVALID\_CANDIDATE: p \notin candidates \rightarrow$
> $\quad err = invalid\_candidate$
> $\quad INVALID\_COMPANY: c \notin \text{dom } vacancies \rightarrow$
> $\quad err = invalid\_company$
> $\quad NO\_VACANCIES: c \in \text{dom } vacancies \land$
> $\quad vacancies(c) = 0 \rightarrow err = no\_vacancies$

Informally, the post-condition specifies what is to happen only if the candidate is valid, the company is valid and the company in question has vacancies. If the candidate is invalid or if the company is invalid, or if the company is valid but has no vacancies, the exceptions associated with these conditions are reported.

The best way of showing how to interpret this extended syntax is to show how it may be translated into the standard pre- and post-condition style of operation specification with no exception clauses. Given the following operation template:

> $ERROR(a: T_a)r: T_r$
> pre p
> post q
> errs $COND1: c_1 \rightarrow r_1$
> $\quad COND2: c_2 \rightarrow r_2$

we may translate it as follows:

> $ERROR\_MEANING(a: T_a)r: T_r$
> pre $p \lor c_1 \lor c_2$
> post $(p \land q) \lor (c_1 \land r_1) \lor (c_2 \land r_2)$

A close examination of this re-formulation of *ERROR* into *ERROR_MEANING* reveals an expanded pre-condition that is made up of a disjunction of p and the error condition guards. The post-condition is potentially a non-deterministic expression unless the disjuncts are mutually exclusive. If they are not mutually exclusive then the specification is satisfied by any true disjunct thus, for example, if c_1 and c_2 are both true then the post-condition will be satisfied by either r_1 or r_2, i.e. by either exception condition.

The convention is often adopted in the error specification predicates, r_1 and r_2, that the state remains *unchanged* unless changes are explicitly specified; thus no state unchanged assertions are usually included.

21.7.3 Structuring VDM specifications

The following example illustrates how VDM data types may be constructed and used as abstract data types within other specifications. We will return to the heat sensor system and specify the entities *Sensor* and *Sensors* as data types; this follows the pattern adopted in the Z specification. We start with *Sensor* by first defining the state and its associated invariant and then specifying one of the operations, *CHANGE_STATUS*. Both the state and the operation will be used in a subsequent specification:

> $Sensor::sensor\_name: Sensor\_id$
> $\qquad status: Status$
> $\qquad upper: \mathbb{Z}$
> $\qquad lower: \mathbb{Z}$
> $\qquad reading: \mathbb{Z}$
> inv $mk\text{-}Sensor(sn,s,u,l,r) \triangleq l \leqslant u$

Next, we require a function that, given an argument of type *Sensor*, yields the name of that sensor. We will require this function in the subsequent specification for, unlike Z, it is not possible to see the structure of states built up in the manner described here. In other words, names only have scope within the data type's specification. Mechanisms are provided for making names visible outside this specification boundary:

$$sensor\_name\_is: Sensor \rightarrow Sensor\_id$$
$$sensor\_name\_is(state) \triangleq sensor\_name(state)$$

Comparing the specification of the following operation with that of the similarly named Z operation reveals how close the styles of specification are in the two notations. The main difference relates to VDM's explicitly identified pre- and post-conditions and the way the operation framing conditions (managing state access, arguments and results) are organized:

CHANGE_STATUS(*newstatus*: *Status*)
ext wr *status*: *Status*
    wr *reading*: $\mathbb{Z}$
    rd *upper*: $\mathbb{Z}$
    rd *lower*: $\mathbb{Z}$
post *status* = *newstatus* $\wedge$
    (($status = enabled \wedge reading \leqslant upper \wedge reading \geqslant lower$)
    $\vee$
    ($status = disabled \wedge reading = \overleftarrow{reading}$))

Next we define the interface for *Sensor*. One operation, *CHANGE_STATUS*, is exported together with the function *sensor_name_is*. Two types, *Status* and *Sensor_name*, are imported from *Sensors* as they are required within the *Sensor* specification. The interface specification is shown in *Figure 21.4*.

module *Sensor*
exports   operations
    CHANGE_STATUS: $Status \xrightarrow{o} ()$
  functions
    sensor_name_is: $Sensor \rightarrow Sensor\_id$
imports from *Sensors*
  types
    Status
    Sensor_id
end

Figure 21.4   Interface specification for the *Sensor* data type

We now specify the data type *Sensors*. As previously we model this as a function from *Sensor_id* to *Sensor* with the same data type invariant. Note that the data type invariant makes use of the function *sensor_name_is* which is defined within *Sensor* and imported into *Sensors*:

Sensors::*sensors*: $Sensor\_id \xrightarrow{m} Sensor$
inv (*sensors*) $\triangleq \forall s \in$ dom *sensors* $\cdot$ *sensor_name_is*(*sensors*(*s*)) = *s*
init (*sensors*) $\triangleq$ *sensors* = {}
Status = {*enabled*, *disabled*}
Sensor_id is not yet defined

We now examine how the *CHANGE_STATUS* operation may be used, or 'quoted', within the *DISABLE_SENSOR*

operation. Intuitively, we first have to establish that the sensor we wish to disable is named correctly, i.e. that it is a valid sensor. We assert this as a pre-condition to the operation. The post-condition then *selects* the named sensor and *quotes* the *CHANGE_STATUS* operation on the selected sensor.

Understanding quotation requires the following insight. Operation pre-conditions and post-conditions may be viewed as functions. A pre-condition is a function from the operations arguments and initial state to a Boolean value which will be true if the pre-condition is satisfied and false otherwise. From this perspective a pre-condition has the following signature:

$$pre\text{-}OP: At_1 \times At_2 \ldots \times State \rightarrow \mathbb{B}$$

Similarly, a post-condition may be viewed as a function with the following signature:

$$post\text{-}OP: At_1 \times At_2 \ldots \times State \times State \times Rt_1 \rightarrow \mathbb{B}$$

that is, it is a function from the operations arguments, initial state, final state and results to a Boolean value which is true if the post-condition is true, and false otherwise.

In the post-condition of the following specification we assert, using existential quantification, that a final sensor state exists which, coupled with the initial state of the selected sensor and a status value, will result in the post-condition being true. The final sensor state is then associated with the sensor's name in the updated value of *sensors*. This manner of using operations defined on complex data types is known as operation quotation derived from our having 'quoted' the pre- and post-conditions. A more extensive discussion of this topic may be found in Jones (1990).

DISABLE_SENSOR(*name*: *Sensor_id*)
ext wr *sensors*: $Sensor\_id \xrightarrow{m} Sensor$
pre *name* $\in$ dom *sensors*
post $\exists$*newsensor*: *Sensor* $\cdot$
    post-CHANGE_STATUS
    ($disabled, \overleftarrow{sensors}(name), newsensor$) $\wedge$
    $sensors = \overleftarrow{sensors} \dagger \{name \mapsto newsensor\}$

The interface definition for the *Sensors* data type, shown in *Figure 21.5*, records information about both imported operations, functions and types and similarly exported objects. Here we see that we need to import the operation *CHANGE_STATUS* and the function *sensor_name_is*. Similarly, we export the user-level operation *DISABLE_SENSOR* and the types *Sensor_id* and *Status*.

module *Sensors*
exports
  operations
    DISABLE_SENSOR: $Sensor\_id \xrightarrow{o} ()$
  types
    Sensor_id
    Status
imports from *Sensor*
  operations
    CHANGE_STATIS: $Status \xrightarrow{m} ()$
  functions
    sensor_name_is: $Sensor \rightarrow Sensor\_id$
end

Figure 21.5   Interface specification for the *Sensors* data type

21.8 Z and BSI/VDM: a comparison

Broadly speaking, both Z and BSI/VDM share a common, model-based, approach to specification. Specifications in either notation introduce functions, types and predicates whose structure is intended to convey the semantics of a particular system. The most interesting general point of similarity is that they have the same view of what a software system consists of.

This shared view says that a software system is a state space together with a series of operations and functions that act upon it. Software specifications express a relation upon the state space, and the intrinsic properties of the operations that are to be implemented. In some sense, a software system is considered to be a kind of state machine in which operations are applied successively one after another to produce outputs in response to input choices.

The BSI/VDM and Z notations have both been given formal semantics (see Larsen *et al.* (1989) and Spivey (1988)) and represent different trade-offs in specification language design, which are discussed here.

21.8.1 Fixed points and definitions by recursion

BSI/VDM gives a least fixed point semantics (based on Scott's domain theory) to both type and explicit function definitions, whereas Z uses the style of loose semantics that is commonly used for logic-based notations. The virtue of least fixed point semantics is that all defined objects (including those defined inductively) are uniformly constrained to be the least objects satisfying the defining property. Moreover, such objects will, as a consequence, be automatically subject to a corresponding induction property.

With loose semantics in Z, the specification determines a class of possible interpretations, according to the predicate constraints imposed within the defining schemas. In this framework, inductive definitions can, of course, be written down just like any other predicate constraint. However, there would be no automatic assumption that an inductive definition specifies a least solution – in Z, this leastness requirement would have to be asserted separately (i.e. as a second-order property) for each definition to which it applied.

It turns out that in using either BSI/VDM or Z, some care is required by the specifier to ensure the consistency of inductive definitions. In either notation, it is possible to write down inductive definitions for which there are no solutions (and hence no least fixed point). Such 'inconsistent' definitions involve writing non-monotonic predicates, perhaps by use of quantification within an inductive definition.

The trade-off between Z and BSI/VDM in respect of inductive definitions lies in either having loose semantics and needing to add leastness assumptions on an *ad hoc* basis (as in Z) or in having the leastness assumptions built-in to the semantics of the notation and so forcing all consistent function and type definitions to uniquely define entities (as in BSI/VDM).

21.8.2 Type invariants

Both methods regard type invariants in terms of logical predicates. In BSI/VDM the invariant is considered as part of the type, including those types that are defined via structural induction. This leads to considerable conciseness in giving type invariants for mutually recursive types since the semantics of BSI/VDM automatically ensures that type invariants will hold for all sub-components of a type and that it is therefore unnecessary to state it specially for each of them.

In Z, types are simply normalized 'maximal' sets (see 'Type structure' section) which can be further constrained by logical predicates given in the corresponding schema. Inductively defined types are only provided via abstract syntax notation and cannot be restricted directly by an invariant predicate.

21.8.3 Type structure and the semantics of types

Both Z and BSI/VDM are strongly typed formal languages. They both have, at least in principle, type systems that can be presented in terms of rules that restrict the way in which declared entities are used to form other compound entities, all based upon the enclosing context of declarations.

It is also true that the notions of type in both Z and BSI/VDM are inherently semantical in nature; both equate the denotation of a type expression with an element of a certain pre-specified and well-defined family of sets (i.e. the Type Model in BSI/VDM (Monahan, 1987) and the World of Sets in the case of Z (Spivey, 1988)). Moreover, if an expression e is said to have type T then this means that the denotation of the expression e belongs to the denotation of the type T.

However, there are also some technical differences in the underlying model of type-checking used. In Z, the process of type-checking expressions reduces to a computation of the form of a 'maximal' type, based upon the form and structure of the expression, together with the types of those declared entities occurring within the expression. If it exists, this maximal type will be expressible in a canonical way in terms of given sets (assumed to be atomic) and the basic type operators such as the (basic) schema type, the power set type or the Cartesian product operation. In general, a process of normalization is performed, based on the syntax of an expression, in order to extract a 'maximal' type that it may possess. If this process fails then the expression also fails to be well typed and so cannot be well formed.

In BSI/VDM, the process of type-checking expressions is concerned with showing that expressions conform to the 'context conditions' expressed as a set of predicates defined over the grammar of the BSI/VDM language. No explicit attempt is made to characterize a 'maximal' type expression for arbitrary expressions; instead, the problem reduces to showing equivalence or sub-type containment between type expressions derived from expressions. In essence, this involves showing that whatever type is provided by an expression meets the constraint imposed by the context.

In both Z and BSI/VDM, there are contexts in which it is possible to perform some kind of type inference process that calculates a most general type possible for a given expression, without needing to specify all of the types of all the entities on which the expression depends. As in the programming languages Standard ML and Miranda, the ability to perform type inference is often needed when writing the right-hand sides of 'let' expressions. However, due to certain fundamental logical difficulties with the semantics of polymorphism, both languages take a conservative approach to polymorphism and have constrained the range of type variables to the set-theoretical denotations for types mentioned above.

21.8.4 Non-determinism and loose specification

In both Z and BSI/VDM, implicit specifications of functions and operations can be expressed using predicates. The semantics of implicitly specified functions is 'loose' in that each possible model of the specification will contain a corresponding function denotation satisfying the implicit specification. Accordingly, the semantics of a function definition is the set of function denotations which logically satisfy the definition. BSI/VDM has the added complication that a least fixed point semantics is required for the inductively defined functions.

On the other hand, the semantics of an operation in either Z or BSI/VDM is a relation on state pairs, with additional provision for input and for output. A process satisfying such a specification may not necessarily be functional in that it is only constrained to satisfy the relation – the process may make an internal choice to select a single state transition from possibly many valid transitions. An internal choice of some object is one that is, for all intents and purposes, non-deterministic since all of the possible influences that may be used to make the choice are otherwise unobservable. Alternatively, if the same circumstances arise repeatedly, it is not possible to guarantee in advance that the same selections will be repeated. A simple, almost canonical example is the specification of a choice operation, called *CHOOSE*, for a non-empty set of values and some state space including the state variable 'possible':

$CHOOSE(s:Value\text{-set})r:Value$
ext wr *possibles*:*Value*-set
pre *possibles* $\cap s \neq \{\}$
post $r \in (possibles \cap s) \wedge$
$\quad possibles = \overleftarrow{possibles} - \{r\}$

The above specification does not say *which* value is returned by the operation, only that some appropriate value satisfying the constraints is returned. Also notice that the state is modified by this operation – as VDM makes use of finite sets only, we know that only a finite number of successful invocations of *CHOOSE* can be made, without the state variable *possibles* being increased by some other operation.

Such flexibility to allow non-determinism is useful when implementing operations. The non-determinism permits the implementer to add some additional (internal) apparatus to make these internal choices, just so long as the resulting selection gives a valid state transition. The fact that these choices are to be made internally by the operation also says that, from an external viewpoint, it is irrelevant what these choices are and that no external agent should ever rely upon the implemented mechanism actually used by the operation to make such choices.

21.8.5 Loose specification and the semantics of 'not yet defined' entities

In BSI/VDM, it is possible to introduce just the *names* of entities (perhaps with additional type information) but with no other defining characteristics. Such entities are said to be *not yet defined* and provides a useful way of reducing the amount of formal detail needed at a particular stage of specification. During development, the *not yet defined* entities are eventually given formal definitions which can, in turn, be refined further, until no further development is necessary. The semantics of *not yet defined* entities is that type identifiers are assigned an arbitrary, but non-empty, type (i.e. an element of the VDM type universe), and value identifiers (including functions and operations) are assigned values that satisfy the appropriate type constraints.

A slightly different approach is taken to this within Z. Definitions are always as loose as the specifier makes them. So to get the effect of a *not yet defined* value, the specifier only introduces the signature (i.e. name and type) of a value, but with no other predicate constraint. The effect of a *not yet defined* type is provided by the introduction of given sets in a Z specification. These act in much the same way as generic parameters or indeterminates, and their semantics is similar to that alluded to above for the *not yet defined* entities.

21.8.6 Pre-/post-condition specification of operations

Both methods view an operation as a relation between the state before the operation and the state arising upon successful termination. However, in Z, a certain economy of notation is achieved by just defining the relation as a logical formula of two states, whereas in BSI/VDM an operation specification is split into an explicit pre-condition formula and a formula describing the transition relation between the before and after states.

However, it is clear that the BSI/VDM form of operation specification is trivially embeddable into an equivalent Z-style schema. In the other direction, it is straightforward to define a general operator in Z that gives the weakest pre-condition for any given relation over state pairs, so allowing a Z-style schema to present the pre-condition information explicitly if so desired.

In system specifications, a non-trivial constraint known as the state invariant is usually placed upon the state space of the system. In both the methods, the result of using a system operation must preserve this invariant. Moreover, it is possible to make use of the properties of the invariant in writing the post-condition of an operation. For example, consider the following fragment of VDM:

$St::var1:\mathbb{N}$
$\quad var2:\mathbb{N}$
inv $mk\text{-}St(v1,v2) \triangleq v2 \leqslant v1$

$ZERO$
ext wr $var1,var2:\mathbb{N}$
post $var1 = 0$

The operation *ZERO* sets '*var1*' to 0, and in order to satisfy the invariant, the variable '*var2*' is implicitly set to 0 as well. Note that 'write' permission is needed for both of the state variables *var1* and *var2* because both variables will need to be updated (see next section).

Finally, the satisfaction relation between relationally specified operations is broadly the same for both Z and BSI/VDM.

21.8.7 The frame problem

The so-called 'frame problem' arises in the following situation. Suppose that you have some process operating upon a given state, which has certain particular components. Now, suppose that during its operation, this process is required to modify some of these components. What should happen (if anything) to the remaining components of the state? The frame problem is concerned with the methods and techniques for stating what is permitted to happen on the state components otherwise unmentioned in the specification predicate.

There are many positions on this issue, and Z and BSI/VDM have taken different views on how to approach the problem.

In Z, the semantics of operations is expressed as a simple logical constraint on state transitions. So, if a particular component is not constrained, arbitrary changes many occur to it during state transitions. Therefore, the basic attitude is that the specifier should always describe what happens to all components of the state, otherwise the semantics would allow arbitrary changes to any components not explicitly mentioned.

This would impose a very tiresome and easily broken obligation on the Z specifier were it not for the schema calculus – see Section 21.5. Using the schema calculus it is easy, for example, to require that certain state components remain unchanged.

This can be done by employing the 'Ξ' convention which, given a (named) schema consisting of state variables, provides the constraint ensuring that these variables remain constant. The 'Δ' convention is similar in that it forms the state space consisting of pairs of states representing the 'before' and 'after' effect of using an operation. As such, the 'Ξ' convention is essentially a restricted use of the 'Δ' convention, and can be defined in terms of it.

In BSI/VDM, the specifier asserts, on an operation by operation basis, which state variables will be modified by giving them 'write' access; other state variables whose value is referred to but not changed by an operation are asserted by the specifier to have 'read' access. The semantics of operations in BSI/VDM then ensures that all state variables without write access are to remain constant for any state transition performed by the given operation. Therefore, the BSI/VDM specifier does not need to ensure that this property holds – it is already a consequence of the semantics of BSI/VDM.

From the BSI/VDM point of view, a Z specification of an operation has all corresponding state variables given write access, but with some additional predicate constraining any components to remain constant that are not otherwise changed explicitly.

In both VDM and Z not only do we specify what changes in the state but we also have to state what remains unchanged. Starting from the premise that what is important in a specification is usually what changes, the object-oriented approach to specification developed at the University of Surrey (Schuman and Pitt, 1987; Schuman et al., 1990) adopts a sound notion of 'the rest stays unchanged'. Thus, to specify:

$$f' = f\dagger\{1\to2\}$$

or:

$$s' = s \cup \{1\}$$

it is sufficient to assert, respectively:

$$f'(1) = 2$$
$$1 \in s'$$

Early experience in the use of this specification style (Colebrook et al., 1990) promises far more concise and readable specifications. While explicitly addressing the frame problem the object-oriented work also aims to capture the semantics of concurrency.

21.8.8 Partiality and logic

Both Z and BSI/VDM allow the specification of partial functions, but they handle the issue differently.

In Z, a partial function is in fact a total function on its domain and range, but whose behaviour is not defined outside its precondition or domain of definition.

In BSI/VDM, partial functions are semantically represented by using (total) Scott continuous functions between Scott Domains (i.e. complete partial orders) that (implicitly) contain a least element, conventionally denoted by $\perp$. The values for which the specified function is taken to be 'undefined' are all mapped into the appropriate least element $\perp$. Since the specifier's concern is to express what the 'good' behaviour of systems should be (i.e. safety properties), BSI/VDM does not need any direct, built-in syntax for values whose denotations is $\perp$. Of course, one can always write 'bad' specifications of things whose denotation would have to be $\perp$ – but it is the specifier's responsibility not to do so.

In addition, BSI/VDM operates semantically using a 3-valued partial function logic (or LPF), whereas Z sticks to conventional 2-valued logic. In actual fact, this 3-valued logic is not a recent innovation and the variant used in BSI/VDM had, for example, been discussed by the logician Kleene in 1952. The application of LPF to software specification has been developed further in Barringer et al. (1984) and in Cheng (1986).

The main advantage of LPF to the specifier is that it allows logical expressions themselves to be partially defined. Further-

more, since the 'and' and 'or' operations are both commutative in LPF, their use does not place unnecessary ordering constraints on the way that logical expressions need to be written for them to be totally defined. It also turns out that the least element $\perp$ will only appear within the semantic interpretation – it need never appear within either specifications or proofs about the entities they define. Finally, the semantics of the logical operations is the greatest monotonic extension of the conventional Boolean operations. This ensures that ordinary 2-valued reasoning about *total* predicates is also valid in the LPF case. This demonstrates that LPF is, as expected, an extension of ordinary Boolean logic.

However, it is also true that there are some 2-valued tautologies which are not tautologies in LPF, such as the law of the excluded middle:

$$\vdash A \vee \neg A$$

This law is so named this because it says that either a proposition or its negation is valid – there is no 'halfway' house. Clearly, this fails in the LPF case because propositions can also be partial. In such cases, a similar LPF tautology can be obtained by merely adding appropriate typing requirements on propositions to the assumptions, as follows:

$$(A \in \mathbb{B}) \vdash A \vee \neg A$$

For similar reasons, the Deduction Inference Rule for Boolean propositional logic cannot hold as it stands for LPF:

2-valued Deduction Theorem $\dfrac{A \vdash B}{\vdash A \Rightarrow B}$

Instead, a similar looking inference property to the Deduction Theorem holds, but again with some extra definedness requirements concerning propositions:

LPF Deduction Theorem $\dfrac{(A \in \mathbb{B}) \quad A \vdash B}{\vdash A \Rightarrow B}$

Moreover, when LPF is used at the level of predicates on values, the usual logical quantifiers are taken to range over the well-defined values of the collection of values, so in LPF the following is valid:

$$\vdash \forall A \in \mathbb{B}. \, A \vee \neg A$$

The property of quantifiers where the bound variable only ranges over denoting (or defined) values is also useful in proving properties concerning partial functions defined by recursion.

Finally, it turns out that the use of LPF does not restrict the kinds of predicates that can be specified. By using the semantics of LPF that has been given in terms of 2-valued logic, it would be possible (although somewhat laborious) to provide an equivalent 2-valued logic specification for every specification in LPF. However, a direct translation of specifications in LPF is likely to produce longer or, at any rate, less concise 2-valued specifications. This is because LPF implicitly handles partially defined logic expressions whereas the translated 2-valued version would need to say how any partial propositions are treated in a uniform way.

21.8.9 Modularity and abstract data types

Neither BSI/VDM nor Z have incorporated a fundamental notion of modularity into their respective core languages.

Within Z, the key notion of 'information hiding' is provided at the schema level in terms of existential quantification. However, it is non-trivial to see how this can solely provide the kind of encapsulation needed to apply the methodology of abstract data types within system development. Hence, it would appear to be necessary to add extra constructs to provide for this style of specification within Z.

In BSI/VDM, there have been several proposals for introducing modularity constructs which provide for some form of 'information hiding' and also parameterization of modules (see Bear (1988), Middleburg (1989)). At the time of writing, there is no clear-cut best solution which provides all the facilities needed for abstract data type methodology.

It should also be noted that both techniques allow the use of operations by reference to the relations that they satisfy. This is useful and naturally arises when building up layers of specifications where one layer refers to the objects of another, prior layer.

In Z, the relation corresponding to an operation is an object just like any other and so can be used directly in expressions with no additional syntax. In BSI/VDM, the operation quotation notation is introduced which permits both the pre- and post-condition to be used as Boolean functions within expressions; this is illustrated in Section 21.7.3.

21.8.10 Auxiliary definitions

In using either Z or BSI/VDM, it is often necessary to specify entities that are not intended to be implemented in their own right, but which serve an auxiliary role in specifying those features that must be implemented. Both techniques permit the definition of these auxiliary entities.

21.8.11 Schema calculus

The schema calculus is unique to Z. It provides an elegant and concise means to compose different pieces of specification together. The semantics of these operators has been given in Spivey (1989).

However, it appears that the semantics of many of the schema combining operators must intrinsically rely upon the way that the declared names in a schema remain part of the schema's denotation. In that case, most of the properties of specifications obtained by the use of schema calculus operations must ultimately rely upon the coincidence of declared names in separate component schemas. Moreover, in common with other name binding mechanisms (such as the lambda calculus), heavy reliance on the subtler features of the schema calculus can make it hard to keep track of which names are significant, where they are bound and to what.

21.8.12 Imperative programming features

BSI/VDM includes a fragment of an imperative programming language that could be used as a pseudo-code for defining algorithmic structure. There are no corresponding features within Z itself, although the recent work of Carroll Morgan (1990) shows how specifications may usefully be embedded within programming languages as part of the structural refinement of program code.

21.8.13 Exceptional conditions

BSI/VDM incorporates two notions of exceptional condition, one for use in implicit specification of operations and the other for use with the imperative programming style; this is illustrated in Section 21.7.2.

The implicit style of exceptional condition specification in BSI/VDM is a way of writing complex pre-/post-condition expressions. A similar style is provided in Z by using schema calculus operations to introduce additional constraints to cover exceptional conditions.

The explicit style of exception handling in BSI/VDM provides a mechanism to break the standard flow of control under exceptional conditions. Z needs no corresponding feature since it does not contain an imperative programming language subset.

21.9 Model-based specifications – some issues

A number of misconceptions and criticisms have arisen concerning what model-based specifications are and what they precisely describe. A number of these points are discussed here.

21.9.1 Operational bias

It is sometimes said that a model-based specification is too operational in the way that the system is described; too much of the design is visible within the abstract specification, distorting the analysis of the 'natural' structure of the system. A potential deleterious effect of such overly prescriptive specifications is that they might prevent (or inhibit) the development of otherwise perfectly good implementations.

This issue is clearly related to the notion of specification bias, discussed by Jones (1980), and also to the process of reification – turning an abstract analysis into a concrete, working system that exhibits or demonstrates the requirements.

21.9.2 Structural bias and over-specification

The model-based descriptions introduce specific structures to represent or model various entities of interest, such as the underlying state space upon which the operations will act. One style of refinement is to exploit the form of the specification in constructing implementations. This gives rise to implementations which 'simulate' the specification by following its syntactic structure.

The complaint here is that, although often manifestly correct, these implementations can easily be impractical and virtually useless for all but the most trivial of input cases. This will be especially true for the more abstract and elegant specifications as these need not contain much in the way of explicit computational or algorithmic content. A further discussion of related issues may be found in Hayes and Jones (1989).

A partial answer is to try to exploit more expressive forms of refinement which permit the implementation to meet functionally the specification without it also having to adopt the same structural form. The remainder of this answer involves a research issue of isolating a rich and varied collection of refinement rules that can be applied to practical specifications whose implementation requires non-trivial algorithm design.

Having said this, there is little in the way of sound practical experience derived from large-scale refinements that provides information on the potential differences between specification and implementation structure. More to the point, active research continues which is aimed at discovering an appropriate taxonomy of useful refinement rules (Fitzgerald and Jones, 1990).

21.9.3 Difficulties in separating different concerns

Model-based specifications necessarily make choices about the structure of a situation, and this may place detailed and specific constraints on the way that design considerations can be met.

Of course, every mathematical model will offer some particular perspective or way of describing a given situation. That is, they discuss situations from a given point of view and assert that the situation has a particular structure from which, it is hoped, relevant conclusions can be drawn and their computational content (in the form of implementations) extracted.

A consequence of this is that a specific view will be presented which selects certain properties and attributes of the situation in terms of which it will be formally characterized. However, this is usually at the expense of other equally relevant properties, which, although perfectly logical and apparently equally fundamental, then appear as derived notions somewhat after the fact.

Indeed, just as a vector space will usually have many spanning sets of vectors to act as bases, so too will there be several collections of properties and relations that capture the same situation. In short, a model-based specification presents a particular and very specific way of characterizing situations and there will be many others (of very different structure) which represent the same situation.

To continue the analogy with vector spaces for a little longer, a model-based specification is analogous to a specific choice of a spanning set of vectors. Other, more property-oriented forms of specification try to achieve a form of presentation that is as independent of modelling choices as possible and therefore only uses characteristic properties that are expressible in a way that is independent of the features of any underlying representation. That approach is somewhat analogous to characterizing a finite dimensional vector space without resorting to the selection of a particular basis for it (i.e. by giving its dimension [an invariant property] and the field of scalars over which it is defined).

Although such 'representation-independent' specifications are very abstract in their formulation, they often have the disadvantage that it is harder to extract any computational content that they might possess. Indeed, it is implied above that every mathematical model must discuss something and inevitably introduces entities in terms of which such a discussion is expressed. Any specification claiming to be 'representation-independent' could only be a certain kind of highly abstract description that only uses very general and universal notions to imply the existence of specific objects. The use of techniques from Category Theory is particularly relevant here (Rydeheard and Burstall, 1988).

21.9.4 Inadequate representation of external concerns

It is sometimes the case that a system specification needs to make reference to entities and notions that the correctness of the software must rely upon, even though these concepts are not to be implemented or even implementable in principle.

A good example is the specification of, say, a process control sensor system which might need to capture certain properties of the physical notion of time. Clearly, although an entity could easily be introduced whose repetitive change in value represents the passage of time, it would certainly be unwise to say that such an entity 'implements' or 'characterizes' time in any fundamental sense. Indeed, implementations of any thing are always definitive whereas time cannot be defined in the same sense, even though the passing of time can obviously be measured.

More generally, certain properties of physical systems must form part of the base of assumptions when formulating the correctness of a system processing physical measurements. In short, a mathematical model of a physical system appears to be necessary in order to express the correctness of process control software.

A possible halfway house is first of all to isolate any relations on the data types and their operators that would result from their supposed correspondence to physical parameters; then, using this information, provide an interpretation of these relations purely in terms of a discrete mathematical model that involves no further justification from, nor reference to, physical

theory. In this sense, the physics will only enter as additional consistency assumptions on the behaviour of the interface to the software which is thereafter assumed to be maintained directly by the external environment.

It should further be emphasized that at all stages of the discussion above, the concern was with various kinds of (mathematical) model and comparisons between the entities that comprise them. Any claimed relationship that these models may or may not have to external physical phenomena will require an appropriate series of experimental tests in order to establish the experimental evidence for such a claim.

21.10 Underlying semantic issues

This section briefly discusses some issues that arise when designing a specification language and in giving it a semantics.

21.10.1 The metacircularity problem

Broadly speaking, a specification language is a mathematical notation for describing the semantics or meaning of a particular software or hardware system. That such a notation must itself possess semantics is a corollary of the fact that it has both the precision and the descriptive power associated with mathematical notations.

This immediately raises the question of how to define the semantics of a notation that is itself capable of defining the semantics of notations and other systems. This issue is known as the metacircularity problem. The immediate technical problem is how to determine consistently denotational spaces that are sufficient for giving a logical interpretation to every well-formed specification.

The heart of this problem concerns showing how to delimit the class of all objects and entities that may populate the denotation of an arbitrary specification. This presents a similar mathematical challenge to that which arises in giving a mathematical definition of the foundations of mathematics itself.

21.10.2 On programming language semantics

In giving the semantics of programming languages, one runs into a problem reminiscent of the metacircularity problem. This is because in many programming languages it is possible to represent reflexive (or circular) programming structures which refer to themselves in some computable manner. This can arise in both a benign form and in a potentially more damaging form.

An example of this benign circularity occurs when giving the semantics of data structures which can contain 'pointers' to themselves. This can be easily modelled by introducing another entity, often called Locations, so introducing an extra level of indirection into the model described. The potential circularity is then tamed by noting that pointers can then be represented in terms of a graph structure involving Locations. The circularity is then only made indirectly via these Locations so preventing any direct circularity from arising.

An example of the potentially more damaging form of circularity occurs when the programming language contains imperative procedures that transform some kind of state space and where these procedures can also be stored as part of the state. There are several ways in which this circularity can be understood and brought under control. One of the most theoretically satisfying involves using Dana Scott's Theory of Domains (Schmidt, 1986). Without going into the technical details here, Scott's Domain Theory provides mathematical techniques for consistently solving the reflexive domain equations corresponding to the implicit self-reference between the store and the procedures that transform the store.

21.10.3 On semantics for concurrency

The semantics of concurrent systems is often expressed in terms of concepts such as evaluation traces or other kinds of observation. It is here that the notion of 'observation' assumes it importance since concurrency is concerned with how individual components of a system can make progress while interacting with one another to achieve some overall goal of the composite system. The semantic problems that arise then revolve around how to model the interaction of components and what observations may be made of such a system (see Chapter 19).

21.11 Proof obligations

A proof obligation is a logical formula which the specifier must show to be a consequence of the specification, so that a specification or more generally, a development, can be taken to be acceptable. The term 'proof obligation' arose because they are often general properties for which a proof cannot always be found by uniform mechanical means (i.e. they belong to a general class of propositions that happens to contain some propositions which are undecidable). In such cases, *ad hoc* techniques involving human guidance can then be applied to help establish these results. In a more pragmatic sense proof obligations may be viewed as what the developer of a specification is obliged to prove in order to confirm that the development or specification is consistent.

21.11.1 Type-checking: proof obligations for consistency

Proof obligations can arise within the context of a particular specification. These are often concerned with ensuring that arguments to functions and operations satisfy any logical constraints such as data type invariants and pre-conditions. The formulae so arising will generally depend upon the context where the entities occur and logical properties involving that context will be required to discharge such obligations.

For example, consider selecting the first element of a list. This operation can only be performed if such a list is not empty, and so a proof obligation would arise wherever such a selection from a list is required. Mathematically speaking, this simply ensures that the partial function for list selection is only applied within its domain of application. More generally, the list selection function requires that the list have as many elements available from which an appropriate selection can be made.

21.11.2 Reification: proof obligations for correct design

As indicated above, proof obligations also arise when reifying one specification into another, more detailed and implementation-oriented version. It is important to realize that such obligations arise purely as a means of establishing a link between one specification and another. As such, these obligations do not lie within either of the specifications but will usually involve concepts and entities from each of them.

For example, consider the reification of a data type specification by its implementation. Associated with this is the requirement that the implementing data type is non-empty and that each abstract value (satisfying the associated type invariant property) can be represented by at least one concrete value (also satisfying a corresponding type invariant on the concrete representation).

The proof obligation to be established is a predicate which 'explains' how the concrete data type represents the values of the abstract type, and will involve entities contained in the defini-tions of the two corresponding data types. This topic is discussed in more detail in Chapter 24.

21.12 VDM and Z – a brief historical perspective

21.12.1 Z historical background

Z originated in the paper 'Specification Language' by Abrial, Schumann and Meyer (1980), used by Abrial as course notes for his lectures in a course given in 1979 at Queen's University Belfast. In late 1979 Jean-Raymond Abrial moved to Oxford and presented a course on the same material to research staff and students at the Programming Research Group (PRG). Rod Burstall observed at the time that the language had a strong flavour of 'Bourbaki' – the goal being to base everything on set theory. Schemas (which were then called 'classes') were presented but without a fully worked-out semantics.

In 1980 Abrial, Tim Clement and Ib Sørensen, all of the PRG, started work on a project suggested by Bernie Cohen, then at Standard Telecommunications Laboratories (later STC Technology Ltd), to specify formally and implement the 'Caviar' (Computer-aided Visitor Information and Reception) system. During this project the notation went through a re-design and the expressive power of classes was developed a little further through the introduction of a class-conjunction operator (which today would be recognized as schema conjunction). Towards the end of the project Abrial (1981) outlined a proof system for the mathematical sub-language (a rudimentary proof system for classes appears in the same document, but was felt at the time to be a little obscure). The language which emerged from the re-design was essentially the same as the mathematical sub-language of Z, but the concrete syntax employed was very much more verbose. It was under the impact of Dana Scott's verdict on the notation 'too long-winded', that the Z group decided to revert to standard mathematical notation.

It was at this point that Cliff Jones and Lockwood Morris joined the PRG. Both were to play an important role in the development of Z; in Morris's case through the constructive criticism of the work of the Z group, and in Cliff Jones's case through the form of competitive collaboration. Impetus for the further development of schemas came from the realization that the standard mathematical forms of extending states and promoting the operations on them were too unwieldy for use in the specification of large-scale systems. What was wanted was a formalism in which extension and promotion were as simply expressible as they were in the VDM meta-language but for which proof rules could be given directly. The nucleus of what later became known as the schema calculus emerged from this effort, and it was Morris's critique of the early attempts to explain conjunction of schemas that forced the first serious attempt at formalizing a proof rule for schema conjunction. It was also in this phase of the development that the idea that a state should contain as little redundancy as possible, then advocated by the VDM school, was rejected (Sufrin, 1983).

Contacts with IBM led to the foundation of the CICS project, the original aim of which was rationally to re-construct IBM's main toolkit for constructing transaction processing systems. Ib Sørensen and Tim Clement joined the project from its inception.

Abrial and Jones left the PRG in the summer of 1981 – Jones having been appointed to a Chair at Manchester; Abrial to take some time away from teaching and research. For the next few years Bernard Sufrin taught Z to students on the Oxford MSc programme and developed an explanation of the type system. Meanwhile, Sørensen and Clement pursued the work at IBM.

The next important step in the development of Z coincided with the arrival of Carroll Morgan at the PRG in 1982. He and

Sufrin worked together on a description of the Unix file system (1984) and it was here that, for the first time, the schema calculus was fully employed. Schemas were used to describe operations as well as describing state and schema disjunction, piping and hiding (all invented by Morgan) were used for the first time.

Following these developments Spivey (1988), in his doctorial thesis, provided Z with a semantic model and Hayes (1987) through his active development of case studies, published a valuable collection of studies in which many of these key ideas appeared. In addition a Z Reference Manual was produced which provides a concise specification of the language (Spivey 1989).

Meanwhile, work at IBM (on which Clement had now been replaced by Hayes) had focused on the development of a 'Z Development Method' to be used on the CICS project. During these investigations a number of disturbing problems concerning the adequacy of the data refinement rules, which had been borrowed from VDM, were discovered. Over a period of three months the whole Z group met regularly at the PRG and formulated answers to these problems (Hoare and Sanders, 1986) and made connection with Milner's and Park's work on simulation.

Hayes was eventually replaced on the IBM project by Jim Woodcock who continued the work on data refinement and proof in Z and started experimenting with describing concurrency. In 1989 a release of CICS was produced with some parts developed using Z. This release showed both a decrease in development cost and an improvement in expected reliability.

21.12.2 VDM – historical background

The origins of VDM lie in the IBM Laboratory in Vienna. The IBM Laboratory originated in a group which Heinz Zemanek brought from the *Technische Hochschule* (now the *Technische Universität Wien*). The group initially worked on hardware projects. A compiler for Algol 60 followed. The recognition that language definition was a crucial issue for the future safe application of computers was emphasized by IBM's creation of the PL/1 language. The Vienna group built on the ideas of Elgot, Landin and McCarthy to create an operational semantics approach capable of defining the whole of PL/1 including its tasking features which involved parallelism. These massive reports were known as the 'Universal Language Document 3' and appeared in three more or less complete versions. The meta-language used was dubbed by outsiders the 'Vienna Definition Language' or VDL. These descriptions were used as the basis for research into compiler design in 1968/70.

The attempt to use the VDL definitions in design were in one sense successful; but they also showed clearly how the operational semantics approach could complicate formal reasoning in an unnecessary way. The Scott/Strachey/Landin work on denotational semantics was taking shape in Oxford. Hans Bekič had long been pressing the Vienna group to adopt a more mathematical approach and Cliff Jones had shown a 'functional semantics' for Algol 60 in a Hursley Technical Report (Jones, 1973). The challenge, starting in late 1972, to design a compiler which translated the evolving ECMA/ANSI standard PL/1 language into the order code of a completely novel machine presented the ideal opportunity to try out the denotational semantics approach. The project was fraught with difficulties and did not result in a finished compiler because of IBM's decision to abandon the machine architecture. It did, however, create VDM.

The formal description of PL/1 in a denotational style is contained in a 1974 Technical Report which was authored by Bekič, Bjørner, Henhapel, Jones and Lucas. The notation used became known as 'Meta IV'.

The diversion of the IBM group to handle more practical problems led to its dissolution. Among others to leave Wolfgang Henhapel became a professor in Darmstadt, Peter Lucas moved to IBM Research in the USA and Dines Bjørner took a visiting chair at Copenhagen and then a permanent one at the Technical University of Denmark. Cliff Jones joined the Programming Research Group at Oxford University and later was appointed to a Chair at Manchester University. Of the key people only Hans Bekič remained at IBM pursuing important research on parallelism until his untimely death in 1982.

Like other dispersions of scientists, this one did not kill the ideas but led to a larger community. The first step was to publish what had been done and Dines Bjørner and Cliff Jones edited Springer's LNCS 61 to this end (1978). Dines Bjørner pursued the language description and compiler development work with Danish colleagues. This led to descriptions of both Ada and CHILL and the first validated European compiler for the Ada language. Cliff Jones picked up on the work he had been doing on formal development methods for non-compiler problems. Five books have been published by Prentice Hall on VDM (Bjørner and Jones, 1978; Jones, 1980, 1986 and 1990; Jones and Shaw, 1990). There are also numerous papers tackling such problems as parallelism and many published case studies.

The English VDM school, inspired by the publication of Jones (1980), resulted in further development impetus for the VDM language. In 1982 ITT IDEC, later to become STC IDEC, evaluated VDM for use in the development of an office automation product. The evaluation report (Hudson, 1982; Jackson *et al.*, 1985) commented favourably on VDM and recommended its use on the project. Amongst its observations were that VDM, as expressed in Jones (1980), was not suitable for large-scale industrial applications as it lacked effective means for structuring specifications, facilities for specifying exceptions, an appropriate pseudo-code into which specifications could be refined and appropriate support tools. Two initiatives sprung from this report. Firstly, a VDM-like language called GREEN was developed along with a syntax and type-checker (Shaw *et al.*, 1984). GREEN was based on a similar language (Beichter *et al.*, 1982) produced by the IBM Laboratory in Boeblingen, Germany. The design and development of GREEN was carried out by Neil Davis, Philip Hudson, Peter Jackson and Roger Shaw. In parallel a separate activity was initiated to develop formally and specify an enhanced version of VDM based on Jones (1980 and 1981). This work resulted in the production of a concrete syntax, an abstract syntax, context conditions, proof obligations, type model (Monahan, 1987) and denotational semantics (Monahan, 1985) for the language. Amongst the new language features developed were means for structuring specifications including the idea of quotation, means for specifying exceptions, higher-order functions (with a restricted form of polymorphism) and 'not yet defined' types and functions. The STC Reference Language (STC-RL), as it was called, became the starting point for the BSI VDM initiative. Work on the development of STC-RL was carried out by Tim Denvir, Mel Jackson, Brian Monahan, Roger Shaw and Ann Walshe and profited from the active involvement, help and support of Cliff Jones.

21.13 Acknowledgements

The authors would like to thank Tim Denvir and Anthony Hall of Praxis Systems and Rosalind Barden of Logical Cambridge for their helpful suggestions and comments regarding this paper. We would also like to thank Bernard Sufrin and Jim Woodcock, both of the PRG, for providing detailed information on the historical background to Z.

21.14 References and bibliography

Abrial, J.-R. (1981) The specification language Z: syntax and semantics, internal teaching notes

Abrial, J.-R., Schuman, S. A. and Meyer, B. (1980) Specification language. In *On the Construction of Programs: An Advanced Course* (R. McKeag and A. Macnaghten, eds), Cambridge University Press

Barwise, J. (1989) Mathematical proofs of computer system correctness. *Notices of the American Mathematical Society*, **36**, 844–851

Barringer, H., Cheng, J. H. and Jones, C. B. (1984) A logic covering undefinedness in program proofs. *Acta Informatica*, **21**, 251–269

Bear, S. (1988) Structuring for the VDM specification language. In *VDM'88: VDM – The Way Ahead* (Bloomfield *et al.*, eds), pp 2–25

Beichter, F., Herzog, O. and Petzsch, H. (1982) *SLAN-4 Reference Manual and Design Rationale*, Technical Report GTR 05.272, IBM Laboratory, Boeblingen

Bjørner, D. and Jones, C. (1978) *The Vienna Development Method – The Meta Language LNCS 61*, Springer-Verlag

Bjørner, D. and Jones, C. B. (1982) *Formal Specification and Software Development*, Prentice Hall International

Bjørner, D., Hoare, C. A. R. and Langmaack, H. (eds) (1990) *VDM'90: VDM and Z – Formal Methods in Software Development*, *Lecture Notes in Computer Science 428*, Springer-Verlag

Bjørner, D., Jones, C. B., Mac an Airchinnigh, M. and Neuhold, E. J. (eds) (1987) *VDM'87: VDM – A Formal Method at Work*, *Lecture Notes in Computer Science 252*, Springer-Verlag

Bloomfield, R., Marshall, L. and Jones, R. (eds) (1988) *VDM'88: VDM – The Way Ahead*, *Lecture Notes in Computer Science 328*, Springer-Verlag

Cheng, J. H. (1986) *A Logic for Partial Functions*, PhD thesis, University of Manchester

Colebrook, A., Pitt, D.H. and Smythe, C. (1990) *A Scheme for Implementing Parallel Search Trees*, Technical Report, Department of Mathematics, University of Surrey

Diller, A. (1990) *Z: An Introduction to Formal Methods*, John Wiley

Ehrig, H. (ed.) (1985) *Formal Methods and Software Development*, *Lecture Notes in Computer Science 186*, Springer-Verlag

Fitzgerald, J. and Jones, C. B. (1990) *Modularizing the Formal Description of a Database System*, Technical Report UMCS-90-1-1, Department of Computer Science, University of Manchester

Gries, D. (1981) *The Science of Programming*, Springer-Verlag

Hall, J. A. (1990) Using Z as a specification calculus for object oriented systems. In *VDM'90: VDM and Z – Formal Methods in Software Development* (Bjørner *et al.*, eds), Springer-Verlag

Hayes, I. (1987) *Specification Case Studies*, Prentice Hall International

Hayes, I. J. and Jones, C. B. (1989) Specifications are not (necessarily) executable. *Software Engineering Journal*, **4**, 320–338

Hoare, C. A. R. and Sanders, J. W. (1986) Data refinement refined. In *Lecture Notes in Computer Science 213*, pp 187–196, Springer-Verlag

Hudson, P. (1982) *Evaluation of VDM*, Technical Report 244 00004-AA, ITT IDEC

Jackson, M. I., Denvir, B. T. and Shaw, R. C. (1985) Experience of introducing the Vienna Development Method into an industrial organisation. In *Formal Methods and Software Development* (H. Ehrig, ed.), Springer-Verlag

Jones, C. B. (1973) *Formal Development of Programs*, Technical Report TR12.117, IBM Hursley

Jones, C. B. (1980) *Software Development, A Rigorous Approach*, Prentice Hall International

Jones, C. B. (1981) *Development Methods for Computer Programs – Including a Notion of Interference*, PhD thesis, University of Oxford

Jones, C. B. (1986) *Systematic Software Development Using VDM*, Prentice Hall International

Jones, C. B. (1990) *Systematic Software Development Using VDM* (2nd edn), Prentice Hall International

Jones, C. B. and Shaw, R. C. (1990) *Case Studies in Systematic Software Development*, Prentice Hall International

King, S. (1990) Z and the refinement calculus. In *VDM'90: VDM and Z – Formal Methods in Software Development* (Bjørner *et al.*, eds), Springer-Verlag

King, S. and Sørensen, I. H. (1989) From specification, through design to code: a case study in refinement. In *Formal Methods: Theory and Practice* (P. N. Scharbach, ed.), Blackwell Scientific

Kleene, S. C. (1952) *Introduction to Meta-Mathematics*, North-Holland

Larsen, P. G., Arentoft, M. M., Monahan, B. Q. and Bear, S. (1989) Towards a formal semantics of the BSI/VDM specification language. In *Information Processing '89* (G. X. Ritter, ed.), Elsevier Science Publishers B.V. (North-Holland), pp 95–100

McMorran, M. A. and Nicholls, J. E. (1990) *Z User Manual*, Technical Report TR12.274, IBM United Kingdom Laboratories Ltd, Hampshire

Middleburg, C. A. (1989) VVSL: A language for structured VDM specifications. *Formal Aspects of Computing*, **1**, 115–135

Monahan, B. Q. (1985) *A Semantic Definition for the STC VDM Reference Language*, Technical Report, STC IDEC Ltd

Monahan, B. Q. (1987) A type model for VDM. In *VDM'87: VDM – A Formal Method at Work* (Bjørner *et al.*, eds), Springer-Verlag

Morgan, C. (1990) *Deriving Programs from Specifications*, Prentice Hall International

Morgan, C. and Sufrin, B. (1984) A formal specification of the Unix file system. *IEEE Software Engineering*, **SE-10**

Rydeheard, D. E. and Burstall, R. (1988) *Computational Category Theory*, Prentice Hall International

Schmidt, D. A. (1986) *Denotational Semantics*, Allyn and Bacon

Schuman, S. A. and Pitt, D. H. (1987) Object-oriented subsystem specification. In *Proceedings IFIP Working Conference on Specification and Transformation*, North Holland

Schuman, S. A., Pitt, D. H. and Byers, P. J. (1990) Object-oriented process specification. In *Specification and Verification of Concurrent Systems*, (ed. C. Rattray), Workshops in Computing, Springer-Verlag

Shaw, R. C., Hudson, P. N. and Davis, N. W. (1984) Introduction of a formal technique into a software development environment. *ACM Software Engineering Notes*, **9**

Spivey, J. M. (1988) *Understanding Z, Cambridge Tracts in Theoretical Computer Science*, Cambridge University Press

Spivey, J. M. (1989) *The Z Notation, A Reference Manual*, Prentice Hall

Sufrin, B. (1983) Formal system specification: notation and example. In *Tools and Notation for Program Construction: An Advanced Course* (D. Neel, ed.), Cambridge University Press

Turski, W. M. and Maibaum, T. S. E. (1987) *The Specification of Computer Programs*, Addison-Wesley

Woodcock, J. (1989a) Calculating properties of Z specifications. *ACM Sigsoft Software Engineering Notes*, **15**

Woodcock, J. (1989b) Structuring specifications in Z. *IEE Software Engineering Journal*, **4**

Woodcock, J. and Loomes, M. (1988) *Software Engineering Mathematics*, Pitman

Wordsworth, J. B. (1987) *A Z Development Method*, Technical Report, IBM United Kingdom Laboratories Ltd

22 Algebraic specifications

M-C Gaudel
LRI, University of Paris-Sud, France

Contents

22.1 Introduction

Algebraic specifications are based on the concept of abstract data types or more precisely, on a way of defining abstract data types which is called algebraic (or, sometimes, axiomatic). This approach was originally introduced by Guttag in his thesis (1975). Since that time this approach has been the subject of theoretical research, with universal algebra, category theory and logic as a common mathematical basis and framework.

Practically, the most important aspect of this work is the design of several algebraic specification languages. Most of these languages have been developed and used experimentally in research laboratories, both public and industrial. In this context, several successful case studies have been performed. Additionally, algebraic data types have been introduced into SDL, the CCITT specification language, in LOTOS, a specification language for protocols which has been submitted to the ISO standardization procedure, and in several specification languages developed in ESPRIT projects.

The first part of this chapter is a presentation of the basic concepts of algebraic data types. The second part lists the main characteristics of some of the most significant algebraic specification languages such as CLEAR, CIP-L, extended-ML, LARCH, OBJ, ACT-ONE and PLUSS. The conclusion gives perspectives on this approach.

22.2 Algebraic data types

22.2.1 Informal introduction

'Types are not sets'. This statement by Morris (1973) is now widely accepted. A data type is characterized by one or more sets of values *and* by the operations which are allowed on the values. For instance, stacks and queues of integers both correspond to lists of integers, but they are different data types since the operations allowed on them are different.

There are different ways of formalizing data types. The algebraic approach defines a data type as *a many-sorted algebra*; a many-sorted algebra is one or several sets of values and some operations on these sets. These sets are named (it is necessary to distinguish them) and their names are called *sorts*.

The *signature of a data type* is made of its sorts, the names of its operations, and the arity of these operations, i.e. the sorts of their domains and co-domain (when there is only one sort, this notion coincides with the definition of a single sorted signature in Chapter 3). Some of the operation names have an arity with a co-domain only: it means that the corresponding operations have no operands; they are constant.

An *abstract data type* is a class of many-sorted algebras with the same signature and some specified common properties. An *algebraic data type* is the definition of an abstract data type by means of a signature and some axioms (logical formulae) that the algebras of the class must satisfy. An example is given in *Figure 22.1*.

Thus the *presentation* of an algebraic data type is a pair $<\Sigma, E>$, where Σ is a signature and E is a set of Σ-axioms.

If the axioms are restricted to equations, the algebraic data type is said to be equational. If the axioms are restricted to implications from conjunctions of equations to one equation (Horn clauses with equality), the algebraic data type is said to be positive conditional. As will be seen later, these two kinds of algebraic data types have interesting properties.

Given a presentation, it is necessary to give it some semantics, i.e. to define what is the class of many-sorted algebras which corresponds to this presentation. There are two main semantic approaches in the field of algebraic data types. The first one is the initial approach, originally developed by the ADJ group

sorts:
Bool, Nat, Set

operations:

true, false: $\to$Bool	_or_: Bool $\times$ Bool$\to$Bool
0: $\to$Nat	s_: Nat $\to$Nat
_eq_: Nat $\times$ Nat $\to$Bool	empty-set: $\to$Set
add_to_: Nat $\times$ Set $\to$ Set	_belongs-to_: Nat $\times$ Set $\to$Bool

axioms:

true or B = true	false or B = B
B or B' = B' or B	0 eq 0 = true
0 eq s(X) = false	s(X) eq 0 = false
s(X) eq s(Y) = X eq Y	X belongs-to empty-set = false
X belongs-to (add Y to S) = (X eq Y) or (X belongs-to S)	

where:
B, B': Bool   X, Y: Nat   S: Set

Figure 22.1   Example of a presentation of an algebraic data type. As introduced for the first time in the OBJ language by Goguen (1978), the syntax of the signature allows infix and even mixfix notation for the operations names. In this case, the operand positions are indicated within the operation name, by the character " _ "

(Goguen *et al.*, 1978). The second one, or more exactly the second ones, are the loose approaches, advocated first by Guttag and formalized later by the CIP group (see for instance Broy *et al.*, 1984) and many others.

Before presenting these approaches, some general definitions are needed. Most of them are just generalization from the definitions of Chapter 3 to the many sorted case.

22.2.2 Basic definitions of the theory of algebraic data types

Definition 1: Σ-algebra

Given a signature $\Sigma = <S,F>$ where S is a *set of sorts*, and F is a set of function names with an arity in $S^* \times S$, a Σ-*algebra A* is:

1. For each s in S, a set of values, denoted A_s; these sets are called carrier sets.
2. For each f in F, with arity $<s1 \ldots sn, s>$, a function f^A from $A_{s1} \times \ldots \times A_{sn}$ into A_s.

An example of a Σ-algebra is the algebra of Σ-terms, often denoted T_Σ (or Σ_T).

Definition 2: Σ-terms and T_Σ

Given a signature $\Sigma = <S, F>$, the set of Σ-terms T_Σ is defined as the smallest set such that:

1. Any c in F with arity $<empty, s>$ (i.e. c is a constant name) belongs to T_Σ, and c is said to be of sort s.
2. For any f in F with arity $<s1 \ldots sn, s>$, for any t_i $(i = 1, \ldots, n)$ of sort si belonging to T_Σ, $f(t_1, \ldots t_n)$ belongs to T_Σ and is of sort s.

The set of Σ-terms of sort s is noted $(T_\Sigma)_s$.

T_Σ is a Σ-algebra where the carrier sets are the $(T_\Sigma)_s$ and the functions are the constructions of a Σ-term from simpler Σ-terms of the right sorts. This algebra is also called the *word algebra* over Σ.

Given a Σ-algebra A and a Σ-term t of sort s, t denotes a value in A_s which is the result of the composition of the various f^A

occurring in t. This value is noted t^A. It is called the *interpretation* of t in A.

Definition 3: *Σ-terms with variables*, $T_Σ(X)$

Given a signature $Σ = <S, F>$, and a set X of variables where each variable is of a given sort in S, the set of Σ-terms with variables in X, $T_Σ(X)$ is defined as the smallest set such that:

1. Any c in F with arity $<empty, s>$ belongs to $T_Σ(X)$ and c is said to be of sort s.
2. Any x in X belongs to $T_Σ(X)$ and is of the sort of x.
3. For any f in F with arity $<s1 \dots sn, s>$, for any t_i $(i = 1, \dots, n)$ of sort si belonging to $T_Σ(X)$, $f(t_1, \dots, t_n)$ belongs to $T_Σ(X)$ and is of sort s.

$T_Σ(X)$ is sometimes noted $Σ_T(X)$.

Given a Σ-algebra A and a Σ-term t of sort s with variables $x_1, \dots x_n$ of sorts $s1, \dots, sn$, t denotes a function from $A_{s1} \times \dots \times A_{sn}$ into A_s which is the composition of the various f^A occurring in t. As above, this function is noted t^A.

Definition 4: *Σ-equations and Σ-axioms*

Given a signature $Σ = <S, F>$, and a set X of variables where each variable is of a given sort in S, a Σ-equation is a formula $t = t'$ where t and t' belong to $T_Σ(X)$ and are of the same sort.

A Σ-axiom is a logical formula built from Σ-equations using the connectives of the propositional calculus: $¬ ∧, ∨, ⇒, ⇔$.

If a Σ-axiom is of the form: $e_1 ∧ \dots ∧ e_n ⇒ e$, where $e, e_1 \dots e_n$ are Σ-equations, it is said to be positive conditional.

Some authors have considered axioms with quantifiers, i.e. first order predicate logic (see for instance Wirsing *et al.*, 1983).

Some inference rules are needed to prove properties of types from their axioms. In the case of positive conditional axioms, the rules are those related to equality (reflexivity, symmetry, transitivity), congruence (substitutivity, see Chapter 3) and implication (*modus ponens*). In more general cases the rules are those of the first order predicate logic.

Incidentally, most of the definitions and results for algebraic specifications are independent of the logic used to write the axioms. The concept of institution introduced by Goguen and Burstall (1984) allows abstraction from the logic. This point is discussed later.

Definition 5: *Σ-algebra satisfying an axiom*

Given a set of Σ-variables X, and a Σ-algebra A, an *assignment* from X into A is a set of functions from X_s into A_s.

A Σ-equation $t = t'$, with its variables in X, is *satisfied* by A, if for any assignment from X into A, t^A and t'^A yield the same result. This notion of satisfaction extends to other axioms by giving the logical connectives their usual interpretations.

A *presentation* $<Σ,E>$ of an algebraic data type defines an interesting class of Σ-algebras: the class $ALG(Σ,E)$ of all the Σ-algebras satisfying the axioms in E. An algebra of this class is called a *Σ,E-algebra*. The various approaches, mentioned above, for defining the semantics of algebraic specifications differ in the subclass of $ALG(Σ,E)$ which is considered to be the semantics of $<Σ,E>$. Putting it in another way, they differ in the class of data types which is stated as corresponding to the presentation of an abstract data type. This class is called the *class of models* of the presentation.

Definition 6: *Σ-homomorphisms*

Given a pair of Σ-algebras A and B, a *Σ-homomorphism* h from A to B is a set of functions $\{h_s: A_s → B_s | s ∈ S\}$ such that for each

f in F with arity $<s1 \dots sn, s>$ and every n-tuple $<a_1, \dots, a_n>$ where $a_i ∈ A_{si}$ for $i = 1, \dots, n$:

$$h_s(f^A(a_1, \dots, a_n)) = f^B(h_{s1}(a_1), \dots, h_{sn}(a_n))$$

Starting from this definition, Σ-isomorphisms can be defined just as in Chapter 3.

22.2.3 Initial approach

In this approach, there is a unique (up to isomorphism) Σ-algebra corresponding to a presentation. This algebra is initial in the category where the objects are the Σ,E-algebras and the arrows are Σ-homomorphisms.

Such an initial algebra always exists when the axioms of the presentation are equational or positive conditional. There is an important theorem on the existence and the construction of this algebra.

Theorem (*Goguen* et al., *1978*): *existence and initiality of* $T_{Σ,E}$

Let $<Σ, E>$ be a positive conditional presentation:

1. There exists a smallest congruence on $T_Σ$ compatible with E, denoted $\sim_E$.
2. The quotient of $T_Σ$ by $\sim_E$ is a Σ,E-algebra which is initial in $ALG(Σ,E)$.

This algebra is noted $T_{Σ,E}$ or $T_{T/E}$.

The construction of $T_{Σ,E}$ is described in Chapter 3, Section 3.3, in the case of single-sorted signatures and equations.

Moreover, it has been proved in Makovsky (1985) that positive conditional axioms are the largest class of axioms which ensures the existence of initial algebras. More precisely, if a presentation admits an initial algebra, it is equivalent (i.e. it has the same initial algebra, up to isomorphism) to a positive conditional presentation.

It is not very difficult to build an example of a presentation without a smallest congruence $\sim_E$. *Figure 22.2* gives such an example: it is impossible to build a smallest congruence on $\{a,b,c\}$ which is compatible with the axiom $a = b ∨ b = c$.

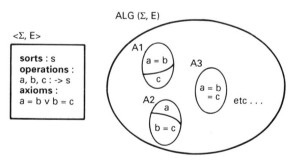

Figure 22.2 A presentation $<Σ,E>$ without initial algebra

Intuitively speaking, $T_{Σ,E}$, when it exists, corresponds to a data type where the values of the carrier sets correspond to equivalence classes in $T_Σ$. Since these equivalence classes are the smallest ones, it means that $T_{Σ,E}$ only satisfies the axioms in E (and their logical consequences using the inference rules mentioned above). There are no additional properties. Moreover, any value of this data type is the interpretation of at least one closed term. There are no additional values.

22.2.4 Loose approaches

The initial approach does not completely match with our intuition of what an abstract data type is: the axioms of a presentation usually express some minimal requirements on the properties of the data type. For instance, in the example of Figure 22.1, it would be interesting to consider those Σ-algebras where the addition operation is permutative: add n to (add n' to s) = add n' to (add n to s). Nothing is said about this property; it is not required by the axioms. However, it is not contradictory to the axioms.

A first idea could be to consider all the Σ,E-algebras. However, there are some clumsy algebras in ALG(Σ,E); one definitely not wanted in the semantics of an abstract data type is the *trivial* Σ-algebra. This algebra satisfies any axiom since there is only one value in each carrier set, and any operation with result in this set returns this value... Note that this algebra is final in the category where the objects are the Σ,E-algebras and the arrows are Σ-homomorphisms.

There are other (less) strange algebras: the ones where the carrier sets contains 'junk', i.e. values which are not computable via the signature. Such models are sometimes interesting. It will be seen later that they are of some use in the case of parameterized specifications. However, most of the time, the only relevant Σ,E-algebras are *finitely generated* with respect to Σ or to a subsignature of Σ.

Definition 7: finitely-generated Σ-algebras, GEN(Σ,E)

Given a signature $\Sigma = <S,F>$, a Σ-algebra A is finitely generated with respect to Σ if for any value v in a carrier set of A, there exists a term t of t_Σ such that $t^A = v$.

The class of finitely generated Σ,E-algebras is called GEN(Σ,E). Algebras of this class are also called term models (cf. Chapter 3).

By construction, $T_{\Sigma,E}$ is finitely generated. Since it is initial in ALG(Σ,E), it is obvious that this algebra is also initial in GEN(Σ,E).

Definition 8: constructors or generators

A Σ-algebra A is finitely generated with respect of a subsignature $\Sigma' = <S,C>$ of Σ if, for any value v in a carrier set of A, there exists a term t of $T_{\Sigma'}$ such that $t^A = v$. The operations in C are called *constructors* or *generators* of A.

One of the advantages of considering the semantics of a presentation to be the class GEN(Σ,E), or the class of Σ,E-algebras finitely generated by some constructors, is the possibility of enriching the inference rules mentioned above by an induction principle.

For instance, in the example of Figure 22.1, it becomes possible to use the following inference rule:

$$[P \text{ (empty-set)} \land (\forall\, X, \forall\, S, P(S) \Rightarrow P \text{ (add X to S))}] \Rightarrow$$
$$[\forall\, S, P(S)]$$

since empty-set and add are the only operations with a result of sort Set.

When the presentation $<\Sigma,E>$ is positive conditional, GEN(Σ,E) has several interesting properties (Broy *et al.*, 1984):

1. Any algebra A in GEN(Σ,E) is isomorphic to a quotient of T_Σ, by a congruence $\sim_A$ which contains $\sim_E$.
2. GEN(Σ,E) is a complete lattice with respect to the inclusion of congruences.

The least element is $T_{\Sigma,E}$. The greatest element is the trivial Σ-algebra.

Let us come back to the problem of removing this uninterest-ing final trivial algebra from the class of Σ,E-algebras associated with a presentation $<\Sigma,E>$. A way to deal with this problem, which seems the most interesting currently, is to introduce a notion of hierarchy in the specification of algebraic data types and to restrict the semantics of a specification SP, which is built above (or is an extension of, or is an enrichment of) a primitive specification SP_p, to a class of algebras which preserve the semantics of SP_p.

For instance, the example of Figure 22.1 can be rewritten in a hierarchical way, distinguishing the Booleans as a primitive part. If the semantics of the Booleans is restricted to the initial algebra, (i.e. true $\neq$ false), then the rule that the algebras associated with the new presentation must preserve this semantics removes the trivial algebra from the models.

The sentence 'the semantics of the primitive part must be preserved' can be interpreted in various ways, depending on the meanings given to the words 'semantics' and 'preserve'.

Definition 9: hierarchical algebraic specifications

A hierarchical algebraic specification is a triple $<\Sigma, E, P>$, where P is a presentation $<\Sigma_p, E_p>$ such that Σ_p is included in Σ and E_p is included in E.

P is called the primitive part of the specification. It may be also a hierarchical specification $<\Sigma_p, E_p, P'>$.

The value of this notion is not limited to the elimination of trivial algebras. It was recognized very early by Burstall and Goguen (1977) to be useful for the composition of specifications in the initial approach, and by Guttag and Horning (1978) for the loose approach.

Definition 10: Σ_p-reduction of a Σ-algebra, Σ-extension of a Σ_p-algebra

Given two signatures Σ and Σ_p such that Σ_p is included in Σ, A a Σ_p-algebra, B a Σ-algebra:

1. A is a Σ_p-reduction of B if $A_s = B_s$ for all sorts s of Σ_p, and $f^A = f^B$ for all functions f of Σ_p.
2. Conversely, B is a Σ-extension of A.

Definition 11: hierarchical models (Wirsing et al., 1983)

Given a hierarchical algebraic specification S = $<\Sigma, E, P>$, a Σ-algebra A is a hierarchical model of S if it belongs to GEN(Σ,E) and if its Σ_p-reduction is a hierarchical model of P. The class of hierarchical models of $<\Sigma,E,P>$ is denoted HMOD(Σ,E,P).

This definition is more a principle than a complete definition; it is meaningless without several comments.

First, if we replace in this definition 'belongs to GEN(Σ,E)' by 'is an initial model of $<\Sigma,E>$' we have a notion of *hierarchy for the initial approach*. This notion allows enrichments only if they follow the rule: *no confusion and no junk* in the primitive data type.

If we now replace in Definition 11 'its Σ_p-reduction is a hierarchical model of P' by 'its Σ_p-reduction is an initial model of P', we have a hierarchy with two levels only, with a combination of initial and loose semantics. This notion of hierarchy was historically the first one and was used for the semantic definition of the CLEAR specification language (Burstall and Goguen, 1980, among others).

The interpretation of Definition 11 followed in the CIP-L language consists in assuming that any specification contains the specification of Booleans and considering only those hierarchical models where true $\neq$ false (Bauer *et al.*, 1985).

The one defined in the PLUSS language (Gaudel, 1985;

Bidoit, 1989) introduces a distinction between basic specifications, without a primitive part, which have an initial semantics, and hierarchical specifications, with basic or hierarchical specification as primitive part, which have a loose semantics, following Definition 11.

In these approaches, if the primitive part of a specification has only non-trivial models, and if there is a final algebra among the hierarchical models, then this algebra is not trivial and is especially interesting; in a final model, all the terms of non-primitive sort in T_Σ are equal unless they are specified different via some operations with different results in the primitive sorts. In some sense, the final algebra is the more abstract one: the interpretation of a term t is independent of the structure of t, and depends only on the observation of t by the operations with primitive co-domain.

In the example of Figure 22.1, if Bool and Nat are considered primitive, the only observation of Set is via the belongs-to operation, and two terms of sort Set are equal if and only if the same natural numbers belong to them. This is perfectly consistent with our intuitive idea of sets.

Some researchers (Wand, 1979, among others) have suggested considering this final algebra as the semantics of a hierarchical specification, with some variants in the choices of the observation contexts (Sannella and Tarlecki, 1987). These approaches are called observational or behavioural semantics. They provide a convenient theoretical framework for the concept of correct representation of an algebraic data type by another one.

Coming back to Definition 11, it is important to note that HMOD(Σ, E, P) can be empty; this is the case when the enrichment includes some contradiction with respect to the primitive specification.

Moreover, when it is not empty, the existence of terminal and final algebras is no longer ensured, even in the positive conditional case (Bernot, 1987). However, some sufficient conditions can be given.

Definition 12: sufficient completeness and hierarchical consistency of a hierarchical specification (Guttag and Horning, 1978)

A hierarchical specification $<\Sigma, E, P>$ is said to be sufficiently complete if:

Every t of T_Σ of primitive sort can be proved equal to a term t_p of $T_{\Sigma P}$.

It is said hierarchically consistent if:

For every t_p and t'_p in $T_{\Sigma P}$, if $t_p = t'_p$ can be proved in $<\Sigma, E, P>$, it can be proved in P (no confusion on primitive terms).

For instance, the example of Figure 22.1, considered as hierarchical with respect to Bool and Nat is sufficiently complete; the only terms of primitive sort, which are not in $T_{\Sigma P}$, are those beginning by 'belongs-to'. It can be proved by induction on Set that such terms are always equal either to true or to false.

Moreover, this specification is hierarchically consistent: the 'or' above can be shown to be exclusive.

We can now give some sufficient conditions for the existence of terminal and final algebras (Broy *et al.*, 1984). A hierarchical positive conditional specification H = $<\Sigma,E,P>$ has an initial model if: P has an initial model, H is sufficiently complete and hierarchically consistent.

A hierarchical positive conditional specification II = $<\Sigma,E,P>$ has a final model if: the premises of the axioms in E are Σ_P-equations, P has a final model, H is sufficiently complete and hierarchically consistent.

22.3 Representation of an algebraic data type, vertical refinements

One of the main interests of algebraic specifications is the possibility of developing a program by starting from a high-level abstract specification and giving successive, more and more detailed representations of this specification. Thus, it is of primary importance to define formally what is a correct representation of an algebraic data type.

Practically, a representation of $<\Sigma, E, P>$ by $<\Sigma', E', P>$ is an enrichment of the second one which defines some simulation of the operations of Σ by the operations of Σ', and possibly some additional ones. For instance the sets of natural numbers of Figure 22.1 can be specified in a less abstract way, as an enrichment of lists of natural numbers, where the operations on sets are defined in terms of operations on lists. The problem is to state a sound definition of the correctness of such a representation.

This notion has been studied a great deal, the difficult points being the vertical composability (if T3 is a correct representation of T2, and T2 is a correct representation of T1, then T3 is a correct representation of T1) and the horizontal composability (compatibility with hierarchy and parameterization; parameterization is discussed later).

This notion is difficult to capture in the initial framework, since an enrichment which is a correct implementation of a data type T, may have an initial algebra which is not isomorphic to the initial algebra of T. This problem was solved in Ehrig *et al.* (1982): a representation is said to be correct if its initial algebra can be made isomorphic to the initial algebra of the represented type via the composition of three functors called 'forget–restrict–identify'. 'Forget' is the forgetful functor and forgets those operations which are used for the representation and which are not in the signature of the represented type; 'restrict' removes the values of the carrier sets which are not actually used to represent a term of the represented type; 'identify' deals with the problem of different equalities in the representation and in the represented type. This definition is not completely satisfactory because the 'restrict' functors do not compose well. Besides, the 'identify' functor expresses the fact that, when they exist, the final algebras of the representation and of the represented type must be isomorphic. This is why it has been claimed that observational semantics is the right framework to deal with the representation correctness problem.

In the loose approach, the definition of this notion is more flexible; a specification SP_r defines a correct representation of SP if any model of SP_r corresponds to a model of SP via some composition of functors called constructor in Sannella and Tarlecki (1988). Depending on the context, it is possible to define specific constructors. For instance, if every value of the representing data type represents a value of the represented data type, the 'restrict' functor is no more necessary in the constructor, and it is possible to define a notion of representation correctness which has good composability properties. This approach unifies and generalizes all the previous ones. However, this definition is model-based rather than proof-oriented; some more work is needed to provide a fully general proof method, in order to automate the correctness proofs.

22.4 Partial functions, exceptions, subsorts, institutions

Until now, total operations have been considered which are defined for all the values of their arguments. This is not always the case in software engineering. Some algorithms do not always terminate, or return error messages in some special cases.

Partial algebraic data types have been investigated by the CIP group in Munich (Broy and Wirsing, 1982). The main definitions and results are given below.

Partial Σ-algebras only differ from the total ones by the possibility of having partial functions as interpretations of the operations of Σ. However, this difference implies a significant revision of the theory above since a way to specify undefinedness is needed, and moreover some terms may be defined or undefined, depending on the algebras.

Definition 13: definedness predicates and equality in partial data types

Given a signature $\Sigma = <S,F>$ of a partial data type, for any sort s in S, there is a predicate D_s called the *definedness predicate* (s is omitted when there is no ambiguity).

If A is a partial Σ-algebra and t belongs to $(T_\Sigma)_s$, $D_s(t)$ is satisfied by A if the term t is defined in A: there exists a value b in A_s such that $t^A = b$.

The equality considered for partial Σ-algebras is *strong equality*: given t and t' in T_Σ, and a partial Σ-algebra A, t = t' is valid in A if t and t' are both undefined or if they are both defined and they have the same interpretation in A:
$$A \models t = t' \text{ iff} (\neg D^A(t) \wedge \neg D^A(t')) \vee (D^A(t) \wedge D^A(t') \wedge t^A = t'^A)$$

The definedness predicate D can occur in the axioms. For instance, positive conditional axioms are of the form:
$$D(t_1) \wedge \ldots \wedge D(t_k) \wedge t'_1 = t''_1 \wedge \ldots \wedge t'_j = t''_j \Rightarrow C$$
where the t_i, t'_i, t''_i belong to $T_\Sigma(X)$ and C is either $D(t)$ or an equation. These axioms have as implicit premises the definedness predicates of all the terms occurring in the equations.

The definitions above make it possible to define the notion of partial Σ-algebra satisfying a set of axioms in a similar way as for total Σ-algebras. The class of all the partial Σ-algebras which satisfy a set of axioms E is noted $PALG(\Sigma,E)$. The class of finitely generated partial Σ,E-algebras is noted $PGEN(\Sigma,E)$.

There are several possibilities for extending the notion of Σ-homomorphisms to partial Σ-algebras depending on the way the definedness of terms is preserved.

Definition 14: Σ-homomorphisms between partial algebras

A *weak* Σ-homomorphism h_w from a partial Σ-algebra A to a partial Σ-algebra B is characterized by:
$$t^B = f^B(h_w(a_1), \ldots, h_w(a_n)) \text{ is defined} \Rightarrow t^A = f^A(a_1, \ldots, a_n) \text{ is}$$
$$\text{defined and } h_w(t^A) = t^B$$
A *strong* Σ-homomorphism h_s is characterized by:
$$t^B = f^B(h_s(a_1), \ldots, h_s(a_n)) \text{ is defined} \Leftrightarrow t^A = f^A(a_1, \ldots, a_n) \text{ is defined}$$
$$\text{and } h_s(t^A) = t^B$$
(exactly the same terms are defined in the source and the target algebras).

When the axioms are positive conditional, there exists an initial algebra in the category $PALG(\Sigma,E)$ with weak Σ-homomorphisms. This algebra is minimally defined: if a term t of T_Σ is defined in this algebra, then it is defined in all the algebras of $PALG(\Sigma,E)$.

A possible choice for the semantics of $<\Sigma,E>$ is to consider only minimally defined algebras of the classes $PALG(\Sigma,E)$ or $PGEN(\Sigma,E)$. The corresponding classes are denoted MDEF $(PALG(\Sigma,E))$ and $MDEF(PGEN(\Sigma,E))$. $MDEF(PALG(\Sigma,E))$ with strong homomorphisms and $PALG(\Sigma,E)$ with weak homomorphisms have the same initial algebra, which is finitely generated by construction.

Considering partial operations is not enough; error messages or exceptions can be returned by some operations. Such features must be explicitly specified in order to be able to describe data types with exceptions or error recovery. This problem was addressed in Goguen *et al.* (1978). It turned out to be particu-

larly difficult. Propagation of errors and recovery mechanisms are onerous to specify and may introduce inconsistencies.

Numerous solutions have been proposed. The more convincing ones avoid the problem of error propagation by characterizing correct values and allow error recovery (Gogolla *et al.*, 1984), (Bernot *et al.*, 1986).

Another important extension of algebraic data types is the notion of subsort. For instance natural numbers are a subset of integers and integers are a subset of real; moreover the addition operation is the same on the common parts. This is the motivation for introducing the so-called 'order-sorted algebraic data types', which are the basis of the OBJ language (Futatsugi *et al.*, 1987).

An order-sorted signature is a triple $<S, \leqslant, F>$ where $\leqslant$ is a partial order on S. An order-sorted algebra A is a many-sorted algebra such that if $s \leqslant s'$, A_s is a subset of $A_{s'}$, and if $s' \leqslant s$, $w \leqslant w'$ and there are two operations of name f with arities $w \to s$ and $w' \to s'$, f^A from $A_{w'}$ into $A_{s'}$ coincides, on A_w, with f^A from A_w into A_s. The initial approach can be generalized to order-sorted data types without too many complications. The loose approach needs some more investigation; the notion of satisfaction of an equation is not straightforward. A difficult point is the definition of a sound deduction system.

All these variants and extensions of algebraic data types have in common a notion of signature, a notion of model (algebra) and functor, a notion of satisfaction of some formulae. A formalization has been proposed in Goguen and Burstall (1984) under the name of institution. It is of primary importance to note that most of the definitions and results introduced for total algebras are institution-independent; thus they can be transposed to partial algebras, exception-algebras, order-sorted algebras, etc.

22.5 Algebraic specification languages

Algebraic specification languages can be classified according to two criteria: their underlying semantics and logic, and their structuring mechanisms.

These structuring mechanisms include, in most of the languages, the following features: enrichment, modularity, renaming and scope rules for identifiers, parameterization and genericity:

1. *Enrichment and modularity* are based on the concept of hierarchy presented above. The enrichment constructs may differ in the hierarchical constraints they require. Some languages such as LARCH (Guttag and Horning, 1986), OBJ2 (Futatsugi *et al.*, 1987) and PLUSS (Gaudel, 1985; Bidoit, 1989) provide several enrichment constructs, from the more permissive (the models of the enriched part may be completely changed) to the more restrictive (any model is an extension of a model of the enriched part and any model of the enriched part is extensible in a model of the new specification). In PLUSS, completed specification components, with a fixed class of models, and specifications under development are distinguished syntactically in order to prevent misuses of permissive enrichment.

2. *Renaming and scope rules for identifiers* are quite similar to the process in modular programming languages. Some specification languages are even reusing these aspects from a programming language. This is the case for LARCH where different interface languages derived from programming languages can be embedded (at this moment it is done for CLU, in LARCH/CLU) and for extended-ML (Sannella and Tarlecki, 1986) which is built on the module constructs of Standard ML.

3. *Parameterization of a specification by another specification*, for instance the specification of sets, parameterized by the

generic spec SET(ELEMENT)
use BOOL
sorts: Set
operations:
empty-set: → Set   add_to_: Elem × Set → Set
belongs-to: Elem × Set → Bool
axioms:
X belongs-to empty-set = false
X belongs-to (add Y to S) = (X eq Y) or (X belongs-to S)
where: X, Y: Elem; S: Set
end SET

par ELEMENT {*specification of the requirements on the parameter*}
use: BOOL
sort: Elem
operations:
 _eq_: Elem × Elem → Bool
axioms:
 eq (X, X) = true   eq (X, Y) = eq (Y, X)
 eq (X, Z) = true ∧ eq (Z, Y) = true ⇒ eq(X,Y) = true
where: X,Y: Elem

Figure 22.3 Example of a parameterized algebraic specification. (The specification language is PLUSS)

specification of elements (see *Figure 22.3*), was first introduced in CLEAR. There are two different approaches for the semantics of parameterized specifications: the meaning of such specifications can be formalized as free functors, while parameter passing is defined in terms of pushouts. This approach is historically the first and is well suited to the initial semantics. A synthetic presentation is given in Ehrig and Mahr (1985). A different approach is taken in ASL (Sannella and Wirsing, 1983): parameterized specifications are formalized as computable transformations on specifications, working at the presentation level; actual parameters can be any non finitely-generated model of the formal parameter.

The most representative specification languages with initial semantics are OBJ2, developed at SRI, AXIS developed at HP Bristol, and ACT-ONE, developed at the Technische Universität Berlin (Ehrig and Mahr, 1985). OBJ allows subsorts, i.e. order-sorted signatures. ACT-ONE provides an elaborate notation for modules. It is interesting to note that very efficient implementations of OBJ and AXIS are available, allowing their authors to use the term 'algebraic programming' rather than algebraic specification.

Representative of the other approaches are CLEAR, CIP-L, and more recently LARCH developed jointly at MIT and DEC Palo Alto, PLUSS from Paris-Sud University and extended-ML from Edinburgh University. These two last languages provide structuring concepts based on ASL, which are institution-independent; the underlying logic may change. Development environments are available for OBJ, AXIS, ACT-ONE, CIP-L, LARCH, PLUSS, etc.

22.5.1 An example

This section presents some parts of a specification of the UNIX file system in the PLUSS specification language. The full specification and its rationale is given in Bidoit *et al.* (1989).

The version of PLUSS which is used here allows one to write any first-order formula as axiom. This makes it possible to define predicates. Operations and predicates may be partial. It is possible to overload operation names and predicate names.

Very briefly, for those who are unfamiliar with Unix, a directory can be seen as a tree, with directories as internal nodes and with files or empty directories as leaves. Each directory or

file has a name. Thus a path in the tree is characterized by a list of names.

The DIRECTORY specification below is an instantiation of the parameterized specification TREE-WITH-PATHS (LEAF), where LEAF is instantiated by FILE:

spec DIRECTORY **as** TREE-WITH-PATHS (FILE)
    renaming Tree **into** Directory
    _is a path to a tree in _**into**_ is a path to a directory in _
end DIRECTORY

Let us consider the LEAF formal parameter and some relevant parts of the FILE specification (see *Figure 22.4*):

param LEAF
    use NAME
    sort LEAF
    operation name: Leaf → Name
end LEAF

Obviously, the FILE specification fits with the requirements of the leaf parameter: it uses the NAME specification; it defines a sort and an operation from this sort into NAME. More formally, the models of FILE are non-finitely generated models of LEAF, up to **renaming**.

When the correspondence is less obvious, it is necessary to specify it via a construct called a 'fitting morphism'. The result of the instantiation above is a specification which is built from the text of TREE-WITH-PATHS (LEAF) by replacing each occurrence of 'Leaf' with 'Name' and each occurrence of 'name' with 'the name of'.

The signature of TREE-WITH-PATHS (LEAF) is given in Figure 22.5. It uses the TREE (LEAF) parameterized specification, which describes labelled trees with any number of sons. Such a specification could be found in a library, but it is not given here.

This signature illustrates several features of the language. As said before, overloading is possible. It is expressed in a profile by a list of sorts between parentheses. For instance, the first line of the operations part in fact defines two operations with the same name and different profiles:

the object at_in_: Path × Tree → Leaf
the object at _in_: Path × Tree → Tree

It is possible to define predicates and to write formulae from them using the **is true** and **is false** suffixes and the usual logical connectives. The **is true** suffix may be omitted if there is no ambiguity.

spec FILE
        use NAME. LIST-OF (CHAR) **renaming** List **into**
        Content
    sort File
    generator
        < _._ > : Name * Content → File
    operations
        the name of   : File → Name
        the content of   : File → Content
    axioms
        na: the name of < n.c > = n
        co: the content of < n.c > = c
    where
        n: Name , c: Content
end FILE

Figure 22.4

proc TREE-WITH-PATH (LEAF) **forget** the son of _named_
    use TREE (LEAF), PATH
  operations
    the object at_in_: Path * Tree → Leaf ∪ Tree
    _plus_added under_: Tree * (Leaf ∪ Tree) * Path → Tree
    pruned at: Tree * Path → Tree
  predicates
    is an existing path of: Path * Tree
    is a path to a tree in: Path * Tree
  preconditions
    obj: the object at p in T **is defined when** p is an existing
      path of T
    plus: T plus LT added under p **is defined when** p is a path
      to a tree in T
    prun: T pruned at p **is defined when** p is a name **is false** ∧
      p is an existing path of T **is true**
  axioms
    exist1: n1 is an existing path of T **iff** n1 = the name of T
    exist2: n1/n2 is an existing path of T **iff** n1 = the name
      of T ∧ n2 belongs to the name set of T
    exist3: n2 belongs to the name set of T **is false** ⇒ n1/n2/p
      is an existing path of T **is false**
    exist4: n2 belongs to the name set of T ⇒ n1/n2/p is an
      existing path of T **iff** n1 = the name of T ∧ n2/p is an
      existing path of the son of T named n2
    path: p is a path to a tree in T **iff** p is an existing path of
      T ∧ the object at p in T is a Tree
    obj: the object at n1 in T = T '*due to the preconditions,*
      n1 is the name of T'
    obj2: the object at n1/p in T = the object at p in the son
      of T named (the first name of p)
    plus1: T plus LT added under n1 = < n1 . the content of
      T plus LT >
    plus2: T plus LT added under n1/n2 = T pruned at n1/n2
        plus (the object at n1/n2 in T
          plus LT added under n2)
        added under n1
    plus3: T plus LT added under n1/n2/p = T pruned at n1/n2
        plus (the object at n1/n2 in T
          plus LT added under n2/p)
        added under n1
    prun1: T pruned at n1/n2 = < n1 . the content of T less
      the object named n2 >
    prun2: T pruned at n1/n2/p = T pruned at n1/n2
        plus (the object at n1/n2 in T
          pruned at n2/p)
        added under n1
  where
    n1, n2: Name , p: Path , T: Tree , LT: Leaf ∪ Tree
end TREE-WITH-PATH

Figure 22.5

spec PATH **as** NON-EMPTY-LIST-OF (NAME)
    renaming   List **into** Path
                add _to_ **into** _/_
                first **into** the first name of
                tail **into** the last part of
                _ is a singleton **into** _ is a name
  operations
    the first part of   : Path → Path
    the last name of   : Path → Name
  preconditions
    fp: the first part of p **is defined when** p is a name **is
      false**
  axioms
    fp1: p is a name **is false** ⇒ the first part of (n/p) =
      n/the first part of p
    fp2: p is a name **is true** ⇒ the first part of (n/p) = n
    ln1: the last name of n = n
    ln2: the last name of (n/p) = the last name of p
  where
    n: Name, p: Path
end PATH

Figure 22.6

An incidental remark for the Unix specialists: at the specification level it is natural to consider two different types, file and directory, since the operations on files and directories are different. It does not mean that files and directories are represented by different types at the implementation level.

22.6 Conclusions and perspectives

The theory of algebraic data types and the semantic bases for the corresponding specification languages are now well established. Such specifications have seemed difficult to put to practical use, maybe because the attempts have been premature. However, the use of good structuring mechanisms seems quite promising and some convincing examples have been recently issued (see for instance Bidoit, *et al.*, 1989).

Besides, applications of such specifications are numerous and very interesting practically: in Bauer *et al.*, (1985) and more recently in Sannella and Tarlecki (1988), the systematic development of programs by successive transformations and refinements of algebraic specifications has been studied. Software reusability (Gaudel and Moineau, 1988; Wirsing, 1988) and automation of program testing (Bougé *et al.*, 1986) are other promising areas. Moreover, several powerful theorem-provers have been developed (cf. Chapter 26)).

It seems sound to conjecture that this kind of specifications will not be put to practical use as they are; the mathematical background is still too visible. Moreover, they must be embedded in (or extended to) a larger framework allowing specification of real-time systems or distributed applications. However, they are among the best candidates to provide a basis for the semantic definition of the next generation of specification languages.

22.7 Acknowledgements

The author is especially indebted to Pascale Le Gall and John McDermid for their careful reading and numerous remarks on the first version of this text. Thanks are due to Gilles Bernot, Pierre Dauchy and Anne Deo-Blanchard for many useful comments.

The definition domains of partial operations are stated in the **preconditions** part. The meaning of the two first preconditions above is straightforward. The third one means that it is not allowed to prune a tree at its root. (If *p* is a single name, it is the name of the root.)

To complete this brief tour of the specification directories, we now give the PATH specification of directories in *Figure 22.6*, which is a good example of the use of renaming.

Using the sorts and operations of DIRECTORY it is possible to specify what is a file system, i.e. a specific directory which can be modified via operations such as mkdir, rmdir, rm, etc. and observed via ls, pwd, etc. see Bidoit *et al.* (1989).

22.8 References

Bauer, F. L., Berghammer, R., Broy, M. *et al.* (1985) *The Munich Project CIP. Volume 1: The wide-spectrum language CIP-L*, LNCS 183, Springer-Verlag

Bernot, G. (1987) Good functors ... are those preserving philosophy. In *Proceedings of the summer Conference on Category Theory and Computer Science*, LNCS 283, Springer-Verlag, pp. 182–195

Bernot, G., Bidoit, M. and Choppy, C. (1986) Abstract data types with exception handling. *Theoretical Computer Science*, **46**, 13–46

Bidoit, M. (1989) PLUSS, un langage pour le développement de spécifications algébriques modulaires, *Thèse d'état*, Université de Paris-Sud

Bidoit, M., Gaudel, M.-C. and Mauboussin, A. (1989) How to make algebraic specifications more understandable? An experiment with the PLUSS specification language. *Science of Computer Programming*, **12**, 1–38

Broy, M., Pair, C. and Wirsing, M. (1984) A systematic study of models of abstract data types. *Theoretical Computer Science*, **33**, 139–174

Broy, M. and Wirsing, M. (1982) Partial abstract types. *Acta Informatica*, **3**, 47–64

Bougé, L., Choquet, N., Fribourg, L. and Gaudel, M.-C. (1986) Test sets generation from algebraic specifications using logic programming. *Journal of Systems and Software*, **6**, 343–360

Burstall, R. M. and Goguen, J. A. (1977) Putting theories together to make specifications. In *Proceedings of the 5th International Joint Conference on Artificial Intelligence, Cambridge*, pp. 1045–1058

Burstall, R. M. and Goguen, J. A. (1980) The semantics of CLEAR, a specification language. In *Proceeding of the Advanced Course on Abstract Software Specifications*, LNCS 86, Springer-Verlag, Copenhagen, pp. 292–332

Ehrig, H., Kreowski, H. J., Mahr, B. and Padawitz, P. (1982) Algebraic implementation of abstract data types. *Theoretical Computer Science*, **20**, 209–263

Ehrig, H. and Mahr, B. (1985) *Fundamentals of Algebraic Specification 1: Equations and Initial Semantics*, Springer-Verlag

Futatsugi, K., Goguen, J. A., Jouannaud, J.-P. and Meseguer, J. (1987) Principles of OBJ2. In *Proceedings of the 12th ACM Symposium on Principles Of Programming Languages*, pp. 51–60

Gaudel, M.-C. (1985) Towards Structured Algebraic Specifications. In *Esprit '85 Status Report*, North-Holland, pp. 493–510

Gaudel, M.-C. and Moineau, Th. (1988) A theory of Software Reusability. In *Proceedings of European Symposium On Programming '88*, LNCS 300, Springer-Verlag, pp. 115–130

Gogolla, M., Drosten, K., Lipeck, U. and Ehrich, H.-D. (1984) Algebraic and operational semantics of specifications allowing exceptions and errors. *Theoretical Computer Science*, **34**

Goguen, J. (1978) Some design principles and theory for OBJ-0, a language for expressing and executing algebraic specifications of programs. In *Proceedings of the International Conference on Mathematical Studies of Information Processing, Kyoto*, pp. 425–473

Goguen, J. A. and Burstall, R. M. (1984) Introducing Institutions. In *Proceedings of the Logics of Programming Workshop, Carnegie-Mellon University*, LNCS 164, Springer-Verlag, pp. 221–256

Goguen, J. A., Thatcher, J. W. and Wagner, E. G. (1978) An initial algebra approach to the specification, correctness and implementation of abstract data types. In *Current Trends in Programming Methodology, Vol. 4: Data Structuring* (ed. R. T. Yeh), Prentice-Hall, pp. 80–149

Guttag, J. V. (1975) The specification and application to programming of abstract data types. *Ph. D. Thesis*, University of Toronto

Guttag, J. V. and Horning, J. J. (1978) The algebraic specification of abstract data types. *Acta Informatica*, **10**, 27–52

Guttag, J. V. and Horning, J. J. (1986) Report on the Larch shared language. *Science of Computer Programming*, **6**, 103–134

Makowsky, J. A. (1985) Why Horn formulas matter in computer science: initial structures and generic examples. In *Proceedings of the International Joint Conference on Theory and Practice of Software Development (TAPSOFT)*, LNCS 185, Springer-Verlag, pp. 374–387

Morris, J. H. Jr (1973) Types are not sets. In *Proceedings of the first ACM Symposium on Principles of Programming Languages*

Sannella, D. T. and Tarlecki, A. (1986) Extended ML: an institution-independent framework for formal program development. In *Proceedings Workshop on Category Theory and Computer Programming, Guilford*, LNCS 240, Springer-Verlag, 364–389

Sannella, D. T. and Tarlecki, A. (1987) On observational equivalence and algebraic specification. *Journal of Computer and System Science*, **34**, 150–178

Sannella, D. T. and Tarlecki, A. (1988) Towards formal development of programs from algebraic specifications: implementations revisited. *Acta Informatica*, **25**, 233–281

Sannella, D. T. and Wirsing, M. (1983) A kernel language for algebraic specification and implementation. In *Proceedings Colloquium on Foundations of Computation Theory, Linkoping*, LNCS 158, Springer-Verlag, pp. 413–427

Wand, M. (1979) Final algebra semantics and data type extensions. *Journal of Computer and System Science*, **19**, 27–44

Wirsing, M. (1988) Algebraic description of reusable software components. In *Proceedings COMPEURO '88, Bruxelles* (ed. E. Milgrom)

Wirsing, M., Pepper, P., Partsch, H., Dosch, W. and Broy, M. (1983) On hierarchies of abstract data types. *Acta Informatica*, **20**, 1–33

23

Formal treatment of concurrency and time

Manfred Broy
Institut für Informatik
Technische Universität München

Contents

23.1 Introduction

What is a distributed, concurrent, reactive system? A simple answer might be that physically (i.e. in the 'real' world) a distributed system is a family of topologically distributed entities which perform actions in parallel (concurrently), and interact (cooperate) mutually and/or with their environment so that there are some causal relationships between their individual actions.

However, this definition immediately seems rather narrow. For instance, is it necessary to have a fixed system structure? In the life cycle of distributed systems new entities may be created, while others may disappear. Therefore it is not possible to characterize a distributed system simply by a set of interacting entities. Moreover, even if it is possible to describe the entities and their connections completely, this may not characterize their interactive behaviour sufficiently (for all purposes).

In traditional engineering disciplines there are a number of techniques for describing physical systems and their dynamic behaviour. In software engineering we are, in general, not so much interested in the physical representation of distributed systems as in their (possible) actions and the causal relationships between those actions which characterize their dynamic behaviour. This leads to a principle that it is the possible actions of the system and their relationships (causality) which are most important for abstract modelling of distributed systems, rather than the entities (individual components).

Note that we always try to distinguish between a distributed system as it is found in the real world, its (informal and necessarily incomplete) description and its (formal) semantic model. The semantic model again is necessarily incomplete as it abstracts away certain (hopefully) unimportant details, and may even be inappropriate for answering certain relevant questions as it may improperly reflect relevant properties. Clearly the appropriateness of a model for a distributed system is not a formal question. Moreover, there is always the danger of confusing (inadequate) properties of the formal model of distributed systems with properties of the real world. This problem can only be avoided by appropriate validation of the formal model.

A special case of a distributed system is that of software structures which use parallelism. These are typically implemented using concurrent programming languages. Behaviour like that of a distributed system is generated whenever such programs are executed on (parallel) hardware.

In software engineering, complex systems often have to be described, analysed or programmed, and these systems have a number of characteristics which are very difficult to treat formally. Typically such systems are distributed. Their components cooperate, communicate or are synchronized. Often their behaviour is non-deterministic and, of course, they run concurrently or in parallel. All the 'buzzwords' used for the characteristics of such systems show particular aspects of this complexity. Descriptive names for such systems include:

1. *Distributed* system, where the system consists of a number of components that are physically (topologically) or conceptually separated.
2. *Parallel* or *concurrent* system, where the system consists of a number of components which operate concurrently or in parallel.
3. *Communicating* system, where a system consists of a number of components which communicate by exchanging messages.
4. *Reactive* or *interactive* system, where the system reacts to actions in its environment or interacts with the environment.
5. *Time-dependent (real-time)* system, where the system behaviour depends essentially on timing.
6. *Cooperating, coordinating* or *synchronized* system, where the

system consists of a number of components which operate in a coordinated way.

Complex systems often show all the characteristics identified above. Further properties which such systems may exhibit are *non-deterministic* and *infinite* behaviours. A system is called non-deterministic if it is likely to have shown a number of different behaviours where the choice of the behaviour cannot be influenced by its environment. The behaviour of a system is called infinite (non-terminating) if it does not terminate, i.e. if it executes indefinitely carrying out an infinite number of actions. For many systems infinite behaviour is intended and welcome, e.g. in a spacecraft flight control system.

The complexity of such distributed systems also arises from the strong interrelationship between these different characteristics. In connection with non-determinism and infinite behaviours, difficult questions, such as those associated with *fairness* arise. Generally, a behaviour is called fair if every action that the system is ready to perform sufficiently often, eventually occurs in its behaviour.

The notion of a component is crucial for structuring systems. Having defined simple components and the modes of composing components we now have a programming language for describing systems in terms of their components. New problems arise for the description of such languages.

This chapter gives a simple introduction to the formal foundations of modelling, specification, analysis and programming of concurrent, communicating, reactive systems. The chapter covers formal models for the description of distributed systems and the semantics of programs that either run on distributed architecture or can be used for controlling distributed systems. In particular, the following formalisms will be considered:

1. Action traces and action structures for representing histories of distributed systems as well as formalisms for specifying sets of those traces and action structures.
2. Properties and concepts of traces and action structures such as safety, liveness, fairness, transactions, states.
3. Programming languages for describing distributed systems.
4. Operational semantics of programming languages for distributed systems based on labelled rewriting systems.
5. Denotational models of programming languages for distributed systems.
6. Logical frameworks for specifying, developing, and verifying distributed programs.

Special characteristics of distributed systems which are covered are the treatment of non-determinism, questions of fairness and modelling of communication. Particular formal models for describing distributed systems and programming languages, that allow the programming of distributed software as well as the control and description of distributed systems, are also discussed.

23.2 Modelling causally connected systems

We consider a simple example for distributed systems and start with its informal description.

Example: Package switch

Throughout this section we study as an example a package switch with two input conveyor belts and two output conveyor belts. Each conveyor belt consists of a sequence of compartments that may be filled with a package or may be empty. Each package carries some address that indicates on which of the output conveyor belts it has to be put by the switch (see *Figure 23.1*).

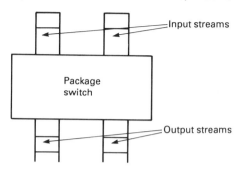

Figure 23.1   Packet switch example

This is a rather informal description of a package switch. However, some ambiguity was admitted deliberately to leave enough freedom for later formalization.

We are interested in the following questions:

1. What is a good formal description of the package switch?
2. What are the relevant properties of a package switch?
3. What is a (good) specification of such properties?
4. How can we verify such properties from a description?

However, before treating the example in detail, we introduce a number of basic formal concepts.

There are dual ways for modelling concurrent systems:

1. Modelling systems by describing their set of actions and their behaviours.
2. Modelling systems by describing their state spaces and their possible sequences of state changes.

These views are dual in the sense that an action can be understood to define state changes, and state changes occurring in state sequences can be understood as abstract representations of actions.

Timing can be added to formal models in several ways. Often the explicit introduction of time makes modelling of particular formal properties simpler. For instance, in the presence of time information many fairness properties can be translated into simple, concrete timing properties. On the other hand, the incorporation of concrete timing properties leads to a considerable loss of abstractness.

23.2.1 Actions

A first step to producing a formal model of a system is the description of its set of possible actions. There are as many techniques for specifying action sets as there are for specifying sets.

Example: Package switch

We assume a given set PKG of packages, including empty packages representing empty slots. The function:

route: PKG → {lft, rgt, empty}

specifies for any package whether it is empty or whether it is labelled by an address for the left or right conveyor belt. Furthermore we define the set:

DCN = {lft, rgt}

The set ACT of actions is defined by:

$$ACT = \{lv(p,d) : p \in PKG \wedge d \in DCN\} \cup$$
$$\{ar(p,d) : p \in PKG \wedge d \in DCN\}$$

Here $lv(p,d)$ stands for the action that the package p leaves at direction d and $ar(p,d)$ stands for the action that the package p arrives on direction d.

On the level of actions, timing can be incorporated in three ways. First, we may associate time intervals with actions, i.e. we may specify how much time an action needs. Then we may introduce certain 'time actions' such as:

1. An action that indicates a 'tick' of the clock (relative timing).
2. An action that indicates that a certain time point has been reached (global timing).

A special action could be 'timeout' as a possible consequence of an action setting a timer.

Here we do not assume any particular properties for a set to be called an action set. Often we may classify the actions according to their effects on the system into:

1. Input actions.
2. Output actions.
3. Synchronization actions.
4. Internal actions.

We shall come back to the implications of such a classification later.

When working towards a state-oriented view of action structures, we associate state changes with actions. This will also be studied later.

23.2.2 Action traces and action structures

Given a set of actions we may specify the behaviour of systems. A system behaviour is understood as a history of an instantiation of a system and can be represented by a family of actions with a causality relation. The causality relation is represented by a partial ordering.

Since particular actions may occur several times in the behaviour of a system, it is not possible, in general, to describe system behaviour simply by establishing a partial ordering on the action set, but rather it is necessary to establish a partial ordering on families of actions represented by a set of events where each event is labelled by some action. This way the concept of an action structure is obtained. In the following, action structures are formalized as descriptions of histories ('runs') of distributed systems.

23.2.2.1 Action structures

Let A be a set of elementary atomic actions and E be a countable set that represents the universe of events. We assume a subset $E_p \subseteq E$ and a total function:

$$\alpha_p : E_p \to A$$

that associates with every concrete event e an action $a = \alpha_p(e)$. Then the event e is called an *instance* or *occurrence* of the action a. Furthermore we assume a partial order '$\leqslant_p$' on E_p. Intuitively for $e, d \in E_p$

$$e \leqslant_p d$$

means that $e = d$ or the event e is causal for (and therefore occurs before) the event d (d cannot start before e has finished).

The triple $(E_p, \leqslant_p, \alpha_p)$ is called an action structure or a process.

Finite action structures can be visualized by acyclic directed graphs, the nodes of which are marked by actions.

Example: Action structure

Let us consider the set of actions $A = \{a,b,c,d\}$. An action structure is given by *Figure 23.2*.

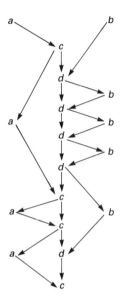

Figure 23.2 Action structure example

An action structure $(E_p, \leqslant_p, \alpha_p)$ is called *sequential* if the ordering $\leqslant_p$ on E_p is linear (total). p_ϕ denotes the empty action structure, i.e. an action structure with an empty set of events.

Next we introduce a number of simple mathematical concepts to talk about relations between action structures. Given an action structure $p = (E_p, \leqslant_p, \alpha_p)$ and a set of events $E_p \subseteq E_p$ then $p|E_q$ the action structure $q = (E_q, \leqslant_q, \alpha_q)$, called a sub-process of p, where:

$$\forall e \epsilon E_q : \alpha_q(e) = \alpha_p(e)$$

$$\forall e,e' \in E_q : e \leqslant_q e' \Leftrightarrow e \leqslant_p e'$$

Two action structures $p = (E_p, \leqslant_p, \alpha_p)$ and $q = (E_q, \leqslant_q, \alpha_q)$ are called *isomorphic* and we write $p \sim q$, iff there exists a bijective mapping:

$$\rho : E_p \to E_q$$

such that:

$$\forall e \in E_p : \alpha_q(\rho(e)) = \alpha_p(e)$$

$$\forall e,e' \in E_p : \rho(e) \leqslant_q \rho(e') \Leftrightarrow e \leqslant_p e'$$

Similarly p is called an *embedding* of q into p iff:

$$\forall e,e' \in E_p : e \leqslant_p e' \Rightarrow \rho(e) \leqslant_q \rho(e')$$

$$\forall e \epsilon E_p : \alpha_p(e) = \alpha_q(\rho(e))$$

If, in addition, $E_q = E_p$ and p is the identity, then p is called a *partial sequentialization* of q. If, in addition, the ordering $\leqslant_p$ is a linear one, we speak of a *(total) sequentialization*. If $E_p \subseteq E_q$ and ρ is the identity on E_p and:

$$\forall e,e' \in E_p : e \leqslant_p e' \Leftrightarrow \rho(e) \leqslant_q \rho(e')$$

then p is a subprocess of the action structure q.

For a given action structure $p = (E_p, \leqslant_p, \alpha_p)$ there are three possible interpretations for the relation:

$$e \leqslant_p e'$$

for events e and e':

1. *Causality*. The event e is causal for event e'.
2. *System constraints on concurrency*. The event e must not happen in parallel with event e'.
3. *Actual timing*. The event e' starts after the event e has been finished.

Of course (1) implies (3), but, the reverse does not generally hold true.

Often the three different sources of the relation are mixed within a model by the partial ordering $\leqslant_p$.

23.2.2.2 Composite actions

So far we have just considered 'atomic' actions and events, but it is also possible to group together a set of events and to call it a composite event. Trivially every composite event also describes a subprocess.

Composite actions and events can also be incorporated into our model via mappings between events. Let $p = (E_p, \leqslant_p, \alpha_p)$ and $q = (E_q, \leqslant_q, \alpha_q)$ be action structures and:

$$\rho : E_p \to E_q$$

be a subjective mapping such that:

$$\forall e, e' \in E_p : \rho(e) \neq \rho(e') \Rightarrow (e \leqslant_p e' \Leftrightarrow \rho(e) \leqslant_q \rho(e'))$$

Then every event $e' \in E_q$ defines a subprocess $p|_{E'}$ of p where $E' = \{e \epsilon E_p : \rho(e) = e'\}$. We call the action structure $(E_p, \leqslant_p, \alpha_p)$ a refinement of the action structure $(E_q, \leqslant_q, \alpha_q)$.

23.2.2.3 Operations and relations on action structures

Now let A be a set of actions and E be a sufficiently large (countably infinite) universe of events. An action structure p is called *finite*, if its set of events E_p is finite. An action structure p is called *finitely based*, if for every event $e \epsilon E_p$ the set $\{e' \in E_p : e' \leqslant_p e\}$ is finite. This means that for an event the set of causal events is finite. We denote the set of all finitely based action structures over E with countable sets of events by $AS(A)$. In this section a number of basic operations and relations on action structures are introduced.

The action structure p is called a *prefix* of q and we write:

$$p \sqsubseteq q \text{ iff} (\forall e,e' \in E_p : e \leqslant_p e' \wedge e' \in E' \Rightarrow e \in E') \wedge p = q|_{E_p}$$

$\sqsubseteq$ defines a partial ordering on the universe of action structures.

It can be used as the approximation ordering for action structures.

In the following, two operations on action structures are characterized by relations (predicates) on action structures. For specifying the *sequential (de-)composition* of action structures we introduce a partial operation:

$$\hat{\ }: AS(A) \times AS(A) \to AS(A)$$

Intuitively, $r = p\hat{\ }q$ means that the action structure r can be seen as a sequential composition of p and q (r can be sequentially decomposed into p and q). It is defined only if $E_p \cap E_q = \emptyset$. Its result r is specified by the following propositions: the event sets are disjoint and E_r is composed from the events of p and q:

$$(E_r = E_p \cup E_q) \wedge (E_p \cap E_q = \emptyset)$$

If we restrict r to the events of p we obtain p, and analogously for q:

$$(r|_{E_p} = p) \wedge (r|_{E_q} = q)$$

Events from p are causal for the events of q:

$$\forall e \in E_p, e' \in E_q : e \leqslant_r e'$$

For specifying the *parallel (de-)composition* of action structures, synchronous with respect to a given set S of actions, we introduce the set-valued ('non-deterministic') operation:

$$.\|..: AS(A) \times \wp(A) \times AS(A) \to \wp(AS(A))$$

The predicate $r \in p\|_S q$ yields true, if r can be decomposed into (considered as being composed of) the action structures p and q where the events labelled by the actions in S are exactly the events that are shared by p and q. The events of r are the events of q and p:

$$(E_r = E_p \cup E_q) \wedge (E_p \cap E_q = \{e \in E_r : \alpha_r(e) \in S\})$$

The labels of r and p as well as q coincide and the causality relation is the transitive closure of the union of the relations on p and q:

$$(a_r|_{E_p} = a_p) \wedge (a_r|_{E_q} = a_q) \wedge (\leqslant_r = (\leqslant_p \cup \leqslant_q)^*)$$

where $(\leqslant_p \cup \leqslant_q)^*$ denotes the reflexive transitive closure over the relation $\leqslant_p \cup \leqslant_q$.

The parallel composition is called *non-deterministic* since, for certain action structures, there may be several ways of obtaining action structures by parallel composition.

For action structures p, q, p', q' we have:

$$p \sim p' \wedge q \sim q' \Rightarrow p\hat{\ }q \sim p'\hat{\ }q'$$

However from $p \sim p'$, $q \sim q'$ and $r \in p\|_S q$ and $r' \in p'\|_S q'$ we cannot conclude $r \sim r'$. This is illustrated by the following example.

Example: Non-determinism in parallel composition

Consider action structures p, p', q, q' with actions a, b, c, $S = \{a\}$ and events $e0, e1, e2, e3$, shown in *Figure 23.3*.

Another problem in the parallel composition is the possibility of a deadlock: we shall come back to this issue later.

It is interesting to see how a given action structure can be understood (modelled) as a sequential or parallel composition of simpler action structures. When designing programs, it is interesting to build up action structures and programs describing them from simpler ones. The study of a given action structure and its decomposition into subprocesses is *analytic* in character, whereas constructing action structures from given subprocesses is *synthetic* in character.

23.2.2.4 Abstract action structures

Generally we are not interested in the concrete event set of an action structure, but rather in its pure action structure, i.e. in the respective isomorphism class. This leads to the concept of an abstract action structure.

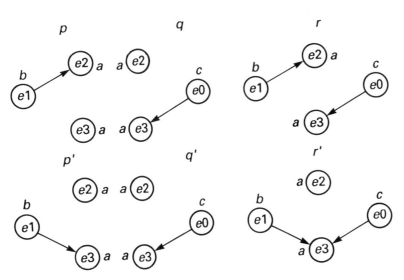

Figure 23.3 Example of non-determinism in parallel composition

A non-empty set $P \subseteq AS(A)$ is called an abstract action structure, if:

1. All action structures in P are isomorphic.
2. If $p \in AS(A)$ and $q \in P$ and $p \sim q$, then $p \in P$.

So the abstract action structures are the isomorphism classes of concrete action structures. The set of abstract action structures will be denoted by AAS(A).

Trivially every concrete action structure p may be mapped onto an abstract action structure by the function abstract:

$$\text{abstract}: AS(A) \rightarrow AAS(A)$$

defined by:

$$\text{abstract}(p) = \{q \in AS(A): p \sim q\}$$

All definitions given so far for concrete action structures immediately carry over to abstract action structures. In particular the predicates defined on concrete action structures may be carried over to abstract action structures: let P0, P1, P2 be abstract action structures. We define:

$$P1 \sqsubseteq P2 \quad \equiv_{df} \forall\, p1 \in P1\; \exists\, p2 \in P2: p1 \sqsubseteq p2$$

$$P0 = P1 \hat{\ } P2 \quad \equiv_{df} \forall\, p0 \in P0\; \exists\, p1 \in P1,\, p2 \in P2: p0 = p1 \hat{\ } p2$$

$$P0 \in P1 \parallel_s P2 \quad \equiv_{df} \forall\, p0 \in P0\; \exists\, p1 \in P1,\, p2 \in P2: p0 \in p1 \parallel_s p2$$

All technical definitions for action structures trivially carry over to abstract action structures.

Two notations for particular abstract action structures will be used in the following. The trivial abstract action structure consisting of exactly one event labelled by the action $a \in A$ is denoted by $P_{(a)}$, i.e.:

$$P_{(a)} = \{(E_p, \leqslant_p, \alpha_p) \in AS(A): \exists\, e \in E: E_p = \{e\} \wedge \alpha_p(e) = a\}$$

and by $P_\emptyset$ we denote the single-element class $\{p_\emptyset\}$ of action structures with the empty set as set of events.

Now we can give a formal definition of a simple mathematical notion of a distributed system.

Definition. A (formal description of a) *distributed system* consists of the specification of an action set and a set of (abstract) action structures.

However, often only those action structures with linear orderings are considered. This simplifies the formal model. However, concurrency is no longer explicitly represented.

23.2.2.5 *Interleaving views of distributed systems*

If only action structures are considered where the causality ordering is linear, we speak of interleaving models. The following lemma is well-known; it uses the fact that a partial order is uniquely determined by all its possible embeddings into linear orders ('topological sorting').

Lemma. A concrete action structure is uniquely determined by its set of sequentializations.

Interestingly, the lemma does not hold for abstract action structures. Let us consider for instance a process p with two events both labelled by action a. The process p has only one

abstract action structure as a total sequentialization, independent of the question of whether the two events are causally related in p or not.

Abstract finitely-based action structures over the set of actions A can be much more conveniently represented by finite and infinite sequences of actions called traces or streams. (In the literature the term trace is sometimes reserved for finite sequences of actions.) The set of streams over the set A is denoted by:

$$A^\omega = A^* \cup A^\infty$$

Here A* denotes the finite sequences of elements from A and A^∞ denotes the infinite sequences of elements of A.

Finitely-based action structures with a linear causality ordering are always isomorphic to total functions on the natural numbers $\mathbb{N}$ with the usual ordering (if they are infinite) or to a total function on a finite subset $\{1, \ldots, n\}$ of $\mathbb{N}$ (if they are finite and contain n events). An infinite sequence s from A^∞ corresponds to a total function:

$$f_s: \mathbb{N} \rightarrow A$$

A finite sequence s corresponds to a total function:

$$f_s: \{1, \ldots, n\} \rightarrow A$$

that can also be seen as a partial function on $\mathbb{N}$.

The prefix ordering on action structures immediately carries over to an ordering on streams. Let $s, s' \in A^\omega$, then we have:

$$s \sqsubseteq s' \text{ iff } s \hat{\ } s'' = s' \text{ for some stream } s''$$

Here $s \hat{\ } s''$ denotes the concatenation of the two streams s and s'', which coincides with its use for denoting sequential composition. Often the following functions on streams (here $A^\perp = A \cup \{\perp\}$) are used:

$$\text{ft}: A^\omega \rightarrow A^\perp$$
$$\text{rt}: A^\omega \rightarrow A^\omega$$
$$.\&.: A^\perp \times A^\omega \rightarrow A^\omega$$

We write these functions in prefix and infix notation. The empty stream will be denoted by ε. The functions above are specified by:

$$a\ \&\ s = \begin{cases} \varepsilon & \text{if } a = \perp \\ <a> \hat{\ }\ s & \text{otherwise} \end{cases}$$

Here $<a>$ denotes the one element stream consisting of a. The special element $\perp$ is introduced to replace undefined:

$$\begin{aligned} \text{ft}.\varepsilon &= \perp \\ \text{ft}(a\ \&\ s) &= a \\ \text{rt}.\varepsilon &= \varepsilon \\ \text{rt}(a\ \&\ s) &= s \text{ if } a \neq \perp \end{aligned}$$

ft, rt, & are monotonic and continuous with respect to the prefix ordering on streams, if we assume that $A^\perp$ is trivially ordered by the so-called *flat* or *discrete* ordering specified as follows:

$$a \sqsubseteq a' \text{ iff } a = a' \vee a = \perp$$

Streams are a very basic concept for modelling sequences of communication and computation steps.

23.2.2.6 *Timed action structures*

As indicated above, special actions concerning timing can be incorporated into a system. Moreover, for modelling timing we may directly incorporate a time concept into action structures. We assume a set TIME which is a linearly ordered set (such as the natural numbers, the rational or real numbers, or some other more abstract structure). A timed action structure is a pair (p, τ) where p is an action structure and all events of p are timed, i.e. we have:

$$\tau : E_p \rightarrow (\text{TIME} \times \text{TIME})$$

with (for all $e, e' \in E_p$):

$$e \leqslant_p e' \Rightarrow \tau_2(e) \leqslant \tau_1(e')$$

$$\tau_1(e) \leqslant \tau_2(e)$$

where τ_1 and τ_2 have the obvious properties of selecting the first and last elements from the pair given by τ.

Note that we do not require the implication in the other direction. This 'model' of time includes actions that take no time by allowing $\tau_1(e) = \tau_2(e)$.

23.2.3 Specification of action structures: safety, liveness, fairness, transactions

A description of a distributed system is given by a set of traces or action structures. Logical formulae, or predicates, are the classical way to specify particular sets. Therefore we may use formulae for action structures to specify properties of systems.

A simple possibility is to use directly the formalism introduced above. For a given process p we may specify the mutual exclusion of actions a and b by the predicate mutex specified as follows:

$$\text{mutex}(p, a, b) =_{df} \forall e, e' \in E_p: \quad \alpha_p(e) = \wedge \alpha_p(e') = b \Rightarrow \\ e' \leqslant_p e \vee e \leqslant_p e'$$

Every logical formula, and every predicate, for an action structure specifies a particular property of a system. Special functions help to formulate such properties. For that purpose we introduce an auxiliary filter function:

$$\mathbb{C}: \wp(A) \times AS(A) \rightarrow AS(A)$$

specified by:

$$\mathbb{C}(x,p) = P_{E'} \quad \text{where } E' = \{e \in E_p: \alpha_p(e) \in x\}$$

We also write $\mathbb{C}(x,p)$ instead of $\mathbb{C}(\{x\},p)$.

We denote the number of events in action structure p by $\#p$. If p has infinitely many events, then $\#p = \infty$.

Example: Sequential subprocess

We may express that the actions a and b form a sequential cyclic subprocess starting with action a by the predicate cycle where:

$$\text{cycle}(p, a, b) =_{df} \forall q: q \sqsubseteq p \wedge \#q < \infty \Rightarrow \\ 0 \leqslant (\#\mathbb{C}(\alpha,q) - \#\mathbb{C}(b,q)) \leqslant 1$$

Note that the predicate cycle applies for concurrent action structures as well as non-concurrent action structures.

For a set of traces or action structures we may classify particular properties into so-called *safety* and *liveness* properties.

A safety property of a distributed system is a property that guarantees that certain unwanted things do not happen, or more strictly speaking cannot be observed in a finite number of observations. This means that particular patterns of actions are not allowed in the corresponding action structure. Safety properties are always invariants; if a safety property holds for an action structure, it holds also for every prefix of that trace or that action structure.

Formally expressed, for a safety property predicate Q on action structures, we generally assume for all action structures p:

$$Q(p) \Leftrightarrow \forall q: q \sqsubseteq p \wedge \#q < \infty \Rightarrow Q(q)$$

Safety properties are closely related to *partial correctness*. A typical example of a safety property for the package switch is given by the predicate 'a package leaves the switch only if it has entered it before' as given in assertion (2) below.

Liveness properties are of a different nature. Liveness properties of a trace or an action structure are characterized by guarantees that certain required actions eventually do happen. A typical liveness property is given by stating that after a particular action another action will happen at some time. In general this property does not hold for prefixes.

An action structure predicate Q defines a pure liveness property if the following proposition holds:

$$\forall p: \#p < \infty \Rightarrow \exists p': p \sqsubseteq p' \wedge Q(p')$$

A typical liveness property for the package switch is given by the predicate 'a package that enters the switch leaves it eventually'.

Neither action structure nor trace views of distributed systems represent certain aspects of systems very explicitly. For instance, in the package switch, arriving packages certainly should be considered as input events, but this hardly can be seen from the causality structure. Note that between successive arrivals at one input belt there is the 'same' causality in our formal model as between the arrival of a package and its action of leaving, although certainly these are relationships ('causalities') of rather different quality. These differences are more adequately modelled in the functional views which are treated later.

Example: Specification of an action structure

The action structure of Section 23.2.2.1 satisfies the following specification. A set of concrete action structures p with actions:

$$A =_{df} \{a, b, c, d\}$$

is specified with the help of the following safety predicate inv:

$$\text{inv}(p) =_{df} (\text{cycle}(p, a, c) \wedge \text{cycle } (p, b, d) \wedge \text{mutex}(p, c, d))$$

The predicate inv represents a typical safety property. A liveness property for the action structure p could read as follows:

$$\#\mathbb{C}(a, p) = \infty \wedge \#\mathbb{C}(b, p) = \infty$$

From this liveness property and the safety property above we can infer immediately:

$$\#\mathbb{C}(c, p) = \infty \wedge \#\mathbb{C}(d, p) = \infty$$

The definitions above do not exclude sequential action structures. In particular, as long as there is no explicit demand for concurrency of events, every specification of action structures can be read as a trace specification, too.

Every predicate Q on action structures can be decomposed into a pure safety predicate S and a pure liveness predicate L:

$$S(p) =_{df} \forall q: q \subseteq p \wedge \#q < \infty \Rightarrow \exists r: q \subseteq r \wedge Q(r)$$
$$L(p) =_{dt} S(p) \Rightarrow Q(p)$$

The definition of L seems somewhat strange. Actually it is the most liberal predicate that, together with the safety predicate, characterizes S.

Particular safety properties may restrict the concurrency of actions. The last part of the formula defining the predicate inv (above) shows an example.

Example: A description of the package switch by action structures

A concrete action structure p satisfies the properties required for a package switch iff:

$$\alpha_p: E_p \rightarrow \text{ACT}$$

and the following conditions hold:

1. On all four belts packages arrive and leave sequentially:

   $$\text{mutex}(p, \text{ar}(k, d), \text{ar}(k', d)) \wedge \text{mutex}(p, \text{lv}(k, d), \text{lv}(k', d))$$

   This is a typical system safety constraint about the concurrency of actions.
2. Invariant property of the action structure p: what came out went in:

   $$q \subseteq p \wedge \text{route}(k) \neq \text{empty} \Rightarrow \#©(\{\text{lv}(k, \text{lft}), \text{lv}(k, \text{rgt})\}, q)$$
   $$\leqslant \#©(\{\text{ar}(k, \text{lft}), \text{ar}(k, \text{rgt})\}, q)$$

   That is a typical safety property.
3. All packages that came in went out:

   $$\text{route}(k) \neq \text{empty} \Rightarrow \#©(\{\text{lv}(k, \text{lft}), \text{lv}(k, \text{rgt})\}, p)$$
   $$= \#©(\{\text{ar}(k, \text{lft}), \text{ar}(k, \text{rgt})\}, p)$$

   This is a typical liveness condition.
4. The routing is correct:

   $$\text{route}(k) \neq \text{empty} \wedge \text{lv}(k, d) = \alpha_p(e) \Rightarrow d = \text{route}(k)$$

With this form of a specification of the package switch a particular question arises: if a package k arrives, must it leave immediately or may it happen that it 'takes a while' until the package leaves the package switch? More precisely, can a number of packages arrive before the package leaves? Of course the arrivals could be empty packages (or more precisely empty slots). Such a property is expressed by the following specification: we replace the condition (2) of the specification above by (with appropriate n):

$$q \subseteq p \wedge \text{route}(k) \neq \text{empty} \Rightarrow \#©\{\text{lv}(k, \text{lft}), (\text{lv}(k, \text{rgt})\}, q) \leqslant$$
$$\#©(\{\text{ar}(k, \text{lft}), \text{ar}(k, \text{rgt})\}, q) \leqslant$$
$$n + \#©(\{\text{lv}(k, \text{lft}), \text{lv}(k, \text{rgt})\}, q)$$

In the specification given so far we have not talked about the role of empty slots.

There are, of course, many different formalisms for describing sets as well as properties of action structures.

In a given action structure we may isolate particular action substructures which correspond to events or actions that together form a conceptually closed activity within the con-

sidered behaviour. Such action structure substructures are also called *transactions*. Transaction-oriented views of concurrent systems are helpful, since they allow us to study particular aspects of a concurrent system. A simple example of a transaction of the package switch can be obtained by considering only those events that concern particular packages. If p is an action structure for the package switch and M is a set of packages, then $p|_s$ denotes a transaction where:

$$S = \{x \in \text{ACT}: \exists\, k \in M, d \in \text{DCN}: x = \text{ar}(k, d) \wedge x = \text{lv}(k, d)\}$$

More complicated transactions cannot be characterized simply by their actions, but, for instance, need to be characterized by certain action patterns forming action substructures.

Example: Timed package switch

For the package switch we may express the property that it takes at least c units of time until a further package enters on the left input belt. This can be formally expressed by a predicate on (p, τ):

$$\alpha(e) = \text{ar}(k, \text{1ft}) \wedge \alpha(e') = \text{ar}(k', \text{1ft}) \wedge t_2(e) - t_1(e') \leqslant c \Rightarrow e = e'$$

We can also formulate other, more tricky, predicates.

For specifying timed action structures we may write predicates working with time information.

Generally, action structures contain more information than is relevant for a distributed system. This leads to the question of what is relevant for a formal model of a distributed system. More precisely we may discuss the concept of *observability* for the action structures occurring in a distributed system.

An important concept of observability in distributed systems is the idea of a state: an action structure is a record of all of the history of a run of a system. For a finite action structure (that started in a certain initial state) a final (or intermediate) state is a record of all effects of actions of an action structure that are 'still observable'.

23.2.4 States in distributed systems

Many descriptions of distributed systems are based on the concept of a state. To make things very simple we can consider a state as a mapping from a given set of components (variables) onto values. A state associates a value with every component. In modelling distributed systems there are many ways of introducing states.

A simple way of introducing a concept of state into a distributed system is to consider the actions as the components of the state and to associate with every action the number of actions performed so far. This gives a first simple example of a state-oriented view of a system. Every finite trace of a finite action structure introduces a state this way, but there are many other conceptual models of states.

Example: States for the package switch

In the example of a package switch we could introduce a state that consists of a pair of sequences of packages – those packages that have entered the switch and have to leave on the right or the left belt of the switch, but have not left the switch so far. We obtain the set STATE, specified by:

$$\text{STATE} =_{df} \text{PKG}^* \times \text{PKG}^*$$

This STATE is used to represent the packages that have entered but not yet left the system.

Every action can be understood to define a state change. This is formalized by a state transition relation.

A state transition relation labelled by actions is given by:

1. A set of states S.
2. A set of actions A.
3. A transition relation $\rightarrow \subseteq$ STATE $\times$ ACTION $\times$ STATE.

We write for states $\sigma, \sigma' \in$ STATE, actions $a \in$ ACTION:

$$\sigma \xrightarrow{a} \sigma'$$

to express that in the state σ the action a is possible and leads to state σ'.

A state σ is called *final* if there is no action α and no state σ' such that $\sigma \xrightarrow{a} \sigma'$.

A state transition relation $\rightarrow$ is called *deterministic*, if for every state σ and action a there is at most one state σ' such that:

$$\sigma \xrightarrow{a} \sigma'$$

Let I be $\mathbb{N}$ or I be $\{k \in \mathbb{N}: 0 \leq k \leq n\}$. A sequence $\{\sigma_i\}_{i \in I}$ of states and a sequence $\{\alpha_i\}_{i \in I}$ of actions is called a *computation* with initial state σ_0 and action trace $\{a_i\}_{i \in I}$, if for all $i, i + 1 \in I$:

$$\sigma_i \xrightarrow{a_i} \sigma_{i+1}$$

The computation is called complete if I is infinite or if σ_n is final for some n. The sequence $\{a_i\}_{i \in I}$ of actions is called an *action trace* and the sequence $\{\sigma_i\}_{i \in I}$ of states is called a *state trace*.

In a state transition system an action a is called *bounded non-deterministic* if, for every state σ the state set:

$$\{\sigma': \sigma \xrightarrow{a} \sigma'\}$$

is finite. If all actions are bounded non-deterministic, then for every state σ and every action a the tree of computations with σ as root and a as labels of arcs leading to successor nodes is finitely branching.

An infinite computation is called *fair*, if every action a that is enabled infinitely often α occurs infinitely often in $\{a_i\}_i \in \mathbb{N}$, i.e. if there exists infinitely many $i \in \mathbb{N}$ with states σ_i such that for some σ':

$$\sigma_i \xrightarrow{a_i} \sigma'$$

Sometimes there are fairness assumptions given, i.e. only (at least with respect to certain actions) fair computations are considered to define behaviour (via action traces) for the system to be modelled. This is a major assumption, which makes it easier to describe certain properties, but makes it more complicated to reason about the description.

We generalize the transition relation on actions to a transition relation on sequential action structures:

$$\rightarrow \in \text{STATE} \times \text{AS(A)} \times \text{STATE}$$

and also write:

$$\sigma \xrightarrow{p} \sigma'$$

for finite action structures p. This relation can be defined in terms of the relation for actions:

$$\sigma \xrightarrow{a} \sigma' \Rightarrow \sigma \xrightarrow{p_{(a)}} \sigma'$$

$$\sigma \xrightarrow{p} \sigma' \wedge r = p\hat{\ }q \wedge \sigma' \xrightarrow{q} \sigma'' \Rightarrow \sigma \xrightarrow{r} \sigma''$$

This way of extending state transition relations to action structures works well for traces, i.e. finite sequential action structures. However, it does not properly reflect the concurrency of action structures.

Example: State transitions for package switches

For the action of the package switch we define the following state transitions:

$$(\text{sl}\hat{\ }<k>, \text{sr}) \xrightarrow{\text{lv}(k,\text{lft})} (\text{sl}, \text{sr})$$

$$(\text{sl}, \text{sr}\hat{\ }<k>) \xrightarrow{\text{lv}(k,\text{rgt})} (\text{sl}, \text{sr})$$

$$\text{route}(k) = \text{lft} \quad \Rightarrow \quad (\text{sl}, \text{sr}) \xrightarrow{\text{ar}(k,d)} (<k>\hat{\ } \text{sl}, \text{sr})$$

$$\text{route}(k) = \text{rgt} \quad \Rightarrow \quad (\text{sl}, \text{sr}) \xrightarrow{\text{ar}(k,d)} (\text{sl}, <k>\hat{\ } \text{sr})$$

$$\text{route}(k) = \text{empty} \quad \Rightarrow \quad (\text{sl}, \text{sr}) \xrightarrow{\text{ar}(k,d)} (\text{sl}, \text{sr})$$

With a concept of state and state transition we can also define the feasible sequential action structures of a system. We define the initial state to be $(\varepsilon, \varepsilon)$. Then a sequential action structure defines a behaviour of the system, if there is a corresponding stream of states such that action sequence and state sequence form a computation. Here again the problem of fairness arises: how often may packages arrive before one leaves?

Given a sequential action structure i.e. a stream of actions $s = a_0 \& a_1 \& \ldots$, we obtain for a given initial state σ_0 streams of states σ_i by the definition:

$$(*) \quad \sigma_i \xrightarrow{a_i} \sigma_{i+1}$$

Every stream of states that fulfills the condition (*) is called an *associated state trace* for the action trace s.

Certainly there are many different ways to choose a state space for a set of actions to define action structures. Abstractly, given a state space, we can relate the actions of the system to the states by giving a state transition relation. A state transition relation is a relation which associates with every state and every action its set of possible successor states. It corresponds to a labelled graph.

Example:

Consider a simple example for states and actions: A is the set of state functions where State $= \{x, y, z, f1, f2\} \rightarrow \mathbb{N}$ and

a: $\quad f1 := x*f1$
c: $\quad x, z := z, z + 1$
b: $\quad f2 := y*f2$
d: $\quad y, z := z, z + 1$

If the initial state is:

$$x, y, z, f1, f2 := 1, 1, 1, 1, 1$$

then the result state (if the system stops as soon as $z > 9$) for the action structure described as an example in Section 23.2.2.1 is:

$$x, y, z, f1, f2 := 9, 8, 10, 6 * 7 * 9, 1 * 2 * 3 * 4 * 5 * 8$$

One can see that this action structure is a run of a program computing the factorial in parallel, as $f1 * f2 = 9!$

However, the concept of a global state seems inappropriate, since highly concurrent systems may never have a consistent global intermediate state, because parts of the system may change at any time. Nevertheless, we talk about 'virtual' intermediate states, and states of the system before it is started and after it has terminated. State transition systems are also called state machines or automata.

Often system descriptions are given in terms of state sequences. State sequences are especially well suited to the concept of *temporal logic*. In temporal logic properties of state sequences are characterized by special logical formulae.

In *linear time temporal logic* we formulate logical predicates on streams of elements from a given set A, according to the following concepts. First, we observe that we can consider every predicate:

$$Q: A \rightarrow \mathbb{B}$$

as a predicate on streams $s \in A^{\omega}$ by defining:

$$Q.s \equiv Q.ft.s$$

Given a predicate R on sequences we may define new predicates on sequences by:

$$(\bigcirc R).s \equiv_{df} R.rt.s \qquad\qquad next\ time$$

$$(\square R).s \equiv_{df} \forall i \in \mathbb{N}: R.rt^i.s \qquad always$$

$$(\diamondsuit R).s \equiv_{df} \exists i \in \mathbb{N}: R.rt^i.s \quad\cdot\quad eventually$$

If we have, for instance, the predicate:

$$is(\alpha): A \rightarrow \mathbb{B}$$

defined by:

$$is(a).x \equiv_{df} (a = x)$$

then the predicate is(a) on traces specifies that the first element of a trace is a. $\bigcirc$ is(a) specifies that the second element of the trace is a. $\square$ is(a) specifies that all elements in the trace are a.

We can include time information in the states by introducing time stamps for states or, equivalently *a* particular variable that has elements of sort TIME as its value. $\diamondsuit$ is(a) specifies that there exists an element a in the trace. We immediately obtain valid formulas such as:

$$\square\ is(a) \Rightarrow \diamondsuit\ is(a)$$
$$is(a) \Rightarrow \diamondsuit\ is(a)$$

A more complicated formula is $\square \diamondsuit$ is(a), which specifies that a occurs infinitely often in the trace.

A temporal formulation of the requirement that every arriving package leaves the package switch again may be formulated as follows (with $k \neq$ empty):

$$\square\ (is(ar(k, d)) \Rightarrow \diamondsuit\ is(lv(k, route(k))))$$

Here we have to assume that packages do not occur several times in the input belts. However, particular properties of traces are difficult to express in the simple temporal logic introduced above.

An example is the specification for the package switch that every outgoing package had previously arrived.

There are also other forms of temporal logic, such as *branching time temporal logic*, that do not consider formulae over sequences but formulae over trees. The advantages of temporal logic are the brevity of formulae and the availability of simple special calculi for their logical manipulations. The major disadvantages are the difficulties of reading and understanding formulae written in temporal logic which have temporal operators nested to several levels, and their limited expressiveness. Certain predicates cannot be formulated in temporal logic. However, to extend the expressiveness of temporal logic additional operators can be introduced (such as the *until*-operator which represents a binary temporal operator). On the other hand this complicates the calculus. Some researchers suggest therefore that temporal formulae should only be used for expressing particular properties, such as liveness, and to use other formalisms, such as state transition relations, for expressing safety properties.

We may include time information into the states by introducing time stamps for states or, equivalently, a particular variable that has elements of sort TIME as its value.

23.2.5 Bibliographical and historical remarks

There are many formalisms, in many variations, that have been suggested for formally modelling systems. First examples were state machines (Rabin and Scott, 1959; Minsky, 1967) and Petri-nets (Petri, 1962; Reisig, 1985). In contrast to state machines, which in general correspond to interleaving views and can be seen as state transition systems, Petri-nets provide a concurrency-oriented model by assuming a distributed state. The semantic meaning of a Petri-net (more precisely a place/transition net) with a particular state can be described by occurrence nets from which action structures can be deduced. Hence, a place/transition net describes a set of action structures where the transitions are playing the role of actions.

Apart from programming language-oriented description, which will be treated separately in Section 23.4, it was not until the 1970s that further formalisms were suggested for specifying systems. Examples are temporal logic (Pnueli, 1977; 1986), path expressions (Campbell and Habermann, 1974), also COSY (Lauer, *et al.*, 1979), traces (Mazurkiewicz, 1977) and event structures (Winskel, 1982; Nielsen *et al.*, 1981).

23.3 Components of causal systems

In a functional, or 'black box', view of a distributed system we are not so much interested in its internal action structure, as in its behaviour seen as an interaction between the system proper and its environment. In particular, a subsystem can be seen as a function from input stimuli to output stimuli. In a functional view a distributed system is understood and described in terms of its interface and its interaction with its environment.

A simple model of interaction between a subsystem and its environment is obtained if we separate the set A of actions into a set I of input actions (also called actions of the environment) and a set O of output actions (also called the system actions) such that $A = I \cup O$. For a state transition system we can then distinguish between the transition steps of the subsystem (which are the actions from O) and the transition steps of the environment which are elements of I. In principle it is also possible to include internal actions.

23.3.1 Functional views

Very generally we may model distributed systems by monotonic functions:

$f: AS(A) \to AS(A)$

mapping the causal structure of input events onto the causality structure of output events.

For a given action structure p and $q = f(p)$ an action structure r is called the *behaviour* of f with input p if the events of r are the union of the input events from p and the output events for q:

$$E_r = E_p \cup E_q$$

The action labelling for r is induced by the action labelling for q and p:

$$\forall e \in E_p: \alpha_r(e) = \alpha_p(e)$$

$$\forall e \in E_q: \alpha_r(e) = \alpha_q(e)$$

The causal structure of r contains all the causalities from p and q and in addition contains causalities between the input and the output:

$$\forall e, e' \in E_r : e \leqslant_r e' \Leftrightarrow (e, e' \in E_p \wedge e \leqslant_p e') \vee (e, e' \in E_q \wedge e \leqslant_q e') \vee (e \in E_p \wedge e \in E_q \wedge \forall p' \subseteq p : e \in E_{p'} \Rightarrow e' \in E_{f(p')})$$

This means that, in addition to the given causal structure on p and q, input events can be causal for output events, but not *vice versa*. An input event e is causal for an output event e' iff whenever e occurs in the input action structure p the event e' occurs in the output action structure $f(p)$.

Considering only monotonic functions as models of distributed systems means that adding input events to a given structure of input events can only add output events to the structure of output events produced so far. Monotonicity also guarantees the existence of a solution for fixpoint equations for action structures (modelling feedback in distributed systems).

Example: Functional specification of the package switch by sequential action structures

We specify a function:

$$f: \{ar(k,d) : k \in PKG \wedge d \in DCN\}^\omega \to \{lv(k,d) : k \in PKG \wedge d \in DCN\}^\omega$$

by the equation:

$$k \neq empty \Rightarrow f(ar(k,d) \ \& \ s) = lv(k, route(k)) \ \& \ f(s)$$

For empty slots there are a number of choices. A simple specification may read:

$$f(ar(empty, k) \ \& \ s) = f(s)$$

Here we have chosen an interleaving view. For a non-interleaving view some complications arise with monotonicity.

A functional view of a system is a first step towards a component-oriented view of a distributed system.

Most abstractly, a component in a distributed system is an entity that may cooperate with the other components of the system. Which particular concept of a component is most appropriate depends on the way a component may cooperate with its environment. A simple idea of a component is obtained by thinking of a component as a function mapping input stimuli onto output stimuli. This is very much in accordance with the example given above.

23.3.2 Forms of compositions

We consider a component as a simple mapping from action

structures to action structures. We study three forms of composition:

1. Sequential composition of such functions.
2. Parallel composition of such functions.
3. Feedback.

For simplicity, we assume that for every function there is a given *alphabet* of actions. In a parallel composition we join the alphabets of the functions both for the input alphabet and for the output alphabet. In a sequential composition we assume that the output alphabet (of the first function) is a subset of the input alphabet of the second function.

Let us consider prefix monotonic functions:

$$f_i: AS(A_i) \to AS(A_i'), \text{ for } i = 1, 2$$

Sequential composition of f_1 and f_2 is defined by (assume $A_1' = A_2$):

$$(f_1 \cdot f_2)(p) = f_2(f_1(p))$$

Parallel composition of f_1 and f_2 is defined by:

$$(f_1 \| f_2): AS(A_1 \cup A_2) \to AS(A_1' \cup A_2')$$

where:

$$(f_1 \| f_2)(p) = q \qquad \text{with } q \in f_1(p|_{A_1}) \|_\emptyset f_2(p|_{A_2})$$

Here we assume for simplicity $A_1' \cap A_2' = \emptyset$.

Feedback of f_1 for the action set $A_1 = A_1'$ is defined by the function:

$$fb(f) \in AS(A_1)$$

where $fb(f)$ is defined by the least fixpoint q of f, i.e. the least solution of the equation:

$$q = f(q)$$

As is well known, for monotonic functions over a domain least fixpoints always exist. In fact AS(A) forms a domain, as will be discussed again in Section 23.4.2.1.

23.3.3 Time information

Again, time information can be incorporated by including special time messages into the streams or by time stamps for the elements of the stream. Using such time information, some funtions can even more easily be specified than without time information. An example is fair merge:

$$merge: T^\omega \times T^\omega \to T^\omega$$

where:

$$T =_{df} D \cup \{\sqrt{}\}$$

Here we use $\sqrt{}$ to represent a tick of the clock. Now a fair merge is easily defined by the equations:

$$merge \ (a \ \& \ x, b \ \& \ y) = a \ \& \ b \ \& \ merge(x,y) \ \vee$$
$$merge(a \ \& \ x, b \ \& \ y) = b \ \& \ a \ \& \ merge(x,y)$$

Here we assume that every input stream for the merge contains many time ticks. Of course we may also specify non-deterministic versions of merge functions.

23.4 Programming languages for describing distributed systems

Concurrent programming languages can be understood to describe distributed systems in the sense of defining sets of action structures. We can see programs written in such languages as descriptions of sets of action structures. Otherwise, though, in a programming language we always have the concept of composition (putting subprograms together to form larger programs) and therefore also the concept of a component. In a programming language used for describing concurrent systems, the notion of component has to be chosen carefully with respect to the notion of connectives. Which properties of a piece of program are semantically important for proper composition concerns which kinds of compositional forms are available in the language. However, this question only arises if one is interested in modular compositional semantics where the meaning of composed programs is to be defined in terms of the meanings of the subprograms. Such a semantics is also called a *denotational semantics*.

In an *operational semantics* this form of modularity is not required. There the meaning of a program is described by referring to the internal structure of the components and associating state transition systems with (concurrent) operations.

23.4.1 Syntactic forms

There are many different concepts of languages for describing concurrent systems. Historically, the first examples of these languages were obtained by extending existing programming languages which were oriented to conventional sequential computer architectures. This is why initially mainly state- and assignment-oriented programming language concepts have been extended by particular forms of cooperation, synchronization and communication for describing concurrent systems.

The idea of shared memory in particular had been used to communicate and to cooperate between distributed components of a system acting in parallel. Later it became apparent that the coordination problems for shared memory systems were difficult to overcome. More explicit and simpler concepts exploit forms of communications where the cooperation and coordination between distributed components of a system executed in parallel are carried out merely by message passing.

23.4.1.1 Shared memory cooperation

Shared memory is memory that can be updated by distinct components that operate in parallel. However, if several components try to access the same component of a shared memory simultaneously and if at least one of these components tries to change the value of this part of the shared memory, this leads to a conflict.

To avoid conflicts, simultaneous mutual access to shared memory has to be prevented. There are many suggestions in the literature for ensuring *mutual exclusion*. One of the first suggestions was the use of *semaphores*. Semaphores are special elements of shared memory that can be accessed exclusively only via very special procedures typically known as P and V. An explanation of the P and V operations is given below.

Later more general mechanisms were suggested such as *conditional critical regions* (Hoare, 1972). A conditional critical region consists of a guard represented by a Boolean expression and a statement. A special predicate is given in the guard, and shared memory can be updated in the statement. The programs executed in parallel only refer to shared memory in the guards and statements within conditional critical regions. A program executes a conditional critical region by testing its guard. If the guard is true and if no other program is executing its conditional critical regions at the same time, then the program is allowed to continue and to execute the statement given in its conditional critical region. Only after the program has finished the execution of the conditional critical region is another program allowed to execute a conditional critical region. If the evaluation of the guard yields false, then the execution waits. If an execution waits in the case where the guard of a conditional critical region is not true, then the guard is re-evaluated after other programs executed in parallel have executed conditional critical regions and it is tested whether the condition is true now. If an execution of a program waits in front of a guard of a conditional critical region which is never changed to true, then the execution of that program waits forever.

The syntax for a simple assignment-oriented language working with conditional critical regions is given by:

```
< action > ::= < assignment > |
               < conditional critical region > | nop
< assignment > ::= < variable > {, < variable > )*
               := < exp > {, < exp > }*
< conditional critical region > ::= await < exp > then
               < assignment > end
< seq program > ::= < action > | < seq program > or
               < seq program > |
               < seq program > ; < seq program > |
               if < exp > then < seq program >
               else < seq program > fi |
               while < exp > do < seq program > od
< par program > ::= < seq program > {|| < par program > }
```

As a side condition ('context condition') we require the Bernstein condition for safe (with respect to mutual access to program variables) parallel programs: if a program variable occurs in different branches of a parallel program, and at least one branch on the left-hand side of an assignment, then it occurs in all parallel branches only within conditional critical regions. Using these rules, read/write conflicts between unguarded statements are prevented.

Example: A program for the package switch

The package switch can be programmed with the following program variables:

lib   sequence of values on left input belt
rib   sequence of values on right input belt
lob   sequence of values on left output belt
rob   sequence of values on right output belt
lsb   sequence of values of internal state waiting to leave on left output belt
rsb   sequence of values of internal state waiting to leave on right output belt

The system of programs reads as follows:

```
input_from_left::  while true do
     await lib ≠ ε then x,lib:= ft.lib, rt.lib end;
     if route(x) = lft then await true then lsb := lsb^<x>
                           end else
     if route(x) = rgt then await true then rsb := rsb^<x>
                           end
                           else nop fi fi
     od
||
input_from_right::  while true do
     await rib ≠ ε then y, rib := ft.rib, rt.rib end;
     if route(x) = lft then await true then lsb := lsb^<y>
                           end else
     if route(x) = rgt then await true then rsb := rsb^<y>
                           end
```

```
        else nop fi fi
    od
    ‖
output_to_left::  while true do
    await lsb ≠ ε then lb, lob : = rt.lsb, (ft.lsb) & lob end
    od
    ‖
output_to_right::  while true do
    await rsb ≠ ε then rb, rob : = rt.rsb, (ft.rsb) & rob end
    od
```

Here states are just mappings from program variables to values. The state changes of assignments are as usual.

We define a state transition for assignments by:

$$\sigma \xrightarrow{x := E} \sigma[d/x]$$

where d denotes the value of E for state σ and $\sigma[d/x]$ represents σ with the value of x replaced by d. Furthermore, we define for conditional critical regions:

$$\sigma \xrightarrow{\text{await C then } x := E \text{ end}} \sigma[d/x]$$

provided the guard C is true in state σ and d denotes the value of E for state σ.

Now we define the set of configurations CF by:

$$\text{CF} = < \text{par program} > \times \text{DATA\_STATE}$$

A configuration defines the state of a computation given the program state and the data state.

We define a configuration transition relation:

$$\rightarrow \subseteq \text{CF} \times \text{ACTION} \times \text{CF}$$

by the axioms (for simplicity we write $c \rightarrow c'$ instead of $c \xrightarrow{\text{nop}} c'$):

$$\sigma \xrightarrow{a} \sigma' \Rightarrow < a, \sigma > \xrightarrow{a} < \text{nop}, \sigma' >$$

$$< \text{nop}; t, \sigma > \rightarrow < t, \sigma >$$

$$< t, \sigma > \xrightarrow{a} < t', \sigma' > \Rightarrow < t; t'', \sigma > \xrightarrow{a} < t'; t'', \sigma' >$$

$$< \text{if C then } t \text{ else } t' \text{ fi}, \sigma > \rightarrow < t, \sigma >$$

if the value of C in state σ is true

$$< \text{if C then } t \text{ else } t' \text{ fi}, \sigma > \rightarrow < t', \sigma >$$

if the value of C in state σ is false

$$< \text{while C do } t \text{ od}, \sigma > \rightarrow$$
$$< \text{if C then } t; \text{while C do } t \text{ od else nop fi}, \sigma >$$

The choice between two statements is expressed by:

$$< t \text{ or } t', \sigma < \rightarrow < t, \sigma >$$
$$< t' \text{ or } t, \sigma < \rightarrow < t, \sigma >$$

For configurations including parallel programs a transition relation is defined by the following rules:

$$< t, \sigma > \xrightarrow{a} < t', \sigma' > \Rightarrow < t \| t'', \sigma > \xrightarrow{a} < t' \| t'', \sigma' >$$

$$< t, \sigma > \xrightarrow{a} < t', \sigma' > \Rightarrow < t'' \| t, \sigma > \xrightarrow{a} < t' \| t'', \sigma' >$$

A parallel program t is called *terminal* in state $\sigma 2$ if there does not exist programs t', actions a, and states σ' with:

$$< t, \sigma > \xrightarrow{a} < t', \sigma' >$$

A parallel program $t (\neq \textbf{nop})$ is said to be in a *deadlock* in state σ if t is terminal in state σ.

By the rules above we can associate with every parallel program t_0 and every initial data state σ_0 finite or infinite computations of the form:

$$< t_0, \sigma_0 > \xrightarrow{a_0} < t_1, \sigma_1 > \xrightarrow{a_1} < t_2, \sigma_2 > \xrightarrow{a_2} < t_3, \sigma_3 > \xrightarrow{a_3} \ldots$$

A computation thus defines a finite or infinite sequence, i.e. stream or trace of actions a_i, a stream of states σ_i and a stream of programs t_i.

More precisely speaking, a finite computation for the parallel program t_0 and the initial state σ_0 is given by the sequences of programs $\{t_i : 0 \leqslant i \leqslant n\}$, by the sequences of states $\{\sigma_i : 0 \leqslant i \leqslant n\}$, and by the sequences of actions $\{a_i : 0 \leqslant i < n\}$ where we have:

$$< t_i, \sigma_i > \xrightarrow{a_i} < t_{i+1}, \sigma_{i+1} > \quad \text{for } 0 \leqslant i < n$$

and t_n is terminal in state σ_n. An infinite computation is given by the infinite sequences of programs $\{t_i : i \in \mathbb{N}\}$, by the sequences of states $\{\sigma_i : i \in \mathbb{N}\}$ and by the sequences of actions $\{a_i : i \in \mathbb{N}\}$ where we have:

$$< t_i, \sigma_i > \xrightarrow{a_i} < t_{i+1}, \sigma_{i+1} > \quad \text{for } i \in \mathbb{N}$$

To characterize the properties of a parallel program we can either characterize the sequences of actions or the sequences of states.

In contrast to the given interleaving view of a parallel program we may also develop a concurrency view: a parallel program t_0 defines for every initial state σ_0 an action structure the actions of which are **nop**, assignments or conditional critical regions. For events labelled by conditional critical regions we require that they are not concurrent; the action substructure consisting of the events labelled by conditional critical regions forms a sequential subprocess. Similarly, we require that every sequential branch of a parallel program forms a sequential subprocess. Moreover, we assume that there exists a sequentialization of the action structure that corresponds to a sequential trace as specified above.

Semaphores (Dijkstra, 1968) can be explained by conditional critical regions. A semaphore is a variable for a natural number for which only two actions are allowed:

$$P(s) : \textbf{await } s > 0 \textbf{ then } s := s - 1 \textbf{ end}$$
$$V(s) : \textbf{await true then } s := s + 1 \textbf{ end}$$

Semaphores can be used to coordinate parallel programs.

A very simple and basic view of reactive systems is found in non-deterministic state transition systems. A prominent example is the formalism called UNITY introduced by Chandy and Misra (1988). There programs consist simply of a collection of assignments and an initialization. Execution is performed by choosing one of the assignments, executing it, choosing another one, and so on. No assumption is made about the choices apart from a fairness assumption; every assignment is chosen infinitely often.

23.4.1.2 Communication-oriented cooperation

In a communication-oriented cooperation the components of a distributed system do not have access to shared memory. Every component running in parallel exclusively uses its local state.

However, components may read messages sent by other components or may produce messages for other components. Two aspects are especially important here. First is the way that messages are addressed and, second, the way that the message transfer is carried out.

The addressing of messages can be achieved, for example, using channel names or the names of components. The concepts are related. In asymmetric communication, the sender may address a particular channel of the receiver. However, the receiver may not know the name of the sender, but the receiver may send a message back to the sender. In this case a communication transaction consists of basically two actions: the sending action and the response to it. We call these 'remote procedure calls'.

The mode of exchange of messages can be as follows. First the receiver of a message can only receive a message after it has been sent. So if an agent wants to receive a message, it has to wait until the message has been sent. For the sender of a message the situation is different. There are two possible modes for the sender. A sender may send its message even in cases where there is no receiver ready to receive it. Then the message has to be buffered (in the channel) and can be received by a potential receiver afterwards. This mode of message passing is called asynchronous. The other possibility is a synchronous mode of message passing (also called rendezvous or handshake). There, a sender is only allowed to send its message when a receiver is ready to receive it. This gives symmetry between sending and receiving such that message passing can be seen as a joint action (a common event) of the sender and receiver.

Related to these different modes of message passing are different possibilities for selecting receivers for a message. If a sender (or receiver) tries to communicate over several channels concurrently by handshake, it is possible to determine which receiver or which sender can exchange a message from their state of readiness. In a buffered communication mode this is not usually possible.

To write communicating programs we redefine the syntax of the language in the preceeding paragraph by defining:

$$< \text{action} > ::= < \text{assignment} > \mid < \text{channel} > < \text{exp} > \mid$$
$$< \text{channel} > ? < \text{variable} > \mid \textbf{nop}$$

Here, for a given channel c we denote by $c\,!\,E$ the sending of the value of E on channel c and by $c\,?\,x$ we denote the receipt of a value from channel c and its assignment to x.

In a *buffered communication* scheme we see channels as variables and associate with every channel in our state a finite sequence (queue) of buffered values. We define:

$$< c\,!E,\sigma > \xrightarrow{c\,!\,E} < \textbf{nop}, \sigma[c\,\hat{}\,<d>/c] >$$

where d denotes the value of E in state σ. Similarly we define:

$$< c\,?\,x,\sigma > \xrightarrow{c\,?\,x} < \textbf{nop}, \sigma[\text{next}(c)/x, \text{rest}(c)/c] >$$

provided the channel c is not empty in state σ. Here, next and rest are assumed to be the classical operations on queues.

For *handshake communication* we do not include channels as variables in states. Instead we use the more complicated action:

$$c\,?\,x{:}d$$

by which we denote the action of receiving the value d on channel c and assigning it to the variable x. We use the rule:

$$< c\,?\,x, \sigma > \xrightarrow{c\,?\,x{:}d} < \textbf{nop}, \sigma[d/x] >$$

For the sending action we use the rule:

$$< c\,!\,E, \sigma > \xrightarrow{c\,!\,d} < \textbf{nop}, \sigma >$$

provided d is the value of E in state σ. We define internal communication by:

$$< t,\sigma > \xrightarrow{c\,!\,d} < t', \sigma > \wedge < u,\sigma > \xrightarrow{c\,?\,x{:}d} < u', \sigma' > \Rightarrow$$

$$< t\|u,\sigma > \to < t'\|u', \sigma > \wedge < u\|t, \sigma > \to < u'\|t', \sigma >$$

This way we obtain another version of a rewriting system for parallel programs.

23.4.2 Semantics of programs describing action structures

So-called concurrent programs describe distributed systems or, following the above, describe sets of action structures. However, generally, programs (or more precisely program fragments) must be seen as more complex objects than just descriptions of (sets of) action structures. They have to be considered as entities that generate an action structure for every given input from some environment.

An environment is formed by other programs executed concurrently and by some initial (global) state (and/or some input). Therefore it is necessary for semantic program-modelling not only to model the action structures, but also to model the relevant aspects of the possible environments and initial states (the input to the system or to the program), so as to predict the way the program behaves when composed with other programs. Only in this way can we achieve a compositional semantic model. Compositionality is the key to modular program design.

A program written in a programming language describing concurrent systems ('action structures') can of course always be understood as describing a set of action structures. More precisely, a complete program (not just a program fragment) can be seen as the description of a set of concrete or abstract action structures. There are, of course, several techniques to give a formal definition for the set of action structures associated with each program.

One can choose a *compositional technique* ('synthetical semantics') where the meaning of a program is defined by composing the meaning of subprograms with appropriate operators attached to the language constructs. Examples of methods of giving synthetical semantics are denotational semantics or algebraic semantics.

Other possibilities are *analytical techniques*, used for the description of the semantics of concurrent programs. Here the explicit syntactic structure of the complete program system is considered to attach a set of action structures to it. Examples of analytical techniques are the many methods of defining the operational semantics of programs.

Independently of the technique that we use for defining the meaning of programs, we can either try to give action structure semantics to concurrent programs, i.e. semantics that define which action structures are attached to a concurrent program, or we can give a semantics that corresponds to a particular abstraction from action structure semantics.

In both cases additional information may have to be added to the semantic representations to ensure compositionality. Nevertheless, action structures can be used directly in a denotational style, since action structures are domains.

23.4.2.1 *Action structures as domains*

The ordering $\sqsubseteq$ on action structures can be used as a partial ordering to turn action structures into complete partially ordered sets.

Theorem. $(AS(A), \sqsubseteq)$ forms a cpo with the empty action structure $p_\emptyset$ as least element.

The domain structure on the set of action structures can be used to give a denotational meaning to concurrent programs. Before demonstrating this we are going to introduce a few additional concepts that are needed for a proper semantic treatment.

23.4.2.2 *Divergence, termination*

For concurrent programs that have to synchronize on a given action set, the notions of divergence and termination are of major importance.

In an action structure p all events labelled by a particular action α may be eliminated; this is expressed by $p\backslash\alpha$ where:

$$p\backslash a = p|_{E'} \text{ where } E' = \{e \in E_p : \alpha_p(e) \neq a\}$$

For action structures, termination can be represented by a special action. Let $\sqrt{}$ denote the action indicating termination. By $AS\sqrt{}(A)$ we denote the set of all action structures p with labels from $A \cup \{\sqrt{}\}$ such that an event is labelled by $\sqrt{}$ only if it is the greatest element (with respect to $\leqslant_p$). By $AAS\sqrt{}(A)$ we denote the set of abstract action structures from $AS\sqrt{}(A)$.

An action structure p from $AS\sqrt{}(A)$ is *terminated* if it includes the action $\sqrt{}$ (which is by definition the label of the largest event). Then we write $\downarrow.p$.

$$\downarrow.p \Leftrightarrow \exists e \in E_p : a_p(e) = \sqrt{}$$

Based on the concept of action structures we can give a formal semantics to a simple programming language for concurrency.

23.4.2.3 *Programming language describing action structures*

Suppose a set A of elementary actions to be given. We define a language CP (communicating processes), which is a simplified version of Hoare's CSP and Milner's CCS.

The syntax is given by the following clauses

< agent > :: = **abort**	non-termination
|**nop**	immediate termination
| < action > → < agent >	elementary action
| < agent > **or** < agent >	non-deterministic choice
| < agent > ⫴ < agent >	dependent choice
| < agent > ‖ < action set >	parallel composition with
< agent >	possible synchronization
| < agent > ; < agent >	sequential composition
| < id >	agent identifiers
| < id > :: < agent >	recursive definition of agents

Examples of agents are:

$$P = p :: a \to c \to p$$
$$Q = q :: b \to d \to q$$
$$R = r :: (c \to r) \mathbin{⫴} (d \to r)$$

By a parallel composition we obtain agents such as:

$$(P\|_{\{c\}}R)\|_{\{c,d\}}(Q\|_{\{d\}}R),$$
$$(P\|_\emptyset Q)\|_{\{c,d\}}R.$$

A special run of the above agents is the example action structure of Section 23.2.2.

Our semantics is purely action structure-oriented. First we define an operational semantics as an example for an analytical method.

23.4.2.4 *Process-oriented operational semantics by rewriting systems for CP*

The operational semantics of CP is given by an inductive definition of a relation between terms labelled by action structures:

$$\to \,\subseteq\, < agent > \times AS\sqrt{}(A) \times < agent >$$

where $t1 \xrightarrow{\ x\ } t2$ means $t1$ may perform a number of actions as indicated in the action structure x and behave like $t2$ afterwards. As the relation we take the least relation for which the following rules are valid (remember that $P_\emptyset$ denotes set of the action structures with the empty event set and $P_{\{a\}}$ the set of action structures with an event set with exactly one event labelled by a):

$$x \in P_\emptyset \Rightarrow \mathbf{abort} \xrightarrow{\ x\ } \mathbf{abort}$$

$$x \in P_{\{\sqrt{}\}} \Rightarrow \mathbf{nop} \xrightarrow{\ x\ } \mathbf{nop}$$

$$x \in P_{\{a\}} \Rightarrow (a \to t) \xrightarrow{\ x\ } t$$

$$t1 \xrightarrow{\ x1\ } t2 \wedge x0 \in P_{\{a\}} \wedge x = x0\,\hat{}\,x1 \Rightarrow (a \to t1) \xrightarrow{\ x\ } t2$$

$$x \in P_\emptyset \Rightarrow t1 \text{ or } t2 \xrightarrow{\ x\ } t1$$

$$x \in P_\emptyset \Rightarrow t1 \text{ or } t2 \xrightarrow{\ x\ } t2$$

$$t1 \xrightarrow{\ x\ } t3 \Rightarrow t1 \text{ or } t2 \xrightarrow{\ x\ } t3$$

$$t2 \xrightarrow{\ x\ } t3 \Rightarrow t1 \text{ or } t2 \xrightarrow{\ x\ } t3$$

$$x \notin P_\emptyset \wedge t1 \xrightarrow{\ x\ } t3 \Rightarrow t1 \mathbin{⫴} t2 \xrightarrow{\ x\ } t3$$

$$x \notin P_\emptyset \wedge t2 \xrightarrow{\ x\ } t3 \Rightarrow t1 \mathbin{⫴} t2 \xrightarrow{\ x\ } t3$$

$$x \in P_\emptyset \wedge t1 \xrightarrow{\ x\ } t3 \Rightarrow t1 \mathbin{⫴} t2 \xrightarrow{\ x\ } t3 \mathbin{⫴} t2$$

$$x \in P_\emptyset \wedge t2 \xrightarrow{\ x\ } t3 \Rightarrow t1 \mathbin{⫴} t2 \xrightarrow{\ x\ } t1 \mathbin{⫴} t3$$

$$t1 \xrightarrow{\ x0\ } t3 \wedge x1 \in P_\emptyset \wedge x \in x0 \|_{c \cup \{\sqrt{}\}} x1 \Rightarrow t1 \|_c t2 \xrightarrow{\ x\ } t3 \|_c t2$$

$$t2 \xrightarrow{\ x1\ } t3 \wedge x0 \in P_\emptyset \wedge x \in x0 \|_{c \cup \{\sqrt{}\}} x1 \Rightarrow t1 \|_c t2 \xrightarrow{\ x\ } t1 \|_c t3$$

$$t1 \xrightarrow{\ x0\ } \mathbf{nop} \wedge t2 \xrightarrow{\ x1\ } \mathbf{nop} \wedge x \in x0 \|_{c \cup \{\sqrt{}\}} x1 \Rightarrow t1 \|_c t2 \xrightarrow{\ x\ } \mathbf{nop}$$

$$t1 \xrightarrow{\ x0\ } t3 \wedge t2 \xrightarrow{\ x1\ } t4 \wedge x \in x0 \|_{c \cup \{\sqrt{}\}} x1 \Rightarrow t1 \|_c t2 \xrightarrow{\ x\ } t3 \|_c t4$$

$$t1 \xrightarrow{\ x\ } t3 \wedge \neg \downarrow.x \Rightarrow t1;t2 \xrightarrow{\ x\ } t3;t2$$

$$t1 \xrightarrow{\ x0\ } \mathbf{nop} \wedge t2 \xrightarrow{\ x1\ } t3 \wedge x = (x0/\sqrt{})\,\hat{}\,x1 \Rightarrow t1;t2 \xrightarrow{\ x\ } t3$$

$$x \in P_\emptyset \Rightarrow q :: t \xrightarrow{\ x\ } t[q :: t/q]$$

$$t[q :: t/q] \xrightarrow{\ x\ } t0 \Rightarrow q :: t \xrightarrow{\ x\ } t0$$

Here, by $t[t'/q]$ we denote the agent in which all free occurrences of q are replaced by t'. It is rather easy to define the set of terminating action structures associated with an agent t based on the induced relation:

$$\text{Cap}_{\text{term}}(t) =_{\text{df}} \{\text{abstract}(x): t \xrightarrow{x} \textbf{nop} \wedge \downarrow.x\}$$

It is also straightforward to define the set of non-terminating or deadlocking finite action structures associated with an agent t:

$$\text{Cap}_{\text{fin}}(t) =_{\text{df}} \{\text{abstract}(x): t \xrightarrow{x} t' \wedge (t' \text{ diverges} \underline{\vee} t' \text{ deadlocks})\}$$

where we define t *diverges* iff there exists a sequence of agents t_n such that:

$$t_0 = t \text{ and } t_n \xrightarrow{x} t_{n+1} \text{ for } x \in P_\emptyset \text{ and all } n \in \mathbb{N}$$

t *deadlocks* iff for all agents t' and action structures x it is not derivable that:

$$t \xrightarrow{x} t'$$

More complicated is the definition of the infinite behaviours of an agent t. Before we state this definition we give a lemma.

Lemma (sequentialization/decomposition)

1. For every action structure x and agents $t0$, $t2$ with $t0 \xrightarrow{x} t2$ and for every non-trivial prefix y of x, $y \sqsubseteq x$ (i.e. $P_\emptyset \neq y$ and $y \neq x$) there exists an agent $t1$ such that:

$$t0 \xrightarrow{y} t1 \wedge t1 \xrightarrow{z} t2$$

and $z = x\big|_{Ex \backslash Ey}$.

2. for all agents $t0$, $t1$, $t2$ and action structures x and y with $t0 \xrightarrow{x} t1$ and $t1 \xrightarrow{y} t2$ there exists an action structure z with

$$t0 \xrightarrow{z} t2 \text{ such that } x \sqsubseteq z \text{ and } z\big|_{Ez \backslash Ex = y}.$$

Based on this lemma we define the infinite capabilities of an agent t; we specify:

$$\text{abstract}(p) \in \text{Cap}^\infty(t) \text{ iff}$$

there exist agents t_n and action structure x_n such that:

$$p = \text{lub}\{x_n\}_{n \in \mathbb{N}}$$

and for all n we have:

$$t \xrightarrow{x_n} t_n$$

and there exist action structures z with:

$$t_n \xrightarrow{z} t_{n+1}$$

and $x_n \sqsubseteq x_{n-1}$ and $z = x_{n+1|En/En+1}$, where E_n is the set of events of x_n.

Finally, we may give the set $\text{Cap}(t)$ of all action structures associated with an agent term t:

$$\text{Cap}(t) = \text{Cap}_{\text{term}}(t) \cup \text{Cap}_{\text{fin}} \cup \text{Cap}^\infty(t)$$

Although the above term rewriting rules gives satisfactory semantics from the point of view of the analytical method, the operational semantics do not support the following compositionality principle: two different agents might have the same capabilities, but behave differently in different contexts, i.e. we cannot replace one for the other when they are occurring as subterms without changing the semantics of the term. Let us consider the following examples:

$$t1 = (a \rightarrow (b \rightarrow \textbf{nop})) \| (a \rightarrow (c \rightarrow \textbf{nop}))$$
$$t2 = a \rightarrow ((b \rightarrow \textbf{nop}) \| (c \rightarrow \textbf{nop}))$$
$$t3 = b \rightarrow \text{nop}$$

It is not difficult to derive that:

1. $t1$ and $t2$ have the same capabilities namely the set $\{\varepsilon, a, ab, ac\}$
2. $t1 \|_{\{b,c\}} t3$ may deadlock
3. $t2 \|_{\{b,c\}} t3$ always terminates successfully.

Informally one might say that $t2$, after having performed the action a is ready to respond to the action b as well as to c when one of them is offered by the environment, whereas $t1$ after having performed a is either ready to respond to b or to c.

23.4.2.5 *Process-oriented denotational semantics for CP*

A careful analysis of the example above may lead to the conclusion that any possible state in a CP program can be characterized by the action structure which has been performed up to now and the set of actions the program is ready to perform next. This will be called again a configuration.

The set of configurations is defined by:

$$\text{CONF} = \{p \in \text{AS}\sqrt{}(A): p \text{ finite}\} \times \wp_{\text{fin}}(A \cup \{\sqrt{}\})^\perp$$

Now, semantically, agents are represented by the elements of the set AGENT, which is the powerset over the set of configurations:

$$\text{AGENT} = \wp(\text{CONF})$$

$< Q, R > \in \text{CONF}$ is a configuration for an agent t if Q is a finite prefix of an action structure in the capabilities of t and R is a set of actions the agent t is ready to do after it had performed Q.

The following simple example may indicate how the semantic representation works:

agent:	$a \rightarrow ((b \rightarrow \textbf{nop}) \text{ or } (a \rightarrow b \rightarrow \textbf{nop}))$	
prefixes Q		ready sets R
$p_\emptyset$		$\{a\}$
$p_{\{a\}}$		$\{b\}$ $\{a\}$
$a \rightarrow b$		$\{\sqrt{}\}$
$a \rightarrow b \rightarrow \sqrt{}$		$\emptyset$
$a \rightarrow a$		$\{b\}$
$a \rightarrow a \rightarrow b$		$\{\sqrt{}\}$
$a \rightarrow a \rightarrow b \rightarrow \sqrt{}$		$\emptyset$

The set of environments is defined by:

$$\text{ENV} = <\text{id}> \rightarrow \text{AGENT}$$

The semantic function associates some set of configurations with every agent in a given environment:

S: $< \text{agent} > \to \text{ENV} \to \text{AGENT}$

The semantic equations for S read as follows:

$S[\textbf{abort}](\sigma) = \{ < P_\varnothing, \bot > \}$
$S[\textbf{nop}](\sigma) = \{ < P_\varnothing, \{\surd\} >, < P_{\{\surd\}}, \varnothing > \}$
$S[a \to t](\sigma) = \{ < P_\varnothing, \{a\} > \} \cup$
$\quad \{ < x, R > : \exists (x0, R0) \in S[t](\sigma) : x = P_{\{a\}} \hat{} x0 \wedge R = R0 \}$
$S[t1 \textbf{ or } t2](\sigma) = S[t1](\sigma) \cup S[t2](\sigma)$
$S[t \parallel t'](\sigma) = \{ < P_\varnothing, \text{join}(R, R', \varnothing) > : < P_\varnothing, R > \in S[t](\sigma) \wedge$
$\quad < P_\varnothing, R' > \in S[t'](\sigma) \} \cup \{ < Q, R > : Q \neq P_\varnothing \wedge$
$\quad (< Q, R > \in S[t](\sigma) \vee < Q, R > \in S[t'](\sigma)) \}$

where the function:

join: $\quad \wp_{fin}(A \cup \{\surd\})^\bot \times \wp_{fin}(A \cup \{\surd\})^\bot \times \wp(A) \to \wp_{fin}(A \cup \{\surd\})^\bot$

is defined by the equations (let R, $A \subseteq R'$):

$\text{join}(R, \bot, c) = \text{join}(\bot, R, c) = \text{join}(\bot, \bot, c) = \bot$
$\text{join}(R, R, c) = ((R \cup R') \backslash c) \cup (R \cap R' \cap c)$

The function join will be also used in the definition of the parallel composition

$S[t; t'](\sigma) =$
$\quad \{ < Q, R > : < Q, R > \in S[t](\sigma) \wedge \neg \downarrow .Q \} \cup$
$\quad \{ < (Q \backslash \surd) \hat{} Q', R' > :$
$\quad \quad < Q, R > \in S[t](\sigma) \wedge < Q', R' > \in S[t'](\sigma) \wedge \downarrow .Q \}$

$S[t \parallel t'](\sigma) = \{ < Q, \text{join}(R, R', c) > :$
$\quad \exists Q1, Q2 : < Q1, R > \in S[t](\sigma) \wedge < Q2, R' > \in S(t'](\sigma) \wedge$
$\quad \quad \quad \quad \quad \quad \quad \quad \quad \quad Q \in Q1 \parallel_{c \cup \{\surd\}} Q2 \}$
$S[\text{id}](\sigma) = \sigma(\text{id})$

Of course, the meaning of $q :: t$ has to satisfy the fixpoint equation:

$S[q :: t](\sigma) = S[t](\sigma[S[q :: t](\sigma)/q])$

The proof of the existence of such a fixpoint and the characterization of an extremal fixed point can be based on different ways for making the powerset of configurations into a domain. For instance, it could be approximated by several iterations along different orderings (Broy, 1984). However, if the recursion is guarded, i.e. if a recursive call is always preceded by one action, then the fixpoint is unique.

A similar, but slightly more abstract, denotational model for CP programs can be obtained by considering interleaving semantics, i.e. only sequential action structures or traces.

23.5 Concluding remarks

It has been the purpose of this chapter to introduce, relate and unify rather distinct ways of formalizing distributed systems and their description. Of course, due to the technically complicated material and the number of different approaches, this could be done only in a very limited way. Depending on the purpose for which a description method is used, different properties and characteristics of the method are important.

The key issues in concurrency are abstraction and compositionality.

23.5.1 Acknowledgement

This work has been developed from joint work with Thomas Streicher within the DFG Projekt Parallelität.

23.6 References and bibliography

André, F., Herman, D. and Verjus, J.-P. (1985) *Synchronization of Parallel Programs.* MIT Press, Cambridge, MA

Astensiano, E. (1984) Combining an operational with an algebraic approach to the specification of concurrency. In *Proceedings of a Workshop on Combining Methods*, D. Bjørner (ed.) Nyborg, Denmark

Alpern, B., Schneider, F. B. (1985) Defining liveness. *Information Processing Letters*, **21**, 181–185

Bernstein, A. J. (1966) Analysis of programs for parallel processing. *IEEE Transactions on Electronic Computing*, **15**, 757–763

Brauer, W. (ed.) (1980) Net theory and applications. *Lecture Notes in Computer Science*, 84, Springer

Brinch Hansen, P. (1978) Distributed action structures: a concurrent programming concept. *Communications of the ACM*, **21**, 934–941

Broy, M. (1980) Transformational semantics for concurrent programs. *Information Processing Letters*, **11**, 87–97

Broy, M. (1984a) Denotational semantics of concurrent programs with shared memory. Proceedings STACS 84. *Lecture Notes in Computer Science*, **166**, Springer, pp 163–173

Broy, M. (1984b) Semantics of communicating processes. *Information and Control*, **61**, 202–246

Broy, M. and Bauer, F. L. (1985) A systematic approach to language constructs for concurrency. SCP

Campbell, R. H. and Habermann, A. N. (1974) The specification of process synchronisation by path expressions. *Lecture Notes in Computer Science*, 16, Springer

Chandy, K. M. and Misra, J. (1988) *Parallel Program Design*, Addison-Wesley

Degano, P. and Montanari, U. (1985) Distributed systems, partial ordering of events, and event structures. In M. Broy (ed.) *Control Flow and Data Flow: Concepts of Distributed Programming. NATO ASI Series, Series F: Computer and System Sciences, Vol. 14*, Springer, pp 7–106

Dijkstra, E. W. (1968) Co-operating sequential processes. In *Programming Languages*, (ed. F. Genuys) Academic Press, New York, pp 43–112

Emerson, E. A. and Clarke, E. M. (1983) Using branching time temporal logic to synthesize synchronization skeletons. *Scientific Computer Programming* 2, 241–266

Francez, N. (1986) *Fairness*, Springer-Verlag, New York

Harel, D. (1987) Statecharts: a visual formalism for complex systems. *Scientific Computer Programming*, **8**, 231–274

Hennessy, M. (1988) *Algebraic Theory of Processes*, MIT Press, Cambridge, MA

Hennessy, M. C. B. and Milner, R. (1980) On observing nondeterminism and concurrency. In J. de Bakker and Jn van Leeuwen (eds) *International Colloquium on Automata, Languages and Programming 80, Lecture Notes in Computer Science*, Springer, pp 299–309

Hennessy, M. and Milner, R. (1985) Algebraic laws for nondeterminism and concurrency. *Journal of the ACM*, **32**, 137–161

Hennessy, M. C. B. and Plotkin, G. D. (1979) Full abstraction for simple parallel programs. *8th Mathematical Foundations of Computer Science, Olomouc, 1979, Lecture Notes in Computer Science*

Hennessy, M. and Plotkin, G. (1980) A term model for CCS. *9th Mathematical Foundations of Computer Science (1980), Lecture Notes in Computer Science 88*, Springer, pp 261–274

Hoare, C. A. R. (1972) Towards a theory of parallel programming. In *Operating Systems Techniques*, (eds. C. A. R. Hoare and R. H. Perott) Academic Press, New York, pp 61–71

Hoare, C. A. R. (1974) Monitors: An operating systems structuring concept. *Communications of the ACM*, **17**, 549–557

Hoare, C. A. R. (1978) Communicating sequential processes. *Communications of the ACM*, **21**, 666–667

Hoare, C. A. R., Brookes, S. D. and Roscoe, A. W. (1981) *A Theory of Communicating Sequential Processes*, Oxford University Computing Laboratory, Programming Research Group, Technical Monograph PRG-21, Oxford. Also (1984) *Journal of the ACM*, **31**, 560–599

Hoare, C. A. R. (1985) *Communicating Sequential Processes*, Prentice Hall

Kahn, G., MacQueen, D. (1977) Coroutines and networks of processes. *Proceedings of IFIP Congress 1977*

Lauer, P. E., Torrigiani, P. R., Shields, M. W. (1979) Cosy – a system specification language based on paths and processes. *Acta Informatica*, **12**, 109–158

Manna, Z. and Wolper, P. (1984) Synthesis of communicating processes from temporal logic specifications. *ACM TOPLAS*, **6,** 68–93

Mazurkiewicz, A. (1985) Traces, histories, graphs: instances of a process monoid. In *MFCS 1984, Lecture Notes in Computer Science*, (eds M. P. Chytil and V. Koubek): **92,** Springer, pp 115–133

Milner, R. (1980) A calculus for communicating systems. *Lecture Notes in Computer Science*, **92,** Springer

Milner, R. (1980) *On Relating Synchrony and Asynchrony*, Internal Report CSR-75-80, University of Edinburgh, Department of Computer Science

Minsky, M. L. (1967) *Computation: Finite and Infinite Machines*, Prentice-Hall, Englewood Cliffs, NJ

Nielsen, M., Plotkin, G. and Winskel, G. (1981) Petri nets, event structures, and domains. Part 1. *Theoretical Computer Science*, **13,** 85–108

Nivat, M. (1979) Infinite words, infinite trees, infinite computations. In J. W. de Bakker (ed.) *Foundations of Computer Science III. 2, Mathematical Centre Tracts 109*, Amsterdam, pp 3–52

Olderog, E.-R. (1985) Specification-oriented programming in TCSP. In *Logics and Models of Concurrent Systems*, (ed. K. R. Apt) Springer-Verlag, pp 397–435

Olderog, E.-R. (1986) Process theory: semantics, specification and verification. In *Current Trends in Concurrency, Lecture Notes in Comput. Sci. 244* (eds J. W. Bakker, W. P. de Roever and G. Rozenberg) Springer, pp 442–509

Olderog, E.-R. and Hoare, C. A. R. (1986) Specification-oriented semantics for communicating processes. *Acta Informatica*, **23,** 9–66

Owicki, S., Lamport, L. (1982) Proving liveness properties of concurrent programmes. *ACM TOPLAS 4*, 199–223

Park, D. (1981) Concurrency and automata on infinite sequences. In *Proceedings 5th GI Conference of Theoretical Computer Science, Lecture Notes in Computer Science 104*, (ed. P. Deussen) Springer

Petri, C. A. (1962) *Kommunikation mit Automaten*, Doctoral Dissertation, Schriften des Institut für Instrumentelle Mathematik, University of Bonn

Plotkin, G. D. (1982) An operational semantics for CSP. In *Formal Description of Programming Concepts 11*, (ed. D. Bjørner) North-Holland, Amsterdam, pp 199–225

Pnueli, A. (1977) The temporal logic of programs. *18th IEEE Symposium on Foundations of Computer Science 224*, Springer-Verlag, pp 403–413

Pneuli, A. (1986) Applications of temporal logic to the specification and verification of reactive systems: a survey of current trends. In *Current Trends in Concurrency, Lecture Notes in Computer Science 224* (eds) J. W. de Bakker, W. P. de Roever and G. Rozenberg Springer, pp 510–584

Rabin, M. O. and Scott, D. S. (1959) Finite automata and their decision problems. *IBM Journal of Research*, **3**

Reisig, W. (1985) *Petri Nets, An Introduction, EATCS Monographs on Theoretical Computer Science*, Springer-Verlag

Rem, M. (1987) Trace theory and systolic computation. In *Proceedings PARLE Conference, Eindhoven, Vol. I, Lecture Notes in Computer Science*, (eds J. W. de Bakker, A. J. Nijman and P. C. Treleaven) Springer, pp 14–33

Robert, P. and Verjus, J.-P. (1977) Toward autonomous descriptions of synchronization modules. In *Proceedings IFIP Information Processing 77*, (ed. B. Gilchrist) North-Holland, Amsterdam, pp 981–986

Rozenberg, G. (1985) Advances in Petri-nets. *Lecture Notes in Computer Science 188*, Springer

Sterling, C. (1987) Modal logics for communicating systems. *Theoretical Computer Science*, **49,** 311–347

Winkowski, J. (1980) Behaviors of concurrent systems. *Theoretical Computer Science*, **11,** 39–60

Winskel, G. (1980) *Events in computation*, PhD Thesis, Department of Computer Science, University of Edinburgh

Winskel, G. (1982) Event structure semantics of CCS and related languages. In *Proceedings 9th Colloqium Automata, Languages and Programming, Lecture Notes in Computer Science, 140*, (ed. E. M. Schmidt) Springer

24

Refinement

Peter Whysall
Department of Computer Science,
University of York

Contents

24.1 Introduction

A specification describes what a system is to do.
An implementation describes how it is to do it.
Refinement produces an implementation from a specification.

These simple statements, though lacking much in detail and substance, provide a good description of the process of refinement. The area of refinement embodies a set of techniques to guide and control the process of producing a piece of software from a description of it; an implementation from a specification.

The aim of this chapter is to familiarize the reader with the concepts of refinement, starting at a high level, with what it is, and why we need it. Second, in a more detailed way, we look at how refinement is performed, what support is available to help perform it, and what problems are still not addressed by the techniques that support it. Refinement can be carried out informally, or formally based on mathematical proof. The principles are the same in each case and will be discussed in general terms, but when we come to look at the technical details, these will be based on the formal techniques. It is therefore expected that the initial sections will be accessible to all readers, while the later, more detailed, sections will require some prior knowledge of the notions of specification and proof, such as can be gained from the earlier chapters on such topics.

The chapter begins (Section 24.2) by describing in more detail what refinement is, looking at the task it performs, and its relationship to our traditional ideas of software development. It goes on (Section 24.3) to discuss why we need refinement: why we need a new technique to perform a task programmers can already do, what we gain that the traditional approaches do not give us, and thus when we might want to use such a technique.

The detail of the chapter begins in Section 24.4, where we consider what refinement means in practice: what information an implementation has that a specification does not have, and where that information comes from. This will lead to the idea of rules to aid in the derivation and checking of the refinement steps that introduce this information, and ultimately to two different approaches to refinement which will be described and contrasted. It will be noticed that the focus is entirely on the technical aspects of performing refinement. This is because the author believes that using refinement during the development process does not introduce any new management problems to the process, but changes only the technical work that must be done.

The following sections (24.5, 24.6) will try to emphasize the practicality of refinement. First we consider a simple example of the practice of refinement, looking at the steps necessary in the refinement of a simple specification. Section 24.6 then looks at the area of support for the theory of refinement, considering first the support ideally necessary to realise the true goals of refinement, and also the support currently available which can go some way to making refinement more practical.

Section 24.7 introduces a little more realism, looking at what refinement can currently achieve, and the costs involved in doing this, and goes on to focus on the problems still not adequately addressed by the researchers, what cannot (yet) be done using refinement.

The chapter ends with an overview of refinement looking at what it aims to achieve, what it can currently achieve, and hence concludes with an analysis of who should consider using refinement, both now, and in the future.

24.2 What is refinement?

In the introduction, we described refinement very simply, as a technique to produce implementations from specifications. The answer to our question 'what is refinement' can hopefully then be clarified, by looking at what we mean by implementation and specification, and what it means to obtain one from the other.

Our ideas of what a specification and implementation are come from our model of the software life cycle, the stages involved in the production of a piece of software, and it is in this framework that it is easiest to describe the role of refinement. This life-cycle model has been discussed in detail in other chapters, but it is useful briefly to re-examine certain key points, in order to highlight their relation to the notion of refinement.

This life-cycle model begins with a phase of requirements analysis, obtaining a first description of what is expected of a system. The result of this work, carried out in conjunction with the customer, is a requirements document, containing two different kinds of information. The first part, often called the functional requirements, describes the basic operation of the system, for example, its inputs and outputs and the relationship between them. The second part contains a set of constraints over the way the functional requirements are achieved, such as the time each operation is allowed to take, or some security rule that it must not breach. This division is not always clear cut, or even possible to make, but it is nevertheless a useful division to consider because, as we shall see later, the two types of information are used in different ways during the process of refinement. The description contained in the requirements will vary in formality, depending on the techniques used, but will typically describe the operation of the system in terms of how it will relate to the 'outside world', that is, how it will communicate with its users and its environment.

The next stage of development involves the production of a specification. This specification provides a clear description of what the system is going to do. The information contained in this specification is essentially the same as that in the functional requirements, although typically it might be in a more system-oriented form, rather than the user- or environment-oriented form of the requirement. For example, our requirements may express properties in terms of relations between actions visible in the real world, whereas our specification will express relationships between data objects manipulated by the system. In fact, if a formal approach is taken to development, and the same notation is used for both functional requirements and specification, then the specification may not include any new information, although there may be information in the requirements (e.g. about the operation of the environment) which will not be included in the specification. This specification, however produced, will form the basis of all the further development.

The design stage of the traditional life cycle involves taking a set of decisions about the way a system is to be implemented. For the majority of current development projects this will involve the (unconstrained) choice of a set of program language data structures and algorithms, to be used to implement the data in the system, and the operations on it. These choices will hopefully be made so as not to breach any of the functional constraints outlined in the requirements document, but there is nothing to enforce such properties in the decisions. This observation reflects common development practice. This state should not hold if effective design reviews are held, or adequate refinement techniques are used. These decisions are then used by the programmer in the next stage – that of implementation. This design stage is rarely given adequate attention, and often only separated from implementation at all so that decisions relevant to several programmers (e.g. choice of main data structures) can be propagated amongst them.

The implementation stage usually consists simply of a programmer writing some piece of code which notionally represents these data structures and algorithms, and implements part of the specification. The combination of these should then produce the final system. In fact, of course, the life cycle then continues with stages of testing and maintenance, but these are not of particular relevance to the concept of refinement.

Even the most informal or *ad hoc* approaches to program development thus involve a design stage (even if it is combined with the implementation stage) and for good reason, since we can see that this is where all the important decisions involved in the transformation from specification to implementation are made. In an informal development strategy these design decisions might typically be represented by a few simple notes, or even ideas in the programmer's head. In a more rigorous approach we might have a design document which describes these important decisions, and perhaps even offers some justification for them. However, we can have no real expectation that such decisions are *correct* or interact correctly. (As a trivial example, decisions to represent some data in a list and to use an array sort algorithm, while perfectly valid in their own right are incompatible if we expect to apply one to the other.)

Refinement takes the notion of a rigorous treatment of design a stage further. Each time a design decision is taken, a new version of the specification, incorporating this new information, is produced. We can now check that the new specification is acceptable with respect to the previous one, or more formally, that it 'satisfies' it. Additionally, this new specification provides the basis for further refinement, so we can also ensure that our separate decisions interact correctly. What actually constitutes such a design decision, and what it means for the new specification to satisfy the old will be discussed in Section 24.4.

This notion of refinement also gives us a framework in which to consider the enforcement of the functional constraints discussed in the requirements document. Ideally, design decisions as to how to represent or implement some part of the specification should be guided by a desire to satisfy these additional constraints. As we make decisions we can now check that this new information is consistent with satisfying the constraints, and finally we can check that the implementation does indeed satisfy them.

The aim of refinement is to produce implementations from specifications. So far we have looked only at producing new specifications from old ones – how do we obtain the implementation? In principle, if we had a suitable language, we could produce the implementation in exactly the same way, repeatedly producing new specifications until finally we obtained an executable specification. In practice, with commonly used languages, this is of course not directly possible (except perhaps for implementations in some functional languages) since we cannot expect the specification language to contain, as a subset, the whole of Ada or Pascal. Typically we will need to use more than one notation in refinement, so we will need to be able to combine and relate notations, for example, to map from a formal definition of a data structure to the programming language declaration. A typical refinement process might thus be as follows, although there could clearly be many more steps in practice:

1. Produce an initial specification in Z.
2. Refine the data structures into more Ada-like types, for example refining mappings into arrays.
3. Refine the operation specifications into algorithms in Dijkstra's guarded command language (GCL).
4. Translate the Z types and GCL algorithms into Ada.

An alternative to this approach is to use a so-called wide spectrum language which includes constructs useful for both the specification and implementation, and which hence allows refinement to take place entirely within one language. A good example of this approach is the CIP language (Bauer *et al.*, 1989) which is discussed in Section 24.6.

Refinement, then, enables us to derive an implementation from a specification by taking a sequence of design decisions and producing new (verified) specifications that incorporate these decisions. We can now go on to see why we might want to do this.

24.3 Why use refinement?

When a system is delivered, a customer wants to have a reasonable expectation that it will work. More specifically he will want to be sure of two things: first that the requirements used in the development process adequately represent what he expects from the system (it does the right thing) and second, that the system that has been delivered correctly implements these requirements (it does the thing right). Achieving the first goal is the province of the customer, aided by a requirements analyst, and where necessary, the producer of the first (top-level) specification. The second goal is the responsibility of the designers and implementors, who must ensure that the final implementation does indeed satisfy the initial specification.

In the real world it is unfortunately true that it is impossible to guarantee that a system is perfect, for the correctness of any system is always dependent on some underlying assumptions which might not be valid. At one level we rely on (assumptions about) the validity of the requirements, but at lower levels we still rely on assumptions such as properties of the hardware, the power supply, or even the laws of physics. Where we cannot validate the assumptions we have residual doubt about the adequacy of the design and implementation. We can attempt to reduce the number of assumptions (but we can never remove them) and can thus reduce the residual doubt about the system. In the domain of design and refinement we are concerned with reducing the residual doubt in the implementation of the system. There are four facets of doubt which we must eliminate during the design stage:

1. *Interpretation.* That the specification produced is based on a correct understanding of the requirements – we are placing the same interpretation on this information as was intended by those who wrote it.
2. *Consistency.* That the specification is internally consistent, that is, it is not contradictory.
3. *Completeness.* That all the information necessary to describe the system is indeed present.
4. *Validity.* That the information contained in the specification 'says the same thing' as the requirements (or whatever the customer really wanted).

Different approaches to design can lead to different degrees of reduction in residual doubt, and from different categories, and hence are appropriate in different circumstances.

24.3.1 *Ad hoc* design

If a system is produced using an *ad hoc* approach to design, then the residual doubt is extremely high, since we rely on the ability of the programmer. A simple mistake could cause complete failure, and we would have no idea of when to expect a problem, nor how to diagnose it when it occurred, especially if the programmer was no longer available. An *ad hoc* approach to design does not lead to reduction in doubt in any of the areas described above. This approach is sometimes acceptable (for example, if only the programmer is likely to use the system developed) but unfortunately this approach to software production is very widespread, even where it is not appropriate.

24.3.2 Informal design

An informal – but planned – approach to software development might enable us to trace, using some design documentation, a piece of the specification through a set of design decisions to the implementation. This does not give any greater expectation that the system will work (no reduction in residual doubt), although it might make the tracing and correction of subsequent faults easier. This is better, but it is still not really enough, for few customers would be willing to accept a system without some evidence of a reasoned approach to design. Testing the system would of course provide some reduction in residual doubt, but by this stage it is really too late. Testing reduces doubt in the completeness and validity of the specification, because we compare it against our expectations, but this of course relies on our understanding of the problem being complete and valid.

24.3.3 Rigorous design

By taking a rigorous approach to design, providing reasoned justifications for design decisions, we can at last start to reduce the residual doubt by design. It is now reasonable to have some expectation that different parts of the implementation achieve their specification, for we have evidence that they were planned and designed.

This rigorous approach to design can be better still if the justification is carried out with respect to a formal specification, for this justification can then be in the form of an outline proof, carefully justifying the implementation against the specification. This use of a formal specification enables us to reduce doubt in the consistency of the design, as there is a formal framework in which to check this. Additionally, if this design was produced with reference to a formal requirements document, then we reduce the doubt involved in interpretation, as we can use the same notion of interpretation as used in the requirements phase. Currently this is perhaps the way formal methods are most often used, for it provides a firm base for further development, without the undoubted additional cost of a full formal development. There have been many cases where comparing specifications with their supposed implementations has led to the detection of flaws, undoubtedly saving much further wasted effort. Clearly, then, such an approach to design can provide a significant reduction in residual doubt, for a modest cost, and the approach is thus likely to become more widespread. Residual doubt does remain, however, and at levels which are sometimes unacceptable.

24.3.4 Formal design

Computer software is increasingly used in applications where its failure is deemed unacceptable. This kind of reliability is required particularly in the domains of the so-called 'safety' and 'security-critical' systems, where failure may, for example, cause loss of life. Even outside these restricted domains high reliability is still often very important, because of the 'significant inconvenience' that failure would cause, and so the need for high-quality software is relatively widespread.

Refinement can do more to reduce residual doubt, because it allows the formal representation of the design decisions as new specifications, and formal proof of the appropriate satisfaction relations between them. This reduces residual doubt, because it is in these satisfaction relations that much of the doubt lies – whether an implementation truly represents its specification or not. This type of proof should be able to remove totally the reliance on the designer's abilities, with respect to interpretation and consistency, for mistakes and flaws will now be detected as failures in the satisfaction relation. (We will of course still rely

on the designer to produce the new specification to check, and will rely on his ability to make a good decision about the way in which to represent a particular part of the specification.) This process thus reduces doubt in the validity of the specification, as it will have been produced directly from earlier specifications, and hence retains their validity. However, this does not, unfortunately, remove all residual doubt, because we must now rely on the ability of the person doing the proof, and any support tools they may use. Refinement cannot then totally remove residual doubt, (as noted earlier this is impossible anyway) but it can reduce it very significantly, because each design decision (and potential error) is scrutinized and analysed formally. The reduction of doubt in the completeness is difficult to assess, for it relies on considering the specification with respect to an understanding of what the whole system is to do, and how it is to interact with its environment. This kind of problem is probably best solved by introducing an independent person who can validate the specification with respect to an understanding of the customer's problem.

Formal specification of a system, especially when followed by a rigorous or formal justification of the design steps leading to an implementation, can therefore lead to a significant reduction in the residual doubt in a system, and a consequent increase in confidence. In particular the use of the process of refinement, involving the proof of these developed steps, can reduce the residual doubt to a very low level, especially if some verified tool support is available to assist in this process.

It should therefore be clear that formal specification techniques can be of general use in the development of systems, and, in particular, that refinement techniques can be of use specifically in the production of safety critical, or high reliability systems. Such systems are referred to generally as high-integrity systems.

24.4 Theory of refinement

Refinement is the production of an implementation from a specification. To understand this claim more fully, and in particular to do so in a formal domain, we must consider first what information is contained in such a formal specification, and second, what further information must be added to turn this into an implementation.

In general a formal specification consists of two sets of information. First, it contains a set of data specifications which are used to represent the data items within the system. Such data specifications exist for all the data to be manipulated by the system, its inputs, outputs, and internal data. Second, it contains a set of operation specifications which describe the way in which the data items are to be manipulated. These operation specifications describe the relationships that hold between different data produced by the system.

There are many possible models for refinement. This section is based on one particular approach, with brief illustrations of some of the other approaches.

24.4.1 What is a specification?

The form and detail with which these data and operations are described will depend on the kind of specification being produced.

If an algebraic specification language like OBJ (Futatsugi, 1985) is used to produce the specification, then the detail given is quite limited. The description of the data may be limited simply to a name, no information about its structure being given at all. Similarly, the operations will be defined implicitly in terms of their relation to other operations on the same datatypes. For example part of a simple specification of a stack in OBJ might be as follows:

```
OBJ stack
SORTS stack
OPS
        empty      : − >stack
        pop        : stack−> stack
        top        : stack−>elem
        push       : elem stack−> stack
        .
        .

VARS
        e          : elem
        s          : stack
EQNS
        (pop(push(e,s)=s))
        (top(push(e,s)=e))
        .
        .
        .

JBO
```

The basic notation used here is discussed briefly in Chapter 22 on algebraic specifications. We name the sort (type) stack that we are creating, and the operations on it, and then define the semantics of the operations and the type using a set of equations. The amount of detail given in the specification is very limited, and in particular no structural or algorithmic information is given.

In a more model-oriented specification, such as one produced using Z (Spivey, 1988) or VDM (Jones, 1986), then a more detailed description is provided. The structure of the data is defined based on certain primitive, but abstract, typing notions such as those of mappings, sets and sequences. These abstract notions allow some detail to be given to the data description but still at a relatively high level, and without a bias towards a particular implementation. The operations can now be defined explicitly, in terms of the changes they make to the data structures. These changes are typically expressed as pre- and post-conditions specified on the data, with little or no information given as to how these conditions should be satisfied. For example, expressing part of our stack example in VDM, we might have:

stack $\overset{\triangle}{=}$ elem-SEQ

pop: stack → stack
pre-pop(s) $\overset{\triangle}{=}$ S ≠ []
post-pop(s,ns) $\overset{\triangle}{=}$ ns = tail(s)

push: elem × stack → stack
pre-push(e,s) $\overset{\triangle}{=}$ true
post-push(e,s,ns) $\overset{\triangle}{=}$ head(ns) = e ∧ tail(ns) = s

We define the state used to represent a stack, a sequence of elements, and then define the operations by describing what the relation is between the new stack (ns) and the old stack (s). Using this kind of specification, we give more structural information about the system (albeit abstract), but still include no algorithmic information about how the particular post-conditions are to be satisfied.

Both algebraic and model-oriented specifications thus give much information about what the system is to do, but give very little information about how this is to be done.

24.4.2 What refinement does

The task of refinement is to add the extra detail to make an implementation. This implementation must include a detailed (concrete) description of the data used by the system, and a detailed concrete description of the algorithms used for performing the operations. A major part of this refinement is thus the process of so-called 'reification', making more concrete, and indeed the term reification is sometimes used instead of refinement. We must expand our specification to include this concrete information about data structures and operation algorithms.

In both the examples above, the data in the system is described in a very abstract way, including only as little about the structure of the data as necessary to be able to represent the appropriate properties. In the algebraic specification it sufficed to name the type, all other information being implicit in the definition of the operations. In the model-oriented specification more detail was used, but only sufficient to be able to describe access to the relevant components of the data. In an implementation this data must be expressed as concrete (perhaps machine-processable) types, and thus the refinement must select suitable representations for this data.

Similarly the operations are expressed at a very high level. We describe what the operations do, either explicitly, in terms of changes to the data (in the model-oriented approach), or implicitly, in terms of their relation to other operations (in the algebraic approach). In an implementation, operations must be algorithms expressed using concrete (possibly machine-processable) instructions, and thus the refinement must choose algorithms capable of producing the required post-conditions. Note that this last statement assumes that we are considering an implementation in an imperative language (e.g. Ada or Pascal), but more generally we might want to consider implementations in functional or logic languages where the properties of the implementation will be different. This discussion will deal mainly with refinement into imperative programs, but it is important to realise that this is not the only possibility.

As was suggested above, refinement of data and operations are distinct and different processes, and will thus be discussed separately. Informally, it has been shown that we must reify and add detail to the specifications, in order to produce 'suitable' data representations, and 'capable' operational algorithms. The next sections will formalize these ideas.

24.4.3 Data refinement

The aim of data refinement is to produce concrete types *adequate* for representing the abstract types of the specification. The first, and most important question that arises is thus 'what do we mean by adequate?'.

Informally, we say that the abstract type is adequate if every value in the abstract type can be represented by the concrete type, and that from this concrete type we can retrieve the abstract value.

We will consider this process of refinement with reference to *Figure 24.1*. In the abstract specification we have definitions for two things: the abstract state, and the operations on it. The aim of this data refinement is to produce a new, concrete state, with which to 'replace' the abstract state.

Clearly the first requirement on such a concrete state is that we can represent all the values possible in the abstract state using the concrete state. In the diagram 'refine' represents a relation between abstract values and concrete values, relating abstract values with their concrete representation. The requirement for this relation expressed formally is:

_ refines _: CS ↔ AS
$\forall a : AS \cdot \exists c : CS \cdot c$ refines a

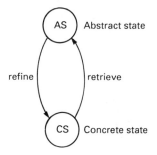

Figure 24.1

For every abstract value there is some concrete value which refines it, and which represents it. In general this is a relation since there might be more than one concrete representation for an abstract value. For example, if we decide to represent a set as a list of its members, then the order of items in the list is not significant, so more than one possible list represents the same set. Note that there are a number of different ways of defining the refines relation, which lead to different properties of implementations. For pedagogical purposes we restrict ourselves to this one simple notion of the refine relation.

In practice it is often simpler to have a unique representation for each abstract value, so we will arbitrarily choose one possible representation as the 'correct one'. For example we might choose the ordered list as the one that correctly represents the set, provided that the members of the set are related by a total ordering. Using this idea we can now represent the notion of refine as a total function (refine):

$$\text{refine} : \text{AS} \rightarrow \text{CS}$$

This representation enforces the above constraint, since a total function must give a result for every value in its domain, but additionally enforces the extra constraint:

$$\forall\, a : \text{AS};\; c,c' : \text{CS} \cdot c \text{ refines } a \text{ and } c' \text{ refines } a \Rightarrow (c = c')$$

If we define the refinement mapping as a total function, then every abstract value will be represented by a unique concrete value.

The second requirement on the concrete state comes from the fact that, having defined the values, we will then want to apply operations on them. However (until we refine them) our operations are defined on the abstract state, and we must therefore 'retrieve' the abstract values before we can apply the operations. We thus define a retrieves relation (similar to the refines relation) which relates a concrete value back to an abstract value. Our requirement is now that we want operations applied to these retrieved values to give the same results as they would if applied to the original abstract values:

$$\_\text{retrieves}\_ : \text{AS} \leftrightarrow \text{CS}$$
$$\forall\, a : \text{AS},\, c : \text{CS} \mid c \text{ refines } a \cdot$$
$$\forall\, a' : \text{AS} \mid a' \text{ retrieves } c \cdot \text{op}(a) = \text{op}(a')$$

An operation applied to a value retrieved from a refined abstract value gives the same result as if applied to the original value. Since the operation has not changed, we achieve this by saying that a and a' must be the same, that is by enforcing:

$$\forall\, a : \text{AS} \cdot \text{retrieves} ([\![\{a\}]\!]) = \{a\}$$

Here we use the relational image brackets '$[\![$' and '$]\!]$' which allow us to apply a relation to a set, and obtain the set of all values which are related to them 'refines$([\![\{a,b\}]\!])$' thus gives the set of all values, which are refinements of either 'a' or 'b'. If we take all the refinements of the value a, and then retrieve all abstract equivalents of these concrete values, we will obtain the single value a. This constraint effectively ensures that retrieve must be a function, since we must only give one result for each possible concrete value. (It need not be a total function, since we need only be able to retrieve from the concrete representations of genuine abstract values.) If refine is also a function, then we can specify the relevant constraints as follows:

$$\text{retrieve} : \text{CS} \rightarrow \text{AS}$$
$$\forall\, a : \text{AS} \cdot \text{retrieve}(\text{refine}(a)) = a$$

This final equation represents our initial informal requirements that we must be able to refine all abstract values into a concrete representation, and retrieve from this concrete value the original abstract one.

What does this mean in practice? When we refine data, we must define the functions (or relations) refine and retrieve, and then prove the relevant properties of them. Doing this is sufficient to prove the adequacy of the representation, and will ensure the correctness of the refinement, as this is the only formal requirement we have of the concrete state. We can use this information to provide guidelines for performing data refinement.

The rules for adequacy here require us to prove properties for all the possible abstract values. If we are refining a model-oriented specification, then this set of values will be very clear, for it will be all the values that can physically be represented by the type structure. In a refinement of the stack example given above, we must be able to give concrete representations for all sequences of elements. If we write the refinement function as a total function over sequences, then this will automatically be true. In the case of an algebraic specification we do not have the necessary information readily available, for our type definition is simply a naming. We must thus deduce the set of possible values from the equations given, which implicitly describe the type. This deduction will usually lead to the derivation of a set of constructor functions, which can be used to produce any possible abstract value. For example, in the case of our stack example again, we deduce that all possible stacks can be produced from the 'empty' stack and applications of 'push' to it. For the refinement to be correct we must show that all stacks can be represented, that is, that the empty stack can be represented, and that any stack constructed using push can be represented.

This assessment of the abstract type effectively tells us what the domain of our refinement function is to be. The next stage is then to define the mapping which is going to produce the concrete type, and the associated retrieve function to reproduce the abstract values. Choosing the basic refinement mapping is a non-trivial operation, for it is this mapping which must introduce the extra detail necessary to implement the type. A document such as this can thus only give guidelines and examples as to how this should be done.

If we want to refine types specified using the abstract notions of a notation like VDM, we must provide methods for refining each of the type structures: mappings, sets, and sequences. For example, consider the refinement of a mapping. A mapping is a data type which associates elements of some domain type with elements of some range type; given an element of the domain, the mapping will give a member of the range. This functional description of a mapping is very similar to that of a programming language array which associates members of an index type with members of the element type. We might thus think that we should be able to refine a mapping into an array. Our refinement function must 'create' an array which represents the information stored in the mapping. This operation hence produces an array of the correct index type (equal to the domain of the function) and stores in each element the result of applying the mapping. Similarly, the retrieve function must produce a mapping which maps members of the array's index type to the correct values stored in the array. Such functions can be defined formally, and the appropriate constraints proved, such that we know that an array can be a genuine refinement of a mapping. Similarly we can prove that a linked list in a programming language can be an adequate implementation of an abstract list (sequence). Finally we will want to define an adequate representation for the abstract set. An example of how this might be done is provided later.

We can define potential (adequate) refinement mappings like this for many different abstract types, and provide a whole library of such mappings, although doing this is not necessarily helpful, as it is not only adequacy which affects our choice of refinement mappings. All refinements must be adequate, but *good* refinements will additionally possess other properties.

There are two additional sources of information which help us to decide whether a particular refinement is good: information we have about what operations will access the data, and also the functional constraints from the requirements document. The task involved is to try to decide whether a particular choice of concrete type is really suitable for representing the abstract type. Unfortunately, there can be no absolute rules for solving this problem and proving suitability. Instead, we must analyse each case individually, and make a choice based on our own experience and judgement.

The sort of information that will be useful here is typically information about speed of access to the data (for inspection and update), the amount of space the data is likely to use, and the pattern of access that is likely to be made to the data. This is best illustrated by means of an example. Consider two concrete representations for a set:

1. Store the elements in a (linked) list.
2. Create a Boolean array indexed by the set's element type.

If a large number of membership tests on the set are likely to be necessary, then using a list will be very inefficient, since a sequential search of the list must be performed for each test. If speed of access is crucial, then using an array would be much more efficient, since this would require a single array lookup for each test. Alternatively, if storage space is more crucial, then we must realise that an array might require a very large amount of space to store a small set (e.g. of integers), whereas the list would use space proportional to the number of elements in the set. In this example, both solutions are adequate, in the sense defined earlier, but we can choose between them for particular applications, based on the type of access (membership tests), and the critical resources (time/memory). This is typical of the sort of decision that might be taken in a traditional design stage, here used to choose between alternate formal refinements.

Data refinement thus uses some of the traditional ideas of design to help guide the choice between concrete types, but additionally enforces the concept of adequacy to ensure that the concrete type will in fact work. More detail of how the refinement step is carried out in practice will be given later.

24.4.4 Operation refinement

Data refinement concerns the implementation of the passive state of the system, and we have to prove that the new concrete state correctly represents the old, that it is adequate. Operation refinement concerns the active part of the system, and we need to prove that new concrete operations *do the same thing* as the

abstract operations. This is known as satisfaction. Although the principle of satisfaction is simple, it is more complicated than adequacy in practice because of the active nature of the operations.

Operation refinements fall into two classes: those which are associated with a data refinement, and those which are not. 'Pure' operation refinement is simply the notion of refinement described earlier, which aims to make an operation more concrete by providing algorithmic details, a description of *how* the specification is to achieve its aim. Those refinements which are associated with a previous data refinement are in two parts: the first to modify the operation to work on the new types, and the second to perform a 'pure' operation refinement of this specification to produce a reasonable implementation. By considering these two stages separately, we deal with both classes of operation refinement.

24.4.1 Dealing with data refinement

The association between operation refinement and data refinement will be described in terms of an extended version of the earlier Figure 24.1 (as shown in *Figure 24.2*).

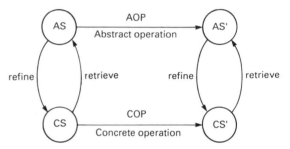

Figure 24.2

The basic notion of satisfaction here is very simple. We want the concrete operation on the appropriate concrete values to give the 'same' result as the abstract operation gave when applied to the abstract value. In particular we require:

$$\text{AOP} : \text{AS} \rightarrow \text{AS}$$
$$\text{COP} : \text{CS} \rightarrow \text{CS}$$

$$\forall\, a : \text{AS} \cdot \text{retrieve}(\text{COP}(\text{refine}(a))) = \text{AOP}(a)$$

While this is a true statement, which must hold between our concrete and abstract operations, it is not actually very helpful, since it is COP which is not yet defined, and it is this which we are trying to specify. We thus want to be able to specify what COP must be, in terms of AOP. Initially we might specify this as:

$$\forall\, c : \text{CS} \cdot \text{COP}(c) = \text{refine}(\text{AOP}(\text{retrieve}(c)))$$

This is not in fact true, because in general our concrete operation might do more than the abstract operation (for example changing some state hidden from the abstract representation) and thus leading to a difference between the two results. In fact what we want to say is that the operation COP is a refinement of the data-refined AOP operation. This ensures that everything that is done by the AOP operation is also done by the COP operation (although it may additionally do more). This part will be the pure operation refinement which was mentioned earlier. Formally we express the required relation as follows, where $\sqsubseteq$ is the relation 'is refined by':

refine ∘ AOP ∘ retrieve ⊑ COP

We can now continue with the pure operation refinement to produce an implementation of COP that satisfies the requirements laid down by the abstract operation, and the data refinement.

24.4.4.2 *Pure operation refinement*

The basic aim of operation refinement is to produce a new concrete operation which 'does the same thing' as an old abstract type. Simplistically, we might try to specify this relationship as we did above (where A ⊑ B means A is refined by B):

A ⊑ B
iff
∀ x · A(x) = B(x)

This is not correct, but it does provide a useful start for deriving a correct understanding of the refinement relation. Notice that the equality we express is not that the operations are the same, but that when applied to the same arguments they give the same results. This equality captures two pieces of information: first, that B is defined exactly when A is (i.e. when A gives a result so does B); second, that when they are defined they give the same result. This can be more clearly expressed as follows: (an operation is only defined when its precondition (pre OP) is satisfied, and if so it terminates with a result satisfying its postcondition (post OP)).

A ⊑ B
iff
pre A = pre B
post A = post B

This definition highlights an additional problem, for this forces A and B to be functionally identical. In fact, the refinement relation is intended to allow B to do more than A, as long as it does at least what A does. In particular, B can be defined on values for which A is not, for these results do not matter – B will only be expected to work on the values for which A does. Additionally B can provide a *stronger* result than A, for example giving values to state not represented in S. In particular we require that:

A ⊑ B
iff
pre A ⇒ pre B
pre A ∧ post B ⇒ post A

Whenever A is defined, so is B (although B may additionally be defined in other cases), and from the result of B (if A was defined) then we can deduce the result that A would have given. In other words our refinement allows us to weaken the precondition and make the operation more deterministic, that is, strengthen the post-condition.

This is a useful definition of refinement, and very widely applicable. However, in deriving it we made a large number of implicit assumptions, so it can in no way be regarded as *the* definition of refinement. The factors which might lead us to derive alternative definitions of refinement will be discussed later in this section.

This satisfaction constraint on the refinement forms the counterpart to the adequacy of data refinement. This constraint will thus form the basis of the refinement process. The task in refining operations is thus to produce new concrete operations which have this relationship to the abstract ones they purport to implement. The earlier description of refinement considered the refinement process to be a sequence of such steps, so an important property to establish at this point is that the refinement relation is transitive. In particular:

A ⊑ B ∧ B ⊑ C
⊢
A ⊑ C

If A is refined by B, and B is refined by C then A is also refined by C. In fact refinement is a partial ordering over specifications. Refinement can thus proceed by producing a series of specifications, each slightly different from the last, each adding more detail about how the 'top-level' specification is to be implemented. The job of the refiner is thus to choose appropriate refinement steps which add such detail, and which additionally satisfy the refinement relation.

The detail which must be added to specifications when refining them comes in two forms. First, we must sometimes add detail to specify things which were not specified (explicitly) in the abstract operation. For example, if refining a set, the implicit information that the set contains no duplicate elements might have to be expressed explicitly in the concrete operation (or in the data definition). There can be few guidelines on how to add such information, because the type of information required will be specific to the particular problem. This information will be necessary, for example, to satisfy the properties of the abstract specification using the new mechanisms (e.g. types) of the concrete representation, and we will thus simply be guided by the need to satisfy this refinement relation. The second kind of information we need to add is algorithmic information on how to produce the results dictated by the abstract specification. The main kinds of algorithmic constructs available in performing refinement are fixed, for example, sequence, choice and iteration. If we can derive refinement rules specifically for introducing particular constructs, and which guarantee the satisfaction relation, then the process of refinement should be made simpler.

Sequence A frequent, simple requirement is to refine a single high-level operation into a sequence of lower level ones. We need to know what properties must hold for this to be a valid refinement step. In particular, we require:

A ⊑ (B;C)
iff
pre A ⇒ pre B
pre A ∧ post B ⇒ pre C
pre A ∧ post (B;C) ⇒ post A

An operation A can be refined by the sequence B followed by C, if the sequence is applicable (pre B); the sequence itself is possible (post B implies pre C), and if the result of the sequence implies the result of the operation A. Here the post-condition of the sequence will be some combination of the post-conditions of the individual operations, depending on how much their operations overlap (i.e. whether C preserves the post-condition of B). This enables us to build up operations from smaller ones in the obvious way. Similarly, we can demonstrate that the elements of these sequences can then be refined independently:

B ⊑ D
C ⊑ E
post B ⇒ pre C
⊢
(B;C) ⊑ (D;E)

This allows the development of an operation by dividing it into a sequence of simpler ones, which are then implemented independently. This simple rule makes several assumptions about the operations (B,C,D, and E), in particular the independence of the operations. More generally we would want to analyse these inter-dependencies explicitly to produce a more widely applicable rule. For a more detailed discussion on these aspects of interdependence, see Dix (1989).

Choice An operation often has to provide different behaviour according to some Boolean condition; for example, performing different actions on some boundary condition, compared to the standard behaviour. This will typically be specified using some Boolean expression, prescribing different results in the different cases. In an implementation we will want to provide this behaviour by means of a conditional statement.

We can express a general form of choice using Dijkstra's Guarded Command Language (1976):

$$\text{if } G_1 \rightarrow B_1 \;[]\; G_2 \rightarrow B_2 \;[]\; \ldots \;[]\; G_n \rightarrow B_n \text{ fi}$$

If guard G_i holds then we execute body B_i; otherwise if guard G_j holds then we execute body B_j, and so on. Clearly this describes a non-deterministic action if more than one of the guards hold, and additionally describes an abort action if none of the guards hold. Often we will want to ensure that the guards are exclusive, and exhaustive, to avoid these problems.

We will now want to derive a refinement rule which describes the conditions which must hold for one of these choice statements to satisfy an (arbitrary) abstract specification:

$$A \sqsubseteq \text{if } G_1 \rightarrow B_2 \;[]\; \ldots \;[]\; G_n \rightarrow B_n \text{ fi}$$
$$\text{iff}$$
$$\text{pre } A \Rightarrow \text{Vi:1..}n\; G_i$$
$$\forall i:1..n \text{ pre } A \wedge G_i \Rightarrow \text{pre } B_i$$
$$\forall i:1..n \text{ pre } A \wedge G_i \wedge \text{post } B_i \Rightarrow \text{post } A$$

This rule essentially says that we can perform the refinement if the following conditions hold.

1. When the pre-condition for A holds then at least one of the guards must be true, one of the actions must be applicable.
2. When the guards for one of the actions hold (and the pre-condition for A holds), then the pre-condition for that action must hold.
3. The results produced by a body (when its guard holds, and the pre-condition for A holds), must imply the results produced by A.

We can thus refine an operation into a choice of actions if we can show that one of the choices is always applicable, and that the choice will achieve the results which the action A would have achieved.

Iteration Often we will specify operations whose results are essentially a whole set of properties, for example one for each of the elements of an array. We will typically want to implement these and other operations by means of an iterative construct.

We can express a general notion of iteration, again using guarded commands:

$$\text{do } G \rightarrow B \text{ od}$$

We can understand the semantics of this construct as, if the guard G holds, then execute the body B, and restart the construct, and if the guard does not hold then finish. The body B thus gets executed zero or more times.

In proving properties about the execution of a loop we want to ensure that each execution of the loop is possible, that is, that its pre-condition holds. We do this by means of a loop invariant, which must be true before the loop starts, is true after each iteration of the loop, and is true after the termination of the loop. This invariant is a predicate over the state used by the loop, and typically also the initial conditions of the loop.

We also want to be able to consider the total correctness of the loop, that it terminates within a finite number of iterations. To enforce this we introduce a (non-negative) bound function which must be reduced by each iteration of the loop, and which must eventually reach some value where the guard fails. This bound function is an additional predicate over the state of the loop, and its initial conditions. For more details of how invariants and bound functions can be used to prove properties of loops, see Gries (1981).

To perform such a refinement we want to enforce the following constraints:

$$A \sqsubseteq \text{do } G \rightarrow B \text{ od}$$
$$\text{iff}$$
$$\text{pre } A \Rightarrow I(s)$$
$$\text{pre } A \wedge G \Rightarrow \text{pre } B$$
$$\text{pre } A \wedge G \wedge \text{post } B \Rightarrow (s')$$
$$\text{pre } A \wedge I(s) \wedge \neg G \Rightarrow \text{post } A$$
$$\text{pre } A \wedge I(s) \wedge G \wedge B \Rightarrow \text{bound}(s) > \text{bound}(s')$$

(where s is the state at the beginning of an iteration, and s' the state at the end of an iteration.) We can understand this rule in terms of the following list of properties which must hold for the refinement to be valid:

1. If A is applicable (its pre-condition holds), then the loop invariant must hold.
2. If the guard G holds (and A is applicable), the body B must be applicable (its pre-condition must hold).
3. If the loop body is executed (because pre A and G hold), then afterwards the invariant I must still hold.
4. If the loop terminates, because G no longer holds (and pre A and I hold), then the required results of A (post A) must be guaranteed.
5. Each time the loop executes the bound function must be reduced, so that we can guarantee eventual termination.

This rule should enable us to introduce iteration into an operation to satisfy a complicated post-condition, providing that we demonstrate the required properties of the loop itself. For more details of these specific rules for refinement, see for example Neilson (1989).

As was the case for data refinement, the rules here only guarantee satisfaction, they do not guarantee a good refinement step. We must still use some design methods to help choose good refinement mappings. It can be noted here that if one of the specific refinement rules (such as introduction of iteration) is applicable, then it is unlikely that such a refinement will be inappropriate. However, we will have had to have done some design already in choosing an appropriate invariant and bound function before we can know that such a refinement would even be possible. Whether using the general or specific refinement rule here, all the design information is being provided by the user, that is the software engineer. One can also envisage more specific rules still, which refine only certain forms of abstract specification, and thus essentially encode certain design information for this particular structure, but as in the case of data refinement such rules are of more limited use, because there will be other factors which will necessarily influence the choice of rule. More detail on how these rules are applied to perform refinement will be given later in this section.

If refining a model-oriented specification, the operation will typically be specified in the form of pre- and post-conditions, or at least in terms of concrete relationships between the input and output variables. To refine such operations, one can consider the application of the refinement rules more or less directly. It is then simply a matter of filling in the detail about how the variables are manipulated to implement the operation. If refining algebraic operations, the pre- and post-conditions are not expressed in such an obvious way, for the relation between input and output is expressed abstractly. In fact, of course, implementations are almost always 'model-oriented' because they deal explicitly with a representation of their input and output variables. To refine the algebraic specification into an implementation of this form, we will probably refine it first into a more model-oriented specification, with explicit definitions of the state, and the pre- and post- conditions over it. This purely abstract refinement will thus typically be of the sort linked with a data refinement. We refine the data, and then we must refine the operations so that they enforce the appropriate properties that were implicit at the higher level. The refinement thus adds more detail, but probably does not introduce explicit algorithmic control structures.

24.4.4.3 Alternative operation refinement rules

As pointed out earlier, the basic refinement rule described above is not the only one possible. Indeed, although this rule is widely applicable, it is also restrictive, describing a limited way in which one operation can refine another. In particular there were several implicit assumptions about the operations and the way they operate. The specification of operations using a pre- and post-condition approach limits refinement to the procedure level. Although this is often appropriate in practice, the limitation this implies must be realised, as in general one might want to refine an arbitrary system.

The basic notion of 'does the same thing' can be expressed in a much more general way which does not restrict the notion of refinement, and this can be used to consider other approaches to the production of refinement rules:

a system B refines a system A if no observation can be made of A that cannot also be made of the new system B.

In the earlier approach to refinement the systems A and B were treated as simple operations, and an observation was considered to involve providing arguments, and examining results. In fact a system is a much more general thing, allowing an arbitrary number of interactions with the environment in which it is operating. The refined system must undergo these same interactions with the environment, irrespective of any changes that might have occurred to the way it operates internally.

In Hoare's CSP (Communicating Sequential Processes) (1985) and Milner's CCS (Calculus for Communicating Systems) (1980), systems are expressed in terms of a sequence of events, some of which are visible to the outside world, and some of which are internal to the process itself. Equivalences are also defined between processes specified in this way, based on the sequences of operations that the processes are prepared to engage in. Milner calls his 'observation equivalence', and defines it in the same way that refinement was defined above. Using CSP or CCS to specify our systems thus provides a very useful way to specify refinement because we can use the notion of observation equivalence to enforce our idea of refinement. Refinement into other specifications in CSP or CCS can thus be carried out relatively easily, and indeed both authors do consider some notion of refinement. Refinement into other notations, and ultimately into programming languages is more

difficult, especially in terms of traditional programming languages, like Ada or Pascal. Using CSP or CCS and associated refinement can thus be useful for certain types of system, or parts of system, particularly with this notion of a sequence of events in the system. For example, this approach might be useful for modelling and refining concurrent aspects of a system, such as the tasks, and associated rendezvous in an Ada program. In such an approach the earlier operation refinement might still be appropriate for the specification of the inter-rendezvous parts of a task, where one must still relate a set of inputs to a set of outputs.

Even this notion of refinement is too limited, for it assumes that the whole environment cannot distinguish the new (refined) system from the old. In a more general framework it might only be required that the individual users of the system could not distinguish between them. For example, if two users are totally independent (except for use of this same system), then it probably does not matter what total view the system presents, as long as the restricted views seen by the users remain unchanged. In particular, one can arbitrarily interleave the interactions with the two users, and they would remain unaffected. Such a view of refinement could be very useful, for it might allow the provision of a more efficient service, for instance by processing calls in parallel.

In a more restricted environment the computing resources might need to be viewed as a transaction-based system. Such a system may vary the order of the individual calls, but must preserve a notion of 'serializability', that is, it must be possible to assign an order in which the transactions (sequences of calls) appear to have occurred. Here the processes tolerate their calls being interleaved, provided that groups of calls that they want to regard as atomic are indeed treated as such.

Jeremy Jacob (1989) provides a set of refinement rules which specify the constraints necessary to enforce these two views of refinement. Note that these rules are weaker (more permissive) than those described earlier.

The earlier view of refinement considered the specification to be a set of simple sequential operations. This extended view considers a specification to be of a single system interacting with an environment. (Even the basic CSP/CCS approach effectively only treats refinement of individual processes, although clearly these approaches are more amenable to considering concurrency.) In practice one might want to consider a refinement which involves an unconstrained change in the 'amount' of concurrency in a system. Consider the following cases:

1. In a simple case one might want to add a notion of concurrency to improve efficiency, for example, by considering the parallel execution of the separate parts of a divide and conquer algorithm.
2. Similarly one might want to remove a notion of concurrency from a specification in order to simplify the implementation, if, for example, it was known that the ultimate execution would be sequential.
3. In a more complicated situation one might want to make an arbitrary change in the 'amount' of concurrency. Consider for example, an abstract specification of a telephone exchange, which is specified to behave as if there was a separate call connecting mechanism for each line on the exchange. One might want to refine this to a specification which stated that in practice there were actually a small number of logical connecting devices, which were attached to individual lines as required.

In general refinement rules are needed which enable one to perform refinements such as these, and verify that the new specifications are indeed satisfactory. He Jifeng (1989) addresses some aspects of the refinement of systems, presenting some refinement rules for CSP. However, this problem is far from solved, with more work being needed to develop refinement rules which enable any of these refinements to be performed.

The earlier part of this section described a basic notion of refinement, and presented some refinement rules that represent the satisfaction relations between specifications. This part has provided some alternate views of what satisfaction should mean for refinement, and references were given for more detail on refinement rules which represent this view. Although by no means exhaustive, this section should have illustrated some of the areas where these alternate views of refinement are appropriate.

24.4.5 Performing refinement

Earlier in this section rules which describe what a refinement actually is were derived and discussed. These rules describe both for data and operations what constraints must hold between the abstract and concrete specifications in order for one to be a refinement of the other. This still leaves the problems of how exactly to go about performing the refinement, how to produce the concrete specification, and how to prove that it is a refinement.

The first, and easiest, way to perform refinement is to treat the refinement rules as a set of transformations. As was suggested earlier, we can use the general refinement rules as the basis for producing a set of specific refinement rules, such as for refining mappings to arrays, or more specific versions of the rules for introducing iteration or choice. For example we might derive the following very simple and naive rule:

$$\forall i{:}m\,..\,n \; P(i) \sqsubseteq (i:=m; \; \text{do } i \leqslant n \rightarrow P(i); \; i:=i+1 \text{ od})$$

This rule states that a property over a range can be enforced by iterating over the range, and enforcing the property individually for each element in the range. The property $P(i)$ can be refined separately. Here we have taken the slight notational liberty of representing a predicate and an associated body as $P(i)$.

We can now consider the use of this refinement rule as a rewrite rule over the abstract specification. If we can find a part of the abstract specification that matches the left-hand side of this rule, then we can replace it by the right-hand side (with the appropriate values for m, n and P). Additionally, we can check any extra constraints that might be included in the rule, for example, in this case this might be on the ranges of m and n, or the type of property P. As the rule is a refinement rule, we know that the new specification satisfied the old, and hence that we have performed a refinement.

The rule given above is a very simplistic and specific one, but in practice many more general rules can be derived for both operation and data refinement, thus providing a large set of potential refinement rules. A refinement can then in principle be carried out relatively automatically by matching and applying these rewrite rules until an implementation is produced.

This approach (unfortunately) suffers from several problems. First the set of refinement rules must be exhaustive; they must say how to refine a specification using any likely formulation and combination of constructs, otherwise the attempt to refine automatically will fail, and we will have to use the other approach (see below), at least for part of the specification. Second, even if a complete set of these refinement rules can be produced, an implementation produced using them is unlikely to be a good one, since it cannot take into account any of the other information available to the designer, but it is limited only to the specification. All the information usually provided at the design stage, including the functional constraints, must therefore be captured in this set of rules. Such an approach is more likely to be successful if applied to a limited problem domain, where a complete set of rules is more likely, especially if it allows

the introduction of new (verified) rules when necessary. Some systems which utilize these techniques are available, and will be discussed later.

The second approach to performing refinement is to use the refinement rule as a means of checking that existing concrete specifications do indeed satisfy their abstract specifications.

Before this kind of checking can take place, a concrete specification must be produced, which supposedly refines some abstract one. This process will be carried out using the traditional design techniques as a basis, using as inputs not only the abstract specification, but also the functional constraints, and any other information available. The designer can also be guided by the refinement rules that he must satisfy, and in particular by any specific refinement rules he may have that are relevent to the specification. Unfortunately the main tool that the designer has in performing this task is simply his ability and experience in performing such design steps. One may think that this is not a problem, since this is what the designer is there for, and he has previously been responsible for this task anyway. There is a disadvantage, however, for the use of refinement enforces the taking of small provable steps, which will not be the style of working that the designer is used to. This stage will, however, lead to the production of a concrete specification which one is now obliged to check using the refinement rules.

The abstract and concrete specifications are matched against a refinement rule, and hence a set of constraints is instantiated which must be satisfiable if the specifications are indeed related by refinement. This set of constraints is called the proof obligations, for one is obliged to prove them to verify the refinement. Here it is useful to use the most specific refinement rule that is appropriate (e.g. an iteration rule rather than a general rule), for this will typically give more but simpler proofs to carry out.

The next stage is to carry out the proofs to complete the formal refinement. Ideally we would have some theorem prover which would carry these out automatically, or at least with only minimal interaction with the user. Unfortunately, good enough theorem provers are not yet widely available, and so most proofs must be carried out manually. It is, of course, at this stage that we rely particularly on the engineer's ability to use the formal mathematical reasoning, and it is at this stage that most mistakes are likely to be made. Certainly some automatic support would be useful for this stage, even if it were only a proof checker, before we can provide a high level of assurance in the validity of the proofs.

This approach to refinement has the advantage that it allows the use of all the available information in performing the refinement, and so should enable the designer to produce better implementations, more appropriate to their intended use. However, this approach also requires much more work on the part of humans, who must carry out the designs and verifications themselves, using the refinement rules merely as guides.

Ultimately, it is likely that transformational approaches to refinement will become widespread because, in principle, many specifications can be implemented automatically. Currently, however, such techniques are not sufficiently well developed to be practical, except in limited domains.

This section has thus described the theory of refinement, what it means to refine, what rules must be used to enforce this refinement, and how we might go about using the rules to perform refinement. The next section will look at these issues more practically, by means of a simple example.

24.5 Example of refinement

The previous section took a fairly theoretical approach to refinement, looking at what information is available in performing a refinement step, and how we can ensure that such a step is indeed valid, (i.e. adequate or satisfactory). This section looks at some of the same issues, but in a more practical way, by means of an example.

Consider for example a refinement which is going to implement a SET using a list. A possible algebraic specification of such a set is as follows:

```
OBJ SET
SORTS set
OPS
            {}              : →set
            {_}             : elem→set
            _U_             : set set→set
            member          : elem set→set
VARS
            e,x : elem
            a,b : set
EQNS
            (a U {} = a)
            (a U b = b U a)
            ((a U b) U c = a U (b U c))
            (a U {e} = a IF member(e,a))

            (member(e,{} = false)
            (member(e,{}) = (e == x))
            (member(e, aUb) = member(e,a) OR
                            member(e,b))
JBO
```

First, we will want to refine the data of the specification. This involves, for an algebraic specification such as this, working out what forms that the data can take. In this case it can be proved that a SET will always take one of the forms:

```
{}              the empty set
{e}             a single element
{e} U a         a union of two sets
```

This last line is possible, rather than the more general (a U b), because of the associativity law expressed for union (U).

We now want to find a refinement mapping and retrieve function for these different forms of set:

```
refine({})      =   []
refine({e})     =   [e]
refine({e} U a) =   union(refine({e}),refine(a))

retrieve([])    =   {}
retrieve(h:t)   =   {h} U retrieve(t)
```

(where *union* is the union function over the list representation of a set). What is not made clear by this definition is that the representation should not allow duplicate elements – that part of the refinement must be enforced by the union function when combining SETS. The data refinement now requires proof that this is adequate by showing that refined values can indeed be retrieved. We must do a proof for each possible form of the set.

```
retrieve(refine({}))    =   retrieve([])
                        =   {}
retrieve(refine({e}))   =   retrieve([e])
                        =   {e}
retrieve(refine({e} U a)) = retrieve(union(refine({e}),
                            refine(a))
                        =   {e} U a
```

The last step of this last proof can only be taken because we are assuming that the operation union is a true refinement of the old operation U. In particular, in the refinement of union we have to show that:

$$a \ U \ b = \text{retrieve(union(refine}(a),\text{refine}(b)))$$

This might seem like the avoidance of a proof, but in fact is is merely being postponed until the operational refinement stage. These simple proofs thus constitute a (conditional) adequacy check for the data refinement.

Proceeding to the refinement of the operations, U, and member, intuition leads to the following definitions (note that U and member are functions on sets, whereas union and mem are the corresponding functions on the list representation):

```
union([]), s)   =   s
union(h:t, s)   =   h : union(t, s)   IF not mem(h, s)
union(h:t, s)   =   union(t, s)       IF mem(h, s)

mem(e,[])       =   False
mem(e,h:t)      =   (e == h) OR mem(e,t)
```

Note that this definition of union does not enforce the property that its two arguments are SETS, that is, have no duplicates. This is assumed as a pre-condition of the function and it must thus be proved that all its arguments will have this property. We do, however, enforce the property described above that (assuming the pre-condition is true), then the result will have no duplicates. We know that the pre-condition will hold, because its arguments will be produced in only a limited number of ways, where the condition is enforced. In particular, the argument will be produced by a direct refinement from a SET, which does enforce the property, or by a previous application of *union*, which, by an inductive assumption, is known to produce only elements with no duplicates.

The proofs must now be carried out to check the satisfaction property necessary for the refinement relation to hold. The proof is actually carried out by showing that the new function is a refinement of the old one applied to the retrieved values. In particular it must be shown that:

$$\text{refine} \circ \text{abstract} \circ \text{retrieve} \sqsubseteq \text{concrete}$$

This can be done by proving:

$$\forall a,b: \text{refine(SET)} \cdot$$
$$\text{union}(a,b) = \text{refine(retrieve}(a) \ U \ \text{retrieve}(b))$$
$$\forall e: \text{elem}; \ a: \text{refine(SET)} \cdot$$
$$\text{mem}(e,a) = \text{refine(member}(e, \text{refine}(a)))$$

Here the notation 'refine(SET)' is used to indicate the type obtained by refining all values of type SET. It is thus the set of all lists that represent a SET. These equations enforce the property that whenever they are both defined (i.e. only on lists which are refined sets) they give the same results. The proofs are carried out by induction over the possible forms of the lists ([], and h:t), for each of the arguments to the function, and demonstrating that the results are the same.

First we treat the simple case with both SETS empty. On the left we use the list representation, rewriting the equations using the function definitions for the lists. On the right we consider the application of the SET version of the function, together with the appropriate use of the retrieve and refine functions, and thus we rewrite the equations using those definitions.

$$union([],[]) = refine(retrieve([]) \cup retrieve([]))$$
$$[] = refine(\{\} \cup \{\})$$
$$= refine(\{\})$$
$$= []$$
TRUE

Now consider the case where the first argument is the empty list, but where the second is a general list. Note that it can be assumed '$t = refine(retrieve(t))$' as the inductive assumption, and also that h is not a member of t, since only lists which represent SETS at the abstract level are being considered:

$$union([],h{:}t) = refine(retrieve([]) \cup retrieve(h{:}t))$$
$$h{:}t = refine(\{\} \cup \{h\} \cup retrieve (t))$$
$$= union([],refine(\{h\} \cup retrieve(t)))$$
$$= union([h],refine(retrieve(t)))$$
$$= union([h],t) \quad \text{(by inductive hypothesis)}$$
$$= h{:}t \quad \text{(since } h \text{ not in } t)$$
TRUE

Similarly, we perform the proof with the second list empty, and the first not, making the same assumptions about h and t.

$$union(h{:}t,[]) = refine(retrieve(h{:}t) \cup retrieve([]))$$
$$h{:}union(t,[]) = refine(\{h\} \cup retrieved(t) \cup \{\}) \ (h \text{ not in } [])$$
$$= union([h]),union(t,[]))$$
$$= h{:}union(t,[]) \quad \text{(since } h \text{ not in } t)$$
TRUE

We must now deal with the most general case in which both lists are non-empty. Here we can make two inductive assumptions, ('$t = refine(retrieve(t))$', and '$y = refine(retrieve(y))$'), one for each of the lists, and again we assume that both lists contain no duplicates (in particular h not in t, and x not in y). Additionally, we must now consider two cases, one in which the element 'h' is not in the list '$x{:}y$', and the second in which it is, and must thus not be included again. Assume h is not in $x{:}y$.

$$union(h{:}t,x{:}y) = refine(retrieve(h{:}t) \cup retrieve(x{:}y))$$
$$h{:}union(t,x{:}y) = refine(\{h\} \cup retrieve(t) \cup \{x\} \cup retrieve(y))$$
$$\quad (h \text{ not in } x{:}y)$$
$$= union([h],union(t,union([x],y))) \quad \text{(induction)}$$
$$= h{:} union(t,x{:}y) \quad \text{(since } x \text{ not in } y)$$
TRUE

In the second case we assume h is in $x{:}y$:

$$union(h{:}t,x{:}y) = refine(retrieve(h{:}t) \cup retrieve(x{:}y))$$
$$union(t,x{:}y) = refine(\{h\} \cup retrieve(t) \cup \{x\} \cup retrieve(y))$$
$$\quad (h \text{ in } x{:}y)$$
$$= union([h],union(t,union([x],y))) \quad \text{(induction)}$$
$$= union(t,x{:}y) \quad \text{(since } x \text{ not in } y)$$
TRUE

The proofs may be a little difficult to follow, as presented above, but it should be possible to see that the proofs can be carried out using a relatively small number of straightforward symbol manipulations. A similar proof can be carried out to demonstrate the correctness of the member function.

These proofs together constitute a proof of our simple refinement. This should have illustrated how the refinement rules of the earlier sections might be applied in practice. What should also be clear is that although the individual manipulations in the proof are straightforward, the overall proof is more difficult, because there is a complex proof management task to perform to ensure that all parts of the proof are indeed discharged, and that there are no circularities in the proof, relying on unproven aspects of the specifications to prove others. This should give the impression that some sort of mechanized support is necessary to enforce the appropriate properties of the proof, and thus help to truly verify the refinement. If support for this stage of proof is not available then there is an advantage in a rigorous approach to refinement, in which one carries out an outline proof, in order to reduce the residual doubt without carrying out a total proof. This is particularly the case if the potential proof is of such a scale that one is unlikely to be able to carry it out correctly (i.e. without error) without the aid of some tool support.

24.6 Support for refinement

The use of formal methods, and in particular, refinement, to aid the software development process is intended to improve the quality and reliability of the software produced. This kind of claim has some validity, as the mathematical formalism on which these techniques are based provides a framework for carrying out proofs of correctness. However, although such proof is possible in principle, we are perhaps equally likely to make mistakes when applying the formal techniques as when carrying out traditional design. These formal techniques can thus only provide real improvement if there is support for them, in the form of tools to verify the accuracy of the formal steps (carried out by fallible humans). It is therefore necessary to ask what tools are available to support the process of refinement.

Consider first the design and proof approach to refinement, based on the idea of a designer producing a concrete specification which is later checked to confirm it satisfies its abstract specification. Two stages must follow a design in this approach: in order to verify the correctness of the refinement step we must first derive a set of proof obligations, and second, discharge these proofs. Ideally there would be automated support for both of these processes, such that these essentially mechanical processes could be carried out without human intervention.

In fact, little work has been done in this area of support for this type of refinement. The task of generating proof obligations is relatively straightforward, for in theory it merely requires the matching of the refinement rule against the two specifications. Despite this, support in the area is limited. This is perhaps not surprising, since automatic generation of proof obligations is of real use only if it is linked to a mechanism to aid in the proof of the obligations. Several so-called verification condition generators are available which form part of program verification systems, like Spade (Carre et al., 1986; Clutterbuck and Carre, 1988) and Gypsy (Good et al., 1978). These systems allow the generation of conditions that must hold if the source code is to satisfy some specified properties. Typically, verification systems such as Gypsy only give adequate support to the final stage of refinement, that is from low-level specifications to programs.

More work has been done in the area of proof, since proof systems are of use in many applications, as well as in refinement. Essentially two different approaches to proof are taken: a fully automated approach, such as that of the Boyer-Moore (1983) theorem prover; or a more interactive approach as taken for example by HOL (Higher Order Logic) (Gordon, 1985). Automatic theorem provers include guidelines about how to prove different kinds of theorem, so that, in principle, a proof can be generated without human intervention. In practice producing such a system is extremely difficult, and provers tend to be geared towards particular types of problem. (For example, the Boyer-Moore theorem prover is particularly good at solving problems involving lists.) Interactive provers also exist which, as the name suggests, perform a proof in conjunction with a user. The system typically understands a series of tactics, each of which perform a particular aspect of a proof (like use induction, or rewrite using a definition), but the user provides the strategy, by telling the system when to apply each of the tactics to accomplish the proof. Interactive theorem provers are thus more generally applicable, since they rely on the user's intuition to guide the proof. The prover itself then provides a proof-checking and proof-management service which should make the user's task simpler, and less error-prone. This approach does produce validated proofs, but the amount of human effort required is not insignificant, and hence until this interaction is cut down performing proofs in this way will still be an onerous task.

More general formal methods tools, such as specification type checkers and animators, also have a place in refinement, for although they do not help perform the actual refinement steps, they do provide some assurance that the specifications themselves are correct.

The second approach to refinement is to refine by transformation. The whole intention of this approach is that it should be automatable, and hence more work has been done in this area, and some genuine refinement tools now exist. In particular Refine and CIP will be looked at here.

24.6.1 Refine

Refine (Abraido-Fandino, 1987) is a software development environment which provides some support for transformational refinement. The environment is based on a language, also called Refine, and encompasses a range of tools necessary in the development of software.

The Refine language is a wide-spectrum language, in that it incorporates both high-level and low-level constructs. At the high level the same kind of abstract concepts can be used as are available in notations like Z and VDM, in particular, sets, sequences, maps, and tuples, together with more basic types such as integers and Booleans. Using these types one can express a wide range of properties in simple predicate calculus, and set theory, typical of the sort of property one might express in a model-oriented specification. One can also define functions over these types in a way typical of functional programming languages, using pattern matching and recursion. At a lower level there are also control structures typical of a more traditional programming language, such as procedures, loops, and choices, together with concrete types.

Of particular interest here, Refine also provides the novel notion of a transformation. Note that this is *not* the same meaning of transformation that was used in the description of the theory of refinement. This transformation describes a relationship between a pre-condition and a post-condition. If the pre-condition holds over some state, then a transformation is carried out to enforce the truth of the post-condition. It can be seen that this is a counterpart for the operations described earlier, and not the refinement rules which the earlier transformation rules represented. As an example consider a simple transformation, such as:

$$x \in R \text{--}{>} f(x) \in S$$

We thus define a transformation that given an x in the set R an appropriate transformation will be carried out to ensure that $f(x)$ is in the set S. Clearly this is a trivial example, but it should illustrate the principle of the transformation. The pre-condition of the transformation can be any arbitrary predicate over the state of the system. Unfortunately however, the post-condition is limited to be a conjunction of the following types of expression:

variable
$\neg$ variable
variable $=$ expression
expression $\in$ variable
expression $\neg \in$ variable

The reason for this limitation will become clear shortly.

The Refine language is a true programming language, in that it is entirely executable. The Refine system includes a compiler, which compiles Refine code directly into (executable) Lisp. Again, the part of this process of interest here is the compilation of the transformations. The compiler includes a set of refinement rules which are applied to the transformations, to make their operation more explicit. Ultimately these transformation rules are refined from the specifications given using pre- and post-conditions, into Lisp statements which will satisfy the post-conditions. Additionally, Refine provides mechanisms to help introduce the appropriate control structure necessary to ensure that the transformations are carried out when required, without the need to call them explicitly.

As was suggested earlier, the transformational approach to refinement is currently only practical in limited problem domains. It can be noted then, that Refine has created itself such a domain by limiting the form of the post-conditions for its operations. For this range of post-conditions Refine can have a complete set of refinement rules, which guarantee implementation of any transformation rule, although the user can add new refinement rules if required. Additionally it can be noted that future versions of Refine intend to extend the range of allowable post-conditions.

The Refine system does, however, consist of more than just a refining compiler for the Refine language; it is intended to provide a whole programming environment. The whole system is based upon an object-oriented knowledge base. This knowledge base is used to store all the information about the system in an integrated way. In particular, it stores source and object code, together with documentation and test data, and can also be used to store and maintain data used by the programs.

The user can query this information directly, using constructs within the Refine language, and can also access it by means of the Refine tool set. This tool set includes the compiler which has already been mentioned, together with editors and browsers, and more specific tools such as document generators, and a debugging system. The aim is thus to provide the whole environment necessary for program development.

Several large companies have used the Refine system, and claim impressive results, not only in terms of improvement of the effort necessary to produce systems, and the size of the code produced, but also in terms of improvements in configuration control, and documentation. Indeed, the Refine system itself was written (at least partially) in the Refine language, using the transformational approach, and using the configuration control mechanism to bootstrap new versions by applying the old object code to the new source code, thereby creating the new system.

24.6.2 CIP

The CIP (Computer-aided Intuition-guided Programming) (Bauer *et al*, 1989) project also considers the construction of programs by transformation.

The CIP project is based on another wide-spectrum language, CIP-L, which aims to be able to capture the specification of a system throughout its life cycle. The life cycle which the CIP project considers is as follows:

1. Formal problem specification (descriptive).
2. Modified specifications (usually descriptive).
3. Non-deterministic implicit recursive solution.

4. Non-deterministic explicit recursive solution.
5. Deterministic tail recursive solution.
6. Ameliorated applicative programs.
7. Efficient procedural or machine-oriented programs.

The motivation for such a wide spectrum language is that program development will proceed by transforming only part of a specification at a time, and hence the various types of specification used cannot be separated, but rather must be integrated into one syntactic and semantic framework.

At the highest level, CIP-L allows algebraic specifications to be written, similar to the OBJ examples seen earlier. These specifications define new sorts, and operations on them, by means of equations called laws. Additionally at this high level, one can express properties of the operations using the traditional notions of set theory, and predicate calculus. This allows one to write more model-oriented specifications by expressing the appropriate conditions over the operations. Specifications at this level are not necessarily expected to be directly executable.

At a lower level, CIP-L introduces more explicit control structure, in a form similar to a functional programming language, defining functions explicitly using conditionals and recursion. Additionally, it represents non-determinism by means of an equivalent to Dijkstra's guarded choice command. This is the applicative level of the language.

At a lower level still, the language allows the use of traditional programming language constructs: variables, assignments, procedures, iteration, and conditional statements. The language even includes a 'machine-oriented' aspect at this level, incorporating jumps, labels and pointers. Additionally, it introduces a notion of parallelism, based on the idea of conditional critical regions.

Finally, the language includes a module structure, called the unit, which allows the construction of separate generic parts of the system, insulated from each other, thus enabling modularization, and re-use.

The CIP approach to program development is through transformation rules, which progressively refine a specification to be more explicit, that is, to be further down this 'language hierarchy', until finally an executable program is achieved. The sort of transformation rule used here is not dissimilar to the specific refinement rules introduced earlier. For example, their system includes a rule which effectively says:

$$\text{if } G \text{ then } B_1 \text{ else } B_2 \text{ fi} \sqsubseteq \text{if } G \rightarrow B_1 \: [] \: \neg G \rightarrow B_2 \text{ fi}$$

This rule is more use than it might at first seem, for we have refined the conditional expression into a conditional statement. The CIP system includes a large set of such rules for performing refinement, but avoids the problems of completeness by allowing the user to devise new rules as and when required.

A simple prototype system based on CIP-L and these transformation rules has been developed to demonstrate the approach, although it is realised that this system is of little practical use. A full transformation system called CIP-S is currently under development, which is intended to be applicable to real world problems. This system will be based around a knowledge base, which will store all the information relevant to the development. This knowledge base will be connected to a system core, which will control access to the database, and will perform transformations and manipulations on the information therein. Between this system core and the user will be a user environment, which will control user interaction, and also translate between internal representations of information, and forms appropriate for visual display.

Due to the ongoing nature of the project, the system has not yet been widely used. However, the prototype system is being used on the project to aid in the development of CIP-S, so it would seem that the techniques do have some applicability.

24.7 Problems with refinement

The previous sections have tried to emphasize the positive side of refinement: that it is a practical method, with a sound basis in theory, and which aims to solve a real problem. Although this is a true description, refinement itself does suffer from a set of problems which means that refinement is not (yet) widely used in practice. This section will examine some of these problems, and look at what solutions to them are likely to be forthcoming.

The first kind of problem reflects non-technical issues, which are limiting the use of refinement. Refinement is currently largely a technique in the province of the academic researcher. These researchers have developed a large body of theory, based on a firm mathematical basis, and applied this theory to a range of 'interesting' examples. However, there have been few applications of refinement techniques to real industrial problems, and hence there is little evidence available to convince workers in industry that these techniques are genuinely useful in practice. Indeed it is striking that, in particular, refinement is perceived as a technique which can help solve the problems of producing so-called high integrity systems. In practice, however, even less work has been carried out to demonstrate that refinement can really be used to produce such safety- and security-critical systems. Until the time that such evidence is available few people will use refinement in industry, and fewer still will use it in safety-critical areas where they must place their reliance on the techniques, and their ability to use them.

Additionally, few people in industry have been trained in the use of such formal methods. The whole concept of refinement is based on the formal manipulation of specifications, and, without a clear understanding of the theory on which these are based, it is unlikely that refinement techniques could be used with any degree of success. Many firms have a formal methods group, where some people are aware of these techniques, but if formal methods are really to become well used, then such expertise must be spread throughout a company, and applied to many projects. These non-technical problems can only be solved by a conscious decision to use formal methods, by giving training to the workers, and finally by applying the techniques to (real) projects, so that their success can be evaluated and disseminated.

There are, however, some technical issues which must also be solved by the refinement researchers, before refinement can be realistically applied to all systems.

The main problem with refinement (as with many formal techniques) is simply the problem of scale. Most techniques have been devised using (relatively) small examples, and unfortunately do not scale easily to larger specifications. This is often not (only) a criticism of the refinement methods themselves, but also of the underlying specification languages on which they are based. Many such notations do not provide adequate structuring methods, so that separate parts of the specification cannot be isolated from each other. Refinement of small examples can thus proceed with some success, but when the size of the specification increases the integration of these separate parts causes both the size and number of the proofs involved in the refinement process to increase considerably.

The second technical problem arises from the functional constraints specified in the requirements. Refinement methods do not adequately describe how one can use these constraints to guide the making of design decisions. In the transformational approach to refinement it is very difficult to utilize this information at all. In the design-and-prove approach such information can be used by the designer in the production of his supposed refinement, and hence be incorporated, but the techniques give no guidance as to how this is to be done. More importantly, the refinement rules do not help in the derivation of proof obligations or the verification that these requirements are indeed satisfied. This is a serious drawback, for the very problems that formal methods aim to address, such as problems of safety and security are often specified as constraints over the functional operation of the system. Indeed, there are cases where refinement of functionality and refinement of functional constraints (e.g. security) are at odds (Jacob, 1989) and it is clear that research is needed to overcome these problems.

A final problem is simply due to the immaturity of the methods, for they have not yet addressed all relevant aspects of specification. For example, as was pointed out earlier, they do not adequately address the problems of refining systems involving concurrency. They also do not deal with issues such as ensuring that atomicity and security guaranteed at one level of specification are not compromised when refinement to a lower level takes place.

Fortunately, none of these problems seem likely to prove insurmountable, so although refinement is not yet as widely applicable as one might like, further research is likely to solve the problems, and speed the spread of the use of formal methods in industrial applications.

24.8 Conclusions

Design and implementation of a system from its specification is usually undertaken by a team of programmers. These programmers will take some joint decisions, then each will proceed independently to implement part of the system. The correctness of such systems, when using conventional development practices, relies entirely on the ability of the programmers. Many programmers are good, and produce good systems, but all are fallible, and so there can be no real assurance of system correctness with this approach.

Computers are increasingly being used in new fields, such as safety- and security-critical applications, where the potential consequences of failure are disastrous, and hence where correctness (with respect to safety or security requirements) is vital. A more formal approach to program development is therefore required which can provide some assurance of correctness for such systems.

Refinement is a technique which produces an implementation from an initial specification by a series of (formally) provable steps, and which can hence provide some assurance that a program does indeed satisfy its specification.

In particular, there is a set of refinement rules which describe the relationships that must hold between a specification and a refinement of it, if one is correctly to implement the other. One can thus use these rules either transformationally to aid the production of a refined specification, or analytically to prove that such a refinement step is correct. In either case such rules enable one to produce a provably correct implementation.

Considerable work has been done on producing notations for the definition and refinement of specifications, and ultimately the production of implementations. Some such techniques have been used on examples to demonstrate their validity and practicality. Additionally, some tool support is available to aid in refinement, particularly in the area of transformational refinement, but also in the area of theorem proving vital to the realistic use of refinement.

It has been seen that formal methods, and in particular refinement, aim to solve a very real problem in the area of program development. Indeed, several such techniques have

been developed and demonstrated to work on some (small) examples. Unfortunately this is not yet enough, for the examples used are usually (relatively) small and simple sequential problems, whereas the problem domains envisaged for refinement involve the production of large and complex real-time concurrent systems such as are needed in many safety-critical environments. More work is needed to ensure the scalability of refinement techniques, and to demonstrate their applicability in the complex domains where the formality is really needed.

In conclusion then, refinement is a technique for producing software which has a realistic chance of assuring its correctness. It is based on a well-established theory, which, given a stronger practical emphasis, will become widely used in the production of reliable software.

24.9 References

Abraido-Fandino, L. M. (1987) *An Overview of Refine 2.0*, Reasoning Systems Inc.

Bauer, F. L., Moller, B., Partsch, H. and Pepper, P. (1989) Formal program construction by transformations – computer-aided, intuition-guided programming, *Transactions on Software Engineering*, **15**

Boyer, R. S. and Moore, J. S. (1983) Proof-checking, theorem-proving, and program verification. *Institute for Computing Science Report 35*, University of Texas at Austin

Carre, B. A, Clutterbook, D. L., Debney, C. W. and O'Neill, I. M. (1986) SPADE – the Southampton Programme Analysis and Development Environment. In *Software Engineering Environments* (ed. I. Sommerville), Peter Peregrinus, pp 129–134

Clutterbuck, D. L. and Carre, B. A. (1986) The verification of low-level code. *Software Engineering Journal, 3*

Dijkstra, E. G. (1976) *A Discipline of Programming*, Prentice-Hall

Dix, A. (1989) Software engineering implications for formal refinement. In *Proceedings of European Software Engineering Conference 89, Lecture Notes in Computer Science 387*, (ed. J. A. McDermid and C. Ghezzi), Springer-Verlag

Futatsugi, K., Goguen, J., Jouannaud, J.-P. and Meseguer, J. (1985) Principles of OBJ2. *Symposium on Principles of Programming Languages*, ACM, pp 52–66

Good, D. L., Cohen, R. M., Hoch, C. G., Hunter, L. W. and Hare, D. F. (1978) A Report on the Language Gypsy, Version 2.0. *Tech Report ICSCA-CMP-10*, University of Texas at Austin

Gordon, M. (1985) HOL: A machine oriented formulation of higher order logic. *Computer Laboratory Report 68*, University of Cambridge

Gries, D. (1981) *The Science of Programming*, Springer-Verlag

Hoare, C. A. R. (1985), *Communicating Sequential Processes*, Prentice-Hall International

Jacob, J. (1989) On the derivation of secure components. In *IEEE Symposium on Security and Privacy*, IEEE Computer Society

Jacob, J. (1989) Refinement of shared systems. In *The Theory and Practice of Refinement*, (ed. J. A. McDermid), Butterworth Scientific

Jifeng, H. (1989) Process refinement. In *The Theory and Practice of Refinement: Approaches to the Formal Development of Large-Scale Software Systems*, (ed. J. A McDermid) Butterworth Scientific

Jones, C. B. (1986) *Systematic Software Development using VDM*, Prentice-Hall International

Milner, R. (1980) A Calculus of Communicating Systems. *Lecture Notes in Computer Science 92*, Springer-Verlag

Neilson, D. (1989) Hierarchical refinement of a Z specification. In *The Theory and Practice of Refinement: Approaches to the Formal Development of Large-Scale Software Systems* (ed. J. A. McDermid), Butterworth Scientific

Spivey, M. (1988) *The Z Notation: A Reference Manual*, Prentice-Hall International

25

Formal implementation

Steven Vickers
Department of Computing, Imperial College of Science, Technology and Medicine, London

Contents

25.1 'Typing is no substitute for thinking'

In Kemeny and Kurtz (1971), the standard beginners' introduction to programming in the 1970s, the above slogan was ascribed to R. J. Hamming. Thus from the earliest days a particularly invidious temptation was recognized – that of typing in a program to see what it does, then typing in something different, to see what *that* does, and so on.

The cure was also known. One must take time to think about programs and understand what they are supposed to be doing. Apart from ideas of structured programming, which clarify the operational structure of the code, the techniques advocated in those days were vague. One was exhorted to write comments, which of course does force one to think a little, but there was little guidance on what the comments should say.

Later experience showed better what made useful comments, and soon some points were well understood. For instance:

1. There is little point in using English to paraphrase operational steps (the COBOL fallacy). It is actually clearer to write 'x := a + b' than 'add b to a giving x'. The role of comments is to incorporate information about the more global behaviour of the algorithm.
2. On the other hand, what *is* useful is a static description of how the variables are supposed to relate to each other and to the original values. Such descriptions can be expressed using the language of logic.
3. A crucially important place for comments is the header of a subroutine. This is the interface between the subroutine and the calling code. The more carefully it is specified, the more effectively the subroutines divide up the program.
4. Comments are especially valuable at the destinations of jumps, where they can say what is being assumed and hence what must be set up before the jump. Jumps are now known to be harmful, but the same principle makes comments useful at the heads of loops (the method of loop invariants).

What emerges from these early insights is that the comments and program code are attempting to describe the algorithm in different ways. The program code describes individual execution steps and the way they are strung together, and this is *how* the algorithm is done. The comments, on the other hand, describe more static conditions, including global behaviour of subroutines – how the outputs relate to the inputs. This is *what* the algorithm is supposed to be doing.

For the computer's sake, the program code must be expressed in uncompromisingly precise terms. This often comes as a shock to the beginner. It is therefore easy to see programming as the transformation of an originally vague requirement into a precise program. However, this overlooks the fact that the program is a precise formulation not of the requirements, but of the computer's execution procedure. Under this view, the programmer is trying at the same time to turn vagueness into precision, and human requirements into computer method. This is a mistake, because the computer operations are not very clearly related to the overall effect of the program, which is what interests humans.

The refined comments mentioned above are a way of dividing up these two parts of the process, because they allow us to give precision to our requirements without mentioning execution steps. This division can be expressed as in *Figure 25.1*.

Returning to the original slogan, the immediate aim is not the program code, but – in effect – the comments. First one tries to make the overall behaviour precise (this is a specification). Then one delves into the structure of the code by making certain design decisions to use subroutines and loops, and formulates specifications and comments for these. At the end one still has to

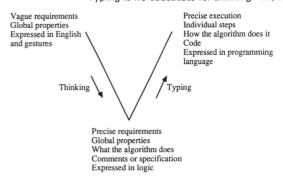

Figure 25.1

make the program code fit between one comment and the next, but this is more or less automatic – it is just *typing*. But because it relates to precise descriptions, it is susceptible to mathematical proof that the relation is sound.

What one ends up with is a combined structure, program = comments + code (*Figure 25.2*).

Just as the human requirements must precede the implementation, so the logical component should precede the code. And although in practice there is some alternation between them, the logic should be the driving force; thinking comes before typing. It is important to grasp this, because a common misunderstanding (the fallacy of the 'well-intentioned hacker') is that after writing some code, one would ideally like to prove it correct. As everyone knows, it is not practically possible to work like this. The coding is not usually completed until after the deadline, leaving negative time for correctness proofs. But the moral is not to dispense with the proof, but in effect to reverse the fallacy; outline the proof first, and *then* write the code that it proves correct. The aim of this chapter is to show how to put this into effect.

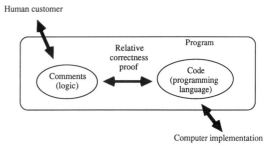

Figure 25.2

25.1.1 Specifications as contracts

The basic problem is this. Suppose there is some unit C of code, whether a simple statement like an assignment, or a compound statement, or a subroutine. The details of its coding may not yet be known, and in fact this methodology will delay this for a while. What is needed here is a way, independent of the coding, of specifying what C is to do.

C is required to do something useful, but it may require something in exchange. For instance, when one calls a square root function, one must ensure that the argument is non-negative before the function can be relied on to give a square root. This contract, a specification, is all that is needed to use the code and reason about it.

Such a specification can be formalized in a pre-condition P, a condition on the initial state before C, and a post-condition Q, relating the states before and after. When coded, C works correctly iff whenever P holds before C is executed, then C will terminate leaving Q holding.

The specification can be seen as a contract between the user of the routine and the implementer, an interlocking system of rights and obligations, and so has two aspects. For the user, it constitutes the instructions: how to use the routine correctly (an obligation), and what it does (a right). This is actually the primary point of view, and is independent of the code. For the implementer, it constitutes a description of what his code is required to do (an obligation), on the assumption that the user calls it correctly (a right).

To compare two states, before and after an operation, one can introduce a notation to distinguish the two. A common one, following the usage of Z (as in Hayes (1987)) and Jones (1980) (but this is different from the more recent VDM notation of Jones (1986)), is to use an unadorned identifier (e.g. x) to mean the value *before* the operation, and the same identifier with a prime (e.g. x') for the value *after*. A specification then looks like:

Pre: P   (a condition involving x)
Post: Q   (a condition involving both
                     x and x')

Although a single identifier x has been used here, it should be thought of as a vector, a list of all the identifiers under consideration.

This scheme is good for subroutines, but cannot be used indiscriminately because of the undisciplined proliferation of primes. Therefore a method will be used that introduces notation for the values stored in the computer. For example, suppose that Sqrt(x) is to replace x by an approximation to its square root, using some fixed error tolerance ε:

First method   *Second method*
Pre: $x \geqslant 0$ Pre: $x \geqslant 0 \wedge x = x_0$
Post: $|(x')^2 - x| < \varepsilon$ Post: $|x^2 - x_0| < \varepsilon$

x_0 is not a computer location, but a logical variable representing the value held by x initially.

Using this technique, we can specify units of code without priming any identifiers. Therefore comments, describing states between actions, will not need directly to mention states at other times. It will be seen later that the first method is more useful when a subroutine is called, but the second is more useful when it is coded.

25.1.2   Outline of the rest of the chapter

Section 25.2 is a theory of the relation between specification and code. It formalizes the two aspects of the specification: for the implementor, the techniques by which one might prove that the implementing code complies with the specification; for the user, the means by which the specification *on its own and independently of the implementing code* can be used in reasoning about the calling program. The theory attacks the same problem as formal logic, that of constructing valid proofs, and is called program logic.

In form, this theory looks like a formalization of the 'well-intentioned hacker's' fallacy, showing what reasoning is needed to prove properties of some written code in terms of properties of its components. However, it goes further in content, because the reasoning represents a deeper understanding of how the program is to work and can be formulated independently of the code. The theory then explains what the components will have to do in order to fit in with the deeper understanding, reducing

the original contract to subcontracts for the components. This gives a precise meaning to the main slogan. The *typing* is the code for the components, the *thinking* is the reasoning. The theory neutrally explains how they they may validly fit together – the 'well-intentioned hacker' types first, while the method urged here is to think first.

Section 25.3 shows the method in action in an example of sorted merge of files. There are a number of different points to be seen here.

First, how does one bring out what is just called 'the reasoning' above? What is the manner in which one brings one's thinking from the back of the mind (the vague ideas present behind even the most slapdash of coding) to the level of precision needed by the formal theory? The 'reasoning' represents the answers to practical programming questions like 'what does this variable do?'

Second, for reasoning to be rigorous it does not need to go to the full degree of formality required by the formal theory. For practical purposes it is acceptable to leave holes where it is obvious how one would fill in the formalities. This is what one does when not putting detailed comments everywhere in the program, but only at crucial points. Of course, what is obvious is not always true, but once one knows where the holes are they are more controllable.

Third, the idea of filling in a hole just to be sure is not so frightening.

Section 25.4 gives some historical notes, and discusses briefly some related approaches to the same problems.

25.2 Program logic

We present a logic that aims at justifying program sequents (or program assertions) of the form:

$\{P\}C\{Q\}$

where P and Q are formulas (logical conditions on the state of the computer), and C is a command in the programming language. (We shall also see how to allow C to be an expression.) This is to mean that if P holds before C is executed, then C will terminate in a state with Q holding.

Such a sequent is often called a Hoare triple after the work of C.A.R. Hoare (1969); but whereas Hoare had a *partial* correctness interpretation – if P holds before C, and *if C terminates*, then Q will hold afterwards – the interpretation here is one of total correctness. (Also, Hoare wrote 'P{C}Q' for his triple.) These concepts were briefly introduced in Chapter 2 but a more complete treatment of the approach is given here, showing how to deal with fairly substantial programs.

Here P and Q are called the premiss and conclusion of the sequent. This is non-standard. They are commonly called the pre-condition and post-condition, for obvious reasons. However, those terms will be reserved for specifications, where they are supposed to describe the full intended behaviour of the routine, and not just a particular true sequent.

25.2.0.1 Sequents and proofs

The word 'sequent' has a precise meaning in formal logic. In ordinary mathematics, there is the notion of proving a formula, Q, possibly starting from an assumption, P. There are various techniques for doing this, depending on the structures of P and Q. For instance, if P is a disjunction $P_1 \vee P_2 (P_1$ *or* $P_2)$, we do a case analysis and prove Q first from P_1 on its own, and then from P_2.

These techniques form what might be described as 'natural deduction', but there is also a formal theory of natural deduction that describes them.

When we have proved Q from P, we express this by the sequent P ⊢ Q. The symbol '⊢' is called a turnstile. Although it carries the exact meaning of 'we have found a proof that . . . ', it is clearly related to the logical connective →. In fact P ⊢ Q if and only if (iff) **true** ⊢ $\forall x_0, x_1, \ldots (P{\rightarrow}Q)$ where the x_is are the free variables of P and Q, i.e. the variables which are not bound to particular values.

This defines the valid sequents in terms of proofs, but there is an independent, more abstract description using the sequent calculus. This gives a set of rules, each one saying that if we have already proved certain sequents (written above a horizontal line), then we can infer another (written below). For instance, our technique of case analysis corresponds to a rule:

$$\text{Lv:} \quad \frac{P_1 \vdash Q, P_2 \vdash Q}{P_1 \vee P_2 \vdash Q}$$

(We give this rule the name Lv because it shows how to deal with ∨ on the left of the turnstile.)

Since the sequent calculus is supposed to agree with natural deduction, each rule had better represent a way of converting proofs of the top sequents to a new proof of the bottom one – the rule above just represents the way that natural deduction combines the ingredients of a case analysis. The rules of the sequent calculus can also be used independently to get valid sequents without reference to the natural deduction proofs. (A clear, careful and entertainingly opinionated account of this is given in Girard *et al.* (1988).)

25.2.0.2 Compositional rules

For the program logic, rules of sequent calculus for {P}C{Q} will be given along similar lines. An informal underlying idea of a proof of {P}C{Q} is, more or less, the annotation of the program C with all the mid-conditions needed to get from P to Q. This provides the rationale for the rules of the sequent calculus. Each one implicitly answers the question, 'Where do you put the mid-conditions for C?'. For instance, when C is of the form $C_1;C_2$, the mid-condition (M, say) goes at the semicolon and divides the proof into two parts, for C_1 and C_2. The rule is:

$$\text{Seq:} \quad \frac{\{P\}C_1\{M\}, \{M\}C_2\{Q\}}{\{P\}C_1;C_2\{Q\}}$$

This rule establishes sequents about a composite command $C_1;C_2$ from sequents about its components C_1 and C_2, and such rules are called compositional. All the rules for composite commands work like this.

25.2.0.3 Top-down programming

So far the proof rules have been described as showing how to arrive at sequents {P}C{Q} where P, Q and C are all known. This represents the intentions of the 'well-intentioned hacker'. What is much more useful is to use the rules *backwards*.

Typically, P and Q are known at an early stage, but not C. Of course, one's programming skills are needed in working C out, but suppose as a first step we decide on a loop structure, with some initialization and finalization:

```
C =
    C₁;          {initialize}
    while B do
        C₂       {loop}
    od;
    C₃           {finalize}
```

The rules tell us how we could prove {P}C{Q}, and by compositionality this will be in terms of similar sequents for the components C_1, C_2 and C_3 (the details will appear in Section 25.2.7 on looping), which arise in effect from putting mid-conditions at key points. In this case, the key point is at the head of the loop, where the mid-condition is supposed to be true on each iteration. This means that the action of the loop body C_2 must not vary the truth of the key mid-condition, and it is called the loop invariant. Let us call it I. Let us also assume that evaluating the loop test B has no side-effects. (We shall actually see how to drop this assumption, but it does simplify the reasoning if it can be arranged.) If the test succeeds, we reach the top of C_2 knowing that I still holds, and B holds too: in other words, we have the conjunction I ∧ B (I *and* B). On the other hand, if the test fails (so we have its negation ¬B, i.e. *not* B), we reach the top of C_3 knowing I ∧ ¬B.

All this is easily seen in terms of flowcharts (*Figure 25.3*).

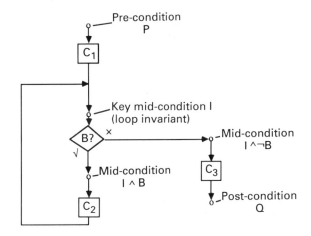

Figure 25.3

Finding a loop invariant, I, requires some programming skill. It describes how we envisage the program working part way through its execution. But by formulating it we reduce the original contract {P}C{Q} for C to some subcontracts for the components C_i, thus simplifying the original problem. In one direction, this is a proof rule:

$$\frac{\{P\}\,C_1\,\{I\}, \{I \wedge B\}\,C_2\,\{I\}, \{I \wedge \neg B\}\,C_3\,\{Q\}}{\{P\}\,C_1; \textbf{while } B \textbf{ do } C_2 \textbf{ od; } C_3\,\{Q\}}$$

and this proof rule derives compositionally from those for i.e.';' and **while**. (This is not quite the whole story, because we must also show that the loop terminates.) The backward direction shows how to put two ingredients – the loop structure and the invariant – into the program and turn the contract into smaller subcontracts. This top-down method is often known as stepwise refinement. It will be seen in detail in the example of Section 25.3.

For informal reasoning one would normally introduce conditions only at key points: the beginning, the end, jump destinations and perhaps some others. That the pre-condition holds is an assumption. But, given that, we can reason to show that the next mid-condition will also hold, and, given that, so will the following one, and so on. Hence we show that each mid-condition will hold whenever program control passes it, and so if the program terminates then the post-condition will hold.

There must also be some argument to show that the program will terminate.

This is the informal scheme, but it can be carried out with reasonable mathematical rigour and is the way the methods are applied in practice. Complete formality requires breaking down the program into its irreducible components, in effect putting a mid-condition at every semicolon. As an example, it would normally be accepted as clear that the sequent:

$$\{x = x_0 \wedge y = y_0\} \ z := x; \ x := y; \ y := z \ \{x = y_0 \wedge y = x_0\}$$

is valid. Such reasoning is rigorous enough. For complete formality, however, you could demonstrate:

$$\{x = x_0 \wedge y = y_0\} \ z := x \ \{z = x_0 \wedge y = y_0\}$$
$$\{z = x_0 \wedge y = y_0\} \ x := y \ \{x = y_0 \wedge z = x_0\}$$
$$\{x = y_0 \wedge z = x_0\} \ y := z \ \{x = y_0 \wedge y = x_0\}$$

The greater formality would also be appropriate in cases of doubt, for instance if x, y and z were not distinct simple variables but involved arrays or aliasing (although it is only fair to say that it is difficult to give valid proof rules to cover these possibilities).

25.2.1 Basic concepts in the logic

It has already been seen that the important units of our reasoning are the program sequents $\{P\}C\{Q\}$ where P and Q are logical formulas, and C is a program command, possibly composite (it will also be seen how C can be an expression). It remains to set out the notation that will be used for the formulae and commands.

The notation for commands is that of computer programming languages. Here it will tend to follow, in a superficial way, Algol 68; but what is really being described is not some minute fragment of Algol 68, but how one reasons about particular kinds of constructs of imperative programming: assignment, iteration, and so on. There is no need to give a formal definition of the syntax here. Each proof rule will implicitly define a syntax for the corresponding construct, as well as semantics (by its logical content, how to reason about the construct).

The notation for the formulas is basically that of standard predicate logic, with the usual distinction between terms (things) and formulae (statements about them). Usage here has the following features:

1. All terms are typed. The type structure should be that of the underlying mathematical structure of the problem rather than a slavish reproduction of the type structure of the programming language, but obviously the two are related. Only two types are explicitly required by the formalism: **bool**, with elements t and f (the Booleans true and false), and **nat**, the type of natural numbers, with elements 0, 1, 2, 3, . . .

   The notation 't:Type' is used to say that a term t has that Type.

2. A distinction is drawn between *identifiers*, which are used in the computer program and stored in the computer (one would normally call these 'variables'), and *variables* in the logical sense, which are not stored in the computer but are introduced in the proof as notation for values. Both can be used as terms in the logic. The distinction will be enlarged upon later.

   Terms and formulae that do not contain any identifiers keep the same value throughout the computation, and are called rigid.

3. There is a special term **result**, which means 'the result of the program expression that has just been evaluated'. This can be thought of as an extra identifier that is accessible from the program only by indirect means, such as assignments. The way this is used will become clear later.

4. All sources of partiality and non-termination are excluded from the logic. User-defined functions and predicates from the program are in general not permitted in terms and formulae, and even some primitive functions, such as division, or Head and Tail for lists, may be excluded; their place is in the commands in program sequents.

   When an expression in the programming language uses only those constructions that are acceptable in the logical language, then that expression is called simple. A simple expression can be used as a term in the logic; by abuse of notation, a simple expression of type **bool** can be used as a formula in the logic.

5. The following standard logical connectives are used:

   (a) **true, false**
   (b) $\wedge$ and (conjunction)
   (c) $\vee$ inclusive or (disjunction)
   (d) $\neg$ not
   (e) $\rightarrow$ implies
   (f) $\leftrightarrow$ implies and is implied by
   (g) $\exists$ existential quantification, 'there exists'
   (h) $\forall$ universal quantification, 'for all'

   For details of the meanings of these connectives see Chapter 1.

6. For both terms and formulae, notation such as 'P[$s, t, \ldots / x_0, y_0, \ldots$]' is used for substitution. It means 'P, but with free (unquantified) occurrences of the variables (or identifiers) x_0, y_0, etc. replaced by the terms s, t, etc.' Read the symbol '/' here as 'for'.

7. When adopting standard mathematical notation, it is important to be imaginative and flexible. For example, if the natural, human view of the computation is that it deals with lists, then do not be afraid to use mathematical list notation in your reasoning, even if the computer sees them as arrays. If it is natural to reason in terms of concatenation of lists, do not be afraid to do so even though for efficiency reasons you would never compute concatenations. Section 25.3 contains an example of reasoning with what are abstractly lists, but concretely (probably) files.

25.2.1.1 Identifiers and variables

To assert a property of the state of the computer, we must make statements about the identifiers that occur in the program. Thus after the assignment x := 2, the state satisfies the formula x = 2 and we can validly assert:

$$\{\textbf{true}\} \ x := 2 \ \{x = 2\}$$

When the identifier x occurs in a formula, it just represents its value at some particular time, although this value may have changed by the next formula (mid-condition). This change can be seen as taking place *with time*.

Although it is common to call the identifiers *variables*, we shall restrict this word for those symbols like y_0 in:

$$\{y = y_0\} \ x := y \ \{x = y_0\}$$

which behave quite differently. y_0 is not stored in the computer, and will not change with time. It is notation introduced to stand in eternity for the value held by the identifier y before the assignment. On the other hand, it can still vary (which is why it is called a variable), but in a way that is perhaps more *spatial*. This is because it does not matter what particular value y had before the assignment; x will have that same value after. y_0 can therefore be seen as a variable parameter for a whole family of more specialized sequents, namely (taking for example the case where y is of type **nat**) the family of sequents, all valid:

$$\{y = 0\}\, x := y\, \{x = 0\}$$
$$\{y = 1\}\, x := y\, \{x = 1\}$$
$$\{y = 2\}\, x := y\, \{x = 2\}$$
$$\vdots$$

Identifiers such as we have described them are sometimes known technically as non-rigid designators. 'Designator', in contrast with 'variable', means something that cannot be varied – at least, not in the 'spatial' way. 'Non-rigid' means that, nevertheless, it can be varied in some other way – over time.

An important use of variables in logic is to make sense of quantification, and this can be understood as taking the potential for variation inherent in the variables, using it in some way and saying something about it. For example, the existentially quantified formula:

$$\exists x_0 : \textbf{nat}.\ 154 = 2 \ast x_0,$$ 'there exists a natural number x_0 such that $154 = 2 \ast x_0$'

says that as you vary x_0 over all possible natural numbers, you will find one which when doubled gives 154. Similarly, the universally quantified statement:

$$\forall x_0 : \textbf{nat}.\ (x_0 \leqslant 9 \vee x_0 \geqslant 10)$$

says that as you vary x_0 over all possible natural numbers, for every single one you will find that it is either at most 9 or at least 10.

The variation exploited here is the 'spatial' one of variables, and not the temporal one of identifiers. It does not make complete sense to quantify an identifier, and it is not allowed.

The variable quantified is said to be bound by the quantifier, which means essentially that its potential for variation has been used up by the quantifier. We may no longer vary it ourselves by substituting other terms for it. If a variable is not bound, then it is free.

What is bound or free is not really the variable, but a given occurrence of it within a formula – the same variable (the same textual symbol) might be reused with a different meaning. For instance, '$n = 5 \vee \exists n.\ (n \leqslant 7 \wedge \forall n.n \geqslant 0)$' is shown in *Figure 25.4*.

The possibility of reuse causes many complications – for example, in the precise definition of substitution, which is explained in standard texts on logic. It is sensible to avoid these by using different variables for different uses.

It will usually be clear from the context whether a symbol is an identifier or a variable, but as a rough guide x, y, z, x', y' and z' will usually be identifiers, and $x_0, y_0, \ldots, r$ and n will usually be variables.

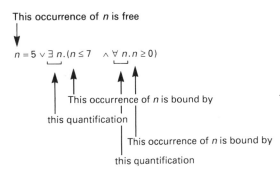

This occurrence of n is free

$n = 5 \vee \exists n.(n \leq 7 \quad \wedge\ \forall n.n \geq 0)$

This occurrence of n is bound by this quantification

This occurrence of n is bound by this quantification

Figure 25.4

A non-rigid designator **result** is used to refer to the result of an expression, so that an expression can also be specified by pre- and post-conditions. For instance, a square root function Sqrt(x) (as opposed to the procedure used in a previous example) might be specified by:

First method	or	Second method
Pre: $\quad x \geqslant 0$		$x \geqslant 0 \wedge x = x_0$
Post: $\quad \lvert \textbf{result}^2 - x \rvert < \varepsilon$		$\lvert \textbf{result}^2 - x_0 \rvert < \varepsilon$

The terms rigid and non-rigid will also be applied to terms and formulae. Something is rigid iff it will not change its value or truth over time, i.e. it contains no non-rigid designators. See *Table 25.1*.

Table 25.1 Summary of the different behaviours of identifiers and variables

	Identifiers (non-rigid designators)	Variables
Typical names	x, y, z, x', y', z' **result**	x_0, y_3, z_2, n
Nature	Known to computer	Names for abstract values
Variation	Over time, as computation proceeds. Non-rigid	By uniformly substituting values. Rigid
Quantifiable?	Not quantifiable	Quantifiable

25.2.2 Pure logic and program sequents

Irrespective of the programming language, there are some proof rules for program sequents that are purely logical in nature. These all derive from the idea that for each command C, the relation between P and Q in $\{P\}C\{Q\}$ is a generalized implication, and hence these rules are analogues of standard ones from the sequent calculus for sequents $P \vdash Q$:

Cons: $\dfrac{P' \vdash P,\ \{P\}C\{Q\},\ Q \vdash Q'}{\{P'\}C\{Q'\}}$ ('rule of consequence')

Rig: $\dfrac{\{P\}C\{Q\}}{\{P \wedge R\}C\{Q \wedge R\}}$ (provided R is rigid)

Subst: $\dfrac{\{P\}C\{Q\}}{\{P[t/x_0]\}C\{Q[t/x_0]\}}$ (provided t is rigid and x_0 is a variable)

R∧: $\dfrac{\{P\}C\{Q\},\ \{P\}C\{Q'\}}{\{P\}C\{Q \wedge Q'\}}$

L∨: $\dfrac{\{P\}C\{Q\},\ \{P'\}C\{Q\}}{\{P \vee P'\}C\{Q\}}$

Lfalse: $\dfrac{}{\{\textbf{false}\}C\{Q\}}$

L∃: $\dfrac{\{P\}C\{Q\}}{\{\exists x_0.P\}C\{Q\}}$ (provided x_0 is not free in Q)

Notes

1. The rule Cons corresponds to a familiar programming phe-nomenon that if one strengthens the pre-condition and weakens the post-condition, then the routine is easier to code – the specification is weakened. In this rule most of ordinary logic is swept under the carpet, since there is no explanation as to how to establish the logical sequents like $P' \vdash P$. Suffice it to say that ordinary mathematical reasoning is used to prove that P' implies P.

2. From Subst, it is clear that when free variables appear in a sequent then they are implicitly universally quantified. (They cannot be explicitly quantified, because the expression '$\forall x_0.\{P\}C\{Q\}$' isn't a sequent.) This is the formalization of the idea that the sequent $\{P\}C\{Q\}$ with free variables is a generic representative of a whole family of more specific sequents, parametrized by the possible values of the free variables.

3. R∧ corresponds to proving a conjunction by proving the two conjuncts separately. Lv corresponds to case analysis, as mentioned earlier. Lfalse corresponds to the idea of being able to prove anything from a contradiction. One might expect a matching rule Rtrue, to prove sequents $\{P\}C\{\textbf{true}\}$, but this would be unsound under our total correctness interpretation; it would make out that every C always terminates.

4. L∃ again is taken from standard logic, but perhaps its use needs explanation. One is trying to show that the mere existence of a value x_0 satisfying P would guarantee C's termination leaving Q. One therefore imagines the ghostly, quantified x_0 having materalized as an actual value called Oscar, say. What is important is that the new name is now a free variable in P, and that it must not clash with any other free variable already existing. One then proves $\{P[Oscar/x_0]\}C\{Q\}$. Oscar is a nice name; but for a systematic reuse of the variables, why not call it x_0 again? It makes no difference, so long as x_0 is not free in Q (so no clash). If there is a clash, if x_0 is free in Q, then you can use Subst to rename it.

   There is an example of reasoning with L∃ in Section 25.2.3 below, showing that two rules Spec1 and Spec2 are equivalent.

25.2.3 Subroutines

Subroutines are the key part of effective reasoning about programs, allowing one to decompose a large problem into smaller ones, and this is reflected in the fact that the head of a subroutine has long been recognized as an essential place to put comments – the specification of the subroutine.

The program sequents for subroutines have two aspects. First, from the point of view of the caller, they are instructions for the correct use of subroutine, showing how to reason with the calls when they are embedded in another program. Second, for the implementor, they are sequents about the implementing code that must be proved to be valid. Because these aspects are rather different in nature, two rules are given which are logically equivalent and convenient for the two different uses.

25.2.3.1 Specification statements

We can specify a subroutine by a pre-condition Pre (involving x) and a post-condition Post (involving x and x') where x and x' represent values before and after execution of the subroutine.

The single identifier x is being used to represent the vector of *all* identifiers. We shall want to use this subroutine in a top-down manner before we have coded it, so let us use a specifica-tion statement [Pre ⇒ Post]. Note that if Post involves the non-rigid designator **result**, then [Pre ⇒ Post] is actually a specifica-tion expression.

The two equivalent rules are:

Spec1:
$$\frac{}{\{\text{Pre} \wedge x = x_0\} \, [\text{Pre} \Rightarrow \text{Post}] \, \{\text{Post}[x_0, x \,/\, x, x']\}}$$

Spec2:

$$\frac{}{\{P \wedge \text{Pre}\} \, [\text{Pre} \Rightarrow \text{Post}] \, \{\exists x_0. \, (\text{Post} \wedge P \wedge \text{Pre})[x_0, x \,/\, x, x']\}}$$
(x_0 not free in Post, P or Pre)

As an implementor you use Spec1. Your aim is to produce code C satisfying:

$$\{\text{Pre} \wedge x = x_0\} \, C \, \{\text{Post}[x_0, x \,/\, x, x']\}$$

where x_0 is chosen so as not to clash with any variable already free in Pre or Post. You therefore gets a single generic pre-condition, parameterized by the possible values of x_0, and you want to compute from that to a single generic post-condition.

For the caller, on the other hand, it is rather inconvenient to have to introduce the logical variables x_0 whenever the subrou-tine is called. The caller will have, just before the call, some mid-condition, which will have to imply Pre (or the specification statement cannot be reasoned with at all), and hence is of the general form P ∧ Pre. Spec2 then says what is known for the next mid-condition.

Note how compositionality works here. [Pre ⇒ Post] is not built up from component statements, and so there are no subordinate sequents, or subcontracts, from which to build up the new sequent. That is why there are no sequents above the line.

Note also a particular case, for a specification expression without side-effects: it can be written in the form [Pre ⇒ Post ∧ x = x'], giving the rule:

Spec3:

$$\frac{}{\{P \wedge \text{Pre}\} \, [\text{Pre} \Rightarrow \text{Post} \wedge x = x'] \, \{P \wedge \text{Pre} \wedge \text{Post}[x \,/\, x']\}}$$

Two early accounts of the specification statement (with weakest pre-condition semantics, see Section 25.4) are given in Morris (1987) and Morgan (1988).

25.2.3.2 Spec1 and Spec2 are equivalent

To deduce Spec1 from Spec2, just set P to be the formula $x = x_0$.

For the converse, P ∧ Pre is equivalent to $\exists x_0.(P \wedge \text{Pre} \wedge x = x_0)$ where x_0 is a new variable (it is really just a notation for the value of x at that time). Therefore, by L∃, it suffices to prove:

$$\{P \wedge \text{Pre} \wedge x = x_0\} \, [\text{Pre} \Rightarrow \text{Post}] \, \{\exists x_0. \, (\text{Post} \wedge P \wedge \text{Pre}) \\ [x_0, x \,/\, x, x']\}$$

We know that:

$$P \wedge \text{Pre} \wedge x = x_0 \vdash \text{Pre} \wedge x = x_0 \wedge (P \wedge \text{Pre})[x_0/x]$$
$$\text{Post}[x_0, x \,/\, x, x'] \wedge (P \wedge \text{Pre})[x_0/x] \vdash \exists x_0. \, (\text{Post} \wedge P \wedge \text{Pre}) \\ [x_0, x \,/\, x, x']$$

so by Cons it suffices to show:

$$\{\text{Pre} \wedge x = x_0 \wedge (P \wedge \text{Pre})[x_0/x]\} \, [\text{Pre} \Rightarrow \text{Post}] \\ \{\text{Post}[x_0, x \,/\, x, x'] \wedge (P \wedge \text{Pre})[x_0/x]\}$$

This follows from Spec1 and Rig, because $(P \wedge \text{Pre})[x_0/x]$ is rigid (because x here is the vector of *all* identifiers).

25.2.4 Assignments

The problem here is to make sequents about an assignment $y := e$, where e satisfies $\{P\}\,e\,\{Q\}$ (recall that Q will contain the non-rigid designator **result**). Let us keep track of two intermediate values of y and **result**, at the point after e has been evaluated but before the assignment, by introducing variables y_{old} and r for them. Then at that point we have:

$$\exists y_{old},\, r.\ Q[y_{old},\, r\,/\,y,\, \textbf{result}]$$

and this is rigid enough to survive the assignment (the identifiers other than y are unchanged). This motivates the rule:

$$\text{Ass:} \quad \frac{\{P\}\,e\,\{Q\}}{\{P\}\,y := e\,\{\exists y_{old},\, r.\,(Q[y_{old},\, r\,/\,y,\, \textbf{result}] \wedge y = r)\}}$$

Ass works forwards from premiss to conclusion, but we can reverse this information flow in the useful special case where e is a simple expression. It then satisfies the sequent $\{P\}e\{P \wedge \textbf{result} = e\}$. Applying Ass, we obtain in this restricted case:

$$\{P\}\,y := e\,\{\exists y_{old}.\,(P[y_{old}/y] \wedge y = e[y_{old}/y])\}$$

Now suppose P takes the form Q[e/y]. Then the conclusion becomes:

$$\exists y_{old}.\,(Q[e[y_{old}/y]\,/\,y] \wedge y = e[y_{old}/y])$$

which implies Q. We deduce a proof rule:

$$\text{Assl:} \quad \frac{}{\{Q[e/y]\}\,y := e\,\{Q\}}$$

This is often presented as the proof rule for assignment, although as we have seen it relies on the simplicity of e. It is clearly much simpler than the more general case, and this illustrates in a formal setting the important idea that programs are easier to reason with if they use simple constructions and avoid side-effects.

25.2.5 Sequencing and skip

We have already seen the proof rules for sequencing:

$$\text{Seq:} \quad \frac{\{P\}\,C_1\,\{M\},\ \{M\}\,C_2\,\{Q\}}{\{P\}\,C_1;C_2\,\{Q\}}$$

The rule for **skip**, like Cons, acts to sweep the details of ordinary logic under the carpet:

$$\text{Skip:} \quad \frac{P \vdash Q}{\{P\}\,\textbf{skip}\,\{Q\}}$$

25.2.6 Conditionals

We take a general conditional, whether a statement or an expression, in the form:

if B then C else D fi

where B is of type **bool**. Then the proof rule is:

$$\text{If:} \quad \frac{\{P\}\,B\,\{M\}\ \ \{M[t/\textbf{result}]\}\,C\,\{Q\}\ \ \{M[f/\textbf{result}]\}\,D\,\{Q\}}{\{P\}\,\textbf{if B then C else D fi}\,\{Q\}}$$

In practical terms this is a computed version of the idea of case splitting in proofs.

When B is a simple expression, the rule can be simplified to:

$$\text{If1:} \quad \frac{\{P \wedge B\}\,C\,\{Q\},\ \ \{P \wedge \neg B\}\,D\,\{Q\}}{\{P\}\,\textbf{if B then C else D fi}\,\{Q\}}$$

25.2.7 Iteration

We consider loops of the form:

while B do C od

Let us first assume that B is a simple Boolean expression, so the necessary reasoning has already been outlined at the start of Section 25.2. We formulate a mid-condition I', say (we called it I before), called a loop invariant, and then the crucial piece of reasoning is to show that it is preserved by the loop code. This can be summarized in the partial correctness rule:

$$\frac{\{I' \wedge B\}\,C\,\{I'\}}{\{I'\}\,\textbf{while B do C od}\,\{I' \wedge \neg B\}} \quad \text{(partial correctness only!)}$$

Unfortunately, this does not guarantee total correctness. The mid-condition reasoning shows that starting from I', *if the loop terminates*, then it leaves $\{I' \wedge \neg B\}$. This is a definite gap in the reasoning, as can be seen by using the invariant P to 'prove' the sequent:

$$\{P\}\ \textbf{while true do skip od}\ \{Q\}$$

In other words, the infinite loop is a partially correct implementation of any specification at all.

To prove termination, we need some measure of how much progress is being made, and this is commonly done by using a value of type **nat** (usually an identifier or calculable from them) that will strictly decrease each time round the loop. This is called a loop variant. Since – as a natural number – the variant can never become negative, this shows that the looping must eventually stop.

Now define a new invariant I with a new variable n: **nat** to represent an upper bound on the variant:

$$I \equiv I' \wedge \text{variant} \leqslant n$$

We can recover I' from I, because $I' \Leftrightarrow \exists n.\,I$. Now the fact that C decreases the variant can be expressed by saying that for all n, if the variant was less than $n+1$ before C than it is less than n after. We also need to specify that C will not be entered if the variant has reached 0. Putting these together gives a rule for total correctness:

$$\text{While1:} \quad \frac{\{I[n+1/n] \wedge B\}\,C\,\{I\},\ \ I[0/n] \vdash \neg B}{\{\exists n.I\}\,\textbf{while B do C od}\,\{\exists n.I \wedge \neg B\}}$$

Note the existential quantifications. Before and after we just know that there is *some* n for which I holds, and it does not have to be the same value in the two cases. In other words, the variant always has some value, but we do not know what. For the purpose of reasoning outside the loop, we do not care.

Let us now drop our assumption about the simplicity of B. We shall therefore need a pair of loop invariants, J for before the calculation of B and I for after:

While:

$$\frac{\{J\}\,B\,\{I\},\ I[0, t/n, \textbf{result}] \vdash \text{false},\ \{I[n+1, t/n, \textbf{result}]\}\,C\,\{J\}}{\{\exists n.J\}\,\textbf{while B do C od}\,\{\exists n.\,I[f/\textbf{result}]\}}$$

25.2.8 Recursion

Sequents for recursively defined subroutines are proved by induction on a value analogous to loop variants. Suppose S is the recursively defined subroutine. We first try to show that it satisfies a sequent {P} S {Q}, where P (but not Q) contains a free logical variable n. If we can show:

1. Base case: {P[0/n]} S {Q}
2. Induction step: for any particular natural number N, if we are given:

   {P[N/n]} S {Q} (induction hypothesis)

then we can show {P[N + 1/n]} S{Q}

then we deduce {P} S {Q} and (by L∃) {∃n.P} S {Q}.

n is most useful as a bound on the depth of recursion. Then for the base we show that if P[0/n] holds before S, then S terminates leaving Q *without making any recursive calls of itself.* Similarly, for the induction step, we show that if P[N + 1/n] holds before S, then all the recursive calls are made with P[N/n] set up for them, so that we can use the induction hypothesis.

25.2.8.1 Tail recursion for loops

As an illustration, suppose S is recursively defined as:

S = **if** B **then** C;S **else skip fi**

This is just the tail recursive definition of **while** B **do** C **od**. It implies a rule:

$$\frac{\{P\} \text{ if B then C; S else skip fi} \{Q\}}{\{P\} S \{Q\}}$$

In other words, you can prove something about the loop by unwinding it by an iteration. Let us now try to prove While from this definition.

Assume we already know:

{J} B {I}
I[0, t/n, **result**] ⊢ **false**
{I[n + 1, t/n, **result**]} C {J}

It suffices by L∃ to show:

{J} S {∃n. I[f/ **result**]}

and we do this by induction on n.

In the Base case, {J[0/n]} B {I[0/n]}, and I[0/n][t/ **result**] ⊢ **false**: so there can't be any more iterations Formally:

{I[0/n][t/**result**]} C;S {∃n. I[f/**result**]}   (Cons and Lfalse)
{I[0/n][f/**result**]} skip {∃n. I[f/**result**]}   (Skip)
{J[0/n]} **if** B **then** C;S **else skip fi** {∃n. I[f/**result**]}   (If)
{J[0/n]} S {∃n. I[f/**result**]}   (definition of S)

For the induction step, suppose we already have {J[N/n]} S {∃n. I[f/**result**]} for a particular value N. We now have:

{J[N + 1/n]} B {I[N + 1/n]}   (Subst)
{I[N + 1/n][t/**result**]} C;S {∃n. I[f/**result**]}
        (by induction and Seq; the mid-condition is J[N/n])
{I[N + 1/n][f/**result**]} skip {∃n. I[f/**result**]}   (Skip)

and again we can put these together using If and the definition of S to get:

{J[N + 1/n]} S{∃n. I[f/**result**]}

25.3 Worked example

This shows the formalism in action, but it also illustrates some other points:

1. Working out specifications and loop invariants is a programming problem, albeit one largely independent of the programming language.
2. Diagrams are valuable. Quite often logic can be seen as formalizing a diagram.
3. An axiomatic method can be useful, basing the reasoning on some axioms. These are not 'so obvious that no sane man could doubt them'. They are the places where the formal reasoning was difficult, so that although the axioms seem obvious, they are spotlighted as clearly as possible to show where problems are most likely to arise.
4. The theory given above usually has a general version and a simple version that can be used in special cases (e.g. when expressions have no side effects). It is worth going for the simple version if you can.

Problem. Given two sorted files as input, output the merged file, still sorted. For the sake of argument, we assume that the entries in the files are natural numbers

Abstraction. For the sake of this reasoning, a file is just a sequence of natural numbers, i.e. a list. The language of lists is therefore used, with **nil** and < > for the empty list and concatenation. Note that although concatenation usually executes less efficiently than the cons operator, that is no cause to avoid it in the reasoning, where it is often clearer.

We can specify the procedure by the specification statement:

[Sorted(In1) ∧ Sorted(In2) ⇒ Sorted(Out′) ∧ Merge
(In1, In2, Out′)]

where In1, In2, Out: List. Anyone who calls our routine should treat it as though it were just this specification statement. It is safer for them not to delve into the code we use to implement it. For various reasons we may subsequently change the code, although it must still conform with the specification.

The specification here uses priming. In our internal reasoning, it will be more convenient to introduce variables $In1_0$ and $In2_0$ for the initial values of the identifiers In1 and In2. Our goal therefore (according to Spec1) is to find some code satisfying:

{Sorted(In1) ∧ Sorted(In2) ∧ In1 = $In1_0$ ∧ In2 = $In2_0$}
   Code
{Sorted(Out) ∧ Merge($In1_0$, $In2_0$, Out)}

25.3.1 Development

Figure 25.5 shows the state part way through the composition. Of the original input file $In1_0$, part (In1read) has been read through, and part (In1cur) is still left. $In2_0$ is similar. We are going to describe in predicate logic what the diagram says statically about intermediate states of the computer. This will form the loop invariant. The dynamic parts, the arrows and 'choose lesser', go into the code.

25.3.1.1 Loop invariant

Loop invariant LI ≡
Sorted(Out < > In1cur)
∧ Sorted(Out < > In2cur)
∧ ∃In1read, In2read: List.
   ($In1_0$ = In1read < > In1cur
   ∧ $In2_0$ = In2read < > In2cur
   ∧ Merge (In1read, In2read, Out))

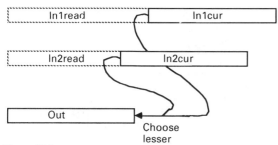

Figure 25.5

Notes:

1. In1cur, In2cur and Out are identifiers. $In1_0$, $In2_0$, In1read and In2read are variables.
2. Sorted (x) can be defined as

Sorted (x) ≡
$\forall i, j$: **nat**. $(0 \leqslant i \leqslant j < \text{length}(x) \rightarrow x[i] \leqslant x[j])$

'Sorted' provides a convenient abbreviation for this.

3. As for Merge, let us not even attempt to define it in predicate logic because it is complicated. We simply say that Merge (x, y, z) means that z is a merge of x and y. Consequently, we ought to be careful to notice what properties of Merge we use in our reasoning – this is the axiomatic approach mentioned above.
4. Sorted(Out < > In1cur) ∧ Sorted (Out < > In2cur) is a slick way of saying that entries are written to Out only when we know that they are no greater than anything yet to be read from In1cur or In2cur.
5. It is easy to miss out something vital from the invariant. This becomes apparent when the reasoning breaks down.

25.3.1.2 *Loop variant*

At every stage, one of In1cur and In2cur is beheaded and the other left unchanged, so the sum of their lengths steadily decreases. This sum is a suitable loop variant:

LV ≡ length (In1cur) + length (In2cur)

We shall go through the problem twice. The first time illustrates a level of reasoning that is at the normal level of mathematical proofs – the 'rigorous' level. This is the practical level at which one can gain the benefits of the method. Of course, even mathematical proofs are known from time to time to contain errors, but this does not mean that one erroneous method is merely replaced with another. As argued in Section 25.1, the logical method lies closer to the underlying idea of what the program is supposed to do. Moreover, the gaps in the rigorous level are intended to represent 'obvious' steps that could be filled in in full formal detail if doubts arose. Section 25.3.2 will give more detail of how the reasoning fits in with the formal rules of Section 2.

We first look at the diagram and its formula (loop invariant) in the two extreme cases.

25.3.1.3 *Initialization*

Initially, we try to set up In1cur = $In1_0$, In2cur = $In2_0$ and Out = **nil**. Under these conditions, the loop variant amounts to:

Sorted(**nil** < > $In1_0$)
∧ Sorted (**nil** < > $In2_0$)
∧ ∃ In1read, In2read: List.
 ($In1_0$ = In1read < > $In1_0$
 ∧ $In2_0$ = In2read < > $In2_0$
 ∧ Merge (In1read, In2read, **nil**))

This holds. The first two conjuncts say Sorted ($In1_0$) ∧ Sorted ($In2_0$), which follows from the pre-condition, and the existence of suitable In1read and In2read for the remainder is shown by taking them both to be **nil**.

Merge was not defined formally because it seemed too difficult, so it should be noted at this point that an axiom is assumed about it: that Merge (**nil, nil, nil**).

The code for the initialization is not difficult, we shall just make the assignments:

In1cur := In1;
In2cur := In2;
Out := **nil**;

25.3.1.4 *Finalization*

The end is reached when In1cur and In2cur are both empty, so we shall continue looping while the loop test LT still holds:

LT ≡ In1cur ≠ **nil** ∨ In2cur ≠ **nil**

When we stop, with LT failing, we have In1cur = In2cur = **nil**. The loop invariant then implies that (i.e. the diagram depicts a situation in which):

Sorted(Out)
∧ ∃ In1read, In2read: List.
 ($In1_0$ = In1read < > **nil** = In1read
 ∧ $In2_0$ = In2read < > **nil** = In2read
 ∧ Merge (In1read, In2read, Out))

In other words, Sorted(Out) ∧ Merge ($In1_0$, $In2_0$, Out)) – the post-condition.

The fact that what is written down so far as the loop invariant already provides this link between the pre- and post-conditions gives grounds to hope that it covers everything of importance that the diagram suggests. Axioms for Merge are dealt with more formally in Section 25.3.2.

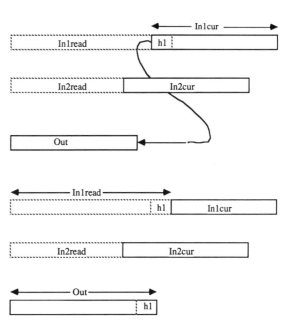

Figure 25.6

25.3.1.5 Re-establishing the invariant

There remains the subcontract for the loop body. This is where the arrows in the diagram are dealt with, and the note 'choose lesser'. We must implement the idea and show that it re-establishes the invariant and decreases the variant.

As long as not both In1cur and In2cur are empty, then we decrease the variant (which is the sum of their lengths) by choosing the head of either In1cur or In2cur, according to which head is smaller, taking that off its list and writing it out to Out. There are two cases, according to which list it is head of.

In Case 1, (see *Figure 25.6*), we take Head(In1cur) (h1, say) if either In2cur is empty, or both are non-empty but In1cur has the smaller head:

Case1 ≡
    In2cur = **nil** ∨∃h1, h2, x1, x2.
    (In1cur = (h1) < > x1 ∧ In2cur = (h2) < > x2 ∧ h1 ⩽ h2)

Note that, either way, (h1) < > In2cur is sorted. h1, x1, h2 and x2 have to be just the heads and tails of In1cur and In2cur, but we avoid mentioning the Head and Tail functions within the logic because they are only partial.

Clearly this idea decreases the loop variant. We must show that it also re-establishes the loop invariant. We know that the invariant held the previous time round; let us write $In1cur_{old}$, Out_{old}, $In1read_{old}$, etc. for the values at that time. Our idea is to make:

Out = Out_{old} < > (h1)   where h1 = Head($In1cur_{old}$)
In1cur = Tail($In1cur_{old}$)
In2cur = $In2cur_{old}$

We therefore want to prove:

Sorted(Out_{old} < > (h1) < > Tail($In1cur_{old}$))
∧ Sorted (Out_{old} < > (h1) < > $In2cur_{old}$)
∧ ∃ In1read, In2read: List.
    ($In1_0$ = In1read < > Tail($In1cur_{old}$)
    ∧ $In2_0$ = In2read < > $In2cur_{old}$
    ∧ Merge (In1read, In2read, Out_{old} < > (h1)))

(Tail has crept into the logic here. Never mind, it will be dealt with later by means of a specification expression.)

The first conjunct is easy. Out_{old} < > (h1) < > Tail($In1cur_{old}$) is equal to Out_{old} < > $In1cur_{old}$, which we know to be sorted from LI the previous time round. For the second, we use the following lemmas, which are both fairly obvious although they could be proved separately:

1. If x < > y < > z is sorted, then so is y.
2. If x < > (a) and (a) < > y are both sorted then so is
   x < > (a) < > y.

Now Out_{old} < > (h1) is a segment of Out_{old} < > $In1cur_{old}$, and hence sorted, and we have already noted that (h1) < > $In2cur_{old}$ is sorted, so it follows that Out_{old} < > (h1) < > $In2cur_{old}$ is sorted as required.

Finally, for the third conjunct, we take In1read = $In1read_{old}$ < > (h1) and In2read = $In2read_{old}$. This again suggests an axiom for Merge:

if Merge (x, y, z) then Merge (x, y < > (a), z < > (a))

(There is not much practical difference between these axioms for Merge and lemmas for Sorted. A definition has been given for Sorted, but if it was found that the definition did not imply a lemma that was wanted one might seriously question whether the definition is right.)

Again, the implementation here is simple:

Out : = Out < > (Head(In1cur));
In1cur : = Tail (In1cur);

This completes the reasoning for Case 1. The principal consequence needed from Case 1 was that (h1) < > In2cur was sorted, but note that it also allowed us to reason – in the presence of LT – that In1cur was non-empty, so that it was indeed valid to ask for its Head and Tail in the implementation.

Case 2 is to be the case when we take the head off In2cur. When Case 1 does not hold, we have:

In2cur ≠ **nil** ∧∀h1, h2, x1, x2.
    (In1cur ≠ (h1) < > x1 ∨ In2cur ≠ (h2) < > x2 ∨ h1 > h2)

In the case where In1cur ≠ **nil**, this implies that Head (In1cur) > Head(In2cur). Hence, eliminating Head as for Case 1, we have that ¬ Case 1 implies:

In1cur = **nil** ∨∃h1, h2, x1, x2.
    (In1cur = (h1) < > x1 ∧ In2cur = (h2) < > x2 ∧ h2 < h1)

This last condition is almost exactly what we get from Case 1 by exchanging In1cur and In2cur, except that it is slightly stronger because ⩽ is replaced by <. This is what would be expected from the symmetry of the problem. The entire reasoning of Case 1 now also works for Case 2, by exchanging 1s and 2s throughout.

25.3.1.6 Coding

We have now demonstrated the correctness of the following pseudocode, which we put together for the first time

```
In1cur : = In1;
In2cur : = In2;
Out : = nil;
while In1cur ≠ nil ∨ In2cur ≠ nil do
    if In2cur = nil
        ∨ (In1cur ≠ nil
        ∧ In2cur ≠ nil
        ∧ Head(In1cur) ⩽ Head(In2cur))
    then {Case1}
        Out : = Out < > Head(In1cur);
        In1cur : = Tail(In1cur)
    else {Case2}
        Out : = Out < > Head(In2cur));
        In2cur : = Tail(In2cur)
    fi
od
```

Converting this into standard programming languages should present no difficulty.

25.3.2 More detailed proof

Using the specification statement given at the start of Section 25.3, and using the rule Spec1 (and also the fact that the original value of Out is never used), the goal is to show:

{Pre ∧ In1 = $In1_0$ ∧ In2 = $In2_0$}
    Code
{Sorted (Out) ∧ Merge ($In1_0$, $In2_0$, Out)}

The code can be written in the form:
```
Code =
    Init;
    while LT do
        Body
    od;
    Final
```

We formulated a loop invariant LI and variant LV, and the reasoning then really proceeds in two stages. The first is that if Init sets up the variables as suggested, and if Body re-establishes the invariant and decreases the variant, and if Final does nothing at all, then Code works as required. In other words, it is enough to use 'sub-specification statements':

Init = [**true** $\Rightarrow$ In1cur$'$ = In1 $\wedge$ In2cur$'$ = In2 $\wedge$ Out$'$ = **nil**]
Body = [LI $\wedge$ LV $\leqslant$ n+1 $\wedge$ LT
$\qquad\qquad\qquad \Rightarrow$ (LI $\wedge$ LV $\leqslant$ n)[In1cur$'$/In1cur etc.]]
Final = **skip**

The second step is to write real code for these specification statements and show that it conforms.

25.3.2.1 Fitting together subspecifications

Lemma. {Pre $\wedge$ In1 = In1$_0$ $\wedge$ In2 = In2$_0$} Init {LI}.

Proof. The immediate application of Spec2 gives:

{Pre $\wedge$ In1 = In1$_0$ $\wedge$ In2 = In2$_0$} Init
{$\exists$ In1$_{old}$, In2$_{old}$, In1cur$_{old}$, In2cur$_{old}$, Out$_{old}$.
(Pre [In1$_{old}$, In2$_{old}$/In1, In2]
$\wedge$ In1$_{old}$ = In1$_0$ $\wedge$ In2$_{old}$ = In2$_0$
$\wedge$ In1cur = In1$_{old}$ $\wedge$ In2cur = In2$_{old}$ $\wedge$ Out = **nil**)}

but the conclusion of this implies:

Pre [In1$_0$, In2$_0$/In1, In2]
$\qquad \wedge$ In1cur = In1$_0$ $\wedge$ In2cur = In2$_0$ $\wedge$ Out = **nil**
which in turn, as argued in Section 25.3.1, implies LI.

Lemma. {LI} **while** LT **do** Body **od** {LI $\wedge \neg$LT}.

Proof. As already mentioned, we combine the invariant and variant into a single formula:

I $\equiv$ LI $\wedge$ LV $\leqslant$ n

Then LI $\Leftrightarrow \exists n$.I, and what we are proving amounts to:

{$\exists n$. I} **while** LT **do** Body **od** {$\exists n$. I $\wedge \neg$LT}

This is now in the form produced in the rule While1:

I[0/n] $\Leftrightarrow$ LI $\wedge$ LV $\leqslant$ 0
$\qquad\quad \Leftrightarrow$ LI $\wedge$ In1cur = **nil** $\wedge$ In2cur = **nil**
$\qquad\quad \Rightarrow \neg$LT

{I[n+1/n] $\wedge$ LT} Body {I} follows directly from the specification statement used for Body.

Lemma. {LI $\wedge \neg$LT} **skip** {Sorted(Out) $\wedge$ Merge(In1$_0$, In2$_0$, Out)}

Proof. LI $\wedge \neg$LT $\vdash$ Sorted(Out) $\wedge$ Merge(In1$_0$, In2$_0$, Out) by the reasoning already given in Section 25.3.1.

We now have two mid-conditions so that we can use Seq to put the three lemmas together and obtain the overall result for Code.

25.3.2.2 Initialization

We now start actual coding, and define:

Init =
In1cur := In1;
In2cur := In2;
Out := **nil**

We must prove (from Spec1):

{In1 = In1$_0$ $\wedge$ In2 = In2$_0$ $\wedge$ In1cur = In1cur$_0$ $\wedge$ In2cur = In2cur$_0$ $\wedge$ Out = Out$_0$}
$\qquad$ Init {In1cur = In1$_0$ $\wedge$ In2cur = In2$_0$ $\wedge$ Out = **nil**}

This is most easily shown by applying Ass1 three times, to obtain:

{In1 = In1$_0$ $\wedge$ In2 = In2$_0$ $\wedge$ **nil** = **nil**}
$\qquad$ Init {In1cur = In1$_0$ $\wedge$ In2cur = In2$_0$ $\wedge$ Out = **nil**}

25.3.2.3 Body of loop

This is defined by:

Body =
$\quad$ **if** In2cur = **nil**
$\quad$ $\vee$ (In1cur $\neq$ **nil**
$\quad\quad$ $\wedge$ In2cur $\neq$ **nil**
$\quad\quad$ $\wedge$ Head(In1cur) $\leqslant$ Head(In2cur)) **then**
$\quad$ Out := Out < > Head(In1cur);
$\quad$ In1cur := Tail(In1cur)
$\quad$ **else**
$\quad$ Out := Out < > (Head(In2cur));
$\quad$ In2cur := Tail(In2cur)
$\quad$ **fi**

Because the post-condition of the specification statement does not refer to the values before, it suffices to prove:

{LI $\wedge$ LV $\leqslant$ n+1 $\wedge$ LT} Body {(LI $\wedge$ LV $\leqslant$ n)}

Now the test in the **if** statement is not actually a simple expression for the condition Case 1, because it uses the partial function Head, but we shall treat it as one. It is worth noting that our care in guarding the calls of Head with tests for emptiness may be wasted with some implementations of some languages (such as Pascal), where the order in which the parts of Boolean expressions are evaluated may be undefined.

As an exercise, one could replace this test by the specification expression:

[LT $\Rightarrow$ (Case1 $\wedge$ **result** = t $\vee \neg$Case1 $\wedge$ **result** = f) $\wedge$ x$'$ = x]

(where x is the vector of all identifiers, so that "x$'$ = x$'$" specifies no side-effects), and use If instead of If1.

Lemma:

{LI $\wedge$ LV $\leqslant$ n+1 $\wedge$ LT $\wedge$ Case1}
$\quad$ Out := Out < > (Head (In1cur));
$\quad$ In1cur := Tail (In1cur)
{LI $\wedge$ LV $\leqslant$ n}

Proof. We treat Head and Tail as being defined by specification expressions:

Head(y: List) = [y $\neq$ **nil** $\Rightarrow \exists$t: List. y =
$\qquad\qquad\qquad\qquad\qquad\qquad$ (**result**) < > t $\wedge$ x = x$'$]
Tail (y: List) = [y $\neq$ **nil** $\Rightarrow \exists$h: **nat**. y = (h) < >
$\qquad\qquad\qquad\qquad\qquad\qquad\qquad$ **result** $\wedge$ x = x$'$]

(Again, x represents the vector of all identifiers.)
Now LI $\wedge$ LV $\leqslant$ n+1 $\wedge$ LT $\wedge$ Case1 $\vdash$ In1cur $\neq$ **nil**, and Head (as also Tail) has no side-effects, so we can use Spec3 to obtain:

{LI $\wedge$ LV $\leqslant$ n+1 $\wedge$ LT $\wedge$ Case1} (Head(In1cur))

$\{LI \wedge LV \leqslant n+1 \wedge LT \wedge Case1 \wedge \exists t1: List. In1cur =$
$$(\textbf{result}) <> t1)\}$$

It follows (although there has not been a thorough enough discussion of expressions to show how formally) that:

$\{LI \wedge LV \leqslant n+1 \wedge LT \wedge Case1\} Out <> (Head(In1cur))$
$\{LI \wedge LV \leqslant n+1 \wedge LT \wedge Case1 \wedge \exists h1:\textbf{nat}, t1:List.$
$$(\textbf{result} = Out <> (h1) \wedge In1cur = (h1) <> t1)\}$$

Now from Ass:

$\{LI \wedge LV \leqslant n+1 \wedge LT \wedge Case1\} Out := Out <> (Head$
$$(In1cur))$$
$\{\exists Out_{old}, r. ((LI \wedge LV \leqslant n+1 \wedge LT \wedge Case1)[Out_{old}/Out]$
$\wedge \exists h1, t1. (r = Out_{old} <> (h1) \wedge In1cur = (h1) <>$
$$t1) \wedge Out = r)\}$$

The conclusion of this is equivalent to the condition X (say), defined as:

$\exists Out_{old}, h1, t1. ((LI \wedge LV \leqslant n+1 \wedge LT \wedge Case1)[Out_{old}/Out]$
$\wedge Out = Out_{old} <> (h1) \wedge In1cur = (h1) <> t1)$

X implies In1cur $\neq$ **nil**, so by a similar argument we get:

$\{X\} In1cur := Tail(In1cur)$
$\{\exists In1cur_{old}, h1x. (X[In1cur_{old}/In1cur] \wedge In1cur_{old} =$
$$(h1x) <> In1cur)\}$$

Expanding X, the conclusion here is equivalent to:

$\exists Out_{old}, h1, In1cur_{old}, h1x.$
$((LI \wedge LV \leqslant n+1 \wedge LT \wedge Case1)$
$$[Out_{old}, In1cur_{old}/Out, In1cur]$$
$\wedge Out = Out_{old} <> (h1)$
$\wedge In1cur_{old} = (h1) <> t1 \wedge In1cur_{old} = (h1x) <> In1cur)$

Using the property of lists that they decompose uniquely into head and tail, this condition is equivalent to:

$\exists Out_{old}, In1cur_{old}, h1. ((LI \wedge LV \leqslant n+1 \wedge LT \wedge Case1)$
$$[Out_{old}/Out, In1cur]$$
$\wedge Out = Out_{old} <> (h1) \wedge In1cur_{old} = (h1) <> In-$
1cur)

We must now show that this implies $LI \wedge LV \leqslant n$; but the argument for this is set out in Section 25.3.1.

Lemma:

$\{LI \wedge LV \leqslant n+1 \wedge LT \wedge \neg Case1\}$
$Out := Out <> (Head (In2cur));$
$In2cur := Tail (In2cur)$
$\{LI \wedge LV \leqslant n\}$

Proof. There is nothing new here.

Finally, we put the two lemmas together to get:

$\{LI \wedge LV \leqslant n+1 \wedge LT\} Body \{LI \wedge LV \leqslant n\}$

as required.

25.4 Notes

Floyd (1967) first proposed the idea of proving properties of flowchart programs by attaching conditions to the edges (as was done at the start of Section 25.2), and Hoare (1969) made the crucial step of applying the idea to structured programs using the program sequents and rules of program logic. Many other systems of program logic are ultimately based on his work, but they differ according to various considerations.

25.4.0.1 Total versus partial correctness

Hoare's original work was a proof system for sequents of partial correctness: 'if P holds before C is executed, *and if C terminates*, then Q will hold afterwards'. The proof rule for **while**-loops is then very simple – it is given in Section 25.2.7. One augments this to total correctness with a termination argument, and in Hoare's system there was a neat division between partial correctness sequents and termination proofs (using loop variants). This neat division gets lost in practice, particularly once subroutines are introduced by specification rather than by coding, and many systems since – e.g. Manna (1974), Gries (1981) – have axiomatized total correctness.

25.4.0.2 Side-effects and partiality in functions

Hoare's original rule for assignment (Ass1) has been quoted as sound, provided that the source expression e is simple, so that it can be used as a logical term. Many treatments omit this proviso and allow the logic to contain partial or divergent expressions of the programming language. Once this is done, ordinary logic no longer works (for instance, is the formula '1/0 = 2/0' true?) and must be replaced. This is the approach adopted in Dijkstra (1976), de Bakker (1980), Goldblatt (1981) and Jones (1986), whose treatment of the logic of partial functions (LPF) is particularly clear.

In contrast, this chapter has retained classical logic by excluding partial or user-defined functions from the logical formulas. Such functions can only be reasoned about indirectly, via logical conditions on the result, and not at all without a termination proof.

25.4.0.3 Variables versus identifiers

The distinction made here between logical variables and computer identifiers (non-rigid designators) is based on discussions with Dr T. Maibaum, for which he is greatly thanked. It is unlikely that the treatment given here is the last word on this particular issue. On the face of it, the distinction is closely connected with that between storage locations and values, and it remains to be seen what happens when one tries to introduce pointers. For similar reasons, the issue of parameter passing has been glossed over. (Another reason is that the reasoning ought to show that you don't mind in what order the parameters are evaluated, and this is intricate.)

25.4.0.4 Guarded Command Language

In Dijkstra's (1976) presentation of a program logic, he introduced the Guarded Command Language, GCL, and many subsequent workers have followed him in this. Guarded commands are of the form B→C where B (the guard) is a Boolean expression, and C is a command. This means, approximately, 'if B holds, then you can do C', but this is only approximate, because guarded commands are used not on their own but as components of conditionals and loops.

A conditional is of the form:

if $B_1{\rightarrow}C_1$ $\square$ ... $\square$ $B_n{\rightarrow}C_n$ **fi**

This means that if one of the guards holds, then the corresponding command is executed. If none of the guards hold, then that is an error. It is not an error if more than one holds. In that case, the computer chooses one of the corresponding commands to execute.

This means that the language is non-deterministic, and hence of some theoretical interest. Its effect on the program logic is that you must prove that, when the computer has a choice, you do not mind which it takes: the rule is:

$$\frac{\{P \wedge B_i\}\, C_i\, \{Q\}}{\{P \wedge (B_1 \vee ... \vee B_n)\}\, \textbf{if}...\textbf{fi}\, \{Q\}}$$

A loop is of the form:

do $B_1 \to C_1\ \square\ ...\ \square\ B_n \to C_n$ **od**

This means that if one of the guards holds, then the corresponding command is executed and the **do** command is repeated. If none of the guards hold, then looping terminates. Again, if more than one guard holds then the computer chooses one of the corresponding commands to execute. The proof rule for partial correctness is:

$$\frac{\{I \wedge B_i\}\, C_i\, \{I\}}{\{I\}\, \textbf{do}...\textbf{od}\, \{I \wedge \neg (B_1 \vee ... \vee B_n)\}}$$

25.4.0.5 Weakest pre-conditions

The ordinary logical sequent $P \vdash Q$, an assertion *about* formulae, is closely related to the formula $P \to Q$, and much of the interest of formal logic derives from the interplay between the 'external' sequents and the 'internal' formulas. In the same way, the program sequent $\{P\}\, C\, \{Q\}$ has an internal version $P \to [C]Q$, where $[C]Q$ is a new logical notation for the weakest precondition for Q after C, the weakest property of the starting state that guarantees that C will terminate leaving Q. $[C]Q$ is also written $wp(C, Q)$.

It sometimes happens that $[C]Q$ can already be expressed in the existing logic. For instance, if e is a simple expression, then $[y := e]Q \Leftrightarrow Q[e/y]$ (see Ass1). In general, $[C]Q$ is something new.

The whole theory of program logic can be rephrased in terms of the weakest pre-conditions, and this is the approach of Dijkstra (1976) (who originated them), Gries (1981), and Goldblatt (1982). Some aspects of the theory are very neat in these terms. For instance, reasoning about sequencing and assignments is determined by the equations:

$[C_1;C_2]Q = [C_1][C_2]Q$
$[y := e]Q = [e](/Q[\textbf{result}/y])$ (or $Q[e/y]$ if e is simple)

Other constructions, such as **while** loops, are harder to handle, although it can be done.

An interesting by-product is the idea that the meaning of a command C is the behaviour of [C] as a function mapping formulas to formulas, Q to $[C]Q$, in other words as a predicate transformer.

25.4.0.6 General reading

In addition to the specific references made already, some more general accounts are as follows. Dijkstra (1976) is the classic text on stepwise refinement, and Dijkstra and Feijen (1988) is a rather pure treatment of it as an undergraduate course. Backhouse (1986) and Dromey (1989) are two readable elementary introductions, Gries (1981) is excellent and practical, and de Bakker (1980) is a heroic account of partial correctness. Hayes (1987) and Jones (1980, 1986) treat particular specification languages, namely Z and VDM.

25.5 References

Backhouse, R. C. (1986) *Program Construction and Verification*, Prentice-Hall, Englewood Cliffs, USA

de Bakker, J. (1980) *Mathematical Theory of Program Correctness*, Prentice-Hall, Englewood Cliffs, USA

Dijkstra, E. W. (1976) *A Discipline of Programming*, Prentice-Hall, Englewood Cliffs, USA

Dijkstra, E. W. and Feijen, W. H. J. (1988) *A Method of Programming*, Addison-Wesley, Wokingham

Dromey, G. (1989) *Program Derivation*, Addison-Wesley, Sydney, Australia

Floyd, R. (1967) Assigning meanings to programs. In *Mathematical Aspects of Computer Science (Proceedings of the Symposia in Applied Mathematics XIX)*, (ed. J. T. Schwartz) American Mathematical Society, Providence, USA, pp. 19–32

Girard, J.-Y., Lafont, Y. and Taylor, P. (1988) *Proofs and Types*. Cambridge Tracts in Theoretical Computing Science 7, Cambridge University Press, Cambridge

Goldblatt, R. (1982) Axiomatizing the logic of computer programming. *Lecture Notes in Computer Science*, **130**, Springer-Verlag, Berlin

Gries, D. (1981) *The Science of Programming*, Springer-Verlag, New York, USA

Hayes, I. (ed) (1987). *Specification Case Studies*, Prentice-Hall, Englewood Cliffs, USA

Hoare, C. A. R. (1969) An axiomatic basis for computer programming. *Communications of the ACM*, **12**, 576-580, 583

Jones, C. B. (1980) *Software Development: a Rigorous Approach*, Prentice-Hall, Englewood Cliffs, USA

Jones, C. B. (1986) *Systematic Software Development Using VDM*, Prentice-Hall, Englewood Cliffs, USA

Kemeny, J. G. and Kurtz, T. E. (1971) *BASIC Programming*, Wiley, New York, USA

Manna, Z. (1974) *Mathematical Theory of Computation*, McGraw-Hill Kogakusha, Tokyo, Japan

Morgan, C. (1988) The specification statement. *ACM Transactions on Programming Languages and Systems (TOPLAS)*, **10**, 403-419

Morris, J. M. (1987) A theoretical basis for stepwise refinement and the programming calculus. *Science of Computer Programming* **9**, 287–306

26

Verification environments

Dan Craigen
Odyssey Research Associates, Ottawa

Contents

26.1 Introduction

Throughout the past two decades of computing science research, there have been significant efforts to increase the degree of mathematical rigour and discipline as applied to the programming process. Examples of such efforts include Hoare's work on proof systems (1969), Dijkstra's work on reasoning about programs (1976), the work on formal specification languages such as Z (Spivey, 1989), VDM (Jones, 1986) and Larch (Guttag *et al.*, 1985), and recent work on constructive type theory (Coquand and Huet, 1985; Constable *et al.*, 1986; Martin-Löf, 1984).

Verification environments are intended to support the application of mathematical principles to program development by harnessing the capabilities of computer systems. Arguably, there are three advantages arising from the application of verification environments (when contrasted with 'pencil and paper' development):

1. An increase in confidence of the programmer's logical reasoning.
2. A magnification of the programmer's ability.
3. The tracking of program development (configuration management).

Verification environments must include an implementation (or, at least, an equivalent formulation) of the logical system to be used for reasoning about programs. Consequently, there will be a mechanization of the basic axioms and of the inference rules of the logic. The mechanization of the logical system leads to a consistent application of the rules and increases confidence in the resulting proof by enforcing the strictures of the logical system. As a program is developed, a form of 'social process' occurs where the programmer describes the reasons why a program is correct and the verification environment rigorously checks each step.

Many of the propositions that arise from a verification effort are textually large yet intellectually shallow. Attempts to manipulate such propositions using 'pencil and paper' are error-fraught activities. Verification environments are better suited to generating and manipulating such propositions. As a result, they support the rigorous development of programs that otherwise would be difficult. The programmer's ability is magnified.

Finally, the tracking of program development, by a verification environment, is a basic database issue. The environment can determine the dependencies between sections of a program. When some program text is modified (and this may include the statements of supporting mathematical lemmata) the environment must recognize what effects the modification will have on other sections of the program and, most importantly, on previously completed proofs.

At present, the existing verification environments only weakly support the above perceived advantages. Existing environments are research prototypes and suffer from various weaknesses and lacunae (discussed later).

26.2 Classical structure of a verification environment

The classical structure of verification environments is based upon the conceptual work of Floyd (1967) and Hoare (1969). The conceptual framework is predicated upon a proof of 'correctness' (more accurately, 'consistency') that a program, written using an imperative language, is consistent with functional specifications describing the intended consequence of executing the program. In the Floyd-Hoare scheme, a program is annotated with Boolean assertions that express properties to be true of the program state when the program reaches the point of the annotation. While there are variations on the theme, the basic property proved is that if a program starts execution in a state satisfying a Boolean pre-condition, then, if the program terminates, it will do so in a state satisfying a Boolean post-condition. (A variation of this theme is to prove, in addition, that the program always terminates.)

A classical verification environment consists of:

1. An imperative programming language.
2. A specification language that is a derivative of first-order, typed, Predicate Calculus.
3. A Verification Condition Generator.
4. A proof checker or theorem prover.

The imperative programming languages are usually of the ALGOL 60, Pascal genre. The most complicated language features that have been supported by the verification environments are concurrency (e.g. the Gypsy Verification Environment's support of process communication via message buffers (Good *et al.*, 1979)), conditions (again, by Gypsy), data structures consisting of pointers (e.g. the Stanford Pascal Verifier (Stanford Verification Group, 1979)), and type abstraction (by various systems).

Since the specification language is a derivative of first-order, typed, Predicate Calculus. one is able to use universal and existential quantification, and function and constant symbols to express a program's putative functionality.

There has not yet been convergence on whether verification environments should present a single linguistic framework that embodies both the specification language and implementation language supported by the environment, or whether the languages should be separate, but related. With a single linguistic framework, there is only the one conceptual framework that need be learned and the integration of specifications and implementations should be fairly clear. The main disadvantage of the single framework is that it is necessary to incorporate constraints from both the specification and implementation components in the language design. With the alternative approach, the single framework is lost and one needs to be concerned about how to relate the specification language to the implementation language, but one gains from the increased flexibility arising from developing the specification and implementation languages independently.

A Verification Condition Generator (VCG) (Igarashi *et al.*, 1975) is the component of a verification environment which generates a set of propositions, usually called verification conditions (VCs), from an annotated program. Successful proof of the VCs is sufficient to show that a program is consistent with its annotations. A VCG eliminates code fragments, using the code specific inference rules of Floyd-Hoare logics and, as a result, the set of propositions is expressed in the environment's variant of the Predicate Calculus.

A proof checker mechanizes the inference rules of the logical system and checks that each of the inference rules of the logic is properly applied during the proof process. A proof checker may be characterized by the following: it is incumbent upon the programmer to describe fully the putative proof; there are no heuristics to help with proof discovery. It is the presence of heuristics (automatic support) which, at least to this writer, distinguishes theorem provers from proof checkers. There is a wide variation in the degree of automatic support that proof checkers and theorem provers make available. For example, some systems require proofs to occur at the most basic levels (e.g. proofs by semantic tableau), whereas other systems have significant heuristics (e.g. for determining induction schemes) and decision procedures for various theories. Some of the more powerful theorem provers actually use proof techniques (e.g. Nelson-Oppen simplification in m-NEVER (Craigen *et al.*,

1988) which stray from the described logical system – but are semantically sound.

Some of the classical verification environments have additional mathematical analysis tools. For example, the Affirm system (Gerhart *et al.*, 1980) also includes tools for checking the consistency (using the Knuth-Bendix algorithm) and completeness of algebraic axioms.

26.3 Maximum element of an integer array

To make the above discussion more concrete, this section consists of the verification of a program that finds the value and location of a maximum element of an integer array. This example has been chosen for pedagogical purposes; significantly more difficult and extensive examples have been successfully proven using m-EVES (described below) and other verification environments. The verification environment used is called m-EVES and was developed under the sponsorship of the Canadian Department of National Defence. (EVES is an acronym for Environment for Verifying and Evaluating Software.) The paper entitled 'm-EVES: a tool for verifying software' presents an overview of the system and cites further references (Craigen *et al.*, 1988).

26.3.1 Introduction to m-EVES

Interaction with m-EVES occurs using a language called ECL (EVES command language). ECL is a derivative of the m-Verdi language to include m-EVES commands (principally theorem prover commands).

m-Verdi is a language which allows for the writing of formal specifications and the implementation of imperative programs. Hence, EVES has merged the two linguistic components of a verification environment. m-Verdi is strongly typed, has constructs for writing annotations (e.g. pre- and post-annotations, loop invariants), identifies those symbols that may be used solely for annotations and those that may, in addition, be used in an executable context; and supports information hiding and abstraction. The language is explicitly defined using denotational semantics (Stoy, 1977).

The m-EVES logic extends the first-order, typed, Predicate Calculus, so that new symbols can be added to a theory (using m-Verdi declarations) and includes proof obligations requiring the 'conservative extension' (from a model theorist's perspective) of theories, and that programs will terminate. m-EVES programs are specified in the Floyd-Hoare style.

By conservative extension it is meant that every mathematical model of the original theory can be extended to model the theory resulting from the addition of the new declaration. The advantages of guaranteeing such an extension are two-fold. First, if the original theory has a model (i.e. is logically consistent), then so has the extended theory. Second, all logical expressions of the theory retain their meaning in the extended theory. Some other systems guarantee a 'proof-theoretic conservative extension' property rather than the 'model-theoretic conservative extension' property described here.

Conceptually, the development of a program is the consequence of the incremental development of a theory. A theory consists of a vocabulary of symbols and axioms relating the symbols. Program development starts from an initial theory which includes symbols and axioms about integers, Booleans, characters and an initial segment of the ordinals. A theory is extended by an m-EVES declaration. In general, each declaration has a proof obligation showing the declaration is a 'conservative extension'.

The m-EVES theorem prover, m-NEVER ('Not the EVEs Rewriter') has powerful automatic capabilities, including the detection of propositional tautologies, reasoning about equality and integer relations, the application of rewrite rules, the application of forward chaining rules; and the Boyer-Moore (Boyer and Moore, 1979) style of automatic induction.

Interaction with m-EVES occurs either through a command processor or through an EMACS editor interface. (Many of the North American verification environments are using variants of EMACS as the principal interface.) m-EVES is implemented in Common Lisp and runs on a variety of hardware.

In the example, all m-EVES commands are bracketed by an exclamation mark and a semi-colon. The exclamation mark is the m-EVES prompt and the semi-colon the terminator for ECL commands.

26.3.2 Verification of program

The first declaration introduces an unspecified constant symbol N, which will be used as the upper bound on indices for the integer array. The prog keyword indicates that N may be used in executable contexts – it is not solely a specification symbol. The subsequent axiom consists of both heuristic and propositional content. Propositionally, it states that N is non-negative and that it is representable; heuristically, as a frule (a mnemonic for 'forward rule'), it states that whenever the constant symbol occurs in a verification condition, then the theorem prover may automatically assume the propositional content of the axiom.

```
!prog const N: INT;

!axiom N_POSITIVE () =
  frule
  triggers (N)
  begin AND (INT'GT (MAXINT, N),
        INT'GE (N, O))
  end N_POSITIVE;
```

The integer array type is now declared. This declaration results in the introduction of symbols and axioms for manipulating integer array values (e.g. indexing into an array and updating an array at a particular index). For this declaration there is a proof obligation of the form that the higher bound on indices is at least as great as the lower bound. The m-EVES command prove results in the non-inductive, automatic, capabilities of the theorem prover being applied to the proof obligation. In this instance, the proof is a simple consequence of the previous axiom and some simple integer inequality reasoning.

```
!prog type ARR = array 0  N of INT;

Beginning proof of ARR .
INT'LE (0, N)
!prove;

Which simplifies
with the assumptions N_POSITIVE to .
TRUE
```

The next two declarations introduce logical variables of the integer array type and of the integers. These declarations do not carry any connotation of program state; they purely extend the theory by adding a set of variable symbols. Further, for technical reasons, each declaration introduces a family of variable symbols. For example, with the first declaration, the symbols, A, A'345 and A'8493 are introduced. The main purpose for these additional variable symbols arises from the need for new symbols to avoid variable capture when performing substitution.

```
!prog var A: ARR;
!prog var VAL, INDEX, UB: INT;
```

To specify the program for determining the maximum element of an integer array, it is necessary to formalize the concept. The function MAXIMUM is defined recursively and captures the concept that VAL is at least as large as any of the values in an integer array A with indices in the range 0..UB. Since MAXIMUM is to be used solely in specification contexts, we do not include the prog keyword with its declaration.

```
!function MAXIMUM (A, UB, VAL): BOOL =
  pre AND (INT'GE (N, UB),
           INT'GE (UB, 0))
  measure ORDINAL'VAL (UB)
  begin if UB = 0
        then INT'GE (VAL, ARR'EXTRACT (A, UB))
        else AND (INT'GE (VAL, ARR'EXTRACT (A, UB)),
                  MAXIMUM (A, MINUS (UB, 1), VAL))
  end if
  end MAXIMUM;
```

All functions are total in m-EVES. However, it is only possible to express strong propositions about function applications which satisfy the pre-condition. Further, to exclude potential inconsistencies, each recursive function must be shown to be well defined. Basically, if one takes an operational view, it must be shown that each function application will terminate (when the function is called with parameters satisfying the pre-condition). An example of an unacceptable definition (in the absence of partial functions) is the function RUSSELL defined by:

```
function RUSSELL(VAL) : BOOL =
begin
  NOT(RUSSELL(VAL))
end RUSSELL
```

RUSSELL is axiomatically equivalent to false. Many of the existing verification environments do not adequately handle such declarations and, consequently, are mathematically unsound.

To accept the function MAXIMUM, it is necessary to exhibit an ordinal expression (of the function's parameters) which is strictly decreasing with each recursive call. In m-EVES, an initial segment of the ordinals (technically, the ordinals up to ω^ω) is supported and since the ordinals are well-ordered by the standard $<$ relation, a decreasing sequence of ordinal expressions must be finite. Hence, from an operational perspective, every call to the recursive function must terminate and return a well-defined value.

```
Beginning proof of MAXIMUM .
IMPLIES (AND
         (INT'GE (VAL, ARR'EXTRACT (A, UB)),
          UB < > 0.
          INT'GE (N, UB),
          INT'GE (UB, 0)).
         ORDINAL'LT (ORDINAL'VAL (MINUS (UB, 1)),
                     ORDINAL'VAL (UB)))
!prove;
```

Which simplifies
when rewriting with ORDINAL'LT_6;
with the assumptions N_POSITIVE to .
TRUE

For MAXIMUM, the parameter UB is decreasing on each recursive call. The appropriate proof obligation is generated by m-EVES and a single prove command is sufficient to show that MAXIMUM is well-defined. In this instance, the theorem prover has used facts about N, integer inequalities, and an axiom (that is a part of the initial theory) relating ordinal inequalities with integer inequalities.

Note that m-EVES has used a rewrite rule called ORDINAL'LT_6, which is one of the axioms of the initial theory. Most verification environments support the printing of introduced events, hence:

```
!print event ORDINAL'LT_6;

axiom  ORDINAL'LT_6
       (ORDINAL'M1, INT'I1, INT'I2) =
rule
begin  ORDINAL'LT
       (ORDINAL'EXTEND (ORDINAL'M1, INT'I1),
        ORDINAL'EXTEND (ORDINAL'M1, INT'I2))
    = AND (INT'GT (INT'I2, 0),
           INT'LT (INT'I1, INT'I2))
end ORDINAL'LT_6;
```

As noted, this is the fact which rewrites an ordinal inequality into a conjunction of integer inequalities. A rewrite rule differs from a forward rule by replacing a sub-expression by a logically equivalent sub-expression; a forward rule adds a known fact to a proposition.

To prove the program, a property about the MAXIMUM function needs to be developed. In particular, the following property is required:

```
!axiom MODIFYING_MAXIMUM_VALUE
       (A, UB, VAL'0, VAL'1) =
begin IMPLIES
      (AND (INT'GE (N, UB),
            INT'GE (UB, 0),
            MAXIMUM (A, UB, VAL'0),
            INT'GE (VAL'1, VAL'0)),
       MAXIMUM (A, UB, VAL'1))
end MODIFYING_MAXIMUM_VALUE;
!prove by induction;
```

This property is proved by induction. The prove by induction command instructs the theorem prover to choose heuristically an induction scheme and then attempt to prove the resulting proposition. The chosen induction scheme is based on the recursive definition of MAXIMUM and results in a scheme which is a minor variation of weak induction. (The induction heuristics used by m-NEVER are based on the work of Boyer and Moore (1979).)

m-EVES first prints the induction scheme to be used and then instantiates the induction to the proposition to be proved, and, in this instance, completes the proof. All that was required was the definition of MAXIMUM, integer reasoning, and the fact about N. (Actually, the fact N is non-negative is not really required; however, the heuristics used it anyway.)

```
Inducting using the following scheme .
AND (IMPLIES
     (NOT (AND(
           INT'GE (VAL'0, ARR'EXTRACT (A, UB)),
           UB < > O,
           INT'GE (N, UB),
           INT'GE (UB, 0),
           INT'GE (VAL'1, ARR'EXTRACT (A, UB)))),
     *P* (A, UB, VAL'0, VAL'1)),
```

```
IMPLIES (AND(
        INT'GE (VAL'0, ARR'EXTRACT (A, UB)),
        UB < > 0,
        INT'GE (N, UB),
        INT'GE (UB, 0),
        INT'GE (VAL'1, ARR'EXTRACT (A, UB)),
        *P* (A, MINUS (UB, 1), VAL'0, VAL'1)),
        *P* (A, UB, VAL'0, VAL'1)))
```

produces ...
```
AND (IMPLIES (NOT(
        AND (INT'GE (VAL'0, ARR'EXTRACT (A, UB)),
        UB < > 0,
        INT'GE (N, UB),
        INT'GE (UB, 0),
        INT'GE (VAL'1, ARR'EXTRACT (A, UB)))),
        IMPLIES (AND (INT'GE (N, UB)),
        INT'GE (UB, 0),
        MAXIMUM (A, UB, VAL'0),
        INT'GE (VAL'1, VAL'0),
        MAXIMUM (A, UB, VAL'1))),
IMPLIES(
        AND (INT'GE (VAL'0, ARR'EXTRACT (A, UB)),
        UB < > 0,
        INT'GE (N, UB),
        INT'GE (UB, 0),
        INT'GE (VAL'1, ARR'EXTRACT (A, UB)),
        IMPLIES (AND (INT'GE (N, MINUS (UB, 1)),
        INT'GE (MINUS (UB, 1), 0),
        MAXIMUM (A, MINUS (UB, 1), VAL'0),
        INT'GE (VAL'1, VAL'0)),
        MAXIMUM (A, MINUS (UB, 1), VAL'1))),
IMPLIES (AND (INT'GE (N, UB)),
        INT'GE (UB, 0),
        MAXIMUM (A, UB, VAL'0),
        INT'GE (VAL'1, VAL'0)),
        MAXIMUM (A, UB, VAL'1))))
```

Which simplifies
with invocation of MAXIMUM
with the assumptions N_POSITIVE to .
TRUE

Having proved the previous result, we are now in a position to present the annotated program:

```
!prog procedure FIND_MAXIMUM_INDEX
                    (lvar A, pvar VAL, pvar INDEX) =
  pre TRUE
  post AND (MAXIMUM (A, N, VAL),
            ARR'EXTRACT (A, INDEX) = VAL)
  begin
  pvar UB := 0
  INDEX := 0
  VAL := ARR'EXTRACT (A, 0)
  loop
    invariant
        AND (INT'GE (N, UB), INT'GE (UB, 0),
             MAXIMUM (A, UB, VAL),
             ARR'EXTRACT (A, INDEX) = VAL)
    measure ORDINAL'VAL (MINUS (N, UB))
    exit when INT'GE (UB, N)
    UB := EPLUS (UB, 1)
    if INT'GT (ARR'EXTRACT (A, UB), VAL)
    then VAL := ARR'EXTRACT (A, UB)
             INDEX := UB
    end if
  end loop
  end FIND_MAXIMUM-INDEX;
```

The post-condition states that VAL is larger than any of the elements in the array A and, further, that there is an index to the array A, such that VAL is the component value.

The bindings of the parameters, lvar and pvar indicate that A may not be modified by the procedure, but that both VAL and INDEX may be modified (by assignment statements and procedure calls). Similarly, the local binding of pvar to the variable UB indicates that UB may be modified. It is with the binding that logical variables are associated with program state.

The loop invariant slightly generalizes the post-condition and asserts that each time the loop body is to be executed, the invariant must be true of the state.

The measure expression is used to prove that the loop will terminate, in much the same sense that measure expressions are used in recursive function definitions. Here, it is claimed that the expression MINUS (N, UB) is decreasing with each loop body invocation.

The Verification Condition Generator produces the following verification condition:

```
Beginning proof of FIND_MAXIMUM_INDEX .
AND (
INT'GE (N, 0),
INT'LE (0, 0),
MAXIMUM (A, 0, ARR'EXTRACT (A, 0)),
ARR'EXTRACT (A, 0) = ARR'EXTRACT (A, 0),
all UB, A'0, VAL, INDEX:
  IMPLIES (
  AND (INT'GE (N, UB),
        INT'GE (UB, 0),
        MAXIMUM (A'0, UB, VAL),
        ARR'EXTRACT (A'0, INDEX) = VAL),
  if INT'GE (UB, N)
   then AND (MAXIMUM (A'0, N, VAL),
             ARR'EXTRACT (A'0, INDEX) = VAL)
   else AND (if INT'GT (ARR'EXTRACT
                      (A'0, EPLUS (UB, 1)), VAL)
     then AND (INT'GE (N, EPLUS (UB, 1)),
           INT'GE (EPLUS (UB, 1), 0),
           MAXIMUM (A'0,
                 EPLUS (UB, 1),
                 ARR'EXTRACT (A'0,
                       EPLUS (UB, 1))),
           ARR'EXTRACT (A'0, EPLUS (UB, 1))
             = ARR'EXTRACT (A'0, EPLUS (UB, 1)))
     else AND (INT'GE (N, EPLUS (UB, 1)),
           INT'GE (EPLUS (UB, 1), 0),
           MAXIMUM (A'0, EPLUS (UB, 1), VAL),
           ARR'EXTRACT (A'0, INDEX) = VAL)
   end if,
   ORDINAL'LT (ORDINAL'VAL
                 (MINUS (N, EPLUS (UB, 1))),
             ORDINAL'VAL (MINUS (N, UB))))
end if))
```

While somewhat complex for the uninitiated, the structure of the VC is determinable from the program structure. The first four conjuncts are the loop invariant on initial entry into the loop. The final conjunct captures the concept of the loop body being executed in an arbitrary state satisfying the loop invariant and, based upon the three possible paths of execution, must end in a state satisfying the post-condition, or end up in a state satisfying the loop invariant. If the program continues execution through the loop then the measure expression must be shown to be decreased by each path; hence, the final ordinal inequality.

This proposition is more difficult to prove than those previously. Here, we first transform the proposition by converting it into prenex normal form (using the prenex command), removing the quantifiers from the resulting proposition (using the open command), and applying the non-inductive portion of the prover to the resulting proposition. Loosely, the prenex command transforms a formula by moving all nested quantifiers, in a logically consistent manner, to the front of the proposition. (See, for example, Smullyan (1971) for the technical details of prenex normal forms.)

For brevity, the results of applying the first two commands are not included.

```
!prenex;
!open;
!prove;
```

Which simplifies
with invocation of EPLUS, MAXIMUM
when rewriting with ORDINAL'LT_6
with the assumptions MAXINT_REQUIREMENT,
MININT_REQUIREMENT, N_POSITIVE to . . .
IMPLIES (AND (INT'GE (N, UB),
         INT'GE (UB, 0),
         MAXIMUM (A'0, UB, VAL),
         ARR'EXTRACT (A'0, INDEX) = VAL),
  OR (INT'GE (UB, N),
        INT'GE (VAL, ARR'EXTRACT
                 (A'0, PLUS (UB, 1))),
      MAXIMUM (A'0, UB, ARR'EXTRACT
                 (A'0, PLUS (UB, 1)))))

The prove command has resulted in a proposition that is significantly simpler than the original verification condition. Analysis of this proposition suggests that the prover was unable to prove the maintenance of the loop invariant when the maximum value is being modified. All other cases, entry into the loop, exit from the loop to the post-condition, transformation from a state satisfying the loop invariant to a new state where the maximum value has not changed, and the termination proof, were all successfully completed.

Consequently, to prove the proposition, we use the 'modifying maximum value' result. The m-EVES use command allows us to use the requisite proposition and allows us to instantiate the axiom to the relevant values:

```
!use MODIFYING_MAXIMUM_VALUE A = A'0,
    UB = UB,
    VAL'0 = VAL,
    VAL'1 = ARR'EXTRACT (A'0, EPLUS (UB, 1));
```

Assuming MODIFYING_MAXIMUM_VALUE
with the instantiations: A = A'0
UB = UB
VAL'0 = VAL
VAL'1 = ARR'EXTRACT (A'0, EPLUS (UB, 1))
generates . . .
IMPLIES (AND (IMPLIES (AND (INT'GE (N, UB),
              INT'GE (UB, 0),
              MAXIMUM (A'0, UB, VAL),
              INT'GE (ARR'EXTRACT (A'0
                     EPLUS (UB, 1)),
                VAL)),
           MAXIMUM (A'0, UB,
             ARR'EXTRACT (A'0, EPLUS (UB, 1)))),
    INT'GE (N, UB),
    INT'GE (UB, 0),
    MAXIMUM (A'0, UB, VAL),
    ARR'EXTRACT (A'0, INDEX) = VAL),
  OR (INT'GE (UB, N),
    INT'GE (VAL, ARR'EXTRACT
                (A'0, PLUS (UB, 1))),
    MAXIMUM (A'0, UB, ARR'EXTRACT
               (A'0, PLUS (UB, 1)))))

Since the prover's heuristics are sensitive to the order in which information is presented in a proposition, we first rearrange the proposition so that simpler information occurs first. (Such rearrangements are one of the penalties arising from the use of heuristic theorem provers.) The proof of the program's correctness is then trivially completed.

```
!rearrange;
```

Rearranging gives .
IMPLIES
    (AND (INT'LT (UB, N),
         INT'GE (UB, 0),
         INT'GE (N, UB),
         INT'LT (VAL, ARR'EXTRACT
                     (A'0, PLUS (UB, 1))),
         ARR'EXTRACT (A'0, INDEX) = VAL,
         MAXIMUM (A'0, UB, VAL),
         IMPLIES
           (AND (INT'GE (UB, 0),
               INT'GE (N, UB),
               INT'GE (ARR'EXTRACT (A'0,
                        EPLUS (UB, 1))),
                       VAL),
             MAXIMUM (A'0, UB, VAL)),
           MAXIMUM (A'0, UB,
             ARR'EXTRACT (A'E,
                   EPLUS (UB, 1)))),
     MAXIMUM (A'0, UB, ARR'EXTRACT (A'0,
                        PLUS (UB, 1))))

```
!prove;
```

Which simplifies
with invocation of EPLUS
with the assumptions MAXINT_REQUIREMENT,
MININT_REQUIREMENT, N_POSITIVE to . . .
TRUE

So, with the completion of this proof, we should be finished with the overall development. To check that nothing has been left undone, we check the status of the system:

```
!print status;
```

Currently proving: FIND_MAXIMUM_INDEX

Proven formula list: ARR, MAXIMUM,
MODIFYING_MAXIMUM_VALUE,
FIND_MAXIMUM_INDEX

Unproven formula list: N_POSITIVE

Only one result has been left unproved and it is to be treated as an axiom – it is an assumption about the value of N. Most verification environments allow for checking the progress of program development.

Finally, verification environments do present varying degrees of online help. In the m-EVES case, there is substantial online documentation. For example, to determine what the functionality of the OPEN command is, one need only type help OPEN; and the relevant information is made available:

```
!help OPEN;
```

OPEN
open ;

If the current formula is contained within a series of universal quantifiers then the universal quantifiers are removed and the quantified variables become free variables. This may reduce the proof effort; however, the automatic part of the prover will not search for some possible refutations. The OPEN is not the exact inverse of CLOSE.

For an overview, see QUANTIFIERS.

The find maximum element example was presented since it is conceptually simple yet indicates some of the facilities to be found in a state of the art verification environment; significantly more difficult problems may be handled.

Further, the proofs made extensive use of the heuristic and automatic capabilities of the underlying theorem prover. In other verification environments, one would expect to interact at much lower levels of logical inference. One of the intentions with the m-EVES development is for the theorem prover to emit a detailed log of the proofs it has discovered. The proof log would then be validated by a separate proof checker. One reason for this proposed division is the view that proof checkers will be more amenable to rigorous analysis than a prover which includes extensive code supporting its heuristic capabilities.

26.4 Gypsy and Affirm

In this section, brief descriptions of two of the more successful North American verification environments are presented. In addition, pointers to other research efforts are listed.

The two verification environments that are described briefly are the Gypsy Verification Environment and Affirm. The descriptions will follow the form of the description of a classical verification environment.

Further, another simple example will be used to demonstrate some of the capabilities of these two systems. The example, drawn from the realm of computer security, is a specification property of a 'flow modulator'. A flow modulator is a message sanitization and downgrading device, i.e. a filter of messages flowing from one computer system to another. If a message satisfies the filter's acceptance test then it will be released to the receiving system; otherwise it is rejected. Here, we restrict ourselves to proving a simple inductive property about a sequence of accepted messages.

26.4.1 Gypsy Verification Environment

The Gypsy Verification Environment (GVE) (Good, 1985) was developed at The University of Texas at Austin, and is under further development by Computational Logic, Inc., also of Austin, Texas. Arguably, the GVE is the most successful of the verification environments and is being extensively used to prove security properties of various computer systems (e.g. Haigh and Young (1987)).

As with the m-EVES system, the GVE presents a single linguistic framework for the imperative specification languages; the language is called Gypsy. The imperative component of Gypsy is modelled after Pascal. The main distinguishing features are the exclusion of global state (state is passed through the parameter lists), of nested declarations, and of pointers. The language supports type abstraction, condition handling, concurrency (through the use of a 'cobegin' statement) and information is shared between processes by the use of message buffers. While pointers are excluded from Gypsy, the language does include sequence and mapping datatypes. Gypsy uses the 'scope' construct to encapsulate related declarations and to limit access to the declarations. Further, Gypsy relaxes the 'declaration before use' requirement that is found in most Pascal-genre languages. There are various linguistic forms for annotating Gypsy programs and there are proof rules supporting the proof

of concurrent programs. The specification language is a variant of first-order, typed, Predicate Calculus.

The GVE has a VCG that determines the appropriate VCs from an annotated GVE program. The GVE supports incremental development of programs and will, if a program is modified, determine those propositions that need to be reproved.

The GVE proof checker, though recently rewritten, is based upon work by Bledsoe and Bruell in the early 1970s. The proof style is of natural deduction and, of the three systems described here (GVE, Affirm and m-EVES), is the least automatic. From this writer's perspective, the GVE's proof checker is the most difficult to use successfully; it is not uncommon to find oneself stuck proving some mathematical trivia. (One of the advantages of semi-decision procedures for various theories is that the verification environment will often complete the trivial steps, and leave the mathematically sophisticated arguments to the program developer.)

The GVE is written in various dialects of Lisp and currently runs on Symbolics Lisp Machines, Suns, and Multics. Compilation of a Gypsy program requires the translation of the Gypsy program into BLISS and then the consequent compilation using a BLISS compiler. The primary interface with the GVE is through an EMACS editor. The GVE also has an information flow analysis tool and has released a version of the system which includes a well-foundedness tool (so that functions, such as the RUSSELL function, are rejected).

As noted, the GVE has been used in specifying the security properties of a number of systems. It has also been used to specify and to prove a realistic flow modulator and to specify and implement a special interface to the ARPAnet. Other pedagogical examples have also been performed.

26.4.1.1 A small example

In this section, a GVE version of the flow modulator is presented. (As with all the examples in this chapter, the transcripts are edited to account for space limitations and formatting requirements; only inessential details have been removed.)

Our first requirement is to load our flow modulator specification into the verification environment. We do this by using the parse command:

```
Gve –> help parse
```

Program units initially enter the system through a translator. The current translator consists of a complete Gypsy parser and semantic checker. A PARSE command is accompanied by a file specification. The specification can be TTY: which accepts input from the terminal. Input is terminated with a control-Z. All program units on the specified file are translated. Then, if they are all syntactically correct, they are entered into the system data base for subsequent reference. Note that external units may or may not be semantically correct.

Example: PARSE NETWORK.GYP

```
Gve –> parse gypsy.flow
```

The Gypsy text is now read into the system. Note the use of the pending keyword in the declarations of message and ok. By the use of this keyword we are deferring the implementations to be associated with these identifiers. Also note that, unlike both Affirm and m-EVES, the GVE includes a predefined concept of sequences.

```
scope flow_modulator =
begin

type message = pending;
type sequence_of_message = sequence of message;

function ok (m : message) : Boolean =
begin
  pending
end;
```

The following function, which is used for specification purposes only, extracts the elements of a sequence that satisfy the ok predicate. The expression null (...) denotes the sequence of message with zero length. The infix operator <: denotes the operation of appending an element to the end of a sequence.

```
function accepted_messages(s : sequence_of_message) :
                                 sequence_of_message =
begin
  exit
  (assume
    result
    = if s = null(sequence_of_message)
      then null(sequence_of_message)
      else if ok (last (s))
        then accepted_messages(nonlast(s)) <: last(s)
        else accepted_messages(nonlast(s))
          fi
      fi);
end;
```

The security property of note is now defined. A sequence of messages satisfies the property if and only if every element of the sequence satisfies the ok predicate.

```
function security_property(s : sequence_of message) :
                                 Boolean =
begin
  exit
  (assume
    result iff if s = null(sequence_of_message) then true
           else security_property(nonlast(s)) & ok(last(s))
           fi);
end;
```

And, finally, we state the lemma of interest:

```
lemma modulator_is_secure(s: sequence_of_message)
  = security_property(accepted_messages(s));

end;
```

> No syntax errors detected
> No semantic errors detected

In this instance, it was possible to load all the declarations without any syntax or semantic errors. If semantic errors had been detected, the declarations would still have been introduced into the GVE, and we would have had the option of either completely clearing the GVE database (and, hence, starting again) or to modify incrementally the incorrect declarations and then resolve the scope. The GVE also supports incremental development by, amongst other capabilities, allowing us to fill in the implementation details pertaining to pending declarations.

As with the other verification environments discussed in this paper, the GVE has commands allowing the system user to determine the status of the effort:

```
Gve -> print
  Object type -> status
  Units and/or VCs -> all
  on file -> tty:
```

The current design and verification status is:

SCOPE FLOW_MODULATOR

```
Waiting for VC generation:
    ACCEPTED_MESSAGES
    MODULATOR_IS_SECURE
    SECURITY_PROPERTY
Waiting for pending body to be filled in:
    OK
For specifications only:
    ACCEPTED_MESSAGES
    SECURITY_PROPERTY
Types, constants:
    MESSAGE SEQUENCE_OF_MESSAGE
```

Having introduced the declarations, we are now in position to generate the proof obligations. We do this by using the generate vcs command. As shown in the example, we can selectively generate the appropriate proof obligations or ask the GVE to generate all obligations. Here we have opted for the latter.

```
Gve -> generate vcS
  Unit names -> ?
Possibilities are:
ACCEPTED-MESSAGES MESSAGE
MODULATOR_IS_SECURE OK
SECURITY_PROPERTY
SEQUENCE_OF_MESSAGE
ALL THEM IT <CR> ? ^E
  Unit names -> all
  more Unit names ->
```

Changing default scope to FLOW_MODULATOR

```
VC for lemma MODULATOR_IS_SECURE:
all S#1 : SEQUENCE_OF_MESSAGE,
SECURITY_PROPERTY(ACCEPTED_MESSAGES(S#1))
```

```
Generating VCs for FUNCTION
                    SECURITY_PROPERTY ...
Generating VCs for FUNCTION
                    ACCEPTED_MESSAGES ...
```

Note: the body of OK is not defined.

Generating VCs for FUNCTION OK ...

```
**** SEQUENCE_OF_MESSAGE is not provable
**** MESSAGE is not provable
```

Note that we only have one interesting proof obligation, and this is confirmed by checking the status again. Besides generating the proof obligations, the GVE's verification condition generator also performs some simplification of the propositions.

```
Gve -> print
  Object type -> statUS
  Units and/or VCs -> all
  on file -> tty:
```

The current design and verification status is:

SCOPE FLOW_MODULATOR

    Waiting to be proved:
        MODULATOR_IS_SECURE
    ...
    Proved in vc generator:
        ACCEPTED_MESSAGES SECURITY_PROPERTY
    ...

Having generated the proof obligation for the lemma, we now move into the prover and try to determine the lemma's validity.

The prover explicitly differentiates between hypotheses and conclusions (unlike m-NEVER which always operates on the proposition as a single entity). In this instance, we have only a conclusion (identified by C1).

Obviously, to prove this proposition, we will need to use a version of sequence induction. The GVE has a collection of induction schemas (depending on the whether one is appending to the head or tail of a sequence, and on whether the sequence is to be bounded or not).

Note that in the induction command there is a change of capitalisation. The GVE supports command completion (unlike m-EVES) and, with lengthy commands such as this, is a useful facility.

Gve –> prove
    Unit or vc names –> modulator_is_secure

Entering Prover with lemma MODULATOR_IS_SECURE
all S # 1 : SEQUENCE_OF_MESSAGE,
SECURITY_PROPERTY(ACCEPTED_MESSAGES(S # 1))

  C1 : SECURITY_PROPERTY
              (ACCEPTED_MESSAGES (S # 1))

Prvr –> indUCT seQUENCE unBOUNDED sinGLE laST

Having generated the base case and the induction step, the GVE puts us in position to prove the base case. Unlike m-EVES and Affirm, the GVE forces us to develop the proof tree in a particular order. So, for example, we could not defer the proof of the base case and proceed with the induction step. (There are, admittedly, some ways around this, but are not as flexible as the m-EVES and Affirm techniques.)

The base case is proven by replacing the two left-most function applications by their definitions. This is performed using the expand command which also results in some simplification.

Proving Base case.
Prvr –> thEOREM
    C1 : SECURITY_PROPERTY(
           ACCEPTED_MESSAGES(
           NULL (SEQUENCE_OF_MESSAGE)))

Prvr –> expand
    Unit name –> accEPTED_MESSAGES

Prvr –> thEOREM

    C1 : SECURITY_PROPERTY

Prvr –> expAND
    Unit name –> secURITY_PROPERTY

Base case proved.

With the base case proven, we are now directed towards the induction step. We use the command theorem to see the current state of the proposition.

The infix operator denotes the operation of joining a sequence (in this case a single element sequence consisting of A # 1) to the end of another sequence.

Proving Induction step 1.
Prvr –> thEOREM

    H1 : SECURITY_PROPERTY
          (ACCEPTED_MESSAGES (S # 1))
  –>
    C1 : SECURITY_PROPERTY
          (ACCEPTED_MESSAGES (S # 1 @ [seq: A # 1]))

Our first step, is to expand the application of the accepted messages function. Since there are two applications of the function, the GVE presents us with the options of which applications to expand. The expansion is followed by a splitting of our analysis based on the truth or falsity of ok(a # 1):

Prvr –> expAND
    Unit name –> accEPTED_MESSAGES
Which ones?
    1. in H1: ACCEPTED_MESSAGES (S # 1)
    2. in C1: ACCEPTED_MESSAGES (S # 1 @ [seq: A # 1])

    < number-list >, ALL, NONE, PRINT, ˆE: 2

Prvr –> casesplit new
CASE: "ok(a # 1);"
CASE: "$done"

Proving Case 1.

Prvr –> thEOREM

    H1 : OK (A # 1)
    H2 : SECURITY_PROPERTY
              (ACCEPTED_MESSAGES (S # 1))
    H3 : SIZE (S # 1) in [0..POSINF]
  –>
    C1 : SECURITY_PROPERTY (if OK (A # 1)
      then ACCEPTED_MESSAGES (S # 1) @ [seq: A # 1]
      else ACCEPTED_MESSAGES (S # 1) fi)

The first case is based on the truth of the ok predicate. The first step is to apply the automatic facilities of the GVE to this proposition. This results in a simplification of the proposition. Note that the automatic facilities are much weaker than with m-NEVER.

Prvr –> qed

12. SIMPLIFY

Ran out of tricks.

Prvr –> thEOREM
    H1 : OK (A # 1)
    H2 : SECURITY_PROPERTY
              (ACCEPTED_MESSAGES (S # 1))
    H3 : SIZE (S # 1) in [0..POSINF]
  –>
    C1 : SECURITY_PROPERTY
          (ACCEPTED_MESSAGES (S # 1) @ [seq: A # 1])

What we need to do is to expand the security property function and then simplify. The proof of this case is then completed.

```
Prvr -> expAND
     Unit name -> securITY_PROPERTY
Which ones?
     1. in H2: SECURITY_PROPERTY
                         (ACCEPTED_MESSAGES (S # 1))
     2. in C1: SECURITY_PROPERTY
                         (ACCEPTED_MESSAGES (S # 1) @ [seq: A # 1])

     < number-list >, ALL, NONE, PRINT,  ˆE: 2

Prvr -> thEOREM
     H1 : SIZE (S # 1) in [0..POSINF]
     H2 : OK (A # 1)
     H3 : SECURITY_PROPERTY
                         (ACCEPTED_MESSAGES (S # 1))
  ->
     C1 : OK (A # 1)
     C2 : SECURITY_PROPERTY
                         (ACCEPTED_MESSAGES (S # 1))

Prvr -> simplify

Case 1 proved.
```

The proof of the second case proceeds requires only a simplification.

Proving Case 2.

```
Prvr -> thEOREM

     H1 : not OK (A # 1)
     H2 : SECURITY_PROPERTY
                         (ACCEPTED_MESSAGES (S # 1))
     H3 : SIZE (S # 1) in [0..POSINF]

  ->
     C1 : SECURITY_PROPERTY (if OK (A # 1)
          then  ACCEPTED_MESSAGES (S # 1)
                              @ [seq: A # 1]
               else ACCEPTED_MESSAGES (S # 1)
          fi)

Prvr -> qed

13. SIMPLIFY
Theorem proved!
```

Having completed the proof, we can look at the resulting proof tree for the lemma, by typing the command 'tree'. In fact, we could have printed the partial proof tree at any time.

```
Prvr -> tree

*1. SEQ-INDUCTION-LAST
     3. EXPAND ACCEPTED_MESSAGES
       6. EXPAND SECURITY_PROPERTY
          8. T
     4. EXPAND ACCEPTED_MESSAGES
       10. CASESPLIT
          12. SIMPLIFY
            15. EXPAND SECURITY_PROPERTY
               17. SIMPLIFY
                 19. T
          13. SIMPLIFY
            21. T
```

A distinction between theorem provers and proof checkers was mentioned earlier. In the author's view, the GVE prover is an example of a proof checker, while m-NEVER is a theorem prover. For the above proof, a single m-NEVER proof command is required (prove by induction).

26.4.2 Affirm

Affirm (Gerhart *et al.*, 1980) was developed at Information Sciences Institute, Marina del Rey, California and at General Electric's research labs in Schenectady, New York, and combines features of two previous research systems: DTVS and XIVUS. DTVS ('Data Type Verification System') focused on the use of algebraic axioms to specify datatypes. XIVUS (a play on the phrase 'x of us') was an earlier classical verification environment.

The imperative programming language supported by Affirm is a variant of Pascal called Affirm Pascal. Affirm Pascal is similar to Pascal except that various simplifying design decisions were made and linguistic forms were added so that programs could be annotated.

The specification language primarily consists of a variant of first-order, typed, Predicate Calculus, with equality, and extended so that algebraic datatypes can be defined. Using ideas reported in Guttag *et al.* (1978), Affirm supports the hierarchical development of abstract datatypes and programs.

Affirm has a VCG which will convert annotated Affirm Pascal programs into verification conditions.

The proof checker (Erickson and Musser, 1980) merges proof capabilities of DTVS and XIVUS. The proof style is that of natural deduction enhanced with unconditional rewrite rules. The natural deduction portion of the prover has the same genesis as the GVE. The rewrite rules are introduced as algebraic equalities in datatype specifications. The Affirm proof checker does not have the same wide range of heuristics that have been exhibited in the 'maximum' example. Analysis tools for determining the consistency (using the Knuth-Bendix algorithm) and completeness of algebraic datatypes are also present.

Further, Affirm supports the testing of specifications by permitting the symbolic execution of specifications. Affirm is implemented using various dialects of Interlisp and runs on DEC VAX machines. The interface to Affirm is via an Mlisp extension to the Unipress EMACS editor. Affirm makes extensive use of the Interlisp programming environment including the spelling checker and history mechanism.

Example verifications using Affirm include the specification and verification of a multiple-user file updating module, a proof of the Schorr-Waite marking algorithm, various protocol specifications and proofs, and a 'shutdown protocol' designed to be used in a redundant computer, fly-by-wire flight control system.

26.4.2.1 A small example

In this section, an Affirm version of the flow modulator is presented.

Our first step is to introduce a datatype that models messages. Here, we introduce the datatype, leaving it underspecified, at this level of abstraction. A logical variable, m 'of type message' is introduced, along with the signature of a function, ok, that will be used to accept or reject messages.

```
type message;

declare m:message;
interface ok(m):Boolean;

end;
```

Having introduced the message datatype, we now need to introduce (a portion of) the concept of sequences. Unlike the GVE, Affirm does not have a built-in concept of sequence. What follows is a fairly typical algebraic datatype specification.

The first part of the sequence theory description introduces the logical variables and the signatures of the functions to be defined, and imports (using the needs clause) the message datatype theory. Note that Affirm allows one to identify functions as to be printed using infix.

```
type sequence_of_message:

needs type message:

declare msg,msg1:message;
declare s,s1,s2,ss:sequence_of_message;

interface new_sequence_of_message : sequence_of_message;
interface s apr msg : sequence_of_message;
interface last(s) : message;
interface less_last(s) : sequence_of_message;

infix apr;
```

Having introduced the logical variables and function signatures, it is now necessary to specify the properties for the functions. What follows is a set of axioms that define these properties.

Besides introducing functional properties, the axioms can also be used as rewrite rules.

```
axiom new_sequence_of_message = s apr msg == FALSE;
axiom s apr msg = new_sequence_of_message == FALSE;
axiom s apr msg = s1 apr msg1 == ((s = s1) and
                                      (msg = msg1));
axiom less_last(s apr msg) == s;
axiom last(s apr msg) == msg;
```

The following declaration introduces an induction schema, defined over finite length sequences, that uses new_sequence_of_message as the base case, and uses the apr function for the induction step. Affirm does not perform any checking on whether the introduced induction schema is, in fact, a valid schema. Consequently, this is a potential source of invalidity.

```
schema induction(ss) ==
    cases(Prop(new_sequence_of_message),
        all s1,msg (IH(s1) imp Prop(s1 apr msg)));
end;
```

With the definitions of message and sequence theories, we are in a position to specify a security aspect of the flow modulator. As with the GVE version of the example, we define the concepts of accepted messages and the security property.

```
type modulator_environment;

needs type message, sequence_of_message;

declare msg:message;
declare s,w,x,y,z:sequence_of_message;

interface accepted_messages(s):sequence_of_message:

define accepted_messages(s) ==
    if s = new_sequence_of_message
    then new_sequence_of_message
    else if ok(last(s))
```

```
    then accepted_messages(less_last(s)) apr last(s)
    else accepted_messages(less_last(s));

interface security_property(s) : Boolean;

define security_property(s) ==
    if s = new_sequence_of_message
    then true
    else security_property(less_last(s)) and ok(last(s));

theorem modulator_is_secure,
    all s (security_property(accepted_messages(s)));

end;
```

What follows is the 'proof tree' for the above theorem. Since the effects of the prover commands are similar to the GVE commands the proof transcript is not included in detail.

The proof proceeds as follows. We first invoke the definition of accepted_messages, i.e. we unwind its definition once. We then employ the induction schema, resulting in the base and induction cases – the deferral of the application of the induction schema, in contrast to the GVE example, is a result of a purely technical point arising from the structuring of the specification.

The base case, starting at step 29, is easily proven by using the definition of the security property.

The induction case, starting at step 12, is rather more complicated. However, the proof requires the explicit invocation of IH, the induction hypothesis, and then some case analysis (using the suppose command). The only notational difficulty below, is the use of, for example, invoke security_property|−1|. This command states that only the last occurrence of the function, in the transformed version of the theorem, is to be invoked. The replace command is used to replace a variable by an expression that is equal in value.

```
3 U: print proof;
theorem modulator_is_secure, all s(security_property
                                    (accepted_messages(s)));

proof tree:
9:!  modulator_is_secure
          invoke accepted_messages
10:  2  employ induction(s')
29:   new_sequence_of_message:
          3 invoke security_property
29:−>    (proven!)
12:   apr:
          4 invoke IH
13:    5  suppose ok(msg')
16:    yes:
            6  invoke security_property|-1|;
17:      8   suppose s1' = new_sequence_of_message
18:      yes:
            9  replace s1'
19:        11 invoke accepted_messages
19:        (proven!)
21:        no:1 invoke accepted_messages|-1|
21:        (proven!)
23:        no: {modulator_is_secure, apr:}
            7  suppose s1' = new_sequence_of_message
24:      yes:
            14 replace s1'
25:        16 invoke accepted_messages
25:        (proven!)
27:        no:15 invoke accepted_messages|-1|
27:        (proven!)
```

While not exhibited by this particular example, the Affirm prover has more automated support than the GVE. Affirm's facility for treating the algebraic axioms of a specification as unconditional rewrite rules is a particular example of this increased support.

26.4.3 Other systems

There are, of course, other significant efforts that have been directed towards verification environments. Some systems of note are:

1. ABEL (Langyhr and Owe, 1978) from the University of Oslo, Oslo, Norway.
2. The Boyer-Moore theorem prover (Boyer and Moore, 1979) from Computational Logic, Inc.
3. EHDM, an abbreviation for Enhanced Hierarchical Design Methodology (von Henke *et al.*, 1988) from SRI International, Menlo Park, California.
4. HOL (Gordon, 1988) from Cambridge University, Cambridge, England.
5. IOTA (Nakajima and Yuasa, 1983), from Kyoto University, Kyoto, Japan.
6. PL–CV (Constable and O'Donnell, 1978) and NuPrl (Constable *et al.*, 1986), from Cornell University, Ithaca, New York.
7. SPADE (Carré *et al.*, 1986), from Program Validation Ltd, UK.
8. Stanford Pascal Verifier (Stanford Verification Group, 1979), from Stanford University, California.

Some of these efforts have strayed from the classical approach that has been described previously. For example, HOL is based on Church's type theory and allows for the definition of higher order functions and type polymorphism. HOL has been successfully used to prove various hardware examples – including portions of the VIPER chip (Cullyer, 1988) designed at Royal Signals and Radar Establishment (RSRE), Malvern, England, for safety critical systems. NuPrL is based on Constructive Type Theory. SPADE, which is based on RSRE's MALPAS (Malvern Program Analysis Suite), and integrates a number of flow analysis tools with some rudimentary verification environment facilities.

Further systems are discussed in Lindsay (1988).

26.5 Problems

While there has been significant progress made during the past 15 years, there are a number of problems associated with a majority of the verification environments.

Probably the most interesting problem is the uncertain mathematical foundation of many of the environments. Earlier in this article, it was noted that in a number of the environments it was fairly easy to introduce declarations which resulted in false being added to the theory. One of the main reasons for this state of affairs is a result of the primary research goal of these environments: the environments were developed to determine whether the verification process could be mechanized. While the eschewing of foundational mathematics may be reasonable in a research laboratory, currently some of these environnments are being applied to critical software systems; in these instances, mathematical soundness is a significant concern. Computer science theory appears to have evolved sufficiently so that the foundations for the verification environments could be significantly improved. For example, NuPrL, the Boyer-Moore theorem prover and m-EVES have solid foundational frameworks.

Applying verification environments to the program development process is expensive. This expense is a consequence, not only of the increased level of analysis that is performed, but also of the weak heuristics embodied in most theorem provers, the predilection to first-order, typed, specification languages (instead of higher-order, polymorphic languages); the lack of reusable mathematical domains of discourse; and the separation of the verification process from the rest of the program development process.

The separation of the verification process from the rest of the program development process is of particular concern and can be resolved. So far, research has been focused on verification environments in isolation. What is now necessary is the merger of verification environments with other tools that are used during the development of programs. It is worth noting that there is nothing inherent in formal verification which is contrary to other good program development techniques. In fact, there is a strong synergism between the various techniques.

Finally, the size of programs that can be adequately handled by the verification environment is still somewhat small, though expanding. Though a measure based on lines of code is rather dubious, the author believes it fair to say that current verification environment technology can handle programs in the low tens of thousands of lines; but certainly not in the hundreds of thousands.

26.6 Areas for future work

Clearly, significant efforts need to be directed at solving the problems outlined in the previous section. However, there is an increasing awareness on the part of researchers and practitioners that software verification is only a portion of the overall problem. To obtain highly trusted systems we need to apply rigorous mathematical techniques to the entire process. This includes the conventional approaches reported above, but also the rigorous mathematical analysis of hardware, and the verification of our tools – including operating systems and compilers.

Consequently, the evolution of verification environments seems to be towards systems that support rigorous mathematical reasoning and allow for the expression of a wide spectrum of properties.

For example, at Computational Logic, Inc., in Austin, Texas, a research project (entitled 'Trusted Systems') is using the Boyer–Moore prover to construct a tower of verified systems (Bevier *et al.*, 1987). At the bottom of this tower is a verified piece of (abstract) hardware; above the hardware is a verified assembler; above the assembler is a verified compiler for a small subset of the Gypsy programming language (called micro-Gypsy). Note, therefore, that it is possible to verify a micro-Gypsy program and, by using the verified compiler, assembler, and hardware, to make some rather strong statements on the actual execution of the program.

The above work is still rather preliminary. The hardware system described has not been manufactured and does not, for example, include I/O. micro-Gypsy is far too small to be a useful programming language. However, as a proof of concept exercise, this work is suggestive of what might be achieved in the foreseeable future.

It is, however, very important that we recognize the theoretical limitations of such efforts. There are, for example, constraints at both the top end and bottom end of the tower. In the first instance, there is a jump from the unformalizable intentions of the client; the formal specifications can never be proved to have completely captured the informal intentions. The best we can do is to show, through testing, proof, and rapid prototyping, amongst other techniques, that we have adequately captured the intent – these are the usual problems of requirements capture. Further, at the bottom end of the tower, we have problems typical to applied mathematics; our formalism of hardware is a model of a slice of physical reality. Consequently, we have an abstraction that excludes some aspects of world behaviour.

It is of crucial importance, especially when applying verification technology to critical systems, that we recognize the limitations of the technology and thereby utilize complementary technologies.

26.7 References

Bevier, W. *et al.* (1987) *Towards Verified Execution Environments*, Symposium on Security and Privacy, Oakland, California

Bledsoe, W. and Bruell, P. (1973) Man–machine theorem proving system. In *Proceedings of Third IJCAL*, Stanford University

Boyer, R. S. and Strother Moore, J. (1979) *A Computational Logic*, Academic Press

Carré, B. *et al.* (1986) SPADE: Southampton Program Analysis and Development Environment. *Software Engineering Environments*, IEE Computing Series 7, Peter Peregrinus

Coquand, Th. and Huet, G. (1985) Constructions: a higher order proof system for mechanizing mathematics. EUROCAL85, Linz, *Lecture Notes in Computer Science*, No. 203, Springer-Verlag

Constable, R. L. and O'Donnell, M. J. (1978) *A Programming Logic*, Winthrop Publishers

Constable, R. L. *et al.* (1986) *Implementing Mathematics with the NuPrl Proof Development System*, Prentice-Hall

Craigen, D. *et al.* (1988) m-EVES: A Tool for Verifying Software. 10th International Conference on Software Engineering (Singapore, April 1988)

Cullyer, J. (1983) Implementing safety-critical systems: the VIPER microprocessor. *VLSI Specification, Verification and Synthesis*, Kluwer Academic Publishers

Dijkstra, E. W. (1976) *A Discipline of Programming*, Prentice-Hall

Erickson, R. W. and Musser, D. R. (1980) The Affirm Theorem Prover: proof forests and management of large proofs. *5th Conference on Automated Deduction, Lecture Notes in Computer Science*, Vol. 57, Springer-Verlag, New York

Floyd, R. W. (1967) Assigning meanings to programs. In *Proceedings of the American Mathematical Society, Symposium in Applied mathematics*, Vol. 19

Gerhart, S. L. *et al.* (1980) An overview of Affirm: a specification and verification system. In *Proceedings of IFIP Congress 80, 8th World Computer Congress* (October 1980)

Good, D. I. *et al.* (1979) Principles of proving concurrent programs in Gypsy. ICSCA-CMP-15 (January 1979), Institute for Computing Science and Computer Applications, The University of Texas at Austin

Good, D. I. (1985) Mechanical proofs about computer programs. In *Mathematical Logic and Programming Languages* (eds C. A. R. Hoare and J. C. Shepherdson), Prentice-Hall

Gordon, M. J. C. (1988) A proof generating system for higher order logic. *VLSI Specification, Verification and Synthesis*, Kluwer Academic Publishers

Guttag, J., Horowitz, E. and Musser, D. (1978) Abstract data types and software validation. *Communications ACM*, **21**, 1049–1064

Guttag, J. *et al.* (1985) Larch in five easy pieces. *Digital Research Report*, No. 5

Haigh, J. T. and Young, W. D. (1987) Extending the noninterference version of MLS for SAT. *IEEE Transactions in Software Engineering*, **SE-13**

von Henke, F. W. *et al.* (1988) EHDM Verification Environment: an Overview. In *Proceedings 11th NBS/NCSC National Computer Security Conference* (Baltimore, Maryland, October 1988)

Hoare, C. A. R. (1969) An axiomatic basis for computer programming. *Communications ACM*, **12**

Igarashi, S., London, R. and Luckham, D. (1975) Automatic program verification I: logical basis and its implementation. *Acta Informatica*, **2**, 335–355

Jones, C. B. (1986) *Systematic Software Development Using VDM*, Prentice-Hall

Langyhr, D. F. and Owe, O. (1978) The programming and specification language ABEL. Research report No. 38, Institute of Informatics, University of Oslo, Oslo, Norway

Lindsay, P. (1988) A survey of mechanical support for formal reasoning. *IEEE Software Engineering Journal*, **3**

Martin-Löf, P. (1984) Intuitionalistic type theory. *Studies in Proof Theory*, Bibliopolis

Nakajima, R. and Yuasa, T. (eds) (1983) The IOTA Programming System. *Lecture Notes in Computer Science*, No. 160, Springer-Verlag

Smullyan, R. (1971) *First-Order Logic*, Springer-Verlag (second printing)

Spivey, J. M. (1989) *Understanding Z: A specification language and its formal semantics*. Cambridge University Press

Stanford Verification Group (1979) *Stanford Pascal Verifier User Manual*. Report No. STANCS-79-731, Computer Science Department, Stanford University

Stoy, J. E. (1977) *Denotational Semantics: The Scott-Strachey Approach to Programming Language Theory*, MIT Press

Software Development Management

27

Project planning and control

Paul Rook
Independent Consultant and Centre for Software Reliability

Contents

27.1 Introduction

The production of a large software system may involve many man-years of skilled effort with correspondingly large budgets. Not only is management of such a project a complex and intrinsically difficult task, but also it is not possible to simply separate project management from the technical work that is being managed. The problems that have to be overcome in a software development project usually arise from technical difficulties or inadequacies in the technical development. They become critical managerial problems if the project control structure is ineffective. The relationship between project management and software technical development has been discussed in Chapter 15 in dealing with software development process models and is also referred to in Section 27.2.4 in this chapter.

It is helpful to draw comparisons with hardware development. Software has no physical existence and, in general, few reliable software metrics have been used. Software may have a much greater complexity than hardware and often includes highly structured data as well as logic. It is deceptively easy to introduce changes into software, the effects of which can propagate explosively. Finally, software developments have traditionally made very little use of pre-existing components. However, software development is like hardware development in many important ways, and can be managed and controlled using very similar techniques to those widely used in other engineering disciplines. The genuine differences listed above are the very factors which make an engineering approach essential for successful software projects.

Improvements in the technology of software development have reached the point where the major issues have been identified and considerable progress has been made in addressing them, as evidenced by other chapters in this book. Software engineering deals with the structuring of a relationship between the technical aspects and the management of the project. For instance, since software is intangible, Chapter 30 describes software metrics that are available and ought to be more widely used in order to achieve a measurable basis for reliable software production. It is also necessary to set out precise definitions of tasks and task-products in the software development process. The satisfactory reviews of task-products against measurable targets then provide unambiguous milestones for measurement of progress. A controllable project is founded on defined baselines for the software specification, design, code and documentation, as discussed in Chapter 15. Software development in such a project can be carried out by professional software staff as reliably as in any other engineering discipline, with a fully and explicitly defined project process, backed by a Code of Practice with standards and procedures.

Section 27.2 describes the structure for control of a project as a primary goal for the project manager. Project control can only be built on an explicit understanding of the software development process, and Section 27.3 discusses the choice of process and phases based on risk management, with reference to the software development process models described in Chapter 15. Section 27.4 then deals with definition and establishment of the chosen process as a firm basis for control. The specific aspects of planning, progress monitoring and reporting for a software project are covered in Sections 27.5 and 27.6. Finally, Section 27.7 deals with the wider management issues of productivity, quality and software development methodology.

The principles covered in the chapter provide the means for overcoming the very real problems in successfully managing the development of a large software product. Some emphases in the chapter are oriented to large software projects, where indeed the problems are such as to require a high degree of explicit definition and formalization of methods of working and responsibilities. However, the principles are still valid for small, or less demanding, projects. The reader should be prepared to glean the principles and tailor their application appropriately. Where the software is being developed as part of a system, an integrated systems approach is essential, with the differences between hardware and software recognized and accommodated in a total system development process.

There is not room to cover all aspects of project management. Instead the chapter concentrates on those aspects which relate specifically to software project control. Those aspects of project management which are equally applicable to any project, such as leadership, people management, decision making, effective communication, etc, are only briefly covered. References are given to papers and books which cover these and other topics in more depth, and Chapter 32 deals with team management, which is an essential part of management of a project. The rest of the chapters in this software development management section of the book deal with the other functions on which project management depends.

27.2 Project control and project management

A control system for a project is based on the common principle of establishing suitable feedback loops to ensure that the controlled system can be guided toward its objective. *Figure 27.1* illustrates, a simplified form, in such a project control system. Technical development is being controlled, with project management as the controller. The feedback loops operate not only directly from technical development, but also through the functions of quality management and configuration management.

The figure illustrates a continuous process, as indicated by the inner loop feeding back intermediate development products as the basis for continuing technical development activities. The quality and configuration management functions operate continuously during the development process, not simply on the products finally delivered to the customer. Quality management is responsible for both measurement of conformance to the procedures defined for the process and measurement of the quality achieved for the products, according to the standards. Configuration management is responsible for the custody of baselined products. Together they can be used to ensure the reliability of the declared achievement of a milestone.

Whilst the inner loop represents the work on the product, the outer feedback loops represent the basis for control. The upper feedback loops will always be present, and represent the paths for changes. The project manager must ensure that they are controlled appropriately; for example, requests for changes to baselined items being handled through a change control procedure. The lower feedback loops represent the progress monitoring functions which will not be present unless established by the project manager. Project control is based on obtaining information to make decisions, replanning as necessary to meet timescale and budget, reassignment of work and feedback to the project manager that the decisions have been implemented and whether the consequences of the decisions have had the desired effect.

Standards and procedures are necessary for the meaningful definition of tasks in software development. Only with such definitions can the project manager be confident that the assigned task is adequately defined and that its completion is unambiguous.

The project control system depends on the existence of clearly defined managerial responsibilities within an organization, related to the four main functions: project management, quality

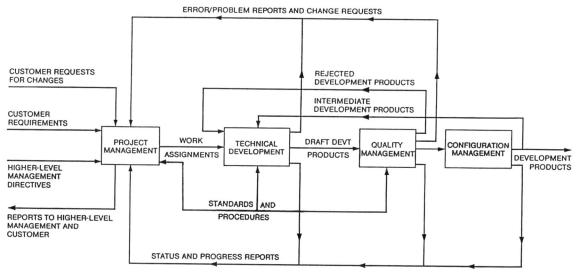

ERROR/PROBLEM REPORTS AND CHANGE REQUESTS

Figure 27.1 Basic operation of a project control system

management, configuration management, and technical development. Figure 27.1 organizes the concepts of project control into an operational structure. The rest of this section deals briefly with the parts of the structure, and the remaining sections of the chapter deal with the various aspects of making the structure work in practice for software development projects.

27.2.1 Project management

Project success is an amalgamation of: meeting the target of developing a particular product on time and within the constraints of resources and budget, meeting the customer's requirements for functionality, performance, reliability and quality and also satisfying the wider objectives of the organization.

Project management technique can be regarded as the set of procedures, rules, practices, technologies and know-how that the manager applies to plan, organize, staff, direct and control an engineering project to achieve success as defined above. The principles and practice can be applied universally to the management of any organisation or activity. The *IEEE Tutorial on Software Engineering Project Management* (Thayer, 1988) is an excellent starting point for reference on all the various aspects of software project management. Thayer's introductory paper on pages 15–53 of the IEEE tutorial gives a comprehensive top-down view of the activities involved. As stated in the introduction, this chapter does not have space to cover all the topics, and concentrates on those aspects which are particular to ensuring control of a software project.

Figure 27.2 shows project management, expanded from the single box in Figure 27.1, as a set of interacting activities relating to project control. This illustrates the principle that the ability to control a project depends on the quality of information that such activities generate and the use made of it.

27.2.1.1 Decision making

The most important aspect of project management consists of making decisions (or ensuring that decisions are made). This includes ensuring that technical decisions are made regarding the product as well as making the more obvious project decisions. Whilst authority and decision making can, and must, be

appropriately delegated, ultimate responsibility for decisions still rests with the project manager. The responsibility includes customer relationship, specification, correctness of design and implementation, quality, use of allocated resources and staff, meeting timescale and budget, standards and procedures, anticipation and resolution of problems and ultimate delivery and acceptance of the product.

All the other activities of project management shown within the outline box in Figure 27.2 should be regarded as providing information on which to make correct decisions, and, even more importantly, early warning triggers that decisions need to be made. Decisions have to be made early while there are still acceptable alternatives to choose. It is an unfortunate aspect of software projects that if difficult decisions are unidentified, ducked or deferred until the 'correct' decision is clear, then the only alternatives left are to try to attempt the impossible, reduce functionality, reduce quality, or accept a slippage in schedule. The result is all too often that the project goes out of control. All the best decisions are made early, based on incomplete but useful data from the other activities of project management. The project manager needs to deploy significant time and resources in looking for trouble rather than waiting for trouble to come looking for the manager. Timely and correct decision making is a necessary pre-requisite for the project manager and the team to be able to work cleverly and effectively. The alternative is to wear blinkers and work hard at the impossible, with failure guaranteed.

For further reading on decision making refer to Bell *et al.* (1988). For decision making in the context of software project management see the papers in pages 349–388 in Thayer (1988) and Boehm (1989), discussed further in Section 27.3.

27.2.1.2 Estimating

Planning and managing the project depend on a method of estimating the development resources required in terms of cost, effort and timescale. The estimating method must be able to take into account the sensitivity of the development cost to various product, project and environmental factors. Cost estimation must also be able to take past experience into account, particularly the relevant experience of the department or business in the development of similar software.

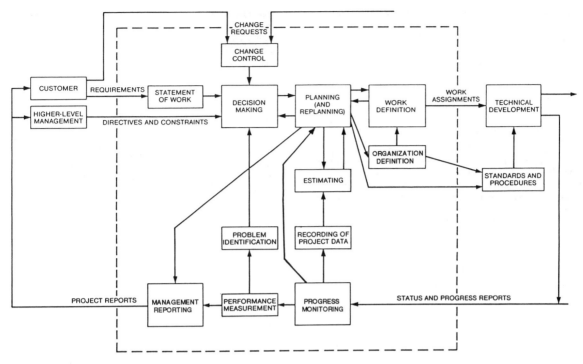

Figure 27.2 Project management

Estimating for software development is rightly regarded as a difficult problem, and for any chance of success must depend on:

1. A trial design.
2. A standard way of organizing a software development project process (right down to task level) and the discipline to stick to this method of working so that assumptions are not invalidated.
3. A trusted estimating method using data from previous projects.

Even with this foundation, there are still problems, and accuracy of estimation is inseparable from risk management, discussed in Section 27.3, and from the need for frequent re-estimation to deal with changing realisation of the scope of the work. For a discussion of software estimating methods and procedure, refer to Boehm (1981).

Reliable estimates for project control are best obtained (and for important projects second-best should be unacceptable) from a combination of the techniques of analogy, expert judgement, summation of effort for individual tasks and metrics-based cost models using data from previous projects. (Chapter 28 deals with software cost estimation models.) All the techniques depend on an understanding of the software development process used for the project as well as on the definition of the software to be implemented.

Estimates obtained in the form of activities and phases of the software development process, as discussed in Chapter 15, lead the project manager to analyse and control the project in a way that builds on the strengths of the phase-based process. The correspondence between the detail of the estimates, the plan, the assignment of work, the team responsibilities in the organization and the measurement of progress strengthens the emphasis on defining the method of working on the project. It also ensures that it corresponds to actual practice rather than just

good intentions. Further, it allows projects to be tracked easily, and facilitates frequent re-estimation, thus giving early warning of the need to re-examine budgets and plans.

27.2.1.3 Planning

Planning includes the activities of defining milestones, assigning resources, scheduling and budgeting. It depends on breaking the overall estimate for the project into task-estimates to fit with the work breakdown structure (WBS). The choice of the WBS is part of planning the use of staff resources and organizational structures. Planning depends on iteration with the activities of work definition, organization definition, estimating and decision making. It is not complete, in the sense of having a plan showing schedules based on planned resources, until all the iterations are complete.

The project manager produces a project plan (to be publicly viewed and reviewed). This shows product and sub-product milestones, schedules and relationships, and the allocation of resources to the tasks. It is accompanied by a definition of the project organization and the standards and procedures to be used in technical development. It is the central, and visible, basis for reference. Work assignments are seen as tasks in the plan, progress is monitored in terms of meeting the planned schedules, and project reporting always refers to the plan.

Work definition, progress monitoring and management reporting are briefly defined below to complete the structure of Figure 27.2. The whole subject of planning and progress reporting is covered in more detail in Sections 27.5 and 27.6.

27.2.1.4 Work definition

The choice of WBS depends fundamentally on the selected technical methods and the software development process chosen for the project (refer to Sections 15.3 and 15.6 in Chapter 15). The detailed work packages (the lowest level of the WBS) define a structure of task-products for project work and management visibility. The WBS not only requires management and customer agreement on the specification of deliverables (final product and subproducts – related to the task-products) but also requires agreement on the methods of working (technical and managerial) to be used for the whole project.

27.2.1.5 *Progress monitoring*

Monitoring involves measuring actual development progress and handling minor revisions to schedule or resource-requirements within the responsibilities of the teams. Project progress is also related to quality assurance through technical reviews and walkthroughs. Based on written reports and meetings, monitoring includes the evaluation of actual progress in producing task-products against expected progress and also the recording of project history in the project data file.

27.2.1.6 *Management reporting*

The project manager reviews the status, progress and identified problems as a foundation for decisions (and replanning if necessary). Comparison of monitored actual progress with expected performance yields relevant information for the project teams, management and customer.

The information for management should be a filtered subset of the information needed by the project manager when tracking progress within the project. The information needed by management is to answer questions such as: 'Is the project on schedule?' and, if not, 'Can the project team handle the schedule slippage within its own area of responsibility, or does management need to do something to help the project return to a controlled state?' The information on measured achievement must be presented effectively to management and the customer so that project progress can be approved at critical points and the correct decisions made. Reporting on risk management forms an important aspect of management reporting. The susceptibility of the project to risks cannot be deduced from reports which only deal with progress and plans.

27.2.2 Quality management

Quality is built into the product by the activities of the technical development staff as a continuous process of producing the product of the specified quality. Quality is everybody's responsibility. It cannot be added by any testing or control on end-products. Verification, validation, testing (VV&T) and quality control on intermediate products as development progresses do, however, provide early warning of problems. Changes can be made at much lower cost than in the later stages of development provided, as always, that proper change control procedures are followed.

Check-out of final products, rejecting those that do not meet quality criteria, does nothing to ensure success of a software development project so the emphasis of quality management in software development is not only on in-process quality control of intermediate products, but also on the development process itself, which is seen as fundamental to the ability of the project to produce products of acceptable quality.

Quality assurance is checking the correctness of the procedures being followed, i.e. whether the development staff are following the intended process (in all their work, not just the VV&T activities) to *assure* the quality of the components produced. VV&T are carried out by technical development staff, but quality assurance is carried out by staff either from a separate QA department or staff specifically assigned to quality assurance work in the project.

Quality management covers the responsibility of obtaining, training (technical skills in quality assurance) and managing the quality assurance staff, and planning and managing the work of:

1. Provision of independent advice on all quality issues, especially on the choice of standards and procedures at the beginning of each project.
2. Preparation of the quality plan (refer to Section 27.4.6 and Chapter 29).
3. Monitoring the process as actually employed on the project.
4. Auditing the quality (conformance to standards and requirements) of products (including the intermediate development products, especially the early ones) as the project progresses to find out if the procedures are being effective.

In a large development project, the quality assurance staff are crucially valuable to the project manager. No-one else will be able to verify that the process is operating as intended and therefore whether it is ensuring the quality intended in the final product. The project manager is not able to do it directly, because of the immediate work he has to do on all the tasks described in Section 27.2.1. In the absence of assurance of quality, project control is open loop as far as the quality of the items that are being produced, with the consequence that the quality of the product in final testing will be a surprise (and unlikely to be a pleasant one). Remedying the deficiencies at this stage is not only costly in resources and budget, but also the timescale to find and reliably fix all the 'bugs' is uncontrollable. Sometimes it is just too late to do anything about it.

Successful quality assurance gives the project manager the means to be sure of both measuring progress through events corresponding to production of items *and* measuring the quality of the items produced, based on the intended process being followed with conformance to standards in the produced items and in the methods of working.

Refer to Chapter 29 for a full discussion of quality control and assurance.

27.2.3 Configuration management

The successful development and maintenance of a large software product requires strict control over the specification, and the documentation and code constituting the product. It is inevitable that these items will be subject to continuous pressure for change; to correct errors, introduce improvements, and respond to the evolving requirements of the customer.

Configuration management (covering identification of versions and variants, physical control of files, change control procedures and build management) supports the disciplines of baselining that are necessary to prevent the chaos of uncontrolled change. The output of each development phase is verified and validated against the relevant preceeding baselines. Configuration management procedures are followed to ensure that this output is, in turn, baselined and that subsequently only up-to-date definitions and baselines are used. The configuration management system must be efficient enough to be able to react to the demands made on it by development staff, and requires not only a separate organizational responsibility, but also automated tool support.

Once a baseline has been formally established, its contents may only be changed by the operation of the formal change control procedure. This has the following advantages:

1. No changes are made thereafter without the agreement of all interested parties.
2. The higher threshold imposed by formal procedures puts a barrier against unconsidered changes.

3. There is always available a definitive version of the product, or of any of the controlled intermediate products (baselines).

Refer to Chapter 34 for a full discussion of configuration management.

27.2.4 Technical development and technical control

The selection, or confirmation, of the technical methods to be used in the project (discussed in Section 15.3 of Chapter 15) together with documentation standards and configuration management and quality assurance procedures, must be matched to the characteristics of the development, the imposed schedules, and other operational considerations. Careful selection of software development techniques is fundamental, since the project cannot succeed without suitable technical skills applied by the staff. The project manager must take responsibility for the decisions which determine the technical basis for the development.

Once selected, the methods must be implemented, supported with tools and training for staff, and integrated into the operational process. No matter how sophisticated the design and programming techniques, they are not sufficient to ensure a successful software project unless the technical development is fully integrated with a systematic approach to software project management.

There is a potential dichotomy between project management and technical development. In most cases the project manager does not have the time, and sometimes also lacks the technical understanding, to be sufficiently involved in the technical work to realise the consequence of technical problems until too late. The danger is that the project manager is only linked through reported progress and even the link between project progress and quality assurance, discussed in Section 27.2.2, is insufficient. Problems may not become apparent until the effects are seen in the phase-products. The technical integrity of a complex development can only be ensured by strategically looking ahead. The activities are performed by members of a number of teams and it is vital to co-ordinate the technical drive to define, design and produce the software. This focus on the central integrity of the technical development is referred to as 'technical control'. The role of technical controller on a large project may be referred to as 'system architect', 'project architect', 'chief engineer' or 'chief programmer' (as used by IBM), or the position may correspond to the leader of the design team.

Primary examples of the responsibilities of technical control are the maintenance of the integrity of the design in the presence of detailed changes after the completion of the structural design phase, and test planning. Test planning is a strategic activity from the very start of the project. It defines and co-ordinates all the test methods, modelling, tools and techniques to be used throughout the life cycle. It also identifies critical components that need the most testing, what test data is required, and when it is to be prepared. The technical controller must determine the verification and validation strategy, and monitor the effectiveness of reviews so that errors are detected and corrected early, and the technical risk is controlled. When subcontractors are involved in the project, technical control becomes even more important in co-ordinating the technical aspects of all work between the subcontractors and the integrity of the subcontract products. In the context of Figure 27.1, technical control is regarded as part of the technical development, and is defined as the continuing activity of making certain that what is being produced is technically correct, coherent and consistent. It can be clearly distinguished from such concerns as schedule, budget, organization, staffing, etc. which are solely the responsibility of project management.

Whilst it is reasonable on very small projects for the project manager to undertake both project management and technical control, on large projects such a combination of roles is not workable. It is rare to find people who combine both the strong management talent and strong technical skills necessary for large projects. More importantly, on a project of even reasonable size, each activity is necessarily a full time job, or more. It is hard for the project manager to delegate the project management tasks to allow time for technical work. It is impossible for the technical controller to delegate technical control work without compromising the conceptual integrity of the product. The bottom line is that for a software project of any significant technical difficulty there *must* be one person fundamentally responsible for technical control, and on a project of sufficient size (it depends on the application, but the boundary is no higher than 5–10 staff) it *cannot* successfully be the same person as is responsible for project management.

Clearly the relationship between the project manager, the technical controller and the project staff can present a problem. There is opportunity for pathological connections (see *Figure 27.5*) and questions to be answered for staff to know who to report to in which context. It is sometimes possible to run a project with the technical control exercised by the senior management in charge of the project and almost all project management tasks delegated to a second-in-command. It is much more usual for the project manager to be in command, with the technical controller having the technical authority. In this case, it is important that the technical controller does have enough authority for decisions without being in the direct management line above all the project teams. Whilst there is no universal solution, the theoretical problems usually have a clear answer in practice in any specific project. Whatever the solution in terms of responsibilities, hierarchy and organization, it must be worked out and made clear to all staff. This is the crucial bridge between software development technique (which sometimes is in danger of being no more than merely technically clever) and software project management (which is concerned with being effective). Brooks (1975) deals with the subject with both humour and insight, comparing the roles of project manager and technical controller to those of producer and director.

27.3 Risk management and choice of process

The software development process is inherently subject to risks, the consequences of which are manifested as financial failures (timescale overrun, budget overrun) and technical failures (failure to meet required functionality, reliability or maintainability). The objectives of risk management are to identify, analyse and give priorities to risk items before they become either threats to successful operation or major sources of expensive software rework, to establish a balanced and integrated strategy for eliminating or reducing the various sources of risk, and to monitor and control the execution of this strategy.

Boehm (1989), from which *Figure 27.3* is taken, gives a full introduction to the subject. As shown, the practice of software risk management involves two primary steps: risk assessment and risk control, each with three subsidiary steps.

Boehm gives a number of risk identification checklists. These checklists can be used by managers and technical staff on a new project to help identify, and suggest resolution techniques for, the most likely serious risks on the project. However, they should be backed up as soon as possible by checklists derived from local experience.

After using all the various risk identification checklists, plus the other risk identification and risk analysis techniques shown in Figure 27.3, one very real risk is that the project will identify so many project risk items that the manager could get bogged down just investigating them. This is where risk priorities become essential. As well as the obvious application of common sense, effective analytical techniques for giving risk priorities involve the quantification of risk exposure (probability of unsatisfactory outcome multiplied by loss level) and risk reduction leverage (reduction of risk exposure divided by cost of risk reduction investment). These techniques are generally necessary to ensure concentration on the key factors. Often there is a great deal of uncertainty in estimating the probability or loss associated with an unsatisfactory outcome. This uncertainty is itself a major source of risk, which needs to be reduced as early as possible. One of the best ways of reducing this uncertainty is to buy information about the actual situation, such as investing in a prototype.

When risk assessment has determined the major risk items for a project and their relative priorities, the next step is to establish risk control. There are two categories of risks to be distinguished: project specific risks and generic risks.

Project specific risks are those which only apply to a particular project, such as:

1. Personnel shortfalls.
2. Unrealistic schedules and budgets.
3. Inappropriate requirements.
4. Shortfalls in externally supplied components and services.
5. Technology shortfalls, unknowns and reliance on advances in the state of the art.
6. User-interface uncertainties.
7. Ambitious performance requirements.

Risks in this category are addressed by the steps in the lower half of *Figure 27.3*, with a set of risk management plans to lay out the activities necessary to bring the risk items under control. The individual risk management plans have to be integrated with each other and with the overall project process and project plan. Once a good set of risk management plans is established, the risk resolution process consists of implementing whatever prototypes, simulations, benchmarks, surveys, or other risk reduction techniques are called for in the plans. Risk monitoring ensures that this is a closed loop process by tracking risk reduction progress and applying whatever corrective action is necessary to keep the risk-elimination process on track (refer to Section 27.6.4.3 for more detail on risk reporting).

Generic risks are those which are common to the generality of software development projects, such as:

1. Costly, late fixes, addressed by early requirements and design verification and validation.
2. Error-prone products, addressed by testing, verification and validation through the life cycle.
3. Uncontrollable process, addressed by planning and control.
4. Uncontrollable product, addressed by configuration management and quality assurance.
5. Poor communication, addressed by documentation, reviews.

The degree to which these are expected to be significant for the particular software development determines the choice of the method of working and the process for the project.

Even for the generic risks, risk management concepts are useful in planning the project, particularly in providing a context and a rationale for software verification and validation

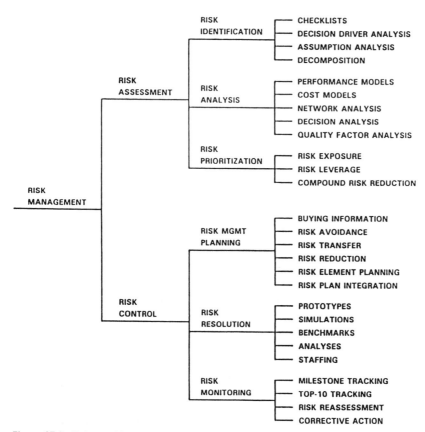

Figure 27.3 Software risk management steps

(V&V) activities, and helps address the key question of 'How much V&V is enough?'. The risk exposure view of software V&V suggests that the level of investment in software V&V should be a function of the relative loss caused by a software error in a system. Also that software V&V should be part of an integrated risk reduction strategy, which includes other error elimination techniques (such as walkthroughs and cleanroom techniques), software fault tolerance techniques, and operational loss limiting techniques.

Risk reduction leverage calculations can be used to assess the relative cost-effectiveness of V&V with respect to other techniques in reducing software risk exposure. These confirm that V&V investments in the early phases of the software life cycle have high payoff ratios, and that V&V is a function which needs to begin early to be most cost-effective. Similar calculations can help a software project determine the most cost-effective mix of defect removal techniques to apply across the software life cycle. Example approaches can be found in Chapter 3 of Jones (1980) and Chapter 24 of Boehm (1981).

As well as using risk assessment to determine the methods of working in the project, risk management is also the basis for the appropriate choice, from the alternative process models, of the specific process for the project. This choice is discussed in Section 15.6 in Chapter 15 in terms of either tailoring the canonical life-cycle model, or making decisions between different models for different circumstances, or using the spiral model to generate an *ad hoc* process chosen phase by phase to reduce and control risks.

The techniques of risk assessment and risk control stimulate a 'no surprises' approach to software management. This improves project management visibility and control, and significantly reduces the cost of software development by discovering and dealing with problems early on rather than having to undertake rework at later stages. Although risk management is the basis for the choice of the software process and, within that process, the determination of which software V&V activities to pursue and at what level of effort, it is still necessary for the project manager to make active use of the process-phases for risk management. The concept of distinct phases of software development (as discussed in Section 15.4 in Chapter 15), representing the achievement of pre-defined states during the development of the product, can be regarded as a device used by project management to deal with risk and to improve visibility. In practice, particularly on large-scale projects, the precise phase-ends depend, to some extent, on management decisions. Milestones are not achieved completely. It is therefore particularly important that status and risk analysis at milestones are obtained from conscientious emphasis on thorough technical and management reviews. The chosen phase definitions are the basis for real control of software development, but that control has to be explicitly planned and based on the methods of working used and applied by development staff. It does not happen naturally. The project manager has to make the chosen process model realistic. The next section deals with the necessary establishment of the specific software development process chosen for the project, which has to be defined at least to the level of detail shown in *Figure 27.6* if it is to be a realistic basis for successful project control.

27.4 Establishing the software development process for the project

Project management depends specifically on project control. As a necessary prerequisite for control, it is the responsibility of the project manager to determine what the process should be, establish it, and ensure that it is really being used, supported and updated as necessary. The project manager must also bridge the gap between technology and management of events, resources and budgets by putting in place a viable basis for determining progress. If this seems an unreasonable, or even impossible, imposition on the shoulders of the manager, then it should be sufficient to point out that if the project manager does not do it then no-one else will. If it is not done, then the project manager cannot manage because the means of management are not there.

In some cases a standard method of working will already be in use, together with the appropriate support facilities. In other cases the project manager will have to select and establish a process specifically for the project. In either event, project management has the final responsibility for ensuring (or confirming) the suitability of the process for the project and defining precisely the details of its operation.

Establishment of the process for the software development project depends on the following five principles:

1. Define the project process for all the work involved, covering technical development, project management, quality assurance and configuration management.
2. Establish the organization to match the process of work on the product.
3. Carry out a project initiation phase to ensure that the process is in place and understood.
4. Use tools to make the work more efficient by automating the tasks and supporting the process.
5. Set the project goals on a contractural basis, with metrics and targets to be achieved, so that effective use can be made of real feedback to control the process.

27.4.1 Definition of the process

It is management's job to steer the individuals and teams on a project in a common direction so that their creativity is productive, the products interface with each other, are finished within the project cost and schedule constraints and together accomplish the project goals. A project can only operate effectively when each member knows the answers to basic questions regarding the job such as:

1. For whom do I work?
2. What is expected of me?
3. Why is it expected of me?
4. What tools and facilities are available to me?
5. How do I do what is expected?
6. What training is available to me?
7. What must I produce?
8. When must it be produced?
9. Who do I give it to?
10. How will my product be evaluated?

Establishment of the relationship between the functions of project management and the technical activities depends on the engineering professionalism of the technical staff. Codes of practice, accepted standards, training in these and professional integrity in working to industry procedures are the mark of a mature engineering discipline. Where these properly exist there is no misconception when a task is assigned and no ambiguity as to whether the product of the task has been completed to the standard required. Answers to the questions above are provided, for each individual on the project, by a combination of the codes of practice and the organizational responsibilities which have to be established by the project manager.

Definition of the overall process for the whole project starts by determining the phases and reviews, and then the software development activities and tasks. The next step is to produce a process definition diagram, showing the relationship of the tasks and the task-products to the phases in the process. An example of such a diagram, for a particular version of a software development process is shown in Figure 27.6. A diagram in this form is an invaluable basis for discussions with senior staff to progressively search out all the tasks and task-products that need to be added to the initial diagram. They thus bring their expertise and share in the decisions that finalize the process. Team leaders are involved in assignment of the tasks on the process definition diagram to teams, thus defining the responsibilities in the organizational structure.

Promulgation of the agreed process definition diagram is the project manager's most effective communication tool for ensuring that everyone on the project understands the process in which they are working and the relationship to the actual tasks in hand. It goes a long way towards answering the questions listed above.

27.4.2 Establishment of the organization

Based on estimates for the sizes of the tasks in the various phases and the defined activities, the work breakdown structure leads to task assignments to teams and a mapping onto an organizational structure. Figure 27.4 shows a generalized software project organization chart which can be tailored to fit particular project needs. The functions can be merged or further divided according to the size and complexity of the work. Chapter 7 in Boehm (1981) gives guidelines for tailoring the organizational structure. The important point is that the precise definitions of the activities and the tasks to produce the phase-products lead naturally to estimates of effort and team sizes which fit into an organizational structure where responsibilities match delegated authority and the principles that enable project control are represented in the structure of the project organization.

Since it is observable that the structure of products display only too well the structure of the organization that produced them, it is generally preferable to set up the organization to correspond to the process for the product that it is wished to produce. *Figure 27.5* illustrates the commonality of principles in good software design and good organizational 'design'. Design of the software development process and of the project organization for a significant software development is a worthwhile intellectual challenge. The same skills and techniques that are used for the design of a significant software system should be applied to the design of the project process and organization. A good design for the organization will bring the immensely useful

Figure 27.5 Common rules for structuring software and organizations

Software	Organization
Each software unit should be small so that it can be easily understood.	Each software team should be small so that it can be effectively controlled.
Each software unit should be only loosely coupled to other software units.	Each software team should be assigned units of work which minimize unnecessary communication among software teams.
Each software unit should be highly cohesive (perform one function).	Each software team should be assigned work units that are highly cohesive.
The scope of effect of a software unit should be a subset of the scope of control.	Software teams should be grouped together (reporting to one manager) in such a way that the decisions made within the managerial group have minimal effect on the work of other managerial groups.
As software is decomposed into a hierarchy of units, higher level units perform decision making and lower level units do the actual work.	In an organizational structure the managerial hierarchy takes the decisions (longer range and more abstract decisions at higher levels of management) and the lower organizational levels perform the actual production work.
'Pathological' connections (communication links not following the hierarchical software structure) should be avoided, or at least fully documented.	Organizations should not have to rely on pathological connections (for instance – dependence on arbitrary communications between programming teams to find out the consequences of design decisions).

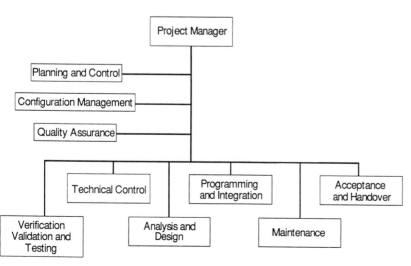

Figure 27.4 Generalized software project organization chart

consequence, from the project manager's point of view, that responsibilities correspond to work assignments and strengthen management's understanding of the structure of the technical work.

27.4.3 Project initiation

Everything that is done right in software development project management is done early. If the process is not adequately established at the beginning, then, on a large project working to meet a deadline, there is never sufficient time subsequently to back-track and set up better means of project control. Establishing a management structure at the earliest possible stage of a project provides the necessary foundation to identify and control problems before they become critical.

The explicit discipline to make visible that the foundation is in place is provided by defining a project initiation phase. At the end of the phase a project initiation review is carried out to check that all the elements necessary for the planned controlled project are in place. The major work in the initiation phase is to define and promulgate the process and to produce the plans for the project through to completion.

The output of each phase of the whole software development project consists entirely of documentation, or of documentation and code. Documents are the sole means by which the successive stages of the design process are recorded, and against which each phase is validated. Thus it is impossible to separate the scheduling of the project from the scheduling of the documentation constituting the baselines. Careful attention, therefore, to the planning, structure, content, preparation, presentation and control of documentation is vital. The documentation plan is completed in the initiation phase, since so much of the structure of the work in the rest of the phases of the project depends on it.

27.4.4 Process definition diagram

The software development process is the basis for a number of diagrams and documents for the project, including the organizational structure diagram, work breakdown structure diagram, timebased networks and bar charts in the project plan, code of practice (standards and procedures) and task definitions. However, none of these gives an easily understood, integrated, overview of the actual project process on which they rely.

A diagram for the specific purpose of displaying the defined process should be drawn as follows:

1. The activities of software development are resolved into tasks. The conclusion of the task being defined by a task-product which passes the criterion of a previously defined standard.
2. The organizational responsibilities are shown for each task-product.
3. The interaction of the tasks, each task depending on products from preceeding tasks, is defined by procedures.
4. The whole project process (either predetermined to completion of the project using a set of phases such as those in the canonical life cycle, or steadily evolving as phases chosen to manage risk) is defined by grouping the task-products and small processes to correspond to the phases. This is done by drawing a diagram showing transition from state to state through the duration of the project, where each state corresponds to the achievement of the end of a phase.

Thus the process definition diagram takes the form of a state-transition diagram linking the different aspects of the process by explicitly showing the top level relationship between:

1. *All* activities involved in the software development process.
2. Top level of the work breakdown structure.
3. Task-products (to be baselined).

4. Standards and procedures.
5. Organizational responsibilities.
6. Phases of the process for the project.

Such a diagram, by integrating the definition of the process for a specific project, facilitates the following:

1. Initial description, argument, resolution and confirmation of completeness of the planned process, between the project manager, senior management, quality assurance, senior technical staff on the project and the customer.
2. Promulgation of the project process, graphically, for all concerned in and with the project, in a way that can be pinned on office walls and readily updated to keep visible the interaction of responsibilities within the process. Its early creation underlines the need to define the process and ensures that everybody understands it.
3. The choice of metrics which are definable as values of attributes of the task-products on the diagram. The values can be set as targets, estimated as the tasks progress and measured as achievements. This gives the data to be collected and analysed, which is part of defining the project process. It must, for a successful product, address the measurement of quality and reliability as well as productivity (project progress against milestones).
4. Derivation of the quality plan for the project. This includes definition of the process and plans for monitoring its quality and reliability as part of assuring the quality and reliability of the product.

The diagram will, inevitably, be different for every project (although in a good organization it will be derivable from existing practice and previous projects) and will need to be updated as the understanding and application of the process evolves. *Figure 27.6* shows a suitable form of the process definition diagram for the canonical life cycle model defined in Section 15.5 of Chapter 15. The diagram is intended to illustrate the sort of visible, straight-forward definition of the process that should be the basis for every project. It must not be confused with the network diagram which may be used as a planning tool (see Section 27.5.4). That is concerned with progress on planned interrelated activities. While it may cover all task interrelationships, it will hardly be involved with invocations of standards and procedures, and is not drawn with the primary aim of illustrating the process and organizational inter-responsibilities.

The form of the diagram emphasizes an object-oriented approach. Each rectangle is an object to be reviewed, with all the overtones implied in referring to object-oriented design of software. The transformations of the design process lead naturally to an object-oriented WBS. The activities of the teams are broken down by the WBS into tasks which produce the objects required for phase-end reviews, which are the major milestones of progress – with the principle of designing the organizational structure in an object-oriented way. The whole drive of the organization, and its motivation to respond to the perceived demands made by the project manager, should be on the basis of producing objects which, within the process structure, progress to combine into the whole product required. So it is not 'I program' (verb intransitive, i.e. for the fun of it or because it seems to be what I should be doing), but 'I program items' (verb transitive, i.e. with the aim of producing a defined object which will be the only way of satisfying the demand made of me by my manager). The logic applies not only to programming but also to all the other activities such as writing documents, reviewing, testing, etc.

Here the term object-oriented is being used not in the sense of applying it to the technical design, but to bring exactly the same principles to the 'design' of the process (as discussed in Section 27.4.2), the organization and the WBS. It is suggested that the 'design' should be an object-oriented design for all the same

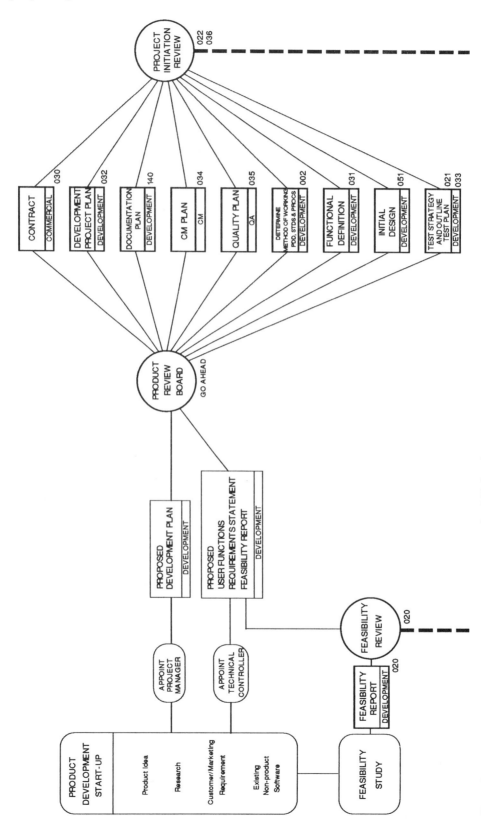

Figure 27.6 Process definition diagram (a) Feasibility study and project initiation phases

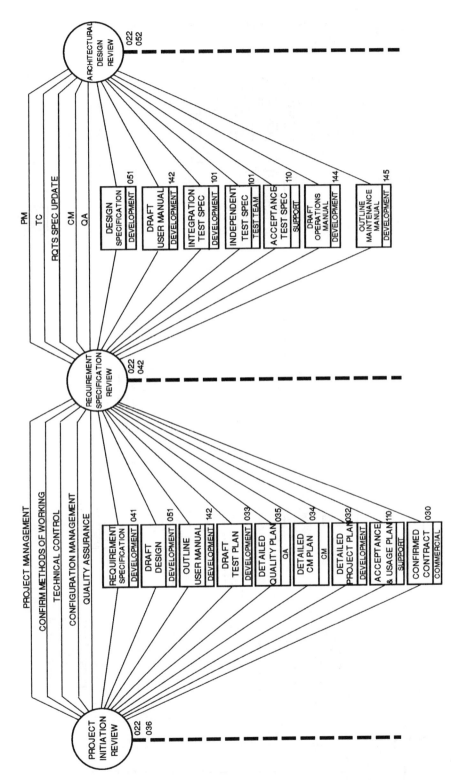

Figure 27.6 (b) Requirement and architectural design phases

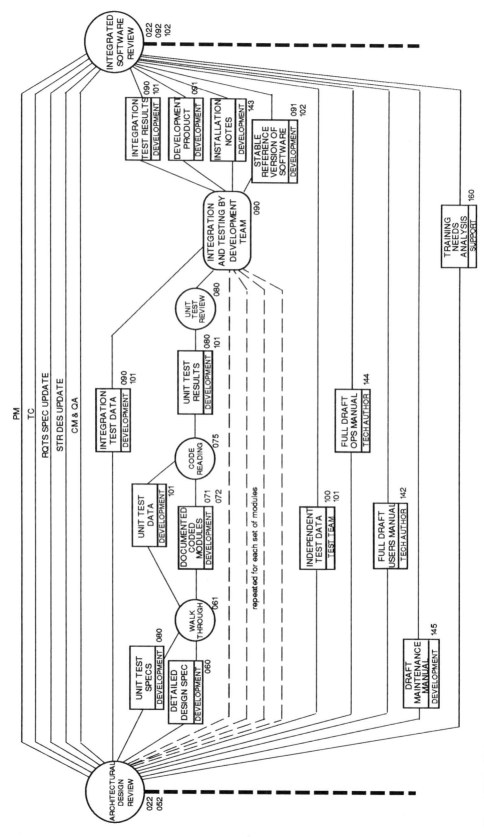

Figure 27.6 (c) Programming and integration phases

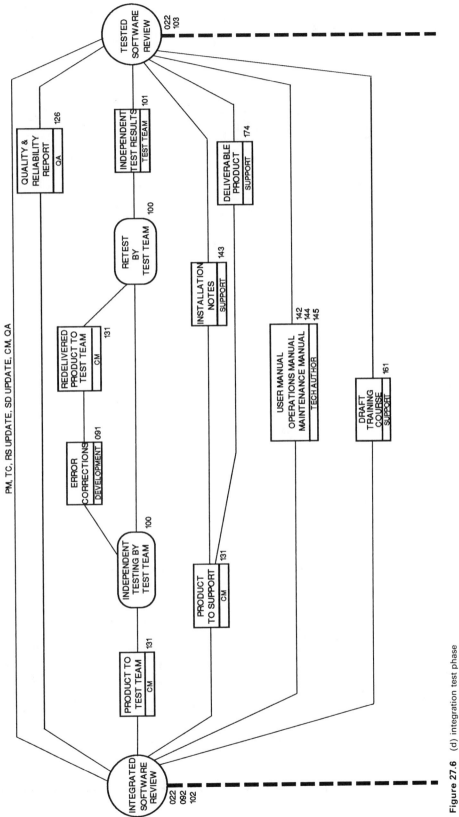

Figure 27.6 (d) integration test phase

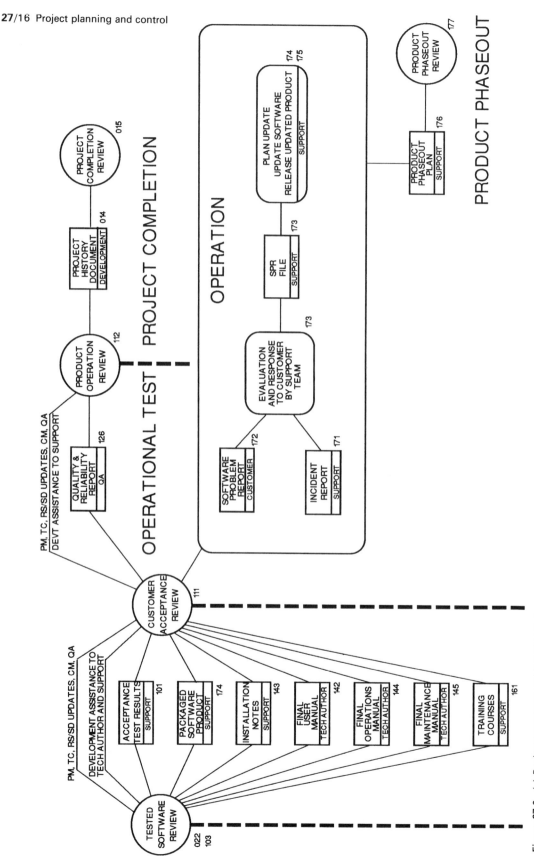

Figure 27.6 (e) Product acceptance and operational phases

reasons that object-oriented design is suitable for complex software systems. Also management of the process is *necessarily* object-oriented. Activities cannot be managed, they are uncontrollable and go on for an indeterminate time. Tasks *are* controllable; they take a finite time with a defined product at the end of the task. Therefore an object-oriented approach to the design of the process ensures its suitability for management control. The goal is explicitly: object-oriented managers, object-oriented processes, object-oriented organizational structures, object-oriented tasks for object-oriented development staff working with object-oriented design techniques and supported by object-oriented environments which possess all the objects within an object management system (OMS). This provides the means of structuring the relationship of technical development to project management to provide the basis for project control.

In *Figure 27.6* the department or team responsible for the production of the item is shown at the bottom of each rectangle. A suitable code of practice is shown in *Figure 27.7* and is referred to in *Figure 27.6* by the numbers against each rectangle (the standard against which the object is judged) and each step in the process (the procedure to be followed). Reviews are shown as circles, each acting as a phase-end focus for the phase-products.

The reader is invited to consider the equivalent diagram for an actual, familiar, project. Completion of the detail of such a diagram may seem to be heavily theoretical, but that is not the intention. What is illustrated on the diagram should correspond to reality. It should be pragmatic not pedantic, though if it is too simple it will not have the value of serving as the fundamental basis for defining the process and achieving project control. There may seem to be a lot of work to complete all the detail of the diagram, but the investment is well worthwhile. It should be developed from discussions with the senior technical staff on the project and used to make clear to all staff what is going on, and therefore has considerable value in bridging the gap between technical development and project management.

001 Index
002 Software development process
003 Glossary of terms and abbreviations
Project management
   010 Project planning and work definition
   011 Estimating and metrics
   012 Progress monitoring/reporting procedure
   013 Change control procedure
   014 Project history document
   015 Project completion review
Technical control
   020 Feasibility report and review
   021 Verification and validation strategy
   022 Procedure for development reviews
Project initiation
   030 Contract standard
   031 Functional definition standard
   032 Project plan standard
   033 Test plan standard
   034 CM plan standard
   035 Quality plan standard
   036 Project initiation review
Requirement specification
   040 Capture of requirements
   041 Requirement specification standard
   042 Requirement specification review
Architectural design
   050 Design techniques
   051 Design specification standard
   052 Architectural design review
Detailed design
   060 Detailed design specification standard
   061 Design walkthroughs
Coding
   070 Structural programming
   071 Module documentation standard
   072 General coding standard
   073 C coding and layout standard
   074 Ada coding and layout standard
   075 Code reading and source code reviews
Unit test
   080 Unit testing and unit test review
Integration
   090 Top-down integration and testing
   091 Development product standard
   092 Integrated software review

Product test
   100 Independent testing
   101 Standard for test specs, data and results
   102 Acceptance of product from development
   103 Tested software review
Customer acceptance
   110 Customer acceptance plan standard
   111 Customer acceptance review
   112 Product operation review
Quality assurance
   120 QA in software development
   121 Creating standards and procedures
   122 Project specific standards and procedures
   123 Concessions procedure
   124 Error data recording and analysis
   125 Quality audit procedure
   126 Quality and reliability reports
Configuration management
   130 CM during software development
   131 Product control (product library operation)
   132 Documentation control
Documentation
   140 Documentation system
   141 Documentation standard
   142 Standard for user manuals
   143 Standard for installation notes
   144 Standard for operations manuals
   145 Standard for maintenance manuals
   146 Documentation production
   147 Documentation review procedure
Development environment
   150 Environment facilities and support
   151 Software tool update procedure
   152 Extraction of files from archive
Training
   160 Training course development procedure
   161 Training course standards
Product support
   170 Product support services
   171 Customer incident handling
   172 Software problem reporting procedure
   173 SPR handling procedure
   174 Deliverable product standard
   175 External product release procedure
   176 Product phaseout plan standard
   177 Product phaseout review

Figure 27.7 Example of standards and procedures covered in a software development code of practice

The process definition diagram should be completed early in project initiation, backed by a code of practice, and fully promulgated well before the project initiation review. The standards, procedures and review check lists are seen to be real and not just a dusty manual on the shelf. If they do not already exist, it should be possible to write them quickly, briefly and to the point. It should be clear that their absence means that the process is undefined and therefore uncontrollable. The overall project process depends on the procedures which are, in turn, smaller processes.

The diagram is not necessarily limited in scope to the relationships between the teams directly involved in the development project. The example in *Figure 27.6* is for a delivery to a specific customer. If the development is an internal one for a product line then the process definition diagram should show all the relationships to the responsibilities and items produced by marketing, sales and commercial departments dealing with market launch, brochures, pricing, sales strategy and general customer training and support.

It is necessary to emphasize that the example shown in *Figure 27.6* is not intended to be seen as the 'correct' set of phases. There is no such thing. As already discussed in Chapter 15 and Section 27.3 in this chapter, there are many ways of constructing the alternative processes suitable for particular projects. It is not possible in the scope of this chapter to work out diagrams for even a selection of the alternative processes, and the canonical life cycle phases have been used as providing the most general reference point from which the reader can translate into the chosen process for a specific project. Each project must ensure that it has its own suitable process. It is not possible to pick a standard process off the shelf and use it without at least some tailoring to local circumstances.

27.4.5 Tools and IPSE support

As well as the definition and establishment of the process discussed in the previous sections, successful control of the project also depends on productivity. So the project manager must not only take responsibility for the methods of working, but also the software development environment – including the software development tools.

To deal effectively with the complexity of significant tasks in software development it is necessary to use really good staff (and as few as possible, to reduce the communication overhead on a complex task) and to equip them with good tools so that they are efficient enough to complete the task in the required timescale. High productivity also gives the staff the chance to give proper attention to quality, instead of having to rush to meet deadlines.

Historically, the earliest tools were concerned with the production of code. These have been followed by tools which assist specification, design, integration testing, data collection and administration, estimating, planning, documentation, and configuration management. Whilst some of these tools are still far from mature, there are now tools available which may be chosen to assist with most of the activities and tasks of software development.

Adequate support for the software development team to produce, review and update documents is very important for project efficiency. The documentation development tools should cover word processing, editing, formatting and printing (including diagrams), which not only work together but are integrated with the configuration management tool(s), e.g. to automatically identify changed sections in reissued documents. Since so much of software development is, in fact, the production of documents, it is very easy to underestimate how much CPU power and disc file space is required compared with that to support coding and testing of the software itself.

However, the first step is not to select tools, but to determine the appropriate techniques and methods to be used in the process. *Then* the appropriate tools are selected to support the methods (although one criterion for choosing a method might be availability of tool support). The methods must be matched to the existing culture, the characteristics of the development, the imposed schedules, and other operational considerations. Some of the technical criteria for selecting methods are discussed in Section 15.3 of Chapter 15, and the STARTS Guide (DTI, 1987) gives some further non-technical criteria for method selection. Once selected, the methods must be properly introduced, supported with training and monitored to ensure that they are really used and that the intended benefits are obtained.

If the software development tools and development environment are not already in use, they will have to be selected and established specifically for the project. Although the technical controller, quality manager and configuration manager will certainly be involved in the decisions, the project manager must ensure (or confirm) the suitability of the development facilities.

When the methods have been chosen, then the right tools not only increase efficiency but also have the further significant advantage of automatically defining part of the method of working, thus simplifying the definition of the process and ensuring conformance. Tools can encapsulate procedures and include tests against standards.

Even with a complete and appropriate set of tools, more is required for an effective software development environment. The tools need to be integrated so that they work together and perform further operations on transferred and shared data based on an object management system (OMS). They also need a common human communication interface so that staff are comfortable that they are working in a coherent environment. This integration into a unified toolset is a primary function of an integrated project support environment (IPSE).

A fully effective IPSE also supports the project process, and is itself a tool to support the method of working for the whole project. Although IPSE support for the process is thus a tool of project management, there will also be other project management tools specifically for the tasks of estimating, planning, work assignment, progress monitoring, analysis and reporting. These functions are supported by the explicit integration of project management tools into the IPSE, often referred to as the project manager's workbench (akin to the configuration manager's workbench, programmer's workbench, etc.).

Some IPSEs define a particular process, which makes them suitable candidates for use on a project for which their in-built process is applicable and sufficient. But note the expressed danger of choosing the IPSE first and then having to force the process and methods of working to conform.

More comprehensive IPSEs provide facilities for tailoring to any required process. This also includes the ability to extend and modify the defined project process as the development progresses and the incorporation of existing or separately supplied third party tools, so that different integrated toolsets can be provided, as required, for different projects supported in the same IPSE.

An IPSE should assist the project manager with the following:

1. Selection and definition of the process suitable for the project.
2. Selection and definition of the organization, methods and tools required.
3. Instantiation of the process, efficiently and completely, by defining it in the IPSE.
4. Integration of all the chosen tools into a unified toolset.
5. Support for inter-staff communication with IPSE facilities.
6. Support for the process in operation, by the combination of the tools and IPSE itself.

7. Automated data collection, which provides the feedback for project control.

Whilst the above functions are only partly achieved in currently available IPSEs, their fuller realisation is the aim of continuing IPSE development. Chapter 33 deals with IPSEs.

27.4.6 Contractural basis for the project

There is a three-way relationship between the project manager, the customer and the quality manager, based on the quality plan:

1. From the customer's point of view, the quality plan defines the process to assure that the product is of the required quality.
2. The quality plan also defines the activities which determine the correctness of operation of the intended process, measurement of the achieved quality against quality targets, and quality reporting mechanisms, all of which are responsibilities of the quality manager.
3. It is the responsibility of the project manager to produce the product with the required quality as well as on-time and to budget. To support this responsibility (and to make sure that quality reporting is as strongly established as progress reporting) the project manager and quality manager jointly use the quality plan as agreed with the customer.

For large bespoke software systems, this is a critical issue. For smaller projects, the issue may be less critical but is still an important aspect of concentrating the direction of the project by prior emphasis on the definition of the success criteria for the project.

An adequately founded project requires all the following plans and contracts:

1. A statement of requirements, defining the required product. This leads to the user manual and the requirement specification.
2. A code of practice, demonstrating ability to produce the product with technical development techniques, tools and trained skilled staff.
3. A quality plan, defining the means of determining the success of the process in operation.
4. A test plan, defining verification, validation and testing throughout the project to determine the correctness of what is being produced.
5. A configuration management plan, defining product possession.
6. A project plan, defining the use of resources against task-estimates for the project.
7. An organizational structure, defining authorities and responsibilities for applying staff resources to the development.
8. A project contract (with the customer, marketing or internally within the business), defining the business success criteria.

In principle, the above contractual basis is no different than that for a project involving any other technology. The difference is that for most engineering technologies, a robust well-defined technical process can generally be assumed for all the plans and contracts. In the case of software development, the technical process is not robust, nor is it sensible to assume it is well-defined in the minds of the generality of software developers. One of the major principles of 'software engineering' is to quantify everything in the software development that affects eventual project success or failure. The principles of this are described in Chapter 30, and a major part of the emphasis and content of the plans and contracts listed above is the setting of targets and defining the means of measurement of success against the targets in order to specify a 'well-defined' process on which the plans can be based.

27.5 Project planning

Section 27.2 introduced the subject of project management and placed it within the context of a system for project control. Project control depends not only on management of risk and the establishment of a suitable software development process as covered in Sections 27.3 and 27.4, but also on an adequate foundation of planning and progress measurement which involves:

1. Definition in detail of the work to be done, how it is to be performed, within what time-scale, and at what cost.
2. Assignment of this work in manageable packages to individuals or small terms.
3. Regular monitoring of the progress of the work packages by both formal and informal means.
4. Dealing with the problems that arise, such as departures from the plan requiring corrective action, technical difficulties or requests for changes impacting schedule or cost.
5. Evaluation of overall project performance and appropriate reporting to higher-level management and the customer.

Figure 27.2 showed the interaction of these activities as part of the function of project management. The principles of the activities have already been covered briefly in Section 27.2. This section and the following section deal in more detail with planning, work definition and assignment, progress monitoring and management reporting.

27.5.1 Planning process

Planning a software development project is a methodological process, starting with a clear statement of the work to be performed and culminating in a detailed project plan, which is a key part of the foundation for project control. The principal steps in the process are:

1. Preparation of the statement of work, ensuring that performance objectives are defined.
2. Preparation of the WBS and development of the work packages.
3. Estimation of the work content of each work package and of the overall project and estimation of total project costs.
4. Development of the scheduled network plans, introducing time and resource constraints.
5. Planning the staffing for the project and developing the project organization structure.
6. Establishing budgets and schedules for tasks and teams.
7. Preparation of supporting plans (quality plan, documentation plan, configuration management plan, risk management plans, reporting plan, etc.).
8. Consolidation of all of the above into a project plan.

Although the steps above are presented sequentially, it will be appreciated that project planning is an iterative process. It is necessary to recycle the various plans and schedules, in increasing detail, to achieve the best (or even possible) resolution of conflicts between availability of resources and budget and the required project time-scales.

Whilst the major effort on planning is required during the project initiation phase, planning continues throughout the project, as it progresses from phase to phase, as further details become apparent, and as changes are introduced.

27.5.2 Statement of work

The statement of work (SOW) defines the scope of the work to be undertaken. It is essential to ensure that all aspects of the customer requirement, as defined by the contract, have been covered and correctly understood. The work should be stated in unambiguous terms so that any work outside the defined scope of the contract can be clearly identified for a possible renegotiation of costs or schedule.

Key elements which must be considered in preparing a SOW are:

1. General scope of the contract (i.e. objectives and related background).
2. Customer specification of requirements.
3. Contractor's tasks.
4. Contract end items.
5. Data requirements.
6. Related studies, documentation and specifications.
7. Customer-furnished documentation.
8. Customer-furnished facilities, equipment and services.

Any intermediate objectives which must be met during the life of the contract should be identified, as well as the contract end items. The customer's priorities for time, technical performance or price must also be stated, enabling the project control system to be tailored to give these items sufficient visibility and the appropriate trade-off decisions to be made where necessary.

In some cases, the project will not have such a clearly identified customer as would appear to be implied above. Where the project does not have a specific customer (for instance, in the case of the development of a product line for the business), then it is very important that a surrogate customer (such as a product manager from marketing) is identified and a clear statement of work thrashed out in the project initiation phase. Otherwise the development project will suffer from moving goal-posts and marketing will suffer from never having a product developed in the required timescale. Obtaining a clear statement of work is *not* the same as obtaining a precise and complete specification. Recognition of the extent to which the latter is not achieved is part of the SOW, and a significant input to the risk management plans and choice of development process. If it is identified as a primary technical risk, then this will probably lead to some element of prototyping in the chosen development process (especially in the case of significant lack of definition of man-machine interfaces). It is necessary to link the identification of such areas in the SOW with early prototype phase products, identification of actual or surrogate customers and resources to work with the prototype(s), assignment of responsibilities to update and complete the specifications, and the contractural basis for the budget and schedule for the project.

27.5.3 Work breakdown structure

The work breakdown structure (WBS) is a product-oriented task hierarchy of all the work to be performed to accomplish the project contractural objectives. The products may be elements of software, hardware, documents, tests, reports, support services, or other quantified elements of the objectives. *Figure 27.8* shows an example of a WBS hierarchy diagram. Use of the term 'product-oriented' does *not* mean (as it is unfortunately sometimes taken to mean) that the WBS should follow a structural decomposition of the functions of the delivered product. It may do so where appropriate, but such a structure is inappropriate for much of a WBS for software development. Many of the most significant activities of software development, such as configuration management, reviewing, production of manuals, test strategy, etc., do not conform to the functional structure of the required product. Even the architectural design for implementation in code will not necessarily conform to the structure of the functions in the specification. If the structure of the WBS is not chosen well to fit the actual work, then key activities will disappear from view and significant amounts of work will be subsumed under the apparent tasks, be overlooked in estimat-

ing, not taken into account in monitoring progresss, and ultimately uncontrollable.

The proper meaning of 'product-oriented' tasks is that of being defined by the object produced, where object is meant in all the generality used in Section 27.4.4.

A WBS element is any one of the individual items in the WBS hierarchy, regardless of level.

A work package is a segment of effort required to complete a specific job or a service which is within the responsibility of a single unit (team or an individual) within the project organization. A work package is usually an element of the lowest level of the WBS.

Work packages are categorized into three types: discrete effort, level of effort and apportioned effort.

Discrete effort is where the work package has a clearly recognizable beginning and end, with a definable end-product. Most of the technical work of software development should be assigned to discrete effort work packages if the project manager is to realistically expect successful project control.

Level of effort is where the work cannot be associated with a definable object or result, but is measured only in terms of the resources consumed, with a time-phased, budgeted rate of consumption (i.e. number of man-months incurred per month). Examples are administration, departmental or team supervision, software development tool support, and some of the routine aspects of configuration management and quality assurance, but *not* the whole of configuration management and quality assurance if the project is adequately defined.

Apportioned effort provides a general service to support the project activities but is carried out by other parts of the organization whose role is not entirely included within the identified work packages. Examples include clerical and data processing services.

The main purpose of the WBS is to identify all the activities and end-items of the development project, and to define the detailed work packages required to enable the production of each end-item. It is a management tool to ensure that all effort contributes directly to the project contractual objectives. The WBS technique is applicable to all types of projects. The extent of its application and level of detail is determined by the scope, complexity and duration of the project. Simple, low-cost projects of short duration do not require a detailed WBS, but it is still worthwhile defining the specific work elements to ensure the production of the contractural end-items.

The primary structure of the WBS is derived from the intersections of the software development activities and the phases of the chosen software development process, as discussed in Chapter 15 and Section 27.3, and the top level of the structure will be closely related to the process definition diagram, as described in Section 27.4.4.

Below the top level, there is no set formula for the construction of the WBS. Project managers must use their own judgement, taking into account the principles of fitting the design of the WBS to the project organization and the suitability of work packages for task assignment. More positively, the project manager should regard the construction of the WBS as a significant opportunity to impose a strong control on the way the project will run. The WBS design will affect the way costs are collected and reported, and must be compatible with accounting constraints as well as with cost reports required by the company and the customer.

Each WBS element should be assigned a coded identification. A simple decimal coding system logically representing the WBS structure is recommended, as illustrated in *Figure 27.8*. However, any alphanumeric or other pre-established coding system may be used if preferred. The WBS element identification is used as a central reference for project control, estimates, cost accumulation and reporting.

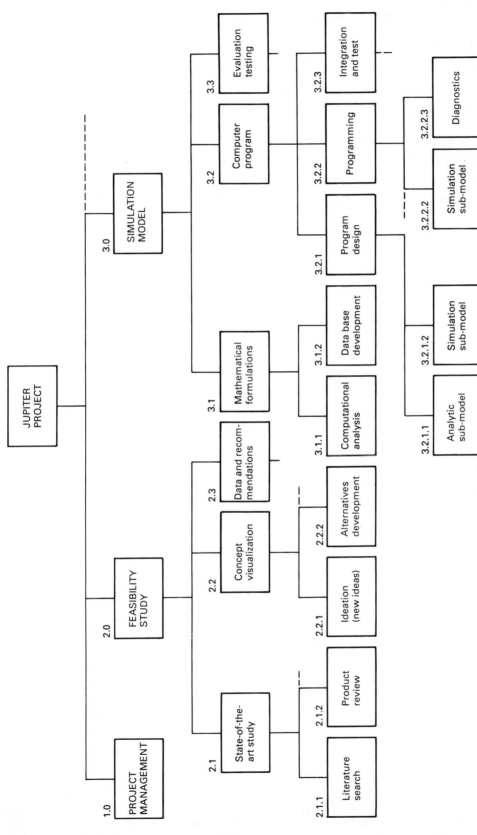

Figure 27.8 Example WBS hierarchy diagram

27.5.4 Estimation, scheduling and logic networks

The principles of estimating have been stated in Section 27.2.1.2. In the context of the WBS, it is tempting to think of estimating primarily in terms of estimates for each work package and then sum all the task estimates to give the project totals. However such an estimating technique is only one of a number that should be used, and a plan based primarily on summation of task estimates with scheduling derived from networking the tasks according to presumptions on precedence relationships and staff availability will generally be inadequate for software development. Experience of such plans shows that they are usually so optimistic that they do not represent an adequate basis for successful project control. The bottom-up estimate needs to be combined with top-down estimates derived from previous projects using the techniques of analogy, expert judgement and metrics-based cost models. Only with such insight is the project cost estimate likely to be valid, and realistic trade-offs able to be made between schedule and staff availability.

It is inevitable that the accuracy of the estimate will depend on the level of detailed knowledge of the software to be developed. This will not be very precise in the early stages of the project, and estimates will have to be based on the high-level WBS elements. As the project proceeds, re-estimates should be performed at lower levels of detail and reflecting any changes in the design which may have occurred.

Scheduling forces the project manager to focus on the timing relationships between the significant tasks necessary for successful completion of the contract objectives. Determination of the optimum order in which tasks should be performed requires the establishment of priorities and interdependencies, and decisions on whether tasks can be performed serially or in parallel. In conjunction with the estimating process, scheduling forces estimates to be quantified in discrete terms and tasks to be placed in proper relationship to each other. Adjustment of scheduling may be required to avoid peaks and troughs in required effort and resources, and make-or-buy decisions may have to be made with regard to tasks which are resource constrained. The final schedules of the tasks in the plan are basic to the measurement of project progress and the prediction of problems.

Logic networks graphically portray the logical relationships between the WBS work elements and their relative timing. Used together with the WBS, networks are particularly useful for the conceptual planning of a project when it is necessary to assess the relative merits of alternative approaches. They enable the build-up of funding to be defined and establish some of the critical areas for risk analysis and margin allocation.

For a software development process based on the phases and activities shown in *Figure 27.9*, a possible top-level structure for the WBS would be that given in *Figure 27.10*, which after estimation and scheduling would result in the network of *Figure 27.11*.

For a small project, a network such as that in *Figure 27.11* would be all that is required, but for a large project a set of networks may be drawn to constitute a hierarchy related to different levels of management. It is important that each level contains only as much detail as is necessary for insight at that level of management. The standard four levels are defined in *Figure 27.12(a)* and Figure 27.12(b) shows the relationship of the levels of networks. Figure 27.12(c) shows a similar set of bar charts which may be used as an alternative way of illustrating the principal project sequences and the timing of the project milestones.

All networks must be drawn on a true time-based grid to give proper visibility to the dates when events are planned to take place. This is particularly true for networks for software development projects. The higher level networks may be quite skeletal in some parts and, if they are laid out for convenience without scrupulous observance of the time base, can give a very false impression to senior management.

Networks facilitate the rapid evaluation of changes and alternative replanning possibilities. They also provide a basis for several forms of analysis, using such techniques as CPM (critical path method) and PERT (programme evaluation and review technique). The networks can be used to define and monitor the critical path to contract completion (i.e. the longest remaining set of serial activities and events which must occur to complete the contract). PERT techniques are widely used to determine the available slack on event completion dates and the effect of slip on events as the project progresses.

However, conclusions drawn purely from analysis of the network of a software development project are generally not as valid as those that can be derived from analysis of networks of hardware manufacturing projects. The precedences and dependencies in software development are much less absolute. (Almost any task in software development can be started without waiting for the 'preceding' tasks to absolutely finish.) The whole drive of defining an object-oriented software development process, and ensuring that it is really carried through to representation in the process definition diagram, is to diminish the fuzziness in relationships between software development tasks. Nonetheless, 'finished' and precedence-dependence relationships still depend on people and reviews, and will not be hard-cast enough to support pure network analysis without insight by the project manager into what is actually being done by the various staff on the project.

This brings us to the next problem with networks. In the case of hardware fabrication, project control can be exerted increasingly tightly by definition of increasingly detailed networks showing precise dependencies between smaller work packages. Whilst it is entirely valid to draw networks at a reasonable level for software development, it does not make sense to try to draw a network for small work packages (such as those assigned to individuals within a team). This is because any attempt to define precise relationships is fictional and would either put an artificial and disabling clamp on the work of the team or would be meaningless as a basis for analysis. In terms of the network levels shown in Figure 27.12(a), it is quite valid to draw networks as appropriate for levels 1 to 3, but, for software projects, no attempt should be made to draw level 4 networks for work packages at team level. The assignment for the team is a set of tasks with estimates and schedules using a form such as that shown in *Figure 27.15*. Analysis of work in progress is based on the information provided by weekly progress summaries such as shown in *Figure 27.16*.

For many projects, particularly those that are technically innovative, it will not be possible at the commencement to plan the complete project in detail. For these cases a 'rolling wave' technique can be used in which those activities that are too small and too distant to be easily defined are initially planned in less detail. Thus the first three months (quarter year) of the project would be planned down to the detail of all assignable work packages, the next quarter planned in less detail, the work being broken down only into planning packages (aggregations of work packages), as represented by level 3 of the network. The third quarter would use even higher level planning packages, and so on.

Planning packages summarize definite work which cannot yet be detailed into assignable work packages. They should be properly scheduled so that they may be mixed with work packages when only part of the work can be detailed, but must be planned as work packages before any of the work in that period commences.

At the end of the first month, the planning detail for the first month of the second quarter is increased to assignable work packages, the first month of the third quarter is increased to level 3, and so on. The process is repeated at the end of each successive month, producing a rolling wave effect. The periods of months/quarters could be changed to longer periods such as

ACTIVITY \ PHASE	PROJECT INITIATION	REQMNT SPECIFICATION	ARCHITECTURAL DESIGN	DETAILED DESIGN	CODE AND UNIT TEST	INTEGRATION & TEST	ACCEPTANCE TEST	MAINTENANCE
Project management	Project estimating, planning, scheduling, procedures, organization etc.	Project management, project planning, contracts, liaison etc.	Project management, status monitoring, contracts, liaison, etc.	Project management, status monitoring, contracts, liaison, etc.	Project management, status monitoring, contracts, liaison, etc.	Project management, status monitoring, contracts, liaison, etc.	Project management, status monitoring, contracts, liaison, etc.	Support management, status monitoring, contracts, liaison, etc.
Technical control	Technical strategy, technical plans, technical standards	System models and risk analysis, appearance test plan, acquire V and V tools for reqmnts and design, top-level test plan	Design quality, models and risk analysis, draft test plans, acquire test tools	Design integrity, detailed test plans, acquire test tools	Design integrity, detailed test plans, install test tools	Design integrity, support test tools, monitor testing	Design integrity, support test tools, monitor acceptance	Design integrity, risk analysis test plans
Requirement specification	Analyse requirements, determine user needs	Analyse existing system, determine user needs, integrate document and iterate requirements	Update requirements	Update requirements	Update requirements	Update requirements	Update requirements	Determine user needs and problems, update requirements
Architectural design	Design planning	Develop basic architecture, models, prototypes	Develop architectural design, models, prototypes	Update design	Update design	Update design	Update design	Update design
Detailed design	Identify programming methods and resources	Prototypes of algorithms, team planning	Models, algorithms investigation, team planning	Detailed design, component documentation	Update detailed design	Update detailed design	Update detailed design	Detailed design of changes and enhancements
Code and unit test	Identify programming methods and resources	Identify programming tools, team planning	Acquire programming tools and utilities, team planning	Integration planning	Code and unit test	Integrate software, update code	Update code	Code and unit test of changes and enhancements
Verification, validation and test	V and V requirements	V and V specification	V and V architectural design	V and V detailed design, V and V design changes	V and V top portions of code, V and V design changes	Perform product test V and V design changes	Perform acceptance test, V and V design changes	V and V changes and enhancements
Manuals	Define users manual	Outline portions of users manual	Draft users, operators manuals, outline maintenance manual	Draft maintenance manual	Full draft users and operators manuals	Final users, operators and maintenance manuals	Acceptance of manuals	Update manual
Configuration management	CM plans and procedures	CM plans, procedures, identify CM tools	CM of requirements, design, acquire CM tools	CM of requirements, design, detailed design, install CM tools, set up library	CM of requirements, design, code, operate library	CM of requirements, design, code, operate library	CM of requirements, design, code, operate library	CM of all documentation, operate library
Quality assurance	QA plans, project procedures and standards	Standards, procedures, QA plans, identify QA tools	QA of requirements, design, project standards, acquire QA tools	QA of requirements, design, detailed design	QA of requirements, design, code	QA of requirements, design, code, testing	QA of requirements, design, code, acceptance	QA of maintenance updates

Figure 27.9 Primary structure of software development work by activity and phase

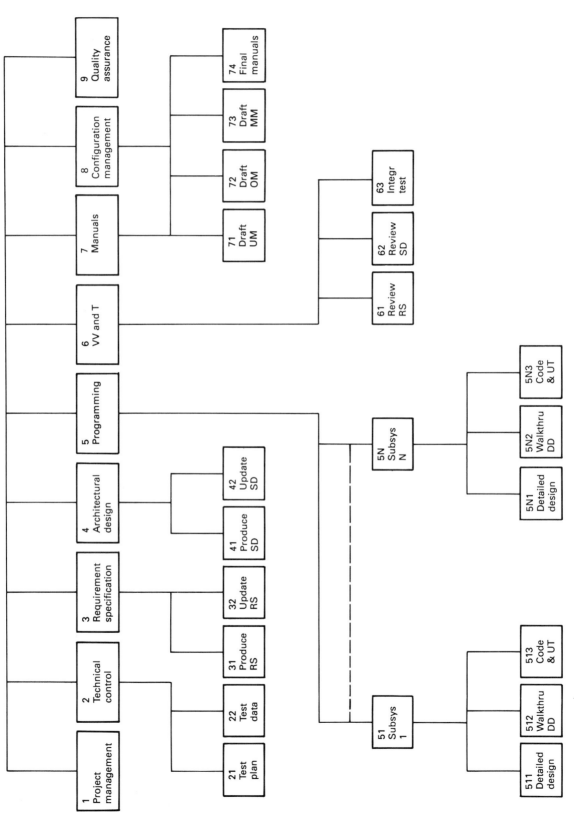

Figure 27.10 Example of a WBS for a software development project

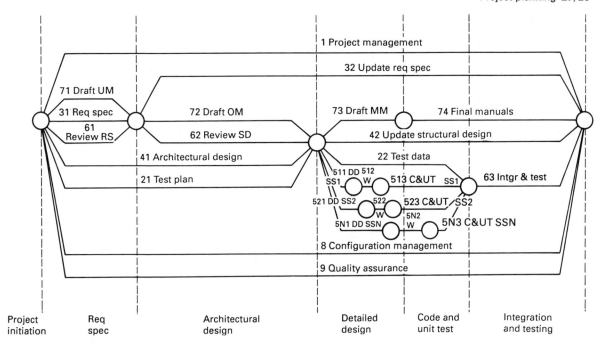

Figure 27.11 Network diagram for the example WBS in Figure 27.10

quarters/years as suitable for the particular project, but should not be any shorter.

The rolling wave technique requires less detailed planning at the commencement of the project, and consequently there is far less documentation to be updated when changes are introduced. However, it is very important to ensure that critical activities and important interdependencies occurring later in the project are explicitly identified. This is done by ensuring that the process definition diagram (Section 27.4.4) is fully drawn out for the project and planning is completed at least to the level corresponding to the PDD though to the end of the project.

27.5.5 Staffing, organization and budgets

The WBS provides a framework for the assignment of responsibilities to the operating units of the project organization. As discussed in Section 27.4.2, the organization for the project is derived from the generalized organization chart (Figure 27.4) by considering the same intersections of the software development activities and the phases of the chosen software development process as for the development of the WBS. This enables the project manager to ensure compatibility, between the work definition structure and the organizational structure. As illustrated in Figure 27.13, these structures will progressively develop as the project progresses through the chosen life cycle phases. Section 7.4 in Boehm (1981) works through a simple example of such a phase-based development of a project organization.

It will take a number of iterations of the plan to converge on a smooth staff loading. Programme changes may be required to use staff efficiently. It may be cost effective to slip certain milestones to avoid difficult staffing peaks. In particular, an incremental developmental strategy can help considerably to produce a flat staff distribution against time.

The WBS elements must be identified with the project organization, with an individual responsible for each element (either doing the work personally, or in the role of team leader). From allocation of staff to specific WBS tasks, a detailed month-by-month staffing plan can be prepared. The staffing plan must be specific, but not to try to be precise on aspects that cannot yet be decided in detail. The rolling wave technique described above should be used. For the programme immediately ahead, the specific activities of each individual or team planned to work on the project should be shown in the form of a bar chart. For the more distant phases, only broad staffing numbers should be allocated to each activity to permit the organization to be planned. How far ahead it is appropriate to plan an individual's assignments will depend on the size of the project, and the staff involved. Probably the most valuable feature of the staffing plan is that it stimulates the project manager's thinking about who will be performing the various tasks on the project. It is also an opportunity to involve the key personnel in the project at an early stage. This enables them to influence and become identified with the project objectives, and increases confidence in the plans.

Budgeted expenditure should, wherever possible, be built up from allocations at work package level. When it is clearly impracticable to plan all the work at the lowest WBS levels, budgets should be identified at higher WBS levels for further subdivision at the earliest opportunity. Such budget allocations must be time-phased and specifically earmarked for the work for which they are intended. Controls must be established to ensure that they are not used to perform any other work.

The budget amounts are formulated in accordance with the business's budget and cost reporting standards, and allocated to the project development phases to produce a budget baseline consistent with the WBS, against which cost and schedule performance will be monitored. The project manager must ensure the commitment of the various team leaders and performing organizations to carry out the assigned work to an agreed budget and timescale. The project budget description consists of a set of expenditure versus time plots. As work is completed or expenses incurred, the amounts are plotted on the same charts and the variations are noted. It is the project manager's responsibility to monitor these variations and understand and justify the reasons for deviations.

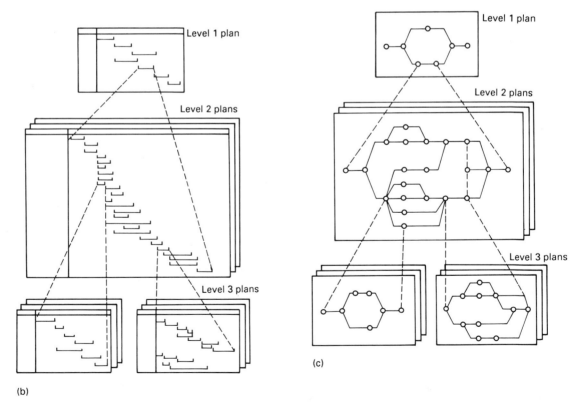

Level of management	Level of information	Level of planning
Customer and senior management	1	
Project manager and management staff	2	
Departments and sub-contractors	3	
Detailed planning and control at work package level	4	

(a)

(b)

(c)

Figure 27.12 (a) Typical relationship between levies of detail and levels of management (b) Hierarchy of bar charts (c) Hierarchy of network plans

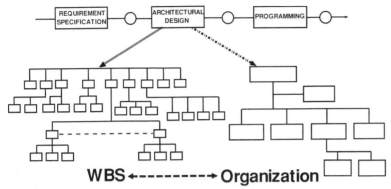

Figure 27.13 Expansion of a phase of the process

27.5.6 Project plan

Whatever the scale of the project, a project plan is required which clearly defines: the project objectives, the necessary work to achieve these objectives, when and by whom this work will be performed, the methods to be employed, how long the project will take, and how much it will cost.

Careful attention must be paid to the potential impact of external constraints on the development schedule. Wherever possible, a tolerance to delays in externally-controlled events should be built into detailed plans. External constraints should be carefully documented as a list of assumptions and shown on the formal schedule as critical events. The customer must be made aware of the impact of each external constraint on the development schedule. Wherever possible, contract provisions should exclude cost or time penalties arising from external causes.

The project plan is supported by a number of specialized plans. These plans will define the approach to documentation, configuration management and development support, quality targets and assurance of achievement of those targets, risk management, etc. They are subject to the appropriate internal and external approvals, and the associated procedures, standards and facilities must be part of the explicit training of project development staff.

Milestones should be identified for each level of the network. All aspects of the project should be covered, including facilities and logistics support. The definition of each milestone should include the associated VV&T, CM and QA activities which confirm the satisfactory completion of the relevant task. Particularly important are the milestones related to the establishment of the baselines at the end of each project phase. Milestone lists should be compiled for each WBS level. Those at the highest level will be used for reporting to upper-level management and the customer.

The project plan is started during the proposal/study period, and refined, established and baselined during the project initiation phase. It is kept up to date with any necessary changes throughout the life of the project. It is required to:

1. Provide the project manager with a reliable basis for allocating resources from start to finish of the project, and for predicting, monitoring and reporting progress and costs.
2. Provide management with a high-level summary of the project and a means of monitoring project status.
3. Provide the customer with the same insight and progress monitoring ability.

An overall format for the project plan is shown in *Figure 27.14*, taken from the IEEE Standard for Software Project Management Plans (IEEE, 1988). For more detailed information, the reader is referred to the standard and also to Fairley (1987).

Title page

Revision chart

Preface

Table of contents

List of figures

List of tables

1. Introduction
   1.1 Project Overview
   1.2 Project deliverables
   1.3 Evolution of the SPMP
   1.4 Reference materials
   1.5 Definitions and acronyms

2. Project organization
   2.1 Process model
   2.2 Organizational structure
   2.3 Organizational boundaries and interfaces
   2.4 Project responsibilities

3. Managerial process
   3.1 Management objectives and priorities
   3.2 Assumptions, dependencies, and constraints
   3.3 Risk management
   3.4 Monitoring and controlling mechanisms
   3.5 Staffing plan

4. Technical process
   4.1 Methods, tools, and techniques
   4.2 Software documentation
   4.3 Project support functions

5. Work packages, schedule, and budget
   5.1 Work packages
   5.2 Dependencies
   5.3 Resource requirements
   5.4 Budget and resource allocation
   5.5 Schedule

Additional components

Index

Appendices

Figure 27.14 Software project management plan format

27.6 Progress monitoring and reporting

27.6.1 Work definition and work assignment

The work packages defined by the WBS are assigned to small development teams, or to individuals. A valid work package must represent a task or job at the performing level, clearly distinguished from all other work packages. Work packages must not straddle the boundaries of phases of the process or activities, but work packages from different activities may be combined into the responsibility of a single team. The size of a work package may reflect the project manager's view of the capabilities of the individuals involved or the desire to monitor work elements more or less closely.

On a large project with a number of levels of management, a work package agreement form may be used to define precisely the work packages, assumptions, areas of risk, key staff, manpower and budget resources, and standards and procedures to be used. It is duly signed by both the senior manager and the work package manager (the individual responsible for completion of the tasks according to the agreement). The work package manager then assigns and monitors weekly progress on the tasks to meet the agreed schedule and budget.

For smaller software development projects the paperwork of such a formal agreement is unnecessary, and the project manager will assign work directly to team leaders (or in some cases individuals) using something similar to the weekly progress summary (WPS) form shown in *Figure 27.15*.

The initial assignment will be a set of tasks, identified in the first columns, with estimated effort (in man-days) and scheduled finish date in the next two columns. No task should be more than two weeks in duration and the pattern of work should be designed to have at least one planned task completion every week for the period scheduled for the set of tasks. The whole period should be of the order of about two months and never more than three months. (Software development at this level of detail will change significantly if an attempt is made to plan more than three months ahead.) Any particular WPS may not survive right through to completion of all the tasks on it. When appropriate, it will be overtaken by a new WPS containing any residue of unfinished tasks that are still relevant, together with changed, new and further tasks which constitute the updated immediate detailed plan for the team over the subsequent period of one to three months.

Although it may not be necessary to use a signed work package agreement form, nonetheless it is important that the team leader, in receiving the assignment defined by the WPS, understands and accepts the commitment to complete the tasks within the agreed budget and schedule.

27.6.2 Progress monitoring

Project control is essentially dependent on integration of technical performance measurement, progress monitoring and cost (expenditure) monitoring. Technical performance measurement is based on technical reviews and walkthroughs. Progress monitoring depends on objective measurement of work accomplishment and is based on the weekly progress summaries and on non-technical project meetings. Costs are recorded on the same basis as budgets so that recorded costs can be related to work performed, with the primary input (man-days) derived from the WPS.

The monitoring system must be established during the project initiation phase, with the project manager making sure that the

WEEKLY PROGRESS SUMMARY

PROJECT: Jupiter

WORK PACKAGE: Simulation Model

NUMBER: 247.3

STATUS AT: _____

DATE OF ISSUE: 01.09.89

SUBTASK NO.	DESCRIPTION	TOTAL SCHEDULED EFFORT (M-DAYS)	SCHEDULED FINISH DATE	EFFORT THIS WEEK (M-DAYS)	EFFORT TO DATE (M-DAYS)	EFFORT TO FINISH (M-DAYS)	ESTIMATED FINISH DATE	COMMENT
3.1.1.1	Update spec from previous version	10	15.09.89					
3.1.1.2	Define computational equations	5	22.09.89					
3.1.1.3	Team Walkthrough of equations	2	25.09.89					
3.1.2.1	Specify form of model database	5	15.09.89					
3.1.2.2	Create initial set of data	5	29.09.89					
3.1.3.1	Draft User Manual for Sim.model	5	29.09.89					
3.1.3.2	Review Math Formulations	2	02.10.89					
3.2.1.1	Analytic Sub-model design	10	13.10.89					
3.2.1.2	Simulation Sub-model design	8	17.10.89					
3.2.1.3	Program Design Review	2	18.10.89					
3.2.1.4	Updated Spec,Design,UM,Testplan	4	20.10.89					
3.2.2.1	Coded Analytic Sub-model	12	03.11.89					
3.2.2.2	Coded Simulation Sub-model	6	03.11.89					
3.2.2.3	Diagnostics Software	5	10.11.89					
3.2.3	Integration and Test	15	17.11.89					
3.3	Evaluation Testing	20	08.12.89					
	PRODUCTIVE TOTALS	116	08.12.89					
	NON - PRODUCTIVE							

Figure 27.15 Assignment of a set of tasks to a team

WEEKLY PROGRESS SUMMARY

PROJECT: ___Jupiter___

WORK PACKAGE: ___Simulation Model___

NUMBER: ___247.3___

STATUS AT: ___03.11.89___

DATE OF ISSUE: ___01.09.89___

SUBTASK NO.	DESCRIPTION	TOTAL SCHEDULED EFFORT (M-DAYS)	SCHEDULED FINISH DATE	EFFORT THIS WEEK (M-DAYS)	EFFORT TO DATE (M-DAYS)	EFFORT TO FINISH (M-DAYS)	ESTIMATED FINISH DATE	COMMENT
3.1.1.1	Update spec from previous version	10	15.09.89		9	-	14.09.89	
3.1.1.2	Define computational equations	5	22.09.89		6	-	22.09.89	
3.1.1.3	Team Walkthrough of equations	2	25.09.89		4	-	26.09.89	
3.1.2.1	Specify form of model database	5	15.09.89		5	-	22.09.89	
3.1.2.2	Create initial set of data	5	29.09.89		3	-	29.09.89	
3.1.3.1	Draft User Manual for Sim.model	5	29.09.89		5	-	05.10.89	
3.1.3.2	Review Math Formulations	2	02.10.89		2	-	06.10.89	
3.2.1.1	Analytic Sub-model design	10	13.10.89		12	-	20.10.89	
3.2.1.2	Simulation Sub-model design	8	17.10.89		10	-	20.10.89	
3.2.1.3	Program Design Review	2	18.10.89		2	-	23.10.89	
3.2.1.4	Updated Spec,Design,UM,Testplan	4	20.10.89	1	1	2	10.11.89	
3.2.2.1	Coded Analytic Sub-model	12	03.11.89	4	10	5	10.11.89	
3.2.2.2	Coded Simulation Sub-model	6	03.11.89	4	6	8	17.11.89	First version for initial integration
3.2.2.3	Diagnostics Software	5	10.11.89		0	5	17.11.89	Replan?
3.2.3	Integration and Test	15	17.11.89		0	15	01.12.89	
3.3	Evaluation Testing	20	08.12.89		0	20	15.12.89	
3.2.2.4	Updated Sim sub-model code				0	5	24.11.89	Second version to complete sub-model
	PRODUCTIVE TOTALS	116	08.12.89	9	75	60	15.12.89	
	NON - PRODUCTIVE			1	5			JPL sick 1 day this week

Figure 27.16 Team progress reporting and estimates to completion

software development staff are comfortable with the procedures and the use of the forms. Any problems should be uncovered and corrected while the team is still small, and data collected from the earliest stages of the project. Too often this data is lost and not available for later use within the same project, or as an input for planning other projects.

27.6.2.1 Weekly progress summary

Weekly reports are prepared by team leaders on the WPS forms. These force the staff in the teams to crystallize their thinking, leading to effective self-assessment and critique of progress. This is a very important part of the measurement of progress as input to the project manager – much more than mere entry of numbers on forms.

For each task on the WPS, an entry is made for the effort this week (in man-days – remembering that this effort may have been contributed by various members of the team), and cumulative effort to date. This information is simply factual and it is *not* sufficient for any assumptions to be made about the proportion of the work performed compared with the total task estimate. The team leader, in discussion with the team members, is required to make an assessment of the number of man-days left to complete each task that is currently open and a commitment to the date of completion (see *Figure 27.16*). This committed date must include the team leader's planning for near-term arrangements for work by team members on the various tasks and any diversion onto non-project work, training or holidays. The most valuable professionals in a software development project are those who can reliably meet their committed short-term dates given to the project manager. The entries for effort to finish and estimated finish date on the WPS must never be lazily derived by subtracting effort and time so far from the original

estimates. It is of course reasonable to see the effort to complete more clearly on tasks that have been started rather than on those which have yet to begin. The size of the latter is not necessarily reconsidered every week, though any schedule implications of slip in present tasks must be thought through and future task schedules updated. This weekly assessment is aided if the tasks are short and clear enough, and this obviously requires careful consideration when the elements of the WBS are planned.

Note that when a task on the WPS is declared to be finished, it *cannot* be restarted. In order to retain a valid basis for project control, where further work is found to be required to update or extend the item previously thought finished, a new task should be created (and added to the WPS with estimate and schedule).

Properly completed on Friday afternoons, and thoroughly studied by the project manager on Monday mornings, with prompt response back to the team leader on matters arising, the WPS forms will ensure that the project manager is continually aware of the status of the project, and able to control its direction. Moreover, the project manager is not faced with a major update for each monthly management report.

The comment column on the WPS may be used to identify current problems, other unplanned activities and potential difficulties. Non-productive effort may also be noted, covering training, leave, sickness, office moves, etc., which although charged to other job numbers, completes the team's work summary for the week. However, the comment columns should not contain significant amounts of text, and any further prose reports should be avoided as being time-consuming, liable to filtering by wishful thinking and often failing to provide useful information. Problems arising requiring a faster response than the WPS should be addressed by an *ad hoc* meeting. Conversely the notes on the WPS ensure that information and events are recorded and not forgotten.

27.6.2.2 *Non-technical project meetings*

As well as the technical review meetings and walkthroughs to ensure correct technical performance, the project manager will need to use the following types of non-technical meetings to monitor and control the project:

1. *Ad hoc* meetings to deal with immediate problems and strategy. The meeting is held for a definite purpose with a view to achieving a specific result. The attendees must be carefully limited, the decisions reached made clear, and follow-up decisions and actions defined.
2. Progress meetings to deal with status, progress and problems with achieving milestones. Working from the WPS forms, the project manager should meet weekly with the team leaders. Bi-lateral progress meetings are recommended in preference to meetings with wider participation, to avoid wasted time and the inclusion of inappropriate subject matter. The one-to-one basis allows concentration on relevant aspects, but it is a difficult discipline to find the time to meet with every team leader every week. Also the project manager must keep key staff fully informed on the status of the project as a whole. It is unrealistic to try to achieve this through the bi-lateral meetings and it is best done at the staff meeting, in relationship to the monthly project review with senior management and the customer.
3. Staff meetings to deal with non-technical matters other than project progress. These may be fortnightly or monthly with the key staff for general communication and to discuss the non-technical aspects of how the work is done, including working methods, allocation of resources, personnel matters, etc. The number of items arising at each meeting serves as a guide to the required frequency. Staff meetings encourage communication on a formal and informal basis throughout the organizations participating in the project. They should be regularly scheduled at a fixed time and not last more than one or two hours.

The total number of the above types of meetings must be kept to a necessary minimum. On most software development projects it will be sufficient to hold weekly bi-lateral meetings and fortnightly staff meetings. When planning meetings, the frequency, format, attendees and subject area must be carefully considered. Due attention must be given to the relationship between technical reviews and non-technical project meetings. The project manager should consider drawing up a project calendar of planned reviews and meetings for the year ahead. This can help ensure that critical meetings are allocated and that provision is made for related costs.

27.6.2.3 *Information feedback*

The collected WPS forms, either as paper or in an automated computer system, serve as one of the primary forms of data collection on the project. Following the collection and analysis of data from the monitoring system, it is extremely important for the project manager to feed back information on overall project status, any replanning, and other decisions, to the project staff. This feedback loop also acts as a check that information is being correctly passed from staff to the project manager. The methods available to document project status and decisions, in ways suitable for keeping all the staff involved include:

1. A weekly consolidated status sheet prepared from the WPS forms.
2. Slip charts (see *Figure 27.17*).
3. Updated and publicly displayed process definition diagrams, showing work completed.

4. Updated and publicly displayed scheduled networks with a 'wavefront' showing progress.

The turnaround of information should be as rapid as possible and is greatly assisted by computer automation for progress reporting.

27.6.3 **Replanning and change control**

It is important to recognize that the project plan must explicitly address risks and contingency and must be dynamic; reference risk management plans discussed in Section 27.3. Through the normal processes of iterative analysis, design and implementation changes, resource problems, customer or environment changes and re-estimates, the project plan will require regular updating and revision. Copies of each version of the project plan should be properly stored in the project history file together with the reasons for revision.

Since the project plan is the basis for management and review of project activities, it should not be changed for every small slippage, since that allows the project to slide imperceptibly one day at a time, until brought up hard against a critical milestone. Nor should the plan be kept unchanged regardless of circumstances, thereby allowing the project to become out of formal control.

There will be numerous occasions when team leaders will wish to recommend changes to the scope and content of their work packages. If such changes affect areas outside their scope of responsibility, for whatever reason, then a change control procedure must be used. Approval for the changes must come from the project manager who is in a position to consider the impact on other areas of the project. The changes will only be permitted after their effect on the project plan have been analysed and they have been budgeted and authorized.

The system for controlling changes usually depends on some change control form, covering technical description, justification, strategy, cost, milestone schedule, key individuals, documents to be produced/changed, resources required, assumptions and dependencies. Such a system must be tailored to provide the project manager with all the necessary information to analyse the project performance, assess any required corrective actions, and make a decision.

The project manager must decide what is a suitable level of detail for such a form after consideration of the size of the project and the likely size of changes. In a large project, if a change has many ramifications or itself significantly impacts cost or schedule, the written submission needs to be virtually a mini-plan. Some formal change control is always necessary but in a small project a simple system, properly used, is quite adequate. It is as important to avoid unnecessary form filling and to expedite rapid processing of requests for changes as it is to avoid inadequate replanning and fuzzy control.

27.6.4 **Management reporting**

The information for reporting to senior management and the customer is obtained from the data collected by the progress monitoring system. It is analysed and reported using the method established and agreed in the project plan. The plan will also state the frequency at which the reviews with senior management and the customer will take place, although it is normal for these to be held monthly.

Before preparing the presentation for the monthly review, it is worthwhile for the project manager to stand back from the project and carry out a private review of the way in which the project is being managed and is progressing. This personal perspective reset is helpful in looking at the project from an overall strategy instead of at the level of tactical detail in which the project manager has been immersed in the previous month. Since the project aim is to complete the development as planned and stated in the contract, the starting point of the perspective reset must be a review of the contract and an analysis of the project activities, plans and problems with respect to the contract. The best method of carrying this out is for the project manager to pose critical questions about the project, the plans, the staff and the understanding of the project tasks and answer the questions from the perspective of senior management and the customer. Thus the project manager is prompted to realise wider implications that might not have been seen in the hurley-burley of detailed project control. Also, the monthly project presentation will be prepared at the level of information and strategic decisions required by senior management rather than fall into the trap of reporting a lot of detailed news on the project which is worse than useless at the monthly meeting.

The simplest method of reporting is to review the milestone list, task list (tasks finished, tasks in progress, tasks not yet started) and the top-level scheduled network, comparing actual progress with planned progress. This may be accompanied by reporting project expenditure, usually by comparing planned and actual cumulative man-months against time, and a chart showing personnel total against time. While these charts provide a good indication of overall project staffing problems, they do not provide any information on how such problems relate to the progress of individual task elements or the overall project. Therefore, it is usually necessary to give details of expenditure for WBS items with special attention drawn to any items with large under-runs or over-runs. This approach identifies the reasons for over-spending against budget, but the form of presentation of the information does not provide much immediate visibility on the project status. Estimates for completion are based on the project manager's perception of current progress

and its effect on future tasks and schedules. The complete set of information is likely to be overwhelming in detail and opaque in providing a view of the significant issues. It is difficult for the project manager to get the essential points across without being sidetracked into issues of detail. The following three techniques are explicitly aimed at clarifying the presentation of the major points at issue for the project.

27.6.4.1 Slip chart

An example of a slip chart is shown in Figure 27.17. Slip charts show graphically the up-to-date history of milestones for a work package or a project and provide a valuable input for decision making and the planning and prediction of future achievement. Their essential value for the monthly review is that they can quickly be appreciated by the reviewers, who have had no contact with the project for the past month, and can see what is going on without having to wade through a lot of detailed charts.

The slip charts are based on significant milestones. Elapsed time is measured vertically and planned time horizontally. Each week new predictions of milestone completion dates are entered from analysis of the WPS sheets. A milestone for which there is no slippage is represented by a line which progresses vertically downwards until, on completion, it reaches the sloping edge of the chart. A line tending to the right represents slippage, and a line tending to the left represents pull-back.

Reviewers are thus presented with a pictorial record of progress showing past, present and expected future performance. This enables them to see quickly what is happening and to identify those tasks requiring corrective action. It is important for the monthly reports that the milestones chosen for the slip charts are not too numerous and concern only those items of

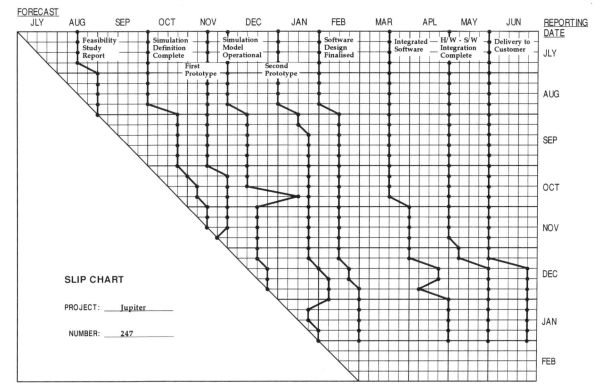

Figure 27.17 Example slip chart

explicit interest to senior management and the customer. It should be pointed out that the slip charts are not only effective in making clear project performance, but also equally make clear the performance of the project manager. Lines which skip along in parallel to the sloping edge show a project manager who is unable to control risk and plan ahead meaningfully.

As well as being used for monthly reporting, slip charts can be used within the project with the following advantages:

1. Ease of communication and comprehension.
2. Reduction in paperwork (updates are easily added, nothing is changed).
3. Management by objectives. Team leaders are involved in setting the objectives, and reported changes are highlighted by the unfolding picture on the slip chart.
4. They provide a means of calibrating an individual's optimism/pessimism over a period of time, which is useful for future planning.
5. Identifying the causes of slippage or pull-back can improve the planning of subsequent tasks. For example, pull-back may be undesirable if excessive resources have been used to the detriment of an equally important task.

27.6.4.2 Earned value system and cumulative performance chart

The earned value system is a technique for assessing the progress, status, and likely final cost of a large, complex software project. The system requires a value to be assigned to each project task. This becomes an 'earned value' as each task is completed. The value assigned to each WBS task must cover all expected direct charges and the appropriate proportion of indirect and overhead costs. At the beginning of the project the planned accumulated earned value for the project is plotted against time, according to the schedule for the completion of each task, and including the amount of level of effort and apportioned effort scheduled to be accomplished within a given time period. The curve, referred to as the budgeted cost of work scheduled (BCWS) (see *Figure 27.18*), is used as the basis of performance measurement, against which project progress will be assessed. The project manager will almost certainly keep some part of the budget as a management reserve, rather than use up the entire budget on planned tasks at the beginning. This will result in the initial BCWS finishing at a lower level than the budgeted cost at completion.

Each month, the earned values of all completed tasks, plus the appropriate portion of the budgets for level of effort and apportioned effort, are summed to give the budgeted cost for work performed (BCWP). The actual costs incurred by the project up to the reporting date, to accomplish the work performed, are derived from the project accounting system to provide the actual cost of work performed (ACWP).

Comparisons between the relative values of BCWS, BCWP and ACWP provides an overview of progress against schedule and actual cost of work performed against budget, as shown in Figure 27.18 which shows a predicted overspend and a schedule slippage. It should be noted that even when a project is proceeding exactly according to plan, project expenditure will always be a few per cent higher than the earned value, due to the cost of work on tasks in progress which make no contribution to the BCWP until they are completed.

Each month, an estimated cost at completion (EAC) is determined and compared with the budgeted cost at completion (BAC) to provide an estimate of project overspend/underspend. The EAC is determined by adding the estimated cost to complete (ETC) of the remaining work to the ACWP. The ETC may be established by:

1. Summing the latest ETCs for each WBS element from the weekly progress summary sheets. For active WBS elements, the weekly progress summary sheets have the advantage of being prepared by those responsible for the work. They are likely to be less valuable for WBS elements not yet started.

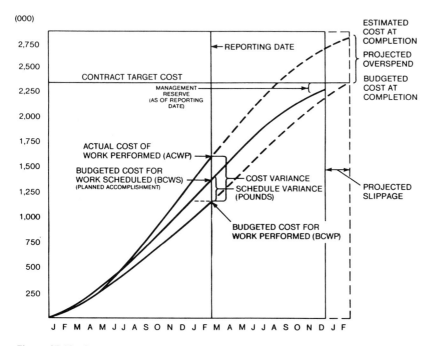

Figure 27.18 Cumulative performance chart

2. Extrapolating the trends in the performance data as follows:
   (a) Current performance factor, CPF = BCWP/ACWP.
   (b) Budgeted cost for remaining work = BAC − BCWP.
   (c) ETC, if same performance continues
   = (BAC − BCWP)/CPF.
   This reflects actual performance against previous estimates but assumes a similar performance for future work, which may not be the case.
3. Re-estimating the remaining work using independent estimating techniques.

The project manager must use a combination of these methods and exercise judgement each month to produce as realistic a prediction of ETC as is possible.

The cumulative performance chart shown in Figure 27.18 allows the BCWP and ACWP curves to be projected to arrive at the BAC and EAC respectively, and displays current overall project status well, but tends to obscure problems as the project progresses, unless they are of major proportions. It is therefore not a good mechanism for providing early warning of problems. A chart showing current trends in cost and schedule variances together with the running value of the management reserve is a better mechanism for highlighting problems in cost and schedule performance, but is only representative of recent effort on a portion of the project. Any major replanning actions earlier in the project involving significant variance adjustments are not displayed. Each method of presentation, cumulative and variance, has its advantages and disadvantages and it is advisable to use both types of chart to obtain a good perspective on project performance.

For small projects a manually calculated earned value system is relatively easy to operate. Such a system will prove well worthwhile if significant changes to the original project plan are subsequently introduced. It will contribute considerably to the understanding of the project at monthly reviews if the reviewers are comfortable with the charts. For large, complex projects, with the likelihood of many changes, an earned value system provides an essential contribution to project visibility and project management. However, in these cases the amount of work involved requires the use of an automated system.

27.6.4.3 Risk reporting

The monthly review should not have to spend much time on normal project progress. Its real function is to look for exceptions; early warnings of problems for which there are still alternatives to be chosen from the perspective of senior management and the customer. In fact, a great deal of the function of the monthly review is to deal with risks, and decisions which ensure that the risks are managed. The traditional method of discovering the risks and what decisions have to be made is to plough through project progress reporting, looking for exceptions which warn of risks. It makes much more sense to present briefly project progress and spend most of the time explicitly on reporting risks, risk resolution and alternatives for which decisions have to be made.

Risk reporting may be tackled by simply reporting progress with respect to the various milestones in an overall risk management plan. Another technique which can be highly successful is to use risk management to drive the monthly management

MONTHLY TOP RISK ITEM REPORT   PROJECT: ___Jupiter___   NO: ___247___   DATE: ___26.01.90___

RANK THIS MONTH	RANK LAST MONTH	MONTHS ON LIST	RISK ITEM	POTENTIAL CONSEQUENCE	RISK RESOLUTION PROGRESS
1	4	2	Replacement for team leader for sensor-control software development team	Lack of expertise in team. Delay in code production, with likelihood of lower quality - less reliable operation even after testing	Chosen replacement unavailable
2	6	2	Requested changes to user-interface	Now realised may impact h/w-s/w interface definition. If not cleared up at next week's user evaluation of prototype, will delay delivery date	User evaluation of latest prototype set for next week - attendance of some key users still to be confirmed
3	2	5	Resolution of compiler problems	Delay in completion of software detailed design and coding	New version of compiler appears to clear most problems but still to be fully checked
4	3	6	Availability of workstations for main test phase	Lack of sufficient workstations will restrict progress on testing	Delay in deliveries being discussed with supplier
5	5	3	Testbed interface definitions	If not finalised by end of next month, will delay availablity of testbed	Delayed items now being worked on, Review meeting scheduled
6	1	3	Tighter fault tolerance requirements impact on performance	Performance problems could require change to h/w-s/w architecture with major impact on cost and schedule	Latest prototype demonstrates performance within specification
7	-	1	Delay in specification of data bus	Could delay availability of hardware subsystems for integration	Meeting scheduled to consider alternatives
8	8	4	Tech author required	Insufficient time for programming staff to produce quality manuals	Requirement with agency
-	7	4	CM assistant required	Inadequate effort for rising CM workload with resulting costly errors	CM assistant joined team full-time
-	9	4	Re-usable database software uncertainties	Potential increase in estimates of coding effort	Uncertainties resolved in latest prototype

Figure 27.19 Example of top-ten risk item list

reviews, by focusing them on assessing the project's top-ten risk items. This concentrates management attention on the high-risk, high-leverage management issues rather than swamping them with large amounts of low-priority detail. *Figure 27.19* shows an example of such a top-ten risk item list. The ranking of the list is determined each month by the project manager, and the review should focus on new entries, items that have been on the list for a long time and those for which there is not yet any credible risk resolution. Some items will be going down in priority or off the list. Those going up the list are generally the ones needing senior management attention to help in getting them resolved quickly. If senior management sees an additional concern, then it is easy to add to the list. The top-ten risk item list is very efficient with respect to management time, as many monthly reviews waste time on things that they do not need to know or can't do anything about. The risk list is a very effective way to focus senior management attention onto the project's critical success factors.

27.7 Productivity, quality and software development methodology

The productivity of software development projects presents a major problem for most organizations. The efficiency of computer hardware continues its spectacular increase, but so often the rate of production and quality of custom-built software continues to be low and notoriously unpredictable. Clearly part of the solution is to increase the use of standard software as far as possible rather than develop bespoke software. However, even if development of new software is unavoidable, a great deal is known about how to improve productivity, and even a doubling of productivity would make a significant difference for most organizations. Instead of being always behind schedule, and then prone to try to meet the impossible, which makes the situation even worse, the software developers would have the time to do the work right, and thereby be able to meet predictions of quality and delivery on time. A major motivation for improving software productivity is that software costs are large and growing larger. Software costs are increasing not because people are becoming less productive, but because of the continuing increase in demand for software and the growing significance of software in the production of complex systems. Any percentage saving from increased productivity will be correspondingly significant.

Software productivity can easily be stated as the quantity of output of software from the development process divided by the cost taken to produce the software. However, this straightforward concept is not so easy to turn into real measurement. The most difficult metric is the 'size' of the product. The traditional measurement in lines of code (LOC) is subject to much criticism but it does have the advantage of being relatively easy to define, its meaning is clear, and it is easy to measure once the software is developed. However, if LOC is to be successfully used in an organization, there must be objective, well-understood counting rules. There must also be a definition of what is delivered in terms of compliance with a set of software quality standards, and definition and tracking of the language level and extent of reuse of source code. Examples of such definitions can be found in Boehm (1981) and Jones (1986). Newer metrics such as function points have been successful in some areas, and many organizations are experimenting with their use, refinement and extension. A further alternative is given in DeMarco (1982), where the principles of software project control are based on size metrics defined for specification weight, design weight and implementation weight. They have the advantage of being predictable and measurable earlier in the project rather than

having to wait until LOC can be measured. Some acceptable size metric has to be used if projects are going to collect data and determine improvements in productivity from introducing better software development practices. Refer to Chapter 30 for a full discussion of metrics.

The expensiveness of software development can be tackled either by reducing the 'size' in the development of the product, or by reducing the 'cost' of producing a product of a particular size. Cost models for software development (derived from analysis of data collected on actual projects) give clear insights into productivity ranges and show the leverage of those factors which are under management control to reduce the costs of producing a required product. They show that 'size' is the most significant influence on software development cost. This therefore leads to cost reduction strategies involving the use of fourth-generation languages, reusable components (see Chapter 41) to reduce the number of source instructions developed, the use of prototyping and other requirements analysis techniques to ensure that unnecessary functions are not developed, and the use of already developed products.

Consideration of reducing the 'cost' of production of a given size of product leads to dealing with two alternative relationships between software development cost and software product quality. The first is that a project can reduce software development costs at the expense of quality, but only in ways that increase the operational and maintenance costs. The second is that a project can simultaneously reduce software development costs and improve software quality by making effective use of modern software techniques, tools and better people. The emphasis is on building quality in from the beginning and early error detection. Getting the right mix of the various components of quality (reliability, efficiency, ease of use, ease of change, etc.) can be a very complex problem. Approaches which have had some success in managing multiple quality objectives are design by objectives in Gilb (1985) and the goals approach in Boehm (1981).

Returning to the insights to be gained from cost models, after the possibility of reduction of the size, the next most significant influence by far on software development productivity is that of the selection, motivation and management of the people involved in the software process. In particular, employing the best people is usually a bargain, because the productivity range for people usually is much wider than the range of people's salaries. The other cost driver factors which are controllable by management are requirements volatility, hardware capacity, use of software tools and modern programming practices. Since large software development projects are highly labour-intensive, there are significant opportunities for the provision of automated aids to make the activities more efficient as well as the implication that human resource and management activities aimed at getting the best from people have high leverage on productivity.

Figure 27.20, from Boehm (1987) shows a comprehensive structure of the major sources of software development cost savings. Boehm's paper gives a thorough discussion of each of these opportunities for improving productivity and a particularly useful list of references for further reading.

In dealing with productivity, it is important to realise that improving software productivity is not an end in itself. It is a means of better expanding the capability of the staff on the project to work effectively in creating a product of the required quality, and must be placed in the context of the wider interests of the organization. Software engineering deals with the structuring of a relationship between technical and management aspects, and this has been the major theme of this chapter in defining the basis for achieving project control. The term 'software development methodology' is used to refer to a systematic set of procedures which integrates the technical

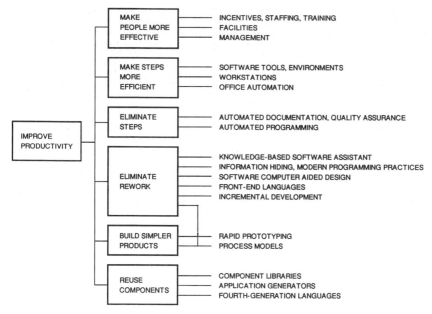

Figure 27.20 Productivity improvement opportunities

development techniques with the management procedures controlling the development process and the deployment of tool support for software development. The managerial and technical aspects of the methodology support and gain strength from each other as shown in *Figure 27.21*, from Freeman and Wasserman (1982). The technical methods provide the basis needed for effective managerial control, while the management procedures provide the organization and resources which enable the technical development to proceed effectively. Tools support the methodology and provide the information needed by project management. The tools provide automated testing, reduce iteration of work and aid improved quality. They also increase visibility of work achieved, provide a source of data, and maintain continuity between projects.

A matrix such as that in Figure 27.9, as well as providing a start for the WBS, also provides the basis for selection of a set of

tools. Every element of the matrix should be provided with tools. The matrix also provides the basis for a code of practice that is complete and non-redundant if it covers every element of the matrix. If any standard or procedure is missing, then there is a hole in the matrix. In fact, the matrix defines a structure which can simplify the presentation of the code of practice.

Training is vital to the success of the programming environment. A defined technique is useless unless every member of the team knows how to use the technique. Training should be provided not only in the technical methods and tools but also in the code of practice.

Procedures and practices need to be backed by a corporate policy, promulgated in a quality manual, which declares the principles of achievement of real quality, backed by management commitment. It sets the quality norm for the organization. It also sets the climate and the leadership style, with an insistence that the standards and procedures are really to be used and that staff are required to be aware of them, responsible for their continued improvement and application in software production.

The effectiveness of software development projects in efficiently producing a quality product depends on the maturity of the technical methods, the coverage of the techniques, tool use and environment support. Methods for technical software development are well defined and practical working tools to support improved software production are commonly available. Experience of large software projects in a number of applications has shown that such projects can be managed successfully and that significant improvements in productivity can be progressively achieved. However, the factor of the greatest importance is the maturity of the process; the extent to which it has been proven over a number of projects, well understood and supported by the standards and procedures and part of the culture for the technical staff, project managers and senior management alike. In turn, software projects depend upon the effectiveness of the organization as evidenced by quality management maturity and software professionalism supported by sufficient development facilities and a good physical environment. This is discussed in Humphrey (1989), which defines five

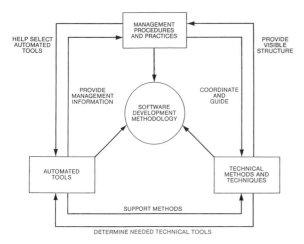

Figure 27.21 Software development methodology

stages of software process improvement: the initial process, the repeatable process, the defined process, the managed process and the optimizing process. The clear message is that improvement in productivity and quality is progressive and that each stage of improvement can only be built on the achievement of the previous stage.

Given that making software engineering really effective is always difficult, it follows that success depends on more than just the wish to improve the control and productivity of software development. Management commitment and active support is necessary in order to achieve successful control of software development projects.

27.8 References

Bell, D. E., Raiffa, H. and Tversky, A. (1988) *Decision Making*, Cambridge University Press

Boehm, B. W. (1981) *Software Engineering Economics*, Prentice-Hall

Boehm, B. W. (1987) Improving software productivity. *IEEE Computer*, Sept, pp 43–57. Reprinted in Thayer R. H. (1988) *Software Engineering Project Management*, IEEE Tutorial, pp 93–107

Boehm, B. W. (1989) *Software Risk Management*, IEEE Tutorial

Brooks, F. P. (1975) *The Mythical Man-Month*, Addison-Wesley, ch 7

DeMarco, T. (1982) *Controlling Software Projects*, Prentice Hall

DTI (1987) *The STARTS Guide* (2nd edn) Department of Trade and Industry. Available from the National Computing Centre

Fairley, R. E. (1988) A guide for preparing software project management plans. In Thayer, R. H. *Software Engineering Project Management* IEEE Tutorial, pp 257–264

Freeman, P. and Wasserman, A. I. (1982) *Software Development Methodologies and Ada; Concepts and Requirements*, Ada Joint Program Office, U.S. Department of Defense

Gilb, T. (1985) *Design by Objectives*, North-Holland

Humphrey, W. S. (1989) *Managing the Software Process*, Addison-Wesley

IEEE (1988: 1058.1) Standard for Software Project Management Plans

Jones, T. C. (1986) *Programming Productivity*, McGraw Hill

Thayer, R. H. (1988) *Software Engineering Project Management*, IEEE Tutorial

28

Software cost estimation models

Chris F Kemerer
Douglas Drane Career Development
Assistant Professor of Information
Technology and Management,
Sloan School of Management,
Massachusetts Institute of Technology

Contents

28.1 Introduction

Practitioners have expressed concern over their inability to estimate accurately costs associated with software development. This concern has become even more pressing as costs associated with development continue to increase. As a result, considerable research attention is now directed at gaining a better understanding of the software development process as well as constructing and evaluating software cost estimating tools.

The purpose of this chapter is to provide practising software development managers with an overview of work in the area of cost estimation models. The chapter is organized as follows. The first sections are a discussion of why estimation is a difficult problem, and why algorithmic models may be of use to the manager. Then an overview of three types of cost estimation models is presented. A review of empirical studies of these models follows this section. Finally, some recent research is summarized, and some suggestions for the practising manager are given. At the end of the chapter is a bibliography of the software cost estimation models literature for the reader who wishes to continue learning about this topic.

28.2 The management problem

It is a rare software development manager who can claim to be able to estimate accurately the costs associated with writing new systems. More likely, he falls into that unhappy category of typical developers who often underestimate large ($>60\,000$ source lines of code) projects by anywhere from 100 to 200% (Jones, 1986b).

There are three main areas of impact of this inability to reliably plan projects: economic, technical and managerial. The economic impacts are most obvious on projects that are grossly mis-estimated. In the case of an internal systems department developing projects for its own firm, the late realization that the project will not be completed anywhere near the budget typically results in the project being cancelled, with the associated waste of all work done to date. Jones (1986b) has estimated that as many as 15% of large systems development projects never deliver anything, and initial misunderstandings of the scope of the project are clearly one cause of these failures. In the case of an outside contractor, underestimates will result in going back to the client, 'hat in hand', in an effort to secure additional funds. If the contract is on a fixed price basis, the contractor will be saddled with the cost of the overrun.

While these economic problems are perhaps the most obvious negative result of underestimates, serious technical problems are also possible. When the budgeted end of the project draws near, but substantial additional work remains, the tendency is to scrimp on the final tasks in order to complete the project at or near the budget. Unfortunately, in the systems development life cycle the last tasks are usually testing, documentation and training. Therefore, the result is systems that are less reliable and less well received by their ultimate users. While underestimation is not the only reason for these problems, it is clearly a contributing factor.

Finally, underestimation leads to a number of managerial problems as well. When an unrealistic deadline draws near additional pressures are brought to bear on the staff to complete the project in a hurry. Besides the likely short-term detrimental effect on the quality of work produced, the long-term effect on morale is also costly. Personnel are pulled from other assignments in order to 'save' the project in trouble, often resulting in a worse problem than the original one – the so-called 'Brooks Law' phenomenon (Brooks, 1975). If this problem is pervasive, then a sort of 'crisis mentality' can develop, where only projects

of this type get any managerial attention. Also, staff turnover due to burnout can only increase.

28.3 Difficulty of software cost estimation

Given the costs associated with chronic underestimation described above, it is clear that management should desire to remedy this unfortunate situation. But to develop better estimates there needs to be some understanding of why software cost estimation is so difficult.

DeMarco has written a very readable book entitled *Controlling Software Projects* (1982), in which he outlines four reasons why software cost estimates are typically not accurate. The first of these is that developing an estimate is a complex task, requiring a significant amount of effort to do correctly. Unfortunately, a number of factors work against this ideal. Estimates are often done hurriedly, without an appreciation for the effort required to do a credible job. In addition, it is too often the case that an estimate is needed before clear specifications of the system requirements have been produced. Therefore, a typical situation is an estimator being pressured to quickly write an estimate for a system that he/she does not fully understand.

A second barrier to good estimates is that fact that the people developing the estimates (typically the project leader) generally do not have much experience at developing estimates, especially for large projects. Compounding this problem is the fact that few firms collect project data with which to check new estimates (more on this below). Therefore, project managers often start by doing a bad job and never get any better.

The third and fourth problems are related. They are an apparent human bias towards underestimation coupled with a management that asks for an estimate but often really desires a goal. One problem is that an estimator is likely to consider how long a certain portion of the system would take, and then to merely extrapolate this estimate to the rest of the system, thereby ignoring the non-linear aspects of systems development including the overhead associated with coordinating a number of interconnected efforts. Another common underestimation problem is that the estimator, often the project manager or senior staff member, estimates the amount of time it would take him/her to do a task, forgetting the fact that in all likelihood, large portions of the system will be written by relatively more junior staff who will require more time. These underestimates are compounded by the fact that management typically tends to want to reduce the estimate to some degree, to make the bid look more attractive or to 'maximize productivity by reducing slack'. Therefore, an estimate that was probably too low to begin with gets further reduced.

28.4 An alternative: algorithmic cost estimate on models

Boehm has defined a set of approaches to software cost estimation (1981). They include: expert judgement, analogy, top-down, bottom-up, and algorithmic models. The first four all suffer from the limits on human decision making capability described above. In situations such as these, explicit decision models are often recommended as an alternative or augmentation to the human decision maker (Tversky and Kahneman, 1974). Moreover, given that accurate software cost estimation is such a universal problem, it is not surprising that a large number of such models have been developed. Of course, the models are still subject to some human limitations in their use and interpretation, but the intent of these models is to provide a more unbiased, relatively independent source of cost estimates.

28.5 Three streams of model development

The first published papers in this area started to appear in the late 1960s and early 1970s, and a good history of some of the earliest models appears in Barry Boehm's book, *Software Engineering Economics* (1981) and see also Boehm (1984). Two types of models emerged from this early work, one of which might be termed the economic stream, represented by the work at TRW and IBM (Woverton, 1974; Walston and Felix, 1977) and the Rayleigh stream, best represented by the work of Putnam (1978 and 1979). A third stream, the function point stream, appears as early as 1979, but the majority of the work by Albrecht and others appears more recently (Albrecht, 1979; Albrecht and Gaffney, 1983; Jones, 1986a).

28.5.1 The economic stream

The economic stream of research is characterized by the development of economic production functions from data on past software development projects. The work on development of software cost is closely related to a number of studies investigating factors which influence software development productivity, such as the early work by Sackman *et al*, (1968), Gayle (1971), and Chrysler (1978). Much of the emphasis in the early cost estimation research was on the variables to be included, with much less emphasis on the input and output metrics or on the functional form of the model. For example, Walston and Felix (1977) investigated the effects of approximately 29 variables. Wolverton's seminal work (1974) might have had greater impact had he not chosen cost in dollars as the input (in contrast to the more common work-hours or work months) and object lines of code (versus source lines of code) as the output.

However, by far the most popular and widely studied of the economic models is the COnstructive COst MOdel (COCOMO), developed by Barry Boehm of TRW and published in 1981. Based on his analysis of 63 software development projects, Boehm developed an easy-to-understand model that predicts the effort and duration of a project, based on inputs relating to the size of the resulting systems and a number of 'cost drivers' that Boehm believes affect productivity.

The popularity of this model in industry can probably be traced to two key factors. The first is that the model is available in the open literature as opposed to other proprietary models such as SLIM (Software Lifecycle Model), Estimacs, and RCA's Price. The second is that Boehm has written a textbook fully detailing the development and justification of the model.

A simplified version of the essential COCOMO effort equation for the basic model (the intermediate and detailed models discussed later) is of the form:

$$WM = C(KDSI)^k$$

where WM = number of work-months (= 152 working hours); C = one of three constant values depending upon 'development mode'; $KDSI$ = thousands of 'delivered source instructions' (DSI); k = one of three constant values, depending upon 'development mode'.

Boehm defines delivered source instructions (DSI) as program instructions created by project personnel that are delivered as part of the final product. They exclude comments and unmodified utility software, and include job control language, format statements, and data declarations.

COCOMO supports three 'development modes' or broad project types. The best case is organic, where relatively small software teams work in a very familiar, in-house environment. The most difficult mode is embedded, where the project must work under severe constraints, such as strict conformance with pre-existing hardware or software. A third mode, which Boehm calls semi-detached, lies between those two extremes.

In Boehm's development of COCOMO he found that the basic model predicted effort within a factor of 1.3 only 29% of the time and within a factor of 2 only 60% of the time for his 63 project database. In an effort to improve the model's accuracy, he refined the equation to include the effects of 15 'cost drivers', which are attributes of the end product, the computer used, the personnel staffing, and the project environment. He believes that these 15 factors affect the project's productivity, and calls this version the intermediate model.

The new equations are:

$$MM = C(WDSI)$$

where

$$WDSI = (KDSI)^{e_i} \prod_{j=1}^{15} EM_j$$

and $WDSI$ = weighted delivered source instructions; e_i = exponent used for the ith development mode; EM_j = effort multiplier determined by the jth cost driver attribute.

The EM_js range from 0.7 (e.g. a product with very low complexity) to 1.66 (e.g., a project developed for a computer with a severe execution time constraint). Essentially, multipliers greater than 1 indicate factors that make the project team less productive than average, and multipliers less than 1 indicate factors that make the team more productive.

The COCOMO detailed model is very similar to the intermediate model except that the project is divided into four phases: product design, detailed design, coding/unit test, and integration/test. The 15 cost drivers are estimated and applied to each phase separately, rather than to the project as a whole.

28.5.2 The Rayleigh stream

The Rayleigh curve has been used by a number of researchers, but has been most widely propagated through the proprietary SLIM estimating method developed in the late 1970s by Larry Putnam of Quantitative Software Management (1978 and 1979). SLIM depends upon a source line of code (SLOC, analogous to Boehm's DSI) estimate for the project's general size, then modifies this through the use of the Rayleigh curve model to produce its effort estimates. The user can influence the shape of the curve through two key parameters: the initial slope of the curve (the manpower buildup index = MBI) and a productivity factor (the technology constant or productivity factor = PF). An important (and somewhat controversial) feature of the model is its strict time/effort trade-offs, where attempts at reducing SLIM's 'minimum' time schedule are met with very large effort increases (Parr, 1980; Boehm 1981; Jeffery, 1987). The Rayleigh curve is a well-known exponentially declining curve used to model a number of developmental processes. Norden of IBM applied the curve to model research and development activities, and Putnam applied it to software development. The curve plots effort on the vertical axis and time on the horizontal axis. The equation describes a build-up followed by a slackening off for the software development cycle, where people are gradually added as they can become useful and then are transferred to other projects when the system is done, except for an ever decreasing maintenance staff.

While the Rayleigh curve describes the theoretical back-

Table 28.1 Function count weighting

	Simple	Average	Complex
External input	× 3	× 4	× 6
External output	× 4	× 5	× 7
Logical internal file	× 7	× 10	× 15
External interface file	× 5	× 7	× 10
External inquiry	× 3	× 4	× 6

ground behind the model, much of the estimating power of SLIM comes from its 'software equation', as follows:

$$S = cK^{1/3}t_d^{4/3}$$

where S = source statements, c = a technology constant (also known as the productivity factor); K = the life cycle effort; t_d = time of peak manpower.

Clearly, a higher value for the technology constant will allow more source statements (source lines of code) to be written with the same amount of effort in the same amount of time. Putnam refers to this technology constant as the 'funnel' through which all system development must pass.

The SLIM user has control over two key variables: the manpower buildup index ($MBI = K/t_d^2$) and the productivity factor ($PF = c$). MBI adjusts the slope of the initial part of the Rayleigh curve. The higher the value, the steeper the curve and the faster the buildup of staff on the project. This number establishes when t_d will be reached, and thus the 'minimum' time in which the project can be completed. The larger the c value, the higher the productivity rate. The SLIM user can choose these values either by calibrating the model with data from completed projects, or by answering a series of 22 questions from which SLIM will provide a recommended PF and MBI.

28.5.3 The function points stream

One criticism of both the economic and Rayleigh type models is that they require the user to estimate the number of SLOC in order to get work-months and duration estimates. The function point measurement method was developed by Allan Albrecht at IBM and first published in 1979 (see also 1983). Albrecht was interested in the general problem of productivity measurement in systems development and created the function point method as an alternative to estimating SLOC. Albrecht's function points are at a more macro level than SLOC, capturing information like the number of input transaction types and the number of unique reports. He believes function points offer several significant advantages over SLOC counts. First, it is possible to estimate them early in the life cycle, about the time of the requirements definition document. This can be an important advantage for anyone trying to estimate the level of effort to be required on a software development project. Second, they can be estimated by a relatively non-technical project member. And finally, they avoid the effects of language and other implementation differences.

There are two steps involved in counting function points: (1) counting the user functions, and (2) adjusting for environmental processing complexity. There are currently five user function categories (although only four in Albrecht's original paper):

1. External input types.
2. External output types.
3. Logical internal file types.
4. External interface file types.
5. External inquiry types.

These are counted and weighted according to complexity, as

shown in *Table 28.1*. The total from this table is the number of function counts (FC).

$$FC = \sum_{i=1}^{5} \sum_{j=1}^{3} w_{ij}x_{ij}$$

where w_{ij} = weights and x_{ij} = counts.

Some guidelines for determining whether a user function is simple, average or complex have been provided by IBM (Albrecht, 1984). For example, for an external input type to be considered simple, it should reference no more than two file types and contain fewer than 16 data elements.

Albrecht also recognized that the effort required to provide a given level of functionality can vary depending upon the environment. For example, input transactions are harder to program if a lot of emphasis is placed on system throughput or end-user convenience. In response to this Albrecht has a list of 14 processing complexity characteristics that are to be rated on a scale from 0 (no influence) to 5 (strong influence). These environmental characteristics overlap only slightly with Boehm's cost drivers, which are heavily focused on project team capabilities and experience. The second step is to sum all the processing complexity points assigned. This number is then multiplied by 0.01 and added to 0.65 to obtain a weighting, as follows:

$$PCA = 0.65 + (0.01) \sum_{i=1}^{14} c_i$$

where PCA = processing complexity adjustment, $0.65 \leqslant PCA \leqslant 1.35$, and c_i = complexity factors, $0 \leqslant c_i \leqslant 5$. This factor is then used in the final equation:

$$FP = FC\,(PCA)$$

where FP = function points and FC = previously computed function counts.

The end result is that the function points can vary ±35% from the original function counts. Once the function points have been computed, they can be used to compare the proposed project with past projects in terms of its size. Through these comparisons an organization can begin to develop cost estimates, first based upon analogies, and later, as additional data are collected, through statistical analysis.

Since the development of function points, a number of proprietary models have adopted a function point type of approach, including Estimacs (Rubin, 1985) and SPQR (Jones, 1986a). Symons has recently provided a critical evaluation of function points (Symons, 1988).

28.6 Model evaluation

The most critical question for a manager interested in using such a model is whether or not the estimates provided are sufficiently useful to justify the cost of using (and in some cases, purchasing) them. Ideally, a model would be easy to use and would provide estimates of sufficient accuracy that no other estimation efforts would be required. However, even models that fall short of this goal can provide sufficient benefits to merit management consideration, whether it be as useful benchmarks for estimates developed in the traditional fashion, or even to the extent that using the model requires the estimator to consider factors about the potential project that may influence his or her thinking.

Nonetheless, it would be useful for managers to understand what the software industry's experience has been with such models, in order to determine what are reasonable expectations in terms of their accuracy and ease of use.

One evaluation standard is the degree to which the model's estimated effort in man-months (MM_e) matches the actual effort (MM_a). If the models were perfect, then for every project, $MM_e = MM_a$. Clearly this will rarely, if ever, be the case.

There are several possible methods for evaluating the man-month estimates. A simple analysis approach would be to look at the difference between MM_e and MM_a. The problem with this absolute error approach is that the importance of the size of the error varies with project size. For example, on a 10-man-month project, an absolute error of 9 man-months would be likely to cause serious project disruption in terms of staffing, while the same error on a 1000-man-month project would be much less of a problem.

In light of this, Boehm and others have recommended a percentage error test, as follows:

$$\frac{MM_e - MM_a}{MM_a}$$

The test eliminates the problem caused by project size and better reflects the impact of any error. However, if one wishes to analyse a model's average performance over the entire set of projects, there is an additional problem. Errors can be of two types, underestimates, where $MM_e < MM_a$, and overestimates, where $MM_e > MM_a$. Both of these errors can have serious impacts on projects. Large underestimates will cause the project to be understaffed, and as the deadline approaches, project management may be tempted to add new staff members despite Brooks's Law. Overestimates can also be costly in that staff members, noting the project slack, become less productive (Parkinson's Law: 'Work expands to fill the time available for its completion') or add so-called 'gold-plating', defined as additional systems features that are not required by the user.

In light of the seriousness of both types of errors, overestimates and underestimates, Conte, *et al.* (1986) have suggested a magnitude of relative error, or MRE test, as follows:

$$MRE = \frac{|MM_e - MM_a|}{MM_a}$$

Since the two types of errors do not cancel each other out when an average of multiple errors is taken, this is a widely-used test.

Still another issue in interpreting the errors concerns bias. For example, a model developed in an environment less productive than the evaluation site, may generate errors that are biased towards overestimation. However, this model may be able to be recalibrated to approximate the evaluation site environment. What is important is that the estimates correlate with the actual results, i.e., bigger projects generate bigger estimates than smaller projects.

Albrecht and Gaffney (1983) and others (Behrens, 1983; Conte *et al.*, 1986) have proposed linear regression as a means of measuring this correlation. Since Albrecht's method does not produce a man-month estimate directly, an alternative was needed to validate the function point method. His proposal was to perform a simple linear regression with man-months as the dependent variable and function points as the independent variable. He also performs regressions with lines of code as the dependent variable to show how function points could be used to generate a lines of code estimate for other models that require it. Regression is often used in this type of research by using actual man-months as the dependent variable and the man-months estimated by each model as the independent variable. The advantage of this method is that it can show whether a model's estimates correlate well with experience even when the MRE test does not. A 'perfect' score on the MRE test would be an error percentage of 0, while a 'perfect' score on Albrecht's test would be an R^2 of 1.00.

28.7 Validation research

A number of empirical studies have been done worldwide to validate the various cost estimation models. Validation is important to determine whether the models are likely to be of value. However, validation is difficult due to the need to capture large amounts of data about completed projects. These data may not have been captured contemporaneously, and therefore data collection may require researching historical projects or putting a mechanism in place to capture information about future projects. Both of these methods are labour- and time-intensive, particularly for larger projects, which happen to be of greatest interest since they are the most difficult to estimate.

Collecting data on large projects is particularly difficult, as most organizations are limited in the number of these projects they can do at one time, which limits the researcher's sample size. The only alternative is to collect data from multiple years, which may raise the issue of whether or not the projects all originate from the same sample. Nevertheless, as shown in *Table 28.2*, a number of researchers have been able to perform such studies.

One of the first independent validations of any of these cost models was Golden *et al.*'s research on SLIM with four projects at Xerox (1981). They found some positive results in terms of SLIM's ability to predict both effort and duration, although the small sample showed a high amount of variance and therefore it is difficult to predict whether these generally positive results would hold for a larger sample. The authors also suggest the development of estimation models that do not require SLOC as an input.

A similar but somewhat more involved study was conducted by a group of researchers associated with Banker's Trust (Wiener-Ehrlich *et al.*, 1984). They tested the fit of the Rayleigh curve (the theoretical basis for the SLIM model, among others) to four data processing projects. In their first test they found that the Rayleigh curve tended to underestimate the time spent in the maintenance phase. Further analysis showed, however, that if maintenance was defined to only include so-called 'corrective' maintenance (Lientz and Swanson, 1980), then the Rayleigh curve predicted the maintenance phase equally well. The authors recommend that organizations collect their corrective maintenance data separately from their perfective and adaptive maintenance work to allow the use of the Rayleigh model, and to treat these latter two forms of maintenance as new projects.

In a series of two articles Kitchenham and Taylor (1984 and 1985) compared the results of the COCOMO and SLIM models on a large dataset of 33 British Telecom and ICL projects. They found that both of the models required calibration in order to accurately predict effort or duration in those environments. They recommended that firms collect sufficient data to allow calibration before implementing the models into their estimation process.

Rubin's research differs from the others in this study in that a hypothetical project was used, and therefore no comparison of estimates with actuals is possible (1985). However, it is an interesting comparison and overview of the inputs and output of these models, and can be seen as an update and improvement to the hypothetical test done by Mohanty (1981). One result was a wide variance in estimates for the same project, suggesting the need for calibration of the models.

Miyazaki and Mori's work (1985) calibrates the COCOMO model for 33 projects at Fujitsu in Japan. They found that COCOMO overestimated their application software projects, which were mostly written in COBOL. In addition to calibrating the major parameters of the model, they also eliminated three of the 15 cost drivers in order to improve the models' historical results.

Caccamese, *et al.* examined the performance of COCOMO

Table 28.2 Cost estimation models validation research

Description	Golden et al.	Wiener-Ehrlich et al.	Kitchenham and Taylor	Miyazaki and Mori	Caccamese et al.	Kemerer	Jeffery
Journal	Database	IEEE Trans on Soft. Engin.	Journals of Systems & Software	Proc. of 8th Intl. Conf. on Soft. Engin.	unpublished	Comm. of the Assoc. for Comp. Mach.	IEEE Trans. on Soft. Engin.
Year	1981	1984	1985	1985	1986	1987	1987
Models used	SLIM	Rayleigh (SLIM)	COCOMO, SLIM	COCOMO	COCOMO, SLIM	COCOMO ESTIMACS, FP, SLIM	Rayleigh (SLIM)
Data source	Xerox	Bankers Trust Company	British Telecom, ICL	Fujitsu	Olivetti	Consulting firm	Software house, government, bank
Data origin	USA	USA	UK	Japan	Italy	USA	Australia
Number of projects	4	4	33	33	3	15	47
Type of projects	—	Data processing	Real time; operating systems	Application software	Systems software	Data processing	Data processing
Language(s) used	—	COBOL, BASIC, FORTRAN, MACRO	S3 (ALGOL), COBOL, Assembler	COBOL, PL/1, Assembler, FORTRAN	PASCAL, PLZ, LIMO	COBOL, Natural, BLISS	COBOL, PL/1
Average size	—	46.4 KSLOC	11.9 KSLOC	—	37 KSLOC	186.6 KSLOC	27.3 KSLOC
Average duration	12.7 months	—	11.7 months	—	24.4 months	14.3 months	15.7 months
Average effort	100 work-months	171 work-months	46.2 work-months	—	104.3 work-months	219.3 work-months	65.3 work-months
Analysis type	Data only	Graphical, regression	Regression	MRE, regression	Graphical	MRE, regression	Regression
Predictions tested	Effort, duration	Effort/phase	Effort, duration	Effort	Effort	Effort	Productivity vs elapsed time
Results	SLIM averaged within 10% of duration, and 42% of effort, with high variance	Rayleigh curve accurate if maintenance defined as corrective only	Calibration required; effort/phase poorly predicted	COCOMO overestimates; 3 cost drivers excluded to improve model	Effort/time not well-modelled; suggest system software development compressed	FP model validated; cost drivers not helpful; SLIM and COCOMO overestimate	No support for notion that productivity is reduced if time is; reduced

and SLIM on three 'systems software' projects at Olivetti in Italy (1986). Like Kitchenham and Taylor, they found that the effort per project phase predictions of both models did not fit their data well. The authors suggest that systems software development is possibly compressed relative to the projects which form the basis of the COCOMO and SLIM databases, even though their small sample does not allow this to be tested.

Kemerer's research (1987) compared both COCOMO and SLIM as well as two newer, non-SLOC models, Estimacs and function points, on a dataset of 15 large data processing projects. Consistent with other researchers, Kemerer found that all of the models require calibration to the target environment, and that both COCOMO and SLIM tend to overestimate data processing applications. An important new result was that the

function point model was validated on an independent dataset. Finally, this research found that the cost drivers and productivity factors of all four models contributed little to their accuracy, and suggests that additional work needs to be done in this area.

Jeffery (1987), working with a relatively large dataset, collected over a ten-year period, suggests that the strict time–effort relationships present in many of the cost estimation models, particularly the Rayleigh curve-based models, is not supported. His data show no support for the notion that productivity decreases as the project's duration is reduced. He suggests that loading (work-months divided by calendar months) may be a better measure than duration for the amount of project 'stress', a result suggested elsewhere as well (Banker et al., 1987).

28.8 Recent research

Some recent research has focused on (1) new methodologies for model development, (2) developing models designed for fourth generation language projects, and (3) new metrics for estimating earlier in the systems life cycle.

Madnick and Abdel-Hamid (1989) propose the use of systems dynamics (SD) to represent explicitly causal relationships in software development, one application of which is as a tool for software cost estimation. They develop an SD model which includes four subsystems: human resource management, software production, controlling, and planning. They propose that their model can be used as a simulation tool to test the estimated effect of changes in project management practices.

Verner and Tate (1988) provide one of the first pieces of research looking at estimation for fourth generation language (4GL) projects. Their case study suggests differences both in total effort and in distribution for 4GL projects.

Wrigley and Dexter (1988) develop an approach that uses some data model metrics and requirements analysis phase data to estimate the size of 4GL systems. In a test on 75 FOCUS programs, they found some statistically significant results in their models of system size.

In the future, one development that will aid the development of new models is the advent of computer-aided software engineering (CASE) tools. These tools designed to aid systems developers (by aiding in the preparation of structured analysis and design deliverables, for example) will greatly assist the cost estimation researcher in collecting design metrics such as the number of processes in a data flow diagram. The automation of such collection should reduce the barriers to new models based on analysis and design metrics.

28.9 Recommendations

Given the previous work in this area and the existence of a number of cost estimation models, how can a firm interested in using these models best proceed? While the exact steps will, of course, differ from firm to firm, the general strategy followed by the firms that have made the initial successes in this area has been to establish a separate team within the department with responsibility for the area of software cost estimation and related tasks (DeMarco, 1982). These permanent teams, variously referred to as the 'metrics council', 'high technology section', 'special studies team', 'productivity tools group', etc. have two broad goals: (1) to measurably improve productivity, and (2) to measurably improve software quality and reliability. To achieve these goals the group has a number of possible tasks related to the measurement and improvement of the management of software development within the firm. These tasks can include:

1. Collect and disseminate project data.
2. Calibrate/develop cost models.
3. Evaluate new technologies.
4. Act as change agents for new tools.
5. Assist/train project managers.
6. Build reusable code libraries.

The overriding concept is that the benefits arising from the investment in this staff group will be able to be leveraged over all of the firm's projects in terms of greater productivity and software quality. By acting as a central resource, the group can both quickly disseminate good ideas and can help project teams to avoid re-inventing the wheel or repeating past mistakes. By specializing in this area, they ensure that promising new ideas or technologies are not missed by the firm's project managers due to their pressing day-to-day concerns. In addition, the tools

group will, over time, develop expertise in these areas which will enable them to evaluate or even develop technologies more efficiently than individual project teams.

The great advantage of such a group is the synergies that develop among all of the tasks. Collecting data on past projects in order to calibrate cost estimation models allows productivity trends to be tracked. The impact of changes in tool or methodology usage can then be measured, which will allow the identification of promising techniques. Tools that allow projects to be done with less effort can also lead to better estimates, since managers' estimation of smaller projects is typically better than larger ones. The typical role of acting as the librarian for the set of reusable code routines fits naturally with acting as the change agents to introduce newer tools, such as object-oriented approaches. Data collection provides a base for evaluating the impact of a change like a new language or something like knowledge-based systems technologies. Firms interested in estimating projects will require data in order to properly evaluate these impacts.

There are a number of guides to developing such a group. DeMarco's book, *Controlling Software Projects* (1982) was among the first to recommend this approach, and remains the most readable. A newer book, *Software Metrics: Establishing a Company-Wide Program* (1987) by Grady and Caswell, describes in great detail the exact process that Hewlett-Packard, one of the 'search for excellence' companies, used to establish their group. While the book's title seems limited to software metrics, all of the examples of the use of metrics are applications to cost estimation, productivity evaluation, and quality improvement.

The authors of these books take care to point out that developing such groups is painstaking and that the group's short term impact is likely to be minimal. However, the ultimate benefit of this approach towards software cost *estimation* improvement is that it will eventually lead to software cost *reduction*, which is a result well worth pursuing.

28.10 References and bibliography

Albrecht, A. J. (1979) Measuring application development productivity. In *IBM Applications Development Symposium*, GUIDE/SHARE, pp. 83–92. [Albrecht's original exposition of the function points method]

Albrecht, A. J. (1984) *AD/M productivity measurement and estimate validation*, CIS & A Guideline 313, IBM Corporate Information Systems and Administration. [Complete guide to using function points. Includes examples and recommendations on use]

Albrecht, A. J. and Gaffney Jr, J. (1983) Software function, source lines of code, and development effort prediction: a software science validation. *IEEE Transactions on Software Engineering*, **SE-9**, 639–648. [Validation and update to the 1979 paper. Adds a fifth category to the four originally espoused]

Bailey, J. W. and Basili, V. R. (1981) A meta-model for software development resource expenditures. In *Proc. 5th International Conference on Software Engineering*, pp. 107–116. [Presentation of a model developed on 18 NASA/Goddard Space Flight Center software projects. Three variables, methodology, complexity, and experience are used to improve the model's ability to do cost estimation]

Banker, R., Datar, S. and Kemerer, C. (1987) Factors affecting software maintenance productivity. In *Proc. 8th International Conference on Information Systems*, Pittsburgh [Preliminary analysis of data on 65 software maintenance projects from a large commercial bank. An economic model of software maintenance is developed, and 15 factors affecting productivity are tested]

Banker, R. and Kemerer, C. Scale economies in new software development. *IEEE Transactions on Software Engineering* (in press, expected to appear in **15** (October 1989)). [Investigation of the effect of project scale on development productivity. It is suggested that *economies* of scale, in addition to the more commonly discussed *diseconomies* of scale, are present in new software development. A methodology for measuring these economies and for identifying the most productive scale size for an environment is presented and tested on eight datasets]

Basili, V. R. (ed.) (1980) *Tutorial on Models and Metrics for Software Management and Engineering*, IEEE Computer Society Press, New York [Useful complement to the Perlis, Sayward, Shaw collection]

Basili, V. R. (1981a) Resource models. In *Software Metrics*, MIT Press, Cambridge, MA., pp. 111–130 [Excellent survey of the software estimation models area]

Basili, V. R. (1981b) Data collection, validation, and analysis. In *Software Metrics*, MIT Press, Cambridge, MA, pp. 143–159 [Clearly addresses need for improved data collection of software metrics. Suggests an approach for implementing these tasks. Practitioner-oriented]

Basili, V. R. and Zelkowitz, M. (1978) Analysing medium-scale software development. In *Proc. 3rd International Conference on Software Engineering*, Institute of Electrical and Electronics Engineers, pp. 116–123 [Discussion of Software Engineering Laboratory at the University of Maryland with a case study applying the Rayleigh curve to two projects]

Behrens, C. A. (1983) Measuring the productivity of computer systems development activities with function points. *IEEE Transactions on Software Engineering*, SE-9, 648–652 [Empirical study within a life insurance organization using function points as output measures]

Boehm, B. W. (1973) Software and its impact: a quantitative assessment. *Datamation*, 19, 48–59 [Interesting survey of the state of the art in 1973. Most of the issues and goals cited remain true today. Another call for software metrics research]

Boehm, B. W. (1981) *Software Engineering Economics*, Prentice-Hall, Englewood Cliffs, NJ [A widely cited text. Approximately divided into two-thirds discussion of Boehm's COCOMO model and other cost estimation topics and one-third other software metrics and application of quantitative methods]

Boehm, B. W. (1984) Software engineering economics. *IEEE Transactions on Software Engineering*, SE-10, 10–21 [A concise summary and update of his 1981 text]

Brooks, F. (1975) *The Mythical Man-month*, Addison-Wesley, Reading, Mass [Classic, very readable book concerning the author's experiences managing the OS/360 project and the lessons imparted on the management of large programming projects]

Caccamese, A., Cappello, L. and Dodero, G. (1986) A comparison of SLIM and COCOMO estimates versus historical man-power and effort allocation. *Unpublished paper* [Test of COCOMO and SLIM against three projects at Olivetti in Italy]

Callisen, H. and Colborne, S. (1984) A proposed method for estimating software cost from requirments. *Journal of Parametrics*, 4, 33–40 [Exposition on preliminary work at developing a requirements analysis document syntax analyser for using an estimating tool]

Chrysler, E. (1978) Some basic determinants of computer programming productivity. *Communications of the ACM*, 21, 472–483 [Empirical study of 36 COBOL programs using regression analysis to determine effects on productivity of programming task attributes and programmer experience levels]

Conte, S., Dunsmore, H. and Shen, V. (1986) *Software Engineering Metrics and Models*, Benjamin/Cummings, Reading, MA [Excellent recent textbook. Useful substitute for the 1981 Boehm text]

Crossman, T. D. (1979) Taking the measure of programmer productivity. *Datamation*, 25, 144–147 [Description of empirical study done in COBOL banking environment. The created micro measure of functionality was a good linear predictor of effort]

DeMarco, T. (1982) *Controlling Software Projects*, Yourdon Press, New York, NY [Excellent, highly readable text for practitioners on how best to do accurate project estimation and to develop a metrics data collection effort within a firm]

Elshoff, J. L. (1976) An analysis of some commercial PL/1 programs. *IEE Transactions on Software Engineering*, SE2, 113–120 [Early quantitative analysis of commercial software]

Ferens, D. V. (1984) Software support cost models: quo vadis? *Journal of Parametrics*, 4, 64–99 [Anecdotal discussion of use of cost estimation models at the Air Force]

Ferens, D. V. and Whetstone, M. J. (1987) Software size estimation, the impossible dream? *Journal of Parametrics*, 7, 57–67 [Results of a research effort directed at estimating eventual source lines of code (SLOC) from a number of functional characteristics such as complexity, reliability, quality of the specification, and the environment.

Four databases containing 7, 26, 25, and 2 projects were used. Only a few statistically significant results were obtained]

Gaffney, J. E. (1984) Estimation of software code size based on quantitative aspects of function. *Journal of Parametrics*, 4, 23–34 [A review of software models with a very general discussion of the possibilities and problems of using expert system technology to perform initial software sizing]

Gaffney, J. E. (1986) The impact on software development costs of using HOLs. *IEEE Transactions on Software Engineering*, SE-12, 496–499 [Brief article illustrating the problems in measuring productivity across projects using different languages and suggests using function points as an alternative measure]

Gayle, J. B. (1971) Multiple regression techniques for estimating computer programming costs. *Journal of Systems Management*, 22, 13–16 [Early attempt at analysis of programming costs based on 18 data points. Significant cost predictors included programmer's experience, number of outputs produced, frequency of operation of the application, and distance of the programmer from the machine]

Golden, J. R., Mueller, J. R. and Anselm, B. (1981) Software cost estimating: craft or witchcraft. *Database*, 12, 12–14 [A test of the SLIM software cost estimating model using four projects at Xerox]

Grady, R. B. and Caswell, D. L. (1987) *Software Metrics: Establishing a Company-wide Program*, Prentice-Hall, Englewood Cliffs, NJ [Recent practitioner-oriented book on Hewlett-Packard's experiences in setting up a corporate database for cost estimation and productivity measurement]

Houtz, C. A. (1985) Anatomy of a cost estimating model. In *Proc. Seventh Annual ISPA Conference* (1985) International Society of Parametric Analysts, pp. 110–123 [Description of a federal government software conversion cost estimating model]

IBM Estimating Application Development Projects Workbook (1980) IBM Corporation, NAD Education Staff Services, East Irving, Texas [A self-paced tutorial on using IBM's Standard Task Method for estimating]

Jeffery, D. R. (1987) Time sensitive cost models in the commercial MIS environment. *IEEE Transactions on Software Engineering*, SE-13, 852–859 [Empirical analysis of time tradeoffs in 47 Australian MIS projects completed in last ten years in four organizations. Uses stepwise regression to determine that projects do not support Rayleigh curve type model. Suggests that it is the maximum number of staff that is important and that loading not duration is the key]

Jones, C. (1986a) *Programming Productivity*. McGraw-Hill, New York [Up-to-date comprehensive survey of the factors affecting programmer productivity. Discussion illustrated with examples generated from Jones's SPQR estimation model]

Jones, C. (1986b) The productivity report card. *Software News*, 6, 19 [Brief article noting some of the important general statistics regarding software development]

Kemerer, C. F. (1987a) An empirical validation of software cost estimation models. *Communications of the ACM*, 30, 416–429 [Empirical test of four algorithmic cost estimating models on a database of 15 large completed software development projects]

Kemerer, C. F. (1987b) Management of software cost estimation. In *Proc. Royal Aeronautical Society's Symposium on Major Software Projects*, London, UK, 1987) [Early version of this chapter. (Helpful comments from S. Madnick and C. Wrigley are gratefully acknowledged)]

Kitchenham, B. and Taylor, N. R. (1984) Software cost models. *ICL Technical Journal*, 5/84, 73–102 [Test of COCOMO and SLIM on a database of 20 projects developed by British Telecom and ICL]

Kitchenham, B. and Taylor, N. R. (1985) Software project development cost estimation. *Journal of Systems and Software*, 5, 267–278 [Further test of COCOMO and SLIM estimation models on a 33 project dataset collected at International Computer Laboratories and British Telecom. Neither model was found to be a good predictor for this dataset]

Lientz, B. P. and Swanson, E. B. (1980) *Software Maintenance Management*, Addison-Wesley, Reading, Mass [Classic book on Software Maintenance]

Madnick, S. and Abdel-Hamid, T. (1989) *The Dynamics of Software Development*, Prentice-Hall, Englewood Cliffs, NJ [Text describing a Systems Dynamics model of the software development process]

Masters, T. F. II. (1985) An overview of software cost estimating at the NSA. *Journal of Parametrics*, 5, 72–84 [Anecdotal discussion of use of parametric software cost estimation models at the National Security Agency]

Miyazaki, Y. and Mori, K. (1985) COCOMO evaluation and tailoring. In *Proceedings of the 8th International Conference on Software Engineering*, pp. 292–299 [Calibration of the COCOMO model using 33 projects at Fujitsu in Japan]

Mohanty, S. (1981) Software cost estimation: present and future. *Software – Practice and Experience*, **11**, 103–121 [A comparison of 12 software cost estimating models on one sample project]

Parr, F. N. (1980) An alternative to the Rayleigh Curve Model for software development effort. *IEEE Transactions on Software Engineering*, **SE-6**, 291–296 [A criticism of Putnam's use of the Rayleigh curve for software development estimating]

Perlis, A., Sayward, F. and Shaw, M. (eds) (1981) *Software Metrics: An Analysis and Evaluation*, MIT Press, Cambridge, MA [Extremely useful collection of articles summarizing the then state of the art. Includes an extensive annotated bibliography]

Pinsky, S. S. (1984) The effect of complexity on software trade off equations. *Journal of Parametrics*, **4**, 23–32 [Comparison of a number of parametric software cost estimation models on their complexity components]

Putnam, L. H. (1978) General empirical solution to the macro software sizing and estimating problem. *IEEE Transactions on Software Engineering*, **4**, 345–361 [Mathematical exposition of Putnam's SLIM model]

Putnam, L. and Fitzsimmons, A. (1979) Estimating software costs. *Datamation*, **25**, Nos. 10, 11, 12 [Non-mathematical exposition of Putnam's SLIM model. Article split over three issues]

Reese, R. M. and Tamulevicz, J. (1987) A survey of software sizing methodologies and tools. *Journal of Parametrics*, **7**, 36–56 [A concise summary of the difficulties involved in estimating the size of a software project. The paper describes the limitations of a number of methods, and illustrates them with examples from DeMarco's Bang, Albrecht's function points and RCA's PRICE-SZ. A combination of methods at different stages in the project is recommended]

Reeves, R. (1986) 2nd Annual COCOMO/WICOMO Software Users Meeting attracts international field to Wang Institute, *Software Engineering Notes*, **11**, No 3, 99, [Press release citing that COCOMO is the currently most widely used software cost estimating model]

Rubin, H. A. (1983) Macroestimation of software development parameters: the Estimacs system. In *SOFTFAIR Conference on Software Development Tools, Techniques and Alternatives*, IEEE [Most comprehensive description of Rubin's Estimacs model in the open literature]

Rubin, H. A. (1985) The art and science of software estimation: fifth generation estimators. In *Proceedings of the Seventh Annual ISPA Conference*, International Society of Parametric Analysts [Overview of estimation process and use of models. Suggests directions for future work in this area]

Rubin, H. A. (chair) (1985) A comparison of cost estimation tools (a panel session). In *Proc. 8th International Conference on Software Engineering*, IEEE Computer Society Press pp. 174–180 [Results of an estimation from a hypothetical system specification by the JS-2, SLIM, GECOMO and Estimacs system. The results were that the estimates varied significantly across models in terms of both effort and duration]

Sackman, H., Erikson, W. J. and Grant, E. E. (1968) Exploratory Experimental Studies Comparing Online and Offline Programming Performance. *Communications of the ACM*, **11**, No 1, 3–11, January (1968) [Seminal research noting the significant performance differences across individual programmers]

Sierevelt, H. (1986) Observations on software models. *Journal of Parametrics*, **6**, 51–74. Calibration of the PRICE-S software cost estimation model on four projects at Philips, Netherlands. Results were improved by not treating all work-months as equal, but rather by taking into account percentage of staff member's time dedicated to the project and the staff loading]

Symons, C. R. (1988) Function point analysis: difficulties and improvements. *IEEE Transactions on Software Engineering*, **14**, 2–11 [A critical evaluation of function points and some suggestions for extensions to address these problems]

Thebaut, S. M. (1983)*The Saturation Effect in Large Scale Software Development: Its Impact and Control*, PhD thesis, Purdue University [This thesis develops a co-operative programming model (COPMO) to demonstrate the effect of larger team sizes on software development projects. A comparison of this model with the COCOMO and SLIM models is also provided]

Tversky, A. and Kahneman, D. (1974) Judgement under uncertainty: heuristics and biases, *Science*, **5**, 1124–1131 [Classic article on the limitations of human information processing]

Verner, J. and Tate, G. (1988) Estimating size and effort in fourth generation development. *IEEE Software*, July, 15–22 [Results of a case study estimating the size and effort of a 4GL project using COCOMO and function points. Relative to a hypothesized COBOL development for the same system, a reduction in effort and a change in its distribution were noted]

Walston, C. E. and Felix, C. P. (1977) A method of programming measurement and estimation. *IBM Systems Journal*, **16**, 54–73 [Important early software estimation model. Uses regression to analyse 60 IBM projects]

Wiener-Ehrlich, W. K., Hamrick, J. R. and Rupolo, V. F. (1984) Modeling software behavior in terms of a formal life cycle curve: implications for software maintenance. *IEEE Transactions on Software Engineering*, **SE-10**, 376–383 [Application of Rayleigh curve to four projects at Bankers Trust. Good fit except for maintenance, which was underestimated. Better fit if maintenance restricted to software repairs (one project's data)]

Wolverton, W. R. (1974) Cost of developing large scale software. *IEEE Transaction on Computers*, **23**, 615–634 [Seminal work for much of the software cost estimation literature. Unfortunately, its use of object lines of code as an output measure has limited its transportability]

Wrigley, C. and Dexter, A. (1988) A model for estimating information systems requirements size: preliminary findings. *Proc 9th International Conference on Information Systems*. November 30–December 3, 1988, 245–255 [Early report on effort to predict software size based on entity – relationship and other data from 15 programs written in a 4GL]

29 Quality control and assurance

Martyn A Ould
Praxis plc

Contents

29.1 Defining quality

This chapter covers a topic that cuts across almost everything else discussed in this book: that of taking action to ensure that the software being engineered is of the required quality. Much has been written of a general nature on the issue of quality, notably by writers such as Crosby (1979). This general material serves as a useful background to a study of quality in software engineering, but this chapter is restricted to the specific approaches that have been developed in software engineering, where, in line with other engineering disciplines, the notions of quality assurance and quality control have been adopted.

This chapter starts by examining the concept of quality. It goes on to deal with the notion of quality assurance – the determination of corporate quality policy and the checking of quality control activities. The next section describes quality control – the techniques available for doing it and how it is planned in individual projects. The chapter finishes with a summary of the main ideas.

29.1.1 A definition of quality

Before considering these two topics one must face the difficult task of defining the notion of quality. Perhaps the best advice is to adopt the standard definition of quality given in ISO 8402: 'The totality of features and characteristics of a product, process or service that bear on its ability to satisfy stated or implied needs.' Fitness for purpose and fitness for use are phrases often used as shorthand, but they still only capture facets of the broader concept defined in ISO 8402. Quality is simply the set of whatever attributes are required in the software. This is a good definition because it says that to control quality one must start by finding a way to define those attributes.

The sort of quality attributes that one might think of generally fall under one of two headings: functional attributes and non-functional attributes.

Functional attributes typically apply to pieces of software, from modules to entire systems. Examples might be:

1. 'When the pressure sensor reading climbs through a pressure level of 3.2 bar, the relief valve control line shall be set to *open*'.
2. 'At the request of the user from a menu, the account status shall be printed with the following data displayed as shown in figure *n.m*: . . .'
3. 'All data shall be secured to disc before any transaction is cleared'.

Non-functional attributes can apply to any product of the development process: specifications, code, manuals, etc. Examples might be:

1. 'With no other load present the system shall complete any type A transaction within 1.5 s, the duration being that time from the operator's pressing the ENTER key to screen acknowledgement.'
2. 'The system shall be capable of operation on a computer with one megabyte of memory.'
3. 'The system shall give uninterrupted service despite any power outages of up to 2 s in duration.'
4. 'The system shall have a failure rate not exceeding one in 10**4 demands under all conditions.'
5. 'A warehouse employee shall be able to use the system confidently after two hours' tuition.'
6. 'The system shall be designed so that the addition of new transaction types does not require changes to type A software.'
7. 'The system shall be constructed so that the language of screen messages can be changed without change to procedural code.'

(Functional and non-functional attributes are concepts discussed in some detail in Chapter 17 of this book.)

So, when someone places an order for a software system, they can therefore expect to describe the quality they expect of it as a collection of attributes, some functional (what they want it to do), and some non-functional (how well they want it to do it, and how they want it to 'look').

When software engineers deliver the system, the user-related attributes will be checked for at some form of system or acceptance test to make sure the quality contracted for has been delivered. They are therefore the software engineers' ultimate target. To achieve them engineers must make sure that every step they make from the start to the end of the development keeps high their chances of successful delivery. So they can expect to be defining developer-related quality attributes for all of the intermediate products of the development process: high-level designs, low-level designs, test plans, project plans, build schema, and so on.

Thus one might require that the code of a particular module is of particular quality in the form of attributes such as:

1. Its functional attributes must be such and such.
2. It must occupy less than 550 bytes of memory.
3. It must in all cases execute in less than 3 ms.
4. It must have been successfully tested on data from all combinations of single samples from the following ranges: . . .
5. The level of annotation must be at least the following: . . .
6. Its McCabe complexity must be less than 12, and so on.

29.1.2 Defining quality attributes

Quality attributes – both at the user level and at the developer level – would be meaningless if one could not test that they had been achieved, so it is important that, when stating what level of quality something should have, software engineers should be able to express that level in a testable form. Attributes such as 'the design must be extensible', 'the code must be easily maintainable and well structured', 'the manual must be easy to use', 'the test plan must be complete', and 'the performance must be acceptable' are all quite useless. One must be precise enough to be able to devise a test to show that the desired value of the attribute has been achieved.

This is potentially easier with functional attributes: provided those attributes can be expressed in a precise and unambiguous fashion (not a trivial matter – see Chapters 16, 21, 22 and 23!) a software engineer will be able to check that the item in question possesses them and is therefore of the requisite quality in that respect at least. Some other quality attributes can be made precise with numerical values, such as 'the software must be less than 320 kbytes when delivered'. In such cases, the necessary precision is there and the engineer simply has to be certain that he or she can actually make the measurement – something that is not always easy with, for instance, performance figures that require the construction of quite elaborate environments to check them out, or with a system in which functions are only loaded when they are called.

So it can be seen that the specification of quality attributes is a non-trivial problem. Indeed, it remains a research topic, but the next two sections of this chapter look briefly at two practical approaches that have been proposed in the past.

29.1.3 The TRW 1973 study

In *Characteristics of Software Quality*, Barry Boehm *et al.* (1978) report on a study done at TRW for the US National Bureau of Standards in 1973. The work is now somewhat dated, and the authors themselves saw it as only a first step, but it still has validity. A number of later authors have offered alternative

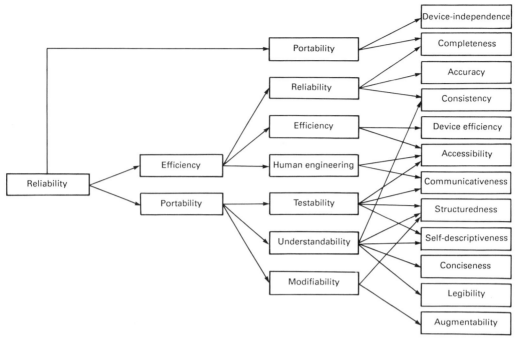

Figure 29.1 Boehm's software quality characteristics tree.
(Reproduced with permission from *Characteristics of Software Quality*, North-Holland)

views but, as this is not a survey of such work, it is sufficient to illustrate the notion of quality by using the TRW study's findings (See *Figure 29.1*).

The study was principally concerned with the delivered software, although this chapter concerns all the outputs of the software development process. One of its results was a hierarchy of 'well-defined and well-differentiated' attributes. The top level attributes relate to the *use* of the software – an important feature – whilst their refinements at the lower levels relate to attributes that can be measured in the software itself. An attribute such as self-descriptiveness could be defined/measured through a checklist of questions such as 'are variable names descriptive of the physical or functional property represented?', and 'where there is module dependence, is it clearly specified by commentary, program data, or inherent program structure?' An algorithm can then be defined to score the module on the answers to these questions. The required quality of a module can then be defined in terms of a minimum score. This clearly requires some experience of the metrics that allows the pass marks to be set, and this calibration – as in all metrics work – requires prior experimentation (see Chapter 12, *Measurement Theory*).

The degree to which numerical values are given to quality attributes is a matter of taste. In some cases it might be very appropriate, such as performance attributes. In other cases, such as the quantity and quality of annotation of a piece of code, some degree of subjective judgement as to the worth of the comments is almost inevitable, though some minima can be set such as the requirement for a positive 'yes' to questions such as 'is reference made to the corresponding issue of the specification?', 'are the units and scale of all floating point variables defined?', and 'are all loop termination conditions explained?'

29.1.4 Gilb's design by objectives

Possibly one of the most pragmatic approaches to the definition,

measurement and achievement of quality attributes is that of Tom Gilb in the techniques he refers to as 'design by objectives' (1987).

Gilb uses a technique whereby unquantifiable and untestable attributes (such as 'the system shall be secure against intrusion') are made testable and qualifiable by refinement. Thus, one measure of a system's security might be in terms of the number of unauthorized intrusions achieved by an 'assault' test team in a certain period *and* the amount of effort that was required to make the first intrusion. An attribute such as 'it shall be easily maintainable' might be first decomposed into the ease with which the system can be changed in the event of an error being found *and* the ease with which an enhancement can be made. The first of these might be further decomposed in terms of the time for the first ten errors found in operation to be corrected. The second might be decomposed in terms of the time taken to add a new transaction and screen to the system *and* the time taken to add a new field to a screen enquiry *and* the time taken to add a new data item to a report.

Once the decomposition has proceeded as far as quantifiable and testable attributes, Gilb recommends that, for each one, the following should be specified: a measuring concept (e.g. number of intrusions in one week); a measuring tool (e.g. the test log); a worst permissible value (e.g. five); a planned value (e.g. two); the best (state-of-the-art) value (zero?); and today's value where meaningful. Gilb provides a number of guidelines for steering this process.

29.1.5 Definitions of quality assurance and quality control

With a clear idea of what quality is and how to go about defining quality attributes, the software engineer is in a position to define how to ensure that the required level of quality has been achieved, i.e. the required level of the quality attributes.

A starting point is the ISO 8402 definitions of quality assurance and quality control. Quality assurance is 'that aspect of the overall management function that determines and implements the quality policy', where a quality policy is the 'overall quality intentions and objectives of an organization as formally expressed by senior management'. So quality assurance includes first, the determination of quality policy – typically through the establishment of a quality management system as will be seen – and second, checking that pre-determined quality control activities are being properly undertaken. It is useful to note the emphasis in the international standard on the need for the quality issue to be addressed from the top of an organization. Whilst individual software engineers might take steps to ensure the quality of their own work, the concept is only truly meaningful if all team members coordinate their quality activities, and if the surrounding corporation is setting targets for all of its teams. The importance of corporate level commitment to quality is stressed further in ISO 9001 (see Section 29.2).

Quality control is the operational techniques and activities that are used to satisfy the quality requirements. So, in particular, quality control is being carried out whenever a check is made that a given item has a pre-determined value or amount of a certain attribute. Anything that could be considered to be testing is a form of quality control, provided it is done against a definition of the attributes being checked for. Checking that a design covers all the requirements in a system's specification, testing a module against its specification, running a spelling checker over a user manual, measuring the response time of a transaction processing system – these are all quality control activities. See Section 29.3 below.

It can be seen from the ISO definitions that, whilst both are planned for, quality assurance and quality control are retrospective actions that in themselves are not enough to produce 'quality software'. Quality always has to be built in at the point of production, and modern methods of software development are largely designed to ensure that the right quality is achieved in the first place (see Birrell and Ould (1988) for a survey). Quality control comes along close behind to check that those methods have been successful and to discover where they have not so that corrections can be made. Quality assurance gives added assurance that the whole producing/checking process is being properly planned and executed and hence is keeping high the chances of producing software of the required quality. The next two sections examine these two concepts in some detail.

29.2 Quality assurance

Remember that quality assurance covers first, the determination of a quality policy, and second, the checking that pre-determined quality control activities are being properly undertaken.

Policy determination happens at the corporate level of organization, and it sets the framework within which the software development team defines and carries out quality control activities. The policy defined by the organization is normally described in a document somewhere – typically a corporate quality manual (see Section 29.3) – and is generally implemented in the form of a quality management system.

29.2.1 Quality management systems (QMSs)

ISO 8402 defines a quality system as 'the organizational structure, responsibilities, procedures, activities, capabilities and resources that together aim to ensure that products, processes or services will satisfy stated or implied needs'. A QMS is something that is set up by an organization to cover a group of projects or departments, on one or more of its sites. It is a statement by management of the strategy and tactics that will be used across the organization to achieve the required quality in whatever is produced.

A great deal of work has been done in industry in general and in the software engineering industry in particular in defining what constitutes a QMS and this has culminated in national and international standards for them. They are of increasing importance to software engineering organizations as many purchasers of software are starting to realise the benefits of requiring that some form of accredited QMS has been used in the development of the software they are buying.

Perhaps the most important general standard for QMSs is ISO 9001 (which is identical to BS 5750 (1987) and the proposed European standard EN29000). Because of its importance we look at it in some detail. (It is important to note that ISO 9001 covers any QMS in any industry, so its requirements need to be carefully interpreted for the software engineering industry. In the UK this interpretation is provided in part by British Standards Institution *Quality Assessment Schedules* which are covered below.)

ISO 9001 defines 20 major requirements on a QMS:

1. *Management responsibility.* The organization must 'define and document management policy and objectives for and commitment to quality' and must 'ensure that this policy is understood, implemented and maintained at all levels in the organization'. In particular the responsibilities of all staff who perform and verify work affecting quality have to be defined, and the senior management must systematically review the operation of the QMS to ensure it remains suitable and effective. Again, there is this emphasis on the need for quality to be addressed from the top of the organization down.

2. *A documented quality system.* This system must cover quality control of all activities in development, and documentation of all the procedures. The documentation will generally take the form of a corporate quality manual (see later).

3. *Contract review.* This is included to ensure that a contract (in this case to produce a software system) starts out with a mutually agreed set of requirements for the system and that the developer is capable of delivering it to the purchaser. Without these safeguards, all else is futile!

4. *Design control.* The standard requires that the developer has, and uses, procedures to control and verify the quality of the design of the system to ensure that it meets its requirements. These procedures should cover planning, identification of the inputs to the design process, identifying what form the design should take and what properties it should have, the verification of the design against the requirements, and how changes in the design will be handled.

5. *Documentation and change control.* This is an especially important area for software development where so much of what is produced takes the form of documents or data in some form: specifications, designs, code, test data, etc. Control of all these generally comes under the heading of configuration management, change management/control, and version control, which are covered in Chapter 34. ISO 9001 calls for procedures for document approval and issue, and for the handling of changes.

6. *Purchasing.* If you plan to incorporate someone else's work in your own system it is clearly important that you satisfy yourself of its quality in some way, and the standard requires, for instance, the assessment of sub-contractors' ability to meet quality requirements, what records should be kept about purchased items, and the verification that bought-in items satisfy the requirements on them.

7. *Purchaser supplied product.* This section of the standard requires procedures for the verification, storage and main-

tenance of bought-in items. At first sight this has little relevance to software engineering, but it is increasingly common for third-party software to be included in a delivered system, and for that third party to issue a stream of new versions, part updates, patches and the like – you need to ensure that you have ways of handling these properly so that the right version is included in the system you release to your client.

8. *Product identification and traceability*. This has always been an important issue for software developers who, like other engineers, build their systems from many small components. Configuration management/control and build control procedures are once more required.

9. *Process control*. This is a general requirement that the production process itself be planned and monitored – see Chapter 27 on project planning and control for techniques in this area.

10. *Inspection and testing*. The standard requires that inspection and testing should take place during the development process, once the system has been completed and before it is delivered for use, and on bought-in-items before they are incorporated. It also requires here, as in most other areas, that records be kept of the results of tests.

11. *Inspection, measuring and test equipment*. Equipment can here be taken to mean software tools in particular. These must themselves be properly controlled with respect to quality, version, etc.

12. *Inspection and test status*. So that the quality of all items at all stages of their development should be clearly known, the standard requires that their test status should be shown in some way at all times. As examples, the design specification of a system should say whether or not it has been reviewed or is only at draft status; a code module should say whether it has been successfully compiled, has passed its tests successfully, or has been frozen as definitive for integration purposes; and so on.

13. *Control of nonconforming products*. This is a requirement that items that do not meet their requirements cannot be inadvertently used.

14. *Corrective action*. If an error is found in an item when a quality control check is carried out on it there are two things that must be done. First, the error must be removed from the item, and second, the processes involved in its production need to be checked to see if they should be changed to avoid such an error appearing in future items of that type.

15. *Handling, storage, packaging and delivery*. Again, this is not obviously of concern to the software engineer but an organization that makes and sells a software product will need to consider its procedures for replicating the software reliably, for ensuring that the correct versions are reaching the correct buyers, that magnetic media – especially those with the product on them – are correctly stored to prevent corruption, and so on.

16. *Quality records*. Here the standard requires the developer to ensure that sufficient records are maintained to demonstrate that the required quality has been achieved and that the QMS is itself operating effectively. The first requirement effectively says that – as far as the purchaser is concerned – unrecorded quality actions never took place; the second requirement ensures that a poor QMS is not followed, lest it become a potential cause of poor quality itself.

17. *Internal quality audits*. This continues the theme that the QMS itself must be subjected to review to maintain its effectiveness, and requires a system of quality audits whose findings are followed up and reported to management.

18. *Training*. If staff are not adequately trained to do their jobs it is unlikely that their work will be of the necessary quality.

This requirement covers the identification of training needs and the training itself.

19. *Servicing*. This is an area that must be subject to the same care as production itself.

20. *Statistical techniques*. The developer is required to 'establish, where appropriate, procedures for identifying adequate statistical techniques required for verifying the acceptability of product characteristics'.

It should be clear from this short coverage of the ISO 9001 standard for QMSs that, taken this seriously, quality requires considerable investment and commitment from the software developer and management.

29.2.2 QMS accreditation

As in many areas of standardization, the effectiveness of a standard for QMSs comes from the existence of bodies able to certify that a given supplier's QMS conforms to the standard: so-called accreditation. Each country has its own national accreditation bodies able to assess QMSs and issue certificates of conformance. In the UK the British Standards Institution (BSI) is amongst such bodies. Accreditation generally requires that the QMS itself is examined against the standard by independent assessors, and that the operation of the QMS is observed to be running effectively over a reasonable period – having a system is not enough; it must be in use and be shown to be effective.

As we have seen, the interpretation of the ISO 9001 standard – which covers QMSs in general across all industries – requires some careful handling. In the UK there are a number of *Quality Assessment Schedule*s prepared by the BSI that provide that interpretation. Of these, QAS3302/79 provides interpretation in the software engineering field. It is worth noting its requirements as it can be seen that many of the other chapters in this book cover precisely these topics, as noted:

1. Management codes of practice requiring the production of a detailed development plan before development starts (Chapter 27).
2. The use of development change control procedures on all development (Chapter 34).
3. Design reviews to highlight and resolve outstanding technical issues (this chapter).
4. Progress reviews to ensure the adequacy of planning and of resources (Chapter 27).
5. Software design to be traceable back to specifications and requirements (Chapter 17).
6. The design to be properly documented and under change control (Chapter 17).
7. Suitable test plans, specifications and records to be produced (Chapter 19).

Once a certificate of conformance has been issued, the accrediting body will make periodic checks to ensure that the QMS remains in force and remains effective. Such a check done by the BSI for instance can result in the assessors making 'observations', or noting 'minor discrepancies' or 'major discrepancies'. Major discrepancies are raised if the QMS or its operation is in some way sufficiently non-conformant to require withdrawal of the certificate unless immediate action is taken to remedy the situation. A minor discrepancy requires the organization to take corrective action before, say, the next visit of the assessor. An observation is precisely that – an observation.

29.2.3 Other QMS standards

For completeness it should be noted that there are a number of other standards for QMSs.

AQAP-1 (1984) is the current NATO standard for Quality Control Systems in general, and AQAP-13 (1981) is the standard for Software Quality Control Systems. Two further documents – AQAP-2 and AQAP-14 – give guidance on their use. (These share a common origin with ISO 9001 – i.e. BS 5750 (1987) – namely an earlier UK defence standard, now no longer used, so there is in fact considerable similarity.) However, the policy of the military regarding these and the international ISO standards may change.

The nuclear industry typically has its own standards, and in the UK the relevant BS is BS 5882 (1980). This covers all quality aspects of nuclear power plants – not just software – in the same way that ISO 9001 covers all industries.

29.2.4 A cautionary note

This constant and independent assessment of an organization's QMS and its operation gives the certificate of conformance a strength that is important to those buying from the organization. It clearly engenders confidence in the latter's commitment to quality. However, it is worth sounding a cautionary note here. An accredited QMS does not itself guarantee quality, nor does the possession of an accredited QMS allow an organization to claim any particular quality in its products. The QMS is a means that still has to be used. Moreover, a QMS is typically a prescriptive thing, telling developers what steps they must take to satisfy the organization's policy on quality. The standards forming the quality manual (see below) should, if they are to be effective and testable, be prescriptive, and this can be counter-productive if certain measures are not taken. As has been stressed, possession of a QMS does not guarantee the quality of the product – the system must be used and used constructively. Following it by rote without an understanding of what it is trying to achieve may not produce any improvement in quality. This is a problem of attitude and culture, rather than a technical problem.

29.3 Quality control

29.3.1 What does quality control look like?

Recapping the ISO definition, quality control is 'the operational techniques and activities that are used to satisfy the quality requirements'. For our purposes here it can be viewed as the action of checking that a given item has a pre-determined value or amount of certain attribute(s).

From this it can be seen straight away that quality control is best carried out on products (things produced during software development) rather than on processes. It would be possible to define the quality of processes: one could check that predefined actions had actually been taken and had been taken in the right order, but this would only say that the 'rule-book' had been followed, so to speak. Checking the quality of the product of those actions is likely to be far more efficient in bringing to our notice any errors introduced by the process.

Of course, we can (and should) use the errors in the product to trace an error in our process. If something keeps coming out wrong it is probably to do with the way it is being produced. (This is a second-order effect, albeit one required by standards for a QMS.)

It can also be seen that the definition of quality control applies to any product. So in what follows it is necessary to try to see what quality control means for system specifications, program specifications, test specifications, code, user manuals, database schema, and every other product produced during software development. This point will be returned to later.

For each product – say, a Pascal module – one will want to apply quality control. What does this mean in practice? It can be viewed in the general case as a five-step process:

1. Define the attribute(s) and level(s).
2. Define the attribute check procedure.
3. Carry out the check procedure.
4. Record the result.
5. Take and record any corrective action taken.

Steps 1 and 2 are planning steps that would be carried out before the product was ready for quality control operations on it – they say what will be done. In step 3 the planned actions are carried out and in step 4 they are recorded. Step 5 is vital: it closes the loop by ensuring that, if the product fails the check, the error is traced, corrected and the corrective action recorded as having been taken. It is all too easy to spot problems and then never quite get round to solving them and correcting the errors. Step 5 ensures that they are solved and that a trace is left to that effect.

As with the corporate QMS (see above) and the project's quality plan (see below): say what you will do, do it, record it and take any necessary actions according to the results.

29.3.2 How much quality control?

There might of course be several non-functional attributes that one would wish to check against. For the Pascal module, these might include memory occupancy and execution speed. The required level of the attribute could take a number of forms e.g. 'the memory occupancy of the module must not exceed 2000 bytes', 'it must execute always in less than 250 ms'. Such attributes are relatively easy to define, and there is a simple method of checking that a given module satisfies them; compile and assemble it to measure its memory occupancy, and time its execution on worst case data to measure its execution speed. Carrying out those methods is straightforward, and checking the actual value of the attribute against the required value equally so.

Conformance to the functional part of the specification is another matter. This problem – the major part of what is normally referred to as verification – is hard and in general there is no guaranteed method of checking for perfection. That is why the above definition in step 1 is so important. For instance, we cannot in general *prove* by testing that a module conforms to its specification. So, if perfection cannot be achieved, it is even more important to define what level of checking will be sufficient for our purposes.

The decision to be made by the software engineer here is 'how much testing should I do to ensure the quality of this system/subsystem/module/procedure?' There is no simple answer to this question (though see Chapter 19), but the responsibility remains with the engineer to decide, at the time that the quality control operations are defined, what level of checking (i.e. testing) is deemed to be sufficient and to record that in the quality control plan. Systems with a high quality requirement, in the sense that they must not fail to behave as specified, will demand more extensive and detailed testing than, perhaps, a test tool for a non-critical system. So, the questions to be asked are: 'how critical is the quality of this product to the overall quality of the final product?' 'how critical is the quality of the overall product?', 'can the quality of this product be most cost-effectively established in this way or that?'

Thus, the quality required from the user interface of a test tool being developed for a project is likely to be less than that required of the final product. Central database functions in an administrative software system are likely to be more thoroughly tested than a little used report facility. Stringent user related quality requirements will generate stringent developer related quality requirements, as we saw above.

29.3.3 How to do quality control

Now we have an understanding of what sorts of activities constitute quality control, it is possible to see that quality control is something that takes place throughout the development of a software system, and, of course, beyond into the maintenance and post-delivery development work that takes place once it is in service. This can be generalized by saying that one should identify quality control on every product at every stage. Every activity should culminate in a quality control activity that establishes – to the degree necessary – that the activity has produced products of the desired quality. This step-by-step approach to quality control underlies the 'building quality in' notion, as opposed to 'building quality on', and is brought out in *Testing in Software Development* (Ould and Unwin, 1987) for instance.

Since one would therefore like to be able to define a quality control activity for every activity during development, it makes sense to look at how the techniques used for each activity can contribute to quality control themselves. Some techniques are good in that they have built-in quality control opportunities. Others do not and one must then apply general quality control actions to make up for this deficiency.

29.3.4 Technique-specific quality control actions

Techniques which specifically support quality control are generally those that are more formal in nature, since that formality means that the semantics of the product are well defined and hence properties of the product can be more easily checked for. As an example, suppose finite state machines (FSM) are being used as a technique for describing how the system will respond to an arbitrary sequence of events. An FSM model describes a system in terms of the different states it can be in and the transitions that occur between states in response to incoming events. With such a model it is easy to check that the proposed system has desirable attributes, such as not reaching certain states under certain input sequences, and not getting into a loop of states. One can also check that the system's response to the arrival of every event in every state has been specified, i.e. that there is some sense in which the model is 'complete'.

Many quality control checks can be automated if the meaning, i.e. semantics, of the representation we are using is well defined. At the very formal end of the spectrum there are methods that use mathematics and logic. Such methods offer mathematical proof as quality control steps on the products, for instance allowing the proof that a refinement of a piece of code preserves its functionality. Simpler cases include the use of static analysis tools (or some compilers) to check for anomalous code, e.g. sections of code that cannot be reached, variables that are never used, or that are read before they are written, and so on. Such analysers rely on the fact that the 'meaning' of a piece of code is formally defined.

29.3.5 Non-technique-specific quality control actions

In many activities in software development, the way the product is produced does not offer clear and reliable quality control actions. This might be either because the method of production we use is not formal (e.g. when writing a user manual) or the resulting product is not amenable to such checks. In these situations one has to fall back on more general, less formal and hence less powerful quality control actions. They generally involve close human analysis of the product (so-called 'eye-balling'), relying on individuals to use their experience and perhaps ingenuity to find errors in it. A number of variations on this common theme have been proposed in the past, and two are covered here, referred to generically as reviews.

29.3.6 Structured walkthroughs

In his book *Structured Walkthroughs* (1979), Ed Yourdon describes a general purpose review technique which has been adopted by many organizations over the years in forms tailored to suit their purposes.

A structured walkthrough is an organized event at which a particular item – a design, a code module, a chapter of a user guide, a test plan, or whatever – is scrutinized by a group of people looking at it from different perspectives and trying to find as many errors as they can in the item. The action centres on the producer of the item who presents it to the other participants who jointly look for errors. Any errors – or possible errors – found are recorded by a coordinator. The group concentrates on error *detection* rather than error *correction*, as it is the producer's responsibility after the walkthrough to take the record of errors found and make sure each is corrected in the item.

Yourdon identifies the following roles as appropriate:

1. *The presenter* – the 'owner' of the item and probably the person who produced it.
2. *The coordinator* – someone to organize the walkthrough and chair it.
3. *The secretary* – who will ensure that the material is issued beforehand and that the records are taken and presented to the presenter.
4. *The maintenance oracle* – who represents the people who will one day be responsible for maintaining the item.
5. *The standards bearer* – who scrutinizes the item for adherence to the local standards that apply to items of that sort.
6. *The user representative* – who checks that the item conforms to the views of its user (who might be the final user of the system or, in the case of a specification say, the 'user' of that specification, namely the designer).
7. Any outsiders who can contribute to the scrutiny.

Crucial to the success of a walkthrough is the prior preparation done by the participants. It is the presenter's responsibility to choose the other participants who could most usefully contribute, to nominate a coordinator who will be able to run the walkthrough effectively, and to choose a time and place. Copies of the item to be reviewed are given to all participants sufficiently in advance for them each to do their own scrutiny of the item. The more individual work done by participants the more productive the walkthrough will be. Participants will take their comments and queries to the walkthrough and, with the guidance of the coordinator, will present these and discuss them sufficiently to decide whether there is an error or likelihood of an error that demands further analysis by the producer of the item.

At the review, the item is scrutinized in whatever way makes most sense; a piece of text can be taken page by page, code procedure by procedure, design diagram by diagram. These are the 'natural' and obvious ways of tackling the problem. However, a number of problems can arise.

First, this serial approach to the walkthrough can lead people towards scrutinizing what is there, and hence away from what is not. In other words, it makes it difficult to see deficiencies and gaps. This can in part be handled by the use of checklists. Many users of walkthroughs and related techniques maintain lists of specific questions that are always asked at such reviews (or, better, by participants during their preparation). Such checklists will generally be specific to particular products: system specifications, module code, test plans, etc. For instance, a checklist used to check the completeness of the coverage of a system specification might contain the following questions:

1. Have all inputs to the system been defined?
2. Have their sources been identified? (human agent, other machine, communications lines, peripheral types . . .)

3. Have their types been specified? (analogue, digital, electrical, acoustical, optical, etc.)
4. Have the range, scaling, format, byte layout etc. been specified?
5. Have validity checks been specified?
6. Have the accuracy levels been defined?
7. Have all outputs from the system been defined? ...
8. Have all aspects of system performance been defined?
9. What is the throughput of the system under different loads?
10. What are the response times in different circumstances?
11. What must be the system's response to failures of software, hardware, power etc?

Such a checklist is designed to help check for completeness – an important quality of any item. Ould and Unwin (1987) and Birrell and Ould (1988) contains extensive checklists for most of the major items produced during software development. These can be used as starting points for your own.

An important aspect of a good QMS is that it is constantly refined by looking to see how it has failed to find errors in past items. This feedback loop helps to reduce the likelihood that similar errors will creep through in the same way in the future. Thus, you might discover as development proceeds that an interface with another system does not operate as expected – this could happen as late as system integration when correction will be expensive. On investigation you find that the error lay originally with the system specification which failed to specify the period for which data on an interface remained valid, and that this was not noticed when the system specification was originally reviewed. This would lead you to add to your checklist a new check for completeness:

12. For how long does the data on the input channel remain valid?

A second problem is that the serial approach to reviewing makes it difficult for errors in the overall approach being taken to be spotted – high-level errors so to speak. This is a particular danger with text which, although it might be divided into chapters and sections, is still a serial thing. Hierarchies of diagrams are less prone to such problems. This can in part be overcome again by the use of checklists that can, for instance, prompt reviewers into checking for the presence of a clear description of the overall strategy in a design, for a single diagram showing the interaction of programs, or for a summary timing diagram of the system's operation.

During the walkthrough it is the coordinator's responsibility to keep the discussion away from possible solutions since it is generally found to be a waste of time if six people argue over what should be one person's job, namely the producer's. It is also the coordinator's job to prevent the discussion from degenerating into arguments about style – all too easy, especially in the area of code!

Once the participants have covered the item in full, it is customary to agree on whether it should be re-reviewed after the producer has corrected any errors detected, or whether the corrections are like to be minor enough to allow the item to be accepted as having passed its quality control checks without a further walkthrough.

In addition to noting the importance of good preparation for walkthroughs if they are to be successful and cost-effective, two other guidelines should be noted that have been adopted by most users of the technique.

First, the item being reviewed should be small enough to be reviewed in no more than, say, two hours. Opinions vary according to people's stamina and concentration span, but this is probably around the limit of the period over which a group can operate effectively. It corresponds to perhaps ten pages of text, five to ten diagrams, or of the order of 200 lines of annotated code.

Second, the item being reviewed should be considered complete by its producer. Finding errors is impossible if the item is incomplete. A participant might spot a problem, but is it just that such and such a section is missing at the moment? This is not to say of course that incomplete documents should not be reviewed informally.

29.3.7 Fagan Inspections

Fagan Inspections (Fagan, 1976) are based on general inspection techniques developed within IBM. The overall principles are similar to those of a Yourdon walkthrough, but Fagan set his inspections in the wider context of planning, measurement and control. They serve two purposes: to find errors in a product, and to give greater control over error detection through the collection of error statistics. As with walkthroughs, the aim is detection and not correction, but errors are now classified in the record by type and severity so that profiles can be maintained to show up the more common types of error and to suggest how they can be avoided in the future. The emphasis, as so often in this area, is on feedback into the development process – learning from mistakes.

A number of 'checkpoints' are defined during the development path. A checkpoint corresponds to the completion of some product or other: a design, some code, a test plan, and so on. For each checkpoint, 'exit criteria' are defined. These are quality levels that need to be reached by the product before it can pass the checkpoint. The inspection is the activity where the quality control check is made.

The original Fagan Inspections do not have the strong social emphasis of Yourdon's book (1979), but an important role is still there: a 'moderator' is responsible for arranging, chairing and following up the inspection, much like Yourdon's 'coordinator'. Around three further participants will be involved including the person responsible for the item being inspected. Fagan describes a four-phase process.

Suppose that an inspection is to be carried out on a piece of design. The procedure would then be as follows:

1. The designer presents the entire inspection team with an overview of the product and distributes the design documentation and any other relevant material.
2. The participants do their own preparation using the material supplied. Besides bringing their own knowledge to bear on their analysis of the design, they use the accumulated experience of past inspections of designs in their part of the organization – in the form of inspection guidelines to concentrate on looking in the areas where errors have most frequently been found in the past. This is designed to optimize the effectiveness of the inspection by concentrating on 'high-yield' problem areas.
3. The inspection itself now takes place. Someone nominated by the moderator walks through the product as for a structured walkthrough, and errors or potential errors are pointed out by the participants. Detection rather than correction being the order of the day, the moderator simply notes things found, and, importantly, assigns it a severity and classifies it by type. As in walkthroughs, strong moderation is necessary if the inspection is not to waste effort and temper on the solution of problems, on issues of style, and so on.
4. After the inspection, the moderator produces the inspection report which then goes back to the item's producer for action. All these issues raised in the report must be resolved, and the moderator has the job of checking that their resolution is complete and satisfactory. Fagan recommends that if the level of reworking involves more than 5% of the item, then the moderator should require another inspection of the item.

Review Report Form   File reference P126.QQ13T/4

Item under review	Code for module QQT13T issue 3.1
Date	25th February 1989
Participants	Pode (author), MAO, ASD, JITB
Re-review required by	No

No.	Location	Severity	Description of problem	Person responsible	Change approved
1	line 63	major	loop bounds incorrectly calculated	Pode	ASD
2	line 71	minor	possibility of invalid data not handled	Pode	ASD
3	line 122	style	variable name non-standard format	Pode	ASD

Figure 29.2 Sample Review Report Form

The notion of feedback is important. The records of errors found, together with their severity and type, (see *Figure 29.2*) allow the organization to refine the inspection guidelines used at step 2 above.

Like walkthroughs, inspections have a number of beneficial side-effects that do not concern us directly here but that are worth noting as part of the justification for installing one of these techniques in your quality control system:

1. They spread understanding and knowledge around the team.
2. They allow easier transfer of ownership should staff leave or change responsibility.
3. They build team strength at the emotional level (if properly managed!).
4. They increase the level of shared ownership of the system by the team, without removing personal responsibility for the individual products.

Organizations often take the good points of Yourdon's and Fagan's techniques and combine the social aspects of the first with the feedback aspects of the second. As always this is an area where an organization can set its own quality control procedural standards.

29.3.8 Quality planning

With a QMS in place – in other words a (corporate) policy defined on how to achieve quality in what is produced – and an idea of the range of quality control activities available, it is necessary to look at the issue of planning quality control at the outset of the project. It is customary to draw up a quality plan to describe the quality control policy of the project. This is a plan that will define quality attributes and levels and will do this by drawing on quality standards from various sources. The QMS has set the framework and the basic procedures. The project must now take that policy and turn it into actions. There are three central notions: say what quality control actions you will take, take them, record the results. These will be taken in turn.

29.3.8.1 Say what you'll do – the quality plan

ISO 8402 defines a quality plan as 'a document setting out the specific quality practices, resources and activities relevant to a particular product, process, service, contract or project'.

When a project is started it will begin by doing a great deal of planning work to ensure that development takes place in an ordered fashion. The normal project plan will identify the products (or deliverables) that the project will produce during development – specifications, designs, code, manuals, proto-

types, etc. – and the activities that will produce them (Chapter 27). The quality plan will follow on by identifying what quality attributes and levels are expected from all these products and what quality control actions will be taken to check that the required quality has been achieved for each.

29.3.8.2 Do it – quality control

For each activity in the development process, a quality control action has been defined that will be carried out on the product of that activity to check it has the required quality attributes to the required level. When the deliverable has been finished it is then submitted to those checks. For example:

1. The system specification is reviewed in a structured walk-through using a checklist drawn from the organization's quality manual, together with additional questions specific to this project.
2. The design is simulated to check that process interactions are correct and that overall timings meet the system requirements. It is then checked to ensure that all the system requirements have been translated into the design in some way.
3. The module design is checked to ensure that it satisfies the specification.
4. The module code is tested against the predetermined test cases; and statistically analysed to check that there are no anomalous data usages.
5. A subsystem is constructed from modules and its memory occupancy checked against the preset maximum.
6. The entire system is timed for the speed of transactions processing on a test database of predetermined size and with a predetermined set of transactions.
7. A novice user is given a preset amount of training and practice and their performance measured to ensure the required usability of the system.

29.3.8.3 Record it – quality control records

Once you have checked an item's quality – and taken any corrective action if it is lacking in some way – you might feel that the job is complete. It is not. It is important to record the results of the check and the fact that the corrective action has been taken. There are two main reasons for this.

First, quality control actions – reviews, module tests, whatever – frequently generate a large number of discrepancies. Each and every one has to be corrected. If a discrepancy is not listed then there is considerable danger that it might be forgotten and hence not corrected, thereby allowing an error to creep through into the next stage of development where it will be much more expensive to correct.

An important feature of any quality system is that it is visibly being used, i.e. that it is auditable. That audit might be carried out by the local quality assurance function who will be checking firstly whether the QMS itself is working effectively, i.e. to the organization's benefit, and secondly whether the organization is carrying out the company's quality policy. An audit might also be carried out by an external assessment function with the task of checking that the certificate of conformance is still justified, i.e. that the QMS is still being operated.

Second, the quality control record is formed from the definition of the check and the required results, the actual results in some form (paper or electronic record), and a record of any corrective action that was required. It is customary for such records to bear signatures (in some form) of those with the authority and responsibility. For instance, a moderator will sign off the report from a Fagan Inspection indicating that all the problems noted were satisfactorily resolved; or a team leader might sign off the record of a successful module test indicating that the module satisfactorily passed the planned test cases and could proceed to, say, integration.

29.3.9 Quality standards and the quality manual

It has been seen how, at the outset of each software engineering project, one will want to identify in the quality plan for the project what quality levels will be required from the various products generated during development. Because such levels are often the same from project to project, it is possible to define quality standards which can be re-used. Such standards are available from a number of sources including national, European and international standardization bodies, trade and professional associations, major purchasers, and other interested groups. Some industries, especially those with stringent quality requirements such as the nuclear power industry, specify their own standards. (Note that the concern here is with quality standards such as those for test plans, as opposed to standards to do with, for instance, communications protocols, languages, or interfaces to graphics packages. These latter standards are more concerned with standardization to reduce barriers to trade and to increase commonality, than with quality.)

The national standards making body in the UK is the BSI. It is DIN in West Germany, ANSI in the USA, and AFNOR in France. At the European level CEN/CENELEC defines standards on behalf of the European Commission. At the world level the International Organisation for Standards (ISO) and the International Electrotechnical Commission (IEC) publish standards. The trend is increasingly for European and international standards to take precedence, and to this end standards at one level are often simply renumberings of standards at another. For instance the ISO standard for QMSs – ISO 9001 – is simply the UK standard BS5750 with an ISO number.

One of the leading bodies in the software engineering scene is the IEEE in the USA. This body supports a number of projects involved in standards making and standards revision. IEEE standards are frequently adopted as US standards by ANSI.

For a comprehensive list of software engineering standards from many sources see Hall (1988) and for further coverage of the bodies involved and the standards see Chapter 50 on standards.

Because of the broadness of the area they try to cover, standards from international and national bodies are frequently general and hence somewhat weak. Many organizations take these standards and then adapt them for their own use, customizing them to their own situation, and thereby giving them a sharper edge. A collection of such local standards typically forms the bulk of an organization's quality manual, complementing descriptions of the overall statement of policy, quality management structures and responsibilities, and so on.

A typical quality manual would contain standards covering all the major products of concern to the organization in question, such as:

1. System specification.
2. System design specification.
3. Module specification.
4. Pascal code (or whatever languages are used locally).
5. Test plans.
6. Acceptance tests.
7. Standards themselves!

Additionally, a quality manual could contain standards on related topics such as:

1. Project plans.
2. Project progress reports.
3. Reviews, walkthroughs and inspections.
4. Project debrief reports.

The quality manual defines the QMS in force in the organization. It is like a top-level quality plan for that organization, which is then refined as necessary for each development project when it draws up its own quality plan.

29.4 Summary

Quality is the totality of features and characteristics of a product, process or service that bear on its ability to satisfy stated or implied needs. Quality attributes are ideally defined in a quantitative fashion and certainly in a way that allows compliance to be checked.

Quality assurance is that aspect of the overall management function that determines and implements the overall quality intentions and objectives of the organization as formally expressed by senior management. The corporate quality assurance policy sets the framework within which each software development team defines and carries out quality control activities. The policy is generally implemented in the form of a quality management system (QMS) and is normally described in a corporate quality manual. Perhaps the most important general standard for QMSs is ISO 9001.

Quality control is made up of all the operational techniques and activities that are used to satisfy the quality requirements of any product. One can view quality control in the general case as a five-step process:

1. Define the quality attribute(s) and level(s).
2. Define the attribute check procedure.
3. Carry out the check procedure.
4. Record the result.
5. Take and record any corrective action taken.

Techniques which specifically support quality control are generally those that are more formal in nature since that formality means that the semantics of the product are well defined and hence properties of the product can be more easily checked for. Many quality control checks can be automated if the meaning, i.e. semantics, of the representation we are using is well defined. In other situations we have to fall back on more general, less formal and hence less powerful quality control actions, such as structured walkthroughs and Fagan Inspections.

Each development project should have its own quality plan identifying how each of the (final and intermediate) products of the project will be checked for quality. The quality plan will often call upon existing standards in the organization's quality manual.

At corporate, project and activity levels the rule is: say what you will do, do it, record it, take any corrective actions. (See *Figure 29.3*.)

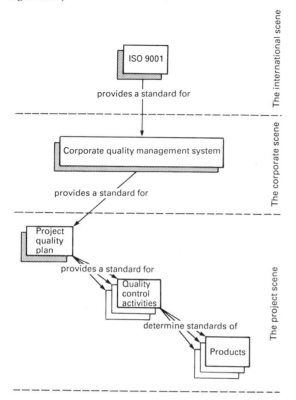

Figure 29.3 Relationships between quality plans

29.5 References

AQAP-1: 1984 NATO requirements for an industrial quality system, Edition 3, NATO

AQAP-2: Guide for the evaluation of a contractor's quality control system for compliance with AQAP-1, NATO

AQAP-13: 1981 NATO software quality control system requirements, NATO

AQAP-14 Guide for the evaluation of a contractor's software quality control system for compliance with AQAP-13, NATO

Birrell, N. D. and Ould, M. A. (1988) *A Practical Handbook for Software Development*, Cambridge University Press

Boehm, B., Brown, J. T., Kaspar, H. *et al.* (1978) *The Characteristics of Software Quality*, North-Holland

BS 5750: Part 1 1987 Quality systems. Part 1. Specification for design/development, production, installation, and servicing, British Standards Institution

BS 5882: 1980 Specification for a total quality assurance programme for nuclear power plants, British Standards Institution

Crosby, P. B. (1979) *Quality is free*, McGraw-Hill

Fagan, M. E. (1976) Design and code inspections to reduce errors in program development. *IBM Systems Journal*, **15**, 182–211

Gilb, T. (1987) *Design by Objectives*, North-Holland

Hall, P. (1988) *Public Domain Standards Listing*, for BCS/IEEE Software Engineering Standards Working Group, The Institution of Electrical Engineers, London (see also Chapter 50)

ISO 8402: Quality assurance – Vocabulary

ISO 9001: Quality systems – Assurance model for design/development, production, installation, and servicing capability

Ould, M. A. and Unwin, C. (eds) (1987) *Testing in Software Development*, BCS Monographs in Informatics, Cambridge University Press

QAS 3302/79 Issue 1 Quality assessment schedule to BS 5750: Part 1 relating to design, replication and distribution of application software for use in electronic computer systems equipment, British Standards Institution

Yourdon, E. (1979) *Structured Walkthroughs*, Yourdon Press, New York

30

Metrics and measurement

Barbara A Kitchenham
Software Metrics Consultant
National Computing Centre, Manchester

Contents

30.1 Introduction

This chapter describes software metrics from the viewpoint of their contribution to project monitoring and control. This means that a number of areas where measurement is used in software production and support are not considered. In particular, readers requiring information about reliability, managing product support, and performance are recommended to Mellor (1987), Grady (1987), and Kobayashi (1978), respectively. Readers who are interested in cost models are advised to consult the chapter on estimation in this book or Conte *et al.* (1986).

This chapter is divided into two parts; the first part being a general introduction to the nature and use of metrics for project control, the second part being an appendix containing detailed descriptions of the compound metrics mentioned in the first part. The appendix includes descriptions of metrics associated with specification notations (i.e., Bang metrics), design structure (i.e., information flow metrics), code structure and text (Cyclomatic Number and Software Science metrics respectively), document readability (i.e., the Fog index).

30.2 Metrics and measurement systems

In this chapter, the term 'software metrics' is used to mean measures (in terms of amounts or counts) related to software products and the process of software production and support. In this context, the 'software products' from which software metrics may be derived should be taken to include all the intermediate products, such as design documents, specifications, code listings, test reports, etc., which are produced during software development and maintenance, not just the final software product.

This fairly loose definition reflects the fact that the term software metrics is used as a general tag to cover all aspects of quantification related to software production and support.

However, to use metrics constructively, it is not enough to measure quantitative attributes; it is necessary to consider a measurement system comprising values obtained in at least three different ways:

1. *By edict.* This occurs when project targets are set, in order to indicate the constraints within which a product is to be developed, or the specific requirements that a product must satisfy. These targets may be set on the basis of commercial decisions such as getting a product into the market before other companies, or obtaining a particular contract.
2. *By estimation.* This occurs when the value of a metric is needed at a stage in the development process when it is not available for direct measurement. Predictions or estimates may be based on estimation models or subjective guesses, but are derived from knowledge of the product to be developed.
3. *By measurement.* This occurs when the value of a metric can be obtained directly.

Targets, predictions and actual values are all needed within the context of project control. Targets provide the constraints within which a project manager must work (i.e., targets are what we want). Predictions provide an indication as to whether a project is likely to achieve its targets (i.e., predictions are what we think we will achieve). Actual values measure attributes of the project directly (i.e., actuals are what we obtained). They also feed forward into both the identification of targets for future projects, and the improvement of estimation methods.

30.3 Nature and use of software metrics

In general, there are two important classes of software metrics:

1. Metrics which assist in the *control* or *management* of the development process.
2. Metrics which are *predictors* (or *indicators*) of either product qualities or control metrics.

In practice, the same metrics may be used for both purposes, but the justification, and hence the criteria by which the metrics should be selected and evaluated, will be different.

30.3.1 Control metrics

Control metrics are not specific to software – any industrial production or manufacturing activity would be managed and controlled by similar 'metrics'.

The metrics which are used most widely for project control are resource-related metrics such as effort, elapsed calendar time, machine usage for particular tasks/activities. These metrics support project control because they may be incorporated into a management planning and monitoring activity, where *estimates* of the effort, timescale and machine usage are made as part of the project planning process and *actual* values are used to monitor progress against those plans.

Other metrics which are used for control are those which are used to estimate task completion, such as percentage of modules coded, or percentage of statements tested. They compare an estimate of the 'size' of the task, in terms of its expected output, with the 'amount' of the task output which has been completed at a particular point in time.

The last category of metrics which is often used in project control is defect-related metrics. From a quality engineering viewpoint, the discovery and elimination of defects is the major project cost. To understand and control such costs it is necessary to record information about the nature and origin of defects and the costs associated with their discovery and removal. From a project management viewpoint, the activity of testing and debugging various intermediate and final products cannot be planned without some estimate of the expected defect rate and effort required to diagnose and fix defects. It is therefore necessary to estimate defect rates based on past projects against both products and testing activities, and monitor current defect rates to ensure that the current product is behaving as expected.

30.3.2 Predictor metrics

Predictor metrics are used to estimate final product characteristics (often called product qualities) or to provide estimates of control metrics. Examples of such metrics are structural metrics which are derived from control flow graphs of programs or data flow diagrams, or readability indexes for software documents which may be based on sentence length and syllable-per-word counts.

The use of metrics as predictors of product qualities rests on three, usually unstated, assumptions:

1. The metric measures some inherent property of the software (or document).
2. The inherent property itself influences the behavioural characteristics (i.e., quality) of the final product.
3. The relationship between the metric and the final quality is understood (at least approximately), and represented in terms of a formula or model.

In practice it is usually only the first two assumptions that are considered. Thus, for example, structural metrics are often assumed to be related to 'complexity', where complexity is meant to imply a subjective assessment of the difficulty to create and/or to understand a piece of code as opposed to any formal notion of computational complexity. The larger the value of the metric, the more complex a program is assumed to be. It is then assumed that complexity is related to various product qualities. For example, complexity is believed to be related to reliability because more complex programs have more chance of containing residual errors. Similarly it is, also, believed to be related to extenciability, since more complex components will be more difficult to understand, and therefore more difficult to amend successfully.

As yet there has been little attempt to formalize such beliefs into general formulae or models, because in practice it is difficult to determine appropriate measurements of final product attributes. However, it remains an obligation on metrics researchers who develop such metrics to validate all their assumptions.

The use of metrics as predictors of control metrics assumes that the metric being measured is related to the control metric, and the relationship can be expressed in terms of a formula or model.

The most common use of control metric predictions is for cost estimates (see Chapter 28 on cost estimation in this volume). An example of this is Albrecht's Function Point metric, which uses a weighted sum of the number of inputs, outputs, master files and commands in a system, as a predictor of development productivity (Albrecht, 1979). Another common example is the use of lines of code to predict effort or schedule in cost models such as COCOMO (Boehm, 1981). It should be noted, however, that for predictions to be made at an early stage of development, cost models use an *estimate* of lines of code as an input to the predictive model.

Relationships between metrics related to product size and various cost metrics have been validated in a number of different studies. However, the specific formula used to express the relationship usually differs from study to study.

There are also attempts to predict the number of faults likely to be found during various testing activities, using metrics based on size, design structure and/or code structure (e.g., Lennselius *et al.*, 1987). Again, relationships (expressed as positive correlations) between size and/or structure metrics and the number of faults found in a piece of code have been observed in a number of investigations, but the formulae are environment dependent.

30.4 Practical constraints

30.4.1 Interpretation of metric values

One of the major problems with the use of software metrics is that they do not, in general, have an interpretation scale, i.e., there is no means of interpreting a value of 100 lines of code in the same way that a value of 100 degrees centigrade can be interpreted. Metrics must usually be interpreted relatively, and there are three ways in which this may be done:

1. *By comparison with plans and expectations.* Formal project constraints, either targets or predictions, may have been specified in a formal project plan. In addition to formal plans, project managers usually have informal expectations about the way a project should progress; for example, it might be expected that the completion of unit testing and the move to integration testing should be accompanied by a reduction in the unit testing fault detection rates.
2. *By comparison with other similar projects.* A metric value may be judged as normal or abnormal by comparison with the values observed for that metric on other similar projects. Data from other projects allow 'baselines' to be established

by which deviations from the expected 'norm' can be detected. It is necessary to have some means of identifying 'similar projects', DeMarco (1982) suggests projects produced by the same company, in the same language, which have the same processing bias (i.e., database-oriented, or function-oriented).

3. *By comparison with other similar components within a project.* This is very similar to comparisons with other projects, but in this case other components, for example modules, are used to set up the baselines. An example of this form of comparison would be to identify modules with unusually large or small error rates, by comparison with the average and range of error rates observed for all the modules in a product.

The methods of metric 'interpretation' suggested above are only suitable for identifying deviations from some agreed standard or norm, be it based on targets, or baselines. It does not provide an interpretation in the real world in the way 100°C is interpreted as the boiling point of water at sea level.

A feature of software projects is that deviations from baselines or norms may be a result of many different underlying causes, some of which may be good, some of which may be bad. For example, a high design to code ratio (i.e., a small number of design statements being expanded to an unusually large number of code statements) may be the result of an incomplete design, but it might also be due to inefficient coding, or alternatively, component re-use. It is usually beyond the scope of the metrics to determine all the possible causes of a particular abnormal value, or to distinguish which cause is operating in any particular circumstances.

30.4.2 Data collection procedures

One of the reasons that metrics are not used more widely in the software industry is that it is difficult in practice to obtain accurate measures. Ideally, metric values need to be repeatable, comparable and verified. Repeatable implies that two independent data collectors would obtain the same value if they were to measure the same item. Comparable implies that metric values are of the same type and are obtained from objects of the same class. In practice, comparability and repeatability are achieved by using well-defined metrics and data collection procedures. Verified implies that values have been checked for clerical errors and inconsistencies. To achieve these requirements, it is necessary to establish data collection procedures and ensure that they are adhered to.

These requirements should not rule out metrics based on subjective assessment, which are often useful (particularly in the context of assessing document qualities, and ranking the effects of various factors on productivity). However, they do suggest that the criteria by which subjective assessments are made should be well-defined.

Data collection procedures must include the following:

1. *Metric definitions.* It is not usually sufficient to define a metric by its name alone. A full definition should identify the units which apply to the metric, the type of software entity to which the metric applies, together with a description of the way in which the metric is to be collected. The need for extended definitions can be appreciated by considering the often quoted 'lines of code' metric. Without specific counting rules for blank lines, comment lines, declarations, multiple statements per line, and executable statements spanning more than one line, there is no way to ensure that values of the metric are repeatable. In addition, without identifying which language the code is written in, it is not possible to know whether values obtained for different programs are comparable. Recently, the ESPRIT-backed REQUEST pro-

ject and the Alvey Software Data Library project have devoted a good deal of effort to the problem of metrics definitions, and have recommended a standard format (Ross, 1986).

2. *Organizational details*. Which should identify the person(s) responsible for collecting data, the person(s) responsible for verifying data, the way in which data is to be recorded, and the way in which data is to be verified and analysed.

In practice, the ways in which data is recorded, verified and analysed are related, and are likely to influence the success or otherwise of any data collection activities. Kitchenham and McDermid (1986) suggest that data collection is unlikely to be successful unless:

1. Data collection is integrated into the development process.
2. It is automated whenever possible.
3. Data which cannot be collected automatically, is collected at the time it becomes available (i.e., is not based on recollection of past events) and is verified immediately.
4. The timescales between data collection and data analysis are minimized.
5. Data is treated as a company resource and facilities are available to keep historical records of projects, not only to monitor current projects.
6. The problem of motivating software engineers to keep accurate records is not underestimated. Proper training in data collection procedures and the use of software metrics, together with quick analysis facilities are essential, but not sufficient requirements.

Examples of existing data collection schemes are given by Basili and Weiss (1982) and Kitchenham (1984).

30.4.3 The analysis of software metrics

The analysis of software metrics data is usually assumed to be a simple matter of utilizing conventional statistical techniques to provide analyses of the following type:

1. Summary statistics indicating the average value and variability of a set of data points.
2. Scatter plots, correlation and regression analysis for investigating the relationship between two metrics.
3. Contingency table analysis to investigate counts and percentages within classification schemes.

However, in practice, software metrics datasets have a number of very undesirable properties. Data values are usually discrete, heavily skewed, non-negative and often contain a substantial number of outliers. In addition, software metrics datasets can seldom be regarded as random samples from a population. This implies that the use of conventional statistical techniques, based on the assumption that the data is a random sample from a Gaussian distribution (i.e., symmetrical, continuous, and possessing a 'bell-shaped' frequency distribution) is a little unrealistic.

Scatter plots and contingency tables are useful methods of analysing and presenting software metrics data because both techniques are minimally affected by the underlying distribution of the data. However, correlation and regression should both be used with caution (and only after looking at the scatter plots), and the conventional summary statistics, i.e., the mean and variance, should be replaced by more robust statistics such as the median and quartiles. In general, the Exploratory Data Analysis (EDA) techniques, pioneered by the statistician J. W. Tukey, seem to be the most suitable for software data analysis (Hoaglin *et al.*, 1983).

30.4.4 The scope of metrics

Currently, software metrics are of limited scope. The majority of metrics apply to only a small part of the overall development process, i.e. code and testing, although recently there have been some suggestions for design metrics (Henry and Kafura, 1981), and specification metrics (DeMarco, 1982). In addition, most of the metrics assume a conventional life cycle, and the conventional third generation languages. Only Albrecht's work on function points (Albrecht, 1979), which is likely to be useful for fourth generation developments, Samson's work on OBJ metrics (Samson *et al.*, 1989), and Markusz and Kaposi's work on PROLOG (Markusz and Kaposi, 1985), have attempted to extend the scope of metrics to more novel software engineering methods.

If metrics are to prove useful for project monitoring and control, then it is essential that metrics be developed and validated which relate to software requirements, specifications and design, and that metrics be developed which are useful for the fourth and fifth generation approaches and novel programming and specification languages.

30.5 A pragmatic approach to metrics

A general approach to using software metrics, applicable to each stage of the life cycle, can be based on a simple process control approach, as found in many industrial situations:

1. Set quantifiable targets for all the activities and outputs associated with a stage. Quantifiable targets permit the amount of work required in each stage to be estimated for budgetary and scheduling reasons, and the percentage of work completed to be assessed at any point during a stage, and establish criteria for determining the completion of a stage.
2. Measure the actual values.
3. Compare the actual values with the target values.
4. Formulate a plan to correct any observed deviations from the targets.

It is somewhat more difficult for software production than for other industries because:

1. There will often be many possible causes for deviations from targets and for each cause there may be several different types of corrective action (see Kitchenham and Walker, 1986). This implies that the project manager will need to institute some additional procedures to determine which, if any, of the possible causes is the actual cause, before any corrective actions can be taken.
2. The targets themselves may be inappropriate, since there are no very accurate models available to establish targets. This again causes complications when attempting to understand the reasons for deviations from targets.

In addition to monitoring with respect to preset targets, metrics may be used to identify anomalous components, which are unusual in comparison with component values rather than with respect to targets. This permits detailed project monitoring to be based on internally generated project norms rather than just on estimates based on other projects.

This general approach can be used for both macro and micro project monitoring. At the macro level this approach is often seen for project cost control; however, the Request project and the Alvey Test Specification and Quality Management (TSQM) project have attempted to use the approach for controlling quality as well, by:

1. Specifying required final product qualities (i.e., non-functional characteristics) in quantitative terms.
2. Developing models to predict final product qualities based on past experience (Petersen, 1987).
3. Collecting metrics to assess final product achievements, and to feed forward into calibrating predictive models for future projects.

The measurements of interest at the macro level include reliability, performance, usability, extendability, reusability, maintainability. Suggestions for how these might be measured, based on Gilb's Design by Objectives approach (Gilb, 1985) are incorporated into a TSQM tool (Walker and Kitchenham, 1989).

At the micro level, a phase-based approach to project monitoring depends on:

1. Identifying metrics for each phase in the life cycle.
2. Identifying how targets and/or norms for the metric values may be established.
3. Identifying statistical methods to analyse metric values in order to detect unusual values, i.e. exceptions, (Kitchenham and Pickard, 1987; Pickard, 1989). Unusual values may be detected in two different ways: firstly, by reference to targets and norms; secondly, by identifying values which are unusual with respect to values observed for similar items, e.g., a module with a low fault rate compared with the fault rates observed for all the modules in a system or subsystem. Deviations from targets are usually fairly simple to detect (using single variate summary statistics), other unusual values may only be detected by bi-variate analysis (e.g. scatter plots). Bi-variate analysis can detect components (usually modules or procedures) which are unusual with respect to a combination of values (e.g., a module with an unusually low number of planned test cases given its number of branches).
4. Identifying the various possible causes for such exceptions, ways of distinguishing between such causes, and the means of responding to the various causes. This is closer to the development of an expert system than conventional software metrics analysis (Basili and Ramsey, 1985).

Metrics which can be used for micro-level project control are discussed in the following section.

30.6 Metrics for project control

The metrics used in the project control can be grouped into five main categories:

1. Metrics relating to specification and design documents.
2. Metrics relating to modules.
3. Metrics relating to checking and testing activities (which may, of course, be cross-referenced to documents or modules).
4. Metrics related to faults and changes (which may be cross-referenced to modules, design and specification documents, and testing activities).
5. Metrics related to resources.

Metrics relating to specification and design documents are similar for both types of document and include:

1. Size, measured using words, sentences, or pages.
2. Structure, derived from graphical representations of specifications or designs. DeMarco identifies a number of basic metrics which may be derived from data flow diagrams and entity-relationship diagrams which he then uses to construct more complex metrics called Bang metrics (analogous to Function Points) for use in cost estimation (DeMarco, 1982), but which are equally useful for project control purposes.
3. Readability, measured using the Fog index (e.g., Gunning, 1962).
4. Stability, assessed from change data (the number, and nature of documents' amendments).
5. Transformation information such as the expansion ratio between specification and design document size.

Module metrics include:

1. Module linkage data, measured by fan-out from (i.e., number of modules called by a particular module), and fan-in to (i.e., number of modules which call a given module) each module, and the number of write accesses and read accesses to common data items.
2. Interface characteristics, such as the number of parameters for each module, and the number of different states or data partitions each parameter could take.
3. Internal characteristics, such as the number of design statements, code size measured by lines of code, control flow, measured by McCabe's metric (McCabe, 1976), data complexity, measured by the number of primitive data items accessed, and transformation characteristics, measured by the expansion ratio from design statements to lines of code.

For project control purposes, it is also important to monitor conformance between phases in the development cycle by noting, for example, the number of modules identified during design that are not implemented and the number of modules implemented but not included in the original design.

Testing metrics include:

1. Test planning metrics such as number of test cases planned, the number of planned and unplanned test cases run.
2. Test coverage metrics, such as the percentage of statements and/or branches covered by a set of test cases (Woodward et al., 1980).

Fault and change metrics include:

1. Fault and change counts classified in terms of the activity (phase) in which the fault was introduced, the activity (phase) in which the fault was detected, and the type of fault, which may be a relatively gross classification as to whether the fault was due to missing or wrong code, or a more detailed classification of the type of processing in which the fault occurred (e.g. I/O, arithmetic calculation etc.).
2. Control information indicating the number of outstanding changes and unresolved faults at the end of a phase.

Resource metrics include:

1. Effort per activity.
2. Elapsed time per activity.
3. Staffing levels throughout development.

These types of metrics can be used to assist project control throughout the phases of the life cycle. Some of the metrics are similar from phase to phase, in particular, fault and change metrics and resource metrics, so in some cases, at least, data collection procedures will be phase-independent. Phase-dependent metrics are the more controversial metrics and need specialized data collection procedures. Therefore, when initiating software data collection, the most cost-effective procedure is to concentrate on fault, change, and resource data, supplemented by a measure of product size, such as lines of code which is relatively simple to collect. The issue of selecting phase-dependent metrics is considered further in Section 30.8.

30.7 An example of metrics analysis and interpretation

Figure 30.1 shows a bi-variate scatter plot of two module linkage metrics. Informational fan-out is the sum of the number of modules called by a given module, and the number of common data structures to which the module writes, and the number of parameters returned by the module; informational fan-in is the sum of the number of modules calling a given module and the number of common data structures from which the module reads data. These metrics are adaptations of the Henry and Kafura information flow metrics (Henry and Kafura, 1981).

It can be appreciated that single variate analysis would identify modules 1 and 2 as unusually large with respect to informational fan-out, and modules 3 and 4 as unusually large with respect to informational fan-in, whereas bi-variate analysis would also indicate modules 5 and 6 as unusual with respect to the combined values.

Once a metric value is identified as abnormal with respect to its norm or target value(s), it is important to determine the possible reasons for the particular abnormality. There are usually favourable and unfavourable interpretations for most exceptions.

A large informational fan-out may indicate that a module contains excessive functionality, or is a simple control module, or writes to a large number of common data items. It has also been observed that modules with a large informational fan-out have a greater likelihood of being particularly error-prone than modules with average or low fan-out values (Kitchenham, 1988). A large informational fan-in usually implies that a module will be re-used frequently, or that a module reads from a large number of common data items. Frequently re-used modules are likely to have stringent reliability and performance requirements, so need to be kept relatively small and simple.

Combinations of metric values may lead to other interpretations – for example, a module with a large informational fan-out, which also exhibits a fairly large informational fan-in would be unlikely to be a simple control module. A simple control module would probably be at the top of a calling hierarchy and therefore have a small or non-existent fan-in. A module with a large informational fan-in and a large informational fan-out is likely to indicate a missing level in the design structure.

Metric values obtained at later stages in the development process can be used to refine an earlier assessment of a module. For example, a module with a large informational fan-in (caused by many module calls rather than many read accesses) may be regarded as particularly problematic, if it is also large or contains a large number of control flow paths. A module which invokes many other modules may not be a problem, if it has a relatively small number of control flow paths. In many cases, however, other information is necessary to assess unusual metric values, for example knowledge about the novelty of the task, and/or the calibre of the staff.

Identification and interpretation of unusual metric values is necessary if appropriate contingency plans are to be developed. For example, if a particular module appears likely to be fault-prone or performance and reliability critical (e.g., has many interconnections with other parts of the system, and/or is particularly large, and/or contains a large number of control flow paths), the short term options may be to re-design the module into smaller components, or extend the timescales for testing the module, or intensify the testing criteria for the module, or use more experienced staff to continue the construction and testing of the module.

30.8 Metrics selection

A number of project control metrics were identified in Section 30.5, and many more exist in the literature, in particular, there are a number of useful survey documents (Höcker *et al.*, 1984; Sherif *et al.*, 1985; Kitchenham, in press). There is, however, less work aimed at metrics evaluation than metrics development, and when such work has been undertaken the metrics have not often proved to be as useful as was first believed (Hamer and Frewin, 1982; Shepperd, 1988).

In general, the following results have usually been found:

1. Most code metrics are strongly correlated with simple size metrics such as lines of code or instruction counts. This is true in particular of Halstead's Software Science metrics (Halstead, 1977), and McCabe's Cyclomatic Number (McCabe, 1976).
2. Provided it is used with caution, lines of code is a reasonable metric for code size. This metric should not be used to compare programs written in different languages, and is sensitive to programming style. It is, however, relatively simple to extract, it is applicable to new and amended code, it is used in most cost models, and it is at least as good an indicator of problem modules as more sophisticated metrics.
3. Composite metrics – metrics made up of a function of a number of simple counts – are difficult to use. Function Points and Bang metrics are weighted sums of primitive metrics and in both cases it is likely that the weights are environment-dependent, so the metrics are meaningless without calibration. In addition, composite metrics cannot be easily interpreted. For example, in Section 30.7, the information fan-in and informational fan-out metric values could not be properly interpreted without knowing how the primitive counts contributed to the metric values. It would have been easier, therefore, simply to have used the primitive counts.
4. Metrics related to the early stages in the development process are the most useful, but also the least well developed. Metrics related to requirements, specifications and design documents

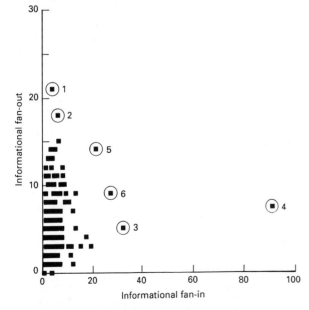

Figure 30.1 Informational fan-out plotted against informational fan-in.

can only be obtained if a formal or semi-formal (structured) method is used to generate such documents, and such metrics are likely to be application- or method-dependent. The primitive counts which are combined to calculate Function Points, Bang metrics and Information Flow metrics provide a number of potentially useful metrics.

Currently, there is no universal consensus about which metrics should be collected in any particular project, however, the following guidelines may be used to assist a project and/or quality manager:

1. Avoid composite metrics, unless they have been properly calibrated and validated for the particular environment.
2. Collect only those metrics which are meaningful in software engineering terms, and, therefore, capable of interpretation.
3. Ensure that metrics of different types are collected, i.e., metrics from each of the five classes discussed in Section 30.6.

30.9 Conclusions

The approach to metrics and measurement described in this chapter is not very original. It has its basis in standard project management techniques which are commonplace outside the software industry. It is, therefore, worth considering why it is not more widely accepted and used in the software industry.

Frühauf (1988) summarizes objections to metrics as follows:

1. There is no generally valid metric for productivity.
2. Software products are all different and are developed differently, so it is impossible to obtain a valid comparative measure of quality.
3. Metric values accepted as 'good' in one environment may be considered 'bad' in another.
4. Evaluation of metrics does not directly improve productivity or quality.
5. Unscrupulous product staff can manipulate metric values (for example, if productivity is used to determine promotion, some staff may introduce unnecessary code).
6. Evaluation of metrics is expensive.

In response to the managerial and economic issues raised by the last three points, Frühauf observes that:

1. Measurement does not directly improve productivity in any other industry, and that does not prevent it being done, and in addition, there is evidence that measuring software characteristics improves quality because people are more careful about them.
2. It is not necessary to use metrics to judge individuals and certainly not necessary to use a single metric value.
3. If managers wish to obtain the information they need to control their projects and understand and improve their development methods they must expect to incur some cost due to data collection and analysis. They need to ensure that, in the long term, they save more money than they spend.

This chapter has tried to address some of the more technical issues raised by the first three points, by suggesting ways in which metric values can be interpreted using locally derived 'norms' if data from other similar projects are available. It has also indicated how module comparisons can be used to identify potential problem modules and to refine detailed project planning even if data are only available from the current development project.

There are problems and limitations with the use of software metrics, of which the lack of validated models relating product metrics to final product qualities, is the most serious. However, the techniques needed to use measurement constructively are available today, and software managers do not need to wait for

some distant future when the 'ideal' metric has finally been discovered, before they can improve their ability to control and monitor their projects.

30.10 Appendix: metrics descriptions

30.10.1 Specification metrics

Until recently, most software metrics have been related to code. It has long been recognized that such metrics are of limited value because they can only be measured at a relatively late stage in the development process. The introduction of structured and formal notations to describe specifications has led to the expectation that more useful metrics related to the early stages of the development process will be identified. DeMarco's Bang metrics, which were originally developed to assist productivity estimation, are the first example of such metrics.

DeMarco's Bang metrics are based on counts derived from data flow diagrams and entity-relationship models. These notations are used to record the specification of a system when De Marco's Structured Analysis and Design method is being used (De Marco, 1978).

The Bang metrics are derived from the following primitives:

1. Number of Functional Primitives (FP) which are the number of circles in a data flow diagram.
2. TC_i, the number of data tokens associated with each FP. Data tokens are the number of data items manipulated by the functional primitive. A compound data item would be treated as 1 token if it was manipulated as a single element and as 2 (or 3, or more) tokens if it was manipulated as 2 (or 3, or more) elements.
3. DEO, the number of output elements crossing the person-machine boundary.
4. OB, number of objects in the retained data model (i.e., the automated part of the data model).
5. RE, the number of inter-object relationships in the retained data model.
6. RE_i, the number of relationships associated with each object in the retained data model.

A 'function strong' project has $RE/FP < 0.7$; a 'data strong' project has $RE/FP > 1.5$; 'hybrid projects' have RE/FP in the range 0.7–1.5.

A Bang metric for a function strong system is derived from data flow metrics. A Bang metric for a data strong system is derived from E-R model metrics. A hybrid system will need both types of Bang metric.

For function strong products, the Bang metric is based on the token count for each functional primitive, TC_i, and an adjustment for complexity based on the type of function (see Table 30.1). The token count is corrected prior to the complexity adjustment using a variant of Halstead's Volume formula (Halstead, 1977):

$$\text{Corrected } TC_i = TC_i \times \log_z(TC_i)$$

The corrected token count CTC_i is multiplied by its relevant complexity weighting w_i and the Bang metric is the sum of the weighted, corrected token counts:

$$\text{Bang} = \sum_{i=1}^{n} w_i \times CTC_i$$

For data strong products, the Bang metric is based on the RE_i count. The correction factor is shown in Table 30.2. DeMarco does not state the basis of the table explicitly, but it appears to be generated by using $RE_i + 1$, in the Halstead Volume formula (Halstead, 1977).

Table 30.1 Complexity weighting factors for various classes of functions (DeMarco, 1982)

Class	Weight	Class	Weight
Separation	0.6	Synchronization	1.5
Amalgamation	0.6	Output generation	1.0
Data direction	0.3	Display	1.8
Simple update	0.5	Tabular analysis	1.0
Storage			
management	1.0	Arithmetic	0.7
Edit	0.8	Computation	2.0
Verification	1.0	Initiation	1.0
Text manipulation	1.0	Device management	2.5

Table 30.2 Weightings for data-strong systems (DeMarco, 1982)

RE_i	Corrected OB
1	1.0
2	2.3
3	4.0
4	5.8
5	7.8
6	9.8

For hybrid systems both Bang metrics should be calculated and cost estimates should treat the database construction activities and the procedure development activities separately.

Bang metrics have some difficulties. They are not simple counts, they are based on complex tables of weights. The complexity weights for the function strong Bang are subjective and environment dependent, and the basic Bang counts make use of the dubious Software Science concepts described later.

30.10.2 Design structure

In an attempt to extend the scope of software metrics, researchers have developed design metrics. Most such metrics are based on the structural relationships observed among modules. The most well-known of these metrics are the Henry and Kafura information flow metrics.

These metrics are counts of the interconnections a module has with other modules in a system. Information flow metrics are based on the information flow between procedures, which includes not only flow based on the fact that one procedure calls another (which Henry and Kafura call 'direct local flow' of information), but also information flow based on return values (which they call 'indirect local flow' of information) and information flow resulting from data being passed between procedures via a global data structure (which they call global flow of information).

Henry and Kafura derive a complexity metric for procedures, based on information flow. They also consider the complexity of modules, where they define a module, in terms of data structures not procedures, to consist of a data structure and those procedures which either directly update it, or directly retrieve information from it.

Information flow fan-in of a procedure is a count of the number of local data flows into the procedure plus the count of the number of data structures from which the procedure retrieves information.

Information flow fan-out of a procedure is a count of the number of local data flows from a procedure plus the number of

data structures which the procedure updates (Henry and Kafura, 1981).

Local data flows occur if any one of the following three conditions hold:

1. A procedure calls another procedure.
2. A procedure calls another, and then makes use of a value returned to it (this is considered to be a fan-in to the calling procedure, and fan-out from the called procedure).
3. A procedure calls two procedures (A and B) and the output from A is passed as input to B (this is considered to be a fan-out from A and a fan-in to B).

Henry and Kafura use the following formula to indicate the complexity of a procedure:

$$\text{length} \times [(\text{fan-in} \times \text{fan-out})^2]$$

where length is any metric of size (e.g., lines of code, or Halstead counts, or McCabe's Cyclomatic Number).

The metrics may be used to identify potentially complex and critical parts of a system.

Henry and Kafura suggest that their complexity metric can be used to identify stress points in a system, and that high information flow fan-out and fan-in counts may indicate procedures which either perform more than one function, or are inadequately refined, in the sense of missing an appropriate level of abstraction.

Henry and Kafura have validated their metrics using the Unix operating system. They found that high values of the formula (fan-in × fan-out) was associated with number of changes (Henry and Kafura, 1981), and that consideration of the complexities of modules could indicate both the need for, and a method of evaluating, a re-design of certain procedures (Henry and Kafura, 1984).

There are some problems with the metrics:

1. The procedural complexity metric is difficult to interpret except in terms of the values of its component metrics. This problem is shared by the information fan-in and fan-out metrics. For example, a procedure which is called by a large number of other procedures is likely to have stringent performance and reliability requirements, whereas this is not likely to be the case for a procedure which reads from a large number of data items, although both types of procedure would have a large informational fan-in value.
2. The procedural complexity metric gives a value of zero for non-trivial procedures if they have no fan-in or fan-out. This occurs in the case of interface procedures which may have a zero fan-in because they are called by system users, not by other system procedures, and in the case of the lowest level system procedures which may have a zero fan-out because they do not call any other procedures.

30.10.3 Code metrics

Most software metrics are derived from source code. The two most well-known metrics (other than lines of code) are Halstead's Software Science metrics which are based on a lexical analysis of source code, and McCabe's Cyclomatic Number which is based on the structural characteristics of source code. Both these metrics are sometimes referred to as 'complexity' metrics.

30.10.3.1 Software Science metrics

Software Science attempts to identify a number of program attributes from a small number of simple metrics derived from the implementation, in a programming language, of an algorithm or program. The attributes of a program include size, mental effort to create the program, time to create the program, and the number of delivered bugs in the program.

Software Science is based on four fundamental measurements:

1. n_1, defined as the number of unique operators in a program.
2. n_2, defined as the number of unique operands in a program.
3. N_1, defined as the total number of operators in a program.
4. N_2, defined as the total number of operands in a program.

From the four basic measures, three other simple metrics are derived:

1. $n = n_1 + n_2$, called the program vocabulary.
2. $N = N_1 + N_2$, called the program length.
3. $V = N. \log_2 n$, called the program volume.

N is a measure of size which is similar to the more conventional count of executable statements. However, Halstead preferred V as a size metric (Halstead, 1977), where V is supposed to measure the number of bits needed to encode the program in a notation with a separate identifier for each operator and operand.

Software Science attempts to characterize a number of program attributes:

1. L, called the level of abstraction, and believed to be the inverse of the difficulty experienced during the coding process.
2. I, called the intelligence content of a program, and meant to be an implementation-independent measure of the functionality of a program.
3. λ, called the language level, and meant to be a program-independent measure of the implementation language used.
4. E, called the mental effort, and believed to measure the number of 'elementary mental discriminations' needed to code a program.
5. T, the time in seconds to code a program.
6. B, the number of 'delivered bugs' in a program, where delivered bugs are those remaining in a program, at the completion of some phase in the development process, which according to Halstead, does not have to coincide with delivery to the ultimate customer.

L is not directly measurable and so is estimated using the following formula:

$$L_{est} = (2/n_1)(n_2/N_2)$$

L_{est} is used to replace L in all the remaining formulas:

$I = LV$
$\lambda = L^2.V$
$E = V/L$

B and T are estimated using the following formulas:

$T_{est} = E/18$
$B_{est} = E^{2/3}/3000$

There have been a large number of evaluation studies of Software Science reported by Halstead (1977) and Fitzsimmons and Love (1978). Unfortunately, the majority of these studies confused correlation, which indicates the existence of a relationship, with regression, which indicates the nature of a relationship. In addition, in many cases there was no attempt to formally test any of the hypotheses under consideration using appropriate statistical methods.

A complete re-evaluation of the initial Software Science evaluation studies has been performed by Hamer and Frewin, (1982). They conclude that 'the claimed experimental support is largely illusionary'.

Other researchers have both criticized the psychological arguments used to derive the equation for T, (Coulter, 1983), and suggested that the Software Science metrics offer no more information about the characteristics of a program than do simple size metrics such as instruction counts, see Kitchenham (1981) or Gremillion (1984).

30.10.3.2 McCabe's Cyclomatic Number

This measure is derived from the control flow graph of a program, and measures the number of linearly independent paths through a program. It is meant to be a measure of the testability and complexity of a program. It may also be used as a control metric to assess the completeness of the testing process.

The cyclomatic number, $V(G)$, is determined from the following formula:

$$V(G) = e - n + 2p$$

where e is the number of edges in the control graph, where an edge is equivalent to a branching point in the program; n is the number of vertices in the control graph, where a vertex is equivalent to a sequential block of code in the program; and p is the number of connected components, usually 1.

In structured programs (i.e., programs which do not permit jumps into and out of the body of loops), $V(G)$ is equivalent to the number of predicates plus 1, where compound predicates such as IF a AND b THEN are treated as two. This is equivalent to the number of decision points in a program.

The metric has a number of difficulties and has been strongly criticized by a number of researchers (see Shepperd, 1988). General problems are:

1. The metric has been shown to be associated with module error rates, but has not been demonstrated to provide much better identification of error-prone modules than LOC. See Kafura and Canning (1985) or Kitchenham (1981).
2. There are practical difficulties sometimes encountered when attempting to determine the flow graph of a program which mean that very often the flow graph of an equivalent program is obtained rather than that of the program as originally written. This must cast some doubt as to what is actually being measured.
3. The metric must be regarded as a very superficial complexity measure since it regards all program structures as equivalent. Thus, a sequence of three loops will provide the same cyclomatic number as three nested loops.
4. A fundamental problem with the use of the metric as a measure of testability is because it is entirely based on control flow and ignores data flow. Many programs can be written to avoid the use of control structures, by the use of look-up tables and arrays and other data-oriented programming practices instead (see Humpphrey, 1986). Thus, the value of the metric may be strongly influenced by programming style, and give very misleading estimates of the amount of testing required.

30.10.4 Document-based metrics

Software documents written in a natural language may be assessed for readability in the same way as any other natural language document. One of the simplest readability indexes is Gunning's Fog Index. This metric assesses the readability of text written in English in terms of the length of sentences and the number of 'hard' words.

The measure is calculated on the basis of sampling text at the rate of about 100 lines per four pages. The characteristics of the text sample measured are as follows:

1. sen, the number of sentences.
2. wrd, the number of words.
3. syl, the number of syllables.

The Fog Index, FI, is calculated as follows:
$$FI = 0.4(wrd/sen + (hrd/wrd)100)$$
where hrd is the number of words of three or more syllables not counting (1) words that are capitalized; (2) combinations of short easy words such as bookkeeper; (3) verbs that are made into three syllables by adding '-ed' or '-es' such as 'programmed'.

The Fog Index is interpreted using the following scale:

$FI \leqslant 5$	fairly easy
$5 < FI \leqslant 8$	standard
$8 < FI \leqslant 11$	fairly difficult
$11 < FI < 17$	difficult
$17 \geqslant FI$	very difficult

This metric can be used to assess the quality of user documentation. It may also be particularly useful for large software projects where many specialists are involved at separate stages in the development process. In this type of project, different staff will be responsible for different stages in the process and will be dependent on written documentation of the previous stages to delineate their required contribution to the project. They will also need to prepare written documentation to record their actual contribution. In this sort of project, a means of assessing the readability and understandability of documents is very important.

30.11 References

Albrecht, A. J. (1979) Measuring application development productivity. *Proc. IBM Applications Development Symposium*

Basili, V. R. and Ramsey, C. L. (1985) Arrowsmith-P – A prototype expert system for software engineering management. *Proc. Symposium on Expert Systems in Government*, pp 252–264

Basili, V. R. and Weiss, D. M. (1982) A methodology for collecting valid software engineering data. *University of Maryland Technical Report*

Boeh, B. W. (1981) *Software Engineering Economics*, Prentice-Hall

Conte, S. D, Dunsmore, H. E. and Shen, V. Y. (1986) *Software engineering metrics and models*, Benjamin/Cummings

Coulter, N. S. (1983) Software science and cognitive psychology. *IEEE Transactions on Software Engineering* SE-9

DeMarco, T. (1978) *Structured analysis and system specification*, Yourdon Press

DeMarco, T. (1982) *Controlling software projects*, Prentice-Hall Inc.

Fitzsimmons, A. and Love, T. A. (1978) Review and evaluation of software science. *Computing Surveys*, **10**, 3–18

Frühauf, K. (1988) Software metrics: facts or dreams. *Proc. of the First European Seminar on Software Quality, Brussels*, pp 437–449

Gilb, T. (1985) Tools for 'Design by Objectives'. In Anderson, T. (ed.), *Software requirements specification and testing*, Blackwell Scientific Publications, pp 50–63

Grady, R. B. (1987) Measuring and managing software maintenance. *IEEE Software*, 35–45

Gremillion, L. L. (1984) Determinants of program repair maintenance requirements. *Communications of the ACM* **27**, 826–832

Gunning, R. (1962) *Techniques of clear writing*, (revised edition) McGraw-Hill

Halstead, M. H. (1977) *Elements of software science*, Elsevier North-Holland

Hamer, P. G. and Frewin, G. D. (1982) M. H. Halstead's Software Science – a critical examination. In *Proc. 6th International Conference on Software Engineering*, pp 197–206

Henry, S. and Kafura, D. (1981) Software structure metrics based on information flow. *IEEE Trans. on Software Engineering*, SE-7, 510–518

Henry, S. and Kafura, D. (1984) The evaluation of software system

structure using quantitative software metrics. *Software Practice and Experience*, **14**, 561–573

Hoaglin, D. C., Mosteller, F. and Tukey, J. W. (1983) *Undertaking Exploratory Data Analysis*, John Wiley & Sons

Höcker, H, Itzfeldt, W. D., Schmidt, M. and Timm, M. (1984) Comparative descriptions of software quality measures. *GMD-Studien*, **81**

Humpphrey, R. A. (1986) Control flow as a measure of programming complexity. *Alvey Club on Software Reliability and Metrics Newsletter*, Issue 4

Kafura, D. and Canning, J. (1985) A validation of software metrics using many metrics and two resources. In *Proc. 8th International Conference on Software Engineering*, pp 378–385

Kitchenham, B. A. (1981) Measures of programming complexity. *ICL Technical Journal*, **2**, 298–316

Kitchenham, B. A. (1984) Program History Records; a system of software data collection and analysis. *ICL Technical Journal*, 103–114

Kitchenham, B. A. (1988) An evaluation of software structure metrics. In *Proceedings of COMPSAC '88*, pp 369–376

Kitchenham, B. A., Metrics for project control. In *Software reliability handbook*, (ed. P. Rook), Elsevier Scientific, in press

Kitchenham, B. A. and McDermid, J. A. (1986) Software metrics and integrated project support environments. *SEJ*, **1**, 58–64

Kitchenham, B. A. and Pickard, L. M. (1987) Towards a constructive quality model, Part II Statistical techniques for modelling software quality. *Software Engineering Journal*, **2**, 114–126

Kitchenham, B. A. and Walker, J. G. (1986) An information model of software quality management. *TSQM report to the Alvey Directorate* A24

Kobayashi, H. (1978) *Modelling and analysis: An introduction to system performance and evaluation methodology*, Addison-Wesley

Lennselius, B., Wohlin, C. and Vrana, C. (1987) Software metrics: fault content estimation and software process control. *Microprocessors and Microsystems*, **11**, 365–375

Markusz, S. and Kaposi, A. A. (1985) Complexity control of logic based programming. *Computer Journal*, **28**, 5

McCabe, T. J. (1976) A complexity measure. *IEEE Trans. Software Engineering*, SE-2, 308–320

Mellor, P. (1987) Software reliability modelling: the state of the art, *Information and Software Technology*, **29**, 81–98

Petersen, P. G. (1987) Software quality: The COnstructive QUAlity MOdelling System. In *ESPRIT '86: Results and Achievements*, Elsevier Science Publications

Pickard, L. M. (1989) Analysis of software metrics. In B. A. Kitchenham and B. Littlewood (eds) *Measurement for Software Quality Assurance and Control*, Elsevier Scientific, pp 335–384

Ross, N. (1987) Data Definitions. *Software Data Library report to the Alvey Directorate* 2.2.2 (1986)

Samson, W. B, Dugard, P. I, Nevill, D. G, Oldfield, P. E, Smith, A. W. and Titterington, G. 1989 The relationship between specification and implementation metrics. In B. A. Kitchenham and B. Littlewood (eds) *Measurement for Software Quality Assurance and Control*, Elsevier Scientific, pp 335–384

Shepperd, M. (1988) A critique of cyclomatic complexity as a software metric. *Software Engineering Journal*, **3**, 30–36

Sherif, Y. S. Ng, E., and Steinbacher, J. (1985) Computer software quality measures and metrics. *Microelectron Reliability*, **25**, 1105–1150

Walker, J. G. and Kitchenham, B. A. (1989) Quality requirements specification and evaluation. In B. A. Kitchenham and B. Littlewood (eds) *Measurement for Software Quality Assurance and Control*, Elsevier Scientific, pp 103–123

Woodward, M. R, Hennell, M. A. and Hedley, D. (1980) Experience with path analysis and testing programs. *IEEE Trans. Software Engineering*, SE-6, 278–286

30.12 Acknowledgements

The approach to metrics described in this chapter evolved from work done as part of the Alvey-backed Test Specification and Quality Management project and the ESPRIT-backed REQUEST project.

The author would like to thank Elsevier Scientific for permission to use some material first presented in two chapters of *Software Reliability Handbook*, P. Rook (ed.).

31

Software reliability modelling

Bev Littlewood
Professor of Software Engineering
and
Director, Centre for Software Reliability,
City University

Contents

31.1 Introduction

This chapter is concerned with evaluation of the reliability of software. It is worth remarking right away that evaluation raises issues quite different from those involved in actually building systems with appropriate functionality, reliability, availability, maintainability, security, etc. Other chapters in this book are concerned with this question of appropriate software engineering methodologies for the achievement of desirable system characteristics, addressing essentially the question of 'how to do it'. This chapter, on the contrary, addresses the question of 'how to know whether it has been done successfully', with particular reference to the achievement of reliability targets.

There are important areas of software engineering where the roles of achievement and evaluation are in almost direct conflict. Consider, as an example, the dual roles of software testing. A common view of testing is that it is a means of identifying faults in the software so that they can be removed and the software thereby becomes more reliable. A good testing procedure is therefore one that does this most efficiently. Unfortunately, such testing procedures are likely to be very different from the kind of use to which software will be subjected during actual operation; in fact they are likely to be more stressful. For this reason they will tend to give a pessimistic view of the reliability of the software, and will not generate data suitable for the statistical models of software reliability which are to be described in this chapter. Random testing, on the other hand, which uses test cases selected randomly from a (real or simulated) user profile, is often regarded as an inefficient way of *finding* faults. The user faces an impasse: using conventional testing may increase the reliability of the product most effectively, but there will be no final measure of what has been achieved; random testing will give a reliability measure for the final product, but the level achieved may be less than would have been achieved with the same effort using a different method.

This conflict of interest between achievement and evaluation is not, of course, restricted to reliability. There are similar problems, for example, in security, where the evaluation problem seems even harder than it is for reliability. This chapter concentrates on reliability evaluation, but the reader should be aware that in most cases there will be a cost overhead involved in making an evaluation. This raises the question of when the extra cost of evaluating the reliability of software is justified. Indeed, it is worthwhile in an introductory chapter like this spending some time discussing the whole issue of why one should want to measure reliability.

In the first place, the most obvious reason why one would want a reliability measure for a program is that it is a formal measure of something which is always of interest, albeit often expressed in informal terms. A user needs a program to be 'sufficiently' reliable for his or her purposes, and will complain (usually rightly) if this informal requirement is not met. Similarly, a vendor who incurs too-high support costs as a result of frequent operational failures, or who merely loses business because of product unreliability becoming known to the community of potential purchasers, has an interest in reliability. In all these cases, it should be noted that quite modest levels of reliability may be involved; the issues of reliability evaluation are not restricted to those dramatic contexts, such as safety-critical systems, where very high reliability may be called for. On the contrary, the reliability evaluation methods described here have been used most widely for fairly mundane applications such as operating systems, telephone switches, etc. More homely examples are likely to become important in future in view of new consumer protection legislation: spreadsheets, word processors, accounting and tax packages.

In all these cases there is a crucial notion of a product being sufficiently reliable for the purpose to which it is to be put. Only with formal measures of reliability is it possible for rational debate to take place between potential adversaries. Thus when vendors routinely quote reliability figures for their products, users will be able to make intelligent decisions between rival products. Reliability may become an important decider of market success, in the way it has for consumer electronics, with buyers prepared to pay a premium for a guaranteed higher reliability.

If one accepts that the reliability of the final product is important and should be evaluated, a second reason for needing an evaluation methodology is to support management of the development process in order to achieve this final goal of a product of sufficient reliability. Only by measurement at intermediate stages of development can one hope to learn of problems sufficiently early that appropriate action can be taken. Control is only possible if one knows the results of design decisions. Of course, reliability will be only one of several metrics which will be used to monitor and control the development of a well-managed software project.

Finally, one needs an evaluation methodology for software reliability as a part of the striving towards a scientific basis for software engineering. At present it is fair to say that software engineering is more of an aspiration than a description of a discipline with a proper scientific support. A necessary (but by no means sufficient) condition for being able to claim that what one does is scientific in that one can measure characteristics of the objects of interest. Although it is unlikely that this will be done to the extent and with the rigour with which it is carried out in, say, mechanical or civil engineering, it seems obvious that one should go as far as one can. Reliability is only one of the things that should become part of a general theory of software metrics. Others include the currently more informal notions of complexity, testedness, maintainability, usability, etc. Nevertheless, simply using reliability evaluation alone it would be possible to make scientifically meaningful comparisons of the efficacy of competing development methods. One could ask questions such as whether it is more cost-effective to achieve a particular reliability using formal methods or fault tolerance, or indeed by heroic testing and debugging; or, more subtly, what is the optimal mix of these approaches in a particular case. Such questions can only be answered if many software projects have been studied, and their results measured. This requires experimentation and instrumented case studies.

In all the foregoing it has been assumed that reliability is of intrinsic interest to a user, because it is directly visible as the system is used, and thus cannot be replaced by an abstract notion such as 'correctness'. This author believes that formal methods may play an important role in the *achievement* of system properties such as reliability and security, but is more sceptical of their contribution to *evaluation*. Leaving aside the continuing technical difficulties involved in the formal verification of large systems, and systems with severe timing constraints, there remains the problem that at best a verification can only confirm that a program is a correct implementation of a formal specification. It seems obvious that, but for a very few cases such as the implementation of mathematical algorithms, the application domains in which we operate are inevitably informal to some degree. Thus a proof of correctness carried out against a formal abstraction of a partially informal requirement will always be open to the charge that a failure may occur as a result of the specification being an inadequate representation of these requirements. In particular, it is likely that formal methods will be of little help in detecting errors of omission in specifications, although they could be valuable in detecting inconsistencies.

Rather than formal verification replacing reliability evaluation, it would seem that final product reliability (along with other measures of dependability) could be used as a means of judging the efficacy of formal methods in competition with other software development methods. Ultimately, the problem to be faced is one of developing systems with a given functionality, and acceptable dependability, at the lowest cost.

31.2 The inevitability of statistical modelling for software reliability

This section motivates the reliability growth models which have been the most successful achievement of the past twenty years' work on software reliability evaluation. It is worth noting that estimating and predicting software reliability is not easy. Perhaps the major difficulty is that we are concerned primarily with design faults. The situation is very different from that tackled by the conventional hardware reliability theory. There the dramatic advances of the past quarter century have resulted from a concentration on the random processes of physical failure. Thus, for example, there is now a good understanding of how the reliabilities of complex hardware systems depend upon, on the one hand, the detailed system structure, and on the other, the reliabilities of the constituent components.

The very success of this physical hardware reliability theory, however, is now revealing the importance of design faults to the overall reliability of complex systems. The very success in devising intelligent strategies to minimize the effects of physical failure of components results in a higher proportion of even 'hardware' failures being caused by flawed designs.

Software, on the other hand, has *no* significant physical manifestation. Software failures are always the result of inherent design faults revealing themselves under appropriate operational circumstances. These faults will have been resident in the software since their creation in the original design or in subsequent changes. It is important to recognize this non-physical nature of the software failure process before attempting to model and predict it.

It will be necessary, though, to ensure that the measures of reliability used for the failures that result from design faults, whether software or hardware, are compatible with those which have traditionally been used for the physical failure process. After all, the objective is always an understanding of the reliability of a total system, which can suffer software and hardware design failures and physical failures.

Table 31.1 shows a subset of some software failure data collected several years ago by John Musa at Bell Labs (Musa, 1979), and since widely used by workers in software reliability modelling. This particular program was part of a real time command and control system for which Musa was project manager, which ensured careful data collection. The observations are the execution times, rounded to the nearest second, between successive failures. Although the data were collected during tests, the environment was carefully contrived to resemble as closely as possible real operational use. Thus the failure behaviour here should be similar to that which will be experienced by the user.

There are several striking features in this data, some of which are typical of software failure data. First, there is obviously growth taking place in the reliability; there is a clear tendency for the times between successive failures to be larger going down the table. On the other hand, there is great variability in these times, with very small times occurring at a late stage, when the average time is perhaps of the order of a few thousand seconds. This variability seems always to be present in such data sets. More worrying, there are several zeros in the table. One might hypothesize that these are the result of bad fixes; i.e. that the program was set running after a botched fault removal, and immediately failed for the same reason as before. In fact, Musa

Table 31.1 Execution times in seconds between successive failures. Read left to right in rows

3	30	113	81	115
9	2	91	112	15
138	50	77	24	108
88	670	120	26	114
325	55	242	68	422
180	10	1146	600	15
36	4	0	8	227
65	176	58	457	300
97	263	452	255	197
193	6	79	816	1351
148	21	233	134	357
193	236	31	369	748
0	232	330	365	1222
543	10	16	529	379
44	129	810	290	300
529	281	160	828	1011
445	296	1755	1064	1783
860	983	707	33	868
724	2323	2930	1461	843
12	261	1800	865	1435
30	143	108	0	3110
1247	943	700	875	245
729	1897	447	386	446
122	990	948	1082	22
75	482	5509	100	10
1071	371	790	6150	3321
1045	648	5485	1160	1864
4116				

claims that this is not the case and that the zeros are small but genuine execution times between failures arising from different faults. The figures in the table are rounded to the nearest second, and thus any execution time less than half a second will appear as a zero.

Musa has, correctly, made much of the fact that he was able to obtain *execution time* data, rather than merely recording calendar time. This is clearly an important issue. Calendar time can be misleading if the usage of the program is not constant in time. The goal should always be to obtain a time variable that represents as closely as possible the extensiveness of the use of the program. This need not be a continuous variable. In a transaction processing system, for example, a count of the number of transactions would generally be an excellent 'time' variable. In cases such as this, where time is really discrete, it is normally possible to use the continuous time reliability models without modification, since the numbers of transactions between failures will be very large.

However, it must be admitted that the collection of the necessary data for reliability prediction is not a trivial exercise. It is invariably necessary to set up a special data collection system in the company (Mellor, 1986; Musa, 1975; Curritt *et al.*, 1986), and it may be necessary to change the inhouse software testing regime. The important point is that the selection of test cases should be carried out to reflect the operational use of the software. The ease with which this can be done clearly varies from one application to another, but there are no shortcuts around this requirement. Even assuming that an accurate reliability model is available for a particular situation, the results will only reflect the type of use to which the program was being put when the data was collected. This requirement may, as was stated earlier, conflict with the requirements of those testers of software who see their goal as finding as many bugs as quickly as possible. A testing regime which is optimized in this way will not generally be typical of operational use and any reliability calculations will be worthless. Unfortunately, at present there is no way to predict the reliability in one environment (e.g. operational use) using testing data from another (e.g. 'conventional' software testing, such as structural testing). It seems that this may eventually be possible in some cases, and this is an active research area.

Table 31.2 shows some data representing failures due to both hardware design faults and software faults for a complex piece of equipment. In both these examples, as failures occur, attempts are made to fix the underlying faults which they reveal. Musa assumes that each fault is successfully removed before the program is set running again. Notice that this is a questionable assumption in many cases. Experience suggests that, not only are fixes 'unsuccessful', but they occasionally cause novel difficulties by inserting new faults.

A cursory inspection of the raw data shows that the reliability is improving, revealed by the tendency for the inter-failure times

Table 31.2 Operating times between successive failures. This data relates to a system experiencing failures due to software faults *and* hardware design faults

39	10	4	36	4
5	4	91	49	1
25	1	4	30	42
9	49	44	32	3
78	1	30	205	5
129	103	224	186	53
14	9	2	10	1
34	170	129	4	4
35	5	5	22	36
35	121	23	33	48
32	21	4	23	9
13	165	14	22	41
12	138	95	49	62
2	35	89	90	69
22	15	19	42	14
11	41	210	16	30
37	66	9	16	14
24	12	159	89	118
29	21	18	2	114
37	46	17	1	150
382	160	66	206	9
26	62	239	13	4
85	85	240	178	34
102	9	146	59	48
25	25	111	5	31
51	6	193	27	25
96	26	30	30	17
320	78	39	13	13
19	128	34	84	40
177	349	274	82	58
31	114	39	88	84
232	108	38	86	7
22	80	239	3	39
63	152	63	80	245
196	46	152	102	9
228	220	208	78	3
83	6	212	91	3
10	172	21	173	371
40	48	126	90	149
30	317	500	673	432
66	168	66	66	120
49	332			

to grow larger in the later stages. However, there is great variability and some small inter-failure times are being observed quite late. The several zeros are rounded down fractions of a second. Musa claims that these features of the data are a natural consequence of the stochastic nature of the failure process and not, for example, a result of bad fixes causing almost immediate failures.

Data of this kind are acquired sequentially as testing progresses. Questions one might ask at each stage of testing include: how reliable is the program now? How reliable will it be at some specified future time? How soon can one expect to achieve a specified target reliability? Before such questions can be answered via models of the failure process, a qualitative understanding of what is happening is needed.

It will be taken that the execution of a program involves the selection of inputs from some input space I (the totality of all possible inputs), and the transformation of these inputs into outputs (comprising *in toto* a space O). It is worth noting that input spaces are typically extremely large and in most cases a complete description will not be available.

The operational profile of the user will determine the probabilities of selection of different inputs during execution. It is often the case that different users of a program have different operational profiles. Remarks here will address a single such profile.

A program fails when an input is selected which cannot be transformed into an acceptable output. The totality of such inputs will be called I_F. In practice a failure will be detected by a comparison between the output obtained by processing a particular input, and the output which ought to have been produced according to the specification of the program. Detection of failures is, of course, a non-trivial task, but is not the concern here.

The conceptual model can be taken a stage further by considering the underlying faults which reside in the program p. If one makes the reasonable assumption that each failure can be said to have been caused by one (and only one) fault, there is then a partitioning of I_F into subsets corresponding to the different faults.

When one successfully removes a fault, and so changes the program p into a new program p', the effect is to remove certain points of I from I_F. Thus the members of the removed fault set now map into 'acceptable' regions of O.

Operational use of a program may be thought of as the selection of a trajectory of points in the space I. Typically many inputs will be successful, i.e. outside I_F, before an input is selected which lies in I_F and so causes a failure. When the failure occurs, an attempt will be made to fix the underlying fault and if this attempt is successful some points are eliminated from I_F. Execution of the program then restarts (most probably in a region outside I_F since I_F is typically very small), and the trajectory of successive inputs continues until the next failure, when the fixing operation is repeated. The result is a sequence of programs, p_1, p_2, p_3, ... and a sequence of successively smaller sets I_F^1, I_F^2, I_F^3, ... Clearly the reliability growth is determined by this sequence $\{I_F^i\}$.

In this chapter it is assumed that the reader is familiar with basic statistical concepts (see Chapter 6). This text is confined to the continuous time case. There is a sense, of course, in which the whole problem is really a discrete time one. (Computer systems are discrete devices; the conceptual model relies on the idea of discrete input cases.) However, the times between successive failures, which will be the random variables of interest, will typically be very much larger than the machine cycle time and the times required to process individual inputs. Therefore a continuous time approach will be a good approximation to what is really happening.

With this proviso, it seems reasonable to assume that the sets I_F are encountered purely randomly in the execution trajectory.

That is, the time to next failure (and so the inter-failure times) has, conditionally, an exponential distribution. If we let T_1, T_2, ... be the successive inter-failure times, we have a complete description of the stochastic process if we know the rates λ_1, λ_2, ...

Clearly these rates, and in particular the successive differences representing the improvements caused by the attempts to remove faults, will depend on the 'sizes' of the subsets representing the faults in I_F. There will be a tendency for the larger faults to be detected, and so removed, earlier. This implies a law of diminishing returns for debugging. However, the failure subset I_F will be encountered randomly and so will its subsets corresponding to the faults. There is no guarantee that faults will be encountered in order of their size. In fact, the sequence of successive fault sizes is a stochastic process, and so, therefore, is the corresponding sequence of rates corresponding to T_1, T_2, ... Call these rates Λ_1, Λ_2, ...

As this model stands, we would expect that $\Lambda_1 > \Lambda_2 > ...$ However, it has so far been assumed that a fix is certain to be effective, and therefore the only uncertainty concerns its magnitude. In fact this may be unrealistic. There is evidence that fix attempts are fallible and that sometimes a program is made less reliable as a result of an attempt to remove a fault. It might be more realistic, therefore, merely to insist that the $\{\Lambda_i\}$ sequence is stochastically decreasing probabilistically to satisfy the relationship $P(\Lambda_i < l) \geqslant P(\Lambda_{i-1} < l)$. This means there is a tendency, but not a certainty, that successive rates become smaller.

To summarize this conceptual model so far, there are two sources of uncertainty in the failure behaviour of software which is undergoing debugging. In the first place there is uncertainty arising from the operational environment, specifically in the sequence of input cases selected for processing by the program. Even if we knew I_F, we would not know when an input would next be selected from here. This uncertainty results in the assumption of conditional exponential distributions for the inter-failure times. Secondly, there is uncertainty arising from the debugging operation itself. Even if we knew the partitioning of I_F, we would not know which fault would be encountered next and so we would be uncertain about the magnitude of the change in the failure rate. We would also be uncertain in many cases whether a particular fix had in fact been successful. The result is that the sequence of rates (parameters of the exponential distributions of the T s) is a stochastic process, that is, we have a doubly stochastic scheme.

31.3 Some software reliability models

The conceptual model described above is, in some ways, too naive. Its problems will be discussed later. However, even this simple doubly stochastic scheme is not followed in all the models which are found in the literature.

Probably the best known model is one of the earliest. The Jelinski-Moranda model (Jelinski and Moranda, 1972), particularly in its extended form as the Musa model (Musa, 1975), is also still one of the most widely used. This model assumes that debugging begins when a program contains N faults, and that each fault contributes the same amount φ, to the overall rate of occurrence of failures. Thus, since the fixes which are carried out at failures are assumed to be perfect, the random variables T_1, T_2, ... are independently exponentially distributed with parameters $N\varphi$, $(N-1)\varphi$, ... successively.

There are two related criticisms of this model. It treats the sequence of rates as purely deterministic and, more importantly, assumes all faults to have equal size. There is plenty of empirical evidence, on the contrary, that faults vary dramatically in their contributions to program unreliability. In some interesting experiments involving replicated runs, a single program was

debugged several times, being restored to its undebugged state for each run (Nagel and Skrivan, 1981). This allowed the experimenters to estimate the size (i.e. rate contribution of the bug to the overall rate of occurrence of failures of the program). They found that these sizes varied by orders of magnitude. In a study of some very large IBM systems, operating in a large world-wide user population, Adams (1984) again managed to estimate the sizes of reported bugs since each had typically been identified on many sites. Once again, these sizes varied by several orders of magnitude. An extraordinary incidental result of the Adams study was the discovery of the large number of extremely small bugs. He showed that 30% of all the bugs that had been discovered, in thousands of years of operational use over many sites, were occurring at frequencies of less than once every 5000 years.

Most importantly from the point of view here is that the reliability predictions obtained from the model are generally too optimistic as a result of these manifestly implausible assumptions (Littlewood et al., 1983), as will be seen in the later analyses of the data shown above.

The Littlewood model (Littlewood, 1981) was designed to overcome this difficulty by allowing rates corresponding to the different faults to have different sizes. There is an obvious unpredictability in these sizes, which becomes reflected in the unpredictability of the improvement in reliability which takes place at a successful fault removal. This is represented here by letting the sizes be independent gamma (α, β) random variables. In this model there is then a tendency for the larger rate faults to be encountered earlier than the smaller ones, but this sequence is itself random. The model therefore represents the diminishing returns in reliability improvement which come from additional testing.

Each of these models is an example of a general class of exponential order statistic models (Miller, 1986a). The faults can be seen as 'competing risks'. A program can be thought of as containing many faults, all waiting to be discovered by causing a program failure. The times to encounter the different faults are independent, identically distributed random variables (exponential for Jelinski-Moranda, Pareto for Littlewood), and the successive inter-failure times seen by the user are the spacings between the order statistics. Competing risk models have been studied widely in the medical statistical literature, where typically a human individual is assumed to be at risk from several competing life-threatening diseases. Unfortunately, this literature does not help us in the software reliability context, since it is usual to be only interested in the (random variable) time to the first infection, whereupon the patient succumbs and the process ends. The case here is closer to a model of childhood infection, where succumbing to a survivable illness (e.g. measles) confers immunity from further infection from that source of risk; the 'bug' of 'measles-susceptibility' has been 'removed'.

A simple early model with a different structure, which still captures the doubly stochastic nature of the conceptual model of the failure process, is due to Littlewood and Verrall (1973). Here the usual assumption is made that the inter-failure times, T_i, are conditionally independent exponentials with rates Λ_i, and the Λ_i are assumed to be gamma ($\alpha,\psi(i)$) random variables. Here $\psi(i)$ is a parametric function which determines the reliability growth (or decay). If $\psi(i)$ is an increasing function of i, it is easy to show that $\{\Lambda_i\}$ is stochastically decreasing and $\{T_i\}$ stochastically increasing. This model differs from the previous one in modelling the successive values of the rate of occurrence of failure of the program itself, Λ_i, rather than the rates of the remaining bugs (which added together give this program rate). Here we shall use $\psi(i) = \beta_1 + \beta_2 i$. Notice that the sign of β_2 then determines whether there is growth or decay in reliability. The data itself, therefore, is allowed to determine whether the reliability is increasing via the estimate of β_2.

The above models have been constructed with the specific intention of capturing the particular characteristics of the failure process of software. Among more standard stochastic processes in the statistical literature, non-homogeneous Poisson processes (Cox and Lewis, 1966) are obvious candidates for modelling the non-stationary behaviour revealed by data like Table 31.1. A minor conceptual drawback is that most such processes have rate functions which change continuously in time. It could be argued that in this case the only changes which take place are the jumps which occur at a fix. However, one way of constructing a non-homogeneous Poisson process is to assume that N (the total number of initial faults) is Poisson distributed in the exponential order statistic models such as Jelinski-Moranda and Littlewood (Miller, 1986a). Thus the Goel-Okumoto model is such a non-homogeneous Poisson process variant of Jelinski-Moranda. It is easy to show that, on the basis of a single realization, it is not possible to distinguish between such an exponential order statistic model and its non-homogeneous Poisson process variant. However, it is hard to give a simple justification for this method of constructing a Poisson process, and it must be admitted that the major advantages for software reliability modelling of the Poisson process are its simplicity and the versatility arising from the freedom to choose the rate function.

Numerous rate functions have been proposed for non-homogeneous Poisson process models in order to model reliability growth. Perhaps most notable is the Duane model (Duane, 1964; Crow, 1977) which was originally devised for *hardware* reliability growth arising from burn-in testing (the elimination of faulty components in complex systems via their early failure).

These are only a few of the models which have been proposed over the years. Although it is possible to argue that some of these are less plausible than others, one is clearly not in a position to select a definitively 'best' one. As will be shown next, the answers obtained from different models on the same data set can differ dramatically. It turns out, also, that the accuracy of models varies from one data set to another (Abdel-Ghaly *et al*, 1986; Littlewood, 1989). All this suggests that we need a mechanism for selecting among the alternative models for each data set.

31.4 Using software reliability growth models

Although one loosely speaks of 'evaluating' or 'measuring' software reliability, it is worth emphasizing that in fact the problem is one of prediction. The objective is to take some data obtained by observing *past* behaviour of the program under study and use this to make predictions about *future* behaviour. Specifically, one wants to be able to make statements about the as-yet-unobserved future inter-failure times T_i, T_{i+1}, ... on the basis of the observed $t_1, t_2, \ldots t_{i-1}$. Clearly, any statements about the future will be expressed in statistical terminology, since there is an intrinsic uncertainty present.

In the previous sections there has been much emphasis on reliability models. In fact making predictions about the future involves three steps:

1. Selecting the reliability growth model itself, such as one of those described above; this allows a complete probabilistic description of the T_js, conditional on some unknown parameters.
2. Applying a statistical procedure for the unknown parameters of the model, using the available data (i.e. the observed t_js).
3. Combining these two pieces of information to make probability statements about the future: the reliability predictions.

All three stages of this prediction system are essential, and inaccurate predictions can be caused by any or all stages. Clearly stage (1), the model itself, is vital. It seems unlikely that good predictions will come from a model which is manifestly implausible. However, a good model is not sufficient and stages (2) and (3) are vital components.

In fact, most reliability growth models are fairly complex mathematically, so our freedom of choice at stages (2) and (3) is generally limited. Worse than this, the standard statistical procedures which one might expect to apply to test the plausibility of the model itself (e.g. goodness-of-fit tests) are also not available, again because of the model complexity. These difficulties arise from the non-stationarity inherent in the data, and, indeed, they make the problem one of interest.

It could be argued that there are models which are 'obviously' better than others because of the greater plausibility of their underlying assumptions, but this is a rather dubious proposition. Certainly, the assumptions of some models seem overtly naive and it might be reasonable to discount them. However, this still leaves others which cannot be rejected *a priori*. Whilst these might differ quite dramatically in their mathematical structure, it is hard to select among them. In fact, it is clear that current understanding of the processes of software engineering is so imperfect that one cannot even choose an appropriate model when one has an intimate knowledge of the software under study. At some future time it may be possible to select the most appropriate reliability model for a program by taking note of the particular characteristics of that program and the process of its creation. This is not currently the case.

Where does this leave a user who merely wants to obtain trustworthy reliability metrics for his or her current software project? It seems that there is no alternative to a direct examination and comparison of the quality of the predictions emanating from different complete prediction systems. Later in this chapter will be shown the beginnings of a set of tools to assist this examination and comparison. Although examples will be shown of these tools applied to the predictions from several prediction systems using real software reliability data, the intention is *not* to recommend particular ways of predicting. Rather, experience teaches that no prediction system can be trusted to be always superior to others (Abdel-Ghaly *et al*, 1986; Littlewood, 1989). The best advice to users, then, is to be eclectic. Try many prediction systems and use the reliability metrics which are the best *for the data under consideration*.

First, consider some competing predictions using the data of Table 31.1. For simplicity only the prediction of the time to next failure, i.e. estimation of the current reliability of the program under test, will be considered, but the general observations to be made here are applicable to other predictions. We want to estimate $F_i(t) \equiv P(T_i < t)$, based on the data $t_1, t_2, \ldots, t_{i-1}$ previously observed.

For each of the models to be used in the following, the prediction system uses maximum likelihood as the method of statistical inference for (2) above, and predictions are made by substitution of these maximum likelihood estimates of the parameters into appropriate expressions obtained from the model. Thus, as an example, for the Jelinski-Moranda model, $F_i(t) = 1 - exp\{N - i + 1)\varphi t\}$, and one would estimate this by substituting estimates of N and φ, based on $t_1, t_2, \ldots t_{i-1}$.

Figure 31.1 summarizes this kind of prediction for various models operating on the data of *Table 31.1*. Here are shown the medians of the times to next failure estimated by the models on the evidence of the inter-failure times so far observed. This is the kind of repeatedly updated calculation that would be carried out if a user was interested in stopping testing and debugging as soon as a pre-specified target reliability had been achieved. Of course the models can present the predictions in other ways (examples are rate of occurrence of failures, reliability function) – medians are shown here only for simplicity.

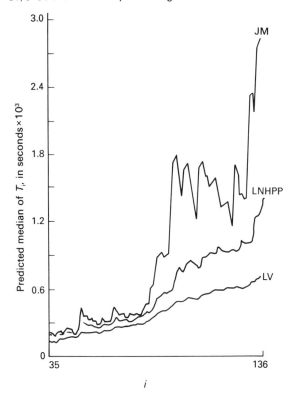

Figure 31.1 Prediction of medians one step ahead, using data of Table 31.1. The models used are: Jelinski-Moranda (JM), Littlewood-Verrall (LV) and the non-homogenous Poisson version of the Littlewood model (LNHPP)

The results shown in *Figure 31.1* seem disappointing. Whilst the models agree that reliability growth is present, they disagree about the nature and extent of that growth. In particular, some models are giving a much more optimistic picture in the later stages of debugging than others. It is also notable that some predictions are more 'noisy' than others. These fluctuations might suggest that there are local set-backs occurring in the overall growth in reliability.

The models are also able (with varying degrees of difficulty) to make longer term predictions. *Figure 31.2* shows an analysis of the same data, where the Jelinski-Moranda and Littlewood-Verrall models are predicting the median 20 steps ahead, that is a prediction is made of the median of T_i at stage i-20, based on $t_1, t_2, \ldots t_{i-20}$. For the JM model, at least, the picture is even bleaker than the previous analysis. There are several excursions to infinity, caused by the model predicting that within the next 20 fixes the last bug will be removed and the program thus become perfectly reliable. Of course, as we know from the raw data, such predictions are simply false and the program continues to fail in each case over 20 more times. The other model does not behave so badly, and *Figure 31.2* shows that at least it is self-consistent. There is close agreement between the predictions of the median of T_i calculated 20 steps before i and 1 step before i. This agreement does not, of course allow one to conclude that these median estimates are necessarily accurate.

A user might reasonably ask after seeing this kind of result which, if any, of these models can be trusted. Unfortunately, this kind of disagreement is typical. Worse, there is evidence that the accuracy of the models varies from one data source to

another (Abdel-Ghaly *et al.*, 1986; Littlewood, 1989), so it is not possible to select a 'universally best' model by comparing different model performances on many data sets. A user is therefore faced with the problem of deciding which, if any, of the reliability predictions he or she can trust *for this particular data source.*

This is the key idea which a potential user of software reliability models should take away from this chapter. *Do not trust any reliability model to give accurate results in all cases.* Nor should it be expected that detailed knowledge of the software under examination will help in identifying the most appropriate reliability model. It is possible that a method of doing this will be developed in the future, but there are currently no such methods available. Fortunately, all is not lost since recent research has made available techniques for analysing the accuracy of the reliability predictions on a particular data source (program) so that it is not necessary to select a model *a priori.* These techniques essentially detect different kinds of disagreement between predicted and actual failure behaviour, and so assist the user to make a decision as to which, if any, of many prediction systems is producing reliability predictions of sufficient accuracy. These techniques use some novel statistical ideas and there is no space to describe them in full here; details can be found elsewhere (Abdel-Ghaly *et al*, 1986; Littlewood, 1989). The following is restricted to describing only one of the techniques, which allows a user to detect consistent bias in a prediction system, and show how it allows the selection of the best of the models in *Figure 31.1*.

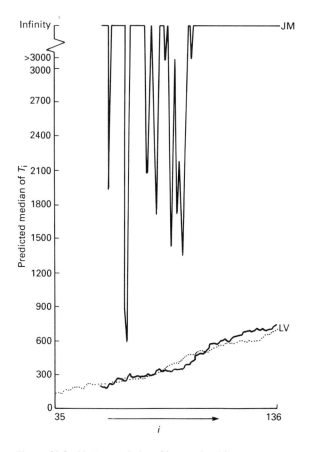

Figure 31.2 Median predictions 20 steps ahead for Jelinski – Moranda (JM) and Littlewood-Verrall (LV) models

31.5 Analysis of the accuracy of reliability measures and model selection

For simplicity this section will concentrate only on the problem of predicting the random variable T_i, having observed $t_1, t_2, \ldots, t_{i-1}$. A good estimate of $F_i(t) \equiv P(T_i < t)$ or, equivalently, of the reliability function $R_i(t) = 1 - F_i(t)$, is required. (Notice that any detailed reliability prediction about T_i can be obtained from this: these include the current rate of occurrence of failures, the mean time to next failure, etc.) From a particular model an estimate $\tilde{F}_i(t)$ is obtained. The user is interested in the closeness of $\tilde{F}_i(t)$ to the unknown true $F_i(t)$. The difficulty is that one never, even after the event, knows the true $F_i(t)$. The most that is seen is a single realization, t_i, of a random variable with distribution $F_i(t)$.

However, since the user will be making a sequence of predictions $\{\tilde{F}_i(t)\}$ as debugging proceeds, he or she can gain information about the accuracy of the model on this data source from the pairs $\{\tilde{F}_i(t), t_i\}$. An informal examination will sometimes be sufficient to detect when the sequence $\{t_i\}$ does not look like a realization from the sequence $\{\tilde{F}_i(t)\}$, i.e. that the model is giving inaccurate answers. More formally, consider the sequence of transformations $u_i = \tilde{F}_i(t_i)$: each u_i is a probability integral transform of the observed t_i using the *previously calculated* prediction, $\tilde{F}_i(t)$. It is easy to see that the u_is should 'look like' a random sample from U(O, 1) since there is a prequential *forecasting system* in the spirit of Dawid (1984). One procedure, then, is to examine the sample distribution function of the sequence of us to see whether there is any evidence of departure from uniformity.

Two such u-plots, for the Jelinski-Moranda and Littlewood-Verrall models, each making 100 predictions using the data source of *Table 31.1*, are shown in *Figure 31.3*. It can be seen that Littlewood-Verrall is closer to the uniform line of unit slope which is the true c.d.f (characteristic distribution function) of a U(0, 1) random variable. There are several formal ways of measuring the distance between the plots and the 'ideal' line of unit slope so as to decide if the deviation is a significant one.

Here the Kolmogorov distance, that is, the maximum deviation between the empirical plot and the line of unit slope, is used. For these two models on the data of *Table 31.1*, the Kolmogorov distances are 0.190 (Jelinski-Moranda), significant at the 1% level, and 0.144 (Littlewood-Verall), significant at the 5% level. There is thus very strong evidence that the Jelinski-Moranda plot is not uniform, indicating that the predictions are inaccurate in some way. There is, likewise, evidence of inaccuracy in the LV predictions, but this is less strong.

More important than the simple evidence of inaccuracy, however, is what the plots say about the detailed nature of the prediction errors. The plot for Jelinski-Moranda is everywhere above the line of unit slope, indicating that there are too many small u values. That is, the model is tending to underestimate the probability of failure before t_i (the later, actual, observed failure time): the model is *too optimistic*. Conversely, there is evidence that Littlewood-Verrall is largely below the line of unit slope and so is *too pessimistic* in its predictions. A user might reasonably conclude that the truth lies somewhere between the Littlewood-Verrall and Jelinski-Moranda predictions. Thus, for example, in Figure 31.1 one might expect the Littlewood non-homogeneous Poisson process predictions to be better than Littlewood-Verrall and Jelinski-Moranda. In fact a u-plot of these predictions is very close to uniform (the Kolmogorov distance, 0.098, is not statistically significant).

A comparison of the performance of ten software reliability models on this data, using u-plots and other criteria (Abdel-Ghaly *et al.*, 1986), shows that in fact the Littlewood non-homogeneous Poisson process is giving the best results overall. In the absence of any other information, a user might conclude that, for *future* predictions on the same data source, this would be the preferred choice. A user therefore has the beginnings of a methodology which enables him or her to compare the accuracy of different models on a particular data source, select the best, and know whether the results are sufficiently accurate.

The calculations involved in this kind of analysis are very extensive. For each model it is necessary to perform a fresh stage (2) of the prediction system, computing the estimates of the unknown parameters of the model, as each new failure time arrives. The whole process is repeated for as many models as are being considered, before the comparison can begin using the methods of evaluating predictive accuracy. Since each of the elementary calculations usually involves a search in the parameter space to find the maximum of the likelihood function, it is important to have an efficient algorithm and implementation if the process is not to be too tedious. Fortunately, such software is available (Reliability and Statistical Consultants Ltd, 1988): the basic calculations on which this paper are based involved fitting nine models to the Musa data of *Table 31.1*, with 100 elementary calculations (reliability predictions) for each, giving 900 elementary reliability predictions altogether. The entire calculation, comprising the reliability predictions and the analysis of their comparative predictive accuracy, ran for about 40 minutes on an IBM PC-AT with maths co-processor, making this kind of analysis practicable in an industrial context. This software is also available for Sun workstations and DEC VAX machines, where it runs correspondingly faster.

31.6 Summary and discussion

The previous sections should give some flavour of what is currently now available to a user who wants to measure the reliability of a program. Briefly, the position is that when fairly modest levels of reliability are required it is generally possible to obtain accurate measures and, just as important, *know* that they are trustworthy. This is achieved by an eclectic policy of applying many of the available models in each application and

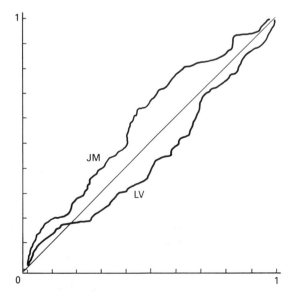

Figure 31.3 *u*-plots for one-step-ahead predict using data from Table 31.1. Models used are Jelinski-Moranda (JM) and Littlewood-Verrall (LV)

using the new evaluation techniques to select one which is giving suitably accurate answers. It cannot be over-emphasized that a user should *not* trust any particular model to be accurate in all circumstances. There is a great deal of evidence that for all models the accuracy varies from one application to another. Although better models are being developed, it is unlikely that this basic situation will change, since the complexity and variability of the underlying processes will preclude the invention of a once-and-for-all definitive model for all circumstances.

Although there are many circumstances where these techniques can be applied successfully, there are equally situations in which they should be used with great care. One example is real-time software which must work continuously in time. Consider, for example, a flight control system for an unstable aircraft, where the software operates in an essentially cyclic manner. In a case like this one has to be careful how one defines software reliability, since the system may have sufficient physical integrity to survive a single isolated failure, but not a succession of failures. The simple conceptual model which underlies the software reliability models described here tacitly assumes that after a failure occurs the program is set running in a different part of the input space from where it failed. In a control system the designer may not have this luxury. After one failed cycle in the avionics example, the next cycle will almost certainly present the program with inputs which are 'close' to the one which has just failed. It seems likely that this new input will be very likely to fail also, and in fact the software might exhibit a large 'cluster' of successive failed inputs.

This is partly a problem of definition. One could choose, conservatively, to assume that any failed input is a possible cause of disaster, and base one's safety case on this. An alternative would be to analyse the nature of the stochastic process of clusters itself, their frequency and their (random variable) sizes. If, for example, it could be shown that clusters were almost always sufficiently small as to present no threat to safe operation, their *frequency* of occurrence could be allowed to be higher. Since, as will be seen later, assuring very low absolute frequencies of failure is extremely hard, this kind of analysis may be of interest in safely-related contexts. Recent work has started to model cluster processes (Csenki, 1989), and there is some intriguing experimental work in which the 'shapes', and so sizes, of faults have been mapped (Knight and Amman, 1987). The idea in this latter study was to take a single failed input, found by chance, and search its locality to determine the boundary between 'failed' and 'non-failed' inputs thus finding the 'shape' of the fault.

As has been suggested earlier, the reliability growth models are not suitable for obtaining assurances that very high reliabilities have been achieved. It is easy to see empirically that there is a potent law of diminishing returns operating during debugging. This is due to the fact that when a program becomes more reliable, after considerable testing has taken place, the faults are being found less frequently *and each such fault is likely to be one with a small rate* and so its removal contributes little to the improvement in the reliability of the program. Clearly, removing a 5000 year bug of the type mentioned earlier (Adams, 1984) will have no perceptible effect on the overall reliability of that program.

Table 31.3 shows this effect quite dramatically for the data of Table 31.1 analysed earlier. It is quite clear that there is a non-linear relationship between what has been achieved (here the mean time to failure) and the effort needed to achieve it (here the testing time).

Figure 31.4 shows an analysis of the data of Table 31.2, this time plotting the estimated achieved rate of occurrence of failures against total elapsed time. It would be rash to predict how this plot would look after very much more testing, but it is again clear that achieving a particular reduction in the rate

Table 31.3 An illustration of the law of diminishing returns in heroic debugging. Here the total execution time required to reach a particular mean time to failure is compared with the mean. The data is from Table 31.1, and the calculations used the Littlewood-Verrall model. Similar results are obtained with other models

sample size, i	elapsed time, t_i	achieved mttf, m_i	t_i/m_i
40	5 324	269.9	19.7
50	10 088	375.0	26.9
60	12 559	392.5	32.0
70	16 185	437.5	37.0
80	20 566	490.4	41.9
90	29 360	617.3	47.7
100	42 014	776.3	54.1
110	49 415	841.6	58.7
120	56 484	896.4	63.0
130	74 363	1 054.1	70.1

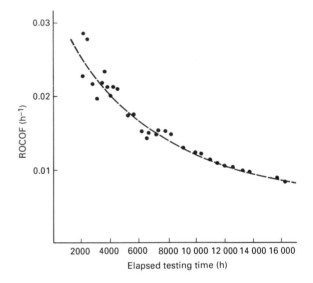

Figure 31.4 Illustration of the law of diminishing returns in heroic testing. Littlewood-Verrall model is applied to data from Table 31.2. Here the rate of occurrence of failures (ROCOF) is plotted against total elapsed testing time

becomes more and more difficult. Indeed it is by no means obvious here that the curve is asymptotic to the axis. This raises the possibility that, for some systems, there may be a level of irreducible unreliability which no amount of testing can eliminate. The evidence of Adams' 5000 year bugs seems to support this, since it is unlikely that the very small improvement in the reliability of the product resulting from the successful removal of such a bug will outweigh the possibly large degradation in reliability caused by a botched attempt.

The major conclusion from these results is that 'heroic' debugging is not a feasible means of achieving very high reliability, because unrealistically long test runs would be needed. Some idea of the problem can be gained by asking how confident we would be in a program *which has never failed*.

Making quite reasonable mathematical assumptions it can be shown that, if x hours of failure-free working have been observed, there is only a 50-50 chance of no failure being seen in the next x hours (Littlewood, 1986). Such a scenario is the most optimistic that can be imagined. If failures *had* been observed in the first x hours, of course, the position would be even worse. Clearly, failure rates such as the oft-quoted 10^{-9} per hour, for flight-critical civil aircraft avionics (RTCA, 1985; Rouquet and Traverse, 1986), which is a median time to failure of the order of 10^9 hours, are far beyond what could be assured even in the lifetime of the entire fleet of aircraft. Of course, this kind of argument only takes account of the observed failure behaviour during some kind of testing activity. In practice, other information about the program will be available. However, it seems unlikely that this could change our confidence in the reliability by the orders of magnitude required. How much, for example, should one be prepared to increase confidence, from what has been learned from testing, upon being told that the software was developed using formal methods and that formal verification had been successfully carried out? Such extra information would make one more confident, but there would remain uncertainty about whether the formal specification was an adequate representation of the informal requirements. An assessment of the impact of specification faults on reliability can only come from testing, and one is back with the original problem.

Similar problems arise with fault-tolerant solutions. Here it is hoped that the development of several diverse versions of a program, with an adjudication mechanism (such as voting) to agree on the output, will result in greater reliability. The success of such an approach depends on the degree of diversity in the failure behaviour of the versions. Roughly speaking, it is required that if one version has failed, there is a low probability of the other version(s) failing. Unfortunately, *assessing* such conditional probabilities turns out to be as hard as simply heroically testing the complete fault-tolerant system as if it were a black box (Miller, 1989).

These problems with formal methods and fault-tolerance illustrate the important distinction between achievement and assessment of reliability with which this chapter opened. It seems clear that both methods are likely to be effective approaches to *achieving* reliability, inasmuch as there is some generic evidence of their success from observation of the reliability of software in operational use. However, this is far from being a *measure* of the extent of success in a particular application. In safety-critical applications, in particular, it would perhaps be irresponsible to regard information about the effectiveness of a development process as a substitute for knowledge of the actual product behaviour in operational use.

Returning now to more modest reliability levels, of the kind where the reliability growth models can operate effectively, it is worth remarking that whenever one speaks of 'the' reliability of a program there is an implicit operational profile over the space of all possible inputs. A reliability measure refers jointly to the program and to this profile. If the latter were to change as a result of a change in the way the software was used, it is likely that the perceived reliability would also change. This problem has been alluded to earlier in the context of test environments and operational use. A reliability measure obtained from testing is a useful prediction of what a user will see only if the testing profile accurately reflects operational use.

In the case of a program which is to run on many sites, there could be many reliability measures of interest. From the point of view of a particular user, the only one of interest is that which refers to his or her own operational profile. For the vendor, interested in the support costs arising from unreliability, a 'meta reliability' for the whole user base is of more interest and this could be represented, for example, by the rate of receipt of software problem reports. In many cases, it will be possible to partition a population of users into groups whose members are similar to one another in their operational profiles, then measure the reliability of each group.

These different perceived reliabilities can contain pitfalls for the unwary. Consider, for example, the Adams (1984) data on a very large world-wide population of users of operating systems. Here the remarkable '5000 year bugs' are probably a result of the differences in the operational profiles from one site to another. If a particular kind of use of the system is exhibited by only a very small number of users, and this type of use alone reveals a particular bug, then that bug will have a very small rate when averaged over the entire population of users. To the vendor the bug could look sufficiently unimportant that a decision is taken not to fix, since this would not cause a perceptible improvement in reliability. To each of the small number of users who see that bug, though, its continued presence could be a serious problem. It is perfectly possible for *every* user to have such bugs, which the vendor does not think worth fixing. In such an extreme scenario, the entire user base is disgruntled, but the vendor believes the product to be a reliable one.

In practice, things are not likely to be as extreme as this, but the general principle is an important one. When there is a large user base for a single product, one needs to worry not only about the 'meta-reliability', averaged over the user base, but also about the disparity of use within that user base.

Notwithstanding these areas where care is needed in the application and use of software reliability models, the author believes that it is possible, in most situations, to obtain accurate reliability estimates. These can be obtained relatively easily with the newly available software and it is to be hoped that the growing interest in using the models in real industrial practice will continue.

31.7 References

Abdel-Ghaly, A. A., Chan, P. Y. and Littlewood, B. (1986) Evaluation of competing software reliability predictions. *IEEE Transactions on Software Engineering*, SE-12, 950–967

Adams, E. N. (1984) Optimizing preventive service of software products. *IBM Journal Research and Development*, **28**, 2–14

Aitchison, J. and Dunsmore, I. R. (1975) *Statistical Prediction Analysis*, University Press, Cambridge

Brocklehurst, S., Chan, P. Y., Littlewood, B. and Snell, J. (1990) Recalibrating software reliability predictions. *IEEE Transactions on Software Engineering* [forthcoming]

Cox, D. R. and Lewis, P. A. W. (1966) *The Statistical Analysis of Series of Events*, Methuen, London

Crow, L. H. (1977) Confidence interval procedures for reliability growth analysis. *Technical Report 197*, US Army Material Systems Analysis Activity, Aberdeen, Maryland

Csenki, A. (1989) Recovery block reliability analysis with failure clustering. In *Proceedings of the Working Conference on Dependable Computing for Critical Applications* (Santa Barbara, August 1989), Springer-Verlag [in press]

Curritt, P. A., Dyer, M. and Mills, H. D. (1986) Certifying the reliability of software. *IEEE Transactions on Software Engineering*, SE-12, 3–11

Dawid, A. P. (1984) Statistical theory: the prequential approach. *Journal Royal Statistical Society, A*, **147**, 278–292

Duane, J. T. (1964) Learning curve approach to reliability monitoring. *IEEE Transactions on Aerospace*, **2**, 563–566

Eckhardt, D. E. and Lee, L. D. (1985) A theoretical basis for the analysis of multi-version software subject to coincident errors. *IEEE Transactions on Software Engineering*, SE-11, 1511–1517

Goel, A. L. and Okumoto, K. (1979) Time-dependent error-detection rate model for software reliability and other performance measures. *IEEE Transactions on Reliability*, R-28, 206–211

Jelinski, Z. and Moranda, P. B. (1972) Software reliability research. In

Statistical Computer Performance Evaluation, (ed. W. Freiberger) Academic Press, New York, USA. pp 465–484

Kalbfleisch, J. D. and Prentice, R. L. (1980) *The Statistical Analysis of Failure Time Data*, Wiley, New York, USA

Keiller, P. A. and Littlewood, B. (1984) Adaptive software reliability modelling. In *Digest 14th International Symposium on Fault-tolerant Computing*, IEEE Press, New York, USA. pp 108–113

Knight, J. C. and Amman, P. E. (1987) Data diversity: an approach to software fault tolerance. In *Digest 17th International Symposium on Fault-Tolerant Computing*, IEEE Press, New York, USA. pp 122–133

Knight, J. C. and Leveson, N. G. (1986) An empirical study of failure probabilities in multi-version software. In *Digest 16th International Symposium on Fault-tolerant Computing*, IEEE Press, New York, USA. pp 165–170

Laprie, J. C. (1988) Dependability: a unifying concept for reliable computing and fault tolerance. In *More Resilient Computing Systems* (ed. T. Anderson) Collins, London [in press]

Littlewood, B. (1981) Stochastic reliability growth: a model for fault removal in computer programs and hardware designs. *IEEE Transactions on Reliability*, **R-30**, 313–320

Littlewood, B. (1986) How reliable is a program which has never failed? *CSR Software Reliability and Metrics Newsletter*, **4**, Centre for Software Reliability, City University, London

Littlewood, B. (1989) Forecasting software reliability. In *Software Reliability, Modelling and Identification* (ed. S. Bittanti) Lecture Notes in Computer Science 341, Springer-Verlag, Heidelberg, FRG. pp 141–209

Littlewood, B., Keiller, P. A., Miller, D. R. and Sofer, A. (1983) On the quality of software reliability predictions. In *Proceedings of NATO ASI on Electronic Systems Effectiveness and Life Cycle Costing*, (ed. J. Skwirzinski) Springer-Verlag, Heidelberg, FRG. pp 441–460

Littlewood, B. and Verrall, J. L. (1973) A Bayesian reliability growth model for computer software. *Journal of the Royal Statistical Society C*, **22**, 332–346

Mellor, P. (1986) Software reliability data collection: problems and standards. In *Software Reliability, Pergamon State of the Art Report* (eds. P. Mellor and A. Bendell), Pergamon, Oxford

Miller, D. R. (1986a) Exponential order statistic models of software reliability growth. *IEEE Transactions Software Engineering*, **SE-12**, 12–24

Miller, D. R. (1986b) Making statistical inferences about software reliability. In *CSR Software Reliability and Metrics Newsletter*, **4**, Centre for Software Reliability, City University, London

Miller, D. R. (1989) The role of statistical modelling and inference in software quality assurance. In *Software Certification* (ed B. de Neumann), Elsevier Applied Science, Barking, pp 135–152

Musa, J. (1975) A theory of software reliability and its application. *IEEE Transactions on Software Engineering*, **SE-1**, 312–327

Musa, J. (1979) Software reliability data. *Technical Report*, available from Data Analysis Center for Software, Rome Air Development Center, NY, USA

Nagel, P. M. and Skrivan, J. A. (1981) Software reliability: repetitive run experimentation and modelling. *Technical Report, BCS-40399*, Boeing Computer Services Company, Seattle, Washington, USA

Reliability and Statistical Consultants Ltd (1988) *Software Reliability Modelling Programs*, available from Reliability and Statistical Consultants Ltd, 5 Jocelyn Road, Richmond, Surrey, TW9 2TJ

Rouquet, J. C. and Traverse, P. J. (1986) Safe and reliable computing on board the Airbus and ATR aircraft. In *Proceedings of Fifth IFAC Workshop on Safety of Computer Control Systems* (ed. W. J. Quirk), Pergamon Press, Oxford, pp 93–97

RTCA (1985) *Software Considerations in Airborne Systems and Equipment Certification*. Radio Technical Commission for Aeronautics, Doc DO178A, Washington, USA

32

Managing software engineering teams

Keith Southwell
Logica Cambridge Ltd

Contents

32.1 Introduction

Few would dispute that people are fundamental to the success of software projects, but much of software engineering pays them little attention, either as producers of software, as users, or in any of the other roles in which they play a part. This is not to play down the role of the technology covered in the rest of this book. However, software is produced by people for people; the technology serves little purpose if it does not help those people. For the most part this chapter leaves aside the technology and concentrates on the people and, in particular, the people who produce the software.

This chapter is concerned with conveying an understanding of how teams operate and explaining how managers can use that understanding to serve their goal, which is to develop software of high quality productively and effectively. In order to do that managers need to:

1. Understand why people do what they do, both as individuals and as groups.
2. Put together and structure development teams.
3. Provide a good working environment for their staff, including not only office facilities but also the organizational, technical, and other aspects of the environment.
4. Plan and delegate work.
5. Motivate people to carry out those plans.
6. Ensure that the plans have been carried out, and take corrective action if they have not.
7. Train and develop their staff.
8. Deal with a variety of people problems which will occur during a project.

In doing these things they will discover that many of the problems they encounter are less amenable to formal treatment than those in the technical domain and, indeed, that people and technical requirements often conflict with each other.

Many of the issues listed above are interlinked. Motivation, for example, can be affected by the way in which most of the other activities are carried out, and motivation is key to the effectiveness of the team. Creating an environment in which people are highly motivated can help to overcome many problems – a highly motivated team will find their own solutions to many deficiencies in a formal organization, whereas no amount of formal organization can get good productive work out of people who are demoralized.

The skills of managing software teams are not particularly different from those of managing other types of people. The issues raised are, however, distinctive enough to make them a fascinating subject in their own right. Getting the people issues right can save a considerable amount of project time and money. It follows that it is worth spending time and money to do so.

The rest of the chapter focuses on:

1. The principles of motivation and delegation.
2. The application of these principles to managing software teams.

32.2 Motivation and delegation

32.2.1 Role of a manager

Managers are appointed to achieve certain goals, in this case typically the completion of a software development project. They are not appointed simply to produce plans and progress reports, or so that they can collect well-reasoned excuses for not achieving their goals.

Because they are managers, they will have to carry out the majority of the tasks needed to complete the project through other people, rather than doing them directly themselves. Some of those people, for example, the main members of the project team, will in principle report to the manager in organizational terms. Others, such as service departments, sub-contractors, users, etc., will not. If managers fail to meet their goals, for example, by completing a project late, they will be seen by all concerned as responsible for the failure, whether or not this is justified. The best way out of this problem is to find ways of ensuring that people do what is needed.

If people are not doing what is needed, there are only two alternatives:

1. The manager can use it as an excuse for his or her failure.
2. The manager can find a way to change the situation.

In the end, it is up to the manager to do something about it.

Management is therefore about getting things done through people. It should be distinguished from the many other things that a manager often has to do; they may well be necessary, but they are not in themselves management. It is, for example, a completely separate activity from 'business', which is about buying and selling things.

Most of this chapter on managing software engineering teams is concerned with groups of people working together. Some of the basic principles, such as those of motivation and delegation are, however, valid even where only one or two people are involved. These are dealt with in the following sections.

32.2.2 Motivation

Managers need to get things done through other people, whether or not they have direct control over them. They therefore have to understand why people do things.

There is reasonable agreement that, within a work context, people are motivated to do things for reasons which fall broadly into three categories:

1. Economic, i.e. they are receiving some kind of compensation.
2. Individual, i.e. in order to satisfy individual physiological and psychological needs – these are classified in a number of ways by different authors.
3. Social, corresponding closely to what is sometimes called a 'psychological contract', which may or may not have been freely entered into.

Anyone who wishes to pursue this in more depth should follow up some of the books covered under 'Further reading'. For the purposes of this chapter, an unsupported leap is now made to assert that the main things affecting the motivation of a software team are:

1. The work they are given and the way in which it is given.
2. The way in which it is checked and monitored.
3. The people they work with.
4. The way in which their manager interacts with them generally.
5. Various aspects of the working environment (the office, the organization, the rules and regulations, etc.).
6. The immediate project organization.
7. The tools (hardware, software, etc.) they are given to do the job.
8. Remuneration and benefits.

A manager should aim to influence as many as possible of these factors in order to provide a framework in which people can be highly motivated, and certainly to address those which are directly controllable. Many of the factors listed will apply equally to motivating other people outside the project team, although the number which can be influenced in this situation is smaller. This does, of course, make it all the more important to get right those factors which are under a manager's control (e.g. how to ask someone to do something).

Most of these topics are dealt with in this chapter, beginning with the way in which work is delegated.

32.2.3 Delegation

In any team which has a manager or leader, the work done by the rest of the team has, strictly speaking, been delegated by the manager or leader. In some environments (e.g. where a strict quality system is operating) this may well be more explicit than in others (e.g. a university research project). Nevertheless, it is always true. This view of life may seem an excessively authoritarian one to some people, but nothing could be further from the truth; it is the style of delegation which is often authoritarian rather than the principle.

Delegation consists of:

1. Making someone responsible for doing something (whilst not in any way lessening one's own responsibility).
2. Giving that person authority to make decisions (e.g. to issue documents, or to spend money without seeking explicit approval) in connection with the delegated task.

The concepts of responsibility and authority will be discussed later, but it is worth noting here that a mismatch of responsibility and authority is a frequent cause of project problems.

Much delegation occurs because convention and expertise cause it to happen anyway. For example, it is rare for managers of large projects to produce code themselves. This can happen without anyone understanding the principles of delegation. In order to manage people well, however, a manager needs to understand the underlying principles.

The principle that managers are personally responsible for the success of their projects was mentioned earlier. Given that they cannot do the whole job themselves, they therefore have to delegate some of the work. There are, however, a number of other benefits of proper delegation:

1. It allows the manager more time to manage properly, as opposed to continual fire-fighting.
2. Members of the team are likely to be highly motivated if work has been properly delegated to them.
3. Members of the team will develop themselves professionally if they are given more complete, responsible, and demanding tasks.

In order to achieve these benefits, work will need to be delegated in a manner which provides the recipient with the right motivating factors. At this level, these tend to be factors which fall into the category of 'individual reasons' referred to in the section on motivation above. Delegated pieces of work should therefore, where possible, provide:

1. Responsibility and scope for decision making.
2. A challenge.
3. Intrinsic interest.
4. A sense of achievement.
5. Scope for creativity.
6. Regular feedback on performance.

All these characteristics are more likely in a task which consists of a complete identifiable piece of work. The concepts of coupling and cohesion used in structured design can provide some interesting analogies when applied to the decomposition of a piece of work. A delegated piece of work should ideally have high cohesion and low coupling to other work packages if it is to meet the above criteria.

Clearly, some jobs will need to be done which fall short of these criteria, but even where characteristics such as interest and scope for creativity are missing, motivation is likely to be higher when carrying out a self-contained job with a clear goal than it is for a job which all appears rather *ad hoc*.

This subject is also addressed from a slightly different viewpoint in Sections 32.2.6, on planning and motivation and 32.3.4 on management styles.

32.2.4 Making things happen

So far, only the initial stages of delegation have been discussed. One of the other motivating factors identified above was the way in which managers interact with their staff. What they say and do, and the way they say and do it, will have a major influence over the motivation of their staff and of other people who are needed to do things for the project.

Again, some people may take the view that this is attributing an excessive degree of omnipotence to managers. However, the most anti-authoritarian software engineer would agree that a bad manager can cause endless problems, whereas the most authoritarian would probably expect that nothing will happen without a good manager. They both therefore agree on the basic premise.

As already discussed, managers are responsible for the success of their projects; they are therefore also responsible for:

1. Ensuring that each team member plays the appropriate part.
2. Getting other people outside the project to collaborate and take notice when important points need to be made.

Blaming people for not doing what was wanted may be satisfying, but it will not solve the problem.

A full discussion of this subject is beyond the scope of this chapter, but the following points should be borne in mind:

1. Software engineers are typically conditioned by their training to expect that all problems can be solved by rational discussion alone (even though they do not always act in a way consistent with this!). This is clearly not true. In the first place, many people do many things for reasons which have more to do with their emotions and which seem to other people irrational. To influence them, you have to take account of the possible emotional reasons. Secondly, in a given case, not everyone necessarily has the same view of the premises on which rational discussion might be based.
2. For these reasons, if for no others, compromises will be needed to secure cooperation and make progress, even if one believes one's case to be 100% sound. Bearing in mind that motivation is a key to effectiveness, it can often be more effective to agree on what appears to be a sub-optimal solution if by doing so one can maintain motivation. There are clearly limits to this process – some compromises on design decisions might destroy the chances of a system ever working, for example. The key is to compromise on the unimportant issues so that one has the psychological 'credit' to be able to stand firm on the important ones.
3. One of the strongest demotivators is when someone is forced to 'lose face'. In situations where one does need to stand firm, therefore one should avoid putting the 'loser' in a situation where they feel they have suffered a crushing defeat. Making a point privately rather than publicly can make an important contribution to this. Apart from anything else, people are more likely to concede a point in private than they are, for example, in a meeting of ten people. (See also Section 32.3.6 on meetings).

32.2.5 Responsibility and authority

To manage well, managers need to have a good understanding both of the motivational factors discussed above and of the more formal concepts of authority and responsibility. Many of the conflicts in organizations occur because of confusion over who is responsible for what and who has what authority. A good understanding of these concepts on the part of everyone concerned is therefore likely to lead to fewer conflicts.

To be *responsible* for something means to be held accountable for it. It should be noted that when managers delegate responsibility, they in no way diminish their own responsibility – they just make it easier to discharge it. To take this point to its logical conclusion, chief executives are responsible for everything which happens in their organizations. Looked at the other way round, it is incorrect for someone to say to their manager: 'You have given me responsibility for this – stop interfering'. Not interfering may be good management practice, but the manager still has overall responsibility for the task, and therefore an entitlement to some visibility.

To have *authority* means to have the right to do something, for example, to spend amounts of company money without asking first. Formally speaking, no-one has any authority unless it has been delegated. In practice, there tends to be an understanding in organizations about what is reasonable for staff to do without explicit authority (e.g. it is conventional to ask permission to take leave, but not for professionals to have to do so before going to lunch). Nevertheless, the question of defined authority for significant technical or management decisions is an important one. For example, a quality plan will normally indicate who is authorized to approve deliverable items; company procedures will normally indicate who is authorized to sign purchase orders. It should also be noted that the fact that someone has taken a decision which they had authority to take does not mean that it cannot be overruled by their manager after the event. It does mean that they cannot be criticized for exceeding their authority.

Authority and responsibility need to be given in appropriate combinations. Authority without responsibility potentially leads to abuse of authority. This can occur in a number of contexts, for example:

1. Over-pedantic quality controls may lead to delays because the quality controller has no responsibility for progress.
2. Over-zealous sales people may sell systems which the customer will find to be inappropriate.

Responsibility without authority makes a job very difficult. A manager who is responsible for a multi-million pound project who nevertheless cannot spend any money without higher approval is operating with his or her hands tied.

Conversely, managers should only have authority over staff for whom they are responsible. It is undesirable for staff to receive orders (however phrased) from several different managers. Conflicting requests may well come from several managers, but staff must have one manager to whom they can refer in order to establish priorities.

While it is important to have an understanding of these concepts, they must be kept in proportion. Whilst people who continually exceed their authority are likely to cause problems, people who always assume they have no authority will rarely achieve much. As always, what is needed is an intelligent understanding and interpretation of the principles.

32.2.6 Planning and motivation

The process of planning and setting targets has both a direct and an indirect effect on the success of the project. The direct effects are obvious – a plan which is self-consistent and achievable but challenging is more likely to lead to success than a plan which falls short on one or more of those characteristics.

The indirect effects have as much to do with the process by which the plan is produced as with the characteristics of the plan itself. A number of studies have been carried out on the effect of estimates and plans on actual performance with the following results:

1. Targets which are realistic are likely to result in better actual performance than targets which are either too tight or too generous.
2. People are more likely to keep to targets which they have played a part in producing than ones which have been presented to them as a *fait accompli*.
3. A given software development task can be carried out in a variety of ways. If one asks people to do it quickly, they will tend to do it quickly; if one asks them to do it with a minimum number of source statements they will do so, and so on.

Giving people excessively tight targets will soon start to have adverse effects. People will be demotivated by continual failure to meet targets and, in turn, they will gradually come to take the plan less seriously. Although to a certain extent people will take as long to do a task as they are given, evidence suggest that, for software development tasks, this only holds within fairly narrow bounds. If the task is seriously underestimated, it will overrun; if it is seriously overestimated then, provided that the task is precisely specified, it will probably be finished early.

It should be added that many projects are specified in such a way that, if more time is available, there is ample scope for improving the original system to fill that time. Alternatively, the time may get used in, for example, producing a few extra utilities to make the next task easier. Both of these ways of filling the time may be perfectly good and in no way imply a criticism of the people concerned, provided that they are as the result of a conscious decision. They do, however, help to explain why it is more usual for projects to overrun rather than underrun.

Plans should therefore be realistic. However, even after acknowledging this, there are two conflicting objectives. The plan which one quotes to a client or user should be one which can be achieved with a high probability. If the timescale and effort quoted are simply the sum of the individual components of the project, however, there is a danger the resulting plan is one which is less likely to be achieved. It was suggested above that it is likely that a few components will overrun, but fewer will underrun. The answer is to retain some contingency (both of effort and of timescale) at project level to allow one or two minor overruns to occur at a lower level without delaying the end date.

32.2.7 Motivation and control

Project and quality control procedures can carry the risk of going against some of the principles of motivation and delegation described above, in that they may appear to give less authority, scope for creativity, and so on to staff than we have been advocating. Demotivated staff, as discussed, are less likely to produce high quality work productively. Project and quality control procedures are nevertheless essential to professional software project management.

The answer is to ensure that a good balance between motivation and control is achieved in defining the procedures:

1. Although regular checking of quality and progress is necessary, it should be at intervals which are consistent with the task in hand and with the person doing it. Breaking work down into five-day packages or even less may be appropriate for an inexperienced programmer (and may indeed give a suitable level of feedback which is also an important motivational factor). For a competent, experienced designer working on a complex creative task, however, it could be both meaningless and almost insulting. Constant checking is a demotivator; regular feedback is a positive motivator. The right balance needs to be achieved.
2. Wherever possible it is desirable for staff to have some scope for creativity and authority to make decisions. Continual

'looking over the shoulder' is likely to be demoralizing, and this in itself is likely to lead to lower quality work. People are less likely to take a pride in their work if they know that, without fail, it will be criticized and modified over their heads. There will, of course, be occasions where, despite the application of all the right principles, the quality of work being produced is not good enough. In such cases, the people concerned should either be given training in order to improve their work or, if this is not successful, they should be found tasks more appropriate to their abilities.

32.3 Managing project teams

32.3.1 Team structure

The preceding section on delegation and motivation dealt with a set of principles which are valid even if only one person is being managed. In managing a team, which is the real subject of this chapter, these principles need to be taken into account, not only in day-to-day dealings with individuals but also in setting up the team.

The organization structure to be used on a project has to take into account:

1. The structure of the work to be carried out.
2. The individuals involved.
3. The relationships between the individuals.

This process of defining the structure inevitably involves iteration on occasions.

A good place to start in devising a project organization is the work breakdown structure. A simple work breakdown structure is shown in *Figure 32.1*.

For a small project, where most of the tasks are carried out by a 3-person software team, the team structure might be a simple one as shown in *Figure 32.2*.

This approach can, however, also be used on larger projects as shown in *Figure 32.3*. In this example, the following people report to the project manager:

1. A project controller (to allow the manager to spend time managing).
2. A three-person team covering analysis, design and implementation.
3. A programming team leader who in turn looks after three small teams.

It is important to maintain a flexible approach to team structures. In addition to fitting the work breakdown structure, they also need to match the people available. Even if there is a good choice of suitable qualified people available, they may well not match exactly what the original project structure specifies.

One subject which repays attention is the depth of the management structure. In a 15-person team, for example, it would at one extreme be possible to have everyone reporting directly to the project manager, which would almost certainly be uncontrollable. At the other extreme, a three-level management structure, where no-one had more than two direct subordinates, would almost certainly lead to inefficient communication and feelings of remoteness.

As a rule of thumb, at any given level of a management structure, managers/team leaders should have between three

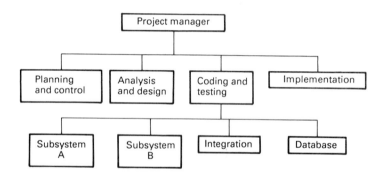

Figure 32.1 Work breakdown structure used as example for project organizations

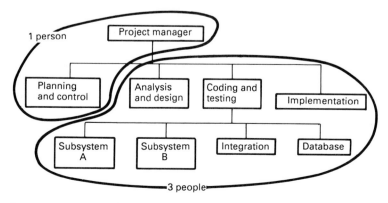

Figure 32.2 Project organization for a small project

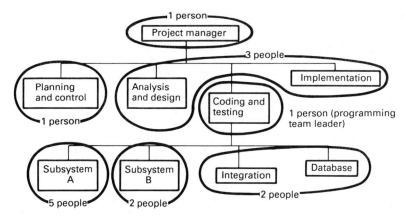

Figure 32.3 Project organization for a larger project

and seven people reporting to them. More than this is difficult to control; fewer than this tends to discourage the manager etc. from delegating properly. There are clearly exceptions to this rule of thumb, for example:

1. Managers who also have significant non-management tasks of their own (e.g. participation in company-wide policy working groups) may have fewer people reporting to them.
2. Some people clearly need more managing than others; some types of task need more managing than others.

The type of project structure which has the whole of the project team reporting to a software team leader, who then reports to a project manager (see *Figure 32.4*), is therefore not a good one if the project manager is not directly supervising anyone else. On the other hand, if the project manager is also supervising, for example a number of sub-contractors, this may be a perfectly good organization.

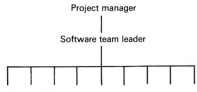

Figure 32.4 Usually unsatisfactory project organization

Recent thinking on organizational structures is tending to favour flatter structures than those described above. It is not clear that software is yet ready for this. There are probably two reasons:

1. The promoters of flatter structures make it clear that the controls thereby removed need replacing in some way, for example, by the integrated manufacturing system in a manufacturing environment. It is not clear that software engineering has reached a state where satisfactory controls exist – replacing line managers by an army of quality checkers is not the answer.
2. The interrelationships between tasks carried out by software developers are complex and can at present only be managed by relatively deep organizational structures. Developments in the technology of software engineering may change this.

To achieve a desirable type of project structure and at the same time to match the project to the staff available, many different roles can be defined, e.g.:

1. Team leaders/managers
2. User liaison manager
3. System architect/design manager
4. Quality manager
5. Integration manager
6. Implementation manager
7. Validation and verification manager
8. Programmer manager/project controller
9. Administration manager
10. Staff manager

On a small project, these jobs would not normally have the title 'manager' associated with them, but on a large project they may well do. Jobs may be combined as shown in Figures 32.2 and 32.3. For example, it might be possible to combine staff manager and integration manager, on the grounds that the main staff management workload was associated with building up the team at the start of the project.

It will also often be the case that the team structure needs to change as the project proceeds from phase to phase, and the emphasis of technical activity shifts (see Chapter 15).

The organization structures discussed so far are all apparently simple hierarchies, although there are certainly some responsibilities which potentially overlap. For example, if a quality manager is appointed on a project, then that responsibility is not a strictly hierarchical one, since everyone on the project is responsible for quality. Many people are tempted to adopt organization structures which depart more fundamentally from a strict hierarchy, in order to ensure that as many aspects as possible are covered, often resulting in some kind of a matrix structure. These do have some potential benefits, but they are rarely fully realised. The key points to bear in mind in designing an organization are:

1. It is important to be clear who has unique line responsibility for the success of the project as a whole and for the success of each part of it. If the parts covered in this way do not add up to the whole project, then the project manager has to look after those parts which are not covered. With a matrix structure, there is a tendency for all of the project to fall into this category.
2. Additional functional responsibilities (e.g. quality, staff, etc.) can often be valuable in reducing the need for line managers (i.e. those with direct responsibility) to be good at everything. However, it should be clear that everyone has one and only one organizational superior. The functional responsibilities are carried out on behalf of the project manager rather than as a right in themselves. Achieving the right combination of

responsibility and authority in functional responsibilities is often difficult.

3. When extra functional responsibilities start accumulating, ways should be sought of simplifying the organization. It is better to start subdividing the main task slightly more in order to make each job slightly less daunting. Jobs in the main management line are usually more 'complete' and therefore more satisfying and motivating than jobs which do not have full responsibility for achieving some goal.

4. Quality controls and reviews are an essential part of the quality management process. In excess they can, however, be demotivating, which will itself impair quality. Occam's razor (the elimination of all unnecessary entities) should be regularly applied to management procedures.

5. Staff are demotivated by the lack of a clearly defined organizational superior who spends sufficient (but not too much) time defining their role and giving them feedback on their performance. The appearance of too many management layers is demotivating. The effects of too few layers can be equally so.

One particular type of hierarchical structure which was fashionable a few years ago was the 'chief programmer team', where the team leader had a more active technical role than is often the case, and had a number of staff with well-defined support roles. The analogy used was that of a surgeon. Although this approach has clearly worked well in some cases, the problem of adhering rigidly to the principle was that it depended very critically on the quality of the 'chief programmer'. It is now best regarded as a useful possible model where the right individual exists. However, what the approach does do is focus on the key role in complex projects of highly competent technical people.

It is essential in a project of any complexity that there exists someone of suitable ability who is the guardian of the technical strategy being adopted, and that that person is able to exercise that guardianship. The role can either be a management role in the software design and development process (as with chief programmers) or a staff position reporting, for example, the project manager. All the principles of authority, responsibility, and organization structure described above still apply, but project managers who attempt to exercise their authority without such a person (who may of course actually be the project manager) will surely not succeed. The management principles expounded in this chapter are intended to support, not to conflict with, the technical principles covered in the rest of the book.

Once the structure has been defined, it should be documented and published. Not only is this important for the smooth running of the project (so that people know who is responsible for what and the scope for misunderstandings is minimized), it is also likely to be essential in any project which is operating under a formal quality system, which is likely to require that organization be documented in the quality plan.

32.3.2 Building a team

Some aspects of building a software engineering team have been covered already in discussing team structures and their dependence on individuals. It is also, however, important that a team should work well as a team, as well as a collection of individuals with defined roles.

The team should ideally have a mix of personalities, which can complement each other. A team where everyone is chosen for their similarity to the project manager probably leaves something to be desired. Equally, studies have shown that attempts to put together teams consisting entirely of 'stars' have often been less successful than teams containing a more balanced mixture; typically an excessive amount of energy gets expended with each of the 'stars' trying to push the project in a particular direction. The following features have emerged as characteristic of unsuccessful teams:

1. Absence of at least one effective team member of clear intellectual ability (a large project would obviously need more than one).
2. Not all team members given well-defined roles appropriate to their capabilities and not in conflict with other roles.
3. Presence of disruptive team members.

If any of these features is present or potentially present, it is likely that firm action will be needed to prevent serious problems arising. Interestingly, good team morale in itself is not sufficient for success – it is not unusual for an unsuccessful project to 'go down smiling'.

Project managers may or may not have responsibility for choosing the members of the team. If they do have that responsibility, they should give the job plenty of attention, at least for the key team members. A project manager is likely to be very busy when a project is starting up, and there is a temptation to pay insufficient attention to staffing. The danger is that if this attention is not paid, they will continue to be very busy for the rest of the project.

The quality and appropriateness of the people on a project can make a massive difference in the ability of the team to produce a high-quality system, on time and budget. There is well-documented evidence that a highly competent, highly experienced team will achieve productivity an order of magnitude higher than a team at the opposite end of the spectrum. In practice, some teams will fail ever to complete tasks which are beyond their ability. Despite a wide recognition of these facts, there is often a reluctance to take the necessary steps to get someone who will carry out a more effective job. These points are particularly true of the key staff in the team. If they are not up to the job, the effects are likely to be felt throughout the project.

In selecting staff, a manager should interview the staff properly, as if they were applying for a permanent job. Apart from helping with the selection process, it is a valuable opportunity to get the working relationship off to a good start. It is also important to try to obtain evidence of real successful work in the past, rather than purely relying on an interview.

Once the team has been selected and structured, the next step is to get the team to work well as a team. Much of this is achieved by paying attention to the topics covered in the rest of this chapter. There is one further key element in getting a team to work well, however, and that is success. It is particularly important to remember this because there is positive feedback at work. If a team meets its deadlines and budgets, makes the system's users happy, and is seen by everyone to be doing so, there is a fair chance that they will continue to do so. Conversely, if things start going wrong, a self-perpetuating spiral can all too easily set in. Thus there is a strong relationship between the realism of the project plan and motivation; this is discussed in Section 32.2.6 (motivation and planning).

32.3.3 The manager's relationships with the team

A good team will acquire a life and momentum of its own. In the best examples of this, the need for 'supervision' as such can almost disappear. A key part of the manager's job is to allow and encourage that to happen, to help it to stay that way, and to avoid actions which destroy that life and momentum.

The relationship between the manager and the team members will therefore play a key role in the success or otherwise of the project. Both the manager and the team members will work better together if they understand how the relationship looks from the other side. Clearly, managers ought to have the advantage here since they will usually have worked in the past as members of project teams. In any case, as discussed earlier, it is the manager's responsibility to bring about that mutual understanding if it does not already exist.

A manager is responsible for the project and therefore has certain rights (e.g. to control what happens, to be kept informed of what is happening, and to expect everyone to do their best). Equally, managers cannot expect these things to happen just because they have that right. As has been seen already, they need to provide the right framework, both from an organizational and from a motivational point of view.

Looked at from the team member's point of view, staff will expect to:

1. Know what is expected of them.
2. Have the opportunity to discuss this.
3. Be given sufficient resources to carry out the task (or at least the scope to acquire those resources).
4. Have an interest shown in what they are doing.
5. Be able to get on with the task without excessive interference, either in the way it is carried out or with the resources (for example staff) which they are using.
6. Be kept informed about what is going on in the project as a whole.
7. Be treated as individuals.

Good managers will aim to maintain all of these features in their relationships with the teams working for them. In particular, they will take care to:

1. Define tasks and roles clearly (although not necessarily in tremendous detail).
2. Discuss these definitions with the people affected before finalizing them, and communicate the results to everyone concerned – team members will be more committed to tasks which they have had a chance to discuss first.
3. Develop clear policies and procedures, at an appropriate level of detail (Occam's razor again).
4. Achieve good results by training and motivation rather than rigid control, whilst not neglecting to maintain a level of visible control appropriate to the type of system being developed.
5. Carry out regular reviews and appraisals of team members' performance.

The question is often asked as to how much time individuals should expect their manager to devote to them. This is a difficult quantity to measure, but some guidance can be arrived at by simple arithmetic. Managers can probably be expected to spend about 25% of their total time in dealing with matters which are directly related to the activities of the staff who report directly to them. The rest of their time will be spent in dealing with organizational superiors and people outside the project, and in doing tasks which are not directly related to these people. If there are five people reporting directly, this implies a total weekly allocation of about two hours per person. Clearly, not all of this will be in direct one-to-one contact – some of the time will be spent in work preparing for or resulting from such meetings (e.g. reading documents to be authorized), and some of the rest will be spent in meetings with a larger number of people.

In larger projects, care is also needed in dealing with relationships between managers and people who do not report directly to them. For example, in a project with several sub-teams, each with a team leader:

1. All the team members will expect and appreciate some contact with the project manager, and an indication that their contribution to the project is visible and appreciated.
2. At the same time, if the manager regularly asks sub-team members to do things directly or formally asks them to report on progress, the delegated authority and responsibility of the team leaders is being eroded.

The project manager should therefore aim to keep a good level of informal contact with all team members, but channel formal tasking and reporting through the team leaders. This should not be too rigid but, when the principle is violated, it is good organizational etiquette for it to be clearly acknowledged that it is an exception to the normal channels. Some readers who are more familiar with less structured organizations may be rather surprised at such formality. If they were to work in a large project, they would almost certainly find that this approach leads to better informal relationships. Much conflict arises from confusion over responsibilities and authority – having a well-understood framework allows everyone to work together more amicably.

32.3.4 Management styles

This chapter has covered a number of topics, some of which concentrate on the formal aspects of organizations, and some of which concentrate on why people do or do not do things irrespective of these formal aspects. A useful approach to looking at ways of bringing these together is the idea of management styles.

One approach distinguishes four styles, characterized as follows:

1. Directing, where the manager provides specific instructions and closely supervises their execution.
2. Coaching, where, in addition to providing specific instructions and closely supervising their execution, the manager also explains decisions, solicits suggestions, and is generally supportive.
3. Supporting, where the manager facilitates and supports a subordinate's efforts and shares responsibility for decision making.
4. Delegating, where the manager turns over responsibility for decision making and problem solving to the subordinate.

A good manager will be able to use each of these styles as appropriate rather than, as some do, always using the same style irrespective of the situation. One way of looking at these styles is on scales of supportive and directive management, as shown in *Figure 32.5*.

	Directive management	
	(low)	(high)
(high)	Supporting style	Coaching style
Supportive management		
(low)	Delegating style	Directing style

Figure 32.5

Not only do different styles need to be used with different people, they also need to be used with the same people at different times. One way of looking at the style needed in a given situation is in terms of the competence and commitment of the individual concerned, for example:

1. A directing approach will be appropriate for people with high commitment but low competence (e.g. with a team of enthusiastic trainees).
2. A coaching approach will be appropriate for people with low commitment but some competence (e.g. with someone who has some experience but has become demotivated for some reason).
3. A supporting approach will be appropriate for people with variable commitment but high competence (e.g. with an expert team pulled together at short notice by taking people away from their normal tasks).

4. A delegating approach will be appropriate for people with high commitment and high competence (e.g. in a well established, highly motivated, well-qualified team).

32.3.5 Relationships within the team

The relationships within the team contribute both to the motivation of the team and to the technical communication which needs to take place if the project is to be a success. Often these relationships will develop spontaneously but, particularly on large projects, there are a number of things which a manager can do to encourage the development and maintenance of good relationships between team members:

1. Events can be organized where team members, particularly those who do not work directly together, will be more likely to get to know each other in the normal work of the project. These events can include both work-related meetings where, for example, progress is presented and discussed, and more purely social activities.
2. Relationships should be taken into account in structuring the project. If there are two otherwise valuable people who find it difficult to work together (either vertically or horizontally in the structure), then finding ways of keeping them apart may save a lot of trouble.
3. The 'informal organization' should not be ignored. In most teams and organizations, there is an informal network of relationships which oils many wheels of day-to-day activity. When this happens, it can be very effective and very cost effective. While there are clearly some activities which must be formalized (e.g. for quality control purposes) it should not be assumed that adding bureaucracy to everything in sight is the right thing to do. In the end, an organization exists to help people, not the reverse.
4. The physical location of the team can, and should, be used to reinforce the effects described above. In particular, geographically dispersed teams make it considerably more difficult to generate momentum. Getting everyone to work in the same geographical location will bring many benefits, although this is not always possible. When it is not possible, other methods of achieving the same ends become doubly important, e.g. electronic mail, project meetings, regular periods when people are able to work together, and so on.

In a large project, different teams will often develop different cultures and feelings of identity. Provided it stops short of destructive conflict, this should be seen as healthy, rather than as a bad thing. People identify more easily with small teams. The identity that they feel with their team will probably outweigh any disturbing feelings the manager may have about lack of unity. Far from encouraging conflict, differentiated teams often allow different types of people to work together on the same project more harmoniously and productively than if they were forced to work next to each other, and the competition between the teams, if properly channelled, can be highly productive.

32.3.6 Meetings

Meetings can serve a number of purposes in the life of a medium or large project, including:

1. Reviewing progress and deliverable items.
2. Dissemination of information.
3. Consultation.
4. Arriving at decisions or approaches where a number of different viewpoints need to be considered.
5. Contributing to 'team spirit'.

Several of these purposes may be satisfied in parallel, of course.

There are no hard and fast rules on the quantity, type, and length of meetings which are desirable. As a general principle, if people feel that there are too many meetings or too few, then it is almost axiomatic that they are right, although in the former case it may also be a reflection of the way in which they are run. A project manager should be sensitive to such reactions and act accordingly.

Meetings should be as focused as possible:

1. Meetings will often be called to address specific issues. In such cases it should be clear what the desired outcome is, e.g. agreement on a specific course of action.
2. Regular review meetings should have a clear purpose and agenda so that they do not degenerate into a useless routine. If this appears to be happening, it is probably better to concentrate on making them short rather than abandoning them, so as to at least retain the possibility of important issues being raised.
3. Where possible, it is often worth saving significant issues for discussion at the next regular review meeting rather than holding a special meeting. This helps both to maintain the sense of purpose of the regular meetings and to keep the total number of meetings within manageable bounds.

Attendance at meetings should be tailored to suit the purpose. Meetings of the whole team, meetings of all team leaders, one-to-one meetings, and meetings of specific individuals all have their place. On a large project, it is usually found that regular meetings are useful. These may include both meetings of all team leaders and one-to-one review meetings between each team leader and the project manager.

Where the objective is to do real work, small meetings are generally likely to be more productive than larger ones, but larger ones also have their place in helping people to get a broader view of the context in which they are working. 'Extras' may well be invited to what is essentially a small working meeting if it will help them to understand the context for their future work. If any of the 'extras' are possibly likely to inhibit the main business, it may be worth explaining beforehand (tactfully) that their role is expected to be that of an observer. If a critical meeting is being called to arrive at a decision on a controversial issue, one-to-one meetings with the key players beforehand may well help to smooth the course of the larger meeting.

Formal review meetings are particular to the software engineering world, and need to be handled with particular care, given that their defined role is to criticize a document produced by one of the attendees. For the review to be constructive, two particular principles must be rigidly enforced:

1. Comments should be made about the object being reviewed, rather than the producer.
2. The review should be carried out within a framework of accepted objective criteria as to the desirable properties of the object being reviewed.

There may also, of course, be issues which need to be addressed which do not fit the above principles (e.g. the fact that this particular programmer has never written a single comment in his or her life). If so, they should be dealt with by the usual management processes, rather than being allowed to disturb the review.

All meetings except those which are largely social in nature should be properly organized and run as follows:

1. The meeting room should be conducive to constructive discussion. Pleasant surroundings, comfortable chairs, reasonable insulation from external distractions, space to organize papers, and so on, are all important.
2. It should be clear who the chairman is, or, if it is a meeting

between two parties (e.g. people from two departments), it should be clear who is taking the lead on each 'side'.

3. The length of the meeting should be defined in advance, at least approximately, if for no other reason than to allow participants to judge the level of their contributions. If a meeting is showing a tendency to wander from the point, a discussion of the timescale for the remainder of the meeting can be helpful in focusing attention.

4. There should be an agenda, even if it is agreed informally at the start of the meeting. Short digressions should normally be allowed unless time is very pressing, but the overall impression should be that the agenda is being followed, that the purpose of the meeting is being addressed, and that the timescale is being followed.

5. When an agreement appears to have been reached, this should be confirmed by repeating it and giving participants the opportunity to dissent. Even if there are known dissenters, it is valuable to confirm the agreement of the others.

6. Minutes (or at least a list of agreed actions and decisions) should be taken and circulated to all participants.

The better these ground rules are understood by all participants, the less need there will be to be over-formal about it.

32.3.7 Staff turnover

On small and medium-sized projects (say up to two years duration) staff turnover should be minimized and ideally completely eliminated, except in the case of staff who are not making an appropriate combination to the team. Team members will have invested a considerable amount of time, and therefore project resource, in learning about the project. A replacement will have to repeat this investment, resulting in a significant direct cost to the project.

On larger projects, however, the answer is less simple. Some projects last for five years or more, and it is often felt that this is too long to spend on one project. Although this should by no means be taken as a fundamental law, turnover will almost certainly occur on projects of this size.

Attention paid to training and career management for project staff on a large project should reduce the level of demand for people to be transferred to a different project. This demand usually occurs because people feel that they are not learning any more and that their careers are not progressing. If attention is paid to training and career progression, then, as well as having the specific needs addressed, people are likely to feel they are being treated as an important, permanent part of the project, and are more likely to want to stay.

Some turnover probably becomes desirable on a long project, however, as relationships may start to stagnate despite the best management practice. A few new faces from time to time can prevent this from happening. If turnover is expected anyway, it should be planned. First, it should happen at times which minimize the damage to the project and, second, an induction process for new staff should be planned to minimize the amount of time they need to get up to speed.

In general, turnover is less likely in a well-structured, well-organized, successful project team where the manager is following the precepts of this chapter than in one which does not satisfy these criteria.

32.3.8 Managing conflicts

A large part of management is about the management of differences – differences of opinion, of priorities, of personality, and so on. Many of these differences, properly managed and exploited, bring benefits, but badly managed they can lead to conflict. One way of looking at the issue is to identify ways in which differences can manifest themselves:

1. Argument.
2. Competition.
3. Conflict.

Of these, competition tends to be seen as usually positive, conflict is seen as negative, argument may be either.

Argument may be either a constructive way of arriving at a better solution, or it may be a symptom of underlying conflict. For argument to be constructive, it needs to concentrate on resolving real differences, and to recognize when the argument is really the result of different underlying premises, or lack of information.

In the world at large *competition* has three principal positive effects:

1. Identifying an appropriately high standard for quality, productivity, etc.
2. Stimulating and channelling energy.
3. Distinguishing the good from the less good.

It is the third of these which is most likely to degenerate into conflict. For competition to be wholly productive, it must be open and have visibly fair rules and procedures. For competition in an organization to be productive, it must be carefully managed.

Conflict can arise from argument or competition which has degenerated, but many of the causes start from two underlying issues: differing objectives/ideologies and competition for territory. Conflict arising from differing objectives or ideologies can arise when:

1. Formal objectives conflict or overlap.
2. Mutual obligations are unclear.
3. A group has several competing roles at once (e.g. service and coordination).
4. True objectives are concealed.
5. Authority and responsibility are not well matched.

The territory analogy arises from studies of animals, but the concepts of territorial violation, overcrowding (too many people chasing too few jobs), and territorial jealousy have clear parallels in organizations.

Conflicts should where possible be turned into either fruitful argument or fruitful competition; failing that, they must be controlled. To achieve fruitful competition, as seen above, it must be open, there must be visibly fair rules and procedures, and there must be agreement on common goals and objectives.

Conflicts can be controlled by:

1. Arbitration.
2. Achieving agreement on a set of working rules.
3. Confrontation (i.e. getting the conflicting parties together to sort out their differences). This is preferable to arbitration if it is possible, because the parties will have participated in finding a solution.
4. Separation – reorganizing so as to reduce the amount of contact between the conflicting parties.

Where possible, an approach which provides a long-term solution is always preferable.

32.3.9 Managing the outside world

As discussed at the start of this chapter, many of the people on whom a project manager relies are not part of the team as such. They include people such as service departments, sub-contractors, users, and so on. They need to be managed in the sense that the manager needs to ensure that they perform, just as much as does the project team proper. It can often be helpful for project managers (and, indeed, everyone in the team) to consider their own line management as falling into the same category!

The image which the team has in the eyes of other people is important. These people will have relatively little knowledge of the team. They will draw conclusions from that small amount of information, and this will influence their willingness to do what is necessary. Even sub-contractors with whom the project has a contractual relationship will perform better if they are properly 'managed'. There is usually a wide range of performance permissible within any given contract without the risk of, for example, legal action becoming likely.

Good relationships need to be maintained with all the external people who contribute to the project, just as they do with the project team. This may involve doing the odd favour. At some point, the project manager may need to call for a contribution beyond the call of duty – if there is a running battle on some other subject, the request is unlikely to be successful, whereas if there has been give and take over the months, the request is likely to be well received.

It is important to get the relationships off to a good clear start. Clear understandings, contractual or otherwise, with the people who need to contribute to the project, should be established at the start. If all parties are very clear where they stand at the start of the project, relationships are less likely to deteriorate.

It is not necessary for all of these relationships to be handled personally by the project manager. In this sense, relationships can be delegated in the same way as other activities. The most appropriate person may be someone who is particularly likely to have a good relationship (e.g. because they already know the people concerned) or the person on the team most affected by the performance of the outside agency.

Of all the external people affected by the project, the users/customers/clients are the most important. Management of this relationship is fundamental to the success of the project. In particular:

1. Clear, well-organized documentary records (in terms of specifications, change control, and so on) provide a firm basis for a good relationship.
2. The value of careful maintenance of the relationship cannot be overemphasized. It is a rare project where the users and project team do not need to ask each other favours from time to time.

This is clearly a subject which goes well beyond the scope of this chapter; suffice it to reiterate that the user/customer/client is the most important part of the 'outside world'.

32.3.10 Managing oneself

Not all readers of this book will be managing software teams, but they will have one thing in common with those who are doing so, namely, the need to manage themselves. Anyone who wishes to succeed in whatever role, whether it is a defined management role or not, needs some management skills in order to do so. Senior technical experts need considerable skill in managing their own time, and in making use of support staff, if they are to be successful (and conversely software managers can rarely succeed in the absence of technical knowledge).

As with a number of the other subjects addressed in this chapter, a full treatment is not possible. The following points provide a good start:

1. Be clear what the key tasks and goals of your job are. It is very easy to spend all your time doing things because they are there rather than because they contribute to your success in your job. Plan your time to ensure that you spend a sufficient proportion of your time on those tasks which do contribute to the success of the job. Failure to do this is certain to limit your success in any job.

2. If you are doing a job which is subject to many interruptions, either by phone or in person, find ways of scheduling periods when you will not be interrupted, to allow you to do the tasks which need more concentration. In order to carry out such tasks well, you need to be in what is known as a state of flow, in which you are fully involved and concentrating on the task in hand. It takes time (maybe 15 minutes) to settle down into this state. If you are constantly being interrupted, you will never reach it, or will only reach it for short periods of time.

3. Pay attention to personal systems for keeping track of documents, meetings, information of various kinds, and so on. There are many different approaches to these problems; the best advice is to look into the alternatives and set up systems which fit your way of working. The investment will be worthwhile, provided one doesn't let the systems themselves take over, and lose track again of what one's real job is.

Being well organized oneself not only brings its own benefits, but also provides an example to the team.

32.4 Providing the environment

At the beginning of this chapter, it was stated that providing a good environment is one of the key things a project manager has to do to contribute to the effectiveness of the software team. The term environment applies to more than just the office accommodation, although this is an important part of it. The term also covers issues such as:

1. The organizational framework within which the project is taking place, including the rules and regulations, procedures, provision of services, ease of getting things done, and so on.
2. The hardware and software environments provided.

32.4.1 Office environment

The office environment will have a significant effect on the effectiveness of the team both directly and indirectly. Attention needs to be paid to:

1. Amount of space
2. Furniture and decoration
3. Noise control
4. Temperature and ventilation
5. Cupboards and filing space
6. Tidiness

Factors such as temperature and noise will certainly have a direct effect, but the indirect effects of getting the above factors wrong will also be very significant. A study carried out by IBM concluded that minimum accommodation requirements were:

1. 100 sq ft of dedicated floor space per person.
2. 30 sq ft of work surface per person.

If standards lower than this have to be tolerated (e.g. in areas where floor space is very expensive), then it is all the more important to pay attention to the other factors.

Some organizations have reported productivity gains as a result of putting system developers in private offices. However, this could also inhibit communication and team spirit. What is important is that people should be able to work for a large part of the time in a pleasant well-furnished environment without excessive distraction. Some of the activities involved in developing systems are carried out far more effectively in an extended period without interruptions. A large proportion of the office environments around fail to provide that possibility for most of their occupants.

32.4.2 Procedures and regulations

Procedures and regulations need to be handled with care. Quite apart from software engineering methods, every organization needs procedures and regulations in order to function properly. Typically they address two issues:

1. What is the easiest/best way to . . . ?
2. Am I allowed to . . . ?

These two motives often get thoroughly confused. Provided they are themselves easy to use, the more there are in the first category the better, whereas those in the second category should be kept to the minimum necessary to ensure adequate control (bearing in mind the issues discussed under 'Motivation and control' above).

32.4.3 Hardware and software environments

The hardware and software environments are dealt with elsewhere in this book. However, a few points are probably worth making from a staff management point of view:

1. The purpose of hardware and software tools is to make it easier for the team to do a good job. This should be remembered both when providing the environment and when presenting it to the users. If the team does not see it in that way, it is unlikely to be well used.
2. In putting together sophisticated combinations of software engineering tools, the provision of good office systems such as word processing, electronic mail, databases, spreadsheets, graphics, and so on, should not be forgotten. They may exist anyway, but if they do not, they need to be provided.
3. The difference in productivity between a well-equipped team and a poorly-equipped team can easily be a factor of 2 or 3. This fact can justify the expenditure of significant amounts of money, but project managers and their teams should not expect these sums of money to be approved without any rational quantitative justification. Although convincing proof of productivity gains is often very difficult to come by, anyone wishing to spend large amounts of money has a duty to put forward a rational quantitative case rather than an emotional one. To do otherwise does software engineering a disservice. The more powerful software tools become, the more capital-intensive the software industry is likely to become, and the more these issues will need to be addressed.

32.5 Software engineering and people

Already discussed is the fact that motivation is affected by factors such as scope for creativity, responsibility and authority, challenge, and job interest. Given that motivation is an important element in the production of high quality systems, what are the implications of all this for software engineering?

Software engineering is concerned, *inter alia*, with:

1. The models and notations used for describing systems and projects.
2. Methods for developing systems (i.e. for moving though a sequence of models, ending up with a working implementable system).
3. Tools and environments to support those models, notations, and methods.
4. Management controls on these processes.

Clearly, if one gets these things wrong and, at the same time, constrains people in such a way that they have no alternative, the possibilities for serious adverse effects on motivation and software development are considerable. It is not at all implausible that, on occasions, experienced system developers have more sophisticated models (even if informally expressed) of the way in which they do their job than those which we might try to impose on them. One therefore needs to tread with care.

32.5.1 Models and notations

With models and notations for describing systems, one is on relatively familiar ground. At a low level, such models and notations have existed for decades in the form of programming languages and the virtual machines defined by operating systems, database management systems and so on. There are lessons which can be learned from this experience:

1. Models and notations are more likely to be seen as helpful if they are supported by good tools – COBOL would have been less successful if there had been no compilers and everyone had been required to translate their COBOL to assembler language by hand.
2. Using the wrong model or notation may be worse than using none (or rather using some lowest common denominator, such as assembler language for programming or natural language for specification). The purpose of models and notations is to provide a precise 'high-level' language for describing systems. If the 'high-level' concepts and precision do not address the problem in hand then a more general approach, even if in some sense lower level and less precise, may well be more illuminating rather than less so.

One therefore needs to be fairly confident of the appropriateness of one's approach before making its use universal and mandatory, otherwise the result is likely to be both ineffective and demotivating. Where a particular notation has been chosen, therefore, an 'open' approach is called for on all but the most predictable system developments, allowing other notations (including natural language) to be used in conjunction with the main one where it is more illuminating.

32.5.2 Methods

When one adopts a defined method or model of system development one is aiming to indicate not the way in which the *system* is described (although this may well be defined by a 'method' as well), but the way in which the developers do their work. One is therefore aiming at the heart of a number of issues which have a fundamental effect on work motivation.

The 'method' aspect of software engineering has probably been less successful to date than the 'notation' aspect. People are probably less likely to adhere to a rigidly defined sequence of tasks than they are to a rigidly defined notation. Furthermore, it is probably less easy to establish whether they have done so. The reason for this may be found in the preceding sections which address motivation, delegation, planning, control, and so on. Whereas, with certain caveats, notations gain from precision and formality, the case for rigidity in methods is less clear cut.

At a high level, there is clearly much to be gained and less to be lost by identifying a model which indicates the sequence in which activities are to be carried out, and imposing that model as far as possible on the projects which we carry out. For several years, it was generally assumed that this model should follow some kind of simple waterfall pattern. The situation is now recognized to be less straightforward. (See Chapter 15 for a full discussion of this point.) The fact remains that some kind of high-level model of the sequence of events to be carried out is essential to the professional execution of system development projects.

At lower levels, however, there is much to be said for considering such prescriptions as advisory rather than mandatory. What does need to be defined is the input to the process, the output from the process, and the relationship between them.

What is then needed is a suggested (almost tutorial) approach to achieving those ends. The requirement to plan and monitor can also remain mandatory but the exact form of the plan can be tailored to the situation. This approach takes more account of the fact that design is a creative process, requiring a significant amount of backtracking and forward looking to achieve the desired end, and allows more scope for decision making and creativity, which are both important motivating factors.

Returning to the discussion of the higher level model, the exact form of development life cycle used for each project may still need to reflect the people involved. A prototyping or incremental approach is usually indicated where the problem is not initially well understood, but this in itself depends on the people involved in the development.

A team which is well experienced in the application and the development tools to be used can probably adopt a fairly conventional sequential approach. A less experienced team might benefit from beginning with a more exploratory approach to build up their understanding. One would expect them to take longer over the project in any case – the only question is how they spend that extra time. It is likely that they will be more motivated by starting with a manageable subset of the problem as opposed to struggling to write a specification for the whole system in the absence of complete understanding.

32.5.3 Tools

Tools can interact with motivational factors in two ways. It has already been suggested that software engineering methods and notations are not yet sufficiently mature to allow them to be specified for mandatory use to the exclusion of all alternatives. The same must therefore also apply particularly to the tools which are so essential to support those methods and notations, particularly because tools have the capability of imposing their rigidity more relentlessly than any human.

Irrespective of the model and notation which they support, tools can interfere in other ways. Tools which suffer from poor performance (irrespective of whether this is a hardware or a software problem) or poor interface may be very frustrating to use. These frustrations may have a negative effect which more than offsets the other benefits arising from the tool.

32.5.4 Software re-use

A further topic of considerable interest at present is software re-use. It is clear that much effort could be saved if a higher degree of re-use and generalization could be achieved, and it is therefore often assumed that all duplication of effort is bad. However, this is by no means always true. Leaving aside the approach to developing critical systems in which a number of independent developments of the same system may take place to increase dependability, there are at least two other reasons why a certain amount of duplication can be permitted without undue concern:

1. As discussed earlier, one function of competition (whether conscious or otherwise) is to set standards. If two people are addressing the same problem, one will almost certainly produce a better solution than the other. If only one person had addressed the problem, it might have been the wrong one.
2. The coordination needed to prevent duplication, the management of reusable objects, and the demotivating effect of extra coordinating activity all cost money. In the short term these costs might well outweigh the savings.

One should certainly continue to pursue the goal of re-use, but one should not necessarily be too concerned at every single example of duplicated effort.

32.5.5 Summary

In summary, therefore:

1. The details of methods should be advisory rather than mandatory.
2. The development life cycle should fit the project team.
3. Notations and tools should be used in an open manner, allowing contained sub-problems to be addressed using a different approach were necessary.
4. Tools which are poorly engineered should be avoided unless the gains really offset the disadvantages.
5. Management controls should not be so overwhelming as to be counter-productive.
6. Duplication of effort is not always wrong.

The focus should be on convincing people of the value of methods, notations, and tools, rather than making them mandatory, if maximum effectiveness is to be achieved. Almost by definition, a good set of tools is one that the staff on the project want to use.

32.6 Further reading

The books quoted here have had a significant influence on this chapter, which could not have been written without them.

Peopleware, by Tom DeMarco and Timothy Lister, is essential reading. It is one of the few books which specifically address the people aspects of system development, and is strong on what makes teams tick and on the working environment. It is anecdotal and readable, but no less useful for that. For people involved in recruitment, the chapter on hiring a juggler is a good one to remember.

In Search of Excellence, by Tom Peters and Robert Waterman, is now seven years old. It had a major impact on management thinking when it first came out, by setting out to demolish the excessively analytical view of what contributes to business excellence (defined as a combination of subject assessment and sustained financial performance). Twelve companies are surveyed, including IBM, Hewlett-Packard, and DEC, to identify eight characteristics which mark them out. Not in principle anything to do with software engineering, but highly relevant. Tom Peters has since written two other books in similar vein: *A Passion for Excellence* (with Nancy Austin) and *Thriving on Chaos*. Both are worth reading.

Understanding Organisations, by Charles Handy, is a standard work and full of valuable insights. The book is at the same time comprehensive, well-organized, and readable. Essential reading for anyone who wants a better understanding of motivation, organizations and teams, both in theory and practice. Thoroughly recommended.

Software Engineering Economics, by Barry Boehm, is still *the* book on productivity and what contributes to it, and pays a considerable amount of attention to the contribution made by people. Productivity and quality are after all the major goals of managing the software team. The book may also help justify the purchase of a development environment.

The Mythical Man-Month, by Fred Brooks, is a classic, having been written in 1972, based on work carried out in the 1960s. However, it has made a permanent contribution to our understanding of the management of large software projects. It places particular emphasis on the importance of maintaining the 'conceptual integrity' of the system being developed.

The Social Psychology of Work, by Michael Argyle, provides a good survey of the principles of psychology as applied to work. It has a particularly useful chapter on their application to specific situations such as appraisal interviews and chairing meetings.

The Psychology of Computer Programming, by Gerald Weinberg, is getting a bit dated now but is still a useful, if sometimes infuriating, antidote to very structured views of life. It rambles rather, and tends to start from the position that programmers would be fine if only managers would not interfere with them.

Although they are not exactly 'further reading', there are a number of training films which succeed in putting across important management principles in a short period of time. The Video Arts films, such as 'The Unorganised Manager' and 'Meetings, Bloody Meetings', which feature John Cleese, are particularly effective.

32.7 References

Argyle, M. (1974) *The Social Psychology of Work*, Pelican

Belbin, R. M. (1981) *Management Teams*, Heinemann

Blanchard, K., Zigarmi, P. and Zigarmi, D. (1986) *Leadership and the One-Minute Manager*, Willow

Boehm, B. W. (1981) *Software Engineering Economics*, Prentice-Hall

Boehm, B. W. (1987) Improving software productivity. *IEEE Computer*, **20**, No. 9, 43

Boehm, B. W., Penedo, M. H. *et al.*, (1986) A software development environment for improving productivity. *IEEE Computer*, **17**, No. 6, 30

Boehm, B. W. and Ross. R. (1989) Theory W software project management. *IEEE Transactions on Software Engineering*, **15**, No. 7, 902

Brooks, F. P. (1975) *The Mythical Man-Month*, Addison-Wesley

Brooks, F. P. (1987) No silver bullet. *IEEE Computer*, **20**, No. 4, 10

De Marco, T. (1982) *Controlling Software Projects*, Prentice-Hall

De Marco, T. and Lister, T. R. (1987) *Peopleware*, Dorset House

Garratt, S. (1985) *Manage Your Time*, Fontana

Handy, C. B. (1981). *Understanding Organisations*, Penguin

Hastings, C., Bixby, P. and Chaudhry-Lawton R. (1986) *Superteams*, Fontana

Jones, T. C. (1986) *Programming Productivity*, McGraw-Hill

Kidder, T. (1982) *The Soul of a New Machine*, Allen Lane

McCue, G. (1978) IBM's Santa Teresa Laboratory – architecture design for program development. *IBM Systems Journal*, **17**, 1

Parnas, D. L. and Clements, D. C. (1986) A rational design process: How and why to fake it. *IEEE Transactions on Software Engineering*, **12**, No. 2, 251

Peters, T. J. (1988) *Thriving on Chaos*, Macmillan

Peters, T. J. and Austin, N. (1985) *A Passion for Excellence*, Random House

Peters, T. J. and Waterman, R. H. (1982) *In Search of Excellence*,- Harper and Row

Weinberg, G. (1971) *The Psychology of Computer Programming*, Van Nostrand Reinhold

33

Integrated project support environments

Anthony Hall
Praxis Systems plc

Contents

33.1 Introduction

Software engineering, like any other engineering activity, requires a combination of creative work with a large amount of tedious administration and control. The mundane aspects of the software engineering task are themselves most appropriately carried out by computers; the software systems used for such tasks as editing, compiling, test administration and so on are referred to as 'software tools'. The development of software tools echoed, in many ways, the history of computer applications in other areas. Initially, there was a period during which individual tools were built to assist with particular software development tasks. It then became apparent that many incompatible tools were being developed, and that it would be much better if a way could be found of bringing together the various tools into a single, integrated, environment. Just as computer applications in commerce were supposed to become centred round the corporate database, so computer applications to support the software engineer were supposed to become centred round the software development environment. This idea was made explicit in two different milieux during the late 1970s and early 1980s.

In the commercial world, the notion of a data dictionary was exploited for software development (De Marco, 1978). A data dictionary was conceived as the corporate database of the computing department, and round it grew a number of tools to support the analysis, design and construction of commercial information systems.

Somewhat later, a similar idea emerged in the technical computing community. The most explicit statement of the idea was a document called Stoneman (Department of Defense, 1980), which was part of the Ada programme undertaken by the US Department of Defense. Stoneman envisaged an Ada programming support environment (APSE). The APSE was to consist of a central database, not unlike a data dictionary, supporting a number of software tools. The term 'integrated project support environment' (IPSE) was coined in the UK to describe the more general notion of an environment of software tools, not necessarily connected with Ada, which would support all the activities within a project. In the US and Europe the terms 'software development environment' and 'software engineering environment' have also been used with the same meaning.

At first, in spite of the similarity of the underlying ideas, practice in the commercial and technical worlds was widely different. More recently the term 'software engineering' has become increasingly used in all types of software development and commercial analysis and design tools are now (1989) being called computer-aided software engineering (CASE) tools. The historical differences are discussed in more detail later. This chapter is concerned with the whole range of environments, whatever they are called. The similarities between the approaches are more important, for the purposes of this discussion, than their differences.

This chapter is not about software tools themselves; it is about the environments within which software tools are used. These environments have a number of objectives:

1. *Productivity.* A central aim is to improve the productivity of a project by automating as much work as possible, and by reducing the risk of error and consequent re-work. A characteristic of IPSEs is that they aim to maximize the productivity of the project as a whole, not just the productivity of any one person or activity.
2. *Reliability.* IPSEs aim to improve the reliability of software through the automation of error-prone processes (such as configuration management) and by the enforcement of standards and good practice.

3. *Visibility.* It is important for a project manager or auditor to be able to see exactly what has really happened on a project and, as far as possible, to see why it has happened. IPSEs aim to capture the information which will make this possible.

The chapter is divided into five main sections after this introduction. Part two discusses why environments are needed, and why the topic of integration is so important. It turns out that building IPSEs is difficult. Part three explains some of the principles that have been used in trying to achieve integration. Part four summarizes the main technologies that are used in current IPSEs. This section does mention some particular IPSE products and indeed some of the precursors to IPSEs. It is not intended, however, as a buyer's guide to IPSEs, but rather as a framework for understanding the various kinds of product available. Part five analyses some of the current trends in IPSE development, on the basis of technical, political and market factors and the likely effect of these on IPSE production and use over the next few years. Part six looks at current research projects and ideas from other areas which can be expected to influence the future course of IPSE development.

33.2 Concepts and requirements

The section identifies the characteristics which are required of a support environment; in particular it concentrates on those characteristics proper to the environment as a whole, as opposed to any particular tool within it. An IPSE must be more than just the sum of its tools.

There are three main requirements that an IPSE must meet:

1. It must support the whole software life cycle.
2. It must support methodical development.
3. It must support development in the large.

These requirements are discussed in the next three sub-sections.

33.2.1 Lifecycle support

No single activity dominates the life cycle of a large software project, so to meet its objectives an IPSE must support the whole life cycle.

There are three important features of the software life cycle which influence the design of IPSEs:

1. The division into phases.
2. The need for iteration.
3. The variety of activities that take place.

33.2.1.1 Life-cycle phases

Almost all life cycle models recognize the existence of phases of development which differ in several important ways:

1. *The representation of the software.* During a design phase, for example, the software may exist as textual documents describing the design, as diagrams, partial specifications and so on. During coding, the same software exists in quite different forms such as source code, object modules and test scripts.
2. *The nature of the development activity.* Some phases (e.g. design) require creative thought; others (e.g. regression testing) can be carried out quite mechanically. Even those that cannot be performed mechanically can sometimes be subjected to mechanical verification.
3. *The scope for tool support.* In the past most tools supported the activities connected with coding. More recently, the emphasis has shifted towards tools to support the earlier phases of the life cycle, such as requirements gathering, analysis and design. These tools are often quite different in nature from coding tools, for example they are often diagrammatic.

33.2.1.2 *Iteration*

The second important feature of the life cycle is that it is iterative. Although there may be more-or-less recognizable phases called 'design', 'code' and so on, development *never* follows a straight line from one to the other. There is always a need to rework the 'earlier' stages in the light of 'later' ones. The extreme example of this is maintenance: many of the changes that take place during maintenance actually arise because of changes to requirements. One of the weaknesses of current development practice is that it fails to take account of this rework. Changes are carried out at the stage the software has reached when the need for change is discovered, rather than the stage at which the error was introduced. The result is that the various representations of the software may start out compatible but they rapidly drift apart, leading to the common observation that 'the only specification of the software is the code'. One of the reasons for this problem is that the different representations of the system are held in different forms, often on different computer systems; another is that there is little help available for making changes in, say, the design and then ensuring that the code changes to match the new design.

An IPSE has to address this problem by close integration of all the representations of the software, by supporting tools to ensure the compatibility of the representations, and by configuration management of the various versions of the software.

33.2.1.3 *Variety of activities*

A third feature of software projects is that, whatever the technical phases through which the software progresses, there are at each stage activities of many different kinds which cut across technical boundaries. Examples of such activities are:

1. Project management.
2. Configuration management.
3. Document production.
4. Reviews and quality assurance.

Each of these activities has its own view of the software under development. However, they are all dealing with the *same objects*. In common practice, however, all these activities will have their own, non-integrated computer support – if indeed they have any at all. Information about the product will be duplicated in several different systems. The consequences are, typically:

1. Management information is notoriously out of date and fails to reflect the true state of the project.
2. Configuration management systems are often burdensome, requiring repetition of information used by development tools; they are also weak, not being able to guarantee that the real development objects are in fact under control.
3. Document production often requires extensive re-input of existing information, and documents quickly become inconsistent with what they purport to describe.

The solution of these problems requires an environment in which the same information can be used by all the different activities within the project. For example, the project plans and work breakdown structures must be directly linked to the actual products developed by the technical activities within that project.

33.2.1.4 *Nature of life cycle support*

There are two characteristics which an environment must have if it is to solve these problems and support the whole lifecycle. The first is coverage; the second integration. Coverage means that the environment must be capable of supporting tools for whatever activities are to be carried on within the project.

Integration means that the tools in the environment must work together and share information.

The fact that an IPSE must support the whole life cycle does not mean that it must be committed to a particular life cycle model. It is true that some IPSEs, for example ISTAR (Dowson, 1987), do work on the basis of a model of a software project. Such models, however, are very generic and can accommodate a wide variety of life cycles. Other IPSEs provide completely general building blocks for putting together life cycle support and do not commit their users to any particular life cycle characteristics at all.

33.2.2 Support for methods

One of the most important characteristics of a large software development is that it must be carried on according to well-defined methods. Some methods do not yet have their own tool support. This can be because they are not well formalized, or because tool support for them is intrinsically difficult. Other methods may need a variety of different tools to carry out different parts of the method. In general terms, it is possible to define what an environment must offer to be capable of supporting methods. There are four aspects to any method, and each aspect makes demands on the facilities of an environment. These aspects are:

1. The underlying model of the method.
2. The views of the model that the method offers to the user.
3. The rules of the method.
4. The procedure to be followed when using the method.

To take Jackson Structured Programming (Jackson, 1975) as a typical example of a method:

1. The model contains entities like data structures, programs, files, correspondences …
2. The views include the various diagrammatic representations of these structures, as well as the corresponding textual representations.
3. The rules include constraints on allowable data structures, rules for program inversion, rules for matching data structures and so on.
4. The procedures include the order in which the six steps of the method are carried out, and the guidance about when, for example, program inversion should be done.

Many current software tools concentrate on the views of a method, and offer little support for the other aspects. In the commercial area, for example, there are many tools which allow the construction of the diagrams associated with various schools of 'structured analysis'. An IPSE must do much more than this. It must capture the underlying model represented by these diagrams, and as far as possible capture the rules of the method as well. The question of how far IPSEs can and should impose the procedures laid down by the method is currently a topic of research and debate, and is discussed in a later section.

There is no one method which covers the whole software life cycle. Any IPSE must therefore support many methods, and it must integrate the methods in exactly the same way that it must integrate different activities. For this integration to be possible, the models underlying the different methods must be able to be related to each other and these relationships must be captured in the IPSE.

Just as commitment to life cycle support does not imply restriction to a particular life cycle model, so commitment to supporting methods means more than simply being a toolset for a particular method or set of methods. New methods are constantly being developed and existing ones improved. Furthermore, very few organizations adopt methods lock, stock and barrel. More often the methods are adapted for individual organizations or even individual projects. This means that the support which the IPSE gives for methods must be very flexible, and it must be possible to define adaptations and extensions of methods within the IPSE.

33.2.3 Support for development in the large

Many of the characteristics of IPSEs derive from the fact that they are aimed at supporting large-scale software development. In particular, this means that:

1. The software products are large.
2. The projects are large.

Support for large-scale products means that IPSEs must include product management methods and tools as well as technical development tools. In particular, configuration management, build control and interface definition and verification must all be provided by the IPSE. These facilities must work across the whole range of information held in the IPSE. For example, configuration management must apply to design information just as much as to code.

The fact that projects are large means that they are carried out by large teams of people, perhaps geographically distributed, and that they last a long time. So if an IPSE is to improve the productivity on such a project it must manage the cooperation between users effectively. This means that information must be communicated between team members, but in a controlled way. On the one hand, as the development progresses all team members should be able to see the most up-to-date state of the project, at least in so far as it affects their own work. On the other hand, they must be insulated from accidental or unapproved changes made by other users which would compromise the integrity of the project as a whole. The IPSE must either prevent, or be capable of resolving, incompatible changes made by different users. The problems here are just the problems faced in other information systems where there is a tension between the need for maximum flexibility for the individual and the need for central control. Commercial organizations, for example, often face the problem of maintaining a corporate information strategy and at the same time giving users flexibility by, say, providing them with their own personal computers.

In this area, as in the previous one, an IPSE must be flexible. There are many different ways of breaking down a software product into components. Indeed, a product will probably be broken down in different ways within a single project. Similarly, project teams can be organized in lots of different ways, with different divisions of responsibility and hence different needs for information flow and control.

The requirement to support large projects makes it imperative that an IPSE be efficient. Otherwise it will act as a bottleneck and lower the productivity of the whole project.

33.3 Principles

There is by no means a single established architecture for an IPSE. Stoneman (Department of Defense, 1980), although a requirements document, did suggest an architecture for an APSE, but many products and proposed environments do not conform to this architecture. On the other hand, it is possible to recognize certain approaches which characterize all IPSEs to a greater or lesser degree, and the author has tried to define these as 'principles' of IPSE design. These principles are:

1. All IPSEs provide some sort of model of the system being produced and, sometimes, of the project which is producing it.
2. An IPSE is more than a collection of tools, because it provides common services over a range of tools and methods.

3. An IPSE offers control over the product and process of development.
4. An IPSE product must be generic, and be capable of being configured for a range of tools, methods and projects.

33.3.1 Modelling

All information processing systems model some aspect of the real world, and it is widely agreed that a good way of designing such systems is to make this model explicit in the structure of the system. (See Jackson, (1983) for example). The 'real world' of an IPSE is the software being developed and the process of its development, and an IPSE embodies a more-or-less complete model of this world. The characteristics of this model determine the possible applications of the IPSE, since if an aspect of reality is not expressed in the IPSE's model, then the IPSE cannot give any support in manipulating that part of the world. In order to offer configuration management, for example, an IPSE must be able to model the notions of 'configuration item', 'version', 'dependency' and so on. The level of detail of the model is also important; an IPSE whose model of a program module is simply at the level of a named file cannot offer language-sensitive editing or static analysis.

The modelling capabilities of an IPSE can cover several areas: product structure, methods and management.

33.3.1.1 Product structure

The most basic need is to have an explicit model of the end product of the IPSE – the software being produced. Software does not, of course, have a single representation. It exists as requirements statements, design documents, code, tests, test results, user manuals and so on. Each of these forms has its own internal structure, and each of them may exist in many versions. The structures are tied together by a complex web of relationships: between design and code, between the different parts of a product, between successive versions of a module, between declarations and uses of names, and many others. Each tool in the IPSE reads a small subset of these objects and relationships and makes its own small additions and changes to the model structure. The structure modelling requirements of IPSEs are very stringent, covering a range of granularities from whole software releases (used by CM tools) down to single program statements (used by program analysers). To cover the whole range is a challenging research issue.

33.3.1.2 Methods

The basic elements of a model of a method have already been discussed. The first component, the objects manipulated by the method, is of course some part of the product structure itself. Methods also require rules to be included in the model. Some of these rules can be captured by some of the so-called semantic data models (Hull and King, 1987; Peckham and Maryanski, 1988). For complete method support, however, an explicit way of representing formulae in logic is required.

Methods also require procedures to be modelled. One way of doing this is to treat procedures as programs (Osterweil, 1987). Other people have proposed modelling procedures by their specifications in terms of pre- and post-conditions (Radice et al., 1985; Ould and Roberts, 1988). An IPSE which contains an explicit model of procedures can enact these procedures itself, or check that they are being carried out correctly.

33.3.1.3 Management

On a larger scale, the IPSE may have explicit models to support management. Such models would include, for example, project structures, responsibilities, access control rules and a model of the project's life cycle. Some IPSEs (Dixon, 1988) take the model of the project, rather than the product, as central; Brooks (1982) points out that the structures tend to be isomorphic.

33.3.2 Common services

An IPSE usually has an identifiable component which is distinct from any of the tools, which is sometimes called a kernel or infrastructure. It is the purpose of this component to provide common services which all the tools in the IPSE can use. There are three distinct reasons for such provision:

1. Economically, if the services are provided once in the infrastructure, rather than being duplicated in each tool, then tools can be simpler to produce, smaller, and cheaper.
2. A related reason is that if the tools are written to use only the services provided by the IPSE, they can be independent of the underlying hardware and operating system. This means that they can be ported to different implementations of the same IPSE kernel, and take advantage of improvements in the underlying hardware as soon as these are supported by the kernel.
3. Provision of services at a sufficiently high level encourages uniformity across the tools, both in their behaviour and in their use of resources. A clear example of this is the Unix operating system: services which are provided by the operating system, like pipes and the file structure, are used uniformly and predictably by tools; services which are provided by the tools themselves, such as parameter analysis and user dialogues, are inconsistent and make the job of learning to use Unix, and the job of combining tools, much more difficult than it need be.

Typically, the common services provided by an IPSE kernel fall into three groups: information management, user interface and process management.

33.3.2.1 Information management

The information management services give the tools access to the stored information that constitutes the project database. The nature of the services directly reflects the nature of the modelling supported by the IPSE. A very simple model might be provided by little more than a structured filing system. A model based on database ideas would be provided by the appropriate kind of database management system. Graph-structured models are supported by graph building and traversal procedures.

33.3.2.2 User interface

User interface services are extremely important in determining the usability of any software. If many tools are used together, it is valuable to provide a high level of common user interface services so as to present a coherent view of the environment as a whole to the user. This is an area which is currently very difficult. This is partly because of the rapidly changing hardware technology. There are as yet no universal standards for communicating with bit-mapped screens, for example. It is also because of the intimate connection between the user interface of a tool and its functionality. There is much research into ways of factoring out user interface design from tool functionality, but as yet no consensus on how this should be done. For a discussion of this issue, see, for example, Young, Taylor and Troup (1988).

33.3.2.3 Process management

One of the ways in which tools can be built economically is to allow them to re-use other tools by invoking them to carry out parts of the job at hand. Uniform tool invocation facilities are therefore a useful service to provide in an IPSE kernel.

In providing these kinds of common service, an IPSE kernel is very like an operating system. Indeed the Unix operating system and its Programmers' Work Bench has been the basis of an important strand of IPSE development. An IPSE kernel differs from an operating system primarily in that it provides a much higher level of services. There is not in fact necessarily any particular bias towards software development applications in the services provided. At present the area where IPSE kernels and operating systems diverge most strongly is in their information handling, with most operating systems offering only a filestore while IPSEs are based on higher level data models.

33.3.3 Control

Provision of common services to tools makes it easier for them to do things right. It is also important, particularly in large projects, to prevent them from doing things wrong. One important principle of IPSE design, therefore, is to ensure that the tools are used under control; that they cannot be used in ways which would damage the integrity of the project. There are three kinds of control which are important for an IPSE: access control, concurrency control and configuration and version control.

33.3.3.1 Access control

This means ensuring that the operations in the IPSE are only carried out by those authorized to do so. For example, it is important in projects where review and sign-off are part of the project management process that these are really done by the proper authorities.

33.3.3.2 Concurrency control

This is the process of ensuring that concurrent operations on the same or related objects are valid and cannot conflict with each other. It is closely related to access control, since an important class of concurrent operations are those carried out simultaneously by different users. Even if each is valid individually, the effect of doing them concurrently will be, at best, to surprise one of the users. Concurrency control in IPSEs is a very difficult topic, for two reasons. First, the objects in an IPSE have very complex relationships, so that changes in one object can have far reaching effects. Second, groups of related changes constituting a 'transaction' typically represent major design changes and therefore can take a very long time – days or weeks, as opposed to the seconds that a conventional database transaction takes.

33.3.3.3 Configuration and version control

A major function of an IPSE is to control the changes that happen as the project proceeds. Version control ensures that changes are noted, that where necessary old versions are kept, and sometimes also that histories of changes and information about reasons for change are preserved. Configuration control is concerned with preserving the integrity of complex collections of objects as the component objects go through many versions. It ensures, for example, that software which is in the field can always be reproduced. In an IPSE, configuration and version control must be built in to the kernel. This ensures that they are not bypassed or forgotten. It also allows the control to be applied in a way which is invisible to the tools, so that tools need not concern themselves with the particular version and configuration regimes in use.

33.3.4 Genericity and tool-building tools

To satisfy the requirements for the IPSE to support many different life cycles, methods and tools, many IPSE providers have adopted the approach of building an IPSE framework which is generic and can be configured to particular projects and methods. An IPSE may be generic in several ways:

1. *Product model.* Many IPSEs have general data modelling capabilities, rather than a fixed data model. The particular types of objects and relationships to be used are set up as part of the IPSE configuration process.
2. *Methods.* All the components of the method definition may be similarly generic: the model, by using the general modelling facilities; the rules, by offering a general method of defining predicates; the views, by offering tailorable user interface facilities; and the process, by offering general process modelling rather than a fixed process definition.
3. *Languages.* Editors, compilers and interpreters can be generated by tools given a non-procedural definition of the language. In more recent IPSEs, the notion of 'language' has been extended to include graphical representations, so that diagram building tools can be built in the same way from definitions of the diagram components and structure.

33.4 Current approaches, technologies and products

33.4.1 Overview and classification

The principles outlined in the last section are now becoming widely accepted as a sound basis for the design of IPSEs. However, it is certainly not true that all current products have been conceived as attempts to embody these principles and thus satisfy a set of requirements such as those in the first section. On the contrary, the majority of products currently available have developed from a more narrow focus: either on solving particular software development problems, or on exploiting particular technologies for software tool production. This section is therefore organized according to the technical approaches that have been adopted, and it concentrates on characterizing the approaches rather than evaluating individual products. This is necessarily an imperfect way of classifying products, since no product demonstrates an approach in its pure form. It does, however, provide a framework which will remain useful in spite of the rapid developments which are taking place in the available products.

The primary distinction which is made in this section is between, on the one hand, environments which have developed from particular tools and technologies and widened their applicability to cover more of the development life cycle; and on the other hand, those environments which have, from the first, been conceived as frameworks capable of incorporating a wide range of tools. The first group can be described, very approximately, as specialized environments: a single tool, or a tightly coupled group of tools sharing some common idea forms the basis for the whole environment. The second group can, equally approximately, be described as general-purpose environments: the possibility of adding new tools and methods is a basic feature of the environment. At the present time, the situation can be summed up as follows:

1. There is a large number of specialized environments available and in use. Many of them offer excellent functionality and real productivity gains, often precisely because they have a single, coherent, approach. In response to the need to extend their coverage, many of these environments are developing beyond their original scope and acquiring more facilities.

Because they *are* specialized, such extensions must be done by extending the design of the environment; they are therefore dependent on the supplier. Where user extensions are possible they are usually strictly confined within, for example, a single programming language.
2. At present there are fewer general-purpose environments, and those that do exist offer very limited functionality. Mechanisms for extensibility, standard interfaces, and so on, are much discussed but as yet little tried in practice. Effective environments of this sort are only just emerging from research projects. There is still a massive effort needed to populate these environments with tools, and it is too early to say whether the theoretical advantages of general-purpose interfaces will be realized in practice.

33.4.2 Specialized environments

Specialized environments all have their roots in systems which are focused on some particular aspect of software development. Some concentrate on a particular phase of the life cycle – e.g. programming. Others support a particular kind of activity within the life cycle – e.g., configuration management. Yet others are based on a particular technology – e.g. workstation-based diagramming tools.

Within their own areas, specialized environments are currently more usable and productive than general-purpose environments. The functions they provide are closely integrated. They offer uniform user interfaces, both at a superficial level and also in the deeper sense that there is a single cognitive model behind the environment.

The problem that all such environments face is that eventually their users reach the limits of their applicability. The users have then to switch to some other tool and they may then experience an abrupt transition to some quite different model. Some specialized environments do not allow export of their information at all; others offer only crude input and output to external systems. Some environments of this sort are, in principle, capable of being extended and their developers are usually working on extensions to turn them into complete environments. Others are by their nature confined to particular applications and require major redevelopment before they could become general purpose environments.

The environments are discussed under the following headings:

1. Programming systems.
2. Design and analysis systems.
3. Project and product management systems.

However, these groups overlap considerably and practical tools often cross boundaries between the groups.

33.4.2.1 Program development environments

It is not surprising that the earliest attempts to improve the production of software concentrated on supporting the programming task. The support developed along various different lines:

1. Interactive code development systems.
2. Integrated mixed-language systems.
3. Generic programming environments and programming environment generators.
4. Programming assistants based on artificial intelligence ideas.
5. Host–target development systems.

33.4.2.1.1 Interactive programming systems

The key idea behind interactive environments is responsiveness. Two important early environments were Dartmouth College

BASIC (Kurtz, 1981) and Teitelman's Interlisp (Teitelman, 1975). In the latter particularly, the emphasis is on supporting a single programmer in exploratory programming: the development of a program by experimenting with it. This idea is extremely attractive and has had a strong influence on the development of environments particularly for artificial intelligence applications.

Environments like Interlisp achieve their power by single-mindedness and responsiveness. Everything is done within a single programming language (Lisp, in the case of Interlisp), and this language is usually interpreted or compiled incrementally. Therefore the programmer can try out the program very quickly and make small changes and test them in a very short time. This makes the environment very productive where such a mode of working is appropriate. The weaknesses of such environments derive from the same causes: they are limited to a particular language; and they do not provide the sort of controls which project teams need.

Following Interlisp, a number of other environments have followed this model. CEDAR (Swinehart, Zellweger and Hagmann, 1985) was an attempt to offer similar responsiveness with a procedural rather than a functional language and an environment used by a large group of people. In most respects CEDAR was successful, but it did not succeed in achieving the same responsiveness because of the longer edit–compile–run cycle demanded by the language implementation.

One single-language, single-user system which has been extremely influential is Smalltalk (Goldberg and Robson, 1983). Smalltalk is the best known example of an object-oriented programming language. The Smalltalk environment is highly significant because the object-oriented paradigm integrates the programming language and the data of the environment in what promises to be a powerful way. It provides a highly extensible environment in which it is very easy for new programs to build on existing ones. Although Smalltalk itself is at present a single-user system, the object-oriented ideas behind it are likely to be influential in large-scale environments.

33.4.2.1.2 Mixed language environments
One of the few multi-language environments is Poplog, (Sloman, Hardy and Gibson, 1983; Hardy, 1984) which was developed to overcome the limitations of a single language. It provides a common, tightly integrated, portable environment for interactive languages of different types including Pop II, Common LISP, Prolog and ML. All the languages are translated to a common Poplog virtual machine which is then compiled to machine code on the host.

33.4.2.1.3 Generic programming environments
A class of programming environments which has received a lot of attention, especially in the USA, is the generic programming environment or programming environment generator. The first such environment was the Cornell Program Synthesiser (Teitelbaum, Reps and Horwitz, 1981), and there have been many similar systems developed. The basic idea of such environments is to provide generic tools for program development, and to instantiate these tools for particular programming languages by providing definitions of the language to be supported. Typically such definitions take the form of an abstract or concrete syntax for the language, plus either an attribute grammar or action routines for expressing the language semantics. The central tool in the environment is usually a structure editor, that is, an editor which manipulates an abstract representation (e.g. a syntax tree) of the program, instead of manipulating the textual form. Other tools, such as incremental compilers, interpreters and debuggers, are driven from the same abstract representation of the program. Some of these systems support programs written in a

variety of languages, by having the abstract program representation common between the languages.

This idea for a generic system can be extended in various ways. Gandalf (Notkin, 1985) adds facilities like modules and version control for programming in the large. In fact any notation – for example, a diagrammatic design notation – can be processed in a similar way, and a number of tools for design in recent IPSEs follow this approach.

33.4.2.1.4 AI-based programming assistants
One of the trends in programming environments has been towards the use of higher level languages. The current limits of this trend are seen in a number of programming environments which use artificial intelligence to support the programming task.

One line of research has been to build programming assistants, for example the Programmer's Apprentice (Waters, 1985). These use knowledge about the programming process in the form of plans for certain programming situations, and in some cases use knowledge about the application domain.

A second, similar approach is the transformational approach. This is based on allowing the user to express the program in a very high-level specification language and transforming this high-level representation to an efficient executable form. The CHI system, developed by the Kestrel Institute (Smith, Kotik and Westfold, 1985) is an example of this approach. There is a commercially available system called Refine from Reasoning Systems based on the CHI system.

A third approach is to provide languages which combine rule-based execution and object-oriented structuring. Such languages provide a powerful environment for exploratory programming using a mixture of paradigms. Examples are LOOPS, FLAVORS, KEE and ART.

33.4.2.1.5 Host-target systems
The final category of programming environments which have influenced IPSE development is that of host-target development systems. These are very different in character and purpose from single-user interactive environments. They are systems for developing on one, powerful, computer programs which are eventually to run on a different, usually less powerful, machine. Typically such environments include cross compilers, emulators, and target debuggers. Because of their widespread use for developing embedded systems, for example in the avionics industry, host-target development systems have sometimes developed into more fully functional programming environments. An example is Perspective Pascal (NCC, 1987), which supports design representation as well as programs and has programming-in-the-large facilities for interface definition and control and for team-wide configuration management.

33.4.2.2 Design and analysis systems

A natural extension of the idea of support for programming is the idea of a tool to support earlier stages of the life cycle–requirements capture (called analysis in commercial systems) and design. Broadly speaking, two approaches have been adopted here.

The earlier systems were essentially tools for recording and analysing requirements and design information. One such system was PSL/PSA (Teichroew and Hershey, 1977), which allowed the entry of requirements in structured textual form and offered a large number of tools to check for completeness and consistency. The CADES system (Snowdon, 1981), developed by ICL, was probably the first example of a real project support environment. It is used to record and control the design and code of the VME operating system. CADES is based round a commercial database system and pioneered the use of database technology for software support. It is still being used for the development and support of VME, which is a very large piece of software, and is possibly the most significant example of IPSE use in existence.

In the commercial world data dictionaries have served the same function for data processing projects. A data dictionary is a database for the data developers and records all the data structures used by an application. Advanced data dictionaries also record details of the real world that is being modelled by the application. Many data dictionaries support application generators which use the data stored in the dictionary to automate much of the task of program production.

More recent systems for design and analysis are often based on particular notations or methods, unlike CADES or PSL/PSA, which are essentially passive repositories. One example in widespread use on technical projects in Europe is EPOS (Lempp, 1986) which is based around a particular design notation. EPOS also offers other functions as configuration management and project management.

Similarly, for commercial developments there are now many CASE systems based on the so-called structured methods of analysis and design. Most of the methods used in this field are based on diagrammatic notations, and the introduction of CASE tools has depended on the availability of low-cost graphics hardware.

CASE tools offer a wide range of functionality:

1. Some of them offer only diagram production; others record the underlying model represented by the diagrams, and sometimes this recording is done directly on a data dictionary.
2. Almost all of them offer some form of rule checking, but this can vary from simple syntactic checks to complete verification of all diagrams against the central data dictionary according to the rules of the method.
3. Most CASE tools are at present single user, but more advanced tools can be used by teams working on a collection of workstations networked together. These systems offer a central data dictionary, configuration management and access control.
4. There are many tools which support just a single part of a method. For example, tools for drawing data flow diagrams are very popular. More advanced tools cover more of the life cycle. Some, such as those supporting the method called Information Engineering (Arthur Young, 1987), start with business analysis; some are able to generate code automatically from the designs.
5. Many CASE products, particularly in the USA, are capable of producing design documents to particular standards, particularly those required by the Department of Defense.

The idea of making a tool generic can be applied to CASE tools, just as it can to programming environments. The tools for design can be configured by providing explicit descriptions of:

1. The diagram shapes (which correspond to the concrete syntax).
2. The formation rules for the diagrams (which correspond to the context conditions of a language definition).
3. Code generation rules (which gives an operational semantics for the diagrams).

There are currently a number of systems offering such generic facilities, including VSF and CADWARE.

33.4.2.3 Project and product management systems

A number of development support systems have concentrated on supporting the management and documentation aspects of projects, rather than on the technical methods used for the development. They are concerned with managing the deliverables of the project but do not necessarily provide support for the production or validation of these deliverables. They may rely on standard text editors or other tools to do any manipulation of their documents. One widely used system is Maestro (Pond, 1988). Maestro is a multi-user system, based on special hardware, which supports the development of code and documents. It provides some development tools but typically relies on a target system for compilations and program builds. The main function of Maestro is to support communication and documentation on large projects. BIS/IPSE (Richardson, 1988) is of similar scope.

In the development of technical software, a major problem has been configuration management (CM), and there are a number of tools which address this aspect of development in the large. These tools typically offer controlled repositories for documents and code, and ensure that:

1. All deliverables are correctly identified.
2. They cannot be changed without authority.
3. Complex objects can be built from their parts dependably.
4. The status of a configuration is known at all times.

Examples of such systems are Changeman, Softool CCC, Lifespan and PCMS (NCC, 1987). They are important because such functions must be part of any IPSE. However, these systems are far from being IPSEs themselves because there is no integration between the management aspects and the technical development. Application of the CM procedures is a separate operation and any correspondence between the models in the CM system and the real dependencies between objects must be maintained by hand. More recently some *ad hoc* combinations of particular method tools with configuration management tools have been developed but these are still a long way from general purpose integrated systems.

33.4.3 General-purpose environments

The environments classified under this heading share one characteristic: they have all been designed, from the start, to be general purpose environments capable of being extended with new tools and new methods. All of them have architectures based on at least some of the principles discussed in Section 33. These architectures can be described as variations on the model first proposed in Stoneman. A generalized form of this architecture is illustrated below in *Figure 33.1*.

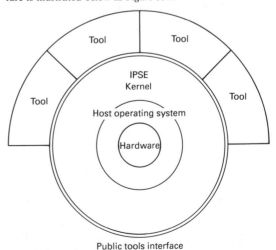

Public tools interface

Figure 33.1 The Stoneman architecture

The architecture is based on the idea of layers, with each layer offering a well defined set of functions used by the layer around it:

1. The innermost layer is the machine or, in a distributed system, a network of machines.
2. There may be a host operating system on top of the machine.
3. There is a kernel which augments the operating system with extra functionality appropriate to software tool support. In particular it is envisaged that the kernel offers a database for storing project information of all sorts.
4. Around the kernel, and using the facilities it provides are the tools. Each tool is envisaged as a self-contained process.

In its idealized form, the architecture has the following features:

1. The kernel offers facilities for:
   (a) data management, modelling, sharing
   (b) user interface
   (c) tool invocation and control
   (d) configuration management
   (e) access control.

2. The tools only use the kernel interface. There is no direct communication from tool to tool.
3. All interaction with users is through kernel facilities.
4. No tool is privileged: all control resides in the kernel, so there is no need for or possibility of a 'controlling' tool which mediates between users and other tools.

In all systems of this type the interface between the kernel and the tools is central to the definition of the environment. Such an interface is called a public tool interface (PTI), since environment suppliers publish the interface definition in the hope that tool suppliers will write tools to use the interface and thus increase the scope of the environment. Much of the debate about the facilities which should be offered by environments can be abstracted into a debate about rival PTI definitions.

Within this overall framework, there are many issues which have been approached in different ways in different projects. These different choices lead to widely different PTIs. An approximate classification of current products divides them into three groups:

1. Some PTIs are very close to operating systems interfaces, and typically the database is actually a file system.
2. Some PTIs are fairly elementary, and in particular lack control facilities. In these cases, the environment needs to contain a privileged tool which enforces the necessary controls.
3. The most advanced IPSEs have PTIs which offer data modelling, advanced user interfaces and control all through the kernel.

The following sections describe examples in each of these groups.

33.4.3.1 Extended operating systems

The model for many IPSEs of this kind was the Unix Programmer's Workbench (PWB) (Mitze, 1981). Key features of Unix which have inspired subsequent similar approaches are:

1. A well-defined operating system interface gives access to all operating system functions. The Unix shell is not a privileged program.
2. The operating system interface offers a layer above the bare machine which means that tools are portable across Unix implementations. The Unix operating system interface is thus an example of a PTI.

3. The hierarchical filing system is a first step towards more powerful data structure.
4. Unix offers good facilities for tool composition, encouraging the idea of a workbench of related tools.

A similar approach to the Unix PWB was taken by TRW, who developed a collection of tools called the Software Productivity System (Boehm *et al.*, 1984).

Unix itself proved adaptable to distributed systems and is widely used as an operating system on workstations. It has been substantially enhanced. The most significant development towards an IPSE is Apollo's Domain Software Engineering Environment (DSEE) (Leblang and Chase, 1987). DSEE extends Unix with facilities for:

1. Version management.
2. Configuration management.
3. Task management.

Although DSEE remains a filing system rather than a database, it is a significant development because it demonstrates the effectiveness of building functionality into the kernel. A tool running on DSEE need have no knowledge of version management built into it, for example. DSEE itself is responsible for selecting the correct version of the file, determined by control structures set up by the user, and presenting it in the form expected by the tool.

A more recent product incorporating similar ideas is Sun's Network Software Environment.

33.4.3.2 Tool-based control

A variation on the idealized architecture is to locate the control functions in a special tool rather than in the kernel. This is considerably less flexible than the ideal, but is more straightforward to implement. It has therefore been used in practical IPSE products which have aimed to provide early availability of a useful subset of the ideal. One such IPSE is GENOS (Higgs and Stevens, 1986). In its early form GENOS did not depend on kernel facilities beyond those of the operating system at all, but imposed control on tools by ensuring that they could only be invoked through a privileged tool. More recently, GENOS has evolved to incorporate a kernel based on the PCTE interface discussed below.

33.4.3.3 Database-based IPSEs

The mainstream of development of general-purpose IPSEs has been based on the replacement of the traditional filing system with a database system. The role of the database is to provide the modelling capabilities and to enforce control over the stored information. Since the idea of a database was first suggested, there has been debate about what form an IPSE database should take. Issues which divide developers include:

1. What is the scope of the model? Does it cover large scale structures such as modules, documents and dependencies, or should it also include fine detail like variables, predicates and individual items on diagrams?
2. What is the best data modelling formalism in which to express the database structure?
3. How should the database incorporate rules, alternative views (e.g., graphical structures) and process structures?
4. How is the database structure to be changed and extended as new tools and methods are added?
5. What controls is the database to impose? In particular, the problem of managing consistency as individuals make changes to the data over long periods has proved intractable.

So far, practical IPSE products have adopted conservative

answers to these questions. All of them use the database to model the project at a fairly coarse level of granularity. There has been remarkable unanimity that the appropriate formalism for the database is Chen's entity-relationship model (Chen, 1976). This has the advantage of being intuitively appealing and widely used as a modelling formalism, although databases outside the area of software development have not implemented this formalism directly. Very little use has been made of rules within IPSEs, and graphical structures have been represented in *ad hoc* ways by file structures stored in or referred to from the database proper.

The main distinctions between the products have been in their approaches to distribution and multi-user working, perhaps because this is where IPSEs differ most drastically from ordinary database applications. In this area they share many problems and approaches with other engineering databases, for example those used for computer-aided design (Katz, Chang and Bhateja, 1986).

33.4.3.3.1 ISTAR and the contractual model

One approach to the problem of control is to build into the IPSE a model of the project which partitions the database in a manageable way. This is the approach taken by ISTAR (Dowson, 1987). ISTAR is based on a model of a project as a hierarchy of contracts. Each contract has inputs and outputs, but is otherwise a completely self-contained piece of work. It may be done by one person, or it may be split into subcontracts, but its internal structure is the responsibility of the contractor, not the client or anyone else. The contract, therefore, is a sound basis both for configuration management and for concurrency control. Because contracts encapsulate pieces of work, they also make a good basis for a distributed system. In ISTAR, a single contract is carried out on one machine, but different contracts may be distributed over different machines on the network.

ISTAR offers tools in integrated groups called workbenches. Within a workbench the tools are closely integrated. The environment can be extended by adding new workbenches.

ISTAR also exploits the idea of generic tools. It has facilities for producing method-specific tools from non-procedural definitions of the method structure.

33.4.3.3.2 IPSEs based on PCTE

Within Europe there has been a major collaborative research and development effort to define an IPSE kernel called the 'portable common tools environment' (PCTE). PCTE adopts the kernel-based architecture. The kernel offers several groups of services:

1. Data management, through a database called the object management system.
2. User interface.
3. Process control.
4. Distribution control.

The object management system implements an approximation to the entity-relationship model. It functions at a coarse level of granularity. In particular it includes Unix files as unanalysed attributes of objects. A design aim of PCTE is in fact to be a superset of the Unix operating system, and PCTE functions like process control are essentially those of Unix. PCTE does, however, have a user interface based on the use of bit-mapped terminals.

In contrast to ISTAR, PCTE adopts a variant of the conventional database approach to concurrency control, using the notion of a database transaction to enforce exclusion between concurrent processes. This approach is consistent with its approach to distribution, which is to make distribution invisible to the user. PCTE is thus logically a single multi-user shared database, which happens to be located on more than one machine.

There are some notable omissions from the functionality of PCTE. For example there are no configuration management facilities at all.

PCTE itself is a definition, not an implementation. There are a number of products available which use it as a base:

1. Emeraude is an IPSE kernel which is a direct implementation of the PCTE definition. It is commercially available on a number of machines.
2. Eclipse (Cartmell and Alderson, 1988) is a complete IPSE based on a PCTE kernel. Eclipse has added to the PCTE object management system a second level of modelling. Within a PCTE file a data model based on the Interface Definition Language (IDL) (Stone and Nestor, 1987) is used to structure the contents, and a uniform interface which hides the differences between the levels is provided. Eclipse can therefore model fine grain structures such as those used in graphical tools.

Like ISTAR, Eclipse exploits the notion of generic tools. It contains a tool called a graphical design editor which allows the construction of interfaces to method tools for a variety of methods.

33.4.3.3.3 Other PCTE projects

Within the Esprit programme there are a number of other projects which are building toolsets to work on PCTE or extending its functionality. One such project, PACT, is adding a further layer of function to offer, for example, configuration management facilities. An extension of PCTE called PCTE + is being developed for military projects; PCTE + includes extensive security facilities absent in PCTE itself.

33.4.3.3.4 Project master database

Most of the work on using databases for IPSEs has been carried on in Europe. One exception is work done by TRW on a project master database (PMDB) (Penedo, 1987). At present the project is prototyping a database designed using the entity-relationship model by implementing it on a commercial database management system.

33.4.4 Conclusions

The environments currently available are still a long way from meeting all the requirements for IPSEs.

Specialized environments concentrate on particular phases of the life cycle and on particular activities within the phases. General-purpose environments do in principle allow the whole life cycle to be supported, but there are no examples yet which have a rich enough set of tools to realize this in practice.

Many specialized environments give excellent support for the models and views of their chosen methods. They are only just beginning to go beyond this to support the rules and the process aspects of the methods, and to support combinations of methods. General-purpose environments offer the hope of method integration, but again this has not yet been realized in practice.

Some environments do address the management of large projects. As yet, however, there are no environments that combine this with excellent support of the development process.

33.5 Current trends

There are three main influences which are dictating current developments in IPSEs:

1. There is growing agreement on the overall requirements that need to be satisfied, leading to convergence between what have historically been very different approaches.
2. There are technological pressures, both from the discovery that present technology is inadequate to solve the problems of IPSE design, and from the desire to take advantage of improvements in hardware and software.
3. There are commercial and political pressures which arise because of the growing importance of software in determining economic and military power.

The following subsections discuss these in turn.

33.5.1 Convergence

A sure sign that IPSEs are important is that almost any software development product is now marketed as an IPSE or a CASE tool. But this marketing hype reflects a reality. Many problems that were previously thought of as different are now regarded as part of the same problem, and many solutions which were previously thought to be distinct are now seen as different approaches to a common end. This can be seen in the breakdown of artificial barriers between, for example:

1. Different application areas.
2. Different kinds of activity.
3. Different technical approaches.

33.5.1.1 Convergence between commercial and technical systems

There used to be a great cultural divide between the practitioners of commercial data processing and the developers of real-time embedded systems. The former were concerned with the problems of managing large amounts of information and were supported by tools like data dictionaries; the latter were more concerned with real-time response and processing structure and had, in fact, very little in the way of tool support. Now, however, commercial systems increasingly rely on real-time transactions over distributed systems and real-time applications increasingly depend on large amounts of complex structured data. The methods used to develop the two kinds of system are correspondingly much more similar than they used to be. For example, the 'structured' methods, like data analysis and data flow, are increasingly relevant to technical developments, and have been extended with real-time analysis tools so that they cover a wide spectrum of applications.

This convergence may go even further in the future, towards integration of hardware and software design. Many of the problems of computer-aided design (CAD) systems are the same as those of IPSEs, and although at the moment the two kinds of system are quite distinct, the idea of a systems factory covering both hardware and software is gaining acceptance.

33.5.1.2 Integration of activities

It is increasingly recognized that the different aspects of a project need to be handled in an integrated way. Tools which started off addressing one aspect have increased their scope to cover other aspects. For example Maestro, which initially was largely a document management and communication system, is acquiring more technical development tools. Similarly, CASE tools which started out offering just diagramming support are increasingly incorporating configuration management and document production, and EPOS, originally a design system, now incorporates project management facilities.

33.5.1.3 Convergence of technical approaches

The convergence of functionality between the various systems

which are evolving into full IPSEs is accompanied by a convergence of their architectures. Tools which started off as specialized systems with limited functionality have increased their coverage and scope. In doing so, they have acquired more and more of the features which characterize general-purpose environments. The more advanced CASE tools, for example, contain data dictionaries which are very like the database kernel of a general-purpose environment. A variety of diagramming tools are provided with the system, all sharing data through the data dictionary. The data dictionary may include configuration control; in distributed systems it may act as a central repository enforcing rules on concurrent access. It may even incorporate rules which must be enforced across the whole tool collection. In future we will see the replacement of product-specific data dictionaries with databases like the object management system of PCTE, originally conceived as the kernels of general-purpose IPSEs.

33.5.2 Trends in technology

33.5.2.1 Knowledge representation

The central technical problem in designing an IPSE is the problem of representing knowledge about the project in a usable form. Specialized systems have adopted *ad hoc* solutions to this problem using representations appropriate to particular kinds of information and particular uses of that information. Attempts to build general-purpose IPSEs, centred on an explicit, comprehensive and general-purpose knowledge repository, have focused attention on the form such a repository should take. One approach, advocated since at least 1983 (Hall, 1984), is to adopt conventional database technology; since, it is argued, this is an accepted way of representing facts in many computer systems, it is a good basis for representing knowledge in an IPSE. The main advantages of using a database management system are:

1. Language-independent data descriptions make the structure of the data explicit and independent of the use to which it will be put.
2. Well-established data manipulation and query languages give ready access to the data.
3. There are existing implementations, representing a considerable investment, which can be used.
4. Mechanisms like views (Brown, Robinson and Weedon, 1986) and sub-schemas (CODASYL, 1971) offer independence between different applications.

However, there are both theoretical and practical difficulties in exploiting conventional database approaches:

1. Data description languages are not very expressive. Although there has been a lot of work on so-called 'semantic' data models (Peckham and Maryanski, 1988; Hull and King, 1987), it is usually only possible to define structures in terms of simple properties and relationships. In particular, databases do not usually support more recent programming language ideas like abstract types. Since the structures needed to represent knowledge about projects are complex and highly interconnected, conventional databases are only capable of representing gross simplifications.
2. The data manipulation languages of databases are also not very expressive. Furthermore, there is a mismatch between programming language data structures and operations on the one hand, and database data structures and operations on the other, which makes applications unnecessarily difficult to write.
3. Existing database implementations are not suited either to the kind of data which are needed for IPSEs or to the kind of use to which the data are put. In particular:

(a) Existing database implementations cannot cope with the complex interrelationships which would be needed to represent a fine-grained analysis of the project data; on the other hand, neither can they support directly large pieces of coarse-grained data stored in files.

(b) Conventional database concurrency control mechanisms are not capable of supporting the patterns of use of data by team members, who typically work on large interconnected collections of information for perhaps weeks at a time.

4. Although a degree of independence between applications is possible, general mechanisms for extending and changing database definitions while preserving existing applications are not yet available in actual implementations.

There have been three responses to these problems. One is to try and build on existing database technology, but to extend and adapt it to IPSE needs. This has been tried in, for example, the Aspect research project (Hitchcock, 1988). A second is to recognize that existing database technology is inadequate and to try and build from scratch a different data model in the same style. Both PCTE and the common APSE interface set (CAIS) are examples of this approach; their data models are unconventional, although related to the entity-relationship model. The third approach is to adopt an altogether more radical solution and to move outside database and file system ideas altogether.

One such radical solution to the mismatch between database structures and programming language structures is to dispense with the database structures altogether. Instead, programming language structures themselves are made persistent, and themselves form the database of the system (Atkinson and Buneman, 1987; Currie, 1985). However, it can be argued that ordinary programming language constructs are even less appropriate for representing project knowledge than are database constructs.

Another approach is to change the programming language to reflect more directly modelling ideas. This is the basis of the object-oriented approach. Object-oriented languages have many features which make them good candidates for knowledge representation:

1. Persistent data structures (objects) are fully integrated into the programming language.
2. Objects have their own identities, independent of the applications which use them.
3. There is no restriction on the complexity of structure or fineness of granularity which can be represented by objects.
4. Objects can represent instances of abstract data types in that they can have their own behaviour, implemented in a way invisible to their clients.
5. Mechanisms like inheritance allow indefinite extension of behaviour while leaving existing applications unchanged.

Object-oriented languages thus represent to some extent a convergence between database and programming language ideas. The disadvantages of the object oriented approach are:

1. Object-oriented languages are currently less powerful than databases in some respects – for example, they do not have non-procedural, set-at-a-time query languages.
2. Multi-user object-oriented systems seem to be very difficult to build.

In spite of these problems, which mean that the method is still evolving and there are no standards in the area, the approach is rapidly gaining ground in many sorts of application, and many software tools and environments are being built using this technology. Examples are:

1. Cépage (Meyer, 1988).
2. Garden (Reiss, 1987) is a prototyping environment which uses object-oriented language for parametrizing a generic design environment.

33.5.2.2 Exploiting new hardware technology

Software engineering has traditionally been a labour-intensive activity and has displayed the common syndrome that the equipment available to the practitioners of computing has been inferior to that available to end users. Two aspects of technology have been under-exploited in IPSEs:

1. User interface developments.
2. Distributed systems.

These two aspects are brought together in the distributed workstation environments that are becoming available.

User interface technology has changed dramatically with the advent of bit-mapped graphics displays and laser printers, and with the development of new user interface paradigms to exploit this hardware. The most prevalent paradigm in end-user computing is now direct manipulation, whereby users interact with computers using physical analogues of the state of the system and the operations they wish to carry out. Software tools are increasingly being written to exploit this hardware and to use this style of user interaction. They are, of course, particularly relevant to those methods which use diagrams. One of the major benefits of having hardware capable of managing and displaying diagrams is that it makes it much easier to keep the diagrams up to date as the project progresses. This meets the requirement for support of iteration in the life cycle, and overcomes one of the major problems that have been found with such methods. The methods work very well at first. Once implementation starts, decisions are made which affect the design but it is very time-consuming to change the diagrams so the code and the diagrams get further and further apart until finally the diagrams are no use because they do not correspond to the system which is actually implemented.

The development of workstations has gone hand-in-hand with the development of networks. The hardware exists to turn single-user workstations into multi-user networks. Current IPSE developments aim to exploit this by developing appropriate multi-user access and concurrency control methods. Two approaches are currently being tried. One is to make distribution invisible, and to treat the information held on the network as a logically unified database. This is the approach taken by PCTE. The other approach is to make the users aware of the distribution, and to have them check out pieces of work to their own workstations, and return them when finished. Strictly speaking, the 'logical' distribution represented by the check out and return mechanism need not correspond to the physical location of the objects – such a system could be implemented on a physically centralized system, for example – but it does lend itself to the obvious implementation of physically copying objects to the workstation when they are checked out by the user. This scheme is the one usually used in CAD systems, where parts of the design are checked out by designers and reintegrated when they have finished. The main difficulty with the scheme is that the complex interconnections in the information make it difficult to find subsets of the information that can be checked out safely. One approach used in CAD systems which is also used in IPSEs is to use optimistic concurrency control. This means that it is accepted that when a designer checks out some information, that does not guarantee that the work will not interfere with other parts of the design. Indeed, in its extreme form no locking at all is done on check out. Instead, when the work is returned, an explicit test is made to see if it is still consistent with the rest of the information. If not, some reconciliation must be done, by backing out or redoing some of the work.

33.5.3 Commercial and political issues

33.5.3.1 General-purpose environments, interfaces and standardization

There are on the market many software tools and environments of the kind described here as 'specialized'. In contrast, almost all the 'general-purpose' environments are the product of government or transnational research funding, and are still some way from the market place. Yet one of the key ideas in general-purpose environments is to offer a way of integrating together tools from different sources and so create a free tools market which will benefit both producers and users.

The problem in achieving this is the following. For there to be a tools market there must be an agreed interface for these tools to exploit. This interface is the public tools interface provided by the IPSE kernel. However, it is no good, from a tool-writer's point of view, having lots of different PTIs. There needs to be one standard one. So far, there are two candidates for such a standard. In Europe, the PCTE definition has been proposed, and is being adopted by a large number of projects, particularly within the Esprit programme. In the USA standards are being developed specifically for Ada support environments – the common APSE interface set (CAIS) (Oberndorf, 1988). In addition to these two official standards, there is a commercial proposal to standardize on an interface for CASE tools based on an existing product called the Software Backplane.

Currently, PCTE is defined in a C language reference, although there is also a formal specification of the interface and an Ada language definition. CAIS is an Ada language definition. It has gone through several very different revisions.

Conceptually, CAIS and PCTE are very close. Both define a database, user interface and process control capabilities. The data model is in both cases an *ad hoc* model of nodes and links related to the entity-relationship model. Nodes have 'contents' which are files, and also other attributes.

While there are obvious advantages in standardizing on one of these definitions, there are also serious objections. Neither system has been proved in use. Both have severe limitations on what they can effectively model. Furthermore, even within the scope of their modelling capabilities, conformance to their interfaces would not by any means be sufficient to guarantee interworking of tools, since in order to interwork, tools need to agree on *what* objects are modelled within an IPSE as well as how they are modelled, and neither standard addresses this. Many people feel that PTI standardization is premature, and that a tools market will not in fact take the form of interchangeable tools working on top of a standard interface. An alternative possibility is that tools will continue to be based on specialized architectures, but they will be able to communicate their results in some standard interchange form. The IRDS proposal (Acly, 1988) for standardizing data dictionary contents is an example of such a standard which would be used more as a repository and interchange medium than as a kernel specification.

33.5.3.2 Populating general-purpose IPSEs

From a potential user's point of view, the major weaknesses of any general-purpose IPSE available is that it contains, so far, very few tools. There are a number of projects which are trying to exploit kernel definitions and produce complete environments with integrated toolsets.

Within Esprit, there are several such projects based on PCTE, for example:

1. *PACT*. The PCTE Additional Common Tools project is building on the PCTE kernel in two ways:
   (a) Adding an extra layer of functionality on top of the basic kernel facilities, to offer common services to all tools.

This layer includes, for example, some configuration management facilities.
   (b) Providing a basic set of tools to work with PCTE, mainly compilers and utilities.
2. *GRASPIN*. This is a project to develop a personal software development workstation for a particular combination of formal and informal graphical development methods.
3. *APHRODITE and HTDS*. These projects aim to provide host-target development environments exploiting PCTE.

There are some very large collaborative projects under the Eureka programme: Eureka Software Factory (ESF), EAST and AIMS, which aim to build very large scale environments on a PCTE base.

33.5.3.3 Procurement pressures

Some of the pressure to adopt IPSEs is not purely commercial but arises from political considerations and from coordinated procurement policies, especially in the public sector. Three particular reasons why IPSEs are being adopted and developed are:

1. *Documentation requirements*. In the USA the Department of Defense requires all projects to produce certain standard forms of documentation. These documents are tedious to produce and very difficult to keep up-to-date. Many CASE products are geared explicitly to the production and maintenance of such documentation.
2. *Configuration management requirements*. Procurement bodies like Ministries of Defence normally mandate certain configuration management standards and procedures. These standards have a considerable influence over the design of configuration management tools. Existence of the standards is itself a pressure for the adoption of tools to support the procedures. It may be that even tools which are difficult to use or offer little real benefit may be adopted because of the existence of such requirements.
3. *Product liability*. Manufacturers of all sorts of products may be required to show that they used the best available technologies in the development of those products. This requirement may force the adoption of more rigorous development methods for software. IPSEs which can support, for example, formal methods, are likely to be more successful because of this pressure.

33.6 Longer term prospects

This section describes some of the work being carried on, largely in research projects, to solve the longer term problems and make major advances in IPSE technology. It describes the area where the IPSEs of five years hence can be expected to be very different from those of today.

In the medium term, the central problem of IPSE development will remain the problem of achieving integration. That problem will never be completely solved, for new ideas and new tools will always make unforeseen demands on whatever environments are in use. However, over the next few years, the coverage and degree of integration of tools will undoubtedly improve. Current research projects are starting to look beyond this problem, and beyond the important but relatively mundane problem of populating IPSEs with tools and information, to major improvements in the functionality of environments.

There are three areas of research which will probably influence the shape of IPSEs in the longer term. These are:

1. Understanding and supporting the *process* of software development.

2. Exploitation of more powerful ways of representing and manipulating knowledge.
3. Use of mathematically based methods of development.

33.6.1. Software development process

There is currently a great deal of research interest in the *process* of software development, in contrast to earlier approaches which have focused on the *products* of development. Such interest is not new, of course. Life cycle models are, to some extent, prescriptive or descriptive statements about the development process. However, recent attention has focused on making such process models more formal and in some cases making them executable. The intention is that an executable model of the development process can form the basis for an active IPSE. Such an IPSE is thought of as one which enacts the development process on behalf of its users, doing as much as it can of the process entirely automatically, driven by the stored process model. Such an architecture for an IPSE has been proposed in Hoffnagle and Beregi (1985).

Two kinds of modelling have been proposed. Procedural modelling (Osterweil, 1987) defines the process like a program, in terms of the steps that are taken and the order in which they are done. Behavioural modelling (Williams, 1988) defines the process like a specification, in terms of the pre-conditions and effects of the subprocesses.

A model of software projects in terms of formal relationships between project activities is described in Bjørner (1987).

Prototypes of active IPSEs of this sort have been built in the UK, by the IPSE 2.5 project (Ould and Roberts, 1988) and in the USA in the MARVEL system (Kaiser and Feiler, 1987).

A joint US-Japanese research project is investigating the use of the behavioural modelling approach to one part of the software life cycle (Kishida *et al.*, 1988).

An active IPSE, based on an explicit process model, can be more powerful than one which is only a passive repository of tools and information. It can, for example:

1. Automatically do things on behalf of the user.
2. Help the user to do the right things in the right order.
3. Prevent the user doing things at inappropriate times.
4. Embody the project plans in its model and guide the development according to the plan.
5. Provide realistic monitoring information to the project manager.

Process modelling is, however, at present still controversial (Lehman, 1987). Two criticisms that have been made are:

1. It cannot be done.
2. It should not be done.

Both these are based on the view that the actual processes that people carry out in doing tasks are poorly understood. Furthermore, even if current processes were understood then formal models might stifle creativity and be counter-productive. There is some support for this view from empirical studies of computer system use in other areas, where users frequently behave in ways not foreseen by developers. On the other hand, these criticisms may be based on a rather naive interpretation of what could be achieved by process modelling. Some researchers see the models as being highly adaptable and evolving as the system is used.

33.6.2 Knowledge-based approaches

An IPSE contains a structured collection of information about a project. In the most current IPSEs this information is held in some sort of database and controlled by some constraints which govern its integrity. Such representations are, however, very weak compared with the ways that people hold and use knowledge. One of the central topics in artificial intelligence is the discovery and exploitation of better means of knowledge representation. There is a lot of research around this topic, and there are some projects which are experimenting with the application of more powerful knowledge representation in software development.

So far, more advanced ways of representing and using knowledge have been applied mainly to the task of programming in the small. These applications are discussed in the section on AI-based programming environments. Here, the knowledge used is knowledge about how to program. Some related projects have also used knowledge about the application domain to guide the development. For example, the ΦNix (Barstow, 1985) project is specialized to developing applications in oil well logging and uses knowledge about physics and geology as well as programming knowledge. Draco (Neighbors, 1984) also makes heavy use of domain knowledge for constructing software from components.

The kinds of knowledge that are used during software development go beyond what can easily be expressed using current technology. Examples are:

1. Knowledge about the development process. Some of the process modelling projects mentioned in the last section are exploring this issue.
2. Knowledge about product management. See Ince (1984) for an application of knowledge representation to the configuration management problem, for example.
3. Knowledge about development methods.
4. Knowledge about aspects of a particular project, for example rationale for decisions.

There are considerable problems in using knowledge of this sort in large scale development. See Barstow (1987) for a summary of the issues. First, the kinds of knowledge needed are not yet well understood and certainly not formalized. Second, algorithms for using explicit knowledge in a general way are very time-consuming and it is impractical to apply them to the enormous amounts of data on a large-scale project. Nevertheless, research into the use of similar ideas on a larger scale is being done in several projects.

The Esprit project ASPIS (Puncello *et al.*, 1988) is building assistants for analysis and design, using knowledge of application domains and of the methods to be used.

CASE/MVS (Symonds, 1988) is an experimental system for using knowledge to support the maintenance and development of existing large-scale software.

33.6.3 Mathematically-based software development

The need for an underlying mathematical basis for software construction is becoming more widely accepted, especially in cases where the cost of software failure is high. IPSEs will, in future, be used for such critical developments, and therefore must provide support for development based on a formal approach.

The central mathematical object in all formal methods is the specification. A specification is a formal statement of what a system must do. From the point of view of an environment it has many similarities to a program: it is a formal text with an abstract underlying structure. It is likely that techniques for storing and manipulating programs, for example using abstract syntax trees, will also be applicable to specifications.

Tools are needed for the activities which are particular to formal methods of development:

1. The specification may be transformed into some less formal notation for discussion with the potential user of the end system. Paraphrasing tools can help with this.

2. Theorems about the specification may be formulated and the environment should provide assistance with proving these theorems.
3. Some specifications can be animated – i.e. prototype implementations can be generated automatically and demonstrated.
4. The specification may be refined into successively more concrete forms. At each step, the user is required to prove that the concrete form implements the more abstract one.
5. The IPSE itself may transform the specification into an executable form.

At present there are few tools to support formal methods at all, and those that exist are not integrated into environments. Formal methods will have to coexist with other methods and any IPSE will have to integrate formal and informal development tools and information.

Some projects are addressing these problems.

There are a number of tools which assist with the development of proofs. See Lindsay (1988) for a survey.

The knowledge-based systems using program transformation are in fact very close to formal method environments. The specifications from which they work are mathematical specifications, and the transformations they apply are mathematically based. For example the Transformation Implementation project at ISI (Balzer, 1985) uses a specification language called GIST from which executable programs can be produced, sometimes with assistance from the user. There is also a paraphraser which helps turn GIST into more readable text.

The Prospectra project (Krieg-Brückner, 1987) is developing a large-scale IPSE for transformation of equational specifications into executable programs. This cannot be done entirely automatically on a large scale, so the environment will function as an assistant. The user will be able to guide the use of transformations and composites of transformations. Even though it uses automatic transformation, Prospectra will depend on proofs. They are needed to validate the original specifications, and also to prove that the specifications meet the conditions governing the applicability of transformations.

The IPSE 2.5 project is researching several aspects of the use of formal methods:

1. Process models of formal development.
2. The integration of formal and informal methods.
3. Proof assistant tools suitable for large-scale development and integrated into the IPSE.

A number of projects are investigating environments which use pictorial techniques to animate formal specifications. These seem particularly appropriate to formal specifications of concurrent systems, since these frequently have an operational semantics which are straightforward to animate. Examples are:

1. An environment for Lotos (Bustard, Norris and Orr, 1988).
2. A programming environment for CSP (Delisle and Schwartz, 1987).

33.7 Conclusions

We are currently seeing a wide range of software tools becoming available. Largely as a result of improvements in hardware, many software engineers have access to powerful workstations and a variety of tools which exploit them. However, there are severe limitations in current tools. Some of the limitations are inherent in the tools themselves, and these are being overcome as we gain a better understanding of development methods, of human–computer interaction and of implementation techniques. On the other hand, some of the limitations are to do with the way tools are integrated together and the way teams can work together using the tools. These problems have been recognized for many years, but progress in solving them has been disappointingly slow. The idea of an integrated environment to overcome these problems dates from at least 1980, and there is still no complete environment which meets the requirements expressed then.

Attempts to provide such an environment have focused on the two approaches described here, either extending particular tools or providing a generalized tool infrastructure. The first approach has, so far, been more successful in offering useful facilities and improving productivity. A number of projects based on the second approach can be expected to show results over the next few years, but at the same time existing tools will be further extended and ultimately the two approaches will converge. This convergence will see highly functional tools sharing information through a knowledge base covering all aspects of a software project, and offering controlled facilities to the whole project team. It is hoped that such environments will offer big improvements in the productivity and quality of large software developments.

33.8 References

Acly, E. (1988) Looking beyond CASE. *IEEE Software*, March, 39–43

Arthur Young (1987) *The Arthur Young Practical Guide to Information Engineering*, Wiley

Atkinson, M. P. and Buneman, O. P. (1987) Types and persistence in database programming languages. *ACM Computing Surveys*, **19**, 105–190

Balzer, R. (1985) A 15 year perspective on automatic programming. *IEEE Transactions on Software Engineering*, SE-11, 1257–1268

Barstow, D. (1985) Domain-specific automatic programming. *IEEE Transactions on Software Engineering*, SE-11, 1321–1336

Barstow, D. (1987) Artificial intelligence and software engineering. In *Proceedings of 9th International Conference on Software Engineering*, IEEE pp. 200–211

Bjørner, D. (1978) On the use of formal methods in software development. In *Proceedings of 9th International Conference on Software Engineering*, IEEE, pp. 17–29

Boehm, B. W., Penedo, M. H., Stuckle, E. D. *et al.*, (1984) A software development environment for improving productivity. *IEEE Computer*, June, 30–44

Brooks, F. P. (1982) *The Mythical Man-Month*, Addison-Wesley

Brown, A. W., Robinson, D. S., and Weedon, E. (1986) Managing software development. In *Software Engineering 86* (eds D. Barnes and P. Brown) Peter Peregrinus, pp. 197–235

Bustard, D. W., Norris, M. T., and Orr, R. A. (1988) A pictorial approach to the animation of process-oriented formal specifications. *Software Engineering Journal*, **3**, 114–118

Cartmell, J. and Alderson, A. (1988) The Eclipse data model – a functional account. In *Software Engineering Environments* (ed P. Brereton) Ellis Horwood, pp. 50–68

Chen, P. P. (1976) The Entity-relationship model: towards a unified view of data. *ACM Transactions on Database Systems*, **1**, 9–36

CODASYL Data Base Task Group (1971) *Report*, ACM

Currie, I. F. (1985) Some IPSE aspects of the Flex Project. In *Integrated Project Support Environments*, (ed J. A. McDermid) Peter Peregrinus, London, pp. 76–85

Delisle, N. and Schwartz, M. (1987) A programming environment for CSP. *ACM SIGPLAN Notices*, **22**, 34–41

DeMarco, T. (1978) *Structured Analysis and System Specification*, Yourdon Inc.

Dixon, D. (1988) Integrated support for project management. In *Proceedings of 10th International Conference on Software Engineering*, IEEE, pp. 49–58

Department of Defense (1980), *Requirements for Ada Programming Support Environments: "Stoneman"*

Dowson, M. (1987) Integrated project support with ISTAR. *IEEE Software*, November, 6–15

Goldberg, A. and Robson, D. (1983) *Smalltalk-80: The Language and its Implementation*, Addison-Wesley

Hall, J. A. (1984) Databases in software development: the Ada programming support environment. In *Lecture Notes in Computer Science 180*, (ed P. J. L. Wallis), Springer Verlag, pp. 115–132

Hardy, S. (1984) A new software environment for list-processing and logic programming. In *Artificial Intelligence: Tools, Techniques, Applications* (eds T. O'Shea and M. Eisenstadt), Harper and Row

Higgs, M. and Stevens, P. (1986) Developing an environment manager for an IPSE. In *Software Engineering Environments*, (ed I. Sommerville), Peter Peregrinus, pp. 39–56

Hitchcock, P. (1988) A Database view of PCTE and ASPECT. In *Software Engineering Environments*, (ed P. Brereton), Ellis Horwood, pp. 37–49

Hoffnagle, G. F. and Beregi, W. E. (1985) Automating the software development process. *IBM Systems Journal*, **24**, 102–120

Hull, R. and King, R. (1987) Semantic database modelling: Survey, applications and research issues. *ACM Computing Surveys*, **19**, 201–260

Ince, D. C. (1984) A source code control system based on semantic nets. *Software – Practice and Experience*, **14**, 1159–1168

Jackson, M. A. (1975) *Principles of Program Design*, Academic Press

Jackson, M. A. (1983) *System Development*, Prentice-Hall

Kaiser, G. E. and Feiler, P. H. (1987) An architecture for intelligent assistance in software development. In *Proceedings of 9th International Conference on Software Engineering*, IEEE, pp 180–188

Katz, R. H., Chang, E., and Bhateja R. (1986) Version modelling concepts for computer-aided design databases. *SIGMOD Record*, **15**, 379–386

Kishida, K. *et al.* (1988) SDA: A novel approach to software environment design and construction. In *Proceedings of 10th International Conference on Software Engineering*, IEEE, pp. 69–79

Krieg-Brückner, B. (1987) Formalisation of developments: an algebraic approach. In *Proceedings ESPRIT Conference 1987*, North Holland, pp. 491–502

Kurtz, T. (1981) BASIC. In *History of Programming Languages*, (ed R. L. Wexelblat), Academic Press, pp 515–537

Leblang, D. B. and Chase, R. P (1987) Parallel software configuration management in a network environment. *IEEE Software*, March, 28–35

Lehman, M. M. (1987) Process models, process programs, programming support. In *Proceedings of 9th International Conference on Software Engineering*, IEEE, pp. 14–16

Lempp, P. (1986) Development and project management support with the integrated software engineering environment, EPOS. In *Software Engineering Environments*, (ed I. Sommerville), Peter Peregrinus, pp. 23–38

Lindsay, P. A. (1988) A survey of mechanical support for formal reasoning. *Software Engineering Journal*, **3**, 3–27

Meyer, B. (1988) Cépage: towards computer-aided design of software. *Journal of Systems and Software*

Mitze, R. W. (1981) The UNIX system as a software engineering environment. In *Software Engineering Environments*, (ed H. Huenke), North-Holland, Amsterdam, pp. 345–357

NCC (1987), *The STARTS Guide* (2nd ed)

Neighbors, J. (1984) The Draco approach to constructing software from reusable components. *IEEE Transactions on Software Engineering*, **10**, 564–574

Notkin, D. (1985) The GANDALF Project. *Journal of Systems and Software*, **5**, 91–105

Oberndorf, P. A. (1988) The Common Ada Programming Support Environment (APSE) Interface Set (CAIS). *IEEE Transactions on Software Engineering*, **14**, 742–748

Osterweil, L. (1987) Software processes are software too. In *Proceedings of 9th International Conference on Software Engineering*, IEEE, pp. 2–13

Ould, M. A. and Roberts, C. (1988) Defining formal models of the software development process. In *Software Engineering Environments* (P. Brereton), Ellis Horwood, pp. 13–26

Peckham, J. and Maryanski, F. (1988) Semantic data models. *ACM Computing Surveys*, **20**, 153–189

Penedo, M. H. (1987) Prototyping a project master database for software engineering environments. *ACM SIGPLAN Notices*, **22**, 1–11

Pond, R. (1988) Maestro and Southern Electricity. In *Software Engineering: Papers presented at the conferences held in London, June 1988*, Blenheim Online, pp. 101–116

Puncello, P. P., Torrigiani, P., Pietri, F. *et al.* (1988) ASPIS: a knowledge-based CASE environment. *IEEE Software*, March, 58–59

Radice, R. A. *et al.* (1985) A programming process model. *IBM Systems Journal*, **24**, 79–90

Reiss, S. P. (1987) Working in the garden environment for conceptual programming. *IEEE Software*, November, 16–27

Richardson, D. (1988) BIS/IPSE – automated support in practice. In *Software Engineering Environments* (ed P. Brereton), Ellis Horwood, pp. 166–173.

Sloman, A., Hardy, S., and Gibson, J. (1983) POPLOG: a multilanguage program development environment. In *Information Technology: Research and Development*, pp. 109–122

Smith, D. R., Kotik, G. B., and Westfold, S. J. (1985) Research on knowledge-based software environments at Kestrel Institute. *IEEE Transactions on Software Engineering*, **SE-11**, 1278–1295

Snowdon, R. A. (1981) CADES and software system development. In *Software Engineering Environments* (ed H. Huenke), North-Holland, Amsterdam, pp. 81–95

Stone, D. L. and Nestor, J. R. (1987) IDL: background and status. *ACM SIGPLAN Notices*, **22**, 5–9

Swinehart, D. C., Zellweger, P. T., and Hagmann, R. B. (1985) The structure of Cedar. *SIGPLAN Notices*, **20**, 230–244

Symonds, A. J. (1988) Creating a software engineering knowledge base. *IEEE Software*, March, 50–56

Teichrow, D. and Hershey, E. A. (1977) PSL/PSA: a computer-aided technique for structured documentation and analysis of information processing systems. *IEEE Transactions on Software Engineering*, **SE-3**, 41–48

Teitelbaum, T., Reps, T., and Horwitz, S. (1981) The Cornell program synthesizer: A syntax-directed programming environment. *Communications of the ACM*, **25**

Teitelman, W. (1975) *Interlisp Reference Manual*, Xerox PARC Technical Report, Palo Alto

Waters, R. C. (1985) The programmer's apprentice: a session with KBEmacs. *IEEE Transactions on Software Engineering*, **SE-11**, 1296–1320

Williams, L. G. (1988) Software process modelling: a behavioural approach. In *Proceedings of 10th International Conference on Software Engineering* IEEE, pp. 174–186

Young, M., Taylor, R. N., and Troup, D. B. (1988) Software environment architectures and user interface facilities. *IEEE Transactions on Software Engineering*, **14**, 697–708

34

Configuration management

Albert Alderson
Software Sciences

Contents

34.1 Introduction

In the context of software development configuration management is defined as the discipline of identifying the components of a continually evolving system for the purposes of controlling changes to those components and maintaining integrity and traceability throughout the life cycle (BSI, 1984).

Software configuration management complements hardware configuration management, contributing to overall system configuration management. Software configuration management is a formal engineering discipline which provides software developers and users with the methods and tools to identify the software developed, establish baselines, control changes to these baselines, record and track status, and audit the product. Software configuration management is the means through which the integrity and continuity of the software products are recorded, communicated and controlled (ANSI/IEEE, 1983a). The software product is not just software but also the documentation necessary to define, develop and maintain that software (Bersoff, 1984).

Software configuration management is not always distinguished from hardware configuration management, which is the older discipline. This has led to the use of inappropriate definitions and procedures in some cases. The two disciplines do share many common aspects, but they are different not least in that hardware has a physical existence. Each copy of a piece of hardware is potentially different because the physical fabrication process can introduce variations. Therefore, each copy must have a serial number to identify it and these serial numbers are an important aspect of hardware configuration management. Fabrication of instances of pieces of software is achieved by a simple copying process which need not introduce variation and so serial numbers are not required. Firmware, computer logic that is hardwired, say by burning it into a PROM, is a special case. The program itself can be managed by using software configuration management, but the pieces of programmed hardware, such as PROMS, must be controlled using hardware configuration management, since the hardwiring is a part of the fabrication of each piece of hardware.

Configuration management benefits all phases of the life cycle of a system, and touches on all aspects of a project. Project control is concerned with planning what the components of a system should be, when they should be delivered, and providing the resources to produce the components. Quality control ensures that the components are fit for their purpose and of the required quality. Configuration management provides stable instances of those components which can be tested and have their quality assessed. Tests and test software themselves should be subject to configuration management. Configuration management interacts with contractual concerns; the contract is usually based around the supply of specified components. Delivery requires goods in/out procedures that are based on the components. Maintenance is concerned with evolving the components in response to requested changes.

Configuration management is often thought to be a concern of large projects. However, every programmer has surely experienced the embarrassment of debugging a previously debugged version of a program. Configuration management is a problem on any scale of project. The basic techniques of configuration management apply to projects of all sizes and kinds. However, the way they are applied can differ considerably between projects, and between different stages of the life cycle.

Configuration management should begin when the first document of the system is written, continue throughout the life cycle, and terminate only when that last release of the system has been decommissioned. Without configuration management the reliability and quality of the software cannot be assured. The consequences of failure of configuration management can be economically and technically severe, and can lead to the complete failure of a project.

Configuration management of documents has generally been considered as another separate discipline. However, the advent of word processing and desktop publishing allows documents and software to be treated in a uniform manner. Documents may be copied onto paper for convenience of access, but this is no longer a necessary process for documents. Software and electronically created documents may be treated as members of a more general class – specifications – to which software configuration management is applicable. A piece of software is an executable specification written in some computer language; a document is a human-processable specification written in some natural language.

34.2 Model of system evolution

To achieve the control required, configuration management must be based on well-founded definitions. Unfortunately there is no consensus in the literature on the necessary definitions. Standards have been promulgated but are not in widespread use, as may be seen from the wide diversity of terms used by the developers of configuration management tools (see later). Definitions of the same term have subtle differences in some cases and exactly opposite meanings in others. Terms such as revision, version and variant are frequently left undefined. However, there does seem to be an underlying model of system evolution upon which there is broad agreement. This model is presented here as a background against which definitions can be made.

A system is the set of all specifications, both executable and otherwise, of a software product. This includes, at least, all requirements, design test and other specifications (usually expressed as documents), all code (usually expressed in some programming language), all that is derived from the foregoing (such as executable binary and printed documents), and all specifications of how to achieve such derivations.

The system is envisaged as having a state. This state changes as the system evolves. The state of the system is only of interest at certain times. It is generally not important to record and store indefinitely the state each time a programmer changes a single line of source text, nor generally would it be practicable to do so, since the storage required would be immense. To control change, at a chosen time, the complete state of the system is recorded. Changes after that time are proposed as changes to that recorded state. Proposed changes must be authorized and the completion of authorized changes must be recorded. When the authorized changes have been completed a new system state is recorded. This process is repeated throughout the life of the system.

The recorded states of a system need not form a single sequence. Two different sets of authorized changes may be applied to the same recorded state to give rise to two new, separate, recorded states. One set of changes may be to correct errors in a system issued to a client, the other set may be to introduce new functionality. This gives rise to a branching tree of recorded states for the system. Later branches of the tree may be merged to give a new state corresponding to the sum of the two sets of changes. Such a state might correspond to the fixing of errors and the addition of new functionality.

The recorded states must be recoverable. Complete or sufficient information must be held to reconstruct them. The times at which these states are recorded are not arbitrary. In practice, they correspond to events in the system life cycle. These events will correspond to the success of some check that the current state represents the completion of some step in the system's life cycle. The check will certainly test that all authorized changes have been made satisfactorily. Certain of these recorded states will be issued to the client for use.

A system is usually complex and is more readily dealt with by decomposing it into components and controlling the evolution of those components. Where the components are complex, heirarchical decomposition into further components is used. Changes are proposed to the components and so on. The decomposition need not be strictly hierarchic; the same components can occur more than once.

Decomposition into components requires control of the interfaces which the components present to each other. An interface has physical and functional aspects. The physical aspect may involve size, performance, language used, and parameters required and returned. The functional aspect concerns the processing undertaken to derive the returned parameter values from the supplied parameter values.

The state of the system at a chosen time is then the sum of the states of its components at that time. The summing process need not be a simple aggregation. Some assembly process may be needed to create the state of the system from the states of its components and of its components' states from their components' states. Where the same component occurs more than once in a system, it is possible for each occurence of that component to be in a different recorded state.

As the system evolves not only may the states of its components change, but the set of components of which it is composed may change. New components may be added and old components removed.

Once a system has been issued for use by a client, it cannot be assumed that the client will be prepared to replace it by its successor. Many successive releases of the system may be in use simultaneously. It is even possible that some release may be removed completely from service before all of its predecessors.

34.3 Definitions

The model given above is, in general terms, the model which underlies most current configuration management systems. There are alternatives (see later). The model does not impose a unique set of definitions of configuration management. Many different consistent sets can be proposed, leading to many different configuration management systems. There is no general consensus on the terms to be used, and the same terms are used differently in different sets of definitions. The following illustrative definitions have been derived from the above model. These definitions have been chosen to encompass the hierarchic software development process.

34.3.1 Configuration item

A configuration item is any system or component whose state is to be recorded and against which changes are to be progressed.

To achieve the required control, it is necessary to formalize the idea of a component. Common practice is to designate certain components as configuration items. A configuration item is the unit for the purposes of configuration management. As such it must be uniquely identifiable.

The configuration items are the only components that are referenced directly in a contract. Not all configuration items are mentioned in the contract, only those which the client can perceive in the delivered system and so can report errors in and request change of, or those to which special contractual terms apply, such as proprietary database interfaces which are charged for separately.

Configuration items must be individually documented and they are the focus of the configuration management procedures.

34.3.2 Version and variant

A version is a recorded state of a configuration item.

The version of a configuration item is the unit against which change is controlled. Changes are proposed to specified versions and approved changes are implemented in succeeding versions. The versions of a configuration item form a tree by virtue of these predecessor–successor relationships.

A variant is a sub-tree of the tree versions of a configuration item.

Variants of a system record the divergence of sets of versions, due to divergence in some physical or functional aspect, such as the target hardware, but in which other aspects stay constant.

Configuration management is based upon the immutability of versions. Once it has been recorded, a version must continue to exist, since it is the reference point for changes and for traceability. The immutability of a version does not imply that the version must be held in an immutable store, although it may be, but it must be possible to reconstruct the precise recorded state of every version.

Many conflicting definitions of version and variant have been proposed in the literature. Generally, standards (BSI, 1984; MOD, 1985) and glossaries (ANSI/IEEE, 1983b) avoid defining these terms, although they may use them. Some definitions consider versions (or revisions) to be states that succeed each other in time, whereas variants are states that exist concurrently in time. Others define versions and variants with reference to the degree or kinds of change of specification giving rise to the version or variant. None of these has found general favour, since examples abound in which successive versions are in use concurrently, while definitions based on difficult-to-measure attributes, such as degree of change, are too imprecise.

34.3.3 Configuration

A configuration is the collection of component configuration items which comprise a configuration item at some stage of its evolution.

As the configuration item evolves in various ways the collection of component configuration items may change, and so the configuration item is described by a tree of configurations. A configuration is in the nature of a template which can apply to a number of versions of the configuration item.

The definition embodies the recursion implicit in hierarchical development. A configuration specifies the components of a configuration item. These in turn have their own configurations. For a system, a configuration is the totality of software, hardware and documents needed to define the system.

This nesting of configurations allows control to be exercised when modular development is occurring. In particular, the formality of nested configurations provides the necessary control when development is distributed and where subcontractor control is required.

34.3.4 An illustration

Figure 34.1 illustrates two configurations, C1 and C2, of item IA. In configuration C1, item IA has component items IB and IC. In configuration C2, item IA has component items IB, IC and ID.

Item IA has four versions defining two variants. Item IB has two versions defining one variant. Item IC has four versions defining two variants. Item ID has one version defining one variant.

The build lists define particular versions of the component items required to build the corresponding versions of item IA. Versions 1, 2 and 3 of item IA have configuration C1. Version 4 of item IA has configuration C2.

Configurations

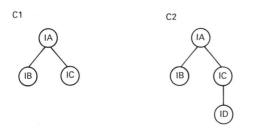

Build lists
For IA(1)-IB(1), IC(1)
For IA(2)-IB(2), IC(2)   For IA(4)-IB(2), IC(4), ID(1)
For IA(3)-IB(1), IC(3)

Items

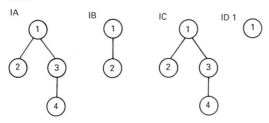

Figure 34.1

Note that the configuration C1 applies to versions of different variants of item IA. These correspond to versions of different variants of item IC.

34.3.5 Building

Building is the process of assembling a version of a configuration item from versions of its component configuration items.

Again there is an implication of recursion, since the versions of the components may themselves require building.

34.3.6 Build list

A build list is the set of versions of the component configuration items used to build a version of a configuration item.

Configuration items progress through versions, and a version of a configuration item is created by choosing versions of each of the component configuration items that contribute to it. These versions are then used in the build process.

The build list also incorporates recursion, leading to a tree structure in which it is possible for different versions of the same configuration item to occur on different branches.

To create a particular version of a configuration item, a particular configuration of that configuration item must be specified and a particular build list supplied. The configuration can be considered as a template into which particular versions of component configuration items are inserted. This process is called binding, the names of the component configuration items being bound to particular versions of those configuration items.

Ensuring that a consistent set of versions are bound to the configuration is a major concern of configuration management. Clearly not every set of selected versions defines a sensible version of the configuration item. This problem is largely unsolved, although languages such as Ada (see later) give assistance.

The scope of the build list might include only the versions of the component configuration items. However, it can be extended to specify the development environment, including, for example, the versions of the tools which are used in the building process, and to specify the run-time environment, including, for example, the version of the run-time kernel and even the expected hardware configuration. In general, the build list could record the version of any item whose change could affect the building process or the run-time behaviour of the built product.

34.4 Procedures

The process of configuration management must be formalized into a set of procedures for communicating between client and contractor concerning required and delivered systems, and controlling the change of such systems.

There is wide scope for defining such procedures and each project will define (or be provided with) procedures. These procedures are embodied in the quality procedures of the project, as are the technical standards to be used. The procedures should address the following:

1. Configuration identification, identifying and documenting the functional and physical characteristics of each configuration item.
2. Configuration control, controlling changes to the configuration items, and, issuing versions of configuration items from the software library (see later) to clients and developers.
3. Configuration status accounting, recording the processing of changes.
4. Configuration audit, controlling the quality of the configuration management procedures.

34.4.1 Configuration identification

Configuration identification is the process of identifying each configuration item and its interface.

The major elements of a system are identified as configuration items at the start of the project. As development progresses through the life cycle further configuration items relevant to the current stage are identified. As hierarchic decomposition proceeds within a life cycle stage, component configuration items are identified, recursively. Normally the source texts of documents and programs will be the ultimate leaves of this component tree, since these are usually the smallest entities that sensibly can be identified separately. The other configuration items will be built from these 'leaf' configuration items. The built configuration items identified will be the high level components of the system, safety critical components, components which are susceptible to change, which are likely to need repair or which may be reused.

Interface identification is the process of identifying all functional and physical characteristics relevant to the interfacing of two or more configurations items.

A configuration item is specified by its interface, defined in terms of its physical and functional characteristics or form, fit and function. Changing the interface of a configuration item will change the contribution it makes to the system, and consequently will change the system.

The configuration items and their interfaces must be recorded and related to the configuration(s) in which they participate.

34.4.2 Configuration control

Configuration control is the process by which a change to a configuration item is proposed, evaluated, approved or rejected, scheduled and tracked.

Configuration control must ensure that:

1. A configuration item is only changed when agreement has been reached on the need for the change and the form that change should take.
2. The changed configuration item is only accepted when it has been shown to conform to the approved change.

Configuration control is applied to versions of configuration items. Development proceeds to a point at which it is sensible to record the state of the configuration item as a version. Changes are then proposed to the version and development proceeds until it is again sensible to record a version. The recording of a version is not arbitrary. The project plan will identify the completion of each version as a project milestone, and the interface of each version must be specified so that achievement of the milestone may be verified.

Where no version of a configuration item exists the specification of its interface will be given by a configuration item from some earlier phase of the life cycle. Where a version does exist, the specification for the new item may be defined as the interface for a previous version together with authorized changes.

34.4.2.1 Baselines

A version of a configuration item serves as a baseline. A baseline is a well-defined point in the evolution of a system. In the early stages of development, a baseline will correspond to a document such as a requirement specification or a design specification. In the later stages a baseline will be a version of the software. A baseline is a basis for further development that can be changed only through formal change control procedures. Completion of the changes authorized to a baseline fixes the new baseline. The baseline of a built configuration item at a specific point in its life cycle is determined by the baselines of its component configuration items at that time.

Baselines serve as milestones for the management of the project. Successful completion of a baseline is established by a formal quality check such as a review or audit. The development process can be planned around standard baselines (Buckle, 1982). Baselines form the agreement between a contractor and a client about a configuration item.

34.4.2.2 Progressing change proposals

Configuration control procedures define the methods to be used to progress change proposals and define the level of authority required to operate those methods.

Configuration control progresses a change through a number of stages. Initially, proposed changes must be recorded, uniquely identified and associated with the proposer and with the version of the configuration item concerned. Each proposed change must then be analysed to determine the nature of each required change, identify all (component) configuration items affected by each change, including documentation, and assess its costs and benefits. Each proposed change must then be reviewed, and approved or rejected by the appropriate authority, which is often called the configuration control board (ANSI/IEEE, 1983b). Once approved a decision must be made about which version(s) to apply it to. Approved changes may be deferred to some later date. The decision and the authorization must be recorded, and details of the change and of the decision must be propagated to those who need to know of the change. Staff must then be authorized to progress approved changes, to maintain records of their status, and undertake re-validation after the changes have been implemented.

34.4.2.3 Controlling the software library

The configuration control procedures must describe the control of the software library. These procedures must include:

1. *Submission.* The entry of approved versions of configuration items into the software library.
2. *Issue.* The copying of versions of configuration items from the software library for use or modification by the developers.
3. *Release.* The transfer of a copy of version of a system (or a configuration item) from the software library of the contractor to the client. Configuration items will usually be released onto some transportable medium, such as magnetic tape. Release usually satisfies some terms of the contract between the client and contractor and so is a formal event. Configuration audit is a prerequisite of release to ensure that the released version is in a fit state for delivery to the client and has been produced with an approved quality control system. Formal certification may be required in the form of a Delivery Note or Certificate of Conformity. A Waiver may be required, documenting an agreement by the client that delivery can occur despite specific non-compliances.

34.4.3 Configuration status accounting

Configuration status accounting is the recording and reporting of information needed for configuration management including the configuration identification, the status of proposed changes, and the implementation status of approved changes. It provides the means by which the history of the system life cycle can be traced.

The configuration status accounting procedures must define how information on the status of configuration items is to be collected, verified, stored, processed, and reported.

Examples of the information required are:

1. The status of proposed changes.
2. The status of approved changes.
3. The baselines and the approved changes associated with each baseline.
4. The date when each version of each configuration item was recorded.
5. Deficiencies identified by the configuration audit.

34.4.4 Configuration audit

Configuration management must be subject to the same standards of quality assurance as other management procedures. Configuration audit is the means of assuring those standards. Configuration audit must check that configuration management responsibilities are clearly defined and accepted, and that configuration management procedures are clear and comprehensive. It must also confirm that those procedures are being applied and are functioning as required.

At any time configuration audit must be able to confirm the validity of the configuration status accounting records. At the end of each life cycle phase, configuration audit must be able to verify that all versions of configuration items required for the baseline have been produced to the specified requirements, that any associated technical documentation completely and accurately describes those versions of the configuration items, and that all approved changes applicable to that baseline have been completed.

34.5 Authorization

Control of change is a fundamental aspect of the software development process. Change involves work and so involves expense. Change modifies the built system and so may have contractual implications. Change alters what is available to users of the changed component; uncontrolled change interferes with the work of the users, so increasing cost. Change may be malicious, intended to gain unauthorized facilities, such as illegal access, or to cause disruption. In order that change be controlled, only authorized change must be permitted.

Configuration management procedures should be specified so that at each stage the appropriate authority has available the necessary information upon which to base authorization, so that what the authority decides can be recorded, and so that the authorization can be proved to have been made. These decisions must be made known to those who are affected by them. Configuration management must then ensure that only authorized actions are undertaken.

Authorization requires security. If configuration management is to be meaningful, access to the configuration items must be controlled. Change control procedures are useless if they cannot be enforced by access controls on the files which contain the software (Huff, 1981).

34.5.1 The software library

The commonest approach to this problem involves the use of controlled and uncontrolled areas. The controlled area, often known as the software library, is accessible only by approved users who may use only approved procedures. The security of this area may be addressed by placing it on a totally separate computer system to which only approved users can gain access. Only approved versions of configuration items are held in the software library.

To apply change to versions of configuration items, a user copies them from the software library into the uncontrolled area, often called the work area. The procedure may require authorization, if only to prevent two users making concurrent modifications to the same version of a configuration item. The user completes the authorized modifications to the versions, and submits them for approval and subsequent storage in the software library. The approval procedure will check that only authorized changes have been made and that all such changes have been completed. Quality procedures will be involved in this.

This approach has a problem when a submitted version of a configuration item has been built from other components in the work area. Unless a configuration item is built only from controlled components, it is not under control. It is necessary to show that a configuration item has not been built using components that are not recorded in the software library. If it has been so built, then it will not be possible to control its change. This requires that all dependencies between objects must be known and recorded. This is a particular problem when the programming language in use provides macro and include facilities. Further, a malicious user will have the opportunity to introduce unauthorized changes by modifying the built component after it has been built from controlled components, but before it is submitted. Rebuilding in the software library is one way to overcome the problem. Where possible, only configuration items which have a human-readable representation should be submitted to the software library, since it is possible to find and review changes. Rebuilding requires recording of a complete description of the build process for the configuration item.

A different approach is to require the user to submit the whole environment in which the change occurred. The whole environment becomes immutable. This overcomes the problem of using uncontrolled components, but not the modification of built components.

The physical isolation provided by the controlled area is expensive in both storage and computational costs, but provides the simplest approach unless adequate access controls are provided. Mandatory integrity controls overcome the problem by enabling the domain of a build to be delineated while maintaining the sharing of objects and tools between domains (NATO, 1988).

34.6 Saving space

The recording of versions can consume a great deal of space, and practical computer-based configuration management systems must address the problem by using space-saving differencing techniques as described here, or by using building techniques as described in the next section.

The key space-saving idea of differencing techniques is that if one version has been derived by applying changes to another, then the two versions probably have a great deal of commonality and a small number of differences. The differences between the two versions should occupy less storage than either of the two versions, so space can be saved by retaining just one version and the differences. Of course it must be possible to re-create the discarded version from the retained version and the differences.

34.6.1 Deltas

The set of differences between two versions is called a delta. Where the differences allow the later version to be recovered from the earlier version, the set of differences is called the forward delta. Where the differences allow the earlier version to be recovered from the later version, the set of differences is called the backward delta.

To hold a sequence of versions, the forward deltas can be calculated between the first and second versions, the second and third versions and so on. Only the first version and the forward deltas are retained. To re-create the n-th version the first, second, ... n-1st forward deltas are applied in turn to the retained first version. Using this approach the time to re-create successive versions increases.

A way to address this problem is to merge the deltas into the first version. This technique is used in SCCS (Rochkind, 1975). The merged technique uses tags to indicate that particular records of the file are to be excluded from a particular version (and from all subsequent versions) while other records are to be included in a particular version (and subsequent versions). Any version can be re-created by a single complete pass through this merged file. The re-creation time is constant for all versions. The technique has the drawback that the creation of the merged file is a complicated process.

In his description of RCS, Tichy (1982) notes that unmerged deltas are conceptually simpler and have a significant performance advantage if arranged properly. The most recent version is accessed much more frequently than earlier versions. Therefore the latest version and the backward deltas should be held. Using backward deltas the latest version is immediately accessible and adding a new version is faster than with merged deltas.

A disadvantage of backward deltas, compared to forward deltas, occurs when the sequence of versions branches to create a tree. With backward deltas the latest version of each branch of the tree is held in full. With forward deltas only the root version of the whole tree is held in full. So forward deltas are more space-efficient in the common, practical case in which there is a tree of versions. The problem is overcome in RCS by using backward deltas for one branch of the tree (the trunk). Other branches use forward deltas. The result is that only the trunk benefits from the use of backward deltas; all other branches suffer the access time deficiencies of forward deltas. This is a problem since it is not plain which branch of the tree will become the main line of development as time passes.

Another technique is to generate the differences between the first and each other version. A single application of the re-creation process is sufficient to create any desired version.

Unfortunately the differences become increasingly great, less space is saved, and the re-creation process takes correspondingly longer.

Schemes as in SCCS and RCS are an attempt to minimize the work needed to re-create a desired version while minimizing the space needed to store all of the versions. However, for any version not held in full, the re-creation process must create a new file containing the full representation of the desired version. Where very large versions are concerned it may not be practicable to create full representations of desired versions.

34.6.2 Computing differences

Differences may be computed in two ways, either by comparing two versions for differences, or by generating the differences as part of the editing process. Comparison techniques are the most commonly used for simple data such as text and byte-oriented data. For data with complex structures, generation as a consequence of editing is common.

A comparison algorithm compares two versions of data at some level of detail, the grain. The grain is typically a character (Wagner and Fischer, 1976) or a line of text (Hunt and McIlroy, 1976), although paragraphs, sections, chapters and so on may also be used (Heckel, 1978). The differences are commonly presented in a human readable form, and preferably in the form of editing commands which generate one version when applied to the other.

Probably the most widely used comparison algorithm is diff (Hunt and McIlroy, 1976). The grain of difference in diff is the line. If any character of a line is changed, the whole line is deemed to have changed. Diff calculates the delta as a sequence of editing commands which when applied to the first file generate the second. These editing commands are readable by humans.

This grain of difference is applicable only to data which can be held in line-based files and is inappropriate in many circumstances. For example, a single character insertion at the start of an object code file, which files are often held as fixed length record files, will cause every line of the new file to be different from its predecessor, according to the diff algorithm.

Obst (1987) reports an algorithm which can be used with byte-oriented data. This algorithm can be used for computing the differences between object code files, executable files, graphic data metafiles, and the like, as well as text files. The computed difference is not easily readable by humans, and so the algorithm is more appropriate as part of a delta storage system. The deltas computed by this algorithm are approximately 30% smaller than those from diff; the processing time is similar to diff.

Few differencing techniques exist for structured data.

Mullin (1981) describes the change area differencing technique for b-trees. The central idea is to record a set of updates to a b-tree without altering the original. Any deletion, insertion or other modification of the b-tree will require any original data block of the b-tree to be copied into the change area before modification. Any blocks on the path from the affected block back to and including the root, must be copied to new blocks and modified to refer to each other. This ensures that every change area contains a b-tree root through which the whole b-tree can be accessed. Blocks already in the change area can be updated *in situ*. The differences, as recorded by the change-area, are generated as a direct consequence of the edit of the b-tree.

The technique uses forward deltas. The original, and the original plus the first forward delta (change area), represent the first and second versions of the b-tree. It can represent any number of versions and branches in the version tree.

Severance and Lohman (1976) describe the differential file

technique for databases. When an update is applied to an original version held in some file, updated data is recorded in a difference file and the original file remains unchanged. The delta is created directly as a consequence of the updating mechanism. The original file plus the difference file jointly represent the second version of the data.

In the differential file method it is not necessary to create a complete representation of a version to access values from it. It is only necessary to check whether the required data item is in the corresponding difference file. If it is, then that value of the data item is used; otherwise the value in the previous version is used (and so on recursively). This property of difference files is critical where each version may be very large, or where only small parts of any version need to be accessed.

The differential file technique uses forward deltas. It can record any number of versions and can be used where there are branches in the tree of versions.

The differential file technique suffers, of course, from the drawback of all forward delta where the deltas are not merged. The time taken to access data in any particular version depends upon how many previous versions exist, and how recently the particular data item sought was modified. A rapid way of locating the required data item from amongst the various files of data is needed.

Severance and Lohman suggested the use of Bloom filters as the means of mapping from an identifier of the required data item to its location in the difference file. The SDS2 differencing technique (Alderson, 1988) differs from that of Severance and Lohman by using change area b-trees rather than Bloom filters.

34.7 Merging

Just as the tree of versions of a configuration item may branch in response to a diverging change request, so there may be a desire to merge two versions to create a single new version combining both sets of change requests.

Simple merge operations can be based upon the differences computed between the two versions. The content of the two versions may be classified as that which is in both, that which is in the first but not the second, and that which is in the second but not the first. Unfortunately the merge cannot be achieved by computing the union of these. A change may be achieved equally by deletion or addition. Further, different changes may affect the same part of the content in different ways.

Because of these difficulties merge operations are usually interactive. The merge operation indicates the differences and the user indicates the action to be taken. The merge operation may proceed by taking merging actions and enabling the user to override those decisions where necessary (Leblang and Chase, 1983).

Greater automation can only be achieved at the expense of holding details of each individual change. The principle is illustrated in the SDS2 system (Alderson, 1988). Here each modification action is recorded in a log of operations, which also records the value of the modified part of the content before and after the modification. True conflicts can be isolated and all other modifications performed automatically by the merge process.

A common case, in which automatic rather than interactive merging may be possible, is error correction propagation. This occurs when an error is found in a version, and that error can be traced back to some ancestor, and forward again from there through other variants. Here we wish the error correction to be propagated to each of the affected variants. It will generally be possible to isolate the change required to correct the error.

34.8 Building a configuration item from its components

Many configuration items are built from component configuration items. The component configuration items required are determined by the configuration, the versions of the component configuration items are determined by the build list. For any given configuration, the instructions to assemble the configuration item will be the same.

The building instructions need not be simple. They can involve macro processing and compilation of many source texts linking with many different object code libraries and many other processes, using many options of the processors in a specific order. If building is to take place in the controlled area, the build instructions must be part of the configuration of the item to be built and they must be precise. Fortunately, because the tools used in the building process are computer-based, it is feasible to formalize the build instructions so that building is automated.

For each configuration item that is built, a formal description of the build instructions is provided. These build instructions are applied to the versions of the component configuration items determined by the build lists to generate a particular version of the built configuration item. The component versions themselves may be built, in which case they will have their own build instructions, and so on recursively. Eventually the recursion must terminate with component versions which are not built. This ability to define the build instructions for a given configuration has two direct benefits:

1. Formal build instructions plus the build list for a version of a configuration item may require considerably less storage space than the version itself. The effect is enhanced where the same build instructions apply to a number of versions. This provides the opportunity to save storage space by saving the build instructions and the build list rather than the version. This of course is at the expense of rebuilding the version when it is needed.

2. When a new version of a component configuration item is created, the new version of the built component can be created automatically whenever its configuration remains unchanged.

The second benefit is obtained by allowing rules to be used in the build list in the place of specific versions. The rules are evaluated at the time that the build instructions are executed and the corresponding configuration item is bound to the selected version. The most common rule is that the most recently created version is to be used. More generally the selection rule may be expressed as a predicate, and the first version found to satisfy the predicate is used (Estublier, 1985; Belkhatir and Estublier, 1987). Even more generally the names used in the build instructions may be purely symbolic. The rules supplied in the build list then select not only the version but the configuration item itself that is to be bound to the symbolic name (Alderson *et al.*, 1986).

Recent systems have taken two approaches to building. One uses the two-stage process of selecting the required versions and then undertaking the build. In the other, the selection of versions occurs dynamically as the build proceeds. Here, the selection of a particular version of a configuration item dynamically constrains the choice of versions of component configuration items. The constraints are expressed as rules.

34.9 Programming in the large

The selection of a consistent set of versions for a build is a key aspect. Proving such consistency is a problem of great difficulty requiring knowledge of the semantics of all of the versions and of the desired system. Approaches to this problem have been made using special languages.

Formal descriptions of the assembly of a configuration item from its components have implicit within them the structure of the configuration item. Just as a compiler can check the internal consistency of a program text, so there is a value in a language to define the structure and a compiler to check that script. Describing such structures has been termed programming in the large and the appropriate languages are module interconnection languages. Programming in the small concerns defining individual components and the appropriate languages are programming languages (DeRemer and Kron, 1976).

A module interconnection language provides facilities to describe decomposition into components and the interfaces provided by and required of those components. It defines the interfaces of the modules so that the consistency may be checked. Where types can be ascribed to components, building rules can be associated with those types. Consequently module interconnection languages should be as rich in type and abstraction definition as other programming languages. Module interconnection languages then form a sound basis for system building when combined with building rules and build lists (Sommerville and Thompson, 1986).

34.9.1 Programming in the large with Ada

The Ada language (ANSI, 1983) has been designed to address the issues of programming in the small and programming in the large.

Ada provides for decomposition and interface specification through the packaging of data types and sub-programs. The separate compilation facility then provides the same degree of checking between packages as within individual packages. The Ada *with* clauses explicitly define dependencies between the packages. A compilation unit depends upon the units mentioned in its with clauses. These dependencies influence the order of compilation (and recompilation) of compilation units. When a compilation unit is compiled, it must be compiled in a context in which the compilation units upon which it depends have already been compiled. The Ada compiler checks the consistency of the interfaces used against those provided.

The context for a compilation is an Ada Program Library. An Ada compilation unit is compiled into a given library. If the compilation unit is changed and then recompiled into the library, any previous compiled version of that unit (the library unit) is overwritten and any library unit which depended upon it is invalidated. Invalidation forces recompilation so that consistency can be checked. An Ada Program Library holds a consistent set of versions of compilation units.

An Ada Program Library system can be constructed which allows compiled units to be shared between program libraries (Pierce, 1987), so avoiding unnecessary compilations. A shared unit must be protected from destruction even if the owner recompiles it. Sharing is achieved by explicitly acquiring the unit. This implies that all the units on which it depends are also acquired, unless this has already happened. The acquire facility is seen as the normal way in which Ada units and subsystems are combined into larger systems and software releases. Acquisition also has the effects that any previous compiled version of an acquired version of an acquired unit in the acquiring library is overwritten and any compiled unit in that library which depended upon it is invalidated.

For Ada it is natural to relate the Ada Program Library to the configuration management system, since the Program Library contains both a record of all of the compiled units of the Ada program and (implicit) instructions on how to build the program. (A correct order of recompilation can be determined.) An

Ada Program Library effectively determines a consistent set of versions of compiled units which are components of some configuration item. It is natural therefore to have versions of Program Libraries.

Ada is deficient in that the Ada Program Library need not include (reference to) the source code, the documentation, the linked system, the test specifications and so on. For configuration management purposes the Ada Program Library should record which (version of the) compilation unit was compiled to create a particular library unit. Further it should be possible to determine which Ada programs were created by linking which Ada Program Library (Pierce, 1987).

There have been proposals for one Ada Program Library to contain a number of consistent sets of versions of the component configuration items (Dausmann, 1987). The required version of the configuration item can be obtained from the library. This proposal follows the configuration management practice of defining a configuration item by a configuration (the Ada compilation units), the build list (the versions of the compilation units) and the build instructions (the order of compilation).

34.9.2 Recording system structure in an object management system

Configuration management must underpin all stages of the life cycle. This is best achieved when the configuration management system is part of the environment in which all development tools are executed. Integrated Project Support Systems (IPSEs) are being developed which enable this (PCTE; NATO, 1988; CAIS, 1988). The object management system at the heart of the IPSE is used to model all of the data manipulated by the development tools. Such modelling can incorporate configurations, versions, change records, and so on. The existence of versions can be made transparent to development tools such as compilers and editors. Special configuration management tools manipulate these configuration management data types (Alderson *et al*, 1986; Thomas, 1988). This provides flexibility to deal with a wide range of structures, to query those structures, and to associate other information with those structures. However the approach does not address the consistency of interfaces within the structure.

34.9.3 Software design methods

A different approach to programming in the large is the use of software design methods such as HOOD (1988) and MASCOT3 (JIMCOM, 1987). Such methods determine and describe the decomposition of the system into a hierarchy of components, and the relationships between those components. Both HOOD and MASCOT3 describe the interface and the body of each component, and can check the consistency of required and provided interfaces. MASCOT3 incorporates a notion of component status corresponding to the degree of consistency between levels of decomposition. Ada compilation units, for example, can be derived automatically from such designs, so that the benefits of the Ada Program Library also accrue.

34.10 Alternative approach to configuration management

The separation into configuration (the template) and build list (the component versions) to define the version of a configuration item is a major feature of current configuration management practice. However, it is not mandatory. Configuration management can be based on just the ideas of a configuration item and the building of a configuration item from its component configuration items.

For example, an Ada Program Library can be considered as a configuration item which is built from component configuration items by the process of compilation. The library contains the consistent set of component configuration items. This uses only the configuration item and the build instructions, and so corresponds to removing the ideas of configuration and build list, and therefore version. This suggests an alternative model of software evolution as follows.

Every system is created by developing a specification of the system and then refining this specification until it is efficiently executable. This system is then released for use by others. Once released, the system becomes immutable.

Errors may be reported in this released system, and enhancements may be requested. These collectively require a new system to be specified. This new system has a specification close to that of the released system. It is a distinct specification in its own right, and is developed as such. The released system is not modified to create the new system. Rather, the new system is developed by reusing components of the releases system (and perhaps other existing systems).

Every system is an independent entity and so there is no problem of name binding and no need to consider the consistency of arbitrary collections of versions. The only relationship it has with other systems is that it may reuse some components of one or more of them, on economic grounds. Reuse is a technique for generating new systems cheaply.

Elements of this approach are discussed in the context of immutable stores by Walpole (1988) and are now appearing in configuration management such as Sun's NSE, Softool's CCC/DM and PACT's VMCS, which are described below.

34.11 Tools

Although configuration management is a problem for every size of project, large scale introduces quantities of data containing complex interrelationships which overwhelm manual procedures. Examples have been reported from the oil industry of a single rig development commonly requiring 50 000 components and 15 000 documents, and from the telecommunications industry of 300 000 documents relating to a switching network product. Such scale demands automated assistance. Tools have been developed and this section describes some of them.

34.11.1 CADES

CADES (McGuffin *et al.*, 1979) was created by ICL to develop and maintain a very large operating system.

CADES consist of a heirarchic design method and tools in support of that method. The method, known as structural modelling, uses top-down data-driven refinement. At each level of refinement, the data of the previous level is partitioned and further refined. The processes which control and use the data, the holons, are then defined. The holon at the previous level is refined into holons each addressing one of the partitions of the refined data. A holon may only manipulate data items which are refinements of data items manipulated by its parent, and which are owned by the holon or by another holon which makes them available through an interface. Only one definition of such interfaces is maintained for use by both called and calling holons.

The hierarchies of data structures and holons, together with any attributes, are represented by records, and these and their relationships are stored in a database. This holds only authorized data. Bulk data, such as source text, might not be held in the database but referenced from it. Each record and each relationship may exist in different versions. A new version inherits the attributes of its predecessor. A new version of a product inherits unchanged versions of its components.

The database is partitioned into regions, in each of which a sub-product can be developed separately. A new version of the total product is created from a version from each of the regions. These regions are subject to access control. Generally users may access only one version from one region.

The refinement of data and holons proceeds until they can be defined using a programming language. These records are the leaves of the decomposition hierarchy. The Environment Processor extracts from the database all holons, data and interfaces necessary for the compilation of a module. Modules are then collected together, as determined by the hierarchy to form products.

Fault reports are held in the CADES database related to the holon in error. Solutions to faults are also recorded and related to the fault and to the holon containing the correction. Changes to the design are approved through a formal change authorization procedure, which requires that the data structures and holons of the parent of those being considered for change are also reviewed.

34.11.2 NSE

NSE (Network Software Environment) is a product from Sun Microsystems Inc., for the Sun Workstation.

NSE is a software development environment, which exploits the parallelism possible in a network of workstations. It prevents concurrent operations from interfering and can distribute multiple builds across multiple workstations.

NSE provides environments which contain typed objects. Objects are manipulated by type-specific tools and type-non-specific commands. NSE also maintains links between objects. The principal object types are:

1. Files, which may be source or derived, and may have versions.
2. Targets, which are compound objects, grouping together a derived file and the files needed to derive it, including a make file.
3. Components, which are compound objects, grouping related objects together making them similar to directories in hierarchical file store.
4. Link databases, which store links.

The types are built-in and new types may be added.

Targets are manipulated using the tools make and dbxtool. Make builds the derived file from the dependency files under control of a make file. NSE maintains targets in response to the addition or deletion of dependency files from which the target is derived. Dbxtool is a symbolic debugger.

Objects can have histories composed of a sequence of immutable revisions. They also have working editions which are modifiable. Files may also have versions, which record a finer grained history of changes.

The user may preserve a working component. This causes creation of a new component revision and (recursively) of a new revision of each object within the working component. Such revisions may be hard (retained forever) or soft (reclaimable when obsolete).

NSE enforces an acquire, modify, reconcile sequence for development. An environment is acquired, creating a new working environment containing working components in the acquired environment. Modifications are made and verified in the context of the new environment. Then the new environment is reconciled with the original environment, creating a new revision containing copies of all modified objects.

This approach allows parallel development of the same

revision of a component. A reconcile is only permitted if it does not conflict with previous reconciles with the same revision. Where there is a conflict with two developers modifying the same object, a resolution must occur. An automatic resolution is provided for conflicting source file objects. This classifies differences as compatible if they do not affect the same region of the file, and conflicting otherwise. All compatible lines are merged into a third file; conflicting lines must be manually resolved.

34.11.3 DSEE

DSEE, the Domain Software Engineering Environment, is a product of Apollo Computer, Inc. for Apollo workstations. DSEE (Leblang and McLean, 1985) is an integrated environment offering source code control, task management and dependency tracking, as well as configuration management.

The source code control, provided by the DSEE History Manager, manipulates versions and variants of elements. An element usually corresponds to a single source module or compilation unit. Elements are grouped into libraries. Each time an element is revised a new version of it is created. The versions of an element are formed into a tree, which has a main branch and variant branches. Each branch consists of a chronological sequence of versions. A merge operation is available to merge the latest versions of two branches. This operation creates a new version of one of these branches and terminates the other branch. The merge is an interactive operation. The merge automates much of the process, but the user can override decisions of the merge process, and edit the resulting file as the merge proceeds.

The versions of an element are stored in a single file using interleaved incremental deltas. Intermixed control records allow the text of any version to be constructed in a single pass over the file. DSEE uses a variation of the difference technique of Heckel (1978). DSEE also saves space by compressing leading blanks in text files. This combination of techniques enables an element with five to ten versions to be stored in the space required by a single clear text copy of the element (Leblang and Chase, 1983).

Operations using the element are given the latest versions of the main branch by default. To access other versions (possibly of other branches) a version map must be created for each process, which specifies the version of each element to be used.

To make changes to an element, a user must reserve it. The reserve operation makes the user a private copy of the latest version of the branch being amended. Having changed this, the user replaces it, creating a new latest version. The reserve and replace operations require the user to give reasons for using the operation. These replies form a history of the element which may be inspected. The ability to determine the differences between versions is also provided.

The DSEE Configuration Manager builds systems from desired element versions. A system is the unit of configuration management. A system is defined using a block-structured system model language. The system model gives a static description of the structure of a system in terms of components and the hierarchical relationships between them. A translation rule defines how a component is built from its constituent elements and from other components. A translation rule is a script specifying the translations (e.g. compilation) that are to be applied to the inputs. The translators can be Apollo- or user-supplied.

The particular versions of elements to be used in a particular build of a system are specified in a configuration thread. A configuration thread is an ordered list of rules. A rule specifies which version of which element is required. The element may be specified absolutely or by pattern matching. The version may be specified absolutely or as the result of evaluating a conditional expression. The Configuration Manager uses the version given by the first rule that it finds to be satisfied. The result of evaluating a configuration thread is a bound configuration thread. This specifies explicit versions for the elements used, and the translation rules for each of the components built. The bound configuration thread is a complete specification for building a configuration of the system.

The built components are stored in derived object pools. The Configuration Manager stores the bound configuration thread with each built component. This enables built components to be reused. The system model and the configuration thread specify the system to be built. The Configuration Manager derives the required bound configuration thread and then undertakes the translations in the order required by the system model. A component is only built if it does not already exist in the derived object pool.

A system model may use the same element many times to build different components. Changes to this element could cause all of those components to be rebuilt. This could be unnecessary. For example, the element may be an 'include' file to which declarations have been added. Only the components which use the new declarations need actually be rebuilt. The user may avoid unnecessary rebuilding by declaring to the Configuration Manager that the new version of the element is equivalent to a previous version for the building of certain components. An element may also be declared to be non-critical for the building of a component. Any built component that differs only in the versions of non-critical elements used to build it, can be reused.

To optimize building performance, the Configuration Manager keeps a record for each user of the most recent version numbers of each element in the system. This is updated whenever a later version is created. The previous desired bound configuration thread is also retained. The new desired bound configuration thread can be derived from the previous one and the record of latest versions.

The DSEE Release Manager is used to produce releases of built components. A release consists of the built components, the bound configuration thread, the versions of the elements used, tools used in the build, and user-supplied information about the release.

34.11.4 Rational's CMVC

CMVC (Morgan, 1988) is a component of the Rational Programming Environment, a product of Rational Inc. The Rational Programming Environment has been designed to provide support for systems written in Ada throughout the life cycle. CMVC addresses system decomposition, library management, configuration control and source control.

In CMVC, systems are decomposed into subsystems that can be developed, tested and released independently. A subsystem is composed of elements, each of which may have mutiple generations. A view specifies the generation of each element in a subsystem. Thus a view specifies the generation of the Ada source of each element in the subsystem.

Each view has an associated Ada Program Library. Compilation in this library ensures the consistency of the generations of the source units. Compilation dependencies are derived from the source units in the view. Changing a view will cause recompilation of the elements whose generation has been changed, and their dependent elements. Where the same generation occurs in more than one view, CMVC will copy the compiled unit from one view to another to reduce recompilations.

Subsystems have spec views and load views. Spec views contain only the Ada specifications exported by the subsystem. Load views contain the specifications and bodies of the subsystem. A view may import a spec view of another subsystem to obtain visibility of its units. Load views may be modified and compiled without causing recompilation of subsystems which imported the related spec view. Subsystem spec and load views extend the Ada distinction between specification and implementation to groups of related units.

Subsystems generally contain multiple load views, each representing an alternative implementation. An activity specifies one load view for each subsystem in a system. The activity is used by the linker-loader when creating programs. Execution is possible provided that each load view implements at least the specifications in the corresponding spec view.

Each element develops through time ordered sequences of generations. There may be many parallel sequences for each element. To produce a new generation of an element, a copy of a generation from a sequence must be checked-out by a view, so establishing an exclusive right to produce a new generation of that sequence. The copy is edited then checked-in as the new generation. The generations of an element form a time ordered sequence. CMVC retains a history of each element, including user comments. Generations are stored using deltas, if they are not used in any view.

A development path is a time ordered sequence of views which represents the development history of a subsystem. The latest view in the sequence is the working view. The previous views, releases, cannot be changed. Parallel development paths are supported. A release may be a released view, which contains both source and executables, a released configuration which contains only source texts, or a code-only view, which contains only executables.

34.11.5 ISTAR

ISTAR (Stenning, 1986) is a product of Imperial Software Technology.

ISTAR is an integrated project support environment based around the contractual model. The contractual model of software development utilizes the hierarchic decomposition of a system into components. A project has a contract to develop the desired system. This project (the client) lets sub-contracts to sub-projects (the contractors) to develop components of the system, and so on recursively.

The client provides the contractor with a specification of the required deliverables. The specification, which may be modified by the client, also contains acceptance criteria. The contractor develops the deliverables, and when they are complete, delivers them to the client. The client then accepts them against the acceptance criteria.

Each contract is represented by one contract database consisting of a contractual area and a number of work areas. The contractual area is the means of communicating between contracts. Development is undertaken in work areas, which are private to a contract.

Configuration items are the units which are passed between contracts. A configuration item is a set of transfer items. The transfer item is the basic unit of information, such as a source text. The specification of the contract and any subsequent change requests are recorded as configuration items. Deliverable configuration items must be recorded in the contractual area before they can be passed to another contract. Within the contractual area, configuration items and transfer items are immutable. A new contract item is created in the contractual area; this may be a successor of an existing configuration item. The transfer items of this contractual item are developed in the work areas, then exported to the contractual area. Existing transfer items may be copied into the work areas.

In ISTAR, tools are organized into workbenches, which can operate on particular transfer item types within a particular type of work area. ISTAR provides two configuration management workbenches. The component management workbench provides submission and control of problem reports, gives access to version histories, and allows control of preferred versions of items. The build workbench enables building of new transfer items from existing transfer items. The required building process is described and a list of the transfer items to be input is provided. The required transfer items are built and a record of that build is stored. This build process can make use of existing transfer items to minimize rebuilding.

34.11.6 EPOS

EPOS (Lempp, 1986) is a product of the University of Stuttgart. This product is marketed by GPP.

EPOS views system development as a sequence of transformations of representations. These transformations may be manual (e.g. editing) or automatic (e.g. compilation). Each representation may have a number of objects, each of which may exist in a number of versions (representing changes through time) and variants (representing different states at the same time). Any object of any degree of simplicity or complexity may be subjected to version and variant control.

EPOS supports the identification of baselines and the control of change to those baselines. A baseline is a recorded state which forms a fixed reference configuration. Consistency, completeness and administrative checks can be applied to a baseline to ensure that all changes applicable to the baseline have been completed. The baseline status accounting includes the documentation of all baselines, all changes proposals and their current status, and identifies individuals responsible. A baseline may be frozen, causing all the baseline items to become read-only.

Change proposals may be recorded. Some automated assistance is provided to identify objects affected by the change. Approval or rejection of a change is recorded. A technical and management framework is then set up within which a new baseline may be developed to reflect the approved changes. A history of all changes is retained.

34.11.7 Adele

Adele (Estublier, 1985; Belkhatir and Estublier, 1987) is a product distributed by the CRIL company, France.

Adele provides a database for holding programs, together with commands for manipulating that database.

Adele is based on the notions of interface, which defines the resources provided, and body, which implements those resources. An interface may have no body, for example, it may define a type or a constant. An interface may depend upon other interfaces, as may a body.

A family is the set of interface versions of the same interface. Each interface versions, may have versions of its implementation. A revision is a minor modification of a version of an implementation. Revisions are held using deltas.

Each interface version may present several interface views, which limit access to some part of the interface or define the same resources in a different programming language.

Families, interfaces and bodies are all composed of objects, which are independent sequential files. For example, an implementation consists of revisions, a history, a manual, documents, and so on. The history of an object records all operations applied to an object, such as the creation of new revisions and modification of documentation, together with the date, user and a comment.

The manual holds user and system defined information about an object. The user information includes a list of constraints that the object places on its environment, and attributes recording characteristics of the object. The system information contains system maintained attributes. Objects are identified by a combination of the family name and a predicate over the attributes. The desired object is identified by evaluating the predicate within the context of the specified family.

Adele enables direct relations to be held between objects. Some relationships, such as the dependency relationship, can be maintained automatically, others must be maintained manually. The dependency relationship defines an acyclic graph. It is used to build configurations and manage side-effects. A configuration is the set of bodies or other configurations needed to implement an interface. A configuration is defined by a composition list. The composition list contains exactly one body or configuration for each family in the transitive closure of the dependency relationship of the interface of the composition. Adele does not require the composition list to be specified explicitly. Rather it may be specified by a mixture of explicit, conditional and default selection.

A side-effect occurs on the source object of a relationship when the target object of the relationship is subject to a modifying or deleting action. The side-effect can be detected before the action occurs, immediately upon completion of the action, or upon access of the source object. The user may request a list of the side-effects pertaining to an object. For each case a response may be invoked, allowing users to be warned of the impact of proposed actions, to cause automatic rebuilding of affected objects, to inform users of changes, and so on.

A key idea, that a configuration is an abstraction, is realised through partitions. A partition is the set of families defined by the transitive closure of the dependency relationship from the partition's root family. A configuration is then a set of versions of the interfaces of the partition. A partition is therefore an abstraction of a configuration. A partition may be considered as a single interface whose versions are its configurations. The visibility of the interfaces of a partition may be controlled, as may the visibility of attributes associated with them.

A work space is a sub-tree of the dependency tree defined by a family. A work space belongs to a user and gives a context within which that user issues commands. The user may operate on local objects, within the work space, or objects visible from the root family. A user may have many work spaces, many of which may apply to the same sub-tree.

Objects are never directly modified in the database. A user must reserve the object; this locks the object and directly dependent objects. The user reads the object into a file, modifies it, then updates the database with the updated object. A list of Adele commands may be applied to all elements of a configuration, for example, to copy all elements into local file store so that they may be link-edited.

34.11.8 Lifespan

Lifespan is a product from Yard available for DEC's VAX/VMS.

Lifespan is based around a database of modules, which may be any material of value to the project, such as documents, source code, and executable code. Modules may be linked together hierarchically into packages. Packages are themselves modules and so may be grouped into hierarchies. The database also contains design change requests and design change orders, for the control of change. Specific users are authorized to propose changes and to approve the entry of modules into approved store. Lifespan provides software production status reports and software defects status reports for tracking the progress of change.

The database retains information about the modules. Each version of each module is held as a separate VMS file; deltas are not used. The database has references to files in a VMS directory structure which contain modules. The names of these files are system-generated. For security purposes, the files are held in encrypted form and Cyclic Redundancy Check numbers for the files are also held in the database. Lifespan provides facilities to track old versions which have been backed up off-line. Lifespan does not support variants.

The database is divided into an unapproved store, which contains all modules under development, and an approved store, which contains all modules passed by quality control.

All modules held by Lifespan have a header. This has a fixed structure and a language of its own. It is initially supplied by the user and subsequently updated by the user, and automatically updated by Lifespan. Data from the header is also recorded in the database. For text files the header is stored at the start of the file. For binary files the header is stored separately. For other modules (e.g. hardware) only the heading is stored by Lifespan. The header provides a unique identifier for the module and fields from it can be used to check that modules are being entered into the approved store correctly.

Lifespan provides software performance reports for reporting problems, design changes for reporting change requests, and software status reports to notify clients of completed changes. A design change is assessed by a user who compiles a list of affected modules on the design change form. Each of these modules has an owner; they are polled by Lifespan for their agreement to the change. The modules to be changed are booked out of the approved store into the unapproved store. There is no locking of such items. The module is changed and then it is booked into the approved store again.

Software is built by users in the unapproved store. The versions of the files to be used are specified in a special source module and Lifespan obtains a copy of all of these versions from approved store into unapproved store. Typically one such file will be a command file to perform the build.

The product has facilities for recording which customers have which versions of which products.

Tools consist of a database server that accesses the Lifespan database and data files, and user processes that interface to the user and communicate with the database server. A procedural interface exists to allow the user to produce further tools. Lifespan provides an internal mail system between Lifespan users.

34.11.9 Expertware's CMF

The Expertware Configuration Management Facility (CMF) is a product of Expertware, Inc., available from Logsys. CMF consists of the Configuration Management Toolkit (CMT) and the Documentation Support Toolkit (DST). CMF is available for Unix and VAX/VMS.

CMF is a set of related tools, which manipulate data within a hierarchic file store divided into five areas:

1. The controlled project area contains all controlled software and inventory lists which define the content of each product.
2. The documentation area, which contains all versions of documents, and system problem reports.
3. The working area contains all developing software and documentation.
4. The test area contains all executable code under test.
5. The configuration management area provides a temporary storage area when transferring files between controlled and working areas.

An end item is built from one or more (hierarchic) levels of components. Components are built from files. Files are either source or binary. Versions of source files are stored using SCCS (Rochkind, 1975). Each version of a binary is stored in a separate file store file. CMT supports branching to form a version tree.

Files can be withdrawn from the controlled area in two modes: for reading or for update. The latter uses locking to prevent further withdrawals for update.

Software will normally be built with the aid of the make tool (Feldman, 1979) in an area within the controlled area. CMT provides some assistance with creating the make files. Uncontrolled files can be included in a build to aid development. The user withdraws a set of files, performs the make and then stores away the by-products. There is a mechanism to store sequences of commands and execute them on request.

CMT provides on-line creation and updating of system problem reports. It is possible to cross refer from system problem reports to one or more configuration items. The relevant system problem report numbers appear in reports concerning those items.

DST provides a means of constructing templates for forms. The user can call-up a particular template and fill in the predefined fields, so creating a computer-based form. The completed forms are held in machine-readable form by DST.

A project may define a set of forms specific to its needs. System-supplied or user written validation rules may be applied to the fields of the forms. There is no supplied interface to aid validation against the CMT file store. It is possible to cause data from selected forms to appear in some reports generated by CMT.

A comprehensive set of form templates and document generation scripts to suit DOD-STD-2167 and NASA standards is provided.

DST also provides an nroff-like (Kernigan et al., 1978) text processing facility for generating documentation. It can include text produced by other means (e.g. another text processor).

34.11.10 Softool's CCC

The CCC Change and Configuration Control Environment is a product of Softool Corporation. It is available for VAX systems. CCC is available in native, command-driven, form and in the menu-driven, CCC/DM form. The CCC/DM form is tailored from the native form, currently omitting tailoring facilities, database integrity checking, and control over compression, encryption and archiving. The CCC/DM form is described here.

The CCC/DM database is a hierarchy consisting of systems composed of releases. Releases may be hierarchically decomposed into (up to 15) levels. Levels are composed of items which contain machine readable data such as source code and executable binary. Each release represents a version of the desired system and the system evolves through a series of releases. Closing a release freezes the current version and creates a new release.

Each release is represented by four parallel configurations. The development configuration contains the development version of the release. The testing configuration contains the version of the release under test. The approved configuration contains the approved version of the release and the production configuration contains the version of the system used in the production environment. When a configuration is closed, all approved changes are incorporated into the production configuration which is preserved, the development and test configurations are deleted, and the approved configuration is copied to form the development, test, approved and production configurations of the new release.

To modify items in the CCC database a project must be created, change requests assigned to that project, and staff assigned to the change requests. Each change request specifies the changes to be made to one or more specified items. Items are checked out into VMS files, where they are modified. The modified items are checked in to the development configuration. When all items relating to a change request have been modified, they are copied into the test configuration from where they may be checked out into VMS files for testing. When a change request is approved, the related items are copied from the test configuration into the approved configuration.

A journal records all transactions against the database and a log file records all responses made by CCC. The database is accessed only through a database server which prevents unauthorized access and modification. Specified users are accorded selected access privileges to each data structure.

A second Softool product, CAC/2167A, provides automated assistance in complying with DOD-STD-2167A and can be used in conjunction with CCC.

34.11.11 PACT's VMCS

PACT (PCTE Added Common Tools) is a project funded under the Esprit initiative of the Commission of the European Community. One problem being addressed by PACT is that of providing a common version management service for tools running on PCTE. This is addressed by the Version Management Common Service (VMCS).

PCTE's object management system records the contents of files as the contents of objects, and allows attributes of objects and relationships between them to be recorded. PACT requires transparency of the version service in which tools may access the contents and attributes of objects and the relationships between them without specifying the desired version. This necessitates that the required versions are implied by the context. Without this property the many existing PCTE tools (and Unix tools) would be unable to benefit from the service unless they were modified.

An object is determined to be a version if it is the destination of a versioned link, a relationship which has the attribute version. Versions are related to each other by predecessor and successor relationships which are set automatically when new versions are created. Versions that are the destinations of predecessor relationships are stable; they cannot be modified.

A composite object is a collection of objects, consisting of an origin object and destination objects. The destination objects are those objects in the transitive closure of the composition relationships from the origin object. All relationships between objects of the composite object are called internal links. All relationships between objects of the composite object and other objects are called external links.

A configuration is a composite object whose relationships are not versioned. Such an object determines particular objects without reference to versioning by virtue of its composition relationships. An object may be a version by virtue of the versioned relationship it has with some object, and it may belong to a configuration by virtue of an unversioned composition relationship. Therefore, a configuration may act as the context which gives transparent access to versions. A version may belong to many configurations. Composite objects themselves may be versions, giving rise to versions of a configuration.

VMCS provides four operations for manipulating composite objects and versions.

The revise operation creates a new version from an existing version. The new version has a copy of the content of the previous version, which becomes stable as a result of the predecessor relationship to it from the new version. The version attribute of any versioning relationship pointing to the new version has a value one greater than for the corresponding relationship of the previous version. If the revised object is a composite object, all of the objects in the composite object are also revised. Internal links in the previous composite object are duplicated in the new composite object, and external links corresponding to those of the previous composite object are established for the new composite object.

The partial revise operation creates a new composite object in which only specified objects are revised.

The snapshot operation is similar to the revise operation except that the newly created version is the destination of the predecessor relationship and so stabilized.

The copy operation is similar to the revise operation in that the object and, if it is a composite object, all of its objects are duplicated, but no versioned relationships are attached to any of the new objects.

VMCS may save storage space by using differencing techniques applied to the content of objects which have predecessor-successor relationships. Where there is no difference the objects may share the content.

34.11.12 SCCS

SCCS (Source Code Control System) is a product of Bell Telephone Laboratories (Rochkind, 1975). It is available for Unix.

SCCS is a tool for controlling changes to text files. It provides facilities to store, update and retrieve any version of a text file, control access to that file, and record which user created each version, when and for what reason.

SCCS stores the versions and all information relating to them in a single file called the s-file. SCCS uses the differencing technique described earlier to reduce the storage space required. SCCS provides operations to:

1. Create an s-file containing the first version of the text file.
2. Read a version from the s-file.
3. Read a version from the s-file and reserve that version for editing (so preventing concurrent editing of that version).
4. Create a new version as a result of that edit.

SCCS also provides reports of the content of an s-file.

The versions are identified by a two part number consisting of the release number and the level number, (e.g. 2.12). Release numbers are allocated sequentially from 1, and level numbers are allocated sequentially from 1 within each release number. Having commenced a new release it is not possible to add a new level to the previous release. However it is possible to create a new branch so forming a tree of versions. The branch is identified by the number of the version from which it commenced (e.g. 2.12). Versions within a branch are again numbered using release and version numbers (e.g. 1.4), the version being identified by the combination of these (e.g. 2.12.1.4). Thus two further numbers are added each time a further branch occurs. A version may also be identified by its date and time of creation.

34.11.13 RCS

The Revision Control System (RCS) [RCS] is available for Unix.

RCS manages the revision of text files using the differencing technique described earlier. RCS provides a facility to check-in a new revision of a file. The user may specify the branch of the revision tree to which the new revision is to be appended. Revisions are given hierarchic numerical identifications (e.g. 2.1.4); the final integer specifies the revision, the preceding numbers specify the branch. RCS supplies the next revision number on the branch, when a revision is checked in. The date and time of the check-in, the user responsible, and a comment solicited from the user are retained with the computed differences. A state is also retained. This state is initially experimental and may be promoted to stable or released.

Revisions are checked-out if they are to be used. The revision number, date, author and state may be used in combination to retrieve a revision. A user must have checked-out a revision to check-in its successor.

34.11.14 Make

Make is a product of Bell Telephone Laboratories, available for Unix.

Make is a program that can generate objects or regenerate them after any of their components have changed. It processes a script, the make file, which describes how to build an object from its components. Make can generate an object that does not yet exist or regenerate an object any of whose components have changed since the object was last generated. Make uses the rules in the make file to regenerate the object. Default rules are provided for some common cases.

The basic mechanism of Make is to examine the components of the target object, ensuring that they exist and are up-to-date by treating each of them as targets, and then generating the target if it is older than any of its components. Make is therefore a recursive process which uses the existence and the time of the most recent modification of each object to determine whether it needs to be generated.

This currency test of Make may not always be the most appropriate. Other implementations of the basic building mechanism using different currency tests are in use.

Make is not aware of versions. However it can be used in conjunction with SCCS. This is achieved by having a Make rule that uses SCCS to create from s-files any text files that do not exist. This rule will read the latest version of each text file. Before termination all such text files should once again be removed so that the next execution of Make will retrieve the latest versions. This has the drawback that any object built in this way will always be rebuilt even when its components have not changed, since the retrieved versions will appear to have been just created.

34.12 Conclusion

As the short survey of tools shows, a wide spectrum of tools is available to assist with, and to varying extents automate, elements of configuration management. These tools have achieved varying degrees of acceptance. Tools such as SCCS and Make, which address lower level concerns, are used far more widely than those which interface with the configuration control procedures of an organization. This might be a reflection of the difficulty of integrating tools with existing procedures when there are no commonly accepted definitions of the concepts that they manipulate.

The availability of object management systems should improve both the degree of automation provided by configuration management tools and ease their integration with existing procedures. Object management systems facilitate the recording and manipulation of the relationships between items and with the change records which are key to successful configuration management. The data modelling capabilities of object management systems will facilitate the integration with existing procedures. These capabilities hold the promise of greatly improved automated support for configuration management.

34.13 References

Alderson, A. (1988) A space-efficient technique for recording versions of data. *Software Engineering Journal*, 3, 240–246

Alderson, A. Bott, M. F. and Falla, M. E. (1986) The Eclipse Object Management System. *Software Engineering Journal*, 1, 39–42

ANSI (1983) *Reference Manual for the Ada Programming Language*, ANSI/MIL-STD 1815A

ANSI/IEEE (1983a) *IEEE Standard for Software Configuration Management Plans*, ANSI/IEEE

ANSI/IEEE (1983b) *IEEE Standard Glossary for Software Engineering Terminology*, ANSI/IEEE

Belkhatir, N. and Estublier, J. (1987) Software management constraints and action triggering in the Adele program database. *1st European Software Engineering Conference, September*, 47–55

Bersoff, E. H. (1984) Elements of software configuration management. *IEEE Transactions on Software Engineering*, **SE-10**, 79–87

BSI (1984) *Configuration management of computer-based systems*, British Standards Institution

Buckle, J. K. (1982) *Software Configuration Management*, The McMillan Press

CAIS (1988) *Common Ada Programming Support Environment (APSE) Interface Set (CAIS), (Revision A)*, Proposed Military Standard DOD-STD-1838A

Dausmann, M. (1987) Version control and separate compilation in Ada. In *Ada components: libraries and tools*, (ed. S. Tafvelin), Proceedings of the Ada-Europe International Conference, Stockholm, 26–28 May 1987, Cambridge University Press

DeRemer, F. and Kron, H. H. (1976) Programming-in-the-large versus programming in the small. *IEEE Transactions on Software Engineering*, SE-2, 80–86

Estublier, J. E. (1985) A configuration manager: the Adele database of programs. Workshop on software engineering environments for programming in the large, Harwichport, Massachusetts

Feldman, S. I. (1979) Make – A program for maintaining computer programs. *Software Practice and Experience*, 9, 255–265

Heckel, P. (1978) A technique for isolating differences between files. *CACM*, April

(1988) *HOOD Manual*, Version 2.2, ESTEC

Huff, K. E. (1981) A database model for effective configuration management in the programming environment. In *International Conference on Software Engineering*, IEEE, pp. 54–61

Hunt, J. W. and McIlroy, M. D. (1976) An algorithm for differential file comparison. *Comp. Sci.Tech.Report. No. 41*, Bell Laboratories

JIMCOM (1987) *The Official Handbook of Mascot*, Version 3.1, Issue 1, June 1987. Issued by JIMCOM and available from the Royal Signals and Radar Establishment, Malvern, Worcestershire

Kernigan, B. W., Lesk, M. E. and Fossanna, J. F. Jr., (1978) Document preparation. *The Bell System Technical Journal*, 57, no 6, pt 2, 2115–2136

Leblang, D. B. and Chase, R. P. (1983) Computer-aided software engineering in a distributed workstation environment. *ACM Software Engineering Notes*, 9, 104–112

Leblang, D. B. and McLean, G. (1985) DSEE: overview and configuration management. In *Integrated project support environments* (ed. J. McDermid) Peter Peregrinus Ltd

Lempp, P. (1986) Development and project management support with the integrated software engineering environment, EPOS. In *Software Engineering Environments* (ed. I. Sommerville), Peter Peregrinus Ltd

McGuffin, R. W., Elliston, A. E., Tranter, B. R. and Westmacott, P. N. (1979) CADES – software engineering in practice. In *Proceedings, 4th International Conference on Software Engineering*, IEEE

MOD (1985) *Configuration Management Policy and Procedures for Defence Materiel*, Ministry of Defence

Morgan, T. M. (1988) Configuration management and version control in the Rational programming environment. In *Ada in Industry* (ed. S. Heilbrunner), Cambridge University Press, pp. 17–28

Mullin, J. K. (1981) Change area b-trees: a technique to aid error recovery. *Computer Journal*, 24, 367–373

NATO (1988) *PCTE+ Functional Specification, Issue 2*, NATO

NSE (1988) Introduction to the NSE *Sun Microsystems*

Obst, W. (1987) Delta technique and string-to-string correction. *1st European Software Engineering Conference*, 69–73

PCTE *A Basis for a Portable Common Tool Environment*, Functional Specifications, Fourth Edition, Bull SA, The General Electric Company plc., ICL International Computers Limited, Nixdorf Computer AG, Olivetti SPA and Siemens AG

Pierce, R. H. (1987) Eclipse – and APSE-based on PCTE. In *Ada components: libraries and tools*, (ed. S. Tafvelin), Proceedings of the ADA-Europe International Conference, Stockholm, 26–28 May 1987, Cambridge University Press

Rochkind, M. J. (1975) The source code control system. *IEEE Transactions on Software Engineering*, SE-1, 364–370

Severance, D. G. and Lohman, G. M. (1976) Differential files: their application to the maintenance of large databases. *ACM Transactions on Database Systems*, 1, 256–267

Sommerville, I. and Thompson, R. (1986) The Eclipse system structure language. *19th International Conference on System Sciences*, Honolulu

Stenning, V. (1986) An introduction to ISTAR. In *Software Engineering Environments* (ed. I. Sommerville), Peter Peregrinus Ltd

Thomas, I. (1988) Writing tools for PCTE and PACT: the how-to-do-it guide. In *Esprit'88*, North-Holland, pp 453–459

Tichy, W. F. (1982) Design, implementation, and evaluation of a revision control system. *Proceedings of 6th International Conference on Software Engineering*, 58–67

Wagner, R. and Fischer, M. (1974) The string-to-string correction. *J.ACM*, **21**, 168–173

Walpole, J. (1988) Maintaining Consistency in Distributed IPSEs. Ph.D. Thesis. University of Lancaster

AI/IKBS
Approaches

35

Functional programming

Hugh Glaser and Peter Henderson
Department of Electronics and Computer
Science, University of Southampton

Contents

35.1 Introduction

This chapter discusses functional programming as a style of programming, and functional programming languages, which have been developed to support the style. Functional languages are a type of programming language generally referred to as declarative languages which provide the user with a descriptive style of notation, where he or she describes the result of the computation, rather than a step-by-step recipe for constructing it. Functional programming languages include Hope, ML, KRC and Miranda. The other major declarative languages are logic programming languages, epitomized by the language Prolog. They are frequently termed non-procedural languages.

Another common characteristic of declarative languages is that they are similar to the various methods used to provide a formal basis for computation. Both functional and logic languages are based on mathematics. Indeed, they grew out of work on the formal basis of programming and on automatic theorem proving. Logic programming is based on predicate calculus and functional programming is based on the lambda calculus. It is believed by their adherents that such rigorous foundations facilitate reasoning about programs written in a declarative style. This is a topic which is now very important to the software engineer. They therefore help to make the task of software engineering a little easier and a little more reliable.

A number of other claims are made for functional programming languages. There are three important attributes which all functional languages share and which are the basis for functional programming:

1. They are higher level than traditional programming languages, in a way which will be illustrated later. As such, they reduce the programming effort required for any particular application.
2. They are closer to specification than imperative programming, and so form a useful bridge between these two stages in a traditional software development process. In other words, functional programs written in a functional language make good prototypes.
3. The absence of side-effects in evaluation is enforced by functional programming languages. This may make them more suitable for parallel evaluation, since independent sub-expressions cannot interfere with each other.

Although functional languages have been promising great advantages for some time, it is hard to find evidence of any direct impact on the life of the software engineer. Although there are some minor reasons, such as a lack of standardization (*cf.* Prolog as the logic programming standard), the major reason has been a lack of effective implementations. Functional languages pay a price for a higher level of programming, in that the implementation must be more sophisticated. It is only now that the implementation techniques are reaching the point where functional languages can be used for large-scale software engineering. For many years Lisp compilers have been giving high performance, but while Lisp supports functional programming in a way that traditional programming languages do not, it does not have the clean and pure attributes of a true functional programming language. More recently, compilers for functional languages, such as the SML compiler from AT&T, have been achieving a similar high performance, and conforming more closely to the characteristics of a functional language as outlined in this chapter.

Before considering exactly what is meant by functional programming, it is important to note that is is not simply the *use* of a functional language, but that it also means a *style* of programming. In particular, the style involves the avoidance of side-effects and the use of abstract data types. Software engineers will be aware that such a style is now recognized as being good practice in any language. Thus an understanding of the functional style of programming is not only an investment for the future, when such languages are likely to be more widely used, but are also a useful focus for consideration of programming style in any language.

35.2 What is meant by functional programming?

As the name suggests, the essence of functional programming is that the method of abstraction used by the programmer is the construction of functions. The use of the word 'function' is more in the mathematical sense than the sense often used in programming languages. In (school) mathematics, a function is an object that provides a list of all the variables for which it varies, together with a formula for actually working out the value. Thus, for example if we write $y = x^2$ we say y is a function of x since, as x varies, y varies as its square. We can emphasize the functional nature of this relationship between x and y by writing $y = f(x)$ and $f(x) = x^2$. Here we have introduced a name f for the function. We say f is the function which squares its argument. However, a function in a language such as Pascal merely denotes a subroutine that returns a value, which can be a pure function of its arguments but may have a side-effect too. Such a function is much harder to reason about.

It is a remarkable discovery (which predates computer programming) that any algorithm can be described as a mathematical function. Functional programming tries to turn this fact into a practical means of software engineering. So, at its most primitive, a functional programming language provides the facility to compute with mathematical functions. Of course, many languages provide support for functions. Functional languages are different because:

1. Functional abstraction is the *only* method of procedural abstraction.
2. Functional languages support functions as fully as possible allowing them to be manipulated as first class values. In other words, they can be passed as arguments, returned as results and stored in data structures, just like any other data value.

In addition to these principal properties, however, a number of other characteristics have become part of the culture of functional programming and functional programming language implementation. The additional facilities usually found in functional languages include:

1. *Garbage collected storage allocation.* This is an important and necessary provision which will be discussed in the next section. Storage management is the principal reason that effective functional programming is difficult in traditional languages.
2. *Pattern matching of function arguments.* This technique leads to more readable code, as will be seen later.
3. *Lazy evaluation.* This is a method of implementation which can support infinite data objects, as long as the program only ever attempts to explore a finite extent of an infinite object.
4. *Abstract data types.* This technique is as important to functional languages as it is to traditional languages. It has, however, a particularly good fit with functional languages.
5. *Polymorphic compile-time type checking.* The simplicity of the semantics of functional languages means that compile-time type checking can be very comprehensive. The support for functions as first-class objects requires this type checking to be parametric with respect to user defined types.

These characteristics are as much part of functional programming as the full support of functions. None of them is exclusive to functional programming – they can all be found in other types of languages – but they are part of functional languages because they fit very well into a system based on functions. Some adherents to functional programming would say that a system which did not provide such facilities would not be considered a *real* functional programming system. Perhaps more reasonably, one can say that the more of these facilities which a particular language provides, the more it supports the techniques of functional programming as we have come to understand them in recent years.

To illustrate the above, we must look at a small example of a program written in functional programming style, but not in any particular functional programming language:

$$factorial\ 0 = 1$$
$$factorial\ n = n * factorial(n - 1)$$
$$map\ f\ nil = nil$$
$$map\ f\ cons(e, rest) = cons(f(e), map(f, rest))$$
$$answer = map\ factorial\ [1,2,3,4,5]$$

We see here three objects defined: *factorial*, *map* and *answer*. Each is defined by equations. Note that the ordering of the equations is not particularly significant, and that there are no 'variables' in the traditional programming language sense. That is, there are no assignments. Nevertheless, this is a complete program for computing the first five factorial numbers. Let us look at each of the objects defined in this program in turn.

The first object is the factorial function:

$$factorial\ 0 = 1$$
$$factorial\ n = n * factorial(n - 1)$$

We have used the case analysis (pattern matching) style which is normal in functional programming. It would have been possible to write the more traditional:

$$factorial\ n = \textbf{if}\ n = 0\ \textbf{then}\ 1\ \textbf{else}\ n * factorial(n - 1)$$

but it is hoped that the reader will agree that the case analysis is a little clearer. Note that it bears a close relationship to the equivalent relation of mathematics:

$$fact_0 = 1$$
$$fact_n = n \times fact_{n-1}$$

The second object is a more complicated map function:

$$map\ f\ nil = nil$$
$$map\ f\ cons(e, rest) = cons(f(e), map(f, rest))$$

Again the pattern matching style of argument definition has been used. This time the patterns are *nil* and *cons(e, rest)*, which denote an empty and non-empty list respectively. The map function takes two arguments. The first is a function which can be applied to each of the elements of the second argument, which is a list.

One can begin to see here how functional languages provide support for computation using functions. Here *map* has a function argument, which is applied in the body of the function to an object of apparently unknown type. It can thus be seen that different calls of *map* will take different types of lists and corresponding functions. Clearly, if the calls are type correct, then the implementation must enforce compatibility between the arguments, and this we assume it does. A function such as *map* whose type is dependent on the types of arguments is called polymorphic. The fact that it takes another function as an argument is usually referred to by saying that *map* is a higher-order function.

The use of the list argument demonstrates the way data objects may be constructed and decomposed. In the body of the function we see the use of the list constructor function, *cons*, to form the new list. In the argument list of the second case, the power of pattern matching is demonstrated. Firstly *cons(e, rest)* says that this case should only be used if the list has at least one element, and secondly the components of the data type are named, without the need for selector functions in the body of the function. Because of this it is a feature of type definitions in functional languages that definition of the type also implicitly defines the selector functions for that type.

It will be noted that there are no explicit storage allocation declarations or instructions in this program. Functional languages rely on automatic storage allocation for constructor functions such as *cons*, and also user-defined data types. Because of this, and because the values in storage are only defined once and then never changed, functional language implementations allocate (and de-allocate) store at a considerable rate. Consequently such implementations provide automatic garbage collection, without the need for routines such as *dispose* or *free*. Storage management is discussed at some length in the next section.

The third and final object defined in this little functional program is *answer*:

$$answer = map\ factorial\ [1,2,3,4,5]$$

This defines a list constructed from the list [1,2,3,4,5] by mapping *factorial* over it. Thus one would expect *answer* to be [1, 2, 6, 24, 120], the first five factorial numbers. In a practical functional programming implementation, typically, one would define a large number of objects like *factorial* and *map* and combine them by function application to construct the results we require as functions of the data we provide. One would use little more paraphernalia than that introduced here. There is little more to functional programming.

Let us look a little more closely at the order in which functions are called. It is widely accepted that functional languages should use a lazy evaluation strategy. This can best be described as 'put off evaluating anything until it is absolutely necessary, and then only evaluate it once'. A direct consequence of this attitude is that functional languages do not evaluate the arguments before calling a function. This is *call-by-name* rather than *call-by-value*, but does not suffer from the inefficiencies normally associated with *call-by-name*, as there cannot be any variables that change, causing the argument to be re-evaluated. It is thus evaluated at most once. Since constructors can also be considered as functions, the elements of a list, and even the structure, will not be evaluated until, and if, required (*cons* should not evaluate its arguments). It is thus possible to compute using unbounded lists and other data structures. The program will terminate as normal, provided the programmer has not asked for the whole list to be evaluated!

As an example of lazy evaluation, consider the following program for computing a list of factorials:

$$ints = cons(1, map\ succ\ ints)$$
$$f = cons(1, tl(ints) * f)$$

This program defines two infinite lists, as follows. The list *ints* is:

$$ints = [1, 2, 3, 4, 5, ...$$

It is constructed recursively using the *succ* function which computes the successor of an integer number. Note that:

$$map\ succ\ ints = [2, 3, 4, 5, 6, ...$$

so that the first equation in our program is correct. This seems tautologous. How does it compute *ints*? In practice the elements of *ints* will be constructed only when needed. When the first element is needed it can be supplied by *cons*(1, ...). When the second element is needed *succ* is applied to the first element, which has already been constructed and does not need to be recomputed. The third element is constructed from the second, and so on.

Now let us determine what the second equation in the lazy program computes. In fact it will be shown that it constructs the infinite list of all factorial numbers as follows:

$$
\begin{aligned}
f &= [1, 2, 6, 24, 120, \ldots . \\
ints &= [1, 2, 3, 4, 5, \ldots \\
tl(ints) &= [2, 3, 4, 5, \ldots \\
tl(ints) * f &= [2, 6, 24, 120, \ldots \\
cons(1, \; tl(ints) * f) &= [1, 2, 6, 24, 120, \ldots
\end{aligned}
$$

We have assumed that multiplication of two lists of integers does element by element multiplication. Again we see that our equations are valid. An argument similar to the one used for *ints* convinces us that the factorial numbers in *f* can be constructed one at a time by the program. This order of evaluation, which delays computation until it is required is called lazy evaluation. In a practical implementation, these two equations would be supplied and then the program invoked by asking, for example, for the first five factorial numbers to be constructed using an invocation such as *first* 5 *f*.

35.3 Functional programming and software engineering

Why is functional programming important in software engineering? Can it only be practised in functional languages? As intimated earlier, its importance stems from its essential simplicity, its proximity to the specification. However, it is difficult to practise functional programming in conventional languages like Pascal and C precisely because of the inadequacy of the storage management normally supplied with implementations of those languages. These issues are addressed more fully in this section.

To some extent, it is remarkable that one can write real programs in a functional style at all. The only computational capability which is supplied is that of applying function. With even quite a modest supply of primitive functions, whole programs can be written using no more than that. Iteration is done by recursive function call. Assignment is replaced by the association of parameters with their corresponding arguments. Data structures are always dealt with as *whole* objects. Selective update, such as assigning to an array element, is unknown in functional programming. Rather, one refers to the *whole* new array constructed from the old array which is identical in all but one location. It is this phenomenon which at the same time gives functional programming its great power despite its simplicity but which leads to the requirement for sophisticated storage management.

How does one program in a functional style? The key concept is to think constructively, to determine how to construct a result from its component parts. Thus, if we want to sum the elements of a list we construct the sum by adding the first element of the list to the sum of the remaining elements in the list:

$$
\begin{aligned}
sum \; nil &= 0 \\
sum \; cons(n, \; r) &= n + sum(r)
\end{aligned}
$$

Similarly, to build a list of the first *n* integers, we construct the result from a list of the first *n* − 1 integers by appending *n* to that list:

$$
\begin{aligned}
integers \; 0 &= nil \\
integers \; n &= integers(n - 1) :: [n], \; n > 0
\end{aligned}
$$

These two operations, built from only a few arithmetic and list primitives have inherited the constructive compositional power of those primitive functions. We can build with these operations in the same transparent way that we build with the given primitives. For example:

$$ sum(integers \; 10) $$

is obviously the sum of the first 10 integers. The call, *integers* 10 constructs (a list of) the first 10 integers and *sum* adds them up.

This is typical of the style adopted in writing functional programs. It is very akin to the style of definition traditionally used in mathematics, and more recently as the basis for formal specification in languages like Z, VDM and OBJ (see Chapters 21 and 22 for a discussion of such languages). In functional programming one restricts oneself to this constructive use of mathematics to achieve reasonable implementations. In fact, functional programming languages can be used for writing specifications, and this has a particular added value in that the specification then becomes executable. This has the advantage that inconsistencies and incompletenesses in the specification may be found at an early stage in the development life cycle. The only reason the functional program cannot then be used as the final product is that the efficiency of the implementation, more often in storage use than CPU use, is not what is desired. Further development effort then needs to be expended to rework the design in some suitable target language, such as Pascal or C.

Where does this inefficiency come from? In fact it is the same problem that makes Pascal and C unsuitable hosts for the functional programming style – specifically, the need for sophisticated storage management. Consider for example the use of function *integers* 10. This builds a list of 10 integers which uses up some storage. Since we apparently wanted to build the list, that seems to present no particular problem. Now consider the function:

$$ sum(integers \; 10) $$

This builds the list of 10 integers, adds them up to compute 55, but then no longer requires the intermediate result, the list of 10 consecutive integers.

Recovery of this storage is necessary. In a functional programming language a garbage collector is invoked periodically, when available (unused) storage gets low, which typically traces all accessible storage and recovers all inaccessible storage for reallocation.

If one naïvely codes up the *integers* function in, say, Pascal, one does not have such a sophisticated storage management system to rely on. Nor is the recovery a simple task for the programmer. One can assume that a simple list processing package has been provided in Pascal, which allows one to declare objects of type *list* and apply the operation *cons* to such objects, without expecting that storage, once allocated, will ever be recovered. Given such a package, the Pascal would look something like the following.

```
function integers(n : integer) : list;
begin
if n = 0 then integers := nil else
integers := append(integers(n − 1), cons(n, nil))
end;
```

Here the construction of *integers*(10) requires us to construct an entire list *integers*(9). Typical implementations of append will copy this intermediate list, thus making the storage which it uses disposable after the outer call has been completed. However, Pascal will not dispose of it. For example, if the append function is programmed, as it usually is, as follows:

```
function append(x, y : list) : list;
begin
if x = then append := y else
append := cons( first(x), append(rest(x), y))
end
```

then the call of *append*(*integers*(9),[10]) duly returns a list of 10 elements but it has made copies of the elements in *integer*(9) in order to do that.

There is no obvious way to use the Pascal memory management routines (dispose, for example) to alleviate this problem, even if their appearance in the code could be tolerated. Alternative strategies can be adopted. For some applications it is possible to determine that data structures, once built, remain throughout the life of the program. They can then be searched very effectively by a functional program. For some applications it is possible to determine at various stages that whole areas of storage can be recovered, so the functional style can be adopted even though it creates inaccessible data, knowing that the storage can be recovered. It may even be possible to organize the program so that at any time (or at least, at frequent moments) it is known where all accessible records are stored. A garbage collector can then be written to take advantage of this fact. This is less trivial than it may sound, because the function calling mechanism in both C and Pascal will leave valid references to data in anonymous places on the activation stack. Only an intimate knowledge of the implementation will allow a reliable garbage collector to be written. The consequence of this is that programming in a functional style in conventional programming languages will never be as effective as in a functional programming language specially developed for the purpose.

35.4 Conclusions

This chapter has shown how powerful and simple functional programming can be. The remarkable fact that entire programs can be built as sets of equations which define functions has been illustrated. Function abstraction is a powerful tool for program decomposition. Combined with techniques such as abstract data types and lazy evaluation, functional programming languages provide a tool for producing very concise programs. The consequence is that such programs are easier to make correct. Functional programming has a simple mathematical basis. Hence functional programs are easier to reason about.

Yet functional programming has not become a major force in the field of software engineering. The reasons are two-fold. First it is difficult to practise functional programming in conventional programming languages because of the rudimentary nature of the storage management provided by those languages. Although some conventional languages (notably ALGOL 68) have provided such facilities, these languages have not superseded C, Pascal, FORTRAN, COBOL and the rest. The second reason

for the comparative obscurity of functional programming has been the lack of standard functional programming languages with efficient implementations. Although functional languages can be implemented efficiently, they have acquired a reputation for being slow because most real implementations are slow (when compared, for example, with C on the same machine). A language such as Lisp, which has efficient implementations and the necessary storage management mechanisms, is generally found unacceptable by software engineers for other reasons. It has a far from friendly (or familiar) syntax and has never really yielded to standardization. In any case, it invites the use of imperative programming by encouraging side-effects and surgery on data.

Perhaps functional programming will become more mainstream when standard functional programming languages with efficient implementations become more widely available. As the discipline has progressed, it has become more acceptable to build systems in the most appropriate language. Thus data processing is done in COBOL, scientific computation in FOR-TRAN, AI in Lisp and Prolog, interactive programs in Smalltalk, and so on. In fact, increasingly, systems are coming to be built in a mixture of languages, so, for example, an interactive AI program may be built partly in Prolog and partly in Smalltalk. Functional programming may yet find its most effective role in such mixed company.

There has recently been a surge in books on functional programming. The authors' own books (Henderson, 1980; Glaser, 1984) are now considerably out of date. Most of the developments in the field have taken place since they were written. Perhaps the most comprehensive survey is given by Field and Harrison (1988) while Bird and Wadler (1988) give a very readable and introductory tutorial. Peyton-Jones (1987) has become a standard work on implementation. Wikstrom (1987) concentrates on ML, which is closest to becoming a *de facto* standard language for functional programming. The relationship between functional and imperative styles of programming is discussed eloquently by both Abelson and Sussman (1985) and by Gordon (1988).

35.5 References

Abelson, H. and Sussman, G. J. (1985) *Structure and Interpretation of Computer Programs*, MIT Press, McGraw-Hill

Bird, R. and Wadler, P. (1988) *An Introduction to Functional Programming*, Prentice-Hall

Glaser, H., Hankin, C. and Till, D. (1984) *Principles of Functional Programming*, Prentice-Hall

Field, T. and Harrison, P. (1988) *Functional Programming*, Addison-Wesley

Henderson, P. (1980) *Functional Programming – Application and Implementation*, Prentice-Hall

Gordon, M. J. C. (1988) *Programming Language Theory and its Implementation – Applicative and Imperative Paradigms*, Prentice-Hall

Peyton-Jones, S. (1987) *The Implementation of Functional Programming Languages*, Prentice-Hall

Wikstrom, A. *Functional Programming Using Standard ML*, Prentice-Hall

36

Logic programming

Christopher John Hogger
Senior Lecturer, Department of Computing,
Imperial College of Science, Technology and
Medicine, London

Contents

36.1 Logic programs for knowledge representation

The choice of logic as a computer programming language implies a commitment to the principle of representing knowledge explicitly, rather than implicitly as in most other programming languages. To solve any particular problem, we have to make use of what we know about the underlying domain. For instance, solving the problem of deciding whether a list is ordered requires knowledge about list structure and about the nature of orderedness. Again, solving the problem of calculating the area of some irregular shape requires general knowledge of how to subdivide shapes into components of greater regularity and of how to calculate and aggregate their individual areas. A key aim of logic programming is to encourage the clear articulation of such knowledge within the program text – indeed, to make such articulation *constitute* the text.

There are many different kinds of logic and many different styles in which to deploy any one of them. Amongst those logics which are sufficiently expressive for dealing with the full range of computationally solvable problems, the most well understood and the most frequently used is first-order logic. It enables us to express, for example, our knowledge that a list L of decimal digits is ordered if every consecutive pair (U, V) of L's members satisfies $U \leqslant V$. In the standard syntax of the language we might express this by a sentence such as the following:

$$(\forall L)(\text{ordered}(L) \text{ if } (\forall U)(\forall V)$$
$$(U \leqslant V \text{ if digit}(U) \text{ and digit}(V) \text{ and pair}(U,V,L)))$$

This can be read literally as saying 'for all L, L is ordered if, for all U and all V, U is less than or equal to V if U and V are decimal digits and (U, V) is a consecutve pair of members in L'.

The primary constituents of the language are predicates, such as pair(U, V, L), which express truth-valued propositions about their arguments. The names used in predicates – such as 'pair', 'U', 'V' and 'L' – are chosen arbitrarily from predetermined vocabularies. As seen in the above example, a complete sentence requires, in general, that predicates or subformulas be subject to quantifiers, such as $(\forall U)$, and that they be composed together using connectives, such as 'if' and 'and', in order to achieve the correct rendition. The freedom to nest quantifiers and connectives to an arbitrary extent enables one to build arbitrarily complicated sentences.

Although there are plenty of precedents for employing the full syntax of first-order logic as a language for problem formulation, the specific discipline of logic programming has concentrated upon a simpler subset of that language known as definite-clause logic. In this language each permitted sentence is a definite clause of the form ε

conclusion if conditions

where the 'conclusion' is a single predicate and where the 'conditions' are predicates joined by the connective 'and'. A logic program is just a set of such clauses, of which the following is a simple example:

ordered(L) if L = nil
ordered(L) if L = U.nil, digit(U)
ordered(L) if L = U.V.T and digit(U) and digit(V)
                    and U $\leqslant$ V and ordered(V.T)

Each clause is implicitly quantified by an outermost $\forall$ for each of its variables (L, U, V and T above), and each one expresses some portion of knowledge about the conclusion predicate. In this example we also see the use of constants – such as 'nil', representing the empty list – and functors – such as the infix dot, representing the list-constructor function symbol. The best-known instance of clausal-form logic deployed as a programming language is Prolog, whose syntax would render the example above slightly differently in the form

ordered(L) :- L = [].
ordered(L) :- L = [U], digit(U).
ordered(L) :- L = [U,V|T], digit(U), digit(V), U = < V,
                                                ordered([V|T]).

Since predicate arguments may consist of any terms comprised of variables, constants and functors, this program could be made even more concise by eliminating the superfluous equality predicates to yield:

ordered([]).
ordered([U]) :- digit(U).
ordered([U, V|T]) :- digit(U), digit(V), U = < V,
                                         ordered([V|T]).

Informally, the first clause says that one way to have an ordered list is to have the empty list; the second says that another way is to have a list containing any single digit U; the third says that another way is to have a list which begins with an ordered pair of digits and which is also ordered beyond its first member. Intuitively the three clauses cover all possible cases. We would describe them as constituting a Prolog program for the 'ordered' relation. To make the program complete we would also need definitions of its auxiliary relations 'digit' and '= <' ('equal to or less than'). Prolog conveniently provides its own built-in definition of '= <'. In order to define 'digit' it would suffice for us to add further clauses:

digit(0).
digit(1).
etc.

explicitly identifying the decimal digits.

36.2 Solving problems with logic programs

We can use a logic program not merely to express the knowledge we already have, but also to derive new knowledge. All forms of problem-solving can be regarded as seeking new knowledge (conclusions) from given knowledge (assumptions). In particular, problem-solving using logic programs derives conclusions which are *logical consequences* of the assumptions expressed by their clauses. For example, the problem of deciding whether the list [2, 3, 5] is ordered can be viewed as querying whether the proposition ordered ([2, 3, 5]) is a logical consequence of the program just presented (which it is). In Prolog we would simply pose the query:

?–ordered([2, 3, 5]).

Execution of this query using the program would generate the answer 'yes'. Had the input list been disordered then Prolog would have answered 'no'. Much more importantly, Prolog can also generate values for query variables. Thus, the query:

?–ordered([2, X, 5]).

asks which values X may take such that [2, X, 5] is ordered, and its execution by Prolog will compute and output all the possible values 2, 3, 4 and 5 in turn.

The classic work on the application of clausal-form logic to problem-solving is the book by Kowalski (1979a).

36.3 Procedural interpretation of logic programs

The syntactical simplicity of clauses favours efficient schemes for storing them in computer memory, renders program texts easier to understand in logical terms and – most important of all – lends itself to a simple procedural interpretation which exposes the pragmatic (algorithmic) content of programs. A satisfactory procedural interpretation is essential to the task of turning any system of logic into a practical computational tool.

In any query of the general form ?–C1, C2, . . . each predicate Ci can be viewed as a procedure call. A set of program clauses sharing a common relation name (predicate symbol) in their conclusion predicates can be viewed collectively as a procedure defining the named relation. In the previous example the program thus contained an explicit procedure, comprising three clauses, for the 'ordered' relation, and another explicit procedure, comprising ten clauses, for the 'digit' relation. Additionally, Prolog contributed an implicit procedure for the '= <' relation.

The basic computational step in logic program execution consists of selecting a call from the query, then identifying its associated procedure in the program, then choosing from that procedure a clause whose conclusion can be matched with the call, and finally replacing the call by the clause's conditions. A conclusion and a call can be matched if and only if they are either already identical or else can be made so by substituting particular values for their variables. For example, a call ordered ([2, X, 5]) can be matched with the conclusion of the clause.

ordered([U, V|T]) :– digit(U), digit(V), U = < V,

ordered([V|T]).

by substituting U:= 2, V:= X and T:= [5]. Consequently, applying one computational step to the query:

?–ordered([2, X, 5]).

would transform it to the new query:

?–digit(2), digit(X), 2 = < X, ordered([X, 5]).

A computation is just a chain of queries each one of which, other than the one initially posed, is derived as above from its predecessor. A computation yields a 'yes' answer if it derives an empty query; it yields a 'no' answer if it derives a query in which some call cannot be matched to any clause; otherwise it fails to terminate and yields no answer. The determination and assigning of values to variables in the course of constructing matching substitutions can be interpreted as data manipulation and communication, and is undertaken automatically by the interpreter (executor).

This account leaves two strategical matters remaining to be articulated – deciding which call to process in the current state of the query, and deciding which program clause to invoke in response to it. In Prolog these matters are decided by simple, fixed selection rules. The call selected is the left-most one in the query. Amongst those clauses which could be matched to this call but which have not yet been invoked by it, the one next invoked is that which appears earliest in the program text. By employing a backtracking mechanism, the matchable clauses for the call are all eventually invoked in turn; a multiplicity of matchable clauses represents a multiplicity of ways to execute the invoking call, each resulting in its own individual outcome.

The significance of the procedural interpretation is that it exposes the algorithmic content of programs, enabling judgement to be exercised during their logical and textual composition by the programmer. Reading programs logically provides insights into their meaning and veracity; reading them procedurally provides insights into their computational utility. Practical procedural interpretations for logic-based formalisms will remain necessary for as long as their execution systems fail to exercise autonomous intelligence over their own behaviour.

The procedural interpretation of logic programs was first articulated by Kowalski (1974), whilst further discussion on this topic can be found in the book by Hogger (1984). Its practical application in the Prolog language is covered comprehensively and with great lucidity in the book by Sterling and Shapiro (1986).

36.4 Logic compared with procedural languages

The chief difference between logic programming and procedural programming is in their relative degrees of flexibility. There are two main senses in which logic programs are more flexible. First, they are not committed to solving any particular problem. Second, even when specific problems are posed, their methods of solution depend upon choices of execution strategy which can be exercised independently of the programs. Logic programs also have other distinctive features which provide for novel methods of implementation and software engineering beyond the scope of procedural programming.

36.4.1 Independence of programs and queries

As a simple example, consider the following logic program which describes lists of even length whose members are either alternating 'ones' starting with a 'one' at the first position, if any, or else alternating 'zeros' starting with a 'zero' at the second position, if any:

ones([]).
ones([1, U|X]) :– ones (X).
zeros([]).
zeros([V, 0|X]) :– zeros(X).

These clauses only *describe* such lists, but in no way do they anticipate the problems we might wish to solve. We can pose any problem we wish, formulated as some query involving either or both of the key relations. Thus, the query:

?–ones([1, 0, 1, 2]).

merely asks whether a given list satisfies the 'ones' property, whilst the query:

?–ones([U, V, 1, 2]).

additionally asks for the determination of some unspecified members; the answer will assign U:= 1 but leave V arbitrary. More elaborate queries might combine references to both relations, as does:

?–ones([1, 0, 1, 2]), zeros([1, 0, 1, 2]).

Changing the *form* of the query in this way, in contrast to merely *altering the data* within one fixed form, is a feature which cannot be achieved in a procedural language without reprogramming to cater for each new form. This is because the operational nature of the coding in such a language inherently drives execution towards some particular end. Perhaps the greatest single weakness and redundancy of procedural languages is this inability to cater economically for a diversity of problem-solving requirements even when the underlying logical laws about the problem domain are fixed and common to them all.

36.4.2 Independence of programs and execution strategies

The Prolog model of program execution outlined earlier is just one of arbitrarily many execution strategies that can be devised for logic programs, though it is arguably the simplest one. Whichever strategy is chosen, however, it cannot intrude upon the logical meaning of programs; a logic program *means* just those propositions which are its logical consequences, irrespective of how execution might demonstrate them to be consequences.

The most important factor determining run-time behaviour is the order in which calls are selected for execution. In standard Prolog the static, text-order basis of call selection provides a simple but somewhat inflexible form of control over the efficiency of execution. Some special-purpose variants of Prolog exist which enable the programmer to make more flexible arrangements for call-selection, typically involving criteria based upon the dynamic state of execution.

Consider the significance of call-order in respect of the query

?–input_list(X), ones(X), zeros(X).

We shall assume that the left-most call is to be executed first in order to access some input list for X. Prolog's sequential strategy would next test whether all the 'ones' were in place, then test whether all the 'zeros' were. This call-order is best-suited to any situation in which the 'ones' call is considered more likely to fail – owing to an anomalous element in an odd position in the list – than the 'zeros' call, since if there *were* such an element then the computation would terminate (in failure) without having had to waste time inspecting elements in even positions. If the balance of probabilities were considered to be the reverse, it would suffice simply to reverse the text-order of the query's last two calls. For a logic program we can be certain that such a modification to the program text cannot alter the answers computed, only the efficiency of computing them. For a procedural program we cannot modify the strategy without modifying the text; nor – in general – can we re-order program statements without affecting, and possibly destroying, the program's meaning.

If the probabilities of failing the 'ones' and 'zeros' calls were known to be equal, then the best call-order arrangement would be a balanced interleaving of the executions of those two calls, thus effectively checking the elements in their natural position-order within the list. Standard Prolog offers no direct means of specifying this requirement. Nonetheless, it can be specified indirectly by the use of meta-programming, which in procedural languages has no practical analogue.

The significance of the separation of logic from control is discussed in detail in a paper by Kowalski (1979b).

36.4.3 Logic for meta-programming

Logic programming provides for remarkably compact and elegant descriptions of how one might go about solving a query. Consider, for instance, how we might express the top-level behaviour of Prolog's method:

```
solve(Query) :– Query = [].
solve(Query) :– Query = [First_call|Other_calls],
        reduce(First_call, Further_calls, Substitution),
        append(Further_calls, Other_calls, Combined_calls),
        apply(Substitution, Combined_calls, Derived_query),
        solve(Derived_query).
```

Informally, the first clause says that the query is immediately solvable in the special case where it is already empty. The second clause deals with the general case where the query is a non-empty list of calls consisting of the first one followed by some others. By invoking some matching clause, this first call is reduced to further calls introduced by that clause, subject to some matching substitution. By appending the other calls of the query on to the *end* of those further calls, and then applying the substitution, one obtains the next derived state of the query.

Besides the two clauses shown above, additional lower-level clauses are necessary to define the auxiliary relations 'reduce', 'append' and 'apply', and these clauses must in turn be able to refer to constituents of whichever object program is provided as data. Executing the complete meta-program under Prolog's strategy merely simulates the behaviour that might otherwise be obtained by executing the object program directly under Prolog.

Now consider the earlier problem of interleaving the executions of the 'ones' and 'zeros' calls. A simple way of achieving this is to put the calls introduced by an invoked clause *after* those calls remaining in the query rather than *before*. So we need only switch the first two arguments of the 'append' call in the meta-program as follows:

append(Other_calls, Further_calls, Combined_calls)

Suppose now that the meta-query:

?–solve([ones([1, 0, 1, 2]), zeros([1, 0, 1, 2])]).

is executed, applying standard Prolog to the modified meta-program and using as object program the clauses given previously for 'ones' and 'zeros'. The following computation will be generated:

?–solve([zeros([1, 0, 1, 2]), ones([1, 2])]).
?–solve([ones([1, 2]), zeros([1, 2])]).
?–solve([zeros([1, 2]), ones([])]).
terminates (with failure).

This clearly alternates its attention between checking the 'ones' and checking the 'zeros' in the manner desired.

Meta-programming plays a major role in Prolog's main application areas, notably in knowledge-based systems, where it facilitates the articulation of problem-solving strategies, the management of programs and data, and the mechanisms of explanation and other forms of interactive dialogue. The fundamental reason why meta-programming is particularly congenial in logic is that the semantics of logic programming can be encapsulated in the single predicate 'solve' – meaning *demonstrate to be a consequence*; moreover, in most practical cases 'solve' is easy to define in logic itself. By contrast, the semantics of a typical procedural language are much more complicated than the simple notion of demonstrating a consequence relation, and are correspondingly more cumbersome to define.

The most up-to-date account of developments in meta-level logic programming is the collection of recent papers Meta88 (1988).

36.4.4 Programming productivity

In principle, logic offers greater productivy in the coding process than do procedural languages. The main argument for this claim is that logic programs are unencumbered by details of run-time control, which are instead consigned, in a once-and-for all fashion, to the responsibility of the interpreter. Consequently they are, in general, far shorter textually than their procedural counterparts.

A striking example of this is given by the path-finding problem. Suppose we have as data a directed graph whose nodes are labelled a, b, c, etc. The arcs of the graph can be represented by unit clauses:

```
arc(a, b).
arc(b, c).
etc.
```

The definition of a path through the graph from any node X to any node Y can now be summed up by just two further clauses:

```
path(X, Z) :- arc(X, Z).
path(X, Z) :- arc(X, Y), path(Y, Z).
```

These are sufficient for solving a straightforward query such as ?–path(a, c). In the process of solving it, a lot more goes on 'behind the scenes' than the clauses alone would suggest. Alternative routes through the graph have to be scheduled for exploration, necessitating the use of internal data structures for recording both the current state of the search and the information needed later on for backtracking. Other internal mechanisms are needed for managing variables – for allocating memory to them, for recording the bindings made to them and for deallocating their memory when appropriate. The interpreter assumes responsibility for all these implementation technicalities. By contrast, the procedural programmer has to spell them out in minute detail, thereby producing code which is longer, more complex, more inscrutable and more error-prone. That code is also less flexible, since the information it contains about the course of execution is necessarily specific to one class of query: a procedural program cannot escape commitment to some intended purpose – it has to 'know where it is going'. The two logic clauses for 'path', however, are adequate for dealing with many kinds of query, such as the following examples:

```
?–path(X, c).
?–path(a, Z).
?–path(X, Y).
?–arc(X, Y), path(Y, X).
?–path(a, X), path(X, c).
```

In the procedural case, dealing with these examples alone would require many hundreds of interdependent statements. The so-called 'high-level' languages are, in reality, very low-level compared to logic because, however sophisticated their constructs might be, they ultimately remain anchored to the detailing of machine transitions. Two benefits which they gain from this proximity to the machine, however, are relative ease of compilation and the fine degree of control they put into the hands of the programmer. Such attributes must be assessed in any particular situation according to the relative priorities assigned to conciseness, lucidity, flexibility, coding productivity and execution performance.

36.5 Logic compared with Prolog

The Prolog formalism includes definite-clause logic as a subset, so that pure logic programming is always an option available to the Prolog programmer. But Prolog provides other features as well, many of which were introduced originally for the purpose of giving programmers more control over run-time behaviour. Others concern the provision in Prolog of mechanisms for default reasoning. Most of these additional features exert a disruptive influence upon the semantics, with the result that the answers computed from Prolog programs are no longer necessarily logical consequences of those programs. In fact the sorts of Prolog program commonly written for real-world applications more closely resemble procedural programs. With hindsight one can adopt the view that the Prolog phenomenon has not necessarily enhanced the cause of pure logic programming because, whilst its proponents may lay claim to Prolog being based upon logical principles, those principles are frequently violated in practice.

Nevertheless, Prolog has served an undeniably useful role in providing a short-term implementation technology for logic programming, notwithstanding its semantic deficits. A good deal of the current research effort in logic programming is directed towards longer-term remedies to the problem of getting better expressiveness and performance out of logic programs, by such means as more intelligent selection strategies, better understanding and support of meta-programming and the development of semantically unintrusive constructs for specifying control requirements. In what follows we examine some of the more notable non-logical features of Prolog. A more wide-ranging analysis of the ways in which Prolog differs from pure logic programming has been given by Kowalski (1981).

36.5.1 Depth-first search

Given a query and a program, the possibility during execution of some call being able to invoke alternative clauses gives rise to alternative computations. In general it is necessary for the interpreter to pursue all these computations in order not to overlook some way of solving the query. The basic computational step by which a call invokes a clause can be viewed as the application of a backward-reasoning inference rule (technically a version of the resolution inference rule). Two important properties are commonly desired of any inference system – completeness and soundness.

Completeness ensures that, for any correct answer to the query, some computation is derivable which leads to that answer. Soundness ensures that any answer derived by a computation must be a correct answer to the query (that is, is a logical consequence of the program). Both properties hold for the inference system which, theoretically at least, is used in logic programming.

However, on any sequential architecture having only a modest amount of memory, practicality requires that the interpreter shall derive computations one at a time, pursuing each one to its termination before backtracking to consider alternatives. This policy is summed up by the term 'depth-first search' and is inherently unfair in that its attention at any time is divided unequally between computations. It is the policy adopted by Prolog. No problems would arise from this if it could always be guaranteed that all computations terminated, but often this is not the case, whether by deliberation or by inadvertence. Consequently, should Prolog enter upon an infinite computation, it will be bound by its depth-first policy to pursue it indefinitely and exclusively, so that any answers which might have been derivable from subsequent alternative computations will be rendered temporally inaccessible. For this reason (as well as for others considered later on), Prolog is effectively incomplete.

One possible remedy (besides writing one's programs more carefully so as to avoid loops in the first place) is to add loop-detection facilities to the Prolog interpreter, but it is well-known from theoretical considerations that a perfect facility for this purpose cannot exist. Another approach to dealing with the problem, in cases where the need is considered to justify the resources required, is to enforce a policy of fair (e.g. breadth-first) search. One way of achieving this, without modifying the interpreter itself, is to interpose an appropriate meta-program along the lines of the 'solve' program shown earlier. In fact that program's use in the 'ones' and 'zeros' example could be regarded as applying a fair policy to the two subcomputations derived from the 'ones' and 'zeros' calls. A fair policy, though it still pursues non-terminating computations in perpetuity, is nevertheless guaranteed to find all answers in finite time, and is therefore effectively complete.

36.5.2 Omission of the occur-check

For a clause to be invokable by a call it is necessary that the interpreter shall first establish that there exists some matching substitution of terms for variables which brings the call and the clause's conclusion into syntactical agreement. (Otherwise, the clause cannot have any relevance to the call.) This is a time-consuming process and hence a significant factor in overall execution performance. In the algorithm customarily employed for seeking such a substitution a crucial test – called the 'occur-check' – is needed in order to prevent self-referential bindings – equivalently, to enforce the usual assumption that one is computing over a domain of finite terms.

Consider the following example in which the standard program for 'append':

append([], Z, Z).
append([U|X], Y, [U|Z]) :- append(X, Y, Z).

is applied to the query:

?–append([], L, [V|L]).

The second clause cannot be invoked because the query's first argument [] cannot be matched to the first argument [U|X] of the clause's conclusion. Thus our attention is fixed wholly upon the first clause. If Prolog attempts to construct a matching substitution in this case, it must make the bindings L:= Z and Z:= [V|L], whose composition is the self-referential binding L:= [V|L]. No such binding is admissible if we assume that L has to be a finite list. On this assumption, then, the query should logically fail. Deployment of the occur-check, whose technical details are unimportant here, ensures that this is indeed the outcome.

However, testing for self-reference is exceedingly expensive in processing time, and for this reason the occur-check is omitted from standard Prolog. The result of its omission when applied to the current example is that the query will succeed, even though the answer is not a logical consequence of our assumptions. (Worse still, any attempt to dereference the bindings in order to report the answer's value for L is liable to send the interpreter into an internal loop of its own.) Thus, even for pure definite-clause logic, Prolog without the occur-check is unsound. Some versions of Prolog include the occur-check as an option that can be enabled by the programmer. Others, notably so-called 'Prolog II', are engineered specifically to cater for computing over infinite terms. An accessible account of this has been given by van Emden and Lloyd (1984). In general the

programmer using standard Prolog simply has to take care not to pose situations which raise these problems.

In summary, even for the unextended kernel language of definite-clause logic, we find that the standard Prolog technology for logic programming is neither sound nor complete, although its deficiencies in these respects arise from comparatively marginal issues. Much more serious are those deficiencies which arise from some of Prolog's language extensions, the more important of which are reviewed below.

36.5.3 The 'cut' primitive

The most well-known means within Prolog of influencing the course of execution, besides the textual ordering of calls and clauses, is the 'cut' primitive (written as '!'), occurrences of which may appear in any positions amongst the calls within any query or any program clause. Operationally the 'cuts' are scheduled and selected just as though they were normal calls.

The basic intention behind any 'cut' is that, when it is selected for execution, it shall dynamically remove certain untried alternative computations from the interpreter's consideration, thus effectively pruning the search space. There are many possible motivations behind such an action. Sometimes the aim is simply to excise some computation which the programmer foresees as being futile – for instance, if it is bound to terminate with failure or if it is bound to loop. More often the 'cut' is used to suppress unwanted solutions, perhaps to force the evaluation of a call to be functional (single-valued) in nature rather than relational (many-valued). In other cases the 'cut' may be used in combination with other non-logical primitives to achieve more elaborate control requirements.

The use of a 'cut' in an otherwise pure definite-clause program never engenders any penalty worse than a loss of completeness – that is, a loss of one or more logically correct answers. If it is used only to prevent the recomputation of identical answers or only to excise futile computations, then it has no effect at all upon completeness and merely serves to improve efficiency.

'Cut' is often used to simulate an 'if ... then ... else' construction, which our first example now demonstrates. Suppose we wished to express the following construction in Prolog:

if T **then** P :– Q
    else P :– R.

One way of achieving this by using a 'cut' is shown below:

P :– T, !, Q.
P :– R.

The idea here is that, to solve a call to P, execution shall first invoke the first clause and apply the test T. If T succeeds then the next call processed will be the 'cut'. In general, any 'cut' excises all those untried computations which have arisen as alternatives upon and since invoking the clause containing the 'cut', which in this particular example has the effect of pruning away the opportunity of invoking the second clause. In summary, if T succeeds then the only way of solving P is by solving Q, as required. On the other hand, if T fails then execution backtracks in the normal fashion and resumes by next invoking the second clause; solving P then only requires solving R, again as required.

Although the above formulation seems to meet the operational requirement both correctly and economically, it is nonetheless vulnerable to very serious logical pitfalls. The issue hinges here upon the interpretation of 'else' in the original specification: does it mean 'if execution fails to show that T holds', or does it mean 'if execution succeeds in showing that the negation of T holds'? The former expresses a step of default inference, and is the one captured by the Prolog clauses above; the latter expresses a step of deductive inference about a negative proposition, which is not wholly realisable in Prolog since the language of definite-clause logic does not allow programs to contain such propositions as elementary facts. In other words, we are commenting here upon the difference between invoking:

```
this      P :- R.
or this   P :- ¬ T, R.
```

and the issue at stake is which of these is consistent with the logical specification of the problem.

Students of Prolog are ritually shown the following variant of the above example, to warn them of the dangers of misusing the 'cut'. Given two numbers X and Y, if $X < Y$ then their maximum is Y else their maximum is X. Suppose we employ the predicate max(X, Y, Z) to express that the maximum of X and Y is Z. The default interpretation of 'else' suggests the following Prolog program which uses a 'cut':

```
max(X, Y, Y) :- X < Y, !.
max(X, Y, X).
```

This works perfectly well for such queries as ?–max(2, 3, Z). and ?–max(3, 2, Z). It does so more efficiently than if we had instead taken the classical interpretation of 'else' and used the program below:

```
max(X, Y, Y) :- X < Y.
max(X, Y, X) :- X > = Y.
```

The point is that the use of 'cut' in the first formulation saves us the redundancy of testing explicitly whether $X > = Y$ holds once we have already shown that $X < Y$ holds. But consider now the use of the first program to solve the new query ?–max(2, 3, 2). The first clause does not match, but the second one does and (incorrectly!) confirms that 2 is the maximum of 2 and 3. Moreover, this conclusion is reached without execution having performed any test at all on the relative magnitudes of X and Y. The diagnosis of this semantically disastrous outcome concerns not so much the 'cut' as the clause:

```
max(X, Y, X).
```

This clause is not consistent with the mathematical specification of the problem – it is not a correct logical law about the 'max' relation. Operationally, its use in the first program is correct in certain contexts but fallacious in others, and the fallacious contexts cannot all be excluded by conditions set by the first clause. In summary, a 'cut' by itself cannot be responsible for unsoundness; but a 'cut' intended to prevent unsound usage of a logically-incorrect clause may fail to do so in some cases. The moral is to use 'cut' for improving efficiency only in combination with logically correct clauses.

36.5.4 Negation-by-failure

Negation-by-failure is arguably the most important, most interesting, most notorious and most problematic of all of Prolog's language extensions. The problems surrounding it are, like the particular use of 'cut' just discussed, concerned ultimately with the logical expression and semantic analysis of default reasoning.

The extension itself consists of allowing calls in queries or program clauses to take the form 'not p', where p is any ordinary call and 'not' is the negation-by-failure operator. The operational interpretation of such a call is as follows: first try to solve the call p; if the attempt finitely fails then 'not p' succeeds, otherwise it fails. This reading corresponds closely to the standard default rule of inference: 'infer that p does not hold, unless it is inconsistent to do so'.

Let us see how negation-by-failure could be put to use in the context of the path-finding problem. Consider the task of expressing that some node Y in the graph is a 'dead end'. For this to be so, Y must be reachable from some other node X, yet no node Z must be reachable from Y. This can be captured in Prolog as follows:

```
dead_end(Y) :- arc(X, Y), not arc(Y, Z).
```

Given some value v for Y execution of the clause's second call will proceed by first trying to solve the query ?–arc(v, Z). If this attempt finitely fails then Prolog infers, by default, that no node Z is reachable from v (since otherwise that attempt must have succeeded, assuming that no loops could ever arise from this example), in which case the desired 'dead end' property of v is established.

Extensive research efforts continue in the search for a wholly logical, consequence-oriented interpretation of negation-by-failure. One route this work has taken is to seek an intuitive logical construction C(P), related to any given program P, such that if a call 'not p' succeeds using negation-by-failure then the classical proposition $\neg p$ is a logical consequence of C(P). The best-known such construction is the so-called 'completed database', denoted by CDB(P). The precise details of this construction are tedious to articulate, but approximately CDB(P) is formed by first changing all of P's occurrences of 'not' to $\neg$, then combining the clauses for each relation into a single conditional sentence and finally changing each such sentence's 'if' connective to 'iff' (if-and-only-if). In the case of our path-finding program together with the 'dead end' definition, CDB(P) would comprise the following logical material:

```
arc(X, Z) iff (X,Z) = (a, b) or (X,Z) = (b, c) or ... etc.
path(X, Z) iff arc(X, Z) or (∃Y)(arc(X, Y), path(Y, Z))
dead_end(Y) iff (∃X)(∃Z)(arc(X, Y), ¬arc(Y, Z))
together with an explicit definition of the '=' relation.
```

It has been argued that the completed database expresses the programmer's supposed intentions more fully than does the corresponding program, by supplementing it with the closed-world assumption. To take a simpler example, suppose that in some program the only clauses for a relation 'A' are these:

```
A :- B.
A :- C.
```

The two clauses are logically equivalent to the single sentence:

```
A :- (B or C)
```

Informally, the closed-world assumption is the assumption that the only condition on which A holds is that (B or C) holds; equivalently, that if (B or C) does not hold then neither does A. Expressed in logic this extra assumption is:

```
¬A :- ¬(B or C)
```

or equivalently:

```
(B or C) :- A
```

which combined with the earlier sentence above gives the completed database:

A iff (B or C)

Exactly the same principles lie behind the completed database presented earlier for the 'dead end' program.

The soundness and completeness properties of fair resolution inference applied to pure definite-clause logic do not extend so as to cover the incorporation of negation-by-failure: in particular a call that succeeds using negation-by-failure is no longer necessarily a logical consequence of the (classical reading of the) program. However, it has a good chance of being a logical consequence of the completed database. This suggests that the correlation of success with logical consequence might be better referred to the completed database rather than to the program alone. In that case we would reformulate the desired soundness property for Prolog with negation-by-failure as follows:

a call is implied by the completed database if that call succeeds.

Unfortunately this does not hold invariably, although certain restrictions are sufficient to make it hold. The best known of these is the so-called safety restriction, which requires that a 'not' call be selectable for execution only if it is ground (that is, contains no free variables). This rule, however, cannot be enforced in all circumstances – execution may derive a query whose calls are all non-ground 'not' calls, in which case execution cannot be continued safely (i.e. soundly); this situation is commonly known as 'floundering' and there is no simple but practical way of preventing it from arising.

Other sorts of restriction attend the satisfaction of the corresponding completeness requirement for Prolog with negation-by-failure, but are qualified by hypothetical assumptions of fair call-selection and fair search which are unlikely to prevail in any practical Prolog environment. Moreover, reference to a completed database is in any case of no significance unless that database is self-consistent, for otherwise it implies *any* proposition and thus forfeits its value as a discriminator. To ensure such consistency one has to impose one or other restrictions upon the syntactical structure of the program; the best known restriction is the stratification property, which prevents a program from defining any ordinary call p in terms of 'not p', directly or otherwise.

Other constructions besides the completed database have been proposed as foundations on which to define consequence-oriented semantics for negation-by-failure. Some researchers have taken a quite different approach, relying upon no such artificial constructions but merely seeking to correlate the operational effects of negation-by-failure with particular preferred models of the programs themselves. These various studies, and the meta-studies of their interconnections, have led logic programming semanticists into labyrinthine complexities which most Prolog programmers – if they were aware of them – would take with a pinch of salt. For the fact of the matter is that negation-by-failure *in practice* is an overtly operational device, the logical meaning of which – if it could ever be formulated satisfactorily – would be unlikely in most circumstances to be genuinely representative of the programmer's conscious intentions. A mathematically tractable semantics would, of course, contribute usefully to formal methodologies for deriving, verifying or otherwise analysing Prolog programs; but, for better or worse, such activities preoccupy academics much more than they preoccupy practitioners.

The first logical analysis of negation-by-failure, and the development of the completed database semantics, was undertaken by Clark (1978). A more recent exposition of the theory of negation-by-failure, and of logic programming in general, is the book by Lloyd (1987).

36.5.5 The 'var' primitive

Although a given program is logically sufficient in principle for answering different queries, it will generally perform much better for some than for others. This is particularly evident when one varies the mode of a query – that is, when one varies the choice of which arguments are variables and which ones are not. For instance, suppose we solve the query ?–path(a, c). using our path-finding program and obtain the answer 'yes'. It does not then follow that the query ?–path(a, Z). can be solved with equal efficiency to yield the answer Z:= c. As a general rule, the more variables there are in a query the less efficient is its execution, due to the greater degree of non-determinism thereby introduced; in the worst case, relaxing the mode of a query – increasing the number of variables within it – may send execution into a loop.

In many cases it is sufficient, in order to cater satisfactorily with a change of query mode, to alter the order in which certain calls are selected for execution. This can be achieved either by altering the program text as the situation demands, or by incorporating language extensions which dynamically test the binding states of variables and thence divert control as appropriate to clauses whose calls are already suitably ordered. The standard Prolog extension for this purpose is the 'var' primitive.

Like the 'cut', this primitive can be inserted anywhere in the form of a call, and its operational effect is as follows: the call var(X) succeeds if, at the moment of its selection, the variable X is unbound, otherwise it fails.

Let us reconsider the earlier definition of the 'path' relation, and in particular the recursive clause:

path(X, Z) :– arc(X, Y), path(Y, Z).

This gives reasonable behaviour if its invocation binds X to a non-variable, but behaves much less efficiently otherwise, for then the ensuing 'arc' will have no values initially assigned to either of its arguments and will therefore present the maximum degree of nondeterminism: it will have to be solved, by repeated backtracking, with respect to every single arc in the database. It is no remedy in this case to reorder the calls in this clause, because that would send execution into a left-recursive loop. A better option for this situation is to use a logically different clause:

path(X, Z) :– arc(Y, Z), path(X, Y).

Thus we have two alternative clauses – one best-suited to the case where X, at least, is bound to a non-variable, and the other best-suited to the case where Z, at least, is bound to a non-variable. The two clauses behave with comparable efficiency in the case where both invoking arguments are variables and also in the case where neither of them are.

To achieve the desired run-time discrimination between the use of the clauses we could use the following Prolog program employing a (risky!) combination of 'var' 'not' and 'cut':

path(X, Z) :– arc(X, Z).
path(X, Z) :– not var(X), !, arc(X, Y), path(Y, Z).
path(X, Z) :– arc(Y, Z), path(X, Y).

Calls such as path(a, d) and path(a, Z) will now use the second clause at the exclusion of the third, whilst calls such as path(X, d) and path(X, Z) will use the third clause at the exclusion of the second. The use of the 'cut' could be avoided at the expense of having a longer program containing multiple occurrences of the two clauses suitably guarded by 'var' and 'not var' calls covering all the possible invocation modes.

Like the 'cut', addition of the 'var' primitive to otherwise pure definite clauses potentially incurs no penalty worse than a loss of completeness – it cannot compromise the soundness of computed answers. But also like the 'cut' and many other non-logical Prolog primitives it can be misused so as to enable the use of clauses which are themselves logically wrong according to the problem specification.

36.5.6 The 'assert' and 'retract' primitives

The execution of a definite-clause program at no stage alters the program itself. Yet there are some circumstances where it is convenient for a program to be modified dynamically. For example, if a large part of a stored database becomes computationally redundant part-way through execution and threatens to compromise the memory demands of the tasks still pending, it is justifiable to delete the unwanted material. In other circumstances one may wish to retain interim computed answers (treating them as lemmas) and access them later on rather than be compelled to recompute them; in this case it is natural, when these answers are first computed, to add clauses representing them to the stored program. The dynamic addition and deletion of clauses are supported in standard Prolog by the 'assert' and 'retract' primitives respectively. Each takes the form of a call whose argument is a term having the syntactic structure of a clause, and can be placed anywhere convenient within the input program. Thus, for instance, successful use of the clause:

father(X, Y) :– parents(X, Y, Z), male(Y),
$\qquad\qquad\qquad\qquad$ assert(father(X, Y)).

in response to a call father(chris, Y), given that the parents of chris are george and amelia and that george is a male, will not merely succeed but will also dynamically add to the program the new clause father(chris, george). In this case the clause added is guaranteed to be a logical consequence of the program, and therefore in no way compromises the soundness of execution. On the other hand, if we used the clause:

father(X, Y) :– parents(X, Y, Z), male(Y),
$\qquad\qquad\qquad\qquad$ assert(mother(X, Z)).

then the added clause mother(chris, amelia) would not necessarily be a logical consequence of the program. Prolog offers no inherent protection against the addition to the program of arbitrary facts, and thus the use of 'assert' is potentially unsound; likewise the use of 'retract' potentially detracts from the completeness of execution.

The 'assert' and 'retract' primitives can be used in combination to simulate the destructive assignment mechanism of procedural languages. Here is such an example, in which the aim is to add up a list of numbers by repeatedly modifying an accumulator represented by a dynamic clause total(T) which records the current total T:

sumlist(L, S) :– assert(total(0)), addup(L), total(S).
addup([U|L]) :– total(T), NextT is U + T,
$\qquad\qquad$ retract(total(T)), assert(total(NextT)), addup(L).

addup([]).

To the logic programming purist this is a horrendous example of misuse of these primitives, since the computed answer represented by the final state of the 'total' clause bears no discernible

logical relationship to the program itself. Such usage is in any case wholly unjustifiable even from an operational viewpoint. The proper way to program this simple problem is by a straightforward recursion:

sumlist(L, S) :– addup(L, 0, S).
addup([], S, S).
addup([U|L], T, S) :– NextT is U + T, addup(L, NextT, S).

Most good Prolog interpreters will execute this recursion iteratively within a fixed allocation of memory and thus intrinsically achieve the space-saving effects which presumably motivated the previous program. Moreover, the new program has the virtues of computing logically sound answers and of catering for a variety of query modes.

There are many other interesting but semantically dubious Prolog extensions which space forbids us to discuss here. Programmers who avail themselves of these facilities without any regard for their logical significance would, in most cases, be better advised instead to use a procedural language, whose operational features might well prove to be more natural and more efficient than their crude Prolog analogues. The only benefit to be had from using Prolog in a grossly procedural style is that it supplies built-in mechanisms for pattern-matching and exhaustive search; were it not for these, procedural Prolog would have far less to offer than any conventional programming language.

36.6 Significance for software engineering

The relationship between logic programming and software engineering is many-faceted. One of the major issues which motivates software engineering is the complexity of software and the consequent need for ways of maintaining intellectual and organizational control over its development. This has led to all sorts of recommendations regarding the features that ought to exist (or ought not to exist) in programming formalisms and also regarding the structural organization of programs written in those formalisms. Another important issue is the veracity and reliability of software in the face of the increasing responsibilities assigned to it. Numerous formalisms have been devised for the purpose of expressing user requirements and specifications, together with associated formal methods of constructing and verifying programs in relation to those specifications.

Much of this effort has been targeted, owing to commercial imperatives, upon conventional (procedural) software. Little analogous effort has so far been made – or been called for – in respect of declarative formalisms such as logic programming. One can suggest a number of reasons for this. In the first place, large-scale applications utilizing logic programming are still comparatively few (although rather more have been undertaken using plain Prolog), so that no widespread demand has arisen for appropriate methodologies. Secondly, logic programs are inherently less complex than their conventional counterparts, so that there is not so much pressure for managing complexity. Thirdly, logic programs ought, in principle, to be more transparent and thus their correctness – or otherwise – more self-evident. Fourthly, even when logic programs require rigorous verification, some aspects of that task are inherently simpler than for procedural programs. Lastly, it has been argued by some that the natural home of logic programming is not in routine application areas but in the specific area of artificial intelligence, where the essentially experimental and heuristic nature of programming does not conform to the basic tenets of the formal methods schools. Most of the above arguments remain matters of opinion, and are open to various interpretations.

In what follows we examine a few of the special features of logic programming which bear upon matters of software engineering.

36.6.1 The matter of complexity

Intuitively, complexity arises from the relationship or dependence between things – in the case of computer programs, from the logical and operational dependences between their statements. In procedural programs the main source of dependence is the use of destructive assignment, which typically makes the execution of one statement contingent upon completing the execution of another. This in turn forces a particular control regime upon the program, so that assignments are performed in the correct order. The complexity is further compounded if the control constructs are themselves sensitive to the current states of assigned variables.

The claim that logic programs are necessarily less complex is based on the fact that individual clauses assume meaning in their own right, independently of the context of their use. This argument needs careful dissection. Suppose we have in some program a clause:

A :– B, C.

as well as other clauses defining the relations B and C. Clearly, what we compute from that clause in response to a call to A must depend upon the program's definitions of B and C. Nevertheless, there are two different and important senses in which the clause does *not* depend upon those definitions. Firstly, the answers computable from it do not depend upon any operational assumption: they are determined by the program's logical content alone, irrespective of how the interpreter might arrange the temporal ordering of call evaluation and clause selection. This fact clearly minimizes the complexity of ascertaining the meaning of the program, because it need take no account of operational considerations; logical analysis alone is sufficient.

Secondly, suppose we have some specification, separate from the program, defining the relations A, B and C. Then the correctness or otherwise of any clause relative to that specification has no dependence upon any other clause. Our clause above for A can be correct as a statement about the logical relationship between A, B and C even if the clauses given elsewhere for B and C are nonsensical – they can play no role in one's judgements about the veracity of the clause for A relative to the specification. This fact clearly minimizes the complexity of the verification process.

Neither of these observations holds for procedural languages, nor can they hold for non-logical, procedural uses of Prolog. Both observations depend critically upon the assumption of pure logic programming.

In principle, such complexity as a logic program may possess should be little more than the inherent complexity of the application it describes (though this may, of course, be very substantial). The weakness of procedural languages is that they add to this natural complexity further complexity of their own making, deriving unavoidably from their machine-oriented semantics.

36.6.2 Logic specifications as programs

The customary restriction of pure logic programming to definite-clause logic often forces a certain amount of procedural bias upon programs. As an example of this, suppose we wished to define the immediate progeny IP of a person P; the immediate progeny is just the set of those persons who are children of P.

The most economical way of expressing this is by a non-clausal sentence as shown below, together with a sample database:

progeny(P, IP) :– (∀X)(member(X, IP) iff child(X, P)).
child(brendon, chris).
child(emlyn, chris).
member(brendon, chris's_progeny).
member(emlyn, chris's_progeny).

Logically this determines that the immediate progeny of chris is the set {brendon, emlyn}.

In many situations it is convenient to use the more flexible non-clausal language of first-order logic in order to set down requirements or preliminary specifications in a neutral fashion without prior commitment to particular problem-solving strategies. Moreover it is desirable that specifications in such a language should be executable, though not necessarily with optimal efficiency, in order to support rapid prototyping. In the case of the example above, we could, in principle, employ some standard theorem-prover for first-order logic in order to execute the 'progeny' specification. But it is cumbersome to employ several technologies when one will suffice. Through the careful use of negation-by-failure it is possible to simplify such specifications syntactically so that they take the form of ordinary Prolog clauses. In the present case we would obtain:

progeny(P, IP) :– not(child(X, P), not member(X, IP)),
                  not(member(X, IP), not child(X, P)).

Executed under standard Prolog for the case P:=chris, IP:=chris's_progeny, the first (compound) call confirms that no child of chris fails to belong to chris's_progeny, and the second (compound) call confirms that no member of chris's_progeny fails to be a child of chris.

Had we expressed the specification in definite-clause logic instead, we would have been compelled to change the data representation to list terms and then devise suitable recursions for scanning them – a much more 'algorithmic' style of programming.

36.6.3 Partial evaluation

The nature of the logical variable, profoundly different from the state variable employed by procedural formalisms, is such as to permit the partial evaluation of queries. Partial evaluation refers in general to the execution of a query in which commitment to values for the query arguments is partially withheld. Partial evaluation enables one to observe how execution proceeds for particular classes of query, and hence how to make certain program optimizations – for instance, in order to eliminate loops or to exclude the computation of unwanted answers.

The flexibility with which logic programs respond to variations in query mode is especially conducive to partial evaluation. Let's look at a simple example concerning who likes whom, for which we are given a database of atomic facts:

likes(brendon, emlyn).
anyone(brendon).
anyone(emlyn).
anyone(chris).
christian(chris).

followed by a general rule saying (approximately) that a Christian likes anyone who is his enemy:

likes(Y, X) :– christian(Y), anyone(X), not likes(X, Y).

Prolog execution of the query

?– likes(Y,X).

yields, in succession, the answers that brendon likes emlyn, chris likes brendon and chris likes emlyn; immediately after this, it becomes trapped in a loop. Partial evaluation can reveal why this is so and suggest a remedy.

It is clear that the loop arises from some use of the general rule, and that the first such use forces Y:=chris by evaluating the call to 'christian'. Thus the loop is instigated by querying, in effect, the proposition likes (chris, X). Let us therefore partially evaluate this less-general query step-by-step using the general rule as follows:

?– likes(chris, X).
?– christian(chris), anyone(X), not likes(X, chris).
?– anyone(X), not likes(X, chris).

first possibility	?– not likes(brendon, chris).
	succeeds for X:=brendon
second possibility	?– not likes(emlyn, chris).
	succeeds for X:=emlyn
third possibility	?– not likes(chris, chris).
	?– likes(chris, chris).
	?– christian(chris), anyone(chris),
	not likes(chris, chris).
	?– anyone(chris), not likes(chris, chris).
	?– not likes(chris, chris).

This clearly shows that for the case X:=chris the original goal of showing that chris likes himself reduces to the derived goal of showing that he does not, and that this goal merely regenerates itself to produce a loop. Thus, all that is needed in order to eliminate the loop is to modify the general rule so that it excludes the case X:=chris, as follows:

likes(Y, X) :– christian(Y), anyone(X), X\=chris,
$$\text{not likes}(X, Y).$$

This leaves the matter of how to deal with the residual case X:=chris. The above computation establishes that the program behaves as if it contained the explicit rule:

likes(chris, chris) :– not likes(chris, chris).

If the 'not' is interpreted classically as $\neg$ then this rule is logically equivalent to the proposition likes(chris, chris). If it is interpreted instead as showing that likes(chris, chris) finitely fails from the given atomic database then, since that call does so fail, a call likes(chris, chris) would succeed from that rule. So under either interpretation we ought to ensure that the fact likes(chris, chris) is derivable from the program; we can do this by simply adding that fact explicitly to the database. The result of these modifications is a program which computes exactly the intended answers and is loop-free.

36.6.4 Verifying the logical content of programs

To verify the logical content of a program requires showing, at the least, that any answer computable from it is in agreement with some independent specification; this property is referred to as the soundness of the program relative to the specification. When dealing with a logic program there is an additional obligation to show the converse – that any answer demanded by the specification is indeed computable from the program. This

property is referred to as the completeness of the program relative to the specification. (These two terms, used here to relate programs to their specifications, must be distinguished – despite the overloading of terminology – from the earlier use of the same terms to denote properties of inference systems.)

The definitions of these two properties use the term 'computable answer' to mean a logical consequence of the program – that is to say, an answer which is computable in principle using some perfect execution strategy. It is a separate issue as to whether the execution strategy actually employed suffers any deficiency – such as occur-check omission or unfairness – which might produce incorrect answers or fail to produce correct ones; neither the program nor its specification has anything to say about the means of execution.

The program property referred to here as soundness is the analogue of that known as partial correctness in the traditional verification theory of procedural formalisms. In applying the latter theory to a procedural program, the task of demonstrating partial correctness has, in general, a complexity which is exponential in the number of program statements, owing to their interdependences. By contrast, demonstrating the soundness of a logic program has a complexity which is only linear in the number of program clauses, since the correctness of any clause with respect to the specification has no dependence upon any other clause. Thus, for the partial correctness property at least, verification of logic programs is inherently less complex than that of procedural programs. In general, of course, verification must also include analysis of whether programs terminate when executed; on the whole, this is not much easier for logic programs than it is for procedural programs.

A specification for a program must fully define all the relations named in the program. It is desirable that such a specification should itself be expressed in logic, for this circumstance opens the possibility of basing verification upon direct deductive relationships between the specification and the program. For instance, if the specification implies the program then (a) the program must be sound and (b) deduction of the program clauses from the specification is sufficient to demonstrate it.

Logical specifications may consist either of other, possibly simpler, logic programs (supplemented by the closed-world assumption, in order to define their relations completely) or of sentences freely expressed in first-order logic, depending upon which is the most convenient for the given situation. Perhaps the best-known tutorial example concerns the 'subset' relation, specified in first-order logic as follows:

subset(X, Y) iff $(\forall U)$(member(U, Y) if member(U, X))
empty(X) iff $(\forall U) \neg$ member(U, X)
select(V, X, Z) iff member(V, Z),
        $(\forall U)$(member(U, Z) iff (member(U, X),
        $\neg$ U = V))

From this it is straightforward to deduce, as consequences, the top-level clauses of the familiar 'subset' program:

subset(X, Y) :– empty(X).
subset(X, Y) :– select(V, X, Z), member(V, Y), subset(Z, Y).

thereby verifying their soundness. Moreover it is easy to show that the exhaustiveness of the deduction method guarantees the clauses' completeness. This (modest) verification task lies within the scope of existing theorem-proving technology for first-order logic.

The use of first-order logic as a specification language from which to derive logic programs by deduction has been examined by Hogger (1981).

36.6.5 Deriving programs from programs

It is often easier to specify relations by means of a naive logic program than by means of the more complex language of unrestricted first-order logic – although it is not hard to find many exceptions to this rule. For this reason alone it is desirable to have procedures for confirming that one program agrees with another. In any case, programs inevitably evolve over time, long after the initial specification phase, so that such procedures are doubly desirable.

The most straightforward way of showing that one program is sound relative to another is to show that the former program is a logical consequence of the other – provided this property does hold in the given situation (it need not). Below is a simple example where the programs do have this property; both of them to serve to compute even and odd numbers represented in Peano notation.

First program   (Prog-1)

        even(0).
        even(s(s(X))) :– even(X).
        odd(s(0)).
        odd(s(s(X))) :– odd(X).

Second program (Prog-2)

        even(0).
        odd(s(0)).
        even(s(X)) :– odd(X).
        odd(s(X)) :– even(X).

Here is a simple deduction from Prog-2 cast somewhat in the style of a partial evaluation:

even(s(X)) :– odd(X).   [third given clause]
even(s(s(Y))) :– odd(s(Y)). [instantiating it with X:=s(Y)]
even(s(s(Y))) :– even(Y).   [invoking fourth given clause by
                              the 'odd' call]

which is just a variant of the second clause of Prog-1.

A virtually identical deduction derives from Prog-2, the fourth clause of Prog-1. The non-recursive clauses are common to both programs. Therefore Prog-1 is a logical consequence of Prog-2, and any answers implied by (computable from) Prog-1 must be implied by (and thus be in agreement with) Prog-2. In short, Prog-1 is sound relative to the specification Prog-2.

The converse also holds – namely that Prog-2 is sound relative to Prog-1 – but deduction alone, using just the clauses as axioms, is insufficient to demonstrate it. Neither can this insufficiency be overcome by adding the closed-world assumption. Stronger techniques are called for – we will consider these presently, after looking further at purely deductive derivation. The form of the deduction shown above is of a kind which has assumed great importance in logic program transformation; it is called 'unfolding'. Associated with it is another form of deduction called 'folding'. Their combination constitutes a very powerful (though not all-powerful) transformation procedure which, in effect, draws extra strength from its reliance upon the closed world assumption.

36.6.6 Unfolding logic programs

Unfolding is a special case of partial evaluation. Suppose we have some program and choose from it a clause, for any relation A, having at least one call B:

A :– calls, B, other-calls.

In normal circumstances the program will contain one or more clauses which can be invoked by that call – suppose, for instance, that there are two:

B :– more-calls
B :– yet-more-calls.

The unfolding at the first level of the clause for A with respect to its B call is defined as the set-of-clauses obtained by partially evaluating the B call using each clause for B. For the present example this unfolding comprises two new clauses for A:

A :– calls, more-calls, other-calls.
A :– calls, yet-more-calls, other-calls.

Two points about this process should be obvious: (a) the unfolding is a logical consequence of the given program and is therefore sound with respect to it, and (b) provided the B call is partially evaluated in every possible way (that is, uses every invokable clause), the original clause for A can be replaced by the unfolding with no loss of completeness. There is a third point to be made which is perhaps less obvious: (c) the execution of any A call will be equal or better in efficiency when using the unfolding than when using the original clause for A. Approximately, this is partly because some of the matching that would have been necessary in order for the A call to invoke the original clause has been effectively compiled into the argument structure of the unfolding's conclusions, and partly because the scheduling overheads originally arising from the intermediate B call have been eliminated. Note that these efficiency improvements are bought at the price of having a longer program. Unfoldings can themselves be unfolded through further levels, so that the growing accumulation of new clauses progressively approximates to a complete execution trace for the call being evaluated.

Let us now return to the program Prog-2 discussed previously:

    even(0).
    odd(s(0)).
    even(s(X)) :– odd(X).
    odd(s(X)) :– even(X).

and construct the (first-level) unfolding of its third clause. The 'odd' call has to be evaluated using two clauses for 'odd', yielding two new clauses for 'even':

    even(s(s(0))).
    even(s(s(Y))) :– even(Y).

Likewise the (first-level) unfolding of the program's fourth clause on its 'even' call is:

    odd(s(s(s(0)))).
    odd(s(s(Y))) :– odd(Y).

Substituting these unfoldings for their originating clauses gives the expanded program:

even(0).   odd(s(0)).
even(s(s(0))).   odd(s(s(s(0)))).
even(s(s(Y))) :– even(Y). odd(s(s(Y))) :– odd(Y).

whose greater efficiency is evidenced, for instance, by the fact that it can show that s(s(0)) is even in just one computation step, whilst the original program required two. The new program suffers a minor redundancy in that the second 'even' clause and the second 'odd' cause are both safely eliminable, for the solutions they afford can in any case be computed from the remaining clauses; this redundancy introduces a slight but unnecessary nondeterminism into most uses of the program. (It is inherited from an analogous minor redundancy in our starting Prog-2.) If we simply remove the two clauses, the result is the former program Prog-1.

Unfolding, and more generally partial evaluation, is a technique which can be implemented using the same core technology as is used in program interpreters. When we unfold a clause A :– B using another clause B :– C to obtain A :– C, this is essentially the same as generating a limited computation from the given clauses:

```
?– A.
?– B.
?– C.
```

which establishes that A holds if C holds – from which it follows that the program implies the clause A :– C. So clearly a Prolog interpreter could be adapted trivially to become a tool for unfolding and partial evaluation, although it should be noted that those techniques are often most effective when pursued using call-selection strategies somewhat more liberal than that of standard Prolog.

36.6.7 Folding logic programs

Folding is similar to unfolding to the extent that it involves replacing calls in clauses by material taken from other clauses, but it does so in a rather more subtle manner. Consider a particularly simple case in which the program contains the clauses:

```
A :– C.
B :– C.
```

Provided the second of these is the *only* clause for relation B in the program, the folding of the first clause on its C call with respect to the second clause is defined as the new clause:

```
A :– B.
```

In most practical circumstances the first clause can be safely replaced by the folding. The second clause stays unchanged.

The folding process relies upon the closed-world assumption and is sound relative to the completed database. In the above example, the assumption that the second clause is the *only* one for relation B determines that its contribution to the completed database of the program is the sentence B iff C which implies C :– B. By using the latter to unfold the C call of the program's first clause, we immediately obtain the desired folding result A :– B. More generally, any folding step applied to a logic program is equivalent to an unfolding step applied to the completed database.

The transformational power of unfolding and folding in combination can be indicated by the following example, which begins with yet another program expressing that a number Y is even if it is twice some natural number X:

```
even(Y) :– nat(X), twice(X, Y).
nat(0).
nat(s(Z)) :– nat(Z).
twice(0, 0).
twice(s(Z), s(s(W))) :– twice(Z, W).
```

First, unfold the first clause on its 'nat' call to produce:

```
even(Y) :– twice(0,Y).
even(Y) :– nat(Z), twice(s(Z), Y).
```

Next, unfold each of these upon their 'twice' calls; this produces just two more clauses:

```
even(0).
even(s(s(W))) :– nat(Z), twice(Z, W).
```

Finally we can fold the latter clause upon the conjunction of its two calls with respect to the first clause of the program, noting that solving those calls is the *only* way of solving even(W). The folding is therefore:

```
even(s(s(W))) :– even(W).
```

This together with the derived fact even(0) can now replace the original clause for 'even', which in turn makes the clauses for 'nat' and 'twice' superfluous and therefore eliminable. The end result of all these steps is a program which is very different in structure from the one we started with, as well as being much more efficient:

```
even(0).
even(s(s(W))) :– even(W).
```

The fold-unfold technique – first developed for functional programming – has since been developed extensively for logic programming, and has been shown capable of effecting many interesting and practical transformations. It has been studied extensively by Sato and Tamaki (1984). It can be viewed as an inference system whose axiom base is the (partly implicit) completed database. Just as for any other inference system, reasonable control strategies are required for its successful exploitation. In principle, all programs which are logical consequences of the completed database are derivable by fold–unfold applied to the given program. However, not all programs which are computationally equivalent to the given one belong to this category – hence our earlier remark that the technique is not all-powerful. It will be argued presently that greater power can be obtained, for the purpose of deriving and comparing programs, by a combination of consistency-analysis and loop-detection (equivalently, induction).

36.6.8 Consistency analysis

Solving a query ?– A. using a program P can be viewed as showing that P and ¬A are mutually inconsistent. (This is in turn equivalent to showing that P implies A.) For example, the successful execution in two steps of ?– A. using as P the clauses:

```
A :– B.
B.
```

can be viewed as a deduction in two steps:

```
¬A, A :– B.   ⇒ ¬B
¬B, B.        ⇒ inconsistency
```

During all stages of software development there are occasions when it is advantageous to perform consistency analysis. For example, one might want to test whether a set of user requirements is consistent, or whether it remains so after some new requirement has been incorporated. Consistency analysis also plays a useful role in the business of comparing programs and specifications. Since the standard execution of a query using a logic program is, in essence, a search for inconsistency, it follows that in order to demonstrate consistency it would be necessary that the search should fail. This means that every individual computation should either finitely fail or else be non-terminating (a loop).

Consider the question of whether the proposition even(a), where a is some constant distinct from 0, is consistent with this program P:

even(0).
even(s(s(X))) :- even(X).

Execution of the query ?- even(a). using P finitely fails, so confirming that even(a) is consistent with P.

Consider next the question of whether even(a) is consistent with the completed database comp(P). It is not necessary to construct comp(P) explicitly in order to do the analysis. This is because comp(P) is invoked implicitly whenever we execute a call using negation-by-failure. So all we need to do is execute, using just the clauses of P, the query ?- not even(a). This execution succeeds; since, in this example, the use of negation-by-failure is *sound* relative to comp(P), we therefore have:

comp(P) implies ¬even(a)

hence:

comp(P) is inconsistent with even(a).

The same result could have been obtained, more laboriously, by making deductions from the explicit formulation of comp(P), which is:

even(Y) iff Y = 0 or (∃X)(Y = s(s(X)), even(X))
together with the properties of '='.

The general point being made here is that standard Prolog technology, oriented to the detection of failure rather than of success, can be employed to test the consistency of propositions relative to both programs and completed databases. It is next shown how this fact can be put to practical use.

36.6.9 Testing for program equivalence

We investigate here the question of whether the two programs examined earlier:

Prog-1	Prog-2
even(0).	even(0).
odd(s(0)).	odd(s(0)).
even(s(s(X))) :- even(X).	even(s(X)) :- odd(X).
odd(s(s(X))) :- odd(X).	odd(s(X)) :- even(X).

agree upon the content of the 'even' relation – that is, whether they are computationally equivalent for that relation. It was shown earlier, using straightforward deduction, that Prog-1 is implied by Prog-2, ensuring that any answer even(t) which is computable from (implied by) Prog-1 is also computable from (implied by) Prog-2.

It was also noted earlier that Prog-2 is *not* implied by Prog-1. Suppose, however, we can show that Prog-2 is consistent with the completed database comp (Prog-1), and that comp(Prog-1) fully defines 'even' (which it does). (Formally, this latter property is called 'ground categorical completeness' and requires that, for any ground proposition A, comp(Prog-1) either implies A or implies ¬A.)

In this event all logical consequences of Prog-2 must also be consistent with comp(Prog-1). In particular, any answer even(t) computed from Prog-2 must then be consistent with comp-(Prog-1). This means that comp(Prog-1) cannot be consistent with ¬even(t) and therefore cannot imply ¬even(t). Due to its ground categorical completeness, comp(Prog-1) must then imply even(t). Finally, since a completed database implies an unnegated proposition if and only if its originating program does, it will follow that Prog-1 implies even(t). In summary, any answer computable from Prog-2 will be computable from Prog-1, the converse of the previous result; hence the two programs will agree exactly upon 'even'.

To show that Prog-2 is consistent with comp(Prog-1) we simply take each clause of Prog-2 in turn, rewrite it in equivalent form as a Prolog query and then show that this query fails when executed using Prog-1. This technique is now illustrated taking the second clause of Prog-2 and rewriting it as the query:

?- odd(X), not even(s(X)).

Execution of this using Prog-1 derives two computations corresponding to the two invokable 'odd' clauses. The first of these is:

?- odd(X), not even(s(X)).
?-not even(s(s(0))).

which finitely fails, whilst the second one is:

?- odd(X), not even(s(X)).
?- odd(Y), not even(s(s(s(Y)))).
?- odd(Y), not even(s(Y)).

which fails due to looping, since the derived query is structurally identical to the top query.

Analogous executions for the other three clauses of Prog-2 likewise all fail. Thus the result is established. Note that all we have relied upon for this exercise is Prolog supplemented by loop-detection.

The role of consistency-checking in program development and its comparison with program transformation is discussed in a paper by Hogger (1988).

36.6.10 Consistency and integrity checking

In a database application it is usual to augment the database with integrity constraints. The aim is to ensure that the (completed) database remains consistent with the constraints in the course of updating it. The same principle extends from databases to programs and specifications undergoing incremental development.

For the 'even and odd' programs a reasonable constraint is that no number shall be both even and odd, which can be represented by the query:

?- even(X), odd(X).

Using the technique just presented, it is easy to show, for

instance, that this is consistent with Prog-1. Suppose we update Prog-1 by adding to it the new clause even(s(0)). Does the result remain consistent with the constraint? To answer this, we begin with the update (since any proof of inconsistency is bound to involve it). From this and the constraint we obtain the derived query ?– odd(s(0)). and this succeeds using Prog-1, signifying an inconsistency. Thus the result of this update has been shown to violate the constraint.

The use of consistency analysis for logic database integrity has been described in detail by Sadri and Kowalski (1988).

36.7 Conclusions

Definite-clause logic programming is the simplest form of logic programming, syntactically, semantically and operationally. It is known to be adequate in theory for expressing and solving all computational problems, and is implementable by the basic Prolog execution strategy. In practice, however, there are many situations in which a restriction to definite-clause logic would result either in cumbersome representation schemes or in poor performance. Such considerations underlie the extensions provided by Prolog, of which the most vital is probably negation-by-failure. These extensions, however, greatly complicate the semantics. Some researchers believe that this dilemma will in time be partly resolved through meta-programming techniques.

A powerful feature of logic programming is its orientation towards the derivation of logical consequences and the relation which this bears to matters of consistency. These issues are central to many software-related activities. Even if logic programming should fail to become widely accepted as a programming language for routine applications, there remain good prospects for its use in software engineering tools and environments, whether these be oriented towards the development of logic-based software or of conventional software.

36.8 References

Clark, K. L. (1978) Negation as failure. In *Logic and Databases* (eds H. Gallaire, and J. Minker), Plenum Press, New York

Hogger, C. J. (1981) Derivation of logic programs. *Journal of the ACM*, **28**, 372–422

Hogger, C. J. (1984) *Introduction to Logic Programming*, Academic Press, Orlando

Hogger, C. J. (1988) Programming environments. In *Proceedings of European Conference on Artificial Intelligence* (Munich, 1988) (eds B. Radig, Y. Kodratoff, B. Ueberreiter, and K-P. Wimmer), Pitman Publishing, London, pp 698–706

Kowalski, R. A. (1974) Predicate logic as a programming language. In *Proceedings of IFIP-74*, North Holland Publishing Company, Amsterdam

Kowalski, R. A. (1979a) *Logic for Problem Solving*, Elsevier-North Holland, New York

Kowalski, R. A. (1979b) Algorithm = Logic + Control. *Communications of the ACM*, **22**, 424–431

Kowalski, R. A. (1981) Prolog as a logic programming language. In *Proceedings of AICA Congress*, Pavia, Italy

Lloyd, J. W. (1987) *Foundations of Logic Programming*, 2nd edn, Springer-Verlag, Berlin

Meta88 (1988) Proceedings of International Conference on Metaprogramming for Logic Programming. Department of Computer Science, University of Bristol. To be published as *Metaprogramming in Logic Programming* (eds H. Abramson and M. H. Rogers), MIT Press, Cambridge, MA

Sadri, F. and Kowalski, R. A. (1988) A theorem-proving approach to database integrity. In *Foundations of Deductive Databases and Logic Programming* (ed. J. Minker) Morgan Kaufmann, Los Altos, CA, pp 313–362

Sato, T. and Tamaki, H. (1984) Unfold/fold transformation of logic programs. In *Proceedings of the Second International Conference on Logic Programming* (ed. S.-A. Tarnlund), Uppsala University Press, Sweden, pp 127–138

Sterling, L. and Shapiro, E. (1986) *The Art of Prolog*, MIT Press, Cambridge, MA

van Emden, M. H. and Lloyd, J. W. (1984) A logical reconstruction of Prolog II. *Journal of Logic Programming*, **1** (2)

37

Development environments

Ruth Aylett
Howard Beck
Paul W H Chung
John L Fraser
John K C Kingston
Knowledge Engineering Group,
Artificial Intelligence Applications Institute,
University of Edinburgh

Contents

37.1 Introduction

An artificial intelligence (AI) system development environment may be defined as a programming environment which consists of an integrated collection of languages and software tools to support the development of AI systems. Before describing any specific development environments, this chapter first gives a brief description of the AI system development cycle, in particular for the development of knowledge-based systems, and then highlights the facilities that may be required in an ideal environment for supporting this style of working. Because of the interactive nature of AI programming, an ideal AI evironment shares many features of an ideal interactive programming environment (Barstow *et al.*, 1984; Sheil, 1987).

The development cycle of a knowledge-based system consists of a number of interconnected tasks, including knowledge acquisition, knowledge representation selection, system implementation, testing and debugging. The process is very complex and ill-defined. It involves gathering raw and unstructured data, and then analysing and representing it in an organized way. The refining and organizing of the data may have to go through several stages before the data can be represented in a formal way that can be used by the computer to draw inferences.

The most prominent characteristic of AI programming is the tendency to use highly interactive incremental development methods. In particular, a widely adopted approach to the development of knowledge-based systems places a great deal of emphasis on repeatedly confronting an expert with the behaviour of an unfinished version of the system which is modified in the light of his or her comments. Each iteration brings the behaviour of the system closer to completion, although, since it is often carried out without a clearly defined notion of completion, it is perhaps better thought of as iteration towards adequate achievement. This process is called rapid prototyping or experimental programming. Thus AI development environments, in contrast with those used in more 'conventional' software engineering, focus largely on support for programming activities.

Despite its detractors, the approach adopted within the AI research community has made its mark, since it has taken computing into new areas. In particular, it has allowed complex problems which cannot be accurately specified to be explored and represented. It gives the ability to see quickly whether a particular computational approach to a problem is working, and to change it or enhance it if it is not, making it possible to tackle problem areas that are too ill-defined to allow a system to be accurately specified in detail, and where the lack of confidence in the usefulness of the result makes committing the resources required for constructing a full system highly questionable.

This chapter illustrates the facilities that would be expected of an 'ideal' development environment, then considers the capabilities of 'state-of-the-art' environments by comparison with the ideal. It also discusses the capabilities of systems for knowledge acquisition (roughly equivalent to requirements analysis).

37.1.1 An ideal development environment

The ideal environment supports the programmer in all aspects of the exploration of problem representation and system implementation. It should be a cooperative and helpful environment in which the programmer can easily:

1. Inspect, modify and test programs.
2. Extend and develop programs incrementally.
3. Identify problems and deficiencies.
4. Dismantle, rebuild and test programs.
5. Work simultaneously on different parts of a program.
6. Change the level of abstraction at which he is working.
7. Use a variety of knowledge representations and inference mechanisms.
8. Get appropriate advice and assistance whenever it is needed.
9. Concentrate on problem solving without having to worry about housekeeping, such as file management.
10. Concentrate on problem solving without having to worry about writing efficient code.
11. Build modules of code that are portable to other applications.
12. Customize the environment.

In addition to the above, there is a growing appreciation that the environment should support the active process of knowledge-based system development; that is, there should be integrated support for both the acquisition and representation of knowledge. Some of the facilities which might make a development environment ideal are discussed below. This conception of an ideal environment is coloured by what is known to be available at present. No adventurous new facilities have been proposed. However, some of those which are not mentioned are not yet commonly available or are not yet in a state of sufficient maturity to be commercially useful.

37.2 Facilities of an ideal environment

37.2.1 Representation and inferencing

The core components of an AI environment are the representation and inferencing facilities. They should not constrain the programmer in his or her thinking about how to solve problems. It should be possible not only to switch from one problem solving paradigm to another but also to integrate several paradigms in the same solution. Different representation and inferencing paradigms are discussed in detail in Chapter 34 of this book.

37.2.2 Presentation

37.2.2.1 Interactive graphical interface

A good development interface lets the programmer see the environment through a collection of display windows, each of which corresponds to a different task or context. Moving from one task to another is simply a case of using a pointer or keyboard input to select the appropriate window.

A simple typical scenario might be to have an editor running in one window and a language interpreter running in another. Experimenting with code changes is done by flitting successively from one window to the other: using the editor to modify source code, using the language interpreter to run some test, using the editor to make further changes and so on.

At the same time the programmer might want to display a graph showing some structure such as a file hierarchy. This is displayed in a third window and is updated dynamically as it changes, for instance, when new files are created. Pointing to the name of a file in this window might allow the contents of the file to be printed or edited in a fourth window, or the file might be 'picked up' with the pointer and moved from one directory to another. Messages offering assistance to the programmer might appear in a fifth window.

One aspect of this style of work is that some mechanism is needed to control the proliferation of windows. Usually it is left to the programmer to manipulate the windows or the contents of a particular window by a combination of keyboard inputs and pointing operations.

One solution is to have each window fill the screen so that the whole window and nothing but the window for the particular task or context is visible while it is current. The drawback is that the programmer can see only one window at a time and all other tasks are hidden.

Perhaps the ideal environment should provide more in the way of support in keeping the workspace tidy but often that is a matter of personal taste and style.

Access to various operations on windows or within tasks is largely through menu selection using a pointer and/or simple keyboard input. Because AI programming is largely concerned with manipulation of symbols, the names of things tend to be long and self-explanatory. The programmer does not want to have to type in these long names in response to prompts from the computer, so the environment is capable of presenting the programmer with a set of options which are meaningful in the current context.

37.2.2.2 *Browsing*

Implicit in what has been said about the graphical interface is that the environment must be able to provide a variety of appropriate ways for the programmer to see quickly what has already been done or what is currently happening. Such browsers then provide easy access into whatever other information, operations or tasks are of interest to the programmer.

Very often it is useful for the programmer to be able to find out which bits of a program affect, or are affected by, which other bits. A program browser advises the programmer of the various dependencies. Knowing such dependencies can help in debugging or, when some design change is being mooted, can suggest whether or not it is feasible.

37.2.3 Editing

The programmer wants an editor to be 'smart' enough to give context-sensitive assistance as code is being written. For instance, it may be useful to have the names of procedures always appearing in a particular style or font. The smart editor will be able to recognize whether something that is typed in is the name of a procedure and change its font accordingly.

The conventions for indenting lines and inserting comments in code vary from language to language and the editor should be aware of that. Syntax checking is also very useful, as anyone who has had to count the brackets in Lisp without the editor's assistance will know.

Some editors are designed so that they allow insertion and manipulation only of structures that are allowable in the syntax of the language. For instance such a 'structure editor' for Lisp will refuse to let you cut-and-paste a portion of code which does not have a consistent set of matching brackets.

37.2.4 Program analysis

37.2.4.1 *Static program analysis*

A more interactive facility is provided by program analysers which build a database about programs or modules that have already been built. This database can be used to monitor the programmer constantly for inconsistent usage or to support some systematic change to all the code that has been written.

37.2.4.2 *Dynamic program analysis: tracing, breaking and debugging*

To identify where a potential solution is going wrong (or to identify why it is succeeding) the programmer needs a step by step description, at an appropriate level, of what the program is doing. Typically this 'trace' indicates which pieces of the program are being run, how they have been invoked, what parameters have been passed to them and what results or side-effects

they produce. In some cases a graphical trace gives a more instructive presentation of what is happening. Sometimes it is more useful to see the trace develop as it happens, other times it is more useful after the event as a record of what did happen.

Often a detailed description of program execution can give more information than the programmer needs and it can be tedious to sift through. So the ideal environment gives the programmer the opportunity to run the program without getting any trace information until the part of particular interest is reached, at which point execution 'breaks'. The programmer can say beforehand where (s)he wants the program to break. (More often it is the system that decides when to break, i.e. when some piece of code is encountered which cannot be executed properly for whatever reason!) So, by setting sensible break points, the programmer can step through execution of the program at whatever grain is appropriate.

We keep stressing the exploratory nature of AI programming. Another valuable source of assistance in exploration is the ability to modify things at a break point, undo part of the execution and redo it having made further changes. Ideally there should be a choice of levels at which changes can be made. For instance, the programmer might merely want to correct a spelling; or the name of some program module might be replaced by the name of another; or some fundamental changes might need to be made within a module that is producing the wrong results; or the same part of a program might need to be run on different sets of data.

37.2.4.3 *Performance monitoring*

The aim of the exploratory programming of AI is usually to come up with the design for a solution to some problem or subproblem. While exploring possible solutions the programmer is usually not too concerned about how efficient the resulting programs are, as long as they do the job. Often however the completed solution has to be applied in the real world and efficient implementation becomes important. The environment should be able to provide tools for performance monitoring and optimization.

37.2.5 Other aids

37.2.5.1 *Interpreted languages and incremental compilation*

The ideal environment supports the exploration of potential solutions while deferring the choice of the 'best' one as long as possible. New potential solutions need to be formulated often and then tested. The use of a language interpreter rather than compiled code allows this to be done speedily and without changing the source code until the programmer is satisfied that the changes are worthwhile.

Some extensions to AI languages such as rule systems require any additional or modified code to be compiled before the changes can be tested. Incremental compilation allows smaller pieces of code to be added and 'compiled in' to existing code without recompiling the existing code itself. Again this means a major saving in time if the programmer wants to explore several different potential changes.

37.2.5.2 *File maintenance*

At some stage the programmer is going to want to save the 'best' set of changes or perhaps several alternative sets of changes. The environment must be capable of maintaining the file system by making sure that changes get stored in the correct files and that old versions of files are saved and numbered as the programmer wishes.

The programmer often requires assistance in remembering the file location of particular bits of code. If the environment does the remembering, e.g. by providing ways of finding programs by function rather than by name, then so much the better.

37.2.5.3 *Help and online documentation*

The programmer often needs help to clarify what the environment's 'rules of combat' are, i.e. how the environment expects, requires or permits certain things to be done. The kinds of questions that are typically asked are: 'What is the possible range of responses to the question I've just been asked?', 'Is there a quick combination of keystrokes that I can use to achieve what I want to do?' 'What arguments does this procedure expect?', 'What is the source code for this procedure?' or 'How do I scroll this window?'.

The environment should be able to present the right kind of information according to the context in which the question is asked. Ideally the environment should also be sensitive to the level of competence of the programmer and to the actual dialogue which led to the current position.

37.2.5.4 *Miscellaneous*

There are further aids which appear in some environments to make the programmer's life a little easier.

One example is a spelling checker. When the programmer types something that is not recognizable as valid input the spelling checker can surmise what was intended by finding closely matching items which could be valid.

Another example is a command editor. This allows the programmer to reduce the amount of typing that has to be done by recalling commands that have already been made and repeating them or executing edited versions of them.

37.2.6 Flexible integrated facilities

37.2.6.1 *Integration of facilities*

Each of the facilities discussed so far is a valuable aid to the programmer. Where the ideal environment really scores is in its ability to integrate them. An example should bring this home. Consider the case where a rule-based system is not working as it should. The program breaks because of some error in a piece of code, say a rule. The debugger allows the programmer to identify where the break occurred and to inspect (perhaps graphically) whatever structures are relevant at the time, such as the rule trace or an object hierarchy. The debugger also identifies where the current definition of the offending rule resides; it could already be in an editor buffer or it could be in some file which has not yet been loaded into the editor. Whichever is the case, the programmer is presented with an editor window ready to accept changes to the rule. The programmer reads the text of the rule and concludes that it is not the rule itself that is the problem, but some piece of data on which the rule acts. A program browser window presents all the data on which the rule acts with their current values. One value is not as it should be. Pointing to the value brings up another program browser which shows all the ways in which the value might have been changed. Inspecting a graphical trace of all rule firings identifies the rule which last changed the value. As before the programmer can browse the rule without knowing its whereabouts beforehand. The rule invokes a couple of procedures unfamiliar to the programmer. One is system-defined. The help facility finds the online documentation which describes what the procedure does. The other procedure has been written by one of the programming team. Again the environment finds its location and loads it into the editor. The procedure needs to be changed. The programmer makes some changes to it but on compiling it the environment discovers that the changes call another procedure with the wrong number of arguments. Having re-made the

required changes, the programmer than compiles the new version of the procedure, without having to re-compile the rest of the program. He then rolls back program execution to the point just before where the rule fired and runs the system forward again from there.

This kind of scenario, in which many activities are invoked within a short space of time and in no predetermined order, frequently occurs during program development. The programmer will be frustrated if there is not a smooth transition from one activity to another. Thus the various activities must be well integrated with each other.

37.2.6.2 *Integration with other applications*

There should also be good integration with other support activities which are not fundamental to program development. For instance, the programmer may want to send an enquiry by electronic mail to a colleague or to a software vendor about some problem that has occurred. It will save a lot of time and possible misunderstanding if the actual input and output associated with the problem can be copied directly from the environment into the mail message while the programmer is still in the debugger. Similarly the preparation of all sorts of documents can be speeded up by having direct access to the original code or screen dumps or records of dialogues. There may well be other applications, such as databases and spreadsheets, with which the AI application will need to communicate. The environment should make it possible for this to happen.

37.2.6.3 *Customization*

Programmers are individuals and will devise their own preferred ways of doing particular tasks, viewing particular pieces of data or conducting dialogue. The environment should allow programmers the flexibility to tailor, and possibly extend, the environment to satisfy their own needs and preferences.

37.3 Current development tools

Knowledge-based system development tools may be broadly divided into three categories: symbolic languages, expert system shells and hybrid toolkits. These will be discussed in turn, with examples given from systems that are commercially available.

37.3.1 Symbolic languages

Before the invention of shells and hybrid toolkits, early AI work was done using symbolic languages. Symbolic languages are preferred because they facilitate easy creation and manipulation of arbitrary symbols and structures. This section considers the two most influential languages: Lisp and Prolog. Another practical language that belongs to this category is POP-11 (Barrett *et al.*, 1985). Since the Lisp and Prolog languages are considered elsewhere in this book, this chapter concentrates on their programming environments.

37.3.1.1 *Lisp*

Lisp (McCarthy, 1960) is one of the oldest high-level programming languages, dating from the early 1960s, which makes it nearly as old as FORTRAN. Its name stands for LISt Processing: giving the programmer the ability to manipulate lists of symbolic information without needing to worry about explicit pointers or store management has turned out to be a basic requirement for a useful AI programming language. Lisp is a flexible and extensible language. Program and data share the same list representation, allowing a program to be used as data and vice versa, so that the language can be extended and reshaped by the programmer. This has allowed, for example, the addition of object-oriented programming extensions.

Most of the early classic systems of AI have been written in Lisp, and it has also been the language for implementing toolkits for building knowledge-based systems (e.g. ART and KEE, which will be described in some detail later).

Lisp development environments A small-scale, widely used example of a Lisp environment is the EMACS screen editor (Stallman, 1987). This is widely available under Unix and other operating systems, and allows multiple windows to be manipulated on ordinary terminals so that for instance, program source and interpreter windows can share a screen. A number of modes appropriate to different languages (including Lisp of course) are provided, supporting intelligent formating and syntax checking facilities. EMACS also contains its own extensive help system and a Lisp interpreter so that a user can write his own commands and tailor the EMACS environment.

At the other end of the scale are those environments mounted on specialized hardware known as Lisp machines – single-user workstations dedicated to the support of programming in Lisp from the hardware level up, such as Symbolics, Xerox 1186, or TI Explorer machines. These systems pioneered graphical WIMP (windows, icons, mouse, pull-down or pop-up menus) interfaces on large bit-mapped screens. They aim to remove the conventionally rigid distinction between the facilities expected of an operating system and those expected of a programming language and offer a complete integration between operating system, interpreter and other facilities, so that everything is accessible and modifiable. Rather than a self-contained piece of code, a program in such a system becomes an extension of the environment for the needs of the programmer, with data-level integration so that functions and data are shared by all processes. All code, including that of the operating system, is therefore reusable. An interpreter, an incremental compiler, a variety of debugging devices, a file handler, an editor, and context-sensitive help facilities are instantly available at any point.

Although the philosophy behind the development of Lisp machines is the same – to provide hardware support for Lisp – the hardware architectures of different machines can be very different (Greenblatt *et al.*, 1987). Of course, the user only sees the software environments, but even then the differences could be quite significant. For example a Symbolics machine would run Common Lisp (Steel, 1984) and provide ZMACS, an EMACS-like text editor. On the other hand, a XEROX 1186 would run InterLisp-D (Xerox, 1985) and provide a structure editor. Though Common Lisp is emerging as a *de facto* language standard, there is no standard Lisp environment. See Barstow *et al.* (1984) for more information on Lisp machines, EMACS, and other programming environments.

Lisp machines are being seriously challenged by more conventional workstations, such as those offered by Sun and Apollo, precisely because conventional workstations have adopted some of the most popular features they pioneered, but at a lower cost and with less specialized hardware. The idea of providing add-on processors for conventional workstations to provide Lisp support may catch on.

Even though the Lisp machines themselves appear to be being displaced by increasingly powerful general-purpose workstations, their software development environments are still among the closest approaches to the ideal presented earlier. For instance, the Genera system, developed for the Symbolics Lisp machines, provides most of the identified desiderata to a significant extent. Context-sensitive help concerning the effect of possible mouse clicks is continually offered. In addition, short documentation of a function or command and the arguments it requires can be obtained with a couple of key strokes, or its program code loaded into the editor. The full manuals for the system can be accessed through a hypertext-style documentation examiner. The system supports very flexible program tracing and breakpointing facilities. There are signs that such environments will be made available on other hardware platforms.

37.3.1.2 *Prolog*

Prolog (PROgramming in LOGic) is based on the Horn clause subset of first order predicate logic (see Chapter 32 for a discussion of Prolog). An efficient compiler and interpreter developed at Edinburgh University first demonstrated Prolog as a practical programming language (Warren, 1977). There are now many implementations of Prolog available on micros, workstations, mainframes and even Lisp machines. The *de facto* standard is a sub-set of the original implementation by Warren *et al.* (1979) described by Clocksin and Mellish (1987). Prolog has received a great deal of attention partly because it has been chosen by the Japanese for their fifth-generation computer project.

Prolog development environments Since Prolog is a relatively new language, there is still much to be learned about it. Hence, the development of environments for Prolog is still in its early stages. The most common facility of this type is for tracing. Most commercial implementations of Prolog adopt the debugging model described by Byrd (1980a, 1980b). The model is based on four kinds of events: call, exit, redo and fail. A call event occurs when Prolog starts trying to satisfy a goal. An exit event occurs when a goal has just been satisfied. A redo event occurs when the system tries to re-satisfy a goal. A fail event occurs when a goal fails. During the execution of a program, the tracer, when enabled, informs the user when events of these four kinds occur.

Quintus Prolog, which runs on workstations and minicomputers, is one of the most advanced commercially available versions of Prolog. It provides an interface with the EMACS editor which allows part of the source code to be incrementally loaded into the system. This is useful when only a small part of the program has been modified. Quintus Prolog has a built-in style checker which warns the user if the source code is written in a way that violates certain style conventions. It also has an extensive help facility allowing the user to get help on Prolog and to access the manual on-line. Quintus Prolog, in contrast to many PC-based Prolog systems, does not have any built-in facilities for manipulating menus or windows, but library routines written in C can be loaded into the system.

Because Prolog employs a very different computational model from other programming languages, using unification and backtracking, some research effort has gone into classifying Prolog bugs and developing novel debugging facilities to help the user to understand or follow the control flow (Brna *et al.*, 1987). There are other research projects that study how different tools may be integrated in a principled way in a Prolog environment (Bowles, 1988; Bowles and Wilk, 1988).

37.3.2 Expert system shells

Many expert systems are developed using expert system shells. A typical expert system shell is a tool which would normally run on a PC and would cost anything from several hundred to a few thousand pounds. A shell will consist of a knowledge representation language, an inference engine and user interface facilities, and usually include interfaces to other software packages or languages.

Shells usually represent knowledge using IF ... THEN rules

and facts, which places some limits on the tasks for which they are useful. There are two types of inference that are used by rule-based systems. Forward chaining means that when all the conditions of a rule are true, the specified conclusion should be drawn. Backward chaining means that, to show that a conclusion is true, show that all of the premises that support it are true.

Expert system shells usually provide some fairly useful interface facilities for program development and applications. For example, a system may provide a template for filling in the details of rules, or have built-in facilities for creating menus and multiple screens which make the application programs attractive and easy to use. Some systems even provide explanation facilities for handling why and how questions. In the expert system context, why questions usually have the restricted meaning 'why are you asking me this question now?' and how questions have the meaning 'how did you conclude *X*?'. Another common feature found in shells is the ability to call procedures that are written in conventional languages like C and Pascal, and the ability to access database packages like dBase III.

There are a variety of advantages to using a shell. These include the following:

1. Cheap to buy and the hardware that it runs on is fairly widely available.
2. Relatively easy to learn and easy to use.
3. Experts often find it easy to express their knowledge in a rule-like format.

The limitations of using a shell become obvious after a few weeks or months to those who use them to write programs. Two main ones are:

1. As the rule base gets bigger, it is difficult to maintain.
2. It is restricted to one way of representing knowledge.

There are a large number of shells on the market today. Two of the most popular shells – Crystal and Xi Plus – will be examined in some detail.

37.3.2.1 Crystal

This brief description is based on Crystal version 3. Crystal is marketed by Intelligent Environments Ltd, and runs on an IBM PC or compatible machine with a minimum of 350 K RAM. It has been available for about five years.

Representation and inferencing Crystal is entirely rule-based; no facilities are available for structuring data in frames, (see below), objects, or any other format. Rules in Crystal have one or more conditions, and one conclusion. Each condition is either a symbolic or numeric expression which is evaluated (perhaps by invoking other rules) to 'true' or 'false'. If all the conditions are evaluated as 'true', the conclusion of the rule is set to be true; otherwise, it is set to be false. Each rule must have a different conclusion, but the rules allow disjunctions ('OR') or in their conditions, so it is possible to specify different ways to reach the same conclusion.

In the conditions of the rule, information may be obtained from the user, and numeric variables can be assigned to, compared or displayed. The values of numeric variables are globally accessible. A wide range of numeric functions are provided: real arithmetic, functions for trigonometric, mathematical, and financial calculations, and a Bayesian probability function. Variables that have symbolic values may also be used.

The inference mechanism used by Crystal is backward chaining. The system attempts to prove the conclusion of a rule, and to do so it attempts to prove the truth of each of the conditions. These conditions can be proved either by investigating further rules whose conclusion proves the truth (or otherwise) of the conditions of the first rule, or by asking the user.

The control strategy is highly procedural, and is fixed by the system; the user cannot alter it. New rules cannot be built and added to the rule base during a run of the system. The system's degree of belief in stored or deduced knowledge can be tuned finely using probability values which are combined using Bayesian probability techniques.

Development facilities Development facilities include:

1. *Presentation.* Crystal, like most systems which run on PCs, displays one window at a time. However, certain other windows (such as a dictionary of terms) are available from menus which are easily accessible to the user. Because its development environment is largely menu-based, Crystal is easy to learn.

   Crystal also offers help in building a system. Users are encouraged to start off by using the Crystal system builder, which provides a template for modifying or adding new rules, and then to save code in compiled form. This is useful for training and for rapid prototyping, since it greatly reduces the number of syntax errors made. A graphic display of the rule base hierarchy is also available if an additional graphics package is purchased. For more complicated systems, rules can be written in files which are then loaded and compiled.

   The user interface of an application developed using Crystal is usually based on forms of text, since these are easy to create and display in Crystal. However, it is possible to display graphics which have been created using GEM or a similar package.

2. *Program analysis.* Crystal provides a rule tracer which can step through rules one at a time, or can step through a rule line by line. At any point, all the currently determined variable values can be viewed and modified. In addition, the Crystal system builder includes a browser and cross-referencer for rules.

3. *External interfaces.* Crystal has a variety of external interfaces. It can call external C code. It can also access spreadsheets (either Lotus 1-2-3 or Symphony), by reading them into a buffer (where they can be both read and updated) and displaying them; the updated buffer can be written back to the spreadsheet. It can also access dBase III files with its own indexing mechanism. The facilities provided for normal database and spreadsheet manipulation are adequate.

37.3.2.2 Xi Plus.

Xi Plus is marketed by Expertech Ltd. It runs on an IBM PC AT or compatible machine with a minimum of 512Kb of memory.

Representation and inferencing Xi Plus stores knowledge in rules, but unlike Crystal it maintains a small database of facts about the world. The rules are written in a form very similar to simple English. Both forward and backward chaining inference methods are available. Xi Plus also incorporates 'demons' or 'active values', which are functions which are attached to a particular fact, and which are executed every time that fact is accessed or changed.

Development facilities Development facilities include:

1. *Presentation.* Xi Plus uses one window at a time. The interface with the application developer is mostly based on menus. It provides a menu-driven interface for building a knowledge base interactively, using the system's editor. Xi Plus is easy to use; the English-like syntax of the rules helps.

   Its main facility for developing interfaces for applications is forms, although it also allows graphics developed using the GEM package to be displayed.

2. *Program analysis.* Xi Plus provides a knowledge base checker, which identifies rules with unused conclusions, statements that cannot be proved, and possibly conflicting values. It also has a tracing facility which traces rules which have been tested and fired, and may display the database of facts and the agenda of rules waiting to fire as well.

3. *External interfaces.* Xi Plus provides interfaces to C and Assembler. It also provides a function for reading from databases, but any other operations have to be done using C or Assembler. However, Xi Plus does have a facility to allow itself to be switched out of memory, and a spreadsheet or database package (such as dBase III) to be switched in, which allows the expert system to make use of the commands provided by the exernal package.

4. *Other aids.* The commands for adding rules and information to the knowledge base can be used during a consultation, if necessary. This means that the knowledge base can be updated dynamically.

Xi provides 'why?' and 'how?' explanations of its reasoning, although these are limited to the knowledge base which is currently loaded; on a smaller PC, several knowledge bases might be needed for an application.

37.3.3 Toolkits

In the development of knowledge-based systems, it quickly became apparent that rules were inappropriate for some types of knowledge-based system. One solution to this problem was to use frames, also known as schemata or units, to represent data, and to perform inference using object-oriented and access-oriented programming. However, frame-based systems also have their limitations (Kingston, 1987), and it is not unusual for different parts of a problem to be best represented using different knowledge representations. This situation has led to the creation of more sophisticated toolkits for building knowledge-based systems, which are multi-paradigm tookits; that is, they incorporate and integrate different methods of representing knowledge and for drawing inferences from that knowledge.

Multi-paradigm toolkits may be designed by providing interfaces for a selection of programming languages which are popular in AI (such as POPLOG or Knowledge Craft), by augmenting an existing system with a new language construct (such as the version of the HOPE functional language which incorporates unification), or by designing a new system that supports different paradigms (such as Inference ART or KEE). In general, toolkits are very useful for designing prototypes of knowledge-based systems rapidly. However, they are more expensive than expert system shells and require more powerful computing resources.

This section reviews two such toolkits: Inference ART and KEE. These two products could be considered as the state-of-the-art commercial multi-paradigm toolkits. Note that this is not intended to be an evaluation of these two systems, since multi-paradigm systems cannot be compared very well by lists of options.

Both toolkits include a frame-based representation of knowledge, forward and backward chaining rules which can make use of this knowledge, and object-oriented and access-oriented programming. They also include facilities for truth maintenance (de Kleer, 1986) using contexts, and sophisticated development environments.

37.3.3.1 Inference ART

This review is based on Inference ART version 3.1 (henceforward called ART in this chapter). ART was originally developed on Symbolics Lisp machine hardware, and is now available on a range of Symbolics and Texas Instruments Lisp-based workstations, SUN 3, Apollo and Hewlett Packard workstations, and a range of DEC VAX hardware.

Representation and inferencing ART works in the following ways:

1. *Frames.* ART can represent data using either frames, which are known as schemata in ART, or arbitrary propositions (known as facts). The value of a slot can be an arbitrary Lisp structure. Inheritance occurs between schemata, and multiple inheritance (inheritance of several values from different schemata) is allowed.

For every slot, a schema exists which defines the behaviour of that slot. This is a powerful feature, because the users can define their own slots, and specify the characteristics of the slot-behaviour schema to themselves. This allows the users to define whether slots can contain one or many values, whether the slot can be inherited, and so on. Some slots are used as relations – links between schemata across which inheritance may occur. Relations may be transitive or reflexive, and ART allows inverse relations to be created automatically.

2. *Rules and rule-based programming.* ART's rule system is similar to the OPS5 production rule system, but has been considerably extended. The conditions of an ART rule may include facts or schemata, assumptive truth maintenance operators (such that the conclusions of the rule are retracted if the stated assumptions are ever falsified), and arbitrary Lisp predicates.

ART allows rule-based programming using either forward or backward chaining, or both. It achieves this by noting the goal patterns which can be satisfied by backward chaining rules; when a goal pattern appears among the conditions of another rule whose other conditions are matched, a backward chaining rule competes for firing in the same way as forward-chaining rules do. ART performs conflict resolution based primarily on user-defined rule priorities. The conclusions and actions of an ART rule allows modifications to facts or schemata, and the execution of arbitrary Lisp functions.

ART also allows the user to improve the efficiency of a system by restricting the invocation of backward-chaining rules, and by optimizing the construction of the join network (into which the conditions of ART rules are compiled). ART's rule-based programming is therefore very powerful.

3. *Object-oriented programming.* Objects in ART are represented using schemata, with some slots which have methods associated with them. ART supports a simple syntax for creating methods and sending messages. The methods themselves (known as actions) are defined using Lisp functions. Actions can be inherited, and the order in which inherited actions and locally-defined actions are executed can be changed.

4. *Access-oriented programming.* ART supports active values which are defined using schemata. They can be executed just before or just after a slot's value is read, asserted, changed, or deleted.

5. *Context manipulation.* ART supports a context mechanism which allows rules to create, delete, or merge hypothesized states, known as contexts. This mechanism is an extension of the Assumption-Based Truth Maintenance System described by de Kleer, (1986). ART tries to match the conditions of rules in any context and, if a rule has conditions which are matched in two or more different contexts, ART will automatically 'merge' those contexts to create a new context in which that rule can fire. Contexts which combine inconsistent information (e.g. multiple inheritance for single-valued slots) are automatically deleted. The user is also allowed to specify

that certain conditions should not occur together, and if they do then that context is to be deleted. ART's context mechanism is very efficient, because it does not actually copy any information into a new context – it simply marks which facts may be inherited into that context from others, and which may not.

ART also supplies the viewpoint mechanism, which allows the user to maintain multiple distinct but interacting context hierarchies. This allows the user to factor out different kinds of knowledge. For instance, a context hierarchy might be used if a stockbroker wanted to examine the consequences of investing in a particular stock, given any one of a number of future economic conditions. If the stockbroker had two clients, one of whom was interested in a very high rate of return, and the other was most interested in protecting an initial investment, then he or she might use viewpoints as a second context tree to allow decisions to be made using two different strategies, based on the same hypothesized future conditions.

Development environment The development environment has the following features:

1. *Presentation.* ART's development is mouse- and menu-based. (ART also provides a 'scrolling studio' for use on text-only terminals which are remotely logged in to a host which runs ART.) The ART interface provides a top-level menu which can be used to access a wide variety of information and optional commands. This information is displayed in several windows which can be drawn out wherever the programmer wants them. Among other options, the user can examine particular rules, examine and modify the knowledge base using an editor, display a diagram of an inheritance hierarchy (schema or context hierarchies) which may be dynamically updateable, and obtain statistics about the program to aid in improving program efficiency.

   The structure of the menus appears to be hierarchical, but in fact it is possible to move around between lower levels of the hierarchy directly. For instance, the user can browse a rule and move to browsing the conditions of a rule in another menu. He or she can then move directly to browsing a schema which matched the conditions of that rule, and can move on to another schema via a menu associated with a slot.

It is possible to select and browse a rule from graphical displays of rules, schemata or viewpoints – full browsing facilities are available on the selected program object. *Figure 37.1* shows part of a viewpoint network with a menu, obtained by clicking the mouse on HYPOTHETICAL-1 in the diagram, which offers access to the information contained in viewpoint HYPOTHETICAL-1. Access to screen editors and various other facilities is also available from various points in the menu system.

As for graphics, the ARTIST icon editor allows icons to be created using the mouse and menu options; schemata are created automatically to represent icons. A variety of graphics can be created and combined. Bitmap graphics and computationally efficient graphics are available. Menus can also be customized for use in the interfaces of applications.

2. *Program analysis.* Other options available from menus include viewing the agenda of rules which are about to fire, asking for rules to be traced or asking for rule firings to be justified. The rule trace provides varying levels of detail; the system may run with no trace at all, or reporting the name of each rule as it fires, or reporting the name of each rule and the facts which matched that rule's conditions as well.

   In addition, ART provides justification of rule firings and facts, which provides detailed answers to 'how?' questions for the application developer.

3. *External interfaces.* The only external interfaces which ART has are those available with Common Lisp, on which ART is based. Sun Common Lisp provides an interface to C.

4. *Other aids.* ART allows the user to create files (and, more importantly, alter and then incrementally recompile rules, facts and schemata) using a conventional screen editor (usually EMACS).

   On-line help is terse. It is desirable for the user to have read the tutorials which accompany the manuals. Fortunately, these tutorials are fairly well written.

37.3.3.2 KEE

This review is based on KEE 3.1. KEE is currently available on most Lisp workstations (Symbolics and TI Explorer/Micro-Explorer), a range of 'engineering' workstations (SUN, Apollo, HP9000 and DEC VaxStation), IBM mainframe and some PCs (IBM PS/2 and Compaq 386 with memory expansion boards).

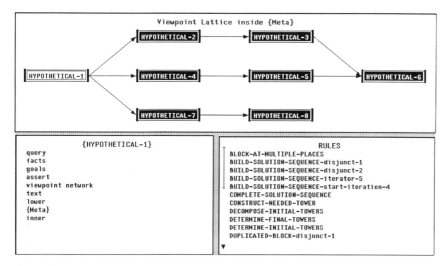

Figure 37.1 Viewpoint network and menu relating to a particular network

Representation and inferencing KEE uses the following features for representation and inferencing:

1. *Frames.* The majority of data in KEE is represented using frames, which are known as units in KEE, although it is also possible to represent unstructured arbitrary facts. KEE supports inheritance and multiple inheritance between units.

   In KEE, each slot is provided with a series of constraints. The constraints on a slot allow the user to control the inheritance of multiple values by the slot, to specify the type or range of a slot value, to put cardinality restrictions on a slot value, to attach active values to monitor a slot value, and attach graphical images which display the slot value and may allow the value to be updated graphically.

2. *Rules and rule-based programming.* KEE incorporates three types of rules – standard rules (used for forward and backward chaining); deduction rules (used for reasoning about beliefs which are dependent on other beliefs in a similar fashion to ART's assumptive truth maintenance system); and new world rules which allow context manipulation.

   Rules are partitioned into rule-sets, and reasoning is restricted to the rules within selected rule-sets. In KEE the same rules can be used for both forward and backward chaining; if a fact is asserted, and a particular rule-set is invoked, then forward chaining may occur; if a query regarding a fact (possibly containing one or more variables) is made, then backward chaining may occur. Intermixing of forward chaining and backward chaining is possible, as is the simultaneous consideration of several rule-sets.

   The KEE user is provided with a number of switches to control the strategies used in rule selection. The search strategy used when backward chaining can be set to be depth-first, breadth-first, or best-first search, or a user-defined strategy. For forward chaining the user can ask the system to prefer the most specific rule, the rule which matches the most recent data, the rule with the highest user-defined priority, or to apply a rule selection stategy defined by the user.

3. *Object-oriented programming.* The object-oriented facilities of KEE are well developed, since KEE's development was based on an object-oriented system. Lisp functions or lambda expressions can be attached to frames as the value of slots. Messages to invoke these methods are sent using a simple command that specifies the unit and the slot to which the message is being sent, as well as any arguments that the method function might require. Inherited methods can be overridden by local methods, or modified by attaching extra local code before, after or 'wrapped around' the inherited code.

4. *Access-oriented programming.* An active value can be defined by creating a unit. This unit can then be attached to the slot(s) to be monitored. The slots of the active value unit define what actions should be taken whenever a monitored slot value is read, asserted, added, or removed.

5. *Context manipulation.* Contexts in KEE are known as worlds. KEE allows worlds to be created, deleted or merged. When a slot value is changed in a world, a new copy of that slot is created, which is considered to exist in the specified world. Slots and values which exist within a world may be inherited by other worlds. The user is allowed to specify that certain worlds may not be merged, or to define rules that detect inconsistent states within a world. KEE will also declare a world to be inconsistent if it violates any restrictions on slots, such as the cardinality, type, or range of slots. KEE allows inconsistent worlds to be 'resurrected' if the inconsistency is removed, which is useful for debugging.

   Chaining of rules can take place within the context of a particular world, and the conclusions of each rule may be asserted, in the same or a newly created world.

Development environment KEE's development environment comprises the following features:

1. *Presentation.* KEE provides an extensive development environment for building knowledge-based systems. It uses multiple windows, available through mouse clicks on menus or on pre-defined icons. It provides a schema and knowledge base browser, a graphics interface development package, diagrams of knowledge bases and rule sets, a language for querying the knowledge base and an EMACS editor.

   The graphics interface development package is mouse- and menu-based. It is based around KEEpictures, an extensive range of pre-defined graphic items which can be defined using units (and animated by changing the values of slots). Examples of KEEpictures are lines, rectangles, curves and bitmaps. Another feature of the package is ActiveImages, which are graphics which allow direct access to the values of slots. An ActiveImage displays a slot value, alerts the user if the value reaches a chosen limit, and allows the user to change the value by clicking the mouse on the graphic. Examples of ActiveImages are gauges and thermometers.

   Almost all interaction with KEE's development tools is performed via menus. KEE menus can be customized for use in the interfaces of applications. *Figure 37.2* shows a menu which has been customized for a particular application: clicking on the taxi icon produces a menu which provides information about the taxi. The diagram also shows three ActiveImages.

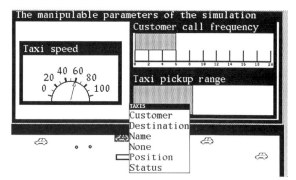

Figure 37.2 Customized menu and ActiveImages developed in KEE

2. *Program analysis.* KEE's debugging information includes a viewer for the agenda of forward chaining rules; dynamic graphic traces for forward chaining rules, backward chaining rules, and worlds; textual traces for rules and methods; a rule cross referencer; and the (machine-dependent) Lisp debugger.

   KEE provides justifications of the derivation of facts after rules have fired. It will also tell the user why the truth maintenance system declared certain facts to be contradictory.

3. *External interfaces.* KEE provides two add-on packages for external interfacing: the KEE-C integration toolkit (a set of Lisp functions for accessing C from KEE or Lisp and C routines for vice versa), and KEEconnection, which allows KEE to interrogate databases using SQL, such as ORACLE or INGRES. KEEconnection is not available on all hardware.

4. *Other aids.* KEE 3.1 provides a rule compiler which permits efficient execution of rule-sets once they have been developed and debugged. As for ART, on-line help is generally terse. One of the add-on packages, called SIMKIT, provides facilities for developing simulation applications.

37.4 Current knowledge acquisition tools

The importance of knowledge acquisition to systems which rely upon the richness of the knowledge embodied within them for their power was recognized very early on. AI/IKBS life cycles typically assume the availability of a knowledge engineer who has a role similar to that of a requirements analyst – facilitating the articulation of knowledge, and organizing and structuring the knowledge so it can be used in the programs to be developed. Knowledge acquisition was also identified as a potential bottleneck within the process of constructing knowledge-based systems (Feigenbaum, 1977; Waterman, 1986), so that the identification and construction of tools and environments which might assist the knowledge engineer – or even remove the need for such an intermediary between expert and system – might appear to be an early priority.

In practice, it turned out to be more difficult to see what would be useful within an as-yet ill-defined process than it was to get on with building tools at the back end to help in system construction. As a result, the number of knowledge acquisition tools commercially available is, at the time of writing (1989), fairly low, reflecting the relative immaturity of this part of the field.

Just as there is no single knowledge representation universally agreed to be ideal for all types of knowledge, there is no single ideal method of knowledge acquisition which could be used as the basis for the ultimate tool or environment. The production of composite tools and environments – a knowledge acquisition toolset – is an active research topic which requires time before it results in stable commercial products.

37.4.1 Rule induction tools

Rule induction tools induce rules from a large set of training cases in which each case can be thought of as an object, described by a set of attributes, together with the object's class. The induction system creates the decision tree by iteratively splitting the cases on a selected attribute until each branch is of only one class. Attributes are selected to distinguish classes from each other most quickly. The limitations of rule induction are manifold, but there are two crucial problems. First is the 'closed world' assumption. The rule induction assumes that all relevant factors are referred to in the examples – if they are not then the rules induced will not deal with all eventualities. Second is the inverse problem to testing. Rule induction systems effectively make assumptions about cases which do not correspond to these examples. Since all cases are not covered explicitly some of the assumptions may prove to be ill-founded when particular examples are encountered.

A number of commercial rule induction systems are now available, for example Crystal Induction and Xi Rule. They generate rules for the previously described expert system shells Crystal and Xi Plus respectively. Both of these induction tools provide a spreadsheet-like template for data entry.

37.4.2 Adoption and computerization of psychometric tools

The most widely-used methods of knowledge elicitation are firstly, those based on interviews of different kinds, and secondly, those involving a record of the expert working at a real problem, from which protocols may be derived. However these methods, especially the first, rely heavily on the ability of experts to articulate their knowledge in a complete and accurate manner.

In fact, it is widely accepted that much expert knowledge is tacit, or compiled, and cannot be easily accessed consciously or articulated (Nisbet and Wilson, 1977). These methods may therefore not only produce an incomplete account, but the phenomena of 'spurious justification', in which experts helpfully speculate about their tacit knowledge, may also make the account inaccurate.

These issues have long been faced by psychologists. Tools which automate or assist the psychometric methods that psychologists have developed form one important subset in this field. Indeed, since psychometric methods were intended to be formal in structure and impartial (as between individual psychologists) in application, they are well-suited to computerization. Just as the original methods aimed to reduce or even render unnecessary the role of the psychologist in the process, so many of the tools research groups have produced are intended to obviate the need for a knowledge engineer, and allow the expert to use the tool directly.

The most widely used basis for this type of tool is the personal construct psychology of Kelly (1955), which had as its goal by-passing cognitive defences in the subject in order to make their implicit knowledge explicit. The technique of repertory grid analysis, which uses statistical techniques to cluster concepts in an *n*-dimensional space, underlies the work of groups such as those at Boeing (Boose and Bradshaw, 1988) and the University of Calgary (Shaw and Gaines, 1988).

An expert using a tool such as ETS (Boose, 1985) or KITTEN (Shaw and Gaines, 1988) would first decide upon a number of significant domain entities. From these, three would be selected, and the expert asked to nominate a domain-significant dimension such that two entities appear at one end, and the third at the other. For example, given entities hay fever, influenza and pneumonia, the expert might categorize the first two as upper respiratory tract diseases and the third as a lower respiratory tract disease. The expert would then be asked to rate all the other entities on the given dimension – a five-or seven-point scale is usually offered with 'not applicable' sometimes included.

This process would continue until the expert felt there were no more meaningful dimensions along which entities could be classified. The system would then perform a cluster analysis, of which a typical output might be a tree diagram showing significant clusters. Some tools also allow rules to be generated automatically at this point. There is currently at least one commercially available tool, NEXTRA, which serves as a front-end to an expert-system shell, NEXPERT, into which the rules thus generated can be incorporated. Both NEXTRA and NEXPERT are marketed by Neuron Data.

Workers using these tools have suggested a remarkable increase in productivity is obtained by comparison with interview-based methods. For instance, it is claimed that ETS, in use in Boeing for more than three years, allows a very rapid prototype to be created in about two hours (Boose and Bradshaw, 1988). However, even the most enthusiastic supporters of this approach to knowledge elicitation agree that in the simple form described above it works much better for classification and diagnosis than for design or planning, and that it is hard to incorporate causal and strategic knowledge (Shaw and Gaines, 1988).

It is also clear that if the number of entities in a domain is high, the comparison of every possible collection of three will lead to a combinatorial explosion. Finally, there is evidence (Schweickart et al., 1987) that experts may find the approach alien to their own ways of thinking and therefore lack enthusiasm for participation.

37.4.3 Knowledge acquisition 'methodologies' and associated tools

Rule induction methods and the adoption of existing psychometric tools have generally been viewed as standalone techniques. These approaches all attempt to bypass the involvement of knowledge engineers. The most commonly adopted approaches to building knowledge-based systems have, however, used informal knowledge elicitation methods which tend to rely heavily on the knowledge engineer. Informal knowledge elicitation procedures generally produce very loosely structured textual information which must be represented by the knowledge engineer. Two of the leading knowledge acquisition research groups in Europe, the KEATS group in Britain and the KADS group mainly based in the Netherlands, take this to be the knowledge acquisition problem and set themselves the task of supporting the activities of the knowledge engineer.

Both groups adopt broadly similar research methodologies in which a model of the knowledge acquisition process is proposed and tools are developed to support the knowledge engineer in managing the various stages of the process.

37.4.3.1 *KEATS*

KEATS (Motta *et al.*, 1988) adopts an approach in which the raw textual data of the expert, possibly the protocol of a talk-through session or an informal interview, is refined and transformed in a stepwise manner through a series of stages. The product or output of each stage is the input to the next stage. The stages are as follows:

1. *Knowledge elicitation.* The process of obtaining raw, unstructured knowledge from a domain expert. This is not supported by KEATS but it does form the input to the KEATS system.
2. *Data analysis.* The process of structuring the knowledge at the linguistic level. This produces so-called 'digested data', an example of which would be a glossary of keywords.
3. *Domain conceptualization.* The process of structuring the data to produce 'an abstract model of the problem'. The form of the abstract model could, for instance, be a semantic network or a flow diagram.
4. *Knowledge representation.* The process of deciding on the appropriate knowledge representation form (e.g. frames, rules).
5. *Implementation.* The process of developing a runnable program.
6. *Debugging.* The process of debugging models. It should be noted that this is a process which occurs at all stages and does not occur just at the implementation stage.

There are two implementations of KEATS. The first implementation, KEATS-1, incorporates widely-available representational aids (e.g. rules and frames), with tools for transcript analysis (CREF) and an intelligent graphical interface to support the analysis and structuring of the domain (GIS).

Because of problems experienced in using KEATS-1, it was decided to design an integrated CREF/GIS tool which supported the smooth transformation of knowledge representations. It was clear that work done in data analysis should be directly accessible to the knowledge engineer currently involved with the domain conceptualization stage. In KEATS-2, a single knowledge acquisition tool, called Acquist, has been developed to support a continuous process through data analysis and domain conceptualization.

Acquist is a hypertext system which allows the knowledge engineer to abstract and structure textual information (i.e. bottom-up acquisition activities). As is the case with CREF, abstraction involves first defining and then structuring segments of text called Fragments. Structuring of the knowledge contained in the fragments occurs in three ways: identifying concepts, grouping of concepts and linking of knowledge items.

Acquist also provides a graphical layout facility called maps, which, like GIS, provides a graphical representation of the structure of the knowledge base as it is being developed. Acquist

allows the knowledge engineer to use the graphical interface to structure all knowledge items, apart from the raw text.

A new facility called Coding Sheets is to be integrated in KEATS. Coding sheets are essentially 'templates defining the structure of a particular task, expert behaviour, or domain'. The intention is to allow top-down and bottom-up approaches to knowledge acquisition to be freely mixed.

37.4.3.2 *KADS*

The KADS (Knowledge Acquisition and Documentation Structuring) methodology has emerged from a group of researchers at the University of Amsterdam (Breuker and Wielinga, 1987) and those associated with them in the Esprit project 'A methodology for the development of knowledge-based systems'. It is the fruit of a conscious attempt to bring knowledge engineering more into line with existing software engineering practice and to separate analysis (in particular) and design from implementation.

The KADS methodology is supported by a set of tools, the KADS Power Tools (Anjewierden, 1987), which currently cover the analysis stage, but which do not extend to support of detailed design and implementation – existing tools and environments were used in KADS-based application development.

KADS, like KEATS, starts from an analysis of the knowledge engineering life cycle, here divided into five stages: knowledge identification, knowledge conceptualization, epistemological analysis, logical analysis and implementation. The first three stages are those on which the methodology concentrates and to which the tools give support; the fourth stage, logical analysis, concerns the choice of knowledge representation and inferencing strategy, and the fifth, implementation, speaks for itself.

While knowledge acquisition and structuring – the content of the first three stages – is seen as highly interactive, the methodology advocates largely completing them before proceeding to the last two. The comprehensive documentation of the knowledge acquisition phase is regarded as central, just as it is in some conventional software engineering methodologies such as SSADM.

A brief description of the KADS power tools is perhaps the easiest way of looking at stages 1–3:

1. *Knowledge identification.* This stage is supported by a dedicated hypertext tool. This assumes that knowledge elicitation is interview-based, with the output transcribed into the tool. An important principle is that the transcript should not be modified, but only annotated, since otherwise some vital piece of knowledge could be lost.

   The transcript is viewed as fragments, which may be any contiguous text from a word to the whole text, and these fragments may then be related in a number of ways. For instance, annotation links connect a fragment to some extra text or a diagram, fragments may be grouped together, a named link may be set up between fragments, or a fragment may be linked to a concept. A set of links can be represented as a web, or an arbitrary selection can be printed out – everything relating to a group, or a particular concept. This tool has many similarities to CREF in KEATS.
2. *Knowledge conceptualization.* A concept editor is supplied for this level, which supports concepts with attributes and values of attributes. Concepts may be linked using domain dependent names, as well as with an *is-a* link which supports inheritance of attributes from classes to sub-classes. The tool also has facilities for formatting and printing the conceptual information. This is intended to support feed-back between knowledge engineer and expert. The concept editor also offers a glossary or lexicon of domain concepts.

3. *Epistemological level*. The third level is supported by two tools, the Interpretation Model Librarian (IML), and the Conceptual Model Editor. Interpretation Models are a component of the KADS methodology, giving a top-down framework for a knowledge domain. The IML provides a library of such models – systematic diagnosis, for instance, would be such a model – in an *is-a* hierarchy. A model defines an inference structure, knowledge sources and meta-classes, which may be mapped onto hierarchies created in the concept editor.

It is envisaged that the knowledge engineer will move between stages 1–3 many times during an analysis. Initially, during the orientation phase, the issues are those of feasibility and defining system boundaries. An Interpretation Model would be at most a weak hypothesis.

Later, the knowledge engineer is concerned with a detailed specification, and with knowledge acquisition proper, which involves both identifying domain concepts and the roles and functions of expert and user, and the analysis of problem-solving strategies. This is seen as fundamentally model-driven, using the idea of the interpretation model.

37.5 Summary

There is now a wide range of tools available for developing AI systems: symbolic languages shells and hybrid toolkits for program development, and systems such as KEATS and KADS which incorporate tools to aid knowledge acquisition as well. Symbolic languages, like Lisp and Prolog, are widely available on a variety of machines. They represent the lowest level but the most flexible tools. The program development environments for these languages depend largely on specific implementations and the hardware that they run on.

The advantage of using shells are that they are cheap, and also easy to learn and use. They are good for developing small-scale, knowledge-based sysems where the expertise can be suitably represented using a single knowledge representation method. If a shell is appropriate for a problem, using a shell will save much development time over using a symbolic language.

Hybrid toolkits allow large problems to be broken down into small parts and the most appropriate representation paradigms to be used for the different sub-problems. They represent the state-of-the-art development environments available today. However, they are relatively expensive and require powerful computing resources. Because a hybrid toolkit is usually very large with many facilities, it requires a considerable learning effort before a programmer is proficient with it.

KEATS and KADS represent the current direction of research on knowledge-based system development environments – the attempt to produce tool sets rather than individual tools and to integrate knowledge acquisition into the overall process of knowledge engineering. Much, however, remains to be done before there is a commercially available knowledge-engineering environment which incorporates aids to knowledge acquisition, knowledge representation, system implementation, testing and maintenance.

37.6 Acknowledgement

The authors would like to thank Robert Inder and Ian Filby for their very helpful comments.

37.7 References

Anjewierden, A. (1987) Knowledge acquisition tools. *AI Communications*, Vol 0, No 1, 29–38

Barrett, R., Ramsay A. and Sloman A. (1985) *POP-II – A Practical Language for Artificial Intelligence*, Ellis Horwood and John Wiley

Barstow, D. R., Shrobe, H. E. and Sandewall, E. (1984) *Interactive Programming Environments*, McGraw-Hill

Boose, J. H. (1985) A knowledge acquisition program for expert systems based on personal construct psychology. *International Journal of Man-Machine Studies*, **20**, 21–43

Boose, J. H. and Bradshaw, J. E. (1988) Expertise transfer and complex problems: using AQUINAS as a knowledge acquisition workbench for knowledge-based systems. In *Knowledge-based Tools for Expert Systems* (eds J. Boose and B. Gaines), Academic Press

Bowles, A. W. (1988) Enhancing Prolog programming environments. *Project Report AIAI-PR-16*, Artificial Intelligence Applications Institute, University of Edinburgh

Bowles, A. W. and Wilk, P. F. (1988) Some design principles for Prolog support environments. *Technical Report AIAI-TR-35*, Artificial Intelligence Applications Institute, University of Edinburgh

Breuker, J. and Wielinga, B. (1987) Use of models in the interpretation of verbal data. In *Knowledge Acquisition for Expert Systems – a Practical Handbook* (ed. A. Kidd) Plenum Press, New York, USA

Brna, P., Bundy, B., Pain, H. and Lynch, L. (1978) Programming tools for Prolog environments. In *Advances in Artificial Intelligence* (eds J. Hallam and C. Mellish) Society for the Study of Artificial Intelligence and Simulation of Behaviour, John Wiley and Sons

Byrd, L. (1980a) Understanding the control flow of Prolog programs. In *Proceedings of the Logic Programming Workshop*, Debrecen, Hungary

Byrd, L. (1980b) Prolog debugging facilities. In *Proceedings of the Logic Programming Workshop*, Debrecen, Hungary

Clocksin, W. F. and Mellish, C. S. (1987) *Programming in PROLOG* 3rd edn, Springer-Verlag, New York

de Kleer, J. (1986) An assumption-based truth maintenance system. *Artificial Intelligence*, **28**, 127–162

Feigenbaum, E. (1977) The art of artificial intelligence: Themes and case studies of knowledge engineering. *IJCAI-77*, 1014–1029

Greenblatt, R., Curet, G. and Kreeger, M. (1987) LISP Machines. In *Encyclopedia of Artificial Intelligence* (ed. S. Shapiro) Wiley-Interscience Publication

Kelly, G. A. (1955) *The Psychology of Personal Constructs*, Norton, New York, USA

Kingston, J. K. C. (1987) Rule-based expert systems and beyond: an overview. Presented at the *British Association of Accountants Conference 1987*, Glasgow Business School, University of Glasgow. Available as an AIAI Technical Report

McCarthy, J. (1960) Recursive features of symbolic expressions and their computation by machine. *CACM*, 7, 184–195

Motta, E., Rajan, T. and Eisenstadt, M. (1988) A methodology and tool for knowledge acquisition in Keats-2. In *Topics in Expert Systems Design* (eds G. Guida and C. Tasso), Elsevier, Amsterdam, The Netherlands

Nisbet, R. E. and Wilson, T. D. (1977) Telling more than we can know how: verbal reports on mental processes. *Psychological Review*, **8**, 231–259

Schweickart, R., Burton, A. M., Taylor, N., Corlett, E. N., Shadbolt, N. R. and Hedgecock, A. P. (1987) Comparing knowledge elicitation techniques: a case study. *Artificial Intelligence Review*, **1**, 245–253

Shaw, M. L. G. and Gaines, B. R. (1988) KITTEN – knowledge initiation and transfer tools for experts and novices. In *Knowledge Acquisition Tools for Expert Systems* (eds J. Boose and B. Gaines), Academic Press

Sheil, B. (1987) Programming environments. In *Encyclopaedia of Artificial Intelligence* (ed S. Shapiro), Wiley–Interscience Publications

Stallman, R. (1987) *GNU Emacs Manual*, Free Software Foundation, Inc., Cambridge, MA, USA

Steel, G. Jr. (1984) *Common LISP: The Language*, Digital Press

Warren, D. (1977) Implementing PROLOG – compiling logic programs. *DAI Research Paper No. 39 and No. 40*, Department of Artificial Intelligence, University of Edinburgh

Warren, D., Pereira, F. and Pereira, L. M. (1979) User's Guide to DECsystem-10 Prolog. *Occasional Paper 15*, Department of Artificial Intelligence, University of Edinburgh

Waterman, D. A. (1986) *A Guide to Expert Systems*, Addison-Wesley

Xerox (1985) *Interlisp-D Reference Manual*, Xerox Artificial Intelligence Systems

38

AI/IKBS development components/ techniques

Helen Sharp
The Open University

Contents

38.1 Introduction

This chapter is intended to introduce the most common elements of intelligent knowledge-based systems (IKBS) development, and to provide references and further reading for those areas of particular interest. There are different reasons for wanting to pursue IKBS issues: a problem which does not easily lend itself to other automation or automated support; unusually sophisticated interface requirements; concern about expertise being lost from an organization; simple curiosity, and so on. Whatever the motivation, however, there are several important questions which should be asked before embarking on what may turn out to be a disappointing journey.

As with all software systems, it is necessary to consider the system's intended role; the level of sophistication aimed for, i.e. background of intended user; whether it should be interactive or embedded; whether it is necessary to build the system from basics or whether short-cuts in terms of off-the-shelf components can be made, and so on. In this sense, skills used for developing conventional software are still relevant to IKBS development. However, since the system is dealing with a different kind of problem and using knowledge, a less tangible commodity than data, there are additional skills required to produce a successful system.

The first and most important point to bear in mind when considering developing IKBS is that it is a long-term activity requiring a large amount of resources. Before embarking on such a project, it is therefore important to understand that although there are techniques and tools to assist in the development, building IKBS requires some different skills and more effort than building conventional software. This chapter will give guidance as to what techniques are available, and what types of problems are suitable areas for IKBS attention. It does not provide a step-by-step guide for producing an IKBS; such an attempt would prove futile, and the result inadequate.

It is tempting to try to provide a definition of IKBS at this point, but this is difficult, since intelligence is a subjective quality, and not an easy property to define. Instead, it is more appropriate to think of IKBS as being systems which are built using techniques to be found in or through references from this chapter which have emerged from the field of artificial intelligence (AI), and related areas. Having said this, however, most systems called IKBS are concerned with tackling problems that are usually considered to require sophisticated knowledge and intelligence if addressed by a human.

This kind of application is so common that it is worthwhile providing a list of general guidelines concerning the problem identified for IKBS treatment, and the resources available for the project. Spending some time comparing these elements to your particular situation before starting development could save a lot of time and agony later on.

38.1.1 The problem

1. The kind of problem being tackled should be one which is often faced by an expert attached to the project. (Indeed, this is the type of problem which would most benefit from IKBS treatment.)
2. The problem should be well-bounded, i.e. it should not take an expert longer than about an hour to solve, and the boundaries of the topic should be well-defined.
3. Problems involving common sense reasoning or requiring further research should be avoided.

38.1.2 The resources

1. Be sure that the appropriate management are committed to the project and that they appreciate the pitfalls associated with a development of this kind.

2. Be sure that the value of the solution is likely to be substantial, i.e. to reflect the effort which will have been input.
3. A rich knowledge source must be available. Suitable sources are discussed in Section 38.2, but typically, the following are needed:
   (a) Either a human expert in the field who is patient, lucid, enthusiastic and dedicated to the project, or
   (b) a collection of case studies covering all essential aspects of the problem which will allow automatic learning of the appropriate knowledge.
4. A large supply of case studies other than those used to obtain knowledge which can be used by the expert to illustrate points, and to test the system at various stages is required.
5. Expectations should not be too high at the start.

Knowledge itself is an elusive entity. People spend many years of their lives collating and categorizing items of knowledge and experience which they have found useful. Problem solving is not well understood, and therefore capturing such information in a piece of software is inevitably a difficult task. Because of these difficulties, IKBS development usually proceeds in an evolutionary fashion, starting with the development of an initial prototype which can be tested by the expert, and refined. It is often only then that the consequences of the expert's captured knowledge becomes clear, and other aspects, conditions and subtleties which were not voiced by the expert are identified (see Chapter 37 on development environments).

Also, people's views vary from day to day or week to week. Any such contradictions must be ironed out satisfactorily before automatic reasoning can be performed. There may, of course, be underlying reasons for the conflict, such as different conditions requiring different treatment, which have not come out before. This leads to possible conflicts in the knowledge contained in the IKBS component, which need to be identified and resolved so as to avoid confusion.

The sections of this chapter address different aspects of IKBS development and, before proceeding, it would be useful to explain the main components of IKBS. Although other, more detailed breakdowns exist, there are three basic components to most IKBS (see *Figure 38.1*):

1. A knowledge base which contains the rules and facts of the domain.
2. An inference engine which processes the system's input and

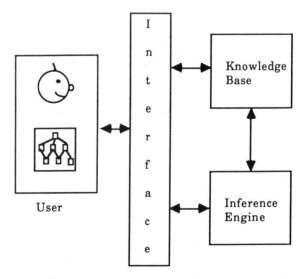

Figure 38.1 Basic components of an IKBS

uses the knowledge base to infer new facts and to produce problem solutions.
3. An interface between the user and the system (the 'user' may, of course, be another software system).

This chapter addresses topics concerned with each of these main components:

1. *Knowledge acquisition.* Before embarking on the design of any software system, it is necessary to know as much as possible about the problem domain. IKBS are no different in this respect, except in the techniques used and the information sought.
2. *Knowledge representation.* As an understanding of the domain emerges, suitable structures for representing the appropriate knowledge must be identified.
3. *Reasoning.* Conventional software consists of algorithms for processing data. Similarly, IKBS must contain mechanisms for processing the knowledge stored in its knowledge base in order to handle the current situation or problem.
4. *Explanation.* Unlike conventional software, the types of tasks being addressed by IKBS require that the system can be queried directly by its user, regarding both its results and its reasoning.
5. *Expert system shells.* Expert system shells are akin to fourth-generation languages (4GLs) in conventional software development in that they are packages for speeding up development of a particular kind of system which can be tailored, to a limited extent, to suit the current situation.

The techniques used in developing the various elements of an IKBS each affect the overall facilities which can be provided by the system. It is therefore beneficial to consider all aspects of the system, if possible, before committing the project to a particular direction. For example, the way that interviews are conducted and recorded during knowledge acquisition may make the provision of a suitable explanation facility easier. Therefore, it is worthwhile at least skipping through all sections in this chapter in case information they contain has a bearing on particular areas currently under consideration by the reader.

Due to space restrictions, some aspects of IKBS development, for example, system evaluation, are not addressed in this chapter. Instead, references to them can be found in the section containing suggested further reading.

38.2 Knowledge acquisition

An IKBS must contain knowledge of the problem domain if it is to provide meaningful solutions, in the same way that any software system must be programmed with algorithms for performing appropriate procedures. This knowledge must be identified, formalized and encoded for automatic processing. That is, the main domain concepts must be identified, and domain knowledge must be structured in a fashion which makes it suitable for automation. A deep understanding of the domain is necessary to achieve this. The activity concerned with this process is called knowledge acquisition or knowledge elicitation (the latter usually referring to acquiring knowledge from a human expert), and a person who is charged with performing this task is called a knowledge engineer. The knowledge engineer's main areas of expertise should be IKBS techniques and the software to be used for developing the system. Ideally, it would be useful if he or she also had a deep understanding of the problem domain itself.

The importance of knowledge acquisition cannot be emphasized enough. Because of the evolutionary nature of IKBS development, knowledge acquisition cannot be a 'one-off' activity which is performed at the beginning of the project. For even the simplest of problems, formalizing knowledge which has hitherto not been formalized is a difficult task. Therefore, you should be prepared for knowledge acquisition resources to be used throughout the life of the system as the knowledge base becomes more and more refined.

The structure of the domain, and the intended use of the system, will affect how the rest of development proceeds, and so it is as well to get as good an understanding of the domain as possible before continuing with development. It is also advisable to ensure that the task selected for IKBS treatment is suitable, and that sufficient resources are available. A set of pointers which provide initial guidelines for this is given in the introduction to this chapter.

There are a number of different kinds of knowledge associated with any domain. First, there is factual knowledge about a particular problem within the domain: this describes the specific problem to be solved, and is necessary for solving any kind of problem. Then there is 'textbook' knowledge, which refers to a collection of information about a domain which is widely accepted, and well-documented, e.g. Newton's laws of motion. Finally, there is knowledge which is gained from experience and is usually not documented but is private to an individual domain specialist, often called 'heuristic' knowledge or 'rules-of-thumb'. If textbook knowledge is sufficient for dealing with the problem domain in hand, for example, if automating a set of building regulations or tax laws which are well-documented, it may not be necessary to consider domain heuristics in order to provide a worthwhile system. However, if dealing with a complex domain based on interpretation of a set of laws, or a domain which is ill-structured, you will probably need to identify domain heuristics.

Systems built using only textbook knowledge are more robust, and take less development effort than those relying on heuristics, since less time needs to be spent on identifying and formalizing appropriate knowledge. They are therefore more commercially viable. However, developing such systems does not fully exploit the ability of IKBS techniques to explore and formalize the deeper structure of the domain, and systems which attempt to capture domain heuristics provide a higher level of sophistication.

This section concentrates on identifying knowledge which has not been formalized previously, since this is the most difficult aspect of knowledge acquisition. It does, however, consider all common sources of knowledge: human experts, case studies, and text books. *Table 38.1* summarizes the use of these different knowledge sources.

38.2.1 Knowledge elicitation from human experts

Acquiring suitable knowledge from human experts is a very common approach, and in some fields may be the only viable one. Human experts are a very rich source of knowledge. They have spent many years dealing with the problem domain, and are very proficient at solving the kinds of problem you might be interested in. However, there are difficulties associated with acquiring knowledge from humans. The main difficulty is that an expert is unlikely to be aware of the heuristics that he or she uses to solve a problem. Experts often refer to 'gut reactions' and 'intuition', and it is difficult for them to identify and express any concrete, formalizeable heuristics or rules. This often leads to them forming a post-rationalization of their actions in an attempt to explain their behaviour. Unfortunately, this does not necessarily reflect their actual performance at all. This is one reason why identifying domain heuristics is such a long and painful activity, but it is also exactly why they have not been well documented before. Using case studies to prompt an expert is a common and invaluable tactic, because they act as a guide and focus for the expert to dig out his or her expertise.

Table 38.1 Suitability of various knowledge sources for knowledge acquisition

	Knowledge source					
	Human expert		Case Studies		Textbook	
	Knowledge engineer	*Direct*	*Automatic*	*Manual*	*Automatic*	*Manual*
Problem Type		Complex Ill-structured		Essential problem characteristics understood		Well-documented Well-structured
Advantages	Expert unaware of technology Discussion Less expert time required	No interpretation by a second human	More effective than human interviews for some problems	No human expert required	No human expert required	
Disadvantages	Knowledge engineer must understand domain Possible communication problems	Domain expert must understand technology Expert isolated Expert needs to formalize own heuristics	Need software capable of learning	Many case studies required	Need software capable of learning Natural language interpretation difficult	Less sophisticated systems can be built May be tedious
Resources Required	Knowledge engineer	Expert-friendly interface software	Learning software	Case studies	Learning software Natural language capability	Good documentation
Questions	One expert or more than one?		All characteristics covered by cases?		Text analysis adequate?	

The most well-known approach to knowledge elicitation from an expert involves the knowledge engineer interviewing the expert, formalizing the knowledge obtained from these interviews, and entering the formalized knowledge into the system. This is not as easy as it sounds. Many interviews will be required before a prototype can be built, and the process will continue for a long time as the knowledge is repeatedly refined and tested in further versions of the system. The use of case studies for illustrating problem-solving strategies and decision making during the interviews is very helpful, as well as being an effective way to test the system as it evolves. As the expert discusses the problem domain, further heuristics can be teased out and formalized. Recording interviews using a tape recorder can prove invaluable since this relieves the knowledge engineer of the need to make notes, and thus frees him or her to concentrate on the expert and the problem. However, it may also have a detrimental effect until both parties become used to the idea and can feel relaxed.

When the knowledge engineer is someone other than the expert, he or she has to interpret what the expert says, and it is possible for misunderstandings to arise. This is one of the main difficulties of such an approach. Before interviewing begins, the knowledge engineer must therefore spend time building up an understanding of the domain, which may include a suitable vocabulary of specialized terms for conversing effectively with the expert. The main advantage of this approach is that the domain expert does not have to be familiar with IKBS techniques or other technical components to be used by the final system. A second advantage is directly related to the knowledge acquisition process of discussion and interviewing, which may help the expert to clarify his or her ideas.

Although this is probably the most common approach for large projects, it may be infeasible for every project to use a knowledge engineer. An alternative approach is to allow the expert to enter knowledge directly into the system, i.e. to rule out the knowledge engineer. This removes the possibility of misinterpretation of the expert's knowledge by a second person, but it means that the expert must be exposed to the technology involved in constructing the system. It is, of course, possible to use front-end software which protects the expert from the details of a specific language or programming system (see Chapter 37). However, it will take time and effort to obtain suitable software, and the amount of protection it provides will be in direct proportion to the amount of tailoring it undergoes. If such software is to be efficient, and truly protect the expert, it must itself be intelligent and understand domain concepts so that the expert does not have to modify his or her language and expression.

The suitability of this approach depends heavily on the expert's willingness to converse with a piece of software, and the availability of suitable interface software. It should be borne in mind that this approach does not involve discussion with another person, and that it will probably require more of the expert's time since he or she has to formalize knowledge as well as enter it into the system. A promising alternative approach which is still being developed, and which requires the expert to interact directly with the system is that of explanation-based learning (DeJong and Mooney, 1986; Kodratoff, 1988). Since it is still at the experimental stage, this is not pursued further in this context.

If it is found that interviewing the expert is unsatisfactory, it may be worthwhile considering using protocol analysis. This involves the expert thinking aloud into a tape recorder whilst solving a problem, and this verbal protocol being analysed for evidence of domain heuristics later on. This could, of course, be used as a technique during interviewing as well.

A significant question connected with acquiring knowledge from human experts is whether to concentrate on just one expert, or to use more than one. It may seem obvious that it is better to consult more than one, since they can check each other's heuristics. However, because heuristics are personal to an individual, and the process of IKBS relies so heavily on evolution, it is advisable to wait until one expert's set of heuristics is reasonably mature and robust before exposing them to the criticism of another expert, whose own heuristics will almost certainly be different. This does not mean that a second expert should not be asked to test the system once the first expert is reasonably happy with a small set of heuristics, since such testing could be very valuable. However, experts are notorious for holding differing opinions on some matters, and one should be prepared for some disagreement if the domain of interest is at all controversial. One way to obtain a more robust system may be to develop two sets of heuristics concurrently using different experts, but only include those heuristics in the final system which are common to both sets. This, of course, requires substantially more resources, and may be impractical except in special circumstances.

Other knowledge elicitation techniques taken from psychology are discussed in Gammack and Young (1985); experiments comparing the efficacy of the different techniques are reported in Schweickert *et al.* (1987).

38.2.2 Knowledge acquisition using other sources

One alternative knowledge source has already been mentioned above, i.e. textbook documentation. Another one is that of previous case studies, i.e. domain problems which have been solved successfully in the past. Both of these knowledge sources can be tapped either using an automatic approach, or a manual approach, none of which relies heavily on a domain expert's time. If an automated approach is to be used, i.e. if a system is to learn its own set of heuristics, then sophisticated software, which is tailored to extract the appropriate information, must be available. If a manual approach is used, the person deriving the heuristics must be familiar with the domain, and must be aware of the needs of the intended system.

Manual acquisition of knowledge from textbook documentation is quite common, and relatively cheap on resources. For example, it has proved useful to encode complicated regulations such as tax laws in an interactive system, thus freeing the user from laboriously searching through complicated, though well-documented, jargon. Assuming that the regulations are consistent, and do not require any kind of 'interpretation', such a system can be constructed easily with great benefits. However, this approach holds less potential for producing sophisticated heuristic-based systems. Automatic learning of knowledge from extracts of textbook documentation is not in common practical use since automatic natural language analysis is difficult, and little success has been achieved in the area.

The use of case studies relies on an analysis of as many different problem-solution pairs as possible and the production of a generalized approach to solving problems from the same domain. For this approach to be most effective, the important characteristics of a problem must be known, so that the analysis concentrates on only significant aspects of the case study. Also, if this is to be achieved automatically, then sophisticated learning software is needed. It is important that there are enough case studies available to cover as many different characteristic value combinations as possible. Ideally, all possible value combinations should be considered, but this may not be feasible. In a complex domain, the important characteristics may be difficult to identify, or there may be a vast number of them. In this case, covering the majority of situations would require a vast number of studies.

In an experiment which compared the relative effectiveness of acquiring heuristics from interviewing a human expert versus automatically deriving them from a set of case studies, it was shown that automatic learning produced a set of rules which could successfully solve the problem in more cases than the set elicited from a human (Michalski, Davis and Bisht, 1982). However, this was a diagnostic problem with identifiable enumerated symptoms and diseases.

Whether an automatic or a manual approach is taken, sets of heuristics can be built up quite effectively by starting with simple case studies which illustrate the basic properties of the domain, and continuing with more and more complex case studies which elaborate certain aspects. This would allow individual problem-solving areas to be targeted and expanded. Alternatively, the same case study could be used a number of times, each time having one aspect of the problem modified slightly; the change in solution strategy needed would then be studied. This technique could also be used during interviews with experts, or when obtaining verbal protocols.

38.2.3 Combined approaches

As already mentioned, combining the use of case studies with interviewing can be most effective. Depending on the resources available, and the problem domain, it may be worthwhile considering other combinations of the approaches described in Sections 38.2.1 and 38.2.2.1.

For example, one such combination is to use a small set of simple case studies to extract and encode a primitive set of rules before interaction with a human expert, and to use this as a prototype for discussion with an expert. In this way, the developer, or knowledge engineer, can become familiar with the problem domain whilst at the same time beginning to tackle representation problems. This also has the advantage of providing a starting point for discussions. The expert can experiment with the system, and may acquire a better understanding of the intentions and limitations of the project. The same result may be obtained by starting with textbook knowledge instead of case studies.

It is likely that this will produce a less sophisticated prototype than the process of interviews described above, but it will be produced faster. Of course, you must be careful not to produce too trivial a system, otherwise the reverse effect may be achieved and people will think that their time is being wasted, and that an intelligent system is not suitable for the problem. This is one of the reasons why it is necessary to ensure that management and experts are committed to the project, and that expectations are not too high at the outset.

38.2.4 Knowledge acquisition and requirements analysis

There are clearly some parallels between knowledge acquisition and requirements analysis. Both activities involve understanding a domain with the aim of producing software to perform functions pertinent to that domain. However, how deep do these similarities go? This question cannot be answered easily, but it is worthwhile passing a few brief comments on the subject in this context.

The first comment which should be made is that although there are some parallels, knowledge acquisition and requirements analysis are clearly different. Extracting heuristics as described above requires different techniques, and tends to be more difficult than conventional requirements analysis.

Requirements analysis aims to discover the best way in which software can be used to meet the needs of an organization or client, and some form of requirements analysis needs to be performed whether a traditional system or an IKBS is to be developed. If a traditional system is to be built, analysis continues by identifying the details of the organization's needs

and operations, including the data being handled and the procedures being performed. For an IKBS, it is the knowledge and heuristics pertinent to the subject domain which need to be studied. The main difference between the aim of knowledge acquisition and the aim of requirements analysis therefore appears to be one of scope – knowledge acquisition must take a more abstract view of the domain under consideration in order to identify and formalize domain concepts. Different techniques need to be used since such concepts are 'less tangible' entities than data and procedures.

The identification of requirements for a conventional system is helped by the fact that data and procedures which already exist within the organization can be observed fairly easily. Although it may be difficult to unearth appropriate requirements for a conventional system, an organization can usually at least say what data it uses, and how it currently processes the data. The underlying knowledge processing activities required in order to solve a problem are less visible. The only evidence of such activity when an expert is solving the problem is his or her explanations and note-making, both of which are open to distortion and interpretation. If a new conventional system is being built, it may be that the systems analyst is free to suggest methods by which the desired functionality can be achieved. In contrast, it is very unlikely that a knowledge engineer who is not an expert in the problem domain would be able to produce a set of heuristics suitable for an IKBS.

The skills required to perform knowledge acquisition and requirements analysis are also similar. Interacting with people, asking them to explain things and rationalizing the information obtained are all important aspects for both activities. Either activity may also include studying documentation and observing work practices. The difference is based on the perspective taken during the investigations due to the fact that different information is being sought, and therefore different goals are in view. Obviously, a knowledge engineer must be conversant with the different knowledge representations available for formalizing the knowledge structure of the domain, whereas a systems analyst must be aware of different programming languages and data structures available. Ideally, the knowledge engineer should understand the domain to a fair level of competence so that he or she can converse easily and unambiguously with the domain expert.

38.2.5 Summary

Knowledge acquisition is the important activity of identifying, formalizing and encoding domain knowledge. A knowledge engineer is someone who performs the task of knowledge acquisition. The most commonly used sources of domain knowledge are human experts, case studies and textbook documentation. Table 38.1 summarizes the use of each of these sources.

Knowledge acquisition has some parallels with requirements analysis, but it differs quite considerably in terms of its intended scope since it handles knowledge and heuristics rather than data and procedures.

38.3 Knowledge representation

The knowledge representation most suitable for the problem under consideration will depend on the inherent structure of the problem domain, and on the processing intended to be performed on it, i.e. on the capabilities required of the system. The representation chosen will have an impact on the system's interface and its learning capabilities. It is therefore important to choose a representation which is appropriate.

As knowledge acquisition progresses, the structure of the knowledge relevant to the system will become clear and it will be easier to decide on an appropriate representation. The complexity of the domain under consideration and the processing to be performed on the knowledge are both relevant factors. It is difficult to say how deep an understanding of the domain is required before a representation should be chosen. Ideally, all the knowledge to be incorporated in this system, all its uses, and all its desired capabilities should have been investigated thoroughly, but this is an unrealistic expectation for data in a conventional software, let alone knowledge in an IKBS! However, if the choice is made too early, then you may discover later on that your understanding of the problem domain was too superficial to have appreciated the important features necessary to be included in the representation. On the other hand, the longer you go without some kind of working prototype, the slower progress will become, and the more disheartened the project team will feel. Obviously, if you are constrained by available development environments, then the choice may be limited. However, it is important to match the representation as closely as possible to the structure of the domain. After all, would you choose the structure of a database before knowing what data it was going to be used for? Other aspects of the system which should also affect the representation chosen are whether you want the system to learn from experience or not and what kind of justification and explanation is required (see Section 38.5).

The design of the knowledge base affects the processing which can be accomplished easily, in just the same way that the design of a database affects a system's performance; aspects of database technology which are relevant to knowledge base technology are discussed elsewhere (Gardarin and Valduriez, 1989).

This section describes the most common representations used in IKBS. The descriptions are not linked to any specific development environment or implementation system, but are intended to be a more general introduction indicating which representations are relevant for which knowledge types.

38.3.1 Production rules

Production rules are a simple but powerful structure which can be used to represent a variety of knowledge types. Basically, a production rule consists of a left side containing a pattern to be matched, and a right side which contains an action to be performed if a match for the left side is found. Such rules are often described in an **if ... then** format. For example:

if income is above limit
then 40% tax is payable

Production rules can be quite complicated with multiple conditions before the **then**, and/or multiple actions after the **then**. The main weakness of production rules is that they can be too general purpose to represent many of the complexities and subtleties found in real-world problems. Production rules are explained in more detail in the chapter on logic programming.

38.3.2 Semantic nets

Every domain consists of two types of entity – classes of items, such as chair, and specific items which belong to one of those classes, such as my favourite chair. In a real-world problem domain, entities are related in some way. This relationship can be via a conceptual link, i.e. two separate classes of items are related, or via a specific link, i.e. a specific instance of one class is related to a specific instance of another class.

Relationships hold not only between items within a particular domain, but also across domains, via such links. For example, consider the library domain. This domain contains classes of items such as books, borrowers and staff members, and it is possible to identify relationships between these classes such as borrowers read books and staff members help borrowers. If a specific borrower reads a specific book, then a specific relationship between that borrower and that book exists.

The concept of a book is not only found in a library domain. It is also found in the publishing domain, the bookshop domain, the school domain, etc. The particular borrower Joe Smith similarly does not only exist in the library domain. He may also be an employee in a specific office domain, a customer in a specific shop domain, a voter in the local elections domain, etc.

Semantic nets were the first structure developed to represent such relationships. They were originally devised for analysing English words, but have since been proved successful in other spheres. *Figure 38.2* shows an example semantic net, describing some of the relationships between items in a simple domain.

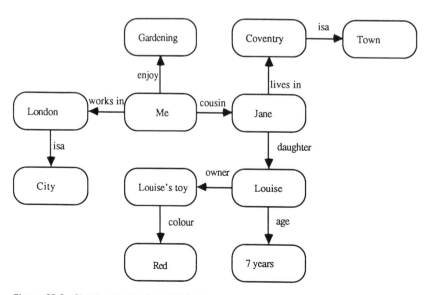

Figure 38.2 Simple example of a semantic net

Nodes represent domain elements, while labelled connecting arcs represent relationships between those elements. Notice that some of the elements are specific items, some are classes of items, some are activities and some are specific values.

The fact that all of these kinds of information can be stored in the net makes it a very flexible notation, but, as ever, this flexibility does have its cost. If semantic nets are used in an IKBS, then it is important to be consistent about the use of nodes and relationships when devising them. If inconsistencies are allowed to creep in, then searching the knowledge base in order to answer queries can be difficult, or misleading. For instance, attributes which in fact relate to a *specific instance* of a class should not be shown in the net as being related to the node representing the *class* of items. For example, the net in Figure 38.2 shows that Louise owns a red toy, while *Figure 38.3* shows that Louise owns all rattles, and all rattles are red, since Rattle represents a class of item; this is obviously not true. Since semantic nets themselves do not impose any kind of restrictions about how to represent different types of elements, it is important for the user to do so.

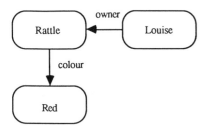

Figure 38.3 A misleading fragment of semantic net

One restriction on the use of the semantic net notation is that the labelled arcs only represent one-way relationships. If a two-way relationship is required, then this must be explicitly allowed for either in the searching method, or in the semantic net itself. For example, if one wanted to find out who lives in Coventry, then either the search strategy must look for nodes with a 'lives in' relationship with Coventry, or a second relationship must be added from the Coventry node to Jane. Which relationships should be stored depends on how the knowledge is to be used, in just the same way that items to be indexed in a database system are influenced by the data access required.

Although semantic nets have proved useful, they are inappropriate for large complex domains. This is firstly because it is difficult to choose initially a suitable set of primitives for such a domain and, secondly, because the nets cannot easily represent quantification information. For example, representing the concept that '*some* rattles are red' could only be provided by introducing a node for each red rattle, while representing the concept that '*all* rattles are red' requires the use of a class node.

38.3.3 Frames

A frame is a mechanism for gathering together a collection of interesting or important attributes which relate to a domain entity. It consists of a name, and a series of slots, each of which can be filled with an attribute value appropriate for the particular entity it represents. Like semantic nets, frames recognize that domains consist of two types of entity – classes of items and specific instances of those classes. Therefore a frame can relate to a class e.g. chair, or a specific item, e.g. my red chair. If a frame representing a specific item is required, it is devised by taking the appropriate class frame and modifying it, as neces-

sary. Such modifications may include instantiating empty slots, or adding new ones relevant to the particular item. Each attribute slot in a class frame may have associated with it a defined set of acceptable values, and/or a default value which is assumed for a specific instantiation if no other one is specified. It is also possible to stipulate that a certain attribute must be filled in, or that it is optional.

A whole domain can be represented by a set of frames which forms a hierarchy, with general class frames such as 'person' at the top of the hierarchy, and specific item frames such as 'my next door neighbour' at the bottom. Frames not at the top of the hierarchy inherit attribute slots and values from their superordinates, i.e. frames immediately above them in the hierarchy; inherited characteristics may need to be modified for a particular instance.

As an example, consider the library domain described above. A set of frames to represent this domain would include one for the class of items called 'Borrowers'. A list of attributes associated with this class includes information about the borrower's name, address, type of borrower, number of tickets, number of books on loan, etc. *Figure 38.4* shows the Borrowers frame. In this particular example, every borrower must be a person, i.e. it is not possible for a company to belong to this library. This class frame would therefore inherit attributes of the class 'person', which might include sex, age, marital status and so on. Notice that the format for the identifier is stipulated and that default values for the type of borrower and the number of tickets are given. The default values here are fairly simple, but it is possible to have more complicated relationships between the different slots, e.g. an ordinary member can have a maximum of ten tickets, while a reference member has no tickets at all. The idea of using default values is useful because it means that properties of a new item can be assumed without them being explicitly observed. So, for example, it can be assumed that a borrower called Edith Jones is an ordinary member with four tickets, although this may not have been directly observed. This concept also allows easy recognition of non-standard objects, i.e. objects which do not use the default value.

Figure 38.5 shows the frame associated with the particular borrower Joe Smith. Notice that although the default value for the type of borrower attribute has been used, the number of tickets attribute has been modified to six.

In a software system, actions are sometimes associated with a slot, so that for example, every time a slot is filled with a value, or its value changes, an action is performed. Using the example above, if the value for the type of borrower is altered, it may be necessary to check the number of tickets slot.

There is a resemblance here between the concept of an object as used in object-oriented programming, and frames. This relationship is not explored here; further discussion can be found in Ramamoorthy and Sheu (1988).

NAME:	BORROWERS	
SLOT 1 (isa):	person	compulsory value;
SLOT 2 (identifier):	\<letter, 5-digits\>	compulsory slot;
SLOT 3 (name):		compulsory slot;
SLOT 4 (address):		compulsory slot;
SLOT 5 (type of borrower):	ordinary	default value;
SLOT 6 (number of tickets):	4	default value;
SLOT 7 (books on loan) :		$0 \leq \text{TICKETS} \leq 10$.

Figure 38.4 Frame representing the class of Borrowers

FRAME:	BORROWERS	
SLOT 1 (isa):	person	;
SLOT 2 (identifier):	A17654	;
SLOT 3 (name):	Joe Smith	;
SLOT 4 (address):	23 The Drive, Swindon	;
SLOT 5 (type of borrower):	ordinary	;
SLOT 6 (number of tickets):	6	;
SLOT 7 (books on loan) :	2	

Figure 38.5 The Borrowers frame instantiated for Joe Smith

38.3.4 Scripts

Scripts are similar to frames, but they are used to hold knowledge about an event rather than an item. They are very useful for describing and predicting events.

The important elements of a script are:

1. *Track*. The specific type of event represented by this script, e.g. church wedding.
2. *Props*. Items which are needed for the events described in the script, e.g. wedding rings, cameras, pen.
3. *Roles*. Entities taking part in the event, e.g. bride, vicar, best man.
4. *Entry conditions*. Conditions which must, in general, be true before the event in the script can happen, e.g. bride and groom are both able to be married.
5. *Result*. Conditions which will, in general, be true after the event described by the script, e.g. bride and groom will be married.
6. *Scenes*. Possible sequences of events which occur as part of the main event, e.g. the procession, exchanging rings, signing the register.

Script:	WEDDING
Track:	Church Wedding
Props:	Rings
	Hymn Books
	Register
	Bells
Roles:	Vicar
	Bride (B)
	Groom (G)
	Best Man
	Bride's Father
	Bridesmaids
	Witnesses
	Guests
Entry conditions:	B is able to be married
	G is able to be married
Result:	B and G are married
	Wedding is registered
	B and G are happy

Figure 38.6 Part of a script representing a church wedding

Figure 38.6 shows part of a script for a church wedding. Knowing that a church wedding is going to take place, it is possible to infer many facts about the event using this information, even though specific details may not be available. For example, if you are invited to a wedding at the local church, you can immediately assume that a bride, a groom and bridesmaids will be present, that rings and a register play an important part in the event, and that afterwards the wedding will be registered and the bride and groom will be happy. Later on you may have to modify these assumptions according to further information, such as discovering that the bride is not having any bridesmaids.

Including descriptions of possible scenes which are part of the main event allows you to predict what can be expected to happen at the event. They easily become complex, however, and it is advisable to use a familiar procedural notation, e.g. flow charts, a modified program design language or similar.

As with frames, a hierarchical set of scripts can be devised to represent events within a domain. This is achieved both by the use of the track element, and by introducing other scripts into the description of possible scenes in the current event.

38.3.5 Summary

The knowledge representation chosen for a system should match the underlying structure of the problem domain as closely as possible. Four common representations are production rules, semantic nets, frames and scripts. Production rules are useful for representing condition-action pairs which can be expressed as 'if ... then' statements; semantic nets represent relationships between items or classes of items; frames and scripts are both useful if it is important to be able to predict properties of a specific entity before specific information is available – frames are used for items, while scripts are used for events. *Table 38.2* contains a summary of the characteristics of these representations.

38.4 Reasoning

If a system is to produce an answer for the current problem, it must have some means of exploiting the knowledge in its knowledge base, i.e. it must be able to reason with that knowledge. Therefore the reasoning strategy chosen for the system is another significant component.

The process of solving a problem involves making a series of decisions in order to arrive at the most appropriate answer. This process can be thought of as navigating through a tree of possible states leading from the initial state, or problem situation, to the goal state, or problem solution. This tree is often referred to as the 'state space' for the problem. Each problem domain has its own state space, with a characteristic structure which can be represented diagrammatically as in *Figure 38.7*. Each node in this diagram represents a possible state. The nodes down the left-hand side of the diagram represent possible initial states, and those down the right-hand side represent possible goal states. Other nodes represent intermediate states which must be passed through to reach the goal state. Lines emanating from one node to another represent the change which must be applied to the first state in order to reach the second. The structure of this state space for a particular problem is significant, as it affects the choice of reasoning strategy, as indicated later in this section.

Of course, if it were possible simply to write down the state space for a problem, then this would imply that all possible solutions were already known. In this case, solving the current problem would simply require that each possibility be considered and the best one chosen using some kind of evaluation function. If all possible solutions were not known, but the state space was understood well enough, then all possible solutions

Table 38.2 Summary of common knowledge representations

	Knowledge Representation			
	Production Rules	*Semantic nets*	*Frames*	*Scripts*
Elements	If... then rules	Nodes and labelled arcs	Attribute slots, default values and conditions	Entry conditions, result, props, roles, track, scenes
Knowledge type	Condition – action pairs	Relationships between concepts or items	Attributes associated with concepts or items	Elements and event sequences associated with common events
Comments	Simple but powerful	Only one-way relationships	Default values allow standard behaviour to be recorded	Can infer actions without specific information
		Keep values for specific items separate from concept nodes		

Initial
States

Goal
States

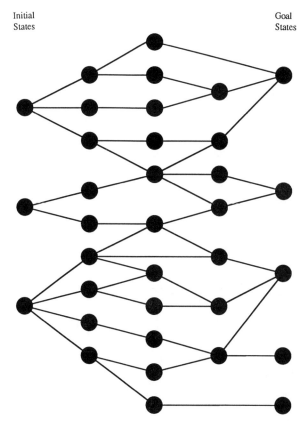

Figure 38.7 A problem state space can be represented using nodes and arcs

could be generated first and then evaluated. Some domains which exhibit these characteristics exist, but both of these approaches have major disadvantages. For non-trivial problem domains, the state space is very large, and exhaustively generating all possible solutions or even just considering all possible solutions may be impractical. In addition, identifying an effective evaluation function is not necessarily a simple task. However, some successful systems have been built using this approach; it has proved to be particularly effective in the sphere of molecule identification (Lindsay *et al.*, 1980).

In reality, problems in a complex domain are not solved by generating and considering a complete set of possible solutions – only a small selection are ever considered. People solving such problems are able to do this because they have developed a set of domain-specific rules of thumb or heuristics which allow them to focus quickly on likely solutions, or alternatively, to rule out large sections of the state space. General-purpose strategies for reaching a solution quickly and effectively have attracted much attention in the field of artificial intelligence. The topic will not be pursued here, since general-purpose searching strategies are less likely to be of interest when developing a specialized IKBS. Heuristics elicited from the expert during knowledge acquisition will contain the necessary knowledge for effectively focusing on the best solutions in the domain of interest. However, the question of how to navigate through the likely paths of the search space, i.e. the reasoning strategy to be used, and how to manage the application of heuristics, including the use of uncertain data, are important decisions.

38.4.1 Reasoning strategies

This subsection describes the three most common approaches to reasoning. The suitability of the first two is closely linked to the structure of the state space, as described above, while the third is a more complex and powerful strategy which requires a greater degree of tailoring than the others. Using just one reasoning strategy may well be considered to be too restrictive. It is common, therefore, to find two or more of these capabilities available in a development environment so that they can be used in combination (see Chapter 37 on development environments).

If justification is required for the system, then it is also necessary to consider how the system's user is likely to reason about the problem. The more closely the system's reasoning steps fit the user's understanding of the problem, the more likely it is that satisfactory justification can be provided. A summary of the main points about these strategies is shown in *Table 38.3*.

38.4.1.1 Forward chaining (data-driven reasoning)

As mentioned above, the suitability of this form of reasoning depends on the structure of the domain's state space. If the problem is associated with a large set of input data, and a relatively small number of solutions, then forward chaining is likely to be an appropriate strategy. A second consideration, however, is the branching factor of the state space, i.e. how many nodes can be reached from one node; it is desirable to move in the direction with the lower branching factor. A suitable state space diagram is illustrated in *Figure 38.8(a)*. An

Table 38.3 Comparison of common reasoning strategies

	Reasoning strategy		
	Forward chaining (Data-driven)	Backward chaining (Goal-driven)	Blackboard model
Description of reasoning	Reasoning proceeds from a set of input data to a solution	Reasoning proceeds from a possible solution towards a set of raw input data	Reasoning is indeterminate and is guided by a domain-dependent control component
Suitable problem type	A large input set with a relatively small solution set	A large solution set with a relatively small data set	Domain with different identifiable areas of expertise
Suitable problem class	Data analysis and interpretation	Diagnostic and classification	Design and synthesis

alternative name for this approach is data-driven, since reasoning starts by examining the input data set, and proceeds by working forwards towards a solution.

For example, a data analysis and interpretation problem such as economic forecasting would be a suitable domain for the use of forward chaining. The initial state would be the set of values for each of a group of significant variables, and the goal state would be the values for these variables in, say, ten years' time. An economic model could be used to modify the initial variable values through a ten-year forecast, producing intermediate states which represent the economic situation at the end of each year, until the tenth year is reached.

38.4.1.2 Backward chaining (goal-driven reasoning)

As you might guess from its name, this strategy is complementary to forward chaining. It starts with a possible solution to the problem, and tries to justify it using the knowledge in the knowledge base to work backwards towards a set of raw input data. This data can then be verified by consulting information about the current situation. If the problem is associated with a small set of input data, and a relatively large number of solutions, then backward chaining is likely to be an appropriate strategy, although the branching factor of the state space should also be considered. A suitable state space diagram is illustrated in *Figure 38.8(b)*. An alternative name for this approach is goal-driven reasoning, since reasoning starts by examining a likely solution, and proceeds by working backwards towards a given input set.

For example, a diagnosis or classification problem such as identifying the cause of machine failure would be a suitable domain for the use of backward chaining. In this example the goal state would be a hypothesis about what might be wrong with the machine, e.g. a leaking valve. To prove or disprove this hypothesis, checks must be made to determine whether the valve is leaking or not. These checks may include measuring the pressure inside the pipe protected by the valve, or searching for escaped fluid outside the pipe. The results of these checks would make up the intermediate states of the problem solution, and the initial state would be a collection of readings which verified that the valve was leaking.

38.4.1.3 Blackboard reasoning

The two strategies described above are fairly straightforward, and are often combined for systems of any complexity. An alternative approach, first introduced to tackle the problem of speech recognition, is that of blackboard reasoning. The easiest way to describe how this strategy works is to use an analogy.

Imagine a group of deaf and dumb individuals, each of whom is an expert in one particular aspect of the current problem domain, standing around a blackboard on which has been written characteristics of the problem under consideration. Each individual (expert) can read the whole blackboard, and each has a piece of chalk, and an area of the blackboard on which to write. A discussion then follows in which each expert can write on the blackboard any relevant information, or partial solution to the problem which arises from using their particular expertise to process the information already on the blackboard. Since all experts can see the whole of the blackboard, ideas can be exchanged, and information from one expert may prompt another one to suggest a possible solution. As the discussion continues, a complete solution to the problem gradually emerges on the blackboard. In practice, such a discussion would often require a chairperson to prevent arguing, or circular reasoning, and to arbitrate over conflicting judgements.

Now think of the blackboard as a partitioned global data structure, the experts as individual knowledge sources, and the chairperson as a controlling strategy with access to higher level domain knowledge. This is the basic structure of the blackboard reasoning strategy. Each of the knowledge sources may be viewed as a small IKBS itself, containing a knowledge base and an appropriate reasoning strategy. Any one of these knowledge sources could therefore use any of the reasoning strategies outlined in this section. Such a structure is illustrated in *Figure 38.9*.

The blackboard approach to reasoning is, however, only a model. It does not specify how to begin developing a blackboard system for any particular problem, and the basic idea requires modifications in order to tailor it to a specific domain. A deep understanding of the problem domain is required to achieve this, especially in order to identify a suitable controlling strategy. Many versions of the blackboard idea have been successfully implemented in a variety of problem domains. Certainly, this strategy is a more powerful one than either forward or backward chaining alone, but implementing such a system requires a larger amount of effort to achieve success.

Describing an implemented system in any detail would require its own section in this book, but a brief description of one blackboard system, Hearsay-II, will help to clarify how the model can work in practice. The problem addressed by Hearsay-II is that of speech recognition. The expertise required for recognizing speech can be divided into distinct, complementary areas. For example, the recognition of segments, phonemes, syllables, words, and phrases is necessary to build a complete picture of a speech fragment. These are complementary in that once a group of segments has been recognized, it is possible to start constructing phonemes, and then syllables and so on. The developers of Hearsay-II exploited this by producing a know-

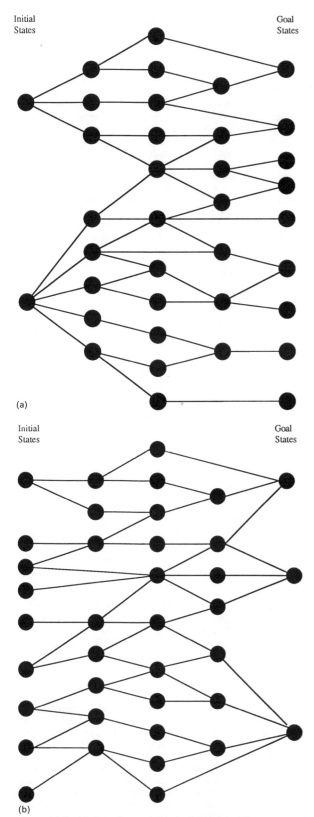

(a)

(b)

Figure 38.8 (a) State space suitable for forward chaining.
(b) State space suitable for backward chaining

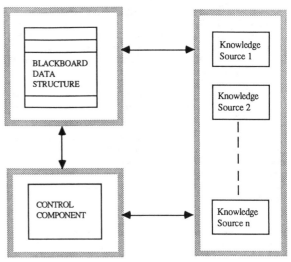

Figure 38.9 Blackboard model of reasoning

ledge source for each level of recognition. Initially, therefore, the knowledge source specializing in segment recognition performs the most work, but once it has written some hypotheses on the blackboard, the phoneme knowledge source can start making suggestions, and so on, until a complete phrase is identified. A mixture of forward and backward chaining was used by the knowledge sources, sometimes working forwards from low-level elements to higher level ones, and sometimes working backwards from possible sentence constructions. The controlling strategy attempted to execute the most productive move at any one stage by using a scheduling system. Although many problems were highlighted during the construction of this system, such a successful early attempt was seen as exciting and encouraging.

Some of the different successful systems are described in detail in Engelmore and Morgan (1988).

38.4.2 Reasoning under uncertainty

Problem solving often involves dealing with information which is not definitely true and is not definitely false, i.e. it may be true, or it may be false. The problem with automated reasoning such as that required by IKBS is that everything must be specified exactly, even if no exact statements can be made easily. This phenomenon presents three major problems to developers of IKBS:

1. When performing knowledge acquisition, an expert may talk in terms of 'sometimes', or 'occasionally'. Such qualifications must be specified more clearly in order for the knowledge to be formalized. In some cases, further discussion reveals an extra condition which can be placed on the situation in order to decide on the suitability of a strategy. However, in many instances this is not the case, and it may be necessary to ask an expert to provide some kind of belief indicator i.e. in 78 cases out of 100, this strategy should be used. Providing such figures accurately is very difficult. Trial-and-error testing and an evolutionary approach to development help to ensure their correctness.
2. How should the lack of evidence be handled? For example, if there are five factors which indicate that a particular fault has occurred in an electronic circuit, and the one which is identified as being the most indicative has not occurred, how much weight, if any, should be placed on the other four?

3. In devising a solution to a particular problem, many elements from the knowledge base are likely to be used. If each if these is associated with a belief indicator of some kind, then there is the problem of how to combine them in a sensible way to associate a further belief indicator for the validity of the solution produced. After all, if you are using uncertain data, and uncertain knowledge to solve a problem, it is unlikely that you will end up with a certain solution. Error factors will increase as more and more imprecise ratings are combined, especially if they are combined in an imprecise way.

The first two problems must be addressed during knowledge acquisition and testing. The figures used will evolve in much the same way as that in which the knowledge itself will evolve as prototypes are developed and refined. If knowledge acquisition is being conducted using a human knowledge source, the knowledge engineer must encourage him or her to suggest appropriate measures where necessary. The form which these indicators should take will be affected by the method chosen to solve the third problem above – that of how to combine them. Their identification and recording will also be affected by the combination method chosen. An awareness of the different ways available for effectively combining the figures acquired during knowledge acquisition in order to guide their identification is therefore important. The most common methods are described below.

38.4.2.1 Probability

It is tempting to argue that there is a well-founded branch of mathematics called probability which has been developed specifically to address these kinds of issues. In particular, Bayes' theorem is a well-known tactic for combining a set of probabilities. This theorem is shown below. Let:

$P(H_i/E)$ = the probability that H_i is true, given that E is true
$P(E/H_i)$ = the probability that event E will happen (i.e. is true), given that H_i is true
$P(H_i)$ = the probability that H_i is true in the absence of any particular evidence (called the *a priori* probability)
k = the number of possible hypotheses H_i

Then:

$$P(H_i/E) = \frac{P(E/H_i) * P(H_i)}{\sum\limits_{n=1}^{k} P(E/H_n) * P(H_n)}$$

Unfortunately, using this theorem in an IKBS has three main drawbacks. First, maintenance of a system using Bayesian inferencing is (computationally) heavy since the sum of the probabilities for all possible hypotheses must be 1, and there is therefore a potential consistency problem. Second, for any kind of substantial problem, computing all the probabilities required to use this formula would use a lot of processing power and time. Finally, the accuracy of the theory depends on knowing all possible hypotheses for a given situation, which may not be feasible. For example, if dealing with a new design for a piece of machinery, an unforeseen fault may occur which has not been diagnosed before.

In order to circumvent these drawbacks, it is often assumed that events are independent, i.e. the probability that E will occur given H_i is the same as the *a priori* probability of E. Using this assumption, the following, simpler formula can be used:

$$P(A + B) = P(A) * P(B)$$

where $P(A + B)$ = the probability that A and B occur.

The weakness of doing this lies in the fact that events are rarely independent, and therefore the desired rigour which should be provided by the use of probability is lost because the basic assumption is invalid.

38.4.2.2 Certainty factors

To overcome the drawbacks of using strict probability theory, some IKBS applications use a modified version, which is derived from probability theory, but which has distinct differences. The belief indicators assigned to facts and rules under this kind of uncertainty reasoning are usually referred to as certainty factors, since this was the term used in one of the earliest and simplest systems to use it (Shortliffe, 1976).

Briefly, the system of certainty factors reasons as follows. Each fact or rule is associated with two figures – a measure of belief and a measure of disbelief, each of which is between 0 and 1. In order to combine evidence to give an overall belief indicator, the measures of belief are added together, the measures of disbelief are added together, and then the latter sum is subtracted from the former. For a more detailed explanation, see Shortliffe and Buchanan (1975).

38.4.2.3 Fuzzy logic

This kind of logic attempts to face the problem of uncertain or 'fuzzy' reasoning head-on. It is an extension of multi-valued logic which allows the user of a system to communicate in terms of vague concepts such as 'good' or 'bad'; quantification can also be specified by vague terms such as 'most of', 'extremely' and 'slightly'. This is achieved by associating each fuzzy term with a special range of values called a fuzzy set. A fuzzy set is a set of values associated with some probability weightings, and fuzzy logic is the logic of fuzzy sets.

For example, if the concept of a 'good' return on an investment was to be represented by a fuzzy set, the following might suffice:

{return ∈ {20..100} 0.6}
{return ∈ {10..19} 0.3}
{return < 10 0.1}

This would be interpreted as saying that if the return is between 20% and 100%, then it would be considered as a good investment with probability 0.6; if return is between 10% and 19% it would be considered as a good investment with probability 0.3; and if return is below 10% the probability of it being considered as a good investment is only 0.1. As with the term 'good' itself, the suitability of the use of this fuzzy set is subjective, and depends on the application being considered.

Fuzzy logic provides rules of inference which incorporate fuzzy ideas such as 'usually' and can be used for handling fuzzy sets. The key ideas of this sophisticated form of logic are summarized in Zadeh (1988).

38.4.3 Summary

The best form of reasoning to use for an IKBS depends on the characteristics of the problem domain. In particular, two main areas of consideration are the shape of the domain state space, which indicates the type of reasoning strategy to be used, and the applicability of uncertain reasoning.

There are three common reasoning strategies: forward chaining, backward chaining and the blackboard approach. The first is suitable for domains where there are many possible solutions but few initial states, the second is most suitable for domains with few possible solutions, but many initial states, and the last one is best suited to a complex domain in which there are a

Table 38.4 Comparison of common uncertain reasoning techniques

	Probability	*Certainty factors*	*Fuzzy logic*
Description of technique	Traditional probability formulae are used	A measure of belief and a measure of disbelief are associated with each piece of knowledge	Fuzzy concepts such as 'good', 'adequate' and 'tall' are represented by means of fuzzy sets
Advantages	Rigorous approach	Allows for the presence of negative information as well as positive	Meets the problem of fuzzy terms head-on Based on sound logic principles
Disadvantages	Assumptions necessary to make calculations feasible may be invalid	Not rigorous	Complex

number of identifiable areas of expertise. *Table 38.3* provides a summary of these approaches.

Most real problem solving is performed using uncertain data. Therefore, it may be important for an IKBS to include facilities for reasoning with uncertain data. To achieve this, uncertainty must be formalized by associating definite figures such as probabilities with any uncertain or fuzzy knowledge elements in the knowledge base. This aspect must be handled during knowledge acquisition while other aspects of formalization are being performed. The identification and recording of these figures is affected by the way in which they are to be combined during reasoning. Three common techniques are the use of traditional probability, the use of certainty factors and fuzzy logic. *Table 38.4* provides a summary of each of these techniques.

38.5 Explanation

General issues regarding the importance of a software system's user interface are addressed in the chapter on interfaces. Clearly IKBS, like other software systems, should be developed with these issues in mind, but the interface for intelligent systems has one important additional requirement. If a system is expected to produce problem solutions, or to give advice in any way connected with unstructured problems, a further aspect of human–computer interaction is introduced – that of explanation and justification. Many traditional computer systems are used 'blindly' in that their operators believe in their accuracy and infallibility almost without question. For example, how often has the retort been that 'the computer says it, so it must be so', when querying outrageous household bills? For an intelligent system, such blind faith is inappropriate, and if an IKBS is to be accepted and used to its full potential, it must be able to justify its decisions for its users. This amounts to being able to explain how a solution has been arrived at, or why a certain line of reasoning is being followed or indeed, is not being followed. This issue goes beyond presentation of information on the screen, and impacts on the initial feasibility investigations.

There is less accepted wisdom in this area than in other topics associated with IKBS, and therefore it is harder to piece together a coherent collection of guidelines. Some of the subjects addressed below are still under discussion and require more investigation. However, it is important to recognize the significance of the explanation facility provided by a system, and the reader therefore urged to look at the following sections, albeit cursorily, so that its impact is understood.

One of the most fundamental questions to be asked regarding the explanation facility is the kind of explanation required. Should the facility provide an interaction in the form of a tutorial, a chat with a colleague, or is the system to be regarded as a wise oracle whose judgement can be explained but not questioned? This may depend on the type of system it is, and the expected set of users. It is important to match the explanation facility with both the system type and its users, since an unhelpful explanation facility will not be used and is a waste of effort.

One way of identifying a suitable explanation style is to keep recordings or transcriptions of the sessions with the expert during knowledge acquisition, if appropriate. The style of explanation used to explain case studies to a knowledge engineer is significant and may be worth building into the system. For example, rules in a rule base may be expressed in the form 'if . . . then . . . because', rather than just 'if . . . then'. The 'because' clause could then be recalled for use in subsequent explanations. By doing this, knowledge of what makes a good explanation is being built into the system as well as knowledge of what makes a good solution. Obviously this possibility must be considered early on so that recordings can be made, and the knowledge engineer can guide the discussion so as to ensure that any explanations are clearly dealt with.

Similarly, if verbal protocols are used for knowledge acquisition, these may also provide useful insights for the explanation facility. Alternatively, studying the explanation style of a popular reference book may help.

The level of detail required in an explanation should also be considered since detailed explanation may be inappropriate. This is particularly true when dealing with uncertain reasoning since the user may not be interested in seeing reams of mathematical data explaining how different facts have been combined. As with other software systems, there are two main groups of people who will need to interact with an IKBS: the system's developers, and the system's users. These two groups require different capabilities, and while it may be appropriate for the developers to see detailed explanations, the users are more likely to be interested in an abstracted form which omits some of that detail. In practice, systems often provide two (or more) styles of interface, one for the developers and one for the end users.

Although the end user(s) of the system may be the same people as those who developed it, the system should, of course, be suitable for use by others. When the system is in real use by someone other than the originator of the knowledge, a different kind of explanation is required involving more general domain knowledge; this is more difficult to provide. This user may be querying not only the system's reasoning, but the validity of the knowledge in its knowledge base. This does not mean that a system should be able to justify the expert's reasoning, but it should be possible for it to explain clearly why it has produced its solution, thus allowing the user to understand its reasoning, even if it does not agree with its underlying assumptions. A truly helpful IKBS would be able to enter into a dialogue with the user to explain its actions, but this is difficult to achieve.

The way that the knowledge base is structured affects the efficacy of the system's access to its own knowledge, and hence its explanation capability. The level of the knowledge contained also affects the explanation possible. For example, an abstract description of the reason for doing something cannot be produced if no knowledge at that level of abstraction has been entered into the knowledge base. At the end of the day, an IKBS is still a piece of relatively dumb software.

38.5.1 Styles of explanation

The following sections discuss the most common approaches which have been considered for providing explanations. *Table 38.5* provides a summary of their characteristics.

38.5.1.1 Rule traces

The simplest form of explanation which a system can provide is that of a rule trace. This is similar to a system log in that every time the system performs an action, a line documenting it is written to a text file. Such rule traces can be very long and are, by their nature, very detailed. An explanation facility which is based on this approach is therefore likely to be detailed and inflexible. The people most likely to benefit from such an explanation facility are the developers of the system.

The developers of an IKBS will typically include a knowledge engineer, and an expert whose knowledge has been encoded in the system (although this will depend on the method of knowledge acquisition used, the following assumes this, common situation). One should remember that the system will be evolving slowly through many versions and prototypes, and will continue to be refined even after it is in heavy use. For this activity, it is important for the consulting expert and the knowledge engineer to be able to understand which elements of knowledge have been used to produce a solution, and how they were combined. In this respect, the activity is very similar to a programmer wishing to step through a program's code in order to understand exactly what it is doing. It is in these detailed investigations that misunderstandings and straightforward errors can be identified. A detailed rule trace is therefore desirable in order for the knowledge engineer to check that the knowledge base is being used as he or she intended, and in order for the expert to check that his or her knowledge has been correctly encoded.

A rule trace is less appropriate for an end user explanation facility, however, since it may provide too much detail or be incomprehensible to a user other than the original expert or knowledge engineer. This would lead to confusion and hence distrust of the system's capabilities. One technique used to get around the problem of incomprehensibility is to provide a natural language description of the meaning of each rule which can then be used for explanation instead of the rule itself. Such explanations are entered into the knowledge base as it is built. It is still possible to provide too much detail using this approach, and so this problem must be addressed by some other means.

38.5.1.2 Canned text

This technique, as the title suggests, involves using sections of canned text to answer user queries, and to justify the system's reasoning. In this case, the system behaves like an online textbook able to produce definitions of terms, and background information for the problem. The main difficulty with this approach is that the answers will inevitably be inflexible, and its efficacy therefore lies in the ability of the developers to foresee as many queries as possible.

Invoking explanations using this method may be based on a rigid query language syntax, such as **explain** < term >, or it may be driven by a keyword search in which the system will search a query for terms or topics referenced in its database.

This approach can be used in conjunction with a rule trace to produce a fairly comprehensive, although inflexible, explanation facility.

38.5.1.3 Natural language

It would, of course, be ideal to be able to produce a system which could hold a conversation with its user, and could explain what it is doing in the same way that a colleague or a teacher might. Unfortunately, such processing requires a great deal of knowledge, and such systems are still very much in the research laboratories. Natural language understanding is a difficult topic

Table 38.5 Comparison of common explanation strategies

	Explanation strategy		
	Rule trace	*Canned text*	*Natural language*
Description of Explanation	A trace of the system's reasoning is kept; like a system log	Pre-stored blocks of text are used to provide term definitions and extra information	Interaction is close to conversation in natural language, e.g. English
User group	Most useful for system developers	End users	End users
Advantages	Easy to implement	Explanations do not need to be constructed dynamically	Easiest approach for users to adapt to since no special syntax required
Disadvantages	Detailed explanation may cause confusion	Inflexible	Natural language understanding is still a research topic
	If using reasoning under uncertainty, how much detail should be given?	Unlikely that all queries can be anticipated	Limited use of natural language may be frustrating
Variations	Canned text and rule trace used together		Keyword search used for 'understanding' natural language input

which has been studied for many years, and although some limited success has been achieved, true conversation with a software system is still far from being a reality. To understand grammatical natural language, the software must be able to analyse sentences input by the user and have enough domain knowledge to make sense of the sentence so that it can react appropriately. Even if the system could handle grammatical sentences, if the interface is to be truly natural, it should be able to understand colloquial commands as well. This would provide further problems.

It is possible to provide interaction using limited natural language by using a keyword search on input, as suggested in the previous section, and providing answers constructed from pre-stored sections of text. Such an approach is not robust, however, and may lead to frustration and hence may not be used.

38.5.2 Level of explanation – novice or expert?

As well as the question of the type of explanation required, and the mechanisms used to provide it, there is also the question of whether the explanation is to be aimed at a novice in the field, or an expert (leaving aside for the moment the problem of defining when a novice becomes an expert). It is significant for the correct level of explanation to be provided, since the system's users would soon lose interest if either the explanation was 'over their heads', or gave so much detail as to be boring. If only experts or only novices are expected to use the system, then providing only one level of explanation facility would be appropriate, but if the group of users contains a mixture of novices and experts, several different explanation facilities will be needed. Actually building these different levels into the system will cause some problems, but another set of problems will arise because it is also necessary to have some mechanism for deciding which level is appropriate for which user, i.e. how does the system tell whether its current user is a novice or an expert? Again, one can imagine an ideal situation where the system knows its user, and hence provides explanations suited to the user's knowledge and background. Unfortunately, this is currently not feasible, for reasons discussed in the chapter on interfaces, concerning adaptive interfaces.

Since truly adaptive interfaces cannot be provided, compromises must be made if mixed groups of users are to be catered for at all. For instance, assuming that different levels of explanation are built into the system, then one way of deciding which is appropriate at any one time is to use a system of self-classification, where the user states whether he or she is a novice, an expert, or some grade in between. Another technique would be for the software to ask pertinent domain questions and to classify the user on the basis of his or her answers. If using self-classification, there is the possibility that the user's idea of 'expert' is different from the system's, and if relying on the system's classification, there is the problem of determining appropriate questions to ask. (These should change each time a user accesses the system, since he or she may have discovered the 'correct' answer to the questions after a previous session.)

38.5.3 Summary

It is important to provide adequate explanation facilities for an IKBS which operates in an unstructured problem domain. This means that the explanation facility should be appropriate for the task, and for the system's user group. The most common approaches to explanation can be divided into three broad styles: rule traces, canned text and natural language. Rule traces are usually most appropriate for the system's developers, but provide too much detail for other users; canned text explanation is relatively easy to provide, but is very inflexible; true natural

language understanding is still a subject for the research laboratories, although keyword search techniques can be used. Table 38.5 summarizes these approaches.

As well as how explanation is to be provided, the level of explanation required must also be decided. This depends on the expected user group for the system; the needs of each element of the group should be catered for.

38.6 Expert system shells

One of the more popular areas of IKBS which has received much attention in the past few years is that of expert systems. Unfortunately, the term has been much over-used and in some cases abused, which has caused some confusion over the term. Some pieces of software which do not strictly belong in the IKBS category at all have been advertised as expert systems. However, an expert system is basically an IKBS with a performance at reasoning about and producing solutions to problems that is comparable to that of a human expert. In addition, most workers in the field would agree that the system must be able to justify and explain its reasoning. For the purposes of this chapter, therefore, the term is synonymous with IKBS.

38.6.1 What is an expert system shell?

It is possible to construct an IKBS from scratch using a purpose-built programming language, such as Lisp, embedded in a development environment (see Chapter 37). This would mean that details of the inference strategies and any uncertain reasoning be incorporated into the system must be explicitly programmed. As already indicated, building an IKBS is a long-term project, but it is possible to cut the development time by employing an 'expert system shell' instead.

Basically, an expert system shell consists of the elements of an IKBS which were introduced at the beginning of this chapter, minus the specific application domain knowledge. That is, a shell provides an off-the-shelf carcass ready to be filled with domain knowledge for a particular problem area. It therefore includes an inference engine, a knowledge representation formalism, an explanation facility, a user interface and a developer interface. If the inference engine has been designed to handle reasoning under uncertainty, then the appropriate mechanisms will also be built in.

There is a fine line dividing expert system shells and development environments, since some systems which began life as simple shells have been expanded to incorporate more facilities, so that more sophisticated systems can be built with them. However, expert system shells are usually much cheaper than full-blown development environments since they provide relatively few facilities and are much less flexible.

38.6.2 Why use an expert system shell?

If a particular problem domain fits into one of the problem categories which have been well tried and tested, and your needs are fairly straightforward, then it is probably worthwhile investigating the use of an expert system shell. Obviously, if you can pick up software which provides the major processing facilities required, then efforts can be concentrated on the crucial task of knowledge acquisition, which will lead to a faster development of an initial prototype. If the system proves to be satisfactory, then the system can be developed through the usual evolutionary cycle.

It may be useful to use an expert system shell as an experimental vehicle for testing out the suitability of IKBS to a particular problem domain. This would allow you to concentrate on the knowledge acquisition activity which can be an enlightening experience in itself, and to produce a small working system fairly quickly.

However, *be warned*. Since shells provide built-in facilities such as reasoning strategy, explanation facility and knowledge representation, it is important to be very careful when choosing one to make sure that those facilities suit the given problem, as described in the earlier sections of this chapter. Buying the cheapest shell on the market, so that cost is kept to a minimum for the initial feasibility study, is not necessarily the best approach. If that shell provides only forward chaining with no uncertainty reasoning, and production rule facilities, whereas the problem is basically backward chaining requiring probabilistic reasoning, a true indication of the suitability of IKBS for the problem will not be achieved.

38.6.3 Summary

An expert system shell provides the framework for constructing an IKBS without the developer having to program it from scratch. A shell consists of all the elements of an IKBS, minus the specific application domain knowledge which must be added by the developer. Since all other facilities are provided, the user of a shell must be sure to buy an appropriate one, as indicated by the earlier sections in this chapter.

Each shell is, of course, accompanied by its own documentation issued by the software producers, e.g. Crystal, Leonardo, Advisor-2, Xi-plus etc. In addition, however, there are some reports which evaluate various expert system shells, (Press, 1989; Gevarter, 1987) and it would be worthwhile spending time ensuring that the system purchased suits your needs.

38.7 Further reading

Other articles and books which are worth further investigation are included in the reference list.

38.7.1 General

Aleksander, I. (1986) *Designing Intelligent Systems,* Kogan Page, London.
Born, G. (ed) (1988). *Guidelines for Quality Assurance of Expert Systems,* Available from Computing Services Association, 73/74 High Holborn, London, WC1V 6LE
Carrico, M. A., Girard, J. E. and Jones, J. P. (1989) *Building Knowledge Systems: Developing and Managing Rule-based Applications,* McGraw-Hill, New York
Forsyth, R. (ed.) (1989) *Expert Systems: Principles and Case Studies* (2nd edn), Chapman and Hall, London
Fox, J. (ed.) (1984) *Infotech State of the Art Report on Expert Systems,* Pergamon
Glorioso, R. M. and Osorio, F. C. C. (1980) *Engineering Intelligent Systems: Concepts, Theory, and Applications,* Digital Press, USA
Hayes-Roth, F., Waterman, D. A. and Lenat D. B. (eds) (1983) *Building Expert Systems,* Addison-Wesley, USA
O'Keefe, R. M., Balci, O. and Smith, E. P. (1987) Validating expert system performance. *IEEE Expert,* **2,** 81–89
Rich, E. (1983) *Artificial Intelligence,* McGraw-Hill Book Co., Singapore
Silverman, B. G. (ed.) (1987) *Expert Systems for Business,* Addison-Wesley, USA

38.7.2 Knowledge acquisition

Cordingley, E. S. (1989) Knowledge Elicitation Techniques for Knowledge-Based Systems. In *Knowledge Elicitation Principles, Techniques and Applications.* (ed. D. Daiper), Ellis Horwood, Chapter 3. London
Hart, A. (1986) *Knowledge Acquisition for Expert Systems,* Kogan Page, London

Kidd, A. L. (ed.) (1987) *Knowledge Acquisition for Expert Systems: A Practical Handbook,* Plenum Press, London
Waldron, V. R. (1986) Interviewing for knowledge. *IEEE Transactions on Professional Communications,* **PC29,** 31–34

38.7.3 Knowledge representation

Brachman, R. J. and Levesque, H. J. (eds) (1985) *Readings in Knowledge Representation,* Morgan Kaufmann, Los Altos
Minsky, M. (1975) Frame-system theory. In *Thinking: Readings in Cognitive Science* (ed. P. N. Johnson-Laird and P. C. Wason), Cambridge University Press, Cambridge, pp 355–376
Ringland, G. A. and Duce, D. A. (eds) (1988). *Approaches to Knowledge Representation: An Introduction,* Research Studies Press Ltd

38.7.4 Reasoning strategy

Mamdani, A. Efstathiou, J. and Pang, D. Inference under uncertainty. In *Expert Systems 85* (ed. M. Merry), Cambridge University Press, Cambridge, pp 181–194
Nii, P. H. (1986) Blackboard systems: the blackboard model of problem-solving and the evolution of blackboard architectures (part one). *The AI Magazine,* **7,** (2), 38–53
Reichgelt, H. and van Harmelen, F. (1985) Relevant criteria for choosing an inference engine in expert systems. In *Expert Systems 85* (ed. M. Merry), Cambridge University Press, Cambridge, pp 21–30

38.7.5 Explanation

Chandrasekaran, B., Tanner, M. C. and Josephson, J. R. (1989) Explaining Control Strategies in Problem Solving. *IEEE Expert,* **4,** 9–24
Ellis, C. (1989) Explanation in intelligent systems. In *Expert Knowledge and Explanation: the Knowledge–Language Interface* (ed. C. Ellis), Ellis Horwood, pp 108–126
Obermeier, K. K. (1989) *Natural Language Processing Technologies in Artificial Intelligence: the Science and Industry Perspective,* Ellis Horwood
Sparck-Jones, K. (1985) Natural language interfaces for expert systems; an introductory note. In *Research and Development in Expert Systems* (ed. M. A. Bramer), Cambridge University Press, Cambridge, pp 85–94

38.7.6 Expert system shells

Murray, J. T. and Murray, M. J. (1988) *Expert Systems in Data Processing: A Professional's Guide,* McGraw-Hill, USA

38.8 References

Bloomfield, B. P. (1986) Capturing expertise by rule induction. *The Knowledge Engineering Review,* **1,** (4), 30–36
DeJong, G. and Mooney, R. (1986) Explanation-based learning: an alternative view. *Machine Learning,* **1,** 145–176
Engelmore, R. and Morgan, T. (eds) (1988) *Blackboard Systems,* Addison-Wesley
Gammack, J. G. and Young, R. M. (1985) Psychological techniques for eliciting expert knowledge. In *Research and Development in Expert Systems* (ed. M. A. Bramer), Cambridge University Press, Cambridge, pp 105–112
Gardarin, G. and Valduriez, P. (1989) *Relational Databases and Knowledge Bases,* Addison Wesley, USA
Gevarter, W. B. (1987) The nature and evaluation of commercial expert system building tools. *IEEE Computer,* **20,** (5), 24–41
Kodratoff, Y. (1988) Applications and prospects of the AI approach to machine learning. *Knowledge Engineering,* **1**
Lindsay, R. K., Buchanan, B. G., Feigenbaum, E. A. and Lederberg, J. (1980) *Applications of Artificial Intelligence for Organic Chemistry: The DENDRAL Project,* McGraw-Hill, New York, USA
Michalski, R. S., Davis, J. H. and Bisht, V. S. (1982) An expert system for the diagnosis of soybean diseases. In *Proceedings of ECAI.* Also in Michalski, R. S. and Chilansky, R. L. (1980) Learning by being

told and learning from examples: an experimental comparison of the two methods of knowledge acquisition in the context of developing an expert system for soybean disease diagnosis. *International Journal of Polray Analysis and Information Systems*, **4**, (2), 125–161

Press, L. (1989) Expert system benchmarks. *IEEE Expert*, **4**, (1), 37–44

Ramamoorthy, C. V. and Sheu, P. C. (1988) Object-oriented systems. *IEEE Expert*, **3**, (3), 9–15

Schweickert, R., Burton, A. M., Taylor, N. K., Corlett, E. N., Shad-bolt, N. R. and Hedgecock, A. P. (1987) Comparing knowledge elicitation techniques: a case study. *Artificial Intelligence Review*, **1**, 245–253

Shortliffe, E. H. (1976) *Computer-based Medical Consultation: MYCIN*, American Elsevier, New York

Shortliffe, E. H. and Buchanan, B. G. (1975) A model of inexact reasoning in medicine. *Mathematical Biosciences*, **23**, 351–379

Zadeh, Lofti A. (1988) Fuzzy logic. *IEEE Computer*, **21**, (4), 83–93

Other Approaches to Software Development

39

Principles of object-oriented systems

**Martin C. Atkins and
Alan W. Brown**
University of York

Contents

39.1 Introduction

In the last few years there has been increasing use of the term 'object-oriented' in many areas of software engineering. There are programming languages, design methodologies, user interfaces, databases and operating systems that have all been described as 'object-oriented'.

While it is exciting to see a common theme linking these disparate areas, it soon becomes evident that the same term is being used in different ways in each of the different application areas. Indeed, a group of leading researchers from one of these domains soon found that there was no common understanding of the term even between themselves (Laguna Beach Participants, 1989).

Therefore, the aim of this chapter is to explain, as far as is possible, the common concepts and principles of object-oriented systems, and to illustrate the use of object-oriented principles in some application domains. It is becoming common to talk about object-oriented design and even object-oriented requirements analysis. These are interesting topics in their own right but the focus here is mainly on object-oriented programming, since the concepts (and systems) are better developed and because the design techniques benefit from the ability to map directly into implementation objects.

39.2 Concepts and terminology

39.2.1 What does 'object-oriented' mean?

A good way of thinking of an object-oriented system is of a space which contains many independent objects. Each object provides a behaviour, which is a set of operations that the object can be requested to carry out. An object's actions are carried out by internal computation and by requesting other objects, which it can name, to carry out operations in turn. This view of a system is intended to match, or in some sense model, the system as it might appear as a collection of cooperating physical objects, or indeed people, in the 'real world'. It is claimed that familiarity with the way the real world operates can then be used to help understand and design object-oriented software systems.

Each object might contain some state, and so the decomposition of a problem into a collection of objects must reflect the relationships between parts of the state of the system. This means that 'object-oriented' inherently implies a 'data-oriented' view of the system.

An alternative is to view each object as presenting a resource to the rest of the system. Usually this resource is simply an abstraction of the state in the object, but objects can also represent real devices, or resources outside the system. The object's operations are provided to allow the rest of the system to use the resource, but limit access so that the object can only be manipulated in ways that the object chooses to allow.

Nothing has been said of the relative sizes of the objects that make up a system, and this is the essential difference between many object-oriented systems. In an object-oriented programming language, such as Smalltalk 80 (Goldberg, 1983) or C + + (Stroustrup, 1986), objects take the place of data structures in traditional languages, and can be very small. For example, in Smalltalk 80 everything is represented as an object, even the integers. More commonly, however, objects take the traditional role of data structures (or records), and so often use a few words of memory. In contrast object-oriented databases such as GemStone (Bretl, 1989) and object-oriented operating systems such as Eden (Black, Lazowska *et al.*, 1986) use objects at a much coarser grain. Here objects provide the behaviour of files, processes, devices, and other services that are in the system. Despite this disparity in scale, these systems have many things in common, and this is what makes them object-oriented.

There have been many attempts to define the properties that make a system 'object-oriented' (Rentsch, 1982; Stroustrup, 1987b; Wegner, 1987) but apart from a consensus that the system should contain 'objects', there is little agreement on an exact definition. A definition will be used here that focuses on the abstract requirements of an object-oriented system, which seems to encompass the notions found in most object-oriented systems. This definition is not quite the same as, but most resembles, that presented by Blair *et al.* (1988).

An object-oriented system is one that contains objects with the following properties:

1. *Encapsulation*. An object's state is only accessible using its nominated operations.
2. *Dynamic lifetimes*. Objects can be created as the system executes.
3. *Identity*. Each object has a name, which can be used to refer to it.
4. *Substitution*. Objects that provide compatible operations can be used interchangeably.

The encapsulation provided by objects is just what is normally meant by saying that an object is an 'instance' of an 'abstract data-type' (Liskov and Zilles, 1974). This does not necessarily mean that an object cannot make its internal state visible from outside, but rather that this is a choice made by the designer of the object, which the rest of the system cannot circumvent. This means that the possible interactions of the object with the rest of the system are limited to those which the designer decides to allow, making it possible for objects to be designed and implemented independently of each other – and of the rest of the system – to a greater extent than is possible with traditional techniques. An object representing a printer spool queue, for example, may be implemented with operators to allow users to add and remove jobs on the queue, and to display a list of those jobs which a user has sent to be serviced. Any other structures and operators required by the object to perform its function remain internal to the object and cannot be accessed from outside the object. Hence, users of the object cannot list all jobs on the queue, nor can they change the order in which those jobs will be serviced. Thus, the degree of access to the printer spool queue is a design decision, enforced by the system through object encapsulation.

The presence of a well-defined interface specification also makes it possible for a variety of implementations to be produced with, say, different performance tradeoffs. If they all provide the same operations then each can be 'slotted in' to the rest of the system to be tested, allowing the most appropriate to be found.

Most modern programming languages provide some support for abstract data-types. Examples are 'packages' in Ada (Ichbiah *et al.*, 1983) and 'modules' in Modula-2 (Wirth, 1980). However, these are instantiated (or in Ada, 'elaborated') statically, at compile time (although run-time initialization is allowed). An object-oriented system is more dynamic, and objects have dynamic lifetimes. One of the actions that an object can carry out as part of its behaviour is to create another object. Conversely, as the system executes, some objects become unnecessary, and the resources associated with them can be reclaimed by the system. This might occur by the explicit action of the programmer, or automatically using some form of 'garbage collection' (Cohen, 1981). Since the reclamation of objects' resources is purely a performance issue, it is not explicit in the definition given above. However, real systems must address this issue in some way.

One of the possible actions of an object is to request another object to carry out an action. This means that it must be possible for one object to contain references to other objects; that is, in some way to name other objects. Some constancy is implied in this naming. Subsequent uses of a name are expected to refer to the same object, at least in some abstract sense. Thus, an object's identity must be consistent throughout its life.

Finally, and most importantly, it should be possible to substitute one object for another in contexts where the substituted object can provide the necessary operations. The substituted object might also allow additional operations, but so long as it provides all the operations that are needed in the context in which it is used, the system will continue to function.

For example, in a document processing system there would appear to be a great similarity in the operators which would be defined for both a text document (e.g. a letter or memo) and for a graphical document (e.g. a diagram or illustration). In particular, one might implement operators that allow text and graphical documents to be edited and printed. Thus, in many situations where a text document is edited and printed one would expect that the same set of operator invocations would be equally valid if a graphical document were to be substituted in its place.

Of course, when one object is substituted for another the system might actually *do* something quite different from what it would have done without a substitution, since the substituted object might have a completely different effect. For example, editing in the context of a text document will clearly have a different effect from editing a graphical document. However, the substitution is still allowed. Careful use of this property is how much of the power of object-oriented systems is gained.

Allowing substitutions seems strange at first, but is actually quite a familiar concept in many contexts. A simple example is the Unix file system (Kernighan, 1979) which provides several operations on open files, such as **read**, **write**, and **close**. However, a file descriptor for a terminal, or some other device, can be substituted for a file descriptor for a file, and these operations will continue to work. The routines executed, and the resulting effects, will be those appropriate to the actual object being used. However, it is important that at a more abstract level the effect is consistent – **write** always 'writes data', regardless of the type of file descriptor it refers to.

The substitution property introduces a form of polymorphism (Cardelli and Wegner, 1985) into object-oriented systems, allowing parts of the system to work successfully on a range of different kinds of object. While substitutability is a fundamental requirement of object-oriented systems, it is also the property that introduces many of the implementation difficulties associated with them.

39.2.2 Terminology for object-oriented systems

Like any other development, object-oriented systems have introduced their own terminology, some of which will be used here. The introduction of terminology specifically related to inheritance and delegation will be postponed until these concepts are described in the next section.

39.2.2.1 Behaviour

Objects are often said to display behaviour. This is interpreted to mean that the object is defined as a collection of operations which selectively reveal or manipulate the state of the object. Different operations on an object can use the state to communicate between operator invocations. Thus, consecutive invocations of an operator might return different results, depending on other operations that may have effected the state of the object.

39.2.2.2 Message

A request to an object to carry out some operation is usually referred to as a message to the object. This may, or may not, imply an underlying communication, depending on the type of system that is involved. However, some transfer of data is normally involved even if this is just in the form of parameters included in the message.

Following this, the request is often referred to as the 'sending of a message to the object', and the object is said to receive the message. This is roughly equivalent to calling a function in traditional systems, since the flow of control goes with the message from the sending, to the receiving object. When the request has been acted on by the receiving object, a reply is returned to the sender of the message, and it can continue to execute.

While the above is true of most object-oriented systems, Actor languages have a different model of message passing, which will be discussed briefly later.

39.2.2.3 Method

The code describing the actions to occur when an object is sent a message is known as a method or, less often, as a script. In C++ it is called a member function, but method will be used uniformly here to avoid a proliferation of equivalent terminology. An object is said to understand a message if it has a method corresponding to that message. Some systems can check that all messages will be understood statically, at compile time, while other systems postpone this check until run time, so that the reception of a message that is not understood causes a run-time error.

39.2.2.4 Receiver and self

The difference between a method and a traditional function (or procedure) is that a method executes 'in the context of' a particular object, that is the object to which the message that requested its execution was sent. This object is called the 'receiver' of the message, and the method has access to its concrete representation. Most languages allow this object to be referred to in the method as **self**, or in C++ **this**.

39.2.2.5 Class and instance

Many objects in a system will differ only in their names and current state, but use the same methods. Consequently, it is often useful to draw together the common methods from such a set of objects, so that they can be referred to collectively. Such a collection of methods is called a class, since it defines the behaviour for a class of objects. The objects are then said to be instances of the class which contains their methods.

Other information that can be shared by all the instances of a class will also be stored in the class. In particular, the class usually contains a description of the construction of its instances, and provides operations that use this information to construct new instances.

In some systems, such as Smalltalk 80, classes are themselves objects, and hence the system is self-describing at this level.

39.2.2.6 Instance variable

The state contained in an object usually consists of a collection of named variables – in this way an object is very much like a traditional structure. These are called instance variables. However, in Lisp-based object-oriented systems they are also known as slots, but are these also (conceptually) contain the methods associated with the object.

39.3 Inheritance and delegation

The substitution property of object-oriented systems is a very powerful system construction principle. Thus, it is very common for many objects in the system to have similar behaviours, so that they can be used interchangeably. As a result, it is important for systems to provide some support for the construction of objects with similar behaviours. To facilitate this, most systems that organize behaviour in classes use inheritance. Delegation is commonly used in systems that do not use classes.

39.3.1 Inheritance

When a class is defined it can, and in some systems must, inherit the behaviour of another class. This means that all the methods in the inherited class, known as its superclass, are implicitly provided in the inheriting class, or subclass. Consequently, any message understood by instances of the superclass will also be understood by instances of the subclass. It also means that any state described by the superclass will be present in instances of the subclass. For example, a class *Person* may be defined with instance variables to record the name and date of birth of *Person* objects, and methods to insert, amend, and display details of a *Person* object. If one now defines a class *Employee* as a subclass of *Person*, then *Employee* would inherit the instance variables and methods of the *Person* class. Hence, the message 'display' when sent to an *Employee* object would have the effect of invoking the display method defined for the *Person* class.

Inheritance is sufficient, but not necessary, to guarantee that an instance of the subclass can be substituted for instances of the superclass, and it will be seen later that this forms the basis of the type system in many object-oriented languages.

Of course, if one is defining a new class, then one does not only want to inherit the behaviour of a superclass, but also to add behaviour, or modify the inherited behaviour in some way. Inheritance mechanisms provide for this by allowing the inheriting class to introduce new behaviour by adding instance variables and methods to those obtained from the superclass. For example, an additional instance variable could be defined for the class *Employee* which records an employee's current salary.

Similarly, most inheritance mechanisms also allow a subclass to override inherited methods, so that new definitions for inherited methods can be provided. Thus, messages associated with the old behaviour can cause parts of the new behaviour to be used instead. For example, having added a new instance variable to the *Employee* class, one may then provide a new 'display' method to take account of this.

It is usually expected that the overriding behaviour will be, in some sense, an extension of the inherited behaviour, and it is common for overriding methods to invoke the methods that they override as part of their actions. This means that it should be possible for a method to use inherited behaviour that is overridden in its class – this is often called 'sending a message to super', the phrase coming from the Smalltalk notation for this action. Thus, the new 'display' method for the *Employee* class need not be written from scratch. Rather, it could perform some of its own actions and then invoke the 'display' method of the *Person* class.

However, the most subtle way in which behaviour can be extended is by 'sending messages to self'. It is common for the evaluation of a method to make use of the actions of other methods defined for the same object. At its simplest this is the same as calling a local function in conventional languages. However, inheritance opens up a new possibility in this situation, which is that a method might cause the invocation of a method defined in a subclass of the class in which it is itself defined. This method will usually have overridden an inherited version that would otherwise have been invoked. Thus, in the

example, another method defined in the class *Person* might send the message 'display' to itself to achieve part of its effect. However, if the object is actually an instance of the subclass *Employee*, then it would be the extended 'display' method defined by *Employee* that would be executed, rather than the original defined in *Person*.

Thus, a method's effect can be modified by overriding the definitions of other methods that it uses, allowing parameterization of behaviours. This means that the interface specification of a class cannot simply consist of the behaviour that it makes available in instances, but must also include the behaviour that it uses by sending messages to self, which might be altered in inheriting classes. The specification of the semantics of a class must provide a way for inherited behaviour to be altered by the inheritance process, as described by Cook (1989).

This parameterization of behaviour can be used in a way that is similar to that provided by higher-order functions in functional languages, but is generally notationally less convenient.

Combined in a single system, these possibilities make inheritance a very powerful way of composing existing, and new, behaviours to construct the desired behaviour. Thus, inheritance is the foundation which encourages a high degree of object reuse in object-oriented systems. However, it can also make the design process more difficult, since the designer of a class should now consider not just the behaviour that is required for the task at hand, but also the interfaces that should be made available to allow this behaviour to be reused through inheritance.

Hence, it is often useful to distinguish two different kinds of classes:

1. *Normal classes*, which describe the behaviour of objects in the system.
2. *Abstract classes*, which describe common behaviour to be inherited by other classes. Such behaviour is not in some sense 'complete', and as a result such classes are not expected to be instantiated directly.

Some object-oriented languages such as Trellis/Owl (Schaffert *et al.*, 1985; Schaffert *et al.*, 1986), Eiffel (Meyer, 1988) and C++ (Stroustrup, 1986) provide mechanisms allowing the programmer to assert that a class is abstract, and the system does not allow instances of these classes to be created. Other languages, such as Smalltalk 80, document abstract classes as a programming technique, but do not provide explicit support for them.

In summary, there are five important characteristics of inheritance mechanisms. An inheritance mechanism may allow a subclass to:

1. Inherit behaviour from a superclass – previously defined behaviour can be used as part of the definition of new behaviour.
2. Provide additional behaviour specific to the subclass – new behaviour can be added to that which was inherited.
3. Override operations inherited from a superclass – inherited operations can be replaced by new behaviour.
4. Access overridden behaviour in the superclass – new behaviour should be able to make use of inherited behaviour that it, or some other new behaviour, hides by overriding.
5. Access overriding behaviour in any further subclasses – inherited behaviour should be able to use overriding behaviour defined when it is inherited.

39.3.2 Multiple inheritance

The discussion above assumes that a class is built by extending the behaviour of another class. In practice there are many situations where the behaviour that is desired is the synthesis of the behaviours of *several* other classes. The restriction that a class can only have one superclass is inconvenient, and can force

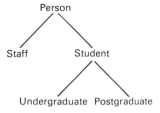

Figure 39.1 Class hierarchy for university example

an unnatural structure on the classes, making them more complicated, and more difficult to reuse. Consider, for example, a University information system which represents University personnel using the class hierarchy illustrated in *Figure 39.1*.

Classes are defined to describe staff and student objects, both inheriting behaviour from the *Person* class. They will additionally have behaviour of their own (e.g. a *Staff* object would have an instance variable to record a staff member's current salary). Then, undergraduate and postgraduate students are represented separately through defining appropriate subclasses of the *Student* class. In addition to inheriting behaviour from the *Student* class, these classes would also have their own behaviour (e.g. a *Postgraduate* object would have an instance variable to record the name of the student's supervisor). However, if it is found that some postgraduate students can be employed as demonstrators on certain courses, it would be appropriate to define a new class of *GraduateDemonstrator* which inherits behaviour from both the *Staff* and *Postgraduate* classes. For example, a *GraduateDemonstrator* object would record both a salary value (inherited from the *Staff* class) and a supervisor's name (inherited from the *Postgraduate* class).

The ability to inherit the behaviours of more than one class is called multiple inheritance and has been implemented by several object-oriented systems, including most of the Lisp-based systems, the Traits system used for the software in the Xerox Star office system (Curry *et al.*, 1982) and more recently in Trellis/Owl, Eiffel, and C++.

In most situations where multiple inheritance is useful there are ways in which the inheritance relationships between classes could be changed to remove the need for multiple inheritance. However, these changes make the classes less general, and so less likely to be useful elsewhere. Hence, this makes multiple inheritance particularly important for encouraging class reuse as it is possible to construct classes describing relatively small behaviours, which are then combined in a 'mix-and-match' style. This is not possible with a single inheritance scheme.

With single inheritance there is no possibility of conflicts, where the inheriting class is inconsistent because of the behaviour it inherits – local definitions of methods clearly override those that are inherited. However, with multiple inheritance the possibility exists that several superclasses might provide methods for the same message, without any 'clearly correct' way to decide between them. This situation gives rise to a conflict. For example, both the *Staff* and *Postgraduate* classes in Figure 39.1 may independently define a method called 'MemberOf' which returns the set of professional societies in which the staff member or postgraduate student is enrolled. Thus, a *Graduate-Demonstrator* object would inherit two different behaviours for the 'MemberOf' method. When the message 'MemberOf' is sent to a *GraduateDemonstrator* object, which inherited method should be invoked?

Similar conflicts arise with inherited instance variables, but here overriding is not useful. Rather, the question is whether two instance variables with the same name and type, inherited from different classes, should be treated as the same instance

variable in the object, or whether there should be two instance variables in the object with a syntax to allow them to be accessed individually.

Different systems have chosen to take different approaches towards resolving multiple inheritance ambiguities. The approach taken often leads to profound differences in the ways in which users make use of inheritance in these systems. For example, some techniques encourage the user towards a 'mix-and-match' approach, while others encourage approaches more like those used with single inheritance.

Figures 39.2 and *39.3* provide two example inheritance graphs which will be used to demonstrate the resolution of conflicts.

In Figure 39.2, class A inherits behaviour for the message m, from both of its superclasses, B and C. If there is also a definition for m in class A, overriding both inherited methods, then there is no conflict. However, if no definition for m exists in A, then one needs a way of deciding which of the inherited methods to invoke when the message m is sent to an instance of class A.

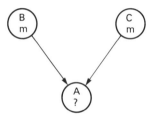

Figure 39.2 Conflicting inheritance of a message

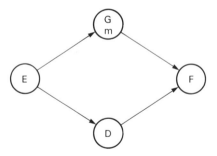

Figure 39.3 Conflicting inheritance of a class

In contrast, in Figure 39.3, the entire behaviour of the class G is inherited twice by class D, and so every message that is understood by instances of G will be in conflict in the definition of class D, unless it is overridden.

There are three main ways to resolve inheritance ambiguities, which have been called linear, graph-oriented, and tree resolution techniques (Snyder, 1986a).

39.3.2.1 Linear resolution

In the linear resolution approach to multiple inheritance, a linear ordering is defined for the inheritance of the superclasses. The ordering preserves as many of the relationships between the classes as possible, and then (in effect) uses single inheritance to construct a class hierarchy with no conflicts.

For example, given the example class definitions of Figures 39.2 and 39.3, the inheritance hierarchies shown in *Figure 39.4* would be constructed.

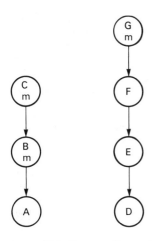

Figure 39.4   Linear conflict resolution

This solution approximates a breadth-first search of the inheritance hierarchy. The problem with this, however, is that it can only give an approximate solution, since it introduces inheritance relationships between classes which were not related in the original inheritance graph. The relationship between classes B and C in Figure 39.4 is an example. Here, attempts by B to communicate with its superclasses, and attempts by C to send messages to self, may be affected.

The advantage of linear resolution is that any inheritance pattern can be accepted by the system. This is useful in the rapid prototyping of systems. A linear resolution technique is used by most of the object-oriented extensions to Lisp including Symbolics' Flavors (Weinreb and Moon, 1981), Common LOOPS (Bobrow *et al.*, 1986), and CLOS (Bobrow *et al.*, 1987).

39.3.2.2 *Graph resolution*

The general philosophy of graph resolution of multiple inheritance conflicts is that a conflict is a programmer error (analogous to a type error) and so rather than attempting to resolve the conflict, the system should refuse to accept classes that introduce conflicts. However, there are some special situations where the system will resolve conflicts automatically. In particular, if the *same* behaviour is inherited more than once, as occurs in Figure 39.3, it is not regarded as a conflict. The resulting class implements the behaviour *once* in the sense that instances of the class will only contain one set of instance variables for the behaviour, regardless of how often it is inherited. As a result, classes that are inherited might communicate via common ancestor classes, reflecting the view of objects as modelling real-world behaviour – a real-world object can only have a behaviour once!

39.3.2.3 *Tree resolution*

Snyder (1986a) suggested tree-based resolution of inheritance conflicts to avoid the ambiguity of other solutions, and improve the encapsulation of classes. In tree resolution the multiple inheritance of a method is an error unless it is explicitly overridden in the inheriting class. However, in contrast to graph resolution, in tree resolution inherited state is always treated as distinct.

Consequently, using tree resolution both of the examples shown in Figure 39.2 and 39.3 are illegal without providing overriding behaviour in the subclass. Then, the conflicting class

example of Figure 39.3 is treated as if it were of the form shown in *Figure 39.5*.

The advantages of the tree resolution approach are:

1. No unexpected sharing can occur between classes because of their choice of instance variable names, or their choice of which classes to inherit. This means that knowledge of the classes that were inherited no longer needs to be part of the specification of a class. With graph resolution this was required in order that communication via common ancestor classes could be predicted by the writer of an inheriting class.
2. All inherited methods can see their instance variables in the same relative positions. This allows more efficient code sharing between classes than would otherwise be possible.

Tree resolution was first used in Snyder's CommonObjects extension to Lisp. This was designed with particular emphasis on the encapsulation of objects and classes, the intention being that classes did not have to include any information about their construction in their externally visible specification. Version 2 of C++ also uses tree resolution for most classes, but acknowledges that graph resolution is sometimes useful, by allowing classes to declare explicitly which of their superclasses can be shared when they are inherited (Stroustrup, 1987a).

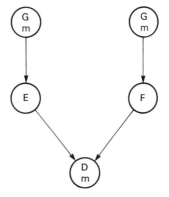

Figure 39.5   Interpretation of Figure 39.3 using tree resolution

39.3.3 Delegation

An alternative to inheritance which has been used in Actor languages is delegation (Lieberman, 1986a). The idea is that an object, when it is asked to carry out some action for which it does not have a method, simply forwards the request to another object, called the delegate. This means that the behaviour of the delegate is visible through those objects which delegate to it. Delegation introduces more possibilities for the sharing of behaviour than are possible with inheritance, since several objects may all delegate messages to a single object, making changes to its state visible through them all. An object can also delegate different messages to different objects, which is the delegation equivalent of multiple inheritance.

There has been much discussion about the exact relationship between inheritance and delegation, in particular see Lieberman (1986a) and Stein (1987), but a fundamental difference is in the value of **self** as seen by a method reached by delegation. Here, **self** refers to the delegate, rather than referring to the object to which the original request was made, making inheritance property 5 (access to overriding behaviour) very difficult to achieve. However, this problem can be avoided if delegation is allowed to use a slightly different mechanism when forwarding messages.

Such an approach is used in Ungar and Smith's language *self* (Ungar and Smith, 1987).

It is worth noting, however, that because it increases the frequency of message sends, it is difficult to provide an efficient implementation of delegation in systems where the cost of sending and receiving messages is high.

39.4 Some object-oriented systems

This section gives a brief survey of some of the more important object-oriented systems that have been developed. The survey is by no means exhaustive – there now being many dozens of systems that are claimed to be 'object-oriented'. However, the systems mentioned have either been particularly influential, or are typical of a particular approach to object orientation.

39.4.1 Simula 67

Object-oriented programming was first supported by Simula 67 (Bertwistle *et al.*, 1973), an extension of Algol 60 specifically intended for the programming of simulations. Simula 67 introduced the *Class* construct, which was intended to reflect program organization techniques that Kristen Nygaard first used in simulations for the Norwegian nuclear power program (Nygaard, 1986). The main motivation behind this approach was that the program structure should parallel that of the system which is being modelled. The class construct allowed objects to be defined to model each real-world object on a one-to-one basis.

A class could be defined with another as its prefix, which is the Simula mechanism for the inheritance of implementations. The term 'prefix' reflects the underlying implementation, where each object contains an instance of its prefix class as its first part. This is the most efficient implementation strategy for object-oriented languages.

Being based on Algol 60, Simula 67 is a statically strongly-typed language. The types of objects are defined by their classes, each class being implicitly a subtype of all its prefix classes – this approach has formed the basis of the type systems for most of the current strongly-typed object-oriented languages, such as C++ and Eiffel.

Simula 67 is most important for its influences on other languages. It introduced most of the concepts central to object-oriented programming, but was never very widely used – perhaps because the system support required by other language features (particularly co-routines) was perceived as being too expensive for a general-purpose language.

The one weak area in Simula 67's support for object-oriented programming is that it did not support the encapsulation of objects in that, while operations can be attached to objects, there was no way to restrict the access that was allowed to an object's state from outside. A directive similar to C++'s 'private' has been added more recently to provide control of the visibility of an object's state.

Nygaard is now involved in the design of a successor to Simula, called *Beta* (Kristensen *et al.*, 1983 and 1985). This language provides a general abstraction mechanism, called a pattern, which can provide the effect of a class, but is more general. For example, functions and co-routines are also described by patterns in Beta.

39.4.2 C++

C++ (Stroustrup, 1986) is an extension of C (Kernighan, 1978) which was (and continues to be) developed by Bjarne Stroustrup of AT&T Bell Laboratories at Murray Hill in the USA. C++ was directly influenced by Simula 67, and development started

when Stroustrup added classes to C using a pre-processor to help him to program some simulations (Stroustrup, 1982).

Although highly compatible with C, C++ is a language in its own right, and, in addition to classes, adds operator overloading, stricter type checking, in-line functions, a less strict declaration syntax, and user-controlled storage management. At the same time many strengths of C are retained, including the possibility of simple, efficient implementations, and low-level access to the machine. Version 2 of C++ (which became available towards the end of 1989) added multiple inheritance, and some other less important facilities, to the previously distributed version (Lippman, 1989).

Being based on C, and having a similar efficiency, C++ has found a widespread acceptance that has not been enjoyed by other object-oriented systems, and many sites are increasingly using it in preference to C. Objects are implemented in the same way as in Simula, and this is extended to multiple inheritance using techniques that were first proposed for Simula by Krogdahl (1984 and 1985).

39.4.3 Smalltalk

The Smalltalk systems developed in the Learning Research Group (which later became the Software Concepts Group, or SCG) at the Xerox Palo Alto Research Center have been most influential in developing the field of object-oriented systems.

Smalltalk was intended to be the software component of the Dynabook, a powerful, portable, personal computer, which turned out to be far more ahead of its time than was perhaps appreciated. Indeed, technologies such as compact high resolution, touch-sensitive displays, and batteries that can provide the power for a powerful system with sufficient memory, are only now beginning to become available. It will probably still be several years before the cost becomes low enough for a Dynabook to be feasible. Fortunately, Smalltalk was developed independently of the Dynabook hardware (Ingalls, 1983):

> The very first Smalltalk evaluator was a thousand-line BASIC program which first evaluated $3 + 4$ in October 1972. It was followed in two months by a Nova assembly code implementation which became known as the Smalltalk-72 system.

Several iterations from this initial design culminated in the Smalltalk 80 system (Goldberg and Robson, 1983). That system was widely distributed outside Xerox PARC, and is the version of Smalltalk that many people now have access to.

Smalltalk was conceived from the start as a complete system, rather than simply a language, and took many ideas from Lisp systems which were also developing in this way. In particular, Smalltalk presents a very dynamic environment and encourages the incremental development of programs. This led to run-time type checking, and a powerful, but potentially expensive mechanism for message dispatch. Unfortunately, while interesting and innovative mechanisms, they were also the cause of the slow acceptance of Smalltalk 80 outside research centres. It is only quite recently that personal computer systems which are powerful enough to support Smalltalk have become generally available, and more sophisticated techniques for the fast execution of Smalltalk have been developed (Deutsch and Schiffman, 1984; Johnson *et al.*, 1988).

The integrated environment provided by Smalltalk 80 is simultaneously both its strongest and its weakest feature, since it provides a highly productive environment for programming, but also restricts Smalltalk applications to situations that can support the whole environment. In particular, it is difficult to write Smalltalk tools that interact conveniently with other tools as is common, say, in Unix. Similarly, it is difficult for companies to distribute Smalltalk programs independently of a particular Smalltalk system.

39.4.4 Lisp-based systems

Many object-oriented systems have been implemented in Lisp. There are several reasons for this:

1. Lisp provides much of the low-level support that is required, and allows the user to construct his or her own higher-level constructs upon those that already exist. Furthermore, such extensions can be implemented in such a way that the additional constructs are no less convenient to use than those in the original system. This means that Lisp is an ideal system for investigating the object-oriented paradigm, with the result that many Lisp prototypes have been developed. Inevitably, a number of these prototypes have been made into practical tools that are used commercially.

2. Lisp does not provide an abstraction mechanism at an intermediate granularity between the function, and the package (where these are provided). Classes and objects fitted nicely into this gap.

3. Many influential people at Xerox PARC worked on both Smalltalk and InterLisp-D, leading to much cross-fertilization of ideas.

The dominant object-oriented extensions to Lisp were Symbolics' Flavors (Weinreb and Moon, 1981) and LOOPS, the Lisp Object-Oriented Programming System (Stefik *et al.*, 1986) for InterLisp-D developed at Xerox PARC. LOOPS developed into Common LOOPS (Bobrow *et al.*, 1986) based on Common Lisp (Steele, 1984). Recently there has been a standardization effort directed at object-oriented extensions to Common Lisp. The result of this is CLOS (The Common Lisp Object System) (Bobrow *et al.*, 1987) which is most closely related to Common LOOPS.

All these object-oriented extensions allow the use of multiple inheritance. LOOPS also introduced multi-methods, which generalize message dispatch, so that the choice of which method is executed for a given message can depend on the types of the parameters as well as the type of the receiver of the message. Message dispatch is normally achieved in these systems by dynamic lookup similar to that in Smalltalk (this is further complicated by multi-methods). As in Smalltalk, the interactive nature of Lisp systems makes the global analysis that would be needed to optimize message lookup very difficult.

Some other Lisp-based object-oriented systems have a rather different philosophy. The best example of this is Snyder's CommonObjects which stresses encapsulation over immediate flexibility (Snyder, 1986b).

Other systems deserve a mention in passing: T (Slade, 1987) and Oaklisp (Lang and Pearlmutter, 1986) are based on the Scheme dialect of Lisp, which is a natural choice for experimenting with novel language constructs (Abelson *et al.*, 1985). T is interesting for its uniformity and run-time efficiency. Oaklisp and ObjVlisp (Cointe, 1987) provide more flexibility in the construction of classes than other systems, by making the equivalent of the Smalltalk Metaclass hierarchy manipulable by the programmer.

39.4.5 Actors

Actor languages model the view of an object-oriented system as a group of communicating objects more closely than other object-oriented languages. In an actor system all objects execute concurrently, and messages between the objects either synchronize the objects' execution, or are queued until the receiving object next attempts to receive a message. Like Smalltalk 80, actor systems are usually uniformly object-objected, so that everything in the system is represented by an object – this unfortunately rules out many opportunities for optimization.

Actor systems were first proposed by Hewitt (1979) and this has led to several actor-based languages, including the Act family (Lieberman, 1986b), Plasma and Acore (Agha and Hewitt, 1987).

39.5 Type systems for object-oriented systems

Type systems are a complex and evolving topic, so we can only briefly address the main issues here. The reader is referred to Danforth and Tomlinson (1988) for a fuller account of types in object-oriented systems.

Many object-oriented languages have used run-time type checking to ensure that the messages that are sent to an object are understood by that object. However, the static use of types to prove that errors of this sort can never occur is the domain of type checking, and is as useful in object-oriented systems as it is in traditional languages. The question arises as to what type model should be used to represent the types of objects.

The important property of objects in this context is the property of substitution (property 4) which says that objects that provide a common set of operations should be able to be used interchangeably in contexts that only require the common behaviour. Inheritance provides a way in which one can guarantee that the inheriting class will have all the behaviour of its superclass. This suggests that the type of an object should be associated with its class, and that instances of a subclass should be able to be used in all the places where instances of the superclass are expected. Such a philosophy has formed the basis of almost every typed object-oriented language, starting with Simula 67, and ranging through C++, Trellis/Owl and Eiffel.

Unfortunately, there is a fundamental flaw with this type system. It is based around an implementation technique for classes, namely inheritance, and not directly around the set of operations that the objects provide – which is ultimately what is important for the substitution property to work.

While the types of objects do follow their class structure much of the time, it is not difficult to find situations where this is inconvenient. As an example, consider a collection of classes defining objects representing geometric figures. One of the most general classes might be *Polygon*, its instances being able to represent any figure made out of straight edges.

Another class might be *Square*, its instances representing squares. Now the substitution property would suggest that, since squares are special cases of polygons, wherever a *Polygon* is expected, it should be possible to use an instance *Square*. In other words, a square *is a* polygon.

If one now considers the implementation of these classes one can see that *Polygon* must have a very general representation, a list of points, say, while squares are completely defined by three points. However, a type system based on inheritance requires that an instance can only be substituted in a context if its class is a subclass of the class expected in that context. Here this means that *Square* must inherit from *Polygon* if one is to be able to substitute squares into contexts expecting polygons. Thus, instances of *Square* must contain (at least) all of *Polygon*'s very general implementation just so that their type has the desired relationship with the type defined by *Polygon*.

In general, the type of an object need have no connection with the way in which it is implemented. This can be achieved in (at least) two different ways:

1. Two different sorts of inheritance could be used, one to define the type of a class, and the other to define the implementation. Where it is convenient, these inheritance hierarchies could be constructed in parallel, giving the same effect as is offered by current systems. However, this would

be a choice that was made by the implementor of the class, on a class-by-class basis.

2. The compatibility check between the types of objects to see if the substitution rule can be used could be based directly on their signatures, rather than the way in which they were constructed (Cardelli, 1984). This is an extension of the use of structural equivalence of types, as used in Algol 68 (Woodward and Bond, 1983) to the type checking of objects, and is usually achieved by introducing a subtype relationship between types.

Both of these solutions can continue to work with an efficient message dispatch scheme (e.g. as used by C + +). The second approach is more general, however, and can be easier to implement, since explicit mechanisms for defining the type hierarchy do not need to be provided. It also corresponds to some of the more recent theoretical work on object-oriented languages, such as that of Cardelli (1988, 1989) and Cook (1990).

This approach, based on structural equivalence, or the conformity of types, has been used for some time by Emerald (Black *et al.*, 1986) which also replaces primitive classes by an object constructor primitive. A function that returns the result of executing an object constructor is similar to a class in other systems, but Emerald does not appear to have explicit mechanisms for the inheritance or composition of object implementations (Black *et al.*, 1987).

39.6 Example

To give an illustration of the development of applications in an object-oriented programming language, this section provides a short example written using the C + + programming language. (The C + + language has been chosen as it is one of the most widely used object-oriented programming languages, and because many people are familiar with the C programming language, the syntax of which it closely resembles. Also note that for convenience of exposition the source lines of the example are numbered. This is not part of the C + + syntax.)

The example is a simple implementation of the classes *Student* and *GraduateStudent* used in Section 39.3, and appearing in Figure 39.1. However, so that the example can be complete, a class *Person* is not included here, and so *Student* will not have any superclasses.

```
1: class Student {
2:     int exams_taken;
3:     float *marks;
4: public:
5:     char *name;
6:     Student(int e, float *m)
7:         {exams_taken = e; marks = m;}
8:     virtual float average_mark();
9:     virtual void format();
10:     virtual void print();
11:     //...
12: };
13: class GraduateStudent :: public Student {
14:     char *supervisor;
15: public:
16:     GraduateStudent(int e, float *m, char *superv)
17:         : (e, m) {supervisor = superv;}
18:     virtual void format();
19:     //...
20: };
```

Figure 39.6 Example class definitions

Figure 39.6 shows the declarations of the two classes. First, class *Student* is declared (lines 1–12). Details of the students' exam results are hidden from other parts of the system by putting their declarations in the 'private' part of the class declaration (lines 2 and 3). The 'public' section allows the name of the student to be accessed, and declares a constructor (lines 6–7) which ensures that new instances of the class are fully initialized. This section also declares some publicly accessible member functions which calculate the student's average mark, write a formatted representation of the student object, and print a slightly more verbose form of the student details.

The declaration of *GraduateStudent* (lines 13–20) inherits from the *Student* class, and then introduces a new private instance variable to contain the name of the graduate student's supervisor. Its constructor must first call the constructor provided by the superclass, using the special ':' syntax on line 17, and then initializes the new instance variable, 'supervisor'.

In this example the bodies of both the constructors appeared with their declarations; this means that they will be expanded in-line when they are used. The member functions' bodies do not appear here, and they must be provided as normal out-of-line functions elsewhere, although they could also be defined in-line if that were desired. They are declared as 'virtual', which means that subclasses are allowed to override their definitions, and indeed one can see on line 18 that *GraduateStudent* is expecting to override the 'format' message inherited from *Student*.

```
21: float Student::average_mark()
22: {
23:     float total = 0.0;
24:     for(int i = 0; i < exams_taken; i + +)
25:         total + = marks[i];
26:     return total/exams_taken;
27: }
28: void Student::print()
29: {
30:     printf("Student called");
31:     format();
32:     print f("\n");
33: }
34: void Student::format()
35: {
36:     printf("%s, average = %g%%", name,
                                average_mark());
37: }
38: void GraduateStudent::format()
39: {
40:     Student::format();
41:     printf("\n\t(Graduate, supervised by %s)",
                                supervisor);
42: }
```

Figure 39.7 Definitions of the member functions

Figure 39.7 shows the definitions of the member functions that were declared in Figure 39.6. The class to which a member function belongs is denoted using the C + + scope operator, '::', and this is also used to access otherwise-hidden variables and functions, such as on line 40, where the definition of 'format' in class *GraduateStudent* calls the member function that it overrides in class *Student*.

These classes are now complete and one can write a main function to test them.

In *Figure 39.8* a main function is defined that creates two student objects – s is a normal student, and gs a graduate student – and then sends a message to each, to ask them to print details of themselves. The output from the program is shown in *Figure 39.9*.

```
43:    float s_marks[ ]={51.2, 65.5, 72.0};
44:    float gs_marks[ ]={72.7, 82.5, 77.1, 93.2, 87.6};
45:    main()
46:    {
47:        Student s(3, s_marks);
48:        s.name = "Fred Bloggs";
49:        GraduateStudent gs(5, gs_marks, "John Doe");
50:        gs.name = "Jane Smith";
51:
52:        s.print();
53:        gs.print();
54:    }
```

Figure 39.8   A main function to test the example classes

Student called Fred Bloggs, average = 62.9%
Student called Jane Smith, average = 82.62%
       (Graduate, supervised by John Doe)

Figure 39.9   Output of the test program

Despite its simplicity, this example illustrates several of the properties of inheritance that have been introduced in this chapter. The important point to note is that the 'format' message is overridden in the class *GraduateStudent* to add the '(Graduate, supervised by . . .)' annotation to the output describing ordinary students. However, the 'format' message is not the message that was sent to the objects to get them to print themselves, rather it was the 'print' message that was used, to put a 'chatty wrapper' around the output of format. When 'print' is sent to the *GraduateStudent* object, it then sends the 'format' message to itself (line 31), causing the overriding definition of 'format' to be executed. Thus, the overriding of the 'format' member function has extended the effect, not just of the 'format' message, but also of the 'print' message.

This example of classes, and inheritance, and in particular the example of overriding, and access to overridden behaviour is, of course, rather contrived. However, these are the kinds of interactions, and possibilities for the extension of the behaviour of classes, which are very common in real programs written using object-oriented techniques, and indeed are fundamental in making programming with objects and inheritance different from simply programming with abstract data types.

39.7 Object-oriented design

As indicated in the introduction, several design and requirements analysis techniques are now being referred to as 'object-oriented'. The motivation appears to be two-fold. The first is to provide design methods which map well into object-oriented implementations, and the second is to gain some of the structuring benefits of object-orientation for the design and requirements notations themselves.

Hence, the past few years has seen increasing interest in object-orientation as it applies to each of the life-cycle phases. For example:

1. Object-oriented requirements analysis (OORA) techniques have been developed which involve early identification of candidate objects and their relationships. The objects are organized into classes, have both state and operational aspects, and so on. The requirements definition consists of documentation describing these objects, together with (graphical) descriptions of their possible interrelationships (Coad and Yourdon, 1990).

2. Object-oriented specification languages are an attempt to try to impose an object-oriented framework onto existing specification languages. For example, the object-oriented approach may be particularly useful as a structuring framework for developing and browsing large specifications in a language such as Z (Carrington *et al.*, 1989).

3. Object-oriented design (OOD) techniques have been under investigation for a number of years. As an extension of the OORA techniques described above, in object-oriented design methods such as HOOD (see Chapter 17 of this book) or Booch's method (Booch, 1982) the notion of an object is used as the primary focus for structuring information.

Clearly, it is not essential to use an object-oriented approach in all of the phases of software development. For example, an object-oriented system design need not necessarily be implemented in an object-oriented programming language. However, by doing so, a cleaner conceptual mapping between the design and coding phases of a software project is provided. Indeed, as it is the management of the relationships between the many system models which is a major factor in the success or failure of a large software project, particularly in the event of errors, omissions, and enhancements to those models, a consistent view of the full software life cycle is particularly important.

However, it is worth noting that while there has been a great deal of interest expressed in object-oriented design techniques, they are much less mature than equivalent implementation techniques, and it still remains to be seen how effective they are in practice. (Space does not permit a detailed review of the techniques, but the interested reader is referred to Chapter 17 for a discussion of HOOD, which is currently one of the most widely used object-oriented design techniques.)

39.8 Comments and conclusions

Having briefly discussed the basic characteristics of object-oriented systems, it is possible to identify a number of general advantages that are commonly claimed for the object-oriented approach. These are particular manifestations of the general principle of support for abstraction – that is, the ability to devise a model of a problem in terms of the data items and operators which are most suited to our needs. The internal details of the data and operators are ignored so that all one needs to know is *what* they do, not *how* they do it.

In addition, by allowing one object to be defined in terms of previously defined objects, a hierarchy is created in which objects are defined and manipulated at increasing levels of abstraction at each level in the hierarchy. The solution to a problem can then be defined at the most appropriate abstract level, using the objects defined at that level. This helps to control the complexity of applications, which is often increased by attempting to define a solution at an inappropriate level of abstraction.

Specific advantages which arise from direct support for abstraction include:

1. *Data hiding.* The internal state of an object is hidden from its users. As a result, the clients of an object need only concern themselves with the service the object provides, not the method by which that service is provided. For example, suppose one wishes to make use of a set of graphical operations for a windowing system. If there is an operator to bring a window to the foreground one only needs to know how to call it, not how it implements its internal algorithms. Thus, not only are clients of an object not distracted by such irrelevant details, they are also unable to attempt to access private parts of the server object's state.

2. *Data independence.* By restricting the use of an object to a
fixed set of operators, one can control the extent to which the
client object relies on the internal details of the server object.
In particular, if the internal algorithms of the server object
are amended, it is possible to insulate the client from those
changes provided the interface to the server object remains
unchanged (i.e. the same operators still exist). Indeed, objects
with the same interface, but different implementations, can
easily co-exist in a system.
3. *Modularity.* The definition of appropriate objects can act as
the focal point for modularizing the implementation of a
large software system, often providing a boundary for distribution or concurrency of objects. The object-oriented approach naturally encourages designs involving a small
number of relatively independent object types interacting in
well-defined ways.
4. *Reuse.* By organizing the classes within a class hierarchy,
common properties of a class can be filtered out and inherited from one class to the next. In this way common state
variables and methods need not be reimplemented, but are
shared between classes. This is an example of component
reuse, providing many benefits to the system implementor
and maintainer, which should ultimately make object-
oriented systems smaller than equivalent systems developed
in conventional systems. In addition, by identifying the main
object classes within an application, the object-oriented
approach lends itself to the creation of object libraries in
which commonly used object classes are maintained. Then,
not only is one encouraged to reuse objects within a single
system through object specialization, but reuse between
different systems is facilitated through shared object libraries.

One of the key characteristics of an object-oriented system is
the flexibility that is provided by allowing new object classes to
be defined which gradually extend the class hierarchy through
the process of specialization. In this way, the different kinds of
objects of interest can be gradually and incrementally extended
as our understanding of the application domain grows. Thus,
the primary benefit of the object-oriented approach is that it
supports directly many of the good practices and goals of
software engineering.

39.9 References

Abelson, H., Sussman, G. J. and Sussman, J. (1985) *Structure and Interpretation of Computer Programs*, MIT Press, Cambridge, MA, USA
Agha, G. and Hewitt, C. (1987) Actors: a conceptual foundation for concurrent object-oriented programming. In *Research Directions in Object-Oriented Programming* (ed. Wegner, Bruce Shriver and Peter.), MIT Press, Series in Computer Science, Cambridge, MA, USA, pp. 49–74
Bertwistle, G., Dahl, O.-J., Myhrhaug, B. and Nygaard, K. (1973) *Simula Begin*, Auerbach, Philadelphia, PA, USA
Black, A., Hutchinson, N., Jul, E. and Levy, H. (1986) Object struc-ture in the Emerald system. *ACM SIGPLAN Notices*, **21**, 78–86
Black, A. P., Lazowska, E. D., Noe, J. D. and Sanislo, J. (1986) *The Eden Project: A Final Report*, 86-11-01, University of Washington, Seattle, Department of Computer Science
Black, A., Hutchinson, N., Jul, E., Levy, H. and Carter, L. (1987) Distributed and abstract types in Emerald. *IEEE Transactions on Software Engineering*, **13**, 65–76
Blair, G. S., Gallagher, J. J. and Malik, J. (1988) *Genericity vs Inheri-tance vs Delegation vs Conformance vs . . . (Towards a Unifying Understanding of Objects)*, Research Report, Department of Com-puting, University of Lancaster
Bobrow, D. G., Kahn, K., Kiczales, G. et al. (1986) CommonLoops: merging Lisp and object-oriented programming. *ACM SIGPLAN Notices*, **21**, 17–29
Bobrow, D. G., DeMichiel, L. G., Gabriel, R. et al. (1987) *Common Lisp Object System Specification*, ANSI X3J13 Document 87-002, American National Standards Institute, Washington, DC, USA

Booch, G. (1982) Object-oriented design. *Ada Letters*, **1**, 64–76
Bretl, R. et al. (1989) The GemStone Data Management System. In *Object-Oriented Concepts, Databases, and Applications* (ed. Lochovsky, W. Kim and F.K.), Addison Wesley, pp. 283–308
Cardelli, L. (1984) A semantics of multiple inheritance. In *Proceedings of the Symposium on the Semantics of Data Types*, pp. 51–67
Cardelli, L. (1988) Structural subtyping and the notion of power type. In *Proceedings of the 15th Annual ACM Symposium on Principles of Programming Languages*, San Diego, CA, USA, pp. 70–79
Cardelli, L. (1989) *Typeful Programming*, Research Report 45, Digital Equipment Corporation, Systems Research Center, Palo Alto, CA, USA
Cardelli, L. and Wegner, P. (1985) On understanding types, data abstraction, and polymorphism. *ACM Computing Surveys*, **17**, 471–523
Carrington, D., Duke, D., Duke, R. et al. (1989) Object-Z; An object-oriented extension to Z. In *Proceedings of Formal Description Tech-niques (FORTE'89)*, Vancouver, Canada
Coad, P. and Yourdon, E. (1990) *Object-Oriented Requirements Analy-sis*, Yourdon Press Computing Series
Cohen, J. (1981) Garbage collection of linked data structures. *ACM Computing Surveys*, **13**, 341–367
Cointe, P. (1987) Metaclasses are first class: the ObjVlisp Model. *ACM SIGPLAN Notices*, **22**, 156–167
Cook, W. (1989) *A Denotational Semantics of Inheritance*, Ph.D. The-sis, CS-89-33, Department of Computer Science, Brown University, Providence, RI, USA
Cook, W. R., Hill, W. L. and Canning, P. S. (1990) Inheritance is not subtyping. In *Proceedings of the 17th Annual ACM Symposium on Principles of Programming Languages*, San Francisco, CA, USA
Curry, G., Baer, L., Lipkie, D. and Lee, B. (1982) Traits – an ap-proach to multiple-inheritance subclassing. In *Proceedings of the Conference on Office Automation Systems*
Danforth, S. and Tomlinson, C. (1988) Type theories and object-oriented programming. *ACM Computing Surveys*, **20**, 29–72
Deutsch, L. P. and Schiffman, A. M. (1984) Efficient implementation of the Smalltalk 80 system. In *Proceedings of the 11th Annual ACM Symposium on Principles of Programming Languages*, Salt Lake City, Utah, USA, pp. 297–302
Goldberg, A. and Robson, D. (1983) *Smalltalk-80: The Language and its Implementation*, Addison-Wesley Publishing Company
Hewitt, C. (1979) Viewing control structures as patterns of passing messages. In *Artificial Intelligence: An MIT Perspective, Volume 2* (ed. Winston, P. H. and Brown, R. H), MIT Press, Cambridge, MA, USA, pp. 433–465
Ichbiah, J. D. et al. (1983) *Reference Manual for the Ada Programming Language*, ANSI/MIL-STD-1815A-1983, US DoD
Ingalls, D. H. H. (1983) The evolution of the Smalltalk virtual machine. In *Smalltalk-80: Bits of History, Words of Advice* (ed. Krasner, Glenn), Addison-Wesley Publishing Company, pp. 9–28
Johnson, R. E., Graver, J. O. and Zurawski, L. W. (1988) TS: an opti-mizing compiler for Smalltalk. *ACM SIGPLAN Notices*, **23**, 18–26
Kernighan, B. W. and Mashey, J. R. (1979) The Unix programming environment. *Software – Practice and Experience*, **9**, 1–16
Kernighan, B. W. and Richie, D. M. (1978) *The C Programming Lan-guage*, Prentice-Hall, Inc, Englewood Cliffs, NJ, USA
Kristensen, B. B., Madsen, O. L., Moller-Pedersen, B. and Nygaard, K. (1983) Abstraction mechanisms in the Beta programming language. In *Proceedings of the 10th Annual ACM Symposium on the Principles of Programming Languages*, pp. 285–298
Kristensen, B. B., Madsen, O. L., Moller-Pedersen, B. and Nygaard, K. (1985) Multi-sequential execution in the Beta programming lan-guage. *ACM SIGPLAN Notices*, **20**, 57–70
Krogdahl, S. (1984) *An Efficient Implementation of Simula Classes with Multiple Prefixes*, 83, Institute of Informatics, University of Oslo
Krogdahl, S. (1985) Multiple inheritance in Simula-like languages. *Bit*, **25**, 318–326
Laguna Beach Participants (1989) Future directions in DBMS re-search. *ACM SIGMOD Record*, **18**, 17–32
Lang, K. J. and Pearlmutter, B. A. (1986) Oaklisp: an object-oriented Scheme with first class types. *ACM SIGPLAN Notices*, **21**, 30–37
Lieberman, H. (1986a) Delegation and inheritance: two mechanisms for sharing knowledge in object-oriented systems. In *3ème Journées d'Etudes Langages Orientés Objets* (ed. Bezivin, J. and Cointe, P.), AFCET, Paris, France, pp. 78–89
Lieberman, H. (1986b) Concurrent object oriented programming in Act 1. In *Object Oriented Concurrent Programming* (ed. Tokoro, A. Y. and Mario), MIT Press, Cambridge, MA, USA, pp. 9–36

Lippman, S. B. (1989) *A C++ Primer*, Addison Wesley

Liskov, B. and Zilles, S. (1974) Programming with abstract data types. *ACM SIGPLAN Notices*, **9**, 50–59

Meyer, B. (1988) *Object-Oriented Software Construction*, Prentice-Hall, Inc, Englewood Cliffs, NJ, USA

Nygaard, K. (1986) History and basic concepts. Object Oriented Programming Society – meeting 3 (20th March 1986)

Rentsch, T. (1982) Object-oriented programming. *ACM SIGPLAN Notices*, **17**, 51–57

Schaffert, C., Cooper, T. and Wilpolt, C. (1985) *Trellis: Object-Based Environment – Language Reference Manual*, DEC-TR-372, Digital Equipment Corporation, Hudson, MA, USA

Schaffert, C., Cooper, T., Bullis, B., Kilian, M. and Wilpolt, C. (1986) An introduction to Trellis/Owl. *ACM SIGPLAN Notices*, **21**, 9–16

Slade, S. (1987) *The T Programming Language: A Dialect of LISP*, Prentice-Hall, Inc, Englewood Cliffs, NJ, USA

Snyder, A. (1986a) Encapsulation and inheritance in object-oriented programming languages. *ACM SIGPLAN Notices*, **21**, 38–46

Snyder, A. (1986b) CommonObjects: an overview. *ACM SIGPLAN Notices*, **21**, 19–28

Steele, G. L. Jr. (1984) *Common LISP: The Language*, Digital Press, Bedford, MA, USA

Stefik, M. J., Bobrow, D. G. and Kahn, K. M. (1986) Integrating access-oriented programming into a multiparadigm environment. *IEEE Software*, **3**, 10–18

Stein, L. A. (1987) Delegation is inheritance. *ACM SIGPLAN Notices*, **22**, 138–146

Stroustrup, B. (1982) Classes: an abstract data type facility for the C language. *ACM SIGPLAN Notices*, **17**, 42–52

Stroustrup, B. (1986) *The C++ Programming Language*. Addison Wesley Publishing Company

Stroustrup, B. (1987a) Multiple inheritance in C++. In *Proceedings of the EUUG Conference*, Helsinki, pp. 189–207

Stroustrup, B. (1987b) What is 'object-oriented programming'? In *Proceedings of ECOOP*, Paris, France

Ungar, D. and Smith, R. B. (1987) Self: the power of simplicity. *ACM SIGPLAN Notices*, **22**, 227–242

Wegner, P. (1987) Dimensions of object-based language design. *ACM SIGPLAN Notices*, **22**, 168–182

Weinreb, D. and Moon, D. (1981) Objects, message passing, and flavors. In *Lisp Machine Manual*, Massachusetts Institute of Technology, pp. 245–275

Wirth, N. (1980) *Modula-2 (second edition)*, ETH Institut für Informatik Report 36

Woodward, P. M. and Bond, S. G. (1983) *Guide to ALGOL 68: for Users of RS Systems*, Edward Arnold (Publishers) Ltd, London

40

Prototyping

Darrel Ince
The Open University

Contents

40.1 Rationale behind prototyping

Software prototyping is a response to major problems which are encountered by software developers during requirements analysis and system specification. During these processes three problems are encountered. First, there is a cultural gap between the developer and the customer. The former is usually proficient at IT skills but may have a hazy view of an application area, while the latter will have a complete view of an application domain but will only have a hazy view of the capabilities of software. Second, the popular notation used for requirements specification, natural language – or at least graphics overloaded with natural language – has the drawback that it is ambiguous and contradictory. Moreover, it is exceptionally difficult to construct any document larger than a few pages which has the desired accuracy required for the description of a complex software system. Third, requirements documents are also very bulky. Even relatively modest software systems are often described by documents hundreds of pages of text in length.

Thus, the developer and the customer have to process bulky documents, in an unsuitable medium, with both sides having major gaps in experience and knowledge. The result of this is, at worst, the cancellation of projects, and at best, project and budget overruns as late changes need to be incorporated into a software system after the customer has seen it in operation during system testing.

Software prototyping has been proposed to overcome this problem. It involves the production of an early version of a software system – usually during requirements specification – which can be shown to the customer, and which acts as a learning medium. Although the major use of prototyping is for requirements clarification, there are a number of other uses:

1. *As a training medium.* Normally, the training of users of a software system tends to be rushed into the later stages of development. A prototype, produced early, allows training to take place in a more planned and considered way. Indeed, this use of a prototype can have the spin-off that the real users of a system may be exposed to it at an early stage in the development process. One of the many difficulties faced by developers during requirements analysis is that the developer rarely meets a real user, who is able to discuss the day-to-day operation of the system. Training enables this meeting to take place, albeit in a semi-clandestine way.
2. *As a medium to evaluate design alternatives.* This can be extremely useful when evaluating human–computer interface design decisions. For example, in a safety-critical system, the quality of an interface can be gauged by producing a prototype of the interface, and by measuring factors such as the number of operator errors that occur during a typical sequence of command initiations.
3. *As a test oracle.* Testing is a major resource consumer on a software project. A large component of testing involves calculating what the response of a system would be to some set of test data. To cut down on this calculation, the prototype of a system can be used to produce test outcomes which can be compared, using an automatic file comparison utility, to the output of the system under test.

Prototypes are produced by compromising on some aspect of the software development process or on some feature of the product to be prototyped. Popular ways of doing this include:

1. Compromising on the quality assurance standards normally used by the developer. Quality assurance activities, by necessity, occupy a large amount of project resource. By compromising on some of these activities, for example, by relaxing the level of unit and integration testing, an early version of a system can be developed.
2. Reducing the non-functional attributes of a system. Usually the non-functional attribute that is reduced is the time-response of the system. A number of tools are now available – discussed later in the chapter – which are capable of producing systems very quickly, but which, unfortunately, result in long response times.
3. Only implementing a subset of functions. Many systems contain requirements which are well defined and understood. A viable strategy for implementing prototypes of such systems is to develop a partial version containing only those requirements for which the developer feels there is a high risk of poor implementation, either because the requirement or implementation options are ill-understood.
4. Omitting functions or the human–computer interface. A common strategy used to implement prototypes is to omit a major component: either the functional part of the system, or its human–computer interface. Implementing the human–computer interface can be combined very easily with top-down development, where elements of the interface tend to lie at the top end of the module hierarchy. Implementing the functional parts of a system can be combined very easily with a bottom-up development strategy. However, this strategy for developing prototypes is normally achieved by the use of software tools. This is discussed later in this chapter.

Contrary to popular belief, there are a number of different ways of categorizing prototyping. The three main categories are: throw-away prototyping, incremental prototyping and evolutionary prototyping

40.1.1 Throw-away prototyping

Throw-away prototyping usually corresponds to the popular view of prototyping. A version of a system is developed which is used for requirements clarification and then discarded, with conventional software development following this process. The conventional development is based on the normal specification documents applied on projects, with the prototype being used to clarify any parts of the specification which might not be clear.

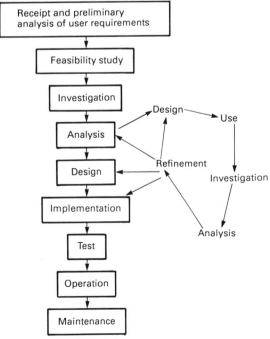

Figure 40.1 Model of throwaway prototyping

The most realistic model of throw-away prototyping is due to Dearnley and Mayhew (1983). It is shown in *Figure 40.1*.

This shows the relationship between throw-away prototyping and conventional phase-oriented software development. The first stage of a project that employs throw-away prototyping involves a preliminary analysis, followed by the development of a feasibility study and an initial investigation into whether prototyping would be a useful technique. If it is found to be useful, the developer enters an iterative process. First, the prototype is designed and implemented. Then it is used. Investigation of the use of the prototype then takes place, followed by further analysis and by refinement of the prototype. This loop continues until the customer is happy with the prototype and an exit to conventional development occurs. Exit can be made before the analysis is required, or to design, if all requirements are incorporated in the prototype, or after design, if the design of the prototype is highly refined.

40.1.2 Incremental prototyping

Incremental prototyping is really another name for staged delivery. What this entails is the developer partitioning the requirements for a system into a number of related subsets. For example, a chemical plant system could be partitioned into functions which monitor pressure and temperature readings, which provide management information, and which carry out the control of reactors.

Once the system requirements have been so partitioned, a series of versions of the system are delivered. Each version implements a new subset of requirements wth, eventually, the full system being delivered.

Incremental prototyping has the advantage that a software project can be split up into a series of mini-projects, each of which delivers a new version of a system. Such mini-projects would have a small number of staff working on them, thus resulting in a low communication complexity and a greater *esprit-de-corps*. This form of development is associated with prototyping because it enables those requirements about which there is some doubt to be included in early versions of the system. The management of this style of development is discussed in Chapter 15.

40.1.3 Evolutionary prototyping

Evolutionary prototyping is a term used to describe the process where the prototype is used as the basis for subsequent development. The prototype is built and then evolved by a process of modification towards a final product. Evolutionary prototyping has arisen in response to the impact of change on large software projects. Change to a software system occurs for a number of reasons:

1. Perfective changes occur when a developer attempts to improve some aspect of a system, for example, by using a fast algorithm in order to improve response time.
2. Corrective changes occur in order to rectify errors created in an earlier part of a project.
3. Adaptive changes occur when system requirements change. An example of this type of change is one which occurs in an accounting system after a company merger, where new or different reporting procedures need to be implemented.

Corrective changes are normally assumed to take place during development, while perfective and adaptive change are assumed to take place during maintenance. Unfortunately, adaptive change can often occur during the duration of a project; for large projects in particular, it is a fact of life. As well as the shifting nature of requirements, there is also the fact that a customer often changes his or her view of what a system is to do when shown part or whole of the system being executed. Evolutionary prototyping is an attempt to ensure that an executable version of a system is available throughout a project.

One of the most realistic models for evolutionary prototyping was developed by Brice and Connell (1989). It is shown as *Figure 40.2*.

The first stage in an evolutionary prototyping project is to derive an outline project plan. This would contain a justification of the development approach to be adopted, the goals of the project, the scope of effort, the development tools to be employed, the responsibilities of the user during the project, a list of deliverables, and a preliminary schedule. This plan would be increasingly refined throughout the project.

The next stage is rapid analysis. The aim of this activity is to produce a starting point for prototype development, rather than

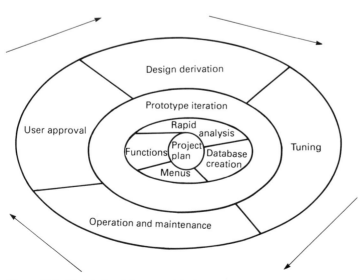

Figure 40.2 Model of evolutionary prototyping

produce an exhaustive specification. This rapid analysis would generate a top-level functional specification of the system. For example, if a data flow diagram was used for specification, this would mean writing down the top two levels of the diagram: an outline description of the data to be manipulated, using a data notation such as an entity-relation diagram, and a design of the interface, usually in the form of some graphical notation such as a control flow graph. Rapid analysis should take no more than a few weeks.

The next stage in the evolutionary prototyping process is the creation of a test database which matches the data description generated during rapid analysis. This is then followed by the development of the system menus and the addition of system functions. Normally, the structure of the system menus provides a good guide to the modular structure of the system.

Once the prototype system has been built, the developer and customer enter an iterative process whereby the prototype is evaluated and modified, until the customer pronounces himself happy with the product. When this happens, the developer derives the design of the system by examining the program code of the prototype.

At this stage, the prototype will be inefficient, so the final stage is to tune the prototype. If a fourth-generation language (4GL) or relational database system is used, a number of options present themselves. The first is to relax the condition that data should be in third normal form; here the developer trades off maintainability against efficiency. Another strategy is to place as much of the stored data as possible into ordinary files. A third strategy – and the least attractive one – is to replace the coding in the prototype by efficient coding. For example, if a fourth-generation language has been employed, this language would be replaced by a conventional programming language.

A further strategy which can be employed, irrespective of the prototyping technique used, is to upgrade the hardware base. This may seem to be a last-ditch strategy. However, it should be remembered that the developer is trading off potentially expensive and hazardous system tuning and future maintenance problems against the simple expedient of buying more powerful hardware.

Testing on a software project is divided into distinct phases. The testing of functions occurs during prototype iteration, while testing of response time and performance occurs during system tuning.

Evolutionary prototyping differs from conventional software development in a number of ways:

1. Often the duration of the prototyping project is much smaller. Experience with projects that have used 4GLs and CASE technology has been that systems can be developed much quicker than with standard programming languages such as COBOL – even when CASE technology has not been used (Connell and Brice, 1989).
2. In general, the milestones in an evolutionary prototyping project tend to be closer together. This is because, first, project duration is reduced, the length of individual tasks is reduced and, hence, milestones come closer. Also, analysis and prototyping tend to be longer activities than analysis on a conventional project, taking over some of the functions of other phases, such as system design. Therefore, some of the tasks between phases will disappear, or at least be minimized.
3. There will be no distinct phase known as analysis. Instead, there is an iteration of a series of analysis and prototyping activities.
4. There is an additional milestone for preliminary requirements. Other milestones in the conventional software project will be replaced by milestones which are preceded by different activities. For example, system design becomes more of a documentation process than a creative one, with the

development team documenting the prototype system.
5. Detailed functional requirements are not finalized until a working prototype is signed off by the customer.
6. In the conventional software project, testing of performance is often intertwined with functional testing. In prototyping, they are distinct processes separated in time.
7. Tuning replaces the conventional implementation phase.

Of the three types of prototyping, evolutionary prototyping is the most difficult to carry out. There are now a large number of tools which enable the developer to produce a prototype very quickly, but attempting to keep an executable version of a system throughout the software project, where that prototype may exist as part functional specification, part design and part program code, is still a subject of long-range research.

40.2 Techniques for prototyping functionality

40.2.1 Early sub-system development

This is probably the least known way of developing a prototype, as the common conception of the prototyping process involves sophisticated tools such as 4GLs. Incremental development involves looking at a customer's statement of requirements and deciding which parts of a proposed system are associated with requirements with some degree of fuzziness.

If the system to be developed contains sub-systems which are relatively isolated, then a developer employing this type of prototyping will produce the sub-system which is least well-defined. There are a number of techniques which can be employed for this. The most common is to relax the quality assurance standards of the project. However, other options are also available, for example, by employing inefficient algorithms which are easy to program, but which may be slow to execute.

40.2.2 Very high-level languages

A very high-level programming language (VHLL) is one in which it is possible to express complicated operations using a small amount of written code. The disadvantage of such languages is that they tend to be inefficient in terms of run time or memory usage. In general, VHLLs are interpretive and interactive, offer a rich set of data objects and corresponding operations, contain a language notation which is short, concise and very expressive, and are normally supported by very powerful programming support environments and debugging facilities. It is the expressive power, together with the ease with which modifications can be carried out, that make such languages ideal for prototyping.

Probably the earliest VHLL to be used for prototyping was APL. This is a language which was very popular in the early 1970s (Tavolato and Vincena, 1984). Its data type is the array, and it provides a whole spectrum of operations for manipulating a large variety of arrays, ranging from conventional Pascal-type arrays up to sparse arrays and triangular arrays. The power of APL makes it possible to carry out very complicated operations in just one line. However, short APL programs can be very difficult to read and understand. This often debars the language from development, but for prototypes which are to be developed in a short time APL would be a good choice. This is especially true for prototypes in the commercial data processing area, particularly because, as compared with other languages described in this section, there are reliable commercial implementations of the language, with full back-up and training facilities.

Another language which has a long history of being used for

prototyping is Lisp (Heitmeyer *et al.*, 1982). Normally, this language is associated with artificial intelligence software development. Because such development is exploratory and experimental, powerful versions of Lisp are available which probably have the best program support environments associated with a VHLL. A second aspect of Lisp which makes it ideal for prototype development is that it is very easy to express short, succinct recursive algorithms in the language. Third, Lisp is based on a very general data structure, the list, and contains a large number of operations which operate on lists (see Chapters 35 and 44 for more detail on functional languages).

A more recent programming language, often associated with artificial intelligence software development, is Prolog (Leibrandt and Schnupp, 1984). This language employs a limited form of predicate calculus consisting of Horn clauses. Such clauses contain a series of conditions which, when they are true, result in a number of outcomes. Prolog is particularly useful in prototyping systems which can be expressed as a number of stimuli and an associated response. For example, a system which contains statements such as:

'When an open signal is received and the subsidiary valve is closed and the reactor is operating at a correct ambient temperature then the main valve is opened.'

'When an open signal is received and the main valve is open and the reactor is operating at the correct ambient temperature then a warning message is displayed on the main operator's console.'

would be a good candidate for prototyping using Prolog. The translation of the first clause into Prolog is:

valve_state(main_vale, open)←signal_received(open),
  valve_state(subsid, closed),
  temp > min_temp,
  temp < max_temp

One of the little-known facilities of Prolog is its ability to produce programming language compilers very quickly. This aspect of the language has been played down in many Prolog texts, in contrast to its capabilities as an artificial intelligence language. Nevertheless, the language contains some of the most powerful facilities for producing a compiler that are available, and which require very little more than the prototyper producing the grammar rules of a language. A description of this approach can be found in Warren (1980) and a detailed description of logic programming is given in Chapter 36.

A little known, but very effective, high-level language is SETL (Schwartz *et al.*, 1986). This contains all the control facilities that one would normally find in a language such as Pascal, plus a very high-level data structure, called a set, together with operations on sets such as forming a set union, checking membership of a set and defining a set by means of constructive definitions. A good account of the use of SETL is contained in Kruchten and Schonberg (1984), which describes the prototyping of a full Ada compiler.

SETL is particularly effective for evolutionary prototyping as it allows the programmer to declare procedures and functions which operate in a simple, succinct way, but which can be refined to make them more and more efficient.

No very high-level language is suitable for prototyping all applications. Normally, a choice has to be made, according to the application area. For example, in prototyping an artificial intelligence application the natural choice would be Lisp, or perhaps Prolog. In prototyping a numerical application, for example a large simulation problem, the natural choice would be APL.

40.2.3 Functional programming languages

Functional programming languages are quite unlike conventional programming languages, such as Pascal, FORTRAN and COBOL. They are mathematical in nature, and are an attempt to overcome the bottleneck problems that occur with conventional languages on multiprocessor computers.

A program in a functional language consists of a series of recursion equations which express an operation in terms of itself. There are a number of good mathematical properties that occur because of this. However, the property that makes such a language useful for prototyping is that, by using such equations, programs can be written very succinctly indeed. An example is an operation, which reverses a list and which would take a number of lines of Pascal code:

reverse [ ] =   [ ]
reverse (x:xs) =   reverse xs + [x]

This is a functional program expressed in a language similar to Miranda (Turner, 1984). The program takes a list and reverses it. The first line states that when an empty list is reversed, the result will be an empty list. The second line states that when one reverses a list containing an element *x* followed by a list *xs*, one gets the reverse of *xs* followed by *x*.

Functional languages available to the prototyper include Miranda, FP, functional variants of Lisp, such as Scheme, and ML. Of these ML (Wikstrom, 1988) is probably the best, as it contains useful facilities for modularization, data encapsulation and exception handling. Unfortunately, the vast majority of functional languages are currently only implemented on conventional, von-Neumann computers; consequently, they suffer from speed problems. Nevertheless, this does not disbar them from being an excellent medium for prototyping. The major disadvantage of such languages is that their facilities for the human–computer interface are very limited indeed, with the designers of the language still adhering to a batch-processing paradigm for input/output.

40.2.4 Specification execution systems

The rationale behind such systems is simple. If it is possible to take a specification and execute it or animate it in some way, then an early version of a software system can be delivered during the requirements analysis phase. This is an attractive idea because the specification of a software system has to be produced, and no extra effort for prototype construction would therefore be needed. This is in contrast to other techniques, such as those using very high-level languages where, after the prototype has been built and agreed with the customer, the specification has to be constructed anew.

The majority of specification execution systems are based on formal notations for the specification of a software system. Such a specification usually relates the functions of a system to the effect of various operations of the system on a state (the system's stored data).

One of the earliest systems for execution specification was based on the Me-Too language developed at Stirling University (Henderson, 1986). This is a functional version of Lisp in which mathematical objects used in formal specification – sets, functions and predicates – can be expressed and the resulting specification prototyped. A much more ambitious system is the EPROS system (Hekmatpour and Ince, 1988). This is based on Unix, and offers a wide spectrum language EPROL as the prototyping medium. A wide-spectrum language typically includes facilities for specification, design, implementation and the man–machine interface. The functional specification part of EPROL is based on META IV, the specification notation associated with the VDM formal software development method. Since EPROL contains facilities for all the development tasks in the software project, it is possible to use it for evolutionary prototyping. A particular feature of EPROS is its ability to carry out functionality prototyping and HCI prototyping, the latter including facilities for specifying forms, state transition diagrams and menus.

Although they have been categorized separately here, functional languages are also a good medium for specification execution prototyping. It is easy to write a mathematical specification using these languages, and then execute it with little further work.

40.2.5 Tool-set approach

This approach uses a software system that provides a series of processors and tools which can be joined together easily and are table-driven. The best system exemplifying the tool set approach is the Unix operating system. This contains utilities such as YACC and LEX, which are capable of processing tables of definitions and producing software very quickly. The use of YACC and LEX is discussed in more detail in Chapter 52.

In Unix chunks of software constructed using processors such as LEX and YACC can be very easily joined together with user-constructed programs, using a facility called the pipe. Piping enables the output of one program to be directly fed in as the input to another program. For example, the compiled code from YACC could be input into a user-written interpreter, which would then execute the compiled program.

A further facility in Unix, which promotes prototyping, is the shell. This is a sort of high-level programming language which provides the control part of the prototype, and acts as the glue which joins each of the processors that make up a prototype.

Although the best example of the tool-set approach is Unix, other tool sets exist. A good example of a tool set for commercial data processing application is TUBA (Van Hoeve and Engmann, 1984). This is a system based on the high-level language, Simula 67, which provides primitives for tasks such as report writing and retrieval of structured data.

40.2.6 Fourth-generation languages (4GLs)

Probably the best known medium which can be used for prototyping – certainly for the prototyping of commercial data processing applications – is the fourth-generation language. The term fourth-generation language is really an artificial one which has really been created for marketing reasons. The best way to describe a 4GL is in terms of the features it offers. Desirable features are (Martin, 1986):

1. The ability to formulate simple and complex queries. A good 4GL should allow non-developmental staff to formulate a query such as:

   LIST ALL PARTS WHICH HAVE BEEN PUT ON THE BACK ORDERS LIST WHICH HAVE BEEN ORDERED BY SUPPLIER JONES IN INCREASING ORDER OF SERIAL NUMBER.

2. The ability to create a database with a particular structure, for example, specifying that records should contain certain fields, and that some fields in records will be used as a key for the file containing that record, or for another file containing different records.
3. The ability to specify exceptions, i.e. actions that should be taken when some relationship between data items holds. For example, when the total number of stock for an item falls below a pre-specified level some warning message would be displayed to the user.
4. A simple procedural language which allows the batch processing of a database. Such a language would contain the normal control constructs found in any programming language, together with sophisticated file manipulation commands, which would provide the user with facilities for reading, writing and updating records held on a database.
5. The ability to create screens for a user, for example, data entry screens in which the entry field corresponds to data items in stored records. This facility should also allow the user to specify the attributes of screen values, for example, whether a value is to be computed or whether the value typed in by a user lies within particular limits.
6. The provision of spreadsheet facilities which allow operations such as adding columns and rows of figures, or finding the maximum or minimum of a row or column figures.
7. The ability to generate reports easily. This would not be via statements equivalent to the print statements in high-level languages, but using non-procedural terms, where the layout of a report may be defined in terms of line formats and exceptions which occur when certain fields contain different values.
8. The ability to produce graphical displays easily. Normally, such facilities are provided by writing the data to be displayed into a matrix and applying some prewritten procedure. The language should contain facilities for generating line graphs, bar charts, column charts and other graphic displays that are normally used for the display of business data.
9. The ability to provide facilities for 'what if' questions, for example, questions such as: 'What if the gross operating profit for the company falls below £1m, and the value of its share holding rises by 10%, and the value of its capital increases by 15%? Does this mean that the liquidity ratio of the company will fall below danger levels?'
10. The ability to analyse – mathematically or financially – figures generated by programs or stored in a database. Such analysis would include facilities such as those for trend calculation and for discounted profit calculation.
11. The ability to enable a user to communicate with other users via electronic mailboxes.

Not all 4GLs support all these features. The reason that 4GLs are such a powerful medium for prototyping is that they offer very high-level facilities which, in a conventional language, might be programmed in a large number of source lines. For example, many 4GLs offer a very sophisticated graphics processing facility. Often all that is needed to use such facilities is to write down one line of program code. Another example of the power of such languages for prototyping lies in their ability to manipulate data stored on databases. There is an increasing trend for such databases to be tabular or relational, and a 4GL offers very powerful facilities for retrieving data based on very complex predicates. Finally, in terms of the ability to produce screens, 4GLs again offer very sophisticated facilities for defining the form of a screen in terms of colour, data entry fields, sophisticated line graphics, and the ability to characterize a field in terms of its contents, its mode and its relationship with other fields.

40.2.7 Application-oriented VHLLs

These are programming languages which are oriented towards one particular application area, for example, stock control or process monitoring. The majority of application-oriented VHLLs are application generators. These are interpretative systems which interactively execute an application description.

Other HLLs are known as program generators. These translate a high level, program-like description of an application into a program expressed in some high-level language such as COBOL.

Probably the best known program generator is Model

(Prywes and Pnueli, 1983), which is aimed at commercial data processing applications. Model is a highly successful system which has produced systems which are five to ten times smaller in textual size than equivalent programs written in conventional programming languages. A Model program consists of descriptions of the data items that are to be manipulated, together with a set of equations which describe the manipulations. This description is then translated into either a PL/1 or COBOL program.

Another typical application oriented very high-level programming language is HIBOL (Mittermier, 1982). A major feature of this system is that it has excellent facilities for the human–computer interface, enabling users to define succinctly graphics such as business forms and transaction screens.

The advantage of these languages is that they can be used by staff with little technical experience. Moreover, they produce very efficient systems. However, their scope is limited to application areas where the underlying domain is well-understood. Considering the fact that prototyping is intended for areas where the domain is fuzzy, this must be counted as a major weakness.

40.2.8 Object-oriented languages

In object-oriented language the first-class entities are objects which usually match objects in the external world – objects such as bank accounts in a commercial data processing system, planes in an air-traffic control system and line-printers in an operating system. Object-oriented languages have a long history, although it is only now that they are coming into prominence. The earliest language with object-oriented properties was Simula 67. However, the most well-known object-oriented languages are Smalltalk (Goldberg and Robson, 1983), Eiffel (Meyer, 1988) and C++ (Stroustrup, 1986).

The importance of object-oriented languages for prototyping lies in a property known as inheritance. This allows the programmer to define a base object, say a plane, and operations on that object, and then with little effort to define new objects based on that object, for example, fighter planes and transport planes.

Object-oriented languages can be used by the developer to build up a library of objects and operations which are required in the application area and then, for each application to be prototyped, to develop the objects in the applications by using the inheritance facilities of the language. This normally requires little programming effort. In essence, prototyping is achieved by a very sophisticated software re-use technology.

40.2.9 Hand translation of specifications into program code

This technique is similar to that of specification execution and mimics what happens when a system is prototyped in an evolutionary manner using 4GL and a relational database system. This method is effective because the programs that are produced manipulate a high-level data structure. This includes the relation and the high-level operators of 4GL such as join, project and select, which are equivalent to many lines of program code, and which can be used in conjunction with each other, to implement very complicated processing in a textually small code size.

Formal specification techniques such as Z are based on another high-level data type – the set. System specifications using these languages involve the specification of a state. The stored data that the system is to operate on, together with the operations that will be required in the system.

These operations are specified as pre- and post-conditions according to their effect on the state. A pre-condition is an expression in predicate calculus which states what must be true before an operations is executed if the operation is to be successfully executed. The post-condition defines what the effect of the operation is in terms of the old value of the state and the new value of the state.

Such formal specification notations can be easily coded up using conventional programming languages, assuming that a basic library of set theoretic operations is available. The only restriction on the programming language used is that it should have some facility for parameterizing types. The ideal language for this would be object-oriented, where an operation such as set union or domain restriction could be defined in terms of a single program unit, which could be instantiated for a wide variety of types.

The initial prototype would then consist of a state, defined in terms of the data structures of the programming language used, and a series of program units, equivalent to operations, consisting of two types of processing statements. The first would implement the pre-condition, and provide diagnostic information if the pre-condition failed, and the second would implement the post-condition which would achieve the processing required. The code corresponding to the post-conditions would make extensive use of the basic library set of operations equivalent to set operations in the formal specification language.

Once such a prototype had been iterated and user agreement obtained it can be tuned. This would consist of replacing simple data types by data types which would increase efficiency, for example, replacing a set by a B-tree. This could be done by hand coding or by using a library of design types. The important point about such a tuning process is that for many applications it can be done gradually, one component of the state at a time. This means that a system can be gradually changed with a test of the slightly more optimal system being made, using the previous version of the system as a test oracle.

The validation of the tuning can be achieved using mathematics, for example, by applying the data reification rules that are part of VDM. However, a valid development strategy would be to use the test strategy described in the previous paragraph. This strategy would prove particularly attractive to developers who might find major problems in training staff in the developmental and specification facilities of a formal method, but have the confidence that their staff would be able to use only the top-level functional specification facilities.

40.2.10 Expert system technology

Another medium which can be used for prototyping is that associated with expert system technology. Expert systems are developed in a similar way to prototypes. An initial working model is produced and then modified in response to the comments of a human consultant. The only difference between the processes is that in the case of expert system construction the person who is shown the system is the human consultant, while with prototyping the customer or his representative is shown the prototype. Software associated with expert system technology such as expert system shells has excellent interactive development facilities and hence is suitable for prototyping. However, the size of prototypes generated is rather limited in that expert system technology has not yet advanced to the point where no more than hundreds of rules can be incorporated in the expert system.

40.2.11 Selecting a prototyping medium for function prototyping

There is quite a wide choice for the developer thinking of carrying out function prototyping. However, some of the tools described in this chapter are still in the research stage. In particular, commercial implementations of executable specification systems and application-oriented very high-level languages, are still a very long way off. Also some are suitable only for certain types of prototyping. *Table 40.1* summarizes the position.

If one is going to prototype a commercial data processing application then the natural choice would be a 4GL. There are many good implementations for almost every range of computer. Moreover, such languages are, on the whole, very easy to learn and also contain sophisticated human–computer interface facilities.

Table 40.1

	Incremental	Throw-away	Evolutionary
Early sub-system development	X	X	
Very high-level languages (VHLLs)	X	X	X
Functional programming languages	X	X	X
Specification execution systems	X	X	X
Tool-set approach	X	X	
Fourth generation languages (4GLs)	X	X	X
Object-oriented languages	X	X	X
Application-oriented VHLLs	X	X	
Hand translation of specifications	X	X	X
Expert system technology			X

For prototyping in other application areas, the choice would be between using Unix as a tool set, or using functional languages. For most developers the former would be the choice. Most developers who use Unix as an operating system usually have a number of staff skilled in using the shell facilities of the language and who are able to interface table-generated software with C programs. What may be lacking is expertise in the more esoteric tools such as LEX and YACC.

Functional programming languages or logic programming languages are a good alternative. However, they do suffer from a skills shortage, particularly in functional languages, where a good understanding of mathematics is required to program using them. Good robust implementations of languages such as ML and Miranda are available and, for the developer with staff expertise, they offer a very good alternative to Unix, especially if he or she is carrying out evolutionary prototyping.

40.3 Techniques for prototyping the human–computer interface (HCI)

In historical terms, techniques and tools for prototyping functionality became available much earlier than those for prototyping the HCI. Even today there is still a tendency for programming language designers to assume the simple input/output model that served them well in the 1970s. However, advances in computer hardware – in particular display technology – has placed powerful, comparatively cheap, graphics workstations on the desks of software developers. This, together with the rise in interest in the HCI – how to specify it, how to measure the ease with which users interact with it and how to build it quickly – has resulted in a large amount of recent work on prototyping the HCI. There are now a number of techniques and tools available.

40.3.1 Simulation

This is probably the oldest technique, and yet has a good history of being very effective, particularly in those application areas where the problem area is ill-structured. A major advantage is that simulation requires very little tool support. Indeed, one of the most impressive simulations of the HCI involved the evaluation of a listening typewriter (Gould *et al.*, 1983).

This was carried out by having a human operator and a user in separated rooms each equipped with a VDU. The user composed his letters by talking into a microphone, and these requests were intercepted by the operator who would carry them out and display the results on the user's VDU. This study allowed experimenters to study aspects such as speech mode, size of vocabulary, composition strategy and the effects of user experience.

Simulation of the HCI aspects of a proposed system can be easily carried out using a 4GL. Such languages have good facilities for defining screens, graphs or business forms. These forms can be linked together by a skeleton program which might provide dummy values for some of the fields. The sequence of screens, perhaps with some branching, can then be shown to a potential user, with the operator carrying out the switching by sensing which keys the user is typing. This technique does not have to be confined to 4GLs. It can be very easily used in conjunction with professional presentation packages or even hypermedia (see Section 40.3.2).

Professional presentation packages allow a speaker to create presentation slides which are displayed on the screen of a graphics computer such as an Apple Macintosh. They allow a wide variety of picture making facilities ranging from the drawing of straight lines to the adjustment of individual pixels.

40.3.2 Hypermedia

Hypermedia is not a new idea, although advances in computer hardware have only recently enabled viable implementations to be constructed. The main idea that lies behind hypermedia documentation is that items in such a document are linked by pointers which are embedded in pages in the document. Thus, a user who is logged into a hypermedia system is able to browse between items in that document either by using key strokes or by manipulating a mouse.

Figure 40.3 gives an idea of the layout of a hypermedia database. It shows a simple example of its use as a browsing tool for extracting articles on computing subjects. The card shown on the front contains a series of keywords which categorize areas of interest. Each field containing the keywords is linked to a series of other fields which contain sub-categories of the keyword. Each field on a sub-categories card contains an author index to the papers.

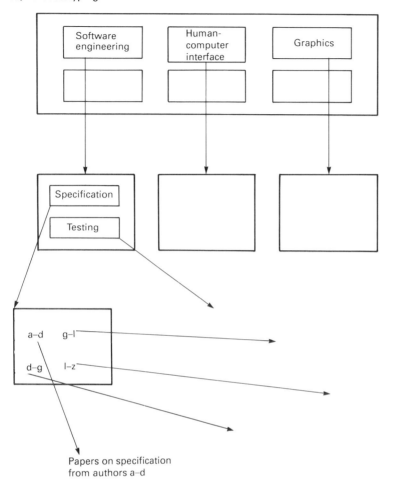

a–d g–l

d–g l–z

Papers on specification
from authors a–d

Figure 40.3   Structure of a hypermedia document

In Figure 40.3 the top level of the hypermedia document contains pointer to categories such as software engineering and graphics. A user who wishes to look at papers on software engineering would usually click the field containing the word 'software engineering', using a mouse. This would bring up the card containing the categories for that subject. If the user was interested in papers on specification then the field with the word 'specification' would be clicked with the mouse. This would bring up an index to papers. The user would then click the range of alphabetic characters required. For example, if he was looking for a paper by Brown he would click the field a–d, and so on.

This is one of the most powerful facilities in hypermedia, and one which is quite useful for the prototyper. However, most hypermedia systems also contain many other facilities which are valuable, for example, the Hyper Talk system, provided with the Apple Macintosh range of computers, provides facilities for defining screens and for switching easily between screens. In this respect, hypermedia systems are an excellent medium for simulation, where the course of a simulation run can be controlled by pointer fields embedded in screens which, when clicked by prototyping staff, will result in the next screen being displayed. Chapter 57 discusses the use of hypermedia for interface prototyping.

40.3.3 Formal grammar processors

A dialogue between a user and a computer can be represented by means of a formal grammar, similar to that used to define programming languages. As an example, consider the grammar shown below:

⟨command⟩ ::= ⟨edit⟩ | ⟨compile⟩ | ⟨run⟩
⟨edit⟩   ::= ed⟨filename⟩
⟨filename⟩ ::= ⟨letter⟩ (⟨letter⟩ | digit)*
⟨letter⟩   ::= A | B | C | D | E . . . . . | X | Y | Z
⟨digit⟩   ::= 0 | 1 | 2 | 3 | 4 | 5 | 6 | 7 | 8 | 9

This describes some commands in a simple operating system. The first line states that a command acceptable to the operating system will either be an edit command, a compile command or a run command. The character | stands for alternatives. The second line states that the edit command is defined to be the two characters *ed*, followed by a file name. The third line states that a filename consists of a letter, followed by 0 or more occurrences of either a letter or a digit. In this line the * symbol is used to represent 0 or more repetitions of the objects enclosed in the round brackets. Inside the round brackets is a choice between a letter or a digit. The fourth line defines a letter to be either an *A* or a *B* or a *C* etc. Finally, the fifth line defines a digit. The full description of the commands would also include lines that define what a compile command is, and the form of the run command. However, these have been omitted.

Descriptions of dialogues, such as the one above, can be processed by software tools which then either produce program code that simulates the interface, or interprets the description directly. Examples of typical formal grammar processors can be found in (Reisner (1981) and Moran (1981).

Unfortunately, such simple descriptions are inadequate for the vast majority of HCIs. The basic idea of a grammar has to be augmented by baroque facilities to handle facilities such as pop-up menus and forms. An example of a more complicated formal grammar processor capable of handling some of these issues can be found in Hekmatpour and Ince (1988).

Formal grammars, although intuitively appealing, suffer from two drawbacks. First, for a system of any size it is very difficult to read a formal grammar description and understand the nature of the interface. Second, formal grammars are particularly weak in describing error cases and help facilities. Often, modifying a formal grammar notation to cater for such facilities means complicating it even further.

40.3.4 State transition processors

State transition diagrams are a graphical notation which describe the states that a dialogue passes through. An example of a small state transition diagram is shown below in *Figure 40.4*. It describes the human–computer interface for a small system for air traffic control. Three commands are allowed in this system. A *position* command, when exercised, returns the position of a specified plane. An *arrival* command displays the identities of planes which have arrived in the last *n* minutes, where *n* can be typed in by the operator. The third command is the *range* command, which displays the identities of planes within a specified range of a particular plane. The state transition diagram in Figure 40.4 omits the dialogue for the last two commands.

In Figure 40.4 the states that the dialogue traverses are shown as bubbles. The switching between states is shown by lines joining the bubbles. State 1 is the first state in which the dialogue finds itself. There are four possible exits from this state. If the user types the command *position*, then the dialogue moves to state 2. If the user types the command *arrivals*, then the dialogue moves to state 5. If the user types in the command *range*, then the dialogue finds itself in state 4. If none of these commands are typed, an error has occurred. This is indicated by the line marked */error message 2. The asterisk signifies that the line is traversed if what is typed in does not match any of the inputs specified on all the exits from that state, the / signals the action

that is to be taken. In the case of a user not typing in a recognized keyword the action is to signal an error by means of error message 2. Such state transition diagrams can be processed by special-purpose software tools which can produce interfaces very quickly (Wasserman, 1985).

40.3.5 Language supported facilities

Until the advent of modern workstations, such as those marketed by Sun and Apple, the facilities offered by programming languages for HCI were rudimentary. The vast majority of language designers adopted a model which was oriented towards stream or batch input/output. However, there is now an increase in languages which feature facilities for menus, overlapping windows and icons. For example, dialects of Pascal for the Apple MacIntosh computer enable the programmer to define sophisticated interfaces which match the level of those provided by the Macintosh system software. However, such interfaces still need to be programmed rather than declared. For a good example of what the ideal language should contain as an HCI facility – certainly for electronic forms – see Gehani (1982).

In terms of HCI facilities, the best is offered by 4GLs, which offer the ability to declare operator screens and sophisticated output facilities, although not the ability to control dialogues.

40.3.6 Selecting a prototyping medium for HCI prototyping

HCI facilities for prototyping lag behind those for function prototyping. However, the facilities that are available now are a major improvement over what was offered four or five years ago. If one is prototyping a commercial data processing system, then the obvious choice is to use a 4GL. For other application areas, the probable choice would be some graphical hypermedia system which contains a programming language and which allows the prototyper to control and sequence a dialogue with the customer. Programming language facilities still requires a large degree of work to produce interfaces and there are few, if any, commercial implementations of state transition processors or syntax directed processors.

40.4 Managing the prototyping project

There is very little written about the management of the prototyping project, for example, there is no coherent management methodology in existence although the issue is discussed in Chapters 15 and 27. What can be written tends to be a list of guidelines. A number of these are:

1. The prototyping objectives for the project should be specified as early as possible. Ideally, they should be written into the project plan, prior to the formal start of a project. These objectives are very important as prototypes can be used for a number of purposes and it should be made clear to the customer what uses are to be made for a project. The objectives should list whether the prototype is to be throwaway, evolutionary or incremental. It should state in what way the prototype will be defective, and whether it is to be used for requirements analysis, training, or as a test comparator. By explicitly stating these objectives the developer will guard himself against occurrences such as the customer demanding that the prototype be used as production software.

2. The project plan should specify exactly the way in which the prototype is to be evaluated, the frequency of evaluation meetings, the staff involved and the tools to be used. In the list of project assumptions the developer should write in some description of what he expects from the customer in terms of availability of personnel.

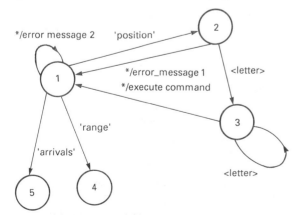

Figure 40.4 State transition diagram

3. Staff who carry out the prototyping process should be chosen on the basis of flexibility, and their willingness to discard their own work.
4. Since change is a matter of course on a prototyping project, a good – preferably automated – configuration management system should be used.
5. The developer should allow enough time for a system specification to be written. An agreed prototype is not the only basis on which subsequent development of a product should be based. A prototype alone is an inadequate overview of the functions and constraints of a system and a normal system specification should also be developed. There are two reasons for this. First, in throw-away prototyping the developer will require this document in order to base subsequent development on. Second, with both evolutionary and throwaway prototyping, there is a need to develop the system specification for maintenance staff.
6. Staff with both technical and interpersonal skills should be chosen to carry out the prototyping. The interpersonal skills are required because of the analyst role the prototyper adopts, while the technical skills are required because the prototyper often has to interact with tools during the prototype building process.
7. All changes should be documented. The documentation should be as short as possible. It should include a technical description of the change, an application-oriented description of the change, the reason for the change and the seriousness of the change. The latter can be specified in a three- or four-point scale ranging from trivial, for example, the movement of a data item on a screen, to the serious: a major change to a top-level function.
8. If the proposed system has strong implications in terms of changing the organization, then an organization development consultant should be used in the prototyping team.
9. A request for an initial version of a prototype or one of the early iterated versions must be resisted. It is one of the commonest reasons for the failure of prototyping projects. Obviously one will have guarded against this in the project plan, by pointing out in the objectives that the prototype will be deficient in some way until comparatively late in a project. However, sometimes the pressure to deliver is so intense that the developer has to hand over. In these circumstances all the developer can do is to agree. However, what should be done at this time is to produce documentation which describes the ways in which the prototype will be deficient. This documentation, usually in the form of memos, will draw upon data in the project plan, and also the log of the prototype iteration phase, and would use phrases such as 'poor response time', 'response time with more than one user cannot be guaranteed', 'our log demonstrates that a number of functions in the system still need to be refined', and 'at this stage only seems to satisfy half of the customer requirements'.
10. Make the prototyping team as small as possible. The major effort in a prototyping project goes into communications. The more staff that are involved in a prototyping project the worse that communication becomes. Rapid analysis can be carried out by one member of staff. For medium-size projects (5–10 man years of conventional effort) which use CASE technology, three or four staff have been found to be the optimum size. In larger prototyping projects it is worth separating out the functions of programming and analysis so that only a relatively small number of staff are involved with specifying a system and taking part in evaluation.
11. It is important to keep track of what happens to the prototype during iteration. One of the problems with this phase of prototyping is that it can so easily go out of control, with the user iterating between different versions of a system, returning to earlier versions, or suddenly demanding huge amounts of new functionality. Attempt to keep track of how the prototype evolves, perhaps by calculating a function count (Albrecht and Gaffney, 1983) after every prototype demonstration.
12. Do not spend a large amount of resources on system and acceptance testing. The process of prototype iteration consist of a large amount of what would be regarded as system testing. System and acceptance testing should concentrate on stress testing the prototype.

40.5 References

Albrecht, A. J. and Gaffney, J. E. (1983) Software function, source lines of code, and development effort predication: a software science validation. *IEEE Transactions on Software Engineering*, **9**, 639–648

Brice, J. L. and Connell, L. B. (1989) *Structured Rapid Prototyping*, Yourdon Press

Dearnley, P. A. and Mayhew, P. J. (1983) In favour of system prototypes and their integration into the system development cycle. *Computer Journal*, **26**, 36–42

Gehani, N. H. (1982) The potential of forms in office automation. *IEEE Transactions on Communications*, **30**, 120–125

Goldberg, A. and Robson, D. (1983) *Smalltalk-80: the Language and its Implementation*, Addison Wesley

Gould, J. D., Conti, J. and Hovanyecz, T. (1983) Composing letters with a simulated listening typewriter. *Communications of the ACM*, **26**, 295–308

Heitmeyer, C., Landwehr, C. and Cornwell, M. (1982) The use of quick prototypes in the Secure Military Message Systems Project, *ACM SIGSOFT Software Engineering Notes*, **7**, 85–87

Hekmatpour, S. H. and Ince, D. C. (1988) *Formal Methods, Software Prototyping and VDM*, Addison-Wesley, London

Henderson, P. (1986) Functional programming, formal specification and rapid prototyping. *IEEE Transactions on Software Engineering*, **12**, 241–250

Van Hoeve, F. A. and Engmann, R. (1984) The TUBA-Project: a set of tools for application development and prototyping. In *Approaches to Prototyping* (eds. R. Budde *et al.*) Springer-Verlag, Berlin, pp. 202–213

Kruchten, P. and Schonberg, E. (1984) The Ada/Ed System: a large-scale experiment in software prototyping using SETL. In *Approaches to Prototyping* (eds. R. Budde *et al.*) Springer-Verlag, Berlin, pp. 398–415

Leibrandt, U. and Schnupp, P. (1984) An evaluation of Prolog as a prototyping system. In *Approaches to Prototyping* (eds R. Budde *et al.*) Springer-Verlag, Berlin, pp. 424–433

Martin, J. (1986) *Fourth Generation Languages*, Prentice-Hall, Englewood Cliffs, New Jersey, USA

Meyer, B. (1988) *Object-oriented Software Construction*, Prentice-Hall, Englewood Cliffs, New Jersey, USA

Mittermeir, R. T. (1982) HIBOL, a language for fast prototyping in data processing environments. *ACM SIGSOFT Software Engineering Notes*, **7**, 133–140

Moran, T. P. (1981) The command language grammar: a representation for the user interface of interactive computer systems. *International Journal of Man–Machine Studies*, **15**, 3–50

Prywes, N. S. and Pnueli, A. (1983) A compilation of non-procedural specifications into computer programs. *IEEE Transactions on Software Engineering*, **9**, 267–279

Reisner, P. (1981) Formal grammar and human factors design of an interactive graphics system. *IEEE Transactions on Software Engineering*, **7**, 229–240

Schwartz, J. T., Dewar, R. B. K., Dubinsky, E. and Schonberg, E. (1986) *Programming with Sets*, Springer-Verlag, New York, USA

Stroustrup, B. (1986) *The C++ Programming Language*, Addison Wesley

Tavolato, P. and Vincena, K. (1984) A prototyping methodology and its tools. In *Approaches to Prototyping* (eds R. Budde *et al.*) Springer-Verlag, Berlin, pp. 434–446

Turner, D. A. (1984) Functional programs as executable specifications. *Phil. Trans Royal Society of London*, **312**, 363–388

Warren, D. H. D. (1980) Logic programming and compiler writing. *Software Practice and Experience*, **10**, 160–201

Wasserman, A. I. (1985) Extending state transition diagrams for the specification of human–computer interaction. *IEEE Transactions on Software Engineering*, **11**, 699–713

Wikstrom, A. (1988) *Functional Programming Using Standard ML*, Prentice-Hall

41

Software reuse

**Patrick Hall and
Cornelia Boldyreff**
Brunel University

Contents

41.1 Introduction

Software has long been the dominant factor in the cost of developing or procuring computer-based systems. There are a number of reasons for this, including the fall in the real cost of hardware, the increase in hardware capability leading to ever more ambitious development projects, and the fact that software development is a labour-intensive process. Software development also dominates the time taken to develop and deploy a new system.

Furthermore, qualified and experienced software development staff are in short supply, and it is necessary to improve productivity significantly, while maintaining or improving quality. One method proposed for making a significant improvement in productivity and quality is software reuse.

What is software reuse? It is the use of a given piece of software in the solution of more than one problem. Frequently this is taken to mean the reuse of program components like library subroutines in more than one application. However, reuse is also applied much more broadly to include the redeployment of designs, ideas, or even the skills and experience of people.

It is possible to further clarify what we mean by reuse by describing what is *not* included within reuse, contrasting the concept with other related ideas: portability, maintenance, and reconfigurability:

1. *Portability*. This is the ability to run an item of software on a number of hardware and operating system platforms, while reusability is the ability to employ an item of software as part of a number of applications. The item of software could be small (e.g. a single library subroutine), or very large (e.g. a complete package).
2. *Maintenance*. Once a piece of software is in use, it may be subject to changes, both to correct defects, and to modify its functions to meet the changing requirements of the users of the software (see Chapter 20 on maintenance). Usually the software is not thrown away and new software produced; instead the existing software is modified. This practice has been described by one author (Wegner, 1984) as an example of reuse, but the view taken here is that this is a misuse of the term.

   However, some of the practices and mechanisms necessary to support maintenance are also necessary to support reuse. These practices are that the software should be well modularized, with consistent specifications and design documentation, supported by library and build tools. The mechanisms that are necessary are flexible module connection methods which, during maintenance, enable the disconnection of faulty modules and their later reconnection following repair, the ability to regression test the system, and where necessary the ability to retrospectively create documentation and restructure the code. During reuse these same mechanisms may make it possible for us to consider reusing a module through examination of its documentation, and enable us to interconnect components to create new applications.
3. *Reconfigurability*. This is used in two senses. The more common usage is as a fault tolerance method, to redeploy and reconnect software in the event of the failure of the underlying hardware (or, indeed, software). The other use is as a method for customizing a piece of software, to include only those facilities required. For both of these senses, we need a flexible interconnection technology, possibly even enabling the dynamic disconnection and reconnection of components, as we saw under maintenance above. Reconfigurability is distinct from reuse as it does not result in software being used in more than one application.

41.1.1 Historical perspective

Of course the reuse of software is not new, and has been with us from the beginning in the form of the publication of algorithms, in the use of high-level programming languages, and in the use of packages, as has been pointed out by many people (e.g. Standish, 1984; Hall, 1987).

Reuse through the publication of algorithms and designs has been very important for the development of computing. The presence of standard textbooks in an area is an indication of the maturity of that area, and is an important vehicle through which the reuse of ideas takes place. Similarly, the procurement of standard packages is an important example of reuse, and the availability of a wide range of products is again an indicator of the maturity of an area of technology. Capers Jones (1984) makes a thorough appraisal of both these areas.

However, it is the consideration of high-level programming languages as examples of reuse that is the most illuminating. In high-level languages, many frequently used combinations of instructions at the assembly level (e.g. for subroutine entry and exit with parameter passing), have been packaged into single constructs at the higher level. The high-level language thus gives a notation for selecting these generic constructs, instantiating them with the appropriate parameters, and then composing them to build software systems. Facilities are provided so that user-created components at the higher level can be stored and incorporated (e.g. via a subroutine library concept). This is not the usual way of viewing programming languages and compilers. These are usually seen as 'tools', rather than as the engineering foundations of software production.

This view of programming languages emphasizes the unique nature of software, the great diversity that its components might take, and the very flexible way they might be interconnected. This flexibility can also be seen in the history of job control languages, which have evolved from very simple-minded methods of sequencing batch jobs passing files from one to the next, to languages with most of the usual programming constructs within them (such as is available in the Unix Shell (e.g. Bourne, 1983)).

Packages have also been an important aspect of the reuse of software. Packages which are rigidly defined are seldom useful – some flexibility is essential. This flexibility is provided through a range of capabilities, from simple parameterization, through configuration following some elaborate build script (as is usually done for operating systems), through to the modification of the package at the source level.

Packages may be thought of as a form of software component. The idea of software components as such was promoted in 1968 by McIlroy (but only published in 1976). Since then many of the other aspects of software reuse outlined above have been subsumed under other software engineering activities, so this chapter will focus on the reuse of software components. However, the term components will be interpreted very widely, to include not only executable code, but also more abstract objects such as designs, specifications, and requirements.

41.1.2 Benefits

The reuse of software means that ideas and code are developed once, and then used to solve many applications problems, thus enhancing our productivity. Some authors have estimated that as much as 60% of the code in data processing applications is (re)developed unnecessarily, and could be standardized and reused (Lagergan and Grasso, 1984). Even allowing for the cost of locating and incorporating the standard components in an application, the productivity gain is worth having. For example, the Japanese reported in 1980 (Yatsumoto *et al.*, 1980) that, through the promotion of reuse, they had achieved an increase in productivity of 14% per year over a number of years (this doubles productivity over five years).

The reuse of software ideas and code has an equally important quality benefit. In developing a reusable item, it is worth devoting more effort to verifying and testing the item as this effort can be amortized over all the item's uses (Lubars, 1986). Further, through wide use and the consequential repair and enhancement, the item should improve in quality and its reliability will be proven in practice. Incorporating a highly reliable item, be it code component, design, algorithm or specification, into a system enhances the reliability of that system. Some work on reliability modelling for software has addressed this issue (Littlewood, 1979), but there needs to be further work done to provide more sophisticated models.

All the available evidence suggests that the exploitation of software reuse is well worth while. However achieving reuse requires that we set about it in a systematic manner, as described in the next section, and employ the appropriate technology, as described in Sections 41.3, 41.4 and 41.5. We should also use various managerial and human factors practices as seen in Section 41.6.

Not all problems associated with software reuse have been solved, and the final section looks at possible future developments in this area by considering current research programmes.

41.2 Reuse processes

The traditional life-cycle model of software development requires an added dimension to accomodate the possibility of software reuse in its various phases. A simple model of the reuse process is discussed below. This model assumes the existence of a library of reusable software components.

To be able to reuse software components, whether code components like subroutines and objects, or ideas like specifications and designs and algorithms, a number of steps need to be taken in proceeding from the recognition of the opportunity for reuse to the actual reuse of the component in new applications. *Figure 41.1* shows these steps in the context of a component catalogue or library.

The reuse process may be viewed from two quite separate perspectives:

1. A building-up phase when reusable software is identified and brought together into a library (shown on the left side of Figure 41.1).
2. A design phase when reusable software is selected from the library on the basis of system requirements and reused in the construction of a new software system (shown on the right side of Figure 41.1).

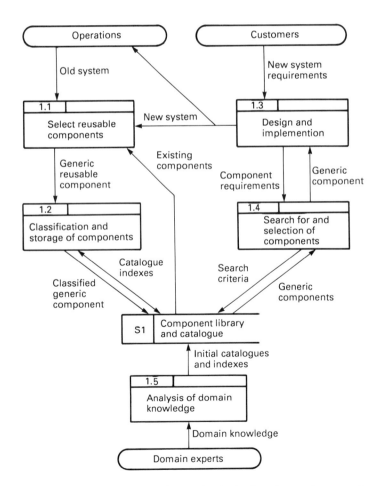

Figure 41.1 The reuse process shown using the dataflow diagramming conventions of Structured Systems Analysis and Design Method (SSADM) (Longworth and Nicholls, 1986)

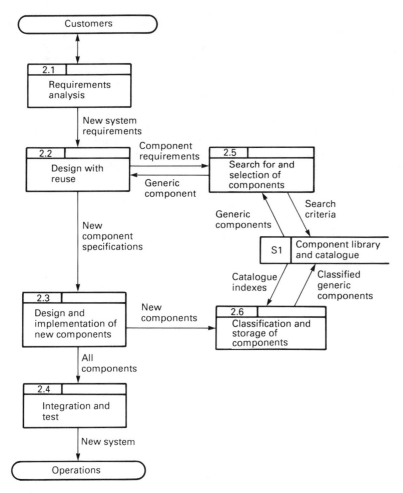

Figure 41.2 Software development life cycle with reuse, shown using the dataflow diagramming conventions of SSADM (Longworth and Nicholls, 1986)

There is also a need to consider more general knowledge about the area of application of the components, as shown at the bottom of Figure 41.1.

Integration of reuse with the traditional life cycle of software development is required. In analysing and designing new systems, the possibility of reuse needs to be considered, and the appropriate library components incorporated. New elements of software that are needed should also be considered as candidates for the library and added to it. This could lead to a variation on the waterfall life cycle as in *Figure 41.2*, a transformation of the reuse process shown in Figure 41.1.

All these technical issues are taken up in more detail below, which should be read in conjunction with Figures 41.1 and 41.2.

41.2.1 Identifying software for the reuse library

To enable reuse, the specification should give a clear statement of the theory and concepts underlying the software, independent of any particular implementation. Even for code, its reuse must be mediated by the existence of specification and design descriptions of the code, which are then used during the early stages of development and ensure the correct incorporation of the code. However, the existence of suitable implementations of the component are not necessary for the successful reuse of the component. Freeman (1983) reiterates this point more strongly, claiming that the reuse of program code alone is of negligible value, and arguing that such an emphasis is inconsistent with the exhortation to put more effort into the analysis and design activities.

Reuse of existing software presents a problem if it is only available as code. One solution is provided by retrofitting specifications to such systems. This strategy has been characterized as re-engineering (Arnold, 1986; Swift, 1987; Sneed and Jandrasics, 1989). Much existing software (so-called 'dusty decks', alluding to its historical origins in the days of punched cards) lacks any systematic documentation from requirements analysis through to specification, design and implementation, although there may be rudimentary documentation describing the software's operational usage. Such software may have evolved over a number of years, and no records may exist of its maintenance and enhancement.

However, it may be that within the organization responsible for such ancient software, there are local experts well versed in the 'folklore' of a particular software system or program. Codifying the expertise of these practising programmers is a first step towards salvaging such software for reuse. This may have the added benefit of leading to the rediscovery of old or lost ideas. In retrofitting a specification to an existing implementation, it is necessary to identify and abstract away from design and implementation decisions. The more abstract specification obtained will allow more flexible reuse of the software.

This reverse engineering, necessary to extract reusable components from existing code, still requires a lot of research. Possible the most promising approach so far comes from the Programmer's Apprenticeship project at MIT (Waters, 1988), where standard 'cliches' or patterns are searched for in the code, thus systematically identifying the design strategies that had been used, enabling us to abstract higher level descriptions of the software.

Alternatively, we could intend only to exploit reusable software when developing new software. This still requires us to be able to identify elements of software that are potentially reusable, and cast them in a sufficiently general form to enable wide reuse. We would then focus extra effort on developing the new reusable parts, to maximize the cost and quality benefits derivable from the reuse of these parts (see the later discussions of languages and existing applications).

In all cases it is essential to create as general a component as possible, while avoiding over-generalization which could make specific uses difficult to instantiate, and inefficient in operation. This requires that generalizations and inductions are made over several more specific components, a process for which no general guidance is available as yet.

41.2.2 Storing and retrieving reusable software

Having identified software which is potentially reusable and described it in such a way that anyone wishing to reuse it would be able to do so, the problem arises as to how to organize the total collection of all such software and related descriptions. Such a library can be structured by classifying the reusable software in various ways. A good system of classification not only provides the basis for cataloguing the software, but it also provides a means for finding a particular piece of software held in the library. Large collections of software present similar problems of classification to those well known in library science. The area of information retrieval (e.g. Salton and McGill, 1983) is well established. Work by Frakes and Nejmeh (1986–7) demonstrates usage of an IR system to support software reuse, and highlights some of the trends in IR research and development.

Prieto-Diaz and Freeman (1987) have surveyed established library classification methods and propounded a scheme for software based on the technique of faceted classification (Vickery, 1960). Faceted classification is essentially a bottom-up approach in contrast to the more traditional hierarchical approach which is top-down. Retrieval is facilitated by ranking facets in citation order.

Prieto-Diaz and Freeman distinguish between the reuse of ideas and knowledge and the reuse of artefacts and components. Although their approach is concerned with the latter, it provides the basis for a more general classification scheme for software concepts and associated specifications as well as other components: designs, source and object code, reference and user manuals, etc. In particular, their integration of faceted classification with the conceptual distance model allows a structuring of terms in a facet. A conceptual graph is constructed by knowledgable experts with terms as leaves, the facet as root, intermediate nodes denoting general concepts relating terms, and weights attached to edges to denote closeness of the term to the concept. These weightings can be used when searching the catalogue to find related entries. Facets used by Prieto-Diaz and Freeman are divided into two classes:

1. Functionality: function, object, medium.
2. Environment: system, area, setting.

A Natural Language approach to cataloguing and retrieval has been developed by Wood and Sommerville (1987) within the ECLIPSE reuse project. They investigated various approaches to development of a software components catalogue, initially limiting themselves to cataloguing primitive software components. They concluded that the functional nature of software components allows a more detailed description than independent keywords; their system is based on the use of conceptual dependencies as a representational system and derives from research in the area of Natural Language understanding/question-answering systems by Schank (1972) and others. The system of classification employed by Wood and Sommerville is based on representations termed software function frames which relate the function performed by a component to the objects it manipulates. This system uses a dictionary of typed verbs and nouns representing classes of functions and objects respectively.

For more formally specified components, Goguen (1986) has suggested a hierarchical library classification scheme in combination with complex indices at different levels of formality ranging from keywords to axioms. He addresses, in addition, the problem of truth management in descriptions, and the use of semantics in library organization as documentation building blocks.

41.2.3 Designing software with reusable parts

Given some statement of requirements, or some detailed specification, or even a high-level design, we will need to match this with the reusable software held in a library. We can identify two types of solution:

1. Finding a single component which will fully, or almost fully, satisfy our requirement.
2. Finding a collection of components, suitably interconnected, which can satisfy the requirement.

The first case is already a common problem in package selection, although this important part of commercial software practice is almost entirely ignored by system development methodologies. What we have to do is match the requirements or specification against the specifications in the library, using the retrieval mechanisms described above. Exact matching of precise (formal) specifications will in general be undecidable, and therefore we must necessarily reduce our descriptions for search purposes, accepting that we can only ever find near matches. Further, even if we could match precisely, we need to recognize that if we get no exact match we can always customize through the addition of extra software 'shells'. Thus we would be quite content to accept partial or approximate matches, with some further manual process required to vet the retrieved components to find the most suitable.

In the second case, only some combination of several components could satisfy our requirements. We therefore need to decompose our requirements in some way. One way is clearly an extension of the first, looking for some sub-match of library components to the requirements, in the manner of searching strings for substrings or graphs for subgraphs.

Alternatively, we must first of all divide the requirements into putative parts, which we then search for in the library. We must first do a high-level design. One approach, being researched by the authors of this chapter, is to use stereotypical high-level designs, these designs being tailored so that appropriate parts are necessarily in the library. These high-level designs are themselves reusable components and are stored in the library: the retrieval of these then reduces to the first case discussed previously.

Having selected a component (or set of components) for reuse, it remains to adapt the component for its intended use, and to compose it with other components and new software to achieve the desired results.

At the code level, adaptation or specialization could vary from modification of sources through to the provision of parameter values to a generic package to instantiate it for a particular use, as in Ada (Ichbiah, 1983) or in fully polymorphic languages such as ML (Wikstrom, 1987). The modification of sources is to be deprecated as an approach of last resort, for this could compromise the quality of the component, and quality was one of the main motivations for software reuse.

In addition there will be a well-defined language for building systems, for connecting components together. This could be the simple linkage mechanisms of the programming language, or could be mechanisms available at the command language level, such as pipes in the Unix shell.

However, the language for system building could also be developed specifically for module interconnection, either as part of a larger programming system such as Conic (Sloman *et al.*, 1985) or C/MESA (Lauer and Satterthwaite, 1979), or could even in principle be independent of the particular underlying programming language, such as INTERCOL (Tichy, 1980). These interconnection languages enable the consistency of interconnection to be assured by strong type checking, but they do not check at any higher level of abstraction or semantics.

When specialized and connected together, the available code components will probably still be insufficient to meet the full requirements, and other original code may be necessary, perhaps to transform the outputs from one component to the required form of inputs to another, or perhaps to add other functions not available from the component library.

At higher levels of abstraction, the same general principles apply. Components might be generic, being instantiated and then connected together, as in the system LIL proposed by Goguen (1986) based on CLEAR (Burstall and Goguen, 1981). The components here are not modified other than through instantiation; in other approaches the components might be treated as 'source' and adapted to the particular needs, then connected together with extra material to meet the particular need. These abstract approaches do in principle allow a more complete check on the consistency of interconnections than is available with code level module interconnection languages.

41.3 Support for reuse by various programming paradigms

The view that conventional high-level languages are collections of programming constructs which may be thought of as reusable components out of which specific programs are developed has already been discussed. Here we examine in more detail the support for reuse in various approaches to programming.

41.3.1 Abstract data types and polymorphism

Most current programming languages allow some form of user-defined type. In progressing up levels of abstraction in programming languages it is necessary not only to represent the basic machine-level types like integers, characters, and strings, but also to permit higher level types like trees. Early developments here were termed 'data structuring' (Hoare, 1972), but later it was realised that types consist of more than just the set of permissible values or members of the type – they also consist of a set of allowable operations upon those values. This then led to the development of 'abstract data types' (ADTs) as the combination of a set of values and set of operations over those values (and possibly other types). These ideas have become embodied in languages like CLU (Liskov, 1981), but are not present in

other languages such as Ada. With abstract data types, libraries of useful types can be built up and reused in the production of new systems. They constitute a component library.

For the ADTs to be really general purpose, it is necessary to be able to parameterize them. For example, we may wish to produce a tree whose nodes can be 'labelled' with elements drawn from some other arbitrary type. Most of the operations on the tree will be independent of the type of the node labels. A generic tree structure parameterized by the type of the node label is necessary.

This need for genericity, plus the need for being able to determine the type of objects in a program at compile time (strong typing), has led to a number of *ad hoc* solutions such as those of Ada, and to the elegant concept of polymorphic types (Cardelli and Wegner, 1985). Variables, particularly parameters to functions and procedures, may take a number of types, and precisely which type is being used may only be resolved at run time. Nevertheless, type consistency can be checked either at compile time or run time, to avoid a whole class of problems that plague languages that are too 'flexible' in their type structures.

Polymorphism complements ADTs; together they enable the construction of libraries of generic functions which may be shared by a number of programs.

41.3.2 Object-oriented programming

This is a natural extension of abstract data types. Two additional abstractions, class and inheritance, allow objects to be grouped into classes, and relations between classes to be specified. Thus a hierarchy is created with objects at the lowest level, classes of objects at the next level and classes of classes at the highest level. Cardelli and Wegner (1985) relate class and inheritance to more general notions of type and polymorphism by identifying the type abstractions: subtype, collection of subtypes and supertype. They characterize inclusion polymorphism as a relation among types that allows the sharing of operations amongst types related by inclusion, i.e. inheritance.

Object-oriented languages provide a powerful basis for reuse – their power is attributed very strongly to the large libraries of objects (components) that are provided with the programming system (e.g. Smalltalk (Goldberg and Robson, 1983)). Problems with using these systems are frequently attributed to inadequate facilities, called in these systems the 'browser', for finding suitable objects for reuse.

41.3.3 Functional programming

One of the barriers to software reuse is the presence of side-effects and subtle interactions between modules. While these can be removed in any language through the application of suitable discipline, functional languages (e.g. Darlington *et al.*, 1982) provide a framework for ensuring that undesired interactions cannot happen. Pure functional languages do not permit interactions other than through explicit mechanisms; for example, functions (procedures) can only affect other parts of a program through their parameters and results. The value of this for reuse has recently been noted by Morrison *et al.* (1987).

41.3.4 Programming in the large – module interconnection languages

To be able to reuse components, particularly code components, it is necessary to be able to connect these together. The general requirements for this were discussed above. The absence of such capabilities in languages like C, and the need for these, underlay the paper by Hall (1986). A number of special languages for module interconnection have been developed in research environments, and facilities for module interconnection have been included in many recent program development systems. A useful survey was published by Prieto-Diaz and Neighbors in 1986.

The languages specifically aimed at module interconnection are exemplified by the INTERCOL system developed by Tichy (1979 and 1980). Modules are interconnected to form systems. Both of these exist as families of versions. Each family has an interface consisting of a number of program resources – the same interface is used by all members of a family, so that members can be freely substituted for each other. These resources may either be provided ('exported') by the family or required ('imported') by the family. The resource specification language is independent of the particular implementation languages in which the modules may be realised. This enables checking for interconnection consistency between modules from whatever source they come.

This system does not offer significantly more than that offered in a number of program development systems. INTERCOL's distinguishing feature is the integration of the interconnection language with a version control system – an integration that one would now expect of any system development system.

The best-known program development systems supporting module interconnection are Unix and Ada, but the facilities here are comparatively crude. The best systems are exemplified by C/MESA (Lauer and Satterthwaite, 1979) and Conic (Sloman et al., 1985; Kramer and Magee, 1985). The facilities available in Conic are indicative of current best practice. Conic provides an extension of Pascal for the implementation of its components or modules, and a Pascal-like language for the connection of these components – the Conic Configuration Language (Dulay et al., 1985). Conic is aimed at the creation of distributed systems. Modules are generic, and have an interface defined for them as a number of 'entryports' and 'exitports' which pass typed data as messages. Module ports may be linked, with the system checking for consistency in doing this. A full hierarchy of modules built from other modules may be constructed, and distributed across a communication system onto a number of processors.

41.4 Examples of reuse in practice

Some examples of reuse in practice are described below. This list is not exhaustive, but typical of practices that are now current or becoming current.

41.4.1 The NAG Library – reuse based on a subroutine library

From its inception, the Numerical Algorithms Group (NAG) has sought not only to provide a balanced, general purpose numerical algorithms library but also to support the library with advice on problem identification and algorithm selection (Ford et al., 1979). Underlying the development of the NAG software is a conceptual machine; software is developed for the conceptual machine, and subsequently tailored for actual machine ranges. The NAG Library and its documentation are organized into chapters which correspond to various areas of mathematics and statistics and contain entries for primary routines which implement the NAG algorithms. The documentation contains an entry for each routine, with 13 sections covering purpose, specification, description, references, parameters, error indicators, auxiliary routines, timing, storage, accuracy, further comments, keywords and an example (NAG 1984). A user of the NAG Library must have some familiarity with the subject areas and the implementation language calling conventions of the

routine. A computerized 'help' system is available for the FORTRAN NAG Library. This describes the subject areas covered by NAG, advises on choice of routines and gives programming details for use of the routine.

Work has been undertaken to assist users of the NAG library with algorithm selection based on a knowledge-based front-end (Mikulecky and Chorvatova, 1986; NAG, 1988).

41.4.2 The Unix shell and software tools – reuse through module interconnection

The Unix philosophy of software development is expounded in the book *Software Tools* by Kernighan and Plauger (1976). Unix epitomizes the constructive approach to software development. Each basic software tool has a well-defined and limited function; tools are provided with uniform interfaces to facilitate tool interconnection. The developer of software tools is exhorted to do small things well, and use proven tools as the basis of more complex tools. The basic software tools aim to solve general problems rather than special cases. The overriding aim in design of the basic tools has been usability. A successful tool must be easier to use than to build from scratch.

The Unix system (*The Bell System Technical Journal*, 1987) consists of a small kernel with most of the conventional operating system functions implemented by small software tools. As the system has evolved, these tools have not been altered to increase their functionality. Instead, new tools have been developed to extend existing tools. For example, the nroff formatter has been extended by the development of various preprocessors and postprocessors.

The Unix shell command language and its associated interpreter provide a uniform mechanism for tool invocation and interconnection. Using the shell several tools may be combined to form a new tool and executed as asynchronous communicating processes. The standard tool interfaces are via byte streams; the Unix input/output (I/O) system is concerned simply with byte streams; structure is imposed on data by the tools that use it, not the I/O system. Thus tools developed to operate on data from files or devices may be reused to process data from a pipe, the Unix mechanism for interprocess communication. The flexibility with which tools may be interconnected using the shell has been an important factor in promoting reuse of tools within Unix (Kernigham, 1984).

The Unix tools are described well in the literature, and by means of an on-line manual system. This manual also describes the library functions employed in the basic tools which are written in C and the Unix system calls which may be accessed via C functions. A conventional format of manual pages imposes some structure on the Unix documentation. The system provides a tool supporting keyword searches of synopsis entries in the manual.

The Unix software tools approach has influenced the specifiers of the ESPRIT Portable Common Tool Environment in the development of the concept of 'granularity' of tools (Software Sciences, 1986). Each tool is characterized as a modular component performing a well defined atomic action. More powerful tools may be assembled from simpler tools, with the new tools becoming new grains in the construction of other tools.

41.4.3 An Ada component collection – An object-oriented approach to reuse

Recent publication of a collection of Ada components by Booch (1987) provides the framework for a basic set of reusable software components useful to any Ada system developer, and represents a foundation upon which more powerful components can be built. The Booch collection contains components listed under the following abstractions: structures, tools and subsystems. The latter are components denoting collections of co-operating structures and tools. Structures are components denoting objects or classes of objects. They are further distinguished as being monolithic: stacks, strings, queues, deques, rings, maps, sets, bags; or polylithic: lists, trees, graphs. Tools are components denoting algorithmic abstractions such as utilities, filters, pipes, sorting, searching and pattern matching. An interesting feature of Booch's collection is the taxonomy he develops and systematically applies in the naming of each components; components under each of the above abstractions may be further distinguished by various categories of forms. These names are carried over into the corresponding Ada package specifications.

41.5 Examples of reuse support systems

In this section work in progress to develop reuse support systems is described. These systems relate to the process of reuse discussed in the sections above although some systems focus on particular aspects of the reuse process such as decomposition, description, classification and selection, whilst others focus on the selection, specialisation and composition phases. In so far as a reuse support system addresses the complete reuse process, it is similar in form to a project support environment (PSE) (see Chapter 33 on integrated project support environments) that provides facilities to support the full project life cycle from capture of requirements through to operational support and maintenance of the project software products.

PSEs are often described as integrated (IPSEs) where tools have compatible interfaces with the users, other tools and the host environment. In most IPSEs the basis of internal tool integration is a database rather than a file system. Not only are database transactions safer and more secure than operations on a file system, but also objects in the database may be structured and classed by their attributes and relations. IPSEs are also integrated by embodying an underlying model of the development process which enforces a uniform discipline on the development even where informal development methods are used.

Similarly, reuse support systems may be characterized by the underlying model of the reuse process, the model of the objects of reuse describable in the system, and the methods employed to support these models. At the centre of these support systems is a library system containing descriptions of the reusable objects and possibly the objects themselves; the library is usually implemented using some form of database or persistent data storage mechanism. The systems described below are representative of research work in this field. Much of this work has been carried out by Peter Freeman and his colleagues at the University of California at Irvine where research in reuse has been in progress for the past ten years.

41.5.1 The Draco system

The Draco system and its approach to the construction of software from reusable components dates from the earlier work on the tranformational approach to software development (Neighbors, 1984). The Draco prototype was originally developed using UCI Lisp, but has been the subject of a project to demonstrate the transformational theory of maintenance based on the reuse of knowledge which involved using Draco to port Draco to Unix systems running Franz Lisp (Arango *et al.*, 1986). Freeman has provided a conceptual analysis of the Draco approach which relates Draco to particular software engineering principles (1987).

The Draco approach is founded on the reuse of analysis information and design information in specific domains. The Draco approach proceeds by a process of domain analysis to identify domain specific objects and operations, followed by domain design of implementations of the objects and operations in *terms of domains already known* to Draco. It follows that underlying the Draco approach is a more fundamental analysis of the division of the universe of discourse into primitive and derived domains.

Reuse is effected by an analyst supplying a specification in a domain language (already known to the Draco system as a result of previous domain analysis). If there is a match between objects and operations required and those of a known domain, a designer interacting with Draco can obtain implementations of these based on refinements of known designs. The designer decides which refinements to use and what kind of structure will result from the refinement chosen. Refinements are recorded and may be replayed.

41.5.2 The Pegasus tool

This tool, also developed at the University of California at Irvine, addresses the acquisition and reuse of software designs. It has been implemented in InterLisp (Kandt, 1984). It essentially consists of a database of software designs, an acquisition subsystem and a retrieval subsystem. The tool is able to handle descriptions in both text and graphic modes. The common description language used to represent designs is based on a subset of the Klone language, a knowledge representation language (Brachman, 1978). Retrieval is effected by means of a query language which allows the user to interactively formulate queries using database instances as templates. It is acknowledged that this system only addresses the design phase of the software development process.

41.5.3 The CATALOG system demonstration

The CATALOG system is an information retrieval (IR) system developed at AT&T Information Systems (Frakes and Leighton, 1985). It was used to construct a demonstration system to illustrate software reuse through IR. Descriptive headers from a set of modules taken from the Bell Laboratories SUPER system provided the basis of information retrieval based on combinations of terms using Boolean operators. The CATALOG system also supported related term matching and phonetic matching.

To promote reuse, a software template for module and function descriptions is proposed by Frakes and Nejmeh; it is suggested that these are included as comments within the C source files contains the reusable code. This system is limited as it only addresses the organization, search and retrieval of reusable C source code.

41.5.4 Reuse library system using faceted classification

Prieto-Diaz and Freeman have constructed a prototype library system based on the classification system reported above with about 200 program descriptors. This system is a Unix-based implementation using the University of California's Troll/USE prototyping tool as the underlying database system. The system does not directly support the phases of adaptation and composition although the system attempts to rank reusable components using a reuse effort estimation metric. This prototype is the basis of a scaling-up exercise to produce a version for use in a production environment at GTE Laboratories.

41.5.5 Reuse support within ECLIPSE

Part of the work on the ECLIPSE project is explicitly concerned with developing methods and tools to support the reuse of existing software. Sommerville and Wood's work on classification described above has been the basis for a prototype implementation of a components catalogue. This prototype has been developed using Prolog and catalogues a set of software components from the Unix operating system. The system components are a dictionary of 300 verbs and nouns describing Unix component functions and objects, a library of 300 or so component descriptions manually produced from the Unix documentation, a user interface which allows the user to form requests by inputting keywords into skeleton frames, and the pattern matching strategies implemented in Prolog. This system is concerned with effective classification to support improved retrieval. It does not address adaptation or composition issues in the reuse of components.

41.5.6 The Library Interconnection Language system

Goguen (1986) has proposed a library interconnection language, LIL, as a means of assembling large programs from existing entities; thus reuse is achieved by interconnecting the same entity in several programs. Reuse in the context of a development environment with a database of entities ranging from requirements, specifications, design histories and code to project status information is not simply limited to reuse of code components. In Goguen's proposal integration of these diverse entities is achieved by describing them all in a common formalism: LIL. This enables the formulation of high level specifications with general parameterization mechanisms. An important feature of LIL is that formal or informal semantics may be associated with entities or entity interfaces. This proposal provides a sound theoretical basis for the development of a reuse support system which addresses a large part of the reuse process.

41.6 Non-technical methods

In order to promote reuse, it is not sufficient merely to establish the correct technical environment. We must also address other non-technical issues, such as managerial practices and the legal constraints of a particular community. We will first of all look at how reuse might be encouraged within the framework of a single company, and then proceed to address how it may be promoted between companies both nationally and internationally.

41.6.1 Individual and organizational reuse

People who work in software production like producing software. That is why they are software engineers. They have a pre-disposition for developing software rather than looking for existing ideas, algorithms, or code. There are all sorts of personally persuasive arguments that they can muster. Reinventing software is fun! Why buy when you can build? Having seen the commercially available product, surely you could build it better? If it was not invented here, could you really trust it? In acquiring software from outside, there is always some compromise required, it never does exactly what is wanted. If you build it yourself, you can control its future development – it will always do what you want.

How can we counter these attitudes?

The ability to build software yourself, be it by an individual software engineer, by a project, or by the organization as a whole, is an enormous barrier to reuse. Contrast this with electronic engineering, where the cost of designing and fabricating your own microprocessor is so enormous, and requires such specialized equipment, that it is only undertaken in very special circumstances: the margin between buying and building is very many orders of magnitude. The margins between buying and building software are not so great, excepting in the large volume microcomputer marketplace; a first shot development could be as cheap as acquiring the software from elsewhere.

For the individual the cost of acquisition consists of the effort of finding the requisite software, and we can address this through the various technical measures discussed above, as well as by the continued training and education of the individual so that more abstract entities will also be reused. A reference book such as this is an important step in that direction.

It is the ratio of cost to benefit that counts, and as well as reducing the cost, we could also increase the benefit. If reuse does enhance productivity, then at least at the project and company levels there are pay-offs, but what about the individual? What extra benefit does he get from reuse?

Here an idea attributed to the Japanese is worth considering – changing the monetary and status rewards for individuals. Firstly, those who provide software for others to reuse could receive some form of royalty for this reuse. This would encourage both the production of general-purpose elements suitably proven and packaged to encourage their reuse, but would also encourage the promotion of the element's availability. The actual reuse should be encouraged, perhaps through piecework where the reward for the job was assessed without reuse in mind, or perhaps through a royalty on reuse for the user as well as the supplier. The status of people who succeed in reuse could be enhanced, possibly with the position of manager of the library of reusable components being made a highly rewarded and sought after post. This status and reward should be comparable with systems architects and database administrators which are highly sought after and respected jobs and are very similar in their intent.

There is no doubt that some form of cultural shift is necessary, with people's and institutional attitudes changing, if reuse is to be successful.

The payoff for reuse occurs only after the item's initial production. Projects are usually established simply to look after the initial development of a software system, with their performance being judged solely by the costs and timescales of the project. Frequently there are quality problems resulting from this practice, for the consequences of low quality are often picked by the follow-on maintenance project – somebody else foots the bill. This management practice does encourage reuse, to reduce project costs, but does not encourage the production of reusable components for other projects, for where is the payoff? Again, some form of royalty payable to the project might be appropriate, if company accounting practices could handle this. Alternatively the reusable components manager could be given a budget to invest in the production of components, either to subsidize their production on projects or to create them speculatively.

41.6.2 National and international reuse

Software reuse between organizations, both nationally and internationally, clearly does currently take place through the production and sale of packages. The experience of the software packages industry is important in understanding how the reuse industry could be expanded to include reusable components.

Illegal copying of software is a problem (Suhler et al., 1986). Copyright protection of software is emerging, but clearly needs to be practised internationally, and much more could be done there. Many producers of software appear to accept this situation, and seek to earn revenue from their software in other ways, by selling manuals or books about using it, or by selling training services.

Frequently software is acquired on the basis of futures, and if the software is bought, its future development may not turn out to be the way you wanted it. If you build it inhouse, you are in total control over its development. This argument ignores all sorts of other costs. Maintenance of inhouse software is likely to be more expensive; the software is likely to be less robust; it may be subject to uncontrolled voluntary 'improvements' that are not required and add to cost.

To maintain competitive advantage, some parts of a company's software may always be proprietary. The proprietary software may not even be particularly sophisticated, but comparable to the way application specific integrated circuits are used in hardware designs to make designs difficult to reproduce from inspection of an example. We must always expect some level of non-reuse.

Software is not a commodity. It does not become an asset of a company that purchases it. Software may be written off in its year of purchase, whereas hardware may be written off over 3–5 years or more. Software may not be allowed to be sold on; a computer manufacturer has required that purchasers of second-hand hardware relicense the software. There is no market in second-hand software: indeed the very idea seems mildly ridiculous. Could this be changed? One could envisage some legal remedies to remove what amount to restrictive and monopolistic practice. Could we get as far as enabling third-party maintenance of software?

Preparing software for reuse as a component does require extra effort. This extra effort needs to be rewarded. In the open market this reward would be some form of royalty or licence fee. There may be problems in enforcing these payments, and disputes within the industry are frequent. However, one person has produced a set of Ada components and is selling these (Booch, 1987).

It is clear that, to avoid some of these problems, a software components industry should be high volume and low cost, producing robust and stable products with low or zero maintenance costs.

41.7 Future directions

We have seen how the reuse of software is already widespread through the use of high-level languages, systems software, packages, and subroutine libraries. The next step is the reuse of software components.

Software components are already in serious use in some Japanese companies, with considerable productivity and quality improvements. There are a number of technical issues that need to be addressed:

1. *Abstraction.* To be able to reuse a piece of software, or the ideas underlying software, we need to be able to abstract a description of the reusable part, making this as generic as possible. Aids for doing this, particularly using informal notations derived from existing code, need to be developed.
2. *Classification.* Software collections, once described, need to be organized for storage and subsequent search and retrieval of the required items by potential reusers: simple applications of library information ideas have been made, but much more development is necessary here.
3. *Composition.* Parts need to be connected together to form solutions: the correctness of proposed connections needs to be checked statically, and further development of formalisms such as that used in LIL need to be made and integrated with other facets of the reuse solution.
4. *Reuse paradigms.* A method for analysing requirements and designing a solution using a body of known parts needs to be developed – current reuse paradigms are too close to the level of code.

5. *Reuse support.* As with other facets of software engineering, software development using reusable components needs to be supported by a comprehensive set of tools.

There are also social and legal problems to be overcome.

Within a single organization, social factors like 'not invented here' can be overcome through organizing the reward structure differently. Between organizations, however, there remain serious legal problems concerned with copyright and accounting practices that will need to be resolved at the level of national and international government.

41.8 References and bibliography

ACARD, Cabinet Office: Advisory Council for Applied Research and Development (1986) *Software A vital key to UK competitiveness*, HMSO, London

Arango, G., Baxter, I., Freeman, P. and Pidgeon, C. (1986) TMM software maintenance by transformation. *IEEE Software*, May

Arnold, R. S. (1986) *Tutorial on Software Restructuring*, IEEE Computer Society, Washington DC, USA

The Bell System Technical Journal (1978), **57**, 6, Part 2.

Boehm, B. (1981) *Software Engineering Economics*, Prentice-Hall

Booch, G. (1987) *Software Components with Ada, Structures, Tools and Subsystems*, Benjamin/Cummings Publishing Company

Bourne, S. R. (1983) *The UNIX System*, Addison-Wesley

Brachman, R. J. (1978) *A Structural Paradigm for Representing Knowledge*, Technical Report 3605, Bolt Beranek & Newman

Burstall, R. M. and Goguen, J. A. (1981) An informal introduction to specifications using Clear. In *The Correctness Problem in Computer Science* (eds R. S. Boyer and J. Strother Moore), Academic Press, pp. 185–214

Cardelli, L. and Wegner, P. (1985) On understanding types, data abstraction, and polymorphism. *ACM Computing Surveys*, **17**, 471–522

Cohen, B., Harwood, W. and Jackson, M. (1986) *The Specification of Complex Systems*, Addison-Wesley

Cox, B. (1986) *Object-Oriented Programming*, Addison-Wesley

Darlington, J., Henderson, P. and Turner, D. A. (eds) (1982) *Functional Programming and its Applications*, Cambridge University Press

Dulay, N., Kramer, J., Magee, J., Sloman, M. and Twidle, K. (1985) *The Conic Configuration Language, Version 1.3*, Research Report DOC 84/20, Imperial College, London

Ford, B., Bentley, J., du Croz, J. J. and Hague, S. J. (1979) The NAG Library 'machine'. *Software Practice and Experience*, **9**, 65–72

Frakes, W. B. and Leighton, W. J. (1985) The catalog information system. In *Proceedings of Symposium on Workstations in the Future Computing Environments*, AT&T Laboratories, Naperville, Illinois

Frakes, W. B. and Nejmeh, B. A. (1986–7) Software reuse through information retrieval, *SIGIR Forum 1986–87*, **21**, 30–36

Freeman, P. (1983) Reusable software engineering: concepts and research directions. In *Proceedings of ITT Workshop on Reusability in Programming, Sept 83*, ITT, pp. 2–16

Freeman, P. (1987) A conceptual analysis of the Draco approach to constructing software systems. In *IEEE Transactions on Software Engineering*, and in *IEEE Tutorial on Software Reusability* (ed. R. S. Arnold), IEEE Computer Society, Washington DC

Goguen, J. A. (1986) Reusing and interconnecting software components. *IEEE Computer*, February, 16–28

Goldberg, A. and Robson, D. (1983) *Smalltalk-80: The Language and Its Implementation*, Addison-Wesley

Hall, P. A. V. (1986) Reusable and reconfigurable software using C. In *Proceedings of the SE86 Software Engineering Conference, Southampton, UK*, IEE UK pp. 164–174

Hall, P. A. V. (1987) Software components reuse – getting more out of your code. *Information and Software Technology*, **29**, 38–43. Reprinted in *Software Reuse: Emerging Technology* (eds W. Tracz), IEEE Computer Society

Heering, J. and Klint, P. (1985) Towards monolingual programming environments. *ACM Transactions on Programming Languages and Systems*, **7**, 183–213

Hoare, C. A. R. (1972) Notes on data structuring. In *Structured Programming* (eds O.-J. Dahl, E. W. Dijkstra and C. A. R. Hoare), Academic Press, pp. 83–174

Ichbiah, J. D. (1983) On the design of Ada. In *Information Processing 83* (ed. R. Mason), North Holland, pp. 1–10

IEEE Transactions on Software Engineering (1984) **SE-10** (5)

Jones, C. B. (1980) *Software Development: A Rigorous Approach*, Prentice-Hall

Capers Jones, T. (1984) Reusability in programming: a survey of the state of the art. *IEEE Transactions on Software Engineering*, **SE-10**, 488–494

Kandt, K. (1984) Pegasus: A tool for the acquisition and reuse of software designs. In *Proceedings of Compsac84 Conference*, IEEE Computer Society Press, Silver Springs, Maryland

Kernighan, B. W. (1984) The UNIX system and software reusability. *IEEE Transactions on Software Engineering*, **SE-10**, 513–519

Kramer, J. and Magee, J. (1985) Dynamic configuration for distributed systems, *IEEE Transactions on Software Engineering*, **SE-11**, 424–436

Lanergan, R. G. and Grasso, C. A. (1984) Software engineering with reusable designs and code. *IEEE Transactions on Software Engineering*, **SE10**, 498–501

Lauer, H. C. and Satterthwaite, E. H. (1979) The impact of MESA on system design. *Proceedings of the 4th International Conference on Software Engineering, Munich, Germany*, IEEE, 174–182

Ledgard, H. (1981) *ADA An Introduction. Ada Reference Manual (July 1980)*, Springer-Verlag

Liskov, B. H. (1981) CLU Reference Manual. *Lecture Notes in Computer Science, vol 114*, Springer-Verlag

Liskov, B. and Guttag, J. (1986) *Abstraction and Specification in Program Development*, The MIT Press, pp. 38–53

Littlewood, B. (1979) Software reliability model for modular program structure. *IEEE Transactions on Reliability*, **R-28**, 241–246

Longworth, G. and Nicholls, D. (1986) *SSADM Manual. Volumes 1 and 2*, NCC Publications

Lehman, M. M. and Stenning, N. V. (1985) Concepts of an integrated project support environment. *Data Processing*, **27** (3)

Lubars, M. D. (1986) Affording higher software reliability through software reusability, *ACM SIGSOFT Software Engineering Notes*, **11**

Mikulecky, P. and Chorvatova, L. (1986) *A Knowledge-based Tool for a Scientific Program Library*, Comenius University, Institute of Computer Science, Bratislava, Czechoslovakia

McIllroy, M. D. (1976) Mass-produced software components. In *Software Engineering Concepts and Techniques*, Petrocelli/Charter, Belgium, pp 88–98

Morrison, R., Brown, A. L., Carrick, R., Connor, R. C. H., Dearle, A. and Atkinson, M. (1987) Polymorphism, persistence and software reuse in a strongly typed object-oriented environment. *Software Engineering Journal*

NAG Ltd (1984) *NAG FORTRAN Mini Manual Mark 11*, Oxford

NAG Ltd (1988) *Logic based front-ends for large software systems with reference to a widely-used statistical GLIM*, Oxford

Neighbors, J. (1984) The Draco approach to constructing software from reusable components, *IEEE Transactions on Software Engineering*, **SE-10**, (5)

Prieto-Diaz, R. and Neighbors, J. (1986) Module interconnection languages. *Journal of System Sciences*, **6**, 307–334

Prieto-Diaz, R. and Freeman, P. (1987) Classifying software for reusability. *IEEE Software*

Schank, R. C. (1972) Conceptual dependency: a theory of natural language understanding. *Cognitive Psychology*, **3**, 552–631

Salton, G. and McGill, M. (1983) *Introduction to Modern Information Retrieval*, McGraw-Hill

Sloman, M., Kramer, J. and Magee, J. (1985) The Conic Toolkit for building distributed systems. *6th IFAC Distributed Computer Control Systems Workshop, Monterey, California, May 1985*, Pergamon Press

Sneed, H. M. and Jandrasics, G. (1989) Inverse transformation from code to specification. In *Software Tools '89*, Blenheim Online, pp 435–448

Software Sciences Ltd (1980) *PCTE and Emeraude – An Overview*, Product literature

Standish, T. A. (1984) An essay on software reuse. *IEEE Transactions on Software Engineering*, **SE-10**, 494–497

Suhler, P. A., Bagherzadeh, N. Malek, M. and Iscoe, N. (1986) Software authorisation systems. *IEEE Software*, 34 et seq

Swift, J. (1987) Software maintenance: defusing the time-bomb. In *Managing Large Projects*, On-Line Software Tools, pp 195–200

Tichy, W. F. Software development control based on module interconnection. In *Proceedings of the 4th International Software Engineering Conference, Munich, Sept 1979*, 29–41

Tichy, W. F. (1980) *Software Development Control Based on Systems Structure Description*, Ph.D. thesis, Carnegie-Mellon University, Computer Science Department

Turski, W. M. and Maibaum, T. S. E. (1987) *The Specification of Computer Programs*, Addison-Wesley

Vickery, B. C. (1960) *Faceted Classification: A Guide to the Construction and Use of Special Schemes*, ASLIB

Waters, R. C. (1988) Program translation vis abstraction and reimplementation. *IEE Transactions on Software Engineering*, **14**, 1207–1228

Wegner, P. (1984) Capital-intensive software technology, *IEEE Software*

Wikstrom, A. (1987) *Functional Programming using ML*, Prentice-Hall

Wood, M. and Sommerville, I. (1988) An information retrieval system for software components. *Software Engineering Journal*, 199–207

Yatsumoto, Y., Sasaki, O. Nakajima, S., Takezawa, K., Yamamoto, S. and Tanaka, T. (1980) SWB system: a software factory. In *Software Engineering Environments* (ed. Huenke) North-Holland, pp. 305–318

Programming
Languages

42

Low-level programming

John Henderson
King's College, London

Contents

42.1 Introduction

This chapter describes the low-level features of current computers from the programmer's viewpoint. It does not describe hardware implementation, but what a machine 'looks like' at the machine code level, and explains some of the reasons why machines are designed as they are. The purpose of this is to increase the programmer's understanding of what may appear to be idiosyncratic features. The hardware view of some of the same features is presented in Chapter 47.

Usually this low-level machine detail is hidden from the user by layers of support software, especially high-level language compilers and operating systems. These are intended to allow a programmer to ignore the details of a particular processor and its input/output (I/O) structure. In practice this goal is only partially achieved and it is often necessary to write some additional code to overcome a shortfall in the support software specification or implementation.

Examples of this include the writing of a driver to control some new type of peripheral device or to write interlude routines to stand between the outputs of compilers for two languages and to convert between their different conventions for parameter passing.

It is unusual today for a complete suite of programs to be written in assembler. The advantages of high-level languages outweigh the benefits that can be achieved by writing at a low level. For example, programmer productivity on a large project, measured in terms of the number of source instructions produced, appears to be independent of the language used. Since a high-level language program to solve a given problem will contain fewer instructions than the same program written in assembler, it is obviously quicker, and therefore cheaper, to use a high-level language. In the past it has often been argued that a program written in a low-level language is much more efficient in terms of memory usage and execution time than the equivalent program written in a high-level language. Whilst this may have been true in the past it is only true now for specialized applications. This is due to a number of features, such as improvements to computer architecture, compiler technology and execution environments. Another reason why high-level languages have gained dominance is that the users of such languages need not be so expert at the low-level details of the particular computer architecture being used. In order to use low-level programming effectively the programmer has to understand thoroughly the machine architecture, which is why an understanding of the low-level details of hardware and software are important. Thus this chapter illustrates the basic properties of machine architectures.

Discussed first are the gross level charateristics of processors (Sections 42.2–42.4), then the specific aspects of typical CPUs. This covers storage of data types (Section 42.5); logical addressing (Section 42.6); physical addressing (Section 42.8); input/output (Section 42.9); and traps (Section 42.10).

The final sections cover more advanced architectures (Sections 42.11 and 42.12). The properties of assemblers are addressed in Section 42.13, and a common use of low-level languages is discussed in 42.7.

42.2 Basic von-Neuman architecture

The basic structure and operation of computers is briefly described in order to set the scene for the rest of the chapter.

42.2.1 Memory, registers and processor flags

The basic von-Neuman machine (Stallings, 1987) is the model for the overwhelming majority of computers in use. This computer comprises a processor which executes instructions and a memory which holds instructions and data. One of the fundamental ideas of the von-Neuman concept is that there is no distinction in memory between instructions and data; they are only distinguished by their use.

The processor and memory represent the absolute minimum components to constitute a computer. With very few exceptions, computers are connected to external devices, traditionally called peripherals.

In addition to the main memory, there are usually a number of extra storage locations, known as registers, many of which reside in the processor. Registers are used to hold intermediate values, a variety of state indicators known as flags, and data necessary to the operation of the processor such as the program counter (that is, the address of the current instruction) and the processor state. The program counter is usually referred to as the PC.

The main memory is likely to be constructed from separate random access memory (RAM) components while the registers are likely to be implemented as part of the central processing unit (CPU).

Main memory can range in size from only a few bytes to many megabytes (MB – millions of bytes). A typical personal computer today will have one or two MB of main memory. The number of registers in the system can vary from a few to several hundred, but typical modern processors have between ten and 50.

Registers are much faster to access than main memory, often because they are implemented using intrinsically faster methods and because they are intimately bound up in the processor implementation and so avoid the overheads of memory access. Registers are used to hold the results of operations on data and to assist in the addressing of memory. Flags are used to indicate conditions caused by operations and to indicate aspects of machine state. These flags can be used to choose various paths through the program code.

42.2.2 Execution cycle

An important machine register is the instruction address register or program counter. This register contains the address of the next instruction to be executed. The basic machine cycle comprises two operations which are continually executed in sequence:

> Read Next Instruction (RNI)
> Execute Instruction

During the RNI operation the CPU fetches from memory the next instruction word and decodes it. This is the process of deciding which operation from the instruction set to perform. The CPU then takes the necessary steps to execute the instruction. This may well involve reading further bytes that are parts of the instruction, and then reading data from the memory or storing data into the memory.

42.2.3 Instruction sets

The collection of instructions which the processor is capable of executing is known as the order code or instruction set. Compatible ranges (families) of processors all share to a greater or lesser extent the same instruction set. 'Compatible' processors may differ in the range of addressing options supported, and some may offer a wider repertoire of instructions. Increasingly, a more advanced member of a family may support the instruction set of an earlier family member as a subset. For example, the Motorola 68030 contains the 68000 instruction set as a subset of its instructions. Incompatibilities sometimes arise because apparently identical instructions are implemented differently and thus have different side effects. Incompatible processors (i.e. from different families) have order codes which, while performing much the same basic operations, are quite different at a detailed level. These differences will include the number of instructions, addressing mechanisms, data types supported, number of registers and the organization of the more complex instructions, i.e. those which combine several basic operations. These differences occur because of the different applications fields of the processors and because of the different ways in which designers perceive the 'best' way to construct the processor.

There are two major classes of order code. The terms used to describe them are not rigorously defined (Colwell *et al.*, 1985).

1. *Complex instruction set computer (CISC)*. This term is used, somewhat disparagingly, to describe computers with a rich and diverse order code. On the face of it the more instructions the better as there is a possibility of the availability of an instruction that will perform exactly what the programmer wants. However, the design of all computers is a compromise and the price to be paid for such an instruction set is in speed of execution and in the complexity of the hardware implementation.

   Moreover, the more abstruse instructions may never be used, certainly in the code generated by compilers, because of the difficulty of recognizing the circumstances which would make the use of such an instruction appropriate.

   It is the intention of the order code designer to simplify the work of the low-level programmer by providing only generally useful instructions. This aim is not always met. Research into actual programs has shown that the designers sometimes provide features which are hardly ever used. The trend in evolving architectures is for the instruction set to become larger and more complex.
2. *Reduced instruction set computer (RISC)*. In direct contrast to the CISC, a RISC instruction set (Stallings, 1986) is designed to be rapid in execution. The instruction set is not intended to be used in low-level programming but to be generated by a compiler from a high-level language program.

   The proponents of such systems argue that the reduced complexity of the hardware and the intrinsic speed of the relatively simple instructions provide the way forward in processor design. It follows that for most programs a RISC program will use more instructions than the same algorithm implemented on a CISC sysem. There are now several RISC based computers on the market, all of them with different order codes. More details of RISC computers are to be found in Chapter 47 Section 5.1.

42.3 CPU characteristics

This section briefly describes those aspects of CPUs which characterize them from the point of view of the low-level programmer. Once programmers understand these characteristics they are in a good position to appreciate the primary constraints on program design.

42.3.1 Variable length versus fixed length

There are two conflicting requirements in order code design – making the order code easy for the programmer to use by including the facilities he or she requires and the production of an order code which is both cheap and easy to implement. The job of the designer consists of a number of tasks. First, there is the need to allocate bits in an instruction word. Second, there is the problem of making the circuits to perform the functions.

It is necessary to have instructions which read data from memory and instructions to write data into memory. The transfers take place into and out of registers. It will be seen that there is a need to define:

1. The operation to be performed.
2. The source address.
3. The destination address.

If there is a large address space, many registers and many instruction types, then the instruction word needs to be large. Word machines, as opposed to byte machines, traditionally hold a complete instruction in a single word. In the case where the instruction length is fixed, say a word, there is a trade-off. More instructions implies less addressability, while more registers mean fewer of the other features. The compromise is because the total number of bits to specify the required instruction, select the appropriate register and to address the memory is fixed. Suppose the number of registers is doubled. Then an extra bit is needed in the register select field. This must be 'stolen' from another field, thus halving the addressability or the instruction repertoire. Many instructions may well not need to address the memory and so mechanisms are developed to avoid wasting the bits reserved for the address and use them instead to extend the order code repertoire. For word machines with fixed length instructions many mechanisms are introduced to minimize the adverse effects of these compromises.

Another technique is to make the instruction length variable. In this case, if there is a need for an address part of the instruction, then it is tagged on the end as extra bytes. The instructions then are of variable length dependent on the address mode. This has implications for execution time as additional memory references need to be made before the complete instruction can be decoded. The programmer need not be aware of the length of the instruction generated, because the assembler will handle that level of complexity. There are problems associated with short skip instructions, which if used carelessly may 'skip' into the middle of an instruction and thus start executing data. It is also more difficult to use a low-level debugger. The advantages seem in practice to be overwhelming as most CISC order codes now implement variable length instructions.

42.3.2 Co-processors

If the facility is included in the original design, the instruction set can be extended by the use of a co-processor (e.g. 80x87 (Ciminiera and Valenzano, 1987)). This technique is used most often to supply additional arithmetic capabilities especially floating point (see Chapter 8). Many order codes do not implement floating-point operations in hardware, but require a software emulation to be used. Often the CPU will trap the missing instructions and automatically invoke a manufacturer supplied software package. The programmer must be aware of the performance differences and of the possibility that the software may not emulate the hardware exactly.

42.3.3 User/supervisor modes

Many machines implement at least two states or modes. One, the 'user', mode is most frequently in use. This mode has restrictions built into it, preventing a user either inadvertently or deliberately interfering with the integrity of the system. Typically in 'user' mode I/O instructions are unavailable and it is impossible to execute the 'halt' instruction. In addition, depending on the processor design, other facilities are denied to a 'user' program.

In 'supervisor', privileged or system mode, it is possible to manipulate all the machine facilities. The supervisor or operating system can then perform I/O, allocate storage and modify the page registers which are used in complex processors to control the allocation and use of physical memory and so control the entire system.

42.3.4 Arithmetic (logical) control

The instruction set is divided into four main parts.

First, there is the arithmetic section. Instructions are implemented to handle addition, subtraction and the testing of values. Associated with the arithmetic unit are the 'carry' and 'overflow' bits. These are necessary to detect certain possible error conditions associated with finite accuracy arithmetic and to implement arbitrary precision arithmetic. Some processors implement condition codes. Condition codes are a set of testable bits which in addition to 'carry' and 'overflow' include 'zero' and 'sign' flags. These flags are set as the result of performing certain instructions. They are not always implemented consistently and it is necessary to check each instruction individually to see whether or not the relevant flags will be altered. Where condition codes are not set as the automatic result of operations there are instructions provided explicitly to test for, and take selective action on, various possible conditions. Multiple register machines usually use a condition code design; it reduces the number of instructions that need to be specified.

Second, there are the logical instructions. These allow the manipulation of byte fields as bits. Typically such instructions include **and, or, exclusive or** and **not**. A variety of logical and arithmetic shift and rotate instructions are usually supplied. These instructions may use the 'carry' bit. They are used for manipulating packed fields and for fast multiplication by manifest constants. Care must be taken when using such instructions to be very clear exactly what happens because there is a wide range of possible outcomes, including sign extension and the use of the carry bit. Some word machines contain byte swap instructions to interchange the bytes in a word, which may make certain operations easier especially in word addressable machines.

The third group of instructions is the set of control instructions. These are used to alter the sequence of instruction execution. They include 'skips' and 'jumps', which are both conditional and unconditional, and 'calls' and 'returns', which are used for procedure invocation.

A further group of instructions is used for controlling the state of the machine and for performing I/O. The sort of internal state flags that can be manipulated are ones for turning the interrupt system off or setting instruction trapping. I/O instructions send and receive control information and data to external devices. Because these instructions can interfere with the basic operation of the processor, they are the ones restricted to the system user, where such a facility is provided. These are typically used by the operating system.

42.3.5 Addressing

Instructions that perform operations on data need to know where to find the data. The data address is sometimes implicit in the instruction, as when the operation can only be applied to the single accumulator. Many instructions involve at least two operands; e.g. addition (of the form $i := i + j$), loading and storing (though the distinction is historical and both are sometimes called moving). In this case the operation will be one of three possible types:

1. Register/register
2. Memory/memory
3. Register/memory

In the first case the operation takes one register as a source

operand and another as a destination. In the second, both operands are in memory, and in the third the operation takes place between a register and memory. By no means all instruction sets offer all three types. Memory-to-memory operations are the least common because they require longer instructions to specify the addresses and so both machine designers and programmers have become used to register-based designs. Some processors have relatively few registers, making register/register instructions relatively useless. All processors which use registers for data manipulation – and nearly all modern order codes do – must at least be able to load from and store to memory.

Processors are seldom consistent or symmetrical in their order codes. There are usually good implementation-dependent reasons why some instructions that might be expected are not provided. Nevertheless, it is essential in all cases to find out exactly what has been provided.

42.4 Hardware implementation

The instruction execution part of the processor can be implemented in several ways. The traditional implementation method is to design a circuit whose function is directly to execute the defined order code. This is known as hard-wired, and its advocates emphasize that it leads to the quickest execution. Errors in its design can only be corrected by re-designing the circuit.

Increasingly the implementation is achieved by means of microcoding (Andrews, 1980; Cline, 1981). The hardware is designed to execute very quickly a highly restricted instruction set. A program is then written in those 'micro' instructions to implement the target or visible instruction code being supported. Microcoding is a relatively arcane art as the micro-instructions operate at a very low level and each instruction may perform several operations at the same time. One approach to microcode implementation is the so called bit-sliced processor. In this case the target processor uses standard chips which support a limited instruction set. These chips operate in parallel and require a microcode program to control them. By using a standard chip the designer does not then have to build all the basic circuits, such as adders, from even simpler circuits himself.

The micro-program itself must be stored in a memory. If that memory is read-only it is described as hard microprogrammed; otherwise, it is known as soft microprogrammed and can in principle be written. Thus the visible instruction set being 'emulated' can be changed.

There are systems which allow a choice of which of several micro-programs is to be used. This allows execution or hardware emulation of different order codes.

A system which depends entirely on a soft micro-program has certain problems in starting itself up and needs appropriate hardware for its initial bootstrapping.

Low-level programming is not usually affected by the implementation technology.

42.5 Data types: internal representation

There have been machines where the data held in memory has associated descriptors for identifying the type of data stored. For the vast majority of processors in common use the interpretation of data is conventional and at the machine language level there is no type checking of the operand, so the types of the operand are assumed by the instructions operating on them. A knowledge of the data types available is critical to low-level program design.

There are usually five types of data conventionally supported:

1. *Bytes/characters.* Bytes are usually eight bits and can therefore store 256 unique values. These are used to store characters. Two conventions are in common use. These are ASCII (American Standard Code for Information Interchange), given as Table 48.3 in Chapter 48, and EBCDIC (Extended Binary Coded Decimal Interchange Code). ASCII is used in many different manufacturers' machines. EBCDIC is largely in use by IBM, although the PC range uses the ASCII character code. ASCII defines 128 7-bit characters, which means that the eighth bit is available for use in a variety of non-standard ways.

   Some older processors used 6-bit character codes and so had a very restricted character set.

2. *Integers.* Fixed-length integers are the basic arithmetic unit. There are two conventions for negative integers: two's complement and one's complement. With one's complement representation zero is represented both by all zeros and by all ones; this latter is known as 'negative zero' and can give rise to programming problems.

   Integers are stored as 8-, 12-, 16-, 18-, 24-, 32- or even 64-bit quantities. With the increasing acceptance of the 8-bit byte as a standard storage unit the most common sizes are 8, 16 or 32 bits. In the case of the two smaller sizes, there is often a need to implement in software multi-length arithmetic to handle values greater than can be held in the basic integer. It is, of course, possible to implement arithmetic of arbitrary precision on any machine with the basic arithmetic facilities.

3. *Addresses.* It is necessary to be able to manipulate addresses. Memory addresses are unsigned integers and it is necessary to be able to perform operations on them and test the results.

4. *Logical variables.* Logical variables can be implemented as single bits in words or bytes. Such 'flags' can usually be conveniently set, reset or tested using the logical instructions.

5. *Floating point/real numbers.* A number of computers have the additional facility of hardware floating point. While there is an international standard for all aspects of floating-point manipulation there exists a wide range of formats between different manufacturers. These differences, often of both magnitude and accuracy, can lead to inconsistent results if applications programs using such arithmetic are not written with care and insight into their particular problem domain.

6. *General data structures.* Low-level programming can use these basic facilities to construct more complex data structures. What the programmer constructs is limited only by his or her ability to manipulate the basic data types available. The most complex structures offered by high-level languages must be mapped by the compiler onto the facilities available for low-level programming. Indeed, the programmer may well be able to use the machine code to implement even more complex structures appropriate to his application.

42.6 Logical addressing

One of the biggest difficulties in producing low-level programs is often caused by trying to find appropriate ways to structure, access and address data. It is therefore important for the programmer to understand the range of addressing modes that are likely to be available.

42.6.1 Direct

The most obvious form of addressing is where the instruction contains a bit pattern which is the address of a storage location. Such an address is called a direct address.

42.6.2 Indirect

An indirect or deferred address is an address generated from (contained in) the instruction points to a location whose contents are the address of the required memory location.

The final address can be held in a register, rather than the main memory. A common use of register-based indirection is the implementation of a stack. Some machines implement a single hardware stack using only one particular register which therefore can be implied rather than explicitly specified in the instruction. Other order codes combine this register indirect addressing with auto-incrementation and auto-decrementation. This can be used to implement a last-in, first-out (LIFO) stack or scan sequentially through an array of characters (a string) or a table of integers.

It is also possible to specify memory indirection, in this case a memory location holds the address of the operand. Some processors implement 'multiple indirection', in this case the top bit of the address word indicates whether or not to take the next address as further indirection or not.

42.6.3 Magic areas or special areas of the address space

The growth in the size of memories fuelled both by the availability of cheap memory chips and the inevitable tendency of programs to get bigger, has made it impracticable to design an order code where each instruction can contain within itself a full memory address. Accordingly a variety of techniques are in use so that the abbreviated address that can be held in an instruction is useful:

1. *Base page.* The idea is that a certain area of memory, starting at location zero, can be addressed by all instructions. This base page can then be used conventionally to allow access to all the address space using some form of indirect addressing.

2. *Current page.* In addition to the base page an instruction can also address the current page. One bit in the address field is used to designate either base or current page. The reference, depending on the machine, may be relative to the current PC value or it may be generated by ignoring the bottom bits of the PC and then adding the displacement. This effectively divides the address space into 'pages' starting on fixed regular boundaries.

   It must be noted that it is only possible to give references to this restricted area of the address space when using basic instructions. Some architectures provide an escape mechanism to use a second word and so generate a double-length instruction. Even when this option is available it uses additional memory space and takes extra cycles to execute.

   The programmer has to organize the data so that most references can be to these easily accessible areas. To access other parts of the address space it is necessary to store in the directly addressable locations pointers to those other areas. This can prove a considerable restriction in practice.

3. *I/O addresses.* In some computers I/O is handled by designating a portion of the address space as I/O registers. Memory addressing instructions can then be used to handle I/O. This reduces the number of instructions to be implemented at the price of losing some addressability. With the large addressing space of modern processors this is rarely a problem.

4. *Registers as memory addresses.* Some processors 'map' the registers onto store addresses. This means that some apparent storage references are in fact referring to registers. These register addresses may be low memory or in the I/O address space. Mapping registers to store addresses allows for a faster context switch mechanism as only the pointer to the registers in memory has to be changed.

5. *Base/base and limits*. Relocation and protection are provided in some processors by the provision of hardware base registers and, sometimes, limit registers. This means that the base register is set to the low address in the real address space and all references, while in user mode, are automaically relocated by this value. A limit register contains the highest address that the program may validly reference.

These registers are usually used by the operating system to provide an area of memory for an application program and/ or to confine it within limits to prevent interference with other programs co-existing within the memory.

42.6.4 Indexing

An extremely powerful addressing mechanism built into most order codes is indexing. In this case the address contained in the instruction is modified by (added to) the value contained in an index register. The number of index registers varies from only one to as many as 128. The more there are, the more bits are needed in the instruction to specify which one is needed.

Typical uses of index registers are for the register to contain the base address of a data structure such as an array and for the elements of that structure to be addressed via off-sets. Alternatively the register can be used to contain the offset of a location which is an element in an array or string.

42.6.5 Hardware stacks

Some architectures implement a hardware stack which is used implicitly in the execution of some instructions. In particular, it is used by the procedure call-and-return mechanism. The same stack may also be used by the interrupt mechanism. It is essential that the stack pointer should be set to a suitable area of memory and that the appropriate disciplines are used if the same stack is used for data storage.

42.6.6 Based addressing

Another technique for constructing addresses dynamically is 'based' addressing. All addresses are constructed by adding the contents of the specified base register to the offset in the instruction. This technique may be combined with indexing, in which case three values are added to produce the effective address.

42.6.7 Segmentation

When segmentation is implemented the total possible address space is regarded as a collection of segments, which are often 64K (works or bytes) in size. An address is then constructed as a displacement within a segment. Additional segment registers are used to indicate within which segment the displacement is to be interpreted. Mechanisms vary as to how the segment is specified. There may be fixed boundaries at segment-sized intervals, or a segment register may contain an address which is the start of the particular segment. One common characteristic of segment-addressing systems is that addresses 'wrap round' within a segment. Thus if a data structure crosses a segment boundary, the program must detect this and change, as appropriate, the relevant segment register. This problem makes the manipulation of large arrays bigger than a segment quite complex.

42.6.8 Modes

The ability of a processor to support user and system modes has been mentioned above. Processors can also support modes in a way that changes the order code in use and so can be used to support hardware emulation of previous order codes. Some processors support a trace mode in which the processor traps after each instruction execution. This allows the implementation of single stepping for debugging purposes, under program control. Programmers need to understand the effect of modes because they may well affect the environment in which their program is to run, or their program may need to manipulate the modes to achieve its goals.

42.6.9 Long/short jumps and calls

Because most programs do not contain many jumps but, in practice, proceed fairly smoothly through the code, many machines provide skips and 'short' jumps and calls. This can give rise to problems when a large program is loaded from a number of separately compiled procedures, each of which is small enough not to exceed segment boundaries, as jumps may need to be converted from short to long form. Long jumps are necessarily slower, requiring more memory accesses, and taking up more space. Thus there is often a mixture of long and short forms of jump in the same program. The ability to force a compiler to generate 'long' form instructions is a common option. This is of concern to the programmer for several reasons. If the program is to form part of a suite of programs it is essential to establish the conventions which will allow inter-module communication to occur. Within a module it might prove acceptable to let the assembler decide the appropriate format of jump. Techniques exist to make the necessary adjustments to jump format if an extra word is introduced or removed, e.g. by changing from a short jump to a long jump, though by no means all assemblers have this facility. It is necessary to use the appropriate conventions when the low-level module has to be called from a high-level compiled program.

The temptation always to use long calls and jumps must be paid for in terms of larger and slower programs.

42.6.10 Relocatability and position independent code

Some order codes which support PC relative memory references allow a program to be written in such a manner that it will run correctly, without modification, wherever it is loaded. This is seldom entirely straightforward at the level of an individual module, which may well have to communicate with global data and call other procedures. For an entire self-contained program, with appropriate hardware facilities, relocatability may be achieved transparently. This has obvious advantages in the allocation of storage where programs may be called into memory on demand.

42.6.11 Code/data areas

The separation of code and data is supported by some architectures and is mandatory in others. Such separation allows the program to be protected by access control hardware from accidental overwriting. It also simplifies the production of re-entrant programs.

42.6.12 Re-entrancy

A re-entrant program is one that does not require initialization and can be run 'simultaneously' as part of separate processes. It is invariant and does not modify itself. For a code section to be simultaneously invoked with different data, that data must be addressed using registers and avoiding any direct, fixed addresses for variables.

42.7 Physical addressing

Associated with every processor is a physical memory. The processor generates logical addresses, which are mapped to actual memory locations. The physical memory is usually a mixture of ROM and dynamic or static RAM. Details of memory systems are to be found in Chapter 47, Section 47.3.2.

The distinction between logical addressability and physical memory must be understood. There is no longer any close relationship between logical and physical addresses. The system must be designed to cope when the addresses generated are greater than those that the hardware supports. The programmer must be aware of the effect of using addresses in such ranges, i.e. of the effect of logical to physical mapping.

42.7.1 Memory sizes

There are two dimensions to the memory size equation. The first is the size of the basic addressable unit. This is likely to be the byte, but may be the word. As most memory chips implement a 1 bit $\times$ 2^n regime there are often multiples of nine chips, the ninth bit being used as a parity bit. In the case of more sophisticated error-correcting memory, the number of additional bits is greater. As chip technology advances the value of n grows rapidly. Originally such a memory chip contained perhaps 1024 bits, (i.e. $n = 10$), but it may now contain a million bits. Thus it is economical to implement a million bytes in a single memory unit, e.g. circuit board, because the price of a chip is not proportional to the number of bits it is capable of storing, and the memory can be constructed on the same number of boards of essentially similar complexity irrespective of the chip capacity. The order codes and their associated addressability were not designed with all these advances in mind. However, the implication now is that physical memories are large and are no longer closely related to the logical address that the order code is capable of generating. Early designs were such that the logical address space and the physical address space were identical.

42.7.2 Bus widths

Memories are conventionally, but not universally, attached to the processor by a bus. This is an interface which permits the parallel transfer of data. The number of bits in parallel is known as the bus width. The bus width is not necessarily the same as the minimum logically addressable unit of storage. It follows that if one byte is requested, then two or more bytes may be transmitted to the processor. The wider the bus, the faster the processor may run, since it is delayed less often waiting for data.

42.7.3 Boundaries

One practical consequence of the bus width being greater than the minimum addressable unit is that wider entities may have to start on specific byte boundaries. Thus, in some machines, instructions and integers must be stored at even addresses, while real numbers occupying four bytes must start on addresses divisible exactly by four. The consequences of this arbitrary rule may be unexpected and undetectable errors.

42.7.4 Paging

Analysis of the behaviour of executing programs shows that neither all the program nor all its data need to be available all the time the program is executing. Paging is a mechanism which allows a program to execute correctly even if not all of its code and its data are resident (Denning, 1970). The hardware detects when a reference is made to an address which is not available in

physical memory, it suspends the executing program and then makes available that (portion of the) program or data from an external device, and the program execution may then continue.

This process makes certain demands on the hardware. It must be able to detect references to 'missing' addresses and to map logical addresses to physical addresses. It is also essential to be able to restart instructions which have been partially executed. This latter criterion has proved to be difficult to meet in the case of variable length instruction sets and in the case of auto-incrementing registers. It is not always easy to undo those steps which have been completed before the missing memory is detected.

Paging was originally used to fit a large program into a small physical memory. Subsequently it has been used to share a relatively large physical memory between several users, none of whom would have been able to address all the memory.

42.7.5 Cache

Because there are hierarchies of memory, where the fastest is the most expensive, the concept of caching has been developed to take advantage of the fast memory without excessive expense (Smith, 1982). The concept works for much the same reason that paging does. Practical experience shows that only a small part of a program or its associated data is active in any particular time slot. Cache memory is used to store recently accessed data and instructions to provide high-speed access. The memory access process looks to see if data is present in the cache before it accesses the main memory. Different manufacturers implement the process each in their own way; the only effect the user should see is improved performance. The process is built into the hardware and is not under programmer control.

42.7.6 R/w/execute protection

Once the hardware implements the complex addressing mechanisms needed for paging or relocation, it is possible to add checks to each access. These checks are usually implemented on page-sized sections of the address space and can be used to prevent accidental overwriting (read-only access), or software theft, by allowing execute only access. It is also possible to mark pages which have been changed, which is significant in a paging environment as it is unnecessary to write out unchanged pages.

Some systems also provide an 'accessed' flag so the system can establish which code and data pages are currently in active use. Again these mechanisms are usually transparent to the low-level programmer.

42.8 Input/output

In nearly all computer systems it is essential to communicate with external devices. This is the process known as I/O. Common external devices are keyboard/screen devices, printers, disc drives and tapes. Nearly all external devices are slow in operation compared with the speed of the processor and memory. Details of the interfacing of I/O devices to a computer are given in Chapter 48. Understanding of I/O is very important as much low-level programming is concerned with peripheral interfacing either exclusively or as part of its task.

42.8.1 Privileged = protected

It has become customary for the vast majority of programs to perform I/O using the facilities provided by an operating system. When privileged instructions are implemented they are used by the operating system to try to provide protection from erroneous I/O operations. Normally, the programmer will access these facilities by calling executive, or supervisor, facilities.

42.8.2 Addressing devices

External devices are assigned addresses. These may be either part of the logical address space or specific I/O port addresses. Such addresses are usually determined by external hardware and as such often assigned conventionally. Whichever method is chosen it is necessary to be able to send commands, read status and transfer data to and from a device. All processors implement mechanisms to achieve this.

42.8.3 Interrupts and polling

Because external devices are slow and unpredictable as to when they have data available, it is necessary to have a mechanism to know when they need attention. There are two principal methods (Chapter 48 Section 48.4).

The first is polling (Stone, 1982). In a polling regime, the controlling program periodically scans the devices which might have some action to report. The status of the device is interrogated and if action is needed, for example, to transfer in the latest keystroke such action is taken. It is important to ensure that the devices are polled often enough to prevent the loss of data and that the control program does not get into a loop and fail to poll at all.

The second method is interrupts (Stone, 1982). In this case, when a device wants attention it raises a hardware flag which alerts the central processor. When the processor acknowledges that flag it interrupts what it is doing, and invokes an interrupt-handling routine. The processor can only accept interrupts at certain points in its execution cycle; RNI time is usual. (Effectively interrupts are techniques for polling at the hardware level where it can be carried out more efficiently.) The processor must have the ability to inhibit further interrupts so that enough of the machine state can be saved so that the process interrupted can be restarted correctly.

The detailed implementation of interrupts varies widely. Some processors have only one interrupt and the handler must identify the interrupting device, others have so-called vectored interrupts where each device invokes its own appropriate handler. Interrupts do not provide a totally secure mechanism to avoid data loss as the interrupt-handling system may be turned off when some crucial event occurs. It is usual for there to be special hardware to handle the priorities of two simultaneous events and to queue those which are pending.

The design of interrupt handlers is rather complex. It is important to ensure that the interrupt system is disabled for as short a period as possible to reduce the risk of data being lost. The handling code must preserve the environment so that it can restore it after handling the interrupt. Broadly, the choice is between completely servicing the interrupt in the handler, or queuing it so that it can be handled later. There is also a problem in loading the interrupt vector with the address of the handler. Some operating systems provide a mechanism to allow the user to provide his own handlers. In such cases there is usually a detailed set of rules to observe to ensure that the overall integrity of the design is maintained.

42.8.4 DMA

When relatively large amounts of data are transferred in a block, e.g. a disc sector or a magnetic tape record, at a fairly high speed, then a device known as a direct memory access controller may well be used (see Chapter 48 Section 48.5). The principle is straightforward; the DMA device is given the position of the data in memory, its length and the device

concerned. It then takes bus cycles to transfer the data directly to memory without going through the central processor at all. An interrupt occurs when the transfer is complete or an error occurs. There are problems in specifying addresses as the cycle stealing process may well bypass any memory protection or relocation hardware. This is a particular problem in time-sharing systems. In such systems a user may have to wait for I/O completion, and another user gains control of the processor. It is very important that the memory concerned with the I/O process is not re-allocated as the DMA is running autonomously.

Sophisticated device controllers may support gather-read and scatter-write. In this case a contiguous disc record is created by reading from different memory areas. The process is reversed on writing back to memory.

42.9 Traps

Traps are internal interrupts. External interrupts are triggered by external events. Traps are caused by internal conditions created by hardware or software. Again traps affect the programmer primarily because he or she may have to handle traps caused by his (or other) programs. Typically traps are 'seen' as interrupts by low-level programs.

1. *Short-call mechanism.* Some processors implement traps as a concise calling mechanism. This can save space if they are used to invoke frequently used services from the operating system. There is also the advantage that the invoking program does not need to know the addresses of the invoked service. This allows a new version of the operating system to be implemented without any change being needed to application programs.
2. *Illegal instructions.* Not all patterns of bits form 'legal' instructions, i.e. defined instructions. Some processors detect this condition and execute an illegal instruction trap.

   Illegal instruction traps can also be used to support missing instructions so that, for example, software floating point emulation code can be automatically entered.
3. *Data errors.* Data errors such as parity faults or division by zero can cause traps.
4. *Paging problems.* A page trap is generated by a reference to a page non-resident in memory. If the system supports demand paging, i.e. it will read from disc the missing portion and carry on, then the instruction so interrupted may be partially complete. This causes considerable difficulties in the design of processors and there are many examples of errors in processor design in dealing with page faults.
5. *Power failure.* For a short time after a power failure in the external supply the processor can still execute. If there is standby power for the memories or core memory it is possible to shut the machine down in orderly fashion so that it can restart properly.
6. *Bootstrapping/IPL.* Many processors can detect an external reset signal; this causes a trap which in turn executes a power up initial program load sequence. This start-up code must be held in some permanent memory, e.g. ROM.

42.10 Pipe-lining/instruction caching

In the constant search for processor speed many machines implement 'pipe-lining' (Stone, 1987; van de Goor, 1989). Using this technique the processor decodes several instructions at a time, the decoding of each being started before the first has finished. Interrupts and jumps cause problems but this overlap does give a speed increase.

Another technique is to hold instructions in a special instruction cache memory. This enables short loops of code to be executed without any instruction fetches from main memory, and thus produces speed improvements.

In both cases the programmer needs to have intimate knowledge of the machine to use the mechanisms safely and efficiently.

42.11 Other architectures

The overwhelming majority of computers in use are based on the above principles. There are other ways to design computers:

1. *P-code machines*. One example of such an approach is to build a machine to do in hardware what is more often done by software. The USCD Pascal system compiles into an intermediate language known as p-code (Nori *et al.*, 1981; Woodman, 1988). This is usually interpreted by software, but processors have been built to execute it directly.
2. *Parallel machines* (Hwang and Briggs, 1986). Most parallel machines are groupings of independently executing von Neumann machines which cooperate on a single task. There are also machines, with array processors, which will perform the same operation simultaneously on all the elements of an array. Details of some of these other architectures are given in Chapter 47, Section 47.5.

42.12 Assemblers and the properties of macro assemblers

In practice most low-level programs are written in assembler. The programmer therefore needs to understand the characteristics of assemblers, as well as the underlying machine. This section summarizes the characteristics of the common forms of assembler.

42.12.1 Basic assembler

Programs written using the mnemonic order code of a particular machine are said to be written in assembler or assembly language. Each processor has its own machine code and associated assembly language, even though some manufacturers try to conceal the fact and persuade users always to program in some higher level language. There are various important characteristics of assemblers (Barron, 1969):

1. *One-for-one*. An assembler allows (or forces!) the programmer to specify each machine instruction individually. This is known as one-for-one.
2. *Syntax*. Most assemblers allow one statement per line. The format is:

LABEL OP-CODE OPERAND Comments

The fields are conventionally separated by at least one blank character. Not all fields have to be present in each statement.

3. *Labels*. Labels are mnemonics which can be associated with instructions and with data. For most assemblers the syntax of labels is that they always start with an alphabetic character. The length of the name depends on the system. Sometimes the name can be long, but only the first few characters are significant. The number of characters allowed in external names, for intermodule communication, is nearly always restricted to six or eight characters. Some-

times $_ and a few other punctuation marks are allowed in a name as well as alphabetic and numeric characters.

Labels are always the first field on a line. There are two common conventions in use. The first is that a field starting in column 1 is a label; the other is that labels are terminated with a colon. This second convention permits multiple labels to be specified on a single statement.

4. *Mnemonic op-codes*. Associated with each instruction in the order code is a mnemonic 'op-code'. Conventions vary, but many systems provide mostly three-letter combinations for each operation. This is not a universal practice. It is the common intention that these letter groupings are meaningful, hence the term mnemonic.
5. *Pseudo ops, comments, lay-out*. In addition to the op-codes which correspond to machine instructions there are usually pseudo-ops. These allow the format of the print-out to be specified, storage locations to be allocated or labels to be assigned to constant values.
6. *Operands*. The third field is the operand field. What this contains is specific to the operation specified in the op-code. It is commonly an address or a constant (also known as a literal value or just literal). The operand can sometimes be modified; indirection or indexing may be specified. Sometimes there may be two fields if the instruction needs both a source and a destination address. It is customary to separate the sub-fields of the operand with commas.

Some limited assembly-time arithmetic capability may be provided on the operand field.

7. *Comments*. The final field on a line is taken to be a comment. Comments are ignored and appear in the file and on listings simply as explanations. Some assemblers require the end of the instruction to be marked with a special character e.g. ; (semicolon). Where this is not the convention an * (asterisk) in column 1 is often used to indicate that the entire line is to be treated as a comment.
8. *Constants*. Facilities are provided for defining constants of all the data types supported, i.e. chars, bytes, integers and reals.

In the case of bytes and integers, especially because they may be used as masks and flags rather than as numbers, it is usual to allow specification of constants in terms of single bits, or in octal, decimal and hexidecimal notations.

Constants can be given a mnemonic name and can often be constructed using assembly time arithmetic and logical operations.

9. *Storage allocation*. Labels can be given to storage locations and blocks of storage. A frequent pseudo-op is block storage start (BSS). In this case the operand is the number of words to be allocated. Zero is permitted which gives a mechanism for multiple labels at a single location in those cases where it is impossible to specify multiple labels on a single line.
10. *Code and data separation*. It is generally desirable to separate code and data storage explicitly and some hardware provides facilities to achieve this. Assemblers supporting these hardware features allow a single program text to be divided into 'Psects' (program sections) and 'Dsects' (data sections). These are loaded separately and the allocation is handled by the loader.

42.12.2 Intermodule communication

Assembly programs lend themselves to modular organization. It is often the case that such programs have to interface with compiled code written in higher level languages. The output of all the different language processors must be expressed in a common relocatable binary language. The crucial point for communication is the concept of entry points and external references. A module can declare one or more of its labels as an entry point. Other modules can declare references to be external. There must be only one entry point declaration of a name but it can be used as an external reference by all the other modules in the system.

In most assembly systems this produces a two-level naming structure. References are either global or local. Some more issues in intermodule communication are discussed in the next section.

42.12.3 Assembly time arithmetic and logic for addresses and data

Constants can be constructed using assembly time arithmetic and logical operations. Not only does this give mnemonic significance to the value, but allows automatic recalculation of that value if one of the component values changes.

Address arithmetic is also possible but it must be noted that while two addresses can be subtracted to provide a constant difference, it is not possible to add two relocatable addresses.

42.12.4 Conditional assembly

An extremely powerful feature of an assembler is a conditional assembly option. By no means all assemblers support such a feature.

Basically, what is provided is a set of 'pseudo-ops' to give an 'if ... then ... else ...' capability. Some value or relationship may be tested and depending on its logical truth or falsity one set of statements will be assembled rather than another.

The capability applies not only to code producing statements but may be used so that, for example, one constant value is used rather than another or one form of data structure is defined rather than another.

Some assemblers allow nesting of conditionals while others implement only a single level.

42.12.5 Macros

A macro (Cole, 1981; Brown, 1975) in this context is a text body into which textual substitutions may be made at assembly time. Once defined it looks like any other op-code. Indeed, it may even be used to redefine an existing order. This contrasts with one-for-one assemblers as a macro instruction may translate to several real machine instructions.

Macros are sometimes provided to simplify the use of operating systems facilities invocation. They may be used to enforce conventions on the accessing of data fields, or in calling procedures and setting up parameter lists.

When invoked, the parameters, which are in the operand field, are substituted textually for the equivalent formal (or dummy) parameters of the definition. The connection between formal and actual parameters is positional.

Macros in some systems can be nested in their expansion so that a macro definition can contain other macros.

It is often the case that the macro expansion can itself be conditional on the number of parameters, so that procedure calls with variable parameter lists can be handled correctly.

42.13 Intermodule communication

From the preceding text it can be seen that there is a rich set of addressing modes which any particular processor may support. A frequent task of the programmer is to write an 'interlude' code section to provide an interface between two modules compiled by different compilers, and probably written in different languages. The need for the interlude code is a result of each compiler designer choosing to use the addressing system in a different way and choosing to represent data in different ways.

What is common to all calling sequences is the need to be able to store a 'return address' so that, when the called module has completed its task, it can then return to the calling program at the correct point. Most modern processors achieve this by pushing the return address onto a stack. It is in the form of an address stored on the stack that one difference between long and short calls manifests itself. This implies that there is a hardware-supported stack and that the user has allowed sufficient space for the stack to grow to save this return address. It is important to realise that the act of making the call has the side-effect of changing the stack pointer. Usually the stack is not used in the strict LIFO way, which allows access only to the top element, but to provide for dynamic local storage. Most languages support the convention that local storage is allocated to a routine when it is called and that it is relinquished at module termination. This implies the existence of a stack frame, a template defining the conventional use of a section of memory. Each level of invoked program will have such a stack frame. There will therefore be conventions so that the local variable space of calling routines can be accessed (see Figure 42.1).

It is often the case that the stack pointer itself cannot be used for accessing stack frame elements, and another register, which will not be automatically altered by the calling hardware instruction, must be explicitly set to contain the value of the base of the stack frame.

This discussion has not included the passing of parameters. Although there are exceptions most languages allow the passing of parameters between modules in one of two ways. Parameters may be passed by value or by reference. Passing parameters by value does not present many theoretical problems. A solution is to place the values on the stack and allow the called routine to address them much as its own local variables. The only complication is passing by value items whose size is not known at compile time or which can be different at each call. Examples of this are strings and arrays. This problem is usually overcome by the use of descriptors which are fixed-size data items describing

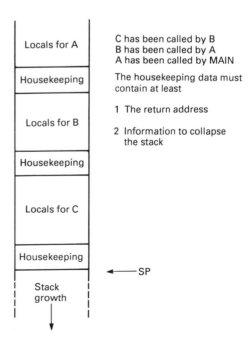

Locals for A	C has been called by B B has been called by A A has been called by MAIN
Housekeeping	The housekeeping data must contain at least
Locals for B	1 The return address
	2 Information to collapse the stack
Housekeeping	
Locals for C	
Housekeeping	◄──── SP
Stack growth	

Figure 42.1 Stack frames

the size and layout of the variable-size data items. Passing parameters by reference is achieved by passing the address of the variable to the called routine. The complications here are two-fold. First, in a segmented addressing scheme it may not be easy to pass the absolute address of a variable which is convention-ally addressed as a register + displacement. The second problem may affect the re-entrancy of the code if the addresses are absolute and not register relative. It is unlikely that the typical low-level program will need to establish its own conventions. The programmer does need to understand the conventions adopted by others, especially compiler writers.

42.14 Conclusions

In practice most low-level programs are written either to inter-face to special-purpose hardware or to interface between pro-grams written in high-level languages. Most low-level programs are written in macro-assembler, and the programmer must be aware of the properties of machines outlined above in order to produce efficient, reliable, modifiable code.

42.15 References

Andrews, M. (1980) Principles of firmware engineering. In *Micropro-gram Control*, Computer Science Press, Silver Spring, Rockville, Maryland, USA

Barron, D. W. (1969) *Assemblers and Loaders*, Macdonald, London

Brown, P. J. (1975) *Macroprocessors and Techniques for Portable Soft-ware*, Wiley, London

Ciminiera, L. and Valenzano, A. (1987) *Advanced Microprocessor Techniques*, Addison-Wesley, Wokingham

Cline, B. (1981) *Microprogramming Concepts and Techniques*, Petro-celli, New York, USA

Cole, A. J. (1981) *Macroprocessors*, Cambridge University Press, New York

Colwell, R. P., Hitchcock, C. Y., Jensen, E. D., *et al.* (1985) Com-puters, complexity and controversy. *Computer*, **18**, 8–19

Denning, P. J. (1970) Virtual memory. *ACM Computing Surveys*, **2**, 153–189

Hwang, K. and Briggs, F. A. (1986) *Computer Architecture and Paral-lel Processing*, McGraw-Hill, New York, USA

Nori, K. V., Ammann, U., Jensen, K., Nageli, H. H. and Jacobi, C. (1981) Pascal-P Implementation notes. In *Pascal – The language and its implementation* (ed. D. W. Barron) Wiley, New York, USA

Smith, A. (1982) Cache memories. *ACM Computing Surveys*

Stallings, W. (1986) *Reduced Instruction Set Computers*, IEEE Com-puter Society Press, Washingon, USA

Stallings, W. (1987) *Computer Architecture and Organisation*, Macmil-lan, New York, USA

Stone, H. S. (1982) *Microcomputer Interfacing*, Addison-Wesley, Read-ing, Mass., USA

Stone, H. S. (1987) *High Performance Computer Architecture*, Addison-Wesley, Reading, Mass., USA

van de Goor, A. J. (1989) *Computer Architecture and Design*, Addison-Wesley, Wokingham

Woodman, M. (1988) The p-System. In *Operating Systems* (ed. L. S. Keller) Prentice Hall, New York, USA

43 Early high-level languages

Brian L Meek
Director of Information Technology
Goldsmiths' College, London

Contents

43.1 Introduction

The development of programming languages has shown gradual trends away from machine dependence and towards greater orientation towards humans – more 'user-friendliness', to use current language. The phrase 'high-level language' originally referred to the first of these, a language not specific to a particular machine architecture. Being more human-oriented came later. However, it is important to recognize that these two trends are distinct, and do not always pull in quite the same direction. It is also important to realise that, while this process has been going on for over 30 years, it is still some way from being completed, and looks set to continue for at least a decade or two more.

The steps taken in this process began with a move from pure machine code to symbolic assembly code, though still with a one-to-one relationship between assembler statements and machine instructions. Then came the addition of extra statements, not directly generating a machine-code instruction, but giving assembler directives, or simply adding comment for the benefit of human readers of the text. Comment remains to this day, which is one indication that the languages themselves are not as fully human-oriented as they might be. Directives also remain, not just in terms of 'pragmas' (assertions to aid program proving, and invocation of compiler options), but in the fabric of the language proper. Type specification statements or declarations are descendants of assembler directives, though admittedly in some languages they do also generate code. For example in FORTRAN, type specification statements are 'non-executable' because they do not generate code directly, but in languages where declarations cause memory to be allocated dynamically when encountered during execution, they do generate code – e.g. to alter the value of a stack pointer – and so are 'executable' in FORTRAN terminology.

So from 'one statement to one machine instruction', languages moved to 'one to one or zero', and the next step was 'one-to-many'. The direct relation, in terms of textual sequence, between what one could now begin to call 'source code' and machine instructions still remained, but some source code statements expanded into several instructions.

An instance of this is the relatively short-lived emergence of 'autocode' as 'high-level assemblers' in the mid-1950s. For example, in Ferranti Pegasus autocode one could write

v1 = v2 + v3

instead of

LOAD v2
ADD v3
STORE v1

This example also displays an element of human-orientation, by the use of conventional infixed notation for dyadic mathematical operations.

One-to-one assembler instructions still lurk not far beneath the surface of many current high-level languages. The unconditional GOTO which many languages retain, despite two decades of vilification, is an obvious example. One-to-many mappings also exist, in forms such as simple conditional GOTOs, surviving curiosities like the FORTRAN statement function, and more sophisticated macro facilities.

Use of single infixed operators, as in the Pegasus autocode example, was quickly followed by use of more general arithmetic expressions, with the development of algorithms to convert conventional-looking mathematical expressions with infixed operators to a form more suitable for translation into conventional, sequential, machine instructions. That form is often known as 'reverse Polish' for historical reasons, but is more usefully and descriptively termed 'postfixed'. The postfixed form of $(a + b)$ is $(ab +)$ and that of $(a - b)/(a + b)$ is $(ab - ab + /)$.

It is interesting to note that direct use of postfixed form survives in the fringe areas of high-level languages on the borders with assembly language, most notably in the language Forth.

Although it can be seen that conversion of a postfixed expression into a sequence of machine instructions is fairly straightforward, already one has moved a long way beyond simple one-to-many assembler or autocode statements. The sequence of symbols–operands and operations–changes greatly. Furthermore, one is not talking of one statement, but of an indefinite and potentially unlimited set of expressions of arbitrary complexity. In effect one has crossed the boundary between simple one-to-many conversion, into a more general form of translation in which any obvious relationship between the sequence of symbols in the source code and the corresponding machine code instructions has disappeared.

For simplicity we shall call this form of translation 'compilation', while recognizing that variations such as 'interpretation' and use of intermediate code exists and that the strict definition of compilation is more specific. For this discussion, the differences between strict compilation and other forms of translation are unimportant. (It can be noted that postfixed expressions can be regarded as an embryonic form of intermediate code, albeit an abstract one.)

Once the direct link between source code form and a sequence of machine instructions has been broken for arithmetic expressions, it is a short step to break that link for other computational processes. The first *successful* high-level language, for production rather than experimental purposes, was designed to bring to scientists and engineers the benefits of being able to write arithmetic expressions in programs in a fairly natural way, as its name FORTRAN (FORmula TRANslation) implies. However, although FORTRAN retained many assembler-like features only very thinly disguised (and indeed retains them to this day) it also exhibited features reflecting the new-found freedom from the constraints of the eventual machine instructions. The design of programming languages was not to look back – or at least, not very much.

Thirty years later, FORTRAN remains one of the main programming languages of the world. It has developed, certainly, and FORTRAN 8X (being finalized as this is written) is a major development, but is still recognizably the same language. There are many reasons for the continued use of FORTRAN – some good, some debatable, some definitely bad. However, one reason must be the scale and nature of the benefits which FORTRAN delivered in usable form, compared with what had gone before, to its target users. Later languages offered further benefits, certainly, but for many those benefits are marginal, or seem so.

Early FORTRAN users found themselves in a land of milk and honey, compared with what they were used to, so they settled down to enjoy it. Later came news that elsewhere there were lands with more milk, sweeter honey, not to speak of new flavours unimaginable unless you tried them. Many pioneered onwards, but many did not attempt the journey. The incentive was simply not great enough. It is dangerous to pursue metaphors too far, but the settlers raised their children in the same tradition . . . and FORTRAN remains a main language.

It is worth pausing here to reflect on the possibilities open at this stage. The technique of compilation (as opposed to conversion) had broken the connection between individual source code statements and corresponding machine code instructions. This, in principle, made possible the writing of programs which were machine-independent. That is, when a program was written the characteristics of the machine it would run on could be forgotten. Further, when it ran after compilation, it would work correctly on any machine, subject only to any limitations resulting from machine capabilities such as memory size or ranges of arithmetic. Since machine independence of programming languages would have been achieved, all programs could be written in the same language, and compiled to run on any (large enough) machine.

Because no dependence on machines would be left, the language for programming computers could be developed to be totally human-oriented. The compilers would convert programs into machine terms.

Three decades on, none of these possibilities has been realised. The twin aims of high-level languages, as indicated earlier, have not pulled in the same directions. All programs are not written in the same language. Programs often cannot be written without reference to machine characteristics. The languages, though human-oriented, are not wholly human-oriented – despite claims to the contrary by devotees of particular ones. Perhaps the difference can best be expressed by saying that, while languages are not machine-specific, they remain machine-dependent. This is because, very often, one cannot be sure whether a program will run, or if it does run, what will happen, if it is transferred from one machine to another.

43.2 Machine dependence: data

In the case of data, high-level languages have steadily moved away from the storage associated models inevitable with assembly language, and the concepts of 'abstract data types' and 'strong typing' (to be dealt with in depth later on) have gradually been developed. Nevertheless residues of machine dependence remain.

43.2.1 Arithmetic types

Assembly languages deal inevitably with storage units like machine words or bytes, and the hardware (or in more recent times, microcoded) operations which are permitted on them. However, high-level languages have allowed programmers to refer to integers, reals and so on, and to mathematical operations on them. (Languages designed for real-time applications or for systems implementation of course have had to retain low-level features but they can be regarded as special cases.)

Interestingly, COBOL, designed for business applications, had a different form of abstraction – a PICTURE. Where the programmer's model of data was not of mathematical domains of numbers, but how the entries would appear as figures on balance sheets, invoices, pay slips etc. Nevertheless, there were limitations of the representation of such abstractions in actual hardware, and of compilers to analyse COBOL source code. These limitations meant that programmers could not think wholly in terms of abstractions, but needed to decide whether the abstraction was actually needed in a particular instance, and cited USAGE IS COMPUTATIONAL – a compiler directive permitting internal representation in any convenient form – if it was not.

More mainstream languages, with their more usual arithmetic types, still show traces of machine dependence. Pascal does not have an exponentiation operator (an incompleteness which is the result of hardware limitations) while in contrast C has some extra operators because they map directly onto machine instructions of the PDP/11 on which the language was first developed. The ability to write $i + +$ instead of $i := i + 1$ can be regarded as a useful abbreviation. Equally a way of making the compiler's job easier at the expense of making the programmer aware

of how the operation works inside the machine. Note that Pascal and C are second-wave, not first-wave, high-level languages. There are many more examples of machine dependencies influencing recent high-level programming languages, so this is still a general limitation.

At least such machine-derived aspects of languages do not harm portability of programs, if they are written in ISO Pascal or C – when the standard is finalized. Much more serious is the fact that the ranges and – in the case of real numbers – precision of arithmetic values, are normally not specified in language definitions and standards. A program using only integer data may run correctly on one system but not on another, even though the system's basic power, in terms of speed and memory, is well capable of the job. The reason is just that this system's language compiler supports a narrower range of integers than the first. Worse, another system may run the program but produce incorrect results, because an arithmetic overflow is commonly regarded by language designers as a fault in the program rather than as a limitation of the processor. Hence it is not generally regarded as necessary for language standards to require compilers to signal overflow, or other undesirable events such as an attempt to divide by zero. Where there is no hardware overflow detector the result may be wraparound.

In some cases, of course, the end results will be only subtly rather than wildly different. Thus it may be hard, if not impossible, to tell without exhaustive tests that the results are wrong. All this means that the programmer cannot act on the assumption that this allegedly machine-independent, high-level language is actually machine-independent. At best the requirements of the program will need to be documented; at worst the program must be self-checking, within the scope permitted to it by the languages, systems and standards which ought to render such self-checking unnecessary.

With real number arithmetic one has not just the range problem. The precision of representation of values, and of the results of operations on values of a given precision, are left undefined, or implementation-dependent, or at best implementation-defined (which at least means that somewhere there should be a specification of what actually happens). The very definition of the familiar mathematical operations of addition, multiplication etc. are normally taken for granted, even though they cannot be taken for granted for real numbers when the domain is granulated rather than continuous (see Chapter 8).

Suppose different chains of calculations can be used to calculate each of two values A and B. These mathematically must yield identical results. A simple example is $A = X*Y + X*Z$ or alternatively $A = X*(Y + Z)$. The effect of granularity – which entails rounding or truncation errors – is that the computed values of the two expressions for A may differ slightly, and the longer the chains of computation the greater the difference is likely to be. This can affect more than just the numerical values of final output. For example, mathematically one set of starting data, like the values of X, Y and Z in the simple example above, may imply that $A > B$. However, if the difference between A and B is close to the granularity then one pair of computational chains may yield approximate values $A1$ and $B1$ where indeed $A1 > B1$, but another may yield $A2$ and $B2$ where instead $A2 < B2$. Hence not just numerical results but the entire program logic can fail – much more subtly than in a simple case of arithmetic overflow and wraparound.

43.2.2 Character data types

The position is no better when character data is considered. Standards for character sets with 7-bit representation have been around for many years e.g. ISO 646. In the English speaking world this is normally referred to by the permitted USA national variant, ASCII language definitions and standards commonly define the set of characters needed to form programs, usually without reference to ISO 646, ASCII, or any permitted variant. Additional characters supported by an implementation are normally left system-dependent, as are characters used in comments or character literals. Worst of all, collating sequences for characters are normally left system-dependent or at best only partially defined. This means that even if a program uses and handles only characters from the language's own basic character set (even if this is a subset of ISO 646/ASCII) it still cannot be guaranteed to produce consistent results when moved between systems.

After primitive beginnings, languages now tend to have reasonably complete facilities for handling both individual characters and character strings. Machine-dependence tends to show through, however, with the provision of built-in functions for mapping the available character set to or from a set of integers. These integers are normally identified with the internal machine representation which also of course provide the basis of variations in collating sequences). This provides some level of portability at the cost of the programmer needing to know about and program investigative and manipulative routines to work around the differences between internal representations. This makes extra work and prevents the programmer from thinking and working wholly in the right level of abstraction. This is all for the sake of ignoring the existence of well-established standards for character sets.

The excuse is, of course, that those not needing portability should not be required to sacrifice efficiency, but it is those who do want portability that tend to pay the price. At least FOR-TRAN 77 provided ASCII-based built-in functions as well as system-dependent facilities. The fault is as much that of the hardware designers as the language designers.

43.2.3 Boolean datatypes

Most languages contain, explicitly or implicitly, the concept of logical or Boolean truth values TRUE and FALSE, and logical operations upon them. Most languages have an explicit data type. Some languages only have Booleans implicitly, and generate Boolean values typically through the use of relational operations like >, < etc. on arithmetic or other values, for use in conditionals etc. These languages do not have the full panoply of a data type, so do not include literal values, variables, parameter passing, built-in functions etc.

Some languages have a bit data type, with values 0 and 1 and operations like logical multiplication, addition and negation to stand in place of the logical operations of Boolean types. There is often confusion between the two even though, at the abstract level, they are undoubtedly distinct despite the very obvious mapping which exists from one to the other. This is compounded by further confusion between the values and their representation. There is no reason, at the abstract level, to assume or need to know whether values like TRUE or 1 are stored as single bits, and certainly no need for language definitions or standards to specify that they must be, unless the language is explicitly designed for 'bit-twiddling' applications.

The distinction between logical and bit types is not very obvious at the single value level; the number of things you can do with a type with only two values is fairly limited. Further, it is easy to fall into the trap of assuming that TRUE and 1, AND and *, are merely alternative syntactic representations of the same concept. The difference becomes clearer when aggregates are considered. Masking and shift operations make sense with bit strings but less sense with vectors of Booleans. However, logical values make more sense than bits when appearing in decision tables.

43.2.4 Derived and user-defined types

Early languages presented the user with some pre-defined types and that was all one had to work with. More modern languages allow programmers to define new types, either derived from built-in types or specified separately. Although derived and user-defined types are logically distinct in nature, they tend not to be so clearly distinct in practice because user-defined types are often derived from some base type that exists anonymously in the language. The only difference between this anonymous type and the built-in types is that the former is not available 'up front' but has to be invoked by a user definition.

Pascal, which pioneered user-defined types, at least in major languages, illustrates this well. One can define a new type:

type *colour*: (*red, blue, black, yellow*)

giving not just this set of values but the ordering

red < blue < black < yellow

whether this is meaningful or not. Also, if we need only four variables of this type we can write:

var *player1, player2, player3, player4*: (*red,blue,black,yellow*)

and this instantiation of the anonymous base type is itself also anonymous. The example above is a Pascal enumerated type (so called because one enumerates each specific value). In Pascal we also have – again, whether relevant or not – explicit type conversions between the values enumerated and a contiguous subset of integers from zero. In our case *yellow*, say, maps onto the integer 3. As well as showing that, in the case of Pascal, the term 'enumerated' can be taken in more than one sense, this demonstrates the 'abstraction' involved is really only a very thin veneer over an explicit hardware-related implementation model.

What makes Pascal enumerated types more than just the result of a sprinkling of syntactic sugar over type integer is that the arithmetic operations are hidden. If one does need them for an enumerated type, one has to use the type conversion functions – and then of course one gets all of the operations, whether meaningful or not.

Derived types from actual (named and usable) types may be new types or subset types. In such cases we might write:

type *temperature* **is new** *integer*

or

type *year* **is** *range* [*1950 . . 1999*] **of** *integer*

Values of the derived type are the same as the values of (or the specified subset of values of) the parent type. A minimal provision of such a facility could simply use the name of the type as a documentation aid but have no other implications, e.g. declaring a variable:

temperature *bath*

would be the same as writing

integer *bath*

Further expressions like

bath + 5   or   *bath* + *index*

(where *index* is an integer variable) would be admissible. However, this delivers only cosmetic benefit to the language user and the strong typing approach normally used requires **temperature** and **year** to be logically and syntactically distinct types from the parent **integer** (and of course each other). The implication is that explicit type conversions have to be provided when needed, e.g.

$$bath + \textbf{temperature}(index)$$

The case of literal values is marginal but strict strong typing principles would require *bath* + **temperature**(*5*) as well.

To date, languages providing such a facility at all tend to take the soft option and assume that the derived type inherits all the properties of the parent type. However, multiplying one integer by another makes sense, but multiplying one year by another does not. In the example cited the safeguard is that the result of such an irrational operation would be outside the specified range of the subset type **year** – but this is not true for **temperature**, where the same arguments apply. Adding one year to another or one temperature to another similarly makes no sense (although in other derived types, such as money in pence or weight in grams, the addition would make sense, since the zero of the counting scale is not arbitrary). However, subtracting two years or two temperatures does make sense, although the results are not of type **year** or **temperature** but are (pure?) integer numbers (of years or degrees).

This suffices to show that the primitive concept of type fostered by conventional languages is deceptively simple – indeed, over-simplified. Inheritance of properties – not just ranges of allowable values – of derived types from their parents is a complicated matter. To date languages which have addressed this issue at all have intended to use rather clumsy 'data-hiding' mechanisms. Here modules define derived types which are exported to the outside world. They also explicitly overload the operators intended to remain valid on inheritance, while hiding the actual parent type and the unwanted operations. This is workable but hardly elegant.

43.2.5 Pointer types

The value of an item of a pointer type is not one of a set of data values but a reference to some other item, which may be of any type (or none), including another pointer. At its crudest and most machine-oriented, the value is a machine address – absolute, or relative to the base address of some allocated area of memory. In languages intended for systems implementation or other applications, like real-time, involving machine-level manipulation, pointers are types in their own right. Alternatively, they appear as an anonymous, basic type – machine memory – from which all others are derived. Languages like Carol 66 underline this by allowing arithmetic operations on address values. Pointers are still effectively types in their own right if they are free pointers, able to reference any other object regardless of type. This occurs in weakly typed languages such as PL/I, or so-called (usually misleadingly) 'untyped' languages. Pointers can be regarded as being of a derived type only if they are constrained to reference items of a specified type, which is the case in more modern languages with strong typing features. The language then has potentially as many 'simple' or direct pointer types as it has ordinary data types, including user-defined, derived and aggregate types. Of course it is possible to allow pointers to point to items of pointer type, to as many levels as needed, i.e. indirect pointers.

43.2.6 Union types

A union (or united) type consists of the union (in the set theoretic sense) of two or more existing types; that is, any value

of any of the types forming the union is a value of the united type. Union types are uncommon if the term is used strictly enough to exclude 'casual' unions resulting from *ad hoc* type conversions in weakly typed languages. Of major languages, Algol 68 is the only one to address them seriously – in terms of providing explicit language features to support them.

Union types create numerous problems. One that is relatively easy to resolve concerns ordering. It could logically be argued that a union type is unordered, but it is probably more useful to regard it as partially ordered (using the ordering within the component types of the union). Further complete ordering is possible where, for example, components of the union are types all derived from the same ordered type. More difficult is the question of whether a permitted operation on values of the component types is valid on values of the united type. However, if, for example, the union is of **character** and **integer**, this applies equally to $x + y$ if + means integer addition or character concatenation, or $x*y$ if y if* is a replication operator which might be used in, say:

$$\text{'GO! '*3} \rightarrow \text{'GO! GO! GO!'}$$

That, however, can be dealt with alongside the operation inheritance problem of derived types. Most difficult is the problem of ambiguity of values, e.g. the status of the value *red* in the union type created from the two user-defined types

type *billiards* = (*red*, *white*, *spot*)

type *croquet* = (*red*, *yellow*, *blue*, *black*)

and the resolution of ambiguity in uniting values of pointers at one level with those at another.

Algol 68 avoided the first by not having subset or enumerated types and resolved the second by banning 'incestuous' types where the components of a union were too closely related. Other languages avoid union types or tend to brush them into well-policed corners like input/output. Effectively they present a problem in language design not yet totally resolved.

43.2.7 Aggregate types

In some discussions, aggregate types, also known as constructed or compound types, are also described as derived types. Since the concept of aggregation already contains the idea of building a new type from components of existing types, it is more helpful to reserve the term 'derived' explicitly for simple types which are monolithic or atomic in structure.

To clarify this point and dispose of a common confusion (although slightly anticipating the discussion below on kinds of aggregates), a set which contains only one element is distinct, structurally and logically, from the element itself. Similarly, string of length 1 is distinct from the single items it contains, as is an array with one element from the element, or a record with one field from the field.

43.2.8 Set types

The value of a set type is, strictly, an unordered collection of values drawn from one or more base types, or one type if unions are included. The usual set theoretic operations and concepts can be provided for such types. In most languages set types have to be simulated by the programmer, using other aggregate types such as arrays or lists, and the only major languages supporting them directly are Pascal and its derivative Modula 2. However, in Pascal, as with various other features, the way it is provided is based on a particular machine-oriented model which results in restrictions both on allowed base types and the sizes of sets. Indeed, a notorious shortcoming of many Pascal implementations is the failure to support even a natural requirement like a set of all the available characters. It is to be hoped that Modula 2, once standardized, will be free of such shortcomings.

43.2.9 Lists

A list is a sequence of elements, which may or may not be homogeneous and may include sub-lists. Here the natural concepts and operations are of (total) ordering, and additions or deletion of elements, including list concatenation. Other features can be added, such as indexing the elements. In most conventional languages lists have to be simulated, e.g. using records linked by pointers, or, if even those are not available, arrays. This is clumsy at best, and often inefficient. However, lists are provided in so-called 'list processing' languages, of which by far the best known is LISP, and rule-based languages like Prolog. In LISP the list is so fundamental that all data and control structures are represented in that form. Hence while lists come naturally, many other things come in a clumsy and unnatural way, or in some versions through 'alien' imports.

43.2.10 Strings

A string is a homogeneous list of simple elements, usually indexed, and often confined to character, or characters and bits. With characters normally represented by a single byte (or two or three in the case of large character sets like Kanji), the machine orientation is clear, although some languages put a thicker veneer over it than others, such as identifying a string with a vector of characters, with a special notation. In such cases, the string 'lemon' is regarded as an abbreviation for the vector ['l', 'e', 'm', 'o', 'n']. In C the distinction is made even clearer, using different delimiters for character and string values, so that "x" denotes a character string of length one containing the character 'x'. This avoids type ambiguities of one-element literals that can occur in other languages.

The machine orientation is also revealed by the limited range of operations available. These are usually confined to concatenation and extraction of single elements, or perhaps substrings, which are easy and efficient to implement.

Character strings are provided in most languages, with various fixes of greater or lesser clumsiness to cope with non-printing characters, especially ⟨CR⟩ (carriage return), ⟨LF⟩ (line feed) and ⟨HT⟩ (horizontal tab). Bit strings are much less common, and even then can come with machine-oriented restrictions such as fixed (byte or word) length. PL/I is the only major language to provide a full range of facilities. However, it does not have a Boolean type (or in PL/I rather a Boolean attribute), bit strings of length one doing duty for the truth values. Other languages identify Boolean with bit types, despite the distinctions mentioned earlier, in the sense of providing bit-string operations on arrays of logicals. Pascal provides very explicitly machine-oriented, and machine-dependent, operations for packing and unpacking arrays, where the intent is to provide efficient storage. This is a point that the programmer must be conscious of and deal with, rather than take for granted as high-level abstraction would demand. Some degree of explicit machine orientation is probably inevitable with bit strings, given the applications that are likely to need them.

43.2.11 Arrays

The array is the oldest and most fundamental data structure. It is an interesting case since, although very little removed from an explicit machine model of storage, it also meets very important application needs. Especially in science and engineering, these arise from mathematical concepts like subscripted variables, vectors and matrices. We thus have the happy, and of course not wholly accidental, situation where machine orientation and application orientation are working together and not in conflict.

An array is a homogeneous structure of elements which are accessed individually, or collectively as sub-arrays or slices (cf. sub-strings) by indices. The dimensionality of an array is indicated by the number of subscripts needed to specify an individual element. A one-dimensional array needs only one index and is often called a vector. This does not, however, imply that such a data structure has the properties of, nor can accept the operations of, vector algebra in mathematics. An array needing N indices (or subscripts) to reference a single element is N-dimensional.

Some discussions treat the case $N = 0$ (no subscripts required), implying a non-aggregated value, as equivalent to the base type of the array. This, however, goes against the way that languages treat arrays, which is based on a more or less explicit implementation model. This consists in general of a storage map containing information about the dimensionality (N) and range(s) of subscripts, followed by a contiguous block of storage containing the elements. Some implementation models are much more explicit than this, especially in older languages. For a scalar (base) value to be regarded as an array of dimension zero, which makes sense at the most abstract or mathematical level, the stub of the storage map, with $N = 0$, would still remain in this case. Also, with scalars as arrays of zero dimension one would expect all types to be 'arrayable', which is not the case in most languages. The only major language which contains explicitly the concept of dimensionality zero is APL, which anyway started its life as a mathematical notation. Algol 68 comes closest of the rest, with its 'rowing' coercion (automatic type conversion) converting a scalar into a vector of length one, though the motivation there seemed mainly to cope with distinguishing characters from strings of length one.

Incidentally, some languages, such as Pascal, and some textbook treatments use the term 'scalar' more restrictively, so that, say, a single record, being an aggregate, could not be so regarded even if the language allows arrays of records. (Pascal does not.)

Others, whether or not containing the concept scalar, regard arrays as possible base types for other arrays so that a two-dimensional array is regarded as a vector of vectors, a three-dimensional array as a vector of two-dimensional arrays, etc. With this treatment, $A[i,j]$ is regarded as equivalent to $A[i][j]$, though this does not necessarily imply that the second form is syntactically acceptable. This could be regarded as merely notational convenience were it not that the implied storage model is that the elements of a 2×2 square array **A** would be stored in the order $A[1,1]$, $A[2,1]$, $A[1,2]$, $A[2,2]$ – something which could be of importance in some circumstances.

The implication of a storage map followed by a contiguous block of homogeneous elements is, of course, that the memory address of a specific element can be simply and quickly calculated from the values of the subscripts. In modern systems the addressing is likely to be logical or virtual, rather than physical, with the actual accesses left to the hardware and/or operating system, but the principle is still clear. In the first FORTRAN standard (1966) this consideration was taken even further; an expression representing an actual subscript could be no more complicated than a linear function of a single simple (integer) variable, on grounds of efficient calculation in hardware registers.

Virtually all languages support arrays of elements of simple base types using integers or subscripts. Strictly, the type of an integer subscript is the derived sub-range type between the lower and upper bounds specified but that implies strict index bound checking, which even now not all languages require. Some languages have a default subscript lower bound (usually 1, occasionally 0) but the practice in older languages of a fixed lower bound has largely been abandoned, as has limiting dimensionality to a small number like $N = 2$ or 3.

However, it is still the case that the facility for addressing cross-sections or slices is not widely available. This is true also for operations on complete arrays, apart from input and output. Where such operations are defined in the language they tend to be element-by-element. (A common mistake of mathematically trained beginners, unless warned, is to assume that $\mathbf{A} \times \mathbf{B}$, where $\mathbf{A}$ and $\mathbf{B}$ are both square $\mathbf{M} \times \mathbf{M}$ arrays, is the matrix product instead of the element by element product.) This reflects the single sequential processor provenance of most major languages, and will doubtless gradually change as vector processors, and data flow and other non-von Neumann architectures become more prominent. Thanks to its foundation in mathematics, APL still has the widest array-based facilities of the major languages.

Most languages still adhere to the basic concept that the index type is integer, and for many of the major applications this reflects the need. However, of the well-known languages Pascal introduced the idea of using other types as index types, provided that these were discrete, and exact. Given the mapping to integers which Pascal built in such types, this was cheap to provide but at the same time gave an improvement in language expressiveness and a liberation from implicit assumptions. Nevertheless, the basic picture of an array is that of a block of contiguous elements of one or more dimensions.

43.2.12 Tables

In this discussion a table is like an array, in that its elements are all of the same type, but indexing is not by a necessarily sequential subscript but by a reference value indicating content. The distinction is perhaps best brought out by an example. Suppose the non-integer index type of an array were a 12-element, user-defined enumerated type representing the months of the year, and a vector were produced of the months in which the birthdays of eight people fell. The vector might look like:

Index	Jan	Feb	Mar	Apr	May	Jun	Jul	Aug	Sep	Oct	Nov	Dec
Birth-days	0	0	1	0	2	1	0	1	0	2	0	1

where the index values Jan–Dec are clearly mapped onto the integers 1–12. A table of the same data might look like:

Index	Mar	May	Jun	Aug	Oct	Dec
Birthdays	1	2	1	1	2	1

although this display has been ordered by the natural ordering of the indices. In contrast to arrays, there is no assumption of contiguity. The indexing in a table is indirect whereas that in an array is direct. Of course, an implementor may choose to map a table of the kind in this example directly onto an array, since this may well be more efficient. However, tables have the capability of handling a potentially unlimited number of different index values which it may be hard to specify in advance. An example is counting the number of occurrences of words used in an arbitrary text written in a given character set.

In almost all languages this kind of aggregate has to be simulated by the programmer, with all the indirect addressing provided explicitly, though Snobol, designed specifically for text handling and analysis, does have some facilities of this kind.

43.2.13 Record types

A record is an aggregate consisting of one or more fields that are in general inhomogeneous. Individual fields are referenced by identifiers, known as field selectors or tags. Indexing is inappropriate because of the inhomogeneity. In principle the fields are unordered, although there are clear implementation advantages to keeping them in a fixed order internally so that tags can be identified with fixed address offsets from the start of the record. This concerns the programmer only in that it is possible to exploit it by allowing a list-like notation for a complete record, e.g. ["*John*", *23*, *male*] to represent the value of a record of a (user-defined) type *person* with fields *name* (string), *age* (subtype of integer) and *sex* (user-defined, two-valued, unordered). Such a record would normally have its own identifier, e.g. *trainee*, and a notation provided to select fields, using the tag identifiers. Most languages use a dot or period notation, so that *trainee.age* (or *age.trainee*, depending on the language) would be of type integer (the specified sub-type) and have the value *23*.

Usually fields are allowed to be of any type, including arrays, other records (permitting nested or hierarchical record structures) or pointers (normally to other records). Use of pointers to other records of the same type allows the construction of linked lists, trees, and other general data structures.

Languages vary considerably in the facilities they provide for manipulating records. Some allow record-to-record assignments. In strongly-typed languages the types would have to match. PL/I, being weakly typed, allows assignments between any records of the same size and shape (including nested sub-records) provided any needed type conversions can be performed. (In PL/I they often can!) PL/I also provides a very useful 'by name' assignment between records totally different in size and shape, where assignments are carried out field by field if the field identifiers are the same (and any needed type conversions can be done).

Assignments and other manipulations can always be done at the individual field level, at least if they themselves are not aggregates, but this can get tedious where many fields are involved, even with the help of program text editors. Though not having record-to-record assignment, Pascal has a WITH statement to ease the burden. Within its scope, field identifiers can be used on their own and automatically associated with the specified record.

In PL/I a field identifier can be used unqualified, as a variable name in its own right. However, this is often less useful than might appear at first sight. To exploit it, field names may need to be specified unnaturally to keep them distinct. However, PL/I does not allow user-defined type names, so multiple records of the same kind have to be specified by declaring one and then creating 'clones' by declaring others to be LIKE that one. So when LIKE is used, the field names are automatically duplicated, entailing some form of qualification when using field names.

Finally, while procedures, and possibly modules, may be used to aid manipulation of records in user-defined ways, many languages place restrictions on what can be done, e.g. returning a record as a function value.

Records first appeared in a major language in COBOL because of the obvious need for them in commercial data processing, but their value is now recognized much more widely. Exceptions among major languages include FORTRAN 77 (but FORTRAN 8X will have them) and APL, although APL arrays are so versatile that the need is less acute. One further development needs to be mentioned – that of the variant record. In this case not all records of a given type have the same structure. There is a common part, which all share, and a variant part, which can differ from record to record according to some selection criterion (the equivalent for data of the case construct in control flow). This concept was introduced in Pascal but has not yet found its way into languages generally. Despite its obvious utility for some applications – e.g., for personnel records where the variant part can contain different fields relevant to different categories of staff – there seems to be no generally agreed feeling within the programming language community that this is a successful feature. Clearly it does increase complexity in handling the records, both for implementors and for programmers, although it could be argued that for programmers using the feature, the complexity is there in the application anyway.

43.3 Control constructs

Conventional languages (sometimes called procedural languages) are essentially flow-of-control driven, based upon von Neumann architecture or elaborations thereof. Languages based upon different approaches, such as dataflow languages or rule-based languages, are dealt with elsewhere (Chapter 36).

Control structures in conventional languages reflect this flow-of-control approach to computing and hence to language design. Machine and assembly languages are ordered sequences of commands. The statements, more accurately termed 'commands', of most high-level languages show that evolving relationships between machine instructions and language statements have in most cases still not gone so far as to break with this underlying assumption of sequentiality.

Given the conventional flow-of-control approach, five general kinds of control flow structure can be distinguished: sequential, parallel, branching, looping, and procedural. There is little to be said about sequential flow, since almost all languages based upon the flow-of-control approach take for granted the rule that program statements will be executed in textual order unless another control flow mechanism is explicitly involved. This discussion will therefore concentrate on the other four mechanisms.

43.3.1 Parallel flow

This kind of flow is the most recent to appear in high-level languages because of the previous assumption of single sequential processors. Hence it is here out of chronological sequence, but is more logically and conveniently dealt with first.

Few current major languages have any explicit parallel processing constructs, although some have had them added as later developments (e.g., concurrent Pascal). Simula 67, as a simulation language, contains features to support the simulation of parallelism. It was nevertheless designed for conventional single processors, as was Algol 60, the algorithmic language on which it was firmly based. Algol 60's successor, Algol 68, did have some primitive constructs to support parallelism.

Early real-time languages such as Coral 66 tended, like Simula, to assume a single processor and mimicked parallelism through interrupts. Often these were not specified in the language but provided instead by dropping down into machine code or assembler. It was not until the late 1970s that major, as opposed to experimental, languages began to emerge which contained genuine parallelism.

The most prominent example is Ada, designed to US Department of Defense (DoD) specifications, with particular emphasis on use in embedded, real-time systems. In Ada, parallel tasks can be programmed as separate modules but can be synchronized through the use of a rendezvous mechanism.

The Inmos language occam, which can be regarded equally as an assembler for the Inmos Transputer as a high-level language, takes a different approach. The programmer explicitly specifies whether a given block of instructions is to be executed SEQ(uen-

tially) or in PAR(allel). Viewed side by side, Ada and occam illustrate the wide range of styles and approaches encompassed by the term 'high-level language', as do – in a different way – COBOL and APL. Ada is a complex, feature-rich language, whereas occam is spartan to the point of asceticism. This is perhaps less surprising when the published views on Ada of the principal designer of occam are taken into account!

Parallelism in languages is, at the time of writing, still in its infancy, studied by numerous researchers but not yet subjected to fierce pressure from the needs of industry. It is the most obvious (to the current observer) growth point in the language design because the present means of expressing parallelism have barely been used so far. Language is a means of formulating thought as well as expressing it and there is little doubt that people will think 'parallelly', or at least think non-sequentially, when languages capable of expressing such thoughts are better developed and more widely available.

43.3.2 Branching

Making a decision between one possible course of action and another is a central feature of automatic computation. From the earliest days machine codes had to have 'jump' instructions, both unconditional and conditional. Hence branching is the earliest and most basic form of flow of control in high-level languages.

In the crudest form of branching, various points in the program are labelled in some way, e.g., by numbering or naming statements, so that they can be branched to from elsewhere. An unconditional branch is then achieved by a statement of the form GOTO *label* and a conditional branch by IF condition THEN GOTO *label*. All early languages contained such facilities and most still retain them. Their assembler level derivation is obvious, a label being a thinly-disguised machine address of an instruction and the term 'high-level' is a dubious epithet. FORTRAN had (and still has) a variation, the 'arithmetic IF' where a jump occurs to one of three labels (numbered statements), depending on whether the value of a given arithmetic expression is negative, zero or positive.

One step away from direct machine language association can be achieved by allowing the IF to control statements other than a GOTO. However, a much bigger step is to have the IF control in a group of statements rather than just one. The move from machine orientation is virtually complete by adding an ELSE part – also controlling a group of statements – as an alternative to be used when the IF condition fails. This can readily be mimicked using IFs and GOTOs – indeed, it can be achieved directly in machine code or assembler – but then it is up to the programmer to build the constructs and maintain their integrity. This means that good program design principles must be adhered to so that casual jumping to labelled statements within the groups – so-called 'spaghetti programming' – is avoided. Machine code and IF/GOTO constructs will not help in this respect, whereas high level IF ... THEN ... ELSE constructs do.

Algol 60 provided the ELSE part of the branch. It also first introduced (in a major language) the concepts of 'statement bracketing', where a sequence of statements is turned into a compound statement by use of the statement brackets BEGIN and END, and of 'blocks' (see below). Hence both the IF/THEN and the ELSE of a logical branch statement could be made to control compound statements. This concept rapidly spread to most other major procedural languages, although it was not until 1977 that it entered standard FORTRAN.

For true integrity of such a construct, entry to a compound statement should only be through the BEGIN, i.e., a jump to a labelled statement within the statement brackets is not allowed from outside. This is to say that the scope of a label is confined to within the BEGIN ... END brackets immediately surrounding the statement which it labels. This was not fully recognized in Algol 60, even though the concept of scope of identifiers was central to the design of the language. For integrity of IF ... THEN ... ELSE, the controlled compound statements should themselves not be labelled, or at least the scopes of any such labels should be confined to that construct. That again was not fully recognized at the time.

By analogy with arithmetic brackets, statement brackets can be nested, allowing arbitrarily large and complex constructs to be formed. Algol 60 was the first major example of what became a huge family of so-called 'block structured' languages which exploited this idea to varying extents. Algol 60 was and remains the single most influential high-level language ever designed, through its exploitation of nested blocks as a means of controlling scopes of identifiers, and hence access to the entities they named. It was two decades before the limitations of this approach seriously began to concern many people in the mainstream of the languages community.

It now seems amusing in retrospect, but one of the things which much exercised the programming language world in those days, the early 1960s, was the so called 'dangling ELSE' problem. This arose from allowing nested IF-THEN-ELSE statements, where in a construction of the form:

IF ... THEN IF ... THEN ... ELSE ...

the 'ownership' of the ELSE is potentially ambiguous. The ambiguity does not exist if the ELSE always has to appear, but always requiring an ELSE part even when it was 'empty' was deemed inelegant. Algol 60 solved the dangling ELSE problem by the rule 'IF must not follow THEN', necessitating the use of statement brackets. Other languages, including PL/I and Pascal, used the rule 'ELSE goes with the last (unpartnered) THEN', necessitating an empty ELSE or statement brackets if something different was intended.

The now obvious solution for major languages – an END IF to match the IF – had to wait until Algol 60's (intended) successor, Algol 68, although the AI language Pop-2, now succeeded by Pop-11, had a CLOSE keyword to match the IF a couple of years earlier. Algol 68 spelt ENDIF as FI, which caused much affront in some quarters, rather diverting attention from far more important matters. Chief of these was that, as well as killing off 'dangling ELSE' as a serious problem, the FI effectively turned IF ... FI (ENDIF) into statement brackets. Thus, IF ... THEN ... ELSE ... ENDIF became a nested bracketing construct, hence removing the necessity for BEGIN ... END as part of the IF construct. The virtues were so obvious that even FORTRAN adopted it in the 1977 standard.

Algol 68 went further, in two respects. It took the affinity between statement brackets and expression brackets to its logical conclusion (far too logical for some) by abolishing the distinction between statements and expressions. Hence every statement potentially had a value, of a given mode. This Algol 68 term took the primitive concept of 'type' as referring merely to the kind of data associated with an object and extended it to something more general and powerful, so that constants, variables, arrays, functions etc. of the same data type nevertheless had different modes. (In that respect it was much more akin to the modern concept of an abstract data type than to that of data types at the time.) The consequences were that not just a condition but a sequence of statements (which were also expressions) could be accommodated between the IF and the THEN, provided the end product was a truth value. Further, the IF construct as a whole also had a value – that of the THEN or the ELSE part, depending on which one was chosen.

With some cleverness, Algol 68 thus imported into, and adapted for a procedural language, a key feature of non-procedural expression languages such as pure LISP, just as those languages have often imported procedural devices from conventional languages.

Algol 68 was not totally successful technically in the way that APL, given its very different approach, might be claimed to be, and certainly not successful in winning enough advocates, for reasons which often seemed little related to technical issues. Ensuring that the IF ... FI construct had a value in all cases entailed a rather delicate process called 'balancing', simply because the whole concept of control-flow branching implies that what happens in the two alternative cases of the IF condition succeeding or failing might be totally different. The connotation of tightrope walking and giddiness was sometimes not far away. In various circumstances a construct could not reasonably be deemed to have a value at all, leading to the concept of VOID, which could be viewed either as a special mode, or the absence of one. VOID had a single special value of EMPTY. This could be regarded as a fudge, though perhaps no more so than the empty set in mathematical set theory, or for that matter the zero in ordinary arithmetic. The concept of zero as a numerical value which could be referred to and manipulated was revolutionary, even heretical in its day, but both it and the empty set have long since proved their worth. The concept of an object of void type, as opposed, diametrically, to an untyped object, may yet prove its value.

Branching unconditionally or by truth value is by far the most common form and usually provided as described, though sometimes notionally very different, e.g., in APL. An interesting variant is Snobol, where every statement is deemed to 'succeed' or 'fail', and branching may be specified as a result of either outcome. A rather horrendous variant of GOTO appears in COBOL, where an ALTER verb can be used to ordain that all commands of the form GOTO WORK (say) shall in the future be treated as if they said GOTO BED. An ALTER command buried in an obscure routine was a palaeolithic version of the modern computer virus.

The next most common forms of branching, are multi-way branches determined not by a condition but a value of some non-Boolean type – usually integer. Algol 60 had a switch where the destination of a GOTO was selected by means of index from a list of labels. Spaghetti code of horrendous complexity could readily be constructed, especially since switch definitions could include recursion. PL/I built on this and the COBOL ALTER, by admitting LABEL as a type attribute and allowing arrays of assignable label variables. FORTRAN had computed and assigned GOTOs which were quite modest and secure in comparison.

Modern case select mechanisms began to come on the major languages scene with, again, Algol 68 and Pascal. By analogy with IF ... THEN ... ELSE ... FI, Algol 68 had CASE ... IN ... OUT ... ESAC. Between the IN and the OUT was a list of simple statements/expressions (though these of course could be larger constructs in brackets) separated by commas. These were implicitly numbered 1,2,3 etc. and the chosen one was selected by the integer value delivered by the value computed (again in general by a sequence of statements) between the CASE and the IN. If the value delivered were outside the implied range (1 to the length of the IN list) the sequence between the OUT and the ESAC was chosen instead.

Pascal varied from this in ways other than just syntactically (OF for IN, END for ESAC, semicolons instead of commas to separate the alternatives). Not sharing Algol 68's view of bracketing, it allowed only an expression after the CASE though as with index selectors for array elements, any discrete scalar type could be used. For example, a user-defined enumerated type, or character type could be used as a selector. Despite the in-built mapping of such types onto integers, the various choices did not have to be given in order, but instead were labelled by selector values. In view of the absence of a defined collating sequence for character type this was probably just as well, but it had two further virtues. First, it was more readable, and, second, if the same action were required in more than one case it could be shown just once (not repeated as in Algol 68) labelled with all of the relevant values.

However, Pascal had no equivalent of the OUT, which meant that all possible values of the selector had to be shown. The action if the selector value was different was undefined. Pascal's enumerated and sub-range types could be used to limit the problem, but it was still a drawback. It was not until Ada that most of the better case select features of both earlier languages were exploited.

43.3.3 Loop constructs

Loop constructs can be regarded as even more fundamental to computing than branch constructs, if only because of the relative cost–benefit ratios between getting a computer to perform a simple task iteratively and getting it to take a complex sequence of decisions. The importance of iterative processes will be reduced by parallel processing, especially when the ready availability of parallelism leads to the development of new parallel algorithms. There is an analogy with the availability of sequential machines which led to the development of iterative algorithms in preference to the 'one-shot' algorithms more suited to hand computation.

Nevertheless, even when this and the growth of non-algorithmic languages are both taken into account, iterative constructs in conventional procedural languages are likely to remain of importance for a good time yet.

At the machine code level, loops can readily be constructed by the use of conditional and/or unconditional jumps. Where the jump to continue the loop is backwards in the sequence of instructions and to the exit is forwards, beyond the range of the loop. This is easy to simulate in simple high level languages with IFs and GOTOs, albeit with the same weaknesses and insecurities as are present at the machine level.

Oddly, the commonality of approach to mainstream aspects of computing, such as branching, found in most conventional high-level languages does not extend to loop constructs. Many variations exist at a more fundamental level than synctactic expression and skirmishes still break out from time to time between supporters of different styles. Part of this can be attributed to the past need for sequential iteration to fill the gap left by the absence of parallelism, but once this is allowed for, unresolved differences remain. The discussion that follows applies when the cyclic nature of the computation in a loop is inherent, rather than merely the consequence of having to do the same thing a number of times using a sequential rather than a parallel machine.

In this case it is worth taking a more general, top-down approach to the question of loop constructs than has applied hitherto. Ignoring for the moment the possibility of nested or multiple loops, the most general form of loop consists of a cycle with multiple entries and multiple exits, rather like a traffic roundabout met by a number of one-way streets.

The smallest number of both entrances and exits is theoretically zero. A loop with no entrances is not very interesting (and not a problem, however specified), so it does no harm to assume at least one entrance. Most loops need some initialization anyway. However, loops with no exits definitely exist, especially for real-time control applications where, once set up, the loop should continue to operate indefinitely, until the process is interrupted by some external agency: operator action, the power failing, the machine wearing out, etc. Some languages contain such facilities explicitly, e.g. Ada and Algol 68, whereas others

leave it to the programmer to use a simple backward GOTO – which at the machine-language level is all it comes to.

Multi-entrance loops can be created by GOTOs but within major high-level languages a single entrance, via a keyword (such as DO, FOR, REPEAT etc.), is virtually universal. APL is different, as usual, but almost everything one might wish to do with loops can be done in APL by using operators – 'functions' as APL prefers to term them. This does, admittedly, sometimes require a certain amount of ingenuity.

This common practice of a single entrance is a consequence of the conventional sequentiality of written text as much as it is of the sequentiality of processors. Of course, in the outer program surrounding the loop, one can always use some construct or another to reach the entrance from several different points in the program. However, as far as the loop is concerned, all processes start at the one entrance.

Given that there is a single entrance, what of the number of exits (assumed non-zero)? The received wisdom of structured programming is that 'single entrance single exit' loops are best since this facilitates the testing of the loop as a single entity. However, it is important to be clear about what 'single exit' means.

Maverick jumps to any accessible label in the surrounding program are clearly excluded (though most languages permit them). What should be made of EXIT statements which transfer control from anywhere in the text of the loop to where the 'actual' exit is? This is equivalent, in the traffic roundabout analogy, of cutting across the central reservation. Viewed from the outside, there is still a single exit, at the textual end of the loop construct, so that the loop can still be regarded as a single entity as far as testing is concerned. However, some purists, or ascetics, argue that a mid-cycle EXIT is analogously dangerous to cutting across a traffic roundabout and should be outlawed accordingly.

Not surprisingly, given these differences of view, different languages resolve these issues in different ways. It often comes down to how the language designers resolve the trade-offs between safety and convenience.

This by no means exhausts the issues surrounding loop constructs, even for the apparently simplest generally useful case of single-entrance, single-exit, single-level (non-nested) loops. One concerns the placement of the single exit in relation to the entrance – immediately after, immediately before, or wherever. Another concerns the number of times a loop is executed and how to control it. The variety of loop constructs in languages reflects differing views of the issues – or, rather, differing priorities between various needs.

The earliest loop mechanisms were conceived in terms of performing the same operation repetitively on each of the elements of an array. Almost inevitably this led to the concept of a 'control variable' to determine progress through a loop, with this variable being closely associated, if not identified, with the index of the relevant array. However, it became rapidly apparent that the concept of repetition – whether or not to ape parallel processes on sequential machines – was far more fundamental to automatic computation than the mere manipulation of array elements.

This was indeed clear even before high-level languages started coming in. Nevertheless, it has been taking a long time for realisation of this to be reflected in languages. The fact that an array is a data structure of major application importance, despite its primitive nature, is presumably a factor in this.

For array handling applications where it is necessary for an index to step through a sequence of values, practice varies between languages from having a loop construct with an explicit control variable, to a more general form where a control variable can be specified if required, with the explicit form being more common. Even here practice varies. In some cases the control variable is confined to that role; in others it is an ordinary variable. The latter is useful if, say, one wishes to carry out of the loop the index value of an element with a particular property that the loop has searched for. The former is more secure but can lead to some clumsiness if an index value is to be preserved.

Although an index is 'naturally' an integer, some languages permit control variables of type real. This has the danger of cumulative errors as the number of increments increases. Of course Pascal allows any discrete type, as it does for array indices, but confines the size of the increment to the value of one (upwards or downwards) or the equivalent in non-integer types (immediate successor or predecessor). It is probably this use of enumerated and other types to control loops that caused in Pascal the restriction for integers to a step length of 1, since anything else would be likely to lead to some rather messy syntax.

Another matter concerns whether the language permits the increment and final value of the control variable to be altered by the code in the body of the loop. For very good and obvious reasons of security, languages have increasingly tended to prohibit this, by various syntactic and semantic means.

One immediate variation of the control variable incremental loop is to make the variable itself implicit rather than explicit if it is not specifically needed in the loop for indexing or other purposes. Examples are COBOL's DO N TIMES, which covers the majority of cases very simply, and Algol 68's rather more flexible but perhaps less graphically expressed method. Here the starting value, finishing value and increment of the control variable can all be specified but the variable itself remains anonymous.

Most control variable loops are of the type where the termination condition 'has the control variable reached or gone beyond its limit value?' is tested on initial entry. This means that the actual loop body may on occasion not be executed at all, e.g. in FOR $i := 1$ TO n DO in Pascal when $n < 1$. This seems to make sense but there was certainly a school of thought in the early days, persisting until quite recent times in some areas, that it was wrong to require the computer to go to the trouble of setting up a loop if it was not to be executed at all, i.e., the 'zero trip loop' should banned. However, zero trip in such cases is undoubtedly the norm.

This can be regarded as a special case of the single-entrance, single-exit loop where the one exit is immediately after the one entrance. The more general form of this kind of loop is usually known as the DO ... WHILE loop, i.e., 'Do what follows WHILE the following condition holds', the implication being that if the condition fails at the outset the loop is not executed at all. Many procedural languages have this in some form or another.

Pascal provides not just the incremental loop and the DO ... WHILE loop but a REPEAT ... UNTIL loop, i.e., 'REPEAT what follows UNTIL this condition is satisfied'. The roundabout model would show this as the single exit appearing immediately before the single entrance, i.e., the loop will always be executed once before the condition is tested. Not many other languages provide this explicitly, perhaps indicating that the zero-trip 'issue' was not really much of an issue.

Issues that do still remain, however, are the number of exits allowed (in the sense of jumps to the one-textual-exit from places textually or logically remote from the end of the loop body), and whether a single exit can be anywhere other than immediately before or after the single entrance. Algol 68 bravely tried to unify all possibilities, particularly to allow the second possibility, though in a way which was never syntactically convincing. A cruder, less structured, but perhaps more effective way is to have an indefinite loop (unconditional DO ... END DO or the like) with one or more EXITs (or, rather, EXIT IFs)

placed in the loop body wherever required. That does exist in one form or another in some languages.

This discussion perhaps indicated why there is such a variety of loop constructs in current major languages and still no settled consensus on some of the issues raised. It also explains why not too much space could be devoted to giving examples of 'typical' constructs! However, one issue still remains – the question of nested loops.

In fact, nested loops do not cause a great problem apart from the question of exits. Should an EXIT other than a 'normal' one (i.e., normal exhaustion of index values or whatever) exit only from the loop in which it occurs, i.e., control is transferred to the next level up, or be free to terminate several levels at once? The argument for the former is that the same result as normal exit is more logical and often what is needed anyway. The argument for the latter is that an 'emergency' in an inner loop probably means that one wants to stop the whole process. A counter-argument is that one cannot always assume that, and what does one do if one wants to continue the outer loop? A third suggestion is that people should be given the choice, but then we are talking about labels and the syntax becomes messy ... Further ramifications can be left to the imagination but this is sufficient to explain why there is no real underlying consensus about how to cope with loop control.

There are some who would argue that this demonstrates that the procedural approach to programming languages must be inadequate and fatally flawed, and that coping with something so fundamental as looping must therefore entail looking at computation in a different way rather than trying to devise better procedural syntax. There are others (apart from those who try to devise better syntax) who would argue that the complexity is inherent in the problem domain and the many possible applications of looping so it cannot simply be removed or obviated. As ever it is probably this last argument that will hold sway until (or unless) someone proves them wrong, whether with a brilliant stroke of procedural syntactic genius, or an effective and comprehensive new approach to the whole area.

43.3.4 Blocks, procedures and modules

The last form of control flow structure in conventional algorithmic-based languages is best described generically as procedural but is conveniently dealt with under the sub-headings of blocks, procedures and modules since the concept of a procedure contains a variety of implications. These map more conveniently (though in some cases by no means exactly) onto the constructs available in actual languages. They also make it possible to separate issues more distinctly.

43.3.4.1 Blocks

In itself a block is not a control flow structure at all, since any change in flow is determined externally to it, but it is worth considering in its various forms because it represents an important stage in the transition from individual statements. The simplest block does no more than parcel together some statements, enabling them to be treated as a single, but compound, entity. Conventionally such a block consists just of a sequence of statements, but letting them be parallel, or a mixture of sequential and parallel, makes no material difference. Most languages display this concept in one form or another even if they do not have the explicit BEGIN ... END statement brackets of Algol 60, or their equivalent. The parcelling has the conceptual if not logical effect of separating off a section of program and giving it, in however tenuous a form, an individual identity.

The next step in separating a block from its environment is to add the concept which might be called (albeit grandiosely) 'access integrity', restricting access to the block to a single entrance – the BEGIN or its equivalent – as already described above. However, this means making GOTO destinations (labels) local to the block, which is merely a special case of making user-defined entities local to the block. If entities are to be referenced, internally or externally, they need identifiers of some kind, so effectively this means limiting the scope of identifiers to the particular block in which they appear. This can be done either implicitly or explicitly. The implicit approach may, for example, be appropriate for GOTO destination labels, since it hardly makes sense to have duplicate labels in the same block and the repetition is easy to detect. The explicit approaches is to have declarations local to the block. This was the line taken in the pioneering and influential language Algol 60, in which the term 'compound statement' was used for parcelling statements and the term 'block' reserved for the case where there were internal declarations whose scope was confined to the block. Many other languages, with variations, have since followed this pattern.

The next issue, perhaps of no great importance on its own but certainly so in conjunction with others, concerns whether a block is open or closed. An open block can include references not only to entities which are within its own scope but to those within the scope of any surrounding block, subject only to name clashes.

This is the classical block-structured pattern adopted by Algol 60 and its many derivatives. However, this assumes a nested block structure. In some languages blocks can be disjoint, in which case the question arises as to whether access to data is global, or local, or can be either. In COBOL the structure of the procedure division is a sequence of paragraphs, which are blocks of a kind, but the data defined in the separate data division is shared globally. In FORTRAN 77, which is not block-structured either, the separate program units are disjoint and symbolic names (i.e. identifiers) and labels are local. Hence by default access to data is local, and data can only be shared by parameter passing in a procedure calling mechanism, or by specifying that data is to be held in COMMON. This FORTRAN concept of COMMON storage, a shared data area, is very machine-oriented and there is no data typing association. Indeed, another of the ideas behind COMMON was that, as well as allowing data sharing, it could be used to allow the same area of storage (then scarce and expensive) to be re-used for different purposes. This is something a simple dynamic stack implementation method for a block-structured language takes care of automatically.

Getting the FORTRAN COMMON storage associations right is entirely the programmer's responsibility, which has led to untold numbers of faults in FORTRAN programs. About the only aid a programmer has is a special BLOCK DATA program unit, the sole purpose of which is to permit areas of COMMON to be named. These names, like the names of the procedure (function and subroutine) program units, are available globally and used at link-edit time to make the requested associations.

Of course, even with a disjoint block structure, the individual blocks can themselves be block-structured on Algol 60 lines. This is the case with PL/I, the classic 'pantechnicon' language which contains almost everything. In FORTRAN 77 program units IF blocks and DO loops can be nested but this has no access implications apart from jumps. In COBOL even that does not arise since a jump is possible only to the start of a paragraph.

The advantages of block structuring are its flexibility and the control over flow of execution and access to data that it affords, without too much need to be aware of machine-level considerations. The advantages of a disjoint structure are that it permits separate compilation and hence the building of libraries of pre-compiled, re-usable routines which can be accessed without the programmer needing to worry about or even be aware of their internal workings. The marriage of these two concepts together with that of procedure calling eventually led to the modern idea of a 'module'.

43.3.4.2 *Procedures*

The basic idea of procedure-calling goes back to the early 1950s, though the germ of the idea can be found even in Ada Lovelace's description of Babbage's Analytical Engine. At its simplest, it consists of a jump which carries with it the memory of where the jump was made from. Thus, when the (appropriately marked) end of the relevant section of code is reached a jump can be made back to immediately after the point of the program from which the jump came. The section of code 'called' in this manner is referred to as a routine. The term 'procedure' is typically reserved for a routine which transfers parameters and a result.

The routine-calling mechanism is easily implemented in machine code by writing the return (jump) address in a special location in the routine. This enables the routine to be called from many different places in the program, and the return to be made to the appropriate place each time. Very early on in computer design machine code instructions, and even special registers, were provided to facilitate routine calling.

In some high-level languages the procedure-calling mechanism is very little removed from this primitive idea. Although some versions of BASIC have more sophisticated procedure calling with parameters the simpler versions of the language e.g. the Minimal BASIC standard have a simple GOSUB ⟨label⟩ statement. This is just a GOTO with a 'come from' link added. After the jump processing continues just as normal until a RETURN statement is reached when the link is invoked and a jump is made back to the statement following GOSUB. Note that if another GOSUB is encountered before RETURN the original link is lost and hence nested procedure calls are not possible though a good BASIC implementation will at least warn if this occurs.

In COBOL each paragraph is named by an identifier, like a heading, and this can be used either as a label for the destination of a GOTO, or to invoke a procedure call. Hence from within a paragraph PARA2 one might either GOTO PARA5, with no return, or PERFORM PARA5 which means that at the end of PARA5 the return is made to the sentence (statement) in PARA2 following the PERFORM command. Note that even this primitive structuring of COBOL is enough to permit nested calls.

COBOL also allows a succession of paragraphs (in textual order) to be called, by naming both the first and the last, e.g., PERFORM PARA5 THRU PARA8. Hence any group of one or more paragraphs in text sequence is potentially callable as a procedure.

These very simple mechanisms work in BASIC and COBOL because in those languages data is shared globally and so parameter passing is unnecessary. However, COBOL does also have a facility, CALL USING, for another complete program to be called. For languages with local data, whether block-structured or not, then parameter passing becomes a virtual necessity. If parameter passing is not available, information has to be passed by global data. It is easy to show that, whether a procedure is confined to just one program or it is to be part of a library, it is preferable for it to have no global references at all and to communicate with the outside world solely through parameters. This sounds rather rigid, and in fact the module concept allows more flexible and powerful means of communication, as we shall see later.

There are many different ways of passing parameters. It is a topic which sometimes gives rise to confusion, usually caused by one of three factors: taking for granted that what one is used to in one language applies to others; taking a model, e.g., a mathematical model, which is inappropriate or inadequate for a computational process; or taking too machine code-oriented a model.

Approaches to parameter passing are strongly interlinked to approaches to data typing. The modern approach is best exemplified by Ada, where parameters are specified as IN, OUT, or INOUT. As the terms imply, IN parameters supply information to the procedure, OUT parameters return results and other information to the outside world at the conclusion of the call, and INOUT parameters do both. Pragmatically, INOUTs are best regarded as the means whereby procedures can be used to update the entities which they name.

The classical form of IN parameter passing is the 'call by value' used in Algol 60 and numerous other languages. The concept here is that the formal parameter used in the definition of the procedure is, in effect, a local variable the value of which is initialized by the actual parameter. This appears to be a more or less direct transfer from the concept of evaluating a function at a given point, e.g., evaluating $\sin(x)$ at $x = 0.5$. However, this overlooks the fact that a procedure in a procedural language is a dynamic object, whereas a mathematical function is static in some sense. Certainly the scientists and engineers for whom procedures were initially mainly put into programming languages viewed functions as static. Hence if the formal parameter called by value is genuinely a variable, its value can be changed during the execution of the procedure body. However, the corresponding actual parameter used to provide the initial value is not changed, so this might appear to be a quibble. It is trivial to rewrite the procedure body so that the integrity of the initial value is maintained, the price being one extra local variable. However, as some have found out the hard way, the problem is that it is possible for the procedure body to alter the value of the parameter through a mistake on the part of the programmer, which it would be impossible for the processor to detect. Essentially it was an unsafe mechanism.

One answer to this is to reject the procedural approach altogether and adopt a functional programming approach where a function call is much more like what it appears to be to scientists and engineers. Within the procedural approach, one answer is to make 'call by value' create a constant for use inside the procedure body, so that assignment to the formal parameter is forbidden. The IN parameter approach has the same effect but with the added advantage that it is more general. An IN parameter can, for example, be a pointer (which cannot be changed even if the object it points to can), or the name of another procedure. Its principal virtue is that it is a clearer concept freed from the associations which words like 'value' might put into people's minds.

For the first two decades of high-level language development the only alternatives to value parameters, and in some languages the only choice available at all, were various forms of INOUT parameters. The most common model was that of passing across a machine address, typically and most commonly that of a simple variable, rather than copying the value held in that address. The procedure could then 'reach back' into the environment which called it and get at the actual parameter directly, using or changing its value (or doing both).

This pure form of INOUT is usually termed 'call-by-reference'. The formal parameter is now not a local variable but a local pointer which is set to point to the actual parameter which in turn can then be accessed through the pointer by indirect addressing.

This is still the basic model for Pascal VAR parameters and the basis of many FORTRAN 77 implementations. However, the FORTRAN ethos has always been machine efficiency, so the

FORTRAN 77 standard is very carefully worded so as not to require call-by-reference. Continual indirect referencing was deemed potentially inefficient and so the standard does not preclude the use of other techniques. The most common alternative is 'copy-in-copy-out', i.e., the value of the actual parameter is copied into the formal parameter (now once again a local variable, not a pointer) on entry, and copied back into the actual parameter when control is returned. This leads to the curiosity that a call of the form F(Q,Q) to a function F(X,Y), i.e. the same actual parameter corresponds to two different parameters, is actually invalid in standard FORTRAN 77 since, for some definitions of F, the result of the call will differ between call by reference and copy-in-copy-out.

Having only INOUT parameters available, as in FORTRAN 77, is clearly potentially insecure if the intended use is only IN. This problem is compounded as it is not necessary, from the implementor's point of view, to check the appropriateness of the address passed across. FORTRAN 'folklore' is full of authenticated instances of the values of literal constants being changed through their being used as actual parameters. Good compilers would of course treat a literal constant as a special case of an expression, and pass across the address of a copy in temporary workspace. However, the FORTRAN standards did not require a conforming implementation to be a good implementation in this sense. Users therefore had to beware of implementors who were willing to cut such corners, whether to squeeze out the last drop of machine efficiency, or for other reasons.

What variations on this form of INOUT parameters have in common is that a reference, once passed, is fixed. Indeed for non-block-structured languages allowing separate compilation of procedures, it would be difficult and expensive to do anything else. However, other forms of INOUT parameter passing are possible.

Typical of the more general forms of parameter passing that are possible is the Algol 60 call-by-name. The concept was that the name of the actual parameter was substituted for that of the formal parameter during the execution of the procedure. This sounds like call-by-reference, and indeed actually is identical in effect to call-by-reference, provided that the name of the actual parameter remains unaltered for the duration of the call. The trouble is that the possibility of side-effects can enter if the actual parameter is other than the name of a simple variable. The classical example of the exploitation of such side-effects, which became part of Algol 60 culture, was Jensen's device. This exploited the possibility of a functional dependence between one parameter and another, both called by name, so that changes in one were reflected in the other. This technique's power was great but was matched by its obscurity even in the simplest case where one parameter was the name of an index variable and another was a subscripted variable indexed by that variable.

Algol 60's call-by-name is actually better thought of as call-by-substitution – the systematic substitution, throughout the source code of the procedure, of the actual parameter in place of the formal parameter. As such it is more akin to a macro and perhaps better suited to an interpretation-oriented language rather than the batch-oriented language that Algol 60 otherwise was in most respects. In mainstream terms it was a rather uneasy amalgam of the much simpler call-by-reference, which was all that was needed most of the time, and call-by-procedure. In this latter case the actual parameter was not simply a reference (a fixed address) but a computation, typically an expression needing to be evaluated each time it is encountered. Algol 68 coped with this distinction between call-by-reference and call-by procedure through its mode concept, which led the way towards the modern concepts of polymorphism and routines as 'first-class values', as described in Chapter 44.

The concept of OUT parameters is a late though logical corollary to that of IN, or value, parameters. The insecurities of using INOUT parameters, where IN is all that is needed, are obvious. There are also less glaring disadvantages in using INOUT parameters when the only purpose is to carry back a result to the surrounding environment. There is always the temptation for the wayward programmer to make use of the IN capacity of the INOUT parameter even though the justification for using it is only its OUT capacity. There is also the fact that, for those trained in the language, the distinction between OUT and INOUT will be blurred.

The point of an OUT parameter is that, although its value might be set in a procedure, that value cannot be *accessed*. The security question is much less acute than with INOUT being used in place of IN, but the availability of OUT as well as INOUT does enable programmers to express and maintain their intent much more precisely. Even the proposals for FORTRAN 8X include INTENT IN, INTENT OUT, and INTENT INOUT statements. However, as the word INTENT implies, it is not the intention of the FORTRAN standards committees to force conforming FORTRAN processors to require programmers actually to write code which accords with their declared INTENT. Nevertheless this would provide both a useful documentation (of intent) aid and open the way for some processors to do some checking.

43.3.4.3 *Functions and subroutines*

In the preceding discussion of procedures, one thing has been left on one side – how the procedure is actually called, which is tied up with what the procedure is supposed to do. The term 'procedure' has been used here for any block of code which can be invoked from elsewhere in a program and can return control there once it has completed its business. Algol 60 and many of its derivations use the term in this generic sense, but others do not use it at all, e.g. FORTRAN 77 distinguishes between FUNCTIONs, which return a value through the function name, and SUBROUTINEs, which do not, and are invoked differently. Pascal, confusingly, uses the term FUNCTION in the FORTRAN sense but uses PROCEDURE for the other cases, that do not return a value. In Algol 68 the distinction is of little significance because of that language's integration of statements and expressions.

At the cost of some redundancy it saves confusion to refer to 'function procedures' and 'subroutine procedures'. The call of a subroutine procedure is then, in conventional languages, a standalone statement in its own right. Calls can take place among assignment statements, I/O statements (which in many languages are in the form of calls of inbuilt procedures) and the rest. In all cases the name of the procedure and the actual parameters to be used in the call have to be supplied.

There are two main variations. Some languages have specific keywords or commands introducing the call, e.g. CALL in FORTRAN or PERFORM in COBOL, whereas in other languages the call is implicit, the name of the procedure being enough. A more modern variation, yet to find its way into the majority of major languages, is to have default settings of parameters specified in the procedure definition, so that in the call only variations from the defaults need be specified. As with operating system commands, from which this idea is derived, this can be done either positionally, or by using the names of the formal parameters as keyword. An example, not taken from any particular language, might be:

PROCEDURE SEARCH (AREA = ALL, KEY = NAME)

where the formal parameters are AREA and KEY with ALL and NAME as the defaults.

Here one might write a call as

CALL SEARCH(,AGE)

or

CALL SEARCH(KEY = AGE)

This is certainly a more user-oriented style of call, especially for procedure libraries, and one that is likely to spread.

Since function procedures return a value, a call is placed where the value is needed, appropriate to the type of the value returned, typically within expressions. Most languages restrict the values returnable in this way to basic simple types like INTEGER, REAL, CHARACTER etc. that are supported by the language, though for full generality this ought to extend to user-defined types, aggregates, pointers, or indeed even procedures, as 'first class values' in the sense of polymorphism. Thoroughgoing polymorphists would extend it to datatypes too.

The greatest dangers of side-effects from the use of non-local variables or non-value parameters within function definitions lurk in function calls that are embedded in expressions. The tenets of structured programming frown on such excesses, but few languages prevent it, and there is a brand of programmer very adept at dreaming up excuses for permissiveness.

In some languages a fragment of program text like F(I,N) might be either a function call or an array reference. The ambiguity can be resolved either by the rule 'declaration before use' or by the use of different brackets for parameter lists and array subscripts. Since arrays do have to be declared, this should not be a problem. In a disjoint structured language like FORTRAN if F has not been declared as an array it must be a function. However, this overlooks the more difficult case of statements like:

CALL G(F,A,B)

where, in FORTRAN, F will be assumed by default to be a REAL variable. Hence, for F to be identifiable as a function name, the declaration:

EXTERNAL F

has to be made in the program unit heading.

Note that this says nothing about the number and types of the parameters of F. A mismatch might be picked up at link-edit time but if the number of parameters is right and parameter passing is by machine address without checking, as happens with FORTRAN 77, then one cannot rely on it being detected – nor of course on any results the program may produce.

The strong typing approach of course requires strict type checking throughout, so any specification of number and types of parameters of an externally defined function would need to be complete. This is the forerunner of one aspect of the module concept. Interestingly, PL/I provides means for complete specification in its rather elaborate ENTRY attribute, which serves the same purpose as FORTRAN's EXTERNAL, to counteract what would otherwise be the effects of its weak typing on parameter passing.

Block-structured languages, with declaration before use, would appear not to have such problems, but the problems do appear sometimes when recursion is involved. Recursive procedures (ones whose definition involves calls of themselves) are allowed in most languages (FORTRAN 77 and COBOL are among the major exceptions though FORTRAN 8X will include them). They are widely available in block-structured languages whose dynamic storage allocation model provides the necessary implementation mechanism. In fact it is not a single recursive procedure that causes a problem, but two or more mutually recursive procedures. The point is that P1 may call P2, and P2 calls P1, but if the definition of P1 precedes that of P2 textually, the rule 'declaration before use' appears to be violated. There are various ways round it, like deeming the declarations of P1 and P2 to be collateral, but they still are sequential textually and this does not satisfy the devotees of single-pass compilation. Another way is to adopt the disjoint structured approach of declaring the procedure heading before the body. This is another trick achievable through Algol 68's mode mechanism, although that has much more power than is necessary, or, possibly wise, to get round this particular problem. Either way it shows the flexibility of the block-structured approach beginning to tear slightly under the strain, and demonstrates that there are limitations to a too strictly purist approach. Again, it is a move towards the development of the module concept.

43.3.4.4 Co-routines

Mutually recursive procedures bring us to the concept of co-routines. This stemmed originally from assembly language routines, and is not much in evidence in major high-level languages, but is mentioned here for completeness. As the term 'subroutine' implies, most procedure-calling assumes a kind of master–slave relationship, with the master calling the slave and giving it a job to do with certain materials (the actual parameters). The slave does its job and the master takes the results.

With co-routines, however, there is no such implied hierarchy. It is simplest to think in terms of just two co-routines but the principles are general. Each routine has the same status, each can call the other, so control is passed backwards and forwards between the two without either being dominant. It is not a question of recursion; there is only one level of call on either side. This may look like a form of parallelism (albeit simulated), but it is not really that. It is more that one routine picks up the ball and runs with it until it decides that it is time for the ball to be passed. In human organization terms it is like a team of people, each with specialist skills, cooperating on a project. Only one can work on the project at a time, and they each do so until it is time to pass on control to someone else.

As with recursion, the point of co-routines as a concept is that some classes of problem are naturally expressed in that way. However, with recursion it is possible to find realistic examples of problems which can only be expressed in a non-recursive way in a very tortuous manner, despite the tortuous arguments used in attempts to prove the contrary by some who dislike recursion. In the case of co-routines it is usually little more difficult to express the problem in terms of two or more subroutines of equal (slave) status and a monitoring (master) program which reassigns control to another subroutine when one relinquishes it, thus obviating the need for an explicit co-routine facility in the language of choice. To go back to the human organization analogy, a group of collaborating people might well be perfectly capable of getting a job done, but it is common for someone to be designated to supervise, and if the supervisor is reasonably competent the work still gets done without much degradation in performance. Hence a problem naturally expressible in co-routine terms might be expressible equally or more 'naturally' in terms of a supervisor program and subroutines. This may help to explain why there has not seemed to be any strong demand from practitioners for the inclusion of co-routine functionality in the major programming languages.

43.3.4.5 Generic procedures, overloading, and user-defined operators

There remains one final area related to procedures which is of importance in some languages. In its basic form a procedure has a fixed number of parameters of fixed type, and if it is a function procedure it returns a value of a fixed type. With a generic procedure, however, the number of parameters and/or types of the parameters, and/or the type of the value returned in the case of a function, can vary from call to call. A simple example of a procedure with a variable number of parameters is MAX, a function procedure returning the largest value from among its set of parameters. A simple example where the datatype of a parameter may vary is ABS, returning the absolute numeric value of its parameter, which may be REAL, INTEGER or COMPLEX. In the final case the result is the absolute magnitude, and of type REAL. Note that in these cases the variation from call to call in the type of the result returned by the procedures.

Such procedures are also termed 'overloaded', a faintly derogatory word no doubt invented by implementors who are faced with a bit more work at the syntax analysis stage if a procedure identifier cannot immediately be designated as being of a specified type.

Generic procedures that are defined as built-in to the language, as the examples MAX and ABS are likely to be, are relatively easy to deal with, but a few languages have gone beyond that to allow programmers to define their own. Algol 68 characteristically does this in its own way, once again through the mode concept as applied to unions and arrays, though uncharacteristically in a rather clumsy way. PL/I, the pantechnicon language, also provides generics, characteristically rather clumsily but fairly effectively. More recently such facilities have tended to become associated with module facilities in languages such as Ada, especially associated with user defined but 'private' types.

The question of so-called 'overloading' also applies to operators as well as procedures. Indeed, in some languages ABS is an operator. Again this is particularly important for user-defined types, where operators like + might have a natural meaning and one might wish to extend their definitions to encompass user-defined types. The separation of the procedure body (or routine text) from the procedure heading in Algol 68 made this a natural possibility, and Ada too allows this. Algol 68 also allows the programmer to create freely new monadic and dyadic operators. Ada is less permissive. Such a facility entails allowing the programmer to set precedence levels (priorities) on dyadic operators, which inevitably complicates parsing of the source text.

43.3.4.6 Modules

If the secret of successful engineering of large, complex artefacts is the availability of tested, reliable components with standard interfaces and properties, then the module is an attempt to provide a mechanism for turning software building from a craft into a genuine engineering discipline.

The modern concept of modules brings together a number of strands from the past, some of them quite old: the separation of procedure heading from procedure body, 'the inheritance by derived types', the inheritance of properties and procedures of parent classes in the class concept of Simula. Even the humble and mundane block data facility of FORTRAN can be seen as having a germ within it of the idea of a module.

Since modules are a comparatively new concept, their form of provision has not yet settled on a commonality of style as with procedures: IF ... THEN ... ELSE, etc. Of the major languages only Ada and Modula 2 fully provide a module facility, though at the time of writing such a facility is planned for inclusion in FORTRAN 8X – a sign of the times. However, in general the main distinguishing features of a module facility are the following:

1. Separation of module specification and module definition.
2. Modules package together type definitions, procedures, operators etc.
3. Modules explicitly export 'public' facilities available to other modules, and import facilities from other modules that they need.
4. Implementation details, which may include further 'private' types, procedures etc., are hidden from the outside world.
5. A 'client' module does not necessarily import all of the facilities of a 'server' module, only those that it needs.

It is clear from this list that the motivation for the module concept is to support and improve good engineering practice so that, for example, the implementation details of a server module can be updated without client modules and application programs using it being affected. For conventional, command-oriented, procedural languages the combination of modules, abstract types and polymorphism currently seems the likely way forward, though it would be foolish to expect that these will be the last word in language design.

43.4 Conclusions

There are those, of course, who would argue that procedural languages have had their day, and that the future will see increased use of functional, declarative, or dataflow languages, or the so-called 'fourth-generation languages' (dealt with elsewhere) and a consequent decrease in the use of procedural languages. In ordinary life, the familiarity of the concept of giving commands, the apparently fundamental nature of the concept of an algorithm, the frequency with which there is a need to explain how to do things, all suggest, however – without denying the importance of new approaches – that there will be room for procedural languages for some time yet. The hope is that they will be better than the ones we have now.

That being so, what is the 'best' language of those currently on offer and readily available? Each language has its proponents, and the only reliable advice is to ignore the advice of those who claim that 'their' language is 'the best' to the exclusion of all others. Different languages have very different design aims, different levels of success in achieving those aims, and different intended areas and circumstances of application. Hence there can be no single answer to the unqualified question 'What is the best language?', even if only technical factors are taken into account. Other factors that may be relevant in making a choice will be costs of acquiring the chosen language, subsequent program development, and later maintenance. It would take too long to explore the possibilities here, and readers are referred for further discussion to, for example, the relevant sections of Barnetson (1985) and Meek, Heath and Rushby (1983) in the bibliography which follows.

43.5 Bibliography

Barnetson, P. (ed.) (1985) *Research and Academic User's Guide to the IBM PC*, IBM United Kingdom Ltd

Ghezzi, C. and Jazayeri, M. (1987) *Programming Language Concepts*, 2nd edn, Wiley

Higman, B. (1977) *A Comparative Study of Programming Languages*, 2nd edn, Macdonald

Hill, I. D. and Meek, B. L., (eds) (1980) *Programming Language Standardization*, Ellis Horwood

Meek, B. L. (1978) *Fortran, PL/I and the Algols*, Macmillan

Meek, B. L., Heath, P. M., and Rushby, N. J. (eds) (1983) *Guide to Good Programming Practice*, 2nd edn, Ellis Horwood

Sammet, J. E. (1969) *Programming Languages: History and Fundamentals*, Prentice-Hall

Tucker, A. B. (1985) *Programming Languages*, 2nd edn, McGraw-Hill

Wexelblat, R. (ed.) (1981) *History of Programming Languages*, Academic Press

Standards

ISO 8652:1987 Programming language – Ada, International Organisation for Standardisation, [Various addenda in preparation 1989]

DIS 8485:1989 Programming language – APL, International Organisation for Standardisation

ISO 1538:1984 Programming language – Algol 60, International Organisation for Standardisation

ISO 6373:1984 Programming language – Minimal Basic, International Organisation for Standardisation

DP 10279:1989, International Organisation for Standardisation. [Draft proposed standard for full Basic, incorporating technical content, conformance rules and subsetting rules of ANS X3-113-1987 and of ECMA-116-1986, the standard produced by the European Computer Manufacturers Association]

DP 9899:1989, International Organisation for Standardisation [Draft proposed standard for C]

ANS X3.23:1985 COBOL, American National Standards Institute. [Endorsed as ISO 1989:1985; previous versions published in 1968 and 1974, various addenda in preparation 1989)]

ANS X3.9:1978 FORTRAN, American National Standards Institute. [Endorsed as ISO 1539:1980; previous version published in 1966, revised version in draft 1989]

BS 6192:1982, British Standard Institution, [Specification for computer programming language Pascal, endorsed as international standard ISO 7185:1982; revised version with minor amendments, and standard for Extended Pascal, in draft 1989]

ANS X3.53:1976 Programming Language PL/I, American National Standards Institute. [Endorsed as international standard ISO 6160:1979, also general purpose subset, ANS X3.74:1981, endorsed as ISO General Purpose PL/I, ISO 6522:1985]

Language definitions

van Wijngaarden, A. *et al.* (1976) *Revised Report on the Algorithmic Language Algol 68*, Springer-Verlag

Wirth, N. (1982) *Modula 2*, 3rd edn, Springer-Verlag

Selected texts on specific languages

Barnes, J. G. P. (1982) *Programming in Ada*, Addison-Wesley

Lindsey, C. H. and van der Meulen, S. G. (1977) *An Informal Introduction to Algol 68*, 2nd edn, North-Holland

Pagan, F. P. (1976) *A Practical Guide to Algol 68*, Wiley

Iverson, K. (1962) *A Programming Language*, Wiley

Kemeny, J. G. and Kurtz, T. (1985) *Back to Basic*, Addison-Wesley

Kernighan, B. W. and Ritchie, D. M. (1978) *The C Programming Language*, Prentice-Hall

Meissner, L. and Organick, E. (1984) FORTRAN 77 – teaching structured programming, Addison-Wesley

McCarthy, J., Abrahams, P. W., Edwards, D. J., Hart, T. P. and Levin, M. I. (1965) *LISP 1.5 Programmer's Manual*, 2nd edn, MIT Press

Steele, Jr., G. L. (1984) *Common LISP: the Language*, Digital Press

Jensen, K. and Wirth, N. (1985) *Pascal User Manual and Report*, 3rd edn, Springer Verlag.

Birwhistle, G. M., Dahl, O.-J., Myrhaug, B. and Nygaard, K. (1973) *SIMULA Begin*, Petrocelli/Charter

Griswold, R. E. and Griswold, M. T. (1973) *A SNOBOL 4 Primer*, Prentice-Hall

44

Modern non-conventional programming language concepts

Carlo Ghezzi
Dipartimento di Elettronica,
Politecnico di Milano, Italy

Contents

44.1 Introduction: what makes a language non-conventional

Considering the evolution of programming languages from a historical perspective, it can be seen that computer architectures restricted programming language designs to what could be efficiently implemented on current machines. Since most architectures have much in common with the original machine designed by John von Neumann in the late 1940s (Burks *et al.*, 1947), they are usually called von Neumann architectures. Accordingly, the languages based on the principles of von Neumann architectures are called von Neumann languages.

Schematically, the von Neumann architecture is based on a central processing unit (CPU), an input/output unit and a memory (see *Figure 44.1*). The memory is a central repository of data and instructions. The CPU provides control facilities for extracting instructions from the memory, one at a time, and executing them. Instructions are very low-level. Basically, they require that data be extracted from memory cells, manipulated by the processing facilities offered by the CPU, and that the results be copied back to memory cells. Data are elementary too; they are extracted from the memory and manipulated one at a time.

Most present-day computers conform to the above abstract scheme, although they differ in many details, such as the repertoire of instructions and the way instructions and data are addressed. Some architectures depart slightly from the above scheme and introduce some degree of parallelism: more than one instruction at a time may be executed, or more than one item of data at a time may be manipulated. However, apart from minor local modifications, the underlying operational structure is still the same as von Neumann's original machine.

Conventional programming languages are abstractions of the behavior of a von Neumann machine. This means that, apart from details, they share some fundamental concepts which reflect the underlying architecture. In particular, they are both characterized by the sequential step-by-step execution of instructions, the modifiable repository of values, and the low level of instructions and data.

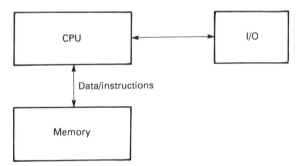

Figure 44.1

The sequential step-by-step execution is reflected by control statements of the programming language. For example, the semicolon control operator of Pascal and Ada is an abstraction of the program counter, which is incremented after an instruction is executed, in order to fetch and execute the next instruction. The **goto** statement is an abstraction of the unconditional branch of underlying von Neumann machine language. Other control statements – such as **if... then ... else, do ... while**, or the procedure call – are higher level abstractions that are ultimately mapped into a straightforward and efficiently executable set of machine-level instructions.

Instructions are executed in a strict sequential order. This leads to a severe bottleneck that limits the speed of program execution. Traditionally, a partial solution to this problem has been to allow the programmer to state explicitly that certain sequential portions of the program may be executed in parallel, by a multi-processor or by a multi-programmed computer. The underlying philosophy of this approach is that the software is mainly sequential, but that a limited amount of parallelism can be introduced although it is the programmer's responsibility to synchronize actions properly.

The concept of a modifiable repository of values is reflected by the concept of variables in conventional programming languages. In a von Neumann machine, values are stored in cells and accessed by addressing such cells. In conventional programming languages, the underlying notions of memory cell and address are reflected by the concept of a variable. A programming language variable is essentially a named memory cell where a value may be stored and accessed. A variable has a name – an abstraction of the cell's address – and can be modified by an assignment operation – an abstraction of the memory copy operation.

The abstract behavior corresponding to the execution of a program written in a conventional programming language may be described as a sequence of state changes of a state machine. Each state is characterized by a set of values, one for reach program variable. The execution of an instruction in a given state may be described as a state transition; the target state is characterized by the same set of values as the source state, except for the variables that are affected by the instruction. The execution of a sequence of instructions on some input values, starting from a given initial state, produces some output values – the results – and, as a side-effect, a state modification. This abstract state machine is an abstraction of the underlying von Neumann architecture.

Finally, conventional programming languages are essentially iterative. Complex operations are accomplished by executing a sequence of elementary steps repeatedly, storing intermediate results in memory. This, again, reflects the von Neumann architecture, in which instructions are stored in the memory, and the only way to accomplish anything complicated is to repeat a sequence of instructions. Actually, most higher level conventional programming languages introduce procedures and functions, together with a way of invoking procedures and functions recursively. Recursive procedure and function calls are another – much more powerful – way to structure complex operations. Procedures and functions are important concepts in conventional languages; they provide invaluable help in writing large programs. However, procedures, functions and recursion do not constitute the essence of conventional programming languages. One could even write a complex, large program without using procedures or functions and recursion. This is probably why it is often observed that conventional programming languages do not provide the best approach to teaching and learning about recursion.

The above characteristics of von Neumann programming languages are emphasized by the following alternative terms that are often used to denote them: procedural languages, statement-based languages and imperative languages.

The proponents of non-conventional programming languages argue that conventional languages are intrinsically low level. Despite any effort to introduce nice new constructs, these languages are reminiscent of the underlying von Neumann architecture. They are still based on low-granularity statements and data, and on iterative, sequential execution of sequences of statements. Understanding the effect of computations requires keeping track of state changes produced by the execution of each of its elementary statements. Finally, the conventional starting point that a language must be an abstraction of the underlying architecture is rejected. Instead, it is claimed that the starting point should be a set of principles upon which the language can be based. The principles should be those that make programs easy to read and write, more reliable, amenable to mathematical reasoning, easy to modify, etc., although different classes of non-conventional languages are based on different sets of principles. In contrast, the main emphasis of the conventional approach is on efficiency. Proponents of non-conventional approaches claim that the premature preoccupation with run-time efficiency is a heritage of the old times, when hardware was the dominant cost factor in a computer-based application. This is certainly no longer the case. However, this does not mean that efficiency is no longer important. It means that the emphasis on structure and readability should come first, while efficiency should come later, in the form of code tuning. Also, they observe that early implementations of non-conventional languages were indeed inefficient. Good implementation techniques are now available to make non-conventional approaches practical. It is also pointed out that conventional programming languages tend to be quite unsuitable for writing software for recently introduced, massively parallel computer architectures. In contrast, most non-conventional approaches intrinsically provide a high degree of parallelism that makes them appealing for such architectures.

How can non-conventional approaches be defined in a precise way? Here the term 'non-conventional programming language' is used to characterize those languages which depart – more or less radically – from conventional, von Neumann programming languages. This definition states what non-conventional languages are not, rather than what they are. In fact, there are different ways in which one can depart from the essence of the von Neumann architecture. One way is not to be strongly biased by the sequential, step-by-step control flow. Another is to do away with the low granularity of instructions and their organization in iterative patterns. Still another is to do away with the low granularity of data. These departures from conventional programming languages result in a number of non-conventional languages that will be described below. This chapter will concentrate mainly on two main categories: functional and logic programming languages. Other approaches, such as rule-based, event-driven, and data intensive will also be covered. The use of such languages is not just a matter of coding the same algorithm in a different syntactic notation. The programming style – or paradigm – is also quite different, if one wants to adhere fully to the principles of such languages.

One further important language category can be introduced – object-oriented languages (Shriver and Wegner, 1987). However, the author decided not to introduce object-oriented languages as a special class of non-conventional languages. Indeed, object-oriented languages support a design method that departs sharply from the traditional functional decomposition. As opposed to conventional languages, where design is based on the recognition of passive operational abstractions (procedures and functions), object-oriented languages structure software as a network of interacting agents or objects. They enforce a programming paradigm based on the recognition of classes of objects, i.e. groups of objects with common properties and operations where the properties may be 'inherited' from one member of a class by another, which typically interact via message passing. They provide a way of modularizing software that is based on the classes and on structural relationships among classes (e.g., 'uses' and 'inherits' relationships).

Thus, basically, one can view object-oriented features as a way of shaping the modular structure of a system. As such, they may be superimposed as a set of programming-in-the-large primitives both 'on top of' conventional, von Neumann-based languages, and on non-conventional ones, such as functional or logic languages. For example, Simula 67 (Birtwistle *et al.*, 1973), Smalltalk 80 (Goldberg and Robson, 1983), C++ (Stroustrup, 1986), Objective C (Cox, 1986), Eiffel (Meyer, 1988) and Trellis/

Owl (Schaffert *et al.*, 1986) may be viewed as von Neumann object-oriented languages. Object-oriented languages that do not inherit the von Neumann paradigm are mentioned here in later sections. Object-oriented languages are discussed in more detail in Chapter 39.

44.2 Functional languages

Functional languages are probably the best known and most widely used family of non-conventional languages. Lisp – the most representative language (from the point of view of use, if not its technical basis) of the family – has been around for about 30 years. Lisp has been a research tool for many years, used mainly in the artificial intelligence research community. More recently, however, the language has gained popularity as a practical development tool, and there are now examples of commercial applications and tools written in Lisp. Other functional languages are also finding their way from research environments into practice.

In addition, there is a school of thought that considers functional programming to be the best vehicle for introducing programming and good programming style to novices. Although this has been a long-standing, controversial issue that will never reach a definite solution, there is an increasing number of computer science schools that teach introductory programming courses using a functional programming language. This will certainly help increase the popularity of such languages.

44.2.1 History

Concepts of functional programming languages sprang up in the late 1950s out of research in artificial intelligence, which was then in its infancy. The ideas of the list data structure and pointers were invented to describe complex structured information. A family of programming languages offering list processing facilities – called IPL – was developed by Newell, Shaw, and Simon for the Rand Corporation's JOHNNIAC computer (Newell and Shaw, 1957).

Quoting McCarthy (1978) – the principal designer of Lisp – 'my desire for an algebraic list processing language for artificial intelligence ... arose in the summer of 1956 during the Dartmouth Summer Research Project on Artificial Intelligence ... (when) Newell, Shaw, and Simon described IPL 2'. Some initial experiments were subsequently made using FLPL, a FORTRAN-based implementation of list processing facilities.

The reason that FORTRAN was chosen as a host for list processing facilities is that it was the only high-level language available at that time. In addition, although being primarily oriented to numerical applications, FORTRAN had a tiny, but seminal, functional component – expressions. Expressions were a fundamental aid to writing programs based on a mathematical notation. They allowed the programmer to abstract away from the sequential, step-by-step fetch, operate and store operations performed by the hardware in order to concentrate on how to compose operators to yield the evaluation of the desired expression (see Section 44.2.2).

As McCarthy started developing a functional recursive notation, however, it became clear that FORTRAN, which does not provide recursion, had to be abandoned. Thus, at the end of 1958, the definition and development of Lisp began.

Lisp is thus the oldest functional language and is probably the best known and most widely used today in that category. The language, unfortunately, was not standardized for a long time. Therefore, many available implementations actually define Lisp dialects that differ from one another in several minor or even major points. There have been two main branches of Lisp –

MacLisp and Interlisp – which in turn spawned their own subdialects. The lack of standardization was a serious obstacle to the industrial success of the language. To tackle this problem, representatives from the various MacLisp groups met in 1981 and decided to define a language, called Common Lisp, which would contain the best known feature of the various dialects. The Interlisp community also joined the effort. All Lisp variants finally converged towards this common language (Steele, 1984), under the active encouragement of the US Defense Advanced Research Projects Agency (DARPA). The standard defines a common language, to which each implementation is free to make extensions. One such extension, for example, is NIL (Burke *et al.*, 1984).

Other functional languages were developed after Lisp. ISWIM is a functional notation introduced by Landin in 1966. Scheme is a dialect of Lisp introduced at MIT and intended primarily as a teaching vehicle for introductory programming (Abelson and Sussman, 1985). SASL (Turner, 1976), KRC (Turner, 1982) and Miranda (Turner, 1985) make up a family of functional programming languages developed by D. Turner in the UK.

ML (Gordon *et al.*, 1979) is a functional language that was first introduced as a metalanguage (hence the acronym) for the LCF theorem prover developed at Edinburgh University. Only later did it evolve into an independent programming language, into which HOPE also converged (Burstall *et al.*, 1980). The result is the SML programming language, or Standard ML (Milner, 1984; Harper *et al.*, 1987; Wikstrom, 1987).

FP is another seminal functional language developed by Backus, the principal designer of FORTRAN (Backus, 1973). Using FP as an exemplifying functional language in his passionate Turing lecture (Backus, 1978), Backus attacked conventional languages on the grounds of unacceptably low reliability of programs, absence of mathematical rigor, and low productivity. He has advocated functional languages as a viable practical alternative since the mid 1970s. Backus' manifesto is important, because it brought serious attention to functional languages, even from the world of software professionals.

Finally, functional features may be found in other languages that depart from the traditional von Neumann style, although in a strict sense such languages cannot be considered functional. The most notable of such languages is probably APL (Iverson, 1962).

44.2.2 Principles

Programming in a conventional language consists of providing for the execution and repetition of certain sequences of individual statements using appropriate control structures. The desired final state is reached by a sequence of intermediate state changes, each caused by the execution of a statement. In contrast, the essence of functional programming is to combine functions in expressions to produce more powerful functions.

44.2.2.1 Referential transparency

In a pure functional programming language, functions behave exactly like mathematical functions. (Existing functional languages may be more or less impure, as will be seen later.) It is commonly said that they preserve referential transparency. Informally, this means that the meaning of a whole – e.g. the value of an expression – can be determined solely from the meaning of its parts – e.g. the value of subexpression – if any. Mathematical expressions are referentially transparent. For example, in the mathematical expression $f(x) + g(x)$, we can take the value of x, evaluate f and g in any order, and then compute the value of the sum based on the value of its subexpressions. Also, we can substitute f' for f, if we know it

produces the same result as f. If the same expression were written in Pascal (or any other conventional language) we would not be assured of these properties. Suppose that f and g receive their parameter by reference and then modify it, or suppose that they modify some global variable that is visible to both. Under these circumstances, we are not assured that $f(x) + g(x) = g(x) + f(x)$, that is, the order of evaluation of subexpressions affects the result.

Conventional programming languages are intrinsically not referentially transparent. The effect of a statement depends on the state in which it is executed and, in turn, the execution of a statement produces a new state in which the next statement is interpreted; computation proceeds by state changes. Assignment statements, parameters passed by reference, and global variables are the main reasons that conventional languages are not referentially transparent. Lack of referential transparency makes programs hard to read, modify and verify. In fact, to understand the effect of a statement (e.g. with the purpose of modifying or verifying it), one must mentally figure out what the state of execution will be when the statement will be executed.

44.2.2.2 Functions are first-class objects

Unlike conventional languages, the essence of functional languages is not in the kind of statements that are part of the language, nor in the way statements are combined to produce compound statements via suitable control structures. Rather, the essence of functional programming is to combine functions to produce more powerful functions. It is commonly said that in functional programming languages functions are first-class objects, i.e. functions have the same status as any other object in the language. Depending on the specific functional language, functions can be the value of an expression, may be passed as arguments of a function invocation, may be inserted as components of a data structure, may be returned from functions, etc.

Functions, as has been said, behave like mathematical functions. This means that they are rules for mapping (or associating) elements of one set (the domain) into elements of another set (the codomain or range). For example, the function square maps elements from the domain of integers to elements of the range of integers.

44.2.2.3 Function definition and application

A function definition specifies the domain, the range and the mapping rule. For example, function *square* may be defined as follows, using a self-explanatory syntax:

square: integer→integer	the set at the left-hand side of the arrow is the domain, the one at the right-hand side is the range.
*square(x) is_defined_as x*x*	this is the mapping rule.

(Using a purely functional syntactic notation, we should write the mapping rule in prefix form as *xx*. The infix notation is used here for readability reasons.)

Once a function is defined, it can be applied to a particular element of the domain set. The application returns the associated element in the range set. In the function definition, a parameter is used to denote any member of the domain set. At application time, a particular member of the domain set is specified. This member, called the argument, replaces the parameter in the definition. The replacement is purely textual. If the definition contains any other function applications, they are applied in the same way, until we are left with an expression that can be evaluated to yield the result of the original application.

Thus, the application *square* (2) yields 2*2 and finally yields 4.

Function application is the essence of the functional programming paradigm. This is why functional languages are also called applicative languages. The parameters of a function are mathematical variables. They are quite different from variables of a conventional von Neumann programming language. In a function definition a parameter – say, *x* – stands for any member of the domain set. It is not a symbolic name for a location where a value will be eventually stored. In the application, *x* is given – bound to – exactly one value. The value bound to a variable does not change thereafter. Thus it can never happen that the value associated with the first occurrence of *x* is different from the value associated to the second in the definition of function *square*, or in the following function *foo*.

> *foo: integer × integer→integer*
> *foo (x, y) is_defined_as x * f (y) * x*

In the case of *foo*, it cannot happen that the application of function *f* to its argument changes the value bound to *x*, as might happen with a conventional programming language.

44.2.2.4 Recursive functions

Functions in a purely functional language do not build their results by iterating executions of simple statements and by storing intermediate results in local storage areas. Rather, they are based on recursion as a mechanism to build complex functions, starting from more elementary ones. As an example, the following recursive function computes *n* – the Fibonacci number:

> *fib: natural→natural*
> *fib(n) is_defined as* **if** *n=0* **or** *n=1* **then** *1*
> **else** *fib(n−1)+fib(n−2)*

A purely functional language intrinsically supports a high degree of parallelism. Since there is no notion of side-effects, subexpressions may be evaluated in any order, possibly in parallel. The choice of what to evaluate in parallel may be entirely left to the underlying language implementation, without any explicit human intervention. For example, in the following function application functions *g*, *h*, and *k* may be evaluated in any order, or even in parallel:

> *f(g (...), h (...), k (...))*

44.2.2.5 Lambda expressions

A common notational device found in functional languages is the lambda expression (λ-expression.) A λ-expression allows function values to be defined. For example, the following λ-expression defines a function that is exactly the same as *square*, except that we do not give a name to it:

> λ*x.x*x*

A function defined by a λ-expression may be applied to arguments, as in the following example:

> (λ*x.x*x*) 2

which yields 4 as result.

We can also name a λ-expression, as in:

> *square is_defined_as* λ*x.x*x*

44.2.2.6 Free and bound variables

Syntactically, the parameters following the 'λ' and before the '.' are called bound variables. Variables appearing in the definition that are not bound are called free variables. Bound variables are like local variables, and free variables are like non-local variables that are bound at an outer level.

A difficulty arises if a lambda expression contains a free variable, as in:

> (λ*x.x*y*)

The value of the formal parameter *x* will become available when the λ-expression is applied, but what is the value of *y*? There are two alternative solutions to this problem. One is lexical (or static) scoping; the other is dynamic scoping. Under lexical scoping the value of the free variable is taken from the static environment in which the function is defined. This is exactly what happens in block-structured programming languages of the ALGOL family, where non-local variables appearing in a procedure or function are bound to the static environment in which the unit is defined, which depends on the nesting unit structure. In the case of dynamic scoping, the value of free variables is taken from the environment that is active at the point of invocation. Note that the two choices have an impact on semantics. The results of a program under one interpretation rule may be different from the results of the same program under the other interpretation rule. Also, it turns out that dynamic scoping has disadvantages in terms of the reliability of the resulting programs. Programs are harder to understand and verify than in the case of lexical scoping.

Unfortunately, not all functional languages adopt the same binding rule. Historically, Lisp implementations adopted dynamic scoping. Recently, however, program reliability concerns have led the trend towards lexical scoping. This is why, for example, Common Lisp requires lexical scoping, although dynamic scoping may be provided optionally as well. Scheme – a Lisp dialect defined for educational purposes – also adopts lexical scoping.

44.2.2.7 Functional forms

New functions may be created by combining existing functions. The most common form of functional combination in mathematics is function composition. If a function *f* is defined as the composition of *g* and *h*, written as *f is_defined_as g∘h*, applying *f* is defined to be equivalent to applying *h* and then applying *g* to the result. Function composition, represented by the function symbol '∘', is an example of a functional form (also called higher order function or combining form). It is a function that takes functions as parameters and yields a function as its result. The ability of a language to define functional forms is an example that shows that functions are treated as first-class objects.

44.2.2.8 Types

An important feature that distinguishes between functional languages is the type system adopted. The type of an expression gives the values it can denote and operations that can be applied to it. For example, integers may be added, while Booleans cannot. The type system of a language is the set of rules that associate a type with expressions of the language. The rules of the type system specify the proper use of each operator in the language. Type checking ensures that each operation in the program is applied correctly according to the types of its operands.

As far as possible programs are checked statically, once and for all, before the program is actually executed. Static checking eliminates the need for error checking during program execution, thus improving run-time efficiency in terms of space and speed. More importantly, it enhances program reliability as it prevents erroneous programs from being released. In fact, large programs tend to have portions that are rarely executed, so programs may be in use for a long time before dynamic checking detects a type violation.

Some functional languages – like Lisp and Scheme – are essentially untyped, and the limited type checking which is possible can only be performed dynamically. In other words, the language does not associate a type with expressions. Thus, programming errors that could be caught by a type checker cannot be detected until a problem arises at run-time, e.g. by trying to add an integer and a string. Other functional languages, like Standard ML, are typed and statically checked. Experiments made with such languages show that it is possible to obtain the benefits of type checking without sacrificing flexibility.

44.2.2.9 Memory management

An important characteristic of existing functional languages is that they provide powerful mechanisms for managing the storage of data automatically, without requiring programmers to deal explicitly with memory allocation and de-allocation. Data is automatically allocated as needed, and storage is automatically released as it becomes inaccessible (garbage collection). Efficient memory management is a crucial factor in functional languages. In fact, since functions behave like mathematical functions, the values they compute cannot be viewed as a modification of some previously stored data items, but rather as fresh, new, values. This means that new storage must be allocated to store the results of functions as they are evaluated. Also, if storage is not released as the values become inaccessible, an enormous amount of memory may be occupied by programs, much of which is actually garbage. The absence of explicit code for memory allocation and de-allocation makes programs shorter, easier to write and understand and more reliable.

44.2.2.10 Interpretive implementation

Most functional languages are implemented by interactive interpreters. In fact, they were some of the first interactive systems in the history of computing. This means that as soon as one types a function name together with a list of arguments, the system responds with the value of the result.

44.2.2.11 Purity of the language

In this introduction to functional languages the term 'purely functional' has been used. Actually, most functional languages are more or less impure, i.e. they depart to a greater or lesser degree from the conceptual integrity of functional style. For example, they may provide some form of assignment to von Neumann-like variables, iterative statements and even gotos. However, these non-functional features have been added because of the need to improve efficiency of implementations; they are not in the intrinsic heart of the language. The programming style is dominated by the purely functional portion of the language, and any abuse of impurities should be viewed as a symptom of bad programming style.

44.2.2.12 Mathematical foundations

Functional languages are based on strong mathematical foundations that make programs and language processors amenable to formal treatment. Theoretically, functional languages are rooted in the theory of recursive functions and the λ-calculus invented by Church (1941). A complete treatment of the topic may be found in Barendregt (1984). For a more introductory treatment, one may refer to Gordon (1988) or Peyton–Jones (1987). McCarthy (1960) is the original paper describing the recursive function theory foundations of Lisp.

44.2.3 Sample languages

44.2.3.1 Lisp

Lisp data objects are symbolic expressions that can be either atoms or lists. An atom is a string of characters (letters, digits, and others). A list is a series of atoms or lists, separated by space and bracketed by parentheses. The empty list () is also called NIL. The list is the only data structuring mechanism available in Lisp.

A Lisp program is itself a list. It is functional in that it is composed of applications of functions that produce results that may be used by other functions. Syntactically, Lisp uses a prefix notation for expressions in which parentheses bracket an operator and its operands. For example (MAX 1 33 5 7) is an expression that evaluates the maximum of a sequence of numbers; its evaluation yields 33. Similarly, (PLUS 3 15) is an expression denoting '3 + 15'; its evaluation yields 18. The general form of an expression is:

$$(E_1 E_2 \ldots E_n)$$

where E_1 represents the operator to be applied to the results of the evaluation of $E_2 \ldots E_n$. Since $E_1 E_2 \ldots E_n$ may themselves be expressions, we can easily write programs where we achieve deep nesting and lots of parentheses. This has often been criticized on the grounds of readability.

However, the syntactic uniformity of the language is an enormous advantage. As programs are represented by lists, it is easy to write programs that manipulate data representing programs, as will be shown below. This is a very useful feature in many practical cases, e.g. if the language is used to implement a programming environment.

There are very few primitive functions in pure Lisp, but existing Lisp systems have added to the basic set considerably. These functions, however, can all be expressed in terms of the original primitive functions. The following gives a brief description of the most notable primitive functions.

QUOTE is the identity function (i.e. (QUOTE A) yields A). It is used to prevent the processor for the language from evaluating its argument.

The most important functions are those that manipulate lists: CAR and CDR are the selection operations, and CONS is the construction operation. CAR returns the first element of a list; CDR returns the tail of a list (i.e. a list composed of all elements, except for the first one); CONS appends an element to a list. For example:

(CAR (QUOTE A B C))) yields A. (If QUOTE were missing, an attempt would be made to evaluate (A B C), which is the operand of CAR. Here A would be interpreted as a function, B and C as its arguments.)

(CDR (QUOTE (A B C))) yields (B C).

(CONS (QUOTE D) (QUOTE (A B C))) yields (DA B C).

A few predicates, i.e. functions returning Boolean values, are also available. A true value is denoted by the atom T; a false value is denoted by NIL (the same as the symbol used to denote the empty list). The predicate ATOM returns T if its argument is an atom; otherwise its value is NIL. The predicate NULL returns T if its argument is an empty list; otherwise it returns NIL. Other predicates are also available to test objects for equality.

Conditional expressions are written using the function COND, which takes as arguments a number of (predicate, expression) pairs. The expression of the first pair (in left-to-right order) whose predicate is true is the value of COND. For example:

(COND ((ATOM (QUOTE (A B))) (QUOTE C))
(T (QUOTE Z)))
yields Z. (Why?)

Functions may be defined using lambda expressions. The function $\lambda x.x*x$ is written in Lisp as:

(LAMBDA (X) (* X X))

A sample application might be:

((LAMBDA (X) (* X X)) 2)

which yields 4

The binding of a name to a function is done by the function DEFUN. For example:

(DEFUN SQUARE (LAMBDA (X) (* X X)))

The ability to name a function and the availability of conditional expressions are the basic mechanisms used to write recursive function definitions. For example, the following function may be used to reverse the elements of a list:

(DEFUN REVERSE (LAMBDA) (L) (REV NIL L)))
To evaluate REVERSE, it evaluates REV with two arguments, the null list and the original list to reverse.

(DEFUN REV (LAMBDA (OUT IN)
COND ((NULL IN) OUT)
(T (REV (CONS (CAR IN) OUT) (CDR IN)))))))

This illustrates the so-called technique of accumulating parameters, which is common in the case of recursive functions. The first parameter of function REV is initially empty and, at each recursive step, accumulates a partially reversed list, until the second parameter, which initially denotes the list to be reversed, becomes empty.

Lisp only has limited power as far as higher order functions are concerned. Among the facilities it provides is the function MAPCAR, which allows a function to be applied to all elements of a list. For example, having defined a function SQUARE, one may write:

(MAPCAR SQUARE L)

to produce a list whose elements are the square of the elements of list L.

Let us return to the observation that Lisp functions are in a list data structure. This means that programs and data are indistinguishable, so that one can write a program to create or manipulate programs. In particular, it is possible to write a function (EVAL e a), where e is an expression to evaluate and a is a list of (variable, value) pairs, in such a way that EVAL yields the result of evaluation of e in environment a. The function EVAL can serve as a formal definition of the language, given in terms of the language itself. Equivalently, it may be viewed as an interpreter for Lisp programs, and Lisp interpreters have actually been implemented by hand-compiling EVAL into machine language.

In order to facilitate programming, existing Lisp systems have introduced a variety of additional features. Also, they depart from the purely functional core of the language and introduce several von Neumann-like language features. They introduce von Neumann-like variables, iterative control structures, explicit control transfer like the goto of conventional languages, and so on. Such features trade the conceptual integrity and purity of the language for execution efficiency.

It has been observed that Lisp programs are viewed uniformly as Lisp data structures, so that tools that manipulate Lisp programs may be written in Lisp. This has been the reason for the earliest examples of advanced programming environments being designed for Lisp. Interlisp is the most notable of such pioneer examples (Teitelman and Masinter, 1981).

44.2.3.2 Standard ML

Many errors that programmers are likely to make when using Lisp, and other untyped languages, involve type inconsistencies. Well-typed expressions cannot go wrong – at least in the sense of applying inappropriate operations to data objects. This is why a powerful type checker provides invaluable help to make programs more reliable. Standard ML (SML) is an interesting functional language, which differs from Lisp mainly through its strong typing. Whenever possible, SML infers types automatically. Type inference in SML is done on the basis of a type checking algorithm developed by Milner of Edinburgh University in the mid 1970s; the algorithm works well even in complex situations.

As a simple example, the inferred type *int* is provided in response to the expression

$2 + 3$;
    5 : int

(Expressions submitted by the programmer are written in plain text, while responses by SML are written in italics.)

Similarly, a type is inferred in response to a function definition:

fun div (x, y) = (y mod x = 0);
    *val div = fn : (int * int) → int*

For some expressions, however, the type checker cannot infer the type. In such a case, types may be explicitly specified by the user. This may happen in the case of overloading, as illustrated by the following example:

fun square (x) = x * x
    unresolvable overloaded identifier: x

In fact, the type inference mechanism cannot derive whether the argument is to be an integer or a real. The user can provide the necessary information by typing:

fun square (x): int = x * x
    *val square = fn : int * int → int*

which specifies the results to be integer or, equivalently;

fun square (x: int) = x * x
    *val square = fn : int * int → int*

which specifies the argument to be integer. In either case the information provides sufficient information to the type inference mechanism, which can infer the type of the whole expression.

Another interesting feature provided by SML is the ability to define polymorphic functions, i.e. functions that can be applied to arguments of several types. Finally, another aspect that gives the language its distinctive flavour if compared to Lisp is the ability to define exceptions and exception handling. These features allow programs to reflect more clearly their intended behavior, instead of hiding it in an obscure implementation. In the absence of explicit exception handling features, for example, a list handling Lisp function which looks for an entry in the list would return the empty list in case the element is not in the list. This might be implemented in SML by raising an exception when the sought entry is not in the list.

44.2.3.3 Miranda

Miranda is a very rigorous, purely functional language. It is deliberately rather terse in its syntax and does not trade purity for more mundane efficiency reasons; there are no side-effects nor imperative features in the language.

Miranda's functions are first-class citizens. They can be both passed as parameters and returned as results from other functions. The language uses the so-called lazy evaluation. This means that expressions are evaluated only when their value is needed. Because of this, it is impossible to write functions that return a value even if some of its arguments are undefined.

As with SML, Miranda is a strongly typed functional language. Apart from simple types, the language provides constructors to build lists and tuples, analogous to Pascal records, whose components are extracted by pattern matching.

Functions may be defined by (possibly recursive) guarded equations. For example:

$$gcd\ x\ y = gcd\ (x-y)\ y,\ x>y$$
$$= gcd\ x\ (y-x),\ y>x$$
$$= x,\ otherwise$$

The language permits the introduction of local definitions in the branches of the guarded form. This allows programs to assume a nested block structure.

Alternative equations defining a function may be selected based on the use of different patterns in the formal parameters. An example is given by the following definition of function 'reverse', which reverses the contents of a list by recursively applying the function to the tail of the list, if it is not empty:

reverse [ ] = [ ]   (reverse of the empty list gives the empty list)
reverse (a : x) = reverse x + + [a]
                                   + + (stands for list concatenation)

44.2.3.4 FP

Backus defined a family of functional programming languages, called FP. Each member of the family provides a choice of functional forms. According to Backus, the more functional forms are in the language, the more expressive it is. Here is just a glimpse of the features of FP.

There are two kinds of data objects: atoms and sequences. Atoms are sequences of characters; a sequence of n objects $x_1, x_2, \ldots, x_n$ is written as $\langle x_1, x_2, \ldots, x_n \rangle$, while the empty sequence is denoted by **nil**. The application of a function f to its parameters x is indicated as $f{:}x$.

Primitive functions include functions for:

1. *Selection*. Useful examples include FIRST (to extract the first example of a sequence), LAST (to extract the last), TAIL (to extract everything except the first element).
2. *Structuring*. These are primitives to manipulate sequences, such as ROTR (rotates the contents right), ROTL (rotates the contents left), LENGTH (computes the length of the sequences), CONS (constructs a sequence, like Lisp's CONS).
3. *Arithmetic operations*.
4. *Predicates*, i.e. functions returning atoms T (for true) or F (for false). Examples are the usual operators $\langle, \rangle, =$, and so on. Also, we have ATOM (returns T if the argument is an atom) and NULL (returns T if the argument is the null sequence).
5. *Logical operations*, such as AND, OR, NOT.
6. *The identity function*, ID.

Among functional forms, the following are suggested as useful by Backus:

7. *Functional composition*, indicated by '∘':

$$(f{\circ}g) : x\ is\_defined\_as\ f : (g : x)$$

8. *Construction*:

$$[f_1, f_2, \ldots, f_n] : x\ is\_defined\_as\ \langle f_1 : x, f_2 : x, \ldots, f_n : x \rangle$$

9. *Insert*:

/f : x is_defined_as **if** x is $\langle x_1 \rangle$ **then** x_1
        else if x is $\langle x_1, x_2, \ldots, x_n \rangle$ **and** $n \geqslant 2$
                then f: $\langle x_1, /f : \langle x_2, \ldots, x_n \rangle \rangle$

This allows us to distribute a binary operator over all elements of a sequence; for example, $/+ : \langle 1, 2, 3, 4 \rangle$ yields 10.

10. *Apply to all*. It applies to all elements of a sequence.

α f : x is_defined_as **if** x is **nil then nil**

        else if x is $\langle x_1, x_2, \ldots, x_n \rangle$
                then $\langle f : x_1, f : x_2, \ldots, f : x_n \rangle$

11. *Condition*:

$$(IF\ p\ f\ g) : x\ is\_defined\_as\ \textbf{if}\ p : x = T\ \textbf{then}\ f : x\ \textbf{else}\ g : x$$

12. *While*. It repeatedly applies a function:

(WHILE p f) : **x** is_defined_as
        if p : x = T **then** (WHILE p f) : (f : x) **else** x

44.2.3.5 Object-oriented functional languages

Finally, there are examples of functional languages blended with features inherited from object-oriented programming: LOOPS (Bobrow and Stefik, 1983), Flavors (Moon, 1986) and CLOS (SIGPLAN, 1988). The idea is that integration of the functional and object-oriented paradigms may lead to languages that mix the mathematical rigor and the flexibility of the functional style with object-oriented structuring mechanisms that help the implementation of large programs. More generally, the ability to take the best from existing programming paradigms is the motivation behind multi-paradigm languages and environments, which represent an important and very active research area (*IEEE Software*, 1986; Zave, 1989).

44.3 Logic languages

Strong mathematical foundations and support of a programming paradigm that does not reflect an underlying, low-level machine architecture are two important factors that are shared by both functional and logic programming. Functional languages are rooted in the theory of Church's lambda calculus. Logic languages are based on predicate calculus. Thus both have strong mathematical foundations that support reasoning about programs in a sound and formally based manner.

44.3.1 History

The origins of logic programming can be traced back to the theory of automatic theorem proving developed by Robinson (1965 and 1971). (See also Robinson (1983).)

The unification operation (see below), which constitutes the basis for the interpretation of logic, is a sophisticated version of pattern matching. Before the advent of logic languages, other languages adopted pattern matching as the main control feature, thus supporting a quite unconventional programming paradigm. Most notable among such languages is SNOBOL4 (an acronym for String Oriented Symbolic Language). SNOBOL4 (Griswold *et al.*, 1971) was introduced as a language supporting complex text processing, such as natural language text manipulations. ICON (Griswold and Griswold, 1983) is a language that combines the interesting concepts of SNOBOL4 with a more traditional syntax and introduces some new concepts of its own.

An example is given here of SNOBOL4 that shows how pattern matching provides powerful capabilities for string processing. We define the structure of a highly simplified subset of the English language by means of the following pattern definitions, which represent a grammar:

```
SUBJECT = "I" | "YOU" | "WE"
VERB = "EAT" | "TAKE"
OBJECT = "FOOD" | "SPOON" | "HER"
SENTENCE = SUBJECT VERB OBJECT
```

If STRING is a variable denoting a string, we can check whether it is a valid sentence according to the above definition by writing:

```
STRING SENTENCE
```

As an example, the result will be a success if the string is 'I EAT FOOD' or "I TAKE HER'. It would be a failure in the case of 'HER SPOON EAT'.

The first examples of logic programming languages were developed in the late 1960s at MIT. Among the initial attempts, one can recall PLANNER (Hewitt, 1969), a simple version of which 'Microplanner' is described in Sussman *et al.* (1970). These languages were defined as research tools for automatic theorem-proving, but never found their way out of research laboratories.

Artificial intelligence research and, in particular, natural language processing were also the motivation behind Prolog. Prolog, an acronym for 'programmation en logique' was developed by a group headed by Colmerauer at the Artificial Intelligence Group (GIA-Group d'Intelligence Artificielle) in Marseilles, France, starting in 1972 (Roussel, 1975).

The relationship between Prolog and classical logic was then investigated by Kowalski (1979a and 1979b). Kowalski's work was extremely important. On the one hand, he stressed the mathematical foundations of the language within logic; on the other he contributed to popularizing logic programming as a new and promising programming paradigm.

In retrospect, Prolog developed slowly in comparison with Lisp. Cohen (1985) offers the following reasons to explain that:

1. The lack of interesting published examples illustrating the expressive power of the language.
2. The lack of adequate implementations.
3. The availability of Lisp to deal with the same class of problems.
4. Efficient Prolog implementations became available in the late 1970s and early 1980s (Warren, 1977). Efficient interpreters and compilers played a major role in the acceptance of Prolog. Another important driving force was the much-publicized Japanese Fifth Generation Computer Project, in which logic programming played a central role (McCorduck and Feigenbaum, 1983; Shapiro, 1983).

Currently, Prolog is a well-established language. As with Lisp, however, it suffers from a lack of standardization. There are many language dialects, and this hampers portability of programs across the various language implementations. Several variants of the Prolog family languages have also been defined and implemented in the research community. Among them are the parallel extensions of the language Parlog (Clark and Gregory, 1986) and concurrent Prolog (Shapiro, 1986 and 1988).

The advent of Prolog has been strongly opposed by several research groups in artificial intelligence, especially advocates of the Lisp programming language. For example, Bobrow (1984) presents a critical view of logic programming, particularly of Prolog, and advocates that none of the known paradigms – von Neumann, logic and functional – is entirely satisfactory if taken alone. His viewpoint is that one should search for integration of the different paradigms. This point will be taken up in Section 44.4.

As will be explained in the Section 44.3.3, the programming style enforced by Prolog may be viewed as an extension of what is currently available for relational database programming. In particular, one can recognize the logic flavor in a relational query language such as SQL. However, Prolog is much more powerful in its deductive features. For these reasons, many interesting research languages are currently being developed to support deductive databases (Ullman, 1987), and one can expect this to be an area where the lesson of Prolog will have a deep impact in the future.

44.3.2 Principles

The basic concepts of logic programming are inherited from logic. However, to understand it in the context of non-conventional languages, one may characterize it by contrasting its principles with those of functional programming.

44.3.2.1 *Relational versus functional programming*

The most striking difference between functional and logic programming is that functional programming is based on mathematical functions, whereas logic programming is based on relations. Functions clearly distinguish between the domain and the range; each value in the domain is mapped into one element of the range. Relations, on the other hand, treat all their arguments uniformly, without distinguishing between inputs and outputs. A relation may be used to describe any given property by grouping tuples that have that property into a set. The grouping does not distinguish between input and output values. This allows a relation to be used in any direction. For example, if there is a relation *father_of* between individuals, described as a set of pairs of names, the relation can be both to evaluate the father of an individual and the individuals with a given father.

44.3.2.2 Facts, rules and queries

Relations in logic programs may be defined extensionally, by listing all tuples that participate in the relation. These are usually called facts. An example might be:

father_of (charles, james)
father_of (charles, martha)
father_of (charles, sylvia)
father_of (john, charles)

Relations may be also defined intensionally, by providing a rule that defines all tuples that participate in the relation, rather than explicitly listing all tuples. For example, based on the definition of *father_of*, one can define the relation *descendant_of* as follows:

descendant_of (X,Y) :– father_of (Y,X)
descendant_of (X,Y) :– father_of (Z,X), descendant_of (Z,Y)

Syntactically, we follow the convention of the most common Prolog dialects. We indicate constants and relation names (called functors) by lower-case identifiers. Identifiers with an initial capital stand for variables. The relation *father_of* is given by a set of facts, separated by a semicolon. The relation *descendant_of* is given by two rules. The symbol ':–' is read as 'if', and the comma stands for 'and'. Variables in a rule are implicitly universally quantified. Thus the two rules defining relation *descendant_of* are read as:

1. For all X and Y, X is a descendant of Y if Y is father of X.
2. For all X, Y, and Z, X is a descendant of Y if Z is father of X and Z is a descendant of Y.

Rules expressed as $P :– Q_1, Q_2, \ldots Q_n$, $n \geqslant 0$, are called Horn clauses, after the logician Horn who studied them.

Facts define properties by listing all tuples that enjoy a property. They are similar to the tuples of a relation in a relational database. Rules do this implicitly, usually in terms of recursion. Logic programs are just a set of facts and rules, to which one can apply queries. Queries may be used to check whether a given tuple is in a relation or, more generally, to deduce new facts from given facts and using rules to apply deductions.

For example, a query against the above relation *father_of* might be:

? father_of (charles, sylvia)

to which we expect the result to be *YES*. Another example is the query:

? descendant_of (james, john)

to which we also expect the answer to be *YES*. Instead the result of the following sample query:

? descendant_of (mary, john)

would be *NO* because there is no fact of this kind that can be deduced from the above relation. This corresponds to the so-called closed world hypothesis, i.e. all truths are only those that can be deduced.

44.3.2.3 Concepts of mathematical logic

To state the above formally, one must refer to a few concepts of mathematical logic.

A *term* is the only kind of data structure available in logic programs. A term is a constant, a variable, or a compound term. A compound term is written as a functor by one or more arguments, which are themselves terms. The number of such arguments is called the arity of the functor. For example, *descendant_of(X,Y)* is a term, as is *descendant_of (X, descendant_of (Y, john))*. A term is *ground* if it does not contain any variables.

A *substitution* is a (possibly empty) finite set of pairs of the form $X_i = t_i$, where X_i is a variable and t_i is a term, $X_i \neq X_j$ for all i, j, and X_i does not occur in t_j for all i, j. The result of applying a substitution μ to term t is denoted by $t\mu$.

A *term* t_1 is said to be an instance of term t_2 if there is a substitution μ such that $t_2\mu = t_1$. If there is a substitution μ such that $t_2\mu = t_1$, but not *vice versa*, one can say that term t_2 is *more general* than term t_1.

We are now in the position to state the rule that is used to apply deductions in logic, called *modus ponens:*

From the rule R: P :– Q_1, Q_2, ... Q_n
and the facts Q'_2, Q'_2, ... Q'_n we can deduce P'
if P' :– Q'_1, Q'_2, ... Q'_n is an instance of R.

This gives a formal justification to our claims that the answer to query:

? father_of (charles, sylvia)

and:

? descendant_of (james, john)

should be *YES*.

Queries can also contain variables, as in:

? father_of (charles, X)

Variables in queries are implicitly existentially quantified. Thus the query reads:

is there an X such that charles is father of X?

In order to accommodate existential queries in the theory of logic programming, we provide a further deduction rule, called generalization. The rule states that an existential query Q is a consequence of an instance of it, Qμ, for any substitution μ. In the example, the answer would be *YES* because we can prove that *charles* is the father of at least one individual.

44.3.2.4 Unification

A procedure to verify mechanically whether a given query is a consequence of a set of facts and rules is based on mechanical deduction. The first landmark paper on this issue was published by Robinson in 1965. This paper introduces the concept of unification, which is the core of the computation model for logic programs. The following illustrates unification in a simple way, without paying any attention to the problem of performing it efficiently. Efficient algorithms can be found in Paterson and Wegman (1978), Martelli and Montanari (1982) and Dwork *et al.* (1984).

Unification may be viewed as a kind of pattern matching that, additionally, performs binding of variables, if any. Formally, we say that two terms t_1 and t_2 unify if there is a substitution μ such that $t_1\mu = t_2\mu$. μ is called a unifier and $t_1\mu$ is called the common instance of t_1 and t_2. The most general unifier (*MGU*) of two terms is a unifier such that the associated common instance is most general. The goal of the unification algorithm is to evaluate the *MGU* of any two given terms t_1 and t_2. It can be shown that the *MGU* is unique up to a renaming of variables.

44.3.2.5 Unification algorithm

The following outlines a unification algorithm, given that t_1 and t_2 find *MGU*.

> Initialize *MGU* to empty, *failure* to false, and the working set S to contain the pair $\langle t_1, t_2 \rangle$.
> **while** S $\neq$ empty **and not** *failure* **do**
> > extract a pair $\langle t', t'' \rangle$ from S
> > **case**
> > > t' is a variable that does not occur in t'':
> > > > substitute t'' for t' in any pair of S and in *mgu*
> > > > and add
> > > > $\langle t', t'' \rangle$ to *mgu*;
> > > t'' is a variable that does not occur in t':
> > > > substitute t' for t'' in any pair of S and in *mgu*
> > > > and add
> > > > $\langle t'', t' \rangle$ to *mgu*;
> > > t' and t'' are two identical constants or variables:
> > > > do nothing
> > > t' is $f(t'_1, t'_2, \ldots, t'_n)$ and t is $f(t''_1, t''_2, \ldots, t''_n)$ for some functor f and $n \geqslant 1$:
> > > > insert $\langle t'_1 = t''_1 \rangle, \langle t'_2 = t''_2 \rangle, \ldots, \langle t'_n = t''_n \rangle$ in S;
> > **otherwise**
> > > *failure* := *true*;
> > **end case**;
> **if not** failure **then** *mgu* is the required unifier
> **else** the algorithm fails without finding a solution

The unification algorithm outlined above can prevent the unification of such terms as $f(\ldots, X, \ldots)$ and X by performing an additional action called occurs check. In fact, there is no finite common instance of these terms.

It is now possible to understand how logic programs may be executed by an abstract interpreter which uses unification as a basic operator. Suppose we are given a query Q and a set of facts and rules constituting a program P. The abstract interpreter starts from Q, which is the initial goal to prove, and progressively decomposes the goal into its subgoals, until no goals remain to be proved. This may be described precisely by an abstract interpretation algorithm.

44.3.2.6 Abstract interpretation algorithm

Given a query Q and a program P, the algorithm answers *YES*, and provides bindings for the variables appearing in Q, or it answers *NO*:

> Initialize the set of goals SG to prove to Q and *failure* to *false*;
> **while** SG $\neq$ empty **and not** failure **do**
> > extract an element G from SG and a (possibly renamed) clause X :– $X_1, X_2, \ldots X_n$, $n \geqslant 0$, from P (note tht the clause is a fact if $n = 0$), such that G and X unify with *mgu* μ;
> > **if** unification algorithm does not fail **then**
> > > insert $X_1, X_2, \ldots, X_n$ into SG; apply μ to all elements of SG and to Q
> > **else** *failure* := *true*;
> **end do**
> **if not** failure **then** the answer is *YES* and Qμ describes the bindings that make the query successful
> **else** the answer is *NO*

Note that the above abstract algorithm may terminate in one of two possible states: success or failure. In addition, the computation may not terminate if the set of goals to prove never becomes empty. Furthermore, a few choices for the interpreter are left unspecified: choosing the next goal to extract from SG and choosing the next clause to match from P. The choice of the goal to prove from SG is immaterial as far as finding a solution is concerned, since all of the goals must eventually be solved. The choice of the clause is much more critical because, even if a solution exists, there are choices that may fail to find a solution and may lead to a search that does not terminate. These choices are discussed in the next section for the case of Prolog.

Interpretation of a logic program is amenable to a highly parallel implementation. This is one of the reasons for the hope that logic programming will become more appealing as new, highly parallel, architectures become available.

44.3.2.7 Negation in logic programming

It has already been observed that logic programming is based on the closed world assumption. False facts are not expressed explicitly; they are exactly those that cannot be proven. Accordingly, logic programming provides a limited form of negation, called negation by failure. In fact, 'not X' is assumed to be a consequence of a given program P if 'X' is not a consequence of P. Unfortunately, it turns out that correct implementation of negation by failure is difficult as well as potentially having undesirable effects in programming.

44.3.2.8 Declarative paradigm

It was observed earlier that logic programming differs from functional programming mainly because it deals with relations (i.e. predicates) rather than functions. Even more striking is the difference between logic and the conventional paradigm of programming in a von Neumann style. Conventional programming is imperative, i.e. it consists of prescribing the exact stepwise sequence of instructions through which a given problem is solved. Logic programming, on the other hand is declarative, i.e. it asserts the properties of a given domain, and lets the interpreter of the language infer solutions to queries by applying inference. To emphasize this fact, one could say that logic programming is closer to specifications than imperative (and even functional) programming is. Descriptions given using imperative programs are implementation-oriented and concentrate on lower level details.

The reader interested in more depth and details on the foundations of logic programming may refer to the first part of Sterling and Shapiro (1986), Lloyd (1984) and Hogger (1984).

44.3.3 Sample languages

44.3.3.1 SQL

The first commercially successful logic languages were database query languages. These languages exhibit very limited logic functionalities, yet they represent a significant departure from the low-level and iterative, step-by-step data manipulation provided by traditional approaches.

An example is the relational database language SQL (Ullman, 1982). Suppose that the database contains a relation *Person* that represents people's personal data along with their birth date and place (city name). Also, suppose that a relation *Geo* exists where city names are listed along with the name of the country of the city. In order to extract all data concerning people born in France we may write the following SQL fragment:

> *select name*
> *from person*
> *where birth_place* =

```
(select town
from geo
where country = "france")
```

We assume here that field *birth_place* of relation *person* contains the name of the place where the people are born; *town* is the field relation *geo* that contains the names of towns, while *country* is the field containing the name of the country to which the town belongs.

By reading the SQL fragment, it is easy to see that the request for the needed information is not given procedurally, but rather in declarative form. The query does not specify how to navigate within the database in order to collect the needed information. It simply defines the logical properties of the output, and leaves the choice of the search strategy to the underlying implementation.

44.3.3.2 Prolog

SQL, and other database query languages, represent a very simple step in the direction of declarative programming and can hardly be classified as fully fledged logic languages. The best known and most widely available logic language is Prolog. Unfortunately, the language has not yet been standardized, and there are many dialects that differ in syntactic and even in semantic details. Among the most notable dialects are Edinburgh Prolog, Micro-Prolog and Prolog II. The first has been popularized by Clocksin and Mellish (1984) and by several available efficient implementations. The second is described in Clark and McCabe (1984). The last has been implemented by the Marseille Group led by Colmerauer, who first introduced the language (Giannessini *et al.*, 1986). In what follows, we will use the notation of Edinburgh Prolog, as we did in the previous section.

Prolog is based on the general concepts of logic programming illustrated in Section 44.3.2. However, to make it a useful and practical language, two important aspects were incorporated. First, particular care has been taken with the strategy followed by the abstract interpreter. Second, a number of extra-logical features, including ways to access some of the facilities provided by the underlying hardware (e.g. arithmetic, input/output, etc.) were added to increase the power of the language.

The interpretation model followed by Prolog solves the two non-deterministic choices on the abstract algorithm of Section 44.3.3 in the following way. First, an ordering relation is imposed on the set of goals SG. The step of the algorithm that states 'extract an element G from SG' is replaced by 'extract the left-most element G from SG'; the step 'insert $X_1, X_2, \ldots, X_n$ into SG' is replaced by 'insert $X_1, X_2, \ldots, X_n$ to the left of the ordered sequence SG'. This choice amounts to handling goals to be solved according to a LIFO policy. Second, the clause to be chosen for unification is selected by sequentially scanning the list of facts and rules that constitutes the program, from top to bottom. Third, to simulate the effect of a non-deterministic algorithm, the interpreter performs backtracking after a failure. That is, if no unifiable clause is found for the chosen goal, the computation backtracks to the last choice made, and the next potential unifiable clause is chosen, if any.

For example, consider the following query to the family program illustrated in Section 44.3.3 and reported hereafter in numbered form for the reader's convenience:

1. *father_of (charles, james)*
2. *father_of (charles, martha)*
3. *father_of (charles, sylvia)*
4. *father_of (john, charles)*
5. *descendant_of (X, Y) :- father_of (Y, X)*
6. *descendant_of (X, Y):- father_of (Z, X), descendant_of (Z, Y)*

Let us consider the effect of the following query:

? descendant_of (james, john)

The unification with the left part of rule 5 yields the *mgu* $\{\langle X, james \rangle, \langle Y, john \rangle\}$ and generates the subgoal *father_of (john, james)*, which eventually fails. Next, backtracking leads to the unification of the goal to prove with the left part of rule 6, which yields the *mgu* $\{\langle X, james \rangle, \langle Y, john \rangle\}$ and generates the subgoals *father_of (Z, james), descendant_of (Z, john)*, to be solved in that order. It is easy to see that eventually, these two goals will succeed, by binding Z to *charles*.

Prolog inherits string handling facilities from Lisp. The term $.(t_1, t_2)$, more conveniently written as $[t_1 \mid t_2)$ corresponds to a CONS pair. The head of the list (i.e. t_1) is what CAR would yield; similarly, CONS would yield the tail (i.e. t_2).

Prolog inherits arithmetic predicates from the underlying machine architecture. The predicate *is* is used for arithmetic evaluation. It corresponds to the familiar von Neumann operator that is usually indicated as ': = '. For example, we may write the predicate:

X *is* $Y + Z$

This requires Y and Z to be bound to a numeric value. The result of $Y + Z$ is then bound to X, if X is unbound.

Finally, Prolog provides a number of extralogical predicates that may help produce useful and more efficient algorithms, but depart from the conceptual integrity of mathematical logic. The two most notable such predicates are *cut* and *fail*. Both may be used to affect the search procedure followed by the abstract interpreter of the language.

The predicate *cut*, denoted by '!', allows us to tell the abstract interpreter that some choices need not be reconsidered upon backtracking. Precisely, it always succeeds when encountered for the first time in a rule. However, it prevents the interpreter from re-satisfying the rule again upon backtracking, should the need arise. The parent goal would fail in such an unfortunate circumstance. The predicate *fail* always fails when encountered. It is a mechanism for explicitly forcing backtracking to occur.

Other extralogical predicates are used to achieve some useful side-effects, such as those concerning I/O and interfacing with the underlying operating system. For example, the predicate *read (X)* reads a value from the input stream and binds it to X; should backtracking occur, it cannot be re-satisfied. Still other predicates are available to access and manipulate programs. Such predicates provide much of the same power that is in Lisp. For example, with such predicates one may access clauses and may add and remove clauses to a program.

44.3.3.3 Other logic languages

Prolog is an untyped language. Correctness of the application of operators to data can only be assessed by the interpreter at run-time, depending on the value that is currently bound to the variable. Indeed, there are some Prolog dialects that introduce some notion of type and type checking, in order to increase the reliability of Prolog programs (for example, see Turbo Prolog from Borland.)

Among current developments in the family of Prolog-based languages, are the efforts aimed at exploiting parallelism in logic programming. The idea is that a subgoal X_i in X :- $X_1, X_2, \ldots,$ X_n may be interpreted as a process, while the goal is a network of processes, and a shared logical variable is an interprocess communication channel.

Actually, in a logic program there are two possible forms of parallelism: AND-parallelism and OR-parallelism. OR-parallelism means that all clauses whose left part unify with a given goal are selected in parallel. AND-parallelism means that all subgoals are solved in parallel. Furthermore, suitable mechanisms are introduced for interprocess communication; in general, they are based on the message-based scheme of CSP (Hoare, 1978).

The first concurrent logic language was IC-Prolog (Clark and McCabe, 1979). Its best known descendants are Concurrent Prolog (Shapiro, 1986 and 1988) and Parlog (Clark and Gregory, 1986). Other proposals are GHC (Guarded Horn Clauses) (Ueda, 1985), P-Prolog (Yang and Aiso, 1986), Delta-Prolog (Pereira and Nasr, 1984) and Strand (Foster and Taylor, 1989). The area is still the subject of much research activity.

Other logic languages incorporate ideas from object-oriented programming, and may be viewed as a more or less integrated mixture of the two paradigms. Among such languages is Vulcan (Kahn *et al.*, 1987). Again, this is an area where language research is extremely active.

44.4 Other approaches

There is a wide variety of non-conventional approaches that have resulted in specific programming languages and language proposals. Some languages commit themselves entirely to a single specific non-conventional approach. More often, however, languages adopt several of them, thus supporting multi-paradigm software development.

44.4.1 Data-intensive languages

Conventional languages and most of the languages examined here may be called computation-intensive. This means that they provide ways to express computations using relatively simple operations on elementary objects. The term data-intensive is used for those languages that provide complex data structuring mechanisms and high-level composite operations to manipulate them.

SQL, introduced in Section 44.3.3, may be considered as an example of a data-intensive language with limited logical capabilities. Apart from the operation of selection, relations in SQL may be projected (e.g. in the case of relation *geo* of Section 44.3.3 one may obtain all cities located in Spain). They may be joined (in the case of relations *geo* and *person*, one might produce a relation where each person has associated the nation, instead of the city, where the person was born). These very-high level operations on complex aggregates reduce the need for expressing navigation among elementary data using lower-level primitives.

Another example of a data-intensive language is APL (Iverson, 1962) which was mentioned earlier and is briefly characterized here. As opposed to SQL, which deals with data stored on secondary storage, APL deals with data – matrixes – stored in main memory. APL may be viewed as a kind of functional language operating on large and complex objects (arrays of many dimensions).

Operators on matrixes provided by APL are so powerful that programs that would otherwise require several lines or even pages of code become extremely compact when coded in APL. This is why they are often called 'one-liners'. Consequently, short APL expressions correspond to long code fragments representing the same computations in other languages. This heavy reliance on expressions allows the language to be classified as a (partially) applicative language.

SETL is yet another data-intensive language. It provides very high-level set manipulation primitives. Its very high level features have led to it being used as a prototyping tool; an example is the construction of the first validated Ada processor (an interpreter rather than a compiler).

SETL's data types include sets (corresponding to the mathematical concept of a set), tuples (corresponding to an ordered collection) and maps (corresponding to a collection of ordered pairs). Such set-theoretic elements may be manipulated in a highly declarative fashion using predicate calculus formulae including the usual Boolean operators and the quantifiers *for each* and *there exists*. Apart from this, however, the language is still imperative and sequential.

44.4.2 Knowledge representation languages

An important and increasingly large class of languages can be classified as knowledge representation languages. Such languages are usually part of a rich environment providing tools that support the development of AI applications, such as expert systems. Their goal is the ability to represent knowledge in particular application domains, and use that knowledge to solve particular problems in that domain.

Although some of the languages discussed in the previous sections may be used for knowledge representation and manipulation (e.g. Lisp and Prolog), there is an increasing interest in languages that incorporate more than one programming paradigm, such as logical, functional, object-oriented, and others. Lisp is often used as the core language of the system. The system is implemented in Lisp, and Lisp is available as a programming tool. In addition to Lisp features, however, others are provided to facilitate software development. Without entering into concepts that are more properly addressed in the context of AI and expert systems, and without aiming at completeness, some language paradigms that are often found in such systems are given below.

44.4.3 Rule-based languages

Rule-based languages are used in many expert systems tools as mechanisms to represent knowledge. Rules provide a formal way of representing recommendations, directives, strategies, and so on. They are expressed as:

if *premisses* **then** *consequences*

Rules resemble their counterpart in logic programming. The basic difference, however, is that rule-based systems take a more pragmatic viewpoint and are not so strongly rooted in theory. In particular, consequences can be any kind of action, not just true facts that are asserted upon the truth of premisses.

In a rule-based system, the set of rules that models the knowledge is checked against a collection of facts representing the database. If the premisses of some rule are found to be true as a result of this matching, then the rule is said to fire (or execute). The consequences of the rule are then executed and their actions may modify the set of facts in the database by, say, adding new facts; more generally, they may perform any action.

For example, the following rules describe hints on how to select wine for a gourmet meal:

if *menu type_1* **then** *red_wine_recommended*
if *menu_type_2* **then** *white_wine_recommended*

Other rules may describe when a given menu is considered to be of one type or the other, depending on the choice of the entries.

The reasoning mechanism in a rule-based system may proceed in two possible ways. One is called forward chaining and the other backward chaining. Consider an initial state consisting of facts A, B, C, D and E, and suppose that rules are as follows:

G & A→X
C & H→G
A→H & U

where X, G, H, and U are all facts to be inserted in the database if their premises are satisfied.

In forward chaining, premises are checked, and a rule may be selected to fire if its premises are found in the database. In the example, rule A→H & U may fire, and this leads to a database containing A, B, C, D, E, H, U. At this stage, the second rule may fire, leading to A, B, C, D, E, H, U, G, and so on. It is easy to see that this approach follows a generative approach, since all facts deriving from the initial facts are progressively derived.

Backward chaining does exactly the opposite. It starts from what one wishes to prove and tries to justify it according to the given facts. Suppose that in the previous case we are asked to prove whether X may occur. This may actually happen if G & A occur; A is in the database, while G is not. G may occur if C and H occur; C is already in the database, while H is not. H can occur if A occurs. Since A is in the database, we may conclude the reasoning by saying that X is verified.

44.4.4 Frame-based languages

Frames are a way to represent knowledge that was introduced by Minsky (1975). Informally, a frame is a chunk of information that represents a concept or a situation. Formally, what a frame really is depends on the specific frame-based language. However, as in the case of object-oriented languages, a frame is usually structured as a set of valued attributes (often called slots).

The most important difference between frame-based and object-oriented languages is that frames are organized in a semantic net. A semantic net is a graph whose nodes are frames and arcs describe the relations between nodes. Common arcs define the relation *is_a*, which correspond to a subclass in object-oriented languages. Other kinds of relation might be *has_part* or *is_agent*.

44.4.5 Access-oriented languages

Access-oriented languages enforce yet another programming paradigm. The idea here is that one can define actions (also called annotations) to be triggered automatically when certain data (called annotated data) is accessed or modified. This allows programs to be designed in a way that certain data may be viewed as active data; as a computation progresses, the actions triggered by active data may be used to monitor the computation. Active data behaves like daemons or 'watchdog units', using the terminology of KEE (IntelliCorp, 1988).

Active values are very useful for modeling reactive systems. For example, one may easily define a module called *cooling_system* to be involved automatically when the value of *temperature* in any of the modules representing physical parts of a plant exceeds a specified limit. This feature is even more useful if it is possible, and easy, to direct the effect of active objects to modify graphical objects. For example, when the value of *temperature* reaches a 'danger level', it would be useful to signal its effect automatically as a flashing image on the screen.

Access-oriented programming has been incorporated as a paradigm in several modern languages, such as Loops (Bobrow and Stefik, 1983), which is based on the earlier research system KRL (Bobrow and Winograd, 1977), and KEE (IntelliCorp, 1988).

44.5 Conclusions

Although most systems are still programmed in conventional, procedural, programming languages, there is an increasing use of non-conventional forms. In particular, functional and logic programming languages are used in a wide number of applications. It seems clear that there are certain classes of problems to which these non-conventional languages are better suited than their procedural counterparts. Consequently, it seems likely that functional and logic languages will continue to be used widely, and it seems probable that their use will increase in these particular application domains. Although researchers have been promising (but not delivering) very high performance implementations of functional and logic languages on parallel machines for some years, it does seem likely that there will be such efficient implementations within the forseeable future. This can only strengthen the trend towards the use of non-conventional languages.

It is clear, however, that there are some applications for which the two main strands of non-conventional languages are not ideally suited. The growth of a number of variants and adaptations of the two prime non-conventional forms, as outlined in Section 44.4, seem set to continue. Taking a broader look at software engineering one can see that 4GLs have been very effective in a particular application domain – they can be thought of as non-conventional languages for a particular problem area. It seems likely that, for well-defined problem domains, there will be an increasing development and application of problem-domain-specific programming languages. In general, these will tend to be non-conventional as the declarative style gives power and succinctness in dealing with application problems and can often be understood by 'end users' without particular programming experience.

All the major programming language styles – procedural, functional and logical – have application domains where they are particularly effective. This suggests that general-purpose programming languages must embrace a number of these different approaches. Consequently, it seems likely that the future of the major general-purpose programming languages will be as multi-paradigm languages. It seems most likely that multi-paradigm languages will be built on a non-conventional basis as it is more practical to build a unified language and integrated environment for a multi-paradigm programming language on a non-conventional, rather than a procedural base. Some of the work described in the previous section already shows the trend towards these multi-paradigm languages.

44.6 References and bibliography

Abelson, H. and Sussman, G. J. (1985) *Structure and Implementation of Computer Programs*, MIT Press

Backus, J. (1973) Programming language semantics and closed applicative languages. *ACM Symposium on Principles of Programming Languages*, Boston, USA

Backus, J. (1978) Can programming be liberated from the von Neumann style?. *Communications of ACM* **21**

Barendregt, H. (1984) *The Lambda Calculus*, North Holland

Birtwistle, G. *et al.* (1973) *Simula Begin*, Studentliteratur and Auerbach Publishers

Bobrow, D. G. (1984) If PROLOG is the answer, what is the question? *Proceedings 5th Generation Computer Systems*, Ohmsa Ltd. Tokyo, Japan and North Holland, Amsterdam, Holland, pp. 138–148

Bobrow, D. J. and Winograd, T. (1977) An overview of KRL, a knowledge representation language. *Cognitive Science*, **1**

Bobrow, D. G. and Stefik, M. (1983) *The LOOPS Manual*, Xerox PARC, Palo Alto, Calif., USA

Burke, G. S. *et al.* (1984) *NIL Reference Manual*, MIT/LCS/TR-311, MIT, Cambridge, Mass., USA

Burks *et al.* (1947) Preliminary discussion of the logical design of an electronic computing instrument. In *John von Neumann: Collected Works*, vol. 5, Macmillan

Burstall, R. *et al.* (1980) HOPE: an experimental applicative language. *Report CSR 62–80, 1980*. University of Edinburgh, Computer Science Dept.

Church, A. (1941) *Calculi of Lambda Conversion*, Princeton University Press

Clark, K. L. and Gregory, S. (1986) PARLOG: Parallel Programming in Logic. *ACM TOPLAS*, **8**, 1–49

Clark, K. L. and McCabe, F. G. (1979) The control facilities of IC-PROLOG. In *Expert Systems in the Microelectronic Age*, Edinburgh University Press, pp. 122–149

Clark, K. L. and McCabe, F. G. (1984) *Micro-PROLOG: Programming in Logic*, Prentice-Hall

Clocksin, W. F. and Mellish, C. S. (1984) *Programming in Prolog*, 2nd edn, Springer-Verlag

Cohen, J. (1985) Describing PROLOG by its implementation and compilation. *CACM*, **28**, 1311–1324

Cox, B. J. (1986) *Objected-Oriented Programming: An Evolutionary Approach*, Addison Wesley

Dwork, C. *et al.* (1984) On the sequential nature of unification. *Journal of Logic Programming*, **1**, 35–50. Also in *Programming Language Theory and Its Implementation*, (ed M. Gordon) Prentice Hall, 1988

Foster, I. and Taylor, S. (1989) Strand: a practical parallel programming language. In *Proceeding 1989 North American Conference on Logic Programming*, Cleveland, USA

Giannessini, F. *et al.* (1986) *Prolog*, Addison Wesley

Goldberg, A. and Robson, D. (1983) *Smalltalk-80: The Language and Its Implementation*, Addison Wesley

Gordon, M. *et al.* (1979) Edinburgh LCF. *Lecture Notes in Computer Science no 78*, Springer Verlag

Gordon, M. (1988) *Programming Language Theory and Its Implementation*, Prentice Hall

Griswold, R. E. and Griswold, M. T. (1983) *The ICON Programming Language*, Prentice Hall

Griswold, R. E., Poage, J. F. and Polonsky, I. P. *The SNOBOL4 Programming Language*, 2nd edn, Prentice Hall

Harper, R. *et al.* (1987) The definition of standard ML-version 2. *Edinburgh University Internal Report ECS-LFCS-87-28*

Hewitt, C. (1969) PLANNER: a language for proving theorems in robots. *Proceedings IJCAI 1969*, Washington DC, USA

Hoare, C. A. R. (1978) Communicating sequential processes. *Communications of the ACM*, **21**, 666–677

Hogger, C. J. (1984) *Introduction to Logic Programming*, Academic Press

IEEE Software (1986) Special Issue on Multiparadigm Languages and Environments, **3**, 1

IntelliCorp (1988) *KEEtutor™: A Basic Course*, Intellicorp, Inc., USA

Iverson, K. E. (1962) *A Programming Language*, J. Wiley & Sons 1962

Kahn, K. E. *et al.* (1987) Vulcan: logical concurrent objects. In *Research Directions in Object-Oriented Programming*, (ed B Shriver and P Wegner), MIT Press

Kowalski, R. A. (1979a) Algorithms = logic + control. *Communications of ACM*, **22**, 424–436

Kowalski, R. A. (1979b) *Logic for Problem Solving*, Springer Verlag

Landin, P. J. (1966) The next 700 programming languages. *Communications of ACM*, **9**, 157–64

Lloyd, J. W. (1984) *Foundations of Logic Programming*, Springer Verlag

Martelli, A. and Montanari, U. (1982) An efficient unification algorithm. *ACM Transactions on Programming Languages and Sytems*, **4**, 1

McCarthy, J. (1960) Recursive functions of symbolic expressions and their computation by machine. *Communications of ACM*, **3**

McCarthy, J. (1978) History of LISP (*ACM SIGPLAN History of Programming Languages Conference*). *SIGPLAN Notices* **13**

McCorduck, P. and Feigenbaum, E. (1963) *The Fifth Generation*, Addison Wesley

Meyer, B. (1988) *Object-Oriented Software Construction*, Prentice Hall

Milner, R. (1984) The standard ML core language. *Edinburgh University Internal Report CSR-168-84*

Minsky, M. (1975) A framework for representing knowledge. In *The Psychology of Computer Vision*, (ed. P. Winston) McGraw Hill

Moon, D. (1986) Object-oriented programming with Flavors. *Proceedings of OOPSLA '86*

Newell, A., and Shaw, J. C. (1957) Programming the logic theory machine. *Procedings of the 1957 Western Joint Computer Conference*, IRE

Paterson, M. S. and Wegman, M. N. (1973) Linear unification. *Journal of Computer and Systems Sciences*, **16**, 158–167

Pereira, L. M. and Nasr, R. (1984) Delta-Prolog: A Distributed Logic Programming Language. In *Proceedings International Conference on Fifth Generation Computer Systems*, Tokyo

Peyton–Jones, S. (1987) *The Implementation of Functional Programming Languages*, Prentice Hall

Robinson, J. A. (1965) A machine-oriented logic based on the resolution principle. *JACM*, **12**, 23–41

Robinson, J. A. (1971) Computational logic: the unification computation. *Machine Intelligence*, **6**, 63–72

Robinson, J. A. (1983) Logic programming: past, present and future. *New Generation Computing*, **1**, 107–124

Roussel, P. (1975) *PROLOG: Manuel de Reference et d'Utilisation*, Group d'Intelligence Artificielle, Université de Marseilles

Schaffert, C. *et al.* (1980) An introduction to Trellis/Owl, (Proceedings OOPSLA 1986) *SIGPLAN Notices 21*, **11**

Shapiro, E. Y. (1983) The fifth generation project: a trip report. *Communications of ACM*, **26**, 637–641

Shapiro, E. (1986) Concurrent Prolog: a progress report. *Computer*, **19**, 44–58

Shapiro, E. (ed.) (1988) *Concurrent Prolog: Collected Papers*, vols 1, 2, MIT Press

Shriver, B. and Wegner, P. (eds.) (1987) *Research Directions in Object-Oriented Programming*, MIT Press

SIGPLAN (1988) Common LISP object system specification. *SIGPLAN Notices* (Sept)

Steele, G. L. (1984) *Common LISP: The Language*, Digital Press

Stefik, M. J. *et al.* (1986) Integrating access-oriented programming into a multiparadigm environment. *IEEE Software*, **3**, 1, 10–18

Sterling, L. and Shapiro, E. (1986) *The Art of Prolog*, MIT Press

Stroustrup, B. (1986) *The C++ Programming Language*, Addison Wesley

Sussman, G. J. *et al.* (1970) *MICROPLANNER Reference Manual*, MIT Artificial Intelligence Laboratory, AI Memo 203

Teitelman, W. and Masinter, L. (1981) The INTERLISP programming environment. *IEEE Computer*, **14**, 25–33

Turner, D. A. (1976) *The SASL Language Manual*, University of St. Andrews

Turner, D. A. (1982) Recursion equations as a programming language. In *Functional Programming and Its Applications* (eds Darlington *et al.*) Cambridge University Press

Turner, D. A. (1985) Miranda – a non-strict functional language with polymorphic types. In *Conference on Functional Programming Languages and Computer Architecture* (ed. Jouannaud), LNCS 201, Springer Verlag

Ueda, K. (1985) Guarded Horn Clauses. *Technical Report TR-103*, ICOT, Tokyo

Ullman, J. D. (1982) *Principles of Database Systems*, 2nd ed., Computer Science Press

Ullman, J. D. (1978) Database theory: past and future. In *Proceedings of 6th ACM Symposium on PODS*

Warren, D. H. D. (1974) Implementing PROLOG – compiling logic programs 1 and 2. *DAI Research Reports 39 and 40*, University of Edinburgh, 1977

Winkstrom, A. (1987) *Functional Programming Using Standard ML*, Prentice Hall

Yang, R. and Aiso, H. (1986) P-Prolog: A Parallel Logic Language Based on Exclusive Relation. In *Proceeding 3rd International Logic Programming Conference*. London

Zave, P. (1989) A compositional approach to multiparadigm programming. *IEEE Software*, **6**, 15–27

45

Features of modern imperative programming languages

I C Wand
Department of Computer Science,
University of York

Contents

45.1 Introduction

Programming languages have developed significantly since early high-level languages in an attempt to address the problems of:

1. Programming in-the-large.
2. Reliability.
3. Wider areas of application.

In addition, semi-political pressure has forced the development of modern 'standard' languages to increase the portability of both programmers and programs. Although, as a result, several new languages have achieved quite widespread use, few, if any, have achieved the popularity of earlier languages such as COBOL and FORTRAN. However, some recent languages, such as Ada, seem destined to achieve wider use in the future.

This chapter does not attempt to build a taxonomy of features in modern programming languages. Instead it concentrates upon the development of features in recent high-level languages in the area of types (which are used to improve the reliability and flexibility of the program), error handling (so that program can either fail gracefully or recover from errors), modularity (the structure of the program above the procedure) and parallelism (the expression of a program in parallel strands either for clarity or to exploit computers with several processors). The overall objective of these developments is to make software both cheaper and more predictable. The above topics are discussed in the order listed, and they are followed by a bibliography. Throughout, a pragmatic approach is taken to the description of languages, concepts and principles.

Many of the examples here are given in Ada – a modern programming language, based upon Pascal, with sophisticated features in all of the areas listed above. Ada was designed on behalf of the US Department of Defense for the programming of so-called embedded computer systems which execute in a real-time environment where there is a high degree of interaction between the surrounding equipment and the computer. In addition to the features listed above, Ada has facilities for direct manipulation of the computer hardware.

In the Ada examples given here, all of the identifiers (names) are written in upper case; all keywords are written in lower case.

45.2 Types

All data objects in a program have an associated type which determines the set of operations that may be performed on the object. The types of objects may be fixed at compile time, run time or a mixture of both. Objects can be placed in either a stack (which mirrors the entry and exit from procedures and blocks) or a heap (in which the creation and destruction of objects is under the control of the programmer). All objects in the stack must have names declared in the program; items in the heap can be referred to indirectly using pointers.

45.2.1 Introduction

Programming languages in which the type of every expression can be determined by static program analysis (at compile time) are said to be statically typed. This property, which protects the programmer from several classes of inadvertent error, insists that all variables and expressions are bound to a type at compile time and occasionally is too restrictive. It is sometimes replaced by the requirement that all expressions are type-consistent, even though the type itself may be unknown at compile time; the validity of the program will then be determined by limited run-time type checking. Languages in which expressions are type-consistent are known as strongly typed languages. The compiler of such languages can guarantee that acceptable programs will execute without type errors. Of course, static typing is to be preferred as it allows a program to execute with maximum efficiency. However, in practice strong typing is necessary to give programs a degree of flexibility.

More recent ideas of typing have refined the idea of strong typing to increase the extent to which types are determined at run time. In such developments, generic procedures, such as those required for sorting which use the same algorithm for a range of types, can be bound to arguments of several types during the running of the program. This facility is called polymorphism.

45.2.2 The concept of type

The characteristics of static typing, following Hoare (1972), are:

1. A type determines the set of values which may be assumed by a value or expression.
2. Every value belongs to one type only.
3. The type of the value denoted by any constant, variable, or expression can be deduced from the context of its use in a program at compile time, and is unaffected by actual value at run time.
4. Each operator expects operands of fixed type, and delivers a result of a further fixed type. If the same symbol (e.g. ' + ') can be applied to operands of several different types, then the operator is said to be overloaded. The resolution of this ambiguity can always be made at compile time.
5. The properties of the values of a type and the primitive operations defined over them can be specified formally, e.g. by means of axioms.
6. Types can be constructed from a number of primitive types by constructors. These include Cartesian products, discriminated unions, sets, functions, sequences and pointers.

Each type defined in a program must be built from previously defined constituent types. The values of the components of this new type are made up of legitimate values of each of the constituent types. If there is only one constituent type it is called the base type. The number of different values a type can take is known as the cardinality; this can be finite, as with enumeration types, or it can be infinite, as with integers. However, in practice an implementation will impose a finite limit on the number of different values of each type.

All programming languages will assume that a number of basic, or primitive, types are available as the building blocks from which further types can be built. These basic types usually include integer, real (fixed or floating point), Boolean and character.

Each type has a range of basic operations associated with it. Usually these are the operations provided by the basic hardware of the computer system and they will apply directly to the basic types. Further operations will be defined in terms of this basic set. More generally, the operations associated with a type are:

1. Assignment and test for equality will be required for both primitive and structured types. For structured types the efficiency will depend upon the representation chosen and may involve operations of considerable complexity. Selective assignment to a component of a large, complex structure is often needed for reasons of efficiency.
2. Transfer or conversion functions are required to convert values of one type to another. This may, or may not, involve a change in representation. In many languages the name of the type required is used to denote the transfer function.
3. Constructors are necessary to denote the construction of a new type from component types.
4. Selectors are required to access the component values of a structured type.

Many types are conveniently regarded as ordered (e.g. Boolean) so that a number of operators have a meaningful interpretation when used with these types. However, from an abstract viewpoint such an interpretation is sometimes unnecessary.

There may be many ways to represent a given type on a particular computer. The representation of the basic types will usually be determined by the hardware and the data handling operations available, but the representation of structured types will usually be determined by considerations such as efficiency. Quite often a range of possible representations may be available; they will have particular time and space characteristics. A representation which attempts to minimize the storage required is described as packed.

Some representations cannot use fixed or stack storage and will require dynamic heap storage with subsequent garbage collection, which may or may not be under the control of the programmer. Different techniques will be appropriate if the values are held on secondary storage.

The following sections will look at the constructors for types using the classification due to Hoare (1972).

45.2.3 Unstructured types

All types are constructed from further types, which ultimately must be either primitive (probably supported directly by the computer's hardware) or are defined by the programmer by listing the set of values the type can take. In practice these types must be represented in terms of the computer's own data types, e.g. integer. However, the programmer may define his own types to take advantages of strong or static typing.

The set of values that can be taken by an unstructured type may be indicated by enumeration. All possible values must be given. An example in Ada is:

    type BUTTON is (UP, DOWN);

In this example it makes little sense to order the values of type BUTTON, even if an implementation chooses to do so. However, the following example shows when an ordering is appropriate:

    type DAYS is (MON, TUE, WED, THU, FRI, SAT, SUN);

so that, for example, TUE is greater that MON. It is often useful to define new or related types which are parts of the range of values allowed by another enumerated type. For example:

    subtype REST_DAYS is DAYS range SAT .. SUN;
    type YEARS is INTEGER range 1900 .. 1999;

Such restricted types enable the programmer to specify exactly the permissible range of values, and are called subtypes or subranges.

The operations on enumerated or unstructured types will be assignment, tests for equality and inequality, discrimination between values (possibly via a case statement), tests for ordering (if this is sensible), selection of the previous or next value in the enumeration, iteration over the values in the enumeration and conversion between both the related types and any subtypes or subranges. Such types may be represented by integers within the computer. The size of integer required will be determined by the number of values in the type.

45.2.4 Cartesian product

The enumerated types, including the ones defined by the programmer, are unstructured – that is, they have no internal structure of direct concern to the programmer (even though

they may be represented by a group of bits). The Cartesian product is a data structuring method which gives the space of possible values of a composite type. Such structures usually have a fixed size and are called records or structures in programming languages, where their components can be named. Here are some examples:

    type COMPLEX_NUMBER is
      record
        REAL: FLOAT;
        IMAG: FLOAT;
      end record;

    type DATE is
      record
        D: DAYS;
        M: MONTHS;
        Y: YEARS;
      end record;

It must be possible to refer to the individual components of a Cartesian product. This is usually done with a dot notation, where the dot separates the name of the variable and the component In some languages, for example in Algol 68 and Ada, it is possible to write down values for the whole object. For example in Ada:

$$Z.REAL := 1.0; \quad Z.IMAG := 2.0;$$

and:

$$Z := (1.0, 2.0);$$

are equivalent, where Z has been declared as a COMPLEX_NUMBER. Some languages (e.g. Pascal) allow references to a structured type to be made without repeated use of the variable name so long as the name is mentioned in a bracketing statement (e.g. with).

A Cartesian product type is represented in store simply by placing the components in consecutive regions of storage. The amount of storage used will be determined by the degree of packing required and by the addressing system used by the computer. As a general rule, the denser the packing used the slower the access will be. In some languages and implementations (e.g. PL/I) the components of the record may be reordered to reduce the padding necessary and to optimize access times.

45.2.5 The discriminated union

It is often necessary to define types which are the union of two or more sets of values, each of which may have components in common. Such a type is known as a discriminated union, and is often called a variant record in programming languages. It is usually specified by listing the components that the sets have in common, followed by the components which differ. When such a type is used either the particular version in use is determined at run time, using a variant tag, or is fixed at compile time. An example in Ada is:

    type PERSON(MARRIED: BOOLEAN) is
      record
        NAME: STRING(10);
        case MARRIED is
          when TRUE => THE_DAY: DATE;
          when FALSE => DIVORCED: BOOLEAN;
        end case;
      end record;

In this example, the variant tag is MARRIED. Depending upon its value, the record has either a FIELD called THE_DAY or a field called DIVORCED. When assigning values to such a record, a value for the variant tag must be given.

The representation of the type will carry a field which gives the current value of the variant tag. It will not allow inappropriate assignments. For example, the field THE_DAY cannot be used if the tag is FALSE. If the tag can be changed when the program is running then the language rules may insist that the whole record is changed by assignment. Several languages demand that the variant part is placed at the end of the record.

45.2.6 The array

In many early languages the array was the only data structure available apart from the basic types. Viewed abstractly it is a mapping between the subscript values and the elements of the array. This mapping will be indicated by a declaration:

A: array S of T;

where S is the subscript range and T is the element type. When a value of the subscript range is applied to the array, a unique element is selected as follows:

M(I) or M[I]

where I must belong to the subscript range. Note that the mapping denoted by the subscript is from a finite range, although the range of values for each element can, in principle, be infinite. An example of the declaration and use of an array is:

type INFLATION is array MONTH of FLOAT;

RATE: INFLATION;

RATE(JAN) := 7.0;

The cardinality of an array type is the cardinality of the element type raised to the power of the cardinality of the subscript type.

Individual elements are selected from an array by subscripting (see above), although some languages allow the programmer to select parts of arrays by indicating a contiguous range of subscripts. This is called slicing. Multi-dimensional arrays can be achieved by viewing the subscript type as a Cartesian product of two or more ranges. However, such subscription is usually expressed directly without the necessity of defining an extra type. Alternatively, the element type may be seen as a further (array) type. Slicing of multi-dimensional arrays is often restricted to the last dimension.

Arrays can be represented in several ways. The most straightforward method is to use a contiguous area of storage in which the elements are placed side by side. The mapping of the subscript on to a position in this storage is calculated by a simple function. The information required by such a function is often collected into a so-called dope vector. Alternatively, arrays of two or more dimensions can be represented as trees. Such a representation is sometimes called an Iliffe vector. Tree representations have the advantage of simple access functions, but they are more expensive in storage. Arrays can be packed or unpacked. In general the more packed they are, the more complex and the slower the access function. Because slicing is restricted to the last dimension, arrays in Ada and Pascal could be implemented by either contiguous storage or Iliffe vectors. However, Algol 68 allows more general slicing, and demands the use of contiguous storage.

45.2.7 The set

A powerset of a given set is the set of all subsets of that set. The values of such a set are selected from a further type called the base. In most languages, such as Pascal, the powerset is simply called a set. An example based upon an earlier declaration of a type DAYS is:

type SICK = set of DAYS;

Each element in the base type (in the above example MON, TUE up to SUN) is either in the set or it is not. The set will contain as many independent values as there are elements in the base type.

Of course, a set can be empty, or can have every element present. Operations will be required to test for membership and equality, and to calculate intersection, union, relative complement and so on. The set can be updated by using join, adding a new member, excluding a member, excluding all members that are in another set and so on. It is sometimes useful to have a mechanism to iterate through the members of a set.

A set can be represented using a bit string with as many bits as there are elements in the set. Operations such as logical intersection, union, complementation, etc., can be implemented with single instructions as long as the set can be represented by a single machine word. This is the system adopted by many Pascal implementations and therefore imposes a strict upper bound on the size of a set. Other implementations allow a variable size set, but with the proviso that smaller sets can be implemented more efficiently. However, programs which need a large set can always be altered so that they use arrays of smaller, more efficient, sets.

45.2.8 The sequence

Unlike the cardinality of the straightforward structured types, that of the sequence cannot be determined at compile time. A sequence of values may be infinitely long and, more practically, may vary as the program executes. If the sequence is long it will be more efficient to update the elements of the sequence individually rather than make a new copy of the entire object. Complicated storage management techniques may be required to manipulate the object. This will be further complicated by the use of backing store or packed representations.

A sequence can be regarded as an arbitrary number of items of a given type placed in a particular order. Such sequences include strings, stacks, queues and so on. The sequence is the abstraction and there are various representations of this abstract notion. Particular examples present in programming languages are the string and the file. Usually restrictions are placed upon the maximum length sequences can take – particularly if it is possible to update elements of the sequence selectively.

The operations on a sequence will usually be empty, extend, shorten, selectively update, assign and compare. A comparison may take a more complex form if the sequence is made up of characters which can be compared with the corresponding position in another sequence. The operations available will depend upon the length and purpose of the sequence in question. So, for example, a stack will only be altered by adding or removing the last element (push and pop), whereas a string must be updatable at any position.

Sequences can be represented as contiguous sections of storage and, indeed, may be declared as arrays in some languages (e.g. STRINGs in Ada), as chained sequences (lists) of single elements or blocks, or as files. Programming languages tend not to treat the sequence as a general linguistic mechanism but to provide specific items for particular purposes. They will then rely upon the programmer to provide other types of sequence by explicit programming. To see how this can be done see, for example, Booch (1988).

45.2.9 Sparse data structures

If the set potentially contains a very large number of elements or if the range of possible subscript values is very large, then the data type is said to be sparse if only a small proportion of possible values are present. Particular examples are the sparse array required by some applications in quantum mechanics, where only a small number of the elements are non-zero, or an array which represents a dictionary and is indexed by character strings corresponding to words. The latter could be declared as:

TYPE dictionary = SPARSE ARRAY word OF definition;

Clearly the range of possible words is infinite, and therefore only a small number of values of word will be required to index the array. However, they will not represent a contiguous section of the array.

Sparse data structures can be represented by keeping tables to map the index values into either main store addresses or positions in a file. In the first case the sophistication of the mechanism will depend upon the number of array elements present. The look-up could be done by sequential searching if the number of elements present is small; otherwise a hashing technique is appropriate. A sparse array represented by a file will be accessed by key, where the key will provide an index into the file.

Sparse data structures, in the general sense, are not recognized in programming languages. Structures such as files will be provided by packages, although the language may recognize the operations required to some degree (e.g. PL/I and direct access files).

45.2.10 Pointers

If T is an expression yielding a type, then a further type can be defined which is a 'pointer to an object of type T'. A pointer can be thought of as the name of the place where an object is kept; usually it will be implemented as an address. Programming languages use a variety of notations to denote pointers. Pascal uses an up arrow thus:

TYPE link = ^cell;

where cell is the type of an object which can be referred to via a link. Other languages use equivalent notations: Ada uses the keyword 'access'; Algol 68 the keyword 'ref'.

Pointers are used to build data structures whose size is, in general, unknown at compile time. Most languages insist that a pointer can only refer to objects in the dynamic storage area (the heap), although a pointer object can be present in either the stack or the heap. Storage from the heap will be reclaimed either automatically (by a garbage collector, which will ensure that space collected can no longer by referenced) or explicitly by the programmer ('dispose' or 'release' in Pascal; UNCHECKED_DEALLOCATION in Ada). The storage is allocated explicitly using a storage allocator (called 'new' in Pascal, Modula 2, Ada and some other languages).

Strongly or statically typed languages insist that the pointer is typed by the type of the object it addresses, unlike earlier languages, such as PL/I, which made no such restriction. This restriction ensures that dynamic data structures are restricted by the requirements of strong typing. Strong typing does not allow the use of a pointer in any general sense.

Pointers can be used in expressions to denote either themselves or the objects at which they point. Furthermore, they can be used in names to indicate a fixed length chain through a number of pointers. This is illustrated by the following fragment of Pascal:

TYPE cell =
  RECORD
    next: link;
    value: data;
  END;

VAR head: link;

{assuming a number of cells have been allocated with the storage allocator, and head is the start of the list, the following statement will assign 'some value' to the field called 'value' in the second item}

head↑.next↑.value := some value;

The use of a pointer within expressions to denote the object at which it points is called de-referencing. In some languages it is explicit (e.g. Pascal where the use of the up arrow after the pointer indicates de-referencing); however, in others it is implicit from the context (e.g. Ada and Algol 68). However, in languages where the de-referencing is implicit, there must be an extra indication when an object, rather than a pointer, is intended (Ada uses the keyword 'all' to denote this).

Some authors have referred to data structures based upon pointers as 'recursive data structures', and have used this device to avoid the definition of pointer types, regarding them as the concern of implementors alone. However, most modern programming languages have pointer types and an associated dynamic storage area. There is little disagreement about the language mechanisms in this area – most modern languages have very similar facilities.

45.2.11 Overloading of function and procedures

An overloaded symbol is one that has different meanings depending upon its context. In most programming languages the operator ' + ' is overloaded because it can be used with both integer and real operands. However, in recent languages it has become possible to add to the existing definitions of the operators with new meanings and, furthermore, to define new functions and procedures with several meanings. An example from Ada is:

function "*" (I, J: INTEGER) return COMPLEX;
function "*" (I, J: COMPLEX) return COMPLEX;

which gives the definition of two functions (without their bodies), using the same operator symbol, to have two different meanings in the same region of the program. The user can apply the same technique to procedures. This is particularly valuable in the definition of procedures for input/output so that PUT, for example, could be used for a wide variety of types.

In itself, overloading is only a notational convenience. However, it does give rise to considerable complications in a compiler, where the process of associating use and declaration of overloaded items is called overload resolution.

45.2.12 Polymorphic functions

An ordinary procedure allows the statements in its body to be executed with arguments of fixed type (overloading extends this to allow several procedures to have the same name). A polymorphic procedure can be executed with arguments of different types. The term polymorphic can be applied to any section of code that can be executed with arguments of different type, so one can have polymorphic procedures, functions and operators.

Polymorphic functions are attractive because they facilitate the implementation of algorithms that manipulate data structures in a manner independent of the element type. Such algorithms include searching, sorting, counting and so on. The following is an example of a polymorphic function in ML which will measure the length of a list, and can be used in lists containing any type of data element:

```
fun length(lptr) =
    if null (lptr) then 0
    else length (tl(lptr)) + 1;
```

The functions 'null' and 'tl' are built into the ML language; null tests if the list is empty and tl delivers the tail of the existing list. The function could be used with both string and numeric data, as follows:

```
length(["able", "baker", "charlie", "dog"]);
length([1, 2, 3, 5, 7, 11]);
```

The square brackets denote the construction of a list from the enclosed constituents.

Polymorphic functions have major advantages over generic functions in Ada, where there may be as many copies of the function as there are possible argument types. However, polymorphic functions will carry a run-time overhead corresponding to the (hidden) data item denoting the type information that must be used inside the function to ensure that its actions are correct for that type of argument.

45.2.13 Types and object-oriented languages

Simula was the first object-oriented programming language. Its notion of type included classes (see Section 45.3 on modularity), the instances of which may persist between the execution of the procedures they contain. The procedures and data declarations of a class constitute the interface and are the parts of the class accessible to users. Classes may inherit properties from their ancestors (the superclass) and can add properties. More recent languages such as Modula 2 and Ada provide weaker mechanisms than Simula for the combination of properties (for example, Ada provides a 'with' statement, so that packages can include the facilities of another, and generics, a mechanism for static parametrization). These mechanisms can lead to inflexibility in the construction of packages or modules which realise composite roles (e.g. if one has packages implementing STACK and another STRING one cannot have a STACK of STRINGs or a STRING of STACKs without considerable difficulty).

Smalltalk introduced an object hierarchy to give some degree of inheritance. It provided some simplicity and polymorphism by factoring out properties common to objects into special types called supertypes. The hierarchy enables superclasses to be shared between subclasses whose attributes they share. Thus polymorphism is related to the notion of inheritance, and the power of object oriented systems is directly related to the polymorphism they display.

Although Smalltalk has been in use for some years, and a number of related experimental object-oriented languages are in use (C + +, Objective-C, etc.), there are a number of issues in the design of the associated type system which are still experimental. In particular, the notion of multiple inheritance, where classes inherit characteristics from a number of ancestors, is still a matter for research.

45.2.14 Summary

Scalar types are now well understood. They conveniently provide an abstract description and map conveniently on to the

computer hardware. However, the balance of facilities in structured types is not so well understood, particularly when the types describe objects whose sizes vary during execution. In addition, the extension of the type system to include modularity (see the next section), including reuse, is a research issue. However, the type systems in use are now sufficiently flexible to make it unnecessary for untyped languages (e.g. BCPL) to be used in the name of efficiency.

45.3 Modularity

45.3.1 Introduction

High-level programming languages have used a number of mechanisms to impose a module structure on the construction of programs. Such modularity may be necessary to restrict the scope of variables (e.g. the block), to define an often-used piece of code (e.g. the procedure or function), to define a section of code suitable for separate compilation (e.g. the Ada package or procedure), or to define some higher-level concept of program structure (e.g. the class or the package). In addition, the module is sometimes used to express the unit of parallelism (e.g. Ada tasks). This is dealt with in a later section.

A module is made up of:

1. The declaration of the interface, which may involve static or dynamic parameterization, and the static import or export of items to or from the module (to control visibility).
2. Declaration of items local to the module.
3. Statements, which may constitute the body of a procedure or the initialization part of a package.

The following issues must be considered when a module structure is designed:

1. Lifetime of the module and of objects declared in that module.
2. How modules are nested.
3. How objects declared in a module, including procedures and functions, are referenced both from inside the module and from outside.
4. How multiple copies of a module can be created.

These mechanisms have been realised in many ways. A review is now given of the major types of modularity used in high-level programming languages.

45.3.2 Blocks

The block was first introduced in Algol 60. It has the following structure:

```
startblock
    declarations
begin
    statements
endblock
```

A block is executed when control reaches its first statement. It has no parameters and cannot be used outside its context. It has two particular advantages:

1. Declarations can be grouped with the statements using them.
2. Demands for storage can be associated with the areas of the program that require them.

The extent of the program in which a declaration is valid is called the scope of the declaration. This is often the whole block in which the declaration is made. Many block structured languages admit nesting (Ada, Algol 60, Pascal, PL/I). However, many do not (C, FORTRAN, RTL/2). The following example shows the nesting of blocks in Ada:

```
declare
   X: INTEGER;
   Y: FLOAT;
begin
   X: = 0;
   declare
      C: CHARACTER;
      X: FLOAT;
   begin
      C := '?';
      X := 1.0;
   end;
   Y := 1.2345;
end;
```

The example also shows how scopes can overlap, i.e. how an object declared in one scope can have the same identifier as another in the same group of nested scopes. Clearly there must be rules to avoid ambiguity so that defining (declaring) and applied (using) occurrences can be linked unambiguously. These rules are:

1. For every applied occurrence there must be a unique defining one.
2. Given a particular applied occurrence, the defining occurrence is found by working outward through the nesting from the point of the applied occurrence, examining each set of declarations, until one with the correct name is found. If one cannot be found, the program is erroneous.
3. Once a declaration in an inner block is given with a name which matches a name in a surrounding block, the outer name is screened and cannot be used in the inner block to denote the outer name.

For example:

```
declare -- block 1
   X: FLOAT;
begin
   -- X from block 1 can be used here
   declare -- block 2
      Z: FLOAT;
   begin
      -- X from block 1 and
      -- Z from block 2 can be used here
      declare -- block 3
         X: INTEGER;
         Y: FLOAT;
      begin
         -- Z from block 2 and
         -- X and Y from block 3 can be used here.
      end;
      -- X from block 1 and
      -- Z from block 2 can be used here.
   end;
   -- X from block 1 can be used here
end;
```

Some languages, e.g. Ada, use a system of block naming (with labels) to overcome the problem of identifier screening. With this system any identifier can be written as:

```
block_name.identifier
```

to identify it uniquely.

Objects declared in blocks are created (allocated memory) when the flow of control reaches the declarations. Because of the properties of nested scope it is possible to make the size of objects depend upon the values of objects declared in surrounding scopes. The storage associated with a block is released when control reaches the end of the block. Normally, the storage required by a block is created afresh each time the block is entered and the storage allocated on a stack with the block currently executing as the top-most item on the stack. The items in the stack will be connected by a chain of addresses; each link in this chain is usually called a dynamic link, and the group of items comprising the declarations for a block is usually called a stack frame. However, there are languages with features which assume that object values will be retained beyond the statements of the block (e.g. own variables in Algol 60). Off-stack storage or heap storage, must be used for such objects.

45.3.3 Procedures and functions

Procedure and functions are blocks with names that can be invoked from any point in the program where their name is visible. Their form is:

```
procedure NAME (optional formal parameters);
   declarations
begin
   statements
end;
```

When a procedure is called, its actual parameters are evaluated and then control is passed to the block representing the body (declarations plus statements) of the procedure. Control is returned to the statement immediately after the call when execution of the block has been completed. Procedures and blocks may be nested in exactly the same way as blocks. Most languages allow a procedure to call itself directly or indirectly. This is called recursion.

The interaction between scope and flow of control can be seen from the following example:

```
procedure ONE is
   X, Y: INTEGER;
   procedure TWO is
      X, Z: INTEGER;
      procedure THREE is
         P,Q: INTEGER;
      begin
         -- ONE, TWO, THREE visible
         -- P and Q from THREE visible
         -- Z and X from TWO visible
         -- Y from ONE visible
      end;
   begin
      -- ONE, TWO, THREE visible
      -- X and Z from TWO visible
      -- Y and Z from ONE visible
      THREE; -- call procedure THREE;
   end;
   procedure FOUR is
      Y, Z: INTEGER;
   begin
      -- ONE, TWO, FOUR visible
      -- Y, Z from FOUR visible
      -- X from ONE visible
      TWO; -- call procedure TWO;
   end;
begin
   -- ONE, TWO, FOUR visible
   -- X, Y from ONE visible
   FOUR; -- call procedure FOUR;
end;
```

Note the calling sequence in the above: ONE→FOUR→ TWO→THREE. Also note the objects that are visible within each of the procedures. This will mean for example that the objects declared in FOUR, although not visible in TWO and THREE, must remain available so that they will be restored when procedure TWO has returned from the call in FOUR. Once again a stack implementation is required. However, the procedure mechanism has introduced an extra complexity (by comparison with blocks) because the visibility of objects is no longer the same as that of the flow of execution (as it was for blocks).

This further requirement demands two mechanisms from the stack storage used by the program. One is the ability to push and pop the storage used by procedures when they are called and when they return (this is the dynamic link described in the last section). A second mechanism is needed to enable a procedure to address the objects currently in scope. This can be done by two equivalent mechanisms: using a static link (which links the items currently in scope) or by a display which is vector of references to the items currently in scope. Both of these mechanisms require code at procedure entry and exit to set/ restore them to appropriate values.

Functions differ from procedures in one major respect only; they return a value through their name to the point of call (which will be within an expression). Some languages require the type of the value returned to be a simple scalar (e.g. an integer). Pascal, PL/I and Algol 60 fall into this category. By comparison Ada and Algol 68 allow structured types to be returned. If the size of an object is unknown at compile time, then it may be created in an off-stack storage area. There are other possible differences between procedures and functions. One of these is that it may not be possible to refer to objects declared with a wider scope than the function – this is to prevent a function having side-effects, that is, depending upon values other than its parameters. The preliminary version of Ada had this restriction.

45.3.4 Parameters

Procedures may be called with parameters which can be used to pass initial values and/or retrieve the subsequent results. Functions use the same parameter mechanism although results are usually passed back to the calling context through the function name only. Quite often functions are restricted in the form of parameter mechanism they are allowed to use (e.g. in Ada functions can use the mode **in** only).

Parameters supplied at the point of call are called actual parameters; those supplied in the procedure declaration are called formal parameters. There are two mechanisms for associating the two sets of parameters in a particular call:

1. *Position*. The parameters are associated on a one to one basis moving from left to right. Normally the number of actuals and formals must be the same.
2. *Keyword*. The parameters are associated by using the names of the formal parameters in the cell to specify the association with a particular actual parameter.

There are hybrid and mixed versions of both systems. In addition C, which uses positional parameters only, allows the number of actuals and formals to differ. This means that one can write variadic procedures in C (for use in input/output, for example). Ada is one of the few high-level languages to use keyword parameters (Job Control Language for OS/360 is another). Furthermore, it allows the two mechanisms to be mixed in a particular call so long as the keyword parameters come first.

There are several methods used for passing parameters. These are usually called the parameter passing modes. The most important ones are:

1. *Call by value*. The values of the actuals, which may be expressions, are calculated in the context of the call and then passed to the formals. In some languages (e.g. Pascal) the actuals then act as variables to the procedure; in others (e.g. Ada – **in** parameters) they can only be used as read-only local variables. Value parameters can be thought of as input-only parameters.
2. *Output parameters*. The actual must define a variable which will be given the final value of the formal on exit from the procedure. There are several minor variations on this basic scheme: the name of the variable may be calculated either at the point of call (as in Ada) or just before exit – the distinction is important if the variable is an element of an array, for example. In addition, it may or may not be possible to use the actual as a local variable prior to the final value being made available to the point of call.
3. *In-out* parameters. This mode acts as both an **in** and an **out** parameter. However, for reasons of efficiency, in-out parameters are often implemented as address or reference parameters.
4. *Address or reference parameters*. The actual parameter must define a variable whose address is computed at the point of call. This address is then used for all references to the actual parameter from the procedure. It is the mechanism used in Pascal and FORTRAN, and is an allowed implementation of the in-out mode in Ada.
5. *Call by name*. This is the mode used in Algol 60. It includes the reference mode as the special case when a simple variable is used as the actual parameter. Call by name allows a full expression as the actual parameter. This expression will then be re-evaluated, in the context of the call, whenever it is referenced. Clearly different forms of expression are appropriate for in and out use. The call-by-name mechanism is complicated and potentially inefficient; however it can be used for various programming 'tricks' such as Jensen's device.
6. *Procedures*. Many programming languages allow procedures to be passed as parameters (e.g. Algol 60 and 68, PL/I and Pascal). This enables the called procedure to call the procedure passed as an actual parameter during its own execution. Such a mechanism is the basis of functional languages. The most important issue is to define the environment (visibility of variables) in which the formal procedure parameter is executed. This will usually be the context of the call: therefore the implementation must pass both the name (i.e. address) of the procedure and its environment (static link) as the value of the actual parameter. Algol 68 uses this method to provide a mechanism equivalent to call-by-name.
7. *Polymorphic parameters*. If the type of the formal parameters is not specified completely in the definition of the procedure, it is said to be a polymorphic procedure. The procedure will then accept a number of types for each parameter position. The code in the procedure body will then need to distinguish between different types of the same parameter. There will be a run-time overhead; each parameter will need to carry information which enables the procedure to distinguish between each possible type supplied.

45.3.5 Packages or modules

A package or module is a mechanism for enclosing a group of declarations, procedures and statements within a static 'fence'. A user of the module can only make use of items within the module which are specifically declared to be accessible. Modules should not be confused with procedures. They are not called, but only exist as static units to break up large programs into manageable units by enforcing separation of concerns.

An example is:

```
package P is
    declaration of external interface,
    including objects and procedures
begin
    statements to initialize objects declared above;
end.
```

The package communicates with the rest of the program through the declared interface which can either list the items available in this package or can, in addition, list the items used by this package which are provided by other packages. Items made available in this package are said to be exported; those brought in from another unit are said to be imported. The statements in the body of the package are executed when the package declaration is elaborated and normally are used to initialize declarations within the package. Note that the lifetime of variables in the package declaration will be that of the innermost block surrounding the declaration.

The module system outlined above is that used in Modula (one), Euclid and CLU (where they are called clusters). However, Ada and Modula 2 have separated the declaration of the interface to the rest of the program from the implementation of the procedures and the statements in the body. In Ada the two parts are called the package and the package body; in Modula 2 they are called the definition module and the implementation module. An example is a package in Ada to maintain a simple counter:

```
package COUNTER is
    procedure AUGMENT(I: in INTEGER);
    procedure VALUE(I: out INTEGER);
    procedure CLEAR;
end COUNTER;

package body COUNTER is
    S: INTEGER;

    procedure AUGMENT(I: in INTEGER) is
    begin
        S := S + I;
    end AUGMENT;

    procedure VALUE(I: out INTEGER) is
    begin
        I := S;
    end VALUE;

    procedure CLEAR is
    begin
        S := 0;
    end CLEAR;

begin
    S := 0;
end COUNTER;
```

Packages and modules cannot be parameterized when their declarations are elaborated (unlike classes). However, some form of parameterization is necessary, given that variants of the same basic module are often needed (e.g. stacks of integers, stacks of reals, etc). In many cases this can be seen as an explicit form of polymorphism introduced at compile time. Ada provides this parameterization using the generic mechanism, which allows packages or procedures to act as a template and be parameterized with values, types and procedures. A particular instance is generated at compile time by instantiation. Such parameterization allows a sophisticated compiler to share the object code between instances of the same generic template.

Packages or modules are broadly equivalent to abstract data types (ADTs), a device for program design and construction in which types and their operators/functions are treated as a unit (e.g. the notion of a stack, the notion of a binary tree, etc.) which has been widely promoted as an effective method of program construction. The user of an ADT is unable to see the way in which the ADT is implemented; some writers call this property the 'separation of concerns'. A truly general language system supporting ADTs should allow the combination of ADTs in a general way. Ada goes some way to achieving this objective (Booch, 1988) although the generic mechanism only allows a restricted form of parameterization. In addition, Ada does not allow the assignment operator to be redefined by the programmer.

Other languages such as Modula 2, Turing and Euclid do not allow parameterized modules and hence cannot be used to construct ADTs of any flexibility.

45.3.6 Classes

Many languages allow pointer types, that is, the use of address variables to reference objects that are placed in a storage area called the heap. Usually the pointers can only address data objects (e.g. in Pascal, Ada, etc). However, Simula introduced the notion of a class in which the object allocated can contain both data objects *and* the procedures/functions which operate on the data. The form of a class is:

```
class P (formal parameters);
    declarations;
begin
    statements;
end P;
```

The class P defines a type P which can have associated pointer types. So, for example, one could declare:

```
var X, Y, Z: P;
```

X, Y and Z are now reference variables which can be used to refer to instances of the type P. Instances may be generated by:

```
X := new P (actual parameters);
```

This statement results in the generation of a new instance of P, the transmission of the actual parameters and the execution of the statements in the body of P. However, this differs from procedures as, when the statements have been completed, the instance of P remains in existence and can be referenced by X. That is, the class instance yields persistent data (plus associated procedures/functions) which can be referenced until it is deallocated explicitly or removed by a garbage collector when it can no longer be referenced.

Items in a class are referenced using the same style of notation as is used for references to objects in records. An example is the following class:

```
class CIRCLE (RAD: FLOAT);

    function AREA returns BOOLEAN is
    begin
        return 3.14159265*RAD**2;
    end;

begin
    if RAD <= 0.0 then
        PUT_LINE("Silly circle");
    end if;
end class;
```

Then instances of the class can be generated and subsequently referenced as follows:

```
X := new CIRCLE (2.0);
Y := new CIRCLE (3.0);
-- now compare the areas
if X.AREA < Y.AREA then
    PUT_("First circle is smaller");
end if;
```

In more complex examples the procedures/functions (such as AREA) can be called with arguments of the class type to, say, compare the value of the argument with that of the class instance.

45.3.7 Summary

The procedure parameter mechanism is now well understood, although there is no widely used technique for providing procedure polymorphism. Program structuring above the procedure level is provided by many mechanisms, which may be related to the type structure of the language. Unfortunately, there is no general agreement about the sort of module-like structuring required to support different methods of program design and construction.

45.4 Exceptions

45.4.1 Introduction

Inevitably faults occur when programs are running. These may be caused by logical errors in the program code, by errors in the data supplied to the program, or by faults detected by the hardware on which the program is running. In many environments (e.g. real-time) it is unacceptable for the program simply to stop with a terse diagnostic. Several programming language mechanisms have been used to provide a framework for detecting and then handling errors so that the program can either fail gracefully or continue after remedial action has been taken.

The requirements for a language mechanism to support error handling are:

1. The code for error handling must not obscure the normal flow of control in the program text.
2. Ideally run-time overheads should only be imposed when an error occurs and is handled.
3. The mechanism should allow a uniform treatment of errors detected by the hardware and by the code of the program itself.
4. The program must be able to detail the recovery action to be taken when an error is detected.

Errors detected during the execution of a program are often called exceptions, and the handling of such exceptions is usually done by a section of program code called an exception handler. One of the most difficult issues in the design of a suitable exception-handling mechanism is the identification of a straightforward error recovery technique.

45.4.2 *Ad hoc* mechanisms

Many early systems attempted to integrate an error handling mechanism into an existing language framework. Examples of these mechanisms are:

1. Procedures or functions returning error values, either via a

special parameter or via their name. This system is used widely in the interface with libraries or operating systems (e.g. the C interface with the Unix operating system).
2. Error returns from procedures. In many systems programmed in assembly language, a call to a procedure can be followed by a series of branches each of which would handle one specific error that can be detected by the procedure; in returning, the procedure would add a value to the return address corresponding to the error it had detected.
3. Passing an error label to a procedure. In this method the label of the error handling code would be passed as a parameter. If the procedure detected an error, then it would perform a non-local goto on that label. This would result in the unwinding of the run-time stack.
4. Passing procedure variables to procedures. The procedure is called when an error is called. This will result in the resumption of the original procedure when the error procedure has completed.

Only (3) and (4) can be seen as programming language mechanisms. They are available in some languages, e.g. RTL/2. Note that (3) can be used when it is not necessary to resume subsequently at the point where the error is discovered, whereas (4) allows resumption. However, these techniques do not allow a straightforward method of integrating errors detected by hardware into the general mechanism. In addition, they suffer from the deficiency of producing obscure programs which are difficult to read and maintain.

45.4.3 Mechanisms in early general-purpose languages

Several early high-level programming languages attempted to provide mechanisms to handle errors or exceptional conditions. A review of these techniques, together with the more general issues, is given by Levin (1977).

The most comprehensive system provided by an early language was PL/I, which was probably the first language to introduce a general error-handling mechanism. The error conditions there are called interrupts or ON-conditions. Such interrupts include both errors detected by the hardware and the software system, together with errors explicitly signalled by the programmer. A number of ON-conditions are built into the environment in which every program runs; this set of ON-conditions can be added to by the programmer and can apply to individual statements or blocks of the program by indicating their names as prefixes. For example:

(SIZE, NOOVERFLOW): B PROCEDURE;

indicates that the built-in ON-condition SIZE is to apply to the procedure B, but that OVERFLOW is not to apply during the procedure. The programmer can declare and raise ON-conditions explicitly:

ON CONDITION (COLLAPSE) on-unit;

and the interrupt can then be signalled with:

SIGNAL CONDITION (COLLAPSE);

An ON-unit may be declared in any block: it can be either related to a built-in ON-condition or it may refer to one declared by the programmer. The previous example shows how an ON-unit may be attached to a user defined condition. The following example shows how an ON-unit can be specified for a built-in condition:

```
(SIZE): B PROCEDURE;
  ON SIZE GO TO BERROR;
  .
  .
  REVERT SIZE;
  .
  .
  .
END B;
```

This example shows that the ON-condition SIZE is enabled for the whole procedure B (it is disabled by default) together with an ON-unit which is executed when the ON-condition is raised. The REVERT statement breaks the connection between the ON-condition and the ON-unit in B, and reverts to any earlier ON-unit for that condition.

When an ON-condition is raised the appropriate ON-unit is found by following the dynamic calling sequence of the program: if no unit is found the program is halted. If the execution of the ON-unit reaches the end of the unit, then the context in which the conditions was raised is resumed. However, an ON-unit can alter the flow of control by executing a GO TO. If a further ON-condition is raised during the execution of an ON-unit, then the ON-unit may be entered recursively. For this reason it is usual to place the single line:

```
ON ERROR SYSTEM;
```

at the head of each ON-unit. This will ensure that the program halts if any error is raised during the execution of the ON-unit.

The PL/I mechanism is elaborate and complicated. It is particularly difficult to define the semantics of resumption after the execution of the ON-unit. The particular circumstances depend critically on the type of ON-condition being handled. Furthermore, the implementation overhead, particularly on procedure entry and exit, is often formidable.

45.4.4 Exceptions in modern languages

It is clear that the PL/I model is too complicated and expensive to satisfy the requirements given earlier. As a result modern programming languages have adopted simpler mechanisms to satisfy the requirements. As far as possible they have separated the exception mechanism from the flow of control within the program.

45.4.4.1 Exception handlers

A handler is the code which is activated when an exception is raised in the area of the program to which that handler applies. The handler must also apply specifically to the given exception. The handler could be attached to statements, blocks, procedures or larger units of a program. In Ada the handler can be attached to any block, procedure or package; in CHILL it can also be applied to any statement. An example of the declaration and use of an exception in Ada is:

```
declare -- start a block
  PRESSURE_TOO_HIGH: exception;
block
  -- statements
  if READING > MAX then
    raise PRESSURE_TOO_HIGH;
  end if;
  -- further statements
exception
  when PRESSURE_TOO_HIGH =>
    STOP_PROCESS;
    PUT("Evacuate boiler house");
end; -- end block
```

This example shows the declaration of an exception, a handler for that exception and the raising of the exception when the program detects an error. The scope rules of the language will determine the area of the program (called the domain by some authors) over which the exception name and the handler can be related correctly. It may be useful to pass parameters when exceptions are raised to avoid the use of global variables, although this cannot be done in Ada.

45.4.4.2 Exception propagation

Once an exception has been raised, either explicitly (for example, by raise) or implicitly (by the run-time system or by the hardware) it must find a handler which will handle the error. Two approaches are possible:

1. To associate the handler with the associated raise at compile time; this will sometimes require extra information with each procedure call (e.g. names of the exceptions that can be raised by that procedure).
2. To associate the handler with the associated raise dynamically. Once an exception is raised, the program is searched for an appropriate handler. This searching is called propagation.

Clearly there is interaction between the scoping rules of a programming language and exception propagation. For example, once an exception has been propagated outside its scope, it will be impossible to find a handler particular to that exception. Furthermore, there will be interactions between exceptions and a mechanism for parallel processing. If an exception is unhandled in either a parallel process or a sequential program, the process or program may be halted.

The dynamic association of handler with an exception gives rise to a more flexible program but with the disadvantage of run-time overhead because of the searching required once an exception has been raised.

45.4.4.3 Resumption and termination

When the handler has been executed and has handled the exception, there are two possible ways in which execution can continue:

1. The area of the program in which the exception is raised can be resumed, possibly by re-executing the statement which gave rise to the error initially or by executing the next statement. This technique is used in PL/I and to a limited degree in PEARL and Mesa. Some writers call this the resumption model.
2. The block or procedure that transferred control to the present context is resumed immediately after the block or call. There will be two forms of return from a block or a procedure – normal or exceptional returns. This is sometimes called the termination model.

An illustration of the termination model with nested blocks in Ada is:

```
declare
  -- declarations
begin
  -- statements
  declare
    VIBRATION_TOO_HIGH: exception;
  begin
    --statements
    if VIBRATIONS > THRESHOLD then
      raise VIBRATION_TOO_HIGH;
  end if;
```

```
--statements, executed if VIBRATION_TOO_HIGH is
-- not raised.
exception
  when VIBRATION_TOO_HIGH =>
    PUT("Close down port engine immediately");
  end;
  -- statements executed when either the nested block
  -- completes normally or after the exception has
  -- been handled
exception
  -- handler for any other exceptions raised
  -- in the nested block or any exception raised
  -- in the outer block
end;
```

45.4.4.4 Exceptions in Ada

The Steelman requirement demanded that Ada have an exception mechanism based upon the termination model. It has the following features:

1. Pre-defined exceptions for error conditions which constitute either faults detected by the hardware or by a run-time violation of the language rules. The built-in exceptions are: CONSTRAINT_ERROR, NUMERIC_ERROR, STORAGE_ERROR, PROGRAM_ERROR and TASKING_ERROR.
2. The user can declare exceptions in the same way as variables. They have the same scope properties as other Ada identifiers.
3. Exceptions can be raised either explicitly in a raise statement or implicitly (by the hardware or run-time system).
4. Exceptions are handled in handlers which can be attached to scopes (see earlier examples). Exception names can be specified either explicitly or as a catch-all (OTHERS).
5. Exceptions are propagated along the dynamic calling sequence until a handler is found. If one cannot be found, the program or task dies.
6. Exceptions raised during the elaboration of declarations cause the block containing the declarations to be abandoned and the exception to be propagated to the context of the caller.
7. The built-in exceptions can be suppressed by use of pragmas (comments that instruct the compiler).
8. Exceptions interact with the Ada model of parallel processing in a complicated way. Full details are not given here. Briefly, a task cannot raise an exception in another. However, if an exception is raised during task communication (rendezvous), then the exception is propagated to both tasks.

Unfortunately, the Ada exception mechanism must give rise to run-time overheads, even when it is not used (hence the requirement for pragma SUPPRESS), because administrative information must be placed at the head of each stack frame for the exceptions handled by code attached to that scope. In addition, the code required to support the parallel processing model is complicated considerably by the interactions between tasking and exceptions. These complications will increase the task switching times even when exceptions are not raised.

45.4.4.5 Exceptions in Modula

Neither Modula (one) nor Modula 2 have an exception mechanism defined in the language, although writers have proposed mechanisms for both languages. However, a recent version, Modula 3, does contain a comprehensive exception mechanism which is, in many respects, similar to Ada. Exceptions can be declared and raised, and then handled in an associated handler. The handler is found, as in Ada, by following the dynamic calling sequence. However, unlike Ada, parameters can be passed from the RAISE statement to the handler. In addition, there is a statement, TRY FINALLY, which allows a group of statements to be executed once an exception has been raised but before the search for a handler begins.

45.4.4.6 Exceptions in Mesa

The exceptions in Mesa are called signals. The language mechanism has the following general characteristics:

1. Mesa exceptions are propagated dynamically.
2. A handler is provided by associating a procedure with the exception at declaration time so they can be passed parameters and can return values.
3. Handlers are associated with blocks.
4. There are two types of exception declaration: signals, which enable the signalling context to be resumed when the handler has completed, and errors which do not.

45.4.5 Summary

An exception mechanism is now included in many modern programming languages, although usually for the handling of errors and not as a general mechanism for controlling the flow of control. Indeed, the use of exceptions for flow control will reintroduce most of the obscure programming techniques which structured programming has attempted to remove. Exceptions work well only when used in a disciplined manner, for the particular purpose for which they are intended.

45.5 Concurrency

45.5.1 Processes or tasks

A sequential program is a section of code where each statement defines a successor either implicitly (next statement) or explicitly (target of a go to, say), with execution starting at the first statement. This model of execution mirrors directly the von Neumann model of computing. Such a unit of code is known as a process or task. A concurrent program specifies two or more sequential programs that can be executed concurrently as parallel processes or tasks. A concurrent program can be executed in two different ways:

1. By multiplexing, through time, the processes on a single processor. This is often called multi-programming.
2. By allocating each process, or group of processes, to a separate processor (computer). If the processors share a common memory this is called multi-processing. If they do not, and the processors are connected by a network (e.g. Ethernet), it is called distributed processing.

One would like to be able to understand the functional behaviour of multi-process programs in terms of the individual processes and their interaction without knowledge of the way in which they are executed, even though such knowledge is essential if performance is to be assessed. Here it is assumed that all processes execute at some finite rate. There is no assumption about the architecture on which they run.

45.5.2 Interactions between processes

Processes must cooperate if they are to achieve some overall goal. To do so they must communicate and synchronize.

Communication allows one process to influence another. This can be achieved by the use of variables shared between processes or by message passing (or the equivalent). Mutual exclusion is a form of communication which ensures that shared variables can only be updated when the updating process has exclusive access to the variables.

Synchronization is necessary to ensure that communication takes place at appropriate points in time. For example, actions (e.g. calculations) may only be carried out when data – perhaps calculated by other processes – is available. In other words, synchronization is a constraint on the ordering of events to ensure that the program proceeds sensibly.

There are three main issues which must be satisfied in the design of a notation for expressing concurrency:

1. How to indicate concurrent execution.
2. Which kind of interprocess communication to use.
3. Which kind of synchronization mechanism to use.

These issues are addressed in many different ways in a wide variety of programming languages. These are now discussed in the order listed.

45.5.3 Concurrent execution

There are many notations for defining the code of a process and for indicating the start of its execution; sometimes these are combined. Notations exist for specifying a fixed or variable number of processes. There may be complex interactions between the scope and lifetime of variables in blocks which contain either the declaration or start of processes because the processes may reference variables in scopes with shorter potential lifetimes than the processes themselves. Such interactions complicate the semantics of any programming language combining these features (e.g. Ada, Modula 2).

Four widely used methods for the declaration and starting of processes are now discussed. There are many others.

45.5.3.1 Coroutines

Coroutines are concurrent processes in which the pattern of process switching has been completely predetermined. Control is passed between coroutines by means of a resume statement, where the resume statement transfers control to the named coroutine – like a procedure call – saving sufficient state for control to be transferred later to the statement after the resume. There is no equivalent to a procedure return. Furthermore, the pattern of resumes need not follow an equivalent pattern of procedure calls and returns. The patterns of resumes completely specifies the pattern of process switching. Coroutines can be seen as processes with each resume causing synchronization.

Coroutines are only suitable for single processors as only one process can run at a time. They are provided in Modula 2 and can be used as the basis of more complex mechanisms.

45.5.3.2 Fork and join

The fork statement indicates that the specified process should start executing concurrently with the process executing the fork; this process can then await the completion of the forked process by executing a join. Quite often the fork statement will return a value identifying the new process; this can then be used by the join statement to identify when the new process has finished. A fork statement can be used in a loop so that many instances of a process can be started.

The fork and join technique was used in Multics (via the PL/I programming language) and is used in Unix (via C). As an example of its use, there follows a section of C which starts a further program as a process, then waits for its completion before resuming. This is the technique used in the Unix 'shell' to run user programs after reading their names from the terminal:

```
#include ⟨stdio.h⟩
main( )
{
int status, pid;
pid = fork( );
if (pid = = 0) {
    /* the child process */
    execl("program file name");
    printf("Error in execl of program");
    exit(1);
    }
else if (pid = = −1) {
    printf("Fork failed");
    exit(1);
    }
else
    /* parent process waits for child to finish */
    wait(&status);
printf("End of program");
exit(0);
}
```

45.5.3.3 Cobegin

The Cobegin is a statement that denotes the concurrent execution of a number of statements or processes. For example, in Algol 68:

```
par (p1, p2, p3);
```

would set procedures p1, p2 and p3 running as separate processes in parallel with the parent. The next statement in the parent cannot execute until all three processes have completed.

45.5.3.4 Process declarations

It is much clearer if processes or tasks are declared as separate entities in programs, distinct from procedures and other items. This declaration may or may not start the process – such separation is necessary if the number of processes is to be dynamic. The following example is from Ada. Declarations and statements have been mixed for ease of explanation:

```
-- declare a task type
task type SIMPLE;

task body SIMPLE is
begin
    -- statements
end SIMPLE;

-- declare and start a single instance
T: SIMPLE;

-- declare and start N instances
-- (where N may be a run-time expression)
T: array (1 .. N) of SIMPLE;

-- now declare a pointer to a task
type REF_SIMPLE is access SIMPLE;

P: REF SIMPLE
-- P may point to a SIMPLE

P := new SIMPLE;
-- create and start a further SIMPLE
-- P can now be used to refer to this instance
```

By comparison Modula (one) and Concurrent Pascal only allow

a fixed number of processes, although they do allow multiple instances of each process to be declared and started.

45.5.4 Synchronization based upon shared variables

Two types of synchronization are useful if shared variables are employed for communication:

1. Mutual exclusion, which ensures that a sequence of statements are treated indivisibly. Such a sequence is called a critical region.
2. Condition synchronization, which ensures that a shared variable is in a state appropriate for an operation e.g. a shared buffer has space available.

Various mechanisms for shared variable synchronization are now surveyed.

45.5.4.1 Busy-wait

A process can set the value of a shared variable to signal a condition. If one process wishes to signal a condition to another, the second process repeatedly tests the variable until it has the desired value. The delay is called busy-waiting and the delayed process is said to be spinning. The variables are sometimes called spin-locks.

Mutual exclusion and synchronization using busy-waiting requires careful protocol design. In addition it suffers from the disadvantage that it wastes processor time during repeated testing of the spin-lock. Also, special indivisible machine operations are necessary for correct operation (e.g. the test and set instruction on the IBM System/370).

45.5.4.2 Semaphores

A semaphore is a low-level sychronization variable, first introduced by Dijkstra, which can be used for process synchronization and mutual exclusion. A semaphore is a non-negative variable, shared between processes, on which two operations are defined:

P (or wait): P(s) means delay the process executing the P until s becomes greater than zero; then execute and decrement s by one. The operation is indivisible.
V (or release): V(s) means increase the value of s by one, possible releasing a waiting process, as an indivisible operation.

Implementations of Dijkstra semaphores often allow the value of the variable to be negative, where the absolute value is the number of processes waiting on the semaphore. Often they are queued in a FIFO manner. Implementations usually ensure fairness so that no process can be blocked for ever if a suitable number of V operations are performed. Semaphores are of two sorts: binary and n-ary. Binary semaphores are suitable when a shared resource of one unit is involved; n-ary semaphores are more convenient when several units are involved (e.g. multiple buffers shared by a producer and a consumer).

The following example shows how a binary semaphore can be used to ensure that only one process can be in a critical region at any one time, hence providing mutual exclusion:

```
program SHARED_RESOURCE
  S: SEMAPHORE := 1;

process A;
begin
  loop
    P(S);
    -- critical region
```

```
    V(S);
    -- non critical code
  end loop;
end A;

process B:
begin
  loop
    P(S);
    -- another critical region
    V(S);
    -- non critical code
  end loop;
end B;
```

The use of the semaphore S makes it impossible for both processes to be in the critical regions at the same time. To understand this, assume that process A executes initially. When it comes to the P, it finds that $S > 0$, S then becomes zero and the critical region executes. If the process is stopped during this section (by the scheduler), then the P operation guarding the second critical region will halt the other process when it tries to execute a P(S) operation (as $S = 0$); it will not be released until the first process is resumed and executes a V.

The semaphore can also be used to achieve synchronization between producer and consumer process (so-called, because one process produces information and another consumes it). An example of a program with two processes one filling and another emptying a shared buffer is:

```
program BUFFERS;
  S1, S2: SEMAPHORE := 0;

process PRODUCER;
begin
  loop
    -- fill buffer will happen first
    fill buffer;
    V(S2);
    P(S1);
  end loop;
end PRODUCER;

process CONSUMER;
begin
  loop
    P(S2);
    process buffer contents;
    V(S1);
  end loop;
end CONSUMER;
```

Note that S2 acts as a 'buffer now full indicator' and S1 as a 'buffer now empty'. The solution can be generalized to deal with N buffers by initializing S1 to $N - 1$ and S2 to zero.

Some authors distinguish between global and private semaphores, where each kind can be associated with a group of processes. If it is private only one process from the group may perform P operations, although all processes can perform V operations. If it is a global semaphore all processes can perform P and V operations. The examples show that global semaphores are used for mutual exclusion, and private semaphores are used for sychronization.

45.5.4.3 Critical regions or sections

Several authors have attributed the unreliability of large systems programs to inadequate methods of program construction. For example, semaphores lead to an unstructured style of programming similar to the effect of gotos in control structures. Critical regions or sections have been proposed to give program structures in which the data shared by concurrent processes is explicitly linked with the operations defined upon them.

A shared variable of type T might be declared as follows:

V: shared T;

Concurrent processes can then only refer to and change a shared variable within a critical region:

region V do S; end region;

which associates a statement S with a shared variable V. Only one process can be inside a critical region with respect to V at any one time. This can be checked easily by a compiler and could be implemented with binary semaphores.

When processes cooperate on a common goal, they must wait until certain conditions have been satisfied by other processes. This can be achieved by conditional critical regions which have the form:

```
region V do
   await B;
   statements;
end region;
```

The await must be enclosed textually by a critical region; the waiting will be carried out until the condition B is satisfied. There are two disadvantages associated with this method:

1. Significant computer time is spent evaluating B repeatedly.
2. The sequence in which waiting processes enter these regions is ignored.

If the resource is used heavily, then control is needed over the scheduling of resources. This can be achieved if event queues are associated with shared variables as follows:

E: event V

A process can leave a critical region associated with V and join the event queue E by executing the statement:

await(E);

Another process can enable all processes in a queue E to re-enter their critical regions by executing:

cause(E);

As an example of these mechanisms, the following is a producer/consumer program in which event queues are used to specify the scheduling:

```
--CONSUMER
region V do
   while not B loop await(E); end loop;
   statements;
end region;

-- PRODUCER
region V do
   statements;
   cause(E);
end region;
```

Conditional critical regions are used in the Edison and Argus programming languages.

45.5.4.4 *Monitors*

Conditional critical regions are both costly to implement and lead to poorly structured programs (as the statements affecting synchronization and mutual exclusion may be scattered throughout the program). A monitor overcomes these problems by encapsulating both the resource definition and the operations that manipulate it; mutually exclusive use of the operations

(procedures) by other processes is guaranteed, thus ensuring that the resource is never accessed concurrently. The structure of a monitor is illustrated by the following example:

M: monitor;

resource definition;

```
procedure P1(formal parameters);
declare local variables for P1;
begin
    code for P1;
end P1;

begin
    code to initialize local variables;
end M;
```

The procedure or operation on the resource guarded by the monitor is invoked by:

M.P1(actual parameters);

Several mechanisms have been used to achieve condition synchronization in monitors:

1. *Condition variables.* Two operations are defined: signal and wait. A wait causes the invoker to be blocked on a condition variable and relinquish mutually exclusive control of the monitor. Signal causes a blocked process to be resumed. Condition variables enable more than one process to be in a monitor. However, all bar one will be delayed at a signal or wait. In some systems it is possible to associate a priority with a wait statement.
2. *Queues.* Concurrent Pascal uses variables of type queue to implement condition synchronization and scheduling. One process only can be suspended on a queue at any given time using the operation delay. Continue is used to resume a previously delayed process. Medium-term scheduling can be achieved using an array of queues.
3. *Other mechanisms.* Several other mechanisms are used including: conditional wait, in which the invoker is delayed until the condition becomes true (no signal is necessary); notify, used in Mesa, in which a process is told that it can resume but the notifying process continues; and time outs in which an event variable is associated with a time-out interval.

Nested monitor calls have been the source of considerable interest. Should monitors be able to call further monitor procedures because, if the second cell is suspended, the first call will remain suspended thus decreasing the amount of parellelism in the system? Some languages prohibit nested calls (e.g. SIMONE); others (e.g. Modula) limited the context of nesting.

45.5.4.5 *Programming languages using monitors*

Both Concurrent Pascal and Modula (one) use monitors. Concurrent Pascal enables the user to declare monitors for the protection of shared data, together with processes for concurrent execution. Queues, signal and delay are used for the control of mutual exclusion and synchronization. The language requires a complex run-time system to support the concurrent 'machine'. Modula, in contrast uses processes, interface modules (which are similar to monitors) and device modules. Signal and wait are used for synchronization: the precise semantics of these statements can only be understood in terms of the implementation where the doio statement acts as a wait pending a hardware interrupt. The run-time system required to support Modula is tiny, although this is achieved by relying upon the hardware for part of the scheduling action.

Modula 2 is a development of Modula which has retained much of the original module mechanism. However, a different, simpler, concurrency model based upon coroutines (and the necessary switching primitives) is used. This new mechanism can be used to construct an equivalent mechanism to that employed in Modula, although without the static checks on the use of concurrent language available in that language.

45.5.5 Message passing

Critical regions and monitors are structured methods of controlling access to shared variables. Message passing is a different approach which can be viewed as extending semaphores to convey data as well as to implement synchronization. Processes send and receive messages instead of reading and writing to shared variables. Data values are sent in the messages, thus achieving communication. Synchronization is accomplished because messages can only be received after they have been sent thus constraining the order of events.

Message passing relies upon two primitive statements:

send MESSAGE to DESTINATION

receive MESSAGE from SOURCE

where MESSAGE may include variable names which will be assigned to and from the message received or sent. The semantics of the message passing statements will define the form of the source and destination used and will specify how communication is synchronized.

45.5.5.1 Channels

The source and destination defines a communications channel which can be named directly in terms of the process names. For example:

send CHARACTER to TERMINAL;

receive CHARACTER from TERMINAL;

Note that receive can only receive a message from the named process.

Process interaction, in terms of a message passing paradigm, is often called a client/server relationship. A client requests service by sending a message to a server which may subsequently send a completion message to the client. Of course, direct naming may inhibit this style of interaction as each server would then need to name each of its clients in a separate receive statement. Conversely, if there are many servers then a client will need to send a message which need only be received by any single server.

This difficulty can be solved by the use of mail boxes, which are global names known to a number of processes. Clients send their messages requesting service to a particular mail box; servers always take their messages from a mail box. If the name of a particular mail box can only appear in the receive statements of one process, then the mail box is called a port. Unfortunately, the implementation of mail boxes can be inefficient without the provision of special purpose hardware.

45.5.5.2 Synchronization

There are a variety of semantics used for message passing synchronization:

1. A statement is said to be blocking if the invoker is delayed; otherwise it is said to be non-blocking.
2. A message may be buffered between sender and receiver. If the buffer capacity is infinite, then the send is called asynchronous message passing or send no-wait; in such a system the sender can get considerably in advance of the server. If there is no buffering, then the send is called synchronous message passing as the sending of the message represents a synchronization point between the client and the server.

3. If the buffer has limited capacity, then there is buffered message passing.
4. A blocking receive may be guarded by a Boolean condition so that a process can receive all available messages and then select one of them to process. This is a form of self-scheduling.

45.5.5.3 Remote procedure call

Any type of process interaction can be programmed using message passing primitives. However, there may be circumstances where the client always uses a send followed by a receive and the server a receive followed by a send. A remote procedure call supports this pattern of interaction directly.

A remote call is executed as follows. The values of the actual parameters to the call are sent to the server named in the call; the calling process then delays until both the service has been completed and the results returned via the parameters. Such a call can be implemented as a send followed by a receive.

The remote procedure can be implemented by a number of mechanisms. It could loop repeatedly waiting for calls; these would then be processed in FIFO order. This could be achieved by placing an accept statement in the server at the point at which the server would wait to receive remote procedure calls demanding services. This is the technique used in Ada; the interaction between caller and server is called a rendezvous. In Ada, the accept statements can be placed at points where the server is willing to provide services. By providing several accept statements, a server can provide several kinds of service and can select between several calls available at any particular instant.

An alternative mechanism is to generate a new process for each server request. However, this is both complicated (what happens if several processes access a common resource?) and expensive to implement.

45.5.6 Programming languages using message passing

45.5.6.1 occam

occam is the language designed to exploit the Inmos transputer; occam 2 is the most recent version. The language is an implementation of CSP embedded within a general-purpose language, which has very restricted type constructors. occam 2 can be viewed as a high-level assembly language for the transputer, where the parallelism in the hardware can be exploited directly. As an example, here is a buffer process in occam 2. Note that the layout of the program defines the statements groupings:

```
VAL INT size IS 100:
INT TOP, BASE, NumberInBuffer:
[size] DATA BUFFER:
SEQ
  NumberInBuffer := 0
  TOP := 0
  BASE := 0
  DATA Any:
  WHILE TRUE
    ALT
      NumberInBuffer < size & APPEND ? BUFFER[TOP]
        SEQ
          NumberInBuffer := NumberInBuffer + 1
          TOP := (TOP + 1) REM size
      NumberInBuffer > 0 & REQUEST ? Any
        SEQ
          TAKE ! BUFFER[BASE]
          NumberInBuffer := NumberInBuffer - 1
          BASE := (BASE + 1) REM size
```

For this buffer process correct functioning is dependent upon correct use by the client processes.

45.5.6.2 *Ada*

Ada has facilities for both multiprogramming and the control of I/O devices. However, it is unclear if the designers meant the language to be suitable for both tightly *and* loosely coupled multi-computer systems because the combined scope and process model assume a common store for all processes.

A process in Ada is called a task. Tasks are declared and activated when either their declaration is elaborated (i.e. executed) or they are activated explicitly. A scope in Ada cannot be left until all tasks that are declared in or depend upon that block have terminated. Tasks can share variables declared in enclosing blocks, although such use will be subject to the usual problems of mutual exclusion unless special care is taken.

Tasks interact principally via the remote procedure call mechanism using entries in the server task called accept statements. Entries are invoked using the procedure-calling mechanism with parameters. Both the call and the accept may block if the server is either not at a corresponding accept statement or is processing another, earlier, call. Such an eventuality can be avoided by using a conditional entry call. Similarly, a server can detect if calls are waiting on a particular entry. A select statement is provided to enable a server to distinguish between alternative calls. Each entry in a select statement can be protected with guards – Boolean conditions which must be true if that entry is to be among those from which a call is selected. If calls are pending on several entries which have guards that are true, then a call is selected arbitrarily. This is intended to ensure fairness. Tasks can suspend execution for at least a given period of time by using a delay statement.

The tasking mechanism is complicated by its use for interaction with I/O devices. Hardware interrupts can be associated with entry calls; the server will then act as an interrupt handler. At present, it is not clear if this mechanism is sufficently efficient for the writing of practical interrupt handlers.

As an example of Ada tasking, the following program is a producer/consumer program with the producer sending characters to a buffer task; the consumer task will then take characters from the buffer task when it requires them. The producer task is prevented from sending characters when the buffer task is incapable of storing them:

```
task BUFFER is
  entry READ(C: out CHARACTER);
  entry WRITE(C: in CHARACTER);
end;

task body BUFFER is
  POOL_SIZE: constant INTEGER := 100;
  POOL: array(1 .. POOL_SIZE) of CHARACTER;
  COUNT: INTEGER range 0 .. POOL_SIZE := 0;
  IN_INDEX, OUT_INDEX: INTEGER
  range 1 .. POOL_SIZE := 1;
begin
  loop
    select
      when COUNT < POOL_SIZE = >
        accept WRITE(C: in CHARACTER) do
          POOL(IN_INDEX) := C;
        end;
        IN_INDEX := IN_INDEX mod POOL_SIZE + 1;
        COUNT := COUNT + 1;
      or
      when COUNT >= 0 = >
        accept READ(C: out CHARACTER) do
          C := POOL(OUT_INDEX);
        end;
        OUT_INDEX := OUT_INDEX mod
        POOL_SIZE + 1;
        COUNT := COUNT + 1;
```

```
    or
      terminate;
    end select;
  end loop;
end BUFFER;
```

45.6 Conclusions

Imperative languages have evolved rapidly during the 1980s, although recent ideas have had little impact on the languages in widespread use. Languages which are strongly typed and have a procedure mechanism are now widely adopted, although the use of structuring techniques, such as the package, are less widely used. Nevertheless, such techniques are essential for large-scale program structuring, for the re-use of software components, and for the construction of reliable software. The recent developments in type models and polymorphism should make reuse possible and bring forward the day when libraries of software components are a practical proposition.

45.7 Bibliography

Andrews, G. and Schneider F. (1983) Concepts and notations for concurrent programming. *Computing Surveys*, **15**, 3–43

Booch G. (1988) *Software Components with Ada*, Benjamin Cummings

Brinch-Hansen, P. (1977) *The Architecture of Concurrent Programs*, Prentice-Hall

Brinch-Hansen, P. (1981) Edison – a multiprocessor language. *Software – Practice and Experience*, **11**, 325–362

Burns, A. and Wellings, A. (1989) *Real-time Systems and Their Programming Languages*, Addison-Wesley

Cardelli, L. *et al.* (1988) Modula-3 report, DEC Systems Research Centre Report 31

Cardelli, L. and Wegner, P. (1985) On understanding types, data abstraction and polymorphism. *Computing Surveys*, **17**, 471–522

Cioni, G. and Salwicki, A. (eds) (1989) *Advanced Programming Methodologies*, APIC Series 30, Academic Press

Dahl, O.-J. *et al.* (1968) The Simula 67 common base language, Norwegian Computing Centre Report

Danforth, S. and Tomlinson, C. (1988) Type theories and object-oriented programming. *Computing Surveys*, **20**, 29–72

Department of Defense (1983) *Reference manual for the Ada programming*, ANSI/MIL-STD 1815A

Goodenough, J. (1975) Exception handling: issues and a proposed notation. *Communications of the ACM*, **18**, 683

Harper, R. Milner, R. and Tofte, M. (1988) The definition of standard ML, version 2, University of Edinburgh Computer Science report ECS-LFCS-88-62

Hoare, C. A. R. (1972) Notes on data structuring. In *Structured Programming*, Academic Press pp 83–174

Jensen, K. and Wirth, N. (1985) *The Pascal User Manual and Report*, (3rd edn) Springer-Verlag

Kaubisch, W. H., Perrott, W. H. and Hoare, C. A. R. (1976) Quasi-parallel programming. *Software – Practice and Experience*, **6**, 341–356

Kernighan, B. and Ritchie, D. (1978) *The C Programming Language*, Prentice-Hall

IBM (1970) PL/I language specification, document number GY33-6003-2

Levin, R. (1977) Program structures for exception condition handling, PhD thesis, Carnegie-Mellon University

Liskov, B. *et al.* (1979) CLU reference manual, MIT report TR-225

Liskov, B. *et al.* (1987) Implementation of Argus. In *Proceedings of the Eleventh ACM Symposium on Operating System Principles*, pp 111–122

Stroustrup, B. (1985) *The C++ Programming Language*, Addison-Wesley

Wijngaarden, A. *et al.* (1975) Revised report on the algorithmic language Algol 68. *Acta Informatica*, **5**, 1–236

Wirth, N. (1977) Modula: a language for modular multiprogramming. *Software – Practice and Experience*, **7**, 3–36

Wirth, N. (1983) *Programming in Modula-2*, Springer-Verlag

46

Practical program development issues

John Henderson
King's College, London

Roy Dowsing
University of East Anglia

Dorothy Graham
Grove Consultants

Contents

46.1 Introduction

There are a number of practical steps to be taken before a program written in a suitable programming language can be implemented on a computer system. Assuming that the program has been written in a high-level programming language, it must first be translated into low-level code. This code must then be loaded into the memory of the computer system and combined with any other code needed for execution – for example, standard library functions – before it can be run. Whilst under development, a program will normally fail to execute correctly and the programmer will have to determine where the error is, what caused it and what modifications are required to remove it.

From this description it can be seen that the implementation of programs on a computer requires a number of complex steps to be performed. Whilst these steps can be carried out manually it is usual to perform them using computer-based tools (Kernighan and Plauger, 1976). For example, the task of converting from a high-level language program to a machine or intermediate code is usually performed by a compiler. It is the provision of appropriate professional tools for each task which can make the implementation less time-consuming and error-prone.

It is inevitable that programs will have to be loaded into the memory of a computer prior to execution. It is almost inevitable that during development programs will fail to execute as intended and one will have to investigate the causes of failure, in a process known as debugging. Thus loaders and debuggers (tools to aid debugging) are two essential tools for the software engineer. Whilst there are other practical program development issues, the focus here is on loading and debugging, as they are essential tools in the program production process. Each topic is dealt with in its own major section.

Loading is essentially a mechanical process. None the less, it is one that the software engineer needs to understand in building programs. The chapter discusses a range of types of loader, but excludes issues such as developing programs for loading into ROM.

Debugging is an intellectual exercise which can be aided by tools. Thus the chapter deals with guidelines on how to approach (and how not to approach) debugging as well as discussing the capabilities of tools.

Loaders are discussed in Section 46.2, and debugging is covered in Section 46.3. Some more minor issues are discussed in Section 46.4.

46.2 Program loading

A major portion of the task of translating a program written in a high-level programming language into a lower level representation is the association of one set of names with another set of names or addresses and bit patterns. This is known as address binding (Jones and Muchnick, 1978). This binding can take place at one of a number of different times, for example, at program writing time, at translation time, at loading time or at execution time. Leaving the binding as late as possible gives greater flexibility but at a higher cost. If a name is associated with an address at program creation time then it will only execute at the addresses built into the code and the program will have to be rewritten to execute at any other address. If the addresses are not decided until load time then the decision on where the program is to be placed in memory can depend on where any other programs are in memory. It is the desire to leave address binding as late as possible which gives rise to the need for some of the software described in this chapter.

This chapter looks at these practical issues of implementing a program on a computer and how this can be aided by a number of software tools. The first software tool considered is the loader

(Barron, 1969; Donovan, 1972; Presser and White, 1972). The language processor which has been used to compile or assemble the source text will produce an intermediate representation of the machine code. This requires further manipulation before it can be executed. At the simplest level it has to be moved into the memory of the computer before it can be executed and this is the function of the loader. At increasing levels of complexity it needs to be combined (linked) with other pieces of code before it can be loaded. This process is handled by a linker and a loader, which may be combined in a single tool or which may be separate tools.

The loader also deals with 'software relocation'. In most order codes, the addresses of both program and data in the running program need to reflect the physical addresses at which the program and data are stored. If several independent compilations are to be combined, or if the locations to be used are not known at compile time, then a program is needed to make the appropriate changes. It is normal for relocation to be carried out by the loader and it is not usual to think of relocation as a separate (separable) activity.

A related topic is that of managing the components which are to be joined together by a linker. This is sometimes called configuration control or management. There is a variety of programs available, often known as MAKE programs, which provide a degree of automatic version control and consistency checking. This topic is dealt with in detail in Chapter 34.

The remainder of this section is mainly concerned with the problems of reusing code (Brown, 1975). It is often the case that parts of a program are written in different programming languages. One reason for this is a deficiency in the facilities provided by one language. Another reason is that library routines may be written by someone else in a different language. The problems that this can cause and ways of identifying them are then discussed in the section on mixed language working. If many different processes wish to use the same code it would be convenient if only a single copy was required. This is the case if re-entrant code is used. This is discussed in the next subsection.

46.2.1 Linking and loading

In order to run a program written in a programming language, a number of different processes have to be applied to the program. A common scheme used by many languages is shown in *Figure 46.1.*

First, the modules of the program have to be translated into low-level code and data by a language translator such as a compiler or assembler. The output of the translator is typically in a form called object module format, which is described later. The object modules are linked together with any library routines or functions required by means of a linker, which fills in the cross-references between the modules. The output from the linker, called a load module, is then loaded into memory, ready for execution, by a program called a loader.

46.2.2 Loaders

46.2.2.1 Bootstrap loader

The simplest but most essential loader is one that will boot the system from start-up. This is known as a bootstrap loader. Early computers had a control panel switch which allowed the operator to toggle into memory a small program in binary which, when run, caused a more complex loader to be read from a standard input device, such as a paper tape reader. The objective in writing one of these small programs was to produce as small a program as possible to do the required job, as loading binary by hand is very tedious and error-prone. Thus these programs used many tricks, such as overwriting the code on execution to

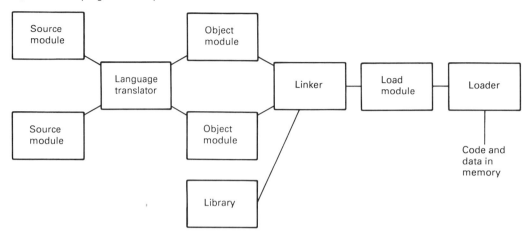

Figure 46.1

transfer control to the loaded program. As the cost of ROMs decreased and their size increased, the practice became to put the bootstrap loader in ROM and to initiate it either by operator action or, later, by automatic means on power up or rebooting. Because the bootstrap loader had to be as small as possible, the code it input had to be in a very simple fixed format. This code was usually a more complex loader to enable input of further programs in more flexible formats.

The number of stages in the bootstrapping process depends on the complexity of software to be loaded. Typically, the bootstrap loader loads another loader which then loads the operating system which contains one or more loaders to load code produced by system software such as compilers and loaders.

Current practice is for the bootstrap loader in ROM to read a more sophisticated loader from one or two blocks on a disc. Control is then transferred to this more sophisticated loader which reads in the operating system from the disc. Some of these operating system loaders expect to find the operating system at a given place on the disc, but most recent loaders interrogate the directory of the disc to look for a specific named file – for example, monitor.sys – and to load that file. This indirect access to the operating system provides a simple method for installing a new one; just rename the old file and install a new one with the appropriate name.

46.2.2.2 Relocating loader

An operating system contains, or has access to, at least one loader, so that a program can be loaded on command. This loader could be one of the two simple ones described above, but they do not usually provide the facilities required to load the output from a translator. A more complex loader is required, which has, amongst other features, the ability to modify the program being loaded so that it will run wherever it is placed.

This process of modification is called relocation. Relocation is achieved by including in the loadable file additional information, in the form of a relocation directory, which the loader can use to make the adjustments to addresses contained in the program appropriate to the locations being used on each occasion. The advantage of relocation is that a program may be run at a different position in memory without it being retranslated; it just has to be reloaded.

Relocation puts additional constraints on the translator, since it has to distinguish between information which *does not* depend on where it is placed in memory, and information which *does*

depend on where it is placed in memory. For example, a numeric constant such as '2' does not depend on where it is placed in memory, but the address of an instruction in the code or of a piece of data depends on where the code or data is placed in memory. For complex expressions it becomes difficult to determine whether the whole expression is or is not dependent on where it is placed in memory, and sets of rules have been developed to enable the mode of any expression to be determined.

The algorithm used by a relocating loader is simple. The input consists of code and data, together with the offset of each item from the nominal start address, which is usually taken to be zero. A relocation constant is provided by the user or the operating system. This constant specifies the actual address in memory where the code and data is to be loaded. The loader then places the code and data at the address given by the sum of the relocation constant and the offset for each item. The loader then uses the information in the relocation dictionary to add or subtract the relocation constant from information in some locations in the program. As a simple example consider the following piece of code:

```
    jmp  L1    ;jump to instruction labelled L1
L1: add  r0,r1  ;add contents of r0 to r1
```

Assume that the jmp instruction is coded in 32 bits, 16 for function and 16 for address, and that the word size is 16 bits, then the assembler will generate code of the form:

```
address  code
0000     xxx    code for jump instruction
0001     2      address of L1 relative to start
0002     yyy    code for add instruction
```

with a relocation dictionary of:

```
0001     +
```

If this code were to be loaded at location 1000 onwards then the loading action would generate:

```
1000     xxx
1001     2
1002     yyy
```

The relocation phase would use the relocation dictionary to

discover that the relocation constant, in this case 1000, has to be added to the information placed at the new address 1001, thus giving:

```
1000    xxx
1001    1002
1002    yyy
```

It should be noted that, using this scheme, once the code has been relocated it will only run at the position to which it has been relocated and, in particular, it cannot be moved during execution.

46.2.2.3 Position-independent code

Another way to produce the same effect as the relocating loader is to force the translator to produce code which can run without modification at any location in memory. This type of code is known as position-independent code (PIC). It can be loaded into any position in memory with a simple loader since it requires no relocation modifications.

It is not always possible to produce PIC, since this can only be written for processors which provide the appropriate addressing mechanisms, for example, relative addressing modes. Thus the simpler microprocessors do not support this type of code.

As an example, consider the generation of code for the example given above. If the address of the instruction labelled L1 was coded into the jmp instruction as a relative address rather than an absolute address, i.e. as a value of 0 rather than 2, then the code would be position-independent. This is because the generation of the effective address to be used in the jump instruction would involve adding the value of 0 to the current value of the program counter which is dependent on where the code is loaded. In order to produce PIC for data access, indexed addressing from a base register is used and the loader has to load the base address of the data segment into the appropriate base register.

46.2.2.4 Dynamic loading

It is possible to leave the process of loading until execution time. This has the advantage that any code or data which is not used in a particular execution does not have to be loaded and therefore does not consume memory. In order to use this technique it must be possible for the processor to determine when reference is made to an entity which has not been loaded. This means making a check on every memory reference against a table of what has been loaded. This requires hardware assistance and is expensive but is used with a paging or segmentation scheme, such as those described in Chapter 49.

In such a scheme a program is considered as a set of pages or segments. Each individual page or segment is normally loaded on demand, i.e. when a reference is made to an address in that page or segment and that page or segment is not currently in memory; hence, the name 'demand loading'. Pages or segments are discarded from memory when the space they occupy is required and access to that page or segment has not been made for some time. The page or segment is left on backing storage, typically disc, so that it may be loaded again if at a later time reference is made to it.

Because the page or segment may not be loaded at the same place in memory at different times, addresses in the code are considered to be virtual addresses which have to be translated by the hardware into real memory addresses on execution. Each virtual address consists of two fields, a page or segment number and an offset within the page or segment. The hardware translates this virtual page or segment number into the start address of the block in memory at which this page or segment resides on every access.

This type of loading is very expensive but it has found favour with many manufacturers of large systems because it is possible to run very large programs on systems with a relatively small amount of physical memory.

46.2.2.5 Downline loading

As has been stated above, a number of different loaders are typically required to load a program into the memory of a computer. If a computer system is being developed from the basic components, then none of these loaders will exist. Also, if the computer system being developed is for an embedded application then the facilities provided may not be suitable for program development; for example, a disc subsystem may not be provided. In these cases it is more convenient to perform the translation and linking on a host computer with the appropriate resources, pass the linked code across a transmission medium, typically a wire using RS232 protocol (see Chapter 44) and to use a small loader on the target machine to accept the transmitted code and load it into its memory.

The target machine loader is very simple and can be stored in a small EPROM. In many cases the link between the host and target computers is also used for program debugging. Instructions are passed across the link to request the small monitor on the target machine to take part in debugging tasks as described later in this chapter.

Although there are no standards for the protocol of connecting together a host and target machine for the purpose of loading code, one of the most common protocols is the Motorola S code format. In this format the code is organized into records. The structure of a typical record is type, two-character byte count, four-character address field, ASCII code for the bytes to be loaded and, lastly, a checksum. One type of record terminates the block of records. From this description it can be seen that the code transmitted by this means must have already been relocated by the sender or the code must be position-independent.

46.2.3 Linkers and link editors

A loader assumes that it is loading a single program and therefore the only concern is where the program should be placed in memory and how it should be modified, if at all, to execute in that position. However, it is often the case that the code produced by a translator refers to other separately compiled modules such as library modules or other program modules.

Before these multi-module programs can be loaded they must be combined to form a single program. This combining process, known as linking (Presser and White, 1972; Beck, 1985) fills in the cross-references between the separately compiled modules. The program which performs this task is called a linker or link editor. Sometimes the linker is combined with a loader and the resulting program is called a linking loader.

There are many reasons why it is preferable to consider a program as a collection of modules. The main reason is that it is then possible for separate people to design and implement the modules without knowing the details of how other modules work, only their interface. Each module can be implemented and tested separately and an error in one module only requires that module to be retranslated, not the whole program.

Another reason is that it may be desirable to produce a program using a number of different languages for different parts of the program. Providing the translators involved produce a common output format then the outputs can be combined by a linker to produce a single unified program.

Furthermore, if a program is written as a set of modules then it is possible to use and include a set of pre-translated library modules. Whilst it is possible to include source code of library routines this is slower and in some cases the library provider may not be willing to let the user see the source code for commercial reasons.

46.2.3.1 Structure and functions of a linker

The process of linking consists of binding externally defined names to addresses. As described previously, this binding can be performed at a number of different times, ranging from translation time to execution time. It has been found that in many cases the most convenient time to perform this binding is just before loading, since this gives flexibility for reasonable cost. Later binding at execution time requires extra hardware which increases the cost substantially.

The primary function of the linker is to bind the externally defined names to addresses. As a secondary function it provides overlay processing, program modification and library access (IBM, undated).

The input to a linker is normally a set of object modules produced from a program by a translator. The output is the code for the program, together with relocation information and a table indicating the definition and use of external symbols. Examples of the formats of the object modules and linker output used in the IBM 360 series are shown in *Figures 46.2* and *46.3*.

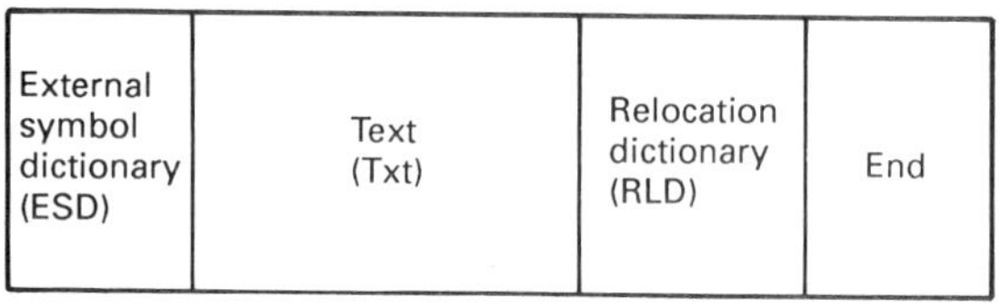

Figure 46.2 Object module format for IBM 360

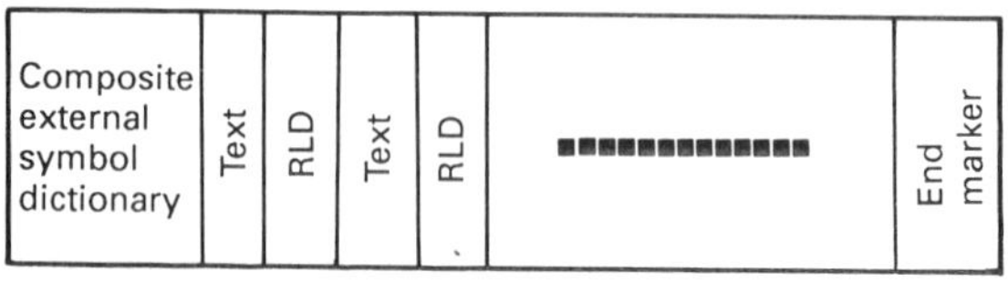

Figure 46.3 Load module format for IBM 360

Using the terminology of the figures, the external symbol dictionary contains the names of symbols defined in this module which can be referenced from another module together with their values. There are usually several different types of external symbols, depending on the type of information which can be communicated, for example, a label definition giving an entry point to that module and a global item of data.

The text portion of the object module contains relocatable code and data. The relocation dictionary contains an entry for each address which has to be relocated when the code is loaded into memory.

The actual contents of a dictionary entry depend on the architecture of the computer in question. Details for the IBM 360 can be found in IBM (undated) and Presser and White (1972). The end record denotes the end of the object module. Many newer object code module formats include extra fields at the front of the module denoting its name, date of creation and other administrative information.

The linker processes a set of object modules to form a load module by merging the external symbol dictionaries to form a composite dictionary. It uses the relocation directory to relocate the required values in each text section. During the relocation it searches the composite external dictionary for external symbols and performs the address binding of external symbols at this point.

The reason for producing a load module which has a similar structure to an object module is that the load module may be reprocessed by the linker, thus allowing a complete program to be created in a hierarchical fashion, so that only the minimum of relinking needs to be performed if the program is modified.

Most linkers use a two-pass algorithm. In the first pass, the definitions of all symbols are collected into a single table and the length of each text segment is found so that the location of each symbol in the load module can be calculated. In the second pass, the code of the object modules is relocated and linked.

The output from a linker is a load map as well as the linked code. The load map gives details of where the various code and data segments have been relocated in memory. As some of these segments are relocatable, the load map cannot give the final position in memory but only an address relative to the relocated constant used by the loader. This load map is useful in debugging as described later.

A crucial feature as far as debugging is concerned is the amount of information which is thrown away at each stage of processing from source code to loadable memory image. If the debugger is to relate errors to the original source code then details such as the source identifiers and the source code line numbers must be kept along with the final code and data. Thus the linker, as one stage in this chain, must retain the correspondence between input tokens and output tokens so that later debugging can refer to source code tokens. This is covered in more detail later in this chapter.

46.2.3.2 Relocatable binary format

The linkage process outlined above is made possible because the language processors communicate with the linker by using a common 'relocatable binary format'. This is highly machine specific. The illustration above uses the IBM 360 format as an example. There are rather more relocatable binary formats than machine types because some compilers will use the format inherited from the machine's original assembler and thus avoid having to re-invent the linker, while others may use their own formats. It may well happen that, during the life-time of a machine/operating system combination, developments put additional demands on the loader and the relocatable binary format may have to be extended.

The requirements of a linker in respect to relocation vary according to machine architectures and source languages. As most formats in use seem to be derived from the hardware manufacturers' original format, which is usually designed to handle all the features of the hardware, this is usually adequate to express the output of most language translators. Other formats are used in general when only a subset of the facilities of the machine are to be used and so a simpler linker using a simpler format is feasible.

46.2.3.3 Selective library searching

From the point of view of a multiple module program, a call to a library function or routine is no different to a call to another module, except that the external reference will not be satisfied from within the program. The linker searches for external references in the composite external symbol dictionary. If the symbol is not in this dictionary then it may be a reference to a library function or routine or it may be an error.

To distinguish between these options, the linker searches any libraries specified by the user. In this activity a file containing pre-translated library routines is consulted. If an unsatisfied external reference is found then the particular library routine or function containing that definition is linked with the current program.

A particular problem with library loading occurs when a routine is loaded which itself requires the loading of further routines from the library. This could be a problem if the library is only searched once sequentially, since the required routine may occur earlier in the library than the routine requesting it.

Various solutions have been adopted. The simplest is to persuade whoever builds the system library to order the files so that the situation cannot arise, or at least to duplicate copies of any anomalous routines in various places in the sequence so that it only requires a single sequential pass. Another variation is to make passes through the library file to collect together all the external references that will be made, but actually link code only on a final pass when all external references can be satisfied. Yet another approach is to scan the library repetitively until a pass is made during which no code is linked.

These different approaches can produce very considerable differences in linking times. For some systems the time taken in the linking process is substantially more than the time in compilation. The differences in linking times are often highly significant in overall program development time, since modification often involves only recompiling a single module which then has to be linked to the rest of the object modules.

46.2.3.4 Librarian

Before a library can be used it has to be built and often a program called a librarian is provided whose role is to build and modify libraries. Computer systems are often provided with a set of 'standard' libraries for common tasks, such as the NAG library for the calculation of mathematical functions. Each compiler will be accompanied by its own libraries for tasks such as input/output.

In addition, users and groups of users may want to build up and maintain their own special libraries. As this is an area where there are no recognized standards, facilities vary. The important function is the one of taking a set of compiled routines and producing from them a single (library) file capable of being selectively loaded.

It is also necessary to be able to replace, delete and add routines to a library.

46.2.3.5 Implementation strategies for linkers

Linker/loaders have two main strategies:

1. The in-core strategy is one where the loader and the loaded program occupy the same logical space. This, of course, implies that the loaded program cannot itself occupy the entire memory space. Traditionally the locations where the loader resides are used for common storage – which cannot be initialized. This strategy simplifies a 'load-and-go' process.
2. The alternative strategy is when the linker writes a file which contains the program memory image which is subsequently loaded by a simple memory-image loader. While this, of course, means that the linker (and its data tables) and the loaded program do not have to compete for space, it is inherently slower as parts of the memory-image file may have to be read back so that relocation and external reconciliation data can be recorded. The effect of this is to require some quite subtle design to avoid the process becoming unacceptably slow.

It is essential that, whichever strategy is adopted, a load-image file can be saved for subsequent execution, by-passing the compilation/linking phase.

46.2.3.6 Inter-module type checking

One task not addressed by many loaders is type checking of inter-module communication at load time. In most relocatable binary formats there is only one 'type' and that is external address. This means that all the strict type checks which can be made within a single text body cannot be applied when those separate modules are combined in the loading process. This problem is often resolved by providing language-specific link loaders. This feature becomes very important in debugging as link-time checks are cheaper than run-time checks.

46.2.3.7 Overlay loading

Memory size limitations can be overcome by the technique of program overlaying. In this technique the program is envisaged as a tree structure where only one complete path from leaf to root need be in memory at any given time.

The design of the layout of such an overlaid program is of the essence as references can only be made up and down a path and not across a path. Equally, a design which required the frequent swapping of overlays would be very time-consuming in execution.

It is a useful technique to include a dummy routine in the root, which is always resident, to make calls on library routines which will be used in several paths to ensure that they are loaded into the root. While there is usually no logical problem if a copy of a library routine is loaded into each of the several overlay paths, it may cause unnecessary disc accesses and make the memory image files larger than necessary.

Some care is needed in the design of programs which are to be overlaid. The flow of program control should be such that each complete overlay follows its predecessor with a minimum of jumps backward and forward between overlays.

Overlaying is now much less widely used as a technique than it was, as computers now have much larger memories. However, a well-designed overlaid program can outperform a less well-designed version where reliance is put on a hardware paging mechanism to remedy the deficiency of having inadequate quantities of real memory.

Overlay loading conventions come in two main flavours:

1. *Transparent overlaying*. Here the calling program uses no special conventions to indicate that the procedure called is not in the same overlay. This allows the design of the tree to be left to load time and indeed for it to be changed without recompiling any component modules.
2. *Explicit overlaying*. Using this approach the user must specify that a called routine is in a particular overlay. This approach requires source code changes to be made to allow a change to be made to the overlay tree.

46.2.3.8 Dynamic linking

The problem of dynamic loading was considered earlier. If the code has been linked before it has been loaded then it is assumed that it will all reside in a contiguous block of memory. However, if use is to be made of the fact that not all code is used on every execution of the program, the program need not be linked before execution; that is, dynamic linking can be used.

One use for dynamic linking is where each program accesses procedures via a linkage segment which contains the name of the procedure and pointers to the address of the procedure – if it has been linked – or an invalid address otherwise. At run time a call to a procedure will succeed if the called routine has been linked, or will trap because of an invalid address if no linking has been performed. This trap causes the linker to be called to link in the required procedure and place its address at the required virtual address. The call instruction is then restarted to continue program execution.

46.3 Debugging

46.3.1 Defining debugging

'Testing and debugging' are often referred to as though they were a single activity. However, they are two distinct and different activities. Testing is the dynamic execution of software under controlled conditions with sample input, in order to compare the output produced with what the software should have done (the expected output). This is done for two purposes: to identify errors (during development) and to give confidence that the system is working (during acceptance testing).

However, testing, especially if it is done well, finds errors and anomalies which then have to be corrected. The correction usually consists of making a change to the software and its associated documentation, but can also consist of changes to the test documentation, user documentation or operational procedures. The process of identifying and correcting errors in software is known as debugging, so-called because one of the earliest faults found in a computer was a suicidal moth (bug) trapped in a relay, causing incorrect operation of the software. This section of the chapter focuses on debugging techniques, but it assumes that testing techniques, such as those described in Chapter 19, are used.

Debugging is a process which is always necessary, yet is rarely anticipated. There is a great chasm between the formality required to produce a machine-executable program and the informality of computerized real-world applications. Errors of translation between the real world and the program are inevitable and often extremely subtle. Finding the causes of faulty computer output or performance requires powers of concentration and insight, and is considerably assisted by software tool support.

46.3.2 Managing debugging

46.3.2.1 Estimation

The effort needed for debugging software systems can be estimated, based on known error rates for similar systems, developed according to similar software engineering standards. Typical figures for the number of bugs (without the use of formal development methods or verification and validation techniques) range from 30 to 85 errors per thousand lines of code (KLOC) (Lauesen, 1979; Boehm, 1981; Beizer, 1983; Kaner, 1988).

The amount of time to allow for identifying and removing each bug is difficult to estimate, as it depends on the following factors:

1. The type of bug. Some are easy to find, others very difficult.
2. The type of automated tool support for the debugging process.
3. The ability of the debug personnel. A range of 18:1 in debug effectiveness is reported by Shooman (1983).
4. The ability of the error report to show the exact conditions under which the bug can be reproduced.

If a bug cannot be reproduced reliably, there is no way for the correction of that bug to be demonstrated. The only way to demonstrate a cure is to input exactly the same test sequence both before and after the fix, with the bug's effect being present before the change and absent after the change.

Initial debugging sessions tend to be quick, with one error being found per session; later sessions find four or five errors each, but take several hours. Finding the final most difficult and elusive errors can be extremely time- and resource-consuming (Lauesen, 1979).

46.3.2.2 Planning

A common planning error for debugging – if planning is done at all – is to schedule too few test cycles. (A test cycle is a thorough test of a version with a report of all known problems with that version.) Two cycles, one to find all the problems and the second to fix them, is typically scheduled. However, eight cycles is a more realistic minimum, and then only if the version testing is thorough; otherwise 20 or 30 cycles is more likely (Kaner, 1988).

An important repercussion for test planning is that the number of errors found can be used as a guide to the number of errors left in a given software module. This can be used to help direct testing effort to the areas where further testing will be most cost-effective. The more errors which have already been found, the more errors are likely to remain (Myers, 1979).

46.3.2.3 Monitoring

The only way to improve the estimation of the cost and time of the debugging process, in order to gain management control of this aspect of software development, is to monitor the debugging process on current development projects, thus building up a picture of what actually happens. There are no global guidelines. Each organization will be different, depending on the software engineering techniques used. However, with the increasing standardization of development methodologies and tools, there should be increased predictability of debug effort.

Error statistics should be collected in the following categories:

1. Severity classification – effect of the bug on the system.
2. Type of error – see error classification below.
3. Where and how found – how effective are different bug-removal methods.
4. Where and how the error was introduced – areas for improved tool support or software engineering techniques.
5. Date of identification of bug and date of final clearance of bug – to monitor bug throughput.

Detailed prescriptive guidance on the content of an error report is given in Kaner (1988).

46.3.2.4 Human considerations

In the management of the debugging process, it is important to remember that the errors which have been introduced are unintentional, and represent deficiencies in the software development process rather than deficiencies in the software developers personally. A great deal of personal antagonism can be generated by reporting errors in the wrong way, and this can considerably decrease productivity. Some organizations have found it effective simply to rename the error reports to something less offensive, such as 'System Query Report'. See also Report type, below. An attitude of 'find the errors before anyone outside can find them' can also be helpful.

46.3.3 Error classifications

46.3.3.1 Severity

When collecting data about software faults found, the most important way to classify them is by their effect, i.e. their severity. One scale gives ten severity levels, ranging from 'mild', e.g. a mis-spelt or misaligned output, through to 'infectious', where the error not only destroys its own system but also affects other systems (Beizer, 1983). However, the cost of very minor errors can in fact be surprisingly high, because of the continuing annoyance and loss of confidence which can result (Kaner, 1988). A three-level scale (minor, serious and fatal) is the minimum which should be used. Note that the repeated occurrence of a minor fault, or a large number of minor faults should be classed as a more serious fault.

46.3.3.2 Report type

Reports can be classified as: definite errors – e.g. coding or design errors; queries – not sure whether it is wrong, but something is not as expected; or suggestions for changes or improvements. The reports can be called fault or error reports (the most aggressive names), item or query reports (neutral names), or possibly suggestion or quality reports (positive connotation). The name of the report does have a subtle influence, and a positive attitude towards improving the quality of the software is more cost-effective than a negative attitude of assigning blame.

46.3.3.3 Taxonomy

Errors can be classified according to different aspects: where the error occurred, the type of error and what can be learned to prevent future errors. There is a good deal of overlap between the classifications; an individual organization should tailor a taxonomy to its own needs.

Errors can be classified into different types, depending on where in the software the error occurs, as follows (Beizer, 1983):

1. *Function-related.* Errors in the requirements specification or test specifications.
2. *System bugs.* Errors in internal or external interfaces, hardware or software architecture, operating system, control and sequence errors, and resource management problems.
3. *Process errors.* Errors of arithmetic or manipulation, initialization errors, control and sequence errors, and static logic errors, e.g. misuse of CASE statement or logical operators.
4. *Data errors.* Information or control data – static and dynamic – can be faulty in contents, structure or attribute.
5. *Other errors.* Code errors (syntax, typographical), style errors. (It is difficult and costly to test software which is not well written.)

A list of errors by type is given in extensive appendices of Kaner's book (Kaner, 1988):

1. *User interface errors.* A total of 140 errors are listed, including errors of functionality, communication, command structure/entry, missing commands, program rigidity, performance and output.
2. *Error-handling faults.* Faults in error prevention, error detection and error recovery.
3. *Boundary-related errors.* Wrong boundary, mishandling of boundary cases, mishandling of cases outside boundaries for numeric, size, time, memory, data, hardware and invisible boundaries.
4. *Calculation errors.* Due to logic errors, arithmetic errors or imprecision.
5. *Initial and later state errors.* Initialization errors, re-initialization errors and follow-on effects.
6. *Control flow errors.* Program control transferred to the wrong place, interrupt handling, crashes, loop errors, control structure errors (IF and CASE statements).
7. *Errors in handling or interpreting data.* When passing data or sending messages between routines, data boundaries and data storage corruption.

8. *Race conditions (timing errors).* Related to processing order, messages, data input and assumptions about program behaviour.
9. *Load conditions.* Resource not available when required, not returned when no longer required, resource shortages, processing priority errors.
10. *Hardware errors.* Wrong device, missing device, misuse, noise problems.
11. *Source, version and ID control errors.* Mismatch errors, lack of information, reappearance of previous errors.
12. *Testing errors.* Failure to find bugs, finding non-existent bugs, poor bug-reporting, poor follow-up of bug reports.

Myers recommends the analysis of all errors in order to improve the software development and testing processes by learning from past errors. The following questions should be asked:

1. Could the error have been detected earlier? The effectiveness of review procedures may need to be improved.
2. When was the error made? An earlier review may have caught errors which have been allowed to slip through. (This is a defect in error management, not in reviewing.)
3. Who made the error? Not as a witch-hunt, but to show a need for further training, for example.
4. What was done incorrectly? These can range from typographical errors to invalid assumptions about the system.
5. How could the error have been prevented? This is part of a quality improvement programme.
6. How was the error found? Capitalize on successful error-finding techniques and reward good testing.

46.3.4 Debug procedure

There are two main aspects to debugging, that of identifying an error and correcting that error. Debug guidelines are described below, giving a four-step procedure to identify (Steps 1 and 2) and correct (Steps 3 and 4) software errors. Within the procedure, different debug methods can be used, as described in the following section.

46.3.4.1 Identifying the fault

The input to the entire debugging process is some indication that all is not well; a report describing something which does happen which should not, or which should happen and does not.

Faults can occur in the requirements specifications, expected results, test plans, test input, comparison of test results with expected results, test running procedures or software operational procedure documentation. One should first eliminate these possibilities before investing effort in investigating the software.

It is psychologically difficult to gather data in a completely objective way; one tends to see what one expects to see, rather than what is actually there. One should look for what has actually happened and gather the evidence. It is important to look at what has happened incorrectly, but also note what has happened correctly, and to look for contradictions or inconsistencies.

Fault evidence can be gathered in two ways:

1. Examining data. Data can be examined by looking at the input and output of the software, by examining any data files or records altered by the software, by examining a memory dump, by running the software with additional printout of data or by using an interactive debug tool to examine data locations either dynamically (animation) or statically (when execution is temporarily halted).

2. Examining logic. Logic can be examined by looking at a trace of the control flow of the software, by running the software with additional printout to trace control flow or by using an interactive debug tool to animate execution, or to step through the code using breakpoints or watchpoints.

46.3.4.2 Proposing hypotheses

When information about the fault has been gathered, then one or more hypotheses should be proposed to explain the evidence gathered. In practice, this step is often done in parallel with the gathering of data. It is useful to propose more than one hypothesis; otherwise the data gathering tends to become 'locked in' to the current hypothesis rather than being objective. Proposing a hypothesis consists of the following steps for each hypothesis:

1. Listing the consequences. Writing down what should happen if a hypothesis is true, both the immediate effects and any consequential effects, e.g. conditions or calculations which depend on a wrong value may give a wrong result.
2. Verifying consequences. Checking the collected data to ensure that the effects of the hypothesis did in fact occur, for both the original and consequent effects.
3. Correcting data manually. If practicable, using an interactive debugging tool to correct the data which has been corrupted by the fault, for both original and consequent effects. If the fault then disappears, reasonable confidence has been established for the hypothesis, i.e. it has been 'proved'. Faulty code can be bypassed or even corrected in order to 'prove' the hypothesis. One should do whatever is necessary to establish the validity of the hypothesis. If the fault has not completely disappeared, then the hypothesis is incorrect or incomplete.
4. Checking for other errors. When a hypothesis has been 'proved', checking all occurrences of the same or similar errors, as the same error may have been made more than once. Also checking for other errors in the same section of code. Errors do tend to cluster, so software in which one error has been found is likely to contain another error.

46.3.4.3 Devising a solution

Once a hypothesis has been 'proved', the error has been identified. The next two steps are concerned with correcting the error. It is in these steps that errors in debugging are often made; a software correction carries a significant risk of containing an error.

Historical evidence indicates that the probability of changing the program correctly on the first try is 50% for a change involving ten or fewer statements, and 20% for a change involving 50 statements (Kaner, 1988). The probability of introducing a new error when changing software is therefore 50% for very small changes, 80% for changes to a small module or part of a module and even less for larger scale changes.

Following a rigorous debug procedure should reduce the incidence of follow-on errors, but there is as yet no empirical evidence to quantify the effects. Steps 3 and 4 ensure that software engineering standards are followed with respect to the changed software.

Devising the change solution consists of the following activities:

1. Producing a draft correction. Writing or typing out the correction to the software neatly. If the corrections are minor, they can be annotated on the documentation, such as the listing, provided that 'reference listings' are part of the current software engineering practices. If the changes are more extensive, re-writing the entire changed section(s) is involved.

2. Reviewing the proposed correction. Applying the same software engineering standards to the correction as apply to the software being corrected. Reviewing the change using manual methods (at the minimum a desk-check with the examples used to 'prove' the hypothesis). If a colleague was involved in identifying the problem, involving the same person in reviewing the solution. If formal reviews are used, they need to be scheduled and carried out.
3. Ensuring no adverse side-effects. Directing the review effort to consider the possibility of adverse side-effects in other parts of the software, and ensuring, as far as possible, that there are none.

46.3.4.4 Implementing the change

The implementation of the reviewed change should also be done with care, as errors are often introduced at this stage, due to carelessness and hurry. Implementing the change is a four-stage process in itself:

1. Changing the code by:
   (a) Saving the current version. The importance of saving the current version of both source and object cannot be over-emphasized. The saving process takes very little time to do, but can save a vast amount of reconstruction time (and embarrassment) for those changes which often seem to go inexplicably wrong in spite of careful preparation.
   (b) Editing source code. With an extensive change, or a change to a large program, preparing the edit instructions off-line for checking before editing. After editing the source, printing it and checking to ensure that no errors have occurred in the editing process.
   (c) Producing object code. Compiling, linking, loading, etc., to produce the changed object code. If necessary, scheduling down-time for changes to systems which are already in use. This may introduce a delay, as users need to be informed in advance.
2. Testing the change. After changing the source and object code, the change needs to be tested, also to the same software engineering standards as the software which is being altered. Testing the change consists of the following steps:
   (a) Testing using hypothesis examples. The examples which were used to 'prove' the hypothesis should be run, in order to demonstrate the 'after' state, i.e. to show that the same input which earlier produced an error does not now produce that error.
      Important note: if the error has not completely disappeared at this point, one should not proceed further, but should replace the original source and object code (which, of course, has been saved) and go back to one of the earlier debugging stages. An inadequate correction of the error indicates either that there is not sufficient information, that the hypothesis was incorrect, or that the implementation of the change contained an error.
   (b) Regression testing. Any additional testing of the system should be run, depending on risk factors such as the extensiveness of the change and the seriousness of any unanticipated side-effects in the system. As a minimum, a selection of the unit test cases should be re-run.
      The test documentation will need to be changed in order to reflect the changes to the software; the new test cases that demonstrate the absence of the known fault need to be added to the test input scripts, expected output, test procedures, etc. The use of software tools to automate the running of regression tests is especially helpful at this stage, particularly for re-testing those parts which should not have changed.
3. Installing the change. Having tested the changed software, there is reasonable confidence that the change has both

corrected the original fault and not introduced any new faults (but by no means is this guaranteed). The final step in the debugging process is the one where the seeds of future problems are often sown. It is important to follow through the implementation of the software change by updating all of the associated documentation, and following the recognized procedures; if this is not done, future changes to this software will be at best confused and time-wasting, and could prove disastrous. The steps in installing the change are:

(a) Observing configuration management procedures. Following the standard change control recording and approval procedures for the change. Ensuring that the change is subject to the same quality assurance as the rest of the system.

(b) Notifying users of the change(s). Nothing is more unsettling to users of an existing system than for something to change without warning, even if it is an improvement. One should ensure that users are notified both of the nature and timing of changes. It may be advisable to implement a number of changes at the same time (all previously tested). The changeover to the new version should be scheduled and publicized.

(c) Update documentation. The software engineering documentation should be updated to reflect the changed software. Documents which may be affected include:
(i) Requirements specifications
(ii) Design documentation
(iii) Code comments (include a new comment for each correction, explaining the error and the change)
(iv) User manuals
(v) Back-up and security copies of source/object code
(vi) Files of paper listings
(vii) System configuration instructions
(viii) Test input cases
(ix) Test expected outputs
(x) Test running procedures

46.3.5 Debug techniques

The following list of debug techniques give a selection of possible ways to organize the information being gathered, and to devise hypotheses. These techniques are not mutually exclusive but complementary. The best way to debug is to use whatever technique seems effective; a combination of techniques will often succeed where an individual technique fails to provide insight.

46.3.5.1 Desk-checking, data-stepping, dry-running

With these techniques, one writes down the names of program variables with space underneath. The flow of control from the source listing is then followed for a chosen value. The value of each data item is written down, with the values which are replaced being crossed out. It is important to follow exactly what the code listing actually says, rather than following what it *should* say. This technique can also be done by a group (e.g. on a whiteboard), and is then known as a walkthrough or data walkthrough.

46.3.5.2 Back-tracking

Starting from a known error, one can track backwards through the code to try to find somewhere that something went wrong (a type of desk-checking). Back-tracking can sometimes show known errors to be consequences of earlier errors, which, in turn, may have been caused by a 'bug'. Back-tracking reduces the likelihood of jumping to the wrong conclusion about the cause of an error.

46.3.5.3 Macroscopic analysis

When large amounts of data are available from identical processes, one can look for patterns (Abbott, 1988) such as:

1. Errors affecting many output types – multiple defects in data or modules.
2. Errors affecting only one output type – fault in that type-processing routine.
3. All occurrences of an output type affected – possible fault in commonly used routine.
4. Only some occurrences of an output type affected – due to data combinations or one module.
5. Persistence of error once set – initialization fault.

46.3.5.4 Testing output data

Based on the principle that 'those who plan for debugging will have less debugging to do', the testing output data technique involves the embedding of output statements within the code when the code is initially designed or written. The test output produced should be concise, but intermingled with real output. Test output is inserted at the beginning and end of modules, at important control points in the program and when important data changes occur. The data which should be output is what would be most useful if the program failed at that point. This technique is reported as cost-effective, as it enables more than one bug to be identified at once, is independent of language used and saves information-gathering time (Lauesen, 1979).

46.3.5.5 Inductive and deductive debugging

Inductive debugging (Myers, 1979) is a process similar to the first two steps of the debug procedure described above, where information is first gathered, then organized, a hypothesis is devised and then proven.

Debugging by deduction (Myers, 1979) proceeds by first enumerating a list of possible hypotheses, then eliminating some of them by using the data collected, refining the remaining one and then proving it.

46.3.5.6 Failure to identify and correct a bug

Debugging is often an unrewarding activity, as some errors in software can be extremely difficult to identify. Once an error is clearly identified, correcting the error is usually reasonably straightforward, although there are always exceptions. Some suggestions for making new progress when the debugging seems to have come to a cul-de-sac are:

1. Using a different debug technique, as above.
2. Trying a different angle:
(a) Has input gone in correctly?
(b) Are expected results correct?
(c) Are the comments or documentation misleading?
(d) Is the correct version of the software being used?
(e) Is the environment set up correctly (including job control language)?
(f) Does the database or file being used contain the correct data?
(g) Is the fault transient or inconsistent?
(h) Are the requirements correct and consistent? (The specification may require one thing in one place and something quite different in another.)
(i) Is there more than one fault, resulting in masking effects?
(j) Is there a physical cause, such as electrical interference at certain times?
(k) As a last resort, are the compiler, system software and hardware working correctly?

3. Reviewing what is known. This involves taking a mental 'step back' from the details, and trying to form a global picture of what is happening. When immersed in detail, patterns can be overlooked.
4. Explaining what is going wrong to a colleague can be very valuable. In many cases, simply the act of organizing one's own thoughts in order to explain what is happening is enough to give an insight, without the colleague having to say a word. On the other hand, a few probing questions from someone who is not as closely involved with the problem can also be very helpful.
5. There is a tendency to try to solve a difficult problem by brute force, staying with it far after meaningful progress has stopped. It is often much more productive to leave the problem completely for hours, days or even weeks. When returning to the problem later, a fresh approach will often be obvious.

46.3.5.7 No short-cuts

Errors are often made in the debugging process because of doing things in the mistaken belief that they will save time. In fact, they inevitably waste far more time than they save.

It is not worth 'just trying a few fixes' to see if they work. It is worth proving a hypothesis even for the one time in a hundred that one may hit on the right solution by chance; at least then first instincts are confirmed.

The object code should not be fixed with the view that the source code can always be tidied up afterwards. The fix should be applied to the highest possible level (except for testing a hypothesis). If 4GL languages are used, the fix should be applied not at the source code, but at the design level, leaving the generation of the changed code to the 4GL tool.

If it becomes evident that a fix is not going to cure the whole problem, there is a great temptation to fix the fix; this should be resisted, as errors are commonly introduced in this way. It is always worth going back to first principles and rethinking the problem, solution and implementation.

The software documentation does not necessarily reflect exactly what is in the software; it represents what the author thought the software would do at the time. This applies to requirements, design, test and user documentation, and fault reports, as well as to source-level program comments.

It is unwise to assume that regression tests will be satisfactory. The only way to ensure that there are no unexpected side-effects of a change is to re-run all the tests on the system. Although this is rarely practicable, some regression testing should always be done for each change.

It is best not to change anything that is not understood. If the nature of the problem is not fully understood, it is extremely unlikely that the solution will fully solve the problem.

Jumping to conclusions is not to be recommended. It is worth investing the time to prove a hypothesis before fixing it, or the effort may well be directed to the wrong problem.

The debug procedure described is a methodical and rigorous error analysis and removal process and should not be rushed. If any of the steps are done less than thoroughly, the probability of introducing a new error arises.

46.3.5.8 Final points

It is worth remembering that there is always a cause for any effect, even though that cause may be far from obvious.

A useful *aide-mémoire* is a notebook in which particulars of errors found are recorded in detail. This can serve as an invaluable reference when future similar errors occur.

46.3.6 Timing errors and other recalcitrant faults

Some of the most difficult bugs to detect and correct are those to do with timing behaviour. This section briefly considers timing errors, then discusses other classes of obscure faults. These types of error are often difficult to find as they relate to interactions and are not usually manifest as direct coding errors. In principle, however, they are amenable to treatment by similar techniques to those classes of bug described above.

46.3.6.1 Timing errors or race conditions

Timing errors (also called race conditions) result when two processes which should proceed in a certain order, proceed in the wrong order. Examples of timing errors are given by Gordon and Finkel (1986).

Information which is received in a buffer area is expected to be processed before the next item of information replaces it; if the processing does not occur on time, then the new information overwrites the previous information, so the old information is lost. (The new information may be processed twice.)

If there is no check on whether requested information has been received into a buffer area, the processing of that data may begin before the data has been put there, or before the transfer of data has been completed, resulting in the use of old data or a mixture of old and new data.

A message from one process to another may arrive in a different order to that in which they were sent, e.g. if more than two processes are involved. A late-arriving message may contain data which should have been included by the receiving program before replying to the early-arriving message, if the messages are received in the wrong order.

Timing errors are often very difficult to reproduce. They can often only be 'caught' by carefully monitoring all issues which may affect timing, e.g. buffer sizes, number of users on system, etc. It is sometimes helpful to instrument programs, but on occasions these program changes eliminate the fault! In practice most timing faults are found by *thinking about* process interactions and interrupts, rather than inspecting details of the code.

46.3.6.2 Memory corruption

Memory corruption errors can be difficult to find, but looking for certain patterns can help to indicate the type of error (Thorpe, 1988).

In trying to resolve these sorts of errors, one should look at:

1. *Structure*. Is there any structure to the corrupted memory area, e.g. does it look like code rather than data?
2. *Size*. How large is the corrupted area? Does it coincide with the size of any known data structure?
3. *Start and end*. Where does the corruption start and end? Does the physical location (and size) correspond to a disc transfer block, for example?
4. *Direction*. What is the direction of corruption? Corruption which spreads backwards could indicate a corrupted program stack, for example.
5. *Recurrence over time*. Can the corruption be reproduced at will? How often does it occur? Can the occurrence be linked with the running of particular modules over time?

Causes of memory corruption include:

1. Data structures out of bounds. The use of a language without bound checking for arrays can lead to memory corruption as a consequent effect of other errors.
2. Misplaced reference structure. If physical addresses are assigned dynamically, a misplaced structure may corrupt the area to which it has been mapped.

3. Logic faults in procedure handling. Procedures or subprograms commonly use the program stack for address and data information. If the stack overflows, corruption of neighbouring memory locations will occur. Using a mixture of high- and low-level language can lead to inadvertently mismanaging procedure information in program stacks.

It can be very difficult to trap memory corruption soon enough to leave enough evidence uncorrupted to enable the cause of the corruption to be found. This is particularly difficult in real-time systems where the corruption may take place at random times and in different memory locations. The following are some ways to trap memory corruption:

1. *Hardware trap.* If data is being corrupted in an area which should not be written to, a hardware trap can be set to stop the computer as soon as one of the forbidden locations is accessed. However, it is not possible to distinguish corruptive changes from legitimate changes to memory locations if write access is permitted.
2. *Rebuilding the software.* This may be achieved by reconfiguring the system so that some software modules run in different physical locations than previously. This may be as simple as loading them in a different order after compilation. Corruption which 'follows' a module through repeated rebuilds is likely to be caused by that module.
3. *Rearranging the data.* This involves changing the location of data structures within a module, so that they are at different physical locations relative to each other. If corruption 'follows' the data (or keeps the same distance away from a changed data structure), then suspicion rests on the handling of that data structure.

If corruption remains in the same physical location when both code and data are moved, then a hardware cause is probably indicated.

46.3.6.3 Heizen-bugs

One of the major problems with debugging real-time systems is that errors tend to disappear when error-finding techniques are used, only appearing again when the bug-finding code is removed. These have been called 'Heizen-bugs' (Neumann, 1987), after the Heizenburg principle of physics that either the mass or location of a small particle can be determined, but never both.

If errors do disappear completely when traps are inserted, one should try different trapping techniques to find out why the trap 'cures' the error. If all else fails, and the error really has disappeared for good, the trap should be left in (with very clear explanations in comments and documentation).

46.3.6.4 Making a bug reproducible

Guidelines given by Kaner (1988) for making a recalcitrant bug reproducible include:

1. Varying the timing. The bug may appear only when data goes in quickly, very slowly, erratically or from more than one input source at once.
2. Error report deficiencies. A detail may have been omitted from an error report because the person making the report considers it 'obvious'. It is easy to think one did something when in fact one did something slightly different. Error reports must contain the minimum information to reproduce the bug exactly, so one should validate the contents of the report by trying to reproduce the error solely from this information.
3. Initialization error. A bug which refuses to reappear may

occur only when the program is first run. Here one should restore to its original state and try again.
4. Hardware failure. Intermittent hardware failures often masquerade as software failures. Since they are intermittent, the hardware usually works when the hardware test programs are run. Such problems can usually only be made reproducible by altering hardware conditions, e.g. temperature or clock rates.
5. Time dependency. Processing which occurs at midnight, week, month or year end is not heavily used, so may contain errors which have not been found by testing or other means. These problems can be investigated by using a software clock and stepping through these periodic activities.
6. Side-effect bugs. An error can occur as a follow-on result of a different error. Trying to reproduce the second error is difficult or impossible in isolation, but easy to reproduce once the earlier error has been reproduced again. For example, denial of a requested resource may cause a software failure after a lengthy wait for a time-out; such errors are said to have a 'long fuse'. The effect of the bug can be much later, and in a different area than the time and location of the cause. For example, if resources such as memory blocks are not returned after use by one program, a completely different program will be denied that resource at a much later time, after they have all been used up. Again, these faults can only be found by carefully logging all information which may affect the faulty behaviour.

46.3.7 Debug tools

Debug tools are programs which act as a harness for the program or programs being debugged. Commands are entered to the tool, which then in turn activates the program, returning control to the tool at points selected, and displaying information as requested through the tool.

Debug tools provide varying facilities, and are of different types.

46.3.7.1 Debug tool facilities

The following are some of the facilities provided by debug tools; the basic facilities are provided by all tools, and more sophisticated facilities by more powerful tools:

1. *Breakpoint.* A breakpoint is a point in a program where the control flow is 'broken', i.e. at a given program instruction, the flow of execution is returned to the debug tool instead of being allowed to continue within the program being debugged.
   The breakpoint location is set within the debug tool when the tool is first invoked and whenever the tool itself is in use. (The debug tool replaces the instruction at the breakpoint with a transfer of control into itself.) The program being debugged is then started under the control of the debug tool, and executes normally until the breakpoint is reached, when control is passed to the debug tool. When a breakpoint is changed or cancelled, the instruction(s) which had been 'broken' is restored.
2. *Watchpoint.* A watchpoint is similar to a breakpoint in the way that control is transferred to the debug tool. The cause of the transfer of control is not reaching a particular instruction, however, but when a particular data location is accessed or overwritten. A watchpoint is set by specifying the address or data name to be 'watched'.
3. *Peek and poke.* When execution has been stopped at some point, using a breakpoint or watchpoint, the values of various locations can then be examined (peeked at) and altered (poked).

4. *Single stepping.* The program can be taken through its execution one statement or instruction at a time, under the control of the debug tool.
5. *Intercepting abnormal termination.* Debug tools can automatically be entered if a program finishes execution with anything other than the normal execution termination code. The program being debugged can then be examined.
6. *Memory protection.* A debug tool can ensure that all data references and transfers of control are within the memory areas permitted for the program, stopping the execution of the program when it violates its protected area and entering the debug tool automatically.
7. *Trace and animation.* Debug tools can show a record of the flow of control through the program, by tracing the execution of each statement in turn. This can be output as a printout (in fact some compilers provide this facility), or by animating the execution on a screen (see screen-based debug tools). This provides information on how the program arrived at a given point.
8. *Stubs.* A debug tool is effectively a 'driver' for the module being tested, but that module may call other modules. In order to simplify the debug testing, those calls can be directed to a 'stub', a simple mimic of the called module with the same interface to the calling module.

46.3.7.2 Types of debug tools

The level at which the debug tool operates reflects the complexity of the tool itself. A sophisticated tool will provide powerful facilities but will also use significant computer resources. In some cases, for example, when debugging software in an embedded environment, a very simple tool may be all that is available.

1. *Machine-level debuggers.* Machine code debuggers are the simplest and earliest debug tools. The tool runs in the same memory space as the program. Addresses and data are displayed in numerical format, and instruction codes may be displayed in mnemonic format. One or more breakpoints can be set. A trace output may be produced.
2. *Mnemonic-level debuggers.* A debug tool at this level allows names to be associated with variables and procedures, although the breakpoints still need to be set with reference to instructions at assembly level.
3. *Source-level debuggers.* A source-level debug tool allows breakpoints to be set within the source code, doing the necessary interpretations from the compiler output so that execution stops at the correct assembly instruction for the relevant compiled statement. Variable names can also be used.
4. *Screen-based debug tools.* Debug tools used from online terminals can allow the use of screen facilities together with either assembler or source-level debugging facilities. Control flow can be 'animated', i.e. the statements being executed can be highlighted or pointed to in sequence on the screen, as the program is executed (slowed down to be visible to the human operator). Data items – e.g. a variable – can be monitored by having each new value shown on the screen whenever it is changed.
5. *Integrated debug tools.* Debug tools can be integrated with source code editors, compilers and configuration management tools, so that changes tried experimentally in the debug tool can be incorporated into the software documentation, with less chance of introducing a clerical-type error.

A debug tool can be linked with analysis and design or CASE tools, so that an error can be corrected at the level at which it occurred, and the relevant documentation kept consistent.

A debug tool can perform some functions which have been regarded as testing. A debug tool which keeps track of the statements executed can produce a statement coverage analysis (percentage of statements exercised), when a set of test data is run through the tool. The same facility can also be used to produce a performance analysis to detect 'hot spots' (frequently exercised code) when normal data is run through the tool.

Some debug tools can also record the commands entered to the tool as a test script, in order to reproduce the same input quickly another time, e.g. to show that a bug has been fixed by a change.

6. *Intelligent debug tools.* An intelligent debug tool can find items which are related to the data or code being altered. For example, if a data structure is the wrong size, it can alert the tool user to other data structures which are copied into or from the affected item, and which may also be the wrong size.

An artificial intelligence 'front end' to a debug tool could assist in guiding the debug effort, and suggest possible errors to look for, debug strategies to try and solutions to errors found.

7. *Debug facilities in other tools.* Facilities which are helpful in debugging can be found in other software tools whose main purpose is another software engineering area. For example, a static analysis (verification) tool which performs information flow analysis can extract a partial program, i.e. those statements of a program which are related only to a particular variable; this can be of great assistance in trying to trace the effect of a change to that variable.

46.3.8 Conclusions

Debugging is an unavoidable activity in software development, but it is often viewed as undesirable. Proper planning can ensure that debugging is not unnecessarily expensive or time-consuming. The use of appropriate tools and error classification schemes as aids to bug location can make debugging a relatively systematic process. In the limit, however, debugging is an intellectual exercise, and one which the software engineer must practise in order to gain skill and expertise.

46.4 Other issues

Three other pragmatic issues which can significantly affect program development are mixed language working, development of re-entrant code and achievement of portability. These are briefly discussed in turn.

46.4.1 Mixed language working

There are sometimes good reasons for combining into one program elements written in several languages. One common reason is the coding of a central routine in assembler to reduce running times. Another reason might be the access to system or library functions that are otherwise unavailable.

Mixed language working is not always as simple as it perhaps ought to be due to incompatible design decisions made by the developers of each language system.

46.4.1.1 Run-time systems and assumptions

Every compiler makes assumptions about the environment in which the code it produces is to run. It is customary for the 'main' program to execute some preamble code to set up registers and initialize various flags to set up this environment and to satisfy these assumptions. The assumptions are seldom the same for two different languages. The problems that arise relate to finding mechanisms such that one language can respect the assumptions of another so that it can run adequately without being able to execute its own preamble code. While many compilers allow the use of other languages, most expect the other language to be subservient. Clearly this is a source of problems.

46.4.1.2 Input/output support

An area where multi-language operations are very difficult is input/output (I/O). To share a device between two different buffering and control systems is seldom possible and never easy. It is advisable, if at all possible, to let one language handle all I/O.

46.4.1.3 Parameter passing

Storage allocation strategies vary widely and so therefore do the conventions for passing parameters. Different languages give different interpretations to parameters. It is often necessary to write intermediate assembly-language programs to allow the successful transmission of parameters.

For example, some languages pass parameters as addresses on a stack, while others may pass values. The format of one parameter list might include 'type' information or a parameter count. Some languages have a list of addresses embedded in the calling routine, and in this case not only do the addresses have to be moved, but the return address itself has to be modified. Such an 'interlude routine' would have to 'understand' both sets of conventions and translate from one to the other. It is necessary that the calls and returns between the 'mixed' languages are both routed through such an interlude. Because of the problems of naming it might prove necessary to provide a routine of this type to handle each called procedure – though not, of course, each call.

46.4.1.4 Memory allocation

Memory allocation conventions vary widely and are seldom well documented in user manuals. Techniques for the storage of dynamic variables and for the allocation and release of storage space are unlikely to be the same for each language. Structured objects, both static and dynamic, can cause confusion. Some languages use 'dope vectors' for array control, other do not. FORTRAN stores the elements of its arrays in quite a different order to many other languages.

There is a problem with architectures where the address may comprise a segment and a displacement. In this case there must be conventions for the called routine to be able to calculate an actual address to reference the value.

46.4.1.5 Stack and register conventions

Many systems expect certain register contents to remain unchanged across procedure calls, while other registers are treated as volatile or are used for the transmission of parameters. Most modern order-codes are stack-oriented, but exactly how stack space is used, what is stored there and the order of storage allocation all vary widely, from language to language.

It will be necessary for the interlude routine to save registers and manipulate stack frames to maintain the integrity of the conventions used by the inter-working languages.

46.4.2 Re-entrant code

Re-entrant code is code that can be shared concurrently between many users. One condition for this is that the code requires no initialization. A rather less demanding requirement is 'serially-

reusable' code, such code can be used repetitively but it is self-initializing.

Although the code itself may be invariant, it must initialize its own data correctly. If the code is shared between multiple tasks, then there must be mechanisms to keep the data of each task inviolate.

46.4.2.1 Advantages of re-entrant code

There are several advantages of re-entrant code:

1. A single copy of such code can be used by several different processes simultaneously.
2. In a swapping environment it need not be swapped out when the space it occupies is needed as the original version on the swapping disc is the same and merely has to be read in again.
3. It must have separate code and data locations and so the code can be run in write-protected memory areas thus shielding it from accidental mutilation.

46.4.2.2 Problems in producing re-entrant code

The advantages of re-entrancy are so manifest it is instructive to investigate why all code is not made re-entrant:

1. The first and most significant reason is that the order code of the computer may make it difficult to achieve. Some instruction sets make access to certain storage addresses relatively easy and so there is a temptation to mix code and data. Secondly, the subroutine call instruction on pre-stack based machines often stored the return address in the called location. Some parameter-calling sequences are stored in locations immediately following the call instruction and these sometimes need to be modified. Most of these hardware-related problems can be solved if they are considered soon enough in the design process of a compiler's code generation strategy or the conventions to be used if the code is written in assembler.
2. Self-modifying programs used to be written to save space and sometimes to exhibit the skill of the programmer. Larger memories and a more responsible attitude may have reduced the temptation.

   However cases do occur, again often to overcome deficiencies in the design of addressing modes, where even high-level languages write addresses into code bodies.

46.4.3 Standards/portability and implementations

It is impossible to ignore the standards for languages if the intention is to write programs so that their source can readily be moved between systems. Each implementation of a particular language will contain different extensions. The temptation to depart from the standard must be resisted.

In programs where such extensions have to be used as they are essential to repair a fundamental deficiency in the language, the use of the extensions should be carefully segregated and annotated. An example is the problem of associating external file names with logical files in Pascal, where each compiler seems to have chosen a different convention from all the others.

The use of options, and taking advantage of hardware-specific features, will further complicate portability. Options – both the facilities supplied and the mechanism for invocation – are usually highly idiosyncratic, and should be used with care.

Often what is offered seeks to overcome particular problems which the language specification has left unsolved. Other options are included because it is difficult but desirable to use some aspects of, say, the addressing scheme of a particular order-code automatically.

There has been relatively little published work on portability.

One useful and general, if a little dated, book is that by Wallis (1982). More specific guidance on developing portable Ada programs is given by Nissen and Wallis (1984).

46.5 Conclusions

Much of this reference book is quite rightly concerned with the principles of designing and developing correct and effective programs. However, it is necessary to be able to put these principles into practice, to be able to develop real programs which execute efficiently despite the constraints of existing hardware and software, and to be able to find and eliminate problems that arise when developing programs. This chapter has been concerned with these latter issues.

In some senses one could regard the topics covered in this chapter as representing 'technician-level' skills, not professional skills for a software engineer. Whilst this may be true it is still essential for the practising software engineer to have these technical skills and the associated knowledge. Even if he or she is not closely involved with developing load maps or debugging programs, the software engineer should be familiar with these issues to ensure that programs he or she designs can readily be mapped on to real machines, are well specified and documented so they can be debugged easily, and so on.

Perhaps one problem in the past has been that the supposed 'professionals' *only* had these technical skills. Whilst it is important to develop new professional skills in formal methods, and so on, it is essential that the basic technical skills of software development are not viewed as 'infra dig' by the professionals.

46.6 References

Abbott, J. (1988) *Unit and Integration Testing Manual*, The National Computing Centre, Manchester

Barron, D. W. (1969) *Assemblers and Loaders*, Macdonald, London

Beck, L. L. (1985) *Systems Software: An Introduction to Systems Programming*, Addison-Wesley, Reading, Mass., USA

Beizer, B. (1983) *Software Testing Techniques*, Van Nostrand Reinhold, NY, USA

Boehm, B. W. (1981) *Software Engineering Economics*, Prentice-Hall, Englewood Cliffs, NY, USA

Brown, P. J. (1975) *Macroprocessors and Techniques for Portable Software*, Wiley, London

Donovan, J. J. (1972) *Systems Programming*, McGraw-Hill, NY, USA

Gordon, A. J. and Finkel, R. A. (1986) TAP: a tool to find timing errors in distributed programs. In *Proceedings of the Workshop on Software Testing, 15–17 July, 1986*, The Institute of Electrical and Electronics Engineers Computer Society, pp. 154–163

IBM (undated) *System/360 Operating System Linkage Editor Program Logic Manual*, IBM Form No Y28-6667-0

Johnson, S. C. (1980) Language development tools on the Unix system. *Computer*, **13**, 16–21

Jones, N. and Muchnick, S. (1978) *TEMPO: A United Treatment of Binding Times and Parameter Passing Concepts in Programming Languages*, LNCS, Springer-Verlag, NY, USA

Kaner, C. (1988) *Testing Computer Software*, TAB Books, Blue Ridge Summit, PA, USA

Kernighan, B. W. and Plauger, P. J. (1976) *Software Tools*, Addison-Wesley, Reading, Mass., USA

Lauesen, S. (1979) Debugging techniques. *Software – Practice and Experience* (Jan.)

Myers, G. J. (1979) *The Art of Software Testing*, John Wiley & Sons, NY, USA

Neumann, P. G. (1987) Risks to the public in computers and related systems. *Association for Computing Machinery Software Engineering Notes*, **12**, 6

Nissen, J. C. D. and Wallis, P. J. L. (1984) *Portability and Style in Ada*, Cambridge University Press

Presser, L. and White, J. R. (1972) Linkers and loaders. *ACM Computing Surveys*, **4**, 149–167

Rustin, R. (1971) *Debugging Techniques in Large Systems*, Prentice-Hall, Englewood Cliffs, NY, USA

Shooman, M. L. (1983) *Software Engineering*, McGraw-Hill, NY, USA

Thorpe, J. (1988) Trouble-shooting main memory corruption on real-time systems. *Computing* (March 31), 20–21

Wallis, P. J. L. (1982) *Portable Programming*, Macmillan

The Operational Environment

47

Computer hardware – introduction and overview

R D Dowsing
Senior Lecturer
Computing School of Information Systems,
University of East Anglia, Norwich

Contents

47.1 History

It is difficult to put an exact date to the first significant event which contributed to the development of computing (Evans, 1981). The person who is recognized as the father of the subject is Charles Babbage. Babbage was the first person to attempt to build an automatic calculating machine, called a Difference Engine, intended for calculating and printing tables of mathematical functions. Although he did build a small machine, the full size machine was never completed. In 1832 he became interested in producing a machine which he called an Analytical Engine. The production of this machine foundered because the engineering skills of the day were not sufficiently advanced to be able to manufacture it. Although it was never built, the Analytical Engine contained many of the essential constituents of present day computers, such as a store, an arithmetic unit, a control unit and input and output devices.

The next significant event in the history of computing was the invention of electromechanical punched card calculating machines by Hermann Hollerith in the late 1880s. Hollerith had noticed that the punched cards used to control Jacquard looms could be used to store the results of census questions. Therefore, if he could invent a machine to sort and count the information stored on the cards he could significantly decrease the time it took to analyse the US census returns. Developments of the machines he produced, for example, to punch holes in the cards, sort them and duplicate them, were in widespread use in the computing industry until about 20 years ago.

In the late 1930s and early 1940s there were a number of efforts in various countries to produce computers. In Germany the inventor Zuse developed a computer system based on mechanical relays which used the binary system. In 1941 his third machine, called Z3, became the first fully operational general-purpose program-controlled computer. He started to build a Z4 machine but this was destroyed in the bombing of Berlin in World War II. Zuse's contribution to the history of computing was not realised until relatively recently because his work has very little influence on the future development of computing.

At about the same time as Zuse's work, Aiken was building the first automatic computer in the USA at Harvard in collaboration with IBM (Goldstine, 1972). This machine was known as the Harvard Mark 1 and it became operational in 1944. It was a mechanical computer and numbers were stored in the machine using wheel positions, each wheel taking one of ten positions and thus representing a digit with groups of wheels representing a number. Addition was performed by connecting the required wheels to a continuously rotating shaft, controlled by a clutch. Electrical contacts on each wheel controlled the clutch operation so that a wheel could be rotated according to the value stored in another wheel. Addition took six seconds and division 12 seconds. Production of Mark 2 was started but never finished as the electronic computer had by now arrived.

Only two years after the Mark 1, the first electronic computer, ENIAC (Electronic Numerical Integrator And Calculator) was developed. The basic ideas behind ENIAC came from pioneering work by Atanasoff, who designed a special-purpose machine to solve simultaneous linear equations in 1939. This machine was dismantled when its creator went to work elsewhere but the ideas were picked up by John Mauchly who, together with John Eckert, was responsible for the design of ENIAC. Production of ENIAC began in 1943 and was completed in 1946. This machine was completely electronic except for the mechanical input and output devices. The reliability of this machine was very poor due to the number and unreliability of the electronic components required. ENIAC took an hour to do work that took Mark 1 a week, being able to make 5000 additions a second. Although produced from completely different technology, this machine used much the same types of facilities as the Mark 1, for example, storage of numbers in decimal form. It was manually programmed by switches and plugging and unplugging wires. ENIAC was dismantled in 1955.

Another significant advance came in 1946 with the work of John von Neumann, a consultant to the ENIAC project, and his co-workers on the theory and design of computers. They put forward the fundamental ideas on which most present day computers are based, for example, the ideas of storing the program in memory prior to execution and making instructions and data in memory only distinguishable by their use. Thus many present day computers are called von Neumann machines. Work was started on the construction of a computer based on these principles called IAS but its completion was delayed until 1952 and several other computers based on the same ideas were completed before it.

The credit for the first stored program computer goes to the Manchester Mark 1 constructed at the University of Manchester (Lavington, 1975). It executed its first program on June 21, 1948. A Williams tube was used for storage and the processor logic was very simple. Several later ideas developed at the University of Manchester were very influential in the development of computing, paging for example.

The 1950s saw the start of commercial computing. The market in this decade was dominated in the USA by IBM and Sperry. Eckert and Mauchly started a company which became the UNIVAC division of Sperry Rand which produced the UNIVAC range of computers. IBM came into the market with the 701 in 1953 and this range of computers first gave the company its dominance of the market.

Developments since this time have become too numerous to chronicle in historical order. Instead the advances made are discussed under various classification and evolution headings.

47.2 Classification

There are many different ways to classify computers.

47.2.1 Technology

The greatest influence on the development of computers has been the rapid advances made in the underlying electronic component technology over the last 30 years. One scheme, shown in *Table 47.1*, classifies computers by the type of technology used in their production. As can be seen from this table, technological improvements have led to the development of larger components. Moore's Law, attributed to the founder of Intel, states that the capacity of an integrated circuit will double each year due to improved definition, leading to smaller components, increased chip sizes and novel circuit and process techniques.

There are a number of reasons why the amount of circuitry which can be held on a single component is important. First, the number of components in a system determines, to a large extent, the reliability of the system; the more components the less reliable. Therefore the more circuits which can be placed on a single component, the smaller the number of components in the system and the more reliable the system will be. Second, the cost of the system is dependent on the number of components, since the mounting of the components and their interconnection and testing is a significant part of the total cost of the system. Last, the cost of a component is only marginally related to its complexity; the fixed costs of the chip production process far outweighs any reduction in yield resulting from the circuit complexity. By far the greatest influence on the cost is the total number of chips produced.

Table 47.1 Generations of technology

	Generation	*Technology*	*Number of transistor equivalents*
1945	First	Valves	
1958	Second	Transistors	1
1965	Third	Small and medium scale integration (SSI and MSI)	1–100
1971	Fourth	Large scale integration (LSI)	100–10 000
1977	Fifth	Very large scale integration (VLSI)	> 10 000

47.2.2 Size

With the increasing size of circuits that can be produced as a single chip, computer designers have been constantly searching for ways of using this extra circuitry to produce higher sales. This has led different manufacturers to concentrate on different markets and to use technology and chip area differently. One possible size classification (Siewiorek, Bell and Newell, 1982) is:

1. *Supercomputers*. The fastest available computers, optimized for particular types of applications such as weather forecasting and mathematical simulation. These machines are built using one of the faster technologies such as emitter coupled logic (ECL).
2. *Maxicomputers*. This is a synonym for mainframe computers. They are fast general-purpose computers aimed at a wide range of applications. They are usually networked to a number of other computers to allow users to access them remotely.
3. *Minicomputers*. These are developments of the small computers which first appeared about 20 years ago, intended for the control of input/output (I/O) peripherals where the amount of computing required was small compared to the amount of device control. They are likely to disappear as a category in the 1990s as maxicomputers or microcomputers take over their role.
4. *Microcomputers*. The first microprocessor, the 4-bit Intel 4004, appeared in 1971 and was designed as a very simple controller rather than a computer (Gupta and Toong, 1983). The latest microprocessors or microcomputers are very sophisticated and some of them approach the power of a minicomputer or maxicomputer. They are usually used in applications where they are embedded in other equipment.

As can be seen by the discussion above, this classification of computers tends to overlap. This is partly because many of the processors in the maxi-, mini- and microcomputer classification use the same technology and have similar architectures and implementation constraints. The main difference between machines in these three categories is the speed of input and output, both to backing storage and to I/O devices. To improve the basic processing speed, instructions and data can be prefetched from memory to buffers in the processor. Output and input can be speeded up by buffering and by the use of intelligent I/O devices.

47.3 Evolution

The evolution of the computer has followed the evolution of the technology. Computers and components have become faster, smaller and cheaper. These improvements have affected the main components of the computer in different ways. The most common structure for computer systems today is a processor, memory and I/O interfaces, attached to a common communication system, a bus. The processor – the CPU – controls access to the shared bus and the other devices act as slave devices, only responding to requests from the processor except for interrupt generation.

47.3.1 Processor developments

The evolutionary trend is for processors to decrease in size and power consumption but to increase in complexity and computing power. For example, the CPU of a typical mainframe computer of the 1960s occupied approximately $3 \, m^3$, but the same computing power can now be obtained from a CPU on an $0.2 \, mm^2$ piece of silicon.

An architectural trend which has accelerated with the increasing complexity of processors is microprogram control. The CPU control unit is a sequential controller, albeit complex, and may be designed using standard logic design techniques, resulting in a hard-wired controller. This uses well-known techniques and produces fast and efficient hardware. The drawback is that it is relatively time-consuming and it is expensive to redesign the hardware if faults are detected or if additions are to be made to the design. An alternative technique is to use microprogramming, first invented by Wilkes (Wilkes and Stringer, 1953). A processor may be thought of as a set of data paths – registers, ALUs (arithmetic logic units) and the buses between them – managed by a control unit. The control unit is a finite state machine (FSM) and can be implemented by a number of different techniques. Before Wilkes' work, the control unit was designed using standard logic design techniques and implemented using hardwired logic. Wilkes' contribution was to see that the FSM could be implemented by another simpler computer that could be programmed to act as the required finite state machine. The programming of this simple processor was called microprogramming. This approach to the implementation of the control unit gains from the use of software development techniques in debugging and modifying the microprogram. Hence complicated controllers are simpler to implement and modifications can be made relatively easily simply by changing the microprogram. The main drawback of this approach is that the microprogrammed processor has to be implemented in faster technology than the higher-level processor to produce acceptable performance. This is both costly and produces a slower processor than a hard-wired one.

The flexibility gained using the microprogrammed approach means that is is now the dominant method of control unit design. Microprogrammable hardware components have been available since the mid 1970s. These devices are known as bit-slice components since they implement a control or data path a few bits – typically 2 or 4 – wide. Processors using wider data or control paths are implemented by stacking several of these components side by side to give the appropriate width of microprogrammed data or control path.

Just as the control unit of a processor can be implemented by a simpler processor, the control unit of this simpler processor can be implemented by an even simpler processor. Whilst, theoretically, this technique can be applied to any level, in practice a maximum of two levels is used. The first level utilizes microprogramming as described above, and the second level uses nanoprogramming. The reason for no more than two levels is that the control unit at the lower level has to be faster than the level above and there are limits to the speed of components.

As a result of technological improvements the number of registers available to the programmer has increased so that a typical processor will have 16 or more general-purpose registers that can be used as accumulators, pointers or temporary storage. Whereas it was possible 20 years ago to classify instruction sets as zero address, one address or two address, this distinction has now become blurred so that it is now usual to find elements of all these three types in a single processor's instruction set. This development has come about partly because of the flexibility of microprogramming which has made it very much easier to decode many different types of instructions. The use of implementation 'tricks' to speed up processing is still widespread as the speed of a processor is still seen as one of the most important measures of its computational power.

The growing use of high-level programming languages has meant that processor design has increasingly been directed to supporting their control and data structures. The support of the control structures is relatively easy and instruction sets have been tailored to this requirement for many years. Using microprogramming, it is relatively easy for the designer to add to the instruction repertoire of the processor, and some processors make use of this by including special instructions in the instruction set to make it easy for the compiler writer to generate code. This same technique also makes the code run faster, since hardware interpretation is generally faster than compilation. Support for data structures is more difficult because of the many different types. More recent processors provide data structure support by including a number of basic types in the instruction set of the processor – for example, the Motorola 68000 provides for operations on 8-, 16- and 32-bit operands – and by including a wide range of addressing modes aimed at optimizing access to data structures. The first processor to become commonly available with a wide range of addressing modes was the Digital Equipment PDP-11 (Bell *et al.*, 1970). This minicomputer provided eight different addressing modes: direct, indirect, auto-increment, indirect auto-increment, auto-decrement, indirect auto-decrement, indexed and indirect indexed. By using the program counter with these modes it was possible to synthesize immediate and relative addressing modes.

The processor structure needed to support high-level languages is still under debate. The argument concerning complex and reduced instruction sets is given later in this chapter.

47.3.2 Memory development

There are two types of memory in a computer system: directly accessible memory and backing storage.

47.3.2.1 *Directly accessible memory*

Directly accessible memory comes in two forms: volatile and non-volatile.

Initially memory was provided in the form of doughnut-shaped ferrite beads called cores. These were expensive to form into a memory and the access time was long. This limited the amount of memory provided with a computer typically to 4 kb in the 1960s. Semiconductor memory was invented by Fairchild in 1970 and its cost fell below that of core memory in 1974. Semiconductor memory prices are still decreasing as larger integrated circuits become available containing more memory

resulting in a typical desktop computer now containing several megabytes of memory. Typical RAM now has a cycle time and an access time of 100 ns.

Another significant development in memory technology was the introduction of associative memory in which access to a memory location is obtained via the contents rather than the address. The first significant use of this type of memory was in the paging system developed for the Atlas machine at Manchester University. Developments of associative memory have led to the production of the content addressable file system (CAFS) developed by ICL and the introduction of new architectures based on this type of memory (Hwang and Briggs, 1986).

The first use of non-volatile memory was to store bootstrap code and this used a diode matrix for storage. With the invention of semiconductor memory, read-only memory (ROM) was used for the same purpose. Its use became more widespread with the invention of microprocessors, used in dedicated applications. More recent developments of EPROM, EEPROM and their derivatives have concentrated on producing memory that is non-volatile, but the contents of which can be changed *in situ* relatively easily.

47.3.2.2 *Backing storage*

Initially backing storage was provided by magnetic drums where information needed to be accessed quickly, and magnetic tape for slower access and archival information. Drums have now been succeeded by various types of magnetic discs with magnetic tape for archival storage. The most common forms of magnetic disc are the floppy disc containing about 1 Mb (megabyte) of information and the Winchester fixed head disc, which comes in sizes from 10 Mb upwards. As well as using normal tape systems for backup, video tapes are now being used because of their high capacity.

Bubble memory, invented by Bobeck in the late 1960s, has also been used for backing storage. Information is stored by magnetic domains in a thin film of magnetic material on application of a magnetic field. Access to the information is via a chain of domains and hence slow. Price has limited its use.

Recently, laser discs have become common for archiving data. These discs use optical technology and have the property, known as WORM, that data can only be Written Once to any part of the disc but can be Read Many times. This property means that these discs are unsuitable for storing ephemeral data and hence are not suitable as general-purpose backing storage.

47.3.2.3 *Memory hierarchy*

Perhaps the most significant development in the architecture of memory was the invention of the one-level storage concept. This was first used in the Atlas computers developed at the University of Manchester and sold commercially by Ferranti (Lavington, 1975). This machine, first operational in 1961, used a paging scheme to implement a virtual memory larger than main memory, with the core store and drum appearing to the programmer as a single large memory. Another similar scheme, called segmentation, has also been used to provide a single-level store, although it has never proved to be as popular. Newer machines, especially high performance ones, use an extended memory hierarchy. Processor registers provide the fastest memory with cache memory providing the next level of the hierarchy. The next level is main memory and discs provide the lowest level. This hierarchy is hidden to the high level language programmer via the translator and operating system.

47.3.2.4 *Memory protection*

With the advent of multiprogramming came the task of ensuring that programs running 'at the same time' did not interfere with one another – for example, by writing to another program's memory area. Some of the simpler schemes developed for providing this protection were based on dividing memory into a number of areas and checking memory access to ensure that a program only referenced its own areas. In most cases hardware is required to perform the checking operation since this has to be applied to each memory access.

The most significant development was the invention of the virtual machine concept. Using this concept each user appears to have access to most of the computer resources. The virtual machine hardware and software is responsible for mapping a number of virtual machines on to the real machine. The basic protection is then provided by the virtual machine mechanism. To make the virtual machine mechanism efficient, the users' address space is normally divided into pages (fixed size) or segments (variable size). Each of these units may have protection bits associated with them so that, for example, a page may be read only if it contains code or constant data.

User programs cannot be allowed unrestricted access to all the computer resources, especially those concerned with the management of the resources. Only the operating system is allowed unrestricted access. The way in which these restrictions are enforced is by the use of a two-state machine; user programs operate in user state and operating system processes operate in supervisor state. In user state, only a subset of the instruction set is available and hence some resources cannot be accessed whilst in supervisor state all the instructions can be used. This scheme is used in the Motorola 68000. Thus if a user program wishes to access restricted resources it has to do so via calls to the operating system. This scheme can be extended to a hierarchy of states with a hierarchy of access privileges, as in the VAX-11 range described later in this chapter.

Like all hierarchical schemes this protection method has drawbacks since each level has a strict subset or superset of the protection at the adjacent levels. Other schemes have been proposed which are not hierarchical but which rely on processes having access rights to the appropriate resources. The access rights are checked whenever the process accesses a resource. The usual way of doing this is to make all access to a resource indirect via an access vector which contains the access rights. The most comprehensive protection methods use a mixture of access lists and capabilities (Peterson and Silberschatz, 1985).

47.3.3 Input/output developments

Most I/O devices still contain some mechanical components and this has hindered both the reduction in cost and the increase in speed of these devices compared to processor and memory. The major trend in I/O processing has been the reduction in the load on the central processor with the increase in intelligence of the I/O interfaces. The first significant development in this area was the introduction of the interrupt method of peripheral control in the Univac 1103 in 1954. Here the central processor is relieved of polling to determine changes of state in the device; instead the device interrupts the CPU when the appropriate change of state takes place. This still leaves the central processor to perform the data transfer and perform any code transformations. Further developments on peripheral handling have concentrated on adding intelligence to the peripheral interface to reduce the load on the processor. This has led to the development of intelligent multiplexers, channels, front-end processors and communication processors (Stallings, 1987). The ultimate here is to have all the peripheral processing performed by computational power in the peripheral, with data transferred to and from the memory using DMA (direct memory access) and an interrupt signalling to the processor when the high level I/O operation has been completed.

47.4 Typical current architectures

As indicated above, the trend in computer architecture over the years, fuelled by the advances in technology, has been increasing complexity and size of the instruction set number of addressing modes, and memory addressing range, and for I/O devices to become more intelligent. This trend has resulted in the typical computer system of today having a complex and large instruction set, a comprehensive set of addressing modes, the capability of accessing large amounts of memory and sophisticated I/O interfaces. Representative architectures of today's state-of-the-art are the Motorola 68000 series (Clements, 1987; Miller, 1988) and the VAX-11 range (Strecker, 1978), which are detailed below.

47.4.1 Motorola 68000

The Motorola 68000 is a range of 32-bit processors from the 68008 – a derivative with an 8-bit external bus used in the Sinclair QL – to the 68030, the highest performance member of the range. The later members of the range have extra instructions and architectural features, but all the members have the same basic architecture. The objective of the 68000 range is to provide the base for the development of complex systems. In order to achieve this the processor is run at a high clock rate, up to 25 MHz for the 68020, and the 68020 and 68030 contain 32-bit wide internal data paths to provide high performance. The processors provide instructions and addressing modes to support the efficient execution of high-level languages and operating system support. Compatibility within the range is achieved by providing object code compatibility.

47.4.1.1 Internal architecture

Internally, the 68000 range of processors have eight general-purpose data registers called D0–D7, each 32 bits wide. These registers may be accessed using byte (8-bit), word (16-bit) or longword (32-bit) instructions that only affect the bits accessed; the other bits are left unaltered. There are additionally eight address registers, A0–A7, also 32 bits wide, that may only be accessed using word or longword instructions. A7 is the system stack pointer. In addition there are two other registers which can be seen by the programmer, the program counter, 32 bits wide in the newer members of the range, and the condition code register. Thus the addressing range of the newer members of the range is 4 Gb (gigabytes). The condition code register holds bits denoting the result of the last instruction, specifically, C (carry), Z (zero), N (negative), V (overflow) and X (extend), the latter being used for extended precision arithmetic.

The 68000 range implements a two-state machine for protecting system resources. In user mode a subset of the instructions is available for user programs, whilst in supervisor mode the full range is available. Access to certain registers – for example, the status register and system stack pointer – is restricted to supervisor mode. The change from user mode to supervisor mode is effected by the occurrence of an exception. External exceptions are normally caused by interrupts generated by hardware and internal exceptions by program. Return to user state is effected by execution of an instruction such as RTE (return from exception).

47.4.1.2 Data types

Three different types of data are supported by the 68000 range: integers, BCD and bits. Integers, which may be signed or unsigned, may be one, two or four bytes long, known as byte, word and longword, respectively. A feature of the 68000 is that byte and word operations on data registers do not affect the rest of the 32-bit register. BCD data can be processed in unpacked form and single bits can be manipulated.

47.4.1.3 Addressing modes

The 68000 range provides a large range of addressing modes in order to support the efficient execution of high level languages. Register and immediate data is supported in byte, word and longword variants. There are two encoding forms for addresses: 16 bit short addresses which are sign extended to 32 bits when used, and 32 bit long addresses. The addressing modes supported by all members of the 68000 ranges are shown in Figure 47.1.

Immediate
Direct or absolute
Register direct
Address register indirect
Address register indirect with postincrement
Address register indirect with predecrement
Register indirect with displacement
Register indirect with index
Program counter relative

Figure 47.1 Motorola 68000 addressing modes

47.4.1.4 Instruction formats

An instruction can take between one and eleven words of storage depending on the addressing mode of each operand. The first word always takes the same format where the bottom six bits represent the mode and register of an operand and the top ten bits represent the opcode. The format of any additional words is complex and contains information such as scale factors, displacement size and index register address.

47.4.1.5 Instruction set

Although the 68000 has a large number of different instructions and addressing modes the instruction set is not orthogonal, that is, not all instructions support all addressing modes. The 68000 range has a conventional instruction set with seven classes of instructions:

1. *Data transfer instructions.* These instructions consist of MOVE instructions and their variants. They allow data to be moved between registers and from registers to memory and *vice versa*. A quick move MOVEQ is provided for byte-sized immediate data and a MOVEM instruction is provided for moving multiple registers, typically used for saving and restoring register contents on entry and exit to subroutines.

2. *Arithmetic instructions.* Arithmetic instructions such as ADD and SUB are provided on all lengths of data and multiply and divide operations operate on 64-bit quantities. The set of arithmetic operations provided includes ADD, SUB, CLR, NEG, MULS and DIVS. Add, subtract and negate operations (ABCD, SBCD and NBCD) are provided on BCD data.

3,4. *Logical and shift instructions.* The standard set of *and*, *or*, *exclusive or* and *not* operations, AND, OR, XOR and NOT, which operate on bytes, words or longwords, are provided. Logical and arithmetic shifts are supported: ASL, ASR, LSR and LSL. Rotate operations are supported with or without the extend condition bit (X) included in the rotation – ROL, ROR, ROXL and ROXR. A

SWAP instruction is provided to swap the word contents of a longword.

5. *Bit instructions.* Bit operations are provided to set, reset, complement and test a bit in a byte – BSET, BCLR, BCHG and BTST.

6. *Program flow control instructions.* A full set of conditional and unconditional branch and jump instructions are provided. Branch instructions use relative addressing whilst jump instructions can use other addressing modes. A set of DBcc instructions are provided which decrement a register and branch if the specified condition is not met. These instructions are provided to implement the test for the end of a loop in WHILE DO, REPEAT UNTIL or FOR loops in high-level languages. BSR and JSR are provided for subroutine calls and RTS for subroutine return. Two instructions, LINK, which reserves stack space, and UNLK, which deallocates stack space, are provided to aid stack management in block structured high-level languages such as Pascal.

7. *CPU control instructions.* The 68000 acts as a two-state machine and a set of instructions are provided to manipulate resources in supervisor state. These consist of specialized move instructions to move data to and from protected registers. The 68000 also includes an instruction in its instruction set to aid in the management of shared memory multiprocessor systems. For a shared memory system a read–modify–write memory cycle is necessary for mutual exclusion to be implemented. This is done on the 68000 by the provision of a TAS (test and set) instruction which returns the value in a memory location and sets it to a known value using a read–modify–write memory cycle provided by the hardware using bus locking. Exceptions may be generated by the user by the use of the TRAP instruction. This instruction takes a 4-bit operand used as a parameter. The action on executing a TRAP is similar to that taken on the receipt of a hardware interrupt. A typical use of the TRAP instruction is to provide direct calls to operating system services from a user program.

47.4.1.6 Exception processing

Exception processing on the 68000 is very similar to interrupt processing on a vectored interrupt machine; that is, the CPU saves the current status, determines the address of the exception processing routine from the exception vector and loads this address into the PC to force the transfer of control. The address of the exception vector is obtained either from internal logic in the case of a software interrupt and from external hardware in the case of an interrupt. Software interrupts are caused by illegal instructions and addressing errors as well as by TRAP instructions. Using software interrupts it is possible to implement breakpoints and tracing.

47.4.1.7 External architecture

Externally the processors have different interfaces. The 68008 has an 8-bit bus and thus allows the use of cheaper 8-bit peripheral interface units. Newer members of the range have 16- and 32-bit external data buses which provide higher performance at higher costs. These larger external data buses can be automatically sized so that 8-, 16- or 32-bit data ports can be handled through the use of control signals. External memory is divided into five subspaces: user program, user data, supervisor program, supervisor data and CPU space. Each processing phase only accesses a single space which is indicated by three output signals from the CPU. It is therefore possible to implement physically discontinuous memory for the separate spaces. Interrupt priority control signals are dealt with by vectored interrupts and bus arbitration signals allow for other devices to obtain control of the bus, that is, to become bus master.

47.4.1.8 Architectural improvements in the 68020

The 68020 (MacGregor, Mothersole and Moyer, 1984) provides a number of features not found in the previous members of the range. For example, it has a 32-bit data and address bus, supports additional instructions, data types and addressing modes and provides support for modular programming and coprocessor interfaces. The objective of these changes is to provide a performance improvement of 4–6 times *vis à vis* the 68000.

The extensions are:

1. 32-bit displacements and 32-bit operands are provided for the few instructions which did not support them in previous processors in the range.
2. Only the 68020 supports variable width bit fields from 1 to 32 bits, packed BCD, quadwords (8 bytes) for long divide and multiply and variable byte operands for the coprocessor interface.
3. The 68020 provides improved support for arrays and lists by expanding the addressing modes to include memory indirection, full 32-bit displacements (which allows branching across the full 4-Gb address space), index scaling and preindexing and postindexing. The new modes make compiler generated code more efficient and faster.
4. The 68020 includes more than 20 new instructions including:
   (a) A set of instructions to manipulate variable width bit fields: clear set, complement, extract, insert, scan and test. These instructions are very useful in graphics and communications applications. The variable width bit fields can span a number of bytes.
   (b) A set of instructions to support the coprocessor (for example, floating point unit, memory management unit) interface. There are seven instructions to communicate instructions and data to the coprocessor and 18 response primitives.
   (c) Modular programming is supported by call module (CALLM) and return from module (RTM). Using this mechanism it is possible to define up to 256 access levels and a protocol for supporting transitions between access levels.

The programmer's model of the 68020 user registers is identical to other members of the range. There are extra registers accessible in the supervisor state to deal with the on-chip instruction cache and process related exceptions.

The extra performance of the 68020 comes about from a number of features of the architecture:

1. *Increased clock frequency.* The 68000 runs at 8 MHz whereas the 68020 can be run at up to 25 MHz.
2. *Increased bus width.* The 68020 has a 32-bit bus whereas older members have a 16-bit bus.
3. *Instruction cache.* If the next instruction is in the cache then access time is reduced by 50% and data and instruction can be simultaneously accessed.
4. *Pipelining.* The micro-machine implementing the processor control is highly pipelined.
5. *Parallelism.* The execution unit can operate in parallel.
6. *New instructions and addressing modes.* High-level language compilers can generate more compact code which runs faster.

47.4.2 VAX-11 range

The DEC VAX-11 is a range of computers which fall into the minicomputer/maxicomputer range. They are a development of the 16-bit PDP-11 range of machines, extended to 32 bits. As the Motorola 68000 range, different models in the VAX-11 range differ in the number of registers and instructions. The details below relate to the basic features of the whole range.

47.4.2.1 Programmer's model

There are 16 32-bit general purpose registers numbered 0 to 15. One of these, R15, is the program counter, while R14 is the stack pointer. R12 and R13 are used as argument pointer and frame pointer respectively to facilitate subroutine calls with parameter passing. A 32-bit status register, called the processor status longword, contains status and control bits. Two input and two output registers are associated with the control console. Four 32-bit clock registers are used for timing purposes and an accelerator control and status word is used to control the floating point accelerator function.

47.4.2.2 Interrupt processing

Two classes of event will cause the VAX CPU to suspend operation and respond to the event: exceptions and interrupts. In both cases the CPU saves the current status and transfers control to a service routine. The CPU responds to events at the end of instructions and at well-defined points in the middle of processing long instructions. Two kinds of interrupts are recognized: hardware interrupts from peripheral devices and software interrupts generated by privileged instructions. The VAX supports 32 priority levels and interrupts will only be serviced if the priority level of the interrupting device is greater than that of the process currently running. The priority of the current process is kept in the status register.

Exceptions are events relating to the current instructions and include page faults, instructions faults such as division by zero and traps used to debug programs. Exceptions do not have a separate priority level but run at the same priority as the current process.

Interrupts and exceptions are vectored with the vectors being stored in the system control block.

47.4.2.3 States

The CPU operates in one of four states which are, in decreasing order of privilege: kernel, executive, supervisor and user. Supervisor state is used to interpret user's commands, executive state to perform file management and kernel state to perform interrupt and exception processing, scheduling, paging and physical I/O. Changes between processing states are effected by a change mode instruction which causes an exception to be generated which transfers control, via the system control block, to a routine in the new access mode. Return to the access mode is made via a return from interrupt (REI) instruction.

47.4.2.4 Addressing

The VAX has one of the most comprehensive sets of addressing modes. In general operands may be 1, 2 or 4 bytes long and the contents of two registers may be used if a 32-bit operand is required.

Two forms of immediate addressing are provided, one for small (<6 bits) operands and one for larger operands. Direct and indirect addressing of registers is supported, together with autoincrement and autodecrement and their deferred analogues. Displacement and displacement deferred addressing is supported for 8-, 16- and 32-bit displacements, and may be used for base register addressing or for indexing. Both absolute and relative addressing is supported as is deferred relative. The VAX processor supports indexing on most of the modes mentioned above, thus giving rise to a wide range of indexed addressing modes. As in the Motorola 68000, the index is scaled by the size of the data being accessed. Branch addressing, identical in action to relative addressing, is provided as a special case since it uses less bits for address encoding. The addressing modes available on the VAX-11 range are shown in *Figure 47.2*. In addition most of these modes are indexable, thus giving rise to many more modes.

Immediate
Absolute
Byte, word or longword relative
Byte, word or longword relative deferred
Indexed
Literal
Register
Register deferred
Autodecrement
Autoincrement
Autoincrement deferred
Byte, word or longword displacement
Byte, word or longword displacement deferred
Branch

Figure 47.2 VAX-11 addressing modes

47.4.2.5 *Instruction formats*

The VAX has a highly variable instruction format, as the designers decided that all instructions should have the 'natural' number of operands and that all operands should have the same generality of specification. The instruction format consists of a 1- or 2-byte opcode followed by from zero to six operand specifiers, each of which may be one or more bytes long, depending on the addressing mode of the operand. Only very few instructions, for example, the string operations, require six operand specifiers; most instructions fall into one or two address formats. Thus the VAX makes the compiler writers task relatively easy at the expense of processor complexity.

Operation types. The instruction set was not designed to be easy to program but rather to generate effective compiler generated code. The aims were therefore a regular and consistent treatment of operators and a large set of instructions to cope with a range of languages. As with Motorola 68000, it is difficult to classify the instructions but they can be roughly classified into nine groups (Stallings, 1987):

1. *Integer arithmetic.* The usual arithmetic operations, addition, subtraction, multiplication and division, are provided

together with some extended precision operations. Each arithmetic and logical operation is provided both in two and three address format.

2. *Floating point arithmetic.* The same set of operations are provided for floating point as for integer arithmetic but operating on longword and quadword formats.
3. *Data move.* A set of MOV instructions are provided to move data between registers, between registers and memory and between memory locations.
4. *Field.* A set of instructions is provided to manipulate variable bit fields including extract, compare and find which finds the first bit in the string which is a 0 or 1.
5. *Control.* A complete set of conditional branch instructions are provided which use 8-bit offset addressing. Jump instructions are also provided and they have a wider addressing range. Two sets of subroutine call and return instructions exist, one of which provides subroutine parameter passing support as well as address linkage.
6. *Queue.* Instructions are provided to manipulate linked lists of data.
7. *Character string.* A set of instructions are provided to manipulate strings, including move, compare, search for single character or substring.
8. *Packed decimal.* Instructions for unpacking, arithmetic and shifting operations on packed decimal values are provided.
9. *Privileged instructions.* A set of instructions are provided which are reserved for operating system use.

In addition, as with the Motorola 68000, the VAX instruction set contains instructions to make the compilation of high-level languages easy, for example, an instruction (AOBLEQ) to implement the end of loop test and a CASE instruction.

The VAX and Motorola architectures are very similar. They are both complex instruction set computers (CISCs) which have a large number of instructions and addressing modes. Each processor is large and was close to the limit of technology when designed. A comparison of the two architectures is given in *Table 47.2*.

47.5 Current architectural trends

During the past two decades a number of important trends have had a significant effect on the development of computer architecture.

47.5.1 Reduced instruction set computers (RISC) (Stallings, 1986)

In the late 1970s computer architects started questioning the apparent trends in the complexity of instruction sets. The conventional reasoning of the day was that programmers worked with high-level languages, so architectures needed to support these languages. The support offered consisted of tailoring the instruction set to the constructs of the language,

Table 47.2 Comparison of Motorola 68000 and VAX-11 architectures

	M68000	VAX-11
Address bus size (bits)	24	32
Data bus size (bits)	32	32
Address space	16 Mb	4 Gb
General registers (32 bits)	16	16
Addressing modes	9	>35
Data types	B,W,L	B,W,L, Q
Processor states	2	4

that is, building higher level constructs into the machine code to lower the semantic gap and to make compilation easier. At the same time the objective was to speed up execution, to be achieved through the provision of special machine code operations, as hardware implementation is generally faster than the equivalent software implementation. This conventional wisdom has been challenged by a number of people who argue that a typical compiler cannot use the special machine code instructions because they are too specialized and that most compilers produce simple machine code. Because of the complexity of the instruction set, the control logic of the processor is very complex, requires a large VLSI chip and operates relatively slowly. Therefore a processor with a reduced instruction set (RISC) should perform as well. Another argument of the CISC designers is that a program compiled for a CISC machine should be smaller – because the instruction set is at a higher level – and faster, because there will be fewer instruction bytes to be fetched from memory. The reply from the RISC designers is that more bits will be required to encode an instruction in a complex instruction set and so although fewer instruction may result, the total number of bits required to store the program may not be much less. Studies have shown that this indeed is the case and typically a program on a RISC only takes about 10% more memory than on a CISC. Hence the conclusion that it is not obvious that a CISC will be 'better' than a RISC.

47.5.1.1 Characteristics of a RISC

A RISC machine must have the following characteristics (Patterson, 1985):

1. All instructions are executed in a single cycle.
2. Operations are generally register to register except for load and store.
3. Only simple addressing modes are supported.
4. Instructions have a simple format and occupy a whole number of words.

Characteristic (1) leads to a simple control structure for the processor, meaning that microcoding is not required and the control logic can be hard-wired, making it fast. Characteristic (2) means that very few variations of instructions are required, for example, only 2 ADD instructions on the Berkeley RISC (Patterson and Sequin, 1982) compared to 25 on the VAX. The third characteristic implies that the control unit can be small and fast and that complex addressing modes have to be simulated in software. The final characteristic implies that memory–processor transfers will be efficient and, if a fixed field format is adopted, concurrent decoding of opcode and operands can be performed speeding up execution.

47.5.1.2 RISC benefits

The benefits of using a RISC design are claimed to be:

1. Better performance, because
   (a) most compilers generate simple code and RISC is smaller and faster for this,
   (b) optimizing compilers can use the simpler structure of a RISC better than a CISC,
   (c) a RISC is more responsive to interrupts since its instructions are shorter.
2. Better use of VLSI chip area, because
   (a) smaller therefore faster,
   (b) control unit area very much smaller (6% as opposed to 50%),
   (c) design and implementation time is very much smaller.

There are three other features which are common in RISC designs but which are not strictly part of the RISC philosophy.

47.5.1.3 Pipelining

In this technique the process of instruction execution is broken down into a number of stages and the execution of these stages for a set of instructions is overlapped. Thus, for example, in the Berkeley RISC (Patterson and Sequin, 1982), instruction execution is broken down into two stages – instruction fetch and execution – and the execution of one instruction is overlapped with the fetch of the next instruction. In the MIPS processor (Przybylsky, 1984) instruction execution is broken down into five stages: instruction fetch, instruction decode, operand decode, operand/store/execute and operand fetch. The first three stages of one instruction are overlapped with the last three stages of the previous instruction. Thus the MIPS processor has more concurrency than the Berkeley machine. The main problem in pipelining is to provide enough resources for concurrent actions, since if two actions can be active concurrently they cannot share resources. This is the reason that the MIPS processor does not implement maximum overlapping; there is only one ALU which is required by both the operand decode and the operand/store/execute stages.

47.5.1.4 Delayed branching

Pipelining causes problems when the next instruction to be executed is not the next in sequence, since the next instruction in sequence will be partially executed before it is discovered that it is not the one to be executed next. Thus there has to be some way in which execution of this partially executed instruction can be aborted and its effects nullified, or of making its effects irrelevant. In most RISC architectures the latter action is taken. For example, in the Berkeley RISC there are only two instructions in the pipeline at once and the code can be arranged so that if the first one is a transfer of control instruction, then the second is a no-op(eration) and thus its execution before the transfer of control has no effect on the program. Thus a compiler for a RISC has to generate a no-op code after each transfer of control. This is not the case for a lot of instances of transfer of control instructions as the code can be reorganized as shown in *Figure 43.3* so that the no-op is not required. In fact studies (Patterson and Sequin, 1982) have shown that only about 3% of the transfer of control instructions cannot be reorganized and have to be followed by a no-op.

47.5.1.5 Register windows

As a consequence of using a RISC architecture, the processor only takes a small amount of silicon area and there is a substantial amount left over when using typical die sizes. This 'spare' area of silicon can be used for a number of different purposes. One common use is to devote the area to implementing a set of registers, only some of which are accessible to the processor at any one time. Since the studies of high-level languages have shown that the most important instruction to support in a processor for efficient language implementation is the procedure call and return, one feature that is necessary is a simple method of parameter transmission between a calling procedure and the called procedure. By the use of a sliding set of register windows, it is possible to provide rapid parameter transmission. At any one time the processor has access to three different sets of registers which are contiguous. One area, at one end of the register set, is used for parameter transmission to a called procedure, and the area at the other end is used for parameter transmission to the calling procedure. The middle area is a local workspace area. Thus to effect a call the register window is moved so that the calling area becomes the new called area and new registers are allocated for local and calling areas.

```
      Load   a              Load   a              Load   a
      Add    b              Add    b              Jmp    L1
      Jmp    L1             Jmp    L1             Add    b
L2:   Add    c              Nop              L2:  Add    c
L1:   Store  d         L2:  Add    c         L1   Store  d
                       L1:  Store  d              ;

        (a)                   (b)                    (c)
```

Figure 47.3 Code reorganization required for a pipelined
architecture; (a) normal code, (b) code with no-operation inserted,
(c) reorganized code

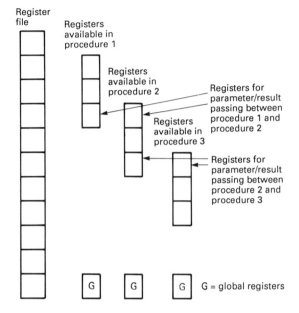

Figure 47.4 Use of register window

A return is effected by moving the register window in the
opposite direction so that the called area becomes the calling
area as shown in *Figure 47.4*. There is also an area which is
common to all procedures which is used for storing global
variables. This is the scheme adopted for the Berkeley RISC and
many others.

It is this feature of many RISCs which has caused some
controversy with CISC designers over the efficiency of CISC
against RISC. CISC designers argue that it is the register
window feature which brings many of the gains of RISC
architectures rather than the RISC features.

47.5.1.6 Some typical RISC processors

One of the first RISC processors was the RISC I developed at
the University of California at Berkeley by Patterson and
Sequin (1982). This processor defined most of the characteristics
of RISC machines, including single cycle execution, few
addressing modes, fixed length instructions, register windows
and pipelining. A second version called RISC II was developed
that included extra addressing modes and a three-stage pipeline,
but with the same basic structure. The Berkeley design is the
basis of the commercially available Pyramid processor which
has a much larger register window.

IBM have developed a RISC machine, the IBM 801 and also
a RISC version of their personal computer called the PC RT
(Waters, 1986). An interesting current commercial RISC design
is the SPARC processor designed by Sun Microsystems and
used in its latest workstations. Interest has been shown by many
firms and there is speculation that this will become a *de facto*
standard. Most major manufacturers have at least one RISC
processor in their current computers. Details of some of the
commercially available RISC machines are given in *Table 47.3*.
A more detailed analysis of current RISC machines is given in
Gimarc and Milutinovic (1987).

47.5.2 Parallelism and distribution

Another major trend which has been discernible in architecture
over the past decade has been the move from uniprocessor
systems to systems with multiple processing elements. Since the
costs of small processors has been decreasing whilst that of high-
performance processors has been increasing, it is possible that
systems consisting of many small, cheap, low-performance
processors may be more cost-effective than a single expensive,
high-performance processor. The multiple processor solution
also gives the possibility of fault tolerant systems and systems in
which the computing power can be incrementally increased by
the addition of more computing elements. The drawback of
using multiple processor systems is that there are problems of
synchronization of both the hardware and the software, and
algorithms for such systems have to be developed rather than
using the conventional uniprocessor ones (Hwang and Briggs,
1986).

47.5.2.1 Classification

One commonly used classification of computer systems is that
developed by Flynn (1972), and is based on the number of
parallel instruction and data streams. In his classification there
are four different types of computer system:

- single instruction single data stream (SISD);
- single instruction multiple data stream (SIMD);
- multiple instruction single data stream (MISD);
- multiple instruction multiple data stream (MIMD).

SISD machines are the 'standard' uniprocessor computers, such
as the Motorola 68000 and VAX 11/780. Array processors fall

Table 47.3 Details of some RISC architectures

Company/university: Chip/computer:	Berkeley RISCI	Inmos T800	MIPS R2000	SUN SPARC
Instructions	31	22	79	89
Registers	138	4	32	120
Pipeline stages	2	0	5	4
Size (transistors)	45 K	238 K	100 K	50 K
Date	1982	1985	1986	1987

into the SIMD class and pipeline processors into the MISD class. Both these types are specialized processors, whereas the MIMD class encompasses general-purpose multiprocessor computers. Within the MIMD class there are two distinct types of computer system: computers which share common memory, known as closely or tightly coupled, and those which do not share memory but communicate via message passing, known as loosely coupled.

47.5.2.2 SIMD processors

SIMD processors are array processors which consist of a set of computing elements that receive a common instruction stream from a special control processor. It is normal for the computing elements to contain some memory and for there to be an interconnection network linking the computing elements together to pass data between them. Thus an array processor is a synchronous array of processing elements designed to perform vector computations on arrays of data. There are two different types of array processor, the most common type using RAM as its storage medium, whilst the other type, called an associative processor, uses associative memory for storage.

There are two basic styles of array processor organization as shown in *Figure 47.5*. In the first type each processing element, P, has its own memory and processors may exchange information by sending information to each other through the interconnection network. In the second type, the memory elements are separate from the processing elements and the interconnections between processing element and memory are made through the alignment network. Thus in both architectures the results of a computation on one processing element may be passed to another processing element using a switching network. In both types of architecture the control unit is responsible for obeying the scalar and control instructions in the program and broadcasting the vector instructions to the processing elements. The control unit is also responsible for setting up the switching network to control data routing. Processing elements may be disabled under software control so that a subset of them can be used in any vector operation. An array processor has to be attached to a host via the control unit. The host is expected to provide the required system software such as compilers and libraries and also to provide the standard operating facilities such as resource management.

The properties which characterize an array processor are the number and type of processing elements, the data routing scheme in the interconnection or alignment network and the masking scheme for the processing elements. Of these properties, the one which has had the most investigation is the routing scheme. In all present SIMD machines the data routing subsystem operates synchronously with the control centralized in the control unit, and circuit switching providing physical paths between the sources and destinations. It is in the routing network topology that there is the greatest difference between architectures. There is a choice of topology (Feng, 1981), static or dynamic. In the static case, the topology is fixed for a program execution, whilst for the dynamic case the topology can change during execution. The other variable is the actual topology used and there are a very large number of possibilities. In the case of static networks one classification is in terms of the number of dimensions required to lay them out. Thus there are one-dimensional topologies – such as a linear array, two-dimensional topologies – such as a ring, star or tree, and three-dimensional topologies – such as a cube or 3-cube-connected cycle. Topologies, such as a hypercube, requiring more than three dimensions are possible. Dynamic networks may be single or multi-stage networks. Single-stage networks comprise two stages, an input stage which is a 1:n multiplexer, and an output stage which is an n:1 multiplexer. By connecting the appropriate

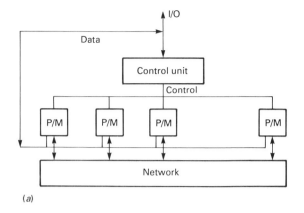

(a)

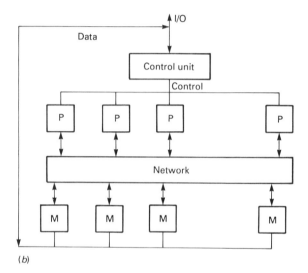

(b)

Figure 47.5 SIMD architectures; (a) direct processing element-memory connection, (b) processor-memory interconnection through network

input multiplexer outputs to the appropriate output multiplexer inputs, all combinations of paths are possible. Multi-stage networks are produced from sets of interconnected switches, often 2×2 switches. These switches are arranged in an array so that in several stages input data may be sent to any output. These types of network have a number of properties. They may be classified as blocking or non-blocking. In blocking networks simultaneous connection of more than one input to more than one output may result in conflict in the use of one or more internal route. In the non-blocking case this will not be true. In a subset of the blocking networks, called rearrangeable networks, it is always possible to rearrange the internal connections so that no internal contention arises. Examples of blocking networks are the data manipulator, baseline and Omega networks. The Benes network is an example of a rearrangeable network and the Clos network and cross-bar switch are examples of non-blocking networks.

Increased flexibility of the network increases the cost and although the interconnection flexibility of the networks is in the order – binary n cube, Omega and data manipulator – so is the cost. For large array processors the cost of the switching network is very significant, hence the use of simple inflexible ones in most commercial machines.

Associative processors use the same basic structure as array processors: a host to provide software and operating system support, a single control unit and multiple processing elements. The main difference is that the memory is associative and each processor can access its memory on the basis of its contents rather than on its address. These machines are built for specialized tasks such as processing radar data.

47.5.2.3 MISD processors

Pipeline processors consist of a number of computing elements or functional units which can be interconnected together to form a pipeline. As an instruction passes along the pipeline it is executed in turn by the functional units it encounters. Pipelining is used in loading and data fetching as well as in execution. To provide efficient pipelining, interleaved memory is required so that concurrent access to consecutive locations is possible for instruction fetching. The main problem in pipelining is the resource contention problem mentioned above in respect to RISC architectures. If several pipeline stages require access to the same resources they cannot be active concurrently. This leads to heavily pipelined processors using large numbers of resources, for example, ALUs, to increase concurrency. This necessitates some form of efficient resource management support in hardware. Another major problem with pipelining concerns how to deal with branching in program code. As discussed in the context of RISCs, the pipeline contains instructions which have been partially executed and when a branch occurs the effect of these instructions must be ignored, either by undoing their effect so far or by ensuring that they have no effect. The solution adopted in most pipeline processors is to fetch the stream of instructions from both possible outcomes of a branch instruction. The effects of the stream not required are then ignored. This solution obviates the need to wait for the correct stream to be loaded if the wrong one has been chosen.

To implement a pipeline processor requires the use of high speed instruction and data buffers. There are two types of MISD architecture: the pipeline processor and the scientific attached processor. The pipeline processor is designed as a supercomputer and the pipelining is intended to provide as much concurrency as possible in executing standard sequential programs. The application area is in applications such as radar and weather forecasting where large arrays or vectors of data have to be manipulated; hence the name vector supercomputers. Only a few of the first generation of pipelined machines such as the Star 100 and Illiac IV were built. The second generation were more successful and machines such as the CRAY 1 (Russell, 1978) and CYBER 200 have sold well. The Cray machine can theoretically process data at a maximum rate of 160 Mflops (million floating point operations/s) although a typical figure in a real application is nearer 24 Mflops. Newer machines have now appeared, such as the Cray X-MP, which is a multiprocessor version of the Cray 1, claimed to be 5 times faster than the single processor. The Cray 2 should be approximately 12 times as powerful as the single processor.

The Cray 1 (Russell 1978) consists of a number of working registers, large instruction and data buffers, and 12 functional pipeline units. The pipeline units may be chained together so that the results of one operation are immediately available to the next operation. It operates at a clock rate of 12.5 ns and has 12 input and 12 output channels that are connected to a front-end machine to perform the required input and output. It may have up to one million words of 64-bit memory which are organized in 8 or 16 banks, thus allowing for concurrent access. The memory is 72 bits wide and the extra eight bits are used for double error detection and single error correction. Data may be transferred from the memory to the processor in 1-, 2- or 4-word parcels per clock period, giving a maximum memory bandwidth of 320 million words/s. Each I/O channel has a maximum transfer rate of 80 Mbytes/s, and four input or output channels operate simultaneously to achieve the maximum transfer of instructions to the computation section.

The structure of the computation section is very complex. There are more than 800 registers and many instruction buffers. The 12 functional units are all pipelines with a delay of between one and 14 clock periods. Arithmetic operations include 24-bit integer and 64-bit floating point computations. The functional units can directly access the eight 24-bit address (A), eight 64-bit scalar (S) and eight sets of 64 vector (V) registers. Intermediate (buffer) registers are provided between these directly accessible registers and memory and block transfers can be performed between these registers.

All instructions are 16 or 32 bits long and are first loaded into one of four buffers, each containing 64 registers, thus substantial program segments can be pre-fetched into the instruction buffers. When an instruction is not in a buffer, the contents of one of the buffers is replaced with a new block of instructions from memory. The Cray 1 has 120 instructions with ten vector types and 13 scalar types, most of which are of the three-address format.

The 12 functional units are organized into four groups: address, scalar, vector and floating point pipelines. Each functional pipe has several stages and thus the delay is variable. The functional units can operate independently of the others, or they can operate concurrently, provided there are no register conflicts. A functional pipe receives its input from two source registers and produces its output in a destination register. As their name suggests, address pipes perform address arithmetic and both take their input from and deposit their output in the A registers. Similarly the vector pipes obtain their inputs from the V and S registers and deliver their results to a V register. Operations available in a vector pipe include add and shift and floating point add and multiply, although these latter two are provided by special floating point pipes. The scalar pipes provide scalar add and shift and logic operations, taking their input from, and delivering their output to an S register. The start-up time for vector operations is very small, thus even small vectors can benefit from using the vector pipeline.

The objective of the Cray's architecture is to process as much data as possible within the processor before returning it to memory. Thus the objective is to process data, preferably vectors, through a set of pipes performing an operation in each pipe. To do this effectively the appropriate registers and functional units have to be reserved so that data is not held up waiting for resources. Data from one functional unit may be fed directly into another functional unit via the register used as the destination of the first unit. This is known as chaining and is used extensively in this architecture.

Scientific attached processors such as the Floating Point Systems AP-120B are intended as back-end arithmetic processors. The host computer provides the operating and system software support as is the case with array processors. The AP-120B gains its speed from pipelined arithmetic units and from the fact that it has multiple memories, many registers and accumulators and seven buses.

Both pipeline and array processors are specialized computers, aimed at particular types of processing, since the algorithms used must be suitable for the particular architecture under consideration. It is the responsibility of the compiler used to optimize the code for the particular array or pipeline architecture. In general these architectures are only suited to particular units of data; for example, an array processor can handle up a given number of data items at the same time but above this number the data has to be split into groups of the appropriate number of items. Also, the execution of any algorithm can be enhanced if the programmer has taken the particular machine architecture into account.

47.5.2.4 General-purpose multiprocessors (MIMD)

Closely-coupled multiprocessor systems share memory. This imposes a constraint on the architecture in that access to the shared memory eventually becomes a bottleneck and hence limits the number of processors. The addition of local memory to each processor for the storage of local code and data allows the common memory to be used solely for communication and the processor limit can be extended, typically to between ten and 20.

Closely-coupled systems are much easier to program than loosely-coupled ones because the system has a global state which can be seen by each processor. Thus synchronization of the processors and hence the processes is much simpler. For the same reason debugging can be much simpler; the system state can be frozen.

The architectural support for programming closely-coupled multiprocessor systems provided by many processors is a test and set instruction. This instruction performs a read–modify– write cycle on the shared memory in mutual exclusion to the other processors which can access the same memory. In effect the instruction returns the value of a flag and sets it to some known value. This instruction can be used as the basis of some other higher level synchronization primitive such as semaphores or monitors which can be provided by software. A test and set instruction is provided in the instruction set of the Motorola 68000 described earlier in this chapter.

In distributed, or loosely-coupled systems, the processors are coupled by communication subsystems and information is exchanged via messages (Sloman and Kramer, 1987). There are two types of distributed system, wide area networks (WANs) and local area networks (LANs). Wide area networks are collections of computer systems which are relatively far apart. Each processor acts as an autonomous system and communicates with another on the same network to share resources and pass messages. These types of system do not have to provide any particular architectural features to support the distribution apart from those needed to support remote communication, for example, a front-end processor for protocol transformations. Local area networks have a much smaller geographical range, typically over a building or site and the collection of computers are thought of and programmed as a single system.

An important property of a distributed system is the cost of communication. If the system is to be successful then the communications bandwidth in the hardware must be able to cope with the peak message transfer rate generated by the software. The partitioning of the problem and the assignment of the individual partitions to hardware units is therefore critical for system performance.

47.6 Future developments

A number of radically different technologies have been proposed for future computers including optical and biological mechanisms. Gallium arsenide, already used for many military applications, has been proposed as a replacement for silicon as an integrated circuit (IC) substrate.

47.6.1 Gallium arsenide

Gallium arsenide was investigated as a substrate for ICs at the same time as silicon, but technology-related problems have stopped its introduction into all but some specialized military applications until the 1980s. Gallium arsenide has a number of advantages over silicon as a substrate (Milutinovic, 1986):

1. Higher resistance to radiation (Helbig, 1986).
2. Tolerance of wider temperature variations about -200 to 200°C.
3. Faster for the same power consumption by about five times.
4. Better suited to electronic/optical component integration.

However it suffers from a number of disadvantages, the most important of which is that a worse yield is obtained for the same circuit complexity. This means that gallium arsenide ICs are about two orders of magnitude more expensive than the equivalent silicon circuits.

The way in which these properties affect the design of computers based on gallium arsenide (Milutinovic et al., 1986) is that ICs have to be small to keep the yield high. This means that system partitioning is crucial, since off chip communication delays are high and must therefore be reduced to a minimum. Thus RISC designs are the only viable ones at present (Fox et al., 1986). Even RISC designs are subject to several constraints due to small chip sizes: no on-chip cache and hardware functions, for example, and memory management relegated to software where possible.

Although some of the problems associated with gallium arsenide are expected to be reduced in the future, one report suggests that circuits produced with this technology will always be about an order of magnitude more expensive than the equivalent silicon circuit.

47.6.2 Optical computing

Optical computing is likely to become one of the most important developments in the future. Research really began in the 1960s with the development of the laser and low-loss optical fibres (Miller, 1969). The fundamental unit of optical computing is the photon and it is the specific properties of the photon which are important in optical computing (Sluss et al., 1987):

1. The speed of the photon is generally faster, typically 1.5 times that of the electron in the usual substrates.
2. Photons may or may not interfere, giving rise to computational properties.
3. Photons can be refracted by lenses and diffracted by slits or pinholes, leading to processing devices.

A stream of photons is normally contained within a waveguide fabricated in a substrate such as silicon. Devices are placed at the ends of the waveguide sections to process the photon stream. Because photons have different properties from electrons there is no reason why an optical computer should duplicate the architecture of a conventional computer; in fact, new architectures are very likely to emerge.

Information may be coded on to the photon beam in a number of ways. The photon beam may be turned on or off to produce representations of the binary digits 0 and 1 or the beam may be modulated in one of a number of ways, similar to analogue data communications, to encode the required bit patterns.

Devices such as modulators, switches and detectors have been fabricated in the technology in an IC on a number of different substrates, including silicon and gallium arsenide. Thus conventional semiconductor processing techniques can be used to fabricate optical circuits and hybrid optical/electronic circuits are possible.

At the present time optical computers are not practical but simple though functionally complex optical circuits are being manufactured for signal processing applications such as high speed spectrum analysis of radar data.

47.7 Computer architecture and software engineering

The architecture of computers has a significant effect on software engineering. All designs have to make trade-offs, and there is a basic conflict in architectural design between producing computers which execute programs as fast as possible and producing computers which make the task of designing and implementing programs simpler. Whilst most designers pay some attention to the latter aim, the main objective of designers is to produce a computer which executes instructions as fast as possible, since this is what the prospective user measures and still regards as the most important requirement. This has led to some of the problems of engineering the software of such systems. There are many facets of this but only two are considered here.

47.7.1 Language implementation

The difficulty of implementing a language depends on the 'semantic gap' between the language being implemented and the language of the intended processor. It is to reduce the semantic gap that the CISC designer has included more complex machine instructions in the instruction set. However, this can lead to inefficient use of the VLSI area and a reduction in the execution speed of the processor. This has led to the development of RISC designs which are simpler processors, easier to implement, but which rely on complicated compiler technology to produce efficient code. Also, most RISC designs are targeted at particular languages rather than being general-purpose. It is likely that the best features of both CISC and RISC designs will be used in the next generation of designs since CISC and RISC are only two points on the design spectrum.

47.7.2 Non-von Neumann machines

It was the search for more computing power and the implementation of other computational models which was and is the driving force for new computer architectures. Most of these new architectures involve multiple processors and many of them have distributed architectures. The main problem at the present time is that they are architectural exercises, that is, they concentrate on what hardware can be built rather than how the software can be built and used. The mapping of a problem specification on to one of these architectures creates a number of problems not encountered in a single-processor machine. For example, algorithms which are efficient on a single processor are not necessarily efficient on a multiprocessor, and hence programs for a single processor cannot simply be ported to a multiprocessor; they have to be re-written. Another problem is that most multiprocessors do not have shared memory, hence programs have to be partitioned into a set of message passing processes. This is complicated since the size of the processes, and hence the number of messages sent, depends on the architecture of the intended computer and so programs become specific to a particular architecture.

There are many problems such as those described above relating to the use of new architectures and it will not be until both architects and software engineers progress further with research that these new architectures will become easy and efficient to use.

47.8 References

Bell, C. G., Cady, R., McFarland, H., Delagi, B., O'Loughlin, J., Noonan, R. *et al.* (1970) A new architecture for minicomputers: the DEC PDP-11. In *Proceedings of the American Federation of Information Processing Systems Spring Joint Computer Conference*, **36**, 657–675

Clements, A. (1987) *Microprocessor System Design: 68000 Hardware, Software and Interfacing*, PWS, Boston

Evans, C. (1981) *The Making of the Micro: A History of the Computer*, Van Nostrand Reinhold, New York

Feng, T. Y. (1981) A survey of interconnection networks. *Computer*, **14**, 12–27

Flynn, M. J. (1972) Some computer organisations and their effectiveness. *The Institute of Electrical and Electronic Engineers Transactions on Computers*, **C-21**, 948–960

Fox, E. R., Kiefer, K. J., Vangen, R. F. and Whalen, S. P. (1986) Reduced instruction set architecture for a GaAs microprocessor system. *Computer*, **19**, 71–81

Gimarc, C. E. and Milutinovic, V. M. (1987) A survey of RISC processors and computers of the mid-1980s. *Computer*, **20**, 59–69

Goldstine, H. (1972) *The computer from Pascal to von Neumann*, Princeton University Press, Princeton

Gupta, A. and Toong, H. (1983) Microprocessors – the first twelve years. In *Proceedings of the Institute of Electrical and Electronic Engineers*, **71**, 1236–1256

Helbig, W. (1986) RISC vs. CISC, GaAs vs. silicon and hardware vs. software. *Invited lecture*, Joint Chapter meeting of IEEE Microwave Theory and Techniques/IEEE Electron Devices societies, Princeton, New Jersey

Hwang, K. and Briggs, F. A. (1986) *Computer Architecture and Parallel Processing*, McGraw-Hill, New York

Lavington, S. (1975) *A History of Manchester Computers*, NCC Publications, Manchester

MacGregor, D., Mothersole, D. and Moyer, W. (1984) The Motorola MC68020. *The Institute of Electrical and Electronic Engineers Micro*, **4**, 101–118

Miller, M. A. (1988) *The 68000 Microprocessor: Architecture, Programming and Applications*, Merrill, Columbus

Miller, S. E. (1969) Integrated optics: an introduction. *Bell Systems Technical Journal*, **48**, 2059–2069

Milutinovic, V. (1986) GaAs Microprocessor Technology. *Computer*, **19**, 10–17

Milutinovic, V., Sibley, A., Fura, D., Keirn, K., Bettinger, M., Helbig, W. *et al.*, (1986) Issues of importance in designing GaAs microcomputer systems, *Computer*, **19**, 45–60

Patterson, D. (1985) Reduced instruction set computers. *Communications of the Association of Computing Machinery*, **28**, 8–21

Patterson, D. and Sequin, C. (1982) A VLSI RISC. *Computer*, **15**, 8–21

Peterson, J. L. and Silberschatz, A. (1985) *Operating System Concepts*, Addison-Wesley, Reading, Massachusetts

Przybylsky, S. A. (1984) Organisation and VLSI implementation of MIPS. *Journal of VLSI and Computer Systems*, **1**, 170–209

Russell, R. M. (1978) The CRAY-1 computer system. *Communications of the Association of Computing Machinery*, **21**, 63–72

Siewiorek, D. P., Bell, C. G. and Newell, A. (1982) *Computer Structures: Principles and Examples*, McGraw-Hill, New York

Sloman, M. and Kramer, J. (1987) *Distributed Systems and Computer Networks*. Prentice-Hall, Englewood Cliffs

Sluss, J. J., Veasey, D. L., Batcham, T. E. and Parrish, E. A. (1987) An introduction to integrated optics for computing. *Computer*, **20**, 9–25

Stallings, W. (1986) *Reduced Instruction Set Computers*, IEEE Computer Society Press, Washington

Stallings, W. (1987) *Computer Organisation and Architecture: Principles of Structure and Funcion*, Macmillan, New York

Strecker, W. D. (1978) VAX 11/780 – A Virtual Address Extension to the DEC PDP-11 Family. In *Proc. National Computer Conference*, 967–980

Waters, F. (ed.) (1986) *IBM RT Personal Computer Technology*, IBM Corporation SA23-1057

Wilkes, M. V. and Stringer, J. B. (1953) Microprogramming and the design of control circuits in an electronic digital computer. *Proc. Cambridge Philosophical Society*, **49**, 230–238

48

Computer interfacing

R D Dowsing
Senior Lecturer
Computing School of Information Systems,
University of East Anglia, Norwich

Contents

48.1 Introduction

An interface defines the outside view of a component or system. Interconnecting subsystems involves connecting interfaces together. Connecting compatible interfaces can be simple but the connection of incompatible interfaces can be much more complex, especially if they were not designed to interact with one another.

Computer interfacing covers a range of topics from the physical construction of the interface, such as the plugs and sockets used, through the electrical characteristics, such as the voltage representation of logic 0 to the protocol used at the interface. This chapter is not concerned with the physical construction of interfaces; interested readers should consult Lesea and Zaks (1977) and Peatman (1977). In some cases, such as memory interfacing, there is little or no software interfacing required whilst in other cases, such as direct memory access (DMA), both software and hardware interfaces are necessary. This chapter will cover both hardware and software interfacing issues.

Standards are important in interfacing so that different manufacturers' components can be connected together simply. With a few notable exceptions, mentioned later, it is only in the last few years that widely recognized standards for many of the interfaces in computers have existed. Many of the standards have evolved from a single manufacturers design rather than being designed specifically as a standard. Most standards are promulgated by the CCITT, IEEE and ISO.

Complexity in the interface arises for a number of reasons. First, the peripheral device and the computer often work at different speeds and hence the interface unit has to provide synchronization. Second, the electrical characteristics of the peripheral device are often very different from those of the computer system and the interface is then responsible for the appropriate conversion. Last, the interface has to provide an appropriate programming interface so that a user (programmer) can effectively control the peripheral and perform the appropriate data transfers.

Most computer systems are organized around one or more bus systems. A bus is a set of parallel communication paths which are shared by the devices connected to the bus. Thus the commonest way to attach a device to a computer system is to attach it to one or more of the buses. Whilst memory is normally designed to interface directly to a bus, peripheral devices are not usually compatible, either at the software or the hardware level, with a computer bus. Compatibility is obtained by interposing an interface unit between the two subsystems, as shown in *Figure 48.1*. Both sides of this interface are electrical and hence any mechanical peripheral devices have to have their mechanical action converted to electrical signals for input and vice versa for output. This is performed by a transducer, usually in the peripheral device. The range of electrical signals accepted by the interface is limited so the input signals have to be conditioned to be in this range and output values converted to be in the desired range. This conditioning is performed by amplifiers if the signal is too small and resistor networks if the signal is too large. Thus some of the problems that occur with floating point number representation occur with signal representation also, for example, granularity of the digital representation, range of values represented and overflow and underflow. The interface contains registers, some of which buffer the data to be transferred and others of which provide control over the transfer. The data transfer registers must buffer the data because of different rates of transfer between the two devices and the interface. The size of the buffers is adjusted to provide an efficient interface by smoothing out the rate of data transfer, for example, to overcome the latency problems with discs. The control and status registers in the interface are used to control the transfer of data,

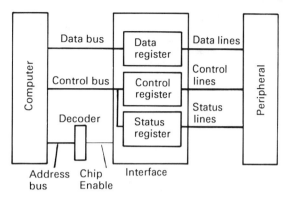

Figure 48.1 Block diagram of peripheral interface

for example, to synchronize the transmitter and receiver so that the transmitter does not transmit until the requisite buffer is empty, and to signal the state of the interface and peripheral, for example by signalling when a buffer is empty.

The typical unit of transfer between a peripheral and the interface is an 8-bit character, and that between the computer and the interface is a word. Thus the interface has to pack and unpack characters into words, if necessary. In many simple interfaces this is unnecessary because the word size of the computer is 8-bits or the computer possesses instructions to transfer bytes rather than words to and from the interface.

Input/output (I/O) devices can be roughly divided into two classes, depending on whether the basic unit of information which they manipulate is a stream of characters, when they are known as character devices, or a block of characters, when they are known as block devices. Tape and disc storage devices are block devices and most other I/O devices are character devices. The essential property of block devices is that they can manipulate blocks independently, whereas character devices can only manipulate characters as part of the character stream. Thus, a disc can read or write any one of its blocks at any time while a computer terminal can only receive and process characters in the order that they are sent. In general, software to control interfaces is divided in the same way; one class to control character devices and one to control block devices.

A device which sends data is known as a transmitter and a device which receives data is known as a receiver. A master device is a device which may initiate a transfer and a slave device is a device which can only respond to a master. In many instances devices may act in more than one role, for example, as transmitter or receiver – a VDU – or as master or slave – a DMA interface. In a typical uni-processor computer system the CPU acts as a master and peripheral devices act as slaves but some interfaces can act as both masters and slaves, depending on the situation. The logic required by a device to act as a master is considerably more complex than that required as a slave. Hence slave devices are cheaper than master devices or those which possess both properties.

For transmission to take place, the master, typically a processor, obtains use of a bus and interrogates the appropriate interface to see if the slave device is in a suitable state to participate in the data transfer. If not the master waits for the slave to attain that state and then begins the transfer using the control registers in the interface to control the transfer and the status registers to monitor the state of the slave device. This imposes a processing overhead on the master and I/O systems are complex because of the need to reduce CPU involvement in the transfer of data. It is cheaper and more cost-effective for the work of transferring data to be relegated to specialized logic or a smaller processor – possibly the peripheral interface itself.

The software to perform I/O tasks is usually organized into device drivers. These device drivers are operating system subroutines which control the data transfer. They are called by the application program whenever I/O processing is required. Internally, these routines control the I/O interfaces directly and only return control to the applications program when the appropriate transfers are complete.

Most books on computer architecture contain a section on I/O interfaces and programming (for example, Stallings (1987), Tanenbaum (1984) and Gorsline (1986)). Books devoted solely to interfacing include Stone (1982) and Artwick (1980)(a). Details of specific interfaces are to be found in the appropriate manufacturers data sheets.

48.2 Address mapping

To connect a component to a computer often only entails adding the required standard interface to the bus of the computer system. Devices attached to the computer bus, for example, the CPU, access the control and data registers in the interface by means of their addresses. The system designer has to map the address of a new interface on to the addressing structure of the system.

Devices such as processors and interfaces are attached to buses which provide the communication media. To address a register in an interface its address is placed on the address bus. If there is only a single address bus then all devices attached to the bus have to share a single address space. This is known as memory mapping since part of the memory address space is allocated to peripheral interfaces. Using this method all the processor instructions and addressing modes can be used to access the registers in the peripheral interface. The other technique is to have multiple buses, for example, a memory bus and an I/O bus, and multiple sets of instructions; one set dedicated to performing I/O and the other set to the normal CPU processing operations in this example. Addresses from the different instruction sets appear on different address buses. The I/O set normally consists of one input and one output instruction, typically IN and OUT, which take a single operand, the address of the interface registers. This method means that only the I/O instructions can be used to perform I/O but that they have their own address space; it is not shared with memory. With the ever-increasing size of memory addressing provided on processors, memory mapping is now the preferred technique.

The address generated on the bus has to be decoded for the correct register to be accessed. Addresses may be either partially or fully decoded. In full decoding all of the address bits are examined and decoded to determine which register or memory location is being addressed. An example of full decoding is given in *Figure 48.2(a)*. The problem with this method is that it requires more logic than the alternative, partial decoding, shown in *Figure 48.2(b)*. In this method only some of the address lines are examined. This method relies on the fact that the address generated is within a subspace of the available address space. A disadvantage with this method is that if access is made outside this subspace then access can still be made to an interface, which can make debugging difficult. In the example given in Figure 48.2, the partial decoding scheme would enable the ROM for a large number of addresses, for example, any address between 8192 (1000000000000) and 12287 (1011111111111), whilst the full decoding scheme would not enable either the ROM or RAM.

To connect a RAM at addresses 4096–8191 and a PROM at 0–4095

Addresses of this form will address the RAM (x is do not care)

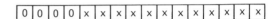

Addresses of this form will address the PROM

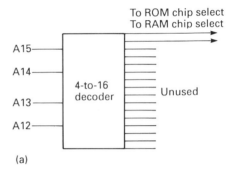

(a)

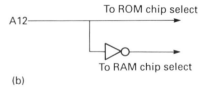

(b)

Figure 48.2 Address decoding (a) full decoding (b) partial decoding

48.3 Computer buses

Most but not all computers communicate internally via one or more bus structures. A bus is a broadcast parallel interface between components of a computer. The components tap on to the bus to provide a communications pathway. A bus only allows a single communication at any one time and this can produce a bottleneck. Thus computers requiring concurrent communication use several buses. The speed of a bus depends on its length, so high-speed buses have to be short. The width of a bus is determined by the size of the data transfer within the computer, typically a word, and the number of control signals required. This has led to the development of many different bus structures for different processors. It is only relatively recently that bus structures have become standardized (Borrill, 1981).

Devices which interface to a bus have to ensure that they only place a load on the bus when they use it, and the common way of ensuring this is to use tristate devices which go into their high impedance state when inactive.

The functions of a bus are to transfer address, data and commands from one module to another, to arbitrate on competing accesses to the bus and to provide handshake signals which control when data transfer take place.

There are three different types of bus, differentiated by the type of handshake protocols used. The simplest type of bus is the synchronous bus. In this type of bus a clock signal dictates when any activity on the bus stops and starts. All activities on the bus take place in a single clock cycle, thus, for example, the write operation is triggered by the leading edge of the clock signal and terminated by the trailing edge. Information on the data and address lines has to be set up before the leading edge of the clock pulse arrives due to the fact that the signals take time to propagate through the logic and reach stability. This is known as the set up time. Similarly, there is a minimum time for which the signals must remain stable after the trailing edge of the clock pulse to take into account the differing delays for clock and information signals. This is known as the hold time. The advantage of this type of bus is simplicity, but it has a major disadvantage in that the clock speed is determined by the time taken to perform the longest transfer and hence slow devices limit the speed of faster devices.

Another type of bus is called a semi-synchronous bus. The operation of this bus is very similar to the synchronous bus except that it is possible for bus transactions to take more than one bus cycle. To do this the device which requires more than one cycle asserts a special signal, often called HOLD or WAIT, which causes the bus to be allocated to that transfer for as long as the signal is asserted. This means that bus transactions can take a varying amount of time. The main drawback is that the HOLD or WAIT signal has to be asserted within a particular time constraint and thus the length of the bus is constrained.

Another method of retaining the simplicity of the synchronous protocol whilst allowing different transaction times is to split the transaction into two parts; the transmission of the relevant address for a read operation followed, some time later, by the transmission of the requested data. This is known as split cycle protocol and has the advantage that the bus is not held for the portion of time that data is being fetched, but it does require more logic since both devices involved in the transfer have to be able to assume the role of both master and slave.

The most flexible bus scheme is an asynchronous bus. In this scheme there is a fully interlocked protocol of control signals which indicates when operations can take place rather than a single bus clock signal. The master signals when the appropriate data and control lines for the transfer have been set up and the slave replies when the data has been read or written. In this bus scheme, each pair of devices operates at its own speed. The scheme is widely adopted in buses due to its reliability and efficiency, even though it is not as fast as a synchronous bus due to the transmission time of the control signals.

48.3.1 Bus hierarchy

There are often several different buses in a computer system. The processor bus usually extends over the printed circuit board containing the processor and other components. A backplane bus is used to connect sets of printed circuit boards together to form a system. These two bus systems are often different, the intraboard bus being a proprietary manufacturer's bus for the particular processor being used, and the interboard bus being a recognized standard. The main reason for using standard backplane buses for interconnection is so that different manufacturer's products can be combined. This hierarchical system

imposes an overhead since signals have to be converted from one bus system to another, but with the growth of standard buses there has been a corresponding growth in the production of interfacing circuits. There are a wide range of standard buses in use because the signals carried by the standard bus depend, to some extent, on the processors used since different processors use different protocols and signals. Thus many standard backplane buses are derived from the buses defined originally by a particular processor manufacturer. Some of the more common standard buses are VME, sponsored by Motorola and standardized as IEEE 1014 (1989), Multibus II (1989), an Intel sponsored bus now being standardized and Nubus (1989), a Texas Instruments sponsored bus used in the Apple Macintosh II. Futurebus, standardized as IEEE 896.1 (1989), is likely to be an important standard in the future.

48.3.2 Bus arbitration

Bus arbitration is required when a system contains more than one bus master to ensure conflict free access to the bus since more than one device may try to access the bus concurrently. The simplest system of arbitration is called daisy-chaining. In the most common implementation of this technique, shown in *Figure 48.3*, a signal called bus grant is connected from the bus arbiter to all of the possible bus masters in some sequence. Two common signals, called bus request and bus busy, are connected from all the possible bus masters to the arbiter. When a bus master requires access to the bus it raises the bus request line. Some time later this is seen by the arbiter which grants the request by setting the bus grant line high, providing that the bus busy line is not asserted, in which case it will delay granting use of the bus since some other module is still using it. The first master in the bus grant chain sees the signal and knows that, if it has requested use of the bus, it may now use it. If it has not requested use of the bus then it passes the grant signal on to the next master in the chain. When a module gains access to the bus it asserts bus busy and this signal is used by the arbiter to reset the bus grant line.

A consideration when selecting an arbitration technique is the reliability of the implementation, for example, will spurious bus transactions take place if one of the bus signals is lost? For the three wire system described above reliability is good and this is one reason why many bus arbitration protocols are based on this method.

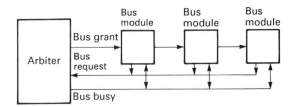

Figure 48.3 Bus arbitration daisy-chaining

48.3.3 A comparison of some buses

There are many different buses and some of the more popular ones are compared in *Table 48.1*. A very recent table (Smolin, 1988) gives more details.

Table 48.1 Comparison of Some Common Buses

Characteristic	Futurebus	Nubus	VMEbus	Multibus II
Performance (M bits/s)	100	37.5	30	35
Synchronous (s)/asynchronous (a)	a	s	a	s
Address width (bits)	32	32	16/24/32	32
Data width (bits)	8/16/24/32	8/16/32	8/16/24/32	8/16/24/32
Block transfer mode	Yes	Yes	Yes	Yes
Broadcast mode	Yes	No	No	Message
Multimaster operation	Yes	Yes	Yes	Yes
Arbitration	Parallel	Parallel	Daisy-chain	Parallel
Priority	Yes	No	Yes	Yes
No. of slots	21-32	16	21	21
IEEE standard No.	896.1	1196	1014	1296

48.4 Polling and interrupts

Data transfers between devices may be controlled by the use of polling or interrupts. In cases where the timing of sender and receiver is synchronized by hardware, for example, in accessing RAM, transmitter and receiver know the state of each other at all times. In other cases where transmitter and receiver are asynchronous, as is the case for most data transfers, status information has to be distributed so that the communicating devices are aware of each other's status and can keep in synchronism.

The simplest technique, known as polling, is to program the master controlling the transfer to monitor continually the state of the device via the status register in the interface. The problem with this approach is that the processor acting as master is generally much faster than the peripheral device it is controlling, so it spends a considerable time continually testing the status register until the data register contains input. This is unproductive work for the processor. One solution to this is to adopt a different approach using interrupts. Here the processor requests input of a unit of data into the interface data register but does not wait until the data is there; instead it carries on with other useful work, if possible. It is the responsibility of the interface to inform the processor, via a signal called an interrupt, that the data is available in the data register. On receipt of an interrupt the processor responds by taking the appropriate action, in this case by moving the data from the interface data register to a processor register or memory.

Using this scheme, which is much more efficient in terms of processor usage, additional hardware is required to deal with interrupt signalling. Interrupt signals from the interface to the processor set a flag in the processor which is checked at the end of every instruction cycle. If the flag is set then the processor knows that an interrupt has been generated and that an interface requires service. An interrupt acknowledge signal generated by the processor completes the handshake. It should be noted that interrupts are really only polling at a lower level, that is, by the hardware of the processor or by microcode. Because interrupts are processed by hardware or firmware they are faster and more efficient than software polling techniques.

On receipt of an interrupt the processor transfers control to the requisite software routine to deal with that particular interrupt. The processor may not wish to respond immediately to an interrupt request because it is performing some higher priority processing. In simple interrupt processing schemes a bit in the processor status word determines whether the processor will respond to interrupts or not. Processes which do not wish to be interrupted set this bit. Interrupt requests are queued until the processor is willing to respond to them, that is, the bit in the processor status word remains set until the device generating the interrupt is serviced.

Many current systems provide for multiple-level interrupts with devices requiring faster service having higher priorities associated with interrupts from their interfaces. In general higher priority interrupts are allowed to interrupt processing of lower priority ones but not *vice versa*. In this system multiple interrupt lines are connected to the processor and the processor determines whether it will respond to an interrupt by comparing the priority of the highest outstanding interrupt request with the priority of the currently running process which is stored in the processor status word.

When a processor has to respond to an interrupt it has to determine which device caused the interrupt and then to execute the appropriate software driver for that device. When there are multiple devices capable of producing interrupts the simplest technique to determine where a particular interrupt came from is for the processor to poll the status registers of all the possible interface units. The appropriate software driver may then be called via a table look-up operation. This is slow and a newer method used almost exclusively on modern processors is called vectored interrupts. The device causing the interrupt generates the address of the device driver, or, more usually, the address of a memory location containing the address of the device driver, on the data bus in response to the interrupt acknowledge signal from the processor. This is loaded, directly or indirectly, into the program counter causing a transfer of control to the appropriate software.

Multiple interfaces may be connected to the same interrupt level and multiple interrupt requests are arbitrated in hardware by daisy-chaining in a very similar manner to bus arbitration, using interrupt request, interrupt acknowledge and busy signals. On receipt of the acknowledge signal an interface places its vector address on the data bus if it has a interrupt request outstanding; otherwise it passes the acknowledge signal to the next interface in the daisy chain. The interface obtains the vector address normally from switch setting made manually on the interface board. The installer has to ensure that the vector address set on the interface board corresponds to the vector address used by the software which uses the interface.

48.5 Direct memory access (DMA)

The CPU is used more efficiently under interrupt control than polling but the CPU is still involved in the transfer of each unit of data to and from peripheral devices. Direct memory access (DMA) interfaces allow the transfer of blocks of data between memory and a peripheral device without CPU intervention. A

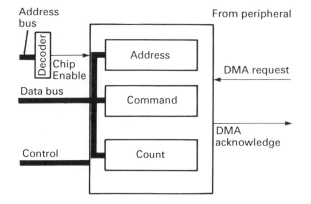

Figure 48.4 DMA interface

48.6 More intelligent interfacing

The continuing trend is for offloading more I/O processing from the central processor to specialized I/O processors. A DMA device is a simple I/O processor in that it only performs I/O transfers; the CPU still has to process the data transferred. More complex I/O schemes provide a more complex processor for the interface which has the task of performing some of the simpler I/O processing tasks such as editing and echoing data and also of multiplexing several I/O devices on to a single fast channel for interaction with the CPU. Using such interfaces the CPU is relieved of most of the task of input-output processing. Such a structure is shown in *Figure 48.5*. In this structure the I/O processor has the various types of interfaces attached to it and it is attached to the CPU by a specially designed fast interface.

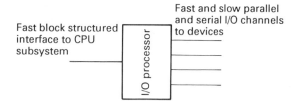

Figure 48.5 I/O subsystem arrangement with I/O processor

typical DMA interface is shown in *Figure 48.4*. The CPU initially sets up the transfer by setting the initial values of registers in the DMA interface to the number of items to be transferred, the starting address in memory from which the data is to be read or written and the type of transfer, read or write, which is to take place. The CPU starts the transfer by setting a bit in the DMA control register and the transfer of data takes place autonomously. The end of the transfer is signalled to the processor by an interrupt. This approach requires more intelligence, and hence more logic, in the DMA interface, thus making such interfaces more expensive.

In a single bus system the DMA controller and the CPU can both be bus masters and therefore contention can occur. A bus arbiter is used to resolve this contention. In simple systems, for example, most 8-bit microcomputers, the arbitration algorithm is to stop the CPU whenever the DMA interface requires use of the bus. This is accomplished by a signal input to the processor, often called HOLD, which causes the CPU to suspend operations when asserted. This solution is inefficient in terms of CPU usage and alternative methods are used for high performance systems. One method is to use a multiple bus architecture with dual-ported memory which allows two concurrent accesses to memory. Another, more common, solution is to use 'cycle stealing'. Here arbitration is performed on each bus cycle. The DMA interface 'steals' a bus cycle from the processor either when it needs it – the most common solution – or when it needs one and the processor does not. The gain in efficiency results from the lower level arbitration and from the fact that the CPU does not access the bus in every machine state of its instruction execution cycle.

48.5.1 Example of a DMA interface – the Motorola 68450

A DMA interface can be complicated especially when it has to be connected to a complex bus structure. The Motorola 68450 DMA controller is an example of such a complex device. It interfaces to a 68000 bus and has all the necessary control signals for data transfers, for example, when it is granted control of the bus it supplies control and timing for the transfer. It has four independent channels which can be connected to different peripheral devices. Each of the channels can be given a priority under program control which determines the order of service of DMA requests from the peripheral device. The maximum data transfer rate between memory and the peripheral device is 4 Mb/s. This DMA interface is expensive because of its complexity and a number of cheaper, simpler, devices have been produced, such as the Signetics SCB68430 (Clements, 1987).

48.6.1 Memory interface

Memory is the simplest component to add to a computer system. It may be added directly to the processor bus on the same printed circuit board as the processor or it may be added as a separate board connected to the processor via a backplane bus. There are many different types of memory which can be added to a computer system, for example, static memory, dynamic memory, RAM, ROM and bubble memory. Whilst each of these different types of memory will require a slightly different interface, for example, ROM does not require a read/write control line, the basic interfacing is the same. Most of the processor manufacturers produce memory circuits that are designed to work with the processor and therefore have a compatible interface. This means that the bus data lines can probably be directly connected to the memory as can the read/write control line. The only line which cannot be directly connected is the chip select line which controls when the chip is active. This line is controlled from a decoding of the address lines via full or partial decoding as explained above in the address mapping section. Memory is the simplest component to add to a computer system because it can often respond in a single bus cycle or, if not, it can respond relatively quickly and the processor can be made to wait via one of the schemes outlined in the bus section. This is not the case with peripheral devices which are often mechanical or dependent on human interaction and therefore truly asynchronous.

48.6.2 Types of peripheral interfaces

There are many different computer interfaces, some of which, like the ones described below, are general purpose and widely available from a range of manufacturers, and others which are individually designed to interface specialized equipment. Only the common, general purpose interfaces are described here, the reader is referred to Artwick (1980) and Stone (1982) for more details on interfacing and to Wilkinson and Horrocks (1980) for details of peripheral operation.

All computer interfaces require the input to conform to both electrical and protocol specifications. The electrical requirements may mean that a signal to or from a peripheral device has to be conditioned to make it acceptable. For example, many interfaces produce output and assume their input to be in the range 0–5 V, thus any input or output signals outside this range will need to be amplified or attenuated. Signals generated by mechanical means are often electrically noisy and have to be filtered before they can be input. Making a peripheral device conform to protocol requirements is more difficult and this is usually dealt with by writing specialized software device drivers.

48.6.3 Parallel interfaces

A parallel interface is the simplest type of interface which connects together the internal parallel control and data bus from the processor with the parallel control and data signals from the peripheral. The general structure conforms to that shown in Figure 48.1. No data manipulation is required in the interface, only synchronization control and status indication. Integrated circuit devices to perform this interfacing function are known as programmable peripheral interfaces (PPIs). The simpler ones consist of a single control and status register and two data registers, one for each direction. Because data transfer can take place in both directions, but not simultaneously, the interface has to be programmed so that it knows which direction is involved in the transfer at any time. Typically, this is performed by sending the appropriate bit pattern, indicating, for each data bit involved, whether it is to be in input or output state. The data transfer takes place by reading or writing to the appropriate data register in the interface. A bit in the status register indicates whether the appropriate data register is full or empty. One or more control bits are used to set up interrupts, for example, whether interrupts are to be edge-sensitive or level-sensitive and whether they are to be triggered by 0 or +5 V. Integrated circuits of this type vary considerably on the exact details of their control and status signals and the flexibility of their interrupt structure.

Parallel interfaces are used in computer systems because they are simple, but their use is limited to relatively short distances due to both cost and timing problems. For a parallel interface one wire is needed for each data bit and at least one wire for timing purposes, together with power lines. This leads to expensive cabling requirements because of size and because care must be taken to ensure that data signals do not interact. The timing problem arises since the data is travelling along different routes and will not take the same time to travel to and from the interface. Thus a timing reference has to be provided and the data rate is constrained by the difference in transmission times of the various signals. A further reason why these interfaces are not widely used is that there are few parallel standards. One notable standard is the IEEE 488 bus (IEEE, 1978), originally designed for connecting measuring instruments together.

48.6.3.1 Example parallel interface – the Motorola 6821

This parallel interface contains two bidirectional 8-bit buses which can be connected to peripheral devices and an 8-bit bus which can be connected to a computer bus. It contains two control registers, two data direction registers, two data registers, four lines for peripheral control and different drive characteristics on the two peripheral buses. The computer interface has been designed to be compatible with the Motorola 6800 bus although it is relatively easy to connect the interface to a Motorola 68000 system.

The control register determines whether interrupts are to be used and, if so, how they are to be configured. The data direction registers are programmed with 0s and 1s so that the corresponding bits in the associated data register are input or output, respectively. On input a voltage greater than 2.0 V is taken to be logic 1 and less than 0.8 V taken to be logic 0. Two of the peripheral control lines, called CA1 and CB1, are input-only and are used to set interrupt flags in the control registers. The other two peripheral control lines may be used as extra interrupt lines or as peripheral control outputs, for example, to provide handshake signals. Their function is controlled by the settings programmed into the control register. The two peripheral buses have different electrical characteristics so that they can be used to interface to different devices without extra interfacing.

48.6.4 Serial interface

This is the most common interface in computer systems since most terminals connected to computers use a serial interface although this is gradually changing to an interface to a local area network (LAN). A serial interface, shown in *Figure 48.6*,

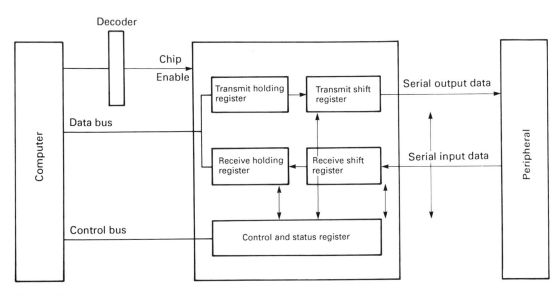

Figure 48.6 Serial interface

implies that the peripheral device sends and receives data as a sequence of bits. This type of interface was first used and standardized by the telecommunications industry and the standard is called CCITT V24. An almost identical one called RS232C was developed by the Electrical Industries Association (EIA) in the USA. These standards define all the characteristics of the transmission, such as the voltages representing each logic state, the ordering of bit transmission and the physical characteristics of the interface, such as the type of plugs and sockets which should be used. Details of the V24 standard are shown in *Figure 48.7* and *Table 48.2*. The data consists of a start bit, followed by up to 8 data bits and 1, 1 1/2 or 2 stop bits. There is a wide variation in the voltages allowed to represented logic 0 and 1 but a sufficient gap between them is required for noise suppression. The reason for the latitude in the number of stop bits is to accommodate devices, mainly mechanical, which require time to recover after transmitting or receiving a character. There have been a number of different codes used to represent characters as a sequence of binary digits although only one code is commonly used now; the ASCII code. This is a 7-bit code and is shown in *Table 48.3*. Since transmission often uses eight bits the eighth bit is sometimes used as a parity bit for error checking. Because there is such widespread use of this interface many manufacturers produce integrated circuits called universal asynchronous receiver/transmitters (UARTS) or universal synchronous/asynchronous receiver/transmitters (USARTS) conforming to these standards.

Serial data transmission requires a minimum of three connections for two-way communication; one signal wire for each direction and a reference. The V24 standard specifies 25 signals for data transmission as shown in *Table 48.4*. This is because this standard was designed for connection via modems and the extra signals are for the transmission of control and status signals between a transmitter/receiver and modem. For example, the RTS (request to send) signal is provided so that the transmitter can indicate to the receiver that it has data to send. The transmitter should not send the data until it receives CTS (clear to send). Direct connection between two devices, for example, processor and terminal does not require these additional modem signals. This has caused problems for computer

Table 48.3 The 7-bit ASCII code

decimal	code hex	character
0–31	0–1F	control codes
32	20	space
33	21	!
34	22	"
35	23	#
36	24	$
37	25	%
38	26	&
39	27	'
40	28	(
41	29	)
42	2A	*
43	2B	+
44	2C	,
45	2D	-
46	2E	.
47	2F	/
48–57	30–39	0 to 9
58	3A	:
59	3B	;
60	3C	<
61	3D	=
62	3E	>
63	3F	?
64	40	@
65–90	41–5A	capital A to Z
91	5B	[
92	5C	\
93	5D	]
94	5E	^
95	5F	—
96	60	`
97–122	61–7A	lower case a to z
123	7B	{
124	7C		
125	7D	}
126	7E	~
127	7F	DEL

manufacturers who do not always implement these additional signals which causes compatibility problems. Additionally, the use of a smaller number of signals allows the use of smaller, cheaper cables and connectors.

A problem with the use of this type of serial interface concerns the use of the terms computer and terminal and relates to the use of the two data transmission lines, receive and transmit. The transmit from one end of the communication must be connected to the receive line at the other and *vice versa*. Unfortunately, there are two ways of doing this which are incompatible. One method is to wire the interconnecting cable so that transmit is connected to receive in both directions. The other method is to internally wire the terminal so that the transmit pin on the socket is internally connected to the receive function. Thus to connect together two devices which act as computers requires a cable with transmit and receive crossed over whilst the interconnection of a computer with a terminal requires a straight through connection. Because no standard has emerged there appears to be little rationale about which method a manufacturer adopts. Trial-and-error is often required to interconnect devices over serial links.

There are two modes in which a serial interface can work: synchronous or asynchronous.

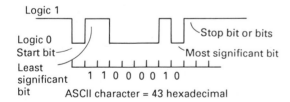

Figure 48.7 Example of the serial bit stream representing the letter 'C'

Table 48.2 Some details of the serial transmission standard

Characteristic	Standard
Representation	
logic 1	−3V to −25V
logic 2	+3V to +25V
Bit transmission order	Least significant bit first
Idle state	Logic 1
Connector	25-way D type connector
Cable length	100 ft (30.48 m) (max)

Table 48.4 CCITT V24 signal assignments on 25-pin connector

Pin	Assignment
1	Chassis ground
2	Transmitted data
3	Received data
4	Request to send (RTS)
5	Clear to send (CTS)
6	Data set ready (DSR)
7	Signal ground
8	Data carrier detect (DCD)
9	Reserved for national use
10	Reserved for national use
11	Select transmit frequency
12	Data carrier detect on backward channel
13	Clear to send on backward channel
14	Transmitted data on backward channel
15	Transmitted clock signal
16	Received data on backward channel
17	Received clock signal
18	Initiate local loopback
19	Request to send on backward channel
20	Data terminal ready
21	Initiate remote loopback
22	Ring indicator
23	Data rate selector
24	External transmitted data clock
25	Test indicator

In the asynchronous mode the receiver interface uses the leading edge of the start signal to trigger an internal clock which operates typically at 16 or 64 times the data transmission rate. This clock is used to sample the data approximately in the middle of each bit so that small variations in the frequency of the transmitter and receiver clocks have no effect on data receipt. The logic required to receive and transmit data is a shift register. Sometimes a second register is used to buffer data so that one piece of data may be transmitted as the next is being received. Input and output from the shift register takes place sequentially or in parallel depending on the direction of data transfer and whether the interface is to the computer bus or to the peripheral device. This type of protocol is called asynchronous since the start of the data can appear at arbitrary times.

In contrast to this synchronous protocols only allow data to be placed on the line at a time relative to a common clock. Thus once the initial connection has been made between transmitter and receiver their clocks are synchronized and data transmission is synchronized to the clocks. Asynchronous protocols are generally slower and more widely used than synchronous ones but they suffer from having an overhead of bits on each character to control the transfer, the start and stop bits in the V24 example. Synchronous protocols on the other hand group characters into blocks with control information at the beginning and end of blocks, thus obtaining better utilization of the transmission medium. Because of this use of blocks the transmitter and receiver have to contain more logic to retain state information and to extract a clock from the data and thus are more expensive. Another difference is in error detection and correction. In asynchronous protocols there is typically no error detection apart from the use of parity bit and correction involves the retransmission of the character. With synchronous protocols more complex error detection capabilities can be built in since these are performed on a per block basis. As explained in Chapter 53 forward error correction can be built into synchronous protocols.

48.6.5 Current loop interfaces

The serial data transmission referred to above, V24 or RS232C, is based on changes in voltage levels to encode binary 0 and 1 and this is by far the most common form of serial transmission. There is another form of serial transmission which is based on the presence or absence of current to encode binary 1 and 0. This type of interface is known as a current loop interface and originated in telephone equipment. The most common implementations of this type of interface use a 20 mA current source thus giving rise to the term '20 mA current loop interface'. A basic block diagram of this type of interface is shown in *Figure 48.8*. This type of serial interface can be used over much longer distances than RS232C since it does not pose the same electrical hazard; the isolation can be greater. It is also less susceptible to noise so has been used satisfactorily in electrically noisy environments such as factories. Recent developments in fibre optics make it likely that current loop interfaces will be replaced by fibre optics in the future.

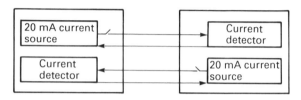

Figure 48.8 Basic bidirectional current loop interface

48.6.6 New standards

The V24 standard and the RS232C standard both contain problems for serial data communication directly without using modems. Both standards restrict the length of cable between the interconnected devices to 100 ft (30.48 m) or less and the maximum data transmission rate to 20 kHz. In fact most of the USARTs produced will allow communication over much longer distances without error but the standard does not guarantee this. Thus there was a need for new standard and three new standards were introduced, RS422, RS423 and RS449 (EIA standards).

RS449 specifies the mechanical connections of the new standard and uses a 37-pin rather than a 25-pin connector, although secondary 9-pin connectors can be used if the primary is a 37-pin one to keep down costs.

The new electrical standard is RS422. RS423 is a new standard which is designed to interface the old standard, RS232C, to the new RS422 standard and its electrical characteristics are virtually identical to RS232C. So far there has been little use of the new RS449 standard, probably because of the additional cost and space requirements of 37-way connectors. However, most manufacturers serial interfaces now conform to RS423 so connection to RS422 systems in the future should be possible.

48.6.6.1 An example serial interface – the Motorola 6850

Serial interfaces have been in existence as single integrated circuits for many years and they are now appearing with multiple interfaces on a single chip. These newer chips tend to be more complex because they multiplex several signals on to a single pin. The Motorola 6850 (Rafiquzzaman, 1984 p. 300) interface is an example of an older interface. The signals on the processor side of the interface are compatible with the Motorola

6800 processor bus to make connection to that processor simple. It is also relatively easy to connect this interface to a Motorola 68000-based system. The connections on the peripheral side are more complex as they correspond basically to the V24 standard. From a programming viewpoint, the device consists of an 8-bit control register, an 8-bit status register and an 8-bit data register. To transmit or receive characters via this interface the control register first has to be set to the required size. This involves deciding whether the transfer is to take place via polling or under interrupt control. The status register shows when one of a number of error conditions has occurred and also when a transfer, receive or transmit, is complete. The data register is either read from or written to depending whether the interface is acting as a transmitter or receiver or both. In fact, there are two sets of registers, one for transmission and the other for receipt. Which set is used depends on whether the program accesses the register with a read or a write operation.

If the programmer performs transfers using interrupts he has to poll the status register to determine whether a transmit or receive operation caused the interrupt since both operations cause an interrupt at the same priority level.

48.7 Analogue/digital converters

Inside a computer information is represented in digital form whilst in the outside world information is often represented in analogue form, for example, the position of a shaft or the voltage from a temperature sensor. Thus there is a need for an interface to convert between analogue and digital representations, and *vice versa*. These two types of interfaces are called analogue- to-digital converters (A/D) and digital-to-analogue converters (D/A).

The problem of translating between digital and analogue values becomes one of approximation, as shown in *Figure 48.11*. Digitizing an analogue value requires that the analogue value be quantized. The error in difference between the two signals then depends on the sampling frequency and the type of analogue waveform. The sampling of an analogue waveform is performed by a sample-and-hold circuit and the encoding to binary is performed by the A/D converter. To convert a digital signal to the corresponding analogue signal involves smoothing out the ramps. This conversion also involves approximations and the error produced depends on the intervals between the digital signals.

These types of interface are more expensive than the simple parallel or serial interfaces and the cost depends on the accuracy and speed required. There are several different types of interface available, depending on the tradeoff between speed, accuracy and price required. In general hardware for A/D conversion is more expensive than for D/A conversion.

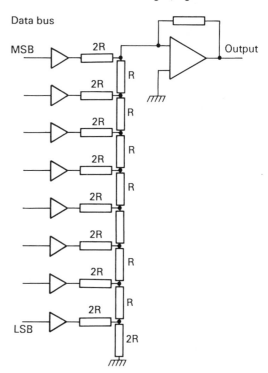

Figure 48.10 R-2R digital-to-analogue converter

48.7.1 Digital-to-analogue conversion

The most common forms of D/A converters use some form of resistor network to perform the transformation. This provides a fast and accurate method of conversion. One form of conversion uses a R/2R resistor network as shown in *Figure 48.10*. The output from the computer may be latched to provide a stable value for the conversion but it is also possible to provide a sample and hold circuit based on the charging of a capacitor which can reduce the amount of logic required and hence the cost.

48.7.2 Analogue-to-digital conversion

For analogue-to-digital conversion, care needs to be taken to condition the input from the transducer to the converter. Firstly, the converter will only accept input in a narrow, well-defined range and so the analogue signal has to be amplified or attenuated to be in this range. Second, raw analogue signals often contain noise due to the method they are generated. This noise has to be filtered out with a suitable filter before conversion.

Conversion can only be performed satisfactorily on a stable signal so a sample and hold circuit is used which often employs a switch and a capacitor charged by the analogue signal. For this sample and hold circuit to work satisfactorily components must be of high quality.

There are several different types of A/D converter. In the servo technique, shown in *Figure 48.11*, a D/A converter is employed and its input is driven from the computer which gradually increases the input value starting from the minimum. The output from the D/A converter is compared with the input analogue voltage in a comparator and the result fed back to the computer. When the output from the comparator signals that

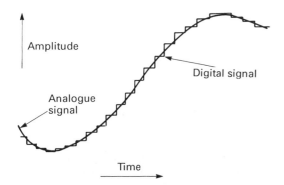

Figure 48.9 Difference between analogue and digital signals

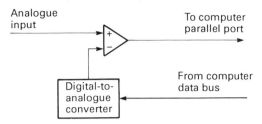

Analogue input

To computer parallel port

From computer data bus

Digital-to-analogue converter

Figure 48.11 Analogue-to-digital converter using the servo technique

the two signals are equal the computer knows that its present output value is the value of the analogue input. This method is simple and cheap but the conversion is relatively slow.

An improvement in this technique can be seen with the use of a better searching technique, such as binary search. This method is known as successive approximation.

A much faster technique is to use parallel conversion. In this scheme there is a separate comparator for each possible digital value. A reference source is used to generate the reference voltages for these comparators via a resistor network and the input analogue voltage is fanned out to all the comparators. The comparator which outputs the smallest difference represents the nearest digital value to the input analogue value. The problem with this technique is the cost since even an 8-bit converter requires 256 comparators.

48.8 Programming I/O devices

Programming devices at the device interface level is difficult to generalize since the different types of interface are significantly different and different manufacturers interfaces differ both in detail and in design philosophy. Hence this section only gives examples of general practice and the details do not apply to all interfaces. For more details on input-output programming see (Stone, 1982 (i)).

There are three main problems which occur in programming I/O interfaces:

1. Interfaces have to be serviced in real time, that is, the processing of I/O instructions has to be synchronized with the action of the peripheral device.
2. The use of interrupts implies concurrent processing which is acknowledged to be difficult to comprehend and debug.
3. The program, including the I/O processing, has to be insensitive to timing since the program cannot, in general, control the timing of operations in the peripheral environment.

There are two methods of controlling I/O interfaces: polling and interrupts. Wherever possible polling is to be preferred since the code is much easier to write, debug and comprehend. In real-time systems its use is often mandatory since the performance of the system, best and worst case, must be able to be computed from the program code and this is not possible for interrupt driven code. However, polling wastes some of the processor time and increases the response time to external events so some devices have to be controlled using interrupts.

Thus the design techniques for programming input-output systems is to divide the interfaces into two classes which can be polled and those which have to use interrupts.

48.8.1 Polling

Using polling the sequence of operations necessary to control an I/O device interface are:

1. *Initialization.* Initialize interface, e.g., set mode – input or output, number of data bits, etc.
2. *Interface use.* Move data to or from interface data register after checking status, if necessary.

48.8.1.1 Example

For the Motorola 6821 PPI described previously the code to control the device in output mode would be (in assembly code):

Initialization

```
clr.b   pacontrol           ; set port a control register for
                              direction register addressing
move.b  #$ff,padirection    ; set port a direction register
                              so all corresponding data
                              bits are in output mode
move.b  #4,pacontrol        ; set port a control for data
                              register addressing
```

Interface use

```
move.b  #data,padata        ; move required data to port
                              data register
```

48.8.2 Interrupts

The general strategy for interrupt processing is to perform as little processing as possible in the interrupt service routines – only the real-time constrained actions – and to perform the rest of the processing of the input or output data at a suitable time later, whenever the processor is free. Interrupt service routines should be made as transparent as possible so that the timing and ordering of interrupts does not matter to the programmer.

The structure of code to control a device using interrupts is:

1. *Initialization.*
   (a) Set up I/O port as necessary, e.g., direction, mode.
   (b) Set up vector address to point to interrupt service routine.
   (c) Enable interrupts – by setting processor priority or enable flag(s) or both.
2. *Interrupt service routine structure.*
   (a) Save status – any registers used by this routine.
   (b) Interrupt processing including any action to clear interrupt, for example.
   (c) Reading the appropriate data register.
   (d) Restore status.
   (d) Return from interrupt instruction.

This general structure will suffice for a multi-level structure. In some systems the priority of the processor is automatically set to the priority of the appropriate interrupt level when the corresponding interrupt service routine is entered, thus only allowing interrupts of higher priority to interrupt that interrupt service routine.

For systems with multiple devices on the same interrupt priority level code it is necessary in the interrupt service routine to poll the device status registers to determine which device caused the interrupt and hence which interrupt service routine needs to be executed.

Interrupts should always be controlled by the use of selective enabling so that they are only enabled when the rest of the program being executed is willing to accept the input or has data to output. Failure to observe this procedure with output interrupts can lead to the processor being continually interrupted by a ready peripheral when it has no output to deliver, thus inhibiting the execution of real work.

48.8.2.1 *Example*

As an example of interrupt processing consider the following fragment of C program which controls the direction of rotation of a stepper motor, reversing it on detection of a key depression which causes an interrupt at priority 4 from a parallel port. The key is attached to the interrupt input of a Motorola 6821 PPI.

Note: the functions DoRTEIns, SetIVec and SetIntLevel are assumed to be in an I/O library. Although most of these can be written in C it is more usual to code them in assembler in a library accessible from C.

Interrupt handler
```
keyhandler()
{dir = dir;          /* change sign of direction flag*/
DoRTEIns();          /* do a return from interrupt via a local
                        library function*/

}
```

Initialization
```
*portbcontrol = 0;   /* set parallel port b control to
                        direction register */
*portdirection = 0;  /* set direction to input */
*portcontrol = 4;    /* set control reg. to data
                        register */
dir = 1;             /* set initial value for direction
                        flag */
SetIVec(4,&keyhandler)  /* load interrupt vector at
                        priority 4 with pointer to
                        keyhandler function */
SetIntLevel(0);      /* set processor priority to
                        zero to allow all interrupts */
```

code to control the stepper motor using dir to control the direction of rotation

48.8.3 Higher level I/O control

One of the structures which can be used successfully to co-ordinate the activities of concurrent processes is the co-routine. In this structure instead of the master–slave relationship associated with a calling routine and the called routine in sequential programming, a peer–peer relationship exists between the two entities. The flow of control between two co-routines is shown in *Figure 48.12*. Initially one of the routines starts execution and proceeds until it calls its co-routine. This routine then proceeds until it reaches a resume for the original routine. The original routine then restarts execution immediately after the first call and this action alternates between the two co-routines. This co-routine structure is typical of many applications where two

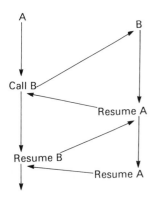

Figure 48.12 Co-routine structure

routines act as producer and consumer. The co-routine structure can be successfully used both in polling and an interrupt environment.

Alternative high-level structures are based on a main process which performs the main processing tasks, including any device polling I/O, with separate transparent interrupt drivers for time critical I/O. The interrupt handlers are decoupled from the main processing routine by the use of a queue of buffers for data transfer, since the exact time and rate of data production or consumption by the peripheral cannot be determined in advance.

48.9 Summary and conclusions

Although the task of interfacing a peripheral device to a computer appears to be simple, there are a number of problems which occur which complicate the task:

1. The computer and peripheral device are asynchronous and have to be synchronized for data transfer to take place. Simple synchronization techniques such as software polling are inefficient and more efficient techniques, such as the use of interrupts and direct memory access, have had to be developed.
2. The lack of standards for interfacing has meant that many manufacturers have developed their own standards and this has caused many problems in interconnecting equipment from different manufacturers.
3. The use of multiple masters on single-bus systems implies that arbitration is necessary to resolve any conflicts on the use of the bus. The need for arbitration circuitry increases the complexity, and hence the cost, of interfaces and computer buses.
4. I/O processing can consume a significant amount of processor time in a system with simple peripheral interfaces. To reduce central processor involvement in I/O tasks interfaces have been made more intelligent, that is, given some processing ability.
5. The most common types of interface are parallel and serial interfaces. Although serial interfaces are slower they have been used frequently because of their lower cabling cost and standardization. Parallel interfaces are faster, but there are few standards so these interfaces tend to be specific to one manufacturers products.
6. The main problems in programming I/O interfaces are the need for real-time programs, concurrent processing of many devices and the need to make the processing programs insensitive to time. All of these tasks are very difficult to solve for the general case and thus I/O programming is very error prone. Additionally, I/O programs are difficult to debug.

Because of these problems I/O interfacing, both software and hardware, is complicated and calls for great care and experience. The quest for ever greater speed and efficiency in I/O means that the task is becoming more complicated.

Looking to the future, there seems to be little change in the nature of interfacing. It will continue the trend set some time ago – interfaces will become more intelligent, more transfers will be performed without direct intervention of the CPU and devices will become faster. The main problem with computer systems at present is that it is both expensive and difficult to produce a system where the I/O subsystem can keep up with the speed required by the CPU. This is likely to get worse with time as the speed of electronic devices is increasing much faster than mechanical devices, thus the speed of the CPU will increase much faster than many peripherals.

To speed up the I/O device a number of techniques are used. The first is buffering. By placing a large amount of buffering –

caches are one form – in the path between the peripheral device and the CPU it is possible to smooth out the rate of requests for I/O, either by pre-fetching input or delaying output until the device is ready. This technique cannot speed up the transfer rate, but it can smooth out the requests to make the best use of the available transfer rate.

A second technique which is now coming back into fashion is not to use a single-bus system but to use multiple buses, some for instructions and some for data. This overcomes the problem of sequential access to a single-bus system. Another similar technique is to couple directly an I/O device directly to a processor rather than going via a bus, with its inherent arbitration overheads and delay. Both these schemes are attempts to reduce the transmission delay between the CPU and the peripheral.

In summary, the trend for interfaces seems to be evolutionary rather than revolutionary. Thus interfaces will become more intelligent, faster and include larger data buffers. The trend is likely to be for more dedicated routes from peripheral to processor, rather than use of a common shared bus as processor become faster and clock speeds increase. Speeds of peripherals are unlikely to increase very much since many contain mechanical parts whose action cannot easily be speeded up.

48.10 References

Artwick, B. A. (1980) *Microcomputer Interfacing*, Prentice-Hall, Englewood Cliffs

Borrill, P. L. (1981) Microprocessor bus structures and standards. *IEEE Micro*, **1**, 84–95

CCITT (1976) *Orange Book, CCITT Sixth Plenary Assembly, Volume VIII.1 Data Transmission over the Telephone Network*, International Telecommunications Union, Geneva, Switzerland

Clements, A. (1987) *Microprocessor System Design: 68000 Hardware, Software and Interfacing*, PWS, Boston

Electronic Industries Association, *EIA Standards, RS Series*, Engineering Department, 2001 Eye Street, Washington DC, 20006, USA

Gorsline, G. W. (1986) *Computer Organisation: Hardware/Software*, Prentice-Hall, Englewood Cliffs

IEEE 488:1978 Standard digital interface for programmable instrumentation, IEEE, USA

IEEE 896.1:1989 Futurebus: a backplane bus specification for multiprocessor architectures, IEEE, USA

IEEE 1196:1989 Nubus: a simple 32-bit backplane bus, IEEE, USA

IEEE 1014:1989 VMEbus, IEEE, USA

IEEE 1296:1989 Multibus, IEEE, USA

Lesea, A. and Zaks, R. (1977) *Microprocessor Interfacing Techniques*, Sybex, Berkeley

Lipovski, G. J. (1980) *Microprocessor Interfacing*, D. C. Heath, Lexington, MA

Miller, M. A. (1988) *The 68000 Microprocessor*, Merrill, Columbus

Motorola (1981) *Motorola 6821 product information sheet*, Motorola Semiconductors, Austin, Texas

Peatman, J. B. (1977) *Microcomputer-based Design*, McGraw-Hill Kogakusha, Tokyo

Rafiquzzaman,M. (1984) *Microprocessors and Micro-computer Development Systems*, Harper and Row, New York

Smolin, M. (1988) IEEE 32-bit backplane bus comparisons. *IEEE Micro*, **8**, 5–7

Stallings, W. (1987) *Computer Organisation and Architecture*, Macmillan, New York

Stone, H. S. (1982) *Microcomputer Interfacing*, Addison-Wesley, Reading, (i) Chapter 9

Tanenbaum, A. S. (1984) *Structured Computer Organisation*, Prentice-Hall, Englewood Cliffs

Wilkinson, B. and Horrocks, D. (1980) *Computer Peripherals*, Hodder and Stoughton, London

49

Operating systems

Laurie S. Keller
The Open University

Contents

49.1 Introduction

An operating system is the software which intervenes, at the lowest level, between the hardware of the machine itself, its peripherals, any applications software, possibly sensors and actuators in the 'real' world and, of course, the 'user'. The 'user' means primarily the software engineer, the programmer, systems programmer or systems manager, but *not* the end user, who often perceives only the 'system' presented by an application. The operating system acts as an intermediary between the requirements of the hardware and the needs of the programmer. It removes from the programmer the need to be concerned with the low-level details of data transfer from main memory to a secondary storage device – and it coordinates the disparate elements of the machine's operating environment, acting as a scheduler of work, an arbiter (on multi-user systems) between the conflicting demands and needs of users and a protector, ensuring that one process cannot corrupt another.

In addition, the operating system presents most users with some kind of interface (unless a more indirect interface is provided for an end user solely by an application program, as is often the case, for example, in form-filling programs for data entry purposes) usually called the command interface, in the form of a set of commands or menu-choices. The command interface in turn arbitrates between the user and a series of general-purpose utility programs (which provide simple, basic services such as a file maintenance, printing services and so on) and those applications programs which can be invoked by the command interface. The command interface which the operating system presents the user gives that user a virtual model of the machine he or she is using. For this reason, dissimilar machines with similar or the same operating system present the user with nearly identical virtual machines. *Figure 49.1* outlines the structure of an operating system.

Of course, hardware is a significant influence on an operating system. For example, if the hardware supports paging structures (see below) then an operating system can use paging to provide a virtual memory (where the size of an application is limited by the structure of the address rather than by the real size of a machine's main memory) for an application or other process. However, if the hardware on which a system will run does not support paging, then the operating system must use some other form of main memory management and cannot provide a virtual memory. Unix 4.3BSD and System V provide an example of this: the operating system provides paging where the hardware has the necessary supporting structures. Direct memory access (DMA) is a hardware facility allowing two or more processors access to the same memory and allows the use of, for example, channels (input/output processors) in conjunction with a main processor. The operating system exploits this in the way it carries out input and output operations. Buffers combined with asynchronous input/output (I/O) – where I/O is carried out by a channel processor and the main processor can be switched to other tasks while the I/O operation is carried out independently – require the use of DMA hardware structures. If these are not present, I/O must be synchronous, that is, the processor must wait for I/O to complete before continuing.

At present, there are three major categories of general-purpose operating system. They are: the simple, single-user operating system, such as is available on micro- and personal computers; the multiprogramming operating system which supports several users simultaneously or allows a single user to run several processes simultaneously, or both, on a single processor; and the multiprocessing, network or distributed operating system. All of the last group are distinct types, but all have features in common in that they allow several processors to cooperate to some degree in providing the user with a service. In addition, there exist special-purpose operating systems particularly designed for critical or high-performance applications such as real-time or transaction processing work. These are often referred to as real-time executives. This text will concentrate on the three major categories of general-purpose operating system.

All operating systems are the result of compromises made by the operating system designer among:

1. The capabilities of the underlying hardware, the needs and demands of the users, where not all classes of user may be in agreement as to what is needed.
2. Mutually exclusive choices among methods and techniques, for example, choosing a particular scheduling technique may make it impossible to do real-time processing.
3. Stringencies of resources – time and money.
4. Marketing considerations such as eventual cost or complexity of the product.

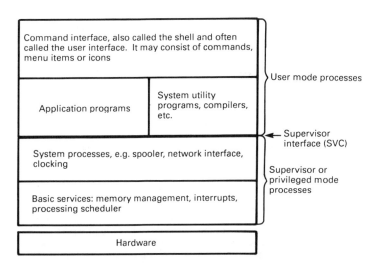

Figure 49.1 A diagrammatic representation of an operating system's architecture, showing the relationship of the command interface, system utility programs, system services and basic services. Application programs are not part of the operating system, but can be invoked by commands in the command interface (or invoked directly when an end user logs on to the system)

For example, choosing to use a round-robin scheduler, where each process is given a discrete time interval in turn in which to use the processor, is suitable for a time-sharing system but cannot be used for a system which must support real-time applications. As a result, no one operating system is suitable for every possible application and one of the choices to be made in designing an application system may be the choice of an operating system.

One can posit broad categories of application: real-time, transaction processing, interactive systems and batch systems. These range from those which are driven by external events (real-time, including networking, and transaction processing) through those which must give precedence to fairness of treatment for all users (interactive multi-user systems) to those which require little or no human intervention but are characterized by a very high volume of repetitive processing work (such as occurs in the preparation of periodic accountancy reports). The requirements of the particular classes of application which dominate may thus dictate the choice of operating system. Many operating systems *can* accommodate more than one type of application, but the application with the most stringent requirements must be given precedence. For example, the Digital Equipment operating system IAS is designed around the provision of real-time services, but time not used for providing such services is available on a lower priority to interactive (or on the lowest priority, to batch) processing applications. On the other hand, Unix is designed for interactive computing use and is wholly unsuitable for real-time applications without considerable modification.

This chapter addresses two objectives: explaining how an operating system works, in fairly general terms, and the significance of different operating system 'styles', explaining how to use an operating system from the point of view of the software engineer and programmer.

Three major classes of operating system are considered in turn. First are the simple, single-user operating systems of the sort popular with personal computers, comparing Digital Research's CP/M, Microsoft's MS-DOS, IBM's PC-DOS and occasionally the UCSD p-System to see how different operating systems designs resulted from a common hardware base. In each case the major parts of an operating system, e.g. memory management and disc and file organization and management, are described. Next, multiprogramming operating systems are looked at, which of necessity are more complex than simple systems, and again the major parts (memory management, storage and file organization and management, process management), three well-known multiprogramming operating systems are reviewed. Unix, VMS, and MVS, are compared. Finally, multiprocessing and distributed systems are reviewed, with examples drawn from MVS (which can also be a multiprocessing system) and a multiprocessing adaptation of Unix. Lastly, the ways the programmer can access operating system services are discussed. The chapter ends with a bibliography and references.

49.2 Simple, single-user operating systems

Originally, all operating systems were single-user and simple. Computers were 'shared' serially by means of booking a unit of time such as an hour and having exclusive use of the machine for that hour. This type of system has returned to prominence with the advent of the micro- and personal computer, although many of these systems have been extended somewhat to allow some degree of multiprogramming (explained below). Popular single-user systems today are CP/M, MS-DOS and PC-DOS. CP/M is primarily known as an eight-bit architecture operating system,

though it has a 16-bit counterpart, CP/M-86. MS-DOS and PC-DOS are very similar systems designed for use on IBM PCs (in the case of PC-DOS) and compatibles (MS-DOS).

Such systems resemble each other in that they all are based on the same fundamental assumptions:

1. That the user 'owns' – or at least has the lion's share of use of – the machine.
2. That shared data is a matter for private arrangements between users.
3. That since only one user at a time will be using the machine, there is no question of having to provide elaborate scheduling facilities or to ensure fairness.

There is also no question of providing real-time services, which is not to say that small machines of this type have not been put to use in real-time applications. There is some need to provide a small amount of multiprogramming, for example, to allow the user to run one application while printing the output from another. Services provided by the operating system for the user are very basic: the operating system manages main memory, provides input and output services to limited numbers and classes of devices such as printer, disc and modem; it manages space on secondary storage media such as discs and provides simple file-handling capabilities (renaming, copying, deleting); it provides for the loading and the start of execution for applications. This last can be organized such that the start of an application is an automatic end to the system's start-up procedures. For example, a PC used by a secretary can automatically be put into a word processing application at the end of system start-up. The operating system usually also provides some form of spooling program so that printing can be carried out without locking the user out of the system.

All other services are generally left to specific applications which the user can purchase or design and develop him- or herself. As a result, most such operating systems are fundamentally similar. All of those mentioned provide a command-based interface to the user: the user types in a short command on the keyboard in order to initiate a response. A few other systems have different interfaces: the UCSD p-System proves a hierarchically arranged menu system where commands are invoked by typing a single letter as shown in a menu; the Apple Macintosh uses a WIMPS interface (windows, icons, mouse, pointer or pull-down menu systems) in which the user is presented with a window – a virtual screen on a visual display unit – which contains icons – pictorial representations of commands and objects such as discs and files – to which the user points by using a mouse.

49.2.1 Memory management in simple systems

One of the primary concerns of an operating system is the management of main memory, which is a limited resource even in single-user simple systems. There are two basic problems to be solved in the management of memory. A primary concern is the protection of different parts of a process (a running program) from each other, the protection of the fundamental parts of the operating system itself (lest the machine be disabled) and the protection of the data in main memory in some measure from inadvertent destruction. (The system generally cannot protect data from a user's stupidity, but it can protect, for example, the program code from being overwritten by data and *vice versa*.) A secondary concern is the loading of program code and data for execution. Given that such systems are very simple, memory management is correspondingly simple.

The operating system of most such systems generally consists of two parts: the essential part which must be resident in order for the system to continue to function, and a 'transient' part which resides in memory only when the operating system is first loaded or when one of the transient functions is invoked by the user. In *Figure 49.2*, certain parts of the command interface and the system processes and basic services must be resident and protected, while less commonly invoked commands, application and utility programs and some of the less frequently used system functions can be transient, and invoked as required and over-written when necessary. At any time, any space in memory occupied by a transient function can be overwritten, that is, used by something else such as a user's data file or an application program. In the case of CP/M, the operating system must be partially reloaded when its transient area has been overwritten. Other systems leave such transient functions to be reinvoked explicitly by the user when he or she issues a transient command or invokes an application program or utility.

The most fundamental parts of the essential portion of these small operating systems are the bootstrap, which is usually in hardware or in firmware in read-only memory (ROM), though parts of a bootstrap program may be software; basic system routines such as memory management; the input/output (I/O) subsystem; and the command interpreter.

The input/output subsystem is normally divided into two parts: one is concerned with character input and output such as keyboard input, screen output and print output, and the other is concerned with devices which handle data in larger blocks – usually discs. The first may be called the basic I/O (sub)system or BIOS, as it is in CP/M. (In other systems, BIOS normally refers to *all* types of I/O.) In either case, a BIOS is machine-dependent; that is, the code must be written afresh for each make and model of machine and is not portable to a dissimilar machine. The second part is called the basic disc operating system (BDOS) in CP/M, where the BIOS and BDOS together are called the fundamental disc operating system (FDOS).

The function of the character-based slow-device BIOS or its analogue is to carry out basic input and output operations to and from slow devices such as keyboards, the character-based screen (although bit-mapped screens are different), and printers or devices made to appear to the system as printers. This is accomplished by the use of printer, serial transmission line, keyboard and screen primitives, special character handling routines, and a small type-ahead buffer or queue on which individual input characters are assembled until they form a meaningful unit (e.g. a command terminated by a carriage-return). The function of the disc management portions of the operating system is to map logical units of data to the cylinder, track and record units of the disc using disc primitives.

The command interface, which is called the console command processor in CP/M, is also an essential part of a small operating system. Without it the system is disabled as it cannot interpret commands and carry out the appropriate actions.

Some commands themselves may also be essential. Generally these are the simple and basic commands which allow the user to access data in files or load application programs or transient commands. Commands which are essential are often called built-in (CP/M) or internal (MS-DOS and PC-DOS). Commands which are not essential, and therefore need not be resident permanently in memory, are called transient or external and are treated differently by memory management routines. Although the 'map' of memory for systems may differ, the philosophy of protecting the essential parts of the operating system from inadvertent over-writing means that these are typically stored in such a way that they are either below (at lower addresses) than the more volatile transient area where applications appear, or they are separated from the transient area by less essential parts of the operating system. Figure 49.2 shows memory use by three such systems.

From the programmer or software engineer's point of view, it is possible to use all of the transient program area (TPA) for an application, though an application can 'steal' space from the console command processor (CCP) in CP/M or from the transient parts of DOS or the transient commands in either of the two DOS systems before a crisis is reached which will cause a system error.

When loading the operating system, most systems, including small systems, begin with a firmware bootstrap which loads a small portion of software which in turn loads further software until all the operating system – or all essential parts of it – are resident. This process usually begins at the lowest address, loading 'upwards', then moves to the highest possible address and loads 'downwards', leaving the portion in between free for applications. When the user invokes an application, the operating system then loads this from the lowest available address above the lower essential parts of the operating system and loads 'upwards' until the application is loaded. Any data files then invoked will be copied in portions into the remaining parts of the transient area above the application program. Data in such buffers may be copied to disc as necessary when more room

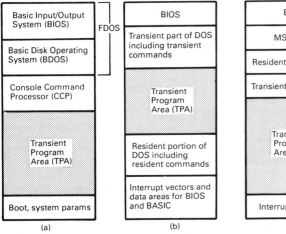
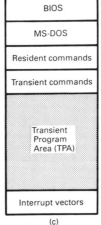

Figure 49.2 Memory maps of small single-user operating systems: (a) CP/M; (b) PC-DOS; (c) MS-DOS. These vary in reality according to hardware factors such as main memory size. The low addresses are shown at the bottom. Applications program (transient) areas are shaded. No scale is implied

is needed for further data in main memory. Such buffer copying is done, not to the original file, but to a temporary work area on disc. It is only when the user signals that the file is to be written, usually by means of a save or quit (with save) command, that the file on disc is written (or overwritten, as the case may be). Thus, space on disc acts as a temporary extension where necessary of main memory. Note that this should not be confused with paging; see below.

49.2.2 Disc and file organization and management

The second major function of a small operating system is to manage disc space and file organization on behalf of the user. Small systems make the assumption that the system user is the owner of the discs and files and has control over who accesses them. Thus, disc and file management is not concerned with identifying ownership nor with protecting data from unauthorized access. This makes such systems very simple, but vulnerable to accident, unauthorized access and malicious mischief.

Disc management is concerned with two things: the identification of free space and the identification of user and system files. At a lower level, this means that space on a disc must be mapped in some way, and the map must be able to identify free space and to indicate where to find the data in named files.

Files are identified by means of a form of record called a file control block (FCB). This will contain, at the minimum, the name of the file and a pointer to the location of the file on disc. File control blocks are concentrated together at a known location on the disc called a file directory. In most systems the disc's primary file directory resides on, say, tracks 1 and 2 of each disc. An entry in this directory may point to a file which is itself a directory, thus achieving an hierarchical arrangement of directories and data files. The FCB entry may, in addition, contain other data useful for the control of files; it may contain the date the file was last accessed or changed, the size of the file and the type of the file. A command to show the contents of a directory will generally display this data, with variations which the user can invoke by means of parameters to the command.

49.2.2.1 CP/M's disc and file management

CP/M's techniques of disc and file management allow data for a single file to be scattered throughout the area of a disc in set-sized sectors. As sectors are assigned to a file, their location is noted in a part of the FCB called the disc allocation map. If a file contains more sectors than can be noted in a single file control block's disc allocation map, the file is allocated more than one FCB. Each disc, in addition, contains an allocation bit map, which records, for each group of eight contiguous sectors (called a cluster) whether that cluster is used or is free space. It does this by having one bit for each cluster; a 1 indicates that the space is used and a 0 indicates that the cluster is free.

When a disc is accessed for the first time in a session, its allocation bit map is copied to main memory. When a file is accessed by means of an 'open', an FCB in main memory is allocated, with the name specified by the user in the command compared with the names in the FCBs in the directory. If a match occurs, the information in the disc's FCB is also copied to main memory. For a new file, the FCB is initialized in the disc's directory. A 'close' operation causes the new information in the main memory FCB to be copied to the disc's corresponding FCB.

When space is allocated or freed, the corresponding bit in the bit allocation map is set and both the main memory and disc copies are kept in step, since the user may remove a disc at any time. When a file needs new space, BDOS searches the bit allocation map to find a free cluster, which is then allocated to the file, with corresponding changes to the bit allocation maps and the main memory copy of the FCB made at the time.

49.2.2.2 MS-DOS and PC-DOS

MS-DOS and PC-DOS use a different technique. Disc space is divided into sectors, and four contiguous sectors are grouped into an allocation unit (AU), as it is called by MS–DOS, or a cluster, as it is called by PC-DOS. Space on the disc is recorded in a file allocation table (FAT). Each FAT entry contains 12 bits. If all bits are set to zero, the AU/cluster is free space. Otherwise, the bits represent either a pointer to another AU/cluster in the list, or, if all bits are set to ones, this indicates that this AU/cluster is the last one in a file. Files are named in FCBs in a directory. This entry contains the file name, an attribute indicator (system or user), the time and date of last update, the number of the first AU/cluster in that file, and the size of the file. To access a file, the FCB is read, the pointer to the first AU/cluster of the file is used to point to the correct entry in the FAT, and that entry in turn points to the next AU/cluster allocated to that file, and so on to the last one. Notice that the FAT does not contain data, merely the address of the next AU/cluster of data. There is a further step required, which is to map the AU/cluster number in the FAT to a real AU/cluster on the disc itself. This technique is known as block-oriented file mapping and is shown in *Figure 49.3*.

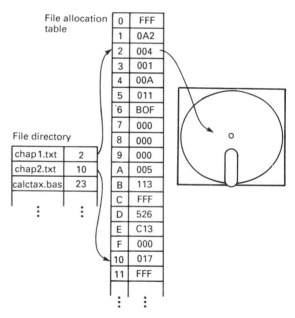

Figure 49.3 Block-oriented file mapping in MS-DOS and PC-DOS. Note that the file 'chap 1.txt' shown in the file directory begins at AU/cluster 2, that the FAT entry at 2 points to the next portion of the file (004) and the file continues from there to 00A, then 005 and ends at 011

Note that direct access to data on any AU/cluster at random requires that the data's position relative to the beginning of the file be known, that the ordinal AU/cluster *within* the file can be determined and that chain of pointers in the file allocation table be followed to find the correct AU/cluster. Only then can the mapping between the AU/cluster number and the actual AU/cluster on disc be made and the data accessed.

49.2.2.3 The p-System

The p-System uses a third strategy, whereby files are stored in contiguous sectors. To find sufficient space for a file, the system looks for the largest available empty space and uses it (the worst fit algorithm). The space for a file is allocated at once when the file is saved, rather than as the file grows. As old files are deleted, areas of free space result into which new – and probably smaller – files will be put and subsequently deleted; the process may eventually clutter the disc with such small free areas that no usable free space remains. It is then incumbent on the user to compact space on the disc. This process groups all files together and all free space together, leaving one large chunk of empty space. Then the process of filling the newly consolidated space with new or growing files begins anew. Thus, when an existing file is changed and grows as a result, it must be allocated new space and the old space it occupied before it 'grew' becomes one of the fragments of free space. The especial advantages of contiguous allocation are the speed with which the file can be accessed, and the ease with which any data can be located directly if its position relative to the beginning of the file is known. The disadvantages are fragmentation resulting from deletions and re-allocations and the consequent need for user intervention to maintain an ample pool of contiguous free space.

49.2.3 Summary and conclusions

The operating system of most simple systems consists of two parts: an essential part which must be resident in order for the system to continue to function, and a 'transient' part which resides in memory only when the operating system is first loaded or when one of the transient functions is invoked by the user. Small operating systems also have three functions: provision of a command interface, the management of main memory and the management of disc space and files. CP/M, MS-DOS and PC-DOS differ in the details of the way in which they manage main memory, but not in their philosophies. The other important function of a simple operating system is the management of disc space and files. Here the three differ more significantly, with CP/M using an allocation bit map to map space on the disc and assign it, and MS- and PC-DOS using four contiguous sectors grouped into an AU or a cluster. Space on the disc is recorded in a FAT. Each FAT entry contains 12 bits. If all bits are set to zero, the AU/cluster is free space. Otherwise the bits represent either a pointer to another AU/cluster in the list, or, if all bits are set to ones, this indicates that this AU/cluster is the last one in a file. The p-System uses a third strategy, whereby files are stored in contiguous sectors. To find sufficient space for a file, the system looks for the largest available empty space and uses it. The space for a file is allocated at once when the file is saved, rather than as the file grows. This necessitates periodic reorganization to recover fragmented space.

From the point of view of the system developer, one is most likely to encounter MS-DOS and PC-DOS systems in the field. CP/M, while not dissimilar, is not as popular a commercial system as these two. The UCSD p-System is largely confined to universities and program development environments where the programs will eventually be 'ported' to dissimilar systems in source language form. In fact, now that there are several good Pascal compilers available for MS- and PC-DOS systems, most Pascal program development is carried out without the intervention of the p-System. For those developing systems to be used on personal computers by 'naive' users, the drawback to the first three systems is the command interface, which is primitive and clumsy and requires some training to use effectively. (However, an application can be provided with its own interface designed according to the principles of HCI, and can be invoked directly at the end of system start-up.) There is a wide range of tools available for both MS- and PC-DOS systems in the form of window and task management, menu interface, compilers, word processors and so on. Fewer such are available for CP/M systems, and very few are available for the p-System.

49.3 Multiprogramming operating systems

For most people who have used any shared computer environment, the multiprogramming operating system will be the most familiar of the three classifications given here. Such systems are available on everything from quite small machines (such as the larger PCs), through the popular and widely available minicomputers to the very large mainframe. The philosophies on which such systems are based, however, vary widely and the various examples show greater diversity than is true of small, single-user operating systems. Three will be considered in some detail: Unix, Digital Equipment's VMS, and IBM's MVS.

Multiprogramming systems make the following assumptions:

1. More than one process will be resident in memory at one time.
2. Each resident process will require some attention from the processor (i.e. the processor itself becomes a resource which the operating system must manage).
3. Simultaneously resident processes will *appear* to execute concurrently.

This means that the operating system must mediate between active processes in the matter of allocating main memory and allocating processor time, and that the latter must be done in a way which guarantees that all processes resident and capable of running share the processor temporally in a reasonably fair way. In addition, most multiprogramming systems are also designed for use by multiple users simultaneously, so that:

1. A process is associated with an owner.
2. Data (in files) has designated owners or authorized users and those owners or users must be able to control access by other users to that data.
3. Users simultaneously 'logged on' must receive service in a way which suggests to each that he or she has control of his or her own virtual machine.

In practice, most systems of this type today are time-sharing or interactive systems, which additionally means that fairness among simultaneous users must also be guaranteed. Additionally, the job of preventing one process from interfering with another becomes much more complex.

49.3.1 Memory management in multiprogramming systems

The problem of protecting the operating system and applications programs also exists in multiprogramming systems, although it becomes more important to guarantee the integrity of the system, because error by one user cannot be allowed to deny service to others. Conceptually, portions of the operating system are usually loaded beginning at the lowest possible address and loaded 'upwards'; these usually constitute the most essential parts of an operating system. The more 'public' services and areas within a multiprogrammed operating system are then usually loaded from the highest address 'downwards'. Examples of such public services are some I/O routines and shared buffers. The area between then becomes available for loading applications and user time-sharing session areas.

In practice, a scarce resource has always been space in main memory. While the scarcity can be relieved partly by adding more memory, as is often the case in microcomputers, there is a ceiling which is imposed by the addressing structure of the hardware – the size of the address registers or sometimes the physical construction of the machine – on how much can easily be added. Most present-day multiprogramming operating systems relieve the scarcity by means of using a high-speed medium such as a drum or fixed-head disc as an extension of main memory. Systems using such approaches are often referred to as paging or virtual memory systems.

'The key to the virtual storage concept is disassociating the addresses referenced in a running process from the addresses available in primary storage [main memory]' (Deitel, 1984). It has long been a practice to disassociate the addresses of an executable (object) program from real addresses by making a program relocatable. This is done by making all address references within a program relative to the start of the program (i.e. the 125th byte or word of a program has a displacement from the start of the program – byte or word zero – of 124), assigning a real address to the start of the program when the program is loaded for execution, and calculating all address references within the process as the starting address plus the displacement. The concept of virtual storage further disassociates addresses from the constraints of real addresses by interposing an additional layer or two of indirection in address translation, as described below.

Observations have shown that programs exhibit a property called locality, that is, frequent reference to the same or closely adjacent instructions such as sequential code execution, the placement of related variables near one another and traversal of arrays (spatial locality) or within a short period of time such as occurs in loops, subroutines, stacks and certain types of variables which are near one another (temporal locality). From these observations developed the theory of a working set of pages (Denning, 1968), which says that any program can be divided into sub-units and some number of sub-units will be referenced repeatedly in such a way that only that group of sub-units will be active and, without seriously affecting efficiency, other sub-units need not be resident in main memory. The sub-units are generally called pages and are small (e.g. 4K), but units of other sizes can be used. It is even possible to use two (or more) different sizes of unit simultaneously, as will be shown. *Figure 49.4* shows a simple scheme for using one level of indirection (pages) in addressing to allow disassociation of one part of a program from another without disturbing the apparent or virtual sequence of addresses.

Figure 49.4 A simple address translation

The practical effect of locality means that only the working sets of active processes need be in memory simultaneously, and memory can be managed as simple, small units allocated to and recovered from active processes as required. In an example of a common memory management scheme, a program is divided into fixed-size sub-units of 4K each, called pages and that these pages are numbered sequentially from zero. It does not matter that pages be in nor that they be adjacent in main memory, so this scheme is called virtual addressing. Any address within a program is thus a virtual address that must be translated to a real address – either on disc or in main memory as described below – by some translation process which maps virtual addresses to real addresses. Further, physical (real) memory itself is also divided into 4K units called page frames, and that an auxiliary medium such as a high-speed fixed-head disc has its space divided into 4K units called page slots. When a program is loaded, all of it is loaded into page frames in memory, and those pages not referenced are gradually marked as 'not needed'. As the operating system requires more space it copies marked pages out to page slots on the disc. When any page not currently in

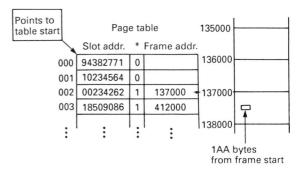

Page table origin register

Figure 49.5 A mapping arrangement for paged memory management. Note that the page number of the page is a number relative to the beginning of the program (or segment,). There needs to be one page table origin register for each active process. A three-digit (hexadecimal) page number with 4K-sized pages allows an exceedingly large program. *Asterisk identifies a bit indicating whether or not a virtual page is in main memory; that is, it indicates whether or not the frame address is valid for this page.

main memory is referenced, a page fault occurs, and the operating system then searches for the true location of the page, fetches it from its slot and finds a frame for it. The mapping of page to frame to slot is accomplished by containing the information in tables. *Figure 49.5* shows one example. To find virtual address 0021AA which consists of page number 002 and a displacement into the page of 1AA bytes, use the page table origin register to find the page table. The virtual address page number (002) gives the displacement into the table, and the pointer at that entry gives the start of the page in main memory or its location (if not in the main memory) on auxiliary storage. If a page is in main memory, simply add the lower-order part of the address, the displacement 1AA, to the starting address of the real page to obtain the real address. If the page is not in main memory, interrupt execution of the current instruction, locate the page on auxiliary storage using the page table, write the page to main memory and re-execute the interrupted instruction.

A variation on paging is the use of segments, which may be of fixed or variable size and are generally larger than pages. The mechanism for mapping segment numbers to actual addresses in main memory (or on auxiliary storage) is very similar, but the segment table contains additional information, on segment size and often on access control information.

A third variant, used by the operating system MVS, combines pages and segments. In MVS, 64K segments contain 16 4K pages, and a program can contain up to 4096 segments (more if run on the newer extended architecture mainframes). A segment table origin register points to the segment table for the program; entries in the segment table point to the appropriate page table, which in turn points to the location of the page. Assistance from hardware structures in the form of additional registers and associative memory make the process efficient.

A system-wide table is used to keep track of each of the running processes, whether they are resident, partly resident or not resident at all. A process likely to have a long wait, for example for some slow peripheral device, is swapped out (removed to auxiliary storage in its entirety) in order to free memory for other processes.

Processes (or in some cases pages) which are read-only (variously termed pure or re-entrant code) can be treated differently from processes which contain internal variables which are modified in the course of execution. Since read-only code is never modified internally, it can be executed apparently simultaneously by several users or parent processes. A frequently used editor or a compiler is one example of this type of code. The advantages of being able to treat such code differently are that only one copy need be resident regardless of how many people are using it (thereby saving main memory space), and since that copy tends to be heavily used, it becomes a working set which remains resident and thereby provides better service. In terms of memory management, systems like Unix handle such code explicitly by maintaining a special table for read-only processes.

49.3.1.1 VMS

As with most modern multiprogramming systems, VMS is paged. Each process in VMS is assigned a limit to the number of pages which can reside in main memory simultaneously – the resident set limit. This limit is adjusted dynamically up to a maximum based on the fault rate. Thus a new process, which will have a high fault rate as frequent references are made to pages not yet resident, will exhibit a rapidly increasing resident set limit.

A reference to a non-resident page results in the pager gaining control of the system and using the virtual address referenced to find the page table entry for the faulted page, as described above. The page is found on the auxiliary storage device and read in, and control is passed back to the instruction which caused the page fault. When the number of pages resident reaches the limit, a page frame is 'stolen' from the process's own set, on a first-in, first-out (FIFO) basis. Pages yielded by a process are put on either a free page list (if they have not been modified) or a modified page list. If a page on either list is referenced, it is simply 'reclaimed', thereby avoiding excessive paging I/O. Pages on the modified list must, of course, be written to auxiliary storage in order for the space they occupy to be moved to the free list and re-allocated. But modified pages are not written out until the list achieves a certain size. This also avoids excessive paging I/O, as pages can be written out in clusters. Further efficiency is achieved when clusters of modified pages belonging to the same process can be written out contiguously.

VMS also uses swapping. When VMS swaps a process in or out, it swaps the entire resident set. (Some systems swap out the entire set but page in pages one-by-one upon reference rather than swap in.) Any newly swapped-in process is guaranteed at least one time-slice before it is eligible to be swapped out again. In order to find the space to swap a process in, VMS looks to the free space list, or may write the modified page list to auxiliary storage in order to free those pages, or it may choose to swap out another process of lower or equal priority.

49.3.1.2 Unix

Unix was not originally a paged system; it used swapping instead. The Unix version BSD 4.0 was the first version to use demand paging. Now versions 4.0 BSD and above, and System V, support paging when installed on machines with memory architecture based on pages and which are capable of re-executing instructions that must be terminated because they reference a page not in main memory. Paging is thus 'grafted onto' an older memory management system based on space occupied by a whole process or space occupied by objects associated with a process.

To understand the way in which Unix manages space in main memory, it is necessary to look at the construction of a process. A program, when compiled or assembled, results in an executable file which consists of headers, program text, a machine representation of any data that has initial values plus an indicator of how much space should be allocated for unitialized data, and other items like the symbol table. When loaded, the

process consists of at least three regions: one for program text, a data region and a stack region. Each process is described to the operating system in a structure called the per process data structure. This in turn points to a region table. The page table for the region is in the region itself. Each page table entry is associated with a disc block descriptor, which points to and describes a 'slot' on auxiliary storage. The page table entry describes a virtual page, points to a page in main memory and to that page's corresponding entry in the page frame table. When a page is paged out, the disc block descriptor associated with the page table entry contains the necessary information for locating the page on auxiliary storage. The structures in the operating system which support paging are shown in *Figure 49.6*.

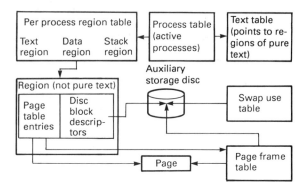

Figure 49.6 Structures for memory management in Unix

49.3.1.3 MVS

MVS maintains the concept of a unitary process, and in fact, of a unitary image of user process and system. Each process, which may be the session of one interactive user, has its own virtual address space which is the maximum 'width' of the addressing structure and thus is 16 Mb (older IBM mainframe architectures) or 2 Gb (extended architectures) in size. The virtual image is one which conceptually contains a complete copy of the operating system and the process, its dependent tasks, buffers and so on. In fact, because the operating system is largely made up of re-entrant code, there is actually only one copy which is shared among all active processes. However, the virtual process image continues to include an apparent private copy. This fiction allows applications to occupy up to 16 Mb or 2 Gb of space including whatever is occupied by the operating system itself.

With the aid of associative memory for efficiency MVS divides the address space (process image, including the virtual private copy of the operating system) into 64 K segments which are further subdivided into 4 K pages. And address space control block (ASCB) describes, at the highest level, the address space occupied by a process, and acts as the entry in the dispatching queue (see below). The ASCB points to the real address of the process's segment table and indicates its length. The segment table in turn points to one page table for each segment, and the page tables point to locations in main memory or auxiliary storage as described above.

Note that MVS maintains information in control blocks which are entities in linked lists rather than use tables, as is done in Unix.

49.3.2 Storage and file organization and management

Because multiprogramming, multi-user systems are shared simultaneously by many people or processes, the problem of identifying files clearly and of assigning ownership and granting the owner rights which he or she can extend to co-workers, and of managing complex arrangements of space on secondary storage devices, needs to be addressed.

The differences between systems are probably their most noticeable to users in this area in particular. Generally, however, systems maintain a two-level structure: one level is directed at devices (such as discs), and the other at files of data.

Structures for devices are analogous to the BIOS portions of small, single-user operating systems. They contain tables of available devices which record device type and status information and point to the appropriate device driver. Each class of device must have a low-level device driver, which is a unit of software or hardware that performs interface functions such as the passing of addresses and interrupts, the buffering of data and the detection of errors; thus it communicates between a peripheral device and the operating system. In Unix, devices are divided into two major classes: character-oriented devices and block-oriented devices and are listed in two tables, the 'cdevsw' and the 'bdevsw'. MVS simply keeps a table of all available devices in order of device number, which dictates paths to a device via channels and relative priority; this contains the necessary descriptive information within each entry in the table. MVS's scheme allows access to a device via more than one channel, thus reducing 'channel busy' wait states.

Structures for keeping track of files may either assign files to definite owners (such as is true of both Unix and VMS) or ignore the question of personal ownership and assume that the organization which controls the system is 'owner' of the files, the strategy adopted by MVS. This has important implications for the sharing of files and for the protection of files against unauthorized access. Where a file has an individual owner, the owner has 'rights' over the file which he or she may then grant, in full or in part, to other users. Both Unix and VMS have a conceptual hierarchy such as that shown in *Figure 49.7*.

In most circumstances, an owner wants to restrict the more powerful permissions; for example by restricting 'delete' and perhaps 'write' to him- or herself, while granting the less powerful permissions of, say, 'read' to his or her working group while allowing the 'world' to have 'execute' permission for files which are executable. In many systems, the more powerful permission implies that the person granted it also had all the permissions below it in the hierarchy, that is, that 'delete' permission implies the ability to write to the file, read and execute it, but the 'write' permission includes only the further right to read a file if that is possible. 'Read' implies character format, while an executable file is unreadable. These two are mutually exclusive categories in most systems, although in some, such as Unix, 'read' allows copying and therefore can be a sensible permission for an executable file.

Other systems, such as MVS, were designed around the notion of an organization being responsible for and therefore 'owning' data in files. MVS does allow an individual to protect his or her files by associating passwords with them. Otherwise, it is assumed that all files are shared by anyone who can name them unless an application provides file control at a different level. Password and other optional security systems (authorized program facility, cryptography), however, are complex and can be used in combination, separately or at different levels. Authorized program facility (APF) identifies 'trustworthy' and 'untrustworthy' programs, for example, and limits the access of the latter to certain parts of the system.

Files are named in a file directory, but the construction of the directory structure again varies from system to system. Both VMS and Unix make possible, and use for their system files, a hierarchical directory structure. Thus the user can organize his or her files under a series of directories, as shown in *Figure 49.8*.

In this case, Andrea, upon logging on, would be 'pointed at'

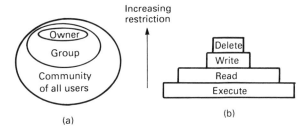

Figure 49.7 Concepts of individual ownership, hierarchy of access and hierarchy of permissions (a) a concept of 'who shares' (b) a concept of how a file can be shared

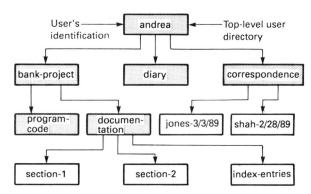

Figure 49.8 A hierarchical directory structure. Shaded boxes are directories, clear boxes are data files

her highest level directory, which is actually a sub-directory of a system master directory. To access her correspondence with Shah from the end of February, she would have to specify a path by noting that the file shah-2/28/89 is to be found by traversing the directory called correspondence. Or, she could change her default directory to correspondence and access the letter shah-2/28/89 directly. If, while accessing this, she wished to refer to something in section-1 of the bank project's documentation, she could specify the full path: up one level to andrea and then traverse, in order, bank-project and documentation to the file section-1.

MVS uses quite a different organization. It has a 'master' directory called the system catalog, which may have subsidiary catalogues. This is a hierarchical arrangement but is invisible to the user, who simply specifies a file name. The catalogue entry contains a pointer to additional information about the file held on the volume table of contents (VTOC) of the disc on which the file actually resides. It is the combination of the entries contained in the catalogue and the VTOC which gives sufficient information to access a file successfully. If a user knows the specific location of a file, i.e. the name of the disc, he or she can access the file directly, circumventing the catalogue. In fact, it is possible to keep files without registering them in any of the catalogues; this can provide a small measure of security. *See Figure 49.9*.

49.3.3 Sharing processor time

To multiprogram efficiently, a system must have:

1. One or more processes ready to run which are resident or can be made resident in main memory.
2. A means of deciding among them which shall run next.
3. A means of pre-empting one running process in favour of another.

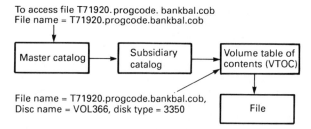

To access file T71920. progcode. bankbal.cob
File name = T71920.progcode.bankbal.cob

File name = T71920.progcode.bankbal.cob,
Disc name = VOL366, disk type = 3350

Figure 49.9 MVS's arrangement of catalogues and VTOCs, and file access. The user sees this not as a means for organizing personal files, but for accessing any file. Some semblance of a hierarchical structure can be made to appear through the use of name levels, but there are no special directories implied at each level, and no 'path' through these to a particular file

The first point implies that the system must maintain the status or state of a process. A process can be:

1. Ready to run and resident;
2. Ready to run but not resident, in which case it must be swapped or paged in, see 'Memory management' above;
3. Not ready (also called blocked);
4. Actually running.

Systems choose which process to run next by choosing from among either the ready and resident, or the ready but not resident. Blocked processes normally are blocked because they are awaiting some event which they have triggered, such as the completion of I/O, or because they have put themselves in a wait state to await some external event, such as the arrival of a message from a network connection.

In addition, systems normally assign a priority to processes and may vary the priority dynamically within limits. Some systems, such as MVS, will also allow the user to request a particular priority in some circumstances, such as in the submission of a batch job, and will allow the system operator to vary priorities manually. A job, in this sense, is defined by the user, who can group one or more programs together for execution, to be executed serially, defining the job with a job statement or card. An end-of-job marker statement defines the end of a job, or if that is missing, the next job statement defines the end of the previous job. The programs within a job so delineated need not be related, but usually are. The job is the unit dealt with by the high-level scheduler; see below. Choice among processes which are of equal status, i.e. there are several processes which are ready and resident, may then be made on the basis of their relative priorities or, if priorities are also equal, on the basis of their position in a queue of ready processes. Priority can also be made the basis by which one process can pre-empt another (see the description of VMS below).

There are a number of commonly used scheduling algorithms. Briefly described, they are:

1. *FIFO.* This implies a queue and the selection of processes in order in the queue.
2. *Round-robin.* Each ready process is given a quantum of time in turn.
3. *Shortest-job-first (or next).* This requires an estimate of the required time to do a job and favours jobs which promise to be quick. A 'guillotine' usually takes care of cheats.
4. *Shortest-remaining-time.* Also requires an estimate of the required time to do a job; the algorithm must also record the time used and in selecting processes favours those which are nearest to finishing.
5. *Highest-resource-ratio-next* (Brinch-Hansen, 1971). Seeks to correct some of the biases of shortest-job-first and does so by

calculating a dynamic priority as a function of the estimated service time (i.e. how much time is required to do the job) and the amount of time the process has already had to wait, such that longer waits will cause the priority to increase.

A system may have scheduling on more than one level and may use more than one of these algorithms. The first 'scheduling barrier' is whether the user or program will be allowed access to the system at all; this is high- or job-level scheduling. Once admitted to the system, the second 'barrier' is whether the program or session will become a process; this is intermediate-level scheduling. Once a process has been formed the final 'barrier' remains, for its lifetime, whether at any opportunity to run it will be granted access to the processor itself; this is low-level scheduling. Different algorithms may apply at each of these levels, and a hierarchical arrangement of several algorithms may apply at any one level. For example, ready processes may be selected by, say, shortest-remaining-time, but if several have equal estimates of remaining time they may then be chosen by either a round-robin arrangement or by the time spent on the queue (FIFO).

49.3.3.1 VMS

VMS divides processes into three major classes which it uses to establish a broad group of priorities. It recognizes time-critical processes (real-time), time-shared (interactive), and background (batch or computation-bound) processes and assigns these, broadly, high, medium and low priorities respectively. On a scale of 32 priorities, the system manager can subdivide time-critical applications into high-priority and low-priority real-time and can control the actual priorities assigned to these groups and to the swapper, which is a system process that frees space in memory by removing inactive processes to secondary memory, or brings such inactive processes back into main memory when they are again ready to run.

An algorithm controls the priorities of time-shared and background processes, subdividing these into I/O bound (requiring higher priority), less I/O bound, and computation-bound (the lowest priority). It then seeks always to provide real-time services for real-time tasks, and then to balance interactive and background work to maximize throughput while providing a good service to highly interactive use (I/O bound). The algorithm varies priorities dynamically within these broader ranges. The scheduler always chooses the process with the highest priority in the ready-and-resident group. Events, such as the completion of I/O, move processes into this group. Each process receives a quantum of time, but real-time processes are exempt from the expiry of their quanta. Processes can be pre-empted before their quanta expire, but until the quantum does expire, a process remains in the set of ready-and-resident processes, with occasional exceptions (such as when swapped out because service is required by a higher priority non-resident process or when entering a wait state).

49.3.3.2 Unix

Unix is a time-sharing system, geared to program development and interactive use. As such, its scheduler is a round-robin scheduler, guaranteeing 'fairness' to each member of a community of interactive users. Background tasks can be started, but have a low priority and run in what is virtually a 'soak up' mode, using time not otherwise devoted to serving interactive users. Processes can voluntarily 'sleep' (enter a wait state) or will be blocked upon issuing an I/O instruction. Then they will be woken up by the occurrence of an event, such as arrival of the type of message they process or the completion of the I/O, and returned to the ready state, from which they will have access to the processor for a quantum, in round-robin fashion. If several processes are asleep awaiting a common event, such as the availability of space in memory, the occurrence of the event wakens *all* of them and the scheduler then chooses one on the basis of priority, which varies dynamically according to the character of the process. Because Unix's scheduler does not allow a process to be awoken and returned to execution immediately the event it awaited occurs, Unix is unsuitable for real-time applications, as no guarantee can be made how soon a process will be scheduled after its waking event occurs.

49.3.3.3 MVS

MVS is a complex and very large operating system, and its scheduling is correspondingly complex. It uses the three levels of scheduler, as described above. Additionally, it divides work which is ready to run into units termed either service requests or tasks. Service requests are small units of work designed to reduce overheads and increase parallelism on multiprocessors where these exist. Service requests have a higher priority than tasks and can be dispatched (selected by the scheduler) to any address space. Tasks, on the other hand, belong to a particular address space, are larger and have a lower dispatching priority.

Work can also be thought of as belonging to a domain, which is similar to the main categories used by VMS (see above); each domain has assigned to it a relative priority. The lowest priority might be batch jobs, the next lowest might be high-priority batch work, then non-trivial interactive use, with the highest priority given to trivial interactive use. (Trivial refers to the resources required, not the perceived importance of the work.) Each unit of activity equivalent to an address space is called a transaction, which for batch jobs is the job as defined by the user's job control language and for interactive use is the time from when a user's address space becomes ready until a terminal-generated wait state occurs, as for example happens when a response is returned to the terminal. The installation defines the transaction types to which each transaction will belong and associates a type with a performance group which is then assigned a performance objective. Each MVS system has an installation performance specification (IPS) which sets installation requirements for each performance objective. The terminology is somewhat confusing, but a domain is a category of work (e.g. interactive, batch), a unit of work (for example a user executing an interactive command) is a service request or a transaction, and a performance group defines a set of performance objectives for a particular domain may give rise to many tasks of various types with each type in turn are associated with a performance group. The complexity, or sophistication, of the scheduling allows for very fine tuning of the system.

A part of the system, called the system resources manager (SRM), uses the IPS to determine which task of all the active tasks should be given access to the system's resources. In addition to attempting to meet the specification set in the IPS, the SRM tries to optimize resource use. The SRM is, however, not a low-level scheduler but an intermediate-level one, as it controls a number of other functions which in turn control resources.

The SRM controls the:

1. Resource manager (RM), which monitors system-wide resource use and determines which resources are under- or over-used.
2. Storage manager (SM), which controls main and auxiliary storage and acts as paging supervisor and swapper.
3. I/O manager, which manages the assignment of devices to a process, builds the control blocks necessary to control I/O and attempts error recovery.

4. Workload manager, which measures resource use and maps the service rate to the service specification in the IPS.
5. CPU manager, which monitors the processor and seeks to reduce delay.

The service rate is a linear combination of the amounts of three basic resources: processor time, an I/O request count, and page-seconds over the lifetime of the transaction. A computer-dependent adjusting factor is included. Each performance objective sets a minimum amount of service that any of its transactions must receive during any processing interval. The resource manager, CPU manager and the workload manager can vote on swap decisions; the SRM controls swapping and vote counting.

The low-level scheduler is the interactive use manager for MVS systems. Choice of a process is based on queues of ready processes; the ASCB (address space control block) which describes the address space also contains pointers to the preceding and following ASCBs in a queue, forming a two-way linked list which comprises a low-level scheduling queue. ASCBs for address spaces which become ready are inserted in the queue according to a priority which changes dynamically, but the queue is serviced by the low-level scheduler in FIFO order.

The high-level scheduler for batch work is software called the job entry subsystem (JES) which exists outside MVS 'proper'. It supports multicomputer systems and some degree of distribution (see below), queues incoming requests, translates and parses job control language, and at the other end controls printing and the punching of cards. Thus it controls entry into and exit from the MVS system 'proper'.

49.3.4 Serialization, concurrency and the prevention and avoidance of deadlock

A problem which arises when several processes execute simultaneously is the possibility of two or more processes seeking to gain access to some unsharable resource at the same time. This is clearly unsatisfiable and access to such a resource must be serialized in some fashion. A greater danger is the possibility of deadlock occurring. A deadlock occurs when one process obtains use of an unsharable resource and needs a second unsharable resource, while a second process has been allocated the second resource but needs the first to continue, see *Figure 49.10*. Neither process can proceed until the other relinquishes the contested resource. Deadlock detection, in this case, is simple but in general the detection of deadlock and the determination as to which proces should 'back off' is difficult. Hence avoidance or prevention is a better solution although some systems do support mechanisms for deadlock detection and recovery.

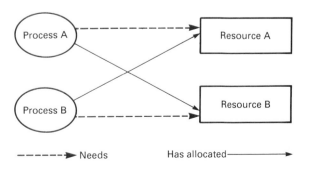

Figure 49.10 A schematic representation of deadlock

There are some resources where concurrent use by different processes do not matter. For example, two or more concurrent processes reading an entry in a database simultaneously is no problem. Since all are reading and none is changing the entry, one can be assured that the information each reads is current and identical to that seen by all other processes. However, should one process want to update an entry, it is wise to ensure that only that process has access to the entry for the duration of the update. Otherwise, reading processes may obtain inconsistent information, or nearly simultaneous updates may corrupt the entry entirely. In this case it is important for the application or the operating system to ensure that the resource is serializable, that is, that concurrency is controlled in each instance where this is necessary.

Another way in which the update of an item of data can become corrupted is when the update is partial or incomplete. For example, a transaction shifting money between one account and another must subtract the amount to be shifted from one account and add it to the other account. Failure part-way through means that one account will lose money but the other will not gain it. Another example is failure part-way through updating the pointers on items in a two-way linked list when inserting or deleting an item from the list. This can cause problems in operating systems which depend on queues and linked lists. To prevent partial update, it is necessary to define atomic actions. These are actions which will either complete with certainty or will return all objects on which they operate to their state before the action started. Thus, failed atomic actions are always restartable, since upon failure of the action to complete all objects return to the state they had before the action began. The system will always be in a known, consistent state. Machine code instructions are atomic. They will always complete or the system will return to the state it was in before the instruction started. Ensuring atomicity means that one must be able to synchronize a given set of events, to make certain that they occur in a particular order. This means being able to serialize sub-actions such as access to any resource (which may be a data item).

To serialize a resource in a shared environment, mutual exclusion can be instituted. This means that whatever process gets hold of a resource which must be serialized, it does so in a way which will exclude access by any other process. To prevent excessive degradation of service, the duration of any period of mutual exclusion should be as short as possible, which means in practice identifying the minimum sub-set of any resource which needs mutual exclusion. Mutual exclusion can be implemented by use of semaphores, which are primitive signals that indicate either that a resource is held under mutual exclusion (in which case processes which need that resource in effect form a queue) or it is not held under mutual exclusion (in which case a process, for example one of a waiting queue, can seek to obtain the resource itself). While a process has a resource under mutual exclusion it should be made uninterruptable. If it is interrupted, the resource it holds becomes unavailable and remains unavailable until such time as the process again becomes active and completes the portion of work which requires mutual exclusion. Semaphores can be simple or more complex. Another method is to establish guards which ensure serialization. A full discussion of methods for mutual exclusion and serialisation can be found in Ben-Ari (1982). These topics, and algorithms for achieving atomicity, are discussed in Chapter 53 on networks and distributed systems, and Chapter 61 on fault tolerant systems.

Deadlock is often caused by allocating resources to processes in a piecemeal fashion in systems which use mutual exclusion. Thus, one method of preventing the possibility of deadlock is to allocate resources to a process in a single act, or if piecemeal allocation seems preferable, to disallow mutual exclusion. A third necessary condition to deadlock is the use of non-pre-emptive scheduling algorithms. Any process allocated a resource under mutual exclusion will be able to hold that resource indefinitely if it is not pre-emptable. However, the apparently obvious solution of designing an operating system without piecemeal allocation, with pre-emptive scheduling and without mutual exclusion is not acceptable in most cases. Pre-emptive scheduling, for example, has a relatively high overhead; mutual exclusion may be a necessity. A number of allocation and deadlock detection and recovery algorithms exist which address the problem of piecemeal allocation. It is the difficulty of avoiding deadlock while satisfying other objectives which forces the use of deadlock detection and recovery mechanisms.

49.3.5 Interprocess communication

It is often desirable to allow processes which share a system to communicate in some way. Among the many possible ways of communicating there are:

1. Message-passing, where one process can send a message to another.
2. Use of common storage or buffers.
3. Use of shared files.
4. The use of signals (software interrupts) and flags.
5. Passed parameters, which can be passed by value or via the medium of a pointer to the location of the parameter.

Of these, the first two allow greatest flexibility and the last is the most static. The interprocess communication facilities of Unix are primitive, limited to parameter passing and signals. Files can be shared, but concurrency control is a matter for voluntary mutual agreement among the users rather than something enforced by the operating system.

VMS allows the use of event flags (a bit which describes status) which processes can use to synchronize themselves, a mailbox facility (message-passing) and shared storage. VMS users can also share files provided all sharers are reading (not writing). Writing on indexed and relative files can be done concurrently, with protection against concurrent access for writing occurring at the record level.

In MVS, tasks can communicate via shared storage – the common system area (CSA) – which is used for communication between tasks which do not share the same address space. Message-passing between sub-tasks and shared buffers are a matter for the application. All three systems make use of parameter passing, but, for example, Unix's 'default' mode is passing by value, while MVS always passes by reference.

Interprocess communication becomes more important when considering distributed systems. See Chapter 53 for a further discussion on this topic.

49.3.6 Summary and conclusions

Multiprogramming systems provide services to multiple users or multiple processes apparently simultaneously. Problems which arise out of this are: the identification of resources, especially of file and processes, and their owners, the protection of parts of the system from each other, the management of space and the management of time on the processor.

49.3.6.1 Unix

Systems like Unix are valuable for developing software because of its array of tools and because the structure of the file system and the assignment of group status and permissions for access promote easy sharing among members of a group working together. However, this very structure conversely makes Unix relatively insecure. It is not a suitable environment for commercial data processing where security is of importance. The voluntary nature of ensuring against double updates is also a severe weakness in an environment where people work in groups on the same programs. Also, its simple file structure makes it unsuitable for database applications, since the serial nature of a file means that direct access is a slow process. Its scheduling algorithms make it unsuitable for real-time applications, since a process may be awoken by an event some indeterminate time before it will again be given the processor. While the software tools are a considerable advantage, using them requires a long learning curve; indeed, most Unix 'experts' know only a relatively small set of these tools (Draper, 1985). Despite its online manual, Unix is not as well documented as MVS and VMS. There is no index and no easy way to find the tool suited to the task.

Debugging programs under Unix also presents difficulties in the event of outright program failure – error messages are very terse, often poor (due to the considerable use of jargon) and are very largely undocumented.

49.3.6.2 VMS

VMS tries to gain some of the advantages for program development that Unix has, but to do so in a more structured way. It also has a file system which provides for sharing, but as access to the system is somewhat more difficult, there is less of a security problem, and file access in shared files is serialized. It also provides tools in the form of system services easily accessible to the programmer, but these are grouped together and amply documented. Because of the organization and grouping of services, the learning curve is shorter and access to information in documentation is simpler. VMS scheduling algorithms are suitable for supporting real-time applications as well. Documentation and a scheme for describing error messages makes debugging easier than it is under Unix.

49.3.6.3 MVS

MVS makes the assumption that it is up to the programmer to learn to use the system to best advantage. Tools are not numerous, but there is a considerable market in add-on tools for the MVS system. The file system structure makes sharing of files among co-workers more difficult, though not impossible. The flexibility of the various access methods for files of different types of use makes MVS extremely powerful for indexed, relative and direct access applications such as the support of databases, especially very large databases. It is relatively easy for the experienced programmer to develop novel file structures and accesses by combining different access methods in building a file. File access is fully serialized unless this is explicitly overridden, as it is for example by database applications.

Debugging is simplified in some senses by the organization of system errors, though the debugger must first acquire the skill of reading hexadecimal memory dumps. This takes about 20 hours with a good teacher. However, because the dumps are comprehensive and messages are thoroughly documented, the condition which causes a failure is rarely hidden from view. The system is comprehensively documented – though the sheer size of the library is daunting (see the entry in the Bibliography). However, it is common for experienced programmers to learn their way around the documentation so that they know which document will tell them what they need to know, and where in the document to look for the information. The scheduling algorithms and interrupt-driven structure of MVS systems makes them suitable for all types of application, though the very considerable overheads of MVS would disqualify it from real-time application. (A transaction processing counterpart, TPF/II, however, is extremely responsive while at the same time capable of supporting thousands of transactions per second.)

49.4 Multiprocessing and distributed systems

Multiprocessing systems are those which include two or more processors working together to accomplish work. MVS, described earlier, is a multiprocessing system as well as a multiprogramming system. Network operating systems are those in which each host computer has its own operating system but also has communications processes which carry out network control functions. Distributed systems can be defined as those where hardware, control or data are distributed geographically, although at least one author (LeLann, 1981) has insisted that all three entities must be distributed. The distinction between these classes of system is often the subject of debate. Generally, network systems can be considered as those where the presence of the network is made visible to users and users must take overt actions to invoke network functions. In distributed systems, and indeed in multiprocessing systems, the fact that there are a number of different processors communicating and cooperating tends to be invisible to the user. Hence the user is very likely to be unaware of which processor is carrying out his or her work.

There is also considerable debate about where the border between multiprocessing and distributed systems lie. A rule of thumb is to consider whether message-passing is the only possible mechanism for cooperating. Message-passing can, of course, be used even in single processor systems as a means of interprocess communication. But as distance increases, the time between sending and receiving communication also increases and at some point this reaches a stage where message-passing becomes the only viable means of communication. For example, two systems closely adjacent can share files by means of a physical switch or direct wiring, but beyond a certain distance, the sharing is more economically and simply accomplished by sending data from a file to a remote processor in the form of a message, however long.

Multiprocessing systems can best be classified according to their relationships, or the closeness of the coupling between them. One possible relationship is that of master and slave, such as that demonstrated by IBM's mainframe attached processor (AP) systems running MVS. Both processors share a single main memory, the master processor provides all the I/O, scheduling and resource management services and the other processor (the attached processor) is devoted to processing work under the direction of the master. Any interrupt occurring in a process in the AP causes a second interrupt in the master processor. Some master-slave arrangements are not so rigid as that of IBM's AP systems; the master may only be the director or dictator, but not have exclusive control of all resources.

Another form of multiprocessing system is called separate executives, whereby each processing element has its own operating system, controls its own I/O devices and files and processes only its own interrupts. I/O devices may be switched between processors through intervention by an operator or a master processor, which may also control access to global data.

Coupling, on the other hand, may range from the very tight (where all processors are semi-independent and have both local memory and shared global memory), to very loosely coupled arrangements where processors have only local memory and share a communications channel.

In symmetrical systems the single operating system floats between identical processors such that only one processor is host to the operating system but any processor is capable of being the host.

MVS, running under the JES3 job entry subsystem, is an example of a separate executives arrangement. (Procesors need not be proximate in JES3 systems, but as the master schedules work for all the other processors, where processors are distant, the 'jobs' are sent in the form of messages.)

There are several possible models of distributed system, including:

1. A local-area network used as a form of 'bus' to connect multiple processors in a multiprocessing-type system.
2. Local processors with local memory sharing discs and files on a network (the 'workstation' model).
3. Personal computers interacting with larger hosts such that smaller applications with a high degree of interaction run on the PCs and larger applications and files reside on a larger host.
4. A community of democratic equal hosts interacting, using an extension to the operating system to provide address extension.

Multiprocessing systems have much in common with multiprogramming systems. In addition, they have added problems of more complex deadlock prevention and concurrency control and load balancing. They are more expensive, but in return offer increased reliability and improved performance, although two processors in a multiprocessing system do not perform at twice the rate of a single processor! The degree of coupling and especially of data sharing dictates to a large extent the degree of performance improvement; unshared data gives the best performance improvement, while global data gives the least.

One of the major objectives of distribution is to render the fact that a system is distributed as transparent as possible. This can be achieved in several ways. For example, Sun Computer's Network File Server attempts to mimic the hierarchical directory and file system of Unix so that the whole distributed file store appears as though it were on a single system. A common mechanism is the remote procedure call (RPC), which attempts to mimic, from the programmer's point of view, an ordinary procedure call statement. However, the procedure call must be 'bundled' into a message along with any parameters to be passed, must be reliably sent to the remote host and reliably invoke the remote procedure, which must then execute and return control and any parameters to the invoking procedure on another machine. These topics are discussed further in Chapter 53 on networks and distributed systems.

Time is of crucial importance in any consideration of distributed systems. Synchronism over considerable distance is difficult, since in a distributed system working over a network using message-passing as an information exchange mechanism there is no common clock. Delays in message transmission do happen, as do failures of hosts and failures in the network. Thus, applications must take into account the possibilities of these occurrences. If distances are very great or the likelihood of delay is great, it may be necessary for the 'working' process to send reassurances to the invoking process as commonly the invoking process must wait a 'reasonable' time before making the assumption that the remote host is unreachable or has failed to complete the transaction. In distributed file systems, a part of the file store may become suddenly unavailable, although this may be compared to a similar problem occurring in a single, centralized file store due to failure of a device or group of devices. A further consideration for many is the security of a distributed system; encryption of messages and other protective measures may be necessary and add to the overhead burden of such a system.

Thus, while distributed systems provide fault tolerance, increased power, and power closer to the user, developers must be aware that the state of the system is not easily determined from any one node and different nodes may simultaneously have different views of the system state. The time taken to pass messages is not insignificant and may add to delay perceived by the user. The working address space available to a user may be smaller than would be the case on a large single system or in a multiprocessing system.

Few commercial examples of truly distributed systems exist at the time of writing (1989). MVS and IBM's VM (Virtual Machine) operating systems support multiprocessor systems, but a job, once assigned to a particular processor or close-coupled processor complex, remains there until completed. Calls to services on other processors outside a close-coupled complex are not supported and hence these do not constitute true distributed systems. Sun Computer's Network File Server, a service added to Unix 4.2 BSD, provides a distributed system of form (2) above. Grapevine was developed at Xerox and is an interesting case study of a distributed system, its advantages and its problems (Coulouris and Dollimore, 1988). A large number of rather *ad hoc* systems of type (3) exist and are rapidly becoming more common. IBM's SNA and SAA network architectures and DECnet support developments of this type. These are *ad hoc* in the sense that organizations are assembling them from a variety of equipment often using or developing a wide variety of applications software designed for distributed use. Thus, each is unique to its organization. As yet, no manufacturer provides a complete system, including applications, which can be purchased entire. Research examples exist of most types.

49.5 Accessing system services

In most systems, requests for system services are provided for applications by code inserted at compilation time by the compiler of high-level language programs. For example, read and write statements call on system I/O services and these calls are inserted into the object program by the compiler when it compiles high-level language statements that are of the read or write type.

In CP/M, MS-DOS and PC-DOS, as well as service requests made by the compiler (or interpreter) from a high-level language on behalf of the programmer, a more direct form of access to system functions is accomplished at the Assembler level by executing an instruction to call the system function, with the required function number in a register designated for the purpose. In MS-DOS the instruction is:

INT 21H

and the function number must be in the AH register. For example, placing 03H in the AH register and executing INT 21H will cause the system to wait for a character from the defined auxiliary port to arrive; when a character does arrive it will be returned to the AL register. Another method used by some programmers is to access directly the system jump table, but this causes problems of portability between versions of MS-DOS and PC-DOS, which have the jump table at different addresses (Lucy, 1984).

In MVS, system services are numerous. Access to such services is normally provided by the compilers for high-level language applications, but more direct access is available at the Assembler level by executing the SVC (supervisor call) instruction, where the operand is the number of the service wanted. For example, SVC 13 opens a file whose identifiers are already established by earlier code. (It is worth noting that most system error codes above 00F in MVS are related to the SVC which detected the error, S013 and S213 errors, for example, are errors which occurred during attempts to open a file and were detected by the SVC 13 routine, while S214 occurs when a file cannot be closed properly – for example, because there is insufficient room to write the end of file marker – and is detected by SVC 14, the file close routine.) Some utility programs, for example the SORT utility, contain numbered 'hooks', often called 'exits', which can be invoked from either high-level or assembler language programs. SORT, for example, contains 'exits' E15 and E35 which allow the programmer control over the input to and output from the sorting process, respectively.

In Unix, which is largely written in a high-level language (C), calls to system services can be made more directly in C or Pascal programs. In this case system services are provided by pre-written modules which can be invoked by calls. For example, in C a 'fork' (which creates a new – child – process) is simply invoked by:

```
main() {
        int ppid;
        signal (SIGINT, signal_monitor);
        if (fork() = = 0)
        {
                /* body of fork code run in child process*
        }
}
```

In this fragment of code two system services have been invoked. Fork has already been mentioned and is invoked in the 'if' statement. The other system service invoked is signal, invoked in the line above. All such system services are documented in the Unix manual which is provided on-line in Unix systems. The most commonly invoked system services are well documented in Kernighan and Ritchie (1978), which is the 'bible' of C programmers. A comprehensive list for System V Unix appears in Thomas *et al.* (1986).

VMS provides system services as functions which can be invoked from high-level languages such as FORTRAN and Modula-2 more directly than is the case with any of the systems above except Unix. The programmer using VAX/VMS utilities must adhere to the VAX Procedure Calling and Condition Handling Standard in order to avoid problems. Utilities are grouped. For example, there is a utility set for: the access control list (ACL), the command language (CLI), conversion (CONV) and data compression and expansion (DCX), and invocation uses these abbreviations in the form:

ACLEDIT$EDIT *item-list*

where ACL is the set, EDIT is the function, and 'item-list' is the parameter.

49.6 Conclusion

Operating systems have existed for nearly 30 years. During that time they have moved from rather simple notions of managing the hardware on behalf of a single user or several users using a machine serially to provision of increasingly complex functions to, first, a number of users sharing a large machine and latterly, to a number of semi-independent users geographically distributed who nevertheless wish to share resources such as data, processes and processing power. Distributed systems are an active area of both research and development as they seek to combine the advantages of simpler, single-user machines with the power, capacity for data and functionality of large centralized machines and systems.

49.7 Bibliography

This bibliography lists some books which are useful in each of the areas noted below. The lists are by no means exhaustive and in most areas new books appear constantly. The exceptions are the documentation for IBM's MVS operating system and DEC's VMS operating system, as noted, where the manufacturer's documentation is the best source of information.

General

Hoare, C. A. R. (1985) *Communicating Sequential Processes*, Prentice-Hall, Englewood Cliffs, New Jersey, USA. [A classic formal discussion of processes, concurrency, non-determinism, communication, sequential processes and shared resources.]

Keller, L. S. (1988) *Operating Systems: Communicating With and Controlling the Computer*, Prentice-Hall, Englewood Cliffs, New Jersey, USA. [The textbook from which this chapter was drawn.]

Maekawa, M., Oldehoeft, A. and Oldehoeft, R. (1987) *Operating Systems: Advanced Concepts*, Benjamin/Cummings, Menlo Park, California, USA. [An extensive text on operating systems with emphasis on advanced features such as virtual memory, distributed systems and distributed concurrency control, deadlock and recovery.]

Concurrency and concurrent programming

Ben-Ari, M. (1982) *Principles of Concurrent Programming*, Prentice-Hall Inc., Englewood Cliffs, New Jersey, USA. [A small but excellent guide to programming parallel structures and achieving mutual exclusion and serialization. Examples are in a Pascal-like language, with a few examples in Ada given where appropriate.]

Lorin, H. (1972) *Parallelism in Hardware and Software: Real and Apparent Concurrency*, Prentice-Hall, Englewood Cliffs, New Jersey, USA. [Though now quite old, this book is one of the best discussions of the principles and details of concurrency and parallelism available.]

CP/M

Waite, M. and Angermeyer, J. (1983) *The CP/M Bible*, Howard Sams & Co., Indianapolis, Indiana, USA. [An extensive users' guide to the CP/M system.]

Waite, M. and Lafore, R. (1983) *Soul of CP/M*, W. Sams & Co., Indianapolis, Indiana, USA. [A guide to CP/M for program developers.]

Distributed systems

Coulouris, G. F. and Dollimore, J. (1988) *Distributed Systems: Concepts and Designs*, Addison-Wesley, Wokingham. [A well-written textbook with ample, detailed case study material, giving it a practical bent.]

Lampson, B. W., Paul, M. and Siegert, H. J. (eds) (1981) *Distributed Systems Architectures and Implementations: An Advanced Course*, Springer-Verlag, New York, USA. [An advanced course on practical issues such as interprocess communication (IPC), distributed control, naming in distributed systems, protection, among other topics. Chapters 11, 12 and 13 on atomic transactions, synchronization and multiple copy update are especially recommended, as is Chapter 15 (error recovery).]

Lorin, H. (1988) *Aspects of Distributed Computer Systems*, 2nd edn, John Wiley & Sons, New York, USA. [A comprehensive view of distributed systems, including hardware and software issues, the distribution of data and distributed databases, and the organization, economics and management of distributed computer systems.]

Sloman, M. and Kramer, J. (1987) *Distributed Systems and Computer Networks*, Prentice-Hall, Englewood Cliffs, New Jersey, USA. [Provides an overview of the principles and concepts of distributed systems.]

MS-DOS

Duncan, R. (ed.) (1988) *The MS-DOS Encyclopedia*, Microsoft Press, Redmond, Washington, USA. [A guide for both users and programmers.]

Jamsa, K. (1988) *Using MS-DOS*, Osborne McGraw-Hill, Berkeley, California, USA. [A comprehensive users' guide to MS-DOS, including advanced features. An optional disc provides online help.]

Lucy, S. (1984) *MS-DOS User Book*, Sigma Press, Wilmslow, Cheshire. [A small but useful book for use of and programming on MS-DOS systems; detail is insufficient for unusual or major development work. The book is not suitable for naive users and may be best used as a quick reference.]

Young, M. J. (1988) *MS-DOS Advanced Programming*, Sybex, San Francisco, California, USA. [A programming guide to MS-DOS, including extensive notes on C and Assembler.]

MVS

IBM provides extensive documentation for its systems. Some manuals which would be useful to the software engineer are listed below. It is best to check with IBM to ascertain the most recent versions. All are published by the IBM Corporation, White Plains, New York, USA.

Bibliography, IBM System/370, 30xx, 4300 and 9370 Processors, order number GC20–0001. [The bibliography contains over 1100 pages, which gives some idea of the scope and complexity of the available documentation. It is divided into three parts. Part 1 has entries grouped by subject and sorted by title key words. Part 2 contains abstracts of all documents listed in Part 1, and Part 3 is a listing by order number.]

An Introduction to MVS, order number GC28–1823.
OS/VS2 MVS Overview, order number GC28–0984.

Documentation below this introductory level is very specific to the part of the system, the processor or peripheral equipment involved, and the options (e.g. cryptography, RACF) installed on a particular system. It is best to consult the *Bibliography* or the IBM Systems Engineer assigned to the installation for further guidance.

PC-DOS

Norton, P. and Wilton, R. (1985, 1988) *The IBM PC & PS/2*, Microsoft Press, Redmond, Washington, USA. [A comprehensive guide to programming on the IBM PC and PS/2 systems with PC-DOS.]

Unix

Bach, M. J. (1986) *The Design of the Unix Operating System*, Prentice-Hall Inc., Englewood Cliffs, New Jersey, USA. [A comprehensive guide to the internal structures of Unix.]

Kernighan, B. W. and Ritchie, D. M. (1978) *The C Programming Language*, Prentice-Hall Inc., Englewood Cliffs, New Jersey, USA. [The C programmer's 'bible'.]

Thomas, R., Rogers, L. R. and Yates, J. L. (1986) *Advanced Programmer's Guide to UNIX System V*, Osborne McGraw-Hill, Berkeley, California, USA. [This guide includes a comprehensive list and description of the system calls and subroutine library of the System V version of Unix.]

VMS

Like IBM, the Digital Equipment Corporation provides extensive documentation of its VMS operating system. Below are listed those parts of the documentation likely to be of most interest to software engineers and programmers developing systems on VAX/VMS systems. All are published by the Digital Equipment Corporation, Maynard, Massachusetts.

Introduction to the VAX/VMS Document Set, order number AA-Z101C-TE. [A guide to the documentation for VMS.]
The VAX/VMS Reference Shelf, in 10 volumes and 19 binders:
    Volume 1 General User, order number QLZZ1-GZ
    Volume 2 Command Language, order number QLZZ2-GZ
    Volume 5 System Management, order number QLZZ5-GZ
    Volume 7 Program Development, order number QLZZ7-GZ
    Volume 8 System Routines, order number QLZZ8-GZ

49.8 References

Brinch-Hansen, P. (1971) Short-term scheduling in multiprogramming systems. In *Third ACM Symposium on Operating Systems Principles, October*, pp.103–5

Coulouris, G. F. and Dollimore, J. (1988) *Distributed Systems: Concepts and Designs*, Addison-Wesley, Wokingham

Deitel, H. M. (1984) *An Introduction to Operating Systems*, Addison-Wesley, Reading, Massachusetts, USA, p.181

Denning, P. J. (1968) The working set model for program behavior. *Communications of the ACM*, **11**, 323–33

Draper, S. (1985) The nature of expertise in UNIX. In *Human-Computer Interaction – Interact '84*, Shakel, B. (ed.), North-Holland

Kernighan, B. W. and Ritchie, D. M. (1978) *The C Programming Language*, Prentice-Hall, Englewood Cliffs, New Jersey, USA

LeLann, G. (1981) Motivations, objectives and characterization of distributed systems. In *Distributed Systems: Architecture and Implementation, An Advanced Course* (ed. B. W. Lampson *et al.*) Springer-Verlag

Lucy, S. (1984) *MS-DOS User Book*, Sigma Press, Wilmslow, Cheshire

Thomas, R., Rogers, L. R. and Yates, J. L. (1986) *Advanced Programmer's Guide to UNIX System V*, Osborne McGraw-Hill, Berkeley, California, USA

50

Standards

Patrick A V Hall
Brunel University

Maurice Resnick
SD-Scicon

Contents

50.1 Introduction

Standards are important in the regulation of the production of software and its deployment. They may be used:

1. In the procurement of individual items of software, to help ensure that they are fit for the purposes that are intended.
2. Across areas of technology to ensure the successful interoperation of independent pieces of equipment, as in communication standards.
3. Within markets to ensure a free market for third party suppliers, as in operating systems and support environments.
4. Within a company to regulate its development of software.

Standards-making and promulgation are generally associated with official bodies, ranging from the quality assurance (QA) department within a company to national and international bodies. The most prominent of these is the International Organization for Standardization (ISO), but there are many other transnational and regional standardization bodies, both military and civil, as well as national bodies in most countries. These various bodies, their inter-relationships, and the way they create and disseminate standards, are described later.

Standards may arise as part of common industrial practice, when they are termed *de facto*. *De facto* standards are usually associated with a dominant commercial interest that determines the structure of a market – such as the use of the MS-DOS or PC-DOS operating system on IBM PCs and compatibles. This form of standard will not be addressed here, though it must be recognized that *de facto* standards frequently themselves become the subject of standardization, as has happened in the transition from Unix to Posix.

In standards there are a number of distinctions:

1. *Reference models* versus actual standards. Some 'standards' do not prescribe particular practices, but instead lay down a framework within which other standards will be formulated. The best known of these is ISO 7498, the Open Systems Interconnection Reference Model (OSI-RM), but there were earlier attempts in the database area (e.g. the ANSI/SPARC report). Other areas of standardization are also attempting to lay down frameworks within which standardization can take place; the ANSI/IEEE 1002 Software Engineering Standards Taxonomy can be viewed as an embryonic reference model for the standards concerned with the software engineering process.
2. *Product* versus *process standards*. Some standards are concerned with specific software products, such as compilers and communications equipment, while other standards are concerned with the process whereby a software product is developed. Process standards (sometimes called method standards) are those concerned with the overall regulation of the development process, such as ISO 9000, or with particular parts of the process such as design (e.g. BS6224) or testing (e.g. IEEE 829). Within product standards one sometimes distinguishes interface standards, which determine purely what happens at the interface and not what happens within the product as a whole. Most communication protocol standards would be viewed as interfaces, while programming language standards would be viewed as product standards since the language semantics determines what should happen within the compiler.
3. *Codes of practice, guidelines, and specifications*. Under the general term of 'standard' a number of levels of enforcement are distinguished, though these do not seem to be officially defined. Broadly speaking, codes of practice and guidelines indicate desirable good practice to which conformance cannot be precisely determined, whereas specifications are precise and conformance is determinable by appropriate tests or analyses. Codes of practice and guidelines are deemed to be worthwhile since

they enable experience within the industry to be passed on in an authoritative manner, enabling economies in future developments.
4. *Prospective* versus *retrospective standards*. There is a strong debate concerning the appropriate time to determine standards. If standardization is undertaken too early, then the technology may not have advanced enough, and standardization may fix on practices which are not adequate, whereas if standardization were undertaken once the technology is advanced, then several incompatible practices may have become established so that the cost of change to conform to a single standard is prohibitive. Standardization activities always face this dilemma, which is further exacerbated by the very long time it can take to formulate a standard. Thus it may be appropriate to develop a standard along with the development of the technology by the industrial concerns involved. The Open Systems Interconnection standards are a pre-eminent example of these prospective standards. Alternatively a standard may be drafted but not fully developed, but still be published as an intercept standard, termed by the BSI a 'draft for development'. Such publication usually arises because insufficient agreement about the standard can be reached due to the immaturity of the technology, or sometimes because the various parties have irreconcilable interests which might be resolved through the passage of time.
5. *Functional standards ('profiles')*. Groups of interrelated standards which together service a user need (function), for example standards for all layers in Open Systems Interconnection, e.g. MAP and TOP.

The consumer's interest in standards is in the quality (fitness for purpose) of the software products that he or she wishes to purchase or use. As such, it is prospective product specification standards that are the concern. All other standards are secondary, a means to an end. Process standards only appear to be of value when there are no product standards or insufficient product standards to enable the proper assessment of the quality of a product. For bespoke development of software, process standards are currently the only way to ensure quality. Of course, the process standards would include processes for specifying the intended software and assessing the successful attainment of these intentions.

Standards, particularly specification standards, bring with them the need to be able to prove conformance with the standard. This proof could be furnished in response to some dispute concerning claims of conformance (labelling a product with the number of a standard would be deemed to be such a claim), but could be furnished independently of any dispute through some certification procedure. Certification requires the participation of some independent organization, which itself will have to be licensed or certified as competent to make certifications. Certification procedures and agencies will be addressed later in this chapter.

50.2 Standards bodies

Standards making today is dominated by the international standards organizations, reflecting the international nature of trade. The most significant of these organizations are:

1. ISO, the International Organization for Standardization, founded in 1947, having the national standards bodies of 73 countries as members, with 14 other countries as corresponding members. These bodies are listed in the ISO Memento (see references).
2. IEC, the International Electrotechnical Commission, founded in 1906, now constituted from the national equivalents of 43 countries.

ISO and IEC have established a formal agreement that their activities should be complementary, so that together they should provide a comprehensive standardization service.

Other international organizations are important in the standards making process, including the CCITT, which is concerned with communications systems.

3. CCITT, the Comité Consultatif International de Télégraphie et Téléphonie, a sub-agency of the United Nations International Telecommunications Union.

Most countries have their own standards bodies, and many groups of countries also have group or regional organizations:

4. CEN, Comité European de Normalisation, and CENELEC, the electrotechnical counterpart of CEN, cover the European Economic Community (EEC) and the European Free Trade Association (EFTA). CEN was founded in 1961 from the national standards bodies of 16 countries of the EEC and EFTA, plus Spain, which was not a member of either of these at that time. CENELEC was founded in 1971 from other groups known as CENEL and CENELCOM.
5. ASMO, the Arab standardization and Metrology Organization founded in 1965 by the Arab League.

There are also regional organizations for Africa (ARSO), Eastern Europe and the communist bloc (CMEA), the Americas (COPANT), and the Pacific area (PASC).

ISO/IEC have made explicit recommendations that appropriate standards should be cited in law, so that legislative work can be simplified and accelerated, barriers to trade can be eliminated, and technical regulations can be updated easily in the face of technological advance.

Most countries have national standards organizations, as shown in *Table 50.1*. It is these national organizations that participate in ISO and in regional standards organizations.

Trade associations and professional societies of various kinds also participate in the formulation and promulgation of standards. In the USA these associations (e.g. IEEE and CBEMA) would typically forward their proposed standards through ANSI into the international arena – see later. Sometimes the associations are *ad hoc*, to defend particular sectional commercial interest, such as the X/Open and Open Software Foundation associations in the general area of open systems interconnection and standard operating systems.

In Europe, ECMA – the European Computer Manufacturers Association – has technical committees covering most areas of potential standardization, and formulates many standards that are then fed forward into wider adoption as appropriate. ECMA has official liaison with both ISO and CCITT. The Standards Promotion and Application Group (SPAG) is an association of 12 leading information technology companies explicitly aimed at promoting the use of standards. EWICS, the European Workshop on Industrial Computer Systems, supported by the European Commission, is also active in preparing pre-standardization proposals and in monitoring other standardization activity.

Military standardization has proceeded largely independently of the civil effort outlined above, and is described in further detail later.

The standards-making organizations and activity outlined above may appear chaotic. There is a concerted attempt to avoid duplication of effort, with many coordination and liaison functions established, as well as much cross-membership of committees. There are also continuing moves towards harmonization, so that where possible a single standard will serve the needs of many industries across many countries, and the needs of both military and civil procurement.

Table 50.1 National standards organizations

Country	Organization Acronym	Title
Albania	KÇSA	Komitet i Çmimeve dhe i Standardeve
Algeria	INAPI	Institut algerién de normalisation et de propriété industrielle
Argentina	IRAM	Instituto Argentino de Racionalización de Materiales
Australia	SAA	Standards Association of Australia
Austria	ON	Österreichisches Normunginstitut
Bangladesh	BST	Bangladesh Standards and Testing Institution
Belgium	IBN	Institut belge de normalisation
Brazil	ABNT	Associação Brasileira de Normas Técnicas
Bulgaria	BDS	Comité de la qualité
Canada	SCC	Standards Council of Canada
Chile	INN	Instituto Nacional de Normalización
China	CSBS	China State Bureau of Standards
Colombia	ICONTEC	Instituto Colombiano de Normas Técnicas
Cuba	NC	Comité Estatal de Normalización
Cyprus	CYS	Cyprus Organization for Standards
Czechoslavakia	CSN	Urad pro normalizaci a mereni Václaské námesti
Denmark	DS	Dansk Standardiseringsraad
Egypt	EOS	Egyptian Organisation for Standardization and Quality Control
Ethiopia	ESI	Ethiopian Standards Institution
Finland	SFS	Suomen Stanardisoimisliitto SFS
France	AFNOR	Association française de normalisation
German Dem. Rep.	ASMW	Amt für Standardisierung, Messwesen und Warenprüfung
Germany, FR	DIN	DIN Deutsches Institut für Normung
Ghana	GSB	Ghana Standards Board
Greece	ELOT	Hellenic Organisation for Standardisation
Hungary	MSZH	Magyar Szabványügyi Hivatal
India	BIS	Bureau of Indian standards
Indonesia	DSN	Dewan Standardization Council of Indonesia

Table 50.1 – *continued*

Country	Organization Acronym	Title
Iran	ISIRI	Institute of Standards and Industrial Research of Iran
Iraq	COSQC	Central Organization for Standardisation and Quality Control
Ireland	NSAI	National Standards Authority of Ireland
Israel	SII	Standards Institute of Israel
Italy	UNI	Ente Nazionale Italiano de Unificazione
Ivory Coast	DENT	Direction de l'environement, de la normalisation
Jamaica	JBS	Jamaica Bureau of Standards
Japan	JISC	Japanese Industrial Standards Committee
Kenya	KEBS	Kenya Bureau of Standards
Korea, D P.R	CSK	Committee for Standardization of the Democratic People's Republic of Korea
Korea, Rep	KBS	Bureau of Standards, Industrial Advancement Administration
Malaysia	SIRIM	Standards and Industrial Research Institute
Mexico	DGN	Direcciáon General de Normas
Mongolia	MSC	State Committee for Prices and Standards of the Mongolian People's Republic
Netherlands	NNI	Netherlands Normalisatie-instituut
New Zealand	SANZ	Standards Association of New Zealand
Nigeria	SON	Standards Organisation of Nigeria
Norway	NSF	Norges Standardiseringsforbund
Pakistan	PSI	Pakistan Standards Institution
Papua New Guinea	PNGS	National Standards Council
Peru	ITINTEC	Instituto de Investigación Tenológica Insutrial y de Normas Técnicas
Philippines	BPS	Bureau of Product Standards
Poland	PKNMiJ	Polish Committee for Standardization
Portugal	IPQ	Instituto Portugués da Qualidade
Saudi Arabia	SASO	Saudi Arabian Standards Organization
Singapore	SISIR	Singapore Institute of Standards and Industrial Research
South Africa	SABS	South African Bureau of Standards
Spain	AENOR	Asociación Española de Normalización y Certificación
Sri Lanka	SLSI	Sri Lankan Standards Institute
Sudan	SSD	Sudanese Standards Department
Sweden	SIS	Standardiseringskommissionen i Sverige
Switzerland	SNV	Swiss Association for Standardization
Syria	SASMO	Syrian Arab Organization for Standardization and Metrology
Tanzania	TBS	Tanzania Bureau of Standards
Thailand	TISI	Thai Industrial Standards Institute
Trinidad & Tobago	TTBS	Trinidad and Tobago Bureau of Standards
Tunisia	INNORPI	Institut national de la normalisation et de la propriété industrielle
Turkey	TSE	Türk Standardlari Enstitüsü
United Kingdom	BSI	British Standards Institute
USA	ANSI	American National Standards Institute
USSR	GOST	USSR State Committee for Standards
Venezuela	COVENIN	Comisión Venesolana de Normas Industriales
Viet Nam	TCVN	Direction générale de standardisation de métrologie et de contrôle de la qualité
Yugoslavia	SZS	Savezni zavod za standardizaciju
Zambia	ZABS	Zambia Bureau of Standards

(Extracted from the *ISO Memento*, which contains full addresses for these organizations)

50.3 ISO, IEC and international standardization

Both ISO and IEC have their headquarters in Geneva. The IEC was established in 1906 to standardize developments in the electrotechnical industries. Attempts to broaden this international standardization activity in the 1930s failed, and it was only in 1947 that international standardization across a broad front was established.

The technical work of ISO is carried out by Technical Committees (TC) which are each responsible for an area of technology. These committees are established by the ISO Council, but thereafter determine their own programme of work. Standardization in the area of information technology is carried out by a joint ISO and IEC committee established in 1987. This is JTC1 Information Technology, which integrates the work of the previous ISO committee TC97 Information Processing Systems and IEC Technical Committee Information Technology Equipment and sub-committee IEC/SC 47B Microprocessor systems. JTC1 is responsible for standardization in the field of information technology systems (including microprocessor hardware and software) and equipment, but does not cover specific applications in areas like banking, industrial automation, and process control.

The Technical Committees in turn establish sub-committees (SC) and working groups (WG) to cover different aspects of their work.

Each Technical Committee and sub-committee has a secretariat assigned to an ISO member body by the ISO Council for Technical Committees or the parent Technical Committee for sub-committees. Each working group has a convenor appointed by the parent Technical Committee. There is some national advantage in having the secretariat of committee, and in consequence there can be competition for these roles. The member bodies that are actively involved in a particular committee are designated participating bodies, and have an obligation to attend meetings and vote.

Most of the sub-committees and working groups of JTC1 are of concern to software engineers, and are listed in *Table 50.2* (adapted from the ISO Memento for 1988).

Altogether there were 164 technical committees in ISO at the end of 1987, some of which do work of interest to the software engineering community. Principal among these are:

1. *ISO/TC46 – Information and documentation* – concerned with the standardization of practices relating to libraries, documentation and information centres, indexing and abstracting services, archives, information science and publishing. Of particular interest are SC4/WG1 on character sets, and SC4/WG6 on electronic publishing.
2. *ISO/TC176 – Quality management and quality assurance* – concerned with standardization of generic quality management, including quality systems, quality assurance, and

generic supporting technologies, including standards which provide guidance on the selection and use of these standards. All work of this committee is of concern in software engineering, and particularly SC2/WG5 on software quality assurance.
3. *ISO/TC184 – Industrial automation systems* – concerned with standardization in the field of industrial automation systems encompassing the application of multiple technologies such as information systems, machines and equipment, and telecommunications. Of particular interest here are SC4 on external representations of product data, including IGES, the Initial Graphical Exchange Specification, for engineering drawings, and MMS, the Manufacturing Message Service, that is part of the MAP system of communication standards.

Most national standards-making bodies will 'shadow' these committees, arranging their internal committee structures so as to relate to them easily.

ISO standards are prepared through a number of stages. A new area of concern is identified and a new work item (NWI) is proposed and agreed at some level within ISO, usually at the Technical Committee level. Usually this work item will propose the development of an international standard, although sometimes it will lead to a number of studies to clarify the area before specific standards-making activities can be begun.

An example of this preliminary study activity is seen in the Special Working Group (SWG) on Systems Software Interfaces (SSI) attached to the Advisory Group of JTC1. This Working Group debates the need for generic interfaces to operating systems and related services, and has to take into account concerns such as attempts to standardize Job Control Languages, and the needs for application portability.

Table 50.2 Principal sub-committees and working groups of JTC1 Information Technology. Secretariat of JTC1 is ANSI

Reference	Secretariat	Title
AG	ANSI	Advisory group
WG2	BSI	Instrumentation magnetic tape
SWG	ANSI	Procedures
SWG	SCC	Strategic planning
SWG	SNV	Registration authorities
SWG	JISC	Systems software interface
SC1	AFNOR	Vocabulary
WG1	SCC	Advisory group for SC1
WG4	ANSI	Fundamental terms and office systems
WG5	DIN	Software
WG6	SCC	Hardware, services and operations
WG7	SCC	Communication
SC2	AFNOR	Character sets and information coding
WG1	SNV	Code extension techniques
WG2	ANSI	Multiple-octet coded character set
WG3	SNV	7-bit and 8-bit codes
WG6		Control functions
WG7		Coded representation of picture and audio information
SC6	ANSI	Telecommunications and information exchange between systems
WG1	ANSI	Data link layer
WG2	BSI	Network layer
WG3	DIN	Physical layer
WG4	AFNOR	Transport layer
SC7	SCC	Software development and system documentation
WG1	ANSI	Symbols, charts, and diagrams
WG2	BSI	Software system documentation
WG3	SCC	Program design
WG5	SCC	Reference model for software development

Table 50.2 – *continued*

Reference	Secretariat	Title
SC11	ANSI	Flexible magnetic media for digital data interchange
SC13	DIN	Interconnection of equipment
WG3	DIN	Lower-level interface functional requirements and lower-level interfaces
SC14	SIS	Representation of data elements
WG1	SIS	Standardization guidelines for the representation of data elements
WG3	SIS	Terminology
WG4	ANSI	Coordination of data element standardization
SC15	SNV	Labelling and file structure
SC17	BSI	Identification and credit cards
WG1	DIN	Physical characteristics and test methods for ID cards
WG4	AFNOR	Integrated circuit card
WG5	ANSI	Registration Management Group
WG7	BSI	Data content, tracks 1 and 2
SC18	ANSI	Test and office systems
WG1		User requirements and SC18 management support
AG	ANSI	Advisory group
WG3	BSI	Document architecture
WG4	AFNOR	Procedures for test interchange
WG5	SCC	Content architectures
WG8	ANSI	Text description and processing languages
WG9	ANSI	User/systems interfaces and symbols
SC20	DIN	Data cryptographic techniques
WG1	BSI	Secret key algorithms and applications
WG2	AFNOR	Public key cryptosystem and mode of use
WG3	ANSI	Use of encipherment techniques in communication architectures
SC21	ANSI	Information retrieval, transfer and management for open systems interconnection (OSI)
WG1	AFNOR	OSI architecture
WG3	SCC	Database
WG4	JISC	OSI management
WG5	BSI	Specific application services
WG6	ANSI	OSI session, presentation and common application services
SC22	SCC	Languages
WG2	BSI	Pascal
WG3	SCC	APL
WG4	ANSI	COBOL
WG5	ANSI	FORTRAN
WG8	SNV	Basic
WG9	ANSI	Ada
WG11	ANSI	Binding techniques
WG12	AFNOR	Language conformity validation
WG13	BSI	Modula 2
WG14	ANSI	C
SC23	JISC	Optical digital data discs
SC24	DIN	Computer graphics
SC47B	JISC	Microprocessor systems
WG1		Definitions of microprocessor instructions and their mnemonic representation
WG3		Bus connector pic assignments
WG4		Architecture
WG5		Guidelines for the technical details
WG6		Revision of Publication 821
WG7		Microprocessor systems quality management
SC83	DKE	Information technology equipment
WG1		Home electronic systems
WG2		Fibre optic connections for local area networks
P&R		Planning and requirements

Once a work item has been agreed and assigned to a particular sub-committee (or a new sub-committee raised to handle it), then its first step towards an international standard is to create a draft proposal (DP) for circulation and study within the Technical Committee. This DP may be written from scratch, but more typically would start with some existing document. This could be a national standard, as happened with ISO 9000 which started from BS5750, and ISO 646 which started from the better known ANSI ASCII standard. Alternatively it could start from some industry standard as has happened with Posix, working from Unix. The DP is debated and modified a number of times until as wide an agreement as possible has been reached (ideally a consensus) and the Technical Committee feels it is suitable to become an official standard of ISO.

At this point the draft proposal is forwarded to the secretariat for registration as a Draft International Standard (DIS). The DIS is circulated to all member bodies for voting. If 75% of the votes cast are in favour of the DIS, it is sent to the ISO Council for acceptance as an international standard. While a consensus is not necessary, it is important that no major disagreements remain, and all issues raised should be answered. The vote in ISO Council provides a final check on this. If the DIS fails in its membership vote, it may have to continue through more draft proposals, although it may also be issued as an intercept standard.

Under special circumstances, standards that have been prepared in organizations other than ISO may be adopted without technical change (but of course with formatting changes to conform to ISO requirements). These procedures are referred to as the abbreviated procedures; the standard effectively enters the ISO procedures at the DIS stage, going straight into voting for acceptance.

All ISO standards are subject to a periodic review at not more than five yearly intervals, when they could be confirmed for a further period, be withdrawn, or be revised. In a rapidly changing technology like computing, such frequent review and revision is essential. In citing standards it is important to indicate which revision of the standard is being referred to. This is done by indicating the year of the revision, as in 'ISO 4057: 1986'.

Functional standards and profiles are handled in a similar manner, with a proposed draft International Standard Profile (pdISP) subject to voting within JTC1, leading to the promulgation of the ISP.

For further details of ISO procedures, the required format of standards, and the various forms used within ISO procedures, the ISO Directives should be consulted.

50.4 Standardization in the UK

Information technology standards in the UK are largely produced through the British Standards Institute (BSI). The BSI originated in 1901 as the Engineering Standards Committee, set up by various professional bodies, and later became the British Engineering Standards Association. A Royal Charter was granted in 1929, and in 1931 the body adopted its present name. It is an independent organization, charged in its charter to draw up standards by voluntary agreement among interested parties, and to promote the adoption of standards once they have been drawn up. The BSI also operates a certification service, particularly well known for its award of 'kitemarks' of quality.

The BSI's standards work is funded largely by sales of standards, the running of specialized information services concerning standards, and by subscription from member organizations, such as firms, trade associations, local authorities, and professional organizations, plus a government grant. Certification work is financed separately through the services provided.

The BSI organizes itself in a manner that more or less 'shadows' the ISO structure, so that it is clear which parts of the BSI liaise with the Technical Committees, sub-committees and Working Groups of ISO.

There are six Councils responsible for the standards-making programme. Some 60 Standards Committees are responsible to these councils for authorizing work on standards. The actual work on standards is undertaken by the numerous Technical Committees. These Technical Committees carry out their detailed work through panels, equivalent to the ISO working groups.

It is the Information Systems Council, designated S/- and its IST standards committee that is responsible for the standards of concern in software engineering. The technical committees and panels responsible to IST are shown in *Table 50.3*. BSI reorganized its committees around 1980, to align these partially with the corresponding ISO committees, and the numbering of committees within IST were made to correspond to those of TC97. With the creation of JTC1 in 1987, some renumbering of committees of the former TC97 took place, but no changes were reflected into the BSI committees of IST. The ISO committees corresponding to the BSI committees are also given in Table 50.3.

Standards for advanced manufacturing technology (AMT) are developed by the AMT Technical Committee, which corresponds to the ISO TC/184. It thus looks after the higher levels of the MAP communications protocols.

Generic engineering standards are the concern of the Quality Management Systems Standards Committee (QMS). QMS has a series of Coordinating and Advisory Committees, of which QMS/2 is responsible for Quality Management Systems through its panels shown in *Table 50.4*. It is the QMS/2/2 Committee that is responsible for BS 5750, the UK equivalent of ISO 9000.

The work on BSI standards is initiated within a Technical Committee, but the initial drafting should preferably be done by a 'responsible body' and not the committee. Existing de facto standards, or documents produced by professional or trade associations, may form a suitable starting point. The Technical Committee, and particularly its BSI secretary, would be responsible for final drafting of the standard in the correct format, ready for public comment. Drafts are circulated for public comment, normally allowing eight weeks. This is usually done once only. All comments must be properly taken into account leading to consensus in the Technical Committee before the standard is published. Note that there is no voting procedure within BSI, unlike the approach taken in ISO and other standards making bodies.

When guidance is required urgently, but it is judged to be too early for satisfactory formulation of a standard, then a Draft for Development (an intercept standard) might be prepared instead.

50.5 Standardization in the USA

Standards-making in the USA follows quite a different pattern. The official standards body in the USA is ANSI, the American National Standards Institute. ANSI represents the USA in international standards bodies.

However, the actual formulation of standards is carried out by a number of accredited agencies. Accreditation is given only if the body can show that all interested parties are permitted to participate unrestricted by membership or financial constraints, and that an appropriate mechanism exists to reach consensus.

ANSI policy in the software engineering area is determined by the Information Systems Standards Board (ISSB). ANSI recognizes two major bodies in this area:

1. IEEE, the Institution of Electrical and Electronic Engineers, Computer Society, which covers the JTC1 areas of work of SC7, SC83, SC47, Posix, and LAN.

Table 50.3 BSI standards committees, panels of the office and Information Systems Technical Committee

Reference	Title	ISO liaison
IST/-	Office and information systems	JTC1
IST/-/1	Management panel for IST	
IST/-/2	European Harmonisation Panel	
IST/-/3	IEC/TC83 monitoring panel	
IST/1	Computer glossary	SC1
IST/2	Coding	SC2
IST/3	Office machines	
IST/3-/1	Steering committee	
IST/3/1	Typewriter	
IST/3/9	Ribbons and spools	
IST/4	Magnetic tape and magnetic disc packs	
IST/5	Programming languages	SC22
IST/5/3	COBOL	
IST/5/4	Pascal	
	Prolog	
	C	
	Modula-2	
IST/5/	VDM Vienna Development Method	
IST/6	Data communications	SC6
IST/6/1	Data link layer	
IST/6/2	Network layer	
IST/6/3	Physical layer	
IST/6/4	Transport layer	
IST/6/6	LAN/PABX interfaces	
IST/8	Instrumentation magnetic tape	
IST/9	Punched cards	
IST/10	Paper tape for ADP	
IST/11	Labelling and file structure	SC15
IST/12	Banking procedures	
IST/13	Interconnection of units of DP equipment	SC13
IST/14	Representation of data elements	SC14
IST/14/-	Dial maintenance advisory panel	
IST/14/1	Guidelines	
IST/14/2	Check character systems	
IST/14/3	Dates and times (drafting)	
IST/15	Software development and documentation of computer-based systems	SC7
IST/15/2	Documentation of computer-based systems	
IST/15/3	Program design	
IST/15/5	Computer systems testing	
IST/15/6	Achievement of quality in software	
IST/17	Identification and credit cards	
IST/17/1	Credit card identifiers	
IST/18	Text preparation and interchange	SC18
IST/18/-/1	User requirements/management support	
IST/18/3	Document structure (NDF)	
IST/18/4	Message transfer (electronic mail)	
IST/18/7	Keyboard layouts for office machines and DP equipment	

Table 50.3 – *continued*

IST/20	Safety of DP and office machines	
IST/20/1	Electrical safety of DPE	
IST/20/2	Electrical safety of office equipment	
IST/20/3	Mechanical safety of DP and OE	
IST/20/4	Acoustic safety	
IST/20/5	Safety from fire in DP installation	
IST/20/6	Information technology equipment (drafting)	
IST/21	Information retrieval, transfer and management for open systems interconnection	SC21
IST/21/-/1	Co-ordination panel	
IST/21/1	OSI architecture	SC7/WG1
IST/21/1/1	Security architecture	
IST/21/1/2	Naming and addressing	
IST/21/1/3	Formal description techniques	
IST/21/1/4	Conformance testing	
	Connectionless mode	
	Multi-peer transmission	
	Distributed application work	
IST/21/2	Graphics	
IST/21/2/1	Metafiles and interfaces	
IST/21/2/2	Language bindings	
IST/21/2/3	3D, GKS-3D and PHIGS	
IST/21/3	Database	SC7/WG3
	Database management reference model	
	Database languages	
	Information resource dictionary system	
	Remote database access	
IST/21/4	OSI management	SC7/WG4
	Management framework	
	Management information systems	
	Directory access	
IST/21/5	Specific application services	SC7/WG5
	File transfer, access and management	
	Virtual terminal	
	Job transfer and manipulation	
	OSCRL	
	Transaction mode	
	Management of distributed applications	
IST/21/6	Session, presentation and common application services	SC7/WG8
IST/21/6/1	Session	
IST/21/6/2	Presentation	
IST/21/6/3	ASN.1	
IST/21/6/4	CASE association control	
IST/21/6/5	Commitment, concurrency and recovery	
	Upper layer architecture	
IST/23	Optical character and mark recognition	
IST/24	Continuous stationery for ADP	
IST/28	Drawing office equipment	

Table 50.4 BSI Coordinating and Advisory Committees of the Quality Management Systems Standards Committee QMS/2

Reference	Title	ISO liaison
QMS/2	Quality Management Systems	
QMS/2/1	Quality Terminology	
QMS/2/2	Quality Management Procedures	
QMS/2/2/7	Software Quality Management Systems	TC176/SC2/WG5
QMS/2/3	Reliability Systems	
QMS/2/4	Metrology Terms	
QMS/2/5	Quality Auditing	

2. The X3 committee, with secretariat CBEMA (the Computer and Business Equipment Manufacturers Association), which covers all other areas of ISO JTC1 work.

The IEEE works through the raising of projects charged with preparing standards and guidelines in their particular area. The IEEE projects active in the software engineering area are shown in *Table 50.5*. As projects complete their standard (see later for lists of IEEE standards), they are closed down, while new projects are raised regularly. The IEEE is very active in standards making, particularly in the development process and communications areas.

The X3 committee has a number of sub-committees charged with standardization in particular areas, and thus is similar in its approach to ISO or BSI. The most relevant sub-committees are shown in *Table 50.6*.

Another important organization is the National Institute for Standards and Technology (NIST) – formerly known as the National Bureau of Standards (NBS) – which through its Institute of Computer Science and Technology (ICST), is charged with developing standards, providing technical assistance and conducting research for computers and related systems. It formulates Federal Information Processing Standards (FIPS) and issues these for conformance in US federal government work. The NIST also represents the US government in other public standards making activity, chairing the activity if the standardization is seen as critical to the US government.

50.6 Military standards

Military systems are very large and complex, typically either custom-built for a particular defence force, or built in relatively small numbers. Military systems frequently have very long lives, continuing in service for perhaps 25 years or more, with later systems being functionally compatible but built on a vastly different technological base.

Quality is a very important issue in military procurement, and most of the concerns about quality systems and project management began in military procurement. A major mechanism in the control of procurement has been the use of standards. The market forces that play an important role in ensuring quality in the civil sector are rarely present in the military sector.

Thus military administrations have established standards making and enforcement mechanisms. All too frequently the separate branches of the armed forces – land, sea, and air – have proceeded independently and duplicated each other's work, though clearly they do have major areas of interest that do not overlap. However, in the area of software they do overlap.

Over many years there has been a strong move to harmonize work on standardization, to bring the separate armed forces within a single defence force together, and to bring separate forces within a military alliance together.

There is no global or international effort in military standardization, but the military alliance NATO (North Atlantic Treaty Organisation) generates standards for use by member countries. Authority for all standards derives from the North Atlantic Council through either the Military Agency for Standardisation (MAS) or the Conference of National Armaments Directors (CNAD).

Standards are published as Allied Publications (APs) and the nature of the AP is indicated by its short title, e.g. Allied Quality Assurance Publications (AQAP), Allied Reliability and Maintainability Publication (ARMP). Agreement to use APs by some or all of the member countries is recorded in the NATO Standardization Agreement (STANAG).

Table 50.5 IEEE projects in software engineering

Reference	Title
P610	Computer dictionary, see 729, P1084–1089
P729	Software engineering terminology
T755	Extended hi-level language implementations
P770	Extended Pascal
P802	Local area networks
P802.1	High level interface working group ('Hi Li')
P802.3	CSMA/CD
P802.2	Logical link control
P802.4	Token bus
P802.5	Token ring
P802.6	Metropolitan area network (a slotted ring)
P802.7	Broadband TAG
P802.8	Fibre optics TAG
P828	Software configuration management plans
P829	Software test documentation
T855	Micro operating systems interface
P982	Standard dictionary for measures to produce reliable software
P1003.0	Guide to Posix-based open system architecture
T1003.1	Portable operating system – Posix
P1003.2	Shell and utility application interface
P1003.3	Test methods: measuring conformance to Posix
P1003.4	Real-time Posix extensions
P1003.5	Ada language binding for Posix
P1003.6	Security interface standards for Posix
P1016.2	Guide to software design descriptions
P1028	Software reviews and audits
P1044	Classification of software errors, faults, and failures
P1045	Software productivity metrics
P1059	A guide for software verification and validation
P1061	Software quality metrics methodology
P1062	Software certification
P1074	Software life cycle process
P1077	A recommended practice for design management
P1078	Information model description language
P1084–9	Computer terminology
P1141	FORTH: a microcomputer language standard
P1151	Modula-2
P1152	Object-oriented programming language

Table 50.6 ANSI X3 sub-committees in software engineering area

Reference	Title
X3H4	Information resources dictionary systems
X3H33	Virtual device interface and virtual device metafile
X3J3	FORTRAN
X3J4	COBOL
X3J11	C
X3L2	Character sets and coding
X3S3	Data communications
X3S3.4	Data link control procedures
X3T5	Open systems interconnection
X3T9	Input/output interfaces
X3T9.3	Intelligent peripheral interfaces
X3T9.5	Fibre distributed interface
X3V1	Office systems
X3V1.3	Message body format
X3V1.4	Message heading format and message related protocols

A key committee in relation to software is the AC/250 Main Group with its sub-groups:

1. SG VIII – review and development of AQAPs.
2. SC IX – reliability and maintainability assurance.
3. SG X – quality assurance of software.

The AC/250 group is responsible for AQAP 1, NATO requirements for Industrial Quality Control Systems and AQAP 13, NATO Software Quality Control System Requirements. Defence suppliers in the software industry are contractually required to comply with these standards. Both AQAP 1 and AQAP 13 are under review, firstly to consider the absorption of AQAP 13 requirements into AQAP 1, and secondly to consider the inclusion of aspects of the international civil quality systems standard ISO 9001 into a revised AQAP 1. In the longer term, a convergence between the military and civil standards is sought with perhaps the acceptance by defence procuring agencies of certification to the international civil standards.

In the UK, the senior Ministry of Defence (MOD) committee on standardization is the Defence Material Standardization Policy Committee, which operates largely through the Defence Engineering and Equipment Standardization Committee (DEESC) and the Defence Electrical and Electronic Standardisation Committee (DELSC). These committees in turn have specialist sub-committees dealing with specific technical topics.

The Directorate of Standardisation (D Stan) is responsible for coordinating and publishing the output of these committees. D Stan also maintains a register of MOD representation of BSI committees, over 400 of which are supported by MOD staff.

MOD standards are published in a variety of guises, the most well-known being Defence Standards (Def Stans), Joint Services Publications (JSPs) and Naval Engineering Standards (NES). Standards in these series applicable to software engineering are included in later sections of this chapter.

The MOD also publishes a number of guides, relevant amongst which are included the *IECCA Guide to the Management of Software-based Systems*, produced by the Inter Establishment Committee on Computer Applications (IECCA), and *Def Stan 00-16, Guide to the Achievement of Quality in Software*.

50.7 Product standards

In procuring equipment containing software, it is clearly the attributes of the product that are of most direct concern. What function does it perform? Will it be able to connect to and interwork with other equipment already installed? Is it sufficiently robust and reliable for the function to be undertaken?

Issues of function can be resolved through the use of product and interface standards, which prescribe the required functions. These functions need to be specified precisely, both to remove possible ambiguities and thus legitimate variations in equipment intended to conform, and to remove intentional loopholes such as those in ISO 646 on 7-bit character codes which leave some codes for national use, and related standards which permit escape sequences to be determined between co-operating users.

There is a growing awareness of the need for mathematical precision in the formulation of standards, though the use of formal description techniques in standards has led to some controversy.

There is legitimate concern that the use of mathematics and related techniques could make the standard unreadable by many of the people for whom it is intended. However, the use of formalisms in standards making has a long way to go; even the use of syntax notations in some areas (e.g. ISO 7889, SGML) has been novel. In many cases the formalisms used are themselves the subject of standardization, as seen in *Table 50.7*.

Table 50.7 Standard covering formal description techniques

Reference	Title and details
BS 6154:1981	Method for defining syntactic metalanguage
ISO DIS 8824	Abstract syntax notation ANS 1 – specification
ISO DIS 8825	Abstract syntax notation ANS 1 – basic encoding rules
ISO DP 8807	LOTOS
ISO DP 9074	Estelle

Other formalisms like VDM, the Vienna Development Method, are undergoing standardization within BSI, and many other formalisms have *de facto* standard forms.

50.7.1 Compilers and programming language standards

Some of the first standardization in software was of programming languages – *see Table 50.8*. The purpose of standardization is to ensure portability of complete software from one hardware environment to another, and of the interworking of separately developed software when brought together for integration into a new system.

Formal definition of languages is becoming increasingly important, as the definition techniques used attain maturity (see earlier). One important distinction in language definition that is beginning to be felt is that between abstract and concrete syntax. In one exercise in the standardization of database languages it was suggested that the important things to standardize were the abstract syntax, and the essential structure and semantics of the language, leaving individual suppliers of products to add their own value through the form of concrete syntax that they offered.

50.7.2 Operating systems and application environments

Several initiatives are under way in the application area to provide standards to assist in application portability, both of programs and of data. Posix is a new arrival, and ISO JTC1 has a study under way to look at systems software interfaces and application portability, effectively an independent and portable operating system interface.

Databases have been considered for a long time, and in the mid 1970s the CODASYL DBTG drew up a standard for a record-oriented database, while an ANSI committee drew up an early reference model for database standardization. Nevertheless there are remarkably few standards for this area.

Documentation standards have been actively pursued, and with large integrated office systems the ability to transfer documents while preserving their structure must be viewed as very important.

Graphics standards are currently focused on the GKS standard, which originated in Germany within the DIN organization. GKS was adopted by ISO in preference to the CORE standard proposed by the USA. GKS has limitations, neither handling hierarchical structures nor graphical interaction. A candidate standard for this has been under development for many years in the USA, PHIGS, the Programmers' Hierarchical Interactive Graphics System.

Table 50.8 Standards for programming languages

Topic	Reference	Standard Title and details
General practices	ECMA 53-1978	Representation of source program for program interchange – APL, COBOL, FORTRAN, minimal Basic and PL/1
	ANSI/ANS 10.2-1982	Recommended programming practices to facilitate the portability of scientific computer programs
	IEEE 693-1984	Standard for microprocessor assembly language
	IEEE 755-1985	Trial use standard for extending high-level language implementations for microprocessors
Ada	ANSI/MIL 1915A 1983	Reference manual for the ADA programming language
Algol 60	ISO 1538:1985	Programming language – Algol 60
Basic	ISO 6373:1984	Data processing – programming languages – minimal Basic. See also ECMA 55-1978 and ANSI X3.60-1978
C	ANSI X3.159-1989	Programming language – C
CHILL	Oct 1984	CCITT high level language (CHILL)
COBOL	ISO 1989:1978	Programming languages – COBOL
CORAL	BS 5905:1980	Specification for computer programming language CORAL 66
	Def Stan 05-47/2 Nov 1983	Computer on-line real-time applications language CORAL 66. Specification for compilers
FORTRAN	ANSI/ISA S61.1-1976	Industrial computer system FORTRAN, procedures for executive functions, process input/output and bit manipulation
	ANSI/ISA S61.2-1978	Industrial computer system FORTRAN, procedures for file access and the control of file contention
	ISO 1539:1980	Programming languages – FORTRAN
MUMPS	ANSI/MDC X11.1 1985	Programming language – MUMPS
Pascal	BS 6192:1982	Specification for computer programming language Pascal
	ISO 7185:1983	Programming languages – Pascal. Endorsement of BS 6192:1982
	ANSI/IEEE 770 X3.97-1983	Specification for computer programming language Pascal, similar but not identical to ISO 7185:1983, BS 6192:1982
PL/1	ISO 6160:1979	Programming languages – PL/I, endorsement of ANSI X3.53-1976. See also ECMA 50-1976
	ANSI/MIL X3.74-1981	Programming language PL/1 general purpose subset
RTL/2	BS 5904:1980	Specification for computer programming language RTL/2

Table 50.9 shows the major standards in this area.

50.7.3 Communications and open systems interconnection

While the need to transfer data and information between systems has long been recognized with early standards like ISO 646, the international version of ASCII, the need for standardization has become imperative with the development of transnational data communications, and commercial and administrative organizations which cross national frontiers. The Open Systems Interconnection standardization activity began in 1977 and published its reference model in 1984, and most of communications standardization is now built around this reference model (see *Table 50.10*).

It is important that groups of standards that together provide a service are identified for particular purposes. These are the functional standards or profiles, and many of these will be promulgated over the next few years.

50.8 Process standards

Regulation of the overall process of software development has drawn upon more general engineering methods, and these have been listed in a separate section later. There has been a persistent concern about the extent to which these do apply, and thus interpretations of the generic standards for use with software have been commonplace. These either take the form of separate standards (such as the UK Def Stan 00-16) or as guides to be used during certification of an organization for software (such as the Quality Assessment Schedules of the BSI).

The more detailed practice of software development has also been directly addressed through standards.

While the ultimate objective of all such standards must be to ensure that high and consistent quality software is produced, the emphasis has been more on bringing managerial control over cost and timescale. Of course the two are related, and with loss of control over cost and timescale, quality is all too frequently also lost.

Table 50.9 Standards for operating systems and application environments

Reference	Title and details
Database	
ISO DIS 8907: 1986	NDL
ISO DIS 9075: 1986	SQL
Operating Systems	
IEEE 1003.1	Portable operating system for computer environments, Posix
Electronic Publishing	
ISO DIS 8613	Office document architecture (ODA) – CCITT T.400 documents
ISO DIS 8613/1	General introduction
ISO DIS 8613/2	Document structure
ISO DIS 8613/3	Document processing reference model
ISO DIS 8613/4	Document profile
ISO DIS 8613/5	Office document interchange format (ODIF)
ISO DIS 8613/6	Character content architecture
ISO DIS 8613/7	Raster graphics content architecture
ISO DIS 8613/8	Geometric graphics content architecture
ISO DIS 8879	Standard generalized mark up language (SGML)
ISO DIS 9069	SGML: document interchange format
ISO DIS 9070	Registration of public contract
Graphics	
ISO 7942: 1985	Graphical kernel system (GKS) – BS 6390: 1985, ANSI X3.124:1985
ISO DP 8651	GKS language bindings
ISO DP 8651/1	FORTRAN
ISO DP 8651/2	Pascal
ISO DP 8651/3	Ada
ISO DP 8805.2	GKS-3D extensions – BSI DD 128: 1986
ISO DP 8806/1	GKS-3D language bindings: FORTRAN
ECMA-96:1986	Graphics data syntax (GDS)
ISO DIS 8632	Computer graphics metafiles
ISO DIS 8632/1	Part 1: Functional description
ISO DIS 8632/2	Part 2: Character encoding
ISO DIS 8632/3	Part 3: Binary encoding
ISO DIS 8632/4	Part 4: Clear text encoding

50.8.1 General engineering standards

A large number of standards has been produced for engineering generally, and is equally applicable for software. These include the generic quality system standards, but also include the standards concerned with project and configuration management and general processes like reviews and documentation. See *Table 50.11*. The major standard for software is ISO 9001, which is identical to BS 5750 Part 1.

50.8.2 Software engineering standards

The many standards available for control of the software engineering process are shown below in *Table 50.12*. Many of the documents listed under 'documentation' attempt to give a complete view of the whole process. However many standards only focus on a part of the overall process.

What is singular about these focused standards is that none of them belong to a cohesive view of the total development process. There is no reference model for software development standards such as that which would be provided by the many commercial 'methods'. The nearest that any collection comes to having cohesiveness is that from the IEEE, which has a taxonomy of software engineering standards, IEEE 1002, and the standard for quality plans, IEEE 730. The rest of the IEEE standards more or less fit into the framework set by these two,

although there are unnecessary differences in details such as the laying out of the common introductory sections.

Of emerging importance are those systems whose failure could lead to loss of life, damage to the environment, or severe financial loss. While the need in these systems is for measurable and consistent quality levels, special standards containing, for example, requirements for formal verification, are currently under development. One such standard, scheduled for issue in 1989, is Defence Standard 00-55 on safety critical systems. Although produced for defence purposes, this standard will undoubtedly have a major impact on the civil market.

50.9 Conformance testing and certification

How does one know whether the manufacturer's claims to conform to a particular standard are correct? Conformance to standards has become an increasing concern:

1. Standards should be formulated so that conformance can be demonstrated.
2. There should be independent certification services to verify conformance, thus saving individual customers the costs of checking conformance themselves.

Table 50.10 Standards covering Communications

Reference	Title and details
General	
ISO 7498	Basic Reference Model for OSI
ISO 7498/DAD1	Connectionless mode addendum
ISO 7498/DAD2	Security architecture
ISO 7498/DAD3	Naming and addressing
ISO 7498/DAD4	Management framework
ISO DP 9595	Management information service
ISO DP 9596	Management information protocol
Electronic Mail	
ISO DIS 8505	MOTIS: functional description. CCITT X.401
ISO DIS 8883	MOTIS: message interchange and transfer protocol. CCITT X.411
ISO DP 9065	MOTIS: user agent. CCITT X.420
ISO DP 9066	MOTIS: reliable transfer service. CCITT X.410 (part)
ISO DP 9072/1	Remote operation service – concepts and model. CCITT X.410 (part)
ISO DP 8072/2	Remote operation service – basic ROS. CCITT X.410 (part)
Applications Layer 7	
ISO DIS 9040	Virtual terminal service: basic class – service definition extended facility addendum
ISO DIS 9040/PDAD1	
ISO DIS 9041	Virtual terminal service: basic class – protocol definition extended facility addendum
ISO DIS 9041/PDAD1	
ISO DIS 8571/1	File transfer and access management. Part 1. General description
ISO DIS 8571/2	File transfer and access management. Part 1. The virtual filestore
ISO DIS 8571/3	File transfer and access management. Part 1. The file service definition
ISO DIS 8571/4	File transfer and access management. Part 1. The file protocol definition
ISO DP 8831	Job transfer and manipulation. Concepts and services
ISO DP 8832	Job transfer and manipulation. Basic class protocol
Common Application Service Elements	
ISO DIS 8649/2	Part 2: Association control – service definition
ISO DIS 8649/3	Part 3: Commitment, concurrency, and recovery – service definition
ISO DIS 8650/2	Part 2: Association control – protocol definition
ISO DIS 8650/3	Part 3: Commitment, concurrency, and recovery – protocol definition
Presentation Layer 6	
ISO DIS 8822	Service definition
ISO DIS 8823	Protocol definition
Session Layer 5	
ISO 8326	Service definition
ISO 8326 PDAD 1	S/L symmetric synchronization service definition
ISO 8327	Protocol definition
ISO 8327 PDAD 1	S/L symmetric synchronization protocol definition
Transport Layer 4	
ISO 8072	Transport service
ISO 8072 PDAD 1	Connectionless service addendum
ISO 8073	Transport protocol
ISO 8073 AD-1	Network connection management sub-protocol
ISO 8073 DAD-2	Class 4 operation over connectionless network service
ISO 8602	Connectionless transport protocol
Network Layer 3	
ISO 8348	Network service
ISO 8348 AD 1	Addressing addendum
ISO 8348 AD 2	Connectionless service addendum
ISO 8878	Use of X.25 to provide OSI connection-oriented network service
ISO DIS 8881	Use of the X.25 packet level protocol in LANs
ISO 8880/1.2 and 3	Specification of protocols to provide and support the OSI network service
ISO 8648	Internal organisation of network layer
ISO 8473	Connectionless network protocol
ISO 8473 AD 1	Provision for underlying service
ISO 8208	X.25 DTE layer 3

Table 50.10 – *continued*

Reference	Title and details
Data Link Layer 2	
ISO DIS 7776	X.25 DTE layer 2
ISO DIS 8886	Data link service
ISO 3309: 1984	HDLC frame structure, BS5397-1:1985, ANSI X3.66:1979
ISO 4335: 1984	HDLC elements of procedures, BS5397-2: 1985, FIPS 71
ISO 7809: 1984	HDLC: unbalanced class, BS 5397-3: 1981, ANSI X3.44: 1974
Local area networks	
IEEE 802.1	Management
IEEE 802.2	Link level control, ISO DIS 8802/2
IEEE 802.3	CSMA/CD ISO DIS 8802/3, ECMA-80.81
IEEE 802.4	Token bus, ISO DIS 8802/4, ECMA-90
IEEE 802.5	Token ring, ISO DIS 8802/5, ECMA-89
IEEE 802.6	Slotted ring, ISO DIS 8802/6, BS6531/2
Physical Layer 1	
ISO 2110: 1984	24-pin connector, BS6623-1: 1985, ANSI EIA RS 232C
ISO 2593: 1984	34-pin connector, BS6623-2: 1986, ANSI EIA RS 449
ISO 4902: 1984	37- and 9-pin connector, BS6623-3: 1986
ISO 4903: 1984	15-pin connector, BS6623-4: 1986
ISO 7480: 1984	Signal quality at DTE/DCE interfaces – start-stop, ANSI EIA RS 404
ISO DIS 8480	Control of standby functions
Character codes	
ISO 646: 1983	7-bit coded character set, ECMA-6:1985, BS4730:1985, CCITT T.50, ANSI X3.4:1977, FIPS 1.1
ISO 2022: 1986	Code extension techniques for 7 and 8-bit codes, ANSI X41:1974
ISO 2047: 1975	Graphical representation of control character of 7-bit code
ISO 2375: 1985	Procedure for registration of character sets
ISO 4873: 1986	8-bit coded character sets, structure
ISO 6429: 1983	Additional controls for character imaging I/O devices
ISO 6937	Text communication code
ISO 6937/1: 1983	Part 1: General introduction
ISO 6937/2: 1983	Part 2: Latin alphabet and non-alphabetic characters
ISO 6937/3:	Part 3: Control functions for page image format (SC2/1426R)
ISO 6937/7: 1986	Part 7: Greek alphabet character set
ISO 6937/8: 1986	Part 8: Cyrillic alphabet character set
ISO 8859	8-bit single byte coded character sets
ISO 8859/1 and 2	Latin alphabets Nos 1 and 2
ISO 8859/5	Latin/Cyrillic alphabet
ISO 8859/6	Latin/Arabic alphabet

The need to formulate standards with conformance certification in mind has already been discussed. This section looks at the actual process of certification, looking at both the certification of products and processes.

Certification is almost uniformly undertaken nationally. Internationally, there does exist an agency for certifying electrical equipment. This is CEE, the International Commission for Conformity Certification of Electrical Equipment, founded in 1946 with 23 European members and observers from Australia, Canada, Hong Kong, Iceland, India, Japan, South Africa, and the USA. It certifies domestic electrical equipment operating the 'E' mark.

More international certification activity can be expected. Already compiler certification is licensed between countries, and the certification of conformance to ISO 9000, although undertaken nationally, will eventually be recognized between groups of countries through memoranda of agreement on accreditation of certifying bodies.

Certification requires the participation of an assessing organization, which may be first, second, or third party.

First party is where a company assesses its own products or processes.

Second party is usually by a purchaser on the supplier or potential supplier, assessing to company, industry or national standard. This is most common for process certification, an example being the assessments carried out at contractors for defence procurer to the AQAP quality system standards, resulting in a certificate of compliance.

Third party assessment is by an independent organization, usually against industry-recognized or national standards. This is most common for product certification, the best known undoubtedly being the BSI 'kitemark' system.

Independent organizations undertaking certification are themselves normally licensed or certified as competent in certification.

50.9.1 Product certification

Conformance to all the product standards listed earlier could in principle be certified. The certification process could be by

Table 50.11 General engineering standards

Reference	Title and details
ANSI/ASME.NQA-1 1983	Quality assurance program requirements for nuclear facilities. American Society of Mechanical Engineers
ANSI/ASME.NQA-2 1983	Quality assurance program requirements for nuclear power plants
ANSI-ASQC:Z-1.15 1979	Generic guidelines for quality systems. American Society for Quality Control
BS 4778:1979	Glossary of terms used in quality assurance (including reliability and maintainability)
BS 4891:1972	Guide to quality assurance
BS 5750	Quality systems – 6 parts. Part 1: Specification for design, manufacture, and installation. Part 4: Guide to the use of part 1
BS 5882:1980	Specification for a total quality assurance programme for nuclear power plants
PD 3542:1979	Operation of a company standards department (BSI)
PD 6489:1980	Guide to the preparations of a company standards manual (BSI)
PD 6495: 1983	IFAN Guide 1. Calculation of the profitability of (company) standardization projects. International Federation for the Application of standards (IFAN). (publ. BSI)
MIL-Q-9858A	Quality Assurance Requirements (US DoD)
ISO 6215	= BS 5882
ISO 9000	Guide to quality management and quality assurance standards
ISO 9001	Quality systems: assurance of design/development, production, installation and servicing capability
ISO 9002	Quality systems: assurance of production and installation capability
ISO 9003	Quality systems: assurance of final inspection and test capability
ISO 9004	A guide to quality management elements
DEF STAN 05-21/1	Quality control system requirements for industry. Superseded by NATO AQAP-1
DEF STAN 05-22/(Part 1)/1	Guide for the evaluation of a contractor's quality control system for compliance with Def Stan 05-21. Superseded by NATO AQAP-2
DEF-STAN 05-62/1	Guidance on quality assurance procedures. Dec. 1983
DEF STAN 05-67	Guide to quality assurance in design
AQAP-1, Sept 1985	NATO quality control system requirements for industry
AQAP-2, Sept 1985	Guide for the evaluation of a contractor's quality control system for compliance with AQAP-1
Reliability	
BS 5760	Reliability of systems, equipments and components
DEF STAN 00-40	Achievement of reliability and maintainability
(Part 1)/1	Part 1: Management responsibilities and requirements for R and M programmes and plans. July 1981
DEF STAN 00-41	MOD practices and procedures for reliability and maintainability
Project Management	
BS 4335:1972	Glossary of terms used in project network techniques
BS 6046	Use of network techniques in project management – 4 parts Part 1: 1984, other parts 1981
MIL STD 499-1974	Engineering management
Configuration Management	
DOD STD 480A-1978	Configuration control – engineering changes, deviations, and waivers
MIL STD 483-1970	Configuration management practices for systems, equipment, munitions, and computer programs
DEF STAN 05-57/2	Configuration management policy and procedures for defence material. (Interim standard)
Specification	
BSI PD 6112:1967	Guide to the preparation of specifications
MIL STD 490A-1968	Specification practices. Oct 1968
Reviews	
MIL STD 1521A-1978	Technical reviews and audits for systems, equipment, and computer programs
Documentation	
ICAM-1	ICAM documentation standards IDS 150120000A Air Force Materials Laboratory, USA. 28 Dec 1981
DEF STAN 05-54/1	NATO guideline for the specification of technical publications. Superseded by AQAP-11
NES 40	Specification for handbook preparation. (UK MOD Navy)
AQAP-11	NATO guideline for the specification of technical publications

Table 50.12 Software development standards

Reference	Title and details
Quality assurance	
MIL S 52779A-1977	Software quality assurance program requirements
TADSTAD9-1978	Tactical digital system standard, software quality assurance testing criteria TADSTAD 9, 1978
ANSI/IEEE 730–1981	IEEE standard for software quality assurance plans. ANSI 12/84
ANSI/IEEE 983-1986	IEEE guide for software quality assurance planning
DEF STAN 00-16/1	Guide to the achievement of quality in software
DEF STAN 05-22/(Part 2)	Guide for the evaluation of a contractor's quality control system for compliance with DEF STAN 05–21. Part 2: supplementary guidance-computer software. Superseded by NATO AQAP-14
AQAP-13	NATO software quality control system requirements, Sept 1985
AQAP-14	Guide for the evaluation of a contractor's software quality control system for compliance with AQAP-13
DOD AFSCP 800-14	Software quality indicators
EEA	Establishing a quality assurance function for software
EEA	A guide to software quality audit
EEA	Software quality plans
HSE (UK)	Programmable electronic systems in safety related applications
Institute of Quality Assurance	A guide to the quality of software
FAA STD 018-1977	Computer software quality program requirements FAA-STD-018, Federal Aviation Administration, USA, May 1977
Management	
MIL STD 1679A-1983	Weapon system software development. Feb 1983
DOD AFSCP 800-43	Software management indicators
DOD STD 2167-1985	Military standard – defense system software development, 31 Jan. 1985. Supersedes MIL STD 1679A and MIL STD 1644B
RADC-1979	RADC computer software development specification CP 07877996100E, Rome Air Development Center, USA. May 1979
IEEE 1058-1987	Software project management plans
ISO/DP 9294	Guide for management of software documentation
DEF STAN 00–22	Firmware management
FIPS 105-1984	Guideline for software documentation management, June 1984
EEA	A guide to the successful start-up of a software project
Software Configuration Management	
BS 6488:1984	Code of practice for configuration management of computer-based systems
ANSI/IEEE 828-1983	IEEE standard for software configuration management plans. ANSI approval 12/84
IEEE 1033-1985	Recommended practice for application of IEEE standard 828 to nuclear power generating plants. Interprets generic requirements of IEEE-828 for nuclear power stations
IEEE 1042-1987	A guide for software configuration management
EEA	Software configuration management
Documentation	
ANSI N413–1974	Guidelines for the documentation for digital computer programs
BS 4884	Guideline for software manuals. Part 1: information to be given in technical manuals explaining use, maintenance, and repair of any material or product. Part 2: requirements for presentation
BS 5515:1984	Code of practice for documentation of computer-based systems
DOD STD 7935-1983	Automated data systems (ADS) documentation. 15-Feb. 1983
IEE	Guidelines for the documentation of software in industrial computer systems, 1985
ICAM-2-1980	ICAM software documentation standards, NBSIR 79-1940(R), Air Force Materials Laboratory, USA. Feb. 1980
IEEE 1063-1987	Software user documentation
DIS 6592	Guidelines for the documentation of computer-based application systems
ISO/DP 9127	User documentation and other information for consumer software packages
ISO/DP 6592	Guidelines for documentation of computer-based application systems
JSP 188 (UK MOD)	Specification for technical publications for the services. Requirements for the documentation of software in military operational real-time computer systems
FIPS 38-1976	Guidelines for documentation of computer programs and automated data systems, Federal Information Processing Standards Publication 38, 15 Feb. 1976
FIPS 64-1979	Guidelines for documentation of computer programs and automated data systems for the initiation phase, Federal Information Processing Standards Publication 64, 1 Aug. 1979

Table 50.12 – *continued*

Reference	Title and details
Charts and symbols	
BS 4058:1973, 1980	DP flowchart symbols, rules and conventions. *Cf* ISO 5807
BS 5476:1982	Specification for program network charts
BS 6224:1982	Guide to design structure diagrams for use in program design and other logic applications
ISO 1028:1979	Information processing – flowchart symbols
ISO 2636:1973	Information processing – conventions for incorporating flowchart symbols in flowcharts
ISO 5807	Documentation symbols and conventions for data, program and systems flowcharts, program network charts, and system resources charts
ISO/DIS 8790	Computer system configuration diagram symbols and conventions
Glossaries	
BS 3527:1976-80	Glossary of terms used in data processing, same as ISO-2382
ANSI/IEEE 729–1983	IEEE standard glossary for software engineering terminology. ANSI approval 8/83
User requirements	
ANSI/ANS 10.5-1979	Guideline for considering user needs in computer program development
BS 6719:1986	Guide to specifying user requirements for computer-based systems
ANSI/IEEE 830-1983	IEEE guide to software requirements specifications. ANSI approval 7/84
Specification	
BS 5487:1982	Specification of single-hit decision tables, see also ISO 5806:1984
BS 6154:1981	Method for defining syntactic metalanguage
CCITT 1984	Functional specification and description language (SDL)
CCITT 1984	Man–machine language (MML)
ISO 5806:1984	Specification of single-hit decision tables, see also BS 5487:1982
Design	
IEEE 990/1987	Recommended practice for Ada as a program design language
IEEE 1016-1987	Software design descriptions
DIS 6593:1984	Program flow for processing sequential files in terms of record groups
DIS 8631	Program constructs and conventions for their use
ISO/DP 6593	Program flow for processing sequential files in record groups
DEF STAN 00-17/1	Modular approach to software construction, operation and test (MASCOT)
Testing and evaluation	
BS 5887:1980	Code of practice for testing of computer-based systems
BS 6238:1982	Code of practice for performance monitoring of computer-based systems
IEE	Guidelines for assuring testability, 1988. Section 4: software testing
ANSI/IEEE 829–1983	IEEE standard for software test documentation. ANSI approval 83
IEEE 1008-1987	IEEE standard for software unit testing. IEEE approved 3/86
IEEE 1012–1986	IEEE standard for software verification and validation plans
ISO/DP 9126	Criteria for evaluation of software
ISO/DP 9241	Methods for evaluation and testing of software usability. Draft
FIPS 99-1983	Guideline: a framework for the evaluation and comparison of software development tools, FIPS PUB 99, March 1983
FIPS 101-1983	Guidelines for life cycle validation, verification, and testing of computer software. FIPS PUB 101, June 1983
N19-1985	NATLAS software unit test standard and method, NAMAS Executive, Edition 1, Dec. 1985
N20-1985	NATLAS accreditation for software testing, NAMAS Executive, Edition 1, Dec. 1985
Other	
BS 6650:1986	Code of practice for the control of the operation of a computer
IEEE 1002	Software engineering standards taxonomy
FIPS 106-1984	Guideline on software maintenance, July 1984

inspection and review (of which formal proofs of correctness would be a special case), or it could be by testing, executing the product with examples of input and required output. Currently testing is the prevalent method, but this has the usual drawbacks of testing, described in the chapter on testing.

Test suites have been developed for most of the currently important programming languages, COBOL and Ada in the US, and Pascal and Coral in the UK. Developing test suites is a highly skilled task, and the test suites have evolved over many years, as experience is gained from the testing of many compilers. The use of conforming compilers is becoming a mandatory requirement in software procurement. Since the number of possible programs is countably infinite, the test suite must necessarily only sample the functions of the compiler, and thus is fallible, particularly with respect to the size of program handled. Nevertheless, the use of test suites does give a good measure of confidence in the acceptability of a compiler and the portability of the code developed using it.

Conformance testing is going to become very important in certifying protocols in open systems interconnection. With the use of formal methods here, there is an opportunity for formal verification of these systems, as well as the use of test suites.

Graphics software claimed to conform to GKS standards has been the source of some difficulty. Conformance to the GKS standard has not been well defined, and implementation of subsets of the facilities is common; the development of software portable across GKS software has not been possible. There is a need for a better definition of conformance, and for the introduction of certification services for GKS.

Certification suites will be developed for Posix. The industry is learning that standards are not enough, and that the certification of products claiming conformance is an equally important part of the package. One can expect certification services to be developed for other standards, such as the electronic publishing SGML and ODA standards.

There has been some certification of packages that do not conform to particular standards. Accounting packages can be certified, and in UK the NCC offers a service here. More generally, for packages that are not aiming to conform to any standards, certification of conformance to intended function has to be made part of the process, and this is essentially what is done in the process standards discussed in other parts of this chapter.

Certification is expensive, and there will always be some reservations about such services, unless the cost of certification can be spread over a large volume of sales.

50.9.2 Process certification

The major process certification activity currently undertaken is conformance with the generic engineering quality standards:

1. Military: AQAP-1, and AQAP-13 for software.
2. Civil: ISO 9000, and BS 5750 in UK. These and the European standard EN29000 are all identical.

Process certification must necessarily be by audit, inspection, and review, and takes the form:

1. A company establishes a quality system that is intended to conform. This quality system will include the complete documentation of the quality system in a quality manual or similar which would be made available for review. The quality manual may itself cite some of the more detailed process standards listed above.
2. A team visits the company for several days, assessing that the quality manual does properly represent practices that conform to the generic quality systems standard, viewing the quality department at work, and viewing projects in progress

that are claiming conformance, to see that the documented practices are being followed.
3. Any appropriate corrective actions to the quality system are made, and the company is registered or certified as conforming to the quality systems standard for the particular branch of engineering concerned.
4. At intervals the company will be audited for continued conformance. In the civil certification system run by BSI and Lloyds, there are several audit visits each year, while for the military system run by the UK MOD assessments occur at two or three year intervals.

When undertaking assessments for the purposes of certification to the above standards, both civil and military organizations use guides to the interpretation of these standards in the software industry. Military publications AQAP 2 and 14 interpret respectively AQAP 1 and 13. Civil publications include several quality assessment schedules (QAS) (see *Table 50.13*) used by BSI QA, and quality system supplements (QSS), used by Lloyds QA. An international guide interpreting ISO 9000 for software is currently in preparation. A complementary activity is also under way in the UK, sponsored by the Department of Trade and Industry, examining the possibility of establishing a Software Sector Certification Scheme.

Table 50.13 BSI quality assessment schedules

Reference	*Title and details*
BSI QAS 3302/40	Quality assessment schedule to BS5750 Part 1: relating to design, manufacture and installation of electronic computer systems equipment (including subsystem equipment). Issue 1, 9 March 1984
BSI QAS 3302/44	Quality assessment schedule to BS5750 Part 2: relating to manufacture and installation of electronic computer systems equipment (including subsystem equipment)
BSI QAS 3302/79	Quality assessment schedule to BS5750 Part 1: relating to design, replication and distribution of application software for use in electronic computer systems equipment, QAS 3302/79 Issue 1, 10 Feb. 84
BSI QAS 3302/80	Quality assessment schedule to BS5750 Part 2: relating to replication and distribution of computer software, QAS 3302/80 Issue 1, 10 Feb. 84
BSI QAS 3302/190	Quality assessment schedule to BS5750 Part 1: relating to the design, manufacture and installation of turnkey systems based on electronic computer systems equipment. Issue 1, 28 Aug. 1985

This form of process certification depends both upon the written guides to the interpretation for software development and upon the individual abilities of the assessors. While the system has been found to be reasonably effective, the main barriers to harmonization of quality systems standards between the civil and military sectors are the difficulties in moving to a single unified certification system.

A step has been made towards the certification of establishments as software test laboratories in the UK. The intention has been to do for software what is established practice in other branches of engineering, such as the testing of materials. Two standards, N19 and N20 (listed in the software development standards given earlier), were developed by the NAMAS Executive, an establishment supported by the UK government Department of Trade and Industry. However, these standards concentrated on unit testing, and on structural testing rather than functional testing, and have not proved successful.

50.10 Useful addresses

Addresses from which standards can be ordered directly, or almost directly, are given below. However, conformance to standards is so commercially important that a number of companies offer information services in the area of standards. Thus in the UK most standards can be obtained from a single company which handles the sale of standards from all around the world: London Information, Index House, Ascot, Berks. SL5 7EU, UK. Tel: (0990) 23377.

Standards can also be obtained from the institutions that promulgate them. The addresses of the most prominent of these are given below – other addresses can be found in the *ISO Memento* and other references cited later.

American National Standards Institute, 1430 Broadway, New York, NY 10018, USA

The British Standards Institute, Marketing Department, Linford Wood, Milton Keynes MK14 6LE, UK

CCITT, rue de Varembe, Geneva 20, Switzerland

Department of Defense, Washington, DC 20330, USA

IEE, Box 96, Stevenage, Herts, SG1 2AY, UK

IEEE Service Centre, Publication Sales Department, Hoes Lane, Piscataway, NJ 08854, USA

International Standards Organisation, Central Secretariat, Assurance, rue de Varembe, Geneva 20, Switzerland

Directorate of Standardization (stan 1), Directorate General of Defence Quality Procurement Executive, Ministry of Defence, Kentigern House, Brown Street, Glasgow G2 8EX, UK

National Bureau of Standards, Technical Information and Publications Division, Washington, DC 20234, USA

Federal Aviation Administration, Department of Transportation, Washington, DC 20591, USA

50.11 References on standardization

Standards-making organizations all have their own documentation on their organization, their rules, and their standards.
BSI BS 0 A standard for standards: Part 1: General principles of standardization. Part 2: BSI and its committee procedures. Part 3: Drafting and presentation of British Standards
BSI Handbook 22, *Quality Assurance*, contains BS 4778, 4891, 5233, 5750, 5760, 6143
BSI Handbook 23, *General Management*, contains BS 3138, 3375, 3811, 4335, 5729, 6046, PD 3542, 6112, 6470, 6489, 6495.
IEEE Computer Society, (1988) *Standards Status Report*
ISO Catalogue, list of all ISO publications, particularly standards.
ISO Directives for the technical work of ISO, gives procedures for the undertaking of ISO work, and the standards for the preparation and layout of ISO standards.
ISO Memento (1988) Describes the structure and administration of ISO and its committees
Ministry of Defence (UK) (1986) Defence Standard 00-00 (Part 3), Section 4/Issue 2, Standards for Defence. Part 3: Index of Standards for defence Procurement. Section 4: Defence Standards Index. Lists all UK MOD defence standards
Andersen, O. and Petersen, P. G. (1986) *Handbook of standards and certification requirements for software*, International Planning Information, Denmark. Contains many useful addresses and listings of process standards for software development
BCS/IEE Software Engineering Working Group *Software Engineering Public Domain Standards*, issue 1.0. Available from the IEE.
Dwyer, J. and Ioannou, A. (1987) *MAP and TOP Advanced Manufacturing Communications*, Kogan Page
Hill, I. D. and Meek, B. L. (1982) *Programming Language Standardization*, Ellis Horwood
ICL (1987) *Standards Directory*. This contains a lot of useful information, broadly paralleling the coverage of this chapter.
Tripp, L. L. (1984) Annotated Software Engineering Standards Bibliography. In *3rd Software Engineering Standards Applications Workshop*.

Part III

Principles of Applications

Introduction and overview to Part III

John A. McDermid

1 Introduction

An engineer requires two kinds of knowledge in order to be successful in developing a software system for some application. First, he must understand the technology for developing and evaluating software systems. Second, he must understand the application domain at least to the extent that he can interpret requirements and understand how the system he will produce should fit into its operational environment. Part II of the reference book focused on this first topic and our aim in Part III is to give some basic information about a number of different application domains, thus addressing the second kind of knowledge.

Achievement of this objective, however, poses a number of problems. The most significant difficulty is the wide range of applications of computers, hence the very wide range of possible application domains that need to be considered. A related, but subsidiary, problem is the rate at which the application of computers is expanding, meaning that it is extremely difficult to avoid rapid obsolescence. The purpose of this introduction and overview is to explain the reaons for selecting the topics to be addressed and to give a brief summary of the twelve chapters in Part III.

1.1 Classification of applications

The introduction to Part I gave a simple classification of application domains in terms of their underlying theory. We will make use of this classification here but go on to refine it taking into account a number of pragmatic issues. First, however, it is worthwhile amplifying on the reasons that software engineers need application domain knowledge.

It has long been recognized that a large proportion of the faults in software systems arise from problems in specification, especially requirements specification. Requirements specifications are communications documents – and they need to provide effective communications between people with differing technical backgrounds, particularly the system's users and the system developers, or software engineers. In the author's view a large proportion of the problems that arise with requirements specifications stem from the need for requirements to be intelligible to two different audiences. Specifically the classes of problem that arise are:

- different interpretations are placed on the specification due to the differing backgrounds of the users and software engineers, in particular the users interpret the specification in terms of their application domain and the software engineers interpret it in computational terms;
- there are often omissions from the requirements which reflect those things that are deemed to be 'obvious' by the users – but

which are not obvious to the software engineers as they do not fully understand the application domain.

The only practical way of overcoming this gulf in understanding is to try to narrow it by suitable training or education. Whilst the onus should not be entirely on the software engineer, he has a responsibility to gain some measure of understanding of the application domain, if only because some 'hidden' requirements often only become manifest part way through the development process, not at the initial requirements analysis stage. The software engineer will require application domain knowledge in order to take appropriate cognizance of this additional information without recourse to the customer.

In the introduction to Part I of the reference book we separated application domain theories into three classes: specialist, self-referential and familiar. Specialist applications are those where there is a particular application domain theory, e.g. fluid dynamics or thermodynamics, which is not directly related to computing as a discipline. Self-referential applications are those where there is a specific application domain theory, but this theory relates to computing or information as processed by computers. Obvious examples in this class are to do with language processing and software engineering itself. The third class, familiar applications, is most similar to the specialist applications but here the theory required for the domain is so simple, or so familiar, that it need not be discussed in depth. Examples of theories which we would classify in this way include simple arithmetic with natural numbers such as might be required for a calculator program.

Following this simple classification it seems appropriate to discuss only specialist and self-referential applications. However, in each of these areas, a further sub-division or classification is appropriate although the boundaries between the classes are not always entirely clear.

With some of the specialist applications there is a very clearly defined problem domain. With the topics we have chosen to cover this is perhaps most clear in the case of symbolic computation, or computer algebra, but computer-integrated manufacture and digital telephony and switching are also fairly well delineated. On the other hand there are broader classes of application such as safety critical or secure applications which really relate to particular facets or characteristics of an application, rather than a specific application domain. However they are properly regarded as specialist applications because the concepts of safety and security are dependent on application and are not intrinsic to computing or software systems.

A similar distinction can be made between different sub-classes of self-referential application. Certain of these self-referential areas, particularly language compilation and databases, are well defined application domains and are largely independent of the specialist application domain. On the other hand there are properties or characteristics of applications, such as the need to interact with users or to respond within real-time constraints, which are less precisely delineated and which really identify broad classes of applications. There is considerable similarity between these classes of self-referential application and the broad classes of specialist applications and, for example, fault-tolerance may be used to achieve safety. A further similarity is that both classifications are generated by the constraints imposed by the working environment on the software system.

Following the above discussion it should be clear that we could categorize the application areas in a different manner, specifically calling them specialist, self-referential and application environment constrained. Philosophically this classification seems rather less satisfactory but, in practice, it can be quite difficult to separate specialist from self-referential applications where there are environmental constraints. As a consequence we do not use this classification to sub-divide Part III of the reference book. Nonetheless we believe that this brief discussion is useful as it gives some indication of the ways that the material covered in this part of the reference book could be applied.

1.2 Criteria for, and choice of, subjects

As has already been mentioned there are many more applications of computer systems than it is possible to address within the space available. It is obviously desirable to have a number of applications from each of the categories identified above, but there are a number of other general criteria which we now briefly discuss.

Any specialist application should have wide relevance and preferably be representative or illustrative of a broad range of application areas to give the widest possible coverage from the limited number of topics it is possible to discuss. From the point of view of self-referential applications the criteria are the commonality of the application or characteristic, and the importance of the application or characteristic, i.e. the extent to which it dominates the development process.

As discussed in the preface to the reference book it is desirable that the material to be discussed is stable and that it should be possible to enunciate clearly principles on which the applications are built. It is also necessary that there should be a coherent and substantive body of knowledge, not just a reliance on common sense. On the other hand it is necessary that the amount of information that has to be presented is reasonably well bounded. For example it would be difficult to deal with a topic such as 'financial services' or 'software reliability' because of the enormous panoply of more specialist applications that are covered by these umbrella topics.

A further set of criteria is that the material should be topical, yet likely to have considerable longevity. In other words the material should currently be of interest and likely to remain of interest for several years to come.

The chosen topics may not exactly match the above criteria but all of them satisfy most of the criteria (although a rather different subset in some of the cases). We briefly discuss the reasons for choosing each subject area.

The chapter on computer-integrated manufacturing is representative of many complex industrial applications and other classes of embedded system. CIM systems are complex, involve the integration of a number of automated systems, are severely constrained by the mechanical components to which they interface and have to comply with a number of relevant standards. This is typical of many other large scale technical applications, e.g. avionics systems.

Digital telephony and switching, e.g. stored program telephone exchanges, represent perhaps the most complex systems made by man. Certainly if the complete world-wide telephone network is considered as a system this must be the most complex man-made artefact. The systems are also representative of a class in that they are largely concerned with processing 'pure' information rather than controlling mechanical or other devices. Again developers of such systems are concerned with system integration and are constrained by applicable standards. From a technical point of view such systems are quite similar to those used by many of the major financial institutions but, of course, the detailed characteristics of the application are very different.

Symbolic computation, or computer algebra as it is sometimes known, is discussed by way of contrast to the other two classes of application. Whilst symbolic computation systems are complex they are self contained and do not have to address issues of system integration. A further reason for including this material is to alert the software engineer to the pitfalls of dealing with numerical applications without the availability of proper guidance from a numerical analyst – this is an area where it is all too easy to produce meaningless results if not guided by the appropriate theory. Thus this chapter serves as something of a cautionary tale.

It is becoming increasingly common to use computers in areas where they are, at least partially, responsible for safety or security. Clearly failure to satisfy safety or security objectives may be catastrophic so these represent a very important generic class of application. In particular material on these two topics is included because the software development, and particularly evaluation, processes have to be adapted for the application areas. Also safety and security requirements can place major constraints on the way the system is designed and implemented thus such requirements are often major drivers in the overall development process.

Turning now to the self-referential applications we can see a rather different application of the above criteria.

Compilation techniques are relevant to a wide class of applications, not just compilers, as very many software systems have to parse and check some textual input from their users. Similarly a very large proportion of major software systems incorporate a database and therefore must be concerned with the associated data design and optimization. It is extremely unlikely that a software engineer would go through a complete working career without needing to use either compiling or database techniques.

Historically many software systems were operated in 'batch' mode although it is now becoming relatively uncommon for major software systems not to have at least a rudimentary interactive interface. Within the next few years it seems likely that the vast majority of new software systems will be developed to exploit the capabilities of interactive bit map graphic workstations and terminals so techniques for the design of interactive systems will become increasingly relevant and prevalent. This is also an extremely pertinent topic because of the importance of user interfaces to the success and viability of a system or product.

Whilst many applications are produced on stand-alone (personal) computers there is an increasing trend for complex systems to employ many processors. Thus an understanding of networks and distributed systems is crucial to many software engineers. This is perhaps the best example of an area where there are now well understood and well articulated principles and concepts which can be used to structure the implementation of applications.

Finally many systems require to be fault tolerant or to respond to external stimuli in real time, i.e. the time frame is dictated by the environment not by the computer system. When an application has to satisfy such requirements the development tends to be dominated by these so-called 'non-functional' properties of the system. These properties may only be relevant to a relatively small class of applications, e.g. safety critical systems, but they are so fundamental that it seems essential to treat them here.

Clearly there are other areas which we could have addressed, e.g. transaction processing systems and scientific visualisation or graphics. However it is hoped that the material covered will prove to be of long lasting value, and that it can be supplemented with material on other important topicas in subsequent editions of the reference book.

1.3 Issues to be addressed

With the sharply focused specialist applications the primary aim is to give the reader a general understanding of the area, particularly covering the vocabulary and general principles of the area, without going into deep technical detail or discussion of theory. A practical aim for these chapters is that a practising software engineer should be able to begin to study the more specialist literature in the field or to hold a reasoned discussion with an expert in the field after having read the relevant chapter.

For the more focused self-referential topics the aim is to give the reader a capability to apply the relevant techniques and to be able to read more detailed papers in the area with a view to comparing and selecting relevant approaches to system development.

The other chapters are concerned with giving the reader a general understanding of the class of application and a knowledge of the ways in which the application characteristics constrain the development of software. This includes discussion both of specialized system architectures for the classes of application and particular development or analysis techniques which have to be used to achieve the desired application characteristics.

2 Overview of the contents of Part III

Although we discussed a categorization of the chapters in this part of the reference book above, there is some difficulty defining the boundaries of the categories and there is no real structure to the categories in the sense of defining the order in which to read the chapters. As a consequence no importance should be attached to the ordering of the following chapters, with the exception of the two chapters on databases (Chapters 54 and 55) which should be read in numerical order.

2.1 Computer-integrated manufacture

It is now quite common to use computers to control certain manufacturing processes, e.g. via computer controlled machine tools. Computer-integrated manufacture relates to the widespread use of automation throughout the factory and, in the limit, implies the integrated control over the complete range of manufacturing processes and the provision of a 'manufacturing information system'.

David Williams sets the scene for the discussion of computer-integrated manufacture (CIM) by discussing approaches to CIM, the industry context and enabling technologies such as industrial robots and computer controlled machine tools. Williams then discusses computer aided design and engineering particularly concentrating on the models and model processing required to design complex mechanical systems. This leads naturally on to a discussion of computer-aided manufacture, ranging from single work cells through to flexible manufacturing systems. Consideration is also given to the managerial aspects of CIM. The chapter concludes with a discussion of software engineering for CIM, the future development of CIM and by presenting a bibliography for the subject.

This chapter can be read independently of the rest of the book but it does have some links with Chapter 53 on networks and distributed systems as these form one of the integrating technologies for CIM.

2.2 Overview of compiler technology

Compilers are the archetypical self-referential application, however, compiler technology is also relevant in a number of other applications, e.g. natural language processing and interpretation of command languages. Thus the material in this chapter is of broad applicability.

Andrew McGettrick gives a general description of the structure of a compiler and then addresses theoretical considerations, e.g. different classes of grammar, building on material set out in Chapter 10. He then discusses the main phases of compilation, specifically lexical analysis, syntax analysis, semantic analysis and code generation, illustrating both the principles and some tools available to support compiler development. The material addresses both conventional programming languages and declarative languages. The chapter closes with a discussion of issues in optimization and a comprehensive set of references.

The chapter builds on the language theory set out in Chapter 10, however, enough of the principles of the language theory are set out here that it is possible to treat the chapter in a stand-alone manner.

2.3 Networks and distributed systems

It is becoming increasingly common to build computer systems containing many processors linked by a variety of communications media. We use the term 'networks' to refer to the communication media and 'distributed systems' to refer to the computing system comprising the processors, memories and network.

Steve Wilbur introduces the basic concepts of networks and discusses models of networks including the ISO OSI model. He discusses wide area and local area networks and gives a summary of the properties of the more common local area networks. He discusses a number of forms of network protocol including those for remote procedure call (RPC). He then discusses issues in developing distributed systems and describes a number of standard solutions, e.g. two phase commit protocols for ensuring consistency in distributed databases, based on top of RPC mechanisms. The chapter also includes a comprehensive set of references, identification of relevant standards and definitions of commonly used abbreviations and terms.

The material in this chapter is largely stand-alone although it does complement other chapters, e.g. Chapters 54 and 55 on database systems, where it discusses distributed concurrency control mechanisms.

2.4 Database systems

Databases are one of the most common components of large scale software systems. This chapter discusses the properties of database systems both from the user's point of view and internal organization.

Dick Whittington outlines the basic properties of conventional databases and identifies the structure of a conventional database management system (DBMS). The discussion covers standard architectures and data models for a DBMS together with the interface between the DBMS and programming language. Whittington then discusses the relational and network models of databases, focusing on the relational model as this is the more widely used data model. He concludes by discussing pragmatic issues of transaction management and the internal organization needed for databases to ensure efficient data access.

This chapter is a companion to Chapter 55 on database system development and it also complements some of the material in Chapter 53 on networks and distributed systems.

2.5 Database system development

Where it is necessary for an application program to manipulate a large quantity of information then it is necessary to design appropriate data structures. There are now well established principles of data design, however these were not addressed in Part II as part of the general discussion of design.

Dick Whittington describes the typical process of database system design and describes techniques for carrying out the primary design processes at each stage. The five stages are: conceptual analysis, i.e. determining the essential data structures for the application; logical design, i.e. developing an implementation independent model of the application data structures; structural design, i.e. organization of data for efficient access; physical design, i.e. mapping of the data structures on to the underlying disc and implementation.

This chapter complements Chapter 54 on database systems and also Chapter 17 on architectural design.

2.6 Real-time systems

Real-time systems are characterized by the need to respond in time-frames dictated by the operational environment for the computer system, rather than by the computer system itself. Special design and implementation techniques are required to guarantee real-time response.

Hermann Kopetz introduces a classification of real-time systems which distinguishes 'hard' from 'soft' real-time systems. In essence the difference is between the need to deal with worst case and average case demands on the system. Kopetz discusses real-time transactions as a way of structuring the design and implementation of real-time systems. He then considers approaches to scheduling processes in order to guarantee satisfaction of deadlines. Finally he discusses achieving real-time performance at the same time as achieving fault-tolerant operation.

This chapter can be read in a stand-alone fashion but it complements Chapter 17 on architectural design and also links to the material in Chapter 61 on fault-tolerant system structuring.

2.7 Design of interactive systems

For many systems the user interface has the most significant effect on usability and aceptability of the system. Consequently it is extremely important for software engineers to understand the principles of interactive system design.

Harold Thimbleby explains some of the fundamental difficulties of designing effective interactive systems and explains the value of being able to evaluate user interface design early in the system life cycle. He then discusses a number of styles of user interface which, loosely, are approaches to structuring and controlling the interaction with the user. He describes a number of principles for designing interactive systems, e.g. minimizing the user's memory load. This leads on to a description of an outline design method for producing interactive systems and a brief example of the application of the approach.

This chapter serves as a complement to Chapter 17 which discussed architectural design but which did not address interface issues in any detail. Although it addresses interface design from the user's perspective it does not explicitly employ the ideas of cognitive psychology so it is complementary to Chapter 13, rather than being dependent upon it.

2.8 Digital telephony and switching

The telephone switching system used on a world-wide basis is probably the most complex artefact produced by man. Conse-quently it is instructive to consider the problems of software engineering for such vast and complex systems.

Malcolm Wardlaw discusses the basic operational characteristics of telephony systems by discussing basic transmission and switching and the principles of controlling and managing telephone calls. The primary software engineering involvement in telephony is in developing programs for stored program telephone exchanges. Wardlaw discusses the computing problems associated with such exchanges including the need to provide real-time response, continuous, i.e. fault-tolerant, operation and the requirement for long term maintenance. The chapter concludes with a discussion of 'intelligent' networks and future trends in telecommunication networks and 'value added' services available over the network.

Again this chapter can be read stand-alone but it acts as a complement to a number of other chapters by setting out the context in which the techniques discussed can be applied. In particular it complements Chapter 53 on networks and distributed systems, Chapter 56 on real-time systems, Chapter 61 on fault-tolerant system structures and, to a lesser extent, Chapter 20 on maintenance.

2.9 Computer security

There are many applications where it is necessary to achieve security, i.e. protection of sensitive civil or military information. Specialized approaches are required to achieve and to demonstrate security.

Chris Sennett first describes the basic functionality typically required of secure systems, including access control and auditing. He then discusses how to achieve assurance, or confidence, in the security functionality dealing especially with specification and evaluation. He then discusses design and development of secure systems, particularly discussing issues of refinement of designs while preserving their relevant security properties.

This chapter can be read stand-alone but it provides an interesting complement to the material on formal development as it illustrates an area where there has been considerable use of formal techniques. It is particularly interesting as a compelement to Chapter 24 on refinement.

2.10 Safety

As with security, the achievement and demonstration of safety requires particular development and assessment techniques. These techniques affect the whole system development life cycle.

Phil Bennett discusses the basic concepts of safety, draws out the distinction between safety and reliability and explains the role of software in safety critical systems. He then discusses approaches to assessing safety including techniques such as fault tree analysis and event tree analysis. He then discusses a typical development process for safety critical systems and surveys evolving standards in the area. He concludes with a discussion of experiences in developing and assessing safety critical systems.

This chapter can be read stand-alone and it complements many of the chapters in Part II dealing with conventional and formal software development. It provides an interesting contrast to Chapter 59 on security as very different techniques for achieving high assurance in critical systems have evolved in the two domains.

2.11 Fault-tolerant system structuring concepts

There are many applications, including safety critical systems, where it is necessary to be able to tolerate faults arising both from design errors and from physical failures. Achievement of fault tolerance influences both the system development process and the system architecture.

Santosh Shrivastava discusses the basic principles of fault tolerance, particularly as they apply to tolerating physical faults. He then discusses methods for developing fault-tolerant software components and illustrates this with a discussion of some standard components such as stable storage. This leads on to a discussion of fault-tolerant distributed systems including the use of concepts such as atomic transactions and conversations to achieve fault-tolerant behaviour. The chapter concludes with a brief discussion of tolerance to design faults.

The material in this chapter complements that in Chapter 53 on networks and distributed systems dealing with communication protocols. It also relates to the material in Chapter 44 on imperative programming languages, particularly the treatment of exception handling. It also describes techniques that are used in safety critical systems and in telephony as discussed in Chapters 60 and 58 respectively.

2.12 Symbolic computation

Computers are obviously forms of calculating engine but one of their powers is that they can manipulate equations symbolically, rather than having to provide solutions in a numerical fashion. Symbolic computation, or computer algebra, is a fascinating and challenging application of computers.

James Davenport introduces the topic by giving an example of the capability of some existing computer algebra systems, e.g. to carry out integration and to solve matrix equations. Davenport then discusses the capability of some of the available computer algebra systems and explains the technical, i.e. mathematical and numerical analysis, pitfalls that await the would-be implementor of such systems. He concludes with a discussion of the capabilities that should be found in a good computer algebra system and indicates some of the resarch problems still to be addressed.

The material in this chapter can be read stand-alone but it provides an interesting contrast to Chapter 8 on numerical computation which discusses the capabilities and limitations of computer arithmetic systems.

3 Conclusions

Almost inevitably treatment of applications of computers will be unsatisfactory because there are such a vast range of current, and possible, applications. However, I hope that the discussion in this part of the reference book is interesting and informative and that it will be of significant practical value by dealing with a representative range of applications and some of the more important characteristics of applications.

It is also interesting to note that we have dealt with a number of issues, e.g. real-time systems and safety, as topics in their own right rather than as part of the treatment of the overall development process in Part II. This was partly a deliberate choice in order to avoid unnecessary complication in, for example, describing architectural design. It also reflects a genuine lack of knowledge and understanding in the software engineering community. We do not, yet, have a good understanding of how to integrate techniques for achieving safety, with those for achieving security, with those for achieving fault tolerance with . . . – and many of the more demanding applications require us to achieve all these properties within the same system. Perhaps the most difficult technical challenge for software engineers over the next few years is to achieve a better understanding of how to take into account all these different facets of a system within one development project.

Finally, we should not forget the epilogue which gives an interesting and challenging analysis of what it means to be truly 'professional' in software development, and of what failure to adopt a professional approach may mean for the future of our industry.

51

Computer-integrated manufacture

David J Williams
University of Technology, Loughborough

Contents

51.1 Introduction

It is essential that the traditionally industrialized countries innovate in manufacturing if they are to survive in the increasingly competitive market place. One of the key technical weapons for this is computer-integrated manufacture (CIM) and its sub-technology, automated manufacture. CIM acts to coordinate and control the activities of the manufacturing business. CIM as a technology has no purpose itself, however, unless it allows manufacturing industry to serve its market worldwide by making its products 'better, faster and cheaper'. Better implies what the customer wants, with the quality and variety that is expected. Faster means that not only must the manufacturing facility go faster to satisfy its growing market, but that to capture that market it must be able to bring products to that market more quickly. Cheaper speaks for itself both to the customer and supplier. CIM can help in all these things when used carefully in conjunction with the talents of people.

51.1.1 Some definitions

CIM is usually regarded as embracing a wide variety of computer-based activities within the manufacturing organization.

There is a continuum of definitions of CIM ranging from 'computer assistance of all the activities carried out within a company' to definitions which imply complete integration and sharing of all the data that can ever be used within the factory. CIM vendors in particular market CIM as a strategy to increase the overall productivity of the manufacturing organization.

CIM is usually considered to encompass three major computer-assisted subsystems. These are briefly discussed to set the scene for the rest of the chapter. The chapter later considers the subsystems in more detail.

51.1.1.1 Computer-aided engineering (CAE)

CAE uses the computer-aided design activity, CAD, to build a product model and may allow the verification of the product design using computer-based analytical packages such as finite element (FE) analysis. It is becoming usual for the analytical packages to take the geometric model of the component directly from its CAD description, provided that this CAD description is sufficiently complete.

51.1.1.2 Computer-aided manufacture (CAM)

CAM is the automated manufacturing facility. It is becoming more usual to have a proportion of the shop floor under direct computer control. This could include a flexible manufacturing system (FMS), a transfer line of computer controlled, automated machines or computer numerically controlled (CNC) machines, arranged as cells or single machines tended by a skilled operator.

51.1.1.3 Computer-aided production management (CAPM)

CAPM encapsulates a number of further sub-systems, the primary aim of which is to provide the high-level ('management') control of the day-to-day activities within the manufacturing enterprise. Key to this are the materials requirements planning (MRP) systems, which projects and plans the delivery of raw materials and bought-out items to the shop floor. This is sometimes extended by a capacity planning system and other utilities into a manufacturing resource planning (MRPII) system. This CAPM activity will also schedule the 'gross' organization of the production on the shopfloor on approximately a weekly basis.

Such systems are sometimes also called manufacturing information systems.

51.1.1.4 Integration of the sub-systems and computer-aided process planning (CAPP)

The above sub-systems are linked, in an ideal world, by a communications sub-system based on, for example, a number of local area networks, and by a CAPP system. CAPP systems do not readily fall into any of the areas above, as they essentially represent the key linking activity between two traditionally distinct empires – that of design and that of manufacture. CAPP is not widely adopted except in the form of CAD/CAM which usually means the generation of part programs (programs for the manufacture of particular parts or components) to control the movement of NC machines from CAD data (particularly for metal cutting) or the generation of process sequences by varying those of a similar design.

It should also be recognized that each CIM subsystem can be applied in the manufacturing business and can be linked with careful use of people to other elements of the operation. This is in contrast to the use of computer communications systems to achieve 'complete' automation and integration.

51.1.2 Advantages of CIM

The discussion above began to outline the key sub-acronyms of CIM. In the ideal CIM system all the above sub-systems would be linked into a seamless factory-wide application and share the same operating data. The key advantages of such a system are reduced manufacturing and design lead times because of the fast and accurate transmission of data. These enable the capture of new marketplaces and customers, and their continued satisfaction with reliable and fast deliveries.

51.1.3 A practical approach to CIM

Innovation in approaches to manufacturing are dominated by those who influence the marketplace: the large vendors, the trade press, the consultants and the academics. For this reason there is a tendency in marketing to generate and use acronyms and jargon. Engineers should note this before they attempt implementations.

Further, it is widely recognized that in many cases it is practically impossible to implement all the technologies that are usually encapsulated by the CIM acronym, and that if such an exercise were possible then the cost would be prohibitive. Thus, complete CIM is rarely financially justifiable at present. This leads to implementation of single elements of the CIM technologies, i.e. CAD, MRP, CAM, where they are financially justified.

Non-strategic implementations with no tailoring to the factory outside the subsystem can, in turn, lead to the problem of the 'island of automation'; a local increase in efficiency which only serves to increase the chaos around it and reduce the overall efficiency of the organization. The CIM implementor must therefore tread a middle path as he or she implements each CIM sub-system as a route to a long-term goal of the integrated factory, and attempt to gain the benefits of each sub-system without perturbing the efficiency of any manual sub-systems that remain around CIM.

CIM systems can frequently enhance the manual systems around them by simplifying data transmission and improving user interfaces.

As a caveat, the systems implied by the descriptions of CIM and CAD/CAM in the literature rarely exist and where the programmable manufacturing technologies exist they are rarely linked to the balance of the CIM systems. The only real links are generally those associated with CAD/CAM. This itself is usually the generation of NC program data from a 2D CAD system and transfer to the machine by direct numerical control (DNC) link.

51.1.4 The balance of the chapter

The balance of the chapter continues the discussion of the CIM sub-systems, after a brief review of the technologies underpinning CIM, and then examines some of the key integrating and computer-based technologies. These technologies will include CAPP, the concepts of hierarchical control for the integration of the automated factory, and standards for data representation and transmission in CIM. The chapter then discusses software engineering practices for CIM and the languages used in the automated factory. A key part of the design of the factory is the simulation of its logical and geometric behaviour, and this is also discussed. The chapter closes with a view of some of the technologies that will affect future CIM applications, and an annotated bibliography.

51.2 Review of the industry context

The purpose of manufacturing is to add value; in the modern manufacturing facility this is carried out by machines and people. The layout of machines and people within a manufacturing plant is therefore particularly important and significantly affected by the volume and value of the parts being manufactured within the plant.

This discussion is included here to focus the attention of the software engineer on the real problems associated with manufacturing that CIM is meant to resolve, when applied with other techniques, and to emphasize that manufacturing problems are not solely solved by the application of software based technologies.

51.2.1 The expediter problem

The traditional factory is typified by a process based layout where machines of a *similar* type are grouped together – all the milling machines are in the same 'section' for example. Such facilities produce a wide variety of parts in one-offs or small batches with the help of skilled labour. Large transport and work-in-progress penalties are usually associated with older facilities of this sort which have grown organically over a number of years. The variability of the skill and amount of attention paid to the manufacturing task by an operator leads to quality variation. Such layouts rely on expediters or progress chasers to push jobs through the factory in an *ad hoc* manner. They therefore have unpredictable and unstable behaviour. Metal cutting plants worldwide have this form of layout and the attendant problems.

51.2.2 Group technology (GT) and the construction of cells

In GT layout, *different* sorts of conventional machines are grouped together into 'GT cells'. Each cell is capable of making a small variety of similar parts and the parts are handled between machines manually and the machines themselves are controlled by an operator. GT cells can reduce work-in-progress and generally increase the operating efficiency of small batch manufacture by reducing handling and transport costs. The design discipline implied by the grouping activity also reduces the proliferation of very similar but different product designs which fulfil essentially the same function. GT and feature-based designs for manufacturing systems are beginning to have a significant effect on the productivity of some innovative companies.

Many flexible factory automation systems are based on groups of parts selected by a GT approach, as are variant process planning systems.

51.2.3 Just-in-time (JIT) manufacture

Many European and US companies are following the Japanese lead to re-group larger manufacturing organizations into small sub-shop floor units, each unit being responsible for its own scheduling and first line maintenance. Such cells are increasingly being linked by paperless Kanban systems. Inventory and work in progress is reduced in Kanban by forcing 'pull-through' production control. Using 'pull-through', the production operation only makes what the customer wants, when he or she wants it, rather than basing production on a forecast of the customer's requirements. This reduces overproduction and surplus capacity in the departments that precede final assembly and dispatch.

Kanban uses containers of inventory as its production control mechanism. The customer will only release a container (i.e. the parts to be made) to carry finished parts to the supplier when the customer needs those parts. The supplier is then allowed to fill the container. In this way, each of the departments in a factory have a customer–supplier relationship. This is a key mechanism in that it ensures that the supplier satisfies the customer in terms of quality and delivery. Most importantly, each cellular unit has 'problem ownership' and therefore the drive to resolve the problems that lead to inabilities to deliver to time or quality. Such systems are usually operated together with a short-term MRP system (as is discussed later).

Kanban style disciplines are sometimes known as Just-In-Time (JIT) or continuous flow manufacture.

There are alternative organizational approaches to complete CIM for factory co-ordination. It must be recognized that it is only appropriate to install high-technology solutions like CIM once the non-functional complexity within the manufacturing activity has been removed by such organizational and 'systems' approaches.

51.2.4 Larger systems

In many plants, subsections of the manufacturing activity are organized as 'lines' of linked processing machines or people. Such layouts usually manufacture a higher volume of parts than the above system. Such complex systems demand control by sophisticated computer systems, as do perhaps the most complex presently practicable flexible manufacturing systems.

However, such complex systems should not be applied until every effort has been made to simplify the mechanical and manual systems even within the most complex of manufacturing businesses such as those found within the aerospace industry.

51.3 Enabling technologies

As indicated in the introduction, there are a number of enabling technologies that underpin the complete CIM architecture. These range from the purely mechanical through to the purely computational.

51.3.1 The machining centre

The machining centre is a particular, but the most well-developed, example of a programmable processing machine. This is a computer-controlled manufacturing device that can be programmed to carry out the metal cutting task, but is flexible enough to produce a wide variety of different components. Contrasting such a machine with a press and its associated die set, which is only able to create a single part geometry, indicates the power of such a flexible manufacturing device.

The programmability of the metal cutting machine tool has led to many of the advances one is familiar with today including the introduction of CAD/CAM systems and flexible manufacturing systems; adding the scheduling and MRP activities to these gives the complete CIM system.

Machining centres have been specially constructed to be suitable for unmanned operation for periods of about a shift. Such tools are most frequently encountered for milling and boring operations where they are called horizontal or vertical machining centres (depending on the direction of the axis of the cutter spindle) and for turning, where they are called turning centres. Turning centres often include facilities for small milling operations and occasionally other more unusual processes such as grinding. A horizontal machining centre is shown in *Figure 51.1*.

Figure 51.1 A horizontal machining centre (courtesy of FMT Ltd)

51.3.2 Computer numerical control (CNC)

Programmable machines are driven by a control program to a position in space, which must be achieved consistently. Servo control is used to achieve this. The axes of the two most commonly encountered programmable automation devices, the machine tool and the robot, have essentially the same feedback servo control hardware. This feedback control technique when used for machine tools is usually known as numerical control (NC).

Such machines are moving objects in space under computer control either as manipulators or to generate a tool cutter path. A simple machine tool consists essentially of a two (x,y) or three (x,y,z) Cartesian axis table being manipulated in front of a single point or multi-point cutter by a 'centre lathe' or 'milling machine'. A robot is a more complex device capable of movement in four or more axes which are not necessarily Cartesian and which are linked and interact in a complex manner.

The axes of these machines are driven usually by DC servo motors and the feedback collected from the rotation of the servo motor – usually measured directly or indirectly using an encoder (robots and machine tools) or inductosyn or resolver (machine tools) – and its speed, measured by a tachogenerator.

CNC implies that the NC servo system is controlled by a microprocessor within the machine. This computer is used to control the sequence activities of the machine tool and its interaction with the outside world including both manual and automatic systems. DNC implies that the machine can take the part program (the computer program describing the sequence of movements made by the machine to create the part) directly from an external store. DNC is discussed later in the chapter.

51.3.3 Transport systems

The discrete manufacturing processes within a plant are linked by a transport system. This may be manually controlled fork lift trucks for example, or automatically controlled in the form of a transfer line. Alternatively it may use a programmable machine such as a robot or automated guided vehicle. An industrial robot is a programmable machine that is used to transport objects around the manufacturing workspace. An automated guided vehicle (AGV) is a transport device that can only move in two dimensions.

51.3.4 The industrial robot

Robots have been applied in industry, for example, for spot and arc welding, spray painting, assembly and metal cutting, as well as the more familiar handling tasks. *Figure 51.2* shows the most commonly encountered robot geometries. The figure also shows the number of axes, usually the number of degrees of freedom that the machine has, and the robot workspace, i.e. the positions that the robot can reach.

51.3.5 Sensing and data collection on the shop floor

Any control system must take real data from sensors on the shop floor. Sensors used include microswitches, proximity sensors and touch trigger probes to measure position. (A touch trigger probe is often fitted to a co-ordinate measuring machine and is a form of very accurate microswitch.) There is an increasing use of machine vision on the shop floor and some use of force sensing. The shop floor is a manual as well as mechanical system and so needs to collect data from people.

One of the most significant sensing based tasks on the shop floor is that of quality assurance which ensures that the manufacturing process does not deviate outside its design capability and generate scrap products. The most powerful tool at present for this is statistical process control which tracks the variation of key process parameters and logs their deviation from the process capability. Computer-based tools are now available to automate the process of data collection and give some assistance in the interpretation of the results.

51.4 Computer-aided engineering (CAE)

51.4.1 CAD and the product model

The most basic form of CAD is interactive computer-aided 2D drafting which uses computer aids to speed the drawing process. This is often said to be automation in the form of a 'drawing processor'; compare this with a word processor.

This drawing becomes part of the CIM database and is perhaps the most significant part of the data stored in the database as it is the data describing the product itself, sometimes called the product model.

51.4.2 3D model

The above form of CAD uses only 2D data, usually as two orthographic views; 3D representations are increasingly being used as representation of the object and as the starting point for control program generation, both for NC and robotics.

A 3D computer model of an object can be built in an imaginary cube which is represented inside a computer memory,

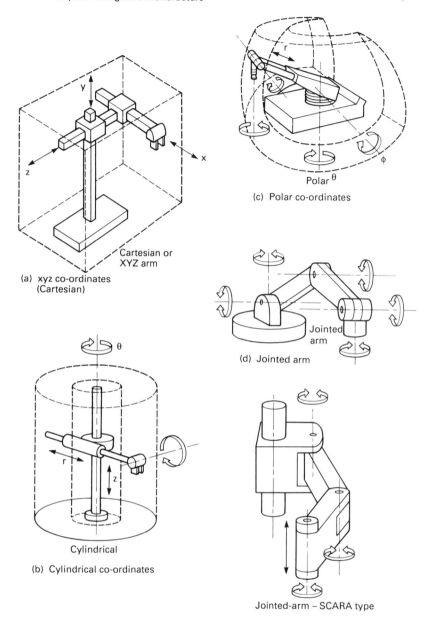

(c) Polar co-ordinates

(a) xyz co-ordinates
(Cartesian)

(d) Jointed arm

(b) Cylindrical co-ordinates

Jointed-arm – SCARA type

Figure 51.2 Robot geometries (courtesy of the British Robot Association)

the size of the cube dictating the limits of the model. The model when built can generally be viewed from any direction and more conventional 2D data extracted from it.

There are a number of significant types of modeller.

51.4.2.1 Wireframe models

A wireframe model of an object, see *Figure 51.3*, is made up of a set of 3D co-ordinates which define the end points of lines in space. The lines can be curved or straight. This type of model, because it is solely described by its edges and vertices, can only provide partial information about the shape of an object.

51.4.2.2 Surface models

Surface models hold the description of an object in terms of points, edges and faces between edges. The models produced by these systems are in the form of a mesh, constructed from a set of measured or calculated co-ordinates. These co-ordinate points, which describe the form of the surface of the object, are input to the CAD system which uses this geometry data to create a meshed surface, as shown in *Figure 51.4*. This form of model is frequently used to generate NC part programs of objects with particularly complex surface profiles such as moulds and dies, and turbine blades.

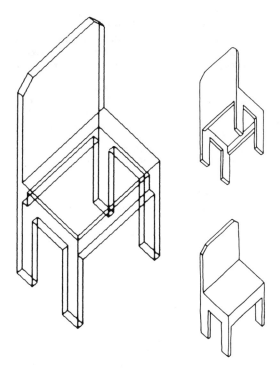

Figure 51.3 A wireframe CAD model

51.4.2.3 Solids models

A solids modeller is probably the most powerful of the 3D modelling techniques as it provides the user with complete information about the outline, surface, volume and mass properties of the model. A solids modeller holds a complete description of an object, in terms of the space which it occupies. The description can indicate whether any point is inside or outside the object and whether it lies on the surface of any object. Solids modellers build up models from primitives that can be described mathematically, usually by one of two methods: constructive solid geometry (CSG) and boundary representation models (BRep).

51.4.2.4 Constructive solid geometry (CSG)

The CSG model models the design as simple primitive solid elements which are built up by operations that combine them. The model is built by the user defining the type of primitive required (cube, cylinder etc.), its key dimensions and position relative to an origin and its relationship with primitives already created. The relationships are usually Boolean operations, such as union, intersection or difference. It is also necessary to use an 'assemble' operator to recognize the difference between the union of two primitives as a single object and the building of the same two primitives into an assembly (as a mechanism for example). *Figure 51.5* shows an example of the primitives used to construct a model, an indication of the Boolean operations and a final model.

CSG models have to be re-evaluated after each design change and therefore interaction with these models can be difficult.

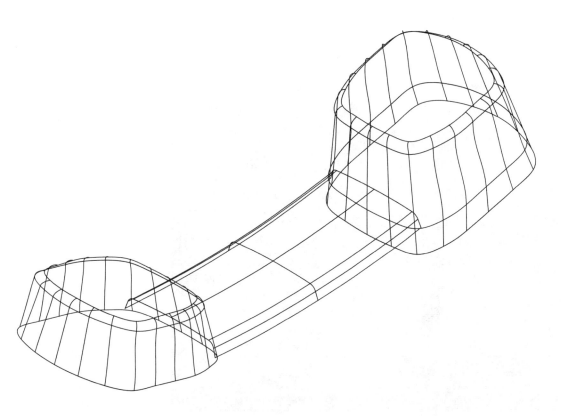

Figure 51.4 A surface CAD model (courtesy of NC Graphics Ltd)

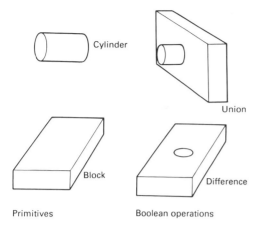

Figure 51.5 Constructing simple CSG solid models

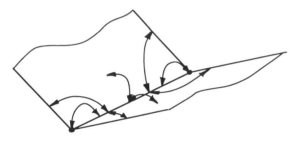

Figure 51.6 The winged edge data structure (after Woodwark (1986) *Computing Shape*, Butterworths)

51.4.2.5 Boundary representation models (BRep)

The BRep model uses a boundary file data structure. In this approach every face edge and vertex of the final object is represented and the data structure defines the geometry of each detail and how the details are connected. The usual data structure used is the 'winged edge' – a directed graph which gives bi-directional pointers from every edge in the model to its two end vertices, two adjacent faces and the four other edges that share a face and a vertex with it. The winged edge data structure is shown in *Figure 51.6*.

The BRep model provided fast image generation, direct user interaction and allows a variety of modelling operations.

51.4.2.6 Mechanical CAD

There are a wide variety of applications of CAD models in manufacturing, for example, as input data for finite element models used for stress or heat flow analysis, or to generate complex cutter paths for machine tools. As a result of this a CAD model using a single representation of the product is not efficient for all purposes. It is therefore necessary to use hybrid modelling schemes where complex surfaces can be abstracted from the single model, for example, when it is necessary to generate blends between solids of complex curvature to create a die or pattern.

51.4.2.7 Electronic computer-aided design (ECAD)

The bulk of the preceding discussion has concentrated on mechanical CAD. It should, however, be recognized that CIM technologies are equally applicable to the manufacture of VLSI or printed circuits. These products are usually inserted into mechanical assemblies at the end of their processing and therefore need to be handled in mechanical CAD systems. They have, however, particular needs which have led to the production of ECAD systems.

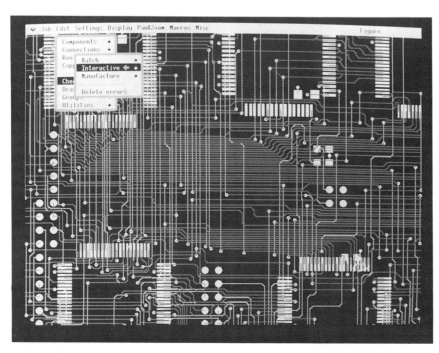

Figure 51.7 ECAD for PCB layout (courtesy of Racal Redac Ltd)

ECAD systems support the designer in creating a design which describes the electrical properties of a circuit, the behaviour of which is then simulated. When the design performs satisfactorily the CAD system will generate a net list which describes the components used in the design and their connectivity. This net list is then used to generate a placement pattern for the physical layout of components on a circuit board. All this can be done automatically, with perhaps a final difficult routing decision being made by a planning engineer, as indicated by *Figure 51.7*. It is a small step in the essentially 2D world of electronics to turn this layout into artwork for PCB manufacture or placement instructions for a component placement machine.

51.5 CAM and automated manufacturing systems

A computer-aided automated manufacturing system can be considered to have three basic elements:

1. The machine tools and manufacturing processes themselves.
2. The transport and handling (including storage) sub-system for parts and tools.
3. The control sub-system which includes the controlling elements and the sensors that feed back the system state.

Both (2) and (3) may be manual.

51.5.1 Direct numerical control (DNC)

One of the precursors of current manufacturing systems approaches is DNC. In DNC installations the individual machines are linked to a central computer which stores part programs on disc. When an operator wishes to run a particular part program he or she can call for it at the individual machine and it is downloaded from the main computer to the particular machine. DNC installations are usually encountered where there are a large number of NC machine tools running a large number of part programs. Such installations are sometimes known as distributed numerical control systems to distinguish them from older DNC installations where programs were downloaded to machines program block by program block.

51.5.2 The manufacturing cell

This can be viewed in an almost biological way as the smallest autonomous unit capable of sustained production. As the cell is automated the cell must be unmanned for extended periods and therefore must be controlled and 'integrated' by a computer system.

A cell is the next level of integration 'up' from single machines and typically consists of a number of machines of different types supplied by different manufacturers. *Figure 51.8* shows a typical multi-machine integrated cell.

The autonomy of a cell requires that there is:

1. Automated or programmable processes; for example, a CNC machine, insertion machine or robot.
2. Automated handling to and from these processes using, for example, a robot.
3. Automated quality control or inspection of the performance of the processes together with rapid feedback of any necessary changes to each process.
4. Supervisory control and sensors to monitor and detect the cell condition and to decide the next activity.

There is some confusion as to the definitions of the expressions cell and workstation. Some US work cells are called workstations, and the workshop level of integration known as a system in the UK is sometimes called a cell.

Figure 51.8 A multi-machine manufacturing cell (courtesy of FMT ltd)

51.5.3 Transfer lines

Flexible transfer lines, sometimes flexible flow lines, generally take one of two forms: either robots carrying out a process linked by a conveyor or pallet shuttle, and/or machining centres, linked in a similar way.

The components in the system always move along the same path. A flexible transfer line usually has limited product variety and is often encountered in automotive applications. They can be reconfigured for another family of components by reprogramming the individual machines. Programmability allows product development and design changes during plant start-up which can dramatically reduce design to product lead times.

51.5.4 Flexible manufacturing systems (FMS)

An FMS consists of three or more machining centres, turning machines, fabricating centres or the like equipped with flexible automatic loading/unloading/transfer devices and a method of monitoring tool conditions and replacement. The entire production scheduling and machining process is automatically supervised by a computer system.

A monolithic FMS consists of programmable machines, a single parts transport sub-system, a tool transport system and storage for tools and components, this all being under the control of a hierarchical computer system. *Figure 51.9* shows such a system. Monolithic implies that the whole system was conceived, built and financially justified at one go. The size and complexity of such systems makes them difficult to design, install, commission and financially justify. These systems are suited, however, to high product variety. Monolithic FMSs usually integrate prismatic machining centres, i.e. centres dealing with essentially box-like components.

Such systems are sometimes called random access systems as they allow access of any component to any machine at any time. Because of this, they have high re-scheduling flexibility. Such systems have been constructed to produce parts for machine tools, automotive engine components, complete valves and prototype parts.

51.5.5 Supercells

Monolithic systems were often conceived before the mechanical and computational complexities of such systems were recognized. Because of the complexity and difficulties associated with the once-off design, financial justification, installation, commissioning, and operation of large systems, FMSs of linked cells have been constructed, see *Figure 51.10*.

These are sometimes called supercells. They can be constructed cell by cell and linked with a transport system at a later date. Such systems are usually constructed for smaller parts families than monolithic FMS and have a number of cells within them carrying out a similar function. They also do not operate on 'batch of one' principles (whereas monolithic FMS do). Batch of one implies that the system performs as efficiently producing a single part as it does when producing a series of the same part, implying that the set-up costs of the system are small. This cannot usually be assumed.

There is redundancy within the system to cope with sub-system failures so, for example, production may be routed to other cells of similar functionality when one particular cell fails. The sub-systems can have a variety of functions such as cutting, welding or assembly.

51.5.6 Automated storage and retrieval system (ASRS)

An ASRS is essentially an automated warehouse system with perhaps some associated AGV or conveyor-based transport system to take parts (or kits of parts) to other areas in the facility. They usually consist of high bay warehouses served by aisle cranes, that are either manned or unmanned. They can be used to store work-in-progress (at a minimum of course), fixtures and tooling, and finished goods. They are widely applied across all industries and are used significantly within the supply industry.

51.5.7 Assembly and test

Much of the discussion within this chapter has confined itself to

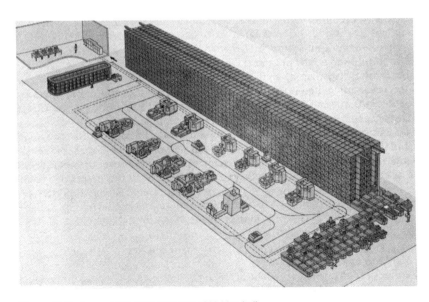

Figure 51.9 A monolithic FMS (courtesy of Makino Ltd)

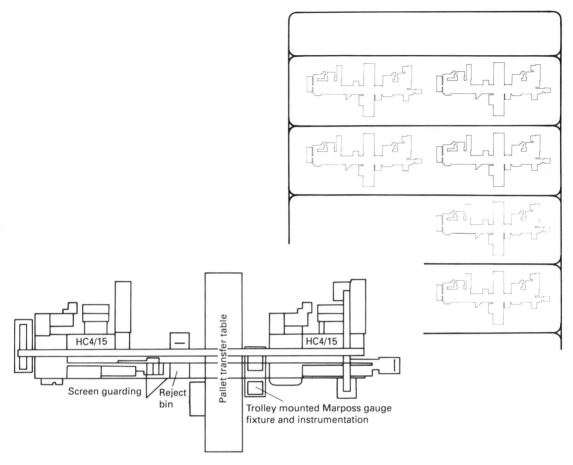

Figure 51.10 Cellular FMS (courtesy of TI Machine Tools Ltd)

the production of components; these components are inevitably assembled to create the final product. Assembly is rarely automated as it is possible to design for ease of assembly and to make careful use of people in such a way that the automation and computer assistance of mechanical assembly is not financially justifiable. It can only usually be justified for annual volumes of the order of a million components, and these volumes are rarely found outside the automotive and electronics sector.

Automated testing of final product assemblies has similar constraints. Tools are, however, now emerging that assist in the statistical process control activity.

51.6 CAPM or manufacturing information systems

There are a number of significant 'managerial' tasks that have to be carried out within a conventional, non automated, manufacturing business. These tasks are closely related and make the following decisions:

1. *Master production scheduling*. Deciding when an order is released to the shop floor.

2. *Materials requirements planning*. Ordering the raw material for manufacture and bought-out components in sufficient time for them to be ready for manufacture.
3. *Inventory management*. The management of the inventory that arises from the above decisions.
4. *Finite capacity planning*. Deciding what jobs to release to the shop floor taking into account a real measure of the capacity of that shop floor.

Such systems may be applied in isolation without, for example, an automated shop floor.

All of the decisions above are made from a knowledge of the product structure information. This is usually the list of the components within a product and is a multi-level 'explosion' of data when components of the product are sub-assemblies. Such data will also include the options and variants on the product, and modifications or engineering alterations. This is sometimes known as the bill of materials (BOM). It will be apparent that for realistically-sized companies with realistically-sized product ranges this represents a considerable amount of data.

Efforts are being made to standardize the manner in which such data is presented. A complete product description will also include a full description of the geometry; perhaps the most significant activity here is the developing ISO standard, Standard for the Exchange of Product Data (STEP), which is likely to subsume all other similar standards efforts.

51.6.1 Master production schedule planning (MPS)

To run the manufacturing business, the first thing it is necessary to generate is a long-term manufacturing plan describing what is to be made and when, and from this to devise an MPS which controls the activity of the shop floor.

This activity uses knowledge of the overall business plan and performance – essentially sales forecasts and firm customer orders, and knowledge of the significant resource constraints of the business (people, machines and money for example) to make its decisions. It should be recognized here that all forecasts are inaccurate, whether they are based on predicted sales or extrapolations of historical demand data. Consideration of this data will indicate where the constraints of the plant are limiting production and allow the planner to circumvent them by calling for extra sub-contracting, or increasing plant capacity by the installation of new equipment.

51.6.2 Materials requirements planning (MRP)

The MRP system ensures that sufficient material is available to allow the overall business plan reflected by the master production schedule to proceed. An MRP system needs the following as its basic input data:

1. A master production schedule.
2. The present stock levels across the whole of the plant.
3. The status of orders (whether they are committed to customers or released to production – the balance being the planning variable).
4. The rules for determining the order quantity and its lead time.
5. The product structure.

The MRP sysem proceeds in its calculations by generating a plan of gross requirements. It then takes stock and safety stock off this plan to generate a net plan and increases this net plan with an allowance for manufacturing scrap. After taking off any orders already committed from this plan it then generates a due date for the order to be finished. Removing the manufacturing lead time or purchase lead time from this gives that date when orders should be released to production or suppliers.

MRP is a large processing activity because of the volume of data involved in the calculation and it is therefore usually run infrequently, for example, monthly or weekly. The re-planning activity occurs because the plan is frequently overtaken by events, the winning of new orders for example. To give more realistic plans with a longer lifetime, the concept of net change MRP has been introduced. Net change MRP re-plans only when there have been changes to the data on which the plan was based, acting to propagate these changes through the system to generate re-evaluated plans.

51.6.3 Capacity planning

Many planning systems assume infinite capacity within the manufacturing plant. However, it is necessary to ensure that there actually is sufficient resource to manufacture the predicted orders. To do this a plan is needed for the actual (finite) capacity of the plant.

This activity is carried out in the following manner. First the system determines the orders being worked on within the factory and the planned orders generated by the MRP system and obtains a description of the path of the product through the facility. This is the process plan (or routing) and includes set-up data and a description of the facility to a necessary level of detail. Such detail could include its capability in production volume terms, and for example, when planned maintenance is to take place. Processing this data by working backwards from

when a due date is required (back scheduling) will indicate problems such as that the capacity of a group of machines is exceeded at certain times or that the manufacture of an order should already be in progress! Sophisticated systems may advise options that will circumvent these problems.

51.6.4 Manufacturing resource planning (MRPII)

MRPII is a complete software system that serves all of the organizational functions required in manufacturing. It consists essentially of MRP extended with finite capacity planning and some ability to rework the overall plan to take into account capacity restrictions.

51.6.5 Comments

It is increasingly recognized in manufacturing where there is not a large product range that there are alternative solutions to the planning problem rather than the application of large software systems like MRPII. In such cases Kanban style scheduling and inventory control disciplines have been applied with short-term MRP systems with some success.

All the software systems above assume the existence of a foreman who has the talent to do short-term job scheduling that ensures the overall schedules and plans are followed. This is not usually the case in automated systems and the controller of the automated system must have facilities to take over from the foreman. Some of the complexity associated with these systems is indicated below.

Although the concepts behind the design of such software systems can be stated simply, as they have been above, it must be recalled that the numbers of products it is necessary to control in such systems for example, in the aerospace business, make the software design problem particularly difficult.

It should be observed that the output from many of the existing CAPM systems are intended to be interpreted by people before the planning decisions that they suggest are implemented. In the future, as the CIM system becomes more integrated and automated, there will not be an opportunity to review the decisions before they are passed to the execution system. This has significant implications for the need to make present generation CAPM systems more robust.

51.7 Integrating technologies

The above text has taken the view that CIM can be resolved into distinct technologies but it cannot always be so considered and CIM must be viewed as a factory-wide strategy. The approach taken here, however, does allow a discussion of the obvious elements of the technology and the manner in which they are linked. Two of the key linking technologies are that of the CAD/CAM link and the single shared database. These technologies have also been supported by the wide adoption of local area networks in manufacturing.

51.7.1 CAD/CAM and CAPP

The key technologies that link CAD and CAM are those that take the representation of the part that is contained in the drawing and facilitate the definition of the manufacturing route. There are two elements in this route: the definition of the sequence of machining activities that are carried out on the part and the generation of the instructions that control the motions of each machine in the route. These are confusingly known by the same acronym – CAPP – which can mean computer-aided process planning or computer-aided part programming.

51.7.1.1 Computer-aided part programming

NC, numerical control, or part programming, is the process of obtaining from the detail drawing of a part, control data which can be used by a numerically controlled machine to produce the part. These instructions are either put into the machine manually by typing directly at its controller (known as manual data input) or are prepared as a punched or magnetic tape and read by a tape reader incorporated in the machine controller.

Computer-aided techniques have therefore been developed, sometimes known as processors. Although still manually extracting the data from an engineering drawing, the programmer specifies the motions required of the tool in a higher level language than the machine tool codes used above. These processors require the use of post-processors to convert the high-level code generated into machine tool code instructions.

Each particular type of machine tool will have its own particular post-processor because of, for example, its particular geometry and the particular actions and number of machine tool codes implemented on that machine.

The most frequently encountered high level programming language or processor used is automatically programmed tools (APT). It is a very large, complex language and many simpler subsets have been developed for more specialized applications such as: ADAPT, for 2.5 axis contour milling and EXAPT 1 (Drilling), II (Turning) and III (Milling). In EXAPT tools, feeds, speeds, and machining sequences can be automatically generated by the processor.

Machine tools are being marketed that allow conversational programming. They are aimed at the small workshop where it is usual for the machine operator to program the machine. This is generally found on machines that do not generate very complex geometries, such as CNC lathes and three axis milling machines.

Conversational part programming is typically supported by a simple graphics screen with menu-driven software.

Machine tool part programs can be generated directly from CAD descriptions of the part. This is what is usually known as CAD/CAM, the link between computer-aided design and computer-aided manufacture. By capturing the engineering drawing there is already a great deal of data representing the form of a product in a computer. It would be sensible to use this data for other tasks within the organization requiring product data, rather than generating this data again by reading the computer-prepared drawing.

Computer-aided part programming, then, can prepare code, often via APT, for metal cutting machine tools. The programmer/designer driving the CAD screen selects a program already developed for a similar object and tailors it to the new part. The prepared code can be transferred to the machine by a data network.

51.7.1.2 Computer-aided process planning

There are essentially three forms of computer-based process planning. These are generative, variant (sometimes called iterative) or constructive. The aim of generative process planning is to generate automatically from a CAD description of the part, a completely new manufacturing route. This is still a major research area. Variant process planning, on the other hand, assists the methods or planning engineer to vary the design of the plan for a master part that has been chosen for its similarity to the new part. This matching of the new part to the master part relies on being able to identify the correct master part. This is usually carried out with a variation of a group technology coding system. A GT code is a string of symbols (usually alphanumeric) which can be used to classify the part for its shape and function and include variable data such as batch size. Constructive process planning emulates the manual planning

approach by constructing a plan from preferred standard operations that have been selected to be desirable after a study of the manufacturing capability of the plant.

51.7.2 The single CIM database

Integrating all the computer-based sub-systems and tools in the manufacturing CIM ensures that all sub-systems within the system use the same data which is held in the same single database. This single database contains static, once per design data (CAE, CAD, CAPP and BOM etc.), and dynamic, once per manufacturing cycle data (CAPM, manufacturing schedules).

This has a number of effects:

1. Data is not duplicated for example; the original design data describing the shape of the component is used to generate the part program.
2. Data errors are not propagated because original data is always used.
3. Data storage is minimized.

51.7.2.1 Practical CIM databases

It must be recognized that in current practical implementations it is impossible to generate a single database that can be used to describe the complete manufacturing facility, the designs within it, and be able to track all the products that are passing through the plant. This leads to the concept of a distributed database – the data being closest to where it is needed. The major problem associated with such an approach is maintaining the consistency of data that is necessarily stored in more than one sub-system. Decisions must also be made on which data should be passed between the sub-systems.

51.7.3 Local area networks (LANs)

The adoption of LANs on the shop floor and in the design and other offices of the manufacturing business has also contributed significantly to the integration of manufacturing. See Chapter 53 for a review of networks and protocols.

There has been a significant standardization effort in LANs for manufacturing resulting in the Manufacturing Automation Protocol (MAP) and Technical and Office Protocol (TOP) standards. These are particular instantiations of the ISO OSI communications model, with the MAP protocol being, for example, a token bus. It should be observed that the robustness of commercially proven, more general-purpose, networks such as Ethernet on the shop floor has reduced the impact of MAP activity. However, the efforts of the MAP community to develop a syntax for manufacturing messages is likely to be a significant long-term contribution to the integration of CIM systems.

51.7.4 Hierarchical control

The task in controlling an automated CIM facility is the management of a complex collection of machines and computer-based activities.

It is usual to control any manufacturing system with a hierarchy of computers, and this control hierarchy is often practically partitioned according to conventional organizational models. An example of such a hierarchy divided to allow the control of a number of cells is shown as *Figure 51.11*.

This hierarchical division is often forced upon manufacturing because of the range of suppliers of equipment at the lower levels and the sophistication required to control these low-level equipments, due to their particular mechanical and electrical design. It is unlikely that such sophistication will be duplicated

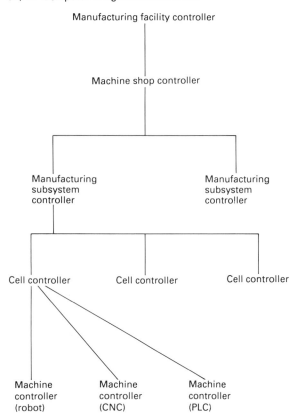

Machine shop controller

Figure 51.11 Hierarchical control

in higher level controllers. The AMRF control system architecture showing the concepts of hierarchical control with single static and dynamic databases, is shown as *Figure 51.12*.

Most conventional automated factory control systems are devolved hierarchically to keep the control problem manageable. A particular model for this decomposition was developed at the Advanced Manufacturing Research Facility (AMRF) at the National Institute of Standards and Technology in the USA. In this model, high-level goals are successively decomposed to lower level control modules until a sequence of coordinated primitive actions is generated. These primitive actions will be simple machine-level commands which can be understood by, for example, a proprietary robot controller or other shop-floor controller. Each control module is implemented as a state table, each line of table effectively representing a condition-action rule.

51.8 Software engineering for CIM

51.8.1 CIM reference models

A number of CIM and factory reference models exist which are intended to allow the structured design and review of CIM systems.

The overall systems view – sometimes known as the physics view – models the enterprise as a small number of simple components: information, control and material, that combine in a number of different ways.

Some of the CIM modelling schemes take software and data modelling techniques as their starting point. Standard software engineering approaches such as Yourdon or Structured Analysis and Design diagrams (see Chapter 17) are frequently used for manufacturing analysis where they are known as ICAM Definition Methodology (IDEF) diagrams. At the implementation level, the three schema database view of an implementation architecture makes the point that there can be three viewpoints on an architecture – the internal schema which describes the physical storage structure, and the conceptual schema – describing an idealized internal representation and the external schema which users construct to suit particular applications (see Chapters 54 and 55 for a fuller discussion on database designs). Other models, for example, those used in DNC, partition themselves as the familiar ISO OSI model of communications.

There are also models of the factory as a control structure. These are usually hierarchical and tend to partition the facility in terms of its organizational or materials-handling structure into enterprise, factory, workshop, cell and machine for example.

51.8.2 Computers for manufacturing

Much of the early experience of CIM technologies was in companies with large CAD or inventory control installations. These were usually centred on a mainframe computer which was accessed via terminals, these being higher performance graphics terminals in the case of the CAD system. The mainframe-centred technology had the advantage that access to files could be controlled easily with, for example, only one designer at a time being allowed to make alterations to a drawing file master, thus implicitly controlling the duplication of data and preventing the propagation of data errors.

The technology, especially in the design and planning area, is now becoming workstation-centred, with these workstations being either engineering workstations or personal workstations. These are usually networked by a proprietary network. The hardware partition between the engineering and personal workstation is becoming less distinct, as the high-end personal machine approaches the functionality of the low-end workstation, and workstations are fitted with personal computer emulations. However, the marketplace is partitioned by the software vendors, with some particularly targeting the personal computer and some the workstation. The implication of this is that more systems of lower functionality are sold to the personal workstation market at a lower price level, while comparatively few, but more expensive, high-function systems are sold to the engineering workstation market.

For the control of the shop-floor devices without their own integral controller and automation systems particular computers are used, known as programmable logic controllers (PLCs). These are ruggedized microprocessors which are programmed via a terminal that is brought to the machine and then removed (thus preventing unauthorized alterations to the program and machine cycle). They are usually of modular mechanical construction and can be configured for particular tasks by the addition of a variety of I/O modules.

51.8.3 Operating systems and open systems

The manufacturing marketplace is very conservative and has been dominated by the major suppliers, who have the commercial structures to support installations in major manufacturing companies. This means that in the past systems have run under the operating system of the selected supplier. Once a manufacturing company has made a choice of this magnitude, the effects of the decision will be felt for many years. This is a result of the life of data within such systems and the need to pass this data

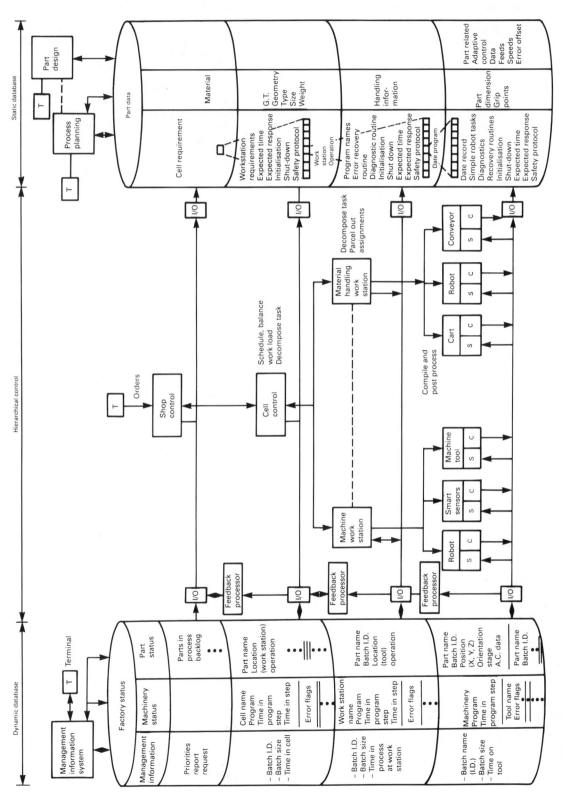

Figure 51.12 The AMRF Control System Architecture at The National Institute of Standards and Technology, Gaithersburg, MA, USA

from system to system when the operating hardware and software are updated. It is usually considered that, for engineering computing, the platform lasts five years, the software system ten years and the data 25 years.

As a result, open systems approaches and Unix are not penetrating the manufacturing market as fast as the academic or other marketplaces. There are, of course, many standardization efforts which seek to allow more open systems, but they are frequently overtaken by the arrival of a new product or the recognition that a mature product, with which many have experience, effectively fulfills the function as a standard.

51.8.4 Data integrity

51.8.4.1 Distributed data storage

As described above distributed data storage causes problems for CIM installations as it can allow the proliferation of different data stores holding the same or similar data, or data describing one entity being scattered through the system. This must be carefully controlled in the design and analysis element of the CIM system. However, it has been recognized that the necessarily distributed nature of the manufacturing shop-floor computing equipment, and hence the data with it, has certain advantages for real-time operation and fault-tolerant operation.

51.8.4.2 Shop-floor data collection

For the management and inventory control elements of the CIM technologies there is a significant problem associated with the collection of data from the shop floor. Data for such systems is usually entered into the system from terminals on the shop floor by an operator who is required to input the changes in status of a set of parts. If this is overlooked for some reason the data within the factory control system will not reflect the true state of the manufacturing facility, with the result that over time the model system, and the decisions made upon it, will considerably deviate from those required by the real system. For this reason it is necessary to have control over data input and periodic audits of inventory to update the data within the computer system.

51.8.5 Integration of shop-floor devices

While many of the devices and sub-systems in CIM systems come from different vendors, the standard activities discussed above have gone some way to allowing their integration. Many of the standards allow the passing of data and messages between systems in standard forms. However, they have not yet standardized the control messages that allow one application to receive data from another or to pass control messages to a device. This is the CIM equivalent of device driving. Solutions are now coming forward, from the academic and commercial community, that will parse output messages in the language of one device into the appropriate instruction string in the input language of another. Such systems are based on rewrite rule-based parsers.

51.9 Languages for CIM

The range of languages used within CIM is very wide. This is a result of the view of many that it is the integration of sub-systems written by different suppliers from different industry groups.

CAD, CAE and simulation systems, for example, have been traditionally written in FORTRAN because of its strength in 'formula translation'; software has grown over time and it is

rare that packages are reimplemented in new languages. Similarly, many of the business systems have their roots in COBOL. Database systems, being a comparatively recent innovation, are more computationally up-to-date and can be addressed by query languages such as SQL.

Shop-floor devices are programmed in a variety of languages, showing the range of suppliers involved and the different roots of the technologies. Machine tools are programmed with machine tool codes, a very basic instruction set. This reflects their early standardized adoption within a conservative industry. Robots and vision systems are programmed in a range of Pascal-like languages or machine-tool code-like languages, the particular language depending on the specific supplier. PLCs are also real-time systems programmed with proprietary machine-level instruction sets. There are, however, a number of graphical programming interfaces often used by inexperienced programmers.

C is becoming all-pervasive, with object-oriented versions beginning to penetrate the research community. Many manufacturing researchers are using artificial intelligence languages.

51.10 Simulation

The systems described here are complex, and it is usual to design them using some form of simulation system.

Computer simulation is experimentation on a computer-based model of a system. The model is used as a vehicle for experimentation, usually in a trial-and-error way, to demonstrate the likely effects of changing design variables. Generally, the problems that simulation is applied to do not yield to the application of more conventional mathematical models, as such models find it difficult to cope with dynamic and transient effects and nondeterministic inputs. However, many of the tasks that simulations are capable of are regarded as operational research (OR) and it is difficult to determine the transition between the design engineering problem and the OR problem. It should be emphasized that simulation should be used alongside more conventional analytical techniques.

The particular design problems here are unstructured and involve quantitative, qualitative and spatial data. Consequently, simulators are usually computer-based, using interactive graphics.

When planning a manufacturing system of any complexity, it is necessary to model the operational behaviour of the system. Discrete event modelling is a well-established tool for this task. Discrete event modelling implies that the behaviour of the system is modelled in a step-by-step, event-by-event way, so that the system has transitions from state to state rather than varying as a continuous function. The most common approach uses a simulation package which provides a 'front-end' language or menu system to ease the process of model building rather than a general-purpose simulation language.

Such systems are used to determine the number of devices within a system and the operating strategy of a system. Such a detailed simulation stage can be preceded by a queuing theory-based modelling stage (see Chapter 6 for details of relevant queuing theory).

Some CAD systems can be used to model and evaluate industrial robot work places and allow the designer to build a static model of the workspace and cell components to check their spatial layout, ensuring that all the elements of the cell fit together and into the appropriate space. He or she can also check that the cell elements are within the reach of the robot. After a static simulation has been drawn, this can be animated to give a 'dyanamic simulation' of the operation of the cell. In such a dynamic simulation the robot is moved around the cell to make an estimation of the cell cycle time and allow checking between the items within the cell. The simulation also ensures that the robot joints are within their limits for the particular cell layout.

In the simulation it is necessary to control the simulated position of the robot. This is done by defining the desired position and orientation of the tool. The simulator can then compute all the joint attitudes using data about the robot given when the model was created. Having developed a program to drive the robot model, a natural development is to provide a post-processor that will produce a usable robot program. It is necessary to adjust this 'theoretical' robot program for errors in the workspace and the robot before the program can be executed safely. This is carried out by a calibration program.

Simulation systems have emerged over the last two years that link the two technologies, allowing the designer to model the geometric aspects of the plant and the logical aspects in one integrated package.

51.11 CIM and factory automation futures

CIM is a fast moving technology, based upon rapidly improving computing platforms and programming environments. It is therefore worth spending the closing part of the chapter examining likely future directions in the technology.

51.11.1 Feature-based design and variant process planning

As mentioned earlier, one of the major research efforts is in generative process planning, that is, the generation of a process route and machine part programs directly from a CAD description of a part. There is now some success in this area for the manufacture of prismatic (box-like) parts.

A significant problem has been the recognition of manufacturing features (for example, holes, surfaces, undercuts) from solid or other CAD model descriptions of the part which contain solely 'position' information. This had led to much work in parsers that are able to recognize such manufacturing features. However, the realisation that feature-based design systems – that is, systems where the designer builds up the design from parametric feature elements rather than using points, lines and intersections – can cut out this step and allow process planning to proceed without difficulty.

However, there is some argument as to whether feature-based design systems will allow the designer to specify geometries that are needed for key functions within a design. If there are constraints then some of the elements of the planning task may still have to be carried out manually.

51.11.2 Concurrent engineering environments

It is becoming increasingly recognized that, for a manufacturer to remain competitive in a world marketplace, design-to-product lead times must become shorter. This has led to the introduction of concurrent, simultaneous engineering concepts. In simultaneous engineering, the product and the manufacturing process (the processes and facility) are designed together instead of sequentially as has been the practice in the past. This has two significant implications for the sorts of CAD environment that will be used in the future. First, designs are likely to be generated with CAD tools that will allow concept design and simulation (rough-and-ready design) before the design is completely worked out. Second, such design environments will need to contain significant software systems that are capable of advising the designer on the manufacturability of the product.

51.11.3 Alternative control schemes

51.11.3.1 System control architectures

The factory floor is a spatially distributed environment which contains specialized machines that carry out particular manufacturing tasks. For efficient manufacture it is necessary to orchestrate the activities of this environment. Within the automated factory this is carried out by an integrating control architecture.

As has been mentioned above, the usual approach to the control task achieves integration by decomposing the control task in a strictly hierarchical manner, the upper levels in the hierarchy being responsible for wider task descriptions and longer control time spans. Such methods rely on centralized data storage within a system, and master–slave relationships between the entities within the system. The advantages of such systems are that control is deterministic and that no data is lost to the higher level computers. Such systems are, however, slow and are not robust to sub-system failure.

The alternative approach couples devices loosely into a heterarchical framework, control proceeding by peer-to-peer communication and negotiation as is indicated by *Figure 51.13*. The advantages of this approach are that it can be fast for large systems, is robust to sub-system failure and requires considerably less software design effort. The disadvantages of this approach are that some hierarchical links are inevitable in a practical implementation and that some data may not be visible to a management control system.

The two approaches are complementary and elements of each solution will be applicable to the control of particular manufacturing tasks. Any final future practical control architecture is therefore likely to be a hybrid, involving some master–slave control and communication, and some negotiation and peer-to-peer communication.

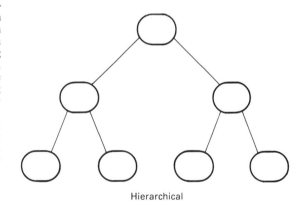

Hierarchical

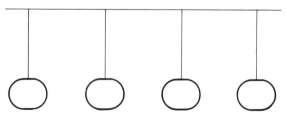

Heterarchical

Figure 51.13 Alternative control architectures

51.11.3.2 *Process control and diagnosis*

There has been a large body of work worldwide on expert control and diagnosis systems for slow, continuous, processes which has moved more and more towards the real-time processes used in discrete manufacture. Examples of the use of such control systems can be found for autoclave control, composite lay up, hot isostatic pressing and spray atomization. These efforts will mean that many more processes become controllable and hence programmable and able to take full advantage of CIM approaches.

Engineering expert systems or toolkits aimed at such control tasks usually include a number of features: object orientation to model the flow of control information in a system; inheritance to fac. :tate rapid prototyping and development from previously successful generalized forms; forward production systems (sets of antecedent → consequent rules); and backward chaining systems, with agenda-based priority scheduling to allow some interruption of the process. The initially purely semantic problem and control model descriptions embodied in the antecedents within conventional expert systems have been extended with the ability to include mathematical models to create 'engineering expert systems'.

The significant contribution of the artificial intelligence approach is that it allows very high-level problem and model descriptions (and rapid prototyping); the disadvantage being that it has to be supported by quantities of low-level code (usually written in the C programming language) to translate the signal data from the plant into semantic primitives.

Such expert controllers include heuristics and mathematical models describing material and process behaviours.

51.11.4 Manufacturing intelligence

As indicated above there are significant opportunities for the application of expert systems and artificial intelligence-based software techniques in manufacturing. Much of the skill of manufacturing engineers has been acquired as a result of the long experience of the manufacturing community. Manufacturing does not have the long and formalized scientific base associated with other engineering disciplines. Because of this, expert approaches are attractive to the manufacturing community. Particular opportunities for this are 'design-for-manufacture' systems which can test a part description for manufacturability, manufacturing system configuration tools and more expert schedulers for small high value facilities.

It is widely considered that the object-oriented programming paradigm will be of significant value to CIM software engineers, promoting as it does the re-use and specialization of code. Much CIM code has to be tailored to particular installations and problems and is constructed in a modular manner. Object-orientation is a natural extension of this approach.

51.12 Concluding comment

CIM is not solely a software technology. It relies on many mechanical engineering skills and is of no value to the manufacturing community unless it solves manufacturing problems.

51.13 Bibliography

CIM General

Wetherall, A. (ed) (1988) *CIM*, Butterworths
[Overview of CIM.]
Rembold, U. and Dillman, R. (eds) (1986) *Computer-Aided Design and Manufacturing*, Springer-Verlag
[Thorough examination of CIM technologies. Second edition of a book based on a short course.]

Ranky, P. G. (1985) *CIM*, IFS Publications
[Perhaps the first CIM book, draws on a wide variety of experience.]

CAD

Woodwark, J. (1986) *Computing Shape*, Butterworths
[First-class short overview of the CAD and modelling technologies.]
Faux, I. D. (1979) *Computational Geometry for Design and Manufacture*, Ellis Horwood
[*The* book on computational geometry – how you represent and process shape in a computer.]

CAM and manufacturing systems

Williams, D. J. (1988) *Manufacturing Systems, an Introduction to the Technologies*, Open University Press
[Bottom-up view of automated manufacture, its control and integration.]
Koren, Y. (1983) *Computer Control of Manufacturing Systems*, McGraw Hill
[Short control engineers view of manufacturing systems.]

Group technology

Gallagher, C. C. and Knight, W.A. (1986) *Group Technology Methods in Manufacturing*, Ellis Horwood

Machine tools and robots

Weck, M. (1984) *Handbook of Machine Tools* (four volumes), Wiley
[Source work for machine tools.]
Boothroyd, G. (1981) *Fundamentals of Metal Machining and Machine Tools*, McGraw Hill
[Overview of the mechanical engineering problems associated with metal cutting.]
Engleberger, J. (1980) *Robotics in Practice*, Kogan Page
[Popular applications book by the 'father' of robotics.]
Appleton, E. and Williams, D. J. (1987) *Industrial Robot Applications*, Open University Press
[Review of robot applications in manufacturing and how to design them.]
Fu, K. S., Gonzalez, R. C. and Lee, C. S. G. (1987) *Robotics – Control, Sensing Vision and Intelligence*, McGraw Hill
[Introduction to advanced robotics.]
Dorf, R. C. (ed.) (1988) *International Encyclopedia of Robotics*, Wiley
[Large source of robotics data.]

MRP and MRPII

Wight, O. W. (1974) *Production and Inventory Management in the Computer Age*, Gower
[MRP straight from the horse's mouth.]
Wallace, T. F. (1985) *MRP II, Making it happen*, Oliver Wight Productions Ltd
[The same for MRPII.]

Hierarchical control and networking

Jones A. and McClean, C. (1986) A proposed hierarchical control model for automated manufacturing systems. *Journal of Manufacturing Systems*, **5**, 15–26
[Paper summarizing the Advanced Manufacturing Research Facility (AMRF) at the National Institute of Standards and Technology (NIST) formerly the National Bureau of Standards, Washington.]
General Motors Technical Center, (1988) *MAP Specification, Version 3.0*
[The full MAP specification.]

Simulation and modelling

Ziegler, B. P. (1976) *Theory of Modelling and Simulation*, Wiley
[The source book on the formal background to simulation.]
Pidd, M. (1984) Discrete Event Simulation in Management Science, Wiley
[Primer in simulation.]

Peterson, J. L. (1981) *Petri Net Theory and the Modelling of Systems*, Prentice Hall, Englewood Cliffs, New Jersey, USA
[Introduction to the application of Petri-nets, a popular way of modelling the logic of simple manufacturing systems.]
Pritsker, A. A. (1986) *Simulation and SLAMII*, 3rd ed, Halsted Press
[The product manual for a favourite simulation system.]
Leimkuhler, F. (1986) Economic analysis of CIM systems. In *Computer-aided Design and Manufacturing* (U. Rembold and R. Dillman (eds)), Springer-Verlag
[A description and listing of CANQ, a fast manufacturing queueing theory model.]

People

Lupton, T (ed) (1986) *Human Factors*, IFS (Publications) Ltd and Springer Verlag
[One of the few people books in this area]

Futures

Wright, P. K. and Bourne, D. A. (1988) *Manufacturing Intelligence*, Addison Wesley
[Very forward-looking book on the factory of the future, concentrating on the replacement of the metal cutting craftsman.]
Duffie, N. A. *et al.* (1986) Hierarchical and nonhierarchical cell control with dynamic part-oriented scheduling, In *Proceedings of NAMRC-XIV, Minneapolis, May, 1986*, Society of Manufacturing Engineers

[Paper reporting the experimental comparison of a variety of small system control architectures.]
Lee, M. H. (1989) *Intelligent Robotics*, Open University and Halsted Press
[Advanced robotics and artificial intelligence with a significant manufacturing applications flavour.]
Kusiak, A. (ed) (1989) *Knowledge-based Systems in Manufacturing*, Taylor and Francis
[Edited text of mostly academic work in KBS applied to manufacturing. The last chapter compares the abilities of existing shells and tools kits for diagnosis and planning tasks.]

Journals

International Journal of Computer Integrated Manufacture.
Computer Integrated Manufacturing Systems.

International Journal of Production Research.
Bulletin of the Japan Society of Precision Engineers.

Harvard Business Review.
Manufacturing Review.
Journal of Manufacturing Systems.

IEEE Journal of Robotics and Automation.

AI in Engineering.
Journal of AI in Engineering Design and Manufacture.
Journal of Intelligent Manufacture.

52

Overview of compiler technology

Andrew D. McGettrick
University of Strathclyde

Contents

52.1 Introduction

As a first approximation a compiler may be described as a program which accepts as input programs written in some source language and produces equivalent programs in some target language.

This initial definition can be faulted on several counts:

1. Many compilers are not programs in the usual sense, but rather a collection of several programs.
2. Given an erroneous program, a compiler should attempt to detect errors and report them in a suitable way to help the programmer.
3. Even with error-free programs a compiler will not merely translate but may also produce a listing of the source program, include checks against run-time errors such as subscripts violating array bounds, perform certain optimizations of the source code, etc.

With these kinds of provisos, the original concept remains valid.

The aim of this chapter is to provide an overview of compiler technology and in so doing to promote the view that compiler building can be best viewed as a software engineering activity.

52.1.1 Structure of a typical compiler

Compilers for different languages will vary in their complexity and in the way they are constructed. This will depend to a large extent on the source language. Even two compilers for the same language may be built in quite different ways. It is usually possible, however, to distinguish a basic strategy common to the construction of all compilers.

The construction of a typical compiler will be described in terms of phases. This should be viewed just as a stage in the compilation process. In reality a phase may be implemented in such a way that:

1. It processes a relatively small fragment of the source program before passing appropriate information to the next stage.
2. It processes the entire text before handing over control to the next phase, and in this case the phase is referred to as a pass.

However, 'phase' encapsulates both notions and is a convenient term for describing different implementations.

There are no hard-and-fast rules about what constitutes a phase in the compilation process. One of the decisions that must be taken during the early stages of the design of any compiler is the precise task to be performed by each phase. There is, of course, interplay between phases; what is not done by one phase must be done by another. These decisions may in turn be determined by the method used in implementing a particular phase of a compiler.

There are (potentially, but not always) six phases of compilation. Each of these involves taking one representation of the source program and producing a different but equivalent representation more closely allied to the ultimate aim of an equivalent machine code version.

52.1.1.1 Lexical analysis

This accepts the original source program as input. Its task is to group together sets of characters which naturally form single entities such as the individual characters which form an identifier, the digits which denote an integer, and so on. Each group is replaced by an individualized token.

The operation can be likened to the process of forming words from the individual characters of a piece of English text. During the lexical analysis process comments and irrelevant spaces will be ignored, listings may be produced, etc.

52.1.1.2 Syntax analysis

The sequence of tokens produced by the lexical analyser is examined for structure, to see if these conform to the syntax rules of the programming language. Thus bracket mismatches, missing semi-colons, etc. are all identified at this stage. The output produced is a parse tree, which characterizes the basic structure of the program.

52.1.1.3 Semantic analysis

The main focus of this phase involves type information. It involves ensuring that identifiers, operators, etc. have been used in a way consistent with that implied by type information (derived from declarations, etc.). In essence, errors of a semantic nature are identified. Alternatively, and for correct programs, the parse tree is augmented with information necessary for the code generation stage.

52.1.1.4 Intermediate code generation

If present, this phase results in the production of code for an intermediate or abstract machine; thus the code is devoid of the peculiar characteristics of any particular machine but easily translatable into machine code or assembly code.

52.1.1.5 Code optimization

If this phase is present, the intermediate code is examined and inefficiencies of various kinds are identified and then removed. Often this involves a process of examining the structure of the code and producing an equivalent but more efficient version by restructuring.

52.1.1.6 Code generation

The final machine code is produced from the optimized intermediate code. This one phase then localizes consideration of the peculiarities of the machine.

Accompanying each of these phases is an associated range of activities. All phases will have access to symbol tables which are used to hold identifiers and information about these. In addition, error handling is a task likely to be undertaken by any phase of the compilation process.

These six phases can be classified in various ways:

1. The first three phases involve a process of analysing the text and are consequently often referred to as the analysis stage; the remaining phases involve the construction of the code and are naturally referred to as the synthesis phase of compilation.
2. Because of their relative independence from the underlying machine, the first five phases can be referred to as the front end of the compiler; the sixth and final phase is often called the back end.

Certain observations can be made about the overall structure. It is quite conceivable that a given compiler will not possess all the distinct phases. For example, the intermediate code generation stage and the code optimization phase could be omitted. In this case, the compiler writer would generate directly from the information supplied by the semantic analysis phase. In the process, of course, certain optimizations would have been lost, but that could be a justifiable decision.

52.1.2 Language design and compiler construction

There is an intimate and delicate relationship between language designs and compiler construction. A role of the compiler is to process a source program with a view to producing an object program which may be executed frequently and perhaps in delicate or sensitive situations, e.g. safety critical applications. Two consequences follow:

1. If the compiler can identify errors in a program this is highly desirable. It reduces the possibility of run-time errors which could be hazardous and it improves the efficiency with which development can take place. What emerges is a philosophy that the earlier an error is caught the better.
2. If some task (such as type checking, for example) can be moved from the run-time system of an object program back to the compilation stage, then a gain in efficiency of the object program can result and can be significant.

The alternative view to (2) above is that flexibility is most important and efficient object code is of secondary importance. This then relates to the purposes for which the language was designed. The key issue here is to stress the need for careful judgement about the facilities offered by the language and the intended supportive role of the compiler.

Traditional approaches to compiler construction lead to an emphasis on the processing of traditional imperative programming languages typified by Pascal, C, Modula 2 and the ALGOLs. With these languages it is then essential to address the handling of a range of:

1. Structuring mechanisms, which include the package concept, subroutines including procedures and functions (all with the associated varieties of parameter passing) and the notion of a block with static or dynamic scoping.
2. Data structures, which include basic or simple types such as integers, reals, characters and Booleans, and include composite types such as string, arrays of different dimensions, records and (possibly recursive) data types.
3. Statements and control structures covering assignments, a range of conditionals and looping mechanisms.

The more recent developments in language design will lead to consideration of the class concept for object-oriented languages, separate compilation, explicit concurrency as in Ada, exception handling, overloading and polymorphism.

Functional programming languages such as Lisp, ML and Miranda are based on the concept of function application. As such they can be viewed as more remote than the imperative languages from the underlying machine. Compilers for these languages have the added degree of complexity brought about by the need to transform from function application into a more sequential form of execution.

Two facts have an impact on compiler technology:

1. There is already an enormous amount of software in existence and already tried and tested.
2. Hardware developments are continuing apace with particular advances being made towards vector and parallel machines.

There is an argument that the compiler is the interface between the programmer and the underlying hardware configuration, and that it ought to protect the programmer from the need to have detailed knowledge either of the hardware or of changes to that hardware. Stated another way, detailed knowledge of the hardware should reside in the compiler and not in the mind of the programmer.

To benefit from the investment that has already taken place in software development and to exploit parallelism in the hardware – specifically without there being any need to recode – it is necessary for compilers to embark upon a new kind of activity. In particular, a two-stage process can be viewed as one route ahead:

1. Seek to analyse programs to identify the concurrency present

in an algorithm and to restructure the program in such a way that the different processes can be identified.
2. With knowledge of the available hardware configurations, explicitly schedule these processes in such a way that they run efficiently; algorithms for this will employ static or dynamic scheduling and can take account of load balancing in distributed systems and other factors.

Analysing programs to extract the inherent parallelism can be viewed as a form of optimization, and these matters will be dealt with at that stage. At the same time, attention will be drawn to different approaches to the scheduling problem.

Despite the wide range of possibilities, there tends to be uniformity in the structure of compilers. This chapter will proceed with a traditional approach, but at an appropriate stage attention will be drawn to the steps that need to be taken to handle functional languages or the problems of extracting the concurrency inherent in a given program.

52.1.3 Related software tools

Although compiling techniques have advanced in harmony with the developments in programming languages themselves, there is now wide recognition that the techniques have greater and wider applicability. Significant utilization of these can be found in:

1. Building interpreters.
2. Building processors for query or command languages.
3. In the construction of calculators.
4. The design and construction of certain kinds of word processors.
5. Natural language processing.
6. The concept of syntax directed editors and syntax directed tools generally.
7. A variety of forms of knowledge representation and processing.

Indeed, it is no exaggeration to say that the development of tools which are used for the processing of information with a well-defined structure will typically lean heavily on a subset of the technique commonly used in the construction of compilers. Typical of this range of software are: cross-reference programs, layout programs (pretty printers), debuggers, theorem provers, automatic verifiers, transformational tools, pattern matching programs and indeed editors, design tools, rewrite systems, and formal specification language tools.

The view expressed above can be reinforced by considering the concept of a program synthesizer. Within the framework provided by a synthesizer, a user is unable to type in a syntactically illegal program. Part of the compiler checking mechanism is integrated into an editor so that checking is then carried out when a program is input via the editor, and corrections can be made immediately. Considerable savings of time and effort are achieved in this way. However, the idea is mentioned merely to indicate that the techniques and mechanisms associated with compilers can be used in less obvious ways and in more interesting settings.

52.1.4 The software engineering view

Producing a compiler can be properly viewed as a software engineering activity. The starting point is typically a specification of a programming language, and this may be formal or informal. In addition, there is a set of user needs, implementation limitations, and aims; there is also the need for a continued maintenance activity. In the course of compiler construction, design decisions have to be made and a variety of factors will influence these decisions. Ultimately, the design should be based on sound foundations, where possible guided by underlying theoretical principles. Finally, software tools have an important role to play in providing automated help with aspects of implementation.

Compiler technology will be looked at from this perspective. Thus there will be an emphasis on practice, guided by an underlying theory or formal framework, accompanied by the appropriate use of tools.

52.2 Engineering a compiler

As with any software engineering projects, a wide range of possible implementation strategies are possible. These are affected by user considerations as well as what is technically possible. In this section some of the options will be examined.

52.2.1 User's view

From a user's point of view there are certain requirements that a good compiler should satisfy. Novice programmers should find the compiler easy to use. On the other hand, more experienced programmers should be blessed with facilities which encourage sensible use of a computer and good programming practice.

Below is an outline of some of the facilities that might be provided. A decision must be taken as to which features are provided automatically (presumably for the novice), and which must be specially invoked or suppressed. Note that the decisions may be affected by the way in which the computer and compiler are being used. Are programs submitted in batch mode for output to a line-printer, or from a graphics terminal, for example?

Each compiler should produce some basic information at each compilation. This includes the source and target languages, the name and version of the compiler, the time and date of the current compilation, and the options that were invoked or suppressed at the time of the compilation. The various options that may be available are now discussed.

52.2.2.1 Listings

All compilers should provide a means of listing the source program. Line numbers (or sometimes statement numbers) are usually provided with listings to act as references for error messages. Other variations are also possible:

1. The various pages may be numbered.
2. Automatic paragraphing may be provided. In block structured languages the blocks can be portrayed by suitably indenting the text.
3. Comments and character strings may be highlighted by producing a 'C' or an 'S' respectively at the right-hand side of the line on which these occur. In this way the programmer can easily detect when comments or strings have not been suitably terminated.
4. The programmer may be permitted to indicate at certain stages that the listing of the program should continue on the next new page, to start from a particular place, or for the numbering to be done in a particular way.
5. There may be available a facility for indicating whether the program is portable, i.e. can easily be moved from one installation to another. If characters are used which are not likely to be available at other installations, these may be distinguished in some way in the listing. Portability problems can also occur in the use of string denotations which span several lines. Such constructions are dangerous since it may not be clear whether the spaces at the end of each line are included in the denotation. Note therefore the relevance of (3) above in this regard.

Another aspect of listings is the provision of summary information. After the initial listing it is possible for the compiler to provide an alphabetic list of, for example, each identifier used by the programmer together with an indication of where it was declared, if this is appropriate, and where it was used. Such a summary is called a cross-reference table. Other forms of summaries might include a note on the number of error or warning messages issued during compilation of the program or an indication of the size of the object program.

52.2.1.2 Errors

All compilers must be able to report errors and possibly provide warnings. These messages should always be 'restrained and polite' and they should provide as much helpful information to the programmer as possible. They should always be phrased in terms of the user program and not in terms of what happpened in the compiler itself. A good compiler should attempt to detect as many errors as possible each time it processes a program. There are four kinds of error that may have to be reported. These are syntax errors, semantic errors, run-time errors and limit errors.

Syntax errors are caused by the program being grammatically incorrect e.g. bracket missing, identifier not declared. The occurrence of these errors in a program should never cause the compiler to go berserk. If possible, it should recover from the error (or possibly repair the error but this is rather ambitious by present day standards) and proceed to find as many other errors as possible.

Semantic errors are typically caused by attempts to use data items of the wrong type, e.g. to add an integer and a string. These should be reported, and recovered from, in a similar manner to syntax errors.

Run-time errors occur when the object program is being executed. They are caused by such eventualities as values being out of range (e.g. subscripts used to index an array or the selecting integer in a case statement or computed GO TO), arithmetic overflow, use of uninitialized variables, etc. So that these errors may be effectively detected the compiler must, at code generation, insert instructions to perform appropriate tests at run time. Less efficient programs result.

When run-time errors do occur there are two standard techniques that can be adopted. Use can be made of program profiles or traces. Profiles provide a listing of each statement together with the frequency with which each has been performed. Traces are used to indicate the path that the program had taken prior to the error together with values of variables. The level of detail in a trace may sometimes be controlled by the programmer.

Limit errors are caused by basic limitations of the compiler. Tables, for example, must have a certain maximum size, determined perhaps by the physical size of the computer. When these boundaries are reached limit errors must be reported. Such errors must eventually occur but when they do they should be genuine and rare. The average programmer should never encounter them.

52.2.1.3 Pragmatic remarks

Basically, pragmatic remarks are instructions of various kinds to the compiler. Through their use it is usually possible to invoke options of the kind discussed in the previous sections. Thus they may be used to switch listings on or off, to include subscript checks, to provide tracing facilities of a certain kind, and so on.

Pragmatic remarks can also be used for other purposes. In a suitable environment it might be possible to invoke library facilities of various kinds, combine different modules of program, temporarily change the type-font, prove properties of programs, etc.

52.2.2 Types of compiler

In the literature on compilers one often sees such terms as multi-pass compiler, in-core batch compiler, cross compiler, etc. These descriptions arise from either the way in which the compiler is constructed or the way in which it operates within a particular installation. A review of the more frequently used terms now follows.

One-pass compilers, as the name suggests, process the source program or a modified version of it just once. In particular, therefore, the lexical analysis phase would act as a routine or co-routine which would be called by the syntax analysis phase; on recognizing various constructions, routines can be called to generate appropriate code. Such compilers tend to have limitations:

1. They are often large, since the code for all phases of the compiler will be present at the same time.
2. Often there are limitations imposed on the source language to simplify the task of writing such a compiler. To give an illustration, one would typically expect that all objects should be declared before being used; this sort of limitation causes problems with mutually recursive constructs.
3. If an error occurs towards the end of a program all the code generation may have been performed needlessly.

However, one-pass compilers do have certain merits. For example, the compiler designer does not have so much worry about the interfaces between the various phases.

Multi-pass compilers aim to overcome the limitations and restrictions of one-pass compilers. They therefore tend to be smaller in size and the nature of the source language might demand many passes. Moreover, if very efficient object code is required, this will usually imply several passes. Often highly efficient code can be obtained by optimizations, which are best implemented using special passes. If the various passes and their interfaces have been clearly specified, the task of implementation can be conveniently tackled by several programmers, e.g. one programmer per pass. This tends to encourage more speedy implementation.

Compile-and-go systems make use of a compiler which generates machine code and places it in the main store of the computer. When the compilation of the source program has ended the machine code program can then be immediately executed. There is no delay.

Compile-and-go systems may use one-pass compilers, and in such cases the compiler will not know in advance what standard procedures, etc., are to be used by the source program. It will then usually happen that the object code for the entire library of standard functions, etc., is first placed in main memory before the compiler starts translating the object program proper. This run-time package, as it is often called, will also contain code for input and output, together with code for producing monitoring information if run-time errors occur, perhaps code for garbage collection should this be necessary, etc. This strategy of course can often lead to object programs which are much larger than might be expected. Libraries other than the standard library may be held in source form. Such a library would then, at a user's request, be incorporated *en bloc* into the source program and compiled before use.

A variation on the above theme is the idea of an in-core batch compiler. Such a compiler would be presented with a batch of programs. Each program in turn would be compiled, its object code placed in main memory and executed. Each program in the batch is thus compiled and run until no program remains. Compilers such as these tend to occupy large amounts of core.

Not only must the entire compiler reside in store but the compiler's lists and tables, together with the object code of a user's program must all be present. With these compilers care must be taken to deal properly with error situations, e.g. if using a monitor the data of the object program may need to be passed over; if run-time errors occur these must not interfere with other programs or with the compiler itself and, again, it may be necessary to skip over data.

The most famous example of an in-core compiler is the WATFOR compiler (FORTRAN compiler designed at the University of Waterloo). To achieve the desired aims of speed and efficient compilation, it is often necessary for the compiler to accept only a subset of the complete language.

The disadvantages of these approaches come from observing the possibilities that arise when some intermediate code (also called relocatable binary, semi-compiled code, etc.) is generated and placed in a file. Contrast this with producing binary in main memory. The intermediate code will be expressed in terms of relative addresses. With this facility:

1. Libraries of standard or user-defined routines can be stored in files in this intermediate code. They can be incorporated into programs as necessary, not *en bloc* but by including only those routines that are required.
2. If all the compilers in a particular system make use of the same intermediate code it becomes possible to write programs using several programming languages; but this can lead to complications since it must be possible for the programmer to specify the necessary interfaces.
3. The compiler requires less space than in a compile-and-go system, since the generated code is not written to main memory but to file and only the necessary standard functions, etc., appear in the final object program.

Now follows a look at other types of compilers. A cross-compiler running on computer A would have a facility for generating object code for a different computer B. This can usefully be employed in at least two situations:

1. When the compiler itself is relatively large and the computer B is small.
2. When the compiler for language L is itself written in L; then the cross compiler can be used to transfer the compiler from machine A to machine B (use the compiler to compile itself on A and produce code for B).

These facilities are usually implemented by linkers and loaders (see Chapter 46).

Sometimes it is desirable to use a compiler to translate into machine code a program which may be used simultaneously by several users. These programs might include editors, compilers or systems software, library routines or programs in application areas such as computer-assisted learning, computer-aided design, etc. In these cases it is important for the proper and sensible management of the computer that the compiler should produce pure or re-entrant code. Then, though ten people simultaneously may be using the computer, there would be only one copy of the program instructions but ten copies of the data, the instructions accessing the data by indirection (see Chapters 42 and 46).

Yet another type of compiler is the incremental or conversational compiler. Such compilers allow the development of programs in an interactive manner. They usually form part of a larger system which might include commands and facilities for editing programs, stopping and restarting programs at particular points in their execution, inspecting values of variables, etc. Usually these compilers will produce a very high level of object code – and therefore the term 'compiler' is somewhat misleading. This code is then usually interpreted. The most common example of conversational compilers are those present in BASIC systems.

The advantage of these compilers is the speed with which a programmer can develop his or her programs. The main disadvantage is the inefficiency of the object code which is produced. To overcome this, it is desirable to have another more traditional kind of compiler to produce efficient code for programs developed interactively. Ideally, both compilers should accept precisely the same source language.

52.2.3 Aims in writing a compiler

Before undertaking the task of producing a compiler, it is important to have certain aims to guide the implementor in arriving at decisions regarding the design of the compiler. Desirable aims might be that:

1. The compiler should be a model of good programming. This implies that it should be robust (i.e. it rarely goes wrong – it would be too ambitious to demand that it should never fault); it should be written using the ideas of structured programming, etc.
2. It should deal sensibly with errors and produce helpful and self-explanatory messages; it should not collapse on encountering an error but should either correct the error and in the process provide an appropriate message, or recover and proceed with compilation.
3. It should represent an implementation of the entire source language; the implementor should not impose unnatural limitations to make this task simpler.
4. The facilities provided should encourage good programming practice.
5. It should achieve an acceptable level of efficiency. One can talk of efficiency in terms of the time taken to implement the compiler, the time taken to compile a program, the time taken to run a program, the store requirements of the compiler or object program, etc.
6. It should be portable. With a portable compiler it is relatively easy to transfer the compiler from one machine to another (this can be achieved, for example, by writing the compiler in a suitable high-level language).
7. It should be adaptable. An adaptable compiler is easily modified so that it can operate in a different environment, e.g. with a different operating system.

This is, then, an incomplete list of possible aims. The set of aims which the compiler writer adopts will be determined by the purpose for which the compiler is being produced. They will have a considerable bearing on the facilities provided, the way the compiler is to be written, etc. Of course, the aims listed above are not independent of each other. There will be trade-offs. Achieving, for example, run-time efficiency of object programs, involves the compiler in extra passes to perform optimization and this leads to slower compile time.

52.3 Theoretical considerations

Many of the basic techniques that underpin compiler construction stem from considerations of a theoretical nature based on the abstract mathematical concept of a grammar (see Chapter 10). Grammars are typically used in defining at least some aspects of programming languages and so provide a sound framework on which to hang the implementation of an associated compiler.

This section gives a brief review of grammars, highlighting not their theoretical properties, but their practical utility and application to the related topics of language definition and compiler construction.

52.3.1 Language definition

Programming languages used for serious software development provide a formal structure of enormous complexity. They typically present a framework within which complex mathematical calculations can be carried out, sophisticated data processing can be performed, real-time control can be described, complex pattern matching can be carried out, and so on. There are typically facilities for branching, looping, routines, modules, exceptions, concurrency, and pattern matching, as well as separate compilation and facilities to support activities performed by groups of programmers. The interaction between these and the consequent scope for uncertainty present a structure of vast complexity. Given the increasing demand for error-free, reliable and safe systems, it is vital that all aspects of programming languages have a clear and unambiguous meaning. Failure to provide this will lead to alternative interpretations and consequently different compiler implementations. This results in the source program producing different effects when processed by different compilers. The basic principles of software engineering demand a sound and agreed basis for the start of any development – and compilers are no different. Yet basic machine limitations and characteristics, together with the wish to free a compiler writer to exploit his or her skills and to design for his or her own particular purpose, produce factors which militate against over prescription.

Completely formal definitions of programming languages, based on mathematical techniques and methods, are likely to produce the most satisfactory definition. In reality, such documents tend to be somewhat opaque and inaccessible to most people because of their excessive formalism. Most programming languages possess a formal syntax which is based on the concept of a grammar. Semantics, on the other hand, tend to be defined more informally in natural language, such as English, although the formal syntax provides a framework on which to hang meaning. The vagaries and imprecisions of natural language mean that ambiguities, inaccuracies, omissions, etc. tend to be present in the semantic issues associated with programming languages. For a discussion of these matters see McGettrick (1980).

52.3.2 Backus-Naur Form

Following its initial use in the definition of ALGOL 60, Backus-Naur Form is a notation commonly used in the description of the syntax of programming languages. Part of the syntax of a Pascal-like language expressed in this way is given in *Figure 52.1*.

The syntax is composed of a set of syntax rules. The first such rule describes a program as:

the word 'program' followed by an ⟨identifier⟩ – since this appears in angle brackets its definition will be given elsewhere – then the symbol '(' followed by an < identifier list > – again defined elsewhere in this syntax – then ')' followed by ';' which in turn is followed by ⟨block⟩ – defined elsewhere – and finally the period '.'

A similar interpretation can be placed on the other syntax rules. To interpret these note that:

::=   denotes 'is defined to be'
| denotes 'or alternatively'

The symbol | is used extensively in the final rule of Figure 52.1, where ⟨statement⟩ can be interpreted in a variety of ways. Indeed, the syntax rule merely lists the alternative kinds of statement that exist within the language.

⟨program⟩ ::= **program** ⟨identifier⟩ (⟨identifier list⟩);
⟨block⟩.
⟨block⟩ ::= ⟨declaration option⟩ **begin** (⟨statement list⟩
end)
⟨statement list⟩ ::= ⟨statement⟩ | ⟨*statement*⟩; ⟨statement
list⟩
⟨statement⟩ ::= ⟨assignment statement⟩
            | ⟨if statement⟩
            | ⟨case statement⟩
            | ⟨while statement⟩
            | ⟨repeat statement⟩
            | ⟨for statement⟩
            | ⟨procedure call⟩
            | ⟨compound statement⟩

Figure 52.1 Grammar in Backus-Naur Form

Legal programs conform to these rules; so they must consist of the word 'program', followed by an identifier, etc. This gives rise to a situation in which parts of a program can be categorized in different ways. A parse tree is thereby associated with a program – akin to what is present in natural language construction.

In the writing of the grammar of Figure 52.1 it is convenient to distinguish two different kinds of symbols:

1. Symbols appearing in angle brackets, e.g. ⟨block⟩, are called non-terminals or non-terminal symbols. These symbols themselves do not appear in programs but they characterize the kinds of construct that can be present.
2. Other symbols such as '**program**', '(' ',' ')' etc., which actually appear in programs. These are called terminals or terminal symbols.

Of the non-terminal symbols one of these is particularly distinguished, i.e. the symbol ⟨program⟩ as this provides the description of the category of objects which are of interest, namely, the set of syntactically legal programs. As such it is usually referred to as the sentence symbol.

Definition. A grammar is a quadruple (V_T, V_N, S, P) consisting of:

1. A finite set V_T of symbols called terminals.
2. A finite set V_N of symbols called non-terminals, with no commonality between V_T and V_N.
3. A distinguished member S of V_N called the sentence or start symbol.
4. A finite set P of productions or rewriting rules of the form:

$$A ::= B_1$$

where each A and B_1 is a (potentially null) sequence of elements from V_T and/or V_N.

A common notation in language definition is to use:

$$A ::= B_1 \mid B_2 \mid \ldots \mid B_n$$

as an abbreviation for:

$$A ::= B_1 \quad A ::= B_2 \ldots A ::= B_n$$

In compiler technology, A is normally restricted to being an element of V_N and then the grammar is referred to as context-free (see Chapter 10).

This brief introduction should have served to introduce the concept of a grammar in a manner which highlights the relevance to language definition. As described above, the names and symbolism associated with the various terminals and non-terminals serve to introduce a vocabulary of terms which are used when talking about the language. In the more abstract world of mathematics such niceties are typically absent; terminals and non-terminals are merely regarded as mutually distinct sets of symbols.

52.3.3 Attribute grammars

In discussing programs, concepts such as identifiers, variables, expressions, functions and so on are part of the common terminology. These terms typically appear, sometimes in disguised forms within the grammar defining the programming language.

It is customary to associate with these same terms qualities such as type, value, scope and so on – thus the type of a variable, the value of an expression, the type of a function. More precisely, these qualities are called attributes. Augmenting the concept of a grammar by associating attributes with nonterminals results in the concept of an attribute grammar.

The concept of an attribute grammar turns out to be a particularly helpful formalism in which to express context-sensitive information or even meaning. Imagine the syntax tree pictured or positioned in such a way that the root is at the top and the leaves are at the foot. Two particular cases emerge.

Consider the value attribute. From the values of variables it is possible to construct the values of expressions in which these variables occur; likewise for type. From the types of variable and constructs the type of the result produced by an expression can be deduced and as a result assignments, for example, can be checked for type compatibility. This situation can be described by saying that the value or type information associated with a larger construct can be constructed or synthesized from the value of lower level constructs. Thus type or value information is typically referred to as a synthesized attribute.

A different set of actions take place if environmental information is viewed as an attribute. Programs are typically executed within an initial or standard environment composed of certain standard identifiers, operations, functions, etc. On entering a program and encountering certain declarations this environmental information needs to be augmented with information about the new declarations; indeed when any new declarations are encountered the environment is augmented, perhaps for a limited part of the program. Another way of viewing this is to say that the environmental information is passed down the syntax tree, being augmented in the process. As such it is referred to as an inherited attribute.

This informal discussion provides the motivation which underlies the following formal concept of an attribute grammar.

Definition. An attribute grammar is a grammar with the following additional property:
To each X in either V_T or V_N is associated two disjoint and finite sets of attributes:

I(X) represents the inherited attributes of X
S(X) represents the synthesized attributes of X

Note that either I(X) or S(X) or indeed both may be empty.

This formalism happens to provide a particularly appropriate framework in which to describe aspects of the compilation process – particularly the semantic analysis phase.

52.4 Lexical analysis

Being the first phase of the compilation process, the lexical analyser has access to the source code as prepared by the programmer.

The process of reading source programs is relatively slow and although other phases of the compilation process are more complex and more interesting, the lexical analysis phase tends to dominate all other phases together from a time point of view. Efficiency is a key consideration during this phase. With this in mind, it may be of interest for the compiler writer to consider experiments aimed at determining the way in which the source language is used. He or she must understand this to perform the task efficiently.

Before getting immersed in the details of programming, it is advisable for the compiler writer to become acquainted with the kind of programs the compiler will have to process. Knuth and others (Knuth, 1971; Partridge and James, 1976) have performed statistical analyses of FORTRAN programs in an attempt to discover some pattern about the way in which people write programs. Knuth reaches many conclusions. From the point of view here there is one which is very significant: 'An average of about 48 blank columns were found per non-comment card. A compiler's lexical grammar should therefore include a high-speed skip over blanks.'

52.4.1 Role of the lexical analyser

Basically, characters are read one at a time. These have to be assembled into symbols. The symbols themselves may typically be interspersed with comments. Commentary followed by a symbol can be regarded as a higher level lexical unit. There are various levels, i.e. character symbol and so on, and this hierarchy should be reflected in the structure of the lexical analyser.

This structure is now examined in more detail. Typically, a case statement is employed, selection of the various alternatives depending on the character which is read in. Within these alternatives additional characters may be absorbed until an appropriate sequence of characters has been grouped and a token produced. Different actions will be taken depending on the nature of the grouping identifiers.

Special symbols, such as operators, brackets, end-of-statement symbols or separators, are replaced by appropriate tokens. In identifying these the lexical analyser may have to look ahead. A colon, for example, can often denote a label, but it might herald the start of the becomes symbol ':='. Thus the lexical analyser needs to separate such uses and return appropriate tokens (so removing the need for resolving such ambiguity again).

Consider the problem of dealing with denotations. These usually include the representation of integers, real numbers and perhaps Boolean characters and strings. Take the case of an integer. The action to be taken is relatively straightforward. The denotation must be read and stored in a table or file, and the token supplied indicates the nature of the denotation and a pointer to where it can be found. At this stage some compilers will try to evaluate the integer and store some internal representation of it. Note, however, that this is contrary to the aim of wishing as much as possible of a compiler to be machine independent, as different machines hold numbers of different magnitudes. So integer denotations and denotations in general will be held in something akin to source format. This has the added advantage that later messages can then be phrased in terms of what the programmer actually wrote.

The situation regarding real denotations is similar, but complicated by the variety of possible forms of real denotations (see Chapter 8 for a discussion of the issues of manipulating floating point numbers). Subject to a mechanism for dealing with this complexity, tokens of an appropriate kind are produced. A mechanism for dealing with this and similar situations is introduced in Section 52.4.3.

String denotations can also be managed in a manner similar to that used for integers. There are no new problems and the same table can even be used.

Other kinds of denotations, e.g. Booleans and characters, are easily processed. The token which replaces them indicates the type of the denotation and, for efficiency, the pointer can take the form of some coding of the Boolean itself or of the character. Indeed, this same scheme can be used to a certain extent for integer denotations. Frequently, single-digit integer denotations occur and these can be treated in the way described. The table of integer denotations would then contain only multi-character symbols. There is, therefore, a saving in table size and in the time taken to access the table.

As for other symbols, identifiers are replaced by tokens in which there is an appropriate token type and there is some other integer giving the details. Identifiers are usually held in tables of some kind and the second part of the token may be a reference to the appropriate place in the table.

The action to be taken on encountering an identifier and the nature of the tables will depend on many factors, including the design of the language being compiled, the amount of information to be held and the number of passes in the compiler. What is certain, however, is that given an identifier, the symbol table will have to be searched to check if that identifier is present. If not, it must be inserted together with the token which will represent it. If it is present, the appropriate token can be extracted from the table. Initially, standard identifiers and their tokens are assumed to be present in the table.

The manner in which reserved words or bold words are treated will depend on the language being compiled. In ALGOL 60, for example, there is only a finite number of reserved words. These can be treated as if they were multiple-character symbols such as ':='. On the other hand, they can be placed in a table together with their tokens; on encountering a reserved word the table would then be searched and the token extracted. In ALGOL 68, however, the programmer can introduce his own reserved words in the form of new modes or operators. In such cases, reserved words can be treated like identifiers, the standard reserved words being entered in the table initially.

Care should be taken when a special symbol can be represented in more than one way. It may be possible, for example, to write the 'less than or equal to' operator as '< =', '⩽' or 'le'. Should the lexical analyser replace these by the same token? The answer to this question depends on the source programming language. In ALGOL 60, for example, the answer would be yes, but in ALGOL 68 operators can be defined and consequently their meaning altered. Altering the meaning of < = would not necessarily alter the meaning of ⩽. Thus the distinction between < = and ⩽ must be preserved and the lexical analyser should replace these with different tokens.

52.4.2 Token structure

During the lexical analysis phase of the compilation process each group of characters is replaced by a token. Each token consists of two fields which represent a token type and data part. The token type will indicate that the particular grouping which the token replaced was, for example, a bold word, etc. The data field will give more specific information about the grouping. When identifiers, for instance, are replaced by tokens it is necessary to remember the identifier usually in some form of table or tree. Each occurrence of that identifier will be replaced by the same token. In this case the data field may be a pointer to that part of the table where the identifier is stored. Integers, real numbers, etc., are dealt with in a similar way. However, in the case of reserved words, or basic symbols, the data field may take the form of a code representing that word or symbol.

The various tokens that are produced will all be of the same size. Thus items of possibly different sizes are replaced by items of one standard size. The tokens themselves often take the form of a pair of integers, one representing the token type and the other representing the data part. Substantial savings in effort and comprehensibility can be obtained by using mnemonics.

52.4.3 Using finite automata

In certain aspects of lexical analysis finite automata (see Chapter 9) are used as a mechanism for resolving the meaning of symbols, for identifying legal denotations and so on. To illustrate their use consider the following example referred to earlier.

In ALGOL 68 the colon might be used in labels, in routines and operators, to separate lower and upper bounds and to start such symbols as ':=', ':=:', and ':/=:'. In all but the last three cases a token for the colon would appear. In the remaining cases appropriate tokens would appear. To distinguish between these the lexical analyser must look at the characters that follow to discover which symbol occurred. The programming for this can be done by means of an if statement. On the other hand, a finite state machine can be used (see *Figure 52.2*).

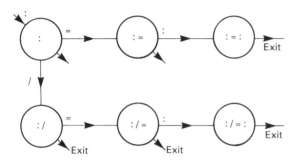

Figure 52.2

The various states are represented by circles and these are labelled with the characters already read. These states could be numbered and with the help of an appropriate matrix the programming can be accomplished simply.

These finite automata can be represented by matrices in which the (i, j) element holds the new state resulting from the appearance of an input i when the system is in the state represented by j. This requires a straightforward numbering of states and symbol kinds.

Another important application of this technique is often used in recognizing real numbers. The precise detail will depend on the particular programming language, but a set of states of the following kind can be envisaged:

1. The state resulting from the reading of an initial sign.
2. The state during which digits before the decimal point are read.
3. The state resulting from the reading of the decimal point.
4. The state during which digits after the point are read.
5. The state resulting from the reading of the exponent 'e'.
6. The state resulting from a reading of the sign in the exponent.
7. The state during which digits within the exponent are being read.

As various symbols are read the automaton can move from one state to (the same or) another state; erroneous symbols produce an error state.

52.4.4 Symbol tables

It has been mentioned that tables are used in the lexical analysis phase to hold, for example, identifiers and the tokens which replace them. If, however, the lexical analysis phase is combined with some other phase of the compilation process, these tables may be required to hold more information and may therefore be more complex.

At some stage tables will have to be built to hold all the necessary information about identifiers (and perhaps reserved words, though without loss of generality one can restrict the discussion to identifiers). Such tables can be fairly complex data structures, usually referred to as a symbol table. Successive phases of compilation result in these tables being more and more complete.

The nature of the symbol table will depend on the language itself and on the design of the compiler. The kind of considerations which must be taken into account and which will affect the final design are:

1. Is there a (reasonable) limit to the maximum number of elements in the table?
2. Does an identifier have an arbitrary number of characters or is its length limited?
3. Is FORTRAN equivalence allowed in the source language?
4. What properties of identifiers are to be stored in the tables?
5. Is there block structure and dynamic storage allocation in the language?
6. What facilities are to be provided for segmentation or modular programming?

The kind of information that may be stored in a symbol table may include:

1. The identifier itself and its token.
2. The mode or type of the identifier.
3. The run-time address.
4. The number of times the identifier was accessed (and possibly the position of these accesses).
5. The scope information.

The mode or type may take the form of some integer code. If the language admits a possible infinity of modes there may be a pointer to a mode table. In summary, the symbol table entry for an identifier typically holds all the information which will be gathered about the identifier during the entire compilation process, i.e. it will hold all the static properties of each identifier.

Of additional interest will be the routines which may access the tables together with the way in which these should be programmed. The processes of inserting and accessing elements in the table are of necessity performed frequently in the compilation process. Consequently, the efficiency of the routines which perform these tasks can have a considerable bearing on the efficiency of the compiler itself.

All of these considerations give rise to a rich range of possible approaches to the implementation of symbol tables. There is complexity caused by multiple occurrences of the one identifier with different meanings. In designing symbol tables consideration needs to be given to:

1. The use of static or dynamic storage allocation mechanisms, with tables or trees being most prominent.
2. Sorting and searching methods giving consideration to efficiency with linear searching or a variety of hashing techniques being important alternatives.
3. The use of a stack mechanism with which to mirror the effect of block structure.

For a reference to these and other possibilities see, for example, Aho *et al.* (1986) and Chapter 11.

52.4.5 Error handling

Various kinds of errors can occur at this stage and, as with all errors, it is important that they are dealt with properly. Examples of these include:

1. Limit errors.
2. Occurrences of illegal characters.
3. Occurrence of characters in illegal positions.
4. Illegal denotations.

Each of these errors must be properly reported. However, it is also important that the compiler should, if possible, take appropriate action and proceed with later phases of compilation. There are two alternatives: the compiler may attempt to correct the mistakes or it can accept the fact that an error has occurred and produce some token indicating an error. If it can be achieved, the former is more desirable since later phases do not have to be specially programmed to deal with error tokens.

Errors of type (1) above include all error situations arising from limitations of the hardware or software systems and should rarely occur. If they do, they can merely be reported and the compilation process terminated. To recover from errors of type (2), the illegal character can be skipped and compilation can proceed as if the offending character had not been present; the user should, of course, be informed of what is happening.

Errors of type (3) are more delicate. A typical problem can be illustrated by considering bold words. In certain ALGOLs these may be represented as a sequence of letters and/or digits starting with a letter, the entire sequence being surrounded by single quotes (thus 'BEGIN'). The language may insist that no spaces, new lines or other characters can appear within the quotes. Suppose the lexical analyser encounters a quote followed by some letters followed by a space. Should one merely ignore the space or should one assume the the final quote is missing? The former strategy leads to an avalanche of errors in

'BEGIN 'INT' X: = 4; PRINT(X) 'END'

and the latter fails in:

'BEG IN' 'INT' X: = 4; PRINT(X) 'END'

If a more sensible stropping convention is adopted, this kind of problem need not arise. Suppose bold words start with an initial period and terminate, not by a matching period, but with any character other than a letter or digit. The correct version of the above piece of program would then appear as:

.BEGIN .INT X: = 4; PRINT(X) .END

Errors of type (4) are relatively common. Typically, erroneous denotations contain periods or special symbols in the wrong position.

The lexical analyser can usually return a sequence of admissible smaller denotations which result in error reporting at the syntax stage. For example '2.3.4' might appear as '2.3' followed by '.4'.

52.4.6 The lex system

lex is a software tool supplied with the Unix system and used for the purpose of generating lexical analysers. Input to the lex system takes the form of a grammar which describes the various symbols. In addition, fragments of C code are typically associated with the recognition of common combinations of characters and upon recognition the C code fragments are executed.

lex is often used in conjunction with Yacc, a complementary tool for producing parsers. Such an approach might be referred to as an automatic approach to compiler construction. The alternative is to produce code by hand in a traditional fashion.

The advantages of the automatic method accrue since this approach tends to be better organized:

1. The programmer is relieved of much of the tedious detail (and can therefore afford to be more ambitious and provide better facilities or perform more tasks during this phase of the compilation process).
2. There is no need to construct finite state machines and corresponding transition matrices.

3. Special cases need not be programmed carefully by hand.
4. It is simple to make dramatic changes such as altering the stropping conventions.
5. Automatic paragraphing can be performed in an orderly manner.

One disadvantage of the automatic approach is that the finished article tends to be larger and less efficient than its hand-coded counterpart. Its efficiency and portability will also depend on the automatic approach used.

52.5 Syntactic analysis

All reasonable approaches to syntax analysis depend heavily on the fact that there is an underlying grammar which defines the syntax, and this framework can be used to determine the structural framework of the parser. The input to this phase of the compilation process is the stream of tokens supplied by the lexical analysis phase; the output will be a parse tree, perhaps accompanied by error messages and/or information to augment the symbol tables.

During this process the underlying structure of the program will be identified and, if no syntax errors are found, the output will take the form of a tree which captures that structure.

A variety of approaches to parsing exist. In discussing these it will be convenient to use capital letters for non-terminal symbols and lower case letters for terminals.

52.5.1 Recursive descent technique

Recursive descent is a simple technique with a certain appeal. Basically, a routine is associated with each non-terminal and that routine recognizes sequences of symbols belonging to the set represented by that non-terminal. The parse is constructed in a very direct way from the grammar rules for the language.

Consider the following:

$$X ::= x\ Y \mid y$$
$$Y ::= \ldots$$

To build a parser there is a routine for X and another for Y. The X-routine is constructed as follows:

if the next symbol is an x,
    absorb it by reading the next symbol again;
call the Y-routine
if on the other hand the symbol is y,
    absorb it by reading the next symbol again

A similar approach would be used for the Y-routine. Note the mutually recursive nature of the various routines, stemming from the recursion inherent in the grammar rules themselves.

This straightforward approach can be extended so that, with grammars of an appropriate kind, parsers can be generated automatically:

1. Non-terminals are replaced by appropriate routine calls.
2. Vertical bars are replaced by **else if** or the equivalent of this.
3. Terminals are replaced by a test to check for their presence (such tests possibly resulting in an error).

When the syntax provides the underlying structure in such a direct way the phrase 'syntax-directed' is often used.

Unfortunately, there are fairly severe limitations on the range of grammars to which the technique can be applied; each alternative in each grammar rule must start with a different terminal. However, the basic notion with its underlying simplicity is attractive and lies at the heart of other more sophisticated techniques.

52.5.2 LL(*k*) parsing

Some of the restrictions that apply to the basic recursive descent approach can be overcome by employing alternative techniques to parsing, techniques of wider applicability.

As before, a syntax-directed approach is involved. The grammar can be pre-processed to determine the range of symbols that can start each alternative in each grammar rule. Provided there is no overlap between the different alternatives in each rule, the parser can decide on the basis of the input which alternative to pursue. If *k* symbols of input have to be looked at, the techniques employed are called LL(*k*) methods. The most popular of this range of techniques uses *k* = 1 (see Chapter 10 for a more detailed treatment of the relevant language theory).

One very definite advantage of this approach is that, in parsing terms, it is efficient. The pre-processing is done once, at the time the parser is first built. Thereafter the sets of symbols are available and can be quickly inspected as parsing progresses. There is no possibility of the parser making an erroneous decision, having to backtrack and therefore reprocess the input. Thus a single pass over the input suffices.

Building LL(*k*) parsers necessitates the development and programming of a set of techniques to identify the sets of symbols referred to above. A good overview of these is contained in Griffiths (1974).

LL(*k*) parsing techniques can be employed only for grammars of a particular kind. Indeed, the grammars are called LL(*k*) grammars. This is still relatively restricting. For example, neither of the rules:

$$X ::= x \, Y \mid x$$
$$X ::= x \mid Xz$$

could occur in such a grammar. Yet these, or equivalent rules, occur frequently in grammars used for describing programming languages. Fortunately there are transformations which can be applied to rules of this kind and render them amenable to LL(*k*) techniques. Again Griffiths (1974) is a good source of reference on this topic.

Finally, it should be noted that much of what has been described here can be automated. In particular, it is possible to build systems which accept grammars of a particular kind, pre-process them, extend the basic recursive descent idea and produce a parser that will recognize and produce a parse tree for properly constructed programs written in the language.

52.5.3 LR(*k*) parsing

To use the terminology of the previous section, LR techniques also offer the possibility of parsing using a single scan of the input (no backtracking) using at most *k* symbols of lookahead. Consequently, they are efficient, and indeed more general than the corresponding LL(*k*) method (see Chapter 10, once more). Again pre-processing of the grammar plays an important role.

LR parsing methods are based on the observation that as parsing progresses, only a finite number of different states can be entered. All the states and all the transitions between them can be calculated in advance by examining the grammar and processing it in particular ways.

As parsing progresses an LR parser will retain information about the text that has previously been read. This information is retained as state information which normally resides on a stack. Thus the parser uses this information as well as the input symbols and a parse table to accomplish its task.

The basic actions of an LR parser can be described by considering a rule such as:

$$A ::= B_1 \, B_2 \ldots B_n$$

1. The process of moving through an alternative, say from B_2 to B_3 is called shifting or a shift.
2. Having recognized $B_1 \, B_2 \ldots B_n$, the parser will have recognized an A and this is referred to as a reduction or a reduce move.
3. Accept moves occur when the parsing has been completed satisfactorily.
4. Error situations provide the fourth alternative.

Each of these (successful) moves results in the construction of part of the parse tree.

A good overview of the techniques that underlie the building of LR parsers is contained in Horning (1974).

The range of languages and grammars amenable to treatment by LR technique is relatively wide, although not universally applicable. In particular, this range tends to include most of the constructs which typically occur in programming languages, there being normally no need to apply transformations to the original grammar. The process of producing an LR parser is relatively complex and normally accomplished by automatic methods. The resulting program is efficient. However, care needs to be taken in representing parse tables, for these can be rather large, but advantage can be taken of their sparseness.

52.5.4 Other parsing techniques

Apart from recursive descent, two important classes of parsing techniques have been discussed. However, these are not the only alternatives. There is a considerable literature on parsing methods with LALR (lookahead LR), SLR (single LR), operator – precedence parsing and other techniques all being prominent and having their advocates.

52.5.5 Yacc system

Yacc is a software tool supplied under Unix to assist with the ready production of parsers. Typically, it is used in conjunction with the lex system described earlier. The origins of the name lies in 'yet-*a*nother-*c*ompiler-*c*ompiler'.

Input to the Yacc system takes the form of an LALR (1) grammar, together with associated fragments of C code representing actions which are executed as recognition progresses. The output is a parser which recognizes legal programs.

52.6 Semantic analysis

One can now assume that the lexical analysis and syntax analysis phases (and any other special phases) have been completed. It is assumed, therefore, that there is available in some form:

1. Symbol tables which contain all the attributes of all the identifiers, bold words, etc.
2. A tree-structure, the parse tree.

The symbol tables have been completed by the syntax analyser. The parse tree is also produced by the syntax analysis phase. It is convenient to think of this parse tree being present explicitly so that one can easily describe actions which will further process the tree. Of course, the tree may be present only implicitly and in this case one can think of the actions which are embedded in the grammar as being the actions which can process the tree.

Until now, no meaning has been associated with the nodes of the syntax tree. Thus if a + appears, there is no mention yet of whether this is the addition of two integers, addition of two reals, or indeed addition at all in the usual sense. The purpose of the semantic analysis phase is to supply this missing information.

52.6.1 Tree transformations

Often programming languages allow the intentions of the programmer to be expressed in several equivalent ways. For example, in some ALGOLs one could write:

real x,y

as:

real x, **real** y

If it is possible to reduce a variety of possible forms to one standard form, it means that the later phases of the compiler have to deal only with the standard form.

The transformation involved here can be described as standardization. This process is performed basically by replacing one subtree by an equivalent subtree. This can be done by a form of pattern matching – when an appropriate pattern is encountered it can be removed and replaced by the standard pattern. If standardization has to be performed to any significant extent, it is important that it be carried out in a bottom-up fashion. If a major portion of the tree has to be standardized, it is usually important that all subtrees of that tree have themselves previously been standardized. A next transformation might involve placing additional information about various identifiers in the symbol table. Thus tokens for the various identifiers now point to entries in the symbol tables and these entries have the attributes of the identifiers present. Indeed, the tokens themselves may be altered by a further transformation so that relevant information such as type or mode may be included in the token itself.

52.6.2 Relevance of attribute grammars

Consider the arithmetic expression:

a + b × c

From the attributes of b and c, obtained in the tokens for b and c or from the appropriate symbol table entries, it will usually be simple to deduce the precise nature of the operator × . If b and c are integers then × denotes integer multiplication, if they are real it denotes real multiplication and so on. So × can be identified easily. The + operator is slightly more difficult to deal with since one must know what the type of the result produced by b × c will be. In more complicated expressions this ad hoc approach will not suffice and it becomes advisable to introduce a semantic stack.

The semantic stack will hold the types of operands. Suppose the syntax tree for an expression is being traversed in postfix order. As operands are encountered their types are placed on the stack. When an operator is encountered, the types of the operands are then in the top two positions on the stack. With this information the operator can be identified properly, the types of the operands removed from the stack and replaced by the type of the result. Continuing in this way allows all operators to be correctly identified.

What has been described above can be regarded in another light. It can be viewed as attribute propagation. The attributes of the leaves have been propagated up the tree from the leaves towards the root of the tree, i.e. they are synthesized attributes.

In general terms, both synthesized and inherited attributes are allowed to permeate through the syntax tree with various checks being carried out in the process or additional information added to the tree to assist with the later code generation activity.

52.6.3 Type checking and coercion

The previous discussion of operator identification and attribute propagation has been rather oversimplified. It frequently happens that the types appearing in a particular place are not quite what is required (e.g. assigning integers to real variables) and type checking or type changes of some kind are required.

Mode changes which have to be inserted automatically by the compiler are called coercions. Often a sequence of coercions are needed to perform the necessary type change. This matter tends to be very language dependent and can be relatively complicated. It is not proposed to delve deeply into this matter. Suffice it to say that the semantic analyser must deduce the coercion sequence required and arrange that the various coercions will be inserted and later performed. This involves intricate aspects of the source language and it is important that its formal definition is very precise in this regard. A typical problem arises from adding the values of two integer variables m and n and assigning this to the real variable x, thus:

$$x := m + n$$

Should the values of m and n be converted to reals and these added or should the values be added under integer addition and the result converted to real? This and similar problems must find their answer in a rigorous formal definition of the programming language.

52.6.4 Type checking in functional languages

In the context of functional programming, type checking can take one of two forms. In one approach it is necessary to check whether the usage of objects is consistent with declarations which flag the intended usage of these objects; this is an approach which mirrors the strong typing regime present in languages such as Pascal, Ada, etc. The second approach involves the execution of an algorithm, the aim of which is to discover the most general type which an expression may have. There are two possible outcomes. One conclusion may be that the expression is invalid or inconsistent and so in error. The happier outcome is an expression to describe a type which is so general that it captures all possible executions of the expression.

The algorithm which underlies the activity described above is typically a type inference system, and involves Robinson's unification algorithm (Robinson, 1965). This is very similar in many respects to theorem proving. For a discussion of such activity see Chapter 7 in Field and Harrison (1988).

52.6.5 The Cornell system

Developed at Cornell University in the USA, the synthesizer generator is a powerful system designed to assist with the production of synthesizers for programming languages. In essence, the system is based on attribute grammars; a program typically supplies an attribute grammar describing a language and is able to provide rules which describe how attributes are to be evaluated as recognition takes place.

The generality of the attribute mechanism means that the system is relatively powerful. Syntax directed editors, parsers, verification condition generators, etc. can all be developed using this system. In addition, since code can be viewed as an attribute, the system permits the development of a compiler. For more details see Reps and Teitelbaum (1989).

52.7 Code generation

In the introduction to this overview it was explained that typically there are two phases concerned with code generation. These relate to the production of an intermediate code, followed later by the production of machine code itself. Of these, the latter tends to be machine dependent and, at least conceptually, straightforward; typically following pattern matching one form of template is replaced by another; in the process, efficient and effective use needs to be made of the target machine.

In this section attention will focus on the issues surrounding the production of the intermediate code, given output from the earlier phases of compilation.

52.7.1 Role of intermediate code

With the end of the analysis phase of compilation there is available a complete parse tree and symbol table augmented with the information necessary for the generation of code. The intermediate code itself must be capable of representing the program in a faithful manner. In addition some basic criteria should be met:

1. It should be relatively easy to generate the code from the input to this phase.
2. Portability should be encouraged.
3. It should be possible to implement the optimization phase that follows efficiently.
4. The generation of actual code should not be difficult.

Most intermediate languages are idealized in some sense, having an abnormally rich set of operations and other features. There are two particular codes which can be mentioned. P-code was specially designed as an intermediate code for Pascal (Barron, 1981); DIANA was designed as an intermediate code for Ada (Goos *et al.*, 1983). A different range of codes is used in other cases.

There are many methods commonly used in representing syntax trees. Three of the more common methods result from the use of:

1. Linked storage
2. Polish notation
3. n – tuples

In the first of these methods the tree is represented as a data structure. Indeed, this is how one would visualize a tree.

Polish notation includes both postfix and prefix forms and can be regarded as a flattening of the tree. Prefix notation is obtained by traversing a tree and printing nodes on the way down the tree; postfix notation results from the nodes being printed on the way up the tree.

For the tree corresponding to $a + b \times c$, the prefix notation is $+ a \times b\ c$, and the postfix notation is $a\ b\ c \times +$.

From the point of view of execution, there are advantages in using either notation. However, the prefix notation tends to be more expensive to produce.

If Polish notation has to be used it will, of course, be necessary to decide on a suitable notation for constructions such as conditionals, loops, subscripts, declarations, etc.

Examples

1. [11 : u1, 12 : u2] a **int** might appear as '11 u1 12 u2 a int dec'. Here a would indicate an entry in the symbol table; dec is an operator implying that a declaration has been encountered.
2. a [p,q] might appear as p q a subs, the subs being an operator implying subscription.

n – tuples take the form:

(operator, operand 1, operand 2, ... operand n)

or:

(operator, operand 1, operand 2, ... operand n, type)

Take the latter case first. The type entry is just the identifica-

tion code for the kind of node that n-tuple represents. The various operands are descendent subtrees. The n-tuples can be of. varying size but it often happens that n is fixed, the most common value being $n = 3$. This results in the use of quadruples.

A variation on this scheme is to regard the type field not as an identification but as a temporary variable in which to hold the result of the operator acting on operand 1 and operand 2. Take again the above example. This could be represented by a set of quadruples:

$\times$ b c T1
$+$ a T1 T2

The use of quadruples is a convenient form from the point of view of optimization. The extra fourth field is in fact unnecessary and adds to the bulk of the intermediate program. This field can be removed by using instead a reference to the number of the triple; thus $a + b \times c$ can be expressed as:

1: $\times$ b c
2: $+$ a (1)

In the second triple the value of a has to be added to the result of evaluating triple 1. This then describes the motivation behind the use of the first of the two kinds of n-tuple.

The methods described above are the more common methods of representing the intermediate program but they are by no means the only methods. Many compiler writers do not restrict themselves to just one of the methods described above. Typically, several of the methods may be interwoven at the whim of the compiler writer.

The intermediate codes for functional languages are typically based on the lambda calculus. Typically the pure lambda calculus is complemented by a set of mechanisms for naming expressions and describing recursion in a convenient form. See, for example, Field and Harrison (1988).

52.7.2 Storage organization

Prior to generating code it is essential to have a preconceived idea of how storage will be utilized. In many ways the complexity of this is reflected in the facilities existing in the programming language. Typically, for languages such as Pascal there will need to be space for code, space for data and space for the run-time system. Of these:

1. The target code is typically of fixed size.
2. The data (i.e. the space allocated for variables, arrays, etc.) is likely to possess one component which is of fixed size and so can be statically allocated at compile time and a separate component whose size will not be known until run time.
3. Run-time systems will be discussed in more detail in Section 52.7.3.

For the purpose of efficiency and simplicity, it is normally desirable to allocate space statically at compile time if possible.

The allocation of static space is conceptually straightforward. For each item of a particular kind, so many memory locations will be utilized, e.g. one for an integer, two for a real number, three for a double precision real, and so on. Such information can be held within a single table. Straightforward arithmetic will provide a measure of the space requirements for records, fixed size arrays and so one. The code generation needs to be aware of these issues as well as issues involving the alignment of objects. In addition, it needs to be able to provide instructions which will access the proper element of one, two, etc. dimensional arrays, given appropriate indices. With these considerations and an indication of what space is allocated and what space is free, the problem of allocating static space at compile time is resolved.

Many of these basic techniques are used when space is

allocated dynamically. Complications occur with nested blocks, dynamic space allocation, recursion, and so on. A stack is typically used in such cases with new space being allocated from the stack at block entry and removed on block exit. A certain amount of housekeeping (e.g. keeping return links on the stack) is necessary for the management of this and code must be provided for this purpose. In addition, activation records store administrative details needed for block exit, etc. Within this broad framework, arrays are handled as before.

The presence of procedures, functions, etc. possibly of a recursive nature, causes this scheme to be augmented. The precise details depend very much on the parameter calling mechanism and, for regimes such as call-by-name (as found in ALGOL 60, for example), can be quite complex. However, procedure calls typically give rise to new activation records and parameters normally appear as additional stack items. Parameters, as well as variables used within the routine, are given an address relative to a position within the stack.

With deeply nested programs or highly recursive routines, the overhead of accessing variables on the stack can be severe. Mechanisms such as displays which are a form of descriptor indicating the layout of the data on the stack, provide one way of reducing these overheads and producing efficient code.

52.7.3 Run-time environments in general

Within the run-time environment, more sophisticated compilation systems typically need to process code which will manage activities of various kinds at run-time, as they arise during computation. The management of stacks is one aspect of this but the problem is more general.

Certain languages permit dynamic stage allocation of a general kind. The 'new' facility in Pascal, 'heap' in ALGOL 68, and so on, are instances of this. There needs to be run-time routines that manage space of this kind, allocating it where it is needed and retrieving it when it is no longer in use. Normally, heap storage is used for this purpose and typically this grows from the bottom of store towards the stack.

The process of retrieving space can produce a considerable overhead. If a user can de-allocate space and thereby return it for re-use there are benefits. However, even this results in fragmentation and the need to monitor what is available or unavailable. Ignoring this problem, the automatic detection of space which is no longer 'live' is important. This is referred to (picturesquely) as 'garbage collection'. Two common approaches are used:

1. Maintaining reference counts, a count of the number of items referring to a particular block of store; when this decreases to zero the space can be released.
2. Marking the blocks which can be reached from elsewhere, so leaving the other blocks available for collection.

Of these, keeping reference counts can be costly, whereas the second is accomplished by suspending the main program until the garbage collection activity has been completed; in real-time systems this is unacceptable.

When parallel processing is present, there can be another important need for run-time support. In particular there can be issues surrounding the scheduling of tasks possibly involving priorities, the maintenance of queues which need to be serviced, as well as the resolution of problems of fairness, liveness, deadlock etc. Finally, the presence of run-time errors gives rise to the need for a monitor to provide information in a user-friendly manner about the circumstances surrounding the error.

52.7.4 Intermediate code generation

Having identified the nature of the intermediate code as well as the storage allocation strategy, the stage is now set for a discussion of code generation techniques. The underlying approach to this phase of compilation is to traverse the parse tree in a particular way and in the process output the necessary code.

Intermediate codes typically include sets of operations that accomplish the following kinds of operations (for a range of operator op, rel):

a: = b op c	a: = op b
a: = b	**goto** L
x: = y [i]	**if** x **rel** y **then goto** L
y[i] : = x	

and using the notation of the C programming language:

x = &y   x: = *y   *x: = y

Additional sets of operations exist for such actions as dealing with scope information, procedure calls, space allocation and de-allocation, accessing records, causing coercions and so on.

All of the above operations can be viewed as single operations that can appear at points within the parse tree. In traversing the parse tree at code generation time, conceptually the lower subtrees are picked off, appropriate code is generated in such a way that the result is held in a temporary stage location t (say), and t then replaces the subtree in the main parse tree. This activity is repeated until the complete parse tree is processed. It demands the presence of a set of temporary locations whose number is controlled by a counter which is increased as code generation progresses.

To be more definite about this activity consider the parse tree for a single arithmetic expression. A postfix traversal of the tree is performed with the output being placed, a symbol at a time, on a stack. Whenever an operation is encountered the operands will be the top two elements on the stack. Thus the appropriate code can be generated with these top two elements being replaced by the appropriate temporary variable. On completing the traversal the entire code will have been produced. The general situation is similar, with calls being made at the appropriate time to the more complex operations described earlier.

52.7.5 Towards the target machine

In translating from intermediate code to machine code there are some issues which stem from the nature of intermediate codes and their contrast with machine codes.

Actual machines have a limited number of registers and a limited amount of memory. Consequently these (relatively scarce) resources must be allocated and used with care during the final stages of code generation. In particular, temporary space should be reused, a requirement that forces the maintenance of a stack-based model of execution.

The range of operators normally available in an intermediate code is larger than that provided by a real machine. These (and related operations associated with such activities as array indexing, field selection, etc.) need to be expressed in an efficient manner.

52.7.6 Code generation for functional languages

Approaches to the implementation of functional languages tend to originate from early work by Landin (1964) on the implementation of an abstract machine which would evaluate lambda expressions. The essential importance of this early work stems from the fact that the effect of functional languages can be simulated in the lambda calculus. In essence, the lambda calculus is equivalent in expressive power to functional languages.

The early implementation of the lambda-calculus was based

on the SECD machine, an abstract machine with four different stacks:

S: the *s*tack of objects.
E: the *e*nvironment, in the form of an association list of identifier – object pairs.
C: for *c*ontrol, the remainder of the expression to be evaluated.
D: for *d*ump, and used on returning from function evaluation.

At any one time the current state would be represented by a quadruple consisting of the state of these four stacks, S,E, C and D. Associated with each type of expression is then a translation which is described as a change from one state to another and expressed as changes to each of the four stacks.

Further details of the implementation can be found in Landin (1964). In Field and Harrison (1988), a variety of other approaches to implementation can be found.

52.8 Optimization issues

To maintain overall efficiency, optimization techniques are normally applied to the intermediate code that has been generated from the parse tree and the symbol table. The purpose is to produce an object program which runs efficiently and accomplishes the task originally described by the programmer.

A serious concern with this exercise is that, after automatic reorganization, a program might fail. The resulting inspection may be meaningless to the programmer who, as a result of the reorganization, is unaware of the order of evaluation of parts of the program. Considerations of this kind lead to optimization phases being optional or to the provision of messages which provide insight.

52.8.1 Sources of optimization

The manner in which optimization is accomplished is normally based upon reorganization or restructuring of the code. A number of general principles can be cited and interpreted in a variety of ways.

If an operation can be performed once and not repeatedly this will lead to savings. In particular:

1. If subexpressions are common to several expressions they can be calculated once only.
2. Statements can be moved out of loops.
3. Declarations can be moved to outer levels.

Certain optimizations can be accomplished by looking at the effect of combinations of statements:

1. Two consecutive assignments may be combined into one assignment thereby removing the need for one variable.
2. Functions and procedures can sometimes be dispensed with by producing code inline; likewise for certain modules.

When two execution sequences achieve the same effect then the more efficient attributes should be selected. Instances of this give rise to:

1. Recursion removal techniques.
2. Expanding loops to remove the need for counters or other controls and so on.

There are many other techniques of the kind described above. For a more complete overview see Aho *et al.* (1986).

52.8.2 Basic block reorganization

This technique potentially results in massive reorganization of a program. It involves the identification of the complete flow of control of a program and a subsequent reorganization.

The term 'basic block' has its origins in FORTRAN 66. The term is used to describe a sequence of statements which possess only one entry point. The basic structure of a program can be represented by its basic blocks together with the set of interconnections between them. This can be viewed as a directed graph.

Stemming from this:

1. The basic blocks themselves can be restructured on an individual basis, especially if these are deeply nested and frequently executed.
2. The overall structure of the program can be modified with a view to improvement.
3. Basic blocks which are never executed can be removed.

52.8.3 Issues involving concurrency

It was stated earlier that extracting the structure from a sequential program in order to identify sections that can be executed in parallel is often an important form of optimization. The majority of this work has been in relation to FORTRAN programs designed for large-scale numerical computation.

The key to identifying concurrency resides in looking at the variables or data accessed by individual statements or groups of them. Concurrent execution is possible if there is no overlap in the data accessed by two sets of statements. These issues can become complex, e.g. when arrays are being processed, and then subsequent analysis is needed. To gain maximum benefit from these notions programs are typically restructured by applying sets of program transformations, such as unrolling, altering or combining loops, interchanging or otherwise reordering statements, replacing procedure calls by in-line code, etc.

A good overview of the possibilities here can be found in Chapter 2 of Polychronopoulos (1988).

The problem of scheduling the processes identified and extracted in the course of program analysis requires attention. One important issue relates to the level of granularity of the concurrency and the extent to which this maps on to the existing hardware. In addition, there are questions about whether the scheduling should be performed in advance by the compiler (the static approach) or whether it should be left until run time, so invoking the operating system or hardware itself.

The difficulties in this area are highlighted by noting the potential inefficiency resulting from a very low level of granularity in the concurrency accompanied by dynamic scheduling of many associated processes.

A good overview of the issues here can be found in Chapter 3 of Polychronopoulos (1988).

52.9 References and further reading

Aho, A. V., Sethi, R. and Ullman, J. D. (1986) *Compilers – Principles, Techniques and Tools*, Addison-Wesley, Reading Mass., USA
Barron, D. W. (1981) *Pascal – The Language and its Implementation*, John Wiley and Son, UK
Bauer, F. L. and Eickel, J. (eds) (1974) Compiler construction: an advanced course. *Lecture Notes in Computer Science, No 21*, Springer Verlag, Berlin, FRG
Field, A. J. and Harrison, P. G. (1988) *Functional Programming*, Addison-Wesley, London
Goos, G., Wulf, W. A., Evans, Jr A., Butler, K. J. (1983) DIANA: an intermediate language for Ada. *Lecture Notes in Computer Science, No 161*, Springer Verlag, Berlin, FRG
Gough, K. J. (1988) *Syntax Analysis and Software Tools*. Addison-Wesley, London
Griffiths, M. (1974) LL(1) parsing. In *Compiler Construction Lecture Notes in Computer Science, No 21* (ed. F. L. Bauer) Springer Verlag, Berlin, FRG
Horning, J. J. (1974) LR grammars and analysers in compiler construction. *Lecture Notes in Computer Science, No 21* (ed. F. L. Bauer) Springer Verlag, Berlin, FRG

Hunter, R. B. (1985) *Compilers: Their Design and Construction using Pascal*, John Wiley and Sons, Chichester

Knuth, D. E. (1971) An empirical study of FORTRAN programs. *Software Practice and Experience*, **1**, 105–133

Landin, P. J. (1964) The mechanical evaluation of expressions. *Computer Journal*, **6**, 308–320

McGettrick, A. D. (1980) *The Definition of Programming Languages*, Cambridge University Press, Cambridge

Partridge, D. and James, E. B. (1978) Compiling techniques to exploit the pattern of language usage. *Software Practice and Experience*, 527–539

Polychronopoulos, C. D. (1988) *Parallel Programming and Compilers*, Kluwer, Dordrecht, The Netherlands

Reade, C. (1989) *Elements of Functional Programming*, Addison-Wesley, London

Rees, M. and Robson, D. (1988) *Practical Compiling with Pascal-S*, Addison-Wesley, Wokingham

Reps, T. W. and Teitelbaum, T. (1989) *The Synthesizer Generator Reference Manual* (3rd edn) Springer Verlag, New York, USA

Robinson, J. A. (1965) A machine-oriented logic based on the resolution principle. *Journal of ACM*, **12**, 23–41

Waite, W. M. and Goos, G. (1984) *Compiler Construction*, Springer Verlag, New York, USA

Watson, D. (1989) *High-Level Languages and their Compilers*, Addison-Wesley, Wokingham

Wilson, L. B. and Clark, R. G. *Comparative Programming Languages*, Addison-Wesley, Wokingham

53

Networks and distributed systems

Steve R. Wilbur
Department of Computer Science,
University College London

Contents

53.1 Introduction

This chapter discusses key developments and concepts relating to distributed systems. However, distribution implies communication. Modern communications systems and networks are quite complex, so they too are covered. This complexity is partly brought about by demands from the users, e.g. the desire for higher data rates and for communications to support the integration of voice, video and data, and partly by the desire of PTTs to provide a hierarchy of digital services.

The present climate is towards open distributed processing, that is, it should be possible to build systems from different vendors' components and they should interwork. To achieve this, standards are vital. Where international standards are not available, *de facto* or industry standards will spring up. This is happening already with distributed file systems where the Sun Microsystems' Network File System (Sun, 1988) is widely adopted.

Early distributed computing focused on a number of specific applications, such as file and job transfer, electronic mail and latterly transaction processing. As the model of user computing moves to distributed systems there is a need to provide familiar mechanisms to programmers to exploit this distribution in their applications. Remote procedure call (RPC) (Wilbur and Bacarisse, 1987) generally meets this need, although proprietary standards abound at present. Tools are also needed to deal with replication and robustness. Few open solutions exist.

This chapter concentrates on issues which affect the construction of distributed systems, especially the RPC style of interprocess communication, atomic transactions, concurrency control, security and replication. These are dealt with in Section 53.5. In order to set these in context, Section 53.3 discusses the communications fabric of local and wide area networks, and Section 53.4 illustrates the issues in developing a virtual communications structure which performs better and is more usable, i.e. aspects of protocol implementation. Communications and distributed systems generally involve parallel activities with asynchronous events. Moreover, because they involve several independent components which must interwork, standards are needed. Many present day standards are only informally specified, but languages such as LOTOS and ESTELLE are beginning to provide the tools needed. The standards aspects are dealt with in Section 53.2. However, before that it is necessary to define a few basic terms.

53.1.1 Terminology

The following is a brief glossary of communications terms:

Circuit. A circuit is a link between two end-systems. It usually has a fixed capacity, e.g. 64 kbs^{-1}, which is available whether or not the applications use it.

Circuit switching. Circuit switching allows circuits to be established between pairs of subscribers. The Public Switched Telephone Network is a circuit switched system.

Multiplexing. Multiplexing provides the ability to share a given circuit between several independent conversations (channels). Frequency division multiplexing uses different carrier frequencies to separate the channels, e.g. radio stations use frequency division multiplexing of the ether. Time division multiplexing provides time slots on the circuit, every nth one being allocated to the same channel. Samples of each conversation are sent in the relevant time slots.

Packet. For data communications, continuous transmission is not generally appropriate. Data can be sent in short bursts or packets, each of which pertains to one conversation. Packets also normally contain some error detection or error correction code, and will contain some indication of the relevant conversation or the end-points. Packet size is usually between a few octets and a few thousand octets, depending on the network. Packets need not all be the same size on a given network. The use of packets allows another form of multiplexing, since packets from different entities can be interleaved arbitrarily over the same link.

Packet switching. A packet switched network can be constructed from a number of links carrying packets connected to nodes to form a mesh. With adequate addressing information in each packet and knowledge of the network topology, the nodes can switch or route incoming packets to the relevant destination.

Connectionless. Connectionless mode is where packets between two entities are completely self-contained, e.g. they contain full addressing information. They can thus pass through the network independent of any previous packet. These packets are sometimes called datagrams by analogy with telegrams.

Connection-oriented. Connection-oriented mode or virtual circuits mode is a long-term interaction between entities. There are three phases: call establishment, data transfer and call termination. Such an association may allow network components such as nodes better to manage buffer resources, and reduce effort on routing.

53.2 Models

53.2.1 Standards bodies

The need for open systems, whereby users can purchase equipment from a number of suppliers knowing that it will interwork, is now generally accepted. Earlier insistence by vendors on proprietary solutions in order to preserve their market niche has largely disappeared now that users insist on heterogeneous distributed systems. To achieve such open systems, standards are needed. What is more they need to be international, agreed by the community of users and suppliers and stable (Knowles *et al.*, 1987). The main relevant international standards bodies are the International Organization for Standardization (ISO) and the International Telephone and Telegraph Consultative Committee (CCITT).

The ISO is organized into Technical Committees (TCs) which are divided into Sub-Committees (SCs) and these are further subdivided into Working Groups (WGs). Open Systems Interconnection (OSI) is covered by TC97, a cross-section of which is:

SC6: Telecommunications and information exchange between systems responsible for lower four layers of the OSI reference model:

    WG1: Physical layer.
    WG2: Data link layer.
    WG3: Network layer.
    WG4: Transport layer.

SC18: Text and office systems.
SC20: Encipherment.
SC21: Information retrieval, transfer and management for OSI responsible for reference model, and upper layers:

    WG1: OSI architecture, formal description techniques.
    WG2: Graphics (not OSI).
    WG3: Database (not OSI).
    WG4: OSI management.
    WG5: Application services.
    WG6: Session and presentation layers, Common Application Service elements.

The CCITT is the international standards-making body which has largely been concerned with standards for the telecommunications industry, with members being the telecommunications carrier for each country. The CCITT works on a four-year cycle, and at the end of each cycle its recommendations are published. Although this may result in incomplete standards, this allows PTTs worldwide to keep in step, even though some details will need further study. The CCITT is divided into study groups (SGs). Those related to OSI are:

SG VII: Data communications networks:

> Facilities, e.g. reverse charging.
> Interfaces.
> Message handling (X.400, X.500).

SG VII: Telematic services:

> Facsimile.
> Teletex.
> Videotex.
> Character sets.

SG XVIII: Digital networks:

> Integrated Services Digital Network.

There is clearly overlap between some of the activities of the CCITT and the ISO. Both are concerned with the lower layers of the reference model, and certain applications like messaging and directory services are common. Recently there has been agreement that for common standards common texts would be produced to reduce diversity, e.g. the X.400 Electronic Messaging Standard.

The processes of the ISO and CCITT are too slow for getting early harmonization between manufacturers, so other bodies also produce standards. One of these is the European Computer Manufacturer's Association (ECMA), which has produced early standards for aspects such as authentication and remote procedure call, following rapidly on the heels of the published research. Typically, these standards later form the basis of input to the ISO.

In the USA, the Institution of Electrical and Electronic Engineers (IEEE) has acted as such a focal point for industry standard electronic interfaces. In the late 1970s it became involved in local area network (LAN) standards and now generally progresses LAN-related standards. Its results are fed through ANSI to ISO. Key standards are:

IEEE 802.1: LAN management.
IEEE 802.2: Link level protocols.
IEEE 802.3: Carrier sense multiple access with collision detect (CSMA/CD) LAN.
IEEE 802.4: Token bus LAN.
IEEE 802.5: Token ring LAN.
IEEE 802.6: Metropolitan area networks (MANs).
IEEE 802.9: Integrated voice and data (IVD).

Protocols tend to be extensive, and because of the consensus procedure there are often several alternatives for particular functions. To reduce the scope of a given implementation, several groups have defined profiles for their purposes. Of particular note are the Manufacturing Automation Protocol (MAP) and Technical and Office Protocol (TOP), which define a specific set of matching standards for their communities. Groups working on office document architecture (ODA) have defined a series of profiles which act as successive annual milestones to allow different vendors' products to keep in step.

53.2.2 Open System Interconnection reference model

The OSI reference model was developed in response to the difficulties being observed in the communications industry over interworking between different proprietary protocol families and the need for a framework in which to develop standards. The structure arrived at is the well-known seven-layer model. It should be emphasized that the layering principle is an important descriptive technique, but that the best performing implementations do not generally implement each layer as a separate process or task. Indeed, the reference architecture and standards are careful to avoid implementation issues, even to the point of specifying only the services performed by layers, not their detailed interfaces.

Ten basic principles were used to define the layers (Knowles *et al.*, 1987):

1. Keep the overall structure simple; keep the number of layers small.
2. Minimize the interactions across boundaries.
3. Ensure that those functions which are very different in nature or purpose are in different layers.
4. Collect similar functions within a layer.
5. Choose boundaries at points which past experience has shown to be successful.
6. Ensure that functions performed by layers are not dependent on a specific implementation choice.
7. Choose boundaries where it may be useful to have a real physical boundary (e.g. front-end processor).
8. Create layers where there is a different level of abstraction in handling data.
9. Do not let changes to functions or protocols within a layer affect other layers.
10. Allow each layer only to interface with its immediately neighbouring layers.

Layer entities at level k communicate with their peers at the same level elsewhere. Thus, k-entities communicate with each other using a k-protocol. The k-protocol is built from services provided at level $k-1$. These are provided via a Service Access Point (SAP) where k-SAPs are defined to be at the layer boundary between layer k and $k+1$. Each SAP has an address and only one entity can exist above a given address. Thus, the k-SAP address identifies a $k+1$-entity (*Figure 53.1*).

The seven layers of the model, starting from the lowest are:

1. Physical.
2. Data link.
3. Network.
4. Transport.

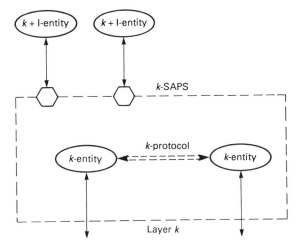

Figure 53.1 Layer entities

5. Session.
6. Presentation.
7. Application.

The physical layer deals with interfacing to the transmission medium. In point-to-point connections, such as leased lines, this will deal with aspects of line signalling. For LANs there will generally need to be some address processing, i.e. to identify which of several nodes are to be addressed. This is because LANs have multiple nodes on a single network, whereas wide area networks (WANs) other than satellite networks usually consist of links between only two end parties.

The data link layer is responsible for reliable communication between adjacent nodes, a 'link'. In particular, it deals with flow control to ensure that data is sent only when the receiver is ready. For a stream of data, where the propagation time over the network is significant, it may be possible for several packets to be 'in flight' simultaneously. As acknowledgements of receipt are received by the sender, more packets can be sent. This is known as a windowed acknowledgement scheme.

The network layer is responsible for building a network out of the individual link. So it is responsible for routing. It also must know about addresses. When independent networks are joined, they are usually joined at the network level. There are other choices, such as at the physical level for LANs (usually called MAC-level bridging) or at the application level (applications level relay). The latter only provides connectivity for specific applications, most commonly electronic mail.

The transport layer provides users with a network-independent view of communications. Above this layer one is more concerned with the attached machines, end-systems; below it the concern is with the communications sub-system. Thus, this layer has responsibility for mapping the user requests (messages and quality of service) into specific network functionality (packets, routes, etc.). It deals with fragmentation and re-assembly of user data, and with attempting to match the user requirements such as maximum error rates to available services. As an example, a mixed-media, voice and data application may need error-free transmission for data with no constraints on arrival rate, but can tolerate a bit-error rate (BER) of 10^{-5} for voice provided the inter-arrival time of voice packets does not vary more than a certain quoted level.

The session layer is concerned with checkpointing and recovery for certain applications. The presentation layer is concerned with the syntax of the messages and the mapping between local and transmitted forms. Abstract Syntax Notation (ASN.1) is used for this. To support applications there are a number of Common Applications Service Elements (CASE). The most notable of these deal with commitment, concurrency and recoverability (CCR) and remote operations (ROS). ROS and presentation level services in combination can provide a basic remote procedure call mechanism.

A number of specific application-layer standards exist or are being developed. These include electronic mail (X.400), directory services (X.500) and file transfer and access (FTAM). Standards for document structures include office document architecture (ODA) and electronic data interchange (EDI) which can be included within the body of X.400 messages.

Increasingly, more formalism is being used to specify standards. ROS and ASN.1 are being used for some applications standards. Two specification languages, LOTOS and ESTELLE, are themselves standards. They are intended to be well-suited to the specification of concurrent systems, such as protocols, but they have only recently become available and have few verification tools at present.

53.2.3 Open distributed processing

The OSI reference model and its associated service definitions and protocols are concerned with peer-based communication. Recently, activity has begun into developing a system view of distributed processing. That work is known as open distributed processing (ODP). It is relatively fluid at this stage.

53.2.4 Other architectures

There are a number of other communications architectures, most notably IBM's Systems Network Architecture (Guruge, 1984; Meijer, 1987), DEC's DECnet (Digital, 1982 and 1987) and the DARPA Internet Protocol suite. Whilst there may be very significant differences in detail between these and the ISO protocols, there is broad similarity in structure. Some vendors have migration strategies for moving from their proprietary architectures towards ISO OSI conformance.

53.2.5 Specification languages

Communications systems typically contain concurrency and are event-driven. As part of the ISO communications standards activities, two languages for formal specification have been developed. These are called LOTOS (ISO 8807) and ESTELLE (ISO 9074). The CCITT has also defined a language called SDL which is very similar to ESTELLE.

LOTOS is intended to be used for behavioural specification of systems. It allows concurrent systems to be specified as a set of communicating processes which communicate through named event gates and the type of data transferred in an event can be used to affect the actions performed in the receiver. Processes implicitly stop at their end unless they re-invoke themselves, so apparently recursive processes run continuously. Processes can be built from other processes by constructs such as sequences, alternates, and parallel activities. LOTOS also allows processes to be completely stopped by another process using the disruption primitive. In addition, LOTOS incorporates ACT1 in order to specify abstract data types, i.e. both the types of variables and the allowed set of operations. A LOTOS specification should emphasize the behaviour of the system in terms of events and actions, rather than detail of the algorithm and other implementation details.

ESTELLE uses a state transition approach to the specification of communication systems. A specification is made up of modules, which interact via channels and interaction points. Channels are essentially buffers and specify which modules will create and which will accept events using them. Modules can be either processes or activities and allow the specification to be split into the continuous and event-driven parts of the system. Process modules can be created and terminated as needed. Interaction points are at the boundaries of modules and channels can be attached to and detached from them as needed. State identifiers are associated with appropriate modules. Transitions between states are specified by transition blocks using a language heavily based on Pascal as the means of specifying the actions performed in response to events. ESTELLE can provide a specification which is much closer to an implementation than LOTOS.

53.3 Networks

53.3.1 Wide area networks

53.3.1.1 Public Circuit Switched Networks

The Public Switched Telephone Network (PSTN) has been used for data communications for many years. Until recently it was an analogue network in that voice was carried using a continuous signal. Over the past 15 years or so most national telephone systems have increasingly become digital in which the analogue voice signal is sampled at a fixed rate. These samples are then sent as a digital data stream, usually at $64\,kb\,s^{-1}$. Generally, at present, digital transmission only occurs on the PTT (telephone company) equipment and trunks and between the exchange and Private Branch Exchanges (PBXs) of business customers, and the circuit to the end customer phone is still analogue. Use of such circuits for digital data transmission requires the use of a modem (modulator/demodulator) to convert between digital and analogue signals at each end. Data transmission rates over the PSTN can be as high as $9.6\,kb\,s^{-1}$ with sophisticated modems, but typical rates are up to $2.4\,kb\,s^{-1}$.

Leased lines can offer higher data rates because they follow a fixed path which can be tuned to provide lower losses and greater bandwidth. The switched telephone network is described more fully in Chapter 58.

As part of the PSTN modernization, the concept of an Integrated Services Digital Network (ISDN) was developed. The aim was to provide circuits to the end user and to provide digital control. In the UK a pilot service known as Integrated Digital Access (IDA) has been available since 1985. Its development pre-dates the ISDN standards and it will be replaced by a conformant ISDN network shortly. The ISDN service (Falek and Johnston, 1987) has several forms. Basic Rate ISDN provides a termination with two $64\,kb\,s^{-1}$ circuits for data (B-channels) and one $16\,kb\,s^{-1}$ channel for signalling (D-channel). The B-channels may be used for data or voice purposes directly and have different addresses ('telephone numbers'). The D-channel provides a packet service (HDLC protocol) to the exchange and is used for dialling and other control purposes. With ISDN, call set-up and close-down take a few tens of milliseconds and so allow data transfers to be organized very differently from that necessitated by the use of current dialled modem access.

Primary Rate ISDN provides a service at $1.544\,Mb\,s^{-1}$ in North America and $2.048\,Mb\,s^{-1}$ in Europe. All channels operate at $64\,kb\,s^{-1}$. In North America the service is structured as 23 B-channels and 1 D-channel, whereas in Europe it comprises 30 B-channels and a D-channel. The spare capacity is used by the service providers for circuit management functions, e.g. diagnostic and timing. There are technical difficulties in arbitrarily combining $64\,kb^{-1}$ channels into channels with larger capacity, but a number of composites are defined. The standard H-channels are:

H0: $384\,kb\,s^{-1}$
H11: $1.536\,Mb\,s^{-1}$ (North America)
H12: $1.920\,Mb\,s^{-1}$ (Europe)
H1: $2.048\,Mb\,s^{-1}$
H4: $140\,Mb\,s^{-1}$

Broadband ISDN will provide a service at rates around $150\,Mb\,s^{-1}$ and is currently a subject of research and standards bodies.

53.3.1.2 Packet-switched networks

There are a vast number of packet-switched wide area networks. Public networks are usually based on the X.25 standard protocols and generally provide data rates at no more than $64\,kb\,s^{-1}$ to the user. Both national and international X.25 public networks exist, including Packet SwitchStream (PSS) offered by BT in the UK and the International Packet Switched Service (IPSS). Such services have been developed for data transmission, and applications range from terminal access and file transfer to transaction processing. Since terminal access is such a common requirement, many public services also offer PAD

(packet assembler/disassembler) services, where a modem is employed by users to access the local PAD and this then uses the packet switched network to access the service required. The protocol between the terminal and the PAD is usually X.28 and that between the PAD and the X.25 network is X.29. Private packet switched networks may be similar, or they may use other protocol families such as IBM's SNA, Digital's DNA, DARPA TCP/IP, etc.

Packet-switched networks have the advantage that they allow several (data) conversations to be multiplexed over a single circuit in an adaptive way based on demand, rather than the fixed sampling which is often employed for circuit switched multiplexing.

53.3.2 Local area networks

Local area networks (LANs) were first developed in the early 1970s, with commercial products appearing in the early 1980s. Such LANs generally operated at data rates between $100\,kb\,s^{-1}$ and $10\,Mb\,s^{-1}$ over distances of a few kilometres. These might be termed first-generation LANs, have now been supported commercially for several years, and have an industry or international standard specification. The most common of these, which will be discussed briefly below, is the ISO 8802/3 CSMA/CD (carrier sense multiple access with collision detection) bus-structured LAN. Although the term Ethernet actually describes a proprietary standard developed by DEC, Intel and Xerox which differs slightly from the ISO standard, it is often colloquially used for any CSMA/CD LAN. Many professional workstations are now sold with Ethernet interfaces as standard, allowing them to work in a distributed computing environment sharing filing and printing services. First-generation LANs are well covered in Stallings (1987).

Experience seems to show that the Ethernet $10\,Mb\,s^{-1}$ capacity is able to support about ten discless workstations working into a shared fileserver, or up to about 30 if much program loading and swapping is only to the workstation's own local discs. However, with applications such as image processing, or in large organizations, a $10\,Mb\,s^{-1}$ network or a $10\,Mb\,s^{-1}$ backbone linking LANs may frequently become congested.

Partly in response to this need for backbone inter-connection, and partly in an attempt to use LAN technology to deal with voice switching, several higher speed LANs (HSLANs) have been developed. These might be termed second-generation LANs. They typically operate in the $50\,Mb\,s^{-1}$ to $150\,Mb\,s^{-1}$ region, over distances of up to $100\,km$. The large distances which are now possible are brought about by the use of optical fibre, but in turn it allows new applications to be considered. For example, PTTs have been investigating the feasibility of such networks for providing high speed data services for customers within a city, the so-called metropolitan area networks (MANs), or even linking company offices over a large geographical area (Mollenauer, 1988). Second-generation LAN products are just becoming available, and the relevant standards are being worked on.

While the need for data transmission related to computation will continue to rise, the integration of communications services into the workstation will place additional demands on the communication infrastructure. Considerable research is underway to investigate the technology, user interfaces, and benefits of integrated voice image (including video), and data for a variety of industrial applications. For certain types of design discussions, data rates of $50-100\,Mb\,s^{-1}$ between user workstations are expected to occur over long periods. Clearly, second-generation LANs will be of limited use with such scenarios. Third-generation LANs are currently in the research stage. They can probably be characterized as having a data rate in excess of $500\,Mb\,s^{-1}$ (typically $1\,Gb\,s^{-1}$), and will certainly be capable of carrying circuit traffic such as voice and video, as well as high bit rate data.

53.3.2.1 CSMA/CD

In CSMA-CD networks all nodes are attached to a single, serial, passive communications bus. Nodes can listen to the bus to determine if data is flowing, and they can transmit on it. Let us suppose that three nodes, A, B, and C are attached as shown in *Figure 53.2*. If A wishes to transmit to B it first listens until the bus is idle and then begins to transmit. The signal travels in both directions from A, being completely absorbed by the terminators at each end. As it passes another node, e.g. B, that node can copy it into local buffers if the transmitted packet's destination matches the node's address. Now assume that as the signal nears C, C, observing an idle bus up to this point, decides to transmit too. Shortly afterwards there will be a collision and the data in the packets from A and C will interfere. C will detect this almost immediately and could stop transmitting, but although A's packet will have been damaged, A will not know about it until the fragment of C's packet has travelled along the cable to A. Thus, the worst case time taken for a collision to be detected occurs when A and C are at extreme ends of the bus, and is equal to twice the propagation time of an electrical signal over the bus length. This parameter is known as the slot time (S) and is important in bus LANs using contention protocols.

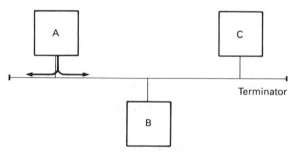

Figure 53.2 CSMA/CD principle

At time S/2 after transmission has begun all nodes are aware that the bus is busy and will not attempt to transmit. Thus, S corresponds to the time taken for any node to be assured that it has transmitted the smallest possible packet without collision; anything smaller is assumed to be a collision fragment and is discarded. For an ISO 8802/3 LAN the slot time is 51.2 μs giving a minimum data size of 46 octets.

When collisions are detected the offending transmitters back off for a random number in the range 1 to 2^N slot times, where N is the number of collisions this packet has been involved in. Thus, the chances of the nodes re-colliding is reduced and the back-off delay increases with network load.

It can be shown that the minimum packet size on a CSMA/CD network is proportional to the product of data rate and the maximum length of the network, its diameter. Thus, as the speed is increased either the diameter must be reduced or the minimum packet size must increase. Experience shows that the majority of packets on LANs carry between one and 64 octets of user data. A larger minimum packet size could prove wasteful of the network capacity.

Some simulation studies have shown that the maximum likely load on CSMA/CD networks before saturation occurs is about 40%. This relates to random source and destination addresses. In practice, there is some concentration of traffic (e.g. several clients of a single file server), so that contention is somewhat limited and the theoretical limit may not be a limitation in practice.

In summary:

Standard: ISO IS8802/3.
Data rate: 10 Mb s^{-1}.
Max. network 'diameter': about 2.5 km.
Control method: CSMA/CD; non-deterministic.
Min. packet size (data): 46 octets.
Max. packet size (data): 1500 octets.
Network connection: passive.
Address size: 16 or 48 bits.
Max. load: random source/destination about 40%.

53.3.2.2 Token ring

Nodes in a token ring are connected cyclically to each other forming a ring. In the quiescent state a recognizable packet circulates, known as the token. A node with data to transmit captures the token as it passes, and then transmits its data packet. When the packet has all travelled back to the originator that node then sends the token, effectively passing it downstream for its neighbour. Thus, there is inherent fairness in the control of access to the network, providing that nodes release the token within an agreed time. Also, knowing the configuration and the maximum token hold time, the maximum delay (latency) between successive transmissions from a given node can be predicted. Typically, the recipient can set response bits, and the packet fully returns to the sender before the token is released for other nodes' use.

In the ISO standard token ring there are a number of priority levels. The transmitting node places its current priority level in the packet header, and as this circulates other nodes with more urgent data can over-write it with a higher priority reservation. If the packet returns to the sender with a higher priority bid, it releases the token with the reserved priority when the packet has fully circulated. Only nodes with data at that priority may then capture the token and transmit. Eventually, the token will return to the original sender which is then responsible for reducing the token's priority to its original level. The scheme can be nested for several priority levels.

The token ring is generally considered to be one of the best LAN structures in terms of throughput. Being deterministic means that there is no bandwidth wasted on collisions. Since packets are generally of sizes up to a few thousand octets, the proportion of the bandwidth used for address and other control purposes is small and there is no lower limit on the packet size. Its main drawback is that the delay in accessing the ring for a given node is the sum of the service times of all the upstream nodes. Because packet sizes can be large, so can the delays. However, the token ring priority schemes do go some way to reducing this problem for certain classes of traffic.

In summary:

Standard: ISO IS 8802/5.
Data rate: 4 Mb s^{-1} and 16 Mb s^{-1}.
Max network 'diameter': unspecified.
Control method: Token with multi-level priority; deterministic.
Min. packet size (data): 2 octets.
Max. packet size (data): 1500 octets.
Network connection: active repeater.
Address size: 16 or 48 bits.
Max. load/efficiency: tends to 98% but latency high.

53.3.2.3 Fibre distributed data interface

The fibre distributed data interface (FDDI) (Ross, 1986; Burr, 1986) began within the ANSI standards body as a network suitable for the interconnection of mainframes and their high-speed peripherals, or as a backbone for first-generation LANs. An enhancement, known as FDDI-II, was developed to address circuit switching. FDDI has now been adopted by ISO, and with the exception of the station management functions, the component standards have reached at least draft international standard status. However, the term FDDI-II has been dropped in favour of the term hybrid ring control (HRC) and those provisions should be balloted shortly.

FDDI consists of two counter-rotating fibre rings which can be wrapped to form a sausage-shaped ring if a node or line fault is detected. The standard assumes a maximum total wiring distance of 100 km, which means a total fibre path of up to 200 km under wrapped conditions. It also allows up to 500 nodes to be attached.

In many token rings the outgoing packet fully returns to the sender before the token is released. With short rings at low data rates this does not significantly consume bandwidth, since the ring delay may be only a few tens of bits. However, as speeds and distances increase the delay will be significant. For example, at 100 Mb s^{-1} a 100 km network would have a delay of 500 μs or about 50 000 bits of delay. Thus, as token rings move to higher speeds early token release is used, where the sender appends the token immediately after their transmitted packet(s). The benefits of response bits (recipient being able to mark the circulating packet as accepted or not) still exist because the packet(s) still return to the sender, but the ring is made available to other nodes much earlier. However, because the head of the packet may not have returned before the token is passed on, the token ring priority scheme described above cannot be used.

The limiting factor in token ring efficiency is determined by the delay between release of the token at one node and capture at the next downstream node (token slack time). This time cannot be recovered, it must always be wasted. For high-speed rings where the nodes may be separated by a kilometre or more, this delay may be about 500 bits.

FDDI operates in two modes: asynchronous and synchronous. Asynchronous working is the normal token ring mode and dynamically allocates any bandwidth remaining after the synchronous requirements have been met. The synchronous mode is for applications which have a requirement where predictable response is needed. A target token rotation time (TTRT) is agreed by all nodes at ring initialization and the token rotation time (TRT) is monitored during operation. If the token returns earlier than TTRT the node can send either synchronous or asynchronous traffic. Synchronous mode is managed by the station management (SMT) layer, which arbitrates bids for bandwidth such that the sum of the allocations, the time for a maximum length packet, and a token circulation must not exceed TTRT.

Asynchronous mode has two forms: non-restricted and restricted tokens. Non-restricted tokens are the norm, and allow even sharing of the bandwidth between nodes. A priority scheme can be used, which is also based on the token rotation time. For those brief occasions when a pair or group of nodes wish to use all the available asynchronous bandwidths the token can be restricted. Higher level protocols are used to establish which nodes are involved in the dialogue, and one of them issues a restricted token.

The difference is that between synchronous and isochronous mode is that with synchronous mode data must be sent in large bursts whereas with isochronous transmission a steady flow of smaller data units is achieved. Synchronous mode provides a bound on the transit delay, but the actual inter-packet arrival time may vary widely depending on the actual instantaneous load. With isochronous forms this delay is virtually constant.

FDDI-II mode is initiated by one node negotiating the right to become cycle master on a ring operating in token mode. This node then has the responsibility for generating an integral number of 125 μs cycles (slots) round the ring and any padding to accommodate them. The cycles are synchronized to an 8 khz clock source, e.g. that used in telephone systems. The main part of the cycle consists of 96 data groups (frames), each containing 16 octets of data (*Figure 53.3*). Essentially, these provide 16 circuit switched channels operating at 6.144 Mb s^{-1} (3×2.048 Mb s^{-1} or 4×1.538 Mb s^{-1}) leaving about 2 Mb s^{-1} of the LAN capacity for control and asynchronous operation. The 16 circuits are controlled by the 16 bits in the template which indicate whether they are in use for circuit data or are free. Thus, circuit N is made up of 96 octets, one from each data group. The 16 octet token group field and any unused channels in the data group are used to provide residual token ring facilities.

In summary:

Standard: ISO 9314.
Data rate: 100 Mb s^{-1}.
Max. network 'diameter': about 100 km.
Control method: token, timed token priority; isochronous, synchronous and asynchronous transfer; deterministic.
Min. packet size (data): 2 octets.
Max. packet size (data): 4096 octets.
Network connection: active repeater.
Address size: 16 or 48 bits.
Max load/efficiency: tends to 99% but latency high.

53.3.2.4 Distributed queue dual bus

The IEEE 802.6 activity on metropolitan area networks is now based on a network known as a distributed queue dual bus (DQDB). The form of the network is very different from those above (Newman *et al.* 1988), and the standards work is at a early stage so this section will concentrate on the principles with a brief look at the salient points of the standard.

The network consists of two uni-directional, serial buses A and B (*Figure 53.4*). The operation of DQDB is symmetric with respect to both these buses, so we shall concentrate on the transmission of data along the A bus. Transmission along the B bus is identical other than interchanging A and B in this description. At the head of each bus is a slot generator and both generate slots at the same rate. Slots are completely absorbed at the tail of each bus. All nodes are connected to both buses and they can read the passing traffic and over-write it as needed. They cannot delete data, though.

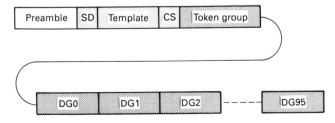

Figure 53.3   FDDI-II cycle-structure

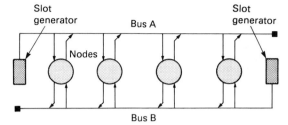

Figure 53.4 DQDB structure

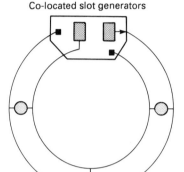

Figure 53.5 DQDB slot generation

Although it is logically a bus structure, physically DQDB is a ring (*Figure 53.5*). The ring is broken at the node providing the slot generators. The slot generators are expected to be synchronized to the 8 Khz PTT reference frequency, so if there should be a break in the cable the nodes either side can act as slot generators and still be synchronized. The slot generation functions migrate automatically to the site of the failure. It is intended to operate at data rates of about 150 Mb s^{-1} over distances of the order of 100 km, using optical fibres as the medium.

DQDB provides a perfect queuing structure. Each slot has a full/empty bit and a request bit together with a data transport field (*Figure 53.6*). Each time a slot passes upstream with a request bit set the node's request queue is incremented. If the node wishes to transmit, it must continue incrementing the queue as requests pass it upstream on B, until a slot without a request arrives. It can now insert its request into the slot, and

add its request into its queue. Other requests continue to arrive, so there are two elements of the queue: the number of requests before the node's own, and the number after. (At any time nodes can only have one of their own requests outstanding.) As empty slots arrive on A these are passed downstream to honour earlier requests and the node's queue is decremented. When the counter reaches zero, the node can transmit its data. Clearly, if the request queue is empty when a node wants to transmit it uses the next free slot after sending a request.

It is straightforward to extend this scheme to allow several priority levels. There needs to be one bit in each slot corresponding to a request at a given level and a similar number of queues in each node. As slots pass downstream the highest priority non-empty queue in each node is decremented.

With DQDB, all nodes are provided an opportunity to transmit based on the time at which they were able to access a request bit in an upstream slot. This scheme does not suffer problems similar to token slack time, because slots can, in principle, be transmitted nose-to-tail. By keeping the slots of fixed, short length the latency for access is kept low, at the cost of fragmentation and re-assembly being needed for large transfers. There is no notion of response bits with DQDB, since the ring is not closed.

Two types of slots are being proposed in the standard: queued-arbitrated (QA) to transfer asynchronous data, and non-arbitrated (NA) to transfer isochronous data. The QA slots are controlled in the way described above. The NA slots are generated by the slot generator at a rate sufficient to satisfy the demands for circuit switched traffic, and nodes are allowed to read and write only agreed portions of such slots, very much like the data groups of FDDI-II. One difference is that NA slots contain an identifier (VCI) which a node can examine to see if the slot relates to its circuits. Both QA and NA segments consist of a four octet header followed by 64 octets of data. The header contains a VCI, data type indication, and priority indication as well as a check sequence.

The basic data packet (MAC frame) is built from QA slots. A MAC frame consists of a header, between 3 and 9188 octets of data and a trailing check sequence.

In summary:

Standard: IEEE 802.6.
Data rate: probably about 2×150 Mb s^{-1}.
Max. Network 'diameter': 100 km or more.
Control method: distributed queue; deterministic.
Packet size (data): 68 octets/9188 octets.
Network connection: passive fibre-optic connection.
Address size: 16, 48 or 60 bits.
Max. load/efficiency: high efficiency, good latency.

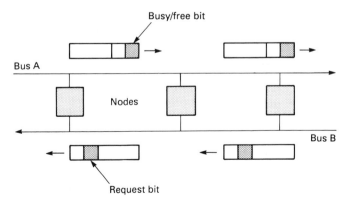

Figure 53.6 DQDB principles

53.4 Protocols

Protocols at or below the transport level are concerned with conveying data between network nodes. As such, they have to provide some or all of the following functions: error control, flow control, congestion control, synchronization, routing and fragmentation and re-assembly. Above the transport level the functions are concerned more with applications (end-systems) and include session management (checkpointing and restart), presentation issues concerned with abstract and machine representations of data and transaction support.

Data in transit is susceptible to corruption. This may occur on random bits or in bursts. By passing the data through a simple mathematical function before transmission, and appending the result to the transmitted data, the receiver can detect whether the data was corrupted. The simplest such function is parity which will detect an odd number of bits in error in the checked sequence, but will not detect an even number of errors. More complex polynomial codes, often known as cyclic redundancy checks are used in most protocols (Lin and Costello, 1981). Such functions provide error detection, and allow the receiving end to discard the incoming packet and if appropriate request the data to be re-sent.

Error-correcting codes or forward error correction use a similar mathematical process but the functions are based on Hamming and related codes in which sufficient redundancy is included in the transmitted message to allow detection and correction of damaged packets by the receiver (Peterson and Welden, 1986). Whereas error detection may include a 32-bit CRC to cover a packet of up to 1500 data bytes, an error correcting code may increase the packet size by 50–100% (often known as 3/4 rate or 1/2 rate encoding) to provide sufficient redundancy for correction. Most conventional data transmission protocols use error detection and re-transmission, but forward error correction is valuable for time-critical situations or satellite links where the round-trip delay is significant (0.5 s for satellite). Some applications may need little error control, e.g. packet voice transmission. A few damaged samples will be heard as distortion or noise, but may not affect intelligibility of the conversation.

Flow control is needed to ensure that the transmitter does not send packets faster than the receiver can pass them on to the application. However, if data is to be transmitted at the maximum rate it is necessary to keep the 'communications pipe' between sender and receiver full of packets. A sliding window protocol is used for this purpose (Tanenbaum, 1988). An initial estimate is made of how many packets may be in flight and this is the window size (w). The sender may transmit up to w packets but can only send further packets when an acknowledgement of arrival of a packet is received from the recipient. Clearly, this scheme needs some refinement as the acknowledgement also takes time to return, leading to 50% link utilization. Most protocols have a means of adjusting the window size during transmission. Another mechanism will be discussed in Section 53.4.2.2.

The network path between end-systems will generally include switching elements which have to deal with many traffic sources. The aggregate traffic may exhaust the buffers in the switching systems causing packets to be discarded. To control this, quench messages are sent from the switches to senders to regulate the congestion.

Routing algorithms are distributed algorithms which identify over which links data should pass to reach a specified destination. In simple cases of fixed routing, each network node knows the best of its links to use for forwarding packets to a given address. Such schemes fail if links fail, so routing protocols are used between the switches (gateways) to produce a distance metric for each destination and to keep this updated. Thus, at any instant a gateway can forward packets down the optimum path even in the face of failures. The algorithms have to be designed with care, otherwise they can become unstable with adjacent gateways routing the same packets to each other.

Different networks are able to deal with different packet sizes. Local area networks typically have a packet size of up to 1500 bytes, X.25 networks may have packet sizes of as little as 128 bytes, whereas packet radio and high speed LANs mave have maximum packet sizes of 30–64 bytes. Thus, a message will need to be fragmented into packets before transmission, and it may be further fragmented during transmission. Intermediate systems (gateways) may re-assemble fragments into larger packets, but they still may not match those used by the transmitter. Typically, fragmentation and re-assembly will be invisible to the end-systems, but message boundaries need to be conveyed from end to end.

53.4.1 X.25

X.25 collectively defines protocols at the physical, link and network layers of the OSI reference model. The physical level protocol is known as X.21 and the Link Level as HDLC, LAP or LAPB depending on the variant used (Tanenbaum, 1988).

The X.21 standard defines how customers' equipment interacts with the network equipment in order to set up calls and transfer data. The terms data terminal equipment (DTE) and data circuit-terminating equipment (DCE) are generally used for the customer's terminal and the network connection, respectively. X.21 is intended to be used in a purely digital network, but in order to allow a transition from existing analogue services based on the old telephone networks, a variant known as X.21 bis also exists. X.21 and X.21 bis define the control protocol and indications for establishing and terminating calls. These are the equivalent of dial-tones, and dialling procedures for a normal telephone. In addition, the standards define the physical characteristics of the data as it passes over the network.

The link level protocols were derived from the earlier IBM Synchronous Data Link Control (SDLC) protocol and are responsible for segmenting the bit stream into packets which may contain an arbitrary number of bits and for controlling data transmission across a link. In order to delimit packets (frames), earlier protocols had used packets composed of an integral number of bytes and used reserved symbols to indicate start and end of the frame. If these symbols occurred in data to be transmitted they had to be 'escaped' by prefixing with a data link escape (DLE) symbol. The receiver would treat 'DLE-x' as 'x', where x was one of the range of reserved control characters, including DLE itself. This is not possible with bit-oriented protocols such as HDLC, since neither octets nor character codes are defined at this level. Instead bit-stuffing is used. A flag sequence (01111110) is used to mark the start and end of a packet. Any user data which contains five successive ones automatically has a zero inserted by the transmitter and removed by the receiver, thus, the data 01111111100 would be transmitted as 011111011100. The frame consists of the following fields:

Flag:	01111110: 8 bits
Address:	8 bits
Control:	8 bits
Data:	0 or more bits
CRC:	16 bits
Flag:	01111110: 8 bits

The address field is principally used on multi-drop lines, i.e. where several terminals share a single line into a computer and a polling mechanism is used to provide orderly sharing of the line. Each terminal will have a unique address. The CRC provides a means of checking for damage to the data. The flag sequence is transmitted continuously on idle lines.

The control field has three forms corresponding to information, supervisory or unnumbered frames. The control field of an information frame contains the sequence number of this frame modulo 8, the sequence number of the next one expected (Next) and a bit indicating polling if appropriate (Poll). Supervisory frames include a type, Next and Poll fields. Type indicates such things as negative acknowledgment, and receiver not ready.

HDLC, LAP and LAPB are very similar in the definitions of information and supervisory frames but differ considerably for unnumbered frames. These latter frames are also used for control purposes, and include functions such as disconnect, reconnect and reset sequence numbers. LAP is unbalanced in that its commands reflect a master-slave approach, e.g. terminal(s) communicating with a computer. HDLC and LAPB are symmetric and allow peers to synchronize. They also allow an extended frame format with 7-bit sequence numbers.

Level 3 maps one or more virtual circuits (vc) onto a physical link at level 2. In order to set up a virtual circuit a call request packet is sent, which contains: the caller's choice of vc number, the calling and called X.25 addresses, a facilities field and, optionally, a small amount of data. The sender chooses a vc number which it is currently not using and there are arrangements to map to another idle value if the receiver's DTE is already using that vc number. The addresses are encoded one digit per 4-bit field, and there is a length indicator for each address field. Facilities include: reverse charging, simplex (one-way) circuits, maximum packet size (default 128 octets) and default window size setting. The data field may be used to convey passwords, or other DTE specific data. In response to this a call accepted packet will normally be returned and the vc can be used for data transfer. Other control packets exist, including clear request and clear confirmation to close down vcs.

Data packets include the virtual circuit number chosen by the sending DTE, a sequence number for the packet, an acknowledgement sequence number (piggy-back), the data and a handful of control bits. The sequence numbers can can be either modulo 8 or 128 depending on the modulo control bits. To allow re-assembly and synchronization of large messages there is a 'more' indicator which is set for all but the last frame of a fragmented packet.

Two forms of datagram service are supported by X.25. In one, the sequence fields of the data packet above are combined with the call request packet and the data portion is expanded to 128 bytes. In the other, known as fast select, the call request and clear request packets include 128 data bytes and fast select is requested as a facility. To the network this looks like an attempt to set up a virtual circuit which is immediately closed down, but with up to 128 bytes passed in each direction.

53.4.2 Lightweight protocols

Flow control and error control are particularly important where a stream of data is being transmitted over a noisy network. Local area networks are relatively error free, typical error rates being 10^{-11}, or one bit in error every eight hours at 10 Mb s^{-1}. This, coupled with high data rates or small messages may mean that simpler retry strategies are appropriate. Three such lightweight protocols are described below.

53.4.2.1 RPC protocol

The concept of remote procedure call (RPC) is described in Section 53.5.2. Essentially it consists of a message initiating the call and passing the procedure parameters, and blocking of the caller until a reply arrives in a second message. The classic approach is developed in Birrell and Nelson (1984).

(a)

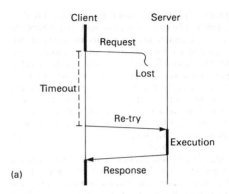

(b)

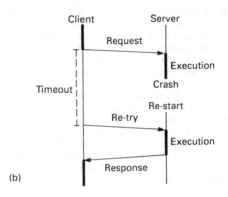

(c)

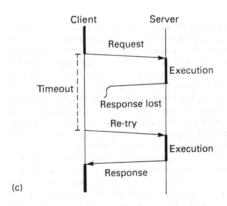

(d)

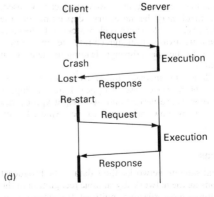

Figure 53.7 Failure modes of simple RPC protocol (a) outbound message lost, (b) Server crash, (c) response lost, (d) client crash

The simplest form of protocol is shown in *Figure 53.7* (Wilbur and Bacarisse, 1987). The call message is sent and a timer is started. If the timer expires before the results are returned, the call is retried. This approach suffers from two problems. First, there may be several reasons for lack of results; it is not clear if the call message was lost, the called process failed, or the results message was lost. Retrying the call may result in multiple executions of the procedure, with attendant problems, e.g. appending another copy of a record to a file with each retry. Secondly, the timeout must be set to be longer than the longest likely execution of the procedure. If there is a failure, the protocol will be slow to recover.

The Birrell and Nelson modifications require that sequence numbers be introduced, so that duplicate requests can be recognized. They also require the called machine to keep the results of a procedure call for some time. Thus, if the caller's timeout expires a duplicate request is sent. If the procedure has finished executing, the stored results are re-transmitted. Otherwise if the computation is still in progress an acknowledgement is sent back and the caller's timeout is restarted. If it should expire again a probe message is sent to check that the computation is still in progress and the acknowledgement is used to restart the timer again. In order to be responsive to failures but to minimize network traffic the caller's timeout value increases rapidly with each probe attempt, saturating at about five minutes after 5–10 minutes. As a final touch, if there is a sequence of calls to the same procedure, the next call message can be used to acknowledge the previous results. If there is no such call an explicit acknowledgement is used. Simple window-of-one flow control is used if call or results messages are longer than the network packet size.

53.4.2.2 *Others*

Other lightweight protocols have been developed, usually where certain controlled conditions hold. For example, bootstrapping a computer via a network may not need flow control, because the machine's memory acts as a large enough buffer for the whole message (e.g. the resident kernel). However, it will need error control. This can be simplified so that when reception has ceased a message containing the addresses of missing packets is sent by the receiver and these are then re-transmitted. If the network is considered to be virtually error-free, an even lighter protocol would send an abort if a damaged packet were received and the whole transmission would be re-started.

There are some applications where packets can be accepted at some guaranteed rate which is less than the transmitter's normal sending rate, e.g. reloading all operational software onto a workstation's disc overnight. Rate-controlled protocols may be used for this where the two ends agree a packet transmission rate and then a protocol without flow-control can be used. Again, error control may be necessary, depending on the application. There is a problem with such protocols. Unless any gateways *en route* are aware of the agreed rate they may bunch successive packets as they pass through, leading to higher than expected loss rates.

As network data rates increase and transmission errors reduce because of the increased use of optical fibres, so higher performance protocols are needed and lightweight approaches can be used. This is now beginning to be explored (van Jacobson, 1988).

53.4.3 Multicast

Some LANs and satellite networks allow data to be broadcast to all destinations on the network. By suitable recognition of the destination address a more selective, multicast, transmission can be achieved whereby a packet is sent to a selected group of recipients. The mechanism can be useful for locating services, or resources such as files in a distributed system, or it may be used to control distributed computations. A lightweight view of multicast is advocated by Cheriton (Cheriton and Zwaenepoel, 1985) in which the relative order of arrival of successive multicast messages at different destinations is immaterial. A very strong form is advocated by Birman (Birman and Joseph, 1987) in which, for a given activity, all participants will see the message sequence in the same order. It appears, however, that the choice is dependent on the nature of the application, and both approaches are valid.

Multicast communication not only involves data transmission, it also involves the management of the groups of participating nodes. Mechanisms are needed for creating groups, assigning a network address to them, adding and deleting members and counting the membership. The protocols for group management generally use multicast protocols to manage a distributed group database.

53.4.4 Network interconnection

Networks are generally interconnected at one of three levels: MAC level (datalink), network or application. Application level gateways or relays are generally used for connecting application systems such as E-mail and providing some protocol conversion at the same time, e.g. conversion from DARPA RFC 822 to X.400 protocol. The MAC level connection is frequently used for LANs and is often termed bridging.

Unlike WANs, where links are generally point-to-point, LANs have multiple nodes connected to the medium, and so each node needs a unique address. Bridges are essentially normal computers attached to two LANs. By listening to all packets passing by on each network (promiscuous mode) the bridge can determine which nodes are on its attached networks (since source and destination addresses are in the packets). Once the bridge learns of the occupants of each LAN it can then forward packets from one LAN to the other if the destination is remote. This scheme only works for LANs directly connected to the bridge. If, instead of forwarding those packets whose destinations were *known* to be remote, all those packets without local destinations were forwarded the scheme would be more flexible. However, a loop (cycle) in the bridge arrangement (*Figure 53.8*) would cause packets destined for an inactive node to circulate forever.

LAN 1

Bridge A

Bridge B

LAN 2

Figure 53.8 Cyclic bridging of two LANS

To remove such cycles the spanning tree algorithm (Backes, 1988) has been developed. Periodically, the bridges poll each other and form a spanning tree. A single route is formed between any pair of nodes, even though there may be cycles in the network. Periodic re-polling allows reconfiguration to occur if a bridge or link fails.

Because MAC level bridges interconnect at the lowest possible level, they allow any LAN protocol to be bridged. Thus, DARPA TCP/IP, DECNet, and OSI protocols which can co-exist on a LAN can all be bridged with one unit. The disadvantage is that the bridge only knows the LAN MAC packet structure and can only control traffic through it on that basis. If access control is required, it is usually done by barring or allowing access based on source and destination machine addresses, rather than process or user identity.

Network level gateways provide a similar function, but are specific to a given protocol family and will use that family's addressing scheme as the basis for routing.

53.5 Distributed systems

53.5.1 Issues

There are several important differences between distributed systems and conventional single or multi-processor operating systems and these give rise to issues which must be resolved in useful systems. Some of these differences are:

1. *Data paths*. In a conventional operating system communication between its constituent parts is via procedure calls, and references to data structures. In a distributed system some communications are via networks, so if good performance is to be obtained the number of messages passed and the size of those messages must be minimized.
2. *Concurrency*. Distributed systems possess true concurrency by virtue of their many processors. Consequently, mechanisms to provide synchronization are vital.
3. *Protection*. Conventional operating systems are encased in a hardware protection mechanism. When the machine is in user mode user processes cannot access operating system data, and can only invoke selected procedures (system calls). In a distributed system the data flows may pass over LANs and be visible to any user. Protection must be provided to ensure that certain data is not observed, data is not corrupted or replayed maliciously, and that the communicating parties are who they claim to be (i.e. they are authenticated).
4. *Consistency*. Transmission of data may be subject to delay and data may suffer damage. Thus, the difference between the real instantaneous state of a given processor and that seen by remote processes may be significant. Without suitable protocols this may lead to different parts of a system making contradictory decisions. This is known as the Byzantine Generals' Problem.
5. *Time*. In a centralized system there is only one reference clock. Clocks are used to avoid deadlock and to protect against replay of messages. For these reasons, clocks in a distributed system must be synchronized. However, this is not a trivial problem and is compounded by clocks which run at different rates, variable delays in networks depending on path and direction of flow, and deliberate attempts to reset clocks to earlier times.
6. *Robustness*. In many operating systems the assumption is that the environment is uniform and reliable. In distributed systems machines may fail independently and networks may fail too. Most networks are complex connections of many LANs and wide area connections, so failures often result in partitioning of the system into independent functioning parts.
7. *Heterogeneity*. Distributed systems often involve different processor types, and a variety of communications facilities. The provision of portable code and the communication of data values, e.g. integers and floating point numbers is made difficult because of this heterogeneity. Heterogeneity also magnifies the problems of managing file space because of multiple copies, managing configuration files, and version control of applications.
8. *Scale*. Many of the problems of scale are related to design,

tuning and operations. Software is generally licensed on a per processor basis. For a mainframe this involves essentially one copy. In a distributed system this may mean many copies of a large (megabyte) binary image, each with a unique machine identifier embedded. There are limits to the number of workstations which can be fed from a file server. Distributed systems can be very sensitive to changes in user work patterns; gateways and bridges may become overloaded making their behaviour erratic. As scale increases good tools are needed to identify and correct these problems.
9. *Autonomy/openness*. Distributed systems need to be constructed so that independent systems can be interconnected and subject to protection controls, they should be able to interwork transparently. This is still a goal rather than an achievement, but agreement of industry standards is a useful step.
10. *Migration*. Standards themselves bring problems. Standards should be stable, but over the years requirements change. It is vital in distributed systems that in migrating from an old standard to a new standard both may co-exist, for a while at least. It is no longer always possible to change all implementations simultaneously.

53.5.2 Remote procedure call

In a distributed system we are forced to use message passing between processes, since in general there is no shared address space. Lauer and Needham (1979) show that message-oriented and shared-memory primitives for operating systems are duals of each other, the one that is chosen for a given job depending on the environment.

Inter-process communications have two components: communication and synchronization. The exchange of data between processes does not necessarily imply synchronization. Where synchronization is not involved one may be able to improve performance because the relevant processes can execute concurrently. Typically, synchronization will be used to ensure controlled access to a resource (monitors, mutual exclusion), or to ensure that a particular sequence is followed. With bilateral communications two common approaches exist. One is based on one-way send/receive primitives, in a variety of flavours, which allow very flexible synchronization options. The second is based on two-way primitives, i.e. sending the message and reception of a reply are part of a single primitive. This usually takes the form of a remote procedure call (RPC) (Birrell and Nelson, 1984) which provides data transfer and synchronization together. Send/receive primitives are documented in many places (Hoare, 1985; Andrews and Schneider, 1983; Sloman and Kramer, 1987) and will not be described further.

Increasingly remote procedure call is being used as an inter-process communication (IPC) mechanism partly because it is a familiar paradigm, partly because it is relatively straightforward to implement and partly because it provides both communication between and synchronization of two processes.

53.5.2.1 RPC mechanism

Remote procedure calls provide an inter-process communication mechanism in which two processes exchange data and are synchronized. The mechanism strongly resembles the procedure call mechanism of conventional programming with a few exceptions, most notably that the caller and callee (usually referred to as the client and server) are in separate processes which are often in different machines. Because of the similarity to a local producer call, a frequent goal is to integrate the RPC mechanism into the user's programming language so as to make local and remote calls syntactically indistinguishable (syntactic transparency). Although syntactic transparency is often achieved, semantic transparency is rarely achieved in present-day programming languages because additional information is often needed for the construction of data types which can be conveyed between machines, because failures of client or server, though rare, have to be coped with and because RPCs are generally orders of magnitude slower in performance than local procedure calls.

The RPC mechanism is usually implemented as follows (*Figure 53.9*). The two parts of the application are split across a procedural boundary, and a dummy procedure with the same name as that in the server is placed in the client process. This dummy procedure, usually known as a stub, is responsible for taking the calling parameters and packing them in a suitable transmission format before sending them to the server. It then merely awaits the server's reply, unpacking the results before passing them in the local representation back to the calling procedure. At the server end the situation is somewhat similar, except that the server may be able to service any one of several call types (service calls to one of several functions). Thus, the main program loop of the server will await an incoming message, decide which function to call, re-format the parameters for local consumption, and call the server procedure. When the procedure returns its results are packed and transmitted back to the client. It can be seen that there is only one thread of control in the application program despite there being two machines and processes in the system. It should also be noted that there is an underlying assumption that the client and server exist in different address spaces, and thus all parameters must be passed by value.

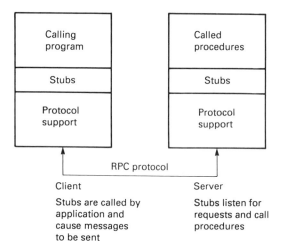

Figure 53.9 RPC stubs

53.5.2.2 Parameters and interfaces

One of the main purposes of the stubs is to translate the representation of data types from that of the local machine into that of the remote machine and vice versa. This is normally accomplished by using an intermediate machine independent representation for transmission and translating to the local conventions at each end. Although this approach leads to two translations being performed for each message sent, the translations can be made relatively efficient taking about 20 μs byte^{-1} on average on modern machines. Even where all machines in the system are identical, the intermediate representation may be valuable, since tags denoting type information may be transmit-

ted with the data itself as an aid to type safety between client and server.

Stubs can be generated either by the programmer or automatically. In the manual case a set of translation functions will be provided from which the user can construct their own stubs. It is the responsibility of the user to translate them correctly for transmission.

Automatic generation of stubs is usually done by having a parameter description language (PDL) which defines the interface between client and server in terms of the procedures and their parameters, constructed from basic types. This PDL is processed to automatically generate appropriate stubs, which can then be compiled and linked in the normal way with the client or server code. The transmitting representation can be either self-describing (tagged, e.g. ASN.1), or untagged. In the latter case some run-time type checking can be done using signatures made up from parameter types and their order. In some cases procedures are grouped into interfaces, where the procedures are related and typically operate on some shared data structure. For example, a file server interface might provide a set of procedures for creating, deleting, reading and writing files. The interface description language (IDL) in such systems allows clients to locate servers by interface rather than procedure name, allow logically related procedures to be grouped, and may allow other attributes such as encryption requirements to be specified. This is the first step towards an object-oriented system, where program objects can only be accessed through a specific set of procedures.

Because the client and server exist in different address spaces, possibly even on different types of machines, passing pointers or passing parameters by reference is meaningless. Most RPC mechanisms therefore pass parameters by value, i.e. all parameters and results are copied between client and server through the intervening network. For simple, compact types, such as integers, counters etc., this poses no problem. Small arrays are also little problem, but larger arrays, and especially multidimensional arrays which would normally be passed by reference can consume much time for transmission of data that may not be used. For example, a 1000-byte array might typically take 20 milliseconds for type conversion and transmission through a LAN.

In some RPC mechanisms there are limitations imposed by the underlying message passing transport service on the actual size of parameters and results passed. This is usually related to some link level packet size and is likely to be of the order of 500–1500 bytes. In some poor implementations these limitations are network dependent, so that an application tailored to exploit the 1500-byte limit of a local network (say) would fail if a link with a 500-byte limit were used. There is, however, an argument in favour of a limited parameter size, and that is that it forces the user to be aware of the expense of remote procedure calls for large parameter lists, and may force a more careful appraisal of the actual interface needed between client and server to minimise the passage of unnecessary data. Thus, a first result of RPC parameter passing semantics is a careful restructuring of application interfaces so that parameters become more specific, with minimal data being transmitted (*cf.* principles of OSI RM layering).

The address space problem also recurs when data types with embedded pointers are to be passed as parameters. A simple, linear linked list is one example of this, and two approaches are possible. The first would be to 'linearize' the list and pass it as an array of list elements. The links themselves have no meaning in the address space of the receiving process, but they can be regenerated relatively easily. In order to perform such regeneration type information must be passed between client and server, indicating not only that a linked list is being passed, but which elements contain pointers and to which elements they point. This process of flattening and shaping of linked lists also extends to other structured data such as trees. However, it is important to note that if the flattening and shaping is to be performed automatically the stubs must be able to trace the links of the structure and translate each element encountered to or from the standardized representation.

The second approach is to inspect the operations performed on the list and provide a more object-based rather than data-based interface. This will tend to produce an interface which is less dependent on the actual machine representation as well as one with smaller parameters. Thus, application of an accepted software engineering principle eases some of the parameter passing problems associated with RPC.

Procedures as parameters also give rise to problems. If the RPC mechanism is being used with an interpreted language then it may be possible to send the code to the server for execution. When compiled procedures are involved in a heterogeneous machine environment then another solution is needed. Provided that the implementation allows a client to act as a server then the client can pass a handle or reference to that required local procedure. This handle will contain the network, machine, interface and procedure identifiers (address) needed to specify the procedure. When the server needs to call the procedure it acts as a client, making a call back to its original client. The semantics of this operation are not the same as passing a procedure across to the server but they are simple to implement and powerful to use. Very large parameters can also be treated in this way, with the recipient getting only a handle on a procedure that can deliver portions of the parameter as they are needed.

The ability for a server to call its client back is very important and care is needed in the design of the RPC protocols to ensure that it is possible.

53.5.2.3 Call execution

A distributed system is prone to partial failures. It is possible in such a system for either the client or server to fail independently, and later to be restarted. The call semantics determine how often the remote function might be performed under fault conditions.

A weak form is at-least-once semantics. In this case the client re-transmits the request if the response does not return within a pre-determined time. Clearly, it is in general impossible to determine whether the failure was due to a server crash, or loss of the request or response. It is thus possible for the procedure in the server to be executed several times or even partially. This behaviour is unlike that of a local procedure call, but can be provided by a very simple protocol. If it is used semantic transparency is lost, and the server must be implemented using idempotent functions, where the programmer must ensure that multiple executions of the same call are identical to that of a single execution with the same parameters.

Acceptable semantics are at-most-once. In this case the server functions are eventually executed once if the server does not crash. The underlying protocol has to be designed to filter out duplicate requests and return the previous results when messages get disrupted. The protocol is more complex, and typically needs to retain results from some previous calls. If the server crashes the procedure may be partially executed, and the application program or an operator would be expected to make the affected data consistent.

The strongest semantics are exactly-once, in which the procedure is guaranteed to be performed exactly once even if the server crashes. This corresponds to the provision of atomic actions, and is rarely found even in non-distributed environments other than through an enhancement package. In the ISO OSI standards, the commitment, concurrency and recoverability mechanisms of the CASE (layer 7) provide this enhancement.

Some RPC mechanisms provide only at-least-once semantics. This is easy to implement over a connectionless protocol, requiring essentially a timer and retry mechanism built into the client transmission routines. The main disadvantage of these cheap semantics are that they force the applications user to design idempotent interfaces, i.e. procedures must produce the same results and side-effects when executed one or more times with the same parameters. For example, a procedure to read successive records might be:

ReadNextRecord(File)

which returns the next record from the named file after each call. Clearly, this is not idempotent and the server needs to keep track of the 'current record' for each client that may be accessing the file. An idempotent interface for sequential file access might be:

ReadRecord(File, N)

which returns record N from the specified file. In this case the server needs to retain no client related state; it is up to each client to keep its own records. However, not all interfaces can be so easily transformed to an idempotent form, e.g. appending a record to the end of a file requires linking of two procedures, one to locate the end of file, the other to write. Typically, a locking mechanism is needed to ensure exclusive access by the client during these two calls.

53.5.2.4 Binding

It is necessary for the client to know the location of the server before the remote procedure call can take place. There are several ways in which this can happen. For example, the server's network address can be compiled into the client code by the programmer, it can be found by looking up the server's name in a file or by soliciting the information from an operator. These methods are not very flexible but are useful in certain limited cases. A more flexible approach is for the client to contact a binding service. Typically the binder will be a server with a well-known address, probably located using one of the simpler methods described above. When a server starts executing it registers its location with the binder together with information about the procedures that it supports. This operation is often called exporting. The client will then contact the binder in order to find the network address of the procedures it requires (importing), and can then use the returned address for the indefinite future. Thus, it is not necessary for the client to consult the binder before each call is made to the server. The binder is a key difference between the local and remote procedure call mechanisms. Several servers may register the same procedures or interfaces; it is up to the client to decide on the most suitable one, or just to choose an arbitrary one.

When servers are about to be withdrawn from service they are usually required to de-register themselves with the binder. De-registration only prevents future attempts at binding to the deceased server from succeeding; existing client–server bindings will still remain. It is therefore important that the underlying transport protocol should be able to detect when the server no longer exists and to inform the client.

53.5.2.5 Server management

In some implementations of RPC several instances of a server may be installed on the same or different machines to provide either load balancing or some measure of resilience to failure.

The binder mechanisms so far described would allow an arbitrary one of these instances to be selected when a client attempts to import the appropriate interface. Such static servers generally remain in existence indefinitely and may retain state between successive procedure calls. Moreover, the server may interleave the requests from a number of clients and thus have to manage concurrently several sets of state information.

In some implementations there is a server manager, which can create servers on demand. The mechanism involves the client contacting the binder in the usual way, but it is returned the address of the server manager. The client contacts the server manager with a suitable CreateServer call, whereupon the server manager passes back the address of a server of the required type to the client for later, private use. In some environments the server manager acts as resource manager and chooses an idle server from an earlier created pool of servers; in others a new server may be spawned on demand. In both cases the client has exclusive use of a server for the duration of a transaction or session. In some cases the server manager can create a variety of servers. Such a server is often known as a generic server.

A third, less common, server management strategy is where each call to the server results in a new server instance. Each instance terminates when its call completes. This might be termed the instance-per-call strategy.

The static server approach is the most rudimentary, but requires the implementor to handle concurrent state management within the server. It is valuable for standard services and may be essential for services controlling physical system resources, but load balancing between different instances is difficult. With server managers, each server normally only services a single client so the need for load balancing disappears, and the code implementing the server only has one set of state to manage. In the final case there is no state retained between calls, even from the same client resulting in a truly stateless server.

Single threaded servers which can only service one client's call at a time are effectively monitors. There is a well-known deadlock problem with nested monitors, and this occurs with nested servers. It has been concluded (Liskov, 1984) that to be generally useful, RPC mechanisms must be implemented in environments which support dynamic process creation, preferably cheaply. Adequate expressiveness and concurrency can normally be obtained with most send/receive primitives in a static process environment.

53.5.3 Atomic transactions

53.5.3.1 Atomic actions

Atomic actions possess the property that if it is impossible to complete the action for some reason, the data items revert to their state before the action was attempted (failure atomicity). If it succeeds the item takes on the new state. This is often referred to as the all-or-nothing property. Thus, with atomic actions it is impossible to observe the data in any intermediate state which might exist during the execution of the action, for any reason.

One is not always provided with suitable primitive actions to maintain consistency of the application data. For example, the implementer of a sort routine may need to interchange two records in a file. If the two records are read into memory, and one is written back in its new position the file is now inconsistent: it contains two copies of one record, and another record is completely missing. Thus, we need constructs for grouping operations or actions together into an atomic transaction. Such atomic transactions have the property that any error during their execution causes the state to revert to that just prior to beginning the transaction. Transactions may contain other atomic transactions, i.e. they can be nested (Moss, 1985). The end of a transaction is known as the commit point, so that once committed there can be no undoing of the transaction.

53.5.3.2 Transactions

A transaction has four basic properties:

1. Atomicity.
2. Durability.
3. Serializability.
4. Isolation.

The atomicity property is that a transaction is either done completely or not at all. If there is a failure of the machine or some of the processing during a transaction's execution, the state of the system reverts to an earlier consistent state, and recovery can take place from there. Normally a transaction completes by the user committing the transaction, but it can be terminated by an abort which reverts to the earlier consistent state. Such aborts may be user-initiated or may be performed by the system as a means removing deadlocks, load balancing, etc.

Durability implies that once a transaction is committed, the system guarantees that the results will not be lost. Stable storage is used to implement this property.

Concurrent transactions must not interfere (the serializability property), i.e. the results must be the same as if the separate transactions were executed serially in any order. This is usually dealt with by some form of concurrency control.

The final property is isolation. This is, it must not be possible to observe the intermediate state of a transaction before it is committed. If it is and the transaction aborts, all other dependent transactions must also abort. This is known as cascading aborts. In systems with real-world effects it may not be possible to abort some actions. An automatic teller machine (ATM) cannot recover money it issued if the transaction were later aborted.

In a centralized environment a transaction manager keeps a commit log, often known as an undo–redo log which accumulates information from the point when a transaction begins until it is committed. It must contain enough information to undo the partial transaction in the case of a crash or abort, and enough information to redo the transaction if a failure occurs immediately after the intention to commit is recorded stably. Because it is possible, but unlikely, that several such crashes may occur, it must be possible for these operations to be executed on several recovery attempts, i.e. the operations must be idempotent. The entries in the log would typically contain:

1. Transaction ID.
2. Record ID.
3. Operation type (insert, delete, modify).
4. Old value.
5. New value.
6. Housekeeping, e.g. linked list of log entries.

There will also be entries in the log corresponding to Begin-Trans operations, i.e. nested transactions. Although the update of a record and its logging in the undo-redo log must appear to be atomic, there is a chance that a crash could occur between the two operations. Thus, the following rules are followed:

1. Before an update is performed, at least the undo part of the log must be in stable storage.
2. Before commitment is recorded, all log records must be on stable storage.

For centralized transactions there are four failure modes which are worth considering:

1. *Failure without memory loss.* This is the case where a transaction is aborted, either by the user or the system. All necessary information is available to recover the system back to an earlier consistent state. The affected transaction is undone using the undo log.
2. *Failure with loss of volatile memory.* Main memory is lost, but

disc contents are still intact, i.e. a system crash. After system re-initialization, but before any application begins executing, it is necessary to run a recovery manager, which scans the logs looking for uncommitted transactions. It also needs to look for all those with a commit record (but not yet fully complete), and then it must undo and redo these transactions respectively. There are techniques for reducing the amount of work to be redone, e.g. by using checkpoints.

3. *Failure with loss of non-volatile memory.* Media failures, head crash. The probability of this is low, but can be improved by use of stable storage. If stable storage is lost it may be possible to partially recover from a previous dump, but this may lead to consistency problems. Loss of the log may well be a disaster.
4. *Failure with loss of stable storage.* The probability of this is never zero but it must be made as small as is affordable.

53.5.3.3 Distributed transactions

For distributed transactions, each machine will have a local transaction manager (LTM) which deals with local transactions. For the remote actions of a transaction the requester gets the relevant LTM to perform the actions and to keep its own log. However, although the LTM must provide local atomicity this is not sufficient, since all participants in a distributed commit need to come to the same conclusion i.e. commit or abort. The simplest approach is the two-phase commit technique. The transaction initiator usually acts as coordinator at the commit point. Phase one begins when all the work of the transaction has been done and the coordinator is requested to commit.

Phase one

1. Coordinator (C) records 'prepare' in its stable storage log together with the identifiers of all the sub-transactions at the other sites.
2. C starts a timeout.
3. C sends 'prepare to commit' to all participants.
4. If any fail to reply before timeout goes off or reply with ABORT then the transaction will be aborted.
5. If all answer READY the transaction *will* eventually be committed. By answering READY a participant has to be able to commit even if there is a site failure from now on. Thus it needs to record on stable storage all logs for this transaction, and the fact that it is now ready (a new log record type) before it returns a READY response.

Phase two

1. C records the result on stable storage, either Global Abort or Global Commit. Despite failures, at some time this will come to pass.
2. C sends notification of this to all participants (Ps).
3. Ps write Global Commit/Abort record to their log and from here on local action can deal with failures.
4. Ps send acknowledgement to C.
5. When all acknowledgements have been received by C, it writes COMPLETE record to log.

The two-phase commit protocol is resilient to all failures which do not result in loss of the log. However, if any participant fails during part of phase 2, all other participants may be delayed until it recovers.

The effects of failure are identified below based on the three types of failures which affect distributed algorithms:

1. Site failures.
2. Lost messages.
3. Network partitioning.

Site failure

1. If P fails before sending a reply in Phase 1, then C will take an ABORT decision, and all other Ps will also abort.
2. If P fails after sending a reply in Phase 1, all other Ps terminate in the ordained way. When P recovers it needs to determine the outcome from C or another P and execute it.
3. If C fails after writing PREPARE it means that the Ps must await C's recovery. On recovery C must issue PREPARE again.
4. If C fails after recording Global Commit or Global Abort, again the Ps have to wait for C to recover, and its decision has to be re-transmitted to all Ps.
5. If C fails after the whole log is written there is no problem, it is all complete.

Lost messages

1. If a READY or ABORT from P is lost C will timeout and issue and ABORT.
2. If a PREPARE message is lost P does not know what is happening and will eventually receive a Global Abort.
3. If a Global Commit or Global Abort is lost P is unclear of the outcome. This can be rectified by P setting a timeout after which it polls C.
4. If an acknowledgement is lost C does not know P's status, so it could timeout and re-send, with P responding with another acknowledgement.

Partitions

A single partition leads to two groups. The one containing the coordinator is known as the Coordinator Group, the other is the Participant Group. For the coordinator group it is similar to site failure cases (1) and (2), and for the Participant Group it is similar to site failure cases (3) and (4).

Until the READY message is issued, any P can unilaterally abort a transaction. It is possible to eliminate the PREPARE message if all operations write the log to stable storage and return READY to C. However, this removes the right to unilaterally abort, and failure of C would cause blocking.

The delays caused by site failures (3) or (4) are the main weakness of the two-phase commit protocol, since all participants are delayed, and transaction resources will generally be locked until the Coordinator recovers. Some refinements of the protocol allow for relocation of the coordinator under these circumstances.

53.5.4 Time

For concurrency control, deadlock detection and security purposes, we need to be able to order events in a distributed system. Generally, the clocks in a system are not synchronized. Methods have been proposed for getting clocks synchronized within limits (Marzullo, 1985; Lamport and Melliar-Smith, 1986) but for many purposes the relative ordering of events is more important than accurate absolute time.

In order to identify the ordering of events and a simpler approach may be taken (Lamport, 1978). All events have a timestamp (TS) attached, and all timestamps are unique; thus TS(A) uniquely identifies event A. For any two events, if A occurred before B, then $TS(A) < TS(B)$. The symbol '$<$' means: 'less than'. We now only need to define 'occurred before' we will use the notation $A \rightarrow B$ to mean 'A occurred before B':

1. If A and B are at the same site, and A occurred before B according to some local clock then, $A \rightarrow B$.

2. If event A sends a message and B receives the same message, then A→B.
3. If A→B and B→C, then A→C.

For some pairs of events there will be no definite ordering, i.e. neither A→B nor B→A, in which case the events are said to be pseudo-simultaneous. Their exact temporal relationship cannot be determined, nor is it relevant.

To restate: the→operator provides a partial ordering. If A→B, then TS(A) < TS(B). If A and B are pseudo-simultaneous there is an arbitrary relation between TS(A) and TS(B). These global timestamps provide a total ordering which is consistent with the partial ordering of the →relation.

Global timestamps must contain the local time and an indicator of the origin site of the timestamp in order to make them unique. (The site identifier is normally in the least significant bits so that arithmetic comparisons of the whole timestamp can be used, i.e. the site identifier is less significant than the time in the comparison process.) Local unique timestamps need to advance by at least one for each event, but may advance faster. Local timestamps keep roughly in step between communicating sites because timestamps are sent in each message. If the time part of an incoming timestamp is greater than the local time then the incoming value is incremented and replaces the local value. If the local part of a received timestamp is less than the local timestamp, then the local timestamp is just incremented.

As an example, suppose A and B at sites 1 and 2 have timestamps set to 0 and 10 respectively. Then initially:

$$TS(A) = <0, 1>$$
$$TS(B) = <10, 2>$$

A and B are pseudo-simultaneous. If B sends a message to A, the message will carry the timestamp < 10, 2> with it, and A will need to update its local timestamp to:

$$TS(A)' = <11, 1>$$

If A sent B a message just before the above message arrived, then it would bear the timestamp <0, 1> which B would inspect and then update its timestamp to:

$$TS(B)' = <11, 2>$$

Note that no two events occur in the same clock grain. This protocol ensures that timestamps are consistent with causality between systems on a pairwise basis, which ensures that the desired partial order is created. Where two events are pseudo-simultaneous, an arbitrary ordering is chosen. Slow clocks will tend to accelerate to the rate of the fastest clock in the system.

53.5.5 Concurrency control

53.5.5.1 Locking

Concurrency control mechanisms are needed to ensure that concurrently executing transactions do not interfere. A number of techniques can be used but one of the most common is locking. Exclusive locks are used by well-formed transactions which update an item, while shared locks are used where an item is only read. Transactions can lock in shared mode if there is no other lock in place, or if the item is already locked in shared mode. They can lock in exclusive mode only if the item is not already locked. In order to maximize concurrency the granularity of the item locked should be as fine as possible; it is better to lock a record than to lock the whole file.

Two-Phase Locking.   It can be shown that concurrent ex-

of transactions is correct provided the following conditions all hold (Ceri and Pelagetti, 1984; Eswaran, 1976):

1. Transactions are well-formed, i.e. use shared and exclusive locks as appropriate.
2. The lock compatability rules are observed.
3. No transaction requests a new lock after it has released any locks.

Condition (3) implies a two-phase locking approach, where in the first phase locks are gradually acquired by a transaction, and in the second phase locks are released. These conditions guarantee the serializability of transactions, but they do not guarantee isolation, i.e. it would be possible for another transaction to observe the effects after the second phase, but before the transaction had committed. Thus, in order to guarantee isolation:

4. All transactions hold all their exclusive locks until commitment. Thus, the general form of locking is as follows:

```
  . . .
Begin Transaction
Acquire locks before reading or writing
Do work
Commit
Release locks
  . . .
```

However, if two concurrent transactions access the same items, but acquire the relevent locks in different orders a deadlock will occur. This problem can be solved in a number of ways:

1. *Deadlock detection.* Deadlock is discovered and one or more transactions are aborted and redone. The expectation is that repetition of transactions will result in locks being acquired in a different order without deadlock arising.
2. *Transaction ordering.* In cases where transactions can be ordered in such a way that deadlock will not occur.
3. *Time limited breakable locks.* Locks which are not freed within an earlier agreed time may be automatically broken on the assumption that a deadlock has occurred.

In the first and third cases above some transactions need to be aborted and redone to eradicate the deadlock.

Distributed two-phase locking   It can be shown that (Ceri and Pelagatti, 1984):

If distributed transactions are well-formed and two-phase locked, then two phase locking is a correct locking mechanism in both distributed and centralized systems.

However, there are difficulties with multiple copies of data.

If two or more copies of a given replicated file acquire locks independently, then it would be possible for a given record of the copies to be locked exclusively by different transactions. The copies might then be updated and conflict with each other, i.e. the replicated file no longer is stored as identical copies everywhere. Even if the conflict were discovered at the commit point, one transaction would need to be redone; if the locks had worked properly that transaction would probably only have been delayed.

In the distributed case locks need to be propagated when they are applied. However, it is only necessary to detect a conflict at any relevant site which leads to three main distributed locking policies:

1. *Write-locks-all/read-locks-one.* Here an exclusive lock is propagated to all sites, so all copies are write locked identically.

For a shared lock, only one arbitrary site is locked. Clearly, any conflict is detected, and read locks are cheap, whereas write locks are expensive.

2. *Majority locking*. Shared and exclusive locks are requested at a majority of copy sites. At least one will show up any conflict.

3. *Primary copy locking*. Here one site is designated as the master copy and all locks are applied to it, and detected there.

A few other points are worthy of note. First, a replicated file may actually reduce the availability of the system depending on the lock propagation policy used. For example, if it is impossible to write lock all copies because of a machine crash, the transaction will have to await recovery or be abandoned. Despite the multiple copies, the data may be less available than without copies.

Secondly, it is often necessary to abort a transaction because a deadlock has been detected, but this cannot be done after the transaction has committed, thus, the growing phase of two phase locking and any deadlock detection must be complete before the participant has declared 'ready to commit'.

Finally, because locks are not released until after commitment, once a participant has answered 'ready to commit' it must hold all locks until it is informed of the decision. If the coordinator fails, then the locks still have to be held until it recovers.

Deadlock. With any locking approach deadlocks will occur when concurrent transactions lock the same resources in different orders. Distributed deadlock is difficult to detect because at no place is there a single list of transaction dependencies. If there were, a deadlock would be observed when the dependencies became circular. In each machine there may be a partial dependency list, often termed the wait-for graph (WFG). By combining these local WFGs it may be possible to discover a deadlock.

An alternative is to use timeouts where long waiting transactions are aborted in the belief that the delay indicates a deadlock. Clearly, there is a balance to be drawn in choosing the timeout period: too short a value will result in unnecessary aborts, too long a value will result in unnecessary waiting during a deadlock. The unpredictable behaviour of communications and remote machines further compounds the problem. There can be another problem with timeouts in that if a short timeout fires in an already heavily loaded system, the abort will cause even more load, which will cause even more transactions to abort, unnecessarily. This timeout-based deadlock detection is best suited to lightly loaded systems, where load effects cannot be mistaken for deadlock.

Centralized or hierarchical approaches can be used for distributed deadlock detection. With them, the local wait-for-graph (LWFG) is propagated to one or a hierarchy of coordinators which combine them to form a global WFG. With such approaches there are problems of node failures and possibilities of the recorded state differing from the actual state due to propagation delays.

A distributed approach, based on the Obermarck Algorithm (Obermarck, 1982) is less prone to these problems. In it, all nodes have the same responsibility for deadlock detection and they build a LWFG in the usual way. The entry and exit nodes of the LWFG are combined into a single external node called EX. Each arc joins dependent transactions, starting first at EX and possibly ending at EX too. If the LWFG is deadlock-free there will not be a complete cycle internally, and there may not even be a cycle including EX. Any cycle which includes EX indicates a potential distributed deadlock, and further action is needed. For the algorithm to work it must always eventually

detect deadlocks, and should minimise transmission. One way of doing this is only to transmit the relevant nodes of the LWFG along both paths; moreover even sending it along, say, the 'forward' arc would produce more messages than needed. Thus, if all sites only send their LWFG to machines containing transactions which they are waiting for, and only when the local transaction identifier is greater than the remote one a minimum of messages will be used.

This approach is iterative, each site building up composite WFGs as necessary and sending potential deadlocks to other sites. The approach is thus:

1. Build LWFG using local information, include EX.
2. For each incoming message:
   (a) Add each transaction in message to LWFG.
   (b) For each transaction in the message starting at EX add an arc to next transaction in message.
3. Cycles in the LWFG which do not involve EX indicate deadlocks. Invoke deadlock resolution.
4. Cycles involving EX are potential deadlocks. Transmit to another site if applicable.

Because such a scheme is distributed with indeterminate delays between transmission of LWFGs and deadlock resolution, it is possible for a transaction to request a resource just after it has been released, but before the release message has been received or processed locally. A false deadlock exists, but is indistinguishable at that point from a real one. Two approaches are possible, either to treat it as real or to validate it. If such occurrences only occur infrequently it may be best to treat it as real and abort a transaction. Validation involves re-collecting the WFG information and may be expensive.

The approach in deadlock prevention is to check to see whether there is a risk of deadlock when a resource is requested, and if so not to let the requesting transaction enter a wait state. Instead one or other of the relevant transactions is aborted. The criteria for detection of possible deadlocks is usually to use a transaction id, based on a timestamp, and to order the transactions accordingly. The two approaches used are: non-pre-emptive and pre-emptive.

With the non-pre-emptive approach, T_i requests a resource held by T_j. T_i is allowed to wait only if T_i is older than T_j, on the basis that it is best to abort a young transaction.

In the pre-emptive approach, T_i is allowed to wait only if it is younger than T_j; otherwise T_j is aborted and the lock is granted to T_i. With this approach T_j cannot be aborted while it is in the second phase of a two-phase commit, but then, since it has all its needed resources at that time it cannot be causing a deadlock, and unless its coordinator crashes it will soon release them.

53.5.5.2 Optimistic concurrency control

As its name suggests, optimistic concurrency control assumes that resources conflicts are unlikely to occur. Only at the commit point is this assumption validated, and if a conflict is observed the transaction is re-started. The approach has also been applied to file updates (Mullender and Tannenbaum, 1985). If updates (new versions) of files do not overlap in time there is little work to be done at the commit point. If two versions proceed in parallel it is necessary to ensure that they are properly serializable.

The classic database approach is covered by Kung and Robinson (1981) and consists of three phases: read, validate, and write. Read is where the old items are accessed and new tentative items are formed. Validate checks for conflicts between the base items and the new ones, and finally the write phase creates the new component (file, database entry, table, etc.). For two transactions T_i and T_j, they are serially equivalent according to Kung if one of the following holds:

1. T_i completes its write phase before T_j begins its read phase.
2. The write set of T_i does not intersect the read set of T_j, and T_i completes its write phase before T_j begins its write phase.
3. The write set of T_i does not intersect the write set or the read set of T_j, and T_i completes its read phase before T_j completes its read phase.

53.5.5.3 *Time-stamp based*

The approach for this method (Ceri and Pelagetti, 1984) is that when each transaction is started it has a timestamp attached to it. Transactions are serialized by ensuring that all transactions are aborted if they attempt to read or write a data item which has been updated by a more recent (younger) transaction. The mechanism must be correct, but may lead to more aborted transactions than necessary. Nonetheless, no locks are involved so the mechanism is deadlock-free.

53.5.6 Security

In a single-computer system, many of the threats to security can be countered by providing special hardware to prevent processes interfering with each other. In communications systems such hardware protection mechanisms cannot be used and cryptographic techniques generally form the basis of any security system. We shall first look at the threats in a distributed system, then look at the basic encryption mechanisms. Cryptographic systems depend on keys, and keys need to be distributed to participants. Key distribution, coupled with key storage, is perhaps one of the hardest problems in communications security. Finally, many systems involve multiple administrations which are autonomous. Coping with this, whilst being sceptical about the trustworthiness of all parts of the system is of growing concern, and has been the subject of a recent paper (Birrel *et al.*, 1986).

There are four broad areas of security in distributed systems:

1. Security threats.
2. Access control.
3. Authentication.
4. Notarization.

53.5.6.1 *Security threats*

Consider a client and server connected by a network link. There are a number of threats posed by such links:

1. Passive tap.
2. Active tap.
3. Denial of service.
4. Faking.
5. Replay.
6. Traffic analysis.
7. Accidental access.

The passive tap allows the interloper to observe traffic passing on the link. Whilst he or she cannot change the observed messages, he may be able to use the information to gain improper access, e.g. if a password is observed it can later be used to log in as someone else. Passive tapping is extremely easy on some networks, e.g. Ethernet.

An active tap is where the interloper can interpose a process between the original client and server. This may be purely for obtaining information such as passwords ('Trojan Horse'), or it may be as a means of changing messages, usually to the benefit of the interloper.

An often forgotten threat is denial of service. In some cases preventing access by a legitimate user can be a serious threat, so very persistent attempts to access a server, although they may be badly formed messages, may jam up the protocol handler and prevent legitimate access.

A process may fake messages and send them to a server. These may be modelled on previous legitimate messages, with key fields changed. If the fields are not changed, it is termed replay, and this may be valuable to the fraud if he can get, say, multiple payments into his bank account. Audit trails are usually used in secure systems to record all transfers, but although the perpetrator may be known, it may be too late to recover the loss. In computer systems, audit trails need to record details of people, processes and machines, although the latter is very difficult on LANs.

Traffic analysis is usually used to infer where and when something is about to happen, based on the assumption that message activity will increase before significant events such as a battle. The usual defence is to keep all links heavily loaded with random (information-free) messages, and when messages need to be sent to transmit them in place of this background traffic.

Accidental access can be caused by a number of failures, e.g. crossed lines, software faults etc. Perhaps the most common on dial-up computer connections is the failure of a call to be completely disconnected by software, and for a subsequent caller to be connected directly to the previous caller's session without any formalities. Similar problems can occur in packet protocols.

53.5.6.2 *Access control*

In a simple client–server interaction the server may wish to limit access to resources. The standard techniques for doing this are:

1. Access control matrix.
2. Capabilities.
3. Labels.

The access control matrix is familiar from many systems, usually splitting the world into the 'owner' of the resource, 'friends' and 'the rest of the world'. The controls may be enforced on a limited number of operations, e.g. Read, Write, Delete, etc. Typically, each resource will hold its access matrix close by, and the client must prove who it is and be classified before access can be granted. It is usually the client's principal, i.e. the person who uses the client process, who is authenticated, but there may be more than one principal.

Capabilities are unforgeable tokens which include indicators as to which functions can be performed on a resource. In a single-machine environment such tokens are never passed to processes, and they are kept securely by the operating system; only references to them are passed out. In a distributed system they must be sent through the network, and it must not be possible to alter them without such changes being detected. Moreover, it is desirable that a process should be able to pass a reduced set of privileges to another process via a capability, preferably without having to consult the original issuer of the capability, i.e. it should be possible for ordinary processes to reduce access rights affected by capabilities but not to enhance them.

Labels are used in so-called mandatory security systems. The techniques above are used in discretionary security systems. Mandatory control is used in military and other high security systems, where classifications such as low, medium, high and top security are used. Information derived from that of other high security information would be classified high security, and only people/processes of suitable clearance could access it. There is a tendency for all new information eventually to migrate to the highest classification, so de-classification has to take place periodically.

53.5.6.3 *Authentication*

Authentication, i.e. proof of identity, of both the client and the server is needed. Client authentication usually involves authentication of the principal. Server authentication is important not only because of the threat of active tapping (Trojan Horse) but also because many methods of binding clients to servers only offer hints as to where a service is located. If it crashes, it may be replaced by another, totally different server, but the client needs to know of this mismatch so that the binder may be consulted again. Cryptography can be used for such purposes.

A related term is message integrity, often called message authentication. It is often important to be sure that a received message has not been tampered with in transcript. Sometimes there is no requirement for secrecy of the message in transit; sometimes there is. A form of strong sumcheck based on cryptographic techniques is appended to messages for such purposes. This is sometimes called a digital signature or a message authentication code (MAC).

53.5.6.4 *Notarization*

Sometimes an even stronger requirement exists, to ensure that the sender cannot deny sending a message. In such cases a notary may be used to register messages such that neither of the participants can back out of a transaction and disputes can be resolved by presenting relevant signatures or encrypted text.

53.5.6.5 *Cryptography*

The purpose of encryption or encipherment is to transform a message or plaintext into an apparently random pattern, the ciphertext, such that decryption of the ciphertext is extremely difficult unless an appropriate algorithm is known. For a normal two-way cipher there will be encryption and decryption algorithms which are complementary; for a one-way cipher the encryption algorithm will have no known inverse, i.e. it is not possible algorithmically to convert ciphertext to plaintext.

To maintain secrecy, it is generally necessary to change the encryption algorithm periodically. If this were to be done on a daily or hourly basis, a large number of algorithms might need to be agreed in advance. For this reason, algorithms can usually be varied by a key. In a good system there will be a vast number of keys to make it difficult to break the code by exhaustive search of the key space, i.e. where the ciphertext is decrypted with every possible key until recognizable cleartext emerges.

In the most common systems, secret key cryptography (SKC), identical or closely related keys are used for both encryption and decryption. Thus knowledge of both the algorithm and the key would breach security. For this reason, although the algorithm may be made public, it is vital that the keys be kept secret. A typical key may be 56 bits long so even if the algorithm is public, exhaustive search will take 11 000 years if the encipherment process only took 5 µs! The most common example of SKC is the FIPS Data Encryption Standard (DES) (NBS, 1977).

A recent development has been public key cryptography (PKC). This is a two-key system where one key is used for encryption and another is used for decryption. Clearly the two keys are related, but the mechanism is designed such that knowing one key yields little clue to the other one. More specifically, to compute the other key with the best of known algorithms would take hundreds or thousands of years. If this is the best case then one key can be published, the public key, and one key is kept by the owner, the personal or secret key. When a message is sent it is encrypted with the public key of the recipient, and only the recipient can decrypt the message. By an interesting twist this mechanism can also be used to prove the authenticity of the sender. If the message is encrypted with the

sender's personal key then anyone can decrypt it by virtue of the published public key. If it decrypts properly, and the published keys are trustworthy then the originator has been authenticated. A combination of the two techniques can be used to provide secrecy and authentication. The most common example of PKC is the Rivest Shamir Adleman algorithm (RSA) (1983).

53.5.6.6 *Techniques*

Capabilities. In an object-based system, access control might be by capabilities which contain some form of object identification, a bit map of the allowed operations, and a random component which is derived from the bits in the capability. If this is to be secure, the algorithm for generating the random component must be kept secret. A public algorithm may be used if the random component (which acts as a means of detecting improper changes) is generated from the other components and a key kept by the server. Since the server generates and checks capabilities before using them there is no difficulty of key distribution. Schemes have been proposed where a client can reduce rights before passing them on the other processes, rather than getting the original issuer to reduce them (Mullender and Tannenbaum, 1984).

Authentication: the SKC approach. Let us suppose that a client, C, wishes to prove its authenticity to a server, S, and also wishes to satisfy itself that S is not a Trojan Horse. The basic scheme for this is due to Needham and Schroeder (1978) and is described below. Modifications are to be found in (Bauer *et al.* 1983; Denning and Sacco, 1981). The scheme includes a trusted authentication server, AS. Before data is transferred between C and S a dialogue of the following form is needed; we shall deal with SKC first.

1. $C \rightarrow AS : A, B, Ia$

2. $AS \rightarrow C : \{Ia, B, K_C, \{K_T, A\} K_B\} K_A$

3. $A \rightarrow B : \{K_T, A\} K_B$

4. $B \rightarrow A : \{Ib\} K_T$

5. $A \rightarrow B : \{f(Ib)\} K_T$

The client sends message (1) to the AS in clear text. This message can be intercepted and replayed, and Ia is included to prevent frauds. Ia and Ib are called nonces and are integers which are not re-used. A and B identify the relevant principals at the client and server.

The authentication server is trusted and contains the keys of all principals. Thus it can generate messages sealed with such keys, and only the relevant principal can unseal the message. Message (2) is sealed (encrypted with the client's personal key) so that only the client can unwrap the outer seal to reveal Ia, B, and K_T. The remainder is sealed for 'the eyes of B only.' At this point the client checks that the values for Ia and B match those of the request and if so it picks up the session or conversation key K_T for later use. The remainder of the message is sent to the server as message (3).

Message (3) allows the server to obtain the name of A and the session key. A's name is included in the wrapping in case a Trojan Horse diverted the message. By using the unwrapped return address rather than the one in the protocol packet header obvious frauds can be minimized.

The server now sends a message (4) back to the client containing a nonce encrypted with K_T. To prove that A is A it returns a message with a simple transformation of Ib. e.g. Ib-1, also encrypted. Only the possessor of K_T would be able to do this, thus proving its identity. Client and server may now exchange data encrypted with K_T.

The reason for the session key is that there is potential for key discovery every time the key is used. Thus the personal keys of users are only used to distribute the session keys to each party. Thereafter the session key is used. For each interaction a different session key may be used for the same reason, i.e. session keys will be changed at irregular intervals.

The above scheme can be extended to multiple authentication servers, for cases where client and server may be in different administrations. In such cases one AS may know the key of the client, another may know the key of the server. We assume that the ASs have already established a secure channel using the session key, K_{AS}. The protocol would be:

1.   A→AS1 : A, B, Ia1.

    (a) AS1→AS2 : {K_T, A, B, Ia2, K_C} K_{AS}.

    (b) AS2→AS1 : { {K_C, A}K_B, Ia2, A} K_{AS}.

2.   AS1→A   : {Ia1, B, K_C, {K_C, A}K_B }K_A.

then, steps (3)–(5) as before. Note that to the client and server this protocol is indistinguishable from the single authentication server case. Note also that AS1 chooses a conversation key and passes it to AS2 which seals it with B's key. Thus, AS2 does not need to trust AS1 with B's key. Different nonces are used for the interactions between A and AS1, and between AS1 and AS2 to minimise the potential for faking.

Authentication: the PKC approach.   The scheme for a single AS using public keys is as follows:

1.   A →AS :   A, B

2.   AS→A   :   {PK_B, B}Sk_{AS}

3.   A →B   :   {Ia, A}PK_B

4.   B →AS :   B,A

5.   AS→B   :   {PK_A, A}SK_{AS}

6.   B →A   :   {Ia, Ib}PK_A

7.   A →B   :   {Ib}PK_B

Data phase:

(a). A →B   :   { {M_{AB}}SK_A }PK_B

(b). B →A   :   { {M_{BA}}SK_B }PK_A

Messages 1, 2, 4 and 5 are given merely to obtain the public key of the other party. The reason for encryption is not for secrecy, since they are public keys, but for *authentication*, i.e. proving that they did actually come from the authentication server whose public key is widely and unforgeably published. Other than that the protocol is straightforward. Double encryption is used in the data phase to both authenticate and seal messages.

The generally accepted method of distribution of public keys is by means of certificates which contain the identity of the key owner, the public key and various other attributes including expiry date. Such values are usually bound together by a cryptographic sumcheck using the secret key of the distribution agency. Thus, the certificate is in clear text but any alterations would be detectable. The standard definition is in the X.400 Security Addendum.

Message integrity. It is often required that a message be verified to be authentic, i.e. that it is intact and has come from the specified source. Depending on the application it may not be necessary to encrypt the whole message, i.e. secrecy is not always required. In order to prove authenticity of messages, a signature is attached to it, often known as a message authentica-

tion code (MAC). Such a MAC can be computed by applying an encryption algorithm such as DES (NBS77) to the message with a key unique to the sender, and choosing the most significant k bits of the last block of the ciphertext. Such a check provides a probability of 2^{-k} that the message is authentic. The exponent k can be chosen to provide the required degree of integrity (Davies and Price, 1984). If secrecy is also required the message may be encrypted again, with a different key.

It is possible that under some circumstances changes may be made to the ciphertext which are normally undetectable when the message is decrypted. To counter this a manipulation detection code (MDC) is appended to the cleartext before encipherment. This may be a simple CRC or similar function. Changes to the ciphertext will produce an invalid MDC when the message is decrypted.

53.5.7 Replication

Replicated files or other objects are usually provided to ensure resilience to node failures or to speed up access by using local copies, e.g. the locally cached copy of a file on a workstation. Replicated data should always appear consistent to the user, even though all the copies may not be identical. Generally, it should be possible to execute any operation on the data at any of the sites holding a copy.

53.5.7.1 Primary site solution

It is possible to nominate one site as the primary site. All updates must take place on the primary copy, but read operations may use either it or a local copy. Clearly all subordinate copies need to be informed of updates, so that read operations on them can recognize that the data is stale and refresh it from the master. Such notification may be significantly faster than updating all copies on every write access. However, a primary site approach is neither resilient to failures of the primary site, nor to network partitions. Replication, here, merely provides better read performance.

53.5.7.2 Weighted voting

The basic ideas of a voting solution are described by Gifford (1979):

1. Every copy of a replicated object is assigned some number of votes.
2. Each transaction must collect a read quorum (r votes) to read a file, or a write quorum (w votes) to write a file, such that $r + w$ is greater than total number of votes for the object.
3. This ensures that there is a non-null intersection between each read and write quorum, i.e. each operation is guaranteed to contain one instance of the most recent version.
4. Version numbers are assigned to identify successive copies.

It is obvious that provided the above requirements are met, it is not necessary to write to the majority of copies.

The basic mechanism is as follows. Irrespective of whether a read or write operation is intended all sites are polled to obtain the version number of the copy they hold and their number of votes. For a write operation, once a quorum has been identified the highest version number is taken. This number is then incremented and used to tag the new version which is written to the quorum. For a read operation the version numbers are first gathered and then the fastest site with a current version is chosen for the read operation itself.

Quorums. In the absence of failures, it is not necessary to establish a quorum prior to each operation. It is sufficient to choose an optimal read and write quorum (based on voting rules and speed) when an object suite is first accessed. Thereafter, the same quorums can be used. (An object suite consists of all replicas of that object.)

Failures. Certain failures may prevent some operations, but it is possible to define the voting configuration so that the suite has a degree of resilience. In such cases, if a node fails during a set of operations, accesses to that node will time out. The client node must then try to establish another suitable quorum and complete the operation. If this is not possible, then the partial operation must be undone. Gifford's paper deals with aspects of locking necessary to maintain consistency.

Config ation changes. It is possible to change the configuration of `le suite. This may be to include new replicas, or to change the voting  `les. It can be shown that provided the new configuration is propagated to the union of a write set in the old configuration and one in the new configuration that the new rules will be obeyed for all future operations.

Limitations. This voting approach is only of value for three or more replicas. Duplex files are not amenable to this approach. The approach relies on numerical assessment to determine set intersection. For a four-file suite this approach, $r + w$ must be greater than 4, but it is possible to identify quorums for which $r + w = 4$, i.e. read quorums are: $R1 + R2$ or $R3 + R4$ and write quorums are; $R1 + R3$ or $R2 + R4$. Clearly, every read set intersects every write set.

53.5.7.3 Generalized quorum consensus

Herlihy (1986 and 1987) has developed a general and systematic approach to dealing with replicated objects. It differs from Gifford's approach in that it derives suitable quorums for arbitrary object types, and is not limited to a simple read-write model of processing. It also provides a methodology for quorum definition. There are also a number of details in which performance can be improved, too.

Replicated objects have state stored redundantly at a number of sites. There are a fixed set of operations for objects of a given type. Object access is split into two components. Repositories are those places where the object state is stored. Front-ends carry out operations for clients. When a client requests an operation to be performed, the chosen front-end will read data from a subset of the repositories and write modified data back to another (possibly identical) subset. Because front-ends do not interact directly with each other, they can be replicated to an arbitrary extent without changing the approach; the degree of replication of the repositories is the important factor.

For each operation, there will be an initial quorum and a final quorum, either of which can be empty. If we consider a simple file object, which has only read and write operations, where read returns the whole file contents and write replaces the whole file contents, then the quorums for these file operations are subject to two constraints:

1. Each final quorum for write must intersect each initial quorum for read.
2. Each final quorum for write must intersect each initial quorum for write.

The first constraint ensures that any front end executing a read will observe at least one copy of the latest update. The second constraint is similar but also ensures that a new version number is contained in the relevant quorum.

A quorum is minimal if no smaller set of repositories is also a quorum for that operation. Thus, for five identical repositories we could have the three minimal arrangements shown in *Table 53.1*, where the first value in each pair is the initial quorum size; the second is the final quorum size.

Table 53.1

	A	B	C
Read	(1, 0)	(2, 0)	(3, 0)
Write	(1, 5)	(2, 4)	(3, 3)

Note that only one of these arrangements would be active at a time, that one being chosen to provide the required performance or resilience. Also the constraints determine the possible availability properties. Thus, there is a direct trade-off between read and write availability due to constraint 1, but a write quorum must encompass a majority of repositories (constraint 2), so write can never be more available than read.

Timestamps. If, instead of attaching version numbers to each copy a unique time stamp is generated at the time of writing, the initial write quorum in the file example can be zero, i.e. there is only one constraint:

1. Every initial read quorum must intersect every final write-quorum.

and the possible arrangements for a 5 repository system are shown in *Table 53.2*.

Table 53.2

	A	B	C	D	E
Read	(1,0)	(2,0)	(3,0)	(4,0)	(5,0)
Write	(0,5)	(0,4)	(0,3)	(0,2)	(0,1)

Because the version number does not have to be found before writing, the number of messages is significantly less than in the earlier case.

Incremental logs. This timestamp approach is still not sufficient to reduce the constraints on some complex operations, e.g. a queue object. Because the *complete* queue state is held at a quorum of replica sites, the Enq operations must read the state before updating it. Using logs rather than versions overcomes this. Logs consist of a record of timestamped operations which have been applied to the object replica. Because each operation is recorded (incremental change) then the Enq operation becomes independent of the previous state of the queue, (ignoring exceptions such as queue full). The constraints can be written as:

1. Every initial Deq quorum must intersect every final Enq quorum.
2. Every initial Deq quorum must intersect every final Deq quorum.

and for 5 repositories, see *Table 53.3*.

Table 53.3

	A	B	C
Enq	(0,1)	(0,2)	(0,3)
Deq	(5,1)	(4,2)	(3,3)

The approach followed above can be used to develop quorums for other object types. It can also be extended to cope with changing the quorums on-the-fly, as might be needed when the bulk of operations change from read to update over a period of time.

53.6 Conclusions

This chapter has shown that there is adequate technology to build distributed systems to meet a wide range of requirements. Data communications technology is now well understood at data rates up to about 2 Mb s^{-1} between organizations and up to 100 Mb s^{-1} within them. Standards exist for protocols to allow interworking between applications over such networks, dealing with the problems of data transmission, representational heterogeneity, security, application service elements such as transactions and fault recovery, and with the conventional file transfer, electronic mail and remote access applications. Techniques for building distributed (operating) systems are well understood, but at present standards tend to be industry-based.

What is missing? Networks are increasing in speed, especially within organizations. 100 Mb s^{-1} networks are available now and 1 GB s^{-1} networks are being developed. However, there are still difficulties in getting virtual circuits between application processes to operate at much greater than a few megabits/sec. Current research (e.g. van Jacobson, 1988) is looking at the architecture of network interfaces for computers and the protocols used between them in order to exploit the available network capacity.

The emphasis until now has been on 'data' communication, where aspects of timeliness, and accuracy of delivery were important but based on messages. Current research is concerned with multi-media communication, involving data, voice and video communication in real-time between users. The desire is for integration, certainly at the physical communications medium, and preferably at the application level so that voice or video messages can be stored and manipulated in similar ways to data. This goal shows up several problems, two of which are: how do applications communicate their needs for different types of channels (quality of service, qos) to the lower layers and how is qos to be specified, and what software infrastructure is needed to deal, with such diverse channels, e.g. to provide voice/data/video synchronization?

Although significant distributed systems have been built for some years, the well-known principles have been incorporated into the code by skilled programmers. There is an increasing tendency to provide toolpacks allowing less skilled users to build distributed applications (Oliver *et al*, 1988). Greater understanding of which tools are required is still needed, as are languages which support presentation standards for interfaces, provide efficient exception and fault recovery mechanisms and provide support for concurrency. Tools which take formal specifications in LOTOS or ESTELLE are beginning to appear, but more emphasis on formal techniques will be needed in future to provide reliable distributed systems. The complexity and scale of many distributed systems can also bring problems of software distribution and version control which are only now beginning to be tackled.

Users of a single processor or parallel processor machine can often ignore the problems caused by processor failures, and communications delays and errors. If software engineers can provide tools and techniques which handle the generality of distributed systems where they cannot be ignored, then these special cases will be covered.

53.7 Standards

The list below is a selection of standards related to the text of this chapter. The reader is advised to check for more recent versions.

CSMA/CD	ISO IS 8802/3 CSMA/CD Local Area Networks
DQDB	IEEE P802.6/D6 Proposed Standard Distributed Queue Dual Bus (DQDB) Metropolitan Area Network (MAN), Unapproved Draft, November 1988
FDDI	ANSI X3T9.5/84-49 FDDI Station Management (SMT), Draft, September 1986
FDDI	ISO/DP 9314/3 Fiber Distributed Data Interface Physical Layer Media Dependent (PMD), August 1987
FDDI	ISO DIS 9314-1 Fibre Distributed Data Interface (FDDI) – Part 1: Physical Layer Protocol (PHY), January 1988
FDDI	ISO DIS 9314-2 Fibre Distributed Data Interface (FDDI) – Part 2: Media Access Control (MAC), January 1988
OSI RM	ISO 7498 Information Processing Systems – Open Systems Interconnection – Basic Reference Model, 1984
Token Ring	ISO DIS 8802/5 Token Ring Local Area Networks

53.8 Abbreviations

ANSI	American National Standards Institution
ASN.1	Abstract syntax notation
b	bit(s)
B	byte(s) or octet(s)
BSI	British Standards Institute
CCITT	International Consultative Committee for Telegraphy and Telephony
CSMA/CD	Carrier sense multiple access with collision detection
DQDB	Distributed queue dual bus
EDI	Electronic data interchange
IEEE	Institute of electronic and electrical engineers
FDM	Frequency division multiplexing
HSLAN	High speed local area network
HRC	Hybrid ring control
IDL	Interface definition language
IPC	Inter-process communication
ISDN	Integrated services digitial network
ISO	International Organisation for Standards
Kb s^{-1}	Kilobits per second
LAN	Local area network
LLC	Logical link control
MAC	Medium access control
MAN	Metropolitan area network
Mb s^{-1}	Megabits per second
Modem	Modulator/demodulator
ms	millisecond
NFS	Network File System
ODA	Office document architecture
PABX	Private automatic branch exchange
PDL	Parameter description language
PSTN	Public switched telephone network
QPSX	*see* DQDB
RM	Reference model
ROS	Remote operations service
RPC	Remote procedure call
s	second
TDM	Time division multiplexing
TRT	Token rotation time
TTRT	Target token rotation time
µs	microsecond
WAN	Wide area network
X.400	Electronic messaging standard
X.500	Directory services standard

53.9 References

Andrews and Schneider, F. B. (1983) Concepts and notations for concurrent programming. *ACM Computing Surveys*, **15**, 3–44

Backes, F. (1988) Transparent bridges for interconnection of IEEE 802 LANs. *IEEE Network Magazine*, **2**, 5–9

Bauer, R. K. Berson, T. A. and Feiertag, R. J. (1983) A key distribution protocol using event markers. *ACM Transactions on Computer Systems*, **1**, 249–255

Birman, K. P. and Joseph, T. A. (1987) Reliable communications in the presence of failures. *ACM Transactions on Computer Systems*, **5**, 47–76

Birrell, A. and Nelson, B. J. (1984) Implementing remote procedure calls. *ACM Transactions on Computer Systems*, **2**, 39–59

Birrell, A. D., Lampson, B. W. *et al.* (1986) A global authentication service without global trust. *IEEE*, 223–230

Burr, W. E. (1986) The FDDI optical data link. *IEEE Communications Magazine*, **24**, 18–23

Ceri, S. and Pelagatti, G. (1984) *Distributed Databases – Principles and Systems*, McGraw Hill

Cheriton, D. R. and Zwaenepoel, W. (1985) Distributed process groups in the V kernel. *ACM Transactions on Computer Systems*, **3**, 77–107

Davies, D. W. and Price, W. L. (1984) *Security for Computer Networks*, John Wiley

Denning, D. E. and Sacco, M. S. (1981) Timestamps in key distribution protocols. *Communications ACM*, **24**, 533–536

Digital (1982) DECnet: Digital Network Architecture (Phase IV), Digital Equipment Corporation, Order No AA-N149A-TC

Digital (1987) DECnet: Digital Network Architecture (Phase V), Digital Equipment Corporation, Order No EK-DNAPV-GD

Eswaran, K. (1976) On the notions of consistency and predicate locks in a relational database system. *Communications ACM*, **19**

Falek, J. I. and Johnston, M. A. (1987) Standard makers cementing ISDN subnetwork layers. *Data Communications*, Oct, 237–255

Gifford, D. K. (1979) Weighted voting for replicated data. In *Proc. 7th ACM Symposium on Operating System Principles*

Guruge, A. (1984) *SNA: Theory and Practice*, Pergamon Infotech

Herlihy, M. (1986) A quorum-consensus replication method for abstract data types. *ACM Transactions on Computer Systems*, **4**, 32–53

Herlihy, M. (1987) Dynamic quorum adjustment for partitioned data. *ACM Transactions on Database Systems*, **12**, 170–194

Hoare, C. A. R. (1985) *Communicating Sequential Processes*, Prentice-Hall International

ISODP8807 LOTOS – A Formal Description Technique Based on the Temporal Ordering of Observational Behaviour

ISODP9074 ESTELLE – A Formal Description Technique Based on an Extended State Transition Model

Joseph, T. A. and Birman, K. P. (1986) Low cost management of distributed data in fault tolerant distributed systems. *ACM Transactions on Computer Systems*, **4**, 54–70

Knowles, T., Larmouth, J. and Knightson, K. G. (1987) *Standards for Open Systems Interconnection*, BSP Professional Books

Kung, H. T. and Robinson, J. T. (1981) On optimistic methods for concurrency control. *ACM Transactions on Database Systems*, **6**, 213–226

Lamport, L. (1978) Time, clocks, and the ordering of events in a distributed system. *Communications ACM*, **21**, 558–565

Lamport, L. and Melliar-Smith, P. M. (1986) Byzantine clock synchronisation. *ACM Operating Systems Review*, **20**, 10–16

Lauer, H. C. and Needham, R. M. (1979) On the duality of operating system structures. Reprinted in *ACM Operating Systems Review*, **13**, 3–10

Lin, S. and Costello, D.J. (1981) Coding for reliable data transmission and storage. In *Protocols and Techniques for Data Communications Networks*, (ed. F. Kuo) Prentice Hall, pp 240–318

Liskov, B. and Scheifler, R. (1983) Guardians and actions: linguistic support for robust, distributed programs. *ACM Transactions on Programming Languages and Systems*, **5**, 381–404

Liskov, B., Herlihy, M. and Gilbert, L. (1984) Limitations of Remote Procedure Call and Static Process Structure for Distributed Computing, Programming Methodology Group Memo 41, MIT

Marzullo, K. (1985) Maintaining the time in a distributed system. *ACM Operating Systems Review*, **19**, 44–54

Meijer, A. (1987) *Systems Network Architecture: a Tutorial*, Pitman

Mollenauer, J. F. (1988) Standards for metropolitan area networks. *IEEE Communications Magazine*, 15–19

Moss, J. E. B. (1985) *Nested Transactions – An Approach to Reliable Distributed Computing*, MIT Press

Mullender, S. J. and Tanenbaum, A. S. (1984) Protection and resource control in distributed operating systems.*Computer Networks*, **8**, 421–432

Mullender, S. J. and Tanenbaum, A. S. (1985) A distributed file service based on optimistic concurrency control. *ACM Operating Systems Review*, **19**, 51–62

NBS (1977) Data Encryption Standard, National Bureau of Standards, FIPS Pub 46

Needham, R. M. and Schroeder, M. D. Using Encryption for Authentication in Large Networks of Computers. *Communications ACM*, **21**, 993–999

Newman, R. M., Budrikis, Z. L. and Hullett, J. L. (1988) The QPSX man. *IEEE Communications Magazine*, **26**, 20–28

Obermarck, R. (1982) Distributed deadlock detection algorithm. *ACM Transactions on Database Systems*, **7**

Oliver, D. *et al.* (1988) ANSA Testbench Manual (Version 2), ANSA Project Report TI.73.01, ANSA, Cambridge

Peterson, W. and Weldon, E. J. (1986) *Error Correcting Codes*, (2nd edn) MIT Press

Rivest, R. L., Shamir, A. and Adleman, L. (1983) A method for obtaining digital signatures and public key cryptosystems. *Communications ACM*, **21**, 120–126, 1978. Reprinted in *Communications ACM*, **26**, 96–99

Ross, F. E. (1986) FDDI – a tutorial. *IEEE Communications Magazine*, **24**, 10–17

Sloman, M. and Kramer, J. (1987) *Distributed Systems and Computer Networks*, Prentice-Hall

Stallings, W. (1987) *Local Networks: An Introduction*, Macmillan

Sun (1988) *SunOS System and Network Administration*, Sun Microsystems, Part 800-1733-10, Rev A, Chp 13

Tanenbaum, A. S. (1988) *Computer Networks*, (2nd edn), Prentice Hall

van Jacobson (1988) Congestion avoidance and control. *ACM Computer Communications Review*, **18**, 314–329. (Also in *Proc. ACM SIGCOMM '88 Symposium*, Stanford, CA, 1988)

Wilbur, S. R. and Bacarisse, B. S. (1987) Building distributed systems with remote procedure call. *IEE Software Engineering Journal*, 148–159

54

Database systems

R P Whittington
Director
Hand, Whittington & Associates Ltd,
York

Contents

54.1 Introduction

This chapter introduces the fundamental concepts of databases and database management systems (DBMSs). It presents and criticizes the approaches taken to database management by current systems, and thus paves the way for a presentation of design techniques in the following chapter.

The material presented is equally relevant to the developer of database system applications, and to the database system administrator (that is, the developer of the database system platform upon which applications will be built), although the former's task requires only a general appreciation of the underlying mechanisms employed by DBMS.

54.1.1 The database concept

The database concept grew from the recognition of two areas of inadequancy in information (or data processing) systems based solely on conventional methods of file handling:

1. *Inadequate productivity.* Programs written against collections of files, which themselves embody the details of the organization of those files, and which manipulate those files by means of rather low-level, record-orientated data manipulation operators, are costly to develop and, more significantly, very costly to maintain. This latter point follows from the bundling together of algorithmic information and data structure information, which means that changes in one often result in the necessity for profound changes in the other.
2. *Inadequate control.* Programs written without any central agency for control of data sharing, recovery from failure, and protection against privacy infringements can result in inconsistent and insecure systems that are costly to manage.

Fundamentally, the database concept rests on the following interrelated ideas:

1. The extraction of data object type descriptions from application programs into a single repository called a database schema (the word schema can be taken to mean a description of form) – an application-independent description of the objects in the database.
2. The introduction of a database management system (DBMS) through which all data definition and manipulation (update and interrogation) occurs – a buffer that controls data access and removes these functions from the applications.

Figure 54.1 illustrates the principle. It shows a database as comprising a schema in addition to the actual (or operational) data objects, and a DBMS as the control point through which all application data manipulation passes.

The database approach to the development and management of information systems concentrates on the inherent data objects involved, in terms of their structures and dynamics, with the view that if these can be captured naturally by means of some representation formalism then systems as a whole are more likely to be efficient and durable. Briefly, the advantages of the approach can be considered under the following headings.

54.1.1.1 Data validation

In principle, validation rules for data objects and interrelationships can be held in the schema and enforced by the DBMS. In addition to providing consistency, and increased maintainability, this reduces the complexity of application code.

54.1.1.2 Data sharing

Changes to the structure of data objects are registered by modifications to the schema. Existing application programs

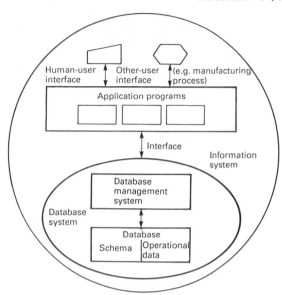

Figure 54.1 Relationships between database and information system concepts

need not be aware of any differences, because a correspondence between their view of data and that which is now supported can also be held in the schema, and interpreted by the DBMS. This concept is often referred to as data independence; applications are independent of the actual representation of their data.

Synchronization of concurrent access, and control of recovery and privacy can be implemented uniformly by the DBMS, because it oversees all database access.

54.1.1.3 Data manipulation

The record-level data manipulation concept of programming languages such as COBOL, PL/1, Fortran, and so on, can be escaped by means of a higher-level (more problem-orientated than implementation-orientated) data manipulation language that is embedded within application programs and that is supported by the DBMS. This allows the productivity of application programmers to be improved.

Furthermore, because the approach involves a central repository of data description, it is possible to develop a mechanism that provides a general enquiry facility to data objects and their descriptions: such a mechanism is normally called a query language.

As well as solving the problems of earlier approaches to system development, the database approach offers opportunities that had not previously been considered. In particular, these include those meta-applications (that is, application programs for use in developing others) that are now generically referred to as fourth-generation languages; forms–input–program generators, report–program generators and the like.

54.1.2 Definitions

A database is defined as an integrated, self-describing repository of data. By integrated we mean that a database has a wholeness: that where cross-references exist they are maintained consistently and are available to be exploited by applications. It is, however, the self-describing nature of a database that is its crucial property; this is the notion of a database schema, or a stored, application-independent database description, referred to earlier. Any collection of data that does not have an associated stored description might be referred to as a data bank, but not as a database.

A DBMS is probably best defined as a sophisticated system that supports the creation, manipulation, and administration of database systems.

A database system comprises a database together with the processing functionality required to access and manage that data. Typically, this means a database and a DBMS, although special-purpose capabilities might be used to replace or supplement a general-purpose DBMS. A database system might in itself constitute an entire information system. Alternatively, and more commonly, it is one component in a larger system, other components of which include programs that make use of its facilities.

54.1.3 Problems with the database approach

These can be addressed under the following headings.

54.1.3.1 Heavy resource usage

DBMSs are required to support:

1. synchronization of concurrent access;
2. privacy protection;
3. audit logging;
4. security against failure; and
5. methods for fast access to high data volumes.

Each of these requirements alone is substantial in its resource implications, and the combination of all inevitably means that DBMSs pose heavy requirements on their host systems. This is the basis of the not uncommon objection to database systems on performance grounds. Any costs incurred in overcoming this objection, however (such as additional memory to reduce paging), must be compared with savings in development costs as a result of the advantages that the database approach brings. The current economics of system development is such that additional costs incurred in overcoming increased resource requirements can normally be justified.

54.1.3.2 Design difficulties

Essentially, the problem here is that database design is a difficult task. Heavy investment in the development of a database system leads to an expectation of the kinds of benefits discussed previously, but these are available only if the design adopted is fundamentally sound. Given the conflicting requirements of different user communities, and the variety of technical factors involved with the physical aspects of system development, there is ample scope for costly errors of judgement.

As with the previous area of problems, however, the response is an admission that additional resources – in this case human and training resources – are required in order fully to benefit from the advantage of database systems.

54.1.3.3 Maintenance difficulties

Having built an integrated database system, it is difficult to disintegrate, where this becomes necessary or desirable. Anticipation of the possibility of such requirements can suggest the choice of federated configurations (see later).

54.1.4 Applicability of the database approach

The database approach is more appropriate for some kinds of systems than for others. The classes of system for which the database approach is widely accepted include those relating to:

1. Commerce (including banking and insurance).
2. Science (including medical, taxonomic and molecular research).
3. Manufacturing (including stock control and production scheduling).
4. Management (including resource management and financial planning).
5. Information services (including libraries, theatres, and travel services).

Systems of these kinds tend to require the handling of large amounts of simple but interrelated data. DBMSs are more suited for the development of such kinds of system than are the filing facilities offered by conventional operating systems.

More recently, the advantages of the approach have been observed to apply to other types of application, especially design systems (Brown, 1990), and even real-time embedded systems (Jervis, 1984). Such applications tend to pose slightly different requirements on the database management functions, and specialized DMBSs have emerged to accommodate these.

54.2 Database management systems

54.2.1 The current DBMS concept

In summary, a DBMS enables its users to perform the following:

1. The creation, and modification, of database structures, and the bulk loading of operational data into these.
2. The simultaneous access to database contents, without fear of conflict, through a number of interfaces, for the purposes of data update and retrieval.
3. The definition and enforcement of security requirements, including user privileges and provision against failure, including the ability to take back-ups.
4. The gathering of statistics that allow system monitoring, and the ability to modify a system to improve its performance in some respect.

The smaller-machine DBMSs tend to support only the first and second of the above. This is sufficient for single-user database systems without the complex interactions of components found in larger computer systems. The full-function systems available today, however, must provide at least the above, and, in order to compete, must offer more besides. Typical extras include the following:

1. Fourth-generation languages to enhance application generation productivity.
2. Data dictionary facilities to support the database system development process.
3. Integrated word processing, spreadsheet, and so on.

An important observation to draw from this list of extras is the trend towards a DBMS supplier as not simply providing facilities for database construction, management, and use, but as providing an entire environment for information system development and management. It is increasingly the case that a DBMS is selected by a user organization not only for the database facilities that it offers, but for its broader information system support.

54.2.2 DBMS components and interfaces

Figure 54.2 details the components of a DBMS and their interfaces with other information system components (the numbers on the arcs refer to interfaces discussed in due course).

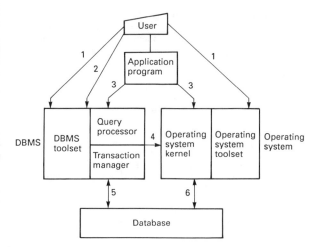

Figure 54.2 Database management system components and interfaces

one operating system file, so as to keep maximum control over how operations are done, and also to enhance portability; and others (such as Empress), which use at least one file per database structure, hence being more integrated with their operating environment.

(b) A set of communication facilities, which, again for the purposes of this section, might further be divided into those concerned with input/output device communication (especially terminal handling), intercomputer communication, and interprocess communication.

2. The operating system toolset, which provides various facilities that are either necessary or useful to supplement the DBMS facilities. Examples are tools such as programming language compilers, where the DBMS toolset does not itself include a complete programming language; text editors, where adequate schema definition facilities are not included in the DBMS toolset; and file protection tools, where the DBMS does not offer this facility.

The arcs in Figure 54.2 indicate where interfaces exist between components, and are explained as follows:

1. A DBMS user, of any class, might access both DBMS and operating system toolsets interactively.
2. A DBMS user, again, of any class, might interactively submit requests to the DBMS query processor.
3. An application program whereby a user interacts with the DBMS will make use of the latter's query processor at some stage in its development, in addition to requiring access to various operating system facilities.
4. A DBMS transaction manager will normally make use of various operating system kernel facilities during the execution of a database transaction. It is often possible, for example, to implement locking schemes using standard operating system facilities. As a further example, when a transaction requires to access data across a communications network, operating system communication facilities will be employed for process invocation and interprocess communication.
5. Some DBMS transaction managers work at the raw device level rather than making substantial use of operating system facilities.
6. The file management system of an operating system kernel can be thought of as providing a high-level interface to stored data.

54.2.3 Levels of abstraction in DBMS

The report of the ANSI/SPARC Study Group on Database Management Systems (ANSI, 1975) was a significant publication in the history of database technology. Essentially, the report presented a framework that acts as both a set of general requirements for a DBMS and as a framework within which systems can be compared and evaluated. According to present terminology, one should probably call the framework a reference model. For purposes here, the most important feature of the Group's proposals is the isolation of three levels of data abstraction; that is, three distinct levels at which data objects can be described.

The three levels, termed respectively the internal, conceptual, and external levels, are illustrated in *Figure 54.3*, which is a considerable simplification of the original framework. It is presumed by the Group that each level of abstraction has an associated schema (or data definition) language (DDL) in terms of which respective schemas are expressed. The meaning and purpose of each level are discussed in terms of these respective schemas:

The components suggested here are not always implemented as isolated functions; for this reason, the decomposition assumed must be interpreted as being logical in nature (i.e. an idealized view that satisfies our present purposes).

A DBMS can be considered to have three components:

1. The query processor, which accepts users' manipulation requests and translates them to a form in which they can be executed; this might involve compilation, or translation to some intermediate form that can be interpreted. This component can be thought of as the DBMS's front-end.
2. The transaction manager, which manages the execution of database manipulation requests. Its tasks are to ensure that concurrent access to data objects does not result in conflict and that failures do not compromise database integrity. This component can be thought of as the DBMS's back-end.
3. The toolset, which provides various facilities for performing tasks such as database creation, database restructuring, performance monitoring and tuning, and application development.

The interactions between operating systems and DBMSs are complex, and not easy to discuss in general. A number of simplifications are made in the following to allow at least a superficial discussion of these interactions. The reader who wishes to read further into this subject will have to specialize, either by DBMS or by operating system; references that might be useful include the work reported in the recent compilation of INGRES papers (Stonebraker, 1986) or, for material specific to the UNIX operating system, Weinberger (1982) is recommended. For the purposes of this section operating systems are considered as consisting of two components:

1. The operating system kernel, which provides, in particular, two services that are normally exploited by DBMSs.

(a) A file management system, which offers a set of general-purpose facilities for creating, modifying, reading, and destroying files. Almost all DBMSs (the exceptions being those that do not assume the existence of a host operating system) make some use of whatever facilities are available. The extent of this varies, however, between those (such as Oracle) that store an entire database as

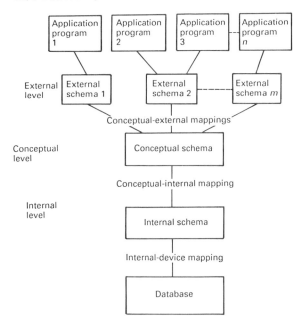

Figure 54.3 The three-level reference model for database management systems

1. An internal schema describes the organization of those data objects that are actually stored in a database. It is intended to reflect efficiency considerations. The description is not presumed to be at the actual device level, but in terms of some abstract device model, and the proposals note that it is necessary to map the internal schema of a database onto specific hardware constructs by means of a device-dependent language.
2. A conceptual schema is an abstract information model of the universe of discourse of the database system. Its purposes are to provide:

    (a) A central control point over the content and use of the database.
    (b) A level of indirection between external and internal schemas.

3. An external schema describes the data objects perceived by a particular application view of a database. A number of external schemas will typically exist in a database system, and these are not necessarily distinct. The proposals allow for external schemas derived from others, provided that consistency with the conceptual schema is maintained.

These levels define broad separations that are desirable within a database system. If the framework is supported in principle by a DBMS, then the following properties of database systems built using that DBMS will apply.

First, it will be possible to modify the stored representation of a database without impinging upon applications that have been developed against it; it will be necessary only to modify the internal schema and the conceptual-internal mapping. This property is often called data independence, or, more precisely, data-storage independence, and is highly desirable owing to the costs of modifying applications.

Second, it will be possible both to add new applications and to modify existing applications against a conceptual schema without detrimental effect to others, even though data might be

shared by applications, and perceived in differing ways by each; it will be necessary only to define a new external schema and an associated conceptual-external mapping. This property might be called data-application independence. Again, this is highly desirable because of the costs involved in modifying applications.

Third, the existence of an explicit conceptual schema ensures an underlying consistency across applications that is a prerequisite for integrity of data, and hence for database system control.

54.2.4 DBMS data models

The concept of a data model is so important that we examine it in itself before moving on to actual models and classes of model. A data model is defined in Kent (1978) as 'a basic system of constructs used in describing reality'. Furthermore, as Kent points out, 'a model is more than a passive medium . . . it shapes our view and limits our perceptions'. That is, a data model is a way of thinking about data and what can be done with it. For any given data model we might define a number of notations that provide a syntax through which to express its concepts.

It has been observed (Codd, 1982) that data models can be thought of as comprising three components, and this observation provides a useful framework for comparing data models:

1. A data structuring concept, which determines what types of data objects may be constructed.
2. A data manipulation concept, which determines what operations may be performed against data objects.
3. A data integrity concept, which imposes restrictions on which operations may be carried out under which circumstances.

A DBMS can be viewed as an implementation of a data model. This is where Kent's second observation comes into play. Because a data model has so profound an effect on our activities as users, any DBMS must be restricted by the quality of its underlying data model. Hence the intensity of work aimed at developing improved data models, especially during the past decade. The following classification of models (and, hence, of DBMSs) is held to be the most useful:

1. *Record-based models.* These include the tabular and navigational models. The former are essentially flat file-based, whereas the latter are characterized by their support of manipulation by navigation through prescribed record structures using visible links. These models are unified through their basis of the record as the unit of structure and manipulation. Systems based on them, however, have in many cases since been enhanced to offer some of the characteristics of the set-orientated models. Record-based models have emerged though implementations (rather than implementations following from the definition of a model), and hence it can be difficult to unearth the underlying model.
2. *Set-orientated models.* These include the relational model, and are characterized by their support of manipulation by set-theoretic operators.
3. *Semantic models.* These include the extended relational, the semantic network, and the functional models. They are characterized by their provision of richer facilities for capturing the meaning of data objects, and hence of maintaining database integrity. Systems based on these models exist in prototype form at the time of writing, and will begin to filter through during the next decade.

54.2.5 DBMS programming language interfaces

Figure 54.4 illustrates four software layers that exist between a database and its users. At the lowest level is the operating

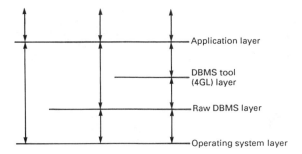

Figure 54.4 Software layers in a database system

system. Interaction with a database at this level is normally only carried out by a DBMS. Above that is the level of direct access to the raw data manipulation facilities of the DBMS, and in particular those that enable the development of software at higher levels. Next is the level of DBMS application-development tools (that is, fourth-generation languages – 4GLs), which generate raw DBMS interface code; and finally there is the level of application code, developed either by means of raw DBMS facilities or by application-development tools.

The early (navigational) DBMSs were little more than programming language interfaces, providing facilities for data definition and management to supplement those provided by the programming languages of the day. It was the emergence of relational DBMSs, together with advances in interactive computing in general, that brought about the concept of interactive query languages. Relational front-ends were later developed to provide comparable facilities for existing systems.

Query languages, although satisfying the requirements for *ad hoc* end-user database access are, however, not generally sufficient in themselves, for the following reasons:

1. Query languages tend not to be functionally complete (i.e., there are operations that they cannot express). This can be (and has been, in some cases) overcome to an extent by allowing functions written using a host programming language to be included within a query language statement.
2. Query languages are unsuitable for certain types of user, including, for example, those responsible for routine data entry. An application program offering *pro forma* screens is more appropriate, and more likely to be productive of the user's time.
3. Some applications, in addition to requiring database access, will require access to other specialist facilities (for example, graphics) that are available only through a particular programming language.
4. Query languages are typically either interpreted or dynamically compiled. With large applications this presents difficulties with regard to response time. Some database management systems overcome this by allowing queries to be compiled and stored in executable form.

The fourth-generation languages that are offered together with many DBMSs at the time of writing universally overcome problem (2) above, and in some cases overcome problems (1) and (4). The author is not aware of any language that solves all of the above, thus obviating the need for any additional database access facilities.

Because of this it remains necessary for a DBMS to provide a more powerful application development language to complement any online query or fourth-generation facilities. This requirement has been met by systems in different ways:

1. Some systems provide a specially designed database pro-

gramming language, providing database manipulation facilities as well as constructs traditionally found in general-purpose programming languages. The work reported by Schmidt (1977; 1985) exemplifies this approach in theoretical terms. Examples of DBMSs that offer such languages are Ashton Tate's dBase products and Software House's DBMS 1032.
2. An alternative (and more commonly used) approach involves providing a mechanism whereby an existing high-level language (usually COBOL, PL/1, FORTRAN, C, Pascal, or Ada) can be augmented to support database manipulation facilities.

The majority of DBMSs that adopt the second of the above approaches in their provision of programming language constructs do so by means of one of the following three mechanisms:

1. A library of standard routines is provided to enhance a host language. Typically, these will be the routines that are used by the DBMS to implement whatever online facilities are offered. This is the approach taken by Concept Asa's db++ (which offers a C library), and by Computer Corporation of America's LDM and DDM (which offer a library of Ada packages).
2. A compiler for a traditional host language is extended to support database manipulation operations.
3. Database manipulation operations are embedded in a host language program and programs are precompiled (that is, run through a program – a precompiler – prior to compilation). During precompilation, database operations are replaced either by assembly code or by calls to executable code stored in the database. This is the approach taken by the majority of the larger DBMSs, including IBM's DB2, Oracle Corporation's ORACLE, and RTI's INGRES, all of which offer precompilers for a variety of programming languages.

If a DBMS aims to offer an interface to only one programming language, then the database language facilities can be designed to be compatible with that language. A DBMS that is written in C, and that will only support C application programs, can, for example, base its data type constructs on those of the C language without fear of conflict. This approach also offers a greater homogeneity of software. A single compiler and linker can be used to install all of the programs involved for a user organization, and any modifications will thus be less expensive to manage.

Unfortunately, the above is not feasible for DBMSs that wish to achieve general adoption. Organizations differ in their programming language expertise, existing software resource, and program development facilities, and hence require the availability of a variety of programming language interfaces. Indeed, many organizations internally make use of more than one programming language for applications of different types, and so will prefer to adopt a DBMS that can support all of these. It is this requirement that causes problems:

1. The cost of supporting interfaces to many languages applies irrespective of which of the interface approaches is taken. The first requires multiple libraries, the second requires multiple extended compilers, and the third requires the development and maintenance of multiple precompilers. This is exacerbated by the need to support different releases and variants of each programming language; the management overheads of controlling the developments are not inconsiderable.
2. The technical problems of reconciling the concepts of a database language with those of a variety of programming languages again apply whichever of the interface approaches is used. Particularly acute problems result from:

(a) Clashes in the various data types supported – for example, because a DBMS supports a FORTRAN interface, and FORTRAN programs tend to be used in scientific applications, it would be useful to allow double-precision numerics; but how would these be interpreted by a Pascal program accessing the same data?

(b) The inability of some programming languages to call separately compiled procedures written in a different language.

54.2.6 Database system configurations

So far it has been tacitly assumed that a database system is a single entity residing on a single computer. Although at one time that would have been a fair assumption, it is increasingly possible to implement other configurations. *Figure 54.5* shows a simple classification of database system configurations into four basic types according to two axes: logical/physical and centralized/distributed. Although the resulting types of system are each suitable for a particular class of applications, most DBMSs are not capable of supporting all four of the types.

The logical configuration of a system is that which appears (at least to its end users) to exist, irrespective of what is in fact implemented; the latter is referred to as the system's physical configuration.

A centralized database system is one that exists in its entirety in one place, whereas a distributed database system, as the term suggests, is one that may span a number of sites. It is often useful to approach this distinction by viewing centralized systems as that special case of distributed systems that arises when a system is distributed across exactly one site.

	Logically-centralized	Logically-distributed
Physically-centralized	Centralized database system	Centralized federation
Physically-distributed	Distributed database system	Distributed federation

Figure 54.5 Classification of database system configurations

54.2.6.1 Centralized database system

This is the normal database system configuration and as such is supported by all DBMSs. These systems reside at a single site, and hence do not have to manage the complexities caused by synchronization over a network. They do, however, need to manage the complexities involved in supporting database integrity, perhaps under conditions of hundreds of transactions per second. This class of systems is suitable for those applications for which the following apply:

1. There exists a consensus among the user community regarding the overall consistency definition.
2. There are good economic reasons for not distributing the data or the transactions that are processed against it (for example, perhaps all of the data is required to be processed and made available at one geographical location).

54.2.6.2 Distributed database system

Distributed database systems differ from their centralized counterparts in that, although a global integrity definition again applies, the system is distributed around a network of computers. This means that the enforcement of the integrity definition is technically much more difficult. In the simplest case, where there is only one node in the network, the database management requirements default to those required for centralized systems. The existence of the global integrity definition makes the system appear centralized to its users (or, at least, its end users: the DBA needs to be aware of its physical distribution for various reasons); we say that the distribution is transparent to these users.

If the computers and DBMSs on the network are identical, then the system is said to be homogeneous, otherwise it is said to be heterogeneous. The reader with special interests in this area is referred to Ceri (1985).

54.2.6.3 Centralized federation

This is a type of database system that has no global integrity definition, but which resides on a single computer system. The term federation (taken from the work reported in Heimbigner and McLeod (1985)) is used to give the impression of a looser, less coherent object than a system. A large organization typically supports a number of distinct database systems on its central computer system. For example, there might be a stock control database system, a marketing database system, a personnel database system, and so on; systems with substantial internal cohesion but only minimal overlap in concerns. For the most part, such a configuration is ideal because the internal politics of the organization almost certainly support such segregation, and all routine database applications will execute against only one database. A centralized federation in a situation such as this allows, in addition to the above, the development of further applications that access multiple database systems.

Thus the concept is not incompatible with centralized database systems. It relates to the possibility of constructing a form of loose superstructure connecting disparate centralized database systems to allow any overlapping concerns to be exploited. Typically this will be for retrieval only, and so the lack of an integrity definition does not give cause for concern.

As above, the terms homogeneous and heterogeneous are used to denote federations of database systems based, respectively, on a single DBMS and on more than one DBMS.

54.2.6.4 Distributed federation

A distributed federation, like a centralized federation, is a loose coupling of database systems that allows some form of access across systems. Unlike the former, however, the database systems involved are distributed across a network of computers. We do not necessarily say that any of the database systems involved must themselves be distributed.

54.2.6.5 Summary

It should be clear from the above that each configuration type of database system poses its own demands on a DBMS. Although a system of any of these types could in theory be constructed using any DBMS (or, indeed, without using a DBMS at all), the amount of work involved would in most cases be prohibitive. The following is a brief summary of what is currently feasible:

1. DBMSs for the construction of centralized database systems are, of course, reasonably mature and a wide choice exists.
2. DBMSs for the construction of distributed database systems (called distributed database management systems) are beginning to emerge – distributed versions of ORACLE, INGRES and DB2 are currently available to support the development of homogeneous and restricted forms of heterogeneous distributed systems.

3. It is possible (albeit clumsily in many cases) to construct homogeneous centralized federations by means of many of the currently available DBMSs, and restricted heterogeneous federations with some.
4. Some of the distributed DBMSs support the development of homogeneous and restricted heterogeneous federations, and multi-database management systems (such as Computer Corporation of America's Multibase) are emerging to support a broader range of such systems.

54.3 The relational model of databases

The relational model was developed during the 1970s through a series of research papers stimulated by Codd's seminal paper (Codd, 1970). This first paper presented the basic core of the model and introduced a wealth of concepts and terminology, many of which remain fundamental to database theory and hence to the current generation of DBMSs. Following that, Codd (1972) offered a substantial development in the manipulation concept of the model, and later (Codd, 1979) formalized what we now understand by the integrity concepts of the model. Finally, Codd (1982) discusses the motivation behind the work and isolates principal objectives in the provision of:

1. A way of looking at (and thinking about) databases independently of the way in which they are physically represented on storage. This is important because it allows the storage representation to be changed without users' perceptions being affected.
2. A simple way of looking at (and thinking about) databases.
3. Powerful, high-level manipulation operators that allow users (i.e., both end users and application developers) to operate on natural, sometimes large, chunks of data at a time.
4. A sound theoretical foundation for database management that allows formalization of the principles involved in designing and using a database system.

In the 1982 paper, Codd uses the general observation, discussed in the previous chapter, that data models can be considered to comprise three components: a structuring concept, a manipulation concept, and an integrity concept.

54.3.1 Structuring concept

The relationship model of databases has a very simple structuring concept, based upon the following principles:

1. A database is a collection of relations.
2. A relation is a time-varying set of tuples (usually pronounced so as to rhyme with couples) with a persistent definition.
3. A tuple is a list of attribute values.
4. Attribute values are taken from named domains.

What in mathematical terms we refer to as the intension of a relation (i.e., its definition), corresponds in the database world to its schema definition – the attribute names and their respective domains. The extension of a relation, on the other hand, corresponds to its operational data – the set of tuples at a given point in time. Consequently, in the terminology of the relational model, a database schema is the combined intensions of the relations comprising the database, and the operational data of a database is the combined extensions of those relations.

In practice, relations have large extensions, and a more manageable way to visualize them is a regular table of values, where the rows correspond to tuples and the columns correspond to the members of those sets over which the relation is defined. One should be careful, however; the extension of a relation, being a set of tuples, is by definition strictly unordered

and contains no duplicate members. Tables, on the other hand, have no such restrictions; Codd (1982) describes tables as important conceptual representations of relations. *Figure 54.6* shows three simple relations, Flights, Airports and (intermediate) Stops, represented as tables.

Flights

flight_number	origin	destin
BA533	Naples	London/Gk
BA528	London/Hw	Pisa
KG2544	Verona	London/Gk
KG2540	Venice/MP	London/Gk
KG946	Venice/MP	Manchester
BR382	London/Gk	Kai Tak
BA019	London/Hw	Kai Tak

Airports

airport_name	country_name
Naples	Italy
London/Gk	England
London/Hw	England
Pisa	Italy
Verona	Italy
Venice/MP	Italy
Manchester	England
Kai Tak	Hong Kong
Dubai	UAE
Changi	Singapore

Stops

flight_number	airport_name	stop_number
BR382	Dubai	1
BA019	Dubai	1
BA019	Changi	2

Figure 54.6 Sample database relations

54.3.1.1 Relation keys

A further structuring concept requires introduction here to prepare for its part in the integrity concept of the model; this is the concept of relation keys. There are two types of key that are of special importance: primary keys and foreign keys.

It has been stressed that the extension of a relation is a set of tuples. By definition, a set cannot contain duplicate members. It follows from this that there must be some collection of attributes that, when taken together, have the property that their values can be used uniquely to identify tuples in that relation. This collection of (one or more) attributes is called the relation's primary key. This designation has no bearing on access to the tuples of the relation in question. A relation's primary key is solely a statement of one or more attributes that are guaranteed uniquely to identify its tuples – access keys should not be confused with this concept.

The attributes in a relation's primary key are called key attributes, and all other attributes are called non-key.

The intension of a database relation is defined by declaring the names and domains of its attributes, and by indicating which of the latter constitute the primary key. As a convention we write relation names with an initial capital, and write attribute and domain names as lower case. We denote the key attributes in the definition of a relation's intension by listing them to the left of a semicolon and underlining them (where a relation is all key we omit the semicolon). When representing a relation in tabular form, we indicate the primary key attributes by a double underline. In the case of the above relations, the definitions might be as follows:

Flights (flight number/flight numbers; origin/names, destin/names)

Airports (airport name/names; country_name/names)

Stops (flight number/flight numbers, airport name/names; stop_number/pos_ints)

Observe that the relation Flights makes two references to airports, one as an origin and one as a destination for a flight. Whenever the primary key of one relation is referred to by any (key or non-key) attribute, or collection of attributes, in another, as is the case with origin and destination here, then the latter is said to be a foreign key. Put simply, a foreign key is a cross-reference from one relation to another. Note that airport-name in Stops is also a foreign key to Airports.

54.3.2 Manipulation concept

Originally, Codd suggested the applicability of a manipulation notation based on an applied predicate calculus, and recognized that such a language would, at least, provide a yardstick of linguistic power for other proposed languages. Codd associated with this language the notion of 'relational completeness'; a language is relationally complete if it can be used to derive any relation that can be derived by means of the relational calculus. Codd also proposed a 'relational algebra' language. The difference between these languages is that:

1. The calculus-based language is non-procedural – it describes a required manipulation by means of a declaration of the relation that will result.
2. The algebra-based language is procedural – it allows the description of a manipulation in terms of a sequence of algebraic operations on relations.

Furthermore, Codd showed that the algebra has equivalent power to the calculus, by providing an algorithm that maps arbitrary operations of the calculus into algebraic operations. Languages based upon the relational algebra are therefore relationally complete, according to Codd's definition.

Underlying both of these approaches to database manipulation is the notion of 'relational closure'. This states that the result of any manipulation of a relation, or collection of relations, will be another relation. Any operation against a relational database is therefore viewed as a transformation of a collection of given relations into another relation that is the desired outcome of the operation.

Of the DBMSs that have been developed upon the relational model, some have implemented algebra-based languages, some have implemented calculus-based languages, and some have implemented hybrids. We consider here only the pure forms of the algebraic manipulation approach. This is sufficient to describe the concepts of relational database manipulation.

Relational algebra languages provide a collection of operators that operate upon (one or more) relations to produce another, without destroying the first. These operators can be divided into those taken from traditional set theory, and a collection of new operators designed specially for use against database relations. We adopt a hypothetical programming-language-like syntax of the form

operator(parameters)

and assume the Flights, Airports, and Stops relations shown previously.

54.3.2.1 Traditional set operators

This category includes four standard set-theoretic operators: Cartesian product, union, difference and intersection. Note that, in each case, an operator takes two relations and produces a third.

1. *The product operator*. A generalized form of the traditional set operator applies to relations. The relation formed by

   product (Flights, Airports)

   includes a tuple included for every pair of tuples in the Flights and Airports relations, tuples being formed simply by concatenating those of the respective pair.
   This operator in isolation is not widely applicable; its results tend not to be, in themselves, of interest. It is in combination with other operators that this operator is often useful.
2. *The union operator*. According to Codd's algebra of relations, this operator only generalizes to relations whose intensions are what he calls 'union compatible' – that is, composed of attributes defined over pairwise-compatible domains. As a consequence we cannot compute, for example,

   union (Flights, Airports)

   The operator acts as a conventional set union, allowing merging of the tuples of two compatible relations.
3. *The difference operator*. The restriction of union compatibility again applies to the definition of this operator. In line with the conventional set difference operator, it allows the construction of a relation whose tuples represent the removal, from one relation, of those tuples that are common between it and the second relation. Unlike the previous and the following, this operator is not commutative.
4. *The intersection operator*. Again, the union compatibility restriction applies. As with traditional set intersection, the operator allows the construction, from two relations, of a relation whose tuples are common to both participating relations.

54.3.2.2 New relational database operators

In the 1972 paper, Codd presented four new relational database operators. Although, strictly speaking, not all of these are necessary to achieve relational completeness, it is convenient to assume all four and so we entertain that luxury.

5. *The restrict operator*. The restrict operator is sometimes called 'select', but we avoid the latter name here because of the confusion that occurs with the SELECT statement in SQL. Its effect is to form a relation whose tuples correspond to those of an input relation, but which have been filtered through a restriction predicate, or condition. The syntax assumed for the operator separates the input relation name from the predicate by a semicolon.
   Figures 54.7(a), (*b*), and (*c*) illustrate restrictions of the Airports relation extension defined previously corresponding, respectively, to the following operations:

1. (b) restrict (Airports; airport_name = London/Gk)
   (b) restrict (Airports; country_name = England)
   (c) restrict (Airports; (country_name = England) or
                             (country_name = Italy))

(a)

airport_name	country_name
London/Gk	England

(b)

airport_name	country_name
London/Gk	England
London/Hw	England
Manchester	England

(c)

airport_name	country_name
London/Gk	England
London/Hw	England
Manchester	England
Pisa	Italy
Verona	Italy
Venice/MP	Italy

Figure 54.7 Illustrations of the restrict operator

The algebra permits restriction predicates of arbitrary complexity, making use of the conventional dyadic predicate constants ($=$, $\neq$, $<$, $>$, $\leqslant$, $\geqslant$) and the logical connectives (and, or, not).

6. *The project operator.* The restrict operator above supports the definition of horizontal partitions of relation (that is, cuts on the horizontal axis). By comparison, the project operator supports the definition of vertical partitions (that is, cuts on the vertical axis).

Projection of a relation over a number of attributes filters out all but those attributes, thus simplifying a relation by reducing its width. The operator can be used also for the permuting of attributes, thus changing column ordering in a table.

As with the previous operator, the assumed syntax separates the input relation from the predicate by a semicolon. *Figures 54.8(a)* and (*b*) show, respectively, the relations resulting from the following four projection operations over the relation Airports:

(a) project (Airports; country_name, airport_name)
 This is an example of the use of project to permute the attributes of a relation, in this case simply swapping them around.

(a)

country_name	airport_name
Italy	Naples
England	London/Gk
England	London/Hw
Italy	Pisa
Italy	Verona
Italy	Venice/MP
England	Manchester
Hong Kong	Kai Tak
UAE	Dubai
Singapore	Changi

(b)

country_name
Italy
England
Hong Kong
UAE
Singapore

Figure 54.8 Illustrations of the project operator

(b) project (Airports; country_name)
 This example illustrates another effect of the closure principle: because all operations produce relations (which are sets), any potentially duplicate tuples (in this case, England) are filtered out as part of any operation. This example also illustrates a unary relation – one defined over a single domain.

7. *The join operator.* In the 1972 paper, Codd presented what he called a θ-join (pronounced 'theta-join'). Various join operators have since been proposed, and of these we adopt here one of the class of so-called natural joins. These are joins that are based only on equality matches.

The join operator allows the construction of relations formed by catenating the tuples of two existing relations according to a join predicate, essentially a foreign key association. We allow for joins over any number of attribute pairs, where any pair may or may not have the same name. In cases where the name is the same the join predicate simply gives that name; in other cases an attribute pair is designated by means of a $\leftrightarrow$ symbol. The ordering of attributes in the resulting relation is that which would result from a product of the relations.

As with the previous operators, a semicolon is used to separate the names of the given input relations from the predicate. *Figures 54.9(a)* and (*b*) show, respectively, the relations produced from the following operations against the Flights, Airports, and Stops relations assumed previously.

(a) join (Flights, Airports; origin $\leftrightarrow$ airport_name)
 This example illustrates a simple join of the two relations over a single pair of attributes – origin in Flights and airport_name in Airports. This introduces the country of the airport of origin of each flight into a relation that otherwise is like the original Flights.

(b) join (Stops, Airports; airport_name)
 This example illustrates the joining of two relations over a pair of identically-named attributes.

flight_number	origin	destin	country_name
BA533	Naples	London/Gk	Italy
BA528	London/Hw	Pisa	England
KG2544	Verona	London/Gk	Italy
KG2540	Venice/MP	London/Gk	Italy
KG946	Venice/MP	Manchester	Italy
BR382	London/Gk	Kai Tak	England
BA019	London/Hw	Kai Tak	England

(a)

flight_number	airport_name	stop_number	country_name
BR382	UAE	1	Dubai
BA019	UAE	1	Dubai
BA019	Changi	2	Singapore

(b)

Figure 54.9 Illustrations of the join operator

The relation produced by joining two relations over some join predicate can always be produced using a combination of product, restrict, and project.

8. *The divide operator*. Like join, the effect of a divide operation can always be produced using a combination of other operators. Also like join, when a direct application of the operator occurs, its availability is greatly appreciated; unlike join, however, such opportunities tend not to be so common.

The divide operator allows the construction of (unary) relations that result from the division of a (binary) relation by another (unary) one. The attribute of the dividing relation must be defined over a domain that is compatible with the domain of whichever of the divided relation's attributes it is to divide into. We call this the divided attribute. And we call the other attribute of the divided relation the undivided attribute. The divided attribute is designated in a divison predicate by means of a ↔ symbol denoting its correspondence with the dividing attribute. The resulting relation's attribute is then defined over the domain of the undivided attribute of the divided relation.

The extension of the resulting relation is a set of those values of the undivided attribute that have matches, in the divided relation, with all values of the attribute in the dividing relation. This is best illustrated by example. Let us suppose that we wish to construct a list of those airports to which we can fly from both London/Gk and London/Hw – that is, we must be able to fly to each of the resulting airports from both London airports.

This is achieved by dividing the origin attribute of a binary relation of flight origins and destinations (shown in *Figure 54.10(a)*) by a unary relation of London airports (shown in *Figure 54.10(b)*). This gives those values of the destin attribute that have matches in the first of the above for both of the entries in the second of the above, that is, that originate at both London airports. The relation resulting from the operation:

divide ((a), (b); origin ↔ airport_name)

is shown as *Figure 54.10(c)*.

(a)

origin	destin
Naples	London/Gk
London/Hw	Pisa
Verona	London/Gk
Venice/MP	London/Gk
Venice/MP	Manchester
London/Gk	Kai Tak
London/Hw	Kai Tak

(b)

airport_name
London/Gk
London/Hw

(c)

destin
Kai Tak

Figure 54.10 Illustration of the divide operator

The relation resulting from changing the designation of the divided attribute in the above division, that is, from the operation:

divide ((a), (b); destin ↔ airport_name)

gives the names of all airports from which it is possible to fly

to both London airports; that is, the relation whose only attribute is origin and whose extension is empty (because there are none in the example data).

54.3.2.3 *Relational update and intension operators*

The manipulation concept discussed thus far relates only to retrieval of data from a database extension. This is not in itself sufficient as a basis for DBMS. Any relational DBMS must, in addition, provide facilities for:

1. Modifying the extension of a database – adding, removing and modifying the tuples of existing relations.
2. Posing queries against the intension of a database, to determine which attributes are in which relations, and are drawn from which domains.
3. Modifying the intension of a database – adding, removing and modifying relations, attributes and domains.

We will now see how these requirements can be met by means of the concepts presented previously. A relational database schema might be formulated in relational terms by means of the following three relations.

Relations(<u>rel name/names, att name/names</u>; dom_name/ names, pkey?/Boolean)

This relation gives, for each database relation (including this one), the names and domains of its attributes, and states whether each attribute is a component of the primary key.

F_Keys(<u>rel name/names, att name/names, xrel name/names, xatt name/names</u>)

This relation holds details of all cross-references between relations; the first pair of attributes describe a foreign key attribute in a relation, and the second pair state the attribute (in another relation) to which it refers.

Domains (<u>dom name/names</u>; dom_defn/text)

This relation captures the definition of each domain used.

One consequence of formulating a database schema in this way is that we can now make enquiries of a database intension in terms of the manipulation concept that has already been discussed: we simply pose queries against the extension of the schema relations. For example, to find the names of the attributes of the Flights relation we can pose the following query:

project (
    restrict(Relations; rel_name = Flights);
    att_name)

As another example, to find the domains of the key attributes of Stops we can pose the following:

project (
    join (
        Domains,
        restrict (Relations;
            rel_name = Stops
            and pkey? = y);
        dom_name);
    dom_name)

Another consequence of implementing a relational schema in this way is that implementations of the relational operators themselves can be based on the manipulation of relational structures (for example, restrict can carry out an operation of itself to check that a restriction predicate is valid), which in turn brings about an economy. Furthermore, by adopting this approach, we force the schema structure itself to be subject to the integrity concept of the model. This ability of the structuring concept of the model to be captured and manipulated by its own primitives is evidence of the elegance and simplicity of the model.

If the intension of a relational database is described by the extension of a collection of schema relations as discussed above, then to update the intension of a database we simply update the extension of the schema relations. For example, to add a new relation to a database:

1. Add any new domains to the Domains relation.
2. Add tuples to Relations to describe the relation's attributes in terms of their domains and whether or not they are key components.
3. Add any tuples to F_Keys necessary to describe cross-references between the relation and existing relations.

The requirements for database updating facilities (for both intension and extension) are, at least, for:

1. Some facility whereby new relations can be defined.
2. An *assignment* operator, of the form:

New_Relation ← Old_Relation,

where the right-hand side can be the result of a relational algebra (or calculus) operation.

Given these, we can make use of the existing manipulation concept to express updating requirements. Commercially available relational DBMSs, however, tend to provide special data *definition* language operators (as opposed to data *manipulation* language operators, which include all of those for extension manipulation), for intension updating. Principally, the reason for this is the practical need to avoid errors when working with intensional data: a tuple mistakenly removed from the schema might have an extraordinarily disastrous effect on the whole of the database.

That is not to say that relational DBMSs do not organize their schemas relationally. Many do, although, again for practical reasons, the relations involved are typically much more complicated than those suggested here.

54.3.3 Integrity concept

The final component of the relational model relates to operators such as those discussed above, and states which rules must be observed when updating a database.

The rules discussed below are called 'general integrity rules' because they are a feature of the relational model itself and not of any particular database system. They are not to be confused with 'specific integrity rules' that relate to a specific application of the model.

There are two general integrity rules, relating respectively to the addition of new data, and the modification (including removal) of existing data.

54.3.3.1 Entity integrity

This rule says that if R is a relation with attributes $a^1, a^2, \ldots, a^n$, and that $a^1, a^2, \ldots, a^i$ constitute its primary key, then for every tuple of R the combination of values of $a^1, a^2, \ldots, a^i$ must be unique. That is to say, a relation must have a primary key, and each value of the primary key (which will be a compound value if the key includes more than one attribute) must be unique over that relation. Without this property, we lose the set-theoretic base (because sets cannot contain duplicates), and hence the manipulation concept as defined previously.

54.3.3.2 Referential integrity

This rule says that, if R and S are relations, and R has an attribute (or compound of two or more attributes) a^j that is a foreign key reference to an attribute a^i (or attribute compound) of S, then, for every value of a^j there must be a matching value of a^i. Essentially, it says that a database must not contain 'dangling' cross-references.

54.3.4 SQL: structured query language

SQL is the most widespread language based on the relational model. Originally offered commercially by IBM as SQL/DS, the language is now supported by most major relational database management systems, including IBMS's DB2, Oracle Corporation's ORACLE, and RTI's INGRES. Furthermore, an International Standard now exists for the language (ISO, 1987), as *the* relational database language. SQL therefore is both formally and *de facto* the standard language for defining and manipulating relational databases.

The SQLs offered by the various products differ in various respects, and are not therefore all identical to the current standard. These differences, however, do not relate to the core of the language, but to the various extensions that they offer above and beyond this.

The language was designed to be used both as a standalone query language and as an extension to conventional high-level programming languages. The commercial implementations and standards activities have both confirmed this dual mode of use. Additional language constructs exist to support the embedding of the language within programming languages (referred to as embedded SQL).

For a tutorial introduction to the standard language and its application, the reader is referred to either VanderLans (1988) or Whittington (1988). The latter also illustrates the relational completeness of the SQL and discusses the weaknesses in its current definition.

54.4 The navigational model of databases

Many writers of database literature differentiate between the *hierarchic* and *network* database models. These models have so much in common that it now seems more appropriate to address them both as special cases of a general class of *navigational* models. The term was first coined by a pioneer of the concept, C. W. Bachman, who entitled his 1973 ACM Turing Award lecture (Bachman, 1973) 'The programmer as navigator'. Navigational models, and record-based models in general, arose through implementations during the 1960s and 1970s. These implementations differ greatly in the facilities they provide, and the restrictions they impose, and are best considered as concrete interpretations of a class of roughly similar database models. The principal attempt at a more abstract, implementation-independent investigation has been the work of the CODASYL DBTG in its work on standard notations for navigational database definition and manipulation. This work has formed the basis of the American standard 'Network Database Language', NDL (ANSI, 1986).

54.4.1 Structuring notion

This involves two concepts:

1. The record type – a collection of records of similar structure.
2. The set type – a collection of cyclic links, each one linking a record of one type (called the owner of the set) with zero or more records of another type (called the member of the set). It is possible for master and members to be of the same type.

A schema for a navigational database is consequently a definition of a collection of each of the above. A diagrammatic notation exists to assist in the conceptualization of navigational databases. A schema thus represented is referred to as a Bachman diagram – the notation was first presented in (Bachman, 1969). *Figure 54.11* shows a Bachman diagram for the sample database that was defined relationally in Figure 54.6.

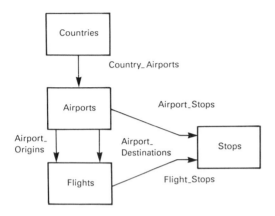

Figure 54.11 Bachman diagram for the example database

54.4.2 Manipulation notion

A central component of the manipulation notion of navigational databases is the concept of currency functions. For any program executing against a navigational database, the following functions are available. Note that if several executions of the same program are in progress concurrently, each executing instance of the program has its own values of these:

1. Current_of_database. This function returns the database key value of the record most recently touched, either for retrieval or update, by an operation of the program.
2. Current_of_record_type (record_type). This function returns the database key value of the most recently touched record of the specified type.
3. Current_of_set_type (set_type). This function returns the database key value of the most recently touched record that participates in a set of the specified type. That is, this function informs us as to the current set of a type, and also of the current position within that set.

In order to retrieve the field values of a record it is necessary for a program to navigate through the database structures to reach that record, and the above functions play a significant part in this. They constitute a dynamic part of the state of a database as it is perceived by each executing program.

The manipulation notion essentially provides for three types of retrieval:

1. Direct-access to an individual record whose database key value is known.
2. Direct-access operator to an individual record of specified type for which a unique key identifier exists, and a relevant value is known.
3. Navigational access to the next record in the current set of a given type.

and for four types of update:

1. Adding a new record of a specified type into a database.

2. Connecting a record of a specified type into a set of a specified type.
3. Disconnecting a record of a specified type from a set of specified type.
4. Removing the current record of a specified type from a database.

All these operators are record-orientated; although the term 'set' is used, its meaning is specific to this model, and it is not possible to process multiple records simultaneously, as it is with the relational model. This is perhaps the most significant difference between the two approaches.

54.4.3 Integrity notion

This can be captured in one simple rule: each record that is a detail of some set must have exactly one (no more and no less) masters in that set. This provides a counterpart to what the relational model calls referential integrity.

There is no explicit concept of what the relational model calls entity integrity, but it is approximated by the facility that allows the specification for a given record type that certain fields must be unique for associative direct access to records. This is not as strong as entity integrity.

54.4.4 The proposals of the CODASYL DBTG

The CODASYL Data Base Task Group (DBTG), and more recently ANSI, have defined languages for the definition and manipulation of navigational databases. For a tutorial coverage of the proposals, the reader is referred to either Olle (1980) or to Date (1986).

Formerly, DBMSs based on the navigational model held a strong position in the commercial world. This reflects the fact that such systems emerged first and, due to the economics of system development in the 1960s and early 1970s, their general efficiency in terms of machine-resource usage supported their continuity despite promises in improved flexibility and development productivity made by the early proponents of the relational approach. Since those days, however, with the shift in the cost equation from machines towards people as the dominant factor, navigational systems have steadily lost their share of the market. It seems unlikely that this demise will one day mean that no navigational systems are in existence, but, by the end of the century, there will be precious few, and these will tend to be for specialist rather than for general-purpose applications.

54.5 Transaction management

54.5.1 The transaction concept

At the centre of database notions of concurrency and recovery management is the concept of a transaction.

A transaction is a unit of work. This might correspond to the execution of a simple query, or of an application program with many DML commands embedded within it. Transactions have the following characteristics:

1. *Independence*. An incomplete transaction does not reveal intermediate results to others. This is the basis of synchronization of concurrent database access.
2. *Failure atomicity*. Either all or none of a transaction's operations are performed.
3. *Permanence*. If a transaction completes successfully, then its effect will never be lost. This, together with the previous characteristic, provides the basis for recovery from failure in database systems.

The concept of transaction is an abstraction that allows the developer of application software (including simple query formulation) to assume the provision of underlying controls. Transactions therefore have two purposes:

1. Application development productivity.
2. Uniformity and predictability in system security.

We now consider briefly the more popular mechanisms used by DBMSs for implementing the transaction concept.

54.5.2 Implementing transaction independence

The following is the most popular correctness criterion for concurrently executing processes:

The concurrent execution of n processes is correct if and only if its effect is the same as that obtained by running those same processes serially in some order.

When a collection of programs executes we refer to the actual sequence of operations that are performed as a schedule for those programs. Clearly there are many possible schedules for any collection of programs, according to the permutations that can be defined by the different interleavings of operations. We say that a schedule is serial if no interleaving of the operations of different programs occurs, and we say that a schedule is serializable if it is equivalent to some serial schedule. Serial schedules are themselves (trivially) serializable – they are equivalent to themselves.

The correctness criterion is satisfied if and only if one permits the execution only of serializable schedules. Although there are many ways in which serializability of schedules can be guaranteed, the majority of DBMSs that are currently available use techniques based upon locking or upon a combination of locking and time-stamping. Most techniques implement the two-phase locking protocol, which says that:

In any process, all lock statements must precede all unlock statements.

The reader with special interests in this area is referred to the following: Ceri and Pelagatti (1985), Date (1983), Garcia-Molina (1983), Gray (1978), Kung and Robinson (1981).

54.5.3 Implementing transaction atomicity and permanence

A transaction can fail for a variety of reasons: erroneous input, requirements for non-existent data, lack of resources, system crash, and so on. These can be classified into the following failure types:

1. Transaction abort (without loss of information).
2. System crash (with loss of main memory contents).
3. Media failure (with loss of disc storage contents).

Implementations of atomicity and permanence in the face of these types of failure are various, and, in general, the greater the reliability that is sought, the greater the complexity that is involved in the implementation, to a point where absolute reliability can be achieved only through absolute complexity. Clearly there are costs associated with complexity, and an appropriate level of reliability for the value of the data (and the value of fast access to it) has to be selected by the database administrator.

Only the principal concepts are examined here; the reader who requires further detail is referred to the references given previously.

The two-phase protocol is the usual basis for guaranteeing permanence and atomicity in the event of failure. During the first phase of execution of a transaction, locks are acquired, data objects are read, and calculations are performed, but no database object is overwritten. A transaction can therefore terminate at any time during this phase of its execution without adverse effect. Upon entering the second phase, a transaction is said to be committed to complete, and during this phase database objects are updated and a failure might result in inconsistencies (i.e. loss of atomicity).

Consequently, there are two cases to accommodate:

1. *Failure prior to the commit point.* Transactions can be terminated and the database rolled back (unlock objects, release storage, and so on) as if the transaction had never been submitted (except for the log entry – see below).
2. *Failure after committing.* Transactions cannot be terminated; they must be restarted at the point of failure, and must run to completion. Various commit protocols exist to guarantee that this is both possible and as efficient as possible.

These cases are independent of the types of failure identified above. There are therefore six failure scenarios for which to make provision. Of these, all but the more serious media failures are normally managed using a logging mechanism. A transaction log or journal is a sequence of records, each corresponding to an operation performed by a transaction. When a transaction fails, for whatever reason, there is sufficient information in the log to undo the operations carried out (for phase one failure) or to restart the transaction at an appropriate point (for phase two failure). Atomicity is implemented in this way by most DBMSs. Permanence is implemented by a combination of logs and periodic database images.

54.5.4 Managing transactions in distributed database systems

The techniques that evolved for use in centralized DBMSs have been generalized for distributed DBMSs, at the expense of increased complexity and communication overheads. It is beyond the scope to enter into detailed examination of those generalizations here and the reader is referred to Ceri and Pelagatti (1985) for coverage of the subject.

Essentially, distributed transaction management operates by imposing a superstructure over a collection of independent local transaction managers. This implements a protocol that restricts the operation of those local systems.

54.6 Internal database organization

54.6.1 File organizations and access methods

Internal organizations for databases are usually described in terms of file organizations. This is because many DBMSs use the filing facilities of a host operating system as a basis for more elaborate facilities, and other systems typically provide similar capabilities. The objective is to support access to data in ways that are compatible with the patterns of access that are required.

A file organization is a collection of manipulation algorithms that determine how records of some type are retrieved, inserted, and deleted. Internally, a database consists of a collection of file organizations, and the compound is referred to as constituting the database organization.

Each file in a database is organized according to one primary organization and zero or more secondary organizations. Primary organizations support insertion and deletion algorithms and some form of primary key retrieval; secondary organizations provide additional access capability beyond that provided by primary organizations. Typically, a DBMS supports a limited number (often one or two) of types of primary organization, and a single secondary organization type.

File organizations can be classified as either static or dynamic. A static organization is one that is loaded as a fixed structure such that:

1. If less data than the maximum provided for exists at any time, the storage allocated to the organization is unused, and unavailable to any other organization.
2. If more data than the maximum provided for exists at any time, the organization treats the additional data as overflow, and organizes it in some other manner, usually to the detriment of the organization as a whole.
3. Periodically, a reorganization is required, to reload the data (including overflow) into a clean structure.

A dynamic organization, on the other hand, expands and contracts with data volumes; space is not wasted when data volumes are lower than expected, no concept of overflow exists, and no periodic reorganization is required. These benefits are paid for by more complex updating algorithms. By way of a comparison with main memory data structures, an array is a static data structure, whereas a linked list is dynamic.

54.6.1.1 Primary organizations

Four standard types of primary file organization have evolved and, for each of these, both static and dynamic forms exist: heaps, sequential organizations, hashed organizations and indexed-sequential organizations. For detailed coverage of the organization types, the reader is referred to Wiederhold (1983), which discusses various organizations and provides cost equations relating to their use. For a more tutorial-like summary, the reader is directed to Whittington (1988).

Of the primary types, most DBMSs offer one serial-access organization, such as the heap, and one direct-access organization, such as indexed-sequential. Of the latter, the most popular are the class of B-Trees. The publication of the original concept (Bayer, 1970) has been complemented by an excellent survey of variants with their respective advantages and disadvantages (Comer, 1979). The most commonly used variant is the B + Tree, in which a file consists of a data part – blocks of data records – and an index part, the leaves of which are connected by a collection of pointers called a sequence set, as illustrated in *Figure 54.12*.

54.6.1.2 Secondary organizations

These provide access capabilities in addition to those supported by the primary organization of a file. They are especially popular in connection with heaps because the resulting organization offers a symmetry of access that is often desirable. Any primary organization can in principle, however, be augmented by secondary capabilities.

A given secondary organization supports access to a given field (or aggregate of fields), by means of a combination of indexing and pointer chains. A secondary index is a file of records, each of which refers to a particular value of the field (or fields) against which the index supports access, and indicates which data records have any value.

A secondary index for a file is sometimes referred to as an inversion, and a file that is fully secondarily indexed (i.e., when one exists for each field) is said to be fully inverted. For storage efficiency, when an inversion exist for a file, there is no strict necessity to hold the corresponding field values in the data records; Wiederhold (1983) calls such non-existent field values phantom data. Some DBMSs (for example, MRI's System 2000) make extensive use of inversions in this manner.

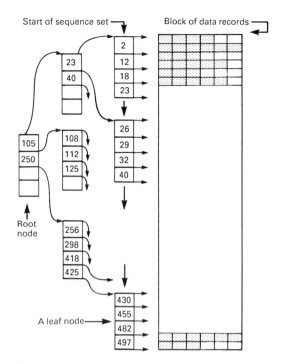

Figure 54.12 A B + Tree

54.7 Summary

This chapter has introduced the fundamental concepts of, and techniques adopted by, current database systems. It has not addressed any particular products in detail, but rather has tended towards generalities, aiming to give a general appreciation, employing particular examples as appropriate.

The coverage has stressed the advantages of certain techniques and the disadvantages of others, thus implicitly also providing criteria for the selection of appropriate packages. In particular, it has stressed the benefits of relational systems and the importance of SQL as an extant and evolving standard language for application development and system administration.

54.8 References

ANSI (1975) *Interim Report of the ANSI/X3/SPARC Study Group on Data Base Management Systems*, ACM SIGFIDET

ANSI (1976) Network Database Language. In *Report of the ANSI X3H2 Technical Committee on Databases*

Bachman, C. W. (1969) Data structure diagrams. *Database*, **1**, 4–10

Bachman, C. W. (1973) The programmer as navigator. *Communications of the ACM*, **16**, 653–658

Bayer, R. and McCreight, E. (1970) Organization and maintenance of large ordered indices. In *ACM SIGFIDET Workshop on Data Description and Access*, pp. 107–141

Brown, A. W. (1990) *Integrated Project Support Environment: the Aspect Project*, Academic Press, London

Ceri, S. and Pelagatti, G. (1985) *Distributed Database Systems: Principles and Systems*, McGraw-Hill

Codd, E. F. (1970) A relational model of data for large shared data banks. *Communications of ACM*, **13**, 377–387

Codd, E. F. (1972) Relational completeness of data base sublanguages. In *Data Base Systems, Courant Comput. Sci. Symp. 6th* (ed. R. Rustin), Prentice-Hall, pp. 65–98

Codd, E. F. (1979) Extending the database relational model to capture more meaning. *ACM Transactions on Database Systems*, **4**, 397–434

Codd, E. F. (1982) Relational database: a practical foundation for productivity. *Communications of the ACM*, **25**, 109–117

Comer, D. (1979) The ubiquitous B-Tree. *ACM Computing Surveys*, **11**, 121–137

Date, C. J. (1983) *An Introduction to Database Systems Volume II*, Addison-Wesley

Date, C. J. (1986) *An Introduction to Database Systems Volume I* (4th edn), Addison-Wesley

Garcia-Molina, H. (1983) Using semantic knowledge for transaction processing in a distributed database. *ACM Transactions on Database Systems*, **8**, 186–213

Gray, J. N. (1978) Notes on data base operating systems. In *Operating Systems: An Advanced Course* (ed. R. Seegmuller, R. M. Bayer, G. Graham), Springer-Verlag, pp. 393–481

Heimbigner, D. and McLeod, D. (1985) A federated architecture for information management. *ACM Transactions on Office Information Systems*, **3**, 253–278

ISO (1987) *Final text of DIS 9075, Information Processing Systems – Database Language SQL*, Report of TC97/SC21/WG3

Jervis, P. (1984) Standards for industrial real-time databases. In *European Workshop on Industrial Computer Systems Spring Workshop*, pp. 1–15

Kent, W. (1978) *Data and Reality*, North Holland

Kung, H. T. and Robinson, J. T. (1981) On optimistic methods for concurrency control. *ACM Transactions on Database Systems*, **6**

Olle, T. W. (1980) *The CODASYL Approach to Database Management*, J. Wiley

Schmidt, J. W. (1977) Some high level language constructs for data of type relation. *ACM Transactions on Database Systems*, **2**, 247–261

Schmidt, J. W. and Linnemann, V. (1985) Higher-level relational objects. In *Proceedings of the 4th British National Conference on Databases*, Cambridge University Press, pp. 1–24

Stonebraker, M. (1986) *The INGRES Papers: Anatomy of a Relational Database System*, Addison-Wesley

VanderLans, R. F. (1988) *Introduction to SQL*, Addison-Wesley

Weinberger, P. J. (1982) Making UNIX operating systems safe for databases. *The Bell System Technical Journal*, **61**, 2407–2422

Whittington, R. P. (1988) *Database Systems Engineering*, Oxford University Press

Wiederhold, G. (1983) *Database Design* (2nd edn), McGraw Hill

55 Database system development

R P Whittington
Director
Hand, Whittington and Associates, York

Contents

55.1 Introduction

The previous chapter introduced the concepts and working of database systems. This chapter builds upon that material and presents a broad methodology and a collection of specific techniques for use in designing the structures and organizations to employ in a database system. It is important to appreciate that the subjects covered here form only one part of the information system development process, and that the development of appropriate database application software is an important parallel activity, the implications of which are considered here, but which is not in itself addressed in detail.

The emphasis throughout is on relational systems, but the techniques presented are equally applicable to other classes of systems (e.g. navigational), and appropriate additional techniques for these are suggested.

The chapter first introduces a general structured methodology, and then addresses applicable techniques for each stage involved, from initial data modelling through to implementation on a database management system.

55.2 Database development methodology

55.2.1 Context

The context of database system development within the broader information system development process, can be interpreted according to *Figure 55.1*.

55.2.2 Models of development

A model of development is a way of thinking about the development process: a broad methodological framework, including techniques and managerial strategy. The database system development process can usefully be viewed as comprising a sequence of stages, of the form shown in *Figure 55.2*. Each stage involves the production of a database system specification, at an increasing level of detail. Associated with that production are methods for design, verification (for internal consistency), and validation (for being a feasible and constructive progression from the previous specification).

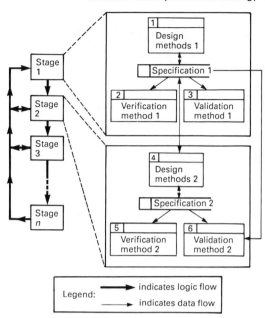

Figure 55.2 Reference model for development models

55.2.3 A development model for database systems

The model adopted here embraces prototyping as a dynamic verification and validation technique, within the context of a structured development framework. It has been developed (and applied extensively) by the author, but is typical of the models assumed by other workers (see, for example, the proposals of Albano and Orsini (1984), Blaha *et al.* (1988), and the approach underlying the ORACLE development tools). The approach is particularly feasible in (although not restricted to) the development of relational database systems, where early relational designs can be implemented rapidly and demonstrated before considering the implementation details – an advantage over navigational systems, which involve physical considerations at an early stage.

The model involves five stages, as shown in *Figure 55.3*. It is possible to loop back from any stage to any previous stage to recognize changed requirements, or to correct any bad decisions. The stages involved are described below.

55.2.3.1 Conceptual analysis

This stage, sometimes called data modelling, involves formulating the data objects of the universe of discourse in terms of a data modelling formalism, to produce a specification of what the required database is to represent. The use of a formal modelling approach makes this stage amenable to automatic verification. The input to this stage is the totality of the results of the systems analysis process that precedes detailed database system development, including application requirements, agreed problems with any existing systems, and the host of other objectives of that exercise (see, for example, Gane and Sarson, 1979; NCC, 1986).

55.2.3.2 Logical design

This stage maps a conceptual description of real-world data objects into a collection of implementation-independent

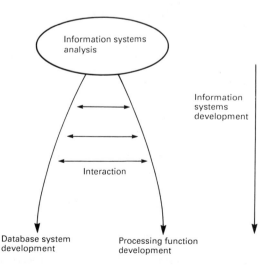

Figure 55.1 Overview of the information systems development process

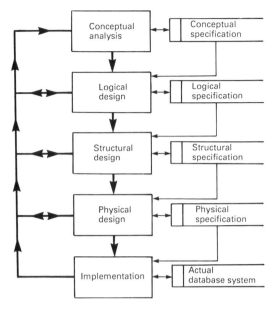

Figure 55.3 Development model for database systems

database structures. These structures are amenable to prototyping, for early feedback to users, and to analytical methods of verification and validation.

55.2.3.3 Structural design

This stage gives a first-cut implementation strategy, by considering the record structures and inter-record links that are to be implemented. Again, the resulting structures might be prototyped, and analytical procedures defined for their verification.

55.2.3.4 Physical design

Having in the previous stage designed implementation structures the next step is to decide upon the representation of those structures in storage, and the methods that are to be provided for accessing them. A physical specification can also be validated through prototyping, and verified analytically. This stage is also the forum for decisions relating to the configuration of the target system.

55.2.3.5 Implementation

This stage involves building the database and making it available to its application users. It is a semi-automatic activity – analogous to program compilation – involving the use of DBMS facilities for structure creation and data loading. Decisions relating to the operation of the system, such as the level and type of recovery from failure that is to be supported, are also made here.

55.2.3.6 Summary

Following the reference model of Figure 55.2, each of the stages of the model is based upon source and target notations, and consists of design, verification and validation techniques. Management procedures follow naturally, and sign-off procedures can be associated with each stage (and, if desired, with detailed steps within stages). Each stage is presented in these terms in the following sections.

55.2.4 Supporting database system development

Consider the development process implied by the model outlined above. The first stage produces a description of a collection of data objects and their interrelationships; the second produces a description of a collection of logical database structures to provide containers for the previous objects; and so on. Each of these products in fact comprises a collection of data objects.

The development of a database system is only one part of the development of an information system. There is a related development exercise involving processing functions and the interfaces that bind them. This exercise will also generate data objects, and, what is more, there will be relationships between its data objects and those of the database system development process (for example, describing the data objects used by a particular program).

The normal means of managing potentially large collections of data is a database system. A database system whose universe of discourse is the information system development process is called a data dictionary system. That is, a data dictionary is a database whose contents describe the data objects of a database system under development, and their interrelationships with related development activities. Data dictionaries are sometimes called meta-databases, because they are databases of meta-data – data about data.

A database schema is one type of data dictionary, but traditional schema languages do not have the capability to provide anything other than run-time support for a DBMS. Nevertheless, some DBMSs refer to their schemas as data dictionaries, but this use of the term should not be confused with the broader interpretation. The current concept of a data dictionary is of a much richer set of facilities capable of supporting the entire development process, including run-time, in four broad and overlapping ways:

1. Generation of system development documentation.
2. Coordination and communication between development activities.
3. Analysis of the impact of altering design decisions.
4. Automatic design and verification.

Data dictionary facilities can be classified in terms of:

1. The levels of support provided for each of the above requirements.
2. Whether the dictionary is active or passive.
3. The extent and nature of any relationship between the facilities and any DBMSs.

An active dictionary is one that is integrated with an operational system to the extent that altering the system in some way is reflected automatically in the dictionary, and *vice versa*; the data dictionary is the sole source of meta-data. A conventional database schema is an active dictionary. A passive dictionary, on the other hand, is one that stands apart from the system that it describes, and has to be maintained independently. If a separate database system were designed solely for the purposes of supporting and documenting a development activity, then that system would provide a passive dictionary.

It is of course possible to construct a data dictionary system making use of whichever DBMS is being used in the development of the database system to which the dictionary refers. The advantages here are that no additional system software is required. Alternatively, one of the data dictionary system products might be used. These are now numerous, and can be classified into those that relate to a specific DBMS and those that are DBMS-independent. Whichever of these is used, there is the advantage that the system will already have a number of useful application programs for reporting, analysing, and designing that would otherwise have had to be developed.

Furthermore, with the progression of data dictionary standardization under the name of 'information resource dictionary systems' (IRDS) – see Gradwell (1987) – there are advantages in meta-data sharing to be gained from the use of standard dictionary structures and interfaces.

Data dictionary systems relating to particular DBMSs (for example, ORACLE's System Development Dictionary) have the advantage of integrating well with the system whose development they support, and can therefore accommodate useful tools such as performance predictions on the basis of that DBMS's operation. On the other hand, DBMS-independent systems are preferable in an organization that uses several DBMSs, or that does not wish to restrict itself to any particular system. Systems such as MSP's DataManager offer facilities for the development of databases for implementation using any of several DBMSs.

There is an overlap in scope between the concept of a data dictionary system (DDS), that has emerged from the world of business information systems, and the concept of an integrated project support environment (IPSE), that has emerged from the world of software engineering. Both are facilities motivated by the need for increased productivity and control in the development process. The principal differences between existing DDSs and IPSEs follow from their orientations. DDSs – and the computer-assisted software engineering (CASE) tools that they support – concentrate on business modelling, database design, and the production of fourth-generation language code modules, whereas IPSEs concentrate on project management, software configuration and version control, and software validation. These differences in emphasis reflect the differing concerns and requirements of system development in the respective contexts.

55.3 Conceptual analysis

55.3.1 Objectives

The objective of this stage is to produce an abstract formulation of the universe of discourse, as delineated by the requirements specification. The results of the exercise should be, on the one hand, a clear, concise and comprehensive description, and, on the other, a workable prescription for system development.

This two-fold objective poses a requirement for a target notation that is at the same time a good common currency with the user and a good working tool for the designer. A number of notations have been proposed over the past decade or so, but of these one class has emerged as dominant: those based on entity–relationship–attribute (ERA) modelling, originally presented in Chen (1976), and enhanced through the work of others, notably Smith and Smith (1977) and Codd (1979). The method presented here is a pragmatic synthesis that is consistent with the mainstream developments in the field.

55.3.2 ERA analysis

The ERA approach adopts the view that the world can be described in terms of entities and entity types, relationships and relationship types, and attributes.

55.3.2.1 Entity types and subtypes

An entity is a 'distinguishable thing of interest': it might be physical, or it might be abstract. By distinguishable we mean that there exists some way of differentiating between any two entities – otherwise they are not two, but one.

Entities are classified into entity types. We can then refer to, for example, London Heathrow as an entity of type Airports (as a convention we write entity type names with initial capitals) or to BA533 as an entity of type Flights.

An entity type can be a subtype of another. This concept allows the factoring out of common characteristics among entity types; subtypes share the characteristics of their mutual supertype, but have additional particular characteristics of their own.

Subtypes of an entity type are in accordance with what Codd has called a category. An entity type might have several groups of subtypes, each group according to a different subtyping category. Subtypes can be exclusive (or disjoint), in that no entity can be classified as more than one of its subtypes, or inclusive, otherwise.

In the notation, individual entities are represented by circles, and entity types are represented by labelled rectangles. Subtypes of an entity type are denoted as entity types in their own right, being attached by arcs to the entity type of which they are subtypes, groups being distinguished by a further arc (drawn roughly perpendicular to the previous one) and labelled with the category of the subtype grouping. The intersections are starred in the case of inclusive subtyping. *Figure 55.4* illustrates the notation. Some entity modelling notations denote subtypes by nested rectangles.

55.3.2.2 Relationship types and roles

Subtyping allows the capture of one form of association between entities; relationships allow the capture of other forms. The hosting of a particular airport by a country can be expressed by means of a relationship. Like entities, relationships are classified into types, and hosting relationships would be classified as constituting a relationship type between the entity types Airports and Countries.

Relationship types between entity types are represented, in the diagrammatic notation, by arcs connecting the participating entity types. The relationship type between Airports and Countries would, therefore, be represented as shown in *Figure 55.5(a)*.

Relationship types are characterized by their degree, which is one of three kinds: one-to-one, one-to-many, and many-to-many. The example above, of Countries containing Airports, is a one-to-many relationship type, because one Country contains many (greater than or equal to zero) Airports but one Airport is in exactly one Country. The relationship type that associates Airports with Flights has degree many-to-many, because one Flight relates to many Airports (of origin, stopover and destination), and one Airport relates to many Flights (which originate, stop over at, or terminate there), as shown in *Figure 55.5(b)*.

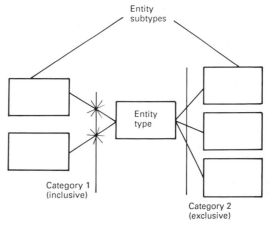

Figure 55.4 Subtyping notation

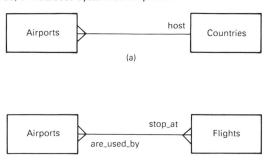

(a)

(b)

Figure 55.5 Relationship types (a) many-to-one (b) many-to-many

True one-to-one relationship types are less common. They are represented simply by connecting the participating entity types.

Entities play roles within relationships and these can sometimes be of interest. One might, for example, choose to capture origin and destination Airports of a Flight by two separate relationship types, as shown in *Figure 55.6*. These are both of degree one-to-many. In one of these relationship types, the Airport entity type plays the role of the origin of the Flight and in the other it plays the role of the destination. The names of these roles are written as shown on the relationship type arcs.

Role names are necessary in cases such as this, where there are multiple relationship types between entity types, otherwise there would be no way of distinguishing between them. They can also be useful, even in cases where they are not strictly needed, for giving clarification of the form of an association being captured (for example, labelling the arc between Countries and Airports in *Figure 55.7(a)* with host indicates clearly that it is the hosting association and not some other that is represented); in such cases their application is optional, according to their usefulness.

55.3.2.3 Attributes of entity types

Entities have attributes that characterize them. Entities of the same type are characterized by the same attributes. Attributes, unlike entities, have values. The acid test for whether an element is an entity or an attribute is the question: 'Does the element take values?'

Each attribute is associated with a named value set that defines the allowable values that it might take. The concept is identical to that of domains in relational databases and types in Pascal-like programming languages. In the diagrammatic notation, the attributes of an entity type are named and attached to it by arcs.

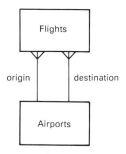

Figure 55.6 The use of role names

55.3.3 Identification and identification dependence

All entities must be individually distinguishable. This is guaranteed for those of some entity types (called kernel entity types in Codd (1979)) by denoting with a double connecting arc some subset of the attributes of an entity type to be the identification key for entities of that type. The concatenated values of the identification key attributes of an entity must guarantee to distinguish that entity from all others of the same type. This is possible in the case of entity types such as Flights, where flight numbers can be guaranteed to distinguish Flights entities.

An entity type is said to be identification-dependent on others if it cannot be uniquely distinguished independently of the identification keys of those others. There are two classes of entity type for which this applies.

For the first of these classes (which Codd has called characteristic), suppose that we have an entity type Times that has the following attributes:

1. Day (for example, Monday).
2. Departure time (for example, 1800).
3. Arrival time (for example, 0645).

Times is associated with Flights by a many-to-one relationship, as illustrated in *Figure 55.7(a)*. For a given Flights entity then, the associated collection of Times gives the applicable departure and arrival times for the days of the week on which the Flight operates. Times entities cannot be distinguished independently, and require, for their complete identification:

1. The identifier of that entity type on which they are dependent (in this case, flight number, the identifier of Flights).
2. The local identifier of the dependent entity type (in this case, day).

Such cases are denoted, as shown in *Figure 55.7(a)* by an elongated 'I' symbol crossing the arc linking the dependent entity type with its superior.

The second case (which Codd has called associative) applies when an entity type in fact represents a many-to-many relationship type between two or more entity types. As an example, suppose that an entity type Stops is used to represent the many-to-many relationship type between Flights and Airports; any Stops entity represents the association between a particular Flight and an Airport, and states by its sole attribute, stop number, the order in which Airports are stopped at by a Flight.

Such entities require, for their complete identification, the identifiers of those entity types on which they are dependent. In this case that means flight number, the identifier of Flights, and airport code, the identifier of Airports. Identification dependencies of this kind are again denoted by an elongated 'I' symbol, but this time crossing the relationship type arcs connecting the dependent entity type with all superior entity types, as in *Figure 55.7(b)*.

55.3.4 A pragmatic analysis method

The above concepts give rise to many possible methods of formulation. Experience shows that iteration is necessary, resulting in a process of gradual refinement, and the following sequence of steps is especially conducive to productive refinement. Together they correspond to the design component of this stage of development.

55.3.4.1 Step 1: Identify entity types and subtypes

This is the most difficult step of all, and is almost invariably done incorrectly during the first iteration. As a first approximation, select as entity types any objects that are associated with identifiers (for example, invoice numbers suggest an entity type

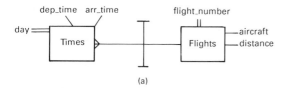

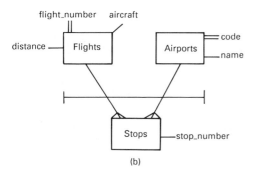

Figure 55.7 Identification dependence (a) on a single entity type (b) on multiple entity types

called Invoices, product codes suggest another called Products, and so on).

55.3.4.2 Step 2: Identify associations between these entity types

As a first cut, it is often useful to construct a matrix listing the names of the selected entity types along both column and row headings. Each intersection should then be considered as posing the question 'Is entity type X associated in some way with entity type Y?' If so, set a mark in the appropriate cell. Note that X and Y here need not necessarily be distinct (for example, People might have relationships with other People, say, by employment or marriage).

Having completed the matrix (which is symmetric, so only entries to one side of the diagonal need be completed), draw the entity types and interconnect them according to the nature of the association.

1. In the case of the association being a supertype-subtype, it is necessary to establish whether this is inclusive or exclusive, and to name the category.
2. If the association is a relationship type, then it is necessary to establish its degree and any identification dependencies, and to mark roles, where appropriate, on the arcs.

55.3.4.3 Step 3: Rationalize the formulation

This step invites verification of what has been achieved so far. It has three sub-steps:

1. Remove any redundant (superfluous) one-to-many relationship types. These can be recognized as follows. There are three entity types, E1, E2 and E3, a one-to-many relationship type between E1 and E2, another between E2 and E3, and yet another type between E1 and E3. If E1 is related to different E3 entity types by its direct E1-E3 relationship type than it is by its indirect E1-E2 and E2-E3 relationship types then there is no redundancy. If this is not the case, then the E1–E3 relationship type is superfluous and should be removed.

2. Remove any redundant (superfluous) entity types. There are two cases to consider:
   (a) There are two entity types related by a one-to-one relationship type and these in fact represent a single entity type. In this case, the two entity types are merged into one (or, equivalently, one entity type is simply removed).
   (b) There are two associative or link entity types between two (or more) others, and these in fact represent the same association. In this case (which is rather like the above, but in a slightly different context), the two entity types are again merged into one.

3. For each many-to-many relationship type introduce a new associative or link entity type to which each of the entity types is related by means of a one-to-many relationship type, and which is identification dependent on the former entity types, as shown in *Figure 55.8*.

Repeat (1) and (2) to deal with any redundancy of relationship or entity types that is introduced as a result.

55.3.4.4 Step 4: Identify attributes of entity types

In doing this be sure that:

1. Each attribute really does characterize only the entity type in question.
2. There are no further attributes of interest that are unassigned.

Assigning a value set to an attribute can reveal difficulties of interpretation that are symptomatic of underlying errors.

55.3.4.5 Step 5: Consider unique identification of entities

For each entity type, other than those that are subtypes of others, mark that subset of attributes that will serve as an identification key. Entity subtypes have the same identification key as their supertypes, and their identification is, consequently, implicit. Review the designated identification dependencies, and be sure that entities of each type can be uniquely distinguished.

Failure to determine a method of distinguishing entities is symptomatic of either a weakness in the universe of discourse, which should be rectified, or an underlying problem of interpretation.

55.3.4.6 Folding

When working with a large universe of discourse (that is, one with more entity types than can be contemplated at any one time), it can be useful to apply the previous method iteratively at increasing levels of detail. The first formulation might yield broad groups of entity types (such as Product, which in fact comprises numerous entity types concerning its manufacture,

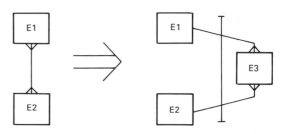

Figure 55.8 Many-to-many relationship type removal

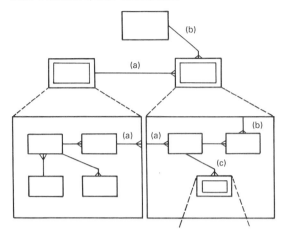

Figure 55.9 Folding of entity-relationship formulations

pricing, and application); and subsequent iterations might refine these into successively smaller units, until base entity types are reached (that is, entity types that require no further refinement).

Entity types that represent abstractions of a more detailed entity type structure are denoted by a double-edged rectangle. In order to retain the relationship type connections between entity types within folded formulations it is useful to adopt a convention of labelling relationship type arcs, as shown in *Figure 55.9*.

The advantages of folding conceptual specifications in this way are that:

1. The design and verification processes can work with manageable-sized problems at any time, while remaining in context with the remainder of the problem.
2. The validation processes, involving discussions with users, can concentrate on areas of individual expertise, without the danger of confusion by additional, irrelevant concepts.

The latter advantage also raises an important general point about the way in which analysis often progresses. In a large organization, a database reflects the combined perceptions of several users, or groups of users. Integrating these views into a coherent conceptual specification can be one of the most taxing tasks at this stage, and the ability to abstract irrelevant details can be of great assistance.

55.3.5 Verification of conceptual specifications

Following the above steps produces a conceptual specification of the data objects of the universe of discourse. The following rules define the conditions for a specification to be internally consistent.

55.3.5.1 Naming rules

1. Entity type names must be unique.
2. Relationship type names must be unique.
3. Attribute names must be unique within entity types.
4. Value set names must be unique.

55.3.5.2 Entity type rules

1. There must be no superfluous entity types (according to the earlier guidelines).
2. Entities of each type must be uniquely distinguishable, either by their own identification keys or by an identification

dependency with another entity type (or types), or a combination of the two.

55.3.5.3 Relationship type rules

1. There must be no hanging relationship types – each must relate one entity type to another (not necessarily distinct).
2. There must be no many-to-many relationship types.
3. There must be no superfluous relationship types (according to the earlier guidelines).

55.3.5.4 Attribute rules

1. Attributes of an entity type must relate specifically to that entity type, and not to any of its associations with others.
2. Each attribute must be associated with a single value set.

Although a formulation satisfying this list of rules is internally consistent, it is not necessarily correct. The resulting specification might be of a hypothetical universe of discourse that has little or nothing to do with the actual problem at hand! This more nebulous issue is the scope of the validation exercise.

55.3.6 Validation of conceptual specifications

A conceptual specification developed using the above method provides a document for discussion with the eventual user of the system, or indeed anyone who has an understanding of the universe of discourse that has been modelled. The purpose of such discussions must be to establish that nothing is incorrect or incomplete. This is the most significant validation exercise that can be applied. Other than agreeing that the formulation is an accurate reflection of the user's perception of the universe of discourse there is little validation that can be performed at this point in the development process.

There are many ways of formulating a universe of discourse, and although all might be argued to be equally correct, not all are necessarily equally useful. The formalization of principles for measuring usefulness of specifications at this level is not yet sufficiently well understood, but the following points are pertinent:

1. The concepts represented in the specification should be natural to the user, and not artificially contrived for the purposes of the exercise – the dangers of introducing conveniences are that misunderstandings between designer and user might easily take root therein, and the user might begin to feel insecure at the disappearance of traditionally held terms.
2. Notwithstanding the above, if two specifications are agreed to be equally correct and friendly to the user, then the simpler of the two is preferable – a specification is simpler than another if it contains fewer concepts (entity and relationship types).

To an extent, the validation procedure of the logical design stage offers a further opportunity for validation of conceptual specifications.

55.3.7 Summary

The end-products from a conceptual analysis exercise include:

1. A diagrammatic specification that describes the universe of discourse in terms of entity types, associations between entity types, and attributes.
2. Textual definitions of the details of the entity types, associations and attributes identified, held as design documentation in the data dictionary.

Examples of the application of the method described previously are given in Whittington (1988).

55.4 Logical design

55.4.1 Objectives

Logical design is the process whereby a conceptual specification of some universe of discourse is transformed into a logical specification of a database. The target of the design is a collection of relation definitions. These are first-cut relation designs, that will be subject to performance analysis during the next stage of the development process. There are two good reasons for adopting the relation as a logical design notation:

1. The simplicity and clarity of relation definitions.
2. The possibility of prototyping a logical design against a relational DBMS.

55.4.2 Deriving a collection of database relations

The following steps guarantee to generate a collection of database relations capable of representing the objects of a universe of discourse, as captured by an ERA formulation. Naming conventions are suggested in each step, principally to allow the method to progress automatically; these conventions need not, of course, be followed.

55.4.2.1 Step 1: First structures

For each entity type in the conceptual specification, define a relation.

1. The name of the relation is the same as that of the entity type.
2. The attributes of the relation include all of those of the entity type, and their names are unchanged.
3. The domains of the attributes are the value sets of the entity type attributes, with names unchanged.

55.4.2.2 Step 2: Establish primary keys

In the following, the identifier of an entity type means its full identifier, including any attributes necessary by virtue of supertypes or identification dependencies. For each relation defined in Step 1:

1. If the relation derives from an entity type that is not identification dependent on any others, then the primary key of the relation is simply the identifier of that entity type.
2. If the relation derives from an identification-dependent entity type, the following apply:

   (a) If the entity type is identification dependent on a single entity type (that is, if it is a characteristic entity type), then the primary key of the relation is the combination of the identifier of the superior entity type and the identifier of the entity type itself. The names and domains of the imported attributes are unchanged.
   (b) If the entity type is identification dependent on two or more entity types (that is, if it is an associative entity type), then the primary key of the relation is the combination of the identifiers of all superior entity types, plus any identification-key attributes of its own (which may or may not exist). As with the previous rule, the names and domains of any imported attributes are unchanged.

3. If the relation derives from an entity that is a subtype of another, then the primary key of the relation derived from the supertype becomes that relation's primary key.

55.4.2.3 Step 3: Establish foreign keys

For each relation defined in Step 1:

1. For each one-to-many relationship type in which the entity type from which the relation derives participates as a 'to' entity type (i.e. at the 'many' end of the relationship type), include the identifier of the 'from' entity type (i.e. at the 'one' end) as foreign-key attribute(s).
2. If, for the relationship type in question, there is a role name for the 'from' entity type and the identifier involved consists of a single attribute, then the foreign-key attribute (with domain unchanged) in the relation should be given that role name; otherwise, the names and domains of imported attributes are unchanged.

55.4.2.4 Step 4: Establish classification keys

Classification keys are attributes that state, for supertype-relation tuples, which of the subtypes that tuple is associated with, and hence in which other relation(s) can be found further applicable details. Values of classification keys are entity sub-type names; hence, the domain of all classification-key attributes is the domain of names. For each category of subtyping:

1. If the category is exclusive (i.e. non-overlapping) then the relation derived from the supertype of the category should be given, as an additional non-primary-key attribute, a classification-key attribute with the same name as the category.
2. If the category is inclusive (i.e. potentially overlapping) then define a new relation as follows:

   (a) The name of the relation is the name of the category.
   (b) The primary key of the relation is the combination of the primary key of the relation derived from the supertype entity type and the classification key resulting from the category, whose name is the name of the category (singularized where possible).
   (c) There are no attributes other than those that comprise the primary key.

55.4.2.5 Step 5: Refinement

It is possible for logically redundant relations to result from applying the above rules in the following instances:

1. When an entity type has been defined even though only an attribute reference to it from some other entity type was in fact required, the relation derived from the entity type will simply duplicate information held elsewhere (because the resulting foreign keys will not lead to anything).
2. When an entity subtype has been defined, but has no attributes of its own (other than its primary-key attributes inherited from its supertype) then again, the relation derived will simply duplicate information contained elsewhere, this time in the relation derived from the supertype.

In such cases the logically redundant relation is removed from the logical specification. Retaining such relations is not erroneous, and they will almost certainly be removed following later design stages in any case, but the designer can be spared some unnecessary effort by this simple filtering process.

55.4.3 Verification of logical specifications

If the above method is applied correctly, then the resulting relations will be internally consistent. Any modifications produced by the validation checks might, however, introduce inconsistencies, and so the following checks for consistency are provided.

55.4.3.1 Naming rules

1. Each relation must have a unique name.
2. Relations must not contain attributes with duplicated names.
3. Each domain must have a unique name.

55.4.3.2 Structuring rules

1. Each attribute must be associated with a single domain.
2. Each relation must have a primary key.
3. Each foreign key in any relation must correspond to a primary key in some other relation.

55.4.4 Validation of logical specifications

55.4.4.1 Normalization of relations

Normalization is a technique that can be used in both the design and validation of logical designs. As a design technique, it encourages a bottom-up approach, in contrast to the top-down approach advocated by the conceptual analysis method used previously, which is sometimes useful for comparison with the results achieved. SSADM (NCC, 1986) advocates the use of both approaches, and the reconciliation of results.

As a validation technique, normalization checks for potential anomalies in the structures designed. Such anomalies in fact reflect an error either in conceptual analysis or in the derivation of relations from a conceptual specification. A correct conceptual specification results in fully normalized relations. Consequently, the technique is a useful second check on the previous stage.

A succession of normal forms have been proposed. For details of the emergence of these the reader is directed to Codd (1971, 1972 and 1974), Fagin (1977) and Date (1986), and for an alternative tutorial, to Kent (1983). Normalization is a refinement process that checks a collection of relations for conformance to each of these. Any relation found not to meet the definition of a normal form is modified accordingly, typically by decomposition into several smaller relations that do satisfy the given rule. A relation that satisfies all of the rules is said to be fully normalized.

The normal forms are, to a large extent, formalizations of common sense; they have been investigated at some length and constitute by now a mature and widely used technique.

55.4.4.2 Functional dependencies

A fundamental concept is that of functional dependence (FD). An attribute a^1 is functionally dependent on another, a^2, if and only if, for a single value of a^2 there is exactly one corresponding value of a^1. We denote a functional dependence by a single-headed arrow from the functional determinant to the dependent attribute, viz:

$$\begin{array}{ccc} & \text{functional} & \\ & \text{dependence} & \\ a^2 & \rightarrow & a^1 \\ \text{(functional determinant)} & & \text{(dependent attribute)} \end{array}$$

For example, there is an FD of country name on airport name, because, for each value of airport name there is exactly one corresponding country name value (viz. airport name→country name).

55.4.4.3 First normal form (1NF)

A relation is said to be 1NF if and only if:

1. All of its non-key attributes are functionally dependent on at least some component of its primary key.
2. All of its attributes are atomic (that is, do not have hidden internal structure).

The relational model is not able to cope with non-first normal form (NF²) relations – its manipulation concept is based on the assumption that such structures are illegal. This assumption is not, however, universally appropriate. The subject of NF² relations has been studied (Hitchcock, 1976; Abiteboul et al., 1984; Afsarmanesh et al., 1985) as a theoretical extension for use in databases for certain application areas (particularly computer-aided design and information retrieval).

A pragmatic design stance apropos 1NF is to view it as a warning of potential difficulties. Attributes that have non-simple values should, however, be examined closely. Because some other normal forms require relations to be 1NF, we taken the view that a relation within which all non-key attributes are dependent upon some component of the primary key, and that has acceptable compound attributes, is 1NF.

55.4.4.4 Second normal form (2NF)

A relation is 2NF if and only if:

1. It is 1NF.
2. All of its non-key attributes are functionally dependent on *the whole* of its primary key.

Consider, for example, the following relation.

Stops (<u>flight_number, airport_ code;</u> stop_number, airport_name)

In this, stop_number is functionally dependent upon the compound (flight_number, airport_code) – because we assume that a Flight only stops once at any given Airport – but airport_name is functionally dependent only on airport_code. The relation is not, therefore, 2NF.

In this relation, the fact that LGW is the code for London Gatwick will be duplicated as many times as there are flights connected with that airport; and the same applies for all other airports. One criticism of the relation might therefore be that of wastefulness. While this would be a valid criticism, it is not the most worrying. Two further problems are of more consequence:

1. The duplication of a fact leaves open the possibility of inconsistency.
2. It is not possible to record the code and name of an airport unless there are flights connected with it – this will cause difficulties with new (planned) airports, or airports to which operations are temporarily suspended.

The above difficulties are typical of non-2NF relations, and result entirely from the existence in a relation of an attribute that is not dependent on the whole of its key. The problems are removed by decomposing the relation into two or more smaller ones that are not at odds with the rule. In the above case, this simply requires that Stops be broken into:

Stops (<u>flight number/codes, airport_code/codes;</u> stop_number/pos_ints)

and:

Airports (<u>airport_code/codes;</u> airport_name/names)

The difficulties are now all resolved:

1. There is no wasted storage.
2. Each fact is recorded exactly once and so there is no possibility of inconsistencies creeping in.
3. We can record Airport details independently of the Flights which operate through them.

The fact that the original Stops relation was derived from a conceptual specification indicates that the latter was erroneous in its formulation of Airports and Stops. Presumably it had been assumed that details of Airports need not be represented by a separate entity type, but by the attributes of the Stops entity type. The incorrectness of this decision has been brought to light through normalization.

55.4.4.5 Third normal form (3NF)

A relation is 3NF if and only if every determinant is a candidate key.

Recall that a determinant is any attribute on which any other is functionally dependent. A candidate key in a relation is a group of (one or more) attributes that will serve as a primary key. A relation might have more than one candidate key.

The corrected relation Stops above in fact has only one candidate key – the compound (flight_number, airport_code), but the relation Airports has two: airport_code and airport _name. In the latter case, either attribute will serve as a primary key.

To see the effect of this rule, suppose, that the rules for logical design produce the following relation:

Airports (airport_code; airport_name, country_name, continent_name)

This relation is 2NF but it is not 3NF because continent _name is functionally dependent on country_name, thus making country_name a determinant, and country_name is not a candidate key (because there is not necessarily only one Airport in any given Country). The only candidate keys in the relation are airport_code and airport_name.

As with the non-2NF relation discussed previously, there is duplication of data – the continent of a country is given for each airport in that country – which in turn brings further problems:

1. There is a danger of inconsistencies entering the relation.
2. The impossibility of associating a country with a continent until that country has an airport with an established code.

These are comparable to the non-2NF problems, and are likewise resolved simply by splitting the relation into smaller relations that satisfy the rule. In this case the following will suffice:

Airports (airport_code/names; airport_name/names, country_name/names)

and:

Countries (country_name/names; continent_name/names)

These relations are 3NF, and can be seen to be free from the above difficulties. As in the non-2NF example, it is apparent that the non-3NF relation originated from an erroneous conceptual specification that did not recognize the need for an entity type to represent Countries, but that attempted to capture country details as attributes of the Airport entities.

55.4.4.6 Fourth normal form (4NF)

In the majority of cases, satisfying the rules of the first three normal forms is sufficient evidence of the validity of a relation design. There are, however, cases of relations which suffer from much the same problems as those shown with non-2NF and non-3NF relations previously, and yet those relations abide by the definition of 3NF. As an example, consider the following relation that holds, independently, the days of the week on which a flight operates, and the seasons during which a flight operates:

Flights (flight_number/codes, day/days, season/seasons)

This relation is all key and so it is 2NF. Furthermore, there are no functional determinants other than the combination of all three attributes, and this combination is a candidate key – in fact it is the only one, and so the relation is 3NF. But an examination of it soon shows that it is a structure that suffers from much the same problems as the undesirable structures met previously.

The relation will involve significant duplication. One might suggest that, because seasons and days are independent, only the first day (or season) value for a flight need be replicated, and the existence of the remaining combinations can be inferred, but such a scheme is open to misinterpretation.

The duplication, as previously, brings with it several problems:

1. There are ambiguities, such as, in the above example, that raised by the presence of Monday tuples for KG2107 for some seasons but not others – how should that be interpreted?
2. We cannot record the seasons for a flight until we know which days it will operate on, and *vice versa*.

So, this example shows a relation design that satisfies 3NF but which nevertheless suffers from the kinds of problems that 3NF attempts to overcome. Such cases are the object of the definition of fourth normal form.

The most useful definition of a 4NF relation is that given in Kent (1983): a relation is 4NF if it is 3NF and contains no more than one *independent, multi-valued fact*. Tuples in the first interpretation of Flights contain two multi-valued facts: one relating a flight with a day on which it operates, and another relating a flight with an applicable season. We can resolve this by decomposing the relation into two projections:

Days (flight_number/codes, day/days)

and:

Fares (flight_number/codes, season/season)

These relations are both all key, but do not suffer from the above kinds of problem. They are 3NF and each contain exactly one multi-valued fact (which, obviously, is independent) and must, therefore, be 4NF.

One must be careful to distinguish between the case of the above example, where the dependencies are independent (that is, where the season does not depend upon, or determine, the day of a flight), and the case where the three attributes are interdependent. If it were the case that the season determines the set of days that a flight operates, then the structure given previously contains only one independent multi-valued fact, and hence would be 4NF. It would not, however, be 5NF – see Date (1986).

55.4.4.7 Prototyping

Normalization is an analytical validation technique. This can be complemented by additional, simulation-based methods.

One reason for adopting relation definitions as a notation for logical database specification is the possibility of prototype database construction. The relations designed by the methods described above can be implemented, probably with small data volumes, without great cost, using a relational DBMS.

Having mounted a prototype database, queries corresponding to the principal retrieval applications can be formulated, perhaps in a simplified form, ignoring output formats, and so on. Furthermore, where such facilities are available, the application generator capabilities of the DBMS can be used to develop sample database update screens.

A working model of the desired system can thus be constructed without significant expense, with the objective of eliciting further response from the eventual users of the system regarding its functional requirements. Such feedback at a stage in the development process before detailed technical decisions have been made can be instrumental in avoiding problems later on, after further development resources have been committed.

55.5 Structural design

55.5.1 Objectives

At this stage in the development process, performance considerations can be introduced. In a case where one is confident that the relations so far achieved satisfy the performance requirements of the database system, this stage is trivial. One can assume a one-to-one correspondence between the relation structures arrived at during logical design and the structures implemented. Such confidence, however, is normally only present when the system in question is small in terms of the number of relations involved, and the requirements are not critical.

On the other hand, if one suspects that the relations so far achieved might result in inefficiencies, or if one at least cannot be sure without further analysis that there will be no such problems, then further effort must be devoted to structural development prior to the choice of appropriate underlying physical access mechanisms.

Furthermore, in cases where one intends to implement the database system by means of a DBMS that supports elaborate inter-record structuring concepts (for example, a navigational DBMS) then the effort involved in designing suitable structures becomes significant. Hence, the design activities of this stage of the development process and, therefore, the classes of techniques that are appropriate, can be divided into:

1. The choice of record type structures for implementation.
2. In the case of navigational DBMS, the choice of (inter-record-type) link types.

55.5.2 Structural design method

The broad logic of the structural stage is as follows:

- *Step 1.* Produce an initial collection of record type structures derived from the relations of the logical specification.
- *Step 2.* If a navigational DBMS is to be used for implementation, produce from the structures a collection of link types, thus giving an initial network design.
- *Step 3.* Apply the verification rules to the design, and make any modifications that are necessary to enforce its internal consistency.
- *Step 4.* Apply the validation rules to the design. If the design achieved is capable of satisfying operational requirements then the structural design stage is complete, otherwise:

    1. Apply the restructuring techniques to generate potential structural redesigns.
    2. If the DBMS in question is navigational, generate corresponding link types.
    3. Go to Step 3.

The steps relating to navigational database design are omitted from the following discussion; the interested reader is referred to Whittington (1988).

55.5.3 Record structures and restructuring operations

Record type definitions are rather like relation definitions in that they are linear structures with cross references (that is, foreign keys). They are unlike relation definitions, however, in that they do not necessarily have unique user identifiers (that is, primary keys). We assume that each record of any type has an internal, system identifier. In most cases however, a user-identification key does exist, and these are of interest.

Record type structures are defined by the fields of which they consist, each of which has an associated data type, together with an indication of any uniqueness or non-null conditions. Field data types are the structural-level equivalent of domains at the logical level: they define, in terms of commonly-supported data types, the internal form of a field. We use the same notation as that used for relations to describe record structures in terms of fields, types, and unique identifiers.

The restructuring of logical relation definitions to produce structures suitable for implementation requires a set of information-preserving operators that define (implicitly) the available options. The following operators combine the capabilities of the traditional relational operators with the new capabilities required of this context, and are guaranteed not to lose any (conceptual) information. They are four in number: composition, vertical decomposition, horizontal decomposition, and flattening. Each transforms one or more structures into one or more others.

55.5.3.1 *Composition*

Two structures can be composed according to a composition predicate (a set of field names), to yield a structure defined by taking a union of the fields of the original structures. The definition of the operator covers both horizontal (*cf.* relational union) and vertical (*cf.* relational join) composition possibilities. It is rather like a generalization covering both union and join operators – it is comparable with the generalized union operator defined in Hall *et al.* (1975) and the outer join operator defined in Codd (1979).

Each record of each participating record type contributes to at least one of the resulting records:

1. In the case of two identical structures this operator defaults to the traditional relational union operator.
2. In cases where the participating structures differ, the effect is more like a relational join: corresponding structures are composed where the composition predicate holds; in other cases a structure is padded out with null values, meaning value inapplicable.

This operator provides a very powerful mechanism for composing normalized logical structures into others, which may or may not be normalized. In the extreme case we can compose a single, universal structure that allows the implementation of a database as a single record type. Clearly, though, there is a need for some mechanism to implement the *value inapplicable* value. Many DBMSs offer direct support for some (*null*) values.

55.5.3.2 *Vertical decomposition*

The vertical decomposition operator allows the decomposition of a structure, along the vertical axis, into a collection of smaller structures, each of which has some subset of the fields of the original structure. To this definition we impose the restriction that each resulting structure must contain the whole of the identifier of the original. It is comparable to repeated application of the projection operator of the relational algebra.

55.5.3.3 *Horizontal decomposition*

The horizontal decomposition operator is analogous to repeated application of the relational restriction operator. It allows a record type structure to be decomposed, along the horizontal axis, into subsets of its records according to a partitioning predicate. Each record of the original structure belongs to at least one of the resulting structures. Partitioning predicates are of two types:

1. General restriction predicates.
2. Uniqueness predicates.

The second type of predicate can be used only when there is a field that can take only a small number of predictable values. This can also be illustrated using the existing Times structure:

Times (flight_number/char(6), day/char(3);
            dep_time/decimal(4,2), arr_time/decimal(4,2))

and the operation:

h_decompose (Times; day)

Times is thereby partitioned into seven separate structures, each of which gives flight times for a different day of the week:

Times_Mon (flight_number/char(6);
            dep_time/decimal(4,2),arr_time/decimal(4,2))
Times_Tue (flight_number/char(6);
            dep_time/decimal(4,2),arr_time/decimal(4,2))
Times_Wed (flight_number/char(6);
            dep_time/decimal(4,2),arr_time/decimal(4,2))

etc.

Note that we have taken information that was previously held as field values and built it into the structure names.

55.5.3.4 *Flattening*

The flattening operator has no analogue in the relational algebra. Rather like the previous one, though, it allows us to move information from one representation to another, in this case from field values to field names; and also, as with the second form of the previous operator, it applies only to fields whose types (domains) are discrete and small in cardinality. It has the effect of flattening out such field types into the structure definition.

For example, consider again the Times structure:

Times (flight_number/char(6), day/char(3);
            dep_time/decimal(4,2),arr_time/decimal(4,2))

The operation:

flatten (Times; day)

has the effect of flattening the day field of that structure to yield:

Flat_Times   (flight_number/char(6);   Mon_dep_time/
            decimal(4,2),
            Mon_arr_time/decimal(4,2),   Tue_dep_time/
            decimal(4,2),
            Tue_arr_time/decimal(4,2),   Wed_dep_time/
            decimal(4,2),
            Wed_arr_time/decimal(4,2), . . .,
            Sun_arr_time/decimal(4,2))

This and the previous example illustrate the fluidity of representation that is possible in database design. Information can equally well be represented as field values, as field names, and as structure names. The combinatorial explosion in possible restructuring choices clearly presents design problems but at the same time presents ample opportunity to the ingenious designer.

55.5.4 Techniques for choosing restructuring operations

We now turn to the examination of techniques that can point towards useful restructurings.

To a large extent these require some knowledge of the application requirements and patterns. In a green-field development, such figures may be difficult to obtain, even as estimates, and in such cases the best strategy is to select the most flexible design available, rather than to make any restricting decisions on the basis of assumptions that may prove false. There is an element of uncertainty in almost all development exercises. This point underlines the requirement to build upon a DBMS that offers the flexibility to modify a design at a reasonable cost after implementation.

A tool on which several techniques are based is the transaction matrix. A transaction matrix is a table whose columns represent transactions – database application requirements – and whose rows represent data fields, as illustrated in *Figure 55.10*.

	Transaction 1 (Frequency)	Transaction 2 (Frequency)	Transaction 3 (Frequency) ...
Field 1	M	R	
Field 2	M		X
Field 3	X	R	R
Field 4	M		C

Figure 55.10 A transaction matrix

A transaction matrix shows, associated with each transaction, a frequency (for example, 1000 per day), as one basis for weighting the importance that is given to respective requirements.

A mark is entered at matrix position (i,j) if field i is manipulated by transaction j. There are four types of mark:

M   signifies that the specified data field is modified by the stated transaction.
R   signifies that the specified data field is output by the stated transaction.
C   signifies that the specified data field is used by the stated transaction for the computation of some other value.
X   signifies that the specified data field is used by the stated transaction, perhaps as an input parameter, or a join predicate, but is not modified, not used in any computation, and not output by the transaction.

The following approach to transaction matrix construction is recommended:

1. Produce the column headings by listing the anticipated transactions of significance (input, update, and retrieval transactions should be included), together with their predicted frequencies.
2. Produce the row headings by anticipating the data fields that are input, used, and output by each transaction listed above; include any requirements for totals, averages, and other derivations.
3. Express each transaction as a relational query against the current structures, and mark the matrix cells accordingly.

Transaction matrices provide a useful basis for a range of design techniques, some of which are discussed below.

55.5.4.1 Field-grouping analysis

A transaction matrix highlights groups of fields that are commonly required together, and which might therefore suggest restructuring. The following rules can be applied to generate restructuring operations that are worthy of further examination:

1. If the frequency with which a group of fields corresponding to a subset of an existing structure is touched, for whatever purpose, is greater than that with which the structure as a whole is required, then a vertical decomposition is worthy of consideration.
2. If the frequency with which a group of fields corresponding to a superset of an existing structure is touched is greater than that with which the individual structures themselves are required, then a composition might be in order.

The most useful interpretation of an apparent grouping is as a prompt, which either confirms or questions an existing structure. The role of the designer at this point cannot be overemphasized.

55.5.4.2 Temporal normal form analysis

It has been observed that data fields with common life-spans often make good groupings for record type structures (Rolland and Richard, 1982). Temporal normal form simply recommends that groups of fields whose values come into being together, and cease to be of interest simultaneously, should be considered as candidate structures.

Transaction matrices assist in temporal normal form analysis by showing the field groupings used by update transactions (that is, groups of fields marked 'M'). From these groupings, any type of restructuring operation might be suggested, but, as with the previous technique, it should be stressed that the approach is again one of throwing up an idea, which may or may not be useful, for further consideration.

In many cases there is more certainty associated with the requirements and frequency of update transactions than with the retrieval details. This, together with its simplicity, makes this technique especially attractive.

55.5.4.3 Key analysis

This technique is not so broad in its scope as are the previous ones. Its scope is restricted to the fields that are used as access keys (that is, those that are marked 'X' for at least one transaction), and it offers a common-sense approach to reducing the storage requirements of a database whilst increasing the reliability of access.

The technique involves considering each access key in turn. If a given key is a compound (that is, consists of two or more fields), then a code might be introduced into the relevant structure, replacing that compound as the access key. Similarly, if an access key comprises a single field, but values of that field are subject to mistyping (which applies especially in the case of text fields), then the possibility of a code should be investigated.

It is sometimes the case that, by replacing an existing, unsuitable access key by a more efficient and reliable code, a vertical decomposition is possible, taking out the previous key into a lexicon structure. For example, suppose that airport codes did not already exist, and we were faced with the following:

Airports (airport_name/char(30); country_name/char(30))

and suppose that airport_name was a commonly used access key. We might then introduce airport_code as a replacement access key, and consider the vertical decomposition resulting in the following pair of structures:

Airports (airport_code/char(3); country_name/char(30))
Airport_Lexicon (airport_code/char(3);
    airport_name/char(30))

The advantages in the above are clear enough:

1. Textual mis-match difficulties are avoided in transactions requiring direct access to Airports.
2. Join operations involving airport_code will be more efficient than they would previously have been involving airport_name.
3. All foreign keys which refer to Airports will be reduced in size, thus saving storage.

These illustrate the advantages of such restructuring in the general case. The disadvantage is that such codes may not be meaningful to users on output, and, if the fields that they replace will often be given as input or required to be output, then there will be additional join operations to recompose the original structures. Indeed, this latter case can be a reason for doing the opposite of the above, and replacing a coded value with a rather more cumbersome field, so as to avoid the cost of a join operation. As with all restructuring considerations, the trade-offs here need to be calculated carefully.

55.5.4.4 Derivation analysis

Systems vary greatly in the extent to which data values are dependent computationally on others. In systems where there are a large number of calculable items, there is a trade-off between the cost of storing values (computing on input) and the cost of calculating values (computing on output).

Derivation analysis involves considering each calculable item, indicated by the existence of fields marked 'C' in the matrix, in terms of:

1. The cost of its derivation.
2. The storage required for values.
3. The cost of computing values on input (that is, whenever parameters are modified).
4. The cost of computing values on output (that is, whenever required in order to satisfy a query).

To quantify the trade-off in a particular case, we need some measure of the relative costs of time and storage. The following cost equations might then be used to measure the strength of each case:

$$\text{computing on input} = (S \times \text{cost of storage})$$
$$+ (T \times \text{cost of computation} \times \text{frequency of recomputation})$$
$$\text{computing on output} = \text{cost of computation} \times \text{frequency of computation}$$

In the first of the above, S and T are constants, where $S + T = 1$, describing the relative costs of storage and response time, respectively.

Thus, the only forms of restructuring suggested by derivation analysis are composition of a structure with a derivable field (to include it as a 'compute on input' field), and vertical decomposition of a structure (to remove from it a field that is to be computed on output).

55.5.5 Verification of structural specifications

The verification of a structural database specification consists of checking its objects for internal consistency. The following groups of rules define the consistency requirements.

55.5.5.1 *Naming rules*

1. Each record type must have a unique name.
2. Fields within record types must have unique names.
3. Each link type must have a unique name.

55.5.5.2 *Record type rules*

1. Each field in each record type must be associated with a defined data type.

55.5.6 Validation of structural specifications

Validation of structural database specifications corresponds to the issue of proving, to a reasonable degree of precision, that a chosen design is capable of satisfying its performance requirements with regard to resource usage and response times. We therefore need techniques that enable us to put fingers on sizes and speeds. We take these separate but related issues in turn.

55.5.6.1 *Estimation of storage requirements*

Given a record type structure we can determine approximate mean and maximum storage requirements for the operational data of that structure under a particular DBMS. What we cannot determine at this stage is the storage requirement for non-operational data, such as indexes, of a structure. We can, however, make assumptions in advance of detailed design work.

The mean storage requirement for the operational data of a record type structure is given by the formula:

record type overhead
+ (mean length of record × expected number of records)

The maximum conceivable size of a record type is also useful:

record type overhead
+ (maximum length of record × maximum number of records).

In these formulae:

1. The 'record type overhead' variables are DBMS constants.
2. The 'record length' variables need to be calculated according to whether the DBMS in question supports fixed- or variable-length fields, taking account of any record overhead that the DBMS requires; and
3. The 'number of records' variables need to be ascertained, either from analysis of existing volumes of data, if the system under development is a replacement for an existing – manual or automated – one; or from user expectation if it is a new system.

One should assume at least a minimal level of indexing of structures and, as a rule of thumb to account for the storage requirements that this poses, one should add one-third to the figures obtained above.

Further to this, one should assume that storage utilization will be in the region of two-thirds (that is, that approximately one-third of the storage apparently occupied by the structure will in fact be unused at any point in time), and hence that a further one-third needs to be added to the storage estimate for indexed, operational data.

Finally, to account for other DBMS storage overheads (schema data, transaction logs, and so on), the DBMS documentation should be consulted. This latter overhead should not be underestimated, and it is important to remember that this is, to a large extent, independent of the actual level of operational data that is stored.

The above considerations enable one to put a reasonable figure (say, plus or minus 10%) on the storage requirements of a given collection of structures, which enables reasonably intelligent assessment whether a given database system will fit on whatever secondary storage may be available. This is not, however, the only storage issue. There are also DBMS storage constraints that have to be considered:

1. Do any structures comprise more fields than the DBMS permits?
2. Are there more structures than the DBMS permits?
3. Are any structures likely to become larger than the maximum size that the DBMS permits (for example, many DBMSs do not permit structures to span discs)?

55.5.6.2 *Estimation of processing performance*

Estimating likely processing speeds for application requirements is a more difficult question. There are two approaches that can be taken: analysis and simulation.

Analytic performance prediction requires figures (say, expected number of disc access operations) for each of the major types of database operations. Such formulae do not exist for the general case, because they are highly dependent on the operating system/DBMS configuration and the values of the DBMS installation parameters (such as memory buffer availability). It is possible, however, to derive such formulae by experiment upon a particular installation, and thus to perform reasonably accurate cost predictions in that particular context.

Alternatively, simplified analytic methods can be adopted that aim not to put precise figures on transaction response, but to indicate the relative workloads involved in processing transactions, and hence to give a broad impression of whether a given transaction will execute quickly, moderately quickly, slowly, or painfully slowly.

The simplest of these methods takes as its unit of database work the relational algebra operation: each transaction is analysed in terms of the number of algebraic operations it logically comprises. An example based upon this approach is given in Whittington (1988). A more sophisticated version of this approach assigns weightings to the various operators (for example, restrict = 2, join = 5) and attempts thereby to give a more accurate ranking.

Accurate analytical response figures are expensive to calculate. The alternative – a simulation-based approach – can be attractive by comparison. The development of a prototype database comprising the structures designed allows the formulation of queries corresponding to the database access elements of the application requirements (retrieval and update), and these in turn allow timings to be carried out, indicating at least the likely order of the performance that will be achieved. Depending on the way that the relevant DBMS operates, it might be necessary to precompile queries in order to yield more realistic estimates.

This latter approach may not, of course, be cost-efficient, especially in a non-relational environment, where considerable effort has to be invested in order to construct the prototype. In such cases one must accept the high (but relatively lower) cost of desk-checking the acceptability of a design in performance terms. The dangers of implementing a structural specification that cannot possibly meet its performance requirements are clear enough. If this is so, then it is as well to be aware at this stage (where compromise might be easier to achieve) than when further resources have been committed.

55.5.7 Summary

Structural design, more than any of the preceding stages, is a balancing exercise. There are three principal areas of trade-off:

1. Normalized relations are highly durable structures; they are based on natural dependencies (which rarely change) and therefore it is unlikely that the introduction (at some later time) of new data items will cause catastrophic restructuring problems. This suggests that the likely stability of a database system must be borne in mind as a broader criterion during this stage of design.

   The trade-off here is short-term efficiency with uncertain durability against medium (or low) efficiency and long-term confidence.

2. Clearly it may be necessary to hold inelegant structures in order to satisfy immutable processing requirements, but whenever such structures are examined it is crucially important that all of their implications are considered. Additional storage volume is an easily-calculated consequence, but the less quantifiable integrity conditions that pose additional updating loads, and risks of unpleasant inconsistency, must not be forgotten.

   The trade-off here is efficiency of certain types of transaction against efficiency of others, and overall throughput.

3. Decisions intended to bring about improvements in processing performance tend to have a detrimental effect on storage requirements, and *vice versa*.

   The trade-off here is simply storage space against processing time.

55.6 Physical design

Broadly speaking, the objective of physical design is to select an implementable organization whereby:

1. The structures thus far designed can be expected to operate according to the performance requirements of the system.
2. The resulting system can be expected to satisfy a range of managerial requirements by virtue of a defined configuration.

Physical database design divides into two areas:

1. *The selection of a database system configuration.* Recall that a configuration for a database system relates to whether it is to be stored in its entirety at a single site or distributed across a network of sites, and whether it is to be implemented as a system or as a federation of independent subsystems. A specific configuration is therefore

   (a) A fragmentation scheme, a mapping of structures to fragments to be held at specified sites
   (b) A decision as to whether these fragments are to be implemented as a single database or as separate databases.

2. *The selection of an appropriate internal organization.* An internal organization consists of, for each record and link type of each fragment:

   (a) An internal representation.
   (b) Access mechanisms to support the manipulation of that representation.

55.6.1 Selecting a database system configuration

55.6.1.1 Database distribution

The reasons for considering a distributed configuration fall into three classes, as follows.

1. Organizational reasons, such as:

   (a) Users consequently having some degree of local autonomy over their data, physically as well as logically.

   (b) Systems exhibiting a high resilience to failure (also referred to as survivability), which enables them to continue to function (albeit to a reduced level of functionality) even in the event of damage to one or more sites.

2. Performance reasons, such as:

   (c) Reduced volumes (and hence faster searching) of local database fragments to which the majority of processing is directed.
   (d) Increased overall processing resources available, and the ability of a distributed system actually to process transactions in parallel.
   (e) Reduced data and/or program transmission costs for remote applications.

3. Evolutionary reasons, such as:

   (f) The pre-existence of some or all components of the system under development as separate systems on different machines.
   (g) The ability to add further sites in the future in a natural way as and when their desirability is dictated by organizational or performance reasons.

Clearly, distributed configurations also have their drawbacks, largely stemming from additional managerial (human and software) overheads, and design difficulties.

The decision of whether or not to distribute seldom reduces to a simple cost–benefit analysis on the basis of the quantifiable (especially performance) criteria. The less quantifiable organizational and evolutionary criteria can easily outweigh any apparent advantages that are to be achieved performance-wise. A distribution criterion is a scheme that reflects the reasoning behind the decision to distribute, and consists of the above factors (a) to (g), each associated with a weighting (the sum of which is equal to 1) that represents its importance.

If a database system is to be distributed, then there are technical decisions to be made regarding the fragmentation of the design over the network – the fragmentation scheme to be adopted. The problem can be stated as follows:

> Given a structural database specification, design a collection of fragments and a mapping of these onto the sites of a network, where each fragment consists of some subset of the structures of the specification, each structure is allocated to at least one fragment, and the chosen fragmentation satisfies the distribution criterion.

55.6.1.2 Fragmentation methods

As with structural design, a useful approach is to adopt techniques that throw up recommended fragmentations, which can then be analysed for their profitability. Also in common with structural design, it is useful to begin with a form of transaction matrix, only in this context we are concerned principally with the sites at which transactions originate. Such matrices are more appropriately called distribution matrices, because they illustrate the logical distribution of processing with reference to the record structures. *Figure 55.11* illustrates a simple distribution matrix.

The term site is used in this matrix. Site can be interpreted logically, as a particular source of transactions within an organization, even if that source is not geographically distinct from others. This broad interpretation makes the techniques appropriate also in the case of non-distributed systems where there are advantages to be gained from internal (physical and/or logical) partitions, as supported by many DBMSs.

For each site, a distribution matrix shows which record structures are processed in any way at all by transactions

	Site 1 (Frequency 1)	Site 2 (Frequency 2)	Site 3 (Frequency 3)
Record Type 1	UH	RV	UH
Record Type 2	BA		
Record Type 3	RH	UA	RV
Record Type 4	RV		UA

Figure 55.11 A simple distribution matrix

submitted at that site, and the total frequency of those transactions. In particular, it shows:

1. Whether a record structure is updated (U), retrieved (R), or both (B).
2. Whether, for any affected record structure, the relevant transactions affect only a horizontal partition (H), only a vertical partition (V), or all of the structure (A).

Such matrices enable the use of techniques analogous to some of those used during structural design.

55.6.1.3 Replication analysis

The principle behind this technique is comparable with that of grouping analysis. We examine the distribution matrix with a view to allocating record types, or, at least, those parts of them – horizontal or vertical – to fragments that reside wherever they are required for processing.

This technique consequently underplays the potential problem of consistency during updates that replicated data introduces. Clearly, this is one criterion that is analysed during detailed consideration of any recommendation.

55.6.1.4 Localization analysis

The principle behind this technique is comparable with that of temporal normal form analysis. We examine the sites of origin of updates to record types, or, at least, parts of them (horizontal or vertical), with a view to holding all types as close as possible to the source of their data.

This technique complements the previous one by putting more stress on update transactions, in recognition of the not-inconsiderable problems that these can bring in distributed systems.

Clearly, any further analysis following from each of these techniques has to address a finer-grained map of the logical distribution (that is, fields rather than record types), but the record type level is appropriate for first-cut analysis.

55.6.2 Verification of a fragmentation scheme

The verification rules for this exercise include equivalents to those of structural design, plus additional rules for fragmentation.

55.6.2.1 Naming rules

1. Each fragment must have a unique name.
2. Each record type within each fragment must have a unique name.
3. Fields within record types must have unique names.
4. Each link type within each fragment must have a unique name.

55.6.2.2 Record type rules

1. Each field in each record type must be associated with a defined data type.
2. Each record type must belong to at least one fragment.

55.6.2.3 Fragment rules

1. Each fragment must be assigned to at least one site.

55.6.3 Validation of a fragmentation scheme

This step is primarily concerned with checking the feasibility of a design with regard to the requirements of the system under development; or, put another way, with seeing whether a given design is a good one. At this stage we are concerned with all types of requirement: information, performance, and managerial. In summary, these consist of the following:

1. The information requirement at this stage requires that no information is lost during fragmentation. All structures of the previous design must be fully represented – horizontally and vertically – in the resulting scheme. This is guaranteed so long as the fragmentation process makes use only of the restructuring operators defined previously.
2. The resource (especially storage) restrictions at individual sites. This requires calculations along the lines of those carried out during structural design.
3. The response time requirements for individual transactions. This again requires calculations similar to those carried out previously, except that here we must take account of the cost of data transfer between sites where the need for this is implied.
4. The distribution criterion, the weighting of which must be represented in the design. This is really the crux of the matter. It steers the decision-making process towards a preferred fragmentation scheme on the grounds of broader organizational objectives.
5. The implementation technology, which must be capable of supporting the chosen design. There are now DBMSs (for example, ORACLE and INGRES) that provide transparent support for a range of distributed configurations, including replicated data, but it is important to check for any restrictions on distributed updates.

55.6.4 Federations versus systems

The decision here, essentially, is whether to impose a global requirement for integrity, or whether individual fragments can be implemented as separate databases, each of which is internally consistent, but between which there is a looser interrelation; a federation rather than a system.

The advantages of a federation, whether distributed or not, over a system divide into the following:

1. Organizational advantages, such as very high (logical or physical) local autonomy – perhaps required for reasons of security – in database management.
2. Performance advantages, such as freedom from the response overheads that result from updates to structures of a separate subsystem.
3. Evolutionary advantages, such as the existence of suitable sub-systems that can be coupled together into a federation.

Clearly, there are disadvantages too, especially where duplicated data is involved, and there might be considerable effort required in maintaining the federation, however loose it might appear on the surface. Because of this it is very unlikely that the decision to implement a federation would be taken purely on the grounds of performance advantages. It is normally the broader concerns expressed through organizational and evolutionary advantages that guide this decision.

55.6.5 Selecting internal organizations

55.6.5.1 Selecting internal representations

DBMSs normally represent records as contiguous collections of field values, each encoded according to one of a small collection of available methods. Individual field values within a record are distinguished by a variety of techniques (normally record maps, delimiter symbols, or some combination of the two), but this is typically fixed by the DBMS and out of the designer's control. The only general decision that is required to be made regarding record representation is therefore the encoding methods to be used for the field values.

Records of a given type are blocked into fixed-size blocks or pages, which are the transfer containers by means of which records will travel from disc into main storage. For some DBMSs there is a degree of flexibility available for the choice of block size, but normally this is set to some operating system default, typically of the order of 2, 3, or 4 kb.

55.6.5.2 Selecting access mechanisms

This task divides into that of choosing a single primary organization and a collection of (zero or more) secondary organizations for each record type. Recall that primary organizations dictate the methods of update and of primary key retrieval, whereas secondary organizations provide additional retrieval capabilities above and beyond this.

55.6.5.3 Primary organizations

Primary organizations are of four types: heaps, hashed organizations, sequential organizations, and indexed-sequential organizations. Particular DBMSs, however, may support different variants of each, or only some, of these organizations. In any development exercise, therefore, it is important to establish precisely the options that are available before considering the issue in detail.

The principal technique for selecting a primary organization is primary-access analysis. This is based on a primary-access matrix, an example of which is shown in *Figure 55.12*.

Primary-access matrices illustrate the pattern of primary-key access to record types by predicted transactions. In particular, for each record type they show whether transactions require:

1. Unique, primary key access (U).
2. Sorted, primary key access (S).
3. No primary key access.

From a primary-access matrix we can calculate for each record type the relative proportions, respectively, of:

1. Unique primary key access.
2. Sorting by primary key.
3. No primary key access.

	Transaction 1 (Frequency 1)	Transaction 2 (Frequency 2)	Transaction 3 (Frequency 3)
Record Type 1	U	U	
Record Type 2	S		U
Record Type 3	S	U	U
Record Type 4	U		S

Figure 55.12 A simple primary-access matrix

The following table then uses that information to direct one towards appropriate primary organization types for each record type.

	Unique access (%)	Sequential access (%)
Heap	< 5	< 5
Hashed	⩾ 50	< 5
Sequential	< 5	⩾ 50
Indexed-sequential	⩾ 5	⩾ 5

This technique is pragmatic in its strong bias towards indexed-sequential organizations, which offer the safest and most dependable solution in cases of uncertainty. In the event of a recommended type of organization not being available, the next best should be adopted; normally this will be indexed-sequential.

Where choice exists between static and dynamic forms of a preferred organization it is necessary to consider the stability of the data.

1. If data volumes are relatively static or growing slowly at a predictable rate, then a static form might produce better response without incurring the problems of poor storage utilization and chaotic degradation. Regular reorganization can be scheduled and managed in such an environment.
2. If, on the other hand, the pattern of updates is less predictable, or update volumes are high, then one should tend towards the dynamic form, which will better be able to handle the changing nature of its contents.

A further consideration – and one that requires interaction with the parallel thread of process development – relates to the update logic that is to be applied. Broadly, there are two options:

1. Interactive update, where additions, deletions, and modifications are applied to live data as they are submitted.
2. Batch update, where additions, deletions, and modifications are batched up in a temporary structure for incorporation at some later time, perhaps on a periodic basis.

Although the database developer may have a strong view on this issue, perhaps by anticipation of unacceptable locking overheads with interactive update strategies, it is a decision that must be taken by a broader authority who can balance such concerns against, for example, the need for currency of information.

Having selected a primary organization type, it is occasionally the case that values need to be chosen for various performance parameters. Some of these are specific to types of organization, such as hashing functions for hashed organizations, but others can apply more generally. Of these latter parameters, probably the most significant performance-wise relates to whether or not the organization is to be clustered. There are DBMSs of all flavours that offer the capability of forcing records of one or more types (and which are frequently required together) to be stored physically close to one another. Clustering offers both primary and secondary access capabilities; in primary terms it increases the performance of serial, or sequential, primary access through a collection of records.

55.6.5.4 Secondary organizations

Secondary organization support, like primary organization types, varies from one DBMS to another. There are two common types of secondary organization:

1. Secondary (or non-unique) indexes.
2. Clustering. This is the same concept as that introduced previously. In addition to offering primary access capabilities it can be interpreted, and used, as a secondary capability to improve the performance of joining structures; clustering the records of two or more types provides for fast linkage between records of those types, and hence improves navigation through a database.

The trade-off when selecting secondary organizations is that, although they can speed up retrieval requests directed at the supported fields, or field combinations, they need to be kept up-to-date, and hence increase the time taken to update records, as well as posing further demands for storage.

The choice of secondary indexes for a record type is guided by a technique called secondary-access analysis, which is based upon the idea of a secondary-access matrix. These show the details of the direct access that is required against non-primary key fields, as illustrated in *Figure 55.13*.

In a secondary-access matrix, the non-key fields of each record type are listed to the left, and 'X's are used to mark those transactions that involve direct access by a particular field. Fields for which there is a direct-access requirement are candidates for secondary indexing, but, as mentioned above, one should always consider the implications of this, especially if fast-reponse, high-volume updating of structures is required by transactions of higher priority.

Useful clusterings of records of more than one type can be identified through clustering analysis, based on a clustering matrix. These show the frequency with which fast reference from the fields of one record type to those of another (as in a relational join operation) are required, and hence which clusterings of structures would result in the greatest performance benefits. *Figure 55.14* illustrates a simple clustering matrix.

In a clustering matrix we list on the left all pairs of structures that could in principle be joined over some collection of common fields, and we mark with an 'X' those transactions that perform that join. Pairs of relations that are joined commonly (and this applies to navigational databases as much as it does to relational ones) are strong candidates for clustering. It must be noted, however, that such decisions may have an impact upon decisions made previously regarding primary organizations and secondary indexes.

55.6.6 Verification of an internal organization

It is difficult to give specific rules for the general case because of the special facilities offered and the restrictions imposed by various DBMSs. The essential rule is that each record type of each fragment must be associated with a single primary organization and zero or more secondary organizations. The special rules governing which organizations (and combinations of organizations) are available are dictated above and beyond this by the DBMS to be used for implementation.

55.6.7 Validation of an internal organization

This is the task of checking that a chosen internal organization is compatible with the operational requirements of the system under development. We are only concerned here with the performance-orientated requirements; in particular, with ensuring that response requirements are indeed met by the organization proposed, and that its overheads do not infringe any resource, especially storage, restrictions.

As with previous validation steps, there are two approaches: analytical and simulation based. Neither is straightforward at this level of detail.

Generalized analytical approaches to evaluating the performance of internal organizations have been developed, and the interested reader is referred to Yao and Merten (1975), Yao (1977), Batory (1982), Batory and Gotlieb (1982), but there is a tendency of such approaches to be either too restricted in terms of the designs that they cover, or too complex to be mathematically tractable. Unfortunately, even tools for performance prediction with particular DBMSs are not widely available (presumably because of the difficulty of producing them).

This leaves, as the only generally available approach, the prototype construction of the chosen internal organization, perhaps with dummy data volumes loaded. Such a prototype could then be used to take advantage of the run-time monitoring facilities offered by the DBMS (and most do offer such tools) under simulated *real* transaction conditions; for example, submitting transactions as sequences of database operations – as relational queries in a relational environment.

The cost of validating a physical design is likely to be considerable. What must be borne in mind, though, is that the cost of re-implementing, following a change to the physical design, is typically higher.

		Transaction 1 (Frequency 1)	Transaction 2 (Frequency 2)	Transaction 3 (Frequency 3)
Rec. Type 1	Field 1.1	X	X	
	Field 1.2		X	X
	Field 1.3	X		X
Rec. Type 2	Field 2.1			
	Field 2.2	X		

Figure 55.13 A simple secondary-access matrix

		Transaction 1 (Frequency 1)	Transaction 2 (Frequency 2)	Transaction 3 (Frequency 3)
Rec. Type 1	Rec. Type 2	X	X	
Rec. Type 1	Rec. Type 3		X	X

Figure 55.14 A simple clustering matrix

55.7 Implementation

Implementation of a database is the production, from a physical specification, of an actual database system that is capable of satisfying its various requirements. The implementation process itself, however, brings further design issues, relating to system performance and management.

In common with previous stages of development, the performance considerations relate to factors that affect transaction response rates and throughputs, and resource utilization. The managerial considerations relate to the ability of the system to support desired levels of:

1. Privacy against unauthorized access.
2. Synchronization of concurrent access.
3. Robustness in the event of failures of various kinds.
4. Audit trailing (i.e. logging from the point of view of being able to investigate access to operational data rather than from the point of view of being able to support recovery in the event of failure).

Implementation can be divided into two broad areas: DBMS installation and database creation. These are not wholly independent, but do allow us roughly to partition the concerns.

55.7.1 DBMS installation

With some DBMSs, all systems developed on a particular machine configuration are perceived as constituting a single system. In other cases this is not necessary, but there are severe performance problems if multiple systems are implemented. Because of these restrictions, the task of implementing a database if a DBMS is already installed, with database systems currently operational under it, may be different from the task if the DBMS has itself to be installed.

It may be, therefore, that no action is required beyond creating the new database as an extension to existing structures. On the other hand, if one does have the option of installing the DBMS or, at least, of setting parameters for the new system, then there are various decisions to be taken, including, typically:

1. Buffer cache size for data blocks and system data.
2. The required level of recovery logging.
3. The required level of audit logging.
4. Whether the system is single- or multi-user.
5. Constant declarations for such issues as the maximum number of concurrent transactions.

The ease of modification of these parameters varies between DBMSs and the parameters involved.

55.7.2 Database creation

The creation of a database divides into three separate concerns:

1. The creation of the structures corresponding to those of the physical specification.
2. The populating of those structures with data.
3. The definition of appropriate access privileges relating to the data.

It is important to appreciate the likely lead time of the data-load process so that it can be put into operation early if necessary, rather than causing unnecessary delays in the availability of the operational system. In this sense, implementation can be viewed as a process that actually progresses in parallel with other development stages, its procedures being carried out as and when they are appropriate.

Privacy definition is an area that is difficult to deal with in the general case – it is an area where DBMSs differ widely in approach. Some systems offer no support at all, relying purely upon whatever is available through the underlying operating system; others include constructs within the definition of database structures that hard code the access privileges; and others, including SQL-supporting systems, provide an interactive facility for granting and revoking privileges.

A discussion of the general problems of privacy protection is not appropriate here; see Wiederhold (1983) for a fairly comprehensive summary of the issues involved. Clearly, there are performance implications of privacy schemes: the complexity of the collection of privileges involved, the time that is necessary for the system to check the correctness of access requests, and maintaining an audit trail adds to the input-output load of each application.

55.8 Summary

The methodology and techniques described in this chapter support the development of the structural and organizational components of a database system. Throughout this process, a parallel development of application procedures is assumed to be active, and the interaction of the two is an important factor that influences design decisions, as discussed particularly during the structural design phase of development.

The methodology described here has been developed (and used) by the author. It is, however, typical of (although notably more comprehensive than) the various methodologies that have been proposed with comparable objectives. The reader who is familiar with the techniques presented here will readily appreciate those adopted by other methodologies, especially where they are orientated towards practical use in systems development with current implementation technology.

55.9 References

Abiteboul, S. and Bidoit, N. (1984) Non-first normal form relations to represent hierarchically organized data. In *Proceedings of the ACM SIGACT-SIGMOD Symposium on Database Systems*, pp. 191–200

Afsarmanesh, H., McLeod, D., Knapp, D. and Parker, A. (1985) An extensible object-oriented approach to databases for VLSI/CAD. In *Proceedings of the 11th International Conference on Very Large Databases*

Albano, A. and Orsini, R. (1984) A Prototyping Approach to Database Applications Development. *IEEE Database Engineering*, **7**, 245–250

Batory, D. S. (1982) Optimal file designs and reorganization points. *ACM Transactions on Database Systems*, **7**, 60–81

Batory, D. S. and Gotlieb, C. C. (1982) A unifying model of physical databases. *ACM Transactions on Database Systems*, **7**, 509–539

Blaha, M. R., Premerlani, W. J. and Rumbaugh, J. E. (1988) Relational database design using an object-orientated methodology. *Communications of the ACM*, **31**, 414–427

Chen, P. P. (1976) The entity-relationship model – toward a unified view of data. *ACM Transactions on Database Systems*, **1**, 9–36

Codd, E. F. (1971) Normalized data base structures: a brief tutorial. In *Proceedings of the 1971 ACM SIGFIDET Workshop on Data Description Access and Control*

Codd, E. F. (1972) Further normalization of the data base relational model. In *Data Base Systems*, (ed. R. Rustin), Prentice-Hall, pp. 33–64

Codd, E. F. (1974) Recent investigations into relational database systems. In *Proceedings of the IFIP Congress*

Codd, E. F. (1979) Extending the database relational model to capture more meaning. *ACM Transactions on Database Systems*, **4**, 397–434

Date, C. J. (1986) *An Introduction to Database Systems Volume I*, 4th edn, Addison-Wesley

Fagin, R. (1977) Multivalued dependencies and a new normal form for relational databases. *ACM Transactions on Database Systems*, **2**, 262–278

Gane, C. and Sarson, T. (1979) *Structured Systems Analysis: Tools and Techniques*, Prentice Hall International

Gradwell, D. J. L. (1987) Developments in data dictionary standards. *Computer Bulletin*, 33–38

Hall, P. A., Hitchcock, P. and Todd, S. J. (1975) An algebra of relations for machine computation. In *Proceedings of the 23rd ACM Symposium on Principles of Programming Languages*, pp. 225–232

Hitchcock, P. (1976) User extensions to the Peterlee relational test vehicle. In *Proceedings of Systems for Large Data Bases* (ed. P. C. Neuhold and F. J. Lockermann), North-Holland

Kent, W. (1983) A simple guide to five normal forms in relational database theory. *Communications of the ACM*, **26**

NCC (1986) *Structured Systems Analysis and Design Method Version 3: Volumes I and II*, NCC Publications

Rolland, C. and Richard, C. (1982) The REMORA methodology for information systems design and management. In *Proceedings of the IFIP Conference on Comparative Review of Information Systems (CRIS 1)*, (ed. T. W. Olle), North-Holland

Smith, J. M. and Smith, D. C. P. (1977) Database abstractions: aggregation and generalization. *ACM Transactions on Database Systems* **2**, 105–133

Whittington, R. P. (1988) *Database Systems Engineering*, Oxford University Press

Wiederhold, G. (1983) *Database Design*, 2nd edn., McGraw Hill

Yao, S. B. and Merten, A. G. (1975) Selection of file organizations using an analytical model. In *Proceedings of the 1st International Conference on Very Large Databases*, pp. 255–267

Yao, S. B. (1977) An attribute-based model for database access cost analysis. *ACM Transactions on Database Systems*, **2**, 45–67

56

Real-time systems

H. Kopetz
Institut für Technische Informatik, TU-Wein, Austria

Contents

56.1 Introduction

The significant decrease of the cost of computer components makes the application of computer technology cost-effective in many new areas. The scope of real-time control systems of the next generation will therefore expand both downwards to instrumentation (sensors and transducers) and upwards to commercial data processing systems. Substantial benefits can be realised by this integration of instrumentation, process control, production control and commercial data processing into a single coherent information system architecture.

The replacement of conventional instrumentation and control technology by distributed computing systems, even in safety-critical applications, has brought the topic of guaranteeing the specified behaviour of a real-time system – both in the domain of value and time – by a systematic and rational design methodology to the forefront of interest (LeLann, 1983).

This chapter deals with the design of hard real-time systems. After a description of the real-time environment and a discussion of the validity of real-time data, the notion of a real-time transaction is introduced. The main focus of this chapter is placed on the problems related to concurrency control and the scheduling of real-time transactions which have to meet their deadlines. In the final section, issues related to the enhancement of the real-time system reliability by fault tolerance techniques are discussed.

56.2 Hard versus soft real-time systems

56.2.1 The real-time environment

In a typical real-time system a control object (the controlled environment) and the control system (the computer) are connected via sensor and actuator-based interfaces. The control system accepts data from the sensors either after periodic intervals or after the occurrence of an external event. It processes the data and outputs the results to the control object via the actuators. The output data influences the control object such that the effects can be observed via the sensors, thus closing the loop.

A real-time system is called a *hard* real-time system if the validity of the results depends not only on the logical correctness of the computations, but also on their timeliness. If a result is not delivered within the specified time interval, the system has failed, with potentially catastrophic consequences. A real-time system is called *soft* if the consequences of a timing failure cannot be catastrophic. *Table 56.1* compares some of the characteristics of a typical hard real-time system with those of a typical soft real-time system.

According to this table, the most important differences between hard real-time and soft real-time systems are:

1. Hard response time.
2. Pacing.
3. Limited validity time of data.
4. Fail-safe operation.

56.2.1.1 Hard response time

A hard real-time system must respond to a stimulus from the control object within an interval dictated by the environment, called the response time. This (maximum) response time must be guaranteed even under peak load conditions (the load hypothesis) and under the anticipated fault conditions (fault hypothesis). On the other hand, the designers of soft real-time systems are normally more concerned about the average than about the maximum response time.

Table 56.1 Characteristics of real-time systems

Characteristic	Hard real-time	Soft real-time
Response time	Hard	Soft
Pacing	By the environment	By the computer
Peak load performance	Predictable	Degraded
Data validity	Time-dependent	Not time-dependent
Data files	Small to medium	Large
Safety	Critical	Not critical
Error detection latency	Bounded by system	Responsibility of user
Redundancy	Active	Standby
Granularity of time base	< 1 ms	About 1 s

56.2.1.2 Pacing

A hard real-time system is driven by the events happening in the environment. It is not possible for the computer to exercise explicit flow control over these events, as is normally assumed in computer communication protocols. A hard real-time system must be designed to handle the maximum rate of event occurrences, i.e. peak load, under all specified conditions.

56.2.1.3 Limited validity time of data

Real-time data is invalidated by the passage of time, i.e. real-time data can lose its meaning to the system waiting to process it. Using real-time data outside the intended interval of time can lead to catastrophic system failures. This topic will be discussed further in the following section.

56.2.1.4 Fail-safe operation

If a serious failure occurs, either in the control system or the control object, such that further continuation of the operation of the control object (plant) is not possible, then the system must switch to a fail-safe mode.

56.2.2 System structure

Most state-of-the-art real-time systems are distributed, i.e. they consist of a set of autonomous components connected by a local area network. The communication between the components is realised solely by the exchange of messages. There are a number of international groups working to standardize the real-time communication system e.g. the MAP group (Rodd and Deravi, 1989). The most common communication system found in real-time applications is a bus or ring system controlled either by a token, time division multiple access or CSMA/CD (Carrier Sense Multiple Access with Collision Detection) protocol.

It is assumed here that all nodes of the distributed system have access to a global time base of bounded and known synchronization accuracy. The granularity of the global time is selected such that a global event, i.e. one which can be observed by all nodes, is never recorded with more than one tick difference (Kopetz and Ochsenreiter, 1987). It should be noted, however, that it is not easy to achieve such a global time base, and provision of such a time base is an important facet of the design of a real-time system.

56.2.3. Validity of real-time data

A real-time control system has to perform real-time control functions and to collect data for archival purposes. It is therefore important to distinguish between two databases which are needed for these two different purposes.

Definition 1: real-time database

The set of all data elements which is needed for the instantaneous real-time control, operator display, alarm monitoring and other real-time functions is called the 'real-time database'.

Definition 2: archival database

The set of all data elements which is required for purposes other than direct real-time functions is called the 'archival database'.

There are important differences between these two databases from the point of view of time and fault tolerance.

The real-time database changes as time progresses, i.e. the information in the real-time database is invalidated by the passage of real time. If the real-time database is lost, the control of the environment is interrupted, possibly leading to a catastrophe.

After an element has been stored in the archival database, it cannot be modified any more, i.e. it does not change as time progresses (the system is not allowed to modify 'history'). If the archival database is lost, there is no immediate effect on the real-time control of the environment.

Experience has shown that in most applications the real-time database is much smaller than the archival database.

The following definitions will be used to refer to the data in the real-time database.

Definition 3: correct information

Information is correct if its values correspond with the intentions of the user.

Definition 4: timely information

Information is timely if it is available within the intended interval of real time.

Definition 5: valid information

Information is valid if it is correct and timely.

To respond correctly to an external or internal stimulus, the real-time database inside the control system must contain a valid image of the external state of the environment.

The concepts of 'strong consistency' and 'weak consistency' between the real-time database and the state of the environment at a given point in time are now introduced.

Definition 6: strong consistency

The real-time database of a control system is strongly consistent with the state of the environment if at time t:

1. Every element of the real-time database is defined.
2. The input values of the real-time database reflect the state of the environment by or after $t - \delta t$.
3. The state of the environment reflects the output values of the real-time database by or after $t - \delta t$.

The interval δt is called the validity time of the information.

Note that the relationship between the state of the environment and the real-time database is symmetric. The same definition can be applied if the environment consists of another information processing subsystem, thus defining strong consistency between two cooperating information processing subsystems which are connected by a two-way communication channel with a bounded delay in each direction.

Definition 7: weak consistency

The real-time database of a control system is weakly consistent with the state of the environment if at time t every value of the real-time database is either:

1. Strongly consistent.
2. Undefined.

Definition 8: inconsistency

The real-time database is inconsistent with the state of the environment at the time t if there is a value in the real-time database which is defined and not strongly consistent.

56.3 Real-time transactions

In the design of hard real-time systems it is necessary to consider the value aspect and the timing aspect of the behaviour simultaneously. The concept of a real-time (RT) transaction is well suited for this purpose.

Definition 9: Real-time transaction

An RT-transaction refers to the execution of a set of correlated actions between a stimulus from the environment and the corresponding time-constrained response indicating the completion of this set of actions.

The notion of an RT-transaction integrates the concerns about the value domain and the time domain into a single concept. Furthermore, it supports the abstraction from the detailed state transformation of its inner actions and thus introduces a powerful mechanism for system structuring. RT-transactions can be used in the requirements specification to express the external requirements. They can also be used to express the behaviour of the system at different levels of detail during the system design.

The expressive power of the transaction concept is well accepted in the database community (Date, 1986). However, there are some important differences between RT-transactions and database (DB) transactions, as is indicated in the *Table 56.2*.

RT-transactions have to interact with the environment and to enforce an intended effect on the environment before a predefined deadline. Only after an observation about the intended effect of the RT-tansaction on the environment is available it can be concluded that the RT-transaction has completed successfully. Thus an RT-transaction has to commit a value to the environment (outside its sphere of control) before its point of termination. After a result has been committed to the environment it cannot be revoked any more. It is thus necessary to associate three visible states with any RT-transaction: the start state, the successful termination state and the safe exit state. As soon as the point of commitment of an RT-transaction has been traversed and a failure occurs, the RT-transaction must terminate in the (externally) visible safe exit state (and no other intermediate state). This is in contrast to a DB-transaction which does not have to commit before the end of the transaction and can thus always return to the start state in case of a failure during transaction execution.

Table 56.2 Real-time versus database transactions

Characteristic	RT-transaction	DB-transaction
Response time	Hard	No concern
Point of commitment	Before termination	At termination
Visible states	Start, termination, safe exit	Start, termination
Data validity	Time-dependent	Not time-dependent
Concurrency conflicts	Immediate resolution	Delay

56.3.1 Concurrency control

In a typical real-time system, many activities take place concurrently within the different nodes, e.g. the control of a set of control loops, communication to the other nodes and to the operator etc. It is the objective of the concurrency control mechanisms to control the concurrent execution of the RT-transactions such that the specified synchronization between the RT-transactions is maintained, the deadlines are met and given consistency constraints are not violated (e.g. access to exclusive resources). In distributed real-time system exclusive access to the individual processors and access to the communication medium by different concurrently executing transactions must be considered (Kopetz, 1986).

In database systems the concurrent access of transactions to a database or other critical resources is controlled such that the combined effects of the executions are the same as those caused by a serialized execution schedule. This is normally achieved by delaying or rolling back those portions of a transaction which are in conflict with another transaction executing in parallel. It is evident that this additional delay of a transaction can lead to a violation of the timing constraints of the RT-transaction and to the invalidation of the RT-data which has been accessed by this transaction. It follows that transaction blockage and rollback have to be analysed carefully before applying them in a hard RT system (Kim, 1989).

Furthermore, total serializability of concurrently executing transactions is not always a desired objective in real-time systems. Depending on the semantic knowledge about the underlying application, it can become necessary to resolve a conflict between competing transactions immediately, e.g. a conflict between an emergency transaction and a 'steady state' transaction. Such a conflict is called a 'semantic conflict'.

Other conflicts, known as 'schedule conflicts', are caused by the execution schedules of particular transaction instances. These conflicts can be avoided if another ordering of the actions of the transactions is realised (provided a conflict-free schedule exists).

56.3.2 Semantic conflicts

As indicated before, a semantic conflict cannot be avoided by any scheduling strategy, since it has its origin in the deep semantics of the given application. If the application semantics requires to execute a RT-transaction with a very short deadline immediately (e.g. an alarm transaction requesting the emergency shut off of the plant) then it is not possible to delay this transaction until the other transactions have released all common resources. Semantic conflicts have to be resolved on the spot (in space and time) in order to meet the specification e.g. by a priority schema, even at the expense of aborting some other transaction or leaving the data in a (transient) inconsistent state.

56.3.3 Schedule conflicts

A schedule conflict, which has its origin in the momentary execution schedule, can be avoided if the execution schedules of the transactions or the access to the common communication medium are modified. There are three possible schedule conflicts between a set of transactions executing in parallel, read-write (rw) conflicts, write-read (wr) conflicts and write-write (ww) conflicts. If more than one version of an object can be provided, the occurrence of rw and wr conflicts can be reduced by limiting the write action to one version (which cannot be read) while leaving the other versions available for reading.

The most serious conflict between RT-transactions executing in parallel, which cannot be handled by introducing object versions, is the ww conflict. In this case the transaction schedules have to be rearranged such that the required consistency constraint on the data is maintained. There are two possible solutions to this problem: static (implicit) synchronization of the transactions at compile time, or dynamic (explicit) synchronization of the transaction at runtime.

56.4 Scheduling issues

Given a set of RT-transactions and a set of hardware resources (processors and communication medium) it must be decided by the scheduling subsystem which RT-transactions or parts thereof – called tasks – should be executed on a particular processor and which tasks may access the communication medium at a point in time. The proper design of the scheduling subsystem is therefore of critical importance for the functioning of the real-time system.

There are basically two different approaches to the solution of the scheduling problem: the dynamic approach and the static approach. In the dynamic approach the scheduling decisions are made at run time on the basis of the momentary system load and some given system parameters. It is up to the run-time scheduler to produce schedules which on the one side will meet all synchronization and mutual exclusion requirements of the transactions and on the other side will meet the given deadlines. A general discussion on scheduling can also be found in Chapter 49 on operating systems.

In the static approach all scheduling decisions are made at compile time and handed over to the run-time dispatcher in the form of a scheduler database, parametrized with the system time. To keep the size of this scheduler database manageable, it is wise to introduce some basic system cycle, after which the schedule is repeated. At any given point in time the run-time scheduler has to look up the scheduler database and schedule the RT-transactions or tasks accordingly. If a transaction, planned for a given point in time, does not require any service, then the reserved time slot on the processor or communication medium will be allocated to a ready soft real-time task. Since all requirements concerning task synchronization and mutual exclusion are already considered implicitly in the scheduler database we call this form of task synchronization implicit synchronization.

A schedule can be defined as optimal if it is equivalent to the best schedule which a clairvoyant scheduler (Mok, 1984), i.e. a scheduler which has complete knowledge about all request times in the future, can find. A schedule is feasible if it will meet all deadline and synchronization requirements but may not be optimal. It has been shown (Garey and Johnson, 1975) that in the general case the decision whether a given set of circumstances a feasible schedule, i.e. one which will meet all specified deadlines, exists is NP hard. Even if it is known that a schedule exists it can be prohibitively expensive to find this schedule. It is thus necessary to introduce simplifying constraints to find feasible schedules quickly.

56.4.1 Dynamic scheduling

Today, most practical real-time systems rely on a simple priority controlled dynamic scheduler for CPU allocation (e.g. Ready, 1986). Communication system access is controlled either by polling, by a token or by CSMA/CD. In many cases the task priorities are static, i.e. they are determined at compile time. Whenever a set of tasks is ready at run time, the run-time scheduler selects the task with the highest static priority. Mutual exclusion and task synchronization are achieved by explicit synchronization between the tasks, e.g. by the use of semaphores or signals. For such a system it is very difficult to guarantee that all hard deadlines will be met. It is even difficult to guarantee the deadline for the highest priority task if task preemption is constrained due to mutual exclusion requirements.

It is evident that this approach is not sufficient for the design of safety critical hard real-time systems, where catastrophic consequences can occur if a deadline is missed. The following section systematically analyses the scheduling problem, starting from the simplest case and continuing to more realistic scenarios.

Let us first consider the simplest case by assuming a single processor with the following set of tasks $M = M_p \bigcup M_a$ where M_p refers to the subset of periodic tasks and M_a refers to the subset of aperiodic tasks. Every task $T_i(c_i, d_i, p_i)$ is characterized by its maximum execution time c_i, its deadline d_i, i.e. the time between the stimulus and the latest response, and the minimum interval between two successive activations p_i. For periodic tasks p_i is equal to the task period. We call $l_i = d_i - c_i$ the laxity of task i. The utilization factor of task T_i is $u_i = c_i/p_i$.

The maximum execution time of a real-time task c_i can only be calculated if a special programming discipline as outlined in Puschner (1988) is observed. For hard real-time programs the upper bound on the maximum execution must be as low as possible, even at the expense of a higher average execution time. This issue of designing algorithms and programs with a low maximum execution time for use in hard real-time system is a topic of very relevant research.

56.4.1.1 Independent periodic tasks

Provided that the set M_a is empty, i.e. there are only periodic tasks, the deadline is equal to the period, i.e. $d_i = p_i$, and all tasks are independent of each other, i.e. every task can preempt every other task at any time, an optimal algorithm for static priority scheduling exists (Liu and Layland, 1973) if:

$$\sum_{i=1}^{k} u_i \leqslant \ln 2$$

This algorithm, which is called the rate monotonic scheduling algorithm, assigns the highest static priority to the task with the smallest period the second highest priority to the next etc. In case the priorities are determined dynamically (i.e. at run time) an optimal scheduling algorithms exist under the given assumptions even if:

$$\ln 2 \leqslant \sum_{i=1}^{k} u_i \leqslant 1$$

Examples of such algorithms are the earliest deadline algorithm or the least laxity algorithm. The earliest deadline algorithm assigns the task with the shortest deadline the highest dynamic priority. The least laxity algorithm assigns the highest priority to the task with the smallest laxity l.

56.4.1.2 Dependent periodic tasks

For real-time systems, the assumption of task independence is too restrictive. To achieve the system objective it is necessary to assume and support some form of inter-task communication. The simplest form of inter-task communication is the exchange of information via access to a common data domain. To avoid any mutilation of this data the mutual exclusion of some of the access operations to this data domain must be enforced by the operating system, e.g. by the use of semaphores. However, as soon as mutual exclusion constraints are introduced it becomes impossible to find an optimal totally online run-time scheduler any more and the solution to the scheduling problem becomes NP-hard (Mok, 1983i). The problem of scheduling a system of nonpreemptive tasks has been analysed in Kim and Naghibadeh (1980).

To simplify the scheduling problem, a further restriction must be introduced. Assume that the system time is quantized such that the maximum execution time of a critical section is always smaller than a granule of time. Then one can be sure that a task, which starts executing a critical section at the beginning of a time granule, will leave the critical section before the end of the time granule. If task pre-emption is only performed at the granule boundary, then no further effect of the mutual exclusion on the scheduling problem has to be considered. However, the resulting slight change to the scheduling problem – tasks may be pre-empted only at granule boundaries instead of at any time – may cause the simple scheduling algorithms introduced before, e.g. earliest deadline scheduling, to fail. Feasible schedules can be found by a technique called 'forbidden regions' (Garey et al., 1981). This technique requires an offline (static) analysis of the scheduling requirements in order to produce a scheduling database which can be used by the run-time scheduler. It is thus not a dynamic scheduling technique any more.

56.4.1.3 Aperiodic tasks

In real-time systems there are situations where a set of tasks will not be activated for most of the time, but as soon as these tasks become ready, they have to be serviced very quickly. An example of such a task is an alarm task for the handling of emergency situations. Consider the situation of a fire developing in an aircraft engine during the critical phases of takeoff. In this situation, emergency actions to extinguish the fire have to be performed concurrently with the delicate engine control. If the highest priority is assigned to the emergency task the deadlines of the flight control might be missed, which is not what is required. Mapping a complex set of deadline and synchronization requirements into a single linear dimension of task priorities is impossible in most cases.

It is obvious that aperiodic tasks, particularly if they have a short laxity, are very difficult to handle. Since one never knows when the stimulus for an aperiodic task will occur one always has to be ready to serve the task within the specified laxity.

One way to solve this problem, as has been shown by Mok (1983ii), is to replace an aperiodic task $T_i(c_i, d_i, p_i)$ by a quasi-periodic task T_i' (c_i', d_i', p_i') such that whenever the quasi-periodic task can be scheduled, then the sporadic task will meet its deadline. The parameters of the quasi-periodic task $T_i'(c_i', d_i', p_i')$ have to be in the following range:

$$c_i' = c_i$$
$$d_i \geqslant d_i' \geqslant c$$
$$p_i' = \text{MIN}(d_i - d_i' + 1, p_i)$$

The period of the quasi-periodic task is basically determined by the latency of the aperiodic task. If this latency is short, the aperiodic task can monopolize the full power of the processor. If the active schedule may not be fully sacrificed in case of emergency situations significant extra resources have to be reserved for the (seldom occurring) aperiodic tasks.

56.4.1.4 Probabilistic dynamic scheduling

If the processing resources for guaranteeing the deadlines of the RT-transactions in all specified scenarios have to be provided all the time, it is very likely that the resource usage will be very low most of the time. It is even controversial whether in any particular stress (peak load) situation all RT-transactions will require serice. Therefore a number of research projects take the view that the dynamic adaptability of the scheduling algorithm to the load scenario developing at a particular instance is more reasonable than the permanent reservation of all resources for the worst case scenario. In these projects e.g. Stankovic and Ramamritham (1987), Levi *et al.* (1989), Tokuda and Mercer (1989), sophisticated dynamic scheduling strategies are proposed, which will try to meet as many deadlines as possible, possibly meeting all critical deadlines most of the time. The processing power required to execute these run-time scheduling algorithms must be deducted from the total processing power available. In the ALPHA project (Northcutt, 1988) a separate processor is provided just for finding a good schedule for a particular scenario. The testing and the evaluation of the performance of these scheduling algorithms is very difficult since peak load is highly correlated and the normal assumptions about the stochastic arrival of input stimuli are seldom valid. Even knowing that a solution exists for a particular scenario is not enough, since there might not be the time to find the solution dynamically.

In practice, many real-time system designers are neither willing to pay the high price for a guaranteed response time nor providing sophisticated run-time schedulers to increase the probability of meeting all deadlines. They rely on simple static priority scheduling for CPU allocation and on a token protocol for access to the communication medium, and hope that under peak load conditions the important transactions will meet their deadline. Since this approach is totally inadequate for life-critical hard real-time systems, these latter systems have to rely on the static scheduling of a set of periodic tasks.

56.4.2 Static scheduling

Given a peak load scenario of a set of periodic and aperiodic transactions, it is necessary to try to find a feasible schedule for CPU allocation and access to the communication medium offline, which is then recorded in a scheduler database for the run-time system (Kopetz, 1986). Since all possible concurrency conflicts and precedence relations between all transactions have been considered implicitly when designing the schedules, no explicit task synchronization or task delay is necessary at run time. Static scheduling is reasonable only if the task set contains periodic or quasi-periodic tasks. However, when transforming aperiodic tasks to quasi-periodic tasks by the techniques introduced before, the problems mentioned, concerning low resource utilization occur as well.

The offline scheduler for static scheduling must produce a feasible, but not necessarily optimal, schedule. Such a schedule can be considered a 'proof by construction' that all critical tasks will meet their deadline. In the MARS system (Kopetz *et al.*, 1989a) the offline scheduler is based on a heuristic search through a schedule tree, to find a feasible schedule which will meet the given synchronization and communication requirements as well as the specified deadlines (Fohler and Koza, 1989).

56.4.2.1 Schedule switch

The problem of giving fast service to aperiodic emergency transactions whenever they occur while still maintaining a reasonable resource utilization in normal situations has led to the concept of a schedule switch in the MARS project (Kopetz *et al.*, 1989a).

Let us assume there exists a set P of operational phases of a system and that at any time the system can only be in any one of these phases, e.g. the startup phase, the normal processing phase, the termination phase, an emergency phase etc. For every phase P_i a corresponding schedule S_i is developed. All these schedules are designed offline and will guarantee the deadlines of all tasks involved. Whenever an aperiodic event occurs which requires immediate service, i.e. transition to another phase, the scheduler will switch to the new schedule which has been designed for this new scenario. However, to maintain the continuity of those transactions which are required in the 'old' and 'new' schedule, any schedule switch must be analysed and designed from the point of view of the application requirements. There are two extreme cases: the immediate switch and the consistent switch. When requesting an immediate switch, all transactions of the 'old' schedule will be abandoned and the 'new' schedule will be started immediately. When requesting a consistent switch, the 'old' schedule will continue until the end of the current scheduling cycle before the 'new' schedule will be considered. In most practical situations, neither the immediate nor the consistent switch are optimal, since some task will have to be serviced continually in both the old and the new schedule. The best switchover between schedules has to be designed according to the particular application context. Take the example of a fire developing in a lift: should the lift stop immediately, should it stop at the next floor or should it finish its present journey? Based on the requirements of a particular application, the full set of static schedules is recalculated to find a good set of schedules meeting all those addition constraints.

It is the author's opinion that the combination of static scheduling with the dynamic schedule switch provides a good compromise in guaranteeing all hard deadlines on one side while still keeping the resource utilization at an acceptable level.

56.5 Fault tolerance

From the point of view of safety, two different types of real-time applications can be distinguished: those for which a safe state can be defined (e.g. a train control system, where all trains can be stopped in an emergency), and those for which a safe state does not exist (e.g. a flight control system). The former are called fail-safe applications while the latter are called fail-operational applications.

After a component has failed a diagnostic program is started to determine the cause of the failure. If no hardware fault can be detected by the offline diagnostic check it must be assumed that the cause of the failure was a transient fault. Experience has shown that most hardware faults of computer systems are of transient nature (Iye *et al.*, 1986). If a permanent hardware fault has been diagnosed, the component must be replaced. In the next phase the re-integration of the (repaired) component can proceed.

Seen from the outside, a failure of a real-time system (or subsystem) will manifest itself by a failure of (at last one of) the current RT-transactions. As mentioned before, there are three distinct states associated with any RT-transactions: the starting state, the successful termination state and the safe exit state. According to its specification, an RT-transaction which is initiated from the starting state has to reach either the successful termination state or the safe exit state by the time of its deadline, even if faults (covered by the specified fault hypothesis) impede the execution of this RT-transaction.

According to the definition of an RT-transaction, it is evident that the classical fault-handling techniques of backward recovery by rollback and retry have only limited relevance for RT-processing. These techniques require substantial additional amounts of time, which normally will not be available within the specified interval until the transaction deadline. If neither the successful termination state nor the safe exit state has been reached by the given hard deadline, the transaction has failed critically.

There are, however, two other fault tolerance techniques appropriate to increase the reliability of RT-transactions in the presence of faults:

1. Fault masking by active redundancy.
2. Forward recovery into the safe exit state by application specific error processing.

The following paragraphs give an overview of these two techniques for fault tolerance in real-time system. For a more detailed analysis, the reader is referred to the standard literature on fault tolerance, e.g. Anderson and Lee (1990) and Johnson (1989), and also to Chapter 61.

56.5.1 Fault masking by active redundancy

If fault masking by active redundancy is selected, then the degree of synchronism between the redundant components must be selected. One can distinguish between instruction synchronism and message synchronism. Instruction synchronism implies that the components operate from a single clock (which must be hardened) and execute the hardware instructions in parallel. Message synchronism refers to a looser type of synchronization at the level of input output messages. This looser synchronism can be achieved without a central clock by distributed clock synchronization (Kopetz and Ochsenreiter, 1987).

From the architectural point of view, a looser synchronism is preferable, since the probability that a single fault event (e.g. spike in the system power) will have the same effect on the redundant components is reduced.

56.5.1.1 Triple modular redundancy

In a triple modular redundant (TMR) architecture, a single component of a non-redundant system is replaced by a fault tolerant unit (FTU), consisting of three components and three voters. Every input message is distributed to the three components in parallel. The three outputs of these three components are compared by three voters, which perform a majority vote. An FTU will thus produce three correct outputs, even if one of the components within the FTU fails. In a TMR system error detection and fault masking is performed in a single step.

The FTMP project (Hopkins et al., 1978) is an example of a TMR system operating in tight synchronism, whereas the VOTRICS (Theuretzbacher, 1986) project is a TMR system based on message synchronism.

56.5.1.2 Fail-silent components

In the following section it is assumed that all components of the system have the 'fail-silent' property, i.e. in case a component failure is detected the component will stop its operation before delivering any invalid (i.e. incorrect or untimely) result to its environment. Under this assumption, an FTU can be constructed out of two fail-silent components operating in message synchronism. As long as only one of these two redundant components of the FTU has failed, the specified service can be delivered in the presence of a fault without a degradation of

performance. It is up to the implementation to guarantee that the property of fail silence is realised with a sufficiently high probability, e.g. by the provision of error detection mechanisms within the component. The tradeoff between complexity at the component level to simplify the component failure modes (fail-silent) versus complexity at the architectural level to detect and handle arbitrary component failures has been analysed in Kopetz (1988). If the fail-silent assumption is not made, the algorithms required to detect and confine erroneous results at the architectural level are very complex (Lamport et al., 1982). Furthermore, these algorithms require an extraordinary amount of resources, communication effort and processing time, such that the goal of timely behaviour is compromised.

In systems based on fail-silent components the error detection coverage of the component is a critical parameter. It is up to the component implementation to provide error detection mechanisms which will assure the specified coverage.

Examples of fail-silent component systems based on tight synchronism are STRATUS (Wilson, 1985) and the BIIN System (Kini, 1989), whereas MARS (Kopetz et al., 1989) is based on loose synchronism.

56.5.2 Forward recovery into the safe exit state

In fail-safe applications – in such an application a safe state is always defined – the error handler of a critical transaction can bring the system into this safe state in case a transaction cannot reach the specified termination state within its deadline. Care must be taken that all nodes of the distributed system agree on the point in time when such a safe exit action has to be taken. A distributed membership protocol, which provides timely and consistent information about the operation of state of each member component, can be of essential service in such a critical situation (Kopetz et al., 1989b).

A typical example of a system with a safe state is a railway application. As soon as a failure of a critical component is detected all signals are switched to red in order to stop the traffic (Hagelin, 1988).

56.6 Conclusion

The design of hard real-time systems with guaranteed performance to meet all critical deadlines of the hard real-time transactions is a challenging and difficult task. If the transactions are scheduled dynamically at run time, it is very difficult to guarantee that the specified deadlines can be met under peak load conditions. On the other hand, if the transactions are scheduled at compile time considering the worst peak load scenario, a very low utilization of the system resources will have to be tolerated. It can be hoped that the improvement in the price performance ratio of the hardware will take away some of the economic pressure for high resource utilization in the future and that a well-chosen compromise between static and dynamic mechanisms, e.g. the concept of a schedule switch, will increase the resource utilization to an acceptable level while still guaranteeing that all hard deadlines can be met.

56.7 Acknowledgement

This work was supported in part by ESPRIT Basic Research Project 3092 on Predictably Dependable Computing Systems (PDCS) and by the FWF-NSF Cooperative Research Project P6010P from the Austrian Foundation for Basic Research.

56.8 References and bibliography

Abbot, R. and Garcia-Molina, H. (1988) Scheduling real-time transactions. *ACM Sigmod Record*, **17**, 71–81

Anderson, T. and Lee, P. (1990) *Fault Tolerance, Principles and Practice*, 2nd edition, Springer Verlag, Vienna

Date, C. J. (1980) *An Introduction to Database Systems*, Addison Wesley

Fohler, G. and Koza, C. (1989) Heuristic scheduling for distributed real-time systems. *MARS Research Report 6/89*, Technical University of Vienna

Garey, M. and Johnson, D. S. (1975) Complexity results for multiprocessor scheduling under resource constraints. *SIAM Journal of Computing*, **4**, 397–411

Garey, M., Johnson, D., Simons B. and Tarjan, R. (1981) Scheduling unit-time task with arbitrary release times and deadlines. *SIAM Journal of Computing*, **10**, 256–269

Hagelin, G. (1988) ERICSSON safety system for railway control. In *Software Diversity in Computerized Control Systems* (ed. U. Voges) Springer Verlag, Vienna, pp.11–22

Hopkins, A. L. *et al.* (1978) FTMP – a highly reliable fault tolerant multiprocessor for aircraft control. *Proceedings of the IEEE*, **66**, 1221–1239

Iyer, R. K., Rossetti and Hsueh, M. C. (1986) Measurement and modelling of computer system reliability as affected by system activity. *ACM Transactions on Computer Systems*, **3**, 214–237

Johnson, B. W. (1989) *Design and Analysis of Fault Tolerant Digital Systems*, Addison Wesley

Kieckhafer, R., Walter, C., Finn, A. and Thambidurai, P. (1988) The MAFT architecture for distributed fault tolerance. *IEEE Transactions on Computers*, **37**, 396–405

Kim, K. H. (1989) An Approach to experimental evaluation of real-time fault-tolerant distributed computing schemes. *IEEE Transactions on Software Engineering*, **15**, 715–725

Kim, K. H. and Naghibadeh, M. (1980) Prevention of task overruns in real-time nonpreemptive multiprogramming systems. In *Proceedings of ACM Performance 80*, ACM Press, pp.112–122

Kini, V. (1989) Fault tolerance in the BIIN computer system. In *Presentation Slides of the International Workshop on Hardware Fault Tolerance in Multiprocessors*, University of Illinois, Urbana, pp.1–6

Kopetz, H. (1986) Scheduling in distributed real time systems. In *Proceedings of the seminar on Real-Time Local Area Networks, Bandol*, INRIA, Rocquencort, France, pp.105–126

Kopetz, H. and Ochsenreiter, W. (1987) Clock synchronization in distributed real time systems. *IEEE Transactions on Computers*, **36**, 933–940

Kopetz, H. (1988) Fehlermodelle in verteilten Echtzeitsystemen, Informatik Fachberichte 187. In *Proceedings of the 18 GI Jahrestagung*, Springer Verlag, Berlin-Heidelberg, pp.56–69

Kopetz, H., Damm, A., Koza, C., Mulazzani, M., Schwabl, W., Senft, C. and Zainlinger, R. (1989). Distributed fault-tolerant real-time systems: the Mars approach. *IEEE Micro*, **9**, pp.25–41

Kopetz, H., Grunsteidl, G. and Reisinger, J. (1989) Fault tolerant membership service in a distributed real-time system. In *Proceedings of the IFIP International Working Conference on Dependable Computing for Critical Applications*. Springer Verlag, Vienna.

Lamport, L., Shostak, R. and Pease, M. (1982) The Byzantine generals problem. *CAM Transactions on Programming Languages and Systems*, **4**, 382–401

LeLann, G. (1983) On real-time distributed computing. In *Proceedings of the IFIP World Congress 1983*, North Holland, pp.741–753

Levi, S., Tripathi, S., Cason, S. and Agrawala, A. (1989). The MARUTI hard real-time operating system. *ACM Operating Systems Review*, **23**, pp.90–105

Liu, C. L. and Layland (1973) Scheduling algorithms for multiprogramming a hard- real-time environment. *Journal of ACM*, **20**, 46–61

Mok, A. (1983) Fundamental design problems of distributed systems for the hard real-time environment. *PhD Thesis*, Report MIT/LCS/TR-297, Massachusetts Institute of Technology, (i) p.46 (ii) p.45

Mok, A. (1984) The design of real-time programming systems based on process models. In *Proceedings of the IEEE Symposium on Realtime Programming*, IEEE Press, Silver Spring, MD, USA, pp 125–134

Northcutt, J. D. (1988) *Mechanisms for Reliable Distributed Real-Time Operating Systems: The Alpha Kernel*, Academic Press, Boston

Puschner, P. and Koza, C. (1989) Calculating the maximum execution time of real-time programs. *Real-Time Systems*, **1**, 159–176.

Puschner, P. and Koza, C. (1990) Calculating the maximum execution time for real time programs. *Real-Time Systems Journal* [to be published]

Ready, J. F. (1986) VRTX: A real-time operating system for embedded microprocessor applications. *IEEE Micro*, **6**, 8–17

Rodd, M. G. and Deravi, F. (1989) *Communication Systems for Industrial Automation*, Prentice Hall

Stankovic, J. A. and Ramamritham, K. (1987) The design of the spring kernel. In *Proceedings of the Real-Time Systems Symposium*, pp.146–157

Theuretzbacher, N. (1986) VOTRICS: Voting triple modular computing systems. In *Proceedings FTCS 16*, IEEE Press, pp.144–150

Tokuda, H. and Mercer, C. W. (1989) ARTS: a distributed real-time kernel. *ACM Operating Systems Review*, **23**, 29–53

Wilson, D. (1985) The STRATUS computer system. In *Resilient Computing Systems* (ed. T. Anderson) Collins Press, London, pp.208–231

57

Design of interactive systems

Harold Thimbleby
Stirling University

Contents

57.1 Introduction

It would be a truism to say that no computer could be used without a user interface, yet the user interface is often an afterthought in the design process. It is tagged on at the end and many opportunities are missed. It has been said – and not in jest – that many user interfaces are outgrowths of the debugging tools built into the prototype program.

Problems first become apparent after systems have been shipped and real use is being made of them. By then it is often too late to change early design commitments, and the best that can be done is to palliate the problem – or offer the user the expense of an alternative system. Various studies have been made of the cost of rectifying design errors in the user interface, and estimates put it around 60% of total software development cost. Of course, end users also have consequential costs that this '60%' does not measure, arising from being trapped into using systems that are not as good as they could be. It has been repeatedly shown that simple improvements to many user interface designs result in increases in productivity and decreases in error rates – and leading to reduced training time, greater job satisfaction and reduced staff turnover.

57.1.1 Overview

This chapter is arranged to be read from start to finish. It starts with an overview – confirming that user interface design is hard – then examines design choices and principles. The principles do not so much answer questions ('should we include this?') as raise important issues. However, design is not just a matter of thinking about principles, but having methods to put them into practice. This chapter therefore describes various design tools, evaluation methods and general approaches. The chapter concludes with a case study: this may be taken either as an example or as an exercise.

57.2 A difficult task

The three laws of interactive systems design are:

1. Know the user.
2. Know the task.
3. Allow for design errors – do not assume one can follow rules 1 and 2.

Rules 1 and 2 are often summarized as 'use the users' models', where the users' models are the users' 'programs' that determine what they do and how they interpret their actions. The users' models, then, are normally established *before* any contact with a computer system, and the designer should go to some lengths to find out how users perform their activities – including error recovery and concealment – prior to computerization.

Rule 3 arises for two reasons. First, one can never really know enough to produce a good design, and second, even if one could, the user will change his or her mind, or the very existence of a system will suggest new ways of doing the job better. Rule 3 suggests an important design strategy, iterative design, which is the *deliberate* attempt to design, test, and design again.

User interface design is only visible when a system can be used, and the standard ways of evaluating interactive systems do not generate useful data for design, as opposed to *re*design.

One can measure the user's training time, error rate, productivity and so on, but if these are unacceptable it is not necessarily clear what part or parts of the design should be reappraised. Besides, once a system has developed far enough to be evaluated, too much software investment has gone into it to make the sorts of radical changes that may be needed.

Given this dilemma, the best two ways to design a system are:

1. To copy or develop an existing system known to be successful. This approach has several merits, not least that of reducing user training.
2. To design the system abstractly, making full use of prototyping tools, to minimize the investment in development before it can be evaluated.

Conventional user interface design relies heavily on evaluation by users. Put cynically, the design is not perfect, but the users will be able to fix it. This tends to result in bottom-up design, as users provide information about isolated aspects of the system: this needs changing, that needs adding. If a design is to survive the insights of evaluation – useful as they may be – it must have a structure by which suggested modifications can be judged. Thus some modifications will be inappropriate, but others may have consequences elsewhere in the system that the users could not have reasonably anticipated. Top-down, principle-led, design is much harder than bottom-up *ad lib* design, and it is only comparatively recently that it has become a plausible way to design interactive systems of any complexity. This advance is primarily because of the leverage provided by formal methods at the early stages of top-down design. At present, much of the application of formal methods in interactive systems design is still at the research stage and probably cannot be used very effectively for large projects. Nevertheless the 'motto' of formal methods – thinking attention to detail – can most profitably be adopted in user interface design. Formal methods are not merely pedantic descriptions, but by expressing ideas lucidly, give an opportunity to test those ideas on paper and, if they fail, to refine them. Without formal methods, or at least a formal inclination, there is no clear expression of ideas, little attempt to prove or refute ideas or to improve on them – and hence none of the improvements (Lakatos, 1976).

57.3 Choice of style

Different applications and different available hardware (and different levels of manpower to implement the system) impose certain constraints on the interface. There are three broad categories of system:

1. *Special-purpose*:
   (a) *Industrial.* Examples are aircraft or military vehicle cockpit control systems. Here special displays (head-up displays, dedicated instruments etc.) and input devices (joysticks, knobs etc.) are developed. An important consideration is that the user is often involved in multiple tasks possibly under extreme pressure and will not be able to handle overly complex systems. Generally, the relevant industry will impose strict standards.
   (b) *Individual.* Examples are systems to help people with special needs. Although special hardware is readily available (micro switches, breath control devices etc.), typically the hardware and software must be tailored to the individual. An important consideration here is that the user will often be exhausted after 'small' efforts to use the system. Paradoxically, predictive systems (that try to anticipate the user's next action, to save him the effort of doing it) can be counter-productive.
2. *Simplified.* Examples are public-operated devices, such as cash-dispensers, travel enquiry booths, arcade games and complex consumer products generally, such as video recorders, music synthesizers, calculators and so on. An important consideration with simplified systems is that users are generally discretionary, that is, they choose to use the system (and probably pay for it), and will only continue to use the system if it does its job well.

3. *Workstation*. An example is any application requiring a general-purpose computer, typically relying on text and hence on typewriter keyboards. Workstations now have *as standard* screen resolutions sufficient for graphic effects, sound output sufficient for acceptable speech, and analogue data entry devices (e.g. a mouse or touch screen) to supplement QWERTY keyboards. An important consideration with workstation systems is the 'obvious' fact that workstations can do practically anything, and therefore they *may* be doing anything. The user therefore requires additional cues as to what is happening – cues that may not have been necessary for special-purpose or simplified designs with characteristic controls.

Workstations provide the greatest range of possibilities. Indeed, they may be used to prototype or simulate interfaces from any other category without the expense of tooling up for special hardware. Conversely, workstations may inhibit better, but more creative, design. Few musicians, for instance, would be satisfied with a workstation style interface instead of a piano-style keyboard.

Within any category of system, there are four broad styles of interaction.

57.3.1 Style 1: the system provides choices for the user

Here the user has little to remember, except how to choose from among the alternatives presented. This style is therefore ideal for infrequent or casual use. For example, in menu systems the system provides a list of alternatives (e.g. destinations for a sight-seeing trip). The user can select from the alternatives in various ways: they may be numbered; they may have buttons adjacent to them; they may be displayed on a touch-sensitive screen. Note that the menu need not be textual, but can be composed of pictograms or even sounds. In the special case that the user is allowed to relocate the menu components, giving a certain sense of physical concreteness, the style is termed *direct manipulation*.

57.3.2 Style 2: the system provides a structure for the user

Here the user is allowed more freedom than merely selecting from alternatives, but nonetheless is 'led through' the interaction, with the computer in control. The user again has little to remember. For example, in form-filling systems the system displays boxes, each of which requires certain data.

It is very useful to distinguish between spatial and temporal structure. A temporal structure usually manifests itself as a series of questions and answers, with the computer asking the questions. The user is very restricted, particularly if he or she notices an earlier mistake that has 'misled' the direction of questioning. Care must be taken to permit the user to go back over earlier answers, unless this style of interaction is employed for security reasons (e.g. what is your name? what is your clearance? what is your password?). In contrast, a spatial structure allows the user to provide answers in any order, and to see all relevant questions (and their answers) at once. (Note that a series of spatial structures can be imposed on the user as a temporal structure.)

The computer can often use the context (e.g. prior knowledge of the user's task, or of his previous answers) to suggest the user's answers. Such suggestions are termed defaults. In a temporal structure, the user will require an 'accept default' button, but in a spatial structure no special provision for defaults is necessary. The user can simply avoid changing the default.

copies? 1 ↩
inches or mm? i ↩
width? 14 ↩
height? 7.75 ↩

Figure 57.1 Temporal structure: question-and-answer style

Figure 57.1 shows a typical temporal structure in the question-and-answer style. The four questions are asked in order, and no question is asked till the previous one has been answered. The question, 'copies?' must be asked first, since if the user answers '0', the other questions need not be asked. Note the arbitrary abbreviation 'i' for inches, and that each answer must be followed by a delimiter, in this case shown as '↩', but often the ASCII character return or escape.

Note that once the user has typed 'i ↩', he or she is not given an opportunity to change to mm. It might have been better to ask the user to type each measurement with its own units, but this would have been not only more tedious but would have relied on the user remembering the more complex form of answers required.

Contrast this with *Figure 57.2* which shows the equivalent spatial structure, in this case a so-called *dialogue box*. The number of copies to be made has not yet been specified; the user can request help, can cancel this paper specification, or can request the computer to proceed (by pressing 'OK'). Note that the fields can be filled in in any order, for example, the user can change the units of measurement before, after or even during entering the numbers. The dialogue box is probably best used with a keyboard (for entering the numbers) in conjunction with a pointing device such as a mouse; however, this is not necessary. For example, pressing 'tab' could move the typing position between the various fields, or alternatives. Since all data the user enters is expected to be numeric, typing 'H', 'C' or 'O' can be used to select help, cancel, or OK as appropriate. There may, of course, be other conventions for help, cancel and OK and these should be used. Note that abbreviations such as 'C' for cancel are language-specific, and may not work if the system is exported to another country.

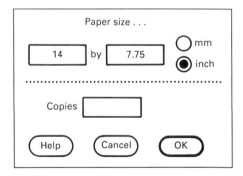

Figure 57.2 Spatial structure: form filling style

57.3.3 Style 3: the user provides 'free-form' input

Here the user is assumed to be skilled in the application. For example, a drawing system allows the user to draw lines and curves freely on the screen; a command-based system allows the user to type statements in some language. In both cases, the computer will impose some syntactical structure (e.g. about how lines may join into polygons) but, in distinction to style 2, the parsing happens *after* the user has submitted input. Since there are so many approaches to parsing, little specific can be said about style 3 in this chapter, except that the designer should take advantage of known parsing algorithms (including language processing tools such as compiler-compilers) wherever possible.

The previous example of paper-size setting is accomplished by the user typing, say, 'papersize 14 7.75' (assuming inches are the default). Note that the command can in principle be entered at any point where a command is expected; the user does not have to wait for questions or a dialogue box to type 'papersize'. On the other hand, the user has to remember the command name for setting paper size (here, 'papersize'), and the correct way to use it. Usually one command, say '?', will print out all available command names, and composite commands like '?pap' will print out information on all commands starting with 'pap', or containing 'pap' in their name.

An alternative way to specify paper size is to use gestural input, rather than by using symbolism which has so far been illustrated. With a gestural interface, the user will provide input by some analogue means, for instance by drawing a full-scale rectangle the size of the required paper (e.g. by using some suitable measuring device, like a tablet) – thus avoiding the question of units of measurement, but introducing potential inaccuracy (or even permitting the user to specify non-rectangular paper!)

57.3.4 Style 4: the user can program the system

A rough distinction is usually made between programming *in* the system (increasing its functionality) and programming *on* the system (merely providing aliases and short-cuts – *accelerators*). Spreadsheets are a good example of programming in; programming on is usually provided by a *macro processing* scheme (and is often also available in spreadsheets) or more simply by customization.

Macros allow the user to define certain symbols (keystrokes or words) to expand to useful sequences, primarily to save typing effort, indeed, to save memorizing long sequences. The advantage of programming on is that it can be implemented separately, as it seems to lie between the user's keyboard and the underlying application. The disadvantage of programming on is that it can interfere with the underlying application, for example, by ignoring any syntactical constraints that should be imposed. In particular, consideration must be given to the manner of handling error messages that arise during the use of a macro – that is, not directly arising from the user's explicit input to the system.

Again, the designer should always take advantage of accepted styles of programming language, and beware of the standard traps (e.g. the 'dangling else' problem). Far too many systems have been marred by *ad hoc* and incomplete languages when a subset of Pascal, Forth or Lisp would have been quite adequate.

Since the four styles of interaction represent increasing flexibility for the user at the expense of greater load on the user's memory, it is sensible to provide 'help', a means to simplify the style of interaction temporarily. For example, in a style 3 interaction, the user may be 'lost for words'. Pressing a help button (preferably one permanently reserved and engraved as such on the keyboard, or 'virtually' displayed on the screen) could bring up a menu of choices, or if this is not possible, of documentation that the user can browse to understand his problem.

57.4 Using principles

It is generally held that using principles in user interface design is better than not using principles, even if these principles are arbitrary. Systems are easier to use if their component parts are usually consistent even when their parts are unconventional; for example, the complete system should only use one algorithm for

abbreviating long names, whatever that algorithm. However, there are plenty of approved principles to deploy (including algorithms for abbreviations) and there is rarely any need to diverge from conventional principles.

The reader is referred to Smith and Mosier (1984) for a substantial collection of principles. Here a very brief list is given omitting such 'obvious' principles as providing rapid feedback to the user's actions. Notice how principles are not necessarily consistent with each other in the limit; the designer has to seek resolutions dependent on the particular circumstances. Also, in certain circumstances there are good reasons to flaunt these principles. For example, if security is an issue, it is better if the user cannot use the system at all than be reminded of the password. Intriguingly, systems that look identical may need quite different design principles; arcade missile games and *real* missile control systems being a case in point. (In this comparison, a careful distinction must be made between *excitement* on the one hand and *alertness* on the other.)

57.4.1 Consistency

Everything should work the same way. This is surprisingly difficult to achieve, not least because it limits the ways in which an existing system can be improved by specific enhancements. Consistent user interfaces avoid the severe problem of *carry-over*, that the user's skills learnt on one system are 'carried over' onto the present system, whether appropriately or not. Carry-over happens particularly when the user is under stress, say, after causing a serious error, and may in turn cause further errors.

Consistency applies to output; the symbols and screen layouts used should be consistent. A good visual consistency is often called a *style* and can be used in a variety of situations; a style may be explicitly designed, e.g. by a typographer.

Consistency also applies to the relation between input and output, which is the next principle.

57.4.2 Enforcing compatibility

Input and output should be compatible, so that in principle the computer's output could be supplied as its own input and *vice versa*. For example, if the system asks for a date in a certain format (e.g. '10 January 1989'), then it should also display dates in this same format throughout.

57.4.3 Using confirmation

1. *Redundant coding.* Contrary to the principle of compatibility, when the user provides input, it is useful if the computer confirms the data *in*compatibly. For example, suppose the preferred date form is '10/1/89', if the user submits '3/7/89' it is useful for the system to confirm the date as 3 July 89, in case the user thought he or she had entered the date March 7 89.
2. *Checkpoint.* The user should be asked whether he or she wishes to proceed with costly or irreversible actions. *Figure 57.2* shows checkpoints 'cancel' and 'OK' in use. The designer should be aware that the user's response may become automatic if he too often needs to reply 'OK'. Some other style of confirmation may be appropriate, or, better still, more actions could be made reversible so that they do not need confirmation.

57.4.4 Clarity in wording

One should be *very* careful about wording. For example, 'Quit without saving data: yes, no or cancel?' is ambiguously worded. Putting the question positively ('Save data before quitting?'), although good practice to improve clarity does not help in this case. The user might say 'no', thinking he did not want to quit, but even so the computer might quit, 'thinking' the user did not want to save! (In this case, it would have been better if confirmation was not a simple answer, but a command, as in 'If you really want to quit without saving data, type REALLY-QUIT'.)

It is advantageous if all phrases can be *configured* in case they later turn out to be inappropriate, e.g. by having a file of standard messages. Incidentally, this simple technique not only makes it easier to export systems to foreign countries but also allows users to work with specialized terminology if necessary. (Consider a stock control program used in different sorts of business.)

57.4.5 Minimizing data entry

The less the user has to enter, the less likely the user is to make mistakes. Nevertheless, errors will still occur, and minimizing data entry should not be taken so far that accidental input has devastating consequences.

57.4.6 Provision for flexibility

It is hard to anticipate the order in which the user will want to accomplish a task. In fact, the user may perform the same task in different ways on different occasions. Systems should therefore not have a fixed order for progressing through a session. Word processors are the classic example of flexibility. A word processor allows the user to write his or her document in any order: starting from the beginning working to the end; starting from headings and fleshing sections out; or even adding bits here and there in any order.

57.4.7 Reducing display clutter

The designer should put as little as possible on the screen. It is unwise to fill the screen with lots of unrelated information (or to use lots of colours – even allowing for colour blindness).

57.4.8 Display inertia

One should change the screen as little as possible (the *principle of display inertia*), and keep regions of it effectively constant (for example, titles). In particular, if menu selection causes side-effects (such as highlighting) then when a menu is redisplayed it should show its last highlighting. This often gives the user a helpful indication of what he has most recently done in that menu.

57.4.9 Exploitation of redundant information

Entries in a menu can be ordered alphabetically, for example, so that the user will be able to locate them faster. Or users can select from menus by alternative means: by typing the entries (abbreviated or in full), by using their key numbers, or by pointing at them.

57.4.10 Allowing for closure

Closure is best illustrated by example. When users go to a cash dispenser (autoteller), they will complete their task – reach closure – when they get their money. The user first has to push a plastic card into the machine, type a few numbers, then get the money. At this point the user will have reached closure, and may walk away *leaving the card behind*. It is therefore essential that the user is given the card back *before* reaching closure; that is, the user should be given the money as the last step after all other details have been completed.

57.4.11 Providing context-sensitive help

'If you want to know what I mean, type "help" ...'

There is a great deal of advice available about writing good and effective help (see the references). Briefly, help should be affirmative or positive, '*do* this, *do* that', rather than negative, '*avoid* this, *never* do that'. It also helps greatly to order actions even within sentences in exactly the order they are required; for example, 'eject the disc after checking you have saved your data', is poor wording, but 'check you have saved your data, then eject the disc', is in the right order.

Note that the author of manuals has a different perspective from that of the user. Typically, the user comes to a manual with a problem and wants to find a solution. That means that indexes, cross-referencing and so on, should tell the user what things *do* as well as what they are called. Who, for instance, would think of looking up 'rm' if they wanted to delete a file?

Users often work in groups, and one may want to provide a specific mechanism in the system so that they can help solve each other's problems, for instance by a simple form of email or 'complaints' field.

The most useful advice is simply to make help as brief as possible (which is, of course, easier than writing copious material) and then simplify the system so that what has been written is sufficient.

57.4.12 Instrumentation

One should provide the means to record what the user is doing, how long it takes, what errors are being made, and so on (with due regard for privacy of personal data). Instrumentation is very useful in identifying bottlenecks in system usage, and may even be retained once a system has been fully released. For example, if a system crashes or has other unusual problems, the logs may provide the designer with useful clues.

57.4.13 Undo

Users make mistakes and will frequently want to undo their actions. The computer, too, may have bugs that cause undesirable effects. In both cases, it is helpful to be able to undo the steps that cause the problem. In the case of computer bugs, the only general way is to keep a log of what the users do: when the system crashes, the log can be replayed just up to the point of disaster. This may then enable users to recover their work by some other method, if the crash was indeed caused by user action, rather than, say, a power failure.

Note that many systems provide a cosmetic undo that has no real power to recover from errors. For example, a drawing program might have a rotation command; although any rotation can be undone by the undo command, the user can 'undo' any rotation merely by rotating backwards, yet may not be able to recover accidental deletions. Note that 'undo' should be able to delete more than just the most recent action; it is probable that after deleting everything the user will panic, and not immediately try the undo command.

57.4.14 Non-preemptive systems

It is not uncommon for dialogue boxes to ask a question while obscuring the information the user needs to answer the question. A *preemptive* system would require the user to answer the question *now*, perhaps even to the extent of not allowing the user to move the dialogue box to reveal the necessary information. A word processor may have a 'check spelling' feature, and as it is running – helping the user to locate spelling mistakes – it should not preempt the user, so stopping him making any other changes he now sees to be appropriate as he fixes spellings. Here preemption is due to the computer only allowing one task (spelling checking), but the user trying to do two (spelling and editing). Preemption may also occur when the user has explicitly embarked on several tasks, say, drawing a picture and printing the previous picture. If the printer runs out of paper, the system can warn the user, but need not preempt the current drawing to tell him.

57.4.15 Allowing interruption

Conversely from Section 57.4.14, if it is a good principle that the system never preempts the user, it is a good principle that the user be able to preempt the system. The system may embark on some long operation, but the user now wants to do something else. The user should be able to interrupt the system at any time, and to resume the interrupted activity when appropriate.

Note that good windowing systems simplify the implementation of non-preemption and interruption principles.

57.4.16 Modes

Each *mode* is a different way of interpreting the same action. The keystroke 'R' may mean run, replace, repeat, rotate, or it may be just the letter 'R' – and then it may mean *insert* the letter 'R' or *overwrite* with the letter 'R'. The more meanings any action has the more likely the user is to misinterpret it. Modes, of course, allow many actions to be made available from a limited symbol set (e.g. the QWERTY keyboard), but great care should be taken that a frequently used symbol in one mode is not overloaded as a dangerous symbol in another mode. It is generally best if non-standard modes are brief, e.g. only active for a short period (e.g. for one keystroke).

Note that different windows strictly represent different modes; the spatial separation of windows is a great aid in reducing mode errors, but it is still a frequent error to 'type into one window while looking at another', that is, to enter data in the wrong mode.

57.4.17 WYSIWYG (what you see is what you get)

Many systems, particularly desk-top publishing and direct-manipulation systems, display a picture representing something real, or potentially printable. At its simplest, WYSIWYG requires that the screen display is an accurate rendition of what will be printed. This is harder than it seems, for instance because of differing resolutions (say, 100 dots/in on a screen against 300 dots/in on a printer), because of different colour schemes (additive on the screen, subtractive on a printer), because of slight differences in font metrics – people being very sensitive to typographical issues. (For example, *Figure 57.3* had to be edited and printed four times to align the grey regions, even though the alignment appeared correct as displayed on screen.) Note that the user may make implicit judgements, say about the alignment of text in certain fonts on the screen, which he expects to work just as well on the printer. More strictly, however, WYSIWYG requires that what the user sees on the screen is *just* what he has, no more and no less. In a word processor, for instance, this would have consequences for the handling of blanks (tabs, newlines and spaces) since they cannot be told apart, all being displayed as nothing. See Figure 57.3, which shows grey regions that the user has *got* but cannot *see* – a common design error that can easily be fixed.

A direct manipulation system adhering to WYSIWYG cannot use accelerators, i.e. keyboard equivalents of certain actions with the mouse on visible objects: the accelerators are not visible, in fact, the entire keyboard is visible, so no *particular* key is visible! This means that an advantage of direct manipulation, visibility of possible operations, is lost with keyboard accelerators.

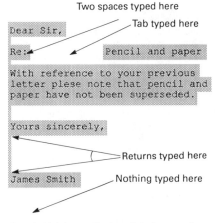

Grey (which is not displayed) indicates where the user may type

Figure 57.3 Incompatibilities with WYSIWYG

Simple hand-held calculators provide another example of failed WYSIWYG. The display shows '84', say. But what is seen does not tell you what you've got: the calculator may have got '84' itself or '84 +' or '84 −' or '84 =' or . . ., and the effect of the next keypress is not determined.

57.4.18 Minimizing user's memory load

It should not automatically be assumed that the user can remember how to use the system – the user may be an infrequent user of the system. Some form of help should always be provided, adopting whatever standard is used in the rest of the user's environment (e.g. hitting the '?' key).

The calculator example above (Section 57.4.17) shows that non-WYSIWYG displays rely heavily on the user's memory to know what keystrokes have gone before.

The use of mnemonics – names – for things in preference to numbers helps here, and a consistent way of naming things (including whether capitalization is significant) is important. There is no excuse to make the user remember 'magic numbers' or numeric IDs. (A macro processor can help sanitize simple interfaces by permitting names to be defined as numbers or other un-mnemonic symbols.)

57.4.19 Providing a sense of progress

Except for skilled users (who were anyway once unskilled), users require 'encouragement' that they are getting closer to achieving their goals. The screen can show how many pages remain to be printed; how many words have been typed; how far the spelling checker has got through the report; how long rendering a car body has yet to take. In some cases absolute measures will be required (e.g. word counts, minutes) while in others a percentage is sufficient. It is, of course, possible to provide both. *Figure 57.4* shows a simple per cent completion bar, shown both graphically and digitally.

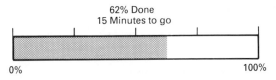

Figure 57.4 Per cent completion indicator

Such indicators also help the user when system limits are reached. Without suitable measures, the user can only guess how to reduce memory loads, but with a memory-remaining indicator, the user has a good idea how effective his 'compaction' is, and also at what stage it is not worth trying to enter more work.

57.4.20 Commensurate effort

Every user action causes a response from the computer, some of which is visible, some of which is (for the moment) internal. The commensurate effort principle requires that the user's effort in getting the computer to do something should be commensurate (roughly, in proportion) to the work the computer does. In particular, it should not be possible to *destroy* information appreciably faster than the user can enter it.

An example that shows using such a principle creatively improves interfaces is a desk-top publishing program that permits the user to change the point size of his or her text. Typically this can be done on letters, words or larger sections. The user may wish to change the type size of a large section, e.g. the entire document. The commands available may permit the user to set the point size to 10, 11, 12 etc. but, if so, then other changes to point size (e.g. in subscripts) within the document will be lost. This is not commensurate effort – information created by many commands (for each of the previous size changes) is lost. Instead, the design should cater for the user to increase or decrease the point size (say by ±1 point). These actions, incidentally, are reversible.

57.4.21 'Can a computer use it?'

Designing systems for fickle people to use is hard. They change their minds, and probably never really know what they want until after the designer has implemented something else. A useful and rigorous test of an interactive system is to try it not on people, but instead on a computer (theoretically or actually). Thus, for the user interface to be usable by a computer, it must not rely on 'insight' or unrevealed knowledge. Any questions asked the user must be computable – if the answer is in principle known by the system (such as the date, or a part number), then it should be accessible for the computer 'user' by some well-defined mechanism. (Thus questions must not be preemptive – for if so, then there is *no* mechanism.) Following a non-procedural programming paradigm, one might further want every 'user' response to be in principle computable from the task that is visible on the *current* screen alone, rather than in addition to information held in the user's memory of past screens.

A word processor, for instance, must not conceal information that it 'expects' its human user to know, e.g. whether a certain region of blank screen is spaces or 'really' empty, for a computer 'user' certainly will not. Of course, a computer *could* know enough to use any system merely by duplicating that system's program, but then that would be like expecting the user to know the system's program by heart, which is an unlikely situation (except for the designer). If the system has reached some limit, e.g. the user has typed six characters into a six character code field, then it should indicate that the limit has been reached. How is the user supposed to know? Would one want to program in all such little details into the test computer program?

The 'Can a computer use it? test' helps remind the designer that the task is not just to design an interactive computer system, but also to 'program' the user – provide good enough documentation – so that the system can be used correctly under all circumstances.

57.4.22 Natural language input

Natural language has the impression of being easy to use, and in

some sense it is. Unfortunately, parsing natural language is extremely costly, slow, and – except in heavily circumscribed applications – subject to âmbiguities. Of course, the system can always ask the user to clarify which of several meanings he or she had in mind (a form of *confirmation*), but too often the apparently unlimited scope of natural language will lead the user to impute impossible skills to the computer. Nevertheless, one should not underrate trivial language processing, as in many adventure games (e.g. 'pick up the red ball'), or basically 'deceptive' language processing, where the computer merely looks for keywords, simply ignoring words not in its vocabulary.

57.4.23 Wider issues

Concessions will generally have to be made for international markets where appropriate, e.g. for date formats and for the language used for any natural language text. Thus standard chess notation, representing Knights by 'Kt' or 'N' (which should be made *aliases* – alternative names for the same thing – in an interactive system) is not the accepted international notation. So-called 'figurine' notation is preferred, where Knights become ♘ and are then unmistakable in any language, and can also be recognized by people unable to read. So, it is important to make full use of *clear* symbols (icons) where possible, whilst noting that the editing and layout of symbols is not so easy as text, e.g. there is no alphabetical order.

A surprising number of users are handicapped in one way or another. Many of us cannot add up numbers accurately; many men are colour blind; many users cannot type very well; many users are doing more than just using the computer – dealing with clients. So providing suitable features enhances the system generally.

Initially, every user of a system is a new user, so one should provide features to support new users. A recommended way to do this is to provide *minimal systems*. These are systems that are syntactically complete but semantically restricted. Thus menus will show the user what he or she can do on a full system, but only safe features are available on the minimal system. The user can use a minimal system quite safely, but is also naturally exposed to the range of features of the full system. Menu entries can be 'greyed-out' if they are inactive, but in general it is better to let the user start advanced features with a warning that they are disabled but would have done these tasks; or perhaps, ask for confirmation, whereby the user may want to learn by exercising on a disabled feature, or may really want to use an 'advanced' feature though still a new user.

57.4.24 Allowing for catastrophes

The computer will crash some day; there may be a power failure, a virus or some hardware failure. So one should build in mechanisms so that the user can recover 'lost' work. Logs should be kept of the user's activities so that they can be replayed on another working system. Users should not be allowed to work for a long time without making backups of the current session. Following the other principles in this list will undoubtedly bring 'percentage' improvements to any interface; following this final principle may save the user weeks' worth of work – and perhaps the user's company as well.

57.5 Gueps: dual principles

Many of the design principles listed above have an uneasy status. It is not *quite* clear what they mean for any particular design, and yet they are undoubtedly 'true'. Some principles relate to the complexities of the real world, e.g. design for international markets, but most concern the inter-relatedness of components of the user interface. As such, they may be formalized and their application in a particular design reasoned through.

In any contractual situation or where a design team of several people is involved, it is essential to identify what such principles really mean. Generative user-engineering principles, *gueps*, are dual principles that have both formal and informal representations. A principle such as WYSIWYG can be expressed as a theorem of the system specification, and can also be expressed colloquially in a form suitable for a user to understand – WYSIWYG itself is practically a colloquial term now. As a theorem it can be shown to hold, or not, as the case may be, or to interact or conflict, or not, with other formalized principles. The advantages that accrue are precisely those of formal methods: the designer knows exactly what is being designed and what its properties are, and furthermore those properties are (presumably) relevant to the user. In particular, the informal expression of the principles can be adopted in the manuals or other user-training material (including on-line help) as 'golden rules' about how the system behaves.

Figure 57.5 indicates the idea. The design principles are first agreed and then expressed as dual principles, both for the software engineering of the computer system design, and for the 'psychological engineering' of all the other materials (training courses, manuals, etc.) that are part of the product. The software engineering and psychological engineering proceed more-or-less in step, although obviously some revisions may be forced from either side. The end results are respectively a computer program, adhering to the principles, and a 'user program' – a manual, for instance – adhering to the *same* principles. The system and its manual therefore agree unusually closely, especially in the nature of limitations, boundary conditions and 'bugs'. In contrast, a conventional design method would have the manual being written by professional documentation writers *after* the system was complete, probably at the last possible moment as this would avoid the cost of revising the manual as the system undergoes its own revisions. This means that insights gained in the 'psychological engineering' of composing good documentation come too late and have to be ignored.

More about gueps can be found in Thimbleby (1990). An application of them is given below in Section 57.7.

57.5.1 Exploiting programming language principles

The first problem with gueps is thinking of them. There are two approaches: invent one's own, or 'steal' some. A fertile area for stealing them from is programming language design, which will now be considered.

Programming languages such as Pascal have come under constructive criticism from denotational semantics. The mathematical way of looking at programming languages means that some things are equally easy to say mathematically, but the language for one reason or another has variations or limitations. Thus, Pascal can only make functions out of commands (so-called procedures) and out of expressions (its so-called functions). But Pascal involves other constructs, such as declarations, and once it has been 'mathematicized', there is no reason in principle not to have functions of declarations – classes, in other words. This is the principle of abstraction: that meaningful syntactic categories (expressions, commands, etc.) can be abstracted, made into procedures. Related programming language design principles are the principle of correspondence, the principle of qualification, the principle of orthogonality and the principle of data-type completeness; see Tennent (1981) for examples. Such principles can be used in user interface design, particularly when the user interface provides a rich variety of features.

The principle of correspondence is perhaps the easiest of these principles to apply to interactive systems design. However, its application is first illustrated below by an example from Pascal. In Pascal there is a semantic correspondence between variable declarations and formal parameter declarations. Thus the two pieces of Pascal code in *Figure 57.6* correspond exactly; both fragments bind the name 'x' to new storage, initialize it to 3, and invoke 'write' (representing the arbitrary body of the block).

In general, the correspondence for any such declarations is exact, assuming only that 'p', the arbitrary name of the procedure, is not otherwise bound. The correspondence could now be 'tidied up', by permitting variables to be initialized when declared (e.g. 'var x: = 3 integer'). Furthermore, the correspondence has not exhausted all declaration and formal parameter mechanisms, and in Pascal there are mechanisms that do not correspond. Thus, 'var' parameters have no corresponding declarative mechanism (though it has semantics similar to 'with' declarations), and 'const' definitions have no corresponding parameter mechanism. Of course, the revised ISO Pascal Standard has addressed some of these issues, for instance providing constant parameter forms, but has not permitted constant definitions with expressions which is immediately suggested by the correspondence of being able to pass constant expressions as actual parameters.

Now consider a user interface such as exhibited by the Macintosh Finder and miniFinder. The Finder is the 'operating system level' of the Macintosh, allowing users to find and open files; the miniFinder is an alternative mechanism that allows

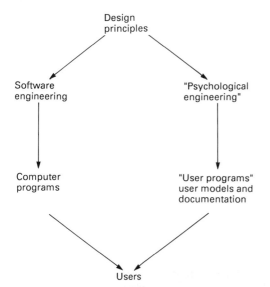

Figure 57.5 Top-down design with dual principles

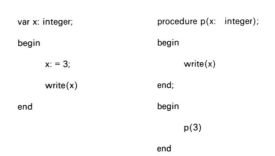

Figure 57.6 Pascal declaration correspondence

Table 57.1 Example miniFinder/Finder correspondences

miniFinder	Finder
New fiile	—
Open file	Open file
Open directory	Open directory
View directory as text	View directory as text
Scroll directory	Scroll directory
—	View directory as icons
View directory alphabetically	View directory alphabetically
—	View directory by date
Go to any parent directory	—
—	Rename existing file
—	Change directory of existing file
—	Copy file
Eject disc	Eject disc
—	Rename disc
—	Use menu bar, run other applications etc.
—	Get information on files
Find file within directory from first character*	—
—	Find file anywhere from full name

*Only when opening an existing file, not when creating or saving a file, when typing changes that file's name.

users to find and open files when they are running an application. Clearly these two schemes correspond – the correspondence is, however, slight, and could easily be completed ('closed'). *Table 57.1* shows the extent of the correspondence, and *some* of the missing possibilities.

Overall, then, adopting programming language principles not only inherits a wealth of powerful research into expressiveness and consistency, but encourages a more systematic interface design.

57.6 Use of tools

So far, the discussion has been conceptual. Practical programming and evaluation tools are now reviewed briefly.

57.6.1 Programming tools

A user interface, say, for a database requires:

1. Basic input/output: graphics, mouse and keyboard event handling.
2. 'Design': what should the screens look like?
3. Semantics: what should it do?
4. Data: what does it do it with?
5. Integration: how does it work with other systems?

Often a 'minor' change in the appearance at the user interface level will require simultaneous changes at all these levels. Obviously this means that one should try to avoid changes by 'getting it right first time', perhaps by adhering closely to standards, *or* one should use a programming environment where there is little overhead moving between the levels.

Object-oriented programming, particularly in Smalltalk, which includes powerful graphics primitives and standard procedures for interaction techniques (such as menus), is an ideal approach. Unless the development is one-off, the disadvantage of Smalltalk is that it requires considerable computing resources which will almost certainly mean that the application has to be recoded in a conventional programming environment once it has been finalized. But this is a very minor cost, given the flexibility available and the ease of getting the first implementation to work well enough for trials. Object-oriented programming for user interfaces has the very significant advantage – for producing quality interfaces – that most user interface features correspond to specific fragments of program – objects, in fact. Thus, improving the program tends to improve the interface, a relation that does not obtain in other programming paradigms.

HyperCard is a simple programmable database with simple bit-mapped graphics and is ideal for developing experimental user interfaces. The major contribution of HyperCard to user interface design is the ease of moving between the various levels of implementation. Furthermore, HyperCard is extensible and can be augmented – programmed *in* – with 'external commands' written in conventional programming languages such as Pascal. Unlike Smalltalk, HyperCard runs well on cheap hardware, such as Apple Macintoshes, and has inspired a number of imitations on other computers. For some applications a Hyper-Card system will be quite adequate as a final system, though error handling is often tricky, if not actually impossible in some cases. Note that in general the chosen programming system's exception handling mechanisms can have a significant effect on the style and quality of the final interface.

There are a number of interface design tools, called user interface management systems (UIMS). These tend to impose a specific style of interaction on applications; they are not equally suitable for all jobs. It will help if the UIMS generates source code, e.g. in Pascal, in case subtle changes need to be made by hand, though this step may compromise maintenance at a later date.

The distinction between UIMS and normal programming support environments is becoming eroded as programming environments become more sophisticated. Thus systems such as interface libraries, MacApp, X/windows, a good Lisp system, and so on, provide many features overlapping with UIMS. A good UIMS, however, should not only provide an environment for rapid prototyping, but should also provide some analysis of the user interface (can the user get trapped? does every subsystem have the same exit command? how many commands are needed to get from here to there?) and be able to generate code that can be incorporated into the rest of the application. *Vice versa*, maybe the application can be incorporated into the UIMS code.

Likewise, the distinction between end user applications and UIMSs is becoming eroded as applications themselves acquire programming facilities. HyperCard, described above, is one such example – it is a programmable database. Some text editors (e.g. EMACS) are programmable and can be extended almost indefinitely, to prototype text processing applications. Many spreadsheets are ideal development tools, not only for financial and numerical applications, but for any interfaces requiring graphical data presentation.

At all levels of design it should go without saying that appropriate programming tools be employed: parser generators, lexical analysers, etc. The power of pencil and paper should not be underestimated, either for thinking or prototyping. Users can often help assess a complex prototype design that is shown to them just using hand-drawn illustrations and hypothetical questions such as, 'You did that, now the computer will show something like this, and ask you to do this.'

57.6.2 Assessment

Most users know more about what they are doing than designers, although designers may have useful insights. Only users know why *they* are puzzled, only users know what they wanted to do, only users know what they *thought* was happening.

A very simple technique, the '*think-aloud method*', is a powerful and cheap way of evaluating user interfaces. Put simply, the think-aloud method is to sit a designer down with a user who is working with the system in question and to encourage the user to think aloud about what he or she is doing. The user is encouraged to say whatever comes into his head as he tries to use the system.

The advantage of sitting with the user and encouraging him to think aloud as he works is that many things would otherwise be quickly forgotten. Giving the user a questionnaire afterwards, which is a standard technique, but requires careful design and administratioin, may be too late. In fact, a new user may not know whether he is making mistakes, but the watchful designer can make a note of any problems.

A few simple rules for the think-aloud method need to be observed:

1. The user must be encouraged to feel at ease thinking aloud. The designer should make it quite clear that this is a test of the system, and not a test of the user. Thus every problem the user has is valuable to hear about.
2. The think-aloud method creates an artificial situation. The designer has to be there, but he must not give special help to the user even if he is asked for it. This may seem rude, and the designer should explain and apologise in advance. The designer should explain that he needs to see how the user sorts out problems for himself. Nevertheless there will be times when the designer needs to intervene and provide hints. This will be when the difficulty has been noted, and it is apparent that the next design can fix the problem. There is no point holding the user up any further.
3. It is useful to remember that being helpful is a temptation to be avoided – especially as the designer knows far more about the system. The more help that is given, the less useful the think-aloud work will be about the *current* design being tested.

Think-aloud can not only be used for helping debug the computer system, but can also help with the design of documentation, and to help discover discrepancies between the documentation structure and the way people use the system to perform their tasks.

Think-aloud is so effective in leading to design improvements that an *n*-person design team will often better split up as an $n-1$ member team, with the 'lost' person doing something else. When the system is almost ready, the 'lost' designer returns to be the 'user' for think-aloud debugging. Because he or she has not seen the system, and has not been party to the reasons – or excuses – why the system has turned out the way it has, he will have startlingly good insights into the user interface design. The end result will be far better, and can be done with fewer man-month's work. (Clearly a designer will tend to generate different sorts of insights about the system than a more typical user. They will still be interesting but may be more technically oriented.)

57.6.3 The Wizard of Oz

Instead of implementing a complete system, for some purposes, particularly during development, it is sufficient to *pretend* to

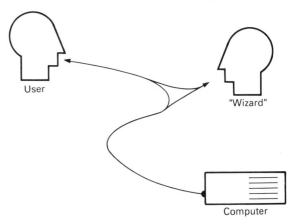

Figure 57.7 The Wizard of Oz

implement a full system. A human, called the wizard, monitors the user's interaction and intervenes as necessary so that the user sees a fully developed system. *Figure 57.7* shows this diagrammatically. A simple application of the *wizard* is to convert prototype error messages (such as 'Error!') into something more relevlant to the user's task (such as 'You can only print one master copy'). Presumably, the human wizard knows that the user is trying to print a master copy, but the prototype system does not yet recognize the context. When the wizard's interventions are examined, various ways of enhancing the interface become apparent. A very powerful way to use the Wizard of Oz technique is to simply place *untrained* users in front of a system and tell them to use it, to print invoices or whatever. Here the users have no preconceptions about the syntax or vocabulary, and the wizard must convert whatever the users generated into valid commands. If many users use similar forms, then these may be candidates for adoption in the final system.

Usually, the wizard should see exactly what the user sees on his or her screen, plus any other useful information. Whenever errors occur, and in certain other situations, the wizard can take control and provide input directly. The wizard will also need to be able to edit unsuitable output from the system before the user sees it. The wizard will probably need to perform experiments, e.g. to find a file the user seems to be referring to, without the user being aware.

Note that the Wizard of Oz is not only a powerful development technique, but in suitable form can also be retained in a final system to enable skilled users to help their colleagues. Here one user might get stuck; he requests help from another user; that user becomes a wizard for the first and helps him out.

57.7 A simple, effective design method

Given the wide range of environments and range of user skills for which systems may have to be developed, it might appear that there would be a correspondingly large range of design methods. However, it is possible to summarize a powerful method for user interface design that applies to the entire range of human–computer interfaces, from programming language designs (not very interactive; user relaxed and alert) to airplane control (real-time and highly interactive; user stressed and fatigued).

The method can be summed up as 'utter honesty plus Occam's razor' and is worked out as follows:

1. Document the intended system from the user's point of view.

The more detailed the documentation the better. If you can't be bothered to document something, take that as an indication that perhaps the feature is not worth having anyway.

2. Describe *all* known bugs, provisos, limitations, side-effects etc. If there are known ways around the bugs ('work-arounds'), write them down too (then ask yourself why the program cannot do them for the user).

3. Improve the *system* by simplifying the *documentation*. In particular, you will improve the system by (truthfully) being able to remove the bug warnings that you entered into the documentation under Rule 2.

(For an essay on utter honesty see Feynman (1985).)

In practice, these steps will be iterated and interleaved with implementation and the development of production documentation. It is possible to compromise the method by designing only the core of the system in the way suggested; this results in a *minimal manual*. Minimal manuals, which correctly describe a subset of the system, have been found to be very effective for user training, but to be effective they require a way to 'block off' the user from the advanced features that are not described in the minimal manual.

For example, one word processor manual warns the user that it is not possible to delete more than 100 paragraphs in one go. But to follow Rule 3, the system should now be changed so that this bug warning is no longer necessary. Maybe the system was written in Pascal with an array of 100 elements, but surely the program could be changed so that if the user tried to delete more than 100 paragraphs, the program would iterate, deleting no more than 100 paragraphs per iteration. This should be easy enough to implement, and doing so would simplify the manual, and improve the system.

Simple, complete documentation is a good thing, and making it so improves the system. In the absence of any agreed ways of evaluation success with design, the length of the documentation is a good indicator. It is useful to reduce the length of documentation, not by glossing bug warnings, but by fixing bugs in the implementation.

This three-step approach is of course facilitated by gueps (Section 57.5), particularly because of the active role of developing documentation enabled by gueps: improvements are led by the documentation, not by the computer implementation.

57.8 Exercise

As an exercise (whether real or imagined) one could consider designing a system to play chess. Although this example has been deliberately kept simple, note:

1. How many alternative design options are available. Trade-offs are not very obvious 'in the abstract', and almost certainly a prototype system must be built and assessed.

2. How many features that are useful for design and evaluation of the system can also form useful features for the user. Notice, too, that a 'simple' self-contained application like chess throws up very many creative possibilities, and that the designer has to make careful tradeoffs.

3. How very soon a very detailed knowledge of the application (in this case chess) is essential to implement a satisfactory system. (Indeed, too many chess programs currently available do not correctly implement the basic rules of chess.)

Chess is a well-known application, and one can assume that users will know how to play the game, but should one provide tuition features? Implementing the chess 'engine' itself is relatively straight-forward. Indeed one may have access to a suitable program whose interface can be modified, either by reprogramming or by filtering the chess program's input and output.

Chess can of course be played on a board with real pieces – a Category 2 interface (Section 57.3) – but more usually one will implement a chess program on a workstation, possibly making use of graphics to provide a display of the board in photographic realism (with perspective and lighting effects?) or in symbolic form (as used in conventional printed chess boards). There are clearly a wide range of choices for the representation of the board, and there is a complex tradeoff between realism and obtaining an adequate speed. There is a subtle tradeoff that the more effort put into the interface, the more the system will exploit idiosyncracies of the hardware it is running on, yet the more the designer may wish to amortize the design effort by making the system portable across many different sorts of hardware.

If the user has few choices for his move (perhaps only one), the system may highlight available alternatives. In fact, the user may want the computer to make the best move, that is, to accept the default offered.

There are many alternatives for input styles. Direct manipulation is feasible. The user simply points at a piece and moves it to its destination square. All moves apart from promoting pawns (the user will normally promote to a queen, but need not do so) are straightforwardly handled by direct manipulation.

Chess has various symbolic notations which suggest alternatives to direct manipulation. Instead of physically moving a pawn, the user might type 'd4', meaning move a piece, e.g. the pawn previously on d2, to square d4. The standard notation provides ample scope for defaults. *Command completion* is a technique where the computer, anticipating what else the user will input, completes the user's command. For example, if the user types 'a' and the only piece he can move on the a file is a pawn at a3, the computer could complete the command with '*a3–a4*', saving the user from typing four characters (or beep if that piece could not be moved). Command completion can be annoying as it doesn't always happen, so it is usual to provide a completion button. Command completion then occurs only when this button is pressed. It amounts to accepting a default given a user-specified prefix.

An equal-opportunity interface would allow the user to move either by direct manipulation or by standard notation. If the user moves a piece by pointing and dragging, then the computer generates the symbolic form. Conversely, if the user types the symbolic form, the computer moves the piece. It will be neat to permit parts of moves to be made either way. Thus, typing 'a4' makes the piece of square a4 flash, just as it would if it had been selected by pointing. Alternatively, selecting a piece by pointing at it, then typing 'a5', moves the selected piece to square a5. In short, equal opportunity removes distinctions between input, e.g. the typed commands, and output (the changes to the board). More generally, equal opportunity suggests allowing the user and computer to exchange sides, viewing the computer's moves as its output responding to the user's moves as its input, which is anyway a useful feature to consider for a chess program.

An advantage of standard chess notation, and written notation in general, is that a log can be kept of the interaction for perusal later. Obviously in chess, a chess player is probably interested in his or her choice of moves that led to a certain outcome, but the designer is also interested in the log, especially if it is annotated with times and errors, to see how the user interface might be improved. The user, too, will want to annotate the log, e.g. with insights about the position, or alternative moves considered, this point confirms the view that designer tools make good user interface features for users. On a workstation it may be desirable to show the complete log of the game at all times. Since this may be too large to fit, there will need to be some mechanism to scroll it (to move it vertically).

People often make mistakes, and although it is strictly illegal in chess, there are cases, e.g. solving set problems, where the user will want to try out moves 'to see what happens', and if the outcome is unwanted to undo his previous move. In general, the user should be able to undo moves right back to the start of a game, and indeed to redo undone moves in case he undoes too far back.

Chess is often played under time constraints. The system should display a time-to-completion indicator. In chess this need only show total time remaining, but in other applications it is more useful to show time remaining before the user next can reply, sometimes as a per-cent-done indicator, as shown in Figure 57.4. In some games, players may be required to move within a certain agreed time per move. It is interesting that on time-shared computers time to completion can be estimated accurately merely by being conservative; any excess time can be spent on other tasks. The user benefits because the time to completion is reliable.

As in many applications, the user may have to suspend a game, for example, while he goes for a cup of tea. The computer may have to be switched off or the session terminated by logging out. In all cases, then, the computer should provide a way of saving and restoring games. In general, a player may want to have more than one game in progress, so there should be a way of identifying suspended games for later recall. This is analogous to, say, word processing where a user may be typing several documents, 'suspended' documents being called files, identified by name. It is good practice to provide an integrated way to save games on alternative media, in case of hardware faults rendering the system inoperable. In particular, hard copy is usually desirable and in the last resort the user can always retype a game by hand – a requirement which in turn requires the user to be able to specify the computer's moves.

Chess provides an obvious application of the use of the Wizard of Oz technique. Instead of playing the computer, the computer merely acts as an intermediary for another human player (perhaps hidden in another room, so that the actual user does not know the difference). The user can be his or her 'own' wizard if the system allows players to change sides.

Chess is a good vehicle for experimenting with the use of speech and sound, to diagnose user errors (illegal moves) and to announce moves, mate and so on. An interesting design principle would be: 'a game can (in principle) be played with your eyes shut', meaning that the sounds provide enough information for the player to know exactly what the board position is. Blind or blindfold chess players might enjoy this, but most players would certainly benefit from the redundant output confirming what they can see happen. If the computer makes moves using 'direct manipulation', speech would dis-ambiguate similar moves such as a bishop or pawn taking a piece.

It is possible that users could be taught playing strategies by viewing, for example, end games animated at high speed. Equally, designers could replay interactions at high speed to identify salient features of interaction. Colour, or grey level, could be used very effectively for indicating certain sorts of positions, e.g. forks, the 'square of the pawn', or the combined force threatening a particular square.

Unusually for such a simple application, chess also provides interesting possibilities for programming. A user may want to play the Sicilian or other book opening, or castle, or to chase the black king into the corner. More interesting possibilities are to change the rules, e.g. to play Scotch chess, or to introduce pieces that move differently.

There are many formal interface design principles applicable to the chess application. Here a few are listed that are readily formalized and are also expressed colloquially as 'golden rules'. Some principles seem obvious, but consider how similar rules are flaunted in many intereactive applications, such as word processors or spreadsheets.

1. The system must have levels, each level selecting a different set of laws of its behaviour. One level certainly has to restrict behaviour to the accepted FIDE tournament rules, while another level allows setting up of arbitrary positions, and another level allows imposing handicaps (e.g. removing a queen), etc.
2. Although the user can change levels at will, it is reasonable to impose laws about level changing. Thus it should not be possible to set the level to tournament rules after 'cheating' by operating at a different level. Nevertheless, the user may want a level so that the system acts as if at the tournament level.
3. All errors are notified by a beep and by an explanatory message on the screen. The message disappears when the cause of the error is rectified.
4. A distinction is made between preemptive and non-preemptive errors/ warnings. At some playing levels, all errors must be preemptive, to stop cheating. At others, some errors, e.g. that a player is in check, may be because the user is constructing a position and further pieces have yet to be placed.
5. The system displays the complete state. That is, it must display: the board; all pieces in their proper places and colours; whether castling and check have occurred for each side; time remaining for each player; move number; moves since a piece has been taken; repetition count etc. If games can be suspended, then their names (or other unique identification) must also be displayed.
6. A saved game saves all the state.
7. Every state must be reachable (at the appropriate playing level). Thus the user must be able to set up any position, including specifying previous castling and checks.
8. Undoing a move always causes the computer to take back the corresponding move; redoing a move causes the computer to replay the original move (and not some alternative). Thus undo-redo are inverse operators.
9. Defaults (command completion) are only suggested when there is exactly one move. Other playing levels may provide 'suggestions' rather than defaults.
10. Abbreviated moves, e.g. 'd4' or 'Nd4' instead of 'Nb2 × d4', are only accepted when unambiguous.
11. Since users make mistakes, and when the playing level permits it, there should be a way to delete typing mistakes. Typically, when the user hits 'DEL', the previous keystroke is deleted. The relevant principle, therefore, is that the system should revert to *exactly* the state it was in before that key was pressed. Thus, any command completion should be taken back; any visual feedback on the board part way through a move showing the selected piece should revert. A second principle – at the appropriate playing level, if any – is that there is no limit on the number of 'DEL's that can be typed, even deleting back through previous moves. (Note that 'DEL' acts at an interface level, undoing actions such as keystrokes, whereas undo acts at an application level, undoing actions such as moves.)
12. Whenever there is a delay, e.g. the computer is considering its move, the screen should show a suitable indication that something is happening. Typically, the cursor will change to a 'watch' or 'hour glass' symbol. This wait symbol is a special case of the percent-done indicator and can be used more generally.
13. If the log is displayed and scrollable, then no changes occur to undisplayed parts of the log. Thus, when either player makes a move, the log must scroll to the appropriate position, presumably the end unless this move is an undo or redo of earlier moves. This is a special case of the rule: when things change, the user can see them change.

57.9 Summary

The user interface is often left till last, as the 'real', underlying part of the system must be implemented first. The user interface tends, then, to be very much an afterthought, and can often be a development from the system debugger. Thus the opportunities for creativity within the constraints of top-down design are lost. User interface design is no less of a challenge than programming the intricate algorithms of the application. Indeed, it is more of a challenge because of the uncertainties of the user's needs and behaviour. It deserves to be designed in step with the rest of the system, with the designs of the underlying application and interface mutually suggesting improvements.

This chapter has raised many of the salient issues in user interface design and suggested various approaches to the effective design of interactive systems. It has not covered psychological techniques, for instance, to find out what users really do or want, or how they really go about using computer systems when nobody is watching them. Instead it has promoted principle-led design, allowed that even with the best intentions bugs and inconsistencies arise, that they must be acknowledged, and their acknowledgement can lead to improvements in the overall system design.

57.10 References and bibliography

Apple (1987) *Human Interface Guidelines: The Apple Desktop Interface*, Addison-Wesley. [Proprietary guidelines for developers of Macintosh applications; much more restricted, then, than Smith and Mosier (1984), but collectively impose a distinctive and effective style. The emphasis is on direct manipulation interfaces.]

Bailey, R. W. (1982) *Human Performance Engineering: a Guide for System Designers*, Prentice-Hall. [Practically all the psychology and ergonomic information that a designer should be aware of.]

Feynman, R. P. (1985) Cargo cult science. In *Surely You're Joking, Mr. Feynman!*, Bantam Books. [The final chapter of this brilliant book is an appeal to do science honestly. It seems to this author that a lot of computer science, particularly user interface design, would be the better for honest standards.]

Harrison, M. D. and Thimbleby, H. W. (1990) *Formal Methods in Human Computer Interaction*, Cambridge University Press. [Summarizes recent research in formal aspects of human–computer interfacing (HCI), in particular bringing software engineering techniques to bear on the HCI design process. Also discusses prototyping and UIMS, etc.]

Helander, M. (ed.) (1988) *Handbook of Human-Computer Interaction*, North-Holland. [A massive guidebook to human factors (psychological/ergonomic) engineering in all aspects oif user interface design; summarizes both research and recommendations. Unfortunately does not discuss implementation issues.]

Lakatos, I. (1976) *Proofs and Refutations*, Cambridge University Press. [A play exploring and developing the creative side of mathematical proof; relevant here for its implications on the creative application of formal methods in 'even' user interface design.]

Levy, D. (1988) *Computer Chess Compendium*, Batsford [A collection of computer chess articles, ranging from the classic Shannon and Turing papers on computer chess, through the de Groot, Chase and Simon psychological studies of skill in chess. Alan Turing mentions paper simulation to help design chess machines, but the only comment about user interfaces as such relates to checking for illegal moves – and is dated 1958, when punched cards were the state-of-the-art user interface.]

Myers, B. (1988) *Creating User Interfaces by Demonstration*, Academic Press [A useful discussion of UIMS, particularly concentrating on the author's system, Peridot. Peridot enables interfaces to be built largely by 'demonstration'.]

Newman, W. M. (1986) *Designing Integrated Systems for the Office Environment*, McGraw-Hill International. [Complements Schneiderman (1987) with very good descriptions of many ofice systems, including networks, graphics, integrated systems.]

Schneiderman, B. (1987) *Designing the User Interface*, Addison-Wesley [A good survey of the human side of interactive systems design. Intermediate between Bailey (1982) and Thimbleby (1990) in orientation towards computers.]

Smith, S. L. and Mosier, J. N. (1984) Guidelines for designing user interface software *Technical Report ESD-TR-84-190*, Hanscom Air Force Base, MA, USA. [A massive compendium of user interface design guidelines. This collection has been repeatedly revised in the light of new studies; more recent editions may be available.]

Tennent, R. D. (1981) *Principles of Programming Languages*, Prentice-Hall. [An introduction to the design principles underlying programming languages.]

Thimbleby, H. W. (1990) *User Interface Design*, Addison-Wesley. [The present chapter is based on this book which is a more abstract survey of user interface design than Schneiderman (1987) promoting formal methods and their creative potential in design.]

58

Digital telephony and switching

Malcolm I Wardlaw
British Telecom

Contents

58.1 Introduction

It bears repeating that the world-wide telephone network is the largest machine that man has ever created. It is perhaps this scale, more than anything else, that generates the most difficulty for the telecommunications software engineer. The magnitude of the problem applies just as much to the physical size (say 10 000–100 000 subscribers) for a modern stored program-controlled (SPC) exchange as it does to the variety of different systems that need to work together. Many of these different systems will have been designed over the last 20 years (before many of the techniques described in this book were commonplace), and this creates another set of compatibility problems as new services are introduced.

The challenge that the exchange designer faces today therefore is the introduction of new exchange features, in commercial timescales, working within an extensive real-time environment, compatible with many older systems and with the management facilities required by the telephone company – all, of course, within budget.

This chapter cannot hope to be a complete guide to writing SPC software, and thus will present an outline of the basic problems that all telephone exchange designers have to solve, and will then describe some of the current problems, architectures and techniques that are being studied today.

58.2 Basic transmission and switching

Before considering the control and management of telephone exchanges, it is important to have a model of the system to be controlled. First the digital exchange will be considered and then this will be developed into the Integrated Services Digital Network (ISDN) concept.

58.2.1 Analogue-to-digital conversion for telephony

The digital transmission and switching of voice signals follows directly from Nyquist's sampling theorem. He showed that if an analogue signal was sampled at a rate at least twice that of the highest baseband signal, the original signal could be perfectly reconstructed (at some distant point) from those samples (see *Figure 58.1*). It has been shown that a baseband signal of 300 Hz–3.4 kHz provides an acceptable telephony system for most users. This signal is then sampled 8000 times per second and the value of the sample is coded into 8 bits, to produce a digitized voice signal of 64 kbit s^{-1}.

It is worth noting that today it is possible to produce very acceptable voice signals using predictive coders at 32 and even 16 kbit s^{-1}. However, Europe has come to standardize on 64 kbit s^{-1}. In the USA, a different voice coding standard has been adopted, resulting in a 56 kbit s^{-1} standard. The remainder of this chapter will assume the European system.

It may also be worth noting that the coding is not linear as more codes are used to cover the quieter signal values (where the subjective effect of a coding error would be greatest) than are used over the greater signal values. An 8-bit code would not be large enough otherwise.

58.2.2 Digital switching

Most telephones remain idle for a large part of the day, and even during the exchange's busiest hour an average residential phone will be busy only 1% of the time and a business line only 10% of the time. In order to provide economically a switching matrix that will deal with a sparse number of active subscribers the architecture of *Figure 58.2* has become very common. This has a concentration switching stage (more inputs than outputs), fol-

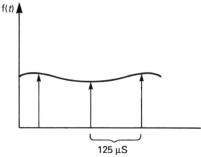

Original analogue signal

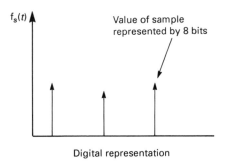

Value of sample represented by 8 bits

Digital representation

Figure 58.1

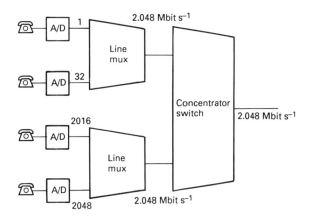

Figure 58.2 Subscriber's concentrator

lowed by a square fully non-blocking switch (any input can reach any output irrespective of the state of the switch).

The usual interface chosen between the concentration stage and the main digital switch will comprise 30×64 kbit s^{-1} circuits time-multiplexed together with an additional two circuits (also of 64 kbit s^{-1} each) carrying timing and signalling information. This will produce an overall bit rate of 2048 kbit s^{-1}.

Thus, the main digital switch has a number of space-divided inputs from the concentrator switches, each carrying 30 time-divided 64 kbit s^{-1} circuits. To connect any subscriber to any other subscriber, it is necessary to be able both to switch one incoming time slot to another outgoing time slot, and to connect spatially one physical circuit to another at any moment in time.

For example, in *Figure 58.3*, to connect A to B, the sample in the first timeslot on circuit 1 has to appear in the third timeslot on circuit *n*. The vast majority of digital switches will be made up of three stages: a time switch followed by a space switch, followed by a time switch (the TST configuration).

Given all the existing paths that are currently in use, the selection of a path through a digital switch is carried out exclusively by software in a modern exchange. A map of the switch is held in the processor and is interrogated by the switch handler in order to select a (pair of) path(s) through the switch. (As most conversations are two-way if A needs a path to B we also need its dual so that B gets a path to A.) If the control processor fails for any reason, this switch map is lost. Most telephone companies require that calls in progress at the time of the crash remain set up in their stable state. This requires that the switch control software is able either to back-up the state of its map periodically to a hard disc or is able to interrogate the actual state of the switch to see what connections are actually set. On the face of it, the latter sounds the safer course. However, it increases the complexity of the switch and the time taken to return the exchange to normal. The former solution runs the risk of breaking, or making, connections that should, or should not, exist.

58.2.3 Signalling

One final concept that needs to be covered in the basic components of an exchange is signalling between both the subscriber and the exchange, and one exchange and another.

Customers will wish to let the processors know that they want to make a call, which directory number they would like to call, that they wish to invoke a new feature, say transfer a call, and finally that they have cleared down the call. For systems employing analogue interfaces between customers and the exchange, two signalling systems are common, one using makes and breaks on the line (loop disconnect) and one using combinations of two from four in band audio frequencies (MF4).

Exchanges also need to communicate call set up and clear down information from one to another in order to route a call across a country or internationally. A whole range of different signalling systems exist for this purpose. However, CCITT Signalling System No 7 has emerged as the clear standard for modern digital exchanges.

58.2.4 A model SPC exchange

Putting all the elements together that have so far been described produces the typical architecture for a digital exchange shown in *Figure 58.4*. It is worth illustrating the functional breakdown of the component hardware and software subsystems by considering the passage of a simple call (A to B) through the exchange.

User A signals that he or she wants to make a call and is allocated a digit receiver in the subscriber's concentrator so that the exchange can receive the dialled digits. This allocation process illustrates that as at any moment only a very small percentage of subscribers are actively dialling, it makes economic sense to use software control to allocate hardware that is only used for a short period of time (resource sharing).

The dialled digits are passed from the subscriber's concentrator over the 2 Mbit s^{-1} link (in the single time slot allocated to signalling -Time slot 16), through a pre-allocated path within the digital switch, to a signalling unit, and then into the exchange processor for reception by the concentrator software. The fact that the concentrator software does not directly control the concentrator hardware by direct input/output allows this unit to be remotely sited from the main exchange.

The dialled digits are then forwarded to the call processing software for analysis. This software will determine that the called subscriber is on this exchange and will issue a series of generic commands to the dependent software subsystems, to 'Connect A to B' through the switches and 'Ring Subscriber B'. The subscribers switch will check if B is able to accept a call and then ring him or her. On receiving an answer condition from B the subscriber's switch will signal to the call processing software that call set-up can be finished. The transmission path between the two subscribers is completed and the call processing software sends a message to the call accounting software to start charging.

The call-processing software will perform a translation function between the directory number that the subscriber dials and the equipment numbers that the exchange understands. The dependent subsystems will thus receive generic messages to connect, ring and clear equipment port numbers. The dependent software, such as the digital switch software, will translate these equipment number-related commands into a series of I/O instructions to set up the required path.

If the call has to be completed on another exchange then the call processing software starts communication with the next exchange in the line to try to complete the call. This is done via the CCITT No 7 signalling software. Only those digits necessary to complete the call are passed on from one exchange to another.

58.2.5 Networks

National networks have traditionally been made up of a number of local exchanges, covering an area of about 2.5 km radius, some sideways links between them to complete local calls, and upward links to main exchanges to complete trunk calls.

Such a scheme has been necessary to provide a fully interconnected network without having much transmission plant lying idle. Thus the switches have acted not only as routing points but

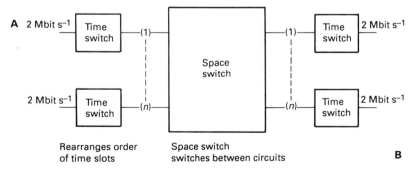

A 2 Mbit s^{-1} — Time switch —(1)— Space switch —(1)— Time switch 2 Mbit s^{-1}

2 Mbit s^{-1} — Time switch —(n)— Space switch —(n)— Time switch 2 Mbit s^{-1}

Rearranges order of time slots   Space switch switches between circuits   **B**

Figure 58.3

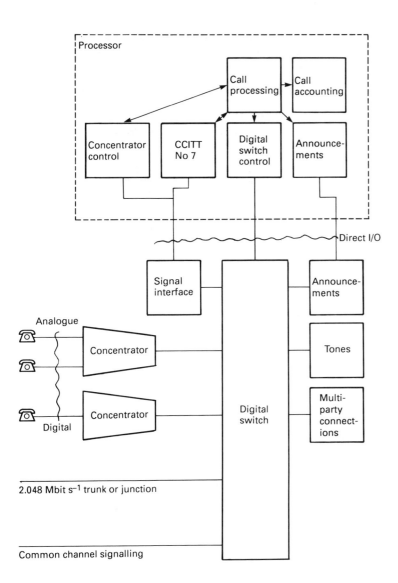

Figure 58.4 Digital exchange

also as points of concentration. In the UK some 6000 local exchanges were required for the network.

Interestingly, the falling cost of transmission has meant that it has been possible to reduce the number of principal local exchanges (carrying the full suite of facility software) by having a larger number of remote concentrator units (RCUs). Because of the problems involved with updating both the program suites and the exchange data online, it has been found operationally safer to have a smaller number of sites worrying about these problems, even though the exchanges are in fact much larger. It also proves economic to maintain a smaller number of large exchanges. Thus, although distributed control exists with microprocessors used in the RCUs, the control has become hierarchical and to a greater extent centralized because of the problems associated with maintenance.

58.2.6 Data and the Integrated Services Digital Network (ISDN)

Completely digital computer-controlled exchanges with analogue interfaces to the telephones can only provide a data path from one customer to another by the use of modems. The ISDN overcomes this problem by extending a digital path all the way down to the telephone. In practice, the owner of an ISDN line has access to two 64 kbit s^{-1} digital circuits which can be used for voice or data, together with a 16 kbit s^{-1} circuit for signalling use. This access is provided over a single pair of wires. The two 64 kbit s^{-1} circuits are switched by the exchanges in the way already described above, although now the signalling system between the exchange and the phone is a digital one (DASS 2).

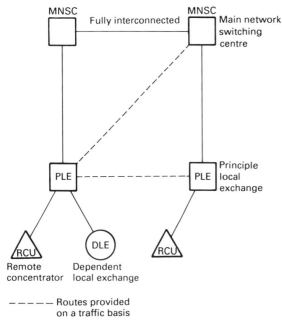

Figure 58.5

58.3 Basic call handling

Having described the telephone exchange in terms of its hardware and function, the next step is to look at some of the problems with which the software designer will have to deal. One can take two views of the problem: that of the call control designer (Section 58.3), and that concerned with the non-stop computing environment (Section 58.4) that this control software has to work in.

58.3.1 Software implications of call handling

Basic call handling has been described above in terms of connecting two subscribers together. Call processing also has to deal with the messages sent from one exchange to another as the call is set up and cleared down. An example set of messages are shown in *Figure 58.6*.

The basic principles that are adopted in such a call set up are:

1. That the call is set up in a step-by-step fashion from one exchange to the next until the final customer's exchange is reached.
2. In this process each exchange only has a limited view of the world around it, i.e. the exchanges to which it is connected.
3. A voice path is set up before the called customer has answered, to return ring tone from the called subscriber's exchange to the caller.
4. An end-to-end message is sent from the called exchange to the calling exchange to start charging when the called subscriber answers.

58.3.2 Real problems

In setting up such a call it is important to realise that the flow of messages in *Figure 58.6* represents the *expected* flow of events. However, in practice a great number of *unexpected* results must be catered for. For example, in a call set up sequence the following may happen:

1. Customers may clear down a call during any stage of dialling and post dialling.
2. Equipment may not be available to complete the call at any stage of call set up.
3. The number dialled may not be valid.
4. The called subscriber may not be able to receive calls as he or she:
   (a) is already busy
   (b) has not paid his bill and temporarily has had the service withdrawn!
   (c) has a phone that has an outgoing calls only capability.
5. There may be no response to a signalling message from a distant exchange (due to say an equipment failure).

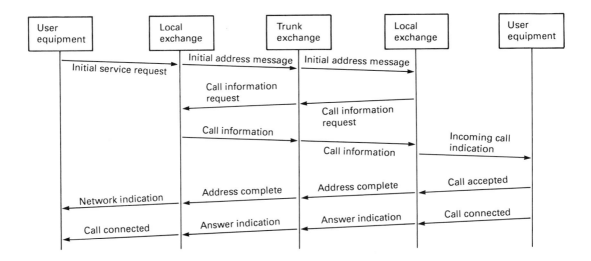

Figure 58.6

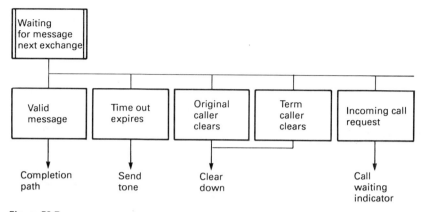

Figure 58.7

Thus, much call control software takes the form of being state-driven with each state having one completion path and many clear down paths from it.

58.3.3 Digit decode

Decoding the digits that the customer dials to determine which outgoing path the call should go out on, and which digits need to be forwarded to the next exchange, represents an interesting problem as there is a reasonable amount of variation in the numbering plans that are used throughout the world. Thus the exchange designer is seeking a solution that can be used in any situation, in any country and in any location within that country.

A common solution is to create a tree structure that has multiple points of entry. It is usual to use a series of pointers in the implementation to produce a quick response (see *Figure 58.8*).

58.3.4 Customer facilities

There is a commercial expectation that modern public exchanges will provide a rich suite of special features such as:

1. Diversion:
   (a) Basic diversion to another national number.
   (b) Diversion on busy or no reply.
2. Super phone:
   (a) Short code dialling.
   (b) Alarm call.
   (c) Call duration and charge advice.
3. Multi-party connections:
   (a) Three-party call.
   (b) Call waiting.
4. Centrex (PABX features from a public switch).

Many facilities are invoked during a call either by the action of one of the subscribers, or by the arrival of another call, or by

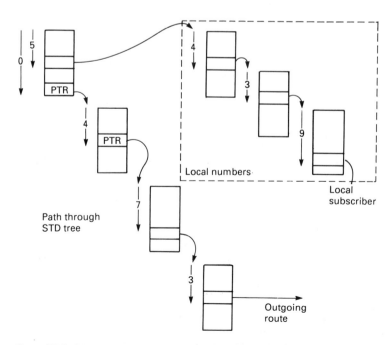

Figure 58.8 Digital decode

some other event. Much of the complexity involved with call-processing software results from the objective of ensuring that new features can be called into play at any time in a call and that they will not interact with each other to create undesirable results.

58.3.5 Network management

Approximately half of all the software loaded in an SPC exchange is devoted to the fundamental requirement of the telephone operating company to be able to administer the exchange automatically through man–machine commands. This may well be done remotely from an operations and maintenance centre, dealing with a number of exchanges for day-to-day management, or locally when dealing with specific faults.

Functionally one can consider the software to be partitioned as follows, although implementation will be different:

1. Control of the exchange database for such purposes as:
   (a) Adding (or deleting) new subscribers.
   (b) Changing the facilities that a subscriber m have or whether he or she may receive calls at all.
   (c) Bringing new parts of the exchange into service.
   (d) Bringing new transmission routes into service.
   (e) Changing the routings and dialling codes.
2. Responding automatically to faults and taking equipment out of service. (This is described in more detail below.)

58.3.6 Billing

Billing software exists within the exchange to receive messages from call processing about the start and finish times of calls, together with the number dialled and the charge-band associated with the call. This information is used either to increment the subscriber's dialled units meter (a software entity), or to keep an itemized record of the call. Whichever mechanism is used, information is ultimately dumped to a tape for processing at a remote billing centre. The exchange only has to keep the records, not process them. The most arduous requirement of the billing software usually specified is that no single (likely) fault will cause a subscriber to be over-charged.

58.4 Computing environment associated with telephone exchanges

Exchange systems need to work in real time, to be able to deal with a very large number of (potential) simultaneous events, and to continue to work even when the system is faulty. The faults may be in the exchange hardware or in the control processor itself, or may be due to software faults in any of the programs running the exchange. Finally, there is a need to be able to take equipment out of service for maintenance purposes.

The operating system, process control module and overload mechanism tend to protect the applications designer from a great number of these problems. However, many of them impinge on the software written to control the essentially simple process of setting up basic calls as described above. This is one reason why exchange software suites are so large.

58.4.1 Real-time systems

Real-time operating systems for exchanges tend to be conventional insofar as they provide the environment to run a set of concurrent processes communicating via tasks. These processes may, of course, be part of the operating system itself, or

application processes. The operating system processes will provide the real-time clock and interrupt handling, backing store and man–machine interfaces, as well as recovery and reload functions.

The part of the operating system that is different from many other real-time systems derives from the fact that the exchange has to recover under all circumstances. This is usually translated into the control computer being either *duplicated* and the operating system providing a worker/hot standby capability, or *replicated* as a multiprocessor. In the former case, the operating system provides the communication mechanisms to keep the standby updated with all the changes to the stable state call records and switch states. In the multi-processor case, the operating systems on each processor need to work together to provide the illusion of a single operating system. The level of sophistication here may vary quite considerably from, at the lowest level, just providing a communication mechanism between independent processors, through to providing the full migration of all processes and functions from one machine to another.

58.4.2 Overload control

Exchanges are designed to provide a statistical performance economically that is acceptable to the customers. That is, the various sizes of each generic exchange design are capable of carrying different amounts of telephone traffic. The processor can handle a maximum number of call attempts per hour. The digital switch can carry a maximum number of calls in the conversation phase. There is only a limited number of outgoing trunk circuits to the other exchanges. If the exchange becomes very busy and is for some reason unable to complete the call, then there is usually a requirement to send a tone to the customer (equipment engaged tone). It is worth noting that a customer's usual reaction to such a tone is to redial, thus increasing the load on the exchange. However, as there is a continuous flow of new calls arriving, stable calls in the conversation phase, and calls clearing down, it is the instantaneous traffic that is important to the exchange designer.

An inability to complete a call because of a lack of exchange plant is usually dealt with by the call processing software and will not be considered further here.

The problem of the processor becoming overloaded is normally dealt with by the operating system. However, as the only way of reducing the load is to make the new call attempts go away, it is necessary to involve other application processes. There are a number of phases in dealing with an overload.

58.4.2.1 Monitoring the load

The load on the machine can be monitored by a number of mechanisms, the most common being to observe the amount of free time the processor has in each 10 ms clock cycle when the background process runs; and to monitor the length of the input queues to the operating system and application processes.

Should a predefined threshold for these measures of free time be exceeded, then the operating system sends commands to the application processes to reduce the load on the machine. This is normally a graduated response, in that, as the load continues to build up, increasingly severe messages are sent to the application processes.

58.4.2.2 Reducing the load

To reduce the load on the machine, the progressive response indicated above may take several forms:

1. 'Do not return dial tone and therefore do not process any new call attempts from the customers on the exchange.'
2. 'Stop processing calls in the dialling phase.'
3. 'Stop processing calls arriving on incoming trunk circuits from another exchange.'
4. 'Stop processing all calls in the setup phase'.

58.4.2.3 *Returning to normal*

As the load reduces, and when the processor activity drops below a given lower threshold (so that there is some hysteresis), commands are sent out by the operating system to increase the load again.

It should be noted that the number of calls being generated will vary quite dramatically throughout any 24-hour period, and everyone calling their mother on Christmas Day may well be the cause of the overload. However, overloads may well occur just because a piece of equipment has failed and the exchange is no longer able to carry the traffic it was designed for.

58.4.3 Non-stop requirement

Exchanges have to meet very demanding mean-time-between-failure (MTBF) conditions, the requirement being a function of traffic carried by the exchange. The first automatic exchanges used distributed control and distributed switch architectures to effect this reliability. The advent of common control (rather than strictly SPC) has meant that the control function has to meet the same order of reliability as the switch. Luckily, the failure requirements are relaxed in line with the performance expected from a computer system, in that more short duration failures are allowed per year than complete failures.

Example failure rates are:

1. 1 min duration: 1/month
2. 10 min duration: 1/year
3. 5 hr duration: 1/decade

With respect to the hardware, replication is used to overcome the effect of any single fault. Thus, most of the equipment is duplicated or triplicated. Usually the amount of logic that will bring the exchange down from a single fault is very small. The most critical areas are in the distribution of common clock signals – which may be triplicated, and all the circuits that have to vote on the sanity of the duplicated or triplicated circuits. As this ultra-critical equipment is minimized, the absolute reliability of the exchange usually depends on the failure of two components. All the reliability calculations assume that the first fault is detected and that the exchange will recover, and, finally, that this fault is corrected in a reasonable time.

One can thus summarize the requirements on the software as:

1. To be able to respond to a number of hardware fault detectors by analysing these signals in order to take out of service a single unit of equipment.
2. To be able to take out of service both the faulty equipment and all that equipment still operational (presumed to be still functioning correctly) but now unable to be used as it depends on the faulty equipment.
3. To be able to restart the exchange from a known and viable state, and to deal with any inconsistencies that may arise. For example, the switch may believe that a call is still in progress (because that was the state before the exchange crashed) and in the meantime the caller cleared.
4. To be able to signal to a remote location that there has been a fault and that the exchange has recovered and be able to list the suspected faulty units.

All of the above should be automatic responses to a given fault.

58.4.4 Maintenance

Equipment will occasionally need to be removed from the exchange to test suspect units, to upgrade existing cards, or to perform routine servicing. Thus, the maintenance software needs to be able to force out of service the required unit and all the dependent units in the exchange. This software usually has the task of checking that the action being requested is sensible. For example, in a duplicated system that has one piece of equipment out of service because it is faulty, a request to force out of service the other working equipment in the duplicated pair should be refused.

The maintenance software also needs to deal with requests to bring equipment back into service. It is usually necessary to attempt to test the new equipment before it is thought safe to rely on it. Once this stage has been passed it is finally necessary to allow the load of the exchange to be transferred to the new equipment.

Much of this software for routine maintenance will be common with that software for dealing with faults.

However, if the exchange is to have a long life, it is important that each subsystem in the exchange (digital switch, subscriber lines and concentrator, signalling subsystems etc.) should have as little knowledge of each other as possible. This allows hardware upgrades to be carried out in one subsystem without affecting the remainder of the exchange software. This usually means that a good deal of maintenance software is, in effect, replicated throughout the exchange.

58.4.5 Software upgrades

As has been suggested above, as much information hiding as is practical is the practice in a modern SPC exchange. However, it is still very difficult to add new features to a suite of programs without making a number of changes to several subsystems, and maybe many processes. The principles described in outline in the next two sections are attempts to create the environment in which new services can be added very much more quickly than today.

However, for the exchange computing environment, the problem of introducing a new suite of software will remain very much the same. The essential problem is how to introduce a set of new processes into a working exchange without the customers realising that the exchange has:

1. Stopped.
2. Restarted.
3. Trialled the new suite of software.
4. Decided that the new suite is acceptable.
5. Made the change permanent.

The simplest class of upgrade occurs when there are no external changes to either the task interfaces to the processes or to the data structures within the exchange. In this case only the new programs need to be trialled. So, with the new suite of software loaded, all that needs to occur is for the new programs to be started together and for the old copies of the processes to remain dormant on the backing store. Should there be a bug in the code and a failure of some kind occurs, the trial is terminated and the old code restarted. It should be possible to design the system so that calls being set up are not lost in this case.

When the interfaces to a number of processes have had to be changed, the above procedure is run as before, but it is important that the suite of processes are trialled together.

Finally, the most difficult case is when the data structures change. Usually this requires that the new programs have access to the old data until the new data is sufficiently mature that it holds all the relevant call information. This involves writing a disposable translation process to form an interface between the old data and the new. It may be very difficult in this case not to lose some calls in the set-up phase at some point in the trial. The case when the trial fails and a return to the old data is necessary (which is now out-of-date) may be even harder to deal with.

58.5 Intelligent networks

58.5.1 Basic principles

Modern SPC exchanges already have a good deal of inbuilt intelligence, both in terms of the customer features that they could potentially offer and, perhaps more importantly, when coupled with operations and maintenance centres in terms of the administration facilities that they provide. However, developing a new customer feature and then deploying it in the field takes a long time in relation to the evolution of the modern marketplace. Much of this time is spent in development testing, ensuring that the new features do not interact with the existing ones. It is also not a trivial task to upgrade in the field each exchange with the new feature. For a network operator using several exchange types from a number of switch suppliers, the problem is compounded and it may be that functionally identical features would work slightly differently in the different designs, which may confuse the customers.

One possible solution is to install a new services network that provides features such as automatic Freephone (0800 calls) by passing new feature class calls from the originating local exchange through to an intelligent overlay network so that the call may be completed. This solution has a number of long-term problems, the most important perhaps being that all feature calls bypass the main network.

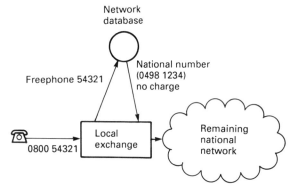

Figure 58.9

An alternative evolution scenario is to arrange for the resident call processing in the local exchange to work in co-operation with a central intelligent network database to modify the routing of the call according to both the definition of that dialled feature and a number of variables, such as time of day and source of the originating call. Essentially, this central database performs a variable translation process to the number dialled. Following this translation, the main network is used to complete the call.

This concept was first deployed in the USA to help implement the 800 service and credit card call verification, and has become known universally as the Intelligent Network (IN). The IN can offer enhanced calling services such as virtual private networking, wide-area Centrex, credit card calling, voice messaging, flexible charging and Freephone.

58.5.2 Freephone example

A good example to consider would be the use of a single national Freephone emergency number for an automobile association. The call processing in the first local exchange would recognize from the dialled digits that this was a call that could only be completed after having sought a translation from the network database. It would thus pass the number dialled and an indication of the location of the calling party to the database. Then, depending on the time of day and the location of the stranded motorist, the network identity of the nearest garage that could deal with the fault would be returned to the parent exchange, so that the call could then be completed in the normal way.

58.5.3 Advantages

Many advantages can be given to customers in terms of more flexible routing of calls depending on who is calling, time of day, called number etc., with the customer receiving the calls determining how these calls should be handled.

58.5.4 Disadvantages

Central databases work very well for calls needing special routing, but they are not very efficient if a great number of calls need to have some form of dialled number translation. Thus, as a longer term option, ways are being explored of decoupling call control software from the hardware and switches, so that new intelligent features can be added to an exchange without having to retest a great deal of existing software.

58.5.5 Intelligent network architecture (IN)

The intelligent network IN should provide an architecture that would:

1. Be open and supplier-independent.
2. Provide standard service-independent interfaces.
3. Allow the rapid deployment of new services.

These requirements have led to a distributed call processing architecture where a specific service is implemented in a service logic program (SLP) that is made up of a number of modular building blocks called functional components (FC). These FCs are programmable subroutines which can be assembled, rearranged and reused in order to create the service. The SLPs reside in a service control point, and interact with the now dumb functions in the exchange via standard signalling components. The architectural model that most people are considering is that developed by Bellcore, shown in *Figure 58.10*.

The basic goal that most designers are striving for is the creation of a set of interfaces and functional components that are independent of all services.

With respect to the IN architecture, the basic components are:

1. Service control point (SCP), which consists of a service logic interpreter (SLI) which executes service logic programs, together with a database and the necessary CCITT No 7 signalling links.
2. Service switching point (SSP), which resides at the local exchange and contains the traditional call processing and signalling functions enhanced to enable it to interwork with the SCP. The SSP also contains a trigger mechanism which determines when IN control is required for a call.
3. Service management system (SMS), which provides the data management system that can be accessed by the network operator and the intelligent network service provider, allowing them to administer and maintain the call processing information.

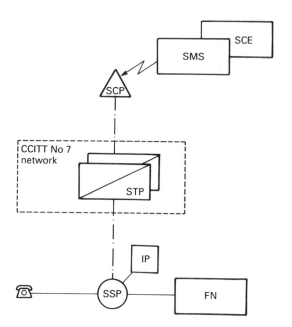

Figure 58.10 Proposed generic architecture for intelligent networks

58.6 Future architectures and networks

The major problems facing the software engineer within the next generation of SPC digital exchanges will be those associated with developing an architecture for software control that will allow new services to be introduced quickly and safely, and those associated with the next major advance of introducing multi-service networks which will transport integrated voice, video and data.

58.6.1 Architectures

Undoubtedly, the advances that have been made possible within the computing industry by having standard languages, operating systems, and the standards developed within the OSI model, have not really been paralleled in the telephony communications world. This difference is becoming even clearer when one looks at the rapid evolution that is obviously possible in the personal computer market.

Within an exchange there are few standards that allow, for example, the application program of one manufacturer to run on the exchange of another. Until such an unbundled architecture is created, progress on adding new features is bound to be slow. The politics of the exchange manufacturers will be one factor in slowing down progress on vendor-independent exchange software. However, the technical problems associated with creating such an architecture are not insignificant.

The two techniques that have received the most attention are perhaps the use of layering and the use of object-oriented techniques. However, coming back to the opening of this chapter, it is perhaps the magnitude of the software problem associated with telephone exchanges that makes the synthesis of such an open model such a difficult research topic.

58.6.2 Multi-service network implications

The next generation of exchanges will be able to switch voice, video and data traffic, as well as a whole range of different integrated services. It is likely that this will be through the use of a subset of fast packet switching where short fixed length packets are used to transport all services. This technique is called asynchronous transfer mode (ATM).

The problem for the software exchange designer will not perhaps be in dealing with the simple call (whether it is voice or video) even though the numbering problems and call set up differences for each service may be very different. The major problem could well come out of the requirement to be able to associate a number of traditional services to create a new integrated service. For example, it may be a requirement starting from a voice call to be able to add a data service during that

4. Service creation environment (SCE), which provides the telephone company with the support system to create its own services.
5. Signal transfer point (STP), which is part of the CCITT No 7 signalling system, being a packet switch providing a routing function for No 7 messages.
6. Intelligent peripheral (IP), which provides the SSP with services that cannot economically be provided on every network switching point, such as voice messaging.
7. Feature node (FN), which provides the link between the intelligent network and the provider of an enhanced service such as credit card validation.

58.5.6 Service creation and IN evolution

Ultimately, it will be the promise of the telephone operating company either being able to procure new services from many suppliers or being able to generate their own which will be the major drive towards the intelligent network.

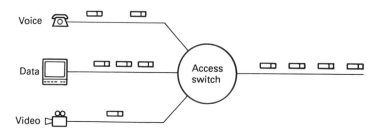

Figure 58.11 Fixed length packets for all information

call so the two subscribers may discuss and edit together a spreadsheet, to finally being able to have a video image of each other on their personal computers so that they can complete their business.

Ultimately, one wonders whether it will be the ability of people's imaginations to conceive new and useful services that will limit the progress of the telephone system, or whether it will be the designer's ability to capture the requirements correctly and implement and maintain a stable system.

58.7 Bibliography

Networks
Ward, K. (1989) The British Telecom Network. *British Tele-communication Engineering*, **8**, 1 (supp)

Switching
SystemX, *Post Office Electrical Engineers' Journal*, Jan 1979–April 1981

Pulse code modulation
Schwartz, M. (1970) *Information Transmission, Modulation and Noise*, McGraw-Hill
CCITT Recommendation G703

ISDN
CCITT Recommendations I420–I450

Broadband ISDN
CCITT Draft Recommendations I113, 121, 150, 211, 321, 311, 326, 327, 361, 362, 413, 432, 610

CCITT No 7
British Telecommunications Engineering, **7**, 1 (1988)
CCITT Recommendations Q701–Q714

59

Computer security

C T Sennett
Royal Signals and Radar Establishment

Contents

59.1 Security functionality

Security, in either a military or commercial sense, is a property of the people and paper world. Ultimately, security nearly always comes down to the question of controlling the ability of a person to transfer information to paper, whether the information is secret or the contents of a payable order. Security functionality in a computer must therefore be designed to support the security policy in the real world. Military security has been an issue from biblical times and the policies which support it have been extensively codified, although they are still changing as a result of the impact of the use of computers to store sensitive information. Commercial security is less well defined, which means that more effort may be needed to formulate security requirements in computer terms. In either case, a fundamental requirement in any secure system is to understand the security policy under which the system is working and relate this to the threat to the system. As the computer aspects of the system design are developed, vulnerabilities, such as the ability of a computer to copy data, are introduced and these must be countered either by security functions in the software of the system or by operational procedures.

The analysis of a system for vulnerabilities demands lateral thought. One approach to this is described in Dobson (1989). Making the choice of software functionality or operational procedures to reduce vulnerability requires a risk analysis to find the counter-measures most cost-effective in reducing the risks to acceptable levels. In any event, security functionality will need to interface to operational procedures and so it will be discussed within the context of existing security policies under the headings of accountability, control of access, audit, least privilege, and denial of service.

59.1.1 Accountability

Accountability lies at the heart of all security functions. Assuming that more than one person is to use the computer, it is necessary to forbid security relevant actions until the person initiating them has been identified. Thus, it is usually necessary to log on to the computer to initiate a session of work and to supply a user name which identifies the person concerned. This identification process must be properly authenticated, usually by means of a password, sometimes by the use of a personal identification device (PID), or sometimes both. In designing an authentication system, the strength of a mechanism, such as the length of the password, should be balanced against the operational procedures, such as the control of physical access. A physically secure system may need a weaker password mechanism than one to which there is public access. Misuse of passwords is a frequent cause of breaches of security (Morris and Thompson 1979; Wood 1977). For all but the weakest requirements, passwords should be generated by the system rather than supplied by the user. It is helpful to make them pronounceable or memorable in some other way, and the password generation algorithm should not allow future passwords to be deduced from current ones.

After logging on, subsequent actions within the computer are carried out by processes on behalf of the user. Consequently, the user name must be associated with the process identity so that it may be used as a basis for access control and as a parameter of the audit mechanism (see below). The control of this association is an important issue of design. Weakness in this area, such as in the Unix superuser mechanism for example, is the basis for many flaws in insecure systems. This association is particularly difficult to maintain in a distributed system and is an important functional aspect to specify in interconnected systems. In this case the security policy in each system must specify the security rules for the interface between the two, which must include the rules for identification and authentication.

59.1.2 Control of access

Control of access in the real world is based on the need-to-know principle and the classification mechanism. Need-to-know expresses the principle that information is only made available to those who have a specific need to use it in the course of their jobs. It carries with it the idea that information is not by default freely available, but that access may be granted by the owner of the information. This idea is modelled in the computer by the discretionary access control (DAC). The word 'discretionary' is used to apply to the owner of the data, who has the right to grant or deny access to it. In the real world, no great distinction is made between the ability to read a file and the ability to expand the contents by adding further items to it. As a general rule, existing material within a file may not be altered. In the computer, overwriting is sometimes a necessary evil and must be controlled, together with the ability to append, from integrity considerations. Consequently, the modes of access controlled should include the ability to read, write or append data to a file. Further modes of access may be distinguished, such as the ability to obey a program or rename or erase a file. In many cases these additional modes form useful controls, but the more general mechanisms discussed under the heading of least privilege below should also be considered.

Access may be granted or denied either to users or groups of users. An example of the latter is that it will nearly always be necessary to give read access to some files for all users of the system. Access control should reflect the roles which users adopt in the real world. For example, all logistics staff will need to update logistics data, so it is useful to have a logistics group and such role groups can simplify the setting and management of the access control mechanisms. In the real world, an individual may have more than one role, but it is important that only one of these should be adopted at a time within the computer, in order to maintain the need to know principle. The role adopted is usually selected when the user logs in, either by default or by an explicit action.

The discretionary access control is usually used to grant access, so the rule is that access is forbidden unless the DAC allows it. In more complicated cases, the DAC may be used to deny access, in which case the rule is that access is forbidden unless the DAC allows it and does not forbid it. Clearly, the latter is a more complicated check to implement.

The other form of access control is based on the classification mechanism. For military systems, and in its simplest form, this consists of a series of labels ('Restricted', 'Confidential', 'Secret' etc.) one of which may be applied to a document to indicate the value of the information in it, or more precisely, the potential harm which could accrue from its unauthorized disclosure. In terms of the value of the information labelled, Secret is more 'valuable' than Confidential, which, in turn, is more 'valuable' than Restricted. The labels are used for two purposes: to control access to the document and to indicate the handling rules which should apply to it. For access control, users are given one of the labels as a clearance; the rule is that a document may not be given to someone if the classification of the document exceeds the user's clearance. Classifications and clearances are not frequently changed, and such changes require special authorization. Classifications affect the handling of a document because the rules call for successively more onerous protective measures to be applied as the classification is increased. This ensures that the more highly classified the information, the less the risk of unauthorized disclosure.

This simple mechanism is made more flexible by the addition of categories and caveats. A category is used to indicate a particular group of people who are privileged to know certain information. The category is given a name which is used as a label and as a clearance. An interesting historical example is the use of the codeword 'Ultra' to indicate information obtained from deciphering Enigma transmissions during the second world war. The addition of a category to a document which is already classified with a category increases the classification of a document, as it requires a reader of the document to be cleared to both categories. This is in contrast to a caveat, which is used to indicate to whom information may be released, but is otherwise used in the same way as a category. The addition of a caveat increases the number of people allowed to see the information classified and so reduces the classification. Caveats are normally used to designate information which may be released to given nations.

Implementation of this policy within the computer is called mandatory access control (MAC) and raises some surprisingly subtle points. It is clearly straightforward to have a representation of labels and to arrange for printed output to bear the correct headings, although even here there are a number of practical problems associated with labelling formatted output and graphical matter. However, the principal problem is to decide what label to apply and how to implement the access control implicit in the labelling. In a simple system, documents will be represented by computer files. It is possible to associate a label with the file to represent the classification and one with the user name to represent the clearance and require that for read access to a file the clearance should be not less than the classification. The printed copy of the file should bear the same label as the file. Complications start to occur when the problem of controlling write access to a file is considered, for in this case it is possible to transfer information into the file from a source of differing classification.

The solution to this problem will depend on whether the process doing the writing can be trusted to uphold the security policy or not. If it can, the process will be able to supply the correct label. For example, a trusted disc management process may be able to produce an unclassified storage report, even for a disc containing classified files. More usually, the trusted part of the system will be quite small and will have the task of constraining the untrusted part of the system to conform to the security policy. This can be achieved by only allowing write accesses when the classification of the file written is not exceeded by the classification of any of the files open for reading or of any data previously read. Consequently, untrusted processes tend to have both a working classification and a working clearance. The classification is that of any data potentially present in the working areas of the process while the clearance is the lower of the user clearance and that of any files open for writing. Manipulation of these working clearances is an important part of the policy which will be discussed below.

Further complications in the implementation of MAC arise from considering the information flows which have been introduced as a result of implementing the file storage system. This is because the supervisory data used to control the filestore, or indeed the running of the computer as a whole, may not bear a classification and can be altered by an untrusted process when it has access to classified files. If this data can be read by a process with lower clearance there is a potential breach of security. Information flows of this nature are called covert channels and will always exist where there is shared, unlabelled data. This will always be the case because of the data needed to implement the mandatory access control itself, but any practical system will have many other items of shared data. The attitude towards covert channels is another part of security policy. In many applications they may safely be ignored because of the extremely unlikely scenarios it is necessary to postulate in order to exploit them. For highly secure systems it may be necessary to identify

them and take steps to reduce the rate of information flow the channel is capable of supporting.

Mandatory access control has so far been discussed in terms of files, but there are many applications where database items contain classified information. This presents a technical problem in that it may be difficult to protect items so small as a database entry, but also a policy problem in that it is sometimes difficult to decide how to carry out the labelling. This arises partly from reasons of inference, that is, it may be possible to deduce classified information from the unclassified result of two queries and partly from the fact that a single unclassified query may require a classified answer. Even returning an error message may result in classified information being deducible. There is no easy solution in this case, but possible approaches will be discussed below.

Discretionary and mandatory access controls have been described largely from the point of view of military security. With commercial systems, the discretionary controls are essentially equivalent to those required for the military, but the mandatory policies are rather different. Commercial documents often carry labels such as 'Personnel', or 'Management in confidence'. However, the structure of labels, that is, the subdivision into categories, caveats and confidentiality, and the associated handling rules, are usually not as well established or clearly defined as in the military case. Thus, although the basic principles of commercial and military access control policies are similar, the detailed implementation may be different.

Commercial policies may also be rather more dynamic. For example, if one part of a financial services company begins to give advice about a takeover of a manufacturing company, then that part should not communicate with its traders dealing in manufacturing shares. This type of policy is usually referred to as 'Chinese walls'. It is clearly dynamic as the actual access control rules in force will vary with the business undertaken by the company.

Historically, commercial security has been rather more concerned with auditing than access control, although this distinction may now be lessening.

59.1.3 Audit

After the complexities of access control, audit is relatively straightforward. In designing audit functions, the need as always is to decide on the threat to which the function is a countermeasure. Audit may be considered necessary for the purposes of monitoring attempts to breach the security of the system or it may necessary for accountability, or it may be necessary for both purposes. Attempts to breach security are likely to involve failed password checks or failures with regard to other access controls, or they may attempt to make use of special functions such as security officer or system manager commands. All of these are likely candidates for events to be monitored. Monitoring a system may be an online function, so that failed log-in attempts, for example, are simply output on a security officer's console, or alternatively, monitoring may consist of recording such events in a short term log or audit trail. The process of monitoring is particularly important for open networks which are subject to hacking attacks and Stoll (1988) gives interesting details of the kind of monitoring functions found necessary to deal with that kind of attack.

Accountability auditing requires a long-term audit trail. The audit trail may be necessary to supplement or replace traditional handling procedures, such as the maintenance of a record of printed output, or it may be used to assess the extent of the material compromised if a user of the system is subverted. This is particularly important in the case of computer controlled financial transactions where the function of audit takes on its traditional context of controlling fraud. In military systems, audit is usually done on the basis of classification, so that, for example, only access to 'Secret' data is recorded. In financial systems it may only be necessary to audit the alteration of data. Selectivity is an important issue in the design of audit mechanisms as audit trails can occupy huge amounts of backing store if all potentially auditable actions are recorded.

In any case, the audit trails will need some form of machine processing. The security officer must be provided with ways of archiving and restoring audit trails and selectively analysing them on the basis of parameters such as the accountable individual, the time of the event, the nature of the event and so on. The audit trails themselves must be protected from alteration and be resistant to machine failures.

59.1.4 Least privilege

The concept of least privilege is another important principle from the people-and-paper world. It expresses the security constraints implicit in the rule that users should have exactly the functions and privileges necessary to carry out their job, and no more. This concept has already been mentioned in connection with discretionary access control, where the control is granted or denied on the basis of the role being exercised. A related concept to least privilege is separation of concerns. Here, jobs should be structured so that critical transactions need to be carried out by more than one person whose interests should conflict if collusion is to be avoided. A typical example is that the person authorized to pay bills should not be the person who accepts goods, as this leads to the possibility of fraud.

This security feature is not well served in current computer architectures. A particularly common failing is that filestores are global and accessed by names which may be constructed by anyone. Thus some operating systems have password files which may be named by any user, thus requiring explicit protection. It is particularly important that databases should be available to those with a need to manipulate the data stored on them. The design of the structure of data to be stored on a system is a very important consideration as it affects both the security and the usability of the system as a whole.

There is also a tendency within standard operating systems to give global privileges to access and change any data on the system to users who have special functions such as the security officer, the system manager or the maintenance engineer. This is rarely necessary. A security officer, when acting as a security officer, should only be allowed to alter passwords, introduce new users, inspect logs and so on, in accordance with the function of the job. It is not necessary for a security officer to see, as of right, data belonging to others. Similarly, the operators and system managers should only be allowed the functions which are necessary to carry out their jobs; and equally, of course, operator and system manager functions should simply not be available to ordinary users.

Because of their ability to access audit trails and change passwords, security officers present a particular vulnerability which may require special counter-measures. The usual approach adopted is to make some of the operations subject to confirmation by another user, thus allowing for separation of concerns. This mechanism may be adopted in an online or an offline mode, depending on the operational requirements.

Least privilege is an important concept in the control of exercises. In this case, the need arises to set up scenarios in which users are allowed to do things which would be forbidden in the real world. The controls required are concerned with integrity rather than security, because the requirement is usually to preserve the real-world data from being corrupted by the exercise. Unfortunately, the requirement is not for a simple separation of data as exercises may involve real world resources. Furthermore, a real world transaction may be initiated from the exercise world and *vice versa*. Separation of real and exercise data is often implemented by means of a mandatory integrity policy. Sessions are initiated either in the real world or in the exercise world and a session integrity clearance calculated appropriately. An object may be over-written only if its integrity classification is dominated by the integrity clearance. The mandatory integrity policy required is not quite the dual of the mandatory security policy described in Section 59.1.2, because the requirement is usually to allow free transfer of information *from* both high and low integrity sources. Thus, although the integrity policy controls write accesses, there is no necessity to control read accesses.

Finally, there is a need for a number of controls which are specific to a given application. A typical example is that release of a message may require authorization, or a command message in a financial system may require non-repudiation.

59.1.5 Denial of service

Denial of service is applied to cases where legitimate access is denied, rather than illegitimate access granted. In military situations this can be the more important issue. Denial of service is applied quite generally to denial of any resource controlled by the computer. Traditional operating systems provide controls in the form of budgets and allowances which will control excessive use of main store, backing store, mill time or excessive output. These are useful controls, but in a military system it is necessary to consider other resources such as use of network capacity or corruption of vital information. The latter is important quite generally, bearing in mind the vulnerability to software viruses.

In all cases the analysis for denial of service is the same. The resources which are vital to the running of the system should be identified and each should then be assessed against the threat of being monopolised or corrupted. The counters to these threats may involve particular controls, but will generally be based on ensuring that processes follow the principle of least privilege, particularly when they have originated from a network connection.

59.2 Assurance of functionality

The specification of security functionality is only the first step towards attaining a secure system and, furthermore, it is not the most difficult step. The main problem with a secure system is not that it should have a given functionality, or even that the functionality is correctly implemented, but rather it should be possible to demonstrate that the functionality cannot be subverted.

The organizational aspect of this has an impact on the software engineering. In military terms, the authority permitting the system to process classified data is called the accreditation authority. Although having an understanding of computer security requirements and of operational needs, the accreditation authority cannot have detailed knowledge about particular systems. This detailed knowledge must be provided by an independent evaluation of the system. Thus, the demonstration of the security of the system is a technical demonstration made to the evaluators, who are independent of the implementation and knowledgeable about its technical details. The evaluators work to standards which enable the demonstration of security provided by the evaluation evidence to be assessed. These standards are defined by a policy authority. For the military this is a government authority charged with the development of handling rules for classified matter. The compliance of a given evaluation with these standards is assured by a certifier, usually an agent of the policy authority. Within this organizational structure, a software engineer may be involved in writing the requirement for the system, in implementing it, or in evaluating it.

The evaluation standards provide for systems which have differing degrees of trustworthiness, ranging from basically sound products to systems for which formal verification is used to obtain the highest assurance level technically possible. Thus the evaluation standards define a scale of assurance levels. The first set of standards was published by the US National Computer Security Center and called the 'Trusted computer system evaluation criteria' (DoD, 1985). It was extremely influential and is commonly known as the *Orange Book*. This was followed in the UK by the publication of UK confidence levels (CESG, 1989) and more recently in Germany by the IT security criteria (GISA, 1989). Other NATO and national standards will no doubt follow. The *Orange Book* differs from the other two standards in specifying levels containing both functionality and assurance criteria, whereas the UK levels are concerned with assurance only and the German document has separate functionality and assurance levels. The German document is interesting as it is intended for civilian as well as defence use.

Because of the less homogeneous policies and security requirements in commercial as opposed to military applications, there are currently no commercial standards which are so well accepted as the *Orange Book*. As well as the GISA criteria, the UK Department of Trade and Industry has sponsored a Commercial Computer Security Centre, which is producing a series of documents setting out the general principles for the specification, design and evaluation of secure systems for the commercial world.

There is much commonality between the available standards, representing some degree of consensus on the factors affecting assurance. Following the UK confidence levels, the factors will be discussed under the following headings, largely from the point of view of military systems:

1. Specification of security requirements.
2. Architectural definition.
3. Implementation.
4. Evaluation.
5. Documentation.
6. Configuration control.

59.2.1 Specification of security requirements

The specification of security requirements is concerned with the precise definition of the trusted functionality and other system requirements. The specification is the basis on which the trustworthiness of the system is founded as it is unlikely that a system will be trustworthy in some aspect which has not been adequately specified. Greater trustworthiness is achieved with greater precision and for the most demanding applications a formal, mathematical specification will be required. The total security requirement is called a system security policy while the precise statement of the rules under which the system operates is often called a security model, a term first used by Bell and LaPadula (1976).

The production of a security policy should follow guidelines laid down by the policy authority, which will give the overall structure to the document. The content of the policy should be formed during the course of risk analysis, to decide what is the most appropriate security functionality to provide in the system. The cost of providing it in the software should be balanced against the cost of providing equivalent measures in physical or personnel security.

At the requirements stage, an informal, but precise, statement of the security policy may be appropriate, with a formal security policy model being provided as part of the procurement specification. At this stage, the major design decisions will have been taken and the formalism can follow, based on these decisions.

Formalizing a security policy at the requirement stage leads to difficulties in maintaining traceability and could pre-empt some implementation decisions, so it is best to postpone this unless the very highest levels of assurance are sought. The production of a security policy is a special application need, not addressed by any of the general requirements analysis methods discussed in Chapter 16. The formalization of security policy is still a subject for research, although some examples can be found in Sennett (1989) and Landwehr (1981).

59.2.2 Architectural definition

The architectural definition is concerned with identifying the trusted functionality and the major breakdown of the system into hardware and software components. The traditional view of this process is that the system will be centralized, with the main security aspects controlled from a large central computer with essentially subservient workstations and networks. However, modern computer systems are nearly always distributed. Modern secure systems often involve trusted network components and in this case one needs a description of the system which can be used to give a breakdown into components, with a clear definition of the trust requirements of each component. These two points of view require rather different approaches and so they will be treated separately.

The traditional view stems from the *Orange Book*, where the architectural definition is called a Descriptive Top-Level Specification (DTLS) and for increased assurance this may be supplemented by a Formal Top-Level Specification (FTLS), which is related to the formal security model. Typically, a security model will be concerned with abstract entities called subjects and objects while the architectural design will be concerned with implementation entities such as processes and files. The key issue as far as security is concerned is maintaining traceability of the security requirements in the security model through the design and on into the implementation. In making the transition from security model to architectural design, many different entities in the design will correspond to objects and subjects, so the transition is akin to the formal process of instantiation in this respect. However, certain minimum features of subjects and objects such as security labels must be present in the design, so in this respect the transition is rather like formal refinement. For these reasons, the transition is usually done by a combination of formal and informal techniques, although there seems to be no reason why it should not be treated completely formally as a data refinement (see Chapter 24). A description of the use of refinement to support traceability is given in Section 59.5.

A distributed system view of an architectural definition is more in keeping with the current approach to computing systems. The problem here is that a state machine description of the world becomes cumbersome and inappropriate. As many security models are expressed in these terms they provide an inadequate basis for expressing the architecture. It seems likely that process and trace oriented security models would more accurately portray distributed architectures, but apart from non-interference assertions (Goguen and Meseguer, 1984) and work at Oxford using CSP (Jacob, 1988) little experience has been gained in their use. A particular problem in this area is concerned with the decomposition of a system into its components. The architectural design should provide a specification for the individual components and make visible the dependencies between them. Work by Neely and Freeman on trust domains (1985) gives an example of a formal approach to this problem.

Much of the general guidance on architectural definition given in Chapter 17 is applicable to secure systems. However, as with requirements, none of the 'standard' techniques deal adequately with the particular requirements of security.

59.2.3 Implementation

Implementation is concerned with the methods of production of module specifications and the actual software which meets these specifications. The assurance factors in the implementation are concerned with the way in which the design has been produced and the amount of testing and analysis applied to the implemented software. The production of module designs can be done either with traditional structured methods or by the use of formal refinement, the latter giving higher assurance. It is important to realise that formal methods may be employed *without* the necessity for mechanical proof of the theorems required. This approach is often called 'rigorous', and has many of the benefits of the use of formal methods in giving greater precision and intellectual control, without the costs of employing a mechanical verification system. Mechanical verification gives an extra level of assurance over the rigorous methods and is required for the most highly trusted systems. Mechanical verification systems are discussed in Chapter 26. Most of the systems described there were initially developed for security applications.

Formal methods do not obviate testing. In many cases they can be used to supplement testing by giving the form for test schedules and oracles. In any case, there will undoubtedly be some aspects of the system which have escaped formalization, so there will inevitably be a need for integrated system testing. A systematic approach to testing will give higher assurance than some arbitrary tests, so it is helpful to have a strategy, either white box or black box testing, supplemented by test coverage monitors. See Chapter 19 for a discussion of approaches to testing.

Apart from test coverage, other forms of analysis may be helpful and required in particular instances. Analysis may be used to show compliance with a specification, to demonstrate lack of exceptions, or to verify information flows or dependencies.

59.2.4 Evaluation

Evaluation has two aspects, concerned with establishing the quality of the implementor's methods of production and with direct assessment of the evaluation evidence within the context of the operational system. The evaluator will certainly need to perform some independent tests, and, for higher assurance, some independent analysis of the delivered software, but it is preferable to have the implementor carry out tests and analysis, with the evaluator assessing the results as part of the evaluation evidence. For this to be acceptable, the development environment must exert some controls over the programmers, discussed in 'Configuration management' below.

The most important part of the evaluation evidence is documentation, also discussed below. Apart from this, the evidence will consist of the source text of the implementation, the formal text of the design specifications and the results of testing. Each of these may be assessed by eye, or with tool support for greater assurance and ease of evaluation. Thus the source text may be independently analysed, proofs required by the formal design can be carried out mechanically and the results of testing checked automatically with a test harness.

59.2.5 Documentation

Documentation is an essential element in any trusted system. Apart from the usual design documentation, which traces the implemented functions through to the original security requirement, trusted software requires additional evidence in the form of a rationale for the division into trusted and untrusted components, the provision of trusted paths and covert channel analysis.

The specification of the documentation requirements can only be done in general terms at the requirement stage, but the detailed documentation requirements will need to be agreed between evaluators and implementors as the design progresses, together with criteria for acceptability. Unlike usual practice, the documentation for trusted software must be produced ahead of the implementation, if it is to meet its purpose. For highly assured systems, the evaluation evidence is more important than the implementation. The uncertified software cannot usefully be used; production of the evaluation evidence on the other hand will result in the implementation task being considerably reduced.

59.2.6 Configuration control

Configuration control, as defined in Chapter 34, is necessary for the maintenance of the status of the evaluated software after hand over of the system. It is also an essential requirement during development, if the system is to be capable of being evaluated. The evaluators must be certain that what they are evaluating is up-to-date and cannot be corrupted after it has been assessed. There are three aspects to configuration control, concerned with the tools for management of the software, the controls required on updating and the management procedures necessary for systems to evolve in sensible ways.

Configuration management tools are necessary to build any large system, but they are essential for trusted systems, as there must be a very tight control over the association of the source text of a module with its code. Systems which allow patching of the object code are unsuitable for trusted use, so the design of the software maintenance system must be done as part of the initial development. It will also be necessary to introduce accountability into the actions of programmers, so the development environment must be capable of controlling their actions in updating, just as the operational users must be controlled when reading classified data in the operational system. Control objectives for a development environment are discussed in Sennett (1987). Finally, the human management of the configuration will need to be carried out by persons who understand the security implications of proposed changes, unless the trusted software is to be invariant with mechanical checks to ensure that it has not been corrupted.

59.3 Designing a secure system

The design of a secure system is an extremely important matter as it governs the feasibility of evaluation and hence the possibility of using the system once it is implemented. The principles governing the design are easy to state, but hard to realize. Given a specification of the security and operational functionality, the design problem is how to distribute this functionality over the hardware and software components available. For any but the smallest systems, there will be a necessity to divide the software into trusted and untrusted elements. The motivation for this is to reduce the evaluation cost of the system, or more realistically, to make it feasible at all. The requirement for trusted software is that it should be sufficiently small to be understandable.

The system must be such that the trusted software can enforce its trust policy over the untrusted software and the enforcement can use either hardware or software mechanisms. Ideally, the hardware should be used to protect the trusted software from corruption and to encapsulate the objects referred to by the security policy, so that the trusted software controls cannot be by-passed. Existing computer systems are unlikely to have the flexibility of hardware protection required to maintain a security policy, so it will nearly always be necessary to rely on software controls as well. This means that the trusted software must be protected from user programming and that the various software components should have well-defined interfaces. The concentration of the trusted software into one hardware regime of protection may have performance penalties, so it is important to consider the implications of this when designing the system.

An important constraint on the design is the granularity of protection. Ideally, the objects in a secure system should map on to the protection mechanisms commonly employed, such as files in an operating system. Unfortunately, user requirements often imply the use of databases, where the object to be protected is not well-defined and the entities in the database are defined by a large amount of untrusted software. This situation calls for a hard-headed analysis of the user requirement. If a database is being interrogated by a number of users, they should have a common need to know the information in it. The only possibility of building security into a database is in terms of the entities it defines, so that a relational database could only be classified at the level of the entity, the domain or range of the relations, the relations as a whole or the database as a whole. By and large, it will be much more satisfactory if the database as whole can be classified at one level and this may well be possible at little operational inconvenience to the users.

Failing this, it is probably best to have classifications at the level of the entities, as this can lead to implementations in which untrusted databases are encapsulated with cryptographic seals. Failing even this, it will be necessary to design a bespoke database system. One such approach is described in Denning *et al.* (1987), which meets security requirements but may be difficult to use in practice.

The other constraint on designs which appears in practical situations is the need to employ existing components, which may be either trusted or untrusted. In the case of an untrusted component, it must be adopted within the protection regime of the trusted system. This will often require it to be adopted in source form, to ensure absence of viruses and to integrate within the configuration management system of the whole. For a trusted component, the issue is whether the trusted functionality maps on to the security requirements and whether the system as a whole can be maintained in the face of changes to the component.

59.4 Writing and responding to a security requirement

A contractual security requirement should cover the security policy and its expression in terms of the boundaries of the machine, the major elements of the security architecture, the security functionality and the degree of assurance required for the trusted security functions. This requirement will have been developed during preliminary design or project definition. It should be the result of a risk analysis leading to a balanced set of measures which implement the user requirement at a reasonable cost.

The security policy, architecture and functionality have been discussed in previous sections. These aspects call for the ability to state the requirements clearly and, in the response, the ability to demonstrate understanding and commitment. This is not greatly different from an ordinary requirement whereas the assurance aspects do require a different approach. This approach will be described from the point of view of the proposer, which implicitly indicates the desirable content of the statement of security requirements.

The assessment of the assurance aspects of a proposal is concerned with judging whether a system will satisfactorily complete its evaluation, and at what cost. The most important evidence which enables this judgement to be made is the design of the trusted mechanisms, so the tender documents must elicit this information. To judge the proposal, it is necessary to understand the hardware and software protection mechanisms and how they will be used to protect the trusted code and encapsulate the subjects and objects. In cases where untrusted code is being encapsulated, the flow of control via the trusted software can become complex and the proposal should be able to make clear exactly what the trusted code is being required to do. This seems rather a lot of design information to appear in a proposal, but it should not be onerous to supply. If the protection mechanism is too complicated for it to be capable of being explained within a page or two, it is unlikely to be able to guarantee a high level of assurance.

The size of the code is a good measure of complexity and the likely difficulty of evaluation so the proposal should contain estimated sizes of trusted code within each of the components of the design, together with the aspect of trust which they enforce. All code that is necessarily trusted by virtue of the hardware protection regime it occupies will need to be included, which will often cause code which is irrelevant to security, schedulers for example, being counted within the trusted software. In this case, the code that is irrelevant to security should be accounted separately, with some indication of the software protection mechanism which will be used to enforce separation.

After the design, the next item of information required in a proposal is the specification of the evaluation evidence which will be produced. This includes the software already listed in the design, the various levels of documentation which will be produced for the evaluators and the degree of testing and analysis which the implementor will use for his own purposes. This again helps to establish the size of the evaluation task and the extent to which it will be possible to use the delivered evaluation evidence rather than the evaluator's own testing and analysis.

The next requirement is the methodology to be used. For very high assurance systems, formal verification will be required, so details of the tools to be used and the manner in which they will be used to provide the evaluation evidence should be given. This enables an assessment of the amount of effort involved in the implementation and subsequent maintenance to be made. For less highly assured systems, a formal methodology can still be used, as described in the next section, and this gives a structure to the documentation and a systematic approach to the system development. Details of the language systems to be used, together with the library and module systems and how the complete system will be built, need to be supplied.

Related to all this are the configuration management procedures to apply and the controls which will be maintained within the development environment to ensure the integrity of the evaluation deliverables and the accountability for alteration. This is related to the changes foreseen for maintenance. For no changes to the trusted code a simple checking program may be enough to guarantee the invariance. More realistically, some changes may be foreseen in the trusted code and the possibilities for change should be included in the security requirements so that they may be taken account of in evaluation.

Finally, the management structure supporting the process of evaluation needs to be specified. The evaluators need access to the implementation as it is being developed and should be consulted about the test schedules and the criteria for acceptability of the evaluation deliverables, particularly documentation standards. To avoid wasteful delays and tiresome disputes, it is as well to agree the structure and content of the deliverables at an early stage.

59.5 Implementing a secure system

The methodology for the production of a secure system will have been defined in the proposal in response to the assurance level required. Similarly, the configuration management tools and languages will already have been fixed. It remains to produce the software itself and the evaluation evidence. As emphasized above, the evaluation evidence should be given the greater prominence and this section will concentrate on the production of documentation to meet the evaluation needs.

The evaluation documentation is required to trace the security requirements from the implementation through to the original security policy. This is best done by following the formal methods of refinement (see Chapter 24). The demonstration of satisfaction of a specification is something which is at the heart of all formal methods, but for this case, the traditional techniques of refinement need to be supplemented. The security requirement is concerned with information flows and this may be expressed as a loose specification and conformance of an implementation may be tested in the usual way. However, the implementation may introduce other information flows using the variables in the implementation state. These may also be significant and must be assessed from the security point of view. Traceability is concerned with keeping track of all these properties and showing how they arise from the combination of the original requirement and the particular implementation chosen.

In analysing security properties, the additional properties required at each stage of the implementation are usually discussed under the headings of 'absence of side-effects' and 'lack of fence penetrability'. The process of formal refinement has a structure, which will be discussed under the headings of 'data', 'transaction' and 'process refinement'. Data refinement means the transformation of the problem – applied to abstract entities such as relations, functions and sets in the specification – into terms of the implementation which will be expressed in terms of arrays, linked lists and other implementation language constructs. Transaction refinement is a term borrowed from Woodcock (1989) and used here to refer to the first level of the decomposition of an operation into components. Finally, process refinement is concerned with combining together the various threads of execution into a system. Each of these stages of refinement gives rise to differing security requirements.

59.5.1 Data refinement

A security model is traditionally defined with a state made up of subjects and objects. The objects represent the labelled items of data whereas the subjects represent the users who move data between the objects. Consequently, an object has a classification and a subject a clearance. Ideally, a security model, as with all specifications, should be expressed at a uniform level of abstraction, and, following this approach, security requirements should be traced back to the user level. To every operation there will be a unique subject corresponding to the user who is accountable for the operation: the security rules are expressed in terms of the subject clearance and the way in which the operation transfers data between objects. Thus, in this example, one could imagine operations such as updating availability information for aircraft or preparing and sending a message. An update is allowed provided the user is cleared both to see and alter the aircraft availability data. Anyone can send a message provided its classification is at least as great as that of the data which made it up.

In implementing such a specification, data refinement provides the first level of traceability. The first necessity is to exhibit the abstraction invariant, which, for an informal development, would be documentation describing precisely what data is used to represent a given type of object or subject. In a simple case,

objects could be represented by named files held in a directory, subjects by processes acting on a user's behalf. Classifications are often represented by bit strings while a user's identity might be represented by an identifier with a mapping from user identifiers to clearances. A practical example would be more complicated than this as the representation of the different types of object would be different. A formal definition of the abstraction invariant would make these representations precise, but even with an informal description, the concept of the abstraction invariant helps in the production of clear and complete documentation.

The next step in the data refinement is to list the implementation operations and the effect they have on the implementation state. For simple cases, one could classify the specification operations as interrogation commands, for which the clearance of the subject must dominate the classification of the objects read, updating commands, for which the classification of the object written must dominate the classification of any object used in the update, and so on. With this classification, it is natural to think in terms of open file operations and associate the security rules with these, rather than the user level operations. This is common practice, but its use obscures the traceability and pre-empts the implementation. For many cases, for example, sending a message, or amending a reference to a classified document, the security rules are not the same as those for reading or writing, and it is better to define the rules explicitly for all transactions for which the system will be used so that user requirement is not confused with the implementation.

The implementation operations can now be analysed to ensure that they conform to the security rules. This corresponds to classical data refinement and given the abstraction invariant it is easy to see how to demonstrate that the security model is satisfied. In particular, the implementation operations must be shown to have equivalent checks to those required by the security model.

The additional requirement it is appropriate to check at this stage is the absence of side-effects. The implementation state introduces more data than is contained in the specification state. In the example, the implementation state will contain information in the directory entries, file names, access control lists and so on, all of which were simply not present in the specification state. The extra items in the state give the potential for information flows which may have a security significance.

The formal definition of the absence of this kind of side-effect has been given by Goguen and Meseguer (1984) in their description of non-interference properties. This uses a simple state machine which is driven by user inputs and produces labelled outputs. One user 'non-interferes' with another user if the outputs available to the second user are unaffected by the inputs of the first user. The formalism in this case is instructive, but usually a simple application of non-interference will be found to be too restrictive and not altogether credible, as it depends on building a formal model of execution of the machine. Nevertheless, the formalism does provide a framework within which the absence of side-effects can be documented. Thus, the documentation describing the analysis for side-effects will cover what elements of the state are observable to a given user, what are the inputs and how they may affect the observables available to other users.

59.5.2 Transaction refinement

The next stage in the refinement is to break down the operation into smaller steps which will ultimately allow the implementation to use processes running in parallel. Each step of the operation accumulates its result into the working space of the process; the refinement obligation is that the accumulation of all the individual steps is equivalent to the specification operation. Formally, transaction refinement is a combination of data refinement and operation refinement. The data refinement is involved because the implementation state contains the working areas used by the process, which are additional to the specification state. This concept of additional working variables in transaction refinement is discussed in Woodcock (1989), where it is shown formally how to capture the simple idea that the intermediate steps to achieve a final state are irrelevant as far as the user-level specification is concerned. Operation refinement is used to show that the combination of the operations defined by the smaller steps achieves the same result as the user operation and may be employed whenever the user operation may be employed.

The most obvious application of this technique for the example is based on the implementation of the user level operations in files, with the smaller steps of the operation being concerned with opening, closing, reading and writing files. This refinement step brings a number of benefits. The first is that it makes clear the distinction between the permanent backing store objects (the files) which are the concern of the security model, and the working storage of the process. It is very important to bear in mind that security is concerned with internal working space only in so far as it has an effect on the external and visible objects. The second benefit of the refinement step is that it introduces some structure into the implementation of trust within the system, so that trusted code is only necessary in the file operations.

Taking the simple example again, an update command would have the security requirement that the classification of the object updated must dominate the classification of the sources of data used for the update. When the transaction refinement rules are applied, this will get translated into the usual security rules for opening files, but will also incur other obligations. These will be requirements that files cannot be altered except through file read and write operations, opening a file is required before it can be accessed at all, and opening in read mode prohibits subsequent write operations. These additional constraints, which are all to do with fence penetrability, are actually made explicit by the formal method and consequently can be traced back to the user level requirement.

Because transaction refinement involves data refinement, one must also consider the question of side-effects. In this case, because the refinement only involves working storage local to the process, and hence available to only one user, only data flows from one transaction to another need be considered. It is usual, at these critical points, to empty all working storage. This points to another benefit in starting from the user level operations, because it makes explicit where one transaction begins and another ends. Without this being explicitly defined, session clearances tend to rise inexorably, resulting in considerable operational difficulties. The isolation of the working storage for a particular transaction can often be guaranteed, either by hardware, or, for a lower assurance level, by a compiler. The latter may be important when considering code which is running in the trusted software's protection domain, but which is otherwise irrelevant to security. For traceability purposes, it is important to make clear not only what is trusted, but precisely what it is trusted to do, or not to do.

The question of initial states can also be discussed under the heading of transaction refinement. It is a requirement of all formal specification methods that one should be able to demonstrate the existence of initial states and say what they are. This question recurs at various levels of refinement. Often the security model is expressed in terms of a single user and in these cases the initial state corresponds to the start of a session. Clearly, therefore, no accountable operation can take place until the subject is defined.

Consequently, the requirement on a standard implementation of a session is that no security object may be inspected or altered before logging in, or after logging out. At further stages in the refinement, the question of initial states for the system as a whole arise. In this case the implementation must recognize the fact that the computer may be switched off and on, and that the initial state achieved before the system is available for use must involve the recovery, without alteration, of the set of security objects which were extant at the time the computer was switched off. By making the requirement for initial states, the formal method provides a basis for documenting these features, which are relevant to the security of the system but are products of the implementation.

59.5.3 Process refinement

Implementations involve more than one process. Usually there will be one or more processes directly associated with the user, together with utility processes providing a service to the user processes. For a distributed system with, say, workstations and a central computer, user processes will appear in both machines. The composition of all the processes must be shown to obey the security requirement, so it is necessary to break down the security requirements at the transaction level to the individual requirements for each of the processes.

The formal treatment of communicating processes involves ideas taken from process algebras such as CSP (Hoare, 1985) and standard sequential specifications. The first step is the identification of the process structure. Each sequential process can be defined by its state and the operations it engages in. Those operations which are events shared by other processes form what in CSP is called the alphabet of the process. The specification of these joint events is particularly well represented in the specification language Z, (see Chapter 21, on model-oriented specification) where a joint event can be defined in terms of the inclusion of the state schemas of the two cooperating processes. The CSP parallel operator is represented by forming a state for the machine as a whole from the product of the states of the individual processes. State changes of the total machine consist of a single process in the machine engaging in one of the events in its alphabet.

Process refinement is again a combination of data and operation refinement. The data refinement occurs because the specification state is spread among two or more processes and the operation refinement occurs because a specification operation will be implemented by operations in the two participating processes. As before, the data refinement allows one to keep track of the security significant data and introduces the requirement to search for side-effects, whereas the operation refinement allows one to break down trust properties and introduces the requirement to check for fence penetrability.

For the example, a typical case of process refinement would be the implementation of file operations by means of a separate backing store server which performed autonomous read and write operations. The previous refinement steps have left open, close, read and write operations with various properties which can be traced back to fence penetrability in the transaction step, the establishment of the initial state, or the original requirement itself. The backing store transfer process is defined in terms of read and write operations only, so some analysis is required to establish the critical directory updating operations and to distinguish alterations to the security object from the alterations to the directory entry which describes it. This is important because even opening a file for reading may involve writing to backing store (the time of last access, for example). In highly trusted systems it may be necessary to structure even the basic device drivers to reflect the security properties they provide.

Because of the data refinement involved, it is necessary to

search for absence of side-effects. A typical element here would be communication channels existing through common data such as lists of free blocks. However, by working down to this operation from the requirement, the necessity for this sort of analysis can be foreseen and superfluous common data hidden into the private work space of the process where it does no harm. Other side-effects which show up at this stage are concerned with object re-use where discarded data from one process is picked up as a newly created object by another.

Another example of process refinement occurs with the introduction of workstations. Here the workstation can be considered as one or more processes running in parallel with the processes in the central machine. With this the security properties required in the workstation software can be found, either from the initial state requirements or the need to separate processes accessing different windows of a display. The analysis of side-effects and fence penetrability for workstations will involve the security properties of the network linking the workstations to the central machine. The formal requirement for non-interference between processes will not be met by broadcast networks but may be enforced by trusted network software. The data refinement of subjects will now include the necessity to identify network addresses and processes within the workstation, both of which have implications for the integrity of the data transmission.

The analysis of the security properties of a network is a good illustration of the need for a combination of formal and informal reasoning. In these cases, the network *could* be modelled formally but it would rarely be profitable to do so. However, the formal refinement process applied to the workstation and central machine supplies the framework within which the appropriate questions may be discussed informally.

The tracing of a security requirement from the user level statement through to the implementation in terms of device drivers, operating system interfaces and the hardware protection mechanisms of a computer is a very difficult task. Without a structure to the description of the steps and evaluation evidence produced in going from requirements to implementation, it is hard to be sure that no security relevant detail has been omitted, or that the security requirements have been correctly captured. The formal refinement process gives intellectual control over the description. Each phase of the process takes place at one level of abstraction. Within this level, the analysis is complete with respect to the requirements above and is sufficiently concise for the extra requirements of fence penetrability and lack of side effects to be addressed systematically. The refinement process can be continued down to a level of detail commensurate with the assurance level required and because of the formal basis, the overall structure of the documentation is almost bound to be logical, which is the prime requirement for understandability.

59.6 Conclusions

Production of secure computer systems is difficult. However, by giving particular attention to certain aspects, the development and evaluation process may be made more manageable.

The first key aspect is that it is essential to identify the security policy for the system as a whole. This issue has been discussed primarily from the point of view of military security, but the ideas translate readily into the commercial domain, apart from details of the security functionality. The security functions which must be implemented by the computer, and which uphold the security policy, must be established by a risk analysis.

Secondly, to achieve assurance in the security of a system it is necessary to have independent evaluation of the system and its development, based largely on the evidence produced in development.

Thirdly, it is important to design the system so that the evaluation will be successful. This leads to the principle of separating trusted and untrusted functionality, together with the need to protect the trusted functions implemented in software from corruption.

Finally, formal methods have a major part to play in structuring the results of the development process to facilitate evaluation. They draw out the explanation of how the design provides a satisfactory implementation of the requisite security functionality and they give a framework for dealing with additional implementation issues such as fence penetrability.

Achievement of security and successful completion of evaluation for a system developed in an *ad hoc* way is practically impossible. Adoption of the principles outlined here will help in making such developments feasible and controllable.

59.7 References

Bell, D. E and LaPadula, L. J. (1976) Secure computer system: unified exposition and Multics interpretation. *Technical Report ESD-TR-75-306*, Mitre Corporation, Bedford, Massachusetts, USA

CESG (1989) UK systems security confidence levels. *CESG Computer Security Memorandum number 3* Communications-Electronics Security Group, Cheltenham, Gloucs

Denning, D. E., Lunt, T. F., Schell, R. R. Heckman, M. and Shockley, W. (1987) A multilevel relational data model. *Proceedings IEEE Symposium on Security and Privacy, Oakland, California, USA*, IEEE Computer Society, USA, pp 220–234

Dobson, J. E. (1989) Modelling real-world issues for dependable software. In *High Integrity Software* (ed C. Sennett), Pitman, London

DoD (1985) Department of Defense trusted computer system evaluation criteria. *Department of Defense 5200.28-STD*

GISA (1989) *IT – Security Criteria*. German Information Security Agency (Zentralstelle für Sicherheit in der Informationstechnik)

Goguen, J. A. and Meseguer, J. (1984) Unwinding and inference control, *Proceedings of Symposium on Security and Privacy, Oakland, California, USA*, IEEE Computer Society, USA

Hoare, C. A. R. (1985) *Communicating Sequential Processes*, Prentice-Hall

Jacob, J. (1988) Security theories: the state of the engineering discipline. *Proceedings of Computer Security Foundations Workshop, Franconia, New Hampshire, USA*, IEEE Computer Society, pp 97–111

Landwehr, C. E. (1981) Formal models for computer security, *Computing Surveys*, **13**, 247

Morris, R. and Thompson, K. (1979) Password security: a case history. *Communications of ACM*, **22**, 594

Neely, R. B., and Freeman, J. W. (1985) Structuring systems for formal verification. *Proceedings of 1985 IEEE Symposium on Security and Privacy*, IEEE Computer Society, pp 2–13

Sennett, C. T. (1987) The development environment for secure software. *RSRE Report 87015*, Royal Signals and Radar Establishment, Malvern, Worcs

Sennett, C. T. (1989) The contractual specification of reliable software. In *High Integrity Software* (ed C. Sennett), Pitman, London

Stoll (1988) Stalking the wily hacker. *Communications of ACM*, **31**, 484–497

Wood, H. M. (1977) The use of passwords for controlling access to remote computer systems and services, *Proceedings of the 1977 National Computer Conference*, AFIPS Press, USA

Woodcock, J. C. P. (1989) Transaction and parallel refinement in Z. *Proceedings of the Second Refinement Workshop, Open University* (to be published). See He, J. (1979) Process refinement. In *The Theory and Practice of Refinement* (1989) (ed. J. McDermid) Butterworths

60

Safety

P A Bennett
The Centre for Software Engineering Ltd

Contents

60.1 Introduction

60.1.1 Background

Industrial companies and their suppliers are increasingly asking software engineers to embed software within the micro-electronics of their product or application in order to maintain a competitive edge. Further, software is being used to achieve the complex control algorithms required by today's computer applications. The use of such embedded software introduces a new set of problems for the software engineer: design, development, quality assurance and *safety*.

Where computer-based systems are integrated into the operation of the control system so that their failure in any way could put life and limb at risk, as well as having significant economic or environmental consequences, they are generically referred to as being 'safety-critical'.

The acknowledgement that software can have a significant effect upon the safety of a system is a recent development that cannot be ignored by engineers. Nor can they ignore a responsibility for the (financial and legal) liabilities attached to such systems.

In the past, there has been a reliance on the education, training, experience and wisdom of engineers to ensure that our systems are safe. In future, engineers will need to be brought up-to-date with the ever-increasing range of tools available to aid the design process involving software. The existence of a pool of experts will be of value in conducting peer reviews of the competence of practising engineers.

60.1.2 Management of risks

In general, the developers of safety-critical systems are concerned with managing risks.

Risk is defined in the IEC standard (IEC, 1989) as 'the combination of the frequency, or probability, and the consequence of a specified hazardous event'. This concept of risk has two elements: the frequency, or probability, with which a hazard occurs, and the consequences of the hazardous event.

In any particular application there will be a level of risk that can be deemed 'tolerable'. In a situation where the level of risk, without precautions, is deemed intolerable, there is a need to ensure that the applied safety-related systems reduce the risk to an acceptable level.

Risks which are taken into account (with safety-critical systems) are those associated with the following consequences or hazards:

1. Loss of human life.
2. Injuries to, or illness of, persons.
3. Environmental pollution.
4. Loss of, or damage to, property.

Risk can be specified as a quantified probability, or as a combination of quantified probabilities. Software safety integrity cannot be specified in the same manner because it is not possible to assess adequately high levels of software reliability (see Chapter 31).

This chapter demonstrates that the development of such software and systems needs additional levels of skill (compared to other types of systems) in order to ensure safe operation. There are a number of standards being developed to aid the developer and there are cost-effective methods of testing and assessing safety without needing recourse to formal mathematical methods in every case. Both these developments will be explored.

60.1.3 Software in safety-critical systems

Software which can put life or valuable resources at risk by the nature of its use and behaviour has become known as 'safety-related'. The most extreme instance of safety-related software is the category which could cause major loss of life if it failed to operate exactly as required. This category is called 'safety-critical'. This provides a finer categorization than the use of 'safety-critical' to classify systems, as indicated above.

The basic principles for the design of control systems, as applied specifically to safety-related applications, have been expressed in existing standards with reference to hard-wired systems.

This chapter seeks to interpret these principles for software in the context of safety-related systems. The chapter covers software in dedicated microprocessors, programmable logic controllers (PLCs), multiprocessor distributed systems, larger scale central processor systems and other forms of safety-related programmable electronic system (PES). It also discusses the principles and requirements for software development and should be read in association with appropriate standards on computer hardware and system integration.

The principles applied in developing safety-related software include:

1. Top-down design methods.
2. Modularity.
3. Verification of each phase.
4. Clear documentation.
5. Auditable documents.
6. Validation testing.

Software design methods, in the sense of software engineering methodology or methods of implementation, are not the principal topic of this chapter. It should be understood here that good practices in software engineering and the application of quality assurance methods, for example as described in the ISO Standard 9000 series, are necessary in safety-related systems. Verified modules, module libraries and strictly defined interfaces should be used. Methods to improve software ergonomics (the human interface) should also be applied to safety-related systems, but are not covered or discussed further in this chapter.

The current state-of-the-art is such that neither the application of quality assurance methods (so-called preventative measures) nor the application of appropriate architectural considerations can guarantee the absolute safety of the system. There is no known way of proving the absence of faults in reasonably complex safety-related software (especially the absence of specification and design faults). Formal methods and tools should be applied where possible, but it must be realised that they do not provide a 'proof of correctness', only a proof of conformance to specification. The bulk of the chapter is concerned with techniques for developing and analysing safety-related and safety-critical software.

60.1.4 Safety and reliability

On a superficial basis, it is sometimes assumed that an operationally reliable system is automatically a safe system. A detailed analysis shows, however, that high reliability, while necessary, is not sufficient to ensure safety and it may be necessary to make a tradeoff between reliability and safety, as will be seen later. The designer must distinguish between reliability and safety. The extent to which reliability, safety or both have to be achieved should be agreed between the customer and the designer of the system in advance.

Reliability is oriented towards the purpose of the system and to the intended action (service); it is the extent to which a system is expected to perform the specified task. Reliability requirements are concerned with the continuous provision of the system service.

Safety, on the other hand, is concerned with the causes and consequences of possible accidents. Safety requirements are concerned with developing a system which does not cause accidents. The safety requirements ensure (require) that the system does not reach a hazardous or unsafe state, where an event may cause an accident. Moreover, it must be transparent from the safety requirements what actions should be taken if an unforeseen event in the environment leads to an unsafe state.

In relation to safety, it does not matter if the system does not serve its purpose, as long as the safety requirements are not violated. (Consider one example from the area of railway signalling, where a switch with a faulty sensor means that the green light for that track will not be set, so the train has to stop.) On the other hand, it is possible that the system is highly reliable, but unsafe; for example, a system with formally verified software where a safety-related situation has not been specified. Furthermore, there may be a tradeoff between reliability and safety, as is illustrated by the following example.

Consider a fail-safe system with two computers operating in active redundancy. The outputs of the two computers are compared in order to detect a possible failure of one of them. After the occurrence of such a failure there are two strategies for handling the situation, depending on whether high reliability or 'high safety' has to be achieved:

1. If a high degree of safety is required, both computers have to be shut down and the process has to be brought into a safe fall-back state. No further service can be provided because there is no way of deciding which of the computers is faulty. Even if there is a high probability that the faulty computer can be identified, it would be impossible to detect further erroneous outputs without redundancy.
2. If a high degree of reliability has to be achieved, there is a probability that the faulty computer can be identified and the operation can be continued without any redundancy with the (probably) intact computer.

There is another difference between safety and reliability. Software has a reliability of its own, that is, the probability of getting the intended result after submitting the input. It is possible to analyse the reliability of software packages. To check the safety of software contained in a safety-related system it is necessary to look at the whole system: the software must be seen in the context of the particular application. It is meaningless to speak about a safe program for sorting or word processing, as there is no possibility of hazard due to an erroneous sorting algorithm (considered in isolation).

60.1.5 The nature of the problem

Safety-critical systems have been in use in nuclear power plants for more than 30 years and in major chemical plants for even longer, so what is new? The answer is the growing use of computers to control such processes. As computer power has increased it has become possible to operate plants by computer with much faster decision-making. This has brought economic benefits but also the need for a more critical appraisal of the whole process, from the specification of what the system is required to do, through the system design phase which identifies how the system may be structured, to its implementation in software. As systems become more complex, each of these phases need codes of practice and, in some cases, regulations to ensure safe operation of the system during its life.

In reliability work it is common to refer to the 'bath-tub curve' to describe a condition where excessive failures occur early in the life of a system, followed by a period of relatively

low failures, later to be followed by an increase in failures. Norman (1986) has likened the development of technological products to this bath-tub curve. When a new technology is introduced into the market it is complex compared to other technologies. As time passes the technology begins to be considered less complex, whereupon the developers begin to increase the complexity once more through applications of the technology. This can be seen in the use of computers to effect control on many industrial processes. When it was introduced, computer control was considered complex and, as a consequence, the extent of the control required of the system was kept within manageable limits. As the use of computers in control became more common, so the perceived complexity reduced, which in turn encouraged the designer of a control system to become more adventurous and once again to increase the complexity. It is this system complexity which now presents the problem of safety in such control systems.

60.1.6 Contents of the chapter

The remainder of the chapter is organized as follows. Section 60.2 discusses the conceptual basis for safety, showing that safety is a subjective concept based on risk assessment. Risk assessment is considered more fully in Section 60.3, which surveys the most commonly used assessment techniques, including fault trees and event trees. Although Section 60.3 discusses assessment techniques for software, much of the material is applicable to any safety-critical system.

Section 60.4 considers the software development life cycle, drawing out those issues which are particular to the development of safety-critical systems. This leads to a discussion of applicable standards in Section 60.5, and of experience in assessing systems in Section 60.6. The conclusions summarize the main points drawn out in the chapter and indicate some directions for research.

60.2 Conceptual model of safety

Safety traditionally refers to a subjective judgement of a potential hazard, within a specified safety criterion, based on personal experience of the assessor and supported by limited measurements of observable parameters. These measurements are currently not possible in the context of software-based systems. systems.

To understand why safety cannot be expressed in terms of a quantitative measurement, the epistemological and logical foundations of measurement need to be examined (see Chapter 12). Before examining the principles of measurement it is necessary to formulate a conceptual model of the problem (see *Figure 60.1*).

A conceptual model is a way of describing the interrelationship of a number of concerns in an abstract way. There are different conceptual models dependent upon the observer: the designer's model, the user's model and the assessor's model.

On one side of the conceptual model a notion of safety comprises ideas of what is 'safe' and what is 'unsafe', probably based upon some value judgement of what is tolerable. This judgement can be expressed in terms of tolerable loss of life, economic loss or environmental damage. To this concept is added a model of the 'real world' which defines the acceptable boundaries of safety applicable to the world model being used. From the concept and the world model a definition can be developed to describe the combination of these two.

On the other side of the conceptual model is some method of instrumentation which provides a measurement and, through pragmatic evaluation, is ordered into some form of index. The ordering of the index is influenced not only by pragmatism but

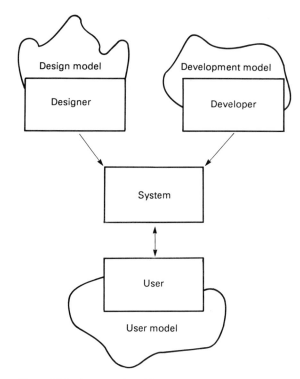

Figure 60.1 Conceptual models

also by both the concept of safety and the world model being used.

To be able to have a quantitative measurement of safety according to the definition derived from the conceptual model, it is necessary to have a mapping between the definition and the index. Finkelstein (1975) defines measurement as being a set of mathematical entities Q, and a set of numbers N, with a mapping function M between the sets, such that M maps the mathematical entities Q onto the set of numbers N: $M:Q \rightarrow N$. A scale of measurement S is given as the triplet $S = \{Q,M,N\}$.

If the class of entities Q is considered to be the definition of safety D in the conceptual model, and the set of numbers N as being the index I, then in order for safety to be expressed in terms of a measurement, a mapping function M which maps the definition D onto the index I, i.e. $M:D \rightarrow I$, is required.

Such a mapping function may be considered as a conjoint measurement which, according to Finkelstein, relates to a set of measurements having the capacity to assign a measure to the object and to order the measure in a set of measures. Conjoint measurement, then, is some form of ordering according to empirical observations (subjective judgement) rather than rankings. Finkelstein describes rankings as being a comparison against defined standards (see also Chapter 12 on measurement theory). Since defined standards for the measurement of software do not exist it is clear that the measurement of the software contained in a safety-critical system cannot be made (at present). Therefore the safety assessment remains, for the present, subjective.

The assessment of a safety-critical system is, then, a subjective judgement about the risk of a hazard materializing and whether that risk is acceptable within the world model being used. It should be noted that the world model, and for that matter the conceptual model, may be subject to change. Following the 1974 Flixborough disaster, when a chemical plant exploded killing many people, a Court of Inquiry was convened and the Report of the Court of Inquiry makes a number of recommendations and comments on the acceptability of risks:

> When Mr Marshall refers to risks exceeding a specific value we understand him to refer to risks which exceed what at a given time is regarded as socially tolerable, for what is and is not acceptable depends in the end upon current social tolerance and what is regarded as tolerable at one time may well be regarded as intolerable at another. Nowhere is this more apparent than in the field of road transport where the construction and use regulations have, over the years, become even more stringent. (DOE, 1975, para. 197)

If it is subjectively asserted that activity X is 'safer' than activity Y, then the judgement may accurately reflect a comparison of some characteristic of the entities. However, the utility of the safeness of entity Y may be greater than that for entity X, since the social and economic consequences of entity Y being unsafe may be greater than for entity X. Therefore, an assessment of the safety of a system must not be considered in isolation from the social and economic costs of the system being unsafe.

Engineers and managers have now begun to realise that with this new technology comes flexibility and additional safety considerations. These considerations include:

1. The knowledge that the correct and safe operation of the business, capital equipment or control system is dependent upon such technology.
2. The risk of causing a loss of human life, economic loss or environmental damage is outside their normal engineering judgement.
3. The concern that conventional safety assessments are insufficient and fail to identify that there are weaknesses in the safe operation of the system.

What is needed now is a structured approach for the assessment of safety-critical systems to which the experienced engineer can turn. In addition to being sufficiently flexible to encompass the latest and more mature techniques the scheme must also be cost-effective.

Until now the only assurance of correct operation of a software-intensive safety-critical system has been by conventional software-testing techniques based on the functional requirements. However, such testing is not without limitations and cannot locate all faults. Faults often only materialize many months or years after a system has been put into operation, possibly leading to very expensive recall procedures or 'retrofits' on site, or even dangerous incidents. Most industries have an urgent requirement for confidence in the correct and safe operation of their computer-based systems. This includes the automotive industry, which is now making extensive use of software in critical applications.

60.3 Approaches to assessment

The structure of the software has an influence on its safety. This section examines the ways in which the software can be structured to ensure safe operation and methods of analysing that safety.

The section begins by examining the use of a set of techniques known generically by the term 'risk' analysis. In particular, the applicability to software of fault tree analysis, Petri Nets and event tree analysis is explored.

State transition diagrams are sometimes considered to be the means of identifying all possible fault conditions. State transition diagrams are examined here with particular reference to the interaction between software, the hardware and the system.

Methods are examined that may be applicable in isolating a fault condition, and then an argument is advanced for weighting failure conditions according to the extent of danger.

The structuring of the software for safety according to the control flow is considered. It is recommended that in safety-related systems the software should be structured into control moduies, safety modules and arbitrator modules. It is also suggested that a system of integrity locks should be used.

'Risk analysis' is used by engineers to describe a group of methods for determining the conditions that will cause a hazardous state to exist, and the associated risk. There is a need to assess the risk resulting from the use of computers as controllers in safety-related processes. The principal cause for concern is the possible number of software errors that can exist and the effects of these errors on the system. Since these techniques are used to analyse the risk associated with industrial processes and its hardware, it follows that control software should also be subject to similar analysis.

Risk analysis comprises a collection of analytical techniques used to examine the design of complex items of equipment within a safety context. The principal risk analysis techniques are fault tree analysis (FTA) and event tree analysis (ETA) (Chelson, 1971). The application of both these risk analysis techniques to software will be discussed later.

60.3.1 Fault tree analysis

Chelson (1971) has shown that fault trees can be constructed by first listing all the possible hazards considered to be present in (or associated with) the system, and then assuming that a particular event has caused one of the hazards and tracing backwards through the logic of the system to find which events could lead to the hazard. Since preceding events may be the logical combination of other events, a set of symbols is used to represent the logical sequence of possible events. As each node in the tree is encountered a decision is made as to whether further investigation is required. As the investigation continues, more symbols are included in the tree until a node is reached where either a failure event or a terminal event (also called a Basic event) is encountered. These symbols are shown in *Figure 60.2*.

Leveson and Harvey (1983) have shown that FTA can be applied to software provided that the catastrophic event which is to be considered can be defined in a precise manner. Since FTA was developed for hardware and has now been applied to software, it is possible to link the two sets of analyses to form a complete set for the total system. FTA applied to software is called software fault tree analysis (SFTA) by Leveson and Harvey.

SFTA, in common with hardware FTA, examines the potentially dangerous conditions called 'catastrophic events' that could occur as a result of 'top events' or 'loss events'. It considers all possible actions that could cause the dangerous conditions to exist. SFTA uses diagrams that are a variation of those used for hardware FTA.

Leveson and Harvey have also shown that SFTA can be performed at various levels and stages of software development. The highest level of analysis is the functional description. At the lowest level of investigation SFTA analyses the program code.

Leveson and Harvey also suggest that it is possible to construct fault trees from a program design language and that the information derived from the tree during the software development phase can be used to aid robust program design. However, SFTA does not cater for the effect of one part of a program influencing another.

In SFTA it is assumed that for a dangerous condition to exist it is necessary for there to be a related output from the computer. Therefore the starting point for SFTA, when work-

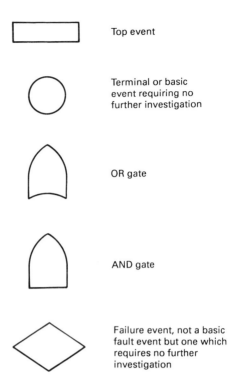

Figure 60.2 FTA symbols

ing at the program level, is the section of code responsible for effecting an output. The analysis then proceeds backwards through the code, determining both how the program arrived at the section of code and the current states of the variables.

Standard forms of symbolism have been proposed by Leveson and Harvey for Pascal-like program statements. The general form for the **if** ... **then** ... **else** statement is shown in *Figure 60.3(a)*. The statement 'if $a > b$ then $x := f(x)$ else $x := 10$' is shown in *Figure 60.3(b)* when analysed for the event '$x > 100$'.

Since the right-most node, stating that $x := 10$ causes $x > 100$, is clearly nonsense, the node can be assigned a zero probability and removed from the tree. Analysing for the top event of $x > 100$ could stop at this point and assertions placed in the code or the preceding code could be analysed for the events '$a > b$' and '$f(x) > 100$'.

Figure 60.4(a) shows the suggested general format for analysing a **while** ... **do** statement and *Figure 60.4(b)* shows the analysis for the loop

```
while b > x do
    begin b: = b − 1
          z: = z + 10;
    end
```

analysed for the top event '$z > 100$'.

Leveson and Stolzy (1987) have suggested that real-time features, such as the concurrency found in the language Ada, can also be analysed using SFTA.

A disadvantage with SFTA is the difficulty in determining all possible top events that may arise and assessing their procedure events (cut sets), and basic failure events (minimum cut sets). SFTA is not exhaustive and relies upon the person analysing the system to identify the 'top events'. Also, there is no check to indicate that the analysis is complete.

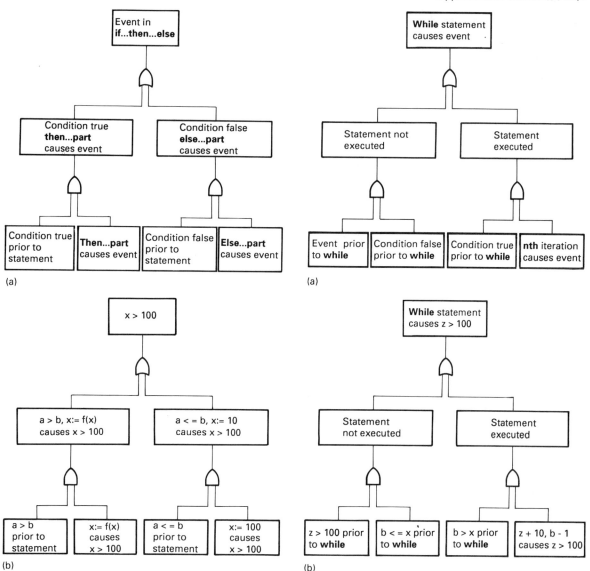

Figure 60.3 SFTA for if ... then ... else

Figure 60.4 Example of SFTA

In the software context, a trace through the data flow of a program and analysis for failure events will identify some hazard situations which can be further examined using SFTA. Data flow can be traced using Petri Nets or event tree analysis.

60.3.2 Petri Nets

The Petri Net, a tool for system modelling, has been developed from the original work of C. A. Petri, who developed a new model of information flow in systems. The model was based on the concepts of asynchronous and concurrent operation by the parts of a system, and the realisation that the relationships between the parts could be represented by a graph or net. Since that time, research has continued into the use of Petri Nets and a number of modifications and enhancements have greatly increased their modelling power.

Petri Nets (Peterson, 1977) are formal methods of represent-ing information flow and can be used to illustrate information flow in a program statement. They are able to represent the information flow at the level of the specification or at the level of the actual program.

Petri Nets are bipartite directed graphs consisting of two basic components: a set of places P, and a set of transitions T. In addition, two functions are created to link transitions to places: the input function I, and the output function O. For each transition t_j, there is a set of output places $O(t_j)$. Formally, a Petri Net is made up of a quadruple $C = (P,T,I,O)$. Since each Petri Net has an initial condition, this needs to be included in the structure, giving a quintuple (P,T,I,O,u). Defining the initial condition of the Petri Net is called 'marking' a Petri Net.

In diagrams, the places in a Petri Net are represented by circles and each transition is represented by a line crossing the arc between two places. A transition is said to be enabled to 'fire' if and only if all the input tokens for that transition (markings) are satisfied and this allows the token at an input place to be transferred to an output place. The transition of the token is, in the abstract, the transfer of information from one place to another place.

When the statement **if** x **then** y **else** z is executed the control will pass to either y or z, according to the truth of x. A Petri Net can be represented graphically for a statement as shown in *Figure 60.5*, where P_i is the initial input place which fires transition t_1. Transition t_2 will only be fired and pass a token to y when t_1 has fired and place x has a token (x is true). Transition t_3 will fire and pass a token to z when t_1 has fired and 'x bar' has a token (x is false). For the **if** x **then** y **else** z statement, places y and z would be the input places for the following statements.

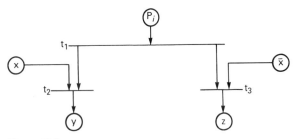

Figure 60.5

The firing of transition t_1 enables the firing of either t_2 or t_3, dependent on the logical state of x. However, when considering a programming statement according to a failure criterion it is important to note that the conditional expression x may also fail. If the possibility of the conditional statement c failing in the statement **if** x **then** y **else** z is included, then the Petri Net changes, as shown in *Figure 60.6*.

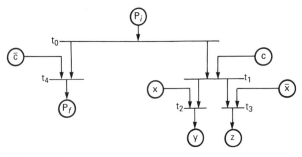

Figure 60.6

The transitions t_1 and t_4 will fire according to the status of the conditional statement c and transitions t_2 and t_3 will fire according to the logical truth of the conditional expression x. The failure of the conditional statement is called the conditional failure, and the logical truth of the conditional expression is called the temporal switch.

Figure 60.7 shows the general form for some Pascal-like programming languages statements using Petri Net diagrams.

Petri Nets of complete programs become unmanageable and need simplification. One method of simplifying the representation of failure events is to use a risk analysis technique called event tree analysis (ETA).

Also, for a graphical representation of an abstract model of information flow to be useful in identifying risks, the probabilities of failure components of the model need to be added. The addition of such probability data to a Petri Net will detract from its function of representing the logical sequence.

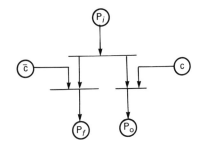

(a)

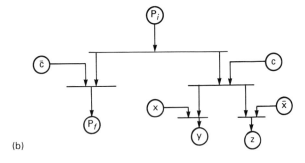

(b)

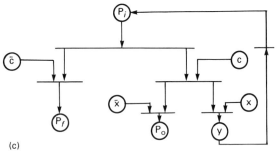

(c)

Figure 60.7 Program statements using Petri Nets: (a) assignment; (b) if ... then ... else; (c) while x do y

60.3.3 Event tree analysis

ETA is less common than FTA but is becoming more frequently used in industry.

Hardware ETA attempts to identify those individual events which may cause a further sequence of events leading to a dangerous condition. It can be considered to be an approach to the task of identifying risks from the lowest event towards the 'top event', and traces back to the lowest event in the sequence examining the causes of events. ETA examines the consequences of possible failure. The use of 'event trees' provides a graphical method of presenting the results of the analysis.

To construct an event tree of failures, each probable failure is considered from the start of the process under analysis to the end. The first stage of the ETA construction is to look at the outcome of each component failure and then represent the outcome as a decision branch. For each outcome of the first stage, consideration is given as to the outcome of each subsequent component failing. The analysis of each susbequent stage is then added to the decision branch of the preceding outcome. The analysis continues until each component in the process has been considered, and its outcome determined and added to the evolving tree structure. Probabilities of failure can then be attached to each outcome of the complete event tree. It is possible to determine the probability of success/failure at any given point in the process.

Figure 60.8 shows an event tree drawn for a parallel pump system employing two water pumps. The failure probabilities are included on the drawing as an example of the calculations.

The application of ETA to software is given the name software event tree analysis (SETA).

Each programming statement in a high-level language is executed according to a set of rules governing the logic of the statement; for example, the statement **if** x **then** y **else** z will execute y or z according to the logical condition of x. Further, the sequence in which the statements are executed is determined according to the logical relationship of one statement to another.

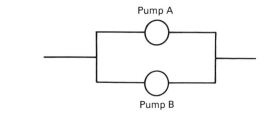

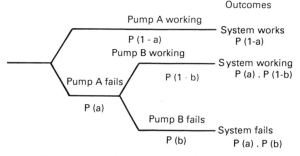

Figure 60.8 ETA analysis of a pumping station

By convention, the failure branch in an ETA diagram is drawn on the lower branch and the success branch is the higher branch. From a single entry to a complete program, there are only two possible exits: success and failure. So for each statement within the program there are also two exits from a single entry. Within the statement the branching strategy continues to a lower level of detail but the respective exits are connected to maintain the higher level strategy of the statement. The respective exits from the statements are connected in order to maintain the strategy of the complete program. Pascal-like programming statements represented in SETA format are shown in *Figures 60.9* and *60.10* where the symbol '*' denotes a terminal failure which would cause an irrecoverable failure to exist. The failures branch can occur on other statements but has been labelled only on this one.

Note that the temporal switch, #, permits the flow to take whichever path is relevant according to the conditional expression, assuming that it has not failed.

Leveson and Harvey observed that SFTA can be combined with FTA to provide a comprehensive analysis of a total system, including hardware and software. The application of ETA to the hardware associated with a computer system can continue to a point where the software element needs to be considered, and SETA can be used to provide a comprehensive analysis.

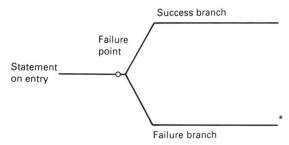

Figure 60.9 Program statement using SETA

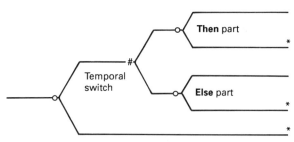

Figure 60.10 if...then...else using SETA

As an example, consider the case where plant sensors are used to pass data to a computer about the functioning of a critical plant area so that optimal control of the plant can be maintained. Using ETA, the sensors, instrumentation, analogue–digital converter and computer I/O mechanisms are considered. However, once the analysis has reached the point where data is requested by the control software from the operating system, device driver or control software, then SETA can be used. SETA can be used to assess the software in the context of programs or programming statements.

A complete ETA/SETA analysis is then possible in order to identify particular items of concern and to seek to reduce the probability of a failure. Assuming an item of concern can be described in terms suitable for analysis using SETA, and that the risk is judged to require further detailed analysis, then additional SFTA can be undertaken.

In summary, the approach is to identify potential failures using ETA/SETA and then to examine the concerns further using SETA.

The application of existing ETA to SETA is possible and provides useful information to the analyst on failure probabilities. By careful identification of the issues raised with SETA, further analysis can be undertaken using what Leveson and Harvey called software fault tree analysis (SFTA) in order to isolate the concerns. Once these concerns have been isolated, suitable remedial action can be taken to eradicate them.

60.3.4 State transition diagrams

The internal state of a process can be modelled in the abstract at any time using graph theoretic methods such as the state transition diagram (STD) which is a special case of the finite state machine (FSM) (see Chapter 9 for a more general discussion of such machines). STDs are commonly used by engineers to assess the behaviour of a given system, which might be an industrial process or the internal function of a computer.

An FSM consists of a finite set of input symbols A, a finite set of internal states S, a finite set of output symbols Z, a next state function f, and an output function g. The machine M is denoted by $M = \{A, S, Z, f, g\}$. Additionally an initial state q_0 may be included when the machine M will be denoted by $M = \{A,S,Z,q_0,f,g\}$.

An example FSM could have three output symbols, three internal states and three output symbols:

$A = \{a,b,c\}$
$S = \{q_0,q_1,q_2\}$
$Z = \{x,y,z\}$

The next state function f could be defined as:

$f(q_0,a) = q_1 \quad f(q_1,a) = q_2 \quad f(q_2,a) = q_0$
$f(q_0,b) = q_2 \quad f(q_1,b) = q_1 \quad f(q_2,b) = q_1$
$f(q_0,c) = q_0 \quad f(q_1,c) = q_0 \quad f(q_2,c) = q_2$

The output function g could be defined as:

$g(q_0,a) = x \quad g(q_1,a) = x \quad g(q_2,a) = z$
$g(q_0,b) = y \quad g(q_1,b) = z \quad g(q_2,b) = y$
$g(q_0,c) = z \quad g(q_1,c) = y \quad g(q_2,c) = x$

A state diagram is one way of representing the machine M (see *Figure 60.11*). A state diagram is a labelled directed graph with the vertices being the states S of M such that an arc can be drawn between state q_0 and q_1 and labelled with the pair a,x representing the next state function $f(q_0,a) = q_1$ and the output function $g(q_0,a) = x$.

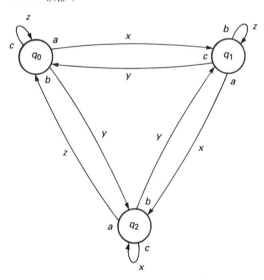

Figure 60.11   State diagram for example machine M

Another way of representing machine M is to use a state table which tabulates the next-state and output for each combination of current state and input. A state table for machine M would be as shown in *Table 60.1*.

Table 60.1

Current state	Input a	Input b	Input c
q_0	q_1, x	q_2, y	q_0, z
q_1	q_2, x	q_1, z	q_0, y
q_2	q_0, z	q_1, y	q_1, x

An STD consists of a set of states S, a set of events E and a transition function t.

The state transition for FSM M can be represented as:

$S = \{q_0,q_1,q_2\}$
$E = \{x,y,z\}$

and the transition functions are:

$t(q_0,x) = q_1 \quad t(q_1,x) = q_2 \quad t(q_2,x) = q_2$
$t(q_0,y) = q_2 \quad t(q_1,y) = q_0 \quad t(q_2,y) = q_1$
$t(q_0,z) = q_0 \quad t(q_1,z) = q_1 \quad t(q_2,z) = q_0$

The STD would be that shown in *Figure 60.12*.

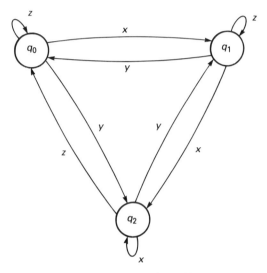

Figure 60.12   STD for the example machine

Industrial control systems can be modelled using both FSMs and STDs, but the use of the STD is more common.

As an example of the use of STD, take a simple control system consisting of a fluid pump P, under the control of a fluid level float F. The control function of F is to maintain the level of liquid within a certain vessel by turning the pump 'on' to lower the level of the liquid when the level is indicated as 'high' by the float. Assuming that the liquid flow into the vessel is constant and not under the control of the system being modelled, the process scheme is shown in *Figure 60.13*.

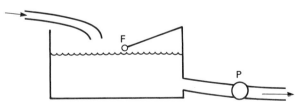

Figure 60.13   Example process

The objective of the control system is to ensure that none of the liquid flows over the top of the vessel. If any liquid does flow over the top of the vessel, the condition is considered to be catastrophic.

To keep the model simple it is assumed that both the float F and the pump P work correctly, even though there is a probability that the control signals may not work. Initially it is further assumed that no such failure of control signals exist.

The pump P is switched on when the float F is indicating 'high' and the pump is switched off when the float indicates 'low'.

The set of states S are:

$$S = \{q_0, q_1, q_2, q_3\}$$

where:

q_0 = level low, pump off.
q_1 = level low, pump on.
q_2 = level high, pump off.
q_3 = level high, pump on.

The set of events E are:

$$E = \{a, b, c, d\}$$

where:

a = float high.
b = float low.
c = pump on.
d = pump off.

The transitions functions t are:

$$t(q_0,a) = q_2 \quad t(q_1,a) = q_3 \quad t(q_2,b) = q_0 \quad t(q_3,b) = q_1$$
$$t(q_0,c) = q_1 \quad t(q_1,d) = q_0 \quad t(q_2,c) = q_3 \quad t(q_3,d) = q_2$$

The STD for the control system is shown in *Figure 60.14*, with the transition T being $T = \{S, E, t\}$ and the initial state q_0 being included to give $T = \{S, E, q_0, t\}$.

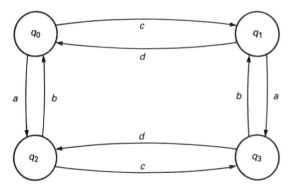

Figure 60.14 STD diagram for the example control system

The transition functions can also be represented by a transition table. *Table 60.2* is a transition table for the control system being considered.

Table 60.2

State	Float	Pump
q_0	Low (0)	Off (0)
q_1	Low (0)	On (1)
q_2	High (1)	Off (0)
q_3	High (1)	On (1)

STDs are deterministic and exhaustive. To demonstrate the exhaustive nature of STDs, consider the control system to have been extended to ignore transient inputs from the float by requiring the float to indicate high for two successive observations before switching the pump on. The control algorithm is expressed as:

$$P_o = (F_s \hat{F_i} \, \mathbf{not} \, P_{oi}) \vee (F_s \vee P_i) \vee P_{oi}$$

where:

P_o is the pump output value according to the logic.
P_{oi} is the initial or correctly stored value for the pump output.
F_s is the stored value for the float.
F_i is the input value for the float.

Assuming no errors are experienced the transient table becomes as shown in *Table 60.3*.

Table 60.3

P_{oi}	F_s	F_i	P_o
0	0	0	0
0	0	1	0
0	1	0	0
0	1	1	1
1	0	0	0
1	0	1	1
1	1	0	1
1	1	1	1

The concern of this chapter is the identification of catastrophic failures/conditions. Such a condition could arise in the control system if the level was high and the pump failed to operate, causing the liquid to overflow. From the transient diagram and the transitions, a catastrophic failure condition can be seen not to occur when all the equipment functions correctly.

So far the concern has been with representing the state transitions when all the equipment is working correctly with no errors. When the control system has the same control algorithm, but uses an industrial controller incorporating software to implement that algorithm, then a catastrophic failure/condition can arise due to the failure of components of the controller, even though the electromechanical equipment may work correctly.

The transition tables for the control system using software considers three error types: stuck at 0, stuck at 1 and inversion. The conditions which are considered to be a catastrophic failure/condition are fluid flowing into the vessel, float fluid level high and pump not on.

The example process modelled for the discussion has been a trivial control system and yet many error conditions can be identified. If the control system was more complex than this one, with many more parameters to consider, then the dimensions of the state diagram would become unmanageable. The number of instances where an error can exist and create a catastrophic failure/condition becomes proportionately greater as the number of parameters increases, making STDs difficult to use for isolating potential hazards.

In many industrial control systems the number of states is so great that exhaustive checking of all conditions would not be practicable.

60.3.5 Recommended approach

It can be seen from the above that there are a number of methods one can use to assess software. The assessor must therefore make a choice as to which of these methods is to be used. The factors influencing this are many, but include the application being assessed, the culture and numeracy of the industry involved and the extent to which software contributes to the criticality within the context of the larger system.

In considering software it is common to limit the scope to the verification and validation of the software against the specification. However, there is an assumption that the specification is itself complete and that it accords with the safety requirements that exist beyond that of the software. For safety-critical systems the assessment must take in these wider issues.

60.4 Development process

Errors in software can affect safety, so the occasions where errors can be introduced in the software development process are now considered. Also discussed are the reasons why it is not practicable to remove all errors from the software. A basis for measuring certain features of the software is introduced. It is suggested that these measures, though not rigorously proved, do give some indication of the scope for error in an individual item of software.

The development and production of 'safe' software systems has five distinct stages, each having a quality assessment part:

1. Requirements specification.
2. System specification.
3. Program specification.
4. Program production.
5. System integration and test.

(See Chapter 15 for a fuller description of the software life cycle.)

Before the software development can begin, the originator of the development, often called the requesting authority, needs to obtain a concise and precise understanding of the requirements. Once the software has been implemented and is in operation the requesting authority may identify what are considered to be short-comings in the system produced. This may necessitate revision of the requirements specification.

The requirements specification may have been prepared by a number of people from differing disciplines and functions within the requesting organization, including the end user. It is therefore necessary for the requirements specification to be unambiguous to all those people involved in its preparation, and the subsequent developers. The removal of ambiguity from the requirements specification is a research topic with no established form. Mathematical methods can be used to formulate the requirements specification but the use of such formal methods presents a paradox: to make the statements unambiguous the axiomatic methods used require a considerable degree of understanding of mathematical logic. This may not present a problem to computer scientists but it may to the requesting authority, which may (in the limit) not understand the requirements specification. If (written) natural language is used for the specification, then the computer scientist may find the specification to be imprecise, while the requesting authority may claim to understand it. At the state of the art there is a risk that ambiguity will persist in requirements specifications for industrial control systems.

The system specification, which follows from the requirements specification, is concerned with the design of the total system against the requirements specification.

Program specifications are concerned with the design of specific programs and the interfaces between them, in order to meet the system specification. The software structure influences the extent to which the system will conform to the requirements specification. If the structuring of the software does not enable the system to conform to the requirements specification, the software may need to be redesigned. So an iterative process is called for, involving all those personnel involved in the requirements specification and system specification. This process is sometimes called the 'design process'.

Once the design process has been satisfactorily completed, the program development can begin. During program development the program is written in accordance with the previously agreed program specification. At the end of program development, the program is tested in isolation from the other programs forming the system.

The stage following program development is called system test and integration, which is when the individually tested programs are tested as a complete system and integrated into a target implementation.

The multi-stage iterative process which describes the development process can be viewed as a directed graph. This is illustrated in *Figure 60.15* where the nodes represent stages of development, each having an associated activity.

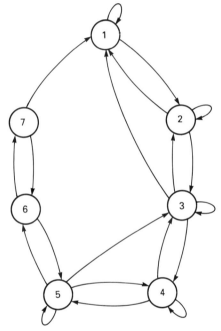

1 – Requirements specification
2 – System specification
3 – Program specification
4 – Program production
5 – System test and integration
6 – Implementation
7 – Operation

Figure 60.15 Software development cycle

Nodes 1–5 in the directed graph of Figure 60.15 each have an arc beginning and ending at that node, to show that progress to the next stage (represented by a node) is not permitted until some form of quality assessment process has been satisfied for that stage. Each normal path between stages, except 7 to 1, has a forward and reverse arc indicating that when the quality assessment cannot be satisfied at a particular node it is necessary to return to the proceeding node and examine the transformation that took place. The arc between stages 7 and 1 is unidirectional, since the logical progression from node 1 is to node 2.

To account for the occasion when the quality assessment

process has shown discrepancies from the specification, such that a radical reconsideration of the design or structure is required, some nodes have additional arcs to nodes other than the succeeding or proceeding node. As an example, if the requirements specification cannot be met in the program specification, it may be necessary to follow the arc from node 3 to 1.

There is a need in all the stages of the development process to analyse errors and to take the appropriate action. Error 'analysis' takes three forms: error prevention, error detection and error correction.

Error prevention implies the use of good software engineering and programming practice: the use of the best known methods of software production, for example, the selection of meaningful variable and constant names, structured programming and other methods of programming.

Finding and removing the cause of errors is an intensive and prolonged activity. Although it is important to correct an error, it is equally important to ensure that the knowledge of the error, its original cause and the correction are recorded in the guide to good programming practice being used by the programmer. Error detection and error correction will be carried out by the programmer in the most efficient way as part of his normal function.

Error determination addresses the following concepts:

1. The software should comply satisfactorily to its specification.
2. The programmer should have completed the test-set provided for the purpose and be satisfied that the tests were as exhaustive as they could be, given the restraints of time, effort and possibly commercial urgency for the software.
3. The development stage when metrics will be used is that stage immediately proceeding the commissioning of the software into operational use, possibly during acceptance testing.
4. Satisfactory test limits will have to be determined for the proposed metrics before the application of these metrics.
5. The test limits and the metrics presented will provide a pass/fail criteria for a Certification Authority seeking to approve the software.

Good software development techniques are considered in detail in Part II of this reference book.

60.5 Developments in standards

In 1974 the issue of industrial safety was brought into sharp focus by two noteworthy events: the Flixborough disaster and the introduction of the Health and Safety at Work Act. Both of these events played a significant role in the development and thinking that has led to further guidance being made available to the engineer. What has happened since?

A recent survey of practices in safety-critical systems has shown that dependence, by the engineer, for safe operation is placed on the use of traditional quality assurance methods, such as BS 5750 and ISO 9000. This is understandable as there are few standards for safety-critical systems and those that there are have only just been published.

The specific concerns of safety-critical and safety-related software began to surface early in the 1980s (Bennett, 1984) and prompted a number of 'standards' activities.

60.5.1 MOD Standards

Many readers will have seen much comment in the press on the Draft Interim Defence Standards 00-55 and 00-56 (MOD, 1989a,b) which place emphasis on the use of formal mathematical methods for defence-procured software. Defence systems continually increase in sophistication to match the greater demands of the armed services and to provide the operational

edge over the opponent's technology. To meet the requirements placed upon modern military equipment in a time- and cost-effective manner, designers are progressively incorporating computer control systems.

Prior to any defence equipment entering service, the manufacturer must demonstrate to the satisfaction of the MOD safety authorities that the item is inherently safe and will not present a hazard to the user. This is particularly important for a system, such as a guided missile, which is designed to inflict serious and widespread damage. The overall safety clearance procedure becomes more complex when the system has embedded control software, for the reasons already discussed.

Hence the MOD has seen a need for greater constraints upon the suppliers of safety-critical software. Through the adoption of tighter controls it was anticipated that future systems would be delivered within timescales and budget and emanate a greater feeling of confidence. The work that was initiated resulted in Draft Defence Standards 00-55 and 00-56, the first parts of an expected series of documents covering the whole of system development to be revised in the future to reflect technology and/or commercial changes.

In future, all MOD projects will be subject to hazard analysis, as defined by the managerial and technical requirements of 00-56. The hazard analysis, started early in the project life cycle, will be used to determine the safety classification of system functions. Software that is identified as being safety-critical will then be bound by the requirements of 00-55.

Draft Defence Standard 00-55 consists of three main sections and a number of annexes, which describe in greater detail the concepts introduced in the main body.

The first of the detailed sections examines the overall management of the safety function. It identifies those organizations and personnel that will be involved in the development of the software and the extent of their responsibilities. Within this definition, the MOD introduce the concept of the Independent Software Safety Assessor (ISSA) and the Independent Verification and Validation Team. These particular parties, appointed by the Design Authority (the organization contracted to undertake the work for the MOD), are responsible for ensuring that the various life-cycle phases have been correctly implemented. On completion of the software, the ISSA is required to sign the Safety-Critical Software Certificate, along with the Design Authority and the MOD project manager. Finally, this section considers the documentation required to accompany the software and its development, and the configuration management of the safety-critical software as defined in Def Stan 05-57.

The second procedural section contains the software engineering practices that must prevail over the software life cycle, so as to reduce the possibility of an undetected error. In this respect, the standard encourages the use of those techniques which are easy to analyse and verify, and proscribes a number of features deemed unsafe or difficult to analyse. In essence, the document tries to identify the practices which will enable a complete verification of the software. The techniques that are strongly endorsed include: formal methods, defensive programming, static code analysis and dynamic testing. Examples of prohibited practices are: recursion, object code patching and dynamic memory management.

The final section relates the requirements as defined in the previous two sections to the project software life cycle. The specified phases are:

1. Concept formulation.
2. Feasibility.
3. Project definition.
4. Full development.
5. Production.
6. In-service.
7. Disposal.

For each phase, the document discusses the necessary inputs and outputs and the roles of the nominated organizations and individuals.

One new area the standard addresses is the training of personnel. Specifying four classes of staff: senior managers, project managers, safety-critical software specialists and software engineers, it provides a brief on the type and level of training, in broad terms, that each should receive. Initially this annex is to stimulate discussion within industry. Surprisingly though, there has been little press interest in the signal work of the professional bodies, like the IEE and I.Gas.E., and trade associations, like EEMUA (1989) in advising their members on this important subject.

60.5.2 Guidelines and international standards

In June 1987 the UK Health and Safety Executive published a document commonly known as the 'PES Guidelines' (HSE, 1987). This document, as its name implies, established guidelines and procedures for the implementation of what are called programmable electronic systems (PES) used in industrial control, instrumentation and consumer products. Similarly, guidelines have been, or are being, developed by trade associations, professional bodies and other UK standards organizations. Similar activity exists in a number of other countries, including France, West Germany, the Scandinavian countries and the USA. In West Germany there is a document from TUV (TUV Rheinland, 1984) of which the reader should be aware.

In parallel with all this activity the International Electrotechnical Commission (IEC) established two working groups with the objective of producing draft international standards in 1989. One working group (SC65A WG9) established in 1984, has been concerned with software for safety-related applications industry and presented its work in Geneva in June 1989 for international comment prior to becoming an international standard. The other working group concerned with generic safety aspects (SC65A WG10) was established in 1987 and submitted its report in Geneva for international consideration in late 1989.

The Instrument Society of America has also formed a committee (SP84) to develop guidance notes on the use of PES-based systems and expects to produce working material during 1990.

The proposed international standard from WG9 (IEC, 1989) is extensive and addresses the full life cycle of software development. The standard is in two parts. Part one contains the normative standard whilst Part two contains an informative annex to expand upon Part one so as to aid the developer of systems. Part two contains, amongst other details, tables to cross-reference particular techniques and software safety integrity levels. Clearly the work of the IEC groups is going to open up a discussion on the subject internationally, and in itself is going to advance the cause for safety in software.

The standard makes very significant technical points. First, the standard advances a five-point scale for the levels of safety integrity to direct the engineer towards a line of thought that safety is not a two-state condition, but one of degree of risk. Second, the standard does not place single emphasis on the use of formal methods for developing and assessing software, unlike Def Stan 00-55. Rather it proposes the use of a 'package' of techniques, chosen from a set, which reflect the system integrity, the application and the industry.

In the proposed IEC standard the required safety integrity level for the software is decided on the basis of the level of risk associated with the system. It is acknowledged that there is not necessarily a direct relationship between the level of risk associated with a system and the level of risk associated with the software. Other non-software components affect the level of risk associated with the software.

Software safety integrity is therefore specified as one or more of five levels:

1: very high
2: high
3: medium
4: low
5: normal

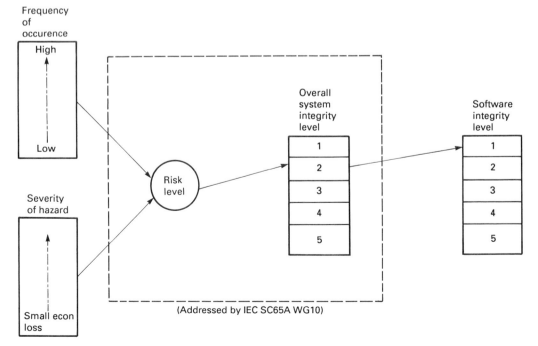

Figure 60.16 Mapping to integrity levels

Compliance with ISO 9000 is a mandatory requirement at all levels of software safety integrity. The base level (normal) represents a system where compliance to ISO 9000 is sufficient and can be considered to be non-safety related.

There is no state-of-the-art method in this standard of mapping the frequency of occurrence and the hazard to the software safety integrity without also considering the risk level to be tolerated and the overall system integrity. The tolerable risk level and the overall system integrity are dealt with by the standard being prepared by IEC SC65A WG10.

To determine the required software safety integrity it is necessary to identify the frequency of occurrence and the severity of hazard which combine to form the risk. As there will be a level of risk which is considered tolerable this is determined as a step to assessing the overall system integrity (which will consider such issues as configuration). From the overall system integrity the software safety integrity can be determined, as in *Figure 60.16*.

For each application a 'package of techniques' can be constructed, which are relevant to the safety integrity level assigned to the software. It should be stressed that the selection of such a package of techniques from tables in the proposed standard do not in themselves ensure that the software is safe at that integrity level.

It is not possible to prove the absence of faults in complex safety-related software, nor is it possible by testing alone to measure the software reliability or integrity. The proposed standard gives recommendations about various approaches to the software development process that could offer confidence that the software is suitable for a given level of integrity. Clearly the higher the integrity requirements, the more onerous the steps involved in developing the software.

Conceptually, the process of producing safety-related software can be considered by reference to *Figure 60.17*. It is not possible to measure the output (safety integrity) at the current state of the art, so the standard concentrates on identifying the key inputs or influencing factors for achieving software safety integrity.

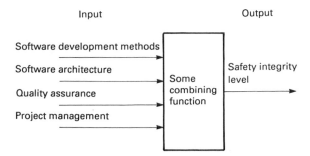

Figure 60.17 Factors affecting safety integrity levels

The next step in the development of this approach is to characterize or find attributes of the influencing factors (for example, rigour of notation is an attribute of the software development process) and then to find measures on and criteria across the safety integrity levels recommended in the proposed standard. *Figure 60.18* gives a representation of how this approach would work, but unfortunately it is not yet possible to achieve this fully.

As a first step, the proposed standard has given a relative ranking of the main software development and safety techniques. Whilst this does not completely meet the attribute-based approach given above, it does indicate those techniques which are more likely to be required at the high integrity levels.

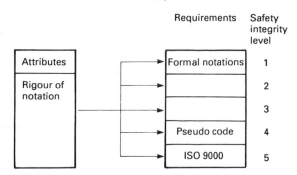

Figure 60.18 Attributes and integrity levels

The tables detailed in the proposed standard are intended to be a design aid to the production of safety-related software, *Figure 60.19*.

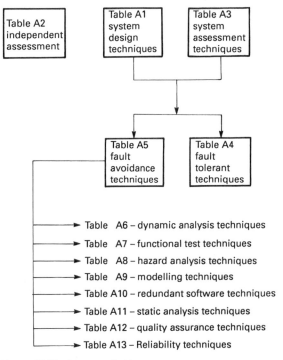

Figure 60.19 Structure of tables

Unlike Def Stan 00-55, the proposed IEC standard does not mandate the use of independent third-party companies for assessing all software. Instead the assessment is still recommended by a third party, but involves varying degrees of independence.

Table 60.4 indicates the degree of independence that is recommended for the assessment of software at each safety integrity level. Each item in the table has a recommendation according to the safety integrity level, from 1 to 5. These recommendations can be:

HR – The technique is highly recommended for a particular safety integrity level.

R – The technique is recommended for a particular safety integrity level only when there is no 'HR' recommendation or where it forms part of package of techniques.

Table 60.4 Independent assessment by integrity level

Technique	Level				
	5	4	3	2	1
Third party (company)		R	HR	HR	HR
Third party (department)	R	R	R	HR	HR
Third party (personnel)	R	R	R		

The above examples are taken from the proposed IEC standard and can only serve to indicate the 'flavour' of the documents and thus the nature of the processes which they may be expected to undertake in developing safety-critical software.

60.5.3 Conclusions

There have been a number of initiatives in the years since the Flixborough disaster and the Health and Safety at Work Act. Some of these are only now becoming common knowledge and more will become known over the next few years. The significance of the two IEC activities must not be overlooked. As proposed international standards, they will have the advantage over national standards of being a reference source across national boundaries and therefore a common basis for determining working practice. Also, both working groups were charged with preparing generic standards which can be tailored for specific industries within the broad scope of being 'civil non-nuclear'. Clearly the IEC work has a real significance to UK industry.

60.6 Experiences in assessing safety-critical systems

As the engineer becomes more aware of needs (contractual, legal and insurance) to assess the computer-based systems for safety he is going to realise the enormous costs that can arise from using formal methods alone on the software. Additionally, the other parts of the system will need to be assessed as well as the software. One solution to this problem is a rational approach to the development of safety-critical systems based on experience with the RISCS approach developed at CSE.

The approach draws on extensive experience in:

1. Developing and applying these methods to evaluate large complex computer systems in many spheres of industry.
2. Those systems which have had a safety-critical or safety-related requirement and have been successfully evaluated.

The combination of this expertise in using advanced verification and validation techniques, coupled with a detailed knowledge of industry, has enabled the methodology to be developed and applied successfully to many systems.

The methodology permits various hazards resulting from the system to be assessed at differing levels of integrity, making use of the most powerful assessment techniques available only when necessary. By this means, a thorough assessment of dependable systems can be achieved in a cost-effective manner. Although it is clearly more cost-effective to apply this standard approach throughout the development stages, it can also be successfully applied to systems already implemented.

The methodology assesses the reliability, system integrity and safety in the context of the complete system and not just the software, although this is an important part of the assessment.

What is more, the client is able to decide on the level of assessment required.

The approach consists of a number of consecutive stages:

1. Hazard criteria selection.
2. Legal/economic considerations.
3. Determination of assessment level.
4. Selection of assessment.
5. Evaluation.

The hazard criteria are established in discussion with the client. These are the criteria by which the system is expected to conform for it to be judged operable. Examples are:

1. No loss of power-assisted braking.
2. No loss of control on the engine management system such that stability is lost.
3. The system shall be capable of fail-safe operation under definable operating parameters.

The hazard criteria differ for each system, industry sector and application because of the way in which the system is to be used, given legal, economic and environmental considerations.

For each hazard criterion a specific assessment level is established after discussion with the client. Since there is no universal technique for making this type of assessment, the criticality of the system, with respect to the client's application, is determined and from this the appropriate technique can be chosen. By means of this consultation the client is assured that the correct emphasis is placed on the application.

Each hazard criterion is evaluated using the selected technique, in terms of the hardware, the software and as a facet of the complete system.

For each hazard criterion, the system will be assessed for conformance to a recognizable standard of safe/reliable operation at the agreed assessment level. If the system passes the assessment, a conformance report is issued. If the system is found to be lacking a deficiency report is issued, suggesting ways in which the system should be changed in order to conform.

Under the methology there are five classes of assessment, increasing in rigour, as will now be described.

60.6.1 Class 0: System Overview

Class 0, System Overview, is characterized by the use of design reviews, often referred to as formal design reviews. A design review is a formal, documented, comprehensive and systematic examination of a design to evaluate the design requirements and the capability of the design to meet those requirements (Fagan, 1976).

A formal design review is an advisory activity with the primary purpose of providing verification by informed engineers of the work of the development team. In general, the review should ensure that a product meets its specified requirements, and that it satisfies customer needs and optimizes costs. Its secondary purpose is to provide input to the creative process, although care must be taken to ensure that the review team does not interfere with the work being undertaken by the design team. In short, a design review should identify problems and propose solutions, where the solutions are likely to be of a general, rather than detailed, nature. Within the context of the methodology, the formal design review should assist in revealing areas where safety-critical features have been overlooked and in highlighting areas where the system can be improved.

60.6.2 Class 1: System Structure Analysis

Class 1, System Structure Analysis, is characterized by the use of checklists, and two types of formal design review, applicable to software development, known as Fagan inspections and structured walkthroughs. Note that these techniques are not necessarily exclusive as Fagan inspections also incorporate the use of checklists.

Checklists are a useful tool in assessing reliability and safety in high-integrity computer systems. They contain a structured set of questions which help the assessor to make a qualitative judgement of the system, and also help to focus the assessment by identifying areas requiring further investigation.

The need to assess safety and reliability of any computer-based system may occur at any stage of the project, where the actual point of assessment will be dependent on the particular project. Furthermore, it is not reasonable to expect that a rigid set of questions will be applicable in every situation. Therefore checklists can be applied in an intelligent manner, adapted to the project under consideration.

To accommodate wide variations in software and systems being validated, these checklists contain questions that are applicable to many types of system. Nevertheless, in some cases it may be desirable to supplement the standard checklist with questions specifically directed at the system being validated.

Structured walkthroughs are a type of technical design review, applicable to software development. During a structured walkthrough, a developer's work, such as program design, program code or documentation, is reviewed by fellow project members. In essence, structured walkthroughs differ little from the formal design reviews described previously. The main difference concerns the duties and responsibilities of the participants.

Structured walkthroughs are arranged and scheduled by the author, that is, the person developing the product to be reviewed, rather than by an appointed chairperson. The author selects the list of reviewers. Furthermore, it is usual for the author to chair the walkthrough meeting, and to compile an action list of all errors, discrepancies and inconsistencies uncovered during the walkthrough.

Software inspections are a form of quality review. Based on well-established review techniques, Fagan inspections provide a more formal and rigorous method of performing technical reviews at the end of development phases.

Because it is a creative activity, the development of software is a process which is prone to error. Testing is the traditional way of reducing software errors, which, if well planned, can be reasonably successful at detecting certain types of error, for example, coding errors. This approach has two distinct disadvantages. Testing can rarely be considered to be completely comprehensive as checking every path, through even a simple program, can be extremely time-consuming and therefore expensive. Secondly, the cost of correcting an error increases as the project life cycle unfolds (that is, the later in the life cycle the error is detected). Testing inevitably detects errors during the later stages of development.

There is therefore a need for a review which can detect errors in the earlier stages of development, and which may improve the quality of the final product, especially by detecting the type of errors which are not easily detected by testing. Fagan's original paper, comparing a team using inspections against a team using less formal reviews, reported a 23% increase in productivity with 38% fewer errors.

60.6.3 Class 2: System Hazard Analysis

The goal of system safety is to incorporate acceptable levels of safety into the system design prior to production and operation. One of the first steps in any attempt to achieve this goal is to perform system hazard analysis. This involves the use of procedures to identify, and assess the criticality levels of, hazards within a design. This facilitates the elimination of those hazards which pose an unacceptable level of risk from the design. Where

elimination may not be possible, the associated risk should be reduced to an acceptable level.

Hazard analysis is characterized by a variety of techniques intended to complement the use of design reviews, walkthroughs and checklists, but which are associated with the previous level, that is, system structure analysis. The particular techniques associated with system hazard analysis can be split into two categories, corresponding to two of the main modes of human reasoning: induction and deduction. These two modes of thought are represented in the different classes of hazard analysis technique.

As already described, one of the most effective, and most commonly used, techniques for performing deductive analysis is fault tree analysis. FTA is widely used within the nuclear industry as a systematic method for acquiring information about a system. Many approaches to the inductive style of systems analysis have been developed, and two approaches are considered to be the most widely used. They are failure modes, effect and criticality analysis (FMECA) and reliability block diagrams (RBD).

60.6.4 Class 3: Rigorous Analysis

This class is characterized by the use of rigorous methods, for example FSMs and timed Petri Nets, which do not require a high degree of mathematical ability. Nevertheless, these methods are generally recognized as part of a wider design approach, commonly referred to as formal methods. Formal methods is a philosophy that places great emphasis on rigour, in particular the use of mathematical modelling, throughout all phases of system development. The following discussion of FSMs and Petri Nets demonstrates that these methods are actually a subset of formal methods, termed dynamic system specifications. This compares with the methods associated with class 4, Formal Mathematical Methods, as described in the following section. These are also considered to be a subset of formal methods, termed model-based specifications.

FSMs provide a method of modelling systems which react to changes in their immediate environment, such that the reaction is recognized by changes in the internal states of the system. A simple FSM consists of a finite set of internal states, a finite set of input symbols and a next state function. At any time, the system will be in one of the internal states. The input symbols represent the environmental influences on the system. The next state function maps the Cartesian product of the set of internal states and the set of input symbols onto the set of internal states.

A more complex finite state machine may be required to include some form of system output in the model, and will thus include a finite set of output symbols and an output function, which maps the Cartesian product of the set of internal states and the set of input symbols onto the set of output symbols (see Section 60.3.4).

60.6.5 Class 4: Formal Mathematical Methods

Level 4 is the most rigorous level of assessment within the methodology, and is characterized by the use of specification methods such as the Vienna Development Method (VDM) and Z. These methods provide a mathematical language in which the developer may describe the system data types and the operations to be performed upon them. The developer is therefore able to build a mathematical model of the system which is exact, free from ambiguity and should therefore be internationally appreciated.

The formal approach is described in more detail in Chapters 21–26.

Having formulated a design specification, the developer is able to proceed with the various stages of system development, and at each stage check that the realized design still meets its specifications. Under certain circumstances, it is possible to verify formally, using formal logical deduction, that a given program is correct, that is, it satisfies its specifications. In most cases, however, it is sufficient to apply less stringent validation techniques, in combination with standard testing methods, to ensure that the design satisfies its specification.

Automated software testing tools such as SPADE and MALPAS may be used to assist in the analysis.

60.6.6 Experience of using RISCS

The methodology has been deployed on many complex embedded control systems, including emergency shutdown systems for oil rigs, fault control for nuclear power and, in the automotive industry, for such applications as anti-lock braking and engine management. In all such cases the client has been an integral part of the assessment: defining the hazard criteria and in determining the assessment level and technique. This has resulted in the client being fully aware of the developing assessment and in the rationale for the outcome. The assessment has in each case been shown to be cost-effective for the client and efficient in staff usage.

With the arrival of international standards many engineers are faced with the need to have assessments conducted on their safety-critical or safety-related systems. As might be expected in a commercial environment the assessment needs to be conducted in a cost-effective way. Within the constraints of developing standards, the methodology is one approach which has been demonstrated to meet these conflicting requirements.

60.7 Conclusions

The control of industrial processes by computer has new risks associated with it. One of the new risks is the incorporation of software into a control system.

It has been shown that measurements of software reliability and measurements of software safety do not have the same goals. Software reliability and software safety have been shown to be related subjects, but software safety is also a separate and distinct subject.

The terms hazard, risk, danger and safe have been defined in terms of industrial control and a relationship between these terms has been postulated. Although an attempt has been made to discuss the philosophy of safety it is evident that there is considerable scope for further work. A formal definition of software safety has been proposed and the terms 'safe' and 'unsafe' have been shown to be subjective judgements.

It has been shown that software influences the safe operation of industrial-based controllers incorporating software and the risk can be assessed and quantified.

The subjectivity of safety has been examined and it is suggested that an assessment of safety is a conjoint measurement.

An examination of the facts affecting the software development process and the metrics available for measuring the influence of these factors, has shown that there are many influences affecting software but that there are few metrics available.

In some systems it will not be possible to determine the unsafe states as the number may be unmanageable. Similarly, it may not be possible to make judgements on the appropriate actions to take as these may be too numerous, may be subject to a large number of variables or may be indeterminate. In such systems some method is required which will allow a judgement to be made based on the current safety practice, the current unsafe state, available states, time available to respond to the current unsafe state and possibly many other variables. The development of what are called intelligent knowledge-based systems may be applicable and research could be conducted into the use of these systems as monitors of safety-related systems.

The subject of assessing and quantifying the safety of software used for industrial control is a controversial topic. The subject areas which, with more research, could produce methods and metrics to quantify the safety of software are still the subject of much study.

60.8 References

Bennett, P. A. (1984) The safety of industrially-based controllers incorporating software. *PhD Thesis*

Chelson, P. O. (1971) *Reliability Computation Using Fault Tree Analysis*, NASA-CR-124740, Jet Propulsion Laboratory, USA

DOE (1975) *The Flixborough Disaster: Report of the Court of Inquiry.* Department of the Environment, HMSO

EEMUA (1989) *Safety Related Instrument Systems for the Process Industries.* Publication No. 160, Engineering Equipment and Materials Users Association

Fagan, M. (1976) Design and code inspections to reduce errors in program development. *IBM Systems Journal*, **15**(3), 182—211 (July, 1986)

Finkelstein, L. (1975) Fundamental Concepts of Measurement: Definition and Scales, *Measurement and Control*, Vol. 8, pp. 105–111

HSE (1987) *Programmable Electronic Systems in Safety Applications.* Health and Safety Executive, HMSO

IEC (1989) BS 33006DC:89, *Software for Computers in the Application of Industrial Safety-Related Systems.* IEC SC65A Working Group 9 (also known as IEC Publication *IEC65A(Secretariat)94*)

Leveson, N. G. and Harvey, P. R. (1983) Analyzing software safety. *IEEE Transactions on Software Engineering*, **SE-9**, No 5, (September 1983)

Leveson, N. G. and Stolzy, J. L. (1983) Safety analysis of Ada programs using fault trees. *IEEE Transactions on Reliability*, **R-32**, No 5 (December 1983)

MOD (1989a) *Requirements for the Procurement of Safety Critical Software in Defence Equipment*, Interim Defence Standard 00-55, Ministry of Defence

MOD (1989b) *Requirements for the Analysis of Safety Critical Hazards*, Interim Defence Standard 00-56, Ministry of Defence

Norman, E. A. (1986) *The Psychology of Everyday Things*. Basic Books

Peterson, J. L. (1977) Petri Nets. *ACM Computing Surveys*, **9**, No 3 (September 1977)

TUV Rheinland (1984) *Microcomputers in Safety Technique*. Verlag TUV Rheinland

61

Fault-tolerant system structuring concepts

S. K. Shrivastava
Computing Laboratory
University of Newcastle upon Tyne

Contents

61.1 Introduction

A fault-tolerant computing system must be capable of providing specified services in the presence of a bounded number of failures. These failures could occur because of faults present in either the components of the system or in the system's design. Building large computing systems is a complex task; fault-tolerance requirements could make the task even more difficult unless appropriate system structuring concepts are utilized. This chapter presents such concepts. The organization of this chapter and the rationale behind it are explained below.

Section 61.2 looks at basic principles. A system fails because it contains faults. This section presents basic concepts of faults, errors and failures and then goes on to discuss principles of fault tolerance.

Section 61.3 develops a methodology – based on programmed exception handling – for the construction of robust software modules with well-defined interfaces. We are now ready to apply the ideas presented so far to construct fault-tolerant computing systems, developing additional techniques and concepts as we go along. It is natural to apply these ideas first to the lower level of the system; this is the topic of the next section.

Section 61.4 considers the construction of fault-tolerant hardware components. A faulty component can behave in many incorrect ways, including exhibiting arbitrary behaviour. By judicious exploitation of redundancy, in the form of replication of components, it is possible to develop abstractions of well-behaved components. This section presents a classification for expressing faulty behaviour of components and then describes, by giving examples (reliable secondary storage, fail-silent processors), how such components can be constructed by implementing fault-tolerant algorithms.

Section 61.5 describes system structuring concepts for distributed and concurrent systems. The underlying hardware base is assumed to be composed from components with well-defined failure modes, as discussed in the previous section. The distributed system is modelled as software modules constructed according to the principles presented in Section 61.3, that interact via the underlying message passing system. Two principal means of structuring distributed systems are presented and the section concludes by describing a fault-tolerant distributed system embodying many of the ideas covered in the section.

Section 61.6 discusses tolerance to design faults. The emphasis so far, particularly in Sections 61.4 and 61.5, has been on tolerating specific types of failures of components. If the building blocks of a system have design flaws, then redundancy, say by replication of components, will not provide tolerance against such faults. What is required is redundancy in the form of design diversity. This subject is discussed in the last major section of the chapter.

61.2 Basic principles

61.2.1 Systems and their failures

Following Laprie (1985) and Anderson and Lee (1981), a system is defined to consist of a set of components together with a design. The components of a system are themselves systems, as is the design. The phrase 'design of a system' is used here to refer to that part of the system which actually supports the interactions of the components, and does not refer to either the abstract notion of a system design or to the process by which the system was designed.

The internal state of a system is the aggregation of the external states of all its components. The external state of a system is an abstraction of its internal state. During a transition from one external state to another, the system may pass through a number of internal states for which the abstraction, and hence the external state, is not defined. We assume the existence of an authoritative specification of behaviour for a system which defines the external states of the system, the operations that can be applied to the system, the results of these operations and the transitions between external states caused by these operations.

In our everyday conversations we tend to use the terms 'fault', 'failure' and 'error' (often interchangeably) to indicate the fact that something is 'wrong' with a system. However, in any discussion on reliability and fault tolerance, a little more precision is called for to avoid any confusion. A failure of a system is said to occur when the behaviour of the system first deviates from that required by the specification. The reliability of the system can then be characterized by a function $R(t)$ which expresses the probability that no failure of the system will have occurred by time 't'. We term an internal state of a system an 'erroneous state' when that state is such that there exists circumstances (within the specification of the use of the system) in which further processing by the normal part of the system will lead to a failure. The phrase 'normal part of a system' is used here to admit the possibility of introducing in the system extra components and design specifically to prevent possible failures. Such additions are referred to as the 'redundant' (exceptional or abnormal) part of the system. The term 'error' is used to designate that part of the internal state that is 'incorrect'. The terms 'error', 'error detection' and 'error recovery' are used as casual equivalents for 'erroneous state', 'erroneous state detection' and 'erroneous state recovery'.

It is instructive to enquire as to why a system might enter an erroneous state (that leads to a failure)? The reason for this could be either a failure of a component or the design (or both). Naturally, a component (or design), being a system, itself fails because of its internal state being erroneous. It is often convenient to be able to talk about causes of a system failure without actually referring to internal states of the system's components and design. We achieve this by referring to the erroneous state of a component or design as a fault in the system. A fault could either be a component fault or a design fault; so a component fault can result in an eventual component failure and similarly a design fault can lead to a design failure. Either of these internal (to a system) failures will cause the system to go from a valid to an erroneous state; the transition from a valid to an erroneous state is referred to as the 'manifestation of a fault'.

In summary, a system fails because it contains faults; during the operations of a system a fault manifests itself in the form of the system stage going into an erroneous state such that – unless corrective actions by the redundant part of the system are undertaken – a system failure will eventually occur.

61.2.2 Principles of fault tolerance

Two complementary approaches have been noted for the construction of reliable systems (Avizienis, 1976).

The first approach, which may be termed fault prevention, tries to ensure that the implemented system does not and will not contain any faults. Fault prevention has two aspects:

1. Fault avoidance techniques are employed to avoid introducing faults into the system (e.g. system design methodologies, quality control).
2. Fault removal techniques are used to find and remove faults which were inadvertently introduced into the system (e.g. testing and validation).

The second approach, which has been termed 'fault tolerance', is of special significance because of the impracticality of ensuring the absence of faults in a system containing a large number of components. Four constituent phases of the fault-tolerance approach have been identified:

1. *Error detection.* For a fault to be tolerated, it must first be detected. Since internal states of components are not usually accessible, a fault cannot be detected directly; rather its manifestations that cause the system to go into an erroneous state can be detected. Thus the usual starting point for fault-tolerance techniques is the detection of errors.

2. *Damage assesment.* Before any attempt can be made to deal with the detected error, it is usually necessary to assess the extent to which the system state has been damaged or corrupted. If the delay involved between the manifestation of a fault and the detection of its erroneous consequences – this delay may be identified as the latency interval of that fault – is large then it is likely that the damage to the system state will be more severe than if the latency interval were shorter.

3. *Error recovery.* Following error detection and damage assessment, techniques for error recovery must be utilized in an attempt to obtain a normal, error-free system state. In the absence of such an attempt (or if the attempt is not successful) a failure is likely to ensue. There are two fundamentally different kinds of recovery technique. The backward recovery technique consists of discarding the current (corrupted) state in favour of an earlier state (naturally, mechanisms are needed to record and store system states). If the prior state recovered to is before the manifestation of the fault then an error-free state will have been obtained. In contrast, a forward recovery technique involves making use of the current (corrupted) state to construct an error-free state.

4. *Fault treatment and continued service.* Once recovery has been undertaken, it is essential to ensure that the normal operation of the system will continue without the fault immediately manifesting itself once more. If the fault is believed to be transient, no special actions are necessary; otherwise, the fault must be removed from the system. The first aspect of fault treatment is to attempt to locate the fault. Following this, steps can be taken either to repair the fault or to reconfigure the rest of the system to avoid the fault.

To illustrate the ideas presented so far, let us examine the recovery block mechanism (Horning *et al.*, 1974, Randell, 1975), a well-known method of constructing fault-tolerant software. The syntax of a recovery block construct is,

ensure⟨acceptance test⟩**by** P_0 **else-by** P_1 **else** fail

which depicts a software system with four components, the two procedures P_0 (the primary) and P_1 (the alternative), the acceptance test and the set of global variables accessible to the procedures (not shown above). The design of the system is the control structure implied by the syntax. Assume that the acceptance test is 'perfect' (i.e. detects all violations of the specification) then the recovery block shown will tolerate all the faults of procedure P_0 (if any) that could lead to its failure. Regarding P_0 as a system, its faults are essentially design faults. So, when it is said that 'a recovery block can tolerate design faults', what is really meant is that it can tolerate faults in some of its components (P_0 in our case) which could fail due to design faults in them. We shall next see how the four aspects of fault tolerance are embodied in a recovery block. The acceptance test (a Boolean expression) is used for detecting errors. Damage assessment is particularly simple; only the program in execution is assumed to be affected. (We are assuming the simple case of a single sequential process; when interacting processes are involved, damage assessment can be quite difficult, see Section 61.5.) Error recovery – backward in this case – consists of recovering the state of the executing program to that at the beginning of the recovery block. Finally, the program in execution (primary or alternative) is assumed to be faulty, so its faults are avoided by executing the next alternative (if any).

The four aspects of fault tolerance form the basis for all fault-tolerance techniques and provide a sound foundation for design and implementation of reliable systems (Anderson and Lee, 1981).

61.3 Software design methodology

This section presents a methodology for the construction of robust software systems based on the treatment presented in Anderson and Lee (1981) and Cristian (1982). Following generally accepted software engineering concepts, we shall assume the use of data abstractions (abstract data types) in program development. This leads to software systems that are structured into a hierarchy of modules (or components). Such a hierarchy may be represented by an acyclic graph (*Figure 61.1*) where modules are represented by nodes and an arrow from a node A to node B means that A is a user of B, that is, there are one or more operations in A such that a successful completion of one such operation depends on the successful completion of some operation provided by B; in other words, B provides certain services to A.

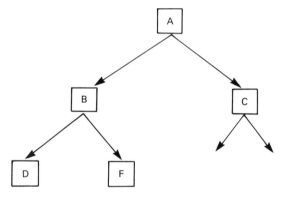

Figure 61.1 Hierarchy of modules

61.3.1 Expected events

The specified services provided by a given module can be classified into normal services (expected and desired) and abnormal or exceptional services (expected but undesired). In programming language terms, when a user module (say A) calls a procedure exported by a lower level module (say B), then either the call terminates normally (expected desired service is obtained) or an exceptional return is obtained. Let us now consider the design of an intermediate nodule such as B (see Figures 61.1 and 61.2).

A normal chain of events might consist of some procedure of 'A' making a call on 'B', as a result of which 'B' calls a lower level module (say F), this call returns normally, and subsequently A's call returns normally. We examine now the two cases that could lead to A's call returning exceptionally.

1. A call to a lower level module (such as F) by B returns exceptionally. In such a case we say that an exception is detected in B (this is synonymous to saying that an error is detected in B; we will use the term 'exception' here because it is more commonly used when talking about software).

   If this exception is not 'handled', then module B would certainly fail to provide the specified service to A. To cope with the detected exceptions, module B therefore contains exception handlers (the handlers thus represent the 'abnormal' part of a system mentioned earlier). If, despite the

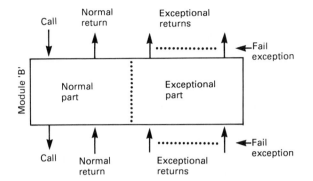

Figure 61.2 Structure of a module

occurrence of a lower level exception return, module B provides a normal service to A, we say that the lower level exception has been masked by the handler in B. On the other hand, if B provides an exceptional return to A, we say that a lower level exception has caused the propagation of a higher level exception.

2. A Boolean expression in B – inserted specifically for detecting an error (exception) – evaluates to false. The treatment of this exception by its handler is similar to the previous case: either that exception is masked, in which case (provided no further exceptions are encountered) B will return normally to A, otherwise an exceptional return is obtained by A.

We thus see that the construction of a robust module requires the provision of (a) exception handlers for coping with exceptions propagated from lower levels; and (b) Boolean expressions for detecting exceptions arising in the module itself, and their exception handlers. Note that it is often possible (and desirable for the sake of simplicity) to map several exceptions onto a single handler.

The need for exception handling facilities in programming languages has now been recognized and many modern languages such as CLU (Liskov and Synder, 1979) and ADA (Luckham and Polak, 1980) contain specific features for exception handling. We shall use here some simple notation that will enable us to illustrate the ideas with the help of a few examples. The following notation will be used to indicate that a procedure P, in addition to the normal return, also provides an exceptional return E:

procedure P(––) **signals** E

The invoker of P can define the exceptional continuation to be some operation H which will be termed the 'handler' of E:

P(––)[E⇒H]

In the body of P, the designer of P can insert the following syntactic constructs (where the braces indicate that the signal operation is optional):

1. [T⇒..;{**signal** E}]
2. 0[L⇒..;{**signal** E}]

Construct (1) represents the case whereby an exception is detected by a run time test T; whilst the second construct represents the case when invocation of an operation '0' results in an exceptional return L which in turn could lead to the signalling of exception E. When an exception is signalled using construct (1) or (2), the control passes to the handler of that exception (H in this case).

Example

We consider the design of a procedure P which adds three positive integers. The procedure uses operation '+' (typically provided by the hardware interpreter) which can signal an overflow exception 'OV'.

> **procedure** P (**var** i:integer; j, k: integer) **signals** OW;
>   **begin**
>   i: = i + j[OV⇒**signal** OW];
>   i: = i + k[OV⇒i: = i − j; **signal** OW];
>   **end**;

It is assumed above that no assignment is performed if an exception is detected during the execution of the operation '+'.

The above example also illustrates an important aspect of exception handling, which is that before signalling an exception it is often necessary to perform a 'clean-up' operation. The most sensible strategy is to 'undo' any side-effects produced by the procedure. If all the procedures of a module follow this strategy, we get a module with the following highly desirable property: either the module produces results that reflect the desired normal service to the caller, or no results are produced and an exceptional return is obtained by the caller.

Example

A file manager module exports a procedure 'CREATE' whose function is to create a file containing a number of blocks, n. Assume that the file manager employs two discs for block allocation such that a given file has its blocks on either disc d_1 or d_2, and that M_1 and M_2 are the disc manager modules for d_1 and d_2 respectively.

> **procedure** CREATE (n : integer) **signals** NS;
>   **begin**
>   -----------
>   M1.AL(n)[DO⇒M2.AL(n)[DO⇒restore; **signal** NS]];
>   -----------
>   **end**;

The above procedure illustrates how an exception may be masked. The 'AL' procedure of a disc manager allocates n blocks, but if the number of free blocks is less than requested, a disc overflow exception (DO) is signalled. The first handler of this exception tries to get space from the second disc manager. If a second DO exception is detected then the procedure is exited with a 'no space' exception NS. The procedure 'restore' recovers the state of global variables accessible to 'CREATE' to that at the beginning of the call (this follows from our philosophy of undoing any side effects before signalling an exception).

61.3.2 Unexpected events

So far we have considered the treatment of 'expected events' (desired or undesired); now we turn our attention to the treatment of unexpected (and therefore undesired) events. Let us assume that the hardware interpreter over which the software under consideration is executing is behaving according to the specification. Then any unexpected behaviour from a software module must be attributed to the existence of one or more design faults in that module or any of its lower level modules. In general, during the execution of a procedure P of a module, a design fault can manifest itself in any of the following ways:

1. The execution of P does not terminate.
2. A lower level exception is detected for which there is no exception handler in P.

3. The execution of P terminates normally (the invoker obtains a normal return) but the results produced by P are not in accordance with the specification.

It is clear that situations (1) and (2) will eventually cause a failure of the module; situation (3) represents the case where the module has failed but this event has not yet been detected by the system. To cope with such cases, we can employ a default exception handler:

```
procedure P (––) signals E;
    begin
        - - -
    end[⇒"default handler"];
```

The control goes to this handler during the execution of P whenever an exception is detected for which there is no handler. Thus, to cope with situation (1) it is possible to start a 'timer' concurrently with the invocation of P; the 'time out' exception will then be handled by the default handler. All the lower level exceptions with no programmed handlers will similarly be handled by the default handler. Finally, we make use of run time checks to detect possible violations of specifications to minimize the danger of undetected failures (case 3).

What strategy should be adopted by the default handler? The simplest thing to do is to undo any side-effects produced by the procedure and to signal a fail exception (see Figure 61.2). When the invoker receives a fail exception, it means that the called module has failed to provide the specified service. Nevertheless, the called module has failed 'cleanly' since no side-effects have been produced. It is also possible for the default handler to mask the (unanticipated) exception by calling an alternative procedure in the hope of circumventing the design fault(s). The similarity with the recovery block approach is not accidental, as the example below shows how a recovery block can be modelled by making use of default exception handlers:

```
ensure⟨acceptance test⟩ by P₀ else-by P₁ else fail
```

The above construct is equivalent to the following one:

$$P_0'[\Rightarrow \text{restore}; P_1'[\Rightarrow \text{restore}; \text{signal fail}]]$$

Where, $P_i', i = 0, 1$ is given by:

```
procedure Pᵢ'
begin
        body of Pᵢ;
    assert⟨acceptance test⟩;
    end[⇒signal fail];
```

The following design methodology has emerged. During the design of a given module, we carefully analyse the cases that could prevent the module from providing the desired normal services. We make use of specific exception handlers either to mask the effects of such undesired, but expected, exceptions or to signal an appropriate exception to the caller of the module. The purpose of signalling an exception is to indicate to the caller that the normal service cannot be provided and also to give an indication of the reason (e.g. arithmetic overflow, disc full, fail etc.). We make use of default exception handlers or recovery blocks to obtain a measure of tolerance against design faults. The capability of tolerating design faults rests largely on the 'coverage' of run-time checks (such as acceptance tests) for detecting errors. Often, for efficiency reasons, it is not possible to check completely within a procedure that the results produced have been according to the specification (e.g. for a routine

that sorts its input, the check that the output has been sorted would be almost as complex as the routine itself). Hence run-time checks are often limited to checking certain critical aspects of the specification (hence the name 'acceptance test'). This means that the possibility of undetected failures cannot be ruled out entirely.

61.4 Constructing fault-tolerant components

The techniques presented in Section 61.3 can be applied to the case when lower level modules have been implemented in hardware (e.g. disc units, processors). If the interfaces of these modules can be structured to provide normal and exceptional services, then the higher level software modules which use them can employ the fault-tolerance techniques discussed previously either to mask a lower level hardware exception or to propagate it as a higher level exception. The term 'software-implemented fault-tolerance' is often used to refer to the software techniques for tolerating hardware faults. The resulting algorithms are termed 'fault-tolerant algorithms'.

The function of a fault-tolerant algorithm of a system is to detect failures of the system's components and to attempt to tolerate these failures so as to provide specified services. One of the problems in constructing these algorithms is finding out the likely failure modes of components, so that specific fault-tolerant measures can be deployed. Of course if a component fails in a manner other than assumed, then no guarantee of fault tolerance can be provided. A failed component, such as a processor, might perform arbitrary state transitions (exhibit uncontrolled behaviour), the effects of which must be prevented from manifesting themselves, in the results delivered by an application program. Ideally one would like to program a system with perfect (failure-free) components. Unfortunately, since all hardware components must eventually fail, such perfection is unattainable. A sensible approach is then to assume that the underlying components, such as processors and communication links, are fail-controlled (do not exhibit arbitrary behaviour under failures) and then to develop programming systems capable of tolerating the assumed faulty behaviour. Intuitively, it should be clear that the task of building such a programming system is considerably simplified if the underlying hardware fails in a 'disciplined manner'. Of course, there is still the task of building hardware components that do indeed fail only as assumed. Fortunately, by judicious utilization of redundancy (e.g. redundant processors and communication channels with independent failure modes), sufficiently realistic approximations to fail-controlled components can be built. First a classification for expressing faulty behaviour of components is presented.

61.4.1 Modelling faulty behaviour of components

Suppose we can classify faulty behaviour of a component, starting from those that are relatively restricted breaches of the specification to those that are increasingly less restrictive breaches of the specification. Then we can design a family of fault-tolerant algorithms – from simple ones tolerating restricted types of faults to increasingly more complex ones tolerating larger classes of faults. Given such a family of algorithms, one can select a particular member depending upon the stated reliability requirements – choosing an algorithm tolerating larger classes of faults (or in the extreme, all types of faults) for a system requiring a very high degree of reliability. In this section, such a fault classification is presented. The treatment presented here is based on Ezhilchelvan and Shrivastava (1988, 1989) where more details can be found.

Following Kopetz (1985), the response of a component for a given input will be said to be correct if the output value is not only as expected, but also produced on time.

61.4.1.1 *Correct and incorrect responses from a component*

Let a component receive at time t_i an input requiring a response from the component and as a result produce an output value v at time t_j. For that input, the response v at time t_j is correct iff:

1. The value is as expected: $v = w$, where w is the expected value consistent with the specification.
2. It is produced on time: $t_{min} \leqslant t_j - t_i \leqslant t_{max}$, where $[t_i + t_{min}, t_i + t_{max}]$ is the interval during which the specified output is expected to be produced.

The values t_{min} and t_{max} are constants of a given component. First, note that the response of a component cannot be instantaneous to a given input, but must experience a finite minimum amount of delay which is specified by the parameter t_{min}. The maximum delay time, t_{max}, indicates the upper bound on the output delay.

A correctly functioning component does not arbitrarily produce responses. In particular, when there is no input (null input) or when no response is expected for an input, naturally no output value is produced (output is null). The values t_{min} *and* t_{max} are meaningful only when a component is expected to produce a response.

If $v \neq w$, then the output value will be termed incorrect; similarly, if $t_j < t_i + t_{min}$ (output produced too early) or $t_j > t_i + t_{max}$ (output produced too late), then the response time will also be termed incorrect.

Given the above definitions of correct and incorrect responses, there are four possible ways in which a response can deviate from that specified. This leads to the following types of faults.

1. *Timing fault.* A fault that causes a component to produce the expected value for a given input either too early or too late is termed a timing fault and the corresponding failure a timing failure. Using our notation:

$$v = w \text{ and } (t_j - t_i < t_{min} \text{ or } t_j - t_i > t_{max})$$

2. *Value fault.* A fault that causes a component to respond for a given input, within the specified time interval, but with a wrong value is termed a value fault and the corresponding failure a value failure:

$$v \neq w \text{ and } t_{min} \leqslant t_j - t_i \leqslant t_{max}$$

3. *Omission fault.* Many fault-tolerant algorithms are designed under a particularly simple failure mode assumption, which is that a component can fail only by producing no response. A fault which causes a component, for a given input requiring a non-null response, not to produce a response is termed an omission fault and the corresponding failure an omission failure.

   We can regard 'not producing a response' as equivalent to 'producing a null value on time', thereby treating an omission fault as a special case of a value fault. We can also treat an omission fault as a special case of a timing fault by regarding 'not producing a response' as equivalent to 'producing a correct value at infinite time'.

4. *Byzantine fault.* A Byzantine (or general) fault is responsible for a Byzantine failure which is *any* violation from the specified behaviour. In particular, it includes the possibility of a component producing a response when no input was supplied. A Byzantine component is customarily considered in the literature to be capable of being 'malicious' in its responses.

61.4.1.2 *Fault/failure lattice*

A Byzantine fault (failure) subsumes all the other three types of faults (failures). The relationships among these four types of faults (failures) can be expressed by the fault (failure) lattice in *Figure 61.3*, where an arrow from A to B, indicates that fault (failure) type A is a special case of fault (failure) type B. (The relation '→' is transitive.) An important observation can now be made. A fault-tolerant algorithm designed to tolerate m, $m > 0$, timing failures (value failures) can also tolerate m omission failures and further that an algorithm designed to tolerate m Byzantine failure can tolerate m failures of any type. The top of the lattice represents the fault type with most restrictions and the bottom with the least.

The above classification is based on the behaviour of a component with respect to a single input. When a sequence of inputs over a given time interval is considered, the type of fault in the component will be taken to be the least restrictive one of which all types of failure occurring during that interval can be considered to be special cases. If a given faulty behaviour persists for a 'sufficiently' long time, then that failure can be considered to be permanent.

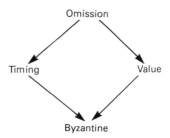

Figure 61.3 Fault/failure lattice

61.4.2 Examples

A processor that, perhaps momentarily, stops functioning, a sensor that occasionally fails to produce output signals and a communication channel that loses messages, are examples of omission failures. A processor producing erroneously computed values on time, and a timely delivery of a corrupted message, are examples of value failures. An overloaded processor producing late responses, and a fast timer which sends an early timeout signal, are examples of timing failures. A failed processor producing arbitrary outputs, a processor 'masquerading' as another processor or altering source/destination of messages it is relaying, are examples of Byzantine failures. Byzantine failures were speculated by Davies and Wakerly (1978), and have been considered in the design of the SIFT computing system (Wensley, 1978) and in the algorithms for reaching agreement in a distributed system (Lamport et al., 1982).

Two examples are now given, illustrating the design of fault-tolerant algorithms capable of tolerating the assumed faulty behaviour from the underlying (hardware) components. The first example illustrates dealing with value failures, and the second one dealing with Byzantine failures.

61.4.2.1 *Construction of stable storage*

This example considers the problem of building a reliable disc storage system out of unreliable ones. A disc can fail due to defective disc surface conditions, failure of the disc drive system or the failure of the read-write electronics. In addition, various other accidents can occur which can cause data stored in one or more pages of a disc to be corrupted. Here is a discussion on tolerance to these latter kind of value failures.

We assume the existence of the following two hardware procedures for accessing a disc:

procedure *write(at : address; data : page)*
procedure *read (at : address;* **var** *data : page)* **signals** *looksbad*

The exception 'looksbad' indicates that the data read could be corrupted. This could either be because the page is really corrupted or some transient failure has occurred – in which case a bounded number of retries should eventually result in good data being read. The effect of a write operation is either (i) the addressed page gets the data; (ii) the addressed page remains unchanged; (iii) the addressed page gets corrupted data.

We next construct fault-tolerant read and write operations using the unreliable operations mentioned above:

procedure *careful-read (at: address;* **var** *data : page)* **signals** *bad-page;*
    begin
           use read operation at most *n* times to obtain good
           data (i.e. **not** *looksbad*) **else signal** *bad-page;*
    end;
procedure *careful-write (at: address; data: page)* **signals** *bad-page;*
    begin
           perform 'write' and then 'careful-read' on the
           same page to check written *data = read data;* **if** the
           check fails even after a few retries **then signal** *bad-*
           page
    end;

One way of guarding against accidental corruption of a page, say due to processor failures, is by making sure that an uncorrupted copy of the page is available somewhere. This can be achieved by employing two discs (with independent failure modes) and by maintaining pairs of pages on these discs. It is then necessary to check at regular intervals that the pairs of pages have identical uncorrupted data stored in them. If not, the corrupted page of a pair is updated by performing a careful read on the paired page followed by a careful write on the corrupted page. The interval of running this checking process is chosen so as to reduce the probability of both the pages of a pair becoming corrupted to an acceptably small quantity (Lampson and Sturgis, 1981). Such a storage system can survive a single disc or processor 'crash' with high probability and is often referred to as 'stable storage'. So far it has been assumed here that a corrupted page can only be made right again by reading from its replica. It is possible to store data on a disc with sufficient structural redundancy that 'minor' corruption of data can be corrected using the redundancy available (e.g. by employing doubly linked lists, for list structured data, certain number of link failures can be recovered from); such techniques have been described in Taylor *et al.* (1980).

61.4.2.2 *Constructing fail-controlled nodes*

The second example illustrates how well-behaved processors, referred to as fail-controlled nodes, can be constructed out of fail-uncontrolled processors (processors with the Byzantine failure mode). A node is assumed to be fail-controlled in the following sense: it has the property of fail-silence, that is, it either works as specified or simply stops working (crash). This section discusses how replicated processing on fail-uncontrolled processors can be exploited to create the abstraction of 'normal processing' on fail-silent nodes.

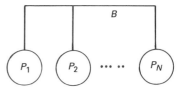

Figure 61.4 *N*-processor distributed system

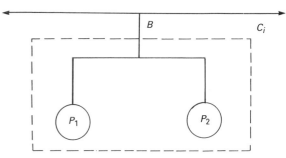

Figure 61.5 2-process node C_i replacing P_i, $1 \leqslant i \leqslant N$ in Figure 61.4

A computing system will be considered to be made up of N, $N > 1$, processors connected by a communications subsystem B as shown in *Figure 61.4*. Then in a redundant, fault-tolerant version of such a system, each processor P_i is replaced by a node C_i as shown in *Figure 61.5*. Each node is composed of two processors P_1, P_2. All the processors are connected by a perfect communication bus B (for the sake of brevity, means of approximating B by redundant communication links will not be examined in this chapter). Each node C_i behaves like a fail-silent node provided no more than one processor in C_i fails. The basic idea is that processors of C_i execute identical programs and compare each other's results. If a disagreement is detected, the non-faulty processor stops further processing.

At this level, computations are structured as concurrent processes interacting via message passing. The bus B will be assumed to deliver messages uncorrupted. It will be assumed that the originator of a message can be authenticated by a non-faulty receiver. Standard techniques employing checksums and message retransmissions are available to ensure that messages are delivered uncorrupted (with high probability); digital signatures (Rivest *et al.* 1978; Okamoto, 1988) implement authentication (with high probability). Since we are achieving fault tolerance by replicated processing, it is also necessary to assume that computations performed by processors are deterministic. This means that if all non-faulty processors of a node have identical initial states and process identical messages in an identical order, then identical output messages in an identical order will be produced.

The clocks of all the non-faulty processors of a node are assumed to be synchronized such that the measurable difference between readings of clocks at any instant is bounded by a known constant. Algorithms for achieving this abstraction exist (see Halpern (1984); Lamport and Melliar-Smith (1985)). Each non-faulty processor of a node is capable of atomically broadcasting a message to all non-faulty processors of that node (including itself). We require the properties of atomicity, validity, termination and order from the atomic broadcast mechanism. When a sender broadcasts a message at its local clock time T, then:

ab1: the message is delivered either to all non-faulty receivers or to none of them (atomicity).

ab2: if the sender is non-faulty then the message is delivered to all non-faulty receivers (validity).

ab3: if the message is delivered then it is delivered to every non-faulty processor (including the sender, if it is non-faulty) at its local clock time $T + \Delta$, where Δ is some known bounded quantity (termination).

ab4: the messages delivered to all non-faulty processors are delivered in an identical order (order).

Algorithms exist for achieving atomic broadcasts in the presence of failures (Cristian *et al.*, 1985). Given that computations have been assumed to be deterministic, it is necessary to ensure that the replicas of computational processes on non-faulty processors within a node process messages in an identical order, to ensure that they produce identical outputs. This is achieved as follows. Each non-faulty processor of a node has four processes:

1. *Sender process*. This takes messages produced by computational processes of that processor, signs them and sends them to the neighbour processor of the node for comparison.
2. *Comparator process*. This process authenticates all incoming messages from the neighbour; an authentic message is compared with its counterpart produced locally. If there is an agreement, then the authenticated message is counter-signed and this double-signed message is sent to its destination node. If a disagreement is detected, the processor stops further processing.
3. *Receiver process*. This process accepts only authentic double signed messages; such valid messages are sent to the local order process for distribution to local destination processes.
4. *Order process*. This process atomically broadcasts valid messages to order processes of that node (including itself). This permits order processes to construct identical queues of valid messages for processing.

Nodes constructed according to the techniques outlined above have the property that functioning nodes interact only by exchanging authenticated double-signed messages. Of course, a failed processor of a node can generate arbitrary messages, but these will be ignored by functioning nodes. Thus, a node with a failed processor appears to behave in a fail-silent manner. The architecture discussed here can be generalized to include more than two processors within a node if tolerance to more than a single processor failure per node is desired. Indeed, it is possible to construct nodes capable of masking processor failures, rather than stopping on a failure. Such, and other, node architectures are discussed in Schneider (1984) and Ezhilchelvan *et al.* (1989).

61.5 Structuring fault-tolerant distributed systems

This section will extend the concepts developed in Section 61.3 to concurrent and distributed systems. Distributed computing systems provide new opportunities for developing flexible and reliable applications. At the same time such systems pose design and implementation problems not normally encountered in more conventional centralized systems. Designing and implementing such systems which continue to provide specified services in the presence of bounded numbers of processor and communication failures is a difficult task. We assume that the main hardware components of the system are workstations (nodes) connected by a communications subsystem. Nodes will be assumed to be fail-silent as discussed previously. It will be assumed that after a crash, a failed node is repaired within a

finite amount of time and made active again. A node can have both stable storage and non-stable (volatile) storage, or just non-stable storage (the former modelling a 'discfull' workstation and the latter a discless one). All of the data stored on volatile storage is assumed to be lost when a crash occurs. Any data stored on stable storage, as stated earlier, remains unaffected by a crash. It is also assumed that faults in the communication subsystem may cause failures such as lost, duplicated or corrupted messages. Well-known network protocol-level techniques are available for coping with such failures, so their treatment will not be discussed further. We will present two different models for structuring distributed systems. In both cases, the elementary building block entities, objects and processes, can be implemented using the methodology presented in Section 61.3. There are three main problems encountered when fault-tolerance is required in distributed systems:

1. *Independent failures*. Independently failing nodes can introduce inconsistencies in a computation executing on multiple nodes (for example a node crash can partly destroy the state of a computation).
2. *Interference*. Concurrently running computations accessing common resources distributed over the system can interfere with each other.
3. *Damage assessment*. Damage assessment in a concurrent system is difficult since any recovery actions of a computation may well affect other computations with which it has interacted. This is particularly so in a distributed system where, in the absence of any centralized control, damage assessment protocols will be required which must themselves be made fault-tolerant.

The following will describe atomic action and conversation-based structuring mechanisms for coping with the above problems. Two canonical models of fault-tolerant distributed systems will be developed. One model employs objects (instances of abstract data types) which are manipulated under the control of atomic actions. The class of applications where such a model has found particular usage include banking, office information and database oriented applications. A number of other applications – typically concerned with real-time control in applications such as avionics, telephone switching – are structured as concurrent processes communicating via messages. Fault tolerance in such systems is introduced through a controlled use of checkpoints (conversations) by processes. The relationship between the two models will be explained.

61.5.1 System structuring with objects and actions

Objects are instances of abstract data types. An object encapsulates some data and provides a set of operations which are the only means of manipulating the data. In most object-oriented fault-tolerant systems an operation is performed by invoking an object with a remote procedure call (RPC), which passes value parameters to the object and returns the results of the operation to the caller. (See ANSA (1989), Powell *et al.*, (1988), Shrivastava *et al.*, (1989), Dixon *et al*, (1989), Gray (1980) and Liskov (1988) for a representative sample.) Programs which operate on objects are executed as atomic actions (atomic transactions) with the properties of (i) 'serializability', (ii) failure atomicity and (iii) permanence of effect. The first property ensures that concurrent executions of programs are free from interference, that is, a concurrent execution can be shown to be equivalent to some serial order of execution (Eswaren *et al.*, 1976; Best and Randell, 1981). The second property ensures that a computation can either be terminated normally, producing the intended results or be aborted, producing no results. This property is obtained by appropriate use of backward errror recovery, which is invoked whenever a failure occurs that cannot be masked.

Typical failures causing an action to be aborted are node crashes and communication failures such as persistent loss of messages. It is reasonable to assume that once a computation terminates normally, the results produced are not destroyed by subsequent node crashes. This is the third property – permanance of effect – which ensures that state changes produced are recorded on stable storage which can survive node crashes with a high probability of success. A commit protocol is required during the termination of an action to ensure that either all the objects updated within the action have their new states recorded on stable storage (normal or committed termination), or no updates get recorded (aborted termination). To facilitate inter-object communications, server processes are associated with objects. An atomic action can then be composed of a client process which performs operations on objects by sending call requests to server processes.

A variety of concurrency control techniques to enforce the serializability property for atomic actions have been reported in the literature. Bernstein *et al.* (1987) describe many concurrency control techniques suitable for distributed systems. There are two widely known techniques: (a) lock-based, where objects to be used are locked for reading or writing – depending upon the type of operation required on objects – and later unlocked when the objects are no longer needed; and (b) time-stamp-based, where atomic actions are assigned unique values (time-stamps) which are utilized for imposing a serial order on their executions. The approach adopted in simple locking is to regard all operations on objects to be of type read or write, which must follow the well known locking rule permitting concurrent reads but only exclusive writes. Eswaren *et al.* (1976) proved that actions must follow a two-phase locking policy (see *Figure 61.6*). During the first phase, termed the growing phase, a computation can acquire locks on objects but not release them. The tail end of the computation constitutes the shrinking phase, during which time locks held can be released but no locks can be acquired. Now suppose that an action in its shrinking phase is to be aborted, and that some updated objects have been released. If some of these objects have been locked by other actions, then abortion of the action will require these actions to be aborted as well. To avoid this cascade abort problem, it is necessary to make the shrinking phase 'instantaneous', as indicated by the dotted lines.

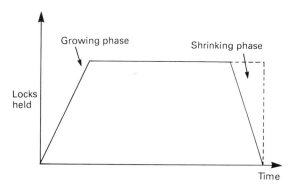

Figure 61.6 Two-phase locking

We will now briefly examine remote procedure calls, whereby a client process can invoke an operation of an object by sending a request to the associated server process. Essentially, in this scheme, a client's remote call is transformed into a request message to the named server who performs the requested work and sends the results back:

Client	Worker
	cycle
send(..)"call msg"	
	receive(..) "get work"
	"work"
	send(..) "send results"
	receive(..)
	end

Both the client and server will contain measures for dealing with failures such as lost messages. The design and implementation of remote procedure calls has been studied extensively in the literature, and the reader's attention is drawn to Birrell and Nelson (1984) and Panzieri and Shrivastava (1988). RPC protocols, in common with other types of protocol, typically employ time-out mechanisms to prevent indefinite (or long) waiting by a process expecting a message. Suppose that a server crashes in the middle of a call, in which case the client will not receive the result message and will eventually be 'timed out'. It is interesting to note that a time-out exception could indicate any one of the following four possibilities:

1. The server crashed during the call.
2. The server did not receive the request (the client's call message got lost).
3. The server's reply did not reach the client.
4. The server is still performing the work (so the time-out interval was not long enough).

The papers cited above discuss the treatment of these and related issues.

The termination of an action is typically carried out under the control of the client process in two phases (the protocol is often referred to as the two-phase commit protocol). The first phase is used to determine the outcome for the action – whether it is to be terminated normally or aborted – and the second phase is used to enforce the decision of the first phase.

> Algorithm (for the client process)
> Phase 1: Send "get ready" command to all the servers
> **if** all reply "yes" **then**
> verdict: = normal **else** verdict: = abort;
> (note: "verdict" is kept on stable storage)
> Phase 2: Send the value of "verdict" to all the servers and get "done" responses from each and every one of them.

> Algorithm (for a server process)
> Phase 1: Wait for "get ready" command from the client;
> **if** none coming **then** abort **else** record state changes on stable storage; send "yes" to the client;
> Phase 2: Wait for the verdict;
> carry out the command and send "done" to the client.

Once a process reaches Phase 2, its state information is made crash-proof on stable storage such that recovery of its node (after a crash) includes starting a recovery process capable of using that information for executing Phase 2 code. Thus repeated crashes of nodes could result in repeated executions of the Phase 2 portions of algorithms. For this reason it is necessary to design this part of algorithms such that the actions that are carried out are *idempotent* (i.e. repeated executions are equivalent to a single execution).

Any atomic action can be viewed at a lower level as constructed out of more primitive atomic actions – this is illustrated

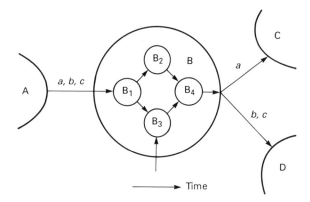

Figure 61.7 Action diagram

in *Figure 61.7*. According to Figure 61.7, action B's constituents are actions B_1, B_2, B_3 and B_4. A directed arc from an action (e.g. A) to some other action (e.g. B) indicates that B uses objects released by A. Optionally, an arc can be labelled, naming the objects used by the action. In Figure 61.7, B uses objects a, b, and c and C uses object a which has been released by B. Actions such as B_2 and B_3 are executed concurrently. Nested actions give rise to nested recovery. Suppose time has advanced up to the point shown by the vertical arrow, and an error is detected in B_3 causing it to be aborted. What happens after B_3's recovery? The question must be resolved within the scope of B – the enclosing action. B can provide a specific exception handler to deal with this particular eventuality; such exception handling techniques have been discussed in Section 61.3. If no programmed handler is available, then a failure of B_3 will cause the default handler of B to be invoked, causing an abortion of B.

The object and action model provides a natural framework for designing fault-tolerant systems with persistent objects. Objects normally reside in object stores – which are designed to be stable. Atomic actions are employed for producing state changes; the properties of atomic actions ensure that only consistent state transformations take place on objects, despite failures. The availability of objects can be increased by replicating them and storing them in more than one object store. Replicated objects must be managed through appropriate replica-consistency protocols to ensure that object copies remain mutually consistent (Bernstein *et al.*, 1987). An example of an object-oriented system will be presented in Section 61.5.4.

61.5.2 System structuring with processes and conversations

Another approach to system structuring will now be discussed. An application is structured out of a number of concurrent interacting processes. The topic of fault tolerance among interacting processes has been studied extensively (Kim, 1982; Koo and Toueg; 1987, Russell, 1980), beginning with the study reported in Randell (1975). The following characteristics will be assumed:

1. Processes do not share memory, at least explicitly, and communicate via messages sent over the underlying communication medium.
2. Appropriate communication protocols ensure that processes can send messages reliably such that they reach their intended destinations uncorrupted and in the sent order.
3. A process can take a checkpoint to save its current state on some reliable storage medium (stable storage). If a process fails, it is rolled back to its latest checkpoint.

The notion of a consistent global state of a system is central when considering the recovery of interacting processes. A global state of a system is the set of local states, one from each process. The interactions among processes can be depicted using a time diagram, such as that shown in *Figure 61.8*. Here, horizontal lines are time axes of processes and sloping arrows represent messages. A global state is a cut dividing the time diagram into two halves. A cut in the time diagram is consistent (consistent global state) if no arrow starts on the right-hand side of the cut and ends on the left-hand side of it. Cut C_1 in the figure is consistent; but cut C_2 is not, since it indicates that process q has received a message which has not yet been sent by r.

In a system of interacting processes, the recovery of one process to its checkpoint can create an inconsistent global state, unless some other relevant processes are rolled back as well. This leads to the notion of a consistent set of checkpoints or a recovery line Randell *et al.* (1978): a set of checkpoints, one from each process, is consistent if the saved states form a consistent global state. *Figure 61.9* illustrates the notions of consistent and inconsistent sets of checkpoints where opening square brackets on process axes indicate checkpoints. Suppose process p fails at the point indicated by the vertical arrow and is rolled back to its latest checkpoint. The global state of the system as represented by cut C_2 is clearly inconsistent; the set of checkpoints on recovery line C_1 is however consistent. Thus a failure of p can cause a cascade rollback of all the four processes – this is the domino effect mentioned in Randell (1975).

The domino effect can be avoided if processes coordinate the checkpointing of their states. A well-known scheme of coordinated checkpoint is the conversation scheme (Randell, 1975, Kim, 1982). The set of processes which participate in a conversation may communicate freely between each other but with no other processes. Processes may enter the conversation at different times but, on entry, each must establish a checkpoint (see *Figure 61.10*). In Figure 61.10, a closing bracket indicates that

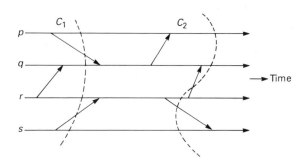

Figure 61.8 Consistent and inconsistent cuts

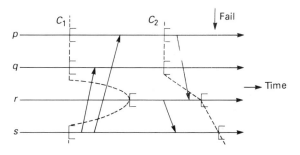

Figure 61.9 Consistent and inconsistent sets of checkpoints

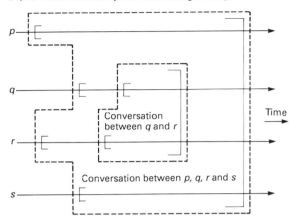

Figure 61.10 Conversations

all participating processes must exit at the same time (brackets will not be explicitly drawn in the subsequent diagrams). If a process within a conversation fails then all the participating processes are rolled back to the respective checkpoints established at the start of the conversation. Conversations can be nested as shown in the figure.

Conversations provide a convenient structuring concept for introducing fault tolerance in a large class of real-time systems (Anderson and Knight, 1983; Tyrell and Holding, 1986). The need to respond promptly to changes in the external environment dictates that most real-time systems have an iterative nature. The model discussed here provides a natural way of expressing such systems in the form of interacting cyclic processes with synchronization points usually associated with timing constraints. A study of real-time system structure for avionic systems (Anderson and Knight, 1983) indicated that synchronization of processes in such a system stems from the need to synchronize with the events in the external environment, rather than from any inherent needs of process themselves. *Figure 61.11* depicts a typical synchronization requirement. An infor-

mal interpretation of such a synchronization graph is as follows: process P_1 repeatedly initiates a computation at time T_1 which must finish by time T_3 ($T_3 > T_1$); processes P_2, P_3 and P_4 complete two iterations in the interval T_1 to T_3. Any interactions between P_2, P_3 and P_4 can be performed within the confines of two conversations: one starting at T_1 and finishing at T_2 and the other starting at T_2 and finishing at T_3. The use of conversations for introducing fault tolerance is discussed at length in Anderson and Knight (1983) and Tyrell and Holding (1986).

61.5.3 Discussion

Basic characteristics of two principal approaches to introducing fault tolerance in distributed systems were reviewed in the previous two sub-sections. The reader may have noticed some similarities in the reliability techniques employed in the two approaches. Thus, atomic actions serve the same purpose as conversations, namely the provision of a control structure within which interactions can take place. Similarly, objects and processes have identical roles (that of repositories for holding system states) and concurrency control for actions corresponds to communication rules for conversations. Indeed we have argued elsewhere (Shrivastava *et al.*, 1987; Mancini and Shrivastava, 1989) that the two models are duals of each other. A given conversation diagram (e.g. *Figure 61.12(a)*), can be translated into an action diagram quite simply (e.g. *Figure 61.12(b)*) by replacing each conversation C_i with a corresponding action A_i, and adding an arrow from A_i to A_j if C_i and C_j have at least one process in common and that process enters C_j after exiting from C_i. An arc from one action to the other is labelled with the objects representing the processes common to the corresponding conversations. A reverse mapping is made possible by replacing distinct objects named in the action diagram by processes. An action is replaced by the corresponding conversation, with the set of processes in the conversation determined by the set of objects named in all the incoming and outgoing arcs of the action. A summary of the various characteristics of the two models for which duality has been established is presented in *Table 61.1*. One of the principal advantages gained from this understanding is that techniques and mechanisms which happen to have been developed within the domain of just one of the

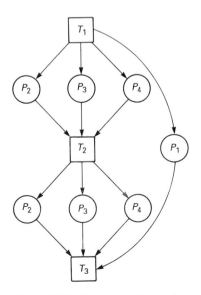

Figure 61.11 A synchronization graph

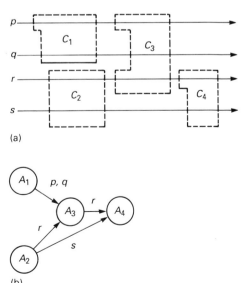

Figure 61.12 Conversations and actions

Table 61.1 Duality mapping

Object Model	Process Model
Objects	Processes
Actions	Conversations
Object invocations	Message interactions
Concurrency control for serializability	Conversation rules preventing no outside communication
Stable objects	Stable processes
Growing phase (two-phase locking)	Processes entering a conversation
Shrinking phase (two-phase locking)	Processes leaving a conversation
Read locks	Read only request messages

models can be mapped and applied to the other model. For example, Mancini and Shrivastava (1989) describe how object replication techniques can be mapped to process replication techniques.

A simple example will be used to illustrate the similarities further by showing how an application may be programmed using objects and actions and then using processes and conversations. The example is often used to illustrate the desirability of fault tolerance in a distributed application and concerns transferring a sum of money from one bank account to another (where the two accounts are assumed to be on two distinct nodes). The failure atomicity property, for example, will ensure that either the sum of money is debited from one account and credited to the other, or no state changes are produced in the event of a failure during a transfer. Two types of objects will be assumed: standing-order, and credit-debit:

```
type standing-order = object
            --object variables--
action transfer (to, from: credit-debit; amount: dollars)
            cobegin
            authority(to, from);
            to.credit(amount);
            from.debit(amount)
            coend
end action
            -- other actions, e.g. authority--
end standing-order;
type credit-debit = object
            --current account variables--
action credit(amount:dollars)
            --add amount--
end action
action debit (amount: dollars)
            --subtract amount--
end action
            --other actions--
end credit-debit;
```

Specific instances of these objects can be created:

order : standing-order
acc1,acc2 : credit-debit

An invocation of *order.transfer* will give rise to a nested computation shown in *Figure 61.13*. Any exceptions during the execution of transfer will cause that action to be aborted.

The same program can be recoded quite easily in terms of communicating processes.

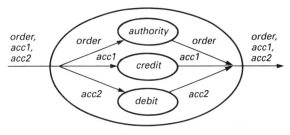

Figure 61.13 A bank action

```
type standing-order = process
            --process variables--
select
conversation transfer (to, from: credit-debit; amount: dollars)
            cobegin
            send(self, authority, to, from);
            send(to, credit, amount);
            send(from, debit, amount)
            coend
end conversation
--other selections, e.g. authority--
end select
end standing-order

type credit-debit = process
            --current account variables--
select
conversation credit (amount: dollars)
            --add amount--
end conversation
--other selections, e.g. debit--
end select
end credit-debit
```

Specific instances of these processes can be created:

order : standing-order
acc1,acc2 : credit-debit

A transfer conversation can be initiated by sending a message to order:

send(order,transfer,parameters)

The transfer conversation is shown in *Figure 61.14*.

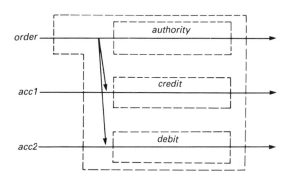

Figure 61.14 A bank conversation

61.5.4 Arjuna

This section concludes with a brief description of an object-oriented distributed system which can serve as an example of a system constructed according to the object model. Arjuna is an object-oriented programming system that provides a set of tools for the construction of fault-tolerant distributed applications (Shrivastava et al, 1990, Dixon et al., 1989). A prototype version has been designed and implemented in C + + (Stroustrup, 1986) to run on a collection of Unix workstations connected by a local area network. Arjuna provides nested atomic actions for structuring application programs. Atomic actions control operations on objects, which are instances C + + classes and RPCs are employed for invoking operations on objects.

The main architectural features of Arjuna are explained with the help of *Figure 61.15* which shows a system with six nodes, out of which one (N_4) is discless, and others have discs organized as object stores. Assume that there are no atomic actions executing in the system. Then all of the objects in the system will be in a passive state, stored in object stores. An object becomes active once an operation is invoked upon it from within an atomic action (say A). It remains active until such time as A either commits or aborts; if A is nested inside other atomic actions, then the object will remain active until either the outermost action commits or else A (or an enclosing atomic action) aborts. Activating an object entails creating a server process on a node and loading the state of the object (the object's image) from the object store into the address space of the server (in volatile store); de-activating an object entails either discarding the current state of the object in the volatile store (if abortion has taken place or the object was not modified) or saving the current state from the volatile store in the object store as the latest version of the object's image (if normal

termination has taken place and the object was modified). An atomic action being executed by client process C_1 (at N_4) is accessing objects O_1 (at N_1), O_2 (at N_2) and O_4 (at N_6). These objects have been activated; for example O'_2 is an active object, with server S_2 associated with it to receive operation invocations from C_1; O_2 represents the old passive copy of the object in the object store. An object can be activated at a node other than its host; for example, O_4 has been activated at N_4. This form of remote activation provides a simple object catching scheme for fast access. Objects can also be replicated, for example in the figure object O_1 is replicated with copies at N_1 and N_3. The activation scheme for replicated objects will depend upon the replication strategy being employed for that object. For example, in the available copy approach (Bernstein et al., 1987), it is possible for all the available copies (i.e. the ones on operating nodes) to be activated (as shown in the figure, where O'_1 is the active replica of O'_1). The figure also shows another client (C_2) accessing some objects. Both C_1 and C_2 have access to O_4. Multiple activations of an object are permitted provided no state changes are involved (this corresponds to the 'shared read' access). Both C_1 and C_2 have cached O_4 at their local hosts. Execution of an operation of an object may involve further operations on other remote objects, which may result in a client–server hierarchy of arbitrary depth, with servers also acting as clients; for the sake of simplicity such a deep hierarchy has not been depicted in the figure. At the time of the termination of the client program, the top level client process, such as C_1, will initiate the commit of the action in which all servers (S_1, S_2, S_3 and S_7 for C_1) will take part. Arjuna employs group communications for invoking replicated objects and for performing commits and aborts. A C + + stub generator hides much of the complications and details of distribution and fault-tolerance from the applications programmer.

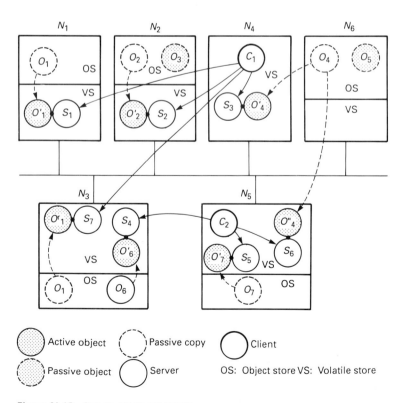

Figure 61.15 Objects, clients and servers

Any distributed object and action based system must provide a number of integrated mechanisms for supporting a variety of system functions. These mechanisms include those for naming, locating and invoking operations on (local and remote) objects, concurrency control, recovery control, managing object states for long-term as well as short-term storage etc. In addition they should be flexible, permitting application specific enhancements of existing mechanisms, for example type-specific concurrency control. Arjuna has been designed to provide such a set of mechanisms through a number of C + + classes which are organized in a class/type hierarchy that will be familiar to the developers of 'traditional' (single node) centralized object-oriented systems. Thus Arjuna illustrates that such an object-oriented design approach can be extended to apply to fault-tolerant distributed systems.

61.6 Tolerance for design faults

The difficulty in providing tolerance for design faults is that their consequences are unpredictable. As such tolerance can only be achieved if design diversity has been built into the system. In Section 61.3, recovery blocks (or default exception handlers) were mentioned as a mechanism for introducing design diversity. In this section the concept of design diversity is explored further. One more proposal, in addition to recovery blocks, has been made for tolerating design faults in software, and is known as N-version programming (Avizienis, 1985). Both the approaches can be described uniformly using the diagram (see *Figure 61.16*) given here (Lee and Anderson, 1985).

Each redundant module has been designed to produce results acceptable to the adjudicator. Each module is independently designed and may utilize different algorithms as chosen by its designer. In the N-version approach, the adjudicator is essentially a majority voter (the scheme is analogous to the hardware approach known as the N-modular redundant technique). The recovery block scheme has an adjudicator which applies an acceptance test to each of the outputs from the modules in turn, in a fixed sequence.

The operational principles of the N-version approach are straightforward: all of the N modules are executed in parallel and their results are compared by a voting mechanism provided by the adjudicator. The implementation of this scheme requires a driver program which is necessary for:

1. Invoking each of the modules.
2. Waiting for the modules to complete their execution.
3. Performing the voting function.

Each module must be executed without interference from other modules. One way of achieving this goal is to physically separate the modules – each module is run on a separate processor.

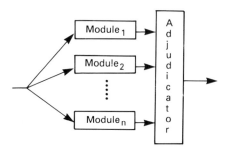

Figure 61.16 Design diversity

A special case of N-version programming is when the degree of replication is just two. In this case the adjudicator provides a comparison check. The Airbus A310 slat and flap control system uses this approach, for driving stepping motors via a comparator (Martin, 1982). In the event of a discrepancy, the motors are halted, the control surfaces locked and the flight crew alerted. With a little care, design diversity can be incorporated in many parts of concurrent and distributed systems; for example, the modules of Figure 61.16 can be structured as atomic actions. Indeed, conversations were originally proposed as a means for tolerating design flaws in concurrent software.

How effective is the design diversity approach? To a large extent the answer hinges on whether independently designed modules can be assured of largely independent failure modes. Experiments conducted at Newcastle and elsewhere suggest that although the occurrence of common mode failures cannot be discounted entirely, design diversity can indeed provide capability for tolerating design faults (Anderson *et al.*, 1985; Knight and Leveson, 1986). There is growing evidence that the approach is being adopted in industry (Voges, 1988).

61.7 Concluding remarks

This chapter began by examining the nature of systems and their faults and developed basic concepts of fault tolerance. These concepts were utilized in the methodology for the development of robust software modules – the building blocks of any software system. Structuring concepts for building fault-tolerant modules and distributed sytems were presented and illustrated with the help of several examples.

61.8 References

Anderson, T. and Lee, P. A. (1981) *Fault-Tolerance: Principles and Practice*, Prentice Hall

Anderson, T. and Knight, J. C. (1983) A framework for software fault-tolerance in real time systems. *IEEE Transaction on Software Engineering, SE-9*, 355–364

Anderson T. et al, (1985) Software fault-tolerance. An evaluation. *IEEE Transactions on Software Engineering, SE-11*, 1502–1510

ANSA (1989) *The ANSA Reference Manual*, available from Architecture Projects Management Ltd., Poseidon House, Castle Park, Cambridge CB3 0RD

Avizienis, A. (1976) Fault-tolerant systems. *IEEE Transactions on Computers, C-25*, 1304–1312

Avizienis, A. (1985) The N-version approach to fault-tolerant software. *IEEE Transactions on Software Engineering, SE-11*, 1491–1501

Bernstein, P. A., Hadzilacos, V. and Goodman, N. (1987) *Concurrency Control and Recovery in Database Systems*, Addison-Wesley

Best, E. and Randell, B. (1981) A formal model of atomicity in asynchronous systems. *Acta Informatica, 16*, 93–124

Birrell, A. D. and Nelson, B. J. (1984) Implementing remote procedure calls. *ACM Transactions on Computer Systems, 2*, 39–59

Cristian, F. (1982) Exception handling and software fault-tolerance. *IEEE Transactions on Computers, C-31*, 531–540

Cristian F., Aghili, H., Strong, H. R. and Dolev, D. (1985) Atomic broadcast: from simple message diffusion to Byzantine agreement. *Digest of Papers, FTCS-15*, Ann Arbor, 200–206

Davies, D. and Wakerly, J. F. (1978) Synchronization and matching in redundant systems. *IEEE Transactions on Computers, C-27*, 531–539

Dixon, G. N., Parrington, G. D., Shrivastava, S. K. and Wheater, S. M. (1989) The treatment of persistent objects in Arguna. *Proceedings of the Third European Conference on Object-Oriented Programming, ECOOP89*, pp. 169–189

Eswaren, K. *et al.*, (1976) On the notions of consistency and predicate locks in a database system, *CACM, 19*, 624–633

Ezhilchelvan, P. and Shrivastava, S. K. (1986) A characterization of faults in systems. *Proceedings of Fifth Symposium on Reliability in Distributed Software and Database Systems*, Los Angeles, pp. 215–222

Ezhilchelvan, P. and Shrivastava, S. K. (1989) A classification of faults in systems. *Technical Report*, Computing Laboratory, University of Newcastle upon Tyne

Ezhilchelvan, P. D., Shrivastava, S. K. and Tully, A. (1989) Constructing replicated systems using processors with point to point communication links, *Proceedings of 16th Annual Symposium on Computer Architecture, Jerusalem, Israel*, pp. 177–184

Gray, J. N. (1986) An approach to decentralized computer systems. *IEEE Transactions on Software Engineering*, SE-12, 684–689

Halpern, J. Y., Simons, B., Strong, H. R. and Dolev, D. (1984) Fault-tolerant clock synchronisation. *Proceedings of Third ACM Symposium on PODC, Vancouver, Canada*, pp. 89–102

Horning, J. J., Lauer, H. C., Melliar-Smith, P. M. and Randell, B. (1974) A program structure for error detection and recovery. *Lecture Notes in Computer Science*, Springer-Verlag, 16, 177–193

Kim, K. H. (1982) Approaches to mechanization of the conversation scheme based on monitors. *IEEE Transactions on Software Engineering*, SE-8, 189–197

Knight, J. C. and Leveson, N. G. (1986) An empirical study of failure probabilities in multi-version software. *Digest of Papers, FTCS-16*, Vienna, 165–170

Koo,, R. and Toueg, S. (1987) Checkpointing and rollback recovery for distributed systems. *IEEE Transactions on Software Engineering*, SE-13, 23–31

Kopetz, H. (1985) Resilient real time systems. In *Resilient Computing Systems*, Collins, London, pp. 91–101

Lamport, L. and Melliar-Smith, P. M. (1985) Synchronising clocks in the presence of faults. *JACM*, 32, 52–78

Lamport, L., Shostak, R. and Pease, M. (1982) The Byzantine Generals Problem. *ACM Transactions on Programming Languages and Systems*, 4, 382–401

Lampson, B. and Sturgis, H. (1981) Atomic transactions *Lecture Notes in Computer Science*, 105, 246–265

Laprie, J. C. (1985) Dependable computing and fault-tolerance: concepts and terminology. *Digest of Papers FTCS-15*, Ann Arbor, Michigan, 2–11

Lee, P. A. and Anderson, T. (1985) Design fault-tolerance. In *Resilient Computing Systems*, Collins, London, pp. 64–77

Liskov, B. (1988) Distributed programming in Argus, *CACM*, 31, 300–312

Liskov, H. and Snyder, A. (1979) Exception handling in CLU. *IEEE Transactions on Software Engineering*, SE-5, 546–558

Luckham, D. C. and Polak, W. (1980) Ada exception handling: an axiomatic approach. *ACM TOPLAS*, 2, 225–233

Mancini, L. V. and Shrivastava, S. K. (1989) Replication within

atomic actions and conversations: a case study in fault-tolerance-duality. *Digest of Papers, FTCS-19*, Chicago, 454–461

Martin, D. J. (1982) Dissimilar software in high integrity applications in flight controls. *AGARD Symposium on Software for Avionics, The Hague, 36:1*

Okamoto, T. (1988) A digital multisignature scheme using bijective public-key cryptosystems, *ACM Transactions On Computer Systems*, 6, 432–441

Panzieri, F. and Shrivastava, S. K. (1988) Rajdoot: a remote procedure call mechanism supporting orphan detection and killing. *IEEE Transactions on Software Engineering*, 14, 30–37

Powell, D. *et al.*, (1988) The Delta-4 approach to dependability in open distributed computing systems. *Digest of Papers, FTCS-18*, Tokyo, 246–251

Randell, B. (1975) System structure for software fault-tolerance. *IEEE Transactions on Software Engineering*, SE-1, 220–232

Randell, B., Lee, P. A. and Treleaven, P. C. (1978) Reliability issues in computing system design. *ACM Computer Surveys*, 10, 123–166

Rivest, R., Shamir, A. and Adleman, L. (1978) A method of obtaining digital signatures and public-key cryptosystems. *Communications of the ACM*, 120–126

Russell, D. L. (1980) State restoration in systems of communicating processes. *IEEE Transactions on Software Engineering*, SE-6, 183–193

Schneider, F. B. (1984) Byzantine Generals in action: implementing fail stop processors. *ACM Transactions on Computer Systems*, 2, 145–154

Shrivastava, S. K. and Banatre, J. P. (1978) Reliable resource allocation between unreliable processes. *IEEE Transactions on Software Engineering*, SE-4, 230–241

Shrivastava, S. K., Dixon, G. N. and Parrington, G. D. (1990) An overview of Arjuna: a programming system for reliable distributed computing. *IEEE Software* (forthcoming)

Shrivastava, S. K., Mancini, L. V. and Randell, B. (1987) On the duality of fault-tolerant system structures. *Lecture Notes in Computer Science, Vol. 309*, Springer-Verlag, pp. 19–37

Stroustrup, B. (1986) *C++ Programming Language*, Addison-Wesley

Taylor, D. J., Black, J. P. and Morgan, D. E. (1980) Redundancy in data structures: improving software fault-tolerance, *IEEE Transactions on Software Engineering*, SE-6, 585–594

Tyrell, A. M. and Holding, D. J. (1986) Design of reliable software in distributed systems using the conversation scheme. *IEEE Transactions on Software Engineering*, SE-12, 921–928

Voges, U. (ed.) (1988) *Software Diversity in Computerised Control Systems*, Springer

62

Symbolic computation

James Davenport
University of Bath

Contents

62.1 Introduction

Symbolic computation, otherwise called computer algebra, is the performance of non-numerical mathematical computations on a computer. This chapter outlines the field, mentions some of the software packages available for computer algebra and the facilities they contain, and warns the reader of some of the pitfalls of trying to develop a symbolic computation facility as part of a more general system.

62.2 Overview

When a mathematician, scientist or engineer says that he is 'calculating something', the layman assumes that he is adding up or multiplying some prodigious list of numbers. In fact, he is far more likely to be multiplying rotation matrices, integrating a complicated function or substituting one formula into another. The nineteenth century produced many prodigious calculations, both numeric (logarithm tables, prime numbers) and non-numeric (Delaunay's formula for the position of the moon, which filled 128 pages). With the advent of electronic computers, though, their use to perform numeric calculations meant that 'scientific computation' has become practically synonymous with 'numeric computation'. Computer algebra is the exception to this identification.

The field is in fact an old one. The first programs were written in 1953. Although it is a gross oversimplification, one can regard the 1960s as the era of discovery, when many small systems or applications were written, and many problems discovered (see, for example, the discussion of greatest common divisors later on). The 1970s were the age when the first great systems (Macsyma, Reduce) were written, and when major new algorithms were discovered, but when the availability of these systems was greatly hampered by their size relative to the memory capacity of existing computers. The 1980s have seen new systems (Maple, Mathematica, Reduce 3 and the new Scratchpad), further advances in algorithms, and widespread application of computer algebra techniques in certain domains (general relativity and geometric reasoning, to name but two). The 1990s will be the decade when computer algebra becomes as ubiquitous as the pocket calculator. That last claim may seem fanciful, but the HP 28-S pocket calculator has incorporated a computer algebra system ever since 1987.

To give the reader a feel for the use of a computer algebra system, *Figure 62.1* presents a brief Reduce session.

We begin with the solution of a fairly complicated integral – complicated in the sense that the amount of work required to get the right answer is greater than most people can do without significant risk of making a slip, followed by a truly difficult integral – the only integral table to contain it has completely the wrong answer (Davenport, 1982). We then perform some matrix algebra, and note that the result contains more digits than most computer 'integer' types can handle, and the result, which is definitely non-zero, would be indistinguishable from zero under single or double precision floating point. This point is stressed later. Reduce is one example – most of the other major systems will provide the same facilities, with slight variations on the syntax required.

62.3 The major systems

The major general-purpose computer algebra systems in existence today are:

1. Macsyma, a commercial products of Symbolics Inc. (Massachusetts).
2. Maple, a product of the symbolic computation group of the University of Waterloo (Canada).
3. Mathematica, a commercial product of Wolfram Research Inc. (Illinois).
4. Reduce, a product of the Rand Corporation (California).
5. Scratchpad, a research product of IBM Research (New York).

Many of these are available from other vendors and retailers as well as the originators. It is worth pointing out that there are a large number of special-purpose sysems, many of which have achieved substantial success in their field, e.g. the system Sheep in general relativity.

One fundamental question that all computer algebra systems or embedded uses of computer algebra in other applications have to solve is that of storage management. In numerical computations, a 10×10 matrix is just that, and occupies 100 units of storage, and the only question one has to ask is whether the numbers are single precision or double precision. But, as seen above, a 'number' in computer algebra can be of almost any size, and the output numbers can be enormously long even when the input numbers are quite small. Hence, it is out of the question to allocate a fixed-size 'results area' for a subroutine. Some kind of dynamic memory allocation is inevitable.

In fact, the demands that computer algebra systems make on memory allocation are immense. Much of the early research on garbage collection was conducted at MIT as an off-shoot of the Macsyma project, and memory allocation is one of the key performance issues for computer algebra systems.

Many computer algebra systems (among them Macsyma, Reduce and Scratchpad) are written in Lisp. This transfers the burden of storage management from the computer algebra system designer to the Lisp system designer, but the two are often the same people, or at least are in very close collaboration. More recently, there has been a trend to write such systems in C (e.g. Maple and Mathematica), although here the designers tend to write in something that macro-expands into C, with the macro-expansion phase taking care of the storage allocation questions.

Although computer algebra systems have been written in many other languages besides Lisp and C (e.g. Pascal, FORTRAN, machine-code and even COBOL), it seems relatively clear that these two are the languages of choice for implementing these large and complicated software systems. If one chooses a Lisp-based implementation, then one requires:

1. Efficiency and robustness of storage allocation and garbage collection.
2. An efficient treatment of multiple-length integers, also an efficient treatment of small integers for modular arithmetic.
3. The ability to deliver a complete system on top of the Lisp, with its own input/output and error-handling facilities.

If one starts from C, then there is more work to be done in implementing these facilities. Regrettably, it is often hard to do this in a machine-independent way. Garbage collection tends to require some way of scanning the stack, which is inherently non-portable. There is also a subtle issue related to the implementation of multiple-length integers. On a 32-bit machine, it would seem natural to use 'digits' base 2^{30} or 2^{31} to represent these integers. However, one needs some way of multiplying two such digits, which would yield a double-length result. Now, most machines actually have such an instruction (and one which divides a double-length integer by a single-length one) but C does not give access to it, unlike its ancestor BCPL. Hence, a small amount of machine code is generally necessary.

1: 1/(x^8 − 1); % the 1: is the system prompt; % introduces comments

$$\frac{1}{X^8 - 1}$$

2: int(ws,x); % ws is the last result

(SQRT(2)*LOG(− SQRT(2)*X + X² + 1) − SQRT(2)*LOG(SQRT(2)*X + X² + 1)

$+ 2*SQRT(2)*ATAN \left(\dfrac{SQRT(2) - 2*X}{SQRT(2)} \right) - 2*SQRT(2)*ATAN \left(\dfrac{SQRT(2) + 2*X}{SQRT(2)} \right)$

+ 2*LOG(X − 1) − 2*LOG(X + 1) − 4*ATAN(X))/16

3: sqrt(x + sqrt(a^2 + x^2))/x;

$$\frac{SQRT(SQRT(A^2 + X^2) + X)}{X}$$

4: int(ws,x);

2*SQRT(SQRT(A² + X²) + X)

+ SQRT(A)*LOG(SQRT(SQRT(A² + X²) + X) − SQRT(A))

− SQRT(A)*LOG(SQRT(SQRT(A² + X²) + X) + SQRT(A)) + SQRT(A)*ATAN((

SQRT(A)*SQRT(SQRT(A² + X²) + X)*SQRT(A² + X²)

− SQRT(A)*SQRT(SQRT(A² + X²) + X)*A

− SQRT(A)*SQRT(SQRT(A² + X²) + X)*X)/(2*A²))

5: matrix hilbert(10,10);
6: for i: = 1:10 do for j: = 1:10 do hilbert(i,j): = 1/(i + j − 1);
7: hilbert;

$$\begin{bmatrix}
1 & \frac{1}{2} & \frac{1}{3} & \frac{1}{4} & \frac{1}{5} & \frac{1}{6} & \frac{1}{7} & \frac{1}{8} & \frac{1}{9} & \frac{1}{10} \\
\frac{1}{2} & \frac{1}{3} & \frac{1}{4} & \frac{1}{5} & \frac{1}{6} & \frac{1}{7} & \frac{1}{8} & \frac{1}{9} & \frac{1}{10} & \frac{1}{11} \\
\frac{1}{3} & \frac{1}{4} & \frac{1}{5} & \frac{1}{6} & \frac{1}{7} & \frac{1}{8} & \frac{1}{9} & \frac{1}{10} & \frac{1}{11} & \frac{1}{12} \\
\frac{1}{4} & \frac{1}{5} & \frac{1}{6} & \frac{1}{7} & \frac{1}{8} & \frac{1}{9} & \frac{1}{10} & \frac{1}{11} & \frac{1}{12} & \frac{1}{13} \\
\frac{1}{5} & \frac{1}{6} & \frac{1}{7} & \frac{1}{8} & \frac{1}{9} & \frac{1}{10} & \frac{1}{11} & \frac{1}{12} & \frac{1}{13} & \frac{1}{14} \\
\frac{1}{6} & \frac{1}{7} & \frac{1}{8} & \frac{1}{9} & \frac{1}{10} & \frac{1}{11} & \frac{1}{12} & \frac{1}{13} & \frac{1}{14} & \frac{1}{15} \\
\frac{1}{7} & \frac{1}{8} & \frac{1}{9} & \frac{1}{10} & \frac{1}{11} & \frac{1}{12} & \frac{1}{13} & \frac{1}{14} & \frac{1}{15} & \frac{1}{16} \\
\frac{1}{8} & \frac{1}{9} & \frac{1}{10} & \frac{1}{11} & \frac{1}{12} & \frac{1}{13} & \frac{1}{14} & \frac{1}{15} & \frac{1}{16} & \frac{1}{17} \\
\frac{1}{9} & \frac{1}{10} & \frac{1}{11} & \frac{1}{12} & \frac{1}{13} & \frac{1}{14} & \frac{1}{15} & \frac{1}{16} & \frac{1}{17} & \frac{1}{18} \\
\frac{1}{10} & \frac{1}{11} & \frac{1}{12} & \frac{1}{13} & \frac{1}{14} & \frac{1}{15} & \frac{1}{16} & \frac{1}{17} & \frac{1}{18} & \frac{1}{19}
\end{bmatrix}$$

8: det hilbert;

$$\frac{1}{46206893947914691316295628839036278726983680000000000}$$

Figure 62.1 Example Reduce session

It was said above that these are large and complex systems. Macsyma was for many years, and may well still be, the largest single Lisp program. Reduce, though smaller, is over 90 000 lines of source code, and has been ported to four different dialects of Lisp, running on 23 different machine ranges. Scratchpad's algebraic programming language represents probably the most complex abstract data-type systems in practical use.

62.4 Pitfalls of computer algebra

One of the major problems with computer algebra is that it is harder than it looks. One thinks to oneself, for example 'Integration of rational functions: I learnt that at school, so it shouldn't be too hard to write a program to do it', but in fact the techniques taught at school assume that the denominator factors completely. Even when the techniques taught are complete, they may well have disastrous performance on non-trivial problems, or give results that are completely useless in practice. These points can be illustrated in turn.

62.4.1 Performance

Consider the problem of taking the greatest common divisor of two polynomials, say:

$$A(x) = x^8 + x^6 - 3x^4 - 3x^3 + 8x^2 + 2x - 5$$

$$B(x) = 3x^6 + 5x^4 - 4x^2 - 9x + 21$$

The first elimination gives $A - (x^2/3 - 2/9)B$, that is:

$$\frac{-5}{9}x^4 + \frac{1}{9}x^2 - \frac{1}{3}$$

and the subsequent eliminations give:

$$\frac{-117}{25}x^2 - 9x + \frac{441}{25}$$

$$\frac{233150}{6591}x - \frac{102500}{2197}$$

and finally:

$$\frac{1288744821}{543589225}$$

Hence, we can deduce that the polynomials are relatively prime; a simple conclusion for so much effort. We can apply the same algorithm to polynomials in several variables, but then every computation with polynomials in n variables would require a large number of g.c.d. calculations in $n - 1$ variables, each of which would in turn require a large number of calculations in $n - 2$ variables, and the whole calculation rapidly becomes infeasible.

We can solve this problem by working in a fraction-free way, i.e. by cross-multiplying in such a way that divisions never introduce fractions. In other words, instead of dividing A by B in $\mathbf{Q}$, we can multiply A by a power (that is with exponent the difference of the degrees plus one) of the leading coefficient of B, so that this multiple of A can be divided by B over $\mathbf{Z}$. For the problem at hand, we get the sequence:

$$-15x^4 + 3x^3 - 9$$

$$15795x^2 + 30375x - 59535$$

$$1254542875143750x - 1654608338437500$$

and:

$$1259333879550074310093115199218750 0$$

which again gives us the conclusion 'relatively prime', at the cost of having to compute a 35-digit number.

There are essentially two ways round this problem. The first, discovered by Collins (1971a), is that certain powers of the leading coefficients from previous steps can be guaranteed to cancel those from later steps. Space, and the mathematical sophistication required to prove this result, does not permit an explanation here. The reader is referred to Loos (1982) for the details. Here are just the corresponding sequence of polynomials when this cancellation has been performed:

$$15x^4 - 3x^2 + 9$$

$$65x^2 + 125x - 245$$

$$9326x - 12300$$

$$260708$$

The second family of methods, due to Brown (1971) and to Collins (1971b), are based on the use of modulo arithmetic. Again, space does not permit a full exposition of the theory, for which the reader is referred to Davenport et al. (1988), especially Chapter 4. Here, we will just show that A and B have no common factor, using only single-digit numbers. Suppose that these two polynomials have a common factor, that is, a polynomial P (of non-zero degree) which divides A and B. Then there is a polynomial Q such that $A = PQ$. This equation still holds if we take each coefficient as an integer modulo 5. If we write P_5 to signify the polynomial P considered as a polynomial with coefficients modulo 5, this equation implies that P_5 divides A_5. Similarly, P_5 divides B_5, and therefore it is a common factor of A_5 and B_5. Calculating the g.c.d. of A_5 and B_5 is fairly easy:

$$A_5(x) = x^8 + x^6 + 2x^4 + 2x^3 + x^2 + 2x$$

$$B_5(x) = 3x^6 + x^2 + x + 1$$

$$C_5(x) = \text{remainder}(A_5(x),B_5(x))$$
$$= A_5(x) + 3(x^3 + 1)B_5(x) = 2x^2 + 3$$

$$D_5(x) = \text{remainder}(B_5(x),C_5(x))$$
$$= B_5(x) + (x^4 + x^2 + 3)C_5(x) = x$$

$$E_5(x) = \text{remainder}(C_5(x),D_5(x)) = C_5(x) + 3xD_5(x) = 3$$

Thus A_5 and B_5 are relatively prime, which implies that $P_5 = 1$. As the leading coefficient of P has to be one, we deduce that $P = 1$.

62.4.2 Utility

Many of the procedures we know produce excellent results when used on the small examples we can do by hand, but rapidly produce unmanageable and useless formulae when applied to more substantial examples. For example, there are formulae for the solution of cubic and quartic equations, analogous to the familiar:

$$-b \pm \sqrt{(b^2 - 4ac)/2a}$$

for quadratic equations. But when we apply them in practice, we find that the results may well be totally unusable. For example, for the case of the general cubic $x^3 + ax^2 + bx + c$, we find that one of the solutions is:

$$\frac{-(\theta^2 \cdot \sqrt{3} \cdot i) - \theta^2 - 2 \cdot \theta \cdot a + \sqrt{3} \cdot a^2 \cdot i - 3 \cdot \sqrt{3} \cdot b \cdot i - a^2 + 3 \cdot b}{6 \cdot \theta}$$

$$(62.1)$$

where:

$$\theta := (\tfrac{1}{2}(9 \cdot \sqrt{(\tfrac{1}{3}(4 \cdot a^3 \cdot c - a^2 \cdot b^2 - 18 \cdot a \cdot b \cdot c + 4 \cdot b^3 + 27 \cdot c^2))}$$

$$- 2 \cdot a^3 + 9 \cdot a \cdot b - 27 \cdot c))^{\frac{1}{3}}$$

$$(62.2)$$

and the solutions of a general quartic are too large to print here.

The same problem arises elsewhere in computer algebra. The problem of characterizing the steady-state behaviour of three communicating enzymes:

$$X_0 \underset{}{\overset{E_0}{\rightleftharpoons}} X_1 \underset{}{\overset{E_1}{\rightleftharpoons}} X_2 \underset{}{\overset{E_2}{\rightleftharpoons}} X_3$$

was long believed to be insoluble by biochemists. In fact, a 10-line Reduce program will solve it, using the method of Gröbner bases (see later), but the solution is four pages of tightly printed equation (not equations – a single equation) (Bennett et al., 1988). Again, we have to ask the question: 'is this really a solution to the problem?' This is an area of current research, but the answer does seem to be 'yes', although the use of the solution most certainly does not consist in looking at it.

For this reason, a computer algebra system must support various forms of output, not only the formulae we saw at the start of this chapter, but also direct output in mathematical notation suitable for use with a typesetting language (the Formulae (62.1) and (62.2) above were typeset by Reduce in T_EX (Antweiler et al., 1988) and output suitable for later numerical evaluation (typically in FORTRAN). The latter is not as easy as it sounds, and substantial work has been done on generating efficient FORTRAN from the computer algebra system (see, for example, Gates and van Hulzen, 1985; van den Heuvel et al., 1989). There is also the problem of generating numerically stable FORTRAN, but this has received less attention.

62.4.3 Completeness

The techniques taught at school or university are not always as complete as one would like, since they are designed to work on the sort of example that one can do by hand. For example, it is not very difficult to see that:

$$\int \frac{5x^4 + 60x^3 + 255x^2 + 450x + 274}{x^5 + 15x^4 + 85x^3 + 225x^2 + 274x + 120}$$

$$= \log(x^5 + 15x^4 + 85x^3 + 225x^2 + 274x + 120)$$

$$= \log(x + 1) + \log(x + 2) + \log(x + 3)$$

$$+ \log(x + 4) + \log(x + 5)$$

but perhaps rather more difficult to see that:

$$\int \frac{5x^4 + 60x^3 + 255x^2 + 450x + 275}{x^5 + 15x^4 + 85x^3 + 225x^2 + 274x + 120}$$

$$= \frac{25}{24}\log(x + 1) + \frac{5}{6}\log(x + 2) + \frac{5}{4}\log(x + 3)$$

$$+ \frac{5}{6}\log(x + 4) + \frac{25}{24}\log(x + 5)$$

(The expression with a single logarithm is too long to write here. It contains the logarithm of a polynomial of degree 120, of which the largest coefficients have 68 decimal places.) In these two cases, the denominator factors completely into linears. If we choose examples where the denominator doesn't factor, e.g.:

$$\int \frac{5x^4 + 1}{(x^5 + x + 3)^2} = \frac{-1}{(x^5 + x + 3)}$$

$$\int \frac{5x^4 + 1}{(x^5 + x + 3)} = \log(x^5 + x + 3)$$

then these examples are easy to spot by hand, but the reader would probably be completely baffled by:

$$\int \frac{5x^4}{(x^5 + x + 3)}$$

In fact, it is possible to factorize a polynomial completely by adding enough new algebraic numbers (four in this case), and then one can write down the integral. This assumes a substantial facility with manipulating algebraic numbers, and also yields a very messy result. Of course, we could apply the same technique to:

$$\int \frac{5x^4 + 1}{(x^5 + x + 3)}$$

which would also give a very messy result, but which we know to be equivalent to a simple result. Might the same be true for:

$$\int \frac{5x^4}{(x^5 + x + 3)}?$$

In fact, it is a consequence of Trager's algorithm (Trager, 1976) that this integral cannot be written in any simpler way than:

$$\sum_y y \log(4xy - 5x + 15y - 15)$$

where

$$y - 253381y^5 \ldots$$
$$+ 1266905y^4 \ldots$$
$$- 2533650y^3 \ldots$$
$$+ 25332250y^2 \ldots$$
$$- 1266250y \ldots$$
$$+ 253125 = 0 \ldots$$

This is certainly a result well beyond the scope of the normal methods of integration.

In short, therefore, it is not sufficient to take the mathematics one learnt at school, and implement that. One needs expert mathematical advice, and this comes generally from 'pure' mathematicians, rather than 'applied' mathematicians, even though the problem to be solved is one of applied mathematics.

62.5 Capabilities of computer algebra systems

Having seen what one cannot expect to do naïvely, let us now see what the main systems can actually do. This will give the reader some idea of what sort of problem it is reasonable to pose one of these systems, and also a 'shopping list' that should be considered in any attempt to incorporate general-purpose symbolic computation in any system.

62.5.1 Manipulation of large numbers, fixed and floating point

Even if there were no external use for this, we would need to implement it in our system, because of the way numerical coefficients can grow unexpectedly fast during a computation. In fact, though, the ability to produce arbitrarily large numbers, or arbitrarily accurate floating-point numbers, is extremely useful. This is often used in the construction of numerical routines, where the constants need to be as accurate as possible, and should therefore be computed to a higher precision than that in which they will be used.

62.5.2 Manipulation of polynomials and rational functions

This is, in general, perfectly straightforward. However, we have seen that the computation of greatest common divisors needs to be handled with care. Factorization of polynomials, though, is an area where we do not know any naïve algorithms, except for polynomials of particular low degrees, such as two or three. Nevertheless, there do exist such algorithms. They are all based on looking at the same factorization modulo a prime number p, for which there are good algorithms, deducing a factorization modulo p^n for a suitably large n, and then deducing from that a solution to the factorization problem over the integers. The first step runs in time cubic in the degree of the polynomial, and the second step in a similar time. The last step is often very easy, but there are polynomials, whose existence was first pointed out by Swinnerton-Dyer (see Berlekamp, 1970), such that their factorization over the integers is arbitrarily different from their factorization modulo p, for all primes p. For example, such a polynomial might be irreducible over the integers but have only quadratic and linear factors modulo every prime. Such a polynomial would require an exponential (with respect to the degree of the polynomial) amount of work to check every possible combination of these quadratics and linears to see if it represented a valid factor over the integers. A recent algorithm by Lenstra *et al.* (1982) gives a polynomial–time algorithm, though with a very large exponent in the polynomial (probably 12).

62.5.3 Manipulation of higher functions, e.g. trigonometic

There are two schools of thought as to how this can be done. One provides special functions, such as Macsyma's trigexpand, which will convert $\sin(a + b)$ into $\sin a \cos b + \cos a \sin b$. The other provides a general rewrite-rule system, in which the user can program such rules for himself, e.g. Reduce's:

for all a,b let sin(a + b) = sin(a)*cos(b) + cos(a)*sin(b)

The trade-off is essentially between the efficiency of the first approach, and the generality of the second. However, there is a further problem (explained by Stoutemyer, 1977): the equation

$\sin^2(x) + \cos^2(x) = 1$. A special program can try to recognize occurrences of the left-hand side, although even this is not easy in large expressions, but it is essentially impossible to write an efficient general-purpose rewriting system which handles addition (or, as it is technically called, the problem of associative–commutative rewriting), and Reduce, for example, will convert:

for all x let sin(x)**2 + cos(x)**2 = 1

into:

for all x let sin(x)**2 = 1 − cos(x)**2

The problem is discussed by Hörnfeldt (1982), but his solutions are not available in any general-purpose system.

62.5.4 Manipulation of matrices

Here, one has to distinguish between *explicit* matrices, such as the matrix **hilbert** in the opening examples, and *implicit* matrices, as one sees when a mathematician says 'let m and n be rotation matrices'. The first is quite easy, and is dealt with by all systems, as we saw in the initial example. The only point to note here is the ease of asking questions whose answer is very large, e.g. writing down a 5×5 generic matrix, then asking for its determinant, or its inverse. The determinant will be a sum of 120 products, and hence occupy at least a printed page, while the inverse will occupy several pages at best.

The treatment of implicit matrices is essentially that of non-commuting variables: $mn \neq nm$. There are two possible syntaxes for handling this in computer algebra systems. Either one declares a special operator for 'non-commutative multiplication', as in Macsyma, or one declares that the elements are non-commutative, as in Reduce. The difference is not particularly profound.

62.5.5 Calculus operations

Differentiation is conceptually simple, but is in fact one of the great uses of symbolic computation as part of a numerical calculation. Many processes, such as minimization and the solution of differential equations, are much more efficient if derivatives of the functions can be provided, as well as the functions themselves. If the problem has many variables, computing these derivatives by hand and coding them in the appropriate programming language can be both tedious and error-prone, whereas a computer algebra system can perform the entire process automatically.

We have already seen some examples of integration. Integration of rational functions and of functions generated by sin, cos, exp and log (the purely transcendental elementary functions) is implemented in all systems, although the case where the denominator does not factorize may not be treated completely. The case of algebraic functions is more difficult, both from a theoretical and from a practical point of view. Two alternative approaches to the theory are described by Davenport (1981) and Trager (1984). There is a partial implementation in Reduce, and a complete one in Scratchpad.

Differential equations are a subject rich both in heuristics and in theory. The heuristics are implemented in many systems, but Macsyma's are among the largest. The theory, which is largely limited to linear equations, has had very few implementations, because of its complexity. There are implementations of Kovacic's algorithm (Kovacic, 1986) for deciding if second-order linear differential equations with rational function coefficients have closed-form solutions.

Limits are an area where heuristics tend to reign. The most complete implementations are probably those of Macsyma and

Maple. This area is closely connected to that of Taylor series and their generalizations, since the limit often has to be discovered to know how to start the series. There are two different ways to represent a power series. The first, and most obvious, is to declare that we wish to have our series up to a certain exponent, say x^{10}, and then the power series function will then return a series up to that exponent. The trouble with this is that one is liable to precisely the same sort of inaccuracies that trouble numerical computations. We can lose significance if we divide such a power series by x, since it will then only be accurate up to x^9, or if we take the square root of a power series that has no constant term, or under various other circumstances.

The second method, pioneered by Norman (1975), represents a series as some terms *and* the rule for generating additional terms, so that additional terms can be computed as and when required, and hence the series are essentially of infinite precision. This method, while substantially more difficult to implement than the straightforward method, has many advantages.

Formal sums are an area where some systems have quite powerful facilities. There are obviously many heuristics that can be applied, and simple sums (e.g. polynomials in n) can be solved readily. There are also two powerful algorithms, due to Gosper (1978) and to Karr (1981) respectively, which can handle many other kinds of summation. Gosper's algorithm is implemented in Macsyma, but there seems to be no implementation of Karr's algorithm.

62.5.6 Solution of equations

Every system has some kind of 'solve' facility, but the capabilities vary widely. At one level, there are a large number of heuristics which can be applied. For certain kinds of equations, or systems of equations, there are algorithms that can be applied to find the solutions. This is obviously true for systems of linear equations. More recently, there has been Buchberger's algorithm, and many developments on it, which can be viewed as doing the same thing for systems of non-linear equations that Gaussian elimination does for systems of linear equations: *viz.* triangularizing the system to produce (assuming that the equations are not under-determined) one equation in the last variable, one (or possibly more) in the last two variables, and so on.

For a concrete illustration of this, consider the equations:

$$0 = x + y + z$$

$$0 = xy + yz + zx$$

$$0 = xyz - 1$$

The corresponding Gröbner base is:

$$\{x + y + z, y^2 + yz + z^2, z^3 - 1\}$$

from which we deduce that z has three possible values, for each of these y has two possible values (in fact, the two other cube roots of unity), and that, for each value of y and z, x is uniquely determined. If we consider a slightly more complicated set of equations, which is in fact under-determined, *viz.*:

$$0 = x + y + z + w$$

$$0 = xy + yz + zw + wx$$

$$0 = xyz + yzw + zwx + wxy$$

$$0 = xyzw - 1$$

we get the Gröbner base:

$$\{w + x + y + z,$$
$$x^2 + 2xz + z^2,$$
$$xy - xz + y^2z^4 + yz - 2z^2,$$
$$xz^4 - x + z^5 - z,$$
$$y^3z^2 + y^2z^3 - y - z,$$
$$y^2z^6 - y^2z^2 - z^4 + 1\}$$

Here we get no polynomial in z alone, so z is a free variable. For every choice of z, y has to satisfy the last polynomial $y^2z^6 - y^2z^2 - z^4 + 1$, unless this vanishes identically, which it will do if z is a fourth root of unity, when y must satisfy the penultimate polynomial: $y^3z^2 + y^2z^3 - y - z$. For such a pair of values for y and z, we must satisfy the appropriate polynomial for x, and then w is determined. In fact, we can simplify this system by noticing that the second polynomial is a perfect square. If we add its square root $x + z$ to the Gröbner base and re-compute, we get the simplified base:

$$\{w + y, x + z, y^2z^2 - 1\}$$

It is now quite obvious that z is undetermined, y is either $1/z$ or $-1/z$, and w and x are determined. Davenport (1987) discusses these equations in more detail, and explains how to perform this sort of simplification automatically.

One problem with this method, and indeed with almost any method of solving systems of equations, is that it inherently looks for complex solutions, whereas the user typically is interested in real solutions only, and maybe only in positive real solutions, or solutions which have a certain physical significance. Some progress on this has been made by Melenk *et al.* (1988).

There is a complete solution methodology for real equations and inequalities, via the theory of *cylindrical algebraic decomposition* (Collins, 1975), but there is only one implementation, in the little-used SAC-2 system, which has not been able to solve substantial problems.

62.6 Conclusions

Symbolic computation is now an important application of computers, and several sophisticated systems exist. Many of the important algorithms are well documented but considerable care is required to produce efficient and effective implementations. This is an area where the software engineer requires specialist advice from mathematicians.

62.7 References and bibliography

Antweiler, W., Strotman, A. and Winkelmann, V. (1988) *A REDUCE \Tex-Interface*, University of Cologne Computer Center Technical Report, April 1988

Bennett, J. P., Davenport, J. H. and Sauro, H. M. (1988) Solution of some equations in biochemistry. *Bath Computer Science Technical Report 88–12*

Berlekamp, E. R. (1970) Factoring polynomials over large finite fields. *Math. Comp.*, **24**, 713–735

Brown, W. S. (1971) On Euclid's algorithm and the computation of polynomial greatest common divisors. *Journal of the ACM*, **18**, 478–504

Collins, G. E. (1971a) Subresultants and reduced polynomial remainder sequences. *Journal of the ACM*, **14**, 128–142.

Collins, G. E. (1971b) Quantifier elimination for real closed fields by cylindrical algebraic decomposition. In *Proceedings 2nd GI Conference Automata Theory and Formal Languages, Springer Lecture Notes in Computer Science 33*, pp. 134–183

Collins, G. E. (1975) *Quantifier Elimination for Real Closed Fields by Cylindrical Algebraic Decomposition*, Proceedings of the 2nd GI Conference on Automata Theory and Formal Languages, Springer Lecture Notes in Computer Science 33, pp. 134–183

Davenport, J. H. (1981) On the integration of algebraic functions. *Springer Lecture Notes in Computer Science 102*, Springer-Verlag, Berlin–Heidelberg–New York (Russian ed. MIR, Moscow, 1985)

Davenport, J. H. (1982) Table erratum 587. *Math. Comp.*, **38**, 335–336

Davenport, J. H. (1987) Looking at a set of equations. *Bath Computer Science Technical Report 87–06*

Davenport, J. H., Siret, Y. and Tournier, E. (1988) *Computer Algebra*, Academic Press, London. Translated from the French *'Calcul Formel'* (Masson, 1986)

Gates, B. L. and van Hulzen, J. A. (1985) Automatic generation of optimized programs. *Proceedings EUROCAL 85, Vol. 2, Springer Lecture Notes in Computer Science Vol. 204*, Springer-Verlag, pp. 583–584

Gosper, R. W. Jr. (1978) A decision procedure for indefinite hypergeometric summation. In *Proceedings Nat. Acad. Sci.*

van den Heuvel, P., van Hulzen, J. A. and Goldman, V. V. (1989) Automatic generation of FORTRAN-coded Jacobians and Hessians. In *Proceedings EUROCAL 87, Springer Lecture Notes in Computer Science 378*, Springer-Verlag, pp. 120–131

Hörnfeldt, L. (1982) A sum-substitutor used as trigonometric simplifier. In *Proceedings EUROCAM 82, Springer Lecture Notes in Computer Science 144*, Springer-Verlag, pp. 188–195

van Hulzen, J. A. and Calmet, J. (1982) Computer algebra systems. In *Symbolic and Algebraic Computation* (Computing Supplementum 4) (ed. B. Buchberger, G. E. Collins and R. Loos), Springer-Verlag, pp. 221–243

Karr, M. (1981) Summation in finite terms. *Journal of the ACM*, **28**, 305–350

Kovacic, J. J. (1986) An algorithm for solving second order linear homogeneous differential equations. *Journal of Symbolic Comp.*, **2**, 3–43

Lenstra, A. K., Lenstra, H. W. and Lovász, L. (1982) Factoring polynomials with rational coefficients. *Math. Ann.*, **261**, 515–534

Loos, R. (1982) Generalized polynomial remainder sequences. In *Symbolic and Algebraic Computation* (Computing Supplementum 4) (ed. B. Buchberger, G. E. Collins and R. Loos), Springer-Verlag, pp. 115–137

Melenk, H., Möller, H. M. and Neun, W. (1988). Symbolic solution of large stationary chemical kinetics problems. *Preprint SC 88–7*, ZIB, Berlin

Norman, A. C. (1975) Computing with formal power series. *ACM Transactions on Mathematical Software*, **1**, 346–356

Stoutemyer, D. R. (1977) sin(x)**2 + cos(x)**2 = 1. In *Proceedings 1977 MACSYMA Users' Conference*, NASA Publication CP-2012, National Technical Information Service, Springfield, Virginia, pp. 425–433

Trager, B. M. (1976) Algebraic factoring and rational function integration. In *Proceedings SYMSAC 76*, ACM, New York, pp. 219–226

Trager, B. M. (1984) *Integration of Algebraic Functions*, PhD Thesis, MIT Dept. of EE&CS

63

Epilogue: future developments

Robert Laurence Baber
Management Consultant and Software
Engineer

Contents

63.1 Introduction 63/3

63.2 The essence of engineering practice 63/3

63.3 Is software development an engineering discipline? 63/4

63.4 Early development of traditional engineering fields 63/6

63.5 Forces and factors influencing development of an engineering discipline 63/7

63.6 Software development tomorrow: possible future worlds 63/11

63.7 Our path to the software engineering future 63/13

63.8 Conclusion 63/14

63.9 Bibliography 63/15

Engineering is born of both practice – *fabrica* – and theory – *ratiocinatio*. Practice is a mechanical facility, developed through study and exercise. Theory is the ability to describe and explain the designed object. (Marcus Vitruvius Pollio, circa 25 BC, paraphrased translation)

The programmer's task is not just to write down a program. His main task is to give a formal proof that the program he proposes meets the equally formal functional specification. (Edsger W. Dijkstra, 1989 AD)

63.1 Introduction

Some 2000 years ago, Vitruvius began his classical work *Ten Books on Architecture* (*De Architectura Libri Decem*) by outlining the wide range of subjects of which the architect and civil engineer must be knowledgeable. He pointed out that both practice – *fabrica* – and theory – *ractiocinatio* – are essential ingredients of the field. Practitioners whose abilities are limited to the mechanical skills (*fabrica*) never achieve much of real significance. Those who, on the other hand, rely only on their knowledge of the theory (*ratiocinatio*) mistake the shadow of the object for the object itself. Only those who are able to apply well developed capabilities in both areas to the job to be done will accomplish it with honour. Both aspects, *fabrica* and *ratiocinatio*, are of equal – and critical – importance in professional practice.

Modern engineers immediately recognize that these comments apply just as much to each of today's engineering sciences as to that engineering field which existed in Vitruvius's time. For an extensive examination of the relevance of Vitruvius's writings to modern information science and technology, the reader is referred to Dijkhuis (1989).

Professor Dijkstra's recent comment cited above seems to be motivated by an observation which has been mentioned by others as well: we software developers today have not achieved the balance of practical skills and theoretical knowledge required of a true professional. The abilities of the typical software developer of today are limited to the *fabrica*. As a result, our possible achievements are significantly – and unnecessarily – restricted.

Dijkstra seems to be going to the other extreme and saying that the *ratiocinatio* is more important than the *fabrica*. Or perhaps he intentionally overemphasizes that which is lacking in order to prod us into giving it sufficient attention.

If software development is to become a true, mature, engineering discipline (and this assumption definitely underlies this reference book, as evidenced by its very title), then the major, overriding developments in the mid- and long-term future of our field must serve to redress this current imbalance and then to maintain the balance called for in Vitruvius's 2000-year old guidelines for an engineering field. Any other pattern of future developments will lead us to a non-engineering state of affairs for our field.

What are the main characteristics and features of engineering practice? How did the other, traditional engineering fields evolve to their respective present states? What forces – technical and socio-economic, internal and external to the field in question – influence the development and evolution of an engineering discipline? These are the main questions we must consider when pondering the probable future of our field, software engineering, and our path thereto. The specific technical developments, discoveries and inventions will be of less direct concern; it is, of course, important that they do occur, but it is not, in the overall scheme of things, so important which particular technical advance is achieved when.

To enable the reader to interpret this chapter optimally and assess possible limitations and even unintentional bias, he or she should be aware of the context in which it is written, i.e. of the author's background. He studied electrical engineering and industrial management. The major part of his professional work involves the application of computing systems in business and industry. He is not a theoretician or mathematician. If he appears occasionally to be enamoured of theory or mathematics, it is only because he (like Vitruvius and many other engineers in the intervening millenia) have found them to be of considerable practical value, enabling him to see, understand and do things which would have otherwise been impossible for him.

Many of the ideas contained in this chapter appeared earlier in the books *Software Reflected* (Baber, 1982) and *The Spine of Software: Designing Provably Correct Software – Theory and Practice* (Baber, 1987), especially Chapters 1 and 7.

63.2 The essence of engineering practice

An engineer applies scientific and theoretical knowledge in designing and constructing structures, machines, systems, etc. of economical value for practical, purposeful use. Especially noteworthy is that he or she uses the theoretical foundation to verify, by systematic calculation and before the object is actually built, that the proposed design will satisfy the specifications. This step gives rise to the high level of reliability to which the engineer, clients and society have become accustomed. It is a prerequisite for the widespread application of potentially dangerous machines, systems, etc. in society. It also enables the engineer to accept responsibility for the correctness, reliability and safety of his or her designs without assuming undue personal risk.

Thus, the two fundamentally important characteristics of engineering practice are:

1. A scientific foundation which the engineer thoroughly understands and continually applies in his work.
2. A highly developed sense of responsibility toward his clients and the public.

In this regard, engineering is directly comparable to other professions such as law and medicine.

What sort of guarantee does the client receive? Typically, the professional guarantees his ability, not a particular result. The lawyer does not guarantee that he or she will win any particular case, only that the lawyer is capable of properly prosecuting it, i.e. in accordance with well-established standards of performance. Similarly, the physician does not guarantee that a particular patient will recover, but rather that the physician is properly qualified to provide medical services of a certain standard of quality. The non-professional supplier of goods or services, on the other hand, guarantees the product or result, not his or her ability or qualifications.

In engineering practice, this distinction is often not of practical consequence, because the engineer's professional ability and the correctness of the design go hand in hand. Properly applied ability implies the correctness of the design, because, as mentioned above, the engineer can – and is expected to – demonstrate that the design satisfies the specifications. If the design turns out to be faulty, the engineer has made a mistake which, in turn, raises serious questions regarding his or her professional ability and the care with which it is applied.

Only those are admitted to ordinary membership in a professional engineering association who can demonstrate that they have a satisfactory working command of a certain body of knowledge and the ability to apply it to practical problems. Usually, this requirement is satisfied by successfully completing a several year long approved academic course of study. At least for some categories of membership, the engineer is also required to formally accept certain responsibilities toward his clients and the public, typically by subscribing to a code of ethics. Most such professional organizations have procedures for reprimanding and even withdrawing the recognition of members whose professional performance does not fulfil the minimum acceptable level of quality or exhibits an unacceptable sense of responsibility.

63.3 Is software development an engineering discipline?

When considering the question whether or not software development is an engineering discipline, we must distinguish between two quite different aspects of this question:

1. Is the field of software development, by its inherent nature, an engineering science?
2. Is software development as currently typically practised an engineering discipline?

We must also beware of a certain misuse of the word 'engineering' in the compound term 'software engineering' as it has come to be commonly used recently. The term software engineering as now frequently used in the technical literature refers to a fairly specific collection of ideas, concepts, methods, etc. pertaining to the management of software development and utilization during the course of its economic life. Most engineers in the traditional engineering disciplines would probably not agree that this material captures the essence of engineering; some quite explicitly do not (Baber, 1989). They would not deny the validity or value of this material, but would argue that it has been misnamed.

Let us compare the essential aspects of engineering as outlined in the above section with the state of software development today. We must consider the following questions. Is there a substantial body of scientific, theoretical knowledge directly relevant to software development? Have software developers learned it thoroughly and do they regularly apply it to their work? Do they take their responsibility to clients and the public for correct, safe designs seriously, e.g. by verifying systematically and analytically that they will satisfy the specifications? What sorts of technical and professional associations exist and what prerequisites do they prescribe for prospective members?

63.3.1 Is there a theoretical foundation for software development?

The question of the existence of a theoretical foundation underlying software development was the subject of some debate in earlier decades, but there appears to be consensus today that such a foundation exists. It is perhaps not as extensive, not as well developed and not as mature as in the cases of the traditional engineering fields, but it does exist. It can certainly be argued that this foundation is now better developed than was the corresponding theoretical foundation of many a classical engineering field when it first began to consider itself a profession (e.g. Nahin, 1988).

The introduction and successful operation of first degree programs in informatics, computing science, software engineering, etc. in many universities in different countries is strong evidence of such a consensus. Few, if any, of these courses suffer from a dearth of material for the curriculum; on the contrary, the problem is more typically lack of time for the desired content (and, of course, availability of qualified teaching staff for the material selected).

Also the existence and content of this reference book are evidence of such a theoretical foundation for software development.

Does this scientific foundation for software development provide an adequate basis for systematically and analytically verifying that a proposed program (design) will fulfil its specification? Some software developers state clearly – from logical conviction as well as own experience – yes, but their number is not yet large enough that one could speak of a consensus. Some others claim to have tried unsuccessfully to apply the theoretical material and have concluded that it is inherently unsuitable for practical application. But most software developers have not attempted to make use of this material, so the question remains unanswered in software development practice.

To someone familiar with the history of other engineering fields, the arguments and conclusions of those who hold the theory of proving programs correct (that is, proving that they satisfy the specifications) to be unsuitable for practical application are quite unconvincing. The experience of other engineering fields belie their conclusions. The early history of electrical engineering, the engineering field with which the author is most familiar, provides many examples of highly regarded practitioners' denying the usefulness of various theoretical analyses which are now common in electrical engineering education and practice. Years after Maxwell's death, for example, his theory of electromagnetism was far from accepted as useful knowledge for the practising electrical engineer. Even after the considerable simplification of this system of equations by Hertz and Heaviside, the theory and its underlying mathematics were still beyond the grasp of most practitioners of the day, including the influential William Preece (appointed engineer-in-chief of the British General Post Office in 1892, elected president of the Institution of Electrical Engineers in 1893) (Nahin, 1988). Today, all this is basic, required material in the electrical engineering curriculum and is taught in the early part of courses.

Among those who seem convinced that the currently existing theoretical foundation for software development enables the programmer to verify analytically that his proposed design will satisfy its specifications are some of our most distinguished experts (e.g. Dijkstra, Hoare, Mills). More widespread indications of growing awareness of the practical potential of this theoretical material can be discerned in the trade and professional literature. Especially in the UK increasing attention is being given to 'formal methods' and 'mathematical verification' as this area is now often called.

Thus, it seems reasonable to conclude that software development is, by its nature at least, an engineering science. But is it practised as such today?

63.3.2 Software development practice today

Does the software developer have a thorough knowledge of the theoretical foundation for his work and does he or she apply it regularly in practice? Here, our answers must be more negative, pointing out areas in which future developments will take place. Only a small fraction of software developers has had an academic tertiary education with a major in computing and has, therefore, been given the opportunity to learn the theoretical foundation essential for professional software development practice. The fraction of such academically educated practitioners varies from country to country but in every country they are in the minority. This fraction is growing, however, and will, it appears, increase more rapidly in the future. Computing departments of academic institutions are doubly challenged by this need and development. They must not only educate increasing numbers of software engineers, they must somehow prepare correspondingly more staff to teach these subjects.

Do software developers take their responsibility to clients and the public for correct, safe designs seriously, for example, by verifying systematically and analytically that they will satisfy the specifications? The typical software developer does not verify his or her designs as traditional engineers do, simply because, lacking the necessary theoretical basis and practice in applying it, he cannot. We still have the infamous 'disclaimer' notices, which are outright denials of responsibility for anything, something unknown in true engineering fields. The failure rate due to software errors (i.e. design errors) is incomparably higher than the error rate in traditional engineering fields (Baber, 1982i; Thomas, 1988). Recent court decisions in suits for damages and movements toward introducing legal liability for injury attributed to software errors suggests that in various countries the public perceives a need for greater corrective action than the software development community is taking. In other words, the software development community is not conducting itself as an engineering profession. The future development of our field will have to include fundamental changes of attitude in this area.

Closely related to the question of the responsibility assumed by the software developer is the matter of the guarantee effectively on offer. For good reason, software developers have historically guaranteed basically nothing. They cannot guarantee their extensive formal qualifications, because they have none. They do not, really, guarantee their product, because they realize that they are not able to convince themselves that it satisfies the specifications. Forced by clients and market forces, the serious software supplier agrees to make reasonable effort to correct those errors which manifest themselves within a certain period of time after installation and which significantly impair the usefulness of the software. But even in this case the value of the 'guarantee' is limited by potential disagreements about what is 'reasonable', what is an 'error', and whether or not the impairment is 'significant'.

63.3.3 Professional associations

What sorts of technical and professional associations exist and what prerequisites do they prescribe for prospective members? If one looks at the computing associations in those countries with the largest activities in the computing field, these associations fall into two main groups.

Associations in the first group (consisting generally of the earliest formed organizations) admit to membership anyone with an interest in computing. Often their members tend to have professional (academic) credentials, including but by no means restricted to the engineering disciplines, but no such requirement is enforced. Among their members are both those providing computing systems and services and those interested primarily in applications from the user's standpoint. Educators, scientists, engineers, technicians and specialists at various levels of expertise are represented. Thus their member body includes a wide variety in terms of levels of qualification, orientation and specific interests. Questions of responsibility or professional ethics are usually handled in an informal, non-binding manner, if at all. Thus, these organizations are not comparable to professional associations in the traditional engineering, legal, medical, etc. fields.

The second group consists of subgroups of long-established engineering (usually electrical) associations. Full membership is granted only to those who satisfy the normal requirements for membership in the parent association itself. A certain anomaly arises here, however. The software developer joining such a computer subgroup may do so on the basis either of a qualification (e.g. academic degree) in the traditional engineering field (e.g. electrical engineering) or in computing, i.e., he or she need not have formal qualifications in computing or software development as a separate field in itself. Initially, members of these subgroups were engineers in the classical field with a special

interest in computing as a subarea, for example, electrical engineers designing computing or telecommunications equipment. Gradually, however, the activities of these computing subgroups expanded to cover ever broader fields, even going into software areas not really related to the original engineering discipline at all.

Examples of associations of the first type are the Association for Computing Machinery (ACM) in the USA, the Gesellschaft für Informatik in the FRG and the British Computer Society in the UK. Among the second group are organizations such as the Computer Society of the Institute of Electrical and Electronics Engineers in the USA and the Informationstechnische Gesellschaft of the Verband Deutscher Elektrotechniker in the FRG.

The British Computer Society in the UK is an interesting and, to the best of my knowledge, currently unique example of a computing association originally of the first type taking definite steps to become a professional organization of the second type. Many years ago it began the transition by introducing the examination requirement. More recently, it continued by starting the process of becoming a member of the Engineering Council with the traditional engineering institutions.

If the field of software development is to become a fully fledged engineering discipline with correspondingly structured professional societies, then computing associations of the first type in other countries will either have to follow the lead of the BCS or else lose ground to computing subgroups of traditional engineering associations which will grow to fill the gap (as some observers believe is happening in the USA). Alternatively, the computing associations of the first type could specialize on computing *science* while computing subgroups of engineering associations or newly formed organizations represent the software *engineering* community.

63.3.4 Other technical factors

A less fundamentally but nonetheless important characteristic of an engineering field is the breadth of related technical subfields which it includes. Only if a sufficiently wide range of technical activities exists can its practitioners develop the theoretical basis and their practical expertise extensively. Such areas include applications (of external interest), various specific technical capabilities (of internal interest), standards, etc.

In this regard, computing in general and software development in particular are off to a good start. Many such areas are already well developed, as evidenced by the contributions in this reference book. Many important questions have been answered, indicating significant progress, and important unanswered questions remain, indicating that there is still much interesting potential for further development.

63.3.5 Summary: software development as an engineering discipline

The current state of software development as pictured above leads to the following conclusions. By its inherent nature, software development is an engineering discipline.

It is not currently practised as such, however. The major barrier to professional practice is the lack of adequately widespread education of software developers. Their command of the relevant theoretical foundation and their ability to apply it to practical software design problems is not up to the standards set by the traditional engineering sciences.

The current structure of technical and professional associations in the computing field shows clear signs of transition to a professional engineering state of affairs.

Thus, we cannot say that software development is today an engineering discipline in the full sense of the term. The stage is set for its becoming one in the near future, however. The main prerequisite is that a sufficient number of software developers want it to become a professional engineering field and are willing to put in the necessary mental effort to make it one.

Lest we become discouraged by the comparison of our young field with mature professions, we should keep in mind that they were not always so advanced as they are today. As will be seen below, the field is now in at least as good a situation as were the traditional engineering fields when they began their transition to professionalism – perhaps even better. Since they made it, so can we. History usually repeats itself.

63.4 Early development of traditional engineering fields

In the above sections, the classical engineering disciplines have been referred to almost as if they are and always were perfect. While they are not, of course, perfect, their practitioners do achieve a very high level of quality in their design work in the sense that the object, when built, almost always meets its specifications. When a building or bridge is built, only very rarely does it collapse. In those unusual cases when it does, a major investigation of the cause is initiated and typically changes in the practice of the field are introduced to prevent comparable events in the future.

This almost ideal situation did not always exist. The classical engineering fields of today also went through their phases of unreliable design work and major failures. In 1628, for example, the Vasa, an expensive warship, sank shortly after launching (Baber, 1987). Apparently her designers were inadequately familiar with the theory of hull stability. Later, in the 1800s, many bridges in Europe collapsed under the weight of the new locomotives, as can be seen in a number of oil paintings in art galleries with collections covering the industrial revolution. Their designers were not able to apply the theory of mechanical statics to their work. Today, with the many software design errors ('bugs') the field of software development is still in this phase (Baber, 1982i; Thomas, 1988i).

In the meantime, hull stability, statics and other relevant theoretical topics have become required components of the curriculum for engineering education. This step has not yet been taken in our field. Our future development as an engineering discipline depends upon it.

The development of many fields of knowledge characteristically has four phases:

1. *Superstition*. Unsystematic explanations of observations of the environment.
2. *Taxonomy*. Organization of observations and objects observed.
3. *Science*. Building models to explain observations and to predict as yet unobserved phenomena.
4. *Engineering*. Applying scientific knowledge from phase 3 to design and construct useful new artifacts, i.e. to modify the environment.

Not all fields of knowledge go through all phases, of course. In some cases, development starts after the first or stops before the last. In one phase development can branch into two or more subfields, etc. In practice, the phases are not temporally mutually exclusive, but overlap, sometimes to a great extent. Perhaps the best known example of development through all four phases more or less linearly is alchemy through chemistry to chemical engineering.

Probably the first field to develop into something like a modern engineering discipline was architecture and civil engineering (as it is now called), i.e. the design and construction of buildings and comparable fixed installations such as dams, bridges, aqueducts, roads, etc. It is difficult to trace its historical

development in a way meaningful for software engineers because this field is so old – the Great Pyramid of Cheops, approximately 230 m × 230 m × 150 m high, was built *circa* 2500 BC and many amphitheatres of quite impressive size were designed and built some 2000 years ago. This field's mathematical basis also dates back to early Greek and Egyptian times.

Engineering disciplines went through a sort of metamorphosis to their current state in the nineteenth century, when essentially all engineering associations were founded. In the UK, for example, the Institution of Civil Engineers was among the first to be established (1818). Among the last to be formed was the Institution of Electrical Engineers (1871). In the other larger European countries and in the USA the pattern was similar, with their electrical engineering associations having been founded by 1900.

Among the various classical engineering fields, electrical engineering is the most relevant to software engineering in terms of its likely historical development. It is the last one to have gone through each stage of development (even aeronautical engineering is slightly older) and it is one of the important roots of the software field. Probably more technical interaction takes place between the software field and electrical engineering than with any other engineering discipline, so that electrical engineering is more likely to serve as a role model than the other fields. To conserve space, this chapter concentrates below on the communications subfield of electrical engineering.

Static electricity and natural magnetism (the loadstone) were known in ancient times. These physical phenomena were, however, little investigated until about 1600 and (except for the magnetic compass) of no significant commercial importance until around 1800.

In the late 1700s and early 1800s a basic knowledge of electrostatics and of magnetism was accumulated which culminated in Maxwell's theory of electromagnetism, published in 1873. Maxwell's equations describe electric and magnetic fields and their interaction and are (in a simpler, better organized form) the theoretical foundation of electrical engineering and practice today.

Parallel to the development of the theory, electricity was applied in commercial ventures. Impressive successes were achieved, but errors were also committed which caused considerable losses. Among the successes were many terrestrial and submarine telegraph cables; by 1895 the telegraph network was so extensive that a message could be transmitted around the world only by electrical means. By 1896 the submarine cable network contained 160 000 nautical miles of cable. Already in 1851 the first successful underwater cable was laid (between Dover and Calais) and in 1858 the first successfully laid transatlantic cable was put into service. Among the catastrophic failures was its destruction a few weeks later, caused by an avoidable error (Nahin, 1988i, ii).

The background of this fiasco warrants looking into in more detail. The person responsible, Edward Whitehouse, chief electrician of the Atlantic Telegraph Company, viewed theory and mathematical analyses as having essentially no practical value. He even went so far as to reject publicly certain theoretical results following from Thomson's already established telegraph equation. In the transatlantic cable incident, Whitehouse decided, presumably on the basis of his experience, to apply a rather high voltage to the cable to ensure that the signal would reach the other end. The unnecessarily high voltage broke down the cable's insulation. After thus destroying the cable and after his opinion regarding the theoretical result mentioned above was proven false, Whitehouse was dismissed. Vitruvius was still right over 1800 years later.

Whitehouse's distaste for theory was not uncommon among the 'practical' men of his day and even years later. Most practitioners probably considered Maxwell's theory to be obviously of no practical value when it was first published. They were right, not because of shortcomings in the theory, but rather because hardly anyone could understand it and the mathematical language which was necessary to express it. Now, every electrical engineering student must acquire a thorough understanding of it as well as demonstrate his ability to apply it to many different types of problems. When complex variables were first introduced into electrical engineering analyses, they were similarly not immediately accepted; only years later did they become a required part of the electrical engineering curriculum (Ryder, 1984, especially i). Many other comparable examples could be cited.

During the early years of the telegraph, a number of phenomena were observed for which no clear explanations existed. After much experimentation and speculation, such problems were often solved by theoretical analyses. One such phenomenon related to the different speeds with which messages could be sent in the two directions over a telegraphic circuit involving a submarine cable. Sometimes, as in this case, the analysis turned out to be short, not particularly complicated, and led to a complete insight into and understanding of the underlying causes of the effects observed. Such situations, as well as some of the errors committed, indicate that practice was often ahead of the development of the theory in these early years.

In some cases, however, theory was ahead of practice. One example was Heaviside's suggestion in 1879, based on theoretical analysis, to insert artificial faults in cables to increase their working speed (Nahin, 1988iii). Only much later was this actually done, with the predicted improvement.

A classic example of theory preceding practice was the celebrated discovery of self-propagating electromagnetic waves in space. For some years it had been recognized by some electrical scientists that Maxwell's equations implied the physical existence of such waves. Finally, Hertz, who knew what to look for on the basis of theoretical analyses, experimentally verified the existence of these waves in 1887–88. In following years wireless telegraphy and telephony covering ever greater distances were developed and put into commercial use.

Thus, one can say that in the time period 1850–1900 the tide began to turn; systematic science and theory began to lead significant practical applications rather than follow them. Scientific theory began to provide the impetus for practical applications rather than simply explaining already existing practical applications. Instead of developing new applications by groping, based on scanty, disconnected pieces of knowledge, one began to design them in a better organized, more systematic way based on a reasonably complete understanding of the underlying physical principles. To be sure, one pressed the limits of knowledge in doing so, but now from within the limits of a more or less closed body of knowledge, extending those limits in the process. Thus, the electrical field became a young engineering discipline.

Related to this shift from a purely 'practical' orientation to a Vitruvian mixture of theory and practice was a corresponding shift in emphasis in the engineering education away from just filling the students' heads with information toward imparting an understanding of the underlying scientific theory. This shift did not, of course, take place suddenly, but rather slowly over time.

From 1900 onward, progress was somewhat more continuous and rapid, with the development and commercial exploitation of long-distance and wireless telegraphy and telephony, national and international telephone networks, radio broadcasting, television, satellite communication, digital communication via all of these media, etc. All of these applications necessitated developing a variety of general-purpose and specialized electrical components, the most advanced today being the VLSI semiconductor chip.

The maturation of the field of electrical engineering was accompanied by a clear shift of influence from the early inventor-entrepreneurs (exemplified by Thomas Edison) to men and women with a solid theoretical education as well as a practical orientation. After the transition of the field to an engineering discipline, practical knowledge alone, no matter how good, was simply not enough to ensure success at the forefront of technical progress. A thorough understanding of scientific fundamentals led to significantly greater overall productivity and enabled engineers to make certain advances which they would otherwise simply not have been capable of achieving. Once again, Vitruvius was right.

Probably the most important task facing the new engineering discipline in its adolescent years was developing the educational infrastructure necessary to pass both the theoretical and the practical knowledge down from generation to generation. Difficult issues regarding what to teach the teachers, financing the educational institutions, etc. had to be resolved. Full-scale departments of electrical engineering did not crop up overnight, of course. The pattern of development varied from university to university, even within one country. Generally typical was the establishment of specialized courses for electrical engineers within existing academic departments, e.g. physics or mechanical engineering. As the number of such courses grew and the number of students specifically interested in electrical engineering increased, subdepartments were organized and, later, spun off to form a new department of electrical engineering. All this took time. To mention one example, the first electrical engineering course at the Massachusetts Institute of Technology was established in 1882 in the Department of Physics. Not until twenty years later, in 1902, was the Department of Electrical Engineering formed (Wildes and Lindgren, 1985).

While the development of other classical engineering disciplines is different in detail from that outlined above, each was similar in general pattern. In this area history has repeated itself many times. To what extent will it do so again in the case of software engineering?

63.5 Forces and factors influencing development of an engineering discipline

What leads to such socio-economic structural changes as the transition from a trade or craft to an engineering discipline? Clearly, the transition must be, on balance, desired; there must be a perceived need or many perceived needs which, in sequence, lead along the path thereto. The transition must also, of course, be technically feasible; an underlying scientific foundation must exist and it must be feasible (technically and economically) to transmit it to an appropriate number of new engineers. In classical economic terms, supply and demand must permit and call for it.

Often in the case of truly fundamental changes, new products or services, etc. the most important needs or demand which are ultimately satisfied are not intitially explicitly perceived but rather are present only latently. To overcome major barriers to the change (costs, investment in a totally new infrastructure, significant modifications to the environment to take advantage of the new service, large scale retraining, etc.), there must be intermediate stages in the transition each of which offers incremental benefits fulfilling perceived needs at acceptable total costs. The introductions of the automobile and the telephone are examples. When initially proposed, the automobile was in the overall social sense, relatively useless, for the necessary roads did not exist and no one really needed to travel so fast anyway; animal-powered transport had sufficed for many centuries. In the early and middle years of the nineteenth century there was, similarly, no concrete need for the telephone, especially not for a nation-wide network. Having managed quite well forever without instantaneous verbal communication over long distances, no one really needed it; and besides, how many people knew anyone to call in a city 200 km away? Intermediate benefits of the telegraph and motorcars for rather specialized users justified the intermediate steps which led to the systems we have today.

Thus, hindrances to progress in the form of lack of awareness of the possibilities of application and potential benefits (latency of need) and lack of awareness and adequate knowledge of the new technical possibilities (latency of supply) are typically overcome in small steps, each of which must exhibit a favourable balance between costs incurred and benefits achieved. Furthermore, this balance must be seen as favourable from both the individual and collective standpoints.

63.5.1 Benefits of the engineering approach

What are the benefits of a professional (e.g. engineering) approach as opposed to that characteristic of crafts or trades? Among the most important is the avoidance of losses attributable to errors in new designs, i.e. a very much higher level of safety. In the pre-engineering days of the nineteenth century, for example, many bridges in Europe collapsed under the weight of the new locomotives with attendant and considerable loss of life and property. After a more professional engineering approach became widespread in civil engineering, structural collapses during and after construction are almost unheard of. When they do occur, they attract much attention both within and outside the field because they are not condoned and they are so rare. In the pre-engineering days of electrical technology, for example, the transatlantic cable was destroyed by improper design of the driving circuits (see earlier); after the field's transition to an engineering discipline, such 'collapses' became rare exceptions to the rule.

Another important benefit of a professional approach is that it enables us, in practice, to exploit the technical possibilities much more thoroughly and to utilize them more efficiently. Without a professional engineering approach electromagnetic waves would have been discovered and exploited practically only much later, if at all. In another example cited above, the engineering approach led to the introduction of artificial faults in cables, with an accompanying increase in efficiency of utilization.

63.5.2 The costs of transition to an engineering discipline

There are significant costs associated with the transition to and maintenance of an engineering discipline, and only if these costs, both individual and collective, are more than offset by benefits will the transition occur. These costs fall into three categories: economic (in the wider sense, i.e. including the investment of people's time), intellectual and psychological.

Psychological factors and fears, while perhaps in a certain sense irrational and in many individual cases unjustified, are real and should not be neglected. They may, in fact, be the most important factor tending to slow down the transition to engineering practice of software development. Engineering practice makes greater intellectual demands on its practitioners than do crafts or trades and many present software developers may wonder if they are capable of meeting those demands. Natural human laziness and convenience cause some to wonder if the benefits are worth the personal trouble and effort and, often only subconsciously, to decide to delay the process, hoping that they can advance into a position immune from the later need to convert to a new way of doing things (or even retire before the transition reaches them). To many, a transition to a software engineering discipline poses a distinct psychological threat to their vocational position and, possibly, to their financial future. Further, if the experienced individual does make the transition successfully, he must then face up to the depressing realization that he or she has been doing things in an inefficient – or perhaps even the wrong – way for years without recognizing it. In extreme cases he might even have to admit to himself that he has wasted a substantial part of his life's effort.

The intellectual cost to the individual already active in software development practice can be substantial, as anyone knows who has taken active part in a serious evening educational program, after putting in full days' work, requiring detailed concentration. In addition, the individual incurs the loss of time and certain costs (professional literature, course fees, registration fees, dues to professional associations, etc.).

The various costs to the individual outlined above represent a barrier which must be overcome. Perhaps the most effective way is the carrot and stick approach – real support from his employer and professional associations, e.g. in the form of recognition, distinction between those who attain the new, higher qualifications and those who do not even bother to try, time from work for training, promotion with a corresponding salary increase, etc. on the one hand and the – equally real – threat of becoming sidetracked on a vocationally stagnant path and, in the long run, being overtaken by colleagues on the other hand. Typical of the development of the classical engineering disciplines was, for example, the introduction of legislation regulating who may practise in the field, especially with regard to safety-critical projects and applications.

Collective costs, i.e. costs borne by society as a whole, constitute a major factor in the transition to and maintenance of a professional state of affairs. In European and many other countries the educational system is the major factor in this category. Also of significance is the legal and public administrative infrastructure concerned with passing and administrating legislation regulating professional practice and education therefore. The required educational and administrative capacity, especially the former, can be established only after the political decision-making processes have run their often lengthy course.

Some observers are convinced that in the Federal Republic of Germany, for example, the establishment of adequate tertiary educational capacity for informatics was delayed by at least a decade by lethargy in the educational/political area. Many politicians could simply not, apparently, believe that the projected and proposed capacity could possibly be really needed. They were forced into action only after it became painfully clear that a large, unsatisfied need already existed which did justify the costs of increasing the educational capacity. It will be years before the consequences of that error are overcome.

63.5.3 Are we ready yet for the transition to software engineering?

As pointed out above, need and technical feasibility are prerequisites for the transition to an engineering discipline. A real need, usually expressible in economic terms, must exist and it must be perceived, not latent. An underlying scientific foundation for the new engineering discipline must exist and it must be feasible (technically and economically) to apply it and to transmit it to an appropriate number of new engineers.

63.5.3.1 The need for software engineering

The first benefit of a professional approach mentioned earlier is the avoidance of losses attributable to design errors. In the pre-professional days of software development, significant losses are attributable to design errors in software (Baber, 1982i). Financial losses of millions of US dollars are not uncommon in businesses and even the loss of human life has been attributed to errors in software (Joyce, 1987), (*IEEE Spectrum*, 1987). Not having completed the transition to a professional state of affairs in normal practice, the field of software development is still characterized by a significant frequency of such events. Such losses have already given rise to lawsuits and to pressure for legal liability for damages caused by errors in software. As these losses and, consequently, pressures increase, so will the perceived need to avoid them by taking an engineering approach to designing software increase.

It appears, however, that the magnitude of these losses has not yet reached a critical level. Dissatisfaction is evident, but the problem has not yet been perceived by the public to be of fundamentally disturbing proportions. Only isolated, individual cases of deaths have been reported and attributed to errors in software, too few, apparently, to give rise to a public outcry and call for action to prevent comparable incidents in the future. Similarly, property loss has apparently not yet reached a critical level in the eyes of the public.

Because computers are capable of analysing large volumes of data and observations and calculating responses much faster (and more rationally) than are human beings, there is a considerable potential for computer applications in safety-critical processes such as monitoring and control of nuclear reactors, air traffic control, instrumentation and flight control in aircraft and space vehicles, etc. Engineers in the classical fields responsible for such systems have, in the past, rejected serious consideration of many such computer applications, however, because they did not have sufficient confidence in the software. More precisely, the freedom from errors in the software could not be demonstrated in a way comparable to that regularly used by engineers to show that the design of some particular mechanism is correct, i.e. meets the specification. Thus, the need for true engineering of such software is today largely latent. Nuclear reactor control applications are, however, under consideration (at least one of which is in the UK (Thomas, 1988ii)) and new aircraft designs include software embedded in subsystems previously implemented only with hardware, so the situation has already begun to change. With continuing advances in the area of safety-critical systems, the need for an engineering approach to software design and analysis will become critical; without it, no one could responsibly approve an application for an operating licence, safety certification, etc.

It was also mentioned previously that an important benefit of a professional approach is that it enables software engineers in practice to exploit the technology in question more thoroughly and more efficiently. We can only guess now about the greatest benefits in this area which a professional engineering approach to software development will bring us in the future. Some current inefficiencies are already apparent (e.g. in finding and correcting errors in software and in the process of setting requirements and specifications for software systems), but it is not yet clear to most practitioners to what extent these inefficiencies can be eliminated by an engineering approach to designing software and to what extent they are inherent in the process. In other words while the need for improved efficiency in the design process is clearly perceived, the need for engineering as a way to achieve it is not so clearly seen. In my opinion, this uncertainty is the major factor, on the benefit side, hindering progress. Furthermore, in the author's opinion, the benefits of increased efficiency in the design and development process are larger than is commonly assumed.

Thus regarding the need for an engineering approach to software development, the situation seems to be just marginally subcritical. While the perceived need alone is not quite enough,

it and the latent need together would seem to be. With growing losses due to software errors and with the increasing attention being given to safety-critical applications, the latent needs will become explicitly recognized, triggering the transition. Only the time which this process will take is uncertain.

63.5.3.2 *The feasibility of software engineering*

What about the supply side? Does an underlying scientific foundation for a software engineering discipline exist, can it be applied to practical design problems and is it possible to transmit it to an appropriate number of new engineers?

Earlier in this chapter it was argued that such a theoretical foundation exists, but experience in applying it as classical engineers apply their corresponding scientific theories is still quite limited. Especially in the UK, one can discern signs of increasing interest in this area coming from the practical (as opposed to the theoretical) side. Standards requiring the use of formal methods when designing software for safety-critical military applications are being seriously considered by the British Ministry of Defence and this interest has attracted attention in the USA (Gruman, 1989). In other countries a few projects involving safety-critical applications are applying relevant theory to verify formally that certain programs satisfy their specifications. Thus, some software developers in responsible and influential positions appear to be convinced that this material is applicable to important practical design problems. While their number may be small, it is growing.

The professional literature contains papers and books arguing that an engineering approach to software design and development is possible and useful in practice, e.g. Hoare (1984, 1987) and showing how the relevant theory can be applied to actual problems arising in software development practice, e.g. Baber (1987).

Papers reporting practical success in applying formal theory and mathematics to large software design and development projects have begun to appear in the professional computing literature, e.g. Mills (1986, 1987 and Selby *et al.* 1987). Other successful applications not reported in the literature have been made.

One could say that the fundamental technical feasibility of software development as a true engineering discipline is, among current practitioners, largely latent, but that their conscious awareness of the practical possibilities is increasing.

It should be pointed out that in one area of computing, the rather extensive practical application of theory is already the norm – compiler design. Initially, before the formal, theoretically based approach was common, this was a rather problematic area, with many errors in compilers. Now, errors in the syntax checking and code translating parts of compilers and interpreters are relatively rare. Those which are present are typically due to mistakes or oversights in formulating the specification, rather than implementing it. Developers of these sections of compilers and interpreters are almost invariably graduates of academic courses in computing science with a strong emphasis on relevant mathematics.

Regarding the education of software engineers, we must distinguish between two areas of concern: educating new entrants to the field and educating (retraining) those already actively engaged in software development.

In many countries, academic programs in computing science have already been established at both the university and polytechnic levels. These courses are, in general, quite successful and are well accepted by students and their subsequent employers alike. Departments of computing science certainly have their problems and difficulties, but these seem to derive ultimately from the courses' popularity, success and newness, not from inherent faults or shortcomings. Where the quality of instruction leaves something to be desired, the cause of the problem is typically an undersupply of adequately qualified staff to teach the large number of students selecting such courses. The various reasons for this shortage are discussed in Baber (1982).

One, from the software *engineering* standpoint perhaps fundamental, shortcoming of the existing computing science courses relates to their orientation and is suggested already by the title computing *science*. Typically, only a minority of the teaching staff has a traditional engineering background and mentality and the courses offered as well as the way they are taught reflect this lack. Students often find that some courses emphasize the theory, not its application, and are most suitable for those intending to pursue careers in research, not commercial software development. They are sometimes left wondering if the material learned can be directly applied at all and if so, how. The problem is not so much the material itself, but rather the flavour and orientation of its presentation. And the other courses which do have a practical orientation are sometimes of a low level, dealing, for example, with a specific programming language and its idiosyncracies. Various proposals for improving the computing science and software engineering curricula have been made, including ones to change the orientation of these courses to bring them more in line with traditional engineering curricula, e.g. (Parnas, 1989; Mills *et al.*, 1989).

Thus, even though some problems exist and changes and improvements are called for, academia is basically prepared to educate new entrants to the software engineering field.

With regard to educating or retraining current practitioners to become properly qualified engineers, however, the situation is much less satisfactory. With insufficient capacity for normal academic programs for full-time day students, there will be little inclination to establish formal evening programs of a high level. Some commercially offered courses are available, but these are typically designed for technician grade personnel. Also, their capacity would be inadequate for a fairly massive, industry-wide retraining effort. A great number of individual seminars on specific topics are available and more could be easily provided to fill in topical gaps, but, while helpful, these would not constitute a complete program for an engineering level qualification.

Unfortunately, we cannot look to other established engineering disciplines for guidance in solving the problem of retraining current software developers to become qualified engineers. Being mature, the other engineering fields have essentially no need for this activity. All of their practitioners entered the discipline through appropriate tertiary educational paths. They have a definite need for continuing education to keep their engineers up to date, but this need can be satisfied by individual seminars.

The problem of retraining current practitioners to become fully qualified engineers was probably the main factor limiting the speed of transition of the classical technical fields to fully developed engineering disciplines and this may very well turn out to be the case for software engineering also. In the long term, however, those who, for whatever reasons, do not acquire the higher engineering qualifications will have to accept technician grade positions in the new scheme of things.

63.5.3.3 Other aspects of the professional engineering infrastructure

In every country in which computing is significant one or more associations of computing specialists exist. As pointed out previously in this chapter, their positions and orientation within the technical/professional community varies considerably from country to country, but many are not directly comparable to professional engineering societies.

Which of these associations will make the transition to a professional engineering society, as the latter are typically structured, is unclear. Some undoubtedly will, some will not. Some will perhaps choose not to become an engineering society, but will rather specialize in, for example, scientific (as opposed to engineering) and research aspects of computing and software.

The future need for software engineering societies can be met in at least three ways:

1. Transformation of existing associations of computing specialists.
2. Establishing subsidiary societies within existing professional engineering societies.
3. Founding new professional software engineering societies.

In some countries, non-specialized engineering societies exist which individual engineers can join (e.g. the *Verein Deutscher Ingenieure* (Society of German Engineers) in the Federal Republic of Germany), so that, in a certain sense at least, a new software engineering society is not actually needed (this is not to say that one would not be desirable in the long term).

The major classical engineering fields did not have such a wide choice in the nineteenth century. They were limited to the third or, in some cases, the first alternative.

Because of the widespread existence both of computing associations and of already established and suitable professional engineering societies, the future software engineering associations will probably be formed in the first two ways mentioned above. There is little need to establish completely new organizations.

Examples of both developmental paths can be observed today. In the UK, for example, the British Computer Society (BCS) is clearly in the process of transforming itself into a professional engineering society as discussed earlier. In the USA, the second approach was taken some time ago when the Computer Society of the Institute of Electrical and Electronics Engineers was formed.

The legal and associated governmental administrative infrastructure for professional engineering was established for the classical engineering fields long ago. This infrastructure is relevant and applicable to the software development field. Some detailed modifications or supplements will undoubtedly prove desirable, but no fundamental structural changes appear to be called for.

Thus, many components of a professional engineering infrastructure for software development are already present and we have an excellent basis for filling in many of those gaps which do still exist. We are certainly in a better position in this regard than were the now classical engineering fields in the nineteenth century when they began their transition to professionalism.

63.5.3.4 Do classical engineers think we are ready to become software engineers?

In discussions with engineer colleagues, an ambivalent attitude toward software development as an engineering discipline usually emerges. They seem to believe that software development is basically a technical field, comparable in a certain general but real sense to their own fields. However, the apparent attitudes of software developers causes these engineers to doubt the viability of software development as an engineering field.

Their reservations derive, in the final analysis, from the high rate of design errors in software delivered to customers for productive use. They complain that software developers with whom they have worked were unable to state unequivocally, before a (software) design was implemented, that it would satisfy the specification or under what conditions it would or would not exhibit the specified behaviour. Furthermore, software developers were unwilling to accept, in any formal manner, responsibility for the correctness of their (software) designs. Engineers in the classical fields consider all three of these points to be antithetical to the very notion of engineering. They conclude from these observations that software developers do not really understand what they are doing, certainly not in an engineering sense, and lack qualifications comparable to those of the engineers. Thus they tend to question whether software development is an engineering discipline and whether software developers are ready to be called engineers.

On the other hand, traditional engineers who design systems with embedded computers and, hence, software, perceive a distinct need to be able to communicate with the software developers as they do with engineering colleagues in other disciplines. They need to be able to agree on specifications of the interfaces between the software and the rest of the system and to have confidence that the software on the other side of the interface will satisfy that interface specification just as reliably as their side of the interface is expected to satisfy the same interface specification. Unless and until this can be done, no engineer can, with good conscience, attest that the entire system will satisfy its specification. And such certification is a normal part of the engineering design process.

When traditional engineers look at our advanced technical literature, they see that there is a highly mathematical and theoretical basis for much of it. Superficially and in general terms, at least, it seems comparable to their own professional literature.

So for these latter reasons, traditional engineers tend to view software development as an engineering discipline or at least as a field ready to become one.

The history of the BCS's relationship with the Engineering Council seems to be another example of an ambivalent attitude on the part of traditional engineers toward computing specialists and software development. The author is not informed about the details of these negotiations, but knows only what has appeared in the trade press. The very willingness to consider the BCS's application seriously and to invest considerable time and effort screening the many applications from BCS members for registration as Chartered Engineers clearly indicates, in the author's view, the basic acceptance by traditional engineers of the position that software development could and should be an engineering discipline. (Computer hardware design was, from its very beginning, a subfield of electrical engineering and, as such, has always been regarded as engineering.) On the other hand, the several delays and postponements of the BCS's final admission as an equal member of the Engineering Council seem to the author to indicate reservation on the part of traditional engineers toward accepting us as engineering colleagues.

Thus, it appears that engineers in the classical fields are basically willing to accept us as fellow members, perhaps even desirous of doing so, but expect us to prove ourselves. In their view, the evidence which we have given to date is not quite complete proof.

63.5.3.5 *Summary: we are ready for the transition to software engineering*

In all respects we are currently in at least as good a position to make the transition to software *engineering* as were the classical engineering fields when they became professions in the nineteenth century. In many respects, our point of departure is more favourable than was theirs. Thus, our chances of success are very good – we only have to really want to become an engineering discipline.

63.6 Software development tomorrow: possible future worlds

What sorts of futures (engineering and non-engineering) of software development are conceivable? What would lead to each of the possibilities and what are the main characteristics of each? The answers to these questions are dealt with in detail in (Baber, 1982ii) and will be summarized in this section.

Depending upon (1) the level of professional competence of software developers and (2) the complexity and size of the computer applications attempted, the success rate and impact upon society as a whole will vary from excellent to disastrous. The spectrum of possibilities can be characterized by three extreme futures:

1. The reckless, audacious Future A.
2. The reactionary, backward Future B.
3. The radical, celestial Future C.

Our actual future will be either one of these or, more likely, an intermediate point somewhere between them.

Each of these future worlds is briefly described below and illustrated with (currently) fictional examples.

63.6.1 The reckless, audacious Future A

The reckless, audacious Future A is largely an extrapolation of our present situation. Enamoured, even infatuated by the possibilities raised by computing systems, much is attempted. Because the technical competence of software developers is limited, failures are common. The consequences of attempting systems beyond the software developers' capabilities are frequently grave, sometimes catastrophic.

Typical of the problematic situations arising in Future A are the following. Errors found in software in air traffic control systems and in onboard subsystems cause an airplane crash killing crew members, passengers and people on the ground. Fires are attributed to errors in software embedded in automatic heating and air conditioning systems installed in warehouses. A large business enterprise becomes unmanageable and, in turn, insolvent because of poorly designed and implemented management information systems.

Even the classical engineering fields, heretofore free of such problems, are affected. A skyscraper collapses during construction because computer programs used for statics calculations contained errors. Errors in a program used to design a nuclear reactor and in the operational program, in combination with a component failure, result in a core melt down and the release of dangerous amounts of radioactive material into the environment.

Another profession, medicine, suffers similarly. A patient dies because a physician could not obtain access to a diagnostic database. A software error caused the malfunction of the data communications network.

Shortly after a new automated driving system was installed in a large section of a country's motorway network, an accident involving hundreds of automobiles occurs. The cause is found to be a mistake in the system's software. A nationwide electrical power failure is caused by a software error introduced when modifying the computerized power distribution control system. A 'bug' in the software in a military defence system leads to the false detection of an enemy attack; the counterattack results in the deaths of the entire population of a small city and lethally high levels of radioactivity in the area for a year. As a result of software errors, an interbank clearing system is inoperative for two days; business is seriously disrupted for even longer. A space vehicle with astronauts on board is lost in deep space.

Future A is a basically unstable situation. The extensive loss of life and other irreversible damage, e.g. to property, cannot, of course, be tolerated. A society facing problems of this type and scale has a choice between two fundamentally different alternatives: (1) restrict application of the new technology to that which is well within the limited capabilities of the practitioners or (2) increase substantially their technical competence. Alternative 1 leads to a reactionary, backward state of affairs (see Future B below), while alternative 2 leads to a radical, more nearly celestial situation (see Future C below).

The history of other technical fields, for example in the nineteenth century, contains situations comparable to or at least clear precursors of Future A. Both reactions outlined above (and mixtures thereof) have occurred, but the second – increasing substantially the technical ability of the responsible designers – has generally dominated. Society, it seems, typically values the potential benefits of new technology highly enough to justify the effort necessary to master it.

63.6.2 The reactionary, backward Future B

In the reactionary, backward Future B, the application of computing systems is limited to those which the not professionally qualified software developers are capable of handling satisfactorily. Widespread scepticism regarding the reliability and safety of proposed software-based systems predominates. Applications involving significant risk to the public are effectively prohibited, either legally, economically or through heavy social pressure.

Typical of the reactionary situations arising in Future B are the following. Legislation requiring unduly lengthy testing of air traffic control software as well as exaggeratedly high liability insurance leads to the scrapping of a newly developed system ready to be installed. Because of serious doubts about the reliability of the software involved, preliminary plans to develop a new temperature control system with embedded microprocessors are dropped in favour of proposals based on traditional technology. In turn, the company reduces sales forecasts and lays off a substantial fraction of its employees.

A trade union prevents the implementation of a new management information system in a large company. Their representative argues that if the system were to turn out a failure, the company would probably collapse. The risk of an ensuing loss of job positions is greater than the union can accept.

Some civil engineers, convinced that programs used by designers of a newly constructed building contain errors, picket the building until all structural computations had been repeated manually. The Anti-Computer League stages demonstrations against an organization doing research on computerized vehicle control systems for motorways. The same organization files a lawsuit against a company developing a computerized control system for a nuclear reactor; the suit delays the project so long that the company finally abandons the project. A pacifist group organizes demonstrations in several countries against a rumored top-secret computerized defence control system, as a result of which the political leaders of the countries affected drop the plans for the system. When plans to connect one bank's computer to an interbank network are announced, most depositors close their accounts.

Particularly characteristic of Future B are the many lost opportunities deriving ultimately from the inability to develop safe and reliable software-based systems. It would, certainly, be expensive to develop the sufficiently widespread ability to design such systems. But how expensive is it not to do so?

63.6.3 The radical, celestial Future C

In the radical, celestial Future C, the professional competence and qualifications of software designers have been developed to such a high level that even very challenging demands can be met reliably and safely. Perhaps equally important, when the specification for a proposed system goes beyond the state of the engineering art at the time, the software developer recognizes and states this fact to his client. The specification and the contractual nature of the project are adjusted accordingly before work is initiated, so that the client knows in advance what he or she will receive as well as how much confidence he can place in the result. Correspondingly, the engineer accepts full responsibility to fulfil the terms of the contract and deliver a design meeting the specification. There are no undue surprises during or after completion of the assignment.

Typical of the situations arising in Future C are the following. They make less exciting reading than the situations arising in Futures A and B, mainly because the results are nearly ideal, with no surprises. The systems function as they should and as expected.

During the transition to Future C, a software developer contracts with a supplier of communications systems to write a software system for a particular customer's needs. The software developer writes all programs and then installs them on a test system. In the meantime, part of the new system's environment has been modified, necessitating corresponding modifications to the design of the new system, which are completed in a short time. The new system is then installed at the customer's site by another specialist only cursorily familiar with the new software. The software developer hears nothing more about the matter until he asks his client several months later how the customer liked the new software. 'Fine' is the answer. The software developer then asks what the customer particularly liked about it. The reply: 'It works'.

Two aircraft nearly collide in flight but are automatically and safely guided apart by the fully automated flight and air traffic control system, which has operated correctly since its installation several years earlier. The system automatically issues a full report to both ground and on-board flight monitors, in which the cause is identified as a traffic volume significantly exceeding design specifications. Furthermore, the system warns that it will prevent higher traffic volumes from arising by limiting take-offs.

The computerized control system of a nuclear reactor responds to a sequence of operator errors by issuing corresponding warnings and finally shutting the reactor down. No injury or damage occurs.

A request to design and implement a fully automatic, computerized language translation system for an international, intergovernmental organization is turned down as being beyond the state of the engineering art at the time. A few gaps exist in the knowledge required to design an efficient and reliable system to translate between ten languages, allowing for all combinations of voice and text input and output.

63.6.4 Whither software?

A society which wishes to take ever greater advantage of the benefits offered by computerized systems will necessarily become more and more dependent upon their correct, reliable and safe functioning. To ensure this, it must place ever more severe demands on the suitability, reliability and correctness of the software controlling them. And this, in turn, can be achieved only if our software developers are professionally qualified and take their responsibility both to clients and the public seriously, as other professionals do.

With regard to other professions and technical fields (e.g. medicine, architecture, civil engineering, electrical engineering, etc.), society has chosen (often after some initial hesitation) to move in the direction of Future C. With regard to computer software, the choice has not yet been finally made, but old precedents and current developments together strongly suggest that the same choice will be made with respect to software.

63.7 Our path to the software engineering future

Will we consciously follow the examples set for us by the classical engineering fields in the last hundred years or so or must we learn again, the hard way, the same lessons? Both paths lead to very similar future worlds, but the first would require less effort and would reach the goal earlier. Knowing that history is likely to repeat itself, we should seek a short cut to a professional state of software engineering. It should be possible for us to avoid most of the mistakes made and the subpaths ultimately rejected by our older engineering brethren.

We have, it seems to the author, a widespread, generally subconscious tendency to reject older ideas and knowledge as being irrelevant to the totally new, unprecedented field of computing and software. Software jargon contains, for example, many newly defined terms with essentially the same meanings as other terms in classical mathematics. We are constantly, it seems, inventing new languages for writing programs, specifications, descriptions of systems, etc. Sometimes these efforts represent an attempt to develop further or improve upon earlier solutions to problems, but all too often they are evidence of lack of familiarity with already existing concepts, knowledge, etc. We talk about 'reusing' things rather than 'reinventing the wheel', but in our upcoming efforts to reshape our field of software development, there is a real danger that we will do the latter – and embark upon an unnecessarily long and expensive journey. Conscious recognition of this danger can enable us to avoid it.

The direction for future development of the software field and its practitioners is outlined well by the statement 'Computer code that is not thoroughly understood by its programmer is not yet complete. If put into use, it leaves a legacy of trouble and disappointment for others. Software engineers are committed to getting the code right the first time.' (McKeeman, 1989). To the last sentence one could add, 'with confidence and accept responsibility therefore'.

A true engineering approach to software development, in which the software engineer does regularly get the code right the first time, will not be trivially easy for many current practitioners to learn. Neither was it easy for the electricians a hundred years ago to learn Maxwell's equations and how to apply them. Neither was it easy for the bridge designers of the nineteenth century to learn higher algebra and calculus and how to apply them in order to get their designs right the first time so that the bridges would stop collapsing. Despite the difficulties, those fields made the transition successfully. We can do it, too.

To progress in the direction of the professional software engineering Future C, all concerned directly or indirectly with software design and development must take certain action. The most important and influential groups are academia, software development management, software developers and purchasers and users of software-based systems. The changes which these groups must implement are described in Baber (1982iii) and are summarized below.

63.7.1 Academia

Probably the most critical prerequisite for any profession is the academic education of its practitioners. Such preparation must convey to the student primarily basic principles which will be of lasting value, validity and relevance throughout his career and which will enable him to learn, on his own, such detailed knowledge as he or she will need from time to time.

This implies that the software engineering student should acquire a sound understanding of mathematics, the basic principles of computing systems and those subjects underlying the likely application areas with which he will be concerned later (e.g. economics, business studies, physics, chemistry, medicine, etc.). As other engineers, he or she need not be a mathematician but must be able to think, write and speak in the language of mathematics and apply it with ease in his or her work. As with other engineers, he need not be an expert in the area in which the objects he designs are applied, but he must have a good understanding of the relevant field and its needs and restrictions and be able to communicate with its experts in their language (*cf.* Vitruvius (circa 25 BCi).

The education of the software engineer, like that of other engineers, must aim at an effective balance between theoretical and practical orientation. The student should appreciate both the theoretical and practical aspects of the field. Currently, this poses a significant problem for many academic departments, most of whose faculty members have lived and worked in only one of these two worlds and are not, therefore, in a position to convey such an attitudinal balance to the students. Conscious awareness of this shortcoming together with an honest desire to overcome it in the interests of the students are promising prerequisites for reducing the severity of the problem in the short term.

Proposals for computing science and software engineering curricula appear more or less regularly in the professional literature. A recent one which emphasizes the *engineering* orientation much more strongly than earlier proposals is Parnas (1989). Coming from a computing and software expert with a classical engineering education, this proposal should be studied carefully and considered seriously, especially by those with no classical engineering background.

63.7.2 Software development management

The problems which the software development manager will face during the transition to software engineering are probably the most difficult ones to overcome. Short-term business pressures and fundamental aspects of human psychology (one's own) act as barriers to the changes which he must, in the long term, implement.

In the face of quantitatively limited programming resources, the software manager facing short-term deadlines is tempted to, and generally does, hire whatever programmers are available. In doing so, he or she effectively encourages new entrants to the field to take a job instead of studying software engineering first. In other cases, students are encouraged to drop out of their academic course of study before completing it and take a highly paid position. These same pressures induce the software development manager to postpone training courses for employees repeatedly and often more or less indefinitely. All of these measures tend to reduce the education and qualification of software development staff. While easing the immediate pressure on the software development manager, they actually serve to create even worse problems in the future, for they leave the manager with underqualified, substandard staff in the future. The solution to this dilemma is clear, but implementing it requires a longer term view and a great deal of will power and foresight. The manager must be willing to accept less quantity and attempt to attract and develop higher quality.

The software development manager, being a human being, will naturally tend to hire software designers and developers whose way of working he or she understands, i.e. the way it was done in his or her own earlier days of programming. In other words, the manager tends to hire people who do things the old way, not the way the new software engineers have been taught to work. Asking the software development manager with no experience with a truly engineering approach to employ the new software engineers and to let them work their way is tantamount to asking him to admit that he has been doing things the wrong way all his career. Psychologically, this tends to destroy his ego and is correspondingly difficult for him to do. Probably, only clear examples of success will enable the typical software development manager to overcome this psychological – but very real – barrier. Only the very unusual manager will be able to overcome the hurdle on the basis of logical conviction alone.

In addition, there is the more technical problem of managing an engineering project. Not being really familiar with an engineering approach to software development, the manager does not know how to organize the work appropriately or how to manage a group of professionally qualified software engineers effectively. This problem, while by no means trivial, can be relatively easily solved by rational means such as learning the new approach (e.g. through study and seminars), working out new organizational forms and procedures for the work cooperatively with the software engineers, etc.

63.7.3 Software developers

With the exception of occasional short-term and regionally localized dips in the job market for software developers, offers of employment have abounded since the field was established. It is very risky, however, to assume – and to gamble one's own financial future – that the current boom market for underqualified software practitioners will last throughout a career lasting another 30–40 years. The individual software developer should carefully assess his or her strengths and weaknesses, measured against standards of professional engineering qualifications, and candidly ask himself if he can reasonably expect to survive to retirement age without significantly upgrading his abilities.

The individual software practitioner can expect assistance and support from the employer, but must be prepared to carry the main burden of acquiring professional qualifications himself. He should place more importance on his medium- and long-term interests and goals than on short-term gains. He should pay more attention to fundamental principles of longer term validity than to technical details of only immediate value. He should try to develop his ability to read the professional, as opposed to the trade, literature.

Most importantly, the prospective new entrant to the field should seriously consider obtaining a professional education first. Starting to work at a high salary a few years earlier may seem appealing, but is a short-sighted way to begin a career lasting almost half a century. Especially the new entrant should weigh the possibilities which a professional preparation will open up to him over the course of his life's work.

63.7.4 Purchasers and users of software based systems

Purchasers and users can help bring about the transformation to software engineering by taking an uncompromising stance on meeting the specifications agreed upon and on quality. In the long run, it is in their own economic interests to do so, for the consequences of the errors in initially cheap software make it, over its lifetime, more expensive than high-quality software. Here again, the analogy with bridge design in the nineteenth century is appropriate. The higher initial cost of professionally designed bridges was more than offset by the losses to life and property avoided by the reliable designs.

Purchasers and users should refuse to accept the argument that software is so fundamentally different from other technical artefacts that it cannot be made to meet specifications reliably. This has been a convenient excuse for sloppiness and carelessness, but it is simply not true. Customers should demand that software developers guarantee either their professional qualifications (as do physicians, lawyers, etc.) or their final products (as do manufacturers, tradesmen, etc.). The current situation, in which software developers and suppliers formally guarantee little or nothing is unique and patently unfair to the customers.

63.8 Conclusion

Software development is 'a tough engineering discipline with a strong mathematical flavour' (Dijkstra, 1982i). Other writers have expressed a similar conviction. There is considerable evidence that software development can and should be an engineering discipline. The history of the classical engineering disciplines and the present and recent past of the software field contain many striking parallel developments, patterns, aspects, incidents, etc.

The history of all classical engineering fields has confirmed Vitruvius. Those who would be or become software *engineers* ignore his advice at their peril. Both practical orientation – *fabrica* – and a thorough understanding of the theoretical foundation of our field and the ability to apply it – *ratiocinatio* – are prerequisites for a software engineering discipline. Neither alone is enough. Neither is it enough that some software developers be well-versed in practice and others well-versed in theory. Each *individual* software *engineer* must have a well-developed capability in both areas and be able to apply his or her skills and knowledge of both types simultaneously to each specific job to be done. Only when he can fulfill this requirement can he justly consider himself to be an engineer.

The level of theoretical knowledge among current software practitioners must be raised, without requiring them to become theoreticians or mathematicians. This is a continuing educational problem. To facilitate this process, the terminology and language in which the theory is expressed should be extended to include simpler forms (e.g. notational conventions) more suited to the orientation, mentality and needs of the engineer, as opposed to those of the scientific researcher. This does not mean proliferation of excessively detailed complexly organized programming and specification languages full of bells and whistles, but rather a lean, to the point, simple terminology. Here again, the classical engineering disciplines offer models worth imitating.

Software developers learning the professional engineering approach often ask, 'But can we afford the extra time – the luxury – required to take this approach?' This very question exposes a short-term view which is one of the causes of the problematic state of affairs of software development today (sometimes called the 'software crisis'). We should be asking ourselves the questions 'How much longer can we afford *not* to take the truly professional approach? How much longer can we afford the "luxury" – the time and cost – of extensive debugging, of the consequences of design errors in software delivered to our clients?'

Again, the experience gained in the classical engineering fields suggests that with software, too, we will soon conclude that we cannot afford the higher costs and losses and the lesser benefits of our current non-engineering approach to software development. If software is to become ever more extensively employed in the technical systems upon which our social organization relies so heavily, if we want to take advantage of the potential software offers, we have no real choice. We must turn software design and development into the same sort of engineering discipline as those which have led to the other technical systems which have served us so effectively in the past and continue to do so today, systems upon which we rely so completely.

Thus, the medium- to long-term future of software development seems clear in general terms. It will be an *engineering* future. Decisions yet to be made will, of course, still influence the details of that future and, most importantly, the *speed* with which we become an engineering discipline. We have an easier task than did our engineering predecessors in other disciplines, for we have their now mature engineering fields as good examples to follow. If we choose to use them consciously as models to imitate, we can save ourselves much time and effort, for they have already solved most of the fundamental problems (albeit in somewhat different contexts) with which we will have to come to grips in the future (see, for example, Butterworth's other Engineer's Reference Books).

The less our individual reluctance and resistance to the forthcoming change, the sooner we stop talking about why it will or won't or can't work and get down to the hard intellectual work of actually making the transition, the easier and quicker will be our metamorphosis from software craftsmanship to software *engineering*.

Many of the steps necessary to transform our field into software engineering have been proposed and discussed before. Talk is, of course, not enough. Concrete action is now required.

63.9 Bibliography

Baber, R. L. (1982) *Software Reflected: The Socially Responsible Programming of Our Computers.*, North-Holland Publishing Co., Amsterdam, New York, Oxford, (i) Chapter 2 (ii) Chapter 4 (iii) Chapter 5

Baber, R. L. (1987) *The Spine of Software: Designing Provably Correct Software – Theory and Practice*, John Wiley & Sons, Chichester

Baber, R. L. (1989) 'Software engineering' vs. software *engineering*. *IEEE Computer*, **22**, No. 5, 81

Dijkhuis, W. (1989) *Vitruvius Revisited: Architecture and Information*, (forthcoming)

Dijkstra, E. W. (1982) *Selected Writings on Computing: A Personal Perspective*. Springer-Verlag, New York. (i) p. 273

Dijkstra, E. W. (1989) Quotation in a press report on the 17th Annual ACM Computer Science Conference, *IEEE Software*, **6**, No. 3, 97

Gruman, G. (1989) Software safety focus of new British standard. *IEEE Software*, **6**, No. 3, 95–96

Hoare, C. A. R. (1984) Programming: sorcery or science? *IEEE Software*, **1**, No. 2, 5–16

Hoare, C. A. R. (1987) An overview of some formal methods for program design. *IEEE Computer*, **20**, No. 9, 85–91

IEEE Spectrum (1987) Lethal dose. (September), 16

Joyce, E. (1987) Software Bugs: A Matter of Life and Liability. *Datamation*, (May 15), 88–92

McKeeman, W. M. (1989) Graduation talk at Wang Institute. *IEEE Computer*, **22**, No. 5, 78–80

Mills, H. D. (1986) Structured programming: retrospect and prospect. *IEEE Software*, **3**, No. 6, 58–66

Mills, H. D., Dyer, M. and Linger, R. C. (1987) Cleanroom software engineering. *IEEE Software*, **4**, No. 5, 19–25

Mills, H. D., Basili, V. R., Gannon, J. D. and Hamlet, R. G. (1989) Mathematical principles for a first course in software engineering. *IEEE Transactions on Software Engineering*, **15**, No. 5, 550–559

Nahin, P. J. (1988) *Oliver Heaviside: Sage in Solitude*, IEEE Press, New York (i) p. 34 (ii) p. 140 (iii) p. 50

Parnas, D. L. (1989) *Education for Computing Professionals*, Technical Report 89–247, Department of Computing & Information Science, Queen's University, Kingston, Ontario, Canada

Ryder, J. D. and Fink, D. G. (1984) *Engineers and Electrons: A Century of Electrical Progress*, IEEE Press, New York. (i) p. 43

Selby, R. W., Basili, V. R. and Baker, F. T. (1987) Cleanroom software development: an empirical evaluation. *IEEE Transactions on Software Engineering*, **SE-13**, No. 9, 1027–1037

Thomas, M. (1988) *Should we trust computers?* The BCS/-UNISYS Annual Lecture 1988, British Computer Society, London, (i) pp 9–13 (ii) pp. 4ff

Vitruvius, M. P. (circa 25 BC) *De architectura libri decem.*, Latin text and English translation by Granger, Frank (1931, 1955) in *Vitruvius: On Architecture*, Volumes 1 and 2, The Loeb Classical Library, Heinemann, London. German translation by Rode, August (1796) in *Vitru: Baukunst*. Volumes 1 and 2, Artemis Verlag für Architektur, Zürich, München, 1987 (i) Bk I. Chapter I

Wildes, K. L. and Lindgren, N. A. (1985) *A Century of Electrical Engineering and Computer Science at MIT, 1882–1982*, MIT Press, Cambridge, Massachusetts, and London

INDEX

Compiled by Paul Nash